CASES AND MATERIALS

PRINCIPLES OF PATENT LAW

FIFTH EDITION

by

F. SCOTT KIEFF
Professor of Law
The George Washington University Law School
Ray & Louise Knowles Senior Fellow
Stanford University Hoover Institution

PAULINE NEWMAN
Circuit Judge
United States Court of Appeals for the Federal Circuit
Distinguished Adjunct Professor of Law
George Mason University School of Law

HERBERT F. SCHWARTZ
Retired Partner
Ropes & Gray, New York
Adjunct Professor of Law
University of Pennsylvania School of Law
New York University School of Law

HENRY E. SMITH
Fessenden Professor of Law
Harvard Law School

FOUNDATION PRESS
2011

THOMSON REUTERS

This publication was created to provide you with accurate and authoritative information concerning the subject matter covered; however, this publication was not necessarily prepared by persons licensed to practice law in a particular jurisdiction. The publisher is not engaged in rendering legal or other professional advice and this publication is not a substitute for the advice of an attorney. If you require legal or other expert advice, you should seek the services of a competent attorney or other professional.

Nothing contained herein is intended or written to be used for the purposes of 1) avoiding penalties imposed under the federal Internal Revenue Code, or 2) promoting, marketing or recommending to another party any transaction or matter addressed herein.

FOREWORD TO THE FIRST EDITION

By
Giles S. Rich *

Don't accept everything you read in this book just because it is in print or written by some court. Judges, like other authors, are not infallible. Controversial and disputed material is included to further one of the objectives of the authors—to make you THINK.

Patent law was long ago referred to as "the metaphysics of the law," suggesting that it is complex, obscure, arcane, and difficult to understand. There is some justification for the charge, but in its essence patent law is quite simple.

Patents are granted to further the constitutional purpose of promoting progress in the useful arts, on *useful* processes, machines, manufactures, and compositions of matter which are *new* and *would not have been obvious* to persons of ordinary skill in the art. (35 U.S.C. §§ 101, 102, 103). That is the essence. The complications arise because the precise meaning of practically every word in the previous sentence and the cited statutes becomes the subject of controversy at one time or another in litigated cases.

Why are patents granted—for what more specific policy reasons? There are several. Basically, they create an incentive system; and its objectives are diverse: (1) to encourage innovation, the creation of new things and processes; (2) to induce inventors to make early public disclosure of their creations and discoveries; (3) most importantly probably, to encourage the investment of risk capital in the commercialization of inventions so that the public gets to enjoy the benefits thereof; and finally, (4) the inducement of "inventing around" the patents on successful inventions to bring even more improvements to the public—a "we can do it differently, or even better," sort of thing.

In what way do patents provide these incentives? In one simple way: by giving to the inventor or inventors or their assignees—whoever owns the patent right—a single, simple thing, *the right to exclude others* from making, using, or selling whatever the patent covers. This legal right the law regards as a "property right." In recent years it has acquired the name of "intellectual property"—one form of it—or "IP." The power of the federal courts is made available to patentees for the enforcement of this *right to exclude others*. Who are these "others"? Competitors, of course. The patent right, while it lasts, because it is limited in time, is an anti-competition device, a limited-in-time monopoly in the limited sense that the patentee has the potential to be the sole seller of what is protected by the patent. This monopoly power is the mainspring that drives the system. We have other laws that frown on monopoly in other forms—the antitrust laws—and this has caused periods of confusion in the courts, persuading them at times to look askance at patents as monopolies. But this attitude seems to have been dissipated. Perhaps the courts have come to see the distinction between the limited power of the patent right and the extensive market power with which antitrust laws are concerned. There is nothing inherently evil about monopoly power. Property rights in general are a form of monopoly. It is simply power which can be put to either good or bad uses. The patent system puts it to good use as an incentive to innovation.

What you hold in your hands—this casebook—is in major part a collection of court *opinions* and commentaries thereon by the authors and others, in cases involving disputes over patent rights, mostly suits by patentees against alleged infringers, those accused of making, using, or selling patented inventions without the permission of the patent owners. Many people, including lawyers and judges, have the careless habit of calling these opinions "decisions," which they are not. The opinions may state, at the end usually, what the decision is, but the decision is a thing apart from the opinion, which is an explanation or rationalization of the decision showing how it was reached. Decisions are usually stated in final judgments, short, concise statements of the result or results reached by the court for the reasons stated in the opinion. Many decisions these days, due to the pressure of heavy case loads, are rendered without opinions.

The named authors of this book represent a rich collection of talent, senior and junior. In the former category are Don Chisum, author of the current leading treatise on patent law; Herb Schwartz, a senior partner at Fish & Neave in New York, law professor at the University of Pennsylvania, and author of a patent law text for judges put out by the Federal Judicial Center (the research and educational branch of the federal judiciary); and Judge Pauline Newman, who has been my colleague on the Federal Circuit since 1984 and is a Distinguished Professor of Law at George Mason University. The juniors are my former law clerk, Craig Nard, a professor of IP law at Marquette Law School and before that at Rutgers, who conceived this casebook; and Scott Kieff, who is my present law clerk, in his second year, and was, for two years, an associate with Pennie & Edmonds in New York. And there are others.

A particularly innovative and intriguing feature of this book is the "*SIDE BAR*" commentaries. They are contributed by judges, including some of my colleagues on the Federal Bench as well as a British IP judge; lawyers, many of whom were former law clerks on the Federal Circuit or its predecessor, the Court of Customs and Patent Appeals; current law clerks; a former Commissioner of Patents and Trademarks; and other professors. There are twenty-two *SIDE BARS*, as of this writing, on as many different topics.

One problem with teaching and learning the law from cases is that the law is not static and to give historical perspective to it both old and new cases are presented. The old cases have often produced opinions the reasoning of which is obsolete. Even some terminology has changed. A warning is therefore in order that in a couple of important respects major changes in patent law have occurred.

The first such major change is with respect to the statutory prerequisite to patentability, now known as non-obviousness and found in Section 103 of the 1952 Patent Act. Section 103 had no statutory predecessor and replaced a judge-made case law requirement for the presence of "invention." It was a sort of mystery. The Supreme Court once said that invention could not be defined. The requirement realistically said nothing more than that to be patentable an invention had to be the result of invention, a sort of "you know it when you see it" proposition. Beware, therefore, of opinions prior to January 1, 1953, when the act took effect, and to be safe, for a decade thereafter, because the courts, the Patent Office, and many lawyers were slow to take in the effect of Section 103. Old habits of thought are broken slowly.

Another source of possible confusion in pre–1953 opinions is with respect to the patent right itself. What did the government grant to the patentee? Before 1953, the old statute, Revised Statutes, § 4884, provided for a grant of "the exclusive right to make, use, and vend the invention or discovery." Just what did that mean? Did the patent grant a right to make etc.? Even the U.S. Department of Justice was misled by that ambiguous language into arguing in a brief that it gives the patentee only the privilege or permission to make, use and vend the invention. However, long before that the Supreme Court had solved the puzzle, holding in *Bloomer v. McQuewan*, 55 U.S. 539, 549 (1852), that "The franchise which the patent grants consists altogether in the right to exclude every one from making, using or vending the thing patented.... This is all that he obtains from the patent." Wherefore, the 1952 Patent Act changed the statute to say that the patent grants "the right to exclude others," thus ridding us of the ambiguous "exclusive right," a term you will still see, however, when people quote old opinions, the old statute, or the patent and copyright clause of the Constitution, Art. I, Sec. 8, Cl. 8, which foisted the term "exclusive right" upon us.

Having posted these warnings about what to watch out for in reading old cases, here is a final thought to ponder in reading any opinion right down to date.

We know that the patent grants the right to exclude, and that is all, and we know that the patent right is limited to what the patent *claims*. The statute providing for claims, § 112, ¶ 2, says that the "specification shall conclude with one or more claims particularly pointing out and distinctly claiming the subject matter which the applicant regards as his invention." That language was carried forward in 1952 from very old statutes enacted when claims were very different from what they are today. It is anachronistic. What the inventor regards as his invention has very little, if anything, to do with most claims. Claims are drafted by attorneys and agents. Their wording ultimately must satisfy patent office examiners that they distinguish, distinctly and with particularity, from all prior art known to them. When litigated, they have to satisfy the judiciary to the same effect and probably with respect to prior art the examiner did not know about, which has been found by the defendant's attorneys. And when all is said and done and the court has spoken, *what is it that the claims point out*? What the inventors invented? Or the scope of the invention? Not likely! It is the claims that have determined what infringes the patentee's right to exclude, construed in the light of the specification—or, more accurately, the "written description" portion of it, because the claims are also a portion of the specification. The prosecution history of the application is also considered in construing the claims. Infringement, in turn, is a violation of the patentee's *right to exclude*—which is all he gets from his patent—so why is it not the reality of the situation that *the claims are the measure of the patentee's right to exclude* rather than the measure of what was invented. Stated another way, aren't the claims *really the measure of the scope of the patent right, which is the right to exclude* rather than definitions of the invention?

And as a kind of postscript to that final point, is it really *the patent* that is infringed? The patent is the government document giving to the patentee the right to exclude others. Isn't it that right to exclude others that is violated by the infringer rather than the patent which granted the right to the patentee? If yes, then "patent infringement" is at least a misnomer. Perhaps, strictly speaking, there is no such thing as patent infringement, but only infringement of the right to exclude, the property right granted by the patent. After all, if someone trespasses on your land, you don't prosecute for violation of your title but for violation of your rights as a property owner. Patent infringement is a form of trespass, a tort. The Black's Law Dictionary (2d ed., 1910) definition of "infringement" is interesting in this connection: "A breaking into; a trespass or encroachment upon; a violation of a law, regulation, contract, or right. Used especially of invasions of the rights secured by patents, copyrights and trademarks."

Read on and learn all about it, but be careful. I believe that progress in legal thinking is not only possible but essential and that this generation should have a clearer understanding of patent law than previous generations, notwithstanding *stare decisis*. So THINK!

Washington, D.C.

22 May 1998

PREFACE TO THE FIFTH EDITION

The Fifth Edition of PRINCIPLES OF PATENT LAW builds on the strengths of prior editions, which served the dual role of a casebook for the teaching environment and a treatise for the practice environment, by offering a unique combination of the law and economic theories of patents, including its foundations in the law of property, contracts, and remedies, with extensive and diverse legal analyses and practical insights for both lawyers and business people. The Fifth Edition also provides a significant update, addressing the many developments that have arisen over the few years since the printing of the Fourth Edition, including the several Supreme Court and Federal Circuit *en banc* decisions. In keeping with valuable feedback from practitioners and educators, the overall length of the text has also been streamlined for the Fifth Edition to focus on those topics that are most instructive and practical.

Students, instructors, and practitioners may be particularly interested in making use of the wealth of supplementary materials that is freely provided through the accompanying website: **innovation.hoover.org/ppl**. Resources available at the site include full versions of background documents such as patents-in-suit, unedited versions of important cases, extra reading, and special materials designed to help students during their studies as well as while seeking a job.

Instructors may be particularly interested in making use of the new Teachers' Manual, sample syllabi, practice exams, and sample answers that are available on the publisher's website behind the customary security wall.

On June 9th, 1999, at the age of 95, the 20th Century's preeminent patent thinker, U.S. Circuit Judge Giles S. Rich passed away. On that day, the nation lost a great asset; and we lost a dear friend. While the patent law community will never be the same, we echo the encouragement he provided us all in his Foreword to this book—to always THINK! This book is dedicated to Judge Rich and his work, which spanned 70 years in the patent field. While it has been over ten years since Judge Rich's passing, his vast work on the patent system continues to be tremendously relevant to today's debates, which feature precisely the same themes from those of the 1940's and '50's that he and other leading centrist thinkers like Judges Learned Hand and Jerome Frank so elegantly guided.

F. SCOTT KIEFF
PAULINE NEWMAN
HERBERT F. SCHWARTZ
HENRY E. SMITH

May, 2011

ACKNOWLEDGMENT

We first and foremost thank Jed Daily, Post-doctoral Research Associate and Administrative Director of the Hoover Project on Commercializing Innovation, member of the Bar of the State of Missouri and the USPTO, and former student of earlier editions of this book, for contributing such outstanding and sustained help toiling so carefully over every production detail. We gratefully acknowledge the support of the Hoover Project on Commercializing Innovation, which studies the law, economics, and politics of innovation. Information about the Project is available on-line at **innovation.hoover.org**.

We also thank the many people who contributed so much to the patent system, generally, and whose excellent work is reproduced, cited, or otherwise reflected herein. The patent system stands today as a testament to their efforts. We thank the prominent members of their professions who generously prepared *SIDE BARS* written especially for this book. The patent system of tomorrow will be shaped by their work. We thank our teachers, advisors, mentors, colleagues, families, and friends, who gave us what we know. We hope to pass the same on to readers of this book. As we worked to do so, we could not have been helped more by any single source, than we were by the vast works of Judge Rich, which span nearly 70 years in the patent law business. Lastly, our acknowledgment would not be complete without also specifically thanking the following individuals and institutions for their critical contributions to this book: Hollie Baker, Roxy Birkel, John Bloomquist, Chris Bracey, Stephen Burbank, Michael Christman, Marie Chow, Laura Coruzzi, Joe Condo, Emil Dabora, Jed Daily, Richard Epstein, Steve Errick, Jonathan Fanton, Gerald Fink, Jennifer Gordon, Bob Gorman, JoAnn Grinstead, Steve Haber, Terri Hitt, Carol Hoffman, Jan Horbaly, George Hutchinson, Paul Joskow, Horace Judson, David Kane, Leo Katz, Seth Kreimer, David Kieff, Elizabeth Kieff, Elliott Kieff, Jacqueline Kieff, Nelson Kieff, Melinda Lindeman, Geoff Manne, Leslie Misrock, Michael Moore, Stephen Morse, Ralph Oman, Troy Paredes, Josephine Pizza, John Raisian, John Reilly, Vince Roccia, Lindsay Russell, Ronald Silverman, Steven Shavell, Michael Schill, Stephen Tapscott, Joel Weiss, Robb Westawker, Miriam Witlin, Henry Wixon, the students and instructors in patent law courses at numerous law schools, The Federal Circuit Bar Association, The Giles S. Rich American Inn of Court, and The Association of Former Law Clerks and Technical Advisors of the Court of Appeals for the Federal Circuit. For those previously unaware of the help they provided, our thanks is overdue. And, to be sure, all errors are our own.

TABLE OF *SIDE BARS*

SUMMARY OF CONTENTS

TABLE OF CONTENTS

TABLE OF CASES

Principal cases are in bold type. Non-principal cases are in roman type. References are to Pages.

TABLE OF OTHER AUTHORITIES

CASES AND MATERIALS

PRINCIPLES OF PATENT LAW

CHAPTER ONE

ORIGINS AND POLICIES

> I don't know what I may seem to the world, but, as to myself, I seem to have been only like a boy playing on the sea-shore, and diverting myself in now and then finding a smoother pebble or a prettier shell than ordinary, whilst the great ocean of truth lay all undiscovered before me.
>
> Isaac Newton[1]

INTRODUCTION

Our patent laws are generally seen to operate as part of an interdependent mix of incentives and restraints that bestow benefits and impose costs on individual people and businesses as well as on society in general. Some see patents as facilitating innovation, access, and competition. Others see patents frustrating these same goals. Most see some mix of these effects but debate about how best to increase the good and decrease the bad. The central means by which the patent system has these varying effects is that it offers some significant economic benefit for patent owners and those with whom they contract. The prospect of receiving this benefit is generally seen as providing positive incentives for various actors to engage in various types of socially constructive behavior, such as inventing, disclosing, investing, commercializing, and the like.

Some think the patent system plays a more important role in some industries (e.g., drugs and medical devices) than others, which may rely more on trade secrecy (e.g., petroleum) or lead time into the market (e.g., software), or both.[2] And some industries seek patent protection with an eye towards commercialization of the patented technology, while others obtain patents to block competitors from developing competing products or to enhance their bargaining position during cross-licensing negotiations, particularly when a "complex" technology (*i.e.*, a product or process that comprises several patented components) is involved.[3] Patent law is not a one size fits all regime. As two commentators recently noted:

---

1. As quoted in JAMES GLEICK, ISAAC NEWTON 4 (2003).

2. See Wesley M. Cohen et al., *Protecting Their Intellectual Assets: Appropriability Conditions and Why U.S. Manufacturing Firms Patent (or Not)* 24 (Nat'l Bureau of Econ. Research, Working Paper No. 7552, 2000) ("We find that the key appropriability mechanism in most industries are secrecy, lead time and complementary capabilities"); WILLIAM M. LANDES AND RICHARD A. POSNER, THE ECONOMIC STRUCTURE OF INTELLECTUAL PROPERTY LAW 312 (2003) ("Many highly progressive, research-intensive industries, notably including the computer software industry, do not rely heavily on patents as a method of preventing free riding on inventive activity").

3. *See* Cohen et al., *Protecting Their Intellectual Assets*, *supra* note 4.

In some areas, patent rights certainly are economically and socially productive in generating invention, spreading technological knowledge, inducing innovation and commercialization, and providing some degree of order in the development of broad technological prospects. However, in many areas of technology this is not the case. In a number of these, strong broad patent rights entail major economic costs while generating insufficient additional social benefits. And in some strong broad patents are simply counterproductive. One needs to be discriminating and cautious on this front.[4]

Thus, a nuanced approach to understanding the costs and benefits of patent law is needed to appreciate its effect on economic welfare. And while the private value of patents increased for some time,[5] our understanding of patent law's relationship to economic welfare, although more sophisticated today than it was 50 years ago, remains incomplete.[6]

To get you started, this chapter is designed to introduce the history, philosophy, and economics of patent law, a basic knowledge of which will, we hope, provide a strong foundation for your understanding and appreciation of patent law and its overall purpose. Before we begin, however, a few introductory remarks are in order about the nature of patents and our patent system.

The term "patent" is short for "letters patent"; derived from the Latin *literae patentes*, meaning open letters.[7] Generally, letters patent were

---

4. Robert Mazzoleni and Richard R. Nelson, *The Benefits and Costs of Strong Patent Protection: A Contribution to the Current Debate*, 27 RESEARCH POLICY 273, 281 (1998).

5. *See* Robert P. Merges, *As Many As Six Impossible Patents Before Breakfast: Property Rights for Business Concepts and Patent System Reform*, 14 BERKELEY TECH. L.J. 577, 603 (1999) (noting the "increase in the private value of patents since the early 1980s"). *See also,* John R. Allison, Mark A. Lemley, Kimberly A. Moore & R. Derek Trunkey, *Valuable Patents*, GEO. L.J.—(2003) (exploring what makes a patent have private value and how to identify those valuable patents).

6. *See* LANDES AND POSNER, ECONOMIC STRUCTURE, *supra* note 4, at 310 ("Although there are powerful economic reasons in favor of creating property rights in inventions, there are also considerable social costs and whether the benefits exceed the costs is impossible to answer with confidence on the basis of present knowledge"); Richard Brunell, *Appropriability in Antitrust: How Much is Enough*, 69 ANTITRUST L.J. 1, 4 (2001) ("[I]f the vast economics literature on intellectual property conveys one message, it is that the relationship between intellectual property protection and economic welfare is unclear"); Adam Jaffe, *The U.S. Patent System in Transition: L Policy Innovation and the Innovation Process* (National Bureau of Econ. Research Working Paper No. 7280, 1999) (stating "despite the significant of policy changes and the wide availability of detailed data relating to patenting, robust conclusions regarding the empirical consequences for technological innovation of changes in patent policy are few").

7. It should be noted that a patent for invention was just one form of "letters patent." In England, the Crown would conduct much of its state business by means of charters and letters patent, including the grant of privileges to inventors to practice their inventions. As William Blackstone writes in his *Commentaries*:

The King's grants are also matter[s] of public record.... These grants, whether of lands, honors, liberties, franchises, or aught besides, are contained in charters, or letters patent, that is, open letters, *literae patentes*: so called, because they are not letters addressed by the sovereign "to all whom these presents shall come," reciting a grant of some dignity, office, franchise, or other privilege that has been given by the sovereign to the patentee.[8]

The modern American patent is a government issued grant, which confers upon the patent owner, from the time the patent issues, the *right to exclude* others from "making, using, offering for sale, or selling the invention throughout the United States or importing the invention into the United States" for a period of 20 years ending from the filing date of the patent application.[9] In return for obtaining this grant, an inventor must describe her invention in some detail so as to give notice to the public and to enable one of ordinary skill in the art to which the invention pertains to make and use the invention. Importantly, the patent document itself is published by the government, thereby placing the teachings of the patent in the public domain, while simultaneously proclaiming the patentee's right to exclude.

The exchange or bargain between the inventor and the public, represented by a government agency (*i.e.*, the Patent and Trademark Office), has been analogized to a contract.[10] Recently, however, courts have frowned upon the contract analogy, positing instead that patents are more akin to a statute, especially with respect to issues of interpretation.[11]

As previously noted, a patent gives an inventor the *right to exclude*. A patent does *not* give the inventor the positive right to make, use, or sell the invention. This is a common misunderstanding of the modern patent grant,[12] perhaps due in part to the language in Article I, Section 8, Clause 8

---

sealed up, but exposed to open view, with the great seal pendant at the bottom; and are usually directed or addressed by the King to all his subjects at large.

WILLIAM BLACKSTONE, 2 COMMENTARIES ON THE LAWS OF ENGLAND 316–17 (1768).

8. ENCYCLOPEDIA BRITANNICA 969–70 (1942).

9. 35 U.S.C. § 154 (1994). Prior to June 8, 1995 (the effective date of the GATT–TRIPS legislation), the term for a United States patent was 17 years from the date the patent *issued*. In April 1994, the United States and several other countries participated in the Uruguay Round Agreements. The Uruguay Round included an "Agreement on Trade–Related Aspects of Intellectual Property" (TRIPS). The TRIPS patent section precipitated the change of the U.S. patent term from 17 years from date of issuance to 20 years from the filing date. As a result, the present patent term for applications filed before June 8, 1995, is (1) 17 years from date of issuance; or (2) 20 years measured from the filing date of the earliest referenced application, whichever is greater. For applications filed on or after June 8, 1995, the patent term is 20 years measured from the earliest claimed application filing date.

10. *See Fried. Krupp Akt. v. Midvale Steel Co.*, 191 F. 588, 594 (3d Cir.1911) ("[A]n American patent is a written contract between an inventor and the government."); *see also, Davis Airfoils v. United States*, 124 F.Supp. 350, 352 (Ct.Cl.1954) ("A patent is a contract between the inventor and the public, the terms of which are formulated by the United States Patent Office. The inventor in such a contract gives as a consideration to the public a new and useful art, machine or composition of matter, and, in return, the public gives as a consideration to the inventor a monopoly expressed by the claims of the patent....").

11. *See Markman, Inc. v. Westview Instruments, Inc.*, 52 F.3d 967, 985–87 (Fed.Cir.1995) (en banc), aff'd, 517 U.S. 370 (1996).

12. For an excellent early 20th century discussion on the confusion that persisted in the lower courts as to what a patent granted to the inventor *see* FRANK Y. GLADNEY, RESTRAINTS OF TRADE IN PATENTED ARTICLES 1–17 (1910).

of the Constitution,[13] wherein Congress is given the power

> [t]o promote the Progress of Science and useful Arts, by securing for
> limited Times to Authors and Inventors the *exclusive* Right to their
> respective Writings and Discoveries.[14]

(emphasis added). As Chief Justice Taney, in the mid–19th century, stated
in *Bloomer v. McQuewan*,[15] "[t]he franchise which the patent grants
consists altogether in the right to exclude everyone from making, using or
vending the thing patented without the permission of the patentee. This is
all that he obtains by the patent."[16] Nearly 75 years later, Justice Taft
remarked in *Crown Die & Tool Co. v. Nye Tool & Machine Works*[17] that in
granting a patent, "the government is not granting the common-law right
to make, use, and vend, but it is granting the incident of exclusive
ownership of that common-law right."[18] In addition, while lecturing at
Columbia University School of Law from 1941–56, Judge Giles S. Rich,
then a New York City patent attorney, offered this pedagogical tool:

> Postulate that there is not now and never was a patent system. A person
> makes an invention. Assuming there is no law prohibiting it, can he make
> it? Can he use it? Can he sell it? Yes. *Without* a patent, he *has* all these
> rights. Now let's write down (on the blackboard) what the statute says the
> patent grants the inventor:

> **A.   THE   EXCLUSIVE   RIGHT TO MAKE, USE, AND SELL**

> and write under it what rights he had without a patent:

> **B.   THE   RIGHT TO MAKE, USE, AND SELL**

---

13. Bruce Bugbee suggests another reason:

> [T]he ancient institution of monopoly, which was also used to reward royal favorites
> or to increase state treasuries through the sale of exclusive privileges to individuals,
> continued to flourish [in the middle ages] in spite of long-standing legal prohibitions.
> Such grants came to be confused with patents on invention when the latter appeared,
> and the onus of monopoly was unjustly shared. In fact, "letters patent" ... were
> issued for all sorts of privileges and grants, as in England, where true patents of
> invention—which were late in appearing—comprised only a very small fraction of the
> total. The exclusive character of both monopolies and patents of invention, and the
> elaborate common procedure by which both were granted, notably in England,
> encouraged this confusion.

BRUCE BUGBEE, GENESIS OF AMERICAN PATENT AND COPYRIGHT LAW 14 (1967). For a thoughtful
discussion of the relationship between the patent laws and antitrust laws, *see* Giles S. Rich's
five-part series, written in 1942, in the Journal of the Patent Office Society. Giles S. Rich, *The
Relation Between Patent Practices and the Anti–Monopoly Laws*, 24 J. PAT. OFF. SOC'Y 85 (1942),
24 J. PAT. OFF. SOC'Y 159 (1942), 24 J. PAT. OFF. SOC'Y 241 (1942), 24 J. PAT. OFF. SOC'Y 328
(1942), and 24 J. PAT. OFF. SOC'Y 422 (1942). *See also*, Louis Kaplow, *The Patent–Antitrust
Intersection: A Reappraisal*, 97 HARV. L. REV. 1813 (1984).

14. Early European and American patent custom defined the patent grant as an
exclusive right to vend and make the invention. For example, the 1870 United States Patent
Act stated that the patentee had "[t]he full and exclusive right and liberty of making using,
and vending to others to be used, the said invention of discovery." R.S. 4884 (1870).

15. 14 How. 539 (1852).

16. *Id.* at 549.

17. 261 U.S. 24 (1923).

18. *Id.* at 36.

Now, let's subtract **B** from **A** and see what the *patent* gave him

EXCLUSIVE

Every business man knows what it means to "have the exclusive" on something. What he gets from the patent—and all he gets—is a right *to exclude*. That's the patent right.[19]

The right to exclude, without the right to use, is somewhat peculiar to patent law (as well as the law of copyright and negative easements). In contrast, the property right in real property (*e.g.*, land) or personal property (*e.g.*, a car or a computer) indirectly but robustly protects a wide range of privileges and interests in use. In this sense, the right to exclude in these contexts is more instrumental in that it exists to ensure the owner's full enjoyment of use. *See* J.W. HARRIS, PROPERTY & JUSTICE 24–27 (1996); J.E. PENNER, THE IDEA OF PROPERTY LAW 68–74 (1997).

While Congress has deemed a patent to be a form of personal property,[20] it, like other types of intellectual property, differs in at least one fundamental way from traditional forms of property. Knowledge and ideas are, to an important extent, non-excludable and non-exhaustible, that is, unlike a car or a computer, the use and enjoyment of knowledge or ideas by one consumer does not deplete the supply for another consumer. As Thomas Jefferson wrote, "[h]e who receives an idea from me, receives instruction himself without lessening mine; as he who lights his taper at mine, receives light without darkening me."[21] With that in mind, we can ask: don't exclusive rights in intellectual property create inefficient and anti-competitive effects because the marginal cost of using intellectual property is zero?[22] On the other hand, will people create, and more

---

19. Taken from the Columbia lecture notes of Judge Rich (on file with the authors). As the patent grant does not give the patentee a right to make, use, or sell the patented invention, one may obtain a patent on an invention and still infringe a preexisting patent. One example in which this phenomenon arises pertains to improvement patents wherein the use of one patented invention requires use of another patented invention. Consider the following: Inventor 1 patents a widget comprising elements A, B, and C. Inventor 2 improves upon inventor 1's invention by adding D, thus giving Inventor 2 a patent on a widget comprising elements A, B, C, and D (assume D is a nonobvious addition to A, B, and C). Although patented, Inventor 2 cannot practice his invention as it would infringe Inventor 1's patent because Inventor 2's invention contains each and every element (A, B, and C) claimed in Inventor 1's patent. On the other hand, Inventor 1 cannot practice Inventor 2's invention without the permission of the latter (assuming consumers demand widgets having element D included). Patents such as these are sometimes referred to as "blocking patents." What may happen in this situation is that inventor 1 and inventor 2 would cross-license each other enabling both to use each other's claimed invention.

20. *See* 35 U.S.C. § 261 ("Patents shall have the attributes of personal property"). Indeed, courts have held that patents are subject to the Fifth Amendment taking provision. *See Hughes Aircraft Company v. United States,* 86 F.3d 1566, 1571 (Fed.Cir.1996) ("The government's unlicenced use of a patented invention is properly viewed as a taking of property under the Fifth Amendment through the government's exercise of its power of eminent domain".) *See also* 28 U.S.C. § 1498.

21. Letter to Isaac McPherson (Aug. 13, 1813), reprinted in JEFFERSON WRITINGS 1291–92 (M. Peterson ed. 1984). Much of this letter was reprinted in *Graham v. John Deere,* 383 U.S. 1, 7–10 (1966), *see* Chapter Five, *infra.*

22. To quote Jefferson once again: "[i]f nature has made any one thing less susceptible than all others to exclusive property, it is the action of the thinking power called an idea,

importantly, will there be sufficient capital investment in one's creation, if third parties can copy the creation with impunity (this is known as the "free rider" effect)? This gets to the non-excludability of informational goods. Thus, there exists a basic tension in patent law between the incentive to create and disseminate these informational goods on the one hand and, on the other, free competition and efficient allocation of these goods. This tension will be explored in detail in Part C, below (Economics of Patent Law), and indeed, throughout the book.

Beyond the economic aspects of patent law, it is also important for us to ask: how does one *philosophically* justify acquiring a proprietary interest in intellectual goods? There are essentially two schools of thought. The first justification, known as the *deontological* or *natural rights* justification, holds that one has a natural or moral right to one's creations regardless of the social or competitive consequences. This is the "just deserts" theory, wherein the inventor is saying, "I worked hard and should be rewarded for my labor; it is a moral imperative." On the other hand, the *consequentialist* or *utilitarian* justification posits that a property right in one's intellectual creations is necessary as a means to a greater end. Thus, the consequentialists tolerate patents as an incentive for the creation, disclosure, and dissemination of technological advances. The consequentialist approach, as we shall see, is at the heart of American intellectual property law and policy. These philosophical themes and their relevance to American patent law will be discussed in Part B, below (Philosophy of Patent Law). For now, you may want to ask yourself which of the two philosophical justifications you think makes the most sense. Or perhaps you can think of others?

With some of these American patent law basics under our belts, we are almost ready for a more detailed discussion of patent law philosophy and economics. However, as is the case throughout most, if not all, of American law, American patent law did not arise in a vacuum. Therefore, we extend our detour from the theory of patent law and turn our attention to its history, for before we delve into the economics and philosophy of patent law, as well as what follows in the subsequent chapters, we think that your understanding of patent law will be enhanced if you have a feel for its past. A study, although brief, of the history of patent law will show it for what it is, an intellectually stimulating body of law in tune with (and at times, at odds with) the human condition.

A.   A HISTORY OF PATENT LAW

1.   THE CLASSICAL PERIOD

Dating back to ancient Greece, one can discern at least the idea of an incentive-based mechanism wherein a potential inventor is encouraged to disclose something new and useful to society. The incentive could take the

---

which an individual may exclusively possess as long as he keeps it to himself; but the moment it is divulged, it forces itself into the possession of every one, and the receiver cannot dispossess himself of it. Its peculiar character, too, is that no one possesses the less, because every other possesses the whole of it." Letter to Isaac McPherson, *supra* note 23.

form of a prize reward or exclusive right in the inventor's contribution. One of the earliest expressions of an incentive-based system can be found in Sybaris, a Greek colony in southern Italy that existed from 720 to 510 B.C. Known for their luxurious and decadent life-style, the Sybarites were said to have enacted a law that gave exclusive rights to those who created certain culinary delights. Quoting from the historian, Phylarcus, the Greek writer, Athenaeus, writes:

> The Sybarites, having given loose to their luxury, made a law that ... if any confectioner or cook invented any peculiar and excellent dish, no other artist was allowed to make this for a year; but he alone who invented it was entitled to all the profits to be derived from the manufacture of it for that time; in order that others might be induced to labour at excelling in such pursuits....[23]

Although the Sybaritic "law" is arguably "apocryphal,"[24] it should give us pause that the very idea of an incentive-based system expressed, remarkably, over two thousand years ago, anticipates some of the very concepts that embody our modern patent code and demonstrates how closely tied patent law is to human nature.

A few centuries after the destruction of Sybaris, Aristotle addressed the notion of an exclusive right for those individuals who discovered something "good" for the state. Specifically, Aristotle addressed Hippodamus of Miletus, a noted city builder and contemporary of Pericles, who proposed that a law be enacted "to the effect that all who made discoveries advantageous to their country should receive honours."[25] Although prize rewards, primarily for aesthetic contributions, were common in classical Greece, Aristotle reacted negatively to Hippodamus' assertion, arguing that it would "lead to alterations to the constitution."[26] While Aristotle's

---

23. Giles S. Rich, *The "Exclusive Right" Since Aristotle*, 2 (1990) (manuscript on file with the authors). According to the intellectual property historian, F.D. Prager, it was said "that the more excellent cooks received golden crowns and other prizes usual in Greek cities." F.D. Prager, *The Early Growth and Influence of Intellectual Property*, 34 J. Pat. Off. Soc'y 106, 114, n. 17 (1952).

24. In his well researched history of American patent and copyright law, Bruce Bugbee writes that the Sybaritic law was "[w]ell-known—but apocryphal." *See* Bugbee, Genesis, *supra* note 15, at 166, n. 5. According to F.D. Prager, the Sybaritic law is a story that "was current in classic times but it was merely a joke. Even if the story was true, it was not taken seriously in the Greek cities or Hellenistic empires." Argues Prager, "[i]t seems that all this was merely in the spirit of revelry and carousing and that no 'law' was involved." Prager, *Early Growth*, *supra* note 25, at 114.

25. Aristotle, Politics II (1268a6) (Penguin Classics 1981).

26. *Id.* at 1268b22. In short, Aristotle preferred political stability, and proposals of the sort made by Hippodamus were suspect. Consider the following language in Politics:

> It is possible for people to bring in proposals for abrogating the laws or the constitution on the ground that such proposals are for the public good. [I]f we look at the other sciences, it has definitely been beneficial—witness the changes in tradition-al methods of medicine and physical training, and generally in every skill and faculty. Now since we must regard statesmanship as one of these, clearly something similar ought to apply there too. And so indeed we could claim to find some indication of that, if we look at the facts and observe how uncivilized, how rough-and-ready, the old laws were.... From these considerations it is clear that there are some occasions that call for change and that there are some laws which need to be changed. But looking at it in another way we must say that there will be need of the very greatest caution. In a

concern was with new political and social ideas and not technological discoveries, he would probably have the same suspicion of the latter because technological change can no doubt alter the political landscape; but perhaps more importantly, Aristotle viewed the "banausic" or useful arts with disdain,[27] writing that they "degrade the mind" and are unworthy of the free and thinking man.[28] Thus, although classical Greece is well known for its prominent scientists and mathematicians and certain inventions have their origins in Greece, the scientific culture placed emphasis on knowledge rather than the application or use of knowledge.[29]

In Greece, exclusive rights were debated and rejected. In classical Rome, monopolies were outlawed. The Emperor Zeno (c. 480 A.D.) proclaimed that

> [n]o one shall exercise a monopoly over any . . . material, whether by his own authority or under that of an imperial rescript heretofore or hereafter promulgated.[30]

Indeed, during the Roman period, with the exception of glassmaking, there

---

particular case we may have to weigh a very small improvement against the danger of getting accustomed to casual abrogation of the laws. . . . A man will receive less benefit from changing the law than damage from becoming accustomed to disobey authority.

Id. at 1268b22, 1268b31, 1269a12.

27. Although, it should be noted that Aristotle is credited for producing *Mechanics*, the world's first engineering text. *See* FRANCIS & JOSEPH GIES, CATHEDRAL, FORGE, AND WATERWHEEL 21 (1994).

28. *Id.* Although for different reasons, Plato too considered the "banausic" as contemptible. F.D. Prager writes:

> [Plato] took no serious interest in any promotion of what is now called the useful arts. He was expressly opposed to most of the fine arts. In his ideal state there was no room for political or industrial development; only scientific research, and that only for few. He held that every craftsman should exercise only one craft, or even part of one craft only, ... His reason for this strange view was metaphysical; he thought that in this manner the artisan might come closer to an eternal "idea" of the goods that he produced.

Prager, Early Growth, supra note 25, at 113. According to Bugbee, "Plato, who regarded the useful arts as 'base and mechanical' and the expression of 'base and mechanical handicraft' as one of reproach, assigned craftsmen and artisans to the lowest stratum of his ideal State." *See* BUGBEE, GENESIS, *supra* note 15, at 166 n. 6.

29. According to F.D. Prager:

> [Aristotle] conceded only incidentally that [Hippodamus'] plan had merits in the "arts and sciences." He hardly included the industrial arts in this concession.

> The leading philosophers considered these arts as unimportant and contemptible. In this their attitude differed radically from the modern one, and from that of the oriental "barbarians." No doubt the work of these philosophers was very constructive for the development of accurate, scientific thinking. However it was destructive for any organized promotion of the useful arts. A society where such attitudes were shown by the foremost leaders of public thought was not likely to follow the advice of Hippodamus. The advice was there, and was seriously debated, but it was clearly rejected.

Prager, *Early Growth, supra* note 24, at 113–14. *See also,* M.I. Finley, *Technical Innovation and Economic Progress in the Ancient World,* ECONOMIC HISTORY REVIEW 32 (1965) (The goal of Hellenistic scientists was "to know, not to do, to understand nature, not to tame her").

30. Prager, *Early Growth, supra* note 24, at 115.

was very little technological advancement.[31] This may be due in part to the lack of a government sponsored incentive-based system, which may have been derived from the anti-technological philosophy inherited from Aristotle and Plato.[32]

Although the ancient Greeks and Romans contributed a great deal to scientific knowledge and left a legacy of impressive structures and design,[33] they clearly did not officially recognize a property interest in intangible goods.[34] There existed no incentive-based legal regime whereby novel and significant contributions to society were encouraged.

2. European Origins

a. THE ITALIAN RENAISSANCE

The Middle Ages (500–1500 A.D.)[35] are widely considered to be a period of technological stagnation and intellectual darkness, or as Edward Gibbon wrote in his *Decline and Fall of the Roman Empire*, a society that witnessed "the triumph of barbarism and religion."[36] But recent scholars have cast this characterization into doubt, arguing that, although the Aristotelian attitude toward the useful arts remained for the most part,

---

31. *See* Gies, Cathedral, *supra* note 29, at 17 ("Nearly everything that sixth-century Europe knew about technology came to it from Rome. Rome, however, invented few of the tools and processes it bequeathed to the Middle Ages. Roman civilization achieved a high level of culture and sophistication and left many monuments, but most of its technology was inherited from the Stone, Bronze, and early Iron Ages."); *see also,* Bugbee, Genesis, *supra* note 15, at 13.

32. *See* Bugbee, Genesis, *supra* note 15, at 13 (Quoting a 20th century scholar's explanation of Rome's poor technological advancement: " 'The central government did nothing to protect Italian industry. There was no legislation in the Imperial period comparable to modern legislation concerning patents. Everybody was free to imitate, and even to counterfeit, the products of a rival.' "); *see also,* Gies, Cathedral, *supra* note 29, at 36–37 ("[F]or the most part theoretical science was underemployed by the Romans in dealing with technical problems. One explanation that had been offered blames the rhetoric-based Roman education system, which in emphasizing composition, grammar, and logical expression rather than knowledge of nature, reflected what Lynn White called 'the anti-technological attitudes of the ruling class.' Yet another problem 'was in the realm of economics.... The economy, in short, was weak in the dynamics that make for the creation and diffusion of technological innovation.' ").

33. For an account of technology and engineering during the classical period, *see* Donald Hill, A History of Engineering in Classical and Medieval Times (1984).

34. *See* Edward C. Walterscheid, *The Early Evolution of the United States Patent Law: Antecedents (Part 1)*, 76 J. Pat. & Trad. Off. Soc'y 697, 702 (1994) ("Despite occasional argument to the contrary, ancient law failed completely to recognize the concept of intellectual property. While accusations of theft and plagiarism were common in both the Greek and Roman worlds, they were almost always tied to concerns about honor, credit or fame."); *see also,* P.O. Long, *Inventions, Authorship, "Intellectual Property," and the Origin of Patents: Notes toward Conceptual History*, 32 Technology and Culture 846, 854 (1991) ("[n]either Greek nor Roman laws included any notion of intellectual property.").

35. For years the starting point of the Middle Ages has been considered to be A.D. 476, marking the formal abdication of the last Roman emperor. However, historians as of late have conceded that there is no official starting date, or for that matter, ending date, which was thought to be 1453, marking the fall of Constantinople and the end of the Hundred Years War. Therefore, we have chosen the round numbers of A.D. 500 and 1500.

36. Edward Gibbon, II Decline and Fall of the Roman Empire 1443 (Modern Library Edition).

technology was beginning to be viewed more favorably,[37] and indeed, several noteworthy technological advancements were made during the Middle Ages.[38] In an attempt to promote technological innovation within the confines of the state or to import such from abroad, several privileges, monopolies, and importation franchises were granted to local guilds or to artisans from afar in an attempt to lure them away from their home state.[39] Nevertheless, any notion of patent-like rights in inventive contributions was lacking.

It wasn't until the Renaissance, specifically Renaissance Italy, that the first true patent was issued; and the first true patent statute was enacted. The former occurred when the Republic of Florence, in 1421, issued a patent to the eminent architect and inventor, Filippo Brunelleschi, for his ship, which transported famed Carraran marble for his famous dome of the Duomo of Florence.[40] However, the granting of patents in Florence, for the most part, ended with Brunelleschi;[41] and the Italian textile guilds, reflecting the growth of commercial activity, filled the void, enacting private rules granting exclusive rights to those members of the guild who invented "certain . . . designs and patterns" of silk or wool.[42] Indeed, in the Renaissance city-states of Italy and most of Europe at that time, commerce and

---

37. *See* JOEL MOKYR, THE LEVER OF RICHES 30–56 (1990) (detailing technological advances during middle ages); NORMAN F. CANTOR, THE CIVILIZATION OF THE MIDDLE AGES 228–29 (1993) (noting technological innovations in horsepower, waterpower, and wind power); GIES, CATHEDRAL, *supra* note 29, at 13 (Middle Age thinkers were beginning to accept "technology as a part of human life, inferior to intellectual and spiritual elements but necessary and natural. Technology made life easier, freeing the mind from material concerns and supplementing man's innate powers.").

38. GIES, CATHEDRAL, *supra* note 29, at 2 ("Today . . . the innovative technology of the Middle Ages appears as the silent contribution of many hands and minds working together. The most momentous changes are now understood not as single, explicit inventions but as gradual, imperceptible revolutions—in agriculture, in water and wind power, in building construction, in textile manufacture, in communications, in metallurgy, in weaponry—taking place through incremental improvements, large or small, in tools, techniques, and the organization of work. This new view is part of a broader change in historical theory that has come to perceive technological innovation in all ages as primarily a social process rather than a disconnected series of individual initiatives.")

39. Walterscheid, *Early Evolution, supra* note 36, at 707; Prager, *Early Growth, supra* note 25, at 117–126; BUGBEE, GENESIS, *supra* note 15, at 12–17.

40. BUGBEE, GENESIS, *supra* note 15, at 17–18; M. Frumkin, *The Origin of Patents*, 27 J. PAT. OFF. SOC'Y 143, 144 (1943); *see also*, GIES, CATHEDRAL, *supra* note 29, at 254 (stating that Brunelleschi "pioneered patent protection for inventors"). *But see* Walterscheid, *Early Evolution, supra* note 35, at 707 ("While it is generally agreed that the custom of granting patents of monopoly, *i.e.*, exclusive right to practice a particular art, in return for its introduction into the state, originated in Italy, there is some question as to whether it began in Venice or in Florence.") Brunelleschi's ship, known as *Il Badalone* (the "Monster" or "water bird") never made it to Florence, sinking in the Arno River near Empoli. For details about Brunelleschi's patent, *see* http://www.stanford.edu/?broich/tamingnature/brunelleschi.htm.

41. Bugbee cites several reasons for this, including "the conflict between the Major Gilds and the Minor Gilds, a decree of 1447 limiting State-governed incentives for new crafts and technological innovations to tax exemptions alone, and the ascendancy of the Medici (and selective patronage) after 1434." BUGBEE, GENESIS, *supra* note 15, at 19.

42. *See* Long, *Inventions, supra* note 36, at 870 ("In promoting attitudes of ownership toward intangible property—craft knowledge and processes as distinct from material products—the guilds developed the concept of 'intellectual property' without ever calling it that.").

the arts were "dominated by guilds,"[43] and these private guild rules led eventually to the first known patent statute, enacted on March 19, 1474, by the Venetian Republic, which had sought to encourage technological advancement by issuing private grants and importation licenses. The statute reads:

> WE HAVE among us men of great genius, apt to invent and discover ingenious devices; and in view of the grandeur and virtue of our city, more such men come to us every day from diverse parts. Now, if provision were made for the works and devices discovered by such persons, so that others who may see them could not build them and take the inventor's honor away, more men would then apply their genius, would discover, and would build devices of great utility and benefit to our commonwealth. Therefore:

> Be it enacted that, by the authority of this Council, every person who shall build any *new and ingenious device* in this City, *not previously made* in our Commonwealth, shall give *notice* of it to the office of our General Welfare Board when it has been *reduced to perfection so that it can be used and operated*. It being forbidden to every other person in any of our territories and towns to make any further device conforming with and *similar* to said one, *without the consent and license of the author, for the term of 10 years*. And if anybody builds it in violation hereof, the aforesaid author and inventor shall be entitled to have him summoned before any magistrate of this City, by which magistrate the said infringer shall be constrained to pay him hundred ducats; and the device shall be destroyed at once. It being, however, within the power and discretion of the Government, in its activities, to take and use any such device and instrument, with this condition however that no one but the author shall operate it.[44]

Many of the basic policies, including the *quid pro quo*, underlying modern patent law regimes are present in the Venetian statute of 1474. That is, the right to exclude is bestowed upon one who discloses a useful invention to society. Remarkably, the statutory requirements set forth in the Venetian statute anticipate by nearly 400 years the requirements articulated in the first United States patent act of 1790 and subsequent acts, as well. For instance, under the Venetian patent statute, the invention must have possessed utility and novelty; and it has been argued that the phrase "ingenious device" was the precursor to our nonobviousness requirement.[45] Furthermore, the statute required that the invention be

---

43. F.D. Prager, *A History of Intellectual Property From 1545 to 1787*, 26 J. PAT. OFF. Soc'y 711, 713 (1944); *see also*, Walterscheid, *Early Evolution, supra* note 36, at 704 ("The example of glassmakers of Venice is particularly instructive. At the time of the Renaissance, Venetian glasswork was recognized as the finest in Europe.... There were detailed guild regulations covering a variety of matters, including legal workdays, election of guild officials, judicial procedures, apprenticeships, and relations between masters and patrons. Selling stolen, defective, or non-Venetian glass products was forbidden."); Prager, *Early Growth, supra* note 25, at 128 ("Over the centuries and in the different countries, the gilds differed greatly in organization and rules. Some were merely instruments of rigid state policies, mainly during times of state absolutism, like the early Middle Ages and the early modern times; others reflected an active life and technical progress of the industry.").

44. Giulio Mandich, *Venetian Patents (1450–1550)*, 30 J. PAT. OFF. Soc'y 166, 176–177 (1948) (emphasis added).

45. *Id.* at 177 ("There is reference to an 'inventive device' (*nuovo et ingegnoso artifico*); in outline, a requirement of inventive merit seems to emerge, according to which the invention must not be a trifling, all too obvious application of known technology."); *see also* Prager,

operable and to have been reduced to practice. There was also a temporal dimension to the exclusive right (*i.e.*, 10 years), and a remedy was provided to the inventor for an infringing act, whereby the inventor could obtain damages from the infringer or could have the latter's infringing device destroyed. Indeed, the Venetian statute of 1474 established a foundation for the world's first patent system and has led one historian to proclaim that "the international patent experience of nearly 500 years has merely brought amendments or improvements upon the solid core established in Renaissance Venice."[46]

Begun in Italy, the European patent custom spread rapidly throughout Europe, due largely to the migration of Venetian artisans and craftsman. As a result, "a patent system almost identical with that of Venice grew up everywhere, before 1600,"[47] including France,[48] Germany,[49] the Netherlands,[50] and England, to which we now turn.

Early Growth, supra note 25, at 139 ("[I]t was clear ... that a patent monopoly required novelty and inventive merit.").

46. BUGBEE, GENESIS, *supra* note 15, at 24. Several patents were granted since the enactment of the 1474 statute. Most notably, Galileo Galilei received a patent in 1594 for a "water-raising and irrigation device." *Id.*

47. Prager, *Early Growth, supra* note 25, at 139. *See also* MOKYR, LEVER OF RICHES, *supra* note 39, at 79 ("Although few patents were actually awarded in Venice, its example was followed widely and by the middle of the sixteenth century the idea had penetrated much of Europe"). It is not surprising that many of the initial patents issued by other European countries were to Italian artisans. *See* Walterscheid, *Early Evolution, supra* note 36, at 710; *see also* CHRISTINE MACLEOD, INVENTING THE INDUSTRIAL REVOLUTION: THE ENGLISH PATENT SYSTEM, 1660–1800, 11 (Cambridge 1988).

48. *See* Prager, *Intellectual Property from 1545 to 1787, supra* note 45, at 723. It has been asserted that the first French patent was granted in 1551 to an Italian inventor for glass making, but Bugbee argues that the grant was more of an importation franchise than a patent, and the first French patent was "probably" given to Abel Foullon in 1551 for a "rangefinder." BUGBEE, GENESIS, *supra* note 10, at 25. Of some significance is the examination procedure adopted by France in 1699 to determine the novelty of an invention. This procedure was known by America's founding fathers and not surprisingly found its way into the 1790 Patent Act. Whereas Venice had a rudimentary examination process, which was not designed for gauging the novelty of an invention, France subjected inventions to the scrutinizing eye of trained examiners under the auspices of the Royal Academy of Sciences and required inventors who received a patent to deposit a model with the Academy. The 1699 French Act stated that:

> The Academy shall, on order of the King, examine all machines for which privileges are solicited from his majesty. It shall certify whether they are new and useful. The inventors of those which are approved shall leave a model thereof.

According to Prager, however, the "basic defect" of the examination procedure was "that it was not obligatory" and "[w]hile it was usual for the king's council and also for the Parliament to consult the academy, no such consultation was strictly necessary for either." Prager, *Intellectual Property From 1545 to 1787, supra* note 45, at 725. Furthermore, even though "the academy scrutinized novelty and 'utility' of the invention, the Parliament was most interested in the competitive chances and prospective tax value of the proposed enterprise" and the technical merits were not examined exclusively. *Id.* at 726.

49. *See* Walterscheid, *Early Evolution, supra* note 36, at 711; *see also,* Hansjoerg Pohlmann, *The Inventor's Right in Early German Law,* 43 J. PAT. OFF. SOC'Y 121, 122–23 (1961); BUGBEE, GENESIS, *supra* note 15, at 26 (asserting that an "advanced patent institution flourished in the German states during most of the sixteenth century and the first three decades of the seventeenth before the destructive Thirty Years War brought its decline.").

50. It is arguable that the patent system of the Netherlands was the most advanced and sophisticated during the 16th and 17th century. *See generally,* GERARD DOORMAN, PATENTS FOR

b. ENGLISH PATENT POLICY AND THE STATUTE OF MONOPOLIES

England was not unlike its European neighbors in its attempt to attract foreign know-how to its shores and to cultivate domestic industry. During the 15th and 16th centuries, the English crown was fairly active in granting importation franchises and monopolistic privileges.[51] But this practice was abused in that it was not uncommon for the crown, specifically Queen Elizabeth I (1558–1603) and James I (1603–1625), to bestow these privileges upon such favorite courtiers as Sir Walter Raleigh.[52] It would not be long before a public outcry ensued leading to several celebrated cases by the Queen's Bench holding that monopolies were against the common law.[53] As a result, the abuses temporarily subsided, but it would not be long before the crown, namely James I, who neither possessed the political savvy nor popularity of Elizabeth I, resumed granting "odious monopolies."[54]

Invention in the Netherlands during the 16th, 17th, and 18th Centuries (The Hague 1942). As one commentator writes:

> From the very beginning of the patent custom in the [Netherlands], the States General required the applicant to clearly delineate the subject matter to be covered by the patent grant. Typically, this was done before a committee appointed for the purpose. Initially, at least, a drawing or a specification had to be submitted. The purpose of the specification, drawing, or model was not to educate the public as to the nature of the invention, but rather solely to provide evidence as to the nature of the invention for purposes of granting the patent or to indicate the nature of the patented matter in the event of later litigation.

Walterscheid, *Early Evolution, supra* note 36, at 714.

51. There were exceptions. For instance, a patent was granted to Giacopo Acontio in 1565 for "the manufacturer of wheeled mechanisms for grinding, crushing, and woodcutting operations" as well as for "furnaces for brewers and dyers." What is important to note is that the patent identified Acontio as the inventor and "source of inspiration." *See* Bugbee, Genesis, *supra* note 15, at 34–35.

52. *See* Charles Eliot Mitchell, Birth and Growth of the American Patent System 43 (1990) ("From the earliest times [in England] the right to grant exclusive privileges had been asserted as a royal prerogative. Sometimes the power had been exercised beneficently. With vastly more frequency it was employed to bring in revenue to the royal coffers. More and more, as the sovereign struggled to govern without the aid of parliament, the power was abused and perverted until, in the days of Elizabeth, monopolies were conferred upon favorites of the court, extending to the most ordinary articles of commerce and consumption."). The historian Bruce Bugbee writes that "[i]n the last twenty years of the [16th] century the Queen's habit of dispensing monopolies became notorious, although the abuses lay chiefly with the grantees. The most objectionable grants were those conferring powers of supervision or control over long-established commercial activities ([Sir Walter] Raleigh received such authority concerning wine-taverns). Also obnoxious were grants of exclusive privileges for making such commodities as salt, salt-peter, and train-oil which bore no relation to the originator or even the introducer (to the country) of the processes concerned." Bugbee, Genesis, *supra* note 15, at 37.

53. *See Davenant v. Hurdis* (1599) and *Darcy v. Allin* (1602) (This case is also known as "The Case of Monopolies").

54. W.S. Holdsworth captures nicely the abusive mind-set of James I:

> James I was always hard up; and for a consideration he was prepared to grant many privileges both of the governmental and of the industrial varieties. . . . Of the second of these varieties of grants the following are a few examples: grant of an exclusive right to export calfskins; grant of an exclusive right to import cod and ling; grant of an exclusive right to make farthing tokens of copper.

This led to yet another public outcry,[55] which ultimately culminated in Parliamentary action. In 1624, Parliament enacted the Statute of Monopolies. Section I of the statute declared all monopolies and grants as void and contrary to law; however, Section VI provided a noteworthy exception:

> Provided also, and be it declared and enacted, that any declaration before mentioned shall not extend to any Letters Patents and grants of privilege for the term of 14 years or under hereafter to be made of the sole working or making of any manner of *new* manufacture within this Realm to the true and first inventor and inventors of such manufactures which others at the time of making such letters Patents and Grants shall not use so as also they be not contrary to law nor mischievous to the State.[56]

The Statute of Monopolies is one of the most famous Parliamentary enactments and is regarded by some as the foundation of the present British patent system. However, the Statute adds very little, if anything, to the Venetian patent statute of 1474. Indeed, it can be argued that the Venetian statute is more advanced in that it provides for a procedural mechanism for obtaining patents, as well as an enforcement scheme. In this light, the Statute of Monopolies, although the first English patent statute, was not so much a statutory advancement in the area of patent law, as it was a response to royal abuses and a confirmation of the common law view that patents should be tolerated only if they serve the public good.[57] The

---

W.S. Holdsworth, *The Common Debates 1621,* in 52 LAW QUARTERLY REVIEW, 481, 487 (1936). In the wake of *Davenant* and *Darcy* (*The Case of Monopolies*), James I, although eventually resuming his proclivity for granting undeserved monopolies, did make certain concessions. For example, he suspended all monopolies with the exception of "awards to corporations and companies of arts and for promoting commerce." BUGBEE, GENESIS, *supra* note 104, at 38. He also issued a declaration called the *Book of Bounty* (1610), which affirmed monopolies were against the common law, but reserved the right to grant monopolies for new contributions. The common law also made its mark in 1615 when the Queen's Bench, in *The Cloth Workers of Ipswich Case*, held that royal grants of a limited duration for *new* manufactures were *not* against the common law.

55. H.G. FOX, MONOPOLIES: A STUDY OF THE HISTORY AND FUTURE OF THE PATENT MONOPOLY 104 (Toronto 1947).

56. Sir William Jarrett, *English Patent System*, 26 J. PAT. OFF. SOC'Y 761, 761 (1944) (emphasis added). According to Edward C. Walterscheid, Lord Coke explained that a patent for invention is valid under Section 6 if seven conditions are met:

> (1) the term of the patent may not exceed fourteen years, (2) the patent "must be granted to the first and true inventor," (3) "it must be of such manufactures, which any other at the making of such Letters Patents did not use," (4) it "must not be contrary to law," (5) it must not be "mischievous to the State by raising of prices of commodities at home," (6) it must not "hurt trade," and (7) it must not be "generally inconvenient."

Edward C. Walterscheid, *The Early Evolution of the United States Patent Law: Antecendents (Part II)*, 76 J. PAT. & TRAD. OFF. SOC'Y 849, 876–880 (1994); *see also* E. Wyndham Hulme, *The History of the Patent System Under the Prerogative and at Common Law*, 12 LAW QUARTERLY REVIEW 141 (1896).

57. *See* MACLEOD, INVENTING THE INDUSTRIAL REVOLUTION, *supra* note 49, at 1, 17–19 ("Contrary to the impression often given, this essentially negative piece of legislation was insufficient by itself to produce an institution at all capable of meeting the needs of the inventors of the industrial revolution.... Evidently, the law was little more than declaratory of preceding practice and common law.... Its importance lay in crystallization, in giving letters patent for invention statutory recognition and hence legal status;.... But in thus codifying, the Act made barely perceptible alterations in the administration of the patent

Statute of Monopolies governed English patent law for more than 200 years, and it was not until the 1852 Patent Law Amendment Act that England witnessed significant patent law legislation.

However, prior to the 1852 Act an important development did take place in English patent law: the *specification*,[58] that is "a full description of the invention and its operation which would show the scope of the patent."[59] Indeed, if we were inclined to isolate a noteworthy English contribution to patent law, it would have to be the development of the patent specification. Although the specification was part of the Continental patent systems, particularly in The Netherlands, it was England in the early 18th century who adopted it as part of patent practice. This practice culminated in the well-known case of *Liardet v. Johnson*, decided in 1778, wherein Lord Mansfield held that the "consideration" for a patent grant was the specification rather than the introduction of a new industry.[60] The role of the specification was, and still is, the dissemination of knowledge. No longer was the law only concerned with the introduction of an actual inventive device or product; rather, the inventor's contribution in the form of *information* assumed center stage. This focus on information still plays an important role in modern patent systems in that one of the primary objectives of patent law is to disseminate knowledge so that others skilled in the art can build upon and advance this knowledge.[61]

3. The American Experience

The influence of the English patent custom on American patent practice is undeniable. There were several American colonies that granted patents;[62] and Colonial patent practice, while limited, due largely to a predominantly agrarian society, influenced the subsequently developed

---

system, ..."). It should be noted that the Statute of Monopolies did not end royal abuses. As Bruce Bugbee writes, "[p]arliamentary supremacy was still a thing of the future, and monopolies did not end with the passage of the Statute." Bugbee, Genesis, *supra* note 15, at 40.

58. *See* Chapters Two and Three, *infra*.

59. Bugbee, Genesis, *supra* note 15, at 41–42 (asserting that a specification "became a standard feature of [English] patents issued after 1734"); *see also*, Doorman, Patents for Inventions in the Netherlands, *supra* note 51, at 22–23.

60. *See* Jarrett, *English Patent System*, *supra* note 58, at 762. *See also*, Edward C. Walterscheid, *The Early Evolution of the United States Patent Law: Antecedents (Part 3)*, 77 J. Pat. & Trad. Off. Soc'y 771 (1995).

61. For an excellent discussion of the role of the patent system in the Industrial Revolution, *see* H. Dutton, The Patent System and Inventive Activity During the Industrial Revolution, 1750–1852 (1984).

62. *See* Bugbee, Genesis, *supra* note 15, at 57–83; V. Clark, I History of Manufactures in the United States: 1607–1860 (1916). America's first colonial patent was issued in Massachusetts in 1641 to Samuel Winslow pertaining to the production of salt for the colony's fishing industry. The most active colonies in issuing patents were Massachusetts, Connecticut, and South Carolina. Bugbee, Genesis, *supra* note 15, at 75–83. It appears that Delaware, New Hampshire, New Jersey, and North Carolina did not issue patents. It is questionable whether Pennsylvania issued any patents during the colonial period, whereas New York, Maryland, Rhode Island, and Virginia issued a combined total of ten. Edward C. Walterscheid, *The Early Evolution of United States Patent Law: Antecedents (5 Part I)*, 78 J. Pat. & Trad. Off. Soc'y 615, 630–31 (1996). Colonial patents were issued through private bills or special enactments, not general or public statutory schemes. *Id.* at 624–25.

patent custom of the states, as well as the federal patent system. The distractions of the American Revolution discouraged notions of "inventive property" at first, but as the revolution continued, victory became less uncertain, and the Confederation witnessed a resumption of issued patents, especially during the 1780s.[63] Indeed, the demands of the Revolution coupled with colonial boycotts of British goods and notions of self-sufficiency stimulated industrial development, leading to the creation of various societies whose purpose was to encourage industry and manufacture.[64] At this increased rate of industrialization coupled with the dissimilarities of state patent customs, it was inevitable that interstate conflicts would occur, thus giving rise to the desirability of a uniform system of patents and copyrights.[65]

Therefore, in response to the driving forces of James Madison and Charles Pinckney, it was proposed, on Wednesday, September 5, 1787,[66]

---

63. In 1784, for example, South Carolina enacted the first American general patent provision, which essentially was a clause in the state's "Act for the Encouragement of Arts and Sciences." The clause read: "The Inventors of useful machines shall have a like exclusive privilege of making or vending their machines for the like term of 14 years, under the same privileges and restrictions hereby granted to, and imposed on, authors of books." BUGBEE, GENESIS, *supra* note 15, at 92–93.

64. *See* INLOW, THE PATENT GRANT 45 (1950); BUGBEE, GENESIS, *supra* note 15, at 85; Walterscheid, *Early Evolution, supra* note 64, at 632 n.80.

65. Prior to the ratification of the Constitution, there was no federal patent system. The states retained the power to issue patents because under Article II of the Articles of Confederation each state retained "every power, jurisdiction and right, which is not by the confederation expressly delegated to the United States, in Congress assembled." *See* Edward C. Walterscheid, *To Promote the Progress of Useful Arts: American Patent Law and Administration, 1787–1836 (Part I)*, 79 J. PAT. & TRAD. OFF. SOC'Y 61, 65 (1997). Furthermore, as Bugbee noted:

> In 1777, when the Articles of Confederation were drafted, patent granting was temporarily in abeyance, and the framers of the Articles made no attempt to transfer the protection of inventive property to the national scene. Had this colonial prerogative been actively exercised at the time by the newly independent states, the Articles would probably have left it to them nevertheless. By 1787, however, the granting of state patents was at a peak, and the need for a centralized system was strongly indicated by the multiple applications of competing inventors. With the emergence of a small but significant class of manufacturers and promoters stimulated by the war, the economic stakes were now considerably greater than had been the case in colonial times. The merits and shortcomings of the state patent practice were therefore clearly visible to those state legislators who were about to transmit this experience to the national scene.

BUGBEE, GENESIS, *supra* note 15, at 103. Take the famed Rumsey–Fitch steamboat dispute as an example. Both John Rumsey and John Fitch lobbied several state legislatures, each having distinct patent customs, for a monopoly for their respective steamboats.

66. The delegates convened in Philadelphia on May 14, 1787. A draft Constitution was reported on August 6 without a patent and copyright clause. However, twelve days later, on August 18, Charles Pinckney of South Carolina, who was serving in the South Carolina legislature when it enacted America's first general patent and copyright provision in 1784, proposed that Congress have the power to enact patent legislation. Also, on August 18, James Madison submitted a similar proposal. David Brearley of New Jersey, a member of the Committee of Eleven, reported to the Convention what is essentially the patent and copyright clause embodied in Article I, Section 8, Clause 8 of the Constitution. *See* BUGBEE, GENESIS, *supra* note 15, at 125–31; *see also* Karl Fenning, *The Origin of the Patent and Copyright Clause of the Constitution*, 17 GEO. L.J. 114 (1929).

during the closing days of the Constitutional Convention, that Congress shall have the power

> [t]o promote the Progress of Science and useful Arts by securing for limited Times to Authors and Inventors the exclusive Right to their respective Writings and Discoveries.[67]

This provision, embodied in Article I, Section 8, Clause 8 of the Constitution, passed unanimously without debate and provides the foundation for American patent and copyright law. Indeed, Madison, in Federalist #43, wrote that

> "[t]he utility of [Article I, Section 8, Clause 8] will scarcely be questioned. The copyright of authors has been solemnly adjudged, in Great Britain, to be a right of common law. The right to useful inventions seems with equal reason to belong to the inventors. The public good fully coincides in both cases with the claims of individuals."[68]

Of particular note is the uniqueness of the intellectual property clause among Congressionally enumerated powers. This clause is the only enumerated power to specifically set forth the means of exercising that power. Consider that pursuant to the Copyright and Patent Clause, Congress may promote the progress of the useful arts (the enumerated power) only by granting *exclusive rights* for *limited times* to *inventors* for their *discoveries*. These limitations were likely crafted in the light of the delegates' knowledge of the Statute of Monopolies.[69]

---

67. The framers, employing colonial syntax as one would expect, were respectively referring to works of authors and inventors when they used the terms "Science" and "useful Arts." In the 18th century, the term "Science," from the Latin, *scire*, "to know," meant learning or knowledge in general and had no particular connection to the physical or biological sciences like it does today. Thus, the operational relationships are between "authors," "science," and "writings" for copyright on the one hand and "inventors," "useful Arts," and "discoveries" for patents on the other. *See* Giles S. Rich, *Principles of Patentability*, in NONOBVIOUSNESS, *supra* note 1; Karl B. Lutz, *Patents and Science: A Clarification of the Patent Clause of the U.S. Constitution*, 18 GEO. WASH. L. REV. 50 (1949); John F. Kasson, *Republican Values as a Dynamic Factor*, in THE INDUSTRIAL REVOLUTION IN AMERICA 6 (1998) (noting that the term "technology" "did not acquire its current meaning until the nineteenth century." In eighteenth century usage, "technology" denoted "a treatise on an art or the scientific study of the practical or industrial arts" or "useful knowledge"). See *generally* Kenneth J. Burchfield, *Revisiting the "Original" Patent Clause: Pseudohistory in Constitutional Construction*, 2 HARV. J.L. & TECH. 155 (1989).

68. THE FEDERALIST, A COMMENTARY ON THE CONSTITUTION OF THE UNITED STATES 278–279 (The Modern Library 1937). The Supreme Court, in *Graham v. John Deere Co.*, 383 U.S. 1, 5–6 (1966), distinguished Article I, Section 8, Clause 8 from English patent custom by stressing that the Constitutional clause was both a grant of and a limitation on Congress's power to make patent policy:

> The clause is both a grant of power and a limitation. This qualified authority, unlike the power often exercised in the sixteenth and seventeenth centuries by the English Crown, is limited to the promotion of advances in the "useful arts." It was written against this backdrop of the practices—eventually curtailed by the Statute of Monopolies—of the Crown in granting monopolies to court favorites in goods or businesses which had long before been enjoyed by the public. . . . The Congress in the exercise of the patent power may not overreach the restraints imposed by the stated constitutional purpose.

69. *See* Robert Patrick Merges and Glenn Harlan Reynolds, *The Proper Scope of the Patent and Copyright Power*, 37 HARV. J. LEG. 45, 52–3 (2000) (asserting that "the constitutional footing for intellectual property protection was constructed with inherent limitations" that

Madison's fellow Virginian, Thomas Jefferson, while no stranger to the inventive process, was skeptical of monopolies and, initially, anything but a *devoteé* of the patent system.[70] Nevertheless, he came to realize the importance of patents[71] and played a prominent role in the early development of American patent law, assuming primary administrative authority of the Patent Act of 1790, America's first patent statute signed into law on April 10, 1790 by President George Washington.[72] The 1790 Act authorized the issuance of patents for "any useful art, manufacture, engine, machine, or device, or any improvement therein not before known or used."[73] The Act

"originated in British analogues that were expressly designed to eliminate rent-seeking abuses"); EDWARD WALTERSCHEID, TO PROMOTE THE PROGRESS OF THE USEFUL ARTS: AMERICAN PATENT LAW AND ADMINISTRATION, 1798–1836, 39 (1998) (noting that "it is precisely because the delegates were familiar with the Statute of Monopolies ... that they were not about to give Congress any general power to create monopolies").

70. *See* MERRILL D. PETERSON, THOMAS JEFFERSON AND THE NEW NATION 450 (1970) ("The first superintendent of patents did not fully subscribe to the principle of the system. He questioned that ingenuity is 'spurred on by the hopes of monopoly,' and thought 'the benefit even of limited monopolies ... too doubtful to be opposed to that of their general suppression.' "). This sentiment was expressed by Jefferson in response to a draft of the Constitution sent to him by Madison. Jefferson wrote:

> I sincerely rejoice at the acceptance of our new constitution by nine states. It is a good canvas, on which some strokes only want retouching. What are these, I think are sufficiently manifested by the general voice from north to south, which calls for a bill of rights. It seems pretty generally understood that this should go to ... Monopolies.... The saying there shall be no monopolies lessens the incitements to ingenuity, which spurred on by the hope of a monopoly for a limited time, as of 14 years; but the benefit even of limited monopolies is too doubtful to be opposed to that of their general suppression.

V WRITINGS OF THOMAS JEFFERSON 45, 47 (Ford ed. 1895).

71. In fact, shortly after the 1790 Act was passed, Jefferson, in a letter to Benjamin Vaughn, wrote:

> An act of Congress authorizing the issue of patents for new discoveries has given a spring to invention beyond my conception. Being an instrument in granting the patents, I am acquainted with the discoveries. Many of them indeed are trifling, but there are some of great consequence, which have been proved of practice, and others which, if they stand the same proof, will produce greater effect.

Tom Arnold, *The Historical Perspective for the Occasion of the Bicentennial of U.S. Patent Law*, in THE BICENTENNIAL OF THE AMERICAN PATENT SYSTEM 309, 317 (1990). It should be noted that there is a great deal of mythology surrounding Thomas Jefferson and his role in American patent law. *See, e.g.,* Anon, *Proceedings in Congress During the Years 1789 and 1790 Relating to the First Patent and Copyright Laws*, 22 J. PAT. OFF. SOC'Y 243 (1940); P.J. Federico, *The First Patent Act*, 14 J. PAT. OFF. SOC'Y 237 (1932). It is widely suggested by commentators that Jefferson strongly influenced the nature of the 1790 Patent Act. *See* Kendall J. Dodd, *Patent Models and the Patent Law: 1790–1880 (Part I)*, 65 J. PAT. & TRAD. OFF. SOC'Y 187, 196 (1983); Levi N. Fouts, *Jefferson the Inventor, and His Relation to the Patent System*, 4 J. PAT. OFF. SOC'Y 316, 322 (1922). *But see* Edward C. Walterscheid, *Patents and the Jeffersonian Mythology*, 29 JOHN MARSHALL L. REV. 269, 276–79 (1995) (questioning the historical scholarship on Jefferson).

72. Act of Apr. 10, 1790, ch. 7, 1 Stat. 109. Indeed, President Washington himself, in his first State of the Union Address, stated: "I cannot forbear intimating to you the expediency of giving effective encouragement, as well to the introduction of new and useful inventions from abroad as to the exertion of skill and genius at home." III Documentary History of the First Federal Congress of the United States of America, House of Representatives Journal 253 (L. G. DePauw et al. eds 1977).

73. A total of 55 patents were issued under the 1790 Act. The Patent Act of 1790 was passed on April 5, 1790, by the Congress of twelve states. Rhode Island did not join the Union

did not create a patent office, but instead designated a patent board that would *examine* patent applications, comprising a specification and drawings, to determine if "the invention or discovery [was] sufficiently useful and important" so as to merit a patent. The board, self dubbed the "Commissioners for the Promotion of the Useful Arts," comprised the Secretary of State (Thomas Jefferson), Secretary of War (Henry Knox), and the Attorney General (Edmund Randolph).[74] The first patent under the 1790 Act issued to Samuel Hopkins[75] for a method of "making Potash and Pearl ash by a new apparatus and Process."[76]

The examination system under the 1790 Act proved to be too burdensome for the three member patent board, and in 1793 a new patent act was on the books. Although the 1793 Act contained several fundamental patent law concepts that are extant today,[77] the Act did away with the patent

---

as the thirteenth state until May 29, 1790, 49 days after President Washington signed the bill. *See* Kenneth W. Dobyns, The Patent Office Pony—A History of the Early Patent Office 22 (1994).

74.   It was said of Jefferson that he "scrupulously guarded the privilege and investigated every claim to satisfy the statutory test of originality." Peterson, Thomas Jefferson, *supra* note 66, at 450. The United States was one of the first countries to enact a statute requiring patent applications to be subjected to an examination so as to ascertain the invention's usefulness and sufficiency. Other countries, most notably England, employed a registration system which is simply ministerial in nature. That is, no examination of the invention's validity or sufficiency is conducted. Although the 1790 Act incorporated parts of the common law, it was no doubt distinctly American. *See* Thomas M. Meshbesher, *The Role of History in Comparative Patent Law*, 78 J. Pat. Trad. Off. Soc'y 594, 595 (1996) ("[T]he 1790 Act was probably the most comprehensive attempt at patent codification that had been seen up to that date."); Bugbee, Genesis, *supra* note 15, at 149 ("The patent examination procedure thus inaugurated was unknown in England, but it had been foreshadowed by the examining committees established by colonial and state legislatures to study and report upon patent petitions....") For a brief, nicely written account of the board's workings, *see* Dobyns, The Patent Office Pony, *supra* note 75, at 21–29.

75.   The original patent document is part of the collections of the Chicago Historical Society. There is presently some dispute as to the origins of Mr. Samuel Hopkins, the first patentee. For years it was thought that Hopkins was from Pittsford, Vermont, but a recent article convincingly argues that he was actually from Philadelphia. *See* David W. Maxey, *Samuel Hopkins, The Holder of the First U.S. Patent: A Study of Failure*, The Pennsylvania Magazine of History and Biography 3–37 (January/April 1998).

76.   Eighteenth century potash was a form of potassium carbonate that had several industrial applications. As David Maxey writes:

> Timber felled in the clearing of land that was not used for lumber or fuel was burned in huge bonfires; the ashes were segregated and saturated with water in a trough, and the resulting mixture was subjected to intense heat in containers that Hopkins and his contemporaries more often than not referred to as pots or kettles, but which actually amounted to cauldrons because of their size. The residue in the pot was potash, a black substance that with refluxing and the application of further heat to eliminate impurities evolved into pearlash.

> One authority would put potash in a class by itself as "America's first industrial chemical." From the vast forests that covered New England and portions of New York and Pennsylvania came the raw material which, through a primitive process accessible to the enterprising farmer or the frontier storekeeper, yielded an ingredient of value in the manufacture of soap, in glassmaking, in dying fabrics, and in the production of saltpeter for gunpowder....

Maxey, *Samuel Hopkins*, *supra* note 77, at 10–11.

77.   For example, Section 6 of the 1793 Act provided an accused patent infringer with certain defenses, namely that the invention was not novel, or was not sufficiently disclosed in

board and the examination proceedings and implemented a registration system, clerical in nature, like that which existed in England.[78] Needless to say, the lack of an examination requirement attracted several fraudulent or duplicative patents.[79] The registration system lasted for 43 years, until July 4, 1836, when Congress enacted what is generally acknowledged to be the foundation of the modern patent system in the United States.[80] The 1836 Patent Act had several features, but most importantly, it reintroduced the requirement under the 1790 Act that patent applications be examined for novelty and utility.[81]

In 1850, the Supreme Court, in *Hotchkiss v. Greenwood*,[82] established what, at the time, was generally considered to be an additional patentability requirement. This requirement eventually became the modern requirement of *nonobviousness*.[83] As one commentator put it, the 1793 Act "may have been good enough for the agricultural country that founded it, but it was not sufficient for the manufacturing nation which had arisen through American ingenuity and intellect."[84] Applicants, as under the 1790 and

---

the patent specification. Other examples are the all too important "public use" or "on-sale" defenses. Lastly, the 1793 Act gave us the four statutory subject matter categories that we use today (*i.e.*, process, machine, manufacture, or composition of matter). The 1793 Act used the term "art," which meant process. The 1952 Act changed "art" to "process," and states that the term process "means process, art, or method." *See* 35 U.S.C. § 101.

78. *See* DOBYNS, THE PATENT OFFICE PONY, *supra* note 73, at 35 ("The Act of 1793 went from the extreme of rigid examination to the opposite extreme of no examination at all. The Patent Board was abolished. The State Department was to register patents, and the courts were to determine whether the patents were valid.").

79. *See* Walterscheid, *To Promote the Progress of Useful Arts*, *supra* note 66, at 73–74; BUGBEE, GENESIS, *supra* note 10, at 150–53.

80. *See* BUGBEE, GENESIS, *supra* note 14, at 152 ("With the act of 1836, the United States patent system came of age."); *see also*, Walterscheid, *To Promote the Progress of Useful Arts*, *supra* note 66, at 61.

81. As noted, the 1793 Act did away with the examination requirement of the 1790 Act which in turn led to fraudulent and duplicative patents. A Senate Report accompanying the 1836 Act cited these fraudulent or duplicative patents as some of the "evils" that existed under 1793 Act. *See* Senate Report Accompanying Senate Bill No. 239, 24th Cong., 1st Sess. (April 1836). *See also*, DONALD S. CHISUM, I CHISUM ON PATENTS OV–5–6 (1997).

82. 52 U.S. (11 How.) 248 (1850).

83. *See* Chapter 5, *supra*.

84. DOBYNS, THE PATENT OFFICE PONY, *supra* note 75, at 100. During the post-bellum era, several patent wars were being waged. For example, Elias Howe, Jr. and Isaac Merrit Singer battled over the sewing machine; Alexander Graham Bell and his telephone went up against Elisha Gray, Thomas Edison, and Emile Berliner and the phonograph; and the reaper saw Cyrus McCormick involved in a patent dispute with Obed Hussey and John H. Manny. *See* DANIEL J. BOORSTIN, THE AMERICANS: THE DEMOCRATIC EXPERIENCE 57 (1973) ("There was hardly a major invention in the century after the Civil War which did not become a legal battlefield"). Of some interest is that Abraham Lincoln was "involved" in the McCormick–Manny case. However, in his wonderful biography of Lincoln, David Herbert Donald explains that although Lincoln was retained by McCormick's eastern lawyers, they rebuffed him and treated him very rudely. DAVID HERBERT DONALD, LINCOLN 186 (1995) ("'[McCormick's] lawyers made it clear to Lincoln that he could not participate in the trial. 'We were all at the same hotel,' [George] Harding recalled; but neither he nor [Edwin McMasters] Stanton 'ever conferred with him, ever had him at our table or sat with him, or asked him to our room, or walked to or from the court with him, or, in fact, had any intercourse with him.'").

1793 Acts, were required to submit a specification, drawings, and models[85] with their application. In addition to the examination requirement, the 1836 Act, *by law,* made the Patent Office a distinct and separate bureau in the Department of State[86] and created the position of Commissioner of Patents.[87] The Act also created the present day patent numbering system[88] and allowed for a patent applicant to appeal an examiner's refusal to issue a patent. The appeal was heard by a three member board appointed by the Secretary of State.

The next major statutory revisions came in 1870 and 1952. The 1870 Act essentially retained the 1836 Act's provisions. However, it is argued that because the courts found it increasingly difficult to discover what the invention was and the distinction between new and old was sometimes blurred, the 1870 Act placed more emphasis on the importance of the patent *claim* and required the patent applicant to define the invention more distinctly.[89]

---

85. Under the 1836 Act the Commissioner of Patent was required to publicly display the models. *See* F.D. Prager, *Examination of Inventions from the Middle Ages to 1836,* 46 J. Pat. Off. Soc'y 268, 289–91 (1964). For many years, patent models were a major tourist attraction in Washington until 1880 when models were no longer required to be submitted with a patent application. Several of these models are now housed in the Smithsonian Institution where they can presently be seen. Also, Judge Giles S. Rich of the United States Court of Appeals for the Federal Circuit has assembled a handsome collection of patent models, which are on display at the Federal Circuit court house.

86. It is difficult to say when exactly the United States Patent Office was created. It was not a part of the Acts of 1790 and 1793. In 1802 Secretary of State James Madison, who was instrumental in the development of patent and copyright law during the early years of the Republic, made the Patent Office a distinct division of the Department of State by appointing the highly regarded Dr. William Thorton, the designer of the U.S. Capitol, at a salary of $1,400 a year to the full-time position of supervising the issuance of patents. Thus, one can argue that it was with this full time appointment of Dr. Thorton in 1802 that the Patent Office was created. It was the 1836 Act, however, that gave the Patent Office legitimacy in the eyes of the law. Furthermore, the 1836 Act provided for the construction of a new building to house the Patent Office. That Patent Office was completely destroyed by fire on December 15, 1836.

87. Henrey Leavitt Ellsworth (1791–1858), one of the twin sons of Justice Oliver Ellsworth, was appointed as the first Commissioner of Patents in 1836.

88. Patent Number 1 was issued to Senator John Ruggles of Maine, who was primarily responsible for the passage of the 1836 Act. Prior to 1836, patents were identified by the date they were issued. The previous name and date of patents were subsequently numbered chronologically and an "X" suffix was added to distinguish them from the new numbered patents. Thus, the first U.S. patent ever issued is number 1X. These older patents are now collectively referred to as the "X-patents"; and much historical research has been accomplished concerning the X-patents in recent years. A notable example is the excellent ongoing research of Jim Davie, et al., much of which has focused on patent drawings.

89. *See* Risdale Ellis, Patent Claims 3 (1949) (Claims under the 1836 Act "served merely to call attention to what the inventor considered the salient features of his invention. The drawing and description were the main thing, the claims were a mere adjunct thereto.... The idea that the claim is just as important if not more important than the description and drawings did not develop until the Act of 1870 or thereabouts.") *See also,* Deller, Patent Claims (2nd ed. 1971) ("Along with the development of the importance of the claim, there was another far-reaching change in the attitude of both the Patent Office and the courts as to the way in which claims should be drawn and interpreted. To appreciate this change, it is necessary to go back to the fundamental principles underlying the definition of what is new and the various modes of distinguishing what is new from what is old. Generally speaking, compliance with the requirements of the early statutes for a distinction between the new and

Before discussing the 1952 Act, a brief discussion of the Supreme Court's attitude towards patents prior to the 1952 Act will shed light on the Act itself, as well as the driving forces behind the Act.[90] From 1890 to 1930, patents were viewed favorably by the Court. But from about 1930 to 1950, the Court approached patents with a great deal of suspicion, emphasizing the monopolistic and social-cost aspects of patents. For example, the Court expanded the patent misuse doctrine (*Mercoid*),[91] did away with the common practice of drafting claims in "means plus function terms" (*Halliburton*),[92] and, most significantly, enhanced the so-called "requirement for invention" by invoking the "flash of genius" test (*Cuno*)[93] and cast doubt on the patentability of "combination" patents (*i.e.*, combination of old elements) by requiring a display of synergism (*Great Atlantic*);[94] that is, the combination, to be patentable, had to equal more than the sum of its parts. Indeed, this anti-patent fervor, led by Justices Douglas and Black, prompted Justice Jackson, in a dissenting opinion, to write that "the only patent that is valid is one which this Court has not been able to get its hands on."[95]

It was inevitable that members of the patent bar would take action. The 1952 Act, drafted primarily by Giles S. Rich, P.J. Federico, Paul Rose, and Henry Ashton, was largely a response to what was perceived to be the Supreme Court's anti-patent attitude. What did the 1952 Act, codified in Title 35 of the United States Code, accomplish? First, section 112 overturned *Halliburton's* invalidation of "means plus function" claims.[96] Second, sections 271(b), (c) and (d) overturned *Mercoid's* broad reading of the misuse doctrine with respect to contributory infringement.[97] Third, section 103 replaced the polysemous "invention" requirement with an objective standard of *nonobviousness*. The *Great Atlantic* synergism requirement and *Cuno's* "flash of genius" test were no more.[98]

---

the old was not perfect. The problem of discovering in the early patents what invention was involved was a burden which was carried by the courts and the public. The desirability of shifting this burden to the Patent Office and to the patentee himself soon became apparent."). *See* Chapter 2 for a discussion on claim drafting.

    90.   For a discussion of the Supreme Court's historical role in the development of patent law, see John F. Duffy, *The Festo Decision and the Return of the Supreme Court to the Bar of Patents*, 2002 SUP. CT. REV. 273.

    91.   *Mercoid Corp. v. Mid–Continent Inv. Co.*, 320 U.S. 661 (1944). *See also, Carbice Corp. v. American Patents Development Corp.*, 283 U.S. 27 (1931).

    92.   *Halliburton Oil Well Cementing Co. v. Walker*, 329 U.S. 1 (1946).

    93.   *Cuno Engineering Corp. v. Automatic Devices Corp.*, 314 U.S. 84 (1941).

    94.   *Great Atlantic & Pacific Tea Co. v. Supermarket Equipment Corp.*, 340 U.S. 147 (1950).

    95.   *Jungersen v. Ostby & Barton Co.*, 335 U.S. 560, 572 (1949).

    96.   *See* 35 U.S.C. § 112, ¶ 6: "An element in a claim for a combination may be expressed as a means or step for performing a specified function without the recital of structure, material, or acts in support thereof, and such claim shall be construed to cover the corresponding structure, material, or acts described in the specification and equivalents thereof." *See* Chapters Two and Nine.

    97.   *See* 35 U.S.C. § 271(d). *See* Chapter Eight.

    98.   *See* Chapter Five. For a history of section 103 of the 1952 Act, *see generally* NONOBVIOUSNESS, THE ULTIMATE CONDITION OF PATENTABILITY (John F. Witherspoon, ed., 1980). *See also* DONALD S. CHISUM, PATENTS, *supra* note 83.

The 1952 Act did a great deal to strengthen our patent system, but problems, mainly procedural in nature, remained. The Evarts Act of 1891 created geographically situated regional circuit courts of appeal. Prior to 1982, regional circuits heard patent infringement appeals from their respective district courts, as they do presently, for example, with most other criminal or civil (e.g., trademark and copyright infringement) cases. But there were large disparities among the regional circuits in the treatment patents received with some circuits viewing patents very favorably, upholding their validity a vast majority of the time, and other circuits displaying a distinct anti-patent bias. This divergent treatment of patents led to forum shopping and a greatly weakened patent system. In response, Congress, in 1982, created the United States Court of Appeals for the Federal Circuit as a unified forum for patent appeals, with the intent of strengthening the American patent system.

Giles Sutherland Rich is widely regarded as the founding father of modern patent law. After establishing a distinguished law practice in New York City, he became a principal architect of the 1952 Patent Act and played an important role in its enactment. In 1956, President Eisenhower appointed Giles Rich to the Court of Customs and Patent Appeals, and he later became a Circuit Judge on the United States Court of Appeals for the Federal Circuit when that court was created in 1982. Judge Rich remained an active member on the Federal Circuit until his death on June 9, 1999, at the age of 95.

Pasquale J. ("P.J.") Federico was the Examiner-in-Chief of the Patent & Trademark Office and one of the primary draftsmen of the 1952 Patent Act. He also played a key role in getting the Act passed in Congress. In fact, his close friend, Giles Rich, has noted that Mr. Federico was the most instrumental person in getting the 1952 Patent Act enacted into law. Mr. Federico's highly regarded and influential *Commentary on the New Patent Act* is, to this day, frequently cited by courts and commentators. The *Commentary* can be found at 35 U.S.C.A. 1 (1954 ed.), reprinted in 75 J. Pat. & Trademark Off. Soc'y 161 (1993).

4.   THE UNITED STATES COURT OF APPEALS FOR THE FEDERAL CIRCUIT

The United States Court of Appeals for the Federal Circuit ("Federal Circuit") was created by Congress in 1982 as our nation's thirteenth federal court of appeals.[99] The creation of the court has been called "perhaps the single most significant institutional innovation in the field of intellectual property in the last quarter-century."[100] As stated above, the court was created primarily in response to a spree of forum shopping in patent litigation, a lack of uniformity in our patent laws, and a high invalidity rate among litigated patents.[101] The Federal Circuit, in its short history, has had a profound effect. The court ushered in a new approach to patent validity and defenses to infringement, resulting in a significant strengthening of the patent grant[102] and a recognition by the Supreme Court of the Federal Circuit's "special expertise" in patent law.[103]

---

99.   Federal Courts Improvement Act of 1982, P.L. 97–164, 96 Stat. 25 (April 2, 1982). This Act merged the Court of Claims, which had seven judges, and the Court of Customs and Patent Appeals, which had five judges. The Federal Circuit came into existence on October 1, 1982. *See* THE UNITED STATES COURT OF APPEALS FOR THE FEDERAL CIRCUIT: A HISTORY (1991). For a discussion of some of the contested issues surrounding the creation of this new nationwide court, *see* Rochelle C. Dreyfuss, *The Federal Circuit: A Case Study in Specialized Courts*, 64 N.Y.U. L. REV. 1 (1989) and sources cited therein.

100.   LANDES AND POSNER, ECONOMIC STRUCTURE, *supra* note 4, at 7.

101.   *See* H.R. REP. No. 312, 97th Cong., 1st Sess. 20–22 (1981) ("'[S]ome circuit courts are regarded as 'pro-patent' and others 'anti-patent,' and much time and money is expended in 'shopping' for a favorable venue." Furthermore, "the validity of a patent is too dependent upon geography (*i.e.*, the accident of judicial venue) to make effective business planning possible.... A single court of appeals for patent cases will promote certainty where it is lacking to a significant degree and will reduce, if not eliminate, the forum-shopping that now occurs."); *see also* S. REP. No. 275, 97 Cong., 1st Sess. 5 (1981) ("The creation of the Court of Appeals for the Federal Circuit will produce desirable uniformity in this area of ... [patent] law. Such uniformity will reduce the forum-shopping that is common to patent litigation.").

The notion of a centralized court of appeals to promote uniformity in patent cases dates to at least 1900 when the American Bar Association's Section of Patent, Trademark and Copyright Law recommended the creation of a "Court of Patent Appeals" with national jurisdiction. See Report of the Committee of the Section of Patent, Trademark and Copyright Law, 23 ABA Rep. 543, 543 (1900).

102.   *See* Donald R. Dunner, J. Michael Jakes, and Jeffrey D. Karceski, *A Statistical Look at the Federal Circuit's Patent Decisions: 1982–1994*, 5 FED. CIRCUIT B.J. 151, 154 (1995) (The authors studied 1307 Federal Circuit cases that spanned an eleven year period (October 1, 1982 through March 15, 1994)). According to the authors, "[t]he most notable trend ... is that, in district court cases, the Federal Circuit was significantly more likely to affirm judgments in favor of patent owners than accused infringers. For example, the court affirmed validity of the patent under 35 U.S.C. § 103 [nonobvious] about 88% of the time while affirming invalidity under the same statutory section only 61% of the time.... The statistics for validity and invalidity determinations under 35 U.S.C. §§ 102 and 112 are similar. Specifically, the affirmance rate for district court holdings of validity under section 102 is 85% as compared to only 62% for invalidity under that section."). *See also* Albert E. Fey, *Fish & Neave: Leaders in the Law of Ideas*, Address at 1996 New York City Meeting of The Newcomen Society of the United States (October 23, 1996) (authored by John E. Nathan, in Newcomen Society of the United States, Pub. No. 1492, at 28–30 (1997).

103.   *Warner–Jenkinson Co. v. Hilton Davis Chem. Co.*, 520 U.S. 17, 20 (1997).

Not only did the Federal Circuit change the legal aspect of patents, but it was partly responsible for altering corporate America's view of patents. After witnessing large damage awards against infringers and upholding preliminary injunctions to protect the inventor's rights while the case was pending, corporations quickly realized that they had valuable patent assets that had been neglected.[104] Moreover, the court "has had a significant positive effect on both the number of patent applications and the number of patent grants."[105] For instance, 109,625 utility patent applications were filed in 1982 with 57,888 issuing, and 326,508 applications were filed in 2001 with 166,039 issuing.[106]

It should be noted that efforts to create a national court for patent appeals began more than 100 years before the creation of the Federal Circuit.[107] Initially, in the days before the regional circuit courts of appeals existed, the desire for a national court for patent appeals was caused by the congested docket of the Supreme Court.[108] Later, after the regional circuit courts were given appellate jurisdiction for cases arising under the patent laws, the desire for a national appellate court was caused by conflicting decisions of the courts of appeals coupled with the unwillingness of the Supreme Court to resolve these conflicts in a timely fashion.[109]

The Federal Circuit is located in Washington, D.C., but may sit any place where the other regional circuit courts may sit pursuant to 28 U.S.C. § 48(a). The court comprises twelve active circuit judges and several senior circuit judges at any given time. Unlike the regional circuit courts, the Federal Circuit has unlimited geographic jurisdiction nationwide with limited subject matter jurisdiction. As such, the court enjoys exclusive jurisdiction over cases arising "under any Act of Congress relating to patents," as well as over cases in several other areas of the law.[110]

---

104. *See* Albert E. Fey, *Fish & Neave, supra* note 104, at 28–30.

105. Landes and Posner, Economic Structure, *supra* note 4, at 340.

106. *See www.*uspto.gov. Indeed, there is a worldwide increase in patent application filings. According to a February 2003 World Intellectual Property Organization announcement, the number of international patent filings (PCT applications) from developing nations has increased from 680 in 1967 to 5,359 in 2002. India (52%), Singapore (19%), and the Republic of Korea (10%) were the top three developing countries. In the developed world, the leading countries in 2002 for international filings were the United States (39%), Germany (13%), Japan (12%), the UK (5%) and France (4%). *See* 34 Int'l Review of Indus. Prop. & Copyright L. 361, 472 (2003).

107. *See* Subcomm. on Patents, Trademarks & Copyrights, Senate Comm. on Judiciary, 85th Cong., 2d Sess., Study No. 20 (1959).

108. *Id.*

109. *See* Frank P. Cihlar, *The Court American Business Wanted & Got: The United States Court of Appeals for the Federal Circuit* 3–4 (1982). The Supreme Court, however, has been more involved in patent law over the last ten years. *See* Duffy, *Return of the Supreme Court to the Bar of Patents, supra* note 92.

110. *See* H.R. Rep. No. 312, *supra* note 103, at 19 ("The proposed new court is not a 'specialized court.' Its jurisdiction is not limited to one type of case, or even to two or three types of cases. Rather, it has a varied docket spanning a broad range of legal issues and types of cases."); S. Rep. No. 275, *supra* note 103, at 6 ("[The Federal Circuit's] rich docket assures

The Federal Circuit's jurisdiction is set forth in the 28 U.S.C. § 1295, which reads in pertinent part:

§ 1295.   Jurisdiction of the United States Court of Appeals for the Federal Circuit

(a) The United States Court of Appeals for the Federal Circuit shall have exclusive jurisdiction—

(1) of an appeal from a final decision of a district court of the United States, the United States District Court for the District of the Canal Zone, the District Court of Guam, the District Court of the Virgin Islands, or the District Court of the Northern Mariana Islands, if the jurisdiction of that court was based, in whole or in part, on section 1338 of this title, except that a case involving a claim arising under any Act of Congress relating to copyrights or trademarks and no other claims under 1338(a) shall be governed by sections 1291, 1292, and 1294 of this title;

* * *

(3) of an appeal from a final decision of the United States Court of Federal Claims

(4) of an appeal from a decision of—

(A) the Board of Patent Appeals and Interferences of the Patent and Trademark Office with respect to patent applications and interferences, at the instance of an applicant for a patent or any party to a patent interference, and any such appeal shall waive the right of such applicant or party to proceed under section 145 or 146 of title 35; or

(B) the Commissioner of Patents and Trademarks or the Trademark Trial and Appeal Board with respect to applications for registration of marks and other proceedings as provided in section 21 of the Trademark Act of 1946 (15 U.S.C. 1071); or

(C) a district court to which a case was directed pursuant to section 145 or 146 of title 35;

(5) of an appeal from a final decision of the United States Court of International Trade;

(6) to review the final determinations of the United States International Trade Commission relating to unfair trade practices in import trade, made under section 337 of the Tariff Act of 1930 (19 U.S.C. 1337);

* * *

(9) of an appeal from a final order or final decision of the Merit Systems Protection Board, pursuant to sections 7703(b)(1) and 7703(d) of title 5;

---

that the work of the ... court will be a broad variety of legal problems. Moreover, the subject matter of the new court will be sufficiently mixed to prevent any special interest from dominating it.'').

(10) of an appeal from a final decision of an agency board of contract appeals pursuant to section 8(g)(1) of the Contract Disputes Act of 1978 (41 U.S.C. 607(g)(1));

* * *

The district courts of the United States, under 28 U.S.C. § 1338, have original jurisdiction in cases relating to the patent laws:

§ 1338. Patents, plant variety protection, copyrights, trade-marks, and unfair competition

(a) The district courts shall have original jurisdiction of any civil action arising under any Act of Congress relating to patents, plant variety protection, copyrights and trade-marks. Such jurisdiction shall be exclusive of the courts of the states in patent, plant variety protection and copyright cases.

(b) The district courts shall have original jurisdiction of any civil action asserting a claim of unfair competition when joined with a substantial and related claim under the copyright, patent, plant variety protection or trade-mark laws.

The Federal Circuit's jurisdiction can be represented by the following schematic:

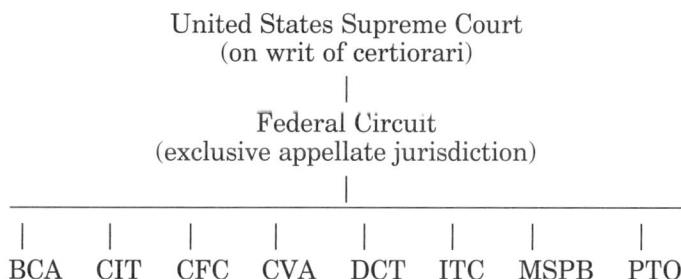

United States Supreme Court
(on writ of certiorari)
|
Federal Circuit
(exclusive appellate jurisdiction)
|

| BCA | CIT | CFC | CVA | DCT | ITC | MSPB | PTO |

Key—These eight sources of jurisdiction comprise approximately 98% of the Federal Circuit's caseload. There is one caveat: although the Federal Circuit has a diverse docket and cases on appeal from the Merit Systems Protection Board (MSPB) are reviewed by the court more frequently than any other type of case, patent law cases take up a greater percentage of the court's time, and the percentage of published opinions pertaining to patent law is significant.

1. BCA—The *Boards Of Contract Appeal* Are Administrative Adjudicative Boards That Were Created By The Contract Disputes Act Of 1978. The Various Boards Hear Cases Pertaining To Contract Disputes Between A Private Contractor And The Government (*e.g.*, Issues Relating To A Defense Contract). *See* 41 U.S.C. § 607(G)(1). The Federal Circuit Has Exclusive Jurisdiction Over Appeals From The Final Decisions Of The Boards. *See* 28 U.S.C. § 1295(a)(10).

2. CIT—The *U.S. Court Of International Trade* Is An Article III Court That Hears Cases Pertaining To, *Inter Alia*, The Classification And Valuation Of Imported Merchandise, The Exclusion Of Merchandise From Entry Into The United States Under The Customs Laws, And Issues Relating To Antidumping And Countervailing Duties. *See* 28 U.S.C. §§ 1581(A)–(i). The Federal Circuit Has Exclusive Jurisdiction Over Appeals From The Final Decisions Of The Cit. *See* 28 U.S.C. § 1295(a)(5).

3. CFC—The *United States Court Of Federal Claims* Has Jurisdiction Over "Any Claim Against The United States Founded Either Upon The Constitution, Or Any Act Of Congress Or Any Regulation Of An Executive Department Or Upon Any Express Or Implied Contract With The United States, Or For Liquidated Or Unliquidated Damages In Cases Not Sounding In Tort" (*e.g.*, Government Contracts, 5th Amendment Taking, Indian Claims, Or Tax). *See* 28 U.S.C. § 1491(a)(1) (The Tucker Act). In Connection With Its Fifth Amendment Taking Jurisdiction, Suits Against The U.S. Government For Patent And Copyright Infringement Are Brought Under 28 U.S.C. § 1498 In The CFC. The Federal Circuit Has Exclusive Jurisdiction Over Appeals From The Final Decisions From The Court Of Federal Claims. *See* 28 U.S.C. § 1295(a)(3).

4. CVA—The *U.S. Court Of Veterans Appeals* Is An Article I Adjudicative Board That Hears Cases Pertaining To Issues That Relate To Or Affect Veterans. Under 38 U.S.C. § 7292(c), The Federal Circuit Has Exclusive Jurisdiction To Review CVA Decisions And "Decide Any Challenge To The Validity Of Any Statute Or Regulation Or Any Interpretation Thereof Brought Under And To Interpret Constitutional And Statutory Provisions, To The Extent Presented And Necessary To A Decision." *See* 38 U.S.C. § 7292(C).

5. DCT—The *United States District Courts* Have *Original* Jurisdiction "Of Any Civil Action Arising Under Any Act Of Congress Relating To Patents." *See* 28 U.S.C. § 1338. The Federal Circuit Has *Exclusive* Appellate Jurisdiction Over Cases That Are "Based, In Whole Or In Part, On Section 1338 Of" Title 28. *See* 28 U.S.C. § 1295(a)(1).[111]

6. ITC—The *International Trade Commission* Has Jurisdiction Over Cases Pertaining To Matters Of Unfair Competition, Specifically Issues Relating To The Importation Of Merchandise That Would "Destroy Or Substantially Injure An Industry In The United States;" Or "Prevent The Establishment Of Such An Industry;" Or "Restrain Or Monopolize Trade And Commerce In The United States" Or Infringe A "Valid And Enforce-

---

111. With respect to the words "arising under" in § 1338, the Supreme Court held that the Federal Circuit's appellate jurisdiction should extend "only to those cases in which a well-pleaded complaint establishes either that federal patent law creates the cause of action or that the plaintiff's right to relief necessarily depends on resolution of a substantial question of federal patent law, in that patent law is a necessary element of one of the well-pleaded claims." *Christianson v. Colt Indus. Operating Corp.*, 486 U.S. 800, 809 (1988). Moreover, the Court has held that the Federal Circuit does not have appellate jurisdiction in cases where the complaint itself does not alleged a claim arising under the federal patent law, even though there is a patent law counterclaim set forth in the answer. *See Holmes Group, Inc. v. Vornado Air Circulation*, 535 U.S. 826, 829 (2002) ("the Federal Circuit's jurisdiction is fixed with reference to that of the district court, and turns on whether the action arises under federal patent law").

able United States Patent." *See* 19 U.S.C. § 1337(A)–(D). The Federal Circuit Has Exclusive Jurisdiction Over Appeals From A Final Decision Of The ITC. *See* 28 U.S.C. § 1295(a)(6).

7. MSPB—The *Merit Systems Protection Board* Is An Administrative Adjudicative Board That Was Created By The Civil Service Reform Act Of 1978. The Board Hears Cases Pertaining To Labor Relations Between Federal Agencies And Their Employees (*e.g.*, When An Employee Is Dismissed Or Disciplined For Misconduct). The Federal Circuit Has Exclusive Jurisdiction "Of An Appeal From A Final Order Or Final Decision" Of The Mspb. *See* 5 U.S.C. § 7703(b)(1) And 28 U.S.C. § 1295(a)(9).

8. PTO—The *Patent And Trademark Office* Has Two Administrative Adjudicative Boards, The Trademark Trial And Appeals Board (Ttab) And The Board Of Patent Appeals And Interferences (Bpai), That Hear Cases Relating To, *Inter Alia*, The Registerability Of Trademarks And The Patentability Of Inventions, Respectively. When Either Of These Boards Denies An Applicant A Trademark Registration Or A Patent, The Applicant May Appeal The Respective Board's Decision To The District Court Or Directly To The Federal Circuit. *See* 28 U.S.C. §§ 1295(a)(4)(B) and 1295(a)(4)(C).[112]

SIDE BAR

The Creation of the Federal Circuit

The Honorable Gerald J. Mossinghoff[*]

The Court of Appeals for the Federal Circuit was established in 1982 in a bipartisan effort to bring certainty and stability to U.S. patent law. Based upon a key recommendation of President Carter's Domestic Review of Industrial Innovation, a centralized national court with exclusive appellate jurisdiction over patent-related cases was viewed in that Review as "a vehicle for ensuring a more uniform interpretation of the patent laws and thus contributing meaningfully and positively to predicting the strength of patents."[1]

One of my highest priorities as a newly appointed Commissioner of Patents and Trademarks in 1981 was to make sure that the Reagan Administration would support that initiative of the Carter Administration. That was by no means assured given the strong opposition of the American Bar Association to the creation of such a "specialized" federal court.

At that time I was teaching patent law at the American University's Washington College of Law and was all too familiar with the chaotic situation that business executives and their counsel faced in deciding how—and most significantly *where*—to enforce their patents. A leader in the research-based pharmaceutical industry summed up that industry's

---

112. With respect to patents only, and instead of appealing directly to the Federal Circuit, an applicant may bring suit against the PTO to obtain the patent in the United States District Court for the District of Columbia. *See* 35 U.S.C. §§ 145–146. Either party may appeal to the Federal Circuit.

support for the Federal Circuit quite succinctly: "to eliminate geography-dependent patent opinions."[2]

The Reagan Administration did strongly support the creation of the Federal Circuit based principally upon the recommendation of then-Secretary of Commerce, the late Malcolm Baldridge. Having served as the very successful Chief Executive of Scovill Industries, Secretary Baldridge often expressed the view that successful business executives are able to "manage around" adversity; they cannot handle uncertainty. And as the several federal circuits drifted farther and farther apart in their interpretations of key sections of the patent code, the inevitable uncertainty actually called into question the viability of an effective U.S. patent system for protecting new technology.

The story is told of then-Second Circuit Court of Appeals Judge Thurgood Marshall when he was visiting Senators in preparation for his confirmation hearing as President Johnson's nominee to the Supreme Court. One well-known Senator asked Judge Marshall what his views were on patents. The Judge reportedly responded, "I haven't given patents much thought, Senator, because I'm from the Second Circuit and as you know we don't uphold patents in the Second Circuit."

The beneficial results of the creation of the Federal Circuit were immediate and felt throughout America's high-technology industries. Forum shopping—or more accurately *circuit* shopping—is a thing of the past. Although in no field of law as dynamic as patent law can there be 100% assurance of the outcome of any case, business executives and their counsel can now look to a coherent and consistent body of case law to guide their fundamental research and development decisions. I now teach patent law at the George Washington University School of Law and the course is entirely different from that which I taught in the late 1970s and early 1980s, thanks to the creation of the Federal Circuit. Then the analysis of most patent issues would depend on what federal circuit one would assume would decide the case, and such an assumption would often be more significant than the facts themselves.

The Reagan Administration can be justly proud of its many achievements in fostering the creation of new technology by enhancing intellectual property protection. But, in my view, no achievement compares in importance with the creation of the Court of Appeals for the Federal Circuit.

* Former Assistant Secretary of Commerce and Commissioner of Patents and Trademarks; currently Senior Counsel to Oblon, Spivak, McClelland, Maier & Neustadt, P.C., Arlington, Virginia. The views expressed herein are solely those of the author and do not necessarily reflect those of the firm or its clients. This *SIDE BAR* was written specially for PRINCIPLES OF PATENT LAW.

1. Hearings on H.R. 6033, H.R. 6934, H.R. 3806 and H.R. 2414 before the Subcommittee on Courts, Civil Liberties and the Administration of Justice, House Committee on the Judiciary, page 797, 96th Cong., 2d Sess. (1980).

2. Statement of Dr. P. Roy Vagelos, then-President, Merck, Sharp & Dohme Research Laboratories, Hearings on H.R. 6033, H.R. 6934, H.R. 3806 and H.R. 2414, *supra* note 2, at page 72.

The Federal Circuit: Judicial Stability or Judicial Activism?

Judge Pauline Newman.
42 Am. U. L. Rev. 683 (1993).

These annual reviews of the jurisprudence of the United States Court of Appeals for the Federal Circuit nicely show the evolution of several important and complex areas of law. Some of this law is of critical importance to the nation's industry, particularly the patent, international trade, and government contract law. Other law assigned to the Federal Circuit serves additional national interests: constitutional takings law; childhood vaccine injuries; veterans appeals; customs law; trademark registration; federal employment law; Native American claims; tax and other claims against the Government; and the newly transferred jurisdiction of the Temporary Emergency Court of Appeals.

Remembrance of the Past

Critical review requires a return to the time of formation of the Federal Circuit, lest we forget the reasons for the judicial restructuring that established this court. These reasons illuminate the court's role in the judicial system, and indeed allow me to presume to the personal role of critic, drawing on my participation during the creation of the court, my knowledge of the problems that this new judicial structure was intended to solve, and my active support for its purposes.

This history has been much explored during this tenth anniversary of the Federal Circuit. It places a spotlight on the court, focused on the national needs that brought it into being. Any examination of the jurisprudence of the Federal Circuit is not complete without evaluation of the extent to which the court has fulfilled the purposes for which it was formed. In brief summary, two distinct paths led to the formation of the Federal Circuit. On one hand there was the growing interest, after a succession of studies of federal judicial structure, in the theory of a national court at the appellate level. This interest is traceable through the studies of the Freund Committee in 1972, the Hruska Commission in 1975, and the studies led by Professor Meador in 1978. In each of these studies, the theoretical benefits of having some form of national court were viewed primarily as providing relief to the Supreme Court, and were countered by a variety of perceived problems. It was not until the coincidence of the Domestic Policy Review of Industrial Innovation, conducted by the Carter administration in 1978–79, that there arose an additional and ultimately controlling reason for establishing a national appellate court. The forceful concern of the nation's technological leadership about the effect on industrial innovation of judge-made patent law brought a new constituency to the rarefied precincts of judicial structure.

The interest of industry was the restoration of the patent system's constitutional and statutory incentive to promote technological progress. That incentive had been diminished by the inconsistencies of judge-made law concerning patent rights and remedies. The concept of a national court that would be free of inter-circuit differences, and thereby provide a stable body of law upon which reliance could be placed by inventors and investors, was intended as a solution to a problem of practical importance to the nation.

Thus the twofold purpose of this novel judicial structure included the experimental one, whereby a national appellate court would receive appeals from all of the district courts of the nation, accompanied by the intended stabilizing effect of this structure on the law supporting industrial innovation. Both of these aspects were premised on the court's patent jurisdiction, for most of the other areas of the Federal Circuit's jurisdiction were already well handled by the two national courts that were melded into the Federal Circuit. The existing jurisdictions of the Court of Customs and Patent Appeals and the Court of Claims, to which had been added appeals from the Merit Systems Protection Board, provided about eighty percent of the Federal Circuit's caseload. The remaining twenty percent were the appeals, transferred from the regional circuit courts, of all cases tried in the district courts under the patent law and the Little Tucker Act.

The idea was ambitious yet simple: the idea that consistent application of the law, achieved by eliminating the opportunity for forum-shopping, would have a direct and salutary effect on industrial innovation, and thereby on the nation's technological strength and international competitiveness. Patent rights are a factor in much of the research, investment, and commercial risk-taking that comprise industrial innovation; yet the marked variations among judicial patent decisions in the regional circuits suggested to the technology community that this aspect was not always well understood.

The shaping of the patent law is to an exceptional degree in the hands of the judiciary, for in patent cases a relatively simple statutory law is applied to an extraordinary complexity of factual circumstances. These encompass the entire range of mechanical, electronic, biological, and chemical subject matter. The entrepreneurial and creative vigor of the nation's technology is metered by the system of laws governing patents. Review of the history of patent law over the economic cycles of the nation, indeed over the nation's evolution from an agricultural to an industrial economy, shows the judiciary reflecting in its patent decisions a variety of perceptions of the place of patents in the nation's economy. Although there was often manifest prescience and great wisdom, increasingly, mirroring society, there appears to have been a failure of the "two cultures" of law and science to understand each other. Today we cannot afford this gap, for scientific and technologic issues underlie large segments of modern jurisprudence, as well as of our economy. As remarked by Professor Teece, "The United States today depends critically on its ability to innovate—and to capture the benefits from invention—for its economic prosperity."

The Federal Circuit was born in the recessive economic period of the late 1970s, and was charged with the expectation that correct and wise judicial application of patent law would support technological innovation, as the law was intended to do, thereby contributing to capital formation and the industrial activity that is the foundation of our nation's economic and political strength. It is not easy to measure the impact of this change in judicial structure, and accompanying changes in jurisprudence, on industrial innovation. I have seen no definitive economic study, and perhaps none is possible, for the nation's economy is not a controlled experiment. However, it is possible to compare the state of patent law today with that of a decade ago, and to evaluate the extent to which the Federal Circuit fulfills these expectations and hopes.

In the first few years of its existence the court resolved major differences among the regional circuits. In decisions of exemplary fidelity to the constitutional and legislative purposes of the patent law, drawing upon the mixture of economic theory and technological practicality that coalesce in the patent law, the Federal Circuit retrieved the law from much of the arcana with which it had been burdened in recent decades. For the first time in many years, the same law was routinely applied in review of patentability in the Patent and Trademark Office and review of patent validity in litigation, because these appeals now resided in the same court. The practical importance of this step is manifest when one considers that over 150,000 patent applications are processed annually by the patent examining system, yet each patented invention that is successful in the marketplace is subject to second-guessing in the courts.

In its early decisions the Federal Circuit returned the patent law to its jurisprudential roots. For example, the measure of recovery for patent infringement was restored to the classical damages principle of making the wronged party whole. The court eliminated special rules such as synergism, and clarified many of the rules of patentability. The court removed many of the artifices and doctrines that had puzzled inventors and confounded jurists. The growing number of jury trials in turn required lawyers and judges to demystify the law. Patent law was placed in the perspective of the marketplace: the destination contemplated in the Constitution.

Patent law is a living law, and the court has advanced the jurisprudence at a rate that would have been impossible were not all appeals concentrated in one court. In so doing, the principles of stare decisis have occasionally been overtaken. This counsels caution, for the value of the court depends on the success with which it provides a stable and consistent law on which the technology community can rely. The most important value of the rule of law is in the provision of a stable and reliable framework for behavior, and the avoidance of litigation.

Patent law is practiced mainly through legal advice and counseling over the course of the commitment of creative and capital resources, to manage legal risk in the already risky business of industrial innovation. Like all commercial law, the cost of guessing wrong about the law and its application is rarely recoverable. The responsibility placed on the Federal Circuit mirrors that placed on all courts, for a useful and reliable law requires that the law is known and knowable. In testifying on behalf of supporters of the court, I said

> [a] centralized court that understands the processes of invention and innovation, and the economic and scientific purposes of a patent system, would be expected to apply a more consistent interpretation of the standards of patentability and the other complex provisions of the patent statute. With a consistent nationwide application of the law, I would hope for and expect a greatly enhanced degree of predictability of the outcome of patent litigation. The predictability that patents improvidently granted will

be held invalid is of no less interest to us as manufacturers and purveyors of goods than the predictability that patents will be held valid if they represent proper protection of a valuable investment in innovative technology. As in all contested situations, a more predictable outcome may encourage the contestants to avoid litigation: the rules of law need not be challenged daily, to reinforce the rule of law. Indeed, unless there can be reasonable reliance on legal advice given during the stages of invention and innovation, unless that advice can correctly predict the legal principles to be applied by the court, the court is not fulfilling its obligations to the public.

Although I have concentrated on the Federal Circuit's patent jurisdiction because of its role in the court's origin, I do not mean to slight our other areas of jurisdiction, for they are not slighted in our daily concern. These areas involve questions of complexity and importance; each field of law requires stability and predictability; and all receive the court's careful attention. All merit critical review, in terms both of the evolution of the law of the Federal Circuit, and in evaluation of the judicial structure to which they are entrusted.

A Caution for the Future

In law, as in science, the most profound of theories is usually the simplest. Simplification requires, demands, the deepest and truest understanding of basic principles; complexity reflects, more often than not, an insufficiency of understanding. The Federal Circuit in its most effective opinions simplified the law so that judges and lawyers, inventors and juries, could understand it and use it. I caution against a retrenchment from that elegant simplicity, into a policy-driven activism whereby the application of the law will not be known until the Federal Circuit hears the case.

The Federal Circuit has been shielded, by its diverse jurisdiction and the breadth of experience of its judges, from the pitfalls of a "specialized" court wherein a cadre of experts, secure in its superior knowledge of the policy that the law should serve, comes to view itself as judge, advocate, and jury. Caution is needed lest our increasing maturity expose us to this pitfall. It is policy choices that lead to departure from precedent, into the judicial activism that weighs against legal stability. Although all judicial decisions reflect, to some degree, the judge's personal predilections, policy choices are not the province of judges. The nature of worldwide competition has changed dramatically, and the need to attune our laws to economic reality is greater than ever. I urge participation of the bar and the interested public in the direction of all of the areas of law assigned to the Federal Circuit. Working together, I am confident that the Federal Circuit will continue to meet its responsibilities with distinction.

NOTES

1. The push to re-strengthen the patent system that culminated in the 1982 Act was very much bi-partisan. It was signed into law by President Reagan but was the direct result of a serious effort launched by President Carter. Pauline Newman, *The Federal Circuit in Perspective*, 54 AM. U. L. REV. 821, 822–23 (2005). By 1978, when the economy had reached such serious disarray, President Carter through his Commerce Department empanelled a group of experts to conduct what was called a

"Domestic Policy Review" to study domestic innovation. Their key findings focused on the destructive impact on commercializing innovation and economic growth caused by unpredictability in the patent system; and their chief recommendations included strengthening the patent system through the increased predictability that could be implemented through a new court. *See generally* Indus. Subcomm. for Patent & Info. Policy, Advisory Comm. on Indus. Innovation, Report on Patent Policy 155 (1979).

2.   The centralization of appellate power for patent cases has raised several issues regarding appellate procedure. One issue of particular importance concerns the net impact of this uniform forum for patent appeals and on patents themselves, generally speaking. This topic has been the focus of several noteworthy studies. *See e.g.,* Donald R. Dunner, J. Michael Jakes, Jeffrey D. Karceski, *A Statistical Look at the Federal Circuit's Patent Decisions,* 5 FED. CIR. B.J. 151 (1995); John R. Allison and Mark A. Lemley, *How Federal Circuit Judges Vote in Patent Validity Cases,* 27 FLA. ST. U. L. REV. 745 (2000); Kimberly A. Moore, *Are District Court Judges Equipped to Resolve Patent Cases,* 15 HARV. J.L. & TECH. 1 (2001); R. Polk Wagner and Lee Petherbridge, *Is the Federal Circuit Succeeding? An Empirical Assessment of Judicial Performance,* 152 U. PA. L. REV. 1105 (2004).

3.   How much deference should the court grant various decision-making bodies it reviews? What deference should be given to a finding of fact by a district court judge, jury, or member of the PTO? *See Dickinson v. Zurko,* 527 U.S. 150 (1999). What deference should be given to conclusions of law by the same players? *See Merck & Co. v. Kessler,* 80 F.3d 1543 (Fed.Cir.1996). *See also* Chapter Two, section B.3, *infra.*

4.   How should the lower tribunals, or components thereof, make decisions so they are accessible for review? To what extent to these tribunals have an incentive to make their own decisions reviewable, or non-reviewable? To what extent do the parties have the same or different incentives? What role should the Federal Circuit have in ensuring reviewability? *See Gechter v. Davidson,* 116 F.3d 1454 (Fed.Cir. 1997). What role should attorneys themselves assume?

SIDE BAR

A Non–Statistical Look at the Federal Circuit's Patent Decisions: 1982–1998

Donald R. Dunner*

During the deliberations that led to the formation of the Court of Appeals for the Federal Circuit, the bulk of the concerns expressed by the participants in the legislative process centered around the need for more uniformity in the application of the patent laws. Proponents of the proposed new court felt, needless to say, that a single appellate court to which all appeals under the patent laws would go would inevitably result in decisional uniformity and eliminate the rampant forum shopping that had pervaded the conduct of patent infringement litigation.

The proposed new court, however, was not without its detractors. Opponents of the court were concerned that appointees to what the regarded as a non-mainstream, "specialized" court would become parochial in its views, ultimately creating a bias either too much in favor of or against the patent owner. Still others expressed concerns that this new court by its very nature would attract lower-quality judges, perhaps serving as a dumping ground for political has-beens or the like.

Conventional wisdom is that the fears of those opposed to the court that became the Federal Circuit were greatly exaggerated. While studies such as that preceding this *SIDE BAR*[1] might be urged to support the notion that the Federal Circuit is pro-patent, that study by its own terms suggests that the results are mixed. Moreover, students of the court know that the court in recent years has been tightening up significantly on the scope of the doctrine of equivalents[2] as was as expanding the reach of prosecution history estoppel,[3] a double whammy militating against the interests of patent owners.

Nor can anyone seriously criticize the quality of the appointments to the Federal Circuit. Indeed, the eleven active judges on the court are all exceedingly bright and hardworking and include two former Supreme Court law clerks; three former patent lawyers (two of whom have Ph. D.'s), two former federal trial judges, and one former law school professor and dean.

How has the Federal Circuit fulfilled the expectations of its proponents? To be sure, the bulk of the pre-Federal Circuit world has changed for the better. Wide variations in the application of the patent law have diminished, as have the number of unresolved conflicts in patent law. And while litigants still shop for the best and friendliest venue, there is not widespread forum shopping that existed pre-Federal Circuit.

There is, however, a new problem: The recently increasing lack of predictability in Federal Circuit decision-making. As the individual Federal Circuit judges have gained judicial experience and increased their comfort levels on the court, they have increased their levels of confidence in and their inclination to advance more forcefully their own views. Since a number of Federal Circuit judges have widely differing views on a number of patent-related topics, decision-making has become highly panel-dependant, even within the confines of the Federal Circuit jurisprudence that compels a given panel to follow the dictates of prior panel and in banc decisions of the court.[4] The end result of this and other factors has been a significant recent increase in the uncertainty of the Federal Circuit judicial process, which—while not nearly as troublesome as the pre-Federal Circuit state of affairs—is not helpful to the court's constituency in its quest for reasonable predictability in its own decision-making process.

Hopefully texts such as this will highlight such problems as they put the spotlight on the court's prodigious legal output. Fortunately, that output has come much closer to fulfilling the dreams of the court's advocates than the fears of its detractors.

* Partner in the firm of Finnegan, Henderson, Farabow, Garrett, & Dunner, L.L.P., resident in the Washington, D.C. office. Former: President of the American Patent Law Association (now American Intellectual Property Law Association), Chair of the ABA Section on Intellectual Property Law, and Chair of the Federal Circuit Advisory Committee. Former law clerk to the Honorable Noble J. Johnson, United States court of Customs and Pat-ent Appeals, predecessor court to the United States Court of Appeals for the Federal Circuit. The views expressed herein are solely the views of the author and do not necessarily reflect those of the firm, the firm's clients, or any other of the listed affiliated organizations. This *SIDE BAR* was written specially for PRINCIPLES OF PATENT LAW.

1. Donald R. Dunner et al., *A statistical Look at the Federal Circuit's Patent*

Decisions: 1982–1994, 5 FED. CIR. B.J. 151 (1995).

2. *See Hilton Davis Chem. Co. v. Warner–Jenkinson Co.*, 62 F.3d 1512 (Fed. Cir.1995) (in banc), *rev'd on other grounds*, 520 U.S. 17 (1997); *Sage Prods., Inc. v. Devon Indus., Inc.*, 126 F.3d 1420 (Fed.Cir.1997).

3. *See Hoganas AB v. Dresser Indus., Inc.*, 9 F.3d 948, 951–53 (Fed.Cir. 1993).

4. *South Corp. v. United States*, 690 F.2d 1368 (Fed.Cir.1982).

Having discussed the history of patent law, we can now ask: what are the philosophical justifications for creating and recognizing property rights in intellectual goods?

B. PHILOSOPHY OF PATENT LAW

Given James Madison's comments in Federalist #43 discussed above, two alternative purposes of Article I, Section 8, Clause 8 have been postulated. One purpose is *consequentialist*[113] or *utilitarian* in nature. This view stems from the Constitutional language "to promote ... the useful Arts." Under this view, the focus is on the consequences the patent law has on the overall public welfare. The second purpose is *deontological*[114] or *natural rights*-based. This view stems from the Constitutional language "securing" rights. Under this view, the rights of inventors are of primary importance, and the patent law exists to protect these rights, irrespective of the consequences the grant of the patent would have on the public welfare. This view is primarily associated with the philosophy of John Locke and G.W.F. Hegel.[115] In this section, we will explore this apparent dual nature of the patent and copyright clause of the Constitution and the various philosophical theories underlying intellectual property.

1. LOCKEAN LABOR THEORY AND NATURAL RIGHTS

The 17th century English philosopher, John Locke (1632–1704), has profoundly influenced our conception of property, particularly how one justifies private ownership. Locke, in his *Two Treatises of Government*

---

113. Consequentialism holds that "all actions are right or wrong in virtue of the value of their consequences." THE OXFORD COMPANION TO PHILOSOPHY 154 (Honderich ed. 1995).

114. Denotology posits that "certain acts are right or wrong in themselves" regardless of their consequences. *Id.* at 187.

115. The philosophy of Hegel as applied to intellectual property is primarily employed in the context of copyright law. Therefore, we thought it best to omit Hegel from the section on the Philosophy of Patent Law. Hegel's philosophy of property is referred to as the "personality theory," which is concerned with "self-actualization," "personal expression," and "notions of dignity." Professor Margaret Radin has described this theory as the "personhood perspective." *See* MARGARET JANE RADIN, REINTERPRETING PROPERTY (1993). One can see how the personality theory has a certain appeal to those concerned with justifying intellectual property, particularly copyright law. The works of both Hegel and Kant were very influential in Continental Europe with respect to copyright law, whereas United States copyright doctrine has drawn more from classical utilitarianism. *See* Neil Netanel, *Copyright Alienability Restrictions and the Enhancement of Author Autonomy: A Normative Evaluation*, 24 RUTGERS L.J. 347, 365 (1993).

(1690),[116] focused on how one can justify having a private property interest in any thing. He answered this question by linking natural rights to a theory of property. Let us review his theory of property before examining its application to intellectual property.

Locke started from the basic natural law proposition that God gave the "world to men in common."[117] This, however, begs the question: How could the existence of a common lead to private ownership? Is the consent of each and every commoner required? Recognizing the impracticality of such consent, Locke's solution was to assert that "every Man has a 'property' in his own 'person' and the 'labour' of his body and the 'work' of his hands, we may say, are properly his."[118] Thus, because one owns his "labour,"

> Whatsoever, then, he removes out of the state that Nature hath provided and left it in, he hath mixed his labour with it, and joined to it something that is his own, and thereby makes it his property. It being by him removed from the common state Nature placed it in, it hath by this labour something annexed to it that excludes the common right of other men.[119]

Locke does impose two conditions on his theory of property. First, Locke states that one's labor leads to a property interest only "where there is enough, and as good left in common for others."[120] The other condition is Locke's non-waste proviso. Accordingly, "[a]s much as any one can make use of to any advantage of life before it spoils, so much he may by his labour fix a property in. Whatever is beyond this is more than his share, and belongs to others."[121]

But, we may ask, what is it about "labour" that justifies the acquisition of private ownership? Locke links labor and property by invoking natural law or God. According to Locke, God gave the earth to "men in common" for "their benefit and the greatest conveniences of life they were capable to draw from it."[122] Therefore,

> it cannot be supposed He meant it should always remain common and uncultivated. He gave it to the use of the industrious and rational (and labour was to be his title to it); not to the fancy or covetousness of the

---

116.   JOHN LOCKE, *Second Treatise on Civil Government*, in TWO TREATISES OF GOVERNMENT (Prometheus Books 1986) (hereinafter *Second Treatise*). All references are to Locke's numbered paragraphs in his *Second Treatise on Civil Government*.

117.   *Second Treatise*, Chapter V at ¶ 25. According to Locke:

The earth and all that is therein is given to men for the support and comfort of their being. And though all the fruits it naturally produces, and beasts it feeds, belong to mankind in common, as they are produced by the spontaneous hand of Nature, and nobody has originally a private dominion exclusive of the rest of mankind in any of them, as they are thus in their natural state, yet being given for the use of men, there must of necessity be a means to appropriate them some way or other before they can be of any use, or at all beneficial, to any particular men.

118.   *Id.* at ¶ 26.

119.   *Id.*

120.   *Id.*

121.   *Id.* at ¶ 30. Although we need not go into it for our purposes, it is worth mentioning that, with respect to the non-waste proviso, Locke recognized that a money economy may lead to an accumulation of non-perishable wealth. *Id.* at 45, 49.

122.   *Id.* at ¶ 33.

quarrelsome and contentious. [F]or it is labour indeed that puts the difference of value on everything.[123]

We can now examine how Locke's natural rights philosophy applies to intellectual property, particularly patent law, but first let's summarize Locke's justification for private ownership:

(1) God gave the earth to people in common;

(2) Every person has a property interest in their own person;

(3) Every person owns their own labor;

(4) Whenever a person mixes their labor with something in the common they make it their property;

(5) The right to private ownership is conditional upon a person leaving in the common enough and as good for the other commoners; and

(6) A person cannot remove more out of the commons that they can make use of.[124]

Although Locke never discussed intellectual property, several scholars have applied Locke's natural rights labor-theory to intellectual property.[125] Most of the scholarship has focused on Locke's conception of labor in the context of intellectual property regimes and whether an inventor has an inherent right to the fruits of her labor. Consider the following excerpt.

The Philosophy of Intellectual Property*

Justin Hughes.
77 GEO. L.J. 287 (1988).

We can justify propertizing ideas under Locke's approach with three propositions: first, that the production of ideas requires a person's labor; second, that these ideas are appropriated from a "common" which is not significantly devalued by the idea's removal; and third, that ideas can be made property without breaching the non-waste condition. Many people implicitly accept these propositions. Indeed, the Lockean explanation of intellectual property has immediate, intuitive appeal: it seems as though people *do* work to produce ideas and that the value of these ideas— especially since there is no physical component—depends solely upon the individual's mental "work."

---

123. *Id.* at 33, 40.

124. This summary was taken from PETER DRAHOS, A PHILOSOPHY OF INTELLECTUAL PROPERTY 43 (1996).

125. *See e.g.,* Justin Hughes, *The Philosophy of Intellectual Property*, 77 GEO. L.J. 287, 296–330 (1988); Wendy Gordon, *A Property Right in Self–Expression: Equality and Individualism in the Natural Law of Intellectual Property*, 102 YALE L.J. 1533 (1993); Edwin C. Hettinger, *Justifying Intellectual Property*, 18 PHIL. & PUB. AFF. 31 (1989); Lawrence C. Becker, *Deserving to Own Intellectual Property*, 68 CHI-KENT L.REV. 659 (1993).

B.   Labor and the Production of Ideas

* * *

Of course, there are some instances in which ideas seem to be the result of labor: the complete plans to a new suspension bridge, the stage set for a broadway show, a scholar's finished dissertation involving extensive research, or an omnibus orchestration of some composer's concertos. The images of Thomas Edison inventing the light bulb and George Washington Carver researching the peanut come to mind as examples of idea-making. As society has moved toward more complicated technologies, the huge scales of activity required by most research, involving time, money, and expertise, have made the autonomous inventor a rarity. This trend strengthens the image of idea-making as labor akin to the mechanical labor that operates industrial assembly lines.

Yet as we move toward increasingly large research laboratories that produce patentable ideas daily, we should not be so entranced by the image of a factory that we immediately assume there is labor in Silicon Valley. Locke, after all, begins his justification of property with the premise that initially only our bodies are our property. Our handiwork becomes our property because our hands—and the energy, consciousness, and control that fuel their labor—are our property. The point here is . . . that Locke linked property to the product of the individual person's labor. We must examine the production of ideas more fully if we expect to show that their creation involves Lockean labor.

1.   The "Avoidance" View of Labor

* * *

[L]abor . . . is something which people avoid or want to avoid, something they don't like, an activity they engage in because they must. Lawrence Becker aptly has described Locke's view of labor as a "proposal" that labor is something unpleasant enough so that people do it only in the expectation of benefits. In fact, Locke himself refers to labor as "pains."

* * *

At this point we can separate the normative proposition of the labor theory from the instrumental argument with which it is usually identified. The normative proposition states: *the unpleasantness of labor should be rewarded with property*. In this proposition, the "should" is a moral or ethical imperative, which is not based on any consideration of the *effects* of creating property rights. In comparison, the instrumental argument is directly concerned with those effects. It proposes that the unpleasantness of labor should be rewarded with property *because people must be motivated to perform labor*. The instrumental claim has a utilitarian foundation: we want to promote labor because labor promotes the public good.

Indeed, when the normative proposition emerges in court opinions it is usually as an adjunct to the instrumental argument. The instrumental argument clearly has dominated official pronouncements on American copyright and patents. . . . The wide acceptance of the instrumental argument suggests wide acceptance of the premise that idea-making is a sufficiently unpleasant activity to count as labor that requires inducement of reward. Admittedly, this hardly is a tight argument. Idea-making just as easily could be a neutral activity or even a pleasant activity whose pursuit individuals covet.

* * *

If we believe that an avoidance theory of labor justifies intellectual property, we are left with two categories of ideas: those whose production required unpleasant labor and those produced by enjoyable labor. Are the latter to be denied protection?

2. The "Value–Added" Labor Theory

Another interpretation of Locke's labor theory can be called the "labor-desert" or "value-added" theory. This position "holds that when labor produces something of value to others—something beyond what morality requires the laborer to produce—then the laborer deserves some benefit for it." This understanding of property does not require an analysis of the idea of labor. Labor is not necessarily a process that produces value to others. It is counterintuitive to say labor exists only when others value the thing produced. It would also be counter to Locke's example of the individual laboring and appropriating goods for himself *alone*. The "labor-desert" theory asserts that labor often creates *social* value, and it is this production of social value that "deserves" reward, not the labor that produced it.

* * *

The value-added theory usually is understood as an instrumentalist or consequentialist argument that people will add value to the common if some of the added value accrues to them. Paralleling the discussion of the avoidance theory of labor, it is possible to treat the value-added theory as a normative proposition: people *should* be rewarded for how much value they add to other people's lives, regardless of whether they are motivated by such rewards.

[Before a patent is granted,] courts [require] a "step forward" or an "advance over prior art." Stated succinctly, they require that an invention be enough of an advance over the previous art so that the average person schooled in the art would not consider the advance immediately obvious, but also would understand how the invention improves upon previously available technology. To require that something be an "advance" over existing technology clearly demands that there be new value added in this item; that the invention be "nonobvious" raises the threshold of the additional value requirement.

* * *

C. Ideas and the Common

It requires some leap of faith to say that ideas come from a "common" in the Lockean sense of the word. Yet it does not take an unrehabilitated Platonist to think that the "field of ideas" bears a great similarity to a common.

The differences between ideas and physical property have been repeated often. Physical property can be used at any one time by only one person or one coordinated group of people. Ideas can be used simultaneously by everyone. Furthermore, people cannot be excluded from ideas in the way that they can be excluded from physical property. These two basic differences between ideas and physical goods have been used by some writers to argue *against* intellectual property, but, if anything, they suggest that ideas fit Locke's notion of a "common" better than does physical property.

The "field" of all possible ideas prior to the formation of property rights is more similar to Locke's common than is the unclaimed wilderness. Locke's common had enough goods of similar quality that one person's extraction from it did not prevent the next person from extracting something of the same quality and quantity. The common did not need to be infinite; it only needed to be practically inexhaustible. With physical goods, the inexhaustibility condition requires a huge supply. With ideas, the inexhaustibility condition is easily satisfied; each idea can be used by an unlimited number of individuals. One person's use of some ideas (prior to intellectual property schemes) cannot deplete the common in *any* sense. Indeed, the field of ideas seems to expand with use.

* * *

1.   The Common and Tempered Property Rights

Existing forms of intellectual property do not countenance complete exclusion of the non-owner. . . . As long as complete exclusion cannot or does not happen, ideas will be available to people in their own thoughts even though these ideas already have become someone else's property. Through this availability, one idea can lead to still more ideas. In other words, once a "new" idea has been put into intellectual commerce, once people know about it, it leads to an "expansion" of the common, or of the accessible common. New idea X may be the key to a whole new range of ideas which would not have been thought of without X. [P]utting X into intellectual commons does not increase the common so much as it enhances the abilities of people to take from the common; it gives people longer arms to reach the ideas on higher branches. In this view, X just makes new ideas Y and Z more easily discovered by a wider range of people. When the range of people and/or ease of discovery is dramatically improved, one can think of the common as being practically enlarged.

* * *

2.   The Common and Ideas That Cannot Be Granted Property Status

Intellectual property systems also are more suitable for a Lockean justification than are physical property systems because a growing set of central ideas are never permitted to become private property and are held in a *permanent common* . . . .

The first is the category of common "everyday" ideas, such as thinking to wash one's car, to add paprika to a quiche for coloring, or to tell mystery stories to your cub scout troop. The second is the category of extraordinary ideas like the Pythagorean theorem, the heliocentric theory of the solar system, or the cylindrical column for architecture.

One reason that we do not permit property rights in either category of ideas may be that doing so would involve tremendous reallocations of wealth toward the property holders of these ideas. If we had to pay a royalty each time we told a ghost story or walked a dog, unprecedented wealth would concentrate in the hands of those "holding" the most common ideas. These common, everyday ideas are too generically useful to allow someone to monopolize them. The common would not have "enough and as good" if they were removed.

* * *

NOTES

1. *The Founding Fathers, Locke, and Intellectual Property.* There is little doubt that the Founding Fathers were aware of Locke and his *Second Treatise.* Indeed, one can argue that the *Second Treatise* profoundly influenced the Founding Fathers' conception of government and the role government should play in the daily affairs of the citizenry.[126] But Locke's natural rights theory and its impact with respect to intellectual property is dubious. Consider a letter Thomas Jefferson wrote to Isaac McPherson in 1813:

> It has been pretended by some, (and in England especially), that inventors have a natural and exclusive right to their inventions, and not merely for their own lives, but inheritable to their heirs. But while it is a moot question whether the origin of any kind of property is derived from nature at all, it would be singular to admit a natural and even an hereditary right to inventors. It is agreed by those who have seriously considered the subject, that no individual has, of natural right, a separate property in an acre of land, for instance. By a universal law, indeed, whatever, whether fixed or movable, belongs to all men equally and in common, is the property for the moment of him who occupies it, but when he relinquishes the occupation, the property goes with it. Stable ownership is the gift of social law, and is given late in the progress of society. It would be curious then, if an idea, the fugitive fermentation of an individual brain, could, of natural right, be claimed in exclusive and stable property. If nature has made any one thing less susceptible than all others of exclusive property, it is the action of the thinking power called an idea, which an individual may exclusively possess as long as he keeps it to himself; but the moment it is divulged, it forces itself into the possession of every one, and the receiver cannot dispossess himself of it. Its peculiar character, too, is that no one possesses the less, because every other possesses the whole of it. He who receives an idea from me, receives instruction himself without lessening mine; as he who lights his taper at mine, receives light without darkening me. That ideas should freely spread from one to another over the globe, for the moral and mutual instruction of man, and improvement of his condition, seems to have been peculiarly and benevolently designed by nature, when she made them, like fire, expansible over all space, without lessening

---

126. But recent scholarship has cast doubt on this proposition, asserting that America's Founders adhered not so much to liberal Lockeanism, as they did to Aristotelian notions of republican civic humanism. *See* GORDON WOOD, THE RADICALISM OF THE AMERICAN REVOLUTION (1991).

their density in any point, and like the air in which we breathe, move, and have our physical being, incapable of confinement or exclusive appropriation. *Inventions then cannot, in nature, be a subject of property. Society may give an exclusive right to the profits arising from them, as an encouragement to men to pursue ideas which may produce utility, but this may or may not be done, according to the will and convenience of society, without claim or complaint from anybody.* Accordingly, it is a fact, as far as I am informed, that England was, until we copied her, the only country on earth which ever, by a general law, gave a legal right to the exclusive use of an idea.

Considering the exclusive right to invention as given not of natural right, but for the benefit of society, I know well the difficulty of drawing a line between the things which are worth to the public the embarrassment of an exclusive patent, and those which are not.

Letter to Isaac McPherson (Aug. 13, 1813), reprinted in JEFFERSON WRITINGS 1291–92 (M. Peterson ed. 1984) (emphasis added). For a discussion of the influence of natural rights theory, see Adam Mossoff, *Who Cares What Thomas Jefferson Thought about Patents? Reevaluating the Patent "Privilege" in Historical Context*, 92 CORNELL L. REV. 953 (2007) (critiquing "[c]onventional [that] wisdom holds that American patents have always been grants of special monopoly privileges lacking any justification in natural rights philosophy"); Adam Mossoff, *Patents as Constitutional Private Property: the Historical Protection of Patents Under the Takings Clause*, 87 B.U. L. REV. 689 (2007) (critiquing "[c]onventional wisdom [that] maintains that early courts never protected patents as constitutional private property under the Takings Clause"); Adam Mossoff, *Rethinking the Development of Patents: An Intellectual History, 1550–1800*, 52 HASTINGS L.J. 1255 (2001). *See also*, Eric R Claeys, *Jefferson Meets Coase: Land–Use Torts, Law and Economics, and Natural Property Rights*, 85 NOTRE DAME L. REV. 1379, 1398–1430 (2008) (exploring Locke's productive labor theory of Locke in application to tangible property); Seana Valentine Shiffren, *Lockean Arguments for Private Intellectual Property* 138–67, in NEW ESSAYS IN THE LEGAL AND POLITICAL THEORY OF PROPERTY (Munzer ed. 2001).

2. *Locke's Labor–Mixing Metaphor.* Why does one acquire a private property interest in an object by mixing one's labor with the object? Indeed, Locke's labor mixing metaphor has not been without criticism. *See e.g.*, Karl Olivecrona, *Locke's Theory of Appropriation*, 24 PHIL. Q. 220 (1974); George Mavrodes, *Property*, 53 PERSONALIST 245 (1972). *But see* Adam Mossoff, *Locke's Labor Lost*, 9 U. CHI. L. SCH. ROUNDTABLE 155 (2002).

If we decide to focus on labor, it is difficult to reconcile the labor-mixing metaphor with the fortuitous invention scenario or what is sometimes referred to as the "eureka" theory of invention. To illustrate this point, let's consider the following example:

> Homer, a cancer research scientist, has been conducting breast cancer treatment experiments with chemicals X and Y for three years and has little to show for it. One day he walks into his laboratory, slips on a wet and dirty floor, and accidentally knocks over a few chemical containing test tubes on a lab bench, not his own, where they are usually stored. The chemicals, A and B, fall to the floor and co-mingle. Homer cleans up the mess and notices that the floor that was covered by A and B just a minute ago is spotless. Further experimentation confirms that A and B react with each other to form a powerful industrial cleaner (let's call it C). Homer decides to file a patent application claiming the industrial cleaner.

In the above example, how would you justify granting Homer a patent under Locke's labor-theory? Does Homer deserve the fruits of his labor? What labor was involved? Does Justin Hughes' "value-added" or "labor-desert" theory help answer the question? According to Hughes, the " 'labor-desert' theory asserts that labor often creates *social* value, and it is this production of social value that 'deserves' reward, not the labor that produced it." Perhaps there is no such thing as fortuitous invention. As historian Felipe Fernández-Armesto writes, "inventions are rarely, if ever, contrived by genuine accident: there is always as shaping imagination at work or a practical observer on hand." FELIPE FERNÁNDEZ-ARMESTO, NEAR A THOUSAND TABLES 9 (2002).

If, as the "value-added" theory suggests, we focus on the *added social value* and not on labor, then it becomes somewhat easier to justify granting Homer a patent and demarcating the boundaries of his right. The industrial cleaner, C, certainly has value. But is it that simple? Natural rights labor-theory of property asserts that property rights are inherent in the laborer (*i.e.*, pre-social). In a market economy, the value of objects is determined by market forces (*e.g.*, subjective consumer demand). With that in mind, we may ask: under the value-added theory, how can a laborer have a natural right in her invention if the value of the invention is determined not by the laborer, but by society?[127] Additionally, recall that Locke posits that we own our labor; however, if labor is no longer a part of the calculus, then, by focusing on "social value," we are moving away from a natural rights justification and towards a consequentialist or utilitarian theory.

Furthermore, instead of acquiring an ownership interest in an object with which one mixes one's labor, why can't one reasonably argue that the opposite is true? Take the example provided by philosopher Robert Nozick:

> If I own a can of tomato juice and spill it in the sea so that its molecules (made radioactive, so that I can check this) mingle evenly throughout the sea, do I thereby own the sea, or have I foolishly dissipated my tomato juice.

ROBERT NOZICK, ANARCHY, STATE, AND UTOPIA 175 (1974). One of the problems seems to be determinacy in one's property interest. In other words, how does labor identify the boundaries or scope of the property right? As Peter Drahos states: "If labor is to form the basis of a natural property right there must be some way in which to demarcate precisely the object of the property right. . . . [W]hat is it that defines the boundaries of the object of property? Labour creates the property right, but what identifies the object of that property right?" PETER DRAHOS, A PHILOSOPHY OF INTELLECTUAL PROPERTY 51 (1996).

Similar problems occur in property under the heading of the general principle of "accession." Many doctrines like the law of increase (under which a baby animal is owned by the mother's owner) help define the scope of a claim to increments of value, and are an important mode of acquisition. See THOMAS W. MERRILL & HENRY E. SMITH, PROPERTY: PRINCIPLES AND POLICIES 165–94 (2007). Under a specific doctrine, also called "accession," an improver can sometimes acquire material used to create a new object, upon payment of damages to the owner of the worked upon material. Does this describe the acquisition of rights in information? See, e.g., Henry E. Smith, *Intellectual Property as Property: Delineating Entitlements in Information*, 116 YALE L.J. 1742, 1766–77 (2007); Christopher M. Newman, Transformation in Property and Copyright (forthcoming, *Villanova Law Review*), http://ssrn.com/abstract=1688585.

There is yet another problem with focusing on value. Can't one argue that Homer is *only* entitled to the value he added and not the total value of C? Isn't there value in the object prior to Homer's labor (A and B). That is, there is pre-

---

127. *See* Hettinger, *Justifying Intellectual Property, supra* note 127, at 38; *see also,* DRAHOS, A PHILOSOPHY OF INTELLECTUAL PROPERTY, *supra* note 126, at 52.

existing value (*i.e.,* A and B) in C. Why is Homer entitled to the entire value of C (*i.e.,* A and B + Homer's added value)? And, if he is entitled only to the added value, how do we measure that value? Can we say that Homer is entitled to the value of the combination?

3. *Just Deserts and Property Rights.* Why is it that the exercise of labor should be rewarded with property rights rather than praise, gratitude, or money? If, as the just deserts argument asserts, an inventor is entitled to the fruits of her labor, should the goal or purpose of the inventor be considered before a patent is issued? What was homer's goal in note 2? Consider the following:

> Are there some types of labor for which property rights are the *only* fitting benefit? Or less strongly, are there some sorts of labor for which property rights are the *most* fitting benefits?

> Suppose we begin by recalling once again that labor (as opposed to random expenditure of effort and play) is goal-directed activity. It is undertaken for some purpose—for the satisfaction of some desire. Now, it is clear that the satisfaction of some such desires might in principle require property rights, while the satisfaction of others does not. If the whole purpose (or an indispensable part of the purpose) of the laborer's efforts is to get and keep as property what the laborer produces, then if the laborer deserves a benefit for his or her efforts, and if property rights in the thing produced do not exceed the proportionality requirement, then they are obviously the only (or part of the only fitting) benefit.

> Note that this does not mean that people can come to deserve property rights by simply having them as part of their goals when they undertake to do something. What they do must deserve a benefit, and a benefit of a size comparable to the value of the property rights they want.... Once this is understood, the labor-desert argument looks quite sound.

LAWRENCE C. BECKER, PROPERTY RIGHTS 52–53 (1977). Do you agree, having read Becker's account, that the labor-desert theory now "looks quite sound?" Becker's "proportionality requirement" holds that the "benefit [conferred on the inventor (e.g., property interest)] must be proportional to the value produced by the labor." As such, aren't we still left with the problem, discussed in note 2, of valuing the inventor's contribution? If labor is a "goal-directed activity," then should an inventor like Homer who is intentionally working on a treatment for breast cancer be entitled to a patent on an industrial cleaner if he discovered the latter by accident? Does Homer have a stronger case if he accidentally discovered a treatment for skin cancer or lung cancer? What if, 10 years after the patent issues to Homer, another inventor discovers that the cure for skin cancer can also be used to treat AIDS? Should Homer have a property interest in this treatment for AIDS? The case law holds that an inventor does not have to appreciate fully the significance of his invention. *See Roberts v. Ryer*, 91 U.S. 150, 157 (1875) ("The inventor of a machine is entitled to the benefit of all the uses to which it can be put, no matter whether he had conceived the idea of the use or not."); *B.G. Corp. v. Walter Kidde & Co.*, 79 F.2d 20, 22 (2d Cir.1935) (Hand, J.).

4. *What Are Just Deserts?* Many of us have at least a visceral understanding of fame and glory. We all know tales of the deserving, but unrecognized and, of the recognized, but undeserving. Or at least we think we do. We would do well to consider the discussion and sources presented by Professor Leo Katz in his book, ILL-GOTTEN GAINS: EVASION, BLACKMAIL, AND KINDRED PUZZLES OF THE LAW (1996). Katz uses societal rules for blame embodied in the criminal law to attempt to derive societal rules for fame. Concerning the distinction between acts and omissions, one might ask what level of contribution is required on the part of a supervising faculty member for co-authorship or co-inventorship. What is sufficient: active advice or passive permission and non-interference where others would have cut off? How should the rules of praise evaluate the problems presented by cases of mere thought, transferred intent, or unreasonable hopes; any of which might nonetheless correlate with inventive success? To what extent should originality, effort, genius, or utility drive our decisions to allocate praise?

5. *Locke's Provisos and the Intellectual Commons.* Locke sets forth two provisos: first, there must be "enough and as good in common for others" after appropriation. Second, one must not appropriate more than one can use (non-waste proviso).

The purpose of Locke's "enough and as good" proviso is to ensure that appropriation of an object by X does not worsen the situation of others; that there be "enough and as good" left for everyone else. This proviso, as Justin Hughes suggests, does not appear to be a concern with respect to intellectual property. The number of ideas, unlike physical objects or land, is seemingly infinite, and, as a result, the "intellectual commons" can never be depleted. Does it follow, therefore, that the issuance of a patent can never worsen the situation of others? Let's revisit the work of Robert Nozick:

> A medical researcher who synthesizes a new substance that effectively treats a certain disease and who refuses to sell except on his terms does not worsen the situation of others by depriving them of whatever he has appropriated. The others easily can [or could have] possess the same materials he appropriated.... An inventor's patent does not deprive others of an object which would not exist if not for the inventor.

NOZICK, ANARCHY, at 181–82. See also, *United States v. Dubilier Condenser Corp.*, 289 U.S. 178, 186 (1933) ("An inventor deprives the public of nothing which it enjoyed before his discovery, but gives something of value to the community by adding to the sum of human knowledge"). In other words, *but for* the inventor, the invention would never have existed. By not selling the invention, the condition of others may not be improved, but, at the same time, their condition is not worsened.[128] Do you agree? Wouldn't the invention have been discovered eventually? What if an inventor refuses to market her invention; that is, she engages in what is sometimes referred to as patent suppression? Consider the following hypothetical put forth by Jeremy Waldron:

> Suppose Q is dying of a disease for which he knows there is no cure; he resigns himself to his fate and prepares for a stoic death. Then the news comes in: a drug has been developed which will remit the disease. The person who made and tested it, P, did so in his own laboratory with his own hands using his own materials. P makes the drug available to a number of his friends, but excludes Q because he dislikes Q's politics. Clearly Q will suffer something as a result of this. Instead of the stoic death he prepared for, it is likely that the rest of his life will be spent in painful bitterness and anger as he endures the thought the he might have

---

128. *See also,* CLARK, ESSENTIALS OF ECONOMIC THEORY 360–61 (1907) ("[The patent owner] is allowed to have an exclusive control of something which otherwise might not and often would not have come into existence at all. If it would not,—if the patented article is something which society without a patent system would not have secured at all,—the inventor's monopoly hurts nobody."); JOHN STUART MILL, PRINCIPLES OF POLITICAL ECONOMY WITH SOME OF THEIR APPLICATION TO SOCIAL PHILOSOPHY, ch. 2, § 6, excerpted in PROPERTY: MAINSTREAM AND CRITICAL POSITIONS 96 (C.B. Macpherson ed., 1978) ("It is no hardship to any one, to be excluded from what others have produced: they were not bound to produce it for his use, and he loses nothing by not sharing in what otherwise would not have existed at all.") We are indebted to Jeremy Waldron, for these sources. *See From Authors to Copiers: Individual Rights and Social Values in Intellectual Property,* 68 CHI.-KENT L.REV. 841 (1993).

lived and flourished but will not, thanks to P's exercise of this exclusionary right.

Jeremy Waldron, *From Authors to Copiers: Individual Rights and Social Values in Intellectual Property*, 68 CHI.-KENT L. REV. 841, 866 (1993). Is Q worse off than he was prior to P's invention? If yes, in what way? Does P's patent suppression violate Locke's non-waste proviso? What if a another medical researcher *independently* invents the same substance as P? Should this researcher be allowed to utilize her invention?

2.   UTILITARIAN THEORY

The philosophical theory of utilitarianism was set forth by the English philosopher, Jeremy Bentham (1748–1832), who once remarked that "natural rights is simple nonsense: natural and imprescriptible rights, rhetorical nonsense—nonsense on stilts."[129] Utilitarianism held that the state should adopt policies (*e.g.*, by enacting legislation) that would maximize the happiness of members of its community. This is what Bentham referred to as maximizing "utility." According to Bentham:

> By utility is meant that property in any object, whereby it tends to produce benefit, advantage, pleasure, good, or happiness (all this in the present case comes to the same thing), or (what comes again to the same thing) to prevent the happening of mischief, pain, evil or unhappiness to the party whose interest is considered: if the party be the community in general, then the happiness of the community: if the particular individual, then the happiness of that individual.[130]

Bentham thereafter refers to a "principle of utility," which "commands a state to maximize the utility of the community."[131] Thus, Bentham writes: "A measure of government . . . may be said to be conformable to or dictated by the principle of utility, when in like manner the tendency which it has to augment the happiness of the community is greater than any which it has to diminish it."[132] The "principle of utility" is Bentham's benchmark for sound and rational legislation. With this in mind, we can see how many have adopted utilitarianism as a basis for justifying our patent laws. Indeed, the predominant justification for American intellectual property law has been, without question, utilitarianism or consequentialism. The patent and copyright clause of the Constitution itself—"[t]o promote the progress of Science and useful Arts"—can be read as predominantly utilitarian in nature. Whereas Locke's natural rights labor—theory posits that property rights are pre-societal and inherent, the utilitarian justification is a matter of positive law (*i.e.*, statutes and cases) concerned with end results and public welfare. According to utilitarianism, but for the prospect of the right to exclude in the form of a patent or copyright, there will be inadequate incentives resulting in a less than "socially optimal output of intellectual products."[133] That is:

---

129.   JEREMY BENTHAM, AN INTRODUCTION TO THE PRINCIPLES OF MORALS AND LEGISLATION (J.H. Burns and H.L.A. Hart, eds.)

130.   *Id.* at ch. 1, § 3, p. 12.

131.   JEAN HAMPTON, POLITICAL PHILOSOPHY 124 (1997).

132.   BENTHAM, PRINCIPLES OF MORALS AND LEGISLATION, *supra* note 132, at § 7, p. 14.

133.   Hettinger, *Justifying Intellectual Property, supra* note 127, at 48.

If competitors could simply copy books, movies, and records, and take one another's inventions and business techniques, there would be no incentive to spend the vast amounts of time, energy, and money necessary to develop these products and techniques. It would be in each firm's self-interest to let others develop products, and then mimic the result. No one would engage in original development, and consequently no new writings, inventions, or business techniques would be developed. To avoid this disastrous result, the argument claims, we must continue to grant intellectual property rights.

Notice that this argument focuses on the users of intellectual products, rather than on the producers [as Locke's natural rights labor-theory]. Granting property rights to producers is here seen as necessary to ensure that enough intellectual products (and countless other goods based on these products) are available to users. The grant of property rights to producers is a mere means to this end.[134]

In short, under the utilitarian theory, the happiness of members of the community is maximized by granting property rights in one's inventive contribution.

Utilitarianism recognizes that intellectual property, like all forms of property, restricts liberty.[135] It seems odd to view intellectual property this way, but one need look no further than the pronounced restrictions imposed by our patent laws. A patent owner (X) has the right to exclude others (Y & Z) from making, using, offering for sale, or selling, her claimed invention. The liberty of Y and Z is constrained because they cannot use X's invention without the latter's consent. However, a utilitarian justification of patent law tolerates this restriction of liberty for the sake of the greater public good. As stated above, utilitarianism holds that but for the prospect of the right to exclude, too few incentives would exist to prompt research and development ventures and capital investment. In the end, fewer members of society would enjoy the fruits of inventive activity than they presently do with a patent system firmly in place.

NOTES

1. *How is Happiness of the Public Good Measured?* Bentham assumed that "happiness" is quantitative. Do you agree? Can you quantify how happy you are right now? Doesn't happiness also have a qualitative component, as John Stuart Mill argued? *See* John Stuart Mill, *Utilitarianism,* in MILL, UTILITARIANISM, LIBERTY, AND REPRESENTATIVE GOVERNMENT 7 (H.B. Acton ed. 1972). Can you quantitatively compare your level of happiness with the person sitting next to you? Would it help you if we thought of our level of happiness with respect to our individual preferences? That is, if I have a particular preference A and you have a particular

---

134. *Id.* at 48. *See also,* Waldron, *From Authors to Copiers, supra* note 131, at 854 (1993) (According to the utilitarian justification, "useful works will be elicited through the rational self-interest of authors [and inventors] up to the point at which their social costs exceed their social benefits.").

135. *See* Joseph William Singer, *The Reliance Interest in Property,* 40 STAN. L. REV. 611, 647 (1988) ("Every entitlement implies a correlative vulnerability of others."); *see also,* Waldron, *From Authors to Copiers, supra* note 131 (Viewing intellectual property from the perspective of those individuals whose liberty is constrained).

preference B, would it be easier to measure our happiness by asking whether my preference A or your preference B has been satisfied?[136]

2. *Property v. Liberty*. We said that intellectual property restricts liberty. If X has a patent on a therapeutic drug, he can, for whatever reason, prevent Y and Z from using the drug. Similarly, if you own a piece of land, you can prevent others from trespassing on your land or you can charge a very high entry fee. Utilitarianism tolerates this constraint on liberty for the sake of the general good. But we may ask: Are the interests of those whose liberty is constrained served by the overall general good that is being promoted? In other words, are people like Y and Z bearing too much of the brunt of our patent system? Or, is this simply the price we have to pay to promote the progress of the useful arts in an optimal fashion?

No doubt, all laws limit liberty in one way or another. You cannot run a red light as you see fit. Thus, it seems that the real question is: Does the liberty that a patent constrains have a certain specialness to it? Consider the following:

From Authors to Copiers: Individual Rights and Social Values in Intellectual Property*

Jeremy Waldron.
68 CHI.-KENT L. REV. 841 (1993).

* * *

If the suggestion is ... that intellectual property infringes a moral right to liberty, then the behavior it constrains must be identified as having a special moral significance.... A law that forbids me from worshiping according to my beliefs is a blow to liberty in a way that a law that regulates traffic at intersections is not. In the latter case, [Charles] Taylor argues, "we are reluctant to speak ... of a loss of liberty at all; what we feel we are trading off is convenience against safety."

Which category do the restrictions imposed by intellectual property fall into? Are they more like restrictions on freedom of worship, or are they like the restrictions that form part of ordinary traffic law. There are a number of different ways of answering this question, a number of ways in which we might try to differentiate between those freedoms that are important enough to be the subject of a right and those that are not.

* * *

C.   Self–Regarding versus Other–Regarding Freedoms

A third approach is to say that there is a special moral presumption in favor of a right to perform actions that do not encroach on the freedom of action of anyone else. This of course is John Stuart Mill's position On Liberty: "The only part of the conduct of anyone for which he is amenable to society is that which concerns others. In the part which merely concerns himself, his independence is, of right, absolute." Actions that impinge on others' actions may be dealt with, quite properly, by ordinary legislation

---

136.   *See* OSKAR MORGENSTERN AND JOHN VON NEUMANN, THEORY OF GAMES AND ECONOMIC BEHAVIOR (1953) and LEONARD SAVAGE, THE FOUNDATION OF STATISTICS (1972). We are indebted to Jean Hampton, *supra* note 134, at 128–29, for these cites.

* Reprinted with the permission of the Chicago–Kent Law Review.

justified on utilitarian grounds. It is only self-regarding actions that attract the special protection of a moral right to liberty. This is also Immanuel Kant's position: the coercion of the law, Kant argued, may be used only to restrain coercion. It follows that if the copier's actions do not impinge on anyone else's freedom, they should not be made the target of coercive laws (such as copyright [and patent]).

Objects of property can be divided into two classes: those that are "crowdable" and those that are "non-crowdable." An object is "crowdable" if one person's use of it is an obstacle to at least one other's use of it. The computer that I am using as I compose this sentence is crowdable; it is a small desk-top machine that can be used for word-processing only by one person at a time. Any attempt by you to use it would interfere with my freedom to use it. The apple that I am eating is crowdable in a slightly different sense; my consumption of it makes it unavailable for others' use forever, not just during the period of my use. The striking thing about intellectual products is that they are non-crowdable. Although only one person can read a given copy of a novel at a given time, any number of people may enjoy the prose contained therein without diminishing anyone else's enjoyment, and of course, it's the prose not the physical book that is the subject of intellectual property. The point seems to apply to copying as much as to reading. Copying a piece of prose does not wear it out; any number of people can copy the same passage (provided they have access to its physical embodiment) at the same time.

It seems to follow from this feature of non-crowdability, that a copier's use of an author's prose [or an inventor's inventive concept] cannot impact on anyone else's actions, and so *a fortiori* cannot impact on the author's [or inventor's] freedom of action. Since all objects of intellectual property have this feature, it seems to follow that all the infringements which intellectual property rules prohibit fall into the Kant/Mill category of acts that have no discernable impact on anyone else's freedom. This conclusion—if it can be sustained—would provide the basis for a powerful libertarian objection to intellectual property rules.

Few people think it can be sustained. In my experience the argument of the previous two paragraphs is viewed by ordinary folks as a piece of academic sophistry. Of course the author's [and inventor's] freedom is affected, they will retort. And many of them add: "he is no longer free to make the profits that he could have made in the absence of the copier's infringement."

* * *

There is no doubt that [a privilege to copy] would undermine the profitability of authorship. But it is much less clear that it does so by restricting freedom. The profitability of authorship needs to be guaranteed by monopoly rules, since absent such rules authors would be unable to convince as many people to pay as much for authorized copies of their works. But inability is not the same as lack of freedom. I may be unable to sell fresh water in Scotland where the stuff falls in bucketfuls from the sky, by my liberty is hardly affected thereby. No doubt, I could make a profit if the Scottish Office granted me a monopoly on water-rights (no one to use any water anywhere without a license purchased from me). Such a monopoly would be coercive so far as other people were concerned, since it would have to prohibit and prevent their free use of water. But the effect it would have on their liberty is not matched by any effect their freedom would have on mine if the monopoly were not established. Though I would receive less money, no assault would be made upon my freedom by the Scottish Office's refusal to give me exclusive water-rights.

* * *

D.   Liberty versus License

Whether or not copiers' actions encroach on liberty, they may still be doing something wrong. Can this be used as a basis for disqualifying their claim to liberty? We often say that freedom of action which violates moral duty is not liberty but license. If the copiers' claim is merely a demand for a license to act wrongly and irresponsibly, it can hardly be used as a basis for imposing a heavier-than-usual burden of justification on those who support intellectual property law.

* * *

It is surely wrong to harm authors [and inventors]. It is morally right perhaps to give authors [and inventors] a reward for their troubles—but we have already seen that the issue is precisely whether a reward for authors [and inventors] should be purchased at the cost of others' freedom. It is no doubt wrong for copiers to impede the progress of the sciences and useful arts—but copiers complain that they are bearing undue costs in the quest of these benefits (and many claim also that exactly the same goal would be better served by the regime they advocate).

—————

The last paragraph nicely captures the patent law dilemma. The granting of patents comes at a price. When does that price become too high? Professor Waldron suggests that permitting one to copy freely a copyrighted work or patented invention does not necessarily restrict the freedom of the author or inventor, respectively; that is, "inability [to make a profit] is not the same as lack of freedom." Do you agree? The patent law does not guarantee a patent owner a profit. The question is if patents were not granted would the progress of the useful arts be impeded? Does Professor Waldron give enough consideration to the incentive arguments? Would you invest in a research project or spend the time conducting the research in a project knowing that someone else will be able to copy it with impunity?

In the computer world, a noteworthy anti-intellectual property or what may be described as a libertarian, sentiment exists. *See* John Perry Barlow, *The Economy of Ideas* 2.03 Wired 84 (March 1984). *See generally*, Tom G. Palmer, *Are Patents and Copyrights Morally Justified? The Philosophy of Property Rights and Ideal Objects,* 13 Harv. J.L. & Pub. Pol'y 817 (1990); J.S.G. Boggs, *Who Owns This?*, 68 Chi.-Kent. L. Rev. 889 (1993) (writing from an artist's perspective of intellectual property law).

C. ECONOMICS OF PATENT LAW

Intellectual property has become increasingly important to American business. This is evidenced by the large sums of money connected to intellectual property, such as the billion-dollar licenses, infringement verdicts, and sales. But the importance of intellectual property is not due merely to individual gains and losses. National intellectual property resources are crucial for long term international economic competitiveness. That is, we want our patent system to create both private value, which it clearly has done, and enhance welfare for society as a whole, an outcome where, some suggest, the patent system's impact is uncertain.

Economic research over the past sixty years has demonstrated the causal link between intellectual property and the growth of our national economy. Intellectual property is an increasingly critical component of United States capital, technology transfer, and foreign trade; and some economic research has demonstrated that changes in intellectual property laws can be used deliberately to promote innovation and national economic development.[137] This research relates back to the Nobel Prize winning work by Professor Robert Solow of MIT in which he demonstrated that most of the economic growth in the United States in the first half of this century could be explained by investments in research and development and education rather than by increases in capital and labor.[138] Professor Solow's work is extended in this connection by Professor Paul Romer of Stanford University, who argues that such investment in research and development and education is unlike other forms of investment in that it does not experience decreasing returns to scale.[139] The more one puts in, the more

---

137. *See generally* the following discussions of the causal link, Ashish Arora, Marco Ceccagnoli, and Wesley M. Cohen, *R & D and the Patent Premium*, (National Bureau of Econ. Research Working Paper No. 9431, 2003) ("Although patent protection is found to provide a positive premium on average in only a few industries, our results also imply that it stimulates R & D across almost all manufacturing industries, with the magnitude of that effect varying substantially"); R & D, PATENTS AND PRODUCTIVITY (Zvi Griliches ed., 1984); Edwin Mansfield, *Unauthorized Use of Intellectual Property: Effects on Investment, Technology Transfer, and Innovation*, in GLOBAL DIMENSIONS OF INTELLECTUAL PROPERTY RIGHTS IN SCIENCE AND TECHNOLOGY 107–145 (Mitchell B. Wallerstein *et al.* eds., 1993); Richard C. Levin, *et al.*, *Appropriating the Returns from Industrial Research and Development*, 3 BROOKINGS PAPERS ON ECON. ACTIVITY 783–820 (1987); Edwin Mansfield, *Patents and Innovation: An Empirical Study*, 1986 MGMT. SCI. 173–81; Robert P. Merges, *Uncertainty and the Standard of Patentability*, 7 HIGH TECH. L.J. 1, 10–12 (1992). A listing of the seminal works in the field would include JOSEPH A. SCHUMPETER, BUSINESS CYCLES (1939); SIMON KUZNETS, SECULAR MOVEMENTS IN PRODUCTION AND PRICES (1936); Robert K. Merton, *Fluctuations in the Rate of Industrial Innovation*, 49 Q.J. OF ECON., 454–474 (May 1935); and Zvi Griliches, *Productivity, R & D, and Basic Research at the Firm Level in the 1970's*, 76 AM. ECON. REV. 141 (1986). For a review of the field, *see* GEOFFREY WYATT, THE ECONOMICS OF INVENTION (1968). For an excellent study of why companies seek patent protection, *see* Wesley Cohen, et al., *Protecting Their Intellectual Assets: Appropriability Conditions and Why U.S. Manufacturing Firms Patent (or Not)*, NATIONAL BUREAU OF ECONOMIC RESEARCH, Working Paper W7552.

138. *See* Robert M. Solow, *Technical Change and the Aggregate Production Function*, 39 REV. ECON. & STAT. 312, 320 (1957).

139. *See* Paul M. Romer, *Increasing Return and Long–Run Growth*, 94 J. POL. ECON. 1002 (1986).

one gets out—and the "bang-for-buck" does not decrease as more and more buck is added. If he is correct, then such investing seems all the more attractive. Therefore, one can argue, intellectual property law is really a public policy tool for promoting industrial growth.

To better understand how this tool can and does operate, we must first understand some basic principles of economics. We begin with the concept of monopolies because patents are often branded with that somewhat value-laden term. But we begin by noting that this is not really correct. In his famous 1942 series of articles on the relations between the patent and anti-monopoly laws, Judge (then attorney) Rich carefully reviews the sources of this confusion.[140] He notes the definition given by Lord Coke:

> A monopoly is an institution ... for the sole buying, selling, making, working, or using, of anything, whereby any person or persons ... are sought to be restrained of any freedom or liberty *that they had before*, or hindered in their lawful trade. (Emphasis in original, quoting 3 Inst. 191, c.85)

He also notes the admonishment by Mr. Justice Clifford:

> *Letters patent are not to be regarded as monopolies ... but as public franchises*, granted ... for the purpose of securing ... as tending to promote the progress of ... the useful arts. (Emphasis in original, quoting *Seymour v. Osborne*, 11 Wall. 516, 533 (1871)).

As we will see below, patents do trigger some key features of monopolies, and do give the potential for market, or even, monopoly power. But patents themselves rarely lead to monopoly power. Indeed, the "average patent ... confers too little monopoly power on the patentee in a meaningful economic sense ... and sometimes it confers no monopoly power at all."[141] While this seems like a game of semantics, it is not. The distinction is well supported by sound economic theory—which we now briefly discuss.

1. A COMPARISON OF PATENT AND MONOPOLY ECONOMICS

The term "monopoly" is used to describe an entire market; like the market for electricity in the typical American city. By definition, a monopoly market is one in which there is only one seller. That seller is termed the monopolist. The markets for most goods and services in the United States

---

140. Giles S. Rich, *The Relation Between Patent Practices and the Anti–Monopoly Laws*, 24 J. PAT. OFF. SOC'Y 85–106 (Feb., 1942); 24 J. PAT. OFF. SOC'Y 159—181 (Mar.); 24 J. PAT. OFF. SOC'Y 241–283 (Apr.); 24 J. PAT. OFF. SOC'Y 329–356 (May); 24 J. PAT. OFF. SOC'Y 423–437 (June). Also consider Kenneth W. Dam, *The Economic Underpinnings of Patent Law*, 23 J. L. STUD. 247, 249–250 (1994):

> Indeed, it had become conventional to say that a patent is a monopoly. Nonetheless, it is readily apparent that the right to exclude another from "manufacture use and sale" may give no significant market power, even when the patent covers a product that is sold in the market. Indeed, without the benefit of empirical research, it is entirely plausible to conclude that in the great bulk of instances no significant market power is granted. We must bear in mind that leading companies may obtain 1,000 or more patents in a single year, and yet many such firms are unlikely ever to obtain even a single monopoly in any market.

141. Landes and Posner, Economic Structure, *supra* note 4, at 374–75.

are not monopolies, but rather are competitive. Competitive markets are characterized by more than one seller, also called a producer, such that the several sellers in the market compete against one another for customers. A typical monopoly market exists because there is some barrier to market entry by potential competitors. Such barriers to entry may be physical, like the wall of a baseball stadium that prevents outside competition in the market for hot dogs; technological, like the secret recipe for Coca Cola; or legal, like the electrical company's exclusive franchise as a regulated utility, or the patent grant of the right to exclude.

Because the term monopoly is applied to an entire market, we begin our analysis of monopolies by looking at markets. Markets tend to order themselves around consumer demand—producers sell what consumers will buy. In general, consumers buy to satisfy their needs or desires. In the context of a particular consumer problem, like mouse infestation, for example, consumers need or want solutions; and producers sell these solutions, perhaps in the form of mouse traps or cats. We already know that a patent excludes others from making, using, selling, or offering for sale a particular invention. We now see that in the context of a market for solutions, a patentee can prevent others from selling a certain solution, though not all solutions to a given problem. Indeed, it is often said that necessity is the mother of invention, and the necessity caused by an inability to gain access to a particular patented solution—perhaps because the price is too high or perhaps because of an injunction—may very well give rise to the development of alternative non-infringing solutions.

It is now apparent that patents share only certain aspects of monopolies. To be sure, in the case of a patented drug for example, the patent term and the state of the evolving art may be such that the patent does provide such an effective barrier to entry for the market in sales to at least a certain class of patients having such an acute illness that they are unable to wait for the development of alternative non-infringing solutions or for patent expiration. In this case, the limited market at this time and for these patients is a monopoly. In the longer term, however, and for less acute patients, the market may be entirely competitive. The so-called incentive to design around theory of patents, which is discussed below, recognizes this feature of the patent system and tries to exploit it to minimize the potential monopolistic effects of patents.

Implicit in all of the discussion of monopolies thus far has been the presumption that monopolies are somehow bad. In certain respects, they are indeed bad, but it is important to understand the nature of the harm caused by monopolies before deciding to intervene against them. Monopolies are bad because they tend to create a market-wide inefficiency called "dead weight loss." In economic terms, the dead weight loss represents a collective loss of societal wealth, *i.e.*, wealth that is not merely shifted from consumers to producers but rather wealth that is altogether lost from producers and consumers collectively. Let us now consider some microeconomics to better understand the creation of dead weight loss in a shift from a competitive to a monopolistic market.

2.   A COMPARISON OF PATENT AND MONOPOLY MICROECONOMICS[142]

Most products sold in the market are termed "goods" by economists because the more money the consumer has, the greater the quantity of the product the consumer will buy.[143] As the price of a good drops, the amount demanded by the consumer will increase, thereby resulting in a downward sloping demand curve.[144] (*See* Figure 1)

Figure 1

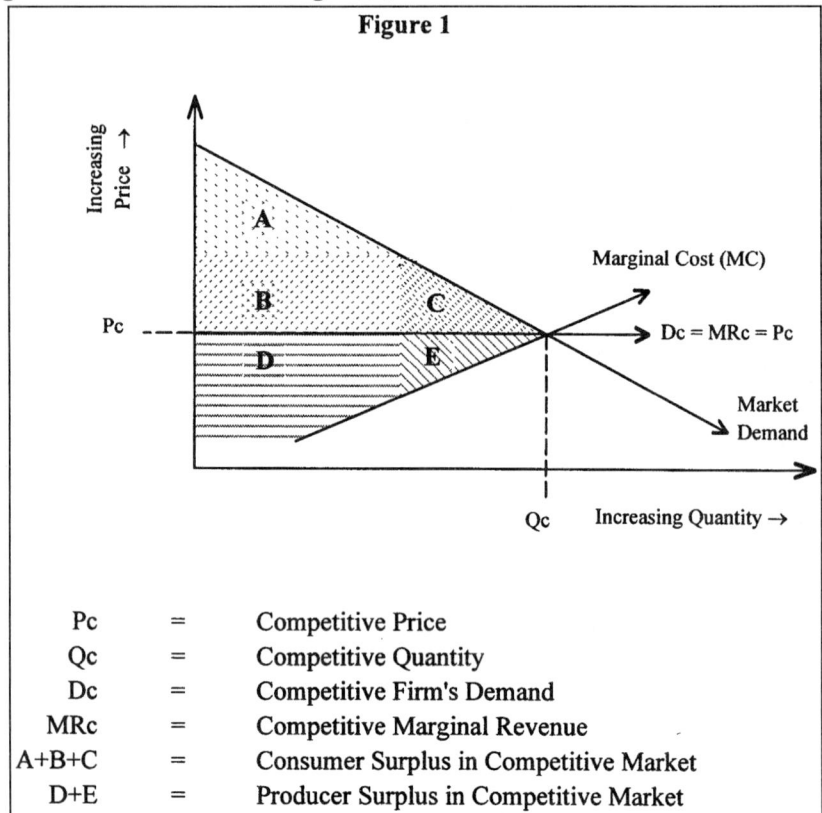

Pc	=	Competitive Price
Qc	=	Competitive Quantity
Dc	=	Competitive Firm's Demand
MRc	=	Competitive Marginal Revenue
A+B+C	=	Consumer Surplus in Competitive Market
D+E	=	Producer Surplus in Competitive Market

It can be demonstrated that a firm selling these goods will maximize

---

142. This section is intended to provide an overview of the microeconomics associated with monopolies and their attendant dead weight loss. A more thorough, but easily readable description can be found in PINDYCK AND RUBINFELD, MICROECONOMICS, 333–352 (1989). The reader with a taste for higher math and multivariate calculus may prefer BRIAN R. BINGER AND ELIZABETH HOFFMAN, MICROECONOMICS WITH CALCULUS 375–385 (1988), or HAL R. VARIAN, MICROECONOMIC ANALYSIS, 79–95 (1984).

143. Some products are termed "bads" because consumption of the product tends to decrease with increasing wealth. Spam is one example of an inferior good, while beef tenderloin is generally thought to be a good.

144. The demand curve can be derived graphically by plotting on the same graph: an individual's consumption mix given a choice between two goods, accompanied by a budget constraint, and a set of indifference curves. The results of this graph can be mapped onto price/quantity space to yield the downward sloping demand curve for one of the goods. For a graphical review of demand theory *see* PINDYK AND RUBINFELD, MICROECONOMICS, *supra* note 145, at 90–91.

its economic profits by selling at a point such that the firm's marginal revenue equals its marginal cost.[145] Marginal revenue is the additional amount a firm earns from the sale of an additional unit of output. Marginal cost is the additional cost incurred by a firm to produce an additional unit of output. If marginal revenue is greater than marginal cost, then the firm can earn more by selling one more unit of output than it costs the firm to produce that unit; and the firm should push output a bit further to capture that added profit between marginal revenue and marginal cost. If, however, marginal revenue is less than marginal cost, then the firm earned less for the last unit of output than it cost the firm to produce that unit; and the firm already went too far—it lost money by producing that last unit of output. In the context of Figure 1, therefore, the profit maximizing output level for a firm is such that the firm's marginal revenue equals its marginal cost: MR = MC.

In a competitive market, the price any one individual firm can charge is capped by market forces. No customer will buy from a firm charging more than the market price. As a result, each firm faces a horizontal demand curve indicating a constant price which is independent of the quantity produced by that firm: Dc = Pc. Such a competitive firm is called a "price taker." Because the price remains fixed regardless of output level, the competitive firm will always charge an amount equal to that fixed price for each additional unit of output.[146] In microeconomic terms, the competitive firm has a fixed marginal revenue, MR, that is set at the market price, Pc, such that MR = Pc. In Figure 1, the competitive firm's marginal revenue is shown to be a horizontal line at the price set by the competitive market.

As discussed above, the competitive firm will maximize profit, as would any other firm, by producing an output level such that marginal revenue equals marginal cost: MR = MC. Figure 1 shows a typical firm's short run marginal cost curve. Because marginal revenue is everywhere Pc, we look to the point on the marginal cost curve that has a price of Pc. We look for MC = Pc. The competitive firm produces at the output level that corresponds to this point, and we designate that output level Qc in Figure 1.

It is important to remember that each individual consumer and producer in the market buys and sells at the prevailing market price. But some consumers value the good at least as much if not more than this market price; they will pay the same or more if they have to. As a result, they receive a benefit beyond what they pay. This should not be surprising, after all, they make the free choice to consume because the purchase makes them better off. Consider, for example, a wealthy adult and a child on a limited allowance who each buy an ice cream cone from the same store. The

---

145. Importantly, economic profits, costs, and benefits are determined by taking account of all costs and benefits—including opportunity costs and so-called "hassle" costs; not merely by measuring simple monetary costs and benefits.

146. Even a seemingly competitive firm will exercise monopoly power if its output becomes a significantly large fraction of total market output. In this case, the demand curve at high levels of output is downward sloping, not horizontal, with marginal revenue even more downward sloping than demand. However, for levels of output such that the individual output of the firm is small as compared to total market output, the firm's demand and marginal revenue curves are both horizontal at Pc.

child may only have been willing to pay the listed price for the treat, while the wealthy adult's purchase decision may have been just as likely if the price were double or even triple. The so-called *consumer surplus* measures how much better off individuals are in the aggregate. More specifically, consumer surplus is the difference between what consumers are willing to pay for a good and what they actually pay when buying it. In the context of Figure 1, the market demand curve represents the price consumers will pay for a given quantity of output. The consumer surplus, A+B+C in Figure 1, represents the additional amount over the competitive price, Pc, that consumers will be willing to pay for the quantity of goods Qc. In an analogous fashion, the so-called *producer surplus* measures the difference between what a producer can collect as payment for a good (the market price) and the marginal cost of production. In the context of Figure 1, the producer would have been willing to accept the schedule of prices indicated by the marginal cost curve. The producer surplus, D+E in Figure 1, represents the additional amount above marginal cost that the producer actually received.

The consumer and producer surpluses together represent the amount by which society as a whole is made better off by the exchanges of the marketplace. Let us see now how society is less well off in a monopoly market than it is in a competitive market.

Unlike the competitive firm, the monopoly firm takes neither price nor output as fixed. The monopoly firm is faced with the total market demand as described by the downward sloping demand function. Marginal revenue for such a linear demand function can be shown to have the same price intercept and twice the downward slope as the demand function.[147]

The resulting marginal revenue curve is below the demand curve itself. This marginal revenue curve for the monopoly is also lower than the marginal revenue curve of the competitive firm, which is horizontal and colinear with competitive demand. Like the competitive firm, the monopoly firm will also maximize profit when marginal revenue equals marginal cost: MR = MC. Therefore, the profit maximizing monopoly produces an output at the intersection of the marginal revenue and marginal cost curves which is lower than the competitive output. The price charged at this output level is then determined by the demand in the market. As Figure 2 shows, the monopoly price for a good with a downward sloping demand curve is higher (and output lower) than competitive levels.

The decreased quantity and increased price of the monopoly regime result in a decrease in net surplus. The consumer surplus is now only area A. While area B is recovered as producer surplus, area C is lost. In addition, the producer surplus in the monopoly regime no longer includes area E. Therefore, the monopoly regime is said to yield a dead weight loss: there is

147. This result can be readily derived from the equation of the demand curve, which can be expressed with price as a function of quantity. Total revenue is price times quantity, which can be expressed mathematically by multiplying the equation for the demand curve by quantity. Marginal revenue is the first derivative with respect to quantity of total revenue. The slope of this curve is twice that of the demand curve but has the same price intercept, as shown in Figure 2.

a net decrease in combined societal wealth represented by the loss of the total area C + E in Figure 2.

The dead weight loss associated with the monopoly model is dependent on the market demand being downward sloping. If, however, the demand curve is perfectly elastic, *i.e.* horizontal, then there is no dead weight loss associated with the monopoly. This case might arise if the product of the monopoly firm is in competition with products from other markets; that is, if there are viable substitutes or, as economists would say, the demand is highly elastic.

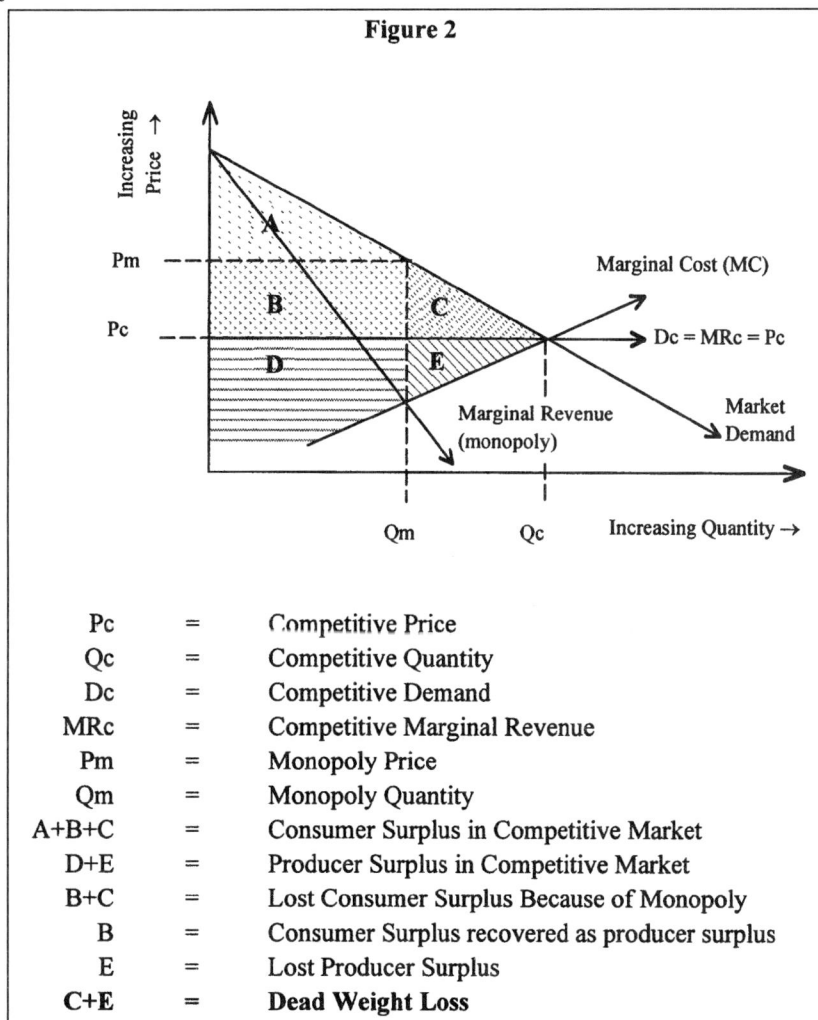

Figure 2

Pc	=	Competitive Price
Qc	=	Competitive Quantity
Dc	=	Competitive Demand
MRc	=	Competitive Marginal Revenue
Pm	=	Monopoly Price
Qm	=	Monopoly Quantity
A+B+C	=	Consumer Surplus in Competitive Market
D+E	=	Producer Surplus in Competitive Market
B+C	=	Lost Consumer Surplus Because of Monopoly
B	=	Consumer Surplus recovered as producer surplus
E	=	Lost Producer Surplus
C+E	=	**Dead Weight Loss**

The important lesson to take from this discussion of monopolies is that no monopoly exists if there is a substitute available to sate consumers' demand. For precisely this reason. Mr. Justice Clark writing for the Supreme Court noted:

> To establish monopolization or attempt to monopolize . . . it would then be
> necessary to appraise the exclusionary power of the . . . patent claim in

> terms of the relevant market for the product involved. Without a definition
> of that market there is no way to measure [the patentee's] ability to lessen
> or destroy competition. It may be that the [patented] device ... does not
> comprise a relevant market. There may be effective substitutes for the
> device which do not infringe the patent.

Walker Process Equip., Inc. v. Food Machinery & Chem. Corp., 382 U.S.
172, 177–78 (1965). For example, people will only buy better mouse traps if
they cost less than cats. Therefore, the patent monopoly is a monopoly on
only one particular solution to the problem, not a monopoly on the problem
itself. The more substitutes there are for the patented product, the higher
the elasticity of demand, the more horizontal will be the patentee's demand
curve, and the closer will be her marginal revenue curve to her demand,
and the smaller will be the dead weight loss she creates.

3.   AN OVERVIEW OF PATENT ECONOMICS

Having concluded that patents do not necessarily create monopolies,
you are now ready to review the ways in which patents do provide economic
aid to their owners. A convenient place to begin in a search for the utility of
the patent is the counterfactual case of no patents. The inventor without
access to a patent faces something often called the *inventor's paradox* or
Arrow's Information Paradox.[148] Imagine, for example, a small inventor in
a world without patents, tinkering away in a garage or basement workshop
before coming upon an invention with large commercial potential. Imagine
further that large capital investment is required before mass production
can be accomplished. Lacking this capital, and most likely the experience
and resources necessary to advertise, distribute, and sell large quantities as
well, the small inventor must find a buyer (or investor) for the inventive
concepts. Perhaps the inventor approaches the leading producer of related
products; or perhaps the inventor shops for venture capital by going door-
to-door on Wall Street. Any potential buyer, of course, will not pay a high
price, or perhaps any price at all, unless sufficient details are disclosed. The
inventor, however, does not want to disclose too much, for fear the would-
be buyer will instead become an independent producer of the invention's
commercial embodiment, and a competitor of the true inventor. The
inventor's paradox may be solved by a patent, which gives the inventor the
freedom to disclose without fear of self-induced competition.

The inventor's paradox is due largely to certain features that are
shared by all forms of information in general. Information is a special type
of economic good, often called a public good, as distinct from so-called
private goods. Public goods have two characteristics. They are nonrival (*i.e.,*
inexhaustable) and nonexclusive. A good is nonrival if consumption by one
person does not leave any less of the good to be consumed by others. In
microeconomics terms, a good is nonrival if for any given level of production, the marginal cost of providing it to an additional consumer is zero. A
good is nonexclusive if people cannot be excluded from consuming it. How

---

148. *See* Kenneth Arrow, *Economic Welfare and the Allocation of Resources for Invention*, in RATE AND DIRECTION OF INVENTIVE ACTIVITY 609 (1962). Perhaps the term "players'
paradox" is more apt because, as we will see later in this section, it may apply to all who play
in the technology transfer game.

does one preclude others from enjoying one's idea for an invention or poem?[149] In addition to information, national defense, television signals, and police protection are generally considered to be further examples of public goods.

The two distinctive features of public goods—nonrival and nonexclusive—suggest that public goods will tend to be under produced, or not produced at all. Indeed, public goods present a special type of problem called the free rider problem or the problem of positive externalities. If a public good is offered for sale, consumers will have a strong incentive to under-represent their personal value for the good, and thereby attempt to pay a low, or no, price for the good. Consider the example of a neighborhood watch program. If a door-to-door collection is undertaken to raise money for the uniforms, flashlights, and communication devices necessary for the program, each resident will have the incentive to pay less than a simple pro-rata share knowing that he will benefit from the program equally whether he pays or not. One can now see why public goods are viewed as a type of market failure.[150] To ensure that an optimal amount of public goods are produced, governments typically intervene in at least one of several ways. A government, funded with tax dollars, may produce the good itself, as with police protection and national defense. A government may also subsidize private production, as with biotechnology research and development.[151] Alternatively, a government may attempt to create a market for the good by establishing new forms of property rights in things related to the good. Patents are often considered to be one such form of intervention.[152]

One may rightly ask whether government intervention is actually necessary in the market for a specific public good, like information or technical know-how. One might wonder to what extent a producer of technical know-how trapped in the inventor's paradox is actually left with no effective way to profit from the information. Surely, such an inventor who is aware of the various financial markets could easily profit through strategic trading in futures contracts. The price for goods that will be needed as production inputs for the invention (like raw materials) will

---

149. Recall Thomas Jefferson's letter to Isaac McPherson, wherein Jefferson writes "[h]e who receives an idea from me, receives instruction himself without lessening mine; as he who lights his taper at mine, receives light without darkening me." Letter to Isaac McPherson (Aug. 13, 1813), reprinted in JEFFERSON WRITINGS 1291–92 (M. Peterson ed. 1984).

150. See U.S. CONGRESS, OFFICE OF TECHNOLOGY ASSESSMENT, FINDING A BALANCE: COMPUTER SOFTWARE, INTELLECTUAL PROPERTY AND THE CHALLENGE OF TECHNOLOGICAL CHANGE 185 (1992) [hereinafter "TECHNOLOGY ASSESSMENT REPORT"] ("Indeed, individuals have an incentive not to pay for the good, or to undervalue it, in hopes of getting access as 'free riders.' The inability to exclude free riders distorts market signals and is thought to result in inefficient allocation of resources to nonexclusive goods and underproduction of them, relative to socially optimal quantities"). For a more detailed discussion of public goods and the market failures associated with them, see ROBERT COOTER AND THOMAS ULEN, LAW AND ECONOMICS, at 46–49, 108–119, and 134–141(1988); PINDYK AND RUBUNFELD, MICROECONOMICS, *supra* note 162, at 617–641; BINGER AND HOFFMAN, MICROECONOMICS WITH CALCULUS, *supra* note 162, at 99–102, 556–585.

151. See Michael Polanyi, *Patent Reform*, 11 REV. OF ECON. STUDIES 61, 65 (1944).

152. TECHNOLOGY ASSESSMENT REPORT, *supra* note 153, at 185 ("In granting a limited monopoly through copyright and patent, the government attempts to compensate for distortions arising from nonexclusivity [of public goods].").

likely increase if the invention becomes a commercial success. Conversely, the price for goods that compete with the invention but are more expensive will likely plummet. While futures trading may seem too speculative, consider the advice offered in FORBES magazine after Pons' and Fleischmann's announcement of cold fusion:

> It sounds too good to be true: an almost limitless source of clean, inexpensive power from a scientific breakthrough which, if fully confirmed, will be as important as the discovery of fire.
>
> Two chemists working at the University of Utah have announced a simple benchtop device which, they claim, produces a thermal output of 4.5 watts on an input of just 1 watt. The scientists, Stanley Pons and Martin Fleischmann, believe the heat arises from nuclear fusion. Laboratories all over the world have been rushing to confirm the experiment, with mixed results.
>
> The Utah discovery is still a very long way from a commercially usable device. But speculators can't wait for scientific proof. They're laying bets now, in, for example, the commodity markets. Because the Utah device uses a palladium electrode, palladium futures have vaulted. One company is making some quick profits selling deuterium to experimenters.
>
> Palladium is the most obvious way to play the cold fusion phenomenon, but there are at least two other metals now known to have potential importance to the process—titanium and lithium. The pure play on titanium, Oregon Metallurgical (OREM), has skyrocketed. An analyst who covers the stock lifted his buy recommendation as it roared through $15—and as I write this, it has crested at $24. This is speculation on a speculation: Ignore it. Palladium and titanium are risky because cold fusion may not depend on either one.
>
> * * *
>
> Maybe palladium is the secret—but maybe it isn't. For investors who are intrigued by the possibility of cold fusion but don't want to bet too heavily on it, I believe lithium is the best choice. We have ourselves followed this course, because I am strongly convinced that lithium is the essential (and commercially most promising) ingredient in the cold fusion process.
>
> Why lithium? I believe lithium–6 is a source in the cell for tritium (just as it is in the nuclear industry) and that the dominant fusion reaction occurs between this tritium and deuterium. Lithium and its other isotopes, notably lithium–7, are implicated in several alternative interpretations as well.
>
> You can play lithium by investing in the stock of FMC Corp. (My firm bought the stock for customer accounts at $33 on Apr. 11.) FMC is a diversified chemical and machinery company that happens to own and produce lithium. It is probably slightly undervalued, so it is thus a fair investment on its other merits. If the cold fusion phenomenon sputters to a dead end—as it certainly could—you would be left with FMC holdings with substantial value. One could not say this of palladium futures.

Michael Gianturco, *A Fusion Flier*, FORBES, May 15, 1989. Curiously, properly-timed trades in palladium futures would have yielded substantial profits even though it was ultimately determined that Pons and Fleischmann's cold fusion proved to be largely nonexistent. Indeed, anyone familiar with the speculative nature of market pricing might have found the following excerpt from the BOSTON GLOBE especially apropos:

> B. Stanley Pons.... He has a wry sense of humor. Asked in Dallas if a cheaper substitute metal for the rare palladium could be used to generate the same effect in his experiment, he replied: "I refuse to say until I sell my futures."

Chris Black, *Pons A "Little Nerdy" Maybe, But He Gives Great Parties*, THE BOSTON GLOBE, April 17, 1989.[153]

A more traditional solution to the inventor's paradox is the governmentally issued patent grant of the right to exclude others from making, using, offering for sale, or selling the patented invention. The patent right is an important tool for establishing market power—it creates a barrier to market entry. It is argued that the patentee will be unable to recoup the costs of the invention without the patent's right to exclude. Consider the costs of inventing, for example. Both the inventor and a competitor will charge a price based on the costs of producing the inventive product. Only the inventor, however, will have borne the additional costs of inventing. The inventor will therefore want to charge a price that also includes this additional cost. In a competitive market, the inventor will face being undersold by the competitor; and thereby never recoup the cost of inventing. The inability to recoup the costs of inventing will discourage inventors from inventing in the first place.

But does this analysis withstand scrutiny? Absent a patent system, would there really be sub-optimal levels of invention? Before deciding to have a patent system, should we not determine whether there is a market failure that the patent system may be designed to correct?[154] More particularly, what will not be produced in the absence of a patent system? Consider open-source software such as the Linux operating system, Apache server software, or PERL language. Open-source software is a classic public good, yet some of the most talented software programmers devote their time and energy to the development and refinement of a software program that anyone can use without paying a fee. What explains this phenomenon? Professors Josh Lerner and Jean Tirole have asserted that what may motivate these volunteer programmers are "signaling incentives," namely,

153. The reader interested in learning more about market pricing behavior may find particularly accessible the discussion by BURTON MALKIEL, A RANDOM WALK DOWN WALL STREET (1996).

154. For some explanations of suggested market failures *see generally*, Wendy Gordon, *Asymmetric Market Failure and Prisoner's Dilemma in Intellectual Property Law*, 17 U. DAYTON L. REV. (1992). In addition, it was suggested that deeper economic analysis may reveal a useful analogy between the markets for research support and technology transfer and a distinct type of market failure called *natural* monopolies. A natural monopoly is characterized by a market in which it is less expensive to have one firm producing a given quantity of output than to have two firms producing the same quantity. The costs of such a market are said to be "subadditive." *See* Kieff, "*Harnessing Law to Promote Corporate Investment: The Expansive Scope of Intellectual Property*", presented to the Faculty of the Legal Studies Department, The Wharton School, University of Pennsylvania, April 30, 1997 (manuscript on file with the authors). For a general discussion of government regulation of natural monopolies *see* Richard Schmalensee, THE CONTROL OF NATURAL MONOPOLIES (1979), and PAUL JOSKOW AND NANCY ROSE, *The Effects of Economic Regulation*, 2 HANDBOOK OF INDUSTRIAL ORGANIZATION (1989).

"ego gratification"—i.e., peer recognition; and "career concern[s]"—i.e., future job prospects or access to venture capital.[155]

With this in mind, let's take a look at the various incentives that the patent system may provide.

4.   ECONOMIC THEORIES UNDERLYING THE AMERICAN PATENT SYSTEM

The American patent system provides several discrete incentives. While each is important, the relative strength of the various incentive based theories remains a topic of much debate. Indeed, it is unclear which, if any, of the postulated incentives is most needed. In addition, a unified theory postulating some primary incentive may emerge with defined subordinate roles for the other incentives.[156] At the moment, however, it is sufficient for the student to appreciate the existence of at least four different incentives that have been postulated to justify the patent system: (1) incentive to invent; (2) incentive to disclose; (3) incentive to commercialize; and (4) incentive to design around. In each case, it is argued that the patent system provides some incentive that would be present at suboptimal levels absent the patent system.[157]

a.   INCENTIVE TO INVENT

The incentive to invent theory suggests that a patent is granted to encourage invention. Under this theory, the original inventor will not be able to recoup the costs of invention, including risk, unless she is ensured "an exclusive" on the product of her inventive efforts. It is postulated that without this reward, the inventor might not invest in the inventive process.

One objection to this theory is that the incentive may be too great, resulting in an inefficiently high level of pre-inventive activity. Patent incentives may cause too many firms to invest in research and development, resulting in duplicative efforts.[158] The result may be a slightly earlier

---

155. Josh Lerner and Jean Tirole, *The Simple Economics of Open Source* 14–15, February 25, 2000, available at http://www. people.hbs.edu/jlerner/simple.pdf; *see also,* David McGowan, *Legal Implications of Open–Source Software*, 2001 Illinois L. Rev. 241; Marcus Maher, *Open Source Software: The Success of an Alternative Intellectual Property Incentive Paradigm*, 10 FORDHAM INTELL. PROP.MEDIA & ENT. L.J. 619 (2000).

156. *But see,* A. Samuel Oddi, *Un–Unified Economic Theories of Patents—The Not–Quite–Holy Grail*, 71 NOTRE DAME L. REV. 267 (1996).

157. Excellent scholarship has been performed to identify and elucidate the several incentive theories of patent protection. The student is well advised to study at least the following representative seminal works in this field, as well as the works cited therein: Giles S. Rich, *The Relation Between Patent Practices and the Anti–Monopoly Laws*, 24 J. PAT. OFF. SOC'Y 85–106 (Feb., 1942); 24 J. PAT. OFF. SOC'Y 159–181 (Mar.); 24 J. PAT. OFF. SOC'Y 241—283 (Apr.); 24 J. PAT. OFF. SOC'Y 328–356 (May); 24 J. PAT. OFF. SOC'Y 423–437 (June); Edmund W. Kitch, *The Nature and Function of the Patent System*, 20 J. L. & ECON. 265, 285 (1977); Rebecca Eisenberg, *Patents and the Progress of Science*, 50 U. CHI. L. REV. 1017 (1989); Robert P. Merges and Richard R. Nelson, *On The Complex Economics of Patent Scope*, 90 COLUM. L. REV. 839 (1990). For an easily accessible review of different patent theories, *see* Pauline Newman, *Legal and Economic Theory of Patent Law*, ABA–IPL Section, July 21, 1994. Much of the discussion presented below is informed by these works, and many others.

158. Duplicative efforts to obtain the same value are often cited as an example of so-called rent-seeking behavior. The social harm from rent seeking is analogized by Professors

discovery but a substantially increased aggregate cost of inventing.[159] This objection, however, ignores the possibility that duplicative efforts may ultimately lead to entirely distinct alternative inventive solutions to the same underlying necessity-creating problem. It also ignores the possibility that some putatively duplicative alternatives might actually be better for some, or all, consumers. Consider the possibility of two drugs able to cure the same illness but each having distinct side-effects. It may be that patients particularly susceptible to one set of side-effects may prefer, if not require, the second, allegedly duplicative drug.[160]

A further criticism of this theory is that it suggests the inventor should be awarded the total social value of the invention. However, the inventor's contribution is often not the invention itself—which would have eventually been invented by someone else—but rather the timing of the invention. In this case, the patent should not reward for the entire value of the invention, but rather for the value of early discovery and disclosure.[161] This criticism does assume that the invention would have been made anyway; perhaps because the institutional norms of science provide adequate incentive.[162] Indeed, some inventors are simply curious, and will go on inventing absent all the external incentives in the world. This assumption is surely valid for fields such as modern biotechnology, or high technology, which have a large number of people with sufficient creative ability seeking to make the invention.[163] Or is it?

Additional criticisms of this theory suggest that other rewards may be available. Perhaps the government could award valuable prizes to inventors in lieu of patents.[164] Fame, alone may be such a prize.[165] The potential for

---

Landes and Posner to the search for lost treasure by anyone interested, leading to a potential waste of scarce resources. William M. Landes and Richard A. Posner, *Trademark Law: An Economic Perspective*, 30 J. L. AND ECON., 265, 267–68 (1987). For a further discussion of rent seeking and patents, *see* Mark F. Grady and Jay I Alexander, *Patent Law and Rent Dissipation*, 78 VA. L. REV. 305 (1992). *But see*, Merges and Nelson, *On The Complex Economics of Patent Scope*, *supra* note 177.

159. *See* RICHARD A. POSNER, ECONOMIC ANALYSIS OF LAW 36 (1986).

160. It has also been argued that the patent system may provide a disincentive for others to make improvements on a patented invention. Professor Eisenberg notes, however, that this argument ignores the value of improvement patents in providing incentives for downstream inventions. Eisenberg, *Patents and the Progress of Science*, *supra* note 20, at n. 177.

161. *See* Kitch, *The Nature and Function of the Patent System*, *supra* note 160, at 285.

162. *See* Robert K. Merton, *The Role of Genius in Scientific Advance*, NEW SCIENTIST, Nov. 2, 1961, at 306. *But see* JACOB SCHMOOKLER, INVENTION AND ECONOMIC GROWTH, 189–195 (1966). Indeed, as recognized by the Supreme Court, serious evidence and scholarly research into the history and sociology of science suggest that "if something is to be discovered, it will likely be discovered by more than one person." *See Kewanee Oil Co. v. Bicron Corp.*, 416 U.S. 470, 490 (1974) (*citing Singletons and Multiples in Science*, (1961) in ROBERT MERTON, THE SOCIOLOGY OF SCIENCE 343 (1973); JONATHON R. COLE AND STEPHEN COLE, SOCIAL STRATIFICATION IN SCIENCE, 12–13, 229–230 (1973); W. F. Ogburn and Dorothy Thomas, *Are Inventions Inevitable? A Note on Social Evolution*, 37 POL. SCI. Q. 83 (1922))

163. *See* Jacob Schmookler, INVENTION AND ECONOMIC GROWTH 215 (1966).

164. *See* Polanyi, *Patent Reform*, *supra* note 154, at 65. *See also* Steven Shavell & Tanguy van Ypersele, *Rewards Verses Intellectual Property Rights*, 44 J.L. ECON. 525 (2001); Michael Kremer, *Patent Buyouts: A Mechanism for Encouraging Innovation*, 113 Q.J. ECON.

fame, however, requires public disclosure, an issue that is the topic of a separate theory of patent incentives.

b.   INCENTIVE TO DISCLOSE

Incentive to disclose suggests that a patent is granted to encourage an "enabling disclosure" that is required to be in the patent application by Section 112 of Title 35. This theory posits that inventors will seek trade secret protection in the absence of a patent system. Such secrecy would interfere with the basic norms of science, including the free and immediate disclosure of information. Moreover, secrecy would deprive the public of the new knowledge and would lead to duplicative work.[166] Under this theory, the patent is offered in return for the "enabling disclosure" in the patent application.

Several objections have been raised against this theory. Most significantly, secrecy is often not a viable alternative to patent protection. Secrecy is especially unavailing if the invention can be easily reverse-engineered. Moreover, it has been argued that the enabling disclosure of the patent application is often not enabling at all.[167] And oftentimes, to practice the disclosed invention, what is needed is an entire "enabling package," which consists of technical know-how not required to be disclosed in the patent document. In addition, many inventors are driven by fame, at least as much as by money, and are already sufficiently motivated to bring their work to the public's attention. Perhaps the rush to announce cold fusion exemplifies this drive. It may also be argued that where long term secrecy is possible, the incentive to disclose is greatly diminished, especially if infringing activities may be kept equally secret.

c.   INCENTIVE TO COMMERCIALIZE

In his 1942 series of articles on the relationship between the patent and anti-monopoly laws, Judge (then attorney) Rich discussed the above theories, but reminded us that they both

> focus primarily on the inventor as though he were the principal character in this economic drama. We think this is a great mistake. He may be an essential party but the emphasis should be placed elsewhere.[168]

Instead, Judge Rich suggested that the focus should be placed on a third theory:

> The third aspect of inducement is by far the greatest in practical importance. It applies to the inventor but not solely to him, unless he is his own capitalist. It might be called *inducement to risk an attempt to commercialize*

1137, 1147–48 (1998); Michael Abramowicz, *Perfecting Patent Prizes*, 56 VAND. L. REV. 115 (2003).

    165.   *See* LEO KATZ, ILL-GOTTEN GAINS: EVASION, BLACKMAIL, AND KINDRED PUZZLES OF THE LAW (1996).

    166.   *See* Eisenberg, *Patents and the Progress of Science, supra* note 160, at 1028.

    167.   *Id.* at 1029.

    168.   Rich, *The Relation Between Patent Practices, supra* note 143, at 175.

the invention. It is the "business" aspect of the matter which is responsible for the actual delivery of the invention into the hands of the public.[169]

Let us return to the inventor's paradox. Potentially, one of the most serious problems facing the inventor is the lack of experience and resources necessary to produce, advertise, distribute, and sell large quantities of the invention's commercial embodiment.

The so-called incentive to commercialize,[170] incentive to invest, incentive to innovate,[171] or prospect theory,[172] offers the patent as a Coasian-type[173] property right placed on the public's auction block by the government.[174] This theory assumes that the rules of the patent system serve to give fixed and public notice to all parties involved in the technology licensing market.[175] Once the property lines are fixed, the parties will bargain toward an efficient result in which the firm that is best able to bring the patented subject matter to market will do so.[176] The patent system achieves this end by awarding publicly announced, exclusive ownership of a prospect shortly after its discovery.[177] The Gordian Knot of the inventor's paradox is thereby cut, and venture capitalists, developers, advertisers, and sellers can all begin to make the necessary investments to ensure that consumers will eventually be offered the invention's commercial embodiment.

---

169. *Id.* at 179.

170. This is the label given by Judge Rich in his 1942 series of articles. For more on the incentive to commercialize theory, and its connections to Judge Rich and the other framers of the 1952 Patent Act, see, generally, F. Scott Kieff, *Property Rights and Property Rules for Commercializing Inventions*, 85 MINN. L. REV. 697 (2001). For more on the importance of property rights in patents for the commercialization of new technologies see, e.g., Ted Sichelman, *Commercializing Patents*, 62 STAN. L. REV. 341 (2010); Richard A. Epstein, *The Disintegration Of Intellectual Property? A Classical Liberal Response To A Premature Obituary*, 62 STAN. L. REV. 455 (2010); Henry E. Smith, *Intellectual Property as Property: Delineating Entitlements in Information*, 116 YALE L.J. 1742 (2007); F. Scott Kieff, *Coordination, Property & Intellectual Property: An Unconventional Approach to Anticompetitive Effects & Downstream Access*, 56 EMORY L. J. 327 (2006).

171. The role of monopolies in fostering innovation is associated with Professor Schumpeter's work on economic development including, Joseph Schumpeter, CAPITALISM, SOCIALISM, AND DEMOCRACY, 81–110 (1950), Joseph Schumpeter, 1 *Business Cycles*, 84–192 (1939), and Joseph Schumpeter, THE THEORY OF ECONOMIC DEVELOPMENT, 61–94 (1983).

172. This is the label given by professor Edmund Kitch in his article, *The Nature and Function of the Patent System*, *supra* note 177, in which he analogizes the United States patent system to the United States mineral claims system.

173. *See generally* Ronald Coase, *The Problem of Social Cost*, 2 J. L. & ECON. 1, 25 (1959) (describing the importance of rules for fixing initial allocations of resources with which parties can bargain for exchanges in order to increase joint profits).

174. Indeed, the several labels for this theory each correspond to a somewhat different approach toward what is generally considered to be the same underlying feature of the patent system. For purposes of this discussion, therefore, we treat these several theories as one.

175. *See* Suzanne Scotchmer, *Standing on the Shoulders of Giants: Cumulative Research and the Patent Law*, 5 J. ECON. PERSP. 29, 32 (1991).

176. *Id.*

177. This is possible because the invention need not actually be reduced to practice before the patent application is filed: filing constitutes a constructive reduction to practice as a matter of law. *See* Kitch, *The Nature and Function of the Patent System*, *supra* note 160, at 266.

For fear that the validity of this theory might lack intuitive appeal, Judge Rich provides the following pointed example:

> Irving Fisher tells the story of Herbert Spencer who invented "an excellent invalid chair, and, thinking to give it to the world without recompense to himself, did not patent it. The result was that no manufacturer dared *risk* undertaking its manufacture. Each knew that, *if it succeeded*, competitors would spring up and rob him of most or all of his profits, while, on the other hand, *it might fail.*"[178]

This lesson may be timely indeed. The vast potential for tort liability in medicine today may already provide a large disincentive to invest in healthcare-related technologies. Moreover, this disincentive may be combined with a reticence to invest in any health-care product (or service) that is not already flagged as billable or reimbursable by today's large managed health-care provider systems.[179]

Under the incentive to commercialize theory, the patent system can be analogized to the mineral prospecting system in which the staking of the claim is the first step in securing the minerals. Like a mineral claim, a patent application need only disclose an invention that is useful, *i.e.* that works, not necessarily one that is in the most marketable form. The analogy to the mineral prospecting system is extended further in the case of inventions for which substitutions are easily found in the marketplace. The demand facing the inventor of such a substitutable invention is not the market demand facing a monopolist, but rather the horizontal demand confronting a competitive firm.[180]

For example, a monopoly on the better mousetrap will not prevent consumers from buying cats. The seller of better mousetraps must still charge a price which is lower than the cost of a cat.[181] Similarly, the gold mined from any one prospect is usually sold on a market with gold from many other prospects.[182] Under this theory, the dead weight loss associated

---

178. Rich, *The Relation Between Patent Practices, supra* note 143, at 179 (emphasis in original) (citations omitted).

179. The publicly spirited inventor has options besides avoiding patent protection altogether. First, it is important to remember at this juncture that the right to exclude others, which is the core of the patent right, does not *require* that there be any exclusion. Indeed, many patentees choose to offer broad-based, non-exclusive licenses to anyone interested in paying a nominal fee. This licensing strategy is common in the biomedical community for basic inventions. For example, the Columbia University patents on transforming cells with foreign DNA and the Stanford University patents on recombinant DNA have been available for licensing by just about anyone, and the fees are commensurate with the intended use: low for academic use and high for commercial use. The universities that own these patents use the revenues to fund new research. Second, in the context of medicine, as suggested in Joseph M. Reisman, *Physicians and Surgeons as Inventors: Reconciling Medical Process Patents and Medical Ethics*, 10 HIGH TECH. L. J. 355, 397–98 (1995), clearinghouse organizations might be established just like ASCAP and BMI, which exist for copyrights. Doctors could be required by state licensing boards to assign all patents to such clearinghouses, who would then monitor use and collect royalties to be distributed to the public, or to fund research, or apportioned among contributing doctors.

180. *See* Kitch, *The Nature and Function of the Patent System, supra* note 160, at 274.

181. Again, the cost here is an economic one. It includes monetary costs as well as other, harder to quantify costs, such as the cost of caring for and cleaning up after a cat.

182. *See* Kitch, *The Nature and Function of the Patent System, supra* note 160, at 266–275.

with the patent's potential monopoly effects is analytically analogous to the transaction costs[183] of building a fence around the prospect and of the sign designating ownership. Both are merely indispensable costs of using the system to allocate resources.[184]

An important implication of the incentive to commercialize theory is the ability of the patent owner (either the original inventor or a subsequent assignee) to coordinate efforts among all players in the relevant market.[185] The signaling function of the patent is especially important. Potential competitors are warned not to invest in making the same patented product;[186] while at the same time are encouraged by the patentee's already established customer base to invent improvements to the patented product. In addition, potential competitors may even be induced to create non-infringing alternatives. This inducement lies at the heart of the fourth theory of patent incentives, the incentive to design around.

d. INCENTIVE TO DESIGN AROUND

The last of the incentives is the incentive to design around. This is really a corollary to the incentive to invest. Incentive to design around proudly offers the patent as forbidden turf, taunting competitors to circumvent its scope by inventing substitutes. Under this theory, one might only condemn the patentee for teasing, and not for taking.

As the market for a patented product becomes tighter and tighter, the patent provides a stronger and stronger incentive for third parties to invent non-infringing substitutes, or even infringing improvements. Simultaneously, it provides stronger and stronger incentives for capitalists to invest in such secondary inventive activity. While at first blush this may seem wasteful, as redundant, it becomes immediately apparent that such secondary inventive activity is usually a very good thing. Often, a second-generation product is better than the first: perhaps being cheaper, more effective, or having fewer collateral costs or side effects. Remember the possibility of two drugs usable to cure the same illness but each having distinct side-effects. Patients particularly susceptible to one set of side effects may prefer, if not require, the second, allegedly duplicative drug.

---

183. As distinct from the costs of raw materials and hired labor. Both of these costs will have allocative effects but do not necessarily decrease net societal wealth.

184. *See* POSNER, ECONOMIC ANALYSIS OF LAW, *supra* note 162, at 37.

185. *See* Kitch, *The Nature and Function of the Patent System*, *supra* note 160, at 276. *See also*, Joseph Schumpeter, CAPITALISM, SOCIALISM, AND DEMOCRACY, 81–110 (1950), Joseph Schumpeter, 1 *Business Cycles*, 84–192 (1939), and Joseph Schumpeter, THE THEORY OF ECONOMIC DEVELOPMENT, 61–94 (1983).

186. *See* POSNER, ECONOMIC ANALYSIS OF LAW, *supra* note 162, at 36.

CHAPTER TWO

OBTAINING THE PATENT GRANT

> [T]he antlike persistency of [patent] solicitors has overcome, and I suppose, will continue to overcome, the patience of examiners, and there is apparently always but one outcome.
>
> —Judge Learned Hand[1]

> The life of a patent solicitor has always been a hard one.
>
> —Judge Giles S. Rich[2]

INTRODUCTION

The previous chapter explained some of the purposes and policies of the patent system and some of the ways a patent can affect the economics of innovation. This chapter will introduce the broad concepts and basic vocabulary involved in the process by which an inventor obtains a patent.[3]

As its name suggests, the United States Patent and Trademark Office (PTO) plays a crucial role in the U.S. patent system. Patent rights do not exist unless granted by the federal government.[4] To obtain a patent, an inventor must file a patent application with the PTO. Then, the Director of Patents and Trademarks is required to "cause an examination to be made of the application and the alleged new invention; and if on such examination it appears that the applicant is entitled to a patent under the law, the Director shall issue a patent therefor." 35 U.S.C. § 131. Examination is conducted to ensure that the claimed invention is adequately disclosed (*see* Chapter Three), new (*see* Chapter Four), nonobvious (*see* Chapter Five),

---

1. *Lyon v. Boh,* 1 F.2d 48, 50 (S.D.N.Y.1924), *rev'd,* 10 F.2d 30 (2d Cir.1926).

2. *In re Ruschig*, 379 F.2d 990, 993 (CCPA 1967).

3. In the United States, unlike most other countries, patents are applied for and issued in the name of the individual inventor or inventors. *See* 35 U.S.C. §§ 111, 115–118, 151–152. To be sure, many inventions are owned by the inventor's employer, often a company, but the actual inventors are required to be named, and incorrect reporting of inventorship in a patent, unless corrected in accordance with statute, can invalidate the patent. *See* 35 U.S.C. §§ 102(f), 256.

4. In contrast, for example, copyright subsists in a work once it is "fixed in any tangible medium of expression", 17 U.S.C. § 102 (a); and federal registration is needed only if the copyright owner wants to bring an infringement action and pursue statutory damages, 17 U.S.C. §§ 411, 412. Similarly, property rights in trademarks are initially created by using the mark in trade, not by governmental grant or registration; while federal registration gives the owner the benefit of additional federal rights and remedies. *See In re DC Comics, Inc.,* 689 F.2d 1042, 1046–55 (CCPA 1982) (opinions by Judges Rich and Nies concurring in result and reviewing the life-cycle of a trademark—beginning with initial use and ending with abandonment or genericness); *see also* Daphne Leeds, *Trademarks—The Rationale of Registrability*, 26 GEO. WASH. L. REV. 653, 666 (1958).

useful (*see* Chapter Six), and within at least one of the statutory classes of patentable subject matter (*see* Chapter Seven). The process of obtaining a patent is called *patent prosecution.*

The writing necessary for a patent application is very technical and a degree in the relevant scientific discipline or other appropriate technical background is helpful. Indeed, the patent prosecutor has an obligation to know and comprehend not only the law, but also the pertinent technology. Thus, specialized training is generally required,[5] with a few notable exceptions, for registration to practice before the PTO.

The patent application, and the resulting issued patent, contains two major components: (1) the *written description*, and (2) the *claims.* These two components together make up the *specification.*[6] The process by which the patent specification and especially the patent claims are shaped is of primary importance because the claims of the issued patent establish the metes and bounds of the patent owner's right to exclude. As described by Judge Rich:

> The U.S. is strictly an examination country and the main purpose of the examination, to which every application is subjected, is to try and make sure that what each claim defines is patentable. To coin a phrase, *the name of the game is the claim* ... [and] the function of claims is to enable everyone to know, without going through a lawsuit, what infringes the patent and what does not.[7]

This chapter is divided into two parts. The first part focuses on the patent application and the steps in the patent prosecution process. In so doing, it also introduces the jargon of patent prosecution. It should be noted, however, entire courses and books are devoted solely to the topic of patent prosecution, and entire legal practices are devoted to this specialty. This chapter merely introduces this complex field of law to the extent necessary to understand the basic principles of patent law.

The second part of the chapter discusses the procedures by which an issued patent may be taken back to the PTO for correction or other modification. These processes are called *reissue* and *reexamination* and have an important role in our patent system.

But before we begin our discussion of the patent document, patent prosecution, and post-issuance procedures, consider the following excerpt by Professors John Allison and Mark Lemley. Professors Allison and

---

5. *See* 37 C.F.R. §§ 10.5, 10.6, 10.7 (2002), wherein the regulations governing individuals practicing before the PTO are set forth. The PTO annually issues a pamphlet entitled "General Requirements for Admission to the Examination for Registration to Practice in Patent Cases before the U.S. Patent and Trademark Office." *See* www.uspto.gov.

6. *See* 35 U.S.C. § 112. Although often, and incorrectly, used interchangeably, the terms "written description" and "specification" are *not* co-extensive. The specification encompasses both the claims *and* the written description.

7. Giles S. Rich, *The Extent of the Protection and Interpretation of Claims—American Perspectives*, 21 Int'l Rev. Indus. Prop. & Copyright L. 497, 499, 501 (1990) as quoted in *Hilton Davis Chem. Co. v. Warner–Jenkinson Co.*, 62 F.3d 1512, 1539 (Fed.Cir.1995) (Plager, Circuit Judge, with whom Chief Judge Archer and Circuit Judges Rich and Lourie join, dissenting) (emphasis in original).

Lemley nicely explore who is obtaining patents, what types of inventions are being patented, and how the patent prosecution process has evolved.

The Growing Complexity of the United States Patent System*
John R. Allison and Mark A. Lemley.
82 B.U. L. REV. 77 (2002).

Introduction

A great deal has been written lately on the growing importance of intellectual property rights to the economy. With this new focus has come increased attention to the patent system. It is well known that the number of patents is increasing rapidly. Scholars offer a variety of explanations for this increase. One explanation is economic: Writers talk of the "new" or "information" economy, in which ideas rather than capital investments are the mainstay of value. As intellectual property becomes more central to a company's value, perhaps companies are willing to spend more to protect it. Another explanation is technological: we are in an era of astounding productivity attributable to technological innovation, and that innovation reflects itself in more patents. A third explanation is legal: the development of the Federal Circuit in 1982 led to stronger patent rights, which encouraged more patenting. There are even cultural explanations: the increasing attention paid to intellectual property in the media and popular press has led people to pay more attention to patents.

However, any focus on absolute numbers obscures a number of interesting facts about the trends in patenting over the past twenty-five years. To understand the significance of this broader trend, we should look not only at how many patents are being issued, but also at who is obtaining them and for what sorts of inventions. Further, we should try to understand how the process of prosecuting patents has changed over time.

In a recent study, we collected and analyzed a random sample of 1000 utility patents issued between 1996 and 1998.[7] We then identified a large number of facts about each of these patents. In that article, we used data from this sample to predict the characteristics of patents being obtained in the entire population of patents issued during that period. We also tested for several relationships in these patents, such as how nationality relates to area of technology and how the size of the patentee relates to the prosecution process. In this Article, we compare that data set to a similar random sample of 1000 patents issued twenty years earlier, between 1976 and 1978. By studying the differences between the groups, we can get a clear picture of how the patent system has changed over time.

The results are dramatic. By almost any measure—subject matter, time in prosecution, number of prior art references cited, number of claims, number of continuation applications filed, number of inventors—the patents issued in the late 1990s are more complex than those issued in the

---

* Reprinted with permission of the authors.

7. *See* John R. Allison & Mark A. Lemley, *Who's Patenting What? An Empirical Exploration of Patent Prosecution*, 53 VAND. L. REV. 2099 (2000) (finding significant variation in the patent prosecution processes of firms in different industries, firms, and nations).

1970s. While some of these effects are attributable to the patenting of new technologies relatively unknown in the early 1970s, like biotechnology and software, the increase in complexity is robust even across areas of technology. Further, the patent system in the 1990s was more heterogeneous than it was in the 1970s. There are far greater differences by area of technology and by nationality in how patents were prosecuted in the 1990s than there were in the 1970s.

We made a number of other interesting findings as well. Among our most important results are the following:

1. There are some radical differences in the nature of the technologies being patented. On the whole, the trend has been towards patenting in industries considered "high–tech," such as software, semiconductors, computers, and biotechnology. Not all increases fit into this category, however, medical devices and automotive technologies also accounted for significantly more patents in the 1990s than in the 1970s. The big losers during this period were the traditional mainstay of patents—mechanical inventions— as well as the somewhat higher–tech category of electronics.

2. U.S. patents are overwhelmingly obtained by inventors in the developed world. Nationality of origin has diversified slightly since the 1970s, but inventorship remains concentrated in North America, Europe, and a small number of Asian countries.

3. Patenting in the united states today is something that is largely done by corporations, not individuals. Further, the trend is clearly continuing in that direction. but the development is not a new one; even in the 1976–78 sample, more than three–quarters of all inventors assigned their patent rights to a corporation.

4. Patent prosecution time has increased substantially over the past twenty years. the increase has occurred across the board, but it is particularly large in fields like pharmaceuticals and biotechnology. this is especially significant given the change in patent term, which is now measured from the filing date and not from the date the patent issued. increased delay in prosecution means that patentees receive less protection, a fact that was politically controversial throughout the 1990s. part of this increase can be attributed to the greater use of continuation practice by patentees, but even when controlling for that practice, patent applications in the 1990s took longer to get through the Patent & Trademark Office ("PTO") than they did in the 1970s. additionally, there is much greater variation by area of technology and by nationality in the time in prosecution than there was in the 1970s.

5. Patents issued in the 1990s cited vastly more prior art than patents issued in the 1970s. overall, patents in the 1996–98 sample cited almost three times as much total prior art, and more than ten times as much non–patent art, as patents in the 1976–78 sample. Industries vary in the amount of prior art they cite much more than they did in the 1970s. Further, U.S. patentees cited the same number of references as their foreign counterparts in the 1970s, but nearly twice as many references in the 1990s.

6. Patents issued in the 1990s contained approximately 50% more claims than patents issued in the 1970s. this means that those patents were somewhat more expensive to prosecute, and it may also indicate that the technology was more complex.

* * *

IV.   Implications of Our Results

A.   Explaining the Results

We have analyzed a great deal of data. Neither the complexity of the relationships we found nor the nature of our methodology lends itself to easy predictions about causation. The reader is cautioned, therefore, that we now leave the hard world of data for the rather more speculative world of theorizing.

At least two themes emerge from the data. First, obtaining a patent was a more complex process in the late 1990s than it was twenty years earlier. Across the board, patent applicants put more claims in their patents, cited more prior art of all types, spent longer in prosecution, and more frequently refiled their applications. Patented inventions tended to be for more complex, "high technology" inventions, and they had more inventors per patent than twenty years before.

Second, patents in the 1990s were much more heterogeneous than their 1970s counterparts. In our prior study, we observed:

> The U.S. patent prosecution system is not unitary. Rather, different entities experience very different sorts of patent prosecution. For example, chemical, pharmaceutical, and biotechnological patents spend much longer in prosecution than other types of patents. Chemical, medical, and biotechnological patents cite much more prior art than other patents, and are abandoned and refiled much more frequently. Our current study demonstrates that this heterogeneity is a product of the last twenty years. None of the factors that today vary so much by country of origin or area of technology was so divided in the 1976–78 sample. Something has happened in the past three decades that caused different pieces of the patent system to move in such different directions.

We can think of several possible explanations for these changes—particularly the increasing complexity of patents—but none is entirely satisfactory. First, it is certainly true that the nature of the technology being patented has changed significantly over this period. Two of the fourteen subject matter categories we used in our 1990s study—software and biotechnology—are not represented at all in the 1970s study. The 1976–78 patents were more likely to be mechanical inventions, which tend to be simpler than other types. This is doubtless a partial explanation for the increased time in prosecution and the increase in prior art citations. Those two factors in turn may influence both the number of applications filed—because applications are more likely to be rejected as more prior art is considered, necessitating more "bites at the apple" by patent applicants—and the number of claims—since patent attorneys may have to draft claims more carefully to avoid the prior art. Technological changes may also explain the increase in heterogeneity; today's inventions simply arise from a wider variety of fields.

Changes in technology cannot explain all the results of our study, however. In particular, the relationship between area of technology and such factors as time in prosecution and number of prior art references cited has itself changed over time. If the overall numbers were simply an artifact of shifts in technology—for example, more patents in the semiconductor category and fewer in mechanics—we would expect the characteristics of patents within those categories to remain stable. . . .

A second hypothesis is that the U.S. PTO conducted much more thorough examinations of patents in the 1990s than it did in the 1970s. Were this true, it would provide an explanation for many of the complexity-related changes. A more thorough examination would cite more prior art and lead to more rejections and thus more refilings, thus causing patents to spend more time in prosecution and possibly causing patentees to write more claims as a safeguard. The problem with the heightened examination process theory is that it does not appear to be borne out by the facts.

The PTO changed the rules in the early 1980s to impose a somewhat higher obligation on patent applicants to disclose prior art of which they are aware. This may account for the aggregate increase in prior art citations. But more prior art disclosed by the applicant does not necessarily imply a more rigorous examination process. PTO examiners spend startlingly little time on a patent—an average total of only eighteen hours over three years. Further, Quillen and Webster have found that once continuation, continuation-in-part, and divisional applications are accounted for as renewed attempts to protect the subject matter of their parent applications, the PTO ultimately granted patents on between 85% and 97% of the applications filed between 1993 and 1998. It is hard to imagine that this is a significantly more rigorous examination than the PTO conducted in the 1970s.

Examination quality might also provide an explanation for heterogeneity, but only if the quality of the PTO examination were thought to vary significantly by subject matter. There is certainly anecdotal evidence to support this proposition; biotechnology attorneys regularly complain that the examiners in their art units are too tough on them, while others complain about the laxity of examination in fields like software. There is also evidence that the law itself varies somewhat by subject matter, with biotechnology patents being read more narrowly than software patents. This evidence is not strong enough to explain our results. The variation occurs across many different fields. Further, it changes over time. Evidence regarding software and biotechnology patents is largely irrelevant to our results, since neither field had any patents in our 1976–78 sample. We know of no evidence—anecdotal or otherwise—to suggest that examination quality has changed radically in different directions in other fields.

Third, it may be that the increase in patenting during the last quarter-century reflects a greater willingness to patent incremental or marginal improvements over the prior art. If this is true in general, it may explain the greater complexity of the patent system; if it is true only in certain industries, it may also explain heterogeneity. The theory is that it is harder to obtain patents for innovations that represent only a slight improvement over the prior art. The PTO may require the applicant to distinguish more and closer prior art, and this may induce applicants to write more claims to ensure that some of those claims survive. Further, examiners may be less willing to grant patents on such marginally improved technologies. This in turn means a tougher prosecution process, which may take longer and require the filing of more continuations. We will call this theory incrementalism.

While incrementalism may explain the growing complexity of the patent prosecution process, it has a harder time explaining industry-specific variation in that process. In particular, the line of reasoning set out above would lead one to conclude that patents were least innovative in the biotechnology and pharmaceutical industries, and most pioneering in the semiconductor industry. This goes against the common wisdom in these fields, as well as the available sector-specific empirical evidence. The evidence suggests just the opposite: semiconductor patents are rarely litigated and are generally used for incremental improvements, while biotechnology and pharmaceutical patents are more frequently litigated than patents in other industries and are often for entirely new products. Thus, incrementalism seems troubling as an explanation for modern changes in patenting.

A fourth possible explanation has to do with search techniques: it is much easier for the PTO and patent applicants to find relevant prior art today than it was in the 1970s. Computer searching in particular may enable examiners to find more non-patent prior art, thus helping to explain the ten-fold increase in citations to such art. It may also enable examiners to find prior art patents that are not classified in the same category as the application, but that have search terms in common. By the chain of reasoning used above, citing more prior art may help explain the other results we found. We do think that the ease of searching is a partial explanation for the dramatic increase in prior art citations, and therefore it may be an indirect explanation for some of the other findings. But we do not believe that is the whole explanation. Although U.S. patent applicants now cite far more art than foreign patent applicants, they did not do so in the 1970s. The ease of PTO searching does not explain why prior art citations tend to show up disproportionately in applications filed by U.S. nationals. Similarly, the search technology theory has difficulty explaining the variation in prior art citations across different areas of technology. It is possible to construct explanations for these differences: for example, U.S. nationals may have better access to technology, or computer searching may work better in some industries than others because of the nature of each industry's prior art. As a result, we don't want to rule this explanation out altogether.

A final hypothesis has to do with the increasing importance of patents to the economy. On this theory, companies have started to pay greater attention to their patent portfolios, making greater use of the patents they have. Certainly there is anecdotal evidence that patents have a higher profile in companies now than they had in the 1970s. Also, patent litigation is increasing; it may be that licensing is increasing too. An increase in the importance of patents may in turn mean that patentees are willing to expend more effort to "get it right," thereby increasing the post-issuance value of their patents. Filing more claims is one way to do that, as it makes it more likely that a patent will "read on" an accused infringer's device. Citing more prior art will also make a patent more valuable in litigation, as it is much harder to prove a patent is invalid if the PTO has already considered and rejected the relevant prior art. More claims and more prior art may mean a longer prosecution process, particularly if the patentee is willing to fight harder to get patent claims with significant scope. Fighting for a broad patent may necessitate refiling, further delaying the issuance of a patent.

The patent value theory may also explain at least some of the heterogeneity we found in the data. First, we found in a prior study that U.S. patentees are far more likely than foreign patentees to enforce their patents in court. Indeed, U.S. patentees accounted for only about half of the total patents issued, but more than 83% of the patents litigated to judgment. Thus, it is plausible that U.S. patentees consider their patents more valuable, at least as litigation or licensing tools, and that they are more willing to spend time and money to improve their patents' quality. This may help explain our findings that U.S. patents cite far more prior art than their foreign counterparts, that they are more likely to be refiled, and that they spend longer in prosecution.

Second, patents are more likely to be used offensively in some industries than in others. In particular, patent litigation is especially likely to occur in the biotechnology and pharmaceutical industries, the two industries whose patentees spent the most time in prosecution and that were the second and third highest citers of prior art. By contrast, litigation is uncommon in the semiconductor and electronics industries, where patent owners frequently engage in royalty-free cross-licensing. Patents in those two industries cited the least prior art in the 1990s, and they were among the quickest patents to issue. While litigation and licensing are not the only measures of patent value—there are lots of other uses for patents—they are certainly indicators of how valuable a patentee considers an invention to be.

A related virtue of this theory is that it can help explain the change in heterogeneity over time. Patents issued in the 1970s arrived at a low point for the patent system. The Federal Circuit did not yet exist. Two-thirds of all patents litigated during that period were held invalid, and relatively few patent lawsuits were filed. By common consensus, patents simply were not very important to business strategy during that period. By contrast, the patent boom of the 1980s and 1990s has led to dramatic changes in the patent system as a whole. But it has been particularly important for U.S. patentees and for patents in certain industries.

If our patent value theory is correct, it implies that litigated patents will on average cite more prior art, have more claims, and spend longer in prosecution than ordinary patents. There is some indirect evidence to support this supposition;[153] we plan to test it more fully in a later study.*

---

153. In 1994, Lemley found that patents issued prior to 1989 and litigated between 1989 and 1994 spent longer in prosecution than a random sample of patents issued in 1994. See

We do not believe that the increasing salience of patents to U.S. business offers a full explanation for our findings. Changes in technology and new search techniques doubtless played a role as well, and there are almost certainly other factors at work. But the patent value theory strikes us as the most plausible explanation for many of the dramatic changes we have seen over the last quarter-century.

* * *

STATUTORY PROVISIONS—35 U.S.C. §§ 111–113, 119, 122, 132, 351

A.   THE PATENT APPLICATION AND ISSUED PATENT[8]

Although the patent application process may be thought of as beginning with the drafting of the application itself, this is usually preceded by other events. For example, an inventor usually documents and records his or her conception of the invention as well as the ensuing development of the invention towards a practical embodiment—this development process is called *"reduction to practice."* Thereafter, it is common practice that the inventor prepares an invention disclosure that is used by the person preparing the application to form the basis of the application. In addition, substantial dialogue may occur between the inventor and the person preparing the application.

Another probable pre-filing event is a *prior art* search. "Prior art" is a term used in patent law to refer broadly to known technical information.[9] Although an applicant is under no obligation to conduct a search prior to filing an application, *see American Hoist & Derrick Co. v. Sowa & Sons,*

Mark A. Lemley, An Empirical Study of the Twenty–Year Patent Term, 22 AIPLA Q.J. 369, 421–22 (1994) ("The patents litigated between 1989 and 1994 spent significantly more time in prosecution on average than did the group of patents issued in December 1994."). Since overall time in prosecution was increasing rather than decreasing during this period, the most plausible explanation is that litigated patents were not a random cross-section of issued patents, but were ones that had spent longer in prosecution. However, the 1994 study did not test that proposition statistically. For other evidence, see Daniel K.N. Johnson, *Forced Out of the Closet: The Impact of the American Inventors Protection Act on the Timing of Patent Disclosure* 6 (2001) (NBER Working Paper 8374). In addition, Lanjouw and Schankerman found that the number of claims in a patent—which they used as a measure of an invention's value—was positively correlated with the likelihood of litigation; accordingly, they concluded that more litigation occurred with more valuable patents. See Jean O. Lanjouw & Mark Schankerman, *Characteristics of Patent Litigation: A Window on Competition*, 32 RAND J. Econ. 129, 137–41 (2001) (finding that the mean number of claims in a patent was larger for litigated patents and concluding that litigated patents were more valuable). Harhoff et al. found that citations to prior art were positively correlated with patent value....

* Editors' footnote: *See* John R. Allison, Mark A. Lemley, Kimberly A. Moore & R. Derek Trunkey, *Valuable Patents*, 435 Georgetown L.J. 92 (2003).

8. Substantive changes in the description and drawing portions of the application are generally not permitted after filing. Thus, the application and final patent share the same structure. References in this chapter to portions of the application also refer to corresponding portions of the patent.

9. To be patentable, an invention must be both new and nonobvious in view of the prior art. *See* Chapter Four "Novelty and Loss of Right," *infra*, and 35 U.S.C. § 102; and Chapter Five "Nonobviousness," *infra*, and 35 U.S.C. § 103.

725 F.2d 1350, 1362 (Fed.Cir.1984), a search is usually done in view of the significant cost associated with preparing and filing a patent application. A thorough search may save the costs of attempting to secure a patent on an unpatentable invention. It may also help give the applicant an opportunity to make informed arguments about the patentability of the invention, and to present the written description and claims in a way favorable to patentability.[10] This search for relevant prior patents and other technical literature may be carried out in the Public Search Room maintained by the PTO in its Arlington, Virginia, location or various satellite search locations scattered throughout the country, or in libraries or other repositories. Today, one may conduct a prior art search using various electronic media, including on-line services and the Internet.

Each application consists of a (1) specification (*i.e.*, the written description and at least one claim), (2) one or more drawings (if necessary), (3) an oath or declaration,[11] and (4) the required filing fees (*See* 35 U.S.C. § 111(a)(2)–(3) (Supp. 2001)). The filing date of such an application, known as a *non-provisional* application,[12] is the date on which the specification and drawings, including at least one claim, are received at the PTO or the date they were deposited in a U.S. post office as Express Mail.

Filing Date ✳

While there is some flexibility as to the presentation of the patent application, the PTO prefers the application to be filed as follows:

1. title;

2. cross-reference to related inventions;

3. statement regarding federally-sponsored research;

4. background of the invention;

5. summary of the invention;

6. brief description of the drawings,

---

10.   Although the search may appear to create added hurdles for the applicant—because it might reveal closer prior art than was known to the inventor, for example—most practitioners actually view these hurdles as an important boost for the patent in several respects. First, previously unknown issues are revealed and can now be addressed in a forum that is more favorable to the patent applicant—i.e., the PTO. Second, the cost of addressing these issues in prosecution is far less than addressing them later in litigation—and it is possible that they might not have otherwise arisen during prosecution, yet still arise in litigation.

11.   The oath or declaration must usually be signed by the inventor, and must state that the inventor has (1) read the application, (2) believes he is the first inventor, and (3) acknowledges the duty to disclose any material information. *See* 37 C.F.R. § 1.63 (b) (2002). 37 C.F.R. § 1.77 (2002); Patent & Trademark Office, U.S. Department of Commerce, MANUAL OF PATENT EXAMINING PROCEDURE [hereinafter MPEP] § 601 (8th ed. 2001, rev. 2003).

12.   Instead of *initially* filing a non-provisional application, an applicant, as of June 8, 1995, may opt to file a *provisional application*. A provisional application does not require claims, it is not examined, and cannot mature into a patent. 35 U.S.C. § 111(b) (2001). Nevertheless, priority can still be claimed from the date of the provisional application under 35 U.S.C. § 119(e) by filing a non-provisional application within one-year from the provisional application's filing date. The advantages of initially filing a "provisional application" instead of a non-provisional application include a slightly lower initial cost and a delay of prosecution costs. However, the provisional application also results in a delay in issuance of a patent, a higher total cost and a risk of inadequate disclosure, which could prove fatal to a claim of priority.

7.   detailed description of the invention;

8.   claims;

9.   abstract of the disclosure;

10.   drawings;

11.   oath or declaration.

The rest of this section will use Sorenson U.S. Patent 5,425,497 to illustrate the different elements of the actual patent. The Sorenson patent describes a popular cupholder for holding cups filled with hot or cold liquids. This cardboard holder insulates against temperature and provides gripability. The cover page for the '497 patent is depicted on the following page.[13]

---

13.   Once cited in full in a document, patents are referred to by their final three numbers throughout the rest of the document.

US005425497A

United States Patent [19]

Sorensen

[11]	Patent Number:	**5,425,497**
[45]	Date of Patent:	Jun. 20, 1995

[54] **CUP HOLDER**

[76] Inventor: **Jay Sorensen**, 3616 NE. Alberta Ct., Portland, Oreg. 97211

[21] Appl. No.: **150,682**

[22] Filed: **Nov. 9, 1993**

[51] Int. Cl.⁶ B65D 3/22

[52] U.S. Cl. 220/738; 220/903; 294/31.2

[58] Field of Search .... 294/27.1, 31.2, 33, 294/149, 152; 220/710.5, 753, 758, 759, 412, 738, 739, 903; 229/1.5 B, 1.5 H, 89, 90

[56] **References Cited**

U.S. PATENT DOCUMENTS

1,632,347	6/1927	Pipkin .	
1,771,765	7/1930	Benson .	
1,866,805	7/1932	Haywood	294/31.2
2,028,566	1/1936	Seipel et al. .	
2,266,828	12/1941	Sykes .	
2,591,578	4/1952	McNealy et al. .	
2,617,549	11/1952	Egger .	
2,661,889	12/1953	Phinney .	
2,675,954	4/1954	Vogel .	
2,853,222	9/1958	Gallagher .	
2,979,301	4/1961	Reveal	229/1.5 H X
3,049,277	8/1962	Shappell .	
3,123,273	3/1964	Miller	229/1.5 B
3,157,335	11/1964	Maier	229/1.5 B
3,908,523	9/1975	Shikaya .	
4,685,583	8/1987	Noon	294/31.2 X
5,092,485	3/1992	Lee .	
5,145,107	9/1992	Silver et al. .	

Primary Examiner—Johnny D. Cherry
Attorney, Agent, or Firm—Kolisch, Hartwell, Dickinson, McCormack & Heuser

[57] **ABSTRACT**

A cup holder is disclosed in the form of a sheet with distal ends. A web is formed in one of the ends, and a corresponding slot is formed in the other end such that the ends interlock. Thus the cup holder is assembled by rolling the sheet and interlocking the ends. The sheet can be an elongate band of pressed material, preferably pressed paper pulp, and is preferably formed with multiple nubbins and depressions. In one embodiment, the sheet has a top and bottom that are arcuate and concentric, and matching webs and cuts are formed in each end of the sheet, with the cuts being perpendicular to the top of the sheet.

6 Claims, 1 Drawing Sheet

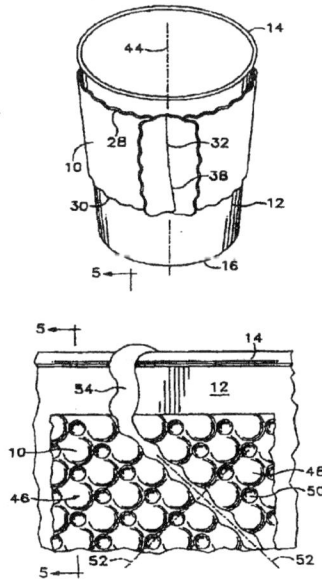

1. THE WRITTEN DESCRIPTION

a. BACKGROUND OF THE INVENTION

The Background of the Invention, together with a short statement about the general Field of the Invention, introduces the reader to the surroundings into which the invention was introduced. In the Sorenson patent, the Background describes the state of the art for cupholders. It also describes certain problems in the state of the art that the patent is intended to solve. Finally, the Background sets forth the objects of the invention which are tailored to fix the problems in the prior art. The background section for the '497 patent follows:

> A cup holder is a removable device that encompasses a cup to provide added features to the cup. These features can include gripability, insulation value, and decoration. By gripability it is meant that the cup and holder combination is easier to hold in a human hand. Insulation value is important if the cup is holding hot or cold liquids, particularly if the cup is a thin disposable paper cup which has little inherent insulation value. Decoration can include features that make the cup more appealing, such as texture or color, or features that communicate to the user of the holder, such as advertising or instructions.

> A conventional cup holder includes a three-dimensional body into which the cup is inserted. These bodies can be in the shape of an annular ring, such as that shown in U.S. Pat. No. 2,028,566, or in the shape of a cup that is oversized relative to the cup to be held, such as that shown in U.S. Pat. No. 2,617,549. In order to provide insulation value from a material that is thermally conductive, such as paper, the cup holders are usually provided with annular grooves or vertical flutes so that the holder is only in contact with the cup at the valleys in the grooves or flutes. These grooves or flutes provide a structural integrity to the cup holders such that they must be packaged in substantially the same form as they will be used. Thus a significant volume is required to store a quantity of the cup holders. Therefore it is cumbersome for a retailer selling drinks in cups to use the cup holders because a significant amount of shelf space is required just to have a sufficient quantity of cup holders accessible for immediate use.

> It is an object of the invention to reduce the volume required to store cup holders.

> Conventional cup holders may also require significant amounts of handling and operations to be assembled. It is a further object of this invention to reduce the number of steps involved in making a cup holder ready for ultimate use by the consumer.

> An object of the invention is to produce a cup holder by bending a sheet and interlocking the ends.

> It is a further object of the invention to improve the gripability of a cup.

> Yet another object of the invention is to thermally insulate the hand of a user from the liquid held in a cup.

> Another object of the invention is to form a cup holder from a substantially flat sheet of pressed paper pulp.

The Background section of the '497 patent accomplished three things: (1) it sets the stage for the applicant's invention by describing the state of prior art; (2) it directly addressed the unsolved problems found in the prior art; and (3) it stated the objects of the invention, and tailored them closely to the stated problems. Skilled practitioners disagree about whether to introduce the invention's objects in the Background section, or whether to limit the Background section to discussion of prior art.

The Background section should use as simple language as the invention permits, especially with respect to commercial issues. Although the law provides that a patent application should disclose technical information to a person of skill in the art to which the invention pertains, some argue that every patent should be written with an eye to the judge, jury, and investment banker, as well as the patent examiner.

b. SUMMARY OF THE INVENTION

The Summary states the invention broadly, tracking the broadest claim, but requires sufficient detail to explain and distinguish from the prior art. The Manual of Patent Examining Procedure[14] (MPEP) § 608.01(d) (8th ed. 2001, rev. 2003) points out, "[s]ince the purpose of the brief summary of invention is to apprise the public, and more especially those interested in the particular art to which the invention relates, of the nature of the invention, the summary should be directed to the specific invention being claimed, in contradistinction to mere generalities which would be equally applicable to numerous preceding patents." The MPEP also suggests that "[t]he brief summary, if properly written to set out the exact nature, operation, and purpose of the invention, will be of material assistance in aiding ready understanding of the patent in future searches."

Although no one particular way to write the Summary exists, it is recommended that § 608.01(d) of the MPEP be followed so that the patent examiner, as well as the public, knows where to look for various kinds of information.

The "Summary of the Invention" section of the '497 patent follows:

The invented cup holder is designed for use with an upright cup. The cup is in turn designed for holding hot or cold liquids, and has an open rim and closed base.

The invented cup holder is formed from a sheet of flat material, preferably pressed paper pulp. The sheet is formed to have a length defined by a first end and a second end. The sheet has a width defined by a top and a bottom. Two cuts are made in the sheet, the first cut extending partially across the width of the sheet and adjacent one end. The second cut also extends partially across the width of the sheet, but is adjacent the end of the sheet opposite from the first cut. Preferably, one of the cuts severs the top of the sheet and the other of the cuts severs the bottom of the sheet. A holder conforming to a cup can then be made by rolling the sheet into a substantially cylindrical shape and interlocking the first end with the second end by interlocking the first cut with the second cut. Once the cylindrically shaped cup holder is made, a cup can be inserted into the cup holder.

The sheet includes a texture to increase the gripability and insulation value of the cup holder. In one embodiment, the texture includes multiple nubbins and depressions interspersed about the sheet, preferably in a uniform repeating geometrical pattern. The depressions can be aligned in rows forming troughs, so that any liquid that should spill on the cup holder will tend to trickle along the troughs.

---

14. The Manual of Patent Examining Procedure (MPEP) is published by the Patent and Trademark Office. It is the main reference work for patent examiners, applicants, attorneys, and agents for the practices and procedures relating to the prosecution of patent applications before the United States Patent and Trademark Office. However, the Manual does not have the force of law or the force of the Patent Rules of Practice in Title 37, Code of Federal Regulations.

If the cup holder is to hold a tapered cup, the holder fits the cup better if the top and bottom of the sheet are arcuate and essentially concentric. Preferably, the first cut is substantially non-parallel to the second cut such that the first cut and the second cut extend along lines that are substantially perpendicular to the arcuate top. When a sheet so formed is made into a cup holder, the resulting holder is tapered with a top and bottom that define planes essentially parallel to the planes defined by the rim and base of the cup to be held. The cuts will also be aligned with the taper of the cup when the holder is assembled, that is, the cuts will extend along a line that is substantially perpendicular to the above planes.

Alternatively, the present invention can be viewed as a combination of a cup and a cup holder. The cup holder is an elongate band having ends that detachably interlock. When the ends are so interlocked, the elongate band extends in a continuous loop. One method of interlocking the ends is by forming interlocking slots in the band. Preferably, the band includes a texture to increase the gripability and insulation value of the combination. The texture can include multiple nubbins and depressions interspersed about the band, preferably in a uniform repeating geometrical pattern. If the cup used as part of the combination is tapered, the upper and lower surfaces of the band can be concentric arcuate shapes so that the continuous loop formed from the band is approximately conformed with the cup.

What is the difference between the primary embodiment and the alternative embodiment? How does this difference manifest itself in the claims set forth below?

c.   DETAILED DESCRIPTION OF THE INVENTION[15]

The Detailed Description focuses on the details of the invention. Because of its comprehensiveness, it constitutes the bulk of the specification. The Detailed Description must contain a *written description* of the invention, if it is not already present, and must be in terms sufficiently full, clear, concise, and exact as to *enable* any person skilled in the art to which the invention pertains to make and use the invention. *See* 35 U.S.C. § 112, ¶ 1 (2001) (*See also* Chapter Three, *infra*). The patent applicant must also disclose the *best mode* of carrying out the invention known to the inventor at the time of filing. *Id.* The best mode is usually described in the detailed description, and may also be represented in the drawings.

The Detailed Description section of the '497 patent is set forth below. The figures are also provided. The reference numbers mentioned in the Detailed Description correspond to the reference numbers in the figures. The drawings have been reproduced here and interspersed with the Detailed Description.[16]

---

15. The section following the Summary of Invention is typically the Brief Description of the Drawings. The Brief Description of the Drawings describes the drawings in the patent, including each of the visible structures. The Brief Description of the Drawings section has been omitted from our discussion.

16. In actual patents, with the exception of the first page, which includes the abstract of the invention and the single drawing corresponding to the broadest claim or claims of the invention, drawings are printed on pages separate from the written portion of the patent.

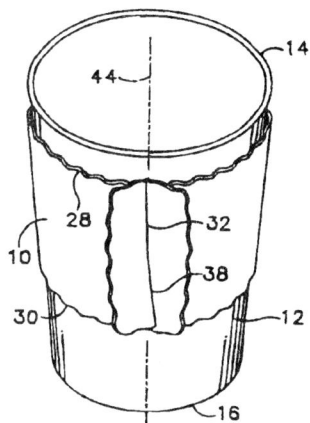

Figure 2

DETAILED DESCRIPTION

Referring to FIG. 1, the cup holder 10 is shown in combination with a cup 12. Cup 12 is usually a tapered paper cup with an open rim 14 and a closed base 16. Cup holder 10 is shown in its assembled state in FIG. 1, and can be described as a continuous loop.

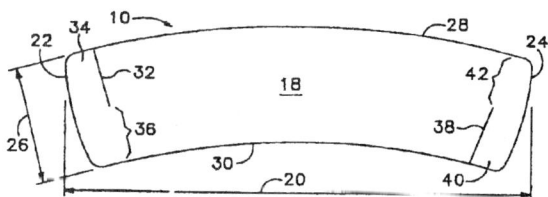

Figure 3

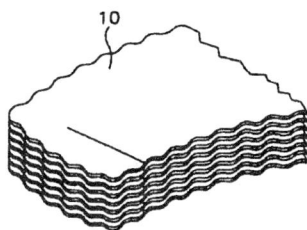

Figure 4 [a]

Cup holder 10 is shown unassembled in FIGS. 2 and 3, and is in the form of a sheet 18, also described as an elongate band having distal ends. Sheet

18 has a length 20 defined by a first end 22 and a second end 24. Sheet 18 also has a width 26, defined by a top 28 and a bottom 30. Top 28 and bottom 30 are preferably arcuate in shape. Thus top 28 can be described as an elongate arcuate surface and bottom 30 can also be described as an elongate arcuate surface. Elongate arcuate surface 28 is essentially concentric with elongate arcuate surface 30, such that the radius of surface 28 is longer than the radius of surface 30 by an amount approximately equal to width 26.

A first cut 32 is made in sheet 18 adjacent first end 22. First cut 32 extends partially across width 26, and preferably severs top 28 such that a first tab 34 and first web 36 are formed. A second cut 38 is made in sheet 18 adjacent second end 24. Second cut 38 extends partially across width 26, and preferably severs bottom 30 to form a second tab 40 and second web 42.

When sheet 18 is configured as described above, a cup holder can be assembled as follows. Sheet 18 is rolled into a substantially cylindrical shape, and cuts 32 and 38 are interlocked with webs 42 and 36, respectively, thereby interlocking first end 22 with second end 24. The resulting cup holder forms a continuous loop as shown in FIG. 1, and can hold cup 12 by inserting cup 12 into cup holder 10. Elongate arcuate surface 28 forms an open annular top that is substantially parallel with rim 14 of cup 12. Elongate arcuate surface 30 forms an open annular bottom that is substantially parallel to base 16 of cup 12. Cup 12 extends through the open top and open bottom and, as shown in FIG. 5, encircles cup 12 so that cup holder 10 has an inner surface 58 (sic) and an outer surface 60. First cut 32 and second cut 38 extend along a line shown generally at 44. Line 44 is substantially perpendicular to rim 14 of cup 12. Alternatively, line 44 can be described as extending along the taper of cup 12.

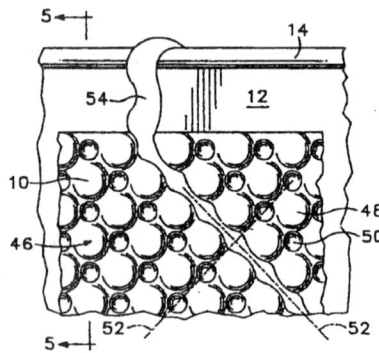

Figure 4 [b]

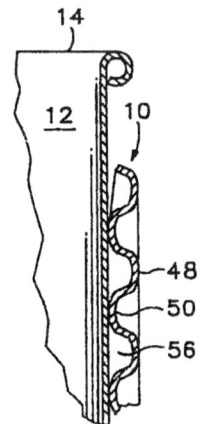

Figure 5

As shown in FIGS. 4 and 5, sheet 18 is provided with a texture indicated generally at 46. Texture 46 includes multiple nubbins 48 and oppositely shaped discrete, approximately semi-spherically shaped depressions 50 distributed on substantially the entire inner surface 58 (sic) of sheet 18. Nubbins 48 and depressions 50 are arranged in a repeating geometrical pattern. Preferably, depressions 50 are aligned in rows forming troughs indicated generally by line 52 in FIG. 4.

Should liquid spill on cup holder 10, as indicated generally at 54 in FIG. 5, liquid 54 will tend to trickle along troughs 52. When the combination of cup holder 10 and cup 12 is held by a human hand, the hand will tend to be held away from troughs 52 by nubbins 48. Thus the hand will be kept out of contact with liquid 54. Furthermore, as shown in FIG. 4, when cup holder 10 is placed on an upright cup 12, troughs 52 extend along lines that intersect both rim 14 and lines extending along the taper of cup 12 at acute angles. Thus the flow of liquid 54 down cupholder 10 is slowed relative to the flow of liquid down vertically oriented flutes.

In addition, texture 46 provides an increased gripability to the cup and cup holder combination. Specifically, nubbins 48 provide a surface texture which is more easily held by a human hand.

Texture 46 also adds an insulation value to the combination because depressions 50 define non-contacting regions 56 of sheet 18, and thus reduce the surface contact between cup holder 10 and the hand of a user and cup 12, respectively. Thus conductive heat transfer is reduced. The insulation value is also increased by air gaps 56 formed by texture 46.

Furthermore, texture 46 is pleasing in appearance, and therefore provides decoration for cup holder 10.

Cup holder 10 as described above and shown in the figures is made from a reversible, two-sided sheet 18. That is, when sheet 18 is rolled to form a continuous loop, either of the textured sides can serve as the outside of cup holder 10. The reversibility of cup holder 10 is particularly evident when, as shown in FIG. 5, inner surface 58 (sic) and outer surface 60 (sic) are mirrored, that is, when each depression 62 (sic) on inner surface 58 (sic) defines a nubbine 48 on outer surface 60 (sic) and each depression 50 on outer surface 60 (sic) defines a nubbin 64 (sic) on inner surface 58 (sic).[17] Non-reversible cup holders are, however, envisioned within the scope of the present invention.

Alternatively, the present invention can be viewed as a method of making a cup and cup holder combination. The method includes the steps of providing a flat sheet with a texture, forming the flat sheet into an elongate band 18 having a top elongate arcuate surface 28 and a bottom elongate arcuate surface 30. Elongate arcuate surface 28 is severed with a first cut 32 extending partially across elongate band 18. Elongate arcuate surface 30 is severed with a second cut 38 extending partially across elongate band 18. Elongate band 18 is then rolled to form a substantially cylindrical shape, and first cut 32 is interlocked with second cut 38 to form a continuous loop. A cup 12 is then inserted into cup holder 10.

Many materials are envisioned for use in making sheet 10, however pressed paper pulp is preferred. Pressed pulp, similar in properties to that used to make semi-rigid paper products such as egg cartons, is pleasing to the touch, partially absorbent, easily formed and relatively inexpensive.

The Detailed Description guides the reader through the invention. It illustrates the best mode and alternate modes, concentrating on the details and pointing out the respective embodiments in the drawings. Notice the differences between the Summary and the Detailed Description.

---

17. Editor's Note—There are numerous errors in identification of the elements of the patent. These errors, however, do not obscure the main idea of the invention.

d. THE DRAWINGS

Title 35, Section 113 requires that the applicant "furnish a drawing where necessary for the understanding of the subject matter sought to be patented." Drawings, like the ones shown in the previous section, are often instructive in teaching the essence of the invention, and are typically necessary for mechanical devices and other forms of invention. If the invention is for a process or method, then drawings usually are not required. If drawings are required, there are formal rules governing their acceptability. Photographs are not accepted, except in limited situations.[18] Would you have understood the patented cup holder without the aid of the drawings? If you would have, then drawings are not required.

2.   THE CLAIMS

The 1790 and 1793 Patent Acts made no mention of claims. The invention was discerned from the written description, often with a claim-like summary at the end, in the English style. It was not until the 1836 Act that "claims" were mentioned by statute. Section 6 of the 1836 Act required the applicant to

> particularly specify and point out the part, improvement, or combination, which he claims as his own invention or discovery.

The claim under the 1836 Act was required in order to facilitate examination, which was concurrently initiated, and served to highlight the inventive contribution. Some commentators suggest that it was the Act of 1870 that elevated the importance of the claim, for the 1870 Act required the applicant to

> particularly point out and *distinctly claim* the part, improvement, or combination which he claims as his invention or discovery.

Our present patent code requires that "[t]he specification shall conclude with one or more claims particularly pointing out and distinctly claiming the subject matter which the applicant regards as his invention." 35 U.S.C. § 112, ¶ 2 (2001). Today, the claim is the most important part of the patent, setting forth the metes and bounds of the patentee's right to exclude. The Federal Circuit has stated time and again, "[i]t is the claims that measure the invention" and "[c]laims are infringed, not specifications." *SRI Int'l v. Matsushita Elec. Corp. of Am.*, 775 F.2d 1107, 1121 (Fed.Cir.1985). Indeed, claim drafting is truly an art, the importance of which cannot be overstated.[19]

Claims are usually made up of three parts: a *preamble*, a *transition phrase*, and a *body*. The preamble identifies the invention or the technical

---

18. A petition must be granted for photographs to be accepted. *See* 37 C.F.R. § 1.84(b). For plant patent applications, color drawings or color photographs are required. *See* 37 C.F.R. § 1.165(b).

19. Books have been devoted to teaching the patent practitioner how best to draft claims. *See, e.g.*, ROBERT C. FABER, LANDIS ON THE MECHANICS OF PATENT CLAIM DRAFTING (4th ed. 1996) [hereinafter MECHANICS OF CLAIM DRAFTING]; THOMAS J. GREER, JR., WRITING & UNDERSTANDING U.S. PATENT CLAIMS (1979); THE ART OF DRAFTING PATENT CLAIMS (Joseph G. Jackson & G. Michael Morris eds., 1966); EMERSON STRINGHAM, PATENT CLAIM DRAFTING (2d ed. 1952).

field of the invention. The transition phrase joins the preamble to the body of the claim, and is usually made up only of the word "comprising,"[20] which means that the invention includes the listed elements, but does not exclude others. *See Moleculon Research Corp. v. CBS, Inc.*, 793 F.2d 1261 (Fed.Cir. 1986) (referring to "the general proposition that a claim employing the transitional term 'comprising' does not exclude additional, unrecited elements").[21] The body of the claim includes a recitation of the *elements*: the steps or parts that make up the invention. It also includes the structural, physical, or functional relationship among the elements. The elements and their relationship usually define the claim, at least for apparatus or device claims. Process claims may require additional detail.

Words in a patent are not necessarily held to their ordinary meaning. Each inventor can be his or her own lexicographer.[22] However, the application must define words being used in an uncommon manner. In addition, words cannot be used in a manner that is repugnant to their accepted meaning.[23] As with the rest of the patent, the author of the patent can punctuate and fashion the claim in whatever manner he or she desires, except that the claim must be one sentence, so there can be only one period, at the end of the sentence.[24]

A patent application generally has more than one claim. The claims of a patent may vary in scope or method of description or expression. Broad claims include fewer limitations than do narrow claims and therefore cover a wider scope. Claims are often arranged in order of decreasing scope, that is, the broadest first and the narrowest last. Can you guess why that is?

Claims can be in independent, dependent, or multiple dependent form. An independent claim is completely self-contained. A dependent claim refers back to an earlier claim and thus it incorporates by reference all limitations of the previous claim and also includes its own limitations. A multiple dependent claim refers back in the alternative to two or more claims and is considered to include all of its own limitations as well as those of any one of the referenced claims.[25]

---

20. "Including" and "having" are sometimes used instead of "comprising."

21. In contrast, use of the phrase "consisting of" as a transition indicates that the claim is closed (that is, that invention is limited to no more and no fewer than the listed elements). *See, e.g., In re Gray*, 53 F.2d 520 (CCPA 1931); *Ex parte Jackson*, 1929 WL 23347 (Pat.Off.Bd. App.1929). Moreover, the phrase "consisting essentially of" has been interpreted to exclude "ingredients that would materially affect the basic and novel characteristics of the claimed composition." *Atlas Powder Co. v. E.I. du Pont De Nemours & Co.*, 750 F.2d 1569, 1574 (Fed.Cir.1984). Yet another phrase, "composed of," as been construed to be synonymous with either "consisting of" or "consisting essentially of," depending upon the written disclosure. *See AFG Indus., Inc. v. Cardinal IG Co., Inc.*, 239 F.3d 1239, 1244–45 (Fed.Cir.2001).

22. *See Lear Siegler, Inc.* v. *Aeroquip Corp.*, 733 F.2d 881, 888 (Fed.Cir.1984); *W.L. Gore & Assocs., Inc.* v. *Garlock, Inc.*, 721 F.2d 1540, 1558 (Fed.Cir.1983); *Autogiro Co. of Am. v. United States*, 384 F.2d 391, 396–397 (Ct.Cl.1967).

23. The latitude given to applicants is limited by MPEP §§ 608.01(*o*), 706.03(d), 2111.01 and 2173.05(a). *See also Lear Siegler*, 733 F.2d at 889.

24. *See* MPEP § 608.01(n) (8th ed. 2001, rev. 2003).

25. For other examples of an independent claim, *see* FABER, MECHANICS OF CLAIM DRAFTING, *supra* note 18, at 17–18. For examples of a dependent claim, *see id.* at 163. For examples of multiple dependent claims, *see* MPEP § 608.01(n) (8th ed. 2001, rev. 2003).

There are five principal ways of claiming the statutory classes of invention set forth in 35 U.S.C. § 101. They include the following:

a. COMPOSITION CLAIMS

Although in practice the usage is not precise, chemical compounds are viewed as "compositions of matter;" whereas chemical combinations or mixtures of ingredients are more accurately simply called "compositions." They may be claimed by naming the compound or the ingredients. If necessary, the proportions or other parameters of the composition are stated. For example:

A plasticizer composition, comprising:

(a) about 50–60% A;

(b) about 20–30% B;

(c) about 15–25% C; and

(d) a pH-modifying substance in an amount sufficient to adjust the pH to a value of about 3 to 4.5.

See ROBERT C. FABER, LANDIS ON MECHANICS OF PATENT CLAIM DRAFTING § 49 (4th ed. 1996).

Alternative expressions are permitted if they present no uncertainty or ambiguity with respect to the question of scope or clarity of the claims. One acceptable form of alternative expression, which is commonly referred to as a *Markush* group, recites members as being "selected from the group consisting of A, B, and C." *See Ex parte Markush*, 1925 C.D. 126 (Comm'r Pat. 1925).

A *Markush* claim is used when there is no generic term that, by virtue of a common characteristic of the things that are being claimed together, encompasses those things that are included in the applicant's invention while excluding those which are not included in the applicant's invention. It creates an artificial "group" of the things claimed, to accommodate the practice that each patent application be directed to one invention only. *See* MPEP § 2173.05(h) (8th ed. 2001, rev. 2003).

Ex parte Markush permits the claiming of a genus expressed as a group consisting of certain members. Inventions in metallurgy, refractories, ceramics, pharmacy, pharmacology and biology are most frequently claimed under the *Markush* formula but purely mechanical features or process steps may also be claimed by using the *Markush* style of claiming, *see Ex parte Head*, 214 USPQ 551 (Bd.App.1981); *In re Gaubert*, 524 F.2d 1222 (CCPA 1975); and *In re Harnisch*, 631 F.2d 716 (CCPA 1980).

b. PROCESS CLAIMS

Process or method claims can be divided into (1) processes or methods of *making*; and (2) processes or methods of *using*. As to the former, the typical method of *making* claim involves acts or steps performed on an object(s) or substance(s) to achieve some result. For example:

A process for making chemical compound X, comprising the steps of:

(a) *mixing* water with compound Z to form a mixture;

(b) *heating* the mixture at a temperature of about 150°–160° C;

(c) *distilling* the mixture; and

(d) *permitting* the mixture to cool to room temperature.

See FABER, MECHANICS OF CLAIM DRAFTING, at § 37. Notice the importance of gerunds in process claims.

It is the combination or sequence of acts or steps that are patented in a process claim, not the resulting product. Where there is a sequence of steps, the sequence should be described. However, non-essential steps and sequences should not be recited in a process claim lest the claim be too easily circumvented. *See id.* at § 39.

The most common way to get effective patent coverage for a new use of an old or new product is in the form of a method claim—this would be a method of *using* claim. Consider this example of a typical method of use claim:

> The method of treating baldness, which comprises applying to the scalp an aqueous solution of sodium chloride having a concentration of 30–40 percent by weight of sodium chloride.

Id. at § 42.

There seems to be some doubt about the availability or effectiveness of a claim directed to a product having a new use. See generally *In re Thuau*, 135 F.2d 344 (CCPA 1943) (collecting cases on both sides of the issue). For example, consider a state of the prior art in which the combination of compounds A, B, and C previously existed, but was not used or was used for some purpose other than treating disease X; and the following patent claim is in issue:

> A treatment for disease X comprising compounds A plus B plus C.

If the phrase, "treatment for disease X," which some might call the "preamble" is interpreted as a limit on the claim, then this claim is directed to the product itself, but only when put to the particular use claimed. Some suggest that such a claim is per se unpatentable. *See* DONALD S. CHISUM, ELEMENTS OF UNITED STATES PATENT LAW 26, n. 91 (2d ed. 2000) ("The 'new use' will not support a claim to the product or substance."). But even the case of *In re Pearson*, 494 F.2d 1399 (CCPA 1974), which is widely cited for having rejected such a composition claim, explicitly acknowledged: "We do not mean to imply that terms which recite the intended use or a property of a composition can never be used to distinguish a new from an old composition." *Id.* at 1403. The court in that case explicitly recited its concerns with such a claim: "It seems quite clear to us that one of the compositions admitted to be old by the appellant would not undergo a metamorphosis to a new composition by labeling its container to show that it is a composition suitable for treating peanuts to avoid the formation of pops and unsound kernels." Wouldn't such a concern be fully addressed if the patent application made explicit that the claim should be read to cover such a compound only when it is actually put to the relevant use instead of merely labeled on its container as intended for such use? Put differently, both anticipation and infringement require all elements of the claim and the use would be an element, making it part of the burden of proof for the party seeking to prove anticipation or infringement. Similarly, while the Federal Circuit has repeatedly held in cases like *In re Gleave*, 560 F.3d 1331 (Fed.Cir. 2009) and *In re Schoenwald*, 964 F.2d 1122 (Fed.Cir. 1992) that a prior art reference need not disclose a use of a compound to fully anticipate a claim to the compound, it is a different question to ask about the patentability of a claim that specifically recites a particular use as one of its elements or limitations when the prior art just does not include that use. Of course, whether the prior art actually fails to include the use is a question of fact, not law, and so will depend entirely on the facts of a given case.

c. APPARATUS CLAIMS

Apparatus claims generally are directed to a mechanical structure. The preamble usually recites the purpose of the apparatus. After the transition (*e.g.*, comprising), each essential element of the apparatus is set forth in outline form. The claim must recite the connection among the elements, sufficiently to clearly define the apparatus. The following example illustrates a simple apparatus claim:

Apparatus for shaking articles, which comprises:

(a) a container for the articles;

(b) a base; and

(c) a plurality of parallel legs, each leg connected pivotally at one end to the container and at the other end to the base to support the container for oscillating movement with respect to the base.

FABER, MECHANICS OF CLAIM DRAFTING § 14.[26]

d. PRODUCT–BY–PROCESS CLAIMS

Product-by-process claims are hybrid claims designed to facilitate the claiming of complex products whose structure or other characteristics are insufficiently known to permit adequate description of the product itself. They indirectly claim a product by reciting the process of creating the product. They usually take the form, "a product 'prepared by a process comprising the steps of . . .' ".[27] For example,

---

26. A useful convention that arose in the context of apparatus claims is the type of claim called the *Jepson* claim. In a *Jepson* claim the preamble sets the invention in the framework of the prior art and the rest of the claim describes an improvement over the prior art. 37 C.F.R. § 1.75(e) (2002) authorizes the use of a *Jepson*-type claim, and explains the structure of the claim as follows:

Where the nature of the case admits, as in the case of an improvement, any independent claim should contain in the following order:

(1) A preamble comprising a general description of all the elements or steps of the claimed combination which are conventional or known,

(2) A phrase such as "wherein the improvement comprises," and

(3) Those elements, steps and/or relationships which constitute that portion of the claimed combination which the applicant considers as the new or improved portion.

27. SHELDON, HOW TO WRITE A PATENT APPLICATION, at § 6.4.5. The PTO views product-by-process claims as product claims. Therefore, the MPEP requires that the product itself meet the requirements of patentability. *See* MPEP § 2113 (quoting *In re Thorpe*, 777 F.2d 695, 698 (Fed.Cir.1985) stating, "[e]ven though product-by-process claims are limited by and defined by

The product of a process comprising the steps of:

(a) *mixing* water with compound Z to form a mixture;

(b) *heating* the mixture at a temperature of about 150°–160° C;

(c) *distilling* the mixture; and

(d) *permitting* the mixture to cool to room temperature.

Consider the following question: If Inventor claims compound X in a product-by-process claim (see above example) and Competitor makes X by a process other than that which is claimed by Inventor, does Competitor infringe? The Federal Circuit recently resolved an inconsistency in its precedents by clarifying that infringement of a product-by-process claim requires the use of the actual claimed process.[28]

e. MEANS–PLUS–FUNCTION CLAIMS

Title 35, Section 112, paragraph six specifically permits "an element in a claim for a combination [to] be expressed as a means or step for performing a specified function." These claim elements are called "*means-plus-function*" elements. Such a claim element defines the function of the element, rather than its structure. The statute then provides that such a claim element "shall be construed to cover the corresponding structure, material, or acts described in the specification and equivalents thereof." Let's take another look at the sample apparatus claim, only now note the added means-plus-function:

Apparatus for shaking articles, which comprises:

(a) a container for the articles;

(b) a base;

(c) a plurality of parallel legs, each leg is connected pivotally at one end to the container and at the other end to the base to support the container for oscillating movement with respect to the base; and

(d) *means for oscillating the container on the legs to shake the articles.*

FABER, MECHANICS OF CLAIM DRAFTING § 14. In the above claim, the means are recited in the written description. The function is "oscillating." Whether a claim element may properly be considered to fall within Section 112, ¶ 6, is sometimes a difficult question, and is studied in Chapter 8, *infra*.[29]

The '497 claims follow. Claim 1 is independent and the other claims are all dependent from claim 1. Identify the preamble, transition phrase, body and type of claim of the independent claim:

---

the process, determination of patentability is based on the product itself. The patentability of a product does not depend on its method of production. If the product in the product-by-process claim is the same as or obvious from a product of the prior art, the claim is unpatentable even though the prior product was made by a different process.")

28. *Abbott Laboratories v. Sandoz, Inc.*, 566 F.3d 1282, 1291–95 (Fed. Cir. 2009) (*en banc*).

29. For a review of some of the difficulties associated with claims having mean-plus-function elements *see* William F. Lee and Eugene M. Paige, *Means Plus and Step Plus Function Claims: Do We Know Them Only When We See Them?*, 80 J. PAT. & TRADEMARK OFF. SOC'Y 4, pp. 241–68 (1998).

CLAIMS

We claim:

1. A cup and holder combination comprising:

    a cup for holding hot or cold liquids; and a holder defined by a band mounted on and encircling the cup, the band having an open top and an open bottom through which the cup extends and an inner surface immediately adjacent the cup with a plurality of discrete, spaced-apart, approximately semi-spherically shaped depressions distributed on substantially the entire inner surface of the band so that each depression defines a non-contacting region of the band creating an air gap between the band and the cup, thereby reducing the rate of heat transfer through the holder.

2. The cup and holder combination of claim 1, wherein the band also has an outer surface opposite the inner surface, with a plurality of discrete, spaced-apart, approximately semi-spherically shaped depressions distributed on substantially the entire outer surface of the band.

3. The cup and holder combination of claim 2, wherein the inner and outer surfaces of the band are mirrored, with each depression on the inner surface defining a nubbin on the outer surface and each depression on the outer surface defining a nubbin on the inner surface.

4. A holder for encircling a liquid-containing cup to reduce the rate of heat transfer between the liquid contained in the cup and a hand gripping the holder encircling the cup, comprising a band of material formed with an open top and an open bottom through which the cup can extend and an inner surface immediately adjacent the cup, the band including a plurality of discrete, spaced-apart, approximately semi-spherically shaped depressions distributed on substantially the entire inner surface of the band so that each depression defines a non-contacting region of the band creating an air gap between the band and the cup, thereby reducing the rate of heat transfer through the holder.

5. The holder of claim 4, wherein the band also has an outer surface opposite the inner surface, with a plurality of discrete, spaced-apart, approximately semi-spherically shaped depressions distributed on substantially the entire outer surface of the band.

6. The holder of claim 5, wherein the inner and outer surfaces of the band are mirrored, with each depression on the inner surface defining a nubbin on the outer surface and each depression on the outer surface defining a nubbin on the inner surface.

The preceding claims demonstrate the relationship between independent and dependent claims. The independent claim states the invention in the broadest scope. Each dependent claim limits the scope of the independent claim in some particular manner.

Review the first claim carefully. What are the elements of the claim? Are all these elements necessary? If someone just makes, sells or uses the cupholder, do they infringe? What about if they sell it to someone else to use with a cup?

How does the first claim compare to the Summary of the Invention? What happened to the preferred embodiment of the invention?

Practical Aspects of the Sorensen Patent
U.S. Patent Number 5,425,497

Katherine Kelly Lutton[1]

The claimed Sorensen cup holder was conceived in the Fall of 1993 when Jay Sorensen, dropping a cup of hot coffee on his lap, was stimulated into thinking about "a better way to get your Joe on the go."[2] After devising an insulative jacket to fit around well-known disposable coffee cups, Mr. Sorensen, who eventually referred to his new product as the "Java Jacket," started selling the Java Jacket® out of his car.[3] After his wife Colleen and he attended a coffee trade show in Seattle, sales, as Mr. Sorensen explains, "percolated."[4] Mr. Sorensen and his family-run business have now sold over 600 million jackets.[5] The jacket is available nation-wide in both small coffee shops as well as large ones such as Noah's Bagels. Mr. Sorensen's patented Java Jacket® is a true commercial success.

The Sorensen Java Jacket®, the patent that arguably covers the Java Jacket®, and the patents' history before the U.S. Patent and Trademark Office, are all ripe with issues that are introduced and discussed throughout this text. For example, as you will discover in Chapter 9 (Defenses and Limitations) and in *Cover v. Sea Gull Lighting*, 83 F.3d 1390 (Fed.Cir. 1996), 35 U.S.C. § 287(a) provides that a patentee may not recover damages for infringement unless (a) the accused infringer was actually notified of infringement or (b) a patented product was marked with the patent number:

> Patentees, and persons making, offering for sale, or selling within the United States any patented article for or under them, or importing any patented article into the United States, may give notice to the public that the same is patented, either by fixing thereon the word "patent" or the abbreviation "pat.", together with the number of the patent, or when, from the character of the article, this can not be done, by fixing to it, or to the package wherein one or more of them is contained, a label containing a like notice. In the event of failure so to mark, no damages shall be recovered by the patentee in any action for infringement, except on proof that the infringer was notified of the infringement and continued to infringe thereafter, in which event damages may be recovered only for infringement occurring after such notice.

35 U.S.C. § 287(a). Mr. Sorensen provides the requisite damages notice by marking his Java Jacket®, seen in Figure 1, with the Sorensen patent number: "Patent #5425497." Although Mr. Sorensen marks the jacket with the patent number, the jacket by itself does not embody (or contain each limitation) of claims 1 or 2 of the patent.

The test for whether a product "embodies" a patent is the same test used for damages, anticipation and infringement: A product embodies a claim (or in other words a claim reads on a product) if the product contains each and every limitation of the claim.[6] In order to embody claims 1 or 2, the Java Jacket® must contain each limitation of claims 1 and 2, including the "cup" limitation: "*a cup* for holding hot or cold liquids; and a holder defined by a band mounted on and encircling the cup. . . ."[7]

Not only does Mr. Sorensen not supply or affix the Java Jacket® to a cup, but neither do many (or any) of the coffee shops that offer the Java Jacket®. At least some of the coffee shops that offer the Java Jacket® offer the jacket in a service station; the coffee shop employees do not actually assemble the Java Jacket® or place the Java Jacket® onto any cups. In fact, if another person, Competitor A, ripped off the Java Jacket®, creating a Coffee Coat that was identical to the Java Jacket®, Company A could avoid *directly* infringing claims 1 and 2 by simply providing the Coffee Coat without the cup.

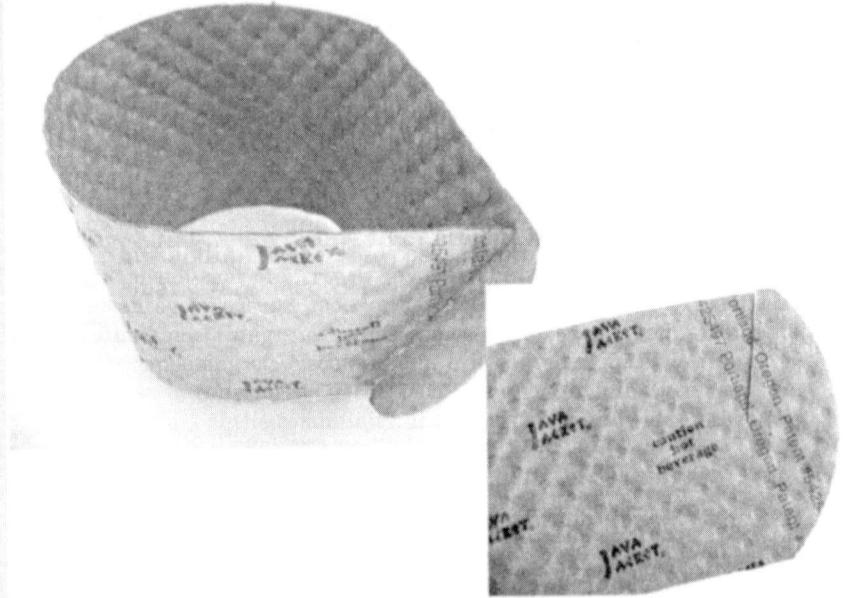

Figure 1. Java Jacket® Marked with Patent Number.

On the topic of infringement, for the same reasons the Java Jacket® does not embody claims 1 or 2, Competitor A would not directly and literally infringe the claims because Competitor A would not, as you will learn in Chapter 8 (Infringement), "make[], use[], offer[] to sell, or sell[] any patented invention within the United States or import[] into the United States any patent invention . . . ."[8] Again, the Coffee Coat does not contain each and every limitations of either of the claims and thus, considering claims 1 and 2 only, the Coffee Coat does not qualify as a patented invention.

But, as you will learn in Chapter 8, "[c]ourts have not always confined patentees to the literal meaning of their claims, sometimes finding infringement when an accused infringing device . . . is an 'equivalent' to that claimed in the patent." Thus, Competitor A may directly infringe under what has become known as the *Doctrine of Equivalents*. Competitor A, however, escapes direct infringement because of at least one doctrine that limits a finding of equivalents: the *All–Elements Rule*. Under the *All–Elements Rule*—which provides that equivalents cannot be found when an entire element is vitiated—the Coffee Coat is arguably not an equivalent because the "cup" limitation is completely missing.

As you will discover in Chapter 8, this is not, however, the end of the infringement analysis as 35 U.S.C. §§ 271(b) and (c) impose liability for indirect infringement. At some point, for Coffee Coat to be of use, someone will have to slip the Coffee Coat onto a coffee cup and will arguably have to "make" and "use" the invention, therefore arguably directly infringing the patent. It is doubtful, however, that these individual users (most likely patrons of coffee shops) would have enough money to satisfy any real judgment. Damages for such a limited use would also not justify the expense of litigation.

The patentee may, however, seek recovery from Competitor A under theories of contributory infringement (35 U.S.C. § 271(c)) and inducement of infringement (35 U.S.C. § 271(b)). Competitor A may contribute to infringement by providing the Coffee Coat which is a component of a patented product that is a non-staple item not "suitable for substantial non-infringing use" and which Competitor A knows is "especially made or especially adapted for us in an infringement of" the Sorensen patent. Competitor A may induce infringement by providing product literature encouraging use of the Coffee Coat with conventional disposable coffee cups.

Under each theory of indirect infringement, infringement may be direct or by equivalents. As seen in Table 1, even though there may be no direct infringe (either literally or by equivalents), if there is contributory or inducement of infringement (either literally or by equivalents), then damages may be recovered.

	Direct	Inducement	Contributory
Literal	NO No infringement without "cup."	Yes? Sleeve is likely sold with product literature demonstrating use with cup.	Yes? Providing sleeve may be sufficient induce infringement.
By Equivalents	NO No infringement without "cup."	Yes? Sleeve is likely sold with product literature demonstrating use with cup.	Yes? Providing sleeve may be sufficient induce infringement.

Table 1. Variations of Infringement of Claims 1 and 2 (by Competitor A)

Inducement of infringement and contributory infringement can only exist, however, if there is direct infringing by someone—if the act of slipping the Coffee Coat onto a cup would itself be an infringing activity. To determine if there is direct infringement, consider issued claim 1:

1. A cup and holder combination comprising: a cup for holding hot or cold liquids; and a holder defined by a band **mounted on** and encircling the cup, the band having an open top and an open bottom through which the cup extends and an inner surface immediately adjacent the cup with a plurality of discrete, spaced-apart, approximately semi-spherically shaped depressions distrib-

uted on substantially the entire inner surface of the band so that each depression defines a non-contacting region of the band creating an air gap between the band and the cup, thereby reducing the rate of heat transfer through the holder.[9]

Claim 1 requires that the holder be "mounted on" the cup. To determine whether there is direct infringement, a court will apply a two-part test: first the claims must be construed; second, a determination must be made as to whether an accused product infringes the claim as properly construed.[10] In order for a court to determine whether an accused holder is "mounted on" the cup, the court must first interpret the term "mounted on."[11] As discussed in Chapter 8, the court will first look to intrinsic evidence—the specification and the prosecution history if in evidence to determine if the inventor defined "mounted." The Sorensen specification and prosecution history does not expressly define "mounted." The specification does, however, include a figure illustrating the use of the holder on the cup. This figure is shown in Figure 3.

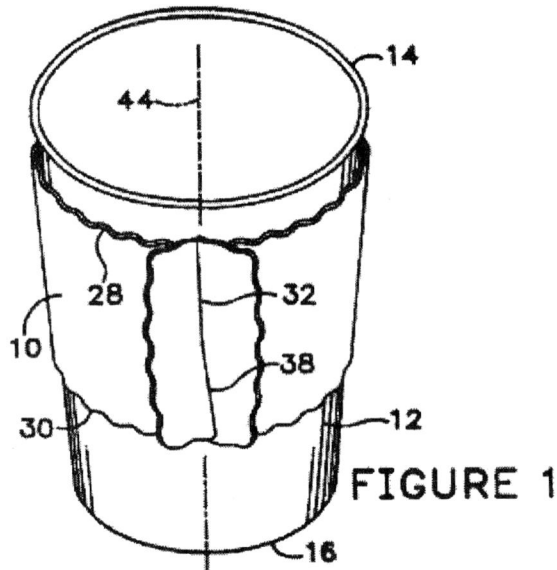

Sorensen Patent, Figure 1.

It is arguably unclear from Figure 1 of the Sorensen patent what the term "mounted on" means as the holder may be affixed to the cup with some type of permanent adhesive or may just be slipped onto the cup. Because the definition is not clear from the intrinsic evidence, a court may consult extrinsic evidence, such as expert testimony as to how one of skill in the art would interpret the drawing. If the court finds that the inventor has not successfully defined the term, the court will rely on the ordinary meaning of the term and will likely turn to dictionary definitions. Webster's Third New International Dictionary defines "mount" as "to attach to a support or assemble for use;" "to attach to a base;" "to attach to a backing for reinforcement or display;" "to glue or paste (as a sheet of paper) upon firm material in bookbinding;" and "to fasten (a stamp) on the page of an album ..."[12] In fact, all definitions in Webster's dictionary imply permanency. Therefore it is arguable that a holder that slips onto a cup and can be slipped off a cup just as easily is not *literally* "mounted on" the cup.

Direct infringement will still exist, however, if the "mounted on" limitation is present by *equivalents* and if the patentee is not barred from asserting such equivalents. In addition to the *All–Elements Rule*, another doctrine referred to as *Prosecution History Estoppel* places limits on equivalents. If a patentee has disclaimed equivalents by amending the claim during prosecution or through arguments made to the Patent Office, *Prosecution History Estoppel* may work to bar equivalents.

In Sorensen's case, he originally filed the following claim 1:

1. A cup holder for use with a cup, the cup holder comprising:

a sheet having distal ends;

a web adjacent one of the ends; and

a slot formed in the sheet adjacent the other end and detachably interlockable with the web to produce a receptacle for holding a cup.

In order to get around prior art cited by the Examiner during prosecution, Sorensen cancelled claim 1 in favor of the claim 1 that issued. Therefore, the term "mounted on" was arguably added in order to secure the patent and, if so, Sorensen is locked into the term and cannot invoke the doctrine of equivalents.

Therefore, it is likely that Sorensen's claim 1 cannot be used to prevent a competitor from making the same exact product Sorensen offers. Fortunately for Sorensen, however, he included within his application claims of varying scope. When Sorensen cancelled originally file claim 1, he also cancelled all claims in the case. He then added claims 1–6, including independent claims 1 and 4. Independent claim 4 provides:

4. A holder for encircling a liquid-containing cup to reduce the rate of heat transfer between the liquid contained in the cup and a hand gripping the holder encircling the cup, comprising a band of material formed with an open top and an open bottom through which the cup can extend and an inner surface immediately adjacent the cup, the band including a plurality of discrete, spaced-apart, approximately semi-spherically shaped depressions distributed on substantially the entire inner surface of the band so that each depression defines a non-contacting region of the band creating an air gap between the band and the cup, thereby reducing the rate of heat transfer through the holder.

Although, like claim 1, claim 4 was added in response to a rejection from the Examiner, and therefore implicates the doctrine of prosecution history estoppel, one need not even reach the equivalents question to find infringement of claim 4 by Competitor A. Unlike claim 1, claim 4 does not require mounting, nor does it require a cup. Therefore Competitor A would be liable for manufacturing the Coffee Coat.

The Sorensen patent illustrates some of the issues involved in prosecution including the importance of including claims of varying scope and the issues that can arise because of representations or claim amendments made during prosecution. The patent also illustrates some of the issues involved in litigation and licensing. Because the term "mounted on" is subject to interpretation, litigation against Competitor A on claim 1 could go either way. And, to avoid the expense and risk of litigation it may be that the hypothetical competitor would be willing to license the Sorensen patent. As you review the concepts in the various chapters of this text, you may want to reflect on the cup holder patent (which is available in its entirety at no charge at www.uspto.gov). You may even want to order the prosecution history to get the rest of the story.

1. Partner with the law firm of Fish & Richardson P.C., Redwood City, California and Adjunct Professor of Patent Law, Santa Clara University School of Law. This Side Bar was written specifically for PRINCIPLES OF PATENT LAW.

2. www.JavaJacket.com/company.php (Sept. 5, 2002).

3. Id.

4. Id.

5. Id.

6. As discuss in Chapter 8 (infringement): "to anticipate a patent, a prior art reference must disclose each and every claim limitation. Thus, the fundamental patent law maxim: 'that which infringes, if later, would anticipate, if earlier.' *See Peters v. Active Mfg. Co.*, 129 U.S. 530, 537 (1889)."

7. U.S. Patent No. 5,425,497, Claim 1 (emphasis added).

8. 35 U.S.C. § 271(a).

9. U.S. Patent No. 5,425,497, Claim 1 (emphasis added).

10. See *Vitronics Corp. v. Conceptronic, Inc.*, 90 F.3d 1576 (Fed.Cir.1996) and Chapter 8 of this Text.

11. The process of determining the meaning of claim terms—which is a question of law for the Judge—is referred to as "claim construction" and is often done is the context of a "Markman hearing." *See Markman v. Westview Instruments, Inc.*, 517 U.S. 370 (1996).

12. Webster's Third New International Dictionary 1477 (Unabridged 1993).

B.   PROCEDURES BEFORE THE PATENT AND TRADEMARK OFFICE

As we noted at the beginning of this chapter, to receive a patent an applicant must file a patent application with the Patent and Trademark Office (PTO).[30] This section explores the portion of the patent prosecution process that occurs *after* the application is received by the PTO.

1.   INITIAL PROCESSING OF THE APPLICATION

All papers arriving at the mail room of the PTO[31] are stamped with the date of receipt. Any papers purporting to be a new application, whether complete or incomplete, are also stamped with an eight-digit application

---

30. The Patent Office, renamed the Patent and Trademark Office in 1975 (Pub. L. 93–596, 93d Cong., 2d Sess. (1975)), is recognized as the oldest federal agency in the United States, created by statute in 1836 and now one of fourteen bureaus in the Department of Commerce. See Chapter One, *infra*.

31. The PTO is, as of the time of this writing, in the process of moving from Arlington, Virginia to Alexandria, Virginia.

number, including a two-digit series code and a six-digit serial number.[32] An application is identified by its application number.

New applications are initially processed by the Application Division, which decides if an application is complete and meets all formal requirements.[33] Any drawings accompanying the application are forwarded to the official draftsman, who checks to see if the drawings comply with the formal requirements. Any assignment of ownership in the application is forwarded to the Assignment Division,[34] which records the assignment in its computer and microfilm records and returns it to the applicant with a notification of the reel and frame numbers in the microfilm records.

The PTO maintains a detailed classification system by which all technologies are broken down into specific categories (*e.g.*, chemical, electrical, etc.). Within the classification system are hundreds of classes, each class having at least dozens of subclasses. The Application Division determines the appropriate technological class and subclass of the application. It then forwards the application to the examining group in charge of that class and subclass. The application and related documents are kept in a file jacket known as a "file wrapper."

2.   Examination and Prosecution

a.   FORMALITIES AND SEARCH BY THE EXAMINER

When an application reaches an examining group, it is assigned to the appropriate art (*i.e.*, technology) unit and then to a particular examiner. The examiner first ascertains that the application contains the elements required to obtain a filing date: (1) written description; (2) claim; and (3) any required drawing. *See* 37 C.F.R. § 1.53(b)(1). The examiner also reads the application to determine whether it is clear enough to be examined[35] and whether it claims more than one invention. If the application contains claims directed to more than one invention, the examiner can require the applicant to elect one of the inventions for prosecution. This is known as a *restriction requirement* and is discussed below. *See infra,* 2(b)(ii).

After determining that an application satisfies these requirements, the examiner conducts a search for prior art relevant to the claimed subject matter. Much of the relevant prior art is usually set forth in the patent applicant's Information Disclosure Statement (recall that it is common for

---

32.   The past practice of the PTO had been to assign each patent a serial number that repeated every few years. This practice required knowledge of the filing date of the application to determine its identity. The PTO has recently added the series code prefix to the serial number, to form a unique "application number" for each patent.

33.   If an application is incomplete, the applicant is notified of the incompleteness and is given time to correct the defect. Depending on the type of defect, the application may or may not be accorded a filing date as of its date of receipt. If a filing date is accorded, it may be lost if the defect is not corrected within the allowed time.

34.   If an applicant transfers all or part of his or her interest in the invention to another, the transferee (or "assignee") has the right to direct the course of the proceedings before the PTO on behalf of the applicant. 37 C.F.R. § 3.71.

35.   For example, an application filed by a foreign applicant may not conform to idiomatic English or U.S. practice. *See* MPEP § 702.01.

an applicant to conduct a prior art search before filing his application) submitted to the PTO along with or shortly after the filing of the application. 37 C.F.R. § 1.56. The quality and thoroughness of the examiner's search is a function of his or her searching skill, the time allocated for the search, and the completeness of the libraries searched. *See* 3 PATENT PRACTICE 11.4, 11.29 (Irving Kayton & Karyl S. Kayton eds., 6th ed. 1995).

SIDE BAR

Searching for Worldwide Prior Art

The Honorable Gerald J. Mossinghoff*

The largest proportion of the work of patent professionals—whether they are in private or corporate practice or examiners in the United States Patent and Trademark Office—centers around the fundamental principle of patent law that an inventor cannot obtain a valid U.S. patent if the invention, or an obvious variation of the invention, was patented or described in a printed publication in this *or a foreign country* either before the invention was made or one year prior to the filing of the patent application in the United States. That requirement, or one similar to it, can be traced back to the very beginning of the U.S. patent system in 1790. But until quite recently, although patent examiners well understood the legal principle, in practice it remained largely theoretical, given the pressures for moving patent applications through the Patent and Trademark Office and the inadequacy of automated worldwide search systems.

When I was a patent examiner in the Patent Office from 1957 to 1961—working in the radar and avionics fields—our searches of the prior art consisted almost exclusively of searches of U.S. patents. Only rarely did we spend time in the Scientific Library searching scientific and technical journals, and we would never go outside of our own "shoe boxes"—which typically contained a small collection of relevant foreign patents—to search foreign patents in any systematic way. We could justify the professional integrity of our searches in the fields I was directly involved in on two grounds: (1) the U.S. clearly was the worldwide leader in avionics and military electronics at that time, and (2) most foreign companies would file patent applications in the United States on virtually all significant inventions in those fields. I suspect, however, that that was not true in many of the thousands of other fields of technology examined in the Patent Office.

All of that has now changed. Given the virtually complete automation of each examiner's work station and the aggressive leadership of the U.S. Patent and Trademark Office in providing examiners access to the most modern automated databases, for the first time examiners are able to test fully the long-standing threshold requirements of §§ 102 and 103 of Title 35 of the U.S. Code by searching in a comprehensive way both technical and scientific literature and foreign patent collections. Perhaps the best example of the effective leadership of the Patent and Trademark Office is in the fast-moving biotechnology sphere where expert specialized searchers are on staff to assist each examiner in conducting comprehensive worldwide searches of genomic and biotechnology prior art. Beyond doubt, such searches compare favorably with those that could be conducted by even the most sophisticated and motivated private concerns.

Moreover, the Patent and Trademark Office has taken the lead in international circles—principally through the World Intellectual Property Organization in Geneva—to connect more effectively all of the major patent databases of the world and place them at the disposal of U.S. patent examiners through their automated systems.

As Assistant Secretary of Commerce and Commissioner of Patents and Trademarks, I was most pleased to play a role in 1983 in establishing what is referred to as Trilateral Cooperation among the European Patent Office, the Japanese Patent Office, and the United States Patent and Trademark Office to assure that the respective efforts of those offices in automation would be tightly coordinated so that each office could benefit from the work of the others. One of the first tangible results of Trilateral Cooperation was providing to U.S. examiners English abstracts of Japanese patents in machine readable form. This opened up in a very practical way an entire field of prior art which otherwise would not have been adequately searched. Now looking towards its fifteenth anniversary, Trilateral Cooperation is forming a solid foundation for those efforts of the U.S. Patent and Trademark Office to extend automated prior art searches worldwide.

All of these efforts of the Patent and Trademark Office are to be warmly applauded. They clearly lead to an increased confidence that a patent, once granted by the U.S. Patent and Trademark Office, will withstand the most intense scrutiny if it is enforced against a competitor. This, in turn, contributes in a tangible way to the overarching goal of the U.S. patent system, namely, "to promote the progress of the ... the useful arts."

* Former Assistant Secretary of Commerce and Commissioner of Patents and Trademark; currently Senior Counsel to Oblon, Spivak, McClelland, Maier & Neustadt, P.C., Arlington, Virginia. The views expressed herein are solely those of the author and do not necessarily reflect those of the firm or its clients. This *Side Bar* was written specially for Principles of Patent Law.

b. OFFICE ACTION

After this initial activity by the examiner, he or she communicates in writing to the applicant or to his or her attorney or agent, if one has been appointed. This communication is called an *Office Action*. The Office Action includes at least two parts: a form cover letter, on which the examiner summarizes the action by checking the appropriate boxes and filling in the correct blanks, and an explanation of the action.

i. *Substantive Actions*. In the first substantive Office action the examiner can allow claims, reject claims,[36] object to claims, or object to the

---

36. Claims may be rejected if they are found not to be novel (35 U.S.C. § 102 (2001 and Supp. 2003)—*see infra* Chapter Four) or made "obvious" by a reference or combination of references (35 U.S.C. § 103 (2001)—*see infra* Chapter Five). Claims may also be rejected under 35 U.S.C. § 112, ¶ 2 if they are vague or indefinite. There are also less common grounds for rejection. For example, a claim will be rejected as being drawn to "nonstatutory subject

written description.[37]

ii.   *Restriction Requirement and Election.* The patent law mandates that a patent applicant can claim only *one* invention per patent. See MPEP, chapter 800. Thus, if the examiner believes that there is more than one invention claimed in the application, the examiner will require the applicant to choose which invention he desires to prosecute. This is accomplished by including in the first Office Action a *restriction requirement.* In response to such a requirement, the applicant must *elect* one invention for prosecution and may thereafter prosecute the nonelected inventions by filing one or more "divisional" applications. *See infra,* § 2(e)(c).

c.   APPLICANT'S RESPONSE

Within the period of time allotted for response, which usually can be extended up to the maximum statutory period of six months upon payment of a fee, the applicant must respond to all of the examiner's rejections and objections or the application will be held abandoned.

Applicants may respond to claim rejections and objections by amendment of the claims and by argument specifically addressing the examiner's Action.[38] Usually, a response includes both claim amendments and arguments designed to distinguish the invention as claimed from any prior art cited by the examiner.[39]

The applicant may also respond by amending the written description to include the language of an originally-filed claim if the examiner rejects or objects to a claim as not being supported by the written description. In addition, the applicant may amend the written description in response to an objection asserting that it does not describe the invention with sufficient clarity, provided that the applicant may not introduce *"new matter."* See 35 U.S.C. § 132 (2001). *New matter is substantive information not contained in the originally filed application.* For the most part, if an applicant wants to retain his original filing date, there is very little he can do to the written description *after* the application is filed.

d.   RECONSIDERATION AND ALLOWANCE

After the applicant submits a response to the first Office Action, the examiner reconsiders the application. If the examiner is satisfied with the response, he issues a *Notice of Allowance.*[40] A Notice of Allowance is a form

---

matter'' if it is drawn to something not enumerated in 35 U.S.C. § 101, § 161, or § 171 (2001).

37.   The written description may be objected to under 35 U.S.C. § 112, ¶ 1 based on, for example, an asserted failure to meet the "enablement" requirement. *See* Chapter Three, *infra.*

38.   Although the amendment may be self-explanatory, as a rule of practice the applicant should accompany the amendment with an explanation of its relevance.

39.   A response may also include affidavits or declarations as to the nonobviousness, operability, or utility of the invention, *see* 37 C.F.R. § 1.132, or as to the applicant's priority of invention, *see* 37 C.F.R. § 1.131. *See also* Chapter Four.

40.   While there is no time-based requirement for the examiner to act on the response filed by the applicant, nevertheless, the patent owner may be granted increased patent term where the examiner has acted with undue delay. The American Inventors Protection Act of 1999 includes the "Patent Term Guarantee Act" which codifies the lengthening of the patent

letter, the primary purpose of which is to inform the applicant of allowance of the application.

If the examiner is not satisfied by a response, he may issue a second Office Action. Unless a second or subsequent Office Action is based on a new ground of rejection, such as newly discovered prior art, the examiner may make it "final."[41]

e. RESPONSES TO A FINAL OFFICE ACTION

After a final rejection by the examiner, the applicant is faced with a choice. The applicant can (1) abandon the application; (2) file an appeal with the Board of Patent Appeals and Interferences;[42] (3) take allowed claims and cancel the others; or (4) file a continuing application.

a. *Appeals.* If the applicant files an appeal with the Board, he is given two months, extendable to seven months, to file an Appeal Brief. After the Appeal Brief has been filed, the examiner must file an Examiner's Answer. There is no statutory or regulatory time limit for filing the Examiner's Answer. Within two months of the Examiner's Answer, the applicant may file a reply brief directed only to any new points that were raised in the Examiner's Answer.

The applicant may request an oral hearing.[43] The appeal is then placed on the Board's calendar and assigned to a panel of three Administrative Patent Judges. When an appeal is set for oral hearing, the applicant is given notice of the date of the hearing and, at that point, may waive the hearing.

After oral hearing, or if no oral hearing is requested, the appeal is considered by the Board. The Board may affirm the decision of the examiner in whole or in part, or may reverse it. If the Board affirms the examiner's decision, the applicant may abandon the application, file a continuing application, bring a civil action to obtain a patent in the District Court for the District of Columbia under 35 U.S.C. § 145, or appeal the Board's decision directly to the Federal Circuit under 35 U.S.C. § 141. If the Board reverses the examiner's decision, the examiner must issue a

---

term in circumstances where the actions of the examiner, or the PTO, have caused undue delay in the patent prosecution process.

41. At any time from the issuance of the first Office Action until the issuance of a final Office Action, the applicant or applicant's representative is entitled to a personal or telephonic interview with the examiner for the purposes of clarifying the issues and of reaching agreement leading to allowance of the application. After a final Office Action is issued, it is within the examiner's discretion to allow interviews and to consider responses. The examiner must make the substance of the interview of record by completing an Examiner Interview Summary Record form and, unless excused by the examiner, the applicant must also file a summary of the interview. 37 C.F.R. § 1.133(b) (2002); MPEP § 713.04. For a discussion of interview practice, *see Magnivision v. Bonneau Co.*, 115 F.3d 956 (Fed.Cir.1997).

42. The Board of Patent Appeals and Interferences is an Article I adjudicative board within the PTO. See generally, Michael W. Bloomer, *The Board of Patent Appeals and Interferences*, AM. INTELL. PROP. L. ASS'N BULL., Dec. 1992, at 188; Paul J. Federico, *The Board of Appeals 1861–1961*, 43 J. PAT. OFF. SOC'Y 691 (1961).

43. The request should be filed within two months of the Examiner's Answer, but it can be filed at any time starting with the filing of the appeal. 37 C.F.R. § 1.194(b) (2002).

Notice of Allowance. The Board can also order further examination or other procedures, if the case warrants.

b.   *Cancellation of Claims*. If an applicant faces final rejection of some claims, but allowance of others, whether or not the result of an appeal, he may decide to take the allowed claims and cancel the others. A notice of allowance would then be issued.

c.   *Continuing Applications*. If an applicant faces a final rejection of all claims in an application; or a final rejection of claims that were canceled to allow other claims to issue; or desires to prosecute claims that were not elected in the face of a restriction requirement; the applicant may wish to file a continuing application. "Continuing application" is a generic term for three types of patent applications that are entitled to the filing date of an earlier ("parent") application. the three types of continuing applications are *continuation applications, continuation-in-part applications,* and *divisional applications*. The requirements for claiming continuing status are that the application be filed while the parent application is still pending ("copendency"), at least one inventor must be common to the two applications, and the text of the second application must refer back to the first. *See* MPEP at §§ 201.06, 201.07, 201.08, and 201.11.

Two types of *continuation applications* exist. Both are filed under 37 C.F.R. § 1.53 (2002). 37 C.F.R. § 1.53(b) (2002) defines an application whose specification is the same as that of the parent application, but whose claims are different from those of the parent application. This type of continuation application is entitled to the parent's filing date as to all subject matter contained in it. There are several reasons for filing a continuation. For example, a continuation under 37 C.F.R. § 1.53(b) (2002) might be filed to obtain further prosecution if all claims are finally rejected in the parent, but the applicant has new amendments or arguments to present. A continuation application is often appropriate if the new amendments or arguments were presented in the parent after final rejection and were not entered because they raised new issues or required further searching, but the examiner gave some indication that the amendments or arguments had merit. A continuation might also be filed if only some claims were finally rejected in the parent. Those claims might be canceled from the parent, allowing the other claims to issue. The canceled claims may then be pursued, with or without change, in the continuation.

A *continuing prosecution application* (CPA) is a special type of continuation application filed under 37 C.F.R. § 1.53(d) (2002). In an application filed under 37 C.F.R. § 1.53(d), the file of the parent is continued and, while the parent is indeed abandoned, the application has the same number as its parent and no reference to the parent is inserted into the specification. An application filed under § 1.53(d) cannot be filed unless the parent is to be abandoned. All papers filed in the parent, except election in a § 1.53(d) divisional application, carry over into the new application. Thus, no separate claim for foreign priority is required in the application filed under § 1.53(d), if a claim has been made in the parent. Also, no reference to the parent has to be inserted to preserve domestic priority. The main differences between the application filed under § 1.53(d) and a continuation application filed under § 1.53(b) are the following: a new file is created for an application filed under § 1.53(b) but not for an application filed under § 1.53(d); a new application number is assigned to a § 1.53(b) application, but not to a § 1.53(d) application; a § 1.53(b) application cannot be filed by Fax, but a § 1.53(d) application can be filed by Fax; a continuation-in-part application (*see next paragraph*) can be filed in a § 1.53(b) application but not in a § 1.53(d) application; a § 1.53(b) application does not automatically abandon the parent application, while a § 1.53(d) application does; and, finally, a § 1.53(b) application must include a reference to parent for domestic priority and must make a claim for foreign priority, while a § 1.53(d) application does not. There are other procedural details concerning filing of the applications that have been omitted for the sake of brevity.

A *continuation-in-part application* is an application that has some subject matter in common with the parent but also has new subject matter. It cannot be filed in a continuing prosecution application. A continuation-in-part is entitled to the parent's filing date as to any subject matter in common, but only to its own filing date as to the new matter. A continuation-in-part might be filed if the applicant wished to add limitations to the parent claims to distinguish a reference or references, but the added limitations were not supported by the written description of the parent, and the examiner would not allow supporting material to be added to the written description because it introduced new matter. The applicant could file a continuation-in-part to include the new matter. A continuation-in-part, including newly developed information, might also be filed if the applicant has improved the invention described in the parent.

A *divisional application* is a continuing application that is based on a parent application and has the same written description except that the claims differ, usually because of a restriction requirement. Recall that a restriction requirement forces the applicant to elect which invention he wants to prosecute. This does not mean that the applicant is precluded from seeking patent protection for the non-elected invention. In fact, the non-elected invention may be prosecuted by filing a divisional application. In essence, the examiner is preventing the applicant from extending his patent rights beyond the statutory term. This type of rejection had significantly more power prior to the GATT amendments to the patent law, which now measure a patent's term from date of filing (*i.e.*, 20 years from date of filing) as opposed to date of issuance (*i.e.*, 17 years from date of issuance). Thus, prior to these amendments, an applicant could overcome a double patenting rejection by filing a *terminal disclaimer* which had the effect of shortening the life of the divisional patent so that it would expire at the same time as the parent application, thus precluding an extension of the patent right. However, since the enactment of the GATT amendments, the terminal disclaimer, in this regard, is no longer needed as patent life is measured from date of filing.

f. PUBLICATION

Prior to the American Inventors Protection Act of 1999 (AIPA), patents were kept secret by the PTO. The AIPA as codified in the United States Code and the Federal Regulations, however, authorizes publication of applications filed on or after November 29, 2000. Pursuant to 35 U.S.C. § 122(b)(1) (2001), subject to some exceptions, "each application for a patent shall be published . . . promptly after the expiration of a period of 18 months from the earliest filing date." The exceptions to publication are set forth in 35 U.S.C. § 122(b)(2) (2001).

1.   *Exceptions to Publication*

a.   *Abandonment.* Section 122(B)(2) excludes applications that are "no longer pending" or "subject to a secrecy order," and provisional and design patent applications.[44]

An applicant may abandon an application to avoid publication. 37 C.F.R. § 1.138(c) (2002) requires a petition "in sufficient time to permit the appropriate officials to recognize the abandonment and remove the application from the publication process." The rule sets forth a four week lead time for assuring non-publication.

In establishing the rule, the PTO stated that "[a]ny applicant seeking to abandon the application for the purpose of avoiding publication must take appropriate action . . . well prior to the projected publication date. If the application is not expressly abandoned at least four weeks prior to the projected publication date, the Office will probably not be able to avoid publication of the application or at least some application information because the Office will place the application (along with the thousands of other applications being published each week) on publication media (*e.g.*, optical disks, magnetic tape) four weeks prior to the projected date. This does not imply that a request to expressly abandon an application to avoid publication (§ 1.138) filed prior to this 'four-week' time frame will ensure that the Office will be able to remove an application from publication. The Office simply cannot ensure that it can remove an application from publication or avoid publication of application information any time after the publication process for the application is initiated."[45]

b.   *Request—No Foreign Filing.* Section 122(B)(2) prohibits publication of an applicant's application if the applicant files a request.[46] In the request, the applicant must certify that "the invention disclosed in the application has not and will not be the subject of an application filed in another country, or under a multilateral international agreement, that requires publication of applications 18 months after filing."[47] (Virtually all patent systems other than that of the United States provide for 18 month publication.)

---

44. 35 U.S.C. § 122(b)(2)(A)(i)–(iv) (2001). See H.R. Rep. No. 106–287, pt. 1, (1999) ("Since design applications do not disclose technology, inventors do not have a particular interest in having them published. The bill as written therefore simplifies the proposed system of publication to confine the requirement to those applications for which there is a need for publication." "Pursuant to 35 U.S.C. § 111(b)(5), all provisional applications are abandoned 12 months after the date of their filing; accordingly, they are not subject to the 18–month publication requirement.").

45. 65 Fed. Reg. at 17951.

46. 35 U.S.C. § 122(b)(2)(B) (2001).

47. 35 U.S.C. § 122(b)(2)(B)(i) (2001).

c. *Rescission—Subsequent Foreign Filing.* An applicant may rescind the request.[48]

An applicant who has made the request but subsequently files an application in a foreign publishing patent system must notify the PTO no later than 45 days after such foreign filing.[49] If the applicant rescinds the request or notifies the PTO of filing in a publishing patent system, the applicant's application is published on the 18 month date "or as soon as is practical after [that] date."[50]

If an applicant fails to make a timely notification, the application is deemed abandoned. The abandoned application is subject to revival if a delay in providing the notification was unintentional.

d. *Redacted Publication.* Section 122(b)(v) provides for publication of a "redacted copy" of a United States application if the corresponding foreign filed application "is less extensive than the application or description of the invention" in the United States application.[51]

Under Rule 217, an applicant desiring redaction must file a redacted copy within 16 months of the earliest filing date.[52] The submitted copy must comply with the PTO's electronic filing system requirements. The applicant must also submit a copy of the corresponding foreign-filed appli-

---

48.   35 U.S.C. § 122(b)(2)(B)(ii) (2001).

49.   35 U.S.C. § 122(b)(2)(B)(iii) (2001):

"An applicant who has made a request under clause (i) but who subsequently files, in a foreign country or under a multilateral international agreement specified in clause (i), an application directed to the invention disclosed in the application filed in the Patent and Trademark Office, shall notify the Director of such filing not later than 45 days after the date of the filing of such foreign or international application. A failure of the applicant to provide such notice within the prescribed period shall result in the application being regarded as abandoned, unless it is shown to the satisfaction of the Director that the delay in submitting the notice was unintentional."

50.   35 U.S.C. § 122(b)(2)(B)(iv) (2001).

51.   35 U.S.C. § 122(b)(2)(B)(v) (2001). See H.R. Rpt. No. 106–287, pt. 1 (1999) ("where an applicant has filed an application in a foreign country, either directly or through the PCT, so that the application will be published 18 months from its earliest effective filing date, the applicant may limit the scope of the publication by the PTO to the total of the cumulative scope of the applications filed in all foreign countries. Where the foreign application is identical to the application filed in the United States or where an application filed under the PCT is identical to the application filed in the United States, the applicant may not limit the extent to which the application filed in the United States is published. However, where an applicant has limited the description of an application filed in a foreign country, either directly or through the PCT in comparison with the application filed in the PTO, the applicant may restrict the publication by the PTO to no more than the cumulative details of what will be published in all of the foreign applications and through the PCT. The applicant may restrict the extent of publication of her U.S. application by submitting a redacted copy of the application to the PTO eliminating only those details that will not be published in any of the foreign applications. Any description contained in at least one of the foreign national or PCT filings may not be excluded from publication in the corresponding U.S. patent application. To ensure that any redacted copy of the U.S. application is published in place of the original U.S. application, the redacted copy must be received within 16 months from the earliest effective filing date. Finally, if the published U.S. application as redacted by the applicant does not enable a person skilled in the art to make and use the claimed invention, provisional rights under [§] 154(d) shall not be available.").

52.   37 C.F.R. § 81.217(a) (2002).

cation together with an English translation if that application is not in English. Also, the applicant must submit desired redactions of the papers in the file wrapper to prevent the redacted material from being made available to the public under Rule 14(c)(2).

2. *Protest Prohibited—Public Submission of Prior Art*

Section 122(c) requires the PTO to establish "appropriate procedures to ensure that no protest or other form of pre-issuance opposition to the grant of a patent on an application may be initiated after publication of the application without the express written consent of the applicant."[53] Protests will be discussed in more detail below in section (i).

Rule 291(a)(1) implements Section 122(c) by providing that a "protest is submitted prior to the date the application was published or the mailing of a notice of allowance ... whichever occurs first."[54] Rule 292 would impose a similar restriction on petitions for public use proceedings.[55]

Rule 99(a) does allow members of the public to submit "patents or publications relevant to a pending published application [for entry] in the application file," but it provides that the involvement of a member of the public in filing a submission under § 1.99 ends with the filing of the submission.[56]

3. *Prior Art Effect*

The AIPA's provisions made published United States applications prior art under Section 102(e) as of their effective United States filing dates.[57] The prior art effect is "vested" on publication and is not affected by a later abandonment of the application.

Section 102(e) into two subparts. Subpart (1) deals with published patent applications. Subpart (2) deals with patents. Subpart (1) includes as prior art descriptions in "an application for patent, published under section 122(b), by another filed in the United States before the invention by the applicant for patent."

Section 102(e) bars carrying back a U.S. patent's prior art effect to its foreign priority filing date.[58] Subpart (1) provides that a person shall be

---

53.   35 U.S.C. § 122(c) (2001). For a discussion of protests, see 4 Donald S. Chisum, Chisum on Patents § 11.03[3][b] (2002).

54.   37 C.F.R. § 1.291(a)(1) (2002).

55.   37 C.F.R. § 1.292(a) (2002).

56.   37 C.F.R. § 1.99(a) (2002).

57.   Pub. L. No. 106–113, § 4505, 113 Stat. 1501 (Nov. 29, 1999). The 1999 Act is effective one year after its enactment date, which was November 29, 1999, and applies "to all applications filed under section 111 of title 35, United States Code, on or after that date, and all applications complying with section 371 of title 35, United States Code, that resulted from international applications filed on or after that date." Pub. L. No. 106–113, § 4508, 113 Stat. 1501 (Nov. 29, 1999). The prior art effect provision will also extend to applications pending on the effective date if the application is "voluntarily published under procedures established" under the legislation.

58.   See H.R. Rpt. No. 106–287, pt. 1 (1999) (the Act "amends § 102(e) of the Patent Act to treat an application published by the PTO in the same fashion as a patent published by the PTO. Accordingly, a published application is given prior art effect as of its earliest effective

entitled to a patent unless the invention was described in "an application for patent, published under section 122(b), by another filed in the United States before the mention by the applicant for patent."[59] Thus, a PCT international application designating the United States becomes prior art as of its international filing date upon its publication—but only if the published application is in English.

Subpart (2) provides that a person shall be entitled to a patent unless the invention was described in "a patent granted on an application for patent by another filed in the United States before the invention by the applicant for patent . . ."[60]

4. *Provisional Compensation Right*

As compensation for the earlier disclosure of an inventor's technology provided by eighteen-month publication, 35 U.S.C. § 154(d) provides for, as an additional right of a patent, a "provisional" right to compensation.

a. *Reasonable Royalty.* The right is to "obtain a reasonable royalty."[61] The royalty is for a period beginning on the date of a patent application's publication and ending on the date of the patent's issuance.[62]

b. *Persons With Actual Notice.* The royalty right extends to "any person" who commits the acts that would otherwise constitute infringement of a patent, that is, making, using, offering for sale, importing, etc.[63] The person must have "had actual notice of the published patent application."[64]

The "actual notice" requirement contrasts with the remedies against direct infringement, as to which there is no knowledge or intent require-

---

U.S. filing date against any subsequently filed U.S. applications. As with patents, any foreign filing date to which the published application is entitled will not be the effective filing date of the U.S. published application for prior art purposes. An exception to this general rule is made for international applications designating the United States that are published under Article 21(2)(a) of the PCT in the English language. Such applications are given a prior art effect as of their international filing date. The prior art effect accorded to patents . . . remain unchanged from present [§] 102(e) of the Patent Act.").

59. 35 U.S.C. § 102(e)(1) (Supp. 2003).

Section 374, on the publication of PCT international applications, was amended to provide that "[t]he publication under the treaty defined in section 351(a) of this title, of an international application designating the United States shall be deemed a publication under section 122(b), except as provided in sections 102(e) and 154(d) of this title." 35 U.S.C. § 374 (Supp. 2003).

60. 35 U.S.C. § 102(e)(2) (Supp. 2003).

61. 35 U.S.C. § 154(d)(1) (2001).

For a discussion of a reasonable royalty, see 7 Chisum on Patents § 20.03[3].

35 U.S.C. Section 184 precludes recovery of increased damages. For a discussion of increased damages under Section 284, see 7 Chisum on Patents § 20.03[4][b].

62. 35 U.S.C. § 154(d)(1) (2001).

63. 35 U.S.C. § 154(d)(1)(A) (2001).

64. 35 U.S.C. § 154(d)(1)(B) (2001). See H.R. Rpt. No. 106–287, pt. 1 (1999) ("The requirement of actual notice is critical. The mere fact that the published application is included in a commercial database where it might be found is insufficient. The published applicant must give actual notice of the published application to the accused infringer and explain what acts are regarded as giving rise to provisional rights.").

ment.[65] The requirement is anomalous in that it tends to reward those who do not take advantage of one of the purposes of eighteen month publication, which is to provide early disclosure of new technology and notice of potential proprietary rights in such technology.

c. *Claim Identity.* The royalty right is "not available ... unless the invention as claimed in the patent is substantially identical to the invention as claimed in the published patent application."[66]

Because the provisional compensation right depends on what claims are in an application as published, patent applicants have an incentive to assure that the published claims are both of appropriately broad scope and are likely to be allowed without substantial change. An applicant may wish to amend or add claims after the original filing with this goal in mind. Rule 215 limits application publication to the application papers on the filing date. The rule gives an applicant an option to have post-filing amendments included but only if the applicant timely supplies a copy of the amended application in compliance with the PTO's electronic filing system.

The "substantially identical" standard will undoubtedly create difficult issues.[67] If prosecution of an application is not substantially complete by the time of publication, the claims in the application may be amended by the addition of narrowing limitations. The claims may also be broadened. To take full advantage of the provisional right, an applicant must make special efforts to avoid amendments to claims that would eliminate the provisional compensation right.

The question of substantial similarity of claimed inventions arises in the context of amendments to claims during reexamination and reissue.[68] It also arises in the context of interferences.[69]

d. *Time Limitation.* The provisional compensation right is "available only in an action brought not later than 6 years after the patent is issued"

65. See 5 Chisum on Patents § 16.02[2].

66. 35 U.S.C. § 154(d)(2) (2001). See H.R. Rpt. No. 106–287, pt. 1 (1999). See also H.R. Rep. No. 106–464, (An "important limitation on the availability of provisional royalties is that the claims in the published application that are alleged to give rise to provisional rights must also appear in the patent in substantially identical form. To allow anything less than substantial identity would impose an unacceptable burden on the public. If provisional rights were available in the situation where the only valid claim infringed first appeared in substantially that form in the granted patent, the public would have no guidance as to the specific behavior to avoid between publication and grant. Every person or company that might be operating within the scope of the disclosure of the published application would have to conduct her own private examination to determine whether a published application contained patentable subject matter that she should avoid. The burden should be on the applicant to initially draft a schedule of claims that gives adequate notice to the public of what she is seeking to patent.").

67. For cases adjudicating the issue of substantial identity for claims altered during reissue and reexamination, see Laitram Corp. v. NEC Corp., 163 F.3d 1342 (Fed.Cir.1998); Bloom Eng'g Co. v. North Am. Mfg. Co., 129 F.3d 1247 (Fed.Cir.1997); Litton Sys., Inc. v. Honeywell, Inc., 87 F.3d 1559 (Fed.Cir.1996), vacated and remanded, 520 U.S. 1111 (1997), *aff'd in part, rev'd in part, vacated in part, & remanded,* 140 F.3d 1449 (Fed.Cir.1998).

68. See 4 Chisum on Patents § 11.07[4][f][ii], § 15.05.

69. See 3 Chisum on Patents § 10.09[4][c].

but is "not ... affected by the duration of the [publication to issuance] period."[70]

This six-year, post-issuance period for enforcement could lead to greatly delayed assertions of a provisional right. For example, a patent application might be filed in June 2002, published in December 2003, and issued only in December 2013. The patentee could file an action regarding the compensation right in December 2019, 16 years after the right accrued.

Presumably, the equitable defenses of laches and estoppel will apply to assertions of the provisional right.[71]

g.   POST–ALLOWANCE ACTIVITY

After a Notice of Allowance is issued, amendments can be made only on a showing of good cause why they were not made earlier. Submissions of additional prior art by the applicant will only be considered if the applicant certifies that the art was not known to the applicant more than three months prior to the date it is submitted. *See* 37 C.F.R. § 1.97(e)(2) (2002). If an applicant's amendment is offered to correct something in an Examiner's Amendment accompanying the allowance, it is usually entered if it does not change the meaning of the allowed application. Similarly, if an amendment is of no substantive consequence, such as an amendment to correct typographical errors in the application, it will be entered. Even new claims may be entered, provided they are of the same scope as allowed claims and are supported by the specification. However, after the issue fee is paid and preparations begin for printing the application as a patent, even simple amendments may be refused.

Side Bar

Opposition Proceedings According to the European Patent Convention

Joel Weiss[*]

The European Patent Convention, the body of law that governs the operation of the European Patent Office, provides for oppositions to granted patents. This sidebar surveys the articles of the European Patent Convention that relate to oppositions. This sidebar also surveys case law from the Opposition Divisions and Technical Boards of Appeal of the European Patent Office.

Within nine months from the publication of the mention of the grant of a European patent, any person may give notice to the European Patent Office of opposition to the European patent. The notice of opposition must include a written reasoned statement as to the grounds for the opposition.[1]

If an opposition is pending against a European patent, any third party who proves that proceedings for infringement of the same patent have been instituted against him may, even after the nine-month opposition period has expired, intervene in the opposition proceedings,[2] if he

---

70.   35 U.S.C. § 154(d)(3) (2001).

71.   See 6 Chisum on Patents § 19.05.

gives notice of intervention within three months of the date on which the infringement proceedings were instituted. Any third party who proves both that the proprietor of the patent has requested that the third party cease alleged infringement of the patent and that it has instituted proceedings for a court ruling that it is not infringing the patent can intervene in a pending opposition under the same rules.[3] The formal rules that apply to a notice of opposition—i.e., that the notice of opposition is not considered to have been filed until the fee has been paid, and the notice of opposition must be accompanied by a reasoned written statement—apply to an intervention as well.[4]

The parties to the opposition proceedings include the opponents as well as the proprietor of the patent. While "any person" may give notice to the European Patent Office of opposition, nevertheless, a European patent cannot be opposed by its own proprietor. Case number G 9/93.[5]

A European opposition is not considered filed until the opposition fee has been paid.[6] Nevertheless, an opposition filed in common by two or more persons[7] is admissible on payment of only one opposition fee. G 3/99.

An opposition pending before the European Patent Office is considered an asset of the opponent. As such, an opposition may be transferred or assigned to a third party as part of a transfer of the opponent's business assets together with the assets in the interests of which the opposition was filed.[8]

An opposition may only be filed if the reasoned statement accompanying the opposition alleges that the subject-matter of the European patent is not patentable within the terms of Articles 52 to 57,[9] the European patent does not disclose the invention in a manner sufficiently clear and complete for it to be carried out by a person skilled in the art, or that the subject-matter of the European patent extends beyond the content of the application as filed, or, if the patent was granted on a divisional application, beyond the content of the earlier application as filed.[10]

Article 82, EPC states that, a "European patent application shall relate to one invention only or to a group of inventions so linked as to form a single general inventive concept." During prosecution of the patent application, the EPO is particularly strict about the unity of invention requirement. Nevertheless, unity of invention is not a ground for opposition. Nor can it preclude the patent proprietor from making amendments during opposition proceedings. Unity of invention is therefore irrelevant in opposition proceedings.[11]

If the opposition is formally admissible—i.e., it is filed by an appropriate party and the grounds for opposition are within the allowable reasons for opposition, and are submitted in a timely manner in writing—the Opposition Division of the European Patent Office examines whether the grounds for opposition prejudice the maintenance of the European patent.[12] In the examination of the opposition, the Opposition Division may invite the parties to file Observations on communications from another party or issued by the party itself within a period to be fixed by the Opposition Division.[13] The parties may be invited to file such Observations by the Opposition Division as often as the Division sees fit. At the conclusion of the written part of the opposition, the Opposition Division conducts Oral Proceedings to allow the parties to the Opposition to argue their case.

The Oral Proceedings are typically heard before a three-member panel. All are examiners in the European Patent Office Examining Division. One member is the Chair-person. He or she presides over and runs the Oral Proceedings. Another member of the panel is the examiner who examined and granted the patent under opposition, if that examiner is available. The third member is usually a more junior examiner. When a legal question is presented in the opposition, the panel will have a fourth, legally-qualified, member.

If the Opposition Division is of the opinion that the grounds for opposition prejudice the maintenance of the European patent, it shall revoke the patent.[14] If the Opposition Division is of the opinion that the grounds for opposition do not prejudice the maintenance of the patent unamended, it shall reject the opposition.[15] If the Opposition Division is of the opinion that, taking into consideration amendments made by the proprietor of the patent during the opposition proceedings, the claimed invention meets the patentability requirements of the European Patent Convention, it shall maintain the patent, as amended, provided that: (a) it is established, in accordance with the provisions of the Implementing Regulations, that the proprietor of the patent approves the text in which the Opposition Division intends to maintain the patent; (b) the fee for the printing of a new specification of the European patent is timely paid.[16] Typically, the Opposition Division announces its decision at the end of the Oral Proceedings. The Opposition Division subsequently issues written reasons for its decision.

Each party to the proceedings shall meet the costs it has incurred unless a decision of an Opposition Division or Technical Board of Appeal, for reasons of equity, orders, in accordance with the Implementing Regulations, a different apportionment of costs incurred during taking of evidence or in oral proceedings.[17]

An appeal may be taken from the decision of the Opposition Division.[18] Appeals may be filed by the patent proprietor if the patent has been revoked or maintained only in amended form. Appeals may be taken by opponents if the patent has been maintained in any form. An appeal may be filed against the decision of the Opposition Division even if the European patent has been surrendered or has lapsed for all the designated States.[19] The Technical Board of Appeal of the European Patent Office hears the appeal.[20]

The appeal procedure is similar to that in the original Opposition. The appellant must file a notice of appeal within two months of the date of the written decision of the Opposition Division. Within two further months, the appellant must file written reasons for the appeal. If the Board finds the appeal formally admissible, it may invite appellees to file Observations against it. Typically, both parties to the appeal file a series of observations before Oral Proceedings.

The appeal is decided by the Technical Board at Oral Proceedings. Like the Opposition Division, the Technical Board is composed of three members (and a fourth legally-qualified member if the appeal presents a legal question). The members of the Board are not examiners or members of the opposition divisions. One member is the chair-person.

Typically, the Board announces its decision on the appeal at the close of the Oral Proceedings. The Board subsequently issues written reasons for its decision.

* Managing Partner, Weiss & Arons, Pomona, New York. This *Side Bar* was written specially for PRINCIPLES OF PATENT LAW.

1. Article 99(1). European Patent Convention. The exact requirements of the notice are set forth in Rule 55 EPC of the implementing regulations to part V of the Convention.

2. It is a prerequisite for intervention in opposition proceedings by an assumed infringer pursuant to Article 105 EPC that there are opposition proceedings in existence at the point in time when a notice of intervention is filed. G 4/91. Nevertheless, intervention of the assumed infringer under Article 105 EPC is admissible during pending appeal proceedings and may be based on any ground for opposition under Article 100 EPC. G 1/94.

3. Article 105(1).

4. Article 105(2).

5. With respect to oppositions filed by a third party: an opposition is not inadmissible purely because the person named as opponent according to Rule 55(a) EPC is acting on behalf of a third party. Such an opposition is, however, inadmissible if the involvement of the opponent is to be regarded as circumventing the law by abuse of process. Such a circumvention of the law arises, in particular, if: the opponent is acting on behalf of the patent proprietor; or the opponent is acting on behalf of a client in the context of activities which, taken as a whole, are typically associated with professional representatives, without possessing the relevant qualifications required by Article 134 EPC. G 4/97. Oppositions are also inadmissible if the named opponent is in fact acting on behalf of an unidentified client. Thus, unlike in Japan, European oppositions must be filed by the true opponent.

6. Article 99(1).

7. In order to safeguard the rights of the patent proprietor and in the inter-ests of procedural efficiency, it has to be clear throughout the procedure who belongs to the group of common opponents or common appellants. If either a common opponent or appellant (including the common representative) intends to withdraw from the proceedings, the EPO shall be notified accordingly by the common representative or by a new common representative determined under Rule 100(1) EPC in order for the withdrawal to take effect.

8. Case number G 4/88—EBA.

9. European Patent Convention Article 52 defines the subject matter of patentable inventions (compare 35 U.S.C. § 101). Article 53 limits the definition of patentable inventions set forth in Article 52 from including immoral inventions or plant or animal varieties or essentially biological processes for the production of plants or animals. This provision expressly does not restrict the patenting of microbiological processes or the products thereof. Article 54 states that an invention shall be considered to be new if it does not form part of the state of the art (compare the novelty requirements of 35 U.S.C. § 102). Article 55 relates to non-prejudicial disclosures. Article 56 relates to inventive step of a patent (compare the nonobviousness requirement of 35 U.S.C. § 103). Article 57 sets forth the requirement of industrial application of the invention.

10. Article 100(a–c).

11. G 1/91–EBA.

12. Article 101(1).

13. Article 101(2).

14. Article 102(1).

15. Article 102(2).

16. Article 102(3).

17. Article 104(1).

18. Article 106(1).

19. Article 106(2).

20. Article 110(1).

h. FOREIGN PRIORITY

An applicant can claim the benefit of the filing date of an application filed abroad. Under the terms of the Paris Convention for the Protection of

Industrial Property[72] (see discussion below), implemented in this country under 35 U.S.C. § 119 (2001 & Supp. 2003), the benefit of the filing date (referred to as "priority") from the first application for an invention filed in any member country can be claimed in a U.S. application as long as it is *filed within one year* of the first application.[73] Priority can be claimed at any time during the pendency of an application. A claim of priority is perfected by filing a certified copy of the foreign application. Whether benefit is claimed from a domestic or foreign application, materials published between the priority date and the application filing date are not prior art to the application. However, the one-year grace period of 35 U.S.C. § 102(b) (2001) is counted from the earliest effective U.S. filing date, not from a foreign priority date.[74] *See* Chapter Four.

There are several international IP agreements and treaties to which the United States is a signatory. Perhaps the three most important with respect to patent law are the Trade–Related Aspects of Intellectual Property Rights (TRIPS Agreement), the Paris Convention for the Protection of Intellectual Property (the Paris Convention), and the Patent Cooperation Treaty (PCT). The TRIPS Agreement is more substantive in nature, and therefore, is discussed throughout the remainder of the book when relevant. Our concern with the Paris Convention and the PCT, while certainly important, is more procedural and will be explored immediately below. In summary, these two treaties help patent applicants who file patent applications in multiple countries to more easily satisfy procedural requirements for filing in other treaty-member countries. What follows is from World Intellectual Property (WIPO) Handbook, reproduced with permission from WIPO:

WIPO Intellectual Property Handbook

The Paris Convention for the Protection of Industrial Property

The Right or Priority

5.20   The right of priority means that, on the basis of a regular application for an industrial property right filed by a given applicant in one of

---

72.   Priority is also available under the GATT–WTO (World Trade Organization) Treaty or under bilateral agreements with individual countries. For example, the United States now has an agreement with Taiwan, as of April 10, 1996, allowing patent applications filed in Taiwan to claim priority based on the filing date of the corresponding U.S. patent applications. *See* Daisy Wang, *Taiwan–U.S. Agreement Permits Claim to Priority Based on U.S. Filing Date*, 10 World Intellectual Property Report 173 (1996).

73.   In addition to the application filed in a member country, an applicant (in certain circumstances) may rely on an "international application" filed pursuant to the Patent Cooperation Treaty (PCT), which is administered by the World Intellectual Property Organization (WIPO). The PCT is a multilateral treaty among more than 50 nations that is designed to simplify the patenting process when an applicant seeks a patent on the same invention in more than one nation. *See* 35 U.S.C. chs. 35–37, and World Intellectual Property Organization, *PCT Applicant's Guide* (1992, rev. 2003).

74.   The exception removing § 102(b) prior art events from the protection of a foreign priority claim is explicitly written into § 119(a) (Supp. 2003). On the other hand, § 119(e), which defines the GATT-based provisional application's domestic priority, includes no such exception. Therefore, the one-year period of § 102(b) is calculated from the provisional application filing date and not the non-provisional application filing date.

the member countries, the same applicant (or its or his successor in title) may, within a specified period of time (six or 12 months), apply for protection in all the other member countries. These later applications will then be regarded as if they had been filed on the same day as the earliest application. Hence, these later applications enjoy a priority status with respect to all applications relating to the same invention filed after the date of the first application. They also enjoy a priority status with respect to all acts accomplished after that date which would normally be apt to destroy the rights of the applicant or the patentability of his invention. The provisions concerning the right of priority are contained in Article 4 of the Convention.

5.21   The right of priority offers great practical advantages to the applicant desiring protection in several countries. The applicant is not required to present all applications at home and in foreign countries at the same time, since he has six or 12 months at his disposal to decide in which countries to request protection. The applicant can use that period to organize the steps to be taken to secure protection in the various countries of interest in the particular case.

5.22   The beneficiary of the right of priority is any person entitled to benefit from the national treatment rule who has duly filed an application for a patent for invention or another industrial property right in one of the member countries.

5.23   The right of priority can be based only on the *first* application for the same industrial property right which must have been filed in a member country. It is therefore not possible to follow a first application by a second, possibly improved application and then to use that second application as a basis of priority. The reason for this rule is obvious: one cannot permit an endless chain of successive claims of priority for the same subject, as this could, in fact, considerably prolong the term of protection for that subject.

5.24   Article 4A(1) of the Paris Convention recognizes expressly that the right of priority may also be invoked by the successor in title of the first applicant. The right of priority may be transferred to a successor in title without transferring at the same time the first application itself. This allows in particular also the transfer of the right of priority to different persons for different countries, a practice which is quite common.

5.25   The later application must concern the same subject as the first application the priority of which is claimed. In other words, the same invention, utility model, trademark or industrial design must be the subject of both applications. It is, however, possible to use a first application for a patent for invention as priority basis for a registration of a utility model and vice versa. The same change of form of protection in both directions may also be possible, in accordance with national laws, between utility models and industrial designs.

5.26   The first application must be "duly filed" in order to give rise to the right of priority. Any filing, which is equivalent to a regular national filing, is a valid basis for the right of priority. A regular national filing means any filing that is adequate to establish the date on which the application was filed in the country concerned. The notion of "national" filing is qualified by including also applications filed under bilateral or multilateral treaties concluded between member countries.

5.27   Withdrawal, abandonment or rejection of the first application does not destroy its capacity to serve as a priority basis. The right of priority subsists even where the first application generating that right is no longer existent.

5.28   The effect of the right of priority is regulated in Article 4B. One can summarize this effect by saying that, as a consequence of the priority claim, the later application must be treated as if it had been filed already at the time of the filing, in another member country, of the first application the priority of which is claimed. By virtue of the right of priority, all the acts accomplished during the time between the filing dates of the first and the later applications, the so-called priority period, cannot destroy the rights which are the subject of the later application.

5.29   In terms of concrete examples, this means that a patent application for the same invention filed by a third party during the priority period will not give a prior right, although it was filed before the later application. Likewise, a publication or public use of the invention, which is the subject of the later application, during the priority period would not destroy the novelty or inventive character of that invention. It is insignificant for that purpose whether that publication is made by the applicant or the inventor himself or by a third party.

5.30   The length of the priority period is different according to the various kinds of industrial property rights. For patents for invention and utility models the priority periods is 12 month, for industrial designs and trademarks it is six months. In determining the length of the priority period, the Paris Convention had to take into account the conflicting interests of the applicant and of third parties. The priority periods now prescribed by the Paris Convention seem to strike an adequate balance between them.

5.31   The right of priority as recognized by the Convention permits the claiming of "multiple priorities" and of "partial priorities." Therefore, the later application may not only claim the priority of one earlier application, but it may also combine the priority of several earlier applications, each of which pertaining to different features of the subject matter of the later application. Furthermore, in the later application, elements for which priority is claimed may be combined with elements for which no priority is claimed. In all these cases, the later application must of course comply with the requirement of unity of invention.

5.32   These possibilities correspond to a practical need. Frequently after a first filing further improvements and additions to the invention are the subject of further applications in the country of origin. In such cases, it is very practical to be able to combine these various earlier applications into one later application, when filing before the end of the priority year in another member country. The combination is even possible if the multiple priorities come from different member countries.

The Patent Cooperation Treaty (PCT)

Introduction

The National Patent System

5.252   The national system requires the filing of individual applications for each country for which patent protection is sought, with the exception of the regional patent systems such as the African Intellectual Property Organization (OAPI) system, the Harare Protocol system established in the framework of the African Regional Industrial Property Organization (ARIPO), the Eurasian patent system and the European patent system. Under the traditional Paris Convention route, the priority of an earlier application can be claimed for application filed subsequently in foreign countries but such later application must be filed within 12 months of the filing date of the earlier application. This involves for the applicant the preparation and filing of patent applications for all countries in which he is seeking protection for his invention within one year of the filing of the first application. This means expenses for translation, patent attorneys in the various countries and payment of fees to the patent Offices, all at a time when the applicant often does not know whether he is likely to obtain a patent or whether his invention is really new compared with the state of the art.

5.253   Filing of patent applications under the national system that every single patent Office with which an application is filed has to carry out a formal examination of every application filed with it. Where patent Offices examine patent applications as to substance, each Office has to make a search to determine the state of the art in the technical field of the invention and has to carry out an examination as to patentability.

5.254   The principal difference between the national patent system and the regional patent systems such as those mentioned above is that a regional patent is granted by one patent Office for several States. Otherwise, the procedure is the same, and the explanations given in the preceding two paragraphs are equally valid.

* * *

Objectives of the PCT

5.257   As its name suggests, the Patent Cooperation Treaty is an agreement for international cooperation in the field of patents. It is often spoken of as being the most significant advance in international cooperation in this field since the adoption of the Paris Convention itself. It is, however, largely a treaty for rationalization and cooperation with regard to the filing, searching and examination of patent applications and the dissemination of the technical information contained therein. The PCT does not provide for the grant of "international patents": the task of and responsibility for granting patents remains exclusively in the hands of the patent Offices of, or acting for, the countries where protection is sought (the "designated Offices"). The PCT does not compete with but, in fact, complements the Paris Convention. Indeed, it is a special agreement under the Paris Convention open only to States which are already party to that Convention.

5.258 The principal objective of the PCT is, by simplification leading to more effectiveness and economy, to improve on—in the interests of the users of the patent system and the Offices which have responsibility to administering it—the previously established means of applying in several countries for patent protection for invention.

5.259 To achieve its objective, the PCT:

- establishes an international system which enables the filing, with a single patent Office (the "receiving Office"), of a single application (the "international application") in one language having effect in each of the countries party to the PCT which the applicant names ("designates") in his application;

- provides for the formal examination of the international application by a single patent Office, the receiving Office;

- subjects each international application to an international search which results in a report citing the relevant prior art (mainly published patent documents relating to previous inventions) which may have to be taken into account in deciding whether the invention is patentable;

- provides for centralized international publication of international applications with the related international search reports, as well as their communication to the designated Offices;

- provides an option for an international preliminary examination of the international application, which gives the applicant and subsequently the Offices that have to decide whether or not to grant a patent, a report containing an opinion as to whether the claimed invention meets certain international criteria for patentability.

5.260 The procedure described in the preceding paragraph is commonly call the "international phase" of the PCT procedure, whereas one speaks of the "national phase" to describe the last part of the patent granting procedure, which is the task of the designated Offices, i.e., the national Offices of, or acting for, the countries which have been designated in the international application. In PCT, terminology, a reference to "national" Office, "national" phase or "national" fees includes the reference to the procedure before a regional patent Office.

5.261 Especially in more developed countries with a greater number of patent applications, patent Offices have been struggling for years with heavy workloads (leading to delays) and with questions of how best to allocate resources, so as to ensure that the patent system yields the greatest return from the available manpower. Under the PCT system, by the time the international application reaches the national Office, it has already been examined as to form by the receiving Office, been searched by the International Searching Authority and possibly examined by an International Preliminary Examining Authority. These centralized procedures of the international phase thus reduce the workload of the national patent offices.

5.262   Further main objectives of the PCT are to facilitate and accelerate access by industry and other interested sectors to technical information related to inventions and to assist developing countries in gaining access to technology.

The Functioning of the PCT System

Filing an International Application

5.263   Any national or resident of a PCT Contracting State an file an international application. International applications can be filed in most cases with the national Office, which will act as PCT receiving Office. In addition, the International Bureau can act as a receiving Office as an option for nationals and residents of all PCT Contracting States.

5.264   An international application has the effect, as of the international filing date, of a national application in those PCT Contracting States which the applicant designates for a national patent in his application. It has the effect of a regional patent application in those PCT Contracting States which are party to a regional patent treaty, providing they are designed for a regional patent (that is, an ARIPO patent, a Eurasian patent, a European patent or a OAPI patent).

5.265   The PCT prescribes certain standards for international applications. An international application which is prepared in accordance with these standards will be acceptable, so far as the form and contents of the application are concerned, to all the PCT Contracting States, and no subsequent modifications because of varying national or regional requirements (and the cost associated therewith) will become necessary. No national law may require compliance with requirements relating to the form or contents of the international application different from or additional to those which are provided for by the PCT.

5.266   Only a single set of fees is incurred for the preparation and filing of the international application and they are payable in one currency and at one Office, the receiving Office. Payment of national fees to the designated Offices is delayed. The national fees become payable much later than for a filing by the traditional Paris Convention route.

5.267   The fees payable to the receiving Office for an international application consists of three main elements:

- the transmittal fee, to cover the work of the receiving Office;

- the search fee, to cover the work of the International Searching Authority;

- the international fee, to cover the work of the International Bureau.

5.268 An applicant who is a natural person and who is a national of and resides in a State whose per capita national income is below a certain level, based on income figures used by the United Nations for determining its scale of assessments for contributions to it, is entitled to a sizable reduction of certain PCT fees, including the international fee. If there are several applicants, each must satisfy the above-mentioned criteria.

5.269 The language in which an international application can be filed depends upon the requirements of the receiving Office with which the application is filed and of the International Searching Authority which is to carry out the international search. The main languages in which international applications may be filed are Chinese, English, French, German, Japanese, Russian and Spanish; other languages also accepted, so far, are Danish Dutch, Finnish, Norwegian and Swedish.

5.270 The receiving Office, after having accorded an international filing date and made a formal check, sends a copy of the international application to the International Bureau of WIPO (the "record copy") and another copy (the "search copy") to the International Searching Authority. It keeps a third copy (the "home copy"). The receiving Office also collects all the PCT fees and transfers the search fee to the International Searching Authority and the international fee to the international Bureau.

The International Search

5.271 Every international application is subjected to an international search, that is, a high quality search of the patent documents and other technical literature in those languages in which most patent application are filed (English, French and German, and in certain cases, Chinese, Japanese, Russian and Spanish). The high quality of the international search is assured by the standards prescribed in the PCT for the documentation, staff qualifications and search methods of the International Searching Authorities, which are experienced patent Offices that have been specially appointed to carry out international searches by the Assembly of the PCT Union (the highest administrative body created under the PCT) on the basis of an agreement to observe PCT standards and time limits.

5.272 The following Offices have been appointed to act as International Searching Authorities: the Australian Patent Office, the Austrian Patent Office, the Chinese Patent Office, the European Patent Office, the Japanese Patent Office, the Russian Patent Office, the Spanish Patent and Trademark Office, the Swedish Patent Office and the United States Patent and Trademark Office.

5.273 Each International Searching Authority is required to have at least the prescribed PCT minimum documentation, properly arranged for search purposes, which can be described in general as comprising the patent documents, as from 1920, of the major industrialized countries, together with agreed items of non-patent literature. The International Searching Authority, in making the search, must make use of its full facilities, i.e., the minimum documentation and any additional documentation it may possess. The obligation to consult at least the PCT minimum documentation guarantees a high level of international searching.

5.274 The results of the international search are given in an international search report, which is normally made available to the applicant by the fourth or fifth month after the application is filed. The citations of documents of relevant prior art in the international search report enable the applicant to calculate his chances of obtaining a patent in or for the countries designated in the international application, and to decide whether it is worthwhile to continue to seek protection for his invention in the designated States.

5.275 An international search report which is favorable, that is, in which the citations of prior art would appear not to prevent the grant of a patent, assists the applicant in the subsequent prosecution of the application before the designated Office. If a search report is unfavorable, the applicant has the opportunity to amend the claims in his international application to better distinguish the invention from the state-of-the-art or to withdraw the application before it is published.

5.276 The international search report assists designed Offices, in particular Offices which do not have technically qualified staff and an extensive collection of patent documents arranged in a manner suitable for search purposes, in examining applications and otherwise evaluating the inventions described.

5.277 The International Searching Authority sends the international search report to the applicant and to the International Bureau. The International Bureau includes the search report in the international publication of the international application and sends a copy to the designated Offices.

International Publication

5.278 International publication serves two main purposes: to disclose to the public the invention (*i.e.*, in general, the technological advance made by the inventor) and to set out the scope of the protection which may ultimately be obtained.

5.279 The International Bureau publishes a PCT pamphlet which contains a front page setting out bibliographic data furnished by the applicant, together with data such as the International Patent Classification (IPC) symbol assigned by the International Searching Authority, the abstract and also the description, the claims, any drawings and the international search report. If the claims of the international application have been amended, the claims are published both as filed and as amended. International publication occurs, in general, 18 months after the priority date of the international application.

5.280 The pamphlet is published in the language of the international application as filed, if that language is Chinese, English, French, German, Japanese, Russian or Spanish. If, however, the international application is published in Chinese, French, German, Japanese, Russian or Spanish, the title of the invention, the abstract and the international search report are also published in English. If the international application has been filed in any other language, it is translated and published in English.

5.281 The publication of each pamphlet is announced in the *PCT Gazette*, which lists the published international applications in the form of entries reproducing data taken from the front pages of the pamphlets. Each issue of the *PCT Gazette* also contains a Classification Index, allowing the selection of the published international applications by technical fields.

5.282 These publications, the pamphlet and the PCT Gazette, are distributed free of charge by the International Bureau on a systematic basis to all PCT Contracting States. They are now also available in CD–ROM format in searchable form. To the public, they are supplied on request, against payment of a fee.

International Preliminary Examination

5.283 Once the applicant has received the international search report, he may make a specific request for international preliminary examination (by filing a "demand" in which designated States are "elected") in order to obtain an opinion as to whether the claimed invention meets any or all of the following criteria—whether it appears to be novel, whether it appears to involve an inventive step and whether it appears to be industrially applicable. A fee for international preliminary examination is due when a demand is filed with the International Preliminary Examining Authority, together with a handing fee to cover the work of the International Bureau. Applicants from certain States are entitled to a sizable reduction of the handling fee (see paragraph 5.268, above).

5.284 As in the case of the International Searching Authorities, the International Preliminary Examining Authorities are appointed by the Assembly of the PCT Union. The offices which have been appointed are the same as those appointed as International Searching Authorities, with the exception of the Spanish Patent and Trademark Office. The results of the international preliminary examination are given in a report which is made available to the applicant and the "elected Offices" (which are the Offices of, or acting for, the elected States) through the International Bureau, which is also responsible for translating the report into English, if required by an elected Office. The opinion on the patentability of the invention, on the basis of the international criteria mentioned above, provides the applicant with an even stronger basis for calculating his chance of obtaining a patent, and the elected Offices have an even better basis for their decision whether to grant a patent. In countries where patents are granted without examination as to substance, the international preliminary examination report will provide a solid basis for parties interested in the invention (e.g., for licensing purposes) to evaluate the validity of such patents.

5.285   Usually upon publication of the international application (but at the latest by the end of the 19th month after the priority date), the International Bureau communicates the international application to the designated Offices. The copy communicated will be used for the subsequent prosecution of the international application before those Offices since, as explained above, the PCT is only a system for filing and not for granting patents, the latter remaining the exclusive task and responsibility of the designated Offices. In practice, more than half of these Offices have waived the weekly communications of copies of published international applications and receive, instead, a free-of-charge complete collection on CD–ROM of all such applications. A CD–ROM workstation is also provided by the International Bureau. The main advantages of the CD–ROM format are rapid access via computer and the limited storage space required. It is noted that, in any case, a designated Office is entitled to receive, upon specific request, copies (on paper) of the international applications, and of related documents, in which it is designated.

5.286   The processing of an international application before the designated (or elected) Offices—the national phase—may not start prior to the expiration of 20 months (or 30 months if Chapter II is applicable) from the priority date of the international application, unless the applicant requests an earlier start.

Prosecution Before the Designated or Elected Offices (the "National Phase")

5.287   After having received an international search report and, where appropriate, an international preliminary examination report, and after having had the possibility of amending his application, the applicant is now in a good position to decide whether he has a chance of obtaining patents in the designated States. If he sees no likelihood, he can either withdraw his application or do nothing; in the latter case, the international application will lose the effect of a national application and the procedure will automatically come to an end. The applicant has in such a case saved himself treat expense, namely, the costs involved in filing separate national applications under the traditional Paris Convention route. He has not paid for applications and translations for the national Offices, he has not paid fees to those Offices, and he has not appointed local agents: all this is required under the traditional Paris Convention route within 12 months from the priority date, and mush be done without having the basis for evaluating the likelihood of obtaining a patent, which is afforded under the PCT by the international search report and, optionally, the international preliminary examination report.

5.288   Where the applicant decides to continue the procedure, and only in that event, he must pay the prescribed national fees to the designated (or elected) Offices and, if required, furnish to these Offices translations of his international application into their official languages; a local agent may also have to be appointed. The furnishing of the translation and the payment of the national fees must be effected within 20 months (or 30 months, if Chapter II is applicable) from the priority date. Once national processing starts, the normal national procedures apply, subject to specific exceptions arising out of the PCT procedure, for example, matters of form and contents of the international application, and the provision of copies of the priority document.

5.289   WIPO has published a *PCT Applicant Guide*. Volume I of this *Guide* contains general information for users of the PCT, relating to the international phase; Volume II contains information on the procedure before the designated and elected Offices, relating to the national phase. Further information is regularly published in the *PCT Gazette*, (Section IV—Notices and Information of a General Character), and in the *PCT Newsletter*, a monthly publication which contains up to date news about the PCT. WIPO's home page on the Internet includes the *PCT Applicant's Guide* and the *PCT Newsletter* as well as other information of a general nature on the PCT. The World Wide Web address is http://www.wipo.int.

3.   Appeals to the Courts

If an applicant is dissatisfied with a decision of the Board of Patent Appeals and Interferences in an appeal from a final rejection by the examiner, he may initiate a civil action against the Director of Patents and Trademarks in the U.S. District Court for the District of Columbia. A party to an interference that is dissatisfied with the decision of the Board may have remedy by civil action against the other party. *See* 35 U.S.C. §§ 145, 146 (2001 & Supp. 2003). In the district court, the question of the applicant's or the interfering parties' right to a patent is tried *de novo*.

The Federal Circuit recently reversed its prior precedent, holding that a patent applicant may introduce new evidence in district court in a § 145 civil action challenging a refusal by the Patent and Trademark Office to grant a patent. *Hyatt v. Kappos*, 625 F.3d 1320 (Fed.Cir. 2010) (*en banc*). The court further held that issues raised by the new evidence must be considered without deference to the Patent and Trademark Office, but if new evidence is not supplied then the court must defer to the agency under the Administrative Procedure Act. Judge Newman dissented on the issue of deference, arguing that the statutory language, precedent, and legislative policy require that a district court always review § 145 cases *de novo*.

Appeal from the decision of the district court is taken exclusively to the Federal Circuit. *See* 28 U.S.C. § 1295 (1993 & Supp. 2003). Alternatively, an applicant may appeal directly from the PTO to the Federal Circuit. *See*

35 U.S.C. § 141 (Supp. 2003). In practice, a vast majority of appeals are taken directly to the Federal Circuit. Decisions of the Federal Circuit are subject to the *certiorari* jurisdiction of the Supreme Court, as are decisions of any regional court of appeals.

In reviewing final decisions of the Board, the Federal Circuit reviews questions of fact under the APA's "substantial evidence" standard of review, *In re Gartside*, 203 F.3d 1305 (Fed.Cir.2000), and questions of law de novo. *See also Dickinson v. Zurko*, 527 U.S. 150 (1999) (holding that APA standards of review apply to factual determinations of Board of Patent Appeals and Interferences). *But see*, Orin S. Kerr, *Rethinking Patent Law in the Administrative State*, 42 WM. & MARY L. REV. 127 (2000) (challenging the assertion that administrative law doctrines should apply to patent law).

C. POST-ISSUANCE PROCEDURES

Upon issuance of a patent, the PTO loses its plenary jurisdiction to determine patentability. Issues pertaining to claim scope and validity are determined by the courts usually during infringement litigation. However, there are procedures whereby a patent may need to be reconsidered by the PTO *after* the patent issues.

The two main procedures that the Patent Act has established to accomplish this renegotiation and correction are *reissue* and *reexamination*. As the "re" suggests, each process requires the PTO to reevaluate an issued patent.

1. REISSUE

Reissue's objective is to allow the patent owner to correct an inadvertent mistake. As such, this process is made available only to the patent owner. Unlike a reexamination proceeding, neither a third party nor the PTO can institute a reissue proceeding.

Section 251 of the Patent Act requires that the mistake sought to be corrected by reissue must be such that its presence causes the patent to be "deemed by the owner wholly or partially inoperative or invalid." The courts have interpreted this requirement to include everything from a typographical error to an error in the scope of the claims.

An inventor is required to show that the mistake was: (1) unintentional or unavoidable; and (2) without deceptive intent. While the government permits the inventor some flexibility in correcting the terms of the patent through reissue, the threshold requirement, in practice, is very high.

As one may expect, the time frame for requesting reissue depends upon the nature of the request itself. After all, an inventor who is further restricting the boundaries of his invention does not harm the public's expectation and should be given more time to do so. Thus, an inventor who wishes to *narrow* his claim scope may do so at any time during the life of the patent. However, an inventor who attempts to *broaden* the scope of his claims through reissue may harm the public's expectations, including competitors of the patentee, who have relied to the original claim language.

As such, a broadening reissue may only be requested within the first two years of the original patent grant.

Even this two-year limitation, however, may unfairly impact a third party's expectations. For example, a patentee's competitor may capitalize on an area left unclaimed by the patent. The competitor may begin to make a significant investment within the first two years of the patent's life, only to have the reissue lay claim to this previously unoccupied area. To guard against such an occurrence, the doctrine of *intervening rights* may protect the competitor's investment.

STATUTORY PROVISIONS—35 U.S.C. §§ 251, 252

a. UNDERLYING POLICIES OF REISSUE

During the period from the enactment of the 1870 Patent Act until the *Topliff* case explored below, the Supreme Court decided a large number of cases in which the scope of original claims had been enlarged through the reissue process. Few of these reissues survived because of problems associated with broadening claims post-issuance, but the Court's attitude toward reissues softened in *Topliff*. In *Topliff*, the Court acknowledged the qualifications that its prior decisions had imposed, and stressed "the obvious intent" of the reissue statute is to avoid "great hardship" to the inventor-patentee and noted that "the specification and claims of a patent, constitute one of the most difficult legal instruments to draw with accuracy." The *Topliff* case marks a greater receptivity to the underlying goals and policies of reissue. The reader should endeavor to notice which policies appear to resonate with the Court, on each side, as well as whether there are yet other policies not expressly addressed in the below excerpt from the Court's opinion.

Topliff v. Topliff

145 U.S. 156 (1892).

■ MR. JUSTICE BROWN delivered the opinion of the court.

The second reissue was applied for a little more than a month after the first was granted, although the patent was not granted upon this application until March 28, 1876,—nearly four years after the application was filed. No change from the first reissue was made in the drawings or specification in this reissue, but the claim was divided and changed....

. . . . There is no doubt, as was said by this court in *Giant Powder Co. v. Cal. Power Works*, 98 U. S. 126, 137, 138, that a reissue can only be granted for the same invention which formed the subject for the original patent, of which it is a reissue, since, as was said by the court in that case, the express words of the act are "a new patent for the same invention." "The specification may be amended so as to make it more clear and distinct; the claim may be modified so as to make it more conformable to the exact rights of the patentee; but the invention must be the same.... This prohibition is general, relating to all patents; and by 'new matter' we suppose to be meant new substantive matter, such as would have the effect of changing the invention, or of introducing what might be the subject of another application for a patent. The danger to be provided against was the temptation to amend a patent so as to cover improvements which might have come into use, or might have been invented by others, after its issue."

In the case of *Miller v. Bridgeport Brass Co.*, 104 U. S. 350, a reissue with expanded claims was applied for 15 years after the original patent was granted. It was held to be manifest upon the face of the patent that the suggestion of inadvertence and mistake was a mere pretense, or, if not a pretense, that the mistake was so obvious as to be instantly discernible on the opening of the patent; and the right to have it corrected was abandoned and lost by unreasonable delay. "The only mistake suggested," said Mr. Justice Bradley, "is that the claim was not as broad as it might have been. This mistake, if it was a mistake, was apparent upon the first inspection of the patent, and, if any correction was desired, it should have been applied for immediately." It was intimated in that case ... that, "if two years' public enjoyment of an invention with the consent and allowance of the inventor is evidence of abandonment, and a bar to an application for a patent, a public disclaimer in the patent itself should be construed equally favorable to the public. Nothing but a clear mistake or inadvertence, and a speedy application for its correction, is admissible when it is sought merely to enlarge the claim." It was further said that the section of the Revised Statutes does not in terms authorize a reissue to enable a patentee to expand his claim, and that it was natural to conclude that the reissue of a patent for such purposes was not in the mind of congress when it passed the laws in question. "At all events," said the court, "we think it clear that it was not the special purpose of the legislation on this subject to authorize the surrender of patents for the purpose of reissuing them with broader and more comprehensive claims, although, under the general terms of the law, such a reissue may be made when it clearly appears that an actual mistake has inadvertently been made.... Now, whilst, as before stated, we do not deny that a claim may be enlarged in a reissued patent, we are of the opinion that this can only be done when an actual mistake has occurred; not from a mere error of judgment, (for that may be rectified by appeal,) but a real, bona fide mistake, inadvertently committed, such as a court of chancery, in cases within its ordinary jurisdiction, would correct.... The granting of a reissue for such a purpose, after an unreasonable delay, is clearly an abuse of the power to grant reissues, and may justly be declared illegal and void."

So, in the case of *Johnson v. Flushing & NSR Co.*, 105 U. S. 539 (1881), the patent was issued in 1857, and at the expiration of the original term of 14 years an extension of 7 years was granted, and a reissue was applied for after a lapse of 15 years, and it was held, upon the authority of *Miller v. Brass Co.*, that, if the patentee had the right to a reissue if applied for in a reasonable time, he had lost it by his unreasonable delay. Said the court, speaking by Mr. Justice Woods: "He has rested supinely until the use of the fish plate joint has become universal, and then, after a lapse of fifteen years, has attempted by a reissue to extend his patent to cover it. We think it is perfectly clear that the original patent could not be fairly construed to embrace the device used by the appellee, which appellants insist is covered by their reissue. If the reissued patent covers it, it is broader than the original, and is, therefore, void."

. . . In the case of *Mahn v. Harwood*, 112 U. S. 354, 5 S.Ct. 174, and 6 S.Ct. 451, a patent reissued nearly four years after the date of the original patent was held to be invalid as to the new claims, upon the ground of unreasonable delay in applying for it; the only object of the reissue being to enlarge the claims. Nothing was changed but to multiply the claims and make them broader, and this was done, not for the benefit of the original patentee, but for that of his assignee. . . . It was held that, while lapses of time might be of small consequence where the original claim was too broad, and the patentee sought to restrict it, there were substantial reasons why the claim could not be enlarged unless the patentee used due diligence to ascertain his mistake. "The rights of the public here intervene, which are totally inconsistent with such tardy reissues; and the great opportunity and temptation to commit fraud after any considerable lapse of time, when the circumstances of the original application have passed out of mind, and the monopoly has proved to be of great value, make it imperative on the courts, as a dictate of justice and public policy, to hold the patentees strictly to the rule of reasonable diligence in making applications for this kind of reissues."

. . . [I]t may be regarded as the settled rule of this court that the power to reissue may be exercised when the patent is inoperative by reason of the fact that the specification as originally drawn was defective or insufficient, or the claims were narrower than the actual invention of the patentee, provided the error has arisen from inadvertence or mistake, and the patentee is guilty of no fraud or deception; but that such reissues are subject to the following qualifications:

First. That it shall be for the same invention as the original patent, as such invention appears from the specification and claims of such original.

Second. That due diligence must be exercised in discovering the mistake in the original patent, and that, if it be sought for the purpose of enlarging the claim, the lapse of two years will ordinarily, though not always, be treated as evidence of an abandonment of the new matter to the public to the same extent that a failure by the inventor to apply for a patent within two years from the public use or sale of his intention is regarded by the statute as conclusive evidence of an abandonment of the patent to the public. . . .

To hold that a patent can never be reissued for an enlarged claim would be not only to override the obvious intent of the statute, but would operate in many cases with great hardship upon the patentee. The specification and claims of a patent, particularly if the invention be at all complicated, constitute one of the most difficult legal instruments to draw with accuracy; and, in view of the fact that valuable inventions are often placed in the hands of inexperienced persons to prepare such specifications and claims, it is no matter of surprise that the latter frequently fail to describe with requisite certainty the exact invention of the patentee, and err either in claiming that which the patentee had not in fact invented, or in omitting some element which was a valuable or essential part of his actual invention. Under such circumstances, it would be manifestly unjust to deny him the benefit of a reissue to secure to him his actual invention, provided it is evident that there has been a mistake, and he has been guilty of no want of reasonable diligence in discovering it, and no third persons have in the mean time acquired the right to manufacture or sell what he had failed to claim. The object of the patent law is to secure to inventors a monopoly of what they have actually invented or discovered, and it ought not to be defeated by a too strict and technical adherence to the letter of the statute, or by the application of artificial rules of interpretation....

NOTES

1. Although *Topliff* was decided long before the current statute was drafted, it still provides a look into the underlying policy concerns of reissue. The product of these policy concerns can be found in 35 U.S.C. §§ 251 and 252.

2. *A Two–Part Test.* In *In re Wilder*, 736 F.2d 1516, 1518 (Fed.Cir.1984), the Federal Circuit identified two "distinct statutory requirements that a reissue oath or declaration must satisfy." First, the oath or declaration "must state that the patent is defective or partly inoperative or invalid because of defects in the specification or drawing, or because the patentee has claimed more or less than he is entitled to." Second, the reissue applicant "must allege that the defective, inoperative, or invalid patent arose through error without deceptive intent." But in *Hewlett–Packard Co. v. Bausch & Lomb, Inc.*, 882 F.2d 1556, 1565 (Fed.Cir.1989), the court noted that the "reissue statute was not enacted as a panacea for all patent prosecution problems." (*quoting In re Wilder*, 736 F.2d at 1582).

b. INTERVENING RIGHTS

A reissue patent is fully effective as of its reissue date. Surrender of the original patent does not affect any pending action or abate any cause of action to the extent that the claims of the original and reissue patents are identical. But when the reissue and original patent claims are sufficiently different, a person may acquire certain "intervening rights" against the reissue patentee on account of prior noninfringing activity under the original patent. The law and policy of intervening rights is the subject of the two *Seattle Box* cases that follow.

Seattle Box Company, Inc. v. Industrial Crating & Packing, Inc. (Seattle Box I)

731 F.2d 818 (Fed.Cir.1984).

■ Before DAVIS, CIRCUIT JUDGE, NICHOLS, SENIOR CIRCUIT JUDGE, and BALDWIN, CIRCUIT JUDGE.

■ NICHOLS, SENIOR CIRCUIT JUDGE.

* * *

I

Background

Plaintiff-appellee Seattle Box Company, Inc. ("Seattle Box") and defendant-appellant Industrial Crating and Packing, Inc. ("Industrial") are

Washington State corporations which provide oil pipe bundling services to oil companies.

Seattle Box filed this action on July 2, 1980, alleging that Industrial infringed U.S. Patent No. 4,099,617 ("the '617 patent") entitled "Shipping Bundle for Numerous Pipe Lengths." Seattle Box brought the action in its capacity as assignee of the rights in the '617 patent. On August 19, 1980, the [United States Patent and Trademark Office] reissued the '617 patent, with broadened claims, in U.S. Patent No. Re. 30,373 ("the '373 reissue patent"). Seattle Box also was the assignee of the rights in this patent. On October 10, 1980, Seattle Box amended its complaint to allege infringement of the '373 reissue patent. Industrial answered and counterclaimed, alleging patent invalidity, noninfringement, and patent misuse.

The district court held in favor of Seattle Box on May 4, 1982, and after an accounting for damages, entered judgment on February 9, 1983. Industrial presses only the issues of patent invalidity and noninfringement here on appeal.

A. The Invention

Until at least 1975, oil companies commonly transported oil pipes of various diameters and with weights upwards of 40 pounds per foot, as loose joints about 40 feet in length. Since no packaging procedure capable of safely and securely handling oil country pipe then existed, many pipes were irreparably damaged in transit and during loading and unloading operations. Rennels, a representative for Atlantic Richfield Company ("ARCO"), in late 1975 recognized ARCO's pipe transport problems and discussed with the patentee, Ferdinand J. Nist, Jr. ("Nist"), ARCO's need for a pipe bundling method which would get oil pipe to the Alaskan North Slope without bends, dents, or damaged ends. . . .

After extensive experimentation, which the district court opinion sets forth in great detail, Nist settled on a system in which he placed a tier of pipes across parallel horizontal wooden beams, or "sleepers." To ensure that adjacent pipes remained separated, Nist placed between them a double-concave wooden spacer block. . . .

Nist stacked several tiers of these crossing rows of sleepers and pipes in order to make one pipe bundle. To prevent the weight of the upper pipes from crushing the lower pipes in either a bundle or a stack of bundles, Nist made his spacer blocks with a height at least equal to the pipe's diameter; the spacer blocks, therefore, absorbed most of the weight of the overhead load. . . .

B. The Patent

Seattle Box filed an application for a patent on Nist's invention on February 17, 1977. Claim 1 of this application stated that the double-concave spacer block had a "height substantially equal to the thickness of the tier of pipe lengths."

Seattle Box's patent attorney, however, narrowed Claim 1 during the application's prosecution so as to specify that the spacer block had a height only "greater than the diameter of the pipe." Soon after the attorney made this narrowing amendment, although not necessarily because of it, the patent examiner allowed each of the application's claims. The '617 patent issued on July 11, 1978.

On December 1, 1978, Seattle Box filed an application to have the '617 patent reissued with broader claims. Nist averred in support of this application that neither the patent examiner nor the cited prior art required the narrow scope of the issued claims, and that the limitation on the height of the spacer block in his Claim 1 was unnecessary and "arose through inadvertence by counsel." Nist additionally stated that "in reality each overlying or superposed sleeper need only be separated from its underlying companion a distance equal to but not less than the diameter (*i.e.*, the thickness) of the pipes in each tier interposed between the sleepers to avoid forces being applied to squeeze the pipe in bundle stacks or handling operations...."

The PTO granted the application for the reissue patent and issued the '373 reissue patent on August 19, 1980. [The PTO allowed] ... Seattle Box to amend Claim 1 to specify a spacer block "of a height *substantially equal to or greater* than the thickness of the tier of pipe length" [emphasis in original]....

* * *

II

Issues

* * *

2.   Did the trial court err in (a) finding that Industrial presently infringes claims of the '373 reissue patent and (b) enjoining that infringement?

3.   Did the trial court err in (a) finding that Industrial infringed claims of the '617 patent before the '373 reissue patent issued and (b) holding Industrial liable for that infringement?

* * *

IV

Liability

The court must consider Industrial's liability for infringement, if any, during two distinct time frames. The first period extends between the date the original patent issued, July 11, 1978, and the date the reissue patent issued, August 19, 1980. Seattle Box's only enforceable patent rights during this period arise from 35 U.S.C. § 252, which allows claims in a reissue patent to reach back under certain circumstances to the date the original patent issued. The second period begins on the date the reissued patent issued, August 19, 1980. During this period, Seattle Box's broadened patent claims cover a double-concave block with a height "substantially equal to or greater than" the diameter of the separated pipes. We consider the two time periods seriatim.

A. *Activities Occurring Before the '373 Reissue Patent Issued.*

Industrial asserts that the district court erred in finding it liable for infringement done before the '373 reissue patent issued. We agree.

An original patent cannot be infringed once a reissue patent has issued, for the original patent is surrendered. At one point in the history of the American patent law, this surrender precluded any action for infringement for acts done prior to the surrender. Courts would not allow a patentee to bring an action in response to acts done before the reissue patent issued since no patent existed upon which one could allege infringement. Courts, moreover, would dismiss for a failure to state a cause of action any action filed before the patent was surrendered since the patent sued on no longer existed. Courts acted, in other words, as if the original patent never was. . . .

To ameliorate the harsh effect of a patent's surrender, Congress has legislated that under certain circumstances claims of the original patent have a form of continuity if carried over to the reissue patent. Congress has incorporated its most recent version of this rule into 35 U.S.C. § 252, the first paragraph of which provides that:

> The surrender of the original patent shall take effect upon the issue of the reissued patent, and every reissued patent shall have the same effect and operation in law, on the trial of actions for causes thereafter arising, as if the same had been originally granted in amended form, but *in so far as the claims of the original and reissued patents are identical*, such surrender shall not affect any action then pending nor abate any cause of action then existing, and the reissued patent, *to the extent that its claims are identical with the original patent*, shall constitute a continuation thereof and have effect continuously from the date of the original patent. [Emphasis supplied.]

Congress, in this statute, has explicitly limited claim continuity to claims in the reissued patent identical to claims in the original patent. The statute does not allow the claims of the original patent some other form of survival. The original claims are dead. The statute permits, however, the claims of the reissue patent to reach back to the date the original patent issued, but only if those claims are identical with claims in the original patent. With respect to new or amended claims, an infringer's liability commences only from the date the reissue patent is issued.

At issue in this case is Congress' meaning of the word "identical." The district court interpreted "identical" to mean "essentially identical," noting that other courts have interpreted the word "identical" in section 252 in a way which does not limit claim continuity to literally identical claims. It cited *Austin v. Marco Dental Products, Inc.*, 560 F.2d 966 (9th Cir.1977), *cert. denied*, 435 U.S. 918, 98 S.Ct. 1477, 55 L.Ed.2d 511 (1978) and *Akron Brass Co. v. Elkhart Brass Manufacturing Co.*, 353 F.2d 704, 147 USPQ 301 (7th Cir.1965).

Akron Brass and *Austin* permitted changes in a reissue patent's claims, however, only if without substance. In *Akron Brass*, a reissued claim substituted the word "outlet" for the word "inlet" in the original claim. Since it was already clear what was intended, the court there noted, substitution of "outlet" for "inlet" in no way enlarged or modified the substance of the claim. In *Austin*, the court found a claim in the reissued patent "identical" to one in the original patent where a modification was made to "make more precise the language used without substantive changes in the claims." 560 F.2d at 973, 195 USPQ at 534.

Since we are not asked to, we do not have to decide exactly what "identical" does mean. It is clear, though, that "identical" means, at most, "without substantive change." Seattle Box, in broadening its claims' scope to cover not only spacer blocks "greater than" but also "substantially equal to" the diameter of the pipes in a bundle, has, in our view, made substantive change to its claims. The original claims cannot reasonably be read as intending, but for some inaccuracy in their expression, the same coverage as the reissue claims. Here, the addition is not a matter of a mere clarification of language to make specific what was always implicit or inherent.

We hold, therefore, that Seattle Box's broadened reissue claims, with the added words "substantially equal to," are not "identical" to its original claims, assuming "identical" means "without substantive change." The district court erred in interpreting "identical" in section 252 to mean "essentially identical." Thus, Seattle Box cannot collect damages for any activities performed before its new and broadened claims issued in the reissue patent. We reverse the trial court's award of damages against Industrial for acts done prior to the date the reissue patent issued.

B. Activities Occurring After the '373 Reissue Patent Issued.

Industrial contends ... that ... the doctrine of intervening rights, 35 U.S.C. § 252, saves Industrial from liability.

* * *

2. Section 252—Intervening Rights

When a reissue patent issues, a new patent with presumably valid claims exists. The reissue patent has "the same effect and operation in law, on the trial of actions for causes *thereafter arising*, as if the same had been originally granted in amended form,...." 35 U.S.C. § 252 [emphasis supplied].

The language quoted above expressly prevents a court from giving any consideration to the protection of intervening rights. The second paragraph of section 252 modifies the first paragraph, however, so as to protect intervening rights. The second paragraph provides, in pertinent part:

> No reissued patent shall abridge or affect the right of any person ... who made ... or used prior to the grant of a reissue anything patented by the reissued patent, to continue the use of ... the specific thing so made ... or used, unless the making [or] using ... of such thing infringes a valid claim of the reissued patent which was in the original patent....

The statute sets forth a single straightforward test for determining whether the doctrine of intervening rights protects an alleged infringer. The only question to ask under this test is whether claims of the original patent which are repeated in the reissue patent are infringed. Section 252 assumes that a patentee having valid claims in a patent will retain those claims in the reissued patent. If valid claims in the original patent appear unaltered in the reissue patent, the doctrine of intervening rights affords no protection to the alleged infringer.

We have already held, however, that the claims appearing in Seattle Box's reissued patent are substantively different than those in the original patent. That is, Seattle Box repeats no claim from its original patent in its reissued patent. Industrial, therefore, may properly raise a defense of intervening rights. *See Cohen v. United States*, 487 F.2d 525, 203 Ct.Cl. 57, 179 USPQ 859 (1973).

When the doctrine of intervening rights is properly raised, the court must consider whether to use its broad equity powers to fashion an appropriate remedy. The second paragraph of section 252 states:

> [The court] may provide for the continued manufacture, use or sale of the thing made ... or used as specified, or for the manufacture, use or sale of which substantial preparation was made before the grant of the reissue, and it may also provide for the continued practice of any process patented by the reissue, practiced ... prior to the grant of the reissue, to the extent and under such terms as the court deems equitable for the protection of investments made or business commenced before the grant of the reissue.

The court is given the discretion to fashion a remedy from a wide range of options available to it. The court may, for example, (1) confine Industrial to the use of those double-concave blocks already in existence, (2) permit Industrial to continue in business under conditions which limit the amount, type, or geographical location of its activities, or (3) permit Industrial to continue in business unconditionally.

The trial court, properly to exercise its equity powers, must carefully weigh standard equitable considerations. Since the trial court incorrectly held section 252 inapplicable here, it has yet to make any findings as to the equities of this case. Accordingly, we vacate this portion of the district court's judgment and remand the case for further proceedings consistent with this opinion.

V

Conclusion

.... We reverse the district court's finding of liability for any activities Industrial performed before the '373 reissue patent issued. Finally, we vacate the district court's conclusions as to the scope of relief to which Seattle Box is entitled for infringement after the '373 reissue patent issued. We remand this case to the district court for further proceedings. Each party to bear its own costs.

Seattle Box Company, Inc. v. Industrial Crating and Packing Inc. (Seattle Box II)

756 F.2d 1574 (Fed.Cir.1985).

■ Before Davis, Circuit Judge, Nichols, Senior Circuit Judge, and Baldwin, Circuit Judge.

■ Davis, Circuit Judge.

This appeal is from a decision, on remand from this court, of the United States District Court for the Western District of Washington, which declined to accord appellants any intervening rights under 35 U.S.C. § 252 as to certain infringing products. We affirm in part and reverse in part.

I.

Background

We have before us a sequel to this court's decision in *Seattle Box Co. v. Industrial Crating & Packing, Inc.*, 731 F.2d 818, 221 USPQ 568 (Fed.Cir. 1984)....

* * *

[T]he district court's finding of liability for pipe bundling activities Industrial performed before the Re '373 patent issued was reversed because under the first paragraph of 35 U.S.C. § 252 the reissue claims were not "identical" to the original claims, and therefore infringement could only be asserted for the Re '373 patent and not the '617 patent.... [W]e vacated the district court's award of post-reissue damages for infringement of the Re '373 patent, holding that the defense of intervening rights under the second paragraph of 35 U.S.C. § 252 was properly raised. Since the district court had not made any findings under § 252, we remanded the case for the district court's consideration of "whether to use its broad equity powers to fashion an appropriate remedy." We declared that such a remedy is discretionary, and suggested a range of options available to the district court.

* * *

On June 12, 1984, the district court held a hearing on the matters remanded from this court. As to the 84 bundles made with spacer blocks 1/4 inch less than the pipe diameter, the district court held that these bundles did not infringe the Re '373 patent. Supporting its assertion that the doctrine of intervening rights applies to the post-reissue bundles (there are 919 bundles in issue), Industrial presented the affidavit testimony of Vernon Zier, Industrial's in-house accountant, who summarized Industrial's business records. Zier averred that on August 19, 1980 (the date of the Re '373 patent), there were orders for 114 bundles which were subsequently completed after that date. In addition, Industrial's inventory of spacer blocks on August 19, 1980 was sufficient to make 224 bundles (this figure incorporates the orders for the 114 bundles). Seattle Box has not contested these facts.

After considering Industrial's argument that intervening rights under 35 U.S.C. § 252 should preclude an award of damages for 224 of the 919 post-reissue bundles, the district court merely stated in its final order on July 19, 1982 that:

> [The 224 bundles] were made after the grant of plaintiff's reissue patent. Defendant has failed to persuade the court that good and valid reasons exist for the court to exercise its discretionary powers in favor of the Defendant as to intervening rights. The Court therefore declines to exer-

cise its discretion in according any intervening rights as to [the 224] bundles.

It is from this order and the ensuing judgment that Industrial appeals.

In the current appeal, Industrial asserts that, contrary to this court's instructions, on remand the district court abused its discretion by not making any findings relating to intervening rights with regard to the pre-reissue spacer block inventory....

II.

The District Court's Action on Remand

A remand from this court to a district court which incorrectly applied the law at the outset should not be casually swept aside in a conclusory fashion. This court in its prior opinion went to considerable length to set out why the lower court erred. We pointed out that the patent claims appearing in Seattle Box's reissued patent are substantively different from those in its original patent, and therefore the doctrine of intervening rights was properly raised. The opinion suggested options available to the district court:

(1) confine Industrial to the use of those double-concave blocks already in existence,

(2) permit Industrial to continue in business under conditions which limit the amount, type or geographical location of its activities, or

(3) permit Industrial to continue in business unconditionally.

731 F.2d at 830, 221 USPQ at 977. Thus, our opinion plainly envisaged a reasoned discussion of the whole matter. We hold (for the reasons expressed below) that the cursory ruling by the district court disregards our prior opinion, and constitutes an abuse of discretion....

* * *

III.

Intervening Rights

The doctrine of intervening rights finds its roots in the second paragraph of 35 U.S.C. § 252:[4]

No reissued patent shall abridge or affect the right of any person or his successors in business who made, purchased or used prior to the grant of a reissue anything patented by the reissued patent, to continue the use of, or to sell to others to be used or sold, the specific thing so made, purchased or used, unless the making, using or selling of such thing infringes a valid claim of the reissued patent which was in the original patent. (2) The court before which such matter is in question may provide for the continued manufacture, use or sale of the thing made, purchased or used as specified, or for the manufacture, use or sale of which substantial preparation was made before the grant of the reissue, and it may also provide for the continued practice of any process patented by the reissue, practiced, or for the practice of which substantial preparation was made, prior to the grant

---

4. .... In the reproduction of the second paragraph at this point, we have numbered the sentences and emphasized some portions.

of the reissue, to the extent and under such terms as the court deems equitable for the protection of investments made or business commenced before the grant of the reissue.

This section provides that when certain conditions are present a reissue shall not abridge or affect certain rights of those who acted before the reissue was granted. *See* Federico, *Commentary on the New Patent Act*, 35 U.S.C.A. 1, 46 (1954). Because of such pre-reissue activity, an infringer might enjoy a "personal intervening right" to continue what would otherwise be infringing activity after reissue. *See* 3 CHISUM, PATENTS, § 15.02[6] (1984). The underlying rationale for intervening rights is that the public has the right to use what is not specifically claimed in the original patent. *Sontag Chain Stores Co. v. National Nut Co.*, 310 U.S. 281, 290, 60 S.Ct. 961, 965, 84 L.Ed. 1204 (1940). Recapture through a reissue patent of what is dedicated to the public by omission in the original patent is permissible under specific conditions, but not at the expense of innocent parties. *Id.* at 293, 60 S.Ct. at 967 (the defendant, who had built and begun to operate its machines in a form not covered by the original patent, was allowed to continue the post-reissue activity which infringed the reissue patent). Therefore, one may be able to continue to infringe a reissue patent if the court decides that equity dictates such a result.[5]

As we said in our first opinion, once the doctrine of intervening rights is properly raised, the court must consider whether to use its broad equity powers to fashion an appropriate remedy.[6] We also held that the second sentence of the second paragraph in 35 U.S.C. § 252 was to be applied in this case in accordance with equity. Accordingly, the district court should have considered the relevant facts as applied to the portion of the statute which questions whether "substantial preparation was made [by the infringer] before the grant of the reissue." Specifically, the district court's inquiry should have been—and it is now our burden to decide—whether the post-reissue use of the 224 bundles which were made from pre-reissue spacer blocks constituted "substantial preparation" to merit the protection afforded by intervening rights, so as to protect "investments made ... before the grant of reissue." We stress that all those spacer blocks were on hand when the reissue patent issued.

Two sets of the district court's factual findings weigh heavily in the present equitable determination of the application of intervening rights.

---

5. Industrial, as it states in the section of its brief entitled "Relief Sought by Industrial Before the District Court," neither sought a continued right to bundle pipe in a manner infringing the reissue patent, nor contended that it should not pay compensation for any of its post-reissue bundling activities. Instead, it urged only that damages should not be awarded for the 224 bundles made from pre-reissue inventory. We limit our inquiry to whether damages may be avoided for these 224 and make no determination as to whether the doctrine of intervening rights would have precluded damages for the remaining 695 bundles (919 less 224) had Industrial set forth adequate equitable factors supporting an application of intervening rights as to all post-reissue activities.

6. In the first *Seattle Box* opinion we set forth a single straightforward test, derived from § 252, for determining when the doctrine of intervening rights might protect an alleged infringer: whether the claims of the original patent repeated in the reissue patent are infringed. Because no claim from the original patent was repeated in the reissue patent, we held that the defense of intervening rights was properly raised. 731 F.2d at 830, 221 USPQ at 576.

First, in the district court's initial findings in its first decision, it was established that, prior to the Re '373 patent, Industrial and its patent attorney were fully aware of the '617 patent. Second, the district court found that Industrial continued manufacturing after reissue on the advice of its patent counsel. *Seattle Box Co.*, 217 USPQ at 349–350. This advice-of-counsel was given to Industrial in April 1980, while the '617 patent was still extant, some 3 months before the Re '373 patent issued (August 17, 1980), and over two months before Industrial's patent counsel was even informed by Seattle Box's patent counsel (July 9, 1980) of the reissue patent claims which had been allowed by the examiner. This pre-reissue advice, followed by Industrial, was to hold the concave block height to about 1/16 of an inch shorter than the pipe diameter. *See* 217 USPQ at 349 (W.D.Wash.); and 731 F.2d at 828–29, 221 USPQ at 576 (Fed.Cir.). From these facts, it is apparent that Industrial was attempting to design its spacer blocks (including those it held on the date of the reissue patent) "around" the original '617 patent claims which called for a spacer block with a height "greater than the diameter of the pipe" (emphasis added). It turned out that these blocks infringed the reissue patent (Re '373), but they plainly did not literally infringe the original '617 patent (and probably did not infringe that patent under the doctrine of equivalents).

To enable Seattle Box now to recapture (in the form of damages for post-reissue use of the 224 bundles made from pre-reissue spacer blocks) matter which Seattle Box had already dedicated to the public in the original patent, at the expense of Industrial which knew of the precise claims of that '617 patent, could open the door to a "gross injustice." *Sontag Stores Co.*, 310 U.S. at 293–94, 60 S.Ct. at 966–67; *see also Gerhardt v. Kinnaird*, 162 F.Supp. 858, 117 USPQ 474 (E.D.Ky.1958) (pre-reissue advice of counsel in building a non-infringing item was one of the equitable factors supporting an application of intervening rights). In these circumstances, the new reissue claims in this case present a compelling case for the application of the doctrine of intervening rights because a person should be able to make business decisions secure in the knowledge that those actions which fall outside the original patent claims are protected.... Here, the spacer blocks involved were made or acquired, before the reissue, so as not to infringe the then existing '617 patent.

Another fact which weighs heavily is that at the time of reissue Industrial had existing orders for 114 bundles. As we have noted, the remedy of intervening rights is calculated to protect an infringer's preexisting investments and business. Prior business commitments, such as previously placed orders and contracts, are one such example. Silverman, *To Err is Human—Patent Reissues and the Doctrine of Intervening Rights*, 48 J.P.O.S. 696 (1966).

Another important factor courts have considered is whether non-infringing goods can be manufactured from the inventory used to manufacture the infringing product. *Plastic Container Corp. v. Continental Plastics of Oklahoma, Inc.*, 607 F.2d 885, 203 USPQ 27 (10th Cir.1979) (Miller, J., sitting by designation), *cert. denied*, 444 U.S. 1018, 100 S.Ct. 672, 62 L.Ed.2d 648 (1980). The cost and ease of converting infringing items to non-infringing items is an important equitable consideration because the "infringer" can then avoid a total loss of his good faith investment. In this case, the district court did not make any finding of the cost of conversion or of possible non-infringing uses. Instead, as previously discussed, a finding was made in its initial order as to non-infringing uses, but then it was retracted. In addition, Industrial has not asked for the continued use (without liability) of goods on hand at the time of ultimate judgment, as did the infringer in the Plastic Container case.[7] In fact, the part of the inventory at issue here had already been fully used before the district court issued its first opinion on May 4, 1982 passing on the issues of validity and infringement.[8]

After weighing the facts and factors, we conclude that Industrial should clearly have been allowed to dispose of old inventory remaining on hand at the time of reissue, without liability to Seattle Box. *Accord Bull Dog Floor Clip Co. v. Munson Mfg. Co.*, 19 F.2d 43 (8th Cir.1927) (product which infringed the reissue but not the original patent was made before the reissue on the advice of counsel and then sold after the reissue). The district court's conclusion to the contrary was an abuse of discretion.[9] We therefore reverse the determination that intervening rights do not protect Industrial from owing damages as to the 224 bundles.

* * *

V.

Conclusion

We reverse the district court's holding that intervening rights does not preclude damages as to the 224 bundles made from pre-reissue spacer blocks, and hold that the doctrine of intervening rights does bar such damages. . . .

Each party to bear its own costs.

■ NICHOLS, SENIOR CIRCUIT JUDGE, concurring and dissenting.

. . . . I do not agree with Parts II and III, The District Court's Action on Remand, and Intervening Rights, and I dissent from those parts.

* * *

As Industrial went right on infringing after filling 114 orders and using up the 12,100 blocks, and other items in its inventory on the reissue date, necessarily purchasing more as needed, it is apparent it never intended to exercise equitable intervening rights as such. It does not come into equity with clean hands. Its attitude was one of complete contempt for both the original patent and the reissue. In these circumstances, I do not think the

---

7. It is interesting to note that the court in Plastic Container found that, although there were non-infringing uses, equity required that the defendant was entitled to recoup its investment of conversion by offsetting any infringement damages.

8. The uncontradicted affidavit of Industrial's accountant, Zier, stated that all 919 post-reissue bundles (including, of course, the 224 bundles made from pre-reissue inventory) were made between August 19, 1980 (the date of the reissue patent) and January 19, 1982.

9. The previous *Seattle Box* opinion listed as an option that the court "confine Industrial to the use of those double-concave blocks already in existence." (See Part II, supra.) This option afforded the narrowest relief to Industrial.

district judge abused his discretion in not making any adjustment for the unfilled orders or the blocks or other inventory items. If he had done so, it would have been, I think, also within his discretion, but if he had given Industrial, as the panel does, a free pass for as many as 224 infringements, I would have thought that an abuse of his discretion. Our suggested possible options in the first opinion respecting application of § 252 were predicated, at least in this author's mind, on Industrial's making a far more impressive show of its equities than it did in fact make. The statute, too, seems to me to visualize equities more impressive than unfilled orders and the mere existence in Industrial's inventory of so many 60 cent blocks, bought in face of the plainest warnings. It seems to contemplate plants built, and matters of that sort.

The statute is so worded that the most obvious equitable adjustment is very likely unauthorized. That would be to credit the infringer with the cost, $7,260, of the blocks in inventory on the reissue date. Assuming, as the panel does, that relief for "intervening rights" must be at a minimum a free license to infringe for some duration, the most equitable duration would be that required to fill the orders for 114 bundles. There would be difficulties in that the customers, who placed the orders, certainly were not asked to excuse Industrial from delivery. If they were asked, persuasion should not have been difficult to obtain since by accepting and using the 114 bundles, they apparently became infringers themselves, a status they might have wished to avoid. I cannot call refusal to make this adjustment an abuse of discretion any more than a decision to make it would be. It is a matter for the district judge to decide, which he has decided.

NOTES

1. *"Identical."* 35 U.S.C. § 252 requires the "claims of the original and the reissued patents ... [to be] identical" in order to preserve the continuity of the patent right. As the previous cases indicate, the meaning of "identical" is based on the public's expectations created by the original patent. On one end of this "identical/not identical" continuum is the mere clarification or explanation of the original claim. On the other end of the continuum is a claim to an entirely different invention.

In the context of intervening rights, if the reissued claims are not "identical" within the meaning of § 252, the defense of intervening rights can be advanced by the alleged infringer. If, on the other hand, the original and reissued claims are "identical" then an infringer cannot raise an intervening rights defense, because there is nothing between which to intervene. The reissue is a seamless continuation of the original, unable to be "wedged open" by intervening rights.

In *Westvaco Corp. v. International Paper Co.*, 991 F.2d 735 (Fed.Cir.1993), the Federal Circuit analyzed the meaning of "identical." This case dealt with the manufacture of a liquid sustaining carton, similar to those used for orange juice. The court held that the reissued and original claims were not identical and were subject to intervening rights, because of the reissue's absence of a limitation which described a polymer as being "coated on" to the carton. The court reasoned that this limitation was important in that it defined the type of structure, i.e. a coated structure, that results from the coating.

2. What would the result have been if the reissue applicant in *Westvaco* had sued on the original patent? Remember, on reissue the original patent will have been offered for surrender at the start of the reissue process and will have been surrendered with the grant of the reissue. Tactically, an applicant will want to sue on the original claim because it is not subject to the intervening rights defense. If the claimant instead chooses to submit the patent for reissue, can one infer from this decision that the claimant believed that the scope of the claims would be enlarged after reissue? What other explanations might there be for this decision?

c.   RECAPTURE

Under the "recapture" doctrine, the deliberate surrender of a claim to certain subject matter during the original prosecution of the application for a patent will not be treated under the Patent Act as "error" of the type that would allow it to be "recaptured" by the patentee. But a patentee may obtain on reissue a claim that varies materially from the claim originally surrendered even though it omits a limitation intentionally added to obtain issuance of the patent. As explored below in the *Mentor* case, the question of whether subject matter may be recaptured through reissue can turn largely on the nature of the error that led to the subject matter's omission from the original claim.

Mentor Corporation v. Coloplast, Inc.

998 F.2d 992 (Fed.Cir.1993).

■ Before LOURIE, CLEVENGER, and SCHALL, CIRCUIT JUDGES.

■ LOURIE, CIRCUIT JUDGE.

* * *

Background

In July 1989, Mentor sued Coloplast for infringement of U.S. Patent 4,475,910, entitled "Male Condom Catheter Having Adhesive on Rolled Portion." While the lawsuit was pending, it was reissued as the '206 patent and Coloplast filed a separate suit for a declaration of invalidity, unenforceability, and noninfringement of that patent. Mentor amended its complaint in the original action to allege infringement of the '206 patent and the two cases were consolidated.

[Mentor's] claimed invention relates to a condom catheter which is used on male patients suffering from incontinence. [T]he '206 patent recite[s] a catheter having a pressure sensitive adhesive on a non-stick (release) layer located on the outer surface of a condom sheath prior to it being rolled up, such that on rolling the sheath outwardly, the adhesive on the outer surface comes into contact with and sticks to the inner surface. When unrolled, the adhesive which was initially applied to the release layer on the outer surface is thereby transferred to the inner surface....

* * *

Coloplast sells the Coloplast Self Sealing Urosheath, which is made by applying adhesive directly to the inner surface, the outer surface being coated with a non-stick, release layer. Use of the Coloplast device does not involve the transfer of adhesive from the outer to the inner surface.

Coloplast admitted that its device was covered by [Mentor's] broadened reissue claims 6–9, but asserted that it had acquired intervening rights and, in any event, that the claims were invalid.

The district court entered judgment according to the jury's answers to special interrogatories, finding, inter alia, that Coloplast infringed ... the '206 patent by the sale of the Coloplast Urosheath, that Coloplast had willfully infringed the '206 patent, that Mentor's broadened reissue claims ... did not recapture any subject matter deliberately canceled by Mentor, and that Coloplast had not acquired intervening rights with respect to [those broadened reissue] claims.... Following Coloplast's post-trial motion for judgment as a matter of law, the court upheld the jury's finding of infringement, but set aside the finding of willfulness.

Discussion

* * *

... Coloplast argues that [the broadened reissue] claims of the reissue patent are invalid because they are not based on "error" within the meaning of 35 U.S.C. § 251 (1988). Coloplast argues that Mentor deliberately and intentionally amended its claims in response to a prior art rejection and that such conduct is not reissuable error. Thus, it asserts, the court erred as a matter of law. We agree.

Whether the statutory requirement of "error" has been met is an issue of law which we review de novo. This legal conclusion is based on underlying factual inquiries which are reviewed for substantial evidence. *See Ball Corp. v. United States*, 729 F.2d 1429, 1439, 221 USPQ 289, 297 (Fed.Cir. 1984) ("On the basis of the facts before us and the reasons given for the cancellation of the claims from the original application, we cannot find, as a matter of law, that [the patentee] is barred from securing reissue....").

Section 251 provides in pertinent part:

> Whenever any patent is, through error without any deceptive intention, deemed wholly or partly inoperative or invalid, by reason of a defective specification or drawing, or by reason of the patentee claiming more or less than he had a right to claim in the patent, the Commissioner shall ... reissue the patent for the invention disclosed in the original patent, and in accordance with a new and amended application, for the unexpired part of the term of the original patent.

Reissue "error" is generally liberally construed, and we have recognized that "[a]n attorney's failure to appreciate the full scope of the invention" is not an uncommon defect in claiming an invention. *In re Wilder*, 736 F.2d 1516, 1519, 222 USPQ 369, 371 (Fed.Cir.1984), *cert. denied*, 469 U.S. 1209, 105 S.Ct. 1173, 84 L.Ed.2d 323 (1985). However, the reissue procedure does not give the patentee "a second opportunity to prosecute de novo his original application," *In re Weiler*, 790 F.2d 1576, 1582, 229 USPQ 673, 677 (Fed.Cir.1986).

> The deliberate cancellation of a claim of an original application in order to secure a patent cannot ordinarily be said to be an "error" and will in most cases prevent the applicant from obtaining the canceled claim by reissue. The extent to which it may also prevent him from obtaining other claims

differing in form or substance from that canceled necessarily depends upon the facts in each case and particularly on the reasons for the cancellation.

In re Willingham, 282 F.2d 353, 357, 127 USPQ 211, 215 (CCPA 1960).

If a patentee tries to recapture what he or she previously surrendered in order to obtain allowance of original patent claims, that "deliberate withdrawal or amendment . . . cannot be said to involve the inadvertence or mistake contemplated by 35 U.S.C. § 251, and is not an error of the kind which will justify the granting of a reissue patent which includes the matter withdrawn." *Haliczer v. United States*, 356 F.2d 541, 545, 148 USPQ 565, 569 (Ct.Cl.1966). "The recapture rule bars the patentee from acquiring, through reissue, claims that are of the same or of broader scope than those claims that were canceled from the original application." *Ball Corp.*, 729 F.2d at 1436, 221 USPQ at 295 (citations omitted). The recapture rule does not apply where there is no evidence that amendment of the originally filed claims was in any sense an admission that the scope of that claim was not in fact patentable, *Seattle Box Co. v. Industrial Crating & Packing, Inc.*, 731 F.2d 818, 826, 221 USPQ 568, 574 (Fed.Cir.1984), but that is not the situation here.

During prosecution of the original patent application, the examiner rejected claim 1 as unpatentable over U.S. Patent 4,187,851 to Hauser in view of U.S. Patent 2,389,831 to Welsh and U.S. Patent 3,403,682 to McDonell. . . .

* * *

. . . Mentor argued that "none of the references relied upon [by the examiner] actually showed the transfer of adhesive from the outer surface to the inner surface as the sheath is rolled up and then unrolled." Mentor characterized the prior art references as disclosing the "transfer" of adhesive from the outer to the inner surface solely by turning the sheath inside out so that the outer surface becomes the inner surface and the adhesive always remains on the same surface. [The] [a]mended claim . . . then issued . . . as a result of Mentor's amendments and argument.

Within two years of issuance, Mentor filed a reissue application accompanied by an attorney declaration, stating that Mentor claimed less than it had a right to claim because the claims of the '910 patent did not "read literally upon male external catheters manufactured using a process in which the adhesive is applied to the inner latex surface of the sheath at the time of manufacture, before the device was rolled." The declaration further stated that "[t]he error arose because [the attorney] assumed that the manufacture of male external catheters by applying the adhesive to the inner latex surface of the catheter was too impractical to be commercially feasible. . . ." Mentor thus added new claims lacking the requirement of transfer of adhesive from the outer to the inner layer. . . . After Mentor submitted detailed information on commercial success, the examiner allowed the claims and the patent was reissued. . . .

Coloplast correctly argues that [the broadened] reissue claim[s], which [do] not include the adhesive transfer limitation, impermissibly recaptures what Mentor deliberately surrendered in the original prosecution. Specifically, the reissue claims do not contain the limitation that, during rolling and unrolling, the adhesive be transferred from the outer to the inner surface of the catheter.

Error under the reissue statute does not include a deliberate decision to surrender specific subject matter in order to overcome prior art, a decision which in light of subsequent developments in the marketplace might be regretted. It is precisely because the patentee amended his claims to overcome prior art that a member of the public is entitled to occupy the space abandoned by the patent applicant. Thus, the reissue statute cannot be construed in such a way that competitors, properly relying on prosecution history, become patent infringers when they do so. In this case, Mentor narrowed its claims for the purpose of obtaining allowance in the original prosecution and it is now precluded from recapturing what it earlier conceded.

Mentor argues that the reissue claims do not recapture subject matter surrendered during the original prosecution. Mentor specifically alleges that recapture is avoided because newly-added reissue claims ... are materially narrower in some respects, albeit broader in others.

Reissue claims that are broader in certain respects and narrower in others may avoid the effect of the recapture rule. If a reissue claim is broader in a way that does not attempt to reclaim what was surrendered earlier, the recapture rule may not apply. However, in this case, the reissue claims are broader than the original patent claims in a manner directly pertinent to the subject matter surrendered during prosecution. Mentor thus attempted to reclaim what it earlier gave up. Moreover, the added limitations do not narrow the claims in any material respect compared with their broadening....

* * *

Thus, since none of [newly-added] reissue claims ... meets the legal requirements for reissue, the court erred in denying the motion for judgment of invalidity as a matter of law. We therefore reverse that part of the court's judgment finding [the newly-added reissue] claims ... not invalid....

* * *

NOTES

1. *Broadening Reissue.* In *In re Clement*, 131 F.3d 1464 (Fed.Cir.1997), the court identified the possible broadening reissue scenarios that one may encounter: "(1) if the reissue claim is as broad as or broader than the canceled or amended claim in all aspects, the recapture rule bars the claim; (2) if it is narrower in all aspects, the recapture rule does not apply ...; (3) if the reissue claim is broader in some aspects, but narrower in others, then: (a) if the reissue claim is as broad as or broader in an aspect germane to a prior art rejection, but narrower in another aspect completely unrelated to the rejection, the recapture rule bars the claim; (b) if the reissue claim is narrower in an aspect germane to prior art rejection, and broader in an aspect unrelated to the rejection, the recapture rule does not bar the claim." Take a minute to consider and map-out these scenarios. The *Clement* court went on to note that "*Mentor* is an example of (3)(a)."

2. *Recapture of Material Surrendered by Argument Alone.* What result for the recapture rule if no claims were amended or canceled, but arguments were made during prosecution history which narrow the claimed invention? Would the recapture rule limit expansion of claims in the same way that prosecution history estoppel limits the doctrine of equivalents? (*See Hester Indus., Inc. v. Stein, Inc.,* 142 F.3d 1472 (Fed.Cir.1998) analogizing the recapture rule to prosecution history estoppel wherein any arguments made during prosecution restrict the permissible range of expansion through reissue just as prosecution history estoppel restricts the permissible range of equivalents under the doctrine of equivalents.)

3. *Reissuable Error.* The court in *Mentor Corp.* draws an interesting line between what is and what is not reissuable error under 35 U.S.C. § 251. Simply stated, this section requires reissuable error be free of deceptive intent. On the one hand, the court held that "[a]n attorney's failure to appreciate the full scope of the invention" is an error that reissue can correct. On the other hand, a patentee (and the attorney) is guilty of deceptive intent if she attempts to recapture the property that was voluntarily surrendered during the attorney's negotiations with the PTO. These two ends of the deceptive intent continuum demonstrate a potential contradiction, i.e., will the strict recapture rule (*i.e.,* you can't recapture that which you've already given up in the patent's prosecution) often prevent the patentee from correcting an error that the liberal construction of deceptive intent (*i.e.,* attorney's failure to appreciate scope) permits? Is there a way to reconcile this seeming discord?

4. *Putting It All Together.* It is important to understand the interplay of the concepts of reissue, recapture, and intervening rights. One may imagine, historically, how these doctrines originated. Reissue was first on the scene with its recognition of the fact that "[t]he specification and claims of a patent ... constitute one of the most difficult legal instruments to draw with accuracy." *Topliff v. Topliff,* 145 U.S. 156, 171 (1892). As a result, reissue developed as an indispensable protection against the "manifestly unjust" situation of not being able to correct such a complex document. *Id.* However, like most equitable doctrines, what reissue gave to the patentee (flexibility to correct errors), it took away from the public (reliance on the original patent grant). As a result, the courts found it necessary to limit this benefit to the patentee to protect "competitors, properly relying on prosecution history, [from] becom[ing] patent infringers when they do so." *Mentor Corp. v. Coloplast, Inc.,* 998 F.2d 992, 996 (Fed.Cir.1993). Recapture and intervening rights are two such protections. These two doctrines protect the public's expectations surrounding the original patent grant. Recapture, by invalidating the reissue, provides full protection to the public. Intervening rights, on the other hand, permits the reissued patent to survive, while providing some protection to the relying public. At a minimum, the public will not be penalized for infringing, and at a maximum the relying public will be able to continue using the property. Therefore, these three doctrines are necessary consequences of the equitable concerns they protect.

2. REEXAMINATION

Reexamination is a procedure whereby the patentee or a third party may request that the PTO reexamine any patent claim in view of cited prior art. A reexamination proceeding may either be ex parte or inter partes. The purpose of the reexamination statute, enacted in 1980, and amended in 1999 to allow for inter partes reexamination,[75] is to strengthen

---

75. The 1999 amendments to the reexamination provisions apply only to issued patents whose filing date was on or after November 29, 1999. However, this includes patents issuing from continuation applications filed after that date, even if the parent application was filed

"investor confidence in the certainty of patent rights by creating a system of administrative reexamination of doubtful patents." H.R.Rep. 96–1307. Unlike a reissue proceeding, a party other than the patentee may request a reexamination, and the claims of the patent may not be broadened.

STATUTORY PROVISIONS—35 U.S.C. §§ 301–05, 311, 314–15, 318

NOTES

1. *Content of Request for Reexamination.* Unlike reissue, reexamination may be requested by a third-party addition to the patentee. 37 C.F.R § 1.510(b) lists the elements required in a request for reexamination: (1) the statement should clearly point out what the requester considers to be the substantial new question of patentability; (2) the request should apply the cited prior art to every claim for which reexamination is requested; (3) a copy of each cited patent or printed publication, as well as a translation of each non-English document is required so that all materials will be available to the examiner for full consideration; (4) a copy of the patent for which reexamination is requested should be provided in a single column paste-up format so that amendments can be easily entered and to ease printing; (5) if the request is filed by a person other than the patent owner, a certification that a copy of the request papers has been served on the patent owner must be included. The PTO encourages the use of Form PTO–1465 when making a request for reexamination. While the form should be helpful to persons filing for reexamination, its use is not a legal requirement.

Under 37 C.F.R § 1.510(e), a patent owner may include a proposed amendment with his or her request, if he or she so desires. The request should be decided on the wording of the claims without the amendments. The decision on the request will be made on the basis of the patent claims as though the amendment had not been presented. However, if the request for reexamination is granted, the *ex parte* reexamination prosecution should be on the basis of the claims as amended.

2. *Notice and Public Access.* Under 37 C.F.R § 1.11(c), reexamination requests made with sufficient fees and any Director initiated orders made without a request will be announced in the Official Gazette in the notice section of the Gazette under the heading of Reexamination Requests Filed and will include the name of any requestor along with the other items set forth in § 1.11(c). With certain limited exceptions, the reexamination file will be made available to members of the public upon request.

3. *Reexamination Ordered at the Director's Initiative.* Under 37 C.F.R § 1.520, "the Director may initiate reexamination without a request being filed and without a fee being paid. Such reexamination may be ordered at any time during the period of enforceability of the patent. If an Office employee becomes aware of an unusual fact situation in a patent which he considers to warrant reexamination, a memorandum setting forth these facts along with the patent file and any prior art patents or printed publications should be forwarded to the Deputy Assistant Director for patents."

4. *Patent Owner's Statement.* Once a reexamination is ordered, a patent owner may file a statement and any amendment that narrow the claims. New matter may not be introduced, but additional claims may be submitted. *See* 37 C.F.R §§ 1.530 and 1.121.

---

prior to that date. *See* Cooper *Technologies Co. v. Dudas*, 536 F.3d 1330 (Fed.Cir.2008). *See supra* note 6 for a further discussion on inter partes reexamination.

Once reexamination is ordered, no further active participation by a reexamination requester is allowed and no third party submissions will be acknowledged or considered unless they are in accordance with 37 C.F.R. § 1.510.

5. *Intervening Rights.* Under 35 U.S.C. § 307, "the situation of intervening rights resulting from reexamination proceedings parallel those resulting from reissue proceedings and the rights detailed in 35 U.S.C. § 252 apply equally in reexamination and reissue situations." *See Kaufman Co. v. Lantech,* 807 F.2d 970 (Fed.Cir. 1986); *Fortel Corp. v. Phone–Mate,* 825 F.2d 1577 (Fed.Cir.1987).

6. *Patent and Trademark Office Authorization Act of 2002.* The Patent and Trademark Office Authorization Act of 2002 (H.R. 2215, Pub. L. No. 107–273) was enacted in 2002 in response to criticism of the earlier Optional Inter Partes Reexamination Procedure Act of 1999. The Optional Inter Partes Reexamination Procedure Act, passed as part of the American Inventors Protection Act of 1999, expanded the role of third-parties in reexamination proceedings. Third-party participation is considered vital to a reexamination proceeding as third-parties possess the most relevant prior art and are the most vigorous opponents of the patent. Prior to passage of the 1999 Act, Ex Parte Reexamination provided, and still provides, third-parties only one opportunity to set forth their opinion concerning the patent with regard to the prior art in the reexamination. The Optional Inter Partes Reexamination Procedure Act permitted third-parties to respond to the patentee throughout the reexamination process through an optional "inter partes" proceeding.

Specifically, inter partes procedures provide that (1) the third-party requester has "one opportunity to file written comments" on each response by a patent owner to a PTO "action on the merits,"[76] and (2) the third-party requester may appeal "any decision favorable to the patentability of any original or proposed amended or new claim of the patent" to the Board of Patent Appeals and Interferences and "be a party to any appeal [to the Board] taken by the patent owner."[77] The rules also prohibit interviews on the merits as part of the Inter Partes reexamination proceeding (though interviews are permitted in Ex Parte Reexaminations).[78] The reasoning for this bar is that, on the one hand, allowing a third party requester to participate along with the patentee in interviews would be too awkward but, on the other hand, barring the requester would be unfair.[79]

---

76. 35 U.S.C. § 314(b)(2). Compare Chisum on Patents § 11.07[4][d][x].

77. 35 U.S.C. § 315(b)(2). Compare Chisum on Patents § 1.07[4][e].

78. 37 C.F.R. § 1.956 (2002).

79. With respect to the rulemaking process that resulted in the prohibition of interviews, the PTO noted:

"The Office has reconsidered its initial position (taken in the August 11, 1995, Notice of Proposed Rulemaking) to permit owner-initiated interviews in which the patent owner and the third-party requester participate. The presence of a third-party requester will complicate the reexamination proceeding and delay it. There is no reason to further complicate and delay the proceeding with inter partes interviews, which past history has shown to be not only resource intensive, but unwieldy. Inter partes interviews are difficult to arrange, control, and conduct. There would be interaction between the patent owner's representative and its experts, the third-party's representative and its experts, the examiner, and the 'senior level official' which would be difficult to regulate and control. It is difficult to record what happened, and cross-transcripts would result in delay and complications. In addition, the time to arrange and conduct the interview would greatly extend the inter partes proceeding time line, and this is clearly contrary to the 'special dispatch' required by 35 U.S.C. 314(c) for the inter partes reexamination proceeding. As to the comments suggesting that the third-party should be permitted to initiate interviews, this would even further complicate the proceeding, adding undue cost to the parties and the Office and further delay to the proceeding.

However, the Optional Inter Partes Reexamination Procedure Act was not without additional limitations that restricted third-party participation. Under the 1999 Act, only the patentee, not the third-party reexamination requester, could appeal the final decision of the Patent and Trademark Office with respect to the Inter Partes Reexamination to the Federal Circuit. In addition, [from the time the reexamination was filed,] third-parties were estopped from later raising in federal court any issue they raised or could have raised in reexamination. Most notably, critics of the Act took issue with its failure to address the Federal Circuit's holding in *In re Portola Packaging*, 122 F.3d 1473 (Fed.Cir.1997) that a reference cited in the original patent examination could not be considered in combination with a new reference to create an issue of obviousness.

The 2002 Act, as codified in Public Law No. 107–273 further expanded the rights of third-parties in inter partes reexamination proceedings and corrected some of the limitations on third party participation set forth in the original Act. For example, Public Law No. 107–273 allows third-parties, as well as patentees, to appeal an adverse decision to the Federal Circuit. Furthermore, Public Law 107–273 overruled *In re Portola* with the addition of the statement "The existence of a substantial new question of patentability is not precluded by the fact that a patent or printed publication was previously cited by or to the Office or considered by the Office." *See also In re Swanson*, 540 F.3d 1368 (Fed.Cir.2008) (affirming legislative overruling of *In re Portola*).

However, Public Law 107–273 did not remove the estoppel provision from inter partes reexamination. While the prohibitive effect of the estoppel provisions are somewhat diminished by the introduction of a right of a third-party to appeal an adverse decision to the Federal Circuit, critics nonetheless note that the estoppel provisions are still a significant obstacle to third-party use of inter partes reexamination that might otherwise afford a more rapid and less costly alternative to litigation.

7. *Reexamination and the Right to a Jury Trial.* In *Patlex Corp. v. Mossinghoff*, 758 F.2d 594 (Fed.Cir.1985), the court held there is no right under the 7th Amendment to a jury for one seeking reexamination.

"Accordingly, the Office has decided that the third-party requester of the inter partes reexamination should neither be permitted to initiate nor be permitted to participate in an interview which addresses the merits of the proceeding. If, however, the patent owner is permitted to initiate and participate in an interview which addresses the merits of the proceeding while the third-party requester is not, this will create an advantage to the patent owner which is contrary to the intent and purpose of the inter partes reexamination addition to the statute. Thus, to 'level the playing field' in the Office, in accordance with the intent and purpose of the statute, the patent owner will neither be permitted to initiate nor be permitted to participate in an interview which addresses the merits of the proceeding. In other words, no interviews which address the merits of the proceeding will be permitted (or held) in an inter partes reexamination proceeding. This offers the additional advantage of further shortening the proceeding, pursuant to the dictates of 'special dispatch' in 35 U.S.C. 314(c). Even further, this deals with the comments which argued that the content of the inter partes interview cannot be adequately captured without the use of expensive and complex transcripts. Anything stated or decided in the proceeding will be on the record, in writing."

65 Fed. Reg. 18162.

CHAPTER THREE

Disclosure Requirements

If I have seen further it is by standing upon the shoulders of Giants.

—Sir Isaac Newton[1]

INTRODUCTION

It would be difficult to overstate the importance of the patent law's disclosure requirements, which are contained in the first two paragraphs of 35 U.S.C. § 112. The patent's disclosure provides the foundation for the claims and hence for the scope of patent protection. The disclosure must support the scope of the patent claim. On the one hand, § 112 requires the patentee to give the public "fair notice of what the patentee and the Patent and Trademark Office have agreed constitute the metes and bounds of the claimed invention."[2] On the other hand, § 112 requires the patentee to disseminate to the public information concerning the patented subject matter. This dual notice/dissemination function allows third parties to avoid conduct that would infringe the patent while providing the interested public with information that enlarges the storehouse of knowledge, and may also help others to improve upon or design around the claimed invention—thus leading to further technological progress. As the Supreme Court stated in *Markman v. Westview Instruments, Inc.*:

> [t]he limits of a patent must be known for the protection of the patentee, the encouragement of the inventive genius of others and the assurance that the subject of the patent will be dedicated ultimately to the public. Otherwise, a zone of uncertainty which enterprise and experimentation may enter only at the risk of infringement claims would discourage invention only a little less than unequivocal foreclosure of the field, and

---

1. Letter of Sir Isaac Newton to Robert Hooke, February 5, 1575/1576, as quoted in Robert K. Merton, On the Shoulders of Giants: A Shandean Postscript 31 (1965). Merton's book unpacks the great deal of historical baggage associated with this famous phrase, which is often attributed to Newton, and demonstrates that Newton may actually have borrowed this phrase from Bernard of Chartres of the early Twelfth Century, who himself may have appropriated the phrase from Priscian, a Sixth Century grammarian, with many other intervening players at each stage. *See also* Suzanne Scotchmer, *Standing on the Shoulders of Giants: Cumulative Research and the Patent Law*, 5 J. Econ. Persp. 29 (1991). Also consider the colorful presentation on derivation by Justice Story in the copyright case of *Emerson v. Davies*, 8 F. Cas. 615, 619 (C.C.D.Mass.1845):

> In truth, in literature, in science and in art, there are, and can be, few, if any, things, which, in an abstract sense, are strictly new and original throughout.... What are all modern law books, but new combinations and arrangements of old materials, in which the skill and judgment of the author in the selection and exposition and accurate use of those materials constitute the basis of his reputation, as well as of his copy-right?

2. *London v. Carson Pirie Scott & Co.*, 946 F.2d 1534, 1538 (Fed.Cir.1991)

[t]he public [would] be deprived of rights supposed to belong to it, without being clearly told what it is that limits these rights.[3]

The first paragraph of 35 U.S.C. § 112 provides three distinct disclosure requirements: **[1]** the written description requirement; **[2]** the enablement requirement; and **[3]** the best mode requirement. In addition, the second paragraph of § 112 provides a fourth requirement; **[4]** that the applicant particularly point out and distinctly claim the invention. This is known as the definiteness requirement. Together, all of this written information comprises what is known as the patent *specification*.[4] Section 112 sets forth, in pertinent part:

> The specification shall contain a **[1]** written description of the invention, and **[2]** of the manner of making and using it, in such full, clear, concise, and exact terms as to enable any person skilled in the art to which it pertains, or with which it is most nearly connected, to make and use the same, and **[3]** shall set forth the best mode contemplated by the inventor of carrying out his invention.

> The specification shall conclude with **[4]** one or more claims particularly pointing out and distinctly claiming the subject matter which the applicant regards as his invention. . . .

The following sections address the requirements of enablement, best mode, written description, and definiteness. There follows a section on complex technologies, which further illustrates the applicability of these requirements to computer-related and biotechnology inventions.

A. ENABLEMENT

Under Section 112, the inventor is required to set forth in a patent specification sufficient information to enable a person skilled in the relevant art to make and use the claimed invention without "undue experimentation." The enablement requirement is often considered to be at the heart of the *quid pro quo* between the government and the inventor. In exchange for the powerful right to exclude, the inventor must inform the public how to make and use the invention so others, namely competitors of the inventor, can improve upon the claimed invention. The enablement requirement also acts as a claim limiting tool in that the enablement must be commensurate with the scope of the claims.

The following sections explore the history, policy, and doctrine of the enablement requirement.

1. HISTORICAL AND POLICY UNDERPINNINGS

The famous telegraph case of *O'Reilly v. Morse* nicely captures patent law's commensurability requirement and the very important issue of optimal claim scope. Although the case reflects many of patent law's policy

---

3. 517 U.S. 370, 390 (1996).

4. It should be noted that, although incorrect, the terms "written description" and "specification" are often (mistakenly) used interchangeably. The specification includes the written description as well as the claims.

tensions, it also deserves at least one important cautionary note: the claims of Morse's patent were written using the now obsolete approach to claiming that was common in the U.S. in the 19th century called "central claiming," in which the claims set forth the core, gist, or heart of the matter. Claiming under the present Patent Act uses an approach called "peripheral claiming," in which the claims set forth the metes and bounds, or outer limits, of the matter.

O'Reilly v. Morse

56 U.S. (15 How.) 62 (1853).

■ MR. CHIEF JUSTICE TANEY delivered the opinion of the court.

... [E]arly in the spring of 1837, Morse had invented his plan for combining two or more electric or galvanic circuits, with independent batteries for the purpose of overcoming the diminished force of electro-magnetism in long circuits, although it was not disclosed to the witness until afterwards; and ... there is reasonable ground for believing that he had so far completed his invention, that the whole process, combination, powers, and machinery, were arranged in his mind, and that the delay in bringing it out arose from his want of means. For it required the highest order of mechanical skill to execute and adjust the nice and delicate work necessary to put the telegraph into operation, and the slightest error or defect would have been fatal to its success. He had not the means at that time to procure the services of workmen of that character; and without their aid no model could be prepared which would do justice to his invention. And it moreover required a large sum of money to procure proper materials for the work. He, however, filed his caveat on the 6th of October, 1837, and, on the 7th of April, 1838, applied for his patent, accompanying his application with a specification of his invention, and describing the process and means used to produce the effect.

* * *

[In a patent issued to Morse in 1840 and reissued in 1848, Morse described "a new and useful apparatus for, and a system of, transmitting intelligence between distant points by means of electro-magnetism, which puts in motion machinery for producing sounds or signs, and recording said signs upon paper or other suitable material, which invention I denominate the American Electro–Magnetic Telegraph...." The patent described "the instruments and ... mode of their operation," including the famed "Code". The patent continued:]

> First. Having thus fully described my invention, I wish it to be understood that I do not claim the use of the galvanic current, or current of electricity, for the purpose of telegraphic communications, generally; but what I specially claim as my invention and improvement, is making use of the motive power of magnetism, when developed by the action of such current or currents, substantially as set forth in the foregoing description of the first principal part of my invention, as means of operating or giving motion to machinery, which may be used to imprint signals upon paper or other suitable material, or to produce sounds in any desired manner, for the purpose of telegraphic communication at any distances.

The only ways in which the galvanic currents had been proposed to be used, prior to my invention and improvement, were by bubbles resulting from decomposition, and the action or exercise of electrical power upon a magnetized bar or needle; and the bubbles and deflections of the needles, thus produced, were the subjects of inspection, and had no power, or were not applied to record the communication. I therefore characterize my invention as the first recording or printing telegraph by means of electro-magnetism.

There are various known modes of producing motion by electro-magnetism, but none of these had been applied prior to my invention and improvement, to actuate or give motion to printing or recording machinery, which is the chief point of my invention and improvement.

* * *

Eighth. I do not propose to limit myself to the specific machinery, or parts of machinery, described in the foregoing specifications and claims; the essence of my invention being the use of the motive power of the electric or galvanic current, which I call electro-magnetism, however developed, for making or printing intelligible characters, letters, or signs, at any distances, being a new application of that power, of which I claim to be the first inventor or discoverer.

* * *

We perceive no well-founded objection to the description which is given of the whole invention and its separate parts, nor to his right to a patent for the first seven inventions set forth in the specification of his claims. The difficulty arises on the eighth.

* * *

It is impossible to misunderstand the extent of this claim. He claims the exclusive right to every improvement where the motive power is the electric or galvanic current, and the result is the marking or printing intelligible characters, signs, or letters at a distance.

If this claim can be maintained, it matters not by what process or machinery the result is accomplished. For aught that we now know some future inventor, in the onward march of science, may discover a mode of writing or printing at a distance by means of the electric or galvanic current, without using any part of the process or combination set forth in the plaintiff's specification. His invention may be less complicated—less liable to get out of order—less expensive in construction, and in its operation. But yet if it is covered by this patent the inventor could not use it, nor the public have the benefit of it without the permission of this patentee.

Nor is this all, while he shuts the door against inventions of other persons, the patentee would be able to avail himself of new discoveries in the properties and powers of electro-magnetism which scientific men might bring to light. For he says he does not confine his claim to the machinery or parts of machinery, which he specifies; but claims for himself a monopoly in its use, however developed, for the purpose of printing at a distance. New discoveries in physical science may enable him to combine it with new agents and new elements, and by that means attain the object in a manner superior to the present process and altogether different from it. And if he can secure the exclusive use by his present patent he may vary it with every new discovery and development of the science, and need place no description of the new manner, process, or machinery, upon the records of the patent office. And when his patent expires, the public must apply to him to learn what it is. In fine he claims an exclusive right to use a manner and process which he has not described and indeed had not invented, and therefore could not describe when he obtained his patent. The court is of opinion that the claim is too broad, and not warranted by law.

No one, we suppose will maintain that Fulton could have taken out a patent for his invention of propelling vessels by steam, describing the process and machinery he used, and claimed under it the exclusive right to use the motive power of steam, however developed, for the purpose of propelling vessels. It can hardly be supposed that under such a patent he could have prevented the use of the improved machinery which science has since introduced; although the motive power is steam, and the result is the propulsion of vessels. Neither could the man who first discovered that steam might, by a proper arrangement of machinery, be used as a motive power to grind corn or spin cotton, claim the right to the exclusive use of steam as a motive power for the purpose of producing such effects.

Again, the use of steam as a motive power in printing-presses is comparatively a modern discovery. Was the first inventor of a machine or process of this kind entitled to a patent, giving him the exclusive right to use steam as a motive power, however developed, for the purpose of marking or printing intelligible characters? Could he have prevented the use of any other press subsequently invented where steam was used? Yet so far as patentable rights are concerned both improvements must stand on the same principles. Both use a known motive power to print intelligible marks or letters; and it can make no difference in their legal rights under the patent laws, whether the printing is done near at hand or at a distance. Both depend for success not merely upon the motive power, but upon the machinery with which it is combined. And it has never, we believe, been supposed by any one, that the first inventor of a steam printing-press, was entitled to the exclusive use of steam, as a motive power, however developed, for marking or printing intelligible characters.

Indeed, the acts of the patentee himself are inconsistent with the claim made in his behalf. For in 1846 he took out a patent for his new improvement of local circuits, by means of which intelligence could be printed at intermediate places along the main line of the telegraph; and he obtained a reissued patent for this invention in 1848. Yet in this new invention the electric or galvanic current was the motive power, and writing at a distance the effect. The power was undoubtedly developed, by new machinery and new combinations. But if his eighth claim could be sustained, this improvement would be embraced by his first patent. And if it was so embraced, his patent for the local circuits would be illegal and void. For he could not take out a subsequent patent for a portion of his first invention, and thereby extend his monopoly beyond the period limited by law.

Many cases have been referred to in the argument, which have been decided upon this subject, in the English and American courts. We shall speak of those only which seem to be considered as leading ones. And those most relied on, and pressed upon the court, in behalf of the patentee, are the cases which arose in England upon Neilson's patent for the introduction of heated air between the blowing apparatus and the furnace in the manufacture of iron.

The leading case upon this patent, is that of *Neilson and others v. Harford and others* in the English Court of Exchequer. It was elaborately argued and appears to have been carefully considered by the court. The case was this:

> Neilson, in his specification, described his invention as one for the improved application of air to produce heat in fires, forges, and furnaces, where a blowing apparatus is required. And it was to be applied as follows: The blast or current of air produced by the blowing apparatus was to be passed from it into an air-vessel or receptacle made sufficiently strong to endure the blast; and through or from that vessel or receptacle by means of a tube, pipe, or aperture into the fire, the receptacle be kept artificially heated to a considerable temperature by heat externally applied. He then described in rather general terms the manner in which the receptacle might be constructed and heated, and the air conducted through it to the fire: stating that the form of the receptacle was not material, nor the manner of applying heat to it. In the action above-mentioned for the infringement of this patent, the defendant among other defences insisted—that the machinery for heating the air and throwing it hot into the furnace was not sufficiently described in the specification, and the patent void on that account—and also, that a patent for throwing hot air into the furnace, instead of cold, and thereby increasing the intensity of the heat, was a patent for a principle, and that a principle was not patentable.

Upon the first of these defences, the jury found that a man of ordinary skill and knowledge of the subject, looking at the specification alone, could construct such an apparatus as would be productive of a beneficial result, sufficient to make it worth while to adapt it to the machinery in all cases of forges, cupolas, and furnaces, where the blast is used.

And upon the second ground of defence, Baron Parke, who delivered the opinion of the court, said:

> It is very difficult to distinguish it from the specification of a patent for a principle, and this at first created in the minds of the court much difficulty; but after full consideration we think that the plaintiff does not merely claim a principle, but a machine, embodying a principle, and a very valuable one. We think the case must be considered as if the principle being well known, the plaintiff had first invented a mode of applying it by a mechanical apparatus to furnaces, and his invention then consists in this: by interposing a receptacle for heated air between the blowing apparatus and the furnace. In this receptacle he directs the air to be heated by the application of heat externally to the receptacle, and thus he accomplishes the object of applying the blast, which was before cold air, in a heated state to the furnace.

We see nothing in this opinion differing in any degree from the familiar principles of law applicable to patent cases. Neilson claimed no particular mode of constructing the receptacle, or of heating it. He pointed out the manner in which it might be done; but admitted that it might also be done in a variety of ways; and at a higher or lower temperature; and that all of them would produce the effect in a greater or less degree, provided the air was heated by passing through a heated receptacle. And hence it seems that the court at first doubted, whether it was a patent for any thing more than the discovery that hot air would promote the ignition of fuel better than cold. And if this had been the construction, the court, it appears, would have held his patent to be void; because the discovery of a principle in natural philosophy or physical science, is not patentable.

But after much consideration, it was finally decided that this principle must be regarded as well known, and that the plaintiff had invented a mechanical mode of applying it to furnaces; and that his invention consisted in interposing a heated receptacle, between the blower and the furnace, and by this means heating the air after it left the blower, and before it was thrown into the fire. Whoever, therefore, used this method of throwing hot air into the furnace, used the process he had invented, and thereby infringed his patent, although the form of the receptacle or the mechanical arrangements for heating it, might be different from those described by the patentee. For whatever form was adopted for the receptacle, or whatever mechanical arrangements were made for heating it, the effect would be produced in a greater or less degree, if the heated receptacle was placed between the blower and the furnace, and the current of air passed through it.

Undoubtedly, the principle that hot air will promote the ignition of fuel better than cold, was embodied in this machine. But the patent was not supported because this principle was embodied in it. He would have been equally entitled to a patent, if he had invented an improvement in the mechanical arrangements of the blowing apparatus, or in the furnace, while a cold current of air was still used. But his patent was supported, because he had invented a mechanical apparatus, by which a current of hot air, instead of cold, could be thrown in. And this new method was protected by his patent. The interposition of a heated receptacle, in any form, was the novelty he invented.

We do not perceive how the claim in the case before us, can derive any countenance from this decision. If the Court of Exchequer had said that Neilson's patent was for the discovery, that hot air would promote ignition better than cold, and that he had an exclusive right to use it for that purpose, there might, perhaps, have been some reason to rely upon it. But the court emphatically denied this right to such a patent. And his claim, as the patent was construed and supported by the court, is altogether unlike that of the patentee before us.

For Neilson discovered, that by interposing a heated receptacle between the blower and the furnace, and conducting the current of air through it, the heat in the furnace was increased. And this effect was always produced, whatever might be the form of the receptacle, or the mechanical contrivances for heating it, or for passing the current of air through it, and into the furnace.

But Professor Morse has not discovered, that the electric or galvanic current will always print at a distance, no matter what may be the form of the machinery or mechanical contrivances through which it passes. You may use electro-magnetism as a motive power, and yet not produce the described effect, that is, print at a distance intelligible marks or signs. To produce that effect, it must be combined with, and passed through, and operate upon, certain complicated and delicate machinery, adjusted and arranged upon philosophical principles, and prepared by the highest mechanical skill. And it is the high praise of Professor Morse, that he has been able, by a new combination of known powers, of which electro-magnetism is one, to discover a method by which intelligible marks or signs may be printed at a distance. And for the method or process thus discovered, he is entitled to a patent. But he has not discovered that the electro-magnetic current, used as motive power, in any other method, and with any other combination, will do as well.

We have commented on the case in the Court of Exchequer more fully, because it has attracted much attention in the courts of this country, as well as in the English courts, and has been differently understood. And perhaps a mistaken construction of that decision has led to the broad claim in the patent now under consideration.

* * *

The two ... patents ..., being both valid, with the exception of the eighth claim in the first, the only remaining question is, whether they or either of them have been infringed by the defendants.

* * *

It is a well-settled principle of law, that the mere change in the form of the machinery (unless a particular form is specified as the means by which the effect described is produced) or an alteration in some of its unessential parts; or in the use of known equivalent powers, not varying essentially the machine, or its mode of operation or organization, will not make the new machine a new invention. It may be an improvement upon the former; but that will not justify its use without the consent of the first patentee.

* * *

The Columbian (O'Reilly's) Telegraph does not profess to accomplish a new purpose, or produce a new result. Its object and effect is to communicate intelligence at a distance, at the end of the main line, and at the local circuits on its way. And this is done by means of signs or letters impressed on paper or other material. The object and purpose of the Telegraph is the same with that of Professor Morse.

Does he use the same means? Substantially, we think he does, both upon the main line and in the local circuits. He uses upon the main line the combination of two or more galvanic or electric circuits, with independent batteries for the purpose of obviating the diminished force of the galvanic current, and in a manner varying very little in form from the invention of Professor Morse. And, indeed, the same may be said of the entire combination set forth in the patentee's third claim. For O'Reilly's can hardly be said to differ substantially and essentially from it. He uses the combination which composes the register with no material change in the arrangement, or in the elements of which it consists; and with the aid of these means he conveys intelligence by impressing marks or signs upon paper—these marks or signs being capable of being read and understood by means of an alphabet or signs adapted to the purpose.

* * *

We deem it unnecessary to pursue further the comparison between the machinery of the patents. The invasion of the plaintiff's rights, already stated, authorized the injunction granted by the Circuit Court, and so much of its decree must be affirmed. But, for the reasons hereinbefore assigned, the complainants are not entitled to costs, and that portion of the decree must be reversed, and a decree passed by this court, directing each party to pay his own costs, in this and in the Circuit Court.

■ MR. JUSTICE WAYNE, MR. JUSTICE NELSON, and MR. JUSTICE GRIER, dissent from the judgment of the court on the question of costs.

■ MR. JUSTICE GRIER.

... The ... point, in which I cannot concur with the opinion of the majority, arises in the construction of the eighth claim of complainant's first patent, as finally amended.

* * *

The great art of printing, which has changed the face of human society and civilization, consisted in nothing but a new application of principles known to the world for thousands of years. No one could say it consisted in the type or the press, or in any other machine or device used in performing some particular function, more than in the hands which picked the types or worked the press. Yet if the inventor of printing had, under this narrow construction of our patent law, claimed his art as something distinct from his machinery, the doctrine now advanced, would have declared it unpatentable to its full extent as an art, and that the inventor could be protected in nothing but his first rough types and ill-contrived press.

* * *

To say that a patentee, who claims the art of writing at a distance by means of electro-magnetism, necessarily claims all future improvements in the art, is to misconstrue it, or draws a consequence from it not fairly to be inferred from its language. An improvement in a known art is as much the subject of a patent as the art itself; so, also, is an improvement on a known machine. Yet, if the original machine be patented, the patentee of an improvement will not have a right to use the original. This doctrine has not been found to retard the progress of invention in the case of machines; and I can see no reason why a contrary one should be applied to an art.

* * *

The word telegraph is derived from the Greek, and signifies "to write afar off or at a distance." It has heretofore been applied to various contrivances or devices, to communicate intelligence by means of signals or semaphores, which speak to the eye for a moment. But in its primary and literal signification of writing, printing, or recording at a distance, it never was invented, perfected, or put into practical operation till it was done by

Morse. He preceded Steinheil, Cook, Wheatstone, and Davy in the success-ful application of this mysterious power or element of electro-magnetism to this purpose; and his invention has entirely superseded their inefficient contrivances. It is not only "a new and useful art," if that term means any thing, but a most wonderful and astonishing invention, requiring tenfold more ingenuity and patient experiment to perfect it, than the art of printing with types and press, as originally invented.

* * *

Now the patent law requires an inventor, as a condition precedent to obtaining a patent, to deliver a written description of his invention or discovery, and to particularly specify what he claims to be his own inven-tion or discovery. If he has truly stated the principle, nature and extent of his art or invention, how can the court say it is too broad, and impugn the validity of his patent for doing what the law requires as a condition for obtaining it? And if it is only in case of a machine that the law requires the inventor to specify what he claims as his own invention and discovery, and to distinguish what is new from what is old, then this eighth claim is superfluous and cannot affect the validity of his patent, provided his art is new and useful, and the machines and devices claimed separately, are of his own invention. If it be in the use of the words "however developed" that the claim is to be adjudged too broad, then it follows that a person using any other process for the purpose of developing the agent or element of electro-magnetism, than the common one now in use, and described in the patent, may pirate the whole art patented.

* * *

[I]t is only where, through inadvertence or mistake, the patentee has claimed something of which he was not the first inventor, that the court are directed to refuse costs.

The books of reports may be searched in vain for a case where a patent has been declared void, for being too broad, in any other sense.

NOTES

1. *The "Lightning Man's" Patent Troubles.* Known as the "Lightning Man" for his work in telegraphy, Samuel Finley Breese Morse expended large sums of money (a "ruinous expense," as Morse said) enforcing and protecting his patent rights, thus prompting him to complain of American patent law: "It is not the way to encourage the Arts, to drive the Artists into exile or to the insane hospital or to the grave." KENNETH SILVERMAN, LIGHTNING MAN: THE ACCURSED LIFE OF SAMUEL F.B. MORSE 319 (2003). Nevertheless, assisted by his business associate and legal counsel, Amos Kendall, Morse, while suffering some set backs, was largely successful in patent litigation. The most important case was *O'Reilly v. Morse*. Henry O'Reilly, a major player in the telegraph industry, was Morse's nemesis. After Morse success-fully enjoined O'Reilly from using the infringing Zook–Barnes Columbian telegraph in Kentucky, an undeterred O'Reilly vowed to appeal to the Supreme Court. Chief Justice Taney and his six colleagues on the Court allowed each side to argue for six hours and to demonstrate the telegraph. According to Morse biographer Kenneth Silverman:

The lawyers covered much familiar ground—the history of electric telegraphy since the eighteenth century, The *Sully* Story. They also presented depositions from prominent scientists (including Joseph Henry, on behalf of O'Reilly), and cited scores of American and English legal precedents. Then as now, legal debate about information technology proved to be of mind-numbing intricacy. In trying to clarify the confusing issues, the lawyers explicated in detail, and often in deadly legalese, the meaning of terms such as "principle" or "improvement"; phrases such as "motive power of the electric current"; dizzying distinctions between "art" and "mode," "arm" and "lever," "characters" and "letters."

SILVERMAN, LIGHTNING MAN, *supra* at 320.

In addition to the issues of commensurability and claim scope, the Court also addressed whether Morse was indeed the "first and original inventor" of the telegraph and whether O'Reilly's use of the Zook–Barnes Columbian telegraph infringed Morse's patent. Despite the argument of O'Reilly's attorney, Salmon P. Chase, the Court, in a thirty-seven page opinion, found that Morse's inventive efforts antedated those of Davy, Steinheil, and Wheatstone and that the Zook–Barnes Columbian telegraph infringed Morse's patent because the former was substantially similar to Morse's claimed invention. A result that, in the eyes of many, seemed justified because:

Morse created a telegraph system that against many competitors repeatedly proved itself to be the cheapest, the most rugged, the most reliable, and the simplest to operate. By perseverance that would not be denied he made it a commercial reality—the catalyst ... of an entire industry and the beginning of a worldwide network.

SILVERMAN, LIGHTNING MAN, *supra*, at 322. Of course, the invalidation of claim 8 denied Morse a total victory. But he subsequently withdrew and narrowed this claim, and successfully secured a seven-year extension for his patent from the Patent Office.

2. *The All–Important Question of Patent Scope*. The *O'Reilly* case involved one of the two great communication inventions of the Nineteenth Century, Morse's telegraph (the other was the telephone). *O'Reilly* demonstrates that the purpose of the disclosure requirement is not only to provide the public with the benefits of a technological disclosure, but also to delineate the proprietary boundaries or scope of the patent owner's rights. The Court was very concerned that Morse's claim 8 would easily capture future improvements or alternatives that Morse did not invent or describe in his patent. But what is the proper scope of Morse's patent? How much improvement activity should the Court have allowed Morse to capture? A patentee cannot foresee every future embodiment or improvement.

Is Chief Justice Taney's reluctance to allow a large patent scope in this case an example of his reluctance to see the government tie its hands in making commitments to private parties, when technological change might require future government flexibility? For a famous debate between Chief Justice Taney in the majority and Justice Story in dissent on this more general question, in the context of a bridge franchise, see *Charles River Bridge v. Warren Bridge*, 36 U.S. 420 (1837)

A critical and difficult balance must be struck. But what considerations guide the determination of optimal claim scope? What incentives and concerns are most important? Incentives to invent, commercialize, coordinate improvement activity, transaction costs? A narrower claim scope may allow for more vigorous improvement activity and competition, but detract from the incentive to invent in the first instance or to see a product through to commercialization. A particular concern is that future innovators may unduly benefit from the first invention's positive externalities that relate to enabling follow-on research and lowering research costs. In contrast, a broader claim scope may lend itself to efficient coordination of improvement activity and allow a patentee to efficiently commercialize the claimed invention, but may limit competition and the pace of technologic advancement due to high transaction costs (e.g., patent license market). This concern is of particular importance for sequential or cumulative technologies. Suzanne Scotchmer succinctly captures the aforementioned scope dilemma when she writes, "the challenge is to reward early innovators fully for the technological foundation they provide to later innovators, but to reward later innovators adequately for their improvements and new products as well." Suzanne Scotchmer, *Standing on the Shoulders of Giants: Cumulative Research and the Patent Law*, 5 J. ECON. PERSPECTIVES 29, 30 (Winter 1991).

Scholars and judges have made an effort to apply an economic analysis to these issues. For arguments advocating narrower claim scope, *see* Robert Merges & Richard Nelson, *On the Complex Economics of Patent Scope*, 90 COLUM. L. REV. 839 (1990); Rebecca S. Eisenberg, *Patents and the Progress of Science: Exclusive Rights and Experimental Use*, 56 U. CHI. L. REV. 1017 (1989); Arti Kaur Rai, *Regulating Scientific Research: Intellectual Property Rights and the Norms of Science*, 94 NW. L. REV. 77 (1999). For arguments supporting a broader claim scope, *see* Edmund W. Kitch, *The Nature and Function of the Patent System*, 20 J.L. & ECON. 265 (1977); F. Scott Kieff, *Property Rights and Property Rules for Commercializing Inventions*, 85 MINN. L. REV. 697 (2001); F. Scott Kieff, *Facilitating Scientific Research: Intellectual Property Rights and the Norms of Science—A Response to Professors Rai and Eisenberg*, 95 NW. L. REV. 691 (2001). *See also Hilton Davis Chem. Co. v. Warner–Jenkinson Co.*, 62 F.3d 1512, 1529 (Fed.Cir. 1995) (Newman, J., concurring) *rev'd and remanded on other grounds*, 520 U.S. 17 (1997).

For a discussion of transaction costs in the context of patent licensing and why parties may have difficulty reaching acceptable terms, *see* Mark A. Lemley, *The Economics of Improvement in Intellectual Property Law*, 75 TEX. L. REV. 989, 1053–61 (1997); and Roberto Mazzeloni and Richard R. Nelson, *The Benefits and Costs of Strong Patent Protection: A Contribution to the Current Debate*, 27 Research Policy 273, 279–80 (1998).

3. *The Telephone, "Undulations," and Light Bulbs.* As noted above, the other great communication device was the telephone. Alexander Graham Bell obtained a patent claiming his invention, and he and his company, the "American Bell Telephone Company," which became AT & T, successfully defended the patent in two cases resolved by the Supreme Court. *Dolbear v. American Bell Tel. Co.*, 126 U.S. 1 (1888); *United States v. American Bell Tel. Co.*, 128 U.S. 315 (1888). Distinguishing the *O'Reilly* telegraph case, the Court upheld as sufficiently enabled Bell's broad claim to the "method of, and apparatus for, transmitting vocal or other sounds telegraphically, as herein described, by causing electrical undulations, similar in form to the vibrations of the air accompanying the said vocal or other sounds, substantially as set forth." The Court wrote:

> What Bell claims is the art of creating changes of intensity in a continuous current of electricity, exactly corresponding to the changes of density in the air caused by the vibrations which accompany vocal or other sounds, and of using that electrical condition, thus created, for sending and receiving articulate speech telegraphically. For that, among other things, his patent of 1876 was, in our opinion, issued; and the point to be decided is whether, as such a patent, it can be sustained. . . . The effect of [the *O'Reilly*] decision was, therefore, that the use of magnetism as a motive power, without regard to the particular process with which it was connected in the patent, could not be claimed, but that its use in that connection could. In

the present case the claim is not for the use of a current of electricity in its natural state as it comes from the battery, but for putting a continuous current, in a closed circuit, into a certain specified condition, suited to the transmission of vocal and other sounds, and using it in that condition for that purpose. So far as at present known, without this peculiar change in its condition it will not serve as a medium for the transmission of speech, but with the change it will. Bell was the first to discover this fact, and how to put such a current in such a condition; and what he claims is its use in that condition for that purpose, just as Morse claimed his current in his condition for his purpose. We see nothing in Morse's case to defeat Bell's claim; on the contrary, it is in all respects sustained by that authority. It may be that electricity cannot be used at all for the transmission of speech, except in the way Bell has discovered, and that therefore, practically, his patent gives him its exclusive use for that purpose; but that does not make his claim one for the use of electricity distinct from the particular process with which it is connected in his patent. It will, if true, show more clearly the great importance of his discovery, but it will not invalidate his patent. . . .

It is true that Bell transmits speech by transmitting it, and that long before he did so it was believed by scientists that it could be done by means of electricity, if the requisite electrical effect could be produced. Precisely how that subtle force operates under Bell's treatment, or what form it takes, no one can tell. All we know is that he found out that, by changing the intensity of a continuous current so as to make it correspond exactly with the changes in the density of air caused by sonorous vibrations, vocal and other sounds could be transmitted and heard at a distance. This was the thing to be done, and Bell discovered the way of doing it.

Dolbear, 126 U.S. at 533–35; 538–39.

Unlike Morse's Eighth claim, the Bell claim was limited to a method and apparatus—that of introducing "undulations" that were "similar in form" to sonar vibrations. This broad claim successfully established Bell's rights over early telephone technology even though Bell's patent only illustrated an electro-mechanical mode for introducing the "undulations," but the industry had adopted a variable resistance mode for the same purpose. Thus, while Bell's claim language was somewhat more restrictive than Morse's, the Court did not limit Bell's claim scope accordingly. How can the two cases be reconciled?

Another interesting 19th century disclosure case is *The Incandescent Lamp Patent,* 159 U.S. 465 (1895). In this case, Thomas Edison sought to invalidate a patent as over broad. The inventors, Sawyer and Man, discovered that "*carbonized* fibrous or textile material" (paper) could be used as incandescent conductors. But two of their patent claims covered all fibrous and textile materials for incandescent conductors, not just carbonized paper. The Court held these claims invalid, stating:

The object of [the enablement requirement] is to apprise the public of what the patentee claims as his own, the courts of what they are called upon to construe, and competing manufactures and dealers of exactly what they are bound to avoid. *Grant v. Raymond*. If the description be so vague and uncertain that no one can tell, except by independent experiments, how to construct the patented device, the patent is void. . . . If Sawyer and Man had discovered that a certain carbonized paper would answer the purpose, their claim to all carbonized paper would, perhaps, not be extravagant; but the fact that paper happens to belong to the fibrous kingdom did not invest them with sovereignty over this entire kingdom, and thereby practically limit other experimenters to the domain of minerals.

Id. at 474, 476.

4. *Chief Justice Marshall and the Disclosure Requirements*. In one of the earliest disclosure cases, *Grant v. Raymond*, 31 U.S. (6 Pet.) 218 (1832), Chief Justice Marshall recognized that a full and enabling disclosure of an invention in the specification was not a mere formality, but rather a fundamental, policy-based requirement of patentability. According to the Court:

> This [enablement requirement] is necessary in order to give the public, after the privilege shall expire, the advantage for which the privilege is allowed, and is the foundation of the power to issue the patent.

The *Grant* opinion addressed a problem created by an ambiguity in the 1793 Act. The Act's third section set forth the enablement requirement in terms similar to those in the present day Section 112:

> . . . [E]very inventor, before he can receive a patent, . . . shall deliver a written description of his invention, and of the manner of using, or process of compounding the same, in such full, clear and exact terms, as to distinguish the same from all other things before known, and to enable any person skilled in the art or science, to which it is a branch, or with which it is most nearly connected, to make, compound, and use the same. And in the case of any machine, he shall fully explain the principle, and the several modes in which he has contemplated the application of that principle or character, by which it may be distinguished from other inventions; and he shall accompany the whole with drawings and written references, where the nature of the case admits of drawings, or with specimens of the ingredients, and of the composition of matter, sufficient in quantity for the purpose of experiment, where the invention is of a composition of matter. . . . And such inventor shall, moreover, deliver a model of his machine, provided, the secretary shall deem such model to be necessary.

The Act's sixth section created a defense of insufficient disclosure, but required proof that the inventor intended to "mislead the public." In *Grant*, the Court held that, despite the language of Section 6 of the 1793 Act, an insufficient specification was grounds for defense on an infringement suit even though the patentee had no intent to deceive the public. Later, the 1952 Act, consistent with *Grant*, recognized that a § 112 enablement deficiency would invalidate a patent claim without regard to intent. *See* P.J. Federico, *Commentary on the New Patent Act*, 35 U.S.C.A. 1, 55 (1954), reprinted at 75 J. PAT. & TRADEMARK OFF. SOC'Y 161 (1993) ("Since intention to deceive the public was an element of this defense it was seldom raised; failure to give a description of the invention as required by Section 112 is a defense without regard to intention.")

5. *Public Disclosure Benefits*. The Court in *Grant* noted that the purpose of the enabling disclosure requirement is "to give the public, after the privilege shall expire, the advantage for which the privilege is allowed." *See also Lowell v. Lewis*, 15 F.Cas. 1018, 1020 (C.C.Mass. 1817) (Story, J.) ("Unless . . . a specification was made, as would at all events enable other persons of competent skill to construct similar machines, the advantage to the public, which the act contemplates, would be entirely lost"). How often will a full enabling disclosure in the specification be important years after the patent issues; or when it expires? The answer must be "Rarely!" The enabling details in a patent will either have been disclosed in other ways, such as through commercialization of the patented invention, or will have become obsolete in view of later technological developments. Does this undermine the *"quid pro quo"* disclosure justification for issuing patents? No. The technical information in the specification may well have immediate value "to the public," for example, by assisting research by others to devise improvements or alternative solutions, or for adaptation to other fields, or simply to add to the general storehouse of knowledge. But oftentimes, to build upon or even satisfactorily practice the claimed invention, a total "enabling package" is needed, which includes technical know-how in addition to an adequate patent disclosure.

2.   STATE OF THE ART AT TIME OF FILING, UNDUE EXPERIMENTATION, AND CLAIM SCOPE

The language of section 112 does not clearly resolve the question of which time frame should serve as the setting for the enablement test. Time frame matters because the enabling quality of a specification can change over time for a number of reasons. First, the level of skill in the art may rise as new information becomes available. Second, important starting materials or other technologies may also become available. Either of these events could render a specification enabling and supportive of a particular claim scope when it was not so before. Indeed, changes in technology may also suggest the opposite. The *Glass* and *Hogan* cases explore the issues of timing, claim scope, and state of the art in the context of the enablement requirement.

In re Glass

492 F.2d 1228 (CCPA 1974).

■ Before MARKEY, CHIEF JUDGE, and RICH, BALDWIN, LANE and MILLER, JUDGES.

■ RICH, JUDGE.

This appeal is from the decision of the Patent Office Board of Appeals affirming the examiner's rejection of all claims remaining in application serial No. 664,879 filed August 31, 1967, entitled "Whiskers." We affirm.

The Invention

The term "whiskers" is the technical name for long, needle-like, linear crystals grown artificially from the vapor phase of such crystal-producing materials as aluminum oxide, silicon nitride, graphite, boron, sapphire, etc.... The appealed claims are directed to both apparatus and method. The whiskers are said to have very high strength and according to one prior art reference ... have utility for reinforcing refractory materials. The application contains the following drawing....

The description in appellant's specification reads:

... there is shown a heated chamber 11 having a mixer chamber 12 which is positioned above a heated vertical cylinder 13. A precipitating zone 14 is formed within cylinder 13, and the temperature within precipitating zone 14 is hotter at the top and cooler at the bottom since a temperature gradient is maintained within precipitating zone 14 by heating means 15 which is positioned along cylinder 13.

The whisker-producing vapor is mixed in a turbulent mixer zone 16 in chamber 12, and the material to be mixed is introduced into chamber 12 through jet nozzles 17–20 which are connected to ingredient containers 23–26 by conduits 27–30 to control the flow of ingredients passing there through.

An electron gun 37, which may be a radioactive cobalt gun, is positioned beneath cylinder 13 and is adapted to discharge electrons into the vapor in precipitating zone 14.

A collector 38 is positioned beneath cylinder 13 for collecting the whiskers formed in precipitating zone 14.

In operation, ingredients A, B, C, and D are passed from ingredient containers 23–26 through metering valves 33–36 and conduits 27–30 and are sprayed through jet nozzles 17–20 into turbulent mixer zone 16 of chamber 12 where the ingredients are thoroughly mixed together. The mixture is then passed downwardly into heated vertical cylinder 13 and precipitating zone 14. Gradient heating means 15 provides a temperature gradient within precipitating zone 14 and forms an optimum supersaturation zone 42 somewhere within precipitating zone 14.

It is to be noted that optimum zone 42 is created within precipitating zone 14 without exactly controlling conditions of temperature, pressure and supersaturation in a selected space. The vapor itself finds the optimum zone 42 by passing through a zone which is above optimum conditions, then passing through the optimum zone 42, and then passing through a zone which is below optimum conditions.

Appellant claims the above described apparatus and the method implicit in said description in claims of varying scope and nothing would be added by setting forth typical claims, particularly in view of the ground of rejection discussed below.

The Rejections

The principal rejection affirmed by the board applies to all claims and is under 35 U.S.C. § 112, first paragraph.[3] It is that the claims are unsupported because the specification contains an inadequate, fatally defective disclosure in that it would not enable any person skilled in the art to practice the invention claimed. In particular, as pointed out by the examiner, appellant acknowledges that at least proper temperature, pressure, and vapor saturation conditions are necessary to precipitate a whisker from a vapor, yet none of these parameters are given in the general description and no specific example is provided. The examiner and the board both felt that appellant had also failed to comply with the "best mode" requirement of § 112, perhaps because there is no specific example. Numerous terms used are alleged to be unclear in their meaning and unexplained, such as "whisker-producing material," "optimum supersaturation," and "above" and "below" optimum supersaturation. Moreover, the examiner felt that the last two terms were used in the opposite senses to what they normally connote and were not only indefinite but confusing. He also found that the terms "A, B, C, and D" describing ingredients are not defined and do not refer to any particular materials. He found the intensity of the electrostatic charge, which he considered to be a matter of importance to whisker growth, if not critical, to be undisclosed. The board reversed as to the term

---

3. "[A] The specification shall contain a written description of the invention, and of the manner and process of making and using it, in such full, clear, concise, and exact terms as to *enable any person skilled in the art to which it pertains, or with which it is most nearly connected, to make and use the same,* and shall [B] set forth the best mode contemplated by the inventor of carrying out his invention." (Emphasis and bracketed letters ours.)

"whisker-producing material," since it felt it would be understood by those skilled in the art, but otherwise affirmed this rejection on the ground of incomplete disclosure....

Opinion

We will first dispose of the last-mentioned argument. The right of the Patent Office to rely on prior United States patents as "prior art" under § 102(e) is pursuant to the rationale of the case of *Alexander Milburn Co. v. Davis–Bournonville Co.*, 270 U.S. 390 (1926), which that section codified. The rationale was that the patentee of the patent in suit could not be the first inventor and have a valid patent if the invention had been described in another's patent, the application for which had been filed before the patentee's date of invention.... There is nothing "unfair" about the situation. The board was right in refusing to consider the patents cited by appellant and we, likewise, refuse to consider them.

Appellant's attempt to use the disclosures of the four patents which issued after his filing date raises a subsidiary question: If a disclosure is insufficient as of the time it is filed, can it be made sufficient, while the application is still pending, by later publications which add to the knowledge of the art so that the disclosure, supplemented by such publications, would suffice to enable the practice of the invention? We think it cannot. The sufficiency must be judged as of the filing date. *Cf. In re Argoudelis*, 434 F.2d 1390, 58 CCPA 769 (1970), particularly Judge Baldwin's concurring opinion, and *In re Hawkins*, 486 F.2d 569 (Cust. & Pat.App.1973). 35 U.S.C. § 132 prohibits adding any "new matter" to the disclosure after filing. Moreover, the filing date becomes a date of constructive reduction to practice in determining priority of invention and this should not be the case unless at that time, without waiting for subsequent disclosures, any person skilled in the art could practice the invention from the disclosure of the application. If information to be found only in subsequent publications is needed for such enablement, it cannot be said that the disclosure in the application evidences a completed invention. We left the above-stated subsidiary question open in *In re Barrett*, 440 F.2d 1391, 58 CCPA 1155 (1971), because decision on it was there unnecessary. It was also unnecessary to decide it in *Argoudelis*.[5] Since it is squarely raised here by appellant's contentions, we now rule that application sufficiency under § 112, first paragraph, must be judged as of its filing date. It is an applicant's obligation to supply enabling disclosure without reliance on what others may publish after he has filed an application on what is supposed to be a completed invention. If he cannot supply enabling information, he is not yet in a position to file.[6]

* * *

---

5. *See* Janicke, *Patent Disclosure: Some Problems and Current Developments*, 53 J. Pat. Off. Soc'y 3, 6–8 (1971).

6. Of course, while later issuing patents or publications may not be relied upon to establish that the specification is enabling under § 112, paragraph one, reference may be made to such publications to construe claim language and in particular to prove the definiteness of claim terminology. As we observed in *In re Fisher*, 427 F.2d 833, 838, 57 CCPA 1099, 1106

Considering the merits of the rejection for insufficiency of disclosure, we agree that it is insufficient to support either the apparatus or the method claims. It does not sufficiently teach how to use the apparatus or how to practice the method. We have quoted above almost all of the substance of the disclosure. While there is more to the specification, it never becomes more specific with respect to process details or apparatus operating conditions. The generality and vagueness of disclosure pervades the summary:

> To summarize, instead of trying to hold exact conditions of supersaturation (as required in the prior art), the present invention provides an optimum supersaturation zone 42 which is located somewhere within cylinder 13, it passes the whisker-producing vapor through cylinder 13 so that it must pass through optimum zone 42, and it provides a copious quantity of nuclei to optimum zone 42 and also to the zones immediately before and after optimum zone 42 to insure that whiskers form and grow with no necessity of having accurate controls.

We are told that cylinder 13 is hotter at the top than at the bottom but not how hot. No temperatures at all are disclosed. We are told that a temperature gradient exists in 13 but not what it is, that "ingredients" A, B, C, and D are mixed in chamber 12 and passed into cylinder 13 but are not told what they are except that one is whisker-producing vapor molecules and another may be "nuclei," comprising particles of barium, calcium, or strontium oxides or carbonates, that free electrons are shot upwardly into cylinder 13 from gun 37 and that all of this makes it unnecessary to exactly control temperature, pressure, and supersaturation because the "vapor itself finds the optimum zone 42" in passing through the cylinder. No pressures or flow rates are mentioned. We are told that an electric discharge point 43 may be placed in wandering zone 42 which "aids in the crystallization of fibers," but not what it discharges or how or in what way it aids crystallization. No example to illustrate the practical operation of the process or the apparatus is given. The strong feeling one gets from reading the entire specification is that either appellant did not have possession of the details of a single operative process or, if he did, he chose not to divulge them. In fact, the deficiencies of the specification are more readily seen by reading it in toto than they are by considering only the specific criticisms the examiner undertook to make.

Basing our decision on the careful consideration of the entire specification and having considered all of appellant's arguments, we are of the opinion that the examiner and the board were fully justified in concluding that the specification leaves too much to conjecture, speculation, and experimentation and is, therefore, insufficient in law to support any of the appealed claims.

The decision of the board is affirmed.

NOTES

1. *The Filing Date Rule.* The language of section 112 does not clearly resolve the question of at what time the disclosure must be "enabling"—that is, sufficient to

---

(1970), "were we to require that the claims speak in the language of the prior art, we would be prohibiting the use of the newer and frequently more precise language of the present art."

enable one with ordinary skill in the art to make and use the claimed invention. Nevertheless, decisions such as *Glass*, have held that the sufficiency of the patent's disclosure "must be judged as of its filing date." Information that is developed or becomes available after that date generally cannot be considered in determining disclosure sufficiency. Similarly, post-filing date developments that enable previously unknown variations generally cannot be relied upon to establish nonenablement. *See United States Steel Corp. v. Phillips Petroleum Co.*, 865 F.2d 1247, 1251 (Fed.Cir.1989).

2. *History—Provisional Specifications—Constructive Reduction to Practice.* The early patent statutes did not require that a fully enabling specification be filed with the initial application. Consider, for example, the 1793 Act, which was interpreted in *Grant v. Raymond*. Section 1 of the Act required that the inventor claim an invention "not known or used before the application," while Section 3 only required the inventor to deliver a specification "before he can receive a patent." Similarly, early English patent practice entailed the filing of a brief "provisional specification" to be followed by a fuller one.

Over time, the Patent Office and the courts put greater emphasis on the disclosure contents of originally filed applications. In 1888, in the *Dolbear* case discussed above, the Supreme Court recognized that an inventor, such as Bell, could apply for a patent even though he had not fully reduced the invention to practice, provided that the application contained a sufficiently enabling disclosure of the invention.

3. *The Deposit Cases.* To comply with § 112, no problem exists when the microorganisms used are known and readily available to the public; however, when a microorganism is not so known and readily available, applicants must take additional steps to comply with the requirements of § 112 such as depositing the microorganism in a recognized central depository. For example, in the case of *In re Lundak*, 773 F.2d 1216 (Fed.Cir.1985), where the inventor had established a necessary cell line culture in a private laboratory but did not make a deposit with a public agency until five days after filing the application, the court held there had been compliance with § 112.

After the enactment of the American Inventors Protection Act of 1999 (AIPA), the biotechnology industry became concerned that biological deposits would have to be made before the end of the 18–month period, rather than at time of issuance. There is certainly a perception that biological deposits are more vulnerable to infringement than other types of patents because third parties can obtain a sample of the deposit and use it to engage in infringing activity. The industry was concerned that if the deposit had to be made prior to the issuance of the patent, third parties would have early access to the deposited material.

Because of this concern, the General Accounting Office (GAO) was charged with studying the risks posed by the AIPA to the "United States biotechnology industry relating to biological deposits in support of biotechnology patents." The GAO initially stated that it was "unable to identify a single case in which a person or organization had gained access to a biological deposit and then used it to infringe the underlying patent." The GAO report concluded that the AIPA 18–month publication requirement does have an effect on the risks for patent infringement because the timing of when the deposit must be made has not changed. Even though the application must be published at 18 months, "the statute does not require the release of a biological deposit that an application refers to but that is neither part of the application nor within the PTO's custody or control." Therefore, "even if the application is published at 18 months, the biological deposit does not have to be released until the patent is granted."

Lastly, it should be noted that the GAO report did express concern about the infringement risk for seed patents, especially with respect to foreign infringers. According to the report, the "seed is its own 'factory' and that a person intent on infringing the patent in question merely has to obtain a sample, plant the seeds, and harvest them at low cost." Exacerbating this concern is the fact that many foreign countries do not issue patents for plant varieties.

The GAO report is available at the General Accounting Office's website (http://www.gao.gov). The report is GAO–01–49.

4. *The Incorporation–By–Reference Cases.* The question of incorporation-by-reference was discussed in the related *Hawkins* cases. *In re Hawkins,* 486 F.2d 569 (CCPA 1973); *In re Hawkins,* 486 F.2d 577 (CCPA 1973); *In re Hawkins,* 486 F.2d 579 (CCPA 1973). Most important is the first *Hawkins* decision. An application was filed disclosing and claiming peroxy-amine compounds and related processes. The sole disclosure for the utility of the compounds was the following statement: "These novel compounds may for example be used in the production of valuable monomers for example by the processes described in co-pending British applications 36107/66, 42756/66, 46971/66, 49699/66, 50324/66, 10070/67, and 10071/67." Adequate disclosure of a utility is required to establish an effective filing date under 35 U.S.C. §§ 101 and 112. *See Brenner v. Manson*, 383 U.S. 519 (1966) (discussed in Chapter Six, *infra*). The patent examiner rejected the application, reasoning that the specification must be complete as of the filing date and a reference to a pending *foreign* application was not effective. The applicant responded by amending its specification to delete the reference to the British applications and to substitute the complete text of those applications (except for cross references and claims). The applicant relied upon § 608.01(p) of the Manual of Patent Examining Procedure (MPEP). The examiner refused to enter the amendments on the ground that they were "new matter"—that is, added information not in the original specification as filed—and continued the inadequate disclosure rejection. The Patent Office Board of Appeals affirmed the rejection. The court reversed. In practice, an application might specifically state: "whenever a reference is cited herein, the entire contents of that reference are hereby incorporated herein by reference as if set forth in their entirety."

5. *How to Use.* The inventor's disclosure must enable one to "use" as well as "make" the claimed invention and to this extent the § 112 enablement requirement supplements the § 101 utility requirement. *See In re Cortright*, 165 F.3d 1353, 1356 (Fed.Cir.1999) ("If the written description fails to illuminate a credible utility, the PTO will make both a section 112, ¶ 1 rejection for failure to teach how to use the invention and a section 101 rejection for lack of utility.... This dual rejection occurs because '[t]he how to use prong of section 112 incorporates as a matter of law the requirement of 35 U.S.C. § 101 that the specification disclose as a matter of fact a practical utility.' ")

6. *Relying on the Prior Art.* The extent to which a patentee may rely on the state of the prior art to "flesh out" an otherwise "bare bones" disclosure may be a practical problem, depending on the nature of the technology. Indeed, it is the law that "a patent need not teach, and preferably omits, what is well known in the art." *See Hybritech v. Monoclonal Antibodies, Inc.*, 802 F.2d 1367, 1384 (Fed.Cir.1986). *But compare, Genentech, Inc. v. Novo Nordisk*, 108 F.3d 1361 (Fed.Cir.1997), where Judge Lourie was critical of attempts to rely on the general knowledge in the prior art for information not provided in the patent disclosure:

> It is true ... that a specification need not disclose what is well known in the art.... However, that general, oft-repeated statement is merely a rule of supplementation, not a substitute for a basic enabling disclosure. It means that the omission of minor details does not cause a specification to

> fail to meet the enablement requirement. However, when there is no disclosure of any specific starting material or of any of the conditions under which a process can be carried out, undue experimentation is required; there is a failure to meet the enablement requirement that cannot be rectified by asserting that all the disclosure related to the process is within the skill of the art.

Id. at 1366. Judge Lourie stressed that "[w]here, as here, the claimed invention is the application of an unpredictable technology in the early stages of development, an enabling description in the specification must provide those skilled in the art with a specific and useful teaching." *Id.* at 1367. Indeed, a patentee cannot "bootstrap a vague statement of a problem into an enabling disclosure sufficient to dominate someone else's solution of the problem." *Id.*

7. *Tension Between Enablement and Obviousness.* Can a claimed invention be nonenabling yet obvious in the light of the prior act? In *Webster*, discussed *supra*, the Supreme Court suggested that there was a potential inconsistency between a patent validity attacker's contentions that a patent claim (1) was not enabled by the disclosure and (2) was obvious over the prior art:

> It is worthy of remark ... that the defendants, in their answer, state it as a fact, that, prior to the alleged invention of Webster, looms containing lays having shuttle-boxes rigidly attached were publicly known and described in certain English patents, which they specify; and that all the other parts and elements mentioned in the fifth claim of Webster's patent (being the claim relied on) were described in another English patent of one Birkbeck; and they aver and insist, as will be more fully noticed hereafter, that the application and use of the two things together, that is, the parts described in Birkbeck's patent, with the rigid lay and shuttle-box described in the other patents, were obvious and required no invention; and that, therefore, the alleged invention of Webster was well known, and constituted a part of the known state of the art. This averment in the answer, which of course is sworn to, does not seem to tally very well with the allegation that Webster has failed to point out, in his patent, how to use and apply his invention, and that it requires further invention to use and apply it.

Webster, 105 U.S. at 587.

The holding in *Glass*—that prior art extant on the filing date may be relied upon to show enablement, while certain obscure or secret prior art cannot be relied on to show enablement—means that arguments for obviousness and nonenablement (or nonobviousness and enablement) are not necessarily inconsistent. For instance, § 102(e) prior art (*i.e.*, disclosures in pending applications by others that later issue as patents) can be used to prove that the claimed invention is obvious, but cannot be used by the applicant to prove enablement; thus, a claimed invention may be obvious but not enabled. Any apparent inconsistency is also undermined by considering claim scope. As the next subsection shows, a broad claim must be enabled to its entire scope. In contrast, a broad claim is unpatentable if it reads on any subject matter that is obvious from the prior art. *See* Donald Chisum, *Comment: Anticipation, Enablement and Obviousness: An Eternal Golden Braid*, 15 Am. Intell. Prop. Law Ass'n. Q.J. 57 (1987).

8. *Tension Between Enablement and Section 102(b).* One could argue that there is also a tension between enablement/best mode and § 102(b). *In Robotic Vision Systems, Inc. v. View Engineering, Inc.*, 112 F.3d 1163, 1168 (Fed.Cir.1997), Judge Lourie discussed this "apparent inconsistency" between § 102(b) and § 112:

> This case presents an interesting situation in which the use of software was sufficiently within the skill of the art as to not run afoul of the best

mode requirement, but it may not have been sufficiently developed by the critical date to cause an offer of the product to constitute an on-sale bar. The reason for this apparent inconsistency is that the relevant statutory provisions have different purposes, one to promote prompt filing of patent applications after commercialization has begun, and the other to compel full disclosure of an invention. Knowledge of one skilled in the art is relevant to satisfaction of the best mode requirement, but such knowledge does not create a completed invention in an on-sale context when the invention at the time of the offer is nothing more than a concept for improving a method of using a prior art machine.

Consider that the focus of § 112 is on a person of skill in the art, whereas § 102(b) is concerned with activities of the inventor (and third-parties). *See also, Lockwood v. American Airlines, Inc.*, 107 F.3d 1565, 1570 (Fed.Cir.1997) ("Lockwood attempts to preclude summary judgment [on the public use issue] by pointing to record testimony that one skilled in the art would not be able to build and practice the claimed invention without access to the secret aspects of [the invention]. However, it is the claims that define a patented invention. As we have concluded earlier in this opinion, American's public use of the high-level aspects of the [invention] was enough to place the claimed features on the '359 patent in the public's possession. Beyond this 'in public use' or 'on sale' finding, there is no requirement for an enablement-type inquiry," *citing In re Epstein*, 32 F.3d 1559, 1567–68 (Fed.Cir.1994)).

In re Hogan

559 F.2d 595 (CCPA 1977).

■ Before Markey, Chief Judge, and Rich, Baldwin, Lane and Miller, Judges.

■ Markey, Chief Judge.

This appeal is from the decision of the Patent and Trademark Office (PTO) Board of Appeals affirming various rejections ... of claims 13–15 in appellants' application No. 181,185 filed September 16, 1971 (the 1971 application) for "Solid Polymers of Olefins."[1] A main issue involves use of a "later state of the art" as evidence to support a rejection. The 1971 application is said to be a continuation of application No. 648,364 filed June 23, 1967 (the 1967 application), in turn a "divisional" of application No. 558,530 filed January 11, 1956 (the 1956 application)[2]. The 1956 application is a continuation-in-part of application No. 476,306 filed December 20, 1954 and application No. 333,576 filed January 27, 1953 (the 1953 application).

We affirm in part, reverse in part, and remand with respect to certain rejections.

The Claims

Although the 1971 application discloses several polymers, the claims are limited:[3]

---

1. The real party in interest is Phillips Petroleum Company.

2. 1956 application is still pending. *See* note 3, *infra*.

3. At oral hearing, appellants' counsel stated that the 1956 application is involved in the "famous" polypropylene interference (*see, e.g., Standard Oil Co. v. Montedison, S.p.A.*, 540

13.   A normally solid homopolymer of 4–methyl–1–pentene....

14.   A polymer of claim 13 having a melting point in the range of 390° to 425° F.

15.   A polymer of claim 13 which is wax-like and thermally stable as evidenced by substantially no decomposition at temperatures below about 700° F....

The Disclosures

Appellants assert that, under the provisions of 35 U.S.C. § 120,[6] claims 13 and 15 are entitled to the benefit of the filing date of the 1953 application and claim 14 is entitled to the benefit of the filing date of the 1956 application.

The 1953 application discloses solid polymers made from 1–olefin monomers having a maximum chain length of eight carbon atoms and no branching nearer the double bond than the 4–position. Several olefin monomers which form such polymers are disclosed: ethylene, propylene, 1–butene, 1–pentene, 1–hexene, and 4–methyl–1–pentene.

A method of making such polymers using a catalyst containing chromium oxide on a silica-alumina support is described. The application includes twenty "examples" and twenty-five "tables" giving detailed information on: how to prepare, activate, use, and regenerate the catalyst; how to influence the molecular weight of the polymer products; what solvents or diluents to use in admixture with the olefin feed; what feed velocities, reaction pressures, reaction temperatures, and reaction times are operative; and certain physical and chemical characteristics of the polymer products.

* * *

The references relied upon by the examiner and board were:

Haven 3,257,367 June 21, 1966 (filed June 3, 1955)

Edwards 3,299,022 January 17, 1967 (filed April 4, 1962)

Edwards 3,317,500 May 2, 1967 (filed October 2, 1963)

Natta et al., Rendiconti dell'Accademia Nazionale dei Lincei, Series VIII, Vol. XIX, No. 6 (December 1955), pp. 397–403.

* * *

Edwards ('022) describes a solid, amorphous, elastomeric homopolymer of 4–methyl–1–pentene.... Edwards ('500) discloses a 1,4–type polymer of

---

F.2d 611 (C.A.3 1976)) and "when that case got into the district court, we gave up on our hope for a generic product claim and filed applications to each one of the several species (of polymers)."

6.   § 120. Benefit of earlier filing date in the United States.

An application for patent for an invention disclosed in the manner provided by the first paragraph of section 112 of this title in an application previously filed in the United States by the same inventor shall have the same effect, as to such invention, as though filed on the date of the prior application, if filed before the patenting or abandonment of or termination of proceedings on the first application or on an application similarly entitled to the benefit of the filing date of the first application and if it contains or is amended to contain a specific reference to the earlier filed application.

4–methyl–1–pentene in a cross-linked form having a molecular weight in excess of 1,000,000.

* * *

The Solicitor

The solicitor ... argues that appellants' claims cover a genus of homopolymers of 4–methyl–1–pentene, including both low and high molecular weight homopolymers; that "at best" appellants teach how to make only low molecular weight homopolymers; that it is possible in view of Natta, Haven, Edwards ('022), and Edwards ('500) to produce homopolymers having high molecular weights; and, therefore, "the enabling disclosure in the specification is not commensurate in scope with the breadth of the claims." ... Thus, the solicitor contends that the examiner and the board made out a prima facie case that appellants' enabling disclosure is not commensurate in scope with the claims.

In response to appellants' argument that their disclosure should be judged by the state of the art as of its effective filing date, the solicitor states:

> The references relied upon by the examiner to demonstrate the shortcomings of appellants' disclosure all have dates prior to the filing date of this [1971] application. Hence, until appellants establish that their present specification is sufficient, there is no need to determine what disclosure might have been sufficient in 1953 and 1954 when appellants' grandparent applications were filed. (Bracketed matter added.)

* * *

Opinion

I. *Disregard of the Effect of 35 U.S.C. § 120*

* * *

We held in *In re Glass*, 492 F.2d 1228, 1232 (CCPA 1974), that an applicant could not rely on what occurred in the art after his filing date because "application sufficiency under § 112, first paragraph, must be judged as of its filing date." ... That principle applies equally to the PTO with respect to a continuing application entitled under § 120 to the benefit of an earlier filing date. No rational distinction can be made in the treatment accorded to the subject matter of an original application and to the same subject matter disclosed in a continuing application. Courts should not treat the same legal question, enablement under § 112, in one manner with respect to the applicant and in a different manner with respect to the examiner.

The examiner and the board, in support of the § 112 rejection, cited Natta, Haven, Edwards ('022), and Edwards ('500), not as prior art, but as evidence to prove appellants' disclosure non-enabling for "other species" of the claimed polymer, in an effort, as judicially required, to show why the scope of enablement was insufficient to support the claims.... As thus implicitly recognized, the references would not have been available in support of a 35 U.S.C. §§ 102 or 103 rejection entered in connection with the 1953 application. To permit use of the same references in support of the 35 U.S.C. § 112 rejection herein, however, is to render the "benefit" of 35 U.S.C. § 120 illusory.[13] The very purpose of reliance on § 120 is to reach back, to avoid the effect of intervening references. Nothing in § 120 limits its application to any specific grounds for rejection, or permits the examiner, denied use of references to reject or to require narrowing of a claim under §§ 102 or 103, to achieve the same result by use of the same references under § 112. Just as justice and reason require application of § 112 in the same manner to applicants and examiners, symmetry in the law, and evenness of its application, require that § 120 be held applicable to all bases for rejection, that its words "same effect" be given their full meaning and intent.

The clear and unambiguous language of § 120 states that "(a)n application ... for an invention disclosed in the manner provided by the first paragraph of section 112 ... in an application previously filed in the United States ... *shall have the same effect, as to such invention, as though filed on the date of the prior application....*" (Emphasis added.) Thus, appellants' 1971 application should have been given "the same effect," *i. e.,* it should have been tested for compliance with § 112, first paragraph, "as though filed on the date of the prior application," to wit, 1953 with respect to claims 13 and 15 ... and 1956 with respect to claim 14.

Because the board did not consider appellants' ancestral applications in affirming the rejections under § 112, first paragraph, in view of the cited references, those rejections must be reversed and the case remanded to permit consideration of enablement questions as of the proper filing date.[15]

II. *Employment of a Later State of the Art in Testing For Compliance With 35 U.S.C. § 112, First Paragraph*

The pendency since 1953 of appellants' applications, giving rise to concern over whether a claim may issue of breadth sufficient to encompass the later existing, "non-enabled" amorphous polymers of Edwards, and the PTO's application to the present facts of this court's statement in *In re Moore,* 439 F.2d 1232, 58 CCPA 1042 (1971) that "the scope of enablement" must be "commensurate with the scope of protection sought," impel clarification.

Citing *Moore,* the examiner stated that the § 112 rejection "is premised on the fact that while the claims are generic in nature, applicants have, at best, only described a very limited species within the generic class." Further, the examiner said "[t]he disclosure ... is non-enabling on how to prepare other species of this (claimed) polymer such as those of (the

---

13. It would also exalt form over substance. If the present appellants had not filed continuing applications, the only filing date involved would be that of the 1953 application. To judge the 1971 application in isolation would have a chilling effect upon the right of applicants to file continuations. The 24 years of pendency herein may be decried, but a limit upon continuing applications is a matter of policy for the Congress, not for us. *See In re Henriksen,* 399 F.2d 253, 262, 55 CCPA 1384, 1395 (1968). As presently constituted, the law as set forth in 35 U.S.C. §§ 112 and 120 is the same for all applications, whether of long or short pendency.

15. It is immaterial under 35 U.S.C. § 120 that the subject matter of claim 13 was not specifically claimed in the 1953 application. *In re Brower,* 433 F.2d 813, 58 CCPA 724 (1970).

four cited references) which, as far as this record is concerned, could not be prepared with the supported chromium oxide catalyst." The board, in adopting the examiner's reasoning, recognized that its primary basis was the Edwards polymer: "The claims on appeal, however, are not limited to a crystalline polymer ... but encompasses [sic] an amorphous polymer (of Edwards) as well which is manifestly outside the scope of the enabling teaching present in the case." Thus, amorphous polymers not having been, on this record, in existence in 1953, the examiner and the board focused on the later state of the art represented by the 1962 filing date of Edwards. . . .

A later state of the art is that state coming into existence after the filing date of an application. This court has approved use of later publications as evidence of the state of art existing on the filing date of an application.[17] That approval does not extend, however, to the use of a later (1967, Edwards) publication disclosing a later (1962) existing state of the art in testing an earlier (1953) application for compliance with § 112, first paragraph. The difference may be described as that between the permissible application of later knowledge about art-related facts existing on the filing date and the impermissible application of later knowledge about later art-related facts (here, amorphous polymers) which did not exist on the filing date. Thus, if appellants' 1953 application provided sufficient enablement, considering all available evidence (whenever that evidence became available) of the 1953 state of the art, *i.e.*, of the condition of knowledge about all art-related facts existing in 1953, then the fact of that enablement was established for all time and a later change in the state of the art cannot change it.

Rejections under § 112, first paragraph, on the ground that the scope of enablement is not commensurate with the scope of the claims, orbit about the more fundamental question: To what scope of protection is this applicant's particular contribution to the art entitled?

Though we do not reach the point on this appeal, we note appellants' argument that their invention is of "pioneer" status. The record reflects no citation of prior art disclosing a solid polymer of 4–methyl–1–pentene, which may suggest that appellants at least broke new ground in a broad sense. On remand, appellants may be found to have been in fact the first to conceive and reduce to practice "a solid polymer" as set forth in claim 13. As pioneers, if such they be, they would deserve broad claims to the broad concept. What were once referred to as "basic inventions" have led to "basic patents," which amounted to real incentives, not only to invention and its disclosure, but to its prompt, early disclosure. If later states of the

---

17. Where, for example, a later publication evidenced that, as of an application's filing date, undue experimentation would have been required, *In re Corneil*, 347 F.2d 563, 568, 52 CCPA 1718, 1724 (1965), or that a parameter absent from the claims was or was not critical, *In re Rainer*, 305 F.2d 505, 507 n. 3, 49 CCPA 1243, 1246 n. 3 (1962), or that a statement in the specification was inaccurate, *In re Marzocchi*, 439 F.2d 220, 223 n. 4, 58 CCPA 1069, 1073 n. 4 (1971), or that the invention was inoperative or lacked utility, *In re Langer*, 503 F.2d 1380, 1391 (CCPA 1974), or that a claim was indefinite, *In re Glass*, supra, 492 F.2d at 1232 n.6, 181 USPQ at 34 n.6, or that characteristics of prior art products were known, *In re Wilson*, 311 F.2d 266, 50 CCPA 773 (1962). Whatever may have been said enroute to decision in these cases, the fact situation in none of them established a precedent for permitting use of a later existing state of the art in determining enablement under 35 U.S.C. § 112.

art could be employed as a basis for rejection under 35 U.S.C. § 112, the opportunity for obtaining a basic patent upon early disclosure of pioneer inventions would be abolished.

The PTO has not challenged appellants' assertion that their 1953 application enabled those skilled in the art in 1953 to make and use "a solid polymer" as described in claim 13. Appellants disclosed, as the only then existing way to make such a polymer, a method of making the crystalline form. To now say that appellants should have disclosed in 1953 the amorphous form which on this record did not exist until 1962, would be to impose an impossible burden on inventors and thus on the patent system. There cannot, in an effective patent system, be such a burden placed on the right to broad claims. To restrict appellants to the crystalline form disclosed, under such circumstances, would be a poor way to stimulate invention, and particularly to encourage its early disclosure. To demand such restriction is merely to state a policy against broad protection for pioneer inventions, a policy both shortsighted and unsound from the standpoint of promoting progress in the useful arts, the constitutional purpose of the patent laws. . . .

Consideration of a later existing state of the art in testing for compliance with § 112, first paragraph, would not only preclude the grant of broad claims, but would wreak havoc in other ways as well. The use of a subsequently-existing improvement to show lack of enablement in an earlier-filed application on the basic invention would preclude issuance of a patent to the inventor of the thing improved, and in the case of issued patents, would invalidate all claims (even some "picture claims") therein. Patents are and should be granted to later inventors upon unobvious improvements. Indeed, encouragement of improvements on prior inventions is a major contribution of the patent system and the vast majority of patents are issued on improvements. It is quite another thing, however, to utilize the patenting or publication of later existing improvements to "reach back" and preclude or invalidate a patent on the underlying invention.

If applications were to be tested for enablement under § 112 in the light of a later existing state of the art, the question would arise over how much later. An examiner could never safely call a halt and pass an application to issue. One who had slavishly copied the disclosed and claimed invention of a patent issued in 1965, for example, could resist an infringement action by insisting that a court hold the patent invalid because it was not enabling with respect to some third product which first came into existence, and thus came within the purview of the claim, in 1975.

The PTO position, that claim 13 is of sufficient breadth to cover the later state of the art (amorphous polymers) shown in the "references," reflects a concern that allowance of claim 13 might lead to enforcement efforts against the later developers. Any such conjecture, if it exists, is both irrelevant and unwarranted. The business of the PTO is patentability, not infringement. Like the judicially-developed doctrine of equivalents, designed to protect the patentee with respect to later-developed variations of the claimed invention,[18] the judicially-developed "reverse doctrine of equivalents," requiring interpretation of claims in light of the specification,[19] may be safely relied upon to preclude improper enforcement against later developers. The courts have consistently considered subsequently existing states of the art as raising questions of infringement, but never of validity. It is, of course, a major and infinitely important function of the PTO to insure that those skilled in the art are enabled, as of the filing date, to practice the invention claimed. If, in the light of all proper evidence, the invention claimed be clearly enabled as of that date, the inquiry under § 112, first paragraph, is at an end.

V. *The Rejections of Claim 15*

Claim 15 presents a situation different from that of claims 13 and 14 because, as appellants acknowledge, the disclosure to support claim 15 appears in the 1953 and the 1967 applications, but not in the 1956 application. . . .

Thus, with respect to the subject matter of claim 15, there is a clear gap in the continuity of disclosure necessary to secure the benefit of § 120. . . .

* * *

MODIFIED AND REMANDED.

■ Miller, Judge, concurring in part.

I join the majority with respect to claim 15. However, I can only concur in the result reached by the majority with respect to claims 13 and 14.

* * *

Contrary to the majority opinion, to permit the "outer boundaries" of a claim to be construed in light of later art, rather than in light of art at the time the patent application was filed, could well impede progress in the useful arts. For example, it would relegate a later species invention (*e.g.*, the solid amorphous homopolymer of Edwards) to a subservient position vis-a-vis an earlier species invention (*e.g.*, the solid crystalline homopolymer disclosed by appellants), even though the earlier inventor did not contemplate, much less enable, a generic invention, merely because the patent application for the earlier invention used a broad term which, at the time, had a meaning to one skilled in the art that was coextensive with the species.

The majority opinion notes that the PTO's arguments evidence a concern that allowance of claim 13 might lead to enforcement efforts against later developers, but states that any conjecture on this point is "both irrelevant and unwarranted," since "(t)he business of the PTO is patentability, not infringement," and "the judicially-developed 'reverse doctrine of equivalents,' requiring interpretation of claims in light of the

---

18. *See Graver Tank & Mfg. Co. v. Linde Air Products Co.*, 339 U.S. 605, 70 S.Ct. 854, 94 L.Ed. 1097 (1950).

19. *See Westinghouse v. Boyden Power–Brake Co.*, 170 U.S. 537, 568–69, 18 S.Ct. 707, 42 L.Ed. 1136 (1898).

specification, may be safely relied upon to preclude *improper* enforcement against later developers." (Emphasis in original. Footnote omitted.) Two comments seem appropriate. First, in saying that "[t]o restrict appellants to the crystalline form disclosed, under such circumstances, would be a poor way to stimulate invention," the majority opinion advocates a double standard: for the inventor, interpret the language of the claims against later developers in light of the later state of the art; but for the PTO, as held here, interpret such language against the inventor only in light of the state of the art at the time the application was filed. I do not agree that such a double standard is needed to spur invention. Second, the PTO, in managing its business of patentability, has a duty to construe the scope of the claims, to interpret the claim language in light of the specification and the art existing at the time the patent application was filed, and to determine whether the scope of enablement is commensurate with the scope of the claims.

If, on remand, the PTO should determine that, at the time appellants' application was filed, one skilled in the art would have interpreted the phrase "solid homopolymer" broadly to include both crystalline and amorphous homopolymers, the PTO could, nevertheless, find that appellants' disclosure was only enabling to make a crystalline homopolymer and could properly reject claims 13 and 14 under the first paragraph of 35 U.S.C. § 112 as of broader scope than the scope of enablement. On the other hand, if the PTO should determine that, at the time appellants' application was filed, one skilled in the art would have interpreted the phrase "solid homopolymer" to include only a crystalline homopolymer, a finding of enablement, at the time appellants' application was filed, to make a crystalline homopolymer would end the inquiry under § 112, first paragraph.

NOTES

1. *The Policy of Enablement.* In many respects, the enablement requirement is at the heart of § 112 and the *quid pro quo* of our patent system. Indeed, it is "arguably the most important patent doctrine after obviousness." *Enzo Biochem, Inc. v. Gen–Probe Inc.,* 323 F.3d 956, 982 (Fed.Cir.2002) (Rader, J., dissenting from the court's decision not to hear the case en banc). On the one hand, the enablement requirement serves to enrich the storehouse of public knowledge, while, on the other hand, it provides for a limitation on claim scope. The scope of the enablement must be commensurate with the scope of the claims. As noted by the Federal Circuit:

> The enablement requirement ensures that the public knowledge is enriched by the patent specification to a degree at least *commensurate* with the scope of the claims. The scope of the claims must be less than or equal to the scope of the enablement. The scope of enablement, in turn, is that which is disclosed in the specification plus the scope of what would be known to one of ordinary skill in the art without *undue experimentation*.

National Recovery Technologies, Inc. v. Magnetic Separation Systems, Inc., 166 F.3d 1190, 1195 (Fed.Cir.1999) (emphasis added).

a. *What is "Undue Experimentation"?* The Federal Circuit, in *In re Wands,* 858 F.2d 731, 737 (Fed.Cir.1988), had this to say about "undue experimentation:"

The determination of what constitutes undue experimentation in a given case requires the application of a standard of reasonableness, having due regard for the nature of the invention and the state of the art. The test is not merely quantitative, since a considerable amount of experimentation is permissible, if it is merely routine, or if the specification in question provides a reasonable amount of guidance with respect to the direction in which the experimentation should proceed.... The term "undue experimentation" does not appear in the statute, ... Whether undue experimentation is needed is not a single, simple factual determination, but rather is a conclusion reached by weighing many factual considerations....

Factors to be considered in determining whether a disclosure would require undue experimentation ... include (1) the quantity of experimentation necessary, (2) the amount of direction or guidance presented, (3) presence or absence of working examples, (4) the nature of the invention, (5) the state of the prior art, (6) the relative skill of those in the art, (7) the predictability or unpredictability of the art, and (8) the breadth of the claims.

See also *Enzo Biochem, Inc. v. Calgene, Inc.,* 188 F.3d 1362, 1371–72 (Fed.Cir.1999) (in applying the *Wands* factors to *inter partes* litigation, the court noted that "[i]n both the *ex parte* and *inter partes* contexts, an enablement determination is made retrospectively, i.e., by looking back to the filing date of the patent application and determining whether undue experimentation would have been required to make and use the claimed invention at that time").

b. *Specification Commensurate With Claims.* To satisfy the commensurate requirement, the scope of the claims must bear a reasonable correlation to the scope of enablement provided by the specification to persons of ordinary skill in the art. *In re Fisher,* 427 F.2d 833, 839 (CCPA 1970). It is common to look at the level of predictability in the relevant art when making this determination. *In re Vaeck,* 947 F.2d 488, 495 (Fed.Cir.1991).

c. *Pioneer Inventions.* The term "pioneer" was defined by the Supreme Court in *Boyden Power–Brake Co. v. Westinghouse,* 170 U.S. 537, 561–62 (1898):

This word, although used somewhat loosely, is commonly understood to denote a patent covering a function never before performed, a wholly novel device, or one of such novelty and importance as to mark a distinct step in the progress of the art, as distinguished from a mere improvement or perfection of what had gone before. Most conspicuous examples of such patents are the one to Howe of the sewing machine; to Morse of the electrical telegraph; and to Bell of the telephone.

In *Hogan,* the Federal Circuit made much of the fact that pioneer inventions "deserve broad claims to the broad concept." But the Federal court has subsequently downplayed the importance of pioneer status, noting that such does not translate into a lower enablement standard. *See Plant Genetic Systems, N.V. v. DeKalb Genetics Corporation,* 315 F.3d 1335, 1339–41 (Fed.Cir.2003) (dismissing statements in *Hogan* that pioneer inventors "deserve broad claims to the broad concept" as "unconvincing" and "extended dicta"). *See* John R. Thomas, *The Question Concerning Patent Law and Pioneer Inventions,* 10 HIGH TECH. L.J. 35 (1995).

2. *Claim Breadth as Leading Edge or Trailing Edge Issue.* The fundamental problem of claim scope, addressed in *O'Reilly* and *Hogan* arises both as a front-end or leading edge problem—how broad a claim should the Patent Office grant and the courts uphold—and as a back-end or trailing edge problem—how broad an interpretation should the courts give to claims in assessing infringement. The first is determined by applying the Section 112 written description or enablement requirements; the second is determined by applying judicially-developed doctrine. Is one context superior to the other? In the second context, the PTO and a reviewing court may not appreciate how broad a claim is in relation to the disclosure, which may become an issue only after subsequent technology developments. In *Hogan*, developments after the original filing but before a final decision on patentability made it clear that a claim to a "solid" plastic, illustrated by a crystalline example, might literally include the later developed amorphous form of the plastic.

3. *The Filing Date Revisited.* The Federal Circuit, in *In re Wright*, 999 F.2d 1557 (Fed.Cir.1993), affirmed the PTO's rejection of a claim pertaining to a "live, non-pathogenic vaccine for a pathogenic RNA virus." The following is an excerpt from the *Wright* opinion:

> The Examiner took the position in her Examiner's Answer that the claims presently on appeal are not supported by an enabling disclosure because one of ordinary skill in the art would have had to engage in undue experimentation in February 1983 (the effective filing date of Wright's application) to practice the subject matter of these claims, given their breadth, the unpredictability in the art, and the limited guidance Wright provides in his application. . . .

> To support the foregoing, the Examiner relied upon an article by Thomas J. Matthews *et al.*, ... [published in 1988]. This article indicates that AIDS retroviruses, which represent only a subset of all RNA viruses, were known even as late as 1988 to show great diversity. . . .

> The Matthews *et al.* article, published approximately 5 years after the effective filing date of Wright's application, adequately supports the [PTO's] position that, in February 1983, the physiological activity of RNA viruses was sufficiently unpredictable that Wright's success in developing his specific . . . virus vaccine would not have led one of ordinary skill in the art to believe reasonably that all living organisms could be immunized against infection by any pathogenic RNA virus by inoculating them with a live virus. . . .

> Wright argues that he has constructed successfully [a] . . . recombinant vaccine according to the present invention, . . . and that these developments illustrate that the art is not so unpredictable as to require undue experimentation. However, all of these developments occurred after the effective filing date of Wright's application and are of no significance regarding what one skilled in the art believed as of that date. [footnote 8: We note . . . that the issue is not what the state of the art is today or what a skilled artisan today would believe, but rather what the state of the art was in February 1983 and what a skilled artisan would have believed at that time].

999 F.2d at 1560, 1562–63.

Is the court in *Wright* consistent, internally, or with *Hogan*, in its treatment of post-filing date evidence? On the one hand, it criticizes the applicant for relying on successful post-filing date experiments showing that his technique for creating a vaccine worked for other animal species and other tumor retroviruses. On the other hand, it approves of the PTO's reliance on the post-filing Matthews article, which described the difficulties in developing vaccines against retroviruses, especially against HIV. Perhaps there is no inconsistency because the PTO used the Matthews article to show state of the art at the time Wright filed his application in 1983. We know from *Hogan* that such use of post-filing information is permissible.

In this case, the applicant claimed a "vaccine", and the court cites a dictionary definition of a vaccine as including the ability to confer immunity. Assume that it was much easier to show that compositions created using Wright's method would cause some immune response (for example, by inducing some antibody production) than to show that the composition would actually confer total immunity. Could the applicant have improved his position with regard to enablement if he only claimed a composition that was capable of causing such an "immunological response" to a pathogenic RNA virus? Would such a claim meet the utility requirement? Would a patent with such a claim be as commercially effective as one directed to vaccines?

4. *The Many Forms of the Enablement Rejection.* The Federal Circuit has noted that the enablement rejection "takes several forms." In *In re Cortright*, 165 F.3d 1353, 1356 (Fed.Cir.1999), the court stated that:

> The PTO will make a scope of enablement rejection where the written description enables something within the scope of the claims, but the claims are not limited to that scope.... This type of rejection is marked by language stating that the specification does not enable one of ordinary skill to use the invention commensurate with the scope of the claims. On the other hand, if the written description does not enable any subject matter with the scope of the claims, the PTO will make a general enablement rejection, stating that the specification does not teach how to make or use the invention.

5. *Examples.* In most fields of science and technology, the practical and accepted way to teach how to make and use an invention is by way of example. Inventors commonly set forth one or more specific examples.

a. Earlier court decisions did not require the inventor to provide a specific example. See e.g, *In re Robins*, 429 F.2d 452, 457 (CCPA 1970) ("[R]epresentative examples are not required by the statute and are not an end in themselves. Rather, they are a means by which certain requirements of the statute may be satisfied."). Nevertheless, the fewer the examples and the less "predictable" and more complex the technology, the more difficult it is to support a broad claim. See e.g., *In re Strahilevitz*, 668 F.2d 1229, 1232 (CCPA 1982) ("We recognize that working examples are desirable in complex technologies and that detailed examples can satisfy the statutory enablement requirement. Indeed, the inclusion of such examples here might well have avoided a lengthy and, no doubt, expensive appeal. As acknowledged by the board, examples are not required to satisfy section 112, first paragraph.") In *Glass*, supra, the specification included no specific example and the claims were held not enabled. In Wright, the specification gave only one example, and the broad claims were held not enabled.

b. Prophetic Examples. Consistent with the constructive reduction to practice theory discussed above, it is presently accepted that, at least in some technologies, an applicant may include "prophetic" or "constructive" examples. To avoid any misrepresentation, constructive examples are required to be written in the present rather than the past tense. See *Atlas Powder Co. v. E.I. du Pont De Nemours & Co.*, 750 F.2d 1569, 1578 (Fed.Cir.1984). Do you think prophetic examples should be permitted? What are the problems associated with them? See S. Leslie Misrock and Stephen S. Rabinowitz, The Inventor's Gamble: Written Description and Prophetic Claiming of Biotechnology Inventions, SIDE BAR, at the end of this Chapter.

6. *The "Famous" Interference Over Plastics. Hogan* dealt with an application that was involved in the truly "famous" four-party interference over the basic plastic, crystalline polypropylene. The interference in the Patent Office, subsequent trial *de novo* in the District Court of Delaware, and appeal to the Third Circuit Court of Appeals stretched on for 28 years and consumed the entire careers of patent lawyers. Phillips eventually won the interference, see *Standard Oil Co. v. Montedison, S.p.A.*, 494 F.Supp. 370 (D.Del.1980), *aff'd*, 664 F.2d 356 (3d Cir.1981), *cert. denied*, 456 U.S. 915 (1982), and in 1980 obtained a patent extending for 17 years based on its 1953 patent application. *See United States Steel Corp. v. Phillips Petroleum Co.*, 865 F.2d 1247 (Fed.Cir.1989). The Polypropylene Interference is often held up as an extreme example of the evils of the United States first-to-invent patent priority system and as a good argument for adopting a simpler "first-to-file" priority system.

B. BEST MODE

The last phrase of the first paragraph of Section 112 provides that the specification "shall set forth the best mode contemplated by the inventor of carrying out his invention." This provision requires the inventor to disclose not only how to make and use the claimed invention, but the *best* way to do so. The purpose of the best mode requirement is to prevent inventors from obtaining patent protection while concealing from the public preferred embodiments of their claimed invention.

The Federal Circuit has constructed a two-part test to determine compliance with the best mode requirement:

> The first is whether, at the time the inventor filed his patent application, he knew of a mode of practicing his claimed invention that he considered to be better than any other. This part of the inquiry is wholly subjective, and resolves whether the inventor must disclose any facts in addition to those sufficient for enablement. If the inventor in fact contemplated such a preferred mode, the second part of the analysis compares what he knew with what he disclosed—is the disclosure adequate to enable one skilled in the art to practice the best mode or, in other words, has the inventor "concealed" his preferred mode from the "public"? Assessing the *adequacy* of the disclosure, as opposed to its *necessity,* is largely an objective inquiry that depends upon the scope of the claimed invention and the level of skill in the art.

Chemcast Corp. v. Arco Industries Corp. Inc., 913 F.2d 923, 927–28 (Fed. Cir.1990) (emphasis in original). The first (or objective) part of the test is explored in *Glaxo, Inc. v. Novopharm, Ltd.* immediately below; and the second (or subjective) aspect of the test is discussed in *Great Northern Corp. v. Henry Molded Products, Inc.*, which follows *Glaxo.*

1. SUBJECTIVE INVENTOR PREFERENCE ON FILING DATE

As noted above, section 112 requires disclosure of the best mode "contemplated by the inventor;" not the "best" mode in any absolute sense. Thus, a best mode attack on a patent will fail absent evidence that the *inventor* knew at the time of application of a best mode and yet concealed it, as explored below in *Glaxo.*

Glaxo Inc. v. Novopharm Ltd.

52 F.3d 1043 (Fed.Cir.1995).

■ Before ARCHER, CHIEF JUDGE, RICH, and MAYER, CIRCUIT JUDGES.

■ Opinion for the court filed by CIRCUIT JUDGE RICH. Dissenting opinion filed by CIRCUIT JUDGE MAYER.

■ RICH, CIRCUIT JUDGE.

Novopharm Ltd. (Novopharm) appeals the judgment of the United States District Court for the Eastern District of North Carolina, *Glaxo, Inc. v. Novopharm Ltd.*, 830 F.Supp. 871, 29 U.S.P.Q.2D 1126 (E.D.N.C.1993), that United States Patent No. 4,521,431 was not invalid and was infringed, and enjoining Novopharm from the commercial manufacture or sale of the patented crystalline form of ranitidine hydrochloride. We affirm.

Background

Glaxo Inc. and Glaxo Group Ltd. (collectively Glaxo) are the owner and exclusive United States licensee, respectively, of United States Patent No. 4,521,431 ('431 patent). The '431 patent claims a specific crystalline form of the compound ranitidine hydrochloride, designated as "Form 2," which Glaxo markets as an antiulcer medication under the brand name Zantac.[1] The '431 patent issued on June 4, 1985.

In 1976, Glaxo chemists investigating potential antiulcer medications synthesized an aminoalkyl furan derivative, later named ranitidine, which proved to be a potent histamine blocker, inhibiting the secretion of stomach acid. Later that year, Glaxo filed an application for a patent on ranitidine in the United Kingdom. It followed with an application for a United States patent, which issued as No. 4,128,658 ('658 patent) on December 5, 1978. The '658 patent claims a number of structurally similar compounds, including ranitidine and its hydrochloride salt. It discloses one method for preparing ranitidine hydrochloride, set forth in the '658 patent as Example 32.[2]

Glaxo prepared large quantities of ranitidine hydrochloride between 1977 and 1980 for use in toxicology and clinical studies. Instead of using the process of Example 32, however, Glaxo's chemists prepared this material using a similar process that they labelled Process 3A. They later developed a more efficient method that they called Process 3B. Until April 15, 1980, both Process 3A and Process 3B yielded ranitidine hydrochloride identical in all respects to that originally produced using the Example 32 procedure.

On that date, however, Glaxo's Derek Crookes used Process 3B to prepare crystalline ranitidine hydrochloride that was visibly different from

---

1. The '431 patent also claims various pharmaceutical compositions and methods of using Form 2 ranitidine hydrochloride. These claims are not at issue in this case. Claims 1 and 2 of the '431 patent, in issue here, read:

1. Form 2 ranitidine hydrochloride characterized by an infra-red spectrum as a mull in mineral oil showing the following main peaks: [list of peaks]

2. Form 2 ranitidine hydrochloride according to claim 1 further characterized by the following x-ray powder diffraction pattern expressed in terms of "d" spacings and relative intensities (1) (s = strong, m = medium, w = weak, v = very, d = diffuse) and obtained by the Debye Scherrer method in a 114.6 mm diameter camera by exposure for 12 hours to CoK_a radiation and for 3 hours to CuK_a radiation.

2. Developed by Glaxo's David Collin in June 1977, that method involves dissolving ranitidine in industrial methylated spirit containing dissolved hydrogen chloride gas. Ethyl acetate is added to the solution, and ranitidine hydrochloride precipitates from solution as a crystalline solid characterized by a melting point of 133°–134° C.

all previous batches of the salt. The difference was confirmed by infra-red (IR) spectroscopy and x-ray powder diffraction, which revealed that the new product was a crystalline form, or polymorph, of ranitidine hydrochloride that differed from the previously known form. Glaxo began to refer to this new polymorph as Form 2 ranitidine hydrochloride (designating the old polymorph as Form 1).

Because Form 2 had better filtration and drying properties, making it better suited for commercial applications, Glaxo decided to proceed with commercialization of Form 2 rather than Form 1. Form 2 was hampered by poor flow properties, however, which made the material difficult to measure and dispense in its pure form. Accordingly, Glaxo scientists developed a novel azeotroping process[3] to granulate the Form 2 salt, which made it much easier to make into pharmaceutical compositions. This process was the subject of a British patent application that Glaxo eventually abandoned without disclosing the process to the public.

Glaxo filed a patent application covering Form 2 ranitidine hydrochloride in the United Kingdom on October 1, 1980. It filed a United States application thereon the next year, which eventually issued as the '431 patent in suit. When George Graham Brereton, Glaxo's patent officer initially charged with pursuing the United States application, learned of the azeotropic granulation process and Glaxo's desire to keep that process secret, he recommended that Glaxo not claim pharmaceutical compositions of the Form 2 salt for fear of violating the best mode requirement. Brereton apparently believed that disclosure of the azeotroping process would be necessary because it was the best way to make the Form 2 salt for use in preparing pharmaceutical compositions. He later moved to another position at Glaxo. The U.S. application was eventually amended to include pharmaceutical composition claims, but Glaxo did not amend the specification to disclose the azeotroping process.

On August 9, 1991, Novopharm Ltd. filed an Abbreviated New Drug Application (ANDA) with the Food and Drug Administration (FDA), seeking FDA approval to manufacture and sell a generic version of Form 2 ranitidine hydrochloride beginning December 5, 1995, the expiration date of the '658 patent, well before the expiration date of the '431 patent in 2002. Glaxo filed this suit for patent infringement on November 13, 1991, alleging technical infringement of claims 1 and 2 of the '431 patent by the ANDA filing as provided in 35 U.S.C. § 271(e)(2) (1988). Novopharm admitted infringement of the claims, but contended that the '431 patent was invalid because it was anticipated by the disclosure of the '658 patent.

---

3. Azeotroping is a technique for separating a chemical mixture, the components of which would otherwise be difficult to separate because of the similarity of their boiling points. An additional substance is added to the mixture, selected for its ability to interact with a component of the original mixture to form an azeotrope—a mixture of substances "the composition of which does not change upon distillation." *See* McGraw–Hill Dictionary of Scientific and Technical Terms 162 (4th ed. 1989). If the proper substance is selected, the resulting azeotrope will have a boiling point that differs substantially from the desired component of the original mixture. The desired component can then be successfully separated from the azeotrope by distillation. See Hawley's Condensed Chemical Dictionary 109 (11th ed. 1987).

Novopharm later amended its answer to add the defense of inequitable conduct arising from alleged false and misleading affidavits provided to the U.S. Patent and Trademark Office (PTO) during prosecution of the applications from which the '431 patent issued. Finally, on June 21, 1993, Novopharm sought summary judgment based on a third defense, Glaxo's alleged failure to disclose the best mode of practicing the claimed invention. The trial court denied the motion, and the case was tried to the court beginning on August 9, 1993.

... The [district] court ... concluded that there was no violation of the best mode requirement because Novopharm had not proved that Crookes, the inventor, knew of the best mode, the statute and this court's precedent providing that knowledge by the inventor himself is required.... [T]he court held that the '431 patent was not invalid, was enforceable and infringed, and ordered that Novopharm refrain from commercial manufacture or sale of Form 2 ranitidine hydrochloride before the '431 patent expires. Novopharm appeals.

Discussion

... Novopharm ... asserts that Glaxo failed to disclose the best mode of practicing the invention, that is, the azeotroping process it uses to formulate the claimed Form 2 ranitidine hydrochloride into pharmaceutical compositions. The best mode defense arose little more than two months before trial just after Glaxo produced documents based on which Novopharm filed a motion for summary judgment of invalidity for failure to disclose the best mode. Less than a week before trial, the district court denied Novopharm's motion stating that "the court cannot hold as a matter of law that Dr. Crookes knew that the azeotroping process was the best mode of manufacturing ranitidine hydrochloride, and summary judgment must therefore be denied." Glaxo, Inc. v. Novopharm Ltd., 830 F.Supp. 869, 871 (E.D.N.C.1993). The district court further stated that it reserved for trial "ruling on the question of whether and to what extent the knowledge of other Glaxo employees and agents may be imputed to Dr. Crookes for purposes of finding a best mode analysis [sic, violation]." *Id.*

At trial, Novopharm produced evidence that officials at Glaxo knew of the azeotroping process and considered it to be the best mode of making Form 2 ranitidine hydrochloride into a pharmaceutical composition. Novopharm argued in district court, as it does here, that the knowledge of the azeotroping process by Glaxo officials should be imputed to inventor Crookes for purposes of finding a best mode violation.

The trial court found Novopharm's argument to have some "intuitive appeal" since Glaxo "has enjoyed the monopoly the issued patent provides." ... Indeed, the trial court stated that if it were to impute the knowledge of others to the inventor of the '431 patent, "then clearly the court would be required to find a best mode violation." ... The trial court concluded, however, that the statute, 35 U.S.C. § 112, first paragraph, and this court's holding in *Texas Instruments Inc. v. United States International Trade Commission*, 871 F.2d 1054, 10 U.S.P.Q.2D 1257 (Fed.Cir.1989) do not permit using imputed knowledge in a best mode analysis. The district court concluded that Novopharm "as a matter of law ... failed to show

the '431 patent should be invalidated based on a best mode violation." ...
On appeal, Novopharm asserts that the district court erred as a matter of
law in holding that a best mode defense cannot be found in the absence of
proof that the inventor knew of that mode.

The statutory provision at issue sets forth that: "The specification ...
shall set forth the best mode contemplated by the inventor of carrying out
his invention." 35 U.S.C. § 112, first paragraph (1988).

The statutory language could not be clearer. The best mode of carrying
out an invention, indeed if there is one, to be disclosed is that "contemplated by the inventor." That the best mode "belongs" to the inventor finds
consistent support in previous statutory language as well.[6] Additionally, the
commentary on the 1952 Patent Act states with respect to the best mode
provision that "[t]his requirement, it should be noted, is not absolute, since
it only requires disclosure of the best mode contemplated by the inventor,
presumably at the time of filing the application." P.J. Federico, *Commentary on the New Patent Act*, 35 U.S.C.A. §§ 1, 25 (1954).

In arguing that Glaxo did not comply with the best mode requirement
of § 112, first paragraph, Novopharm relies on *Amgen, Inc. v. Chugai
Pharmaceutical Co.*, 927 F.2d 1200, 18 U.S.P.Q.2D 1016 (Fed.Cir.), *cert.
denied*, 502 U.S. 856, 112 S.Ct. 169, 116 L.Ed.2d 132 (1991), for the
proposition that the best mode requirement lies at the heart of the
statutory *quid pro quo* of the patent system. This is true enough. However,
Amgen, consistent with the statute, speaks of the best mode requirement in
terms of the best mode contemplated by the inventor.... In fact, as we
have previously stated, the sole purpose of the best mode requirement "is
to restrain inventors from applying for patents while at the same time
concealing from the public preferred embodiments of *their inventions* which
they have in fact conceived." *Chemcast Corp. v. Arco Indus. Corp.*, 913 F.2d
923, 926, 16 U.S.P.Q.2D 1033, 1035 (Fed.Cir.1990) (emphasis added) (*quoting In re Gay*, 309 F.2d 769, 772, 135 USPQ 311, 315 (CCPA 1962))....

The best mode inquiry focuses on the inventor's state of mind at the
time he filed his application, raising a subjective factual question.... The
specificity of disclosure required to comply with the best mode requirement
must be determined by the knowledge of facts within the possession of the
inventor at the time of filing the application....

That the best mode inquiry is grounded in knowledge of the inventor is
even more evident upon contrasting the best mode requirement of § 112
with the enablement requirement of that section.... "Enablement looks to
placing the subject matter of the claims generally in the possession of the

---

6. The 1793 Act stated: "in the case of any machine [the inventor] shall fully explain the
principle, and the several modes in which he has contemplated the application of that principle
or character, by which it may be distinguished from other inventions." Act of Feb. 21, 1793,
ch. 11, § 3, 1 Stat. 318.

The 1836 Act stated: "in case of any machine, [the inventor] shall fully explain the principle,
and the several modes in which he has contemplated the application of the principle or
character by which it may be distinguished from other inventions." Act of July 4, 1836, ch.
357, § 6, 5 Stat. 117.

The Act of 1870 changed the "several modes" provision of the previous Acts to the present-day
"best mode" Act of July 7, 1870, ch. 230, § 26, 16 Stat. 198.

public." ... Best mode looks to whether specific instrumentalities and techniques have been developed by the inventor and known to him at the time of filing as the best way of carrying out the invention.... The enablement requirement, thus, looks to the objective knowledge of one of ordinary skill in the art, while the best mode inquiry is a subjective, factual one, looking to the state of the mind of the inventor. Indeed, recently this court in addressing whether an applicant's best mode had to be updated upon filing a continuation application affirmed that the best mode requirement "focuses on what the *inventor* knows." *Transco Prods. Inc. v. Performance Contracting, Inc.*, 38 F.3d 551, 558, 32 U.S.P.Q.2D 1077, 1083 (Fed.Cir.1994) (emphasis added), cert. denied, ___ U.S. ___, 115 S.Ct. 1102, 130 L.Ed.2d 1069 (1995).

Based on the clear wording of the statute and our case law, the trial court properly rejected Novopharm's "imputed knowledge" best mode defense. As the trial court correctly noted, we held in *Texas Instruments* that there was no violation of the best mode requirement of § 112 by reason of knowledge of the purported best mode on the part of T.I. employees, other than the inventor, in the manufacturing group when the inventor did not know of or conceal this best mode....

There is simply no evidence in the record before us, indeed Novopharm points to none, that the inventor of the '431 patent knew of and concealed the azeotroping process when his application was filed. Inventor Crookes in a declaration in opposition to Novopharm's best mode summary judgment motion stated "I did not know of any azeotroping of ranitidine hydrochloride, or of its benefits, prior to commencement of this litigation. I did not—indeed, could not—consider the azeotrope process a 'best mode' of making ranitidine hydrochloride tablets at the time of filing any patent application." Crookes indicated that he worked in a different department than those who developed the azeotroping process.

As the district court observed, the record does indicate, however, that others at Glaxo knew of the azeotroping process and knew that this process would be used commercially to produce pharmaceutical forms of the claimed product.[7] The record also indicates that these individuals as well as their English patent agent were concerned that failure to disclose the azeotroping process may present a best mode problem. However, in neither instance did Glaxo nor its patent agent appropriately consider that inventor Crookes knew nothing of the azeotroping process. That Glaxo thought it may have a best mode problem either because of its incorrect or incomplete consideration of U.S. patent law does not make it so.

Novopharm maintains that Glaxo intentionally isolated Crookes from knowledge of the azeotroping process leaving "it to others to commercialize and reduce the invention to practice." Thus, Novopharm fears that Glaxo purposefully prevented the inventor from gaining knowledge of the most advantageous application for his invention, the azeotroping process, so that

---

7. The claims at issue are not directed to a pharmaceutical compound. Therefore, there may be a question whether the azeotroping process is indeed the best mode of carrying out the claimed invention. *See Chemcast*, 913 F.2d at 927, 16 U.S.P.Q.2D at 1036. In view of our decision, however, it is not necessary for us to reach this issue.

that process could be maintained as a trade secret. That fear does not equate with a best mode violation.

In this case, Crookes was unconcerned with the commercialization of the claimed compound. It is undisputed that Crookes invented a compound and was not involved in whatever processes were to be used to commercially produce it. Therefore, whether Glaxo deliberately walled off the inventor is irrelevant to the issue of failure of his application to disclose the best mode known to him.

In arguing that Crookes was screened from knowledge, Novopharm relies on testimony of Glaxo's in-house patent agent that Crookes was not consulted "at any time" during the preparation of the application that matured into the '431 patent. This however, completely ignores the requirement that patents are applied for "in the name of the actual inventor or inventors" according to 37 C.F.R. § 1.41(a) (1983). The inventor(s) must submit an oath or declaration attesting that they have "reviewed and understand[ ] the contents of the specification" and believe "the named inventor or inventors to be the original and first inventor or inventors of the subject matter which is claimed and for which a patent is sought." 37 C.F.R. § 1.63(b)(1), (2) (1992); see also 37 C.F.R. § 1.51(a)(2) (1992). Moreover, this court in *Sun Studs, Inc. v. Applied Theory Associates, Inc.*, 772 F.2d 1557, 1568, 227 USPQ 81, 89 (Fed.Cir.1985), recognized that 35 U.S.C. § 111 (1988) "requires that the *inventor* must apply for the patent ...." (emphasis in original). Novopharm has not alleged that these requirements were violated.

It is therefore presumed that Crookes, the inventor and applicant, must have reviewed the specification and signed the required declaration before the application was filed. Without more, Novopharm is simply wrong when it alleges that Crookes had nothing to do with determining what needed to be disclosed in his patent application.

Novopharm additionally contends that looking solely to the inventor's knowledge in a best mode analysis "makes a mockery of the best mode requirement, and fosters a 'head in the sand' mentality for corporate applicants."

However, the practical reality is that inventors in most every corporate scenario cannot know all of the technology in which their employers are engaged. Therefore, whether intentionally or not, inventors will be effectively isolated from research no matter how relevant it is to the field in which they are working. Separating scenarios in which employers unintentionally isolate inventors from relevant research from instances in which employers deliberately set out to screen inventors from research, and finding a best mode violation in the latter case, would ignore the very words of § 112, first paragraph, and the case law as it has developed, which consistently has analyzed the best mode requirement in terms of knowledge of and concealment by the inventor. Congress was aware of the differences between inventors and assignees, see 35 U.S.C. §§ 100(d) and 152, and it specifically limited the best mode required to that contemplated by the inventor. We have no authority to extend the requirement beyond the limits set by Congress.

The dissent argues that imputing knowledge of others than the inventor to the inventor for purposes of considering what was "contemplated by the inventor" in a best mode analysis "may be necessary under appropriate circumstances, to protect the public's 'paramount interest in seeing that patent monopolies spring from backgrounds free from fraud or other inequitable conduct.' " The dissent contends that such knowledge can be imputed to the inventor under principles of agency law stating that, "[a]n agent's acts and knowledge can be imputed to the principal when necessary to protect the interests of others, so long as the acts or knowledge in question fall within the scope of the agent's authority," *citing* Restatement (Second) of Agency, § 261.

The Restatement defines agency as "the fiduciary relation which results from the manifestation of consent by one person to another that the other shall act on his behalf and subject to his control, and consent, by the other so to act." Restatement (Second) of Agency, § 1.

The flaw in the dissent's analysis is that a patent attorney[8] does not enter into an agency relationship with the inventor for purposes of what is disclosed in the inventor's patent application. Simply, the inventor never authorizes his patent attorney to "act on his behalf" with respect to disclosing the invention. Or, in the terms used by the dissent, the scope of the patent attorney's authority does not include inventing, *i.e.*, either supplementing or supplanting the inventor's knowledge of his own invention. Rather, the information disclosed in the inventor's patent application must be that which is actually known to him. The statute requires that he submit an oath to this effect. *See* 35 U.S.C. § 115 (1988).

An agency relationship may exist during prosecution before the PTO where the patent attorney is acting on the inventor's behalf. *See* 37 C.F.R. § 1.56(a) (1992). An agency relationship does not exist, however, with respect to what an inventor must disclose in order to obtain a patent on his invention, which includes, of course, any best mode under § 112. Therefore, in addition to being inconsistent with § 112, as explained above, because an agency relationship does not exist for purposes of what is disclosed in a patent application, it would be improper to impute a patent attorney's knowledge of a best mode to the inventor for purposes of finding a best mode violation.

In any case, the dissent's application of general agency principles to the analysis of best mode disclosure under § 112 is an entirely new idea and is not existing law.

* * *

AFFIRMED.

■ MAYER, CIRCUIT JUDGE, dissenting.

With this case, the court blesses corporate shell games resulting from organizational gerrymandering and willful ignorance by which one can

---

8. A "patent agent" is subsumed within this term as a patent agent acts as the inventor's attorney before the PTO. The label "patent agent" does not mean there is an agency relationship, rather than an attorney-client relationship, between the inventor and such individual for all purposes.

secure the monopoly of a patent while hiding the best mode of practicing the invention the law expects to be made public in return for its protection. Because I believe this is a perverse interpretation of the law, I dissent.

* * *

Glaxo first suggests that the azeotropic granulation process was not an appropriate candidate for disclosure because it fell outside the scope of the claimed invention. Rather, Glaxo says the process is simply a production technique useful in the formulation of ranitidine hydrochloride into pharmaceutical compositions. It says the process is therefore relevant, if at all, only to the claims of the '431 patent that cover such compositions. No such claims are at issue here, so Glaxo says the best mode should not be considered.

But the statutory language demands that the patent disclose the best mode of "carrying out" the claimed invention. As the district court recognized, this language encompasses not only modes of making the invention, but of using it as well. *See Christianson v. Colt Indus. Operating Corp.*, 822 F.2d 1544, 1563, 3 U.S.P.Q.2D 1241, 1255 (Fed.Cir.1987), *vacated on other grounds*, 486 U.S. 800 (1988). The azeotroping process was the best way to formulate raw ranitidine hydrochloride into pharmaceutical compositions suitable for use as a drug in human patients, the only use Glaxo contemplated for the invention. Glaxo admits the process was not generally known to those skilled in the art. Accordingly, the court could have found that disclosure of the process was required by section 112, so long as the other, subjective, elements of the best mode test were met....

The best mode inquiry begins with what the inventor knew when he filed his application. This subjective part of the inquiry traditionally rests on the factual question whether the inventor actually contemplated a preferred mode. *Chemcast*, 913 F.2d at 928, 16 U.S.P.Q.2D at 1036. But the inquiry is not limited to the inventor's actual knowledge.

* * *

... *Texas Instruments* stands only for the unremarkable proposition that there is no best mode violation where the inventor knew of the alleged mode and did not consider it to be a part of the preferred embodiment. It says nothing about whether specific knowledge of a best mode by a corporate assignee/employer may be imputed to the inventor/employee. Nor does any other precedent of this court.

As the district court recognized, "Glaxo, and not Crookes individually, ... both directed the patent prosecution and has enjoyed the monopoly the issued patent provides." ... Glaxo employees acted as agents for inventor Crookes during prosecution of the U.S. application. They were also agents for Glaxo, the assignee of the application and later the owner of the '431 patent. And that is the crucial point: Glaxo, not Crookes, brought this suit against Novopharm for infringement of the patent. Accordingly, Glaxo's conduct and knowledge during prosecution is important to the resolution of this case; it is not irrelevant, as the court says.

Glaxo says, and the court agrees, that it did not have to disclose the azeotroping process because Crookes did not know of that method of preparing pharmaceutical compositions of Form 2 ranitidine hydrochloride. On the record before us, one wonders how Glaxo could have been sure of what Crookes knew. Brereton, the Glaxo employee charged with initiating the application for the '431 patent, testified that he did not consult Crookes, the named inventor, at any time. Instead, in accordance with Glaxo's standard patent policy, Brereton conferred with Crookes' superiors to obtain all of the information necessary to secure a patent on the invention. It strikes me as incongruous to rely on the inventor's actual knowledge here if Glaxo indeed thought that knowledge was so insignificant that it did not even merit consultation during preparation of the application.[9] At the very least, the district court should have given Novopharm the chance at discovery about just what Crookes in fact knew.

But I believe that even absent further discovery the district court could have found a best mode violation in this case. As the district court stated,

> [i]t is undisputed, however, Brereton and other officers within Glaxo believed azeotroping was the best mode of preparing ranitidine hydrochloride for pharmaceutical use, and Glaxo actually utilized this method in the commercial production of ranitidine hydrochloride. These officials within Glaxo made a deliberate choice not to reveal what they believed to be the best mode of making the patented invention, but instead to protect the knowledge as a trade secret.

830 F.Supp. at 881. This recitation suggests that Glaxo set out to isolate Crookes from any knowledge about the azeotroping technique specifically to avoid the best mode disclosure requirements. If true, these circumstances would justify imputing knowledge to Crookes from Brereton and the other Glaxo employees who acted as agents for Crookes during the application process. I would remand to allow the district court to make the necessary factual findings and decide whether to impute that knowledge.

Imputing knowledge to an inventor may be necessary under appropriate circumstances, to protect the public's "paramount interest in seeing that patent monopolies spring from backgrounds free from fraud or other inequitable conduct." *Precision Instrument Mfg. Co. v. Automotive Maintenance Mach. Co.*, 324 U.S. 806, 816 (1945) (endorsing equitable doctrine of unclean hands in patent suits). "The possession and assertion of patent rights are 'issues of great moment to the public.'" . . . And the best mode requirement lies at the heart of this public interest. It is a vital part of the statutory quid pro quo that justifies a patent. . . . In return for a seventeen year monopoly the patentee must disclose his invention to the public. But he must go beyond simply informing the public of the bare outlines of the invention. He must also tell what he believes to be the best embodiment of the invention, and he must do so in a way that allows the public to practice that embodiment. This prevents the inventor from obtaining patent protection with a minimal disclosure that reveals only inferior forms of the

---

9. The court finds comfort in the regulations requiring that the inventor sign an oath attesting that he has reviewed the application, 37 C.F.R. §§ 1.41(a), 1.51(a)(2) & 1.63(b)(1), (2), reasoning that Glaxo must have at least let Crookes review the application before it was filed. But none of these regulations speaks to the best mode requirement. Nor are we told how Crookes could sign such an oath if he was never consulted before the application was filed. Perhaps the court has hit upon grounds for a charge of inequitable conduct against Glaxo that everyone else missed.

invention, while retaining for himself the most advantageous modes of carrying the invention into practice.... The court's pinched reading of the best mode requirement surely violates at least the spirit of this rule at the public's expense.

Imputing an agent's knowledge to the principal has sound roots in law and equity. An agent's acts and knowledge can be imputed to the principal when necessary to protect the interests of others, so long as the acts or knowledge in question fall within the scope of the agent's authority. Restatement (Second) of Agency, § 261 (principal liable for agent's fraud within scope of agency), § 274 (knowledge of agent acquiring property for principal imputed to principal); *see also American Soc. of Mechanical Engineers, Inc. v. Hydrolevel Corp.*, 456 U.S. 556, 566 (1982) (principal liable for antitrust violation based on agent's fraud within apparent authority). This precept is firmly rooted in patent law as well, in the traditional doctrine of inequitable conduct, whereby the inventor's duty to disclose material information to the Patent Office is extended to all those involved in the filing and prosecution of a patent application. See 37 C.F.R. § 1.56 (1994); *Fox Indus. v. Structural Preservation Sys.*, 922 F.2d 801, 804, 17 U.S.P.Q.2D 1579, 1581 (Fed.Cir.1990).

The fact that Crookes' agents knew about the process does not by itself justify imputing that knowledge to him. If he really was unfamiliar with the azeotroping process, that unfamiliarity may simply have resulted from the normal division of labor necessary within a large corporate enterprise. But the district court appears to have inferred a darker subtext—that Glaxo may have deliberately set out to screen this inventor from the azeotroping technique to conceal the process for itself.

The problem is that Glaxo's version of best mode, which the court now adopts, would allow, if not encourage, employers to isolate their employee/inventors from research directed to finding the most advantageous applications for their inventions, knowledge that the inventors would probably have had but for the employer's efforts to keep the work secret. As a result, inventors may have only limited perspective on the real value of their inventions, and can accordingly share only this limited perspective with the public. All the while, the employer/assignee will have a view of the big picture, fully aware, through its other employees, of superior modes of practicing the invention. But the assignee will be under no obligation to disclose those modes to the public. This deliberate subversion of the statutory disclosure would deprive the public of the benefits of the best mode of practicing the invention. There is no reason why this court should condone such abuse of the public trust....

I would hold that if there truly was such a pattern of deliberate concealment of information that would otherwise have been known to the inventor, the knowledge of those who sought to conceal that information and who now attempt to enforce the patent may be imputed to the inventor. The district court can refuse to enforce the patent and should be given the opportunity to do so with a correct understanding of its powers.

NOTES

1. *Timing and the Need to Update.* The critical time for complying with the best mode requirement is the filing date of the application. An inventor need not amend an application to add a best mode discovered after the filing date. Best mode compliance for a continuation application will be measured as of the filing date of the original application. *See Transco Products Inc. v. Performance Contracting, Inc.*, 38 F.3d 551, 557–58 (Fed.Cir.1994). The same is true of reissue applications, *see Dow Chemical Co. v. American Cyanamid Co.*, 615 F.Supp. 471, 482 (E.D. La. 1985), *aff'd*, 816 F.2d 617 (Fed.Cir.1987); and for U.S. applications claiming priority, the date of compliance is the foreign filing date. *See Tyler Refrigeration Corp. v. Kysor Indus. Corp.*, 601 F.Supp. 590, 605 (D.Del.1985), *aff'd*, 777 F.2d 687 (Fed. Cir.1985). Thus, if an inventor files an application promptly after preparation, he will avoid the risk that a specific better mode will be developed at some point after the preparation of an application, but before filing. Presumably, for continuation-in-part applications, the applicant must update the best mode for the new matter that is added. *See Applied Materials, Inc. v. Advanced Semiconductor Materials Am., Inc.*, 98 F.3d 1563, 1566 (Fed.Cir.1996) (see concurring opinion of Judge Mayer).

2. *Concealment—Intent.* Language in many judicial opinions suggests that a best mode violation only occurs if there was an "intent" to conceal. *See e.g., Hybritech Inc. v. Monoclonal Antibodies, Inc.*, 802 F.2d 1367 (Fed.Cir.1986), *infra.* Does this require proof of anything beyond (1) a subjective preference for a mode, and (2) an objective failure to disclose the mode? In *U.S. Gypsum Co. v. National Gypsum Co.*, 74 F.3d 1209 (Fed.Cir.1996), Judge Lourie gave a qualified answer, explaining that a manifestly inadequate disclosure of the best mode will violate the statute:

> Although it has been said that "[i]nvalidity for violation of the best mode requires intentional concealment of a better mode than was disclosed," *Brooktree Corp. v. Advanced Micro Devices, Inc.*, 977 F.2d 1555, 1575, 24 U.S.P.Q.2D 1401, 1415 (Fed.Cir.1992), the rule is not so limited. *Graco, Inc. v. Binks Mfg. Co.*, 60 F.3d 785, 789–90, 35 U.S.P.Q.2D 1255, 1258 (Fed.Cir.1995) (rejecting argument that intentional concealment is required for a best mode violation). A best mode violation may occur if the disclosure of the best mode is so objectively inadequate as to effectively conceal the best mode from the public. *Transco Prods.*, 38 F.3d at 560, 32 U.S.P.Q.2D at 1084 ("Even where there is a general reference to the best mode of practicing the claimed invention, the quality of the disclosure may be so poor as to effectively conceal it."); *Spectra–Physics, Inc. v. Coherent, Inc.*, 827 F.2d 1524, 1535 (Fed.Cir.1987) ("[O]nly evidence of 'concealment,' whether accidental or intentional, is considered.")....
>
> The "concealment" language of our case law originated in *In re Gay*, 309 F.2d 769, 135 USPQ 311 (CCPA 1962). In *Gay*, the Court of Customs and Patent Appeals (CCPA) explained that "the sole purpose of [the best mode] requirement is to restrain inventors from applying for patents while at the same time concealing from the public preferred embodiments of their inventions which they have in fact conceived." ... Subsequently, the CCPA clarified that "only evidence of concealment (whether accidental or intentional) is to be considered. That evidence, in order to result in affirmance of a best mode rejection, must tend to show that the quality of an applicant's best mode disclosure is so poor as to effectively result in concealment." *In re Sherwood*, 613 F.2d 809, 816, 204 USPQ 537, 544 (CCPA 1980).... We consider *Sherwood* to be binding precedent, and that, by its reference to "accidental" concealment, it holds that failure to find intentional concealment does not preclude a finding that the best mode requirement has been violated. We also note that the second inquiry concerning best mode compliance is an objective one, relating to whether the inventor effectively enabled his best mode of practicing the claimed invention. Inquiry into an intent to conceal, being subjective, is inconsistent with the objective nature of the second aspect of best mode compliance. It is not part of that analysis.

3. *Trap for the Unwary*? Is it wise policy to impose a requirement that makes so much (*i.e.*, the validity of a patent right) depend on what individuals contemplate at a precise point in time? Should a deliberate infringer of a patent on a pioneering invention be able to escape all liability by convincing a trier of fact (*e.g.* a jury), years after the patent application was filed and the patent issued, that a patent attorney neglected to include in the patent's specification a "mode" subjectively preferred by an inventor (who was technically brilliant but ignorant of the requirements of patent law)—even though the "mode" was fully disclosed to the public by other means soon after the patent application was filed? Should there be a means whereby an applicant, upon discovering an inadvertent best mode violation, could add the disclosure without losing the benefit of the original application filing date? Consider the implications of the "two function" theory regarding enablement, discussed *supra*.

4. *Who's Contemplation Counts*? As *Glaxo* notes, § 112 refers to the best mode "contemplated by the inventor." Often, in patent law, when the inventor assigns patent rights, usually to an employer, the assignee is deemed to assume the inventor's obligations. The *Glaxo* decision applies the best mode requirement literally. Why? Compare the judicial treatment of the § 102(b) "on sale" and "public use" bars, discussed in Chapter Four. Would you rely on the *Glaxo* case to advise a corporate client to set up a formal system for deliberately keeping the inventors of a basic technology ignorant of development efforts taking place before the filing date in order to be able to omit from the patent specification "modes" that are potentially valuable trade secrets?

5. *Foreign Inventors Seeking U.S. Patents.* *Glaxo* illustrates the difficulties that non-U.S. inventors and companies face in pursuing U.S. patents. The intricate best mode disclosure requirement is unique to the United States, but, to establish a right of priority in the United States, an applicant filing an application in another country must fully comply with U.S. disclosure requirements, including the best mode requirement. This means that an applicant who intends to pursue patent rights in the U.S. must, before filing a priority application in his own country, predict what must be disclosed to comply with the U.S. best mode requirement. In *Glaxo*, the assignee filed initially in Great Britain and deliberately omitted reference to the preferred process for converting the compound into a pharmaceutical composition based on its patent counselor's prediction that the U.S. best mode requirement would not require disclosure of the process so long as the application contained only claims to the compound and not to compositions or therapeutic methods. This advice may or may not have been accurate, but, years later, the patent escaped a best mode violation for a different reason (no personal knowledge by the inventor).

2.   ADEQUATE DISCLOSURE

The second prong of a best mode inquiry focuses on the adequacy of the disclosure. As explored in the *Great Northern* case below, analysis of this issue is very similar to the analysis under the enablement requirement discussed earlier.

Great Northern Corp. v. Henry Molded Products, Inc.

94 F.3d 1569 (Fed.Cir.1996).

■ Before MICHEL, CIRCUIT JUDGE, SMITH, SENIOR CIRCUIT JUDGE, and CLEVENGER, CIRCUIT JUDGE.

■ CLEVENGER, CIRCUIT JUDGE.

Henry Molded Products, Inc. (Henry Molded) seeks review of the decision of the United States District Court for the Eastern District of

Wisconsin ... which held that ... the 5,080,314 patent (the '314 patent) is invalid for failure to disclose the best mode.... We affirm....

I

Great Northern is the assignee of the '732 patent which discloses elongated bar members [made of expanded foam] that may be used to support rolls of material such as cellophane or steel.

* * *

Since about 1978, Great Northern has marketed and sold the ROLL-GUARD product embodying the invention claimed in the '732 patent.

Given the characteristics of expanded foam, a need arose to make a roll stacker of more environmentally friendly material. In response to this need, Henry Molded developed a molded pulp roll support called the STAKKER and received the '314 patent thereon. At about the same time, Great Northern developed and marketed its own molded pulp roll support called ROLLGUARD II.

Shortly after Henry Molded was issued the '314 patent, Great Northern filed suit alleging that Henry Molded's STAKKER product infringed Great Northern's '732 patent. Henry Molded counterclaimed alleging that Great Northern's ROLLGUARD II product infringed Henry Molded's '314 patent. After a two week trial, the jury issued the following special verdicts: (1) Henry Molded's STAKKER product does not infringe Great Northern's '732 patent; (2) claim 1 of Henry Molded's '314 patent is invalid due to anticipation; (3) the '314 patent is invalid for failure to disclose the best mode; (4) the '314 patent is not unenforceable due to inequitable conduct; and (5) Great Northern's ROLLGUARD II product infringes the '314 patent.

Upon completion of the jury trial, both parties renewed their motions for judgment as a matter of law. After considering these motions and hearing oral argument, the district court upheld the jury verdicts in all respects except for the jury's verdict that Great Northern's ROLLGUARD II product infringes the '314 patent, which the district court set aside....

II

By special verdict, the jury concluded that Great Northern proved by clear and convincing evidence that Henry Molded's '314 patent is invalid due to failure to disclose the best mode of carrying out the invention because the '314 patent does not disclose the use of diamond indentations (diamonds).[2] Henry Molded asserts that this verdict is erroneous. As explained below, we disagree because substantial evidence supports the jury's verdict on this issue.

---

2. These diamond-shaped indentations (or ribs) provide strength to the molded pulp, in part to prevent it from collapsing while still wet.

Title 35, section 112 provides, in pertinent part, that the specification "shall set forth the best mode contemplated by the inventor of carrying out his invention." 35 U.S.C. § 112 (1994). Evaluation of whether the best mode requirement has been satisfied entails two underlying factual inquiries. One must first determine whether the inventor subjectively contemplated a best mode of practicing the claimed invention at the time the patent application was filed.... If the inventor contemplated such a best mode, one must then determine whether, objectively, the specification adequately discloses that best mode such that those having ordinary skill in the art could practice it.... Because this best mode inquiry is a question of fact, ... our scope of review is limited to deciding whether substantial evidence supports the jury's verdict on this issue,....

A

As an initial matter, Henry Molded notes that the best mode requirement relates only to the best mode for practicing the invention and not to "production details." *See Transco Prods. Inc. v. Performance Contracting, Inc.*, 38 F.3d 551, 560 (Fed.Cir.1994); *Wahl Instruments, Inc. v. Acvious, Inc.*, 950 F.2d 1575, 1579–80 (Fed.Cir.1991). Seizing upon this language, Henry Molded contends that because the diamonds are added during the production process to maintain the shape of the unit while it is still wet so that it does not collapse, the diamonds merely constitute a production detail rather than the best mode of practicing the claimed invention.

Henry Molded is correct that our precedent recognizes the distinction between production details and the best mode of practicing the claimed invention. Our cases, however, employ the term "production detail" in two senses, neither of which supports Henry Molded's argument. We have used the term to refer to commercial considerations such as the equipment on hand, or prior relationships with suppliers that were satisfactory. *See Wahl*, 950 F.2d at 1581. Such commercial considerations do not constitute a best mode of practicing the claimed invention because they do not relate to the quality or nature of the invention. Our cases have also used "production details" to refer to details which do relate to the quality or nature of the invention but which need not be disclosed because they are routine—*i.e.*, details of production about which those of ordinary skill in the art would already know. In this latter scenario, the omitted detail constitutes a best mode but the disclosure is deemed adequate because the detail is routine.

According to our precedent, then, we cannot decide whether the diamonds constitute a best mode merely by examining whether the diamonds relate to the production process. Instead, we must determine whether the diamonds relate to the claimed invention or to commercial considerations. The invention claimed in the '314 patent is a molded pulp member for supporting rolls of material. The record makes clear that, at a minimum, STAKKERs designed to support large-diameter rolls could not be produced without the diamonds. This demonstrates that the diamonds are critical to practicing the claimed invention rather than simply a commercial consideration, such as which supplier to use. *Cf. Dana Corp. v. IPC Ltd. Partnership*, 860 F.2d 415, 418–19, 8 U.S.P.Q.2D 1692, 1695 (Fed.Cir.1988) (best mode violated when specification did not disclose surface treatment necessary for performance of claimed invention), *cert. denied*, 490 U.S. 1067, 109 S.Ct. 2068, 104 L.Ed.2d 633 (1989). Therefore, we conclude that the diamonds relate to the best mode for practicing the claimed invention.[3]

B

We must next determine whether the inventors contemplated this best mode when they filed their patent application. Henry Molded argues unsuccessfully that the inventors did not contemplate the use of diamonds until after the filing date, April 6, 1990. Michael Grubb testified, however, that as of April 6, 1990, the preferred way of making the STAKKER product was to use diamonds. This testimony is supported by Henry Molded's production drawing dated April 6, 1990, which shows diamonds being used on the STAKKER. This constitutes substantial evidence in support of the jury's implicit finding that the inventors contemplated use of the diamonds as of the patent application filing date. . . .

C

Finally, we must determine whether the specification adequately discloses the best mode such that those having ordinary skill in the art could practice it. Both parties concede that the specification makes no mention of the diamonds, and that therefore there is no disclosure of the best mode. Despite this lack of disclosure, Henry Molded argues on appeal that the best mode requirement is satisfied because the diamonds are a routine detail—*i.e.*, those of ordinary skill would have known to employ such diamonds even without being explicitly told to do so.

The record before us, however, reveals that Henry Molded never raised this argument at the trial level. We can find no testimony from trial which indicates whether or not the diamonds are routine and known to those of ordinary skill in the art.[4] At oral argument, this court asked Henry Molded's counsel for any record citations which supported its argument. Henry Molded provided none. . . . From this silence, we can only conclude that Henry Molded chose not to litigate this issue at trial and therefore waived it.[5]

---

3. Whether the diamonds constitute the second type of production detail, *i.e.,* a routine detail, relates to the adequacy of the disclosure, which we address below in subsection C.

4. In its appeal brief, Henry Molded asserts that "[c]o-inventor Moyer testified that it was obvious to add a rib to increase the strength in a molded pulp product." Because Henry Molded does not direct us to a record citation, we can only assume it refers to Mr. Moyer's testimony at pages 1363–64 of the joint appendix where the following dialogue appears:

Q: So it would be obvious to one skilled in the art that's involved here in this patent of Exhibit No. 2, the Henry patent, to add the depressions 30 and 31 and the lands 32 and 33 at the time that you came up with your device?

A: I would say yes. Adding ribs to the part would be a simple, common step, yes.

This testimony, however, relates to the lands and depressions indicated on Fig. 6 of the '314 patent and not to the diamonds.

Therefore, contrary to Henry Molded's assertion in its appeal brief, this testimony is not directed at whether one of ordinary skill in the art would know to employ the diamonds.

5. We are comforted in this conclusion by the fact that Henry Molded consented to (and does not challenge on appeal here) jury instructions which stated: "The best mode requirement is not satisfied by reference to the level of skill in the art or to what the prior art

In this case, we decline to adjudicate arguments which have not been first presented to the district court.... This approach is needed to ensure that "parties may have the opportunity to offer all the evidence they believe relevant to the issues ... [and] in order that litigants may not be surprised on appeal by final decision there of issues upon which they have had no opportunity to introduce evidence." ... The time to prove that diamonds are routine was with evidence at trial, not with lawyer's argument in the appeal brief. Such an explanation simply comes too late and is offered in the wrong form to the wrong audience.

* * *

We affirm the decisions of the district court that (1) Henry Molded's patent is invalid for failure to disclose the best mode and (2) Henry Molded's STAKKER product does not infringe Great Northern's '732 patent. Accordingly, we need not comment on the remaining jury verdicts. AFFIRMED.

NOTES

1. *Leave Out the Kitchen Sink.* For purposes of satisfying the best mode requirement, the Federal Circuit makes a distinction between "production details" and the best mode of practicing the claimed invention. In a case decided five years before *Great Northern*, the Federal Circuit discussed the policy underlying this distinction:

> A description of particular materials or sources or of a particular method or technique selected for manufacture may or may not be required as part of a best mode disclosure respecting a device.... Thus, the particulars of making a prototype or even a commercial embodiment do not necessarily equate with the "best mode" of "carrying out" an invention. Indeed, the inventor's manufacturing materials or sources or techniques used to make a device may vary from wholly irrelevant to critical. For example, if the inventor develops or knows of a particular method of making which substantially improves the operation or effectiveness of his invention, failure to disclose such peripheral development may well lead to invalidation.... On the other hand, an inventor is not required to supply "production" specifications.... Under our case law, there is no mechanical rule that a best mode violation occurs because the inventor failed to disclose particular manufacturing procedures beyond the information sufficient for enablement. One must look at the scope of the invention, the skill in the art, the evidence as to the inventor's belief, and all of the circumstances in order to evaluate whether the inventor's failure to disclose particulars of manufacture gives rise to an inference that he concealed information which one of ordinary skill in the art would not know....

> Any process of manufacture requires the selection of specific steps and materials over others. The best mode does not necessarily cover each of these selections. To so hold would turn a patent specification into a detailed production schedule, which is not its function. Moreover, a re-

---

disclosed." Pursuant to this instruction's statement of the pertinent law, the jury was directed to ignore whether use of diamonds was well known to those of ordinary skill in the molded pulp art. Given that our precedent requires the adequacy of disclosure to be measured from the perspective of one of ordinary skill in the art, we can only surmise that Henry Molded failed to object to this instruction for the same reason it presented no testimony on the issue: it made a decision that its best arguments lay elsewhere.

quirement for routine details to be disclosed because they were selected as the "best" for manufacturing or fabrication would lay a trap for patentees whenever a device has been made prior to filing for the patent. The inventor would merely have to be interrogated with increasing specificity as to steps or material selected as "best" to make the device. *A fortiori*, he could hardly say the choice is not what he thought was "best" in some way. Thus, at the point he would testify respecting a step or material or source or detail which is not in the patent, a failure to disclose the best mode would, ipso facto, be established. However, the best mode inquiry is not so mechanical. A step or material or source or technique considered "best" in a manufacturing circumstance may have been selected for a non-"best mode" reason, such as the manufacturing equipment was on hand, certain materials were available, prior relationship with supplier was satisfactory, or other reasons having nothing to do with development of the invention.

Wahl Instruments, Inc. v. Acvious, Inc., 950 F.2d 1575, 1579–81 (Fed.Cir.1991).

2. *Enabling Exact Duplication*? Cases dealing with inventions requiring the use of biological materials and software confirm that, to be adequate, a best mode disclosure need not necessarily enable the public to duplicate *exactly* the patentee's preferred implementation of the invention. *See Fonar Corp. v. General Elec. Co.*, 107 F.3d 1543 (Fed.Cir.1997), discussed *infra* (software discussed by function); *Amgen, Inc. v. Chugai Pharmaceutical Co., Ltd.*, 927 F.2d 1200 (Fed.Cir.1991); *Scripps Clinic & Research Foundation v. Genentech, Inc.*, 927 F.2d 1565 (Fed.Cir. 1991), discussed *infra*. For example, in *Amgen*, the patent claimed cells transformed with DNA to encode production of erythropoeitin (EPO). The inventor's best mode of practicing the claimed invention was a specific Chinese hamster ovary (CHO) cell line, developed with a technique, gene amplification, that multiplied the cells' copies of the gene and, therefore, their ability to produce EPO. In his patent specification, the inventor identified the CHO cell line and the method of making it but did not deposit the preferred cell line with a public depository. The court found no best mode violation even though, without access to the inventor's cell line, one could not exactly duplicate it. "What is required is an adequate disclosure of the best mode, not a guarantee that every aspect of the specification be precisely and universally reproducible." *Amgen*, 927 F.2d at 1212.

C. WRITTEN DESCRIPTION

The first paragraph of Section 112 provides that the "specification shall contain *a written description of the invention*...." The written description requirement largely serves a signaling function, permitting third parties to read the patent document and understand with a substantial degree of certainty where the patentee's proprietary boundaries reside. This requirement allows other inventors to develop and obtain patent protection for later improvements and subservient inventions that build upon the patentee's teachings. At the same time, the written description requirement limits the patentee's ability to file subsequent applications claiming broader subject matter while retaining the original application's filing date.

Vas–Cath Inc. v. Mahurkar

935 F.2d 1555 (Fed.Cir.1991).

■ RICH, MICHEL and PLAGER, CIRCUIT JUDGES.

■ RICH, CIRCUIT JUDGE.

Sakharam D. Mahurkar and Quinton Instruments Company (collectively Mahurkar) appeal from the September 12, 1990 partial final judgment ... of the United States District Court for the Northern District of Illinois, Easterbrook, J., sitting by designation ... Granting partial summary judgment to Vas–Cath Incorporated and its licensee Gambro, Inc. (collectively Vas–Cath), the district court declared Mahurkar's two United States utility patents Nos. 4,568,329 ('329 patent) and 4,692,141 ('141 patent), titled "Double Lumen Catheter," invalid as anticipated under 35 U.S.C. § 102(b). In reaching its decision, ... the district court concluded that none of the twenty-one claims of the two utility patents was entitled, under 35 U.S.C. § 120, to the benefit of the filing date of Mahurkar's earlier-filed United States design patent application Serial No. 356,081 ('081 design application), which comprised the same drawings as the utility patents, because the design application did not provide a "written description of the invention" as required by 35 U.S.C. § 112, first paragraph. We reverse the grant of summary judgment with respect to all claims.

BACKGROUND

Sakharam Mahurkar filed the '081 design application, also titled "Double Lumen Catheter," on March 8, 1982. The application was abandoned on November 30, 1984. Figures 1–6 of the '081 design application are reproduced below.

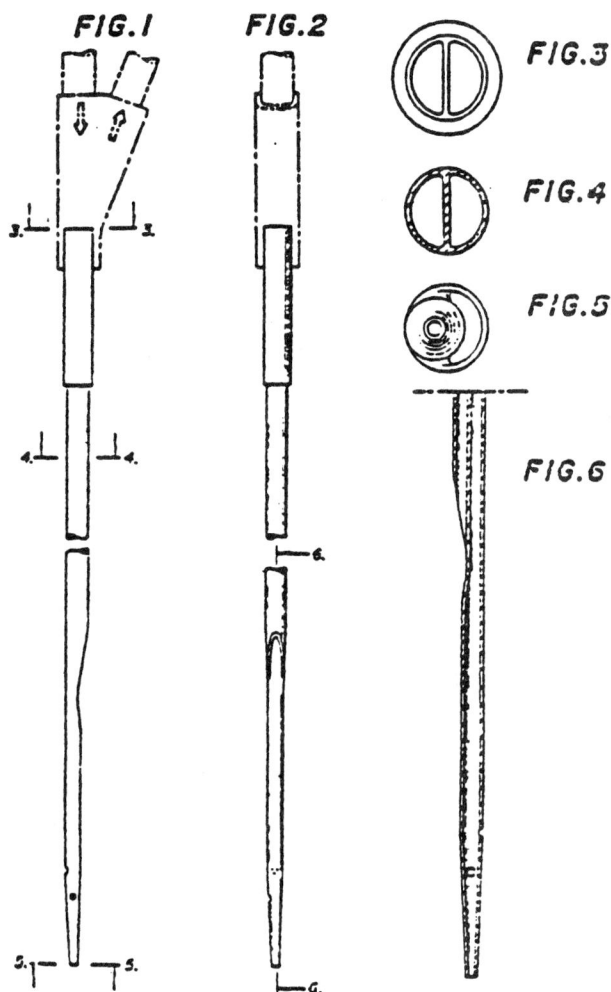

FIG.1   FIG.2   FIG.3

FIG.4

FIG.5

FIG.6

As shown, Mahurkar's catheter comprises a pair of tubes (lumens) designed to allow blood to be removed from an artery, processed in an apparatus that removes impurities, and returned close to the place of removal. Prior art catheters utilized concentric circular lumens, while Mahurkar's employs joined semi-circular tubes that come to a single tapered tip. Advantageously, the puncture area of Mahurkar's semicircular catheter is 42% less than that of a coaxial catheter carrying the same quantity of blood, and its conical tip yields low rates of injury to the blood. The prior art coaxial catheters are now obsolete; Mahurkar's catheters appear to represent more than half of the world's sales....

After filing the '081 design application, Mahurkar also filed a Canadian Industrial Design application comprising the same drawings plus additional textual description. On August 9, 1982, Canadian Industrial Design 50,089 (Canadian '089) issued on that application.

More than one year later, on October 1, 1984, Mahurkar filed the first of two utility patent applications that would give rise to the patents now on appeal. Notably, both utility applications included the same drawings as the '081 design application.[2] Serial No. 656,601 ('601 utility application) claimed the benefit of the filing date of the '081 design application, having been denominated a "continuation" thereof. In an Office Action mailed June 6, 1985, the Patent and Trademark Office (PTO) examiner noted that "the prior application is a design application," but did not dispute that the '601 application was entitled to its filing date. On January 29, 1986, Mahurkar filed Serial No. 823,592 ('592 utility application), again claiming the benefit of the filing date of the '081 design application (the '592 utility application was denominated a continuation of the '601 utility application). In an office action mailed April 1, 1987, the examiner stated that the '592 utility application was "considered to be fully supported by applicant's parent application SN 356,081 filed March 8, 1982 [the '081 design application]." The '601 and '592 utility applications issued in 1986 and 1987, respectively, as the '329 and '141 patents, the subjects of this appeal. The independent claims of both patents are set forth in the Appendix hereto.

Vas–Cath sued Mahurkar in June 1988, seeking a declaratory judgment that the catheters it manufactured did not infringe Mahurkar's '329 and '141 utility patents.[3] Vas–Cath's complaint alleged, inter alia, that the '329 and '141 patents were both invalid as anticipated under 35 U.S.C. § 102(b) by Canadian '089. Vas–Cath's anticipation theory was premised on the argument that the '329 and '141 patents were not entitled under 35 U.S.C. § 120[4] to the filing date of the '081 design application because its drawings did not provide an adequate "written description" of the claimed invention as required by 35 U.S.C. § 112, first paragraph.

Mahurkar counterclaimed, alleging infringement. Both parties moved for summary judgment on certain issues, including validity. For purposes of the summary judgment motion, Mahurkar conceded that, if he could not antedate it, Canadian '089 would represent an enabling and thus anticipating § 102(b) reference against the claims of his '329 and '141 utility patents.... Vas–Cath conceded that the '081 design drawings enabled one skilled in the art to practice the claimed invention within the meaning of 35 U.S.C. § 112, first paragraph.... Thus, the question before the district court was whether the disclosure of the '081 design application, namely, the drawings without more, adequately meets the "written description" re-

---

2. The utility patent drawings contain additional but minor shading and lead lines and reference numerals not present in the design application drawings.

3. Vas–Cath's apprehension of suit apparently arose from a 1988 Canadian action instituted by Mahurkar for infringement of Canadian '089.

4. Section 120, titled "Benefit of Earlier Filing Date in the United States," provides (emphasis ours):

An application for patent for an invention *disclosed in the manner provided by the first paragraph of section 112 of this title* in an application previously filed in the United States, or as provided by section 363 of this title, which is filed by an inventor or inventors named in the previously filed application shall have the same effect as to such invention, as though filed on the date of the prior application, if filed before the patenting or abandonment of or termination of proceedings on the first application or on an application similarly entitled to the benefit of the filing date of the first application and if it contains or is amended to contain a specific reference to the earlier filed application.

quirement also contained in § 112, first paragraph, so as to entitle Mahurkar to the benefit of the 1982 filing date of the '081 design application for his two utility patents and thereby antedates Canadian '089.

Concluding that the drawings do not do so, and that therefore the utility patents are anticipated by Canadian '089, the district court held the '329 and '141 patents wholly invalid under 35 U.S.C. § 102(b), ... and subsequently granted Mahurkar's motion for entry of a partial final judgment under Fed. R. Civ. P. 54(b) on the validity issue. This appeal followed.

DISCUSSION

The issue before us is whether the district court erred in concluding, on summary judgment, that the disclosure of the '081 design application does not provide a § 112, first paragraph "written description" adequate to support each of the claims of the '329 and '141 patents. If the court so erred as to any of the 21 claims at issue, the admittedly anticipatory disclosure of Canadian '089 will have been antedated (and the basis for the court's grant of summary judgment nullified) as to those claims.

* * *

The "Written Description" Requirement of § 112

The first paragraph of 35 U.S.C. § 112 requires that:

> [t]he specification shall contain a *written description of the invention*, and of the manner and process of making and using it, in such full, clear, concise, and exact terms as to enable any person skilled in the art to which it pertains, or with which it is most nearly connected, to make and use the same, and shall set forth the best mode contemplated by the inventor of carrying out his invention.

(Emphasis added). Application of the "written description" requirement, derived from the portion of § 112 emphasized above, is central to resolution of this appeal. The district court, having reviewed this court's decisions on the subject, remarked that "[u]nfortunately, it is not so easy to tell what the law of the Federal Circuit is." ... Perhaps that is so, and, therefore, before proceeding to the merits, we review the case law development of the "written description" requirement with a view to improving the situation....

The cases indicate that the "written description" requirement most often comes into play where claims not presented in the application when filed are presented thereafter. Alternatively, patent applicants often seek the benefit of the filing date of an earlier-filed foreign or United States application under 35 U.S.C. § 119 or 35 U.S.C. § 120, respectively, for claims of a later-filed application. The question raised by these situations is most often phrased as whether the application provides "adequate support" for the claim(s) at issue; it has also been analyzed in terms of "new matter" under 35 U.S.C. § 132. The "written description" question similarly arises in the interference context, where the issue is whether the specification of one party to the interference can support the claim(s) corresponding to the count(s) at issue, *i.e.*, whether that party "can make the claim" corresponding to the interference count.

To the uninitiated, it may seem anomalous that the first paragraph of 35 U.S.C. § 112 has been interpreted as requiring a separate "description of the invention," when the invention is, necessarily, the subject matter defined in the claims under consideration.... One may wonder what purpose a separate "written description" requirement serves, when the second paragraph of § 112 expressly requires that the applicant conclude his specification "with one or more claims particularly pointing out and distinctly claiming the subject matter which the applicant regards as his invention."

One explanation is historical: the "written description" requirement was a part of the patent statutes at a time before claims were required. A case in point is *Evans v. Eaton*, 20 U.S. (7 Wheat.) 356 (1822), in which the Supreme Court affirmed the circuit court's decision that the plaintiff's patent was "deficient," and that the plaintiff could not recover for infringement thereunder. The patent laws then in effect, namely the Patent Act of 1793, did not require claims, but did require, in its 3d section, that the patent applicant "deliver a written description of his invention, and of the manner of using, or process of compounding, the same, in such full, clear and exact terms, as to distinguish the same from all things before known, and to enable any person skilled in the art or science of which it is a branch, or with which it is most nearly connected, to make, compound and use the same...." ... In view of this language, the Court concluded that the specification of a patent had two objects, the first of which was "to enable artizans to make and use [the invention]...." ... The second object of the specification was

> to put the public in possession of what the party claims as his own invention, so as to ascertain if he claims anything that is in common use, or is already known, and to guard against prejudice or injury from the use of an invention which the party may otherwise innocently suppose not to be patented. It is, therefore, for the purpose of warning an innocent purchaser, or other person using a machine, of his infringement of the patent; and at the same time, of taking from the inventor the means of practising upon the credulity or the fears of other persons, by pretending that his invention is more than what it really is, or different from its ostensible objects, that the patentee is required to distinguish his invention in his specification....

A second, policy-based rationale for the inclusion in § 112 of both the first paragraph "written description" and the second paragraph "definiteness" requirements was set forth in *Rengo Co. v. Molins Mach. Co.*, 657 F.2d 535, 551, 211 USPQ 303, 321 (3d Cir.), *cert. denied*, 454 U.S. 1055 (1981):

> [T]here is a subtle relationship between the policies underlying the description and definiteness requirements, as the two standards, while complementary, approach a similar problem from different directions. Adequate description of the invention guards against the inventor's overreaching by insisting that he recount his invention in such detail that his future claims can be determined to be encompassed within his original creation. The definiteness requirement shapes the future conduct of persons other than the inventor, by insisting that they receive notice of the scope of the patented device.

With respect to the first paragraph of § 112 the severability of its "written description" provision from its enablement ("make and use") provision was recognized by this court's predecessor, the Court of Customs and Patent Appeals, as early as *In re Ruschig*, 379 F.2d 990, 154 USPQ 118 (CCPA 1967). Although the appellants in that case had presumed that the rejection appealed from was based on the enablement requirement of § 112, . . . the court disagreed:

> [T]he question is not whether [one skilled in the art] would be so enabled but whether the specification discloses the compound to him, specifically, *as something appellants actually invented* . . . . If [the rejection is] based on section 112, it is on the requirement thereof that "The specification shall contain a written description *of the invention* . . . ." (Emphasis ours.)

Id. at 995–96, 154 USPQ at 123 (first emphasis added). The issue, as the court saw it, was one of fact: "Does the specification convey clearly to those skilled in the art, to whom it is addressed, in any way, the information that appellants invented that specific compound [claimed]?" . . .

In a 1971 case again involving chemical subject matter, the court expressly stated that "it is possible for a specification to enable the practice of an invention as broadly as it is claimed, and still not describe that invention." *In re DiLeone*, 436 F.2d 1404, 1405, 168 USPQ 592, 593 (CCPA 1971) (emphasis added). As an example, the court posited the situation "where the specification discusses only compound A and contains no broadening language of any kind. This might very well enable one skilled in the art to make and use compounds B and C; yet the class consisting of A, B and C has not been described." . . . *See also In re Ahlbrecht*, 435 F.2d 908, 911, 168 USPQ 293, 296 (CCPA 1971) (although disclosure of parent application may have enabled production of claimed esters having 2–12 methylene groups, it only described esters having 3–12 methylene groups).

The CCPA also recognized a subtle distinction between a written description adequate to support a claim under § 112 and a written description sufficient to anticipate its subject matter under § 102(b). The difference between "claim-supporting disclosures" and "claim-anticipating disclosures" was dispositive in *In re Lukach*, 442 F.2d 967, 169 USPQ 795 (CCPA 1971), where the court held that a U.S. "grandparent" application did not sufficiently describe the later-claimed invention, but that the appellant's intervening British application, a counterpart to the U.S. application, anticipated the claimed subject matter. As the court pointed out, "the description of a single embodiment of broadly claimed subject matter constitutes a description of the invention for anticipation purposes . . . , whereas the same information in a specification might not alone be enough to provide a description of that invention for purposes of adequate disclosure . . . ."

The purpose and applicability of the "written description" requirement were addressed in *In re Smith and Hubin*, 481 F.2d 910, 178 USPQ 620 (CCPA 1973), where the court stated:

> Satisfaction of the description requirement insures that subject matter presented in the form of a claim subsequent to the filing date of the application was sufficiently disclosed at the time of filing so that the prima facie date of invention can fairly be held to be the filing date of the

application. This concept applies whether the case factually arises out of an assertion of entitlement to the filing date of a previously filed application under § 120 ... or arises in the interference context wherein the issue is support for a count in the specification of one or more of the parties ... or arises in an ex parte case involving a single application, but where the claim at issue was filed subsequent to the filing of the application....

Id. at 914, 178 USPQ at 623–24 (citations omitted).

The CCPA's "written description" cases often stressed the fact-specificity of the issue.... The court even went so far as to state:

[I]t should be readily apparent from recent decisions of this court involving the question of compliance with the description requirement of § 112 that each case must be decided on its own facts. Thus, the precedential value of cases in this area is extremely limited.

In re Driscoll, 562 F.2d 1245, 1250, 195 USPQ 434, 438 (CCPA 1977).

Since its inception, the Court of Appeals for the Federal Circuit has frequently addressed the "written description" requirement of § 112. A fairly uniform standard for determining compliance with the "written description" requirement has been maintained throughout: "Although [the applicant] does not have to describe exactly the subject matter claimed, ... the description must clearly allow persons of ordinary skill in the art to recognize that [he or she] invented what is claimed." *In re Gosteli*, 872 F.2d 1008, 1012, 10 U.S.P.Q.2D 1614, 1618 (Fed.Cir.1989) (citations omitted). "[T]he test for sufficiency of support in a parent application is whether the disclosure of the application relied upon 'reasonably conveys to the artisan that the inventor had possession at that time of the later claimed subject matter.'" *Ralston Purina Co. v. Far–Mar–Co, Inc.*, 772 F.2d 1570, 1575, 227 USPQ 177, 179 (Fed.Cir.1985) (*quoting In re Kaslow*, 707 F.2d 1366, 1375, 217 USPQ 1089, 1096 (Fed.Cir.1983)). Our cases also provide that compliance with the "written description" requirement of § 112 is a question of fact, to be reviewed under the clearly erroneous standard. *Gosteli*, 872 F.2d at 1012, 10 U.S.P.Q.2D at 1618; *Utter v. Hiraga*, 845 F.2d 993, 998, 6 U.S.P.Q.2D 1709, 1714 (Fed.Cir.1988).

There appears to be some confusion in our decisions concerning the extent to which the "written description" requirement is separate and distinct from the enablement requirement. For example, in *In re Wilder*, 736 F.2d 1516, 1520, 222 USPQ 369, 372 (Fed.Cir.1984), *cert. denied*, 469 U.S. 1209, 105 S.Ct. 1173, 84 L.Ed.2d 323 (1985), we flatly stated: "The description requirement is found in 35 U.S.C. § 112 and is separate from the enablement requirement of that provision." However, in a later case we said, "The purpose of the [written] description requirement [of § 112, 1st ¶] is to state what is needed to fulfill the enablement criteria. These requirements may be viewed separately, but they are intertwined." *Kennecott Corp. v. Kyocera Int'l, Inc.*, 835 F.2d 1419, 1421, 5 U.S.P.Q.2D 1194, 1197 (Fed.Cir.1987), *cert. denied*, 486 U.S. 1008, 108 S.Ct. 1735, 100 L.Ed.2d 198 (1988). "The written description must communicate that which is needed to enable the skilled artisan to make and use the claimed invention." *Id.*

To the extent that *Kennecott* conflicts with *Wilder*, we note that decisions of a three-judge panel of this court cannot overturn prior precedential decisions. *See UMC Elec. Co. v. United States*, 816 F.2d 647, 652 n. 6, 2 U.S.P.Q.2D 1465, 1468 n. 7 (Fed.Cir.1987), *cert. denied*, 484 U.S. 1025, 108 S.Ct. 748, 98 L.Ed.2d 761 (1988). This court in *Wilder* (and the CCPA before it) clearly recognized, and we hereby reaffirm, that 35 U.S.C. § 112, first paragraph, requires a "written description of the invention" which is separate and distinct from the enablement requirement. The purpose of the "written description" requirement is broader than to merely explain how to "make and use"; the applicant must also convey with reasonable clarity to those skilled in the art that, as of the filing date sought, he or she was in possession of the invention. The invention is, for purposes of the "written description" inquiry, whatever is now claimed.

The District Court's Analysis

* * *

... [U]nder proper circumstances, drawings alone may provide a "written description" of an invention as required by § 112. Whether the drawings are those of a design application or a utility application is not determinative, although in most cases the latter are much more detailed. In the instant case, however, the design drawings are substantially identical to the utility application drawings.

Although we join with the district court in concluding that drawings may suffice to satisfy the "written description" requirement of § 112, we cannot agree with the legal standard that the court imposed for "written description" compliance, nor with the court's conclusion that no genuine issues of material fact were in dispute.

With respect to the former, the district court stated that although the '081 design drawings in question "allowed practice" [*i.e.*, enabled], they did not necessarily

> show what the invention is, when "the invention" could be a subset or a superset of the features shown. Is the invention the semi-circular lumens? The conical tip? The ratio at which the tip tapers? The shape, size, and placement of the inlets and outlets? You can measure all of these things from the diagrams in serial '081 and so can practice the device, but you cannot tell, because serial '081 does not say, what combination of these things is "the invention", and what range of variation is allowed without exceeding the scope of the claims. To show one example of an invention, even a working model, is not to describe what is novel or important.

745 F.Supp. at 522, 17 U.S.P.Q.2D at 1356.

We find the district court's concern with "what the invention is" misplaced, and its requirement that the '081 drawings "describe what is novel or important" legal error. There is "no legally recognizable or protected 'essential' element, 'gist' or 'heart' of the invention in a combination patent." *Aro Mfg. Co. v. Convertible Top Replacement Co.*, 365 U.S. 336, 345 (1961). "The invention" is defined by the claims on appeal. The instant claims do not recite only a pair of semi-circular lumens, or a conical tip, or a ratio at which the tip tapers, or the shape, size, and placement of the inlets and outlets; they claim a double lumen catheter having a combination of those features. That combination invention is what the '081 drawings show. As the district court itself recognized, "what Mahurkar eventually patented is exactly what the pictures in serial '081 show." ...

We find the "range of variation" question, much emphasized by the parties, more troublesome. The district court stated that "although Mahurkar's patents use the same diagrams, [the claims] contain limitations that did not follow ineluctably [*i.e.,* inevitably] from the diagrams." ... As an example, the court stated (presumably with respect to independent claims 1 and 7 of the '329 patent) that

> the utility patents claim a return lumen that is "substantially greater than one-half but substantially less than a full diameter" after it makes the transition from semi-circular to circular cross-section, and the drawings of serial '081 fall in this range. But until the utility application was filed, nothing established that they had to—for that matter that the utility patent would claim anything other than the precise ratio in the diagrams....

Id. at 523, 17 U.S.P.Q.2D at 1357. Mahurkar argues that one of ordinary skill in this art, looking at the '081 drawings, would be able to derive the claimed range.

The declaration of Dr. Stephen Ash, submitted by Mahurkar, is directed to these concerns. Dr. Ash, a physician specializing in nephrology (the study of the kidney and its diseases) and chairman of a corporation that develops and manufactures biomedical devices including catheters, explains why one of skill in the art of catheter design and manufacture, studying the drawings of the '081 application in early 1982, would have understood from them that the return lumen must have a diameter within the range recited by independent claims 1 and 7 of the '329 patent. Dr. Ash explains in detail that a return (longer) lumen of diameter less than half that of the two lumens combined would produce too great a pressure increase, while a return lumen of diameter equal or larger than that of the two lumens combined would result in too great a pressure drop.[7] "Ordinary experience with the flow of blood in catheters would lead directly away from any such arrangement," Ash states.

Although the district court found this reasoning "logical," it noted that later patents issued to Mahurkar disclose diameter ratios closer to 1.0 (U.S. Patent No. 4,584,968) and exactly 0.5 (U.S. Des. Patent No. 272,651). If these other ratios were desirable, the district court queried, "how does serial '081 necessarily exclude the[m]?" ...

The district court erred in taking Mahurkar's other patents into account. Mahurkar's later patenting of inventions involving different range limitations is irrelevant to the issue at hand. Application sufficiency under § 112, first paragraph, must be judged as of the filing date.

The court further erred in applying a legal standard that essentially required the drawings of the '081 design application to necessarily exclude

---

7. Higher pressure drops are associated with smaller cross-sectional areas for fluid flow. Mahurkar's opening brief to this court states that by applying well-known principles of fluid mechanics (*i.e.,* the work of Poiseuille and Hagen), it can be calculated that the diameter of the circular (return) lumen would have to be in the range of 0.66 times the diameter of the two lumens combined in order to achieve proper blood flow at equal pressure drop. The 0.66 ratio falls within the noted claim limitation.

all diameters other than those within the claimed range. We question whether any drawing could ever do so. At least with respect to independent claims 1 and 7 of the '329 patent and claims depending therefrom, the proper test is whether the drawings conveyed with reasonable clarity to those of ordinary skill that Mahurkar had in fact invented the catheter recited in those claims, having (among several other limitations) a return lumen diameter substantially less than 1.0 but substantially greater than 0.5 times the diameter of the combined lumens. Consideration of what the drawings conveyed to persons of ordinary skill is essential. *See Ralston Purina*, 772 F.2d at 1575, 227 USPQ at 179 (ranges found in applicant's claims need not correspond exactly to those disclosed in parent application; issue is whether one skilled in the art could derive the claimed ranges from parent's disclosure).

Mahurkar submitted the declaration of Dr. Ash on this point; Vas–Cath submitted no technical evidence to refute Ash's conclusions. Although the district court considered Dr. Ash's declaration, we believe its import was improperly disregarded when viewed through the court's erroneous interpretation of the law.[8] We hold that the Ash declaration and Vas–Cath's non-refutation thereof, without more, gave rise to a genuine issue of material fact inappropriate for summary disposition. *See Hesston Corp. v. Sloop*, 1988 U.S.Dist. LEXIS 1573, *13 (D.Kansas) (summary judgment on § 112 "written description" issue inappropriate where resolution of what parent disclosure conveyed to those skilled in the art may require examination of experts, demonstrations and exhibits).

Mahurkar urges that at least some of the remaining claims do not contain the range limitations discussed by the district court, and that the presence of range limitations was not a proper basis for invalidating those remaining claims. For example, claim 8 of the '141 patent requires, *inter alia*, a smooth conical tapered tip and "the portion of said tube between said second opening and said conical tapered tip being larger than said first lumen in the transverse direction normal to the plane of said septum." Vas–Cath counters that claim 8 of the '141 patent is just as much a "range" claim as claims 1 and 7 of the '329 patent, albeit one having only a lower limit and no upper limit.

Absent any separate discussion of these remaining claims in the district court's opinion, we assume that the court applied to them the same erroneous legal standard. Summary judgment was therefore inappropriate as to the remaining claims. Additionally, the possibility that the '081 drawings may provide an adequate § 112 "written description" of the subject matter of some of the claims but not others should have been

---

8. The following colloquy at oral argument before the district court supports our view:

Counsel for Mahurkar: "So the only evidence that we have on this subject from people of ordinary skill in the art is that the drawings do communicate these range limitations, and given the procedural posture of this case, the Court has to accept that evidence...."

District Court: ... "And if you could have written a large number of things that were different from what was actually filed in 1984, then the diagram isn't enough. And that seems to me something that can't be resolved by ogling the Ash declaration. It's really a pure question of law."

considered. *See, e.g., In re Borkowski*, 422 F.2d 904, 909 n. 4, 164 USPQ 642, 646 n. 4 (CCPA 1970) (on review of § 112 non-enablement rejection: "A disclosure may, of course, be insufficient to support one claim but sufficient to support another.") On remand, the district court should separately analyze whether the "written description" requirement has been met as to the subject matter of each claim of the '141 and '329 patents.

CONCLUSION

The district court's grant of summary judgment, holding all claims of the '329 and '141 patents invalid under 35 U.S.C. § 102(b), is hereby reversed as to all claims, and the case remanded for further proceedings consistent herewith.

* * *

REVERSED and REMANDED.

APPENDIX

Independent Claims of the '329 Patent:

1.   A double lumen catheter having an elongated tube with a proximal first cylindrical portion enclosing first and second lumens separated by an internal divider, the proximal end of said elongated tube connecting to two separate connecting tubes communicating with the respective first and second lumens for the injection and removal of fluid, the first lumen extending from the proximal end of said elongated tube to a first opening at the distal end of said elongated tube, and the second lumen extending from the proximal end of said elongated tube to a second opening at approximately the distal end of said first cylindrical portion, wherein the improvement comprises:

said elongated tube having at its distal end a smooth conical tapered tip that smoothly merges with a second cylindrical portion of said elongated tube, and said second cylindrical portion enclosing the first lumen from the conical tapered tip to approximately the location of said second opening, wherein said second cylindrical portion has a diameter substantially greater than one-half but substantially less than a full diameter of said first cylindrical portion.

7.   A double lumen catheter having an elongated tube with a proximal first cylindrical portion enclosing first and second lumens separated by an internal divider, the proximal end of said elongated tube connecting to two separate connecting tubes communicating with the respective first and second lumens for the injection and removal of fluid, the first lumen extending from the proximal end of said elongated tube to a first opening at the distal end of said elongated tube, and the second lumen extending from the proximal end of said elongated tube to a second opening at approximately the distal end of said first cylindrical portion, wherein the improvement comprises:

said elongated tube having at its distal end a smooth conical tapered tip that smoothly merges with a second cylindrical portion of said elongated tube, and said second cylindrical portion enclosing the first lumen from the conical tapered tip to approximately the location of said second opening, said second cylindrical portion having a diameter substantially greater than one-half but substantially less than a full diameter of said first cylindrical portion, said divider in said first cylindrical portion being planar, the lumens being "D" shaped in cross-section in said first cylindrical portion, the elongated tube being provided with a plurality of holes in the region of the conical tapered tip, and said first cylindrical portion of the elongated tube smoothly merging with said second cylindrical portion of the elongated tube.

Independent Claims of the '141 Patent:

1. A double lumen catheter having an elongated tube with a proximal first cylindrical portion enclosing first and second lumens separated by an internal divider, the proximal end of said elongated tube connecting to two separate connecting tubes communicating with the respective first and second lumens for the injection and removal of fluid, the first lumen extending from the proximal end of said elongated tube to a first opening at the distal end of said elongated tube, and the second lumen extending from the proximal end of said elongated tube to a second opening at approximately the distal end of said first cylindrical portion, wherein the improvement comprises:

said elongated tube having at its distal end a smooth conical tapered tip that smoothly merges with a second cylindrical portion of said elongated tube, and said second cylindrical portion enclosing the first lumen from the conical tapered tip to approximately the location of said second opening, wherein said second sylindrical [sic] portion has a diameter substantially less than a full diameter of said first cylindrical portion but larger than said first lumen in the transverse direction normal to the plane of said flat divider.

7. A double lumen catheter comprising an elongated cylindrical tube enclosing first and second lumens separated by a flat longitudinal internal divider formed as an integral part of said tube, said tube and said divider forming said first and second lumens as semi-cylindrical cavities within said tube, the proximal end of said elongated tube connecting to two separate connecting tubes communicating with the respective first and second lumens for the injection and removal of fluid, the first lumen extending from the proximal end of said elongated tube to a first opening at the distal end of said elongated tube, said distal end of said tube forming a smooth conical tapered tip and the second lumen extending from the proximal end of said elongated tube to a second opening spaced a substantial distance away from said first opening toward the proximal end of said tube, the distal end of said divider being joined to the outside wall of said tube distal of said second opening, and the outside wall of said tube forming a smooth transition between said conical tapered tip and the outer circumference of the tube proximal of said second opening, said transition being larger than said first lumen in the transverse direction normal to the plane of said flat divider.

8. A double lumen catheter comprising an elongated cylindrical tube having a longitudinal planar septum of one-piece construction with said tube, said septum dividing the interior of said tube into first and second lumens, said lumens being D-shaped in cross-section, the proximal end of said tube connecting to two separate tubes communicating with the respective first and second lumens for the injection and removal of fluids, the lumen extending from the proximal end of said tube to a first lumen extending from the proximal end of said tube to a first opening at the distal end of said tube, and the second lumen extending from the proximal end of

said tube to a second opening axially spaced from the distal end of said tube, said tube having at its distal end a smooth conical tapered tip that merges with the cylindrical surface of said tube, said first lumen, including the internal wall thereof formed by said septum extending continuously through said conical tapered tip, and the portion of said tube between said second opening and said conical tapered tip being larger than said first lumen in the transverse direction normal to the plane of said septum.

13.   A double lumen catheter comprising an elongated cylindrical tube enclosing first and second lumens separated by a flat longitudinal internal divider formed as an integral part of said tube, said tube and said divider forming said first and second lumens as semi-cylindrical cavities within said tube, the proximal end of said elongated tube connecting to two separate connecting tubes communicating with he [sic] respective first and second lumens for the injection and removal of fluid, the first lumen extending from the proximal end of said elongated tube to a first opening at the distal end of said elongated tube, said distal end of said tube forming a smooth conical tapered tip defining the distal portion of said first lumen and said first opening, said first opening and an adjacent portion of said first lumen having a circular transverse cross-sectional configuration, and the second lumen extending from the proximal end of said elongated tube to a second opening spaced a substantial distance away from said first opening toward the proximal end of said tube, the inside walls of said tube forming a smooth transition between said semicylindrical and circular transverse cross-sectional configurations of said first lumen, the outside dimension of said transition being larger than said first lumen in the transverse direction normal to the plane of said flat divider.

NOTES

1. *Mahurkar's Persistence.* To save Dr. Mahurkar's patent rights, the courts resolved a number of close questions in his favor. In addition to the above decision on the description requirement, consider the later decisions on an apparent "on sale" bar, *In re Mahurkar Double Lumen Hemodialysis Catheter Patent Litigation,* 71 F.3d 1573 (Fed.Cir.1995), and on proof of a pre-filing invention date to avoid a publication bar, *Mahurkar v. C. R. Bard, Inc.,* 79 F.3d 1572 (Fed.Cir.1996). What explains this apparent judicial lenience? Was the fact that Mahurkar was a "small" inventor and not a large corporate entity a factor? Is the answer in the objective considerations?

> Advantageously, the puncture area of Mahurkar's semicircular catheter is 42% less than that of a coaxial catheter carrying the same quantity of blood, and its conical tip yields low rates of injury to the blood. The prior art coaxial catheters are now obsolete; *Mahurkar's catheters appear to represent more than half of the world's sales....* (Emphasis added).

Should the courts give weight to the evidence of the marketplace in evaluating inventions, and determining their pioneer status?

The district court, on remand, found compliance with the written description requirement. The opinion, written by Circuit Judge Easterbrook of the Seventh Circuit, sitting by designation, also covers a wide spectrum of other patent law issues and includes analytic insights from a "law and economics" perspective. *In re Mahurkar Patent Litigation,* 831 F.Supp. 1354 (N.D.Ill.1993), aff'd 71 F.3d 1573 (Fed.Cir.1995).

Can you guess why enablement did not seem to feature prominently in this phase of the case? Would the party challenging the patent have an incentive to concede enablement with respect to the originally filed application? If that disclosure enabled, then it would be a stronger piece of prior art when used to attack the patent under the prior art rules, which generally require disclosure of each and every element of the claim as well as enablement. By focusing on inadequacy of description, the challenger was trying to ensure that the patent would not enjoy the benefit of the earlier filing date, thereby making the inventor's own document count as prior art.

2. *The Purpose for Requiring "Support" for Claim Language—Contexts of "Written Description" Problems.* Two central purposes have been postulated for the written description requirement. First, the requirement serves "to buttress the original filing date of the application as the prima facie date of invention." DONALD S. CHISUM, CHISUM ON PATENTS § 7.04 (1997). It ensures that the applicant conveyed to a person having ordinary skill in the art that the applicant fully possessed the claimed subject matter on the application filing date. Second, the requirement helps ensure that the property rights in the patent are fixed and publicly noticed. Thus, investors, potential infringers, those who would design around, and those who would improve upon, can all be certain of the precise details and limits of the patentee's right to exclude. It allows other inventors to develop and to obtain patent protection on later improvements and subservient inventions that build on the teachings of the earlier patentee.

The written description requirement most frequently comes into play when a patent applicant files an amendment to his patent application adding claim language or files a continuation application with new claim language. The issue is whether the new claim language has support in the specification; or, in other words, is the new claim language entitled to the original file date, which, as discussed in Chapter 4, is the prima facie date of invention. If support is lacking, the claims may be unpatentable. Thus, the principal role of the written description requirement is to ensure that later added claim language has support in the specification as originally filed.

In *Ariad Pharmaceuticals, Inc. v. Eli Lilly and Co.,* 598 F.3d 1336 (Fed.Cir. 2010) (en banc), the Federal Circuit reaffirmed that the written description requirement is separate from the enablement requirement. The court also affirmed the "fairly uniform standard" of *Vas–Cath Inc. v. Mahurkar. Ariad Pharmaceuticals, Inc.,* 598 F.3d at 1351 (quoting *Vas–Cath Inc. v. Mahurkar,* 935 F.2d 1555, 1562–63 (Fed.Cir.1991)). The court clarified that "the test requires an objective inquiry into the four corners of the specification from the perspective of a person of ordinary skill in the art. Based on that inquiry, the specification must describe an invention understandable to that skilled artisan and show that the inventor actually invented the invention claimed." *Id.*

The claimed invention does not have to be described *ipsis verbis* in order to satisfy the written description requirement. *Application of Wertheim,* 541 F.2d 257, 265 (CCPA 1976). In *Wertheim,* the patent claimed a range that was narrower than what was disclosed in the specification (claimed "at least 35%" and the specification disclosed a range of "25 to 60%"). The CCPA held that the specification supported the claim even though the precise range claimed was not exactly set forth in the specification. *See also, Union Oil Co. v. Atlantic Richfield Co.,* 208 F.3d 989, 1000–01 (Fed.Cir.2000).

The Federal Circuit has also applied the written description requirement to originally filed claims that were never amended. *See Regents of the Univ. of California v. Eli Lilly & Co.,* 119 F.3d 1559 (Fed.Cir.1997). Some have argued that this application takes the requirement out of its original context because there is no after-filing amendment or continuation application at issue in this scenario. In other words, *Eli Lilly* did not involve a priority date issue.

Although the *Eli Lilly* case is considered in greater detail later in this chapter under "Complex Technologies," for present purposes, it should be noted that the opinion has invited controversy. *See, e.g., Enzo Biochem, Inc. v. Gen–Probe Inc.*, 323 F.3d 956, 979–80 (Fed.Cir.2002) (rehearing en banc denied) (Rader, J., dissenting) (asserting that *Eli Lilly* is inconsistent with precedent because "for the first time, this court purported to apply [written description] as a general disclosure doctrine in place of enablement, rather than as a priority doctrine"); *Moba, B.V. v. Diamond Automation, Inc.*, 325 F.3d 1306, 1327–28 (Fed.Cir.2003) (stating that *Eli Lilly* did not constitute "a departure from prior law when it applied the written description requirement in a non-priority context"). For more on the recent debates on surrounding the written description requirement, see the materials at the end of this chapter on biotechnology.

The *Eli Lilly* opinion has also caused some confusion about the purpose of the written description requirement, prompting the Federal Circuit to clarify that the requirement actually has two applications:

> First, in 1967, this court's predecessor inaugurated use of § 112 to prevent the addition of new matter to claims. *In re Ruschig,* 379 F.2d 990 (1967). As this court's predecessor noted, "[t]he function of the description requirement is to ensure that the inventor had possession, as of the filing date of the application relied on, of the specific subject matter later claimed by him." *In re Wertheim,* 541 F.2d 257, 262 (CCPA 1976). Although the statute proscribes addition of new matter to a specification or claims under § 132, the United States Court of Customs and Patent Appeals decided to police the addition of new matter to claims separately using § 112. *In re Rasmussen,* 650 F.2d 1212, 1214 (CCPA 1981). This court's predecessor explained that the use of § 132 or § 112 was synonymous because "a rejection of an amended claim under § 132 is equivalent to a rejection under § 112, first paragraph." *Id.* Since then, this court has continued to use § 112 to ensure that a patentee had possession at the time of filing of subject matter subsequently claimed. In this court's most recent application of the written description doctrine, it noted: "The purpose of the written description requirement is to prevent an applicant from *later* asserting that he invented that which he did not; the applicant for a patent is therefore required 'to recount his invention in such detail that his *future* claims can be determined to be encompassed within his *original* creation.' " *Amgen Inc. v. Hoechst Marion Roussel Inc.*, 314 F.3d 1313, 1330, (Fed.Cir.2003) (citing *Vas–Cath Inc. v. Mahurkar*, 935 F.2d 1555, 1561 (Fed.Cir.1991)). In that setting, the written description is the metric against which a subsequently added claim is measured to determine if it is due the priority date of the original patent. *Id.* at 1560 ("The question raised by these situations is most often phrased as whether the application provides 'adequate support' for the claim(s) at issue; it has also been analyzed in terms of 'new matter' under 35 U.S.C. § 132."); *In re Wright,* 866 F.2d 422, 424, 9 USPQ2d 1649, 1651 (Fed.Cir.1989) ("When the scope of a claim has been changed by amendment in such a way as to justify an assertion that it is directed to a different invention than was the original claim, it is proper to inquire whether the newly claimed subject matter was described in the patent application when filed as the invention of the applicant. That is the essence of the so-called 'description requirement' of § 112, first paragraph.").

The second application of the written description requirement is reflected in *Regents of the University of California v. Eli Lilly & Co.*, 119 F.3d 1559 (Fed.Cir.1997). There, this court invoked the written description requirement in a case without priority issues. Invoking § 112, *Lilly* required a precise definition of a DNA sequence in the patent specification.

Moba, B.V. v. Diamond Automation, Inc., 325 F.3d 1306, 1319–20 (Fed.Cir.2003). For a discussion of how the Federal Circuit has since distinguished *Lilly* in *Enzo Biochem, Inc. v. Gen–Probe Inc.*, 323 F.3d 956 (Fed.Cir.2002) and *Amgen Inc. v. Hoechst Marion Roussel, Inc.*, 314 F.3d 1313 (Fed.Cir.2003), *see* Section E.2, *infra*. *See also* F. Scott Kieff, *Blame within the Patentee's Domain? Failing the Patentability Requirements of Written Description and On–Sale Bar*, at the end of this chapter.

3. *Claims Dominating "Unsupported" Subject Matter.* Another distinction is between the ability of a specification to support a claim to specific subject matter and its ability to support a broader claim that covers or dominates that same subject matter. In *Ethicon Endo–Surgery, Inc. v. United States Surgical Corp.*, 93 F.3d 1572 (Fed.Cir.1996), the court distinguished "a claim not supported by the specification, which is not allowable, with a broad claim, which is." In *Ethicon*, an examiner rejected a claim with a specific limitation on the location of an element (on a stapler) because the specification only showed the element in another location (on a cartridge).

> It does not follow ... that [applicant's] disclosure could not support claims sufficiently broad to read on [the element not in the disclosed location, *i.e.* on the cartridge.] *See, e.g., In re Vickers,* 141 F.2d 522, 525 (CCPA 1944) ("an applicant is generally allowed claims, when the art permits, which cover more than the specific embodiment shown.").... If [the applicant] did not consider the [element's] precise location ... to be an element of his invention, he was free to draft [a] claim ... broadly (within the limits imposed by the prior art) to exclude the [element's] exact location as a limitation of the claimed invention. *See* 35 U.S.C. § 112 (1994) (allocating to the *inventor* the task of claiming what "the [inventor] regards as *his invention.*" (emphasis added)).... Such a claim would not be unsupported by the specification even though it would be literally infringed by undisclosed embodiments.

Id. at 1582, n.7. *But see Tronzo v. Biomet, Inc.*, 156 F.3d 1154, 1159 (Fed.Cir.1998) (holding that under the written description requirement claims 1 and 9, which claimed a generic shape of a cup, are not entitled to an earlier filing date because the specification disclosed "only two species of cups"). Compare *Ethicon* to *Gentry Gallery, Inc. v. Berkline Corp.*, 134 F.3d 1473 (Fed.Cir.1998) (the sofa case). Gentry's invention related to a "unit of a sectional sofa in which two independent reclining seats ('recliners') face in the same direction." The recliners had a console situated between them, which "accommodate[d] the controls for both reclining seats." Berkline asserted that the patent was invalid under 35 U.S.C. § 112 because the claims at issue

> are directed to sectional sofas in which the location of the recliner controls is not limited to the console. According to Berkline, because the patent only describes sofas having controls on the console and an object of the invention is to provide a sectional sofa "with a console ... that accommodates the controls for both the reclining seats," '244 patent, col. 1, ll. 35–37, the claimed sofas are not described within the meaning of § 112, ¶ 1. Berkline also relies on [the inventor's] testimony that "locating the controls on the console is definitely the way we solved it [the problem of building a sectional sofa with parallel recliners] on the original group [of sofas]." Gentry responds that the disclosure represents only [the inventor's] preferred embodiment, in which the controls are on the console, and therefore supports claims directed to a sofa in which the controls may be located elsewhere. Gentry relies on *Ethicon Endo–Surgery, Inc. v. United States*

Surgical Corp., 93 F.3d 1572, 1582 n. 7 (Fed.Cir.1996), and *In re Rasmussen*, 650 F.2d 1212 (CCPA 1981), for the proposition that an applicant need not describe more than one embodiment of a broad claim to adequately support that claim.

The court agreed with Berkline "that the patent's disclosure does not support claims in which the location of the recliner controls is other than on the console." According to the court:

It is a truism that a claim need not be limited to a preferred embodiment. However, in a given case, the scope of the right to exclude may be limited by a narrow disclosure. For example, as we have recently held, a disclosure of a television set with a keypad, connected to a central computer with a video disk player did not support claims directed to "an individual terminal containing a video disk player." *See id.* (stating that claims directed to a "distinct invention from that disclosed in the specification" do not satisfy the written description requirement); *see also Regents of the Univ. of Cal. v. Eli Lilly & Co.*, 119 F.3d 1559, 1568 (Fed.Cir.1997) (stating that the case law does "not compel the conclusion that a description of a species always constitutes a description of a genus of which it is a part").

In this case, the original disclosure clearly identifies the console as the only possible location for the controls. It provides for only the most minor variation in the location of the controls, noting that the control "may be mounted on top or side surfaces of the console rather than on the front wall ... without departing from this invention." '244 patent, col. 2, line 68 to col. 3, line 3. No similar variation beyond the console is even suggested. Additionally, the only discernible purpose for the console is to house the controls. As the disclosure states, identifying the only purpose relevant to the console, "[a]nother object of the present invention is to provide ... a console positioned between [the reclining seats] that accommodates the controls for both of the reclining seats." *Id.* at col. 1, ll. 33–37. Thus, locating the controls anywhere but on the console is outside the stated purpose of the invention. Moreover, consistent with this disclosure, [the inventor's] broadest original claim was directed to a sofa comprising, *inter alia*, "control means located upon the center console to enable each of the pair of reclining seats to move separately between the reclined and upright positions." Finally, although not dispositive, because one can add claims to a pending application directed to adequately described subject matter, [the inventor] admitted at trial that he did not consider placing the controls outside the console until he became aware that some of Gentry's competitors were so locating the recliner controls. Accordingly, when viewed in its entirety, the disclosure is limited to sofas in which the recliner control is located on the console.

Gentry's reliance on *Ethicon* is misplaced. It is true, as Gentry observes, that we noted that "an applicant ... is generally allowed claims, when the art permits, which cover more than the specific embodiment shown." *Ethicon*, 93 F.3d at 1582 n. 7 (*quoting In re Vickers*, 141 F.2d 522, 525 (CCPA 1944)). However, we were also careful to point out in that opinion that the applicant "was free to draft claim[s] broadly (within the limits imposed by the prior art) to exclude the lockout's exact location as a limitation of the claimed invention" only because he "did not consider the precise location of the lockout to be an element of his invention." *Id.* Here, as indicated above, it is clear that [the inventor] considered the location of the recliner controls on the console to be an essential element of his invention. Accordingly, his original disclosure serves to limit the permissible breadth of his later-drafted claims.

Similarly, *In re Rasmussen* does not support Gentry's position. In that case, our predecessor court restated the uncontroversial proposition that "a claim may be broader than the specific embodiment disclosed in a specification." 650 F.2d at 1215. However, the court also made clear that "[a]n applicant is entitled to claims as broad as the prior art and his disclosure will allow." *Id.* at 1214. The claims at issue in *Rasmussen*, which were limited to the generic step of "adheringly applying" one layer to an adjacent layer, satisfied the written description requirement only because "one skilled in the art who read [the] specification would understand that it is unimportant how the layers are adhered, so long as they are adhered." Here, on the contrary, one skilled in the art would clearly understand that it was not only important, but essential to [the inventor's] invention, for the controls to be on the console.

It seems that a key factor for the court in *Gentry*, and what distinguished *Gentry* from *Ethicon*, was that the patentee considered the location of the controls on the console to be an "essential element of his invention."

In *Johnson Worldwide Associates, Inc. v. Zebco Corp.*, 175 F.3d 985, 993 (Fed.Cir.1999), the Federal Circuit distanced itself from *Gentry*, stating that "*Gentry Gallery* ... considers the situation where the patent's disclosure makes crystal clear that a particular (*i.e.*, narrow) understanding of a claim term is an 'essential element of [the inventor's] invention.' Here, however, the patent disclosure provides ample support for the breadth of the term 'heading'; it does not unambiguously limit[ ] the meaning of 'heading.' " In fact, the court, in *Cooper Cameron Corp. v. Kvaerner Oilfield Products, Inc.*, 291 F.3d 1317, 1323 (Fed.Cir.2002), stated that there is no "essential elements" test:

> [In *Gentry*,] we did not announce a new "essential element" test mandating an inquiry into what an inventor considers to be essential to his invention and requiring that the claims incorporate those elements. Use of particular language explaining a decision does not necessarily create a new legal test. Rather, in *Gentry*, we applied and merely expounded upon the unremarkable proposition that a broad claim is invalid when the entirety of the specification clearly indicates that the invention is of a much narrower scope.

See also, Amgen Inc. v. Hoechst Marion Roussel, Inc., 314 F.3d 1313, 1333 (Fed.Cir.2003) (discounting significant of *Gentry Gallery*).

4. *Written Description v. Enablement.* What is the difference between the written description requirement and the enablement requirement? Can you think of a scenario where a claimed invention is enabled but fails the written description requirement? Consider the following example: Inventor files a patent application disclosing in the specification a method of making a square table with four legs. But Inventor generically claims a method of making a table. While the specification may enable a person with ordinary skill in the art to make a round table with fewer than four legs, the Inventor's broad claim arguably does not satisfy the written description requirement because the specification does not show that the Inventor was in possession of round tables with fewer than four legs. In other words, the specification indicates that the invention was of "much narrower scope" than what was claimed.

In addition, consider an art such as modern biotechnology, in which the repertoire of experimental techniques is fairly diverse and sophisticated. Imagine further that a researcher has conceived of a particular invention—perhaps an isolated gene encoding a physiologically important protein, like insulin. To be sure, this conception may be in sufficient detail to be an invention, especially if followed by either actual or constructive reduction to practice. But at this stage of the project two contrasting facts are likely to exist: although the researcher may still not know a great deal about the precise details of the gene and its encoded protein, both can be isolated and placed in an appropriate, publicly accessible, depository. Therefore, the deposited material combined with the advanced state of the art may make a non-enablement argument difficult to mount. But what about written description? Can the researcher at this stage describe the invention? Perhaps the details of the one version of the gene and protein that happened to have been used in the experiment can be adequately described (and thus are similarly adequately conceived—but more on the tie between conception and written description later in this Chapter. *See Fiers v. Revel*, 984 F.2d 1164 (Fed.Cir.1993)). Yet, what if that one version happens to be merely one member of a large family of such genes and proteins? This possibility is indeed quite likely. Often the biotechnology researcher begins the research with a version of the gene and its encoded protein isolated from one animal, sometimes a mammal, and then looks to identify each corresponding version of that gene and protein in each experimentally or commercially significant species of animal—one might start with a gene in mice (because mice have become a common and available experimental model), and then find the corresponding versions in cows (for marketing to the dairy and beef industries), monkeys (for further experimentation leading to human use), and humans (for actual human use). So where is the written description problem? What if the actual precise sequences of the genes and protein in this family differ slightly from species to species? What if they are the same, but none is commercially significant until just one slight change is made to the sequence, and then the biological activity of the protein increases a million fold? Given the advanced state of the art, finding each version of the gene and protein may be enabled, but perhaps the genes and proteins themselves will not be described.[5]

Judge Rader has argued that the written description is not distinct from the enablement with respect to *disclosure* requirements. Under this view, the written description requirement is seen to be priority focused and preventing applicants from claiming new matter in subsequently filed applications that seek to obtain an earlier filing date. *See Enzo Biochem, Inc. v. Gen–Probe Inc.*, 323 F.3d 956, 976–87 (Fed.Cir.2002) (Rader, J., dissenting from denial to hear en banc). For a position contra, *see* Judge Newman's opinion in *Enzo Biochem*, 323 F.3d at 975 (concurring in denial to hear en banc).

5. *Role of the Prior Art.* As with the enablement and best mode requirements, questions arise as to the role of the prior art and the knowledge of persons skilled in the art in determining compliance with the written description requirement. *See In re Hayes Microcomputer Products, Inc. v. Hayes Microcomputer Products, Inc.*, 982 F.2d 1527, 1534 (Fed.Cir.1992) (in discussing the written description requirement, the court stated that "an inventor is not required to describe every detail of his invention. An applicant's disclosure obligation varies according to the art to which the invention pertains.").

Does the *Mahurkar* decision mean that a later claimed invention is supported whenever one of ordinary skill in the art would find that claim as obvious from the original specification disclosure? In *Lockwood v. American Airlines, Inc.*, 107 F.3d 1565 (Fed.Cir.1997), Judge Lourie rejected that implication.

---

5. *See New England Med. Ctr. Hosps., Inc. v. Peprotech, Inc.*, 29 U.S.P.Q.2d 1852 (D.N.J.1993) *appeal dismissed by joint request* 111 F.3d 141 (Fed.Cir.1997).

It is the disclosures of the applications that count. Entitlement to a filing date does not extend to subject matter which is not disclosed, but would be obvious over what is expressly disclosed. It extends only to that which is disclosed. While the meaning of terms, phrases, or diagrams in a disclosure is to be explained or interpreted from the vantage point of one skilled in the art, all the limitations must appear in the specification. The question is not whether a claimed invention is an obvious variant of that which is disclosed in the specification. Rather, a prior application itself must describe an invention, and do so in sufficient detail that one skilled in the art can clearly conclude that the inventor invented the claimed invention as of the filing date sought. . . . Lockwood argues that all that is necessary to satisfy the description requirement is to show that one is "in possession" of the invention. *Lockwood* accurately states the test, *see Vas–Cath Inc. v. Mahurkar*, 935 F.2d 1555, 1563–64 (Fed.Cir.1991), but fails to state how it is satisfied. One shows that one is "in possession" of the invention by describing the invention, with all its claimed limitations, not that which makes it obvious. . . . One does that by such descriptive means as words, structures, figures, diagrams, formulas, etc., that fully set forth the claimed invention. Although the exact terms need not be used in *haec verba*, *see Eiselstein v. Frank*, 52 F.3d 1035, 1038 (Fed.Cir.1995) ("[T]he prior application need not describe the claimed subject matter in exactly the same terms as used in the claims. . . ."), the specification must contain an equivalent description of the claimed subject matter. A description which renders obvious the invention for which an earlier filing date is sought is not sufficient.

6. *Investing and Divesting Descriptions.* Assume that, in *Mahurkar*, the court concluded that the "invention" (*i.e.* the functioning catheter) later claimed was *not* described in the original design application filed in 1982, and, therefore, that the 1982 application failed to provide priority support for the later 1984 utility application. Would it be inconsistent to conclude further that the published 1982 Canadian design registration was an adequate description of the "invention" within the meaning of § 102(b), the one-year bar rule—given that the 1982 application and the 1982 Canadian publication were the same? The answer is that there would not necessarily be an inconsistency. In *Mahurkar*, the court noted that "subtle distinction between a written description adequate to support a claim under § 112 and a written description sufficient to anticipate its subject matter under § 102(b)."

> The difference between "claim-supporting disclosures" and "claim-anticipating disclosures" was dispositive in *In re Lukach*, 442 F.2d 967 (CCPA 1971), where the court held that a U.S. "grandparent" application did not sufficiently describe the later-claimed invention, but that the appellant's intervening British application, a counterpart to the U.S. application, anticipated the claimed subject matter. As the court pointed out, "the description of a single embodiment of broadly claimed subject matter constitutes a description of the invention for anticipation purposes . . . , whereas the same information in a specification might not alone be enough to provide a description of that invention for purposes of adequate disclosure. . . ."

7. *The Role of Design Patent Applications.* Why did Mahurkar originally file a design patent application for what is clearly a functional invention? A design patent provides protection only for the ornamental features of an article of manufacture, 35 U.S.C. § 171, and case law makes clear that features dictated by function cannot be protected by a design patent. One answer is that it is considerably cheaper and easier to file a design application. The disclosure consists almost entirely of a drawing of the design in question.

8. *Original Claims Described Only By Biological or Other Function.* The traditional role of the description requirement is to prevent inventors from manipulating claim language by a post-filing amendment or in later continuing applications to cover inventions not fairly described in the specification as originally-filed. "Original" claims, that is, claims in the specification as filed with the application, are part of the specification and constitute their own description. It would seem to follow that an original claim cannot be rejected for noncompliance with the description requirement. *E.g. In re Koller*, 613 F.2d 819 (CCPA 1980).

In recent cases dealing with biotechnology inventions, the Federal Circuit has indicated that a specification describing a gene or DNA sequence only in terms of its biological function, *e.g.*, to encode for a known protein, does not comply with the written description requirement even as to an original claim directed to the functionally-defined DNA sequence. *See The Regents of the University of California v. Eli Lilly and Company*, 119 F.3d 1559 (Fed.Cir.1997); *Fiers v. Revel*, 984 F.2d 1164 (Fed.Cir.1993). Identifying the DNA solely by reference to its biological function shows neither a complete conception nor an adequate written description of the invention but rather merely a "wish" or "research plan."

9. *PTO's New Written Description Guidelines.* On January 5, 2001, the PTO issued new written description guidelines. *See* 66 Fed. Reg. 1099 or the PTO's website at www.uspto.gov. These guidelines do not constitute substantive rulemaking, and thus do "not have the force and effect of law." What follows are some excerpts from the guidelines:

> An applicant shows possession of the claimed invention by describing the claimed invention with all of its limitations using such descriptive means as words, structures, figures, diagrams, and formulas that fully set forth the claimed invention. Possession may be shown in a variety of ways including description of an actual reduction to practice, or by showing that the invention was "ready for patenting" such as by the disclosure of drawings or structural chemical formulas that show the invention was complete, or describing distinguishing identifying characteristics sufficient to show that the applicant was in possession of the claimed invention.

> A description as filed is presumed to be adequate unless or until sufficient evidence or reasoning to the contrary has been presented by the examiner to rebut the presumption.... The examiner has the initial burden of presenting by a preponderance of evidence why a person skilled in the art would not recognize in an applicant's disclosure a description of the invention defined by the claims.

66 Fed. Reg. at 1104, 1107.

Fujikawa v. Wattanasin

93 F.3d 1559 (Fed.Cir.1996).

■ Before MAYER, CLEVENGER, and RADER, CIRCUIT JUDGES.

■ CLEVENGER, CIRCUIT JUDGE.

Yoshihiro Fujikawa *et al.* (Fujikawa) appeal from two decisions of the Board of Patent Appeals and Interferences of the United States Patent & Trademark Office (Board) granting priority of invention in two related interferences to Sompong Wattanasin, and denying Fujikawa's motion to add an additional sub-genus count to the interferences. We affirm.

I

These interferences pertain to a compound and method for inhibiting cholesterol biosynthesis in humans and other animals. The compound count recites a genus of novel mevalonolactones. The method count recites a method of inhibiting the biosynthesis of cholesterol by administering to a "patient in need of said treatment" an appropriate dosage of a compound falling within the scope of the compound count.

The real parties in interest are Sandoz Pharmaceuticals Corporation (Sandoz), assignee of Wattanasin, and Nissan Chemical Industries, Ltd. (Nissan), assignee of Fujikawa.

* * *

V

Fujikawa ... appeals the Board's decision denying Fujikawa's motion to add a sub-genus count to the interference. The Board denied the motion because it found that Wattanasin's disclosure did not sufficiently describe Fujikawa's proposed count. Whether a disclosure contains a sufficient written description to support a proposed count, is a question of fact which we review for clear error. *Ralston Purina Co. v. Far–Mar–Co, Inc.*, 772 F.2d 1570, 1575, 227 USPQ 177, 179 (Fed.Cir.1985). We affirm the Board's denial of Fujikawa's motion because we do not believe it was clearly erroneous.

Wattanasin's application disclosed compounds of the following structure:

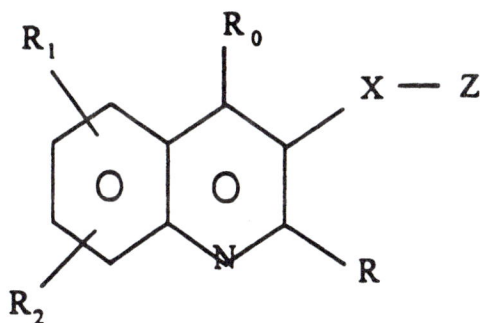

wherein each of R and R_0 is, independently, C_{1-6} alkyl (primary, secondary, or tertiary), C_{3-7} cycloalkyl, or the following ring,

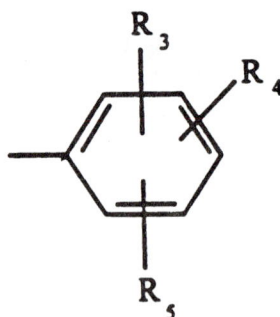

and each of R_1, R_2, R_3, R_4, and R_5 is, independently, hydrogen, C_4 alkyl, C_4 alkoxy, trifluoromethyl, fluoro, chloro, phenoxy, benzyloxy, or hydroxy.

In addition to this genus of compounds, Wattanasin disclosed as his preferred embodiments that: R_1 and R_2 are most preferably hydrogen, R_0 is most preferably phenyl, 4–fluorophenyl, or 3,5–dimethylphenyl; and R is most preferably methyl[10] or isopropyl.[11] Essentially, Fujikawa's proposed sub-genus is directed to compounds of the above structure in which R is cyclopropyl[12] and R_0 is 4–fluorophenyl. In other respects, the parties do not dispute that the particular constituents recited in Fujikawa's proposed count are adequately disclosed in Wattanasin's application. Thus, for example, both Wattanasin's most preferred embodiment and Fujikawa's proposed count describe R_1 and R_2 as hydrogen.

In denying Fujikawa's motion, the Board first noted that the proposed sub-genus was not disclosed *ipsis verbis* by Wattanasin. Specifically, the Board noted that Wattanasin preferred methyl and isopropyl for R, rather than cyclopropyl as in the proposed count. In addition, Wattanasin listed three preferred choices for R_0 only one of which was 4–fluorophenyl and gave no indication in his application as to whether he would prefer any one of the choices over the other two.

As the Board recognized, however, *ipsis verbis* disclosure is not necessary to satisfy the written description requirement of section 112. Instead, the disclosure need only reasonably convey to persons skilled in the art that the inventor had possession of the subject matter in question. . . . In other words, the question is whether Wattanasin's "application provides adequate direction which reasonably [would lead] persons skilled in the art" to the sub-genus of the proposed count. . . .

Many years ago our predecessor court graphically articulated this standard by analogizing a genus and its constituent species to a forest and its trees. As the court explained:

It is an old custom in the woods to mark trails by making blaze marks on the trees. It is no help in finding a trail . . . to be confronted simply by a

---

10.   Methyl is another name for C_1 alkyl.

11.   Isopropyl is another name for C_3 alkyl.

12.   Cyclopropyl is another name for C_3 cycloalkyl.

large number of unmarked trees. Appellants are pointing to trees. We are looking for blaze marks which single out particular trees. We see none.

In re Ruschig, 54 C.C.P.A. 1551, 379 F.2d 990, 994–95, 154 USPQ 118, 122 (1967).

In finding that Wattanasin's disclosure failed to sufficiently describe the proposed sub-genus, the Board again recognized that the compounds of the proposed count were not Wattanasin's preferred, and that his application contained no blazemarks as to what compounds, other than those disclosed as preferred, might be of special interest. In the absence of such blazemarks, simply describing a large genus of compounds is not sufficient to satisfy the written description requirement as to particular species or sub-genuses. *See, e.g., id.* 379 F.2d at 994, 154 USPQ at 122 ("Specific claims to single compounds require reasonably specific supporting disclosure and while ... naming [each species] is not essential, something more than the disclosure of a class of 1000, or 100, or even 48 compounds is required.").

Before this court, Fujikawa challenges the Board's denial of its motion on two grounds. First, Fujikawa persists in arguing that its proposed count is disclosed *ipsis verbis* in Wattanasin's application. The basis for this contention seems to be that Wattanasin lists cyclopropyl as one possible moiety for R in his disclosure of the genus. Clearly, however, just because a moiety is listed as one possible choice for one position does not mean there is *ipsis verbis* support for every species or sub-genus that chooses that moiety. Were this the case, a "laundry list" disclosure of every possible moiety for every possible position would constitute a written description of every species in the genus. This cannot be because such a disclosure would not "reasonably lead" those skilled in the art to any particular species. We therefore reject Fujikawa's argument on this point.

Second, Fujikawa claims that the Board erred in finding that Wattanasin's disclosure contained insufficient blazemarks to direct one of ordinary skill to the compounds of its proposed count. Specifically, Fujikawa points out that with respect to practically every position on the compound, the proposed count recites at least one of Wattanasin's preferred choices. Even with respect to position R, Fujikawa further explains, one of ordinary skill would have been moved by Wattanasin's disclosure to substitute cyclopropyl for isopropyl because the two substituents are isosteric.

While Fujikawa's arguments are not without merit, we cannot say, on this record, that the Board's decision was clearly erroneous. As the Board pointed out, Fujikawa's proposed sub-genus diverges from Wattanasin's preferred elements at least with respect to position R. Although, in hindsight, the substitution of cyclopropyl for isopropyl might seem simple and foreseeable, Wattanasin's disclosure provides no indication that position R would be a better candidate for substitution than any other. Thus, faced with Wattanasin's disclosure, it was not clear error to hold that one of ordinary skill would not be led to Fujikawa's sub-genus in particular.

Were we to extend *Ruschig*'s metaphor to this case, we would say that it is easy to bypass a tree in the forest, even one that lies close to the trail, unless the point at which one must leave the trail to find the tree is well marked. Wattanasin's preferred embodiments do blaze a trail through the forest; one that runs close by Fujikawa's proposed tree. His application, however, does not direct one to the proposed tree in particular, and does not teach the point at which one should leave the trail to find it. We therefore affirm the Board's denial of Fujikawa's motion.

VI

For the reasons we set forth above, the decision of the Board is, in all respects,

AFFIRMED.

NOTES

1. *Why Did Fujikawa Rely on Wattanasin's Written Description?* We can only speculate, but there may be a few reasons. First, Fujikawa wanted the PTO to rule that Wattanasin's specification did not support Fujikawa's subgenus so that when Fujikawa, down the road, filed a patent application on the subgenus, the PTO would find it difficult to use Wattanaisin's patent as prior art. Second, if the PTO agreed to add the subgenus count, Fujikawa would be confident that it could prove priority because Fujikawa worked on the subgenus and Wattanasin did not. Therefore, Fujikawa wanted the PTO on record that Wattanasin's specification did not provide adequate support for Fujikawa's subgenus, thus neutralizing the prior art and the PTO; or, third, Fujikawa wanted a victory during the interference proceeding there and then.

2. *Fujikawa* illustrates the limiting effect that the written description requirement can have on strategies in an interference (a proceeding to determine which of two parties has priority as to a given invention). To alter the facts for education purposes (and, hopefully, to simplify matters a bit), assume that: (1) the invention is a class of chemical compounds, "mevalonolactones," which we shall refer to as M/1–10,000, the class encompassing 10,000 related specific compounds; (2) both parties, Wattanasin (W) and Fujikawa (F), have discovered that M compounds have important cholesterol inhibiting qualities; (3) W's earliest research involved compound M/5; (4) F's later work involved M/2523; and (5) W's subsequent work has shown that compound M/2912 is by far the most effective and least toxic and, therefore, the only one that is commercially valuable. If the "invention" is defined as the M class, W will prevail because it was the first to invent (and to disclose in a patent application) a compound falling within that class. It will follow that, after winning the interference, W obtains a broad patent claiming M and can exclude F from the marketplace. As a strategy to obtain some patent leverage, F may assert that the subclass of M/2500–3000 is a separate invention. In interference terms, M/2500–3000 would be a separate "count." F could establish priority as to this count (being the first to develop a compound within the count). A patent claiming the subclass would be commercially valuable, covering M/2912. With separate patents, each covering the M/2912 compound, the parties might negotiate some type of cross-license. The strategy failed because F could not establish "written description" support in W's specification.

D.   DEFINITENESS: PARTICULARLY POINTING OUT AND DISTINCTLY CLAIMING

Section 112, paragraph 2 requires that the patent applicant particularly point out and distinctly claim the invention. The primary purpose of this requirement, known as the definiteness requirement, is to provide an explicit notice to others as to what constitutes infringement of the patent. A secondary purpose is to provide a clear measure of the invention in order to facilitate determinations of patentability.

On occasion, courts have failed to distinguish carefully among the definiteness, written description, and enablement requirements. One way to think about these three requirements is that definiteness and written description work hand in glove to assure that the boundaries of the patent applicant's proprietary interest are clearly demarcated. The definiteness requirement insures that a patent claim, which comprises a single sentence, is clear on its face. The written description requirement allows the inventor to provide a long and detailed lexicon for interpreting every word in that single sentence—that is the claim—but requires that the lexicon itself be clear. Enablement means that the specification must describe the manner of making and using the invention in such clear terms as to enable any person skilled in the art to make and use it. The scope of enablement must be commensurate with the scope of the claims, but this is a problem of the sufficiency of the specification, not the clarity of the claim language.

Athletic Alternatives, Inc. v. Prince Mfg., Inc.

73 F.3d 1573 (Fed.Cir.1996).

■ Before Michel, Circuit Judge, Nies, Senior Circuit Judge,* and Clevenger, Circuit Judge.

■ Michel, Circuit Judge.

Athletic Alternatives, Inc. ("AAI") appeals from the June 29, 1994 order of the U.S. District Court for the District of Arizona, No. CIV–92–176–PHX–RGS (SLV), granting summary judgment of noninfringement in favor of Prince Manufacturing, Inc. ("Prince"). [footnote omitted] Because AAI cannot lawfully prevail on its infringement allegations against Prince when the asserted patent claim is correctly construed, we affirm.

BACKGROUND

AAI designs athletic products, including string systems for sports rackets, and Prince manufactures and distributes tennis rackets. In February 1990, after entering into a confidentiality agreement, the parties began a collaborative effort to develop a commercially available tennis racket with splayed strings, *i.e.*, with string ends anchored to the racket frame alternately above and below its central plane. AAI had already conceived of and applied for a patent covering its prototype "Redemption Stringing System" in August 1988, and it shared the prototype with Prince under the confidentiality agreement. During the course of their collaboration, Prince and AAI shared other designs and ideas but ultimately failed to reach a mutually satisfactory licensing agreement.

Prince abandoned work on AAI's prototype in favor of an alternative splayed string system. In February 1991, it placed a racket with this system

---

* Judge Nies took senior status on November 1, 1995.

on the market under the model name "Vortex." The sides of the Vortex frame include strings splayed from the central plane at two, and only two, distinct offset distances: a distance of 2 millimeters at the upper and lower corners, and a distance of 4.5 millimeters along the sides of the frame.

AAI, meanwhile, continued to prosecute its splayed string system patent application. As originally filed, the application contained 19 claims, the first of which broadly claimed "[a] sports racket ... wherein at least some of [the] ends of [the] string segments are successively and alternately secured to [the] frame at locations a distance d_i in front of and behind [the] central plane." Claim 5 of the application, depending from Claim 1, recited a racket "wherein d_i is uniform for all strings." Claim 7, also drafted in dependent form, recited a racket "wherein [the] distance d_i ... varies continuously between minimums as small as about zero for the lateral strings near the tip and the heel portions of said frame, and a maximum of up to about 1/2 inch for the ends of the lateral string segments through the center of the side portions of [the] frame." This language, unlike that of Claim 1, closely tracked the specification's description of the preferred embodiment.[2]

In a May 1989 office action, the examiner rejected, inter alia, Claims 1 through 5 and objected to Claim 7. Specifically, the examiner rejected Claims 1 and 5 as anticipated by British Patent No. 223,151 to Lewis ("Lewis"). Like AAI's Claim 5, Lewis discloses a racket in which all the string ends are offset from the central plane by a uniform distance. Having rejected Claim 1, the independent claim from which it ultimately depended, the examiner objected to Claim 7. At the same time, however, the examiner indicated that Claim 7 contained patentable subject matter and thus "would be allowable if rewritten in independent form."

In response to this office action, AAI filed a set of amendments to the application in October 1989. First, AAI canceled Claim 1 in favor of a new Claim 20, reciting "[a] sports racket ... where [the offset] distance d_i varies between a minimum distance for the first and last string ends in [the] sequence [of adjacent string ends] and a maximum distance for a string end between [the] first and last string ends in [the] sequence." After noting that it "rewrote Claim 1 to more succinctly define the present invention ... [in] Claim 20", AAI explained the responsiveness of the new claim to the rejection on Lewis as follows:

> Lewis is primarily concerned with the problem of splitting of wooden frames where all holes are located in the center plane of the frame. Another objective is to stabilize the frame against twisting. He places the holes somewhat away from and alternately above and below the center plane. Consequently, the stringing surface superficially resembles the present string suspension arrangement. However, we do not believe that the degree of splay or separation is sufficient to achieve the present effect of improved performance and feel of the string surface. Moreover, the Lewis

---

2. According to the specification, "[s]ince the important objective is to correct for elevational trajectory errors, it is preferred to flare the ends of lateral strings only, most preferred is that d_i vary continuously between a maximum of $d_i = 1/2$ inch in the center, to zero for the last lateral strings near the tip and the heel of the frame."

racket is structurally different in that it maintains the same [s]play (d_i) all the way around.

Claim 1 has now been rewritten and resubmitted as Claim 20 to positively recite the feature of the splay (d_i), varying between a minimum and a maximum for a series of adjacent parallel strings, to thus clearly distinguish over Lewis.

In other words, according to this portion of the record, AAI drafted Claim 20 in a manner calculated to retain as much of the scope of Claim 1 as possible while still avoiding the Lewis reference.

Consistent with the examiner's suggestion, AAI also redrafted Claim 7 in independent form and submitted it as Claim 21. It recited "[a] sports racket ... wherein [the] distance d_i ... varies continuously between minimums as small as about zero for the ends of laterial [sic, lateral] strings near the tip and heel portions of [the] frame, and maximum of up to about 1/2—inch for the ends of lateral string segments near the center of [the] side portion of [the] frame." As with Claim 7, the language of Claim 21 closely tracks that of the specification's description of the preferred embodiment. Claim 21 thus differed from Claim 20 in two ways: first, with respect to the limitation directed to the pattern of splay, Claim 20 recited an offset distance that "varies between" minimum and maximum values, whereas Claim 21 recited an offset distance that "varies *continuously* between" such values (emphasis added); second, Claim 21 recited particular numerical values for the minimum and maximum offset distances, whereas Claim 20 did not. Finally, AAI added a new claim that, like the rejected Claim 1, broadly covered any pattern of splayed string ends.[3]

The examiner's Interview Summary Record indicates that the parties discussed proposed Claims 20 and 21 during a personal interview on November 16, 1989. In sharp contrast to the explanation AAI offered with the amendments that it filed, the summary notes that AAI's "[a]ttorney explained how cl. 20 is directed to [the] preferred embodiment and how [its] recitation distinguishes over [the] cited references." This notation calls into serious doubt the premise that AAI drafted Claim 20 with the sole purpose of overcoming the Lewis-based rejection of Claim 1.

After reviewing the submitted amendments, the examiner rejected Claims 20 through 22 in the final office action of January 29, 1990. Specifically, the examiner concluded that all three claims would have been obvious from Lewis in view of U.S. Patent No. 4,664,380 to Kuebler. AAI contested the rejection, arguing that the Kuebler patent, directed to improving the stiffness of racket frames, teaches nothing at all about splayed string ends and reiterating that "Lewis ... exhibits splay, but uniform splay all the way around the racket frame." According to AAI, its "previous amendment ... introduced the structural limitations of variously specifying the non-uniform splay characteristics which clearly differentiate the present invention from the 1924 wooden tennis racket art represented by the Lewis reference." The examiner nevertheless adhered to his final rejection of the claims by notice dated April 17, 1990.

---

3. Styled Claim 22, it recited the improvement in a sports racket "comprising that a part of the total number of the strings are secured to the frame alternately in front of and behind the central plane in a splayed configuration to improve playing characteristics of [the] racket."

AAI appealed the final rejection to the Board of Patent Appeals. Consistent with the Interview Summary Record discussed above, and in contrast to the supporting explanation filed with the amendments, AAI implied in its appeal brief that Claims 20 and 21 had the same scope with respect to the claimed pattern of splay. First, early in its appeal brief, AAI noted that "Claims 20 and 21 represent independent claims based on rewritten dependent claim[ ] 7 ... which [was] formerly held to be allowable if rewritten in independent form." Second, in explaining the nature of the invention, AAI stated that "[i]n the preferred embodiment, best seen in Fig. 4a, the distance d_i varies between minima for the first and last lateral strings near the tip section 12 and heel section 13, respectively, and a maximum in the central region of the lateral section of the frame." AAI thus described the preferred embodiment as a pattern in which the offset distance "varies between" a minimum and a maximum without using the intervening modifier "continuously." Finally, AAI affirmed that "Claim 20 requires the distance d_i (the degree of splay) to vary between a minimum ... and a maximum," and that "Claim 21 ... recites the same element of varying splay of the ends of lateral string segments." After further communication between AAI and the examiner, as well as an amendment deleting Claim 22, the examiner withdrew the final rejection and issued a Notice of Allowability in December 1990.

AAI was accordingly granted U.S. Patent No. 5,037,097 (the '097 patent) on August 6, 1991. It then filed the infringement suit at bar in January 1992. Claim 1 of the '097 patent, formerly Claim 20 of the application, was the only claim AAI asserted against Prince. It reads as follows:

1.   A sports racket, comprising:

a peripheral frame having a tip, heel, and side portions disposed in and about a central plane of symmetry; said tip, heel, and side portions having a width in a direction perpendicular to said plane of symmetry;

a handle with a grip thereon extending from and secured to the heel of said frame;

a first plurality of string segments extending across said central plane between opposite locations of said frame in a first direction;

a second plurality of string segments extending across said central plane between opposed locations of said frame in a second direction;

said first and second direction being at an angle with respect to each other, and said first and second plurality of string segments being interwoven into a planar webbing defining a ball contact area in said central plane within said frame;

each of said string segments having two ends, a first of said ends extending in a first direction between the periphery of said contact area and a proximate location on said frame, and the second of said ends extending between the opposite side of the periphery of said ball contact area to a proximate location on said frame in a direction opposite to said first direction;

where at least said first ends of at least said first plurality of string segments are secured to said frame at a distance d_i, where d_i is the perpendicular distance between the central plane and the location on said frame to which the ith string end is secured, i designating the order of the ith string end in the sequence of adjacent first string ends of said first plurality of string segments, the distance d_i being alternately measured in opposite directions from said central plane, and *where said distance d_i varies between minimum distances for the first and last string ends in said sequence and a maximum distance for a string end between said first and last string ends in said sequence.*

The language critical to this appeal has been emphasized. Claim 14 of the '097 patent, formerly Claim 21 of the application, is the patent's only other independent claim. Again, it covers AAI's preferred pattern of variation in the string offset distances, according to which distance d_i "varies continuously between minimums as small as about zero for the ends of lateral strings near the tip and heel portions of said frame, and a maximum of up to about 1/2–inch for the ends of lateral string segments near the center of said side portions of said frame."

On December 7, 1992, Prince moved for summary judgment of noninfringement on the grounds that (a) Claim 1 of the '097 patent, which, according to its construction, requires that the offset distance d_i take on at least three values (*i.e.*, a minimum, a maximum, and at least one intermediate value), does not read on the Vortex racket, which has only two offset distances; and (b) the prosecution history of the '097 patent, during which AAI amended Claim 1 to require this minimum of at least three values for d_i in order to overcome the rejection on Lewis, estops AAI from attempting to hold Prince liable for infringement under the doctrine of equivalents.[4]

The district court granted Prince's motion for summary judgment over AAI's opposition in its June 29, 1994 order, adopting the substance of Prince's arguments as to both claim construction and prosecution history. Specifically, the court concluded that "according to the plain language of Claim 1, d_i must change at a point that is in an intermediate position in relation to the minimum distances for the first and last string ends and the maximum distance for a string end between the first and last string end. Consequently, there must be more than two values for d_i." The court further concluded that AAI was estopped from alleging that the Vortex racket infringes Claim 1 under the doctrine of equivalents, having already sacrificed coverage of a splay pattern with less than three offset distances in order to overcome the rejection on Lewis. Providing an alternative ground for its decision of noninfringement under the doctrine of equivalents, the district court also concluded that AAI's failure to respond to Prince's motion for summary judgment with citation to "specific facts from which a factfinder could conclude that Defendant's racket 'performs substantially the same function in substantially the same way to obtain the same result'" entitled Prince to summary judgment in its favor on the issue.

---

4. Prince's answer to AAI's complaint set up certain affirmative defenses but did not include invalidity of the '097 patent as an affirmative defense. Prince's prayer for relief contained a single reference to invalidity, in praying for a decree and judgment "[d]eclaring United States patent 5,037,097 to be invalid and not infringed." Prince's motion for summary judgment was not styled as a partial motion, and the issue of validity was not raised on summary judgment or in the appeal to this court.

AAI appeals from the district court's decision, contending that Claim 1, when properly construed, reads on the splay pattern with two offset distances used in the Vortex racket. In other words, according to AAI, the district court erred in construing Claim 1 to require that the offset distance d_i take on at least three values. AAI further contends that the district court repeated its error in claim construction when it undertook its prosecution history estoppel analysis and erred by entering judgment against AAI for failure to point to specific record evidence of the fact of equivalence at a time when AAI was not on notice that such citation to specific evidence was required to resist an adverse summary judgment.

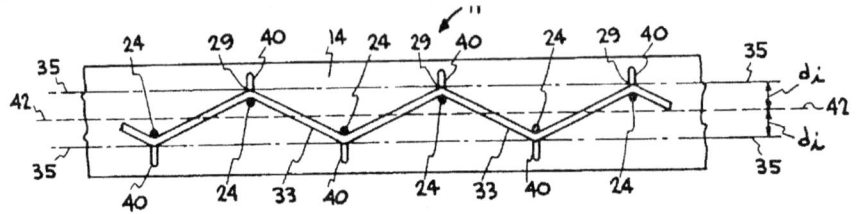

FIG. 2

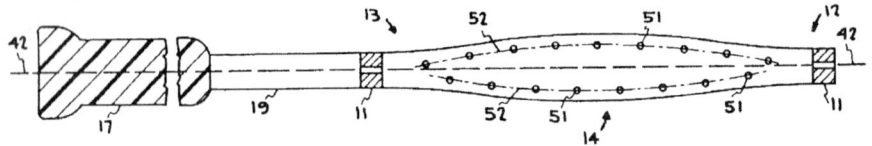

FIG. 4A

[Editors' Note—Quote from the specification of the '097 patent]

[The principal feature of the invention becomes more apparent from inspection of **FIG. 2**, which is a cross-section [of the tennis racket].... Dotted line **42** indicates the location of the center plane through the racket. The numerals **24** indicate the lateral strings contacting the last longitudinal string **33** next to the side of frame **11**, forming nodes **29** defining the ends **40** of the string segments. The ends **40** of the lateral strings **24** are alternately anchored to the frame **11** at points above and below the center plane **42** at a distance d_i therefrom. The distance d_i is thus the measure of the distance from the center plane at which the ith string end is anchored. Since the important objective is to correct for elevational trajectory errors, it is preferred to flare the ends of lateral strings only, most preferred is that d_i vary continuously between a maximum of $d_i = 1/2$ inch in the center, to zero for the last lateral strings near the tip and the heel of the frame. Col. 4, l. 57 to col. 5, l. 7.

FIG. 4a is a cross-section of a preferred racket frame through its central axis **42**, having a handle **17**, arms **19** extending from said handle to generally elliptical racket frame **11**. The significant feature of the racket frame **11** is that its side sections **14** are widened in order to permit a pattern of drillings **51** at a greater distance from the center plane than would be possible with the racket frames of conventional width,.... The width contour of the side sections **14** of the racket frame preferably corresponds to the distance contour **52** of the chosen pattern of flare for the drillings **51** for receiving the string segment ends, i.e., widest in the center of the side sections, up to about the width of the handle, and gradually diminishing in width of the frame towards the tip and heel sections **12** and **13** respectively." Col. 5, ll. 51–68]

ANALYSIS

* * *

A. Literal Infringement

Patent infringement analysis involves two steps: the threshold construction of the meaning and scope of the asserted claim, followed by the determination whether the accused product infringes the properly construed claim. *Id.* at 976. Where, as here, the parties do not dispute any relevant facts regarding the accused product but disagree over which of two possible meanings of Claim 1 is the proper one, the question of literal infringement collapses to one of claim construction and is thus amenable to summary judgment. *See, e.g., Chemical Eng'g Corp. v. Essef Indus.*, 795 F.2d 1565, 1572–73 (Fed.Cir.1986).

The task of claim construction requires us to examine all the relevant sources of meaning in the patent record with great care, the better to guarantee that we determine the claim's true meaning. As we have often noted, these sources include the patent's claims, specification, and, if in evidence, its prosecution history. *Markman*, 52 F.3d at 979–80, 34 U.S.P.Q.2D at 1329–30. In addition, a number of canons, such as the doctrine of claim differentiation, guide our construction of all patent claims. Finally, we have a rich body of case law on which to rely.

1. The Claim Language

We begin with the language of Claim 1 itself. As was noted above, Claim 1 of the '097 patent recites a pattern of splay "where [the offset] distance d_i varies between minimum distances for the first and last string ends in [the] sequence and a maximum distance for a string end between [the] first and last string ends in [the] sequence." Because the specification contains neither a definition of the phrase "varies between" nor a suggestion that AAI sought to assign to claim terms anything but their ordinary and accustomed meanings, those are the meanings we must give them. *Intellicall, Inc. v. Phonometrics, Inc.*, 952 F.2d 1384, 1388 (Fed.Cir.1992); *Envirotech Corp. v. Al George, Inc.*, 730 F.2d 753, 759 (Fed.Cir.1984).

AAI contends, citing a number of dictionary definitions of "between" in its favor, that "the plain meaning of the words 'varies between minimums ... and a maximum' is that the distance of string splay must change ... [but] nothing in Claim 1 prescribes (or limits) how much or how many times the distance must change."[5] Prince, for its part, cites alternative and equally valid dictionary definitions of "between" in an effort to demonstrate that the trial court properly construed the claim to require that the offset distance d_i take on at least three values, i.e., a minimum, a maxi-

---

5. Were the claim to be so construed, it would cover any splay pattern with more than one offset distance and would thus read on the Vortex racket.

mum, and at least one intermediate value.[6] A comparison of these definitions with those relied upon by AAI suggests that the claim phrase "varies between" is, at best, equivocal.

According to one ordinary sense of "between"—"in the space that separates: BETWIXT <an alleyway—two tall buildings> <a vacuum—two electrodes>: in the midst of : surrounded by <a lion rampant—eight crosses>," WEBSTER'S THIRD NEW INTERNATIONAL DICTIONARY OF THE ENGLISH LANGUAGE 209 (1976) (definition 2b of preposition "between")—only a splay pattern in which the offset distance takes on more than two values has an offset distance that varies between minimum distances and a maximum distance. According, however, to another equally ordinary sense of "between"—"from one to the other of <air service—the two cities>," *id.* (definition 3a of preposition "between")—a splay pattern in which the offset distance takes on only two values has an offset distance that varies between minimum distances and a maximum distance. In sum, the dispositive claim language on its face is susceptible to two equally plausible meanings, under one of which the Vortex racket literally infringes Claim 1, and under the other of which it does not. As a result, the scope of Claim 1 cannot be defined by resort to the ordinary and accustomed meanings of its terms alone, and the specification is completely silent with regard to the meaning of "varies between."

2.   The Prosecution History

Because the disputed claim and its specification do not establish the meaning of the operative claim language, we turn to the prosecution history for guidance. Our reading of the prosecution history is informed by the understanding that the documents recording this history are created by persons schooled in the art of patent prosecution.

To the trained eye, the prosecution history of the '097 patent presents a muddled and self-contradictory story. As originally filed, independent Claim 1 broadly claimed a racket with any pattern of splay, while dependent Claims 5 and 7 each claimed a particular pattern of splay. Specifically, Claim 5 recited the pattern of uniform splay, while Claim 7 recited the pattern of splay described as the preferred embodiment in the patent's specification. Thus, as originally filed, Claim 1 was certainly broad enough to cover a racket with a pattern of splay containing less than three offset distances. The examiner initially rejected Claims 1 and 5 as anticipated by Lewis, a reference teaching the pattern of uniform splay. Such a rejection was, of course, appropriate as to Claim 1 because the pattern of uniform splay taught by Lewis surely anticipates a claim broadly covering a pattern with "at least some" splay.

Before focusing on AAI's response to this rejection, we pause to note a practical aspect of patent prosecution. Specifically, when amending a claim so as to avoid a rejection based on a particular reference, the skilled patent prosecutor usually seeks to draft an amendment that narrows the claim only as much as is thought necessary to overcome the rejection. Prior to looking at AAI's response to the initial rejection, an experienced patent

---

6.   According to this construction, the Vortex racket cannot literally infringe the claim.

prosecutor might thus have expected AAI to attempt to overcome Lewis by amending Claim 1 to cover all patterns of non-uniform splay, including those with only two offset distances.

AAI's written response to the first office action does not disappoint this expectation. As was discussed above, AAI's response included two distinct amendments. First, AAI rewrote Claim 1 as new Claim 20, expressly stating that it was doing so in a manner calculated to overcome the Lewis rejection. Second, AAI rewrote Claim 7 as new Claim 21. Since the subject matter of this latter claim had already been deemed allowable by the examiner, AAI did not discuss Claim 21 beyond briefly remarking that it was an independent version of Claim 7. This brief remark sharply contrasts with AAI's detailed explanation of why, in its view, Lewis did not anticipate Claim 20, thereby lending strong support to the conclusion that AAI drafted Claim 20 to be broader in scope than Claim 21. We might well conclude that Claim 20 was directed to any non-uniform splay pattern, including a pattern having only two offset distances, were this the only evidence in the file history. It is not.

The record also contains documents clearly indicating that, with respect to the pattern of splay, AAI understood the scope of Claim 20 to approximate that of Claim 21, which both parties concede recites a pattern of splay containing at least three offset distances. The first such document is the examiner's Interview Summary Record of November 16, 1989, in which the examiner noted that AAI's "[a]ttorney explained how cl. 20 is directed to [the] preferred embodiment and how [its] recitation distinguishes over [the] cited references." In other words, according to this summary, the intended scope of Claim 20 was not the broadest scope that would nonetheless overcome the Lewis reference, but was instead the same as that of Claim 21, at least with respect to the basic pattern of splay. On this reading, Claims 20 and 21 differed only in that Claim 21, unlike Claim 20, recited specific numerical values for the minimum and maximum offset distances.

AAI's appeal brief, like the interview summary, features the same characterization of Claim 20. There, as outlined above, AAI stated that *both* Claims 20 and 21 were based on the allowable subject matter that had originally appeared in Claim 7, reciting the pattern of splay in the preferred embodiment. Furthermore, AAI used the phrase "varies between" to describe the variable splay of the preferred embodiment and maintained that the "element of varying splay" was the same in Claims 20 and 21. Again, these assertions indicate that the scope of Claims 20 and 21 differed only with respect to the particular numerical embodiment described in Claim 21, but not with respect to the basic pattern of splay.

Two strong and contradictory interpretive strands thus run through the patent's prosecution history. According to the first, Claim 20 was drafted simply to avoid the Lewis reference and differs significantly in scope from Claim 21. According to the second, Claims 20 and 21 recite the same basic pattern of splay, while Claim 21 adds a numerical value limitation. Each strand, considered alone, leads to a coherent and distinct meaning of the disputed claim. One does not prevail over the other, and together they are irreconcilable. The prosecution in this case is thus unhelpful as an interpretive resource for construing the "varies between" claim limitation.

3.   Claim Differentiation

Neither the claim, the specification, nor the prosecution history establishes the meaning of the phrase "varies between" in Claim 1. AAI, resorting to an interpretive guide for secondary support of its position regarding the meaning of "varies between," contends that the doctrine of claim differentiation compels us to interpret the claim as it does, *i.e.*, to require that the offset distance take on two or more, rather than three or more, values. According to AAI, while "[t]here is no question Claim 14 requires three or more different distances of string splay," it would constitute legal error to read the "continuously" limitation of Claim 14 into Claim 1.

AAI's argument overlooks the fact that Prince does not contend that Claim 1, like Claim 14, requires that the offset distance recited therein vary continuously between minimums and a maximum. Continuous variation, as AAI itself concedes, requires a continuous gradual change in the offset distance of parallel strings; this implies that the offset distance for each string differs from that of both adjacent strings. In contrast, Prince contends only that Claim 1 requires that the offset distance take on three or more values, a potentially broader limitation. For example, suppose a tennis racket were to employ seventeen horizontal strings but only four offset distances. Under Prince's construction, this arrangement would infringe Claim 1 because it employs more than three offset distances, but would not infringe Claim 14 because the offset distances do not vary continuously. Therefore, assent to Prince's contention that Claim 1 requires three or more offset distances would not render the "continuously" limitation in Claim 14 superfluous. In short, the choice between Prince's and AAI's construction of Claim 1 simply does not implicate the doctrine of claim differentiation, and we are left with two equally plausible meanings of Claim 1. We must therefore pursue the interpretive process to state which of the two meanings is correct.

4.   Section 112

In order to decide which of the two senses of "varies between" to employ in construing the '097 patent, we refer to the statutory provision that prescribes the would-be patentee's claim drafting burden, 35 U.S.C. § 112 (1988). Specifically, paragraph 2 of section 112 requires that the "specification shall conclude with one or more claims particularly pointing out and *distinctly* claiming the subject matter which the applicant regards as his invention." (Emphasis added). As courts have recognized since the requirement that one's invention be distinctly claimed became part of the patent law in 1870,[7] the primary purpose of the requirement is "to guard against unreasonable advantages to the patentee and disadvantages to others arising from uncertainty as to their [respective] rights." *General*

---

7. Patent Act of 1870, ch. 230, § 26, 16 Stat. 198, 201 ("[B]efore any inventor or discoverer shall receive a patent ... he shall particularly point out and distinctly claim the part, improvement, or combination which he claims as his invention or discovery....").

Electric Co. v. Wabash Appliance Corp., 304 U.S. 364, 369 (1938). *See, e.g., McClain v. Ortmayer*, 141 U.S. 419, 424 (1891) ("The object of the patent law in requiring the patentee [to distinctly claim his invention] is not only to secure to him all to which he is entitled, but to apprise the public of what is still open to them."); *Rengo Co. v. Molins Mach. Co.*, 657 F.2d 535, 551 (3d Cir.) ("Its purpose is to demarcate the boundaries of the purported invention, in order to provide notice to others of the limits beyond which experimentation and invention are undertaken at the risk of infringement.") (internal quotation omitted), *cert. denied*, 454 U.S. 1055 (1981); *Hoganas AB v. Dresser Indus.*, 9 F.3d 948, 951, (Fed.Cir.1993) (function of claims is "putting competitors on notice of the scope of the claimed invention"). Were we to allow AAI successfully to assert the broader of the two senses of "between" against Prince, we would undermine the fair notice function of the requirement that the patentee distinctly claim the subject matter disclosed in the patent from which he can exclude others temporarily. Where there is an equal choice between a broader and a narrower meaning of a claim, and there is an enabling disclosure that indicates that the applicant is at least entitled to a claim having the narrower meaning, we consider the notice function of the claim to be best served by adopting the narrower meaning.

We conclude that Claim 1 of the '097 patent includes the limitation that the splay-creating string end offset distance take on at least three values, i.e., a minimum, a maximum, and at least one intermediate value. We thus affirm the district court's conclusion that Claim 1 does not literally read on the Vortex racket.

* * *

CONCLUSION

Because AAI cannot lawfully prevail on its infringement allegations against Prince when the asserted patent claim is correctly construed, summary judgment for Prince was proper. Accordingly, the district court's order and the judgment of noninfringement are

AFFIRMED.

COSTS

Each party to bear its own costs.

■ NIES, SENIOR CIRCUIT JUDGE, concurring in result.

I concur in the result of the majority opinion.

I do not agree that the adoption of the narrower of two equally plausible interpretations somehow flows from the requirement of section 112 ¶ 2 that the patentee must particularly point out and distinctly claim the subject matter which he regards as his invention. The majority analysis is illogical to me. Narrowness can not be equated with definiteness. *Cf. In re Robins*, 429 F.2d 452, 458, 57 CCPA 1321 (1970) (" 'Breadth is not indefiniteness.' *In re Gardner*, 427 F.2d 786 (1970)."). The majority, in effect, eviscerates the requirement of section 112, ¶ 2 for the patentee to particularly point out and distinctly claim his invention while purporting to rely on it.

In any event this new basis for construing a claim is unnecessary in this case. The claims must be construed to require at least three offset distances (d_i) based on the prosecution history, the other claims, and the prior art. Respecting the meaning of the phrases "varies continuously between" (Claim 14) and "varies between" (Claim 1), AAI concedes that "[t]here is no question that Claim 14 requires three or more different distances of string splay," but argues that Claim 1 requires only two. Yet, it is not the word "continuously" which indicates "three or more distances" of splay in Claim 14. The word "continuously," as the majority holds, merely suggests the arrangement of the various d_i along the sides of the racket. Thus, it can only be the phrase "varies ... between" which leads one to conclude that Claim 14 requires at least three distances of splay. Therefore, the word "continuously" need not be read into Claim 1 in order to construe Claim 1 as also requiring at least three distances of splay. Giving the words "varies between" the same interpretation in Claim 1 as in Claim 14, one must conclude that at least three distances are required in both. This interpretation is buttressed by the patentee's statement during prosecution that the claim that became Claim 1 is directed to the preferred embodiment which showed at least three d_i. AAI never withdrew that statement. The prosecution history is not as equivocal as the majority posits.[1]

* * *

NOTES

1. *The Policies Underlying 112, ¶ 2.* Section 112, ¶ 2 requires that the patent particularly point out and distinctly claim the invention. This requirement, known as the "definiteness" requirement, serves two purposes. First, a distinctly drafted claim puts the public, particularly the patentee's competitors, on notice of where the patentee's proprietary boundaries reside thereby informing the competitors of what activity may constitute infringement; and second, a distinctly drafted claim distinguishes the invention from the prior art, in other words, it sets forth what exactly the invention is. An assertion of indefiniteness "requires an analysis of whether those persons skilled in the art would understand the bounds of the claim when read in light of the specification," *Credle v. Bond*, 25 F.3d 1566, 1576 (Fed.Cir.1994), and the "degree of precision necessary for adequate claims is a function of the nature of the subject matter." *Miles Laboratories, Inc. v. Shandon Inc.*, 997 F.2d 870, 875 (Fed.Cir.1993). As one district court noted, citing *Miles Laboratories*, "[p]recision should ... not be equated with quantification. Not every claim must be expressed in terms of specific numerical values." *Bausch & Lomb, Inc. v. Alcon Labs., Inc.*, 79 F.Supp.2d 243, 246 (W.D.N.Y.1999). Indeed, terms of degree such as "substantially" are frequently used in claim drafting. *See Andrew Corp. v. Gabriel Electronics, Inc.*, 847 F.2d 819, 821 (Fed.Cir.1988). In the late 19th century, the Supreme Court captured the policies underlying the notice function:

> Accurate description of the invention is required by law, for several important purposes: 1. That the government may know what is granted, and what will become public property when the term of the monopoly

---

1. I find no reason for an extended analysis of the doctrine of claim differentiation which is a trivial issue in this case. Claims 1 and 14 are of different scope by reason of the numerical limitations set forth in Claim 14.

expires. 2. That licensed persons desiring to practise the invention may know during the term how to make, construct, and use the invention. 3. That other inventors may know what part of the field of invention is unoccupied.

Bates v. Coe, 98 U.S. 31, 39 (1878).

Thus, patent claim drafting is serious business and many pitfalls can be labeled under the rubric of indefiniteness. An excellent review of some typical formal indefiniteness problems can be found in Robert C. Faber, Landis on Mechanics of Patent Claim Drafting § 23 (4th ed., 1996). For example, the first time an element or part is mentioned in a claim it should be introduced with an indefinite article "a" or "an" and then in all subsequent appearances the element should be referred to with the definite article "the", or by "said". Similarly, it is considered indefinite to positively recite a hole, grove, aperture, slot, etc. Instead such voids should be recited inferentially, such as "a door having a peep-hole there through." Faber, Landis on Mechanics of Patent Claim Drafting § 26. To avoid the possibility that claims may be held invalid under § 112, ¶ 2, they should be devoid of vague and indefinite language—they should be certain as to what they cover and how they relate to the entire written description, including any examples therein. Faber, Landis on Mechanics of Patent Claim Drafting § 68.

Summarizing indefiniteness, the Federal Circuit recently had this to say: "When a claim is not amenable to construction or [is] insolubly ambiguous it is indefinite. However, a claim is not indefinite merely because it poses a difficult issue of claim construction. Rather, if the meaning of the claim is discernible, even though the task may be formidable and the conclusions may be one over which reasonable persons will disagree, we have held the claim sufficiently clear to avoid invalidity on indefiniteness grounds." *Power–One, Inc. v. Artesyn Tech., Inc.* 599 F.3d 1343, 1350 (Fed.Cir.2010) (citations and quotations omitted).

2. *Narrowing the Scope to Save the Claim.* The majority opinion in the *AAI* case makes much of the notice function of patent claims. At issue in the *AAI* opinion, is the part of this notice function that is played by the requirement of Section 112, second paragraph. (Remember, the written description requirement also plays an important part in the notice function of patent claims). According to the majority

> Where there is an equal choice between a broader and a narrower meaning of a claim . . . we consider the notice function of the claim to be best served by adopting the narrower meaning.

Other Federal Circuit panels have endorsed this as a canon of claim construction. *See, e.g., Ethicon Endo–Surgery, Inc. v. United States Surgical Corp.,* 93 F.3d 1572, 1581–82 (Fed.Cir.1996); *Digital Biometrics, Inc. v. Identix, Inc.,* 149 F.3d 1335, 1344 (Fed.Cir.1998).

Do you think that the result reached by the majority best serves the overall public policies underlying the patent system? Is it compelled by an analysis that is based on the notice function of patent claims? When we discuss notice in this context, it is notice to whom? The majority is focusing on specific notice to actual potential infringers who might read a specific patent and rely on that reading. Is there another form of notice? How about notice to all of the participants in the patent system: such as patentees, infringers, those who would design around, and those who would learn from the disclosed knowledge? Is it possible that Judge Nies, in her concurring opinion, is concerned with this general form of notice? Indeed, according to Judge Nies, the majority opinion "in effect, eviscerates the require-ment of section 112, ¶ 2." If the concurring opinion were the law, then it would give broad general advice on how to draft, read, and act upon, patent claims: don't be ambiguous, or your claim is invalid. But what do you think of such a rule? Is there any text that is completely lacking in ambiguity? Consider Chief Justice Marshall's statement in *Evans v. Eaton*, 16 U.S. 454, 506, 3 Wheat. 454 (1818):

> The construction of the patent must certainly depend on the words of the instrument. But where, as in this case, the words are ambiguous, these may be circumstances which ought to have great influence in expounding them. The intention of the parties, if that intention can be collected from sources which the principles of law permit us to explore, are entitled to great consideration.

To ask these questions in a slightly different way: In a choice between these two views—ambiguous terms get their narrower meaning or ambiguous terms invalidate the claim—which result better serves the policies of the patent system? Some might argue that the result that saves the patent seems attractive, because it protects all of those who have invested in the commercial activity surrounding a patent: factories may have been built, labor hired, advertising campaigns started, etc. But what about the investment backed expectations of the alleged infringer? Others might argue that the result that invalidates all such ambiguous patent claims purges the system of sloppy patents. *See Process Control Corp. v. HydReclaim Corp.*, 190 F.3d 1350 (Fed.Cir.1999) (Where "claims are susceptible to only one reasonable interpretation and that interpretation results in a nonsensical construction of the claim as a whole, the claim must be invalidated, thus preventing unduly burdening competitors who must determine the scope of the claimed invention based on an erroneously drafted claim.")

3. *Invalidating a Claim Under the Definiteness Requirement.* The court in *AAI* points out in footnote 4 that validity was not before the court. Do you think the court would have reached a different result if validity under the definiteness requirement had been "in play" in that case? Consider the court's decision to hold claims invalid under the definiteness requirement because of the use of the word "about" in the case of *Amgen, Inc. v. Chugai Pharm. Co.*, 927 F.2d 1200 (Fed.Cir. 1991). The claims at issue in this part of the court's analysis were claims 4 and 6 of GI's '195 patent, which were directed to a purified protein called EPO having a specific activity of "at least about 160,000" units. The appellate court pointed out that:

> The district court found that "bioassays provide an imprecise form of measurement with a range of error" and that use of the term "about" 160,000 IU/AU, coupled with the range of error already inherent in the specific activity limitation, served neither to distinguish the invention over the close prior art (which described preparations of 120,000 IU/AU), nor to permit one to know what specific activity values below 160,000, if any, might constitute infringement. It found evidence of ambiguity in the fact that Chugai, GI's partner, itself questioned whether the specific activity value of 138,000 IU/AU for its own rEPO was within the claim coverage.

> In prosecuting the '195 patent, GI disclosed to the examiner a publication by Miyake et al., which discloses a uEPO product having an in vivo specific activity of 128,620 IU/AU. When the examiner noticed this disclosure late in the prosecution, he rejected the '195 claims with a specific activity limitation of "at least 120,000" as anticipated by the Miyake et al. disclosure. It was only after the "at least 120,000" claims were cancelled that GI submitted the "at least about 160,000" claim language.

> The court found the "addition of the word 'about' seems to constitute an effort to recapture ... a mean activity somewhere between 120,000, which the patent examiner found was anticipated by the prior art, and [the] 160,000 IU/AU" claims which were previously allowed. Because "the term 'about' 160,000 gives no hint as to which mean value between the Miyake

et al. value of 128,620 and the mean specific activity level of 160,000 constitutes infringement," the court held the "at least about" claims to be invalid for indefiniteness. This holding was further supported by the fact that nothing in the specification, prosecution history, or prior art provides any indication as to what range of specific activity is covered by the term "about," and by the fact that no expert testified as to a definite meaning for the term in the context of the prior art. In his testimony, Fritsch tried to define "about" 160,000, but he could only say that while "somewhere between 155[,000] might fit within that number," he had not "given a lot of direct consideration to that...."

When the meaning of claims is in doubt, especially when, as is the case here, there is close prior art, they are properly declared invalid. *Standard Oil Co. v. American Cyanamid Co.*, 774 F.2d 448, 453 (Fed.Cir.1985). We therefore affirm the district court's determination on this issue. We also note that, in view of our reversal of the district court's holding that claims 1 and 3 are valid, it is clear that claims 4 and 6 would also be invalid without the "about" limitation. In arriving at this conclusion, we caution that our holding that the term "about" renders indefinite claims 4 and 6 should not be understood as ruling out any and all uses of this term in patent claims. It may be acceptable in appropriate fact situations, *e.g., W.L. Gore & Assocs., Inc. v. Garlock, Inc.*, 721 F.2d 1540, 1557 (Fed.Cir.1983) ("use of 'stretching ... at a rate exceeding about 10% per second' in the claims is not indefinite"), even though it is not here.

927 F.2d 1200, 1217–1218.

E. COMPLEX TECHNOLOGIES—BIOTECHNOLOGY

Several areas of modern technology, such as computer hardware and software, semiconductors, chemistry, and biotechnology, raise some especially difficult disclosure problems for inventors and their patent attorneys. Focusing on biotechnology, in particular, as a representative example, the materials in this section are offered to explore some of these problems in more depth as well as some suggested tools for their mitigation.

In the later chapters on the "nonobviousness" requirement for patentability (Chapter Five), and infringement, especially under the doctrine of equivalents (Chapter Nine), we will return to these and similar technologies and, in some instances, to the same cases.

Developments in biotechnology have provided special challenges for patent law. Prior to 1980, case law focused on whether patent claims could be obtained for newly-discovered uses for natural substances, including microorganisms, *In re Bergstrom*, 427 F.2d 1394 (CCPA 1970), and on public deposits as a means for complying with the disclosure requirements, *In re Argoudelis*, 434 F.2d 1390 (CCPA 1970).

In the 1980's the courts addressed whether genetically-altered living organisms were patentable subject matter under Section 101. *E.g. Diamond v. Chakrabarty*, 447 U.S. 303 (1980), *see* Chapter Seven. The "patenting life" controversy, which continues, overshadows other problems in determining the appropriate scope of patent protection for the fruits of biotechnology research that are, arguably, of greater technological and commercial importance. These problems include adequate disclosure (Section 112), patentability under the nonobviousness condition (Section 103), *see* Chapter Five, and the interpretation of patent claims to determine infringement, *see* Chapter Nine. Like the Federal Circuit's first real biotechnology case, Hybritech Inc. v. Monoclonal Antibodies, 802 F.2d 1367 (Fed.Cir.1986), some focus on immunology-based technologies like monoclonal antibodies. Others focus on nucleic acids. Many involve both.

In re Wands

858 F.2d 731 (Fed.Cir.1988).

■ Before SMITH, NEWMAN, and BISSELL, CIRCUIT JUDGES.

■ SMITH, CIRCUIT JUDGE.

This appeal is from the decision of the Patent and Trademark Office (PTO) Board of Patent Appeals and Interferences (board) affirming the rejection of all remaining claims in appellant's application for a patent, serial No. 188,735, entitled "Immunoassay Utilizing Monoclonal High Affinity IgM Antibodies," which was filed September 19, 1980. . . . The rejection under 35 U.S.C. § 112, first paragraph, is based on the grounds that appellant's written specification would not enable a person skilled in the art to make the monoclonal antibodies that are needed to practice the claimed invention without undue experimentation. We reverse.

* * *

II. *Background*

A. *The Art*

The claimed invention involves immunoassay methods for the detection of hepatitis B surface antigen by using high-affinity monoclonal antibodies of the IgM isotype. Antibodies are a class of proteins (immunoglobulins) that help defend the body against invaders such as viruses and bacteria. An antibody has the potential to bind tightly to another molecule, which molecule is called an antigen. The body has the ability to make millions of different antibodies that bind to different antigens. However, it is only after exposure to an antigen that a complicated immune response leads to the production of antibodies against that antigen. For example, on the surface of hepatitis B virus particles there is a large protein called hepatitis B surface antigen (HBsAg). As its name implies, it is capable of serving as an antigen. During a hepatitis B infection (or when purified HBsAg is injected experimentally), the body begins to make antibodies that bind tightly and specifically to HBsAg. Such antibodies can be used as regents for sensitive diagnostic tests (*e.g.*, to detect hepatitis B virus in blood and other tissues, a purpose of the claimed invention). A method for detecting or measuring antigens by using antibodies as reagents is called an immunoassay.

Normally, many different antibodies are produced against each antigen. One reason for this diversity is that different antibodies are produced that bind to different regions (determinants) of a large antigen molecule such as HBsAg. In addition, different antibodies may be produced that bind to the same determinant. These usually differ in the tightness with which they bind to the determinant. Affinity is a quantitative measure of the strength of antibody-antigen binding. Usually an antibody with a higher affinity for an antigen will be more useful for immunological diagnostic tests than one with a lower affinity. Another source of heterogeneity is that there are several immunoglobulin classes or isotypes. Immunoglobulin G (IgG) is the most common isotype in serum. Another isotype, immunoglobulin M (IgM), is prominent early in the immune response. IgM molecules are larger than IgG molecules, and have 10 antigen-binding sites instead of the 2 that are present in IgG. Most immunoassay methods use IgG, but the claimed invention uses only IgM antibodies.

For commercial applications there are many disadvantages to using antibodies from serum. Serum contains a complex mixture of antibodies against the antigen of interest within a much larger pool of antibodies directed at other antigens. These are available only in a limited supply that ends when the donor dies. The goal of monoclonal antibody technology is to produce an unlimited supply of a single purified antibody.

The blood cells that make antibodies are lymphocytes. Each lymphocyte makes only one kind of antibody. During an immune response, lymphocytes exposed to their particular antigen divide and mature. Each produces a clone of identical daughter cells, all of which secrete the same antibody. Clones of lymphocytes, all derived from a single lymphocyte, could provide a source of a single homogeneous antibody. However, lymphocytes do not survive for long outside of the body in cell culture.

Hybridoma technology provides a way to obtain large numbers of cells that all produce the same antibody. This method takes advantage of the properties of myeloma cells derived from a tumor of the immune system. The cancerous myeloma cells can divide indefinitely in vitro. They also have the potential ability to secrete antibodies. By appropriate experimental manipulations, a myeloma cell can be made to fuse with a lymphocyte to produce a single hybrid cell (hence, a hybridoma) that contains the genetic material of both cells. The hybridoma secretes the same antibody that was made by its parent lymphocyte, but acquires the capability of the myeloma cell to divide and grow indefinitely in cell culture. Antibodies produced by a clone of hybridoma cells (*i.e.*, by hybridoma cells that are all progeny of a single cell) are called monoclonal antibodies.[2]

B. *The Claimed Invention*

The claimed invention involves methods for the immunoassay of HBsAg by using high-affinity monoclonal IgM antibodies. Jack R. Wands and Vincent R. Zurawski, Jr., two of the three coinventors of the present application, disclosed methods for producing monoclonal antibodies against HBsAg in United States patent No. 4,271,145 (the '145 patent), entitled "Process for Producing Antibodies to Hepatitis Virus and Cell Lines Therefor," which patent issued on June 2, 1981. The '145 patent is incorporated by reference into the application on appeal. The specification

---

2. For a concise description of monoclonal antibodies and their use in immunoassay *see Hybritech, Inc. v. Monoclonal Antibodies, Inc.*, 802 F.2d 1367, 1368–71, 231 USPQ 81, 82–83 (Fed.Cir.1986). . . .

of the '145 patent teaches a procedure for immunizing mice against HBsAg, and the use of lymphocytes from these mice to produce hybridomas that secrete monoclonal antibodies specific for HBsAg. The '145 patent discloses that this procedure yields both IgG and IgM antibodies with high-affinity binding to HbsAg. For the stated purpose of complying with the best mode requirement of 35 U.S.C. § 112, first paragraph, a hybridoma cell line that secretes IgM antibodies against HBsAg (the 1F8 cell line) was deposited at the American Type Culture Collection, a recognized cell depository, and became available to the public when the '145 patent issued.

The application on appeal claims methods for immunoassay of HBsAg using monoclonal antibodies such as those described in the '145 patent. Most immunoassay methods have used monoclonal antibodies of the IgG isotype. IgM antibodies were disfavored in the prior art because of their sensitivity to reducing agents and their tendency to self-aggregate and precipitate. Appellants found that their monoclonal IgM antibodies could be used for immunoassay of HbsAg with unexpectedly high sensitivity and specificity. Claims 1, 3, 7, 8, 14, and 15 are drawn to methods for the immunoassay of HBsAg using high-affinity IgM monoclonal antibodies. Claims 19 and 25–27 are for chemically modified (*e.g.*, radioactively labeled) monoclonal IgM antibodies used in the assays. The broadest method claim reads:

> 1. An immunoassay method utilizing an antibody to assay for a substance comprising hepatitis B-surface antigen (HBsAg) determinants which comprises the steps of:
>
> contacting a test sample containing said substance comprising HBsAg determinants with said antibody; and
>
> determining the presence of said substance in said sample;
>
> wherein said antibody is a monoclonal high affinity IgM antibody having a binding affinity constant for said HBsAg determinants of at least 10^9 M^{-1}.

Certain claims were rejected under 35 U.S.C. § 103; these rejections have not been appealed. Remaining claims 1, 3, 7, 8, 14, 15, 19, and 25–27 were rejected under 35 U.S.C. § 112, first paragraph, on the grounds that the disclosure would not enable a person skilled in the art to make and use the invention without undue experimentation. The rejection is directed solely to whether the specification enables one skilled in the art to make the monoclonal antibodies that are needed to practice the invention. The position of the PTO is that data presented by Wands show that the production of high-affinity IgM anti-HBsAg antibodies is unpredictable and unreliable, so that it would require undue experimentation for one skilled in the art to make the antibodies.

III. *Analysis*

A. *Enablement by Deposit of Microorganisms and Cell Lines*

* * *

Where an invention depends on the use of living materials such as microorganisms or cultured cells, it may be impossible to enable the public to make the invention (*i.e.*, to obtain these living materials) solely by means of a written disclosure. One means that has been developed for complying with the enablement requirement is to deposit the living materials in cell depositories which will distribute samples to the public who wish to practice the invention after the patent issues.[7] Administrative guidelines and judicial decisions have clarified the conditions under which a deposit of organisms can satisfy the requirements of section 112.[8] A deposit has been held necessary for enablement where the starting materials (*i.e.*, the living cells used to practice the invention, or cells from which the required cells can be produced) are not readily available to the public.[9] Even when starting materials are available, a deposit has been necessary where it would require undue experimentation to make the cells of the invention from the starting materials.[10]

In addition to satisfying the enablement requirement, deposit of organisms also can be used to establish the filing date of the application as the prima facie date of invention,[11] and to satisfy the requirement under 35 U.S.C. § 114 that the PTO be guaranteed access to the invention during pendency of the application.[12] Although a deposit may serve these purposes, we recognized, in *In re Lundak*, . . . that these purposes, nevertheless, may be met in ways other than by making a deposit.

A deposit also may satisfy the best mode requirement of section 112, first paragraph, and it is for this reason that the 1F8 hybridoma was deposited in connection with the '145 patent and the current application. Wands does not challenge the statements by the examiner to the effect that, although the deposited 1F8 line enables the public to perform immunoassays with antibodies produced by that single hybridoma, the deposit does not enable the generic claims that are on appeal. The examiner rejected the claims on the grounds that the written disclosure was not enabling and that the deposit was inadequate. Since we hold that the written disclosure fully enables the claimed invention, we need not reach the question of the adequacy of deposits.

---

7. *In re Argoudelis*, 434 F.2d 1390, 1392–93, 168 USPQ 99, 101–02 (CCPA 1970).

8. *In re Lundak*, 773 F.2d 1216, 227 USPQ 90 (Fed.Cir.1985); *Feldman v. Aunstrup*, 517 F.2d 1351, 186 USPQ 108 (CCPA 1975), *cert. denied*, 424 U.S. 912, 96 S.Ct. 1109, 47 L.Ed.2d 316 (1976); Manual of Patent Examining Procedure (MPEP) 608.01(p)(C) (5th ed. 1983, rev. 1987). *See generally* Hampar, Patenting of Recombinant DNA Technology: The Deposit Requirement, 67 J. Pat. Trademark Off. Soc'y 569 (1985).

9. *In re Jackson*, 217 USPQ 804, 807–08 (Bd.App.1982) (strains of a newly discovered species of bacteria isolated from nature); *Feldman v. Aunstrup*, 517 F.2d 1351, 186 USPQ 108 (uncommon fungus isolated from nature); *In re Argoudelis*, 434 F.2d at 1392, 168 USPQ at 102 (novel strain of antibiotic-producing microorganism isolated from nature); *In re Kropp*, 143 USPQ 148, 152 (Bd.App.1959) (newly discovered microorganism isolated from soil).

10. *In re Forman*, 230 USPQ 546, 547 (Bd. Pat. App. & Int.1986) (genetically engineered bacteria where the specification provided insufficient information about the amount of time and effort required); *In re Lundak*, 773 F.2d 1216, 227 USPQ 90 (unique cell line produced from another cell line by mutagenesis).

11. *In re Lundak*, 773 F.2d at 1222, 227 USPQ at 95–96; *In re Feldman*, 517 F.2d at 1355, 186 USPQ at 113; *In re Argoudelis*, 434 F.2d at 1394–96, 168 USPQ at 103–04 (Baldwin, J. concurring).

12. *In re Lundak*, 773 F.2d at 1222, 227 USPQ at 95–96; *In re Feldman*, 517 F.2d at 1354, 186 USPQ at 112.

B. *Undue Experimentation*

Although inventions involving microorganisms or other living cells often can be enabled by a deposit, ... a deposit is not always necessary to satisfy the enablement requirement.[15] No deposit is necessary if the biological organisms can be obtained from readily available sources or derived from readily available starting materials through routine screening that does not require undue experimentation. . . . Whether the specification in an application involving living cells (here, hybridomas) is enabled without a deposit must be decided on the facts of the particular case. . . .

Appellants contend that their written specification fully enables the practice of their claimed invention because the monoclonal antibodies needed to perform the immunoassays can be made from readily available starting materials using methods that are well known in the monoclonal antibody art. Wands states that application of these methods to make high-affinity IgM anti-HBsAg antibodies requires only routine screening, and that does not amount to undue experimentation. There is no challenge to their contention that the starting materials (*i.e.*, mice, HBsAg antigen, and myeloma cells) are available to the public. The PTO concedes that the methods used to prepare hybridomas and to screen them for high-affinity IgM antibodies against HBsAg were either well known in the monoclonal antibody art or adequately disclosed in the '145 patent and in the current application. This is consistent with this court's recognition with respect to another patent application that methods for obtaining and screening monoclonal antibodies were well known in 1980.[18] The sole issue is whether, in this particular case, it would require undue experimentation to produce high-affinity IgM monoclonal antibodies.

Enablement is not precluded by the necessity for some experimentation such as routine screening. . . . However, experimentation needed to practice the invention must not be undue experimentation. . . . "The key word is 'undue,' not 'experimentation.' " . . .

> The determination of what constitutes undue experimentation in a given case requires the application of a standard of reasonableness, having due regard for the nature of the invention and the state of the art. *Ansul Co. v. Uniroyal, Inc.* [448 F.2d 872, 878–79; 169 USPQ 759, 762–63 (2d Cir.1971), *cert. denied*, 404 U.S. 1018, 92 S.Ct. 680, 30 L.Ed.2d 666 (1972)]. The test is not merely quantitative, since a considerable amount of experimentation is permissible, if it is merely routine, or if the specification in question provides a reasonable amount of guidance with respect to the direction in which the experimentation should proceed. . . .[22]

The term "undue experimentation" does not appear in the statute, but it is well established that enablement requires that the specification teach those in the art to make and use the invention without undue experimentation. . . . Whether undue experimentation is needed is not a single, simple factual determination, but rather is a conclusion reached by weighing many factual considerations. The board concluded that undue experimentation

---

15. *Tabuchi v. Nubel*, 559 F.2d 1183, 194 USPQ 521 (CCPA 1977).

18. *Hybritech*, 802 F.2d at 1384, 231 USPQ at 94.

22. *In re Jackson*, 217 USPQ at 807.

would be needed to practice the invention on the basis of experimental data presented by Wands. These data are not in dispute. However, Wands and the board disagree strongly on the conclusion that should be drawn from that data.

Factors to be considered in determining whether a disclosure would require undue experimentation have been summarized by the board in *In re Forman*.[24] They include (1) the quantity of experimentation necessary, (2) the amount of direction or guidance presented, (3) the presence or absence of working examples, (4) the nature of the invention, (5) the state of the prior art, (6) the relative skill of those in the art, (7) the predictability or unpredictability of the art, and (8) the breadth of the claims.

In order to understand whether the rejection was proper, it is necessary to discuss further the methods for making specific monoclonal antibodies. The first step for making monoclonal antibodies is to immunize an animal. The '145 patent provides a detailed description of procedures for immunizing a specific strain of mice against HBsAg. Next the spleen, an organ rich in lymphocytes, is removed and the lymphocytes are separated from the other spleen cells. The lymphocytes are mixed with myeloma cells, and the mixture is treated to cause a few of the cells to fuse with each other. Hybridoma cells that secrete the desired antibodies then must be isolated from the enormous number of other cells in the mixture. This is done through a series of screening procedures.

The first step is to separate the hybridoma cells from unfused lymphocytes and myeloma cells. The cells are cultured in a medium in which all the lymphocytes and myeloma cells die, and only the hybridoma cells survive. The next step is to isolate and clone hybridomas that make antibodies that bind to the antigen of interest. Single hybridoma cells are placed in separate chambers and are allowed to grow and divide. After there are enough cells in the clone to produce sufficient quantities of antibody to analyze, the antibody is assayed to determine whether it binds to the antigen. Generally, antibodies from many clones do not bind the antigen, and these clones are discarded. However, by screening enough clones (often hundreds at a time), hybridomas may be found that secrete antibodies against the antigen of interest.

Wands used a commercially available radioimmunoassay kit to screen clones for cells that produce antibodies directed against HBsAg. In this assay the amount of radioactivity bound gives some indication of the strength of the antibody-antigen binding, but does not yield a numerical affinity constant, which must be measured using the more laborious Scatchard analysis. In order to determine which anti-HBsAg antibodies satisfy all of the limitations of appellants' claims, the antibodies require further screening to select those which have an IgM isotype and have a binding affinity constant of at least 10^9 M^{-1}.[26] The PTO does not question

---

24. *In re Forman*, 230 USPQ at 547.

26. The examiner, the board, and Wands all point out that, technically, the strength of antibody-HBsAg binding is measured as avidity, which takes into account multiple determinants on the HBsAg molecule, rather than affinity. Nevertheless, despite this correction, all parties then continued to use the term "affinity." We will use the terminology of the parties.

that the screening techniques used by Wands were well known in the monoclonal antibody art.

During prosecution Wands submitted a declaration under 37 C.F.R. § 1.132 providing information about all of the hybridomas that appellants had produced before filing the patent application. The first four fusions were unsuccessful and produced no hybridomas. The next six fusion experiments all produced hybridomas that made antibodies specific for HBsAg. Antibodies that bound at least 10,000 cpm in the commercial radioimmunoassay were classified as "high binders." Using this criterion, 143 high-binding hybridomas were obtained. In the declaration, Wands stated that[27]

> It is generally accepted in the art that, among those antibodies which are binders with 50,000 cpm or higher, there is a very high likelihood that high affinity (Ka [greater than] 10^9 M^{-1}) antibodies will be found. However, high affinity antibodies can also be found among high binders of between 10,000 and 50,000, as is clearly demonstrated in the Table.

The PTO has not challenged this statement.

The declaration stated that a few of the high-binding monoclonal antibodies from two fusions were chosen for further screening. The remainder of the antibodies and the hybridomas that produced them were saved by freezing. Only nine antibodies were subjected to further analysis. Four (three from one fusion and one from another fusion) fell within the claims, that is, were IgM antibodies and had a binding affinity constant of at least 10^9M^{-1}. Of the remaining five antibodies, three were found to be IgG, while the other two were IgM for which the affinity constants were not measured (although both showed binding well above 50,000 cpm).

Apparently none of the frozen cell lines received any further analysis. The declaration explains that after useful high-affinity IgM monoclonal antibodies to HBsAg had been found, it was considered unnecessary to return to the stored antibodies to screen for more IgMs. Wands says that the existence of the stored hybridomas was disclosed to the PTO to comply with the requirement under 37 C.F.R. § 1.56 that applicants fully disclose all of their relevant data, and not just favorable results.[28] How these stored hybridomas are viewed is central to the positions of the parties.

The position of the board emphasizes the fact that since the stored cell lines were not completely tested, there is no proof that any of them are IgM antibodies with a binding affinity constant of at least 10^9 M^{-1}. Thus, only 4 out of 143 hybridomas, or 2.8 percent, were proved to fall within the claims. Furthermore, antibodies that were proved to be high-affinity IgM came from only 2 of 10 fusion experiments. These statistics are viewed by the board as evidence that appellants' methods were not predictable or

---

Following the usage of the parties, we will also use the term "high-affinity" as essentially synonymous with "having a binding affinity constant of at least 10^9 M^{-1}."

27. A table in the declaration presented the binding data for antibodies from every cell line. Values ranged from 13,867 to 125,204 cpm, and a substantial proportion of the antibodies showed binding greater than 50,000 cpm. In confirmation of Dr. Wand's statement, two antibodies with binding less than 25,000 cpm were found to have affinity constants greater than 10^9 M^{-1}.

28. *See Rohm & Haas Co. v. Crystal Chem. Co.*, 722 F.2d 1556, 220 USPQ 289 (Fed.Cir.1983).

reproducible. The board concludes that Wands' low rate of demonstrated success shows that a person skilled in the art would have to engage in undue experimentation in order to make antibodies that fall within the claims.

Wands views the data quite differently. Only nine hybridomas were actually analyzed beyond the initial screening for HBsAg binding. Of these, four produced antibodies that fell within the claims, a respectable 44 percent rate of success. (Furthermore, since the two additional IgM antibodies for which the affinity constants were never measured showed binding in excess of 50,000 cpm, it is likely that these also fall within the claims.) Wands argues that the remaining 134 unanalyzed, stored cell lines should not be written off as failures. Instead, if anything, they represent partial success. Each of the stored hybridomas had been shown to produce a high-binding antibody specific for HBsAg. Many of these antibodies showed binding above 50,000 cpm and are thus highly likely to have a binding affinity constant of at least 10^9 M^{-1}. Extrapolating from the nine hybridomas that were screened for isotype (and from what is well known in the monoclonal antibody art about isotype frequency), it is reasonable to assume that the stored cells include some that produce IgM. Thus, if the 134 incompletely analyzed cell lines are considered at all, they provide some support (albeit without rigorous proof) to the view that hybridomas falling within the claims are not so rare that undue experimentation would be needed to make them.

The first four fusion attempts were failures, while high-binding antibodies were produced in the next six fusions. Appellants contend that the initial failures occurred because they had not yet learned to fuse cells successfully. Once they became skilled in the art, they invariably obtained numerous hybridomas that made high-binding antibodies against HBsAg and, in each fusion where they determined isotype and binding affinity they obtained hybridomas that fell within the claims.

Wands also submitted a second declaration under 37 C.F.R. § 1.132 stating that after the patent application was submitted they performed an eleventh fusion experiment and obtained another hybridoma that made a high-affinity IgM anti-HBsAg antibody. No information was provided about the number of clones screened in that experiment. The board determined that, because there was no indication as to the number of hybridomas screened, this declaration had very little value. While we agree that it would have been preferable if Wands had included this information, the declaration does show that when appellants repeated their procedures they again obtained a hybridoma that produced an antibody that fit all of the limitations of their claims.

We conclude that the board's interpretation of the data is erroneous. It is strained and unduly harsh to classify the stored cell lines (each of which was proved to make high-binding antibodies against HBsAg) as failures demonstrating that Wands' methods are unpredictable or unreliable.[29] At

29. Even if we were to accept the PTO's 2.8% success rate, we would not be required to reach a conclusion of undue experimentation. Such a determination must be made in view of

worst, they prove nothing at all about the probability of success, and merely show that appellants were prudent in not discarding cells that might someday prove useful. At best, they show that high-binding antibodies, the starting materials for IgM screening and Scatchard analysis, can be produced in large numbers. The PTO's position leads to the absurd conclusion that the more hybridomas an applicant makes and saves without testing, the less predictable the applicant's results become. Furthermore, Wands' explanation that the first four attempts at cell fusion failed only because they had not yet learned to perform fusions properly is reasonable in view of the fact that the next six fusions were all successful. The record indicates that cell fusion is a technique that is well known to those of ordinary skill in the monoclonal antibody art, and there has been no claim that the fusion step should be more difficult or unreliable where the antigen is HBsAg than it would be for other antigens.

When Wands' data is interpreted in a reasonable manner, analysis considering the factors enumerated in *In re Forman* leads to the conclusion that undue experimentation would not be required to practice the invention. Wands' disclosure provides considerable direction and guidance on how to practice their invention and presents working examples. There was a high level of skill in the art at the time when the application was filed, and all of the methods needed to practice the invention were well known.

The nature of monoclonal antibody technology is that it involves screening hybridomas to determine which ones secrete antibody with desired characteristics. Practitioners of this art are prepared to screen negative hybridomas in order to find one that makes the desired antibody. No evidence was presented by either party on how many hybridomas would be viewed by those in the art as requiring undue experimentation to screen. However, it seems unlikely that undue experimentation would be defined in terms of the number of hybridomas that were never screened. Furthermore, in the monoclonal antibody art it appears that an "experiment" is not simply the screening of a single hybridoma, but is rather the entire attempt to make a monoclonal antibody against a particular antigen. This process entails immunizing animals, fusing lymphocytes from the immunized animals with myeloma cells to make hybridomas, cloning the hybridomas, and screening the antibodies produced by the hybridomas for the desired characteristics. Wands carried out this entire procedure three times, and was successful each time in making at least one antibody that satisfied all of the claim limitations. Reasonably interpreted, Wands' record indicates that, in the production of high-affinity IgM antibodies against HBsAG, the amount of effort needed to obtain such antibodies is not excessive. Wands' evidence thus effectively rebuts the examiner's challenge to the enablement of their disclosure. . . .

IV. *Conclusion*

Considering all of the factors, we conclude that it would not require undue experimentation to obtain antibodies needed to practice the claimed

---

the circumstances of each case and cannot be made solely by reference to a particular numerical cutoff.

invention. Accordingly, the rejection of Wands' claims for lack of enablement under 35 U.S.C. § 112, first paragraph, is reversed.

■ NEWMAN, CIRCUIT JUDGE, concurring in part, dissenting in part.

A

I concur in the court's holding that additional samples of hybridoma cell lines that produce these high-affinity IgM monoclonal antibodies need not be deposited. This invention, as described by Wands, is not a selection of a few rare cells from many possible cells. To the contrary, Wands states that all monoclonally produced IgM antibodies to hepatitis B surface antigen have the desired high avidity and other favorable properties, and that all are readily preparable by now-standard techniques.

Wands states that his United States Patent No. 4,271,145 describes fully operable techniques, and is distinguished from his first four failed experiments that are referred to in the Rule 132 affidavit. Wands argues that these biotechnological mechanisms are relatively well understood and that the preparations can be routinely duplicated by those of skill in this art. . . . I agree that it is not necessary that there be a deposit of multiple exemplars of a cell system that is readily reproduced by known, specifically identified techniques.

B

I would affirm the board's holding that Wands has not complied with 35 U.S.C. § 112, first paragraph, in that he has not provided data sufficient to support the breadth of his generic claims. Wands' claims on appeal include the following:

> 19.   Monoclonal high affinity IgM antibodies immunoreactive with HBsAg determinants, wherein said antibodies are coupled to an insoluble solid phase, and wherein the binding affinity constant of said antibodies for said HBsAg determinants is at least 10^9 M^{-1}.

> 26.   Monoclonal high affinity IgM antibodies immunoreactive with HBsAg determinants wherein said antibodies are detectably labelled.

Wands states that he obtained 143 "high binding monoclonal antibodies of the right specificity" in the successful fusions; although he does not state how they were determined to be high binding or of the right specificity, for Wands also states that only nine of these 143 were tested.

Of these nine, four (three from one fusion and one from another fusion) were found to have the claimed high affinity and to be of the IgM isotype. Wands states that the other five were either of a different isotype or their affinities were not determined. (This latter statement also appears to contradict his statement that all 143 were "high binding.")

Wands argues that a "success rate of four out of nine," or 44.4%, is sufficient to support claims to the entire class. The Commissioner deems the success rate to be four out of 143, or 2.8%; to which Wands responds with statistical analysis as to how unlikely it is that Wands selected the only four out of 143 that worked. Wands did not, however, prove the right point. The question is whether Wands, by testing nine out of 143 (the Commissioner points out that the randomness of the sample was not established), and finding that four out of the nine had the desired properties, has provided sufficient experimental support for the breadth of the requested claims, in the context that "experiments in genetic engineering produce, at best, unpredictable results," quoting from *Ex parte Forman*, 230 USPQ 546, 547 (Bd. Pat. App. and Int.1986).

The premise of the patent system is that an inventor, having taught the world something it didn't know, is encouraged to make the product available for public and commercial benefit, by governmental grant of the right to exclude others from practice of that which the inventor has disclosed. The boundary defining the excludable subject matter must be carefully set: it must protect the inventor, so that commercial development is encouraged; but the claims must be commensurate with the inventor's contribution. Thus the specification and claims must meet the requirements of 35 U.S.C. § 112. . . .

As the science of biotechnology matures the need for special accommodation, such as the deposit of cell lines or microorganisms, may diminish; but there remains the body of law and practice on the need for sufficient disclosure, including experimental data when appropriate, that reasonably support the scope of the requested claims. That law relates to the sufficiency of the description of the claimed invention, and if not satisfied by deposit, must independently meet the requirements of Section 112.

Wands is not claiming a particular, specified IgM antibody. He is claiming all such monoclonal antibodies in assay for hepatitis B surface antigen, based on his teaching that such antibodies have uniformly reproducible high avidity, free of the known disadvantages of IgM antibodies such as tendency to precipitate or aggregate. It is incumbent upon Wands to provide reasonable support for the proposed breadth of his claims. I agree with the Commissioner that four exemplars shown to have the desired properties, out of the 143, do not provide adequate support.

* * *

. . . Wands must provide sufficient data or authority to show that his results are reasonably predictable within the scope of the claimed generic invention, based on experiment and/or scientific theory. In my view he has not met this burden.

NOTES

1. In 1930, Congress enacted the "Plant Patent Act", now at 35 U.S.C. § 161, authorizing patents for asexually reproduced plants. The statute recognized that new plants cannot be "enabled" by a written description. Accordingly, Section 162 provides that "No plant shall be declared invalid for noncompliance with section 112 of this title if the description is as complete as reasonably possible." The Plant Patent Act is limited to asexually reproduced plants (that is, seeds are excluded) and also does not encompass bacteria or other cellular material. *In re Arzberger*, 112 F.2d 834 (CCPA 1940). The relationship between "utility" patents on biological material and the Plant Patent Act is discussed in the Supreme Court's 1980 *Chakrabarty* decision, in Chapter Seven.

2. *Public Deposits of Biological Material as Compliance with the Enablement Requirement.* In *Wands* the court discussed "enablement by deposit of microorganisms and cell lines.'' The practice of using public deposits to comply with patent law requirements grew up without statutory authority but is now well-established in the rules of the PTO, *see* 37 C.F.R. §§ 1.801–809, and in judicial decisions, *see In re Lundak*, 773 F.2d 1216 (Fed.Cir.1985). *See* Donald S. Chisum, Chisum on Patents § 7.03[5][b]. Could and should similar rules be used for computer software patent applications? If so, should deposit be made of the human-readable source code, or the machine-readable object code?

3. As *Wands* illustrates, if enablement is limited to a specific monoclonal antibody on deposit, the scope of the enabled subject matter may be quite narrow, leading to a patent that may have little commercial value.

The following cases pertain to recombinant DNA technology. The first case, *In re O'Farrell*, is here to provide a lucid explication of the technology. As *O'Farrell* is essentially a nonobviousness case, we will revisit it in Chapter Five.

In re O'Farrell

853 F.2d 894 (Fed.Cir.1988).

■ Before Markey, Chief Judge, and Rich and Nies, Circuit Judges.

■ Rich, Circuit Judge.

* * *

The claimed invention is from the developing new field of genetic engineering. A broad claim on appeal reads:

Claim 1. A method for producing a predetermined protein in a stable form in a transformed host species of bacteria comprising, providing a cloning vector which includes at least a substantial portion of a gene which is indigenous to the host species of bacteria and is functionally transcribed and translated in that species, said substantial portion of said indigenous gene further including the regulatory DNA sequences for RNA synthesis and protein synthesis but lacking the normal gene termination signal, and linking a natural or synthetic heterologous gene encoding said predetermined protein to said indigenous gene portion at its distal end, said heterologous gene being in proper orientation and having codons arranged in the same reading frame as the codons of said indigenous gene portion so that readthrough can occur from said indigenous gene portion into said heterologous gene in the same reading frame, said heterologous gene portion further containing sufficient DNA sequences to result in expression of a fused protein having sufficient size so as to confer stability on said predetermined protein when said vector is used to transform said host species of bacteria.

* * *

Although the terms in these claims would be familiar to those of ordinary skill in genetic engineering, they employ a bewildering vocabulary new to those who are not versed in molecular biology. An understanding of the science and technology on which these claims are based is essential before one can analyze and explain whether the claimed invention would have been obvious in light of the prior art.

I. Background

Proteins are biological molecules of enormous importance. Proteins include enzymes that catalyze biochemical reactions, major structural materials of the animal body, and many hormones. Numerous patents and applications for patents in the field of biotechnology involve specific proteins or methods for making and using proteins. Many valuable proteins occur in nature only in minute quantities, or are difficult to purify from natural sources. Therefore, a goal of many biotechnology projects, including appellants' claimed invention, is to devise methods to synthesize useful quantities of specific proteins by controlling the mechanism by which living cells make proteins.

The basic organization of all proteins is the same. Proteins are large polymeric molecules consisting of chains of smaller building blocks, called *amino acids*, that are linked together covalently.[2] The chemical bonds linking amino acids together are called *peptide* bonds, so proteins are also called *polypeptides*.[3] It is the exact sequence in which the amino acids are strung together in a polypeptide chain that determines the identity of a protein and its chemical characteristics.[4] Although there are only 20 amino acids, they are strung together in different orders to produce the hundreds of thousands of proteins found in nature.

To make a protein molecule, a cell needs information about the sequence in which the amino acids must be assembled. The cell uses a long polymeric molecule, DNA (deoxyriboneucleic acid), to store this information. The subunits of the DNA chain are called *nucleotides*. A nucleotide consists of a nitrogen-containing ring compound (called a *base*) linked to a 5–carbon sugar that has a phosphate group attached.[5] DNA is composed of

---

2. There are twenty amino acids: alanine, valine, leucine, isoleucine, proline, phenylalanine, methionine, tryptophan, glycine, asparagine, glutamine, cysteine, serine, threonine, tyrosine, aspartic acid, glutamic acid, lysine, arginine, and histidine.

3. Proteins are often loosely called *peptides*, but technically proteins are only the larger peptides with chains of at least 50 amino acids, and more typically hundreds of amino acids. Some proteins consist of several polypeptide chains bound together covalently or noncovalently. The term "peptide" is broader than "protein" and also includes small chains of amino acids linked by peptide bonds, some as small as two amino acids. Certain small peptides have commercial or medical significance.

4. Polypeptide chains fold up into complex 3–dimensional shapes. It is the shape that actually determines many chemical properties of the protein. However, the configuration of a protein molecule is determined by its amino acid sequence. [Alberts, Bray, Lewis, Raff, Roberts and Watson, *The Molecular Biology of the Cell*, 111–12 (1983)] [hereinafter *The Cell*]; [Watson, Hopkins, Roberts, Steitz and Weiner, *The Molecular Biology of the Gene* Vol. 1 (4th ed., 1987) 50–54] [hereinafter *The Gene*].

5. The sugar in DNA is deoxyribose, while the sugar in RNA, *infra*, is ribose. The sugar and phosphate groups are linked covalently to those of adjacent nucleotides to form the backbone of the long unbranched DNA molecule. The bases project from the chain, and serve as the "alphabet" of the genetic code. DNA molecules actually consist of two chains tightly entwined as a double helix. The chains are not identical but instead are complementary: each A on one chain is paired with a T on the other chain, and each C has a corresponding G. The chains are held together by noncovalent bonds between these complementary bases. This

only four nucleotides. They differ from each other in the base region of the molecule. The four bases of these subunits are adenine, guanine, cytosine, and thymine (abbreviated respectively as A, G, C and T). The sequence of these bases along the DNA molecule specifies which amino acids will be inserted in sequence into the polypeptide chain of a protein.

DNA molecules do not participate directly in the synthesis of proteins. DNA acts as a permanent "blueprint" of all of the genetic information in the cell, and exists mainly in extremely long strands (called *chromosomes*) containing information coding for the sequences of many proteins, most of which are not being synthesized at any particular moment. The region of DNA on the chromosome that codes for the sequence of a single polypeptide is called a gene.[6] In order to *express* a gene (the process whereby the information in a gene is used to synthesize new protein), a copy of the gene is first made as a molecule of RNA (ribonucleic acid).

RNA is a molecule that closely resembles DNA. It differs, however, in that it contains a different sugar (ribose instead of deoxyribose) and the base thymine (T) of DNA is replaced in RNA by the structurally similar base, uracil (U). Making an RNA copy of DNA is called *transcription*. The transcribed RNA copy contains sequences of A, U, C, and G that carry the same information as the sequence of A, T, C, and G in the DNA. That RNA molecule, called *messenger RNA*, then moves to a location in the cell where proteins are synthesized.

The code whereby a sequence of nucleotides along an RNA molecule is translated into a sequence of amino acids in a protein (*i.e.*, the "genetic code") is based on serially reading groups of three adjacent nucleotides. Each combination of three adjacent nucleotides, called a codon, specifies a particular amino acid. For example, the codon U–G–G in a messenger RNA molecule specifies that there will be a tryptophan molecule in the corresponding location in the corresponding polypeptide. The four bases A, G, C and U can be combined as triplets in 64 different ways, but there are only 20 amino acids to be coded. Thus, most amino acids are coded for by more than one codon. For example, both U–A–U and U–A–C code for tyrosine, and there are six different codons that code for leucine. There are also three codons that do not code for any amino acid (namely, U–A–A, U–G–A, and U–A–G). Like periods at the end of a sentence, these sequences signal the end of the polypeptide chain, and they are therefore called *stop codons*.

The cellular machinery involved in synthesizing proteins is quite complicated, and centers around large structures called *ribosomes* that bind to the messenger RNA. The ribosomes and associated molecules "read" the information in the messenger RNA molecule, literally shifting along the strand of RNA three nucleotides at a time, adding the amino acid specified

double helical structure plays an essential role in the replication of DNA and the transmission of genetic information. *See generally The Cell* at 98–106; *The Gene* at 65–79. However, the information of only one strand is used for directing protein synthesis, and it is not necessary to discuss the implication of the double-stranded structure of DNA here. RNA molecules, *infra*, are single stranded.

6. Chromosomes also contain regions of DNA that are not part of genes, *i.e.*, do not code for the sequence of amino acids in proteins. These include sections of DNA adjacent to genes that are involved in the control of transcription, *infra*, and regions of unknown function.

by that codon to a growing polypeptide chain that is also attached to the ribosome. When a stop codon is reached, the polypeptide chain is complete and detaches from the ribosome.

The conversion of the information from a sequence of codons in an RNA molecule into the sequence of amino acids in a newly synthesized polypeptide is called *translation*. A messenger RNA molecule is typically reused to make many copies of the same protein. Synthesis of a protein is usually terminated by destroying the messenger RNA. (The information for making more of that protein remains stored in DNA in the chromosomes.)

The translation of messenger RNA begins at a specific sequence of nucleotides that bind the RNA to the ribosome and specify which is the first codon that is to be translated. Translation then proceeds by reading nucleotides, three at a time, until a stop codon is reached. If some error were to occur that shifts the frame in which the nucleotides are read by one or two nucleotides, all of the codons after this shift would be misread. For example, the sequence of codons [C–U–C–A–G–C–G–U–U–A–C–C–A ...] codes for the chain of amino acids [... leucine-serine-valine-threonine-...]. If the reading of these groups of three nucleotides is displaced by one nucleotide, such as [... C–U–C–A–G–C–G–U–U–A–C–C–A ...], the resulting peptide chain would consist of [... serine-alanine-leucine-proline ...]. This would be an entirely different peptide, and most probably an undesirable and useless one. Synthesis of a particular protein requires that the correct register or *reading frame* be maintained as the codons in the RNA are translated.

The function of messenger RNA is to carry genetic information (transcribed from DNA) to the protein synthetic machinery of a cell where its information is translated into the amino acid sequence of a protein. However, some kinds of RNA have other roles. For example, ribosomes contain several large strands of RNA that serve a structural function (*ribosomal* RNA). Chromosomes contain regions of DNA that code for the nucleotide sequences of structural RNAs and these sequences are transcribed to manufacture those RNAs. The DNA sequences coding for structural RNAs are still called genes even though the nucleotide sequence of the structural RNA is never translated into protein.

Man, other animals, plants, protozoa, and yeast are *eucaryotic* (or eukaryotic) organisms: their DNA is packaged in chromosomes in a special compartment of the cell, the nucleus. Bacteria (*procaryotic* or prokaryotic organisms) have a different organization. Their DNA, usually a circular loop, is not contained in any specialized compartment. Despite the incredible differences between them, all organisms, whether eucaryote or procaryote, whether man or mouse or lowly bacterium, use the same molecular rules to make proteins under the control of genes. In all organisms, codons in DNA are transcribed into codons in RNA which is translated on ribosomes into polypeptides according to the same genetic code. Thus, if a gene from a man is transferred into a bacterium, the bacterium can manufacture the human protein. Since most commercially valuable proteins come from man or other eucaryotes while bacteria are essentially little biochemical factories that can be grown in huge quantities, one strategy for manufacturing a desired protein (for example, insulin) is to transfer the gene coding for the protein from the eucaryotic cell where the gene normally occurs into a bacterium.

Bacteria containing genes from a foreign source (*heterologous* genes) integrated into their own genetic makeup are said to be *transformed*. When transformed bacteria grow and divide, the inserted heterologous genes, like all the other genes that are normally present in the bacterium (*indigenous* genes), are replicated and passed on to succeeding generations. One can produce large quantities of transformed bacteria that contain transplanted heterologous genes. The process of making large quantities of identical copies of a gene (or other fragment of DNA) by introducing it into procaryotic cells and then growing those cells is called *cloning* the gene. After growing sufficient quantities of the transformed bacteria, the biotechnologist must induce the transformed bacteria to *express* the cloned gene and make useful quantities of the protein. This is the purpose of the claimed invention.

In order to make a selected protein by expressing its cloned gene in bacteria, several technical hurdles must be overcome. First the gene coding for the specific protein must be isolated for cloning. This is a formidable task, but recombinant DNA technology has armed the genetic engineer with a variety of techniques to accomplish it. Next the isolated gene must be introduced into the host bacterium. This can be done by incorporating the gene into a cloning vector. A *cloning vector* is a piece of DNA that can be introduced into bacteria and will then replicate itself as the bacterial cells grow and divide. Bacteriophage (viruses that infect bacteria) can be used as cloning vectors, but plasmids were the type used by appellants. A *plasmid* is a small circular loop of DNA found in bacteria, separate from the chromosome, that replicates like a chromosome. It is like a tiny auxilliary chromosome containing only a few genes. Because of their small size, plasmids are convenient for the molecular biologist to isolate and work with. Recombinant DNA technology can be used to modify plasmids by splicing in cloned eucaryotic genes and other useful segments of DNA containing control sequences. Short pieces of DNA can even be designed to have desired nucleotide sequences, synthesized chemically, and spliced into the plasmid. One use of such chemically synthesized linkers is to insure that the inserted gene has the same reading frame as the rest of the plasmid; this is a teaching of the Bahl reference cited against appellants. A plasmid constructed by the molecular geneticist can be inserted into bacteria, where it replicates as the bacteria grow.

Even after a cloned heterologous gene has been successfully inserted into bacteria using a plasmid as a cloning vector, and replicates as the bacteria grow, there is no guarantee that the gene will be expressed, *i.e.*, transcribed and translated into protein. A bacterium such as *E. coli* (the species of bacterium used by appellants) has genes for several thousand proteins. At any given moment many of those genes are not expressed at all. The genetic engineer needs a method to "turn on" the cloned gene and force it to be expressed. This is the problem appellants worked to solve.

* * *

Amgen, Inc. v. Chugai Pharmaceutical Co., Ltd.

927 F.2d 1200 (Fed.Cir.1991).

■ Before MARKEY, LOURIE and CLEVENGER, CIRCUIT JUDGES.

■ LOURIE, CIRCUIT JUDGE.

This appeal and cross appeal are from the March 4, 1990, judgment of the United States District Court for the District of Massachusetts, *Amgen, Inc. v. Chugai Pharmaceutical Co.*, 13 U.S.P.Q.2D 1737, 1989 WL 169006 (1989), and involve issues of patent validity, infringement, and inequitable conduct with respect to two patents: U.S. Patent 4,703,008 ('008), owned by Kirin–Amgen Inc. (Amgen), and U.S. Patent 4,677,195 ('195), owned by Genetics Institute, Inc. (GI). Chugai Pharmaceutical Co., Ltd. (Chugai) and Genetics Institute, Inc. (collectively defendants) assert on appeal that the district court erred in holding that: ... 3) the failure of Amgen to deposit the best mode host cells was not a violation of the best mode requirement under 35 U.S.C. § 112; and 4) claims 4 and 6 of GI's '195 patent are invalid for indefiniteness under 35 U.S.C. § 112.

On cross appeal, Amgen challenges the district court's holdings that: 1) claims 1 and 3 of the '195 patent are enabled; ... and 4) claims 7, 8, 23–27 and 29 of the '008 patent are not enabled by the specification.

We affirm the district court's holdings in all respects, except that we reverse the court's ruling that claims 1 and 3 of the '195 patent are enabled.

BACKGROUND[1]

Erythropoietin (EPO) is a protein consisting of 165 amino acids which stimulates the production of red blood cells. It is therefore a useful therapeutic agent in the treatment of anemias or blood disorders characterized by low or defective bone marrow production of red blood cells.

The preparation of EPO products generally has been accomplished through the concentration and purification of urine from both healthy individuals and those exhibiting high EPO levels. A new technique for producing EPO is recombinant DNA technology in which EPO is produced from cell cultures into which genetically-engineered vectors containing the EPO gene have been introduced. The production of EPO by recombinant technology involves expressing an EPO gene through the same processes that occur in a natural cell.

THE PATENTS

... U.S. Patent 4,703,008, entitled "DNA Sequences Encoding Erythropoietin" (the '008 patent), issued on October 27, 1987, to Dr. Fu–Kuen Lin, an employee of Amgen. The claims of the '008 patent cover purified and isolated DNA sequences encoding erythropoietin and host cells transformed or transfected with a DNA sequence. The relevant claims are as follows:

---

1. The district court, in a detailed opinion, fully sets out the scientific and historical background relating to the patents at issue. *See Amgen*, 13 U.S.P.Q.2D at 1741–58. Familiarity with that opinion is presumed.

2. A purified and isolated DNA sequence consisting essentially of a DNA sequence encoding human erythropoietin.

* * *

4. A procaryotic or eucaryotic host cell transformed or transfected with a DNA sequence according to claim 1, 2 or 3 in a manner allowing the host cell to express erythropoietin.

* * *

7. A purified and isolated DNA sequence consisting essentially of a DNA sequence encoding a polypeptide having an amino acid sequence sufficiently duplicative of that of erythropoietin to allow possession of the biological property of causing bone marrow cells to increase production of reticulocytes and red blood cells, and to increase hemoglobin synthesis or iron uptake.

DISCUSSION

* * *

C. *Best Mode*

Defendants argue that the district court erred in failing to hold the '008 patent invalid under 35 U.S.C. § 112, asserting that Lin failed to disclose the best mammalian host cells known to him as of November 30, 1984, the date he filed his fourth patent application.

The district court found that the "best mode" of practicing the claimed invention was by use of a specific genetically-heterogeneous strain of Chinese hamster ovary (CHO) cells, which produced EPO at a rate greater than that of other cells. It further found that this strain was disclosed in Example 10 and that Lin knew of no better mode. GI argues that Lin's best mode was not adequately disclosed in Example 10 because one skilled in the art could not duplicate Lin's best mode without his having first deposited a sample of the specific cells in a public depository. The issue before us therefore is whether the district court erred in concluding that Example 10 of the '008 patent satisfied the best mode requirement as to the invention of the challenged claims[5] and that a deposit of the preferred CHO cells was not necessary.

A determination whether the best mode requirement is satisfied is a question of fact, *DeGeorge v. Bernier*, 768 F.2d 1318, 1324, 226 USPQ 758, 763 (Fed.Cir.1985); we therefore review the district court's finding under a clearly erroneous standard. 35 U.S.C. § 112 provides in relevant part:

> The specification shall contain a written description of the invention, and of the manner and process of making and using it, in such full, clear, concise, and exact terms as to enable any person skilled in the art to which it pertains, or with which it is most nearly connected, to make and use the

---

5. Defendants assert that all the claims should be invalid for failure to disclose the best mode. We perceive that the best mode issue only relates to the host cell claims, 4, 6, 23–27, and 29. Absent inequitable conduct, a best mode defense only affects those claims covering subject matter the practice of which has not been disclosed in compliance with the best mode requirement. *See Northern Telecom, Inc. v. Datapoint Corp.*, 908 F.2d 931, 940, 15 U.S.P.Q.2D 1321, 1328 (Fed.Cir.), *cert. denied*, 498 U.S. 920, 111 S.Ct. 296, 112 L.Ed.2d 250 (1990).

same, and shall set forth the best mode contemplated by the inventor of carrying out his invention.

(Emphasis added).

This court has recently discussed the best mode requirement, pointing out that its analysis has two components. *Chemcast Corp. v. Arco Indus. Corp.*, 913 F.2d 923, 927, 16 U.S.P.Q.2D 1033, 1036 (Fed.Cir.1990). The first is a subjective one, asking whether, at the time the inventor filed his patent application, he contemplated a best mode of practicing his invention. If he did, the second inquiry is whether his disclosure is adequate to enable one skilled in the art to practice the best mode or, in other words, whether the best mode has been concealed from the public. The best mode requirement thus is intended to ensure that a patent applicant plays "fair and square" with the patent system. It is a requirement that the quid pro quo of the patent grant be satisfied. One must not receive the right to exclude others unless at the time of filing he has provided an adequate disclosure of the best mode known to him of carrying out his invention. Our case law has interpreted the best mode requirement to mean that there must be no concealment of a mode known by the inventor to be better than that which is disclosed. *Hybritech Inc. v. Monoclonal Antibodies, Inc.*, 802 F.2d 1367, 1384–85, 231 USPQ 81, 94 (Fed.Cir.1986), *cert. denied*, 480 U.S. 947, 107 S.Ct. 1606, 94 L.Ed.2d 792 (1987). Section 282 imposes on those attempting to prove invalidity the burden of proof. We agree that the district court did not err in finding that defendants have not met their burden of proving a best mode violation.

As noted above, the district court found that the best mode of making the CHO cells was set forth in Example 10. As the district court stated, while it was not clear which of two possible strains Lin considered to be the best, the cell strain subjected to 1000 nanomolar MTX (methotrexate) or that subjected to 100 nanomolar MTX, the best mode was disclosed because both were disclosed.[6] Defendants argue that this disclosure is not enough, that a deposit of the cells was required.

Defendants contend that "[i]n the field of living materials such as microorganisms and cell cultures," we should require a biological deposit so that the public has access to exactly the best mode contemplated by the inventor. This presents us with a question of first impression concerning the best mode requirement for patents involving novel genetically-engineered biological subject matter.

For many years, it has been customary for patent applicants to place microorganism samples in a public depository when such a sample is necessary to carry out a claimed invention. This practice arose out of the development of antibiotics, when microorganisms obtained from soil samples uniquely synthesized antibiotics which could not be readily prepared

---

6. In its opinion, the district court stated that "the best way to express EPO was from mammalian cells ... and that a cell line derived from 11 possible clones from the CHO B11 3, 1 cell strain was to be used for Amgen's master working cell bank, which was expected to be started on November 26, 1984." 13 U.S.P.Q.2D at 1772. At another point, the court stated that Amgen "did disclose the best mode in Example 10 of the invention, when it described the production rates of the 100 nanomolar-amplified cells (the B11 3,.1 cell strain) and one micromolar-treated cells." *Id.*

chemically or otherwise. *In re Argoudelis*, 434 F.2d 1390, 168 USPQ 99 (CCPA 1970). Such a deposit has been considered adequate to satisfy the enablement requirement of 35 U.S.C. § 112, when a written description alone would not place the invention in the hands of the public and physical possession of a unique biological material is required. *See, e.g., In re Wands*, 858 F.2d 731, 735–36, 8 U.S.P.Q.2D 1400, 1403 (Fed.Cir.1988) ("Where an invention depends on the use of living materials ... it may be impossible to enable the public to make the invention (*i.e.*, to obtain these living materials) solely by means of written disclosure."); *In re Lundak*, 773 F.2d 1216, 1220, 227 USPQ 90, 93 (Fed.Cir.1985) ("When an invention relates to a new biological material, the material may not be reproducible even when detailed procedures and a complete taxonomic description are included in the specification."); *see generally* Hampar, *Patenting of Recombinant DNA Technology: The Deposit Requirement*, 67 J. Pat. & Trademark Off. Soc'y 569, 607 (1985) ("The deposit requirement is a nonstatutory mechanism for ensuring compliance with the 'enabling' provision under 35 U.S.C. § 112.").

The district court found that the claims at issue require the use of biological materials that were capable of being prepared in the laboratory from readily available biological cells, using the description in Example 10. The court also found that there were no starting materials that were not publicly available, that were not described, or that required undue experimentation for their preparation in order to carry out the best mode. The court noted that Lin testified that the isolation of the preferred strain was a "routine limited dilution cloning procedure[ ]" well known in the art. Dr. Simonsen, GI's own expert, testified that the disclosed procedures were "standard" and that:

> with the vectors and the sequences shown in Example 10, I have no doubt that someone eventually could reproduce—well, could generate cell lines [sic, strains] making some level of EPO, and they could be better, they could be worse in terms of EPO production.

The district court relied on this testimony, and, upon review, we agree with its determination. The testimony accurately reflects that the invention, as it relates to the best mode host cells, could be practiced by one skilled in the art following Example 10. Thus, the best mode was disclosed and it was adequately enabled.

These materials are therefore not analogous to the biological cells obtained from unique soil samples. When a biological sample required for the practice of an invention is obtained from nature, the invention may be incapable of being practiced without access to that organism. Hence the deposit is required in that case. On the other hand, when, as is the case here, the organism is created by insertion of genetic material into a cell obtained from generally available sources, then all that is required is a description of the best mode and an adequate description of the means of carrying out the invention, not deposit of the cells. If the cells can be prepared without undue experimentation from known materials, based on the description in the patent specification, a deposit is not required. *See Feldman v. Aunstrup*, 517 F.2d 1351, 1354, 186 USPQ 108, 111 (CCPA 1975), ("No problem exists when the microorganisms used are known and readily available to the public."), cert. denied, 424 U.S. 912, 96 S.Ct. 1109, 47 L.Ed.2d 316 (1976). Since the court found that that is the case here, we therefore hold that there is no failure to comply with the best mode requirement for lack of a deposit of the CHO cells, when the best mode of preparing the cells has been disclosed and the best mode cells have been enabled, *i.e.*, they can be prepared by one skilled in the art from known materials using the description in the specification.

Defendants also contend that the examiner's rejection of the application that matured into the '008 patent for failure to make a publicly accessible biological deposit supports its argument. U.S. Patent Application Serial No. 675,298, Prosecution History at 179 (First Rejection July 3, 1986). However, that rejection was withdrawn after an oral interview and a written argument that the invention did not require a deposit. Id. at 208.

We also note that the PTO has recently prescribed guidelines concerning the deposit of biological materials. *See* 37 C.F.R. § 1.802(b) (1990) (biological material need not be deposited "if it is known and readily available to the public or can be made or isolated without undue experimentation"). The PTO, in response to a question as to whether the deposit requirement is applicable to the best mode requirement, as distinct from enablement, said:

> The best mode requirement is a safeguard against the possible selfish desire on the part of some people to obtain patent protection without making a full disclosure. The requirement does not permit an inventor to disclose only what is known to be the second-best embodiment, retaining the best.... The fundamental issue that should be addressed is whether there was evidence to show that the quality of an applicant's best mode disclosure is so poor as to effectively result in concealment. *In re Sherwood*, 615 [613] F.2d 809, 204 USPQ 537 (CCPA 1980). If a deposit is the only way to comply with the best mode requirement then the deposit must be made. 52 Fed.Reg. 34080, 34086 (Sept. 8, 1987).

We see no inconsistency between the district court's decision, which we affirm here, and these guidelines.

Defendants also assert that the record shows that scientists were unable to duplicate Lin's genetically-heterogeneous best mode cell strain. However, we have long held that the issue is whether the disclosure is "adequate," not that an exact duplication is necessary. Indeed, the district court stated that

> [t]he testimony is clear that no scientist could ever duplicate exactly the best mode used by Amgen, but that those of ordinary skill in the art could produce mammalian host cell strains or lines with similar levels of production identified in Example 10.

What is required is an adequate disclosure of the best mode, not a guarantee that every aspect of the specification be precisely and universally reproducible. *See In re Gay*, 309 F.2d 769, 773, 135 USPQ 311, 316, 50 CCPA 725 (1962).

Defendants finally argue that Lin's failure to deposit the transfected cells notwithstanding the fact that he was willing to deposit essentially worthless cell material was evidence of deliberate concealment. We have already stated that deposit of the host cells containing the rEPO gene was not necessary to satisfy the best mode requirement of Section 112. The best mode was disclosed and a deposit was not necessary to carry it out. Therefore, the fact that some cells were deposited, but not others, is irrelevant.

D. *Enablement of claims 7, 8, 23–27, and 29*

Amgen argues that the district court's holding that GI "provided clear and convincing evidence that the patent specification is insufficient to enable one of ordinary skill in the art to make and use the invention claimed in claim 7 of the '008 patent without undue experimentation" constituted legal error. 13 U.S.P.Q.2D at 1776. Amgen specifically argues that the district court erred because it "did not properly address the factors which this court has held must be considered in determining lack of enablement based on assertion of undue experimentation," citing this court's decision in *In re Wands*, 858 F.2d at 737, 8 U.S.P.Q.2D at 1404.

Claim 7 is a generic claim, covering all possible DNA sequences that will encode any polypeptide having an amino acid sequence "sufficiently duplicative" of EPO to possess the property of increasing production of red blood cells. As claims 8, 23–27, and 29, dependent on claim 7, are not separately argued, and are of similar scope, they stand or fall with claim 7. *See In re Dillon*, 919 F.2d 688, 692, 16 U.S.P.Q.2D 1897, 1900 (Fed.Cir. 1990) *(in banc)*.

Whether a claimed invention is enabled under 35 U.S.C. § 112 is a question of law, which we review de novo. *Moleculon Research Corp. v. CBS, Inc.*, 793 F.2d 1261, 1268, 229 USPQ 805, 811 (Fed.Cir.1986), *cert. denied*, 479 U.S. 1030, 107 S.Ct. 875, 93 L.Ed.2d 829 (1987). "To be enabling under § 112, a patent must contain a description that enables one skilled in the art to make and use the claimed invention." *Atlas Powder Co. v. E.I. duPont De Nemours & Co.*, 750 F.2d 1569, 1576, 224 USPQ 409, 413 (Fed.Cir.1984).

That some experimentation is necessary does not constitute a lack of enablement; the amount of experimentation, however, must not be unduly extensive. *Id.* The essential question here is whether the scope of enablement of claim 7 is as broad as the scope of the claim. *See generally In re Fisher*, 427 F.2d 833, 166 USPQ 18 (CCPA 1970); 2 D. Chisum, Patents § 7.03[7][b](1990).

The specification of the '008 patent provides that:

> one may readily design and manufacture genes coding for microbial expression of polypeptides having primary conformations which differ from that herein specified for mature EPO in terms of the identity or location of one or more residues (*e.g.*, substitutions, terminal and intermediate additions and deletions).

* * *

> DNA sequences provided by the present invention are thus seen to comprehend all DNA sequences suitable for use in securing expression in a procaryotic or eucaryotic host cell of a polypeptide product having at least a part of the primary structural conformation and one or more of the biological properties of erythropoietin, and selected from among: (a) the

DNA sequences set out in FIGS. 5 and 6; (b) DNA sequences which hybridize to the DNA sequences defined in (a) or fragments thereof; and (c) DNA sequences which, but for the degeneracy of the genetic code, would hybridize to the DNA sequences defined in (a) and (b).

The district court found that over 3,600 different EPO analogs can be made by substituting at only a single amino acid position, and over a million different analogs can be made by substituting three amino acids. The patent indicates that it embraces means for preparation of "numerous" polypeptide analogs of EPO. Thus, the number of claimed DNA encoding sequences that can produce an EPO-like product is potentially enormous.

In a deposition, Dr. Elliott, who was head of Amgen's EPO analog program, testified that he did not know whether the fifty to eighty EPO analogs Amgen had made "had the biological property of causing bone marrow cells to increase production of reticulocytes and red blood cells, and to increase hemoglobin synthesis or iron uptake." Based on this evidence, the trial court concluded that "defendants had provided clear and convincing evidence that the patent specification is insufficient to enable one of ordinary skill in the art to make and use the invention claimed in claim 7 of the '008 patent without undue experimentation." 13 USPQ at 1776. In making this determination, the court relied in particular on the lack of predictability in the art, as demonstrated by the testimony of both Dr. Goldwasser, another scientist who worked on procedures for purifying urinary EPO (uEPO), and Dr. Elliott. After five years of experimentation, the court noted, "Amgen is still unable to specify which analogs have the biological properties set forth in claim 7." *Id.*

We believe the trial court arrived at the correct decision, although for the wrong reason. By focusing on the biological properties of the EPO analogs, it failed to consider the enablement of the DNA sequence analogs, which are the subject of claim 7. Moreover, it is not necessary that a patent applicant test all the embodiments of his invention, *In re Angstadt*, 537 F.2d 498, 502, 190 USPQ 214, 218 (CCPA 1976); what is necessary is that he provide a disclosure sufficient to enable one skilled in the art to carry out the invention commensurate with the scope of his claims. For DNA sequences, that means disclosing how to make and use enough sequences to justify grant of the claims sought. Amgen has not done that here. In addition, it is not necessary that a court review all the *Wands* factors to find a disclosure enabling. They are illustrative, not mandatory. What is relevant depends on the facts, and the facts here are that Amgen has not enabled preparation of DNA sequences sufficient to support its all-encompassing claims.

It is well established that a patent applicant is entitled to claim his invention generically, when he describes it sufficiently to meet the requirements of Section 112. *See Utter v. Hiraga*, 845 F.2d 993, 998, 6 U.S.P.Q.2D 1709, 1714 (Fed.Cir.1988) ("A specification may, within the meaning of 35 U.S.C. § 112 p 1, contain a written description of a broadly claimed invention without describing all species that claim encompasses."); *In re Robins*, 429 F.2d 452, 456–57, 166 USPQ 552, 555 (CCPA 1970) ("[R]epresentative samples are not required by the statute and are not an end in themselves."). Here, however, despite extensive statements in the specification concerning all the analogs of the EPO gene that can be made, there is little enabling disclosure of particular analogs and how to make them. Details for preparing only a few EPO analog genes are disclosed. Amgen argues that this is sufficient to support its claims; we disagree. This "disclosure" might well justify a generic claim encompassing these and similar analogs, but it represents inadequate support for Amgen's desire to claim all EPO gene analogs. There may be many other genetic sequences that code for EPO-type products. Amgen has told how to make and use only a few of them and is therefore not entitled to claim all of them.

In affirming the district court's invalidation of claims 7, 8, 23–27, and 29 under Section 112, we do not intend to imply that generic claims to genetic sequences cannot be valid where they are of a scope appropriate to the invention disclosed by an applicant. That is not the case here, where Amgen has claimed every possible analog of a gene containing about 4,000 nucleotides, with a disclosure only of how to make EPO and a very few analogs.

The district court properly relied upon *Fisher* in making its decision. In that case, an applicant was attempting to claim an adrenocorticotrophic hormone preparation containing a polypeptide having at least twenty-four amino acids of a specified sequence. Only a thirty-nine amino acid product was disclosed. The court found that applicant could not obtain claims that are insufficiently supported and hence not in compliance with the first paragraph of 35 U.S.C. § 112. It stated:

> Appellant's parent application, therefore, discloses no products, inherently or expressly, containing other than 39 amino acids, yet the claim includes all polypeptides, of the recited potency and purity, having at least 24 amino acids in the chain in the recited sequence. The parent specification does not enable one skilled in the art to make or obtain ACTHs with other than 39 amino acids in the chain, and there has been no showing that one of ordinary skill would have known how to make or obtain such other ACTHs without undue experimentation. As for appellant's conclusion that the 25th to 39th acids in the chain are unnecessary, it is one thing to make such a statement when persons skilled in the art are able to make or obtain ACTH having other than 39 amino acids; it is quite another thing when they are not able to do so. In the latter situation, the statement is in no way "enabling" and hence lends no further support for the broad claim. We conclude that appellant's parent application is insufficient to support a claim as broad as claim 4.

* * *

> [Section 112] requires that the scope of the claims must bear a reasonable correlation to the scope of enablement provided by the specification to persons of ordinary skill in the art.

Fisher, 427 F.2d at 836, 839, 166 USPQ at 21–22, 24.

Considering the structural complexity of the EPO gene, the manifold possibilities for change in its structure, with attendant uncertainty as to what utility will be possessed by these analogs, we consider that more is needed concerning identifying the various analogs that are within the scope of the claim, methods for making them, and structural requirements for producing compounds with EPO-like activity. It is not sufficient, having made the gene and a handful of analogs whose activity has not been clearly ascertained, to claim all possible genetic sequences that have EPO-like activity. Under the circumstances, we find no error in the court's conclusion that the generic DNA sequence claims are invalid under Section 112.

NOTES

1. *A Plethora of Disclosure Problems. Amgen* posed a number of interesting patent disclosure problems arising from the development of purified and recombinant versions of natural proteins, such as erythropoietin (EPO). The portions of the opinion set forth above concern best mode and enablement issues with Amgen's '008 patent, which claimed DNA sequences that encode for EPO or EPO-like proteins. It is important to understand that the '008 patent did not claim the end product itself (EPO), but rather a product, a DNA sequence, that is useful for making the end product. In a sense, the '008 patent claimed a starting material for making a therapeutic product.

2. *Best Mode: Cells and Software.* The *Amgen* case involved biotechnology, and the *Fonar* case involved computer technology. Notice how these opinions apply section 112 to these different technologies.

3. *Enablement—Scope of Amgen's '008 Patent Claim 7.* The court holds claim 7, which covered DNA sequences encoding for any protein that had the important biological properties of EPO, invalid for lack of enablement. What would the patentee have had to disclose in order to "justify" such a broad claim? Five examples? 50?

4. *Enablement—Operability of Genetic Institute's '195 Patent Claim.* In *Amgen*, the Chugai–Genetics Institute (GI) side accused the Amgen–Kirin side of infringing GI's '195 patent. Unlike the '008 patent, which claimed DNA sequences, the '195 patent claimed purified EPO itself with a "specific activity of at least 160,000 IU per absorbance unit at 280 nanometers." The district court held both this patent and Amgen's '008 patent valid and infringed.

a. As matters stood in the district court, both sides held valid patents that covered aspects of the technology necessary to produce and market EPO. Had the district court's ruling become final, what would have been the legal and commercial impact on the parties? Were the only options a cross-license or a stand-off? If you were counseling Amgen, would you have advised the company to appeal?

b. Amgen appealed and convinced the Federal Circuit that its patent was valid and infringed and that GI's '195 patent was invalid for lack of enablement. The methods disclosed in GI's patent were not operable to produce EPO with the claimed activity level (160,00 IU/AU). The court's reasoning is set forth below. (Note that "uEPO" refers to EPO extracted and purified from urine whereas "rEPO" refers to EPO produced by the recombinant DNA process described in O'Farrell and Amgen.)

> Defendants have produced no evidence that it ever prepared EPO with a specific activity of at least 160,000 IU/AU in vivo using the disclosed methods. In its report to the FDA, GI stated that it had purified uEPO material "to homogeneity" by subjecting partially purified uEPO material to reverse phase high performance liquid chromatography (RP–HPLC), the technique taught by [the inventor] Hewick in the '195 patent. The district court found that GI reported to the FDA that the specific activity of uEPO, based on in vivo bioassays, was only 109,000 IU/AU.... GI originally arrived at the figure of 160,000 IU/AU by calculation, before it had the

capacity to derive quantitative information from bioassays. Hewick subjected the EPO to RP–HPLC, the EPO having an actual value of 83,000 IU/AU. After weighing the chromatograph, he found that "at least fifty percent" of the area under the chromatograph curve was attributable to something other than EPO. He then doubled the 83,000, and arrived at a theoretical specific activity of "at least about 160,000 IU/AU." That procedure, while possibly valid as a means for estimating the specific activity of a pure sample, does not establish that GI had a workable method for actually obtaining the pure material that it claimed.

Moreover, the work of others shows that Hewick did not enable the preparation of uEPO having an in vivo specific activity of at least 160,000, as the claims required. Dr. Kawakita, a scientist at Kummamoto University in Japan, reported an in vivo specific activity of 101,000 IU/AU when using RP–HPLC according to Hewick's method. This is similar to the 109,000 value reported to the FDA by GI. Kawakita did report a value of 188,000, but did not follow the teachings in the '195 patent. Defendants also rely on the testimony of Fritsch that "I've also seen further data in Chugai's PLA indicating additional urinary EPO preparation that had activities of 190,000, I believe, units per absorbance unit." However, the document to which Fritsch referred was not offered into evidence by GI after Amgen objected to its introduction and is not before us.

Defendants argue that Dr. Kung's uEPO test result of 173,640 IU/AU in an in vitro test supports the enablement of its claims. Amgen argues that an in vivo test result would only have been 65 percent of the in vitro result and thus would not have met the 160,000 IU/AU limitation of the claims. The district court relied on Kung, despite the demonstrated disparity between the results of in vitro and in vivo testing.

It is not absolutely clear to us that, for uEPO, the in vivo specific activity is 65 percent of the in vitro specific activity. Nonetheless, Kung's measurement, being in vitro, does not demonstrate enablement of the claimed invention, and that fact means that the court erred in finding enablement. Added to this fact is the difference that exists between the in vivo results for rEPO and uEPO . . ., and the other lack of support for the 160,000 limitation. Under these circumstances, we hold that the district court erred in accepting the in vitro data as support for claims containing what has been found to be an in vivo limitation.

In addition to the question of enablement regarding uEPO, the district court found that the only purification attempt on rEPO in the manner set out in the '195 patent failed to provide homogeneous EPO. The patent itself, in Example 2, discloses GI's purification efforts on rEPO and indicates that GI did not obtain purified rEPO. As the district court found, "[t]he patent does not contain any procedures . . . for purifying rEPO to the point that RP–HPLC will be successful." 13 U.S.P.Q.2D at 1758. Thus, the patent fails to enable purification of either rEPO or uEPO. . . . *See In re Rainer*, 377 F.2d 1006, 1012 (CCPA 1967) ("specification is evidence of its own inadequacy").

The burden of showing non-enablement is Amgen's, not GI's, but in the case of a challenged patent, when substantial discovery has occurred, and there is no credible evidence that the claimed purified material can be made by those skilled in the art by the disclosed process, and all evidence from both the inventor and his assignee and from third parties is to the contrary, we conclude that Amgen has met its burden to show that the claims have not been adequately enabled. We do not hold that one must always prove that a disclosed process operates effectively to produce a claimed product. But, under these circumstances, we conclude that the court erred in holding that claims 1 and 3 were properly enabled.

The "enablement" issue with regard to the '195 patent is quite different from that for Amgen's '008 claim 7. How would you articulate the difference?

c. Financial Consequences. The Federal Circuit's 1991 Amgen decision had immediate financial and commercial consequences. See Rundle & Stipp, Amgen Wins Biotech Drug Patent Battle—Genetics Institute's Shares Plunge on Court Ruling As Victor's Stock Surges, Wall Street Journal, 1991 WL–WSJ 617341 (March 7, 1991). GI's stock dropped 35%; Amgen's rose 12%. The stock of Upjohn, GI's partner, fell $3.125 a share. The Wall Street Journal article reported that "The ruling was a knock-out punch that even Amgen's most optimistic followers hadn't forecast" and added:

> ... Amgen learned late Tuesday that a decision had been reached, but couldn't find out what it was. Officials huddled around a fax machine early yesterday as pages of the document trickled in from a Washington law firm.

> "Eventually folks will get back to work around here," quipped company spokesman Mark Brand. Especially jubilant are "the chemists, attorneys and others who devoted the bulk of the last several years of their lives to EPO," he said. The company has spent more than $10 million in legal fees fighting Genetics Institute.

d. GI's Continuing Application. After its unsuccessful appeal in Amgen, GI used a pending "continuing" application containing the same disclosure as the '195 patent to obtain a second patent claiming purified EPO without a limitation to an activity level of 160,000. Is this claim broader in scope than the claim in the '195 patent? Is this claim enabled by GI's teaching of purified EPO with an activity level lower than 160,000. Should this patent be held invalid, based on the res judicata or collateral estoppel effect of the first Amgen case? See Amgen, Inc. v. Genetics Institute, Inc., 98 F.3d 1328 (Fed.Cir.1996).

5. *Invention Priority—Conception.* The 1991 *Amgen* decision dealt with yet another issue, the conception of DNA inventions, which has had an impact on the written description requirement, as the following two decisions, *Fiers* and *Regents*, illustrate. The conception issue arose because GI contended that Amgen's '008 patent, based on the work of its scientist Dr. Lin, was invalid because of the prior invention by GI's scientist Dr. Fritsch. As discussed below in Chapter 4, Section B.10., an invention date depends on "conception" and "reduction to practice." Amgen's Lin "reduced to practice" the EPO–DNA invention by cloning and sequencing the DNA (gene) in September 1983. GI's Fritsch did not successfully clone and sequence the gene until 1984, but GI contended that Fritsch had an earlier 1981 "conception" of the invention in the form of a strategy or method for isolating the gene. The Federal Circuit held that Fritsch did not have a sufficient conception.

> Prior to 1983, the amino acid sequence for EPO was uncertain, and in some positions the sequence envisioned was incorrect. Thus, until Fritsch had a complete mental conception of a purified and isolated DNA sequence encoding EPO and a method for its preparation, in which the precise identity of the sequence is envisioned, or in terms of other characteristics sufficient to distinguish it from other genes, all he had was an objective to make an invention which he could not then adequately describe or define.

> A gene is a chemical compound, albeit a complex one, and it is well established in our law that conception of a chemical compound requires that the inventor be able to define it so as to distinguish it from other materials, and to describe how to obtain it.... Conception does not occur unless one has a mental picture of the structure of the chemical, or is able to define it by its method of preparation, its physical or chemical properties, or whatever characteristics sufficiently distinguish it. It is not sufficient to define it solely by its principal biological property, e.g., encoding human erythropoietin, because an alleged conception having no more

specificity than that is simply a wish to know the identity of any material with that biological property. We hold that when an inventor is unable to envision the detailed constitution of a gene so as to distinguish it from other materials, as well as a method for obtaining it, conception has not been achieved until reduction to practice has occurred, i.e., until after the gene has been isolated.

Fritsch had a goal of obtaining the isolated EPO gene, whatever its identity, and even had an idea of a possible method of obtaining it, but he did not conceive a purified and isolated DNA sequence encoding EPO and a viable method for obtaining it until after Lin. It is important to recognize that neither Fritsch nor Lin invented EPO or the EPO gene. The subject matter of claim 2 was the novel purified and isolated sequence which codes for EPO, and neither Fritsch nor Lin knew the structure or physical characteristics of it and had a viable method of obtaining that subject matter until it was actually obtained and characterized.

Defendants further argue that because the trial court found that the probing and screening method employed by Lin is what distinguished the invention of the '008 patent over the prior art, Fritsch's strategy in 1981 had priority over Lin's use of that strategy. We disagree. The trial court found that Fritsch's alleged conception in 1981 of an approach that might result in cloning the gene was mere speculation. Conception of a generalized approach for screening a DNA library that might be used to identify and clone the EPO gene of then unknown constitution is not conception of a "purified and isolated DNA sequence" encoding human EPO. It is not "a definite and permanent idea of the complete and operative invention." Fritsch's conception of a process had to be sufficiently specific that one skilled in the relevant art would succeed in cloning the EPO gene. See Coleman, 754 F.2d at 359, 224 USPQ at 862. Clearly, he did not have that conception because he did not know the structure of EPO or the EPO gene.

The record indicates that several companies, as well as Amgen and GI, were unsuccessful using Fritsch's approach. As the trial court correctly summarized:

> Given the utter lack of experience in probing genomic libraries with fully degenerate probes and the crudeness of the techniques available in 1981, it would have been mere speculation or at most a probable deduction from facts then known by Dr. Fritsch that his generalized approach would result in cloning the EPO gene. 13 U.S.P.Q.2D at 1760. As expert testimony from both sides indicated, success in cloning the EPO gene was not assured until the gene was in fact isolated and its sequence known. Based on the uncertainties of the method and lack of information concerning the amino acid sequence of the EPO protein, the trial court was correct in concluding that neither party had an adequate conception of the DNA sequence until reduction to practice had been achieved; Lin was first to accomplish that goal.

927 F.2d at 1206–07.

Fiers v. Revel

984 F.2d 1164 (Fed.Cir.1993).

■ Before MICHEL, CIRCUIT JUDGE, COWEN, SENIOR CIRCUIT JUDGE, and LOURIE, CIRCUIT JUDGE.

■ LOURIE, CIRCUIT JUDGE.

Walter C. Fiers, Michel Revel, and Pierre Tiollais appeal from the June 5, 1991 decision of the Patent and Trademark Office Board of Patent

Appeals and Interferences, awarding priority of invention in a three-way interference proceeding, No. 101,096, to Haruo Sugano, Masami Muramatsu, and Tadatsugu Taniguchi (Sugano). We affirm.

BACKGROUND

This interference among three foreign inventive entities relates to the DNA which codes for human fibroblast beta-interferon (B–IF), a protein that promotes viral resistance in human tissue. It involves a single count which reads:

> A DNA which consists essentially of a DNA which codes for a human fibroblast interferon-beta polypeptide.

The parties filed U.S. patent applications as follows: Sugano on October 27, 1980, Fiers on April 3, 1981, and Revel and Tiollais (Revel) on September 28, 1982. Sugano claimed the benefit of his March 19, 1980 Japanese filing date, Revel claimed the benefit of his November 21, 1979 Israeli filing date, and Fiers sought to establish priority under 35 U.S.C. § 102(g) based on prior conception coupled with diligence up to his British filing date on April 3, 1980.

Sugano's Japanese application disclosed the complete nucleotide sequence of a DNA coding for B–IF and a method for isolating that DNA. Revel's Israeli application disclosed a method for isolating a fragment of the DNA coding for B–IF as well as a method for isolating messenger RNA (mRNA) coding for B–IF, but did not disclose a complete DNA sequence coding for B–IF. Fiers, who was working abroad, based his case for priority on an alleged conception either in September 1979 or in January 1980, when his ideas were brought into the United States, coupled with diligence toward a constructive reduction to practice on April 3, 1980, when he filed a British application disclosing the complete nucleotide sequence of a DNA coding for B–IF. According to Fiers, his conception of the DNA of the count occurred when two American scientists, Walter Gilbert and Phillip Sharp, to whom he revealed outside of the United States a proposed method for isolating DNA coding for B–IF brought the protocol back to the United States.

Fiers submitted affidavits from Gilbert and Sharp averring that, based on Fiers' proposed protocol, one of ordinary skill in the art would have been able to isolate B–IF DNA without undue experimentation. On February 26, 1980, Fiers' patent attorney brought into the United States a draft patent application disclosing Fiers' method, but not the nucleotide sequence for the DNA.

The Board awarded priority of invention to Sugano, concluding that (1) Sugano was entitled to the benefit of his March 19, 1980 Japanese filing date, (2) Fiers was entitled to the benefit of his April 3, 1980 British filing date, but did not prove conception of the DNA of the count prior to that date, and (3) Revel was not entitled to the benefit of his November 21, 1979 Israeli filing date. The Board based its conclusions on the disclosure or failure to disclose the complete nucleotide sequence of a DNA coding for B–IF.

DISCUSSION

Revel bears the burden of proving entitlement to the benefit of his earlier-filed Israeli application date. *Utter v. Hiraga*, 845 F.2d 993, 998 (Fed.Cir.1988). To meet this burden, Revel must prove that his application meets the requirements of 35 U.S.C. § 112, first paragraph, which provides in pertinent part:

> The specification shall contain a written description of the invention, and of the manner and process of making and using it, in such full, clear, concise, and exact terms as to enable any person skilled in the art to which it pertains, or with which it is most nearly connected, to make and use the same....

Revel thus must show that the Israeli application contains a written description of the DNA of the count and that it is enabling. The Board held that Revel's Israeli application did not contain a written description of a DNA coding for B–IF since it did not disclose the nucleotide sequence or "an intact complete gene." The Board, in denying Revel's request for reconsideration, rejected the argument that it is only necessary to show some correspondence between the language in the count and language in the Israeli application to satisfy the written description requirement. The Board stated:

> Moreover, what is needed to meet the description requirement will necessarily vary depending on the nature of the invention claimed. The test for sufficiency of support is whether the disclosure of the application relied upon "reasonably conveys to the artisan that the inventor had possession at that time of the later claimed subject matter." As is apparent from our decision, we found the description in Revel's Israeli application inadequate to reasonably convey to the artisan that Revel was in possession of the invention of beta-interferon DNA [citations omitted].

Relying on *Amgen*, the Board concluded that the Israeli application was not enabling since Revel had not yet conceived the DNA of the count and "[l]ogically, one cannot ... enable an invention that has not been conceived." Slip op. at 13.

Revel argues that the disclosure of his Israeli application satisfies the written description requirement because it contains language of similar scope and wording to that of the count. Revel cites the following passages from the Israeli application:

> The invention thus concerns also said purified m-RNAs which comprises normally up to 900–1000 nucleotides.... In the same manner it also concerns the corresponding c-DNA which can be obtained by transcription of said RNAs [emphasis added]; It is a further object of the present invention to provide a process for the isolation of genetic material (DNA) containing the nucleotide sequence coding for interferon in human cells.

Revel points to a claim in the original Israeli application that corresponds substantially to the language of the count. According to Revel, since the language of the count refers to a DNA and not to a specific sequence, the specification need not describe the sequence of the DNA in order to satisfy the written description requirement. Revel thus urges that only similar language in the specification or original claims is necessary to satisfy the written description requirement.

We disagree. Compliance with the written description requirement is a question of fact which we review for clear error. *See Vas–Cath Inc. v. Mahurkar*, 935 F.2d 1555, 1563 (Fed.Cir.1991); *Utter*, 845 F.2d at 998. On reconsideration, the Board correctly set forth the legal standard for sufficiency of description: the specification of Revel's Israeli application must "reasonably convey[ ] to the artisan that the inventor had possession at that time of the ... claimed subject matter." Slip op. at 3 *(citing Vas–Cath, 935 F.2d at 1563)*.

An adequate written description of a DNA requires more than a mere statement that it is part of the invention and reference to a potential method for isolating it; what is required is a description of the DNA itself. Revel's specification does not do that. Revel's application does not even demonstrate that the disclosed method actually leads to the DNA, and thus that he had possession of the invention, since it only discloses a clone that might be used to obtain mRNA coding for B–IF. A bare reference to a DNA with a statement that it can be obtained by reverse transcription is not a description; it does not indicate that Revel was in possession of the DNA. Revel's argument that correspondence between the language of the count and language in the specification is sufficient to satisfy the written description requirement is unpersuasive when none of that language particularly describes the DNA.

As we stated in Amgen and reaffirmed above, such a disclosure just represents a wish, or arguably a plan, for obtaining the DNA. If a conception of a DNA requires a precise definition, such as by structure, formula, chemical name, or physical properties, as we have held, then a description also requires that degree of specificity. To paraphrase the Board, one cannot describe what one has not conceived.

Because the count at issue purports to cover all DNAs that code for B–IF, it is also analogous to a single means claim, which has been held not to comply with the first paragraph of section 112. *See In re Hyatt*, 708 F.2d 712 (Fed.Cir.1983) ("the enabling disclosure of the specification [must] be commensurate in scope with the claim under consideration.") Claiming all DNA's that achieve a result without defining what means will do so is not in compliance with the description requirement; it is an attempt to preempt the future before it has arrived.

The Board's determination that the Israeli application does not contain a written description of a DNA coding for B–IF was thus not clearly erroneous. The Board correctly determined that Revel is not entitled to the benefit of his November 1979 Israeli application since it fails to satisfy the written description requirement of section 112.

Sugano's Case for Priority

The Board held that Sugano established entitlement to his March 19, 1980 Japanese filing date because the disclosure of his Japanese application contains the complete and correct sequence of the DNA which codes for B–

IF, along with a detailed disclosure of the method used by Sugano to obtain that DNA. The Board rejected Fiers' argument that Sugano's March 1980 application is not enabling, since Fiers presented only attorney argument that was "unsupported by competent evidence, entitled to little or no weight and [was] unpersuasive in any event." Slip op. at 12.

Fiers argues that Sugano failed to prove that his application is enabling because he did not produce extrinsic evidence showing enablement. Fiers also argues that the Board erroneously imposed a burden on him to show that Sugano's application is not enabling when, in fact, Fiers had no right to submit rebuttal evidence once Sugano elected to rely solely on his Japanese application.

Enablement is a question of law that we review de novo. *Amgen*, 927 F.2d at 1212. Enablement requires that the application " 'contain a description that enables one skilled in the art to make and use the claimed invention.' " *Id.*, (citing *Atlas Powder Co. v. E.I. duPont De Nemours & Co.*, 750 F.2d 1569, 1576 (Fed.Cir.1984)). "[A] specification disclosure which contains a teaching of the manner and process of making and using the invention in terms which correspond in scope to those used in describing and defining the subject matter sought to be patented must be taken as in compliance with the enabling requirement of the first paragraph of § 112 unless there is reason to doubt the objective truth of the statements contained therein which must be relied on for enabling support." *In re Marzocchi*, 439 F.2d 220, 223 (CCPA 1971). "[A]ny party making the assertion that a U.S. patent specification or claims fails, for one reason or another, to comply with § 112 bears the burden of persuasion in showing said lack of compliance." *Weil v. Fritz*, 601 F.2d 551, 555 (CCPA 1979). Thus, once the examiner accepted the sufficiency of Sugano's specification, Sugano had no further burden to prove by extrinsic evidence that his application was enabling; the Board correctly determined that it was Fiers (or Revel) who then had to prove that Sugano's application was not enabling. Even if Fiers had no opportunity to cross-examine Sugano because Sugano elected to stand on his filing date, Fiers had other opportunities, including during the motion period, to challenge Sugano's entitlement to his Japanese application filing date. Thus, he did not lack opportunity to challenge.

We conclude that Sugano is entitled to rely on his disclosure as enabling since it sets forth a detailed teaching of a method for obtaining a DNA coding for B–IF and the Board did not err in determining that Fiers presented no convincing evidence impeaching the truth of the statements in Sugano's patent specification. We also conclude that Sugano's application satisfies the written description requirement since it sets forth the complete and correct nucleotide sequence of a DNA coding for β–IF and thus "convey[s] with reasonable clarity to those skilled in the art that, as of the filing date sought, [Sugano] was in possession of the [DNA coding for B—IF]." *See Vas–Cath*, 935 F.2d at 1563. The Board correctly determined that Sugano's March 19, 1980 Japanese application satisfies the requirements of section 112, first paragraph, and that Sugano thus met his burden to establish entitlement to that filing date.

NOTES

1. *Amino Acid and DNA Sequences.* A number of issues and case holdings on biotechnology patents cannot be understood without appreciating the relationship between the sequences of (a) the amino acids making up a protein, and (b) the nucleotide sequence of a gene that encodes for the protein. In addition to the discussions of the genetic code's "degeneracy" in *O'Farrell* and *Amgen*, the distinction is reviewed in a series of decisions applying the obviousness requirement. *E.g. In re Deuel*, 51 F.3d 1552 (Fed.Cir.1995). *See* Chapter 5, Section F.2. Some have analogized the relationship between DNA and an amino acid sequence to a program for controlling a computer and the output the program causes. Many different programs (and DNA sequences) can produce the same output (and amino acid sequences); a given program (and DNA sequence) produces only one output (and amino acid sequence).

2. *Linking Conception and Written Description—Original Claims.* Fiers links the invention date concept of "conception" to the Section 112 written description requirement: "one cannot describe what one has not conceived."

3. *Enablement and Novelty.* Are the concerns with a conception, a written description or an original claim to a structure or class of structures stated solely in terms of biological function best viewed as "written description," or as enablement or novelty (and/or obviousness)? For example, is it likely that it was known that there was a gene, some gene, that encodes for EPO or human fibroblast interferon? The problem was that no one yet knew the specific DNA structure. See the SIDE BAR following the *Regents* case below.

4. *Three Foreign Inventive Entities.* Fiers is an "interference," a proceeding for determining who is the first inventor. At the time, 35 U.S.C. Section 104 barred proof of invention dates by reference to activity outside the United States. (As we will see, Section 104 was significantly altered in 1995 and 1996.) Yet all three parties in *Fiers* were "foreigners," who, ordinarily, can rely only on their priority filing dates, *i.e.*, priority is determined by "first-to-file", not "first-to-invent." *Fiers* demonstrates that determining who was actually the first to file can be a more complicated inquiry than might be initially supposed. Determining "first to file" may require that invention disclosure adequacy issues be resolved.

5. *Linking Amgen, Fiers, and Lilly.* The next major biotechnology case focusing on disclosure problems was *The Regents of the University of California v. Eli Lilly and Company*, 119 F.3d 1559 (Fed.Cir.1997), and many commentators and practitioners merely saw it as naturally following from the *Amgen* and *Fiers* cases. All three of these cases—*Amgen*, *Fiers*, and *Lilly*—teach a number of important lessons about the interaction among a number of the validity rules discussed in this Chapter (enablement, best mode, written description, and definiteness) and other validity rules discussed in Chapter 4, particularly the conception doctrine, which helps establish when an invention should be considered to have been made for purposes of applying patent law's novelty requirement. In a portion of *Amgen* not included in this chapter because it relates to issues studied in Chapter 4, the court was wrestling with the validity of the claims directed to a purified and isolated DNA sequence encoding human EPO in Amgen's '008 Patent to Lin over an alleged prior invention by GI's Dr. Fristch under 35 U.S.C. § 102(g). The court rejected GI's argument on this issue because "until Fritsch had a complete mental conception of a purified and isolated DNA sequence encoding EPO and a method for its preparation, in which the precise identity of the sequence is envisioned, or in terms of other characteristics sufficient to distinguish it from other genes, all he had was an objective to make an invention which he could not then adequately describe or define." 927 F.2d 1206. In *Fiers*, the court explicitly linked its reasoning on the issue of conception from *Amgen* with the issue of written description that was to be decided in *Fiers*. The court pointed out that a written description of a DNA requires "a description of the DNA itself" and not merely of a method for isolating it. In *Lilly*, the court reaffirmed this view, stating that a "written description of an invention involving a chemical genus, like a description of a chemical species, 'requires a precise definition, such as by structure, formula, [or] chemical name,' of the claimed subject matter sufficient to distinguish it from other materials." Thus, "the description requirement ... requires a description of an invention, not an indication of a result that one might achieve if one made that invention."

6. *Lasting Lessons and Wrap–Up.* The cases in this Chapter suggest a number of lasting lessons, many of which are explicitly set forth in the material thus far. But the strategic and practical implications continue to be a topic of great attention in the government and the practicing Bar. Remember, the PTO issued new written description guidelines on January 5, 2001, *see* Note 9 in section C, *infra*, and these guidelines will most likely affect biotechnology patents. Moreover, the judges on the Federal Circuit itself seem to be divided on the topic, as well. For some practical responses to these issues, see the following SIDE BAR by Misrock and Rabinowitz and excerpts.

SIDE BAR

The Inventor's Gamble: Written Description and Prophetic Claiming of Biotechnology Inventions

S. Leslie Misrock and Stephen S. Rabinowitz*

"The prophets prophesy falsely ... and what will ye do in the end thereof?"
Jeremiah v:31

In a series of cases culminating in *Regents of the University of California v. Eli Lilly and Co.*,[1] the Federal Circuit has clarified how the written description requirement of section 112 applies in the field of biotechnology. The *Lilly* court emphasized that a DNA invention is not adequately described by reciting the biological function of a gene—what the DNA *does* (*e.g.* encoding protein x). Rather, the inventor must say what the gene *is* by disclosing its chemical structure or its defining physical or chemical properties.

Some have viewed these decisions as making new law, or as imposing a special rule in DNA cases. But that is not so. In fact, these cases merely apply the long-established principle that an invention cannot properly be described in purely functional terms.

For example, in the famous case of *O'Reilly v. Morse*, 56 U.S. (15 How.) 62 (1853), the Supreme Court held that the inventor of the telegraph could not validly claim all other machines that transmitted written characters by electromagnetism. More recently, the Court applied this principle in striking down a claim to a starch-based glue "having substantially the properties of animal glue". *Holland Furniture Co. v. Perkins Glue Co.*, 277 U.S. 245 (1928). As the *Holland* Court explained:

> [T]he attempt to broaden product claims by describing the product exclusively in terms of its use or function is subject to the same vice as is the attempt to describe a patentable device or machine in terms of its function. As a description of the invention it is insufficient and if allowed would extend the monopoly beyond the invention.

Id. at 257–258.

Properly read, *Lilly* is less about how to *describe* DNA inventions than about how to *claim* them. A simple example will show that the *Lilly* rule has desirable practical consequences because it requires claims to be drafted in such a way that the inventor, and not the public, bears the risk that a prophetic teaching may turn out to be wrong.

Suppose a scientist has isolated a valuable gene (say, the gene encoding insulin in mice). The scientist files a patent application that discloses the sequence of the mouse gene and recites a hypothetical example in which a portion of the mouse gene is used to probe for and isolate the corresponding gene in humans.[2] Prophetic teachings of this kind are quite proper and are often relied on in biotechnology, as in other technical fields. The application contains three claims:

1. An isolated human gene encoding insulin.

2. The gene according to claim 1, wherein the gene hybridizes to [a specified nucleic acid] under "moderately stringent" conditions.[3]

3. The gene according to claim 1, wherein the gene comprises a subunit that hybridizes under highly stringent conditions to a nucleic acid selected from the group consisting of [a list of nucleic acids][4]

Given the advanced state of the art, most scientists (and patent examiners) would presume that all these claims are enabled, unless there is a particular reason to doubt this for the gene in question. Let's assume that all three claims issue and are asserted in litigation. The accused infringer has evidence that the human insulin gene—unexpectedly—does not hybridize under the usual conditions, *i.e.*, that the prophetic teaching of the patent happens to be incorrect. Under these hypothetical facts, the "hybridizing" element of claims 2 and 3 is not satisfied and accordingly, claims 2 and 3 are not infringed. Thus, the outcome of the litigation may depend on whether claim 1—the only claim that might be infringed—is tested under *Lilly*.

Under *Lilly*, claim 1 is invalid because it is directed to a gene described only by its function ("encoding insulin"). Claims 2 and 3 pass muster because they are directed to genes defined by recited physical properties (hybridizing to specified nucleic acids under defined conditions), but these claims are not infringed. Accordingly, the defendant is free from liability. The *Lilly* rule forces applicants to make their gamble explicit in the claims and to bear the risk of their own false prophecy.

Without cases like *Lilly*, the outcome may be different. Claim 1 is infringed, since it reads on any isolated human gene that encodes insulin. To escape liability, the defendant must overcome the statutory presumption of validity by persuading the fact finder (perhaps a lay jury) by clear and convincing evidence that the claim is not enabled. Given the high standard of proof, the defendant may not succeed. If the claims were not tested under *Lilly*, the public would bear at least some of the risk of the inventor's false prophecy—surely an unsatisfactory result.

Lilly shows how patent law adapts as a field of technology matures. Gene cloning techniques were once finicky and difficult, and the enablement requirement was a substantial obstacle for claims directed to genes that had not actually been isolated. Nowadays, these techniques are robust and reliable, and enablement is easily satisfied. The limiting factor will frequently be description: can the applicant give enough specific details about the claimed subject matter to justify the claim?

The principle at stake here is hardly unfamiliar, and will readily be acknowledged by just about anyone who has lost an item (a watch, say) in a public place and has gone to retrieve it from the lost-and-found department. The claimant will expect to be asked: what does your watch look like? And the person in charge ought to insist on structural detail, and should not accept the answer that it tells the time. So let it be with patents.

* S. Leslie Misrock was the Senior Partner of the firm of Pennie & Edmonds LLP, New York, New York. Stephen S. Rabinowitz is a partner, Fried Frank, New York, New York. The views expressed herein are solely those of the authors and do not necessarily reflect those of the firms or their clients. This *SIDE BAR* was written specially for PRINCIPLES OF PATENT LAW.

1. 119 F.3d 1559 (Fed.Cir.1997). The other cases in this series are *Amgen, Inc. v. Chugai Pharmaceutical Co.*, 927 F.2d 1200 (Fed.Cir.1991) and *Fiers v. Revel*, 984 F.2d 1164 (Fed.Cir.1993).

2. As explained in the portion of *In re O'Farrell* that is set forth earlier in this chapter, a gene is a stretch of DNA that encodes the information for making a given protein. DNA consists of subunits ("nucleotides") joined end-to-end; and the information content of a piece of DNA is encoded in the sequence of the four possible nucleotides (A, G, C, and T). Each nucleotide can pair up with only one other "complementary" nucleotide. DNA generally occurs in the form of two strands that selectively stick to each other because they are complementary in the sequence of their nucleotides. Because of this property, one piece of DNA (a "probe") can be used to fish out a second DNA containing a stretch that is complementary to the probe. Perfect complementarity along the

entire length of the probe is not required; but the better the match, the more tightly they will stick ("hybridize"). For any pair of DNA's, whether they hybridize will depend upon experimental conditions such as temperature and salt concentration. "Highly stringent" conditions permit only highly complementary strands to hybridize; while "moderately stringent" conditions are less demanding. Starting with a probe that is perfectly complementary to part of a known gene, one can choose conditions so that the probe will selectively hybridize to unknown genes that are imperfectly complementary to the probe. Thus, a scientist who possesses DNA from one gene can find genes of varying degrees of similarity to that starting gene by varying the stringency of the hybridization conditions.

3. Here, the inventor is gambling that the human gene will be at least somewhat similar to the mouse gene and that a DNA probe for the mouse gene will fish out the human gene under "moderately stringent" conditions (which are defined in the application).

4. Here, the inventor predicts that certain parts of the gene are so important for biological function that they will not vary much between mouse and man, and gambles that well-chosen probes will stick to the human gene under defined "highly stringent" conditions.

Blame within the Patentee's Domain? Failing the Patentability Requirements of Written Description and On–Sale Bar

F. Scott Kieff.*
July 15, 2003.

Writing for the Federal Circuit in *Vas–Cath* in 1991 and relying on his earlier opinion for the CCPA in *In re Ruschig* in 1967, Judge Rich told us

* Excerpted from presentation to the "Second Annual Symposium on Hot Topics in Patent Law," sponsored by George Mason University School of Law and Banner & Witcoff, Ltd., in Arlington, Virginia.

that Section 112 provides a separate written description requirement that is distinct from the enablement requirement and operates to ensure the patentee had possession of the claimed invention at the time of filing the application.[6] Five years later in *Fujikawa*, he told us that the standard for satisfaction of this requirement is whether the disclosure as filed conveys to a PHOSITA that the inventor had possession of the claimed invention at that time, and that *ipsis verbis* disclosure is not needed.[7] For cases involving "a genus and its constituent species" and claims to certain of those species, the analogy he offered was "to a forest and its trees . . .:"

> It is an old custom in the woods to mark trails by making blaze marks on the trees. It is no help in finding a trail . . . to be confronted simply by a large number of unmarked trees. Appellants are pointing to trees. We are looking for blaze marks which single out particular trees.[8]

The well known biotechnology cases of *Amgen*, *Fiers*, and *Lilly*, gave some teaching about how to satisfy this standard: the applicant must give details about the physical or chemical structure of the claimed invention; and merely describing it by function does not suffice.[9] The furniture and computer cases of *Gentry* and *Lockwood* let us all know this standard is not technology-specific.[10]

But some questions came to the forefront in the July 15, 2002 reissued opinion from earlier that year in *Enzo* as to whether things were so settled.[11] The claimed genetic construct in that case was described by its ability to selectively hybridize to a genetic sequence in a public depository. In an opinion authored by Judge Lourie, the court decided that this was not a merely functional description but rather may have provided sufficient details of the physical or chemical structure of the claimed subject matter to serve the blaze mark function. Dissenting from the denial of rehearing in banc, Judge Rader, joined by Judges Gajarsa and Linn, suggested that the written description requirement "operate[s] solely to police priority" and should not be treated as a separate validity requirement. Judge Linn, joined by Judges Rader and Gajarsa, suggested that the enablement requirement

6. Vas–Cath Inc. v. Mahurkar, 935 F.2d 1555, 1561 (Fed.Cir.1991) (Rich, J.) (citing In re Ruschig, 379 F.2d 990, 995–96 (1967)) ("[T]he question is not whether [one skilled in the art] would be so enabled but whether the specification discloses the compound to him, specifically, *as something appellants actually invented . . . .*") If [the rejection is] based on section 112, it is on the requirement thereof that "The specification shall contain a written description *of the invention . . . .*" (Emphasis ours.) (first emphasis added). Other cases since Rushig that develop the separate written description requirement include In re Wertheim, 541 F.2d (CCPA 1976); In re Barker, 559 F.2d 588 (CCPA 1977); In re Kaslow, 707 F.2d 1366, 1375 (Fed.Cir.1983); Ralston Purina Co. v. Far–Mar–Co., Inc. 772 F.2d 1570 (Fed.Cir.1985); and In re Alton, 76 F.3d 1168 (Fed.Cir.1996).

7. Fujikawa v. Wattanasin 93 F.3d 1559, 1570 (Fed.Cir.1996) (quoting In re Ruschig, 379 F.2d 990, 994–95 (CCPA 1967)).

8. Id.

9. Amgen, Inc. v. Chugai Pharmaceutical Co., Ltd., 927 F.2d 1200 (Fed.Cir.1991); Fiers v. Revel, 984 F.2d 1164 (Fed.Cir.1993); and Regents of the University of California v. Eli Lilly & Co., 119 F. 3d 1559 (Fed.Cir.1997).

10. Gentry Gallery, Inc. v. Berkline Corp., 134 F.3d 1473 (Fed.Cir.1998); Lockwood v. American Airlines, Inc., 107 F.3d 1565 (Fed.Cir.1997).

11. In Enzo Biochem, Inc. v. Gen–Probe, Inc., 285 F.3d 1013 (Fed.Cir.2002), replaced on rehearing, 323 F.3d 956 (Fed.Cir. July 15, 2002).

would do the necessary work. Concurring in the denial of rehearing in banc, Judge Lourie and Judge Newman each pointed out that the statute and precedent dictate that the written description requirement is not and should not be limited as Judge Rader suggests. Also concurring in the denial of rehearing in banc, Judge Dyk suggested that further development of the case law, especially relating to *Lilly*, might help resolve these issues.

While this diversity of viewpoints remains the news today, the Federal Circuit has issued opinions in the written description area over the past year that at least appear on their face to be less controversial. For example, at the end of July 2002, the court issued its decision in *New Railhead*, which simply points out that evidence of enablement is unpersuasive on the issue of written description for the reasons explored in *Vas–Cath*: the written description requirement is distinct from the enablement requirement.[12] Similarly, in September of 2002, in *PIN/NIP*, the court simply reminded that the test for compliance with the written description requirement requires a comparison of the claims as issued against the disclosure as originally filed, and held invalid a claim not supported by the disclosure of the un-amended application.[13] And in October of 2002, in *All Dental Prodx*, the court reminded, as in *Fujikawa*, that the test does not require the disclosure to provide the identical words of the claims, *ipsis verbis*; the test only requires disclosure to convey the substance of the claim to a PHOSITA.[14] The court applied the same rules in *Singh* in January of 2003.[15]

But, also in January of 2003, the court issued its opinion in *Amgen v. HMR*, which suggests a split in views on written description that is somewhat different from the disagreements highlighted in *Enzo*.[16] The majority opinion, written by Judge Michel and joined by Judge Schall, at some length considers a number of specific written description arguments but the common theme it reiterates for each is relatively uncontroversial: that the test for compliance is measured against the actual subject matter as claimed, not against it's precursors, parts, or gist.[17] In dissent, Judge Clenvenger expressed concern that the majority's approach elevates form over substance and would allow the crafty patentee to avoid the need to disclose as much detail by drafting a broader claim.[18] It seems that the nature of this disagreement centers on the amount of detail that is needed to comply with the written description requirement. If so, then the lesson for the patentee is disclose as much as possible paying particular attention

---

12.   New Railhead Mfg., L.L.C. v. Vermeer Mfg. Co., 298 F.3d 1290, 1295–96 (Fed.Cir. July 30, 2002).

13.   PIN/NIP, Inc. v. Platte Chem. Co., 304 F.3d 1235, 1246–47 (Fed.Cir. Sept. 4, 2002).

14.   All Dental Prodx, LLC v. Advantage Dental Prods., Inc., 309 F.3d 774, 779 (Fed.Cir. Oct. 25, 2002).

15.   Singh v. Brake, 317 F.3d 1334, 1344 (Fed.Cir. Jan. 29, 2003).

16.   Amgen Inc. v. Hoechst Marion Roussel, Inc., 314 F.3d 1313 (Fed.Cir. Jan. 6, 2003).

17.   Id. at 1330–34.

18.   Id. at 1358–61 (Clevenger, J., dissenting in part). The dissent seems to suggest the claims to the product in that case required greater disclosure of the details needed to make the product since the product claims recited some process limitations and that the disclosure of some species of those methods is inadequate to describe the genus of all such methods.

to the claim as drafted. This is not new. It has long been known that all patentees face a similar tension because a broader claim may be easier to describe in some senses, but it may be harder in others, and it may also be harder to enable, and it most certainly will be less likely to avoid the prior art.[19] Importantly, however, if the disagreement between the majority and the dissent in this case suggests a view under which no disclosure could have complied, then that view of the law is of serious note.[20]

Finally, in April of 2003, in *MOBA*, a panel of Judges Rader, Schall, and Bryson issued a *per curiam* opinion that seems unremarkable in applying the written description test that looks to whether the disclosure in the application as filed would convey to a PHOSITA the substance of the claims as issued.[21] But this opinion is noteworthy in drawing a distinction between the cases that apply this test to determine validity under Section 112 as in *Lilly*, and those that apply this test to determine a claim for priority to an earlier-filed application, which often have outcomes driven by some issue of validity over intervening prior art.[22]

Furthermore, in a concurring opinion, Judge Rader reiterated the argument from his dissent in *Enzo*, that the written description requirement should only be used to provide priority protection, and not as a "free-standing disclosure doctrine," but went further to point out exactly why this matters: "each time a claim encompasses more than the preferred embodiment of the invention described in the specification, a defendant can assert that the patent is invalid for failure to describe the entire invention."[23] That is, he is suggesting that the requirement should be given a lesser substantive role to avoid the dire consequences of it being enforced as strongly as suggested by the dissenting opinion of Judge Clevenger in *Amgen v. HMR*, which in turn relies upon a strong reading of *Lilly*.[24]

In response, Judge Bryson offered a concurrence to point out that the concern expressed by Judge Rader might require more than a rejection of *Lilly*.[25] As a member of the *Lilly* panel, he views the reasoning of the *Lilly* case as entirely consistent with the statute and precedent including *In re Ruschig* in holding that the written description is distinct from the enablement requirement and not merely a limit on priority claims.[26]

As a commentator and a former practitioner, my personal views are that the conflict here may be a bit illusory.[27] Most of the written descrip-

---

19. This dilemma facing every patentee is central to U.S. patent law and was long recognized by Judge Rich. *See, e.g.,* Giles S. Rich, *The Proposed Patent Legislation: Some Comments*, 35 GEO. WASH. L. REV. 641, 644 (1967) (explaining patentee's dilemma, or "puzzle" as: "the stronger a patent the weaker it is and the weaker a patent the stronger it is").

20. See discussion regarding Judge Rader's concurrence in *MOBA infra* at note 23.

21. MOBA, B.V. v. Diamond Automation, Inc., 325 F.3d 1306, 1319–21 (Fed.Cir. Apr. 1, 2003).

22. Id.

23. Id. at 1322–27 (Rader, J., concurring).

24. *See supra* notes 18–20 and accompanying text.

25. MOBA, at 1327–28 (Bryson, J. concurring).

26. Id.

27. Most of the academic commentators have taken one of two opposing views on this point: on the one hand arguing that the requirement is rightly so severely strict that nothing

tion opinions can be read to suggest a standard for compliance with the written description requirement that is attainable by a well drafted application as filed—give as much detail as possible to provide the needed blaze marks. If so, then application of that requirement as an independent test for validity may not be as pernicious as Judge Rader's opinions correctly notes they otherwise could be. And adherence to this view would not require a jettisoning of an entire line of cases as Judge Bryson correctly notes might otherwise be needed.

* * *

Property and Biotechnology

F. Scott Kieff.*
October 24, 2003.

As Judge Giles S. Rich often said about patents under the present system, *"the name of the game is the claim* ... [and] the function of claims is to enable everyone to know, without going through a lawsuit, what infringes the patent and what does not."[1] Patent claims under the present U.S. system can be thought of as a simple logical list in which each word (or perhaps phrase, for convenience) in the claim is thought of as a single item on that list. The tests for patentability over the prior art [as discussed in Chapters 4 and 5] require that this set of items not be found in the prior art—as a set. As a logic problem, this means that the patentee will be motivated to add items to the list until the list as a whole avoids the prior art. Of course [as discussed in Chapter 8], claims are interpreted the same for purposes of both validity and infringement; and so concerns about the ability to capture as much as possible in an infringement suit will also motivate the patentee to remove items from the list because infringement properly exists only when each and every element of the claim—item on the list—can be found in the allegedly infringing product or process.

This approach to claiming that presently exists in the U.S. is generally known as "peripheral claiming," as distinct from "central claiming."

---

but the narrowest of claims should be able to satisfy it and on the other hand arguing that the requirement has become so lax that it or some other requirement such as utility must be sharply ratcheted up to prevent "overly broad" patents. I have not embraced either pole. See F. Scott Kieff, *Perusing Property Rights in DNA* in F. SCOTT KIEFF, PERSPECTIVES ON PROPERTIES OF THE HUMAN GENOME PROJECT 125 at 138–142 (2003, Academic Press, an imprint of Elsevier) (citing F. Scott Kieff, *Facilitating Scientific Research: Intellectual Property Rights and the Norms of Science—A Response to Rai & Eisenberg*, 95 Nw. U. L. REV. 691, 699–700 (2000) (showing how a more middle ground reading of the Federal Circuit's written description cases such as *Amgen, Fiers,* and *Lilly* help ensure proper breadth of patent claims even for controversial technologies such as gene fragments and citing F. Scott Kieff, *Property Rights and Property Rules for Commercializing Inventions*, 85 MINN. L. REV. 697 (2001))).

* Excerpted from presentation to the conference "The Biotechnological Revolution: Scientific and Societal Aspects," sponsored by the Alexander von Humboldt Foundation, in Potsdam, Germany.

1. *See, e.g.,* Giles S. Rich, *The Extent of the Protection and Interpretation of Claims—American Perspectives*, 21 Int'l Rev. Indus. Prop. & Copyright L. 497, 499, 501 (1990), *quoted in* Hilton Davis Chem. Co. v. Warner–Jenkinson Co., 62 F.3d 1512, 1539 (1995) (Plager, J., dissenting, joined by Archer, C.J., and Rich & Lourie, JJ.), *rev'd*, 520 U.S. 17 (1997).

Under a central claiming approach, the claims set forth the "core," "heart," "essence," or "gist," of the protected area and courts must determine how close or how far both the prior art and the alleged infringement must be to that core as a matter of law to trigger a judgment based on the facts. Under a peripheral claiming approach, courts need only determine the outer boundary as a matter of law and then the facts will turn out to indicate whether the prior art or alleged infringement each lie inside or outside.[2]

For this reason, according to Judge Rich, claims present a fundamental dilemma for every patentee because "the stronger a patent the weaker it is and the weaker a patent the stronger it is."[3] By this he meant that a broad patent claim is strong on offense because it covers more and, therefore, is more likely to be infringed, but it also is weak on defense because it may cover something in the prior art or fail to be supported by a sufficiently detailed disclosure in the rest of the patent, and, therefore, is more likely to be invalid. In contrast, a narrow claim is weak on offense, because it covers less and, therefore, is less likely to be infringed, but it also is strong on defense because it is likely both to avoid the prior art and to be supported by a sufficiently detailed disclosure, and, therefore, also is less likely to be invalid.[4]

At bottom, all of this suggests several practical insights for both putative patentees and putative infringers. First, the differences between peripheral and central claiming can be seen according to the following schematic, where the elements of the claim are set forth as items E_1 through E_n both as a list and as a set of boundaries, that define a closed space (the box in the below schematic). Then, the legal tests for both patentabililty over the prior art and infringement are based on whether something is in or out of that boundary, as a matter of fact, not whether it is judged to be near enough or far enough to some region judged to be its core.[5]

---

2. See generally, F. Scott Kieff, *The Case for Registering Patents and the Law and Economics of Present Patent—Obtaining Rules*, 45 B.C. L. Rev. 55, 99–105, 109–114 (2003) (discussing the normative—case for the disclosure rules and showing how they are a better institutional choice—in terms of minimizing aggregate social costs—for allowing both patentees and third parties to manage the problem of claim breadth than other techniques including the so-called "doctrine of equivalents").

3. *See* Giles S. Rich, *The Proposed Patent Legislation: Some Comments*, 35 Geo. Wash. L. Rev. 641, 644 (1967) (emphasis omitted) (responding to proposed legislation S. 1042, 90th Cong. (1967) and H.R. 5924, 90th Cong. (1967) and President's Comm'n on the Patent Sys., "To Promote the Progress of . . . Useful Arts" in an Age of Exploding Technology (1966)).

4. *Id.* (explaining patentee's dilemma, or "riddle").

5. Indeed, because these determinations under the present system end of turning on relatively simple facts, such as whether a particular prior art reference is in our out of the boundary, even lay judges and juries are able to make the seemingly technologically complex determinations of patentability over the prior art. F. Scott Kieff, *How Ordinary Judges and Juries Decide the Seemingly Complex Technological Questions of Patentability over the Prior Art* in F. Scott Kieff, Perspectives on Properties of the Human Genome Project 471 (2003, Academic Press, an imprint of Elsevier).

I claim (or what is claimed is)

A (an) E comprising
E_2
$E_{...}$
E_n

E_1

In | Out

E_n E_2

Core?

$E_{...}$

?

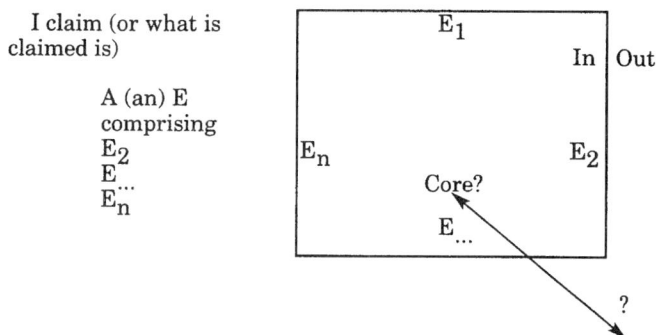

In biotechnology, for a typical patent that relates to a particular genetic sequence, the way patentees often strike this balance is shown in the below example where the schematic list of claim elements is filled-in with typical real-world representative terms. A brief explanation is given for the main purpose of each term and of course a detailed disclosure will need to be provided in the original application, as filed, so that the enablement and written description requirements of Section 112 are met for the claim as a whole.

Claim Language	Explanation
I claim (or what is claimed is)	
a heterologous DNA	"heterologous" is to avoid prior art
comprising	this means "including"
sequence that hybridizes	this is to provide flexibility (alleles & species)
under high (or medium) stringency conditions	this is to satisfy § 112, ¶ 2
to SEQ ID #___	the discovered sequence

Importantly, such a disclosure can be drafted if the applicant has indeed provided enough raw data. Each term must be defined. In addition, under a peripheral claiming system, it is only necessary for the patentee to describe and enable the class that corresponds to the area circumscribed by the claim. Each member of the class need not be disclosed. For example, the patentee can disclose a member of that class while indicating what allows one of skill in the art to determine what all members of the class share with each other so as to make them members of the same class and what distinguishes them from everything outside of that class.[6]

Indeed, the famous litigation of *Amgen v. Chugai*, over the patents relating to erythropoetin ("EPO"),[7] the ultimate judgments of on each patent can seen as not surprising when measured against the basic tests for compliance with the positive law rules for patentability including disclosure under Section 112, as well as validity over the prior art under Sections 102

---

6. *See* Kieff, *supra* note 1 at 111–114.

7. 927 F.2d 1200 (Fed.Cir.1991).

and 103 [as discussed in Chapters 4 and 5].* Both sides of the suit had a patent to assert against the other and the results on appeal are summarized below:

Amgen had patent entitled "DNA Sequences Encoding Erythropoietin" (the '008 patent) The relevant claims are:	The outcome on appeal was:
2. A purified and isolated DNA sequence consisting essentially of a DNA sequence encoding human erythropoietin.	Infringed by Chugai's side (including a company called Genetics Institute, or "GI") Not invalid:
4. A procaryotic or eucaryotic host cell transformed or transfected with a DNA sequence according to claim 1, 2 or 3 in a manner allowing the host cell to express erythropoietin.	—Under §§ 102(g) (GI's guy did not have sequence first so no conception first) —Under § 103 (process did not obviate product made by it)
6. A procaryotic or eucaryotic host cell stably transformed or transfected with a DNA vector according to claim 5.	—Under § 112 (best mode—a deposit was not required because the disclosure was enough)
7. A purified and isolated DNA sequence consisting essentially of a DNA sequence encoding a polypeptide having an amino acid sequence sufficiently duplicative of that of erythropoietin to allow possession of the biological property of causing bone marrow cells to increase production of reticulocytes and red blood cells, and to increase hemoglobin synthesis or iron uptake.	Invalid under § 112 (enablement—these claims are directed to broad classes and using language that sounds like it relates to written description-type concerns, the court relied on the patent's failure to show how to make

* Casebook Editors' Note: the pertinent portions of the *Amgen* decision relating to nonobviousness are set forth and discussed at some length in Chapter 5. Readers may wish to refer back to this summary when studying that portion of the text.

8. A cDNA sequence according to claim 7.	the many members of the class in a way that will predictably be similar to each other and different from what is outside the claim: how do you know get to have EPO-like activity and how do you know you have it?)
23. A procaryotic or eucaryotic host cell transformed or transfected with a DNA sequence according to claim 7, 8, or 11 in a manner allowing the host cell to express said polypeptide.	
24. A transformed or transfected host cell according to claim 23 which host cell is capable of glycosylating said polypeptide.	
25. A transformed or transfected mammalian host cell according to claim 24.	
26. A transformed or transfected COS cell according to claim 25.	
27. A transformed or transfected CHO cell according to claim 25.	
29. A procaryotic host cell stably transformed or transfected with a DNA vector according to claim 28.	
Chugai and GI had patent entitled "Method for the Purification of Erythropoietin and Erythropoietin Compositions" (the '195 patent) Representative claims are:	The outcome on appeal was:
1. Homogeneous erythropoietin characterized by a molecular weight of about 34,000 daltons on SDS PAGE, movement as a single peak on reverse phase high performance liquid chromatography and a specific activity of at least 160,000 IU per absorbance unit at 280 nanometers.	Invalid under § 112¶ 1(enablement—disclosed process did not work to generate enough activity)
3. A pharmaceutical composition for the treatment of anemia comprising a therapeutically effective amount of the homogeneous erythropoietin of claim 1 in a pharmaceutically acceptable vehicle.	
4. Homogeneous erythropoietin characterized by a molecular weight of about 34,000 daltons on SDS PAGE, movement as a single peak on reverse phase high performance liquid chromatography and a specific activity of at least	Invalid under § 112¶ 2 (indefiniteness—"at least about")*

about 160,000 IU per absorbance unit at 280 nanometers.	
6. A pharmaceutical composition for the treatment of anemia comprising a therapeutically effective amount of the homogeneous erythropoietin of claim 4 in a pharmaceutically acceptable vehicle	

* Casebook Editors' Note: The debate on the written description requirement continues among the judges of the Federal Circuit. In particular, in at least two recent cases the court seems to be suggesting that when a claim is viewed to cover a class defined by functional aspects, it may be necessary for the original disclosure to specifically recite several members of that class. As of this writing it remains to be seen whether this trend is in conflict with reversal of Enzo I by Enzo II on allowing functional language in claims as long as the functional characteristic of the claimed class is coupled with a disclosed correlation between that function and a structure that is sufficiently known or disclosed; or whether this requirement is a mere formality that can be satisfied by recitation of commercially insignificant members of the class. see Noelle v. Lederman, 355 F.3d 1343 (Fed.Cir. Jan. 20, 2004) (class of human and mouse antibodies found not supported by disclosure of mouse antigen); Univ. Rochester v. G.D. Searle, 358 F.3d 916, 2004 WL 260813 (Fed.Cir. Feb. 13, 2004) (class of methods for selectively inhibiting one pathway over another found not supported by disclosure that did not recite a specific compound that performed the method).

CHAPTER FOUR

NOVELTY AND LOSS OF RIGHT

> Every carving, every mask, served a specific religious purpose, and could only be made once. Copies were copies; there was no magical feeling or power in them; and in such copies Father Huismans was not interested. He looked in masks and carvings for a religious quality; without that quality the things were dead and without beauty.
>
> —V.S. Naipaul[1]

> [S]o shall my anticipation prevent your discovery.
>
> —William Shakespeare[2]

INTRODUCTION

Many suggest that it is best to think of § 102 not so much as a simple series of patentability hurdles, one after the next; but rather as a statutory mine field through which patent applicants must navigate in order to obtain a patent. Indeed, § 102 is often seen as being riddled with pitfalls and disabling subtleties. This chapter is designed to serve as a map to help identify these statutory land mines and guide you through § 102's convoluted maze.

Section 102 requires a patent applicant to contribute something *new* to society.[3] The novelty requirement, as it is appropriately known, is embodied in subsections (a), (e), and (g). The reason for this novelty requirement is straightforward: it makes no sense to grant someone a patent on an invention that already exists. If an invention isn't new, it is said to be *anticipated* by the prior art.[4] For example, if an inventor claims an invention comprising elements A, B, and C and a certain relationship among these three elements and if the prior art discloses explicitly or inherently the same invention comprising the same elements in the same relationship, the invention is said to be *anticipated* by the prior art. Of

---

1. *A Bend in the River*, Vintage Press (1989).

2. *Hamlet* (Act II, Scene II).

3. A novelty requirement is itself nothing new. As set forth in the Venetian patent statute of 1474 (see Chapter One), what is considered by many to be the first modern patent statute, "every person who shall build any new and ingenious device in this City, not previously made in our Commonwealth," shall be granted an exclusive right to use and operate the device.

4. Under Section 103, the invention may still be unpatentable if, although new, it would have been obvious in view of the the prior art. Section 103 and obviousness are discussed in Chapter Five.

particular importance with respect to § 102(a) prior art is that it must be "publicly accessible" (more on this later).

Under § 102(e), prior art may assume two forms: (1) Pursuant to 35 U.S.C. § 122(b), subject to a few exceptions,[5] each patent application filed on or after November 29, 2000 will be published "after the expiration of a period of 18 months" from its earliest filing date. Section 102(e)(1) allows for a *published* patent application, filed in the United States, to serve as prior art from the time of publication;[6] (2) Unlike "publicly accessible" prior art under § 102(a), an applicant may be the victim of so-called secret prior art under § 102(e)(2) (as well as § 102(g), discussed *infra*). If an application is not published, it will be kept confidential pursuant to § 122(a). But the confidential application may nevertheless serve as prior art under § 102(e)(2) if the application discloses the claimed subject matter and ultimately issues as a patent. The effect of this section is best illustrated by an example. Consider the following: if Homer (a third party) files a patent application in the United States before Mary files her application, and if Homer's application *discloses* (but does not claim) the claimed subject matter of Mary's application *and* ultimately issues as a patent, Mary will be denied a patent even though Mary had no way of knowing about Homer's application.

Section 102(g) serves dual purposes. First, it is the basis for what is known as a priority dispute or "interference." When an application is made for a patent claiming the same subject matter as another application or an issued patent, an interference may be declared by the Patent & Trademark Office. An interference is a procedural mechanism to determine who is the first inventor (*i.e.*, who has priority of invention). See Section B–10, *infra*. *See* also 35 U.S.C. § 135 (1994). Second, § 102(g) provides statutory grounds for "secret" prior art that may have a patent-defeating effect. For instance, § 102(g)(1) permits an applicant to use foreign-based inventive activity to *obtain* patent rights, but not defeat patent rights (more on this later), as long as the invention was not abandoned, suppressed or concealed. Section 102(g)(2), however, allows for patent-defeating inventive activity that is not subject to an interference, but the inventive activity must be "in this country" (*i.e.*, the United States). For example, imagine that Homer, instead of filing a patent application, practices his invention, that he made *in the United States*, as a trade secret. A third party can use Homer's trade secret as a prior art reference against Mary's claimed invention, if Homer invented Mary's claimed invention before she did. While § 102(g) does not require that prior art be publicly known, as in

---

5. The most noteworthy exception to publication is when an applicant certifies that the disclosed invention "has not and will not be the subject of an application filed in another country, or under a multilateral international agreement." 35 U.S.C. § 122(b)(2)(B)(i). Other exceptions are set forth in 35 U.S.C. § 122(b)(2)(A)(i)–(iv).

6. Also, Patent Cooperation Treaty applications can serve as prior art as of their international filing date, but these applications must be published in English to serve as prior art or to have patent-defeating effect under § 102(e)(1). Thus, for a non-English language patent application to have prior art effect under § 102(e)(1), the application must ultimately be filed in English. Importantly, the application never has to be filed in the United States to serve as prior art. See notes in Section B–6, *infra*.

§ 102(a), a limitation on § 102(g) prior art is that the invention not be abandoned, suppressed, or concealed.

In addition to the novelty requirement, § 102 sets forth several *statutory bars*. Under § 102(b), even when an inventor is the first to invent something new, she may be statutorily barred under subsection (b) if she or a *third party* sells, offers for sale, publicly uses, patents, or describes in a printed publication the claimed invention more than one year before the filing date of the patent application. There is a geographic distinction between printed publications and patents on the one hand and on-sale and public-use activity on the other. The former can be published anywhere, whereas the latter must occur in the United States. For example, Inventor offers for sale a product embodying elements A, B, and C on January 1, 1997 in the United States, and, 15 months later, on April 1, 1998, a patent application is filed claiming elements A, B, & C. Inventor is barred from obtaining a patent under § 102(b). The statutory bars may be viewed as a back-handed grant of a one-year grace period "during which an inventor may perfect his invention and prepare and file his application, testing it in public, if necessary." *See Palmer v. Dudzik*, 481 F.2d 1377, 1387 (CCPA 1973). The objective of § 102(b) is to "encourage[ ] earlier disclosure, publication, or public use of the invention, through which the public may gain knowledge of it." *Id.*[7]

As you proceed through this chapter, the logic of § 102 will become apparent. Before we delve into the caselaw, however, it may be helpful, for purposes of understanding § 102, to highlight some of the more salient differences between novelty and statutory bars. Statutory bars focus on when the applicant *filed* the patent application. Recall, an inventor has one year to file her patent application with the PTO after the invention was sold, offered for sale, publicly used, patented, or described in a printed publication. Novelty, on the other hand, concerns itself with when the applicant actually *invented* the claimed invention. Novelty simply asks: is the applicant's invention *new*. Think of novelty as focusing on just one applicant and asking whether some third person, who is not seeking a patent, previously disclosed or invented what the applicant is seeking to patent. The novelty provisions ((a), (e), and (g)) only pertain to third-party activity prior to the date of invention. But under subsection (b) or (d), both the activity of a third party *and* the inventor are relevant. Indeed, an inventor can statutorily bar herself from obtaining a patent, even though she is the first to invent under subsections (a), (e), and (g). Subsections (a), (b), (e), and (g) are the most important subsections in § 102.

There is one more § 102 sub-section we should mention in this introduction. Section 102(f), known as the "derivation" provision, holds that a person is entitled to a patent unless "he did not himself invent the subject matter sought to be patented." In other words, the named inventor is actually not the inventor because he *derived* the claimed subject matter from someone else.

---

7. Section 102(d) is another statutory bar provision with a focus on foreign patent applications. See *In re Kathawala*, 9 F.3d 942 (Fed.Cir.1993), discussed *infra*.

Moreover, two terms of art must be introduced. The date attributed to a piece of prior art for purposes of patentability determinations is called the *effective date*. The earliest date of which the inventor may claim the benefit under the statute is called the *critical date*. In a typical § 102(a) case, the critical date is the date of invention; and the invention is anticipated if the effective date of the reference is earlier than this critical date. In a typical § 102(b) case, the *critical date* is not the date of invention, but is one year prior to the filing of the patent application. So under § 102(b), the question is: did the inventor or a third party sell, offer for sale, publicly use, patent, or describe in a printed publication the claimed invention or an obvious variation thereof before the *critical date*. If the answer is in the affirmative, the inventor may be barred from obtaining a patent.

In sum, you should keep in mind that section 102 serves two practical purposes for lawyer and decision-maker alike. First, it sets the standard for determining *which* items (*e.g.*, references and sample products) must be considered as prior art. Second, section 102 sets the standard for determining *whether* a given item identified as prior art discloses enough information to render the claimed invention anticipated or statutorily barred. Importantly, even if the disclosure is insufficient to anticipate or statutorily bar the claimed invention, the item identified as prior art under section 102 must still be analyzed under section 103 to determine whether it renders the claimed invention obvious. Obviousness is discussed in Chapter Five, *infra*.

The Who, What, When, and Where of § 102

Subsection	Who	What	When	Where
a	third-party	knew or used invention	before date of invention	USA
	third-party	patented/described invention in printed publication	before date of invention	USA/foreign country
b	inventor/third-party	patented/described invention in printed publication	more than one year before filing date of patent application	USA/foreign country
	inventor/third-party	offered for sale, sold, or publicly used invention	more than one year before filing date of patent application	USA
c	inventor	abandons invention	——	USA
d	inventor	patents invention	more than one year before filing USA patent application	foreign country
e	third-party	describes invention in patent application that ultimately issues or PCT application is published in English	filed before date of invention	USA/foreign country
f	inventor	derived invention from third-party	before date of invention	USA/foreign country
g	third-party	invented invention	before date of invention	USA

STATUTORY PROVISION—35 U.S.C. § 102

A. TIMELY APPLICATION—LOSS OF RIGHT

The statutory bar provisions of section 102 do not in and of themselves require an inventor to file an application for a patent within any certain period of time. But the statutory bar provisions do prescribe a time period within which to file a patent application, and do provide a set of events that will trigger the start of this time period. The statutory bar triggering events can result from actions of the inventor or actions of third parties. Therefore, the statutory bar provisions can be seen as giving the inventor a grace period in which to file his patent application after the occurrence of a triggering event. The present grace period is one year.

1. HISTORICAL AND POLICY UNDERPINNINGS

The following case, though of relatively ancient origin, had a remarkable impact on the subsequent legislative and judicial development of United States patent law. It distinguished between the concepts of *novelty* (now Sections 102(a), (e), and (g)), which is triggered by the anticipatory work of others and *loss of right* (now in Sections 102(b) and (d)), which is triggered by the actions of the inventor (as well as, possibly, by others). It also identified the policy underpinnings for the loss of right provisions, which, to this day, heavily influence the interpretation of those provisions. Finally, the case illustrates the most common cause for inventors losing potential patent rights in otherwise novel, unobvious and commercially valuable inventions: failure to take timely steps to apply for a patent.

Pennock v. Dialogue

27 U.S. 1, 2 Pet. 1 (1829).

THIS case was brought before the Court, on a writ of error to the circuit court* for the eastern district of Pennsylvania.

In that court, the plaintiffs in error had instituted their suit against the defendants, for an infringement of a patent right, for "an improvement in the art of making tubes or hose for conveying air, water, and other fluids." The invention claimed by the patentees, was in the mode of making the hose so that the parts so joined together would be tight, and as capable of resisting the pressure as any other part of the machine.

... The invention, for which the patent right was claimed, was completed in 1811; and the letters patent were obtained in 1818. In this interval, upwards of thirteen thousand feet of hose, constructed according to the invention of the patentees, had been made and sold in the city of Philadelphia. One Samuel Jenkins, by the permission of, and under an agreement between the plaintiffs as to the price; had made and sold the

---

* Casebook Editors' Note: The trial courts were called circuit courts at the time this opinion was written.

hose invented by the plaintiffs, and supplied several hose companies in the city of Philadelphia with the same. Jenkins, during much of the time, was in the service of the plaintiffs, and had been instructed by them in the art of making the hose. There was no positive evidence, that the agreement between Jenkins and the plaintiffs in error was known to, or concealed from the public. The plaintiffs, on the trial, did not allege or offer evidence to prove that they had delayed making application for a patent, for the purpose of improving their invention; or that from 1811 to 1818, any important modifications or alterations had been made in their riveted hose. The plaintiffs claimed before the jury, that all the hose which had been made and sold to the public, prior to their patent, had been constructed and vended by Jenkins under their permission.

Upon the whole evidence in the case, the circuit court charged the jury:

> We are clearly of opinion that if an inventor makes his discovery public, looks on and permits others freely to use it, without objection or assertion of claim to the invention, of which the public might take notice; he abandons the inchoate right to the exclusive use of the invention, to which a patent would have entitled him, had it been applied for before such use. And we think it makes no difference in the principle, that the article so publicly used, and afterwards patented, was made by a particular individual, who did so by the private permission of the inventor. As long as an inventor keeps to himself the subject of his discovery, the public cannot be injured: and even if it be made public, but accompanied by an assertion of the inventor's claim to the discovery, those who should make or use the subject of the invention would at least be put upon their guard. But if the public, with the knowledge and the tacit consent of the inventor, is permitted to use the invention without opposition, it is a fraud upon the public afterwards to take out a patent. It is possible that the inventor may not have intended to give the benefit of his discovery to the public; and may have supposed that by giving permission to a particular individual to construct for others the thing patented, he could not be presumed to have done so. But it is not a question of intention, which is involved in the principle which we have laid down; but of legal inference, resulting from the conduct of the inventor, and affecting the interests of the public. It is for the jury to say, whether the evidence brings this case within the principle which has been stated. If it does, the court is of opinion that the plaintiffs are not entitled to a verdict.

To this charge the plaintiffs excepted, and the jury gave a verdict for the defendant.

Mr. Webster, for the plaintiff in error, contended,

1.   That the invention, being of such a nature that the use of it, for the purpose of trying its utility and bringing it to perfection, must necessarily be open and public; the implication of a waiver or abandonment of the right, furnished by such public use, is rebutted by the circumstance that the article was made and sold only by one individual; and that individual was authorized and permitted so to do by the inventors.

2.   That the use of an invention, however public, if it be by the permission and under the continual exclusive claim of the inventor; does not take away his right, except after an unreasonable lapse of time, or gross negligence, in applying for a patent.

3. That the jury should have been instructed, that, if they found the riveted hose, which was in use by the hose companies, had been all made and sold by Jenkins, and by no one else, prior to the grant of the patent; and that he was permitted by the inventors, under their agreement, so to make and sell the same; that such use of the invention, not being adverse to their claim, did not take away their exclusive right, nor imply an abandonment of it to the public.

* * *

Mr. Sergeant, for the defendant, insisted,

1. That mere invention gives no right to an exclusive use, unless a patent is obtained; and that if at a time when no right is infringed, the public fairly acquire possession of it, the inventor cannot, by subsequently obtaining a patent, take it away.

2. That the inventor, by abstaining from getting a patent encouraged the public to use the article freely, and thus benefitted his own manufactory. And he is not at liberty, when this advantage is exhausted, to turn round, and endeavor to reach another and a different kind of advantage, by appropriating the use exclusively to himself.

* * *

■ MR. JUSTICE STORY delivered the opinion of the Court.

* * *

The single question ... is, whether the charge of the court was correct in point of law. It has not been, and indeed cannot be denied, that an inventor may abandon his invention, and surrender or dedicate it to the public. This inchoate right, thus once gone, cannot afterwards be resumed at his pleasure; for, where gifts are once made to the public in this way, they become absolute. Thus, if a man dedicates a way, or other easement to the public, it is supposed to carry with it a permanent right of user. The question which generally arises at trials, is a question of fact, rather than of law; whether the acts or acquiescence of the party furnish in the given case, satisfactory proof of an abandonment or dedication of the invention to the public. But when all the facts are given, there does not seem any reason why the court may not state the legal conclusion deducible from them. In this view of the matter, the only question would be, whether, upon general principles, the facts stated by the court would justify the conclusion.

In the case at bar, it is unnecessary to consider whether the facts stated in the charge of the court would, upon general principles, warrant the conclusion drawn by the court, independently of any statutory provisions; because, we are of opinion, that the proper answer depends upon the true exposition of the act of congress, under which the present patent was obtained. The constitution of the United States has declared, that congress shall have power "to promote the progress of science and useful arts, by securing for limited times, to authors and inventors, the exclusive right to their respective writings and discoveries." It contemplates, therefore, that this exclusive right shall exist but for a limited period, and that the period shall be subject to the discretion of congress. The patent act, of the 21st of

February, 1793, ch. 11, prescribes the terms and conditions and manner of obtaining patents for inventions; and proof of a strict compliance with them lies at the foundation of the title acquired by the patentee. The first section provides, "that when any person or persons, being a citizen or citizens of the United States, shall allege that he or they have invented any new or useful art, machine, manufacture, or composition of matter, or any new or useful improvement on any art, machine, or composition of matter, not known or used before the application; and shall present a petition to the secretary of state, signifying a desire of obtaining an exclusive property in the same, and praying that a patent may be granted therefor; it shall and may be lawful for the said secretary of state, to cause letters patent to be made out in the name of the United States, bearing teste by the President of the United States, reciting the allegations and suggestions of the said petition, and giving a short description of the said invention or discovery, and thereupon, granting to the said petitioner, & c. for a term not exceeding fourteen years, the full and exclusive right and liberty of making, constructing, using, and vending to others to be used, the said invention or discovery, & c." The third section provides, "that every inventor, before he can receive a patent, shall swear, or affirm, that he does verily believe that he is the true inventor or discoverer of the art, machine, or improvement for which he solicits a patent." The sixth section provides that the defendant shall be permitted to give in defense, to any action brought against him for an infringement of the patent, among other things, "that the thing thus secured by patent was not originally discovered by the patentee, but had been in use, or had been described in some public work, anterior to the supposed discovery of the patentee."

These are the only material clauses bearing upon the question now before the court; and upon the construction of them, there has been no inconsiderable diversity of opinion entertained among the profession, in cases heretofore litigated.

* * *

Justice Joseph Story (1779-1845) was one of the most influential architects of American patent law in the 19th century. As Gerald T. Dunne noted in his 1970 biography, Justice Story approached patent law with

> a creative balancing of incentive for enterprise on one hand and pro-tection of public interest on the other…. His efforts here were per-haps the most luminous vindication of his many-sided talents, for he started with a taste for books rather than things, and at times he complained of his lack of mechanical aptitude. Nonetheless, he laid the cornerstone of American patent law.

GERALD T. DUNNE, JUSTICE JOSEPH STORY AND THE RISE OF THE SU-PREME COURT 112 (1970). For further reading on Justice Story's in-fluence on patent law, *see* Frank D. Prager, *The Influence of Mr. Jus-tice Story on American Patent Law*, 5 Am. J. Leg. Hist. 254 (1961) and Frank D. Prager, *The Changing Views of Justice Story and the Con-struction of Patents*, 4 Am. J. of Leg. Hist. 1 (1960).

By the very terms of the first section of our statute, the secretary of state is authorised to grant a patent to any citizen applying for the same, who shall allege that he has invented a new and useful art, machine, & c. & c. "not known or used before the application?" The authority is a limited one, and the party must bring himself within the terms, before he can derive any title to demand, or to hold a patent. What then is the true meaning of the words "not known or used before the application?" They cannot mean that the thing invented was not known or used before the application by the inventor himself, for that would be to prohibit him from the only means of obtaining a patent. The use, as well as the knowledge of his invention, must be indispensable to enable him to ascertain its competency to the end proposed, as well as to perfect its component parts. The words then, to have any rational interpretation, must mean, not known or used by others, before the application. But how known or used? If it were necessary, as it well might be, to employ others to assist in the original structure or use by the inventor himself; or if before his application for a patent his invention should be pirated by another, or used without his consent; it can scarcely be supposed, that the legislature had within its contemplation such knowledge or use.

We think, then, the true meaning must be, not known or used by the public, before the application. And, thus construed, there is much reason for the limitation thus imposed by the act. While one great object was, by holding out a reasonable reward to inventors, and giving them an exclusive right to their inventions for a limited period, to stimulate the efforts of genius; the main object was "to promote the progress of science and useful arts;" and this could be done best, by giving the public at large a right to make, construct, use, and vend the thing invented, at as early a period as possible; having a due regard to the rights of the inventor. If an inventor should be permitted to hold back from the knowledge of the public the secrets of his invention; if he should for a long period of years retain the monopoly, and make, and sell his invention publicly, and thus gather the whole profits of it, relying upon his superior skill and knowledge of the structure; and then, and then only, when the danger of competition should force him to secure the exclusive right, he should be allowed to take out a patent, and thus exclude the public from any farther use than what should be derived under it during his fourteen years; it would materially retard the progress of science and the useful arts, and give a premium to those who should be least prompt to communicate their discoveries.

A provision, therefore, that should withhold from an inventor the privilege of an exclusive right, unless he should, as early as he should allow the public use, put the public in possession of his secret, and commence the running of the period, that should limit that right; would not be deemed unreasonable. It might be expected to find a place in a wise prospective legislation on such a subject. If it was already found in the jurisprudence of the mother country, and had not been considered inconvenient there; it would not be unnatural that it should find a place in our own.

Now, in point of fact, the statute of 21 Jac. ch. 3, commonly called the statute of monopolies, does contain exactly such a provision. That act, after prohibiting monopolies generally, contains, in the sixth section, an exception in favour of "letters patent and grants of privileges for fourteen years or under, for the sole working or making of any manner of new manufactures within this realm, to the true and first inventor and inventors of such manufactures, which others, at the time of making such letters patent and grants, shall not use." Lord Coke, in his commentary upon this clause or proviso, (3 Inst. 184,) says that the letters patent "must be of such manufactures, which any other at the time of making such letters patent did not use; for albeit it were newly invented, yet if any other did use it at the making of the letters patent, or grant of the privilege, it is declared and enacted to be void by this act." The use here referred to has always been understood to be a public use, and not a private or surreptitious use in fraud of the inventor.

In the case of *Wood vs. Zimmer*, 1 Holt's N. P. Rep. 58, this doctrine was fully recognised by lord chief justice Gibbs. There the inventor had suffered the thing invented to be sold, and go into public use for four months before the grant of his patent; and it was held by the court, that on this account the patent was utterly void. Lord chief justice Gibbs said, "To entitle a man to a patent, the invention must be new to the world. The public sale of that which is afterwards made the subject of a patent, though sold by the inventor only, makes the patent void." By "invention," the learned judge undoubtedly meant, as the context abundantly shows, not the abstract discovery, but the thing invented; not the new secret principle, but the manufacture resulting from it.

The words of our statute are not identical with those of the statute of James, but it can scarcely admit of doubt, that they must have been within the contemplation of those by whom it was framed, as well as the construction which had been put upon them by Lord Coke....

* * *

The only real doubt which has arisen upon this exposition of the statute, has been created by the words of the sixth section already quoted. That section admits the party sued to give in his defence as a bar, that "the thing thus secured by patent was not originally discovered by the patentee, but had been in use anterior to the supposed discovery of the patentee." It has been asked, if the legislature intended to bar the party from a patent in consequence of a mere prior use, although he was the inventor; why were not the words "anterior to the application" substituted, instead of "anterior to the supposed discovery?" If a mere use of the thing invented before the application were sufficient to bar the right, then, although the party may have been the first and true inventor, if another person, either innocently as a second inventor, or piratically, were to use it without the knowledge of the first inventor; his right would be gone. In respect to a use by piracy, it is not clear that any such fraudulent use is within the intent of the statute; and upon general principles it might well be held excluded. In respect to the case of a second invention, it is questionable at least, whether, if by such second invention a public use was already acquired, it could be deemed a case within the protection of the act. If the public were already in possession and common use of an invention fairly and without fraud, there might be sound reason for presuming, that the legislature did not intend to grant an exclusive right to any one to monopolize that which was already common. There would be no quid pro quo—no price for the exclusive right or monopoly conferred upon the inventor for fourteen years.

Be this as it may, it is certain that the sixth section is not necessarily repugnant to the construction which the words of the first section require and justify. The sixth section certainly does not enumerate all the defences which a party may make in a suit brought against him for violating a patent. One obvious omission is, where he uses it under a license or grant from the inventor. The sixth section in the clause under consideration, may well be deemed merely affirmative of what would be the result from the general principles of law applicable to other parts of the statute. It gives the right to the first and true inventor and to him only; if known or used before his supposed discovery he is not the first, although he may be a true inventor; and that is the case to which the clause looks. But it is not inconsistent with this doctrine, that although he is the first, as well as the true inventor, yet if he shall put it into public use, or sell it for public use before he applies for a patent, that this should furnish another bar to his claim. In this view an interpretation is given to every clause of the statute without introducing any inconsistency, or interfering with the ordinary meaning of its language. No public policy is overlooked; and no injury can ordinarily occur to the first inventor, which is not in some sort the result of his own laches or voluntary inaction.

It is admitted that the subject is not wholly free from difficulties; but upon most deliberate consideration we are all of opinion, that the true construction of the act is, that the first inventor cannot acquire a good title to a patent; if he suffers the thing invented to go into public use, or to be publicly sold for use, before he makes application for a patent. His voluntary act or acquiescence in the public sale and use is an abandonment of his right; or rather creates a disability to comply with the terms and conditions on which alone the secretary of state is authorized to grant him a patent.

The opinion of the circuit court was therefore perfectly correct; and the judgment is affirmed with costs. . . .

NOTES

1. *The Policies of Loss of Right.* In his opinion for the Court, Justice Story, a noted lawyer, author, and teacher, as well as judge, provided a guiding policy-based rationale for a vague statutory phrase—"known and used." Specifically, Justice Story identified the encouragement of early disclosure and protection of the public interest as policies served by the loss of right provision, policies that are grounded in the utilitarianism of Article I, Section 8, Clause 8 of the Constitution. As Justice Story stated:

> While one great object [of the loss of right provision] was, by holding out a reasonable award to inventors, and giving them an exclusive right to their inventions for a limited period of time, to stimulate the efforts of genius; the main object was "to promote the progress of science and useful arts."

These policies have been adopted by the Federal Circuit, with one addition that resulted from the introduction of a grace period. According to a Federal Circuit predecessor court:

> Legislative history and case law reveal four identifiable policies underlying the "on sale" bar. First, there is a policy against removing inventions from the public which the public has justifiably come to believe are freely available to all as a consequence of prolonged sales activity. *See* S.Rep.No.

876, 76th Cong., 1st Sess. 1–2 (1939); H.R.Rep.No.961, 76th Cong., 1st Sess. 1–2 (1939). Next, there is a policy favoring prompt and widespread disclosure of new inventions to the public. The inventor is forced to file promptly or risk possible forfeiture of his invention rights due to prior sales. A third policy is to prevent the inventor from commercially exploiting the exclusivity of his invention substantially beyond the statutorily authorized 17–year period. The "on sale" bar forces the inventor to choose between seeking patent protection promptly following sales activity or taking his chances with his competitors without the benefit of patent protection. The fourth and final identifiable policy is to give the inventor a reasonable amount of time following sales activity (set by statute as 1 year) to determine whether a patent is a worthwhile investment. This benefits the public because it tends to minimize the filing of inventions of only marginal public interest. The 1–year grace period provided for by Congress in § 102(b) represents a balance between these competing interests.

General Electric Co. v. United States, 654 F.2d 55, 61 (Ct.Cl.1981). Keep these policies in mind as we proceed through § 102(b). Interestingly, one commentator writes that these policies were "lifted from a student law review note." Thomas K. Landry, *Certainty and Discretion in Patent Law: The On Sale Bar, the Doctrine of Equivalents, and Judicial Power in the Federal Circuit*, 67 S. Cal. L. Rev. 1151, 1164 (1994).

2. *Absolute Novelty v. Grace Period.* The *Pennock* holding would bar an inventor from obtaining a patent if the inventor made or authorized any public use or sale of an embodiment of his invention (except possibly for purposes of experimentation) even one day before the inventor filed an application for a patent. This strict approach, sometimes referred to as "absolute novelty," is the law throughout most of the world, including Japan and the countries of the European Patent Convention. For example, Article 54(2) of the European Patent Convention states:

> The state of the art shall be held to comprise everything made available to the public by means of a written or oral description, by use, or in any other way, before the date of filing of the European patent application.

See also Section 29 of the Japan Patent Law; Christopher Heath's *Side Bar, Grace Periods in the World, infra.*

The 1836 Act essentially codified *Pennock* by barring a patent if the invention was "at the time of his application, in public use or on sale with consent or allowance." 5 Stat. 117. But the 1839 Act broke new ground, and introduced a period of "grace" by providing that pre-application purchase, sale or use would not invalidate a patent "except on proof of abandonment of such invention to the public; or that such purchase, sale, or prior use has been for more than two years prior to such application for a patent." 5 Stat. 353.

Two changes brought the statutory provision into its current form. In 1897, Congress specified that a barring public use or sale must be "in this country," but added patenting and description in a printed publication anywhere as bars. 29 Stat. 692. In 1939, exactly a century after the two-year grace period was introduced, Congress lowered the period to one year. 53 Stat. 1212. What basis is there for choosing one-year? What length of time do you think is appropriate? Should it be the same for all technologies? Why?

For more on the theory and empirics of grace periods consider the following:

> The pre-filing grace period is the source of great debate among those interested in the patent systems of the world. That a grace period can make quite a difference to a patent system is a topic of substantial

agreement. It is the degree and nature of its impact that are topics of substantial disagreement.

According to some, a patent system in which there is no grace period may provide incentives for decreased rate of disclosure of new technologies and a decrease in the over-all value of patents. The decreased rate of disclosure under a system lacking a grace period would be due to the need to keep potentially patentable information unpublished before filing the patent application. Under such a system, any such pre-filing publication would be treated as prior art. The decrease in over-all value of patents under such a system would be due to the fear of unavoidable pre-filing disclosures lurking in the history of every patent.

According to others, a patent system in which there is a grace period may provide incentives for decreased early investment in using new technologies. This decreased investment under a system having a grace period would be due to potential fear that such new technology might later become subject to someone else's patent application, which might in time issue as a valid patent.

* * *

Straus' discussion brings into sharp focus the central themes and key implications of the debate. He provides full, but not burdensome, citations to both the arguments and the facts. In addition, he provides a very good overview of the normative arguments for and against grace period adoption and tests each major view against the empirical data drawn from systems that have a grace period and those that do not have a grace period. More specifically, for systems that do not have a grace period provided by statute, Straus shows through his careful collection of court cases how judges in those systems can, and often do, effectively gave grace period treatment under particular facts of the case despite the absence of national statutory law permitting a grace period. Similarly, for systems that do have a grace period provided by statute, Straus reviews a wealth of empirical data about who benefits from the grace period and how.

F. Scott Kieff, *Book Review: Joseph Straus, Grace Periods and the European and International Patent Law: Analysis of Key Legal and Socio–Economic Aspects*, 34 INT'L REV. INDUS. PROP. & COPYRIGHT L. (IIC) 347 (2003), and also 4 ENGAGE 160 (2003).

3. *A Prelude to Third–Party Activity.* The language of the 1836 Act raised the question of whether sales or uses without the inventor's "consent or allowance" would bar a patent before or after the two-year grace period. The 1839 Act eliminated any reference to consent or allowance. In *Andrews v. Hovey*, 123 U.S. 267, 274 (1887), the Supreme Court noted: "The evident purpose of the section was to fix a period of limitation which should be certain, and require only a calculation of time, and should not depend upon the uncertain question of whether the applicant had consented to or allowed the sale or use. Its object was to require the inventor to see to it that he filed his application within two years from the completion of his invention...." Despite the 1839 Act, and the 1870 Act, which is consistent with the 1839 Act in this regard, the policy considerations identified in *Pennock*, such as the policy of not allowing undue extension of the patent term, do not apply in the same way to activity by persons other than the inventor-applicant, and to this day courts struggle with whether and how to apply concepts that involve third-party activity. *See infra* Section A.5 for a discussion of third-party use.

4. *Defining "Invention" for Public Use and On–Sale Purposes.* This issue is explored in detail when we discuss *Pfaff v. Wells Electronics* in Section A.4, but it is worth highlighting here. In discussing Chief Justice Gibbs' opinion in the English case of *Wood v. Zimmer*, Justice Story stated: "By 'invention,' the learned judge undoubtedly meant, as the context abundantly shows, not the abstract discovery, but the thing invented; not the new secret principle, but the manufacture resulting from it." For now ask yourself, why an "abstract discovery" or "secret principle" does not, in the view of Justice Story, invoke the loss of right provision?

SIDE BAR

Grace Periods In the World

Christopher Heath*

1. Outside the United States of America, the world is an amazingly graceless place. Similar provisions to the grace period of one year[1] that is currently granted under US law can only be found in Canada (here the grace period is even two years),[2] and in Thailand.[3] Other national patent laws offer grace periods that are considered as not novelty destroying under particular circumstances only. Japan provides a grace period of six months under any of the following circumstances: publication by the inventor himself, publication against the will of the inventor or display at a recognised exhibition.[4] Malaysia provides a one-year grace period in similar circumstances.[5] Even more limited are the exceptions recognised by the European Patent Convention in Art. 55 and the corresponding provision under the domestic laws of Germany,[6] France,[7] the United Kingdom,[8] Italy,[9] and others: grace period of six months for cases of publications against the inventor's will only.

2. From a historical perspective, Sec. 6 of the **English** Statute of Monopolies 1624 granted patents for "the sole working or making of any manner of new manufacture within this realm, to the true and first inventor and inventors of such manufactures which others at the time of making such letters patent and grants shall not use". The novelty requirement expressed therein should ensure that "a patent takes absolutely nothing away from the public which it had the right to use before the grant of the absolute rights conferred upon the patentee."[10] For that reason, it was held immaterial by whom the patented invention was made public prior to the application for a patent:

> "If the public once becomes possessed of an invention by any means whatever, no subsequent patent can be granted for it, either to the true and first inventor himself, or to any other person, for the public cannot be deprived of the right to use the invention and a patentee of the invention could not give any consideration to the public for the grant, the public already possessing everything that he could give."[11]

In a later case, it was held:

> "Public use . . . means a use in public, not by the public, I think there is no room for doubt that the use by the defender of his own paint was of this character. It is quite true that, in order to obtain letters patent, the inventor must disclose his secret to the public in return for the monopoly conferred upon him. But such a disclosure as that is not necessary to the prior use, which will anticipate and so avoid a patent."[12]

Subsequently, however, a number of circumstances would allow for a certain grace period, e.g., necessary public use for experimental purposes,[13] and use of a provisional specification similar to the US instrument of a provisional filing.[14] The provisional filing preserved novelty if a proper specification was made within 12 months, yet initially allowed the inventor to file only a rough sketch of the invention. This instrument was scrapped and the novelty requirements harmonised in accordance with the EPC in the UK Patents Act 1977.

The **French** position under the Patent Act 1844 was also hostile to a grace period, yet for different reasons. Under Sec. 31 of this Act, any form of "publicité antérieure" was novelty destroying. While some French academics argued that publication by the inventor was, strictly speaking, not "antériorité" but rather "divulgation",[15] this distinction was widely rejected, as the fact of publication could not be made subject to the question of who had published due to the principle under Roman law that *"protestatio non valit contra factum"*.[16]

As a starting point, the **US** patent system took the English position that publication by the inventor would amount to an "abandonment" of the patent right.[17] Yet this stance was soon modified in favour of publications due to misappropriation or other unlawful acts by third parties.[18] The U.S. Patent Acts of 1836 and 1839 broadened this exception to a grace period of two years in cases of acts of prior use by the inventor or third parties.[19] The revisions of 1870 and 1897 dropped any limiting requirements of the grace period.

Finally, the **Canadian** grace period of two years was introduced under the Canadian Patent Act 1935 in an apparent wish to harmonise its system with that of the United States.[20]

The **German** Patent Act of 1877 also did not provide for any grace period.[21] Some academics found this lamentable, in particular in cases of publications against the inventor's will.[22] This was amended in 1891 to allow for a three month grace period in case of publications and on condition of reciprocity.[23] This provision, of course, was no longer relevant after Germany joined the Paris Convention. A general grace period of six months was introduced in Sec. 2(2) German Patent Act 1936, which just as the US Patent Revision one hundred years earlier, was the result of an inventor friendly climate.[24] This general grace period of six months was maintained until the Patent Act 1981 was harmonised with the EPC.

3. Given the importance of the question, a number of attempts for international harmonisation of the grace period were made, two at revision conferences of the Paris Convention. At the revision conference in London, some of the discussion focussed on improving the position of the inventor. Under the heading "nouveau droit morale de l'inventeur", the right of the inventor's nomination in the patent was discussed together with aspects of employees' inventions and a grace period for publications prior to the first filing. The Italian and Dutch delegates proposed a grace period of 12 months for presentations before an academic forum (Italy) and six months in general (the Netherlands). The Dutch delegation highlighted the problem of hastily drafted patent applications, legally untrained inventors and the necessity of a grace period for academia.[25] While this proposal apparently fizzled out in the course of several committee meetings, a similar proposal made at the Lisbon Conference was supported by the US and Germany. The proposal was particularly aimed at clarifying the relationship between a grace period and a priority filing.

It should be clarified that the grace period should not only become generally available for a period of six months but that this grace period could also be combined with the priority period of 12 months, thus covering publications up to six months prior to the first filing as non-novelty destroying. The discussions concerned two scenarios: first, a third party publication against the inventor's intentions, and, second, a publication by the inventor himself. The proposal was ultimately defeated by Austria, France and the Netherlands.[26] Within AIPPI the problem was discussed at a number of annual meetings: so in Prague 1938,[27] and in particular in Vienna in 1952.[28] The Vienna congress came out in favour of a grace period in the case of publications against the inventor's will. The last attempt to harmonise the grace period to date was made within the framework of the proposed Patent Law Treaty of 21 December 1990. According to Art. 12, disclosure by a third party, who obtained information directly or indirectly from the inventor, would not affect patentability during the 12 months preceding the filing date or, where priority is claimed, the priority of the application. However, agreement on the overall framework of the Patent Law Treaty has not yet been reached. The problem is further aggravated by the fact that most countries do not allow for a combination of grace period (where applicable) with the priority rights under the Paris Convention. Should a novelty destroying publication (e.g., one against the inventor's will) appear abroad, even countries which allow for a grace period under these circumstances would require domestic filing within the period of time specified by domestic legislation, rather than by combining this period with the one year period of the Paris Convention.[29] The opposite stance was taken by the Dutch Supreme Court, yet in interim procedures.[30] The European Patent Office in an action before the Enlarged Board of Appeal ultimately rejected this broader interpretation, largely based on the wording of Arts. 89, 55(1) European Patent Convention[31].

While a good many member states to the Paris Convention seem to favour the interpretation of the German, Swiss and Japanese courts,[32] and the Paris Convention strictly speaking does not cover acts before the first filing date, the underlying and almost forgotten objective of the Paris Convention, that of properly protecting the inventor, would favour an interpretation which allowed for the combination of both grace period and priority interval.[33] The more so since relying on a priority filing by now has become the norm rather than the exception. In other words, limiting the application of the grace period to the actual filing date deprives a huge number of filings of the benefit of a domestic grace period.[34]

4.   The pros and cons of introducing a grace period have been discussed at length in a number of studies.[35] Empirical studies are hard to come by.[36] The opponents of a grace period point out in particular the factual extension of the patent monopoly, the loss of legal certainty and the difficulty of proving the proper date of publication. On the other hand, it is indisputable that the introduction of a grace period in the United States, Canada or Germany has confirmed none of these arguments. Further, it has to be pointed out that legal uncertainty and difficulty in proving the relevant date of publication encounters the same problems in systems that allow for a grace period only in case of a publication against the inventor's will. That a publication has been made under such circumstances is often far from evident. Legal uncertainty should also rule out a piecemeal approach which would allow a grace period only under certain circumstances.[37] Just as an example of the difficulties encountered in this respect, a Japanese decision denied patentability in a case where the

inventor could neither prove that the written publication had been by himself, nor against his will.[38] Introducing a general grace period would not only help the legally untrained inventor, but also large-scale enterprises.[39] The increasing importance of university inventions and the necessity for academics to publish first and patent later would require a general grace period.[40] To make the introduction of a grace period dependant upon a world-wide harmonisation treaty, as seems to be the EC position, is thus unhelpful not least for European industry. "No convincing evidence has been offered that a patent system with a general grace period would substantially or even at all increase the legal uncertainty which doubtless exists, for instance, under the EPC. Assumptions to the contrary find no empirical justification."[41] Finally, it should not be forgotten that law is meant to serve mankind and not vice versa. Yet trying to explain to a legally untrained inventor why his own publication should destroy novelty is a well nigh impossible endeavour.

* Head of the Asian Department, Max–Planck Institute for Foreign and International Patent, Copyright and Competition Law, Munich, Germany. This SIDE BAR was written specially for PRINCIPLES OF PATENT LAW.

1. Two years until 1940 under Sec. 4886 of the US Patents Act 1870. Current rules under Sec. 102(b) and (d) of the US Patents Act 1952.

2. Sec. 28(2) Canadian 1952 Patents Act.

3. Sec. 6(2) Thai Patent Act 1999.

4. Sec. 30 Japanese Patent Act 1959.

5. Sec. 14(3) Malaysian Patents Act 1983.

6. Sec. 3(4) German Patent Act 1981.

7. Sec. 9 French Patent Act 1968.

8. Sec. 2(4) UK Patents Act 1977.

9. Sec. 15 Italian Law on Patents for Inventions of 1939.

10. G. Amdur, *Patent Fundamentals*, New York 1956, 50.

11. English Court of Appeal, *Patterson v. Gaslight & Coke*, 3 Appeal Cases 244 [1875].

12. Scottish Court of Session, *Gill v. Coutts*, [1896] RPC125.

13. Sec. 51(3) UK Patents Act 1949.

14. Sec. 52 UK Patents Act 1949.

15. Roubier, *Le Droit de la Propriété Industrielle*, Vol. 2, Paris 1954, 141.

16. E.g., Cour de Cassation, Annales 1866, 289; Cour de Cassation, Annales 1885, 59; Cour de Cassation, Annales 1967, 3.

17. *Pennock v. Dialogue*, 7 L.Ed. 327 (U.S.1829).

18. *Shaw v. Cooper*, 8 L.Ed. 689 (U.S. 1833).

19. Sec. 6 Patent Act 1836, Sec. 7 Patent Act 1839 and *Andrews v. Hovey*, 31 L.Ed. 557.

20. Vojáek, *A Survey of the Principal National Patent Systems*, London 1936, 133.

21. Sec. 2 of the German Patent Act 1877 merely stated that "An invention is not considered as new if at the date of filing the application according the provisions of this present law, the same has been so described in public prints, or so publicly employed in the country that the use of the same by other competent persons appears possible."

22. Criticism particularly by J. Kohler, who had done so much to interpret patent law as a proper protection for the inventor's rights. He criticised in particular that "the inventor loses unaccountable wealth without deeper justification" if a law did not come to the inventor's rescue in case of such unauthorised publications: J. Kohler, *Handbuch des deutschen Patentrechts*, Mannheim 1900, 199.

23. Sec. 2(2) German Patent Act 1891. Comparable provisions could be found in a number of national laws before these countries joined the Paris Convention. Grace periods in cases of foreign publications were contained in the German–Austrian Trade Agreement of 1881, in the Austrian Patent Act of 1899 (Sec. 3), in the Finnish Patent Act of 1898 and the Mexican Patent Act of 1890.

24. Glorification of inventors had become fashionable in the Third Reich, not least because Hitler had mentioned them in his book, *Mein Kampf*, as some academics of that period were anxious to point out: Ristow, *Die Praxis und das neue Patentgesetz*, Juristische Wochenschrift 1936, 1492.

25. Actes de la Conference de Londres (1935), 260.

26. Actes de la Conference de Lisbonne (1963), 349–364.

27. AIPPI Annuaire 1938, 188.

28. AIPPI Annuaire 1952, 133.

29. This at least is the interpretation by the German Bundesgerichtshof, GRUR Int. 1971, 399; Swiss Bundesgericht, GRUR Int. 1992, 293; and Tokyo High Court, 13 March 1997, 30 IIC 449 [1999].

30. Hoge Raad of 23 June 1995, OJ EPO 1998, 278—Follicle Stimulation Hormone II.

31. Decision G 2/99 of 12 July 2000, OJ EPO 2001, 83.

32. Actes de la Conference de Londres (1935), 375.

33. This also seems to be the opinion taken by P. Mathély, *Le Droit française des Brevets d'Invention*, Paris 1974, 149, although most other French academics seem to take the view that both periods cannot be cumulated.

34. This appropriately mentioned by Loth, Münchner Gemeinschaftskommentar, Art. 55 EPC, marginal note 65.

35. E.g., H.F. Loth, *Neuheitsbegriff und Neuheitsschonfrist im Patentrecht*,

Köln 1988; M.-A.Houtmann, *Brevet et Delai de Grace en Droit International*, Strasbourg 1988; M. Koktvedgaard, *A Novelty Grace Period for Patent Applications*, Study for the EC Commission, 1984; J. Straus, *Grace Period and the European and International Patent Law*, IIC Studies Vol. 20, Munich 2001.

36. But see, J. Straus, *Die Bedeutung der Neuheitsschonfrist für die ausserindustrielle Forschung in den Ländern der europäischen Wirtschaftsgemeinschaft*, 1986.

37. As is advocated by, e.g., M. Koktvedgaard, Brussels 1984, 136.

38. Tokyo High Court, 16 March 1992, 1993 Tokkyo Kanri 869—"Concrete Enforcement". In this case, the inventor had made test data available and was acknowledged in the publication.

39. As a matter of fact, the German company Bayer could only narrowly uphold its patent for the Adalat pharmaceutical because of a prior publication.

40. R. Krasser, *The Importance of an Extensive Research Period of Grace for the Commercial Exploitation of the Results of Scientific Research*, in: *European Research Structures: Changes and Challenges, The Role and Function of Intellectual Property Rights*, Max Planck Society, E2/94, Munich 1994, 169.

41. J. Straus, *Grace Period and the European and International Patent Law*, Munich 2001, 95.

2. PUBLIC USE

Section 102(b) provides that one is not entitled to a patent on an invention if the invention was in public use more than one year before the filing date of the patent application. In *Egbert v. Lippmann*, which is one of patent law's few humorous interludes, the Court takes a decidedly minimalist approach to what constitutes a "public use." After carefully reading the majority and dissenting opinions, ask yourself what are the policy advantages and disadvantages of such an approach.

Egbert v. Lippmann

104 U.S. 333 (1882).

■ MR. JUSTICE WOODS delivered the opinion of the court.

This suit was brought for an alleged infringement of the complainant's reissued letters-patent, No. 5216, dated Jan. 7, 1873, for an improvement in corset-springs.

The original letters bear date July 17, 1866, and were issued to Samuel H. Barnes. The reissue was made to the complainant, under her then name, Frances Lee Barnes, executrix of the original patentee.

* * *

The evidence on which the defendants rely to establish a prior public use of the invention consists mainly of the testimony of the complainant.

She testifies that Barnes invented the improvement covered by his patent between January and May, 1855; that between the dates named the witness and her friend Miss Cugier were complaining of the breaking of their corset-steels. Barnes, who was present, and was an intimate friend of the witness, said he thought he could make her a pair that would not break. At their next interview he presented her with a pair of corset-steels which he himself had made. The witness wore these steels a long time. In 1858 Barnes made and presented to her another pair, which she also wore a long time. When the corsets in which these steels were used wore out, the witness ripped them open and took out the steels and put them in new corsets. This was done several times.

... [T]hese steels embodied the invention afterwards patented by Barnes and covered by the reissued letters-patent on which this suit is brought.

Joseph H. Sturgis, another witness for complainant, testifies that in 1863 Barnes spoke to him about two inventions made by himself, one of which was a corset-steel, and that he went to the house of Barnes to see them. Before this time, and after the transactions testified to by the complainant, Barnes and she had intermarried. Barnes said his wife had a pair of steels made according to his invention in the corsets which she was then wearing, and if she would take them off he would show them to witness. Mrs. Barnes went out, and returned with a pair of corsets and a pair of scissors, and ripped the corsets open and took out the steels. Barnes then explained to witness how they were made and used.

* * *

We observe, in the first place, that to constitute the public use of an invention it is not necessary that more than one of the patented articles should be publicly used. The use of a great number may tend to strengthen the proof, but one well-defined case of such use is just as effectual to annul the patent as many. . . .

We remark, secondly, that, whether the use of an invention is public or private does not necessarily depend upon the number of persons to whom its use is known. If an inventor, having made his device, gives or sells it to another, to be used by the donee or vendee, without limitation or restriction, or injunction of secrecy, and it is so used, such use is public, even though the use and knowledge of the use may be confined to one person.

We say, thirdly, that some inventions are by their very character only capable of being used where they cannot be seen or observed by the public eye. An invention may consist of a lever or spring, hidden in the running gear of a watch, or of a rachet, shaft, or cog-wheel covered from view in the recesses of a machine for spinning or weaving. Nevertheless, if its inventor sells a machine of which his invention forms a part, and allows it to be used without restriction of any kind, the use is a public one. So, on the other hand, a use necessarily open to public view, if made in good faith solely to test the qualities of the invention, and for the purpose of experiment, is not a public use within the meaning of the statute. *Elizabeth v. Pavement Company*, 97 U.S. 126; *Shaw v. Cooper*, 7 Pet. 292.

Tested by these principles, we think the evidence of the complainant herself shows that for more than two years before the application for the original letters there was, by the consent and allowance of Barnes, a public use of the invention, covered by them. He made and gave to her two pairs of corset-steels, constructed according to his device, one in 1855 and one in 1858. They were presented to her for use. He imposed no obligation of secrecy, nor any condition or restriction whatever. They were not presented for the purpose of experiment, nor to test their qualities. No such claim is set up in her testimony. The invention was at the time complete, and there is no evidence that it was afterwards changed or improved. The donee of the steels used them for years for the purpose and in the manner designed by the inventor. They were not capable of any other use. She might have exhibited them to any person, or made other steels of the same kind, and used or sold them without violating any condition or restriction imposed on her by the inventor.

According to the testimony of the complainant, the invention was completed and put into use in 1855. The inventor slept on his rights for eleven years. Letters-patent were not applied for till March, 1866. In the mean time, the invention had found its way into general, and almost universal, use. A great part of the record is taken up with the testimony of the manufacturers and venders of corset-steels, showing that before he applied for letters the principle of his device was almost universally used in the manufacture of corset-steels. It is fair to presume that having learned from this general use that there was some value in his invention, he attempted to resume, by his application, what by his acts he had clearly dedicated to the public.

* * *

We are of opinion that the defense of two years' public use, by the consent and allowance of the inventor, before he made application for letters-patent, is satisfactorily established by the evidence.

■ Mr. Justice Miller dissenting.

The sixth section of the act of July 4, 1836, c. 357, makes it a condition of the grant of a patent that the invention for which it was asked should not, at the time of the application for a patent, "have been in public use or on sale with the consent or allowance" of the inventor or discoverer. Section fifteen of the same act declares that it shall be a good defense to an action for infringement of the patent, that it had been in public use or on sale with the consent or allowance of the patentee before his application. This was afterwards modified by the seventh section of the act of March 3, 1839, c. 88, which declares that no patent shall be void on that ground unless the prior use has been for more than two years before the application.

This is the law under which the patent of the complainant is held void by the opinion just delivered. The previous part of the same section requires that the invention must be one "not known or used by others" before the discovery or invention made by the applicant. In this limitation, though in the same sentence as the other, the word "public" is not used, so that the use by others which would defeat the applicant, if without his consent, need not be public; but where the use of his invention is by his consent or allowance, it must be public or it will not have that affect.

The reason of this is undoubtedly that, if without his consent others have used the machine, composition, or manufacture, it is strong proof that he was not the discoverer or first inventor. In that case he was not entitled to a patent. If the use was with his consent or allowance, the fact that such consent or allowance was first obtained is evidence that he was the inventor, and claimed to be such. In such case, he was not to lose his right to a patent, unless the use which he permitted was such as showed an intention of abandoning his invention to the public. It must, in the language of the act, be in public use or on sale. If on sale, of course the public who buy can use it, and if used in public with his consent, it may be copied by others. In either event there is an end of his exclusive right of use or sale.

The word public is, therefore, an important member of the sentence. A private use with consent, which could lead to no copy or reproduction of the machine, which taught the nature of the invention to no one but the party to whom such consent was given, which left the public at large as ignorant of this as it was before the author's discovery, was no abandonment to the public, and did not defeat his claim for a patent. If the little steep spring inserted in a single pair of corsets, and used by only one woman, covered by her outer-clothing, and in a position always withheld from public observation, is a public use of that piece of steel, I am at a loss to know the line between a private and a public use.

The opinion argues that the use was public, because, with the consent of the inventor to its use, no limitation was imposed in regard to its use in public. It may be well imagined that a prohibition to the party so permitted against exposing her use of the steel spring to public observation would have been supposed to be a piece of irony. An objection quite the opposite of this suggested by the opinion is, that the invention was incapable of a public use. That is to say, that while the statute says the right to the patent can only be defeated by a use which is public, it is equally fatal to the claim, when it is permitted to be used at all, that the article can never be used in public. . . .

Metallizing Engineering Co. v. Kenyon Bearing & Auto Parts Co.

153 F.2d 516 (2d Cir.1946).

■ Before L. HAND, AUGUSTUS N. HAND, and CLARK, CIRCUIT JUDGES.

■ L. HAND, CIRCUIT JUDGE.

The defendants appeal from the usual decree holding valid and infringed all but three of the claims of a reissued patent, issued to the plaintiff's assignor, Meduna; the original patent issued on May 25, 1943, upon an application filed on August 6, 1942. The patent is for the process of "so conditioning a metal surface that the same is, as a rule, capable of bonding thereto applied spray metal to a higher degree than is normally procurable with hitherto known practices" (p. 2, lines 1–5). It is primarily useful for building up the worn metal parts of a machine.

The greatness of Learned Hand as a jurist is well known, but perhaps less appreciated is his contribution to patent law. As Gerald Gunther wrote regarding Hand's approach to patent cases, "Year after year, his pre-conference memos reveal a remarkable understanding of the contraptions before him, a mastery gained through careful study, hard work, and lucid, forceful explanations of his modifications of received legal wisdoms." GERALD GUNTHER, LEARNED HAND: THE MAN AND THE JUDGE 311 (1994). It should come as no surprise then that Learned Hand's "patent-law opinions the most cited by other circuit courts and the most quoted by commentators." *Id.* at 315. *See also*, PAUL H. BLAUSTEIN, LEARNED HAND ON PATENT LAW (1983).

* * *

The only question which we find necessary to decide is as to Meduna's public use of the patented process more than one year before August 6, 1942. The district judge made findings about this ... The kernel of them is the following: "the inventor's main purpose in his use of the process prior to August 6, 1941, and especially in respect to all jobs for owners not known to him, was commercial, and ... an experimental purpose in connection with such use was subordinate only." Upon this finding he concluded as matter of law that, since the use before the critical date—August 6, 1941—was not primarily for the purposes of experiment, the use was not excused for that reason.... Moreover, he also concluded that the use was not public but secret, and for that reason that its predominantly commercial character did prevent it from invalidating the patent. For the last he relied upon our decisions in *Peerless Roll Leaf Co. v. Griffin & Sons*, 29 F.2d 646, and *Gillman v. Stern*, 114 F.2d 28. We think that his analysis of *Peerless Roll Leaf Co. v. Griffin & Sons*, was altogether correct, and that he had no alternative but to follow that decision; on the other hand, we now think that we were then wrong and that the decision must be overruled for reasons we shall state. *Gillman v. Stern, supra*, was, however, rightly decided.

* * *

... [I]n *Peerless Roll Leaf Co.* ..., where the patent was for a machine, which had been kept secret, but whose output had been freely sold on the market, we sustained the patent on the ground that "the sale of the product was irrelevant, since no knowledge could possibly be acquired of the achine in that way. In this respect the machine differs from a process ... or from any other invention necessarily contained in a product" 29 F.2d at page 649. So far as we can now find, there is nothing to support this distinction in the authorities, and we shall try to show that we misapprehended the theory on which the prior use by an inventor forfeits his right to a patent.... In *Gillman v. Stern, supra*, 2 Cir., 114 F.2d 28, it was not the inventor, but a third person who used the machine secretly and sold the product openly, and there was therefore no question either of abandonment or forfeiture by the inventor. The only issue was whether a prior use which did not disclose the invention to the art was within the statute; and it is well settled that it is not. As in the case of any other anticipation, the issue of invention must then be determined by how much the inventor has contributed any new information to the art. *Gayler v. Wilder*, 10 How. 477, 496, 497.

* * *

... [I]t appears that in *Peerless Roll Leaf Co.*... we confused two separate doctrines: (1) The effect upon his right to a patent of the inventor's competitive exploitation of his machine or of his process; (2) the contribution which a prior use by another person makes to the art. Both do indeed come within the phrase, "prior use"; but the first is a defence for quite different reasons from the second. It had its origin—at least in this country—in ... *Pennock v. Dialogue* ...; *i.e.*, that it is a condition upon an inventor's right to a patent that he shall not exploit his discovery competitively after it is ready for patenting; he must content himself with either secrecy, or legal monopoly. It is true that for the limited period of two years he was allowed to do so, possibly in order to give him time to prepare an application; and even that has been recently cut down by half. But if he goes beyond that period of probation, he forfeits his right regardless of how little the public may have learned about the invention; just as he can forfeit it by too long concealment, even without exploiting the invention at all. *Woodbridge v. United States*, 263 U.S. 50; *Macbeth–Evans Glass Co. v. General Electric Co., supra*, 6 Cir., 246 F. 695. Such a forfeiture has nothing to do with abandonment, which presupposes a deliberate, though not necessarily an express, surrender of any right to a patent. Although the evidence of both may at times overlap, each comes from a quite different legal source: one, from the fact that by renouncing the right the inventor irrevocably surrenders it; the other, from the fiat of Congress that it is part of the consideration for a patent that the public shall as soon as possible begin to enjoy the disclosure.

It is indeed true that an inventor may continue for more than a year to practice his invention for his private purposes of his own enjoyment and later patent it. But that is, properly considered, not an exception to the doctrine, for he is not then making use of his secret to gain a competitive advantage over others; he does not thereby extend the period of his monopoly. Besides, as we have seen, even that privilege has its limits, for he may conceal it so long that he will lose his right to a patent even though he does not use it at all. With that question we have not however any concern here.

Judgment reversed; complaint dismissed.

NOTES

1. *How Public Must "Public Use" Be?* It is clear from the pertinent Supreme Court decisions that very little use and very little publicity are required to constitute a public use under 35 U.S.C. § 102(b). In *Egbert*, the use was by a donee of apparently a single embodiment of the invention. The Court emphasized that "one well defined case of public use is just as effectual to annul the patent as many." The Federal Circuit has also adopted this minimalist approach to public use. *See, e.g., In re Smith*, 714 F.2d 1127 (Fed.Cir.1983).

"Public" use means use of the product or process "in its natural and intended way"—even though the invention may in fact be hidden from public view with such use. Again, in *Egbert*, corset steels were apparently hidden inside the corset, and of course, the corset in use was hidden from truly public view by the woman's clothing. At least one person other than the inventor knew of the invention.

2. *Private Uses.* To escape the public use bar the utilization must be private, under the inventor's control, and not for commercial purposes. Despite *Egbert*, courts continue to exclude, under § 102(b), purely private uses of an invention by the inventor or uses under the conditions of confidentiality. In *Moleculon Research Corp. v. CBS, Inc.*, 793 F.2d 1261 (Fed.Cir.1986), the invention was a puzzle, popularly known as "Rubik's Cube." While a graduate student, the inventor had constructed several models of his invention, which he displayed and explained to roommates and another graduate student. Later, after beginning employment, he showed another model to his employer. Upholding the district court's finding that the uses were private, the Federal Circuit distinguished *Egbert*: the uses were either by or under the inventor's control and the inventor "had not given over the invention for free and unrestricted use by another person." Id. at 1266. Would the result in *Moleculon* have changed if the inventor had displayed his invention to guests at a private party? *See Beachcombers v. WildeWood Creative Products, Inc.*, 31 F.3d 1154 (Fed.Cir.1994) (distinguishing *Moleculon* and upholding a jury verdict of public use).

3. *Commercial Products, Secret Production.* What if the invention is used for a commercial purpose but under conditions of deliberate secrecy? Judge Hand faced this question in *Metallizing*, which established that *commercial* exploitation by the inventor of a machine or process constitutes a public use even though the machine or process is held secret. As Judge Hand stated in this regard, an inventor "forfeits his right regardless of how little the public may have learned about the invention." As a result of Judge Hand's opinion in *Metalallizing*, it is now well established that commercial exploitation by the inventor of a machine or process constitutes a public use even though the machine or process is held secret. *See TP Laboratories v. Professional Positioners, Inc.*, 724 F.2d 965, 972 (Fed.Cir.1984) (public use may bar patent "if the inventor is making commercial use of the invention under circumstances which preserve its secrecy"); *Torpharm, Inc. v. Ranbaxy Pharmaceuticals, Inc.*, 336 F.3d 1322 (Fed.Cir.2003) (stating that if the patentee owner "sold improved Form 1 ranitidine made by the claimed process, then its process claims would be invalid under section 102(b)—regardless of whether the process was disclosed to the public or not"). But third-party use of a secret process without the consent of the inventor may lead to a different result. *See infra*, Section A.5 for a discussion of third-party activity.

4. *Policies and Interpretations.* Interpreting "public use" in light of policy may lead to at least two different nonliteral interpretations, with the statutory provision meaning both more and less than its "ordinary meaning." In *Metallizing*, a secret use of the invention, a process, was treated as a public use because the use was commercial rather than experimental. The Court seems to have been moved by the policy concern of discouraging inventors from delaying commencement of the statutory term of protection. As will be seen below, experimental uses are not counted as public uses even though they are in fact perceptible by the public. This alternative nonliteral approach to Section 102(b) is based on ancient authority, beginning with *Pennock*, and seems to be motivated by the policy concern of allowing inventors to field test their own inventions.

3.   EXPERIMENTAL USE

In many cases, the existence of a public use prior to the critical date will be clear and undisputed. In some of these, the focus of attention is on the principal exception to the public use bar—the experimental use doctrine. This doctrine provides that activity that would otherwise constitute "public use" will not trigger the § 102(b) statutory bar if the use was incidental to experimentation. This doctrine, frequently invoked by patent holders, is not reflected in the Patent Act. But the Supreme Court recognized the validity of experimental use in the leading case of *City of Elizabeth v. American Nicholson Pavement Company*, explored below, and it has been the subject of judicial development ever since.

City of Elizabeth v. American Nicholson Pavement Company

97 U.S. (7 Otto) 126 (1878).

APPEAL from the Circuit Court of the United States for the District of New Jersey.

■ Mr. Justice Bradley delivered the opinion of the court.

This suit was brought by the American Nicholson Pavement Company against the city of Elizabeth, N. J., George W. Tubbs, and the New Jersey Wood–Paving Company, a corporation of New Jersey, upon a patent issued to Samuel Nicholson, ... for a new and improved wooden pavement ... [I]n the specification, it is declared that the nature and object of the invention consists in providing a process or mode of constructing wooden block pavements upon a foundation along a street or roadway with facility, cheapness, and accuracy, and also in the creation and construction of such a wooden pavement as shall be comparatively permanent and durable, by so uniting and combining all its parts, both superstructure and foundation, as to provide against the slipping of the horses' feet, against noise, against unequal wear, and against rot and consequent sinking away from below.... The patent has four claims, the first two of which, which are the only ones in question, are as follows:

I claim as an improvement in the art of constructing pavements:

1.   Placing a continuous foundation or support, as above described, directly upon the roadway; then arranging thereon a series of blocks, having parallel sides, endwise, in rows, so as to leave a continuous narrow groove or channel-way between each row, and then filling said grooves or channelways with broken stone, gravel, and tar, or other like materials.

2.   I claim the formation of a pavement by laying a foundation directly upon the roadway, substantially as described, and then employing two sets of blocks: one a principal set of blocks, that shall form the wooden surface of the pavement when completed, and an auxiliary set of blocks or strips of board, which shall form no part of the surface of the pavement, but determine the width of the groove between the principal blocks, and also the filling of said groove, when so formed between the principal blocks, with broken stone, gravel, and tar, or other like material.

The bill charges that the defendants infringed this patent by laying down wooden pavements in the city of Elizabeth, N. J., constructed in substantial conformity with the process patented, and prays an account of profits, and an injunction.

The defendants answered in due course, admitting that they had constructed, and were still constructing, wooden pavements in Elizabeth, but alleging that they were constructed in accordance with a patent granted to John W. Brocklebank and Charles Trainer, dated Jan. 12, 1869, and denied that it infringed upon the complainant.

* * *

They also averred that the alleged invention of Nicholson was in public use, with his consent and allowance, for six years before he applied for a patent, on a certain avenue in Boston called the Mill-dam; and contended that said public use worked an abandonment of the pretended invention.

* * *

To determine this question, it is necessary to examine the circumstances under which this pavement was put down, and the object and purpose that Nicholson had in view. It is perfectly clear from the evidence that he did not intend to abandon his right to a patent. He had filed a caveat in August, 1847, and he constructed the pavement in question by way of experiment, for the purpose of testing its qualities. The road in which it was put down, though a public road, belonged to the Boston and Roxbury Mill Corporation, which received toll for its use; and Nicholson was a stockholder and treasurer of the corporation. The pavement in question was about seventy-five feet in length, and was laid adjoining to the toll-gate and in front of the toll-house. It was constructed by Nicholson at his own expense, and was placed by him where it was, in order to see the effect upon it of heavily loaded wagons, and of varied and constant use; and also to ascertain its durability, and liability to decay. Joseph L. Lang, who was toll-collector for many years, commencing in 1849, familiar with the road before that time, and with this pavement from the time of its origin, testified as follows:

> Mr. Nicholson was there almost daily, and when he came he would examine the pavement, would often walk over it, cane in hand, striking it with his cane, and making particular examination of its condition. He asked me very often how people liked it, and asked me a great many questions about it. I have heard him say a number of times that this was his first experiment with this pavement, and he thought that it was wearing very well. The circumstances that made this locality desirable for the purpose of obtaining a satisfactory test of the durability and value of the pavement were: that there would be a better chance to lay it there; he would have more room and a better chance than in the city; and, besides, it was a place where most everybody went over it, rich and poor. It was a great thoroughfare out of Boston. It was frequently traveled by teams having a load of five or six tons, and some larger. As these teams usually stopped at the toll-house, and started again, the stopping and starting would make as severe a trial to the pavement as it could be put to.

This evidence is corroborated by that of several other witnesses in the cause; the result of the whole being that Nicholson merely intended this piece of pavement as an experiment, to test its usefulness and durability. Was this a public use, within the meaning of the law?

An abandonment of an invention to the public may be evinced by the conduct of the inventor at any time, even within the two years named in the law. The effect of the law is, that no such consequence will necessarily follow from the invention being in public use or on sale, with the inventor's consent and allowance, at any time within two years before his application; but that, if the invention is in public use or on sale prior to that time, it will be conclusive evidence of abandonment, and the patent will be void.

But, in this case, it becomes important to inquire what is such a public use as will have the effect referred to. That the use of the pavement in question was public in one sense cannot be disputed. But can it be said that the invention was in public use? The use of an invention by the inventor himself, or of any other person under his direction, by way of experiment, and in order to bring the invention to perfection, has never been regarded as such a use. CURTIS, PATENTS, sect. 381; *Shaw v. Cooper*, 7 Pet. 292.

Now, the nature of a street pavement is such that it cannot be experimented upon satisfactorily except on a highway, which is always public.

When the subject of invention is a machine, it may be tested and tried in a building, either with or without closed doors. In either case, such use is not a public use, within the meaning of the statute, so long as the inventor is engaged, in good faith, in testing its operation. He may see cause to alter it and improve it, or not. His experiments will reveal the fact whether any and what alterations may be necessary. If durability is one of the qualities to be attained, a long period, perhaps years, may be necessary to enable the inventor to discover whether his purpose is accomplished. And though, during all that period, he may not find that any changes are necessary, yet he may be justly said to be using his machine only by way of experiment; and no one would say that such a use, pursued with a bona fide intent of testing the qualities of the machine, would be a public use, within the meaning of the statute. So long as he does not voluntarily allow others to make it and use it, and so long as it is not on sale for general use, he keeps the invention under his own control, and does not lose his title to a patent.

It would not be necessary, in such a case, that the machine should be put up and used only in the inventor's own shop or premises. He may have it put up and used in the premises of another, and the use may inure to the benefit of the owner of the establishment. Still, if used under the surveillance of the inventor, and for the purpose of enabling him to test the machine, and ascertain whether it will answer the purpose intended, and make such alterations and improvements as experience demonstrates to be necessary, it will still be a mere experimental use, and not a public use, within the meaning of the statute.

Whilst the supposed machine is in such experimental use, the public may be incidentally deriving a benefit from it. If it be a grist-mill, or a carding-machine, customers from the surrounding country may enjoy the use of it by having their grain made into flour, or their wool into rolls, and still it will not be in public use, within the meaning of the law.

But if the inventor allows his machine to be used by other persons generally, either with or without compensation, or if it is, with his consent, put on sale for such use, then it will be in public use and on public sale, within the meaning of the law.

If, now, we apply the same principles to this case, the analogy will be seen at once. Nicholson wished to experiment on his pavement. He believed it to be a good thing, but he was not sure; and the only mode in which he could test it was to place a specimen of it in a public roadway. He did this at his own expense, and with the consent of the owners of the road. Durability was one of the qualities to be attained. He wanted to know whether his pavement would stand, and whether it would resist decay. Its character for durability could not be ascertained without its being subjected to use for a considerable time. He subjected it to such use, in good faith, for the simple purpose of ascertaining whether it was what he claimed it to be. Did he do any thing more than the inventor of the supposed machine might do, in testing his invention? The public had the incidental use of the pavement, it is true; but was the invention in public use, within the meaning of the statute? We think not. The proprietors of the road alone used the invention, and used it at Nicholson's request, by way of experiment. The only way in which they could use it was by allowing the public to pass over the pavement.

Had the city of Boston, or other parties, used the invention, by laying down the pavement in other streets and places, with Nicholson's consent and allowance, then, indeed, the invention itself would have been in public use, within the meaning of the law; but this was not the case. Nicholson did not sell it, nor allow others to use it or sell it. He did not let it go beyond his control. He did nothing that indicated any intent to do so. He kept it under his own eyes, and never for a moment abandoned the intent to obtain a patent for it.

In this connection, it is proper to make another remark. It is not a public knowledge of his invention that precludes the inventor from obtaining a patent for it, but a public use or sale of it. In England, formerly, as well as under our Patent Act of 1793, if an inventor did not keep his invention secret, if a knowledge of it became public before his application for a patent, he could not obtain one. To be patentable, an invention must not have been known or used before the application; but this has not been the law of this country since the passage of the act of 1836, and it has been very much qualified in England. *Lewis v. Marling*, 10 B. & C. 22. Therefore, if it were true that during the whole period in which the pavement was used, the public knew how it was constructed, it would make no difference in the result.

It is sometimes said that an inventor acquires an undue advantage over the public by delaying to take out a patent, inasmuch as he thereby preserves the monopoly to himself for a longer period than is allowed by the policy of the law; but this cannot be said with justice when the delay is occasioned by a bona fide effort to bring his invention to perfection, or to ascertain whether it will answer the purpose intended. His monopoly only continues for the allotted period, in any event; and it is the interest of the public, as well as himself, that the invention should be perfect and properly tested, before a patent is granted for it. Any attempt to use it for a profit, and not by way of experiment, for a longer period than two years before the application, would deprive the inventor of his right to a patent. . . .

Lough v. Brunswick Corporation

86 F.3d 1113 (Fed.Cir.1996).

■ Before PLAGER, LOURIE, and CLEVENGER, CIRCUIT JUDGES.

■ LOURIE, CIRCUIT JUDGE.

Brunswick Corporation, d/b/a Mercury Marine, appeals from the final judgment of the United States District Court for the Middle District of

Florida in which the court denied Brunswick's Motion for Judgment as a Matter of Law and its Motion for New Trial after a jury verdict of infringement of U.S. Patent 4,848,775, owned by the inventor Steven G. Lough.... Because the court erred in denying Brunswick's Motion for Judgment as a Matter of Law, we reverse in part and vacate in part.

BACKGROUND

Stern drives are marine propulsion devices for boats in which the engine is located inside the boat and is coupled to an outdrive, which includes a propeller located outside the boat ("inboard/outboard boat")....

In 1986, Steven G. Lough worked as a repairman for a boat dealership in Sarasota, Florida. While repairing Brunswick inboard/outboard boats, he noticed that the upper seal assembly in the stern drives often failed due to corrosion....

Lough determined that the corrosion in the upper seal assembly occurred due to contact between the annular seal ... and the bell housing aperture.... He designed a new upper seal assembly that isolated the annular seal ... from the aluminum bell housing ... in order to prevent such corrosion.

After some trial and error with his grandfather's metal lathe, he made six usable prototypes in the spring of 1986. He installed one prototype in his own boat at home. Three months later, he gave a second prototype to a friend who installed it in his boat. He also installed prototypes in the boat of the owner of the marina where he worked and in the boat of a marina customer. He gave the remaining prototypes to longtime friends who were employees at another marina in Sarasota. Lough did not charge anyone for the prototypes. For over a year following the installation of these prototypes, Lough neither asked for nor received any comments about the operability of the prototypes. During this time, Lough did not attempt to sell any seal assemblies.

On June 6, 1988, Lough filed a patent application entitled "Liquid Seal for Marine Stern Drive Gear Shift Shafts," which issued as the '775 patent on July 18, 1989....

After learning of Lough's invention, Brunswick designed its own improved upper seal assembly.... In addition to a bushing with an upper and lower portion, Brunswick's upper seal assembly included its own patented gap technology.... Brunswick incorporated its new upper seal assembly in its "Alpha One" inboard/outboard boat. In addition, it sold this seal assembly as a replacement part under its "Quicksilver" line of replacement parts.

Lough sued Brunswick on June 12, 1993, alleging infringement of the '775 patent. Brunswick counterclaimed for a declaratory judgment of patent noninfringement, invalidity, and/or unenforceability. A jury found that Brunswick failed to prove that Lough's invention was in public use before the critical date on June 6, 1987, one year prior to the filing date of the '775 patent. The jury also found that Brunswick infringed claims 1–4 of the '775 patent, both literally and under the doctrine of equivalents. Based on its infringement finding, the jury awarded Lough $1,500,000 in lost profits. After trial, Brunswick filed a Motion for Judgment as a Matter of Law in which it argued, inter alia, that the claimed invention was invalid because it had been in public use before the critical date. Brunswick also filed a Motion for New Trial on damages. The court denied Brunswick's motions without any comment. . . . Brunswick appeals.

DISCUSSION

* * *

Brunswick challenges, *inter alia*, the court's denial of its motion for JMOL on the issue of public use. Brunswick argues that the district court erred in denying its motion for JMOL because the uses of Lough's prototypes prior to the critical date were not experimental. Brunswick asserts that Lough did not control the uses of his prototypes by third parties before the critical date, failed to keep records of the alleged experiments, and did not place the parties to whom the seals were given under any obligation of secrecy. Based on this objective evidence, Brunswick argues that the uses of Lough's prototypes before the critical date were not "experimental." Therefore, Brunswick contends that the jury's verdict was incorrect as a matter of law and that the court erred in denying its JMOL motion.

Lough counters that the tests performed with the six prototypes were necessary experiments conducted in the course of completing his invention. He argues that when the totality of circumstances is properly viewed, the evidence supports the jury's conclusion that those uses were experimental. Lough maintains that a number of factors support the jury's experimental use conclusion, including evidence that he received no compensation for the prototypes, he did not place the seal assemblies on sale until after he filed his patent application, and he gave the prototypes only to his friends and personal acquaintances who used them in such a manner that they were unlikely to be seen by the public. He further argues that, to verify operability of the seal assemblies, prototypes had to be installed by mechanics of various levels of skill in boats that were exposed to different conditions. Thus, he asserts that the court did not err in denying Brunswick's JMOL motion. We disagree with Lough.

One is entitled to a patent unless, inter alia, "the invention was . . . in public use . . . in this country, more than one year prior to the date of the application for patent in the United States." 35 U.S.C. § 102(b) (1994). We have defined "public use" as including "any use of [the claimed] invention by a person other than the inventor who is under no limitation, restriction or obligation of secrecy to the inventor." *In re Smith*, 714 F.2d 1127, 1134, 218 USPQ 976, 983 (Fed.Cir.1983) (*citing Egbert v. Lippmann*, 104 U.S. 333, 336 (1881)). An evaluation of a question of public use depends on "how the totality of the circumstances of the case comports with the policies underlying the public use bar." *Tone Bros. v. Sysco Corp.*, 28 F.3d 1192, 1198, 31 U.S.P.Q.2D 1321, 1324 (Fed.Cir.1994), *cert. denied*, ___ U.S. ___ (1995). These policies include:

> (1) discouraging the removal, from the public domain, of inventions that the public reasonably has come to believe are freely available; (2) favoring the prompt and widespread disclosure of inventions; (3) allowing the inventor a reasonable amount of time following sales activity to determine

the potential economic value of a patent; and (4) prohibiting the inventor from commercially exploiting the invention for a period greater than the statutorily prescribed time.

Id., 28 F.3d 1192, 1198, 31 U.S.P.Q.2D at 1324–25. A patentee may negate a showing of public use by coming forward with evidence that its use of the invention was experimental. *See TP Lab. v. Professional Positioners, Inc.*, 724 F.2d 965, 971, 220 USPQ 577, 582 (Fed.Cir.) ("[I]f a prima facie case is made of public use, the patent owner must be able to point to or must come forward with convincing evidence to counter that showing."), *cert. denied*, 469 U.S. 826 (1984).

Neither party disputes that Lough's prototypes were in use before the critical date. Thus, both parties agree that the issue presented on appeal is whether the jury properly decided that the use of Lough's six prototypes in 1986, prior to the critical date, constituted experimental use so as to negate the conclusion of public use.[4] Whether an invention was in public use prior to the critical date within the meaning of § 102(b) is a question of law. *Manville Sales Corp. v. Paramount Sys., Inc.*, 917 F.2d 544, 549, 16 U.S.P.Q.2D 1587, 1591 (Fed.Cir.1990).

"The use of an invention by the inventor himself, or of any other person under his direction, by way of experiment, and in order to bring the invention to perfection, has never been regarded as [a public] use." *City of Elizabeth v. American Nicholson Pavement Co.*, 97 U.S. 126, 134, 24 L.Ed. 1000 (1877). This doctrine is based on the underlying policy of providing an inventor time to determine if the invention is suitable for its intended purpose, in effect, to reduce the invention to practice. . . .

To determine whether a use is "experimental," a question of law, the totality of the circumstances must be considered, including various objective indicia of experimentation surrounding the use, such as the number of prototypes and duration of testing, whether records or progress reports were made concerning the testing, the existence of a secrecy agreement between the patentee and the party performing the testing, whether the patentee received compensation for the use of the invention, and the extent of control the inventor maintained over the testing. . . . The last factor of control is critically important, because, if the inventor has no control over the alleged experiments, he is not experimenting. If he does not inquire about the testing or receive reports concerning the results, similarly, he is not experimenting.

---

4.   The trial judge instructed the jury as follows:

* * *

The law requires that an inventor must file a patent application within one year after his invention is publicly used. Public use means any use of Mr. Lough's invention by any person other than Mr. Lough who was not limited or restricted in their activities regarding the invention, or not obligated to secrecy by Mr. Lough. Such use, however does not invalidate Mr. Lough's patent if the use was primarily for bona fide experimental purposes.

. . . The parties do not dispute that the five seal assemblies were used by others before June 6, 1987. The only dispute is whether these uses qualify as experimental uses. The law places the burden on Mr. Lough to come forward with convincing evidence showing that these uses were experimental uses [emphasis added].

In order to justify a determination that legally sufficient experimentation has occurred, there must be present certain minimal indicia. The framework might be quite formal, as may be expected when large corporations conduct experiments, governed by contracts and explicit written obligations. When individual inventors or small business units are involved, however, less formal and seemingly casual experiments can be expected. Such less formal experiments may be deemed legally sufficient to avoid the public use bar, but only if they demonstrate the presence of the same basic elements that are required to validate any experimental program.... The question framed on this appeal is whether Lough's alleged experiments lacked enough of these required indicia so that his efforts cannot, as a matter of law, be recognized as experimental.

Here, Lough either admits or does not dispute the following facts. In the spring of 1986, he noted that the upper seal assembly in Brunswick inboard/outboard boats was failing due to galvanic corrosion between the annular seal and the aperture provided for the upper seal assembly in the aluminum bell housing. He solved this problem by isolating the annular seal from the aluminum bell housing in order to prevent corrosion. After some trial and error, Lough made six prototypes. He installed the first prototype in his own boat. Lough testified at trial that after the first prototype had been in his boat for three months and he determined that it worked, he provided the other prototypes to friends and acquaintances in order to find out if the upper seal assemblies would work as well in their boats as it had worked in his boat. Lough installed one prototype in the boat of his friend, Tom Nikla. A prototype was also installed in the boat of Jim Yow, co-owner of the dealership where Lough worked. Lough installed a fourth prototype in one of the dealership's customers who had considerable problems with corrosion in his stern drive unit. The final two prototypes were given to friends who were employed at a different marina in Florida. These friends installed one prototype in the boat of Mark Liberman, a local charter guide. They installed the other prototype in a demonstration boat at their marina. Subsequently, this boat was sold. Neither Lough nor his friends knew what happened with either the prototype or the demonstration boat after the boat was sold. After providing the five prototypes to these third parties, Lough did not ask for any comments concerning the operability of these prototypes.

Accepting that the jury found these facts, which either were undisputed or were as asserted by Lough, it cannot be reasonably disputed that Lough's use of the invention was not "experimental" so as to negate a conclusion of public use. It is true that Lough did not receive any compensation for the use of the prototypes. He did not place the seal assembly on sale before applying for a patent. Lough's lack of commercialization, however, is not dispositive of the public use question in view of his failure to present objective evidence of experimentation. Lough kept no records of the alleged testing. *See Paragon Podiatry Lab., Inc. v. KLM Lab., Inc.,* 984 F.2d 1182, 1188, 25 U.S.P.Q.2D 1561, 1566 (Fed.Cir.1993) ("[W]hen further combined with other factors, such as the inventor's failure to keep test records, the entire surrounding circumstances point to only one possible legal conclusion—that the sales [of the patented device] were commercial in nature and fall within the statutory bar."); *Sinskey,* 982 F.2d at 499, 25

U.S.P.Q.2D at 1294 (relying on patentee's failure to introduce medical records that would likely indicate that use of medical device was experimental). Nor did he inspect the seal assemblies after they had been installed by other mechanics. *See In re Hamilton*, 882 F.2d 1576, 1581–83, 11 U.S.P.Q.2D 1890, 1894–96 (Fed.Cir.1989) (lack of involvement by inventor in alleged testing is an important factor in determining that use was not experimental). He provided the seal assemblies to friends and acquaintances, but without any provision for follow-up involvement by him in assessment of the events occurring during the alleged experiments, and at least one seal was installed in a boat that was later sold to strangers. Thus, Lough did not maintain any supervision and control over the seals during the alleged testing. . . .

Lough argues that other evidence supports a finding that his uses were experimental, including his own testimony that the prototypes were installed for experimental purposes and the fact that the prototypes were used in such a manner that they were unlikely to be seen by the public. However, "the expression by an inventor of his subjective intent to experiment, particularly after institution of litigation, is generally of minimal value." *TP Laboratories*, 724 F.2d at 972, 220 USPQ at 583. In addition, the fact that the prototypes were unlikely to be seen by the public does not support Lough's position. As the Supreme Court stated in *Egbert v. Lippmann*:

> [S]ome inventions are by their very character only capable of being used where they cannot be seen or observed by the public eye. An invention may consist of a lever or spring, hidden in the running gear of a watch, or of a rachet, shaft, or cog-wheel covered from view in the recesses of a machine for spinning or weaving. Nevertheless, if its inventor sells a machine of which his invention forms a part, and allows it to be used without restriction of any kind, the use is a public one.

104 U.S. at 336. Moreover, those to whom he gave the prototypes constituted "the public," in the absence of meaningful evidence of experimentation. Thus, we find Lough's reliance on this additional evidence to be of minimal value when viewed in light of the totality of the other circumstances surrounding the alleged experimentation.

We therefore hold that the jury had no legal basis to conclude that the uses of Lough's prototypes were experimental and that the prototypes were not in public use prior to the critical date. Our holding is consistent with the policy underlying the experimental use negation, that of providing an inventor time to determine if the invention is suitable for its intended purpose, *i.e.*, to reduce the invention to practice. Lough's activities clearly were not consistent with that policy. We do not dispute that it may have been desirable in this case for Lough to have had his prototypes installed by mechanics of various levels of skill in boats that were exposed to different conditions. Moreover, Lough was free to test his invention in boats of friends and acquaintances to further verify that his invention worked for its intended purpose; however, Lough was required to maintain some degree of control and feedback over those uses of the prototypes if those tests were to negate public use. . . . Lough's failure to monitor the use of his prototypes by his acquaintances, in addition to the lack of records or reports from those acquaintances concerning the operability of the devices, compel the conclusion that, as a matter of law, he did not engage in experimental use. Lough in effect provided the prototype seal assemblies to members of the public for their free and unrestricted use. The law does not waive statutory requirements for inventors of lesser sophistication. When one distributes his invention to members of the public under circumstances that evidence a near total disregard for supervision and control concerning its use, the absence of these minimal indicia of experimentation require a conclusion that the invention was in public use.

We conclude that the jury's determination that Lough's use of the invention was experimental so as to defeat the assertion of public use was incorrect as a matter of law. The court thus erred in denying Brunswick's JMOL motion on the validity of claims 1–4 of the '775 patent under § 102(b).[5]

* * *

■ PLAGER, CIRCUIT JUDGE, dissenting.

I respectfully dissent. In my view, the panel majority confuses its role as law-giver and law-reviewer with the role of fact-weigher and fact-decider. The majority and I agree that the issue is not whether the trial court applied the wrong law (it did not), or whether the jury was wrongly instructed (it was not). . . .

This is not a contest between Evinrude (Outboard Marine Corporation) and Mercury Marine (Brunswick), the two big competitors in this field, to see who can market a better engine. If it were, we could expect the combination of engineering and legal staffs on each side to be punctilious about observing the niceties of our prior opinions on how to conduct experiments so as to avoid any possible running afoul of the public use bar. No, this is a home-made improvement by a man with only a high school education who worked on boats and boat engines, including his own, where he kept encountering the problem with these shaft seals that Mercury Marine had failed to solve. He solved it by trial and error, with an ingenious bushing of his own design, and, on his grandfather's metal lathe, after several tries, fashioned a half-dozen prototype seals that looked like they might do the job.

* * *

Of course it would have been better for all concerned (except perhaps for Mercury Marine) if Mr. Lough had read our prior opinions before he became an inventor. Then he might have kept detailed lab notes setting out the problem and the possible solutions, and he wisely would have obtained written confidentiality agreements from those allowed to see or use his prototypes. Had he studied our cases first, he no doubt would have

---

5. Each claim of the patent must be considered individually when evaluating a public use bar. However, Lough did not argue lack of public use on a claim-by-claim basis at trial. Nor does he do so on appeal. Moreover, section 102(b) may create a bar to patentability either alone, if the device used in public is an anticipation of the later claimed invention or, in conjunction with 35 U.S.C. § 103, if the differences between the claimed invention and the device used would have been obvious to one skilled in the art. *See LaBounty Mfg., Inc. v. United States Int'l Trade Comm'n*, 958 F.2d 1066, 1071, 22 U.S.P.Q.2D 1025, 1028 (Fed.Cir. 1992). Thus, our holding with regard to the public use of the invention applies equally to all of the claims of the '775 patent.

developed a detailed questionnaire for the persons to whom he provided the seals, and he would have insisted on periodic written reports. In other words, he would have put in the set of tight controls the majority would have wanted. Instead, he did what seemed appropriate in the setting in which he worked: he waited to hear from his test cases what problems might emerge, and, hearing none, at least none that convinced him he was on the wrong track, he accepted some friendly advice and proceeded to patent his invention.

Yes, he failed to conduct his testing, his experiments, with the careful attention we lawyers, with our clean and dry hands, have come to prefer. But, under all the facts and circumstances, it is more likely than not that he was testing and perfecting his device, rather than simply making it available gratis to members of the general public for what the law calls "public use." The most that can be said for the majority view is that this is a close question under the totality of circumstances. The ultimate question of what is public use under 35 U.S.C. § 102(b) may be a question of law, but in a given case in which the issue is whether in fact the challenged use was experimental (a complete answer to an infringer's defense based on a § 102(b) violation), the issue involves a blend of law and fact. This issue, unlike claim construction, is one in which a jury fully participates. Thus the question before us is not whether, on the facts, we are persuaded Lough retained all the control a well-designed test of the seals would have afforded, but whether a reasonable jury, on all the evidence before it, could have arrived at the conclusion it did. . . . The jury chose to accept Lough's view of the events, and under that view there was more than enough evidence to support a jury finding that he was testing and perfecting his invention during much of the period leading up to the time he applied for his patent. . . . As we said in *Manville Sales Corp. v. Paramount Systems, Inc.*, 917 F.2d 544, 551, 16 U.S.P.Q.2D 1587, 1592 (Fed.Cir.1990): "When durability in an outdoor environment is inherent to the purpose of an invention, then further testing to determine the invention's ability to serve that purpose will not subject the invention to a section 102(b) bar." (*citing City of Elizabeth*, 97 U.S. at 133–34).

Many of the cases cited by the majority in support of their position are cases in which the inventor made a sale or an offer to sell the product prior to the critical date. . . . The record in this case is undisputed that Lough made no sales of his invention until after his patent application was filed. Nor was this simply market testing, rather than product testing, as in *In re Smith*, 714 F.2d 1127, 218 USPQ 976 (Fed.Cir.1983); and in any event, that was part of the issue presented to the jury.

There is no dearth of cases in this court in which inventors tested their products in various ways before various audiences, and in which we have held that such testing, when it made sense in light of the circumstances, did not constitute public use under section 102(b). *See, e.g., Tone Bros. v. Sysco Corp.*, 28 F.3d 1192, 31 U.S.P.Q.2D 1321 (Fed.Cir.1994) (students asked to test functional features of spice containers prior to the critical date; summary judgment of invalidity reversed), *cert. denied*, ___ U.S. ___ (1995); *TP Lab., Inc. v. Professional Positioners, Inc.*, 724 F.2d 965, 220 USPQ 577 (Fed.Cir.) (orthodontic devices tested on patients prior to critical date; held not invalid even though a fee paid by the patients), *cert. denied*, 469 U.S. 826 (1984); *Manville Sales Corp.*, 917 F.2d 544, 16 U.S.P.Q.2D 1587 (testing of streetlight, conditionally approved for sale, at outdoor site held experimental); *see also Moleculon Research Corp. v. CBS, Inc.*, 793 F.2d 1261, 229 USPQ 805 (Fed.Cir.1986) (inventor of puzzle showed it to a few close colleagues, and allowed one person to use it, prior to the critical date; held not invalid.), *cert. denied*, 479 U.S. 1030 (1987)....

NOTES

1. *Distinguishing Between Public and Experimental Use.* The experimental use doctrine seeks to balance two policies. The first is to allow the inventor time to test and perfect his invention and to assess its utility in operation, which results in social benefits. The second is to prevent inventors from extending the statutory period of exclusivity by delaying filing for a patent while commercially exploiting the invention. Under this view, this balance is achieved through application of a "reasonable purpose" test: the inventor's *purpose* in undertaking activity that would otherwise constitute a public use must be one of experimentation, not commercial exploitation; and, further, the scope and length of the activity must be reasonable in terms of that purpose. If the purpose was experimental and the activity reasonable, it does not matter that the inventor benefits incidentally from the activity. *See* DONALD S. CHISUM, 6 CHISUM ON PATENTS (2003).

Given the broad definition of public use, it is not surprising that disputes about application of the public use bar focus more often on the experimental use issue than on whether a use was otherwise public. The statutory language ("public use") does not exclude experimental uses, but beginning with *Pennock* in 1829 and later *City of Elizabeth*, the courts recognized that such use by an inventor should not create a bar. The doctrine is a difficult one to apply to actual cases. It is frequently invoked by patent holders to avoid the statutory bar, but is rarely sustained by the courts. (In fact, *City of Elizabeth* is the only Supreme Court case in which the Court excused public use or on-sale activity on the basis of the experimental use doctrine.)

2. *Defining and Applying Standards for Experimentation.* Applying the experimental use doctrine is no simple task, as the many cases cited in *Lough* illustrate. Consider the list of experimental factors set forth in *Lough*, such as [1] "number of prototypes and duration of testing" [2] "whether records or progress reports were made concerning the testing" [3]"the existence of a secrecy agreement between the patentee and the party performing the testing" [4] "whether the patentee received compensation for the use of the invention" and [5] "the extent of control the inventor maintained over the testing." The court emphasized that the control factor "is critically important, because if the inventor has no control over the alleged experiments, he is not experimenting." Importantly, the experimental use exception only applies to claimed features of the invention. *See In re Brigance*, 792 F.2d 1103, 1109 (Fed.Cir.1986).

More recently, the Federal Circuit has found an implied understanding of confidentiality in certain cases. "[T]he fact that the inventors revealed the prototype to a select group of individuals without a written confidentiality agreement is not dispositive. When access to an invention is clearly limited and controlled by the inventor, depending upon the relationships of the observers and the inventor, an understanding of confidentiality can be implied." *American Seating Co. v. USSC Group, Inc.*, 514 F.3d 1262, 1268 (Fed.Cir.2008).

A number of factors contributed to the holding in *City of Elizabeth*. First, the nature of the invention (road paving) was such that any testing necessarily had to be to some extent in public. Second, for similar reasons, the testing had to be for a substantial period of time (long term durability being the object of road paving). Third, the section of paving was at least to some extent under the control of the inventor. It was laid on private land belonging to a company of which the inventor was an officer. Fourth, the inventor regularly inspected the road during the period of use to determine its performance. In *Lough*, experimental use was not found because the court thought that, despite lack of commercialization efforts (which cut in favor of the patentee), the lack of record keeping and inventor control were outcome-determinative in that case.

3. *When Does Experimental Use End?* The Federal Circuit has stated on numerous occasions that experimental use ends when the invention is reduced to practice. *See, e.g., New Railhead Mfg. v. Vermeer Mfg.*, 298 F.3d 1290, 1297–8 (Fed.Cir.2002); *RCA Corp. v. Data General Corp.*, 887 F.2d 1056, 1061 (Fed.Cir.1989). And a public use bar may not be overcome even though the invention may be later refined or improved. But the environment in which the invention will be used must be taken into consideration. For example, in the *City of Elizabeth*, Nicholson had to test the pavement in its intended environment. As Judge Hand noted in *Aerovox Corp. v. Polymet Mfg.*, 67 F.2d 860, 863 (2nd Cir.1933), "it did not appear that Nicholson, the inventor, delayed for any other reason than to learn how well his pavement would wear; apparently it was already as good as he hoped to make it." In this regard, consider *Manville Sales Corp. v. Paramount Systems, Inc.*, 917 F.2d 544 (Fed.Cir.1990). In *Manville*, the court held that a public use bar did not arise when the inventor installed the invention, an iris arm luminaire pole, in a highway rest stop for testing in Wyoming winter weather conditions, even though the inventor previously tested the invention in a R & D center. According to the court: "Prior to its testing in the winter environment, there really was no basis for confidence by the inventor that the invention would perform as intended, and hence no proven invention to disclose.... When durability in an outdoor environment is inherent to the purpose of an invention, then further testing to determine the invention's ability to serve that purpose will not subject the invention to a section 102(b) bar." *Id.* at 550–51.

4. *Market Testing.* Experimental use does not include market testing or attempts to develop buyer demand for the invention. Such a purpose falls into the category of commercial exploitation, rather than experimentation. *See, e.g., Western Marine Electronics, Inc. v. Furuno Electric Co., Ltd.*, 764 F.2d 840, 846 (Fed.Cir.1985). But compare *In re Smith*, 714 F.2d 1127 (Fed.Cir.1983) with *Grain Processing Corp. v. American Maize–Products Corp.*, 840 F.2d 902 (Fed.Cir.1988). In *Smith*, the invention in question was a vacuumable, powdered, carpet and room deodorizer. Prior to the critical date, the inventor's assignee conducted a test that involved having 76 customers try two versions of the product (one granular and one powdered) in their homes for a two week period. The Federal Circuit held that the test was a public use because it was designed primarily to gauge consumer preference and reaction. Data on the operation and usefulness of the product could have been obtained at the assignee's own facilities; and the consumers were placed under no restrictions as to use or confidentiality.

In contrast, the Federal Circuit, in *Grain Processing*, affirmed the district court's finding that the patentee's acts of shipping samples of the patented product (a starch hydrolysate) to a few food manufacturers did not constitute a public use. It was an "industry custom" to submit samples of proposed products to food manufacturers for determination of the product's utility; this testing was necessary because such products may interact adversely with other food ingredients in the manufacturers' products. Moreover, the testing "was short, very small quantities of the samples were shipped, and they were free of charge." *Id.* at 906.

5. *Burden of Proof.* Who bears the burden of proof on experimental use—the patentee or one challenging the validity of a patent? Generally, the burden of proving invalidity of a patent rests on one who challenges the validity of a patent claim, and this is extended to issues of public use and sale—even though the patentee's own, often private, acts are at issue. One school of thought is that experimental use is an exception or excuse for conduct by the inventor-patentee that otherwise would constitute a barring public use. From this it follows that the burden should be on the patentee to rebut any showing of public use more than a year before the patent application filing date with evidence of experimentation. Another school of thought is that experimentation "negates" public use, from which it would follow that the burden remains on the validity challenger. The Federal Circuit follows the negation school, but, as noted in *Lough*, a *prima facie* showing of public use by a challenger will shift to the patentee the burden of producing evidence of experimentation. This issue was discussed in *TP Laboratories supra*, 724 F.2d at 971–72, which both the majority and dissent cited in *Lough*:

> Under this analysis, it is incorrect to impose on the patent owner, as the trial court in this case did, the burden of proving that a "public use" was "experimental." These are not two separable issues. It is incorrect to ask: "Was it public use?" and then, "Was it experimental?" Rather, the court is faced with a single issue: Was it public use under § 102(b)?

> Thus, the court should have looked at all of the evidence put forth by both parties and should have decided whether the entirety of the evidence led to the conclusion that there had been "public use." This does not mean, of course, that the challenger has the burden of proving that the use is not experimental. Nor does it mean that the patent owner is relieved of explanation. It means that if a *prima facie* case is made of public use, the patent owner must be able to point to or must come forward with convincing evidence to counter that showing.

6. *The Uncertainty of the Experimental Use Doctrine.* Is the law relating to experimental use so complex that it creates an unacceptably high degree of uncertainty, thereby impeding planning and fostering litigation? This is a question that may well be asked about many areas of patent law. In *Lough*, can one argue that due to the unsophisticated nature of the inventor, the underlying policies of the on-sale bar were not threatened; that Lough was, as Judge Plager notes, not "market testing," but "product testing." The major policy concern on the minds of the majority was removing inventions from the public which the public has come to think were freely available. Does the majority give an adequate reason as to why this policy consideration outweighs the other policy considerations underlying the public use or on-sale bar (*e.g.* preventing the inventor from commercially exploiting his invention beyond the statutory time period)? Is the majority placing too much emphasis on the utilitarian justifications underlying our patent laws?

4.   ON-SALE BAR

In addition to barring a patent for an invention that was in public use, § 102(b) prevents one from obtaining a patent on an invention that was "on sale" for more than one year before the patent application filing date. Thus, public use and on-sale activities are separate events and one may occur without the other. In *Pfaff v. Wells Electronics*, explored below, the Supreme Court devoted its attention solely to the on-sale bar.

Pfaff v. Wells Electronics

525 U.S. 55 (1998).

■ STEVENS, J., delivered the opinion for a unanimous Court.

Section 102(b) of the Patent Act of 1952 provides that no person is entitled to patent an "invention" that has been "on sale" more than one year before filing a patent application. We granted certiorari to determine whether the commercial marketing of a newly invented product may mark the beginning of the 1–year period even though the invention has not yet been reduced to practice.[2]

I

On April 19, 1982, petitioner, Wayne Pfaff, filed an application for a patent on a computer chip socket. Therefore, April 19, 1981, constitutes the critical date for purposes of the on-sale bar of 35 U.S.C. § 102(b); if the 1–year period began to run before that date, Pfaff lost his right to patent his invention.

Pfaff commenced work on the socket in November 1980, when representatives of Texas Instruments asked him to develop a new device for mounting and removing semiconductor chip carriers. In response to this request, he prepared detailed engineering drawings that described the design, the dimensions, and the materials to be used in making the socket. Pfaff sent those drawings to a manufacturer in February or March 1981.

Prior to March 17, 1981, Pfaff showed a sketch of his concept to representatives of Texas Instruments. On April 8, 1981, they provided Pfaff with a written confirmation of a previously placed oral purchase order for 30,100 of his new sockets for a total price of $91,155. In accord with his normal practice, Pfaff did not make and test a prototype of the new device before offering to sell it in commercial quantities.[3]

The manufacturer took several months to develop the customized tooling necessary to produce the device, and Pfaff did not fill the order until July 1981. The evidence therefore indicates that Pfaff first reduced his invention to practice in the summer of 1981. The socket achieved substantial commercial success before Patent No. 4,491,377 (the '377 patent) issued to Pfaff on January 1, 1985.[4]

---

2. "A process is reduced to practice when it is successfully performed. A machine is reduced to practice when it is assembled adjusted and used. A manufacture is reduced to practice when it is completely manufactured. A composition of matter is reduced to practice when it is completely composed." *Corona Cord Tire Co. v. Dovan Chemical Corp.*, 276 U.S. 358, 383, 48 S.Ct. 380, 72 L.Ed. 610 (1928).

3. At his deposition, respondent's counsel engaged in the following colloquy with Pfaff:

"Q. Now, at this time [late 1980 or early 1981] did we [sic] have any prototypes developed or anything of that nature, working embodiment?

"A. No.

"Q. It was in a drawing. Is that correct?

"A. Strictly in a drawing. Went from the drawing to the hard tooling. That's the way I do my business.

"Q. 'Boom-boom'?

"A. You got it.

"Q. You are satisfied, obviously, when you come up with some drawings that it is going to go—'it works'?

"A. I know what I'm doing, yes, most of the time." App. 96–97.

4. Initial sales of the patented device were:

After the patent issued, petitioner brought an infringement action against respondent, Wells Electronics, Inc., the manufacturer of a competing socket. Wells prevailed on the basis of a finding of no infringement. When respondent began to market a modified device, petitioner brought this suit, alleging that the modifications infringed six of the claims in the '377 patent.

After a full evidentiary hearing before a Special Master, the District Court held that two of those claims (1 and 6) were invalid because they had been anticipated in the prior art. Nevertheless, the court concluded that four other claims (7, 10, 11, and 19) were valid and three (7, 10, and 11) were infringed by various models of respondent's sockets. App. to Pet. for Cert. 21a–22a. Adopting the Special Master's findings, the District Court rejected respondent's § 102(b) defense because Pfaff had filed the application for the '377 patent less than a year after reducing the invention to practice.

The Court of Appeals reversed, finding all six claims invalid. 124 F.3d 1429 (C.A.Fed.1997). Four of the claims (1, 6, 7, and 10) described the socket that Pfaff had sold to Texas Instruments prior to April 8, 1981. Because that device had been offered for sale on a commercial basis more than one year before the patent application was filed on April 19, 1982, the court concluded that those claims were invalid under § 102(b). That conclusion rested on the court's view that as long as the invention was "substantially complete at the time of sale," the 1–year period began to run, even though the invention had not yet been reduced to practice. *Id.*, at 1434. . . .

Because other courts have held or assumed that an invention cannot be "on sale" within the meaning of § 102(b) unless and until it has been reduced to practice, *see, e.g., Timely Products Corp. v. Arron,* 523 F.2d 288, 299–302 (C.A.2 1975); *Dart Industries, Inc. v. E.I. du Pont De Nemours & Co.,* 489 F.2d 1359, 1365, n. 11 (C.A.7 1973), *cert. denied,* 417 U.S. 933, 94 S.Ct. 2645, 41 L.Ed.2d 236 (1974), and because the text of § 102(b) makes no reference to "substantial completion" of an invention, we granted *certiorari.* 523 U.S. ___, 118 S.Ct. 1183, 140 L.Ed.2d 315 (1998).

II

The primary meaning of the word "invention" in the Patent Act unquestionably refers to the inventor's conception rather than to a physical embodiment of that idea. The statute does not contain any express requirement that an invention must be reduced to practice before it can be patented. Neither the statutory definition of the term in § 100[8] nor the

---

1981 $350,000

1982 $937,000

1983 $2,800,000

1984 $3,430,000

App. to Pet. for Cert. 223a.

8. Title 35 § 100, "Definitions," states:

"When used in this title unless the context otherwise indicates—

"(a) The term 'invention' means invention or discovery. . . ."

basic conditions for obtaining a patent set forth in § 101[9] make any mention of "reduction to practice." The statute's only specific reference to that term is found in § 102(g), which sets forth the standard for resolving priority contests between two competing claimants to a patent. That subsection provides:

> In determining priority of invention there shall be considered not only the respective dates of conception and reduction to practice of the invention, but also the reasonable diligence of one who was first to conceive and last to reduce to practice, from a time prior to conception by the other.

Thus, assuming diligence on the part of the applicant, it is normally the first inventor to conceive, rather than the first to reduce to practice, who establishes the right to the patent.

It is well settled that an invention may be patented before it is reduced to practice. In 1888, this Court upheld a patent issued to Alexander Graham Bell even though he had filed his application before constructing a working telephone. Chief Justice Waite's reasoning in that case merits quoting at length:

> It is quite true that when Bell applied for his patent he had never actually transmitted telegraphically spoken words so that they could be distinctly heard and understood at the receiving end of his line, but in his specification he did describe accurately and with admirable clearness his process, that is to say, the exact electrical condition that must be created to accomplish his purpose, and he also described, with sufficient precision to enable one of ordinary skill in such matters to make it, a form of apparatus which, if used in the way pointed out, would produce the required effect, receive the words, and carry them to and deliver them at the appointed place. The particular instrument which he had, and which he used in his experiments, did not, under the circumstances in which it was tried, reproduce the words spoken, so that they could be clearly understood, but the proof is abundant and of the most convincing character, that other instruments, carefully constructed and made exactly in accordance with the specification, without any additions whatever, have operated and will operate successfully. A good mechanic of proper skill in matters of the kind can take the patent and, by following the specification strictly, can, without more, construct an apparatus which, when used in the way pointed out, will do all that it is claimed the method or process will do. . . .

> The law does not require that a discoverer or inventor, in order to get a patent for a process, must have succeeded in bringing his art to the highest degree of perfection. It is enough if he describes his method with sufficient clearness and precision to enable those skilled in the matter to understand what the process is, and if he points out some practicable way of putting it into operation. *The Telephone Cases*, 126 U.S. 1, 535–536, 8 S.Ct. 778, 31 L.Ed. 863 (1888).

When we apply the reasoning of The Telephone Cases to the facts of the case before us today, it is evident that Pfaff could have obtained a patent on his novel socket when he accepted the purchase order from Texas

---

9. Section 101, "Inventions patentable," provides: "Whoever invents or discovers any new and useful process, machine, manufacture, or composition of matter, or any new and useful improvement thereof, may obtain a patent therefor, subject to the conditions and requirements of this title."

Instruments for 30,100 units. At that time he provided the manufacturer with a description and drawings that had "sufficient clearness and precision to enable those skilled in the matter" to produce the device. The parties agree that the sockets manufactured to fill that order embody Pfaff's conception as set forth in claims 1, 6, 7, and 10 of the '377 patent. We can find no basis in the text of § 102(b) or in the facts of this case for concluding that Pfaff's invention was not "on sale" within the meaning of the statute until after it had been reduced to practice.

III

Pfaff nevertheless argues that longstanding precedent, buttressed by the strong interest in providing inventors with a clear standard identifying the onset of the 1–year period, justifies a special interpretation of the word "invention" as used in § 102(b). We are persuaded that this nontextual argument should be rejected.

As we have often explained, most recently in *Bonito Boats, Inc. v. Thunder Craft Boats, Inc.*, 489 U.S. 141, 151, 109 S.Ct. 971, 103 L.Ed.2d 118 (1989), the patent system represents a carefully crafted bargain that encourages both the creation and the public disclosure of new and useful advances in technology, in return for an exclusive monopoly for a limited period of time. The balance between the interest in motivating innovation and enlightenment by rewarding invention with patent protection on the one hand, and the interest in avoiding monopolies that unnecessarily stifle competition on the other, has been a feature of the federal patent laws since their inception. As this Court explained in 1871:

> Letters patent are not to be regarded as monopolies ... but as public franchises granted to the inventors of new and useful improvements for the purpose of securing to them, as such inventors, for the limited term therein mentioned, the exclusive right and liberty to make and use and vend to others to be used their own inventions, as tending to promote the progress of science and the useful arts, and as matter of compensation to the inventors for their labor, toil, and expense in making the inventions, and reducing the same to practice for the public benefit, as contemplated by the Constitution and sanctioned by the laws of Congress. *Seymour v. Osborne*, 11 Wall. 516, 533–534.

Consistent with these ends, § 102 of the Patent Act serves as a limiting provision, both excluding ideas that are in the public domain from patent protection and confining the duration of the monopoly to the statutory term. *See, e.g., Frantz Mfg. Co. v. Phenix Mfg. Co.*, 457 F.2d 314, 320 (C.A.7 1972).

We originally held that an inventor loses his right to a patent if he puts his invention into public use before filing a patent application. "His voluntary act or acquiescence in the public sale and use is an abandonment of his right" *Pennock v. Dialogue*, 2 Pet. 1, 24, 7 L.Ed. 327 (1829) (Story, J.). A similar reluctance to allow an inventor to remove existing knowledge from public use undergirds the on-sale bar.

Nevertheless, an inventor who seeks to perfect his discovery may conduct extensive testing without losing his right to obtain a patent for his invention—even if such testing occurs in the public eye. The law has long recognized the distinction between inventions put to experimental use and products sold commercially. In 1878, we explained why patentability may turn on an inventor's use of his product.

> It is sometimes said that an inventor acquires an undue advantage over the public by delaying to take out a patent, inasmuch as he thereby preserves the monopoly to himself for a longer period than is allowed by the policy of the law; but this cannot be said with justice when the delay is occasioned by a bona fide effort to bring his invention to perfection, or to ascertain whether it will answer the purpose intended. His monopoly only continues for the allotted period, in any event; and it is the interest of the public, as well as himself, that the invention should be perfect and properly tested, before a patent is granted for it. *Any attempt to use it for a profit, and not by way of experiment, for a longer period than two years before the application, would deprive the inventor of his right to a patent. Elizabeth v. American Nicholson Pavement Co.*, 97 U.S. 126, 137, 24 L.Ed. 1000 (1877) (emphasis added).

The patent laws therefore seek both to protect the public's right to retain knowledge already in the public domain and the inventor's right to control whether and when he may patent his invention. The Patent Act of 1836, 5 Stat. 117, was the first statute that expressly included an on-sale bar to the issuance of a patent. Like the earlier holding in *Pennock*, that provision precluded patentability if the invention had been placed on sale at any time before the patent application was filed. In 1839, Congress ameliorated that requirement by enacting a 2–year grace period in which the inventor could file an application. 5 Stat. 353.

In *Andrews v. Hovey*, 123 U.S. 267, 274, 8 S.Ct. 101, 31 L.Ed. 160 (1887), we noted that the purpose of that amendment was "to fix a period of limitation which should be certain"; it required the inventor to make sure that a patent application was filed "within two years from the completion of his invention," *ibid*. In 1939, Congress reduced the grace period from two years to one year. 53 Stat. 1212.

Petitioner correctly argues that these provisions identify an interest in providing inventors with a definite standard for determining when a patent application must be filed. A rule that makes the timeliness of an application depend on the date when an invention is "substantially complete" seriously undermines the interest in certainty.[11] Moreover, such a rule finds no support in the text of the statute. Thus, petitioner's argument calls into question the standard applied by the Court of Appeals, but it does not persuade us that it is necessary to engraft a reduction to practice element into the meaning of the term "invention" as used in § 102(b).

---

11. The Federal Circuit has developed a multifactor, "totality of the circumstances" test to determine the trigger for the on-sale bar. *See, e.g., Micro Chemical, Inc. v. Great Plains Chemical Co.*, 103 F.3d 1538, 1544 (C.A.Fed.1997) (stating that, in determining whether an invention is on sale for purposes of 102(b), " 'all of the circumstances surrounding the sale or offer to sell, including the stage of development of the invention and the nature of the invention, must be considered and weighed against the policies underlying section 102(b)' "); see also *UMC Electronics Co. v. United States*, 816 F.2d 647, 656 (1987) (stating the on-sale bar "does not lend itself to formulation into a set of precise requirements"). As the Federal Circuit itself has noted, this test "has been criticized as unnecessarily vague." *Seal–Flex, Inc. v. Athletic Track & Court Construction*, 98 F.3d 1318, 1323, n. 2 (C.A.Fed.1996).

The word "invention" must refer to a concept that is complete, rather than merely one that is "substantially complete." It is true that reduction to practice ordinarily provides the best evidence that an invention is complete. But just because reduction to practice is sufficient evidence of completion, it does not follow that proof of reduction to practice is necessary in every case. Indeed, both the facts of the Telephone Cases and the facts of this case demonstrate that one can prove that an invention is complete and ready for patenting before it has actually been reduced to practice.[12]

We conclude, therefore, that the on-sale bar applies when two conditions are satisfied before the critical date. First, the product must be the subject of a commercial offer for sale. An inventor can both understand and control the timing of the first commercial marketing of his invention. The experimental use doctrine, for example, has not generated concerns about indefiniteness, and we perceive no reason why unmanageable uncertainty should attend a rule that measures the application of the on-sale bar of § 102(b) against the date when an invention that is ready for patenting is first marketed commercially. In this case the acceptance of the purchase order prior to April 8, 1981, makes it clear that such an offer had been made, and there is no question that the sale was commercial rather than experimental in character.

Second, the invention must be ready for patenting. That condition may be satisfied in at least two ways: by proof of reduction to practice before the critical date; or by proof that prior to the critical date the inventor had prepared drawings or other descriptions of the invention that were sufficiently specific to enable a person skilled in the art to practice the invention.[14] In this case the second condition of the on-sale bar is satisfied

---

12. Several of this Court's early decisions stating that an invention is not complete until it has been reduced to practice are best understood as indicating that the invention's reduction to practice demonstrated that the concept was no longer in an experimental phase. *See, e.g., Seymour v. Osborne*, 11 Wall. 516, 552, 20 L.Ed. 33 (1870) ("Crude and imperfect experiments are not sufficient to confer a right to a patent; but in order to constitute an invention, the party must have proceeded so far as to have reduced his idea to practice, and embodied it in some distinct form"); *Clark Thread Co. v. Willimantic Linen Co.*, 140 U.S. 481, 489, 11 S.Ct. 846, 35 L.Ed. 521 (1891) (describing how inventor continued to alter his thread winding machine until July 1858, when "he put it in visible form in the shape of a machine.... It is evident that the invention was not completed until the construction of the machine"); *Corona Cord Tire Co. v. Dovan Chemical Corp.*, 276 U.S., at 382–383, 48 S.Ct. 380 (stating that an invention did not need to be subsequently commercialized to constitute prior art after the inventor had finished his experimentation. "It was the fact that it would work with great activity as an accelerator that was the discovery, and that was all, and the necessary reduction to use is shown by instances making clear that it did so work, and was a completed discovery").

14. The Solicitor General has argued that the rule governing on-sale bar should be phrased somewhat differently. In his opinion, "if the sale or offer in question embodies the invention for which a patent is later sought, a sale or offer to sell that is primarily for commercial purposes and that occurs more than one year before the application renders the invention unpatentable. *Seal–Flex, Inc. v. Athletic Track and Court Constr.*, 98 F.3d 1318, 1325 (Fed.Cir.1996) (Bryson, J., concurring in part and concurring in the result)." It is true that evidence satisfying this test might be sufficient to prove that the invention was ready for patenting at the time of the sale if it is clear that no aspect of the invention was developed after the critical date. However, the possibility of additional development after the offer for

because the drawings Pfaff sent to the manufacturer before the critical date fully disclosed the invention.

The evidence in this case thus fulfills the two essential conditions of the on-sale bar. As succinctly stated by Learned Hand:

> [I]t is a condition upon an inventor's right to a patent that he shall not exploit his discovery competitively after it is ready for patenting; he must content himself with either secrecy, or legal monopoly. *Metallizing Engineering Co. v. Kenyon Bearing & Auto Parts Co.*, 153 F.2d 516, 520 (C.A.2 1946).

The judgment of the Court of Appeals finds support not only in the text of the statute but also in the basic policies underlying the statutory scheme, including § 102(b). When Pfaff accepted the purchase order for his new sockets prior to April 8, 1981, his invention was ready for patenting. The fact that the manufacturer was able to produce the socket using his detailed drawings and specifications demonstrates this fact. Furthermore, those sockets contained all the elements of the invention claimed in the '377 patent. Therefore, Pfaff's '377 patent is invalid because the invention had been on sale for more than one year in this country before he filed his patent application. Accordingly, the judgment of the Court of Appeals is affirmed.

It is so ordered.

NOTES

1. *It Has Been Some Time.* The 1998 *Pfaff* decision is the first Supreme Court decision on the Section 102(b) statutory bars to patenting since 1939, see *Electric Storage Battery v. Shimadzu*, 307 U.S. 5 (1939), and the first ever to focus specifically on the "on sale" bar. The Federal Circuit has considered the "on sale" bar many times in recent years, and its opinions reflect deep divisions among the court's judges.

2. *The "On–Sale" Bar—The Test.* In *Pfaff*, the Supreme Court set forth a two-part test. First, "the product must be the subject of a commercial offer for sale;" second, "the invention must be ready for patenting."

    a.   *"Commercial Offer for Sale."* Prior to Pfaff there was some confusion as to what constituted an offer under § 102(b). See *RCA Corp. v. Data General Corp.*, 887 F.2d 1056 (Fed.Cir.1989) and *Evans Cooling Systems, Inc. v. General Motors Corp.*, 125 F.3d 1448 (Fed.Cir.1997). But in *Group One, Ltd. v. Hallmark Cards, Inc.*, 254 F.3d 1041, 1046–7 (Fed.Cir.2001), the Federal Circuit, applying contract principles, attempted to resolve this issue:

> [T]o the extent it was believed that something less than an offer to sell as understood in general commercial transactions was sufficient to trigger the on-sale bar, it is likely that such belief can no longer be the law. The Supreme Court in *Pfaff v. Wells Electronics,* swept away this court's "totality of the circumstances" analysis of the on-sale bar and replaced it with a two-part test: "First, the product must be the subject of a commercial offer for sale.... Second, the invention must be ready for patenting." *Id.* at 67. Though the Court did not elaborate on what was meant by "a

---

sale in these circumstances counsels against adoption of the rule proposed by the Solicitor General.

commercial office for sale"—the issue not being directly presented—the language used strongly suggests that the offer must meet the level of an offer for sale in the contract sense, one that would be understood as such in the commercial community. Such a reading leaves no room for "activity which does not rise to the level of a formal 'offer' under contract law principles."

Effective January 1, 1996, "offer to sell" was added as an act of patent infringement. 35 U.S.C. § 271(a). It will be interesting to see whether courts will apply the policy-driven standards for "on sale" under Section 102(b) to determining what constitutes an infringing "offer to sell" under Section 271(a).

(i) *Subject Matter of the Sale.* It is important to remember that *Pfaff* "did not remove the requirement that the subject matter of the commercial offer for sale 'be something within the scope of the claim.' " *Scaltech Inc. v. Retec/Tetra, L.L.C.*, 178 F.3d 1378, 1383 (Fed.Cir.1999). The Federal Circuit has elaborated upon the test set forth in *Pfaff*. According to the court, the party invoking the on-sale bar:

> must demonstrate by clear and convincing evidence that ... the subject matter of the sale or offer to sell fully anticipated the claimed invention or would have rendered the claimed invention obvious by its addition to the prior art.

Tec Air, Inc. v. Denso Mfg. Michigan, Inc., 192 F.3d 1353, 1358 (Fed.Cir.1999).

The Federal Circuit has also distinguished between the sale of, on the one hand, tangible items such as a product or composition of matter and, and on the other hand, the sale of a process, which is a series of steps. *See In re Kollar*, 286 F.3d 1326 (Fed.Cir.2002). According to the court:

> A process ... is a different kind of invention; it consists of acts, rather than a tangible item. It consists of doing something, and therefore has to be carried out or performed. A process is thus not sold in the same sense as is a tangible item. "Know-how" describing what the process consists of and how the process should be carried out may be sold in the sense that the buyer acquires knowledge of the process and obtains the freedom to carry it out pursuant to the terms of the transaction. However, such a transaction is not a "sale" of the invention within the meaning of §§ 102(b) because the process has not been carried out or performed as a result of the transaction. The same applies to a license to a patent covering a process.

Id. at 1332. The court noted that it could not "articulate in advance what would constitute a sale of a process" for 102(b) purposes. What it did say, however, was that while the sale of a product made by the process or performing the process itself for consideration would trigger the on-sale bar, "licensing the invention, under which development of the claimed process would have to occur before the process is successfully commercialized" would not. *Id.* at 1333.

(ii) *Assignments and Licenses.* An inventor who sells his patent rights (assigns the invention) to raise money to develop and perfect the invention does not invoke the on-sale bar. *See Moleculon Research Corp. v. CBS, Inc.*, 793 F.2d 1261, 1267 (Fed.Cir.1986) ("an assignment or sale of the rights in the invention and potential patent rights is not a sale of 'the invention' within the meaning of 102(b).... Such a result comports with the policies underlying the on sale bar ... and with the business realities ordinarily surrounding a corporation's prosecution of patent applications for inventors."); *United States Electric Lighting Co. v. Consolidated Electric*, 33 Fed. 869, 870 (C.C.S.D.N.Y. 1888) ("what was put on sale, if anything was, was the patent itself, and not the thing patented. The patent is the mere right to exclude others from practicing the invention. The invention itself is another thing"). Also, a transfer of know-how requiring further development or an offer to license the patent does not typically give rise to the on-sale bar because 102(b) bars a sale, not a license, of the patented product, and a license usually involves prospective activity. *See In re Kollar*, 286 F.3d 1330–31 ("We have held that merely granting a license to an invention, without more, does not trigger the on-sale bar") (citing *Mas–Hamilton Group v. LaGard, Inc.*, 156 F.3d 1206, 1216–7 (Fed.Cir. 1998)). Moreover, the Federal Circuit has held that there was no commercial offer for sale where the patentee had provided potential customers with samples of a product, without providing any contract terms, because the patentee had not manifested sufficient willingness to be contractually bound under general contract law. *See 3M v. Chemque*, 303 F.3d 1294 (Fed.Cir.2002).

The *Kollar* court was quick to point out, however, that not all licenses are exempt from the on-sale bar:

> We use the term "license" here to refer to rights under a patent, not to describe a commercial transaction arranged as a "license" or a "lease" of a product or a device that may or may not have been patented. *See Group One, Ltd. v. Hallmark Cards, Inc.*, 254 F.3d 1041, 1049 n.2,(Fed.Cir.2001) (distinguishing between "rights in a patent" and the "sale of an interest that entitles the purchaser to possession and use" of an embodiment of an invention that is unrelated to any patent). In certain situations, a "license" in the latter sense of the word may be tantamount to a sale (*e.g.*, a standard computer software license), whereupon the bar of § 102(b) would be triggered because "[t]he product is ... just as immediately transferred to the 'buyer' as if it were sold." Id. at 1053 (Lourie, J., concurring). However, as explained below, a "license" that merely grants rights under a patent cannot *per se* trigger the application of the on-sale bar.

Id. at 1331, n.3. For a case distinguishing *Kollar, see Minton v. National Ass'n of Securities Dealers, Inc.*, 336 F.3d 1373 (Fed.Cir.2003) ("Whereas Kollar merely conveyed know-how to Celanese, Minton conveyed to Starks a fully operational computer program implementing and thus embodying the claimed method. Also, Minton conveyed with TEXCEN a warranty of workability, whereas Kollar's process had to be developed for commercialization").

b. *"Ready for Patenting."* The Supreme Court affirmed that an invention need not be reduced to practice in order to be subject to the on-sale bar. But the Court disapproved of the Federal Circuit's "totality of circumstances" and "substantial completion" tests, suggesting that these tests were impermissibly indefinite. Rather, the invention has to be "ready for patenting," and this can be shown by proof of (1) reduction to practice, or (2) a description of the claimed invention that was sufficiently specific to enable a person skilled in the art to practice the invention.

In a post-*Pfaff* case, the Federal Circuit has rejected the notion that conception alone is enough to prove "ready for patenting," despite *Pfaff's* language that "invention ... unquestionably refers to the inventor's conception rather than to a physical embodiment of [the] idea." *Pfaff*, 525 U.S. at 60. In *Space Systems/Loral, Inc. v. Lockheed Martin Corp.*, 271 F.3d 1076, 1080 (Fed.Cir.2001), the court stated:

> [T]he [Supreme] Court did not hold that a conception, having neither a reduction to practice nor an enabling description, is ready for patenting as a matter of law. To be "ready for patenting" the inventor must be able to prepare a patent application, that is, to provide an enabling disclosure as required by 35 U.S.C § 112. For a complex concept.... a bare conception that has not been enabled is not a completed invention ready for patenting. Although conception can occur before the inventor has verified that his idea will work, *see Burroughs Wellcome Co. v. Barr Labs., Inc.*, 40 F.3d 1223, 1228 (Fed.Cir.1994), when development and verification are needed

in order to prepare a patent application that complies with § 112, the invention is not yet ready for patenting.

3. *Seller's Knowledge.* With respect to the inventor's (or seller's) knowledge of the product offered for sale, the Federal Circuit has adopted more of an objective test. In *Scaltech Inc. v. Retec/Tetra*, 178 F.3d 1378, 1383 (Fed.Cir.1999), the Federal Circuit held that "there is no requirement that the offer specifically identify these [claim] limitations.... Nor is there a requirement that [the patentee] must have recognized the significance of these limitations at the time of offer." In *Abbott Laboratories v. Geneva Pharmaceuticals, Inc.*, 182 F.3d 1315, 1318–19 (Fed.Cir. 1999), the patentee argued that the on-sale bar does not apply because the seller did not have knowledge of the exact nature of the invention sold, and therefore, there was no conception. The Federal Circuit disagreed:

> The fact that the claimed material was sold under circumstances in which no question existed that it was useful means that it was reduced to practice. In any event, this is not a priority dispute in which conception is a critical issue. The sale of the material in question obviates any need for inquiry into conception.... It is well settled in the law that there is no requirement that a sales offer specifically identify all the characteristics of an invention offered for sale or that the parties recognize the significance of all these characteristics at the time of the offer.

Moreover, inventor confidence or lack thereof in whether the invention would work for its intended purpose is irrelevant in determining whether the invention is "ready for patenting." *See Robotic Vision Systems, Inc. v. View Engineering, Inc.*, 249 F.3d 1307, 1312 (Fed.Cir.2001) ("notably absent from [the *Pfaff*] test is a requirement that an inventor have complete confidence that his invention work will work for its intended purpose").

4. *Is the "Ready for Patenting" Test Any More Definite than the Federal Circuit's "Substantial Completion" Test?* Why is certainty so important with respect to § 102(b)? Consider Judge Smith's dissent in *UMC Electronics Co. v. United States*, 816 F.2d 647, 664 (Fed.Cir.1987), wherein he expressed concerns about the majority's holding that reduction to practice of the claimed invention is not required to invoke the on-sale bar:

> It is the users of the patent system who will suffer the impact of the panel majority decision. The question is not theoretical; it is of great practical importance.

> Those inventors who have sought financing, or who have contacted potential customers, or who have engaged in other normal business activities before they have made a workable device will not know how the time limit for filing a patent application will be measured or where the line will be drawn between raw idea and proved invention. Inventors do not normally try to patent something they have not yet found workable. The patent law, and particularly section 112, does not favor it. Most inventors do not hire a patent lawyer until they have something that works, by which time, according to the panel majority, it may be too late.

> * * *

> It is not clear why this change is being wrought on the community of inventors and the public without providing some alternative measure of certainty. The "all circumstances" rule evoked by the panel majority means that the critical question in more and more cases can only be answered with finality by a judicial determination in which there is no further appeal.

What do you think Judge Smith's reaction would have been to Justice Stevens's opinion in *Pfaff*?

5.   *Experimental Use as Applied to the On–Sale Bar.* The Supreme Court in *Pfaff* preserved the experimental use doctrine. *Pfaff*, 525 U.S. at 64 ("[A]n inventor who seeks to perfect his discovery may conduct extensive testing without losing his right to obtain a patent for his invention—even if such testing occurs in the public eye. The law has long recognized the distinction between inventions put to experimental use and products sold commercially"). Thus, although the experimental use doctrine usually arises in connection with the public use bar, it may also extend to the on-sale bar, provided that the inventor exercise control over the invention and the transaction is a reasonable means of testing the invention. Moreover, one may "escape the on-sale bar if the sale was 'merely incidental to the primary purpose of experimentation.'" *Aqua Marine Supply v. Aim Machining, Inc.*, 247 F.3d 1216, 1218 (Fed.Cir.2001); *In re Theis*, 610 F.2d 786, 793 (CCPA 1979). If experimental use is found, it follows that the invention was not "ready for patenting" under step two of *Pfaff*.

The court has identified 13 factors for assessing experimental use. These include: (1) the necessity for public testing, (2) the amount of control over the experiment retained by the inventor, (3) the nature of the invention, (4) the length of the test period, (5) whether payment was made, (6) whether there was a secrecy obligation, (7) whether records of the experiment were kept, (8) who conducted the experiment, ... (9) the degree of commercial exploitation during testing[,] ... (10) whether the invention reasonably requires evaluation under actual conditions of use, (11) whether testing was systematically performed, (12) whether the inventor continually monitored the invention during testing, and (13) the nature of contacts made with potential customers.... *EZ Dock v. Schafer Sys., Inc.*, 276 F.3d 1347, 1357 (Fed.Cir.2002) (Linn, J., concurring).

Although the court first determines whether a device sold was an embodiment of a claimed invention, in *Allen Engineering Corp. v. Bartell Industries, Inc.*, 299 F.3d 1336 (Fed.Cir.2002), the Federal Circuit began its analysis of the on-sale bar issue by pointing out that "in some cases, it may be more efficient to first assess experimental use negation of sales allegedly made, as 'adequate proof of experimentation negates a statutory bar.'" *Id.* at 1353 (quoting *EZ Dock v. Schafer Sys., Inc.*, 276 F.3d 1347, 1352 (Fed.Cir.2002)). According to the court:

> [W]hat is important to an assessment of the commercial versus experimental significance of a sale is not necessarily the posture of the invention's overall development, but the nature or purpose of the particular use to which the invention that is the subject of that sale is to be put....
>
> Thus, the question posed by the experimental use doctrine, assessed under the first prong of the two-part on-sale bar test of *Pfaff*, is not whether the invention was under development, subject to testing, or otherwise still in its experimental stage at the time of the asserted sale. Instead, the question is whether the transaction constituting the sale was "not incidental to the primary purpose of experimentation," i.e., whether the primary purpose of the inventor at the time of the sale, as determined from an objective evaluation of the facts surrounding the transaction, was to conduct experimentation.... As noted, once the invention is reduced to practice, there can be no experimental use negation. But up to that point, regardless of the stage of development of the invention, and quite apart from the possible satisfaction of the second prong of the *Pfaff* test, the inventor is free to experiment, test, and otherwise engage in activities to determine if the invention is suitable for its intended purpose and thus satisfactorily complete.

Id. at 1354.

See also Atlanta Attachment Co. v. Leggett & Platt, Inc., 516 F.3d 1361 (Fed.Cir. 2008).

6. *Commercialization Versus Experimentation.* Was the Supreme Court naive in assuming, apparently, that there is a clear distinction between commercialization, on the one hand, and experimentation and development on the other hand? Often the two go hand-in-hand, especially when an inventor is working with a particular customer. In *Weatherchem Corp. v. J.L. Clark, Inc.*, 163 F.3d 1326 (Fed.Cir.1998), the first Federal Circuit decision to consider *Pfaff*'s impact, the court held that the "ready for patenting" test was met, even though the patentee "continued to fine-tune features not claimed in the patent," because the patentee had produced drawings that showed all the limitations of the patent claims that were specific enough to enable an art-skilled person to practice the invention and because a customer had ordered a commercial quantity of the invention before the critical date, "showing its confidence that the invention was complete and operative."

Is there a viable or useful distinction between (a) holding that there is no on-sale bar because there is not yet an "invention" to be offered, that is, the invention is not "complete" as that term is used in *Pfaff* and (b) holding that there is no on-sale bar because the invention is undergoing experimentation? In *Seal–Flex, Inc. v. Athletic Track and Court Construction*, 98 F.3d 1318 (Fed.Cir.1996), there was clearly experimental activity but there may also have been purely commercial activity (the offer to sell) that was not related to the experimentation. The majority refused to apply the on-sale bar because the invention was in development at the time of the sale. In a concurrence, however, Judge Bryson observed that

> [a]n inventor should not be able to sell his invention for commercial purposes, but avoid the on-sale bar by separately conducting tests on his invention. As I view the case, it is therefore irrelevant to the status of the Logan transaction that Maxfield was continuing to evaluate the performance of the Seal–Flex process at the Beloit track. If the Logan transaction constituted an offer to make a commercial sale of a product made by the later-patented process, the on-sale bar should be triggered even if Maxfield was concurrently conducting tests on his process at another facility.

98 F.3d at 1325. Does Judge Bryson do away with this distinction and get to the heart of the matter? In a post-*Pfaff* case, the Federal Circuit seems to have put the experimental use defense to rest. *See Scaltech Inc. v. Retec/Tetra*, 178 F.3d 1378, 1384 n.1 (Fed.Cir.1999) ("Scaltech argues that its invention was still experimental at the time Scaltech was soliciting an opportunity to practice the invention. This argument fails because it is premised on the 'experimental stage' doctrine which has been rejected by both this court and the Supreme Court. Commercial exploitation, if not incidental to the primary purpose of experimentation, will result in an on sale bar, even if the invention was still in its experimental stage.").

7. *Joint Development—Offer to Independent Entity.* An offer or sale transaction may be between related entities, for example, a manufacturer and its wholly—or partially—owned distributing subsidiary or between parties to a joint development agreement. For demonstrative cases that draw fine distinctions as is typical in the on sale and public use law, compare *Buildex Inc. v. Kason Industries, Inc.*, 849 F.2d 1461 (Fed.Cir.1988) (customer under exclusive supply contract in which the customer contributed to development expenses is a bar; "this court has never recognized a 'joint development' exception") with *Continental Can Company USA, Inc. v. Monsanto Co.*, 948 F.2d 1264 (Fed.Cir.1991) (a device produced as part of a later-terminated manufacturer-customer joint development project and "cloaked in confidentiality" was not "on sale"). In a post-*Pfaff* case, the Federal Circuit reiterated that it has " 'never recognized a "joint development" exception to the "on-sale" bar.' " In *Brasseler, U.S.A. v. Stryker Sales Corp.*, 182 F.3d 888 (Fed.Cir.1999), the patentee argued that the on-sale bar should not apply because the buyer and the inventor were joint developers and that both entities employed one or more of the named inventors. The court rejected this argument and declined "to establish a new exception" to the on-sale bar. The court, citing *Buildex*, stated that "we have 'never recognized a joint development exception to the on sale bar.' " *Id.* at 890. There is also no "supplier" exception. *See Special Devices, Inc. v. OEA, Inc.*, 270 F.3d 1353, 1355 (Fed.Cir.2001).

Blame within the Patentee's Domain? Failing the Patentability Requirements of Written Description and On–Sale Bar

F. Scott Kieff.*
July 15, 2003.

As with written description, to best understand the recent evolution in the case law of the on-sale bar, it is important to see that rule in context. As part of the core requirement in 35 USC § 102 that the claimed invention not be within the prior art, the U.S. patent system allows patentees a grace period for their own disclosures to be disclosed to the public for one year before the filing of a patent application: such a disclosure is not treated as being within the prior art.[28] The beginning of this grace period is triggered by public use or sale.

The question for this part of the essay is what the recent case law tells us about how to determine whether the on-sale bar has been triggered. The central lesson for the savvy strategist is rather old and simple: be absolute-

---

* Excerpted from presentation to the "Second Annual Symposium on Hot Topics in Patent Law," sponsored by George Mason University School of Law and Banner & Witcoff, Ltd., in Arlington, Virginia.

28. For a thorough review of the rules governing novelty over the prior art and the various statutory bars see [the rest of the materials in Chapter 4]. For a brief overview of the theory and comparative law aspects of such grace periods, see F. Scott Kieff, *Book Review: Joseph Straus, Grace Periods and the European and International Patent Law: Analysis of Key Legal and Socio–Economic Aspects*, 34 INT'L REV. INDUS. PROP. & COPYRIGHT L. (IIC) 347 (2003), and also 4 ENGAGE 160 (2003):

> According to some, a patent system in which there is no grace period may provide incentives for decreased rate of disclosure of new technologies and a decrease in the over-all value of patents. The decreased rate of disclosure under a system lacking a grace period would be due to the need to keep potentially patentable information unpublished before filing the patent application. Under such a system, any such pre-filing publication would be treated as prior art. The decrease in over-all value of patents under such a system would be due to the fear of unavoidable pre-filing disclosures lurking in the history of every patent.

> According to others, a patent system in which there is a grace period may provide incentives for decreased early investment in using new technologies. This decreased investment under a system having a grace period would be due to potential fear that such new technology might later become subject to someone else's patent application, which might in time issue as a valid patent.

For a more detailed, but still conveniently short, discussion including a collection of sources and empirical data see JOSEPH STRAUS, GRACE PERIODS AND THE EUROPEAN AND INTERNATIONAL PATENT LAW: ANALYSIS OF KEY LEGAL AND SOCIO-ECONOMIC ASPECTS, Published by the Max Plank Institute for Foreign and International Patent, Copyright, and Competition Law, Printed by Verlag C.H. Beck, Munich, 2001, ISBN 3–406–47667–8.

ly certain to file a patent application—of course in view of the earlier discussion with adequate disclosure to support the claims that may be eventually desired—within one year of any activity that might trigger the on-sale bar.

The recent chapter in the long story relating to the on-sale bar begins with the 1998 Supreme Court decision in *Pfaff*, which held that the on-sale bar is triggered when more than one year before filing of the patent application, the claimed invention was both (1) the subject of a "commercial" offer for sale, and (2) "ready for patenting," which may be shown either by an actual reduction to practice or by proof of the preparation of an enabling description of the invention.[29]

Over the past year, there have been relatively few of Federal Circuit decisions applying *Pfaff*. Some issues have been resolved. Others remain open.

In July of 2002, in *Netscape*, the court continued its practice of looking to the "principles of general contract law" to determine prong 1, commercial offer for sale, of the test from *Pfaff*.[30] The court also continued its practice of looking to determine whether there fairly can be said to have been two distinct parties to the putative commercial offer for sale.[31] To answer that question the court looked to "whether the seller so controls the purchaser that the invention remains out of the public's hands."[32]

In early August of 2002, in *Allen Engineering*, the court began its analysis of the on-sale bar issue by pointing out that "in some cases, it may be more efficient to first assess experimental use negation of sales allegedly made, as 'adequate proof of experimentation negates a statutory bar.' "[33] According to the court,

> [W]hat is important to an assessment of the commercial versus experimental significance of a sale is not necessarily the posture of the invention's overall development, but the nature or purpose of the particular use to which the invention that is the subject of that sale is to be put.

---

29. Pfaff v. Wells Electronics, Inc., 525 U.S. 55 (1998) (rejecting the Federal Circuit's subjective "totality of the circumstances" test). It must be kept in mind that art determined to satisfy any subsection of § 102 is available for consideration of whether it alone fully discloses the claimed subject matter and therefore invalidates under § 102 or whether its disclosure can be combined with other prior art to invalidate under § 103. In addition, although outside of the twelve month window of this essay, note should be made of the decision from the Federal Circuit in February of 2002 in *Dana*, which held that before any meaningful validity analysis of this type can be conducted the patent claim in issue must be construed. Dana Corp. v. American Axle & Manufacturing, Inc., 279 F.3d 1372 (Fed. Cir, Feb. 12, 2002).

30. Netscape Communications Corp. v. Konrad, 295 F.3d 1315, 1323–25 (Fed.Cir. Jul. 9, 2002) (citing Group One, Ltd. v. Hallmark Cards, Inc., 254 F.3d 1041, 1048 (Fed.Cir.2001)).

31. Id. at 1324 (citing In re Caveney, 761 F.2d 671, 676 (Fed.Cir.1985)).

32. Id. (citing Ferag v. Quipp, Inc., 45 F.3d 1562, 1567 (Fed.Cir.1995) (citing In re Caveney, 761 F.2d at 676)). Although outside of the twelve month window of this essay, note should be made of the Federal Circuit decision from April 2002 in *In re Kollar*, which held that a mere license of the claimed invention may not count as a "sale." In re Kollar, 286 F.3d 1326 (Fed.Cir., Apr 11, 2002).

33. Allen Engineering Corp. v. Bartell Industries, Inc., 299 F.3d 1336, 1353 (Fed.Cir. Aug. 1, 2002) (quoting EZ Dock v. Schafer Sys., Inc., 276 F.3d 1347, 1352 (Fed.Cir.2002)).

Thus, the question posed by the experimental use doctrine, assessed under the first prong of the two-part on-sale bar test of *Pfaff*, is not whether the invention was under development, subject to testing, or otherwise still in its experimental stage at the time of the asserted sale. Instead, the question is whether the transaction constituting the sale was "not incidental to the primary purpose of experimentation," *i.e.*, whether the primary purpose of the inventor at the time of the sale, as determined from an objective evaluation of the facts surrounding the transaction, was to conduct experimentation. As noted, once the invention is reduced to practice, there can be no experimental use negation. But up to that point, regardless of the stage of development of the invention, and quite apart from the possible satisfaction of the second prong of the *Pfaff* test, the inventor is free to experiment, test, and otherwise engage in activities to determine if the invention is suitable for its intended purpose and thus satisfactorily complete.[34]

The court admonished that a determination of the experimental use negation requires consideration of the thirteen factors reviewed in Judge Linn's concurring opinion in *EZ Dock*.[35] Such a multi-factorial test may leave some room for further development.

At the end of August in 2002, in *3M v. Chemque*, the Federal Circuit held that there was no commercial offer for sale sufficient to trigger the on-sale bar where the patentee had provided potential customers with samples of a product, without providing any contract terms, because the patentee had not manifested sufficient willingness to be contractually bound under general contract law principles.[36] The court relied upon the somewhat similar case from the end of December in 2001, *Micrel*, in which no commercial offer was found because although the patentee had distributed data sheets to potential customers listing many of the features of the later-patented product; conducted a sales conference to provide information regarding the upcoming product; and received purchase orders offering to buy the devices before their official release date, none of these facts, taken alone or together, established the basic components of a willingness to be bound under general principles of contract law and instead were merely indications of "preliminary negotiations."[37] Petitions for certiorari were filed in both cases but *3M v. Chemque* was dismissed after settlement in April of 2003[38] and certiorari was denied in *Micrel* in May of 2003.[39]

34. Id. at 1354 (quoting EZ Dock, 276 F.3d at 1356–57) (Linn, J., concurring) (internal citations omitted).

35. Id. These factors are: "(1) the necessity for public testing, (2) the amount of control over the experiment retained by the inventor, (3) the nature of the invention, (4) the length of the test period, (5) whether payment was made, (6) whether there was a secrecy obligation, (7) whether records of the experiment were kept, (8) who conducted the experiment, and (9) the degree of commercial exploitation during testing.... (10) whether the invention reasonably requires evaluation under actual conditions of use, (11) whether testing was systematically performed, (12) whether the inventor continually monitored the invention during testing, and (13) the nature of contacts made with potential customers." EZ Dock, 276 F.3d at 1357 (Linn, J., concurring) (internal citations omitted).

36. Minnesota Min. & Mfg. Co. v. Chemque, Inc., 303 F.3d 1294, 1307–08 (Fed.Cir. Aug. 30, 2002).

37. Linear Technology Corp. v. Micrel, Inc., 275 F.3d 1040, 1049–52 (Fed.Cir.2002).

38. Chemque, Inc. v. Minnesota Min. & Mfg. Co., 123 S.Ct. 1779 (U.S. Apr. 9, 2003) (dismissing certiorari under Supreme Court Rule 46.1 for settlement).

Importantly, this emphasis on general contract law principles that look to a willingness to be bound differs from some prior Federal Circuit case law that had focused on overall commercial activity.[40]

In March of 2003 in *Lacks Industries*, the Federal Circuit signaled that there may be some diversity in viewpoints about how to implement the general contract law principles-based approach discussed above.[41] The court made clear that this question of general contract law would be a matter of Federal Circuit law, not state law.[42] But it is not entirely clear how exactly that test will be applied. The majority opinion, authored by Judge Michel and joined in pertinent part by Judge Clevenger, remanded the case for further fact finding about industry practice to help decide whether there was a commercial offer for sale.[43] In dissent, Judge Newman argued that "industry-specific, local, and subjective criteria are a regression toward the imprecision of the discredited 'totality of the circumstances,' a standard purposefully rejected by the Supreme Court in *Pfaff*."[44] To the extant general contract law principles require consideration of industry practice the disagreement between the two opinions in this case is illusory. To the extent the majority is urging some greater role for industry practice the disagreement is alive and might be outcome determinative in some cases.

SIDE BAR

The Stage of Development of an Invention Subject to the On–Sale Bar to Patentability

Manya S. Deehr & William C. Rooklidge*

I. INTRODUCTION

We are all too aware of the fundamental law of thermodynamics predicting the ineluctable flow of the universe toward entropy. Nothing in patent law demonstrates this principle more clearly than a review of the common law that has developed around the on-sale bar of 35 U.S.C. Section 102(b). This statute requires an inventor to file a patent application within one year after placing the invention on sale in the United States. Specifically, the "on sale bar" provision of the Patent Act provides that "[a] person shall be entitled to a patent unless ... (b) the invention was ... on-sale in this country, more than one year prior to the date of the application for patent in the United States...."[1] In other words, if the inventor delays filing for more than a year after an on-sale activity,

---

39. Micrel, Inc. v. Linear Technology Corp., 123 S.Ct. 2129 (U.S. May 19, 2003) (denying certiorari).

40. *Compare*, RCA Corp. v. Data General Corp., 887 F.2d 1056 (Fed.Cir.1989) (less than a commercial offer may suffice), *with* Group One, Ltd. v. Hallmark Cards, Inc., 254 F.3d 1041, 1046 (Fed.Cir.2001) (commercial contractual indicia required under *Pfaff*). *See also*, Micrel, 275 F. 3d at 1048 (recognizing that *Group One* effectively over-rules *RCA* based on *Pfaff*).

41. Lacks Industries, Inc. v. McKechnie Vehicle Components USA, Inc., 322 F.3d 1335, 1347–48 (Fed.Cir. Mar. 13, 2003).

42. Id. at 1347.

43. Id. at 1348.

44. Id. at 1352 (Newman, J., concurring in part and dissenting in part).

she loses the right to a United States patent on the invention subject to the activity.

While the language of the statute is quite simple, application of the on-sale bar has proven quite complicated. In part, this complexity stems from the competing policies underlying the bar. The Federal Circuit has identified the policies underlying the on-sale-bar as: (1) discouraging the removal from the public domain of inventions that the public reasonably has come to believe are freely available; (2) favoring the prompt and widespread disclosure of inventions; (3) allowing the inventor a reasonable amount of time following the public use or sales activity to determine the potential economic value of patent protection; and (4) prohibiting the inventor from commercially exploiting the invention for longer than the statutorily defined one-year grace period.[2] Courts have long struggled to reconcile these policies with the language of the statute. The focal point of that struggle has been on interpreting the meaning of the term "invention" for the purposes of the statute.

The term "invention" has been attributed many different interpretations even in the relatively narrow confines of patent law. The Patent Act sheds little light on the issue; it defines "invention" as "invention or discovery."[3] Courts and commentators alike have labored to settle on a universally applicable definition of "invention."[4] As a result, one could find support for almost any interpretation of "invention" for the purpose of applying the on-sale bar. The term could, and has been argued to, mean anywhere from the subject matter of the barring activity to any of a number of stages of development of the invention, including conception, reduction to practice, ready for patenting and commercial availability. The courts have attempted to identify the earliest stage of development at which the on-sale bar may be applied—a stage that balances the policies underlying the on-sale bar and, at the same time, provides a bright-line standard. Over a hundred years of reasoning have, however, resulted in a complicated knot of logic and abandoned rationalization, ultimately resulting in what amounts to a highly subjective case-by-case determination.

In an apparent attempt to cut the Gordian knot of uncertainty, the United States Supreme Court in *Pfaff v. Wells Electronics, Inc.*[5] introduced a new test identifying that an invention is an "invention" for the purposes of the on-sale bar when it was "ready for patenting"[6], not surprisingly, the test quickly became known as the "ready for patenting test." As with most other approaches, however, the ready for patenting test has proven in application just as subjective as the predecessor tests rejected by the courts. It finds no support in the policies underlying the on-sale bar, cannot be applied universally and appears to require nothing more than a documented conception—a standard which courts previously considered and rejected. In order to understand the difficulties of establishing a stage of development in the spectrum of invention, and, hence, the challenges of implementing the ready for patenting test, it is important to first revisit the development of the on-sale bar doctrine.

II. THE DEVELOPMENT OF THE DOCTRINE

Before the twentieth century, the on-sale bar did not impose a "stage of development" requirement for application of the on-sale bar. Patent protection was barred if the subject matter was the subject of sale or offer for sale more than a year before the patent application was filed, regard-less of the stage of development of that subject matter.[7] If the inventor—or anyone else—sold an embodiment of her invention, regardless of how crudely constructed and poorly tested, and then delayed filing a patent application for more than a year, she could not obtain a patent. As one court explained, "when an inventor puts his incomplete or experimental device upon the market and sells it, as a manufacturer, more than two years before he applies for a patent, he gives to the public the device in the condition or stage of development in which he sells it."[8]

Nineteenth century courts developed an exception to the on-sale bar, allowing certain activities—even offers or sales—if they were conducted by the inventor for the purpose of reducing the invention to practice.[9] This was not, however, a blanket exception for any commercial activities undertaken prior to reduction to practice; the activities had to constitute an experimental use.[10] Indeed, in the Supreme Court's seminal experi-mental use case, the Court cautioned that "[a]ny attempt to use [an embodiment of the invention] for a profit, and not by way of experiment, for a longer period than two years before the application, would deprive the inventor of his rights to a patent."[11]

Soon after the turn of the century, however, courts parlayed the "experimental use exception" into a requirement that the on-sale bar could not be invoked before the "invention" was actually reduced to practice. To the extent these courts identified a basis for this reduction to practice requirement, they relied on either a stray statement in 1939 congressional reports accompanying a minor amendment to the on-sale bar,[12] misapplication of dicta in earlier cases,[13] or on the meaning of the word "invention," reasoning that there could be no invention until the invention was reduced to practice.[14] The font of this latter analysis is *McCreery Engineering Company v. Massachussetts Fan Company*,[15] where the court interpreted "invention" to require not only conception, but reduction to practice, and reversed the judgment of invalidity under the on-sale bar because of "the absence of evidence that the invention had been reduced to practice at the time of the executory contract."[16]

Indeed, the *McCreery* court did not stop after imposing the reduction to practice requirement. The court went on to lay the foundation for requiring a physical embodiment of the invention. In dicta, the *McCreery* court speculated that the words "on-sale" required "a present offer of existing goods."[17] In 1916 the Second Circuit followed this dicta in *Burke Electric Co. v. Independent Pneumatic Tool Co.*[18], holding that "if [patent-ed articles] are not [on hand ready to be delivered to any purchaser], they cannot be said to be on-sale within the meaning of the act, though the invention itself has ceased to be experimental and is complete." Thus, *Burke* established the "on hand" doctrine, requiring that the inventor have a physical embodiment of the invention on hand and ready for delivery to the customer at the time the invention was sold or offered for sale.[19]

The courts soon recognized, however, that the on hand doctrine actually enabled an inventor to extend her period of commercial exclusivi-ty, by allowing her to market her invention for months or years before filing a patent application and initiating commercial production. These courts recognized that while this rule had the advantages of certainty, it did not serve the underlying policies of the on-sale bar. Thus, the courts sought to strike a balance between the prohibition of extending the patentee's period of exclusivity and allowing the inventor a reasonable amount of time following the commercial activity to evaluate the potential economic value of patent protection. In *Timely Products*,[20] the Second Circuit acknowledged the policies underlying the on-sale bar and rejected the on-hand requirement. In doing so, however, the *Timely Products Court* reverted to *McCreery*'s reduction to practice requirement.[21]

Shortly after its creation in 1982, the Federal Circuit recognized the policies relied on in *Timely Products*, but foreshadowed its imminent rejection of the reduction to practice requirement.

The *Timely Products* standard, while requiring less for "on-sale" activity than the "on hand" test, is, nevertheless, restrictive in that an offer to sell, without the existence of a physical embodiment of what is offered, does not start the running of the time period. It is not difficult to conceive of a situation where because commercial benefits outside the allowed time have been great, the technical requisite of *Timely Products* for a physical embodiment, particularly for a simple product, would defeat the statutory policy and we, therefore, do not adopt the *Timely Products* test as the answer in all cases.[22]

Essentially, the Federal Circuit envisioned situations where the policies underlying the on-sale bar could be violated without triggering the bar; for example, an inventor could potentially prepare all of the component parts of an invention, with the intention of combining the parts and, by simply not combining the parts until the inventor was ready to commercialize the invention. Five years later, in *UMC Electronics*,[23] the Federal Circuit encountered those exact circumstances, and held that an invention need not be reduced to practice in order to invoke an on-sale bar.[24]

After rejecting the reduction to practice requirement, the *UMC* court speculated in dicta that "[i]f the inventor had merely a conception or was working towards development of that conception, it can be said there is not yet any 'invention' which could be placed on-sale."[25] The court found that at the time of the offer for sale, the patentee's aviation counting accelerometer existed as a "substantial embodiment" of the claimed invention,[26] and was "far beyond a mere conception."[27] An engineering prototype had been built and the novel analog sensor portion, though not installed, had been separately tested to the inventor's satisfaction.[28] The two parts of this simple invention merely had to be combined. The court concluded that the invention was sufficiently developed to invoke the on-sale bar.

This began the Federal Circuit's struggle to determine at what stage in the spectrum of development an invention would be an "invention" for the purposes of the on-sale bar. The answers range from "conception" to "substantial embodiment" to "actually reduced to practice".[29] The *UMC* court had not defined what constituted a "substantial embodiment" or otherwise attempt to identify any precise point on the spectrum where an "invention" could invoke the on-sale bar. The *UMC* dicta, however, provided the bases for numerous tests to come. In *Micro Chemical v. Great Plains Chemical*,[30] the court adopted a standard of a "substantially completed invention" with "reason to expect that it would work for its intended purpose upon completion" under "the totality of the circumstances."[31] By adopting "substantially completed" as the requisite level of development, the *Micro Chemical* court presumably intended to echo *UMC*'s characterization of the bar triggering *UMC* device as the "substantial embodiment" of the invention ultimately patented.[32]

In *Robotic Vision Systems v. View Engineering*,[33] the court refined the substantially completed invention standard by adding an operability qualification. The *Robotic Vision* court held that an invention can not be "substantially completed", if elements necessary to operability of the invention have not yet been developed—even where those elements are not recited in the patent claims in question.[34] The *Robotic Vision* panel reasoned that although commercial exploitation before the critical date is improper, resolution of on-sale questions must not be so narrowly focused as to mandate the premature filing of patent applications on incomplete inventions.[35] The panel emphasized that collaboration between potential inventor-suppliers and customers would be chilled if the law treated "mere discussions," or even agreements to develop and provide a device not yet invented, developed, or completed, as triggering the on-sale bar.[36]

As the tests grew increasingly complex, and yet remained entirely subjective, the Federal Circuit repeatedly tried to clarify the issue, always eliciting a wave of commentary.[37] Its opinion in *Pfaff v. Wells Elec., Inc.*[38] was to represent its final attempt before the Supreme Court opted to address the problem and offer its solution. Pfaff was in the business of developing sockets for testing leadless chip carriers. More than a year before filing its patent application, Pfaff received a verbal purchase order from a customer for over 30,000 sockets for production use, prepared detailed engineering drawings of the requested socket, and received a written purchase order, confirming the verbal purchase order and referencing the engineering drawing Pfaff had prepared for the socket.

When Pfaff attempted to enforce its issued patent against Wells, Wells challenged the validity of the patent, claiming that Pfaff had offered the socket for sale more than one year before filing his patent application, thus triggering the on-sale bar. The U.S. District court held that the claimed invention was not on-sale within the meaning of Section 102(b) because, while there were drawings of the sockets, there were no physical embodiments at the time that Pfaff offered the socket for sale.[39]

The Federal Circuit held the invention embodied in the majority of the claims was on sale because it was "substantially complete" based on "all of the circumstances" surrounding the sale or offer for sale.[40] The Federal Circuit treated the embodiments of the invention offered for sale before the critical date as 102(b)/103 prior art to the claimed invention of two of the claims, and hence concluded that the claims that were not anticipated were invalid for obviousness under Section 103.[41] The Federal Circuit rejected the argument that the invention must have demonstrable suitability for its intended purpose, relying instead on its finding that Pfaff apparently felt confident that the invention would work based on the engineering drawings, as it was his business practice to go directly from engineering drawings to tooling and production without a prototype.

III. READY FOR PATENTING

The Supreme Court granted certiorari and, in a unanimous decision in *Pfaff v. Wells Electronics, Inc.*,[42] held Pfaff's patent claims invalid under the on-sale bar because the claimed socket (1) was "the subject of a commercial offer for sale," and (2) was "ready for patenting" at the time of the offer.[43] The Court promulgated the concept that an invention is "ready for patenting" if there is "[(1)] proof of reduction to practice before the critical date, or [(2) there is] proof that prior to the critical date the inventor had prepared drawings or other descriptions of the invention that were sufficiently specific to enable a person skilled in the art to practice the invention."[44] This tests fails for a number of reasons. First, despite touting the importance of certainty, the Court's test is no less subjective than its predecessors. Second, the Court appears to have reverted to a standard of documented conception. Finally, the Court's test does not account for the use of its newly minted definition in the context of an embodiment of the invention used as 102/103 prior art.

The Court rejected the "substantially complete" test, promulgated by the Federal Circuit, in part because "[a] rule that makes the timeliness of an application depend on the date when an invention is 'substantially complete' seriously undermines the interest in certainty."[45] In promulgating the "ready for patenting" test, the Court did create some certainty by eliminating any remaining vestiges of the reduction to practice requirement. However, the Court held that an invention will invoke the on-sale bar if, at the time it is sold or offered for sale, there is "proof that prior to the critical date the inventor had prepared drawings or other descriptions of the invention that were sufficiently specific to enable a person skilled in the art to practice the invention."[46] This standard provides no guidance as to what would be required beyond the minimum documentation or drawings of an embodiment of the invention.

In fact, the standard will only serve to promulgate more confusion on fundamental issues that the Federal Circuit has spent years attempting to clarify. The ready for patenting test does not overtly undermine the policies underlying the on-sale bar. It encourages inventors to file patent applications as soon as possible after conception, it discourages removal from the public domain of inventions that the public reasonably has come to believe are freely available (through commercial activities involving a conceived invention) and it encourages prompt and widespread disclosure of inventions through issued patents. The ready for patenting test is consistent with the policy of allowing the inventor a reasonable amount of time following commercial activity to determine the potential economic value of patent protection, because that policy is implemented by the one-year grace period which may be triggered by any commercial activity involving a conceived invention. The ready for patenting test is irrelevant to the policy of allowing the inventor an opportunity to reduce the invention to practice, because that policy is implemented by the experimental use exception.

The Court has, however, promulgated a test that, instead of examining the totality of the circumstances in light of the underlying policies, focuses on the sufficiency of the documentation of conception. Abandoning the broader concepts of patent law and policies, the court had shifted the focus away from the patent claims and onto the commercial embodiment of the invention. The "ready for patenting" test encourages the comparison of the prior art, in the form of the inventors early drawings or "other descriptions" of the invention, and the commercial product-not the patent claims which may be invalidated.[47] In fact, the ready for patenting test has created a standard that requires little more than documented conception of the invention. Indeed, an invention is ready for patenting upon conception because a party may file a U.S. patent application immediately upon conception—a fact the Court relied on in rejecting the reduction to practice requirement.[48]

What the Court failed to reflect in the ready for patenting test is that, for the purposes of application of section 102(b), every element of the invention must be reflected in the patent claim.[49] Thus, the spectrum of development from conception to reduction to practice can not be considered as reflecting the development of a single invention, but rather as a series of conceptions of different inventions and subsequent reductions to practice. For example, an inventor may first conceive of a widget and then subsequently conceive of an incremental improvement to the widget. Then the inventor might be issued a patent that includes a claim to the improved widget, but not the original widget. Assume that the inventor had offered the original widget for sale before the critical date, providing the potential customer with drawings of the original widget. According to the ready for patenting test, the Court would potentially review the drawings for the original widget to determine if the improved widget was "ready for patenting" for the purposes of section 102(b). But the analysis of whether an invention has been conceived or reduced to practice, by its very nature, cannot be applied to an incomplete iteration of the invention, because the invention, for purposes of section 102(b), has not yet been conceived when it is incomplete.

In fact, this analysis is not properly considered under section 102 at all, this analysis properly falls within the purview of section 103. An invention that has been offered for sale or sold, but does not embody the claimed invention, can be considered technical prior art for the purposes of a 102(b)/103 obviousness analysis. In this context, there is no requirement that section 102(b) prior art be at any particular stage of development. For example, in *Pfaff*, the invention claimed in two of the patent claims included an additional element, a hook, that was not included in the original invention offered for sale before the critical date. Thus, even though the original invention was not the "invention" for the purposes of those two claims, it was nonetheless considered as technical prior art under section 102(b), because Pfaff offered it for sale more than a year before filing its patent application. When it was combined with other prior art under a section 103 analysis, the original invention rendered the two claims invalid as obvious. The analysis should be simple. If the original invention is not identical to the claimed invention, it becomes prior art for the purposes of an obviousness analysis. If the original invention is identical to the claimed invention, it should invalidate the applicable patent claims under a section 102(b) analysis.

* Manya S. Deehr is a Chief Legal Officer, General Counsel, and Secretary, Eurand, Philadelphia, Pennsylvania and formerly served as a law clerk to the Honorable Giles S. Rich of the United States Court of Appeals for the Federal Circuit. William C. Rooklidge is a partner at Jones Day in Irvine, California and formerly served as a law clerk to the Honorable Helen W. Nies of the United States Court of Appeals for the Federal Circuit. The views expressed herein are solely those of the authors and do not necessarily reflect

those of Eurand, or Jones Day, or their clients.

1. 35 U.S.C. § 102(b).

2. *King Instrument Corp. v. Otari Corp.*, 767 F.2d 853 (Fed.Cir.1985). The history of this particular statement of the policies has been traced and the statement itself has been criticized for ignoring the policy underlying experimental use negation. *See* William C. Rooklidge and Mathew F. Weil, *The Application of Experimental Use to Design Patents: A Square Peg in a Round Hole*, 77 J. Pat. & Trademark Off. Soc'y 921 (1995). These policies were first identified in *Note, New Guidelines for Applying the On-sale Bar to Patentability*, 24 Stan. L. Rev. 730, (1972), and were comprehensively reexamined in William C. Rooklidge, *The On-sale and Public Use Bars to Patentability: Policies Reexamined*, 1 Fed.Cir.B.J. 7 (1991).

3. 35 U.S.C. § 100(a) (1994).

4. See, e.g., Paul M. Janicke, *The Varied Meanings of "Invention" in Patent Practice: Different Meanings in Different Situations*, in Dunner, Gambrell & Kayton, Patent Law Perspectives (1970); J. Hayes, Invention (1942).

5. 525 U.S. 55 (1998).

6. *Id.*

7. *See Lyman v. Maypole*, 19 F. 735, 736–737 (C.C.N.D.Ill.1884); *Henry v. Francestown Soap–Stone Co.*, 2 F. 78, 80–81 (C.C.D.N.H.1880). *See also Bradley v. Eccles*, 138 F. 911, 915–916 (C.C.N.D.N.Y. 1905) (Public Use).

8. *Lyman v. Maypole*, 19 F. at 736–37.

9. The history, policies and application of the experimental use exception is analyzed in William C. Rooklidge & Stephen C. Jensen, *Common Sense, Simplicity and Experimental Use Negation of the Public Use and On-sale Bars to Patentability*, 29 J. Marshall L. Rev. 1 (1995).

10. *See Swain v. Holyoke Mach. Co.*, 109 F. 154, 158–59 (1st Cir.1901) (for a sale during the "experimental stage," "the primary and governing consideration is the purpose and object of the inventor in making such a sale")

11. *City of Elizabeth v. American Nicholson Pavement Co.*, 97 U.S. 126, 137 (1877). *See also Smith & Griggs Mfg. Co. v. Sprague*, 123 U.S. 249, 256 (1887) ("Where the substantial use is not [substantially for purposes of experiment], but

is otherwise public, and for more than two years prior to the application, it comes within the prohibition" of the public use bar).

12. *E.g., Stewart–Warner Corp. v. City of Pontiac*, 717 F.2d 269, 273 (6th Cir.1983); *Austin v. Marco Dental Prods.*, 560 F.2d 966, 970 (9th Cir.1977).

13. An example of this misapplication of dicta flowed from *Wende v. Horine*, 225 F. 501, 505 (7th Cir.1915), where the court affirmed a judgment of invalidity under the on-sale bar and explained that "an offer to sell, made to a prospective purchaser after the experimental stage has been passed, the invention reduced to practice, and the apparatus manufactured in its perfected form, is placing on-sale within the statute." The *Wende* court stated that the invention had been reduced to practice and manufactured in its perfected form to refute the allegation of experimental use, not to imply that reduction to practice or manufacture in perfected form was in any way required for application of the on-sale bar. Nevertheless, later courts interpreted this *Wende* statement as establishing as a requirement for application of the on-sale bar that the invention be not only reduced to practice, but manufactured in its completed form. E.g., *Galland–Henning Mfg. Co. v. Dempster Bros., Inc.*, 315 F.Supp. 68 (E.D.Tenn. 1970). Likewise, this statement from *Wende* was quoted in the same context in subsequent cases holding patents invalid, including *Magee v. Coca–Cola Company*, 232 F.2d 596, 600 (7th Cir.1956), which were themselves interpreted as establishing a requirement for application of the on-sale bar. *See Langsett v. Marmet Corp.*, 231 F.Supp. 759 (W.D.Wis.1964) (holding patent invalid but relying on *Magee* for proposition that "[w]hat is required [for application of the on-sale bar], after the experimental stage has been passed, is that the invention be reduced to practice and the device manufactured in its perfected form").

14. *E.g., Dataq, Inc. v. Tokheim Corp.*, 736 F.2d 601, 605 (10th Cir.1984); *McCreery Engineering Co. v. Massachusetts Fan Co.*, 195 F. 498 (1st Cir.1912).

15. 195 F. 498, 503 (1st Cir.1912).

16. *Id. See, also e.g., Stewart–Warner Corp. v. City of Pontiac*, 717 F.2d 269, 273 (6th Cir.1983) (requiring a "completed device"); *Digital Equip. Corp. v. Dia-*

mond, 653 F.2d 701, 718 (1st Cir.1981) (stating that "an invention cannot be 'on-sale' until it is operable and 'reduced to practice'"); *CTS Corp. v. Piher Int'l Corp.*, 527 F.2d 95, 103 (7th Cir.1975) (requiring invention be "complete in the sense that it represented a reduction of the invention to practice"). An invention has been actually reduced to practice when it has been "sufficiently tested to demonstrate that it will work for its intended purpose." *Barmag Barmer Maschinenfabrik AG v. Murata Machinery, Ltd.*, 731 F.2d 831, 838 (Fed.Cir.1984). An invention is "complete" if reduced to practice. Id.

17. *Id*. at 502–03.

18. 234 F. 93 (2d Cir.1916).

19. *Id*.

20. *Timely Prods. Corp. v. Arron*, 523 F.2d 288 (2d Cir.1975).

21. Rejecting the restrictive "on hand" requirement of earlier cases, the *Timely Products* court held that an inventor's pre-critical date solicitation of an order for electrically heated socks, which were not actually available for delivery until after the critical date, nevertheless triggered the on-sale bar. Although the socks were not "on hand" prior to the critical date, and existed then only in sample form, the *Timely Products* court concluded that the bar was triggered because the offer of the socks satisfied the following three requirements:

> (1) The complete invention claimed must have been embodied in or obvious in view of the thing offered for sale. . . .

> (2) The invention must have been tested sufficiently to verify that it is operable and commercially marketable. This is simply another way of expressing the principle that an invention cannot be offered for sale until it is completed, which requires not merely its conception but its reduction to practice. . . .

> (3) Finally, the sale must be primarily for profit rather than for experimental purposes. . . .

523 F.2d at 289.

22. *Id*.

23. 816 F.2d 647 (Fed.Cir.1987), cert. denied, 484 U.S. 1025 (1988).

24. It supported its position by relying on three basic precepts (1) Section 101 allows an inventor to file a patent application on an invention upon conception, without an actual reduction to practice; (2) Section 102 would be internally inconsistent if "invention" included an actual reduction to practice in this subsection; and (3) Section 102(g) defines priority among inventors in an interference proceeding, not the term "invention."

25. *UMC*, 816 F.2d at 655.

26. *Id*. at 657.

27. *Id*.

28. *Id*.

29. The exception being the panel majority in *Seal–Flex, Inc. v. Athletic Track and Court Constr.*, 98 F.3d 1318 (Fed.Cir.1996), identified a "complete" invention as the prerequisite for placement on-sale, stating that "the general rule is that the on-sale bar starts to accrue when a completed invention is offered for sale." *Id*. A "complete" invention is one that is "known to work for its intended purpose without further testing or evaluation." *Id*. This definition comports with an actual reduction to practice. *Id*. Thus, the majority's opinion in Seal–Flex harkened back to pre-UMC doctrine requiring an actual reduction to practice before an invention can be placed on-sale.

30. 103 F.3d 1538 (Fed.Cir.), cert. denied, 117 S.Ct. 2516 (1997).

31. *Id*. at 1545.

32. The claimed invention in *Micro Chemical* was directed to a machine for adding small amounts of supplements to animal feed. *Id*. at 1540. Accurate measurement of added ingredients was facilitated by the presence of means for isolating the weighing mechanism from vibrations. *Id*. at 1541–42. At the time of the alleged offer for sale, the inventor had developed a prototype of the weighing system, had made only a sketch of the mixing system, and had not yet even designed the isolating elements. *Id*. at 1544–45. The *Micro Chemical* majority held that there was no offer for sale under Section 102(b), as the invention was "not close to completion" and the inventor was not confident that it would work for its intended purpose. *Id*. at 1545. The dissent in *Micro Chemical* is significant for its overriding concern with the policy against commercial exploitation outside the grace period. In the dissent's view, this "singularly important" policy of preventing inventors from extending the exclusivity period should trump the majority's concerns over the less-than-completed status of the invention. See *Id.* at 1553 (Mayer, J., dissenting).

33. *Robotic Vision Sys., Inc. v. View Eng'g, Inc.*, 112 F.3d 1163 (Fed.Cir.1997). Judge Lourie, author of the *Micro Chemical* majority, also authored the opinion in *Robotic Vision*.

34. *Robotic Vision's* patent in suit claimed a method for scanning the leads of integrated circuit chips by employing a "full-tray scanning" three-dimensional sensor. Id. at 1164. The Federal Circuit held that software for controlling a computer interfaced to the scanner, though not recited in the claims nor expressly disclosed in the written description of the patent, was the best mode for carrying out the claimed scanning method. When the patentee offered to supply Intel with a full-tray scanner several months before the critical date, that software was still in a mere "developmental" stage. See Id. at 1164. The *Robotic Vision* court rejected the defendant's argument that because the patentee was not working on a part of the invention recited in the claims, the experimentation cannot prevent imposition of the on-sale bar. Id. at 1167. Because workable software was necessary to operation of the scanner, the on-sale bar could not have been triggered at a time when the software was "not even close to completion" and was "nothing more than a concept." Id. at 1168.

35. *Id.*

36. *Id.*

37. *See, e.g.,* David W. Carstens and Craig A. Nard, Conception and the "On Sale" Bar, 34 WM & MARY L. REV 393 (1933); James S. Jorgenson, Note, Environmentally Dependent Inventions and the "On Sale" and "Public Use" Bars of 102(b): *A Proffered Solution to the Statutory Dichotomy*, 49 U. MIAMI L. REV. 185 (1994); Thomas K. Landry, *Certainty and Discretion in Patent Law: The On Sale Bar, the Doctrine of Equivalents, and Judicial Power in the Federal Circuit*, 67 S. CAL. L. REV. 1151 (1994); R. Carl Moy, *Jurisprudential Implications of the Federal Circuit's Decisions Regarding the On Sale Bar*, address at the ABA/ALI Advanced Course of Study, "Patent Law and Litigation" 3 (Dec. 4, 1991) (describing

the totality of the circumstances approach as "the legal-reasoning equivalent of a Quija Board").

38. *Pfaff v. Wells Elec., Inc.*, 124 F.3d 1429 (Fed.Cir.1997).

39. *Id.* at 656 (stating that a "reduction to practice of the claimed invention has not been . . . an absolute requirement of the on-sale bar.") However the Federal Circuit stated the importance of a reduction to practice in analyzing the on-sale bar by stating: A holding that there has or has not been a reduction to practice of the claimed invention before the critical date may well determine whether the claimed invention was in fact the subject of the sale or offer to sell or whether a sale was primarily for an experimental purpose. *Id.* The Federal Circuit also stated that "reduction to practice" is a term of art used in interference proceedings to determine the first to invent. *Id.* at 655. However, if the invention is actually reduced to practice prior to the sale or offer for sale and a patent application is not filed within a year of the sale or offer for sale, a patent will likely be barred. *Id.* at 656. The court stated that reduction to practice is "an important analytical tool in an on-sale analysis." *Id.* For more information on the UMC Electronics case, see; William C. Rooklidge & Stephen C. Jensen, *Common Sense, Simplicity and Experimental Use Negation of the Public Use and On-sale Bars to patentability*, 29 J. MARSHALL L. REV. 1 (1995). In *UMC Electronics Co. v. United States*, 816 F.2d 647, UMC Electronics brought suit against the United States for infringement by the Navy of UMC's patent for an aviation accelerometer after the Navy awarded a contract to UMC's competitor, Systron–Donner Corp. Weaver, an inventor working for UMC, invented an improved accelerometer in an effort to secure a contract with the Navy. *Id.* at 649. UMC filed a patent application for Weaver's accelerometer on August 1, 1968. *Id.* The trial court found that UMC submitted a bid to the Navy for the claimed accelerometer on July 27, 1967, four days prior to the critical date. *Id.* at 650. The trial court also found that prior to the critical date, Weaver had tested to his satisfaction the part of the accelerometer that he improved. *Id.* However, the trial court found that the prototype built by UMC did not embody the claimed invention; therefore, prior to the critical date, no physical embodiment of the invention existed. *Id*. at 651.

40. *Pfaff* at 1433.

41. *Pfaff* at 1424 (stating that "[t]he general rule is that the on-sale bar starts to accrue when a completed invention is offered for sale.... The trier of fact must determine whether the invention was completed and known to work for its intended purpose, or whether the inventor was continuing to develop and evaluate the invention.").

42. 525 U.S. 55 (1998).

43. *Pfaff*, 119 S.Ct. at 311 (stating that "[t]he evidence in this case thus fulfills the two essential conditions of the on-sale bar").

44. *Pfaff*, 119 S.Ct. at 312. Thus, the Supreme Court found that Pfaff's invention was "ready for patenting" because Pfaff had sent completed drawings of the invention to the manufacture prior to the critical date. *Id*.

45. *Pfaff*, 525 U.S. at 64.

46. *Pfaff*, 119 S.Ct. at 312. Thus, the Supreme Court found that Pfaff's invention was "ready for patenting" because Pfaff had sent completed drawings of the invention to the manufacture prior to the critical date. *Id*.

47. Furthermore, because of the ambiguity as to what constitutes a sufficient description to trigger the on-sale bar, the inventor is more likely than ever to inadvertently trigger the grace period when aspects of the invention are discussed with potential customers. U.S. patent law has been pushed one step closer to the absolute novelty approach of the European community.

48. The Court did not address, however, the policy that formed the basis of the reduction to practice requirement, that encouraging an inventor to actually reduce the invention to practice before filing a patent application. See McCreery Engineering, 195 F. at 501 ("the law

should encourage the inventor to embody his invention in practical form, even though it excuses him from doing so if he files his application in the Patent Office"). That is likely because that policy is already served by the experimental use exception, which allows the inventor the opportunity to undertake activities for the purpose of reducing the invention to practice.

49. The Court rejected the test proposed by the Solicitor General that would have addressed the 102(b)/103 prior art issue.

> The Solicitor General has argued that the rule governing on-sale bar should be phrased somewhat differently. In his opinion, "if the sale or offer in question embodies the invention for which a patent is later sought, a sale or offer to sell that is primarily for commercial purposes and that occurs more than one year before the application renders the invention unpatentable. *Seal–Flex, Inc. v. Athletic Track and Court Constr.*, 98 F.3d 1318, 1325 (Fed. Cir.1996) (Bryson, J., concurring in part and concurring in the result)." It is true that evidence satisfying this test might be sufficient to prove that the invention was ready for patenting at the time of the sale if it is clear that no aspect of the invention was developed after the critical date. However, the possibility of additional development after the offer for sale in these circumstances counsels against adoption of the rule proposed by the Solicitor General.

525 U.S. 55, 66. If an element of the claimed invention was developed after the critical date, the claimed invention could not have been conceived or reduced to practice before the critical date.

5. THIRD–PARTY ACTIVITY

Whether public or commercial use by one without the consent or under the control of the inventor constitutes public use or an on-sale event under § 102(b) is a question that escapes easy resolution. In grappling with this issue consider the policies underlying § 102(b) and the policy considerations discussed in the following two cases, *Lorenz v. Colgate Palmolive* and

Baxter International v. COBE Laboratories. Also revisit Justice Story's and Judge Hand's respective opinions in *Pennock* and *Metallizing*, and ask how these jurists would view the third-party activity in *Lorenz* and *Baxter*.

Lorenz v. Colgate–Palmolive–Peet Co.

167 F.2d 423 (3d Cir.1948).

■ Before BIGGS, GOODRICH, AND MCLAUGHLIN, CIRCUIT JUDGES.

■ BIGGS, CIRCUIT JUDGE.

... In the District Court Lorenz and Wilson (Lorenz), persons interested in Lorenz Patent No. 2,084,446, one of two interfering patents, brought suit under R.S. Sec. 4918, 35 U.S.C.A. § 66, against Colgate–Palmolive–Peet Company (Colgate), the owner of the other interfering patent, Ittner, No. 1,918,603.... Both patents cover a process for the manufacture of soap and the recovery of glycerine....

The interference between Lorenz and Ittner in the Patent Office arose under the following circumstances. Lorenz had filed an application for his process in the Patent Office on January 24, 1920. Shortly thereafter he communicated the substance of the disclosures of his application to Ittner, who was Colgate's chief chemist, in order that Colgate might exploit the process if it so desired. After examination Ittner expressed himself as uninterested in the process. Next, the Patent Office rejected Lorenz's application and he abandoned the prosecution of the application. On July 18, 1933, Patent No. 1,918,603 was issued to Ittner on an application filed by him on February 19, 1931. Lorenz, learning of the Ittner patent, filed a petition in the Patent Office to revive his original application. This petition was rejected. On November 8, 1934, more than a year after the issuance of the Ittner patent, Lorenz filed a new application in which he adopted as his own nineteen claims of Ittner's patent, asserting that the subject matter of Ittner's patent had been disclosed by him to Ittner in 1920. The Patent Office declared an interference. The examiner of interferences decided in Lorenz's favor and for reasons which need not be gone into here no appeal was taken.

* * *

We proceed immediately to an examination of the defense of prior public use....

The court below found that:

It clearly appears from the undisputed testimony and the documentary evidence offered in support thereof that the process of the patent was in public use in the factory of the defendant from November 1931 until November 1932, approximately one year, but more than two years prior to the Lorenz application of November 8, 1934. This use was preceded by several months of experimentation, but commercial production of soap and glycerine by the process of the patent was accomplished in November of 1931 and continued thereafter until 1932, when the use of the process was either discontinued or abandoned. This public use, although it did not enrich the art, was sufficient under the statute to preclude the issuance of a valid patent....

... Agreeing with Lorenz that under the peculiar circumstances of this case an unusually heavy burden rests upon Colgate in order to prove prior public use, we have made generous allowance for the difficulties which Lorenz encountered in procuring evidence to rebut Colgate's proof of prior public use. But we cannot say that the court below erred in finding that the process of Lorenz's patent was in public use in Colgate's plant for a period of a year more than two years preceding the filing of Lorenz's second patent application on November 8, 1934. . . .

We come then to the question whether the public use under the circumstances was such as to be within the purview of R.S. Sec. 4886. Lorenz contends that it was not such a use; that Congress did not intend the provision of the statute to bar the grant of a valid monopoly to an inventor whose disclosures have been "pirated" by the person to whom he confided them. . . .

Colgate asserts that its use was neither fraudulent nor piratical and that the disclosures made by Lorenz to Ittner in 1920 carried no pledge, express or implied, that Ittner or Colgate should not make use of Ittner's invention; that Lorenz had filed a patent application and that Ittner knew this and that otherwise Ittner would have refused to receive the disclosures; that since these were made under a then pending application Ittner and Colgate were at liberty to make use of Lorenz's process and answer to Lorenz in a patent infringement suit for profits or damages; that no confidential or trust relationship in Lorenz's favor was or could be imposed on either Ittner or Colgate under the circumstances. We are aware of the ordinary practice under which manufacturers refuse to receive an inventor's disclosures unless there is a pending patent application which covers the discovery. This proper practice is one which usually inures to the benefit of both inventor and manufacturer since it settles in written terms the nature of the disclosure and lessens the probability of future disputes. In the case at bar, however, Ittner immediately rejected Lorenz's disclosures as commercially impractical only to make substantial commercial use of them some eleven years later. The circumstances of the instant case are therefore unusual and reflect a very different pattern from that which customarily ensues when an inventor makes a disclosure to a manufacturer. Usually if the manufacturer declares himself interested in the process a contract is drawn up whereby the rights of the parties are fixed for the periods of manufacture both prior to the issuance of the patent as well as thereafter. No such opportunity was given to Lorenz in the case at bar because of Ittner's rejection of the process as soon as it had been disclosed to him.

We do not doubt that Lorenz's disclosures were made to Ittner with the implicit understanding that if Ittner was to make use of them an arrangement was to be effected whereby Lorenz was to be compensated. Certainly Lorenz was not offering his process to Ittner gratis. Under these circumstances we cannot say that an inventor may not invoke the aid of a court of equity to impose an accounting on the manufacturer, provided the inventor moves to protect his rights with reasonable promptness. *Cf. Bohlman v. American Paper Goods Co.*, D.C.N.J., 53 F.Supp. 794. We have found no case which is on all fours with the circumstances at bar but a helpful analogy is supplied by *Hoeltke v. C. M. Kemp Mfg. Co.*, 4 Cir., 80 F.2d 912, 922–924. In this case Hoetlke disclosed his invention to Kemp after he had filed an application but before the issuance of a patent to him Kemp made use of the device, claiming to have developed it independently. The court had no difficulty in holding Kemp liable. It stated, 80 F.2d at page 923: "It would be a reproach to any system of jurisprudence to permit one who has received a disclosure in confidence to thus appropriate the ideas of another without liability for the wrong." *See also Chesapeake & O.R. Co. v. Kaltenbach*, 4 Cir., 95 F.2d 801, and *Booth v. Stutz Motor Car Co. of America*, 7 Cir., 56 F.2d 962. We think it clear that Ittner received the disclosures *cum onere* and that Colgate cannot now be heard to assert that it owes no duty to Lorenz.

But Colgate's position in this regard is not really an issue in the instant case. The scope which Congress intended the public use statute to have is the important question. Here the defense of prior public use in reality is asserted on behalf of the public, albeit by Colgate. Was it the intention of Congress that public use by one who employs a process in breach of a fiduciary relationship, who tortiously appropriates it or who pirates it, should bar the inventor from the fruits of his monopoly? Lorenz asserts that there is no case in point and that the question is an original one. He relies on certain cases beginning with *Pennock v. Dialogue*.

* * *

On consideration of these authorities, and we can find no others even as pertinent, and weighing the policy embodied in the statute we are forced to the conclusion that the decisions of the Supreme Court in *Klein v. Russell* [19 Wall. 433 (1874)] and in *Andrews v. Hovey* on rehearing [123 U.S. 267 (1887)], and that of the Circuit Court of Appeals for the Second Circuit in *Eastman v. Mayor of New York* [134 F. 844 (2d Cir.1904),] point the way to the ruling which we must make on this point. The prior-public-use proviso of R.S. Sec. 4886 was enacted by Congress in the public interest. It contains no qualification or exception which limits the nature of the public use. We think that Congress intended that if an inventor does not protect his discovery by an application for a patent within the period prescribed by the Act, and an intervening public use arises from any source whatsoever, the inventor must be barred from a patent or from the fruits of his monopoly, if a patent has issued to him. There is not a single word in the statute which would tend to put an inventor, whose disclosures have been pirated, in any different position from one who has permitted the use of his process.... As Judge Coxe said in the *Eastman* case, isolated instances of injustice may result if the law be strictly applied, but the inventor's remedy is sure. He is master of the situation and by prompt action can protect himself fully and render the defense of prior public use impossible: "If (the inventor) fails to take so simple and reasonable a precaution why should it not be said that the risk is his own and that he cannot complain of the consequences of his own supineness?" Moreover, it is apparent that if fraud or piracy be held to prevent the literal application of the prior-public-use provision a fruitful field for collusion will be opened and the public interest which [the statute] is designed to protect will suffer. While we cannot fail to view Lorenz's predicament with sympathy, we may not render our decision on such a basis. For these reasons we hold, as did the court below, that the Lorenz patent is void by reason of prior public use.

The judgment of the court below will be affirmed.

Baxter International, Inc. v. COBE Laboratories, Inc.

88 F.3d 1054 (Fed.Cir.1996).

■ Before NEWMAN, LOURIE, and SCHALL, CIRCUIT JUDGES.

■ LOURIE, CIRCUIT JUDGE.

Baxter International, Inc. and Baxter Healthcare Corporation (collectively "Baxter") appeal from the decision of the United States District Court for the Northern District of Illinois holding on summary judgment that the asserted claims of U.S. Patent 4,734,089 are invalid under 35 U.S.C. § 102(b) on the ground of a prior public use.... Because the district court did not err in holding that there were no genuine issues of material fact regarding the disputed public use and because COBE was entitled to judgment as a matter of law, we affirm.

BACKGROUND

The '089 patent concerns a sealless centrifuge for separating blood into its components. The application for the patent was filed on May 14, 1976 and it therefore had a critical date of May 14, 1975 for purposes of 35 U.S.C. § 102(b). The alleged prior public use involved the activities of Dr. Jacques Suaudeau, ... who was a research scientist for the National Institutes of Health (NIH). Suaudeau was studying isolated heart preservation by perfusion, which involved the pumping of whole blood and platelet-rich plasma that had been separated from whole blood through a heart. The centrifuge he had been using damaged platelets in the blood and he found that the damage was caused by rotating seals in the centrifuge. He approached Dr. Yoichiro Ito, another scientist at NIH, for advice in solving this problem, and Ito recommended that Suaudeau try using a sealless centrifuge that Ito had designed. Neither Suaudeau nor Ito had any relationship or connection with Herbert M. Cullis, the inventor named in the '089 patent.[2]

Suaudeau had the centrifuge built by the machine shop at NIH using Ito's drawings. Suaudeau balanced the centrifuge with water and then with blood, and tested it, all before the critical date. It was immediately apparent to Suaudeau that the centrifuge worked properly for its original purpose, as a separator, and that the centrifuge separated blood into its components. He also tested the suitability of the centrifuge for his own purposes, by performing experiments in order to determine if the centrifuge would produce platelet-rich plasma with a platelet count satisfactory for perfusion. These tests involved operating the centrifuge for as long as forty-three hours. All of this occurred in Suaudeau's laboratory at the NIH

---

2. Ito later filed his own patent application for the centrifuge and that application was placed in interference with Cullis's application. However, the claims of the '089 patent at issue in this case were not part of the interference.

campus in Bethesda, Maryland. Suaudeau also balanced and tested the centrifuge at Massachusetts General Hospital, where he went to work after leaving NIH.

Baxter sued COBE Laboratories, Inc. for infringement of the '089 patent. . . .

COBE filed a motion for summary judgment of invalidity, asserting that there were no genuine issues of material fact and that the claimed invention had been in public use before the critical date. On December 21, 1994, the district court conducted a hearing on COBE's motion. It then held that Suaudeau had publicly used the claimed invention before the critical date and that the use was not experimental. The court stated that "a use by a single person not under the control of the inventor and in public, as that term of art is used, is a [use] sufficient" to invalidate a patent. The court found that the invention here had been reduced to practice before the critical date, and that others at NIH and Mass. General had observed the centrifuge in operation. Regarding Baxter's assertion that Suaudeau's use was experimental, the court stated that "the experimental use exception is limited to the inventor or people working for the inventor or under the direction and control of the inventor," but that neither Suaudeau nor Ito were acting under the direction or control of Cullis, the inventor. Furthermore, the court found that Suaudeau was not experimenting to perfect or test the invention but, rather, was making modifications for his own particular requirements. Accordingly, the district court held that there were no genuine issues of material fact, that the claimed invention had been in public use before the critical date, and that the asserted claims of the '089 patent were invalid. Baxter now appeals.

DISCUSSION

Baxter argues that the district erred by not considering the totality of the circumstances or the policies underlying the public use bar. According to Baxter, Suaudeau's use of the centrifuge was not publicly known or accessible, and ethical constraints would have limited or precluded those who saw the centrifuge in operation from disclosing their knowledge of it. Baxter asserts that the most applicable policy involved here is the removal of inventions from the public domain that the public believes are freely available; according to Baxter, the public had no reason to believe that the centrifuge was freely available.

COBE responds that the district court correctly applied the law, considering the relevant policies underlying the public use bar. According to COBE, the centrifuge in Suaudeau's laboratory at NIH and at Mass. General was publicly accessible and those who saw it in operation were under no duty of confidentiality. Furthermore, COBE argues that the relevant policies support the district court's decision, as those who saw the centrifuge in operation would have reasonably believed the centrifuge was publicly available. COBE also asserts that NIH had an interest in continuing to use the technology that its employees, Ito and Suaudeau, began using without restriction before the critical date.

* * *

We agree with COBE that there were no genuine issues of fact, that Suaudeau publicly used the invention before the critical date, and that COBE was entitled to judgment as a matter of law. We do agree with Baxter that the most applicable policy underlying the public use bar here is discouraging removal from the public domain of inventions that the public reasonably has come to believe are freely available. However, invalidation of the Cullis patent is not inconsistent with that policy. Suaudeau's use was public, and it was not experimental in a manner that saves Cullis's patent.

The centrifuge that Suaudeau was using met all the limitations of the representative claims of the '089 patent. Suaudeau testified that the centrifuge worked as a separator as soon as he operated it, which verified that it would work for its intended purpose as a centrifugal blood processing apparatus and method as recited in the claims. Suaudeau further testified that others at NIH came into his laboratory and observed the centrifuge in operation, including co-workers, who were under no duty to maintain it as confidential. Nor did Suaudeau make any discernible effort to maintain the centrifuge as confidential. His laboratory was located in a public building, and he testified that he recalled "people coming and looking, people flowing into the lab" before the critical date. He even testified that NIH had an anti-secrecy policy.

Suaudeau's lack of effort to maintain the centrifuge as confidential coupled with the free flow into his laboratory of people, including visitors to NIH, who observed the centrifuge in operation and who were under no duty of confidentiality supports only one conclusion: that the centrifuge was in public use. The record contains clear and convincing evidence to support the conclusion that the asserted claims of the '089 patent are invalid on the ground of Suaudeau's prior public use.

Baxter asserts that those who observed the centrifuge were under an ethical obligation to keep it secret. However, there was no evidence that this was so. According to unrefuted testimony by Suaudeau and Dr. Ronald Yankee, any relevant ethical obligation that existed was to refrain from taking credit for the work of others, or publishing the work of others without permission. Those who observed the centrifuge in operation were under no duty to maintain it as confidential.

Baxter also argues that Ito and NIH did not consider Suaudeau's use to have been a public use. Baxter cites the declaration in Ito's own patent application on the sealless centrifuge, filed under the auspices of NIH. In his declaration, Ito averred that the invention had not been in public use more than one year before the filing date of his patent application. The district court discounted the declaration, stating:

> I regard Ito's declaration as a groundless statement insofar as the evidence before me bears upon its truth or falsity. I don't mean to say that Dr. Ito made a false declaration. That issue is not before me. All I can say is that on the basis of the evidence which is before me, which has been submitted by both sides here, he was clearly wrong when he said that there had been no use of the invention during the period exceeding a year prior to his own application.

The court was correct in discounting this declaration. Ito's averment was a statement of his own appraisal of the relevant facts, made in relation to his own application for patent. It does not bind a court later evaluating those facts, especially in relation to a third party's application for patent. Moreover, the declaration was only one factor to be considered under a totality of the circumstances evaluation. Ito's conclusory statement does not preclude the district court from deciding that the undisputed facts indicated a public use of the claimed invention before the critical date; the court thus did not err in discounting it.

Baxter argues that any alleged public use by Suaudeau is negated by the fact that it was experimental use. According to Baxter, Suaudeau's use was not for commercial purposes; it was to determine whether the invention would function as intended. Baxter also argues that Cullis was entitled to the benefit of Suaudeau's experimental use, even though Suaudeau was not acting under the control or direction of Cullis.

* * *

The district court determined as a matter of law that Suaudeau's use was not experimental. It properly determined that Suaudeau was not experimenting with the basic features of the invention, stating:

> Furthermore, the work that they [Suaudeau and Ito] were doing was not experimental as to the invention. They were not trying to further refine the invention and prove that it would work for its intended purpose. They would not have been using it if it was not suitable for its intended purpose. They would have found something else to use instead. What they were doing was making modifications that would satisfy their particular requirements, much as one might modify the engine of an automobile to produce a speed greater than that afforded by the engine that came with the automobile. That doesn't mean that the modifier is experimenting with the basic invention represented by the engine, or at least not doing so within the meaning of the public use exception.

The district court did not err in this conclusion. Neither the basic purpose of the invention, which had previously been realized by others, nor the representative claims required obtaining platelet-rich plasma suitable for preservation of hearts, which was the purpose of Suaudeau's experiments. These experiments, which Baxter alleges constituted experimental use, were directed to fine-tuning the centrifuge to work for Suaudeau's particular purpose of heart preservation, not to determining if it would work as a centrifugal blood processing apparatus, or perform a method of centrifugally processing blood, as recited in the claims and which he had already verified. Further refinement of an invention to test additional uses is not the type of experimental use that will negate a public use. *Brigance*, 792 F.2d at 1109, 229 USPQ at 991; *see also Harrington Mfg. Co. v. Powell Mfg. Co.*, 815 F.2d 1478, 1481, 2 U.S.P.Q.2D 1364, 1366–67 (Fed.Cir.1986) (stating that testing a tobacco harvester to harvest lower leaves of a tobacco plant was not experimental use where the claim broadly recited removing leaves from part of a tobacco stalk and prior testing had shown efficacy in harvesting upper leaves).

The inventor's lack of direction or control over Suaudeau's use of the invention also supports a conclusion that the use was not experimental. One of the policies underlying experimental use as a negation of public use is allowing an inventor sufficient time to test an invention before applying for a patent.... Providing Cullis, the inventor, with the benefit of Suaudeau's testing is thus contrary to this policy, as Suaudeau was not using or testing the invention for Cullis.... Accordingly, we hold that public testing before the critical date by a third party for his own unique purposes of an invention previously reduced to practice and obtained from someone other than the patentee, when such testing is independent of and not controlled by the patentee, is an invalidating public use, not an experimental use.

* * *

■ NEWMAN, CIRCUIT JUDGE, dissenting.

This case relates to the status as "public use" of unpublished information used for research purposes by a person who was completely independent of the inventor of the patent-in-suit. Can such private laboratory research use, if it occurs after a laboratory "reduction to practice," serve as an invalidating "public use" bar to the patented invention of another? The panel majority so holds.

The panel majority holds that since the reduction to practice of the similar device assertedly occurred more than a year before the filing date of the patent in suit, the ensuing laboratory use of that device was a "public use" and a bar under 35 U.S.C. § 102(b). This new rule of law, that unpublished laboratory use after a reduction to practice is a public use, creates a new and mischievous category of "secret" prior art. I respectfully dissent from the court's ruling, for it is contrary to, and misapplies, the law of 35 U.S.C. § 102.

* * *

The issue here is not that of an Ito/Suaudeau personal defense as a prior user, a matter of current discussion among policy-makers. On the panel majority's ruling it is irrelevant whether Cullis or Ito was the first inventor, for the Cullis patent is now held to be barred by the Suaudeau laboratory use of the Ito device, before the date of any reference publication or the filing date of any patent application. This is not a correct reading of the law. Suaudeau's use in his laboratory did not become a public use under § 102(b) as soon as the Ito centrifuge was reduced to practice. *Cf. W.L. Gore & Assoc., Inc. v. Garlock Inc.*, 721 F.2d 1540, 1550, 220 USPQ 303, 310 (Fed.Cir.1983) (a third person's secret commercial activity, more than one year before the patent application of another, is not a § 102(b) bar to the patent of another), *cert. denied*, 469 U.S. 851 (1984).

* * *

... This use of unknown, private laboratory work to create a new bar to patentability as of the date of laboratory reduction to practice is a distortion of the law and policy set forth in 35 U.S.C. § 102. Sections 102(a) and (b) establish that prior art is prior knowledge that meets specified requirements. This new category of internal laboratory use is immune to the most painstaking documentary search. The court thus produces a perpetual cloud on any issued patent, defeating the objective standards and policy considerations embodied in the § 102 definitions of prior art.

* * *

Heretofore, § 102(e) was the only source of so-called "secret prior art": the patent text remains secret while the patent application is pending, but after the patent is issued its subject matter is deemed to be prior art as of its filing date.... Thus the term "secret prior art" is used for prior art under § 102(e). This law reflects a careful balancing of public policies, for it is an exception to the rule that "prior art" is that which is available to the public.... This retroactive effect does not reach back to the underlying research or to the date of reduction to practice of the reference patented invention. See § 102(e) (the patent applicant may show that his invention predates the filing date of the reference patent). It is irrelevant, as well as usually unknown, when the invention of the reference patent was reduced to practice. Such information is not discernable from the issued patent. Thus the court's ruling today adds an omnipresent pitfall to the complexities of the patent system.

* * *

Cullis and Ito were engaged in an interference proceeding in the PTO, in which Ito prevailed. Elaborate rules and extensive precedent govern the determination of reduction to practice under § 102(g). *See, e.g., Schendel v. Curtis*, 83 F.3d 1399, 38 U.S.P.Q.2D 1743 (Fed.Cir.1996) (illustrating rigorous requirements for reduction to practice in patent interferences). Today's acquiescence in Suaudeau's purported reduction to practice, based on credibility determinations and other findings unwarranted in a summary proceeding, is unburdened by the usual rigors of this determination.

The record does not explain the relationship between the Ito patent, the lost counts of the interference, and the patent in suit. However, it is not irrelevant that the PTO issued the Cullis patent despite the Ito patent, and that the information that is deemed invalidating by the panel majority was not so viewed by the PTO. The panel majority's holding today is dramatically new law. Indeed, the panel majority suggests that since Suaudeau's use after reduction to practice is public use, the Ito patent is also invalid. Ito, not a party to this case, had no chance to dispute this result....

NOTES

1. *Third–Party Secret Use and the Policies of 102(b).* Whether secret commercial use by one without the knowledge or consent of the first inventor constitutes "on-sale" or "public use" activity is a question of considerable difficulty. Regarding such use or knowledge, Justice Story, in *Pennock*, stated that "it can scarcely be supposed, that the legislature had within its contemplation such knowledge and use." And Judge Hand, in *Metallizing*, distinguished between inventor and third-party "exploitation."

But *Pennock*, which was decided in 1829, was interpreting the 1793 Patent Act. The 1836 Act codified *Pennock* in this regard by adopting the "consent and allowance" language, perhaps to offset the harshness of result from the lack of a grace period. Since that time, the Supreme Court, on numerous occasions, indicated that the statutory bar standards are the same, whether the use or sale is by the inventor or by someone else without the inventor's consent. Notably, these cases were decided after the 1839 Act, which adopted a two-year grace period and eliminated the "consent and allowance" language of the 1836 Act. For example, the

Court in *Andrews v. Hovey*, 123 U.S. 267 (1887), cited in *Lorenz*, noted that Congress, by eliminating the "consent or allowance," intended to adopt a certain standard requiring only a calculation to time:

> It is very plain that under the act of 1836, if the thing patented had been in public use or on sale, with the consent or allowance of the applicant, for any time, however short, prior to his application, the patent issued to him was invalid. Then came section 7 of the act of 1839, which was intended as an amelioration in favor of the inventor, in this respect, of the strict provisions of the act of 1836 [because it introduced a two-year grace period]....
>
> [But by eliminating the "consent or allowance" language,] [t]he evident intention of congress was to take away the right (which existed under the act of 1836) to obtain a patent after an invention had for a long period of time been in public use, without the consent or allowance of the inventor; it limited that period to two years, whether the inventor had or had not consented to or allowed the public use. The right of an inventor to obtain a patent was in this respect narrowed, and the rights of the public as against him were enlarged, by the act of 1839.

Id. at 274. Perhaps Congress felt comfortable eliminating the "consent and allowance" language because it introduced a two-year grace period, thus retaining a degree of protection for inventors from third-party activity, but one based on time, not consent. Does a grace period or inventor consent offer the inventor more protection against third-party activity? Which one offers the public greater protection? Is it easier to determine whether two years transpired or whether an inventor has given consent?

The Federal Circuit has followed *Andrews*, stating that "it is of no consequence that the sale was made by a third party, not by the inventor." *Zacharin v. United States*, 213 F.3d 1366, 1371 (Fed.Cir.2000); *Abbott Laboratories v. Geneva Pharmaceuticals, Inc.*, 182 F.3d 1315 (Fed.Cir.1999); *In re Epstein*, 32 F.3d 1559, 1564 (Fed.Cir.1994) ("The section 102(b) 'public use' and 'on sale' bars are not limited to sales or uses by the inventor or one under the inventor's control, but may result from activities of a third party which anticipate the invention, or render it obvious"). But a third-party sale of a product made from a patented process is treated differently. See *TorPharm, Inc. v. Ranbaxy Pharmaceuticals, Inc.*, 336 F.3d 1322, 1327 (Fed.Cir.2003) (stating "if the product were sold by one other than the patentee, and the process of making remained unknown, then sale of the product would not pose a statutory bar to a claim on the process"); *W.L. Gore & Associates, Inc. v. Garlock, Inc.*, 721 F.2d 1540 (Fed.Cir.1983) (court indicated that secret third-party use of a process was not a bar).

The language of section 102(b) does not distinguish between inventor-applicant-patentee activity and third-party activity. But what about the underlying policies of this section? In *General Electric v. United States*, 654 F.2d 55, 61 (Ct.Cl.1981), the court discussed third-party use:

> Where the sale is by one other than the inventor (one not under the inventor's control), it would seem that the policy against extended commercial exploitation and the policy favoring the filing of only worthwhile inventions could be said not to apply. Nevertheless, it is well established that a placing of the invention "on sale" by an unrelated third party more than 1 year prior to the filing of an application for patent by another has the effect under § 102(b) of invalidating a patent directed to that invention. Accordingly, Congress should be held to have concluded, at the least, that the policy against removing inventions from the public domain and the policy favoring early patent filing are of sufficient importance in and of

themselves to invalidate a patent where the invention is sold by one other than the inventor or one under his control.

In *Baxter,* Judge Lourie wrote that "the most applicable policy underlying the public use bar here is discouraging removal from the public domain of inventions that the public reasonably has come to believe are freely available." According to the court, a finding of public use was not inconsistent with this policy, mainly because of the lack of secrecy in the NIH lab. A few questions are in order. First, was the invention really in *public* use and did the public believe that the invention was freely available? Second, what about the other policies underlying 102(b)? Did the inventor in *Baxter* attempt to exploit commercially his invention beyond the statutory patent term? Is the holding in *Baxter* consistent with the policy favoring prompt disclosure? Does the court's holding place too much emphasis on its assertion that the public has come to believe that the invention is freely available and too little emphasis on the patent system's incentive functions. Do you agree with Judge Newman that the majority created "a new and mischievous category of 'secret' prior art" that is "immune to the most painstaking documentary search."

2. *"Pirated" Inventions.* Assuming that public commercialization of an inventor's idea by one who "pirated" the idea will be a bar, what remedies are available to the inventor? *Lorenz* suggests that the inventor should file a timely application in order to preserve his rights to a patent and that the inventor may have other monetary and injunctive remedies based on tort law or fiduciary duties rather than the patent laws. Note that in *Lorenz,* the "pirate," Colgate, did file a timely application. Should the true inventor, Lorenz, be able to obtain ownership of that application, or any patent issuing thereon, or correct the designation of inventorship on that application? *Cf. Richardson v. Suzuki Motor Co., Ltd.,* 868 F.2d 1226 (Fed.Cir.1989).

In *Evans Cooling Systems, Inc. v. General Motors Corp.,* 125 F.3d 1448 (Fed.Cir.1997), the patentee argued that the on-sale bar should not apply when its invention was misappropriated by the alleged infringer which led to an offer for sale by third parties not involved in the theft. The Federal Circuit disagreed. Quoting from *Lorenz,* the court held that a patent is barred when " 'a public use arises from any source whatsoever.' " But the court was particularly persuaded by the fact that the offers were made by innocent third-parties:

> Even if we were to create an exception to the on sale bar such that third parties accused of misappropriating an invention could not invalidate a patent based upon sales by the guilty third party, GM correctly asserts that . . . activities of third parties uninvolved in the alleged misappropriation raise the statutory bar, even if those activities are instigated by the one who allegedly misappropriated the invention.

Id., at 1453. *See also, Abbott Laboratories v. Geneva Pharmaceuticals, Inc.,* 182 F.3d 1315, 1318 (Fed.Cir.1999) (stating "the statutory on-sale bar is not subject to exceptions for sales made by third parties either innocently or fraudulently"). With respect to available remedies for the inventor, the court indicated that a state law cause of action for misappropriation of trade secrets can be pursued. State law causes of action also may lie under the general property law theories of conversion and waste.

3. *Imputing Third–Party Experimental Use to the Inventor.* In *Baxter,* the patentee argued that Cullis was entitled to the benefit of Suaudeau's experimental use. The court rejected this argument because "Suaudeau was not using or testing the invention for Cullis." Should the experimental use doctrine apply to independent third-party activity? But if you do not require the consent or control of the patentee when invoking the public use bar for third-party activity, why should control be required to impute the third-party's experimental use?

The court also stated that "[f]urther refinement of an invention to test additional uses is not the type of experimental use that will negate public use." Do the policy considerations supporting the experimental use doctrine apply with equal force—or at all—to activity by a third party, when the third-party's work perfecting the invention will not enhance the information that appears in the inventor's patent?

4. *Prior User Rights.* In her dissent, Judge Newman stated that "[t]he issue here is not that of an Ito/Suaudeau personal defense as a prior user, a matter of current discussion among policy-makers." In 1999, Congress enacted the American Inventors Protection Act, of which the "First Inventor Defence Act of 1999" was a part. However, this defense is limited to a "method of doing or conducting business." 35 U.S.C. § 273(a)(3). Senator Lott, however, noted during the introduction of the legislation that the word "method" is to be given an expansive meaning. This issue is discussed, *infra*, in Chapter Nine.

6.   FOREIGN ACTIVITY AS A STATUTORY BAR

Section 102(d) incorporates another statutory bar, this one having its focus on foreign patent applicants. This section bars a foreign patent applicant (which may be an American company) from obtaining a United States patent if (1) the foreign application is filed more than one year before the U.S. application is filed *and* (2) the foreign patent issues before the U.S. patent is filed. Thus, even if a foreign applicant files in the U.S. more than one year after the foreign filing he may still obtain a U.S. patent if the foreign patent issues after the U.S. patent. Consider the following case where the court held that the foreign applicant was barred under § 102(d) from obtaining a U.S. patent.

In re Kathawala

9 F.3d 942 (Fed.Cir.1993).

■ Before LOURIE and RADER, CIRCUIT JUDGES, and WOODS, DISTRICT JUDGE.

■ LOURIE, CIRCUIT JUDGE.

Kathawala filed the instant application on April 11, 1985, more than one year after he filed counterpart applications in Greece and Spain on November 21, 1983. Kathawala initially filed an application in the U.S. on November 22, 1982, claiming most of the same compounds as in the instant application. When he filed abroad, however, in 1983, he expanded his claims to include certain ester derivatives of the originally claimed compounds. It is claims to those esters, which Kathawala made the subject of a subsequent continuation-in-part application, the application now before us, that are at issue here.

Both foreign patents issued prior to the instant application in the U.S., the Greek patent on October 2, 1984, and the Spanish patent on January 21, 1985. The specifications of the Greek and Spanish patents are substantially the same as that of the U.S. application, both disclosing the same compounds, compositions, and methods of use. The Greek patent contains claims directed to the compounds, compositions, methods of use, and processes for making the compounds. The Spanish patent contains only "process of making" claims.

Because Kathawala filed his U.S. application claiming the esters more than one year after he filed his corresponding foreign applications, and those foreign applications issued as patents prior to the U.S. filing date, the examiner rejected the claims under 35 U.S.C. § 102(d), which precludes issuance of a patent when the invention was first patented or caused to be patented ... by the applicant or his legal representatives or assigns in a foreign country prior to the date of the application for patent in this country on an application for patent ... filed more than twelve months before the filing of the application in the United States. 35 U.S.C. § 102(d). The examiner rejected each of the claims over the Greek patent, and claims 1 and 2, the compound claims, over the Spanish patent.

Kathawala appealed to the Board, arguing with respect to the rejection over the Greek patent that his invention was not "patented" in Greece under section 102(d) because the compound, composition, and method of use claims in the Greek patent were invalid under Greek law as directed to non-statutory subject matter. Kathawala also argued that the examiner's rejection based on the Spanish patent was erroneous because, although that patent issued and was enforceable prior to the U.S. filing date, the specification was not publicly available until August 1, 1985, the date on which the notice of the Spanish patent grant was officially published, which was after the U.S. filing date. Thus, Kathawala argues, the compositions were not "patented" for purposes of section 102(d). Kathawala further argued that the "invention ... patented" in Spain was not the same "invention" claimed in the U.S. application because the Spanish patent claimed processes for making the compounds, and claims 1 and 2 were directed to the compounds themselves.

The Board affirmed the examiner's rejections over both foreign patents. With regard to the Greek patent, the Board concluded that the validity of the Greek claims was irrelevant for purposes of section 102(d), the controlling fact being that the Greek patent issued containing claims directed to the same invention as the U.S. application. With regard to the Spanish patent, the Board concluded that Kathawala's invention was "patented" when the patent was granted and Kathawala's rights became fixed. The Board also concluded that the "invention ... patented" in Spain was the same "invention" claimed in the U.S. application. Kathawala appealed.

DISCUSSION

The issue before us thus is whether the Board properly determined that the Greek and Spanish patents bar issuance of Kathawala's U.S. application under section 102(d). We must interpret the phrase "invention ... patented" under § 102(d) and determine whether Kathawala's "invention" was first "patented" in Greece and in Spain within the meaning of that provision.

Statutory interpretation is a question of law which we review de novo. *In re Carlson*, 983 F.2d 1032, 1035 (Fed.Cir.1992) (citations omitted). Turning first to the Greek patent, there is no dispute that it contains claims directed to the same invention as that of Kathawala's U.S. application. Kathawala argues, however, that his invention was not first "patented" in Greece under section 102(d) because the compound, composition, and method of use claims are invalid under Greek patent law as directed to non-statutory subject matter. According to Kathawala, only his process claims are valid under Greek law. Kathawala thus argues that the validity of his claims under Greek patent law determines whether his invention was "patented" in Greece within the meaning of section 102(d) prior to his U.S. filing date.

We disagree. Even assuming that Kathawala's compound, composition, and method of use claims are not enforceable in Greece, a matter on which we will not speculate, the controlling fact for purposes of section 102(d) is that the Greek patent issued containing claims directed to the same invention as that of the U.S. application. When a foreign patent issues with claims directed to the same invention as the U.S. application, the invention is "patented" within the meaning of section 102(d); validity of the foreign claims is irrelevant to the section 102(d) inquiry. This is true irrespective of whether the applicant asserts that the claims in the foreign patent are invalid on grounds of non-statutory subject matter or more conventional patentability reasons such as prior art or inadequate disclosure.

Kathawala does not dispute that the Greek patent issued containing claims directed to the same invention as that of his U.S. application. Kathawala sought and obtained the claims contained in the Greek patent and cannot now avoid the § 102(d) bar by arguing that that which he chose to patent abroad should not have been allowed by the foreign patent office. Acceptance of such a position, as the Board stated, would place an " 'unrealistic burden' on the courts and PTO to resolve 'esoteric legal questions which may arise under the patent laws of numerous foreign countries[.']" Slip op. at 21. The PTO should be able to accept at face value the grant of the Greek patent claiming subject matter corresponding to that claimed in a U.S. application, without engaging in an extensive exploration of fine points of foreign law. The claims appear in the Greek patent because the applicant put them there. He cannot claim exemption from the consequences of his own actions. The Board thus correctly concluded that the validity of the Greek claims is irrelevant for purposes of section 102(d). Accordingly, the Board properly affirmed the examiner's rejection over the Greek patent.

Also before us is the rejection of claims 1 and 2, the compound claims, based on the Spanish patent. Kathawala argues that this rejection was erroneous for two reasons. First, Kathawala asserts that although the Spanish patent was granted and enforceable prior to the U.S. filing date, it was not published until after that date. Kathawala thus argues that his invention was not "patented" in Spain until the publication date of the Spansh patent. Second, Kathawala argues that the "invention" of claims 1 and 2, the compounds themselves, is not the same "invention . . . patented" in Spain under section 102(d), that compositions are a separate invention from processes.

We reject both arguments of Kathawala. With regard to the first argument, Kathawala concedes that the Spanish patent issued and was enforceable on January 21, 1985, a date prior to the U.S. filing date. Kathawala nevertheless asserts that the effective date of a foreign patent for purposes of § 102(d), the date on which an invention is "patented," is not the date the foreign patent issues and becomes enforceable, but the date on which it becomes publicly available.

The law on this issue was well established by our predecessor court in *In re Monks*, 588 F.2d 308, 200 USPQ 129 (CCPA 1978), and *In re Talbott*, 443 F.2d 1397, 170 USPQ 281 (CCPA 1971). In Monks, the court considered the date on which an invention was "patented" in Great Britain under § 102(d), and inquired whether the effective date for purposes of that section was the date on which the complete specification was published, a date prior to the U.S. filing date, or the date on which the patent was "sealed" under British law, which occurred after the U.S. filing date. After reviewing the legislative history of section 102(d), the court concluded that "patented" means "a formal bestowal of patent rights from the sovereign to the applicant such as that which occurs when a British patent is sealed." 588 F.2d at 310, 200 USPQ at 131. It was on the "sealed" date that the patentee's rights became fixed and settled and the rights of the patent accrued, not the later publication date. The court thus reversed the examiner's rejection, since the applicant's British patent was not sealed and hence "patented" until after his U.S. filing date. In *Talbott* the court held that a foreign patent need not be publicly available to be "patented" under section 102(d). The court rejected the applicant's argument that the statutory bar did not apply because he had kept his German patent secret until after his U.S. filing date. 443 F.2d 1397, 170 USPQ 281. *See also Duplan Corp. v. Deering Milliken Research Corp.*, 487 F.2d 459, 179 USPQ 449 (4th Cir.1973), cert. denied, 415 U.S. 978, 94 S.Ct. 1565, 39 L.Ed.2d 874 (1974) (An invention is "patented" in France under section 102(d) on its "delivery" date, the date on which the inventor's exclusive rights formally accrue, not on the later publication date when the patent is made publicly available.).

The import of the decisions in *Monks* and *Talbott* is that, contrary to Kathawala's argument, it is irrelevant under section 102(d) whether the Spanish patent was publicly available prior to the U.S. filing date. Rather, the Board correctly concluded that an invention is "patented" in a foreign country under section 102(d) when the patentee's rights under the patent become fixed. *See* Marina V. Schneller, *Patenting and Filing Abroad as a Bar to U.S. Patent Grant—History, Purpose and Sanctions of 35 U.S.C. § 102(d)*, 11 INT'L REV.INDUS.PROP. & COPYRIGHT L. 324, 345 (1980) ("[T]he date upon which the foreign patent is 'patented,' within the meaning of 35 U.S.C. s 102(d), is the date upon which the rights to enforce the foreign patent first accrue to the U.S. applicant ... [and] the publication date of the foreign patent is irrelevant...."). In the instant case, Kathawala stipulated that the Spanish patent was enforceable on January 21, 1985, the date the patent was granted and a date prior to the U.S. filing date. Hence, the Board correctly concluded that Kathawala's invention was "patented" in Spain prior to his U.S. filing date.

Kathawala's second argument is that the "invention" patented in Spain is not the same "invention" claimed in claims 1 and 2. Kathawala argues that each claim defines a separate invention, and since the Spanish claims are directed to processes for making the subject compounds, and claims 1 and 2 of the instant application are directed to the compounds themselves, the "invention" patented in Spain is not the same "invention" as that of claims 1 and 2. Hence Kathawala urges that the rejection of claims 1 and 2 under section 102(d) based on the Spanish patent was erroneous.

We do not agree. It is a truism that a claim defines an invention, and a claim to a composition is indeed different from a claim to a process. However, we cannot let rigid definitions be used in situations to which they don't apply to produce absurd results. The word "invention" in the Patent Act has many meanings depending on the context. *See* Paul M. Janicke, *The Varied Meanings of "Invention" in Patent Practice: Different Meanings in Different Situations*, in PATENT LAW PERSPECTIVES App.1 (Donald R. Dunner *et al.* eds., 1970). In the present context, it must have a meaning consistent with the policy and purpose behind section 102(d), which is to require applicants for patent in the United States to exercise reasonable promptness in filing their applications after they have filed and obtained foreign patents. *See* DONALD S. CHISUM, PATENTS § 6.04[1] (1993).

Kathawala made an "invention" relating to a group of new compounds. He filed applications in Greece and Spain disclosing his invention as consisting of four different aspects: compounds, compositions, methods of use, and processes of making the compounds. While Kathawala had the potential to claim each of those aspects, and did so in his Greek application, he chose to claim only the processes in Spain because, he asserts, pharmaceutical compositions and methods of use were not patentable under Spanish patent law during the relevant time period.

Kathawala's understandable decision not to claim the compounds in Spain, however, does not permit him to evade the statutory bar by arguing that the Spanish Patent Office would not have allowed such claims. Similarly, neither would it have mattered if Kathawala had applied for compound claims and the Spanish Patent Office had rejected them. What is controlling is that the application that Kathawala filed in Spain disclosed and provided the opportunity to claim all aspects of his invention, including the compounds.

It would be contrary to the policy of the statute to permit an applicant to file a foreign application on an invention that may be claimed by four related types of claims, obtain a grant of whatever patent rights were available in the foreign country, and then file an application in the United States, after the foreign patent has issued and more than one year after the foreign filing date on the same invention, with claims directed to those aspects of the invention which were unpatentable in the foreign country. That would permit grant of a U.S. patent on what is essentially the same "invention" as that patented in the foreign country and would frustrate the policy underlying section 102(d), which is to encourage the filing of applications in the United States within a year of the foreign filing of a counterpart patent application. An applicant cannot evade the statutory bar by citing alleged defects of foreign law concerning scope of patentable subject matter.

We thus hold that when an applicant files a foreign application fully disclosing his invention and having the potential to claim his invention in a number of different ways, the reference in section 102(d) to "invention . . . patented" necessarily includes all disclosed aspects of the invention. Thus, the section 102(d) bar applies regardless whether the foreign patent contains claims to less than all aspects of the invention.

* * *

CONCLUSION

Because Kathawala filed Greek and Spanish applications on his "invention" more than one year before he filed an application on the same invention in the United States, and the foreign applications issued as patents prior to his U.S. filing date, Kathawala is barred under 35 U.S.C. § 102(d) from obtaining a U.S. patent. Accordingly, the decision of the Board is affirmed.

NOTES

1. *The Policy of § 102(d).* The general purpose of section 102(d) is to require persons who obtain patent protection abroad to apply promptly for patent protection in the United States. But assuming this policy is valid, some commentators have noted that it may make greater sense to focus on the foreign filing date, rather than on date of patenting:

> Most countries measure the period of a patent from the filing date. . . . Thus, the focus should be on the foreign filing date. The most logical approach would be to make any foreign patent fully prior art against the patentee as of one-year after its filing date. Thus, unless the applicant promptly files in the United States within one year and obtains the right of priority under Section 119, his own foreign patent would operate as prior art against him in the United States.

Donald S. Chisum, *Foreign Activity: Its Effect on Patentability under United States Law*, 11 Int'l Rev. Indus. Prop. & Copyright L. 26, 47 (1980).

2. *Is a Separate Provision Needed?* Arguably, a separate provision on foreign patenting such as § 102(d) seems unwise in terms of policy. It tends to operate only as a technical map for insufficiently advised foreign inventors. There exist many other incentives for prompt filing in the United States. Section 102(d) aside, a foreign applicant must file within twelve months to retain the benefit of the priority filing date, a matter of some importance to many applicants. The applicant must also file within 12 months of patenting or publication of the patent application or be barred under § 102(b).

B. Novelty

Independent of the statutory bar provisions, which focus on the date of filing and on triggering events, the novelty provisions of section 102 operate to prevent a patent from issuing on claimed subject matter that was not new at the time of invention. More specifically, while the statutory bar provisions create a one-year grace period starting from the occurrence of a triggering event, the novelty provisions have no grace period; the claimed subject matter is either new or not new at the time of invention.

Claimed subject matter that is not new at the time of invention is said to be *anticipated*.

The materials that follow explore two important aspects of the novelty provisions. First, they explore how one determines date of invention; second, they explore how one determines which items (*e.g.*, references and sample products) can act as prior art; that is, items that came into existence before the date of invention that can be used against the claimed invention.

These materials also discuss the central analytical tool for every section 102 analysis, whether it relates to a statutory bar or novelty. For a prior art reference to render the claimed subject matter unpatentable under any part of section 102, the reference must contain a disclosure that sets forth each and every element of the claimed invention and enables a person of ordinary skill in the art to make and use the claimed invention. The following materials explore how to determine whether a reference contains such a sufficient disclosure.

1. PROVING DATE OF INVENTION

The novelty provisions of §§ 102(a), (e), and (g) focus on events prior to the date of invention of the applicant or patentee (in contrast to the focus on filing date in §§ 102(b) and (d)). Moreover, the United States is the only industrialized country to award patent rights to the first person to invent (rather than the first to file). Thus, proving date of invention can be an undertaking of extreme importance, as explored in the following case.

Mahurkar v. C.R. Bard, Inc.

79 F.3d 1572 (Fed.Cir.1996).

■ Before ARCHER, CHIEF JUDGE, MICHEL, and RADER, CIRCUIT JUDGES.

■ RADER, CIRCUIT JUDGE.

Dr. Sakharam D. Mahurkar sued C.R. Bard, Inc., Davol Inc., and Bard Access Systems, Inc. (Bard) for infringing U.S. Patent No. 4,808,155 (the '155 patent).

On appeal, the parties raised numerous issues to which this court gave full consideration. As to validity, Bard appeals the trial court's grant of Dr. Mahurkar's motion for judgment as a matter of law at the close of the evidence on anticipation. Because the district court correctly granted Dr. Mahurkar's motion on anticipation, this court affirms in part.

The '155 patent discloses a simple double-lumen catheter. A double-lumen catheter simultaneously removes and restores fluids to the human body during a transfusion. To accomplish this mission, this flexible surgical instrument uses two channels—one to withdraw fluids, another to inject fluids.

Dr. Mahurkar created the claimed invention to treat chronic dialysis patients whose veins usually will no longer tolerate acute catheters. Dr. Mahurkar's invention does not traumatize sensitive veins, yet still supports maximum blood flow with a minimum catheter cross section. After a chronic patient's veins have deteriorated from frequent transfusions, this catheter permits insertion into a major vein—percutaneous insertion—without expensive cut-down surgery.

Dr. Mahurkar filed an initial patent application on his invention on October 24, 1983. After two continuations, the United States Patent and Trademark Office (PTO) issued the '155 patent on February 28, 1989.

In May 1990, Dr. Mahurkar granted Bard a limited license under the '155 patent. This license limited Bard to non-hemodialysis applications. Dr. Mahurkar asserts that Bard made and sold infringing hemodialysis catheters in violation of that license. Specifically, Dr. Mahurkar claims that Bard's "Hickman I" and "Hickman II" hemodialysis catheters infringe the '155 patent.

Bard argues that the '155 patent is invalid under 35 U.S.C. § 102(a). In July 1983, Cook, Inc. published a nationwide catalog (the Cook catalog) disclosing a Cook Double Lumen Subclavian Hemodialysis Catheter. At the conclusion of the evidence at trial, Bard moved for judgment as a matter of law (JMOL) that the Cook catalog anticipated the '155 patent. Dr. Mahurkar cross-moved. The district court granted Dr. Mahurkar's motion for JMOL. According to the district court, no reasonable jury could find the Cook catalog anticipated claim 1 of the '155 patent.

* * *

At trial, Bard sought to show that the Cook catalog anticipated claim 1 of the '155 patent. The catalog's July 1983 publication date preceded the filing of the '155 patent by about three months. The parties disputed only the status of the Cook catalog as prior art under 35 U.S.C. § 102(a). By challenging the validity of the '155 patent, Bard bore the burden of persuasion by clear and convincing evidence on all issues relating to the status of the Cook catalog as prior art.

Section 102(a) of Title 35 defines one class of prior art. As a printed publication, the Cook catalog fits within some terms of 35 U.S.C. § 102(a). Section 102(a) also requires, however, that the catalog description appear before the invention.

In *ex parte* patent prosecution, an examiner may refer to a document published within one year before the filing date of a patent application as prior art. However, this label only applies until the inventor comes forward with evidence showing an earlier date of invention. Once the inventor shows an earlier date of invention, the document is no longer prior art under section 102(a).

Any suggestion that a document is prior art because it appears before the filing date of a patent ignores the requirements of section 102(a). Section 102(a) explicitly refers to invention dates, not filing dates. Thus, under section 102(a), a document is prior art only when published before the invention date. For the Cook catalog to constitute prior art, therefore, it must have been published before Dr. Mahurkar's invention date.

Resolution of this point turns on procedural rules regarding burdens of proof as well as several rules of law borrowed from the interference context. Bard offered into evidence at trial a document published about

three months before the filing date of Dr. Mahurkar's patent disclosing each and every element of the claimed invention. Dr. Mahurkar then had the burden to offer evidence showing he invented the subject matter of his patent before the publication date of the document. *Innovative Scuba*, 26 F.3d at 1115; *see generally Director, Office of Workers' Compensation Programs v. Greenwich Collieries*, 512 U.S. 267, 114 S.Ct. 2251, 2255–57, 129 L.Ed.2d 221 (1994) (discussing burden of persuasion and burden of production). Had Dr. Mahurkar not come forward with evidence of an earlier date of invention, the Cook catalog would have been anticipatory prior art under section 102(a) because Dr. Mahurkar's invention date would have been the filing date of his patent, *Vas–Cath Inc. v. Mahurkar*, 935 F.2d 1555, 1562, 19 U.S.P.Q.2D 1111, 1115 (Fed.Cir.1991).

However, Dr. Mahurkar offered evidence at trial to show that he invented the subject matter of the patent before publication of the Cook reference. He met his burden of production. Consequently, this court turns to an evaluation of the evidence offered by Dr. Mahurkar under the proper burden of persuasion in this infringement action and the rules of law relating to invention dates.

Section 102(g) of Title 35 contains the basic rule for determining priority. 35 U.S.C. § 102(g). Section 102(g) also provides basic protection for the inventive process, shielding in particular the creative steps of conception and reduction to practice. In the United States, the person who first reduces an invention to practice is "prima facie the first and true inventor." *Christie v. Seybold*, 55 F. 69, 76 (6th Cir.1893) (Taft, J.). However, the person "who first conceives, and, in a mental sense, first invents ... may date his patentable invention back to the time of its conception, if he connects the conception with its reduction to practice by reasonable diligence on his part, so that they are substantially one continuous act." *Id.* Stated otherwise, priority of invention "goes to the first party to reduce an invention to practice unless the other party can show that it was the first to conceive the invention and that it exercised reasonable diligence in later reducing that invention to practice." *Price v. Symsek*, 988 F.2d 1187, 1190, 26 U.S.P.Q.2D 1031, 1033 (Fed.Cir.1993).

To have conceived of an invention, an inventor must have formed in his or her mind "a definite and permanent idea of the complete and operative invention, as it is hereafter to be applied in practice." *Burroughs Wellcome Co. v. Barr Labs., Inc.*, 40 F.3d 1223, 1228, 32 U.S.P.Q.2D 1915, 1919 (Fed.Cir.1994), *cert. denied*, 516 U.S. 1070, 116 S.Ct. 771, 133 L.Ed.2d 724 (1996) (citations omitted). The idea must be "so clearly defined in the inventor's mind that only ordinary skill would be necessary to reduce the invention to practice, without extensive research or experimentation." *Id.*

This court has developed a rule requiring corroboration where a party seeks to show conception through the oral testimony of an inventor. This requirement arose out of a concern that inventors testifying in patent infringement cases would be tempted to remember facts favorable to their case by the lure of protecting their patent or defeating another's patent. *Eibel Process Co. v. Minnesota & Ontario Paper Co.*, 261 U.S. 45, 60, 43 S.Ct. 322, 327, 67 L.Ed. 523 (1923). While perhaps prophylactic in application given the unique abilities of trial court judges and juries to assess credibility, the rule provides a bright line for both district courts and the PTO to follow in addressing the difficult issues related to invention dates.

In assessing corroboration of oral testimony, courts apply a rule of reason analysis. Under a rule of reason analysis, "[a]n evaluation of all pertinent evidence must be made so that a sound determination of the credibility of the inventor's story may be reached." (citation omitted).

This court does not require corroboration where a party seeks to prove conception through the use of physical exhibits. The trier of fact can conclude for itself what documents show, aided by testimony as to what the exhibit would mean to one skilled in the art.

Reduction to practice follows conception. To show actual reduction to practice, an inventor must demonstrate that the invention is suitable for its intended purpose. *Scott v. Finney*, 34 F.3d 1058, 1061, 32 U.S.P.Q.2D 1115, 1118 (Fed.Cir.1994). Depending on the character of the invention and the problem it solves, this showing may require test results. *Id.* at 1062; *Manville Sales Corp. v. Paramount Sys., Inc.*, 917 F.2d 544, 550, 16 U.S.P.Q.2D 1587, 1592 (Fed.Cir.1990). Less complicated inventions and problems do not demand stringent testing. In fact, some inventions are so simple and their purpose and efficacy so obvious that their complete construction is sufficient to demonstrate workability. *Id.*

Where a party is first to conceive but second to reduce to practice, that party must demonstrate reasonable diligence toward reduction to practice from a date just prior to the other party's conception to its reduction to practice. *Griffith v. Kanamaru*, 816 F.2d 624, 625–26, 2 U.S.P.Q.2D 1361, 1362 (Fed.Cir.1987).

Bard bears the burden of persuasion on the status of the Cook catalog as prior art. Bard must persuade the trier of fact by clear and convincing evidence that the Cook catalog was published prior to Dr. Mahurkar's invention date.

At trial, Dr. Mahurkar offered evidence to demonstrate prior invention in two ways. He offered evidence to show he conceived and reduced to practice his invention before publication of the catalog. He also offered evidence to show that he conceived of his invention prior to the date of publication of the Cook catalog and that he proceeded with reasonable diligence from a date just prior to publication of the catalog to his filing date. Bard, in turn, challenged Dr. Mahurkar's evidence.

With all of the evidence from both sides before the jury, Bard must persuade the jury by clear and convincing evidence that its version of the facts is true. In other words, Bard must persuade the jury that Dr. Mahurkar did not invent prior to publication of the catalog. This is because (1) he did not conceive and reduce his invention to practice before the publication date and (2) he did not conceive and thereafter proceed with reasonable diligence as required to his filing date. If Bard fails to meet this burden, the catalog is not prior art under section 102(a).

Viewing the evidence of record below in the light most favorable to Bard, this court concludes that no reasonable jury could have found clear and convincing evidence that the Cook catalog was prior art. Dr. Mahurkar testified that he conceived and began work on dual-lumen, flexible, hemodialysis catheters, including the '155 catheter, in 1979. From late 1980 through early 1981, Dr. Mahurkar constructed polyethylene prototype catheters in his kitchen. He bought tubing and various machines for making and testing his catheters.

During this time period, he also tested polyethylene prototypes and used them in flow and pressure drop tests in his kitchen. These tests used glycerine to simulate blood. These tests showed, to the limit of their design, the utility of his claimed invention. Dr. Mahurkar designed these tests to show the efficiency of his structure knowing that polyethylene catheters were too brittle for actual use with humans. But, he also knew that his invention would become suitable for its intended purpose by simple substitution of a soft, biocompatible material. Dr. Mahurkar adequately showed reduction to practice of his less complicated invention with tests which "[did] not duplicate all of the conditions of actual use." *Gordon v. Hubbard*, 347 F.2d 1001, 1006, 146 USPQ 303, 307 (CCPA 1965).

Dr. Mahurkar provided corroboration for his testimony. Dr. Mahurkar confidentially disclosed the catheter prototype tips of his '155 invention to Geoffrey Martin, President of Vas–Cath Inc. in 1981, and Brian L. Bates of Cook, Inc. Mr. Martin testified that he received the polyethylene prototype tips from Dr. Mahurkar in 1981. Dr. Mahurkar also produced a letter from Stephen Brushey, an employee of Vas–Cath, dated April 21, 1981, that described several of his catheters. Additionally, Dr. Mahurkar presented a letter from Brian L. Bates of Cook, Inc., dated October 23, 1981. In this letter, Cook was "impressed with the thought and technology which has gone into the fabrication of the prototype material."

In addition to evidence of actual reduction to practice before publication of the Cook catalog, Dr. Mahurkar also showed reasonable diligence from his conception date through the filing of his patent application. From conception to filing, Dr. Mahurkar continuously sought to locate companies capable of extruding his tubing with the soft, flexible materials necessary for human use.

On this record and with the applicable burden of persuasion, no reasonable jury could have found that Bard proved the Cook catalog was prior art. Consequently, the court properly granted Dr. Mahurkar's motion for JMOL of non-anticipation of claim 1 of the '155 patent.

Affirmed-in-part, Vacated-in-part, and Remanded

NOTES

1. *Date of Invention as Critical Date.* As the court in *Mahurkar* stated, "a document is prior art only when published before the invention date." Thus, the critical date under § 102(a) is the inventor's *date of invention*.

Proving date of invention for novelty purposes (as well as for determining who is entitled to a patent between two or more parties claiming the same invention) is unique to American patent law. Other industrialized nations are first-to-file countries, which means that they look to the *priority date* (not date of invention), which is the earliest filing date of the patent application. For example, the novelty provision of the European Patent Convention, section 54(2), looks to the "state of the art ... *before the date of filing* of the European patent application." (Emphasis added). And Article 29(1) of the Japanese Patent Law recites that one is entitled to a patent unless the invention was "publicly known in Japan or elsewhere *prior to the filing* of the patent application." (Emphasis added). As we discussed in Section A, *supra*, there is no grace period under the European Patent Convention. Thus, not only is the filing date under the EPC important for novelty purposes, but it dictates when inventors can begin exploiting their inventions.

2. *Burden of Proof. Mahurkar* made clear that the party challenging the validity of a patent has the burden of persuasion by clear and convincing evidence on all issues relating to "the status of the" prior art (Cook catalog). Once the challenger presented prior art evidence, the burden shifted to the patentee, or the patent applicant, "to offer evidence showing he invented the subject matter of his patent before the publication date of the [prior art reference]."

3. *Proving Date of Invention.* The court borrowed extensively from § 102(g) interference practice (which we will cover in Section B–10, *infra*). To summarize, (1) the first to reduce to practice is the prima facie first inventor, but a party who was second to reduce to practice will be considered the first inventor if he can show that he was the first to conceive and exercised reasonable diligence in reducing his invention to practice; (2) reduction to practice is shown if the inventor can prove that the invention works for its intended purpose and there is a contemporaneous appreciation of such; and (3) conception is proved through the presentation of corroborated evidence that the inventor formed in his mind "a definite and permanent idea of the complete and operative invention, as it is thereafter applied in practice."

There are two types of reduction to practice (RTP): (1) Constructive, which the date of filing the patent application regardless of whether anything is physically constructed; and (2) Actual, which occurs when the invention is shown to be suitable for its intended purpose and there is a "contemporaneous recognition and appreciation of the invention represented by the claims." *Purdue Pharma L.P. v. Boehringer Ingelheim,* 237 F.3d 1359, 1365 (Fed.Cir.2001). As the Federal Circuit, in *Estee Lauder Inc. v. L'Oreal, S.A.,* 129 F.3d 588 (Fed.Cir.1997), explained:

> [I]n addition to preparing a composition, an inventor must establish that he "knew it would work," to reduce the invention to practice.... This suggests that a reduction to practice does not occur until an inventor, or perhaps his agent, knows that the invention will work for its intended purpose.... [U]ntil he learns that threshold information, there can be no reduction to practice. Moreover, *Burroughs Wellcome* [see Section B–10, *infra*] states that a reduction to practice requires "the discovery that an invention actually works." ... This suggests that until that "discovery" is actually made, there is no reduction to practice. These cases trumpet, therefore, the principle that a reduction to practice does not occur until the inventor has determined that the invention will work for its intended purpose. "It is well-settled that conception and reduction to practice cannot be established nunc pro tunc. There must be *contemporaneous recognition and appreciation* of the invention represented by the counts." *Breen v. Henshaw,* 472 F.2d 1398, 1401 (CCPA 1973) (emphasis added) (holding no reduction to practice during lab experiments because there was no "indication in the contemporaneous record" that utility "was recognized *at that time*" (emphasis added)).

Id. at 593–4. *See* Section B–10, *infra*.

4. *Foreign Inventive Activity and § 104.* Prior to the implementation of NAFTA and the international agreement on the Trade–Related Aspects of Intellectual Property Rights (TRIPS) of GATT, inventive activity (*i.e.*, conception and reduction to practice) outside of the United States could not be used to prove date of invention under 35 U.S.C. § 104. This pro-American bias has historically been a part of American patent law. For instance, foreign applicants were not permitted to obtain U.S. patents under the 1793 Patent Act, and while foreigners could obtain patent rights under the 1836 Act, British citizens were required to pay $500 and other aliens had to submit $300.

The later twentieth century witnessed a strong push towards harmonization. Consistent with this trend, § 104 was amended to permit patent applicants to rely on inventive activity in any NAFTA or World Trade Organization (WTO) member country. The amendments to § 104 became effective for NAFTA and WTO countries on *December 8, 1993* and *January 1, 1996*, respectively. Inventive activity occurring before December 8, 1993 in NAFTA countries and before January 1, 1996 in WTO countries cannot be used to prove date of invention.

NAFTA and GATT/TRIPS did not amend § 102(g), which, prior to American Inventors Protection Act of 1999, limited inventive activity for priority purposes (*i.e.*, obtaining a patent) to acts *"in this country."* Thus, there was an inconsistency between §§ 104 and 102(g), wherein the former permitted foreign-based inventive activity to be used in an interference proceeding, but § 102(g) appeared to prevent the applicant from relying on that activity. The American Inventors Protection Act amended § 102(g) to allow foreign-based inventive activity to be used in an *interference*, thus making § 102(g) consistent with § 104. Section 102(g) now reads:

A person shall be entitled to a patent unless—

(g)(1) during the course of an interference conducted under section 135 or section 291, another inventor involved therein establishes, to the extent permitted in section 104, that before such person's invention thereof the invention was made by such other inventor and not abandoned, suppressed, or concealed, or (2) before such person's invention thereof, the invention was made in this country by another inventor who had not abandoned, suppressed, or concealed it....

Thus, there is a distinction between *patent-obtaining* and *patent-defeating* activity. One may use foreign-based inventive activity to *obtain* a patent under § 102(g)(1). However, foreign-based inventive activity cannot be used as prior art to *defeat* patent rights outside of the interference context. Although such prior art is defeating in the sense that an applicant can use it to obtain a patent over another, thereby defeating another's quest to obtain patent rights, it is important to note again that the use of foreign-based inventive activity is limited to the interference context (*i.e.*, obtaining rights). Inventive activity that can be used as prior art to defeat patent rights is limited under § 102(g)(2) to activity "in this country."

Does this dichotomy violate the spirit, if not the letter, of Article 27(1) of TRIPS, the non-discrimination provision? This article reads:

Subject to the provisions of paragraphs 2 and 3, patents shall be available for any inventions, whether products or processes, in all fields of technology, provided that they are new, involve an inventive step and are capable of industrial application. Subject to paragraph 4 of Article 65, paragraph 8 of Article 70 and paragraph 3 of this Article, patents shall be available and patent rights enjoyable without discrimination as to the place of invention, the field of technology and whether products are imported or locally produced.

5. *Proving Date of Invention for Chemical/Biological Compounds.* In *Amgen, Inc. v. Chugai Pharmaceutical Co., Ltd.*, 927 F.2d 1200 (Fed.Cir.1991), the patent related to DNA sequences for encoding erythropoietin (EPO). The court defined conception in the same manner as did the court in *Mahurkar*, but went on to say that

[i]n some instances, an inventor is unable to establish a conception until he has reduced his invention to practice through a successful experiment. This situation results in simultaneous conception and reduction to practice....

A gene is a chemical compound, albeit a complex one, and it is well established in our law that conception of a chemical compound requires that the inventor be able to define it so as to distinguish it from other materials, and to describe how to obtain it. Conception does not occur unless one has a mental picture of the structure of the chemical, or is able to define it by its method of preparation, its physical or chemical properties, or whatever characteristics sufficiently distinguish it. It is not sufficient to define it solely by its principal biological property, *e.g.*, encoding for [EPO], because an alleged conception having no more specificity than that is simply a wish to know the identity of any material with that biological property. We hold that when an inventor is unable to envision the detailed constitution of a gene so as to distinguish it from other materials, as well as a method for obtaining it, conception has not been achieved until reduction to practice has occurred, *i.e.*, until after the gene has been isolated.

Id. at 1206.

6. *Rule 131—"Swearing Behind the Reference."* 37 C.F.R. 1.131 allows an applicant to "swear behind" the effective date of a reference. Date of invention, as discussed, is proved by showing reduction to practice prior to the effective date of the prior art reference, or conception of the invention prior to the effective date and due diligence. *See* 37 C.F.R. 1.131(b). A Rule 131 affidavit only applies to references that *disclose*, but do not claim, the subject matter claimed in the patent application. It should also be pointed out that Rule 131 affidavits can not remove references whose effective date is "more than one year prior to the date on which the application was filed in this country." Thus, Rule 131 cannot be used to overcome statutory bars under Section 102(b).

2. IDENTITY OF INVENTION AND ANTICIPATORY ENABLEMENT

As explored in *Paulsen*, below, for a reference to anticipate, in addition to being prior, it must also have an adequate disclosure as measured under a standard similar to the enablement requirement explored in Chapter Three.

In re Paulsen

30 F.3d 1475 (Fed.Cir.1994).

■ Before NIES, MICHEL, and LOURIE, CIRCUIT JUDGES.

■ LOURIE, CIRCUIT JUDGE.

AST Research, Inc., (AST) appeals from the July 23, 1993 decision of the United States Patent and Trademark Office (PTO) Board of Patent Appeals and Interferences sustaining the final rejection upon reexamination of claims 1–4, 6, 9–12, and 18–34 of U.S. Patent 4,571,456. We affirm.

BACKGROUND

The '456 patent, entitled "Portable Computer," was issued to David C. Paulsen *et al.*, on February 18, 1986. The claims of the patent are directed to a portable computer contained within a compact metal case. A salient feature of the claimed invention is its "clam shell" configuration, in which the computer's display housing is connected to the computer at its midsection by a hinge assembly that enables the display to swing from a closed, latched position for portability and protection to an open, erect position for viewing and operation. Computers consistent with this design are commonly referred to as "laptop" computers.

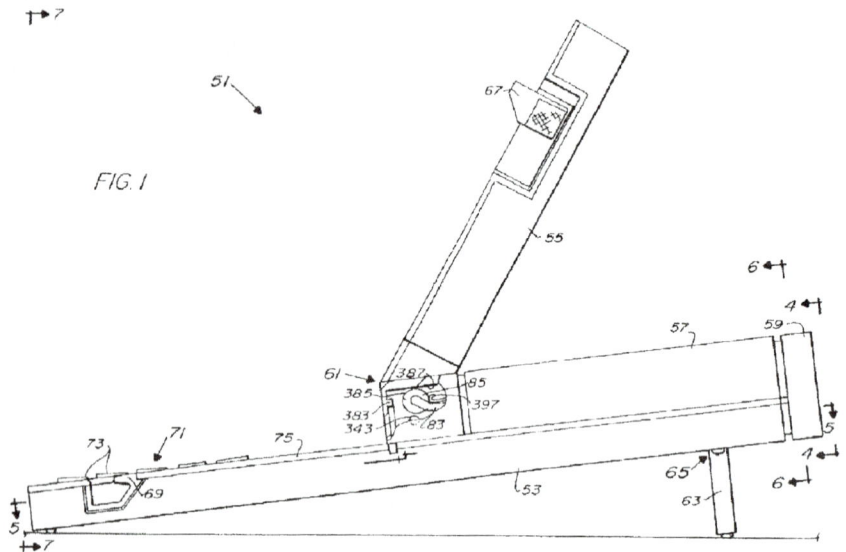

FIG. 1

On April 27, 1990, and subsequently on June 12, 1990 and October 22, 1990, requests were filed in the PTO for reexamination of the '456 patent. See 35 U.S.C. § 302 (1988). The requests were consolidated into a single proceeding for the reexamination of claims 1 through 34. On August 9, 1991, the examiner issued a final office action in the reexamination rejecting claims 1–4, 6, 7, 9–12, and 18–34. Independent claims 1 and 18 were rejected under 35 U.S.C. § 102(b) (1988) as being anticipated by Japanese Application 47–14961 to Yokoyama.

On appeal, the Board affirmed the examiner's rejections except as to claim 7. In sustaining the rejections of claims 1 and 18, the Board rejected the appellant's argument that Yokoyama is a non-enabling reference. AST, the present assignee of the '456 patent, now appeals from the Board's decision.

DISCUSSION

We first address AST's challenge to the Board's determination that claims 1 and 18 are anticipated by the Yokoyama reference. Anticipation is a question of fact subject to review under the "clearly erroneous" standard. *In re King*, 801 F.2d 1324, 1326, 231 USPQ 136, 138 (Fed.Cir.1986). A rejection for anticipation under section 102 requires that each and every limitation of the claimed invention be disclosed in a single prior art reference. In addition, the reference must be enabling and describe the applicant's claimed invention sufficiently to have placed it in possession of a person of ordinary skill in the field of the invention.

The Yokoyama reference discloses a desktop calculator contained within a housing having the form of a portable attache case. The front half of the case consists of a lid that is hinged at the midsection of the case. Connected to the inside of the lid is a display which is able to be viewed when the lid is opened to a vertical position. A keyboard is also exposed for operation when the lid is opened. When the device is to be transported, the lid is closed and latched to protect the display and the keyboard.

AST asserts that Yokoyama does not anticipate claims 1 and 18 because it is not enabling. AST argues that Yokoyama only discloses a box for a calculator and thus does not teach how to make and use a portable calculator. This argument, however, fails to recognize that a prior art reference must be "considered together with the knowledge of one of ordinary skill in the pertinent art." *In re Samour,* 571 F.2d 559, 562, 197 USPQ 1,3–4 (CCPA 1978); *see also DeGeorge,* 768 F.2d at 1323, 226 USPQ at 762 (Fed.Cir.1985) (a reference "need not, however, explain every detail since [it] is speaking to those skilled in the art"). As the Board found below, the level of skill to which Yokoyama is addressed was "quite advanced" at the time the '456 patent was filed and that "one of ordinary skill in the art certainly was capable of providing the circuitry necessary to make the device operable for use as a computer." We discern no clear error in the Board's findings and conclude as a matter of law that Yokoyama is sufficiently enabling to serve as a section 102(b) reference.[9] See *Gould v. Quigg,* 822 F.2d 1074, 1077 (Fed.Cir.1987) (ultimate issue of enablement is one of law based on underlying factual findings).

Accordingly, we affirm the Board's rejection of claims 1 and 18 as being anticipated by Yokoyama.

NOTES

1. *The Identity Requirement.* To anticipate an invention, a *single* prior art reference must disclose each and every limitation of the claimed invention. In other words, anticipation cannot be shown by combining two or more references. *See In re Bond,* 910 F.2d 831, 832 (Fed.Cir.1990) ("For a prior art reference to anticipate in terms of 35 U.S.C. § 102, every element of the claimed invention must be identically shown in a single reference"). It should be noted that the single source rule does not preclude the use of extrinsic evidence to prove what a reference discloses to one of ordinary skill in the art. *See Scripps Clinic & Research Foundation v. Genentech, Inc.,* 927 F.2d 1565 (Fed.Cir.1991) (It "is sometimes appropriate to consider extrinsic evidence to explain the disclosure of a reference. [However,] [s]uch factual elaboration is necessarily of limited scope and probative value, ... a finding [of anticipation] is not supportable if it is necessary to prove facts beyond those disclosed in the reference in order to meet the claim limitations."). In essence,

---

9. We also note that under the enablement standard that AST would have us apply to Yokoyama, the '456 patent itself would be non-enabling. The '456 patent similarly relies on the knowledge and skill of those skilled in the art. If detailed disclosure regarding implementation of known electronic and mechanical components necessary to build a computer were essential for an anticipating reference, then the disclosure in the '456 patent would also fail to satisfy the enablement requirement.

extrinsic evidence may be used to "explain, but not expand," what a reference means. *See In re Baxter Travenol Labs.*, 952 F.2d 388, 390 (Fed.Cir.1991). Moreover, if a claim covers several compositions, "by recitation of ranges or otherwise, . . . a claim is 'anticipated' if *one* of them is in the prior art." *Titanium Metals Corp. of America v. Banner*, 778 F.2d 775, 782 (Fed.Cir.1985) (emphasis in original).

2. *Anticipatory Enablement v. § 112 Enablement.* As *In re Paulsen* states, for a prior art reference to anticipate a claimed invention, the reference must *enable a person of ordinary skill in the art* to produce the claimed invention. In other words, prior art under § 102:

> must sufficiently describe the claimed invention to have placed the public in possession of it. Such possession is effected if one of ordinary skill in the art could have combined the publication's description of the invention with his own knowledge to make the claimed invention. Accordingly, even if the claimed invention is disclosed in a printed publication, that disclosure will not suffice as prior art if it is not enabling. It is not, however, necessary that an invention disclosed in a publication shall have actually been made in order to satisfy the enablement requirement.

In re Donohue, 766 F.2d 531, 533 (Fed.Cir.1985). The Federal Circuit, borrowing from the § 112 enablement requirement, has held that a skilled artisan must be able to make and use the invention without undue experimentation, and "[t]he determination of what constitutes undue experimentation in a given case requires the application of a standard of reasonableness, having due regard for the nature of the invention and the state of the art." *In re Wands*, 858 F.2d 731, 737 (Fed.Cir. 1988). *See, e.g., American Medical Systems, Inc. v. Medical Engineering Corp.*, 794 F.Supp. 1370, 1383 (E.D.Wis.1992), *aff'd in part, rev'd in part & remanded*, 6 F.3d 1523 (Fed.Cir.1993) (The experiments of Dr. Austad were not prior art because "while various persons may have entered Dr. Austad's lab, the concept of how the filled tissue expanders were stored were not public. For one thing, persons having access to the lab would not know the import of the jars until someone explained it to them.").

When patent attorneys speak of the "enablement requirement," they are usually referring to § 112, which requires a patent applicant to sufficiently describe her invention so as to "enable any person skilled in the art to which it pertains, . . . to make and use" the invention. Compare the requirements of § 102 with those of § 112. Can you discern any differences? What is the policy behind these requirements? Both serve to place the subject matter at issue into the possession of the public. Why is that important? Under 37 C.F.R. § 1.132, an inventor can argue that a prior art reference is not anticipatory (or perhaps even not relevant) because it discloses an inoperable invention. Should a patent applicant that discloses no more in her specification than what is disclosed in a prior art reference assert that the latter is non-enabling? What did the court in *In re Paulsen* hold? *See also, In re Epstein*, 32 F.3d 1559, 1568 (Fed.Cir.1994) ("With respect to the [applicant's] argument that the publications lack diagrams, flow charts, and source codes that would enable one of ordinary skill in the art to practice the systems described in the publications, we find that the disclosure of appellant's system fails to provide the same detailed information concerning the claimed invention. In the absence of such a specific description, we assume that anyone desiring to carry out such computerized . . . systems would know of the equipment and techniques to be used.").

It is important to note that while a reference must be enabling to anticipate under § 102, "a non-enabling reference may qualify as prior art for the purpose of determining obviousness under § 103." *See Symbol Technologies, Inc. v. Opticon, Inc.*, 935 F.2d 1569, 1578 (Fed.Cir.1991). All this means is that a non-enabling disclosure can act as prior art under § 103 for what it *discloses* and *teaches*; and therefore can be combined with other references. *See* Chapter Five.

3. *Inherency and Knowledge of Persons of Ordinary Skill in the Art.* In *Minnesota Mining & Mfg. Co. v. Johnson & Johnson Orthopaedics*, 976 F.2d 1559, 1565 (Fed.Cir.1992), the Federal Circuit explained that anticipation of a patent claim must be proven by showing that "each element of the claim in issue is found, either expressly or under principles of inherency, in a single prior art reference." What is meant by "principles of inherency?" In *Glaxo Inc. v. Novopharm Ltd.*, 52 F.3d 1043 (Fed.Cir.1995), the Federal Circuit affirmed a lower court's finding of no anticipation based on inherency. According to the district court:

> If an inventor seeks to claim an advantage or modification that flows necessarily from a prior art reference, the reference inherently anticipates the inventor's claim ... even if the advantage was not appreciated by the inventor of the prior art.... In order for a claim to be inherent in the prior art it is not sufficient that a person following the disclosure sometimes obtain the result set forth in the claim, it must invariably happen.

830 F.Supp. 871, 874 (E.D.N.C.1993). *See also, In re Robertson*, 169 F.3d 743, 745 (Fed.Cir.1999) ("To establish inherency, the extrinsic evidence 'must make clear that the missing descriptive matter is necessarily present in the thing described in the reference, and that it would be so recognized by persons of ordinary skill.'" *Continental Can Co. v. Monsanto Co.*, 948 F.2d 1264, 1268 (Fed.Cir.1991)). Inherency, however, may not be established by probabilities or possibilities. The mere fact that a certain thing may result from a given set of circumstances is not sufficient. "We also note that under the enablement standard that AST would have us apply to Yokoyama, the '456 patent itself would be non-enabling. The '456 patent similarly relies on the knowledge and skill of those skilled in the art. If detailed disclosure regarding implementation of known electronic and mechanical components necessary to build a computer were essential for an anticipating reference, then the disclosure in the '456 patent would also fail to satisfy the enablement requirement." *Id.* at 1269.

How do you reconcile the concept of inherency with the famous Supreme Court case of *Tilghman v. Proctor*, 102 U.S. 707 (1880), wherein the Court held that "If the [claimed invention] were accidentally and unwittingly produced, whilst the operators were in pursuit of other and different results, without exciting attention and without it even being known what was done or how it had been done, it would be absurd to say that this was an anticipation...."? *Id.* at 711. *See also, International Nickel Co. v. Ford Motor Co.*, 166 F.Supp. 551, 560–61 (S.D.N.Y.1958) ("[A] prior use of a product deliberately created may constitute an anticipation, though the full benefits accruing therefrom may not be fully appreciated or even recognized. The prior user may have been in complete ignorance of the scientific phenomenon involved.... [However,] [w]here the allegedly anticipating product was produced merely by chance and never recognized nor appreciated, one who later discovers and recognizes the product may patent it.").

What is the relationship between inherency and knowledge of persons of ordinary skill in the art? Recall that in *In re Paulsen*, the court noted that in determining anticipation, not only must a court consider what the prior art discloses, but also the knowledge of one of ordinary skill in the art. In *Atlas Powder Co. v. Ireco, Inc.*, 190 F.3d 1342, 1347 (Fed.Cir.1999), the Federal Circuit elaborated on the relationship between inherency and knowledge of one of ordinary skill in the art:

> Under principles of inherency, if the prior art necessarily functions in accordance with, or includes, the claimed limitations, it anticipates. Inherency is not coterminous with knowledge of those of ordinary skill in the

art. Artisans of ordinary skill may not recognize the inherent characteristics or functioning of the prior art. However, the discovery of a previously unappreciated property of a prior art composition, or of a scientific explanation for the prior art's functioning, does not render the old composition patentably new to the discoverer.

* * *

The public is free to make, use, or sell prior art compositions or processes, regardless of whether or not they understand their complete makeup or the underlying scientific principles which allow them to operate. The doctrine of anticipation by inherency, among other doctrines, enforces that basic principle.

See also Schering Corp. v. Geneva Pharmaceuticals, 339 F.3d 1373 (Fed.Cir.2003) (stating "this court rejects the contention that inherent anticipation requires recognition in the prior art.... Contrary to Schering's contention, *Continental Can* does not stand for the proposition that an inherent feature of a prior art reference must be perceived as such by a person of ordinary skill in the art before the critical date.... Read in context, *Continental Can* stands for the proposition that inherency, like anticipation itself, requires a determination of the meaning of the prior art. Thus, a court may consult artisans of ordinary skill to ascertain their understanding about subject matter disclosed by the prior art, including features inherent in the prior art").

4. *"That Which Will Infringe If Later, Will Anticipate, If Earlier."* This maxim, first articulated by the Supreme Court in *Knapp v. Morss*, 150 U.S. 221 (1893), is known as the "classic infringement test for anticipation." For example, A invents and publishes a description of a device comprising X, Y, and Z and, thereafter, B invents and files a patent application on a device comprising X, Y, and Z. Does A's device anticipate B's claimed invention? Under the classic test, we would ask: if A's invention had come after B's, would it have infringed B's claims? What if B claimed X, Y, and Q? Even with Q in her claim, A may still infringe under the doctrine of equivalents, which we will discuss in Chapter Eight. That is, Z may be "equivalent" to Q. Therefore, the classic test must be modified to read as follows: "That which would *literally* infringe if later in time anticipates if earlier than the date of invention." *Lewmar Marine, Inc. v. Barient, Inc.*, 827 F.2d 744, 747 (Fed.Cir.1987).

5. *Genus and Species Claims.* One may not claim a genus if the prior art discloses a species of the claimed genus. *See In re Gosteli*, 872 F.2d 1008 (Fed.Cir.1989). Recall our maxim in note 4, "that which will infringe if later, will anticipate if earlier." Clearly, the species would infringe the genus claim if the species would have come later. What if a patentee secures a patent on a species and, thereafter, files for a patent on the genus? The same result. *See Eli Lilly & Co. v. Barr Laboratories, Inc.*, 222 F.3d 973, 987 (Fed.Cir.2000) ("Our law firmly establishes that a later genus claim is not patentable over an earlier species claim.").

But when "the only pertinent disclosure in the reference is a single species of the claimed genus, the applicant can overcome the rejection directly under 37 C.F.R. 1.131 by showing prior possession of the species disclosed in the reference." § 715.03 MPEP. But a reference "which discloses several species of a claimed genus can be overcome directly under [rule 131] *only* by a showing that the applicant completed, prior to the date of the reference, all of the species shown in the reference." *Id.*; *In re Stempel*, 241 F.2d 755 (CCPA 1957).

What about when a reference discloses the genus and a species of that genus is later claimed? Should this situation be treated differently than where the species is disclosed prior to the later claimed genus? Consider the following example: Inventor claims a composition of matter comprising element X having a melt index of *less* than 5 grams. The patent specification showed that many pre-existing problems were solved by keeping the melt index less than 5, and demonstrated how similar compositions of matter with melt indexes of greater than 5 had significant short-comings. The prior art disclosed an identical composition of matter and stated that the preferred melt index should be between 0.1 and 40. Does this prior art reference anticipate Inventor's patent claim? Does your answer change if Inventor performed a great deal of experimentation, picking, choosing, and selecting various melt indexes before arriving at the claimed invention? *See Ex Parte Lee*, 31 U.S.P.Q.2d 1105 (Bd.Pat. App. and Int'f 1993). Courts have held that a prior genus does not always anticipate a later claimed species, but *may* render the later claimed species obvious under 35 U.S.C. § 103. *See In re* Baird, 16 F.3d 380 (Fed.Cir.1994) and *In re Jones*, 958 F.2d 347 (Fed.Cir.1992). *See also, Eli Lilly & Co. v. Barr Laboratories, Inc.*, 222 F.3d 973, 986 (Fed.Cir.2000) ("Lilly's reliance on *In re Baird* and *In re Jones* is unavailing. In those cases, we held that a species claim is not necessarily obvious in light of a prior art disclosure of a genus.... The present case, however, in which the same party *claims* a genus in an earlier patent and then *claims* a species in a later patent is entirely different from cases such as *Baird* and *Jones*, in which the prior art merely *discloses* a genus and a later patent claims a species.") (emphasis in original).

3. "KNOWN OR USED"

The issue here is whether a use will trigger the "known or used" provision of § 102(a) if the use is not accessible to the public. Although the statutory phrase itself does not mention "in public," some "publicity" dimension has been read in through the case law. As explored in the materials that follow, the use must be in a manner that is accessible to the public in the U.S. for it to trigger this provision of the statute.

Gayler v. Wilder
51 U.S. (10 How.) 477 (1850).

■ MR. CHIEF JUSTICE TANEY delivered the opinion of the court.

The [assignee, Wilder, of the patent-in-suit] brought an action against Gayler and Brown, for an alleged infringement of a patent right for the use of plaster of Paris in the construction of fire-proof chests. In the declaration, it was averred that one Daniel Fitzgerald was the original and first inventor of a new and useful improvement in fire-proof chests or safes, and that letters patent were granted him therefor, bearing date the 1st day of June, 1843.

* * *

The remaining question is upon the validity of the patent on which the suit was brought.

It appears that James Conner, who carried on the business of a stereotype founder in the city of New York, made a safe for his own use between the years 1829 and 1832, for the protection of his papers against fire; and continued to use it until 1838, when it passed into other hands. It was kept in his counting-room and known to the persons engaged in the foundery; and after it passed out of his hands, he used others of a different construction.

It does not appear what became of this safe afterwards. And there is nothing in the testimony from which it can be inferred that its mode of construction was known to the person into whose possession it fell, or that any value was attached to it as a place of security for papers against fire; or that it was ever used for that purpose.

Upon these facts the court instructed the jury, "that if Connor had not made his discovery public, but had used it simply for his own private purpose, and it had been finally forgotten or abandoned, such a discovery and use would be no obstacle to the taking out of a patent by Fitzgerald or those claiming under him, if he be an original, though not the first, inventor or discoverer."

The instruction assumes that the jury might find from the evidence that Conner's safe was substantially the same with that of Fitzgerald, and also prior in time. And if the fact was so, the question then was whether the patentee was "the original and first inventor or discoverer", within the meaning of the act of Congress.

The act of 1836, ch. 357, § 6, authorizes a patent where the party has discovered or invented a new and useful improvement, "not known or used by others before his discovery or invention." And the 15th section provides that, if it appears on the trial of an action brought for the infringement of a patent that the patentee "was not the original and first inventor or discoverer of the thing patented", the verdict shall be for the defendant.

Upon a literal construction of these particular words, the patentee in this case certainly was not the original and first inventor or discoverer, if the Conner safe was the same with his, and preceded his discovery. But we do not think that this construction would carry into effect the intention of the legislature. It is not by detached words and phrases that a statute ought to be expounded. The whole act must be taken together, and a fair interpretation given to it, neither extending nor restricting it beyond the legitimate import of its language, and its obvious policy and object. And in the 15th section, after making the provision above mentioned, there is a further provision, that, if it shall appear that the patentee at the time of his application for the patent believed himself to be the first inventor, the patent shall not be void on account of the invention or discovery having been known or used in any foreign country, it not appearing that it had been before patented or described in any printed publication.

In the case thus provided for, the party who invents is not strictly speaking the first and original inventor. The law assumes that the improvement may have been known and used before his discovery. Yet his patent is valid if he discovered it by the efforts of his own genius, and believed himself to be the original inventor. The clause in question qualifies the words before used, and shows that by knowledge and use the legislature meant knowledge and use existing in a manner accessible to the public. If the foreign invention had been printed or patented, it was already given to the world and open to the people of this country, as well as of others, upon reasonable inquiry. They would therefore derive no advantage from the invention here. It would confer no benefit upon the community, and the inventor therefore is not considered to be entitled to the reward. But if the foreign discovery is not patented, nor described in any printed publication, it might be known and used in remote places for ages, and the people of this country be unable to profit by it. The means of obtaining knowledge would not be within their reach; and, as far as their interest is concerned, it would be the same thing as if the improvement had never been discovered. It is the inventor here that brings it to them, and places it in their possession. And as he does this by the effort of his own genius, the law regards him as the first and original inventor, and protects his patent, although the improvement had in fact been invented before, and used by others.

So, too, as to the lost arts. It is well known that centuries ago discoveries were made in certain arts the fruits of which have come down to us, but the means by which the work was accomplished are at this day unknown. The knowledge has been lost for ages. Yet it would hardly be doubted, if any one now discovered an art thus lost, and it was a useful improvement, that, upon a fair construction of the act of Congress, he would be entitled to a patent. Yet he would not literally be the first and original inventor. But he would be the first to confer on the public the benefit of the invention. He would discover what is unknown, and communicate knowledge which the public had not the means of obtaining without his invention.

Upon the same principle and upon the same rule of construction, we think that Fitzgerald must be regarded as the first and original inventor of the safe in question. The case as to this point admits, that, although Conner's safe had been kept and used for years, yet no test had been applied to it, and its capacity for resisting heat was not known; there was no evidence to show that any particular value was attached to it after it passed from his possession, or that it was ever afterwards used as a place of security for papers; and it appeared that he himself did not attempt to make another like the one he is supposed to have invented, but used a different one. And upon this state of the evidence the court put it to the jury to say, whether this safe had been finally forgotten or abandoned before Fitzgerald's invention, and whether he was the original inventor of the safe for which he obtained the patent; directing them, if they found these two facts, that their verdict must be for the plaintiff. We think there is no error in this instruction. For if the Conner safe had passed away from the memory of Conner himself, and of those who had seen it, and the safe itself had disappeared, the knowledge of the improvement was as completely lost as if it had never been discovered. The public could derive no benefit from it until it was discovered by another inventor. And if Fitzgerald made his discovery by his own efforts, without any knowledge of Conner's, he invented an improvement that was then new, and at that time unknown; and it was not the less new and unknown because Conner's safe was recalled to his memory by the success of Fitzgerald's.

We do not understand the Circuit Court to have said that the omission of Conner to try the value of his safe by proper tests would deprive it of its priority; nor his omission to bring it into public use. He might have omitted both, and also abandoned its use, and been ignorant of the extent of its value; yet, if it was the same with Fitzgerald's, the latter would not upon such grounds be entitled to a patent, provided Conner's safe and its mode of construction were still in the memory of Conner before they were recalled by Fitzgerald's patent.

The circumstances above mentioned, referred to in the opinion of the Circuit Court, appeared to have been introduced as evidence tending to prove that the Conner safe might have been finally forgotten, and upon which this hypothetical instruction was given. Whether this evidence was sufficient for that purpose or not, was a question for the jury, and the court left it to them. And if the jury found the fact to be so, and that Fitzgerald again discovered it, we regard him as standing upon the same ground with the discoverer of a lost art, or an unpatented and unpublished foreign invention, and like him entitled to a patent. For there was no existing and living knowledge of this improvement, or of its former use, at the time he made the discovery. And whatever benefit any individual may derive from it in the safety of his papers, he owes entirely to the genius and exertions of Fitzgerald.

Upon the whole, therefore, we think there is no error in the opinion of the Circuit Court, and the judgment is therefore affirmed.

Rosaire v. Baroid Sales Division

218 F.2d 72 (5th Cir.1955).

■ Before HOLMES and TUTTLE, CIRCUIT JUDGES, and ALLRED, DISTRICT JUDGE.

■ TUTTLE, CIRCUIT JUDGE.

In this suit for patent infringement there is presented to us for determination the correctness of the judgment of the trial court, based on findings of fact and conclusions of law, holding that the two patents involved in the litigation were invalid and void and that furthermore there had been no infringement by defendant.

The Rosaire and Horvitz patents relate to methods of prospecting for oil or other hydrocarbons. The inventions are based upon the assumption that gases have emanated from deposits of hydrocarbons which have been trapped in the earth and that these emanations have modified the surrounding rock. The methods claimed involve the steps of taking a number of samples of soil from formations which are not themselves productive of hydrocarbons, either over a horizontal area or vertically down a well bore, treating each sample, as by grinding and heating in a closed vessel, to cause entrained or absorbed hydrocarbons therein to evolve as a gas, quantitatively measuring the amount of hydrocarbon gas so evolved from each sample, and correlating the measurements with the locations from which the samples were taken.

Plaintiff claims that in 1936 he and Horvitz invented this new method of prospecting for oil. In due course the two patents in suit, Nos. 2,192,525 and 2,324,085, were issued thereon. Horvitz assigned his interest to Rosaire. Appellant alleged that appellee Baroid began infringing in 1947; that he learned of this in 1949 and asked Baroid to take a license, but no license agreement was worked out, and this suit followed, seeking an injunction and an accounting.

In view of the fact that the trial court's judgment that the patents were invalid, would of course dispose of the matter if correct, we turn our attention to this issue. Appellee's contention is that the judgment of the trial court in this respect should be supported on two principal grounds. The first is that the prior art, some of which was not before the patent office, anticipated the two patents; the second is that work carried on by one Teplitz for the Gulf Oil Corporation invalidated both patents by reason of the relevant provisions of the patent laws which state that an invention is not patentable if it "was known or used by others in this country" before the patentee's invention thereof, 35 U.S.C.A. § 102(a). Appellee contends that Teplitz and his coworkers knew and extensively used in the field the same alleged inventions before any date asserted by Rosaire and Horvitz.

On this point appellant himself in his brief admits that "Teplitz conceived of the idea of extracting and quantitatively measuring entrained or absorbed gas from the samples of rock, rather than relying upon the free gas in the samples. We do not deny that Teplitz conceived of the methods of the patents in suit." And further appellant makes the following admission: "We admit that the Teplitz–Gulf work was done before Rosaire and Horvitz conceived of the inventions. We will show, however, that Gulf did not apply for patent until 1939, did not publish Teplitz's ideas, and did not otherwise give the public the benefit of the experimental work."

In support of their respective positions, both appellant and appellee stress the language in our opinion in the case of *Pennington v. National Supply Co.*, 5 Cir., 95 F.2d 291, 294, where, speaking through Judge Holmes, we said: "Appellant insists that the court erred in considering the prior use of the Texas machine, because that machine was abandoned by the Texas Company and was not successful until modified and rebuilt. As to this, it does not appear that the Texas machine was a failure, since it drilled three wells for the Texas Company, which was more than was usually accomplished by the rotary drilling machines then in use."

"An unsuccessful experiment which is later abandoned does not negative novelty in a new and successful device". *T. H. Symington Co. v. National Malleable Castings Co.*, 250 U.S. 383, 386, 39 S.Ct. 542, 63 L.Ed. 1045; *Clark Thread Co. v. Willimantic Linen Co.*, 140 U.S. 481, 489, 11 S.Ct. 846, 35 L.Ed. 521. Nevertheless, the existence and operation of a machine, abandoned after its completion and sufficient use to demonstrate its practicability, is evidence that the same ideas incorporated in a later development along the same line do not amount to invention. *Corona Cord Tire Co. v. Dovan Chemical Corporation*, 276 U.S. 358, 48 S.Ct. 380, 72 L.Ed. 610; *Jones v. Sykes Metal Lath & Roofing Co.*, 6 Cir., 254 F. 91. If the prior machine does not anticipate, it would not have done so if it had been neither unsuccessful nor abandoned. Novelty is ascribed to new things, without regard to the successful and continued use of old things. Correlatively, it is denied to old things, without regard to the circumstances which caused their earlier applications to be unsatisfactory or their use to be abandoned.

The question as to whether the work of Teplitz was "an unsuccessful experiment", as claimed by appellant, or was a successful trial of the method in question and a reduction of that method to actual practice, as contended by appellee, is, of course, a question of fact. On this point the trial court made the following finding of fact: "I find as a fact, by clear and substantial proof beyond a reasonable doubt, that Abraham J. Teplitz and his coworkers with Gulf Oil Corporation and its Research Department during 1935 and early 1936, before any date claimed by Rosaire, spent more than a year in the oil fields and adjacent territory around Palestine, Texas, taking and analyzing samples both over an area and down drill holes, exactly as called for in the claims of the patents which Rosaire and Horvitz subsequently applied for and which are here in suit. This Teplitz work was a successful and adequate field trial of the prospecting method involved and a reduction to practice of that method. The work was performed in the field under ordinary conditions without any deliberate attempt at concealment or effort to exclude the public and without any instructions of secrecy to the employees performing the work."

As we view it, if the court's findings of fact are correct then under the statute as construed by the courts, we must affirm the finding of the trial court that appellee's patents were invalid. As to the finding of fact we are to affirm unless we conclude that it is "clearly erroneous." Rule 52, Fed.Rules Civ.Proc., 28 U.S.C.A.

A close analysis of the evidence on which the parties rely to resolve this question clearly demonstrates that there was sufficient evidence to sustain the finding of the trial court that there was more here than an unsuccessful or incomplete experiment. It is clear that the work was not carried forward, but that appears to be a result of two things: (1) that the geographical area did not lend itself properly to the test, and (2) that the "entire gas prospecting program was therefore suspended in September of 1936, in order that the accumulated information might be thoroughly reviewed." It will be noted that the program was not suspended to test the worth of the method but to examine the data that was produced by use of the method involved. The above quotation came from one of the recommendations at the end of Teplitz's report, and was introduced on behalf of the appellant himself. Expert testimony presented by witnesses Rogers, Eckhardt and Weaver supported appellee's contention.

With respect to the argument advanced by appellant that the lack of publication of Teplitz's work deprived an alleged infringer of the defense of prior use, we find no case which constrains us to hold that where such work was done openly and in the ordinary course of the activities of the employer, a large producing company in the oil industry, the statute is to be so modified by construction as to require some affirmative act to bring the work to the attention of the public at large.

While there is authority for the proposition that one of the basic principles underlying the patent laws is the enrichment of the art, and that a patent is given to encourage disclosure of inventions, no case we have found requires a holding that, under the circumstances that attended the work of Teplitz, the fact of public knowledge must be shown before it can be urged to invalidate a subsequent patent. The case of *Corona Cord Tire Co. v. Dovan Chemical Corporation, supra,* is authority for the opposing view, that taken by the court below. In that case the Supreme Court said: "In 1916, while with the Norwalk Company, Kratz prepared D.P.G. and demonstrated its utility as a rubber accelerator by making test slabs of vulcanized or cured rubber with its use. Every time that he produced such a slab he recorded his test in cards which he left with the Norwalk Company and kept a duplicate of his own. . . . This work was known to, and was participated in, by his associate in the Norwalk Company, his immediate superior and the chief chemist of the company, Dr. Russell, who fully confirms Kratz's records and statement." *Corona Cord Tire Co. v. Dovan Chemical Corporation*, 276 U.S. 358, 378, 379, 48 S.Ct. 380, 386, 72 L.Ed. 610.

The court further states in the *Corona* case at page 382 of 276 U.S., at page 387 of 48 S.Ct.: "But, even if we ignore this evidence of Kratz's actual use of D.P.G. in these rubber inner tubes which were sold, what he did at Norwalk, supported by the evidence of Dr. Russell, his chief, and by the indubitable records that are not challenged, leaves no doubt in our minds that he did discover in 1916 the strength of D.P.G. as an accelerator as compared with the then known accelerators, and that he then demonstrated it by a reduction of it to practice in production of cured or vulcanized rubber. This constitutes priority in this case."

Concluding, as we do, that the trial court correctly held that patents invalid, it is not necessary to consider the question of infringement. The judgment of the trial court is affirmed.

NOTES

1. *"A Manner Accessible to the Public."* When we ask whether the invention was "known or used" under § 102(a), we are really asking whether the invention was "known or used" by someone other than the inventor. As Justice Story explained in *Pennock v. Dialogue*, 27 U.S. (2 Pet.) 1, 18 (1829):

> What then is the true meaning of the words "known or used before the application?" They cannot mean that the thing invented was not known or used before the application by the inventor himself, for that would be to prohibit him from the only means to obtain a patent. . . . These words, then, to have any rational interpretations, must mean, not known or used by others before the application.

As *Gayler* points out, however, an invention may have been known or used by others, but such knowledge or use will not anticipate the claimed invention if the prior knowledge or use is not publicly accessible. Why? One reason may be the public policy favoring the person who is the first to disclose the invention to the public, even though someone else may have made the discovery earlier. Public disclosure is a firmly embedded policy underlying our patent system. Recall, the Court in *Gayler* stated that "[i]t is the inventor here that brings [the invention] to [the public], and places it in their possession." In the eyes of our patent law, the prior user in *Gayler* did not contribute anything to the public; and although the patentee's invention was not novel in the strictest sense of the word, he was the first to disclose the invention to the public, and "the law regards him as the first and original inventor." But what if the first, and secret, inventor had made substantial efforts to commercialize the invention for public distribution—building a factory, hiring labor, etc.—but happened not to have finished his efforts, even though he is still years closer to delivery of an actual good to the hands of the public then is anyone else, including the patent applicant?

2. *Does "Accessible to the Public" Really Mean Absence of Concealment?* How accessible to the public was the invention in *Rosaire*? According to the court § 102(a) does not "require some affirmative act to bring the work to the attention to the public at large." Does accessible to the public simply mean not secret? For all practical purposes, wasn't the subject matter in *Rosaire* secret? *See W.L. Gore & Associates, Inc. v. Garlock, Inc.*, 721 F.2d 1540 (Fed.Cir.1983), *appeal after remand*, 842 F.2d 1275 (Fed.Cir.1988) ("The nonsecret use of a claimed process in the usual course of producing articles for commercial purposes is a public use."); *Egbert v. Lippmann*, 104 U.S. 333 (1881) ("public use" found where the invention was corset steels which were hidden from public view by the clothing worn over the corset); *National Research Development Corp. v. Varian Associates, Inc.*, 822 F.Supp. 1121 (D.N.J.1993) ("A prior use is public even if there is no effort to show the invention to the public at large, ... even if the invention is completely hidden from view.... There is simply no requirement that the prior user make an effort to make the invention publicly accessible, so long as he or she uses it in the ordinary course of business without efforts to conceal it.").

It is somewhat premature to ask the following question, but you should keep it in mind: With respect to prior art, what is the difference between § 102(a) and § 102(g)? We explore section 102(g) below.

3. *Defining Prior Art and Geographical Limitations: American v. European/Japanese Views and Bioprospecting.* Section 102(a) says that an invention will be anticipated if it was "known or used *in this country.*" Recall that § 104 was amended so that one may use foreign inventive activity to prove date of invention in the obtainment of patent rights, but foreign knowledge and use cannot act as prior art to defeat patent rights. This geographic disparity differs sharply with the European Patent Convention (Article 54(2)) and the Japan Patent Law (Section 29(1)), both of which treat public foreign knowledge and use as prior art.

Why is knowledge and use limited to the United States? This geographic limitation did not make its way into our patent law until 1836, but the Senate Report accompanying the 1836 Act offers little if any explanation. Common sense tells us that unpublished knowledge and use are less difficult for a U.S. inventor to discover in the U.S. as opposed to Europe or Japan. How does one search for unpublished knowledge in foreign lands without incurring a great deal of expense or "search costs." It is difficult enough to obtain such knowledge in the United States, let alone a foreign country. At least with many foreign publications and most foreign patents, there exist databases that one can search relatively cheaply today. Foreign patents and publications may be anticipatory under § 102(a) and § 102(b) (we will discuss patents and printed publications in detail in the next section). Furthermore, as a matter of policy, it is difficult for Americans to enjoy unpublished knowledge and uses if they are extant only in a foreign land. The Court in *Gayler* addressed the geographic issue:

> If the foreign invention had been printed or patented, it was already given to the world and open to the people of this country, as well as of others, upon reasonable inquiry. They would therefore derive no advantage from the invention here. It would confer no benefit upon the community, and the inventor therefore is not considered to be entitled to the reward. But if the foreign discovery is not patented, nor described in any printed publication, it might be known and used in remote places for ages, and the people of this country be unable to profit by it. The means of obtaining knowledge would not be within their reach; and, as far as their interest is concerned, it would be the same thing as if the improvement had never been discovered.

But our world today is much smaller than it was in 1850. As such, does the geographic distinction still make sense? Consider the concern of developing nations and their inability to do much to prevent American patents from issuing (or from securing compensation from commercial exploitation of such patents) on inventions derived from indigenous flora and fauna, what is sometimes referred to as "biopiracy" or "bioprospecting." Indeed, § 102(a) provides refuge for inventors who seek to patent inventions based on foreign knowledge. A prominent example is the neem tree controversy. The leaves and bark of the neem tree, which is indigenous to India, have been used as natural pesticides and fuel by the people of India for years. In the early 1990s, a multi-national company, W.R. Grace, obtained United States and European patents on pesticide products derived from the neem tree. The patents were challenged by two Indian non-governmental organizations, resulting in one of the European patents being invalidated a lacking novelty. But the validity of the American patents remained intact. The central reason for this difference in result is that unlike the European Patent Convention, namely Article 54(2), American patent law, specifically section 102(a), distinguishes between domestic knowledge and use and foreign knowledge and use. Notably, Section 29 of the Japan Patent Law, like Article 54(2) of the EPC, does not distinguish between domestic and foreign knowledge in this regard.

For competing views on this issue, *see* Margo A. Bagley, *Patently Unconstitutional: The Geographical Limitation on Prior Art in a Small World*, 87 MINN. L. REV. 679 (2003) (asserting geographic distinction of § 102(a) is unconstitutional); Craig Allen Nard, *In Defense of Geographic Disparity*, 88 MINN. L. REV. 221 (2003) (asserting geographic distinction fosters innovation in the pharmaceutical industry and calls for keepers of traditional knowledge to be compensated, thus "the problem is not the availability of patent protection as it is the lack of an adequate compensatory mechanism for developing nations and indigenous peoples"); F. Scott Kieff, *The Case for Registering Patents and the Law and Economics of Present Patent–Obtaining Rules*, 45 B.C. L. REV. 55, 98 (2003) ("By making prior foreign use that occurs within a country with whom we are a trading partner under either of these treaties available to support a claim to a patent, these revisions protect those investment-backed expectations made abroad that are sufficiently serious to have led to the filing of a patent application. By leaving all other foreign prior use unavailable to defeat a patent, these revisions protect the investments of the one who filed the patent application and disregard those of others whose use is not corroborated by a printed publication."); F. Scott Kieff, *Patents for Environmentalists*, 9 WASH. U. J.L. & POL'Y 307 (2002) (showing how the commercialization of products derived from biodiversity can, under a patent system, benefit the custodians of the biodiversity). *See also* Keith Aoki, *NeoColonialsim, Anticommons Property, and Biopiracy in the (Not–So–Brave) New World Order of International Intellectual Property Protection*, 6 IND. J. GLOBAL LEGAL STUD. 11 (1998) and sources cited therein, including; VANDANA SHIVA, BIOPIRACY: THE PLUNDER OF NATURE AND KNOWLEDGE (1996); VANDANA SHIVA, MONOCULTURES OF THE MIND: PERSPECTIVE ON BIODIVERSITY AND BIOTECHNOLOGY (1993); INTELLECTUAL PROPERTY RIGHTS AND INDIGENOUS PEOPLES: A SOURCEBOOK (Tom Greaves ed., 1994); JACK R. KLOPPENBERG, JR., FIRST THE SEED: THE POLITICAL ECONOMY OF PLANT BIOTECHNOLOGY (1988); Ruth L. Gana, *The Myth of Development, The Progress of Rights: Human Rights to Intellectual Property and Development,* 18 LAW & POL'Y 315 (1996).

For a nice overview of these issues, see Kamal Puri's SIDEBAR immediately below.

SIDE BAR
Biodiversity and Protection of Traditional Knowledge
Kamal Puri*

Definitions

Biodiversity connotes biological diversity.[1] It encompasses the variety of all life forms: the different plants, animals or microorganisms, the genes they contain and the ecosystems of which they form a part. There are three general kinds of biodiversity: habitat diversity, genetic diversity, and species diversity. The survival of each is linked to the health of the other two, and together they comprise the wealth of ecosystems.[2]

Bioprospecting refers to a form of research science; the search for biological and genetic resources for potentially useful and marketable products and processes such as pharmaceuticals, pesticides and cosmetics. Critics dub it "biopiracy".

Ethno-pharmacology is a type of bioprospecting using indigenous knowledge as a guide in search for new medicines. Human Genome Diversity Project is an example of bioprospecting for genetic material in human populations. Its aim is to draw blood and tissue samples from as many diverse indigenous groups worldwide as possible. It is criticised as a commodification and exploitation of indigenous peoples by "gene hunters".

Significance of traditional knowledge

Indigenous people have for millennia played a significant role in maintaining the diversity of environments that are important to global ecologically sustainable development. Traditional knowledge, which is ingrained in a spiritual understanding of the world, has historically been dubbed as folklore with disapproving connotations.[3] Australia is a mega-diverse region of the world with richest sources of novel species and compounds and the greatest diversity and wealth of fauna and flora. For indigenous peoples, heritage is a bundle of relationships, rather than a bundle of economic rights.[4] Existing Australian heritage protection legislation is limited in its capacity to protect indigenous knowledge, as it protects only physical heritage. Unlike NZ, Canada, and the US, Australia has never signed a single treaty with indigenous people.

Traditional knowledge is a rich and diverse source of creativity and innovation. It is a framework for continuing source of information in most fields of technology, ranging from traditional medicinal and agricultural practices to music, design, and the graphic and plastic arts. There is a lack of legal recognition of indigenous peoples' rights in their medicinal knowledge, and the absence of a requirement for prior informed consent[5] in current laws and practices.

With the recent increased interest in natural remedies, pharmaceutical companies are keen to use traditional knowledge.[6] It has been estimated that 25% of prescription drugs (about 7000) in the U.S. have active ingredients that are extracted or derived from plants. In the chemical field, extracts from particular plants have been used as a natural insecticide by environmentally friendly pest controllers. A Brazilian fungus has been patented as a natural fire ant control and genetically modified organism—the potential seems unlimited. Biotics, a U.K. company, is conducting literature searchers of anthropological, medical and scientific texts for information about the uses of plant and animal extracts in traditional medicine for the purpose of providing this "common knowledge" to pharmaceutical companies such as SmithKline Beecham for use in new drug development. Another useful drug derived form a plant in Madagascar is *rosy periwinkle* that is used against childhood leukaemia. In Australia, Amrad has signed an agreement with Tiwi Land Council to enable it to conduct research with rare Northern Territory plants with the assistance of Tiwi Aborigines.

Again, a new painkiller is currently being developed in Queensland from the bark of a native tree, which appears to have the same potency as morphine. The idea for using the bark came after observing the actions of an Aboriginal man involved in an accident while trying to catch a crocodile. The crocodile attacked the man and severed a finger. The Aborigine, while in significant pain, stripped some bark from a particular tree, chewed it, and put the chewed mass on the severed finger, which miraculously appeared to stop the pain.

The Convention on Biological Diversity 1992[7]

The Convention on Biological Diversity (CBD) is the most important international instrument with respect to protection of traditional knowledge. It was signed by 169 nations, including Australia, U.K., and U.S. The Convention came into force on 29 December 1993. The U.S. has not ratified the Convention yet.

The reasons that led to the Convention included the following:

♦ the need to introduce standards and measures to encourage countries to conserve their biological diversity through conservation and sustainable use;

♦ to restrain the unregulated and out-of-control international trade in genetic materials and species; and

♦ to provide a firm international basis for balancing the competing concerns which arise from bio prospecting.

It was agreed that states should have ownership of the natural biological resources in their territories, including their genetic resources. The Convention imposes obligations with regard to conservation of biodiversity, recognizes the value of intellectual property rights, and seeks to address the needs of developing countries by requiring technology transfer and equitable sharing in the results of research and development.

Main provisions of the Convention

Article 8(j) encourages member states to "respect, preserve and maintain knowledge, innovations and practices of indigenous and local communities" and recommends establishment of measures for conserving biological diversity and sustainable use of its components. It recognises the sovereign right of states to exploit their natural resources and to determine access—this is a fundamental shift from previous concept of genetic resources being the "common heritage of mankind".

The Convention bids developed nations to involve developing countries in biotechnology research activities arising from the use of their natural resources. It further encourages them to facilitate access and transfer to other countries of technologies relevant to the conservation and sustainable use of biological diversity.

Some countries have already enacted laws declaring the physical property of flora and fauna to be the property of the state. For example, in 1992, Costa Rica enacted a wildlife protection law and established the National Bio-diversity Institute (INBio) to take charge of naturally occurring and traditionally bred plant genetic resources. Australia has recently enacted the *Environment Protection and Biodiversity Conservation Act 1999* (Cth) to harmonise its law with the CBD. The Act provides for indigenous representation on the statutory Scientific and Biodiversity Committees, as well as establishes a statutory Indigenous Environment Advisory Committee.

Mention should also be made of the *Draft Declaration on the Rights of Indigenous Peoples* that has been developed by the UN Working Group on Indigenous Populations. Article 24 of the *Draft Declaration* provides for indigenous peoples' rights to their traditional medicines and health practices, including the right to the protection of vital medicinal plants, animals and minerals.

Is there a conflict between TRIPS Agreement and CBD?

Protagonists of the CBD have argued that there is a serious conflict on the rights and obligations of member-states between the two treaties, particularly between Article 8 (j) of the CBD and Article 27.3.(b) of the Agreement on Trade–Related Aspects of Intellectual Property Rights (TRIPS) 1995. Article 8 (j) calls on governments to respect, preserve, and maintain knowledge, innovations, and practices of indigenous and local communities in biodiversity conservation and encourage equitable sharing of benefits arising from the utilization of such knowledge. On the other hand, Article 27.3.(b) of TRIPS legitimise private property rights in the form of intellectual property over life and processes entailed in modifying life forms. But these are rights for individuals, corporations, and states, not for indigenous peoples and local communities. The major suggestions/criticisms are outlined below:

♦ That TRIPS should be revised to explicitly protect indigenous peoples' traditional knowledge and intellectual property rights.[8] In particular, steps should be taken to provide for the introduction of indigenous collective certifications and geographical indications to protect indigenous arts, cultural expressions, and traditional knowledge, innovation and practices;

♦ That the patent legislation should be amended under Article 27(2) of TRIPS to prevent patenting of indigenous knowledge and resources;

♦ That measures should be introduced under Article 39(2) to protect secret, sacred and confidential information, knowledge, practices and representations by and of indigenous peoples;

♦ That to avoid cause further disintegration of indigenous communal values and practices, a distinction should be drawn between private property rights and indigenous knowledge and cultural heritage that collectively evolves through generations;[9]

♦ That all biodiversity related issues are removed from TRIPS to CBD, as the former is ill equipped to deal with these matters with the right understanding and sensitivity. These would include matters relating to plants, animals, micro-organisms, community intellectual rights, and plant varieties;

♦ That patenting of varieties of genetic material developed over generations by indigenous communities is undermining the concept of equitable benefit-sharing envisaged in the CBD;

♦ That Article 27.3(b) of TRIPS should be amended to take into account the CBD and the need to clarify that all living organisms and their parts cannot be patented; and to ensure the protection of innovations of indigenous and local farming communities and the continuation of traditional farming practices;

♦ That any discussion on traditional and indigenous knowledge should always refer to the *Draft Declaration on the Rights of Indigenous Peoples*, particularly Articles 24, 25, 26, and 29 which clearly established that rights to indigenous knowledge, innovations, and practices (referred to as intellectual and cultural heritage) cannot be discussed in isolation from indigenous peoples' rights to their territories and resources; and

♦ That the definitional constructs of patents for life forms or a sui generis system for protection of plant varieties preclude recognition of innovations that are inter-generational, collective and for social good.[10]

Major examples of biopiracy

Basmati rice

Basmati is a long grain, superior rice of Indian origin. Produced in both India and Pakistan, it is one of India's growing export earners.[11] The Texas based RiceTec, Inc., has obtained a patent on this "Basmati" type of rice. The patent allows as many as 20 claims—eleven relating to the plant, five to the grain, three to breeding methods and one to the seed. RiceTec has presently graduated from marketing rice under spurious names like "Texmati" and "Kasmati" to breeding its own "Basmati" which it claims is superior to the original Indian and Pakistani variety.[12] RiceTec also claims in its patent application that its rice can be grown outside sub-Himalayan India and Pakistan and still use the "Basmati" name on the plea that it is a generic appellation and not a trademark. The issue regarding the usage of the name "Basmati" is a matter of separate debate and is the subject matter of cases before the British Courts filed by India.

The Indian Government has sought to impeach the RiceTec's patent by arguing that the knowledge of Basmati constitutes prior art. It is also argued that no patents should be granted for items, which are inherent and inalienable part of Indian traditional knowledge and biodiversity. None of the twenty claims is valid since they do not state anything that is new.

Another facet of the Basmati litigation is that it is a clear violation of the geographical indication clause of TRIPS. The latter provides that the quality, reputation or other characteristics of a good can each be a sufficient basis for eligibility as a geographical indication, where they are essentially attributable to the geographical origin of the good.[13] Further, registration of a trade mark which uses a geographical indication in a way that misleads the public as to the true place of origin must be refused or invalidated *ex officio* if the legislation so permits or at the request of an interested party.[14] However, the only limitation to this strategy is that India is yet to have a geographical indications law.

Neem Patents[15]

In the U.S., a patent was obtained by W.R. Grace & Co. to manufacture a pesticide with an active ingredient that naturally occurs in the neem seeds. This patent has been challenged on the ground that no naturally occurring substance should be allowed to be patented.[16]

Patent law requires something more than just the discovery of a naturally occurring product. A legally significant amount of human innovation must be involved for it to be patented.

For times immemorial, farmers in India have used the neem's pesticidal qualities for many beneficial purposes. The neem tree (*Azirdirachta Indica*) is a tropical evergreen indigenous plant/tree to the Indian subcontinent. The biological properties of its seeds are well established, including the pesticidal activity of compound called *azadirachtin*.

W.R. Grace's claims relate to storage of *azadirachtin* in solutions that stabilise this ingredient's pesticidal activity, since the use of this compound was limited by the degradation that occurred in solutions. A typical claim of the patent requires an extraction of *azadirachtin* from a neemseed, combined with several solvents in specific proportions to obtain storage-stable solutions.

W.R. Grace's claim does not pertain to a naturally occurring plant part. Instead, its claim relates to a purified form of a naturally occurring compound in combination with solvents that extend the shelf life of the purified compound.

Recently, the European Patent Office (EPO), Munich, has revoked a patent granted earlier to a fungicide derived from the Indian medicinal tree, Neem. The patent had been challenged on the ground, inter alia, that the fungicide qualities of the neem and its use has been known in India for over 2000 years, and for use to make insect repellants, soaps, cosmetics and contraceptives.

In accepting the challenge, the EPO conceded that the patent amounted to bio-piracy and that the process for which the patent had been granted had been actually in use in India from time immemorial.[17]

It is noteworthy that in the United States, prior existing knowledge to deny a patent is accepted in terms of publication in any journal, but not of knowledge known and available in oral or folk traditions. This narrow view of prior knowledge has been responsible for any number of patents for processes and products derived from biological material, or their synthesis into purer crystalline forms.

Turmeric Patent[18]

In 1995, the United States Patent and Trademark Office (USPTO) had granted a patent to the University of Mississippi Medical Centre (UMMC) for the use of turmeric powder as a wound-healing agent.[19] Two years later, the Indian government's Council of Scientific and Industrial Research (CSIR) challenged the patent on the ground that it lacked novelty. Turmeric has been used as a wound-healing property in India for centuries. It also submitted relevant documents to prove this assertion.[20] The US Patent Office upheld the objection and canceled the patent.

Conclusion and Recommendations

Except in limited instances, current forms of intellectual property protection, such as patents and plant breeders' rights are not adequate for the protection of traditional knowledge. The challenge is to develop a system that satisfies the needs of industry, achieves conservation goals, and recognises and protects the rights of indigenous peoples. A special legislation should be developed to protect the knowledge associated with genetic resources separate from the existing intellectual property rights systems. The new law should provide for indigenous peoples to share equitably in benefits resulting from the use by the wider community of their traditional knowledge, innovation and practices, and for prior informed consent to be obtained from indigenous knowledge holders as a condition of use of their knowledge, innovation and practices.

The CBD vests sovereignty over natural resources and the right to grant access to genetic resources to national governments. The knowledge, innovations and practices of indigenous and local communities are considered key to the conservation, and sustainable use of biodiversity. Governments are required to respect, preserve and maintain these elements, to protect customary use of bio-resources, to act according to national law to develop and use traditional and indigenous technologies, and to adopt economically and socially sound measures that act as incentives for the conservation and sustainable use of components of biological diversity. The cumulative effect of these provisions is to make it mandatory for governments to enact a law recognizing indigenous and local community knowledge systems.

Member countries of the CBD are obliged to ensure that patents and other intellectual property rights are supportive of the objectives of the Convention and do not undermine them. It follows that TRIPS under the World Trade Organisation[21] and the CBD should be mutually supportive. TRIPS sets out a set of minimum obligations in each area of intellectual property laws, viz., copyright, trademarks, geographical indications, industrial designs, patents, layout designs of integrated circuits and "undisclosed information".

One possible way of protecting traditional knowledge may be to improve the private law rights of the creators or custodians of such knowledge. This could be achieved either by modifying current copyright law or by creating sui generis traditional knowledge rights.

Alternatively, traditional knowledge may be protected as a public law right either by creating a statutory authority or by establishing a domain public payment right or by empowering indigenous peoples themselves to take charge of the situation under their customary Aboriginal law.[22]

It has also been proposed that under the TRIPS Agreement, patent applicants should be required to disclose the source of origin of the biological material utilised in their invention. Applicants should also be required to obtain prior informed consent of the country of origin. If this were done, it would enable domestic institutional mechanisms to ensure sharing of benefits of such commercial utilization by the patent holders with the indigenous communities whose traditional knowledge has been used.

* Professor of Law, Queensland University of Technology; President, Australian Folklore Association Inc.; Winner of the Canadian Studies Faculty Research Award 1995. This *SIDE BAR* was written specially for PRINCIPLES OF PATENT LAW.

1. Article 2 of the *Convention on Biological Diversity 1992* reads: " 'Biological diversity' means the variability among living organisms from all sources including, inter alia, terrestrial, marine and other aquatic ecosystems and the ecological complexes of which they are part; this includes diversity within species, between species and of ecosystems." For the full text of the Convention, see http://www. unep.ch/bio/conv-e.html, visited 9 August 2000. See further, *Background of the Convention*, http://www.biodiv.org/conv/ BACKGROUND.HTML (visited 10 August 2000).

2. See, generally, J. Harte, *The Green Fuse: An Ecological Odyssey* (1993, University of California Press). See also http://www.twnside.org.sg/access_7.htm, (visited 9 August 2000) and http://www. cwis.org/fwdp/International/grouprt.txt, visited 10 August 2000.

3. For a detailed analysis of the relevant legal issues, see K. Puri, "Legal Protection of Expressions of Folklore" (1998) XXXII UNESCO's Copyright Bulletin 5 and "Cultural Ownership and Intellectual Property Rights Post *Mabo*: Putting Ideas into Action" (1995) 9 Intellectual Property Journal 293 (Canada). See generally, R. Coombe, "Intellectual Property, Human Rights and Sovereignty: New Dilemmas in International Law posed by the Recognition of Indigenous Knowledge and the Conservation of Biodiversity", http://www. law.indiana.edu/glsj/vol6/no1/coom.html (visited 10 August 2000).

4. See K. Puri, "The Meaning of Ownership" *UNESCO Sources* No. 117, November 1999, at 6.

5. "Prior informed consent" is defined to mean that indigenous peoples and local communities will be consulted, informed and their full consent obtained before any appropriation or research of their knowledge is undertaken: see M. Khor, "Indigenous People Criticise WIPO Approach" http://www.twnside.org.sg/ title/wipo2–cn.htm (visited 9 August 2000).

6. See S. Singh, "Traditional Knowledge under Commercial Blanket" http:// www.twnside.org.sg/title/wipo2–cn.htm (visited 9 August 2000), where it is stated that in 1995, the estimated market value of pharmaceutical derivatives from indigenous peoples' traditional medicine was $43 billion worldwide.

7. See http://wwww.unep.ch/bio/ conv-e.html (visited 9 August 2000).

8. For a fiery comment, see "Biopiracy and Intellectual Property Rights" http://www.heureka.claim.net/gaia/ gentetix.htm, (visited 7 August 2000) and *Indigenous Peoples' Seattle Declaration*, http://www.ldb.org/indi99.htm (visited 10 August 2000).

9. Martin Khor, "Indigenous People Criticise WIPO Approach" http://www. twnside.org.sg/title/wipo2–cn.htm (visited 9 August 2000) Leaders of indigenous people's organisations attending a WIPO Roundtable meeting on intellectual property and traditional knowledge have criticised the WIPO approach in attempting to impose an intellectual property rights regime on traditional knowledge. They called on WIPO, governments and other multilateral organisations to explore other ways to protect and promote indigenous and traditional knowledge outside of the traditional IPR regime. More than a hundred indigenous people's organisations separately issued a statement calling on governments to amend the TRIPS Agreement, Article 27.3 (b), to mandatorily ban the patenting of all life-forms, all naturally occurring processes, and of traditional knowledge on the use of biological resources.

10. Speaking at an *International Seminar on Biodiversity Law* in Brasilia (11–14 May 1999), G.S. Nijar stated that the concept of patenting and owning life was antithetical to all cultures in the Third World. He observed that, "Indigenous knowledge has fed, clothed and healed the world for millennia". http: //www.twnside.org.sg / title / input-cn.htm (visited 7 August 2000). See also, by the same author, "Legal and Practical Perspectives on Sui Generis Options", where he cites some interesting statistics. For example, it is estimated that three-quarters of the plants that provide active ingredients for prescription drugs came to the attention of researchers because of their use in traditional medicine: http://www.twnside.org.sg/title/generis-cn.htm (visited 10 August 2000).

11. Each year India sells approximately $300 million' worth of Basmati rice and it is counted among the nation's fastest growing exports: http://www.twnside.org.sg/title/generis-cn.htm. See also, M. Khor, "A worldwide fight against biopiracy and patents on life" http://www.twnside.org.sg/title/pat-ch.htm

12. Thailand is also worried that its famed jasmine is the next to be patented. Thai legislators are working to protect the nation's fragrant rice under a trademark before RiceTec or another foreign company acquires such certification.

13. Article 22.1, TRIPS Agreement.

14. Article 22.3, TRIPS Agreement.

15. See, V. Shiva, "The neem tree—a case history of biopiracy" http://www.twnside.org.sg/title/pir-ch.htm (visited 7 August 2000).

16. It is noteworthy that more than 40 patents have been awarded worldwide for inventions directed at some compound found naturally within neem seeds or for novel uses of such compounds.

17. See C. Raghavan, "Neem Patent Revoked by European Patent Office," http://www.twnside.org.sg/title/revoked.htm (visited 7 August 2000).

18. *See V. Shiva, "The turmeric patent is just the first step in stopping biopiracy"* http://www.twnside.org.sg/title/tur-cn.htm (visited 7 August 2000).

19. US Patent No.5401504, 28 March 1995.

20. The USPTO expunged the patent by applying 35 USC102(b) and 35 USC 103(a).

21. The WTO now has 134, with a further 32 countries in the process of negotiating their accession to the WTO. See generally, K. Ferguson, "The World Trade Orgainization (WTO) and its Multilateral Trade Agreements (GATT, GATS, TRIPS, TRIMS, etc.)" http://www.peacecenter.com/issues/global/gl_wto2.html (visited 10 August 2000).

22. *See C. Raghavan, "Neem patent revoked by European Patent Office"* http://www.twnside.org.sg/title/revoked.htm (visited 7 August 2000).

---

4. "Described in a Printed Publication"

The issue here is what constitutes a "printed publication." As explored below in the cases *In re Hall* and *In re Cronyn*, to be treated as a printed publication, a document must be both physically and logically available to a hypothetical member of the interested public.

In re Hall

781 F.2d 897 (Fed.Cir.1986).

■ Before Baldwin, Circuit Judge, Nichols, Senior Circuit Judge, and Kashiwa, Circuit Judge.

■ Baldwin, Circuit Judge.

This is an appeal from the decision of the U.S. Patent and Trademark Office's (PTO) former Board of Appeals, adhered to on reconsideration by the Board of Patent Appeals and Interferences (board), sustaining the final rejection of claims 1–25 of reissue Application No. 343,922, filed January 29, 1982, based principally on a "printed publication" bar under 35 U.S.C. § 102(b). The reference is a doctoral thesis. Because appellant concedes that his claims are unpatentable if the thesis is available as a "printed publication" more than one year prior to the application's effective filing date of February 27, 1979, the only issue is whether the thesis is available as such a printed publication. On the record before us, we affirm the board's decision.

A protest was filed during prosecution of appellant's reissue application which included in an appendix a copy of the dissertation "1,4–a–Glucanglukohydrolase ein amylotylisches Enzym ..." by Peter Foldi (Foldi thesis or dissertation). The record indicates that in September 1977, Foldi submitted his dissertation to the Department of Chemistry and Pharmacy at Freiburg University in the Federal Republic of Germany, and that Foldi was awarded a doctorate degree on November 2, 1977.

Certain affidavits from Dr. Erich Will, who is the director and manager of the Loan Department of the Library of Freiburg University, have been relied upon by the examiner and the board in reaching their decisions. One document, styled a "Declaration" and signed by Dr. Will, states that:

> [I]n November 1977 copies of the dissertation Foldi ... were received in the library of Freiburg University, and in ... December 1977 copies of the said dissertation were freely made available to the faculty and student body of Freiburg University as well as to the general public.

In an August 28, 1981 letter responding to an inquiry from a German corporation, Dr. Will said that the Freiburg University library was able to make the Foldi dissertation "available to our readers as early as 1977."

The examiner made a final rejection of the application claims. He said: "On the basis of the instant record it is reasonable to assume that the Foldi thesis was available (accessible) prior to February 27, 1979." He also pointed out that there was no evidence to the contrary and asked the appellant to state his "knowledge of any inquiry which may have been made regarding 'availability' beyond that presently referred to in the record." Appellant did not respond.

By letter, the PTO's Scientific Library asked Dr. Will whether the Foldi dissertation was made available to the public by being cataloged and placed in the main collection. Dr. Will replied in an October 20, 1983 letter, as translated:

> Our dissertations, thus also the Foldi dissertation, are indexed in a special dissertations catalogue, which is part of the general users' catalogue. In the stacks they are likewise set apart in a special dissertation section, which is part of the general stacks.

In response to a further inquiry by the PTO's Scientific Library requesting (1) the exact date of indexing and cataloging of the Foldi dissertation or (2) "the time such procedures normally take," Dr. Will replied in a June 18, 1984 letter:

> The Library copies of the Foldi dissertation were sent to us by the faculty on November 4, 1977. Accordingly, the dissertation most probably was available for general use toward the beginning of the month of December, 1977.

The board held that the unrebutted evidence of record was sufficient to conclude that the Foldi dissertation had an effective date as prior art more than one year prior to the filing date of the appellant's initial application. In rejecting appellant's argument that the evidence was not sufficient to establish a specific date when the dissertation became publicly available, the board said:

> We rely on the librarian's affidavit of express facts regarding the specific dissertation of interest and his description of the routine treatment of dissertations in general, in the ordinary course of business in his library.

On appeal, appellant raises two arguments: (1) the § 102(b) "printed publication" bar requires that the publication be accessible to the interested public, but there is no evidence that the dissertation was properly indexed in the library catalog prior to the critical date; and (2) even if the Foldi thesis were cataloged prior to the critical date, the presence of a single cataloged thesis in one university library does not constitute sufficient accessibility of the publication's teachings to those interested in the art exercising reasonable diligence.

The statutory phrase "printed publication" has been interpreted to give effect to ongoing advances in the technologies of data storage, retrieval, and dissemination. Because there are many ways in which a reference may be disseminated to the interested public, "public accessibility" has been called the touchstone in determining whether a reference constitutes a "printed publication" bar under 35 U.S.C. § 102(b). The § 102 publication bar is a legal determination based on underlying fact issues, and therefore must be approached on a case-by-case basis. The proponent of the publication bar must show that prior to the critical date the reference was sufficiently accessible, at least to the public interested in the art, so that such a one by examining the reference could make the claimed invention without further research or experimentation.

Relying on *In re Bayer*, appellant argues that the Foldi thesis was not shown to be accessible because Dr. Will's affidavits do not say when the thesis was indexed in the library catalog and do not chronicle the procedures for receiving and processing a thesis in the library.

As the board pointed out in its decision, the facts in *Bayer* differ from those here. Bayer, who was himself the author of the dissertation relied upon by the PTO, submitted a declaration from the university librarian which detailed the library's procedures for receiving, cataloging, and shelving of theses and attested to the relevant dates that Bayer's thesis was processed.

The evidence showed that cataloging and shelving thesis copies routinely took many months from the time they were first received from the faculty and that during the interim the theses were accumulated in a private library office accessible only to library employees. In particular, processing of Bayer's thesis was shown to have been completed after the critical date.

On those facts the CCPA held that Bayer's thesis was not sufficiently accessible and could not give rise to the § 102(b) publication bar. But the court did not hold, as appellant would have it, that accessibility can only be shown by evidence establishing a specific date of cataloging and shelving before the critical date. While such evidence would be desirable, in lending greater certainty to the accessibility determination, the realities of routine business practice counsel against requiring such evidence. The probative value of routine business practice to show the performance of a specific act has long been recognized. *See, e.g.,* 1 WIGMORE, EVIDENCE § 92 (1940); rule 406, Fed.R.Evid.; 2 WEINSTEIN, EVIDENCE §§ 406[01], 406[03] (1981). Therefore, we conclude that competent evidence of the general library practice may be relied upon to establish an approximate time when a thesis became accessible.

In the present case, Dr. Will's affidavits give a rather general library procedure as to indexing, cataloging, and shelving of theses. Although no specific dates are cited (except that the thesis was received on November 4, 1977), Dr. Will's affidavits consistently maintain that inasmuch as the Foldi dissertation was received by the library in early November 1977, the dissertation "most probably was available for general use toward the beginning of the month of December, 1977." The only reasonable interpretation of the affidavits is that Dr. Will was relying on his library's general practice for indexing, cataloging, and shelving theses in estimating the time it would have taken to make the dissertation available to the interested public. Dr. Will's affidavits are competent evidence, and in these circumstances, persuasive evidence that the Foldi dissertation was accessible prior to the critical date. Reliance on an approximation found in the affidavits such as "toward the beginning of the month of December, 1977" works no injustice here because the critical date, February 27, 1978, is some two and one half months later. Moreover, it is undisputed that appellant proffered no rebuttal evidence.

Based on what we have already said concerning "public accessibility," and noting that the determination rests on the facts of each case, we reject appellant's legal argument that a single cataloged thesis in one university library does not constitute sufficient accessibility to those interested in the art exercising reasonable diligence.

We agree with the board that the evidence of record consisting of Dr. Will's affidavits establishes a prima facie case for unpatentability of the claims under the § 102(b) publication bar. It is a case which stands unrebutted.

Accordingly, the board's decision sustaining the rejection of appellant's claims is affirmed.

In re Cronyn

890 F.2d 1158 (Fed.Cir.1989).

■ Before FRIEDMAN, SENIOR CIRCUIT JUDGE, and ARCHER and MAYER, CIRCUIT JUDGES.

■ FRIEDMAN, SENIOR CIRCUIT JUDGE.

The sole question in this case is whether the Board of Patent Appeals and Interferences (Board) correctly held that three undergraduate theses were "printed publications" under 35 U.S.C. § 102(b) (1982), which anticipated the invention for which a patent was sought. We hold that the theses were not "printed publications," and we therefore reverse the Board.

The facts in this case are undisputed. The patent application was for a chemical compound that apparently may be useful in cancer treatment. The appellant, the applicant for the patent, is a professor of chemistry (and Vice President/Provost) at Reed College, a liberal arts college in Portland, Oregon. Reed College is solely an undergraduate institution, and does not have any graduate programs for research or scholarship.

As a requirement for graduation with a Bachelor of Arts degree, Reed College requires each of its students to prepare a senior thesis. The student presents the thesis to a Thesis Oral Board, composed of four faculty members including the student's faculty sponsor and another faculty member from the student's department. The appellant states that the "purpose of the thesis requirement is to give the student the opportunity to carry out laboratory or scholarly research and to present the work in a more thorough and formal manner than is normally possible with the usual term paper," and that the "thesis requirement is purely educational and the students are not required by general college policy to produce original or publishable research or scholarship."

A copy of each thesis is filed in the main college library and in the library of the particular department in which the student's work was done. The theses are listed on individual cards which show the student's name and the title of the thesis. The cards are filed alphabetically by the author's name.

The titles of the theses may be descriptive, as were the titles of the three theses involved in this case. One of these is entitled "Synthesis of Cyclic Methanedisulfonate Esters by Silver Salt Method." Other theses on file in the chemistry department library, however, have more fanciful titles, such as "Make My Func. the P–Func"; "Close to the Edge"; "Evolution and Lucifer"; "Easy Come, Easy Go"; "Hunan's Thanatopsis: Haecceity, Tathat, and Doedecahedrane".

In the main library, there are approximately 6,000 cards listing theses. In the chemistry department library there are approximately 450 cards contained in a shoebox. At oral argument the appellant stated that both the listing cards and the theses themselves are available for public examination.

In neither the main library nor the chemistry department library are the theses generally indexed or cataloged. They are not assigned Library of Congress catalog numbers.

The appellant stated that "occasionally a student's thesis is published, in whole or part, in a professional journal." He further stated, however, that although the thesis research projects were carried out in his laboratory, "none of the students involved have presented their senior theses or pertinent parts thereof in any professional journal or to any professional society, or in any other professional setting." The appellant also stated that prior to the filing of the patent application he had not "made any publication in a professional journal, or presentation to a professional society, or any other disclosure or presentation in the fields" involved in or related to the senior theses that "would associate my research interests with the field of the invention."

The Board affirmed the examiner's rejection of the application under 35 U.S.C. § 102(b) as anticipated by the three student theses. The Board stated that the "sole issue before us is whether" the three theses "are printed publications within the meaning of" 35 U.S.C. § 102(b), since the appellant had "conceded ... that if they are, the subject matter of the claims is unpatentable to him." The Board found that there was "no significant distinction between the facts here and those in" *In re Hall*, 781 F.2d 897, 228 USPQ 453 (Fed.Cir.1986). It concluded that "reasonable diligence" by a researcher in the field "would have uncovered the documents."

In cases like the present one, where there are no disputed factual issues, the question whether particular material is a "printed publication" is a question of law. "[T]he printed publication provision was designed to prevent withdrawal by an inventor, as the subject matter of a patent, of that which was already in the possession of the public." *In re Wyer*, 655 F.2d 221, 226, 210 USPQ 790, 794 (CCPA 1981). "The statutory phrase 'printed publication' has been interpreted to mean that before the critical date the reference must have been sufficiently accessible to the public interested in the art; dissemination and public accessibility are the keys to the legal determination whether a prior art reference was 'published.'" *Constant v. Advanced Micro–Devices, Inc.*, 848 F.2d 1560, 1568, 7 U.S.P.Q.2D 1057, 1062 (Fed.Cir.), *cert. denied*, ___ U.S. ___, 109 S.Ct. 228, 102 L.Ed.2d 218 (1988).

This court and its predecessor twice recently have considered the status as printed publications of academic papers filed in a university library. In *In re Bayer*, 568 F.2d 1357 (CCPA 1978), the Board held that a master's thesis became a printed publication upon its receipt by a university library because the three-member faculty committee that had approved the thesis "could have located his thesis in the library where it was available to them on request," so that the thesis "was capable of providing wide public access to the information it contained." 568 F.2d at 1359. On the critical date the library had received the thesis but had not yet cataloged it or placed it on the library shelves in bound form as it ultimately would do.

The Court of Customs and Patent Appeals reversed. The court first held that "a printed document may qualify as a 'publication' under 35 U.S.C. § 102(b), notwithstanding that accessibility thereto is restricted to a 'part of the public,' so long as accessibility is sufficient 'to raise a presumption that the public concerned with the art would know of [the invention].' Accessibility to appellant's thesis by the three members of the graduate committee under the circumstances of the present case does not raise such a presumption." 568 F.2d at 1361.

Moreover, since appellant's thesis could have been located in the university library only by one having been informed of its existence by the faculty committee, and not by means of the customary research aids available in the library, the "probability of public knowledge of the contents of the [thesis]," was virtually nil.

The court rejected the Commissioner's argument that the student's defense of his thesis before the faculty committee reflected an intent to make the result of his research available to the public. The court stated: "[W]e are unconvinced that appellant's thesis defense before the graduate committee in its official capacity as arbiter of appellant's entitlement to a master's degree was somehow transmuted into a patent-defeating publication merely by depositing the thesis in the university library where it remained uncatalogued and unshelved as of the critical date in question." 568 F.2d at 1362.

In re Hall involved a doctoral dissertation filed in the library of a German university. A university official, Dr. Will, submitted letters, which the court described as affidavits, stating that "[o]ur dissertations ... are indexed in a special dissertations catalogue...." 781 F.2d at 898. In affirming the Board's ruling that the dissertation was a printed publication, the court rejected the contention that the dissertation "was not shown to be accessible because Dr. Will's affidavits do not say when the thesis was indexed in the library catalog and do not chronicle the procedures for receiving and processing a thesis in the library." 781 F.2d at 899. The court stated:

> The only reasonable interpretation of the affidavits is that Dr. Will was relying on his library's general practice for indexing, cataloging, and shelving theses in estimating the time it would have taken to make the dissertation available to the interested public. Dr. Will's affidavits are competent evidence, and in these circumstances, persuasive evidence that the Foldi dissertation was accessible prior to the critical date.

Id.

As the opinions in *Bayer* and *Hall* indicate, the critical difference between the cases that explains the different results is that on the critical date in *Bayer* the thesis was "uncatalogued and unshelved" and therefore not accessible to the public, whereas in *Hall* the "dissertation was accessible" because it had been indexed, cataloged and shelved.

We conclude that in the present case, as in *Bayer* and unlike *Hall*, the three student theses were not accessible to the public because they had not been either cataloged or indexed in a meaningful way. Although the titles of the theses were listed on 3 out of 450 cards filed alphabetically by author in a shoebox in the chemistry department library, such "availability" was not sufficient to make them reasonably accessible to the public. Here, the only research aid was the student's name, which, of course, bears no relationship to the subject of the student's thesis.

Considering all the facts of this case, we hold that the three student theses were not "printed publications" under 35 U.S.C. § 102(b).

The decision of the Board of Patent Appeals and Interferences is Reversed.

■ MAYER, CIRCUIT JUDGE, dissenting.

In my view, the papers at issue here were sufficiently available to the public to qualify as "printed publications" within the meaning of 35 U.S.C. § 102(b). The nature and quality of the index in the Reed College chemistry department library are not determinative of whether the theses were publicly available. Neither *Bayer* nor *Hall* turned solely on the existence, absence, or character of an index. Indeed, the result in both cases is not inconsistent with the notion that merely shelving a single copy of a work in a publicly accessible area of a library is sufficient for publication under the statute. Earlier decisions of the Patent Office Board of Appeals, interpreting the predecessor to section 102(b), were to the same effect: shelving a thesis in a university library is alone sufficient to render it a "printed publication". *Gulliksen v. Halberg v. Edgerton v. Scott*, 75 USPQ 252, 257 (Pat.Tr.Off.Bd.App. 1937); *Ex parte Hershberger*, 96 USPQ 54, 56 (Pat.Tr. Off.Bd.App. 1953).

Of course, the "shoebox" author index in this case is relevant to the question of publication. When considered together with the shelving of the theses in publicly accessible areas of the Reed College libraries, the presence of even this "noncustomary" index convinces me that these works were published as contemplated by the statute. But the existence or nature of an indexing system is only one factor to be considered in assessing the public availability of a work; it is neither a necessary nor a sufficient condition for publication.

NOTES

1. *"Public Accessibility."* The court in *In re Hall* called public accessibility the "touchstone in determining whether a reference constitutes a 'printed publication.'" In the above cases, a doctoral thesis deposited *and indexed* (in some meaningful way) in a German library was sufficiently accessible, whereas an undergraduate thesis deposited, but not indexed did not constitute a "printed publication." The focus of the inquiry is not whether a person of ordinary skill in the art would have come across the prior art reference or in fact did; rather, the question is whether the reference was sufficiently accessible. *See Constant v. Advanced Micro–Devices, Inc.*, 848 F.2d 1560, 1568–69 (Fed.Cir.1988) ("The statutory phrase 'printed publication' has been interpreted to mean that before the critical date the reference must have been sufficiently accessible to the public interested in the art; dissemination and public accessibility are the keys to the legal determination whether a prior art reference was published. . . . If accessibility is proved, there is no requirement to show that particular members of the public actually received the information."); *In re Bayer*, 568 F.2d 1357 (CCPA 1978) (thesis catalogued but not indexed before the critical date is not sufficiently accessible to constitute a "printed publication"). What if the reference is improperly indexed? Do you agree with Judge Mayer's dissent in *Cronyn* that "the existence or nature of an indexing system is only one factor to be considered in assessing the public availability of a work?" It would seem that a subject index should be sufficient, but what about an author index? Does your answer change if the author is so famous in her field that her name alone is effectively synonymous with the subject itself?

For more discussion of public accessibility, see *SRI International, Inc. v. Internet Security Systems, Inc.*, 511 F.3d 1186 (Fed.Cir.2008) (holding that a document on an uncatalogued, unindexed but open-access FTP server that was not intended for dissemination to the public was not publicly accessible). *See also In re Lister*, 583 F.3d 1307 (Fed.Cir.2009) (holding that copyright registration submissions prior to the availability of keyword searching by text and title were not sufficiently accessible to constitute printed publications. Note, however, that such searches are now available).

2. *Date of Publication.* The date the relevant public (*i.e.*, persons of ordinary skill in the art) can actually gain access to the publication is the date of publication for prior art purposes. *See In re Bayer,* 568 F.2d 1357 (CCPA 1978) ("The date on which the public actually gained access to the invention by means of the publication is the focus of the inquiry"). With respect to a thesis, for example, does this mean the date it is catalogued and put in the private faculty reserve room, or the date it is eventually put on a publically accessible shelf or database?

3. *Limited Access/Secrecy Order.* Consider the following examples: (1) A document on a military system was distributed to 50 persons involved in the management and construction of the military system. The document was not under a secrecy order but it had stamped on the margin "reproduction or further dissemination is not authorized-not for public release." The document was housed in a library of a corporation primarily responsible for the development of the system. Access to the library was restricted to "authorized personnel." Is this document a "printed publication?" (2) A memorandum that is listed on a library's database, but is located in a part of the library that is inaccessible to the public?

4. *"Printed."* In 1836, when the term "printed" first appeared in § 102(a), actual printing was the only known means for disseminating or making information available. Today, however, there are obviously other means available such as computer storage or microfilm. Does storage on a computer satisfy the "printed" requirement under § 102? In *In re Wyer,* 655 F.2d 221, 226 (CCPA 1981), the Court of Customs and Patent Appeals stated that:

> The traditional dichotomy between "printing" and "publication" is no longer valid. Given the state of technology in document duplication, data storage, and data-retrieval systems, the "probability of dissemination" of an item very often has little to do with whether or not it is "printed" in the same sense of that word when it was introduced into the patent statute in 1836. In any event, interpretation of the words "printed" and "publication" to mean "probability of dissemination" and "public accessibility," respectively, now seems to render their use in the phrase "printed publication" somewhat redundant.

Thus, it appears that the term "printed" is interpreted to mean that which is available to the public in tangible form. Should our analysis here be influenced by the view under copyright law that copyright subsists in a work once it is "fixed in any tangible medium of expression?" 17 U.S.C. § 102(a); *see also,* 17 U.S.C. § 101 (defining fixation). Or are copyrightability requirements irrelevant here? What are the implications for information available through the Internet—perhaps fleetingly?

5. "PATENTED"

The issue here is what does it mean for something to be treated as though it has been "patented." As explored below in the case *In re Carlson,* the focus in this analysis is not on the entire content of the putative prior art document, but on the legal rights it conveys.

In re Carlson

983 F.2d 1032 (Fed.Cir.1992).

■ Before NIES, CHIEF JUDGE, LOURIE and CLEVENGER, CIRCUIT JUDGES.

■ CLEVENGER, CIRCUIT JUDGE.

The two issues raised in this appeal are whether the design protected by a German Geschmacksmuster constitutes an "invention ... patented ... in ... a foreign country" within the meaning of 35 U.S.C. § 102(a)

(1988) and thus may be considered prior art, and whether Des. 289,855 is unpatentable under 35 U.S.C. § 103 (1988) as obvious in light of the pertinent prior art. The application that culminated in issuance of Des. 289,855 on May 19, 1987 was filed with the PTO by Carlson on November 19, 1984. The claim of Des. 289,855 covers the ornamental design for a dual compartment bottle as depicted in the six figures included in the design patent.

On April 6, 1990, the PTO granted a request for reexamination of Des. 289,855 filed by Revlon, Inc. and Smiletote, Inc., whom Carlson had accused of infringing Des. 289,855. During the reexamination, several references were considered which had not been before the examiner during prosecution of the initial application. The new references were (i) German Geschmacksmuster No. 4244, issued to Firma Frankenwald–Presserei Horst Rebhan on May 9, 1984; (ii) U.S. Design Patent No. 86,749, issued to Salvatore Scuito on April 12, 1932, and entitled "Design for a Combined Flask and Drinking Glass Holder" (Scuito); and (iii) a magazine article entitled "News in Packaging," Drug & Cosmetic Industry (July 1978) (Redken article), illustrating the type of bottle cap used in Des. 289,855.

A Geschmacksmuster is a design registration obtained by an applicant from the German government after performing certain registration procedures. Professor Chisum, in a nutshell, thus describes the registration process in effect in 1984:

> [A] person may register an industrial design or model by depositing with a local office an application with a drawing, photograph or sample of the article. Registration is effective on deposit, and lists of registered designs are published a short time after registration.

1 DONALD S. CHISUM, PATENTS § 3.06[2], at 3–107 (1992).

The local office of deposit of a Geschmacksmuster in a city is the Amtsgericht, which is the local courthouse or seat of government of that city. The published list, which discloses certain particulars of each registration, is contained within the Bundesanzeiger, or Federal Gazette. The information typically disclosed in the Bundesanzeiger, with respect to a registered design, consists of a general description of the deposited design and the class of articles deposited, identifying numbers of the deposited designs, the name and location of the registrant, the date and time of registration, and the term of protection. In addition, the city location of the deposited design is also known because the published list is organized under city headings.

Certified copies of Geschmacksmuster are available from the Amtsgericht in which the registered designs are deposited. Such copies typically include the same information regarding the Geschmacksmuster as provided in the Bundesanzeiger, *supra*, including the city of deposit, and a copy of the drawing or photograph deposited. In the case of deposited sample articles, certified copies of Geschmacksmuster contain photographs of the sample articles.

The Geschmacksmuster in this case embraces three different bottle designs, Nos. 3168–3170. Only Model No. 3168 is pertinent to the design claimed in Des. 289,855. That model is a bottle design consisting of two attached container portions divided by a striking, asymmetrical zig-zag line of demarcation. Each container portion has an externally threaded neck with an associated screw-on cap. As translated, both the Bundesanzeiger publication referring to the Geschmacksmuster and the certified copy of the Geschmacksmuster state, in relevant part: "An open package with plastic or synthetic bottles with stoppers.... Model for plastic products." The description as "open" signifies that the deposited materials are available for public inspection. In addition, the certified copy of the Geschmacksmuster, which was supplied to the examiner as relevant prior art, includes a series of photographs of the three deposited designs taken from various orientations. The Bundesanzeiger identifies the German city of Coburg, Bavaria as the location of the registered design.

Upon reexamination, the examiner rejected Carlson's argument that the Geschmacksmuster should not qualify as prior art under section 102(a), and found that the design protected by Des. 289,855 would have been obvious under section 103.

On appeal, the Board cited as its guide and authority *In re Talbott*, 443 F.2d 1397, 170 USPQ 281, 58 C.C.P.A. 1374 (1971) (German Geschmacksmuster constitutes a "foreign patent" for purposes of 35 U.S.C. § 102(d) (1988)), and *In re Monks*, 588 F.2d 308, 200 USPQ 129 (CCPA 1978) (no reason to distinguish between sections 102(a) and 102(d) in determining what constitutes a "foreign patent"). Based on those cases, the Board concluded that a Geschmacksmuster constitutes a patent for purposes of section 102(a).

Assuming no other bar to patentability, a person is entitled to a patent under U.S. law unless the same invention was patented by another person in a foreign country prior to the invention thereof by the U.S. applicant. 35 U.S.C. § 102(a) (1988). The potential bar thus created by the existence of a patent issued in a foreign country gives rise to the availability of such a foreign patent as a prior art reference for the purpose of determining the validity of the claims in a U.S. patent or pending patent application.

A further bar to patentability arises if an applicant for a U.S. patent has been granted a patent in a foreign country on the same invention more than twelve months prior to the date the patent application is filed in the United States. 35 U.S.C. § 102(d) (1988). With respect to design patents, however, Congress has provided that the time bar in section 102(d) is six months. 35 U.S.C. § 172 (1988).

In *In re Talbott*, our predecessor court decided, as a matter of first impression, that a design protected by a Geschmacksmuster qualifies under section 102(d) as an invention patented in a foreign country for purposes of applying the statutory time bar against an application for a U.S. design patent covering the same subject matter. 443 F.2d at 1398–99, 170 USPQ at 282. The court rejected the argument that a Geschmacksmuster should not be deemed to fall within section 102(d) because the copyright nature of the rights protected by the Geschmacksmuster is substantially different from the rights inherent in a U.S. design patent. *Id.*, 443 F.2d at 1398–99, 170 USPQ at 281–82. This rejection was based on reasoning adopted in the case by the Board, which in turn relied upon the opinion of Examiner-in-Chief P.J. Federico in *Ex Parte Weiss*, 159 USPQ 122 (Pat.Off.Bd.App.

1967). With regard to construing "patented . . . in a foreign country" under section 102(d), Federico concluded that the rights and privileges attaching to the protection granted by foreign governments need not be coextensive with the exclusive rights granted under U.S. law, so long as the foreign rights granted are both substantial and exclusive in nature. *Id.* at 123–24. *Cf. In re Howarth,* 654 F.2d 103, 105 n. 3, 210 USPQ 689, 690 n. 3 (CCPA 1981) ("Not every foreign document labelled a 'patent' is a patent within the meaning of 35 U.S.C. § 102(a) or (b)." (*citing In re Ekenstam,* 256 F.2d 321, 323, 118 USPQ 349, 351, 45 C.C.P.A. 1022 (1958))). Because a Geschmacksmuster conveys substantial and exclusive rights in the design, the Board in Weiss held that a Geschmacksmuster qualifies as prior art under section 102(d). 159 USPQ at 124. The court in *Talbott* expressly "adopt[ed] as our own, the reasoning set out so completely in [*Weiss*]." 443 F.2d at 1399, 170 USPQ at 282.

Our predecessor court also had occasion to consider whether the phrase "patented . . . in . . . a foreign country," as used in section 102(a), should have a different meaning from the same language used in section 102(d). The issue arose in *In re Monks,* a case concerned with the bar to patentability under section 102(d). The Solicitor contended that the date upon which an invention is patented in a foreign country should differ for the purposes of section 102(a) versus section 102(d). At stake was whether the British patent date should be the date the patent finally issued, or an earlier date when the contents of the patent were initially published. 588 F.2d at 309, 200 USPQ at 130. Emphasizing that section 102(d) relates to foreign patents of the U.S. applicant (of which the U.S. applicant must necessarily be aware), whereas section 102(a) relates to foreign patents of others, the Solicitor argued that the foreign patent date under section 102(d) could properly precede the like date under section 102(a). The court refused to draw such a distinction:

> First, there is no basis in the [Patent] Act or its legislative history for making such a distinction. The statute uses the identical phrase, "patented . . . in a foreign country," in each of these sections. Nowhere in the legislative history is there the slightest suggestion that these same phrases be interpreted differently. *Id.* at 310, 200 USPQ at 131. Although this observation was made with respect to the date on which a foreign patent becomes "patented" within the meaning of section 102(d), the language applies equally as well to the present issue of whether a distinction should be drawn between subsections (a) and (d) of section 102 when considering whether a Geschmacksmuster is a foreign patent citable as prior art in a section 103 analysis.

Whether a Geschmacksmuster is a foreign patent under section 102(a) is a question of first impression. That a Geschmacksmuster qualifies as a patent for section 102(d) purposes is settled law, embraced by the Solicitor, unchallenged by Carlson, and a proposition with which we do not disagree.

Notwithstanding the holding in *Talbott* and the strong conclusion in *Monks* that the test for determining what constitutes a foreign patent should not differ between subsections (a) and (d) of section 102, Carlson invites this court to deny Geschmacksmuster the status of patents under section 102(a).

Carlson first points to language in *Talbott* that recognizes the different situations addressed by subsections (a) and (d) of section 102 and states that the policy considerations underlying the different subsections, "while overlapping to some extent, are not necessarily identical." 443 F.2d at 1399, 170 USPQ at 282. Carlson claims to base his argument on this premise.

We do not dispute that section 102(a), relating to potential prior art in the form of patents issued in a foreign country and held by persons other than the U.S. patent applicant, serves a purpose akin to, but different from, section 102(d), which specifies the time within which the owner of a foreign patent must apply for a U.S. patent on the same invention. That distinction, however, does not suggest that a Geschmacksmuster lacks the necessary credentials to qualify as a patent under section 102(a).

Nevertheless, Carlson asserts that the correct interpretation of section 102(a) requires that a foreign patent only serve as prior art if it discloses its invention in a readily-accessible fashion. In essence, Carlson argues that the embodiment of foreign protection must take a form that fully discloses the nature of the protected design in a medium of communication capable of being widely disseminated. Because this requirement is clearly not satisfied by depositing a model in a city courthouse in a foreign land, the embodiment cannot constitute an invention patented in a foreign country for purposes of section 102(a) because it is incapable of providing detailed instruction to a large enough number of persons remote from the location of deposit. Moreover, Carlson argues, since the Bundesanzeiger entry does not explicitly refer to dual-compartment containers, it cannot provide notice of the existence of the pertinent model of the Geschmacksmuster to a designer of such containers.

Carlson correctly surmises that section 102(a) contains a requirement that a foreign patent be disclosed in order to qualify as prior art under section 102(a). The requirement, however, is only that the patent be "available to the public."

Because the description of the Geschmacksmuster in the Bundesanzeiger does not specifically refer to a multicompartment container, Carlson would have us deem the designs incorporated therein outside of the relevant field of prior art. His argument, however, represents an overly narrow view of the prior art germane to his invention. *See, e.g., In re Deminski*, 796 F.2d 436, 442, 230 USPQ 313, 315 (Fed.Cir.1986) (reference must be "within the field of the inventor's endeavor," or if not, "reasonably pertinent to the particular problem with which the inventor was involved.").

The Bundesanzeiger entry regarding the Geschmacksmuster at issue in this appeal clearly refers to a single package incorporating multiple plastic bottles, thereby alerting the public to potentially relevant designs, and directs the notified reader to proceed to Coburg to obtain the actual design. Once in Coburg, the protected design is completely "available to the public" through the certified copy of the Geschmacksmuster.

We recognize that Geschmacksmuster on display for public view in remote cities in a far-away land may create a burden of discovery for one without the time, desire, or resources to journey there in person or by agent to observe that which was registered and protected under German law. Such a burden, however, is by law imposed upon the hypothetical person of ordinary skill in the art who is charged with knowledge of all the contents of the relevant prior art. *Kimberly–Clark Corp. v. Johnson & Johnson,* 745 F.2d 1437, 1454, 223 USPQ 603, 614 (Fed.Cir.1984); *see also In re Hall,* 781 F.2d 897, 899–900, 228 USPQ 453, 456 (Fed.Cir.1986) (doctoral dissertation, catalogued and available at Freiburg University, Germany, provides sufficient "public accessibility" for a printed publication under section 102(b)).

Moreover, actual knowledge of the Geschmacksmuster is not required for the disclosure to be considered prior art. To determine patentability, a hypothetical person is presumed to know all the pertinent prior art, whether or not the applicant is actually aware of its existence. *In re Nilssen,* 851 F.2d 1401, 1403, 7 U.S.P.Q.2D 1500, 1502 (Fed.Cir.1988); *see also In re Howarth,* 654 F.2d 103, 106, 210 USPQ 689, 692 (CCPA 1981) ("Section 102 has as one objective that only the first inventor obtain a patent. . . . Foreign 'patents' and foreign 'printed publications' preclude the grant of a patent whether or not the information is commonly known. Under [section] 102 a conclusive presumption of knowledge of such prior art is, in effect, a statutorily required fiction.").

In conclusion, we hold that because the Geschmacksmuster fully discloses the design upon which German law conferred the exclusive rights attendant to the registration, the Geschmacksmuster qualifies as a foreign patent for purposes of section 102(a). . . .

Affirmed.

NOTES

1. *The Difference Between a Patent and a Printed Publication.* In the United States a patent is published the date it is issued and therefore is both a patent and a printed publication under § 102(a). Therefore, one may think that the distinction between patents and printed publications is irrelevant. As we saw in *In re Carlson,* however, most of the problems with respect to prior art patents concern foreign patents. This is because although many countries do not actively disseminate the contents of a patent specification, the contents are made available by the government patent office for public inspection. Indeed, many private companies take advantage of this public access to provide the private service of public dissemination, for a fee, of course.

Recall that Carlson argued that for a foreign patent to be prior art under § 102(a), the "foreign protection must take a form that fully discloses the nature of the protected design in a medium of communication capable of being widely disseminated." The court agreed with Carlson that a foreign patent must be "disclosed" for § 102(a) purposes, but stated that disclosure is satisfied when the patent is "available to the public." The court, citing *In re Hall,* stated:

> We recognize that [a Geschmacksmuster] on display for public view in remote cities in a far-away land may create a burden of discovery for one without the time, desire, or resources to journey there in person or by agent to observe that which is registered and protected under German law. Such a burden, however, is by law imposed upon the hypothetical person of

ordinary skill in the art who is charged with knowledge of all the contents of the relevant prior art.

2. *Geschmacksmuster v. Gebrauchsmuster.* We must distinguish between a *geschmacksmuster* and a *gebrauchsmuster*. The former, discussed in *In re Carlson*, is a design registration that is obtained after satisfying certain registration procedures. The latter, in contrast, is more akin to the United States utility patent and is sometimes referred to as a "petty patent" because, unlike a regular German patent, it is not subject to a novelty search and there is no requirement of nonobviousness. The duration of the gebrauchsmuster is also shorter than a regular German patent. The purpose of a gebrauchsmuster "is to enable the applicant to obtain a speedy protection for a new article and if desirable, to concurrently seek a regular patent, a procedure which would consume much more time." *Reeves Bros., Inc. v. United States Laminating Corp.*, 282 F.Supp. 118, 134–36 (E.D.N.Y.1968).

Nevertheless, a gebrauchsmuster is a prior art patent under § 102, but only for that which it claims, not for what is disclosed in the specification. *See Bendix Corp. v. Balax, Inc.*, 421 F.2d 809, 811–13 (7th Cir.1970) ("[A]ll parties agree that only that which is 'patented' by a [gebrauchsmuster] may be considered as prior art under Section 102(b). Subject matter which is ancillary to, but not a part of, the patented subject matter may not be considered.... The *Reeves* court had said 'for anticipation purposes under Section 102 a [gebrauchsmuster] is a reference only for what is patented, *i.e.*, for what it claims and not for what is disclosed in its specifications.'.... Each case will, of course, turn on its own facts. In each case the question will be 'What is patented?' The specifications of the [gebrauchsmuster] may be resorted to if necessary to clarify the meaning of the words of the claim—to determine what it is that the claims 'patent' but not to add to what they patent"). The role of the specification as prior art is not necessarily clear. How would you apply §§ 102(a) and (b) in the light of the policies underlying our patent system?

6. "SECRET" PRIOR ART—§ 102(e)

As with § 102(a), § 102(e) is also a novelty provision. But it differs from § 102(a) in that the prior art under (e) can defeat novelty even though the prior art is essentially inaccessible to the public, including the inventor. As explore below in *Alexander Milburn v. Davis–Bournonville* the particular problem raised by § 102(e) is the effective date that should be attributed to the disclosure in a patent application that later issues as a patent—the filing date, issue date, or some other date?

Alexander Milburn Co. v. Davis–Bournonville Co.

270 U.S. 390 (1926).

■ MR. JUSTICE HOLMES delivered the opinion of the Court.

This is a suit for the infringement of the plaintiff's patent for an improvement in welding and cutting apparatus alleged to have been the invention of one Whitford. The suit embraced other matters but this is the only one material here. The defense is that Whitford was not the first inventor of the thing patented, and the answer gives notice that to prove the invalidity of the patent evidence will be offered that one Clifford invented the thing, his patent being referred to and identified. The application for the plaintiff's patent was filed on March 4, 1911, and the patent was issued on June 4, 1912.

There was no evidence carrying Whitford's invention further back. Clifford's application was filed on January 31, 1911, before Whitford's, and his patent was issued on February 6, 1912. It is not disputed that this application gave a complete and adequate description of the thing patented to Whitford, but it did not claim it. The District Court gave the plaintiff a decree, holding that while Clifford might have added this claim to his application, yet as he did not, he was not a prior inventor. 297 F. 846. The decree was affirmed by the Circuit Court of Appeals. 1 F.(2d) 227. There is a conflict between this decision and those of other Circuit Courts of Appeal, especially the sixth. *Lemley v. Dobson–Evans Co.*, 243 F. 391, 156 C. C. A. 171. *Naceskid Service Chain Co. v. Perdue*, 1 F.(2d) 924. Therefore a *writ of certiorari* was granted by this Court. 45 S. Ct. 93, 266 U. S. 596, 69 L. Ed. 459.

The patent law authorizes a person who has invented an improvement like the present, "not known or used by others in this country, before his invention," etc., to obtain a patent for it. Rev. Sts. § 4886, amended by Act March 3, 1897, c. 391, § 1, 29 Stat. 692 (Comp. St. § 9430). Among the defences to a suit for infringement the fourth specified by the statute is that the patentee "was not the original and first inventor or discoverer of any material and substantial part of the thing patented." Rev. Sts. § 4920, amended by Act March 3, 1897, c. 391, § 2, 29 Stat. 692 (Comp. St. § 9466). Taking these words in their natural sense as they would be read by the common man, obviously one is not the first inventor if, as was the case here, somebody else has made a complete and adequate description of the thing claimed before the earliest moment to which the alleged inventor can carry his invention back. But the words cannot be taken quite so simply. In view of the gain to the public that the patent laws mean to secure we assume for purposes of decision that it would have been no bar to Whitford's patent if Clifford had written out his prior description and kept it in his portfolio uncommunicated to anyone. More than that, since the decision in the case of the Cornplanter Patent, 23 Wall. 181, it is said, at all events for many years, the Patent Office has made no search among abandoned patent applications, and by the words of the statute a previous foreign invention does not invalidate a patent granted here if it has not been patented or described in a printed publication. Rev. Sts. § 4923 (Comp. St. § 9469). *See Westinghouse Machine Co. v. General Electric Co.*, 207 F. 75, 126 C. C. A. 575. These analogies prevailed in the minds of the courts below.

On the other hand publication in a periodical is a bar. This as it seems to us is more than an arbitrary enactment, and illustrates, as does the rule concerning previous public use, the principle that, subject to the exceptions mentioned, one really must be the first inventor in order to be entitled to a patent. *Coffin v. Ogden*, 18 Wall. 120, 21 L. Ed. 821. We understand the Circuit Court of Appeals to admit that if Whitford had not applied for his patent until after the issue to Clifford, the disclosure by the latter would have had the same effect as the publication of the same words in a periodical, although not made the basis of a claim. 1 F.(2d) 233. The invention is made public property as much in the one case as in the other. But if this be true, as we think that it is, it seems to us that a sound distinction cannot be taken between that case and a patent applied for before but not granted until after a second patent is sought. The delays of the patent office ought not to cut down the effect of what has been done. The description shows that Whitford was not the first inventor. Clifford had done all that he could do to make his description public. He had taken steps that would make it public as soon as the Patent Office did its work, although, of course, amendments might be required of him before the end could be reached. We see no reason in the words or policy of the law for allowing Whitford to profit by the delay and make himself out to be the first inventor when he was not so in fact, when Clifford had shown knowledge inconsistent with the allowance of Whitford's claim, *Webster Loom Co. v. Higgins*, 105 U.S. 580, 26 L.Ed. 1177, and when otherwise the publication of his patent would abandon the thing described to the public unless it already was old, *McClain v. Ortmayer*, 12 S.Ct. 76, 141 U.S. 419, 424, 35 L.Ed. 800. *Underwood v. Gerber*, 13 S.Ct. 854, 149 U.S. 224, 230, 37 L.Ed. 710.

The question is not whether Clifford showed himself by the description to be the first inventor. By putting it in that form it is comparatively easy to take the next step and say that he is not an inventor in the sense of the statute unless he makes a claim. The question is whether Clifford's disclosure made it impossible for Whitford to claim the invention at a later date. The disclosure would have had the same effect as at present if Clifford had added to his description a statement that he did not claim the thing described because he abandoned it or because he believed it to be old. It is not necessary to show who did invent the thing in order to show that Whitford did not.

It is said that without a claim the thing described is not reduced to practice. But this seems to us to rest on a false theory helped out by the fiction that by a claim it is reduced to practice. A new application and a claim may be based on the original description within two years, and the original priority established notwithstanding intervening claims. *Chapman v. Wintroath*, 40 S.Ct. 234, 252 U.S. 126, 137, 64 L.Ed. 491. A description that would bar a patent if printed in a periodical or in an issued patent is equally effective in an application so far as reduction to practice goes.

As to the analogies relied upon below, the disregard of abandoned patent applications however explained cannot be taken to establish a principle beyond the rule as actually applied. As an empirical rule it no doubt is convenient if not necessary to the Patent Office, and we are not disposed to disturb it, although we infer that originally the practice of the Office was different. The policy of the statute as to foreign inventions obviously stands on its own footing and cannot be applied to domestic affairs. The fundamental rule we repeat is that the patentee must be the first inventor. The qualifications in aid of a wish to encourage improvements or to avoid laborious investigations do not prevent the rule from applying here.

Decree reversed.

NOTES

1. *§ 102(e) and Prior Art.*

a. *Section 102(e)(1) and Publication.* The American Inventors Protection Act of 1999 amended the patent code to require, with certain exceptions, patent applications filed on or after November 29, 2000, to be published "promptly after the expiration of a period of 18 months from the earliest filed date." 35 U.S.C. § 122(b). (Under 37 C.F.R. 1.219, an applicant can have his application published "earlier" than 18 months from the earliest filing date.) As such, § 102(e)(1) was added to permit published applications to serve as prior art. This subsection reads:

> A person shall be entitled to a patent unless—
>
> (e)(1) an application for patent, published under section 122(b), by another filed in the United States before the invention by the applicant for patent, except that an international application filed under the treaty defined in section 351(a) [Patent Cooperation Treaty] shall have the effect under this subsection of a national application published under section 122(b) only if the international application designating the United States was published under Article 21(2)(a) of such treaty in the English language.

Under § 102(e)(1), once a United States patent application is *published* in the United States, its prior art effect is triggered, and its effective date reverts to its date of filing.

Of perhaps greater significance, however, is that an international patent application filed pursuant to the Patent Cooperation Treaty (PCT) that designates the United States and is ultimately published in English will have prior art effect under § 102(e)(1) as of its international filing date, which is the date the PCT application is filed. The international filing date is no more than 12 months from the priority date (*i.e.*, the date of first filing in a PCT member country); and, under Article 21(2)(a) of the PCT, a PCT application is published 18 months after its priority date. Of note is that a PCT application, which satisfies the English language and designation requirements, can serve as a prior art reference as of its international filing date, even though an application is never subsequently filed in the United States. *See* 35 U.S.C. § 374. Consider the following example:

> Inventor files a patent application in France on January 2, 2001. Ten months later, on November 2, 2001, he files a PCT application designating the United States and several other PCT member countries. The PCT application will be published on July 2, 2002—18 months after the priority date (*i.e.*, French filing date). If the PCT publication is in English, it can serve as prior art under § 102(e)(1) as of its international filing date (not the priority date), which is November 2, 2001, even though Inventor may choose not to file an application in the United States.

b. *Section 102(e)(2) and Confidentiality.* Under § 102(e)(2), international (or PCT) applications have no prior art effect; but United States patent applications are certainly eligible. A United States patent application that is not subject to publication (because, for example, the applicant certifies that he is not filing in a foreign country) is "kept in confidence by the PTO" under 35 U.S.C. § 122(a). As a result, pending patent applications are not "known" (*i.e.*, "publicly accessible" in the § 102(a) sense); yet, such applications can serve as prior art references as of their filing date under § 102(e)(2) if the application eventually issues as a patent. Why? According to Justice Holmes, "delays in the Patent Office ought not to cut down the effect of what has been done." That is, but for the administrative delays present within the PTO in examining and ultimately issuing the patent, the basic fact is that someone other than the inventor disclosed the inventor's invention. Is this fair to the inventor? Isn't § 102(e) prior art "immune to the most painstaking documentary search." Cf., Baxter Int'l, Inc. v. COBE Laboratories, Inc., 88 F.3d 1054 (Fed.Cir.1996) (Newman, J., dissenting opinion) (discussing other inaccessible information). The inventor (and everyone else) is statutorily precluded from accessing pending patent applications. Why must the pending patent application issue before it can become a prior art reference? Perhaps there is a publicity requirement to § 102(e), but it simply comes later in the game, acting as a condition precedent.

2. *§ 102(e)(2) is Limited to U.S. Patent Applications.* Unlike § 102(e)(1), prior art under § 102(e)(2) is limited to United States patent applications that ultimately issue as patents. Consider the following: One month before inventor Y files her U.S. patent application, X files a patent application in France disclosing inventor Y's claimed invention. X eventually receives a French patent. Why isn't X's French patent prior art as of its filing date? Given the policy of *Milburn*, what is the difference between X filing his application in France or the U.S.? *See In re Hilmer*, 359 F.2d 859 (C.C.P.A. 1966) (*Hilmer I*) and *In re Hilmer*, 424 F.2d 1108 (C.C.P.A. 1970) (*Hilmer II*) discussed *infra*, Section B–8. Is there a U.S. bias in § 102(e) or are we simply unwilling, regardless of geography, to extend the secret prior art provision of § 102(e)? Should a manuscript be considered prior art when it is submitted to the journal; when it is sent out for editorial or peer review; or when the journal is ultimately published?

3. *§ 102(e)(2) and Provisional Patent Applications.* The Federal Circuit recently made clear that the effective prior art date of a patent claiming priority to an earlier provisional application is the date the provisional patent application was filed. *In re Giacomini*, 612 F.3d 1380, 1383–85 (Fed.Cir.2010).

4. *That Which is Disclosed, Not Claimed.* It is important to remember that patents and published patent applications under § 102(e) are prior art only for what they disclose, not what they claim. If a previously filed patent application claims the same subject matter as a later filed application, § 102(g) would be applicable because now we are talking about who *invented* first. Remember, it is the claims that define the property interest.

7. "SECRET" PRIOR ART—§ 102(g)

As with §§ 102(a), and (e), § 102(g) is also a novelty provision. But similar to § 102(e), § 102(g) art can defeat novelty even though it is virtually inaccessible to the public, including the inventor. As explored below in *Thomson v. Quixote*, all that is required is that the use not be "abandoned, suppressed, or concealed." The reader should be careful to compare the level of "publicity" required under this provision with that required under other the provisions of Section 102, including (a).

Thomson, S.A. v. Quixote Corp.

166 F.3d 1172 (Fed.Cir.1999).

■ Before RICH, SCHALL, and GAJARSA, CIRCUIT JUDGES.

■ RICH, CIRCUIT JUDGE.

Thomson, S.A. ("Thomson") appeals from the June 24, 1997 order of the United States District Court for the District of Delaware in an action for patent infringement. The court denied Thomson's motion for Judgment as a Matter of Law or in the alternative for a new trial, and sustained the jury verdict that U.S. Patent Nos. 4,868,808, 5,182,743, 4,961,183, and 5,175,725 are invalid for lack of novelty under 35 U.S.C. § 102(g). We affirm.

BACKGROUND

Plaintiff–Appellant Thomson is the assignee of the patents in suit, which are directed to optical information-storage devices, such as compact discs ("CDs"). Thomson makes and markets machines that "read" or "play" CDs, and grants licenses under the patents in suit to companies which produce CDs. Defendants–Appellees, Quixote Corp. and Disc Manufacturing, Inc. (collectively, "Quixote") make CDs.

Thomson sued Quixote for patent infringement. The parties agreed to base the outcome of the trial on three representative claims: claims 1 and 13 of U.S. Patent No. 4,868,808, and claim 1 of U.S. Patent No. 5,182,743. Before the full trial, the district court conducted a *Markman* hearing and issued a written opinion construing the representative claims.

At trial, the parties stipulated that Thomson's invention date for the patents in suit is August 25, 1972. Quixote's defense included evidence purporting to show that the representative claims are anticipated by an unpatented laser videodisc developed before August 1972 by a non-party, MCA Discovision, Inc. ("MCA"). After trial, the jury found in special verdicts that all of the representative claims were literally infringed, but that those claims are invalid due to lack of novelty (*i.e.*, anticipated) under 35 U.S.C. § 102(g).

Thomson submitted a motion requesting that the district court either set aside the jury's verdict of invalidity and enter Judgment as a Matter of Law ("JMOL") holding the patents not invalid, or grant a new trial on the lack of novelty issue. Thomson argued that JMOL was proper because there was insufficient evidence in the record to support the jury's anticipation verdict concerning certain claim limitations the court had held to be present following the *Markman* hearing.

In its opinion denying Thomson's motion, the district court described evidence in the record supporting the jury's finding of anticipation for each of the limitations that Thomson asserted had not been proven to be present in the MCA videodisc. The court noted that the evidence supporting the anticipation finding came from one or more sources: the live testimony of two people who had worked on the MCA laser videodisc project; an expert's report and portions of his deposition testimony, both of which were read into the record; the expert's exhibits; and certain MCA documents that the expert had reviewed. The court concluded that substantial evidence supports the jury's finding that Quixote had shown, by clear and convincing evidence, that every limitation in the representative claims was anticipated by the MCA device.

Thomson appeals the district court's denial of its motion for JMOL.

ANALYSIS

* * *

Thomson's core argument in support of reversing the district court's denial of its motion for JMOL is based on its assertions that (1) the jury verdict rests upon mere testimonial evidence by the two non-party MCA employees who worked on the videodisc project, and (2) this evidence is insufficient as a matter of law to support a holding of invalidity under subsection 102(g), because such testimonial evidence by inventors of their prior invention requires corroboration. Even if we accept Thomson's first assertion, and further assume that the MCA employees were acting as inventors in the laser videodisc project, Thomson's argument fails because this case does not present circumstances in which there is a need for corroboration, as hereinafter explained.

We begin with the language of 35 U.S.C. § 102(g):

A person shall be entitled to a patent unless....

(g) before the applicant's invention thereof the invention was made in this country by another who had not abandoned, suppressed, or concealed it. In determining priority of invention there shall be considered not only the respective dates of conception and reduction to practice of the invention, but also the reasonable diligence of one who was first to conceive and last to practice, from a time prior to conception by the other.

We have interpreted the first sentence of subsection 102(g) to permit qualifying art to invalidate a patent claim even if the same art may not qualify as prior art under other subsections of § 102. *See, e.g., Checkpoint Sys., Inc. v. United States Int'l Trade Comm'n*, 54 F.3d 756, 761, 35 U.S.P.Q.2D 1042, 1046 (Fed.Cir.1995); *Amgen, Inc. v. Chugai Pharm. Co.*, 927 F.2d 1200, 1205, 18 U.S.P.Q.2D 1016, 1020 (Fed.Cir.1991).[3] Art is not qualified under subsection 102(g) unless, viewed under a rule of reason, the totality of the evidence that the art satisfies the requirements of subsection 102(g) is clear and convincing. *See Price v. Symsek*, 988 F.2d 1187, 1194–95, 26 U.S.P.Q.2D 1031, 1036–37 (Fed.Cir.1993). We have also often held, in both interference and infringement lawsuits, that an inventor's testimony alone respecting the facts surrounding a claim of derivation or priority of invention cannot satisfy the clear and convincing standard without corroboration. *See, e.g., Cooper v. Goldfarb*, 154 F.3d 1321, 1330, 47 U.S.P.Q.2D 1896, 1903 (Fed.Cir.1998) (interference); *Woodland Trust v. Flowertree Nursery, Inc.*, 148 F.3d 1368, 1371, 47 U.S.P.Q.2D 1363, 1366 (Fed.Cir. 1998) (infringement). Although courts have reviewed infringement suits in which the defendant had attempted to prove subsection 102(g)-type antici-

3. The interpretation of subsection 102(g) to provide a prior art basis for invalidating a patent claim in infringement litigation was not intended by the drafters of the 1952 Patent Act. As the second sentence in the subsection indicates, 102(g) was written merely to provide a statutory basis for determining priority of invention in the context of interference proceedings before what was then the United States Patent Office. *See* P.J. Federico, Commentary on the New Patent Act at 19, in 35 U.S.C.A. (1954 ed., discontinued in subsequent volumes) (reprinted in 75 J. Pat. Trademark Off. Soc'y 161, 180 (1993)). Nevertheless, the first sentence is clear and, as the cases show, has been taken to have independent significance as a basis for prior art outside of the interference context.

This result makes sense. The first to invent who has invested time and labor in making and using the invention—but who might have opted not to apply for a patent—will not be liable for infringing another's patent on that same invention, while the public will have benefitted because the invention was not abandoned, suppressed or concealed. However, in view of these and other related policy concerns, and amendment of the statute, we have made clear that art qualifying only under subsection 102(g) may not be used under § 103 to invalidate other patents of fellow employees engaged in team research. *See Oddzon Prods., Inc. v. Just Toys, Inc.*, 122 F.3d 1396, 1402–03 (Fed.Cir.1997) (discussing *Application of Bass*, 59 C.C.P.A. 1342, 474 F.2d 1276, 1290 (1973) and the 1984 amendments to § 103).

pation by a non-party inventor at trial, *see, e.g., Eibel Process Co. v. Minnesota & Ontario Paper Co.*, 261 U.S. 45, 43 S.Ct. 322, 67 L.Ed. 523 (1923); *Washburn & Moen v. Beat'Em All Barbed–Wire*, 143 U.S. 275, 12 S.Ct. 443, 36 L.Ed. 154 (1892); *New Idea Farm Equip. Corp. v. Sperry Corp.*, 916 F.2d 1561, 16 U.S.P.Q.2D 1424 (Fed.Cir.1990), neither the Supreme Court nor we have directly held whether the corroboration rule must be applied to testimony by non-party inventors that is directed to establishing their invention as anticipating the claims at issue.

The cases that discuss skepticism of uncorroborated inventor testimony directed to establishing priority over an opponent's patent claim involve situations where the inventor is self-interested in the outcome of the trial and is thereby tempted to "remember" facts favorable to his or her case. *See, e.g., Barbed–Wire*, 143 U.S. at 284–85, 12 S.Ct. 443 (indicating that testifying non-party inventors' patents would increase in value if patent claims at issue were invalidated); *Price v. Symsek*, 988 F.2d at 1194, 26 U.S.P.Q.2D at 1036 (showing that testifying inventor's interfering patent claims would be invalidated if he could not establish priority; and holding that board extended corroboration rule beyond reasonable bounds).

The clear and convincing standard of proof required to establish priority, along with the numerous methods in the Federal Rules of Civil Procedure and Evidence by which a party may test, challenge, impeach, and rebut oral testimony, normally protects patentees from erroneous findings of invalidity. *See Price v. Symsek*, 988 F.2d at 1192–94, 26 U.S.P.Q.2D at 1035–36 (discussing standards of proof and requiring interference junior party to establish priority by clear and convincing evidence). Thus, the corroboration rule is needed only to counterbalance the self-interest of a testifying inventor against the patentee. We therefore hold that corroboration is required only when the testifying inventor is asserting a claim of derivation or priority of his or her invention and is a named party, an employee of or assignor to a named party, or otherwise is in a position where he or she stands to directly and substantially gain by his or her invention being found to have priority over the patent claims at issue.

In the current case, the purported inventors who testified were non-parties and their testimony concerned an unpatented prior invention. Although Thomson argues that the corroboration rule is justified here because both testifying witnesses were involved in businesses that supplied goods and services to Quixote, this does not rise to the level of self-interest required to justify triggering application of the corroboration rule. In fact, Thomson's only reference to the record showing this potential source of bias is a transcript of Thomson's cross examination of one of the witnesses, which means that the jury had the necessary facts to assess the credibility of the witnesses.

We therefore conclude that the district court was correct in holding that substantial evidence supports the jury's finding that Quixote showed, by clear and convincing evidence, that every limitation in the representative claims was anticipated, and that the district court was correct in denying Thomson's motion for JMOL.

* * *

NOTES

1. *§ 102(g) Prior Art—A History Lesson.* Prior to *Thomson*, there was some uncertainty as to whether § 102(g) could be used for prior art purposes. As noted in footnote 3 of the *Thomson* opinion, the drafters, including Judge Rich, of the 1952 Patent Act did not intend § 102(g) to act as a prior art section. In a speech delivered by Judge Rich to the New York Patent Law Association after the enactment of the 1952 Act, he stated:

> The purpose of paragraph (g) is to codify the law on determining priority, and it also preserves in the statutes a basis for interferences. It uses the words (which are new in this connection in this statute) "abandoned, suppressed, or concealed."

Giles S. Rich, Speech to the New York Patent Law Association (Nov. 6, 1951)(The effective date of the 1952 Act was January 1, 1953). Furthermore, in his well known commentary on the 1952 Act, P.J. Federico, the other primary drafter, wrote:

> Paragraph (g) relates to prior inventorship by another in this country as preventing the grant of a patent. It is based in part on the second defense in old R.S. 4920 [that the patentee "had surreptitiously or unjustly obtained the patent for that which was in fact invented by another, who was using reasonable diligence in adapting or perfecting the same"], and retains the rules of law governing the determination of priority of invention developed by decisions.

P.J. Federico, *Commentary on the New Patent Act* at 19, 35 U.S.C. §§ 1 *et. seq.* (1954 ed., discontinued in subsequent volumes) (reprinted in 75 J. PAT. TRADEMARK OFF. SOC'Y 161, 180 (1993)).

2. *§ 102(a) v. § 102(g).* It should be clear by now that the "publicity" requirement of § 102(a) as set forth in *Gayler* cannot be taken at face value. Even if use or knowledge of the claimed invention is not publicly accessible, anticipation may nevertheless reside in § 102(g). *See Thomson, S.A. v. Quixote* Corp., 166 F.3d 1172 (Fed.Cir.1999) (and cases cited therein). In *International Glass Co. v. United States*, 408 F.2d 395, 402 (Ct.Cl.1969), the Court of Claims, a Federal Circuit predecessor, makes the following distinction between §§ 102(a) and (g):

> [U]nlike a defense under section 102(a) where prior knowledge and use must be "public" at the time the patented invention is made, ... prior invention under section 102(g) requires only that the invention be complete, *i.e.*, conceived and reduced to practice, and not abandoned, suppressed or concealed.... Section 102(g) most commonly applies to priority disputes in U.S. Patent Office interference proceedings. However, it may also be an appropriate defense to patent validity in infringement litigation where a patent application was never filed by the prior inventor.

Does § 102(g) eviscerate § 102(a)? Doesn't § 102(g) incorporate public and secret knowledge and use? One basic distinction is that although § 102(a) has a publicity requirement, it does not require continued use like § 102(g); that is, under § 102(g), the invention must not be abandoned, suppressed or concealed. Given the Constitutional mandate to "promote the progress of the useful Arts" and our patent system's emphasis on disclosure, why shouldn't the second inventor who took the necessary steps to disclose her invention to society be entitled to a patent? Although there is no requirement that one obtain a patent, *see Checkpoint Systems, supra*; *Dunlop Holdings Ltd. v. Ram Golf Corp.*, 524 F.2d 33, 37 (7th Cir.1975), is there any reason to protect the first inventor who did not seek a patent? One can imagine a situation where an inventor does not apply for a patent, yet practices her invention (*e.g.*, process for making widgets) in such a way that, while not informing the public of the invention, allows the public to benefit from it in that the public has access to the widgets. In this scenario, the prior user has invested time and money in a process invention and is commercializing it. If a second inventor were permitted to obtain a patent, the prior user will, literally overnight, turn into an infringer. Thus, it seems that the prior art provision in § 102(g) focuses on the first inventor who, although failing to obtain a patent, invested time and labor in her invention. See footnote 3 in *Thomson* wherein the court set forth the policy for using § 102(g) as a prior art section: "The first to invent who has invested time and labor in making and using the invention—but who might have opted not to apply for a patent—will not be liable for infringing another's patent on that same invention, while the public will have benefitted because the invention was not abandoned, suppressed or concealed." *See also,* DREYFUSS AND KWALL, INTELLECTUAL PROPERTY 646–47 (1996).

a. *Prior User Rights—Sort Of.* In 1999, the American Inventors Protection Act (AIPA) was enacted. One of the more significant changes to Title 35 was the inclusion of the "First Inventor Defense Act of 1999,"[8] which is a mild form of prior user rights. Under newly created § 273,

> It shall be a defense to an action for infringement under section 271 of this title with respect to any subject matter that would otherwise infringe one or more claims for a *method* in the patent being asserted against a person, if such person had, acting in good faith, actually reduced the subject matter to practice at least 1 year before the effective filing date of such patent, and commercially used the subject matter before the effective filing date of such patent.

35 U.S.C. § 273(b)(1) (emphasis added). Note that the defense is limited to method patents, but § 273(a)(3) limits the defense even more by defining "method" as "a method of doing or conducting business." There are several provisions and subsections that need to be explored, but we will save that until Chapter Nine. For purposes of this chapter, particularly § 102(g) prior art, it is important to note that § 273(b)(6) states that the first inventor defense "may be asserted only by the person who performed the acts necessary to establish the defense" and this defense, absent a transfer or assignment of patent rights, "cannot be licensed or assigned or transferred to another person." Furthermore, § 273(b)(9) states a "patent shall not be deemed to be invalid under section 102 or 103 of this title solely because a defense is raised or established under this section." Thus, establishment of the first inventor defense does not invalidate the patent-in-suit. See Chapter 9, Section H for a more detailed discussion of the First Inventor Defense.

What are the advantages and disadvantages of the first inventor defense, from both practical and policy viewpoints? Consider the alternatives that a court, as in *Thomson*, faces without a prior use right. The court can (1) invalidate the patent based on the prior use and thrust the claimed subject matter into the public domain; or (2) maintain the validity of the patent and enjoin the prior user. These two alternatives lead to a "winner take all" situation. With the first inventor defense, however, the court has a third option: maintain the patent's validity but exempt the prior user from infringement liability. Thus, the prior use cannot act as prior art. *See* 35 U.S.C. § 273(b)(9). The public continues to benefit from the prior user's domestic investment and commercialization of the invention *and* obtains an enabling disclosure of the claimed subject matter from the patent. So why not expand the first inventor defense to other types of inventions as is done in

---

8. The first inventor defense is effective as of November 29, 1999 and is retroactive. But the defense is not available for any infringement action that was pending on November 29, 1999 or "with respect to any subject matter for which an adjudication of infringement, including a consent judgment, has been made before such date of enactment." Section 4303 of the AIPA.

European patent law? Why allow an alleged infringer who is not a prior user to cite another's prior use to invalidate a patent under § 102(g)? Under the scenario envisioned by the First Inventor Defense Act, the validity of the patent is maintained and the prior user may continue to practice the invention because both parties have contributed something to society—what has the alleged infringer contributed?

Are there any disadvantages to prior user rights? Would they encourage the first user to avoid disclosure via the patent system? Would the second inventor also avoid the patent system, having lost the possibility of exclusivity? Are prior user rights a form of compulsory licensing? Should they be *in personam*, non-transferrable rights? Would prior user rights benefit larger corporations at the expense of small inventor patentees in that the former can use its resources to tie up the latter in court?

By way of a representative European example, the prior use defense in the United Kingdom can only be invoked if the prior acts are committed in the UK and carried out in good faith. Moreover, the "defense is available where the defendant had done the acts or made 'serious and effective preparations' before the priority date of the patent to do an act which would be infringing if it was carried out after the grant of the patent." LIONEL BENTLY AND BRAD SHERMAN, INTELLECTUAL PROPERTY 508–09 (2001). Importantly, the right can be assigned to an entity that acquires "that part of the business in the course of which the act was done or the preparations were made." *Id.* at 509. But licensees are excluded from enjoying the defense. For a discussion of prior user rights, see Gary L. Griswold, *Prior* User Rights—*A Necessary Part of a First-to-File System*, 26 J. MARSHALL L. REV. 567 (1993).

b. *Abandonment, Suppression, or Concealment.* Given the secret nature of § 102(g) prior art, how does one prove that an invention was not abandoned, suppressed, or concealed? The court in *Oak Industries, Inc. v. Zenith Electronics Corp.,* 726 F.Supp. 1525 (N.D.Ill.1989), stated that a:

> Court may find that an invention was abandoned, suppressed or concealed if within a reasonable time after the invention was reduced to practice the inventor took no steps to make the invention publicly known. Factors supporting a finding of abandonment, concealment or suppression include not filing a patent application, not publicly disseminating documents describing the invention, and not publicly using the invention.

> We believe that in order to avoid a finding of suppression or concealment, [the challenger] need only show that the public enjoyed the use and benefits of the [invention].

The last sentence of the *Oak Industries* opinion is of particular significance. How does one show that the "public enjoyed the use and benefits" of one's secret use of an invention? Does it matter whether the prior user commercializes the invention? Should the nature of the defendant make a difference (*i.e.*, is the defendant the actual prior user of the invention or an ordinary infringer who is relying on third-party secret use of the invention)?

In *Oak Industries*, the court stated that the use of the invention did not rise "to the level of public use or benefit necessary to defeat an allegation of concealment under § 102(g). The converters (*i.e.*, the invention) were not 'freely accessible to the public at large,' so potential competitors could not discover the invention." The court went on to say that the use is "quite different from the sale of large quantities of products to the general public, which courts have found sufficient to show non-concealment and non-suppression." The court relied on *Friction Division Prod., Inc. v. E.I. DuPont de Nemours & Co.*, 658 F.Supp. 998 (D.Del.1987), *aff'd* 883 F.2d

1027 (Fed.Cir.1989) and *Dunlop Holdings Ltd. v. Ram Golf Corp.*, 524 F.2d 33 (7th Cir.1975). In both cases, the invention was commercialized prior to the patentee's date of invention. However, in *International Glass Co. v. United States,* 408 F.2d 395 (Ct.Cl.1969), the invention was never commercialized. The court stated that the invention "lay dormant, did not enrich the art, and thus 'remained secret, effectively concealed and suppressed until exhumed by . . . (defendant) for the defense of this case.' " *Id.* at 403–04.

Why should commercialization of the secret prior user be an important factor under § 102(g)? The obvious answer appears to be that the public has access to the invention or product embodying the invention and therefore benefits, even though the public may not be informed as to what the invention is. Does this distinction make sense given that both uses are noninforming? In both types of uses, the public is completely unaware of the invention. The court's language about "potential competitors" discovering the invention is somewhat puzzling given the fact that we are talking in *Oak Industries* about noninforming secret use. Would it make greater sense if courts spoke in terms of commercialization rather than secret and/or noninforming uses?

What about the nature of the defendant? This seems to be an important factor under § 102(g) in that courts appear to be less inclined to find concealment or suppression if the defendant is the actual prior user; whereas concealment or suppression is more likely to be found when the defendant is an ordinary infringer relying on third-party prior use. In both *Dunlop,* which explicitly acknowledged the importance of the nature of the defendant, and *Friction Products,* the defendant was the prior user and no concealment or suppression was found. In contrast, the defendants in *Oak Industries* and *International Glass* were ordinary infringers and the court held that the invention was concealed and suppressed by the prior third-party user. Thus, a prior secret user defendant who commercialized the patentee's invention may have a greater chance of proving lack of suppression and concealment than a defendant who did not commercialize the invention and relies on a third-party's secret use.

3. *How Much Corroboration is Required Under § 102(g)?* For corroboration purposes, the use of third-party prior art can be beneficial to the defendant. For example, in *Thomson,* the court stated:

> [T]he corroboration rule is needed only to counterbalance the self-interest of a testifying inventor against the patentee. We therefore hold that corroboration is required only when the testifying inventor is asserting a claim of derivation or priority of his or her invention and is a named party, an employee of or assignor to a named party, or otherwise is in a position where he or she stands to directly and substantially gain by his or her invention being found to have priority over the patent claims at issue.

Do you think MCA had an interest in seeing the patents-in-suit invalidated? Wouldn't MCA become an infringer if the patents were found not invalid?

The Federal Circuit further expounded generally on the issue of corroboration and § 102(g):

> The law has long looked with disfavor upon invalidating patents on the basis of mere testimonial evidence absent other evidence that corroborates that testimony. The Supreme Court recognized over one hundred years ago that testimony concerning invalidating activities can be "unsatisfactory" due to "the forgetfulness of witnesses, their liability to mistakes, their proneness to recollect things as the party calling them would have them recollect them, aside from the temptation to actual perjury." Accordingly, "[w]itnesses whose memories are prodded by the eagerness of interested

parties to elicit testimony favorable to themselves are not usually to be depended upon for accurate information," and therefore such testimony rarely satisfies the burden upon the interested party, usually the accused infringer, to prove invalidity by clear and convincing evidence.

Mere testimony concerning invalidating activities is received with further skepticism because such activities are normally documented by tangible evidence such as devices, schematics, or other materials that typically accompany the inventive process. *See Woodland Trust v. Flowertree Nursery, Inc.*, 148 F.3d 1368, 1373 (Fed.Cir.1998) (noting that the skepticism with which mere testimony of invalidating activity is received is "reinforced, in modern times, by the ubiquitous paper trail of virtually all commercial activity. It is rare indeed that some physical record (e.g., a written document such as notes, letters, invoices, notebooks, or a sketch or drawing or photograph showing the device, a model, or some other contemporaneous record) does not exist."); *Eibel Process Co. v. Minnesota & Ontario Paper Co.*, 261 U.S. 45, 60, 43 S.Ct. 322, 67 L.Ed. 523 (1923) (holding that the oral testimony of prior public use "falls short of being enough to overcome the presumption of novelty from the granting of the patent" when "there is not a single written record, letter or specification of prior date to [the patentee's] application that discloses any such discovery by anyone. . . .").

While this court has in the past applied the requirement of corroboration more often in the context of priority disputes under § 35 U.S.C. § 102(g), [e.g., *Thomson*] corroboration has been required to prove invalidity under other subsections of § 102 as well. In the context of § 102(f) (derivation) and § 102(g) (priority), we have stated that "the case law is unequivocal that an inventor's testimony respecting facts surrounding a claim of derivation or priority of invention cannot, standing alone, rise to the level of clear and convincing proof." *Price v. Symsek*, 988 F.2d 1187, 1194 (Fed.Cir.1993). No principled reason appears for applying a different rule when other subsections of § 102 are implicated: a witness's uncorroborated testimony is equally suspect as clear and convincing evidence if he testifies concerning the use of the invention in public before invention by the patentee (§ 102(a)), use of the invention in public one year before the patentee filed his patent (§ 102(b)), or invention before the patentee (§ 102(g)).

Moreover, the need for corroboration exists regardless whether the party testifying concerning the invalidating activity is interested in the outcome of the litigation (e.g., because that party is the accused infringer) or is uninterested but testifying on behalf of an interested party. That corroboration is required in the former circumstance cannot be debated. Uninterested witnesses are also subject to the corroboration requirement. For example, in *Barbed–Wire Patent*, some twenty-four witnesses, all apparently uninterested in the outcome of the case, testified on behalf of the accused infringer that they had seen the patented fence exhibited by a third party, Mr. Morley, at a county fair more than two years prior to the filing of the patent. *See Barbed–Wire Patent*, 143 U.S. at 286–87, 12 S.Ct. 443. That the witnesses themselves were not interested did not immunize their testimony from the corroboration requirement. *See Barbed–Wire*, 143 U.S. at 284, 12 S.Ct. 443 ("[w]itnesses whose memories are prodded by the eagerness of interested parties to elicit testimony favorable to themselves are not usually to be depended upon for accurate information."). It is not surprising that the cases have held that testimony concerning a witness's own anticipatory activities must be corroborated. A witness who testifies to antedating the invention of the patent-in-suit can be expected to derive a sense of professional or personnel accomplishment in being the first in the field, and in this sense is not uninterested in the outcome of the litigation, even if that witness is not claiming entitlement to a patent. Of course, the need for corroboration takes on special force when an otherwise uninterested witness shows some reason to be biased in favor of the interested party.

* * *

In the final analysis, the Supreme Court has defined the necessity of corroboration not with reference to the level of interest of the testifying witness, but rather because of doubt that testimonial evidence alone in the special context of proving patent invalidity can meet the clear and convincing evidentiary standard to invalidate a patent. *Thomson* is not to the contrary. The *Thomson* court did opine on the necessity of corroboration, stating that "corroboration is required only when the testifying inventor is asserting a claim of derivation or priority of his or her invention and is a named party, an employee of or assignor to a named party, or otherwise is in a position where he or she stands to directly and substantially gain by his or her invention being found to have priority over the patent claims at issue." *Thomson*, 166 F.3d at 1176. However, *Thomson* did not involve uncorroborated testimony of a single witness. Indeed, the district court in that case "noted that the evidence supporting the anticipation finding came from one or more sources: the live testimony of two people who had worked on [the project that was alleged to anticipate]; an expert's report and portions of his deposition testimony . . .; the expert's exhibits; and certain . . . documents that the expert had reviewed." *See id.* at 1174. Therefore, the facts of *Thomson* did not present the question of the necessity of corroboration vel non, but rather the sufficiency of the corroborating evidence, a distinct inquiry involving an assessment of the totality of the circumstances, including consideration of "the interest of the corroborating witness in the subject matter of the suit." *See Woodland Trust*, 148 F.3d at 1371. Cases like *Thomson* and *Woodland Trust* correctly recognized that the level of interest of the testifying witness is an important consideration when such testimony is offered to corroborate another witness's testimony. Those cases, however, do not stand for the proposition that only an interested witness's testimony requires corroboration. In any event, corroboration is required of any witness whose testimony alone is asserted to invalidate a patent, regardless of his or her level of interest.

Finnigan Corp. v. International Trade Comm'n, 180 F.3d 1354, 1366–69 (Fed.Cir. 1999). How does this law impact litigation strategy? Pre-litigation investigation strategy? What witnesses should litigators interview?

8.   USING FOREIGN PRIORITY FOR PRIOR ART PURPOSES UNDER §§ 102(e) AND (g)

Remember that we studied in Chapter 3 the ways in which a patent applicant can have her patent application treated as though it were filed on an earlier filing date. She accomplishes this by using the priority provisions of § 119 and § 120, both of which require that the original application to which she claims priority provide sufficient § 112, ¶ 1, disclosure of the claims now in issue.

The two cases that follow, *Hilmer I* and *Hilmer II*, explore a similar set of priority claims, but in these cases the person making the argument is someone who wants to challenge patent claims, not defend them. The challenger in these cases is using the patent in issue as a prior art document to attack a different patent and wants to have the patent in issue be treated as available as prior art on some date earlier than the date on which the patent is published. As seen in the cases that follow, these efforts failed, and so patents are only available as prior art on the dates expressly provided under the prior art provisions of § 102(e). Put differently, these cases reject arguments that § 119 impacts the date on which one patent is available as prior art to attack another patent. More specifically, *Hilmer I* rejects an argument about a connection between § 119 and § 102(e). *Hilmer II* rejects a similar argument about a connection between § 119 and § 102(g).

In re Hilmer (Hilmer I)

359 F.2d 859 (CCPA 1966).

■ Before WORLEY, CHIEF JUDGE, and RICH, MARTIN, SMITH and ALMOND, JUDGES.

■ RICH, JUDGE.

The sole issue is whether a majority of the Patent Office Board of Appeals erred in overturning a consistent administrative practice and interpretation of the law of nearly forty years standing by giving a United States patent effect as prior art as of a foreign filing date to which the *patentee* of the reference was entitled under 35 U.S.C. § 119.

Because it held that a U.S. patent, cited as a prior art reference under 35 U.S.C. § 102(e) and § 103, is effective as of its foreign "convention" filing date, relying on 35 U.S.C. § 119, the board affirmed the rejection of claims 10, 16, and 17 of application serial No. 750,887, filed July 25, 1958, for certain sulfonyl ureas.

This opinion develops the issue, considers the precedents, and explains why, on the basis of legislative history, we hold that section 119 does not modify the express provision of section 102(e) that a reference patent is effective as of the date the application for it was "filed in the United States."

The two "references" relied on are: Habicht 2,962,530 Nov. 29, 1960 (filed in the United States January 23, 1958, found to be entitled to priority as of the date of filing in Switzerland on January 24, 1957) and Wagner et al. 2,975,212 March 14, 1961 (filed in the United States May 1, 1957).

The rejection here is the aftermath of an interference (No. 90,218) between appellants and Habicht, a *priority* dispute in which Habicht was the winning party on a single count. He won because appellants conceded priority of the invention *of the count* to him. The earliest date asserted by appellants for their invention is their German filing date, July 31, 1957, which, we note, is a few months later than Habicht's priority date of January 24, 1957.

After termination of the interference and the return of this application to the examiner for further ex parte prosecution, the examiner rejected the appealed claims on Habicht, as a primary reference, in view of Wagner *et al.*, as a secondary reference, holding the claimed compounds to be "unpatentable over the primary reference in view of the secondary reference which renders them obvious to one of ordinary skill in the art."

Appellants appealed to the board contending, *inter alia*, that "The Habicht disclosure cannot be utilized as anticipatory art." They said, "The rejection has utilized ... the disclosure of the winning party as a basis for the rejection. The appellants insist that this is contrary to the patent statutes." Explaining this they said:

> ... the appellants' German application was filed subsequent to the Swiss filing date (of Habicht) *but prior to the U.S. filing date of the Habicht application.* The appellants now maintain that the Habicht disclosure *cannot* be utilized as anticipatory in view of 35 U.S.C. 119 which is entitled "Benefit of Earlier Filing Date in Foreign Countries: Right of Priority." This section defines the rights of foreign applicants and more specifically defines those rights with respect to dates to which they are entitled if this same privilege is awarded to citizens of the United States. There is no question (but) that Section 119 only deals with "right of priority." The section does not provide for the use of a U.S. patent as an anticipatory reference as of its foreign filing date....

* * *

The second restriction in the board's fourth statement of the issue is that "the reference patent is found to be entitled to the date of a prior foreign application under 35 USC 119...." To some degree this loads the question. There is in it an implicit assumption that if the patent is "entitled to the date of a prior foreign application," it is entitled to it, and that is that. But one must examine closely into what is meant by the word "entitled." In essence, that is the problem in this appeal and we wish to point to it at the outset to dispel any mistaken assumptions. A patent may be "entitled" to a foreign filing date for some purposes and not for others, just as a patent may be "used" in two ways. A patent owner uses his patent as a legal right to exclude others, granted to him under 35 U.S.C. § 154. Others, wholly unrelated to the patentee, use a patent, not as a legal right, but simply as evidence of prior invention or prior art, *i.e.*, as a "reference." This is not an exercise of the patent right. This is how the Patent Office is "using" the Habicht patent. These are totally different things, governed by different law, founded on different theories, and developed through different histories.

* * *

We can now summarize the issue and simultaneously state the board's decision. Continuing the above quotation, the board said:

> The Examiner insists, however, that the effective date of the Habicht patent is January 24, 1957, the date of an application filed in Switzerland which is claimed by Habicht under 35 USC 119. Appellants have not overcome this earlier date of Habicht. The issue is hence presented of whether the foreign priority date of a United States patent can be used as the effective filing date of the patent *when it is used as a reference.* (and this is the second statement of the issue by the board.) Our conclusion is that the priority date governs.

This is the decision alleged to be in error. We think it was error.

* * *

Turning from the general to the specific, we will now consider our specific reasons for construing the applicable statutes as they have for so long been construed, contrary to the recent innovation of the Patent Office.

OPINION

* * *

The board's construction is based on the idea that the language of the statute is plain, that it means what it says, and that what it says is that the application filed abroad is to have the same *effect* as though it were filed here—*for all purposes*. We can reverse the statement to say that the actual U.S. application is to have the same effect as though it were filed in the U.S. on the day when the foreign application was filed, the whole thing being a question of effective date. We take it either way because it makes no difference here.

Before getting into history, we note first that there is in the very words of the statute a refutation of this literalism. It says "shall have the same effect" and it then says "but" for several situations it shall not have the same effect, namely, it does not enjoy the foreign date with respect to any of the patent-defeating provisions based on publication or patenting any-where in the world or public use or being on sale in this country *more than one year before the date of actual filing in this country.*

As to the other statute involved, we point out that the words of section 102(e), which the board "simply" reads together with section 119, also seem plain. Perhaps they mean precisely what they say in specifying, as an express patent-defeating provision, an application by another describing the invention but only as of the date it is "filed *in the United States.*"

The great logical flaw we see in the board's reasoning is in its premise (or is it an *a priori* conclusion?) that "these two provisions must be read together." Doing so, it says 119 in effect destroys the plain meaning of 102(e) but the board will not indulge the reverse construction in which the plain words of 102(e) limit the apparent meaning of 119. We see no reason for reading these two provisions together and the board has stated none. We believe, with the dissenting board member, that 119 and 102(e) deal with unrelated concepts and further that the historical origins of the two sections show neither was intended to affect the other, wherefore they should not be read together in violation of the most basic rule of statutory construction, the "master rule," of carrying out the legislative intent. Additionally, we have a long and consistent administrative practice in applying an interpretation contrary to the new view of the board, con-firmed by legislation ratification in 1952. . . .

Section 119

* * *

This priority right was a protection to one who was trying to *obtain* patents in foreign countries, the protection being against patent-defeating provisions of national laws based on events intervening between the time of filing at home and filing abroad. . . .

* * *

We need not guess what Congress has since believed to be the meaning of the disputed words in section 119, for it has spoken clearly. World wars interfere with normal commerce in industrial property. The one-year period of priority being too short for people in "enemy" countries, we had after World War I a Nolan Act (41 Stat. 1313, Mar. 3, 1921) and after World War II a Boykin Act. Foreign countries had reciprocal acts. One purpose was to extend the period of priority. House Report No. 1498, January 28, 1946, by Mr. Boykin, accompanied H.R. 5223 which became Public Law 690 of the 79th Cong., 2d Sess., Aug. 8, 1946, 60 Stat. 940. Section 1 of the bill, the report says, was to extend "the so-called period of priority," which then existed under R.S. 4887. On p. 3 the report says:

> In this connection, it may be observed that the portion of the statute which provides that the filing of a foreign application—shall have the same force and effect as the same application would have if filed in this country on the date on which the application for patent for the same invention, discovery, or design was first filed in such foreign country—is intended to mean "shall have the same force and effect," etc., insofar as applicant's right to a patent is concerned. This statutory provision has no bearing upon the right of another party to a patent except in the case of an interference where the two parties are claiming the same patentable invention. U.S.Code Congressional Service 1946, p. 1493.

We emphasize none of those words because we wish to emphasize them all. We cannot readily imagine a clearer, more definitive statement as to the legislature's own view of the words "same effect," which now appear in section 119. This statement flatly contradicts the board's views. The board does not mention it.

* * *

For the foregoing reasons, we are clearly of the opinion that section 119 is not to be read as anything more than it was originally intended to be by its drafters, the Commission appointed under the 1898 Act of Congress, namely, a revision of our statutes to provide for a right of priority in conformity with the International Convention, for the benefit of United States citizens, by creating the necessary reciprocity with foreign members of the then Paris Union.

* * *

Section 102(e)

We have quoted this section above and pointed out that it is a patent-defeating section, by contrast with section 119 which gives affirmative "priority" rights *to applicants* notwithstanding it is drafted in terms of "An application." The priority right is to save the applicant (or his application if one prefers to say it that way) *from patent-defeating provisions* such as 102(e); and of course it has the same effect in guarding the validity of the patent when issued.

Section 102(e), on the other hand, is one of the provisions which defeats applicants and invalidates patents and is closely related in fact and in history to the requirement of section 102(a) which prohibits a patent if

> (a) the invention was known or used by others in this country, or patented or described in a printed publication in this or a foreign country, *before* the *invention* thereof by the applicant for patent, . . .

*   *   *

We will not undertake to trace the ancestry of 102(e) back of its immediate parentage but clearly it had ancestors or it would never have come to the Supreme Court. We will regard its actual birth as the case of *Alexander Milburn Co. v. Davis–Bournonville Co.*, 270 U.S. 390, 46 S.Ct. 324, 70 L.Ed. 651 (March 8, 1926), which we shall call *Milburn*. It is often called the *Davis–Bournonville* case. It was an infringement suit on a patent to Whitford and the defense, under R.S. 4920, was that he was not the first inventor. . . .

We need not go into the reasoning of the *Milburn* case, which has its weaknesses, because all that matters is the rule of law it established: That a complete description of an invention in a U.S. patent application, filed before the date of invention of another, if it matures into a patent, may be used to show that that other was not the first inventor. This was a patent-defeating, judge-made rule and now is section 102(e). The rule has been expanded somewhat subsequent to 1926 so that the reference patent may be used as of its U.S. filing date as a general prior art reference. . . .

What has always been pointed out in attacks on the *Milburn* rule, or in attempts to limit it, is that it uses, as prior knowledge, information which was secret at the time *as of which* it is used—the contents of U.S. patent applications which are preserved in secrecy, generally speaking, 35 U.S.C. 122. This is true, and we think there is some validity to the argument that that which is secret should be in a different category from knowledge which is public. Nevertheless we have the rule. However, we are not disposed to extend that rule, which applies to the date of filing applications *in the United States*, the actual filing date when the disclosure is on deposit in the U.S. Patent Office and on its way, in due course, to publication in an issued patent.

The board's new view, as expressed in this case . . . has the practical potential effect of pushing back the date of the unpublished, secret disclosures, which ultimately have effect as prior art references in the form of U.S. patents, by the full one-year priority period of section 119. We think the *Milburn* rule, as codified in section 102(e), goes far enough in that direction. We see no valid reason to go further, certainly no compelling reason.

*   *   *

Section 104

This brings us to another related section of the statute. We noted above that section 102(a) refers to knowledge of an invention *in this country* as a patent-defeating provision. This had been interpreted, long before the 1952 codification, to mean public knowledge....

* * *

The "elsewhere" is section 104 which has also superseded section 9 of the 1946 Boykin act, above discussed. Before quoting it, we will mention another patent-defeating provision, 102(g) which says a patent may not be obtained on an invention if "before the applicant's invention thereof the invention was made *in this country* by another who had not abandoned, suppressed, or concealed it." The first sentence of section 104 reads:

> § 104, Inventions made abroad.
>
> Inventions made abroad and in the courts, an applicant for a patent, or a patentee, may not establish a date of invention by reference to knowledge or use thereof, or other activity with respect thereto, in a foreign country, except as provided in section 119 of this title.

The second sentence is an exception not relevant here.

It seems clear to us that the prohibitions of 104, the limitations in sections 102(a) and 102(g) to "in this country," and the specifying in 102(e) of an application filed "in the United States" clearly demonstrates a policy in our patent statutes to the effect that knowledge and acts in a foreign country are not to defeat the rights of applicants for patents, except as applicants may become involved in *priority* disputes. We think it follows that section 119 must be interpreted as giving only a positive right or benefit to an applicant who has first filed abroad to *protect him* against possible intervening patent-defeating events in *obtaining* a patent. Heretofore it has always been so interpreted with the minor exceptions, of little value as precedents, hereinafter discussed. So construed, it has no effect on the effective date of a U.S. patent as a reference under section 102(e).

* * *

The simple observable fact, therefore, is that the effect of section 102(e) is to make a U.S. patent *available* as a reference, as of its U.S. filing date, and that thereafter the rejection of an application, or the holding of invalidity in the case of a patent, is *predicated on* some other section of the statute containing a patent-defeating provision to which the reference applies. Much confused thinking could be avoided by realizing that rejections are based on statutory provisions, not on references, and that the references merely supply the evidence of lack of novelty, obviousness, loss of right or whatever may be the ground of rejection of the board's decision.

Section 120

At oral argument the Patent Office Solicitor argued by "analogy" from 35 U.S.C. § 120 (a section which he said gives one U.S. application the benefit of an earlier U.S. application under specified circumstances *for all purposes*) that section 119 should similarly give to a patent, used as a reference under section 102(e), effect as of an earlier *foreign* filing date.

* * *

We find no substance in this argument because: (1) as above pointed out, our statute law makes a clear distinction between acts abroad and acts here except for patents and printed publications. Section 120, following policy in sections 102(a), (e) and (g) and 104, contains the limitation to applications "filed in the United States," excluding foreign applications from its scope. (2) Use of the same expression is mere happenstance and no reason to transfer the meaning and effect of section 120 as to U.S. filing dates to section 119 with respect to foreign filing dates. Section 120 was not drafted until 49 years after the predecessor of section 119 was in the statute.

* * *

The decision of the board is reversed and the case is remanded for further proceedings consistent herewith.

In re Hilmer (Hilmer II)

424 F.2d 1108 (CCPA 1970).

■ Before RICH, ACTING CHIEF JUDGE, ALMOND, BALDWIN, and LANE, JUDGES, and MATTHEWS, SENIOR JUDGE, United States District Court for the District of Columbia, sitting by designation.

■ RICH, ACTING CHIEF JUDGE.

This is a sequel to our opinion in *In re Hilmer*, 359 F.2d 859, 53 CCPA 1288, (1966) (herein *"Hilmer I"*), familiarity with which is assumed.

* * *

In *Hilmer I*, the question we decided was whether the Habicht patent was effective as a prior art reference under 35 U.S.C. § 102(e) as of the Swiss filing date. We held that it was not and that it was "prior art" under 102(e) only as of the U.S. filing date, which date Hilmer could overcome by being entitled to rely on the filing date of his German application to show his date of invention. This disposed of a rejection predicated on the disclosure of the Habicht patent, as a primary reference, coupled with a secondary prior art patent to Wagner *et al.*, No. 2,975,212, issued March 14, 1961, filed May 1, 1957 (herein "Wagner").

* * *

The board's conclusion was that the subject matter of claim 1, the compound claimed, is prior art against Hilmer. As to the basis on which it can be considered to be, or treated as, prior art, the board divided. Two members stated that the statutory basis is 35 U.S.C. § 102(g) combined with § 119 and read in the light of § 104. The third member declined to accept this, concurred only in the result, and said, "I see no reason to go beyond the concession of priority filed by Hilmer *et al*...." Since his view was not determinative of the appeal, we consider that what we have before us for review is only the correctness of the reasoning of the majority.

Note must be taken of the fact that the rejection here is under 103 for obviousness wherefore it is clear that the subject matter of the appealed claims is different from the subject matter of Habicht's claim 1, allegedly, however, only in an obvious way by reason of the further disclosures of Wagner. Were the appealed claims to the *same* subject matter, it seems clear that Hilmer, because he conceded *priority* to Habicht, would not be entitled to them and Hilmer appears to have admitted as much throughout this appeal. But, it is contended, the situation is different when the claims on appeal are to different subject matter. We confess to some difficulty in determining just what appellants' view is but it seems to come down to this:

> Appellants are entitled to the benefit of their German filing date and this antedates Habicht's U.S. filing date, which is the earliest date as of which Habicht's claim 1 invention can be "prior art." The words appellants use, referring to Habicht's U.S. filing date, are, "the only possible date that can be considered for anticipation purposes." Appellants appear to use the term "anticipation" in the broad sense to mean "prior."

We turn now to the reasoning by which the board majority arrived at the conclusion that the compound of Habicht claim 1 is in the prior art— *i.e.*, ahead of Hilmer's German filing date—and usable with the Wagner patent to support a section 103 obviousness rejection. We note at the outset that the board majority in no way relied on what occurred in the interference, on the concession of priority, or on any estoppel growing out of the interference.

Before examining the board majority's statutory theory, we will recall the fact that in *Hilmer I* we dealt with another statutory theory that by combining § 102(e) and § 119 a U.S. patent had an effective date as a prior art reference for all it discloses as of its foreign convention filing date. We reversed that holding and remanded. We now are presented with another theory that by combining § 102(g) with § 119 at least the claimed subject matter of a U.S. patent is prior art as of the convention filing date. The crux of the matter lies in § 102(g), which we must have before us.

* * *

The board majority's rationalization begins thus:

> Section 102(g) of the statute refers to the prior invention of another as a basis for refusing a patent. Inasmuch as the subject matter of the claim of the Habicht patent is patented to another, it must be recognized as an invention of another, and being the invention of another, some date of invention must be ascribed to it. When nothing else is available, the date of filing the application [in the United States] is by law taken as the date of invention since the invention obviously must have been made on or before the day the application for a patent for it was filed.

But this much, assuming its correctness, would not sustain the rejection because appellants are entitled to a date of invention which is earlier than the day the Habicht application was filed in the United States, the date obviously referred to in the above quotation. To sustain the rejection it was necessary for the board to accord an earlier date to Habicht's invention, the only such date available being the date Habicht filed his application in *Switzerland*. This, however, is not in compliance with the provision of 102(g) that the invention be "made" (or at the very least *be*) "in this country." The board majority attempted to vault this hurdle as follows:

> While Section 102(g) refers to the prior invention as made "in this country", this limitation is removed as to application filing date by Section 119 of the statute which provides that an application for a patent for an invention shall have the same effect as though filed in this country on the date a prior application was filed in a foreign country, under the conditions prescribed. That this is the effect of Section 119 is also evident from Section 104.... The Habicht invention is ... entitled to the filing date of the application in Switzerland as its date of invention in this country. Hence, we conclude on the basis of Section 102(g) and Section 119 that the claimed subject matter of the Habicht patent is available for use against the present application (as patent-defeating prior art) as of the date of the application filed in Switzerland.

We disagree with this line of reasoning.

In *Hilmer I* we explained at length why we could not accept similar reasoning about § 119 which was there alleged to remove or qualify the limitation in § 102(e) to the date when an application was filed "in the United States." For the same reasons we hold, contrary to the *ipse dixit* of the board, that § 119 does not remove the limitation of § 102(g) found in the phrase "in this country."

We disagree with the board that such an effect "is also evident from Section 104." Section 104 merely states that, except as provided by § 119, an applicant or patentee may not establish a date of invention "by reference to knowledge or use thereof, or other activity" in a foreign country. Thus § 119 and § 104 relate, respectively, only to what an applicant or patentee may and may not do to protect himself against patent-defeating events occurring between his invention date and his U.S. filing date. Moreover, we discussed § 104 and § 102(a), (e), and (g) in *Hilmer I* and there showed that they indicate an intention on the part of Congress that knowledge and acts in a foreign country are not to defeat the rights of an applicant for a patent, except as the applicant may become involved in a priority dispute with another applicant entitled to § 119 benefits. The present appeal does not involve a priority dispute. We repeat what we said at the end of that discussion in *Hilmer I*:

> We think it follows that section 119 must be interpreted as giving only a positive right or benefit to an applicant who has first filed abroad to protect *him* against possible intervening patent-defeating events in obtaining a patent.

That Habicht, as an applicant, was entitled to the benefit of his Swiss filing date does not mean that his invention acquires that same date under § 102(g) as patent-defeating prior art, in direct contravention of the "in this country" limitation of the section.

* * *

As we understand the meaning of the term "priority," it refers either (a) to the issue which exists in the interference proceedings, namely, which of two or more rival inventors *attempting to patent* the *same* invention shall be deemed prior or first in law and *entitled to the patent* or (b) preservation of an effective filing date during a period such as the "convention" year as against acts which would otherwise bar the grant of a patent, for the protection *of an applicant* against loss of right *to a patent*. Nothing we have seen tends to indicate that this matter of "priority" has ever been intended to modify the long-standing provisions of our statutes as to what shall be deemed "prior art" under § 103.

* * *

Reversed.

NOTES

1. *Obtaining v. Defeating.* Despite the "same effect" language of Section 119, the *Hilmer I* decision makes clear that a foreign filing date (unlike a domestic filing date) does not make the foreign application prior art in determining the patentability of later inventions by others. Do you agree with the court's conclusion that foreign priority dates can be used to obtain patent rights, but not to defeat patent rights? What is the rationale for this distinction? Recall Justice Holmes' statement in *Milburn* that delays in the patent office "ought not to effect what has been done." Holmes' statement and § 102(e) pertain to ministerial delay in the PTO. Shouldn't the same concerns apply to foreign patent offices? Certainly, if the foreign patent had issued the same day it was filed no one would argue that it isn't prior art.

Importantly, the American Inventors Protection Act of 1999 (AIPA) did not alter in any way the *Hilmer* decisions. The *priority* date of a U.S. patent cannot serve as the effective prior art date. But a PCT application published in English can serve as prior art as of its *international* filing date, which is no more than 12 months from the priority date. See note 1 in Section B–5, supra. Lastly, foreign-inventive activity cannot be used for patent-defeating purposes; rather, such activity is limited to obtaining patent rights in the context of an interference. *See* §§ 102(g) and 104.

2. *Hilmer, TRIPS, and the Paris Convention.* The United States is a signatory to both the Paris Convention and the Trade Related Aspects of Intellectual Property Rights (TRIPS). Article 27(1) of TRIPS states that "patents shall be available and patent rights enjoyable without discrimination as to the place of invention." And Article 4 states that "With regard to the protection of intellectual property, any advantage, favour, privilege or immunity granted by a Member to the nationals of any other country shall be accorded immediately and unconditionally to the nationals of all other Members." Article 4 of the Paris Convention sets forth the priority provision that entitles a U.S. patent applicant to a filing date of up to 12 months earlier than its U.S. filing date. Do the *Hilmer* decisions violate these articles? Some commentators think so. *See* Toshiko Takenaka, *Rethinking the United States First-to-Invent Principle from a Comparative Law Perspective: A Proposal to Restructure § 102 Novelty and Priority Provisions*, 39 HOUS. L. REV. 621, 659 (2002) ("The *Hilmer* doctrine also has been extensively criticized by foreign legal commentators for violating the priority right provision under the Paris Convention, as well as the non-discrimination policy provision regarding the place of invention under the TRIPS Agreement"); Heinz Bardehle, A New Approach to Worldwide Harmonization to Patent Law, 81 J. PAT. & TRADEMARK OFF. SOC'Y 303, 309 (1999) ("A particularity in a continuing program of patent harmonization, of course, would be the Hilmer Doctrine applied in the USA, which—as is also not denied there—represents a discrimination against foreigners that, however, despite contradicting the spirit of the Paris Convention, does not violate the fundamental right of national treatment").

3. *Hilmer, Interferences, and the Notions of Estoppel.* The right to a patent in the United States is based on a first to invent system. Thus, a party who is second to file a patent application may nevertheless be awarded the patent if he can prove that he was the first to invent. (*See* Section B–10, *infra*). The procedure by which priority is determined is called an *interference*. A "count" is the procedural vehicle used in an interference proceeding for defining the invention common to the parties. If priority is awarded against an applicant as to a certain count, the "doctrine of lost counts" would allow use of that count as prior art against that applicant's claims to related subject matter. What if the winning party bases its priority claim on a foreign filing date (*i.e.*, the invention defined in the count is based on foreign activity)? Can the PTO use such a count as prior art? The CCPA in *In re McKellin* answered in the negative. *See In re McKellin*, 529 F.2d 1324 (CCPA 1976) (relying in part on *In re Hilmer*).

But see *In re Deckler*, 977 F.2d 1449 (Fed.Cir.1992), wherein, in facts similar to *McKellin*, the applicant Deckler sought a patent for an improved seed planter. In an interference proceeding, the PTO awarded priority to the opposing party Grataloup. Deckler was the first to reduce his invention to practice, but he suppressed his invention (*see* Section B–10, *infra*) until after Grataloup's priority date established by a *foreign* patent application filing. Grataloup obtained a patent with claim 11 corresponding to the lost interference count. Thereafter, Deckler returned to *ex parte* prosecution and the PTO rejected his application based on the subject matter disclosed in Grataloup's patent. On appeal, Deckler conceded that the claims were not patentably distinct. The Federal Circuit affirmed the rejection:

> Under [res judicata and collateral estoppel] principles, a judgment in an action precludes relitigation of claims or issues that were or could have been raised in that proceeding.... Similarly, this court has applied interference estoppel to bar the assertion of claims for inventions that are patentably indistinct from those in an interference that the applicant lost.

> The interference judgment conclusively determined that, as between Deckler and Grataloup, Grataloup was entitled to claim the patentable subject matter defined in the interference count. It is therefore proper, and consistent with the policies of finality and repose embodied in the doctrines of res judicata and collateral estoppel, to use that judgment as a basis for rejection of claims to the same patentable invention.

Does *Deckler* conflict with the *Hilmer* cases concerning the relationship of foreign filing dates and patent rights? The *Deckler* court distinguished the *Hilmer* cases and *McKellin*:

> The issue is each of those cases was the validity of an obviousness rejection based upon the Board's holdings, on various grounds in the different cases, that under the governing statute the foreign filing date could not be used to make patent prior art for obviousness purposes.

> In the present case, in contrast, there was no obviousness rejection. The Board's sole ground of rejection was that under principles of res judicata and collateral estoppel, Deckler was not entitled to claims that were patentably indistinguishable from the claim on which he lost the interference....

> Unlike the situation in those three cases, here the Board did not use the interference count as prior art in making an obviousness determination, but based its decision on a wholly different theory.

Deckler, 977 F.2d at 1453. What is the court's distinction between *Deckler* and *Hilmer*? Is there a difference between priority claims in the interference context and, for example, antedating a reference?

9.   DERIVATION—§ 102(f)

Patent law requires that a patent application be filed in the name of the "true" inventor. In other words, the named inventor must not have derived the claimed invention from another source. The *Gambrio Lundia* case discusses what is referred to as "derivation."

Gambro Lundia AB v. Baxter Healthcare Corp.

110 F.3d 1573 (Fed.Cir.1997).

■ Before ARCHER, CHIEF JUDGE, LOURIE, and RADER, CIRCUIT JUDGES.

■ RADER, CIRCUIT JUDGE.

In this patent infringement case, Gambro Lundia AB (Gambro) appeals and Baxter Healthcare Corporation (Baxter) cross-appeals a final judgment of the United States District Court for the District of Colorado. The patent at issue, U.S. Patent No. 4,585,552 ('552 patent), claims a "system for the measurement of the difference between two fluid flows in separate ducts." This invention recalibrates sensors during hemodialysis to accurately measure the impurities removed from a patient's blood. Due to error in the district court's analyses of invalidity, unenforceability, and infringement, this court reverses.

BACKGROUND

Hemodialysis, commonly called dialysis, removes contaminants and excess fluid from the patient's blood when the kidneys do not function properly. Hemodialysis works by passing a dialysate solution through a machine, called a dialyzer, which functions as an artificial kidney. In the dialyzer, the dialysate passes on one side of a porous diffusion membrane, while the patient's blood passes on the other side. Because of the pressure differential across the membrane, blood contaminants and excess fluid diffuse through the membrane from the patient's blood into the dialysate. These impurities diffused from the patient's blood are known as ultrafiltrate.

After hemodialysis, the volume of the dialysate is greater. The difference between the initial and end volumes of dialysate can be used to calculate the amount of the ultrafiltrate removed from a patient's blood. This calculation is critical to the success of hemodialysis. Removal of too much or too little ultrafiltrate may lead to severe medical problems or even death.

Repgreen Limited (Repgreen), a British bioengineering company, improved ultrafiltrate calculation. Keith Wittingham, Repgreen's chief designer, introduced the Repgreen monitoring system, the UFM 1000, in late 1977. Wittingham's development relied on the research of Professor Michael Sanderson.

The UFM 1000 used two electromagnetic flow sensors to measure the difference between the rate of dialysate flow into and out of the dialyzer. The difference in flow rates indicated the quantity of ultrafiltrate leaving the system. To calibrate the system for an accurate measurement of dialysate flow rates, the operator would direct clean dialysate through both sensors before dialysis. This calibration method, however, could not account for clogging in the outflow sensor during dialysis. Over time, the ultrafiltrate would build up behind the outflow sensor and disrupt the accuracy of the measurements. Experts refer to this increasing inaccuracy as "drift."

In the late 1970s, Gambro sought to improve ultrafiltrate monitoring. During 1979, Wittingham met with Gambro engineers on two occasions to discuss Repgreen's development of an ultrafiltrate monitor for Gambro. In July 1979, after Repgreen went bankrupt, Gambro purchased Repgreen's hemodialysis technology, including the rights to the UFM 1000 monitor. After acquiring Repgreen's technology, Gambro's research team worked for three years on improving ultrafiltration monitors. In June 1982, four Gambro engineers, including Bengt–Ake Gummesson, refined the monitoring system. Their invention ultimately issued as the '552 patent.

Gambro filed its initial patent application in Sweden on September 28, 1982. Gambro followed up with a U.S. application in September 1983. Gunnar Boberg, Repgreen's in-house patent counsel, and Arnold Krumholz, Repgreen's U.S. patent counsel, prosecuted the U.S. application. The examiner rejected claim 1 as anticipated by a German patent application (German '756). In response, Gambro provided the examiner with a German-language copy of German '756, along with arguments prepared by Boberg (who is fluent in German). Based on this submission, the examiner withdrew the rejection. The '552 patent issued on April 29, 1986.

The Gambro invention uses valves to direct clean dialysate around the dialyzer to recalibrate the sensors during dialysis. The invention's valve system can direct clean dialysate through the first flow sensor, around the dialyzer, and through the second flow sensor. To recalibrate, the invention momentarily blocks passage of contaminated dialysate through the outflow sensor. Instead, clean dialysate flows through the outflow sensor and recalibrates the detectors with the same clean dialysate flowing through both intake and outflow sensors. After the brief recalibration, the hemodialysis continues with contaminated dialysate flowing through the second sensor.

In 1984, Baxter acquired the dialysis equipment division of Extracorporeal, Inc. Dissatisfied with the accuracy of the Extracorporeal technology, Baxter developed the Baxter SPS 550 and began marketing the device in December 1987. Gambro filed suit against Baxter in the District Court for the District of Colorado in March 1992 claiming the Baxter SPS 550 infringed the '552 patent. In defense, Baxter asserted the invalidity and unenforceability of the '552 patent.

After a ten-day bench trial on the issues of infringement, validity, and unenforceability, the district court held claim 1 of the Gambro '552 patent invalid for obviousness and derivation, and unenforceable for inequitable conduct.

DISCUSSION

I. *Derivation*

The trial judge found that Gambro had derived the '552 invention from a Wittingham proposal left in the files when Gambro acquired Repgreen's dialysis technology. This court reviews a finding of derivation as a question of fact. *Price v. Symsek*, 988 F.2d 1187, 1190, 26 U.S.P.Q.2D 1031, 1033 (Fed.Cir.1993). This requires acceptance of the district court's findings unless clearly erroneous or predicated on an improper legal foundation. *Raytheon Co. v. Roper Corp.*, 724 F.2d 951, 956, 220 USPQ 592, 596 (Fed.Cir.1983). To show derivation, the party asserting invalidity must prove both prior conception of the invention by another and communication of that conception to the patentee. *Price*, 988 F.2d at 1190. This court reviews a determination of prior conception, which must be proven by facts supported by clear and convincing evidence, as a question of law based on underlying factual findings. *Id.* at 1190–92.

Turning first to conception, the district court found that Wittingham had conceived the invention no later than July 1979. The court based this finding on Wittingham's testimony and the Wittingham proposal left in the Repgreen file. Although the district court found Wittingham highly credible, an inventor's testimony, standing alone, is insufficient to prove conception. *See Price*, 988 F.2d at 1194. Conception requires corroboration of the inventor's testimony. *Id.*

Thus, this court must weigh whether the Wittingham proposal, prepared in 1979, corroborates Wittingham's testimony of conception. The proposal is a four-page document alluding to an ultrafiltration monitor with valves that automatically zero the sensors upon start-up. The proposal briefly discusses the Auto Zero/Start feature: "To ensure ease of operation the process of shunting the kidney in order to zero monitor will be done automatically on pressing of the start button. This will also initiate the automatic zeroing of unit."

Baxter contends that this document also discloses the concept of recalibration (or zeroing) during dialysis. In support of this contention, Baxter identifies the following passage from the proposal: "A zero button may also be necessary in order to zero Ultrafiltration Monitor but not start the automatic control (start signal cannot be allowed till 20 minutes after switch on?)."

Baxter argues that the only reason to zero the monitor without starting the automatic control is to zero the monitor when it is already started—in other words, during dialysis.

Baxter's novel interpretation of this single ambiguous passage in the Wittingham proposal, however, lacks sufficient support to corroborate Wittingham's conception testimony. First, the reference is so unclear that even Wittingham conceded that this single sentence does not state expressly the concept of recalibration during dialysis. In fact, the parenthetical within the sentence suggests that the device should not be in use "till 20 minutes after switch on." For this reason, among others, Professor Sanderson, an expert in dialysis whose early research formed the basis of Wittingham's work, testified that one of ordinary skill in dialysis in 1982 would not have understood this obscure passage to disclose recalibration during dialysis. Professor Sanderson noted that the Repgreen monitor needed twenty minutes to stabilize before use. Therefore, this obscure sentence more reasonably suggests the use of the zero button during the pre-dialysis warm-up period.

In addition, the obscure sentence states that depressing the button calibrates the monitor, but does "not start the automatic control." In its ordinary start-up operation, the Repgreen monitor would calibrate the monitor, start the automatic control, and finally automatically begin the dialysis. The reference to "zeroing" before the automatic control phase thus suggests calibration before dialysis, not during dialysis. Further, if Wittingham had conceived of recalibration during dialysis—an important advance in the dialysis art—the four-page Wittingham proposal would surely contain more than a single cryptic sentence memorializing the advance. Accordingly, this court determines that the Wittingham proposal does not corroborate conception. The only other evidence offered by Baxter to corroborate conception is the testimony of Mr. Smith, Wittingham's supervisor at Repgreen. Referring to the ambiguous sentence, Smith testified that the Wittingham proposal included the idea of calibration during dialysis. The trial judge, however, did not rely on this self-serving testimony in finding prior conception. Moreover, as noted above, the language of the Wittingham proposal itself belies Smith's testimony about calibration during dialysis. In sum, this court concludes that Baxter failed to meet its burden of proving by facts supported by clear and convincing evidence that Wittingham conceived the invention of the '552 patent.

The second prong of the derivation test—communication of the prior conception to the named inventor—poses similar difficulties for Baxter. As an initial matter, the district court applied the wrong legal standard. Citing *New England Braiding Co. v. A.W. Chesterton Co.*, 970 F.2d 878, 23 U.S.P.Q.2D 1622 (Fed.Cir.1992), the district court concluded that Baxter did not need to prove communication of the entire conception, but rather only so much of the invention "as would have made it obvious to one of ordinary skill in the art." *Gambro Lundia AB v. Baxter Healthcare Corp.*, 896 F.Supp. 1522, 1540 (D.Colo.1995) (*citing New England Braiding*, 970 F.2d at 883). Based on this reasoning, the district court applied the obviousness standard in 35 U.S.C. § 103 (1994) to determine that the named inventors received enough information to make the invention obvious to one skilled in the dialysis art. This reasoning, however, misconstrues the dictum in *New England Braiding* and introduces incorrectly an obviousness analysis into the test for derivation.

The Supreme Court announced the standard for finding communication of a prior conception over 125 years ago in *Agawam Woolen v. Jordan*, 74 U.S. (7 Wall.) 583, 19 L.Ed. 177 (1868). The Court required a showing that the communication "enabled an ordinary mechanic, without the exercise of any ingenuity and special skill on his part, to construct and put the improvement in successful operation." *Id.* 74 U.S at 602–03 (emphasis added). This court's predecessor consistently applied this Supreme Court standard. *See, e.g., Hedgewick v. Akers*, 497 F.2d 905, 908, 182 USPQ 167, 169 (CCPA 1974) ("Communication of a complete conception must be sufficient to enable one of ordinary skill in the art to construct and successfully operate the invention."); *DeGroff v. Roth*, 56 C.C.P.A. 1331, 412 F.2d 1401, 1405, 162 USPQ 361, 365 (CCPA 1969).

This court recognizes that the district court's incorrect derivation standard springs from dictum in this court's *New England Braiding* decision. In that case, this court noted: "To invalidate a patent for derivation of invention, a party must demonstrate that the named inventor in the patent acquired knowledge of the claimed invention from another, or at least so much of the claimed invention as would have made it obvious to one of ordinary skill in the art." *New England Braiding*, 970 F.2d at 883. This dictum did not in fact incorporate a determination of obviousness into a Section 102(f) analysis.

Indeed, this court in *New England Braiding* did not apply such a test. The *New England Braiding* court upheld the denial of a preliminary injunction because the record showed a likelihood that New England Braiding's patent was invalid under 35 U.S.C. § 102(f). The record showed that George Champlin, the named inventor, worked for the A.W. Chesterton Co. (Chesterton) and participated in experiments that developed the invention. One Chesterton employee testified that Champlin had said, when he left to start his own company, that he wanted to patent the experimental braiding if Chesterton decided not to do so. Champlin denied these allegations. *Id.* at 883–84. The key issue was a credibility determination between the witnesses for the two parties. The sufficiency of the communication, particularly whether the invention was obvious in light of such disclosure, was not at issue. Thus, *New England Braiding* did not incorporate an obviousness test into the § 102(f) analysis.

Applying the correct standard—whether the communication enabled one of ordinary skill in the art to make the patented invention—this court discerns insufficient evidence of communication. Wittingham testified that he was not sure that he had discussed calibration during dialysis with anyone at Gambro, and he did not discuss the sensor contamination problem. The trial judge based his finding of communication solely on Wittingham's written proposal. Gambro acquired this document when it acquired Repgreen's technology. During discovery, the proposal appeared in the files of one of the named inventors. However, as discussed above, the proposal does not disclose recalibration during dialysis to one skilled in the art at the relevant time. If the proposal does not disclose recalibration during dialysis, it cannot serve as the basis for a communication of that idea. Thus, under the correct legal standard, the record evidence is insufficient to support a finding of communication. The district court erred in finding communication and conception, and, hence, the finding of derivation is also clearly erroneous.

Because this court reverses the district court's ruling of invalidity based on derivation, it need not reach the issue of correction of inventorship under 35 U.S.C. § 256 (1994).

REVERSED.

NOTES

1. *§ 102(f) and Derivation*. Section 102(f) is known as the "derivation" provision. It provides that a person is entitled to a patent unless "he did not himself invent the subject matter sought to be patented." In other words, the named inventor *derived* the claimed subject matter from a third party. Consider the following scenario: You are sitting next to a stranger on a bus somewhere between Pittsburgh and Philadelphia. Out of the blue, he begins to convey to you a "wonderful invention" that he has been developing over the past few months. The information that he gives you is enough so as to enable you to make the invention. Should you be able to receive a patent on this invention?

It is clearly improper to issue a patent to one who has taken the invention of another. The Federal Circuit in *Gambro* held that the party asserting invalidity under § 102(f) must prove both prior conception of the invention by another and communication of that conception to the patentee. The *Gambro* court also stated that the communication must be such that it *enables* one of ordinary skill in the art to construct and operate the invention. Even if the prior art reference does not enable, and therefore, does not anticipate under section 102, the reference may still be used for an obviousness analysis under section 103. *See OddzOn Products, Inc. v. Just Toys, Inc.*, 122 F.3d 1396 (Fed.Cir.1997) (discussing §§ 102(f)/103 prior art). For more on obviousness generally, *see infra*, Chapter Five.

2. *A Bus Ride Abroad.* Let's return to the bus ride scenario; but instead of being between Pittsburgh and Philadelphia, you are now touring Burgundy, France. Should this change in geography make a difference under § 102(f)? The answer is no. Section 102(f) denies a patent to one who derived the invention from another in the U.S. or in a foreign country. *See* P.J. Federico, *Commentary on the New Patent Act*, 35 U.S.C.A. (1952), at 24.

10. PRIORITY—§ 102(g)

Priority of invention in the United States is based on a *first to invent* system. The United States is unique in this regard among industrialized nations in that other countries have adopted a *first to file* system of priority.[9] Thus, a party who is second to file may nevertheless be awarded the patent if he can prove that he was the first to invent. The procedure by which priority is determined is called an *interference*.

Priority is given to the first to reduce the invention to practice, except: (1) an inventor who was second to reduce to practice but first to conceive can still get priority if he or she exercised *reasonable diligence* in reducing to practice from a time just prior to conception by the person who first reduced to practice; and (2) a second inventor will be awarded priority where the first inventor *abandoned, suppressed, or concealed* the invention after reducing it to practice.

a. CONCEPTION

The following two cases, *Fiers* and *Burroughs Wellcome*, explore what is required to prove conception. Patent law requires more proof than simply, "I had the idea first."

---

9. There has been much discussion in recent years among commentators and members of the bar as to whether the United States should adopt a first-to-file system. *See, e.g.,* Mark A. Lemley and Colleen V. Chien, *Are the U.S. Patent Priority Rules Really Necessary?*, 54 HASTINGS L.J. 1299 (2003) (conducting extensive empirical study of priority disputes); Dana Rohrabacher & Paul Crilly, *The Case for a Strong Patent System*, 8 HARV. J.L. & TECH. 263 (1995) (advocating first-to-invent system); Toshiko Takenaka, *Rethinking the United States First-to-Invent Principle From a Comparative Law Perspective*, 39 HOUS. L. REV. 621 (2002) (advocating global patent systems should harmonized to include first-to-file system). *See also* Professor Marco Ricolfi's *SIDE BAR* at the end of this chapter for discussion of the first-to-file and first-to-invent systems.

Fiers v. Revel

984 F.2d 1164 (Fed.Cir.1993).

■ Before MICHEL, CIRCUIT JUDGE, COWEN, SENIOR CIRCUIT JUDGE, and LOURIE, CIRCUIT JUDGE.

■ LOURIE, CIRCUIT JUDGE.

Walter C. Fiers, Michel Revel, and Pierre Tiollais appeal from the June 5, 1991 decision of the Patent and Trademark Office Board of Patent Appeals and Interferences, awarding priority of invention in a three-way interference proceeding, No. 101,096, to Haruo Sugano, Masami Muramatsu, and Tadatsugu Taniguchi (Sugano). We affirm.

BACKGROUND

This interference among three foreign inventive entities relates to the DNA[1] which codes for human fibroblast beta-interferon (B–IF), a protein that promotes viral resistance in human tissue. It involves a single count which reads:

> A DNA which consists essentially of a DNA which codes for a human fibroblast interferon-beta polypeptide.

The parties filed U.S. patent applications as follows: Sugano on October 27, 1980, Fiers on April 3, 1981, and Revel and Tiollais (Revel) on September 28, 1982. Sugano claimed the benefit of his March 19, 1980 Japanese filing date, Revel claimed the benefit of his November 21, 1979 Israeli filing date, and Fiers sought to establish priority under 35 U.S.C. § 102(g) based on prior conception coupled with diligence up to his British filing date on April 3, 1980.

Sugano's Japanese application disclosed the complete nucleotide sequence of a DNA coding for B–IF and a method for isolating that DNA.[4] Revel's Israeli application disclosed a method for isolating a fragment of the DNA coding for B–IF as well as a method for isolating messenger RNA (mRNA) coding for B–IF, but did not disclose a complete DNA sequence coding for B–IF.[5] Fiers, who was working abroad, based his case for priority on an alleged conception either in September 1979 or in January 1980, when his ideas were brought into the United States, coupled with diligence toward a constructive reduction to practice on April 3, 1980, when he filed a British application disclosing the complete nucleotide sequence of a DNA coding for B–IF. According to Fiers, his conception of the DNA of the count

---

1. DNA is deoxyribonucleic acid, a generic term encompassing the many chemical materials that genetically control the structure and metabolism of living things.

4. Sugano's method involved the preparation of two populations of radioactivity-labelled cDNA probes prepared from the mRNA of fibroblast cells. One population of probes was prepared from the mRNA of induced fibroblast cells and the other population from the mRNA of non-induced cells. These probes were then exposed to a cDNA library prepared from induced cells, and the clones that only hybridized with the first probe were selected. The selected clones were then used as probes to select the full-length DNA sequence encoding β–IF, which was then sequenced.

5. Revel's method involved preparing a cDNA library of clones from the mRNA of cells induced to produce B–IF, screening each clone for hybridization to mRNA from induced cells, eluting the hybridized mRNA, and assaying the eluted mRNAs for B–IF activity.

occurred when two American scientists, Walter Gilbert and Phillip Sharp, to whom he revealed outside of the United States a proposed method for isolating DNA coding for β–IF brought the protocol back to the United States.[6] Fiers submitted affidavits from Gilbert and Sharp averring that, based on Fiers' proposed protocol, one of ordinary skill in the art would have been able to isolate B–IF DNA without undue experimentation.[7] On February 26, 1980, Fiers' patent attorney brought into the United States a draft patent application disclosing Fiers' method, but not the nucleotide sequence for the DNA.

The Board awarded priority of invention to Sugano, concluding that (1) Sugano was entitled to the benefit of his March 19, 1980 Japanese filing date, (2) Fiers was entitled to the benefit of his April 3, 1980 British filing date, but did not prove conception of the DNA of the count prior to that date, and (3) Revel was not entitled to the benefit of his November 21, 1979 Israeli filing date. The Board based its conclusions on the disclosure or failure to disclose the complete nucleotide sequence of a DNA coding for B–IF.

DISCUSSION

Fiers' Case for Priority

The Board held that Fiers failed to establish conception in the United States prior to his April 3, 1980 British filing date. Specifically, the Board determined that Fiers' disclosure of a method for isolating the DNA of the count, along with expert testimony that his method would have enabled one of ordinary skill in the art to produce that DNA, did not establish conception, since "success was not assured or certain until the [B–IF] gene was in fact isolated and its sequence known." The Board relied on our opinion in *Amgen Inc. v. Chugai Pharmaceutical Co.*, 927 F.2d 1200, 18 U.S.P.Q.2D 1016 (Fed.Cir.1991), in which we addressed the requirements necessary to establish conception of a purified DNA sequence coding for a specific protein. Accordingly, the Board held that Fiers was entitled only to the benefit of his April 3, 1980 British application date because only that application disclosed the complete nucleotide sequence of the DNA coding for β–IF. That date was subsequent to Sugano's March 1980 Japanese priority date.

Fiers argues that the Board erroneously determined that *Amgen* controls this case. According to Fiers, the Board incorrectly interpreted *Amgen*

---

6. Fiers presented his protocols and progress to date toward isolating DNA coding for B–IF at a September 21, 1979 meeting in Paris at which Sharp and Gilbert were present. Sharp and Gilbert returned to the United States on September 23 and 24, respectively. Fiers made a second presentation in Martinique on January 12, 1980. Gilbert and Sharp were both present and returned to the United States on January 15 and 17, respectively. On March 25, 1980, Fiers disclosed by telephone to his patent attorney that he had determined the entire nucleotide sequence of a DNA coding for B–IF. Fiers presented that nucleotide sequence along with a protocol for preparing the complete DNA in Switzerland on March 28, 1980. Fiers and his attorney worked from March 31 until April 2 in Ghent drafting the final portion and claims of the British application that Fiers filed on April 3, 1980.

7. Fiers' proposed protocol involved preparing a cDNA library from the mRNA of cells induced to produce B–IF mRNA, and screening the cDNA library for a cDNA that, when introduced into a cell, would cause it to display B–IF activity.

as establishing a rule that a DNA coding for a protein cannot be conceived until one knows the nucleotide sequence of that DNA. Fiers argues that this court decided *Amgen* on its particular facts and that this case is distinguishable. Fiers' position is that we intended to limit *Amgen* to cases in which isolation of a DNA was attended by serious difficulties such as those confronting the scientists searching for the DNA coding for erythropoietin (EPO), *e.g.*, screening a genomic DNA library with fully degenerate probes. According to Fiers, his method could have been easily carried out by one of ordinary skill in the art.[9] Fiers also argues that *Amgen* held that a conception of a DNA can occur if one defines it by its method of preparation. Fiers suggests that the standard for proving conception of a DNA by its method of preparation is essentially the same as that for proving that the method is enabling. Fiers thus urges us to conclude that since his method was enabling for the DNA of the count, he conceived it in the United States when Gilbert and Sharp entered the country with the knowledge of, and detailed notes concerning, Fiers' process for obtaining it.

Conception is a question of law that we review *de novo*. Although *Amgen* was the first case in which we discussed conception of a DNA sequence coding for a specific protein, we were not writing on a clean slate. We stated:

> Conception does not occur unless one has a mental picture of the structure of the chemical, or is able to define it by its method of preparation, its physical or chemical properties, or whatever characteristics sufficiently distinguish it. It is not sufficient to define it solely by its principal biological property, e.g., encoding human erythropoietin, because an alleged conception having no more specificity than that is simply a wish to know the identity of any material with that biological property. We hold that when an inventor is unable to envision the detailed chemical structure of the gene so as to distinguish it from other materials, as well as a method for obtaining it, conception has not been achieved until reduction to practice has occurred, i.e., until after the gene has been isolated.

927 F.2d at 1206, 18 U.S.P.Q.2D at 1021.

We thus determined that, irrespective of the complexity or simplicity of the method of isolation employed, conception of a DNA, like conception of any chemical substance, requires a definition of that substance other than by its functional utility.

Fiers' attempt to distinguish *Amgen* therefore is incorrect. We also reject Fiers' argument that the existence of a workable method for preparing a DNA establishes conception of that material. Our statement in *Amgen* that conception may occur, inter alia, when one is able to define a chemical by its method of preparation requires that the DNA be claimed by its method of preparation. We recognized that, in addition to being claimable by structure or physical properties, a chemical material can be claimed by means of a process. A product-by-process claim normally is an after-the-

---

9. Fiers' method involved screening a cDNA library which he maintains is smaller and less complex than a genomic DNA library. Fiers also contends that his screening techniques were routine to those skilled in the art, while those skilled in the art lacked experience screening with fully degenerate probes. Fiers also notes that, in contrast to the situation with EPO in which erroneous amino acid sequence information had been published, the first thirteen amino acids of B–IF were known to the art.

fact definition, used after one has obtained a material by a particular process. Before reduction to practice, conception only of a process for making a substance, without a conception of a structural or equivalent definition of that substance, can at most constitute a conception of the substance claimed as a process. Conception of a substance claimed per se without reference to a process requires conception of its structure, name, formula, or definitive chemical or physical properties.

The present count is to a product, a DNA which codes for B–IF; it is a claim to a product having a particular biological activity or function, and in *Amgen*, we held that such a product is not conceived until one can define it other than by its biological activity or function. The difficulty that would arise if we were to hold that a conception occurs when one has only the idea of a compound, defining it by its hoped-for function, is that would-be inventors would file patent applications before they had made their inventions and before they could describe them. That is not consistent with the statute or the policy behind the statute, which is to promote disclosure of inventions, not of research plans. While one does not need to have carried out one's invention before filing a patent application, one does need to be able to describe that invention with particularity.

Fiers has devoted a considerable portion of his briefs to arguing that his method was enabling. The issue here, however, is conception of the DNA of the count, not enablement. Enablement concerns teaching one of ordinary skill in the art how to practice the claimed invention. *See* 35 U.S.C. § 112 (1988); *Amgen*, 927 F.2d at 1212, 18 U.S.P.Q.2D at 1026. Since Fiers seeks to establish priority under section 102(g), the controlling issue here is whether he conceived a DNA coding for β–IF, not whether his method was enabling.

We conclude that the Board correctly decided that conception of the DNA of the count did not occur upon conception of a method for obtaining it. Fiers is entitled only to the benefit of his April 3, 1980 British filing date, since he did not conceive the DNA of the count under section 102(g) prior to that date.

Burroughs Wellcome Co. v. Barr Laboratories, Inc.

40 F.3d 1223 (Fed.Cir.1994).

■ Before MAYER, LOURIE, and SCHALL, CIRCUIT JUDGES.

■ MAYER, CIRCUIT JUDGE.

Barr Laboratories, Inc., Novopharm, Inc., and Novopharm, Ltd., appeal the order of the United States District Court for the Eastern District of North Carolina, *Burroughs Wellcome Co. v. Barr Lab., Inc.*, 828 F.Supp. 1208 (E.D.N.C.1993), granting the motion of Burroughs Wellcome Co. for judgment as a matter of law that six United States patents were not invalid and were infringed. We affirm in part, vacate in part, and remand.

Background

Burroughs Wellcome Co. is the owner of six United States patents that cover various preparations of 3'-azidothymidine (AZT) and methods for using that drug in the treatment of persons infected with the human immunodeficiency virus (HIV).[1] Each of these patents names the same five inventors—Janet Rideout, David Barry, Sandra Lehrman, Martha St. Clair, and Phillip Furman (Burroughs Wellcome inventors)—all of whom were employed by Burroughs Wellcome at the time the inventions were alleged to have been conceived. The defendants-appellants concede that all five are properly named as inventors on the patents.

Burroughs Wellcome's patents arise from the same parent application filed on September 17, 1985. Five of the patents relate to the use of AZT to treat patients infected with HIV or who have acquired immunodeficiency syndrome (AIDS).[3] The other patent, the '750 patent, covers a method of using AZT to increase the T-lymphocyte count of persons infected with HIV.[4]

In the early 1980s, scientists began to see patients with symptoms of an unknown disease of the immune system, now known as AIDS. The disease attacks and destroys certain white blood cells known as CD4 T-lymphocytes or T-cells, which form an important component of the body's immune system. The level of destruction eventually becomes so great that the immune system is no longer able to mount an effective response to infections that pose little threat to a healthy person.

In mid–1984, scientists discovered that AIDS was caused by a retrovirus, known as HTLV III or, more commonly today, HIV. After the identification of HIV, Burroughs Wellcome began to search for a cure, screening compounds for antiretroviral activity using two murine (or mouse) retroviruses, the Friend leukemia virus and the Harvey sarcoma virus.

At about this time, scientists at the National Institutes of Health (NIH), led by Samuel Broder, were looking for effective AIDS therapies as well. Unlike Burroughs Wellcome, Broder and his colleagues used live HIV, and were able to develop a test that could demonstrate a compound's effectiveness against HIV in humans using a unique line of T-cell clones (the ATH8 cell line). The NIH scientists began to seek compounds from private pharmaceutical companies for screening in their cell line. After Burroughs Wellcome contacted Broder in the fall of 1984, he agreed to accept compounds from Burroughs Wellcome under code for testing against live HIV.

---

1. Although two of the patents claim pharmaceutical compositions of AZT, not methods of treatment per se, the parties treat all of the patents as covering the particular use of AZT as a treatment for AIDS and its symptoms. The district court adopted this interpretation and applied the patents as though all claimed methods of treatment; no party argues for another interpretation, so we do the same.

3. Claim 1 of the '232 patent covers "[a] method of treating a human having acquired immunodeficiency syndrome comprising the oral administration of an effective acquired immunodeficiency syndrome treatment amount of–azido–3'–deoxythymidine to said human.".…

4. Claim 1 of the '750 patent covers "[a] method of increasing the number of T-lymphocytes in a human infected with the HTLV III virus comprising administering to said human an effective amount of–azido–3'–deoxythymidine or a pharmaceutically acceptable alkali metal, alkaline earth or ammonium salt thereof."

Burroughs Wellcome's Rideout selected AZT and a number of other compounds for testing in the murine screens on October 29, 1984. The tests, performed at Burroughs Wellcome facilities by St. Clair, showed that AZT had significant activity against both murine retroviruses at low concentrations. In light of these positive results, the Burroughs Wellcome inventors met on December 5, 1984, to discuss patenting the use of AZT in the treatment of AIDS. Burroughs Wellcome's patent committee thereafter recommended that the company prepare a patent application for future filing. By February 6, 1985, the company had prepared a draft application for filing in the United Kingdom. The draft disclosed using AZT to treat patients infected with HIV, and set out various pharmaceutical formulations of the compound in an effective dosage range to treat HIV infection.

Two days earlier, on February 4, 1985, Burroughs Wellcome had sent a sample of AZT, identified only as Compound S, to Broder at NIH. In an accompanying letter, Lehrman told Broder of the results of the murine retrovirus tests and asked that he screen the compound for activity against HIV in the ATH8 cell line. Another NIH scientist, Hiroaka Mitsuya, performed the test in mid-February 1985, and found that Compound S was active against HIV. Broder informed Lehrman of the results by telephone on February 20, 1985. Burroughs Wellcome filed its patent application in the United Kingdom on March 16, 1985.

After Burroughs Wellcome learned that AZT was active against HIV, it began the process of obtaining Food and Drug Administration (FDA) approval for AZT as an AIDS therapy. As a part of the clinical trials leading to FDA approval, Broder and another NIH scientist, Robert Yarchoan, conducted a Phase I human patient study which showed that treatment with AZT could result in an increase in the patient's T-cell count. Broder reported this result to Lehrman on July 23, 1985. In 1987, the FDA approved AZT for marketing by Burroughs Wellcome; Burroughs Wellcome markets the drug for treatment of HIV infection under the trademark Retrovir.

On March 19, 1991, Barr Laboratories, Inc. (Barr) sought FDA approval to manufacture and market a generic version of AZT by filing an Abbreviated New Drug Application (ANDA) pursuant to 21 U.S.C. § 355(j) (1988). As part of the process, Barr certified to the FDA that Burroughs Wellcome's patents were invalid or were not infringed by the product described in its ANDA. After Barr informed Burroughs Wellcome of its action, Burroughs Wellcome commenced this case for patent infringement against Barr on May 14, 1991, alleging technical infringement of its patents under 35 U.S.C. § 271(e)(2)(A) (1988).

Barr filed a counterclaim under 35 U.S.C. § 256 (1988) seeking correction of the patents to list Broder and Mitsuya as coinventors. Barr admitted that its AZT product would infringe the patents, but contended that it did not because Barr had obtained a license to manufacture and sell AZT from the government, which should be deemed the owner of the interest of coinventors Broder and Mitsuya in the AZT patents. Burroughs Wellcome denied that Broder and Mitsuya were coinventors and also responded that the assertion of any rights of Broder, Mitsuya, or the government in the patents was barred by laches, estoppel, and waiver.

Thereafter, Novopharm, Ltd. filed an ANDA of its own, seeking approval to manufacture and market its generic version of AZT. Burroughs Wellcome filed infringement suits against Novopharm, Ltd. and its American subsidiary Novopharm, Inc., which were consolidated with the suit against Barr. Like Barr, Novopharm, Ltd. admitted that its AZT product would infringe the claims of the six patents, but for the failure of Burroughs Wellcome to name the NIH scientists as coinventors of the subject matter of the patents. Although Novopharm, Inc. agreed to be bound by any injunction issued against its parent, it argued that it had not infringed the patents because it had not filed an ANDA and had no AZT product of its own. Novopharm contended that Broder and Mitsuya should have been named as inventors on five of the patents, and contended that Broder and Yarchoan were coinventors of the '750 patent. It maintained that the patents were invalid because of the alleged nonjoinder, and because Burroughs Wellcome had omitted the coinventors with deceptive intent, the patents were unenforceable for inequitable conduct.

After more than three weeks of trial, while Burroughs Wellcome was still in the process of presenting its case, the district court granted Burroughs Wellcome's motion for judgment as a matter of law against all of the defendants, concluding that the Burroughs Wellcome inventors had conceived of the subject matter of the inventions at some time before February 6, 1985, without the assistance of Broder, Mitsuya, or Yarchoan. The court rejected the arguments of Barr and Novopharm that they should be allowed to present evidence that the Burroughs Wellcome inventors had no reasonable belief that the inventions would actually work—that AZT was in fact active against HIV—until they were told the results of the NIH testing.

The court also rejected Novopharm's argument that the Burroughs Wellcome inventors had not conceived the invention of the '750 patent— the use of AZT to increase a patient's T-cell count—before July 23, 1985, when Broder reported the results of the NIH patient study to Lehrman. The court concluded that the increase in T-cell count was an obvious phenomenon known to the inventors that would result from administration of AZT. And the district court denied Barr's renewed motion for partial summary judgment on Burroughs Wellcome's equitable defenses to its counterclaim for correction of the patents under section 256.

Discussion

The arguments of both Barr and Novopharm are directed to when the inventors conceived the invention. Burroughs Wellcome says it was before they learned the results of the NIH tests; Barr and Novopharm say that confirmation of the inventions' operability, which came from the NIH tests, was an essential part of the inventive process. If Burroughs Wellcome is right, then the patents name the proper inventors, they are not invalid, and the appellants are liable for infringement. If Barr and Novopharm are correct, then Broder, Mitsuya, and Yarchoan should have been named as joint inventors and the resolution of Burroughs Wellcome's infringement suits is premature.

* * *

A joint invention is the product of a collaboration between two or more persons working together to solve the problem addressed. 35 U.S.C. § 116 (1988); *Kimberly–Clark Corp. v. Procter & Gamble Distrib. Co.*, 973 F.2d 911, 917, 23 U.S.P.Q.2D 1921, 1926 (Fed.Cir.1992). People may be joint inventors even though they do not physically work on the invention together or at the same time, and even though each does not make the same type or amount of contribution. 35 U.S.C. § 116. The statute does not set forth the minimum quality or quantity of contribution required for joint inventorship.

Conception is the touchstone of inventorship, the completion of the mental part of invention. *Sewall v. Walters*, 21 F.3d 411, 415, 30 U.S.P.Q.2D 1356, 1359 (Fed.Cir.1994). It is "the formation in the mind of the inventor, of a definite and permanent idea of the complete and operative invention, as it is hereafter to be applied in practice." *Hybritech Inc. v. Monoclonal Antibodies, Inc.*, 802 F.2d 1367, 1376, 231 USPQ 81, 87 (Fed.Cir.1986) (citation omitted). Conception is complete only when the idea is so clearly defined in the inventor's mind that only ordinary skill would be necessary to reduce the invention to practice, without extensive research or experimentation. *Sewall*, 21 F.3d at 415, 30 U.S.P.Q.2D at 1359; *see also Coleman v. Dines*, 754 F.2d 353, 359, 224 USPQ 857, 862 (Fed.Cir.1985) (conception must include every feature of claimed invention). Because it is a mental act, courts require corroborating evidence of a contemporaneous disclosure that would enable one skilled in the art to make the invention. *Coleman v. Dines*, 754 F.2d at 359, 224 USPQ at 862.

Thus, the test for conception is whether the inventor had an idea that was definite and permanent enough that one skilled in the art could understand the invention; the inventor must prove his conception by corroborating evidence, preferably by showing a contemporaneous disclosure. An idea is definite and permanent when the inventor has a specific, settled idea, a particular solution to the problem at hand, not just a general goal or research plan he hopes to pursue. *See Fiers v. Revel*, 984 F.2d 1164, 1169, 25 U.S.P.Q.2D 1601, 1605 (Fed.Cir.1993); *Amgen, Inc. v. Chugai Pharmaceutical Co.*, 927 F.2d 1200, 1206, 18 U.S.P.Q.2D 1016, 1021 (Fed.Cir.1991) (no conception of chemical compound based solely on its biological activity). The conception analysis necessarily turns on the inventor's ability to describe his invention with particularity. Until he can do so, he cannot prove possession of the complete mental picture of the invention. These rules ensure that patent rights attach only when an idea is so far developed that the inventor can point to a definite, particular invention.

But an inventor need not know that his invention will work for conception to be complete. *Applegate v. Scherer*, 332 F.2d 571, 573, 141 USPQ 796, 799 (CCPA 1964). He need only show that he had the idea; the discovery that an invention actually works is part of its reduction to practice. *Id.*; *see also Oka v. Youssefyeh*, 849 F.2d 581, 584 n. 1, 7 U.S.P.Q.2D 1169, 1171 n. 1 (Fed.Cir.1988).

Barr and Novopharm suggest that the inventor's definite and permanent idea must include a reasonable expectation that the invention will work for its intended purpose. They argue that this expectation is of paramount importance when the invention deals with uncertain or experimental disciplines, where the inventor cannot reasonably believe an idea will be operable until some result supports that conclusion. Without some experimental confirmation, they suggest, the inventor has only a hope or an expectation, and has not yet conceived the invention in sufficiently definite and permanent form. But this is not the law. An inventor's belief that his invention will work or his reasons for choosing a particular approach are irrelevant to conception. *MacMillan v. Moffett*, 432 F.2d 1237, 1239, 167 USPQ 550, 552 (CCPA 1970).

To support their reasonable expectation rule, Barr and Novopharm point to a line of cases starting with *Smith v. Bousquet*, 111 F.2d 157, 45 USPQ 347 (CCPA 1940), establishing the so-called doctrine of simultaneous conception and reduction to practice. *Smith* was an interference priority contest between alleged inventors of the use of two known compounds as insecticides. Both parties asserted priority based on testing of the compounds against selected insect species. Noting the unpredictability of the experimental sciences of chemistry and biology, in particular the uncertain relationship between chemical structure and biological activity, *Smith* declined to find conception until the invention had been reduced to practice by the filing of the first patent application. *Id.* at 162, 45 USPQ at 352. Barr and Novopharm read this and subsequent cases to establish, or at least support, their rule that conception of an invention in an unpredictable field occurs only when the inventor has reasonable grounds to believe the invention will work.

But these cases do not stand for the proposition that an inventor can never conceive an invention in an unpredictable or experimental field until reduction to practice. In rejecting the asserted evidence of conception, *Smith* said as to one of the compounds:

> it is apparent from the record that neither [party] had in mind at the time the suggestions were originally made, nor at any time thereafter, until successful tests, if any, were made, what insects, if any, it might be effective against, or how it might be applied to produce the desired results. Accordingly, neither party had a definite idea of the "complete and operative invention" here involved prior to a successful reduction—actual or constructive—of it to practice.

Thus, in awarding priority to Smith based on his constructive reduction to practice, the court relied not on the inherent unpredictability of the science, but on the absence of any evidence to corroborate an earlier conception for either of the parties.

It is undoubtedly true that "[i]n some instances, an inventor is unable to establish a conception until he has reduced the invention to practice through a successful experiment." *Amgen*, 927 F.2d at 1206, 18 U.S.P.Q.2D at 1021; *Alpert v. Slatin*, 305 F.2d 891, 894, 134 USPQ 296, 299 (CCPA 1962) (no conception "where results at each step do not follow as anticipated, but are achieved empirically by what amounts to trial and error"). But in such cases, it is not merely because the field is unpredictable; the alleged conception fails because, as in *Smith*, it is incomplete. Then the event of reduction to practice in effect provides the only evidence to corroborate conception of the invention.

Under these circumstances, the reduction to practice can be the most definitive corroboration of conception, for where the idea is in constant flux, it is not definite and permanent. A conception is not complete if the subsequent course of experimentation, especially experimental failures, reveals uncertainty that so undermines the specificity of the inventor's idea that it is not yet a definite and permanent reflection of the complete invention as it will be used in practice. *See Amgen*, 927 F.2d at 1207, 18 U.S.P.Q.2D at 1021 (no conception until reduction to practice where others tried and failed to clone gene using suggested strategy); *Rey–Bellet v. Engelhardt*, 493 F.2d 1380, 1387, 181 USPQ 453, 457–58 (CCPA 1974) (focusing on nature of subsequent research as indicator that inventors encountered no perplexing intricate difficulties). It is this factual uncertainty, not the general uncertainty surrounding experimental sciences, that bears on the problem of conception.

Barr and Novopharm argue for a broader reading of *Amgen* and *Fiers* in support of their reasonable expectation rule. Both of these cases involve conception of a DNA encoding a human protein—a chemical compound. Conception of a chemical substance includes knowledge of both the specific chemical structure of the compound and an operative method of making it. *Fiers*, 984 F.2d at 1169; *Amgen*, 927 F.2d at 1206; *Oka*, 849 F.2d at 583. The alleged inventors in *Fiers* and *Amgen* claimed conception of their respective inventions before they knew relevant chemical structure—the nucleotide sequence—so the courts found no conception until experimentation finally revealed that structure. Here, though, Burroughs Wellcome's inventions use a compound of known structure; the method of making the compound is also well known.

We emphasize that we do not hold that a person is precluded from being a joint inventor simply because his contribution to a collaborative effort is experimental. Instead, the qualitative contribution of each collaborator is the key—each inventor must contribute to the joint arrival at a definite and permanent idea of the invention as it will be used in practice.

Nor do we suggest that a bare idea is all that conception requires. The idea must be definite and permanent in the sense that it involves a specific approach to the particular problem at hand. It must also be sufficiently precise that a skilled artisan could carry out the invention without undue experimentation. And, of course, the alleged conception must be supported by corroborating evidence. On the facts before us, it is apparent that the district court correctly ruled against Barr and Novopharm as to five of the patents, but that the court's judgment as to the sixth, the '750 patent, was premature.

The '232, '838, '130, '208, and '538 patents encompass compositions and methods of using AZT to treat AIDS. The Burroughs Wellcome inventors claim conception of these inventions prior to the NIH experiments, based on the draft British patent application. That document is not itself a conception, for conception occurs in the inventors' minds, not on paper. The draft simply corroborates the claim that they had formulated a definite and permanent idea of the inventions by the time it was prepared.

The Burroughs Wellcome inventors set out with the general goal of finding a method to treat AIDS, but by the time Broder confirmed that

AZT was active against HIV, they had more than a general hope or expectation. They had thought of the particular antiviral agent with which they intended to address the problem, and had formulated the idea of the inventions to the point that they could express it clearly in the form of a draft patent application, which Barr and Novopharm concede would teach one skilled in the art to practice the inventions. The draft expressly discloses the intended use of AZT to treat AIDS. It sets out the compound's structure, which, along with at least one method of preparation, was already well known. The draft also discloses in detail both how to prepare a pharmaceutical formulation of AZT and how to use it to treat a patient infected with HIV. The listed dosages, dose forms, and routes of administration conform to those eventually approved by the FDA. The draft shows that the idea was clearly defined in the inventors' minds; all that remained was to reduce it to practice—to confirm its operability and bring it to market. *See Haskell v. Colebourne*, 671 F.2d 1362, 1365–66, 213 USPQ 192, 194 (CCPA 1982) (enabling draft patent application sufficient to corroborate conception).

An examination of the events that followed the preparation of Burroughs Wellcome's draft confirms the soundness of the conception. Broder and Mitsuya received from Burroughs Wellcome a group of compounds, known to Broder and Mitsuya only by code names, selected for testing by the Burroughs Wellcome inventors. They then tested those compounds for activity against HIV in their patented cell line. The test results revealed for the first time that one of the compounds, later revealed to be AZT, was exceptionally active against the virus.

Here, though, the testing was brief, simply confirming the operability of what the draft application disclosed. True, the science surrounding HIV and AIDS was unpredictable and highly experimental at the time the Burroughs Wellcome scientists made the inventions. But what matters for conception is whether the inventors had a definite and permanent idea of the operative inventions. In this case, no prolonged period of extensive research, experiment, and modification followed the alleged conception. By all accounts, what followed was simply the normal course of clinical trials that mark the path of any drug to the marketplace.

That is not to say, however, that the NIH scientists merely acted as a "pair of hands" for the Burroughs Wellcome inventors. Broder and Mitsuya exercised considerable skill in conducting the tests, using their patented cell line to model the responses of human cells infected with HIV. Lehrman did suggest initial concentrations to Broder, but she hardly controlled the conduct of the testing, which necessarily involved interpretation of results for which Broder and Mitsuya, and very few others, were uniquely qualified. But because the testing confirmed the operability of the inventions, it showed that the Burroughs Wellcome inventors had a definite and permanent idea of the inventions. It was part of the reduction to practice and inured to the benefit of Burroughs Wellcome.

Barr and Novopharm allege error in the district court's refusal to hear their evidence of the poor predictive value of the murine retrovirus screens for activity against HIV. Regardless of the predictive value of the murine tests, however, the record shows that soon after those tests, the inventors determined, for whatever reason, to use AZT as a treatment for AIDS, and they prepared a draft patent application that specifically set out the inventions, including an enabling disclosure. Obviously, enablement and conception are distinct issues, and one need not necessarily meet the enablement standard of 35 U.S.C. § 112 to prove conception. *See Fiers*, 984 F.2d at 1169, 25 U.S.P.Q.2D at 1605. But the enabling disclosure does suffice in this case to confirm that the inventors had concluded the mental part of the inventive process—that they had arrived at the final, definite idea of their inventions, leaving only the task of reduction to practice to bring the inventions to fruition.

The question is not whether Burroughs Wellcome reasonably believed that the inventions would work for their intended purpose, the focus of the evidence offered by Barr and Novopharm, but whether the inventors had formed the idea of their use for that purpose in sufficiently final form that only the exercise of ordinary skill remained to reduce it to practice. *See MacMillan v. Moffett*, 432 F.2d at 1239, 167 USPQ at 552 (Inventor's "reasons or lack of reasons for including U–5008 are not relevant to the question of conception. The important thing is that he did think in definite terms of the method claimed."). Whether or not Burroughs Wellcome believed the inventions would in fact work based on the mouse screens is irrelevant.

We do not know precisely when the inventors conceived their inventions, but the record shows that they had done so by the time they prepared the draft patent application that thoroughly and particularly set out the inventions as they would later be used. The district court correctly ruled that on this record, the NIH scientists were not joint inventors of these inventions.

The '750 patent is another question. It claims "[a] method of increasing the number of T-lymphocytes in a human infected with the [HIV] virus comprising administering to said human an effective amount of" AZT. Novopharm argues that there is no evidence, under any test of inventorship, that the Burroughs Wellcome inventors conceived of this invention until after the Phase I patient study conducted by Broder and Yarchoan revealed that AZT could lead to increased levels of T-cells in AIDS patients.

Novopharm is right that the record is devoid of any statement that the inventors thought AZT could raise a patient's T-cell levels, but evidence need not always expressly show possession of the invention to corroborate conception. The district court held that the record supported conception as a matter of law, concluding that "an increase in T-lymphocyte count was an 'obvious,' natural phenomenon known to the [Burroughs Wellcome] inventors that would result from the inhibition of a retrovirus." *Burroughs Wellcome Co. v. Barr Lab., Inc.*, 828 F.Supp. at 1213. Burroughs Wellcome argues that this conclusion was proper because increased T-cell count is simply an obvious property or use of the greater discovery at issue here, the treatment of HIV infection with AZT. Because an increase in T-lymphocytes follows inevitably from treatment of AIDS patients with AZT, Burroughs Wellcome says, Broder and Yarchoan merely observed that the method invented by the Burroughs Wellcome inventors had qualities that the inventors failed to perceive. Burroughs Wellcome says this is not an inventive contribution to the claims of any of the AZT patents.

* * *

The alleged conception is supported by testimony of Burroughs Wellcome's experts, Burroughs Wellcome's draft Phase I protocol, and the same draft patent application that corroborates conception of the other five inventions. The experts testified that those skilled in the art at the time expected increased immune function to accompany inhibition of HIV. The draft patent application discloses that HIV preferentially destroys T-cells, that AIDS is associated with progressive depletion of T-cells, and that AZT is an effective treatment for HIV infection. Finally, the draft protocol directs the administrators of the Phase I study to monitor patients' T-lymphocyte count. This evidence supports an inference that the Burroughs Wellcome inventors did have the necessary definite and permanent idea, for, given the virus' effect on T-lymphocytes, it seems logical to conclude that stopping the virus might reverse the process of T-cell destruction and restore the body's immune system to a pre-infection state. If this were the only evidence in the record, the court's judgment would be sustained.

But Novopharm offered evidence suggesting that one skilled in the art would not have expected T-cell count to rise. On deposition, Broder testified that prior to the first patient study, "no one knew whether there was such a thing as recovery" of T-cells, based on the NIH's experience with suramin, a drug that entered clinical trials before AZT. Although suramin showed some activity against HIV, inhibition of the retrovirus apparently was not accompanied by increases in T-cell count or restoration of immune functions. Of course, there might be any number of other explanations for the results of the suramin trials; but they might suggest that although those skilled in the art recognized the significance of T-lymphocyte levels in HIV infection and AIDS, they might have expected inhibition of the virus simply to halt the continuing destruction of T-cells, not to increase T-cell count and restore immune function. This could support an inference that the inventors themselves did not conceive the invention prior to the Phase I study.

Novopharm also contends that Burroughs Wellcome prepared its Phase I protocol in collaboration with Broder and the NIH, possibly from a draft protocol prepared by Broder and Yarchoan pursuant to their study of suramin. These contentions are relevant to the conception inquiry for they tend to undermine the corroborative value of the draft protocol, and might even support joint inventorship based on that draft. *See Coleman v. Dines*, 754 F.2d at 360, 224 USPQ at 863 (document's co-author cannot be considered sole inventor of invention disclosed in document without further proof). Because under Rule 50(a) all inferences must be taken against the moving party, the court's ruling on the '750 patent was inappropriate, and we vacate the judgment to that extent and remand for further proceedings.

■ LOURIE, CIRCUIT JUDGE, concurring-in-part and dissenting-in-part.

I concur in the majority's decision with respect to the '232, '838, '130,-'208, and '538 patents, and join the opinion except for the following: I do not agree that reduction to practice is corroboration of conception and that the completeness of a conception is affected by subsequent experimental success or failure. These statements confuse the idea of conception with both corroboration and reduction to practice. A conception must be judged as to its completeness in relation to the invention being claimed. It must also be corroborated by evidence independent of the inventor. If subsequent experimentation shows that an invention that was only conceived does not work, that fact does not vitiate the earlier conception. A conception not later reduced to practice may have little significance, but it is important that we not confuse concepts. The conception was still a conception. It is of course possible for an invention to be reduced to practice constructively, *i.e.*, by filing a patent application, rather than actually, by doing the work, in which case the reduction to practice clearly says nothing about the completeness of the conception. Moreover, what matters, in addition to the completeness of a conception, is its date. Corroboration must be of the date of the conception. If the only "corroboration" of the conception is its reduction to practice, corroboration has not occurred concerning the alleged date of conception. Finally on this point, reduction to practice by the inventor is not corroboration because corroboration must be independent of the inventor. Corroboration is not a demonstration that the conceived invention works; it is evidentiary proof that the mental act of invention occurred on a certain date.

I also believe that the issue of joint inventorship is irrelevant here and therefore confusing. If the Burroughs Wellcome inventors had a complete conception, as we hold, then the NIH scientists were not inventors because the invention had already been made, not because of any shortcomings in their inventive contributions. Thus, there is no need to discuss joint inventorship at all.

I respectfully dissent from the vacating of the court's judgment concerning the '750 patent. I believe that the method of the '750 patent is an inherent, inevitable result of the practice of the other method patents claiming treatment of HIV or AIDS. It seems to be the (or a) mechanism by which the other methods find their use.

Even if it is true that the first verification or articulation of the increase in the T-cell count occurred in the hands of NIH scientists, this finding inures to the benefit of those who conceived the method of treatment that led to it. The method of the '750 patent is merely a refined definition of the method of the '232 patent, which issued from the original application. The '130 and '208 patents, which also came from applications later filed with the '750 and the composition patents, are also modifications of the original filing.

It is common practice for applicants to claim all aspects of their invention and that is what appears to have happened here. An inventor is entitled to the inherent benefits that flow from his or her invention. It is improper to split the inventorship of what is one invention merely because the means by which it was achieved was later verified by scientists acting pursuant to the original conceivers.

The PTO of course issued these patents. During its examination, it determined that the '750 method was obvious over the '232 method. Given a terminal disclaimer, this led to the grant of the patent. More than being obvious, however, the method was inherent in the '232 method and therefore lacking in novelty. See 35 U.S.C. § 102 (1988). If, as I believe, the '750 invention does lack novelty over the other patents, its validity may be in question on the ground of double patenting because a terminal disclaimer is not effective to cure a double patenting problem when the inventions are the same. As long as the inventive entities are also the same, however, it doesn't really matter.

Even assuming that the '750 method is a separate invention, the majority concedes that evidence supports an inference that the Burroughs Wellcome inventors alone conceived the method. The majority goes off the track, however, in relying on Novopharm's offer of evidence that one would not have expected the T-cell count to rise. This is irrelevant if Burroughs Wellcome's inventors had the conception, because the opinion earlier correctly holds that a reasonable expectation of success is not necessary to a conception.

The majority here is inviting the trial court on remand and motion, see 35 U.S.C. § 256 (1988), to partially split the inventorship, and presumably also the ownership, of this related collection of patents claiming the physical act of "treating" and the result which the treatment accomplishes. This makes no sense. It amounts to deciding that treating a person in pain with aspirin is one invention and invoking the pain-relieving mechanism by means of that treatment is another. One cannot apparently treat HIV-infected humans with AZT without also increasing the level of T-lymphocytes. The panel is thus inconsistent in upholding the conclusion of the trial court that Burroughs Wellcome's scientists alone conceived the invention of using AZT to treat HIV infection, but then failing to arrive at the same conclusion regarding a patent claiming one of the sequelae of that use.

The real result of the majority's vacating the court's decision on the '750 patent is that, while it may believe that it is affirming the decision on the other patents, it may in practical effect be destroying Burroughs Wellcome's exclusivity for its invention and creating a whole new set of questions. If the trial court joins the NIH inventors, and NIH has licensed the patent to companies intending to sell AZT, will those companies infringe the '232 and other patents? Is the terminal disclaimer still valid, lacking the consent of one of the assignees? Without a valid terminal disclaimer, is the '750 patent valid? While these questions are not before us, exploring them illustrates the strange consequences of the majority's decision. On the other hand, if the trial court confirms its finding that the T-lymphocyte "invention" was essentially the same invention and inured to the benefit of Burroughs Wellcome, the remand will have been superfluous. Useless and inefficient litigation and burdening of the courts will have resulted.

The trial court's decision should be affirmed across the board because it correctly found that the Burroughs Wellcome inventors solely conceived and are entitled to the inventive benefit of all the claimed inventions.

NOTES

1. *Defining Conception.* As the court stated in *Mahurkar, supra* Section B–1, the person "who first conceives, and, in a mental sense, first invents ... may date his patentable invention back to the time of its conception, if he connects the conception with its reduction to practice by reasonable diligence on his part, so that they are substantially one continuous act." How should conception be defined?

In the 1897 case of *Mergenthaler v. Scudder*, 1897 C.D. 724, 731 (1897), the Court of Appeals for District of Columbia laid down a definition that has been adopted by the Federal Circuit:

> The conception of the invention consists in the complete performance of the mental part of the inventive act. All that remains to be accomplished in order to perfect the act or instrument belongs to the department of construction, not invention. It is, therefore, the formation in the mind of the inventor of a definite and permanent idea of the complete and operative invention as it is thereafter to be applied in practice that constitutes an available conception within the meaning of the patent law.

In *Mahurkar v. C.R. Bard, supra*, the Federal Circuit stated:

> To have conceived of an invention, an inventor must have formed in his or her mind "a definite and permanent idea of the complete and operative invention, as it is hereafter to be applied in practice." [citing *Burroughs Wellcome*]. The idea must be "so clearly defined in the inventor's mind that only ordinary skill would be necessary to reduce the invention to practice, without extensive research or experimentation."

In *Amgen, Inc. v. Chugai Pharmaceutical Co., Ltd.*, 927 F.2d 1200 (Fed.Cir. 1991), the Federal Circuit addressed what is needed to prove date of invention for chemical/biological compounds. The patent related to DNA sequences for encoding Erythropoietin (EPO). The court defined conception in the same manner as did the court in *Mahurkar, supra*, but went on to say that

> [i]n some instances, an inventor is unable to establish a conception until he has reduced his invention to practice through a successful experiment. This situation results in simultaneous conception and reduction to practice....
>
> A gene is a chemical compound, albeit a complex one, and it is well established in our law that conception of a chemical compound requires that the inventor be able to define it so as to distinguish it from other materials, and to describe how to obtain it. Conception does not occur unless one has a mental picture of the structure of the chemical, or is able to define it by its method of preparation, its physical or chemical properties, or whatever characteristics sufficiently distinguish it. It is not sufficient to define it solely by its principal biological property, *e.g.*, encoding for [EPO], because an alleged conception having no more specificity than that is simply a wish to know the identity of any material with that biological property. We hold that when an inventor is unable to envision the detailed constitution of a gene so as to distinguish it from other materials, as well as a method for obtaining it, conception has not been achieved until reduction to practice has occurred, *i.e.*, until after the gene has been isolated.

Id. at 1206.

2. *Corroboration.* As the court stated in *Burroughs Wellcome*, because conception "is a mental act, courts require corroborating evidence of a contemporaneous disclosure that would enable one skilled in the art to make the invention." 40 F.3d at 1228. In *Mahurkar v. C.R. Bard*, 79 F.3d 1572, 1577 (Fed.Cir.1996), the Federal Circuit addressed why corroboration is required and how the court analyzes corroborating evidence:

This court has developed a rule requiring corroboration where a party seeks to show conception through the oral testimony of an inventor. This requirement arose out of a concern that inventors testifying in patent infringement cases would be tempted to remember facts favorable to their case by the lure of protecting their patent or defeating another's patent. While perhaps prophylactic in application given the unique abilities of trial court judges and juries to assess credibility, the rule provides a bright line for both district courts and the PTO to follow in addressing the difficult issues related to invention dates.

In assessing corroboration of oral testimony, courts apply a rule of reason analysis. Under a rule of reason analysis, "[a]n evaluation of all pertinent evidence must be made so that a sound determination of the credibility of the inventor's story may be reached."

This court does not require corroboration where a party seeks to prove conception through the use of physical exhibits. The trier of fact can conclude for itself what documents show, aided by testimony as to what the exhibit would mean to one skilled in the art.

Indeed, the *Mergenthaler* court stated that without such a requirement, there would be a "great temptation to perjury." 1897 C.D. at 732.

3. *Inventive Activity Abroad: Post–GATT and Post–NAFTA.* Recall that in *Fiers*, the inventor attempted to prove the date in which his invention was "brought into the United States." Prior to 1994, § 104 of the Patent Act precluded an inventor from using inventive activity abroad (*i.e.*, conception and reduction to practice) to establish priority under § 102(g). However, GATT/TRIPS (Trade Related Aspects of Intellectual Property Rights) and NAFTA amended § 104 to allow applicants to rely on foreign inventive activity to prove a date of invention. Section 104 now reads:

§ 104.   Invention made abroad

(a) In General—

(1) Proceedings. —In proceedings in the Patent and Trademark Office, in the courts, and before any other competent authority, an applicant for a patent, or a patentee, may not establish a date of invention by reference to knowledge or use thereof, or other activity with respect thereto, in a foreign country other than a NAFTA country or a WTO country member country, except as provided in sections 119 and 365 of this title.

(2) Rights. —If an invention was made by a person, civil or military—

(A) while domiciled in the United States, and serving in any other country in connection with operations by or on behalf of the United States,

(B) while domiciled in a NAFTA country and serving in another country in connection with operations by or on behalf of that NAFTA country, or

(C) while domiciled in a WTO member country and serving in another country in connection with operations by or on behalf of that WTO member country,

that person shall be entitled to the same rights of priority in the United States with respect to such invention as if such invention had been made in the United States, that NAFTA country, or that WTO member country, as the case may be.

(3) Use of Information.—To the extent that any information in a NAFTA country or a WTO member country concerning knowledge, use, or other activity relevant to proving or disproving a date of invention has not been made available for use in a proceeding in

the Patent and Trademark Office, a court, or any other competent authority to the same extent as such information could be made available in the United States, the Commissioner, court, or such other authority shall draw appropriate inferences, or take other action permitted by statute, rule, or regulation, in favor of the party that requested the information in the proceeding.

(b) Definitions. —As used in this section—

   (1) the term "NAFTA country" has the meaning given that term in section 2(4) of the North American Free Trade Agreement Implementation Act; and

   (2) the term "WTO member country" has the meaning given that term in section 2(10) of the Uruguay Round Agreements Act.

35 U.S.C. § 104 (as amended by P.L. 103–182, Dec. 8, 1993, § 331, 107 Stat. 2113; P.L. 103–465, Dec. 8, 1994, § 531(a), 108 Stat. 4982).

It is important to note the *effective date* of the changes to § 104. Under § 531(b) of the Uruquay Round Agreements Act (URAA) the amendment to § 104 "shall apply to all patent applications that are filed on or after the date that is 12 months after the date of entry into force of the WTO Agreement with respect to the United States." The WTO Agreement went into effect in the United States on January 1, 1995. Therefore, the effective date of the amendments to § 104 is *January 1, 1996*. Section 531 is not retroactive, and thus, applicants can only rely on foreign inventive activity on or after January 1, 1996.

The effective date with respect to NAFTA is *December 8, 1993*. Therefore, applicants may rely on inventive activity in a NAFTA country on or after December 8, 1993.

4. *§ 104 and § 102(g)*. NAFTA and GATT/TRIPS did not amend § 102(g), which, prior to American Inventors Protection Act of 1999 (AIPA), limited inventive activity for priority purposes (*i.e.,* obtaining a patent) to acts "*in this country*." Thus, there was an inconsistency between §§ 104 and 102(g), wherein the former permitted foreign-based inventive activity to be used in an interference proceeding, but § 102(g) appeared to prevent the applicant from relying on that activity. Was this an oversight or is the United States playing unfairly? Although it was a subject of debate, it is clear that GATT/TRIPS did not intend, with the exception of interferences, to permit unpublished, secret foreign activity to act as prior art. Consider the following scenario:

Inventor A conceives and reduces to practice XYZ in France on January 2, 1996. Inventor B conceives and reduces to practice XYZ in the United States on May 1, 1996. Both inventors apply for a patent in the United States.

Under amended § 104, inventor A will now be awarded priority. But prior to enactment of the AIPA, inventor B could argue that he is also entitled to a patent because under § 102(g), inventor A did not invent "in this country?" The legislative history of the URAA suggests that this problem can be solved by resort to the doctrine of interference estoppel (*see* 37 C.F.R. § 1.658(c) and MPEP § 2363.03), which states:

The implementing bill does not change present practice regarding the effect of a determination that establishes which of two or more inventors was first. This practice precludes the losing party from separately patenting the invention in dispute, even if the invention of the winning party was not made "in this country", pursuant to application of section 102(g) of Title 35, U.S. Code. Thus, a losing party is and will continue to be precluded through interference estoppel from separately patenting the invention in dispute or an invention that is not patently [sic] distinguishable from the invention in dispute.

The Uruguay Round Agreements Act Statement of Administrative Action, 103rd Cong., 2d Sess. 1001 (1994), *reprinted in* 1194 U.S.S.C.A.N. 4040, 4294–95. The *Statement of Administrative Action* is regarded as an "authoritative expression by the United States concerning the interpretation and application of the Uruguay Round Agreements and this Act in any judicial proceeding in which a question arises concerning such interpretation or application." § 102(d) of URAA. Thus, if the losing party's claims are not patentably distinct from those of the winning party, the losing party will continue to be estopped from obtaining a patent. *See In re Deckler*, 977 F.2d 1449 (Fed.Cir.1992), *infra* Section B–8, note 3.

The American Inventors Protection Act recognized this inconsistency and amended § 102(g) to allow foreign-based inventive activity to be used in an interference, thus making § 102(g) consistent with § 104. Section 102(g) now reads:

A person shall be entitled to a patent unless—

(g)(1) during the course of an interference conducted under section 135 or section 291, another inventor involved therein establishes, to the extent permitted in section 104, that before such person's invention thereof the invention was made by such other inventor and not abandoned, suppressed, or concealed, or (2) before such person's invention thereof, the invention was made in this country by another inventor who had not abandoned, suppressed, or concealed it....

Thus, there is a distinction between *patent-obtaining* and *patent-defeating* activity. One may use foreign-based inventive activity to *obtain* a patent under § 102(g)(1). But foreign-based inventive activity cannot be used as prior art to *defeat* patent rights outside of the interference context. Although such prior art is defeating in the sense that an applicant can use it to obtain a patent over another, thereby defeating another's quest to obtain patent rights, it is important to note again that the use of foreign-based inventive activity is limited to the interference context (*i.e.,* obtaining rights). Inventive activity that can be used as prior art to defeat patent rights is limited under § 102(g)(2) to activity "in this country."

-----

b.   REDUCTION TO PRACTICE

There are two types of reduction to practice: (1) constructive, which occurs when a patent application is filed; and (2) actual. The following case address the latter. What exactly is needed to prove that an invention was actually reduced to practice? Does something physical have to be constructed? Does it have to be commercially viable, or merely work?

DSL Dynamic Sciences Limited v. Union Switch & Signal, Inc.

928 F.2d 1122 (Fed.Cir.1991).

■ Before RICH, PLAGER, and CLEVENGER, CIRCUIT JUDGES.

■ RICH, CIRCUIT JUDGE.

DSL Dynamic Sciences Ltd. (DSL) appeals from the March 28, 1990 decision of the United States District Court for the Western District of

Pennsylvania in a patent interference proceeding under 35 U.S.C. § 146, awarding priority of invention to Union Switch & Signal, Inc. (Union Switch). We affirm.

BACKGROUND

The present case relates to "coupler mount assemblies," which are essentially clamps, used to attach various equipment to a railway car coupler. The assembly engages relief holes located in the side of a standard railway car coupler so as to grasp the side of the coupler without interfering with the ability to use the coupler to attach the railway car to another railway car. An example of the type of equipment mounted on the coupler mount assembly is a brake pressure monitor, which measures the brake pressure at the end of a train and transmits the brake pressure measurement to a receiver located in the locomotive.

DSL is the assignee of U.S. Patent No. 4,520,662 (Schmid patent), which issued on June 4, 1985 to Hartmut Schmid, and is based on an application filed on September 9, 1983. Union Switch is the assignee of U.S. Patent Application serial No. 593,778 (Blosnick application), which was filed on March 27, 1984 in the names of Robert Blosnick and James Toms. On April 4, 1986, the Patent and Trademark Office (PTO) declared interference No. 101,561 between the Schmid patent and the Blosnick application. The sole count remaining when the case was heard by the Board of Patent Appeals and Interferences (Board) was the following:

> A coupler mount assembly for use with a railway vehicle coupler including a side wall having a convex exterior surface that is provided with a first pair of vertically aligned and spaced-apart relief holes adjacent the coupler tip, and a second pair of vertically aligned and spaced-apart relief holes adjacent the coupler base, said coupler mount assembly being adapted to mount an equipment housing on the coupler and comprising:
>
> first and second jaw means, each of which includes a hook; support means to which the equipment housing may be secured, said support means additionally supporting said first and second jaw means for movement relative to each other and so that the hooks thereof project from said support means and face each other; and clamping means supported by said support means for drawing said first and second jaw means toward each other, whereby said hooks of said first and second jaw means clamp an intermediate portion of the coupler sidewall between the first and second relief hole pairs when said hook of said first jaw means has been inserted into one hole of the first relief hole pair and said hook of said second jaw means has been inserted into a corresponding hole of the second relief hole pair.

Because the activity relating to conception and reduction to practice by Schmid was performed in Canada, DSL is prevented by 35 U.S.C. § 104 from establishing an invention date earlier than its filing date of September 9, 1983, and that is the date it has relied on throughout the proceedings. Union Switch, on the other hand, maintained before the Board a conception date of January, 1983, and a reduction to practice date of no later than May, 1983. As evidence to support its claim of reduction to practice, Union Switch presented evidence that around April 1, 1983, the inventors Blosnick and Toms tested a prototype of their invention by mounting the prototype on a railway car coupler and stepping on it. It also presented evidence of tests that were performed on actual moving trains during May of 1983. Three of these tests, which are referred to in the record as "Test Nos. 3, 4 and 5," involved the use of a prototype of the coupler mount assembly on cabooses of trains over distances of 144 miles (Test No. 3), 457 miles (Test No. 4), and 108 miles (Test No. 5). The performance of the prototype in each case was documented with pictures and written reports.

Before the Board, DSL argued that the prototypes used by Union Switch in early 1983 did not fall within the scope of the count and therefore were insufficient to reduce to practice the invention of the count. The Board disagreed, and in a decision dated March 29, 1989, found that Union Switch had established an invention date of no later than May of 1983, and therefore was entitled to priority of the invention of the count.

DSL sought review of the Board's decision via an action under 35 U.S.C. § 146 in the district court. Before the district court, DSL continued to attack the sufficiency of Union Switch's evidence of its reduction to practice, but presented a new theory in doing so. Specifically, DSL argued that the tests were not performed in the intended environment of a coupler mount assembly, and therefore were not sufficient to establish reduction to practice.

In support of this argument, DSL offered testimony, not previously presented to the Board, including the testimony of Hartmut Schmid as an expert in the field. According to DSL, Schmid would have testified that the purpose of the equipment supported by a coupler mount assembly is to obviate the need for a caboose at the end of a train, and that, therefore, the coupler mount assemblies of the count would never in reality be attached to a caboose, but generally would be attached to the coupler of a freight car. Schmid further offered to testify that the suspension system is much better on a caboose, which is intended to carry passengers, than that on a freight car, and that consequently while the devices tested by Union Switch in May of 1983 performed satisfactorily when attached to cabooses, those devices would have failed if attached to a freight car.

DSL also offered the testimony of Michael Starr, an employee of Southern Pacific Railroad. According to DSL, Starr would have testified to the failure of several coupler mount assemblies sold to Southern Pacific by Union Switch in 1985, and to the fact that major modifications of those assemblies were required before they were found suitable for use.

Union Switch objected to the newly proffered evidence on various grounds, and a hearing was held to determine the admissibility of the evidence. Subsequently, the district court ruled to exclude the evidence. Schmid's testimony was excluded on the grounds that 35 U.S.C. § 146 only allows for the introduction of evidence not presented to the Board if that evidence was unavailable despite diligence by the proponent of the evidence in obtaining it.

The district court found that DSL must have known of the expert testimony of Schmid, the inventor of the Schmid patent, and that DSL deliberately withheld this testimony from the Board. Starr's testimony was excluded as irrelevant because, in the district court's opinion, such evidence concerning commercial failures two years after reduction to practice was not relevant as to reduction to practice.

Having excluded the new evidence, the district court merely reviewed the Board decision, and found no "definite and thorough conviction" that the Board erred.

Therefore, the district court affirmed the award of priority to Union Switch. DSL appealed here.

OPINION

DSL argues strenuously that the district court erred in its interpretation of 35 U.S.C. § 146, causing the testimony of Schmid to be erroneously excluded. DSL also argues that the exclusion of Starr's testimony was error. We, however, do not reach either issue because it is our opinion that even if this testimony had been presented, Union Switch would still have been entitled to the award of priority of invention. The issue of reduction to practice is a question of law which this court reviews de novo. *Hybritech Inc. v. Monoclonal Antibodies, Inc.*, 802 F.2d 1367, 1376, 231 USPQ 81, 87 (Fed.Cir.1986), *cert. denied*, 480 U.S. 947, 107 S.Ct. 1606, 94 L.Ed.2d 792 (1987).

It is true, as DSL points out, that proof of actual reduction to practice requires a showing that "the embodiment relied upon as evidence of priority actually worked for its intended purpose." *Newkirk v. Lulejian*, 825 F.2d 1581, 1582 (Fed.Cir.1987). This is so even if the "intended purpose" is not explicitly set forth in the counts of the interference. On the other hand, tests performed outside the intended environment can be sufficient to show reduction to practice if the testing conditions are sufficiently similar to those of the intended environment. *Tomecek v. Stimpson*, 513 F.2d 614, 618 (CCPA 1975).

The burden of proof here was initially on Union Switch to prove an actual reduction to practice. *See id.* at 618, 185 USPQ at 238. Thus, for Union Switch to prevail, it must show one of two things: (1) that use of a coupler mount assembly with a caboose is an intended purpose of the coupler mount assembly, or (2) that if use with a caboose is not an intended use of a coupler mount assembly, the tests performed on a caboose coupler sufficiently simulated the conditions present on a freight car coupler to adequately show reduction of the invention to practice.

The tests performed by Union Switch were extensive. The reports prepared after each test show in detail the distance travelled between various checkpoints and the average speed between the checkpoints. The total distance travelled by the trains in Tests Nos. 3, 4 and 5 was over 700 miles. The average speed was often over 40 miles per hour, and for one 30 minute period was 56 miles per hour. Importantly, a unit was mounted on the coupler mount assembly to measure the forces applied to the assembly. The report for Test No. 4 indicates that the "vibration equipment showed shocks of over 15 G's," but that the coupler mount assembly still operated successfully.

Thus, even accepting DSL's argument that coupler mount assemblies are not intended for use on cabooses, we are convinced that the train tests were sufficient to reduce the invention to practice. Included in DSL's offer of proof is a report by Schmid which compares the device disclosed in the Blosnick application and tested by Union Switch with the device of the Schmid patent. The report indicates that a coupler mount assembly must be able to withstand "continuous shock and vibration at low frequencies and high amplitude with peak loads to 20 g." We are of the opinion that Union Switch's train tests, which applied forces "in excess of 15 G's," sufficiently approximated the condition of "loads to 20 g" which Schmid indicates a coupler mount assembly must withstand on a non-cushioned rail car such as a freight car.

The Schmid report also concludes with the following:

> [The tests performed by Union Switch] are inadequate. They covered a total of only 414 miles at an average speed of 34 MPH (MAX 56 MPH) over flat terrain. I understand the Blosnick–Toms unit was never attached to a regular rail car, but was only tried on a caboose. A caboose rides smoother than a regular rail car, especially compared with an extended-length platform car at 70 or 80 MPH.

First, we note that the statement that the tests covered "only 414 miles" appears to be an error, since the record clearly shows that Test Nos. 3, 4 and 5 covered over 700 miles. Secondly, and more importantly, the other factors referred to in Schmid's report relate to how well the device works, not to whether it works at all. DSL does not contend that the device of the Blosnick application was only intended for use with an extended-length platform car or at speeds of 70 or 80 miles per hour, nor do we think it could reasonably so contend. The essence of Schmid's report is that the device he invented works better than the device invented by Blosnick and Toms. That may well be the case. However, that does not change the fact that (1) the device tested by Union Switch in May of 1983 fell within the scope of the count (a finding made by the Board, affirmed by the district court, and not contested here) and (2) the tests performed by Union Switch sufficiently establish that the device would work to hold equipment on a moving rail car, even if that rail car was not a caboose. This is sufficient to establish actual reduction to practice. *See Tomecek*, 513 F.2d at 618, 185 USPQ at 239.

With respect to the proffered testimony of Mr. Starr, some cases have held that events occurring after an alleged actual reduction to practice can call into question whether reduction to practice has in fact occurred. *See, e.g., Brown–Bridge Mills, Inc. v. Eastern Fine Paper, Inc.*, 700 F.2d 759, 765–66, 217 USPQ 651, 657 (1st Cir.1983). However, there is certainly no requirement that an invention, when tested, be in a commercially satisfactory stage of development in order to reduce the invention to practice. *King Instrument Corp. v. Otari Corp.*, 767 F.2d 853, 861, 226 USPQ 402, 407 (Fed.Cir.1985), *cert. denied*, 475 U.S. 1016, 106 S.Ct. 1197, 89 L.Ed.2d 312 (1986); *Randolph v. Shoberg*, 590 F.2d 923, 926, 200 USPQ 647, 649–50 (CCPA 1979). A failure of several commercial devices allegedly made according to the Blosnick application long after the reduction to practice is insufficient to convince us that a device, meeting the limitations of the count, was not adequately tested to establish a reduction to practice.

NOTES

1. *Actual v. Constructive Reduction to Practice.* There are two types of reduction to practice (RTP): actual and constructive. *Actual* RTP occurs when the invention is shown to be suitable for its intended purpose, that is, when the invention is physically made and tested (*e.g.*, a prototype). *See DSL, supra* ("[P]roof of actual reduction to practice requires a showing that 'the embodiment relied upon as evidence of priority actually worked for its intended purpose....' On the other hand, tests performed outside the intended environment can be sufficient to show reduction to practice if the testing conditions are sufficiently similar to those of the intended environment.")

Constructive RTP happens when the patent application is filed. Constructive RTP may occur even if the applicant never built or tested his invention as long as the applicant satisfies § 112. The policy behind constructive RTP is to encourage early disclosure of the invention. Requiring actual testing may delay disclosure. Nevertheless, § 112 must be satisfied. *See Fiers v. Revel, supra* ("While one does not need to have carried out one's invention before filing a patent application, one does need to be able to describe that invention with particularity.")

2. *Actual RTP and Testing.* To prove actual RTP, an inventor must construct the invention (*e.g.*, prototype) and test the invention to determine if it works for its intended purpose. The Federal Circuit, in *Estee Lauder Inc. v. L'Oreal, S.A.*,129 F.3d 588, 593 (Fed.Cir.1997), has held that there must some recognition of successful testing for an invention to be actually reduced to practice:

> [*Hahn v. Wong*] requires that in addition to preparing a composition, an inventor must establish that he "knew it would work," to reduce the invention to practice.... This suggest that a reduction to practice does not occur until an inventor, or perhaps his agent, knows that the invention will work for its intended purpose. Indeed, ... the "utility requirement is satisfied when an inventor has learned enough about the product to justify the conclusion that it is useful for a specific purpose."... But until he learns that threshold information, there can be no reduction to practice. Moreover, *Burroughs Wellcome* states that a reduction to practice requires "that discovery that an invention actually works."... This suggests that until that "discovery" is actually made, there is no reduction to practice. These cases trumpet, therefore, the principle that a reduction to practice does not occur until the inventor has determined that the invention will work for its intended purpose.

What type of testing is required? It is clear that actual working conditions may not be required. Indeed, laboratory tests may be sufficient if they simulate actual working conditions. In the Federal Circuit case of *Scott v. Finney,* 34 F.3d 1058 (Fed.Cir.1994), the court stated that cases dealing with the sufficiency of testing in proving actual RTP "share a common theme." The court wrote:

> In each case, the court examined the record to discern whether the testing in fact demonstrated a solution to the problem intended to be solved by the invention.... In tests showing the invention's solution of a problem, the courts have not required commercial perfection nor absolute replication of the circumstances of the invention's actual use. Rather, they have instead adopted a common sense assessment. This common sense approach prescribes more scrupulous testing under circumstances approaching actual use conditions when the problem includes many uncertainties. On the other hand, when the problem to be solved does not present myriad variables, common sense similarly permits little or no testing to show the soundness of the principles of operation of the invention.

Id. at 1063. *See also, Mahurkar v. C.R. Bard, Inc.,* 79 F.3d 1572, 1578 (Fed.Cir. 1996) ("To show actual reduction to practice, an inventor must demonstrate that the invention is suitable for its intended purpose.... Depending on the character of the invention and the problem it solves, this showing may require test results.... Less complicated inventions and problems do not demand stringent testing.... In fact, some inventions are so simple and their purpose and efficacy so obvious that their complete construction is sufficient to demonstrate workability.")

3. *Commercial Viability.* There is a difference between proving that the invention works for its intended purpose and proving that the invention works in the commercial sense. Neither perfection nor commercial viability is required to show actual RTP. As the Federal Circuit stated in *DSL*:

> [S]ome cases have held that events occurring after an alleged actual reduction to practice can call into question whether reduction to practice has in fact occurred. However, there is certainly no requirement that an invention, when tested, be in a commercially satisfactory stage of development in order to reduce the invention to practice.... A failure of several commercial devices allegedly made according to the [applicant's] application long after the reduction to practice is insufficient to convince us that a device, meeting the limitations of the count, was not adequately tested to establish a reduction to practice.

DSL, 928 F.2d at 1126.

4. *Corroboration.* As with conception, an inventor must be able to corroborate independently his actual reduction to practice. This can be done through the submission of affidavits analyzing and describing the experiments, the dates of the experiments, etc. The Federal Circuit applies a "rule of reason" standard when evaluating the sufficiency of the corroborating evidence:

> This court applies a "rule of reason" standard when reviewing the sufficiency of evidence about reduction to practice.... This rule requires the Patent and Trademark Office to examine, analyze, and evaluate reasonably all pertinent evidence when weighing the credibility of an inventor's story.... Under the rule of reason, this court cannot ignore the realities of technical operations in modern day research laboratories.... Recognizing these realities, a junior technician performing perfunctory tasks under the supervision of a senior scientist is not generally necessary to verify the reliability of evidence about scientific methods or data. In the absence of indicia calling into question the trustworthiness of the senior scientist's testimony, the rule of reason permits the Board to rely on the trained supervisor's testimony to ascertain scientific methods or results.

Holmwood v. Balasubramanyan Sugavanam, 948 F.2d 1236, 1238 (Fed.Cir.1991). The law also makes clear that some evidence beyond mere testimony or documents authored by an inventor is required. The interested statements of an inventor must be corroborated by either testimony from an uninterested witness or some tangible evidence such as exhibits. *See* Singh v. Brake, 317 F.3d 1334, 1341 (Fed.Cir.2003). A mosaic of contemporaneous written documents and physical evidence, even when some was authored by the inventor, may be sufficient. Such "[d]ocumentary or physical evidence that is made contemporaneously with the inventive process provides the most reliable proof that the inventor's testimony has been corroborated." Sandt Technology, Ltd. v. Resco Metal & Plastics Corp., 264 F.3d 1344, 1350–51 (Fed.Cir.2001).

c.   ABANDONMENT, SUPPRESSION, AND CONCEALMENT

The first person to reduce an invention to practice (and therefore presumptively the first inventor) loses the right to priority of invention if that person thereafter abandons, suppresses or conceals (ASC) the invention. The same holds true if the inventor was second to reduce to practice, but the first to conceive, but also abandoned, suppressed or concealed. The policy behind the ASC requirement is the encouragement of prompt public disclosure of the invention. The *Fujikawa v. Wattanasin* case explores what constitutes abandonment, suppression or concealment.

Fujikawa v. Wattanasin

93 F.3d 1559 (Fed.Cir.1996).

■ Before MAYER, CLEVENGER, and RADER, CIRCUIT JUDGES.

■ CLEVENGER, CIRCUIT JUDGE.

Yoshihiro Fujikawa *et al.* (Fujikawa) appeal from two decisions of the Board of Patent Appeals and Interferences of the United States Patent & Trademark Office (Board) granting priority of invention in two related interferences to Sompong Wattanasin, and denying Fujikawa's motion to add an additional sub-genus count to the interferences. We affirm.

I

These interferences pertain to a compound and method for inhibiting cholesterol biosynthesis in humans and other animals. The compound count recites a genus of novel mevalonolactones. The method count recites a method of inhibiting the biosynthesis of cholesterol by administering to a "patient in need of said treatment" an appropriate dosage of a compound falling within the scope of the compound count.

The real parties in interest are Sandoz Pharmaceuticals Corporation (Sandoz), assignee of Wattanasin, and Nissan Chemical Industries, Ltd. (Nissan), assignee of Fujikawa.

The inventive activity of Fujikawa, the senior party, occurred overseas. Fujikawa can thus rely only on his effective filing date, August 20, 1987, to establish priority. 35 U.S.C. § 102(g) (1994). Whether Wattanasin is entitled to priority as against Fujikawa therefore turns on two discrete questions. First, whether Wattanasin has shown conception coupled with diligence from just prior to Fujikawa's effective filing date until reduction to practice. *Id.* Second, whether Wattanasin suppressed or concealed the invention between reduction to practice and filing. *Id.* With respect to the first question, Fujikawa does not directly challenge the Board's holdings on Wattanasin's conception or diligence, but rather contends that the Board incorrectly fixed the date of Wattanasin's reduction to practice. As for the second question, Fujikawa contends that the Board erred in concluding that Wattanasin had not suppressed or concealed the invention. Fujikawa seeks reversal, and thus to establish priority in its favor, on either ground.

II

The Board divided Wattanasin's inventive activity into two phases. The first phase commenced in 1979 when Sandoz began searching for drugs which would inhibit the biosynthesis of cholesterol. Inventor Wattanasin was assigned to this project in 1982, and during 1984–1985 he synthesized three compounds falling within the scope of the compound count. When tested *in vitro*, each of these compounds exhibited some cholesterol-inhibiting activity, although not all the chemicals were equally effective. Still, according to one Sandoz researcher, Dr. Damon, these test results indicated that, to a high probability, the three compounds "would be active when administered *in vivo* to a patient to inhibit cholesterol biosynthesis, *i.e.* for the treatment of hypercholesteremia or atherosclerosis." Notwithstanding these seemingly positive results, Sandoz shelved Wattanasin's project for almost two years, apparently because the level of *in vitro* activity in two of the three compounds was disappointingly low.

By January 1987, however, interest in Wattanasin's invention had revived, and the second phase of activity began. Over the next several months, four more compounds falling within the scope of the compound count were synthesized. In October, these compounds were tested for *in vitro* activity, and each of the four compounds yielded positive results. Again, however, there were significant differences in the level of *in vitro* activity of the four compounds. Two of the compounds in particular, numbered 64–935 and 64–936, exhibited *in vitro* activity significantly higher than that of the other two compounds, numbered 64–933 and 64–934.

Soon after, in December 1987, the three most active compounds *in vitro* were subjected to additional *in vivo* testing. For Sandoz, one primary purpose of these tests was to determine the *in vivo* potency of the three compounds relative to that of Compactin, a prior art compound of known cholesterol-inhibiting potency. From the results of the *in vivo* tests, reproduced in the margin,[1] Sandoz calculated an ED_{50}[2] for each of the compounds and compared it to the ED_{50} of Compactin. Only one of the compounds, compound 64–935, manifested a better ED_{50} than Compactin: an ED_{50} of 0.49 as compared to Compactin's ED_{50} of 3.5. All of the tests performed by Sandoz were conducted in accordance with established protocols.

1.

Compound	dosage	% change
64–933	1.0	–36.3%
	0.3	–17.0%
	0.1	–18.6%
64.935	1.0	–65.8%
	0.3	–29.7%
	0.1	–36.3%
64.936	1.0	–9.0%
	0.3	–39.2%
	0.1	–22.5%

2. The ED_{50} of a compound represents the effective concentration, measured in milligrams of compound per kilogram of laboratory specimen, which inhibits cholesterol biosynthesis by 50%.

During this period, Sandoz also began to consider whether, and when, a patent application should be filed for Wattanasin's invention. Several times during the second phase of activity, the Sandoz patent committee considered the question of Wattanasin's invention but decided that it was too early in the invention's development to file a patent application. Each time, however, the patent committee merely deferred decision on the matter and specified that it would be taken up again at subsequent meetings. Finally, in January 1988, with the *in vivo* testing completed, the Committee assigned Wattanasin's invention an "A" rating which meant that the invention was ripe for filing and that a patent application should be prepared. The case was assigned to a Ms. Geisser, a young patent attorney in the Sandoz patent department with little experience in the pharmaceutical field.

Over the next several months the Sandoz patent department collected additional data from the inventor which was needed to prepare the patent application. This data gathering took until approximately the end of May 1988. At that point, work on the case seems to have ceased for several months until Ms. Geisser began preparing a draft sometime in the latter half of 1988. The parties dispute when this preparation began. Fujikawa contends that it occurred as late as October, and that Ms. Geisser was spurred to begin preparing the draft application by the discovery that a patent to the same subject matter had been issued to a third party, Picard. Fujikawa, however, has no evidence to support that contention. In contrast, Sandoz contends that Ms. Geisser began the draft as early as August, and that she was already working on the draft when she first heard of Picard's patent. The evidence of record, and in particular the testimony of Ms. Geisser, supports that version of events. In any event, the draft was completed in November and, after several turn-arounds with the inventor, ultimately filed in March of 1989.

Both Wattanasin and Fujikawa requested an interference with Picard. The requests were granted and a three-party interference between Picard, Fujikawa, and Wattanasin was set up. Early in the proceedings, however, Picard filed a request for an adverse judgment presumably because he could not antedate Fujikawa's priority date. What remained was a two-party interference between Fujikawa and Wattanasin. Ultimately, for reasons not significant to this appeal, the interference was divided into two interferences: one relating to the method count and one relating to the compound count. The Board decided each of these interferences adverse to Fujikawa.

With respect to the compound count, the Board made two alternative findings regarding reduction to practice. First, it found that the in vitro results in October 1987 showed sufficient practical utility for the compound so as to constitute a reduction to practice as of the date of those tests.[3] In the alternative, the Board held, the in vivo tests which showed significant activity in the 64–935 compound at doses of 1.0 and 0.1 mg were sufficient to show practical utility. Consequently, Wattanasin had reduced the compound to practice, at the latest, as of December 1987. Since Fujikawa did

---

3. As explained more fully below, reduction to practice requires a showing of practical utility, which may be satisfied by an "adequate showing of any pharmacological activity." *Nelson v. Bowler*, 626 F.2d 853, 856, 206 USPQ 881, 883 (CCPA 1980).

not challenge Wattanasin's diligence for the period between Fujikawa's effective filing date of August 20, 1987 and Wattanasin's reduction to practice in either October or December 1987, the Board held that Wattanasin was de facto the first inventor of the compound count. Finally, the Board found that the seventeen month period (counting from the in vitro testing) or fifteen month period (counting from the in vivo testing) between Wattanasin's reduction to practice and filing was not sufficient to raise an inference of suppression or concealment given the complexity of the invention, and therefore awarded priority of the compound count to Wattanasin. In reaching this conclusion, the Board rejected Fujikawa's argument that Wattanasin was spurred to file by Picard because it held that spurring by Picard, a third party, had no legal effect in a priority dispute between Fujikawa and Wattanasin.

With respect to the method count, the Board determined that Wattanasin reduced to practice in December 1987 on the date that *in vivo* testing of the 64–935 compound was concluded. In reaching that conclusion, the Board first noted that a reduction to practice must include every limitation of the count. Consequently, Wattanasin's early *in vitro* testing could not constitute a reduction to practice of the method count, since that count recites administering the compound to a "patient." The *in vivo* testing, however, met the limitations of the count since the word "patient" was sufficiently broad to include the laboratory rats to whom the compounds were administered. The *in vivo* testing also proved that 64–935 had practical utility because the compound displayed significant cholesterol inhibiting activity at doses of 1.0 and 0.1 mg. Given this date of reduction to practice, the Board again held that Wattanasin was the *de facto* first inventor of the count and that the delay in filing of fifteen months was not sufficient to trigger an inference of suppression or concealment. The Board therefore awarded priority of the method count to Wattanasin.

Before this court, Fujikawa seeks review of these adverse priority determinations.... We have jurisdiction to hear this appeal under 28 U.S.C. § 1295(a)(4)(A) (1994).

III

* * *

B

Turning to the method count, the Board found that Wattanasin reduced the method to practice in December 1987 when successful *in vivo* testing of the compound was completed. This finding, too, was based on testimony that the *in vivo* data for one of the compounds tested, 64–935, showed significant cholesterol inhibiting activity in the laboratory rats tested.

Fujikawa challenges the Board's holding by referring to an anomaly in the test data of the 64–935 compound which it contends undercuts the reliability of the *in vivo* tests. In particular, Fujikawa points to the fact that the compound's potency was less at a dosage of 0.3 mg than it was at a dosage of 0.1 mg. On the basis of this aberration, Fujikawa's expert, Dr.

Holmlund, testified that this test data was unreliable and could not support a finding that the compound was pharmacologically active.

It is clear from the Board's opinion, however, that to the extent Dr. Holmlund was testifying that this aberration would lead one of ordinary skill to completely reject these test results, the Board did not accept his testimony. This decision of the Board was not clear error. Admittedly, the decreased potency at 0.3 mg is curious. The question remains, however, as to how much this glitch in the data would undercut the persuasiveness of the test results as a whole in the mind of one of ordinary skill. Each party presented evidence on this point and the Board resolved this disputed question of fact by finding that the test results as a whole were sufficient to establish pharmacological activity in the minds of those skilled in the art. In doing so, the Board properly exercised its duty as fact finder, and we therefore affirm its finding on this point.[7]

As noted above, Fujikawa does not challenge the Board's conclusions that Wattanasin conceived prior to Fujikawa's effective date or that Wattanasin pursued his invention with diligence prior to Fujikawa's date until his reductions to practice in October and December 1987. Consequently, we affirm the Board's finding that Wattanasin has shown conception coupled with diligence from just prior to Fujikawa's effective date of August 20, 1987 up to the date he reduced the invention to practice in October 1987, for the compound, or December 1987, for the method.

IV

Having determined that Wattanasin was the de facto first inventor, the remaining question before the Board was whether Wattanasin had suppressed or concealed the invention between the time he reduced to practice and the time he filed his patent application. Suppression or concealment of the invention by Wattanasin would entitle Fujikawa to priority. 35 U.S.C. § 102(g).

Suppression or concealment is a question of law which we review *de novo*. *Brokaw v. Vogel*, 57 C.C.P.A. 1296, 429 F.2d 476, 480, 166 USPQ 428, 431 (1970). Our case law distinguishes between two types of suppression and concealment: cases in which the inventor deliberately suppresses or conceals his invention, and cases in which a legal inference of suppression

---

7. Before the Board, Fujikawa additionally argued that *in vivo* testing cannot establish reduction to practice of the method count because it does not fulfill every limitation of the count. In particular, Fujikawa argued that only human beings can be considered "patients in need of" cholesterol biosynthesis inhibition, as required by the count. As noted above, the Board rejected this argument and held that the term "patient" in the count is broad enough to encompass mammals, such as the laboratory rats tested *in vivo*.

In its brief to this court, Fujikawa renews this argument. In the process, however, Fujikawa seems to add an additional ground which it did not argue before the Board below. We are not absolutely certain, but it appears that Fujikawa is now contending that *in vivo* testing cannot constitute a reduction to practice because the rats tested were, from all that would appear, healthy animals, rather than animals in need of cholesterol biosynthesis inhibition. To the extent that Fujikawa's argument before this court is directed to this novel ground not raised below, we consider the argument waived and decline to address it. To the extent that Fujikawa is still arguing that the count requires administration of the compound to a human, we disagree, and affirm the Board's decision on this point.

or concealment is drawn based on "too long" a delay in filing a patent application. *Paulik v. Rizkalla*, 760 F.2d 1270, 1273 (Fed.Cir.1985) (*in banc*).

Fujikawa first argues that there is evidence of intentional suppression or concealment in this case. Intentional suppression refers to situations in which an inventor "designedly, and with the view of applying it indefinitely and exclusively for his own profit, withholds his invention from the public." *Id.* (*quoting Kendall v. Winsor*, 62 U.S. (21 How.) 322, 328, 16 L.Ed. 165 (1858)). Admittedly, Sandoz was not overly efficient in preparing a patent application, given the time which elapsed between its reduction to practice in late 1987 and its ultimate filing in March 1989. Intentional suppression, however, requires more than the passage of time. It requires evidence that the inventor intentionally delayed filing in order to prolong the period during which the invention is maintained in secret. *Cf. Peeler v. Miller*, 535 F.2d 647, 653–54 (CCPA 1976) (implying that intentional suppression requires showing of specific intent). Fujikawa presented no evidence that Wattanasin delayed filing for this purpose. On the contrary, all indications are that throughout the period between reduction to practice and filing, Sandoz moved slowly (one might even say fitfully), but inexorably, toward disclosure. We therefore hold that Wattanasin did not intentionally suppress or conceal the invention in this case.

Absent intentional suppression, the only question is whether the 17 month period between the reduction to practice of the compound, or the 15 month period between reduction to practice of the method, and Wattanasin's filing justify an inference of suppression or concealment. *See id.* The Board held that these facts do not support such an inference. As the Board explained: "In our view, this hiatus in time is not sufficiently long to raise the inference that Wattanasin suppressed or concealed the invention considering the nature and complexity of the invention here."

Fujikawa attacks this finding of the Board on two grounds. First, it contends that the Board should not have held that a 15 or 17 month delay is *per se* insufficient to raise an inference of suppression or concealment without examining the circumstances surrounding the delay and whether, in view of those circumstances, Wattanasin's delay was reasonable. Second, Fujikawa argues that the Board failed to consider evidence that Wattanasin was spurred to file by the issuance of a patent to a third party, Picard, directed to the same genus of compounds invented by Wattanasin. Evidence that a first inventor was spurred to disclose by the activities of a second inventor has always been an important factor in priority determinations because it creates an inference that, but for the efforts of the second inventor, "the public would never have gained knowledge of [the invention]." *Brokaw*, 429 F.2d at 480, 166 USPQ at 431. Here, however, the Board expressly declined to consider the evidence of spurring because it held that spurring by a third party who is not a party to the interference is irrelevant to a determination of priority as between Wattanasin and Fujikawa. We first address Fujikawa's arguments concerning spurring.

A

We are not certain that the Board is correct that third party spurring is irrelevant in determining priority. After all, "[w]hat is involved here is a policy question as to which of the two rival inventors has the greater right to a patent." *Brokaw*, 429 F.2d at 480, 166 USPQ at 430. Resolution of this question could well be affected by the fact that one of the inventors chose to maintain his invention in secrecy until disclosure by another spurred him to file, even when the spurrer was a third party not involved in the interference. We need not resolve that question here, however, because we hold that no reasonable fact finder could have found spurring on the facts of this case. The only evidence in the record on the question of spurring is the testimony of Ms. Geisser who expressly testified that she had already begun work on the Wattanasin draft application before she learned of Picard's patent, in other words, that she had not been spurred by Picard. Consequently, we leave the question of the relevance of third-party spurring for another case.

B

Fujikawa's other argument also requires us to examine the evidence of record in this case. As Fujikawa correctly notes, this court has not set strict time limits regarding the minimum and maximum periods necessary to establish an inference of suppression or concealment. *See Correge v. Murphy*, 705 F.2d 1326, 1330, 217 USPQ 753, 756 (Fed.Cir.1983). Rather, we have recognized that "it is not the time elapsed that is the controlling factor but the total conduct of the first inventor." *Young v. Dworkin*, 489 F.2d 1277, 1285, 180 USPQ 388, 395 (CCPA 1974) (Rich, J., concurring). Thus, the circumstances surrounding the first inventor's delay and the reasonableness of that delay are important factors which must be considered in deciding questions of suppression or concealment. *See, e.g., id.* at 1281–82, 180 USPQ at 392–93.

Fujikawa again correctly notes that the Board's opinion gives short shrift to the question of whether this delay on the facts of this case was reasonable. In seeking reversal of the Board's decision, Fujikawa asks us to assess the factual record for ourselves to determine whether Wattanasin engaged in sufficient disclosure-related activity to justify his 17–month delay in filing.

The facts of record, however, do not support Fujikawa's position.

In our view, the circumstances in this case place it squarely within the class of cases in which an inference of suppression or concealment is not warranted. We acknowledge, of course, that each case of suppression or concealment must be decided on its own facts. Still, the rich and varied case law which this court has developed over many years provides some guidance as to the type of behavior which warrants an inference of suppression or concealment. *See Paulik*, 760 F.2d at 1280, 226 USPQ at 231–32 (Rich, J., concurring). In this case Wattanasin delayed approximately 17 months between reduction to practice and filing. During much of that period, however, Wattanasin and Sandoz engaged in significant steps towards perfecting the invention and preparing an application. For example, we do not believe any lack of diligence can be ascribed to Wattanasin for the period between October and December 1987 when *in vivo* testing of the invention was taking place. See *Young*, 489 F.2d at 1281, 180 USPQ at 392. Similarly, at its first opportunity following the *in vivo* testing, the

Sandoz patent committee approved Wattanasin's invention for filing. This takes us up to the end of January 1988.

Over the next several months, until May 1988, the Sandoz patent department engaged in the necessary collection of data from the inventor and others in order to prepare Wattanasin's patent application. We are satisfied from the record that this disclosure-related activity was sufficient to avoid any inference of suppression or concealment during this period.[8] *Cf. Correge*, 705 F.2d at 1330–31, 217 USPQ at 756 (five significant acts of disclosure-related activity over the course of seven months sufficient to rebut any inference of suppression). Also, as noted above, the record indicates that by August 1988, Ms. Geisser was already at work preparing the application, and that work continued on various drafts until Wattanasin's filing date in March 1989. Thus, the only real period of unexplained delay in this case is the approximately three month period between May and August of 1988.

Given a total delay of 17 months, an unexplained delay of three months, the complexity of the subject matter at issue, and our sense from the record as a whole that throughout the delay Sandoz was moving, albeit slowly, towards filing an application, we conclude that this case does not warrant an inference of suppression or concealment. Consequently, we affirm the Board on this point.

C

Finally, Fujikawa contends that assuming *in vitro* tests are sufficient to establish reduction to practice, Wattanasin reduced the compound count to practice in 1984 when he completed in vitro testing of his first three compounds falling within the scope of the count. If so, Fujikawa argues, the delay between reduction to practice and filing was greater than four years, and an inference of suppression or concealment is justified.[9]

We reject this argument in view of *Paulik v. Rizkalla*, 760 F.2d 1270, 226 USPQ 224 (Fed.Cir.1985) (*in banc*). In *Paulik*, we held that a suppression or concealment could be negated by renewed activity prior to an opposing party's effective date. There, inventor Paulik reduced his invention to practice and submitted an invention disclosure to his employer's patent department. For four years the patent department did nothing with the disclosure. Then, just two months before Rizkalla's effective date, the patent department allegedly picked up Paulik's disclosure and worked diligently to prepare a patent application which it ultimately filed. *See id.* at 1271–72, 226 USPQ at 224–25. We held that although Paulik could not rely on his original date of reduction to practice to establish priority, he

---

8. Our conclusion in this regard is based, in small part, on the testimony of Mr. Melvyn Kassenoff, a lawyer in Sandoz's patent department. Before the Board, Fujikawa challenged large parts of this testimony as inadmissible. In this opinion we therefore rely only on those portions of the testimony which even Fujikawa concedes are admissible, *i.e.*, testimony relating to Mr. Kassenoff's legal services rendered in connection with the prosecution of Wattanasin's application.

9. This argument, of course, relates only to the compound count, since, as explained above, the method count was not reduced to practice until the in vivo testing in December 1987.

could rely on the date of renewed activity in his priority contest with Rizkalla. In large measure, this decision was driven by the court's concern that denying an inventor the benefit of his renewed activity, might "discourage inventors and their supporters from working on projects that had been 'too long' set aside, because of the impossibility of relying, in a priority contest, on either their original work or their renewed work." *Id.* at 1275–76, 226 USPQ at 227–28.

Paulik's reasoning, if not its holding, applies squarely to this case. A simple hypothetical illustrates why this is so. Imagine a situation similar to the one facing Sandoz in early 1987. A decisionmaker with limited funds must decide whether additional research funds should be committed to a project which has been neglected for over two years. In making this decision, the decisionmaker would certainly take into account the likelihood that the additional research might yield valuable patent rights. Furthermore, in evaluating the probability of securing those patent rights, an important consideration would be the earliest priority date to which the research would be entitled, especially in situations where the decisionmaker knows that he and his competitors are "racing" toward a common goal. Thus, the right to rely on renewed activity for purposes of priority would encourage the decisionmaker to fund the additional research. Conversely, denying an inventor the benefit of renewed activity would discourage the decisionmaker from funding the additional research.

Here, Wattanasin returned to his abandoned project well before Fujikawa's effective date and worked diligently towards reducing the invention to practice a second time. For the reasons explained above, we hold that, on these facts, Wattanasin's earlier reduction to practice in 1984 does not bar him from relying on his earliest date of renewed activity for purposes of priority.

NOTES

1. *Abandonment, Suppression, and Concealment ("ASC").* Consistent with the patent policy favoring prompt disclosure, an inventor who was the first to reduce to practice may lose his right of priority if he abandons, suppresses, or conceals his invention. Consider the following scenario:

> Inventor 1 reduces to practice invention X, but neither files a patent application, nor markets invention X. Two years later, inventor 2, ignorant of inventor 1 and his invention X, invents X and files a patent application. Upon learning of inventor 2, inventor 1 is "spurred" into activity and claims that he is the first to invent X.

The law favors inventor 2 in this instance because it is he who brought invention X to the public whereas inventor 1 abandoned, suppressed, and concealed invention X and only came to the fore once he found out about inventor 2. But under § 102(g), if inventor 2 never came into the picture, inventor 1 may still apply for and obtain a patent, even though there was a delay. Indeed, there is no duty to file a patent application.

There are two types of ASC: (1) explicit or active; and (2) inferential based on delay. With respect to inferential ASC, there are no set time limits on when an inventor must publicly disclose his invention having first made it. The Federal Circuit has stated that after first making the invention, an inventor's failure to file a patent application, describe the invention in a published document, or publicly use the invention may within a "reasonable time" may result in ASC. *See Dow Chemical v. Astro–Valcour,* 267 F.3d 1334, 1342 (Fed.Cir.2001). But the court has also stated that "mere delay, without more, is not sufficient to establish" ASC. *Young v. Dworkin,* 489 F.2d 1277, 1281 (CCPA 1974).

Is there a difference among "abandon," "suppress," and "conceal?" Consider the following discussion:

> The three words—"abandon," "suppress," and "conceal"—are perhaps misleading in suggesting that there are three separate and independent possibilities. In fact, the three words reflect a unitary concept, focusing on the failure of the person who was the first to reduce the subject matter to practice to either apply for a patent or commercialize the invention or both. The concept is figuratively speaking a "putting the invention in the drawer" and doing nothing with it, at least not until spurred into action by the appearance of a rival inventor. . . .

> In determining what kind of delaying conduct constitutes abandonment-suppression-concealment, three factors are especially pertinent: (1) length of the delay-period from reduction to practice to either an application for patent or commercialization; (2) the existence and nature of any activity during the delay-period; and (3) the cause of the resumption of activity (including the first inventor's contemporaneous characterizations of that resumption). . . .

> As to the length of the delay period, the notion is that delay alone is not conclusive on the issue of abandonment, suppression, and concealment. However, if the delay period is long enough, then it provides the basis for an inference of abandonment-suppression-concealment.

> * * *

> As to the cause of resumption of activity, if the first inventor is "spurred" into renewed activity immediately upon learning of the activity of the second inventor, then that is very strong evidence of abandonment-suppression-concealment. This makes sense. A common sense inference is that but for the appearance of the second inventor, the first inventor would have allowed the potentially valuable idea to lie fallow indefinitely. Contrawise, if the first inventor for its own reasons and truly spontaneously resumes activity, that tends to mitigate against a finding of abandonment-suppression-concealment. The absence of "spurring" is by no means conclusive however.

CHISUM, 3 CHISUM ON PATENTS § 10.08[1]. *See also, Mason v. Hepburn,* 13 App.D.C. 86 (1898).

2. *Diligence.* Diligence only comes into play when a party is the first to conceive, but the second to reduce to practice. The patent law favors prompt disclosure, and therefore, wants to know what this party was doing given the fact that another was the second to conceive, but the first to reduce to practice. The junior party (*i.e.,* the party who was the first to conceive but second to reduce to practice) must show continuous and reasonable diligence from a date just prior to the senior party's (*i.e.,* the party who was the first to reduce to practice) conception to the junior party's its reduction to practice. As the Board of Patent Appeals & Interferences explained:

> A party that seeks to establish reasonable diligence must account for the entire period during which diligence is required; that period commences from a time just prior to the senior party's [date of conception] to the junior party's reduction to practice, either actual or constructive. . . .

Public policy favors early disclosure, . . . and thus the law is reluctant to displace an inventor who was the first to disclose to the public his invention . . . During this period there must be "reasonably continuous activity." . . . Evidence which is of a general nature to the effect that work was continuous and which has little specificity as to dates and facts does not constitute the kind of evidence required to establish diligence in the critical period.

Hunter v. Beissbarth, 230 USPQ 365, 368 (Bd.Pat.App. & Int'f 1986).

While a showing of constant effort is not required to prove diligence, the inventor must account for the entire critical period. The activities that tend to prove diligence "take a variety of forms" and are on a "continuum between, on the one hand, ongoing laboratory experimentation, and on the other hand, pure money-raising activity that is entirely unrelated to practice of the process." *Scott v. Koyama,* 281 F.3d 1243, 1248 (Fed.Cir.2002). The question is whether the applicant was pursuing his goal "in a reasonable fashion." *Hybritech Inc. v. Abbott Laboratories,* 4 U.S.P.Q.2d 1001, 1006 (C.D.Cal.1987), *aff'd,* 849 F.2d 1446 (Fed.Cir.1988). Thus, periods of inactivity may not be fatal to a showing of diligence if the inventor has an adequate excuse such as (1) poverty or illness of the inventor, *Christie v. Seybold,* 55 F. 69, 77 (6th Cir.1893) ("the sickness of the inventor, his poverty, and his engagement in other inventions of similar kind are all circumstances which may affect the question of reasonable diligence."), (2) obligations of the inventor's regular employment, *Gould v. Schawlow,* 363 F.2d 908, 919 (CCPA 1966) ("reasonable diligence does not require that one abandon his means of livelihood to further his reduction to practice."), or (3) excessive workload of the inventor's patent attorney provided the attorney "takes up work in a reasonable order—for example, handling applications in the chronological order in which they are submitted." DONALD S. CHISUM, 3 CHISUM ON PATENTS § 10.07[4][e]. In the end, while each piece of evidence standing alone, or even small groups of them together, might have been insufficient to meet the appropriately demanding evidentiary standards for a Junior Party to prove that a reduction to practice actually occurred, the burden may be met where as a set they leave the only reasonable inference that logically follows from the set of facts in this case to be that the Junior Party did, in fact, reduce to practice by the critical date. *See* Kridl v. McCormick, 105 F.3d 1446, at 1450 (Fed.Cir.1997) (quoting Berges v. Gottstein, 618 F.2d 771, 775 (CCPA 1980)) (" 'relevant related independent events' served to corroborate the inventor's allegations"); Cooper v. Goldfarb 154 F.3d 1321, 1329–30 (Fed.Cir.1998) (proof of reduction to practice from "evidence as a whole" based on interaction among different pieces of corroborating evidence).

3. *Doctrine of Prosecution Laches.* This equitable doctrine renders a patent unenforceable if it was obtained after unreasonable and unexplained delay in prosecution. *See Woodbridge v. United States,* 263 U.S. 50 (1923); *Webster Electric Co. v. Splitdorf Electrical Co.,* 264 U.S. 463 (1924); *In re Bogese,* 303 F.3d 1362 (Fed.Cir. 2002). The policy underpinning the doctrine is grounded in both utilitarianism and public notice. The former relates to the patentee's failure to disclose his patented invention to the public in a timely fashion, whereas the latter is concerned with the potential adverse consequences suffered by competitors who invested in a product while that patent application was pending in confidence, a product that would infringe the patent upon issuance. This type of patent is also known as a submarine patent because it remains unknown (submerged) during prosecution and surprisingly surfaces to capture a competitor's investment. The submarine patent is less of a concern today because of the 18–month publication rule, as well as the rule that patent term is measured from filing date in contrast with issue date, but some suggest that abusive continuation practice remains.

A recent example of so-called submarine patents is Jerome Lemelson's patents on machine vision and automatic identification bar code technology. Fourteen of Lemelson's patents related to this technology were invalidated under the doctrine of prosecution history laches. *See Symbol Technologies, Inc. v. Lemelson Medical Education & Research Foundation*, 301 F.Supp.2d 1147 (2004) (finding 19 to 36 year delay in prosecution unreasonable and unexplained). Jerome Lemelson was one of the most prolific inventors in history, amassing over 550 patents in various fields of technology.

SIDE BAR

Patent Harmonization: First to File v. First to Invent

Marco Ricolfi*

In all the countries of the world, except in the United States, the novelty of a patent for which an application is made is measured as to the *filing* date; as a consequence the question of who invented first is, for most purposes,[1] irrelevant. In the U.S., on the contrary, the critical date is the date of invention. Specifically, the novelty of a patent is measured as of the date of invention. Disputes over the question who was the first inventor are resolved through an interference proceeding, discussed in this chapter. It is therefore said that the U.S. follows a first-to-invent system, the rest of the world a first-to-file system.

What are the reasons of this striking difference?

Arguably the first-to-file principle is much more certain and precise, while first-to-invent takes into greater account notions of fairness. Indeed, under the former principle there is not much room for debate, as the conflict between two parties claiming priority is resolved simply by comparing two dates and those dates are officially certified by public or quasi-public bodies, such as patent offices around the world. Interference proceedings, on the other hand, require a complex assessment of arcane concepts, such as conception, reduction to practice, continuous diligence, all of which are decided by the U.S. Patent and Trademark Office and by courts on the basis of cumbersome evidence derived from laboratory notebooks, testimony by coworkers and the like. Yet the U.S. adopted principle gives the first inventor a chance to obtain patent rights over an invention that he first reduced to practice, even though he failed to be the first to rush to the Patent Office to file an application. Such a possibility seems to respond to some fundamental principle of fairness; and even more so in the case of the U.S. where preference for the first inventor is combined with the rule that requires patent applications to be filed by the individual inventor (or inventors), rather than by the corporation which employs them.

Japan, Canada and the Philippines originally adopted the U.S. principle, but eventually went the other way, mainly to put themselves in line with the practice of the rest of the world.[2] But the U.S. has adamantly refused to align itself in this regard. This refusal has continued in spite of the reiterated efforts directed towards international patent harmonization. The U.S. did not make concessions on the first-to-invent issues either in the process which finally led to the adoption of the WIPO-sponsored Patent Law Treaty (discussed since 1985 and signed in 2000) or during Uruguay Round negotiations, which lead to the adoption in 1993 of the GATT/TRIPs Agreement. Even though the U.S. PTO has been cooperating with the EU and Japanese Patent Offices in matters which in fact implicate the choice between first-to-invent and first to rule, this exercise has not led yet to a change of mind in this connection.

The American opposition appears to come from all quarters, including individual inventors, business circles, universities and patent professionals; and seems to have begun quite a long time ago.[3] What are the components which explain the decision of the U.S. to stick to the first-to-invent principle in spite of universal adoption of the opposite principle? Certainly the preservation of a first-to-invent system is driven by the desire to keep a principle believed to be just and fair. But additional considerations may have proved as important. I will list a few.

(1) The first-to-invent principle may assist the original inventor not only against an unrelated party, coming later to the invention but filing earlier. It may also protect the genuine inventor against a variety of forms of misappropriation or even theft, e.g. through industrial espionage, by a business associate, an unfaithful contractor or a partner. Even though a similar protection may also be obtained in first-to-file systems,[4] it is reasonable to assume that a legal environment based on a first-to-invent system may provide the optimal background to make good the claims of the true inventor.

(2) The American patent system grants inventors a "grace period"— whereby description in the year prior to the date of the application does not destroy the novelty of the invention. Such a grace period may be important for inventors operating in a university or public research context, where the imperative to publish is felt as keenly as the drive to obtain patent protection. Even though this may not always be fully perceived, the operation of a grace period is much more germane to a first-to-invent than to a first-to-file system. In fact, in a first-to-file system it is possible to accommodate a grace period for selected disclosures by an inventor (e.g. in academic conferences, proceedings and publications) by providing that these are not deemed novelty destroying; but it is much harder to deal with intermediate disclosures by third parties based on the original disclosure by the inventor itself. It is unclear how these should be treated under a first-to-file system; if it were provided that even third-party disclosures based on the inventor's disclosure were to be assimilated to the latter, still the inventor would have the burden to prove the connection between the two or, more likely, that the latter was "based"— in some meaning of the word—on the former.[5] Moreover, in the event the third-party filed, the original inventor would in most cases have no remedy. The same problems are much better taken care of by a first-to-invent system: proof of prior inventive activity before the third-party disclosure is sufficient under § 102(a) and (b).

(3) Certain applications of the first-to-file principle proved apt to give distinctive advantages to American applicants over their foreign rivals. There are three separate, yet interrelated, advantages:

(i) In the past, and until the coming into force of the 1994 Patent Act implementing TRIPs,[6] under 35 U.S.C. § 104 inventors filing in the U.S. were not permitted to prove a date of invention abroad (*i.e.*, conception and reduction to practice activity) which antedated their foreign filing date. At that time only evidence of prior inventive activity in the U.S. (or, after Dec. 8, 1993, in NAFTA countries) could be used against a third-party patent filing for the same invention in order to prove that the claimed invention was novel in that it was made earlier than the third-party filing itself, while in corresponding circumstances evidence of prior foreign inventive activity did not qualify and was therefore not admitted.

(ii) In the U.S. under § 102(e), a patent X filed at time T, when issued, may invalidate a different patent Y, filed at time T + 1, by disclosing (without claiming) prior art anticipating the Y invention as of the date of the filing of the application of X (and in spite of the fact that patent X had yet to be published). But a so-called Rule 131 Affidavit enables the holder of patent Y to prove that his invention (if not the filing of the corresponding filing) was reduced to practice at a time earlier than the filing of X, and therefore, antedates X. However, if the inventive activity concerning Y was carried out abroad, a Rule 131 Affidavit would not be available.

This list may assist us in giving a more realistic explanation of the reasons why the peculiar U.S. principle has been preserved for such a long time, even though the rest of the world had in the meantime moved in the opposite direction. It may be argued that the principle was looked upon favorably by a variety of constituencies for different reasons: its fairness was highly rated by the (decreasing in numbers, but still vocal) class of individual inventors; its contribution to the dissemination of knowledge was viewed favorably by public sector researchers. It may well be expected that corporate R & D has in turn been more than willing to exploit the competitive edge over foreign rivals afforded by the mechanisms described above. The three groups together have proved a formidable obstacle to legislative innovation in the field. Indeed, they could combine the rhetorical ammunition provided by the former two groups with the negotiating and lobbying clout of the third one.

There seems to be some empirical evidence confirming this reasoning.[7] It would appear that each year there is a quite small number of interference proceedings, up to 100; maybe 25 or 30% of these have success. But it seems that the typical interference proceeding, which is quite expensive as far as legal costs are concerned, is reserved for important patents. Several of those are reported to originate from a foreign filing; so that, if the interference is successful, the world is divided up in two: the U.S. and the rest of the world. A subsequent cross-licensing may well ensue, to overcome the rift.

A few years ago, the U.S. was compelled to introduce several changes to their patent laws with an eye towards harmonization. For the present purposes, it should be noted that § 104, which unequivocally favored inventive activity carried out in the U.S. over foreign inventive activity and thus had been contrary to the National Treatment obligation in the Paris Convention, additionally ran counter Art. 3 of TRIPs. Moreover, as foreign inventive activity in NAFTA countries, after Dec. 8, 1993, had in the meantime obtained a privileged status identical to U.S. activity, also the Most Favored Nation Treatment under Art. 4 of TRIPs was violated. An amendment of to section 104 was therefore mandated.

What remains puzzling to a non-American observer is the way the U.S. decided to comply with their international obligations. A first alternative would have consisted in relinquishing the first-to-invent principle and joining the rest of the world in following the first-to-file principle. It may be argued that such a move would have had various long term-advantages. First, a step towards the uniformity of patentability requirements might have helped the U.S. PTO to play a larger role in global patent procurement.[8]

Second, as a condition to adopt the first-to-file principle, the U.S. might have bargained for reciprocal concessions. Third, U.S. corporations might have profited by advancements toward a seamless patent procurement system, the importance of which is increasing as the global scope of American business abroad is expanding and has in some cases—as in the field of digital technology—become a precondition for success.

But this route has not been followed. The first-to-invent principle is still followed, except as noted above, that under the present text of § 104 evidence of foreign inventive activity has the same value as evidence of U.S. (or NAFTA) activity to prove date of invention. Moreover, a Rule 131 Affidavit may also be used to establish a date of invention abroad. At the same time, a simplified provisional application was introduced, to provide an incentive to earlier filings.

The American system still contains a few provisions that may discriminate against foreign residents. Under Art. 102(a) an invention is not considered novel only if it was "known or used by others" in the U.S.; knowledge or use abroad still being irrelevant for the purpose of destroying novelty.[9] Even after the amendments made by the American Inventors Protection Act of 1999, foreign inventive activity, which as just indicated may preserve patentability of foreign inventions, still may not as a rule be used under Art. 102(g) to attack the validity of a U.S. patent for the same invention.[10] Both of these provisions may well be subject to attack under Arts. 4 and 5 of TRIPs.

Should we conclude that the U.S. sticks to the first-to-invent principle to preserve a few advantages for American inventors? This explanation seems rather unconvincing. The allegedly discriminatory rules might quite easily be modified in a TRIPs-compliant way, without the need to abandon the first-to-invent principle. It may therefore be that the above mentioned advantages of adopting a first-to-file principle have been deemed vague and speculative; and that time is not yet ripe to abandon an old principle and the opportunity for fairness it may still entail.

This is hardly surprising. As old Goethe said: *"es erben sich Gesetze und Rechte/wie eine ewige Narrheit fort,"* "the Eternal Madness of the Past we inherit in the form of old Laws and Acts." Still, it may be questioned whether the present solution is stable: the current negotiations for the Substantive Patent Law Treaty and the ongoing cooperative activity among major Patent Offices around the world, in which the U.S. PTO is intensively taking part, may in the end lead to the disappearance of the "American anomaly" in patent law.

* Professor of Intellectual Property Law, Torino Law School, LL. M. Yale 1976. This *Side Bar* was written specifically for Principles of Patent Law.

1. Except as indicated in note 4, *infra.*

2. For Japan, which changed its principles back in 1921, see H.C. Wegner, *Patent Harmonization*, Sweet & Maxwell,

London, 1993, 44; for Canada, which did so in 1980, see G.F. HENDERSON, *An Introduction to Patent Law,* in (G.F. HENDERSON-H.P. KNOPFF-J.R. RUDOLPH eds.), *Patent Law of Canada,* Carswell, Scarborough, Ontario, 1994, 14. Even the Philippines made the change as of Jan. 1, 1998: see M. NOLFF, *TRIPs, PCT and Global Patent Procurement,* Kluwer Law International, 2001, 159.

3. *See, e.g.* H.C. WEGNER, *Patent Harmonization,* above at note 2, at 55, indicates that the *Report of the Commission on the Patents System, "To Promote the Progress * * * of Useful Arts" in an Age of Exploding Technology,* Government Printing Office 1966, met opposition both by grass-roots organisations and by business circles. On opposition to the first-to-file feature of WIPO led patent harmonization efforts by American patent professionals see M. NOLFF, *TRIPs, PCT and Global Patent Procurement, supra* note 2, at 167.

4. See Art. 55(1)(a) of the European Patent Convention (EPC), providing that in the event of evident abuse towards the inventor a disclosure shall be disregarded, on condition that the original inventor files a European patent application within 6 months and Art. 61 determining the impact of a national Court's final and binding decision as to the ownership of an invention on a European patent application or grant.

5. It has been proposed by M. NOLFF, *TRIPs, PCT and Global Patent Procurement, supra* note 3, at 163 to amend Art. 27(1) TRIPs to provide for a grace period for "disclosures made directly or *indirectly* by applicant during the 12 months preceding the date of filing" of the application. It would appear to me

that the notion of an indirect disclosure is too vague: does it cover disclosures improving on the original invention? Disclosures generalizing more limited teachings of the original disclosure? What to say if inventor A discloses to a conference to which B assists; and B in turn refers to the original disclosure in a subsequent conference to which C assists, prompting C to teach his class about this recent development? For a full treatment of the issue see S.J.R. BOSTYN, *International Harmonization of the Patent System,* II in 27 *Journal of The Japanese Group of the AIPPI,* 2002, 384 ff.

6. Pub. L. No. 103–465, 108 Stat. 4809.

7. The data reported in this paragraph are drawn from H.C. WEGNER, *Patent Harmonization,* above at note 2, 43, 56 ff.

8. It might have been envisaged, for instance, that a search by the US PTO might have automatic recognition by other important patent offices, as the EPO and Japanese Patent Office.

9. On this issue see C.A. NARD, *In Defense of Geographic Disparity.* 88 MINN. L. REV. 221 (2003).

10. See the *Hilmer* cases discussed in this chapter. It should be added that, even after the adoption of the American Inventors Protection Act (AIPA), a foreign priority date under the Paris Convention of a U.S. patent cannot serve as prior art date; rather, it is only a PCT application published in English and designating the U.S. which can serve as prior art as of its international filing date (which is to be no more than 12 months from the original priority). In other words: AIPA does not suppress *Hilmer* I and II.

The following excerpt from an article on the so-called "registration theory" of patents provides a useful discussion of an over-arching normative, or policy, basis for the prior art rules. It is hoped that this single policy based approach is more helpful to students than sheer memorization by showing how these rules work together and make sense as a set. In addition, this excerpt provides a practical schematic chart to help show how a patent claim may be easily evaluated against the prior art. Versions of this schematic claim chart can also be useful in determinations of obviousness, as discussed in Chapter 5, and infringement, as discussed in Chapter 8.

The Case for Registering Patents and the Law and Economics of Present Patent–Obtaining Rules

F. Scott Kieff.
45 B.C. L. Rev. 55 (2003).

1. Novelty and Bar

The patent system's patent-obtaining rules relating to the prior art begin with those in § 102 of the statute, which relate to novelty and bar.[123] "Anticipation by the prior art" is the phrase in patent law used to describe the case where a patent claim is directed to subject matter that is not new.[124] "Statutorily barred" is the phrase in patent law used to describe the case where a patent claim is directed to subject matter that, even if new at the time of invention, was exposed to the public more than a year before the application was filed.[125] The registration view elucidates why it makes sense for the patent system to have evolved these doctrines in all their detail.[126]

In accordance with the registration view, printed publications describing a technology count as prior art under the novelty provisions because publicly available documents are good evidence of investment by their authors and of something on which others could rely.[127] Any printed publication will count, even if in a foreign country, as long as it is verifiably the type of publication on which a member of the public could rely.[128] Indeed, even pending patent applications that later issue as patents, but

---

123. 35 U.S.C. § 102 (2000) ("Conditions for patentability; novelty and loss of right to patent"). The mention in § 101 of the word "new" has not been read to provide any separate novelty requirement. See [P.J. Federico, *Commentary on the New Patent Act, in* Title 35, United States Code Annotated 1 (West 1954), *reprinted in* 75 J. Pat. & Trademark Off. Soc'y 161 (1993)], at 178 ("The general part of the Committee Report states that section 102 'may be said to describe the statutory novelty required for patentability, and includes, in effect, an amplification and definition of "new" in section 101' "); *see also In re* Bergy, 596 F.2d 952, 960 (1979) ("Notwithstanding the words 'new and useful' in § 101, the invention is not examined under that statute for novelty because that is not the statutory scheme of things or the long-established administrative practice."), *dismissed as moot*, 444 U.S. 1028 (1980).

124. The maxim setting forth the so-called "classic infringement test for anticipation," which also applies to analysis under the statutory bar, is "[t]hat which will infringe if later, will anticipate, if earlier." *See* Donald S. Chisum, Craig A. Nard, Herbert F. Schwartz, Pauline Newman, & F. Scott Kieff, Principles of Patent Law (2d ed. 2001), at 414 (citing Knapp v. Morss, 150 U.S. 221 (1893)). For more on how this test is applied in practice, see *infra* notes 19–28 and accompanying text.

125. For a discussion of the bar, which also operates as a one-year grace period for filing, see *infra* notes 137–140.

126. *Compare* [rent dissipation and reward theories].

127. *See* 35 U.S.C. § 102(a)–(b) (referring to printed publications).

128. *See In re* Hall, 781 F.2d 897, 898–900 (Fed.Cir.1986) (counting a single cataloged student thesis at Frieburg University in Germany as prior art because it was, inter alia, physically available to the public); *In re* Cronyn, 890 F.2d 1158, 1161 (Fed.Cir.1989) (not counting three student theses at an American university as prior art, even though they were physically accessible to the public, because there was no evidence they were logically accessible to the interested public by, for example, being indexed in the library's subject catalog). Under the registration theory these publications should count as prior art because they might lead to third-party reliance, not because they might somehow fairly be said to have been available to the patentee.

that are not yet published, count as prior art as of their filing date because
their inventors have invested in the verifiable contents of these govern-
ment-stored documents and those in confidential relationships with their
inventors could rely on them as well.[129]

Similarly, uses of a technology only count as prior art if corroborated
by someone other than the one claiming prior invention because verifiable
public use may induce investment in the technology by observers of this
use.[130] Although § 102(a) only expressly provides, in pertinent part, that
the invention must not have been "known or used by others," the word
"public" has been read into that statutory language through case law.[131]
Use that is not public, yet also is not abandoned, suppressed, or concealed,
may also count as prior art under § 102(f) and § 102(g), but only if
corroborated by evidence other than inventor testimony.[132]

---

129. *See* Alexander Milburn Co. v. Davis–Bournonville Co., 270 U.S. 390, 399–402 (1926)
(Holmes, J.) (counting so-called secret prior art as prior art as of the application's filing date).
The present version of this rule is codified in § 102(e)(2). *See* 35 U.S.C. § 102(e)(2). For the
same reasons, an application filed in foreign patent offices will also count as prior art as of its
filing date with one of the international Patent Cooperation Treaty-designated patent offices,
if filed according to the procedural rules of the treaty, and as long as the application is
eventually published in English and designates that it should be sent to the United States
Patent Office. *Id.* Also for the same reasons, under § 102(e)(1), prior art effect is extended to
pending applications that do not issue as a patent but do get published under the rule of
publishing eighteen months after filing, which was part of the 1999 American Inventors
Protection Act and is codified in § 122(b). *Id.* §§ 102(e)(1), 122(b). Applications not published
pursuant to § 122(b), however, such as those abandoned, do not count as prior art. The
authors of these documents are able to maintain their information as a trade secret but the
documents themselves will not preclude patentability for others. To be sure, the use by these
authors may in certain circumstances preclude patentability under § 102(a) or (g), as discussed *infra* at notes 130–132 and accompanying text.

130. The registration protects against the risk of these investments being later subject
to a patent right to exclude by enforcing the rule that they destroy patentability.

131. Gayler v. Wilder, 51 U.S. (10 How.) 476, 494–98 (1850) (not counting use of a
technology relating to a safe as prior art unless it is accessible to the public). *See* 35 U.S.C.
§ 102(a).

132. Section 102(f) is the provision governing cases of derivation, where the party
claiming the patent right derived the claimed information from someone else. 35 U.S.C.
§ 102(f); *see* Gambro Lundia AB v. Baxter Healthcare Corp., 110 F.3d 1573, 1576–78
(Fed.Cir.1997) (holding that § 102(f) prevents patentability if there can be shown to be both
prior, corroborated, conception of the claimed invention, and its communication to the one
claiming to be the first inventor). Where the prior inventor turns out to have sought its own
patent, the Patent Office conducts something called an "interference proceeding," which is the
quasi-litigation process initiated when a patent application claims the same subject matter as
another application or an issued patent to determine who is the first inventor. Section 102(g)
is generally understood to govern interference proceedings but also has been held to be a
provision under which information may be treated as prior art just like under the other
subsections of § 102. *See* 35 U.S.C. § 102(g). *See generally* Donald S. Chisum, Craig A. Nard,
Herbert F. Schwartz, Pauline Newman, & F. Scott Kieff, Principles of Patent Law (2d ed.
2001), at 441–51 (describing evolution of case law treating 35 U.S.C. § 102(g) as a provision
under which prior use may count as prior art even if not public, as long as it is not abandoned,
suppressed, or concealed, as well as the amount of evidence needed to satisfy that provision).
For more on the rules governing priority disputes, see *infra* Part III.A.3. Where the prior
inventor turns out to have been outside the United States, the rules become more complicated,
as discussed *infra* Part III.A.4. For more on why the use of priority of invention as a test to
determine who wins a patent right as between two or more claimants makes more sense under
the registration and commercialization theories than the use of filing date, because when

Verifiable public use or sale sufficiently in advance of patent application filing, even if by the one seeking a patent, can count as prior art against that application under certain circumstances because it may induce investment in the technology by observers of this use.[133] For this reason, the statutory bar provisions treat sale or use in public by either the inventor or a third party as prior art against the inventor's claim to a patent.[134]

The patent system even protects the inventor's own investments to some extent through allowance of a one-year grace period in which to file a patent application before the on-sale and public use bars are triggered. This is important because a patent system in which there is no grace period may provide incentives for decreased rate of disclosure of new technologies, and a decrease in the overall value of patents. The decreased rate of disclosure under a system lacking a grace period would be due to the need to keep potentially patentable information unpublished before filing the patent application.[135] The decrease in overall value of patents would be due to the fear of unknown but unavoidable pre-filing disclosures lurking in the history of every patent.[136]

But the inventor's own investments have to be balanced against the reasonable reliance interests of others. For this reason, the grace period is limited to one year, which allows others to rely on essentially any public evidence of a technology that is beyond the time of the grace period.[137] As soon as an inventor's use of the technology becomes available to the

---

invention date is used it is more likely that a valid patent claim will emerge than when filing date is used, see *infra* notes 183–186 and accompanying text.

133. *See* 35 U.S.C. § 102(b). The policy goal of protecting investment has been recognized in the case law associated with this prior art provision. *See* General Elec. Co. v. United States, 654 F.2d 55, 61 (Ct. Cl. 1981) ("First, there is a policy against removing inventions from the public [that] the public has justifiably come to believe are freely available to all as a consequence of prolonged sales activity.").

Often described as a statutory bar to the patenting of inventions publicized for more than a year, this provision operates to provide a one-year grace period for publicity that will not bar patentability. The grace period entered the U.S. patent system in 1839 as a period of "grace" lasting two years. Act of March 3, 1839, 5 Stat. 353. The period was shortened to one year in 1939. Act of August 5, 1939, Pub. L. No. 76–288, 53 Stat. 1212. It remains so in the present 35 U.S.C. § 102(b).

Not all patent systems in the world provide a statutory grace period, although it is not exactly clear whether most systems end up providing one through case law. *See generally* Joseph Straus, Grace Period and the European and International Patent Law (2001) (study commissioned by the European Patent Organization to examine whether European patent law should provide a pre-filing grace period) (collecting sources).

134. *See* Baxter Int'l, Inc. v. COBE Labs., 88 F.3d 1054, 1058–59 (Fed.Cir.1996) (third-party use may raise statutory bar).

135. *See* Straus, *supra* note 133, at 80–81, 93 (discussing incentives to suppress publication under a regime of no grace period).

136. *Id.* at 95–96 (discussing decrease in value of patents under absolute novelty regimes, which do not have a grace period).

137. Under the registration theory, the specific amount of time is arbitrary as long as it is fixed and knowable ex ante and as long as it is both long enough to allow some grace-period effect and not long enough to unduly frustrate investment in recently public technologies. For some history of the various grace periods, see *supra* note 133.

public,[138] or is on sale at any stage past when it is "ready for patenting," the clock on the one-year window begins.[139] The subsequent one year provides time for the inventor to decide whether to prepare and file a patent application, and then to take these steps if elected.[140]

Taken together, these rules about what counts as prior art allow every patent claim to be judged as of its "critical date" against a piece of prior art's "effective date."[141] The critical date is either the verifiable date of invention, or one year before the application's filing date, depending upon whether the invention is being analyzed for anticipation or bar.[142] The effective date is the date the piece of prior art is allowed to count as prior art, as discussed above.[143]

Under § 102, patentability is precluded if any single item that is determined to count as prior art under any single subsection of the statute is found to fully disclose the claimed invention.[144] Importantly, case law has provided a remarkably easy test for determining whether an invention is fully disclosed for purposes of this analysis, which can be seen through the use of the schematic claim chart in Table 1, below.[145,146]

Table 1: Analysis Under § 102

	PAR_1
E_1	✓
E_2	✓
$E_{...}$	✓
E_n	✓
E_*	✓

---

138. *See* Egbert v. Lippmann, 104 U.S. 333, 333–38 (1882) (holding use even in a private undergarment, here corset steels, can count as prior art). *Compare* Metallizing Eng'g Co. v. Kenyon Bearing & Auto Parts Co., 153 F.2d 516, 517–20 (2d Cir.1946) (Hand, J.) (use will count if it is commercial), *with* Elizabeth v. Pavement Co., 97 U.S. 126, 134 (1878) (use will not count if merely experimental). To whatever extent potential third-party reliance is a serious theoretical matter, actual third-party public use as in *Baxter*, 88 F.3d at 1058–59, counts as prior art because it shows actual reliance.

139. Pfaff v. Wells Elecs., 525 U.S. 55, 67–68 (1998) (holding the year begins when the technology is "subject to a commercial offer for sale" and "ready for patenting").

140. The importance of taking the time to prepare a good application is discussed *infra* Part III.A.3.

141. Donald S. Chisum, Craig A. Nard, Herbert F. Schwartz, Pauline Newman, & F. Scott Kieff, Principles of Patent Law (2d ed. 2001), at 326 (providing sample analysis using these terms).

142. Anticipation occurs when the claimed invention is found to have been in the art that existed prior to the putative invention. *See supra* notes 118–132 and accompanying text. A statutory bar occurs when the application is not filed within one year of a bar-triggering event. *See supra* notes 133–139 and accompanying text.

143. This is either the date of use, publication, or filing, depending upon which part of § 102 is triggered. *See supra* notes 118–132 and accompanying text.

144. *See supra* note 124 (discussing basic statement of test for anticipation).

145. *See infra* notes 146–150 (discussing application of this test).

146. E_1 through E_n represent the elements of the claim arbitrarily assigned numbers 1 through n. E_* represents enablement of the entire claim. PAR_1 represents any single prior art reference, such as a journal article, sample product, student thesis, etc.

Table 1 compares the elements of a stylized claim against the prior art for a determination of potential unpatentability or invalidity under § 102.[147] The substantive requirement for determining no valid patent claim under § 102 is triggered only if a single prior art reference discloses, either expressly or under principles of inherency, each and every element of the claim, plus enablement.[148] When mapped onto this table, this means that a proper holding of invalidity will only lie if a check mark can be found as a matter of fact for every row.[149] And to achieve a check mark there must be admissible evidence that as a matter of fact the pertinent content is present in the piece of prior art.[150]

---

147. The term invalidity refers to the failure of a claim in an issued and successfully examined patent to satisfy one of the substantive patent-obtaining rules. The term unpatentability refers to the failure of a claim in a patent application to satisfy one of the substantive patent-obtaining rules. These terms are interchangeable if operating under a soft-look system like the registration model that does not involve any examination.

The representation of a claim as a listing of its several elements in claim charts like Table 1 has become so common in patent cases that the local rules of some courts that hear many patent cases, like the Northern District of California, have for some time required their use. Donald S. Chisum, Craig A. Nard, Herbert F. Schwartz, Pauline Newman, & F. Scott Kieff, Principles of Patent Law (2d ed. 2001), at 848–49 (discussing local rules for claim charts). The identification of these elements turns largely on the interpretation, or construction, of a patent claim, which is treated as a matter of law for decision by the court, and which is the first step in any analysis of either validity or infringement because the claim must be construed the same for both purposes. *See generally id.* at 829–73 (discussing the substantive and procedural law of claim interpretation after the Supreme Court decision in Markman v. Westview Instruments, Inc., 517 U.S. 370 (1996)). The great degree of debate over the law of claim construction itself injects a degree of uncertainty into this otherwise relatively crisp analysis. Recent empirical work by Wagner suggests that this uncertainty may lessen over time as the Federal Circuit develops predictable trends in its case law. *See* R. Polk Wagner & Lee Petherbridge, *Is the Federal Circuit Succeeding? An Empirical Assessment of Judicial Performance*, 152 U. Penn. L. Rev. 1105 (discussing empirical work relating to trends in the Federal Circuit's law of claim construction).

148. *See* Minn. Mining & Mfg. v. Johnson & Johnson, 976 F.2d 1559, 1565 (Fed.Cir. 1992) (Rich, J.) (invalidity under § 102 is "a question of fact, and one who seeks such a finding must show that each element of the claim in issue is found, either expressly or under principles of inherency, in a single prior art reference"); *In re* Paulsen, 30 F.3d 1475, 1479 (Fed.Cir.1994) ("In addition, the reference must be enabling and describe the applicant's claimed invention sufficiently to have placed it in possession of a person of ordinary skill in the field of the invention."); *see also In re* Robertson, 169 F.3d 743, 745 (Fed.Cir.1999) ("To establish inherency, the extrinsic evidence 'must make clear that the missing descriptive matter is necessarily present in the thing described in the reference, and that it would be so recognized by persons of ordinary skill. Inherency, however, may not be established by probabilities or possibilities. The mere fact that a certain thing may result from a given set of circumstances is not sufficient.' " (citation omitted) (quoting Cont'l Can Co. v. Monsanto Co., 948 F.2d 1264, 1268, 1269 (Fed.Cir.1991))). The inherency and enablement doctrines make sense under the registration theory because a disclosure may induce third-party reliance based upon its ability to enable those in the art to practice its teachings, even if those teachings do not contain all the words that might appear in some patent claim. What matters for purposes of such reliance is substance, not form.

149. This represents the presence of each element in the claim, plus enablement, which as discussed in the case law *supra* note 148, is required for a finding of invalidity under § 102.

150. As discussed in the case law, *supra* note 148, invalidity under § 102 requires the prior art disclosure to be in a single reference.

* * *

3. First-to-Invent

The patent system's rules governing priority contests between two or more claimants to a patent right protect investment by awarding the patent to the one who was first to invent, not first to file.[183] As recognized by the commercialization theory, a shift to a first-to-file system may lead to an increased likelihood that neither party in a priority dispute will remain with a valid patent because the increased incentive to file early that may operate to make one party a winner on priority might also have caused that party to file an application with inadequate disclosure.[184]

In contrast, under a first-to-invent system there is less of an incentive to rush to file because priority is not determined by filing and, as a result, there is a lower likelihood that the winner on priority will be left with a patent that fails to meet the disclosure requirements.[185] The first-to-invent

---

183. Whereas priority under a first-to-file system is awarded to the application that is filed first regardless of priority of invention, under a first-to-invent system like the present patent system, priority is awarded to the first inventor. *See* F. Scott Kieff, *Property Rights and Property Rules for Commercializing Inventions*, 85 Minn. L. Rev. 697 (2001), at 749–50 (discussing differences between these two types of priority regimes and collecting sources).

184. As explained by the commercialization theory when discussing incentive to file early and its interaction with the disclosure requirements:

> A hastily filed application is more likely to be found invalid for nonenablement or lack of written description under recent Federal Circuit case law. *See* Amgen Inc. v. Chugai Pharm. Co., 927 F.2d 1200, 1213–18 (Fed.Cir.1991) (applying the statutory requirement that the text of the patent application as filed contain sufficient disclosure to enable one in the art to make and use whatever is covered by patent claims as eventually issued and applying separate written description requirement to claims in the field of biotechnology); Vas–Cath Inc. v. Mahurkur, 935 F.2d 1555, 1563–67 (Fed.Cir.1991) (holding that the statute also requires the text of the patent application as filed to satisfy the separate and distinct written description requirement so as to reasonably convey to those in the art exactly what is covered by the patent claims as eventually issued); Amgen v. Chugai, 927 F.2d 1200, 1213–18 (applying separate written description requirement to claims in the field of biotechnology); Fiers v. Revel, 984 F.2d 1164, 1170–71 (Fed.Cir.1993) (solidifying the court's position on a separate written description requirement); Regents of the Univ. of Cal. v. Eli Lilly & Co., 119 F.3d 1559, 1566–69 (Fed.Cir.1997) (further solidifying the court's position on a separate written description requirement); Lockwood v. Am. Airlines, Inc., 107 F.3d 1565, 1572 (Fed.Cir.1997) (applying the same written description requirement to the field of computer software); Gentry Gallery, Inc. v. Berkline Corp., 134 F.3d 1437, 1479–80 (Fed.Cir.1998) (indicating that the written description requirement is not limited to complex technologies but applies equally to simple technologies, like sofa recliners). . . .

F. Scott Kieff, *Property Rights and Property Rules for Commercializing Inventions*, 85 Minn. L. Rev. 697 (2001), at 750 n.239; *see also* S. Leslie Misrock & Stephen S. Rabinowitz, *Side Bar: The Inventor's Gamble: Written Description and Prophetic Claiming of Biotechnology Inventions*, *in* Donald S. Chisum, Craig A. Nard, Herbert F. Schwartz, Pauline Newman, & F. Scott Kieff, Principles of Patent Law (2d ed. 2001), at 319, 319–22 (discussing the application of the separate written description requirement to claims in the field of biotechnology).

185. The reasoning here is similar to that for the one-year grace period. *See supra* note 140 and accompanying text (discussing the importance of the grace period to allow time to file

system thereby at least protects the investments of one of the claimants.[186] In addition, first-to-file may lead to a winner-take-all mindset for those seeking patents. This, in turn, may cause a reduction in the beneficial inducing power of the reward because each potential claimant may find the possibility of winning the race to be too low. Alternatively, it may cause the harmful, rent-dissipating power to increase as the increase in uncertainty causes even more individuals to gamble on winning the race.[187]

A first-to-invent regime does increase litigation frequency by bringing priority disputes to available contests, but this is beneficial because such disputes can also reach issues of validity.[188] The costs of determining validity in such a proceeding are likely to be less than in a hard-look examination because the opponent in such a priority dispute is like the alleged infringer in litigation in its ability to more cheaply obtain and evaluate the information needed to determine validity.[189] The registration theory thereby explains the persistence of the first-to-invent aspect of the present patent system despite harmonization efforts to have the United States match the rest of the world, which uses first-to-file.[190]

4. Prior Foreign Use

Like the rules governing novelty generally, the rules about prior foreign use make sense under the registration theory as tools for protecting

---

a properly drafted application when measured under the disclosure requirements of § 112). For more on the disclosure requirements, see *infra* Part III.B.

186. The investments of the one who wins the priority dispute are protected. This thereby provides for some commercialization benefit, which is important under the commercialization theory, and some protection of investment-backed expectations on the part of at least one of the parties, which is important under the registration theory. Furthermore, it is generally agreed that under the present system most interference proceedings are won by the first to file anyway. *See* Edwards v. Strazzabosco, 58 U.S.P.Q.2d (BNA) 1836, 1840 (Board of Patent Appeals and Interferences 2001) (approximate 75% success rate for the first to file); Charles R.B. Macedo, *First-to-File: Is American Adoption of the International Standard in Patent Law Worth the Price?*, 18 Am. Intell. Prop. L. Ass'n Q.J. 193, 217 (1990) (same); Gerald J. Mossinghoff, *The U.S. First-to-Invent System Has Provided No Advantage to Small Entities*, 84 J. Pat. & Trademark Off. Soc'y 425, 427 (2002) (between 1983 and 2000, the first to file won 1917 of the 2858 interference cases). *But see* Charles L. Gholz, *A Critique of Recent Opinions in Patent Interferences*, 84 J. Pat. & Trademark Off. Soc'y 163, 181 (2002) (suggesting that the U.S. Patent and Trademark Office ("PTO") data reports that the first to file has recently been winning in only 52.5% of the cases).

187. *See* F. Scott Kieff, *Property Rights and Property Rules for Commercializing Inventions*, 85 Minn. L. Rev. 697 (2001), at 711 (discussing Mark F. Grady & Jay I. Alexander, *Patent Law and Rent Dissipation*, 78 Va. L. Rev. 305, 305–10 (1992), and the problem of rent-seeking and rent-dissipating effects in patent law).

188. *See* Charles L. Gholz, *Side Bar: Interferences*, *in* Donald S. Chisum, Craig A. Nard, Herbert F. Schwartz, Pauline Newman, & F. Scott Kieff, Principles of Patent Law (2d ed. 2001), at 511–13 (describing the interference process and its ability to reach issues of validity).

189. The parties to the priority dispute either have the information relating to the prior art themselves because their own work is being used as prior art against each other or they at least have the same if not greater incentives to find that information as does an ordinary defendant in a litigation who is serving the screening function identified by the commercialization theory. *See supra* notes 59–64 and accompanying text (discussing the screening function).

190. *See* F. Scott Kieff, *Property Rights and Property Rules for Commercializing Inventions*, 85 Minn. L. Rev. 697 (2001), at 748–50 (discussing harmonization efforts in relation to first-to-file and first-to-invent).

verifiable investment-backed expectations.[191] For most of the past century, prior use that was outside of this country would not count for purposes of either staking a claim to priority for purposes of obtaining patent rights in a priority contest or defeating patent rights in a challenge to validity.[192] But since 1994, uses that occur in countries that are members of the North American Free Trade Agreement ("NAFTA") or the World Trade Organization ("WTO") will be available when seeking to obtain a patent in a priority dispute against another claimant—as a sword—but not when seeking to defeat a patent owned by another—as a shield.[193]

By making prior foreign use that occurs within a country with whom we are a trading partner under either of these treaties available to support a claim to a patent, these revisions protect those investment-backed expectations made abroad that are sufficiently serious to have led to the filing of a patent application.[194] By leaving all other foreign prior use unavailable to defeat a patent, these revisions protect the investments of the one who filed the patent application and disregard those of others whose use is not corroborated by a printed publication.[195] The registration theory's focus on verifiable evidence of potential investment-backed expectations thereby explains what may otherwise appear to be an intricate effort to favor domestic interests.

SIDE BAR

Interferences

Charles L. Gholz*

Your professor may tell you that interferences are priority contests. If so, don't you believe her (or him)! That's what they were in historical origin, but that's not what they are today. Today they are *inter partes* proceedings before highly skilled administrative patent judges in which the parties can raise *any* validity or unenforceability issue that they could raise in a patent infringement action. That includes unpatentability under 35 U.S.C. § 102(g) (*i.e.*, lack of priority), but it also includes unpatentability under 35 U.S.C. § 102(f) (*i.e.*, derivation from an opposing party or a stranger to the interference), all of the other sections of 35 U.S.C. § 102, 35 U.S.C. § 103, 35 U.S.C. §§ 135(b) and (c), etc., etc., etc. The overall

---

191. *See supra* note 112 and accompanying text (discussing registration theory on prior art rules and the goal of protecting investment-backed expectations based on objective verifiable evidence).

192. This is in contrast with the impact of prior use as discussed *supra* notes 130–132 and accompanying text (discussing rules relating to prior use).

193. *See* 35 U.S.C. §§ 102(g), 104 (2000) (as amended by Uruguay Round Agreements Act, Pub. L. No. 103–465, § 531(a), 108 Stat. 4809, 4982–83 (1994); North American Free Trade Agreement Implementation Act, Pub. L. No. 103–182, § 331, 107 Stat. 2057, 2113–14 (1993)). For more on the operation of these new provisions, see Donald S. Chisum, Craig A. Nard, Herbert F. Schwartz, Pauline Newman, & F. Scott Kieff, Principles of Patent Law (2d ed. 2001), at 489–91 (discussing legislative changes and explaining their practical impact).

194. *See supra* note 112 (discussing registration theory on prior art rules and the goal of protecting investment-backed expectations based on objective verifiable evidence).

195. *See supra* notes 127–128 and accompanying text (printed publications anywhere in the world may be available as prior art because they are verifiable).

effect of that is that a company can use the interference system to take down a competitor's patent, to prevent a competitor's patent from ever issuing, or to defend its own patent or patent application in a jury-free environment, before technically trained triers of fact who understand the patent law—at approximately a tenth of the cost of accomplishing the same result in a patent infringement action and with considerably more certainty of obtaining a rational result.[1] Moreover, the result obtained before the board is binding in a subsequent patent infringement action against one's erstwhile opponent in the interference![2]

What transformed patent interferences from proceedings of limited scope to the proceedings of choice for rational parties to determine validity and unenforceability was Pub. L. 98–622, §§ 105 and 202, 98 Stat. 3385–86 (Nov. 8, 1984). That statute authorized the board to "determine questions of patentability." At first there was considerable confusion over how the board would go about doing that. *Chester v. Miller*, 906 F.2d 1574 (Fed.Cir.1990),[3] suggested that the Federal Circuit would handle patentability issues arising in an interference just as it handles patentability issues arising during ex parte prosecution, creating no troublesome distinctions between how such issues are handled in ex parte and inter partes appeals from the PTO. However, the board developed a labor saving device: it would look at the patentability of each count, considered as if it were a claim, and, if it held that the count was unpatentable, it would then hold that all of the claims designated as corresponding to the count were likewise unpatentable without considering them on a claim-by-claim basis. In *In re Van Geuns*, 988 F.2d 1181 (Fed.Cir.1993),[4] the court partially (but only partially!) approved that labor saving device, indicating that the claims designated as corresponding to a count fall with the count if the count is anticipated by the prior art, but that, if the subject matter defined by the count would only have been obvious from the prior art, the patentability of the claims designated as corresponding to the count had to be determined on a claim-by-claim basis. That holding was a disaster. However, the Federal Circuit ignored *Van Geuns* in *Eiselstein v. Frank*, 52 F.3d 1035 (Fed.Cir.1995),[5] and, in *Rowe v. Dror*, 112 F.3d 473 (Fed.Cir.1997),[6] it emphatically required treatment of patentability issues arising in interferences on a claim-by-claim basis in *all* cases.

One of the biggest open questions in interference law now is whether a party against which a judgment is going to be entered has a right to stay in the interference to present evidence to take down its opponent's claims. *Wu v. Wang*, 129 F.3d 1237 (Fed.Cir.1997),[7] says that it is not an abuse of discretion for the board to allow such a party to stay in an interference for that purpose, but it does not say the converse—i.e., that it *would* be an abuse of discretion for the board to enter judgment against such a party before it has the opportunity to introduce the evidence needed to takes its opponent down as well.[8] Obviously, if the court says that, it will strengthen the effectiveness of interferences as a substitute for infringement litigation—and per contra per contra. Thus, I hope that we will have a case saying that by the time that the second edition of this case book comes out!

Your professor also may say that interference law is dry and boring. It is not! It is a fascinating, dynamic, important area of patent law. Come on in!

* Partner in and head of the Interference Section of Oblon, Spivak, McClelland, Maier & Neustadt, P.C., Arlington, Virginia. The views expressed herein are solely those of the author and do not necessarily reflect those of the firm or its clients. This *SIDE BAR* was written specially for PRINCIPLES OF PATENT LAW.

1. This is particularly important because, as I hope that your professor will have explained to you, (1) our current reexamination system is dysfunctional and nearly worthless and (2) the proposed amendments to the reexamination system, while some improvement, will not begin to make reexaminations as useful as interferences for taking down a competitor's patent rights. See generally Kelber, *To Reexamine is Humanly Possible—To Interfere is Divine* in the proceedings of the American Bar Association's Section of Intellectual Property Law's annual continuing legal education program for 1997.

2. *See* generally Gholz, *Collateral Estoppel Effect of Decisions by the Board of Patent Interferences*, 65 JPOS 67 (1983), and see particularly *Coakwell v. United States*, 292 F.2d 918 (Ct.Cl.1961)

(which is, of course, binding precedent in the Federal Circuit).

3. *Chester* is discussed in Gholz, *A Critique of Recent Opinions of the Federal Circuit in Patent Interferences*, 73 JPTOS 700 (1991) at 703–05.

4. *Van Geuns* is criticized in Gholz, *A Critique of Recent Opinions of the Federal Circuit in Patent Interferences*, 76 JPTOS 649 (1994) at 654–57.

5. *Eiselstein* is discussed in Gholz, *A Critique of Recent Opinions of the Federal Circuit in Patent Interferences*, 78 JPTOS 550 (1996) at 558–59.

6. *Rowe* is discussed in Gholz, *A Critique of Recent Opinions of the Federal Circuit in Patent Interferences*, 80 JPTOS 321 (1998) at 342–43.

7. *Wang* is discussed in Gholz, *A Critique of Recent Opinions of the Federal Circuit in Patent Interferences*, 80 JPTOS 321 (1998) at 354–58.

8. The law is clear that the board can enter a judgment against both or all parties. In fact, that is a fairly common result.

CHAPTER FIVE

NONOBVIOUSNESS

As we refrain from granting patents on those inventions that are not new, we must also refrain from granting patents on those inventions which would arise spontaneously, given the need or desire for them, as the yelp of the dog surely follows from stepping on his tail.

Judge Giles S. Rich[1]

[A]ll improvement is not invention, and entitled to protection as such.

Justice William Strong[2]

INTRODUCTION

In addition to the other requirements for patentability such as novelty and utility, an invention must also be nonobvious. The nonobviousness requirement, embodied in section 103 of the patent code, lies at the heart of our patent system and, in many ways, is the most significant obstacle that a patent applicant faces. Indeed, it has been called the "final gatekeeper of the patent system."[3] Why do we have a nonobviousness requirement? Although the novelty requirement of § 102 casts a watchful eye over the public domain so as to prevent a patent applicant from obtaining protection on an invention that a person of ordinary skill in the art could retrieve from the technical literature or other available source, the test for novelty is rather confining in that each and every limitation of the claimed invention must be present in a single prior art reference.[4] The nonobviousness requirement, on the other hand, cast a broader net and recognizes that the limitations of a claimed invention may be scattered throughout more than one prior art reference, and it would be "obvious" to a person of ordinary skill in the art to assemble these elements in the form of the claimed invention. In such a situation, it could reasonably be said that the claimed invention was already in the public domain, albeit not in one single prior art reference.[5] Thus, even if an invention is novel, it may nevertheless

---

1. Giles S. Rich, *The Vague Concept of "Invention" as Replaced by Section 103 of the 1952 Act* [or the "Kettering Speech"] in NONOBVIOUSNESS—THE ULTIMATE CONDITION OF PATENTABILITY 1:401, 1:404 (John Witherspoon ed. 1980). The *Vague Concept of Invention* was the title of the "Charles F. Kettering" speech delivered by Giles Rich in 1964 at the Award Dinner of the Eighth Annual Public Conference of The Patent, Trademark, and Copyright Research Institute. Judge Rich received the Institute's "Charles F. Kettering Award for Meritorious Work in Patent, Trademark, and Copyright Research and Education."

2. *Pearce v. Mulford*, 102 U.S. 112, 118 (1880).

3. ROBERT PATRICK MERGES & JOHN FITZGERALD DUFFY, PATENT LAW AND POLICY 612 (4th ed. 2007).

4. *See* Chapter Four.

5. *See* ROCHELLE COOPER DREYFUSS and ROBERTA ROSENTHAL KWALL, INTELLECTUAL PROPERTY 648 (1996).

497

fail to meet the statutory requirements if it is not significantly different from the prior art.[6] Note that the claimed invention must be significantly *different*, not necessarily better, than the prior art to satisfy § 103. As a co-author of § 103 frequently admonished, we must avoid "the unsound notion that to be patentable an invention must be better than the prior art."[7] In this regard, Judge, soon to be Chief Justice, Warren Burger, stated, quoting Judge Giles Rich:

> Progress is most effectively promoted by protecting those who enrich the art as well as those who improve it. Even though their inventions are not as good as what already exists, such inventors are not being rewarded for standing still or for retrogressing, but for having invented something. The system is not concerned with the individual inventor's progress but only with what is happening to technology.[8]

But how do we know when an invention is obvious or nonobvious? This question, which is much more complex than meets the eye, is the focus of this chapter. But first a little history, which hopefully will shed some light on just how complex and difficult an obviousness inquiry can be.

The nonobviousness requirement did not originate with the 1952 Patent Act, for it is considered to have been a common law principle since 1850. In that year, the Supreme Court decided *Hotchkiss v. Greenwood* (the "doorknob case").[9] In *Hotchkiss*, the invention related to an old method of making doorknobs whereby the doorknob had a certain shaped hole for the fastening of a shank. The only difference was that the inventor substituted a clay or porcelain knob for a metallic knob. Although the invention was technically new, the Court denied the patent, stating that:

> The difference is formal, and destitute of ingenuity and invention . . . ; for unless more ingenuity and skill in applying the old method of fastening the shank and the knob were required in the application of it to the clay or porcelain knob than were possessed by an ordinary mechanic acquainted with the business, there was an absence of that degree of skill and ingenuity, which constitute essential elements of every invention.[10]

The *Hotchkiss* case is widely regarded as creating an additional patentability hurdle, above and beyond novelty and utility, which required an inventor to display "more ingenuity and skill" than that possessed by the "ordinary mechanic." This hurdle, needless to say, was ambiguous, and subsequently led to two successive interpretations.

---

6. *See* P.J. Federico, *Commentary on the New Patent Act*, 75 J. PAT. TRAD. OFF. SOC'Y 160, 179–80 (1993) ("An invention which has been made, and which is new in the sense that the same thing has not been made before, may still not be patentable if the difference between the new thing, and what was known before is not considered sufficiently great to warrant a patent.").

7. Giles S. Rich, *Principles of Patentability*, in NONOBVIOUSNESS, *supra* note 1, at 2:1.

8. This language is from Giles S. Rich, *Principles of Patentability*, in NONOBVIOUSNESS, *supra* note 1, and was quoted with approval by then Judge Warren Burger in the case of *Commissioner of Pats. v. Deutsche Gold-und-Silber–Scheideanstalt*, 397 F.2d 656, 667 (D.C.Cir.1968).

9. 52 U.S. (11 How.) 248 (1850).

10. *Id.* at 266. The phrase "ordinary mechanic" is from the district court's charge to the jury.

First, a group of cases arose asserting a "requirement for invention," and attributed this requirement to *Hotchkiss*. For nearly a century, there existed this vague and malleable requirement of patentability that judges, depending upon their particular view of a patent, could manipulate to mean whatever they wanted it to mean.[11] So nebulous was this standard that it has been called the "plaything of the judiciary;"[12] and a "fugitive, impalpable, wayward, and vague a phantom as exists in the whole paraphernalia of legal concepts."[13] Members of the patent bar, especially in New York, realized that something had to be done about the so-called "requirement for invention." The problem is nicely captured in the following:

> It has generally been stated to be the law that, in addition to being new and useful, an invention, to be patentable, must involve "invention." Merely to state that proposition, . . . sounds ridiculous. A neophyte might well ask, "What do you mean, an invention must involve invention."[14]

This realization was intensified in the light of the Supreme Court's antagonistic view of patents during the 1930s and 40s. Representative of this attitude towards patents was the Supreme Court decision of *Cuno Engineering Corp. v. Automatic Devices Corp.*,[15] wherein the Court, in applying *Hotchkiss*, stated that to be patentable, an invention had to be the result of a "flash of creative genius." It was perceived by many in the patent community that *Cuno* raised the hurdle of patentability above and beyond the "requirement for invention."

In the same year *Cuno* was decided, President Roosevelt appointed a National Patent Planning Commission. This Commission issued a report in 1948, which reads in part:

> One of the greatest technical weaknesses of the patent system is the lack of a definitive yardstick as to what is invention. To provide such a yardstick and to assure that the various courts of law and the Patent Office shall use the same standards, several changes are suggested. It is proposed that Congress shall declare a national standard whereby patentability of an

---

11. *See* Giles S. Rich, *The Vague Concept of "Invention" as Replaced by Section 103 of the 1952 Patent Act*, in NONOBVIOUSNESS, *supra* note 1, at 1:409 (The requirement for invention "left every judge practically scott-free to decide this often controlling factor according to his personal philosophy of what inventions should be patented, whether or not he had any competence to do so or any knowledge of the patent system as an operative socioeconomic force. This was too great a freedom because it involves national policy which should be declared by Congress, not by individual judges or even groups of judges."); *See also* P.J. Federico, *A Commentary on the New Act*, *supra* note 6, at 183 (the requirement for invention "is an unmeasurable quantity having different meanings for different persons.").

12. Giles S. Rich, *Why and How Section 103 Came to Be*, in NONOBVIOUSNESS, *supra* note 1, at 1:208.

13. *Harries v. Air King Products Co.*, 183 F.2d 158, 162 (2d Cir.1950) (Hand, J.). Also, during Senate testimony pertaining the American patent system, Judge Hand had this to say about the courts' treatment of the "requirement for invention": "You could find nearly anything you liked if you went to the opinions. It was a subject on which judges loved to be rhetorical." Giles S. Rich, *The Vague Concept of "Invention" as Replaced by Section 103 of the 1952 Patent Act,* in NONOBVIOUSNESS, *supra* note 1, at 1:405.

14. Giles S. Rich, *Principles of Patentability*, in NONOBVIOUSNESS, *supra* note 1, at 2:10.

15. 314 U.S. 84 (1941).

invention shall be determined by the objective test as to its advancement of the arts and sciences.[16]

Nine years after *Cuno* and the formation of the Presidential Commission, the Court decided *The Great Atlantic Tea & Pacific Tea Co. v. Supermarket Equipment Corp.* (the "A & P" case).[17] In *A & P*, the invention (a check out stand as used in a supermarket) was a combination of known elements, as mostly all inventions are,[18] which, stated the Court, yielded no "unusual or surprising consequences."[19] In other words, each element of the invention performed exactly as one would expect it to perform, or as the Court said, "two plus two have been added together, and still they make only four."[20] As such, the invention was unpatentable because "[t]he conjunction or concert of known elements must contribute something; only when the whole in a way exceeds the sum of its parts is the accumulation of old devices patentable" (the so-called "synergism requirement").[21] Justice Douglas, in a concurring opinion, stated that an "invention, to justify a patent, had to serve the ends of science—to push back the frontiers of chemistry, physics, and the like."[22] According to one drafter of the 1952 Act, "[t]hat reasoning is what clinched the decision to enact a statutory substitute that would make more sense, would apply to all kinds of inventions, would restrict the courts in their arbitrary, *a priori* judgments on patentability, and that, above all, would serve as a uniform *standard of patentability.*"[23]

This sense of urgency led to the second line of interpretation relating to *Hotchkiss*. A group of prominent members of the New York patent bar seized upon the "ordinary mechanic" language of *Hotchkiss* in an effort to rein in legislatively the "requirement for invention." This legislative effort ultimately led to Section 103 of the 1952 Act, which reads:

> A patent may not be obtained though the invention is not identically disclosed or described as set forth in section 102 of this title [*i.e.*, the invention is novel], if the differences between the subject matter sought to be patented and the prior art are such that the subject matter as a whole would have been obvious at the time the invention was made to a person having ordinary skill in the art to which said subject matter pertains. Patentability shall not be negatived by the manner in which the invention was made.[24]

---

16. REPORT OF THE NATIONAL PATENT PLANNING COMMITTEE, June 18, 1943, H. Doc. 239, 78th Cong., pp. 6, 10.

17. 340 U.S. 147 (1950).

18. *See Safety Car Heating & Lighting Co. v. General Elec. Co.*, 155 F.2d 937, 939 (2d Cir.1946) (Hand, J.) ("Substantially all inventions are the combination of old elements; what counts is the selection, out of all their possible permutations, of that new combination which will be serviceable.").

19. *A & P, supra* note 17, at 152.

20. *Id.*

21. *Id.*

22. *Id.* at 154–155.

23. Giles S. Rich, *Laying the Ghost of the "Invention" Requirement*, in NONOBVIOUSNESS, *supra* note 1, at 1:508 (emphasis in original).

24. With respect to the enactment of § 103, P.J. Federico, one of the drafters of the 1952 Act, wrote in his *Commentary on the New Patent Act*:

In an attempt to foster consistency and stability, the drafters sought to provide a judge with a clearly marked road map to follow when deciding whether an invention is obvious.[25] Indeed, "[s]ection 103 was a whole new way of thinking and a clear *directive* to the courts to think that way."[26] But section 103 received an inconsistent judicial reception. Despite the fact that the vague term "invention" was purposely omitted from § 103,[27] some circuit courts (First, Sixth, Eighth, and Ninth) viewed § 103 as a mere codification of the "requirement for invention." However, other circuit courts (Second, Third, Fourth, Fifth, Tenth, and the District of Columbia), most notably Judge Learned Hand of the Second Circuit, recognized what it was attempting to accomplish,[28] "namely, to restore the law to what it had

> While it is not believed that Congress intended any radical change in the level of invention or patentable novelty, nevertheless, it is believed that some modification was intended in the direction of moderating the extreme degree of strictness exhibited by a number of judicial opinions over the past dozen or more years; that is, that some change of attitude more favorable to patents was hoped for. This is indicated by the language used in section 103 as well as by the general tenor of remarks of the Committees in the reports and particular comments. Weight should be given to the terms used in the section since a variety of expressions used in decisions were available, including some stated with an extreme degree of strictness, which could have been used as the model for the phraseology to be adopted, but the language selected was of the more moderate variety. The Committee Report, in the general part, states that the section "should have a stabilizing effect and minimize great departures which have appeared in some cases"; the departures of which complaint has been made in the recent past are all departures in the direction of greater strictness and hence these would be what the report indicates should be minimized.

P.J. Federico, *Commentary on the New Patent Act*, *supra* note 6, at 183–84. For a nicely written discussion of the history and current application of § 103, including sample jury instructions and a foreword by Judge Giles Rich, *see* George M. Sirilla, *35 U.S.C. § 103: From Hotchkiss to Hand to Rich, the Obvious Patent Law Hall-of-Famers*, 32 J. MARSHALL L. REV. 437 (1999).

25. Giles S. Rich, *Laying the Ghost of the "Invention" Requirement*, in NONOBVIOUSNESS, *supra* note 1, at 1:508 ("The first policy decision underlying Section 103 was to cut loose altogether the century-old term 'invention.' So Section 103 speaks of a condition of *patentability* instead of 'invention.' The condition is *unobviousness*, but that is not all. The unobviousness is *as of a particular time* and *to a particular* legally fictitious, technical *person*, analogous to the 'ordinary reasonable man' so well known to courts as a legal concept. To protect the inventor from hindsight reasoning, the time is specified to be *the time when the invention was made*. To prevent the use of too high a standard—which would exclude inventors as a class and defeat the whole patent system—the invention must have been obvious at that time to 'a person having ordinary skill in the art to which said subject matter (*i.e.*, the invention) pertains.' But *that* is not all; *what* must have been obvious is '*the subject matter as a whole.*' That, of course, is the invention as defined by each patent claim.") (emphasis in original); *see also*, P.J. Federico, *Commentary on the New Patent Act*, *supra* note 6, at 181 ("[§ 103] is added to the statute for uniformity and definiteness ... and with the view that an explicit statement in the statute may have some stabilizing effect ....").

26. Giles S. Rich, *Laying the Ghost of the "Invention" Requirement*, in NONOBVIOUSNESS, *supra* note 1, at 1:508 (emphasis in original).

27. As a drafter of § 103 stated: "Nowhere in the entire act is there any reference to a *requirement* of 'invention' and the drafters did this deliberately in an effort to free the law and lawyers from bondage to that old and meaningless term...." Giles S. Rich, *Principles of Patentability*, in NONOBVIOUSNESS, *supra* note 1, at 2:10.

28. *See Lyon v. Bausch & Lomb Optical Co.*, 224 F.2d 530, 535 (2d Cir.1955) (Hand, J.) ("[h]ad the case come up for decision within twenty, or perhaps, twenty-five years before the Act of 1952 ... it is almost certain that the claims would have been held invalid. The Courts

been 20 or 30 years earlier and, ... 'to change the slow but steady drift of judicial decisions that had been hostile to patents.' ''[29]

In the light of this circuit conflict, the Supreme Court granted certiorari in 1965, and in 1966, decided *Graham v. John Deere; Calmar, Inc. v. Cook Chemical Co; Colgate–Palmolive Co. v. Cook Chemical Co.; and United States v. Adams,* the seminal cases in modern nonobviousness jurisprudence.

A.   THE *GRAHAM* FRAMEWORK

In 1965, the United States Supreme Court ended a fifteen-year silence on the issue of the standard of invention by granting certiorari in *Graham, Calmar,* and *Colgate* to consider the questions (1) "what effect the 1952 act had upon traditional statutory and judicial tests of patentability," and (2) "what definitive tests are now required." In two opinions of the Court written by Mr. Justice Clark, the Court formulated a general approach to the issue of patentability under Section 103, invalidated the patents in *Graham* and *Calmar,* and upheld the validity of the patent in *Adams.* Most importantly, the Court embraced the 1952 Act's "nonobviousness" standard over the previous "requirement for invention."

Graham v. John Deere Co.

383 U.S. 1 (1966).

[Together with *Calmar, Inc. v. Cook Chemical Co.* and *Colgate–Palmolive Co. v. Cook Chemical Co.*]

■ MR. JUSTICE CLARK delivered the opinion of the Court.

After a lapse of 15 years, the Court again focuses its attention on the patentability of inventions under the standard of Art. I, § 8, cl. 8, of the Constitution and under the conditions prescribed by the laws of the United States. Since our last expression on patent validity, *A. & P. Tea Co. v. Supermarket Equipment Corp.,* 340 U.S. 147, 71 S.Ct. 127, 95 L.Ed. 162 (1950), the Congress has for the first time expressly added a third statutory dimension to the two requirements of novelty and utility that had been the sole statutory test since the Patent Act of 1793. This is the test of obviousness, *i.e.,* whether "the subject matter sought to be patented and the prior art are such that the subject matter as a whole would have been obvious at the time the invention was made to a person having ordinary skill in the art to which said subject matter pertains. Patentability shall not be negatived by the manner in which the invention was made." § 103 of the Patent Act of 1952.

of Appeal have very generally found in the recent opinions of the Supreme Court a disposition to insist upon a stricter test of invention than it used to apply—indefinite it is true, but indubitably stricter than that defined in § 103."); *See also, Reiner et al. v. I. Leon Co.,* 285 F.2d 501 (2d Cir.1960).

29.   Giles S. Rich, *The Vague Concept of "Invention" as Replaced by Section 103 of the 1952 Patent Act,* in NONOBVIOUSNESS, *supra* note 1, at 1:412.

The questions, involved in each of the companion cases before us, are what effect the 1952 Act had upon traditional statutory and judicial tests of patentability and what definitive tests are now required. We have concluded that the 1952 Act was intended to codify judicial precedents embracing the principle long ago announced by this Court in *Hotchkiss v. Greenwood*, 11 How. 248, 13 L.Ed. 683 (1851), and that, while the clear language of § 103 places emphasis on an inquiry into obviousness, the general level of innovation necessary to sustain patentability remains the same.

I.

The Cases.

(a). No. 11, *Graham v. John Deere Co.*, an infringement suit by petitioners, presents a conflict between two Circuits over the validity of a single patent on a "Clamp for Vibrating Shank Plows." The invention, a combination of old mechanical elements, involves a device designed to absorb shock from plow shanks as they plow through rocky soil and thus to prevent damage to the plow. In 1955, the Fifth Circuit had held the patent valid under its rule that when a combination produces an "old result in a cheaper and otherwise more advantageous way," it is patentable. In 1964, the Eighth Circuit held, in the case at bar, that there was no new result in the patented combination and that the patent was, therefore, not valid. We granted *certiorari*, 379 U.S. 956, 85 S.Ct. 652, 13 L.Ed.2d 553. Although we have determined that neither Circuit applied the correct test, we conclude that the patent is invalid under § 103 and, therefore, we affirm the judgment of the Eighth Circuit.

(b). No. 37, *Calmar, Inc. v. Cook Chemical Co.*, and No. 43, *Colgate–Palmolive Co. v. Cook Chemical Co.*, both from the Eighth Circuit, were separate declaratory judgment actions, but were filed contemporaneously. Petitioner in *Calmar* is the manufacturer of a finger-operated sprayer with a "hold-down" cap of the type commonly seen on grocers' shelves inserted in bottles of insecticides and other liquids prior to shipment. Petitioner in *Colgate–Palmolive* is a purchaser of the sprayers and uses them in the distribution of its products. Each action sought a declaration of invalidity and noninfringement of a patent on similar sprayers issued to Cook Chemical as assignee of Baxter I. Scoggin, Jr., the inventor. By cross-action, Cook Chemical claimed infringement. The actions were consolidated for trial and the patent was sustained by the District Court. 220 F.Supp. 414. The Court of Appeals affirmed, 8 Cir., 336 F.2d 110, and we granted *certiorari*, 380 U.S. 949, 85 S.Ct. 1082, 13 L.Ed.2d 967. We reverse.

Manifestly, the validity of each of these patents turns on the facts. The basic problems, however, are the same in each case and require initially a discussion of the constitutional and statutory provisions covering the patentability of the inventions.

II.

At the outset it must be remembered that the federal patent power stems from a specific constitutional provision which authorizes the Congress "To promote the Progress of . . . useful Arts, by securing for limited

Times to ... Inventors the exclusive Right to their ... Discoveries." Art. I, § 8, cl. 8. The clause is both a grant of power and a limitation. This qualified authority, unlike the power often exercised in the sixteenth and seventeenth centuries by the English Crown, is limited to the promotion of advances in the "useful arts." It was written against the backdrop of the practices—eventually curtailed by the Statute of Monopolies—of the Crown in granting monopolies to court favorites in goods or businesses which had long before been enjoyed by the public. *See* MEINHARDT, INVENTIONS, PATENTS AND MONOPOLY, pp. 30–35 (London, 1946). The Congress in the exercise of the patent power may not overreach the restraints imposed by the stated constitutional purpose. Nor may it enlarge the patent monopoly without regard to the innovation, advancement or social benefit gained thereby. Moreover, Congress may not authorize the issuance of patents whose effects are to remove existent knowledge from the public domain, or to restrict free access to materials already available. Innovation, advancement, and things which add to the sum of useful knowledge are inherent requisites in a patent system which by constitutional command must "promote the Progress of ... useful Arts." This is the *standard* expressed in the Constitution and it may not be ignored. And it is in this light that patent validity "requires reference to a standard written into the Constitution." *Great A. & P. Tea Co. v. Supermarket Equipment Corp., supra,* 340 U.S. at 154, 71 S.Ct. at 131 (concurring opinion).

Within the limits of the constitutional grant, the Congress may, of course, implement the stated purpose of the Framers by selecting the policy which in its judgment best effectuates the constitutional aim. This is but a corollary to the grant to Congress of any Article I power. *Gibbons v. Ogden,* 9 Wheat. 1, 6 L.Ed. 23. Within the scope established by the Constitution, Congress may set out conditions and tests for patentability. *McClurg v. Kingsland,* 1 How. 202, 206, 11 L.Ed. 102. It is the duty of the Commissioner of Patents and of the courts in the administration of the patent system to give effect to the constitutional standard by appropriate application, in each case, of the statutory scheme of the Congress.

Congress quickly responded to the bidding of the Constitution by enacting the Patent Act of 1790 during the second session of the First Congress. It created an agency in the Department of State headed by the Secretary of State, the Secretary of the Department of War and the Attorney General, any two of whom could issue a patent for a period not exceeding 14 years to any petitioner that "hath ... invented or discovered any useful art, manufacture, ... or device, or any improvement therein not before known or used" if the board found that "the invention or discovery (was) sufficiently useful and important...." 1 Stat. 110. This group, whose members administered the patent system along with their other public duties, was known by its own designation as "Commissioners for the Promotion of Useful Arts."

Thomas Jefferson, who as Secretary of State was a member of the group, was its moving spirit and might well be called the "first administrator of our patent system." *See* Federico, *Operation of the Patent Act of 1790,* 18 J.PAT.OFF.SOC. 237, 238 (1936). He was not only an administrator of the patent system under the 1790 Act, but was also the author of the 1793

Patent Act. In addition, Jefferson was himself an inventor of great note. His unpatented improvements on plows, to mention but one line of his inventions, won acclaim and recognition on both sides of the Atlantic. Because of his active interest and influence in the early development of the patent system, Jefferson's views on the general nature of the limited patent monopoly under the Constitution, as well as his conclusions as to conditions for patentability under the statutory scheme, are worthy of note.

Jefferson, like other Americans, had an instinctive aversion to monopolies. It was a monopoly on tea that sparked the Revolution and Jefferson certainly did not favor an equivalent form of monopoly under the new government. His abhorrence of monopoly extended initially to patents as well. From France, he wrote to Madison (July 1788) urging a Bill of Rights provision restricting monopoly, and as against the argument that limited monopoly might serve to incite "ingenuity," he argued forcefully that "the benefit even of limited monopolies is too doubtful to be opposed to that of their general suppression," V Writings of Thomas Jefferson, at 47 (Ford ed., 1895).

His views ripened, however, and in another letter to Madison (Aug. 1789) after the drafting of the Bill of Rights, Jefferson stated that he would have been pleased by an express provision in this form:

> Art. 9. Monopolies may be allowed to persons for their own productions in literature, & their own inventions in the arts, for a term not exceeding— years, but for no longer term & no other purpose. *Id.*, at 113.

And he later wrote:

> Certainly an inventor ought to be allowed a right to the benefit of his invention for some certain time.... Nobody wishes more than I do that ingenuity should receive a liberal encouragement. Letter to Oliver Evans (May 1807), V Writings of Thomas Jefferson, at 75–76 (Washington ed.).

Jefferson's philosophy on the nature and purpose of the patent monopoly is expressed in a letter to Isaac McPherson (Aug. 1813), a portion of which we set out in the margin. He rejected a natural-rights theory in intellectual property rights and clearly recognized the social and economic rationale of the patent system. The patent monopoly was not designed to secure to the inventor his natural right in his discoveries. Rather, it was a reward, an inducement, to bring forth new knowledge. The grant of an exclusive right to an invention was the creation of society—at odds with the inherent free nature of disclosed ideas—and was not to be freely given. Only inventions and discoveries which furthered human knowledge, and were new and useful, justified the special inducement of a limited private monopoly. Jefferson did not believe in granting patents for small details, obvious improvements, or frivolous devices. His writings evidence his insistence upon a high level of patentability.

As a member of the patent board for several years, Jefferson saw clearly the difficulty in "drawing a line between the things which are worth to the public the embarrassment of an exclusive patent, and those which are not." The board on which he served sought to draw such a line and formulated several rules which are preserved in Jefferson's correspondence. Despite the board's efforts, Jefferson saw "with what slow progress a system of general rules could be matured." Because of the "abundance" of cases and the fact that the investigations occupied "more time of the members of the board than they could spare from higher duties, the whole was turned over to the judiciary, to be matured into a system, under which every one might know when his actions were safe and lawful." Letter to McPherson, *supra*, at 181, 182. Apparently Congress agreed with Jefferson and the board that the courts should develop additional conditions for patentability. Although the Patent Act was amended, revised or codified some 50 times between 1790 and 1950, Congress steered clear of a statutory set of requirements other than the bare novelty and utility tests reformulated in Jefferson's draft of the 1793 Patent Act.

III.

The difficulty of formulating conditions for patentability was heightened by the generality of the constitutional grant and the statutes implementing it, together with the underlying policy of the patent system that "the things which are worth to the public the embarrassment of an exclusive patent," as Jefferson put it, must outweigh the restrictive effect of the limited patent monopoly. The inherent problem was to develop some means of weeding out those inventions which would not be disclosed or devised but for the inducement of a patent.

This Court formulated a general condition of patentability in 1851 in *Hotchkiss v. Greenwood*, 11 How. 248, 13 L.Ed. 683. The patent involved a mere substitution of materials—porcelain or clay for wood or metal in doorknobs—and the Court condemned it, holding:

> [U]nless more ingenuity and skill ... were required ... than were possessed by an ordinary mechanic acquainted with the business, there was an absence of that degree of skill and ingenuity which constitute essential elements of every invention. In other words, the improvement is the work of the skillful mechanic, not that of the inventor. At p. 267.

Hotchkiss, by positing the condition that a patentable invention evidence more ingenuity and skill than that possessed by an ordinary mechanic acquainted with the business, merely distinguished between new and useful innovations that were capable of sustaining a patent and those that were not. The *Hotchkiss* test laid the cornerstone of the judicial evolution suggested by Jefferson and left to the courts by Congress. The language in the case, and in those which followed, gave birth to "invention" as a word of legal art signifying patentable inventions. Yet, as this Court has observed, "[t]he truth is, the word ['invention'] cannot be defined in such manner as to afford any substantial aid in determining whether a particular device involves an exercise of the inventive faculty or not." *McClain v. Ortmayer*, 141 U.S. 419, 427, 12 S.Ct. 76, 78, 35 L.Ed. 800 (1891); *A. & P. Tea Co. v. Supermarket Equipment Corp., supra*, 340 U.S., at 151, 71 S.Ct. at 129. Its use as a label brought about a large variety of opinions as to its meaning both in the Patent Office, in the courts, and at the bar. The *Hotchkiss* formulation, however, lies not in any label, but in its functional approach to questions of patentability. In practice, *Hotchkiss* has required a comparison between the subject matter of the patent, or patent application, and the background skill of the calling. It has been from this comparison that patentability was in each case determined.

IV.

The 1952 Patent Act.

The Act sets out the conditions of patentability in three sections. An analysis of the structure of these three sections indicates that patentability is dependent upon three explicit conditions: novelty and utility as articulated and defined in § 101 and § 102, and nonobviousness, the new statutory formulation, as set out in § 103. The first two sections, which trace closely the 1874 codification, express the "new and useful" tests which have always existed in the statutory scheme and, for our purposes here, need no clarification. The pivotal section around which the present controversy centers is § 103. It provides:

§ 103. *Conditions for patentability; non-obvious subject matter*

A patent may not be obtained though the invention is not identically disclosed or described as set forth in section 102 of this title, if the differences between the subject matter sought to be patented and the prior art are such that the subject matter as a whole would have been obvious at the time the invention was made to a person having ordinary skill in the art to which said subject matter pertains. Patentability shall not be negatived by the manner in which the invention was made.

The section is cast in relatively unambiguous terms. Patentability is to depend, in addition to novelty and utility, upon the "non-obvious" nature of the "subject matter sought to be patented" to a person having ordinary skill in the pertinent art.

The first sentence of this section is strongly reminiscent of the language in *Hotchkiss*. Both formulations place emphasis on the pertinent art existing at the time the invention was made and both are implicitly tied to advances in that art. The major distinction is that Congress has emphasized "nonobviousness" as the operative test of the section, rather than the less definite "invention" language of *Hotchkiss* that Congress thought had led to "a large variety" of expressions in decisions and writings. In the title itself the Congress used the phrase "Conditions for patentability; *non-obvious subject matter*" (italics added), thus focusing upon "nonobviousness" rather than "invention." The Senate and House Reports, S.Rep. No. 1979, 82d Cong., 2d Sess. (1952); H.R.Rep. No. 1923, 82d Cong., 2d Sess. (1952), U.S.Code Congressional and Administrative News 1952, p. 2394, reflect this emphasis in these terms:

Section 103, for the first time in our statute, provides a condition which exists in the law and has existed for more than 100 years, but only by reason of decisions of the courts. An invention which has been made, and which is new in the sense that the same thing has not been made before, may still not be patentable if the difference between the new thing and what was known before is not considered sufficiently great to warrant a patent. That has been expressed in a large variety of ways in decisions of the courts and in writings. Section 103 states this requirement in the title. It refers to the difference between the subject matter sought to be patented and the prior art, meaning what was known before as described in section 102. If this difference is such that the subject matter as a whole would have been obvious at the time to a person skilled in the art, then the subject matter cannot be patented.

That provision paraphrases language which has often been used in decisions of the courts, and the section is added to the statute for uniformity and definiteness. This section should have a stabilizing effect and minimize great departures which have appeared in some cases. H.R.Rep., *supra*, at 7; S.Rep., *supra*, at 6.

It is undisputed that this section was, for the first time, a statutory expression of an additional requirement for patentability, originally expressed in *Hotchkiss*. It also seems apparent that Congress intended by the last sentence of § 103 to abolish the test it believed this Court announced in the controversial phrase "flash of creative genius," used in *Cuno Engineering Corp. v. Automatic Devices Corp.*, 314 U.S. 84, 62 S.Ct. 37, 86 L.Ed. 58 (1941).

It is contended, however, by some of the parties and by several of the *amici* that the first sentence of § 103 was intended to sweep away judicial precedents and to lower the level of patentability. Others contend that the Congress intended to codify the essential purpose reflected in existing judicial precedents—the rejection of insignificant variations and innovations of a commonplace sort—and also to focus inquiries under § 103 upon nonobviousness, rather than upon "invention," as a means of achieving more stability and predictability in determining patentability and validity.

The Reviser's Note to this section, with apparent reference to *Hotchkiss*, recognizes that judicial requirements as to "lack of patentable novelty (have) been followed since at least as early as 1850." The note indicates that the section was inserted because it "may have some stabilizing effect, and also to serve as a basis for the addition at a later time of some criteria which may be worked out." To this same effect are the reports of both Houses, *supra*, which state that the first sentence of the section "paraphrases language which has often been used in decisions of the courts, and the section is added to the statute for uniformity and definiteness."

We believe that this legislative history, as well as other sources, shows that the revision was not intended by Congress to change the general level of patentable invention. We conclude that the section was intended merely as a codification of judicial precedents embracing the *Hotchkiss* condition, with congressional directions that inquiries into the obviousness of the subject matter sought to be patented are a prerequisite to patentability.

V.

Approached in this light, the § 103 additional condition, when followed realistically, will permit a more practical test of patentability. The emphasis on non-obviousness is one of inquiry, not quality, and, as such, comports with the constitutional strictures.

While the ultimate question of patent validity is one of law, *A. & P. Tea Co. v. Supermarket Equipment Corp., supra,* 340 U.S. at 155, the § 103 condition, which is but one of three conditions, each of which must be satisfied, lends itself to several basic factual inquiries. Under § 103, the scope and content of the prior art are to be determined; differences between the prior art and the claims at issue are to be ascertained; and the level of ordinary skill in the pertinent art resolved. Against this background, the obviousness or nonobviousness of the subject matter is determined. Such secondary considerations as commercial success, long felt but unsolved needs, failure of others, etc., might be utilized to give light to the circumstances surrounding the origin of the subject matter sought to be patented. As indicia of obviousness or nonobviousness, these inquiries may have relevancy. *See* Note, *Subtests of "Nonobviousness": A Nontechnical Approach to Patent Validity*, 112 U.PA.L.REV. 1169 (1964).

This is not to say, however, that there will not be difficulties in applying the nonobviousness test. What is obvious is not a question upon which there is likely to be uniformity of thought in every given factual context. The difficulties, however, are comparable to those encountered daily by the courts in such frames of reference as negligence and scienter, and should be amenable to a case-by-case development. We believe that strict observance of the requirements laid down here will result in that uniformity and definiteness which Congress called for in the 1952 Act.

Although we conclude here that the inquiry which the Patent Office and the courts must make as to patentability must be beamed with greater intensity on the requirements of § 103, it bears repeating that we find no change in the general strictness with which the overall test is to be applied. We have been urged to find in § 103 a relaxed standard, supposedly a congressional reaction to the "increased standard" applied by this Court in its decisions over the last 20 or 30 years. The standard has remained invariable in this Court. Technology, however, has advanced—and with remarkable rapidity in the last 50 years. Moreover, the ambit of applicable art in given fields of science has widened by disciplines unheard of a half century ago. It is but an evenhanded application to require that those persons granted the benefit of a patent monopoly be charged with an awareness of these changed conditions. The same is true of the less technical, but still useful arts. He who seeks to build a better mousetrap today has a long path to tread before reaching the Patent Office.

VI.

We now turn to the application of the conditions found necessary for patentability to the cases involved here:

A.   *The Patent in Graham v. John Deere Co.*

This patent, No. 2,627,798 (hereinafter called the '798 patent) relates to a spring clamp which permits plow shanks to be pushed upward when they hit obstructions in the soil, and then springs the shanks back into normal position when the obstruction is passed over. The device, which we show diagrammatically in the accompanying sketches [See Graham '798 Patent in Fig. 1(a)], is fixed to the plow frame as a unit. The mechanism around which the controversy centers is basically a hinge. The top half of it, known as the upper plate (marked 1 in the sketches), is a heavy metal piece clamped to the plow frame (2) and is stationary relative to the plow frame. The lower half of the hinge, known as the hinge plate (3), is connected to the rear of the upper plate by a hinge pin (4) and rotates downward with respect to it. The shank (5), which is bolted to the forward end of the hinge plate (at 6), runs beneath the plate and parallel to it for about nine inches, passes through a stirrup (7), and then continues backward for several feet curving down toward the ground. The chisel (8), which does the actual plowing, is attached to the rear end of the shank. As the plow frame is pulled forward, the chisel rips through the soil, thereby plowing it. In the normal position, the hinge plate and the shank are kept tight against the upper plate by a spring (9), which is atop the upper plate. A rod (10) runs through the center of the spring, extending down through holes in both plates and the shank. Its upper end is bolted to the top of the spring while its lower end is hooked against the underside of the shank.

When the chisel hits a rock or other obstruction in the soil, the obstruction forces the chisel and the rear portion of the shank to move upward. The shank is pivoted (at 11) against the rear of the hinge plate and pries open the hinge against the closing tendency of the spring. [See Graham '798 Patent in Fig. 1(b)]. This closing tendency is caused by the fact that, as the hinge is opened, the connecting rod is pulled downward and the spring is compressed. When the obstruction is passed over, the upward force on the chisel disappears and the spring pulls the shank and hinge plate back into their original position. The lower, rear portion of the hinge plate is constructed in the form of a stirrup (7) which brackets the shank, passing around and beneath it. The shank fits loosely into the stirrup (permitting a slight up and down play). The stirrup is designed to prevent the shank from recoiling away from the hinge plate, and thus prevents excessive strain on the shank near its bolted connection. The stirrup also girds the shank, preventing it from fishtailing from side to side.

Figure 1(a)—'798 Graham Patent

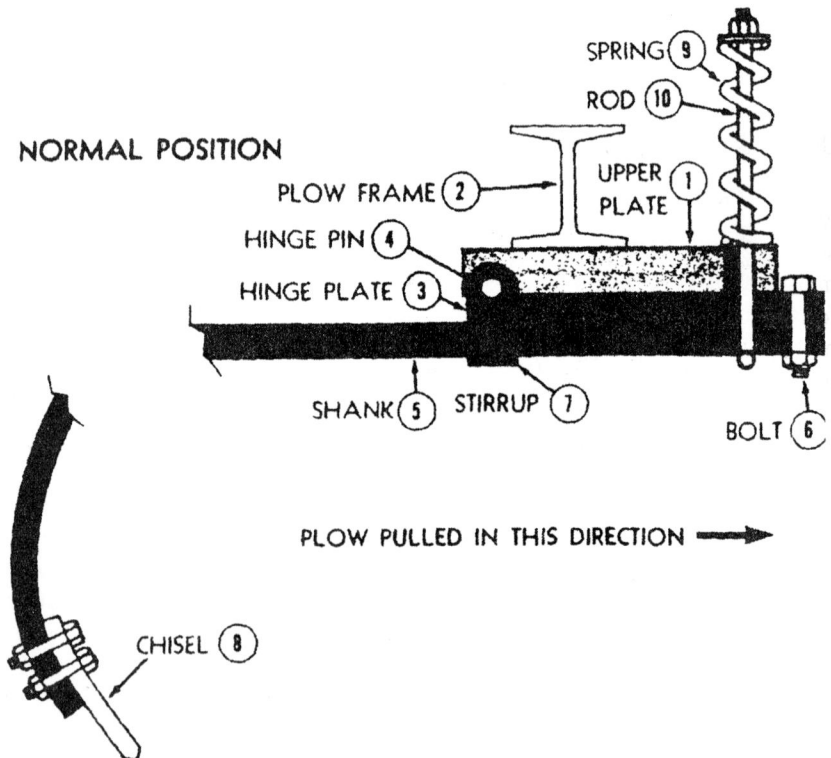

In practical use, a number of spring-hinge-shank combinations are clamped to a plow frame, forming a set of ground-working chisels capable of withstanding the shock of rocks and other obstructions in the soil without breaking the shanks.

Figure 1(b)—'798 Graham Patent

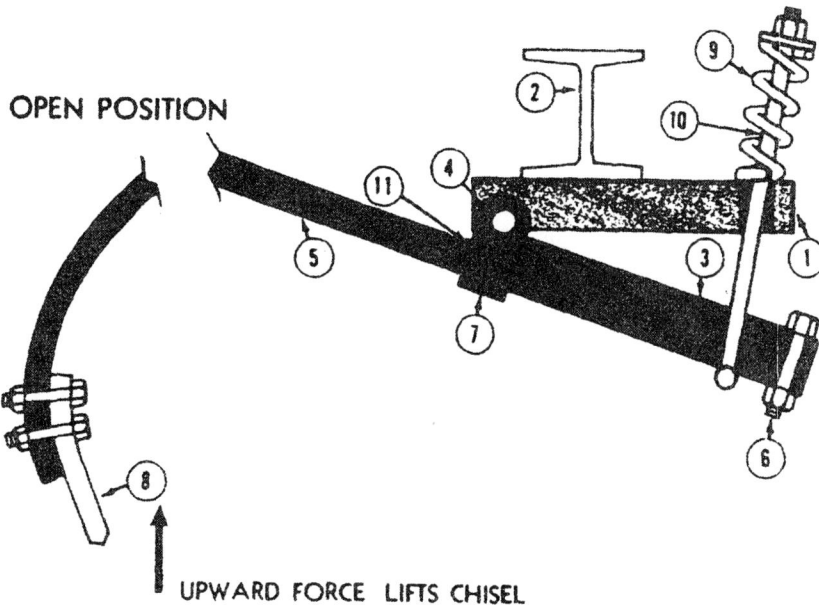

Background of the Patent.

Chisel plows, as they are called, were developed for plowing in areas where the ground is relatively free from rocks or stones. Originally, the shanks were rigidly attached to the plow frames. When such plows were used in the rocky, glacial soils of some of the Northern States, they were found to have serious defects. As the chisels hit buried rocks, a vibratory motion was set up and tremendous forces were transmitted to the shank near its connection to the frame. The shanks would break. Graham, one of the petitioners, sought to meet that problem, and in 1950 obtained a patent, U.S. No. 2,493,811 (hereinafter '811), on a spring clamp which solved some of the difficulties. Graham and his companies manufactured and sold the '811 clamps. In 1950, Graham modified the '811 structure and filed for a patent. That patent, the one in issue, was granted in 1953. This suit against competing plow manufacturers resulted from charges by petitioners that several of respondents' devices infringed the '798 patent.

The Prior Art.

Five prior patents indicating the state of the art were cited by the Patent Office in the prosecution of the '798 application. Four of these patents, 10 other United States patents and two prior-use spring-clamp arrangements not of record in the '798 file wrapper were relied upon by respondents as revealing the prior art. The District Court and the Court of Appeals found that the prior art "as a whole in one form or another contains all of the mechanical elements of the '798 Patent." One of the prior-use clamp devices not before the Patent Examiner—Glencoe—was found to have "all of the elements."

We confine our discussion to the prior patent of Graham, '811, and to the Glencoe clamp device, both among the references asserted by respondents. The Graham '811 and '798 patent devices are similar in all elements, save two: (1) the stirrup and the bolted connection of the shank to the hinge plate do not appear in '811; and (2) the position of the shank is reversed, being placed in patent '811 above the hinge plate, sandwiched between it and the upper plate. The shank is held in place by the spring rod which is hooked against the bottom of the hinge plate passing through a slot in the shank. Other differences are of no consequence to our examination. In practice the '811 patent arrangement permitted the shank to wobble or fishtail because it was not rigidly fixed to the hinge plate; moreover, as the hinge plate was below the shank, the latter caused wear on the upper plate, a member difficult to repair or replace.

Graham's '798 patent application contained 12 claims. All were rejected as not distinguished from the Graham '811 patent. The inverted position of the shank was specifically rejected as was the bolting of the shank to the hinge plate. The Patent Office examiner found these to be "matters of design well within the expected skill of the art and devoid of invention." Graham withdrew the original claims and substituted the two new ones which are substantially those in issue here. His contention was that wear was reduced in patent '798 between the shank and the heel or rear of the upper plate.[11] He also emphasized several new features, the relevant one here being that the bolt used to connect the hinge plate and shank maintained the upper face of the shank in continuing and constant contact with the underface of the hinge plate.

Graham did not urge before the Patent Office the greater "flexing" qualities of the '798 patent arrangement which he so heavily relied on in the courts. The sole element in patent '798 which petitioners argue before us is the interchanging of the shank and hinge plate and the consequences flowing from this arrangement. The contention is that this arrangement—which petitioners claim is not disclosed in the prior art—permits the shank to flex under stress for its entire length. As we have sketched [See Graham '798 Patent in Fig. 2], when the chisel hits an obstruction the resultant force (A) pushes the rear of the shank upward and the shank pivots against the rear of the hinge plate at (C). The natural tendency is for

---

11. In '811, where the shank was above the hinge plate, an upward movement of the chisel forced the shank up against the underside of the rear of the upper plate. The upper plate thus provided the fulcrum about which the hinge was pried open. Because of this, as well as the location of the hinge pin, the shank rubbed against the heel of the upper plate causing wear both to the plate and to the shank. By relocating the hinge pin and by placing the hinge plate between the shank and the upper plate, as in '798, the rubbing was eliminated and the wear point was changed to the hinge plate, a member more easily removed or replaced for repair.

that portion of the shank between the pivot point and the bolted connection (*i.e.*, between C and D) to bow downward and away from the hinge plate. The maximum distance (B) that the shank moves away from the plate is slight—for emphasis, greatly exaggerated in the sketches. This is so because of the strength of the shank and the short—nine inches or so—length of that portion of the shank between (C) and (D). On the contrary, in patent '811 [See Graham '811 Patent in Fig. 2], the pivot point is the upper plate at point (c); and while the tendency for the shank to bow between points (c) and (d) is the same as in '798, the shank is restricted because of the underlying hinge plate and cannot flex as freely. In practical effect, the shank flexes only between points (a) and (c), and not along the entire length of the shank, as in '798. Petitioners say that this difference in flex, though small, effectively absorbs the tremendous forces of the shock of obstructions whereas prior art arrangements failed.

Figure 2—'798 and '811 Graham Patents (Flex Comparison)

GRAHAM '798 PATENT

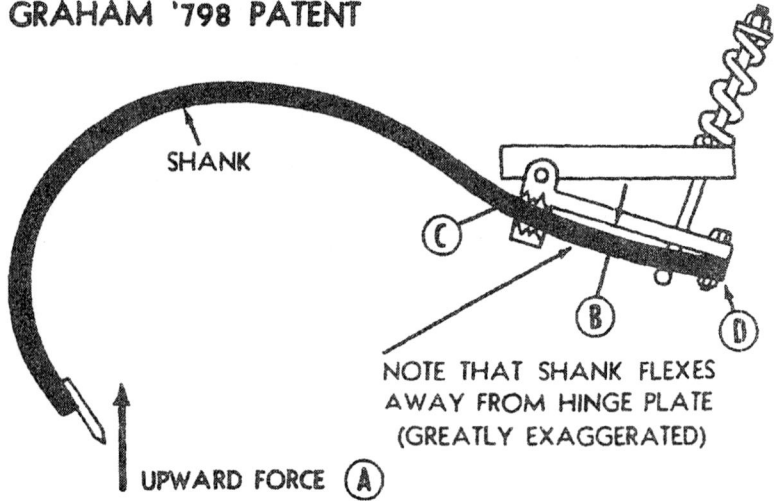

SHANK

C

B

D

NOTE THAT SHANK FLEXES
AWAY FROM HINGE PLATE
(GREATLY EXAGGERATED)

UPWARD FORCE (A)

GRAHAM '811 PATENT

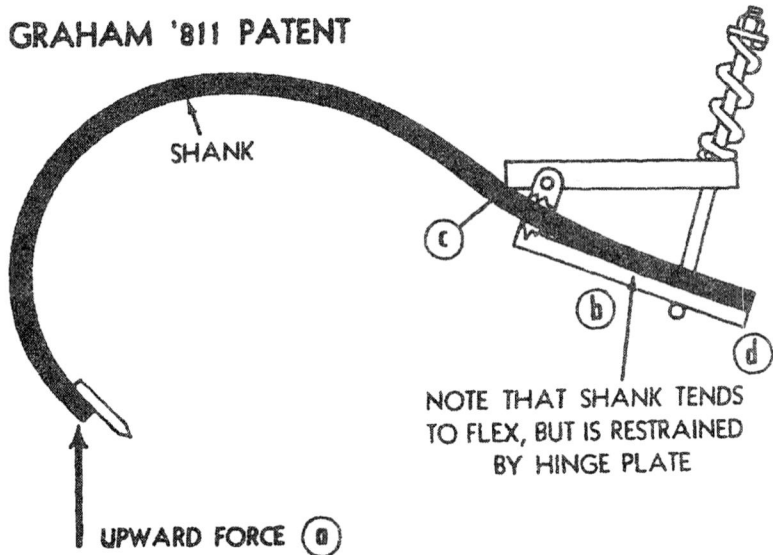

SHANK

c

b

d

NOTE THAT SHANK TENDS
TO FLEX, BUT IS RESTRAINED
BY HINGE PLATE

UPWARD FORCE (D)

The Obviousness of the Differences. *

We cannot agree with petitioners. We assume that the prior art does not disclose such an arrangement as petitioners claim in patent '798. Still

---

* Casebook Editors' Note: Students should note that the wording of this heading is not consistent with the wording of the statute, which refers to the obviousness of the invention as a whole.

we do not believe that the argument on which petitioners' contention is bottomed supports the validity of the patent. The tendency of the shank to flex is the same in all cases. If free-flexing, as petitioners now argue, is the crucial difference above the prior art, then it appears evident that the desired result would be obtainable by not boxing the shank within the confines of the hinge. The only other effective place available in the arrangement was to attach it below the hinge plate and run it through a stirrup or bracket that would not disturb its flexing qualities. Certainly a person having ordinary skill in the prior art, given the fact that the flex in the shank could be utilized more effectively if allowed to run the entire length of the shank, would immediately see that the thing to do was what Graham did, *i.e.*, invert the shank and the hinge plate.

Petitioners' argument basing validity on the free-flex theory raised for the first time on appeal is reminiscent of *Lincoln Engineering Co. of Illinois v. Stewart–Warner Corp.*, 303 U.S. 545 (1938), where the Court called such an effort "an afterthought. No such function . . . is hinted at in the specifications of the patent. If this were so vital an element in the functioning of he apparatus, it is strange that all mention of it was omitted." At p. 550. No "flexing" argument was raised in the Patent Office. Indeed, the trial judge specifically found that "flexing is not a claim of the patent in suit . . ." and would not permit interrogation as to flexing in the accused devices. Moreover, the clear testimony of petitioners' experts shows that the flexing advantages flowing from the '798 arrangement are not, in fact, a significant feature in the patent.

We find no nonobvious facets in the '798 arrangement. The wear and repair claims were sufficient to overcome the patent examiner's original conclusions as to the validity of the patent. However, some of the prior art, notably Glencoe, was not before him. There the hinge plate is below the shank but, as the courts below found, all of the elements in the '798 patent are present in the Glencoe structure. Furthermore, even though the position of the shank and hinge plate appears reversed in Glencoe, the mechanical operation is identical. The shank there pivots about the underside of the stirrup, which in Glencoe is *above* the shank. In other words, the stirrup in Glencoe serves exactly the same function as the heel of the hinge plate in '798. The mere shifting of the wear point to the heel of the '798 hinge plate from the stirrup of Glencoe—itself a part of the hinge plate—presents no operative mechanical distinctions, much less nonobvious differences.

B. *The Patent in Issue in Calmar, Inc. v. Cook Chemical Co., and in Colgate–Palmolive Co. v. Cook Chemical Co.*

The single patent[14] involved in these cases relates to a plastic finger sprayer with a "hold-down" lid used as a built-in dispenser for containers or bottles packaging liquid products, principally household insecticides.

---

14. The patent is U.S. No. 2,870,943 issued in 1959 to Cook Chemical Co. as assignee of Baxter I. Scoggin, Jr., the inventor. In [Calmar v. Cook Chemical], Calmar is the manufacturer of an alleged infringing device, and, in [Colgate–Palmolive v. Cook Chemical], Colgate is a customer of Calmar and user of its device.

Only the first two of the four claims in the patent are involved here and we, therefore, limit our discussion to them.

In essence the device here combines a finger-operated pump sprayer, mounted in a container or bottle by means of a container cap, with a plastic overcap which screws over the top of and depresses the sprayer [See Scoggin '943 Patent in Fig. 3]. The pump sprayer passes through the container cap and extends down into the liquid in the container; the overcap fits over the pump sprayer and screws down on the outside of a collar mounting or retainer which is molded around the body of the sprayer. When the overcap is screwed down on this collar mounting a seal is formed by the engagement of a circular ridge or rib located above the threads on the collar mounting with a mating shoulder located inside the overcap above its threads.[15] The overcap, as it is screwed down, depresses the pump plunger rendering the pump inoperable and when the seal is effected, any liquid which might seep into the overcap through or around the pump is prevented from leaking out of the overcap. The overcap serves also to protect the sprayer head and prevent damage to it during shipment or merchandising. When the overcap is in place it does not reach the cap of the container or bottle and in no way engages it since a slight space is left between those two pieces.

Figure 3—'943 Scoggin Patent

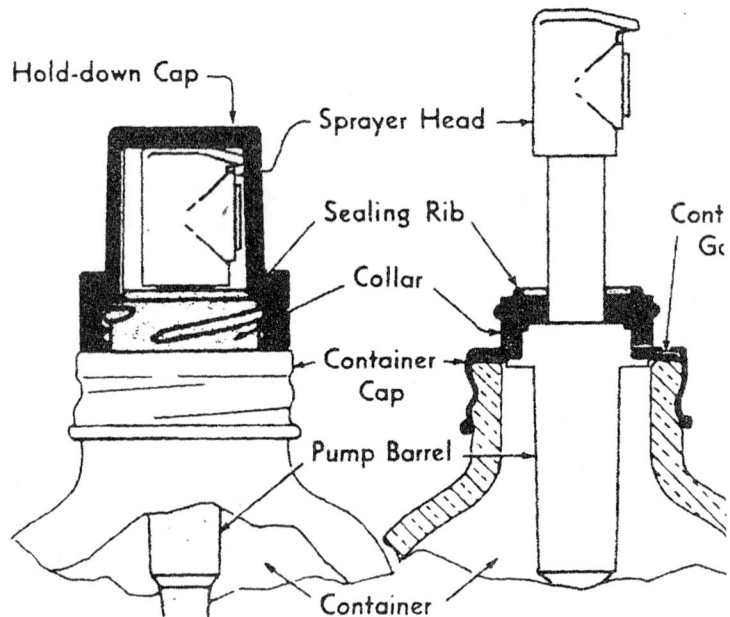

The device, called a shipper-sprayer in the industry, is sold as an integrated unit with the overcap in place enabling the insecticide manufac-

---

15. Our discussion here relates to the overcap seal. The container itself is sealed in the customary way through the use of a container gasket located between the container and the container cap.

turer to install it on the container or bottle of liquid in a single operation in an automated bottling process. The ultimate consumer simply unscrews and discards the overcap, the pump plunger springs up and the sprayer is ready for use.

The Background of the Patent.

For many years manufacturers engaged in the insecticide business had faced a serious problem in developing sprayers that could be integrated with the containers or bottles in which the insecticides were marketed. Originally, insecticides were applied through the use of tin sprayers, not supplied by the manufacturer. In 1947, Cook Chemical, an insecticide manufacturer, began to furnish its customers with plastic pump dispensers purchased from Calmar. The dispenser was an unpatented finger-operated device mounted in a perforated cardboard holder and hung over the neck of the bottle or container. It was necessary for the ultimate consumer to remove the cap of the container and insert and attach the sprayer to the latter for use.

Hanging the sprayer on the side of the container or bottle was both expensive and troublesome. Packaging for shipment had to be a hand operation, and breakage and pilferage as well as the loss of the sprayer during shipment and retail display often occurred. Cook Chemical urged Calmar to develop an integrated sprayer that could be mounted directly in a container or bottle during the automated filling process and that would not leak during shipment or retail handling. Calmar did develop some such devices but for various reasons they were not completely successful. The situation was aggravated in 1954 by the entry of Colgate–Palmolive into the insecticide trade with its product marketed in aerosol spray cans. These containers, which used compressed gas as a propellent to dispense the liquid, did not require pump sprayers.

During the same year Calmar was acquired by the Drackett Company. Cook Chemical became apprehensive of its source of supply for pump sprayers and decided to manufacture its own through a subsidiary, Bakan Plastics, Inc. Initially, it copied its design from the unpatented Calmar sprayer, but an officer of Cook Chemical, Scoggin, was assigned to develop a more efficient device. By 1956 Scoggin had perfected the shipper-sprayer in suit and a patent was granted in 1959 to Cook Chemical as his assignee. In the interim Cook Chemical began to use Scoggin's device and also marketed it to the trade. The device was well received and soon became widely used.

In the meanwhile, Calmar employed two engineers, Corsette and Cooprider, to perfect a shipper-sprayer and by 1958 it began to market its SS–40, a device very much similar to Scoggin's. When the Scoggin patent issued, Cook Chemical charged Calmar's SS–40 with infringement and this suit followed.

The Opinions of the District Court and the Court of Appeals.

At the outset it is well to point up that the parties have always disagreed as to the scope and definition of the invention claimed in the patent in suit. Cook Chemical contends that the invention encompasses a unique combination of admittedly old elements and that patentability is found in the result produced. Its expert testified that the invention was "the first commercially successful, inexpensive integrated shipping closure pump unit which permitted automated assembly with a container of household insecticide or similar liquids to produce a practical, ready-to-use package which could be shipped without external leakage and which was so organized that the pump unit with its hold-down cap could be itself assembled and sealed and then later assembled and sealed on the container without breaking the first seal." Cook Chemical stresses the long-felt need in the industry for such a device; the inability of others to produce it; and its commercial success—all of which, contends Cook, evidences the nonobvious nature of the device at the time it was developed. On the other hand, Calmar says that the differences between Scoggin's shipper-sprayer and the prior art relate only to the design of the overcap and that the differences are so inconsequential that the device as a whole would have been obvious at the time of its invention to a person having ordinary skill in the art.

Both courts accepted Cook Chemical's contentions. While the exact basis of the District Court's holding is uncertain, the court did find the subject matter of the patent new, useful and nonobvious. It concluded that Scoggin "had produced a sealed and protected sprayer unit which the manufacturer need only screw onto the top of its container in much the same fashion as a simple metal cap." 220 F.Supp., at 418. Its decision seems to be bottomed on the finding that the Scoggin sprayer solved the long-standing problem that had confronted the industry. The Court of Appeals also found validity in the "novel 'marriage' of the sprayer with the insecticide container" which took years in discovery and in "the immediate commercial success" which it enjoyed. While finding that the individual elements of the invention were "not novel per se" the court found "nothing in the prior art suggesting Scoggin's unique combination of these old features . . . as would solve the . . . problems which for years beset the insecticide industry." It concluded that "the . . . [device] meets the exacting standard required for a combination of old elements to rise to the level of patentable invention by fulfilling the long-felt need with an economical, efficient, utilitarian apparatus which achieved novel results and immediate commercial success." 336 F.2d, at 114.

The Prior Art.

Only two of the five prior art patents cited by the Patent Office Examiner in the prosecution of Scoggin's application are necessary to our discussion, *i.e.*, Lohse U.S. Patent No. 2,119,884 (1938) and Mellon U.S. Patent No. 2,586,687 (1952). Others are cited by Calmar that were not before the Examiner, but of these our purposes require discussion of only the Livingstone U.S. Patent No. 2,715,480 (1953). Simplified drawings of each of these patents are reproduced in [Figs. 4 & 5], for comparison and description.

The Lohse patent [See Lohse '884 Patent in Fig. 4] is a shipper-sprayer designed to perform the same function as Scoggin's device. The differences, recognized by the District Court, are found in the overcap seal which in Lohse is formed by the skirt of the overcap engaging a washer or gasket which rests upon the upper surface of the container cap. The court emphasized that in Lohse "[t]here are no seals above the threads and below the sprayer head." 220 F.Supp., at 419.

Figure 4—'884 Lohse Patent

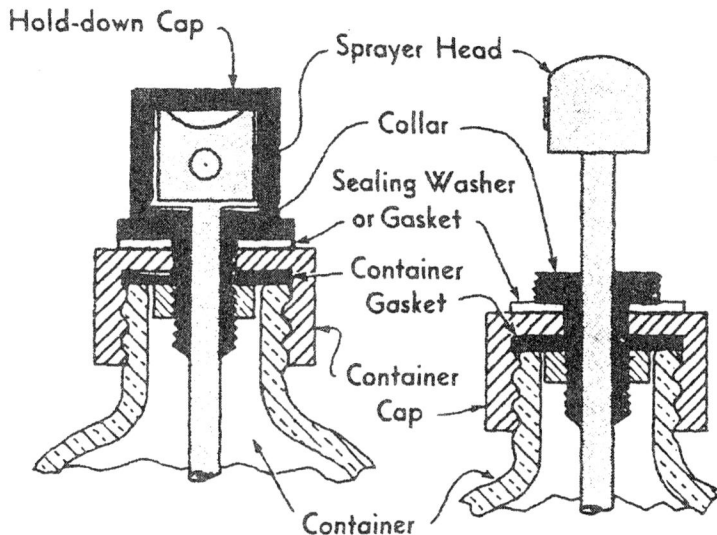

The Mellon patent [See Mellon '687 Patent in Fig. 5], however, discloses the idea of effecting a seal above the threads of the overcap. Mellon's device, likewise a shipper-sprayer, differs from Scoggin's in that its overcap screws directly on the container, and a gasket, rather than a rib, is used to effect the seal.

Finally, Livingstone [See Livingstone '480 Patent in Fig. 5] shows a seal above the threads accomplished without the use of a gasket or washer. Although Livingstone's arrangement was designed to cover and protect pouring spouts, his sealing feature is strikingly similar to Scoggin's. Livingstone uses a tongue and groove technique in which the tongue, located on the upper surface of the collar, fits into a groove on the inside of the overcap. Scoggin employed the rib and shoulder seal in the identical position and with less efficiency because the Livingstone technique is inherently a more stable structure, forming an interlock that withstands distortion of the overcap when subjected to rough handling. Indeed, Cook Chemical has now incorporated the Livingstone closure into its own shipper-sprayers as had Calmar in its SS–40.

**Figure 5—'687 Mellon Patent (above) and '480
Livingstone Patent (below)**

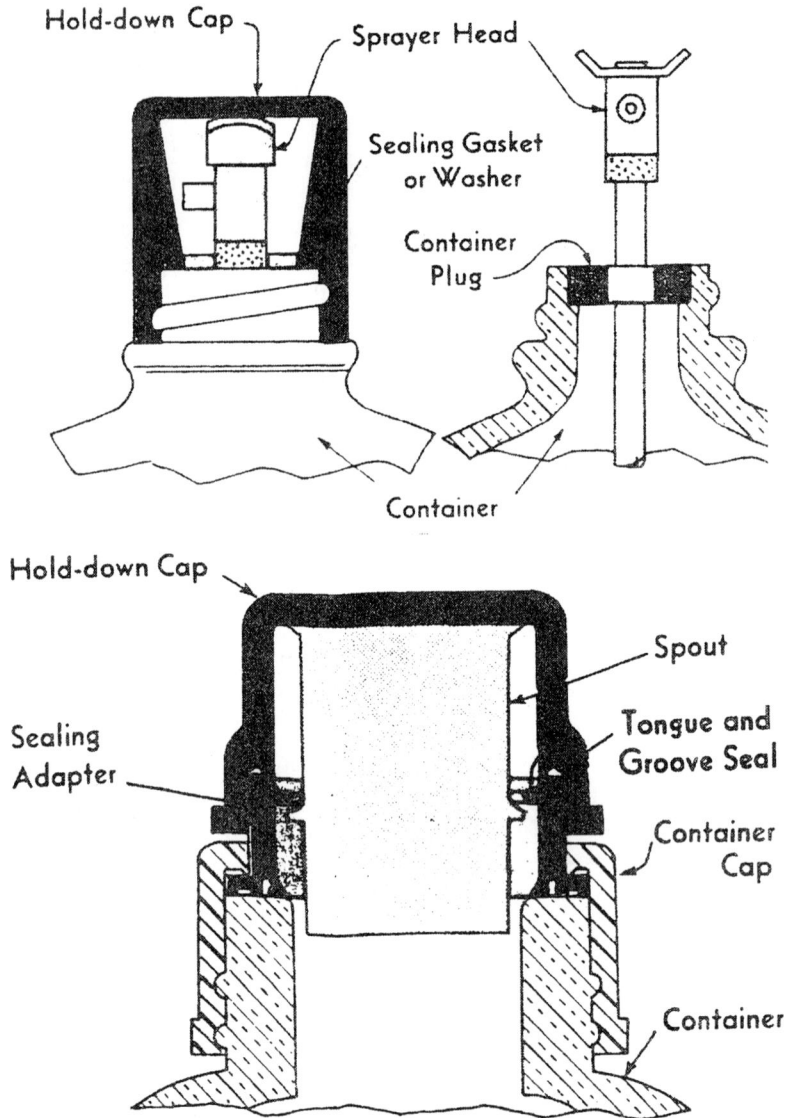

The Invalidity of the Patent.

Let us first return to the fundamental disagreement between the parties. Cook Chemical, as we noted at the outset, urges that the invention must be viewed as the overall combination, or—putting it in the language of the statute—that we must consider the subject matter sought to be patented taken as a whole. With this position, taken in the abstract, there is, of course, no quibble. But the history of the prosecution of the Scoggin application in the Patent Office reveals a substantial divergence in respondent's present position.

As originally submitted, the Scoggin application contained 15 claims which in very broad terms claimed the entire combination of spray pump and overcap. No mention of, or claim for, the sealing features was made. All 15 claims were rejected by the Examiner because (1) the applicant was vague and indefinite as to what the invention was, and (2) the claims were met by Lohse. Scoggin canceled these claims and submitted new ones. Upon a further series of rejections and new submissions, the Patent Office Examiner, after an office interview, at last relented. It is crystal clear that after the first rejection, Scoggin relied entirely upon the sealing arrangement as the exclusive patentable difference in his combination. It is likewise clear that it was on that feature that the Examiner allowed the claims. In fact, in a letter accompanying the final submission of claims, Scoggin, through his attorney, stated that "agreement was reached between the Honorable Examiner and applicant's attorney relative to *limitations* which must be in the claims in order to define novelty over the previously applied disclosure of Lohse when considered in view of the newly cited patents of Mellon and Darley, Jr." (Italics added.)

Moreover, those limitations were specifically spelled out as (1) the use of a rib seal and (2) an overcap whose lower edge did not contact the container cap. Mellon was distinguished, as was the Darley patent on the basis that although it disclosed a hold-down cap with a seal located above the threads, it did not disclose a rib seal disposed in such position as to cause the lower peripheral edge of the overcap "to be maintained out of contacting relationship with [the container] cap . . . when . . . [the overcap] was screwed [on] tightly. . . ." Scoggin maintained that the "obvious modification" of Lohse in view of Mellon would be merely to place the Lohse gasket above the threads with the lower edge of the overcap remaining in tight contact with the container cap or neck of the container itself. In other words, the Scoggin invention was limited to the use of a rib—rather than a washer or gasket—and the existence of a slight space between the overcap and the container cap.

It is, of course, well settled that an invention is construed not only in the light of the claims, but also with reference to the file wrapper or prosecution history in the Patent Office. *Hogg v. Emerson*, 11 How. 587 (1850); *Crawford v. Heysinger*, 123 U.S. 589 (1887). Claims as allowed must be read and interpreted with reference to rejected ones and to the state of the prior art; and claims that have been narrowed in order to obtain the issuance of a patent by distinguishing the prior art cannot be sustained to cover that which was previously by limitation eliminated from the patent. *Powers–Kennedy Contracting Corp. v. Concrete Mixing & Conveying Co.*, 282 U.S. 175, 185–186, (1930); *Schriber–Schroth Co. v. Cleveland Trust Co.*, 311 U.S. 211, 220–221 (1940).

Here, the patentee obtained his patent only by accepting the limitations imposed by the Examiner. The claims were carefully drafted to reflect these limitations and Cook Chemical is not now free to assert a broader view of Scoggin's invention. The subject matter as a whole reduces, then, to the distinguishing features clearly incorporated into the claims. We now turn to those features.

As to the space between the skirt of the overcap and the container cap, the District Court found:

> Certainly without a space so described, there could be no inner seal within the cap, but such a space is not new or novel, but it is necessary to the formation of the seal within the hold-down cap.

> *To me this language is descriptive of an element of the patent but not a part of the invention.* It is too simple, really, to require much discussion. In this device the hold-down cap was intended to perform two functions—to hold down the sprayer head and to form a solid tight seal between the shoulder and the collar below. In assembling the element it is necessary to provide this space in order to form the seal. 220 F.Supp. at 420. (Italics added.)

The court correctly viewed the significance of that feature. We are at a loss to explain the Examiner's allowance on the basis of such a distinction. Scoggin was able to convince the Examiner that Mellon's cap contacted the bottle neck while his did not. Although the drawings included in the Mellon application show that the cap might touch the neck of the bottle when fully screwed down, there is nothing—absolutely nothing—which indicates that the cap was designed at any time to engage the bottle neck. It is palpably evident that Mellon embodies a seal formed by a gasket compressed between the cap and the bottle neck. It follows that the cap in Mellon will not seal if it does not bear down on the gasket and this would be impractical, if not impossible, under the construction urged by Scoggin before the Examiner. Moreover, the space so strongly asserted by Cook Chemical appears quite plainly on the Livingstone device, a reference not cited by the Examiner.

The substitution of a rib built into a collar likewise presents no patentable difference above the prior art. It was fully disclosed and dedicated to the public in the Livingstone patent. Cook Chemical argues, however, that Livingstone is not in the *pertinent* prior art because it relates to liquid containers having pouring spouts rather than pump sprayers. Apart from the fact that respondent made no such objection to similar references cited by the Examiner, so restricted a view of the applicable prior art is not justified. The problems confronting Scoggin and the insecticide industry were not insecticide problems; they were mechanical closure problems. Closure devices in such a closely related art as pouring spouts for liquid containers are at the very least pertinent references. *See,* II WALKER ON PATENTS § 260 (Deller ed. 1937).

Cook Chemical insists, however, that the development of a workable shipper-sprayer eluded Calmar, who had long and unsuccessfully sought to solve the problem. And, further, that the long-felt need in the industry for a device such as Scoggin's together with its wide commercial success supports its patentability. These legal inferences or subtests do focus attention on economic and motivational rather than technical issues and are, therefore, more susceptible of judicial treatment than are the highly technical facts often present in patent litigation. *See* Judge Learned Hand in *Reiner v. I. Leon Co.,* 285 F.2d 501, 504 (1960). *See also* Note, *Subtests of "Nonobviousness": A Nontechnical Approach to Patent Validity,* 112 U. PA. L. REV. 1169 (1964). Such inquiries may lend a helping hand to the judiciary which, as Mr. Justice Frankfurter observed, is most ill-fitted to discharge the technological duties cast upon it by patent legislation. *Marconi Wireless Telegraph Co. of America v. United States*, 320 U.S. 1, 60 (1943). They may also serve to "guard against slipping into use of hindsight," *Monroe Auto Equipment Co. v. Heckethorn Mfg. & Supply Co.*, 332 F.2d 406, 412 (1964), and to resist the temptation to read into the prior art the teachings of the invention in issue.

However, these factors do not, in the circumstances of this case, tip the scales of patentability. The Scoggin invention, as limited by the Patent Office and accepted by Scoggin, rests upon exceedingly small and quite nontechnical mechanical differences in a device which was old in the art. At the latest, those differences were rendered apparent in 1953 by the appearance of the Livingstone patent, and unsuccessful attempts to reach a solution to the problems confronting Scoggin made before that time became wholly irrelevant. It is also irrelevant that no one apparently chose to avail himself of knowledge stored in the Patent Office and readily available by the simple expedient of conducting a patent search—a prudent and nowadays common preliminary to well organized research. *Mast, Foos & Co. v. Stover Mfg. Co.*, 177 U.S. 485 (1900). To us, the limited claims of the Scoggin patent are clearly evident from the prior art as it stood at the time of the invention.

We conclude that the claims in issue in the Scoggin patent must fall as not meeting the test of § 103, since the differences between them and the pertinent prior art would have been obvious to a person reasonably skilled in that art.

The judgment of the Court of Appeals in [*Graham v. John Deere*] is affirmed. The judgment of the Court of Appeals in [*Calmar v. Cook Chemical*] and [*Colgate–Palmolive v. Cook Chemical*] is reversed and the cases remanded to the District Court for disposition not inconsistent with this opinion. It is so ordered.

United States v. Adams

383 U.S. 39 (1966).

■ MR. JUSTICE CLARK delivered the opinion of the Court.

This is a companion case to *Graham v. John Deere Co.*, decided this day along with *Calmar, Inc. v. Cook Chemical Co.* and *Colgate–Palmolive Co. v. Cook Chemical Co.* The United States seeks review of a judgment of the Court of Claims, holding valid and infringed a patent on a wet battery issued to Adams. This suit under 28 U.S.C. § 1498 (1964 ed.) was brought by Adams and others holding an interest in the patent against the Government charging both infringement and breach of an implied contract to pay compensation for the use of the invention. The Government challenged the validity of the patent, denied that it had been infringed or that any contract for its use had ever existed. The Trial Commissioner held that the patent was valid and infringed in part but that no contract, express or implied, had been established. The Court of Claims adopted these findings, initially reaching only the patent questions, 330 F.2d 622, 165 Ct.Cl. 576, but subsequently, on respondents' motion to amend the judgment, deciding the contract claims as well. 330 F.2d, at 634, 165 Ct.Cl., at 598. The United

States sought *certiorari* on the patent validity issue only. We granted the writ, along with the others, in order to settle the important issues of patentability presented by the four cases. 380 U.S. 949, 85 S.Ct. 1090, 13 L.Ed.2d 968. We affirm.

I.

[The Court addressed jurisdictional issues]

II.

The Patent in Issue and Its Background.

The patent under consideration, U.S. No. 2,322,210, was issued in 1943 upon an application filed in December 1941 by Adams. It relates to a nonrechargeable, as opposed to a storage, electrical battery. Stated simply, the battery comprises two electrodes—one made of magnesium, the other of cuprous chloride—which are placed in a container. The electrolyte, or battery fluid, used may be either plain or salt water.

The specifications of the patent state that the object of the invention is to provide constant voltage and current without the use of acids, conventionally employed in storage batteries, and without the generation of dangerous fumes. Another object is "to provide a battery which is relatively light in weight with respect to capacity" and which "may be manufactured and distributed to the trade in a dry condition and rendered serviceable by merely filling the container with water." Following the specifications, which also set out a specific embodiment of the invention, there appear 11 claims. Of these, principal reliance has been placed upon Claims 1 and 10, which read:

> 1.   A battery comprising a liquid container, a magnesium electropositive electrode inside the container and having an exterior terminal, a fused cuprous chloride electronegative electrode, and a terminal connected with said electronegative electrode.

> 10.   In a battery, the combination of a magnesium electropositive electrode, and an electronegative electrode comprising cuprous chloride fused with a carbon catalytic agent.

For several years prior to filing his application for the patent, Adams had worked in his home experimenting on the development of a wet battery. He found that when cuprous chloride and magnesium were used as electrodes in an electrolyte of either plain water or salt water an improved battery resulted.

The Adams invention was the first practical, water-activated, constant potential battery which could be fabricated and stored indefinitely without any fluid in its cells. It was activated within 30 minutes merely by adding water. Once activated, the battery continued to deliver electricity at a voltage which remained essentially constant regardless of the rate at which current was withdrawn. Furthermore, its capacity for generating current was exceptionally large in comparison to its size and weight. The battery was also quite efficient in that substantially its full capacity could be obtained over a wide range of currents. One disadvantage, however, was that once activated the battery could not be shut off; the chemical reactions in the battery continued even though current was not withdrawn. Nevertheless, these chemical reactions were highly exothermic, liberating large quantities of heat during operation. As a result, the battery performed with little effect on its voltage or current in very low temperatures. Relatively high temperatures would not damage the battery. Consequently, the battery was operable from 65E below zero Fahrenheit to 200E Fahrenheit.

Less than a month after filing for his patent, Adams brought his discovery to the attention of the Army and Navy. Arrangements were quickly made for demonstrations before the experts of the United States Army Signal Corps. The Signal Corps scientists who observed the demonstrations and who conducted further tests themselves did not believe the battery was workable. Almost a year later, in December 1942, Dr. George Vinal, an eminent government expert with the National Bureau of Standards, still expressed doubts. He felt that Adams was making "unusually large claims" for "high watt hour output per unit weight," and he found "far from convincing" the graphical data submitted by the inventor showing the battery's constant voltage and capacity characteristics. He recommended, "Until the inventor can present more convincing data about the performance of his [battery] cell, I see no reason to consider it further."

However, in November 1943, at the height of World War II, the Signal Corps concluded that the battery was feasible. The Government thereafter entered into contracts with various battery companies for its procurement. The battery was found adaptable to many uses. Indeed, by 1956 it was noted that "[t]here can be no doubt that the addition of water activated batteries to the family of power sources has brought about developments which would otherwise have been technically or economically impractical." *See* Tenth Annual Battery Research and Development Conference, Signal Corps Engineering Laboratories, Fort Monmouth, N.J., p. 25 (1956).

Surprisingly, the Government did not notify Adams of its changed views nor of the use to which it was putting his device, despite his repeated requests. In 1955, upon examination of a battery produced for the Government by the Burgess Company, he first learned of the Government's action. His request for compensation was denied in 1960, resulting in this suit.

III.

The Prior Art.

The basic idea of chemical generation of electricity is, of course, quite old. Batteries trace back to the epic discovery by the Italian scientist Volta in 1795, who found that when two dissimilar metals are placed in an electrically conductive fluid an electromotive force is set up and electricity generated. Essentially, the basic elements of a chemical battery are a pair of electrodes of different electrochemical properties and an electrolyte which is either a liquid (in "wet" batteries) or a moist paste of various substances (in the so-called "dry-cell" batteries). Various materials which may be employed as electrodes, various electrolyte possibilities and many combinations of these elements have been the object of considerable experiment for almost 175 years. *See generally*, Vinal, Primary Batteries (New York 1950).

At trial, the Government introduced in evidence 24 patents and treatises as representing the art as it stood in 1938, the time of the Adams invention. Here, however, the Government has relied primarily upon only six of these references which we may summarize as follows.

The Niaudet treatise describes the Marie Davy cell invented in 1860 and De La Rue's variations on it. The battery comprises a zinc anode and a silver chloride cathode. Although it seems to have been capable of working in an electrolyte of pure water, Niaudet says the battery was of "little interest" until De La Rue used a solution of ammonium chloride as an electrolyte. Niaudet also states that "[t]he capital advantage of this battery, as in all where zinc with sal ammoniac [ammonium chloride solution] is used, consists in the absence of any local or internal action as long as the electric circuit is open; in other words, this battery does not work upon itself." Hayes likewise discloses the De La Rue zinc-silver chloride cell, but with certain mechanical differences designed to restrict the battery from continuing to act upon itself.

The Wood patent is relied upon by the Government as teaching the substitution of magnesium, as in the Adams patent, for zinc. Wood's patent, issued in 1928, states: "It would seem that a relatively high voltage primary cell would be obtained by using ... magnesium as the ... [positive] electrode and I am aware that attempts have been made to develop such a cell. As far as I am aware, however, these have all been unsuccessful, and it has been generally accepted that magnesium could not be commercially utilized as a primary cell electrode." Wood recognized that the difficulty with magnesium electrodes is their susceptibility to chemical corrosion by the action of acid or ammonium chloride electrolytes. Wood's solution to this problem was to use a "neutral electrolyte containing a strong soluble oxidizing agent adapted to reduce the rate of corrosion of the magnesium electrode on open circuit." There is no indication of its use with cuprous chloride, nor was there any indication that a magnesium battery could be water-activated.

The Codd treatise is also cited as authority for the substitution of magnesium. However, Codd simply lists magnesium in an electromotive series table, a tabulation of electrochemical substances in descending order of their relative electropositivity. He also refers to magnesium in an example designed to show that various substances are more electropositive than others, but the discussion involves a cell containing an acid which would destroy magnesium within minutes. In short, Codd indicates, by inference, only that magnesium is a theoretically desirable electrode by virtue of its highly electropositive character. He does not teach that magnesium could be combined in a water-activated battery or that a battery using magnesium would have the properties of the Adams device. Nor does he suggest, as the Government indicates, that cuprous chloride could be substituted for silver chloride. He merely refers to the cuprous ion—a generic term which includes an infinite number of copper compounds—and in no way suggests that cuprous chloride could be employed in a battery.

The Government then cites the Wensky patent which was issued in Great Britain in 1891. The patent relates to the use of cuprous chloride as a depolarizing agent. The specifications of his patent disclose a battery comprising zinc and copper electrodes, the cuprous chloride being added as a salt in an electrolyte solution containing zinc chloride as well. While Wensky recognized that cuprous chloride could be used in a constant-current cell, there is no indication that he taught a water-activated system or that magnesium could be incorporated in his battery.

Finally, the Skrivanoff patent depended upon by the Government relates to a battery designed to give intermittent, as opposed to continuous, service. While the patent claims magnesium as an electrode, it specifies that the electrolyte to be used in conjunction with it must be a solution of "alcoline, chloro-chromate, or a permanganate strengthened with sulphuric acid." The cathode was a copper or carbon electrode faced with a paste of "phosphoric acid, amorphous phosphorous, metallic copper in spangles, and cuprous chloride." This paste is to be mixed with hot sulfuric acid before applying to the electrode. The Government's expert testified in trial that he had no information as to whether the cathode, as placed in the battery, would, after having been mixed with the other chemicals prescribed, actually contain cuprous chloride. Furthermore, respondents' expert testified, without contradiction, that he had attempted to assemble a battery made in accordance with Skrivanoff's teachings, but was met first with a fire when he sought to make the cathode, and then with an explosion when he attempted to assemble the complete battery.

IV.

The Validity of the Patent.

The Government challenges the validity of the Adams patent on grounds of lack of novelty under 35 U.S.C. § 102(a) (1964 ed.) as well as obviousness under 35 U.S.C. § 103 (1964 ed.). As we have seen in *Graham v. John Deere Co.*, novelty and nonobviousness—as well as utility—are separate tests of patentability and all must be satisfied in a valid patent.

The Government concludes that wet batteries comprising a zinc anode and silver chloride cathode are old in the art; and that the prior art shows that magnesium may be substituted for zinc and cuprous chloride for silver chloride. Hence, it argues that the "combination of magnesium and cuprous chloride in the Adams battery was not patentable because it represented either no change or an insignificant change as compared to prior battery designs." And, despite "the fact that, wholly unexpectedly, the battery showed certain valuable operating advantages over other batteries [these advantages] would certainly not justify a patent on the essentially old formula."

There are several basic errors in the Government's position. First, the fact that the Adams battery is water-activated sets his device apart from the prior art. It is true that Claims 1 and 10, *supra*, do not mention a water electrolyte, but, as we have noted, a stated object of the invention was to provide a battery rendered serviceable by the mere addition of water. While the claims of a patent limit the invention, and specifications cannot be utilized to expand the patent monopoly, *Burns v. Meyer*, 100 U.S. 671, 672 (1880); *McCarty v. Lehigh Valley R. Co.*, 160 U.S. 110, 116 (1895), it is fundamental that claims are to be construed in the light of the specifications and both are to be read with a view to ascertaining the invention, *Seymour v. Osborne*, 11 Wall. 516, 547 (1871); *Schriber–Schroth Co. v. Cleveland Trust Co.*, 311 U.S. 211 (1940); *Schering Corp. v. Gilbert*, 153 F.2d 428 (2d Cir.1946). Taken together with the stated object of disclosing a water-activated cell, the lack of reference to any electrolyte in Claims 1 and 10 indicates that water alone could be used. Furthermore, of the 11 claims in issue, three of the narrower ones include references to specific electrolyte solutions comprising water and certain salts. The obvious implication from the absence of any mention of an electrolyte—a necessary element in any battery—in the other eight claims reinforces this conclusion. It is evident that respondents' present reliance upon this feature was not the afterthought of an astute patent trial lawyer. In his first contact with the Government less than a month after the patent application was filed, Adams pointed out that "no acids, alkalines or any other liquid other than plain water is used in this cell. Water does not have to be distilled. . . ." Letter to Charles F. Kettering (January 7, 1942), pp. 415, 416. Also see his letter to the Department of Commerce (March 28, 1942), R., p. 422. The findings, approved and adopted by the Court of Claims, also fully support this conclusion.

Nor is *Sinclair & Carroll Co. v. Interchemical Corp.*, 325 U.S. 327 (1945), apposite here. There the patentee had developed a rapidly drying printing ink. All that was needed to produce such an ink was a solvent which evaporated quickly upon heating. Knowing that the boiling point of a solvent is an indication of its rate of evaporation, the patentee merely made selections from a list of solvents and their boiling points. This was no more than "selecting the last piece to put into the last opening in a jig-saw puzzle." 325 U.S., at 335. Indeed, the Government's reliance upon *Sinclair & Carroll* points up the fallacy of the underlying premise of its case. The solvent in *Sinclair & Carroll* had no functional relation to the printing ink involved. It served only as an inert carrier. The choice of solvent was dictated by known, required properties. Here, however, the Adams battery is shown to embrace elements having an interdependent functional relationship. It begs the question, and overlooks the holding of the Commissioner and the Court of Claims, to state merely that magnesium and cuprous chloride were individually known battery components. If such a combination is novel, the issue is whether bringing them together as taught by Adams was obvious in the light of the prior art.

We believe that the Court of Claims was correct in concluding that the Adams battery is novel. Skrivanoff disclosed the use of magnesium in an electrolyte completely different from that used in Adams. As we have mentioned, it is even open to doubt whether cuprous chloride was a functional element in Skrivanoff. In view of the unchallenged testimony that the Skrivanoff formulation was both dangerous and inoperable, it seems anomalous to suggest that it is an anticipation of Adams. An inoperable invention or one which fails to achieve its intended result does not negative novelty. *Smith v. Snow*, 294 U.S. 1 (1935). That in 1880 Skrivanoff may have been able to convince a foreign patent examiner to issue a patent on his device has little significance in the light of the foregoing.

Nor is the Government's contention that the electrodes of Adams were mere substitutions of pre-existing battery designs supported by the prior art. If the use of magnesium for zinc and cuprous chloride for silver chloride were merely equivalent substitutions, it would follow that the resulting device—Adams'—would have equivalent operating characteristics. But it does not. The court below found, and the Government apparently admits, that the Adams battery "wholly unexpectedly" has shown "certain valuable operating advantages over other batteries" while those from which it is claimed to have been copied were long ago discarded. Moreover, most of the batteries relied upon by the Government were of a completely different type designed to give intermittent power and characterized by an absence of internal action when not in use. Some provided current at voltages which declined fairly proportionately with time. Others were so-called standard cells which, though producing a constant voltage, were of use principally for calibration or measurement purposes. Such cells cannot be used as sources of power. For these reasons we find no equivalency.

We conclude the Adams battery was also nonobvious. As we have seen, the operating characteristics of the Adams battery have been shown to have been unexpected and to have far surpassed then-existing wet batteries. Despite the fact that each of the elements of the Adams battery was well known in the prior art, to combine them as did Adams required that a person reasonably skilled in the prior art must ignore that (1) batteries which continued to operate on an open circuit and which heated in normal use were not practical; and (2) water-activated batteries were successful only when combined with electrolytes detrimental to the use of magnesium. These long-accepted factors, when taken together, would, we believe, deter any investigation into such a combination as is used by Adams. This is not to say that one who merely finds new uses for old inventions by shutting his eyes to their prior disadvantages thereby discovers a patentable innovation. We do say, however, that known disadvantages in old devices which would naturally discourage the search for new inventions may be taken into account in determining obviousness.

Nor are these the only factors bearing on the question of obviousness. We have seen that at the time Adams perfected his invention noted experts expressed disbelief in it. Several of the same experts subsequently recognized the significance of the Adams invention, some even patenting improvements on the same system. Fischbach *et al.*, U.S. Patent No. 2,636,-060 (1953). Furthermore, in a crowded art replete with a century and a half of advancement, the Patent Office found not one reference to cite against the Adams application. Against the subsequently issued improvement patents to Fischbach, *supra*, and to Chubb, U.S. Reissue Patent No. 23,883 (1954), it found but three references prior to Adams—none of which are relied upon by the Government.

We conclude that the Adams patent is valid. The judgment of the Court of Claims is affirmed.

■ MR. JUSTICE WHITE dissents.

NOTES

1. *Section 103 and the Constitution.* Article I, Section 8, Clause 8 can be properly viewed as not only an enabling provision, but also a limitation on Congressional power to formulate patent policy. The Court in *Graham* discussed Congress' role in promoting "the progress of . . . useful Arts:"

> The clause is both a grant of power and a limitation. . . . The Congress in the exercise of the patent power may not overreach the restraints imposed by the stated constitutional purpose. Nor may it enlarge the patent monopoly without regard to the innovation, advancement or social benefit gained thereby. Moreover, Congress may not authorize the issuance of patents whose effects are to remove existent knowledge from the public domain, or to restrict free access to materials already available. Innovation, advancement, and things which add to the sum of useful knowledge are inherent requisites in a patent system which by constitutional command must "promote the Progress of . . . useful Arts." This is the *standard* expressed in the Constitution and it may not be ignored. . . .

383 U.S. at 5–6 (emphasis in original).

2. *The Factual Inquiries*. The *Graham* Court stated that although "the ultimate question of patent validity is one of law, . . . the § 103 condition . . . lends itself to several basic factual inquiries." 383 U.S. at 17. According to the Court:

> [1] the scope and content of the prior art are to be determined; [2] differences between the prior art and the claims at issue are to be ascertained; [3] and the level of ordinary skill in the pertinent art resolved. Against this background, the obviousness or nonobviousness of the subject matter is determined.

Id. The Federal Circuit has emphasized to district courts the need for express findings of the *Graham* factual inquiries in an ordered and systematic manner. *See Specialty Composites v. Cabot Corp.*, 845 F.2d 981, 990 (Fed.Cir.1988) ("Failure to base an examination of obviousness on the factual findings required by *Graham* can require that the case be remanded for those findings to be made. . . . In this case the district court's discussion of obviousness does not mention *Graham*. It would have been preferable if the court had enumerated the *Graham* factors and systematically presented its analysis in terms of these factors."); *see also, Loctite Corp. v. Ultraseal Ltd.*, 781 F.2d 861, 873 (Fed.Cir.1985). These factual inquires are discussed below. *See* Sections B–D, *infra*.

Although not defined by § 103, the words "prior art" clearly refer to section 102 prior art. As P.J. Federico stated in his commentary on the 1952 Act, "[t]he antecedent of the words 'prior art,' which here appear in a statute [§ 103] for the first time, lies in the phrase 'disclosed or described as set forth in section 102' and hence these words refer to material specified in section 102 as the basis for comparison." P.J. Federico, *Commentary on the New Patent Act*, 35 U.S.C.A. 1, 20 (1954). Of course, as we know from the previous chapter, not all of the § 102 subsections are prior art provisions. As Judge Rich explained in *In re Bass*, 474 F.2d 1276, 1290 (CCPA 1973) (emphasis in original):

> The anatomy of § 102 is fairly clear. As forecast in its heading, it deals with the two questions of "novelty and loss of right." It also deals with originality in subsection (f) which says that one who "did not himself invent the subject matter" (*i.e.*, he did not originate it) has no right to a patent on it. Subsections (c) on abandonment and (d) on first patenting the invention abroad, before the date of the U.S. application, on an application filed more than a year before filing in the U.S., are loss of right provisions and in no way relate to prior art. Of course, (c), (d), and (f) have no relation to § 103 and no relevancy to what is "prior art" under § 103. Only the remaining portions of § 102 deal with "prior art." Three of them, (a), (e), and (g), deal with events prior to applicant's *invention* date and the other,

(b), with events more than one year prior to the U.S. *application* date. These are the "prior art" subsections.

3. *Secondary Considerations.* In addition to the "basic factual inquiries," the Court mentioned the importance of what are known as secondary considerations to the question of obviousness:

> Such secondary considerations as commercial success, long felt but unresolved needs, failure of others, etc., might be utilized to give light to the circumstances surrounding the origin of the subject matter sought to be patented. As indicia of obviousness or nonobviousness, these inquiries may have relevancy....

> These legal inferences or subtests do focus attention on economic and motivational rather than technical issues and are, therefore, more susceptible of judicial treatment than are the highly technical facts often present in patent litigation.... Such inquires may lend a helping hand to the judiciary which, as Mr. Justice Frankfurter observed, is most ill-fitted to discharge the technological duties cast upon it by patent litigation. They may also serve to "guard against slipping into use of hindsight," and to resist the temptation to read into the prior art the teachings of the invention in issue.

Graham, 383 U.S., at 17–18, 35–36. The Federal Circuit has certainly taken note of the importance of the so-called secondary considerations. *See Stratoflex, Inc. v. Aeroquip Corp.*, 713 F.2d 1530 (Fed.Cir.1983) (secondary considerations should be appraised in every case). Secondary considerations are discussed below. *See* Section E, *infra*.

4. *Synergism, Combination Patents, and a Flash of Creative Genius.* It is now well-settled, nearly 50 years after the enactment of the 1952 Patent Act, that a lack of synergism, a combination of known elements in a patent, or the manner in which an invention was made will not preclude patentability under § 103. As the Federal Circuit stated in *Stratoflex,*, 713 F.2d at 1540:

> A requirement for "synergism" or a "synergistic effect" is nowhere found in the statute, 35 U.S.C. When present, for example in a chemical case, synergism may point toward nonobviousness, but its absence has no place in evaluating the evidence on obviousness.

> The reference to a "combination patent" is equally without support in the statute. There is no warrant for judicial classification of patents, whether into "combination" patents and some other unnamed and undefined class or otherwise. Nor is there warrant for differing treatment or consideration of patents based on a judicially devised label. Reference to "combination" patents is, moreover, meaningless. Virtually all patents are "combination patents," if by that label one intends to describe patents having claims to inventions formed of a combination of elements. It is difficult to visualize, at least in the mechanical-structural arts, a "non-combination" invention, *i.e.*, an invention consisting of a single element. Such inventions, if they exist, are rare indeed.

With respect to the "flash of creative genius" issue, the last sentence of section 103(a) explicitly states that "[p]atentability shall not be negatived by the manner in which the invention was made." *See also, Life Technologies, Inc. v. Clontech Laboratories, Inc.*, 224 F.3d 1320, 1325 (Fed.Cir.2000) (asserting that the "path that leads an inventor to the invention is expressly made irrelevant to patentability by statute" citing § 103(a)); *Standard Oil Co. v. American Cyanamid Co.*, 774 F.2d 448, 454 (Fed.Cir.1985) ("A person of ordinary skill in the art is also presumed to be one who thinks along the line of conventional wisdom in the art and is not one who undertakes to innovate, whether by patient, and often expensive, systematic research or by extraordinary insights, it makes no difference which."). This rejection of the "flash of genius" test is consistent with the pre-*Hotchkiss* era. As Justice Story noted in *Earle v. Sawyer*, 8 F. Cas. 254, 256 (C.C. Mass. 1825):

> It is of no consequence, whether the thing be simple or complicated; whether it be by accident, or by long, laborious thought, or by an instantaneous flash of mind, that it is first done. The law looks to the fact, and not to the process by which it is accomplished. It gives the first inventor, or discoverer of the thing, the exclusive right, and asks nothing as to the mode or extent of the application of his genius to conceive or execute it.

5. *Section 103's European Counterpart: The "Inventive Step."* The European Patent Convention (EPC) requires that an invention claim an "inventive step," which is comparable to the nonobviousness requirement embodied in § 103. Specifically, Article 56 of the EPC states:

> An invention shall be considered as involving an inventive step if, having regard to the state of the art, it is not obvious to a person skilled in the art. If the state of the art also includes documents within the meaning of Article 54, paragraph 3. these documents are not to be considered in deciding whether there has been an inventive step.

While there are many parallels between the EPC's "inventive step" and § 103, there are also important differences. For instance, the EPC employs the "problem and solution approach" to the inventive step analysis. The basis is that an invention presumably provides a solution to a problem, and thus "inventive step" can be viewed as "a step from the technical problem to its solution." LIONEL BENTLY AND BRAD SHERMAN, INTELLECTUAL PROPERTY LAW 440–41 (Oxford 2001). According to Professors Bently and Sherman:

> [R]ather than asking whether an invention is obvious, the European Patent Office asks whether the solution that an invention provides to the problem being addressed would have been obvious to the person skilled in the art. In more positive terms, this means that for an invention to be patentable, the solution must *not* have been obvious to the person skilled in the art at the priority date of the invention in question.

Id. at 441 (emphasis in original).

Moreover, unlike the American system, patent applications that have been previously filed, but have not issued, cannot be used as prior art under the EPC. This rule is stated in the second sentence of Article 56. But these applications can be used as prior art for determining novelty. In other words, the EPC does not follow *In re Bass, infra,* but does adhere to *Alexander–Milburn, supra* Chapter Four.

SIDE BAR

The Way the Law of Section 103 Was Made

Tom Arnold*

You should know that for some years prior to the 1952 Patent Act, the actions of the Supreme Court had become so doctrinaire against all patents as to induce Mr. Justice Jackson to opine in his 1949 dissent in *Jungersen v. Ostby*[1] that,

> ... the only patent that is valid is one which this court has not been able to get its hands upon.

Understandably, patent law revision bills appeared in the 79th, 80th and 81st (HR 4061, HR 4798 and HR 6436) Congresses, and the first hearings relating to the test "for determining invention" (that was the phraseology used at that time) were held in 1948 and 1949. Of particular significance in these bills to amend patent statutes was one presented in two successive Congresses to reestablish the doctrine of contributory infringement, drafted by The New York Patent Law Association, represented at hearings by Giles S. Rich.[2]

The hearing on these bills gave the House Subcommittee on Patents, which was also the Committee on Codification of the Laws, the incentive to suggest that they undertake the codification of the patent statutes, and the Patent Office offered to draft a bill to that end, assigning P.J. (Pat) Federico, an Examiner-in-Chief, to that job. The patent bar thought it should have a hand in the task and a meeting of the National Council of Patent Law Associations was called. On February 8, 1950, those present at the meeting constituted themselves a Coordinating Committee[3] under the chairmanship of Henry Ashton of New York who then appointed a two-man drafting committee consisting of Paul Rose of Washington, D.C. and Giles S. Rich of New York. From that day forward, the drafting of the 1952 Act was jointly done by Federico, Ashton, Rich, and Rose with much input of suggestions and advice from all over the country. The whole Coordinating Committee, to which several significant organizations were added, met from time to time to consider, revise, and vote on redrafts.

I became acquainted with then-attorney and now-Judge Giles Rich when my employer, the Department of Justice, designated me as liaison from the Department to the Bar's legislative activity in patent law, *e.g.*, to the bar's Coordinating Committee.

This Committee was in a drafting session on December 4, 1950, when it got a call that the Supreme Court decision in *A & P v. Supermarket Equipment Company* had been rendered. They stopped their work until they could get a copy of the opinion and Giles Rich, sitting on the corner of a table, read it to the others. Instantly they all knew positively, absolutely, what this group had apparently already more or less concluded far ahead of the bar as a whole, that the new bill absolutely had to abandon the idea of defining what is "invention", and must rather define what is patentable, and it must be damn sure they reversed the philosophy of *A & P* as well as Douglas's "flash of genius" test. *A & P* became the third major driving force for them and the bar as a whole, (1) to codify the then disjointed patent law, (2) to correct the law of induced/contributory infringement fouled up or obliterated in the *Mercoid Cases*,[4] and (3) to correct what inventions are patentable.

And so, to work they went on what in Pat Federico's prior bills had been Section 23, which became Section 103 of the 1952 Act.

Years passed with no good word from the Supreme Court and precious little from other courts (the Fifth and Tenth Circuits being the leading exceptions to anti-patent bias). It was appalling. Philosophic inertia supported by continued citations to prior case law as though nothing was changed, and a continued anti-patent bias, were almost completely frustrating implementation of the new statute. Then in early 1965 came the grant of *certiorari* in *Graham v. John Deere* and *Calmar,*

Inc. v. Cook Chemical Co.[5] (*Certiorari* in the third case in this trilogy, *U.S. v. Adams*,[6] came a little later.)

By coincidence, Judge Rich and I ran into each other at a bar meeting shortly after *cert.* was granted in *Calmar* and *Graham*.[7] Judge Rich said words to the effect, "Tom, given the nature of those two cases (neither of them seemed to have any real 'sex appeal' in favor of the patentee's innovation, like *Graver Tank*[8] had in spades) and given the way the Supreme Court is now so strongly biased against patents, the entire patent system is going to be effectively repealed in those cases if we can't somehow get a law clerk on the court who knows something about patents." I agreed, but my response was to the effect that I had no "in" with anybody, and had no idea how I could contribute to that effort.

Then it happened, as if delivered from heaven.

I was by then a patent trial lawyer and an adjunct professor of patent law. I was in Dallas trying a patent infringement suit before Judge Sarah Hughes. During that trial she told counsel that Mr. Justice Tom Clark of the Supreme Court was in town and had come by to see her, and would we, the counsel in the case, like to join her in her chambers during the afternoon recess to meet Mr. Justice Clark. Of course we said, "yes."

During that short recess visit, Justice Clark, upon being told that I was from Houston, volunteered to me that one Charles Reed was to be his law clerk in the next term of Court beginning in September. "Magnificent," I exclaimed, "He is a client of mine, an inventor, a student in my current patent law class at the University of Texas, and far and away the most brilliant student in the entire school." He truly was.

Justice Clark said, "Well, I'm glad you know him and can give him such a recommendation, but he doesn't know he's got the job yet, so don't tell him. The letter from me to him likely won't get out for another couple or three weeks, and I'd like him to learn it from me rather than from what he would see as some rumor mill."

The last class of the semester, the early May review before the final examination in my patent law class, was held perhaps ten days later. And you should know that far and away the most learned and most excellent writing that had ever been written about the section 103 nonobviousness standard of the 1952 Patent Act, which Judge Rich had earlier co-authored, was the published version of the "Kettering Award Speech" (*The Vague Concept of "Invention" as Replaced by Section 103 of the 1952 Act*).[9] This speech was delivered by Judge Rich on June 18, 1964, upon the occasion of his receiving the Charles F. Kettering Award for Meritorious Work in Patent, Trademark an Copyright Research and Education.

When my law school class convened, Charlie Reed did not yet know what I knew, that he was to be Mr. Justice Clark's clerk, and that two patent cases (soon to be three when *cert.* was granted on *U.S. v. Adams*) were to be decided during his watch on the Court. He sat in the back of the room as usual and stayed completely silent, as was his style.

I prompted questions from the students about the course and the examination to be held in a few days. One student asked some kind of question I don't now recall, but the answer I recall very vividly. Said I, "Well, I see that though I cited it to you during the course, you have not committed to memory and full understanding Judge Giles Rich's Kettering Award speech. No student can pass this course without committing that paper to memory and full understanding. This is what Judge Rich said by way of answer to your question:...." And then I proceeded to answer his question more or less as it was presented by Judge Rich in his published speech.

Another student asked a question. Said I, "Well, I see that you too have not committed to memory Judge Rich's Kettering Award speech. I say again, no student can pass my final examination without committing to memory and full understanding everything in that paper. This is what Judge Rich said by way of answer to your question...." And then I recited Judge Rich's speech material on that topic.

I was able in a two hour session, again and again to recite that same theme: You don't pass my examination unless you know and understand all, absolutely all, of the Kettering Award paper.

Charlie Reed never said a word. But, straight up and legitimately, he made the highest grade I ever gave a student in over half a dozen years of teaching as an adjunct professor of law—as he did in most of his other courses.

By coincidence, on the morning the Supreme Court opinions came down, I had breakfast with Charlie Reed at the Mayflower Hotel in Washington, D.C. The opinions being not yet out, of course he neither told me who wrote the opinions nor what the result was. But he reported two generalities about the opinions which he could not resist leaking to his old professor: (1) He got as much of the Kettering Award speech into the opinions as a mere law clerk for one Justice could get in, and (2) I was going to be mad as hell at one sentence, a sentence that was inserted at the last minute in order to get a unanimous court and avoid a dissent.

Of course I could not wait to get my hands on a copy of the opinions at noon that day, and find that the author was reported to be Mr. Justice Tom Clark. And as I read, I found also that the essence of Judge Rich's Kettering Award speech was the backbone of the opinions. That was at least a pair of jacks for openers, encouraging my warm and fuzzy feelings. I scanned rapidly until I found the sentence. Ugh! There it was. "The law is the same." *I.e.*, the law of what is patentable since the 1952 Patent Act is the same as before that act. How totally silly! How ridiculous!

That of course was a surprise to Giles Rich, Pat Federico, Henry Ashton, and Paul Rose, who had revised Federico's prior draft section 23 into section 103 essentially as it became law, on the 1950 afternoon of the Supreme Court decision in *A & P*. They expressly intended to overturn that law and the "flash of genius" test previously authored by Mr. Justice Douglas. It just had to be, I thought, it just had to be that it was Mr. Justice Douglas who required that sentence in order that he would sign the opinion. Blessedly, the rest of the judiciary since then has not followed that horrible unconscionable little sentence, but mostly has given a fresh, if unfortunately variable, look at section 103 in the determination of their subsequent cases—led of course by the opinions of the CCPA on which Giles Rich by then was serving.

Mr. Justice Clark travelled with Charlie Reed to several law review or seminar banquets very soon after the trilogy was decided, and was quite candid in telling us about Charlie's role in drafting those opinions. Now,

Justice Clark's generous portrayal was somewhat of a surprise to Charlie; but much of what I've told you earlier in this *SIDE BAR* was truly news to Charlie when he learned about it a decade later. At that time, he responded thusly:

> Tom Arnold's introduction of me comes as a revelation.... [U]ntil today, I had always assumed that I played a *deus ex machina* part in the *Graham, Calmar,* and *Adams* cases. Now I learn that my role was more like that of the robot R2D2 from the movie Star Wars. I was preconditioned and programmed, sent forward to the Supreme Court to get the word across. The "word," of course, was what was truly intended by the drafters of Section 103.

* * *

> .... In discussing this background, which was obtained in my role as a law clerk for Mr. Justice Clark, I do so with a great sensitivity to unwritten but heavily felt obligation to respect the confidences of the Court's internal processes.... Indeed, one purpose of my remarks must be to point out that the Justice, in his typical generosity and self-effacement, was overly generous in describing my so-called role. He has said I wrote the opinions, a not uncommon task for a law clerk, although Justices vary in the degree to which their law clerks assist in opinion drafting. Actually, what I did was prepare a first draft. The Justice's revisions were extensive. What emerged was both substantively and stylistically his (except as to errors, for which I must take the blame).[10]

Out of such coincidences as a Justice Department liaison, becoming a trial lawyer and a law professor, being in trial in Dallas, when a Supreme Court justice visited, a trial judge's invitation to meet the justice, the professor just then having a student in his class, who ..., was the patent law saved from what I then perceived as almost certain oblivion for some indeterminate, but long time.

Or would it have all turned out the same as it did anyway, given the quality of Charlie Reed and the appeal of facts in *U.S. v. Adams*?[11]

---

* Founder, Arnold White & Durkee. Former President/Chairman of American Intellectual Property Law Association, IP Section of the American Bar Association, National Council of Patent Law Associations, Houston Bar Association, Houston Executives Association, A. A. White Dispute Resolution Institute, and others. AAA Panel for Large Complex Cases; Advisory Board, Institute for Transnational Arbitration, Fellow, and Executive Committee of the North American Branch, of the Chartered Institute of Arbitrators, London; Advisor to CPR, AAA, WIPO on alternative dispute resolution matters. This *SIDE BAR* was written specially for PRINCIPLES OF PATENT LAW.

1. *Jungersen v. Ostby & Barton Co.,* 335 U.S. 560, 572 (1949).

2. Indeed, the Rich testimony before Congress concerning efforts to revive contributory infringement featured promi-

nently in the Supreme Court's decision in *Dawson Chem. Co. v. Rohm and Haas Co.,* 448 U.S. 176, 206–214 (1980).

3. To coordinate the efforts of, and the dissemination of information to, the 25 or so local patent law associations in the country at that time.

4. 320 U.S. 661 and 320 U.S. 680 (1944).

5. The Supreme Court wrote only one opinion for *Graham v. John Deere Co., Calmar v. Cook,* and *Colgate–Palmolive Company v. Cook Chemical Company,* 383 U.S. 1 (1966).

6. 383 U.S. 39 (1966).

7. 383 U.S. 1 (1966).

8. *Graver Tank v. Linde Air Products,* of 1949 and 1950, can be cited as the notable if erratic exception to the almost uniform series of anti-patent actions by the Supreme Court in the 35 years I will call the 30's through '65. *Graver* involved a truly great and dramatic invention by *any* measure. The Supreme Court held invalid most of the significant claims including claims reading literally upon the accused product, in one opinion, 336 U.S. 271, then granted rehearing on infringement issues and there held remaining claims infringed under the doctrine of equivalents by the admitted copyist using novel subject matter taught in the patent. 339 U.S. 605.

9. The Kettering Award Speech, formally *The Vague Concept of "Invention" as Replaced by Section 103 of the 1952 Act*, was published in IDEA, the Journal of the George Washington University Research Foundation, 1964 p. 136, again in 46 J. PAT. OFF. SOC'Y. 855–876 (Dec. 1964), and in a book edited by John F. Witherspoon, III, NONOBVIOUSNESS, THE ULTIMATE CONDITION OF PATENTABILITY, Bureau of National Affairs, Inc., 1980, at 1:401.

10. *See* Charles Reed, *Some Reflections on Graham v. John Deere Co.*, in NONOBVIOUSNESS, *supra* note 10, at 2:301–02.

11. Or perhaps victory is due to the rhetorical and forensic skills of one John A. Reilly, who argued the *Adams* case in a way that surely must be legendary in the Supreme Court. As Charlie Reed told the story a decade later:

> [I]t was a classic of effectiveness. John brought a working model of the battery at issue to the argument. The model was an unpretentious glass of water, electrolyte, chemicals, and a Rube

Goldberg combination of flimsy wire electrodes and lightbulb. John argued that the Army had scoffed at his client, claiming that the battery wouldn't work. As he argued, he fidgeted with his model. I recall Mr. Justice Black cracking a joke (perhaps not intentionally) by asking whether the contraption was going to explode. John assured him it was safe. I didn't know it at the time, but John had experimented with different temperatures of electrolyte to control the rate at which current was to be generated. On that day, he used a colder solution. The result was that when John's oral argument had ended, his battery had not. His opponent had to argue as all the while John's (or Mr. Adams's) battery powered that tiny, but attention-gathering, lightbulb. Indeed, the demonstration sputtered on into the next case quietly yet eloquently mocking the Army's lack of confidence.

Charles Reed, *Some Reflections on Graham v John Deere Co.*, in NONOBVIOUSNESS, *supra* note 10, at 2:303–304. The entire transcript of John Reilly's oral argument in *Adams* is found in the appendix of that book at A:6–15. Not surprisingly, in view of his argument in *Adams*, John Reilly's career appears to have continued rather well; and an endowed chair for visiting professors at The Harvard Law School now exists in his name.

Today, the method for conducting an obviousness analysis is a relatively straightforward analytical road map based on complex factual determinations. As we saw in Chapter Four, the gravamen of a section 102 analysis was the disclosure in a single reference determined to be available under any 102 subsection that sets forth each and every element of the claimed invention and that enables a person of ordinary skill in the art to make and use the claimed invention. In contrast, an obviousness analysis under section 103 allows one to look for the same disclosure spread among more than one reference, as long as the references are analogous, include a teaching or motivation for them to be combined, and convey to a person having ordinary skill in the art a reasonable expectation of success that the claimed invention would result from the combination. Remember, section 102 determines what can be used as prior art for analysis under both sections 102 and 103. We now turn to the many complex factual determinations that support an obviousness analysis.

B.   THE SCOPE OF THE PRIOR ART

The *Graham* decision requires the courts and the PTO to make several "factual inquires." One of the most important of these factual determinations is the ascertainment of the "scope and content of the prior art." Prior art "scope" and "content" are different inquires. With respect to scope, we have to make the initial foundational determination of what exactly *is* the prior art to which to compare the subject matter sought to be patented. Only when the prior art is identified for § 103 purposes can we then explore the content question, which focuses on what the prior art discloses.

1.   ANALOGOUS v. NON-ANALOGOUS ART

A long line of cases have struggled with the question of what *is* the prior art under § 103, all the art that is available under § 102, or only some subset? The issue explored below in *In re Clay* and *In re Paulsen* is whether art that is said to be "non-analogous" can be kept out of the substantive analysis under § 103. Under this view, art is considered "analogous" if it is in the same field as the invention or in some other field, but still germane to the problem facing the inventor before making the invention.

In re Clay

966 F.2d 656 (Fed.Cir.1992).

■ Before PLAGER, LOURIE, and CLEVENGER, CIRCUIT JUDGES.

■ LOURIE, CIRCUIT JUDGE.

Carl D. Clay appeals the decision of the United States Patent and Trademark Office, Board of Patent Appeals and Interferences, Appeal No. 90–2262, affirming the rejection of claims 1–11 and 13 as being unpatentable under 35 U.S.C. § 103. These are all the remaining claims in application Serial No. 245,083, filed April 28, 1987, entitled "Storage of a Refined Liquid Hydrocarbon Product." We reverse.

Background

Clay's invention, assigned to Marathon Oil Company, is a process for storing refined liquid hydrocarbon product in a storage tank having a dead volume between the tank bottom and its outlet port. The process involves preparing a gelation solution which gels after it is placed in the tank's dead volume; the gel can easily be removed by adding to the tank a gel-degrading agent such as hydrogen peroxide.

Two prior art references were applied against the claims on appeal. They were U.S. Patent 4,664,294 (Hetherington), which discloses an apparatus for displacing dead space liquid using impervious bladders, or large bags, formed with flexible membranes; and U.S. Patent 4,683,949 (Sydansk), also assigned to Clay's assignee, Marathon Oil Company, which discloses a process for reducing the permeability of hydrocarbon-bearing formations and thus improving oil production, using a gel similar to that in Clay's invention.

The Board agreed with the examiner that, although neither reference alone describes Clay's invention, Hetherington and Sydansk combined support a conclusion of obviousness. It held that one skilled in the art would glean from Hetherington that Clay's invention "was appreciated in the prior art and solutions to that problem generally involved filling the dead space with *something*." (emphasis in original).

The Board also held that Sydansk would have provided one skilled in the art with information that a gelation system would have been impervious to hydrocarbons once the system gelled. The Board combined the references, finding that the "cavities" filled by Sydansk are sufficiently similar to the "volume or void space" being filled by Hetherington for one of ordinary skill to have recognized the applicability of the gel to Hetherington.

Discussion

The issue presented in this appeal is whether the Board's conclusion was correct that Clay's invention would have been obvious from the combined teachings of Hetherington and Sydansk. Although this conclusion is one of law, such determinations are made against a background of several factual inquiries, one of which is the scope and content of the prior art. *Graham v. John Deere Co.*, 383 U.S. 1, 17, 86 S.Ct. 684, 693–94, 15 L.Ed.2d 545, 148 USPQ 459, 467 (1966).

A prerequisite to making this finding is determining what is "prior art," in order to consider whether "the differences between the subject matter sought to be patented and the prior art are such that the subject matter as a whole would have been obvious at the time the invention was made to a person having ordinary skill in the art." 35 U.S.C. § 103. Although § 103 does not, by its terms, define the "art to which [the] subject matter [sought to be patented] pertains," this determination is frequently couched in terms of whether the art is analogous or not, *i.e.*, whether the art is "too remote to be treated as prior art." *In re Sovish*, 769 F.2d 738, 741, 226 USPQ 771, 773 (Fed.Cir.1985).

Clay argues that the claims at issue were improperly rejected over Hetherington and Sydansk, because Sydansk is nonanalogous art. Whether a reference in the prior art is "analogous" is a fact question. *Panduit Corp. v. Dennison Mfg. Co.*, 810 F.2d 1561, 1568 n. 9, 1 U.S.P.Q.2D 1593, 1597 n. 9 (Fed.Cir.), *cert. denied*, 481 U.S. 1052, 107 S.Ct. 2187, 95 L.Ed.2d 843 (1987). Thus, we review the Board's decision on this point under the clearly erroneous standard.

Two criteria have evolved for determining whether prior art is analogous: (1) whether the art is from the same field of endeavor, regardless of the problem addressed, and (2) if the reference is not within the field of the inventor's endeavor, whether the reference still is reasonably pertinent to the particular problem with which the inventor is involved. *In re Deminski*, 796 F.2d 436, 442, 230 USPQ 313, 315 (Fed.Cir.1986); *In re Wood*, 599 F.2d 1032, 1036, 202 USPQ 171, 174 (CCPA 1979).

The Board found Sydansk to be within the field of Clay's endeavor because, as the Examiner stated, "one of ordinary skill in the art would certainly glean from [Sydansk] that the rigid gel as taught therein would have a number of applications within the manipulation of the storage and processing of hydrocarbon liquids ... [and that] the gel as taught in Sydansk would be expected to function in a similar manner as the bladders in the Hetherington patent." These findings are clearly erroneous.

The PTO argues that Sydansk and Clay's inventions are part of a common endeavor—"maximizing withdrawal of petroleum stored in petroleum reservoirs." However, Sydansk cannot be considered to be within Clay's field of endeavor merely because both relate to the petroleum industry. Sydansk teaches the use of a gel in unconfined and irregular volumes within generally underground natural oil-bearing formations to channel flow in a desired direction; Clay teaches the introduction of gel to the confined dead volume of a man-made storage tank. The Sydansk process operates in extreme conditions, with petroleum formation temperatures as high as 115E C and at significant well bore pressures; Clay's process apparently operates at ambient temperature and atmospheric pressure. Clay's field of endeavor is the *storage* of refined liquid hydrocarbons. The field of endeavor of Sydansk's invention, on the other hand, is the *extraction* of crude petroleum. The Board clearly erred in considering Sydansk to be within the same field of endeavor as Clay's.

Even though the art disclosed in Sydansk is not within Clay's field of endeavor, the reference may still properly be combined with Hetherington if it is reasonably pertinent to the problem Clay attempts to solve. *In re Wood*, 599 F.2d at 1036, 202 USPQ at 174. A reference is reasonably pertinent if, even though it may be in a different field from that of the inventor's endeavor, it is one which, because of the matter with which it deals, logically would have commended itself to an inventor's attention in considering his problem. Thus, the purposes of both the invention and the prior art are important in determining whether the reference is reasonably pertinent to the problem the invention attempts to solve. If a reference disclosure has the same purpose as the claimed invention, the reference relates to the same problem, and that fact supports use of that reference in an obviousness rejection. An inventor may well have been motivated to consider the reference when making his invention. If it is directed to a different purpose, the inventor would accordingly have had less motivation or occasion to consider it.

Sydansk's gel treatment of underground formations functions to fill anomalies so as to improve flow profiles and sweep efficiencies of injection and production fluids through a formation, while Clay's gel functions to displace liquid product from the dead volume of a storage tank. Sydansk is concerned with plugging formation anomalies so that fluid is subsequently diverted by the gel into the formation matrix, thereby forcing bypassed oil contained in the matrix toward a production well. Sydansk is faced with the problem of recovering oil from rock, *i.e.*, from a matrix which is porous, permeable sedimentary rock of a subterranean formation where water has channeled through formation anomalies and bypassed oil present in the matrix. Such a problem is not reasonably pertinent to the particular problem with which Clay was involved—preventing loss of stored product to tank dead volume while preventing contamination of such product. Moreover, the subterranean formation of Sydansk is not structurally similar to, does not operate under the same temperature and pressure as, and does not function like Clay's storage tanks. *See In re Ellis*, 476 F.2d 1370, 1372, 177 USPQ 526, 527 (CCPA 1973) ("the similarities and differences in structure and function of the invention disclosed in the references . . . carry far greater weight [in determining analogy]").

A person having ordinary skill in the art would not reasonably have expected to solve the problem of dead volume in tanks for storing refined petroleum by considering a reference dealing with plugging underground formation anomalies. The Board's finding to the contrary is clearly erroneous. Since Sydansk is non-analogous art, the rejection over Hetherington in view of Sydansk cannot be sustained.

In re Paulsen

30 F.3d 1475 (Fed.Cir.1994).

■ Before Nies, Michel, and Lourie, Circuit Judges.

■ Lourie, Circuit Judge.

AST Research, Inc., (AST) appeals from the July 23, 1993 decision of the United States Patent and Trademark Office (PTO) Board of Patent Appeals and Interferences sustaining the final rejection upon reexamination of claims 1–4, 6, 9–12, and 18–34 of U.S. Patent 4,571,456. We affirm.

Background

The '456 patent, entitled "Portable Computer," was issued to David C. Paulsen *et al.*, on February 18, 1986. The claims of the patent are directed to a portable computer contained within a compact metal case.[2] A salient feature of the claimed invention is its "clam shell" configuration, in which the computer's display housing is connected to the computer at its midsec-

---

2. Claim 1 is the broadest claim in the '456 patent and is illustrative of the claimed invention. The claim reads as follows:

    1. A portable computer constructed to be contained within an outer case for transport and to be erectable to a viewing and operating configuration for use, said computer comprising

a base,

a display housing,

a top cover,

a rear cover,

hinge means for permitting swinging movement of the display housing about an axis of rotation adjacent the rear end of the display housing and from a closed and latched position of the display housing on the base to an erected position for viewing by an operator, and including stop means for holding the display housing at the desired angle for viewing, the hinge means being located in a mid portion of the base and wherein the hinge means permit swinging movement of the display housing to an erected position in which the inner surface of the display housing is held in an upward and rearwardly inclined angle for viewing by an operator in front of the computer, and including a keyboard in the portion of the base which is exposed by the movement of the display housing to the erected position.

tion by a hinge assembly that enables the display to swing from a closed, latched position for portability and protection to an open, erect position for viewing and operation. Computers consistent with this design are commonly referred to as "laptop" computers.

Discussion

Obviousness is a question of law to be determined from the facts. *In re Fine*, 837 F.2d 1071, 1073, 5 U.S.P.Q.2D 1596, 1598 (Fed.Cir.1988). Thus, the Board's conclusion of obviousness is reviewed for error as a matter of law, *In re De Blauwe*, 736 F.2d 699, 703, 222 USPQ 191, 195 (Fed.Cir. 1984), and underlying factual inquiries are reviewed for clear error, *In re Caveney*, 761 F.2d 671, 674, 226 USPQ 1, 3 (Fed.Cir.1985).

1. Non–Analogous Art

AST argues that claims 2, 6, and 28–34, which add particular features to the hinge and latch means of the display housing, were erroneously rejected over non-analogous references directed to hinges and latches as used in a desktop telephone directory, a piano lid, a kitchen cabinet, a washing machine cabinet, a wooden furniture cabinet, or a two-part housing for storing audiocassettes. AST maintains that because the references pertain to fields of endeavor entirely unrelated to computers and are not pertinent to the problems faced by the present inventors, they do not render the claims obvious. It argues that the cited references, dealing with such articles as cabinets and washing machines, do not deal with the particular environment presented in portable computers. This argument rests on too narrow a view of what prior art is pertinent to the invention here.

Whether a prior art reference is "analogous" is a fact question that we review under the "clearly erroneous" standard. *In re Clay*, 966 F.2d 656, 658, 23 U.S.P.Q.2D 1058, 1060 (Fed.Cir.1992). Although there is little dispute that the prior art references cited here are not within the same field of endeavor as computers, such references may still be analogous if they are "reasonably pertinent to the particular problem with which the inventor is involved." *Id.*; *see also Heidelberger Druckmaschinen AG v. Hantscho Commercial Prods., Inc.*, 21 F.3d 1068, [1071]–1072, 30 U.S.P.Q.2D 1377, 1379 (Fed.Cir.1994) ["References that are not within the field of the inventor's endeavor may also be relied on in patentability determinations, and thus are described as 'analogous art,' when a person of ordinary skill would reasonably have consulted those references and applied their teachings in seeking a solution to the problem that the inventor was attempting to solve"]. The problems encountered by the inventors of the '456 patent were problems that were not unique to portable computers. They concerned how to connect and secure the computer's display housing to the computer while meeting certain size constraints and functional requirements. The prior art cited by the examiner discloses various means of connecting a cover (or lid) to a device so that the cover is free to swing radially along the connection axis, as well as means of securing the cover in an open or closed position. We agree with the Board that given the nature of the problems confronted by the inventors, one of ordinary skill in the art "would have consulted the mechanical arts for housings, hinges, latches, springs, etc." Thus, the cited references are "reasonably pertinent" and we therefore conclude that the Board's finding that the references are analogous was not clearly erroneous.

NOTES

1. *Analogous v. Non–Analogous Art.* Even though § 102 is the only source of prior art for § 103 determinations, not just any § 102 reference can be used for § 103 purposes. Throughout the years, beginning with the Supreme Court case of *C & A Potts & Co. v. Creager*, 155 U.S. 597, 607–08 (1895), courts, most recently the Federal Circuit as we have seen, have developed what is known as the doctrine of analogous and nonanalogous art. Only prior art that is considered to be analogous to the subject matter sought to be patented can be used under § 103, although, as we saw in *In re Paulsen*, the technological relationship between the prior art (*e.g.,* mechanical hinges and laches) and the claimed invention (*e.g.,* personal computer) does not have to be as direct as one would initially think.

This analogous art requirement highlights a key distinction between a § 102 novelty determination and a § 103 obviousness inquiry. With respect to the former, a reference's analogous nature or lack thereof to the claimed subject matter is entirely irrelevant. To prove anticipation under § 102, one could point to *any* single prior art reference so long as it discloses the same invention including each and every limitation of the claimed invention; not so for § 103 purposes. Why do we require art to be analogous for § 103 purposes, but not for § 102? The answer to this question may be driven by a practical concern. To prove obviousness under § 103, one can combine the teachings of several prior art references. In contrast, anticipation under § 102 must reside in a *single* prior art reference. Therefore, while it is a difficult enough burden to presume that an inventor is knowledgeable of prior art in his own inventive field and fields related thereto, it is not only unfair but also unrealistic to require an inventor to be presumptively aware of non-analogous prior art. As the Court of Customs and Patent Appeals stated in *In re Wood*, 599 F.2d 1032, 1036 (CCPA 1979):

> In resolving the question of obviousness under 35 U.S.C. § 103, we presume full knowledge by the inventor of all the prior art in the field of his endeavor. However, with regard to prior art outside the field of his endeavor, we only presume knowledge from those arts reasonably pertinent to the particular problem with which the inventor was involved. The rationale behind this rule precluding rejections based on combination of teachings from references from non-analogous arts is the realization that an inventor could not possibly be aware of every teaching in every art. Thus, we attempt to more closely approximate the reality of the circumstances surrounding the making of an invention by only presuming knowledge by the inventor of prior art in the field of his endeavor and in analogous arts.

See also, Union Carbide Corp. v. American Can Co., 724 F.2d 1567, 1572 (Fed.Cir. 1984) (quoting *In re Wood*).

2. *When is Art Pertinent?* Section 103 states that the subject matter sought to be patented is compared with prior art "to which said subject matter pertains." Professor Kitch identifies two ways in which one can ascertain whether art is pertinent. He writes:

> One is to define the "pertinent art" as the art of the industry for which the innovation is designed. This can be called the "product-function" approach. The second is to define the "pertinent art" as the art of dealing with the

kind of problem which the innovation is designed to solve. This is the "problem-solving" approach.

Edmund Kitch, *Graham v. John Deere Co.: New Standards for Patents,* 1966 Sup. Ct. Rev. 293, 336 (1966). What are the pros and cons of each approach? The Federal Circuit has, with some consistency, adopted the "problem-solving" approach. *See In re Clay*, 966 F.2d, at 659 ("A reference is reasonably pertinent if, even though it may be in a different field from that of the inventor's endeavor, it is one which, because of the matter with which it deals, logically would have commended itself to an inventor's attention in considering his problem. Thus, the purposes of both the invention and the prior art are important in determining whether the reference is reasonably pertinent to the problem the invention attempts to solve."); *see also, Shatterproof Glass Corp. v. Libbey–Owens Ford Co.,* 758 F.2d 613, 620 (Fed.Cir. 1985) ("The jury was correctly advised to look first to the nature of the problem confronting the inventor. . . . If the reference is not within the field of the inventor's endeavor, one looks at whether the field of the reference is reasonably pertinent to the problem the inventor is trying to solve.")

2.   § 102/103 PRIOR ART

The following discussion elucidates the problems that have arisen when the prior art reference is only available as prior art under particular subsections of § 102, namely subsections (e), (f), and (g).

a.   § 102(e)/103 PRIOR ART

The issue here is whether art that is only available under § 102(e) is also available under § 103. As explored below in the *Hazeltine* case, such art is available for an obviousness analysis.

Hazeltine Research, Inc. v. Brenner

382 U.S. 252 (1965).

■ MR. JUSTICE BLACK delivered the opinion of the Court.

The sole question presented here is whether an application for patent pending in the Patent Office at the time a second application is filed constitutes part of the "prior art" as that term is used in 35 U.S.C. § 103 (1964 ed.), which reads in part:

> A patent may not be obtained . . . if the differences between the subject matter sought to be patented and the prior art are such that the subject matter as a whole would have been obvious at the time the invention was made to a person having ordinary skill in the art. . . .

The question arose in this way. On December 23, 1957, petitioner Robert Regis filed an application for a patent on a new and useful improvement on a microwave switch. On June 24, 1959, the Patent Examiner denied Regis' application on the ground that the invention was not one which was new or unobvious in light of the prior art and thus did not meet the standards set forth in § 103. The Examiner said that the invention was unpatentable because of the joint effect of the disclosures made by patents previously issued, one to Carlson (No. 2,491,644) and one to Wallace (No. 2,822,526). The Carlson patent had been issued on December 20, 1949, over eight years prior to Regis' application, and that patent is admittedly a part of the prior art insofar as Regis' invention is concerned. The Wallace patent, however, was pending in the Patent Office when the Regis application was filed. The Wallace application had been pending since March 24, 1954, nearly three years and nine months before Regis filed his application and the Wallace patent was issued on February 4, 1958, 43 days after Regis filed his application.

After the Patent Examiner refused to issue the patent, Regis appealed to the Patent Office Board of Appeals on the ground that the Wallace patent could not be properly considered a part of the prior art because it had been a "co-pending patent" and its disclosures were secret and not known to the public. The Board of Appeals rejected this argument and affirmed the decision of the Patent Examiner. Regis and Hazeltine, which had an interest as assignee, then instituted the present action in the District Court pursuant to 35 U.S.C. § 145 (1964 ed.) to compel the Commissioner to issue the patent. The District Court agreed with the Patent Office that the co-pending Wallace application was a part of the prior art and directed that the complaint be dismissed. . . . On appeal the Court of Appeals affirmed *per curiam*. 119 U.S.App.D.C. 261, 340 F.2d 786. We granted *certiorari* to decide the question of whether a co-pending application is included in the prior art, as that term is used in 35 U.S.C. § 103. 380 U.S. 960, 85 S.Ct. 1108, 14 L.Ed.2d 152.

Petitioners' primary contention is that the term "prior art," as used in § 103, really means only art previously publicly known. In support of this position they refer to a statement in the legislative history which indicates that prior art means "what was known before as described in section 102." They contend that the use of the word "known" indicates that Congress intended prior art to include only inventions or discoveries which were already publicly known at the time an invention was made.

If petitioners are correct in their interpretation of "prior art," then the Wallace invention, which was not publicly known at the time the Regis application was filed, would not be prior art with regard to Regis' invention. This is true because at the time Regis filed his application the Wallace invention, although pending in the Patent Office, had never been made public and the Patent Office was forbidden by statute from disclosing to the public, except in special circumstances, anything contained in the application.

The Commissioner, relying chiefly on *Alexander Milburn Co. v. Davis–Bournonville Co.*, 270 U.S. 390, 46 S.Ct. 324, 70 L.Ed. 651, contends that when a patent is issued, the disclosures contained in the patent become a part of the prior art as of the time the application was filed, not, as petitioners contend, at the time the patent is issued. In that case a patent was held invalid because, at the time it was applied for, there was already pending an application which completely and adequately described the invention. In holding that the issuance of a patent based on the first application barred the valid issuance of a patent based on the second application. Mr. Justice Holmes, speaking for the Court, said, "The delays of the patent office ought not to cut down the effect of what has been done. . . . (The first applicant) had taken steps that would make it public as soon as the Patent Office did its work, although, of course, amendments might be required of him before the end could be reached. We see no reason in the words or policy of the law for allowing (the second applicant) to profit by the delay. . . ." At p. 401, 46 S.Ct. at p. 325.

In its revision of the patent laws in 1952, Congress showed its approval of the holding in *Milburn* by adopting 35 U.S.C. § 102(e) (1964 ed.) which provides that a person shall be entitled to a patent unless "(e) the invention was described in a patent granted on an application for patent by another filed in the United States before the invention thereof by the application for patent." Petitioners suggest, however, that the question in this case is not answered by mere reference to § 102(e), because in *Milburn*, which gave rise to that section, the co-pending applications described the same identical invention. But here the Regis invention is not precisely the same as that contained in the Wallace patent, but is only made obvious by the Wallace patent in light of the Carlson patent. We agree with the Commissioner that this distinction is without significance here. While we think petitioners' argument with regard to § 102(e) is interesting, it provides no reason to depart from the plain holding and reasoning in the *Milburn* case. The basic reasoning upon which the Court decided the *Milburn* case applies equally well here. When Wallace filed his application, he had done what he could to add his disclosures to the prior art. The rest was up to the Patent Office. Had the Patent Office acted faster, had it issued Wallace's patent two months earlier, there would have been no question here. As Justice Holmes said in *Milburn*, "The delays of the patent office ought not to cut down the effect of what has been done." P. 401, 46 S.Ct. at p. 325.

To adopt the result contended for by petitioners would create an area where patents are awarded for unpatentable advances in the art. We see no reason to read into § 103 a restricted definition of "prior art" which would lower standards of patentability to such an extent that there might exist two patents where the Congress has plainly directed that there should be only one.

1. *Alexander Milburn Holds Sway.* The Court relied on the opinion of Justice Holmes in *Alexander Milburn*, quoting Holmes's famous line: "The delays in the patent office ought not to cut down the effect of what has been done." When deciding to invoke 102(e) as a prior art section, the Court saw no difference between anticipation and obviousness. But did the Petitioner here have a more persuasive argument than the patentee in *Milburn*, namely that the Regis invention is not precisely disclosed in the Wallace patent?

2. *Compare Milburn, Bass, and Hilmer I & II.* Compare *Milburn* to *In re Bass*, which is immediately below, and ask how inaccessible must a prior art reference be before rendering §§ 102(e) and (g) off limits. Also, compare *Milburn* and *Bass* to the *Hilmer* decisions, discussed in Chapter Four, where the CCPA did draw a line: foreign filing dates and inventive activity cannot be used to defeat patent rights. Was the prior art in *Milburn* (and ask the same in *Bass*) any more accessible than the references in *Hilmer I* and *II*?

b. § 102(g)/103 PRIOR ART

The issue here is whether information that is only available under § 102(g) is also available under § 103. As explored below in *In re Bass*, such art was available for an obviousness analysis; but because this holding raised important concerns for large research teams the statute was amended to make 102(g)/103 art essentially unavailable under a § 103 analysis against an invention that is owned by the same person who owns the art. The notes following *In re Bass* explore this issue in greater detail.

In re Bass

474 F.2d 1276 (CCPA 1973).

■ Before RICH, ACTING CHIEF JUDGE, ALMOND, BALDWIN and LANE, JUDGES, and ROSENSTEIN, JUDGE, UNITED STATES CUSTOMS COURT, sitting by designation.

■ RICH, ACTING CHIEF JUDGE.

This appeal is from the decision of the Patent Office Board of Appeals affirming the examiner's rejection of claims 1–9 of application serial No. 623,721, filed March 16, 1967, for "Air Control System for Carding Machines." All claims are rejected on the ground of obviousness in view of the following references:

Holden	1,612,581	Dec. 28, 1926
Reiterer	3,115,683	Dec. 31, 1963
Bass, Jr. et al. (Bass)	3,315,320	Apr. 25, 1967 (filed Aug. 23, 1965)
Jenkins, Sr. (Jenkins)	3,348,268	Oct. 24, 1967 (parent filed Oct. 13, 1964)
Fuji	Japanese Patent Application No. 1025/63, published Feb. 14, 1963.	

. . . . The statutory basis of this rejection is primarily 35 U.S.C. § 103, which requires unobviousness of the claimed subject matter in view of "the prior art" of "the subject matter as a whole . . . at the time the invention was made to a person having ordinary skill in the art to which said subject matter pertains." Additionally, however, 35 U.S.C. § 102(g) is relied on to establish that the prior inventions of Bass and Jenkins, as shown in their patents, are "prior art."

* * *

The issues raised by this appeal are, first, whether § 102(g) makes available as "prior art," within the meaning of § 103, the prior invention of another who has not abandoned, suppressed or concealed it. The remaining issues are the obviousness of the subject matter of the several claims in view of the available prior art.

The Invention

The joint invention of Bass, Jr., Jenkins, Sr., and Horvat is a vacuum system for controlling and collecting waste on carding machines. Carding is the process of cleaning, straightening, aligning, and forming textile fibers into slivers preparatory to spinning. . . .

* * *

. . . [A]ppellants describe their invention in general terms as follows:

. . . There is provided a unique combination of elements which cooperate with each other to minimize the air pressure beneath the main cylinder without reducing its speed and to control the disposition of waste in the area beneath the main cylinder. More specifically, the invention comprises [1] an enclosure for the area beneath the main cylinder whereby it is rendered as airtight as practical, [2] means closely adjacent the transfer points of the web from the lickerin to the main cylinder and [3] from the main cylinder to the doffer for relieving or drawing off air pressure created through rotation of the main cylinder and lickerin to reduce the air pressure beneath the main cylinder and while also drawing off fly and lint released at said transfer points and, preferably, [4] means carried by the screen beneath the main cylinder for controlling the flow of air currents toward the center of the carding machine and away from its edges whereby to further minimize the danger of "blowouts" carrying waste into the atmosphere. [Bracketed numbers ours.]

* * *

Claims 1 [is] representative (emphasis added):

1. A vacuum system for controlling and collecting waste on carding machines of the type having a lickerin, a main cylinder, a *screen* beneath the main cylinder, and a doffer roll; said device comprising:

(a) *a source of suction*;

(b) *a first suction nozzle* disposed above the lickerin and arranged adjacent the point where the surfaces of the lickerin and cylinder diverge to draw off surface air currents created through rotation of the lickerin and main cylinder;

(c) *a second suction nozzle* disposed between the main cylinder and the doffer adjacent the point where the surfaces of the doffer and main cylinder converge to draw off surface air currents generated through rotation of the main cylinder as well as lint and fly released at the transfer point of the web between the main cylinder and the doffer;

(d) *said screen comprising*:

i.) a frame having a longitudinal axis and including a pair of longitudinally extending parallel side members spaced from each other and on opposite sides of said longitudinal axis; and

ii.) channeling means extending between said side members channeling more of said air currents through said screen intermediate said side members than at said side members, said channeling means comprising a plurality of air obstructing elements, each element having a face, the faces of said air obstructing elements being narrower adjacent said longitudinal axis than adjacent said side members; and

(e) [sic] whereby air pressure in the area beneath the main cylinder is minimized and waste passing through the screen is collected in the central portion of the area beneath the main cylinder.

* * *

The References
* * *

Reiterer discloses the use of a suction nozzle adjacent the point where the lickerin and main cylinders diverge.

Bass essentially describes the [lickerin] suction nozzle used by appellants. The patentees are the present appellants Bass and Horvat.

Jenkins essentially shows the main cylinder screen used by appellants and the patentee is appellant Jenkins.

Fuji discloses the use of a suction nozzle at the point where the main cylinder and the doffer converge. . . .

* * *

. . . . As to the Bass and Jenkins references, the examiner said in his final rejection that while the affidavits may overcome them so far as 35 U.S.C. § 102(e) is concerned, because the affidavits antedate the *filing dates* of those two patents, they are not overcome as disclosing *prior inventions* of "another" under 35 U.S.C. § 102(g). He relied on the Board of Appeals decision in *Ex parte Robbins and Porter*, 156 USPQ 707 (1967), from which he quoted as follows, the opinion being by Federico, Examiner-in-Chief:

> However, assuming that the affidavits were sufficient, the reference is *not necessarily removed* (emphasis added) in view of the relationship of the parties and the common ownership. There is still section 102(g) to consider. Under this provision the prior invention of another, meeting the conditions specified [in § 102(g)], is prior art with respect to a later invention. The invention claimed in the Porter *et al.* patent is taken as having been made prior to the date the invention claimed in the present application was made. . . .

That is the end of the examiner's quotation but the board opinion continued, saying, "in view of the facts present in this case, and hence is available as prior art." Applying the *Robbins* statement to the case before him, the examiner held:

> Therefore, under 35 U.S.C. § 102(g), the affidavits do not remove either Jenkins, Sr., or Bass, Jr., *et al.* as a reference.

In his Answer, the examiner adhered to this position, adding the following:

> Further, it should be noted that the structure of the screen in claims 1, 6, and 7 of the present application is defined word for word as the screen defined in claims 6 and 1 of the Jenkins, Sr. patent.

> The practice of antedating a reference is directed to proving that applicant's invention is of earlier date than the invention of the reference and this could not be the case when both are of identical origin. The nature of the subject matter claimed in the patents and present application, the relationship of the parties and the apparent common ownership, and the respective order of the filing dates of the applications involved indicate the order in which the inventions were made.

* * *

Appellants' argument in this court is along three lines. They argue unobviousness of the inventions of the appealed claims over all the references, unobviousness over the references exclusive of Bass and Jenkins, and the impropriety of using Bass and Jenkins as prior art under § 102(g). The last point certainly is the point principally argued.

Appellants' brief refers to the rejection in this case as "a section 102(g) rejection," which it is not, and we therefore clarify that matter at the outset. The rejection is for obviousness under § 103 based in part on alleged prior inventions of others which are deemed to be "prior art" within the meaning of that term in § 103 by virtue of § 102(g). The essence of appellants' argument against this use of § 102(g) is that it is concerned only with "identity of invention." They say, "The applicants' invention must be *the same* as the invention of another." Since that is obviously not the case here, so their argument runs, § 102(g) "is out and Rule 131 is in." Appellants argue that the *Robbins* case is distinguishable because it was a case of identical inventions. This, however, is not so. The examiner had rejected the claims, *inter alia*, for obviousness. . . .

* * *

Rejections are not based on § 103 when they are identical with the prior art. They rest, in such a case, on § 102 alone.

In addition to contending that § 102(g) "is out" because the application is claiming separate and distinct inventions from what is claimed in the Bass and Jenkins patents, appellants argue that they are not proper references "since applicants [Bass, Jenkins, and Horvat] were working together on a common project, as evidenced by the facts in the Rule 131 affidavit. . . ." They then add that "the appellants freely admit that they did not invent the claimed subject matter of the Bass, Jr. patent or the Jenkins, Sr. patent. . . ."

OPINION

§ 102(g) Prior Invention as "Prior Art" under § 103

Narrowly considered, the issue presented by the facts of this case is one of first impression in this court. This is by no means the first time we have passed on whether § 102(g) prior invention of another is prior art, as will be shown, or even the first time we have considered whether such prior invention can be combined with other prior art to sustain a § 103 obviousness rejection. However, it is the first time we have considered combining § 102(g) and § 103 in the context of an *ex parte* rejection entirely divorced from the award of priority in an interference which established the prior inventorship relied on in rejecting.

* * *

This court has several times approved of rejections based on a combination of § 102(g) with § 103. [The court goes on to discuss its precedent in this regard].

* * *

[I]t is clear beyond question that in using § 102(g) prior art to support a rejection it has not been limited to situations involving "identity of invention," as appellants contend, but has repeatedly been used to support the rejection of claims to different but obvious inventions under § 103.

As a general proposition of law, and particularly considering the way in which full anticipation situations under § 102 shade into obviousness rejections under § 103 because of discernable differences, we cannot sanction an interpretation of the statute under which a prior invention is "prior art" under the former situation but not under the latter.

The situation presents a close parallel to the situation under § 102(e) which was dealt with by this court in *In re Harry*, 333 F.2d 920, 51 CCPA 1541 (1964), and by the Supreme Court a year later in *Hazeltine Research, Inc. v. Brenner*, 382 U.S. 252, 86 S.Ct. 335, 15 L.Ed.2d 304 (1965). In *Hazeltine* the patentee tried in vain to do the very thing appellants attempt here, namely, to distinguish between § 102 full anticipation and § 103 obviousness rejections. A parallel attempt was made in *Harry* with respect to § 102(e). In *Hazeltine* the Court gave this answer (emphasis added):

> Petitioners suggest, however, that the question in this case is not answered by mere reference to § 102(e), because in *Milburn* [*Alexander Milburn Co. v. Davis–Bournonville Co.*, 270 U.S. 390, 46 S.Ct. 324, 70 L.Ed. 651], which gave rise to that section, the co-pending applications described the same *identical invention*. But here the Regis invention is not precisely the same as that contained in the Wallace patent, but *is only made obvious* by the Wallace patent in light of the Carlson patent. We agree with the Commissioner that *this distinction is without significance here*.

In *Harry* [333 F.2d 920 CCPA 1964], in discussing the § 102(e)/§ 103 rejection our summation reads (emphasis added):

> In our opinion, the *"prior art" referred to in § 103 includes* along with the patents, printed publications, public uses and sales of paragraphs (a) and (b) of section 102, *prior invention* as established by a copending application, *if* it becomes a patent, as contemplated by paragraph (e) and as held in the *Milburn* case. Such *prior invention*, as prior art, *may be combined with other references to sustain a rejection for obviousness* under section 103.

Such being the law as to prior invention established under § 102(e), as it surely is with the Supreme Court's approval, we see no reason a different rule should prevail when the prior invention is otherwise established, as by the circumstances of the case, an adverse ruling in an interference, admissions by the applicant, or otherwise, the statutory basis for using the prior invention being § 102(g).

It is not a new idea that what is prior art for one purpose is prior art for all purposes. Judge Learned Hand, speaking for the Second Circuit Court of Appeals in *Western States Mach. Co. v. S. S. Hepworth Co.*, 147 F.2d 345 (1945), said, at the end of a long discussion of the "plausible" argument that there should be a distinction between a prior invention under the *Milburn* rule which fully anticipates and one which merely makes obvious,

> ... once the first application is treated as prior art when it *fully anticipates*, there seems to be no reason to deny it *whatever effect it would have as prior art*, if it were literally such. [Emphasis added.]

It is our view that the law as applied in the Patent Office must be uniform with the law as applied in the courts in passing on patent validity. It is our belief that that is what it is doing in this case.

* * *

In view of the foregoing decisions and principles, we rule against appellants and hold that the use of the prior invention of another who had not abandoned, suppressed, or concealed it under the circumstances of this case which include the disclosure of such invention in an issued patent, is available as "prior art" within the meaning of that term in § 103 by virtue of § 102(g).[7]

Prior Invention

Having settled the question of law, it remains to determine what the evidence shows as to the priority of the Bass and Jenkins inventions, upon which their availability as prior art depends.

* * *

The earliest date of invention alleged by appellants for their combination is the date of conception, February 10, 1964. Reduction to practice is alleged in April 1964. Their effective filing date is October 11, 1965.

First, we consider Jenkins, asserted to be the prior inventor of the tapered bar screen element of the claimed combination. The affidavit evidence asserts that the screen was conceived "before December 6, 1963" and built according to a drawing dated December 5, 1963. It was installed in the first prototype of appellants' combination about April 17, 1964. Assuming that to be the first reduction to practice of the screen, as well as of the combination, the record contains an admission of its conception by Jenkins about two months before appellants claim to have conceived the combination. The Jenkins invention would appear, *prima facie*, to be prior on the basis of prior conception and simultaneous reduction to practice, which makes diligence irrelevant. *Whittier v. Borchardt*, 154 F.2d 522, 33 CCPA 1023 (1946), *Lassman v. Brossi*, 159 USPQ 182 (Bd.Pat.Int'f.1967). In the absence of any traverse, even in appellants' brief, this screen appears to be a prior invention under § 102(g). While we have said that there is no necessary relationship between the order of making inventions and the order of filing applications on them, *In re Land and Rogers*, 368 F.2d 866, 54 CCPA 806 (1966), we think there is further evidentiary significance in the fact that Jenkins filed October 13, 1964, and appellants did not file for nearly a year thereafter, on October 11, 1965. On the basis of all the evidence of record, we accept the Jenkins screen as described in his patent, to which reference is made in the application at bar, as prior art.

We turn now to the Bass and Horvat reference (Bass). The invention of these patentees is the "first suction nozzle," element "(b)" in claim 1, located at the lickerin end of the machine. The only argument the solicitor makes on the priority issue is that "the affidavits make no attempt to show that the invention of Bass and Horvat was not prior to the invention of appellants." We do not think it was incumbent on the applicants to prove it was *not* prior, merely because the Patent Office thinks it might have been. . . .

---

7. It may be wondered why, in the twenty years since § 102(g) came into effect, there have not been more adjudicated cases reported relying on it to show "prior art" in support of a § 103 rejection. The answer probably is that there are many other defenses much easier to establish and it is a rare case where the effort of going back to the date of invention of a prior inventor is worth the cost. In particular, § 102(e) makes patents unquestioned prior art for all purposes as of their United States filing dates and the date of invention is usually not enough earlier to make a difference in the result.

Appellants' position with respect to Bass is "that the Bass, Jr. *et al.* lickerin plenum and the instant combination were part of the same research and development program and were invented simultaneously, as opposed to the Patent Office's position that the Bass, Jr. *et al.* lickerin plenum was invented previous to the combination merely because it was filed first." Finding no substantial evidence of record tending to indicate priority in Bass, we believe the appellants' position to be sound. In fact, it appears as logical on the facts of this case to find that the claimed combination was conceived before the Bass plenum as described in the reference patent. We therefore exclude Bass from consideration as prior art in passing on the obviousness rejection.

The Rejections of Claims

Claims 2, 3, 4, and 5 were rejected as obvious in view of Reiterer and Fuji. We have carefully considered appellants' argument but agree with the decision on obviousness and this rejection is affirmed.

The rejection of all remaining claims, 1, 6, 7, 8, and 9, was predicated on Bass combined with Fuji, Jenkins being added in rejecting claims 1, 6, 7, and 9. With the elimination of the Bass reference, there is no suggestion in the remaining references applied of the suction means at the lickerin side of the carding machine and no basis for a holding of obviousness of the combination of which it is a principal element. It is, therefore, necessary to reverse the rejection of these claims.

Comments on Judge Baldwin's Concurring Opinion

This concurring opinion is in reality a dissent. The only concurrence is with the final disposition of the claims. On the principal point of law involved in this case there is total disagreement. The concurring opinion expresses the view that prior invention under § 102(g) is not "prior art" under § 103 *unless* the priority happens to have been established in an interference, when it *is* "prior art" under § 103. Since there has been no interference here, the position taken is that the Bass patented suction nozzle and the Jenkins patented main cylinder screen would not be "prior art" under § 103 even if the priority of these inventions were firmly established by evidence, and so these inventions must be ignored in determining obviousness under § 103, on which basis the same result is reached that we reach. It also expresses the view that although prior inventions under § 102(g) are prior art which can be used to sustain a full anticipation rejection under § 102, they cannot be used to sustain an obviousness rejection under § 103—that prior art is not prior art for all purposes. We consider this position anomalous.

* * *

In short, prior art for one purpose is prior art for all purposes and in all courts and in the Patent Office. On one matter the concurrence maintains a significant silence. Throughout, it takes it for granted that prior invention under § 102(g) *is* prior art which will support a rejection of claims to the same or substantially the same invention. Without emphasis on the fact, the entire concurrence carefully limits its discussion to the status of "a non-anticipatory reference." It attempts to develop, as an assumed part of the law, a spurious distinction between "prior art" and "prior invention," a *"prior art* defense" and a *"prior invention* defense." Regardless of what may have been said in three opinions written in 1902, 1912, 1916, long before *Milburn* and *Hazeltine*, prior invention is prior art and always has been. The only distinction which exists is between anticipation and obviousness and the determination of either depends on what is in the prior art. Its status as prior art is not determined by whether it fully discloses or only partially discloses the claimed invention.

The concurrence also admits that lost counts in interference—which is but one way of establishing prior invention—are properly used as the basis for rejections, not only of the *same* invention but also of those obvious in view of the prior invention thus established.... [I]t makes no sense to distinguish one prior invention from another according to the *manner* in which its priority has been established. This brings us to an error of reasoning in the concurrence which treats what we are doing as "pushing back" the effective dates of references and to the use made of our remarks in the first *Hilmer* opinion. We are not pushing back the dates *of references*. As shown above, the *evidence* of *prior* invention in this case was not found *in the references* but in affidavits, admissions, and circumstances taken together with the disclosures of the references identifying the prior *subject matter*. *Hilmer* was a different situation altogether where we *were* asked to push back reference dates by reason of 35 U.S.C. § 119 to events taking place abroad, contrary to what we found to be the express desire of Congress and statutory limitations to events in the United States.

* * *

The concurrence worries about our decision making a lot of issued patents invalid, which presumably would not otherwise be. The concern is misdirected. Since we are making no change in the law—certainly no change as it is applied by other courts in infringement suits—no more patents will be invalid than is already the case. (The Patent Office never has and never will be able to examine applications as to all defenses to validity). *See* 35 U.S.C. § 282(2). However, should the law be as the concurrence would have it, the Patent Office would be compelled to issue *more* invalid patents by being barred from applying the law as other courts apply it. This is the amazing choice the concurrence makes out of fear of nightmarish situations of its own imagining. In all the years we have had the law as we now declare it to be none of them has materialized.

The concurrence makes the erroneous statement that in past cases we have based our thinking on "the proposition that *everything* in section 102 is prior art" (original emphasis). The anatomy of § 102 is fairly clear. As forecast in its heading, it deals with the two questions of "novelty and loss of right." It also deals with originality in subsection (f) which says that one who "did not himself invent the subject matter" (*i.e.*, he did not originate it) has no right to a patent on it. Subsections (c) on abandonment and (d) on first patenting the invention abroad, before the date of the U.S. application, on an application filed more than a year before filing in the U.S., are loss of right provisions and in no way relate to prior art. Of course, (c), (d), and (f) have no relation to § 103 and no relevancy to what is "prior art" under § 103. Only the remaining portions of § 102 deal with "prior art." Three of them, (a), (e), and (g), deal with events prior to applicant's invention date and the other, (b), with events more than one year prior to the U. S. *application* date. These are the "prior art" subsections.

* * *

■ BALDWIN, JUDGE, concurring, with whom ALMOND, J., joins.

On the basis of the *Milburn* case, which changed the effective date of a U.S. patent from its issue date to its filing date, the principal opinion would change the effective date of all U.S. references to the unknown point in time when their subject matter was invented. On the basis of cases dealing with the rejection of a losing interference party's claims over the lost counts, the principal opinion condones the rejection of one applicant's claims over the contents of a patent where the parties' cases had never been in interference and in fact could not be put into interference under well established law. Further, the principal opinion fails to follow our previous cases which have decided the identical point of law.

* * *

The principal opinion takes the position that the term "prior art" as it is used in 35 U.S.C. § 103 should include all inventions which were made in this country before an applicant or patentee made his invention, regardless of when those inventions are made public or patent applications on them are filed, so long as those inventions are found not to have been abandoned, suppressed or concealed. I disagree with that conclusion for the reasons stated hereinafter.

* * *

II. The Statute

* * *

The statute does not contain a definition of the term "prior art." Nor does section 103 require that *everything* referred to in section 102 must be considered as "prior art" as that term is used therein. Indeed, using the "common meaning of the words" approach to ascertain the meaning of section 103, one might easily conclude that the "prior art" was intended to include only that material in section 102 in which something is "disclosed or described." However, the history of section 103 contains indications that such an interpretation would be too restrictive. We are not called upon here to consider all aspects of the interrelationships between 102 and section 103. Our task is rather to decide whether a secret invention is within the meaning of "prior art," as that term is used in section 103, by virtue of section 102(g). Before dealing specifically with section (g), a short discussion of secret prior knowledge is in order.

III. Prior Public Knowledge or Use

The doctrine that prior knowledge or use of an invention must be *public* before it can prevent the issuance of, or invalidate, a patent to another for that invention is an old one in patent law. It was firmly adopted as a ruling doctrine of United States law in the case of *Pennock v. Dialogue*, 27 U.S. (2 Pet.) 1, 7 L.Ed. 327 (1829). The statute governing that case was the Act of 1793, Ch. 11, 1 Stat. 318, section 1 of which provided for the grant of a patent for a:

> New and useful art ... not known or used before the application.

The court held that "not known or used" meant not *publicly* known or used *by others*:

> What then is the true meaning of the words "not known or used before the application?" They cannot mean, that the thing invented was not known or used before the application, by the inventor himself, for that would be to prohibit him from the only means of obtaining a patent.... The words, then, to have any rational interpretation, must mean, not known or used by others, before the application. But how known or used? If it were necessary, as it well might be, to employ others to assist in the original structure or use by the inventor himself, or if before his application for a patent, his invention should be pirated by another, or used without his consent, it can scarcely be supposed, that the legislature had within its contemplation such knowledge or use.

> We think, then, the true meaning must be, not known or used by the public, before the application.

The validity of the above reasoning has not diminished one scintilla in the 143 years since it was put down on paper. To be sure, there has been an exception created to the rule that the prior knowledge must be public, in the case of an application for a United States patent. Under 35 U.S.C. § 102(e), which was derived from *Alexander Milburn Co. v. Davis–Bournonville Co.*, 270 U.S. 390, 46 S.Ct. 324, 70 L.Ed. 651 (1926), a U.S. patent is effective as a reference as of its application date, even though the knowledge contained in the application was not made public until the patent issued. *Hazeltine Research, Inc. v. Brenner*, 382 U.S. 252, 86 S.Ct. 335, 15 L.Ed.2d 304 (1965); *In re Harry, supra.* But as this court said in *In re Hilmer*, 359 F.2d 859, 877, 53 CCPA 1288, 1311 (1966):

> What has always been pointed out in attacks on the *Milburn* rule, or in attempts to limit it, is that it uses, as prior knowledge, information which was secret at the time *as of which* it is used—the contents of U.S. patent applications which are preserved in secrecy, generally speaking, 35 U.S.C. § 122. This is true, and we think there is some validity to the argument that that which is secret should be in a different category from knowledge which is public. Nevertheless we have the rule. However, we are not disposed to extend that rule, which applies to the date of filing application *in the United States*, the actual filing date when the disclosure is on deposit in the U.S. Patent Office and on its way, in due course, to publication in an issued patent.

> The board's new view, as expressed in this case ..., has the practical potential effect of pushing back the date of the unpublished, secret disclosures, which ultimately have effect as prior art references in the form of U.S. patents, by the full one-year priority period of section 119. We think the *Milburn* rule, as codified in section 102(e), goes far enough in that direction. We see no valid reason to go further, certainly no compelling reason.

To push the effective date of a non-anticipatory reference backwards beyond the point where the knowledge it contains was made public to the time when its author obtained that knowledge, as we are asked to do here, would be to extend the exception to the point where it essentially swallows the rule. Section 102(e) would be turned into mere surplusage, for the application date of the patent would no longer be important, except as showing a constructive reduction to practice and except insofar as it evidences an intent not to suppress, conceal or abandon.

The *Milburn* and *Hazeltine* decisions are strictly limited to applications for U.S. patents. The question in *Milburn* was whether unclaimed anticipatory disclosure in an earlier filed application was a bar to the claims in the later filed application. The Court held that it was, stating:

> We understand the Circuit Court of Appeals to admit that if Whitford had not applied for his patent until after the issue to Clifford, the disclosure by the latter would have had the same effect as the publication of the same words in a periodical, although not made the basis of a claim.... The invention is made public property as much in the one case as in the other. But if this be true, as we think that it is, it seems to us that a sound distinction cannot be taken between that case and a patent applied for before but not granted until after a second patent is sought. The delays of the patent office ought not to cut down the effect of what has been done. The description shows that Whitford was not the first inventor. Clifford had done all that he could do to make his description public. He had taken steps that would make it public as soon at [sic] the Patent Office did its work, although, of course, amendments might be required of him before the end could be reached. We see no reason in the words or policy of the law for allowing Whitford to profit by the delay and make himself out to be the first inventor when he was not so in fact, when Clifford had shown knowledge inconsistent with the allowance of Whitford's claim, [*Webster*] *Webster Loom Co. v. Higgins*, 105 U.S. 580, 26 L.Ed. 1177, and when otherwise the publication of his patent would abandon the thing described to the public unless it already was old.

The Court in *Hazeltine Research, Inc. v. Brenner*, 382 U.S. 252, at pages 255–256, 86 S.Ct. 335, at page 338, 15 L.Ed.2d 304 (1965) expressly followed the identical reasoning as that in *Milburn*, stating:

> The basic reasoning upon which the Court decided the *Milburn* case applies equally well here. When Wallace filed his application, he had done what he could to add his disclosures to the prior art. The rest was up to the Patent Office. Had the Patent Office acted faster, had it issued Wallace's patent two months earlier, there would have been no question here. As Justice Holmes said in *Milburn*, "The delays of the patent office ought not to cut down the effect of what has been done."

In neither case did the Court push the effective date of a U.S. patent backward in time any further than its filing date. Both of the cases rely on the proposition that a prior applicant when he filed his application "had done what he could to add his disclosures to the prior art." They did nothing to extend the effective date to a point *before* the inventor filed his application—a point in time when he has done absolutely nothing towards "adding his disclosures to the prior art." Such a result conflicts with the rationale behind those cases. How can filing an application be a step towards adding an invention "to the prior art" if the invention itself *is* prior art at the moment it is conceived?

* * *

VII.   *Practical Considerations*

* * *

If we allow this subjective, secret knowledge to become the standard against which patentability is judged, we will do the public a disservice by watering down the incentive that the patent system provides for the advancement of the useful arts. Very few inventions are arrived at by a "flash of genius" or accidently, for example, by spilling a rubber composition onto the stove. Most are the result of carefully planned scientific research, often with numerous persons working on various aspects of a given problem. Invention is often reached via a large number of small steps forward. Given the possibility that the special knowledge of the inventor's coworkers developed during the pursuance of the invention would be usable against any patent based on the invention which is the end result of the research effort, investors and corporate management would, or should, be most wary of using the patent system to protect any commercially valuable invention, rather than following the trade secret route. The problems presently faced under section 102(e), *see, e.g.*, Franz, *Prosecution Problems with a Plurality of Inventions From a Single Project*, 51 J.P.O.S. 559 (1969), are nothing compared to the problems which would ensue if the effective date of a patent were changed from its filing date, which is at least a definite date, to the date of "invention."

* * *

NOTES

1. *More on § 102(g)/103 Prior Art.*

a. *In re Clemens.* Seven years after *Bass*, the CCPA decided another § 102(g)/103 prior art case, *In re Clemens*, 622 F.2d 1029 (CCPA 1980). In *Clemens*, the court, in less than lucid fashion, reaffirmed the principle stated in *Bass* that § 102(g) can be used as prior art under § 103. The PTO rejected Clemens' patent application in the light of a patent issued to Barrett (filed on April 16, 1973), who was doing research for the same company as Clemens. Because Clemens filed on December 23, 1973, after Barrett, Clemens, in order to remove Barrett as a § 102(e) reference, submitted a Rule 131 affidavit (*See* Chapter Four) showing date of invention prior to Barrett's filing date. That was not the end of the story in that the PTO reasoned that Barrett could still be prior art under § 102(g) if it could be shown that Barrett invented prior to Clemens. Ultimately, however, the Barrett reference failed under § 102(g) because of insufficient evidence that Barrett invented before Clemens.

Also of some note is that the *Clemens* court distinguished *Bass* on the § 102(g)/103 issue by suggesting that an applicant must have actual knowledge of the prior invention, as in *Bass*, before § 102(g)/103 can be invoked. According to the court:

> Where an applicant begins with knowledge of another's invention that will be available to the public at a later date as a result of an issued patent,

treating this other invention as prior art is justified under facts such as those in *Bass*. No such consideration is present when the applicant does not begin with such knowledge. To the contrary, where this other invention is unknown to both the applicant and the art at the time the applicant makes his invention, treating it as 35 U.S.C. 103 prior art would establish a standard for patentability in which an applicant's contribution would be measured against secret prior art. Such a standard would be detrimental to the innovative spirit the patent laws are intended to kindle.

622 F.2d at 1039–40. Based on what you know about § 102(g), is the *Clemens* court knowledge requirement sustainable? Did the *Bass* court discuss the knowledge of the applicants? Recall, the only reason that knowledge existed in *Bass* is because the prior inventor was a later *joint* inventor, which evoked a practical concern for Judge Baldwin with respect to organized research efforts. Does the knowledge requirement in *Clemens* address the organized research concern? Do you see why it is a concern? The *Clemens* court also states that secret prior art is "detrimental to the innovative spirit" of the patent law. Does this concern echo Judge Baldwin's words in *Bass* (*see* "VII. Practical Considerations" of Judge Baldwin's concurrence), wherein he states that "[i]f we allow this subjective, secret knowledge to become the standard against which patentability is judged, we will do the public a disservice by watering down the incentive that the patent system provides for the advancement of the useful arts."

b. *Kimberly–Clark Corp. v. Johnson & Johnson.* In *Kimberly–Clark Corp. v. Johnson & Johnson*, 745 F.2d 1437 (Fed.Cir.1984), the *Bass–Clemens* issue of § 102(g)/103 prior art made its way to the Federal Circuit. Judge Rich, author of *Bass*, wrote for the majority, holding that § 102(g) prior art is available for § 103 purposes, and that § 102(g) contains "no personal knowledge requirement;" language in *Clemens* to the contrary was mere "dictum." *Id.* at 1445.

The inventor in *Kimberly–Clark* was Roeder, a researcher at Kimberly–Clark (K–C), whose application was filed on May 8, 1970. The accused infringer cited as prior art against K–C the work of Mobley and Champaigne, who were also researchers employed by K–C. The work of Champaigne was disclosed in a patent application filed on February 5, 1970 and subsequently issued as a patent. Mobley's work was never embodied in a patent application. The court found that there was insufficient evidence of reduction to practice by Mobley and therefore § 102(g) did not apply to Mobley's work. The accused infringer, relying on *Clemens*, nevertheless argued Roeder had actual knowledge of Mobley's work and therefore asserted that Mobley can be used as prior art. The majority dismissed this argument:

As § 102(g) contains no personal knowledge requirement, the [*Clemens*] court's sole discussion of personal knowledge was dictum in the course of a discussion which distinguished the facts before it from those in a previous opinion of the court also dealing with § 102(g)/103, namely *In re Bass*.

745 F.2d at 1445. As to the Champaigne reference, the court found that it satisfied the requirements of § 102(g) (*i.e.*, the invention was not abandoned, suppressed or concealed).

c. *E.I. du Pont de Nemours & Co. v. Phillips Petroleum Co.* In 1988, the Federal Circuit decided *E.I. du Pont de Nemours & Co. v. Phillips Petroleum Co.*, 849 F.2d 1430 (Fed.Cir.1988), and, like *Kimberly–Clark*, dismissed the *Clemens* knowledge requirement as dictum and reaffirmed the use of § 102(g) as prior art under § 103:

Kimberly–Clark distinguished as dictum the *Clemens* requirement of applicant's personal knowledge because "§ 102(g) contains no personal knowledge requirement." ... Nor does § 102(g) contain a "known to the art" requirement apart from the requirement of no abandonment, suppression or concealment. Hence, the alternative *Clemens* requirement that the prior work be "known to the art" is also implicitly dismissed as dictum....

Certainly the court in *Kimberly–Clark* was concerned about "secret prior art,".... Nevertheless the requirement of proving no abandonment, suppression, or concealment does mollify somewhat the "secret" nature of § 102(g) prior art. Despite its concern over "secret prior art," the court in *Kimberly–Clark* allowed prior work to be used as prior art in a § 103 context so long as it satisfied the requirements of § 102(g).

849 F.2d at 1437.

It is well settled now that § 102(g) prior art can be used for § 103 purposes. But there are some lingering questions. First, when does secret prior art under § 102(g) become abandoned, suppressed, or concealed? Neither the secret nature of the prior art, nor the failure to file a patent application results in abandonment, suppression, or concealment. *E.I. du Pont*, 849 F.2d at 1436–37. What does? Second, the *Kimberly–Clark* and *E.I. du Pont* decisions did not address the organized research problem that we saw in *Bass, Clemens,* and *Kimberly–Clark*, and that was a concern of Judge Baldwin's in *Bass*. That is, research conducted by different inventive entities working for the same company where the work of one inventive entity may be cited as prior art against another inventive entity thus resulting in diminished communication among members of research teams. Recall from Chapter Four, section 10, that for prior art purposes, two or more inventive entities (*e.g.*, (1) A; (2) A and B; and (3) A, B, and C) are treated as legally distinct even though they may have common members.

Eleven years after Judge Baldwin's concurrence, Congress addressed this problem.

d. *The Patent Law Amendments Act of 1984.* In 1984, Congress added the following sentence to what is now § 103(c):

Subject matter developed by another person, which qualifies as prior art only under subsections (f) and (g) of section 102 of this title, shall not preclude patentability under this section where the subject matter and the claimed invention were, at the time the invention was made, owned by the same person or subject to an obligation of assignment to the same person.

P.L. 98–622, § 104, 98 Stat. 3384. The legislative history nicely illustrates the purpose behind the 1984 amendment:

"Prior art" is the existing technical information against which the patentability of an invention is judged. Publicly known information is always considered in determining whether an invention is obvious. However, under *In re Bass* and *In re Clemens*, an earlier invention which is not public may be treated under section 102(g), and possibly under 102(f), as prior art with respect to a later invention made by another employee of the same organization.

New technology often is developed by using background scientific or technical information known within an organization but unknown to the public. The bill, by disqualifying such background information from prior art, will encourage communication among members of research teams, and patenting, and consequently public dissemination, of the results of "team research."

"Section-by-Section Analysis of H.R. 6286, Patent Law Amendments Act of 1984," 130 Congressional Record, Oct. 1, 1984, H10527. *See also, Kimberly–Clark Corp. v.*

Procter & Gamble Dist. Co., Inc., 973 F.2d 911, 917 (Fed.Cir.1992) (stating the purposes behind the 1984 amendment to § 103).

2. *§ 102(e)/103 Prior Art and the 1984 Amendment to § 103.* How does the 1984 amendment affect § 102(e)/103 prior art? In *In re Bartfeld*, 925 F.2d 1450 (Fed.Cir. 1991), the court stated that the 1984 amendment *only* applies to §§ 102(f) and (g) prior art even though the patent applications in issue were under common ownership and despite applicant's argument that corporate assignees would be "forced to use burdensome and costly procedures such as abandoning both applications and refiling a combined application." *Id.* Does this make good policy? Doesn't the common ownership problem apply to § 102(e)? It does. *See In re Land and Rogers*, 368 F.2d 866 (CCPA 1966) (holding that Edwin Land's first-filed application served as prior art under § 102(e)/103 against a subsequent application filed by Land and a co-inventor, Rogers). However, the text of the 1984 amendment omits § 102(e), and the legislative history states that prior art subject matter is "strictly limited" to §§ 102(f) and (g). Why do you think that § 102(e) was excluded in the 1984 amendment to § 103? Was it just an oversight?

In the end and 33 years after *In re Land and Rogers*, § 103(c) was amended to include § 102(e). *See* Section 4807 of the American Inventors Protection Act of 1999. Section 103(c) now reads in relevant part:

> Subject matter developed by another person, which qualifies as prior art only under one or more of subsections (e), (f), and (g) of section 102 of this title, shall not preclude patentability under this section were the subject matter and the claimed invention were, at the time the invention was made, owned by the same person or subject to an obligation of assignment to the same person.

The new § 103(c) applies to any application filed on or after November 29, 1999.

c. § 102(f)/103 PRIOR ART

The issue here is whether information that is only available under § 102(f) is also available under § 103. As explored below in *Oddzon*, such art is available for an obviousness analysis.

OddzOn Products, Inc. v. Just Toys, Inc.

122 F.3d 1396 (Fed.Cir.1997).

■ Before MICHEL, LOURIE, and RADER, CIRCUIT JUDGES.

■ LOURIE, CIRCUIT JUDGE.

OddzOn Products, Inc. appeals from the decision of the United States District Court for the Northern District of California granting summary judgment in favor of defendants Just Toys, Inc., Lisco, Inc., and Spalding & Evenflo Companies, Inc. (collectively "Just Toys") on OddzOn's claims of design patent infringement, trade dress infringement, and state-law unfair competition. Just Toys cross-appeals from the decision granting summary judgment in favor of the patentee OddzOn on Just Toys' claim of patent invalidity. *OddzOn Prods., Inc. v. Just Toys, Inc.*, No. 95–CV–1077 (C.A.Fed.1997). Because OddzOn has failed to demonstrate that a reasonable jury could find that Just Toys' tossing balls infringe OddzOn's design patent or protectable trade dress, and, derivatively, that there was unfair competition, we affirm the district court's judgment in favor of the defendant Just Toys. Because no reasonable jury could conclude other than that the patented design is ornamental, novel, and nonobvious, we affirm the district court's judgment that the patent was not proved invalid.

Background

OddzOn is a toy and sporting goods company that sells the popular "Vortex" tossing ball, a foam football-shaped ball with a tail and fin structure. The Vortex ball is OddzOn's commercial embodiment of its design patent, U.S. Patent D 346,001, which issued on April 12, 1994. . . .

* * *

Just Toys, Inc., another toy and sporting goods company, sells a competing line of "Ultra Pass" balls. . . .

OddzOn sued Just Toys for design patent infringement. Just Toys denied infringement and asserted that the patent was invalid. On cross-motions for summary judgment, the district court held that the patent was not shown to be invalid and was not infringed. . . .

The district court determined that two confidential designs that had been disclosed to the inventor qualified as subject matter encompassed within the meaning of 35 U.S.C. § 102(f) (1994) and concluded that these designs could be combined with other prior art designs for purposes of a challenge to the validity of the patent under 35 U.S.C. § 103 (1994). Nonetheless, the district court held that the patented design would not have been obvious in light of the prior art, including the two confidential designs. . . .

* * *

Discussion

* * *

A. The Prior Art Status of § 102(f) Subject Matter

The district court ruled that two confidential ball designs (the "disclosures") which "inspired" the inventor of the OddzOn design were prior art for purposes of determining obviousness under § 103. The district court noted that this court had recently declined to rule definitively on the relationship between § 102(f) and § 103, see *Lamb–Weston, Inc. v. McCain Foods, Ltd.*, 78 F.3d 540, 544, 37 U.S.P.Q.2D 1856, 1858–59 (Fed.Cir.1996), but relied on the fact that the United States Patent and Trademark Office (PTO) interprets prior art under § 103 as including disclosures encompassed within § 102(f). OddzOn challenges the court's determination that subject matter encompassed within § 102(f) is prior art for purposes of an obviousness inquiry under § 103. OddzOn asserts that because these disclosures are not known to the public, they do not possess the usual hallmark of prior art, which is that they provide actual or constructive public knowledge. OddzOn argues that while the two disclosures constitute patent-defeating subject matter under 35 U.S.C. § 102(f), they cannot be combined with "real" prior art to defeat patentability under a combination of § 102(f) and § 103.

The prior art status under § 103 of subject matter derived by an applicant for patent within the meaning of § 102(f) has never expressly been decided by this court. We now take the opportunity to settle the persistent question whether § 102(f) is a prior art provision for purposes of § 103. As will be discussed, although there is a basis to suggest that § 102(f) should not be considered as a prior art provision, we hold that a fair reading of § 103, as amended in 1984, leads to the conclusion that § 102(f) is a prior art provision for purposes of § 103.

Section 102(f) provides that a person shall be entitled to a patent unless "he did not himself invent the subject matter sought to be patented." This is a derivation provision, which provides that one may not obtain a patent on that which is obtained from someone else whose possession of the subject matter is inherently "prior." It does not pertain only to public knowledge, but also applies to private communications between the inventor and another which may never become public. Subsections (a), (b), (e), and (g), on the other hand, are clearly prior art provisions. They relate to knowledge manifested by acts that are essentially public. Subsections (a) and (b) relate to public knowledge or use, or prior patents and printed publications; subsection (e) relates to prior filed applications for patents of others which have become public by grant; and subsection (g) relates to prior inventions of others that are either public or will likely become public in the sense that they have not been abandoned, suppressed, or concealed. Subsections (c) and (d) are loss-of-right provisions. Section 102(c) precludes the obtaining of a patent by inventors who have abandoned their invention. Section 102(d) causes an inventor to lose the right to a patent by delaying the filing of a patent application too long after having filed a corresponding patent application in a foreign country. Subsections (c) and (d) are therefore not prior art provisions.

In *In re Bass*, 474 F.2d 1276, 1290 (CCPA 1973), the principal opinion of the Court of Customs and Patent Appeals held that a prior invention of another that was not abandoned, suppressed, or concealed (102(g) prior art) could be combined with other prior art to support rejection of a claim for obviousness under § 103. The principal opinion noted that the provisions of § 102 deal with two types of issues, those of novelty and loss-of-right. It explained: "Three of [the subsections,] (a), (e), and (g), deal with events prior to applicant's *invention* date and the other, (b), with events more than one year prior to the U.S. *application* date. These are the 'prior art' subsections." *Id.* (emphasis in original). The principal opinion added, in dictum (§ 102(f) not being at issue), that "[o]f course, (c), (d), and (f) have no relation to § 103 and no relevancy to what is 'prior art' under § 103." *Id.* There is substantial logic to that conclusion. After all, the other prior art provisions all relate to subject matter that is, or eventually becomes, public. Even the "secret prior art" of § 102(e) is ultimately public in the form of an issued patent before it attains prior art status.

Thus, the patent laws have not generally recognized as prior art that which is not accessible to the public. It has been a basic principle of patent law, subject to minor exceptions, that prior art is

> technology already available to the public. It is available, in legal theory at least, when it is described in the world's accessible literature, including

patents, or has been publicly known or in . . . public use or on sale "in this country." That is the real meaning of "prior art" in legal theory—it is knowledge that is available, including what would be obvious from it, at a given time, to a person of ordinary skill in the art.

Kimberly–Clark Corp. v. Johnson & Johnson, 745 F.2d 1437, 1453 (Fed.Cir. 1984) (citations omitted).

Moreover, as between an earlier inventor who has not given the public the benefit of the invention, *e.g.*, because the invention has been abandoned without public disclosure, suppressed, or concealed, and a subsequent inventor who obtains a patent, the policy of the law is for the subsequent inventor to prevail. *See W.L. Gore & Assocs., Inc. v. Garlock, Inc.*, 721 F.2d 1540, 1550 (Fed.Cir.1983) ("Early public disclosure is a linchpin of the patent system. As between a prior inventor [who does not disclose] and a later inventor who promptly files a patent application . . ., the law favors the latter."). Likewise, when the possessor of secret art (art that has been abandoned, suppressed, or concealed) that predates the critical date is faced with a later-filed patent, the later-filed patent should not be invalidated in the face of this "prior" art, which has not been made available to the public. Thus, prior, but non-public, inventors yield to later inventors who utilize the patent system.

However, a change occurred in the law after *Bass* was decided. At the time *Bass* was decided, § 103 read as follows:

> A patent may not be obtained though the invention is not identically disclosed or described as set forth in section 102 of this title, if the differences between the subject matter sought to be patented and the prior art are such that the subject matter as a whole would have been obvious at the time the invention was made to a person having ordinary skill in the art to which said subject matter pertains. Patentability shall not be negatived by the manner in which the invention was made.

35 U.S.C. § 103. The prior art being referred to in that provision arguably included only public prior art defined in subsections 102(a), (b), (e), and (g).

In 1984, Congress amended § 103, adding the following paragraph:

> Subject matter developed by another person, *which qualifies as prior art only under subsection (f) or (g) of section 102* of this title, shall not preclude patentability under this section where the subject matter and the claimed invention were, at the time the invention was made, owned by the same person or subject to an obligation of assignment to the same person.

35 U.S.C. § 103 (now § 103(c)) (emphasis added). It is historically very clear that this provision was intended to avoid the invalidation of patents under § 103 on the basis of the work of fellow employees engaged in team research. *See* Section-by-Section Analysis: Patent Law Amendments Act of 1984, 130 Cong. Rec. 28069, 28071 (Oct. 1, 1984), reprinted in 1984 U.S.C.C.A.N. 5827, 5833 (stating that the amendment, which encourages communication among members of research teams, was a response to *Bass* and *In re Clemens*, 622 F.2d 1029 (CCPA 1980), in which "an earlier invention which is not public may be treated under Section 102(g), and possibly under 102(f), as prior art"). There was no clearly apparent purpose in Congress's inclusion of § 102(f) in the amendment other than an attempt to ameliorate the problems of patenting the results of team

research. However, the language appears in the statute; it was enacted by Congress. We must give effect to it.

The statutory language provides a clear statement that subject matter that qualifies as prior art under subsection (f) or (g) cannot be combined with other prior art to render a claimed invention obvious and hence unpatentable when the relevant prior art is commonly owned with the claimed invention at the time the invention was made. While the statute does not expressly state in so many words that § 102(f) creates a type of prior art for purposes of § 103, nonetheless that conclusion is inescapable; the language that states that § 102(f) subject matter is not prior art under limited circumstances clearly implies that it is prior art otherwise. That is what Congress wrote into law in 1984 and that is the way we must read the statute.

This result is not illogical. It means that an invention, A', that is obvious in view of subject matter A, derived from another, is also unpatentable. The obvious invention, A', may not be unpatentable to the inventor of A, and it may not be unpatentable to a third party who did not receive the disclosure of A, but it is unpatentable to the party who did receive the disclosure.

The PTO's regulations also adopt this interpretation of the statute. 37 C.F.R. § 1.106(d) (1996) ("Subject matter which is developed by another person which qualifies as prior art only under 35 U.S.C. §§ 102(f) or (g) may be used as prior art under 35 U.S.C. § 103."). Although the PTO's interpretation of this statute is not conclusive, we agree with the district court that it is a reasonable interpretation of the statute.

It is sometimes more important that a close question be settled one way or another than which way it is settled. We settle the issue here (subject of course to any later intervention by Congress or review by the Supreme Court), and do so in a manner that best comports with the voice of Congress. Thus, while there is a basis for an opposite conclusion, principally based on the fact that § 102(f) does not refer to public activity, as do the other provisions that clearly define prior art, nonetheless we cannot escape the import of the 1984 amendment. We therefore hold that subject matter derived from another not only is itself unpatentable to the party who derived it under § 102(f), but, when combined with other prior art, may make a resulting obvious invention unpatentable to that party under a combination of §§ 102(f) and 103. Accordingly, the district court did not err by considering the two design disclosures known to the inventor to be prior art under the combination of §§ 102(f) and 103.

* * *

NOTES

1. *§ 102(f)/103 Prior Art?* As discussed in Chapter Four, *supra*, § 102(f) embodies the originality requirement. Recall that this requirement means that if a person acquires an entire idea for an invention from another person or source he cannot obtain a patent on that invention because he is not the original inventor. The issue of whether § 102(f) can be used in combination with § 103 is slightly different. Consider the following example: X obtains information about an inventive concept from another source, his friend, Y, but the information that Y conveys to X is incomplete. Therefore, § 102(f) *by itself* does not apply. However, what if the incomplete information is coupled with relevant prior art so as to make the inventive concept obvious under § 103? *Can the incomplete information derived from another source be used as prior art for § 103 purposes?* Remember in the *Bass* case, Judge Rich wrote that § 102(f) had "no relation to § 103." The Federal Circuit, on the other hand, saw things differently. Although the court initially did not directly hold that § 102(f) may be used for § 103 purposes, it certainly had suggested as much in *Lamb–Weston, Inc. v. McCain Foods, Ltd.*, 78 F.3d 540, 544 n* (Fed.Cir.1996):

> The dissent [written by Judge Newman] has provided certain citations of authority for the proposition that section 102(f) may not be used as prior art under section 103. However, the following contrary authorities should also be considered. [citing the 1984 amendment to § 103]; ... *New England Braiding Co., Inc. v. A.W. Chesterton, Co.*, 970 F.2d 878, 883 (Fed.Cir.1992) ("To invalidate a patent for derivation of invention, a party must demonstrate that the named inventor ... acquired knowledge of the claimed invention from another, or at least so much of the claimed invention as would have made it obvious to one of ordinary skill in the art.") ...

In *OddzOn*, the court spoke definitively on the issue, holding that § 102(f) can be used for § 103 purposes. How did the court reconcile Judge Rich's comments in *Bass*? The answer, according to *OddzOn*, is the 1984 amendment to § 103. On its face, the 1984 amendment to § 103 appears to be strong evidence that § 102(f) prior art can be employed under § 103 except in circumstances where the derived information and the invention are subject to common ownership. According to the court, if § 102(f) cannot be used in common ownership situations, one can argue, by negative implication, that, like § 102(g), it can be used in situations where there isn't common ownership. Do you agree? Can you think of any reasons why § 102(f) should not be used as prior art for purposes of § 103?

2. *OddzOn and Inter–Institutional Collaborative Research.* Does *OddzOn* pose a threat to patent rights for collaborative inventors employed by different institutions, which frequently occurs among academic researchers employed by different universities and research initiatives between a university and a private concern? Recall that the 1984 amendment to section 103(c) requires that, "at the time the invention" is made, the "subject matter and the claimed invention" be "owned by the same person or subject to an obligation of assignment to the same person." Presumably, this means that researchers at different institutions would be well advised to work out who is going to own patent rights before embarking on common research goals lest the resulting patent be susceptible to the obviousness requirement under § 103(c)? But isn't a negotiation of this sort cumbersome and likely to impede collaborative efforts? Is *OddzOn* contrary to the spirit of the 1984 amendments? In a reaction to the *OddzOn* decision, the "Cooperative Research and Technology Enhancement (CREATE) Act of 2004" extended the common ownership safe harbor to parties to a joint research agreement. See § 103(c)(2) and (3).

3. *§ 102(b)/103 Prior Art.* Should § 102(b) prior art also be used for purposes of § 103? The CCPA addressed this question in *In re Foster*, 343 F.2d 980 (CCPA 1965). In *Foster*, the applicant argued that § 102(b) had no applicability if the claimed invention was not disclosed in a single prior art reference. The CCPA did not agree:

> First, as to principle, since the purpose of [§ 102(b)] has always been to require filing of the application within the prescribed period after the time the public came into possession, whether by a public use, a sale, a single

patent or publications, or by combinations of one or more of the foregoing. In considering this principle we assume, of course, that by these means the invention has become obvious to that segment of the "public" having ordinary skill in the art. Once this has happened, the purpose of the law is to give the inventor only a year within which to file and this would seem to be liberal treatment. Whenever an applicant undertakes, under Rule 131, to swear back of a reference having an effective date more than a year before his filing date, he is automatically conceding that he made his invention more than a year before he filed. If the reference contains enough disclosure to make his invention obvious, the principle of the statute would seem to require denial of a patent to him. The same is true where a combination of two publications or patents makes the invention obvious and they both have dates more than a year before the filing date.

As to dealing with the express language of 102(b), for example, "described in a printed publication," technically, we see no reason to so read the words of the statute as to preclude the use of more than one reference; nor do we find in the context anything to show that a "printed publication" cannot include two or more publications. We do not have two publications here, but it is a common situation.

Id. at 988.

C.   The Content of the Prior Art

Having discussed what may qualify as prior art for § 103 purposes, we can now ask what the prior art must contain so as to render an invention obvious under § 103. In the process, we will highlight another key distinction between § 102 anticipation and § 103 obviousness. Recall that under § 102, an invention is anticipated if only a *single* prior art reference discloses each and every limitation of the claimed invention. That is, one cannot combine references under § 102. There is no such restriction imposed upon § 103. In fact, an overwhelming majority of obviousness decisions involve more than one prior art reference. As such, there is usually a combination of references that, when read together, present § 103 problems for an inventor. But the Federal Circuit and its predecessor, the CCPA, have made it perfectly clear on numerous occasions that before prior art references can be combined under § 103, the references must *suggest* to a person of ordinary skill in the art that he should make the invention and, once made, would have a *reasonable expectation of success*. Thus, although § 103, unlike § 102, permits one to combine prior art references, one must have a reason to do so.

McGinley v. Franklin Sports, Inc.

262 F.3d 1339 (Fed.Cir.2001).

■ Before Mayer, Chief Judge, Michel and Clevenger, Circuit Judges.

■ Clevenger, Circuit Judge.

This is a patent infringement suit in which Michael L. McGinley charges Franklin Sports, Inc. ("FSI") with infringement of claims 1, 2, 6, and 7 of U.S. Patent No. 5,407,193 ("the '193 patent"). On summary judgment, the United States District Court for the District of Kansas ruled in favor of McGinley on the issue of infringement, and the case proceeded to trial on the issues of validity. The jury found that the asserted claims were not invalid. On a subsequent motion filed by FSI for judgment as a matter of law ("JMOL"), the trial court set aside the jury verdict on validity, holding that the asserted claims of the '193 patent are invalid as obvious pursuant to 35 U.S.C. § 103(a).

McGinley appeals the district court's grant of JMOL of invalidity. . . .

Because we conclude that the district court erred in finding that no reasonable jury could have reached a verdict of nonobviousness, we reverse the JMOL of invalidity. . . .

I

Background

The application for the '193 patent was filed on July 3, 1991, and the patent issued on April 18, 1995. In general terms, the '193 patent discloses and claims an instructional pitching device in the form of a regulation baseball with specific "finger placement indicia" for teaching students how to grasp a baseball for throwing different types of pitches. With the endorsement of a famous professional baseball pitcher, McGinley's invention was marketed and distributed as the Roger Clemens Instructional Baseball ("RCIB"). FSI also manufactured and sold a baseball designed to teach students to throw different types of pitches. The accused device in this case, the Franklin Pitch Ball Trainer 2705 ("FSI's 2705 baseball"), was sold in the United States from at least as early as April 1995 to March 1999.

In the preferred embodiment of the claimed invention, an aspect of which is illustrated in the following figure, three sets of finger placement indicia 11 are positioned on the cover 17 of a regulation baseball 10. Each set of indicia 11 is intended to illustrate the placement of a student pitcher's index and middle fingers so as to throw a particular type of pitch (*e.g.*, two-seam fast ball, slider, curve ball, etc.).

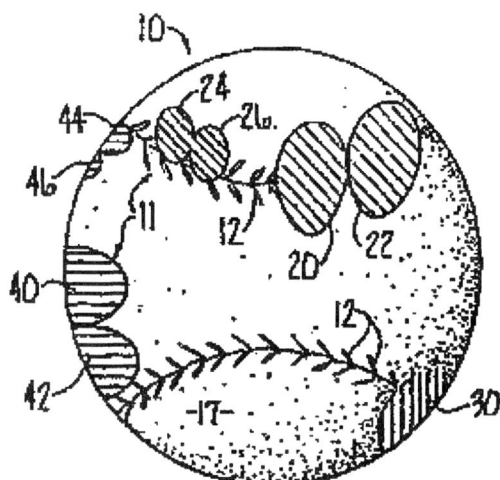

Indicia 11 are presented in two sizes, to allow the indicia intended for a left-handed student to be easily distinguished from the indicia intended for a right-handed student. The smaller indicia, exemplified by indicia 24 and 26, are intended for use by left-handed pitchers, while the larger indicia, as represented by indicia 20 and 22, are intended for use by right-handed pitchers. Moreover, indicia 11 are coded by coloring all indicia which are representative of a certain type of pitch in one color and indicia representative of another type of pitch in a different color. To further assist a student in learning how to throw a particular pitch, the indicia are shaped so as to indicate the relationship of the palm of the hand in grasping the ball. Specifically, the portion of each "egg-shaped" indicium to be situated closest to the palm is slightly tapered so as to indicate the correct orientation of the baseball in the palm. Although the preferred embodiment of the '193 patent makes no provisions for "thumb placement indicia," the written description of the '193 patent repeatedly states that the thumb is generally to be positioned on the baseball at a location opposite the corresponding set of finger placement indicia.

As originally filed in 1991, the claims of the '193 patent required that eight sets of finger placement indicia be provided on a single baseball pitching training device. Specifically, the four original claims all required the presence of indicia demarcating the placement of fingers for four specific types of pitches (i.e., curve ball, two-seam fast ball, slider, and four-seam fast ball), for both left-handed and right-handed students. These claims were rejected on obviousness grounds in view of U.S. Patent No. 2,925,273 ("Pratt"), which had issued on February 16, 1960, more than thirty years before McGinley's filing date. Pratt was brought to the attention of the Patent and Trademark Office ("PTO") via an Information Disclosure Statement ("IDS") filed concurrently with McGinley's priority patent application by McGinley's counsel.

Like the claims originally filed by McGinley, Pratt disclosed, inter alia, a conventional baseball having multiple sets of finger placement indicia for teaching baseball players to throw different types of pitches. Specifically, in the embodiment illustrated in Figure 4 (shown below), Pratt's written description disclosed the placement of finger and thumb placement indicia for three types of pitches (*i.e.,* fast ball, curve ball, and screw ball). Equatorial band 17 was an important feature of Pratt's claimed invention. When a student threw Pratt's baseball correctly, bands of complementary colors in the equatorial band would blend into a single color to provide a visual indication to the student that the ball had been thrown with proper rotation.

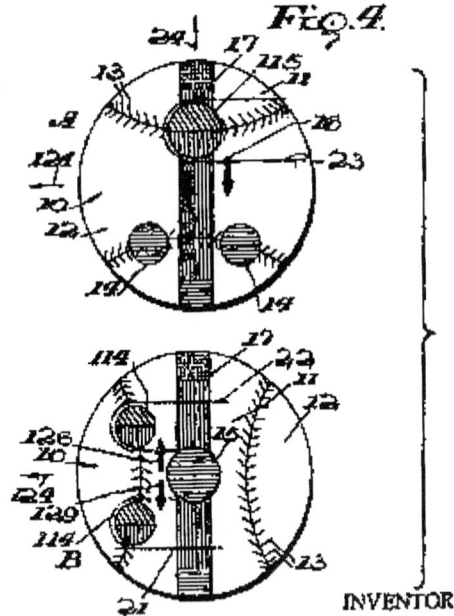

Fig. 4.

INVENTOR

Although the similarities between Pratt's disclosure and McGinley's then-existing claims are striking, there are also a few differences between Pratt's teachings and McGinley's initially claimed invention. First, Pratt did not provide for different sets of indicia on a single ball for distinguishing between left-handed and right-handed students. Also, Pratt's finger placement indicia were described and illustrated as being circular, but "phantom lines" illustrating the placement of fingers 21, 22 and thumb 23 were included in the patent figures. These phantom lines, however, are not described in Pratt as actual markings on the baseball. In contrast, the finger placement indicia in the preferred embodiment of McGinley's invention are actually marked on the ball, and are "egg-shaped" and slightly tapered at one end to indicate the proper orientation of the ball with respect to the student's palm.

Another prior art reference which was brought to the attention of the PTO via McGinley's IDS was U.S. Patent No. 3,110,494 ("Morgan"), which issued on November 12, 1963. In contrast to Pratt and the '193 patent, which are based on using a conventional regulation baseball, Morgan describes a baseball training device using a lightweight and inexpensive baseball "replica" fabricated in the form of plastic or metallic hemispherical shells which occupy a minimum of space before use, but which can be easily assembled by gluing the two hemispherical halves together. In Figure 6 of Morgan (shown below) and the accompanying written description, a single set of finger-shaped marks "D", "E", and "L" (for teaching proper placement of the forefinger, middle finger, and thumb, respectively) are provided on the baseball training device to teach a student how to throw a baseball with a particular curve or break.

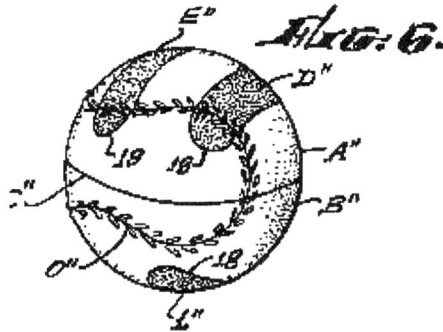

Throughout the prosecution history of the '193 patent, McGinley's claims at issue in this case were rejected in view of Pratt on anticipation grounds. With respect to Morgan, although this reference was before the PTO during the entire pendency of McGinley's patent application, it was never explicitly relied upon as a basis for a rejection based on a prima facie case of anticipation or obviousness.

Ultimately, in 1995, after a series of rejections, amendments, and responses (including a partially successful appeal to the Board of Patent Appeals and Interferences and the filing of a continuation application), the '193 patent issued with 14 claims. Ten of the issued claims (*i.e.,* claims 3–5 and 8–14) explicitly retain the original limitation requiring the inclusion of finger placement indicia on a single baseball pitching training device for both left-handed and right-handed students. These claims were not asserted in this case. Instead, McGinley asserted the remaining four claims (*i.e.,* independent claim 1 and dependent claims 2, 6, and 7) against FSI, alleging willful infringement by making and selling the 2705 baseball. The asserted claims read as follows in their entirety:

1. A baseball pitching training device for duplicating finger placement on a baseball by a student comprising:

a baseball cover;

a plurality of sets of finger placement indicia on said cover, said sets of indicia comprising:

a first set of indicia demarcating the placement of finger [sic] for throwing a first pitch;

a second set of indicia demarcating the placement of fingers for throwing, [sic] a second pitch;

a third set of indicia demarcating the placement of fingers for throwing a third pitch;

means for indicating the orientation of the baseball relative to the palm of the hand; and

means for coding said finger placement indicia sets for identification of each of said indicia associated with any one of said sets.

2. The device as claimed in claim 1 wherein said means for coding comprises a color for association with each indicia of a particular set.

6. The device as claimed in claim 1, wherein said means for indicating orientation comprises shaping said indicia to distinguish that portion of the baseball to be located proximate to the palm of the hand.

7. The device as claimed in claim 1 wherein said indicia are shaped to indicate a correct orientation of the baseball with respect to the palm of the hand.

'193 patent, col. 5, ll. 29–48; col. 5, ll. 61–64; col. 6, ll. 1–3.

.... [T]he district court denied FSI's motion for partial summary judgment on validity, finding disputed issues of material fact with respect to the obviousness issue. The case proceeded to trial, and on January 19, 2000, the jury returned a verdict in favor of McGinley, finding the '193 patent not invalid and willfully infringed.

FSI then filed a post-trial motion, seeking JMOL on the issue of validity. In the alternative, FSI also moved for a new trial. On April 5, 2000, the district court set aside the jury's verdict and granted FSI's motion for JMOL on invalidity, concluding that "as a matter of law, plaintiff's patent is invalid as obvious in light of Pratt or the combination of Pratt and Morgan." Judgment was entered in favor of FSI, and this appeal followed, vesting us with jurisdiction pursuant to 28 U.S.C. § 1295(a)(1).

* * *

IV

Obviousness

A patent is invalid for obviousness if "differences between the subject matter sought to be patented and the prior art are such that the subject matter as a whole would have been obvious at the time the invention was made to a person having ordinary skill in the art to which said subject matter pertains." 35 U.S.C. § 103(a) (1994). "Throughout the obviousness determination, a patent retains its statutory presumption of validity, *see* 35 U.S.C. § 282, and the movant retains the burden to show the invalidity of the claims by clear and convincing evidence as to underlying facts." *Rockwell Int'l. Corp. v. United States,* 147 F.3d 1358, 1364 (Fed.Cir.1998).

Although it is well settled that the ultimate determination of obviousness is a question of law, it is also well understood that there are factual issues underlying the ultimate obviousness decision. *Richardson–Vicks Inc. v. Upjohn Co.,* 122 F.3d 1476, 1479 (Fed.Cir.1997). Specifically, the obviousness analysis is based on four underlying factual inquiries, the well-known *Graham* factors: (1) the scope and content of the prior art; (2) the differences between the claims and the prior art; (3) the level of ordinary skill in the pertinent art; and (4) secondary considerations, if any, of nonobviousness. *Graham v. John Deere Co.,* 383 U.S. 1, 17–18 (1966).

At trial, FSI argued, inter alia, that the asserted claims of the '193 patent were obvious in view of either Pratt alone, or in view of Pratt in combination with Morgan. FSI's obviousness theories are best summarized in its own words from its opening brief on appeal:

> The only element of the asserted claims that is not clearly anticipated by the Pratt patent is the finger shaped marks that orient the ball with respect to the palm of the user's hand. However, this feature is obvious in light of the lines indicating finger placement on the drawings of the Pratt patent. Moreover, the concept of a set of finger marks to orient the ball is clearly taught in the Morgan patent. It would have been obvious to one of ordinary skill in the art to substitute the finger marks of the Morgan patent for the marks of the Pratt patent. Or, stated another way, it would have been obvious to place three sets of marks on the Morgan ball in light of the teaching of Pratt.

In other words, FSI argued to the jury that the "missing element" in Pratt (*i.e.,* the "means for orientation") can be found either in the "phantom lines" of Pratt or in Figure 6 of Morgan. McGinley argued at trial that there was no motivation to combine the prior art as suggested by FSI. . . .

The jury agreed with McGinley. Specifically, in the special verdict form used in this case, the jury answered three questions that are relevant to this appeal in favor of McGinley. First, the jury found that FSI had not proven by clear and convincing evidence that each of the elements of the invention defined in claims 1, 2, 6 and 7 of the '193 patent is disclosed in Pratt. This was a factual finding. *In re Beattie,* 974 F.2d 1309, 1311 (Fed.Cir.1992) ("What a reference teaches is a question of fact.").

Second, the jury found that FSI had not proven by clear and convincing evidence that any of the asserted claims were invalid as being obvious in view of Pratt alone. Finally, the jury found that FSI had not proven by clear and convincing evidence that any of the asserted claims were invalid as being obvious in view of a combination of Pratt and Morgan. These latter two findings by the jury are directed to the ultimate legal issue of obviousness, and provide no insight as to the jury's findings with respect to the underlying factual underpinnings. . . .

In its motion for JMOL, FSI argued that no reasonable jury could have concluded that the asserted claims were not obvious in view of either Pratt alone or in view of Pratt in combination with Morgan. The district court agreed, and granted FSI's motion for JMOL. Specifically, the court found that "no reasonable jury could conclude that the motivation to combine Pratt and Morgan did not exist." . . . .

* * *

Whether a patent claim is obvious under section 103 depends upon the answer to several factual questions and how the factual answers meld into the legal conclusion of obviousness *vel non*. In this case, we think that the central question is whether there is reason to combine the Pratt and Morgan references, because if the references are properly combined, it is certain that the claims are prima facie invalid for obviousness. If the jury was entitled to conclude that these two references should not be combined, then the asserted claims of the '193 patent cannot be invalid for obviousness in the light of the proposed combination. If those claims are not invalid under a combination of Pratt and Morgan, then, as a matter of logic, those claims cannot be invalid in the light of Pratt alone. We thus turn first to the issue of whether Pratt and Morgan must be combined.

The genius of invention is often a combination of known elements which in hindsight seems preordained. To prevent hindsight invalidation of patent claims, the law requires some "teaching, suggestion or reason" to combine cited references. *Gambro Lundia AB v. Baxter Healthcare Corp.,* 110 F.3d 1573, 1579 (Fed.Cir.1997). When the art in question is relatively simple, as is the case here, the opportunity to judge by hindsight is particularly tempting. Consequently, the tests of whether to combine references need to be applied rigorously.

Whether a motivation to combine prior art references has been demonstrated is a question of fact. *Winner Int'l Royalty Corp. v. Wang,* 202 F.3d 1340, 1348 (Fed.Cir.2000). The assessment of whether to combine references in a given case has sometimes been viewed conceptually as a subset of the first *Graham* factor, the scope and content of the prior art. Although that view is not incorrect, accurate assessment of whether to combine references may require attention to other *Graham* factors. For example, the level of skill in the art may inform whether the artisan would find a suggestion to combine in the teachings of an exemplar of prior art. Where the level of skill is high, one may assume a keener appreciation of nuances taught by the prior art. Similarly, appreciation of the differences between the claims in suit and the scope of prior art references—a matter itself informed by the operative level of skill in the art—informs the question of whether to combine prior art references. At bottom, in each case the factual inquiry whether to combine references must be thorough and searching.

There is no question here that FSI presented sufficient evidence at trial from which a jury could have decided that one of ordinary skill in this case would have been motivated to combine Pratt and Morgan to produce a prima facie obvious invention. Specifically, FSI argued to the jury that the only elements of the asserted claims that are not clearly anticipated by Pratt are the finger-shaped marks that orient the ball with respect to the palm of the user's hand. Referring to the "phantom lines" in Pratt as suggestive of finger placement on the ball, FSI argued that one of ordinary skill would have been motivated to substitute the finger marks from the Morgan ball for the circular marks on Pratt, or alternatively to place three sets of marks on the Morgan ball in the light of Pratt's teachings. In addition, FSI argued that one of ordinary skill would have known to add the finger orientation means of the Morgan patent to Pratt by "filling in" the phantom lines in Pratt's drawings and treating them as finger orientation means.

But the jury did not hear a one-sided case on the issue of obviousness, generally and in particular on whether to combine Pratt and Morgan. As FSI conceded at oral argument, McGinley presented reasons to the jury to reject a combination of the references. McGinley argued many grounds to support his contention that the asserted claims are not obvious in the light of Pratt and Morgan. To counter FSI's claim that those references should be combined to render McGinley's "means for orientation" obvious, McGinley pointed to specific differences between the prior art and the asserted claims. For example, Morgan does not disclose the required markings for at least three different kinds of pitches, as do the asserted claims. And Morgan does not disclose markings on a real baseball, as do Pratt and the asserted claims. We recount the gist of this testimony below.

> The jury heard from Mr. Charles Quinn, FSI's vice president of marketing and corporate representative at trial. Quinn testified in detail as to the express teachings of Pratt and Morgan, and as to the differences between these references and the asserted claims. For example, he conceded that the markings on the baseball in Pratt's invention were circular, and therefore incapable of indicating orientation. He also acknowledged that the "phantom lines" in Pratt's drawings were not actually markings on a baseball. Quinn also pointed out that Morgan did not discuss implementing a baseball training device using a regulation baseball. Moreover, he acknowledged that Morgan taught only the provision of indicia for throwing a single type of pitch on each training device, instead of three sets of indicia as required in the asserted claims.

The jury also heard from Mr. Richard Stitt, the attorney who prosecuted the '193 patent. Stitt testified at length about the prosecution history of the '193 patent and the fact that Pratt and Morgan were considered by the PTO throughout the entire pendency of McGinley's application. He confirmed that the "phantom lines" in Pratt's drawings were not actually marked on a baseball. Stitt also pointed out that the PTO never rejected the asserted claims as obvious in view of Pratt, and that it was never suggested by the PTO that the phantom lines of Pratt could easily be transferred to the actual baseball to arrive at McGinley's claimed invention.

Stitt testified that the PTO never rejected McGinley's claims by saying that one could substitute the "elongate finger-shaped markings" shown in Figure 6 of Morgan in place of the "circular dots" in Pratt. He also pointed out that the PTO could have issued an obviousness rejection of the asserted claims based on a theory of transferring Pratt's phantom lines onto the baseball, but never did so. Similarly, he testified that the PTO could have issued an obviousness rejection of the asserted claims based on a theory of combining Pratt with Morgan, but never did so either.

Stitt also testified that he flew to the Patent Office in Washington, D.C., with McGinley for an interview with the Examiner to discuss the differences between Pratt and Morgan and the claimed invention. Finally, he explained in detail why neither Pratt nor Morgan alone or in combination with each other would provide the claimed "means for orientation."

In addition, McGinley relied heavily on the presumption of validity to which his patent is entitled by the terms of 35 U.S.C. § 282, mainly in the context of Stitt's tutorial concerning how McGinley's patent was prosecuted, and in McGinley's opening statement and closing argument to the jury. As noted above, throughout the trial, McGinley pointed out that both the Pratt and Morgan references were before the examiner who tested McGinley's patent for validity. Indeed, those two references were discussed in an interview between the applicant and the examiner. The examiner rejected McGinley's claims as anticipated by Pratt, and made no mention of any concern as to obviousness in view of Pratt alone or of a combination of Pratt and Morgan. The Board of Patent Appeals and Interferences reversed the examiner's anticipation rejection, holding that Pratt failed to teach McGinley's means for orienting the baseball relative to the palm of the hand. In due course, McGinley's patent issued and became clothed with the statutory presumption of validity, with no obviousness challenge having been mounted against it, either on the basis of Pratt alone, or of Pratt in combination with Morgan.

The jury in this case was expressly charged that the patent in suit is entitled to the presumption of validity, and that FSI could only overcome that burden with clear and convincing evidence to the contrary. It is well established in our case law that FSI's burden in this case was especially heavy:

> When no prior art other than that which was considered by the PTO examiner is relied on by the attacker [FSI], he has the added burden of overcoming the deference that is due to a qualified government agency presumed to have properly done its job, which includes one or more examiners who are assumed to have some expertise in interpreting the references and to be familiar from their work with the level of skill in the art and whose duty it is to issue only valid patents. In some cases a PTO board of appeals may have approved the issuance of the patent.

American Hoist & Derrick Co. v. Sowa & Sons, Inc., 725 F.2d 1350, 1359 (Fed.Cir.1984), *cert. denied,* 469 U.S. 821 (1984).

Perhaps McGinley's best argument to save his claims from prima facie obviousness in the light of Pratt and Morgan is his contention that those references together teach away from their combination. We have noted elsewhere, as a "useful general rule," that references that teach away cannot serve to create a prima facie case of obviousness. *In re Gurley,* 27 F.3d 551, 553 (Fed.Cir.1994). If references taken in combination would produce a "seemingly inoperative device," we have held that such references teach away from the combination and thus cannot serve as predicates for a prima facie case of obviousness. *In re Sponnoble,* 405 F.2d 578, 587 (1969) (references teach away from combination if combination produces seemingly inoperative device).

McGinley argues in his brief that Pratt itself teaches away from combining the finger orientation of Morgan, because Pratt, by teaching only the placement of finger tips on the baseball, leads away from placing a full finger orientation on the ball. Such may be the case, but we have no assurance that the jury heard that argument. At oral argument in this court, however, FSI confirmed that McGinley argued to the jury that adding the finger marks of Morgan to Pratt's baseball, by "filling in" the phantom marks to create structure that defines orientation as claimed, would require obliteration of the claimed rotation arrows, a feature that is necessary in order to permit the Pratt invention to operate properly. FSI also confirmed at oral argument that the jury heard McGinley's argument that to combine the finger placements of Morgan onto the Pratt ball would also render the Pratt ball inoperable, by eliminating the multi-colored equatorial band, a claimed feature of the Pratt patent also required for successful operation of Pratt's invention.

We are satisfied that McGinley presented sufficient evidence as well to counter FSI's alternative argument that it would have been obvious to place three sets of marks on the Morgan ball in light of the teaching of Pratt. First, a reasonable jury could have determined from examining the Morgan reference that the finger placement indicia on Morgan are too large to allow the inclusion of more than a single set of markings. This point is important, because Morgan expressly requires markings on the ball to accommodate the placement of two full fingers and a thumb to simulate throwing a single pitch. The jury could have certainly concluded that one of ordinary skill would not attempt to place markings for two additional pitches on Morgan's ball. Two more sets of markings as shown by Morgan itself would require markings for two additional sets of fingers and thumbs. On the other hand, two sets of markings as shown by Pratt would lead to confusion as to the correct means for orientation on Morgan's ball. Any such configurations, *i.e.,* Morgan's invention with markings for throwing three different pitches, would risk, if not achieve, obliteration of the clear and unmistakable markings shown on Morgan's ball to teach the throwing of a single curving pitch. Moreover, a reasonable jury could have considered that all of the embodiments described and illustrated in the Morgan reference are expressly limited to teaching a student pitcher to throw a baseball with a "particular curve or break," and that none of the embodiments discuss or suggest using a conventional baseball as opposed to a hollow shell comprising two metallic or plastic hemispheres glued or otherwise bonded together. The jury also could have concluded that Morgan—with its full finger and thumb imprint markings on the ball—teaches away from a means for orientation using the smaller tear-drop markings disclosed by McGinley or the small truncated finger-shaped markings used in FSI's accused baseballs.

Given the strength of the teaching away point, we think it remarkable that FSI makes no attempt whatsoever in its brief to counter McGinley's argument. The jury's verdict that the claims in suit are not obvious is supported by the evidence brought forward by McGinley to resist FSI's contrary evidence. Here we have the classic example of sufficient evidence to support each position argued to the jury. The key issue, namely what the references teach and whether they teach the necessity of combination or the requirement of separation, is a fact issue. When the jury is supplied with sufficient valid factual information to support the verdict it reaches, that is the end of the matter. In such an instance, the jury's factual conclusion may not be set aside by a JMOL order.

Given the multiple bases upon which the jury's verdict in favor of McGinley can be sustained over FSI's arguments for combining the references, we must conclude that FSI fares no better in arguing a combination of Pratt into Morgan than it does in arguing a combination of Morgan into Pratt. The jury was thus entitled to reach its verdict of nonobviousness on the ground that one of ordinary skill in the art would not deem the asserted claims of the '193 patent obvious in light of Pratt and Morgan in combination. That being the case, it is illogical to think that one of ordinary skill in the art would have deemed McGinley's claims obvious in the light of Pratt alone. If one of ordinary skill is not taught by Morgan to extend Pratt's circular markings into the phantom lines, that person would not be taught by the phantom lines alone to do so.

Nonetheless, we think the district court erred as well in its decision that McGinley's asserted claims were obvious as a matter of law in view of Pratt alone. According to the district court's reasoning, no reasonable jury could have failed to conclude that an ordinarily skilled artisan would have been motivated to transfer the finger-shaped "phantom lines" shown in the Pratt reference onto the actual Pratt baseball itself, thus providing the missing "means for orientation" that is admittedly otherwise missing in Pratt.

It should be noted that the "phantom lines" shown in Pratt are virtually identical to the finger-shaped markings on Fig. 6 of the Morgan reference, except that the Morgan markings are "filled-in" and actually marked on the ball. Therefore, many of the arguments mentioned above with respect to Morgan apply with equal force with respect to the Pratt phantom lines. Specifically, as FSI conceded at oral argument before this court, the jury heard McGinley's argument that transferring large finger-shaped markings (such as those illustrated in Fig. 6 of Morgan or in the phantom lines of Pratt) would render the Pratt invention inoperable by interfering with the multi-colored equatorial band. Thus, according to this evidence, one of ordinary skill in designing baseballs for use as pitching trainers would not be motivated to modify Pratt by filling in the phantom lines to express palm-oriented finger placement on the ball. As mentioned above, the jury also heard extensive testimony concerning the prosecution history of the '193 patent, including the critical facts that (1) Pratt was before the PTO during the entire pendency of the patent application, and (2) although the PTO continued to reject the asserted claims as anticipated by Pratt until McGinley won an appeal before the Board on that point, the PTO never rejected the asserted claims as obvious in view of Pratt alone. Surely, relying on the presumption of regularity that applies to all administrative agencies such as the PTO, the jury could have reasonably concluded that if the PTO believed that an obviousness rejection based on Pratt alone was warranted, such a rejection would have been promptly been made. Also, just as was the case with the Morgan markings, the jury could have reasonably concluded from an examination of the references that the Pratt phantom lines are so large that it would not be feasible to include three sets of them on a single baseball, as required by the asserted claims. Because substantial evidence supports the jury's implicit factual finding that no motivation to modify Pratt in that manner has been demonstrated in this case, the district court's ruling that Pratt alone renders the asserted claims obvious as a matter of law was erroneous.

Due to the "black box" nature of the jury's verdict, it is impossible to determine which of the above pieces of evidence, alone or in combination, carried the day in the jury room, and how much weight was assigned to each piece. All that can be said with certainty is that—as a whole—the evidence enumerated above (all of which was admittedly before the jury) constitutes substantial evidence to support the jury's verdict....

For the reasons set forth above, we conclude that the district court erred when it ruled on JMOL that no reasonable juror could have ruled that FSI failed to make out a case of obviousness by clear and convincing evidence.

NOTES

1. *The Two–Part Test.* An obviousness rejection requires both a suggestion in the art to combine the references and a reasonable expectation of success once combined.

a. *A Suggestion in the Art.* A finding of obviousness requires that there be a suggestion, teaching, or motivation to combine the prior art references. The policy behind this requirement was stated by the Federal Circuit in *McGinley*: "The genius of invention is often a combination of known elements which in hindsight seems preordained" and "[t]o prevent hindsight invalidation of patent claims, the law requires some 'teaching, suggestion or reason' to combine cited references." 262 F.3d at 1531.

The source of the suggestion may come (1) "from the references themselves;" (2) "from knowledge of those skilled in the art that certain references, or disclosures in the references, are known to be of special interest or importance in the particular filed;" and (3) "from the nature of a problem to be solved, leading inventors to look to references relating to possible solutions to that problem." *Pro–Mold & Tool Company v. Great Lakes Plastics, Inc.*, 75 F.3d 1568, 1573 (Fed.Cir. 1996). Thus, the suggestion does not have to be explicit. *See In re Nilssen*, 851 F.2d 1401, 1403 (Fed.Cir.1988) ("[F]or the purpose of combining references, those references need not explicitly suggest combining teachings, much less specific references."). In *In re Oetiker*, 977 F.2d 1443, 1447 (Fed.Cir.1992), Judge Nies, in an interesting concurring opinion, sought to clarify this notion of suggestion in the prior art, noting that "it would better reflect the concept of obviousness to speak in terms of *'from the prior art'* rather than *'in the prior art.'* " She added:

> The word "from" expresses the idea of the statute that we must look at the obviousness issue through the eyes of one of ordinary skill in the art and what one would be presumed to know with that background. What would be obvious to one of skill in the art is a different question from what would be obvious to a layman. An artisan is likely to extract more than a layman from reading a reference.

> While there must be some teaching, reason, suggestion, or motivation to combine existing elements to produce the claimed device, it is not necessary that the cited references or prior art specifically suggest making the combination.... Such suggestion or motivation to combine prior art teachings can derive solely from the existence of a teaching, which one of ordinary skill in the art would be presumed to know, and the use of that teaching to solve the same or similar problem which it addresses.

> In sum, it is off the mark for litigants to argue, as many do, that an invention cannot be held to have been obvious unless a suggestion to combine prior art teachings is found *in* a specific reference.

Id. at 1448 (emphasis in original). All of this having been said about the debates over how to combine prior art for the suggestion, it is clear that the source of the suggestion may not be the applicant's own disclosure. *See In re Dow*, 837 F.2d 469 (Fed.Cir.1988).

b. *A Reasonable Expectation of Success.* In addition to proving that the prior art suggests to a person of ordinary skill in the art to make the claimed invention, one must also show that once the invention is made the person with ordinary skill in the art would have a reasonable expectation of success; absolute predictability is not required.

2. *Prior Art as a Whole.* In an obviousness determination, it is impermissible to "pick and choose" from a prior art reference only that which will lend support to your position. As the Federal Circuit has stated: "We do not 'pick and choose among the individual elements of assorted prior art references to recreate the claimed invention,' but rather, we look for 'some teaching or suggestion in the references to support their use in the particular claimed combination.'" *Symbol Technologies, Inc. v. Opticon, Inc.*, 935 F.2d 1569, 1576 (Fed.Cir.1991). *See also, SmithKline Diagnostics, Inc. v. Helena Laboratories Corp.*, 859 F.2d 878, 887 (Fed.Cir.1988).

3. *Hindsight Prohibited.* The court in *Dow* wrote of the inappropriateness of "hindsight" in making obviousness determinations. Indeed, there is a temporal dimension to a § 103 determination in that the decision-maker is required to ask whether the invention was obvious "at the time the invention was made." What is obvious today was not necessarily obvious yesterday. As such, the Federal Circuit has repeatedly stated that the use of "hindsight" is prohibited in determining obviousness. The inappropriateness of hindsight was discussed in *Panduit Corp. v. Dennison Mfg. Co.*, 774 F.2d 1082, 1090–91 (Fed.Cir.1985), in an opinion by the Federal Circuit's first Chief Judge, Howard Markey:

> It is not appropriate for the Court to engage in hindsight. Furthermore, it is not appropriate for the Court to pick and choose isolated elements from various prior art references and combine them so as to yield the invention in question when such combining would not have been an obvious thing to do at the time in question.

* * *

> The record compels the conclusion that the district court ... was unable to cast the mind back to the "time the invention was made." 35 U.S.C. § 103. The court did not, as the statute requires, view the prior art from the perspective of one skilled in the art and uninformed by [the inventor's] testimony.... In deciding the obviousness question, the district court looked to knowledge taught by the inventor, ... in his patents and in his testimony, and then used that knowledge against its teacher. The test is whether the subject matter of the claimed invention would have been obvious to one skilled in the art at the time the inventions were made, not what would be obvious to a judge after reading the patents in suit and hearing the testimony.

See also W.L. Gore & Assoc., Inc. v. Garlock, Inc., 721 F.2d 1540, 1553 (Fed.Cir. 1983) ("It is difficult but necessary that the decision-maker forget what he or she has been taught at trial about the claimed invention and cast the mind back to the time the invention was made (often as here many years), to occupy the mind of one skilled in the art who is presented only with the references, and who is normally guided by the then-accepted wisdom of the art."); *In re Shuman*, 361 F.2d 1008, 1012 (CCPA 1966) ("It is impermissible to first ascertain factually what appellants did and then view the prior art in such a manner as to select from the random facts of that art only those which may be modified and then utilized to reconstruct appellants' invention from such prior art."). It is also worth mentioning that Judge Rich invoked Milton's PARADISE LOST, Part VI, L. 478–501, which "so aptly described" this notion of "hindsight reconstruction":

The invention all admired, and each how he To be the inventor missed; so easy it seemed, Once found, which yet unfound most would have thought, Impossible!

Gillette Co. v. S.C. Johnson & Son, Inc., 919 F.2d 720, 726 (Fed.Cir.1990).

Lastly, as Judge Markey's words in *Panduit* indicate, it is impermissible to use the inventor's patent disclosure itself as prior art because such did not exist "at the time the invention was made." *See Interconnect Planning Corp. v. Feil*, 774 F.2d 1132, 1138 (Fed.Cir.1985) ("The invention must be viewed not with the blueprint drawn by the inventor, but in the state of the art that existed at the time."); *see also, Grain Processing Corp. v. American Maize–Products Co.*, 840 F.2d 902, 907 (Fed.Cir.1988) ("Care must be taken to avoid hindsight reconstruction by using 'the patent in suit as a guide through the maze of prior art references, combining the right references in the right way so as to achieve the result of the claims in suit.' "). In this regard, it is important to keep in mind that even the known solvability of a problem can make the problem easier to solve; and the patentee's own success in achieving the claimed invention makes it easier for us now to look back at the prior art and think it would have been easy to combine all of its diverse teachings to reach the claimed invention. Perhaps for this reason, the Federal Circuit has cautioned against hindsight bias when considering a large number of complex possibilities. Ortho–McNeil Pharmaceutical v. Mylan Labs., 520 F.3d 1358 (Fed.Cir. 2008) (distinguishing "the easily traversed, small and finite number of alternatives that *KSR* suggested might support an inference of obviousness"). For a discussion of nonobviousness in the context of psychological research on the "hindsight bias," see Jeffrey J. Rachlinski, *A Positive Psychological Theory of Judging in Hindsight*, 65 U. Chi. L. Rev. 571, 613–15 (1998).

4. *Teaching Away and Inconsistent Teachings.* If the prior art, as in *McGinley*, is not only silent, but actually discourages a person of ordinary skill in the art to combine the references in a way that would render the claimed invention obvious, then can one conclude that the requisite teaching or suggestion is not present? While the Federal Circuit believes this to be "a useful general rule," it has warned that "such a rule can not be adopted in the abstract, for it may not be applicable in all factual circumstances. Although a reference that teaches away is a significant factor to be considered in determining unobviousness, the nature of the teaching is highly relevant, and must be weighed in substance." *In re Gurley*, 27 F.3d 551, 553 (Fed.Cir.1994). *See also, United States v. Adams*, 383 U.S. 39, 52 (1966) ("This is not to say that one who merely finds new uses for old inventions by shutting his eyes to their prior disadvantages thereby discovers a patentable innovation. We do say, however, that known disadvantages in old devices which would naturally discourage the search for new inventions may be taken into account in determining obviousness").

In *Gurley*, the patent applicant claimed a flexible *epoxy-based* printed circuit material. The PTO found applicant's invention to be obvious in the light of the Yamaguichi reference, which disclosed a printed circuit material comprised of a *polyester-imide,* not an epoxy-based substance. The Yamaguichi reference recognized the usefulness of an epoxy-based material, stating that it had "some degree of flexibility," but ultimately regarded it as inferior to that of a polyester-imide resin. The court in *Gurley*, 27 F.3d at 553, discussed what is meant by teaching away:

> A reference may be said to teach away when a person of ordinary skill, upon reading the reference, would be discouraged from following the path set out in the reference, or would be led in a direction divergent from the path that was taken by the applicant. The degree of teaching away will of course depend on the particular facts; in general, a reference will teach away if it suggests that the line of development flowing from the reference's disclosure is unlikely to be productive of the result sought by the applicant.

The court then specifically addressed applicant's assertion that Yamaguichi teaches away from his claimed invention:

[E]poxy was known, the structure of these circuit boards was known, and epoxy had been used for [the applicant's] purpose. We share [applicant's] view that a person seeking to improve the art of flexible circuit boards, on learning from Yamaguichi that epoxy was inferior to polyester-imide resins, might well be led to search beyond epoxy for improved products. However, Yamaguichi also teaches that epoxy is usable and has been used for [applicant's] purpose. The board recognized Yamaguichi's teaching of the deficiencies of epoxy-impregnated material, but observed that [applicant] did not distinguish his epoxy from the product described by Yamaguichi.... Even reading Yamaguichi's description as discouraging use of epoxy for this purpose, [applicant] asserted no discovery beyond what was known to the art.

Gurley, 27 F.3d at 553. Is the court saying that a reference will teach away when a person of ordinary skill in the art, having made what the reference discloses, would not have a "reasonable expectation of success?" Do you think that if one followed Yamaguichi's description, one would have a reasonable expectation of success no matter if the epoxy or polyester-resin were used?

What happens when the prior art discloses inconsistent or conflicting teachings? Consider the following example: X files a patent application claiming an apparatus having elements A, B, and C. The invention pertains to a seismograph to be used in mountainous regions like the Alps, and the addition of C is thought, by the applicant, to yield greater accuracy. Prior art reference number 1 (PR#1), relating to an underwater seismograph, discloses A and B, but suggests that the addition of C lends itself to a more accurate device. However, prior art reference number 2 (PR#2), which evaluated PR#1, states that the addition of C in PR#1 yields no improvement in accuracy. Would you grant X a patent knowing what you do about PR#1 and PR#2? The Federal Circuit was faced with a similar situation in *In re Young*, 927 F.2d 588 (Fed.Cir.1991):

Even if tending to discredit [PR#1], [PR#2] cannot remove [PR#1] from the prior art. Patents are part of the literature of the art and are relevant for all they contain.

When prior art contains apparently conflicting references, the Board must weigh each reference for its power to suggest solutions to an artisan of ordinary skill. The Board must consider all disclosures of the prior art, ... to the extent that the references are ... in analogous fields of endeavor and thus would have been considered by a person of ordinary skill in the field of the invention. The Board, in weighing the suggestive power of each reference, must consider the degree to which one reference might accurately discredit another.

Id. at 591.

D.   JUST WHO IS THIS PERSON HAVING ORDINARY SKILL IN THE ART?

A § 103 obviousness determination is based on whether a person having ordinary skill in the art (PHOSITA)[30] to which the claimed inven-

---

30. The acronym, PHOSITA, was coined by Cyril A. Soans in his article *Some Absurd Presumptions in Patent Cases*, 10 IDEA 433, 436 (1966). Soans referred to the person having ordinary skill in the art as "Mr. Phosita."

tion pertains would have found the claimed invention obvious. But just who is this person with ordinary skill? What is *ordinary* skill in the art? What is the breadth of this person's knowledge?

Who is the "Person Having Ordinary Skill in the Art"? It is well settled that we are not talking about the inventor or any particular expert or handyman, but rather a *hypothetical* person who has ordinary skill in the art to which the claimed invention pertains. Thus, "subjective motivations of inventors is not material." *Life Technologies, Inc. v. Clontech Laboratories, Inc.*, 224 F.3d 1320, 1325 (Fed.Cir.2000). Consider the Federal Circuit's discussion in *Kimberly–Clark Corp. v. Johnson & Johnson, Co.*, 745 F.2d 1437, 1453–54 (Fed.Cir.1984) (emphasis added):

> Since January 1, 1953, the effective date of the 1952 Patent Act, ... courts [no longer made] use of the legal fiction that an *inventor* must be presumed to know the "prior art." The inventor, for purposes of legal reasoning, has been replaced, as some courts have discovered, by the statutory hypothetical "person of ordinary skill in the art" who has been provided by 35 U.S.C. § 103. Since that date, there has been no need to presume that the inventor knows anything about the prior art.

> Since we believe that progress in legal thinking is not only possible but highly desirable when it simplifies such thinking, we believe the time has come to discontinue this particular fiction of the patent law. Congress has given us in § 103 a substitute for the former "requirement for invention," which gave rise to the presumption, and that substitute being statutory, should be used exclusively. We hereby declare the presumption that the *inventor* (emphasis added) has knowledge of all material prior art to be dead.

> What controls the patentability of the fruits of the inventor's labors are the statutory conditions of novelty, utility, and unobviousness "to a person having ordinary skill in the art to which said subject matter pertains" as stated in § 103. *It should be clear that that hypothetical person is not the inventor, but an imaginary being possessing "ordinary skill in the art"* created by Congress to provide a *standard of patentability*, a descendant of the "ordinary mechanic acquainted with the business" of *Hotchkiss v. Greenwood*. Realistically, courts never have judged patentability by what the real inventor/applicant/patentee could or would do. Real inventors, as a class, vary in their capacities from ignorant geniuses to Nobel laureates; the courts have always applied a standard based on an imaginary worker of their own devising whom they have equated with the inventor.

See also, Standard Oil Co. v. American Cyanamid Co., 774 F.2d 448, 454 (Fed.Cir.1985) ("Inventors, as a class, according to the concepts underlying the Constitution and the statutes that have created the patent system, possess something—call it what you will—which sets them apart from the workers of ordinary skill, and one should not go about determining obviousness under § 103 by inquiring into what patentees ... would have known or would likely have done, faced with the revelations of references.").

What Level of Skill is "Ordinary?" The term "ordinary" was placed in § 103 to curb those judges who had a penchant for permitting too high of a skill level (*e.g.*, extra-ordinary skill). But how does one determine what is "ordinary skill?" The Federal Circuit has set forth several factors that should be considered. In *Environmental Designs, Ltd. v. Union Oil Co.*, 713 F.2d 693, 696 (Fed.Cir.1983), the court noted:

Factors that may be considered in determining level of ordinary skill in the art include: (1) the educational level of the inventor; (2) type of problems encountered in the art; (3) prior art solutions to those problems; (4) rapidity with which innovations are made; (5) sophistication of the technology; and (6) educational level of the workers in the field.

According to the court in *Custom Accessories, Inc. v. Jeffrey–Allan Industries, Inc.*, 807 F.2d 955, 963 (Fed.Cir.1986), "[n]ot all such factors may be present in every case, and one or more of them may predominate." For specific examples, *see Orthopedic Equip v. All Orthopedic*, 707 F.2d 1376, 1382 (Fed.Cir.1983):

> The district court specifically found that the level of ordinary skill at the time of the invention was that of an engineer having at least a few years of design experience working in the field of developing orthopedic soft goods. Appellant attacks this finding as lacking evidentiary support and setting the level of skill at an unnecessarily high level. It, however, points to no evidence in the record establishing that the district court's finding is clearly erroneous, although the inventor himself was not an engineer. Although the educational level of the inventor may be a factor to consider in determining the level of ordinary skill in the art, it is by no means conclusive. Other factors which may be relevant in ascertaining the level of ordinary skill in the art include "the various prior art approaches employed, the types of problems encountered in the art, the rapidity with which innovations are made, the sophistication of the technology involved, and the educational background of those actively working in the field ..."

See also, Medtronic Inc. v. Intermedics, Inc., 799 F.2d 734, 739 n.14 (Fed.Cir.1986) ("The 'level of skill' as set by stipulation of the parties was a 'person having the combination of skill and knowledge of a cardiac surgeon together with the expertise of biomedical engineer having a mechanical or electrical aptitude or engineering degree.' "); *Geo M. Martin Co. v. Alliance Machine Systems Int'l LLC*, 618 F.3d 1294 (Fed.Cir.2010) (" '[T]hough not determinative of statutory obviousness, [simultaneous invention is] strong evidence of what constitutes the level of ordinary skill in the art.' ") (quoting *Ecolochem, Inc. v. Southern California Edison Co.*, 227 F.3d 1361, 1379 (Fed.Cir.2000)).

What is the Breadth of the Hypothetical Person's Knowledge? Although the level of skill in the art is ordinary, the breadth of our hypothetical person is perfect. Complete knowledge of all pertinent art is presumed, despite that such a presumption is unrealistic. As Judge Learned Hand stated, "[w]e must suppose the inventor to be endowed, as in fact no inventor is endowed; we are to impute to him knowledge of all that is not only in his immediate field, but in all fields nearly akin to that field." *International Cellucotton Prod. Co. v. Sterilek Co.*, 94 F.2d 10, 13 (2d Cir.1938). *See also, Custom Accessories, Inc. v. Jeffrey–Allan Industries, Inc.*, 807 F.2d 955, 962 (Fed.Cir.1986) ("The person of ordinary skill is a hypothetical person who is presumed to be aware of all the pertinent prior art.").

Judge Rich has portrayed the person of ordinary skill in the art "as working in his shop with the prior art references—which he is presumed to know—hanging on the walls around him." *In re Winslow*, 365 F.2d 1017, 1020 (CCPA 1966) (the workshop analogy is sometimes referred to as the "*Winslow* Tableau"). The following cases have evoked the workshop analogy. *See Para–Ordnance Manufacturing, Inc. v. SGS Importers International, Inc.*, 73 F.3d 1085, 1088 (Fed.Cir.1995); *Allen Organ Co. v. Kimball International, Inc.*, 839 F.2d 1556, 1564 (Fed.Cir.1988); *Liberty Leather Products, Co. v. VT International Ltd.*, 894 F.Supp. 136, 140 (S.D.N.Y. 1995); *General American Transportation Corp. v. Cryo–Trans, Inc.*, 893 F.Supp. 774, 792 (N.D.Ill.1995); *Nordberg, Inc. v. Telsmith, Inc.*, 881 F.Supp. 1252, 1293 (E.D.Wis.1995).

What is the policy behind this presumption? What are the potential complications or problems, if any, with presuming that a person of ordinary skill has perfect knowledge of the pertinent art? As one of us wrote, "[t]he policy behind this presumption of knowledge is clear enough. In order to discourage wasteful or duplicative original inventive activity, the patent laws impose an absolute duty to research the entire pertinent prior art for a solution to a problem at hand. However, the presumption ... dilutes the weight of both expert testimony and evidence of prior failures in the art— since both are often predicated on less-than-perfect knowledge of the prior art." Chisum, 2 Patents § 5.04[1] (1997).

Furthermore, consider the following comments from the prominent patent practitioner, Tom Arnold:

> The inventor sometimes works without his end function in mind or his problem clearly defined. He has available in his mind and handy in references he considers "a likely place to look" thousands of ideas, elements, thoughts,.... 99 44/100ths of his information is chaff information, totally unuseful for his purpose. And often he does not know where the wheat information is.... The inventor at the time of his entry into the very high economic risk venture that is R & D, even though knowing of all the references, had difficulty selecting which references to try to combine together because he didn't yet know which combinations would work. Once his references were selected he had the foresight and the determination that they would, only to find his choice of references was in error because the ones he had selected wouldn't combine properly. He has to go back and start his selection process again and then foresee the manner of combining his new choice of references. Again and again.

* * *

> Even assuming knowledge of every relevant reference, they don't all come to mind in pre-assembled order when the invention has not yet been made. The man of ordinary skill works in context of the haystack of chaff art. Pick out the three closest references, set them up side by side, remind him of the *applicability here* known but forgotten things like magnetism as a means for detachable connecting metal parts, and of course the invention is obvious. Not so, when the nature of the reference, the utility of the reference, the applicability of the references, the location of the reference, are all obscured in the haystack of chaff knowledge.

> When infringers start a search to prove patent invalidity, ... they know what elements to look for, and what combination to look for. They search the scrap heap of ideas that failed, resurrect abandoned dreams never enjoyed or used by anybody, using the knowledge of the invention's value and success to screen the chaff art out, retaining only the three or four gems of most relevant art.

* * *

It is quite clear that *Winslow* is in error when it suggests that only the references screened out by the hindsight use of the workability of the invention as a screen, have been selected from the masses of the references in the art and put in physical juxtaposition one to another on the wall in front of the inventor. That physical juxtaposition of only the most closely related references is a totally unnatural and improper description of the environment in which the inventor must work. . . .

Tom Arnold, *Converting Hindsight to Foresight Judgment*, 12 (1972) (emphasis in original). In the end, the CCPA, particularly Judge Rich, in *In re Antle,* somewhat revised the workshop analogy of *Winslow*:

In *Winslow* we said that the principal secondary reference was "in the very same art" as appellant's invention and characterized all the references as "very pertinent art." The language relied on by the solicitor, quoted above, therefore, does not apply in cases where the very point in issue is whether one of ordinary skill in the art would have selected, without the advantage of hindsight and knowledge of the applicant's disclosure, the particular references which the examiner applied. As we also said in *Winslow,* "Section 103 requires us to presume full knowledge by the inventor of the prior art in the field of his endeavor", but it does not require us to presume full knowledge by the inventor of prior art outside the field of his endeavor, *i.e.,* of "non-analogous" art. In that respect, it only requires us to presume that the inventor would have that ability to select and utilize knowledge from other arts reasonably pertinent to his particular problem which would be expected of a man of ordinary skill in the art to which the subject matter pertains.

In re Antle, 444 F.2d at 1171–72.

SIDE BAR

Two Thoughts About 103

John F. Witherspoon*

The first thought concerns language. Perhaps we should delete from Section 103 language having nothing to do with its essence and unnecessarily suggesting the importance of method. The substantive inquiry is whether the subject matter sought to be patented, as a whole, would have been obvious at the time the invention was made to a person having ordinary skill in the art. If it were not, of course it was because of the *differences* between that subject matter and the prior art. How else could it have been nonobvious? Thus, the following language in Section 103 is not needed: "the differences between the subject matter sought to be patented and the prior art are such that." More important, that language can be mischievous, by directing attention to differences rather than to results. Note, for example, the Supreme Court's concern with "The Obviousness of the Differences" in *Graham v. John Deere Co.*, 383 U.S. 1 (1966). "The gap," the Court said later, "is simply not so great as to render the system nonobvious. . . ." *Dann v. Johnston*, 425 U.S. 219 (1976).

The second thought relates to substance. Section 103 identifies two bodies of subject matter: the subject matter sought to be patented and the prior art. Obviousness, we are told, is to be determined from the standpoint of a person having ordinary skill in the art to which the subject matter sought to be patented pertains. Is this not an invitation for hindsight? Should not the determination always be made from the standpoint of a worker in the *prior* art? It is as though the inventor had been walking around the mainland (the prior art), ventured out to sea, made his invention (the island), and we are now asked to decide whether the island would have been obvious. According to the statutory language, we should stand on the island and determine whether a person having ordinary skill in the art of the island (the invention) would have done what the inventor has done. But at the time the invention was made the inventor was working not on the island (which didn't exist) but on the mainland, and it is from the latter that obviousness is to be viewed. In practical application, it seems to me, the person having ordinary skill in the art should be the person having ordinary skill in whatever art (that portion of the mainland) upon which an examiner or party litigant relies in a given case to allege that the invention would have been obvious.

* Member of the District of Columbia Bar and editor of the book NONOBVIOUSNESS—THE ULTIMATE CONDITION OF PATENTABILITY, BNA (1980). Mr. Witherspoon practices patent law in Washington, D.C., and is Distinguished Professor of Intellectual Property Law and Coordinator of the Specialty Track in Intellectual Property Law at George Mason University School of Law, as well as Adjunct Professor of at Georgetown University Law Center. From 1971–1978 he was an Examiner-in-Chief and member of the Patent and Trademark Office Board of Appeals (a predecessor to the present Board of Patent Appeals and Interferences). From 1964 to 1966 he was a law clerk to Judge Giles Rich. This SIDE BAR was adapted specially for PRINCIPLES OF PATENT LAW.

KSR v. Teleflex

550 U.S. 398 (2007).

■ KENNEDY, J., delivered the opinion for a unanimous Court.

Teleflex Incorporated and its subsidiary Technology Holding Company—both referred to here as Teleflex—sued KSR International Company for patent infringement. The patent at issue, United States Patent No. 6,237,565B1, is entitled "Adjustable Pedal Assembly With Electronic Throttle Control." The patentee is Steven J. Engelgau, and the patent is referred to as "the Engelgau patent." Teleflex holds the exclusive license to the patent.

Claim 4 of the Engelgau patent describes a mechanism for combining an electronic sensor with an adjustable automobile pedal so the pedal's position can be transmitted to a computer that controls the throttle in the vehicle's engine. When Teleflex accused KSR of infringing the Engelgau patent by adding an electronic sensor to one of KSR's previously designed pedals, KSR countered that claim 4 was invalid under the Patent Act, 35 U. S. C. § 103, because its subject matter was obvious.

* * *

In Graham v. John Deere Co. of Kansas City, 383 U. S. 1 (1966), the Court set out a framework for applying the statutory language of § 103, language itself based on the logic of the earlier decision in Hotchkiss v. Greenwood, 11 How. 248 (1851), and its progeny. See 383 U. S., at 15–17. The analysis is objective:

> "Under § 103, the scope and content of the prior art are to be determined; differences between the prior art and the claims at issue are to be ascertained; and the level of ordinary skill in the pertinent art resolved. Against this background the obviousness or nonobviousness of the subject matter is determined. Such secondary considerations as commercial success, long felt but unsolved needs, failure of others, etc., might be utilized to give light to the circumstances surrounding the origin of the subject matter sought to be patented." Id., at 17–18.

While the sequence of these questions might be reordered in any particular case, the factors continue to define the inquiry that controls. If a court, or patent examiner, conducts this analysis and concludes the claimed subject matter was obvious, the claim is invalid under § 103.

Seeking to resolve the question of obviousness with more uniformity and consistency, the Court of Appeals for the Federal Circuit has employed an approach referred to by the parties as the "teaching, suggestion, or motivation" test (TSM test), under which a patent claim is only proved obvious if "some motivation or suggestion to combine the prior art teachings" can be found in the prior art, the nature of the problem, or the knowledge of a person having ordinary skill in the art. See, e.g., Al–Site Corp. v. VSI Int'l, Inc., 174 F. 3d 1308, 1323–1324 (CA Fed. 1999). KSR challenges that test, or at least its application in this case. Because the Court of Appeals addressed the question of obviousness in a manner contrary to § 103 and our precedents, we granted certiorari. We now reverse.

* * *

The District Court granted summary judgment in KSR's favor. After reviewing the pertinent history of pedal design, the scope of the Engelgau patent, and the relevant prior art, the court considered the validity of the contested claim. By direction of 35 U. S. C. § 282, an issued patent is presumed valid. The District Court applied *Graham*'s framework to determine whether under summary-judgment standards KSR had overcome the presumption and demonstrated that claim 4 was obvious in light of the prior art in existence when the claimed subject matter was invented. See § 102(a). The District Court determined, in light of the expert testimony and the parties' stipulations, that the level of ordinary skill in pedal design was " 'an undergraduate degree in mechanical engineering (or an equivalent amount of industry experience) [and] familiarity with pedal control systems for vehicles.' " 298 F. Supp. 2d, at 590. The court then set forth the relevant prior art, including the patents and pedal designs described above.

Following *Graham*'s direction, the court compared the teachings of the prior art to the claims of Engelgau. It found "little difference." 298 F. Supp. 2d, at 590. Asano taught everything contained in claim 4 except the use of a sensor to detect the pedal's position and transmit it to the computer controlling the throttle. That additional aspect was revealed in sources such as the '068 patent and the sensors used by Chevrolet. Under the controlling cases from the Court of Appeals for the Federal Circuit, however, the District Court was not permitted to stop there. The court was required also to apply the TSM test. The District Court held KSR had satisfied the test. It reasoned (1) the state of the industry would lead inevitably to combinations of electronic sensors and adjustable pedals, (2) Rixon provided the basis for these developments, and (3) Smith taught a solution to the wire chafing problems in Rixon, namely locating the sensor on the fixed structure of the pedal. This could lead to the combination of Asano, or a pedal like it, with a pedal position sensor.

The conclusion that the Engelgau design was obvious was supported, in the District Court's view, by the PTO's rejection of the broader version of claim 4. Had Engelgau included Asano in his patent application, it reasoned, the PTO would have found claim 4 to be an obvious combination of Asano and Smith, as it had found the broader version an obvious combination of Redding and Smith. As a final matter, the District Court held that the secondary factor of Teleflex's commercial success with pedals based on Engelgau's design did not alter its conclusion. The District Court granted summary judgment for KSR.

With principal reliance on the TSM test, the Court of Appeals reversed. It ruled the District Court had not been strict enough in applying the test, having failed to make " 'finding[s] as to the specific understanding or principle within the knowledge of a skilled artisan that would have motivated one with no knowledge of [the] invention' . . . to attach an electronic control to the support bracket of the Asano assembly." 119 Fed. Appx., at 288 (brackets in original) (quoting In re Kotzab, 217 F. 3d 1365, 1371 (CA Fed. 2000)). The Court of Appeals held that the District Court was incorrect that the nature of the problem to be solved satisfied this requirement because unless the "prior art references address[ed] the precise problem that the patentee was trying to solve," the problem would not motivate an inventor to look at those references. 119 Fed. Appx., at 288.

Here, the Court of Appeals found, the Asano pedal was designed to solve the " 'constant ratio problem' "—that is, to ensure that the force required to depress the pedal is the same no matter how the pedal is adjusted—whereas Engelgau sought to provide a simpler, smaller, cheaper adjustable electronic pedal. Ibid. As for Rixon, the court explained, that pedal suffered from the problem of wire chafing but was not designed to solve it. In the court's view Rixon did not teach anything helpful to Engelgau's purpose. Smith, in turn, did not relate to adjustable pedals and did not "necessarily go to the issue of motivation to attach the electronic control on the support bracket of the pedal assembly." Ibid. When the patents were interpreted in this way, the Court of Appeals held, they would not have led a person of ordinary skill to put a sensor on the sort of pedal described in Asano.

That it might have been obvious to try the combination of Asano and a sensor was likewise irrelevant, in the court's view, because " ' "[o]bvious to try" has long been held not to constitute obviousness.' " Id., at 289 (quoting In re Deuel, 51 F. 3d 1552, 1559 (CA Fed. 1995)).

The Court of Appeals also faulted the District Court's consideration of the PTO's rejection of the broader version of claim 4. The District Court's role, the Court of Appeals explained, was not to speculate regarding what the PTO might have done had the Engelgau patent mentioned Asano. Rather, the court held, the District Court was obliged first to presume that the issued patent was valid and then to render its own independent judgment of obviousness based on a review of the prior art. The fact that the PTO had rejected the broader version of claim 4, the Court of Appeals said, had no place in that analysis.

The Court of Appeals further held that genuine issues of material fact precluded summary judgment. Teleflex had proffered statements from one expert that claim 4 " 'was a simple, elegant, and novel combination of features,' " 119 Fed. Appx., at 290, compared to Rixon, and from another expert that claim 4 was nonobvious because, unlike in Rixon, the sensor was mounted on the support bracket rather than the pedal itself. This evidence, the court concluded, sufficed to require a trial.

II

A

We begin by rejecting the rigid approach of the Court of Appeals. Throughout this Court's engagement with the question of obviousness, our cases have set forth an expansive and flexible approach inconsistent with the way the Court of Appeals applied its TSM test here. To be sure, *Graham* recognized the need for "uniformity and definiteness." 383 U. S., at 18. Yet the principles laid down in *Graham* reaffirmed the "functional approach" of Hotchkiss, 11 How. 248. See 383 U. S., at 12. To this end, *Graham* set forth a broad inquiry and invited courts, where appropriate, to look at any secondary considerations that would prove instructive. Id., at 17.

Neither the enactment of § 103 nor the analysis in *Graham* disturbed this Court's earlier instructions concerning the need for caution in granting a patent based on the combination of elements found in the prior art. For over a half century, the Court has held that a "patent for a combination which only unites old elements with no change in their respective functions ... obviously withdraws what is already known into the field of its monopoly and diminishes the resources available to skillful men." Great Atlantic & Pacific Tea Co. v. Supermarket Equipment Corp., 340 U. S. 147, 152 (1950). This is a principal reason for declining to allow patents for what is obvious. The combination of familiar elements according to known methods is likely to be obvious when it does no more than yield predictable results. Three cases decided after *Graham* illustrate the application of this doctrine.

In United States v. Adams, 383 U. S. 39, 40 (1966), a companion case to *Graham*, the Court considered the obviousness of a "wet battery" that varied from prior designs in two ways: It contained water, rather than the acids conventionally employed in storage batteries; and its electrodes were magnesium and cuprous chloride, rather than zinc and silver chloride. The Court recognized that when a patent claims a structure already known in the prior art that is altered by the mere substitution of one element for another known in the field, the combination must do more than yield a predictable result. 383 U. S., at 50–51. It nevertheless rejected the Government's claim that Adams's battery was obvious. The Court relied upon the corollary principle that when the prior art teaches away from combining certain known elements, discovery of a successful means of combining them is more likely to be nonobvious. Id., at 51–52. When Adams designed his battery, the prior art warned that risks were involved in using the types of electrodes he employed. The fact that the elements worked together in an unexpected and fruitful manner supported the conclusion that Adams's design was not obvious to those skilled in the art.

In Anderson's–Black Rock, Inc. v. Pavement Salvage Co., 396 U. S. 57 (1969), the Court elaborated on this approach. The subject matter of the patent before the Court was a device combining two pre-existing elements: a radiant-heat burner and a paving machine. The device, the Court concluded, did not create some new synergy: The radiant-heat burner functioned just as a burner was expected to function; and the paving machine did the same. The two in combination did no more than they would in separate, sequential operation. Id., at 60–62. In those circumstances, "while the combination of old elements performed a useful function, it added nothing to the nature and quality of the radiant-heat burner already patented," and the patent failed under § 103. Id., at 62 (footnote omitted).

Finally, in Sakraida v. AG Pro, Inc., 425 U. S. 273 (1976), the Court derived from the precedents the conclusion that when a patent "simply arranges old elements with each performing the same function it had been known to perform" and yields no more than one would expect from such an arrangement, the combination is obvious. Id., at 282.

The principles underlying these cases are instructive when the question is whether a patent claiming the combination of elements of prior art is obvious. When a work is available in one field of endeavor, design incentives and other market forces can prompt variations of it, either in the same field or a different one. If a person of ordinary skill can implement a predictable variation, § 103 likely bars its patentability. For the same reason, if a technique has been used to improve one device, and a person of ordinary skill in the art would recognize that it would improve similar devices in the same way, using the technique is obvious unless its actual application is beyond his or her skill. Sakraida and Anderson's–Black Rock are illustrative—a court must ask whether the improvement is more than the predictable use of prior art elements according to their established functions.

Following these principles may be more difficult in other cases than it is here because the claimed subject matter may involve more than the simple substitution of one known element for another or the mere application of a known technique to a piece of prior art ready for the improvement. Often, it will be necessary for a court to look to interrelated teachings of multiple patents; the effects of demands known to the design community or present in the marketplace; and the background knowledge possessed by a person having ordinary skill in the art, all in order to determine whether there was an apparent reason to combine the known elements in the fashion claimed by the patent at issue. To facilitate review, this analysis should be made explicit. See In re Kahn, 441 F. 3d 977, 988 (CA Fed. 2006) ("[R]ejections on obviousness grounds cannot be sustained by mere conclusory statements; instead, there must be some articulated reasoning with some rational underpinning to support the legal conclusion of obviousness"). As our precedents make clear, however, the analysis need not seek out precise teachings directed to the specific subject matter of the challenged claim, for a court can take account of the inferences and creative steps that a person of ordinary skill in the art would employ.

B

When it first established the requirement of demonstrating a teaching, suggestion, or motivation to combine known elements in order to show that the combination is obvious, the Court of Customs and Patent Appeals captured a helpful insight. See Application of Bergel, 292 F. 2d 955, 956–957 (1961). As is clear from cases such as Adams, a patent composed of several elements is not proved obvious merely by demonstrating that each of its elements was, independently, known in the prior art. Although common sense directs one to look with care at a patent application that claims as innovation the combination of two known devices according to their established functions, it can be important to identify a reason that would have prompted a person of ordinary skill in the relevant field to combine the elements in the way the claimed new invention does. This is so because inventions in most, if not all, instances rely upon building blocks long since uncovered, and claimed discoveries almost of necessity will be combinations of what, in some sense, is already known.

Helpful insights, however, need not become rigid and mandatory formulas; and when it is so applied, the TSM test is incompatible with our precedents. The obviousness analysis cannot be confined by a formalistic conception of the words teaching, suggestion, and motivation, or by over-emphasis on the importance of published articles and the explicit content of issued patents. The diversity of inventive pursuits and of modern technology counsels against limiting the analysis in this way. In many fields it may be that there is little discussion of obvious techniques or combinations, and it often may be the case that market demand, rather than scientific literature, will drive design trends. Granting patent protection to advances that would occur in the ordinary course without real innovation retards progress and may, in the case of patents combining previously known elements, deprive prior inventions of their value or utility.

In the years since the Court of Customs and Patent Appeals set forth the essence of the TSM test, the Court of Appeals no doubt has applied the test in accord with these principles in many cases. There is no necessary inconsistency between the idea underlying the TSM test and the *Graham* analysis. But when a court transforms the general principle into a rigid rule that limits the obviousness inquiry, as the Court of Appeals did here, it errs.

C

The flaws in the analysis of the Court of Appeals relate for the most part to the court's narrow conception of the obviousness inquiry reflected in its application of the TSM test. In determining whether the subject matter of a patent claim is obvious, neither the particular motivation nor the avowed purpose of the patentee controls. What matters is the objective reach of the claim. If the claim extends to what is obvious, it is invalid under § 103. One of the ways in which a patent's subject matter can be proved obvious is by noting that there existed at the time of invention a known problem for which there was an obvious solution encompassed by the patent's claims.

The first error of the Court of Appeals in this case was to foreclose this reasoning by holding that courts and patent examiners should look only to the problem the patentee was trying to solve. 119 Fed. Appx., at 288. The Court of Appeals failed to recognize that the problem motivating the patentee may be only one of many addressed by the patent's subject matter. The question is not whether the combination was obvious to the patentee but whether the combination was obvious to a person with ordinary skill in the art. Under the correct analysis, any need or problem known in the field of endeavor at the time of invention and addressed by the patent can provide a reason for combining the elements in the manner claimed.

The second error of the Court of Appeals lay in its assumption that a person of ordinary skill attempting to solve a problem will be led only to those elements of prior art designed to solve the same problem. Ibid. The primary purpose of Asano was solving the constant ratio problem; so, the court concluded, an inventor considering how to put a sensor on an adjustable pedal would have no reason to consider putting it on the Asano pedal. Ibid. Common sense teaches, however, that familiar items may have obvious uses beyond their primary purposes, and in many cases a person of ordinary skill will be able to fit the teachings of multiple patents together like pieces of a puzzle. Regardless of Asano's primary purpose, the design provided an obvious example of an adjustable pedal with a fixed pivot point; and the prior art was replete with patents indicating that a fixed pivot point was an ideal mount for a sensor. The idea that a designer hoping to make an adjustable electronic pedal would ignore Asano because Asano was designed to solve the constant ratio problem makes little sense. A person of ordinary skill is also a person of ordinary creativity, not an automaton.

The same constricted analysis led the Court of Appeals to conclude, in error, that a patent claim cannot be proved obvious merely by showing that the combination of elements was "obvious to try." Id., at 289 (internal quotation marks omitted). When there is a design need or market pressure to solve a problem and there are a finite number of identified, predictable solutions, a person of ordinary skill has good reason to pursue the known options within his or her technical grasp. If this leads to the anticipated success, it is likely the product not of innovation but of ordinary skill and common sense. In that instance the fact that a combination was obvious to try might show that it was obvious under § 103.

The Court of Appeals, finally, drew the wrong conclusion from the risk of courts and patent examiners falling prey to hindsight bias. A fact finder should be aware, of course, of the distortion caused by hindsight bias and must be cautious of arguments reliant upon ex post reasoning. See Graham, 383 U. S., at 36 (warning against a "temptation to read into the prior art the teachings of the invention in issue" and instructing courts to " 'guard against slipping into the use of hindsight' " (quoting Monroe Auto Equipment Co. v. Heckethorn Mfg. & Supply Co., 332 F. 2d 406, 412 (CA6 1964))). Rigid preventative rules that deny fact finders recourse to common sense, however, are neither necessary under our case law nor consistent with it.

We note the Court of Appeals has since elaborated a broader conception of the TSM test than was applied in the instant matter. See, e.g., DyStar Textilfarben GmbH & Co. Deutschland KG v. C. H. Patrick Co., 464 F. 3d 1356, 1367 (2006) ("Our suggestion test is in actuality quite flexible and not only permits, but requires, consideration of common knowledge and common sense"); Alza Corp. v. Mylan Labs., Inc., 464 F. 3d 1286, 1291 (2006) ("There is flexibility in our obviousness jurisprudence because a motivation may be found implicitly in the prior art. We do not have a rigid test that requires an actual teaching to combine . . ."). Those decisions, of course, are not now before us and do not correct the errors of law made by the Court of Appeals in this case. The extent to which they may describe an analysis more consistent with our earlier precedents and our decision here is a matter for the Court of Appeals to consider in its future cases. What we hold is that the fundamental misunderstandings identified above led the Court of Appeals in this case to apply a test inconsistent with our patent law decisions.

III

When we apply the standards we have explained to the instant facts, claim 4 must be found obvious. We agree with and adopt the District Court's recitation of the relevant prior art and its determination of the level of ordinary skill in the field. As did the District Court, we see little difference between the teachings of Asano and Smith and the adjustable electronic pedal disclosed in claim 4 of the Engelgau patent. A person having ordinary skill in the art could have combined Asano with a pedal position sensor in a fashion encompassed by claim 4, and would have seen the benefits of doing so.

* * *

. . . Accordingly, Teleflex has not shown anything in the prior art that taught away from the use of Asano.

Like the District Court, finally, we conclude Teleflex has shown no secondary factors to dislodge the determination that claim 4 is obvious. Proper application of Graham and our other precedents to these facts therefore leads to the conclusion that claim 4 encompassed obvious subject matter. As a result, the claim fails to meet the requirement of § 103.

We need not reach the question whether the failure to disclose Asano during the prosecution of Engelgau voids the presumption of validity given to issued patents, for claim 4 is obvious despite the presumption. We nevertheless think it appropriate to note that the rationale underlying the presumption—that the PTO, in its expertise, has approved the claim— seems much diminished here.

IV

A separate ground the Court of Appeals gave for reversing the order for summary judgment was the existence of a dispute over an issue of material fact. We disagree with the Court of Appeals on this point as well. To the extent the court understood the *Graham* approach to exclude the possibility of summary judgment when an expert provides a conclusory affidavit addressing the question of obviousness, it misunderstood the role expert testimony plays in the analysis. In considering summary judgment on that question the district court can and should take into account expert testimony, which may resolve or keep open certain questions of fact. That is not the end of the issue, however. The ultimate judgment of obviousness is a legal determination. Graham, 383 U. S., at 17. Where, as here, the content of the prior art, the scope of the patent claim, and the level of ordinary skill in the art are not in material dispute, and the obviousness of the claim is apparent in light of these factors, summary judgment is appropriate. Nothing in the declarations proffered by Teleflex prevented the District Court from reaching the careful conclusions underlying its order for summary judgment in this case.

* * *

We build and create by bringing to the tangible and palpable reality around us new works based on instinct, simple logic, ordinary inferences, extraordinary ideas, and sometimes even genius. These advances, once part of our shared knowledge, define a new threshold from which innovation starts once more. And as progress beginning from higher levels of achievement is expected in the normal course, the results of ordinary innovation are not the subject of exclusive rights under the patent laws. Were it otherwise patents might stifle, rather than promote, the progress of useful arts. See U. S. Const., Art. I, § 8, cl. 8. These premises led to the bar on patents claiming obvious subject matter established in *Hotchkiss* and codified in § 103. Application of the bar must not be confined within a test or formulation too constrained to serve its purpose.

KSR provided convincing evidence that mounting a modular sensor on a fixed pivot point of the Asano pedal was a design step well within the grasp of a person of ordinary skill in the relevant art. Its arguments, and the record, demonstrate that claim 4 of the Engelgau patent is obvious. In rejecting the District Court's rulings, the Court of Appeals analyzed the issue in a narrow, rigid manner inconsistent with § 103 and our precedents. The judgment of the Court of Appeals is reversed, and the case remanded for further proceedings consistent with this opinion.

It is so ordered.

NOTES

1. *A Change in the Law or Not?* Can it be fairly said that the Court's cases before the 1952 Act roughly split into two lines of reasoning: those based on *Hotchkiss*, which focused on facts about the state of the art; and those related to *A & P*, which focused on synergism? Did the '52 Act pick only one of these: *Hotchkiss* and facts? Did subsequent cases like the *Graham* Trilogy, *Black Rock*, and *Sakraida* vary this approach? Some leading judges like Giles Rich, Learned Hand, and Jerome Frank, as well as Patent Office authorities thought not. See, e.g., Safety Car Heating & Lighting Co. v. General Elec. Co., 155 F.2d 937, 939 (2d Cir. 1946) (Hand, J.); Giles S. Rich, "Laying the Ghost of the 'Invention' Requirement," 1 Am. Pat. L. Ass'n Q. J. 26, 44 (1972); Picard v. United Aircraft Corp., 128 F.2d 632, 643–644 (2d Cir. 1942) (Frank, J. dissenting); C. Marshall Dann, Examination of Claims for Patentability Under 35 U.S.C. § 103, 949 U.S. Pat. & Trademark Off. Gazette 3 (1976); Rene D. Tegtmeyer, Commercial Success and Other Considerations Bearing on Obviousness, 973 Official Gazette 34 (1978). Did *KSR* change things? The Federal Circuit decision in that case was not precedential. The Federal Circuit decisions on § 103 that were issued after the Court granted cert but before it issued its opinion in *KSR* were expressly embraced by the Court's *KSR* opinion. And the Court expressly recognized that the fact-based TSM test was "a helpful insight," warned against "mere conclusory statements," and called for both "articulated reasoning" and consideration of "when prior art teaches away." Indeed, don't all claims combine old elements? Otherwise the inventor would have to invent the elements in the claim to then invent the claim, etc. And won't 2 + 2 always equal 4 in the real world?

2. *To What Extent Has the Court Slipped into Tautologies?* The Court wrote: "When there is a *design need or market pressure* to solve a problem." When do people in business invent for no reason, or for some reason other one such as these? The Court continued: "and there are a *finite* number of *identified, predictable* solutions." What is not finite? If the solutions are identified, then isn't this a § 102 case, not a § 103 case? If the solutions are predictable, then isn't this a conclusion on the ultimate question of obviousness? The Court continued: "a person of ordinary skill has *good reason* to pursue the *known* options *within* his or her technical grasp." Aren't these also conclusions on the ultimate question? The Court continued: "If this leads to the *anticipated* success." How is this not either a conclusion on the ultimate question of obviousness, or a conclusion that this is a § 102 case of anticipation? The Court continued by concluding that in such cases: "it is likely the product not of innovation but of ordinary skill and common sense. In that instance the fact that a combination was obvious to try might show that it was obvious under § 103." Hasn't the Court reached a conclusion premised on the same conclusion? Has the Court embraced a broad "obvious to try" standard; or by tying its conclusion to "in that instance" has the Court made clear that only in cases in which there essentially is anticipation is it fair to say it was "obvious to try?"

3. *The Impact of KSR.* Following the *KSR* decision, the Federal Circuit's obviousness jurisprudence has broadened considerably. For example, in *Muniauction, Inc. v. Thomson Corp.,* 532 F.3d 1318, 1326–27 (Fed.Cir.2008), the court stated that "adapting existing electronic processes to incorporate modern internet and web browser technology was similarly commonplace [in 1997]." This passage from *Muniauction* suggests a skepticism towards patents based primarily on bringing pre-existing electronic inventions onto the internet.

KSR has also increased the reliance of what some call "common sense" in the determination of obviousness. In *Perfect Web Tech., Inc. v. Infousa, Inc.,* 587 F.3d 1324, 1328–31 (Fed.Cir.2009) the court discussed the use of common sense at length and noted that "on summary judgment, to invoke 'common sense' or any other basis for extrapolating from prior art to a conclusion of obviousness, a district court must articulate its reasoning with sufficient clarity for review." For further discussion of so-called "common sense," see *Wyers v. Master Lock Co.,* 616 F.3d 1231 (Fed. Cir. 2010); *The Western Union Co. v. MoneyGram Payment Systems, Inc.,* 626 F.3d 1361 (Fed.Cir.2010). A central concern with reliance on so-called "common sense" is that it can be hard to prove what exactly is within "common sense." Some also wonder who gets to make that determination.

E. Secondary Considerations

Secondary considerations are relevant to, and sometimes determinative of, a § 103 obviousness determination. The "real world" considerations, thought to be objective in nature, include *commercial success, long-felt need, failure of others,* and *licensing/acquiescence.* As the *Graham* Court noted, these considerations "focus our attention on economic and motivational rather than technical issues and are, therefore more susceptible of judicial treatment than are the highly technical facts often present in patent litigation." 383 U.S. at 35–36. Indeed, the Federal Circuit, perhaps more adamantly than the Supreme Court, has clearly recognized the importance of secondary considerations, sometimes elevating them to a fourth *Graham* factor. For example, in *Stratoflex, Inc. v. Aeroquip Corporation,* 713 F.2d 1530, 1538–39 (Fed.Cir.1983) (emphasis in original), the court stated:

> It is jurisprudentially inappropriate to disregard any relevant evidence on any issue in any case, patent cases included. Thus evidence rising out of the so-called "secondary considerations" must always when present be considered en route to a determination of obviousness. *In re Sernaker,* 702 F.2d 989, 217 USPQ 1 (Fed.Cir.1983) *citing In re Fielder and Underwood,* 471 F.2d 640, 176 USPQ 300 (Cust. & Pat.App.1973), *see In re Mageli et al.,* 470 F.2d 1380, 1384, 176 USPQ 305, 307 (Cust. & Pat.App.1973) (evidence bearing on issue of nonobviousness "is never of 'no moment', is always to be considered and accorded whatever weight it may have.") Indeed, evidence of secondary considerations may often be the most probative and cogent evidence in the record. It may often establish that an invention appearing to have been obvious in light of the prior art was not. It is to be considered as part of all the evidence, not just when the decision maker remains in doubt after reviewing the art.
>
> En route to a conclusion on obviousness, a court must not stop until *all* pieces of evidence on that issue have been fully considered and each has been given its appropriate weight. Along the way, some pieces will weigh more heavily than others, but decision should be held in abeyance, and doubt maintained, until all the evidence has had its say. The relevant evidence on the obviousness-nonobviousness issue, as the Court said in *Graham, supra,* and as other courts had earlier emphasized, includes evidence on what has now been called "secondary considerations." It is error to exclude that evidence from consideration.

However, the Federal Circuit has held that even a combination of multiple objective indicia of nonobviousness may be unable to defeat a strong prima facie case of obviousness. In *Agrizap, Inc. v. Woodstream Corp.,* 520 F.3d 1337 (Fed.Cir.2008), the court held the patent obvious despite showing of commercial success, copying by others, and long-felt need, stating: "This is a textbook case of when the asserted claims involve a combination of familiar elements according to known methods that does no more than yield predictable results.... [T]he objective evidence of nonobviousness simply cannot overcome such a strong prima facie case of obviousness." *See also Leapfrog Enterprises, Inc. v. Fisher–Price, Inc.,* 485 F.3d 1157 (Fed.Cir.

2007) (holding patent obvious despite showing of substantial evidence of commercial success, praise, and long-felt need).

1.   COMMERCIAL SUCCESS

Pentec, Inc. v. Graphic Controls Corp.

776 F.2d 309 (Fed.Cir.1985).

■ Before MARKEY, CHIEF JUDGE, BENNETT, CIRCUIT JUDGE, and HARVEY, SENIOR DISTRICT JUDGE.

■ MARKEY, CHIEF JUDGE.

Appeal from a judgment of the United States District Court for the Central District of California declaring claims 1–4 of U.S. Patent No. 3,983,569 to James Hubbard and Charles Erdman ('569 patent) invalid for obviousness and not infringed and dismissing the counterclaims of Graphic Controls, Inc. (GC) for infringement and unfair competition. We affirm.

Background

Pentec, Inc. and Bob Allen (Pentec) sued for a declaration of invalidity and noninfringement of the '569 patent. GC, as assignee of the patent, counterclaimed for infringement of claims 1–4 and for unfair competition. After a nonjury trial, the district court adopted in full the findings and conclusions submitted by Pentec, and declared the claims in suit invalid and not infringed. . . .

A.   Prior Technology

The recording instruments here involved are formed of thin, very light, and small elements. Before 1970, recording instruments included metal "bucket" pens, each affixed permanently to a pen arm, with refillable liquid ink supplies. Users experienced difficulties in maintaining ink flow and refilling.

During the 1970's, the industry developed disposable pens with fibrous ink reservoirs, solving the flow and refill problems. However, frequent replacement of the disposable pen risked upsetting or damaging the delicate pen arm. During the early 1970's, GC and its competitors used folded-over metal tabs to attach the pen.

In 1973, GC introduced its first disposable "Series 10" pen for use on round chart recorders. That pen had the same fastening means as GC's earlier "MARK–TROL" pen. The Sanford Corporation (Sanford) sought to develop disposable pens with a better fastening means. Sanford's efforts produced U.S. Patent No. 3,893,130 to Charles Browning and Gilbert Perrigo (Browning) which issued July 1, 1975. That patent disclosed a plastic channel on the pen as a means for attaching it to the arm. However, that means proved insecure. An improved version was disclosed in U.S. Patent No. 3,934,255 to Guy Taylor (Taylor) which issued January 20, 1976 on an application filed June 3, 1974.

On September 28, 1976, the '569 patent issued from a continuation-in-part application to Hubbard and Erdman who assigned it to GC. The date of the original application, January 10, 1975, has been stipulated to have been the date of invention.

B. The '569 Patent

In 1977, GC introduced to the market its "Series 39" pen, which embodied the Hubbard invention disclosed in the '569 patent. The Hubbard invention includes a pen arm having an "integrally molded hinge member" for folding over against the pen body. Claim 1, the only independent claim in issue and from which claims 2–4 depend, is in *Jepson* form. It reads:

> In an instrument marker pen body [**10**] including an ink reservoir [**12**] and means for receiving a writing tip [**30**], the improvement comprising a pen arm [**22**] holding means consisting of an integrally molded hinged member [**14**] [with ridges **20, 24**] adapted to fold against a surface of the pen body [**10**] and to be locked against said surface by engageable locking means [**26, 28**] and to receive and secure in place against said surface a pen arm when said hinged member is in its folded and locked position.

* * *

* * *

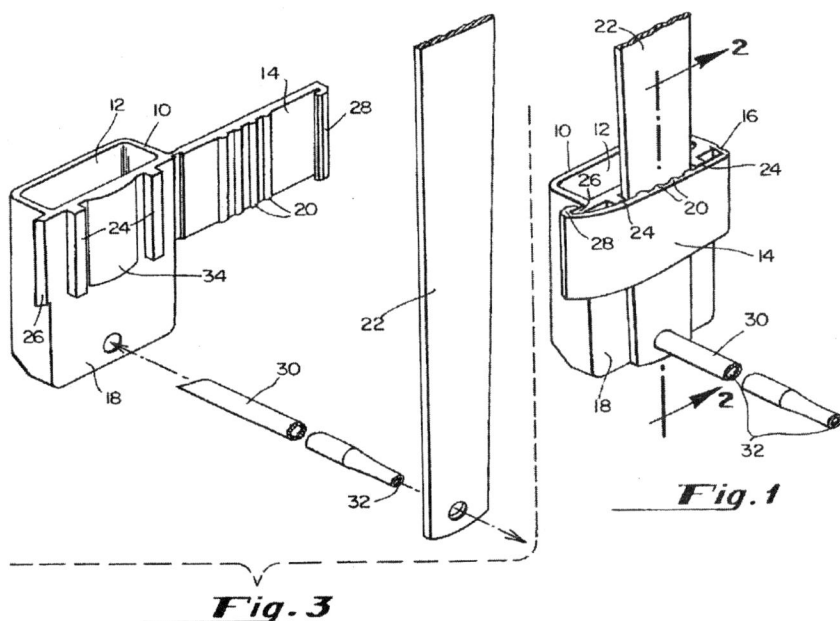

Fig. 1

Fig. 3

GC successfully marketed under its "Series 39" designation many models of its "snap-on" recording instrument pens embodying the inventions claimed in the '569 patent.

C. Pentec's Actions

Shortly after setting up his wholly owned Pentec corporation in 1979, Allen requested, and GC refused, a license under the '569 patent. Pentec tried to compete with its first "Series 390" pen. However, Pentec withdrew that pen from the market because it did not mount securely to the arm.

In 1982, Pentec introduced a second "Series 390" pen. It has a hinged clasp attached to the side of the pen and is the product accused as an infringement in GC's counterclaim. It differs from the invention claimed in '569 patent solely in that its hinged clasp is separately molded and ultrasonically welded in a separate process rather than being "integrally molded" in one step.

Pentec introduced the accused pen without advice of counsel. Bob Allen testified that he believed the '569 patent to be invalid and that Pentec's pen did not infringe it. When GC charged it with infringement of the '569 patent, Pentec sought counsel and initiated this declaratory judgment action in 1983.

D.   District Court Proceedings

Trial was held on June 5, 7, 8, 11, 12, and 13, 1984. On November 13, 1984, the district court issued judgment in favor of Pentec. The record indicates that the court crossed out "proposed" from the title page of the findings and conclusions submitted by Pentec and adopted them verbatim.

The adopted findings and conclusions relating to validity say: (1) Pentec rebutted the presumption of validity by clear and convincing evidence; (2) the '569 patent was invalid in light of the prior art because the Hubbard invention would have been obvious to one of ordinary skill in the art; (3) GC had not clearly established a nexus between the commercial success of its patented pen and the claimed invention; and (4) GC had not shown existence of a long felt need for a hinged fastener.

* * *

Issues Presented

Whether the district court erred in: (1) declaring claims 1–4 invalid for obviousness under § 103. . . .

Opinion

* * *

B.   Obviousness

[The court discussed the scope and content of the prior art; level of ordinary skill in the art; differences between the claimed invention and the prior art; and affirmed the district court's decision holding the '569 patent invalid under 35 U.S.C. § 103.]

(4) Objective Evidence

Objective evidence of nonobviousness, when present, must always be considered before reaching a legal conclusion under § 103. *Stratoflex, Inc. v. Aeroquip Corp.*, 713 F.2d 1530, 1538, (Fed.Cir.1983). "Indeed, evidence of secondary considerations may often be the most probative and cogent evidence in the record. It may often establish that an invention appearing to have been obvious in light of the prior art was not." *Id.*

For a claimed invention's commercial success to be given substantial weight, a nexus must be established between it and the merits of the claimed invention. *Cable Electric Prods. v. Genmark, Inc.*, 770 F.2d 1015, 1026 (Fed.Cir.1985); *Solder Removal Co. v. United States Int'l Trade Comm'n.*, 582 F.2d 628, 637 (CCPA 1978). The district court found that GC failed to prove that the undisputed commercial success of its "Series 39" pen was attributable to the claimed invention. The district court based that finding on the testimony of the inventor and Adams, GC's former general manager. They testified that when the plastic hinge was combined with nondisposable pens, that combination was received "coolly" in the market-place. It was only when the plastic hinge was combined with disposable pens that that combination was received "extremely warmly." The district court concluded that the success of the latter combination was caused by the marketplace's readiness for disposable pens and the great sums spent by GC in advertising its "Series 39" pen.

That the structure of claims 1–3 was received "coolly" when the "pen body" of those claims was nondisposable does not preclude GC from reliance upon the success achieved with the structure of claim 4, in which the "pen body" of that claim is, as set forth in the claim, "disposable." It is undisputed that the structure of claim 4 was commercially successful, that GC's share of the recorder pen market grew between 1980 and 1983, and that GC sold about twice as many pens as the rest of the industry combined. Nonetheless, GC's showing of commercial success on this record falls just short of a showing sufficient to tilt toward a required conclusion of non-obviousness the scales on which rests all the evidence.

The record is clear that, upon introducing the claimed invention in 1977, GC launched an extensive advertising campaign and continued that campaign for three years. That GC reduced its advertising budget in 1980–1983 is of little moment, absent a showing that continued high sales volume was not due to the extensive campaign of 1977–1980. The district court's finding that GC's promotional campaign contributed to the patented pen's commercial success has not been shown to have been clearly erroneous.

The record shows that GC was the leader in the recording pen field well before the issuance of its '569 patent. During the 1970's, GC had greatly increased the number of its personnel and the size of its facilities. A former regional sales manager for GC testified that it was selling in the early 1970's its "MARK–TROL" pen at levels similar to those achieved with the "Series 39" pen. Because GC was clearly the market leader well before the introduction of the "Series 39" pen, its sales figures cannot be given controlling weight in determining the effect of commercial success in this case on the question of obviousness. *Cf. Schwinn Bicycle Co. v. Goodyear Tire & Rubber Co.*, 444 F.2d 295, 300 (9th Cir.1970) (sponsorship by market leader "may be largely responsible for the success of the design"). On the present record, it cannot be said that the commercial success here may not have been due in large part to "other economic and commercial factors unrelated to the technical quality of the patented subject matter." *Cable Electric, supra,* 770 F.2d at 1027 (Fed.Cir.1985). In sum, GC has simply failed on this record to show the required nexus.

* * *

NOTES

1. *Commercial Success—The Argument.* Commercial success is the most important and most often asserted of the secondary considerations. Why is commercial success indicative of nonobviousness? If an invention does *not* enjoy commercial success, does it necessarily mean that the invention is obvious?

When a patentee asserts commercial success, he is essentially saying, "if my invention is obvious, why didn't any of my competitors have success making the invention given its significant consumer demand?" The reason, the argument goes, is that the competitors tried and failed, thus leading to the conclusion that the invention was nonobvious. Is this true? Do researchers have the market in mind when they toil away in their laboratories? Can you think of reasons why a firm would not research and develop an invention even if a market existed? Indeed, many commentators have criticized the Federal Circuit's reliance on and treatment of commercial success. *See* Robert P. Merges, *Commercial Success and Patent Standards: Economic Perspectives on Innovation,* 76 CALIF. L. REV. 803, 838–39 (1988):

> Commercial success is a poor indicator of patentability because it is indirect; it depends for its effectiveness on a long chain of inferences, and the links in the chain are often subject to doubt. This was one of the central insights of a seminal article on patentability written in 1966 by Edmund Kitch [*see Graham v. John Deere Co.: New Standards for Patents,* 1966 SUP. CT. REV. 293, 332]. Kitch argued that commercial success was an unreliable indicator of nonobviousness. To illustrate his point, Kitch identified four inferences a judge must make to work backward from evidence of market success to a conclusion of patentable invention:
>
>> First, that the commercial success is due to the innovation. Second, that . . . potential commercial success was perceived before its development. Third, the potential commercial success having been perceived, it is likely that efforts were made [by a number of firms] to develop the improvement. Fourth, the efforts having been made by men of skill in the art, they failed because the patentee was the first to reduce his development to practice.
>
> With only the fact that one company has successfully innovated as a starting point, a court is asked to reconstruct a long series of events and, more importantly, to decide how much of the final success is attributable to each factor introduced along the way. Each inference is weak, because there are almost always several explanations why a product was successful or why other firms missed a market opportunity. Only the last piece of the puzzle—the failure of others independently to produce this innovation—is indisputably established. This "objective evidence" requires an extraordinary job of factual reconstruction.

2. *The Nexus.* Of course, commercial success may be due to, and consumer demand may be a result of, factors unrelated to the technical quality of the claimed invention (*e.g.,* clever advertising, aggressive marketing, business acumen, or significant market share). In fact, the Federal Circuit has held that raw sales data is insufficient to prove commercial success, *Vandenberg v. Dairy Equip. Co.,* 740 F.2d 1560, 1567 (Fed.Cir.1984). For evidence of commercial success to be persuasive, the patentee must show comparative success with other products on the market, *In re Mageli*, 470 F.2d 1380, 1384 (CCPA 1973), *and* "a nexus must be established between [commercial success] and the merits of the claimed invention." *Pentec*, *supra*.

Consider the following discussion of the nexus issue in *Windsurfing International Inc. v. AMF, Inc.*, 782 F.2d 995 (Fed.Cir.1986). In *Windsurfing*, the party challenging the patent introduced a great deal of evidence, like the challenger in *Pentec*, to show that the commercial success of the patent was due to factors other than the merits of the claimed invention. The court was not persuaded:

> Before concluding that the combination of the universal joint with the wishbone rigging would not have been obvious, the district court reviewed the objective evidence, *Stratoflex, Inc. v. Aeroquip Corp.*, 713 F.2d 1530, 1538, 218 USPQ 871, 879 (Fed.Cir.1983), and correctly sought a nexus between WSI's commercial success and the merits of the claimed invention. *Cable Electric Prods. v. Genmark, Inc.*, 770 F.2d 1015, 1026, 226 USPQ 881, 887 (Fed.Cir.1985). In essence, AMF says that the commercial success found by the district court was due in large part to "other economic and commercial factors unrelated to the technical quality of the patented subject matter." *Id.* at 1027, 226 USPQ at 888. Particularly, AMF argues that the great commercial success found by the district court was due to: (1) sales of accessories amounting to 10–15 percent of the gross receipts; (2) an extensive advertising campaign and European promotional effort; and (3) more efficient manufacturing and design changes. They argue that WSI's commercial success is of little probative value because it occurred so many years after the date of invention and was not the result of providing any solution to some existing problem or long-felt want.

> Having carefully reviewed the record before us, we conclude that the district court did not impermissibly credit the evidence of commercial success. It specifically found that WSI's commercial success should not be "significantly diminished" by testimony that 10–15 percent of gross receipts are from paraphernalia. 613 F.Supp. at 948 n. 84, 227 USPQ at 938 n. 84. The court accorded some weight to motivational factors leading to German licenses, but concluded that "widespread recognition and use of the invention" indicated that it would not have been obvious. *Id.* at 949, 227 USPQ at 938–39. The commercial success of the invention was found to have been "well beyond the effect" of WSI's promotional efforts. *Id.*, 227 USPQ at 939.

> Absent some intervening event to which success must be attributed, the delay in achieving the great commercial success of the claimed invention in this case does not detract from the probative value of the evidence of that success.

Id. at 999–1000.

At what point with respect to the standard of proof does the patentee establish the requisite causal nexus? Can you discern a standard in *Pentec* or *Windsurfing*? *See* Merges, *Commercial Success* 76 CALIF. L. REV. at 824 (bemoaning the inconsistent application of the commercial success doctrine, stating that "[p]artly as a result of the malleable nexus standard, the court in some cases has used commercial success and other secondary factors to override strong evidence that an invention was obvious."); *see also*, Reed W.L. Marcy, *Patent Law's Nonobviousness Requirement: The Effect of Inconsistent Standards Regarding Commercial Success on the Individual Inventor*, 19 HASTINGS COMM/ENT L.J. 199, 199 (1996) (arguing that "inconsistent [commercial success] standards employed by the Federal Circuit and the district courts have created a measure of uncertainty that may handicap the individual inventor and entrepreneur."). Do you think there is a danger that courts would place too much emphasis on commercial success (or other secondary considerations) when the technology is particularly complex?

3.   *The CCPA v. Federal Circuit Nexus Standard.* The CCPA appeared to have a significantly stronger nexus standard than that adopted by the Federal Circuit, despite the fact that the latter's standard is somewhat vague. In *In re Heldt*, 433 F.2d 808, 812–13 (CCPA 1970), the CCPA stated that it must be "positively clear . . . that the commercial success asserted was the direct result of the unique characteristics of the claimed invention. . . ." According to Professor Merges, contrary to its predecessor, the Federal Circuit "has softened [the commercial success] requirement considerably by demanding that a patentee show only a 'nexus' between the commercial success and the patented invention. In contrast to the former 'direct result' standard, the nexus standard simply requires some connection between the invention and the success. Although it is difficult to pin down the exact differences between the standards, it is clear that they lead to different outcomes in some (and perhaps many) cases." Merges, *Commercial Success*, 76 CALIF. L. REV. at 824–25.

Other secondary considerations are: (1) long-felt need and failure of others; (2) copying; and (3) license requests or acquiescence. Let's take a closer look at each of these.

2.   LONG–FELT NEED AND FAILURE OF OTHERS

a.   *The Rationale.* The fact that there is a long-felt need in an industry and others in the industry have tried and failed to satisfy that need may imply nonobviousness. Consider Judge Easterbrook's comments in *In re Mahurkar Patent Litigation*, 831 F.Supp. 1354, 1377–78 (N.D.Ill.1993), *aff'd*, 71 F.3d 1573 (Fed.Cir.1995):

> The existence of an enduring, unmet need is strong evidence that the invention is novel, not obvious, and not anticipated. If people are clamoring for a solution, and the best minds do not find it for years, that is practical evidence—the kind that can't be bought from a hired expert, the kind that does not depend on fallible memories or doubtful inferences—of the state of knowledge.

In *Uniroyal, Inc. v. Rudkin–Wiley Corp.*, 837 F.2d 1044 (Fed.Cir.1988), the Federal Circuit addressed the issue of long-felt need and failure of others:

> The [district] court also did not take into account other objective evidence of long felt need and failure of others. The Maryland study, by itself, is strong evidence of both. The fact that such an extensive study was performed in 1953 shows a significant interest in drag reduction techniques long before fuel consumption became a critical concern. In addition, the record does not contain any indication that in the approximately ten years between the Maryland study and Saunders' invention any solution to the air resistance problem of tractor-trailers was forthcoming, particularly a solution of such effectiveness, and of such ease of use and manufacture, as the claimed invention.

> The district court did not consider the failure of the Maryland study to produce an effective solution to the wind resistance problem as an indica-

tion of long felt need. Instead, it viewed that failure as an indication that a later invention, based on a different principle, would have been obvious, because the inventor would know from such failure that he should try some other approach. Under this reasoning, it would be progressively more difficult, after a succession of failures, to secure a patent or an invention that provided a solution to a long felt need. This is contrary to the well established principle that the failure of others to provide a feasible solution to a long standing problem is probative of nonobviousness. *In re Piasecki*, 745 F.2d 1468, 1473–75, 223 USPQ 785, 790 (Fed.Cir.1984).

b. *Looking Behind the Need and Failure.* Does a long-felt need and failure of others necessarily imply nonobviousness? The fact that there was a failure to achieve the patented solution may simply be the result of a company's complacency towards its existing technology even though such technology is not state of the art. Furthermore, certain firms may not be willing to commit the time and resources to solving identified problems within the industry. That is, economic and business decisions must be considered when one analyzes long-felt need and failure of others.

c. *Identifying the Need.* Defining what the need is can be particularly problematic; yet, it is also crucial to the analysis. This problem, and what's at stake, were nicely articulated by Judge Feikens in *Indian Head Industries, Inc. v. Ted Smith Equipment Co.*, 859 F.Supp. 1095, 1107–08 (E.D.Mich.1994) (emphasis in original):

> Disputes about the appropriate level of generality always carry with them a certain degree of arbitrariness. Stating the problem broadly enough, almost any step forward can be said to address a long-felt need. Defining the problem narrowly, however, makes it possible to describe any need in such a way that the claimed invention does not solve it. Defining a need or problem narrowly also tends to make most solutions appear obvious: the mere fact that there is an articulable need for a *precise* product is evidence that an alleged invention is obvious.

Do you agree with the statement that "an articulable need for a *precise* product is evidence that an alleged invention is obvious?"

d. *Timing.* Determination of a long-felt unmet need is based on the filing date of the challenged invention, not the time that the invention is actually available on the market. *Procter & Gamble Co. v. Teva Pharmaceuticals USA*, 566 F.3d 989, 998 (Fed.Cir.2009). *See also Monarch Knitting Mach. Corp. v. Sulzer Morat GmbH*, 139 F.3d 877 (Fed.Cir.1998). This approach is consistent with the view that the long-felt unmet need is evidence of the nonobviousness of the invention itself.

e. *Actual Failures and Incomplete Prior Art.* Identification of the need is done from an objective standpoint (*i.e.*, the hypothetical person). Recall, the hypothetical person of ordinary skill in the art is deemed to have perfect knowledge of the prior art. In *Hodosh v. Block Drug Co., Inc.*, 786 F.2d 1136, 1144 (Fed.Cir.1986), the Federal Circuit noted that

> [e]vidence of secondary considerations is considered independently of what any real person *knows* about the prior art. These considerations are *objective* criteria of obviousness that help illuminate the subjective determination involved in the hypothesis used to draw the legal conclusion of obviousness based upon the first three factual inquires delineated in *Graham*. Thus, to require that actual inventors in the field have the

omniscience of the hypothetical person in the art is not only contrary to case law ... but eliminates a useful tool for trial judges faced with a nonobviousness determination.

(Emphasis in original).

Does it make sense to consider long-felt need and failure of others "independent of what any real person *knows* about the prior art?" How much emphasis should be placed on actual failures if such failures were based on an incomplete picture of the relevant prior art? In other words, if the industry were aware of all of the prior art, perhaps the long-felt need would be easily satisfied, thus making the claimed invention obvious. On the other hand, maybe the claimed invention would be nonobviousness. The point is that evidence of actual failures is diminished when all of the prior art, or a crucial portion thereof, was not available or known.

3. COPYING

Frequently, patentees assert that a competitor copied the claimed invention, thus manifesting nonobviousness. This argument is perhaps strongest, however, when there is evidence that the competitor initially attempted to design around the patent, as in *Vandenberg v. Dairy Equipment Co.*, 740 F.2d 1560 (Fed.Cir.1984):

> There is one aspect of the evidence, however, that at first appears to weigh rather heavily in appellants' favor. Appellants accuse DEC of "slavishly copying" their patented device after being unable to design a satisfactory system on their own. Indeed, the evidence shows that after Jack Johnson was assigned the task of designing a support system for DEC in 1980, he became aware of the '575 patent, and ultimately used the exact dimensions from that patent in designing DEC's system. The copying of an invention may constitute evidence that the invention is not an obvious one. *Troy Co. v. Products Research Co.*, 339 F.2d 364, 367, 144 USPQ 51, 53 (9th Cir.1964), *cert. dismissed*, 381 U.S. 930, 85 S.Ct. 1762, 14 L.Ed.2d 689 (1965). This would be particularly true where the copyist had itself attempted for a substantial length of time to design a similar device, and had failed.

> There are several reasons, however, why this principle should not be a decisive factor in this case. First, while DEC had worked on a new design for a support system for several years, the district court found that the project was given a low priority. DEC employees would from time to time submit proposed improvements for milk hose supports, but there is no evidence of a concerted effort to design a new device until Jack Johnson was given the task in 1980.

> Second, DEC's efforts cannot be characterized as total failures with respect to the question of obviousness. Although no commercially viable system was designed, DEC engineers did sketch a design for a plastic support device using a ball and socket joint prior to assigning the task to Johnson, as noted above.

> This would tend to suggest that the basic concepts employed by the '575 patent were obvious to those skilled in the art.

> Third, appellants' accusation of "slavish copying" overstates the case. Johnson testified that not only had DEC engineers sketched a ball and socket design prior to 1980, but that he himself had begun working on a

prototype employing a ball and socket joint before becoming aware of the '575 patent. After learning of the patent, he incorporated the dimensions (which were not claimed) from the device corresponding to the '575 patent into his own design. Viewed in this context, the copying of the '575 patent may be construed as an admission that appellants' device was perhaps mechanically superior to DEC's own device, but it is not strong evidence of nonobviousness. The basic concept of the invention occurred independently to DEC's staff.

4. Licensing/Acquiescence

Lastly, a patentee may assert that the acceptance of a license by the defendant or other competitors is an implicit recognition that the patent is nonobvious. The rationale is that firms would not pay royalties on a patent unless it thought the patent was valid. As the Federal Circuit stated, "such real world considerations provide a colorful picture of the state of the art, what was known by those in the art, and a solid evidentiary foundation on which to rest a nonobviousness determination." *Minnesota Mining & Mfg. Co. v. Johnson & Johnson Orthopaedics, Inc.*, 976 F.2d 1559, 1575 (Fed.Cir. 1992).

Can you think of reasons, other than an implicit affirmation of the patent's validity, as to why a firm may accept a license? In *EWP Corp. v. Reliance Universal Inc.*, 755 F.2d 898, 907–08 (Fed.Cir.1985), the Federal Circuit noted that:

> [Licensing] programs are not infallible guides to patentability. They sometimes succeed because they are mutually beneficial to the licensed group or because of business judgments that it is cheaper to take licenses than to defend infringement suits, or for other reasons unrelated to the unobviousness of the licensed subject matter.

In other words, sometimes it just makes business sense not to contest the validity of a patent even though you may have strong evidence of obviousness. As a result, the patentee must show a "nexus between the merits of the invention and the licenses of record." *In re GPAC, Inc.*., 57 F.3d 1573, 1580 (Fed.Cir.1995). Similarly, this is the very reason why courts refuse to apply the so-called doctrine of licensee estoppel which would prohibit the licensee from challenging the validity of the licensed patent. *See Lear v. Adkins*, 395 U.S. 653 (1969).

But before getting too deep into these complex determinations, another excerpt from the article on the so-called "registration theory" of patents is presented below to provide a useful discussion of an over-arching normative, or policy, basis for the prior art rule on nonobviousness. Again, it is hoped that this single policy based approach be more helpful to students than sheer memorization by showing how these rules work together and make sense as a set. In addition, as before, this excerpt provides another practical schematic chart to help show how a patent claim may be easily evaluated against the prior art for an obviousness determination. Versions of this schematic claim chart can also be useful in determinations of novelty or statutory bar, as discussed in Chapter 4, and infringement, as discussed in Chapter 8.

The Case for Registering Patents and the Law and Economics of Present Patent–Obtaining Rules

F. Scott Kieff.
45 B.C. L. Rev. 55 (2003).

Although this determination of novelty is relatively easy, the registration theory recognizes that it may not go far enough in that parties may invest in a technology before it fully exists.[151] As a result, the patent system may have to go beyond merely requiring inventions be new, or not fully disclosed in a single prior art reference; it may also have to prevent valid patents from covering what anyone is investing towards, if such a determination can be made inexpensively.[152] Under the registration theory, this is the role played by the nonobviousness requirement, discussed below.[153]

2.   Nonobviousness

The patent system has long demanded something more than mere novelty when determining patentability over the prior art. This additional requirement is called "nonobviousness" in the present system.[154] It has been given labels in previous systems that are as tautological as "the requirement for invention;" and its various forms have generated great difficulty for the courts for over a century.[155] It also raises significant

---

151.   Indeed, the likelihood of these investments is logically closely tied to the presence in the art of a specific teaching, suggestion, or motivation to combine elements in the prior art to work towards the claimed invention. The registration view thereby provides a justification for the case law that requires these elements as part of a nonobviousness analysis. For more on the law of nonobviousness, see *infra* Part III.A.2.

152.   The ultimate question of whether it goes far enough will turn on whether these investments can be efficiently identified and protected. As discussed *infra* in Part III.A.2, although it is clear that the nonobviousness test does a better job on this score than the former "requirement for invention," it is not entirely clear whether the case law relating to the test of nonobviousness has implemented the test optimally.

153.   *See supra* note 86 (the registration theory helps explain the intricacies of the patent-obtaining rules whereas the other theories do not).

154.   For history of the nonobviousness requirement in patent law, see generally [Nonobviousness—The Ultimate Condition of Patentability 2:1, 2:9 (John F. Witherspoon ed., 1980)]; [George M. Sirilla, *35 U.S.C. § 103: From* Hotchkiss *to Hand to Rich, the Obvious Patent Law Hall-of-Famers*, 32 J. Marshall L. Rev. 437 *passim* (1999)].

155.   During the first half of the 1900s when called the requirement for invention, before the 1952 Patent Act, it had become known as "the plaything of the judiciary." Giles S. Rich, *Why and How Section 103 Came to Be, in* [Nonobviousness—The Ultimate Condition of Patentability 2:1, 2:9 (John F. Witherspoon ed., 1980)], at 1:208. Even after Congress wrote the § 103 nonobviousness into the statute in the 1952 Patent Act, over ten years passed before the Supreme Court applied the new standard of nonobviousness in *Graham* and its companion cases. 383 U.S. at 12–37 (consolidated with *Calmar* and *Colgate–Palmolive*); *Adams*, 383 U.S. at 48–52. For an inside look at the *Graham* decision, see Tom Arnold, *Side Bar: The Way the Law of Section 103 Was Made, in* [Donald S. Chisum, Craig A. Nard, Herbert F. Schwartz, Pauline Newman, & F. Scott Kieff, Principles of Patent Law (2d ed. 2001)], at 549, 549–54. Soon afterwards, the Court re-injected confusion by writing about synergism and combinations. *See* Sakraida v. Ag Pro, Inc., 425 U.S. 273, 282 (1976) (holding patent invalid because it was a mere combination of old elements and had no synergistic effect); Anderson's–Black Rock, Inc. v. Pavement Salvage Co., 396 U.S. 57, 61 (1969) (holding patent invalid because "No such synergistic result is argued here"). These terms were not weeded back out of the law until the creation of the Federal Circuit in 1982. *See* [George M. Sirilla, *35 U.S.C. § 103: From*

problems for the patent theories in the literature.[156]

The version of this requirement called nonobviousness was written into the patent system through the 1952 Patent Act to statutorily jettison the prior case law associated with the former, vague and anti-patent, requirement called "the requirement for invention."[157] Even the drafters of this new standard recognized that it did not, on its face, appear to be any more precise in application than the former requirement.[158] Nevertheless, as the registration theory would predict, the case law interpreting this new standard correctly has provided an objective and practicable framework tied to third-party investments.[159]

The analysis for a nonobviousness determination under § 103 begins with the entire body of prior art determined to be available under § 102.[160]

Hotchkiss *to Hand to Rich, the Obvious Patent Law Hall-of-Famers*, 32 J. Marshall L. Rev. 437 *passim* (1999)], at 543. As the Federal Circuit has reminded:

A requirement for "synergism" or a "synergistic effect" is nowhere found in the statute, 35 U.S.C. When present, for example in a chemical case, synergism may point toward nonobviousness, but its absence has no place in evaluating the evidence on obviousness. . . .

The reference to a "combination patent" is equally without support in the statute. There is no warrant for judicial classification of patents, whether into "combination" patents and some other unnamed and undefined class or otherwise. Nor is there warrant for differing treatment or consideration of patents based on a judicially devised label. Reference to "combination" patents is, moreover, meaningless. Virtually *all* patents are "combination patents," if by that label one intends to describe patents having claims to inventions formed of a combination of elements. It is difficult to visualize, at least in the mechanical-structural arts, a "non-combination" invention, i.e., an invention consisting of a *single* element. Such inventions, if they exist, are rare indeed.

Stratoflex, Inc. v. Aeroquip Corp., 713 F.2d 1530, 1540 (Fed.Cir.1983).

156. *See supra* notes 30–49 and accompanying text (other theories merely point out rent-seeking concerns that are implicated by patents and at best suggest that ex ante determinations be made about which patents turn out to be better at decreasing the rent-seeking type of social cost).

157. *See generally* Giles S. Rich, *Laying the Ghost of the "Invention" Requirement*, 1 Am. Pat. L. Ass'n Q.J. 26 (1972), *reprinted in* [Nonobviousness—The Ultimate Condition of Patentability 2:1, 2:9 (John F. Witherspoon ed., 1980)], at 1:501 [hereinafter Rich, *Laying the Ghost*] (discussing the great lag between the arrival of the new standard in the statute and its adoption by the courts); Giles S. Rich, *The Vague Concept of "Invention" as Replaced by Section 103 of the 1952 Patent Act*, 46 J. Pat. Off. Soc'y 855 (1964), *reprinted in* [Nonobviousness—The Ultimate Condition of Patentability 2:1, 2:9 (John F. Witherspoon ed., 1980)], at 1:401 (Judge Rich's speech upon receipt of the Kettering Award in which he discusses the role of nonobviousness in § 103 as the replacement for the so-called requirement for invention).

158. *Compare* [P.J. Federico, *Commentary on the New Patent Act, in* Title 35, United States Code Annotated 1 (West 1954), *reprinted in* 75 J. Pat. & Trademark Off. Soc'y 161 (1993)], at 183 (the requirement for invention "is an unmeasurable quantity having different meanings for different persons"), *with id.* at 184 ("The problem of what is obvious and hence unpatentable is still of necessity one of judgment.").

159. *See supra* notes 151–153 and accompanying text (discussing role of nonobviousness analysis according to registration theory).

160. *See* [P.J. Federico, *Commentary on the New Patent Act, in* Title 35, United States Code Annotated 1 (West 1954), *reprinted in* 75 J. Pat. & Trademark Off. Soc'y 161 (1993)], at 180:

But important areas of the prior art are then carved out so they can be excluded from the nonobviousness analysis.[161] First, only art considered to be analogous may be considered under the nonobviousness analysis.[162] Under the registration theory, which looks to protect the reasonable investment-backed expectations of third parties, non-analogous art is properly discarded because it is not likely to be the basis for any such reliance.[163] Importantly, as would be predicted by the registration theory, the distinction between analogous and non-analogous art is viewed as important, not as evidence of what the inventor himself or herself could have known about the art, but rather what was knowable to a hypothetical third party having ordinary skill in the art ("PHOSITA").[164] Second, secret

---

> In form this section is a limitation on section 102 and it should more logically have been made part of section 102, but it was made a separate section to prevent 102 from becoming too long and involved and because of its importance. The antecedent of the words "the prior art," which here appear in a statute for the first time, lies in the phrase "disclosed or described as set forth in section 102" and hence these words refer to the material specified in section 102 as the basis for comparison.

Id.

161. Although all of the § 102 art is initially available for analysis under § 103, certain types of prior art are excluded. According to the registration theory, these carve outs exist to remove from consideration the prior art for which the inference of possible innocent third-party reliance is not reasonable. *See infra* notes 162–166 and accompanying text (discussing carve outs).

162. The statute provides that the analysis should look to a hypothetical "person having ordinary skill in the art to which [the claimed] subject matter pertains" and ask whether to that person "the [invention] as a whole would have been obvious" given the "differences between the subject matter sought to be patented and the prior art." 35 U.S.C. § 103 (2000). This in turn requires that several factual inquiries be made: "the scope and content of the prior art are to be determined; differences between the prior art and the claims at issue are to be ascertained; and the level of ordinary skill in the pertinent art resolved." *Graham*, 383 U.S. at 17. A person having ordinary skill in the art according to this framework is sometimes called a PHOSITA, thanks to the coining of that term by Soans. Cyril A. Soans, *Some Absurd Presumptions in Patent Cases*, 10 IDEA 433, 438–39 (1966). The "pertinent art" is selected from among the entire set of prior art identified by § 102 depending upon whether it is analogous or non-analogous. According to the Federal Circuit:

> Two criteria have evolved for determining whether prior art is analogous: (1) whether the art is from the same field of endeavor, regardless of the problem addressed, and (2) if the reference is not within the field of the inventor's endeavor, whether the reference still is reasonably pertinent to the particular problem with which the inventor is involved.

In re Clay, 966 F.2d 656, 658–59 (Fed.Cir.1992) (citations omitted); *see also Paulsen*, 30 F.3d at 1475 (affirming Patent Office rejection under § 103 because references from the fields of cabinetry and desktop accessories are properly considered to be analogous art to a patent claim directed to a clamshell case for a laptop computer under the second of these two alternative criteria).

163. *See supra* notes 95–96 and accompanying text (discussing purpose of the prior art rules under the registration theory).

164. *See* Soans, *supra* note 162, at 438–39 (coining the term PHOSITA). Indeed, Judge Rich, who co-authored § 103, has portrayed this PHOSITA "as working in his shop with the prior art references—which he is presumed to know—hanging on the walls around him." *In re* Winslow, 365 F.2d 1017, 1020 (C.C.P.A. 1966) (Rich, J.) (this metaphor is referred to as the "*Winslow* Tableau"); *see also* Custom Accessories, Inc. v. Jeffrey–Allan Indus., Inc., 807 F.2d 955, 962 (Fed.Cir.1986) ("The person of ordinary skill is a hypothetical person who is presumed to be aware of all the pertinent prior art."); Int'l Cellucotton Prods. Co. v. Sterilek Co., 94 F.2d 10, 13 (2d Cir.1938) (Hand, J.) ("[W]e must suppose the inventor to be endowed,

prior art that would count only under § 102(e), (f), and (g) has been statutorily excluded from the nonobviousness analysis if it is owned by the same entity whose patent claim is at issue.[165] The exclusion of this art also makes sense under the registration theory because no third-party investments will have been made in art that is commonly owned and kept secret.[166]

The content of the remaining prior art as a whole must then be surveyed to determine whether it may have reasonably triggered investment-backed expectations in achieving the subject matter of the patent claim in issue.[167] Such investments are most likely to have existed only when there can be found among these many remaining pieces of art each and every element of the claimed subject matter along with sufficient teaching, motivation, or suggestion for the pieces that contain those elements to be combined such that there would be a reasonable expectation of success in establishing the claimed subject matter when they are com-

---

as in fact no inventor ever is endowed; we are to impute to him knowledge of all that is not only in his immediate field, but in all fields nearly akin to that field."). Judge Rich improved upon the *Winslow* Tableau in *In re Antle*:

> In *Winslow* we said that the principal secondary reference was "in the very same art" as appellant's invention and characterized all the references as "very pertinent art." The language relied on by the solicitor, quoted above, therefore, does not apply in cases where the very point in issue is whether one of ordinary skill in the art would have *selected*, without the advantage of hindsight and knowledge of the applicant's disclosure, the particular references which the examiner applied. As we also said in *Winslow*, "Section 103 requires us to presume full knowledge by the inventor of the *prior* art *in the field of his endeavor*" (emphasis, except of "prior," added), but it does not require us to presume full knowledge by the inventor of prior art *outside* the field of his endeavor, i.e., of "non-analogous" art. In that respect, it only requires us to presume that the inventor would have that ability to select and utilize knowledge from other arts reasonably pertinent to his particular problem which would be expected of a man of ordinary skill in the art to which the subject matter pertains.

444 F.2d 1168, 1171–72 (C.C.P.A. 1971).

165. *See* 35 U.S.C. § 103(c) (providing carve outs). The carve outs for § 102(f) and (g) were added in 1984 to reverse the holding in *In re Bass*, 474 F.2d 1276, 1288–91 (Fed.Cir. 1973). *See* Patent Law Amendments Act of 1984, Pub. L. No. 98–622, § 103, 98 Stat. 3383, 3384 (1984). The carve out for § 102(e) was added in 1999 through § 4807 of the American Inventors Protection Act of 1999. American Inventors Protection Act of 1999, Pub. L. No. 106–113, § 4807, 113 Stat. 1501A–552, 1501A–591 (1999). For a discussion of the history of these carve outs, see [Donald S. Chisum, Craig A. Nard, Herbert F. Schwartz, Pauline Newman, & F. Scott Kieff, Principles of Patent Law (2d ed. 2001)], at 575–78.

166. No carve out is needed for the novelty analysis because the co-owner can keep the information sufficiently secret before the later claim that the reference will not trigger any of the subsections of § 102, except perhaps § 102(f). *See* 35 U.S.C. § 102. For this subsection, derivation, the co-owner can seek a claim by naming the first inventor, whose activity is co-owned. If the earlier reference does not disclose enough to invalidate under a novelty analysis then it would not have been possible for the subject matter to have been claimed at the time of the earlier reference, and the only opportunity to claim the subject matter is at the later time. The exclusion of the prior art from a nonobviousness analysis at that later time helps ensure the possibility of it being covered by a claim. Because the subject matter is co-owned with the prior art and is not otherwise available under any of the other subsections of § 102, it also is not the target of third-party investment.

167. *See supra* note 115 and accompanying text (discussing the goal of the nonobviousness requirement according to the registration theory).

bined.[168] The practical operation of this analysis can be seen through the use of the schematic claim chart in Table 2, below.[169]

Table 2: Analysis Under § 103

	PAR_1	PAR_2
E_1		✓
E_2	✓	
$E\ldots$		✓
E_n	✓	
E_*		✓
TMS	✓	
RES		✓

Like Table 1 [in the excerpt from this article that appears in Chapter Four of this book], Table 2 compares the elements of a stylized claim against the prior art, but this time for a determination of nonobviousness under § 103.[170] Invalidity under this rule of nonobviousness also requires

---

168. According to the Federal Circuit:

> The consistent criterion for determination of obviousness is whether the prior art would have suggested to one of ordinary skill in the art that this process should be carried out and would have a reasonable likelihood of success, viewed in the light of the prior art. Both the suggestion and the expectation of success must be founded in the prior art, not in the applicant's disclosure.

In re Dow Chem. Co., 837 F.2d 469, 473 (Fed.Cir.1988) (citations omitted); *see also* [Donald S. Chisum, Craig A. Nard, Herbert F. Schwartz, Pauline Newman, & F. Scott Kieff, Principles of Patent Law (2d ed. 2001)], at 584–97 (discussing contours of this analysis in practice and collecting sources).

169. As in Table 1, E_1 through E_n represent the elements of the claim arbitrarily assigned numbers 1 through n; and E_* represents enablement of the entire claim. *See supra* note 24 and accompanying text. In this table, PAR_1 and PAR_2 each represent any single prior art reference, such as a journal article, sample product, student thesis, etc. The key to the analysis under § 103 is that it permits the looking to more than one reference in the prior art to find all the elements of the claim plus enablement but only if in those references there can also be found (1) a teaching, motivation, or suggestion (TMS in the table) for those references to be combined to form the claimed subject matter as well as (2) a reasonable expectation of success (RES in the table) that the claimed subject matter will result when the references are so combined.

The apparent crispness of this framework may be somewhat illusory for several reasons. First, as with Table 1, there is some uncertainty regarding claim construction. *See supra* note 147 (discussing uncertainty about the law of claim construction and its application in any given case). Second, as discussed, *supra* note 162, the determination of obviousness is to be done from the perspective of a PHOSITA, and the case law leaves some substantial uncertainty as to how this hypothetical person is to be conceptualized. The Federal Circuit has provided a number of factors to consider when determining the characteristics of the PHOSITA:

> Factors that may be considered in determining level of ordinary skill in the art include: (1) the educational level of the inventor; (2) type of problems encountered in the art; (3) prior art solutions to those problems; (4) rapidity with which innovations are made; (5) sophistication of the technology; and (6) educational level of the workers in the field.

Envtl. Designs, Ltd. v. Union Oil Co., 713 F.2d 693, 696 (Fed.Cir.1983); *see also* [Donald S. Chisum, Craig A. Nard, Herbert F. Schwartz, Pauline Newman, & F. Scott Kieff, Principles of Patent Law (2d ed. 2001)], at 597–600 (discussing the case law relating to the determination of the PHOSITA).

170. *See supra* note 147 (discussing the validity and patentability analyses).

the presence in the prior art reference, either expressly or under principles of inherency, of each and every element of the claim, plus enablement. But, unlike the analysis under § 102, the analysis under § 103 allows the elements to be spread among two or more individual pieces of prior art, as long as some additional facts are present: teaching, motivation, or suggestion to combine those references to obtain the subject matter of the claim as a whole ("TMS"), plus a reasonable expectation of success in achieving the claimed subject matter upon the combination ("RES").[171] When mapped onto this table, this means that a proper holding of invalidity or unpatentability under § 103 will only lie if a check mark can be found as a matter of fact for every row and at least some tie can be made across all columns using the TMS and RES that must be found in at least one of the rows.[172]

Unfortunately, the appropriateness of the nonobviousness requirement is not entirely clear under the registration theory. To the extent that the analysis operates as crisply as suggested by Table 2, it makes sense as a reasonably inexpensive way to protect against verifiable investments that may have been made towards a technology.[173] The practice may deviate some from this framework, however, when requiring that in every case some weight be attributed to the so-called secondary considerations of nonobviousness: chiefly, commercial success and long-felt need and failure of others.[174] Long-felt need and failure by others may not represent a

171. For a discussion of the case law leading up to this composite test, see *supra* notes 162–168.

172. The nonobviousness analysis is presently pertinent when determining patentability before the Patent Office and when determining validity in litigation, but under a soft-look system would only be relevant in litigation. *See supra* note 147.

173. *See supra* notes 151–153 (discussing role of nonobviousness under registration theory).

174. As the Court in *Graham* stated when describing these secondary considerations and their purpose:

Such secondary considerations as commercial success, long felt but unsolved needs, failure of others, etc., might be utilized to give light to the circumstances surrounding the origin of the subject matter sought to be patented. As indicia of obviousness or nonobviousness, these inquiries may have relevancy....

. . . .

... These legal inferences or subtests do focus attention on economic and motivational rather than technical issues and are, therefore, more susceptible of judicial treatment than are the highly technical facts often present in patent litigation. Such inquires may lend a helping hand to the judiciary which, as Mr. Justice Frankfurter observed, is most ill-fitted to discharge the technological duties cast upon it by patent legislation. They may also serve to "guard against slipping into use of hindsight," and to resist the temptation to read into the prior art the teachings of the invention in issue.

383 U.S. at 17–18, 35–36 (citations omitted). It is important to realize that even this initial Supreme Court statement of the secondary considerations raises the specter of endeavoring to judge the technological merit of the record rather than its factual content, as the registration theory would require. That is, under the registration theory, the framework is a factual one that anyone well skilled in trial and appellate practice can use, whereas the Court seems to be suggesting a deeper foray into the technological merit by speaking of "technological duties."

The Federal Circuit has gone further than the Supreme Court in *Graham* by requiring: "evidence rising out of the so-called 'secondary considerations' must always when present be

deviation and may instead fit well within the registration theory's framework as outlined in Table 2 because they may be probative evidence of a lack of TMS and RES, in which case the art may fairly be said to "teach away" from the failed approaches.[175]

In contrast, commercial success may deviate materially from the framework of the registration theory, although for reasons different than identified in the literature.[176] Exemplifying the literature critical of the commercial success factor, Robert Merges urges that the system will operate better when "focus returns to the invention's technical merits" because we should question "the spurious inferential connection between success and significant technical advance."[177] In his work on the prospect theory, Kitch takes a different view of commercial success arguing that this factor matters under the prospect theory because it shows that the patent has become "the foundation for a series of now valuable contract rights."[178] On first blush it may appear that the commercialization theory would view commercial success the same way, for similar reasons. That is, commercial success might be seen as relevant not because it says something about how hard it was to make the invention, but only because it says something about how commercially relevant the subject matter has become.[179]

Although the commercial success consideration may seem to map on to the incentive to commercialize discussed earlier, it is not clear that this

---

considered en route to a determination of obviousness." *Stratoflex*, 713 F.2d at 1538–39; *see also* [Donald S. Chisum, Craig A. Nard, Herbert F. Schwartz, Pauline Newman, & F. Scott Kieff, Principles of Patent Law (2d ed. 2001)], at 601–12 (discussing the case law and commentary on the secondary considerations and collecting sources).

175. *See supra* note 171 and accompanying text (discussing TMS and RES); *see also In re* Gurley, 27 F.3d 551, 553 (Fed.Cir.1994):

> A reference may be said to teach away when a person of ordinary skill, upon reading the reference, would be discouraged from following the path set out in the reference, or would be led in a direction divergent from the path that was taken by the applicant. The degree of teaching away will of course depend on the particular facts; in general, a reference will teach away if it suggests that the line of development flowing from the reference's disclosure is unlikely to be productive of the result sought by the applicant.

Id.

176. In his work pre-dating the prospect theory, Kitch pointed out that commercial success may be a poor indicator of the nonobviousness of an invention because it relies upon too long of a chain of doubtful inferences between the original state of the art and the eventual success. Edmund Kitch, Graham v. John Deere Co.: *New Standards for Patents*, 1966 Sup. Ct. Rev. 293, 331–33. Commercial success, however, may operate as a good proxy for what was not being done by others to the extent it can be determined that its primary cause is the invention itself, as opposed to other factors such as marketing or happenstance. One problem with making such determinations is that they easily can be influenced by reward theory and thereby become as indeterminate as the reward theory.

177. Robert P. Merges, *Commercial Success and Patent Standards: Economic Perspectives on Innovation*, 76 Calif. L. Rev. 803, 838–42 (1988) (citing Kitch, *supra* note 176, at 330–35).

178. [Edmund W. Kitch, *The Nature and Function of the Patent System*, 20 J.L. & Econ. 265, 265–67 (1977)], at 282–83.

179. *See* [F. Scott Kieff, *Property Rights and Property Rules for Commercializing Inventions*, 85 Minn. L. Rev. 697 (2001)], at 707–10 (discussing the commercialization theory's focus on providing incentives for commercialization).

factor should be considered if minimizing social cost is the goal.[180] With the benefit of the registration and commercialization theories combined, commercial success may turn out to be properly ignored as a potential factor of nonobviousness because the factor places too much focus on the merits of the invention, which leads to it not being workable, and not enough focus on the investment-backed expectations by third parties, which is what matters under these theories.[181] Therefore, in the final analysis, it may not be advisable to abandon the § 103 requirement of nonobviousness in its entirety because most of the nonobviousness framework is shown both to work well according to the registration theory and be well explained by the registration theory.[182]

F. COMPLEX TECHNOLOGIES

Technology and the patent law are interrelated and inseparable. This is particularly true with respect to the fields of chemistry and biotechnology, for they present unique problems for obviousness determinations and thus, as with the chapter on "Disclosure Requirements," we decided to address them in a separate section. The uniqueness of these technologies stems primarily from their volatile and unpredictable nature. Chemical compounds which are structurally similar possess, for the most part, similar properties (structure dictates properties); however, there are occasions where a slight change in structure may lead to a significantly different and unexpected property. With respect to biotechnology, the properties of a specific protein may lead a researcher to the protein's amino acid sequence, which in turn may shed light on the DNA sequence that encodes for the protein. At the same time, the manner of producing or isolating a DNA sequence is often times unpredictable. For this reason, Congress enacted the Biotechnological Process Patents Act of 1995 (*see*

---

180. *See supra* notes 85–86 and accompanying text (discussing registration theory's goals of minimizing social cost).

181. *See supra* notes 27, 81, 106–107 and accompanying text (discussing problems with focus on the merits of the inventions); *see also supra* notes 93–103 and accompanying text (discussing importance of investment-backed expectations by third parties). In cases where enough time has gone by for there to be evidence of commercial success, there is usually an infringer or two and then the court is left trying to determine whether to decide in favor of the coordination benefits of patents or in favor of protecting the investments of the infringers. In a single-cycle game it may be easy to decide in favor of protecting the infringer's investment. But in a multi-cycle game such a rule would provide incentives to infringe too much and in an uncoordinated fashion and so instead the coordination benefits dominate and evidence of commercial success, or lack thereof, should be ignored, not required.

182. Only to the extent the secondary factors so soften the crispness of the framework modeled in Table 2 that the net benefits of the entire nonobviousness standard fade should it then be abandoned in its entirety. *See supra* note 46 (suggesting that the registration theory may not require the nonobviousness standard and noting that [Edmund W. Kitch, *The Nature and Function of the Patent System*, 20 J.L. & Econ. 265, 265–67 (1977)], may not be to the contrary). This conclusion, although admittedly not this reasoning, accords with the views of at least one framer of the 1952 Patent Act who described nonobviousness as "the heart of the patent system and the justification of patent grants." Rich, *Laying the Ghost, supra* note 48, at 1:501.

infra). This Act, embodied in § 103(b), acknowledges the unique nature of biotechnology as it relates to the patent law.

We begin with the chemical cases and then proceed to discuss the cases pertaining to biotechnology. However, the first case we address under the heading "Chemical Inventions" is actually a mechanical case. The reason that we included it is to show how, as many commentators suggest, the Federal Circuit has come to distinguish non-chemical from chemical cases under § 103.

1. Chemical Inventions

a. STRUCTURAL SIMILARITY AND THE PRESUMPTION OF OBVIOUSNESS

In re Wright

848 F.2d 1216 (Fed.Cir.1988).

■ Before Friedman, Newman, and Mayer, Circuit Judges.

■ Newman, Circuit Judge.

The judgment of the Board of Patent Appeals and Interferences of the United States Patent and Trademark Office, rejecting claims 1 through 8 of patent application Serial No. 399,850 of Randall J. Wright for "Level Vial with Extended Pitch Range", is reversed.

The Invention

Instruments that are commonly called carpenter's levels have long been known. They use small liquid-filled transparent vials with an entrained gas bubble; the vials function by gravity, the bubble automatically seeking the highest point within the vial. The vial is attached to a support, such that when the surface on which the support is placed is level, the bubble is centered. Thus, the position of the bubble shows the orientation of the vial and of the support.

Levels in common use today are made from barrel-shaped vials, mounted so that the bubble may be viewed from either side of the vial. An example of a barrel-shaped vial set in a molded plastic housing is shown in Vaida U.S. Patent No. 3,871,109, of record:

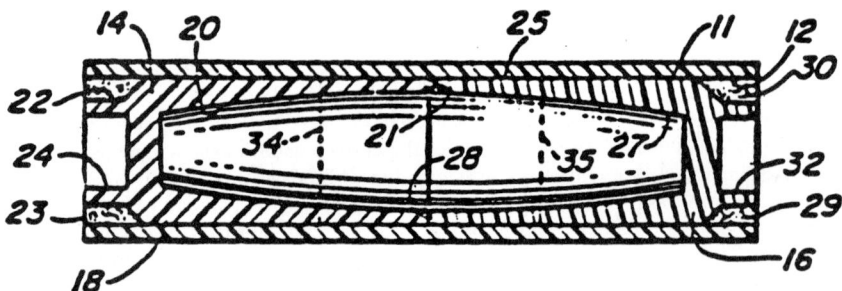

These levels of the prior art are limited in their pitch measuring capability because of the limited amount of curvature that can be formed in the molded barrel vial shape.

The Wright invention is a level-measuring instrument that has an increased range of pitch measurement capability, yet retains the advantages of the barrel vials of the prior art. . . .

* * *

The Wright structure is illustrated as follows:

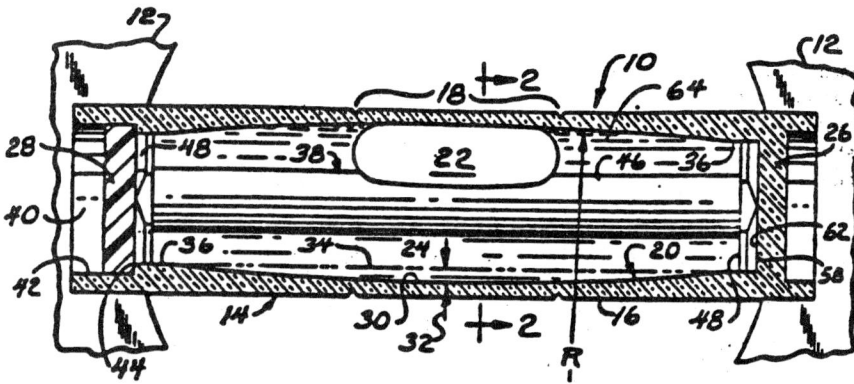

According to the Wright disclosure, by combining a core pin (46) and a barrel vial (14), the indicator bubble (22) does not move as far along the barrel with a given change in pitch, compared with the barrel vials of the prior art. Wright illustrates this phenomenon in his specification (showing a pitch change of 3/8 inch per 12 inches):

Thus the Wright level can measure greater changes of pitch before the bubble reaches the end of the vial.

The Rejection

The Board agreed with Wright that his claimed combination was new. However, because it was known to place a core pin in a cylindrical vial in order to increase the visibility of the bubble, as shown in Bishop U.S. Patent No. 771,803:

the Board held that it would have been obvious to construct a level having a core pin in the barrel-shaped vial of Vaida, irrespective of the purpose. The Commissioner on appeal argued that the Bishop and Vaida references presented, in combination, a *prima facie* case of unpatentability, stating:

> [A] claimed invention may be unpatentable if it would have been obvious for reasons suggested by the prior art, even though those reasons may be different from the reasons relied upon by the inventor and may result in a different advantage.

The PTO position is that since it would have been obvious to make the Wright combination in order to improve visibility of the bubble, it is immaterial that Wright's combination improves pitch measurement.

Discussion

The Commissioner argues that if it is obvious to combine the teachings of prior art references for any purpose, they may be combined in order to defeat patentability of the applicant's admittedly new structure. The PTO states that "a claimed invention may be unpatentable if it would have been obvious for reasons suggested by the prior art, even though those reasons may be different from the reasons relied upon by the inventor and may result in a different advantage." The PTO position is that it is irrelevant that Wright's structure was for a purpose, and has properties, that are neither obtainable from the prior art structures, nor suggested in the prior art. In this lies the PTO's error.

We repeat the mandate of 35 U.S.C. § 103: it is the invention as a whole that must be considered in obviousness determinations. The invention as a whole embraces the structure, its properties, and the problem it solves. *See, e.g., Cable Electric Products, Inc. v. Genmark, Inc.*, 770 F.2d 1015, 1025, 226 USPQ 881, 886 (Fed.Cir.1985) ("In evaluating obviousness, the hypothetical person of ordinary skill in the pertinent art is presumed to have the 'ability to select and utilize knowledge from other arts reasonably pertinent to [the] particular problem' to which the invention is directed"), *quoting In re Antle*, 444 F.2d 1168, 1171–72, 58 CCPA 1382, 170 USPQ 285, 287–88 (CCPA 1971); *In re Antonie*, 559 F.2d 618, 619, 195 USPQ 6, 8 (CCPA 1977) ("In delineating the invention as a whole, we look not only to the subject matter which is literally recited in the claim in question ... but also to those properties of the subject matter which are inherent in the subject matter *and* are disclosed in the specification") (emphasis in original).

The determination of whether a novel structure is or is not "obvious" requires cognizance of the properties of that structure and the problem which it solves, viewed in light of the teachings of the prior art. *See, e.g., In re Rinehart*, 531 F.2d 1048, 1054, 189 USPQ 143, 149 (CCPA 1976) (the particular problem facing the inventor must be considered in determining obviousness); *see also Lindemann Maschinenfabrik GMBH v. American Hoist and Derrick Co.*, 730 F.2d 1452, 1462, 221 USPQ 481, 488 (Fed.Cir. 1984) (it is error to focus "solely on the product created, rather than on the obviousness or nonobviousness of its creation") (*quoting General Motors Corp. v. U.S. Int'l Trade Comm'n*, 687 F.2d 476, 483, 215 USPQ 484, 489 (CCPA 1982), *cert. denied*, 459 U.S. 1105, 103 S.Ct. 729, 74 L.Ed.2d 953 (1983)).

Thus the question is whether what the inventor did would have been obvious to one of ordinary skill in the art attempting to solve the problem upon which the inventor was working. *Rinehart*, 531 F.2d at 1054, 189 USPQ at 149; *see also In re Benno*, 768 F.2d 1340, 1346, 226 USPQ 683, 687 (Fed.Cir.1985) ("appellant's problem" and the prior art "present different problems requiring different solutions").

The problem upon which Wright was working was improving the pitch-measuring capability of the level, not the visibility of the bubble. The PTO, having conceded that Wright's structure was unobvious for his intended purpose, erred in holding that this was not relevant. The problem solved by the invention is always relevant. The entirety of a claimed invention, including the combination viewed as a whole, the elements thereof, and the properties and purpose of the invention, must be considered.

Factors including unexpected results, new features, solution of a different problem, novel properties, are all considerations in the determination of obviousness in terms of 35 U.S.C. § 103. When such factors are described in the specification they are weighed in determining, in the first instance, whether the prior art presents a *prima facie* case of obviousness. *See, e.g., In re Margolis*, 785 F.2d 1029, 1031 (Fed.Cir.1986) (comparative data in the specification must be considered in PTO determination of unexpected results, as part of "the entire body of evidence ... which must be weighed in the first instance by the PTO.") When such factors are brought out in prosecution before the PTO, they are considered in determining whether a *prima facie* case, if made based on the prior art, has been rebutted. *See, e.g., In re Piasecki*, 745 F.2d 1468, 1472 (Fed.Cir.1984) (rebuttal evidence is considered along with all other evidence of record). In either case, the requisite view of the whole invention mandates consideration of not only its structure but also its properties and the problem solved.

Applicant Wright agrees that he has combined old elements. The Commissioner agrees that Wright has achieved a new combination, and that the result obtained thereby is not suggested in the references. The patentability of such combinations is of ancient authority. *See, e.g., Prouty v. Draper*, 41 U.S. (16 Pet.) 336, 341, 10 L.Ed. 985 (1842); *Eames v. Godfrey*, 68 U.S. (1 Wall.) 78, 79–80, 17 L.Ed. 547 (1863); *Gill v. Wells*, 89 U.S. (22 Wall.) 1, 25, 22 L.Ed. 699 (1874); *see also* H.T. Markey, *Why Not the Statute?*, 65 J.Pat.Off.Soc'y 331, 333–34 (1983) ("virtually all inventions are 'combinations', and ... every invention is formed of 'old elements'.... Only God works from nothing. Man must work with old elements").

The PTO position that the claimed structure is *prima facie* obvious is not supported by the cited references. No reference shows or suggests the properties and results of Wright's claimed structure, or suggests the claimed combination as a solution to the problem of increasing pitch measurement capacity. It is not pertinent whether Wright's new structure also has the prior art attribute of increased visibility of the bubble, for that is not his invention.

The Commissioner on appeal defends the fact that the Board and the examiner never reached this analysis. The Board relied on *In re Wiseman*, 596 F.2d 1019, 201 USPQ 658 (CCPA 1979), to support the Board's statement:

> If the claimed subject matter would have been obvious from the references, it is immaterial that the references do not state the problem or advantages ascribed thereto by appellant.

Wiseman does not support the generalization that the Board attributes to it. In *Wiseman* the prior art reference showed a similar problem and suggested a similar solution to that of the applicant. Specifically, the prior art showed a disc brake having grooves for the purpose of venting dust generated during use; the applicant showed a disc brake having grooves for the purpose of venting steam generated during use. The applicant asserted no results or properties that were not fairly suggested by the prior art. The court's discussion in *Wiseman* must be viewed in context, and as with all section 103 decisions, judgment must be brought to bear based on the facts of each case.

In re Dillon

919 F.2d 688 (Fed.Cir.1990) (*en banc*).

■ Before NIES, CHIEF JUDGE, RICH, CIRCUIT JUDGE, COWEN, SENIOR CIRCUIT JUDGE, MARKEY, NEWMAN, ARCHER, MAYER, MICHEL, PLAGER, LOURIE, CLEVENGER, and RADER, CIRCUIT JUDGES.

■ LOURIE, CIRCUIT JUDGE.

Diane M. Dillon, assignor to Union Oil Company of California, appeals the November 25, 1987, decision of the Board of Patent Appeals and Interferences (Board) of the United States Patent and Trademark Office (PTO), rejecting claims 2–14, 16–22, and 24–37, all the remaining claims of patent application Serial No. 671,570 entitled "Hydrocarbon Fuel Composition." We affirm the rejection of all of the claims.

The Invention

Dillon's patent application describes and claims her discovery that the inclusion of certain tetra-orthoester compounds in hydrocarbon fuel compositions will reduce the emission of solid particulates (*i.e.*, soot) during combustion of the fuel. In this appeal Dillon asserts the patentability of claims to hydrocarbon fuel compositions containing these tetra-orthoesters, and to the method of reducing particulate emissions during combustion by combining these esters with the fuel before combustion.

Claim 2 is the broadest composition claim:

2. A composition comprising: a hydrocarbon fuel; and a sufficient amount of at least one orthoester so as to reduce the particulate emissions from the combustion of the hydrocarbon fuel, wherein the orthoester is of the formula:

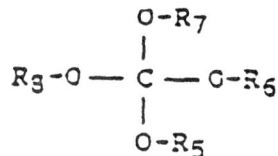

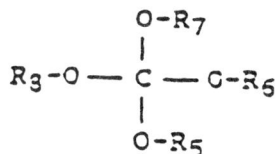

```
           O-R7
           |
R3-O — C — O-R6
           |
           O-R5
```

```
           O-R7
           |
R3-O — C — O-R6
           |
           O-R5
```

wherein R_5, R_6, R_7, and R_8, are the same or different monovalent organic radical comprising 1 to about 20 carbon atoms.

* * *

The tetra-orthoesters are a known class of chemical compounds. It is undisputed that their combination with hydrocarbon fuel, for any purpose, is not shown in the prior art, and that their use to reduce particulate emissions from combustion of hydrocarbon fuel is not shown or suggested in the prior art.

The Rejection

The Board held all of the claims to be unpatentable on the ground of obviousness, 35 U.S.C. § 103, in view of certain primary and secondary references. As primary references the Board relied on two Sweeney U.S. patents, 4,390,417 ('417) and 4,395,267 ('267). Sweeney '417 describes hydrocarbon fuel compositions containing specified chemical compounds, viz., ketals, acetals, and tri-orthoesters,[2] used for "dewatering" the fuels, particularly diesel oil. Sweeney '267 describes three-component compositions of hydrocarbon fuels heavier than gasoline, immiscible alcohols, and tri-orthoesters, wherein the tri-orthoesters serve as cosolvents to prevent phase separation between fuel and alcohol. The Board explicitly found that the Sweeney patents do not teach the use of the tetra-orthoesters recited in appellant's claims.

The Board cited Elliott U.S. Patent 3,903,006 and certain other patents, including Howk U.S. Patent 2,840,613, as secondary references. Elliott describes tri-orthoesters and tetra-orthoesters for use as water scavengers in hydraulic (non-hydrocarbon) fluids. The Board stated that

---

2. Tri-orthoesters have three-OR groups bonded to a central carbon atom, and the fourth carbon bond is to hydrogen or a hydrocarbon group (-R); they are represented as $C(R)(OR)^3$. Tetra-orthoesters have four-OR groups bonded to a central carbon atom, and are represented as $C(OR)^4$.

the Elliott reference shows equivalence between tetra-orthoesters and tri-orthoesters, and that "it is clear from the combined teachings of these references ... that [Dillon's tetra-orthoesters] would operate to remove water from non-aqueous liquids by the same mechanism as the orthoesters of Sweeney."

The Board stated that there was a "reasonable expectation" that the tri-and tetra-orthoester fuel compositions would have similar properties, based on "close structural and chemical similarity" between the tri-and tetra-orthoesters and the fact that both the prior art and Dillon use these compounds as "fuel additives." The Commissioner argues on appeal that the claimed compositions and method "would have been *prima facie* obvious from combined teachings of the references." On this reasoning, the Board held that unless Dillon showed some unexpected advantage or superiority of her claimed tetra-orthoester fuel compositions as compared with tri-orthoester fuel compositions, Dillon's new compositions as well as her claimed method of reducing particulate emissions are unpatentable for obviousness. It found that no such showing was made.

The Issue

The issue before this court is whether the Board erred in rejecting as obvious under 35 U.S.C. § 103 claims to Dillon's new compositions and to the new method of reducing particulate emissions, when the additives in the new compositions are structurally similar to additives in known compositions, having a different use, but the new method of reducing particulate emissions is neither taught nor suggested by the prior art.

The Broad Composition Claims

* * *

The Board found that the claims to compositions of a hydrocarbon fuel and a tetra-orthoester were *prima facie* obvious over Sweeney '417 and '267 in view of Elliott and Howk. We agree. Appellant argues that none of these references discloses or suggests the new use which she has discovered. That is, of course, true, but the composition claims are not limited to this new use; *i.e.*, they are not physically or structurally distinguishable over the prior art compositions except with respect to the orthoester component. We believe that the PTO has established, through its combination of references, that there is a sufficiently close relationship between the tri-orthoesters and tetra-orthoesters (see the cited Elliott and Howk references) in the fuel oil art to create an expectation that hydrocarbon fuel compositions containing the tetra-esters would have similar properties, including water scavenging, to like compositions containing the tri-esters, and to provide the motivation to make such new compositions. Howk teaches use of both tri-and tetra-orthoesters in a similar type of chemical reaction. Elliott teaches their equivalence for a particular practical use.

Our case law well establishes that such a fact situation gives rise to a *prima facie* case of obviousness. *See In re Shetty*, 566 F.2d 81, 85, 195 USPQ 753, 755–56 (CCPA 1977); *In re Albrecht*, 514 F.2d 1385, 1388, 185 USPQ 590, 593 (CCPA 1975); *In re Murch*, 464 F.2d 1051, 1054, 59 CCPA

1277, 175 USPQ 89, 91 (CCPA 1972); *In re Hoch*, 428 F.2d 1341, 1343, 57 CCPA 1292, 166 USPQ 406, 409 (CCPA 1970).

Appellant cites *In re Wright*, 848 F.2d 1216, 1219, 6 U.S.P.Q.2D 1959, 1961 (Fed.Cir.1988), for the proposition that a *prima facie* case of obviousness requires that the prior art suggest the claimed compositions' properties and the problem the applicant attempts to solve. The earlier panel opinion in this case, *In re Dillon*, 892 F.2d 1554, 13 U.S.P.Q.2D 1337 (now withdrawn), in fact stated "a *prima facie* case of obviousness is not deemed made unless both (1) the new compound or composition is structurally similar to the reference compound or composition and (2) there is some suggestion or expectation *in the prior art* that the new compound or composition will have the *same or a similar utility as that discovered by the applicant.*" *Id.* at 1560, 13 U.S.P.Q.2D at 1341 (emphasis added).

This court, in reconsidering this case *in banc*, reaffirms that structural similarity between claimed and prior art subject matter, proved by combining references or otherwise, where the prior art gives reason or motivation to make the claimed compositions, creates a *prima facie* case of obviousness, and that the burden (and opportunity) then falls on an applicant to rebut that *prima facie* case. Such rebuttal or argument can consist of a comparison of test data showing that the claimed compositions possess unexpectedly improved properties or properties that the prior art does not have (*In re Albrecht*, 514 F.2d 1389, 1396, 185 USPQ 585, 590 (CCPA 1975); *Murch*, 464 F.2d at 1056, 175 USPQ at 92), that the prior art is so deficient that there is no motivation to make what might otherwise appear to be obvious changes (*Albrecht*, 514 F.2d at 1396, 185 USPQ at 590; *In re Stemniski*, 444 F.2d 581, 58 CCPA 1410, 170 USPQ 343 (CCPA 1971); *In re Ruschig*, 343 F.2d 965, 52 CCPA 1238, 145 USPQ 274 (CCPA 1965)), or any other argument or presentation of evidence that is pertinent. There is no question that all evidence of the properties of the claimed compositions and the prior art must be considered in determining the ultimate question of patentability, but it is also clear that the discovery that a claimed composition possesses a property not disclosed for the prior art subject matter, does not by itself defeat a *prima facie* case. *Shetty*, 566 F.2d at 86, 195 USPQ at 756. Each situation must be considered on its own facts, but it is not necessary in order to establish a *prima facie* case of obviousness that both a structural similarity between a claimed and prior art compound (or a key component of a composition) be shown and that there be a suggestion in or expectation from *the prior art* that the claimed compound or composition will have the same or a similar utility *as one newly discovered by applicant.* To the extent that *Wright* suggests or holds to the contrary, it is hereby overruled. In particular, the statement that a *prima facie* obviousness rejection is not supported if no reference shows or suggests the newly-discovered properties and results of a claimed structure is not the law.[3]

---

3. . . . [T]his opinion and the dissent cite and rely on cases involving claims to chemical compounds, whereas this case involves compositions. The reason for this reliance is that, in this case, the principal difference between the claimed and prior art compositions is the difference between chemical compounds, viz., tri-orthoesters and tetra-orthoesters. Cases dealing with chemical compounds are therefore directly analogous here and, in view of the

Under the facts we have here, as described above, we have concluded that a *prima facie* case has been established. The art provided the motivation to make the claimed compositions in the expectation that they would have similar properties. Appellant had the opportunity to rebut the *prima facie* case. She did not present any showing of data to the effect that her compositions had properties not possessed by the prior art compositions or that they possessed them to an unexpectedly greater degree. She attempted to refute the significance of the teachings of the prior art references. She did not succeed and we do not believe the PTO was in error in its decision.

Appellant points out that none of the references relates to the problem she confronted, citing *In re Wright*, and that the combination of references is based on hindsight. It is clear, however, that appellant's claims have to be considered as she has drafted them, *i.e.*, as compositions consisting of a fuel and a tetra-orthoester, and that Sweeney '417 and '267 describe the combination of a liquid fuel with a related compound, a tri-orthoester. While Sweeney does not suggest appellant's use, her composition claims are not limited to that use;[4] the claims merely recite compositions analogous to those in the Sweeney patents, and appellant has made no showing overcoming the *prima facie* presumption of similar properties for those analogous compositions. The mention in the appealed claims that the amount of orthoester must be sufficient to reduce particulate emissions is not a distinguishing limitation of the claims, unless that amount is different from the prior art and critical to the use of the claimed composition. *See In re Reni*, 419 F.2d 922, 925, 57 CCPA 857, 164 USPQ 245, 247 (CCPA 1970). That is not the case here. The amount of ester recited in the dependent claims can be from 0.05–49%, a very broad range; a preferred range is .05–9%, compared with a percentage in Sweeney '417 approximately equimolar to the amounts of water in the fuel which the ester is intended to remove (.01–5%).

Appellant attacks the Elliott patent as non-analogous art, being in the field of hydraulic fluids rather than fuel combustion. We agree with the PTO that the field of relevant prior art need not be drawn so narrowly. As this court stated in *In re Deminski*, 796 F.2d 436, 442, 230 USPQ 313, 315 (Fed.Cir.1986) (*quoting In re Wood*, 599 F.2d 1032, 1036, 202 USPQ 171, 174 (CCPA 1979)):

> [t]he determination that a reference is from a nonanalogous art is therefore two-fold. First, we decide if the reference is within the field of the inventor's endeavor. If it is not, we proceed to determine whether the reference is reasonably pertinent to the particular problem with which the inventor was involved.

---

history of this case and its *in banc* status, we will make much comment on these cases in this opinion. We do not, however, intend to imply that in all cases involving claimed compositions, structural obviousness between involved chemical compounds necessarily makes the claimed compositions *prima facie* obvious.

4. The dissent misinterprets this comment as indicating that claims to new compounds and compositions must contain a limitation to a specific use, and states that past cases have rejected this proposition. Our comment only points out that the composition claims on appeal are not structurally or physically distinguishable from the prior art compositions by virtue of the recitation of their newly-discovered use.

Following that test, one concerned with the field of fuel oils clearly is chargeable with knowledge of Sweeney '417, which discloses fuel compositions with tri-orthoesters for dewatering purposes, and chargeable with knowledge of other references to tri-orthoesters, including for use as dewatering agents for fluids, albeit other fluids. These references are "within the field of the inventor's endeavor." Moreover, the statement of equivalency between tri-and tetra-orthoesters in Elliott is not challenged. We therefore conclude that Elliott is not excludable from consideration as non-analogous art. It is evidence that supports the Board's holding that the prior art makes the claimed compositions obvious, a conclusion that appellant did not overcome.

Appellant urges that the Board erred in not considering the unexpected results produced by her invention and in not considering the claimed invention as a whole. The Board found, on the other hand, that no showing was made of unexpected results for the claimed compositions compared with the compositions of Sweeney. We agree. Clearly, in determining patentability the Board was obligated to consider all the evidence of the properties of the claimed invention as a whole, compared with those of the prior art. However, after the PTO made a showing that the prior art compositions suggested the claimed compositions, the burden was on the applicant to overcome the presumption of obviousness that was created, and that was not done. For example, she produced no evidence that her compositions possessed properties not possessed by the prior art compositions. Nor did she show that the prior art compositions and use were so lacking in significance that there was no motivation for others to make obvious variants. There was no attempt to argue the relative importance of the claimed compositions compared with the prior art. *See In re May*, 574 F.2d 1082, 1092–95, 197 USPQ 601, 609–11 (CCPA 1978).

Appellant's patent application in fact included data showing that the prior art compositions containing tri-orthoesters had equivalent activity in reducing particulate emissions (she apparently was once claiming such compositions with either tri-orthoesters or tetra-orthoesters). She asserts that the examiner used her own showing of equivalence against her in violation of the rule of *In re Ruff*, 256 F.2d 590, 596, 45 CCPA 1037, 118 USPQ 340, 346 (CCPA 1958). While we caution against such a practice, it is clear to us that references by the PTO to the comparative data in the patent application were not employed as evidence of equivalence between the tri-and tetra-orthoesters; the PTO was simply pointing out that the applicant did not or apparently could not make a showing of superiority for the claimed tetra-ester compositions over the prior art tri-ester compositions.

* * *

The Dissent

The strong assertions by the dissent and its treatment of some of the case law impel us to make the following comments.

The dissent argues that our decision is "contrary to the weight and direction of . . . precedent, as embodied in over three decades of decision";

that we are resurrecting the *"Hass–Henze"* Doctrine, which was "discarded thirty years ago"; and that our holding today "changes what must be proved in order to patent a new chemical compound and composition and its new use, and thus changes what is patentable." We have done none of the above.

What we have done is to decide the case before us on the basis of long-established principles which had provided a stable understanding of the chemical patent law until the issuance of the original panel opinion in this case which we have now vacated. Our intent is to restore the law to its state existing before that panel opinion.

The length of the dissent and the number of cases it discusses may convey the impression that the weight of past jurisprudence is contrary to our holding today. That is not the case. The cited cases are simply not controlling on the facts of the present case or they are not contrary. Many do not deal with the requirements of a *prima facie* case. Some involve process claims, not compound or composition claims. Others are not pertinent for other reasons.

In brief, the cases establish that if an examiner considers that he has found prior art close enough to the claimed invention to give one skilled in the relevant chemical art the motivation to make close relatives (homologs, analogs, isomers, etc.) of the prior art compound(s), then there arises what has been called a presumption of obviousness or a *prima facie* case of obviousness. *In re Henze*, 181 F.2d 196, 37 CCPA 1009, 85 USPQ 261 (CCPA 1950); *In re Hass*, 141 F.2d 122, 127, 130, 31 CCPA 895, 60 USPQ 544, 548, 552 (CCPA 1944). The burden then shifts to the applicant, who then can present arguments and/or data to show that what appears to be obvious, is not in fact that, when the invention is looked at as a whole. *In re Papesch*, 315 F.2d 381, 50 CCPA 1084, 137 USPQ 43 (CCPA 1963). The cases of *Hass* and *Henze* established the rule that, unless an applicant showed that the prior art compound lacked the property or advantage asserted for the claimed compound, the presumption of unpatentability was not overcome.

Exactly what facts constituted a *prima facie* case varied from case to case, but it was not the law that, where an applicant asserted that an invention possessed properties not known to be possessed by the prior art, no *prima facie* case was established unless the reference also showed the novel activity. There are cases, cited in the dissent, in which a *prima facie* case was not established based on lack of structural similarity. *See In re Grabiak*, 769 F.2d 729, 732, 226 USPQ 870, 872 (Fed.Cir.1985); *In re Taborsky*, 502 F.2d 775, 780–81, 183 USPQ 50, 55 (CCPA 1974). Some of the cited cases also contained language suggesting that the fact that the claimed and the prior art compounds possessed the same activity were added factors in the establishment of the *prima facie* case. *E.g., In re Zeidler*, 682 F.2d 961, 966, 215 USPQ 490, 494 (CCPA 1982); *In re Grunwell*, 609 F.2d 486, 491, 203 USPQ 1055, 1058 (CCPA 1979); *In re Payne*, 606 F.2d 303, 314, 203 USPQ 245, 255 (CCPA 1979); *In re Swan Wood*, 582 F.2d 638, 641, 199 USPQ 137, 139 (CCPA 1978); *In re Lamberti*, 545 F.2d 747, 751, 192 USPQ 278, 281 (CCPA 1976); *In re Susi*, 440 F.2d 442, 445, 58 CCPA 1074, 169 USPQ 423, 426 (CCPA 1971). Those cases did not say, however, as the dissent asserts, that, in the absence of the similarity of activities, there would have been no *prima facie* case.

For example, the dissent quotes a statement in *Grabiak* that "[w]hen chemical compounds have 'very close' structural similarities and similar utilities, without more a *prima facie* case may be made." 769 F.2d at 731, 226 USPQ at 871. That case does not state, as implied by the dissent, that without the similarity of utilities, there would not have been a *prima facie* case. A conclusion based on one set of facts does not necessarily rule out a similar conclusion with slightly different facts.

One case cited by the dissent as "rejecting the PTO's interpretation of *Henze* as establishing a 'legal presumption' of obviousness" was *In re Mills*, 281 F.2d 218, 47 CCPA 1185, 126 USPQ 513 (CCPA 1960). All that case decided, however, was that a one-carbon member of a homologous series is too far from the prior art disclosure of 8 to 12 members to justify the presumption. *Id.* at 223–24, 126 USPQ at 517–18.

We will not review all the cases cited in the dissent, but *Stemniski* is an important case, for it overruled *Henze* and *In re Riden*, 318 F.2d 761, 50 CCPA 1411, 138 USPQ 112 (CCPA 1963) (a case similar to *Henze*), "to the extent that [they] are inconsistent with the views expressed herein." 444 F.2d at 587, 170 USPQ at 348. The views that were expressed therein were that:

> [w]here the prior art reference neither discloses nor suggests a utility for certain described compounds, why should it be said that a reference makes obvious to one of ordinary skill in the art an isomer, homolog or analog or related structure, when that mythical, but intensely practical, person knows of no "practical" reason to make the reference compounds, much less any structurally related compounds?

Id. at 586, 170 USPQ at 347. Thus, *Stemniski*, rather than destroying the established practice of rejecting closely-related compounds as *prima facie* obvious, qualified it by holding that a presumption is not created when the reference compound is so lacking in any utility that there is no motivation to make close relatives.

* * *

Properties, therefore, are relevant to the creation of a *prima facie* case in the sense of affecting the motivation of a researcher to make compounds closely related to or suggested by a prior art compound, but it is not required, as stated in the dissent, that the prior art disclose or suggest the properties newly-discovered by an applicant in order for there to be a *prima facie* case of obviousness.

The dissent cites the seminal case of *Papesch,* suggesting that it rejected the principle that we now "adopt," thereby implying that we are weakening *Papesch*. We are doing nothing of the sort. *Papesch* indeed stated that a compound and all of its properties are inseparable and must be considered in the determination of obviousness. We heartily agree and intend not to retreat from *Papesch* one inch. *Papesch,* however, did not deal with the requirements for establishing a *prima facie* case, but whether the examiner had to consider the properties of an invention at all, when there was a presumption of obviousness. 315 F.2d at 391, 137 USPQ at 51. The reference disclosed a lower homolog of the claimed compounds, so it was clear that impliedly a *prima facie* case existed; the question was whether, under those circumstances, the biological data were admissible at all. The court ruled that they were, *id.* at 391, 137 USPQ at 51, and we agree with that result. The dissent quotes the brief passage at the end of the *Papesch* opinion to the effect that the prior art must "at least to a degree" disclose the applicant's desired property, *id.* at 392, 137 USPQ at 52, but this brief mention was not central to the decision in that case and did not refer to the requirements of a *prima facie* case. *Papesch* is irrelevant to the question of the requirements for a *prima facie* case, which is the question we have here.

The dissent refers to a number of cases, including *In re Lunsford*, 357 F.2d 380, 53 CCPA 986, 148 USPQ 716 (CCPA 1966), stating that the court had rejected the Patent Office's position of "structures only." That case must be understood in the context of the refusal of the examiner to consider any showing of improved properties, not in the context of a discussion whether a *prima facie* case was created. The compounds were conceded to be sufficiently close to the prior art that, without a showing of a significant difference in properties, they would have been obvious. *Id.* at 381, 148 USPQ at 717.

The dissent asserts that the *Shetty* case "diverg[ed] from the weight of [the court's] precedent" in holding that a *prima facie* case was made based on similarities of structure. The court, in that opinion, accepted the *prima facie* case and concluded that "appellant ha[d] offered no evidence of unobviousness, as by showing an actual difference in properties." 566 F.2d at 86, 195 USPQ at 756 (*citing Hoch*). The opinion does not suggest that the court was diverging from the weight of precedent.

The dissent mentions positions advanced by the Commissioner, including citing the *In re Mod*, 408 F.2d 1055, 56 CCPA 1041, 161 USPQ 281 (CCPA 1969) and *In re De Montmollin*, 344 F.2d 976, 52 CCPA 1287, 145 USPQ 416 (CCPA 1965) decisions. We do not, however, in today's decision necessarily adopt any positions of the Commissioner other than those stated in our opinion and note that neither *Mod* nor *De Montmollin* dealt with the requirements of a *prima facie* case. They concerned the question whether the existence of a new property for claimed compounds in addition to a property common to both the claimed and related prior art compounds rendered the claimed compounds unobvious. We are not faced with that question today.

* * *

Another example of the lack of direct pertinence of a case quoted in the dissent is *May*, which the dissent cites as an example of the consistent line of decisions to the effect that "both structure and properties must be suggested in the prior art before a *prima facie* case of obviousness was deemed made." This case does not state that both structure and properties "must" be suggested. The claimed and prior art compositions were both disclosed as having analgesic activity; it was conceded that a *prima facie* case was made out, but the court concluded that applicants had rebutted the presumed expectation that structurally similar compounds have similar properties with a showing of an actual unexpected difference of properties between the claimed compound and the prior art. 574 F.2d at 1095, 197 USPQ at 611. The applicant in that case thus made a showing that Dillon did not make in this case.

Properties must be considered in the overall evaluation of obviousness, and the lack of any disclosure of useful properties for a prior art compound may indicate a lack of motivation to make related compounds, thereby precluding a *prima facie* case, but it is not correct that similarity of structure and a suggestion of the *activity of an applicant's compounds* in the prior art are necessary before a *prima facie* case is established.

* * *

■ NEWMAN, CIRCUIT JUDGE, with whom COWEN, SENIOR CIRCUIT JUDGE, and MAYER, CIRCUIT JUDGE, join, dissenting.

The court today resolves certain disparities in the extensive body of precedent on the question of obviousness of new chemical compounds and compositions. However, these disparities are resolved in a way that is contrary to the weight and direction of this precedent, as embodied in over three decades of decision. The court departs from its considered development of the law governing patentability of new chemical compounds and compositions, and reinstates a rule of "structural obviousness". In so ruling the court not only rejects the weight of precedent, but also errs in the application of 35 U.S.C. §§ 101, 102, and 103.

The majority's holding that *prima facie* obviousness of new chemical compounds and compositions is determined based only on structural similarity to prior art compounds and compositions having a known use is reminiscent of the "*Hass–Henze* Doctrine" of earlier days. This doctrine was discarded thirty years ago, and although it resurfaced on occasion, its original sweep was superseded by many years of judicial analysis. Review of this analysis shows the courts' evolving understanding of the characteristics of chemical inventions, particularly the inseparability of chemical properties and chemical structure, and the legal consequences of this scientific fact.

Judicial decisions over the past three decades established the general rule that the determination of *prima facie* obviousness of new chemical compounds and compositions and their uses can not be based on chemical structure alone, but must also include consideration of all their properties, including those discovered by the applicant. This rule had important procedural and substantive consequences during patent examination, for it determined the kind of evidence and proof that was required of a patent applicant. The ruling of this *in banc* court changes what must be proved in order to patent a new chemical compound or composition, and thus changes what is patentable.

The body of precedent establishing the burdens of modern patent examination was developed in judicial decisions applying the 1952 Patent Act. As I shall discuss in greater detail, when patent examination showed that the prior art suggested the inventor's new chemical structure and the inventor's newly discovered property and use, a *prima facie* case of obviousness of the new chemical compound or composition and its use was deemed made.

The inventor could, of course, argue that the differences from the prior art were such that a *prima facie* case was not made. And the inventor could rebut the *prima facie* case of obviousness, by showing some unexpected difference in structure or properties and use, not apparent from the teachings of the prior art. Such rebuttal was generally presented in the form of comparative experimental data, whereby the inventor demonstrated that the properties of his or her new chemical compound or composition achieved some unobvious or unexpected result or advantage, as compared with the actual properties of the prior art structure. This rebuttal often required the inventor to go beyond the general teachings in the prior art, and prove that the prior art compound did not, in fact, possess the specific property and advantage of the new compound or composition. Such proofs were invariably required when the prior art suggested the general property and use discovered by the applicant. Many dozens of decisions of the CCPA and this court illustrate this procedure, and the variety of factual circumstances in which it has been invoked.

In accordance with the court's *in banc* holding,[2] a new chemical compound or composition is not patentable even when the prior art does not suggest that the new chemical compound or composition would have the applicant's newly discovered property and use, unless the applicant makes the same showing that is required when the prior art does suggest the applicant's new property and use.

The applicant is thus required to show "unexpected" properties and results, *whether or not* the prior art provides an expectation or suggestion of the properties and results disclosed in the patent application. And unless the applicant proves that the prior art structure does not actually possess the same unobvious property that the applicant discovered for the new structure, the court holds today that the new chemical compound or composition is not patentable. This is an incorrect application of the patent

---

2. The majority holds that a *prima facie* case of obviousness is made whenever the structure of the applicant's new compound or composition (or mechanical device) is "obvious" from that shown in the prior art, independent of whether the prior art suggests or makes obvious the applicant's newly discovered property and use. The majority allows an exception for situations where the prior art gives no "reason or motivation to make the claimed invention", and duly makes clear that this means motivation to make the new compound or composition for the prior art use, not for the applicant's newly discovered use. This exception comes into play only when the prior art structure has no known utility; and a few such situations are reported, *e.g. In re Stemniski*, 444 F.2d 581, 58 CCPA 1410, 170 USPQ 343 (CCPA 1971) (prior art compounds used only as intermediates), and *In re Albrecht*, 514 F.2d 1389, 185 USPQ 585 (CCPA 1975) (no practical utility). Thus, according to the majority, when the prior art chemical compound or composition has no known use, the prior art provides no "reason or motivation" to make a structurally similar new compound or composition; and in such case the prior art would not make a prima facie case of obviousness based on structural similarity alone.

While I welcome any reduction in the sweep of the court's holding, this exception is of trivial impact. In most cases the prior art compound or composition has some known use; and thus for most cases the majority's "motivation" test would be met based solely on similarity of structure. This is an important change of law. While the holdings of the prior law were not entirely consistent—see the various CCPA opinions discussed post—this *in banc* court now establishes the rule that will control all cases in the future.

statute, and a rejection of the wisdom of precedent. Therefore, respectfully, I dissent.

I
The Law

A
The In Banc Issue

.... The Commissioner, asking the court to choose between divergent decisions of the CCPA, stated the PTO position that *prima facie* obviousness should be based on chemical structure alone:

> [I]f the prior art suggests an inventor's compound or composition *per se,* that compound or composition would be *prima facie* obvious, regardless of the properties disclosed in the inventor's application.

The majority of the *in banc* court adopts the Commissioner's position, expressly rejecting the panel's position that the properties and use discovered by the applicant must be considered in connection with determination of the *prima facie* case under section 103, thereby overruling all prior decisions that so held.

I would hold that determination of whether a *prima facie* case of obviousness has been made requires consideration of the similarities and differences as to structure and properties and utility, between the applicant's new compounds or compositions and those shown in the prior art....

Structure alone, without consideration of the applicant's newly discovered properties, is an incomplete focus for consideration of these factors.

B
The Prima Facie Case

* * *

The initial determination by the patent examiner is critical to further proceedings, for the presence or absence of a *prima facie* case of obviousness controls the need for the applicant to adduce rebuttal evidence of unobviousness. The procedure serves to clearly allocate the burdens of going forward and of persuasion as between the examiner and the applicant. *In re Johnson,* 747 F.2d 1456, 1460, 223 USPQ 1260, 1263 (Fed.Cir. 1984). It determines what the applicant must prove, and the kind of evidence the applicant must provide. Thus it determines what is patentable under the statute.

While many judicial decisions turn on the question of adequacy of the rebuttal evidence, the concern of the *in banc* court today is the issue of the *prima facie* case. For when, as here, no rebuttal evidence is presented, determination of the *prima facie* case is decision of the question of patentability.

As illustrated in Dillon's case, the question of whether there is a *prima facie* case of obviousness controls whether Dillon is required to prove that her newly discovered property of particulate (soot) reduction during combustion is not actually possessed by the prior art composition, when the prior art composition was not known or suggested to have this property. Dillon did not so prove, and the Commissioner urges that since Dillon's specification itself discloses that the prior art composition does possess this newly discovered property, the *prima facie* case based on structural similarity was not rebutted.

Heretofore, the courts generally recognized a controlling distinction between the two principal types of factual situations that arise when a patent applicant's new chemical compound or composition has a structure that is "similar" to chemical structures shown in the prior art: (1) those where the prior art suggests, at least in general terms, that the new chemical compound or composition will have the applicant's newly discovered property and use; and (2) those where it does not. These factual situations have had different consequences with respect to whether a *prima facie* case of obviousness was made. The difference turned on whether or not the structure and properties and use of a new chemical compound or composition were suggested in the prior art. The distinction determined whether the applicant was required to come forward with rebuttal evidence, which often was in the form of new technological information not known to the prior art, in order to establish an "unexpected" difference between the properties discovered by the applicant and those actually possessed by the prior art structure.

This distinction brought a consistent application of the law of 35 U.S.C. § 103 to the examination of chemical inventions, for it established the framework wherein the law was applied to the facts of each case. The court today rejects this distinction, holding *in banc* that it suffices to show *prima facie* obviousness whenever the prior art describes a similar chemical structure, provided only that the prior art gives some "reason or motivation" to make the claimed chemical structure, "regardless of the properties disclosed in the inventor's application", in the Commissioner's words. This position is contrary to the weight and direction of precedent, as I shall illustrate, and is contrary to the statutory imperatives of Title 35.

* * *

D

The Merits

Applying the guidance of precedent to Dillon's invention: the compositions are new, and their property and use of reducing particulate emissions is not taught or suggested in the prior art. There is no objective teaching in the prior art that would have led one of ordinary skill to make this product in order to solve the problem that was confronting Dillon: to reduce soot from combustion of hydrocarbon fuels. There is no reasonable basis in the prior art for expecting that Dillon's new compositions would have the particulate-reducing property that she discovered. Structure, properties and use must be considered in determining whether a *prima facie* case under section 103 has been made.

The Sweeney references show the water-sequestration property of triorthoesters in hydrocarbon fuels, and the Elliott reference shows the water-sequestration property of tri-and tetra-orthoesters in hydraulic fluids (which are not hydrocarbons and not fuels). There is no suggestion in the prior art that would have led one of ordinary skill to make Dillon's new compositions in the expectation that they would reduce particulate emissions from combustion. No reference suggests any relationship between the properties of water-sequestration and soot-reduction. All this is undisputed.

* * *

The board stated that it is inherent in Dillon's compositions that they would reduce particulate emissions, that Dillon "merely recited a newly discovered function inherently possessed" by the prior art. Arguments based on "inherent" properties can not stand when there is no supporting teaching in the prior art. . . .

When the PTO asserts that there is an explicit or implicit teaching or suggestion in the prior art, the PTO must produce supporting references. *In re Yates,* 663 F.2d 1054, 1057, 211 USPQ 1149, 1151 (CCPA 1981).

The applicant's newly discovered properties must be considered in determining whether a *prima facie* case of unpatentability is made, along with all the other evidence. Neither structure nor properties can be ignored; they are essential to consideration of the invention as a whole. But Dillon's own discovery of the soot-reducing property of the tri-orthoester fuel composition is not evidence against her in determining whether the prior art makes a case of *prima facie* obviousness. *In re Wertheim,* 541 F.2d 257, 269, 191 USPQ 90, 102 (CCPA 1976) (applicant's own disclosures can not be used to support a rejection of the claims "absent some admission that matter disclosed in the specification is in the prior art"); *In re Ruff,* 256 F.2d at 598, 118 USPQ at 347 ("The mere statement of this proposition reveals its fallaciousness").

* * *

The Commissioner raised the policy argument that Dillon is simply removing from the public an obvious variant of Sweeney's and Elliott's compositions, one that might be useful to scavenge water in fuels. In *Ruschig* the court had considered the argument, and remarked that the provision of adequate patent protection for the applicant's new compounds, not previously in existence and having a new and unobvious use, was favored over the "mere possibility that someone might wish to use some of them for some such [other] purpose." 343 F.2d at 979, 145 USPQ at 286. *See also, e.g., Chupp,* 816 F.2d at 647, 2 U.S.P.Q.2D at 1440, wherein the court expressed a similar view. This practical wisdom has been tested by long experience. It accords with judicial recognition that:

> Although there is a vast amount of knowledge about general relationships in the chemical arts, chemistry is still largely empirical, and there is often great difficulty in predicting precisely how a given compound will behave.

In re Carleton, 599 F.2d 1021, 1026, 202 USPQ 165, 170 (CCPA 1979).

Granting Dillon a patent on her invention takes away nothing that the public already has; and the public receives not only the knowledge of Dillon's discovery, for abandoned patent applications are maintained in secrecy, but Dillon is not deprived of an incentive to discover and to commercialize this new product for this new use.

Conclusion

Following the weight of precedent, I would hold that a *prima facie* case of obviousness of a new chemical compound or composition requires consideration of not only the chemical structure but also the newly discovered properties, in light of the teachings and suggestions of the prior art. I would expressly reject the Commissioner's position that determination of the *prima facie* case is made regardless of the properties disclosed in the inventor's application.

Since there is no suggestion in the prior art references, alone or in combination, of the particulate-reducing property and use discovered by Dillon for her new compositions, a *prima facie* case of obviousness has not been made. Thus it is not necessary to patentability that Dillon establish that the prior art compositions do not possess the same soot-reduction property and use.

NOTES

1. *Pre–Dillon: The Hass–Henze Doctrine and its Progeny*. Prior to *Dillon*, there existed a line of cases with respect to the issue of *prima facie* obviousness that, as illustrated in *Dillon*, are subject to conflicting interpretations. A good place to begin is a series of three cases, *Hass I, II, and III*, decided by the Court of Customs and Patent Appeals in 1944; and the case of *In re Henze*, handed down in 1950. These early cases stood for the proposition that structural similarity *alone* between a prior art compound and the claimed composition created a presumption of obviousness. This presumption could be rebutted if the applicant came forward with evidence showing that the claimed compound possessed unexpected properties not present in the prior art compound. As expressed by the court in *Henze*:

> In effect, the nature of homologues and the close relationship the physical and chemical properties of one member of a series bears to adjacent members in [sic] such that a presumption of unpatentability arises against a claim directed to a composition of matter, the adjacent homologue of which is old in the art. The burden is on the applicant to rebut that presumption by a showing that the claimed compound *possesses* unobvious or unexpected beneficial properties not actually *possessed* by the prior art homologue. It is immaterial that the prior are homologue may not be recognized or *known* for the same purpose or to possess the same properties as the claimed compound.

In re Henze, 181 F.2d at 201 (emphasis in original).

The CCPA's decision in *In re Papesch*, 315 F.2d 381 (CCPA 1963), affirmed the reasoning of the *Hass–Henze* doctrine, but appeared to have tempered it somewhat, stating that "[p]atentability has not been determined on the basis of the obviousness of structure alone. . . . From the standpoint of patent law, a compound and all of its properties are inseparable." *Id.* at 391. With *Papesch* appearing more receptive to the patent applicant, the dissent in *Dillon* relied heavily on it for the proposition "that the prior art disclosure should be 'at least to a degree, of the same desired property.' " The majority dismissed this statement as not central to the *Papesch* court's analysis, and insisted that it "intend[s] not to retreat from *Papesch* one inch" because, according to the majority, *Papesch* held nothing more than "that a compound and all of its properties are inseparable and must be considered in the determination of obviousness."

2. *Dillon and Prima Facie Obviousness.* In *Wright*, Judge Newman, who wrote the dissent in *Dillon*, emphasized the many factors that should be taken into consideration when making a § 103 nonobviousness determination:

> The entirety of a claimed invention, including the combination viewed as a whole, the elements thereof, and the properties and purpose of the invention, must be considered. Factors including unexpected results, new features, solution of a different problem, novel properties, are all considerations in the determination of obviousness in terms of 35 U.S.C. § 103.

Read the following excerpt from the majority in *Dillon* and ask yourself what is left of *Wright*?

> Appellant cites *In re Wright*, 848 F.2d 1216, 1219 (Fed.Cir.1988), for the proposition that a *prima facie* case of obviousness requires that the prior art suggest the claimed compositions' properties and the problem the applicant attempts to solve. The earlier panel opinion in this case, *In re Dillon*, 892 F.2d 1554 (now withdrawn), in fact stated "a *prima facie* case of obviousness is not deemed made unless both (1) the new compound or composition is structurally similar to the reference compound or composition and (2) there is some suggestion or expectation *in the prior art* that the new compound or composition will have the *same or a similar utility as that discovered by the applicant.*" *Id.* at 1560, 13 U.S.P.Q.2D at 1341 (emphasis added).
>
> This court, in reconsidering this case *in banc*, reaffirms that structural similarity between claimed and prior art subject matter, proved by combining references or otherwise, where the prior art gives reason or motivation to make the claimed compositions, creates a *prima facie* case of obviousness, and that the burden (and opportunity) then falls on an applicant to rebut that *prima facie* case. Such rebuttal or argument can consist of a comparison of test data showing that the claimed compositions possess unexpectedly improved properties or properties that the prior art does not have that the prior art is so deficient that there is no motivation to make what might otherwise appear to be obvious changes or any other argument or presentation of evidence that is pertinent. There is no question that all evidence of the properties of the claimed compositions and the prior art must be considered in determining the ultimate question of patentability, but it is also clear that the discovery that a claimed composition possesses a property not disclosed for the prior art subject matter, does not by itself defeat a *prima facie* case. Each situation must be considered on its own facts, but it is not necessary in order to establish a *prima facie* case of obviousness that both a structural similarity between a claimed and prior art compound (or a key component of a composition) be shown and that there be a suggestion in or expectation from *the prior art* that the claimed compound or composition will have the same or a similar utility *as one newly discovered by applicant.* To the extent that *Wright* suggests or holds to the contrary, it is hereby overruled. In particular, the statement that a *prima facie* obviousness rejection is not supported if no reference shows or suggests the newly-discovered properties and results of a claimed structure is not the law.

919 F.2d at 692 (emphasis in original).

What was so significant about the holding in *Dillon*? How is the analysis in *Dillon* different from that of *Wright*? According to one commentator:

Prior to *Dillon*, a long line of conflicting cases had steadily moved from a presumption of *prima facie* obviousness, when the claimed compound had a structure similar to that of the prior art compound, to proof of structural similarity and a suggestion in the prior art that the claimed composition would have the new property. Because it is far more difficult to prove that the prior art suggested any new or unexpected properties than it is to prove that, due to structural similarity, the prior art suggested "old" or expected properties, a higher burden of proof in order to create a *prima facie* case of obviousness existed before *Dillon*. In other words, after *Dillon*, it is easier to prove a *prima facie* case of obviousness because all the Examiner has to do is demonstrate structural similarity and some motivation for combining or modifying references where there was the suggestion in the prior art that the claimed compound would have the same expected benefit or utility as the prior art compound.

For example, assume the claimed compound is Compound A, similar in structure to Compound B, a previously patented compound used as a cough suppressant. The prior art would suggest that Compound A would have similar cough-suppressant properties. If Compound A's only property is that of a cough suppressant, all prior case law would be in accord that a *prima facie* case has been established because "(t)he art provided the motivation to make the claimed compositions in the expectation that they would have similar properties." *Dillon*, 919 F.2d at 693. However, if Compound A had both the expected cough-suppressant property and an unexpected property such as that of a decongestant (assume Compound B did not have, nor suggest, a decongestant property), *Dillon* would demand a *prima facie* case whereas the prior trend of cases would not.

Todd R. Miller, *Motivation and Set–Size: In re Bell Provides a Link Between Chemical and Biochemical Patent Claims*, 2 U. BALT. INTELL. PROP. L.J. 89, 93 n. 20 (1993).

b. UNEXPECTED PROPERTIES AS EVIDENCE OF NONOBVIOUS-NESS

In re Soni

54 F.3d 746 (Fed.Cir.1995).

■ Before MICHEL, LOURIE, and BRYSON, CIRCUIT JUDGES.

■ Opinion for the court filed by CIRCUIT JUDGE LOURIE. Dissenting opinion filed by CIRCUIT JUDGE MICHEL.

■ LOURIE, CIRCUIT JUDGE.

Pravin L. Soni, Ceinwen Rowlands, Larry Edwards, and Mark Wartenberg (collectively "Soni") appeal from the decision of the U.S. Patent and Trademark Office ("PTO") Board of Patent Appeals and Interferences affirming the examiner's final rejection of claims 1–6, 8–12, and 21 of application Serial No. 07/462,893, entitled "Conductive Polymer Compositions," as unpatentable on the ground of obviousness under 35 U.S.C. § 103 (1988). Because the PTO's conclusion that unexpected results were not shown was clearly erroneous, we reverse.

Background

The claimed invention relates to conductive polymer compositions. Claim 1 is illustrative:

1. A melt-processed composition which comprises

(i) an organic polymer which is not crosslinked and has a molecular weight which is greater than 150,000 when measured by high temperature gel permeation chromatography, and

(ii) a particulate conductive filler which is dispersed in the polymer and which is present in [an] amount sufficient to render the composition electrically conductive (emphasis added).

Soni's patent specification states that the claimed compositions have significantly improved physical and electrical properties compared to compositions using polymers having a molecular weight below 150,000. To illustrate this point, the specification describes a number of tests comparing the properties of a composition of the invention composed of polyethylene having a molecular weight of 203,000 with a comparative composition composed of polyethylene having a molecular weight of 148,000. The data show at least a fifty-fold increase in tensile strength for the higher molecular weight composition compared to the lower molecular weight composition. The data also show at least a five-fold increase in peel strength as well as improved resistivity and recovery behavior properties. From these data, the specification concludes that "[t]he tensile, peel, resistivity behavior and recovery tests show significantly improved properties for a polymer having a molecular [weight] of 203,000 compared to one having a molecular weight of 148,000, which are much greater than would have been predicted given the difference in their molecular weights."

During prosecution, the examiner rejected the claims over the following prior art:

Rosenzweig et al.	U.S. Patent 4,775,501
Soni et al.	U.S. Patent 4,921,648
Lunk et al.	U.S. Patent 4,624,990
Taylor	U.S. Patent 4,426,633
Wu et al.	U.S. Patent 4,228,118
Capaccio et al.	U.S. Patent 4,268,470
Ward et al.	U.S. Patent 3,962,205

The examiner first rejected claims 1–6, 8–12, and 21 under 35 U.S.C. §§ 102 or 103 as being anticipated by or obvious from the disclosures of the Rosenzweig or Soni patents. The examiner took the position that each of these references discloses all of the limitations recited in the claims. Second, the examiner rejected claims 1–6, 8–12, and 21 under § 103 as being unpatentable over Lunk or Taylor, taken alone or in combination with Rosenzweig, Soni, Wu, Capaccio, or Ward. The examiner asserted that each of Lunk and Taylor discloses a melt-processed composition comprising an organic polymer and a particulate conductive filler. While acknowledging that Lunk and Taylor are silent as to the molecular weight of the polymers used, the examiner argued that a person of ordinary skill in the art would have selected a polymer having a molecular weight within the claimed range. Wu, Capaccio, and Ward were cited for their disclosures of melt-processable organic polymers having molecular weights within the claimed range.

The rejections were subsequently made final, and Soni appealed to the Board. The Board affirmed the first rejection on the ground of § 103, but reversed it with respect to § 102. The Board found that the parent application commonly shared by Soni and Rosenzweig did not disclose the specific molecular weight limitation found in the claims and thus the claims were not anticipated by Soni or Rosenzweig under § 102(a) or (e). The Board found, however, that

> [i]f higher molecular weight melt-processable polymers were not available at the time the parent application was filed, they certainly became available by the time of appellants' invention, as evidenced by appellants' acknowledgments in the present specification, *i.e.*, that the compositions in the appealed claims are based on commercially available polymers. *It is also acknowledged on this record that one of ordinary skill in the relevant art would have expected higher molecular weight polymers to result in better composition properties.* See the present specification at page 17, lines 22 to 28. On this record, it would have constituted nothing more than the exercise of ordinary skill for one to have selected commercially available higher molecular weight polymers to use in the melt-processes of the references to obtain advantageous physical properties in the resulting product (emphasis added).

In response to Soni's argument that its specification describes unexpected results, the Board stated:

> In the referenced portion of the present specification, it is also asserted that the improvement in properties resulting from the use of the specific class of molecular weights set forth in appellants' claims was "much greater than would have been predicted." However, *this record appears to be devoid of any evidence to support that conclusion.* Thus, *to whatever extent* it may be considered that *there is any evidence of unobviousness, it is clearly insufficient* to outweigh the evidence of obviousness of record (emphasis added).

The Board also affirmed the § 103 rejection based on Lunk or Taylor, taken alone or in combination with the other references cited by the examiner. The Board found that Lunk would have anticipated the claimed invention except that the reference does not explicitly disclose polymers having a molecular weight greater than 150,000. The Board further found that

> selection of a specific molecular weight from within the very high molecular weight class disclosed by Lunk would have been obvious to one of ordinary skill in the relevant art, and there is no convincing evidence that unobvious results are associated with the specific molecular weight limitation in question. Similarly, there is no evidence that substitution of other well-known melt-processable polymers in the Lunk composition produces unobvious results.

The Board noted that this analysis applied equally to the Taylor reference and found the remaining references essentially superfluous in view of Lunk or Taylor.

Soni requested reconsideration of the Board's decision, arguing that the Board ignored the evidence of unexpected results disclosed in the specification. On reconsideration, the Board adhered to its decision:

> That which appellants characterize as "evidence" consists of conclusory statements made in the original specification concerning unpredictable differences, which statements are *unsupported by any factual data*. In a given case, this could conceivably be adequate; however, where as here the evidence of obviousness found in the references is quite strong, this type of unsupported conclusion is inadequate to outweigh it (emphasis added).

Soni now appeals.

Discussion

* * *

The question whether an applicant made a showing of unexpected results is one of fact, subject to the clearly erroneous standard of review.

On appeal, Soni concedes that the prior art relied upon establishes a *prima facie* case of obviousness. Thus, the sole question for resolution is whether Soni carried its burden of rebutting the *prima facie* case of obviousness. *See In re Rijckaert*, 9 F.3d 1531, 1532, 28 U.S.P.Q.2D 1955, 1956 (Fed.Cir.1993) (*prima facie* case of obviousness shifts burden to applicant to come forward with rebuttal evidence or argument).

The references cited describe relevant compositions containing polyethylene and a conductive filler. We need not focus on the specific disclosures of the references since it is conceded that the correctness of the rejections boils down to the question whether the data in Soni's patent specification show that the compositions of the claims exhibit unexpectedly improved physical and electrical properties compared to lower molecular weight compositions.

Soni argues that it overcame the *prima facie* case of obviousness because its patent specification contains data showing that the claimed compositions do exhibit unexpectedly improved properties. Soni further argues that the Board ignored these data, pointing to the Board's statements that Soni's claim of unexpected results was "unsupported by any factual evidence" and that "this record is devoid of any evidence."

In reply, the PTO maintains that Soni has not met its burden of rebutting the *prima facie* case of obviousness. Specifically, the PTO contends that the Board did in fact consider the data in Soni's specification, but found the data unpersuasive. The PTO points out that Soni's statement that the results were unexpected is conclusory and that the record lacks any evidence or explanation why the results were unexpected. The Board, the PTO notes, found that Soni had acknowledged that improved properties would have been expected for higher molecular weight compositions. The PTO contends that, because Soni did not prove, or even state, how much improvement would have been expected, there is no factual basis for analyzing whether Soni's data show unexpected results. Thus, in the PTO's view, the comparative data are entitled to little probative weight. The PTO also contends that any showing of unexpected results made by Soni was not commensurate in scope with the appealed claims.

The patent statute provides that "[a] person shall be entitled to a patent unless" any of the §§ 102 or 103 bars applies. 35 U.S.C. § 102. When a chemical composition is claimed, a *prima facie* case of obviousness under § 103 may be established by the PTO's citation of a reference to a similar composition, the presumption being that similar compositions have similar properties. *See In re Dillon*, 919 F.2d 688, 692, 16 U.S.P.Q.2D 1897, 1901 (Fed.Cir.1990) (*en banc*) ("structural similarity between claimed and prior art subject matter, . . . where the prior art gives reason or motivation to make the claimed compositions, creates a *prima facie* case of obviousness"), *cert. denied*, 500 U.S. 904, 111 S.Ct. 1682, 114 L.Ed.2d 77 (1991). One way for a patent applicant to rebut a *prima facie* case of obviousness is to make a showing of "unexpected results," *i.e.*, to show that the claimed invention exhibits some superior property or advantage that a person of ordinary skill in the relevant art would have found surprising or unexpected. The basic principle behind this rule is straightforward—that which would have been surprising to a person of ordinary skill in a particular art would not have been obvious. The principle applies most often to the less predictable fields, such as chemistry, where minor changes in a product or process may yield substantially different results.

Consistent with the rule that all evidence of nonobviousness must be considered when assessing patentability, the PTO must consider comparative data in the specification in determining whether the claimed invention provides unexpected results. *In re Margolis*, 785 F.2d 1029, 1031, 228 USPQ 940, 941–42 (Fed.Cir.1986). However, "[i]t is well settled that unexpected results must be established by factual evidence. Mere argument or conclusory statements in the specification does not suffice." *In re De Blauwe*, 736 F.2d 699, 705, 222 USPQ 191, 196 (Fed.Cir.1984); *see also In re Wood*, 582 F.2d 638, 642, 199 USPQ 137, 140 (CCPA 1978) ("Mere lawyer's arguments and conclusory statements in the specification, unsupported by objective evidence, are insufficient to establish unexpected results."); *In re Lindner*, 457 F.2d 506, 508, 173 USPQ 356, 358 (CCPA 1972) ("[M]ere conclusory statements in the specification . . . are entitled to little weight when the Patent Office questions the efficacy of those statements.").

Here, Soni's specification contains more than mere argument or conclusory statements; it contains specific data indicating improved properties. It also states that the improved properties provided by the claimed compositions "are much greater than would have been predicted given the difference in their molecular weights." The Board inferred from this statement a concession that a person of ordinary skill in the art would have expected a composition using a higher molecular weight polymer to yield better results than one using a lower molecular weight polymer. Further, while the Board accepted this part of the statement as true, it declined to accept the statement's conclusion that the improvements were much greater than would have been predicted. We think the Board read too much into the statement in concluding that it amounted to a concession that one skilled in the art would have expected improved properties. One can just as readily interpret the statement as meaning that one would not have expected the improvement that was realized, given the molecular weights, not that the improvement was expected. Moreover, it is illogical for the

Board, without reason, to accept as true only that part of Soni's statement which supports the PTO's theory of unpatentability, while rejecting the remainder of the statement.

The Board further stated that it could have taken judicial notice of the fact that higher molecular weight polymers would have been expected to tolerate higher filler loadings without degradation in properties and that it could have taken notice of the fact that it is the polymer *per se* that primarily determines the mechanical properties of a filled polymer composition. To support the latter principle, the Board cited a technical dictionary, which states that "[t]he polymer matrix primarily determines the mechanical properties of the composite system." The dictionary does not state, however, that higher molecular weight polymers form improved conductive polymer compositions. Thus, we find the Board's reliance on judicial notice to be no more convincing than its reliance on Soni's alleged admission.

Mere improvement in properties does not always suffice to show unexpected results. In our view, however, when an applicant demonstrates *substantially* improved results, as Soni did here, and states that the results were *unexpected*, this should suffice to establish unexpected results *in the absence of* evidence to the contrary. Soni, who owed the PTO a duty of candor, made such a showing here. The PTO has not provided any persuasive basis to question Soni's comparative data and assertion that the demonstrated results were unexpected. Thus, we are persuaded that the Board's finding that Soni did not establish unexpected results is clearly erroneous.

The cases cited by the dissent are not to the contrary. Neither *De Blauwe*, nor *Wood*, nor *Lindner* requires a showing of unexpectedness separate from a showing of significant differences in result. Nor does *Merck*, which involved compositions understood to differ only in "a matter of degree." Those are not the facts here, where substantially improved properties were shown. Given a presumption of similar properties for similar compositions, substantially improved properties are *ipso facto* unexpected. The difficulty postulated by the dissent in distinguishing substantial from insubstantial improvement is no greater than the PTO and the courts have encountered, successfully, for many years in making judgments on the question of obviousness. It is not unworkable; it is simply the stuff of adjudication. Nor does it change established burdens of proof. The PTO here established a *prima facie* case, the applicant responded to it with a showing of data, and the PTO made an inadequate challenge to the adequacy of that showing.

On appeal before us the PTO raises for the first time the argument that Soni's showing of unexpected results is not commensurate in scope with the claims. *See In re Dill*, 604 F.2d 1356, 1361, 202 USPQ 805, 808 (CCPA 1979) ("The evidence presented to rebut a *prima facie* case of obviousness must be commensurate in scope with the claims to which it pertains."). Here, claim 1 broadly encompasses all melt-processed compositions comprising a polymer having a molecular weight greater than 150,-000. The proof of unexpected results, on the other hand, is limited to a single species within the claimed range, polyethylene having a molecular weight of 203,000. The same deficiency is said to apply to the dependent claims. Claim 6, for example, recites a composition in which the polymer is polyethylene having a molecular weight of 200,000 to 400,000.

We will not consider this argument for the first time on appeal. *See De Blauwe*, 736 F.2d at 705 n. 7, 222 USPQ at 196 n. 7 ("[T]he Solicitor cannot raise a new ground of rejection or *apply a new rationale* to support a rejection in appeals from decisions of the board.") (emphasis added). Since the only rejection made and argued in the PTO was based on the asserted failure of the data concerning the 203,000 molecular weight composition to evidence unexpected properties, and we have concluded that that rejection was erroneous, we must reverse the rejection of all of the claims. If, following return of this case to the PTO, the PTO considers that a new obviousness rejection should be made of claims broad enough to encompass compositions that have not been held in this decision to have unexpected superiority, it is free to do so.

* * *

■ MICHEL, CIRCUIT JUDGE, dissenting.

As the majority observes, the question presented by Soni's appeal is a narrow and factual one: namely, "whether the data in Soni's patent specification show that the compositions of the claims exhibit unexpectedly improved physical and electrical properties compared to lower molecular weight compositions." Slip op. at 749. I am unable to answer this controlling question in the affirmative. But, in reversing the Board's decision, the majority overturns a well-settled facet of the law of rejections for obviousness by eliminating altogether one of the two requirements of a successful rebuttal case of unexpectedly improved results—namely, *objective* proof that the observed improvement was indeed unexpected. Having so amputated the applicable legal rule, the majority finds clear error where, applying precedent, I see no error at all. I therefore respectfully dissent.

Discussion

According to Soni's specification, the claimed invention derives entirely from the "discover[y]" that use of "a melt-processable polymer having a molecular weight greater than 150,000" yields a conductive filler-polymer composition with "significantly improved physical and electrical properties, compared to those [made with] polymers of lower molecular weight, for the same filler loading." These improvements are, according to Soni, both "valuable and surprising."

The specification supports the assertion of significantly improved properties with data from a set of tests comparing two compositions. According to the specification,

> A number of physical tests were carried out on samples of polyethylene to show the significant improvement in the physical properties that is [sic, are] observed at a molecular weight value of 150,000. Tensile tests, peel tests, resistivity behavior tests and recovery behavior tests were carried out. Each test was carried out on samples of Marlex HXM 50100 (Polyethylene, molecular weight 203,000, a composition according to the invention) and also on comparative samples of Marlex 6003 (polyethylene, molecular weight 148,000, outside the scope of the present invention).

After detailing the results of these comparative tests, the specification continues with the following, ostensibly summary, assertion:

> The tensile, peel, resistivity behavior and recovery tests show significantly improved properties for a polymer having a molecular [weight] of 203,000 compared to one having a molecular weight of 148,000, which are much greater than would have been predicted given the difference in their molecular weights.

It is critically important to note that the final phrase of this sentence, an assertion made without objective support, is the *only* evidence Soni has *ever* offered to show that the variety of improvements observed in the change from a 148,000–molecular–weight to a 203,000–molecular–weight polymer were "much greater than would have been predicted"—that is, were unexpectedly large. It is also important to note that the majority concedes that the data show the observed degree of improvement but not that the observed degree of improvement was unexpected. Slip op. at 750 (Soni indicates improvements by "specific data," but only "states" unexpectedness).

The examiner rejected Soni's claims as anticipated by or obvious from a number of prior art references, and the Board affirmed the rejection on obviousness grounds. During the course of its analysis, the Board focused on the specification's assertion "that the improvement in properties ... was 'much greater than would have been predicted'," but found the record "devoid of any evidence to support that conclusion." The Board found that this statement, while some evidence of unobviousness, was "clearly insufficient to outweigh the evidence of obviousness of record." It adhered to this view on reconsideration, observing that the only evidence of unexpectedness Soni brought forward "consists of conclusory statements made in the original specification concerning unpredictable differences, which statements are unsupported by any factual data."

On appeal, Soni "concede[s] that the claimed invention would be *prima facie* obvious under 35 U.S.C. § 103, but contend[s] that the evidence in the specification clearly rebuts the *prima facie* case and establishes the patentability of the claims." Soni's contention persuades me no more than it did the Board.

The applicable legal rules are both clear and longstanding. First, as we noted in *In re Oetiker*, "[t]he *prima facie* case [of obviousness] is a procedural tool of patent examination, allocating the burdens of going forward as between examiner and applicant.... As discussed in *In re Piasecki* [, 745 F.2d 1468, 1472, 223 USPQ 785, 788 (Fed.Cir.1984)], the examiner bears the initial burden, on review of the prior art or on any other ground, of presenting a *prima facie* case of unpatentability. If that burden is met, *the burden of coming forward with evidence or argument shifts to the applicant*." 977 F.2d 1443, 1445, 24 U.S.P.Q.2D 1443, 1444 (Fed.Cir.1992) (emphasis added) (citations omitted). Soni concedes that the examiner properly made out a *prima facie* case of obviousness, and thus concedes that it bore the burden of coming forward with evidence to rebut that case. Second, "whether [the applicant's] rebuttal evidence is sufficient to persuade the examiner that unexpected results exist is an evidentiary matter left for the trier of fact," *In re Johnson*, 747 F.2d 1456, 1460, 223

USPQ 1260, 1263 (Fed.Cir.1984), and reversed on appeal only where clearly erroneous, *In re Caveney,* 761 F.2d 671, 674, 226 USPQ 1, 3 (Fed.Cir.1985). Far from clearly erring, the Board correctly evaluated Soni's rebuttal evidence, according to the controlling cases, as slight and insufficient.

One way for an applicant to satisfy the burden of coming forward with evidence to rebut the *prima facie* case of obviousness is to demonstrate that the claimed invention yields unexpected results. *In re Davies,* 475 F.2d 667, 670, 177 USPQ 381, 384 (CCPA 1973). As *In re Lindner* makes clear, the applicant's rebuttal evidence of unexpectedness must be objective:

> The affidavit and specification do contain *allegations* that synergistic results are obtained with all the claimed compositions, but ... mere lawyers' arguments unsupported by *factual* evidence are insufficient to establish unexpected results. Likewise, mere conclusory statements in the specification and affidavits are entitled to little weight when the Patent Office questions the efficacy of those statements.... [W]e agree with the board that there is insufficient evidence to overcome the case of *prima facie* obviousness found to exist here.

457 F.2d 506, 508–09, 173 USPQ 356, 358 (CCPA 1972) (emphasis added) (citations omitted). *See also In re De Blauwe,* 736 F.2d 699, 705, 222 USPQ 191, 196 (Fed.Cir.1984) ("It is well settled that unexpected results must be established by factual evidence. Mere argument or conclusory statements in the specification does not suffice."); *In re Wood,* 582 F.2d 638, 642, 199 USPQ 137, 140 (CCPA 1978) ("Mere lawyer's arguments and conclusory statements in the specification, unsupported by objective evidence, are insufficient to establish unexpected results."). *See also In re Carabateas,* 357 F.2d 998, 1001, 149 USPQ 44, 46–47 (CCPA 1966) (Rich, J., concurring in the judgment) ("[T]he art makes no suggestion whatever that a reversal of the ester linkage would result in an increased activity *approximating the nineteen-fold increase found by appellant.* At the very best, the art suggests an increase of the order of four to eight times.... The question is not, it seems to me, whether the art suggests *an* improvement, but rather whether it reasonably suggests *the particular* improvement relied upon for patentability in both its qualitative and quantitative sense."). The majority acknowledges this principle but declines to apply it to the case at bar.

Soni failed to come forward with factual evidence tending to establish the unexpectedness of the observed degree of improvement in the claimed composition's physical properties, choosing instead to rely on the combined force of its data about the improvements and the subjective conclusory statement that such improvements "are much greater than would have been predicted given the difference in their molecular weights." The Board read this statement, quite naturally, as a concession that some *lesser* degree of improvement in properties would have been predicted from the difference in molecular weights alone, or, in the Board's words, as an "acknowledge[ment]" that "one of ordinary skill in the relevant art would have expected higher molecular weight polymers to result in better composition properties."[1] In light of the concession, the lack of objective evidence of the

---

1. Indeed, Soni continued to make this same concession on appeal before us, albeit implicitly. *See, e.g.,* Reply Brief at 4–5 ("As to the results which would be expected with polymers of molecular weight less than 203,000, one of ordinary skill in the art, having learned

unexpectedness, as distinct from the magnitude, of the improvements proved fatal to Soni's appeal before the Board, just as cases such as *Lindner* require. The majority, however, now excuses Soni by eliminating the requirement that the improvement's unexpectedness be demonstrated objectively.

The majority claims that "the Board accepted this [concessionary] part of the statement as true, [but] it declined to accept the statement's conclusion that the improvements were much greater than would have been predicted," and then criticizes this reasoning as "illogical." Slip op. at 750–51. There is nothing in the Board's opinion, however, to suggest that it failed to credit Soni with the statement's full worth—namely, the worth of a candid report of Soni's sincere subjective belief that he would not have predicted the changes in properties that he observed on the basis of the difference in the polymers' molecular weights. Of course, such a conclusory statement reporting the inventor's subjective belief has virtually no worth at all as evidence of unexpectedness; despite the majority's appeal to them, Soni's actual candor is not doubted and his duty of candor is not relevant. Slip op. at 750–51. Our cases require objective rebuttal evidence of unexpectedness. Thus, far from falling prey to faulty reasoning, the Board correctly found that Soni's conclusory statement regarding the unexpectedness of the improvements, however heartfelt, was "clearly insufficient to outweigh the evidence of obviousness of record."

Indeed, the Board's approach would have been proper even if Soni had never conceded that a lesser degree of improvement would have been predicted based on the change in molecular weights alone. Neither the specification nor any post-rejection submission contains objective evidence tending to establish either (1) a baseline of expected improvements against which to measure the observed improvements, or (2) the lack of any such baseline expectation in the relevant prior art, as a result of which all degrees of improvement would be unexpected. Without establishing a baseline or the unavailability of one, however, unexpectedness cannot be proved.

Our decision in *In re Merck & Co., Inc.*, 800 F.2d 1091, 231 USPQ 375 (Fed.Cir.1986), illustrates the point. Merck was the assignee of a patent claiming a method of treating depression in humans comprising oral administration of amitriptyline, or its non-toxic salts, in a daily dosage of 25 to 250 milligrams. During reexamination, the examiner rejected the relevant claims on both anticipation and obviousness grounds, and the Board sustained the rejection for obviousness on review. The prior art taught, *inter alia*, that (1) amitriptyline is psychoactive, (2) imipramine, which differs from amitriptyline only in the replacement of the unsaturated carbon atom in its central ring with a nitrogen atom, is a highly effective antidepressant, (3) the replacement of the nitrogen atom in the central ring of a phenothiazine compound with an unsaturated carbon atom yielded a

of the surprising good results provided by a molecular weight of 203,000 as compared to a molecular weight of 148,000, and knowing that molecular weight is a continuously variable quantity, would expect that the improvements would continue to be observed as the molecular weight was reduced below 203,000, by a degree which was diminishing, but nonetheless surprising.").

thioxanthene derivative with strongly similar pharmacological properties, and (4) imipramine and amitriptyline have a variety of similar pharmacological properties unrelated to the treatment of depression. *Id.* at 1094–95, 231 USPQ at 377–78. On appeal, we affirmed the Board's conclusion that "one of ordinary skill in the medicinal chemical arts ... would have expected amitriptyline to resemble imipramine in the alleviation of depression in humans." *Id.* at 1097, 231 USPQ at 379. Merck contended, as it had before the Board, that amitriptyline had unexpectedly more potent sedative and anticholinergic effects than imipramine, supporting its contention with an affidavit from a professor of psychiatry and the published record of a symposium of physicians and psychiatrists concerned with the treatment of depression. *Id.* at 1098, 231 USPQ at 380. Both the affidavit and the symposium, however, merely noted the difference in effects between imipramine and amitriptyline without touching on the unexpectedness of the fact of or degree of difference. *Id.* We rejected Merck's theory, reasoning as follows:

> The core of it is that, while there are some differences in degree between the properties of amitriptyline and imipramine, the compounds expectedly have the same type of biological activity. In the absence of evidence to show that the properties of the compounds differed in such an appreciable degree that the difference was really unexpected ... appellants' evidence was insufficient to rebut the *prima facie* case. The fact that amitriptyline and imipramine, respectively, helped some patients and not others does not appear significant. As noted by the Board, a difference in structure, although slight, would have been expected to produce some difference in activity.

Id. at 1099, 231 USPQ at 381. In short, where an applicant fails to establish the relevant baseline according to which the Board can evaluate the unexpectedness of any observed improvements, he has failed to come forward with effective rebuttal evidence. It is true that *Merck* does not explicitly hold that unexpectedness must be proved separately by objective evidence. Nor do the earlier cited cases. But that, I submit, is their logic. Otherwise, an ostensibly two-part inquiry collapses in effect to a one-part inquiry.

According to the majority, "an applicant [who] demonstrates *substantially* improved results, as Soni did here, and states that the results were *unexpected* ... establish[es] unexpected results *in the absence* of evidence to the contrary." Slip op. at 751. This new rule for assessing an applicant's rebuttal evidence eliminates what I take to be the applicant's burden of coming forward with objective evidence of unexpectedness and thus directly contradicts the holdings I discern from the controlling cases. Quite apart from the quick work it makes of cases such as *Lindner* and *Merck*, however, the majority's new rule may be inherently unworkable. For example, one may well ask how large improvements in results must be before the Board must consider them to be "*substantially* improved results" such that they amount to an effective rebuttal of a *prima facie* case of obviousness. The majority provides no guidance on the question, despite how critical it is to the workings of the new rule.

Perhaps the majority means to say little more than that, for claims drawn to polymer compositions, a 50–fold improvement in tensile strength after a 37% increase in the polymer's molecular weight requires the conclusion that the claimed invention is unobvious, limiting the effect of this case largely to the world of conductive polymer composition technologies. This reading would make the majority's decision relatively innocuous but all the more mysterious a departure from the two-part requirement of the governing cases. Or perhaps the majority means to say, more generally, that examiners, Board members, and Federal Circuit judges will know "substantial" improvements when they see them. Disagreements among these evaluators are, of course, inevitable, and will likely be frequent. This reading, though less perplexing, would have far broader implications: unhindered by any objectively established baseline of expected improvement in the relevant art, the assessment of an applicant's unsupported assertion that the observed degree of improvement was unexpected can flex to suit the taste of the assessor, thus destabilizing the obviousness inquiry and virtually ensuring litigation through final appeal to us in most every case of allegedly unexpected improvement. The resulting loss of objectivity and predictability bodes ill for patentability determinations.

Similarly perplexing is the majority's reference to *"the absence of evidence to the contrary."* Slip op. at 751. First, this eliminates the *applicant's* obligation to come forward with evidence, the obligation that was the heart of the established rule. Second, it assumes that an unfair burden has been placed on the applicant. If the burden were one of persuasion, perhaps. But a mere burden of coming forward?

Conclusion

I question the desirability of the majority's new rule for assessing an applicant's rebuttal evidence of unexpectedness, according to which there need not be *any* objective evidence of unexpectedness other than the inventor's unsupported assertion that an artisan would not have expected so great an improvement in light of the changes made. Even if desirable, such a rule is certainly not the one our cases have established. Nor does the majority merely create an exception to the settled rule; it altogether abolishes the rule in favor of a "substantially improved results" standard that will often be met. Many cases will be decided differently in the future as a consequence.

Because of dramatic improvements here, the majority sets off on a dramatic departure from the law as it stood before this case, a departure I do not think it either explains or justifies. Nor will the new rule be easy to apply or predictable in its application. If the old rule is too harsh here, then at most a narrowly defined exception could perhaps be crafted. Instead, the majority upends settled law for all cases in all arts. Like the Board, I would follow the rule of cases such as *Merck* and *Lindner* and would thus affirm the Board's rejection of Soni's application.

NOTES

1. *The Policy of Unexpected Properties.* The court in *Soni* explained the premise underlying the doctrine of unexpected properties:

One way for a patent applicant to rebut a *prima facie* case of obviousness is to make a showing of "unexpected results," *i.e.*, to show that the claimed invention exhibits some superior property or advantage that a person of ordinary skill in the relevant art would have found surprising or unexpected. The basic principle behind this rule is straightforward—that which would have been surprising to a person of ordinary skill in a particular art would not have been obvious. The principle applies most often to the less predictable fields, such as chemistry, where minor changes in a product or process may yield substantially different results.

2. *Proving Unexpected Properties?* We know from *Dillon* that once a *prima facie* case of obviousness is established, the applicant, in order to overcome the obviousness rejection, must come forward with evidence demonstrating that the claimed invention possesses unexpected properties. But what kind of evidence is required in order to prove unexpected properties. The majority in *Soni* stated:

> Mere improvement in properties does not always suffice to show unexpected results. In our view, however, when an applicant demonstrates substantially improved results, as Soni did here, and states that the results were unexpected, this should suffice to establish unexpected results in the absence of evidence to the contrary. Soni, who owed the PTO a duty of candor, made such a showing here. [Furthermore,] "[i]t is well settled that unexpected results must be established by factual evidence. Mere argument or conclusory statements in the specification does not suffice." [The applicant's] "specification contains more than mere argument or conclusory statements; it contains specific data indicating improved properties.... Given the presumption of similar properties for similar compositions, substantially improved properties are *ipso facto* unexpected."

The dissent challenged what it perceived to be an unwarranted and unworkable subjectivity in the majority's analysis or what may be called the "know it when I see" attitude towards "substantial improvement." Instead, Judge Michel argued that an applicant must prove "objective rebuttal evidence of unexpectedness" meaning that the applicant must "establish either (1) a baseline of expected improvements against which to measure the observed improvements, or (2) the lack of any such baseline expectation in the relevant prior art, as a result of which all degrees of improvement would be unexpected; ... to be objective, the evidence must justify, rather than merely report, the subjective experience of surprise at an observed degree of improvement."

Do you think Soni satisfactorily proved unexpected properties? Is the majority's test too subjective in nature?

2. BIOTECHNOLOGY INVENTIONS

The biotechnology industry is devoted to the development of commercially valuable therapeutic, biochemical, and pharmaceutical products and processes, among others. Many of these products and processes revolve around the manipulation of DNA molecules and their encoded proteins. In the last thirty years, great strides have been made in the field of biotechnology, particularly recombinant DNA research, the technology which we will explore and discuss below. However, with this progress has come a degree of uncertainty regarding the obviousness of certain biotechnological inventions.

For example, methods of cloning genes and shuttling them between organisms have become common place. Such methods are practiced with a certain expectation of success. The ready availability of these methods, coupled with the central dogma of molecular biology (*i.e.*, DNA is transcribed into RNA, which in turn is translated into functional or structural protein molecules), has created a somewhat muddled legal standard of obviousness in the PTO and the Federal Circuit, which has led to, at times, a difference in views between the agency and the court. Students unfamiliar with the basic science of recombinant DNA technology might study the overview provided in *In re O'Farrell*, 853 F.2d 894 (Fed.Cir.1988).

Amgen, Inc. v. Chugai Pharmaceutical Co., Ltd.*

927 F.2d 1200 (Fed.Cir.1991).

■ Before MARKEY, LOURIE and CLEVENGER, CIRCUIT JUDGES.

■ LOURIE, CIRCUIT JUDGE.

Chugai Pharmaceutical Co., Ltd. (Chugai) and Genetics Institute, Inc. (collectively defendants) assert on appeal that the district court erred in holding that: 1) Amgen's '008 patent is not invalid under 35 U.S.C. § 103....

* * *

Background

Erythropoietin (EPO) is a protein consisting of 165 amino acids which stimulates the production of red blood cells. It is therefore a useful therapeutic agent in the treatment of anemia or blood disorders characterized by low or defective bone marrow production of red blood cells.

The preparation of EPO products generally has been accomplished through the concentration and purification of urine from both healthy individuals and those exhibiting high EPO levels. A new technique for producing EPO is recombinant DNA technology in which EPO is produced from cell cultures into which genetically-engineered vectors containing the EPO gene have been introduced. The production of EPO by recombinant technology involves expressing an EPO gene through the same processes that occur in a natural cell.

The Patents

On June 30, 1987, the United States Patent and Trademark Office (PTO) issued to Dr. Rodney Hewick U.S. Patent 4,677,195, entitled "Method for the Purification of Erythropoietin and Erythropoietin Compositions" (the § 195 patent). The patent claims both homogeneous EPO and compositions thereof and a method for purifying human EPO using reverse phase high performance liquid chromatography. The method claims are not before us. The relevant claims of the § 195 patent are:

1. Homogeneous erythropoietin characterized by a molecular weight of about 34,000 daltons on SDS PAGE, movement as a single peak on reverse

---

* Casebook editors' note: Readers are reminded to refer back to the summary of all of the outcomes under sections 112, 102, and 103 in the *Amgen* case at the end of **Chapter Three**.

phase high performance liquid chromatography and a specific activity of at least 160,000 IU per absorbance unit at 280 nanometers.

* * *

The other patent in this litigation is U.S. Patent 4,703,008, entitled "DNA Sequences Encoding Erythropoietin" (the '008 patent), issued on October 27, 1987, to Dr. FuBKuen Lin, an employee of Amgen. The claims of the '008 patent cover purified and isolated DNA sequences encoding erythropoietin and host cells transformed or transfected with a DNA sequence. The relevant claims are as follows:

2. A purified and isolated DNA sequence consisting essentially of a DNA sequence encoding human erythropoietin.

* * *

7. A purified and isolated DNA sequence consisting essentially of a DNA sequence encoding a polypeptide having an amino acid sequence sufficiently duplicative of that of erythropoietin to allow possession of the biological property of causing bone marrow cells to increase production of reticulocytes and red blood cells, and to increase hemoglobin synthesis or iron uptake.

* * *

Discussion

I. Amgen's '008 Patent (Lin)

* * *

B. Alleged Obviousness of the Inventions of Claims 2, 4, and 6

Claim 2, as noted above, recites a purified and isolated DNA sequence, and claims 4 and 6 are directed to host cells transformed with such a DNA sequence. The district court determined that claims 2, 4, and 6 are not invalid under 35 U.S.C. § 103, concluding that the unique probing and screening method employed by Lin in isolating the EPO gene and the extensive effort required to employ that method made the invention nonobvious over the prior art.

Obviousness under Section 103 is a question of law. *Panduit Corp. v. Dennison Mfg. Co.*, 810 F.2d 1561, 1568, 1 U.S.P.Q.2D 1593, 1597 (Fed. Cir.), *cert. denied*, 481 U.S. 1052, 107 S.Ct. 2187, 95 L.Ed.2d 843 (1987). The district court stated that one must inquire whether the prior art would have suggested to one of ordinary skill in the art that Lin's probing and screening method should be carried out and would have a reasonable expectation of success, viewed in light of the prior art. *See In re Dow Chemical Co.*, 837 F.2d 469, 473, 5 U.S.P.Q.2D 1529, 1531 (Fed.Cir.1988). "Both the suggestion and the expectation of success must be founded in the prior art, not in applicant's disclosure." *Id.*

The district court specifically found that, as of 1983, none of the prior art references "suggest[s] that the probing strategy of using two fully-redundant [sic] sets of probes, of relatively high degeneracy [sic], to screen a human genomic library would be likely to succeed in pulling out the gene of interest."[4] 13 U.S.P.Q.2D at 1768. While it found that defendants had shown that these procedures were "obvious to try," the references did not show that there was a reasonable expectation of success. *See In re O'Farrell*, 853 F.2d 894, 903–04, 7 U.S.P.Q.2D 1673, 1680–81 (Fed.Cir.1988).

Defendants challenge the district court's determination, arguing that, as of September 1983, one of ordinary skill in the art would have had a reasonable expectation of success in screening a gDNA library by Lin's method in order to obtain EPO. We agree with the district court's conclusion, which was supported by convincing testimony. One witness, Dr. Davies of Biogen, another biotechnology company that had worked on EPO, stated that he could not say whether Biogen scientists would have succeeded in isolating the EPO gene if Biogen had the EPO fragments that were available to Lin in 1983. Dr. Wall, a professor at UCLA, testified that it would have been "difficult" to find the gene in 1983, and that there would have been no more than a fifty percent chance of success. He said, "you couldn't be certain where in the genomic DNA your probe might fall." The court found that no one had successfully screened a genomic library using fully-degenerate probes of such high redundancy as the probes used by Lin. In the face of this and other evidence on both sides of the issue, it concluded that defendants had not shown by clear and convincing evidence that the procedures used by Lin would have been obvious in September 1983. We are not persuaded that the court erred in its decision.

Defendants assert that whether or not it would have been obvious to isolate the human EPO gene from a gDNA library with fully-degenerate probes is immaterial because it was obvious to use the already known monkey EPO gene as a probe. Defendants point out that, in the early 1980s, Biogen did significant work with an EPO cDNA obtained from a baboon, and that they used it as a probe to hybridize with the correspond-

---

4. At this point, some explanation of the involved technology may be useful, consistent with that expressed in the district court opinion. DNA consists of two complementary strands of nucleotides, which include the four basic compounds adenine(A), guanine(G), cytosine(C), and thymine(T), oriented so that bases from one strand weakly bond to the bases of the opposite strand. A bonds with T, and G bonds with C to form complementary base pairs. This bonding process is called hybridization and results in the formation of a stable duplex molecule. The structure also includes 5–carbon sugar moieties with phosphate groups. The genetic code for a particular protein depends upon sequential groupings of three nucleotides, called codons. Each codon codes for a particular amino acid. Since there are four nucleotide bases and three bases per codon, there are 64 (4x4x4) possible codons. Because there are only 20 natural amino acids, most amino acids are specified by more than one codon. This is referred to as a "redundancy" or "degeneracy" in the genetic code, a fact that complicates and renders more difficult the techniques of recombinant DNA. In order to prepare a protein using recombinant DNA technology, the gene for the protein must first be isolated from a cell's total DNA by screening a library of that cell's DNA. The DNA library is screened by use of a probe, a synthetic radiolabelled nucleic acid sequence which can be used to detect and isolate complementary base sequences by hybridization. To design a probe when the gene has not yet been isolated, a scientist must know the amino acid sequence, or a portion thereof, of the protein of interest. Because some amino acids have several possible codons and the researcher cannot know which of the possible codons will actually code for an amino acid, he or she may decide to design a set of probes that covers all possible codons for each amino acid comprising the protein, known as a "fully-degenerate" set of probes. A library to be screened can be a genomic library (gDNA), which contains a set of all the DNA sequences found in an organism's cells or a complementary DNA (cDNA) library, which is much smaller and less complex than a gDNA library, and is used frequently when the tissue source for a given gene is known.

ing gene in a human gDNA library. However, this technique did not succeed until after Lin isolated the EPO gene with his fully-degenerate set of probes.

To support its obviousness assertion, defendants rely upon the testimony of their expert, Dr. Flavell, who testified that the overall homology of baboon DNA and human DNA was "roughly 90 percent". While this testimony indicates that it might have been feasible, perhaps obvious to try, to successfully probe a human gDNA library with a monkey cDNA probe, it does not indicate that the gene could have been identified and isolated with a reasonable likelihood of success. Neither the DNA nucleotide sequence of the human EPO gene nor its exact degree of homology with the monkey EPO gene was known at the time.

Indeed, the district court found that Lin was unsuccessful at probing a human gDNA library with monkey cDNA until after he had isolated the EPO gene by using the fully-degenerate probes. Based on the evidence in the record, the district court found there was no reasonable expectation of success in obtaining the EPO gene by the method that Lin eventually used. While the idea of using the monkey gene to probe for a homologous human gene may have been obvious to try, the realization of that idea would not have been obvious. There were many pitfalls. Hindsight is not a justifiable basis on which to find that ultimate achievement of a long sought and difficult scientific goal was obvious. The district court thoroughly examined the evidence and the testimony. We see no error in its result. Moreover, if the DNA sequence was not obvious, host cells containing such sequence, as claimed in claims 4 and 6, could not have been obvious. We conclude that the district court did not err in holding that the claims of the patent are not invalid under Section 103.

* * *

Side Bar

Two Hundred Year Old Legal Principles Meet A New Technology

William F. Lee*

The high stakes trial over the right to market erythropoietin ("EPO") in the United States pitting Amgen against Genetics Institute began in August 1989 amid much fanfare. The legal and scientific communities recognized the trial as one of the first opportunities for the courts to attempt to apply centuries old patent law concepts to a very new technology: biotechnology and, in particular, the emerging science of recombinant genetic engineering. Nor was the significance of the proceedings lost on the public at large. The very day the trial began the New York Times included an extensive opinion piece on the implications of the proceedings about to commence.

The parties opened to Magistrate (now District Court Judge) Patti B. Saris and a completely packed courtroom. Sitting in the audience were some of the true pioneers in the field of recombinant genetic engineering. Professors Axel Ulrich, Tom Maniatis, Richard Flavell, Randy Wall and Julian Davies were not only there, but prepared to testify. Of course, the audience was also populated by various investment analysts and arbitrageurs, all seeking insights from the opening statements that any experienced trial lawyer could have told them would not be available.

As one might anticipate, as the legal system attempts to adapt to a new and emerging technology, the legal issues to be tried ran the gamut. Novelty, nonobviousness, enablement, best mode, inequitable conduct, conception, diligence, reduction to practice and utility were all questions to be decided. Was there simultaneous conception and reduction to practice? Were deposits required to satisfy the enablement and best mode requirements of section 112? Could a product patent claiming a purified protein and based only on work with the natural protein cover a purified recombinant protein? All new and novel questions.

What was truly remarkable about the trial was the ability of the parties to introduce the evidence necessary to resolve these complex legal issues while focusing the themes of the trial on the equitable and morally persuasive facts that would make a fact finder want to find for a particular party. Thus, Amgen devoted much of its evidence to the scientific and medical importance of its invention, to the many patients throughout the world whose lives had been made better by recombinant EPO, and to the toil and effort that had enabled it to unlock a puzzle others had not been able to solve. Similarly, Genetics Institute focused upon its own independent research and development, its own substantial scientific advances, its own contributions to the well being of patients and the fortuity of who happened to reduce to practice first. The testimony was at times moving, at others plodding, but always relevant.

After forty days of trial, Magistrate Judge Saris rendered an extensive opinion addressing many issues of first impression. All the parties and lawyers had been informed that her opinion would be rendered on a specific day at a specific hour. Clients, scientists, lawyers and others gathered in conference rooms across the country awaiting the opinion. When it arrived in a brown envelope, we quickly moved to the last page and found that the court had held each parties "patent not invalid and infringed." *Amgen, Inc. v. Chugai Pharmaceutical Co., Ltd.* 706 F.Supp. 94, 9 USPQ2d 1833 (D.Mass.1989) *aff'd in part, rev'd in part*, 927 F.2d 1200 (Fed.Cir.), *cert. denied*, 502 U.S. 856 (1991).

Magistrate Judge Saris' opinion sparked a flurry of reaction and activity. Stock prices rose and fell as the market and investing community endeavored to comprehend the opinion's ramifications and implications, not only for the EPO controversy, but for the industry at large. The litigators similarly studied the opinion in an effort to determine who, if anyone, now had the advantage. Genetics Institute decided to assume the initiative and moved for a permanent injunction. Because Amgen was on the market in the United States and Genetics Institute was not, the obvious hope was to provide Amgen a draconian incentive to bring the dispute to a quick resolution. Amgen, of course, opposed.

The motion for permanent injunction was heard by District Judge William G. Young. Judge Young fashioned an extraordinary and creative remedy. After providing the parties full opportunity to be heard, he ordered entry of permanent injunctions against both Amgen and Genetics Institute; however, he then stayed the entry of the injunction for ten days and ordered that the injunction would be stayed indefinitely if the parties agreed to cross license each other.

In the next ten days, businessmen negotiated, and lawyers lawyered. Amgen moved before the Court of Appeals for the Federal Circuit to stay Judge Young's order. Everyone tried to determine whether Judge Young had the authority and discretion to do what he had done. Several days before the permanent injunctions were to become effective, Amgen returned to Judge Young to request that he stay his order until the Federal Circuit had ruled. He refused.

As the parties left the courtroom, a consensus seemed to emerge. A cross license agreement had to be reached, and now. The permanent injunction could not become effective. The case appeared resolved.

But no one had had an opportunity to tell the Federal Circuit. A mere two hours later, the Federal Circuit announced that it had determined to stay Judge Young's order. There would be no settlement and the battle was joined again. Much of the rest is reported history. The Federal Circuit affirmed the finding that Amgen's patent was not invalid and infringed, but reversed and held Genetics Institute's patent invalid. Amgen had won the United States EPO market.

While the EPO litigation was the subject of much commentary, what the litigation really demonstrated was the inherent flexibility and adaptability of our system of justice and our patent system in particular. Neither discouraged nor daunted by a new area of technology, the courts and the litigants stepped to the proverbial "plate" to once again demonstrate the resiliency and timelessness of our patent law system.

* Managing Partner, Hale and Dorr, LLP and John A. Reilly Visiting Professor from Practice at Harvard Law School.

This *SIDE BAR* was written specially for PRINCIPLES OF PATENT LAW.

In re Deuel

51 F.3d 1552 (Fed.Cir.1995).

■ Before ARCHER, CHIEF JUDGE, NIES and LOURIE, CIRCUIT JUDGES.

■ LOURIE, CIRCUIT JUDGE.

Thomas F. Deuel, Yue–Sheng Li, Ned R. Siegel, and Peter G. Milner (collectively "Deuel") appeal from the November 30, 1993 decision of the U.S. Patent and Trademark Office Board of Patent Appeals and Interferences affirming the examiner's final rejection of claims 4–7 of application Serial No. 07/542,232, entitled "Heparin–Binding Growth Factor," as unpatentable on the ground of obviousness under 35 U.S.C. § 103 (1988). *Ex parte Deuel*, 33 U.S.P.Q.2D 1445 (Bd.Pat.App.Int.1993). Because the Board erred in concluding that Deuel's claims 5 and 7 directed to specific cDNA molecules would have been obvious in light of the applied references, and no other basis exists in the record to support the rejection with respect to claims 4 and 6 generically covering all possible DNA molecules coding for the disclosed proteins, we reverse.

Background

The claimed invention relates to isolated and purified DNA and cDNA molecules encoding heparin-binding growth factors ("HBGFs"). HBGFs are proteins that stimulate mitogenic activity (cell division) and thus facilitate the repair or replacement of damaged or diseased tissue. DNA (deoxyribonucleic acid) is a generic term which encompasses an enormous number of ...leotide units. DNAs consist of four ...rogenous bases adenine, guanine, ...ping of three such nucleotides (a ...DNA's sequence of codons thus ...assembled during protein synthe- ...but only 20 natural amino acids, ...han one codon. This is referred to ...he genetic code.

...rganism's genetic information. It ...e located on chromosomes in the ...osomal DNA encodes functional

...) is a similar molecule that is ...he process of protein synthesis. ...plementary copy ("clone") of ... transcription of mRNA. Like ...coding regions of DNA. Thus, ...n, the amino acid sequence of ...dicted using the genetic code ...ids. The reverse is not true, ...any other DNAs may code for ...ships between DNA, mRNA, ...ressed as follows:

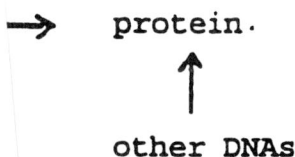

...NA molecules derived from ...boratory or obtained from ...aries contain a mixture of the mRNAs found in a specific tissue ...s are tissue-specific because proteins and their corresponding ...... only made ("expressed") in specific tissues, depending upon the protein. Genomic DNA ("gDNA") libraries, by contrast, theoretically contain all of a species' chromosomal DNA. The molecules present in cDNA and DNA libraries may be of unknown function and chemical structure, and the proteins which they encode may be unknown. However, one may attempt to retrieve molecules of interest from cDNA or gDNA libraries by screening such libraries with a gene probe, which is a synthetic radiolabelled nucleic acid sequence designed to bond ("hybridize") with a target complementary base sequence. Such "gene cloning" techniques thus exploit the fact that the bases in DNA always hybridize in complementary pairs: adenine bonds with thymine and guanine bonds with cytosine. A gene probe for potentially isolating DNA or cDNA encoding a protein may be designed once the protein's amino acid sequence, or a portion thereof, is known.

As disclosed in Deuel's patent application, Deuel isolated and purified H–GF from bovine uterine tissue, found that it exhibited mitogenic activity, and determined the first 25 amino acids of the protein's N-terminal sequence. Deuel then isolated a cDNA molecule encoding bovine uterine HBGF by screening a bovine uterine cDNA library with an oligonucleotide probe designed using the experimentally determined N-terminal sequence of the HBGF. Deuel purified and sequenced the cDNA molecule, which was found to consist of a sequence of 1196 nucleotide base pairs. From the cDNA's nucleotide sequence, Deuel then predicted the complete amino acid sequence of bovine uterine HBGF disclosed in Deuel's application.

Deuel also isolated a cDNA molecule encoding human placental HBGF by screening a human placental cDNA library using the isolated bovine uterine cDNA clone as a probe. Deuel purified and sequenced the human placental cDNA clone, which was found to consist of a sequence of 961 nucleotide base pairs. From the nucleotide sequence of the cDNA molecule encoding human placental HBGF, Deuel predicted the complete amino acid sequence of human placental HBGF disclosed in Deuel's application. The predicted human placental and bovine uterine HBGFs each have 168 amino acids and calculated molecular weights of 18.9 kD. Of the 168 amino acids present in the two HBGFs discovered by Deuel, 163 are identical. Deuel's application does not describe the chemical structure of, or state how to isolate and purify, any DNA or cDNA molecule except the disclosed human placental and bovine uterine cDNAs, which are the subject of claims 5 and 7.

Claims 4–7 on appeal are all independent claims and read, in relevant part, as follows:

4. A purified and isolated DNA sequence consisting of a sequence encoding human heparin binding growth factor of 168 amino acids having the following amino acid sequence: Met Gln Ala ... [remainder of 168 amino acid sequence].

5. The purified and isolated cDNA of human heparin-binding growth factor having the following nucleotide sequence: GTCAAAGGCA ... [remainder of 961 nucleotide sequence].

6. A purified and isolated DNA sequence consisting of a sequence encoding bovine heparin binding growth factor of 168 amino acids having the following amino acid sequence: Met Gln Thr ... [remainder of 168 amino acid sequence].

7. The purified and isolated cDNA of bovine heparin-binding growth factor having the following nucleotide sequence: GAGTGGAGAG ... [remainder of 1196 nucleotide sequence].

Claims 4 and 6 generically encompass all isolated/purified DNA sequences (natural and synthetic) encoding human and bovine HBGFs, despite the fact that Deuel's application does not describe the chemical structure of, or tell how to obtain, any DNA or cDNA except the two disclosed cDNA molecules. Because of the redundancy of the genetic code, claims 4 and 6 each encompass an enormous number of DNA molecules, including the isolated/purified chromosomal DNAs encoding the human and bovine proteins. Claims 5 and 7, on the other hand, are directed to the specifically disclosed cDNA molecules encoding human and bovine HBGFs, respectively.

During prosecution, the examiner rejected claims 4–7 under 35 U.S.C. § 103 as unpatentable over the combined teachings of Bohlen and Maniatis. The Bohlen reference discloses a group of protein growth factors designated as heparin-binding brain mitogens ("HBBMs") useful in treating burns and promoting the formation, maintenance, and repair of tissue, particularly neural tissue. Bohlen isolated three such HBBMs from human and bovine brain tissue. These proteins have respective molecular weights of 15 kD, 16 kD, and 18 kD. Bohlen determined the first 19 amino acids of the proteins' N-terminal sequences, which were found to be identical for human and bovine HBBMs. Bohlen teaches that HBBMs are brain-specific, and suggests that the proteins may be homologous between species. The reference provides no teachings concerning DNA or cDNA coding for HBBMs.

Maniatis describes a method of isolating DNAs or cDNAs by screening a DNA or cDNA library with a gene probe. The reference outlines a general technique for cloning a gene; it does not describe how to isolate a particular DNA or cDNA molecule. Maniatis does not discuss certain steps necessary to isolate a target cDNA, *e.g.*, selecting a tissue-specific cDNA library containing a target cDNA and designing an oligonucleotide probe that will hybridize with the target cDNA.

The examiner asserted that, given Bohlen's disclosure of a heparin-binding protein and its N-terminal sequence and Maniatis's gene cloning method, it would have been *prima facie* obvious to one of ordinary skill in the art at the time of the invention to clone a gene for HBGF. According to the examiner, Bohlen's published N-terminal sequence would have motivated a person of ordinary skill in the art to clone such a gene because cloning the gene would allow recombinant production of HBGF, a useful protein. The examiner reasoned that a person of ordinary skill in the art could have designed a gene probe based on Bohlen's disclosed N-terminal sequence, then screened a DNA library in accordance with Maniatis's gene cloning method to isolate a gene encoding an HBGF. The examiner did not distinguish between claims 4 and 6 generically directed to all DNA sequences encoding human and bovine HBGFs and claims 5 and 7 reciting particular cDNAs.

In reply, Deuel argued, *inter alia*, that Bohlen teaches away from the claimed cDNA molecules because Bohlen suggests that HBBMs are brain-specific and, thus, a person of ordinary skill in the art would not have tried to isolate corresponding cDNA clones from human placental and bovine uterine cDNA libraries. The examiner made the rejection final, however, asserting that

> [t]he starting materials are not relevant in this case, because it was well known in the art at the time the invention was made that proteins, especially the general class of heparin binding proteins, are highly homologous between species and tissue type. It would have been entirely obvious to attempt to isolate a known protein from different tissue types and even different species.

No prior art was cited to support the proposition that it would have been obvious to screen human placental and bovine uterine cDNA libraries for the claimed cDNA clones. Presumably, the examiner was relying on Bohlen's suggestion that HBBMs may be homologous between species, although the examiner did not explain how homology between species suggests homology between tissue types.

The Board affirmed the examiner's final rejection. In its opening remarks, the Board noted that it is "constantly advised by the patent examiners, who are highly skilled in this art, that cloning procedures are routine in the art." According to the Board, "the examiners urge that when the sequence of a protein is placed into the public domain, the gene is also placed into the public domain because of the routine nature of cloning techniques." Addressing the rejection at issue, the Board determined that Bohlen's disclosure of the existence and isolation of HBBM, a functional protein, would also advise a person of ordinary skill in the art that a gene exists encoding HBBM. The Board found that a person of ordinary skill in the art would have been motivated to isolate such a gene because the protein has useful mitogenic properties, and isolating the gene for HBBM would permit large quantities of the protein to be produced for study and possible commercial use. Like the examiner, the Board asserted, without explanation, that HBBMs are the same as HBGFs and that the genes encoding these proteins are identical. The Board concluded that "the Bohlen reference would have suggested to those of ordinary skill in this art that they should make the gene, and the Maniatis reference would have taught a technique for 'making' the gene with a reasonable expectation of success." Responding to Deuel's argument that the claimed cDNA clones were isolated from human placental and bovine uterine cDNA libraries, whereas the combined teachings of Bohlen and Maniatis would only have suggested screening a brain tissue cDNA library, the Board stated that "the claims before us are directed to the product and not the method of isolation. Appellants have not shown that the claimed DNA was not present in and could not have been readily isolated from the brain tissue utilized by Bohlen." Deuel now appeals.

Discussion

Obviousness is a question of law, which we review *de novo*, though factual findings underlying the Board's obviousness determination are reviewed for clear error. *In re Vaeck*, 947 F.2d 488, 493, 20 U.S.P.Q.2D 1438, 1442 (Fed.Cir.1991); *In re Woodruff*, 919 F.2d 1575, 1577, 16 U.S.P.Q.2D 1934, 1935 (Fed.Cir.1990). The examiner bears the burden of establishing a *prima facie* case of obviousness. *In re Rijckaert*, 9 F.3d 1531, 1532, 28 U.S.P.Q.2D 1955, 1956 (Fed.Cir.1993); *In re Oetiker*, 977 F.2d

1443, 1445, 24 U.S.P.Q.2D 1443, 1444 (Fed.Cir.1992). Only if this burden is met does the burden of coming forward with rebuttal argument or evidence shift to the applicant. *Rijckaert*, 9 F.3d at 1532, 28 U.S.P.Q.2D at 1956. When the references cited by the examiner fail to establish a *prima facie* case of obviousness, the rejection is improper and will be overturned. *In re Fine*, 837 F.2d 1071, 1074, 5 U.S.P.Q.2D 1596, 1598 (Fed.Cir.1988).

On appeal, Deuel challenges the Board's determination that the applied references establish a *prima facie* case of obviousness. In response, the PTO maintains that the claimed invention would have been *prima facie* obvious over the combined teachings of Bohlen and Maniatis. Thus, the appeal raises the important question whether the combination of a prior art reference teaching a method of gene cloning, together with a reference disclosing a partial amino acid sequence of a protein, may render DNA and cDNA molecules encoding the protein *prima facie* obvious under § 103.

Deuel argues that the PTO failed to follow the proper legal standard in determining that the claimed cDNA molecules would have been *prima facie* obvious despite the lack of structurally similar compounds in the prior art. Deuel argues that the PTO has not cited a reference teaching cDNA molecules, but instead has improperly rejected the claims based on the alleged obviousness of a method of making the molecules. We agree.

Because Deuel claims new chemical entities in structural terms, a *prima facie* case of unpatentability requires that the teachings of the prior art suggest *the claimed compounds* to a person of ordinary skill in the art. Normally a *prima facie* case of obviousness is based upon structural similarity, *i.e.*, an established structural relationship between a prior art compound and the claimed compound. Structural relationships may provide the requisite motivation or suggestion to modify known compounds to obtain new compounds. For example, a prior art compound may suggest its homologs because homologs often have similar properties and therefore chemists of ordinary skill would ordinarily contemplate making them to try to obtain compounds with improved properties. Similarly, a known compound may suggest its analogs or isomers, either geometric isomers (cis v. trans) or position isomers (*e.g.*, ortho v. para).

In all of these cases, however, the prior art teaches a specific, structurally-definable compound and the question becomes whether the prior art would have suggested making the specific molecular modifications necessary to achieve the claimed invention. *See In re Jones*, 958 F.2d 347, 351, 21 U.S.P.Q.2D 1941, 1944 (Fed.Cir.1992); *In re Dillon*, 919 F.2d 688, 692, 16 U.S.P.Q.2D 1897, 1901 (Fed.Cir.1990) (*en banc*) ("structural similarity between claimed and prior art subject matter, . . . where the prior art gives reason or motivation to make the claimed compositions, creates a *prima facie* case of obviousness"), *cert. denied*, 500 U.S. 904, 111 S.Ct. 1682, 114 L.Ed.2d 77 (1991); *In re Grabiak*, 769 F.2d 729, 731–32, 226 USPQ 870, 872 (Fed.Cir.1985) ("[I]n the case before us there must be adequate support in the prior art for the [prior art] ester/[claimed] thioester change in structure, in order to complete the PTO's *prima facie* case and shift the burden of going forward to the applicant."); *In re Lalu*, 747 F.2d 703, 705, 223 USPQ 1257, 1258 (Fed.Cir.1984) ("The prior art must provide one of ordinary skill in the art the motivation to make the proposed molecular modifications needed to arrive at the claimed compound.'').

Here, the prior art does not disclose any relevant cDNA molecules, let alone close relatives of the specific, structurally-defined cDNA molecules of claims 5 and 7 that might render them obvious. Maniatis suggests an allegedly obvious process for trying to isolate cDNA molecules, but that, as we will indicate below, does not fill the gap regarding the subject matter of claims 5 and 7. Further, while the general idea of the claimed molecules, their function, and their general chemical nature may have been obvious from Bohlen's teachings, and the knowledge that some gene existed may have been clear, the precise cDNA molecules of claims 5 and 7 would not have been obvious over the Bohlen reference because Bohlen teaches proteins, not the claimed or closely related cDNA molecules. The redundancy of the genetic code precluded contemplation of or focus on the specific cDNA molecules of claims 5 and 7. Thus, one could not have conceived the subject matter of claims 5 and 7 based on the teachings in the cited prior art because, until the claimed molecules were actually isolated and purified, it would have been highly unlikely for one of ordinary skill in the art to contemplate what was ultimately obtained. What cannot be contemplated or conceived cannot be obvious.

The PTO's theory that one might have been motivated to try to do what Deuel in fact accomplished amounts to speculation and an impermissible hindsight reconstruction of the claimed invention. It also ignores the fact that claims 5 and 7 are limited to specific compounds, and any motivation that existed was a general one, to try to obtain a gene that was yet undefined and may have constituted many forms. A general motivation to search for some gene that exists does not necessarily make obvious a specifically-defined gene that is subsequently obtained as a result of that search. More is needed and it is not found here.

The genetic code relationship between proteins and nucleic acids does not overcome the deficiencies of the cited references. A prior art disclosure of the amino acid sequence of a protein does not necessarily render particular DNA molecules encoding the protein obvious because the redundancy of the genetic code permits one to hypothesize an enormous number of DNA sequences coding for the protein. No particular one of these DNAs can be obvious unless there is something in the prior art to lead to the particular DNA and indicate that it should be prepared. We recently held in *In re Baird*, 16 F.3d 380, 29 U.S.P.Q.2D 1550 (Fed.Cir.1994), that a broad genus does not necessarily render obvious each compound within its scope. Similarly, knowledge of a protein does not give one a conception of a particular DNA encoding it. Thus, *a fortiori*, Bohlen's disclosure of the N-terminal portion of a protein, which the PTO urges is the same as HBGF, would not have suggested the particular cDNA molecules defined by claims 5 and 7. This is so even though one skilled in the art knew that some DNA, albeit not in purified and isolated form, did exist. The compounds of claims 5 and 7 are specific compounds not suggested by the prior art. A different result might pertain, however, if there were prior art, *e.g.*, a protein of sufficiently small size and simplicity, so that lacking redundancy, each possible DNA would be obvious over the protein. *See In re Petering*, 301

F.2d 676 (CCPA 1962) (prior art reference disclosing limited genus of 20 compounds rendered every species within the genus unpatentable). That is not the case here.

The PTO's focus on known methods for potentially isolating the claimed DNA molecules is also misplaced because the claims at issue define compounds, not methods. *See In re Bell*, 991 F.2d 781, 785, 26 U.S.P.Q.2D 1529, 1532 (Fed.Cir.1993). In *Bell*, the PTO asserted a rejection based upon the combination of a primary reference disclosing a protein (*and its complete amino acid sequence*) with a secondary reference describing a general method of gene cloning. We reversed the rejection, holding in part that "[t]he PTO's focus on Bell's method is misplaced. Bell does not claim a method. Bell claims compositions, and the issue is the obviousness of the claimed compositions, not of the method by which they are made." *Id.*

We today reaffirm the principle, stated in *Bell*, that the existence of a general method of isolating cDNA or DNA molecules is essentially irrelevant to the question whether the specific molecules themselves would have been obvious, in the absence of other prior art that suggests the claimed DNAs. A prior art disclosure of a process *reciting a particular compound* or obvious variant thereof as a product of the process is, of course, another matter, raising issues of anticipation under 35 U.S.C. § 102 as well as obviousness under § 103. Moreover, where there is prior art that suggests a claimed compound, the existence, or lack thereof, of an enabling process for making that compound is surely a factor in any patentability determination. *See In re Brown*, 329 F.2d 1006, 141 USPQ 245 (CCPA 1964) (reversing rejection for lack of an enabling method of making the claimed compound). There must, however, still be prior art that suggests the claimed compound in order for a *prima facie* case of obviousness to be made out; as we have already indicated, that prior art was lacking here with respect to claims 5 and 7. Thus, even if, as the examiner stated, the existence of general cloning techniques, coupled with knowledge of a protein's structure, might have provided motivation to prepare a cDNA or made it obvious to prepare a cDNA, that does not necessarily make obvious a particular claimed cDNA. "Obvious to try" has long been held not to constitute obviousness.* *In re O'Farrell*, 853 F.2d 894, 903, 7 U.S.P.Q.2D 1673, 1680–81 (Fed.Cir.1988). A general incentive does not make obvious a particular result, nor does the existence of techniques by which those efforts can be carried out. Thus, Maniatis's teachings, even in combination with Bohlen, fail to suggest the claimed invention.

The PTO argues that a compound may be defined by its process of preparation and therefore that a conceived process for making or isolating it provides a definition for it and can render it obvious. It cites *Amgen Inc. v. Chugai Pharmaceutical Co.*, 927 F.2d 1200, 18 U.S.P.Q.2D 1016 (Fed. Cir.), *cert. denied*, 502 U.S. 856, 112 S.Ct. 169, 116 L.Ed.2d 132 (1991), for that proposition. We disagree. The fact that one can conceive a general process in advance for preparing an *undefined* compound does not mean that a claimed *specific* compound was precisely envisioned and therefore

* Casebook Editors' Note: The Supreme Court has since held in *KSR v. Teleflex* that "obvious to try" may be proper grounds for an obvious rejection in some cases. See the notes following this case for more discussion.

obvious. A substance may indeed be defined by its process of preparation. That occurs, however, when it has already been prepared by that process and one therefore knows that the result of that process is the stated compound. The process is part of the definition of the compound. But that is not possible in advance, especially when the hypothetical process is only a general one. Thus, a conceived method of preparing some undefined DNA does not define it with the precision necessary to render it obvious over the protein it encodes. We did not state otherwise in *Amgen*. *See Amgen*, 927 F.2d at 1206–09, 18 U.S.P.Q.2D at 1021–23 (isolated/purified human gene held nonobvious; no conception of gene without envisioning its precise identity despite conception of general process of preparation).

We conclude that, because the applied references do not teach or suggest the claimed cDNA molecules, the final rejection of claims 5 and 7 must be reversed. *See also Bell*, 991 F.2d at 784–85, 26 U.S.P.Q.2D at 1531–32 (human DNA sequences encoding IGF proteins nonobvious over asserted combination of references showing gene cloning method and complete amino acid sequences of IGFs).

Claims 4 and 6 are of a different scope than claims 5 and 7. As is conceded by Deuel, they generically encompass all DNA sequences encoding human and bovine HBGFs. Written in such a result-oriented form, claims 4 and 6 are thus tantamount to the general idea of all genes encoding the protein, all solutions to the problem. Such an idea might have been obvious from the complete amino acid sequence of the protein, coupled with knowledge of the genetic code, because this information may have enabled a person of ordinary skill in the art to envision the idea of, and, perhaps with the aid of a computer, even identify all members of the claimed genus. The Bohlen reference, however, only discloses a partial amino acid sequence, and thus it appears that, based on the above analysis, the claimed genus would not have been obvious over this prior art disclosure. We will therefore also reverse the final rejection of claims 4 and 6 because neither the Board nor the patent examiner articulated any separate reasons for holding these claims unpatentable apart from the grounds discussed above.

* * *

We have considered the PTO's remaining arguments and find them not persuasive. The Board's decision affirming the final rejection of claims 4–7 is reversed.

NOTES

1. *For Whom the Bell Tolls: The PTO's Position.* The issue in *Bell* was whether the Board correctly determined that the amino acid sequence of a protein in conjunction with a reference indicating a general method of cloning renders the gene *prima facie* obvious. The claims in *Bell* were directed to nucleic acid molecules containing human sequences which code for human insulin-like growth factors I and II (IGF), single chain serum proteins that play a role in the mediation of somatic cell growth following the administration of growth hormones. The examiner rejected the claims as obvious over the combined teachings of Rinderknecht and Weissman asserting that it would have been obvious, "almost tedious," from the teachings of Weissman to prepare probes based on the Rinderknecht amino acid sequences to obtain the claimed nucleic acid molecules. According to the Examiner:

> [I]t is clear from Weissman that the ordinary artisan knows how to find the nucleic acid when the amino acid sequence is known, and that the claimed sequences and host would have been readily determinable by and obvious to those of ordinary skill in the art at the time the invention was made.

The Board affirmed the Examiner's rejection, holding that the examiner had established a *prima facie* case of obviousness for the claimed sequences "despite the lack of conventional indicia of obviousness" (*e.g.*, structural similarity between the DNA which codes for IGFBI). The Board reasoned that "although a protein and its DNA are not structurally similar, they are correspondingly linked via the genetic code."

The issues in *Deuel* were quite similar to those presented in *Bell*. According to the Board, the issue is "whether or not knowledge of the partial amino acid sequence of a protein, in conjunction with a reference indicating a general method of cloning, renders the invention as a whole, *i.e.*, the gene, *prima facie* obvious." The invention in *Deuel* pertained to genomic and complementary DNA molecules encoding heparin-binding proteins. Again, the Examiner had combined two references, the first (Bohlen) setting forth a partial amino acid sequence of the protein encoded by the claimed nucleic acid, and the second (Maniatis, *et al.*) providing general cloning methods for the cloning of any foreign gene of interest. It was the Examiner's position that the combination of these two references rendered the claimed invention obvious. Certain differences existed between the sources of the proteins disclosed in Bohlen and Deuel. Bohlen taught that the heparin-binding factors were localized in brain tissue. Deuel screened bovine and human placental cDNA libraries to isolate the claimed nucleic acid sequences. It was Deuel's position, therefore, that Bohlen taught away from the claimed invention because of the difference in tissue source.

The Board was not persuaded by this argument, stating that "the claims before us are directed to the product and not the method of isolation." In affirming the Examiner's obviousness rejection, the Board further noted that it is

> constantly advised by the patent examiners, who are highly skilled in the art, that cloning procedures are routine in the art. The examiners urge that when the sequence of a protein is placed into the public domain, the gene is also placed into the public domain because of the nature of cloning techniques.

Deuel, 33 U.S.P.Q.2D at 1447. See *also, In re Hudson*, 18 U.S.P.Q.2d 1322, 1324 (Bd. Pat. App. & Int'f 1990) ("Once the amino acid sequence of a known useful protein is discerned, there is motivation for one of ordinary skill in the art to construct a biosynthetic gene or biosynthesis of that protein.").

2. *The Federal Circuit's Position.* The Federal Circuit has repeatedly overturned Board decisions such as *Bell* and *Deuel*. The court has rejected the PTO's reasoning that the correspondent link between a gene and its encoded protein via the genetic code renders the gene obvious when the amino acid sequence (or partial sequence) is known, and the "implicit ... proposition that this relationship raises a *prima facie* case of structural obviousness" similar to the relationship between "closely related homologs, analogs, and isomers in chemistry." *Bell,* 991 F.2d at 784. According to the court, general knowledge of methodology utilized to isolate nucleic acids encoding desirable proteins is not enough to render the claimed nucleic acid sequences obvious despite the fact that the partial amino acid sequence of the protein is known. In *Deuel*, the court stated:

> Because Deuel claims new chemical entities in *structural* terms, a *prima facie* case of unpatentability requires that the teachings of the prior art suggest *the claimed compounds* to a person of ordinary skill in the art.... Here the prior art does not disclose any relevant cDNA molecules, let alone close relatives of the specific, structurally defined cDNA molecules of claims 5 and 7 that might render them obvious.

Deuel, 51 F.3d at 1557–58.

Furthermore, the court reaffirmed its position in *Bell*, asserting that the "PTO's focus on known methods for potentially isolating the claimed DNA molecule is misplaced because the claims at issue define compounds not methods." *Bell*, 991 F.2d at 1532. Thus, the Board's rejection of Deuel's argument pertaining to the methods used to isolate the claimed DNA was the very same argument used to overturn the obviousness rejection. In other words, the court turned the tables, taking the position that the rejection was erroneously based on the obviousness of the methods used to isolate the DNA and not the actual obviousness of the structural features of the claimed nucleic acid sequence.

3. *A Matter of Structural Chemistry or Biology?* The Federal Circuit's decisions in *Bell* and *Deuel* are consistent with each other; but are they consistent with biological methodology? Does the court, in holding nucleic acids nonobvious when complete or partial amino acid sequences encoded by the gene are known, improperly apply principles of structural chemistry while ignoring the fundamental biological link provided by the genetic code? In explaining why the relationship between related homologs, analogs, and isomers is not the same as the relationship between a gene and the protein for which in codes, the court in *Bell* stated that "because of the degeneracy of the genetic code, there are a vast number of nucleotide sequences that might code for a specific protein." While it is true that degeneracy (recall, degeneracy refers to the fact that several different codons or nucleotide sequences may encode for the same amino acid) of the genetic code gives rise to a vast possibility of encoding nucleic acids, biological investigators have devised certain experimental strategies to facilitate the isolation of the desired gene once the amino acid sequence is known. For example, different species preferentially use one codon as opposed to another. Thus, while some amino acids may be encoded by up to six (6) different codons, organisms preferentially use one codon over another. This information is particularly relevant when designing probes for screening cDNA or genomic libraries. Additionally, several recombinant DNA technology manuals are available to those of ordinary skill in the art. *See generally,* CURRENT PROTOCOLS IN MOLECULAR BIOLOGY, eds. Frederick M. Ausubel, *et al.* (1995). The ready availability of such information removes a great deal of the guess work.

Given the fact that the chemical structure of a DNA sequence is not known, when will a structural analysis (*i.e., Dillon* analysis) lead to a finding of obviousness? You can't compare something to nothing. *See* Sean Johnston, *Patent Protection for the Protein Products of Recombinant DNA*, 23 INTELL. PROP. L.REV. 185, 204 (1991).

4. *Market Power and Technological Development.* The Board in *Deuel* expressed its concern with the breadth of protection that is afforded a patentee of a particular DNA sequence:

> When a patentee issues on the DNA which codes for the protein, the patent owner receives the exclusive right to the DNA and, practically speaking, to the preparation of commercial quantities of the protein which requires the DNA for its production. This is true whether or not isolation of the DNA is accomplished via routine or extraordinary techniques.

Deuel, 33 U.S.P.Q.2D at 1447. *See also*, Anita Varma & David Abraham, *DNA is Different: Legal Obviousness and the Balance Between Biotech Inventors and the Market*, 9 HARV. J.L. & TECH. 53, 55 (1996) (with respect to "the obviousness relationship between DNA and proteins, the Federal Circuit's guidance has upset the delicate balance between patentees and the market, and threatens the development of DNA-based technology."). Do you think the Federal Circuit or the PTO fails to appreciate the market balance? Both? Neither?

5. Deuel, KSR, *and* Kubin. The court in *Amgen* and *In re Deuel*, refers to "obvious to try" as an impermissible ground for rejection under § 103. Yet in *KSR* the Supreme Court embraced "obvious to try," writing: "When there is a design need or market pressure to solve a problem and there are a finite number of identified, predictable solutions, a person of ordinary skill has good reason to pursue the known options within his or her technical grasp. If this leads to the anticipated success, it is likely the product not of innovation but of ordinary skill and common sense. In that instance the fact that a combination was obvious to try might show that it was obvious under § 103." 550 U.S. at 421. To what extent do you think this language from *KSR* has overruled *In re Deuel*, 51 F.3d 1552 (Fed.Cir.1995)? In a post-*KSR* decision, *In re Kubin*, 561 F.3d 1351 (Fed.Cir.2009) the Federal Circuit wrote: "Insofar as *Deuel* implies the obviousness inquiry cannot consider that the combination of the claim's constituent elements was 'obvious to try,' the Supreme Court in *KSR* unambiguously discredited that holding." 561 F.3d at 1358. But in *Kubin* the Federal Circuit also wrote:

> The Supreme Court's admonition against a formalistic approach to obviousness in this context actually resurrects this court's own wisdom in *In re O'Farrell,* which predates the *Deuel* decision by some seven years. This court in *O'Farrell* cautioned that "obvious to try" is an incantation whose meaning is often misunderstood:

>> It is true that this court and its predecessors have repeatedly emphasized that "obvious to try" is not the standard under § 103. However, the meaning of this maxim is sometimes lost. Any invention that would in fact have been obvious under § 103 would also have been, in a sense, obvious to try. The question is: when is an invention that was obvious to try nevertheless nonobvious?

In re O'Farrell, 853 F.2d 894, 903 (Fed.Cir.1988). To differentiate between proper and improper applications of "obvious to try," this court outlined two classes of situations where "obvious to try" is erroneously equated with obviousness under § 103. In the first class of cases,

>> what would have been "obvious to try" would have been to vary all parameters or try each of numerous possible choices until one possibly arrived at a successful result, where the prior art gave either no indication of which parameters were critical or no direction as to which of many possible choices is likely to be successful.

Id. In such circumstances, where a defendant merely throws metaphorical darts at a board filled with combinatorial prior art possibilities, courts should not succumb to hindsight claims of obviousness. The inverse of this proposition is succinctly encapsulated by the Supreme Court's statement in *KSR* that where a skilled artisan merely pursues "known options" from a "finite number of identified, predictable solutions," obviousness under § 103 arises. 550 U.S. at 421.

The second class of *O'Farrell*'s impermissible "obvious to try" situations occurs where what was "obvious to try" was to explore a new technology or general approach that seemed to be a promising field of experimentation, where the prior art gave only general guidance as to the particular form of the claimed invention or how to achieve it.

853 F.2d at 903. Again, *KSR* affirmed the logical inverse of this statement by stating that § 103 bars patentability unless "the improvement is more than the predictable use of prior art elements according to their established functions." 550 U.S. at 417.

This court in *O'Farrell* found the patentee's claims obvious because the Board's rejection of the patentee's claims had not presented either of the two common "obvious to try" pitfalls. Specifically, this court observed that an obviousness finding was appropriate where the prior art "contained *detailed enabling methodology* for practicing the claimed invention, a suggestion to modify the prior art to practice the claimed invention, and evidence suggesting that it would be successful." 853 F.2d at 902 (emphasis added). Responding to concerns about uncertainty in the prior art influencing the purported success of the claimed combination, this court stated: "[o]bviousness does not require absolute predictability of success ... *all that is required is a reasonable expectation of success.*" *Id.* at 903–04 (emphasis added). The Supreme Court in *KSR* reinvigorated this perceptive analysis.

Id. at 1359–60. In view of the Federal Circuit's detailed discussion in *Kubin*, how far has the obviousness standard really shifted as a result of *KSR*? How far should it?

3. BIOTECHNOLOGY PROCESSES—METHODS OF MAKING AND METHODS OF USING A NEW PRODUCT

In re Durden

763 F.2d 1406 (Fed.Cir.1985).

■ Before MARKEY, CHIEF JUDGE, RICH, CIRCUIT JUDGE, and NICHOLS, SENIOR CIRCUIT JUDGE.

■ RICH, CIRCUIT JUDGE.

This appeal is from the decision of the U.S. Patent and Trademark Office (PTO) Board of Appeals (board) affirming the examiner's rejection of the single claim remaining in application serial No. 148,557, filed May 9, 1980, for a process of making certain compounds as obvious under 35 U.S.C. § 103 in view of a U.S. patent to Punja, No. 3,843,669. We affirm.

Background

Quoting appellants' brief, they filed a parent application June 21, 1976, "claiming novel oxime compounds, novel insecticidal carbamate compounds and a novel process for producing the carbamate compounds, employing the novel oxime compounds as the starting materials." A patent issued in 1980 on the parent application claiming carbamate compound products. A divisional application was filed claiming the oxime compound starting materials, and another patent issued thereon. The application at bar, which is another division, claims the process of making the novel carbamate products from the novel oxime starting materials and the one remaining claim now before us stands rejected as directed to obvious subject matter in view of the single reference patent to Punja, assigned to Imperial Chemical Industries.

In his answer to appellants' brief before the board, the examiner said:

> .... While the instant starting material and instant product may be patentable, the instant process and the process of Punja are drawn to [the] same process, reacting an oxime group to form a carbamate ester.

Against this background, appellants' brief in this court makes the following express concession:

> To simplify the issues in this appeal appellants concede that the claimed process, apart from the fact of employing a novel and unobvious starting material and apart from the fact of producing a new and unobvious product, is obvious. Appellants do not argue that differences in the chemical structure of either the starting oxime compound or the product produced would be expected to affect the reaction in any way which might render the claimed process unobvious.

Appellants' "Summary of the Argument" states:

> A chemical process which (a) employs a novel and unobvious starting material *or* (b) is for the production of a novel and unobvious product compound or (c) which employs a novel and unobvious starting material *and also* is for the production of a novel and unobvious product compound, is patentable, regardless of the extent of other similarities to prior art processes. [Emphasis ours.]

This clear statement is made even clearer by appellants' concise statement of the issue, which we repeat as our own.

The Issue

"The issue to be decided is whether a chemical process, otherwise obvious, is patentable *because* either or both the specific starting material employed and the product obtained, are novel and unobvious." [Emphasis ours.]

Opinion

Of course, the appellants say the process is patentable. But with the issue that broadly stated, the answer must be "Not necessarily." For reasons unknown to us, the board convened a 16–member panel to hear the appeal. It then split 9 to 7 in deciding it. The issue is far from new....

* * *

.... Though the burden is on appellants on this appeal to persuade us that the board majority is wrong, they have not even mentioned the CCPA precedent principally relied on by the board majority, the *Albertson* case hereinafter discussed. No reply to the PTO's brief citing added precedent was filed. Their other main argument is that § 103 requires their claimed invention to be considered "as a whole," a proposition with which we agree, and that so considering it, "both the starting materials and the final products individually constitute a part of '... the subject matter as a whole ...' sought to be patented, which must be considered in assessing the obviousness of the claimed process." ...

The board majority relied on *In re Albertson*, 332 F.2d 379, 141 USPQ 730 (CCPA 1964). It saw no way to distinguish *Albertson* from the present case, nor do we. This court is bound by clear precedents in the CCPA. *South Corp. v. United States*, 690 F.2d 1368, 215 USPQ 657 (Fed.Cir.1982). The same arguments appellants are making here were made in *Albertson*. The starting materials used in and the product produced by the claimed process were the subjects of allowed claims; the process claims were rejected as obvious in view of references showing the same chemical reduction process applied to other materials. The board affirmed the rejection and the CCPA affirmed the board. *Larsen* was relied on by the *Albertson* board and the appellant attempted to distinguish it, together with two similar CCPA decisions, on the ground that "the specific reactants in a process 'are a vital, significant part of any process,' and therefore the 'use of an unobvious starting material renders a process unobvious.'" The CCPA said:

> We do not agree with appellant's proposition that the "use of an unobvious starting material renders a process unobvious." Were this true, every step, for example, dissolving or heating, when performed on a new compound would result in a patentable process. We reiterate that all of the evidence must be considered on the "subject matter as a whole," from the viewpoint of one skilled in the art, in the determination of obviousness, and not simply the patentability of one of the starting reactants in a process.

The CCPA there also made clear its approach to the issue, which is the same approach we take here and in all like cases, namely, "that each statutory class of claims should be considered independently on its own merits. *In re Wilke et al.*, 50 CCPA 964, 314 F.2d 558, 136 USPQ 435; *In re Adams et al.*, 50 CCPA 1185, 316 F.2d 476, 137 USPQ 333."

We reiterate another principle followed in obviousness issue cases, which is to decide each case on the basis of its own particular fact situation. What we or our predecessors may have said in discussing different fact situations is not to be taken as having universal application.

The opinion joined by the dissenting board members states that they, like the majority, were unable to distinguish *Albertson*, but that they "consider it no longer viable." They had convinced themselves that in view of subsequent CCPA decisions, on other fact situations, "*Albertson* would be decided differently today." Even were that so, the case still stands as a precedent until overruled. Their principal support for that erroneous surmise appears to have been the CCPA opinion in *In re Kuehl*, 475 F.2d 658, 177 USPQ 250 (CCPA 1973). The board majority also considered *Kuehl* at length and found it distinguishable on the ground that the process there claimed and found to be unobvious was a process of cracking hydrocarbons by means of the newly invented catalyst ZK–22, which cracking process was not predictable on the basis of mere possession of the catalyst, whereas the process claimed in *Albertson*, like the process claimed here, was predictable and obvious to those of ordinary skill in the art from the "prior art." The board majority found the distinction between the cases "readily apparent," and so do we.

We find it unnecessary to discuss the other cases cited by the dissenters on the board. We suspect the possibility, in connection with these highly debatable matters, that there has been a failure to distinguish between novelty and unobviousness. Of course, an otherwise old process becomes a new process when a previously unknown starting material, for example, is used in it which is then subjected to a conventional manipulation or reaction to produce a product which may also be new, albeit the *expected* result of what is done. But it does not necessarily mean that the whole process has become *unobvious* in the sense of § 103. In short, a new process may still be obvious, even when considered "as a whole," notwithstanding the specific starting material or resulting product, or both, is not to be found in the prior art.

To conclude, and possibly to put an end for now to this potentially endless debate on what the "law" is, which is not unlike sitting under a tree discussing good and evil with Socrates, we revert to appellants' statement of the issue, *supra*, and the use of the word "because" therein.

A process, after all, is a manipulation according to an algorithm, as we have learned in recent years—doing something to or with something according to a schema. The argument is that an otherwise old process with a predictable outcome is *unobvious because* it is applied to a new material, notwithstanding the new material is similar or analogous to materials identically manipulated or treated before. To anyone other than a patent lawyer and therefore unfamiliar with the mysteries of patent claims, this would make little sense, we believe. Appellants conclude their argument with the assertion that they "are entitled to claim their invention as they see fit," which is indisputable. 35 U.S.C. § 112, second paragraph. But when it comes to determining whether their claim is allowable under § 103, as was said in *Albertson* and elsewhere, we must treat the claim as we find it. We hold the process claim before us to be directed to obvious subject matter in view of Punja. We do not find that *Albertson* has been previously overruled *sub silentio*, as the dissenters believe, and we do consider it a viable precedent which fully supports this decision.

We are sure that there are those who would like to have us state some clear general rule by which all cases of this nature could be decided. Some judges might be tempted to try it. But the question of obviousness under § 103 arises in such an unpredictable variety of ways and in such different forms that it would be an indiscreet thing to do. Today's rule would likely be regretted in tomorrow's case. Our function is to apply, in each case, § 103 as written to the facts of disputed issues, not to generalize or make rules for other cases which are unforeseeable. The task may sometimes be easy and sometimes difficult; and as this case shows, not all of those required to decide may agree. But such is the way of the "law."

In re Pleuddemann
910 F.2d 823 (Fed.Cir.1990).

■ Before RICH, CIRCUIT JUDGE, FRIEDMAN, SENIOR CIRCUIT JUDGE, and MILLS, DISTRICT JUDGE.

■ RICH, CIRCUIT JUDGE.

This appeal is from the March 3, 1989, decision of the United States Patent and Trademark Office (PTO) Board of Patent Appeals and Interferences (board) affirming the examiner's rejection of claims 8–16, 18–21, 26, and 27 of Pleuddemann's application serial No. 917,950, a division of serial No. 803,043, filed November 29, 1985, for "Silane Coupling Agents." The real party in interest is Dow Corning Corporation, Midland, Michigan. We reverse.

The rejection of the above claims is predicated solely on 35 U.S.C. § 103 on the ground of obviousness in view of the disclosure of a single reference, Pleuddemann *et al.* patent No. 3,258,477 ('477 patent), issued June 28, 1966, to Dow Corning Corporation, together with admissions in appellant's specification.

The application at bar incorporates by reference the disclosure of the '477 patent which also discloses organosilane coupling agents. Appellant says that the different coupling agents of the '477 patent have been "an industry standard for fiberglass-filled unsaturated polyesters for many years." It is explained that the silane compounds couple or bond the polyester resins to the fiberglass filling material, improving the mechanical properties of the resulting products. The specification of the application at bar further says that "[t]hese low molecular weight compounds are believed to form chemical links between filler particles and polymer molecules, and as such, they must incorporate functional groups capable of reacting with filler and resin alike." Disclosed are many suitable resins, all well known in the art, and a large number of suitable fillers of the general class of mineral fillers, likewise well known.

The Claimed Invention

Pleuddemann's present invention is broadly stated to be as follows:

> It has now been found that a silane coupling agent, comprising the reaction product of an isocyanatoalkyl ester with an aminoorganosilane, can impart superior moisture resistance to mineral-filled unsaturated polyesters, as well as other unsaturated resin composites.

There then follows a structural formula purporting to define the class of organosilane reaction products which, with all of its substituent (R, R', R" etc.) definitions, occupies half a page, which it is unnecessary to repeat here in order to deal with the legal problems before us.

Next follows the statement, in two separate paragraphs, that the invention also relates to (1) a *process for bonding* a polymerizable material to a mineral filler and (2) a *method for priming* a surface to improve its bonding to certain organic resins. The claims on appeal are all directed to these *processes or methods*. All but two are dependent claims. Independent claim 26 is directed to the process of bonding and independent claim 27 is directed to the method for priming and both recite the elaborate structural formula of the class of organosilanes which do the bonding or priming, described in the specification.

The specification also states:

> Methods of incorporating silane coupling agents to improve performance of filled resins are well known in the art.

It then explains how several of such methods are carried out.

The two representative independent claims on appeal are set forth below, omitting the formula contained in them which defines the class of coupling agents used (emphasis ours):

26. A *process for bonding* a polymerizable material to a mineral filler *comprising*: (a) mixing an organosilane with a polymerizable material having aliphatic unsaturation and a filler having hydroxyl functionality thereon, to obtain a uniform dispersion of the components; *and* (b) *polymerizing* the material to form a solid composite, wherein said organosilane is represented by the formula.

27. A *method for priming* a surface having hydroxyl functionality thereon to improve its bonding to organic resins containing aliphatic unsaturation in the uncured state, *comprising wetting* the surface with a solution of an organosilane *and then drying* said surface, wherein said organosilane is represented by the formula.

* * *

The Rejection

In his Answer on appeal to the board, the examiner stated that the Pleuddemann *et al.* '477 patent

teaches the same process of bonding a polymerizable material to a filler containing hydroxy functionality using an analogous silane containing both unsaturation and hydrolyzable groups. The appellant further admits that silane coupling agents are well known in the art to improve mechanical properties of filled resins.

The examiner then stated that it was his position

that it would have been obvious to one skilled in the art to use one silane compound in place of another in the process ... and in the method ... since the silane compound coupling agent acts as a coupling agent in the process and method.

In support of his rejection, the examiner cited *In re Durden*, 763 F.2d 1406, 226 USPQ 359 (Fed.Cir.1985).

In affirming, the board likewise relied on *Durden* and in an extensive opinion responding to appellant's legal arguments added two more cases, decided by our predecessor court, which it said it was unable to distinguish from the present case, namely, *In re Kanter*, 55 CCPA 1395, 399 F.2d 249, 158 USPQ 331 (1968), and *In re Neugebauer*, 51 CCPA 1138, 330 F.2d 353, 141 USPQ 205 (1964).

Appellant's Contentions

First, we need to know a little prosecution background. The patent application (803,043) contained three groups of claims: (1) to the new group of aminoorganosilanes; (2) the process and method claims at bar; and (3) to the new articles of manufacture produced by using the new coupling agents. Restriction was required by the examiner and group (1) was elected. The claims were allowed and on March 17, 1987, Patent No. 4,650,889 was issued thereon. The claims in group (3), which were all dependent claims, were stated by the examiner to be allowable if rewritten in independent form and are not involved in this appeal. They are still pending in the application at bar in their conditionally allowed status. The patenting of the compounds claimed in group (1) provides us with the premise that they are new and unobvious compounds, which we take as a given in further discussion.

In essence, appellant contends that in addition to the claims on the new class of coupling *agents* which the PTO has granted, and the allowed claims on the *articles* made by using said agents in the usual way, he is also entitled to the appealed claims on the *process or method of using* those agents—in the usual way—for bonding or priming. It is contended that such method of use claims should be allowed because the *articles* made by using the new bonding agents have superior moisture resistant properties.

The shibboleth which appellant hopes will get the claims at bar into the golden realm of patentability, notwithstanding precedents cited by the PTO, is that they are "method of use" rather than "method of making" claims. It is further emphasized that the claims call for the use of a novel and nonobvious class of organosilane compounds and that is not disputed.

Opinion

When a new and useful compound or group of compounds is invented or discovered having a *particular use* it is often the case that what is really a single invention may be viewed legally as having three or more different aspects permitting it to be claimed in different ways, for example: (1) the compounds themselves; (2) the method or process of making the compounds; and (3) the method or *process of using* the compounds for their intended purpose. *In re Kuehl*, 475 F.2d 658, 177 USPQ 250 (CCPA 1973), was such a case. Our predecessor court so analyzed it. The case dealt with a new zeolite catalyst useful in the hydrocarbon cracking process in which other zeolite catalysts had been used before. The then Patent Office had allowed claims to the new zeolite, ZK–22, and to the method of making it, but balked at allowing claims to the method of using ZK–22 as a catalyst in hydrocarbon cracking. The appellant argued that allowance of claims to ZK–22 *necessarily* entitled him to claims on the method of use because the catalyst was a new and useful compound.

The court said the proposition was "too broadly stated," citing *In re Albertson*, 51 CCPA 1377, 332 F.2d 379, 141 USPQ 730 (1964), where claims to the process of preparing certain compounds were rejected as obvious notwithstanding the compounds themselves were the subject of allowed claims. In *Albertson*, in affirming the rejection, the court said:

> We are of the opinion that each statutory class of claims should be considered independently on its own merits. *In re Wilke et al.*, 50 CCPA 964, 314 F.2d 558, 136 USPQ 435 [1963]; *In re Adams et al.*, 50 CCPA 1185, 316 F.2d 476, 137 USPQ 333 [1963]. The fact that the starting materials and the final product are the subject matter of allowed claims does not *necessarily* indicate that the process employed [to *make* the compounds] is patentable. [Emphasis ours.]

In *Kuehl*, however, we stated, as we often had before:

The unobviousness of the herein claimed method of cracking hydrocarbons *using* ZK–22 must be judged by applying to the facts of this case the statutory standard for unobviousness of § 103. [Our emphasis.]

* * *

In discussing prior cases in *Kuehl*, the court observed that there is a distinction which may be of significance between claims to a method of *making* a novel compound, which can be obvious though the compound itself is not, and claims to a method of *using* the compound. See the extended discussion under the heading "The Prior Cases," at the end of which it was said:

> We have concluded, for reasons stated above, that the process-of-use claims are patentable and that it is not necessary to show unexpected utility in order to show unobviousness. We would add, moreover, that in our view it is in the public interest to permit appellant to claim the process [of use] as well as the product. The result is to encourage a more detailed disclosure of the specific methods of using the novel composition he had invented in order to have support for the process claims.

> We believe the constitutional purpose of the patent system is promoted by encouraging applicants to claim, and therefore to describe in the manner required by 35 U.S.C. 112, *all aspects of what they regard as their inventions, regardless of the number of statutory classes involved.* [Emphasis ours.]

Twelve years after *Kuehl*, we again reviewed the case law in *Durden*, on which the PTO here relies, involving claims to a process of *making* a novel compound and a process *using* a novel compound and reiterated that, whatever process is claimed, its obviousness is to be determined under § 103 in *light of the prior art*, each case to be decided on the basis of its own fact situation. We declined to lay down any general rule and explained why. The examiner and board appear to have regarded *Durden*, or something said therein or to be deduced therefrom, as "controlling" of the present case. However, the facts here are not the facts of *Durden*. The single appealed claim in *Durden* was for a method of *making* a compound. The board majority rejected it for obviousness in view of a prior art patent and we affirmed. The appealed claims here are for methods of bonding/priming by the use of novel agents invented by appellant for that particular use. We repeat that the controlling law is in § 103 of the statute, which must be applied to the facts of this case.

"From the standpoint of patent law, a compound and all of its properties are inseparable; they are one and the same thing." *In re Papesch*, 50 CCPA 1084, 315 F.2d 381, 391, 137 USPQ 43, 51 (1963). It is the properties of appellant's compounds as bonding/priming agents for certain polymers and fillers or support surfaces that give them their utility. As stated above, the compounds and their use are but different aspects of, or ways of looking at, the same invention and consequently that invention is capable of being claimed both as new compounds or as a new method or process of bonding/priming. On the other hand, a process or method of making the compounds is a quite different thing; they may have been made by a process which was new or old, obvious or nonobvious. In this respect, therefore, there is a real difference between a process of making and a process of using and the cases dealing with one involve different problems from the cases dealing with the other. *Durden* was a case involving only the patentability of a process of making a novel insecticide and the single claim on appeal was held to be directed to obvious subject matter in view of a prior art patent disclosing a very similar process using similar reactants notwithstanding the facts that there were unobvious starting materials used and unobvious products obtained. We are not here concerned with a process of making bonding/priming agents but with the agents themselves in which the bonding/priming properties are inherent, for which reason we do not find *Durden* a controlling precedent as did the examiner and the board.

* * *

We deem the present case to resemble *Kuehl* wherein we held the use of the new catalyst, ZK–22, claimed as a method of cracking hydrocarbons, to be unobvious, for which reason we reverse the rejection.

The board was aware of *Kuehl* and sought to distinguish it on the ground that the *result* of the claimed process or method should be *unpredictable* before nonobviousness can be found. This involves, it seems to us, the same flaw we found in *Kuehl* in that it presumes appellant's new group of silane compounds to be prior art. In *Kuehl* the court said, 475 F.2d at 664–665, 177 USPQ at 255:

> The test under § 103 is whether *in view of the prior art* the invention as a whole would have been obvious at the time it was made, *and the prior art here does not include the zeolite, ZK–22.* The obviousness of the process of cracking hydrocarbons with ZK–22 as a catalyst must be determined *without reference to knowledge of ZK–22 and its properties.* So judged, the process of the appealed claims would not have been obvious. [Emphasis ours.]

In the present case likewise, § 103 obviousness of claims 26 and 27 depends on the obviousness of using appellant's new compounds, which constitute the essential limitation of the claims, in light of the prior art. That being so, the board's hindsight comparison of the functioning of the new compounds with the functioning of the compounds of the prior art was legal error. It uses appellant's specification teaching as though it were prior art in order to make claims to methods of bonding/priming using his admittedly novel compounds appear to be obvious. We hold that appellant is entitled to his method of use claims 8–16, 18–21, 26, and 27, together with the already allowed article of manufacture claims.

---

a.   CONGRESS RESPONDS TO *DURDEN*

The implications of *Durden* for the biotechnology community were cause for concern. Although products (*e.g.*, isolated and purified genes) of biotechnological research are often patentable, there are many occasions where patent protection for the product is not available. As a result, the inventor must rely on process patent protection. Prior to 1988, competitors could practice a patented process outside of the United States and import the non-patented product into the United States and sell it. Infringement did not exist because the product was not patented and the process was used outside of the United States. Infringement occurs only when the patented invention is used in the United States. 35 U.S.C. § 271(a). In 1988, however, Congress enacted the Patent Process Amendments Act, which essentially made it an act of infringement to import a non-patented product made by a patented process. 35 U.S.C. § 271(g). *See* Chapter Eight, *infra. See also*, David L. Hitchcock and Craig Allen Nard, *The Patent Process Amendments Act: The Labyrinth*, 3 FORDHAM INTELL. PROP. L.J. 441 (1993). This explains why *Durden* was very troubling for the biotech industry: process patent protection was crucial. *See Amgen v. United States Int'l Trade Comm'n*, 902 F.2d 1532 (Fed.Cir.1990).

In 1995, Congress responded by amending § 103, breaking it down into three distinct sections: section (a) became the former first paragraph that was drafted in 1952; section (c) embodied the second paragraph drafted in 1984; and section (b), which addressed the concerns of the biotechnology industry:

(b)(1) Notwithstanding subsection (a), and upon timely election by the applicant for patent to proceed under this subsection, a biotechnological process using or resulting in a composition of matter that is novel under section 102 and nonobvious under subsection (a) of this section shall be considered nonobvious if—

(A) claims to the process and the composition of matter are contained in either the same application for patent or in separate applications having the same effective filing date; and

(B) the composition of matter, and the process at the time it was invented, were owned by the same person or subject to an obligation of assignment to the same person.

(2) A patent issued on a process under paragraph (1)—

(A) shall also contain the claims to the composition of matter used in or made by that process, or

(B) shall, if such composition of matter is claimed in another patent, be set to expire on the same date as such other patent, notwithstanding section 154.

(3) For purposes of paragraph (1), the term "biotechnological process" means—

(A) a process of genetically altering or otherwise inducing a single-or multi-celled organism to—

(i) express an exogenous nucleotide sequence,

(ii) inhibit, eliminate, augment, or alter expression of an endogenous nucleotide sequence, or

(iii) express a specific physiological characteristic not naturally associated with said organism;

(B) cell fusion procedures yielding a cell line that expresses a specific protein, such as a monoclonal antibody; and

(C) a method of using a product produced by a process defined by subparagraph (A) and (B), or a combination of subparagraphs (A) and (B).

This new subsection of § 103 provides that a process is nonobvious if the composition of matter, which serves as either the starting material in the process or its end product, is nonobvious. There are the additional requirements of common ownership of the process and composition of matter and the simultaneous filing (or same effective filing date) of the composition of matter and process claims.

b. THE FEDERAL CIRCUIT STEPS BACK FROM *DURDEN*

In re Ochiai

71 F.3d 1565 (Fed.Cir.1995).

■ Before ARCHER, CHIEF JUDGE, MICHEL, CIRCUIT JUDGE, and CARRIGAN, DISTRICT JUDGE.

■ PER CURIAM.

This appeal is from the July 8, 1992, decision of the United States Patent and Trademark Office (PTO) Board of Patent Appeals and Interferences (Board) affirming the examiner's rejection of claims 6 through 10 of Michihiko Ochiai *et al.* (collectively "Ochiai") application serial no. 07/462,-492, claiming priority from parent application serial no. 642,356, filed December 19, 1975, now U.S. Patent No. 4,098,888 (methods for the manufacture of cephems). *Ex parte Ochiai*, 24 U.S.P.Q.2D 1265 (Bd.Pat. App. & Int.1992). The real party in interest is Takeda Chemical Industries, Ltd., the assignee of any patent issuing from the application.

The rejection of the above claims was predicated on an asserted view of the law of obviousness, per 35 U.S.C. § 103, in view of the combined teaching of six references. Because, under the legally correct method for determining obviousness, the claimed process is not obvious in view of the cited prior art references, we reverse.

The Invention

Ochiai's application is directed to a process for using an acyl side chain from a particular type of organic acid having a 2–aminothiazolyl group, and a particular type of amine to make a particular cephem compound having antibiotic properties. Claim 6, the principal claim on appeal, is as follows:

6. A process for preparing a cephem compound of the formula:

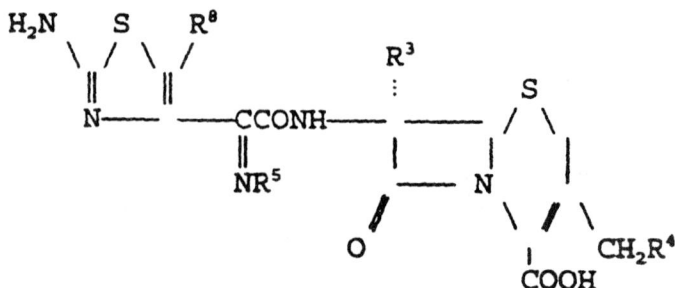

wherein R3 is hydrogen or methoxy, R4 is hydrogen or a residue of a nucleophilic compound, R5 is hydroxyl or a protected hydroxyl, and R8 is hydrogen or a halogen, or a pharmaceutically acceptable salt or ester thereof, which comprises introducing an acyl group of the formula:

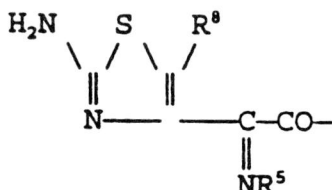

$$H_2N \quad S \quad R^8$$
$$N--- \quad ---C-CO-$$
$$NR^5$$

wherein R5 and R8 are as defined above into the amino group of the molecule of the formula:

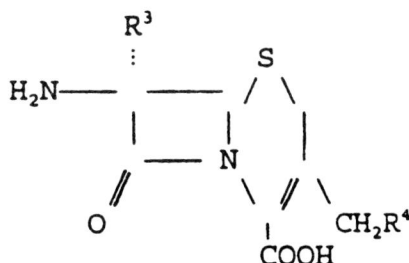

$$R^3$$
$$H_2N--- \quad --- \quad S$$
$$--- N$$
$$O \qquad COOH \qquad CH_2R^4$$

wherein R3 and R4 are as defined above or a salt or ester thereof.

Id. at 1266.

Ochiai's U.S. Patent No. 4,298,606 covers the cephem compound resulting from the process of claim 6, and Ochiai's U.S. Patent No. 4,203,899 covers the organic acid used in the process of claim 6. *Id.* at 1267. In other words, viewed as of the time the claimed process was invented, claim 6 recites a process of using a new, nonobvious acid to make a new, nonobvious cephem. The '606 and '899 patents, like the application at bar, claim priority from the December 1975 parent application.

The Rejection

The examiner rejected claims 6 through 10 as obvious in light of the combined teaching of the six references noted above. All six references, as Ochiai acknowledges, teach the use of a type of acid to make a type of cephem by a standard acylation reaction with the very same amine recited in claim 6. The examiner explained the rejections thusly in his answer to Ochiai's appeal to the Board:

> It must again be stressed that the citation of six references is to demon-strate convincingly that a *standard, conventional* process of preparing cephalosporin compounds is being claimed. The *only* difference between what is being claimed and the prior art is the selection of a *slightly* different acylation agent [*i.e.,* acid] to result in a slightly different final product. The *closest* prior art of the six references is represented by the

Cook *et al.* 4,024,133 and, Gregson *et al.* patent 4,024,134. These two references use [sic, are] quite similar in their disclosure, Cook being the *most* [sic, more] relevant. Both of these references *generically* disclose the "2–amino–thiazolyl" group which appellants seek to introduce....

The examiner recognizes that the *specific* "2 amino thiazolyl" moiety has *not* been *specifically* named in [the] Cook *et al*[.] patent. However, Cook *et al.* when viewed from the standpoint of one skilled in the art would recognize the use of "2–aminothiazolyl" if the final products sought were to contain this moiety. This merely states the obvious....

* * *

The facts presented here are *identical* to those that occurred in the *Durden* decision (*In re Durden* [763 F.2d 1406] 226 USPQ 359). The *acylating* agent herein being used has been patented by appellants, see *Ochiai et al.* 4,203,899. The final products have also been patented by appellants which appellants acknowledge, brief page 5 footnote 4. The *only* difference between the facts in *Durden* ... and the instant situation is that appellants have not *admitted* on the record that the process is obvious. Appellants seek to distinguish the *Durden* decision based on this difference. However, the *Durden* decision is believed to be controlling because of the *reasoning* used therein and not an admission or lack of admission of the obviousness of the process. The references discussed above abundantly demonstrate the *routineness* of the claimed process. Thus, the Court rejected the argument that a conventional manipulation or reaction was *unobvious* "notwithstanding the specific starting material or resulting product or both, is not to be found in the prior art". (Emphasis in original). Importantly, the examiner conceded the total absence from the prior art of both the acid used and the cephem made in the process recited in claim 6. In addition, the examiner discussed no references containing any suggestion or motivation either (a) to reject known acids and select instead the particular one used in claim 6, or (b) to obtain the particular cephem made according to the process of claim 6.

On appeal, the Board affirmed the examiner's rejection. After reviewing the examiner's reliance on *In re Durden*, 763 F.2d 1406, 226 USPQ 359 (Fed.Cir.1985), and the "standard" nature of the acylation reaction disclosed in the rejected claims, the Board acknowledged Ochiai's contention that the fact that "neither the final product nor the method of introducing the particular [acid] component were known, obvious or even remotely suggested in the prior art ... should be dispositive of the obviousness of the invention" recited in claim 6. *Ochiai*, 24 U.S.P.Q.2D at 1267. The Board did not, however, find Ochiai's contention persuasive. According to the Board,

> [w]e are not here concerned with the patentability of the starting materials, the final compounds or other processes of making the [cephem] compounds. We are concerned only with the claimed process and the patentability thereof. Cases such as *In re Larsen*, 292 F.2d 531, 49 CCPA 711, 130 USPQ 209 (CCPA 1961); *In re Albertson*, 332 F.2d 379, 51 CCPA 1377, 141 USPQ 730 (CCPA 1964) and, particularly, *In re Durden, supra*, all of which were directed to processes of making chemical compounds, are controlling herein.... In each case, a material A, either known or novel, was subjected to a standard process of reacting with a standard reactant, B, in order to produce the result expected from the reaction of A with B.

Indeed in *Albertson* as in the instant case, the only manipulative step of the process is that which is embodied in the word "reacting."

Id. The Board also rejected Ochiai's assertion that cases such as *In re Pleuddemann*, 910 F.2d 823, 15 U.S.P.Q.2D 1738 (Fed.Cir.1990), *In re Mancy*, 499 F.2d 1289, 182 USPQ 303 (CCPA 1974), and *In re Kuehl*, 475 F.2d 658, 177 USPQ 250 (CCPA 1973), are in tension with *Durden* and *Albertson* and counsel allowance of the rejected claims. Distinguishing *Pleuddemann, Mancy, and Kuehl* as "method of using" rather than "method of making" cases, the Board summarized its decision as follows:

> In the case before us, appellants have admitted the claims are directed to a process of making a desired AB product. The process steps, "introducing" A into AB or "reacting" A with B are standard processes used by practitioners in the prior art for reacting similar A moieties with the same B moiety. We are in agreement with the examiner that there is nothing unobvious in the particular *process* chosen and claimed by the appellants.

Ochiai, 24 U.S.P.Q.2D at 1270 (emphasis in original).

Ochiai appeals, contending that both the examiner and the Board failed to apply the proper test for obviousness established by *Graham v. John Deere Co.*, 383 U.S. 1, 86 S.Ct. 684, 15 L.Ed.2d 545, 148 USPQ 459 (1966), and its progeny. Specifically, according to Ochiai, both the examiner and the Board, on the assumption that our decision in *Durden* controlled the outcome of the instant case, failed to weigh the specific differences between the claimed invention—with all its limitations—and the prior art references, the so-called "second *Graham* factor." *See id.* at 17, 86 S.Ct. at 693–94 ("Under § 103 ... differences between the prior art and the claims at issue are to be ascertained[.]"). In addition, Ochiai contends that the decisions in *Mancy* and *Kuehl*, which, like all Court of Customs and Patent Appeals decisions, were *in banc*, limit the decision in *Albertson* to its facts.

The Solicitor, while defending the correctness of the Board's conclusion and, unlike the Board itself, doing so in the familiar terms of *Graham*, also asserts that a supposed irreconcilable conflict in our cases—between *Albertson* and *Durden*, on the one hand, and *Pleuddemann*, on the other— "makes it very difficult for patent attorneys to give cogent advice to clients or for patent examiners to render consistent decisions on the patentability (under § 103) of processes involving the use of new and unobvious starting materials." Unlike Ochiai, however, the Solicitor asks us to take the opportunity to reaffirm the vitality of *Albertson* and *Durden* in the course of deciding this appeal.

The Issue

The issue before this court is whether the Board erred in upholding the examiner's rejection of claim 6 as obvious under 35 U.S.C. § 103 in view of *Larsen, Albertson*, and *Durden* as interpreted by the PTO when neither the particular acid used nor the particular cephem produced is either taught or suggested by the art that predates the parent application.

The Analysis

The test of obviousness *vel non* is statutory. It requires that one compare the claim's "subject matter as a whole" with the prior art "to which said subject matter pertains." 35 U.S.C. § 103. The inquiry is thus highly fact-specific by design. This is so "whether the invention be a process for making or a process of using, or some other process." *Kuehl*, 475 F.2d at 665, 177 USPQ at 255. When the references cited by the examiner fail to establish a *prima facie* case of obviousness, the rejection is improper and will be overturned. *In re Fine*, 837 F.2d 1071, 1074, 5 U.S.P.Q.2D 1596, 1598 (Fed.Cir.1988).

Applying this statutory test to the art of record, we conclude that Ochiai's process invention as claimed is not *prima facie* obvious. The process invention Ochiai recites in claim 6 specifically requires use of none other than its new, nonobvious acid as one of the starting materials. One having no knowledge of this acid could hardly find it obvious to make any cephem using this acid as an acylating agent, much less the particular cephem recited in claim 6. In other words, it would not have been obvious to those of ordinary skill in the art to choose the particular acid of claim 6 as an acylating agent for the known amine for the simple reason that the particular acid was unknown but for Ochiai's disclosure in the '429 application. As one of our predecessor courts had occasion to observe, in a case involving a highly analogous set of facts, "one cannot choose from the unknown." *Mancy*, 499 F.2d at 1293, 182 USPQ at 306.

In addition, although the prior art references the examiner discussed do indeed teach the use of various acids to make various cephems, they do not define a class of acids the knowledge of which would render obvious the use of Ochiai's specifically claimed acid. The Board noted that Ochiai's specifically claimed acid is "similar" to the acids used in the prior art. Likewise, the examiner asserted that the claimed acid was "slightly different" from those taught in the cited references. Neither characterization, however, can establish the obviousness of the use of a starting material that is new and nonobvious, both in general and in the claimed process. The mere chemical possibility that one of those prior art acids could be modified such that its use would lead to the particular cephem recited in claim 6 does not make the process recited in claim 6 obvious "unless the prior art suggested the desirability of [such a] modification." *In re Gordon*, 733 F.2d 900, 902, 221 USPQ 1125, 1127 (Fed.Cir.1984). As we noted above, the examiner discussed no references containing any suggestion or motivation either (a) to modify known acids to obtain the particular one recited in claim 6, or (b) to obtain the particular new and nonobvious cephem produced by the process of claim 6. In short, the prior art contains nothing at all to support the conclusion that the particular process recited in claim 6 is obvious.

In light of the above, the examiner's errors are evident. First, the examiner concluded that one of ordinary skill in the art would "recognize the use of '2–aminothiazolyl' if the final products sought were to contain this moiety." The prior art, however, contains nothing at all to suggest that one seek this concededly nonobvious final product. The examiner erred by indulging in an essentially hindsight comparison of the functioning of the new acid in claim 6 as a precursor to the claimed cephem with that of other acids in the prior art processes that produced other cephems. Such a comparison uses Ochiai's specification as though it were prior art in order to make the claim to a method that uses the nonobvious acid to make the nonobvious cephem appear to be obvious. Second, the examiner incorrectly drew from *Durden*, a case turning on specific facts, a general obviousness rule: namely, that a process claim is obvious if the prior art references disclose the same general process using "similar" starting materials.[5] No such *per se* rule exists. Mere citation of *Durden, Albertson*, or any other case as a basis for rejecting process claims that differ from the prior art by their use of different starting materials is improper, as it sidesteps the fact-intensive inquiry mandated by section 103. In other words, there are not "*Durden* obviousness rejections" or "*Albertson* obviousness rejections," but rather only section 103 obviousness rejections.

The Board essentially repeated the examiner's error of sidestepping the particularized inquiry required by section 103 by grounding the rejection on the supposedly "controlling" effect of "[c]ases such as *In re Larsen, In re Albertson*, and, particularly, *In re Durden*, all of which were directed to processes of making chemical compounds." *Ochiai*, 24 U.S.P.Q.2D at 1267 (citations omitted). After categorizing the process recited in claim 6 as a "process of making" rather than as a "process for using," the Board reached its conclusion according to the following syllogism: (a) "process of making" claims have led to rejections, as in *Larsen, Albertson*, and *Durden*, whereas "process for using" claims have led to allowances, as in *Kuehl, Mancy*, and *Pleuddemann*; (b) Ochiai's claim is directed to a "process of making"; (c) therefore, the rejection should be affirmed. *Id.* at 1268–70. This method of analysis is founded on legal error because it substitutes supposed *per se* rules for the particularized inquiry required by section 103. It necessarily produces erroneous results. Moreover, the Board indulged a *non sequitur* when it grounded its conclusion of obviousness on the assertion that the starting materials recited in claim 6 are "similar" to those of the prior art. The recited acid is nonobvious, having itself been patented based on the parent application. Nor did the Board justify its characterization of "similar[ity]" in any other manner. Similarity is, as we noted above, not necessarily obviousness.

The Alleged Conflict in Our Case Law

Both the Solicitor and Ochiai devote substantial portions of their briefs to purported demonstrations that our precedents on the obviousness *vel non* of chemical processes are, if not in conflict, at least in severe tension with one another and thus create unnecessary confusion. Both parties identify the same two sets of three cases as presenting the conflict: *Larsen, Albertson*, and *Durden*, upholding rejections on appeal, are said to be inconsistent with *Kuehl, Mancy*, and *Pleuddemann*, reversing rejections on appeal. While we agree that some generalized commentary found within several of these decisions may present minor tensions, both Ochiai and the Solicitor draw far too bleak a picture of the state of our case law. Other

---

5. This is most apparent from the examiner's baffling assertions that "a standard, conventional process . . . is being claimed" and that "[t]he references . . . abundantly demonstrate the routineness of the claimed process." Because the claimed process includes as a limitation the use of an acid unknown in the prior art, the prior art can only demonstrate the routineness of a process similar to the claimed one. Similarity is, of course, not necessarily obviousness.

language in these cases, like their actual holdings, obviates any real inconsistency.

In *Albertson,* the court "reiterate[d] that all of the evidence must be considered on the 'subject matter as a whole,' from the viewpoint of one skilled in the art, in the determination of obviousness, and not simply the patentability of one of the starting reactants in a process." *Albertson,* 332 F.2d at 382, 141 USPQ at 732. Thus, the Board in this case looked to the general result in *Albertson* while ignoring the *Albertson* court's explicit methodology. Every subsequent case that the parties discuss has been grounded on the same analytic principle: namely, that section 103 requires a fact-intensive comparison of the claimed process with the prior art rather than the mechanical application of one or another *per se* rule. *See Pleudde-mann,* 910 F.2d at 827, 15 U.S.P.Q.2D at 1741 ("We repeat that the controlling law is in § 103 of the statute, which must be applied to the facts of this case."); *Durden,* 763 F.2d at 1411, 226 USPQ at 362 ("Our function is to apply, in each case, § 103 as written to the facts of disputed issues, not to generalize or make rules for other cases which are unforeseeable."); *Mancy,* 499 F.2d at 1292, 182 USPQ at 305 ("[T]he statutory standard of § 103 for determining obviousness of an invention is whether in view of the prior art the invention as a whole would have been obvious at the time it was made."); *Kuehl,* 475 F.2d at 665, 177 USPQ at 255 ("The test of unobviousness is a statutory test and requires comparison of the invention with the prior art in each case. . . ."). As a consequence, these cases do not—indeed, cannot—present or create conflicting legal rules. They present, instead, applications of a unitary legal regime to different claims and fields of art to yield particularized results. It is thus surprising that the Board relies on *Durden* for a general rule when the *Durden* court expressly cautioned the bar "not to generalize or make rules for other cases."

Because the regime of section 103, much like the Fourth Amendment proscriptions against "unreasonable" searches and warrants issued upon less than "probable cause," mandates that legal outcomes turn on the close analysis of facts, reasonable persons may well disagree about the outcome of a given obviousness determination. These disagreements over the application of a legal rule can, however, be transformed into perceived "irreconcilable conflicts" between legal rules only when, as occurred here, examiners, members of the Board, and patent lawyers purport to find competing *per se* rules in our precedents and argue for rejection or allowance of a particular claim accordingly. We acknowledge that some generalized commentary found in these cases reviewing rejections of claims directed to chemical processes may, if viewed in isolation, have inadvertently provided encouragement to those who desire *per se* rules in this area. For example, one case includes an extensive discussion of the conceptual link between the obviousness *vel non* of a chemical composition and the obviousness *vel non* of a process for making the composition.[6] Such discussion, while

---

6. *See Pleuddemann,* 910 F.2d at 827, 15 U.S.P.Q.2D at 1741 (" 'From the standpoint of patent law, a compound and all of its properties are inseparable; they are one and the same thing.' *In re Papesch,* 315 F.2d 381, 391, 50 CCPA 1084, 137 USPQ 43, 51 (1963). It is the properties of appellant's compounds as bonding/priming agents for certain polymers and fillers or support surfaces that give them their utility. As stated above, the compounds and their use

entirely accurate, may have contributed to the erroneous view that one may determine the obviousness of a chemical process merely by determining whether it is a process for making a composition. As the cases noted above make clear, however, this is not and has never been the law of section 103. Indeed, *Durden*, the very case relied on by the examiner and the Board for a purported *per se* rule, clearly states that there are no such *per se* rules.

The use of *per se* rules, while undoubtedly less laborious than a searching comparison of the claimed invention—including all its limitations—with the teachings of the prior art, flouts section 103 and the fundamental case law applying it. *Per se* rules that eliminate the need for fact-specific analysis of claims and prior art may be administratively convenient for PTO examiners and the Board. Indeed, they have been sanctioned by the Board as well. But reliance on *per se* rules of obviousness is legally incorrect and must cease. Any such administrative convenience is simply inconsistent with section 103, which, according to *Graham* and its progeny, entitles an applicant to issuance of an otherwise proper patent unless the PTO establishes that the invention as claimed in the application is obvious over cited prior art, based on the specific comparison of that prior art with claim limitations. We once again hold today that our precedents do not establish any *per se* rules of obviousness, just as those precedents themselves expressly declined to create such rules. Any conflicts as may be perceived to exist derive from an impermissible effort to extract *per se* rules from decisions that disavow precisely such extraction.

In sum, as we clearly indicated in *In re Dillon*, a recent *in banc* decision, "[w]hen any applicant properly presents and argues suitable method claims, they should be examined in light of all ... relevant factors, free from any presumed controlling effect of *Durden*" or any other precedent. 919 F.2d 688, 695, 16 U.S.P.Q.2D 1897, 1903 (Fed.Cir.1990) (*in banc*), *cert. denied*, 500 U.S. 904, 111 S.Ct. 1682, 114 L.Ed.2d 77 (1991). Having compared Ochiai's claims, limited as they are to the use of a particular nonobvious starting material for making a particular nonobvious end product, to the prior art of record, we reverse the rejection of claims 6 through 10 as an incorrect conclusion reached by incorrect methodology.

NOTES

1. *Claiming Products, Processes, and So Forth.* We know from our discussion in Chapter Two that an applicant may claim a product (or apparatus) or process (or method). For example, an applicant may claim a composition of matter X comprising elements A, B, and C. He may also claim a method of using X and a method of making X. The nonobviousness standard must be applied to each of these claims.

---

are but different aspects of, or ways of looking at, the same invention and consequently that invention is capable of being claimed both as new compounds or as a new method or process of bonding/priming. On the other hand, a process or method of making the compounds is a quite different thing; they may have been made by a process which was new or old, obvious or nonobvious. In this respect, therefore, there is a real difference between a process of making and a process of using and the cases dealing with one involve different problems from the cases dealing with the other").

2.   *The Path to Durden.*

a.   *The Early Cases.* A good place to begin our journey is with *In re Larsen*, 292 F.2d 531 (CCPA 1961). The issue in *Larsen* was "whether a process for making a patentable compound is, *ipso facto*, a patentable process." *Id.* at 532. The applicant claimed several novel/nonobvious organic compounds (esters of benzoic acids) and a process of preparing them. The claims to the compounds were allowed; but the PTO rejected the process claims under § 103. The CCPA affirmed the PTO and was of the opinion that the "inventive concept is that of the compounds themselves." *Id.* at 533. Indeed, applicant conceded that "if the products made by his process were not novel and patentable, the process might not be patentable." *Id.* at 532. Once the compounds were invented, according to the court, the process by which they are made became obvious. *Id. See also, In re Neugebauer*, 330 F.2d 353 (CCPA 1964); *In re Kanter*, 399 F.2d 249 (CCPA 1968). Judge Smith dissented. He viewed the

> process and product claims as but different ways of claiming the disclosed invention. At the time this invention was made, the prior art did not disclose either the claimed product or the claimed process for making that product.... The prior art, "at the time the invention was made," must, in my opinion, exclude applicant's new compounds. It is only as the prior art is viewed *after* applicant's invention of the new compounds that the process claimed has been found by the majority ... to be obvious to a person of ordinary skill in the art.

Id. at 536 (emphasis in original).

The next major case was *In re Albertson*, 332 F.2d 379 (CCPA 1964). The process claim pertained to the use of a novel/nonobvious claimed organic compound to produce a novel/nonobvious claimed organic compound. Thus, the starting material and end product were both novel and nonobvious. The process, however, was similar to a conventional reaction present in the prior art. Applicant argued that its claimed process was distinguishable from the claimed process in *Larsen* in that applicant's process employed a novel/nonobvious starting material and produced a novel/nonobvious starting material. According to the applicant, "the specific reactants in a process 'are a vital, significant part of any process,' and therefore the 'use of an unobvious starting material renders a process unobvious.'" *Id.* at 381. The court was not persuaded:

> The fact that starting materials and the final product are the subject matter of allowed claims does not necessarily indicate that the process employed is patentable.... We do not agree with appellant's proposition that the "use of an unobvious starting material renders a process unobvious." Were this true, every step, for example, dissolving or heating, when performed on a new compound would result in a patentable process.

Id. at 382. Judge Smith once again dissented.

b.   *Methods of Using v. Methods of Making.* The process claim issue resurfaced in 1973 in the case of *In re Kuehl*, 475 F.2d 658 (CCPA 1973). The claimed invention in *Kuehl* had three aspects: (1) a composition of matter called ZK–22, which was a solid crystalline aluminosilicate zeolite catalyst; (2) a method of making ZK–22; and (3) method of using ZK–22 to crack hydrocarbons. The examiner allowed the claims directed to (1) and (2), but rejected the claims pertaining to (3) as obvious. The prior art disclosed a method of cracking hydrocarbons using known crystalline aluminosilicate zeolite catalysts with properties not unlike ZK–22.

The CCPA reversed. Initially, the court rejected, as too broadly stated, applicant's assertion that "the allowance of the composition of matter claims here *necessarily* entitles him to claims in the same application directed to the method of using the" composition of matter. *Id.* at 661 (emphasis in original). The court then focused on the meaning of the term "prior art," and concluded that the examiner "incorrectly" used applicant's claim composition of matter (*i.e.*, ZK–22) as prior art. Viewing the invention "as a whole," the court concluded that the process "includes the use of the ZK–22 zeolite and one having no knowledge thereof would not find it obvious to crack hydrocarbons using it as a catalyst." *Id.* at 663. How does the court reconcile *Kuehl* with *Larsen* and *Albertson*? Consider the following language:

> The alleged analogous circumstance is where the court or the Patent Office has found that a composition or product is new and unobvious but has refused to allow claims to the *process for making* the unobvious product. [citing *Larsen* and *Albertson*]. The solicitor maintains by this reasoning that the claims calling for a *process using* an unobvious composition ought to be treated identically with claims calling for the process of making an unobvious composition. We disagree. The test of unobviousness is a statutory test and requires comparison of the invention with the prior art in each case, whether the invention be a process for making or a process of using, or some other process.

> [T]he principle opinion in *Larsen* ... appears to have erroneously approached the § 103 obviousness question by asking whether "*given* the idea of the compound" the process for making it is obvious. To this extent, at least, *Larsen* and its progeny, *Albertson*, are inconsistent with the statutory standards of § 103.

Id. at 665–66 (emphasis in original). The court distinguished *Larsen* and *Albertson* as involving claims directed to methods of making as opposed to methods of using.

Lastly, the court cited the policy underlying its decision:

> We believe the constitutional purpose of the patent system is promoted by encouraging applicants to claim, and therefore to describe in a manner required by 35 U.S.C. § 112, all aspects of what they regard as their inventions, regardless of the number of statutory classes involved.

Id. at 666.

One year later, in *In re Mancy*, 499 F.2d 1289, 1293 (CCPA 1974), the CCPA adopted the *Kuehl* rationale:

> We think that there is significant difference between a method of making a novel product and a method of using a novel product.... [U]nder § 103 neither a novel product made by, nor a novel starting material used in, the process can be treated as prior art. In the method-of-use cases, such as *Kuehl*, the novelty of the starting material may lend unobviousness to the process. In the cases where the invention is a process for making a new product, however novel the product may be, the claimed process steps and starting material may themselves still be old and the process therefore obvious.

Do you think that the distinction is artificial? By denying patent protection on method of making claims, is the PTO and the court, contrary to their assertion, impermissibly using the claimed invention as prior art? In any event, can't a clever patent attorney draft claims that would easily circumvent this distinction?

3. *The Stage is Set for Durden.* The decision in *Durden* did much to perpetuate this distinction by holding that a claim to a method of making a compound with a starting material may or may not be obvious even though the starting material and compound itself are nonobvious. The court viewed the confusion surrounding the method of using/making distinction as "a failure to distinguish between novelty and unobviousness." According to the court, "a new process may still be obvious, even when considered" as a whole, "notwithstanding the specific starting material or resulting product, or both, is not to be found in the prior art." 763 F.2d at 1410.

4. *Retreating From Durden.* It can be argued that the retreat from *Durden* began in earnest with the *Pleuddemann* decision wherein the court distinguished between methods of using and making and refused to apply *Durden* to so-called method-of-use claims:

> It is the properties of appellant's compounds as bonding/priming agents for certain polymers and fillers or support surfaces that give them their utility. As stated above, *the compounds and their use are but different aspects of, or ways of looking at, the same invention and consequently that invention is capable of being claimed both as new compounds or as a new method or process of bonding/priming.* On the other hand, a process or method of making the compounds is a quite different thing; they may have been made by a process which was new or old, obvious or nonobvious. In this respect, therefore, there is a real difference between a process of making and a process of using and the cases dealing with one involve different problems from the cases dealing with the other. *Durden* was a case involving only the patentability of a process of making a novel insecticide and the single claim on appeal was held to be directed to obvious subject matter in view of a prior art patent disclosing a very similar process using similar reactants notwithstanding the facts that there were unobvious starting materials used and unobvious products obtained. We are not here concerned with a process of making bonding/priming agents but with the agents themselves in which the bonding/priming properties are inherent, for which reason we do not find *Durden* a controlling precedent as did the examiner and the board.

910 F.2d at 827 (emphasis added). Did Judge Rich adopt Judge Smith's reasoning in *Larsen*? We should ask again whether you find the distinction between methods of making and using convincing? Wasn't the starting material in *Durden* also novel and nonobvious? Is the court exalting form over substance with respect to how it characterizes a process claim, which in turn prompts patent practitioners to simply engage in clever claim drafting?

Yet another step back from *Durden* came with *In re Dillon.* Recall that although the *Dillon* court refused to rule on the patentability of the applicant's claims directed to a method of using the novel composition, Judge Lourie nevertheless had this to say about *Durden*:

> [W]e do not regard *Durden* as authority to reject as obvious every method claim reading on an old *type of process,* such as mixing, reacting, reducing, etc.... The materials used in a claimed process as well as the result obtained therefrom, must be considered along with the specific nature of the process, and the fact that new or old, obvious or nonobvious, materials are used or result from the process are only factors to be considered, rather than conclusive indicators of the obviousness or nonobviousness of a claimed process. When any applicant properly presents and argues suitable method claims, they should be examined in light of all these relevant factors, from any presumed controlling effect of *Durden. Durden* did not hold that all methods involving old process steps are obvious;....

919 F.2d at 695 (emphasis in original). The retreat continued with the uproar from the biotechnological community, which led to the 1995 Congressional amendment to § 103 overruling *Durden.*

The latest judicial salvo launched on *Durden* came from *In re Ochiai,* 71 F.3d 1565 (Fed.Cir.1995), and *In re Brouwer,* 77 F.3d 422 (Fed.Cir.1996). *Ochiai* was a decision, ironically, handed down shortly after the 1995 amendment to § 103. As one of us stated, *"In re Ochiai* ... virtually emasculated the *Durden* case, which was the impetus from the [1995] Act." 2 D. Chisum, Chisum on Patents § 5.04[8][b] 46 (Supp. 1997). Even though the Ochiai application used a novel/nonobvious starting material, which resulted in a novel/nonobvious final product, the Board rejected the process claim because *it was* directed to a "method of making." The Board in *Ochiai* relied on *Larsen, Albertson,* and *Durden* as support for its rejection. Consider the following language of the Board:

> We have reviewed [the relevant CCPA and Federal Circuit cases] for guidance.... When the process claimed was considered to be one of "using" a novel material, patentability of the process was linked to the patentability of the material used. However, when the process claimed was considered to be directed to a "method of making" a novel material, patentability of the process was determined based on the inventiveness of the process steps themselves. Selection of a novel starting material was not considered dispositive of patentability if, indeed, an element of the process. Linkage between product and use thereof is logical because the obviousness of a process of using a novel product must be ascertained without knowledge of the thing used and its properties. In chemical cases, a compound and its properties are inseparable. Logic dictates that one cannot use a novel material without prior knowledge of the specific material and its properties.... While linkage of the starting material selected and patentability may *seem* equally logical, this is not the case.

24 U.S.P.Q.2d 1265, 1268–70 (Bd. Pat. App. & Int'f 1992) (emphasis in original).

On appeal, the parties argued that there existed a tension in the Federal Circuit cases pertaining to method of making/using claims in the chemical and biotechnological fields. The court agreed, to a certain extent, and appeared to retreat from *Durden*:

> The process invention Ochiai recites in claim 6 specifically requires use of none other than its new, nonobvious acid as one of the starting materials. One having no knowledge of this acid could hardly find it obvious to make any cephem using this acid as an acylating agent, much less the particular cephem recited in claim 6. In other words, it would not have been obvious to those of ordinary skill in the art to choose the particular acid of claim 6 as an acylating agent for the known amine for the simple reason that the particular acid was unknown but for Ochiai's disclosure in the '429 application. As one of our predecessor courts had occasion to observe, in a case involving a highly analogous set of facts, "one cannot choose from the unknown." *Mancy,* 499 F.2d at 1293, 182 USPQ at 306.

* * *

> The Board essentially repeated the examiner's error of sidestepping the particularized inquiry required by section 103 by grounding the rejection on the supposedly "controlling" effect of "[c]ases such as *In re Larsen, In re Albertson*, and, particularly, *In re Durden*, all of which were directed to processes of making chemical compounds." *Ochiai,* 24 U.S.P.Q.2D at 1267 (citations omitted). After categorizing the process recited in claim 6 as a "process of making" rather than as a "process for using," the Board reached its conclusion according to the following syllogism: (a) "process of making" claims have led to rejections, as in *Larsen, Albertson*, and *Durden*, whereas "process for using" claims have led to allowances, as in *Kuehl, Mancy,* and *Pleuddemann;* (b) Ochiai's claim is directed to a "process of making"; (c) therefore, the rejection should be affirmed. *Id.* at 1268–70.

> This method of analysis is founded on legal error because it substitutes supposed *per se* rules for the particularized inquiry required by section 103. It necessarily produces erroneous results.

Ochiai, 71 F.3d at 1569–70. As for the apparent tension in the case law:

> We acknowledge that some generalized commentary found in these cases reviewing rejections of claims directed to chemical processes may, if viewed in isolation, have inadvertently provided encouragement to those who desire *per se* rules in this area. For example, one case includes an extensive discussion of the conceptual link between the obviousness *vel non* of a chemical composition and the obviousness *vel non* of a process for making the composition. Such discussion, while entirely accurate, may have contributed to the erroneous view that one may determine the obviousness of a chemical process merely by determining whether it is a process for making a composition. As the cases noted above make clear, however, this is not and has never been the law of section 103. Indeed, *Durden*, the very case relied on by the examiner and the Board for a purported *per se* rule, clearly states that there are no such *per se* rules.

Id. at 1572.

Lastly, the Federal Circuit, two days after *Ochiai*, was handed down decided *In re Brouwer*, 77 F.3d 422 (Fed.Cir.1996). The facts of *Brouwer* were similar to those in *Larsen* in that the claimed process (claim 8) was for making a novel/nonobvious compound (*i.e.*, sulfoalkylated resins) and the process, commonly known as a "Michael addition" reaction, was *only generically* disclosed in the prior art. The invention covered the making of these resins by a process "of reacting a crosslinked resin with an ester of an alkenesulfonic acid to make a new, nonobvious" compound (*i.e.*, sulfoalkylated resins). The Board rejected the process claim, and the Federal Circuit reversed using language reminiscent of Judge Smith's dissent in *Larsen*:

> Although the prior art references the examiner cited teach a generic chemical reaction of a compound containing an active methylene group with an ester of vinylsulforic acid, we have made clear that "the mere fact that a device or process utilizes a known scientific principle does not alone make the device or process obvious" [citations omitted]. Moreover, the mere possibility that one of the esters or the active methylene group-containing compounds disclosed in [the prior art] could be modified or replaced such that its use would lead to the specific sulfoalkylated resin recited in claim 8 does not make the process recited in claim 8 obvious "unless the prior art suggested the desirability of [such a] modification" or replacement. Without first knowing of Brouwer's claimed process steps or the composition resulting from those steps, there is simply no suggestion in the references cited by the examiner to practice the claimed process. It is therefore not *prima facie* obvious.

Id. at 425.

What is left of *Durden*? What test should be applied to other technological fields (*e.g.*, mechanical): *Durden* or *Ochiai*?

CHAPTER SIX

UTILITY

> "Practical Utility" is a shorthand way of attributing "real-world" value to claimed subject matter.
>
> —Judge Giles S. Rich[1]

INTRODUCTION

In order to be patentable, a claimed invention must be "useful." But what is the meaning of this term, which is found in our Constitution ("*useful* arts") and the patent code (35 U.S.C. § 101)? At first glance, the utility requirement in patent law appears to be somewhat superfluous. Why would anyone make or buy a useless invention? Indeed, for many years since the creation of the Federal Circuit, it was a rare occasion that lack of utility was raised as an invalidating defense in a patent litigation context. However, the courts have more recently looked to the utility requirement as a tool for helping secure a *quid pro quo* for society. The thinking goes that we require the claimed invention to be operative; in other words, the invention must function for its intended purpose. Thus, before we grant to an inventor the right to exclude others from making, using, or selling her invention, she must provide society with an invention that operates in accordance with its intended purpose or a purpose discernible by a person of ordinary skill in the art. As the noted 19th century patent law scholar, William C. Robinson stated:

> In order that an invention may be patentable it must not only be bestowed upon the public by its inventor, but when bestowed it must confer on them a benefit.... No recompense can properly be made to one from whom the community receives no consideration.[2]

But against the background of a well functioning set of disclosure requirements, especially the enablement requirement, some have wondered why an additional type of utility is needed. How would a claim that describes something that does not operate meet the enablement requirement? And if it fails the enablement requirement then why look to a separate utility requirement?

Among the cases raising serious utility challenges, so far they have been least successful in mechanical and electrical applications. These types of inventions have a certain physicality, the utility of which is manifested through the use of drawings and diagrams. In contrast, utility challenges have met with greater success when raised against chemical and biological inventions. First, it is difficult to convey the utility of a chemical composition or a pharmaceutical invention by employing drawings, diagrams, or

---

1. *Nelson v. Bowler*, 626 F.2d 853, 856 (CCPA 1980).
2. 1 WILLIAM ROBINSON, TREATISE ON THE LAW OF PATENTS 462–63 (1890).

formulae. Second, unlike mechanical and electrical inventions, which usually have a specific end result and use in mind that involves some consumer or manufacturer, chemical and pharmaceutical inventions often have a range of utilities, and often an evolving range. Some also see inventions in these areas as somehow more like building blocks than completed buildings. Some see a spectrum of utility, whose breadth is especially apparent in the case of chemical and biological inventions. At one end of the spectrum, some of these inventions may be viewed as having a general usefulness in basic research; while at the other end, some may provide specific and immediate societal utility.

Constitutional Provision—U.S. Const. Art. 1, § 8, cl. 8

Statutory Provision—35 U.S.C. § 101

A.   The Utility Doctrine in Historical Context

Brenner v. Manson
383 U.S. 519 (1966).

■ Mr. Justice Fortas delivered the opinion of the Court.

[The patent examiner and the CCPA both denied Manson's request for an interference because Manson did not satisfy the utility requirement. The CCPA reversed, stating that " 'where a claimed process produces a known product it is not necessary to show utility for the product.' " Brenner (the Commissioner of Patents) successfully petitioned the Supreme Court to grant certiorari.]

In December 1957, Howard Ringold and George Rosenkranz applied for a patent on an allegedly novel process for making certain known steroids. They claimed priority as of December 17, 1956, the date on which they had filed for a Mexican patent....

In January 1960, Manson, a chemist engaged in steroid research, filed an application to patent precisely the same process described by Ringold and Rosenkranz. He asserted that it was he who had discovered the process, and that he had done so before December 17, 1956. Accordingly, he requested that an "interference" be declared in order to try out the issue of priority between his claim and that of Ringold and Rosenkranz.

A Patent Office examiner denied Manson's application, and the denial was affirmed by the Board of Appeals within the Patent Office. The ground for rejection was the failure "to disclose any utility for" the chemical compound produced by the process. This omission was not cured, in the opinion of the Patent Office, by Manson's reference to an article in the November 1956 issue of the Journal of Organic Chemistry, 21 J.Org.Chem. 1333–1335, which revealed that steroids of a class which included the compound in question were undergoing screening for possible tumor-inhibiting effects in mice, and that a homologue[3] adjacent to Manson's

---

3. "A homologous series is a family of chemically related compounds, the composition of which varies from member to member by CH(2) (one atom of carbon and two atoms of

steroid had proven effective in that role. Said the Board of Appeals, "It is our view that the statutory requirement of usefulness of a product cannot be presumed merely because it happens to be closely related to another compound which is known to be useful."

The Court of Customs and Patent Appeals (hereinafter CCPA) reversed[.] The court held that "where a claimed process produces a known product it is not necessary to show utility for the product," so long as the product "is not alleged to be detrimental to the public interest." *Certiorari* was granted to resolve this running dispute over what constitutes "utility" in chemical process claims.

II.

Our starting point is the proposition, neither disputed nor disputable, that one may patent only that which is "useful." [U]tility has maintained a central place in all of our patent legislation, beginning with the first patent law in 1790 and culminating in the present law's provision that

> Whoever invents or discovers any new and useful process, machine, manufacture, or composition of matter, or any new and useful improvement thereof, may obtain a patent therefor, subject to the conditions and requirements of this title.

As is so often the case, however, a simple, everyday word can be pregnant with ambiguity when applied to the facts of life. That this is so is demonstrated by the present conflict between the Patent Office and the CCPA over how the test is to be applied to a chemical process which yields an already known product whose utility—other than as a possible object of scientific inquiry—has not yet been evidenced. It was not long ago that agency and court seemed of one mind on the question. In *Application of Bremner,* 182 F.2d 216, 217, the court affirmed rejection by the Patent Office of both process and product claims. It noted that "no use for the products claimed to be developed by the processes had been shown in the specification." It held that "It was never intended that a patent be granted upon a product, or a process producing a product, unless such product be useful."

The Patent Office has remained stead-fast in this view. The CCPA, however, has moved sharply away from *Bremner*. The trend began in *Application of Nelson,* 280 F.2d 172, 47 CCPA (Pat.) 1031. There, the court reversed the Patent Office's rejection of a claim on a process yielding chemical intermediates "useful to chemists doing research on steroids," despite the absence of evidence that any of the steroids thus ultimately produced were themselves "useful." The trend has accelerated, culminating in the present case where the court held it sufficient that a process produces the result intended and is not "detrimental to the public interest."

Respondent does not—at least in the first instance—rest upon the extreme proposition, advanced by the court below, that a novel chemical process is patentable so long as it yields the intended product and so long

---

hydrogen).... Chemists knowing the properties of one member of a series would in general know what to expect in adjacent members."

as the product is not itself "detrimental." Nor does he commit the outcome of his claim to the slightly more conventional proposition that any process is "useful" within the meaning of § 101 if it produces a compound whose potential usefulness is under investigation by serious scientific researchers, although he urges this position, too, as an alternative basis for affirming the decision of the CCPA. Rather, he begins with the much more orthodox argument that his process has a specific utility which would entitle him to a declaration of interference even under the Patent Office's reading of § 101. The claim is that the supporting affidavits filed pursuant to Rule 204(b), by reference to Ringold's 1956 article, reveal that an adjacent homologue of the steroid yielded by his process has been demonstrated to have tumor-inhibiting effects in mice, and that this discloses the requisite utility. We do not accept any of these theories as an adequate basis for overriding the determination of the Patent Office that the "utility" requirement has not been met.

Even on the assumption that the process would be patentable were respondent to show that the steroid produced had a tumor-inhibiting effect in mice, we would not overrule the Patent Office finding that respondent has not made such a showing. The Patent Office held that, despite the reference to the adjacent homologue, respondent's papers did not disclose a sufficient likelihood that the steroid yielded by his process would have similar tumor-inhibiting characteristics. Indeed, respondent himself recognized that the presumption that adjacent homologues have the same utility has been challenged in the steroid field because of "a greater known unpredictability of compounds in that field." In these circumstances and in this technical area, we would not overturn the finding of the Primary Examiner, affirmed by the Board of Appeals and not challenged by the CCPA.

The second and third points of respondent's argument present issues of much importance. Is a chemical process "useful" within the meaning of § 101 either (1) because it works—*i.e.*, produces the intended product? or (2) because the compound yielded belongs to a class of compounds now the subject of serious scientific investigation? These contentions present the basic problem for our adjudication. Since we find no specific assistance in the legislative materials underlying § 101, we are remitted to an analysis of the problem in light of the general intent of Congress, the purposes of the patent system, and the implications of a decision one way or the other.

In support of his plea that we attenuate the requirement of "utility," respondent relies upon Justice Story's well-known statement that a "useful" invention is one "which may be applied to a beneficial use in society, in contradistinction to an invention injurious to the morals, health, or good order of society, or frivolous and insignificant"—and upon the assertion that to do so would encourage inventors of new processes to publicize the event for the benefit of the entire scientific community, thus widening the search for uses and increasing the fund of scientific knowledge. Justice Story's language sheds little light on our subject. Narrowly read, it does no more than compel us to decide whether the invention in question is "frivolous and insignificant"—a query no easier of application than the one built into the statute. Read more broadly, so as to allow the patenting of any invention not positively harmful to society, it places such a special meaning on the word "useful" that we cannot accept it in the absence of evidence that Congress so intended. There are, after all, many things in this world which may not be considered "useful" but which, nevertheless are totally without a capacity for harm.

It is true, of course, that one of the purposes of the patent system is to encourage dissemination of information concerning discoveries and inventions. And it may be that inability to patent a process to some extent discourages disclosure and leads to greater secrecy than would otherwise be the case. The inventor of the process, or the corporate organization by which he is employed, has some incentive to keep the invention secret while uses for the product are searched out. However, in light of the highly developed art of drafting patent claims so that they disclose as little useful information as possible—while broadening the scope of the claim as widely as possible—the argument based upon the virtue of disclosure must be warily evaluated. Moreover, the pressure for secrecy is easily exaggerated, for if the inventor of a process cannot himself ascertain a "use" for that which his process yields, he has every incentive to make his invention known to those able to do so. Finally, how likely is disclosure of a patented process to spur research by others into the uses to which the product may be put? To the extent that the patentee has power to enforce his patent, there is little incentive for others to undertake a search for uses.

Whatever weight is attached to the value of encouraging disclosure and of inhibiting secrecy, we believe a more compelling consideration is that a process patent in the chemical field, which has not been developed and pointed to the degree of specific utility, creates a monopoly of knowledge which should be granted only if clearly commanded by the statute. Until the process claim has been reduced to production of a product shown to be useful, the metes and bounds of that monopoly are not capable of precise delineation. It may engross a vast, unknown, and perhaps unknowable area. Such a patent may confer power to block off whole areas of scientific development, without compensating benefit to the public. The basic *quid pro quo* contemplated by the Constitution and the Congress for granting a patent monopoly is the benefit derived by the public from an invention with substantial utility. Unless and until a process is refined and developed to this point—where specific benefit exists in currently available form—there is insufficient justification for permitting an applicant to engross what may prove to be a broad field.

These arguments for and against the patentability of a process which either has no known use or is useful only in the sense that it may be an object of scientific research would apply equally to the patenting of the product produced by the process. Respondent appears to concede that with respect to a product, as opposed to a process, Congress has struck the balance on the side of nonpatentability unless "utility" is shown. Indeed, the decisions of the CCPA are in accord with the view that a product may not be patented absent a showing of utility greater than any adduced in the present case. We find absolutely no warrant for the proposition that although Congress intended that no patent be granted on a chemical compound whose sole "utility" consists of its potential role as an object of use-testing, a different set of rules was meant to apply to the process which yielded the unpatentable product. That proposition seems to us little more than an attempt to evade the impact of the rules which concededly govern patentability of the product itself.

This is not to say that we mean to disparage the importance of contributions to the fund of scientific information short of the invention of something "useful," or that we are blind to the prospect that what now seems without "use'" may tomorrow command the grateful attention of the public. But a patent is not a hunting license. It is not a reward for the search, but compensation for its successful conclusion. "(A) patent system must be related to the world of commerce rather than to the realm of philosophy. * * * "

The judgment of the CCPA is reversed.

■ MR. JUSTICE HARLAN, concurring in part and dissenting in part.

* * *

What I find most troubling about the result reached by the Court is the impact it may have on chemical research. Chemistry is a highly interrelated field and a tangible benefit for society may be the outcome of a number of different discoveries, one discovery building upon the next. To encourage one chemist or research facility to invent and disseminate new processes and products may be vital to progress, although the product or process be without "utility" as the Court defines the term, because that discovery permits someone else to take a further but perhaps less difficult step leading to a commercially useful item. In my view, our awareness in this age of the importance of achieving and publicizing basic research should lead this Court to resolve uncertainties in its favor and uphold the respondent's position in this case.

This position is strengthened, I think, by what appears to have been the practice of the Patent Office during most of this century. While available proof is not conclusive, the commentators seem to be in agreement that until *Application of Bremner,* 182 F.2d 216, 37 CCPA (Pat.) 1032, in 1950, chemical patent applications were commonly granted although no resulting end use was stated or the statement was in extremely broad terms.[4] Taking this to be true, *Bremner* represented a deviation from established practice which the CCPA has now sought to remedy in part only to find that the Patent Office does not want to return to the beaten track. If usefulness was typically regarded as inherent during a long and prolific period of chemical research and development in this country, surely this is added reason why the Court's result should not be adopted until Congress expressly mandates it, presumably on the basis of empirical data which this Court does not possess.

---

4. See, *e.g.*, the statement of a Patent Office Examiner-in-Chief. "Until recently it was also rather common to get patents on chemical compounds in cases where no use was indicated for the claimed compounds or in which a very broad indication or suggestion as to use was included in the application. (*Bremner* and another later ruling) * * * have put an end to this practice." ...

Fully recognizing that there is ample room for disagreement on this problem when, as here, it is reviewed in the abstract, I believe the decision below should be affirmed.

NOTES

1. *Substantial Utility.* The majority in *Manson* places a great deal of emphasis on the "basic *quid pro quo* contemplated by the Constitution." For Justice Fortas, the *quid pro quo* is "derived by the public from an invention with substantial utility." The Court states that there is substantial utility "where specific benefit exists in currently available form." Until this occurs the "metes and bounds" of the claimed invention "are not capable of precise delineation." Is the Court confusing the disclosure requirements of § 112 with the utility requirement of § 101? Section 101 says nothing about precisely delineating one's invention or enabling one to use the invention. It is § 112 that requires a patent applicant to (1) "enable" one skilled in the art to practice the invention and (2) "particularly point out and distinctly claim the subject matter" of her invention. The policy behind these requirements is to facilitate full disclosure of the claimed invention and to prevent the applicant from "engross[ing] a vast, unknown, and perhaps unknowable area." For a well written explication and distinction between §§ 101 and 112, *see In re Nelson*, 280 F.2d 172, 182 (CCPA 1960).

On the other hand, "questions of whether a specification provides an enabling disclosure under § 112, ¶ 1, and whether an application satisfies the utility requirement of § 101 are closely related." *See In re Swartz*, 232 F.3d 862, 863 (Fed.Cir. 2000). According to the Federal Circuit

> To satisfy the enablement requirement of § 112, ¶ 1, a patent application must adequately disclose the claimed invention so as to enable a person skilled in the art to practice the invention at the time the application was filed without undue experimentation. The utility requirement of § 101 mandates that the invention be operable to achieve useful results. Thus, if the claims in an application fail to meet the utility requirement because the invention is inoperative, they also fail to meet the enablement requirement because a person skilled in the art cannot practice the invention.

Id. See also, Process Control Corp. v. HydReclaim Corp., 190 F.3d 1350, 1358 (Fed.Cir.1999).

2. *Promoting the Useful Arts.* By requiring that the invention "exists in currently available form," does the Court further the Constitutional goal of promoting the progress of the useful arts? In his dissent, Justice Harlan wrote: "What I find most troubling about the result reached by the Court is the impact it may have on chemical research. Chemistry is a highly interrelated field and a tangible benefit for society may be the outcome of a number of different discoveries, one discovery building upon the next." One year after *Manson*, the Court of Customs and Patent Appeals decided *In re Kirk*, 376 F.2d 936 (CCPA 1967) and *In re Joly*, 376 F.2d 906 (CCPA 1967). Both decisions relied upon and extended the reasoning in *Manson* to affirm patent office rejections based on lack of utility. However, in a lengthy and cogently written dissent, Judge Rich, in *In re Kirk*, relied on case law and chemical industry practice, when he wrote:

> I believe ... that usefulness, *to* chemists doing research on steroids, *as* intermediates to make other compounds they desire to make is sufficient [to satisfy the utility requirement]. I further believe that this is the law as to the meaning of "useful" in 35 U.S.C. § 101 as it was applied for decades and reaffirmed by the 1952 codification.... From a practical administrative standpoint, the best rule, which is what we had in substance until 1950, is that chemical compounds are per se "useful" within the meaning

of 35 U.S.C. § 101.... [Such a rule] would have the salutary effects of ... (5) increasing the incentives to produce and disclose new compounds, (6) encouraging the production and marketing of new compounds for experimental purposes which will develop new uses for them, thus advancing the art and advantaging the public.

In re Kirk, 376 F.2d at 946, 949, 957 (emphasis in original).

Furthermore, consider the following statement in *Nelson v. Bowler,* 626 F.2d 853, 856 (CCPA 1980) (Rich, J.):

> Knowledge of the pharmacological activity of any compound is obviously beneficial to the public. It is inherently faster and easier to combat illnesses and alleviate symptoms when the medical profession is armed with an arsenal of chemicals having known pharmacological activities. Since it is crucial to provide researchers with an incentive to disclose pharmacological activities in as many compounds as possible, we conclude that adequate proof of any such activity constitutes a showing of practical utility.

Given the concerns of Justice Harlan and Judge Rich, should the utility standard be dictated by industry custom? It should be noted that Judge Smith, with whom Judge Rich joined, also dissented in *Kirk* and *Joly.* Of particular interest is that Judges Rich and Smith were the only judges on the CCPA with patent law experience at the time *Kirk* and *Joly* were decided.

3. *An introduction only?* In 1979, the CCPA in *Bergy* wrote that "in 1952 Congress voiced its intent to consider the novelty of an invention under § 102 where it is first made clear what the statute means by 'new', notwithstanding that this requirement is first named in § 101." *In re Bergy,* 596 F.2d 952, 959–64 (C.C.P.A. 1979) (Rich, J.), *dismissed as moot,* 444 U.S. 1028 (1980) (companion case to *Diamond v. Chakrabarty,* 447 U.S. 303, 309–18 (1980)). Put differently, for purposes of interpreting the novelty requirement, the CCPA was in effect reading § 101 as a mere introduction to the other sections in the Patent Act that set forth the conditions for patentability, including the specifics of the novelty requirement that are set forth in § 102. If § 101 is merely an introduction to § 102 then why is it not also a mere introduction to § 112, which after all sets forth the specifics of the disclosure requirements including written description, enablement, best mode, and definiteness? See F. Scott Kieff, *The Case for Registering Patents and the Law and Economics of Present Patent–Obtaining Rules,* 45 B.C. L. Rev. 55, 106–07 (2003).

B. A MODERN APPROACH TO UTILITY

In re Brana

51 F.3d 1560 (Fed.Cir.1995).

■ Before PLAGER, LOURIE, and RADER, CIRCUIT JUDGES.

■ PLAGER, CIRCUIT JUDGE.

Background

On June 30, 1988, applicants filed [a] patent application (the '690 application) directed to 5–nitrobenzo[de]isoquinoline–1,3–dione compounds, for use as antitumor substances....

* * *

The specification states that [the] non-symmetrical substitutions produce compounds with "a better action and a better action spectrum as anti-tumor substances" than known benzo[de]isoquinolines, namely those in K.D. Paull *et al.*, Computer Assisted Structure–Activity Correlations, Drug Research, 34(II), 1243–46 (1984) (Paull). Paull describes a computer-assisted evaluation of benzo[de]isoquinoline–1,3–diones and related compounds which have been screened for anti-tumor activity by testing their efficacy *in vivo*[3] against two specific implanted murine (*i.e.*, utilizing mice as test subjects) lymphocytic leukemias, P388 and L1210.[4] These two *in vivo* tests are widely used by the National Cancer Institute (NCI) to measure the antitumor properties of a compound. Paull noted that one compound in particular [NSC 308847], was found to show excellent activity against these two specific tumor models. Based on their analysis, compound NSC 308847 was selected for further studies by NCI. In addition to comparing the effectiveness of the claimed compounds with structurally similar compounds in Paull, applicants' patent specification illustrates the cytotoxicity of the claimed compounds against human tumor cells, *in vitro, and concludes that these tests "had a good action."*

The examiner initially rejected applicants' claims in the '690 application as obvious under 35 U.S.C. § 103 in light of U.S. Patent No. 4,614,820, issued to and referred to hereafter as Zee–Cheng et al. Zee–Cheng et al. discloses a benzo[de]isoquinoline compound for use as an antitumor agenst with symmetrical substitutions on the 5–position and 8–position of the quinoline ring; in both positions the substitution was either an amino or nitro group.[7] Although not identical to the applicants' claimed compounds, the examiner noted the similar substitution pattern (*i.e.*, at the same positions on the isoquinoline ring) and concluded that a mixed substitution of the invention therefore would have been obvious in view of Zee–Cheng et al.

In a response dated July 14, 1989, the applicants rebutted the § 103 rejection. Applicants asserted that their mixed disubstituted compounds had unexpectedly better properties than the symmetrically substituted compounds in Zee–Cheng et al. In support of this assertion applicants attached the declaration of Dr. Gerhard Keilhauer. In his declaration Dr. Keilhauer reported that his tests indicated that applicants claimed compounds were far more effective as antitumor agents than the compounds

3. *In vivo* means "[I]n the living body, referring to a process occurring therein." Steadman's Medical Dictionary 798 (25th ed. 1990). *In vitro* means "[I]n an artificial environment, referring to a process or reaction occurring therein, as in a test tube or culture media." *Id.*

4. The analysis in Paull consisted of grouping the previously-tested compounds into groups based on common structural features and cross-referencing the various groups, in light of the success rates of the group as a whole, to determine specific compounds that may be effective in treating tumors.

7. The chemical compound in Zee–Cheng et al. is labeled a 3,6–disubstituted–1,8–naphthalimide and uses different numbering for the positions on the isoquinoline ring. The structure of this compound, however, is identical to that claimed by the applicants except for symmetrical substitutions at the 5–position and the 8–position of the isoquinoline ring. Zee–Cheng et al. teaches identical substitutions of amino or nitro groups while applicants claim a nitro group substitution at the 5–position and an amino group substitution at the 8–position.

disclosed in Zee–Cheng et al. when test, *in vitro*, against two specific types of human tumor cells, HEp and HCT–29. Applicants further noted that, although the differences between the compounds were slight, there was no suggestion in the art that these improved results (over Zee–Cheng et al.) would have been expected. Although the applicants overcame the § 103 rejection, the examiner nevertheless issued a final rejection, on different grounds, on September 5, 1989. . . .

In his answer to the applicants' appeal brief, the examiner stated that the final rejection was based on 35 U.S.C. § 112 ¶ 1.[9] The examiner first noted that the specification failed to describe any specific disease against which the claimed compounds were active. Furthermore, the examiner concluded that the prior art tests performed in Paull and the tests disclosed in the specification were not sufficient to establish a reasonable expectation that the claimed compounds had a practical utility (*i.e.* anti-tumor activity in humans).

In a decision dated March 19, 1993, the Board affirmed the examiner's final rejection. The three-page opinion, which lacked any additional analysis, relied entirely on the examiner's reasoning. Although noting that it also would have been proper for the examiner to reject the claims under 35 U.S.C. § 101, the Board affirmed solely on the basis of the Examiner's § 112 ¶ 1 rejection. This appeal followed.

Discussion

At issue in this case is an important question of the legal constraints on patent office examination practice and policy. The question is, with regard to pharmaceutical inventions, what must the applicant prove regarding the practical utility or usefulness of the invention for which patent protection is sought. This is not a new issue; it is one which we would have thought had been settled by case law years ago.[11] We note the Commissioner has recently addressed this question in his Examiner Guidelines for Biotech Applications, *see* 60 Fed.Reg. 97 (1995); 49 Pat.Trademark & Copyright J. (BNA) No. 1210, at 234 (Jan. 5, 1995).

The requirement that an invention have utility is found in 35 U.S.C. § 101: "Whoever invents . . . any new and *useful* . . . composition of matter . . . may obtain a patent therefor. . . ." (emphasis added). It is also implicit in § 112 ¶ 1, which reads:

> The specification shall contain a written description of the invention, and of the manner and process of making and using it, in such full, clear, concise, and exact terms as to enable any person skilled in the art to which it pertains, or with which it is most nearly connected, to make and use the same, and shall set forth the best mode contemplated by the inventor of carrying out his invention.

Obviously, if a claimed invention does not have utility, the specification cannot enable one to use it.

---

9.   The examiner's answer noted that the final rejection also could have been made under 35 U.S.C. § 101 for failure to disclose a practical utility.

11.   *See, e.g, Cross v. Iizuka,* 753 F.2d 1040 (Fed.Cir.1985); *In re Langer,* 503 F.2d 1380 (CCPA 1974); *In re Krimmel,* 292 F.2d 948 (CCPA 1961); *In re Bergel,* 292 F.2d 958 (CCPA 1961).

As noted, although the examiner and the Board both mentioned § 101, and the rejection appears to be based on the issue of whether the compounds had a practical utility, a § 101 issue, the rejection according to the Board stands on the requirements of § 112 ¶ 1. It is to that provision that we address ourselves.[12] The Board gives two reasons for the rejection; we will consider these in turn.

1.

The first basis for the Board's decision was that the applicants' specification failed to disclose a specific disease against which the claimed compounds are useful, and therefore, absent undue experimentation, one of ordinary skill in the art was precluded from using the invention. *See Hybritech Inc. v. Monoclonal Antibodies, Inc.,* 802 F.2d 1367, 1384 (Fed.Cir. 1986), *cert. denied,* 480 U.S. 947 (1987). In support, the Commissioner argues that the disclosed uses in the '944 application, namely the "treatment of diseases" and "antitumor substances," are similar to the nebulous disclosure found insufficient in *In re Kirk,* 376 F.2d 936 (CCPA 1967). This argument is not without merit.

In *Kirk* applicants claimed a new class of steroid compounds. One of the alleged utilities disclosed in the specification was that these compounds possessed "high biological activity." *Id.* at 938. The specification, however, failed to disclose which biological properties made the compounds useful. Moreover, the court found that known specific uses of similar compounds did not cure this defect since there was no disclosure in the specification that the properties of the claimed compounds were the same as those of the known similar compounds. *Id.* at 942. Furthermore, it was not alleged that one of skill in the art would have known of any specific uses, and therefore, the court concluded this alleged use was too obscure to enable one of skill in the art to use the claimed invention. *See also Kawai v. Metlesics,* 480 F.2d 880 (CCPA 1973).

Kirk would potentially be dispositive of this case were the above-mentioned language the only assertion of utility found in the '944 application. Applicants' specification, however, also states that the claimed compounds have "a better action and a better action spectrum as antitumor substances" than known compounds, specifically those analyzed in Paull. As previously noted, *see supra* note 4, Paull grouped various benzo[de]isoquinoline–1,3–diones, which had previously been tested *in vivo* for antitumor activity against two lymphocytic leukemia tumor models (P388 and L1210), into various structural classifications and analyzed the test results of the groups (*i.e.* what percent of the compounds in the particular group showed success against the tumor models). Since one of the tested compounds, NSC 308847, was found to be highly effective against these two lymphocytic leukemia tumor models, applicants' favorable comparison im-

---

12. This court's predecessor has determined that absence of utility can be the basis of a rejection under both 35 U.S.C. § 101 and § 112 ¶ 1. *In re Jolles,* 628 F.2d 1322, 1326 n. 11 (CCPA 1980); *In re Fouche,* 439 F.2d 1237, 1243 (CCPA 1971) ("[I]f such compositions are in fact useless, appellant's specification cannot have taught how to use them."). Since the Board affirmed the examiner's rejection based solely on § 112 ¶ 1, however, our review is limited only to whether the application complies with § 112 ¶ 1.

plicitly asserts that their claimed compounds are highly effective (*i.e.* useful) against lymphocytic leukemia. An alleged use against this particular type of cancer is much more specific than the vaguely intimated uses rejected by the courts in *Kirk* and *Kawai. See, e.g., Cross v. Iizuka,* 753 F.2d at 1048 (finding the disclosed practical utility for the claimed compounds—the inhibition of thromboxane synthetase in human or bovine platelet microsomes—sufficiently specific to satisfy the threshold requirement in *Kirk* and *Kawai.*)

The Commissioner contends, however, that P388 and L1210 are not diseases since the only way an animal can get sick from P388 is by a direct injection of the cell line. The Commissioner therefore concludes that applicants' reference to Paull in their specification does not provide a specific disease against which the claimed compounds can be used. We disagree.

As applicants point out, the P388 and L1210 cell lines, though technically labeled tumor models, were originally derived from lymphocytic leukemias in mice. Therefore, the P388 and L1210 cell lines do represent actual specific lymphocytic tumors; these models will produce this particular disease once implanted in mice. If applicants were required to wait until an animal naturally developed this specific tumor before testing the effectiveness of a compound against the tumor *in vivo,* as would be implied from the Commissioner's argument, there would be no effective way to test compounds *in vivo* on a large scale.

We conclude that these tumor models represent a specific disease against which the claimed compounds are alleged to be effective. Accordingly, in light of the explicit reference to Paull, applicants' specification alleges a sufficiently specific use.

2.

The second basis for the Board's rejection was that, even if the specification did allege a specific use, applicants failed to prove that the claimed compounds are useful. Citing various references, the Board found, and the Commissioner now argues, that the tests offered by the applicants to prove utility were inadequate to convince one of ordinary skill in the art that the claimed compounds are useful as antitumor agents.[16]

This court's predecessor has stated: "[A] specification disclosure which contains a teaching of the manner and process of making and using the invention in terms which correspond in scope to those used in describing and defining the subject matter sought to be patented must be taken as in compliance with the enabling requirement of the first paragraph of § 112 unless there is reason to doubt the objective truth of the statements contained therein which must be relied on for enabling support." *In re Marzocchi,* 439 F.2d 220, 223 (CCPA 1971). From this it follows that the PTO has the initial burden of challenging a presumptively correct assertion of utility in the disclosure. Only after the PTO provides evidence showing that one of ordinary skill in the art would reasonably doubt the asserted

---

16. As noted, this would appear to be a § 101 issue, rather than § 112.

utility does the burden shift to the applicant to provide rebuttal evidence sufficient to convince such a person of the invention's asserted utility.

The PTO has not met this initial burden. The references cited by the Board, Pazdur and Martin, do not question the usefulness of any compound as an antitumor agent or provide any other evidence to cause one of skill in the art to question the asserted utility of applicants' compounds. Rather, these references merely discuss the therapeutic predictive value of *in vivo* murine tests—relevant only if applicants must prove the ultimate value in humans of their asserted utility. Likewise, we do not find that the nature of applicants' invention alone would cause one of skill in the art to reasonably doubt the asserted usefulness.

The purpose of treating cancer with chemical compounds does not suggest an inherently unbelievable undertaking or involve implausible scientific principles. *In re Jolles,* 628 F.2d at 1327. Modern science has previously identified numerous successful chemotherapeutic agents. In addition, the prior art, specifically Zee Cheng *et al.,* discloses structurally similar compounds to those claimed by the applicants which have been proven *in vivo* to be effective as chemotherapeutic agents against various tumor models.

Taking these facts—the nature of the invention and the PTO's proffered evidence—into consideration we conclude that one skilled in the art would be without basis to reasonably doubt applicants' asserted utility on its face. The PTO thus has not satisfied its initial burden. Accordingly, applicants should not have been required to substantiate their presumptively correct disclosure to avoid a rejection under the first paragraph of § 112.

We do not rest our decision there, however. Even if one skilled in the art would have reasonably questioned the asserted utility, *i.e.,* even if the PTO met its initial burden thereby shifting the burden to the applicants to offer rebuttal evidence, applicants proffered sufficient evidence to convince one of skill in the art of the asserted utility. In particular, applicants provided through Dr. Kluge's declaration[19] test results showing that several compounds within the scope of the claims exhibited significant antitumor activity against the L1210 standard tumor model *in vivo.* Such evidence alone should have been sufficient to satisfy applicants' burden.

The prior art further supports the conclusion that one skilled in the art would be convinced of the applicants' asserted utility. As previously mentioned, prior art—Zee Cheng *et al.* and Paull—disclosed structurally similar compounds which were proven *in vivo* against various tumor models to be

---

19. The declaration of Michael Kluge was signed and dated June 19, 1991. This declaration listed test results (*i.e.* anti-tumor activity) of the claimed compounds, *in vivo,* against L1210 tumor cells and concluded that these compounds would likely be clinically useful as anti-cancer agents. Enablement, or utility, is determined as of the application filing date. *In re Glass,* 492 F.2d 1228, 1232, 181 USPQ 31, 34 (CCPA 1974). The Kluge declaration, though dated after applicants' filing date, can be used to substantiate any doubts as to the asserted utility since this pertains to the accuracy of a statement already in the specification. *In re Marzocchi,* 439 F.2d at 224 n. 4, 169 USPQ at 370 n. 4. It does not render an insufficient disclosure enabling, but instead goes to prove that the disclosure was in fact enabling when filed (*i.e.,* demonstrated utility).

effective as chemotherapeutic agents. Although it is true that minor changes in chemical compounds can radically alter their effects on the human body evidence of success in structurally similar compounds is relevant in determining whether one skilled in the art would believe an asserted utility.

The Commissioner counters that such *in vivo* tests in animals are only preclinical tests to determine whether a compound is suitable for processing in the second stage of testing, by which he apparently means *in vivo* testing in humans, and therefore are not reasonably predictive of the success of the claimed compounds for treating cancer in humans.[20] The Commissioner, as did the Board, confuses the requirements under the law for obtaining a patent with the requirements for obtaining government approval to market a particular drug for human consumption. *See Scott v. Finney,* 34 F.3d 1058, 1063 (Fed.Cir.1994) ("Testing for the full safety and effectiveness of a prosthetic device is more properly left to the Food and Drug Administration (FDA). Title 35 does not demand that such human testing occur within the confines of Patent and Trademark Office (PTO) proceedings.").

Our court's predecessor has determined that proof of an alleged pharmaceutical property for a compound by statistically significant tests with standard experimental animals is sufficient to establish utility. *In re Krimmel,* 292 F.2d 948, 953 (CCPA 1961). In concluding that similar *in vivo* tests were adequate proof of utility the court in *In re Krimmel* stated: "We hold as we do because it is our firm conviction that one who has taught the public that a compound exhibits some desirable pharmaceutical property in a standard experimental animal has made a significant and useful contribution to the art, even though it may eventually appear that the compound is without value in the treatment in humans." *Krimmel,* 292 F.2d at 953. Moreover, NCI apparently believes these tests are statistically significant because it has explicitly recognized both the P388 and L1210 murine tumor models as standard screening tests for determining whether new compounds may be useful as antitumor agents.

In the context of this case the Martin and Pazdur references, on which the Commissioner relies, do not convince us otherwise. Pazdur only questions the reliability of the screening tests against lung cancer; it says nothing regarding other types of tumors. Although the Martin reference does note that some laboratory oncologists are skeptical about the predictive value of in vivo murine tumor models for human therapy, Martin recognizes that these tumor models continue to contribute to an increasing human cure rate. In fact, the authors conclude that this perception (*i.e.* lack of predictive reliability) is not tenable in light of present information.

On the basis of animal studies, and controlled testing in a limited number of humans (referred to as Phase I testing), the Food and Drug Administration may authorize Phase II clinical studies. Authorization for a

---

20. We note that this discussion is relevant to the earlier discussion as well. If we were to conclude that these in vivo tests are insufficient to establish usefulness for the claimed compounds, that would bear on the issue of whether one skilled in the art would, in light of the structurally similar compounds in Paull and Zee Cheng *et. al.*, have cause to doubt applicants' asserted usefulness for the compounds.

Phase II study means that the drug may be administered to a larger number of humans, but still under strictly supervised conditions. The purpose of the Phase II study is to determine primarily the safety of the drug when administered to a larger human population, as well as its potential efficacy under different dosage regimes. *See* 21 C.F.R. § 312.21(b).

FDA approval, however, is not a prerequisite for finding a compound useful within the meaning of the patent laws. Usefulness in patent law, and in particular in the context of pharmaceutical inventions, necessarily includes the expectation of further research and development. The stage at which an invention in this field becomes useful is well before it is ready to be administered to humans. Were we to require Phase II testing in order to prove utility, the associated costs would prevent many companies from obtaining patent protection on promising new inventions, thereby eliminating an incentive to pursue, through research and development, potential cures in many crucial areas such as the treatment of cancer.

In view of all the foregoing, we conclude that applicants' disclosure complies with the requirements of 35 U.S.C. § 112 ¶ 1.

NOTES

1. *The Brana Two–Step.* The Federal Circuit in *Brana* articulated a two-step test for determining whether the utility requirement has been met. First, the PTO "has the initial burden of challenging a *presumptively* correct assertion of utility in the disclosure." Second, "[o]nly after the PTO provides evidence showing that one of ordinary skill in the art would reasonably doubt the asserted utility does the burden shift to the applicant" to prove utility. *Brana*, 51 F.3d at 1566 (emphasis added). How far does Judge Plager's "presumptively" language satisfy Judge Rich's *per se* utility proposal in *In re Kirk?* How much evidence of utility must the PTO provide to prove that a person of ordinary skill in the art has a "reasonably doubt" about the asserted utility? What must the applicant show?

In *In re Swartz*, 232 F.3d 862 (Fed.Cir.2000), the Federal Circuit held that the applicant failed to satisfy the utility requirement; and citing *Brana*, stated that

> the PTO provided several references showing that results in the area of cold fusion were irreproducible. Thus the PTO provided substantial evidence that those skilled in the art would 'reasonably doubt' the asserted utility and operability of cold fusion. The examiner found that Mr. Swartz had not submitted evidence of operability that would be sufficient to overcome reasonable doubt.

Similarly, in *Process Control Corp. v. HydReclaim Corp.*, 190 F.3d 1350, 1359 (Fed.Cir.1999), the court held that the claims were in inoperable because they required a violation of the principle of conservation of mass. And in *Newman v. Quigg*, 877 F.2d 1575 (Fed.Cir.1989), the court held that claims to a perpetual motion machine were inoperable. The court reached a similar result in *In re Ferens*, 417 F.2d 1072, 57 C.C.P.A. 733 (1969), in which the claims were directed to a cure for baldness.

In *Cross v. Iizuka*, 753 F.2d 1040, 1050 (Fed.Cir.1985), the Federal Circuit held that *in vitro* testing of a claimed invention coupled with *in vivo* testing of structurally similar compounds satisfied the utility requirement. According to the court, *in vitro* data is

[p]resumably . . . the accepted practice in the pharmaceutical industry, . . . and we note that this practice has an inherent logical persuasiveness. In vitro testing, in general, is relatively less complex, less time consuming, and less expensive than in vivo testing. Moreover, in vitro results with respect to the particular pharmacological activity are generally predictive of in vivo test results, *i.e.*, there is reasonable correlation there between. Were this not so, the testing procedures of the pharmaceutical industry would not be as they are. [We agree with the Board that] there is a reasonable correlation between the disclosed in vitro utility and an in vivo activity, and therefore a rigorous correlation is not necessary where the disclosure of the pharmacological activity is reasonable based upon the probative evidence.

The court in *Cross* seems to rely on industry practice and "pharmacological activity." How important is industry custom in determining utility? Recall the dissents of Justice Harlan in *Manson* and Judge Rich in *Kirk*.

The *Cross* court held that the utility requirement was satisfied because the *in vitro* data possessed "pharmacological activity," which in turn is "generally predictive" of *in vivo* test results. That is, utility is satisfied if there is a "reasonable correlation between the disclosed *in vitro* utility and an *in vivo* activity." Keeping *Brana* in mind, can anything which "reasonably correlates" with the asserted utility be "reasonably doubted" by the PTO? If the answer is no, can you imagine a situation where a patent applicant would have to put on rebuttal evidence under step two of *Brana*? *See also, In re Krimmel,* 292 F.2d 948 (CCPA 1961) ("[I]t is our firm conviction that one who has taught the public that a compound exhibits *some* desirable pharmaceutical property in a standard experimental animal has made a significant and useful contribution to the art, even though it may eventually appear that the compound is without value in the treatment of humans.") Are the standards set forth in *Brana* and *Krimmel* too lax? Should the applicant be required to submit evidence of utility that is "convincing" to a person of ordinary skill in the art? *See In re Buting,* 418 F.2d 540, 543 (CCPA 1969) (applying the "convincing" standard).

2. *Is Brenner v. Manson Still Good Law?* Can *Brana* and *Cross* be reconciled with *Manson*? Did the invention in *Manson* possess "pharmacological activity"? The Federal Circuit in *Cross* embraced *Manson,* stating that the "starting point for a practical utility analysis is [*Manson*]." *Cross,* 753 F.2d at 1046. *Manson* was concerned that there exist an immediate benefit to society, and therefore eschewed intermediate chemical compounds. With this concern in mind, the court in *Cross* stated that "[s]uccessful *in vitro* testing will marshal resources and direct the expenditure of effort to further *in vivo* testing of the most potent compounds, thereby providing an immediate benefit to the public." *Cross,* 753 F.2d at 105. *See also, Nelson v. Bowler,* 626 F.2d 853, 856 (CCPA 1980) ("Knowledge of the pharmacological activity of any compound is obviously beneficial to the public."). Do *Nelson* and *Cross* adopt the dissents of Justice Harlan in *Manson* and Judge Rich in *Kirk?* Recall that we mentioned in the introduction section of this chapter that the utility requirement can be viewed as covering a spectrum. It seems that there has been a shift in where the utility of the claimed invention may lie on the spectrum. Do you agree? Or do you think that the Federal Circuit is being less than faithful to *Manson?*

The NIH has argued that *Manson* remains applicable to situations where utility is asserted based on homology in an unpredictable art such as biotechnology, particularly DNA and protein technology. For example, there remains a lack of predictability between DNA/protein sequence polymorphisms and functional activity. Thus, to establish the function of a gene not only is the structure and sequence of the gene needed, but the gene itself must be expressed. In short, structural homology in biotechnology may not be enough to predict biological function. *See* NIH commentary on PTO Utility Guidelines at www.uspto.gov.

3. *Is Brana Still Good Law?* The Federal Circuit takes a relatively generous approach to 101 utility in *Brana*. But in *In re Fisher*, 421 F.3d 1365 (Fed. Cir. 2005), involving a patent owned by Monsanto that claimed "expressed sequence tags" for identifying nucleic acid sequences in maize genes, the court held the claim to be unpatentable for lack of utility and lack of enablement. Writing for the majority, Chief Judge Michel, joined by Judge Bryson, agreed with the appellant that the utility standard is not high; but applying a deferential "substantial evidence" standard of review, the court affirmed the PTO's rejection. Returning to some of the text in *Brenner*, the court in *Fisher* argued:

> The basic *quid pro quo* contemplated by the Constitution and the Congress for granting a patent monopoly is the benefit derived by the public from an invention with *substantial* utility. Unless and until a process is refined and developed to this point-where *specific benefit exists in currently available form*-there is insufficient justification for permitting an applicant to engross what may prove to be a broad field.

421 F.3d at 1371 (quoting *Brenner*, 383 U.S. at 534–35, (emphases added by *Fisher*)). Why is use by researchers not a sufficiently specific benefit? The court in *Fisher* continued by stating that the utility must be such that: " 'one skilled in the art can use a claimed discovery in a manner which provides some *immediate benefit to the public*.' " *Id*. (quoting Nelson, 626 F.2d at 856 (emphasis added by *Fisher*)). Why are researchers not members of the public? Or does this mean that unless the patent claims a technology that is available to mass market consumers it is not patentable? The dissenting opinion, by Judge Rader, pointed out that:

> These research tools are similar to a microscope; both take a researcher one step closer to identifying and understanding a previously unknown and invisible structure. Both supply information about a molecular structure. Both advance research and bring scientists closer to unlocking the secrets of the corn genome to provide better food production for the hungry world. If a microscope has § 101 utility, so too do these ESTs.

Id. at 1380 (Rader, J., dissenting). Focusing on precedent and procedure, judge Rader pointed out that:

> Rather than fault Fisher for not presenting evidence it was prevented from offering, this court should instead observe that the Board did not satisfy its burden of challenging Fisher's presumptively correct assertion that the ESTs were capable of performing those functions. See MPEP § 2107.02(IV) at 2100–40 (noting that the initial burden is on the office to establish a prima facie case as to lack of utility and to provide evidentiary support thereof); *In re Brana*, 51 F.3d 1560, 1566 (Fed.Cir.1995) (where an applicant has asserted utility in the disclosure, the Patent Office has the initial burden of challenging this presumptively correct assertion of utility).

Id. at 1381 (Rader, J., dissenting). Can you reconcile *Fisher* with *Brana*?

4. *"Reason to Doubt the Objective Truth" and the Use of the In Vitro/In Vivo Test.* The court in *Brana* states that a statement in the specification pertaining to "the manner and process of using the invention . . . must be taken as in compliance with the 'how to use' requirement of 35 U.S.C. § 112 *unless* there is a reason to doubt the objective truth of the statement." 51 F.2d at 1566. The same is true with respect to statement of utility in the specification. *See Ex parte Bhide*, 42 U.S.P.Q.2d 1441, 1447 (Bd.Pat.App. & Int'l 1996); *In re Langer*, 503 F.2d 1380, 1391 (CCPA 1974). In *Bhide*, the Board doubted the objective truth of the applicant's statements made in the specification with respect to both utility and § 112 enablement because of the "speculative" nature of applicant's evidence. The court further stated that "[w]hile *in vitro* or *in vivo* tests would not be the only possible way to overcome our basis for questioning applicants' utility, *in vitro* or *in vivo* tests certainly would provide relevant evidence." *Bhide*, 42 U.S.P.Q.2d at 1448. Compare this to the § 112 written description analysis that is conducted in cases like *Fiers* and *Eli Lilly v. Regents of California*, *supra* Chapter Three.

5. *Illegal or "Immoral" Inventions—Gambling Devices.* The unpatentability of immoral subject matter seems to have originated with Justice Story's opinion in *Bedford v. Hunt*, 3 F.Cas. 37, 37 (C.C.D.Mass.1817):

> By useful invention, in the statute, is meant such a one as may be applied to some beneficial use in society, in contradistinction to an invention, which is injurious to the morals, the health, or the good order of society.

Prior to 1977, the courts and the PTO frequently barred the patentability of gambling inventions pursuant to § 101 as immoral, despite their obvious utility. *See, e.g., Reliance Novelty Co. v. Dworzek*, 80 Fed. 902 (C.C.N.D.Cal.1897) (denial of preliminary injunction where the allegedly infringed patent pertained to a "card-playing slot machine" because the invention has no utility except for its immoral gambling purposes); *Schultze v. Holtz*, 82 Fed. 448 (N.D.Cal.1897) (patent denied for coin return device because of its application to coin operated slot machines); *Brewer v. Lichtenstein*, 278 Fed. 512 (7th Cir.1922) (patent for "punch board" held invalid because the invention had no apparent utility except as a lottery device). By the mid–1970s, however, courts had begun questioning their ability to invalidate patents on the ground that the subject matter of the invention was perceived as immoral. In 1977, in *Ex parte Murphy*, 200 U.S.P.Q. 801 (Bd.Pat.App. & Int'l 1977), the Board of Patent Appeals and Interferences upheld a patent which covered a "one arm bandit" slot machine. The Board held that "while some may consider gambling to be injurious to the public morals and the good order of society, we cannot find any basis in [§ 101] which justifies a conclusion that inventions which are useful only for gambling *ipso facto* are void of patentable utility." For a more recent pronouncement on utility and morality, *see Juicy Whip, Inc. v. Orange Bang, Inc.*, 185 F.3d 1364, 1366 (Fed.Cir.1999) ("To be sure, since Justice Story's opinion in *Lowell v. Lewis*, 15 F.Cas. 1018 (C.C.D.Mass.1817), it has been stated that inventions that are 'injurious to the well-being, good policy, or sound morals of society' are unpatentable.... [But this principle] has not been applied broadly in recent years.... As the Supreme Court put the point more generally, 'Congress never intended that the patent laws should displace the police powers of the States, meaning by that term those powers by which the health, good order, peace and general welfare of the community are promoted.' ").

Should an invention that is perceived as "immoral" be patentable? What if the patentee views the claimed invention as immoral and wishes to preclude others from using them? Remember, patent law does not give the inventor any right to use the claimed invention, but only the right to exclude others. Don't other laws already operate here? Who should make these determinations? The PTO? The courts? The legislature? What types of modern inventions, if any, do you think should be unpatentable as "immoral"? Radar detectors? Nuclear Weapons technology? Condoms? Abortion pills? *See Juicy Whip, supra*, 382 F.3d at 1368 ("Of course, Congress is free to declare particular types of inventions unpatentable for a variety of reasons, ... Cf. 42 U.S.C. § 2181(a) (exempting from patent protection inventions useful solely in connection with special nuclear material or atomic weapons.")).

6. *The PTO's Final Utility Examination Guidelines for Gene-related Inventions.* Despite numerous concerns expressed by various individuals and organizations, the

PTO, on January 5th, 2001, issued final utility examination guidelines for gene-related inventions that, while raising the utility bar, leave no doubt about the patentability of isolated and purified genes and Expressed Sequence Tags. The guidelines do not discuss the ethical or moral issues associated with patenting genes or ESTs. Contrary to the United States patent code, the European Patent Convention ("EPC") addresses the morality issue as it pertains to the patenting of all inventions. In particular, the EPC, in addition to requiring utility, novelty, and nonobviousness (what is referred to as "inventive step"), also states that "European patents shall not be granted in respect of: (a) inventions the publication or exploration of which would be contrary to the 'ordre public' or morality, provided that the exploration shall not be deemed to be so contrary merely because it is prohibited by law or regulation in some or all of the Contracting States." EPC Article 53 (1973).

The new guidelines require a patent examiner to "review the claims and the supporting written description" and states that the examiner should not issue a rejection based on lack of utility "if 'at any time during the examination, it becomes readily apparent that the claimed invention has a well-established utility,' which means that '(1) ... a person of ordinary skill in the art would immediately appreciate why the invention is useful based on the characteristics of the invention (*e.g.*, properties or applications of a product or process), and (2) the utility is specific, substantial, and credible.' The skilled artisan assesses credibility based on the disclosure and 'any other evidence of record.' If the examiner finds that 'specific and substantial utility' is lacking credibility, he must reject the application under §§ 101 and 112."

There were 23 concerns raised about the patentability of genes and ESTs that were rejected by the PTO. Here are a few of them:

1. Genes are discoveries, not inventions;

2. Genes are naturally occurring;

3. The sequence of the human genome is at the core of what it means to be human and no person should be able to own or control something so basic;

4. The patenting of genes and ESTs is contrary to indigenous law and the 13th Amendment;

5. Gene patents delay medical research and deprives others of incentives and the ability to continue exploratory research and development.

See http://www.uspto.gov/web/offices/com/sol/notices/utilexmguide.pdf to read the guidelines in their entirety. See also 60 Fed.Reg. 1092 (2001).

7. *The Biotechnology/Pharmaceutical "Catch–22."* Traditionally, biotechnology and pharmaceutical companies and research institutions have experienced a "catch–22," in that if the company only tested its claimed product *in vitro* or on animals the PTO would reject the application for lack of utility. On the other hand, if the claimed invention were tested on humans, the PTO would base its rejection on § 102(b) (*i.e.*, the invention was on-sale or in public use more than one year prior to the filing of the patent application). For example, universities and other non-profit entities frequently publish the results and methodologies pertaining to their research efforts for obvious reasons. Publishing, prestige, promotion, and the dissemination of knowledge are usually inextricably linked. However, many of the advances realized by these research facilities do not have an immediate end use or are simply irreplaceable pieces of an overall puzzle. In short, these advances do not have *Manson*-like utility. Furthermore, small or start-up companies may have difficulty attracting venture capital without some insurance in the form of a patent application or otherwise full disclosure. Does the holding in *Brana* remedy these problems?

8. *Is There a Need For a Utility Standard?* What is the harm in granting a patent on a useless invention? Who is harmed by such a patent? On one hand, if the invention is truly useless, would anyone want to practice it; and if no one would want to practice it, is the public harmed in anyway? On the other hand, if folks are lining up to practice the invention, then perhaps it really is useful after all. Thus, what is wrong with leaving the problem of utility to the market that may or may not exist after the patent issues? *See* B. Zorina Khan, *Innovations in Law and Technology, 1790–1920* IN CAMBRIDGE HISTORY OF LAW (2003) (noting that in the 19th century, "the judiciary treated the utility requirement as merely nominal, since it was the function of markets, not courts, to determine the value of patents. Infringers who tried to undermine the validity of the original patent on the grounds of utility were reminded that their very use of the item overturned any allegation of lack of utility"). Indeed, are there not some collateral benefits to the issuance of useless patents? If the lack of utility is due to lack of practical application, then they may still impart new knowledge. And if the lack of utility is absolute—perhaps because the logic is faulty, or the state of related arts is insufficiently advanced to permit utility—then at least the patent teaches others what *not* to do. Even that seems worth something.

9. *Patents and Putative Problems with "Upstream" Biomedical Research.* Professors Michael A. Heller and Rebecca Eisenberg of the University of Michigan School of Law have suggested that the privatization of intellectual property rights in biomedical research has created a "tragedy of the anticommons" in which patents on what they call "upstream" technologies unduly tax and retard production of what they call "downstream" technologies. Heller and Eisenberg write:

> . . . . Responding to a shift in U.S. government policy in the past two decades, research institutions such as the National Institutes of Health (NIH) and major universities have created technology transfer offices to patent and license their discoveries. At the same time, commercial biotechnology firms have emerged in research and development (R & D) niches somewhere between the proverbial "fundamental" research of academic laboratories and the targeted product development of pharmaceutical firms. Today, upstream research in the biomedical sciences is increasingly likely to be "private" in one or more senses of the term—supported by private funds, carried out in private a institution, or privately appropriated through patents, trade secrecy, or agreements that restrict the use of materials and data.

> * * *

> The problem we identify is distinct from the routine underuse inherent in any well-functioning patent system. By conferring monopolies in discoveries, patents necessarily increase prices and restrict use—a cost society pays to motivate invention and disclosure. The tragedy of the anticommons refers to the more complex obstacles that arise when a user needs access to multiple patented inputs to create a single useful product. Each upstream patent allows its owner to set up another tollbooth on the road to product development, adding to the cost and slowing the pace of downstream biomedical innovation.

> * * *

> *Concurrent fragments.* The anticommons model provides one way of understanding a widespread intuition that issuing patents on gene fragments makes little sense. Throughout the 1980s, patents on genes generally correspond closely to foreseeable commercial products, such as therapeutic proteins or diagnostic tests for recognized genetic diseases. Then, in 1991,

NIH pointed the way toward patenting anonymous gene fragments with its notorious patent applications and now takes a more hostile position toward patenting ESTs and raw genomic DNA sequences. Meanwhile, private firms have stepped in where NIH left off, filing patent applications on newly identified DNA sequences, including gene fragments, before identifying a corresponding gene, protein, biological function, or potential commercial product....

Although a database of gene fragments is a useful resource for discovery, defining property rights around isolated gene fragments seems at the outset unlikely to track socially useful bundles of property rights in future commercial products. Foreseeable commercial products, such as therapeutic proteins or genetic diagnostic tests, are more likely to require the use of multiple fragments. A proliferation of patents on individual fragments held by different owners seems inevitably to require costly future transactions to bundle licenses together before a firm can have an effective right to develop these products.

Michael A. Heller and Rebecca Eisenberg, *Can Patents Deter Innovation? The Anticommons in Biomedical Research*, 280 SCIENCE 698 (1998). But recent empirical scholarship has challenged the anticommons thesis. *See* John P. Walsh, Ashish Arora, and Wesley M. Cohen, *Effects of Research Tool Patents and Licensing on Biomedical Innovation*, in PATENTS IN THE KNOWLEDGE-BASED ECONOMY 285–340 (The National Academies Press 2003):

[W]e report the results of 70 interviews with personnel at biotechnology and pharmaceutical firms and universities in considering the effects of research tool patents on industrial or academic biomedical research.... [W]e consider whether biomedical innovation has suffered because of either an anticommons or restrictions on the use of upstream discoveries in subsequent research. Notwithstanding the possibility of such impediments to biomedical innovation, there is still ample reason to suggest that patenting benefits biomedical innovation, especially via its considerable impact on R & D incentives or via its role in supporting an active market for technology.... To prefigure our result, we find little evidence of routine breakdowns in negotiations over rights, although research tool patents are observed to impose a range of social costs and there is some restriction of access.

Id. at 287–89.

Also consider the following:

To what extent can advocates for policy change through court or legislative action use the labels "upstream" and "downstream" merely as synonyms for the things they buy and the things they sell, respectively? Since these are relative terms that describe a transaction between players, for everyone who sees something as upstream there is someone else who sees the same thing as downstream. If so, then it would be totally rational—if not a bit self-involved—for a party to view everything for which they would have to buy a license as "upstream" and everything for which they would like to sell a license as "downstream." There is not much room for a patent system if we as a society decide there should not be patents on things for which someone might want to buy a license. In the final analysis, the upstream/downstream debate may tell us something (but not much in a market system) about whether we should have patents at all, but not which patents we should deem "better" or "worse." Indeed, the core work on anti-commons, Michael A. Heller, *The Tragedy of the Anticommons: Property in the Transition From Marx to Markets*, 111 HARV. L. REV. 622 (1998), nicely elucidates a problem where the right to exclude cannot legally and openly be used to sell licenses. Too many rights of that type do have an anti-commons effect. But in contrast to the problem of having to trade—or even bribe—with one who cannot openly sell to you, if a patent license is what you seek then you are most likely to find that patentees are often eager, and certainly are allowed to be open, in their desire to find licensees at the right price.

F. Scott Kieff, *Property and Biotechnology*, presented October 24, 2003, to the conference "The Biotechnological Revolution: Scientific and Societal Aspects," sponsored by the Alexander von Humboldt Foundation, in Potsdam, Germany. For some further samples of the debate on the general question of patents in biotechnology—including many more issues than merely the positive law question of utility—compare the SIDE BAR below with the article excerpt that follows. Although not written in direct response to each other, these two pieces nicely capture two different views on the relationship between patents and biotechnology generally.

SIDE BAR

Patents, Upstream Research, and Biopharmaceutical Innovation

Arti K. Rai*

In recent years, patent policy debates have been dominated by the question of whether too many patents are being issued, with the possible result that patents are impeding rather than incentivizing innovation.[1] Nowhere has this concern been more salient and widely discussed than in biopharmaceutical innovation. In this arena, commentators have identified two sets of concerns. The first is that widely enabling upstream research—in other words, research that is far removed from a therapeutic end product but, rather, represents the foundation for a wide variety of follow-on research—is the subject of broad patents.[2] Although widespread use of such research would be desirable, the transaction costs associated with licensing may limit use. For example, the owner of a broad patent that can block all further research may engage in strategic behavior, demanding an unduly large share of the surplus to be gained from subsequent research. Alternatively, to the extent that the patent owner is also a product developer, it may be reluctant to license a potential competitor. A second concern is that the upstream research discoveries necessary for follow-on research are the subject of multiple patents, each of which has to be licensed.[3] In this "anticommons" or "patent thicket" scenario, transaction costs are also likely to be high.[4] Notably, the two scenarios are not mutually exclusive: because of the doctrine of blocking patents, the existence of a broad patent in a given area of research does not preclude the availability of additional patents.

Although transaction costs are of concern, there is reason to be wary of measures that diminish upstream patent protection too dramatically. Although established pharmaceutical companies that produce end products typically do not rely on such protection, this is not the case for small biotechnology firms. For these capital-poor firms, upstream patents appear to be necessary for attracting investment, either directly or through inter-firm alliances.[5] To the extent that we want small firms to remain viable (for example, because we think they are uniquely positioned to generate innovative ideas), at least some upstream patenting may be useful. Additionally, in the case of some widely enabling research tools, patents may be necessary to motivate the substantial investment necessary for reliable mass production. For example, in the case of the major DNA sequencing technology, an automated sequencer that relies on optical scanning and four-color fluorescent technology, patents on the initial prototype were necessary to incentivize the development that preceded mass dissemination[6] Such development was costly and could not be induced by the possibility of additional downstream patents.

Of the two potential difficulties—broad patents and numerous patents—broad patents pose the more acute problem. There is a well-documented history of broad upstream patents encouraging strategic behavior and delaying research in a number of important industries.[7] Narrow patents increase the bargaining power of the follow-on researcher vis a vis the original inventor, thereby decreasing the likelihood that the original inventor will be able to engage in strategic behavior.

Narrow patents can also mitigate considerably concerns over upstream patent thickets. The case of gene fragment, or expressed sequence tag ("EST"), patenting, represents an example of a situation where narrow scope played a critical role in averting transaction cost problems for follow-on researchers. When EST patent applications were first filed, they often claimed not only the fragment but also the full gene of which the fragment was a part. Commenting on these applications, the Patent and Trademark Office ("PTO") initially suggested that EST patents would exist in a blocking relationship with any subsequent patents on the full gene.[8] Under this approach, a researcher who wanted to do research on a gene might have to seek licenses from multiple holders of EST patents as well as the holder of the gene patent. In response to pressure from researchers who feared patent thickets, the PTO subsequently reversed itself. It determined that, to the extent patent applications on ESTs were granted at all, the grant would be strictly limited to the fragment. Those who wanted to do research on the full gene would therefore not have to negotiate with multiple EST patent holders.

Of course, the Federal Circuit rather than the PTO is primarily responsible for making patent law and policy.[9] To some extent, Federal Circuit case law also suggests that patents on upstream biopharmaceutical innovation should be relatively narrow. Several Federal Circuit decisions, most prominently its 1997 decision in *Regents of California v. Eli Lilly*[10] and its 2002 decision in *Enzo Biochem, Inc., v. Gen–Probe*,[11] indicate that certain types of broad claiming with respect to chemicals such as DNA sequences—specifically claiming by method of isolation or function rather than structure—is susceptible to rejection for failure to meet the Section 112 written description requirement. Although the court's strict interpretation of the written description requirement has rightly been questioned by commentators as failing to apprehend the relevant technology[12] (and perhaps also the relevant law),[13] this flawed jurisprudence may have the virtue of keeping claims on at least some research platforms narrow.

Consider, for example, the prominent patent issued to Harvard, MIT, and the Whitehead Institute that effectively claims all compounds that work by inhibiting a complex biological pathway, the NF-kB pathway, that regulates the transcription of multiple genes and has been implicated in diseases ranging from cancer and osteoporosis to atherosclerosis and rheumatoid arthritis.[14] Under Federal Circuit case law, it is unlikely that this broad patent, which describes the pathway, but does not identify the structure of any compounds that could inhibit it, would be upheld. Indeed, in the recent case of *University of Rochester v. G.D. Searle & Co., Inc.*,[15] the district court relied on the *Eli Lilly* line of cases to strike down a patent that was substantially narrower in scope. This patent claimed all compounds that could inhibit the cox–2 enzyme (which is associated with pain and inflammation) without inhibiting the cox–1 enzyme (which protects against stomach irritation). According to the *Rochester* court, it was inappropriate for the patentee to make this claim when it had not identified these compounds structurally but, rather, had only suggested an assay that might be used to identify the compounds.

As an instrument of patent policy, the Federal Circuit's case law ultimately has serious drawbacks, however.[16] As an initial matter, given the Federal Circuit's recent *Amgen v. Hoechst Marion Roussel, Inc.* decision,[17] in which the court refused to apply *Eli Lilly* and its progeny in the context of cell biology,[18] it is not clear that restrictions on claim scope in biotechnology will extend beyond the context of DNA sequence claims. In addition, the proferred reason for keeping claim scope narrow—that DNA sequences can only be claimed by structure, or perhaps more broadly, that scientific progress in the area of biotechnology is uncertain and unpredictable—does not readily allow for meaningful distinctions between upstream and downstream research. While the scope of upstream patents should be narrow, narrow scope is more problematic for downstream work. For example, suppose a patentee wanted to claim a gene sequence that coded for a particular therapeutic protein. If a patentee were allowed to claim only those gene sequences it had actually isolated, a rival could "invent around" the gene patent by making trivial base-pair changes to the patented sequence. Given that strong patent protection for therapeutics is generally necessary in order to make the FDA approval process an economically feasible undertaking, further development of the therapeutic might be stymied. Finally, because the *Eli Lilly* line of cases is based on a misapprehension of the relevant technology, it has problematic repercussions in other areas of patent doctrine. Specifically, the Federal Circuit's refusal to consider tried and true methods of isolation as sufficient to describe DNA sequence claims also plays out in its refusal to consider such methods as relevant prior art. Hence DNA sequences are considered by the Federal Circuit to be nonobvious even when the methods for isolating them are routine in the art.[19]

A more promising approach would involve some explicit recognition by the Federal Circuit that, as a matter of patent policy, determinations of claim scope can and should encompass some evaluation of the following considerations: 1) is the invention a widely enabling research tool; 2) can the tool be readily disseminated "as is," without the need for expensive development; and 3) is follow-on research using the tool likely to be incentivized through the availability of downstream patents. To the extent tool meets these criteria, the court should err on the side of narrow claim scope.

* Professor of Law, Duke University School of Law. This SIDE BAR was written specially for PRINCIPLES OF PATENT LAW.

1. See, e.g., Wesley M. Cohen and Stephen A. Merrill, Introduction, in NATIONAL RESEARCH COUNCIL, PATENTS IN THE KNOWLEDGE-BASED ECONOMY (Wesley Cohen & Stephen Merrill, eds., 2003).

2. See, e.g., Arti K. Rai, Fostering Cumulative Innovation in the Biopharmaceutical Industry: The Role of Patents and Antitrust, 16 BERKELEY TECH.L.J. 813 (2001); John Walsh, Ashish Arora and Wesley Cohen, Effects of Research Tool Patents and Licensing on Biomedical Innovation, in NATIONAL RESEARCH COUNCIL, PATENTS IN THE KNOWLEDGE-BASED ECONOMY (Wesley Cohen & Stephen Merrill, eds., 2003).

3. See Michael A. Heller and Rebecca S. Eisenberg, Can Patents Deter Innovation: The Anticommons in Biomedical Research, 280 SCIENCE 698 (1998).

4. See id.

5. F.M. Scherer, The Economics of Human Gene Patents, 77 ACADEMIC MEDICINE 1348, 1363–54 (2002).

6. See NATIONAL RESEARCH COUNCIL, INTELLECTUAL PROPERTY RIGHTS AND RESEARCH TOOLS IN MOLECULAR BIOLOGY 46–48 (1997).

7. Robert Merges and Richard Nelson, On the Complex Economics of Patent Scope, 90 COLUM.L.REV. 839 (1990).

8. See John J. Doll, The Patenting of DNA, 289 SCIENCE 689 (1998).

9. See Arti K. Rai, Engaging Facts and Policy: A Multi–Institutional Approach to Patent System Reform, 103 COLUM.L.REV. 1035, 1132–33 (2003) (noting that under the Supreme Court decision in United States v. Mead, 533 U.S. 218 (2001), the PTO's current decisionmaking procedures probably do not merit Chevron deference).

10. 119 F.3d 1559 (Fed.Cir.1997).

11. 285 F.3d 1013 (Fed.Cir.2002), vacated on rehearing by 323 F.3d 956 (Fed.Cir.2002).

12. See Janice Mueller, The Evolving Application of the Written Description Requirement to Biotechnological Inventions, 13 BERKELEY TECH.L.J. 615 (1998).

13. See Mark Janis, On Courts Herding Cats: Contending with the "Written Description" Requirement and Other Unruly Patent Disclosure Doctrines, 2 WASH.U.J.L. & POL'Y (2000).

14. Nuclear Factors Associated with Transcriptional Regulation, Patent NO. 6,410,516, issued June 25, 2002.

15. 249 F.Supp.2d 216 (W.D.N.Y. 2003).

16. Some of this discussion is based on Rai, Engaging Facts and Policy, supra note 9.

17. 314 F.3d 1313 (Fed.Cir.2003).

18. Id. at 1332.

19. See, e.g., In re Deuel, 51 F.3d 1552 (Fed.Cir.1995).

Facilitating Scientific Research: Intellectual Property Rights and the Norms of Science—A Response to Rai & Eisenberg

F. Scott Kieff.
95 NW. U. L. Rev. 691 (2001).

I. Introduction

Arti Rai's article in the Fall 1999 issue of the *Northwestern University Law Review* explores the proper use of both legal rules and prescriptive norms to shape behavior in the basic biological research community.[1] Rai's article builds upon the extensive work in this area by Rebecca Eisenberg, which first attained prominence through Eisenberg's article in the Decem-

---

1. Arti Kaur Rai, *Regulating Scientific Research: Intellectual Property Rights and the Norms of Science*, 94 Nw. U. L. Rev. 77 (1999).

ber 1987 issue of the *Yale Law Journal*.[2] Eisenberg concludes that the use of patents in the area of basic biological research may frustrate central norms of the community.[3] Rai prescribes concerted public and private action as the best tools for avoiding patents and the problems Eisenberg attributes to them.[4] This Essay responds to patent critics like Rai and Eisenberg by showing how patents are essential for promoting the central norms of the basic biological research community.

Rai begins her argument by painting a portrait of the basic biological research community before 1980 as a benchmark against which to measure the relative performance of that same community today. She analyzes the traditional prescriptive norms of the earlier community and argues that they "discouraged property rights in scientific invention and discovery."[5] Against this benchmark, she criticizes the shift in the statutory and case law around 1980 that increased availability of patents in this community.[6] According to Rai, this legal change triggered a cascade of selfish behavior among those in the community that caused a significant erosion of the community's central norms, replacing them instead with property interests.[7] Rai then provides an economic analysis to justify her argument that patents should be avoided in this community.[8] In the end, Rai recommends the creation and implementation of new laws and prescriptive norms to avoid patents and the problems they purportedly cause for the basic biological research community.[9]

* * *

II. Setting a Proper Benchmark

The norms of the basic biological research community that are the focus of arguments by patent critics like Rai and Eisenberg are termed

---

2. Rebecca S. Eisenberg, *Proprietary Rights and the Norms of Science in Biotechnology Research*, 97 YALE. L.J. 177 (1987) (exploring the potential negative impact of patent rights on scientific norms in the field of basic biological research) [hereinafter Eisenberg, *Proprietary Rights*]; *see also, e.g.*, Rebecca S. Eisenberg, *Patents and the Progress of Science: Exclusive Rights and Experimental Use*, 56 U. CHI. L. REV. 1017 (1989) [hereinafter Eisenberg, *Progress of Science*] (exploring an experimental use exemption from patent infringement as a device for alleviating potential negative impact of patent rights on scientific norms in the field of basic biological research); Rebecca S. Eisenberg, *Public Research and Private Development: Patents and Technology Transfer in Government–Sponsored Research*, 82 VA. L. REV. 1663 (1996) (offering preliminary observations about the empirical record of the use of patents in the field of basic biological research and recommending a retreat from present government policies of promoting patents in that field); Michael A. Heller & Rebecca S. Eisenberg, *Can Patents Deter Innovation? The Anticommons in Biomedical Research*, 280 SCIENCE 698 (1998) (arguing that patents can deter innovation in the field of basic biological research).

3. Eisenberg further recommends various avenues for retreating from strong patent enforcement. *See* sources cited *supra* note 2.

4. Rai, *supra* note 1, at 152.

5. *Id.* at 88.

6. *Id.* at 115.

7. *Id.*

8. *Id.* at 80.

9. *Id.* at 152.

"prescriptive norms," or "normative norms."[10] These are "socially inculcated beliefs within the research science community about how scientists *should* behave, as opposed to descriptions of how they actually *do* behave."[11] These prescriptive norms of the basic biological research community closely track the traditional prescriptive norms of basic science as they are generally explored in the works of sociologists Barnard Barber, Warren Hagstrom, and Robert Merton.[12] Eisenberg focuses on the following four interrelated prescriptive norms: universalism, communism, disinterestedness, and organized skepticism.[13] Universalism means that the veracity of claimed scientific observations should be determined by universal criteria without regard to the particular attributes of the claimant, such as reputation, institutional affiliation, or nationality.[14] Communism means that scientific advances should be a product of the community and for the benefit of the community.[15] Disinterestedness means that scientific effort should be expended for the purpose of seeking generally applicable scientific truth, rather than some personal interest.[16] Organized skepticism means that claimed scientific observations should be subject to empirical scrutiny.[17]

Rai expands the focus to include two additional prescriptive norms: independence and invention.[18] Independence means that scientists should be "free to set their own research agendas and to criticize the work of others."[19] Invention means that scientists should "make original contributions to the common stock of knowledge."[20]

This set of prescriptive norms may be an accurate accounting of the consensus goals of the basic biological research community and a proper statement of what those goals should be.[21] Nevertheless, each of these prescriptive norms is relatively abstract. Moreover, even as a set they fail to give clear guidance about the merits of specific behaviors, like seeking patents. Rai asserts that before 1980 these prescriptive norms interacted in

---

10. *Id.* at 81; *see also, e.g.*, Eisenberg, *Proprietary Rights*, *supra* note 2, at 179 n.5.

11. Eisenberg, *Proprietary Rights*, *supra* note 2, at 179 n.5.

12. *See* BERNARD BARBER, SCIENCE AND THE SOCIAL ORDER (1953); WARREN O. HAGSTROM, THE SCIENTIFIC COMMUNITY (1965); ROBERT K. MERTON, THE SOCIOLOGY OF SCIENCE (1973).

13. Eisenberg, *Proprietary Rights*, *supra* note 2, at 183 (citing MERTON, *supra* note 12, at 270–77).

14. *Id.* (citing MERTON, *supra* note 12, at 270–73).

15. *Id.* (citing MERTON, *supra* note 12, at 273–75).

16. *Id.* (citing MERTON, *supra* note 12, at 275–77).

17. *Id.* (citing MERTON, *supra* note 12, at 277).

18. Rai, *supra* note 1, at 90–94.

19. *Id.* at 91 (citing BARBER, *supra* note 12, at 89–90, 144 and HAGSTROM, *supra* note 12, at 88).

20. *Id.* at 92 (citing HAGSTROM, *supra* note 12, at 13, 23–42, 69–85). Eisenberg also discusses this norm, but she does so in a way that does not expressly identify it as a norm. Eisenberg, *Proprietary Rights*, *supra* note 2, at 183–84 (citing MERTON, *supra* note 12, at 286, 325–27).

21. For purposes of this Essay, the prescriptive norms discussed thus far are not disputed, and so for convenience are referred to collectively as the "consensus set" of prescriptive norms.

a way that "discouraged property rights in scientific invention and discovery."[22] More specifically, Rai argues that in light of the prescriptive norm of communism, scientists in this community did not seek property rights in their inventions, but were instead rewarded merely with recognition and esteem.[23] Thus, Rai essentially argues that there existed an additional, more specific, prescriptive norm directly targeted against the seeking of intellectual property, and that this additional prescriptive norm can be derived from the consensus set of more abstract prescriptive norms discussed above.

Yet, no such additional specific prescriptive norm against seeking intellectual property existed in the basic biological science community before 1980, or thereafter. Furthermore, to the extent that additional prescriptive norms about seeking patents or other forms of intellectual property can be derived from the consensus set of more abstract prescriptive norms, such a derivative prescriptive norm should not be directed against patents, as urged by Rai. A prescriptive norm in favor of patents will better promote the consensus set of more abstract prescriptive norms.

The pre–1980 basic biological research community did not have a prescriptive norm against seeking intellectual property. Rai's argument that scientists sought merely recognition and esteem rather than property ignores the ability for recognition and esteem to function as forms of property. It is well recognized that scientists generally have treated reports of a scientist's work as a form of intellectual property, serving as one type of currency in the market for scientific kudos.[24] And scientists have demonstrated countless ingenious methods for staking out, defending, and even pirating this form of intellectual property.[25] The persistence and prevalence of this form of intellectual property in the scientific community strongly suggests that its use was at least countenanced, if not encouraged, by applicable prescriptive norms.[26]

It is not even clear that the pre–1980 basic biological research community had a prescriptive norm that specifically rejected patents, as distinct from other forms of intellectual property. In arguing that the presently-observed desire for patents in the basic biological research community was sparked by a change in applicable patent law, Rai presumes that there was a lack of desire for patents before 1980.[27] But the nature and direction of the causal link between prescriptive norms and changes in law are not clear in this area. The fact that few patents were obtained during the early days

---

22. Rai, *supra* note 1, at 88.

23. *Id.* at 90 (citing MERTON, *supra* note 12, at 273 (discussing the proper behavior of a scientist)).

24. *See e.g.,* JEROME R. RAVETZ, SCIENTIFIC KNOWLEDGE AND ITS SOCIAL PROBLEMS 245 (1996). For more on the market for kudos, see *infra* notes 34–35, 68 and accompanying text.

25. *Id.* at 245–72 (reviewing the evolution of socially accepted practices for protecting this form of property in the scientific community including the present method of journal publication and citation thereto).

26. Rai herself recognizes that scientists sought recognition and esteem under the prescriptive norms of the basic biological research community. Rai, *supra* note 1, at 90.

27. According to Rai, recent changes in patent law caused changes in attitudes towards obtaining patents in basic biological research. *Id.* at 94.

in molecular biology does not necessarily mean that they were not desired. Patents may not have been sought because, as Rai correctly points out, a number of hurdles to such patents existed as a matter of positive law during this time.[28] Many federal courts, including the Supreme Court, were hostile towards patents and promulgated a variety of limits on patentability, including an enhanced utility requirement and the treatment of algorithms as excluded from patentable subject matter.[29] While positive law became more favorable to these types of patents, to the extent that the desire for patents preceded this change in the law, law can be viewed as having caught up with prescriptive norms, rather than as having spurred changes in them.

Furthermore, the breakdown in prescriptive norms that Rai attributes to patents in the post–1980 basic biological research community actually occurred well before 1980 as a result of several factors other than patents, which were largely unavailable in that community before 1980. Patents are not assigned any of the blame for the breakdown in the community of science that began long before 1980, in Jerome Ravetz's detailed account of the social problems in science after World War II.[30] Instead, Ravetz ties this breakdown to what he terms the "industrialization of science."[31] By this he means the dominance of capital-intensive research and the concomitant reliance of science on government and industry for massive sums of money to fund this research.[32] According to Ravetz, these changes brought a sudden increase in the size of the scientific community, which caused differentiation and stratification within the community.[33] This in turn caused a concentration of power to distribute kudos in small numbers of the most prestigious individuals and institutions.[34]

---

28. The term "positive law" refers to the set of currently binding statutes, judicial decisions, and administrative rules. The term "normative law" includes accepted and theoretical principles about what those binding statutes, decisions, and rules should be.

29. *See generally* Donald S. Chisum, Craig Allen Nard, Herbert F. Schwartz, Pauline Newman & F. Scott Kieff, Principles of Patent Law 729–812 (1998) (reviewing shifts in the positive law of utility and statutory subject matter). In preparation for his confirmation hearing as President Johnson's nominee to the Supreme Court, Thurgood Marshall reportedly responded to a question from a well-known Senator about his views on patents by saying: "I haven't given patents much thought, Senator, because I'm from the Second Circuit and as you know we don't uphold patents in the Second Circuit." Gerald Mossinghoff, *The Creation of the Federal Circuit in* Chisum et al., *supra*, at 29–30. Similarly, as Rai recognizes, Justice Jackson noted a "strong passion in this Court for striking down [patents,] so that the only patent that is valid is one which this Court has not been able to get its hands on." Rai, *supra* note 1, at 102 n.133 (quoting Jurgenson v. Otsby & Barton Co., 335 U.S. 560, 572 (1949) (Jackson, J., dissenting)).

30. Ravetz, *supra* note 24, at 30–68.

31. *Id.* at 30.

32. *Id.*; *see also* Marshall S. Shapo, A Nation of Guinea Pigs 7 (1979) (noting enormous growth in the number of scientists by 1979 and reporting an estimate "that about 85 percent of all the scientists who ever lived" were living at that time).

33. Ravetz, *supra* note 24, at 30.

34. *Id.* Kudos can take many forms, including publication in prestigious journals, citation by peers, general prestige, the award of research grants, academic appointments and tenure, and salary. *Id.* at 245–72 (reviewing the evolution of the forms of kudos in the scientific community).

Frustration of the prescriptive norms should not be unexpected in such a stratified community engaged in a highly competitive market for kudos.[35] Desire for recognition and prestige can function like desire for property in frustrating the prescriptive norms. By focusing so heavily on property, Rai glosses over the powerful role generally played by descriptive norms, sometimes called "regularities," which describe tendencies, habits, inclinations, proclivities, or preferences.[36] Scientists are burdened with the same basic tendencies experienced by everyone. Some of these tendencies may be seen as relatively benign, such as the desire to like and to be liked by members of our communities. Other tendencies may be seen as more pernicious, such as ego, hubris, and desire for fame. Some may be seen as more ambiguous in their net impact, such as ambition and desire for accomplishment. In the context of science, these descriptive norms are manifested in the ways that scientists treat recognition and esteem, similar to the ways others treat more tangible forms of property.

The interaction between descriptive norms and prescriptive norms is complex. In some cases descriptive norms are the very devices that operate to make humans responsive to prescriptive norms.[37] In other cases, descriptive norms are the very sources of frustration for prescriptive norms. In the hypothetical case of a more-established scientist who is prestigious and closely associated with a particular theory, consider the possible frustrations of the prescriptive norms that might be wrought in a putative utopia of no patent property.[38] The scientist may manifest various combinations of the many descriptive norms—benign, pernicious, and ambiguous. As an established and prestigious member of the academic community, this scientist is likely to sit on committees that review applications for funding, manuscripts submitted to prominent journals for publication, and the candidacies of less-established scientists for promotion. In this hypothetical case, a less-established scientist with a competing theory who is aware of the descriptive norms and who is interested in funding, publishing, and obtaining promotion may rationally experience apprehension about offending the descriptive norms of the more-established scientist. The more-established scientist might even act in accordance with pernicious descrip-

---

35. While kudos can function as a form of property, the markets for kudos differ from markets for other forms of property in important respects. Markets for kudos are especially complex, and while markets for kudos do involve transfers of money, such transfers in the kudos markets often do not involve ordinary market prices. As discussed below, markets for kudos are likely to have a greater propensity for failure than markets for other forms of property. *See infra* notes 68–69 and accompanying text.

36. *See* Robert D. Cooter, *Decentralized Law for a Complex Economy: The Structural Approach to Adjudicating the New Law Merchant*, 144 U. Pa. L. Rev. 1643, 1656–57 (1996) (contrasting use of the word norm to refer to an obligation rather than to a regularity in behavior).

37. For example, an individual's desire to be liked by the community may motivate individuals to behave in accordance with the prescriptive norms of the community. *See* Robert C. Ellickson, *Law and Economics Discovers Social Norms*, 27 J. Legal Stud. 537 (1998) (arguing that founders of classical law and economics implicitly placed too much stress on an individual's hunger for material, as opposed to status, rewards).

38. This hypothetical case is also useful for fully evaluating the relative performance of a state of the world in which patents are available in the basic biological research community and one in which they are not. *See infra* note 65 and accompanying text.

tive norms in a way that directly influences the less-established scientist's research agenda.

A resulting change in the research agenda of the less-established scientist could offend each of the prescriptive norms. For instance, such a change could offend the norm of independence—the less-established scientist's research agenda would have been influenced by something other than desire for scientific truth. Likewise, the norm of organized skepticism also would be offended if research into a competing theory were foregone. If the change in the less-established scientist's agenda embraced the more-established scientist's theory, and that theory happened to be wrong, then the norm of universalism would be offended because the less-established scientist would have subscribed to a theory precisely because of its proponent's personal attributes rather than its scientific truth. The disinterestedness norm would be offended because the less-established scientist would have selected a research agenda that would benefit the less-established scientist's career instead of the public storehouse of scientific knowledge. Further, the communism norm would be offended if limited resources were directed in a way that would benefit the two scientists rather than the public storehouse of scientific knowledge. Finally, the invention norm would be offended because the public storehouse of scientific knowledge would not have been enhanced.

Thus, the portrait painted by Rai of the early days of the basic biological research community is not the appropriate benchmark against which to measure the performance of the current patent system. The benchmark offered by Rai is a utopian vision characterized by specific prescriptive norms against intellectual property generally and patents in particular, but devoid of descriptive norms such as selfish behavior, which enjoys no frustration of the consensus set of abstract prescriptive norms.

This utopia, however, never existed. Contrary to Rai's assertion, it is not clear that the pre–1980 basic biological research community had a prescriptive norm specifically discouraging patents. In fact, the community did have a prescriptive norm that at least permitted, if not encouraged, seeking other forms of intellectual property, such as scientific kudos. Furthermore, descriptive norms such as selfish behavior have been, and remain, a significant presence in the real biological research community made up of real humans engaged in the highly competitive market for kudos. Descriptive norms have frustrated the prescriptive norms of the basic biological research community since long before the general availability of patents in that community.

Indeed, it is not clear that any historical benchmark would be a proper basis for comparison against the present basic biological research community because the community has enjoyed such rapid and enormous advances in technology and overall prosperity, even since 1980.[39] Rather, a proper

---

39. *See generally* OFFICE OF TECHNOLOGY ASSESSMENT, BIOTECHNOLOGY IN A GLOBAL ECONOMY 1–33 (U.S. Government Printing Office, OTA–BA–495, Washington, DC, 1991) [hereinafter BIOTECH-NOLOGY IN A GLOBAL ECONOMY] (reviewing changes in biotechnology, defined to be only the "new biotechnology," which refers to the recombinant DNA, cell fusion, and bioprocessing techniques that did not come into regular use until around 1980, or thereafter); *see also infra* notes 54–59 and accompanying text.

evaluation of the impact patents have had on the basic biological research community requires a comparison of the present state of the world, where patents are available, with the realistic alternative state, which differs solely in that patents are not available.[40] The operative questions explored below are whether the potential breakdown in prescriptive norms would be greater in one of these states of the world, and if so, in which one.

III. Making a Proper Comparison

To compare properly the present state of the world where patents exist to the alternative state where patents do not exist, it is first necessary to understand the theory, design, and operation of the patent system. The focus of Rai's argument is a purported shift in patent theory from one that views patents as providing incentives for engaging in inventive activity to one that views patents as providing incentives for engaging in subsequent commercialization.[41] There was no such shift. The changes in positive patent law discussed by Rai marked important components of a larger effort to help positive law catch up with normative theory and to bring the patent system more in line with its design.

As I explain at length in a separate paper, the key to understanding the intended operation of the patent system is to consider a normative theory that views patents as providing incentives for commercialization.[42] According to the commercialization theory, the treatment of patents as property rights enforceable by property rules—as distinct from liability rules[43]—is necessary to facilitate investment and coordination around the complex, costly, and risky commercialization activities required to turn nascent inventions into new goods and services.[44] Thus, the power to *restrict use* that is conferred by a patentee's property right is paradoxically essential to *avoiding underuse*. Not only are property rights of exclusion

---

40. For a proper comparison, the set of prescriptive norms discussed by critics of the patent system is assumed to be a constant, shared by both states of the world. The set of descriptive norms discussed above is also assumed to be a constant, shared by both states of the world. The relevant inquiry, then, is not whether a patent system has problems, but rather how it compares to other available alternative institutions. *See* Harold Demsetz, *Information and Efficiency: Another Viewpoint*, 12 J.L. & Econ. 1, 14 (1969) (critiquing the so-called nirvana approach to institution analysis in favor of a comparative institution approach).

41. Rai, *supra* note 1, at 96–97.

42. F. Scott Kieff, *Property Rights and Property Rules for Commercializing Inventions*, 85 Minn. L. Rev. 697.

43. An entitlement enjoys the protection of a property rule if the law condones its surrender only through voluntary exchange. The holder of such an entitlement is allowed to enjoin infringement. An entitlement has the lesser protection of a liability rule if it can be lost lawfully to anyone willing to pay some court-determined compensation. The holder of such an entitlement is only entitled to damages caused by infringement. *See* Guido Calabresi & A. Douglas Melamed, *Property Rules, Liability Rules, and Inalienability: One View of the Cathedral*, 85 Harv. L. Rev. 1089 (1972); *see also* Jules L. Coleman & Jody Kraus, *Rethinking the Theory of Legal Rights*, 95 Yale. L.J. 1335 (1986).

44. *See* Kieff, *supra* note 42, at 707–12 (showing how a patent right to exclude those who have not shared in the commercialization costs provides incentives for the patentee and other players in the complex process of technological progress to come together and incur such commercialization costs, thereby facilitating the social ordering and bargaining around inventions that are necessary to generate output in the form of information about the invention, a product of the invention, or a useful embodiment of the invention).

advantageous, they must also be enforced by a property rule, not a liability rule. The use of liability rules would lead to a net increase in social cost and frustrate the very efforts for ordering and bargaining around patents that are necessary to generate output of patented inventions.[45] Furthermore, the ability to use price discrimination gives the patentee a strong financial incentive to maintain output at competitive levels thereby avoiding the dead-weight loss potentially caused by a property owner's power over price.[46]

The commercialization view also shows how the changes in positive patent law discussed by Rai are improvements. For example, patents should be available for subject matter such as living organisms, gene fragments, computer software, and financial services, which many like Rai previously considered to be ineligible for patent protection.[47] Protection is necessary to permit recovery of commercialization costs in markets such as these precisely because they are characterized by a particularly large difference between average cost and marginal cost.[48] Indeed, the need for protection is especially strong in such markets because commercialization costs represent a significant component of average cost.[49] Furthermore, the categories of patents in the field of basic biological research that Rai considers to be pernicious simply cannot, under applicable law, have the very broad impact she ascribes to them. For example, Rai raises the problem of patents on multiple gene fragments, such as ESTs, blocking the use of a larger DNA sequence of which they can be a part.[50] As the law currently stands, a patent claim directed to a gene fragment like an EST cannot be construed to cover a larger DNA sequence, such as a substantial portion of an entire gene.[51]

---

45. *Id.* at 732–36 (showing how the potential infringements induced by a liability rule will discourage investment in the commercialization process ex ante and may even result in a net destruction of social wealth if the collective costs of entry and exit across infringers exceeds the social surplus otherwise created by the invention).

46. *Id.* at 727–732 (showing how the patent system's facilitation of tie-ins and other forms of price discrimination where technological and economic factors alone might prevent price discrimination provides incentives for the patentee to elect to keep output at competitive levels).

47. *Id.* at 701 n.9 (collecting sources of criticism of present patentable subject matter); *see also* Rai, *supra* note 1, at 100–09 (criticizing the change in positive patent law regarding patentable subject matter).

48. Kieff, *supra* note 42, at 724–26, 747–48. Average cost per unit of output includes both a pro rata share of total fixed costs, like the costs of building a factory, and marginal costs, which are the incremental costs of inputs like raw materials and labor that are needed to make each unit of output.

49. *Id.*

50. *See* Rai, *supra* note 1, at 126–29 (citing Heller & Eisenberg, *supra* note 2). ESTs are only small fragments of full-length genes. They are not usually useful in making the product that is encoded by the gene and instead are often used as tags, or markers, to identify whether a particular gene is present. Typically, the full-length gene, or a substantial portion of it, is needed to make the product encoded by that gene. For most pieces of DNA, their biological significance is due mostly to the product they encode.

51. *See* Kieff, *supra* note 42, at 721–22 (noting that if the patentee attempts to argue that the claim to the smaller fragment covers the fragment within the environment of the larger DNA, then the claim is likely to be held invalid over the prior art or for lack of adequate disclosure because to be valid, the claimed subject matter must be new and nonobvious, and

In addition, according to the commercialization view of patents, these changes bring the present patent system in line with design. Although the commercialization view of the patent system had not been previously articulated, collective writings of those involved in framing our current patent system demonstrate that the commercialization theory's link among patents, property rights, and price discrimination informed and motivated their efforts to frame the system.[52]

The actual operation of the patent system presents an even greater obstacle for patent critics. Regardless of normative theory, the very real beneficial impact of patents in the basic biological research community evidences the enormous expansion of the entire biotechnology industry that has occurred since the 1980 changes in positive patent law discussed by Rai. The unique growth in the biotechnology industry in the United States has directly benefited both the basic biological research community, by providing expanded resources like funding; and the general public, by providing better goods and services in important industries like health-care.[53]

Critics of the use of patents in the basic biological research community must acknowledge the immense amounts, and diversity in sources, of funding and other resources that patents have brought to this community. A decade after the 1980 changes in positive patent law discussed by Rai, the United States continued to make the largest commitment to basic research in biological sciences worldwide.[54] And by 1990, the single largest source of funding for research and development in this field in the United States was private industry, not the federal government.[55] According to a recent collection of studies by the National Research Council, the unique growth of biotechnology in the United States, as compared with other countries, is due largely to the link between industry and academic science that was facilitated by the same intellectual property laws that Rai discusses, which were implemented since 1980 in the United States but not in other countries.[56] The study also credits these unique features of United States patent law for allowing the United States to make better comparative use

the patent application must disclose the metes and bounds of the claimed subject matter with physical and chemical detail as well as how to make and use it; and alternatively pointing out that since ESTs exist in nature in the company of the other DNA of the genome, a typical EST claim must be limited in order to overcome this prior art to a version of the EST in some specific environment other than its natural one, such as isolated from all other DNA or inserted into an artificially engineered piece of DNA, and the details of the degree of isolation or of the engineered piece of DNA must also be provided so as to satisfy the disclosure requirements).

52. *Id.* at 736–46 (reviewing writings of the framers of the present patent system and showing the importance of the commercialization view of patents to the design of the system).

53. *See* Ian Cockburn et al., *Pharmaceuticals and Biotechnology, in* U.S. INDUSTRY IN 2000 STUDIES IN COMPETITIVE PERFORMANCE 389–92 (David C. Mowery ed., 1999) (reviewing relative performance of the United States biotechnology industry).

54. *See* BIOTECHNOLOGY IN A GLOBAL ECONOMY, *supra* note 39, at 163.

55. *Id.* at 164 (noting that despite growth in Federal Government funding for research and development since 1980, only since 1980 has industry spent more than the Federal Government on research and development).

56. *See* Cockburn, *supra* note 53, at 390–92.

of biotechnology as a research tool.[57] Not surprisingly, many researchers and industrialists regard patent protection as the most important factor in preserving the United States's competitiveness in biotechnology.[58] According to Dr. William Raub, then of the National Institutes of Health, "many biological scientists, perhaps most, regard the patent process as a means of institutionalized secrecy, whereas it is in fact a time-tested way to assure broad and ready access to proprietary information."[59]

Despite the unmatched growth of United States biotechnology industry and research since 1980, Rai criticizes any theory of the patent system that focuses on the development of nascent inventions, like the commercialization theory.[60] Patent critics like Rai and Eisenberg argue that the patent right to exclude actually interferes with commercialization in the field of basic biological research and thereby frustrates the prescriptive norms.[61] The patent right to exclude may allow a patentee of a basic research tool— like a particular cell line or DNA construct—to exert control over others interested in using those tools to conduct subsequent research. According to patent critics, the patent holder may elect to exercise such control in a way that will reduce total creative output "by refusing to license those who have different theoretical perspectives, or more generally, those who present a professional threat."[62] Rai correctly points out that in such situations the potential social benefits of licensing are high but would not be realized through a voluntary license agreement because they would inure to the benefit of the would-be licensee and society, but to the detriment of the would-be licensor.[63]

Such a refusal to license would offend the consensus set of prescriptive norms. The independence norm would be offended because the would-be licensee's research agenda would have been influenced by something other than the desire for scientific truth. Similarly, the norm of organized skepticism would be offended because research into a competing theory would have been foregone. The universalism norm would be offended because the would-be licensee's theory would have been abandoned not because of scientific merit, but rather because of the attributes of the would-be licensor. The norm of disinterestedness would be offended because the would-be licensee's theory would have been abandoned not for the benefit of public storehouse of scientific knowledge, but rather for the

---

57. *Id.* at 392–95.

58. *See Europe Lags Behind in Biotech Commercialization?*, BIOTECH. BUS. NEWS, Jan. 17, 1992; *see also* Reid Adler, *Genome Research: Fulfilling the Public's Expectations for Knowledge and Commercialization*, 257 SCIENCE 908, 909 (1992) (noting that the United States biotechnology industry is critically dependent on patent protection to maintain its leadership in world markets).

59. *Commercialization of Academic Biomedical Research: Hearings Before the Subcomm. on Investigations and Oversight and the Subcomm. on Science, Research and Technology of the House Comm. on Science and Technology*, 97th Cong. 79 (1981) (testimony of Dr. William Raub).

60. Rai, *supra* note 1, at 120–29.

61. *Id.*; *see also, e.g.*, Eisenberg, *Progress of Science*, *supra* note 2.

62. Rai, *supra* note 1, at 124 (citing Eisenberg, *Progress of Science*, *supra* note 2, at 1057–61).

63. *Id.*

benefit of the would-be licensor's career. The norm of communism would be offended because failure to license would prevent society from realizing a potential benefit so as to prevent the would-be licensor from suffering a detriment. The invention norm would be offended because the would-be licensee's efforts would not come to fruition and enhance the public storehouse of scientific knowledge.

But such an account of this potentially bad outcome is not complete. The descriptive norms suggest that a patentee might be motivated to suppress subsequent work in order to avoid criticism or discredit. Alternatively, the descriptive norms also suggest that a patentee might respond to the prescriptive norm of organized skepticism and thereby be selfishly motivated to encourage subsequent work in the hope of obtaining peer confirmation and acceptance of the patentee's work and theories. The patentee may be motivated to have even large numbers of subsequent users by a desire for fame, which in academic circles may come in the form of a high number of citations to the scientist's publications describing the subject matter of the patent.[64] The relative strengths of these competing motivations are unclear, but by failing to address one entire set, the patent critics fail to offer any reason why their net impact is expected to be negative.

Furthermore, the patent critics' evaluation of this potentially bad outcome fails to compare the patent regime with the alternative regime of no patent availability in view of the same motivations for suppression of subsequent work. Consider again the case discussed earlier of a prestigious, more-established scientist who is closely associated with a particular theory, and a less-established scientist with a competing theory, who is interested in funding, publishing, and promotion.[65] The more-established scientist may be motivated to suppress subsequent work by the less-established scientist just like the patentee in Rai's example may be motivated to suppress.[66] The availability of patent protection may provide the less-established scientist with sources of funding and promotion alternative to those guarded by the more-established scientist. With a patent obtained on some product or method tied to the competing theory, the less-established scientist can turn to the capital and industrial markets for funding or employment. It may be socially desirable for the less-established scientist's theory to be evaluated by those best able to do so. But while the capital and industrial market participants, themselves, may have less expertise in evaluating technical issues than the more-established scientist, they may be able to cover for this deficiency by hiring technical consultants. Furthermore, the market participants are less likely than the more established scientist to have cognitive and emotional biases in evaluating issues in the scientist's own technical field. Patents can therefore be necessary to allow the less-established scientist to further the consensus set of prescriptive norms.

---

64. Citation analysis as a measure of kudos is not limited to science. Indeed, it is a topic of great interest to communities in other disciplines, including law. *See, e.g.,* Symposium, *Trends in Legal Citations and Scholarship*, 71 CHI.-KENT L. REV. 743 (1996).

65. *See supra* note 38 and accompanying text.

66. Rai's example is discussed *supra* at note 62 and accompanying text.

Rai suggests that negotiations between a would-be licensee and a would-be licensor are likely to face valuation problems.[67] Especially for patents in basic biological research, objective indications of value may be hard to find because full commercial markets may not yet have blossomed, and the patent holder might exhibit a cognitive bias towards overvaluation if the original inventor has not yet sold the patent. Valuation problems of this type can plague negotiations in any market. But, again, Rai fails to compare the potential for these problems to operate in the market characterized by patents on the one hand and the market characterized by kudos for scientific achievement on the other hand. Important differences between the two markets suggest that these problems will actually be worse in the market for scientific kudos. Kudos are not fungible, and the number of potential valuators in the kudos market is relatively small.[68] In contrast, scientists are given unfettered access to the entire worldwide financial community through the patent market, and, as discussed above, this ability for patents to bring immense amounts of, and diversity in sources of, funding and other resources to the basic biological research community is recognized as a critical factor in the great success the community has enjoyed since 1980.[69]

Rai also advances the argument articulated by Eisenberg and Michael Heller that even if patentees are willing to license, the transaction costs of licensing patents in basic biological research will unduly tax and retard subsequent research.[70] But the basic biology research process, like any process, can be viewed as one that requires inputs and generates outputs, and experience shows that patents on inputs generally do not prevent the production of outputs.[71]

Thus, a comparison between the state of the world in which patents are available for basic biological research and one in which they are not suggests that the patent state of the world better promotes the consensus set of prescriptive norms. Just as the descriptive norms suggest that a patentee may be motivated to suppress subsequent work in order to avoid criticism or discredit, they also suggest that a patentee may be selfishly motivated to encourage subsequent work in the hope of obtaining peer confirmation and acceptance of the patentee's work and theories. In addition, the availability of patent protection for those who want to do subsequent work may alleviate harm otherwise caused by those who might

---

67. Rai, *supra* note 1, at 126.

68. *See* RAVETZ, *supra* note 24, at 30 (describing the market for scientific credit as one in which power to give desired credit is concentrated in small numbers of the most prestigious individuals and institutions).

69. *See supra* notes 53–59 and accompanying text.

70. Rai, *supra* note 1, at 126–29 (citing Heller & Eisenberg, *supra* note 2).

71. *See* Kieff, *supra* note 42, at 720–21 (noting that entire industries have come and gone using scores of patented inputs and that even in the specific case of the basic biological research community, scientists routinely use a variety of patented machines, reagents, and equipment in the ordinary course of research; and pointing out that this argument also goes too far and would require that members of the basic biological research community should not have to pay the licensing fee for too many other patented inputs, including, for example, the intermittent windshield wiper subsystems on the cars they drive to the laboratory in the morning).

withhold kudos in an attempt to suppress subsequent work. While all markets experience some extent of market failures and transaction costs, the relatively large number of participants and the fungibility that are characteristic of a patent market suggest that it is likely to function better than the corresponding market for kudos, which is significantly smaller and more subjective. The ability for patents to bring immense amounts of, and diversity in, sources of funding and other resources to the basic biological research community is recognized as a critical factor in the great success the community has enjoyed since 1980. In view of the superiority in promoting the consensus set of abstract prescriptive norms that is enjoyed by a state of the world in which patents are available as compared to one in which they are not, the basic biological research community would be better off with a specific prescriptive norm in favor of obtaining patents.

IV.   Conclusion

Rai and Eisenberg make important contributions by elucidating several problems that can potentially arise from patents in the field of basic biological research. But as shown above, many such problems would be paradoxically worse for that community if patents were not available at all. Patents increase community output simply by increasing input. Patents also increase community output by improving efficiency. Patents overcome the frustration of the community's prescriptive norms that would otherwise be caused by selfish behavior in a market for only scientific kudos.

While public coercion against obtaining patents in the form of new laws or prescriptive norms would prevent both beneficial effects of patents, many of the problems that Rai and Eisenberg associate with patents may be avoided through selfish private action. Rai, herself, points out that universities such as MIT have developed patent acquisition and technology transfer practices that tend to maintain the tightest private control over the inventions that can be most efficiently utilized from a societal point of view if subject to a single rights-holder.[72] This behavior is in the commercial self-interest of the universities because obtaining and enforcing patents in this area is an extremely expensive and risky investment. Rai's own account thereby shows the emergence of a new descriptive norm among individual actors in the community that avoids frustration of the consensus set of abstract prescriptive norms without public action to create and enforce a new, more specific prescriptive norm.

This result should not be surprising. Consider the ordinary practice among owners of prime real estate in the most expensive parts of Manhattan who rationally elect to license freely the public to use plazas and expanded sidewalks while simultaneously reserving uncluttered title to their land by relying on carefully placed anti-adverse possession plaques.[73]

---

72.   Rai, *supra* note 1, at 112–13 (describing practices); *id.* at 145 (noting practices to be efficient).

73.   These metal plaques implanted in the sidewalks usually state that the real estate is the property of a private landowner and that permission is granted for members of the public to make limited use of it, but that such permission is revocable at the sole discretion of the owner. The assertion of ownership combined with a grant of permission prevents anyone else from acquiring title through adverse possession or an easement by prescription. All of this is

Rather than implement new prescriptive norms or laws against patents, the community should rest assured that new descriptive norms that will emerge because individual community members acting rationally within their own self-interest will tend to maintain the tightest private control over only those inventions that can be most efficiently utilized if subject to a single rights-holder.

Certainly, this private action will be imperfect—holdouts and strategic behavior, for example, will continue—but the above discussion shows that it is better than the alternative of broad restrictions on patents publicly imposed by new laws or prescriptive norms. Recent actions by the governments of the United States and England show that even the mere suggestion of the unavailability of patents in the basic biological research community can cause a devastating reduction in the crucial sources of funding and other resources that the community enjoys from the private sector.[74] Therefore, the public should not adopt Rai's prescription for the imposition of new prescriptive norms and laws to prevent the use of patents in the basic biological research community.

---

accomplished without costly and obtrusive fences, thereby leaving the thoroughfares of a very crowded city relatively open to the flow of pedestrian traffic.

74. *See* Robert Langreth & Bob Davis, *Press Briefing Set Off Rout in Biotech*, WALL ST. J., Mar. 16, 2000, at A19 (reviewing aftermath of announcements by the President of the United States and the Prime Minister of England that stock markets understood to be signals that both countries would not allow patents on the results of the human genome project); *see also* Robert Langreth & Ralph T. King Jr., *Biotechnology, Genomics Stocks Plunge on Fear U.S. May Curb Gene–Data Sales*, WALL ST. J., Mar. 15, 2000, at A3 (reporting announcement and initial market reaction).

CHAPTER SEVEN

STATUTORY SUBJECT MATTER

> The question here, as it has always been, is: are the inventions claimed of a *kind* contemplated by Congress as possibly patentable *if* they turn out to be new, useful, and unobvious within the meaning of those terms as used in the statute.
>
> —Judge Giles Rich[1]

> [I]nventions are rarely, if ever, contrived by genuine accident: there is always a shaping imagination at work or a practical observer on hand.
>
> —Felipe Fernandez–Armesto[2]

INTRODUCTION

This chapter discusses the *kinds* of things that may be patented. Setting aside the other requirements for patentability (adequacy of disclosure, novelty, nonobviousness, and utility), to be patentable, the invention must fall within at least one of the four classes of statutory subject matter set forth in 35 U.S.C. § 101: processes, machines, manufactures, or compositions of matter. But, according to the Federal Circuit, the "question of whether a claim encompasses statutory subject matter should not focus on *which* of the four categories . . . a claim is directed to."[3] Rather, the inquiry should be on "the essential characteristics of the subject matter, in particular, its practical utility."[4]

The Supreme Court in *Diamond v. Chakrabarty* interpreted these statutory classes expansively to "include anything under the sun that is made by man."[5] But the Court was quick to note the old patent law saying that "laws of nature, physical phenomena, and abstract ideas" are not patentable.[6] So, while Einstein might have been able to patent a specific method for converting mass into energy, his scientific law $E=mc2$, in and

---

1. *In re Bergy*, 596 F.2d 952 (CCPA 1979) (emphasis in original).

2. FELIPE FERNANDEZ–ARMESTO, NEAR A THOUSAND TABLES: A HISTORY OF FOOD 9 (2002).

3. *State Street Bank and Trust v. Signature Financial Group, Inc.*, 149 F.3d 1368, 1375 (Fed.Cir.1998) (emphasis in original).

4. *Id.*

5. Diamond v. Chakrabarty, 447 U.S. 303, 309 (1980) (citing the Committee Reports, S.Rep. No. 1979, 82d Cong., 2d Sess., 5 (1952); H.R. Rep. No. 1923, 82d Cong., 2d Sess., 6 (1952) and the testimony of P.J. Federico, Hearings on H.R. 3760 before subcommittee No. 3 of the House Committee on the Judiciary, 82d Cong., 1st Sess., 37 (1951)); *In re Bergy*, 596 F.2d 952, top of column 1 (patentable subject matter "may include *anything under the sun made by man*.") (Rich, J., emphasis his) (citing same Committee Reports and testimony).

6. *Id.*

of itself, is not patentable. As the materials that follow demonstrate, however, it is not clear whether this saying stands for little more than what logically follows from the other requirements for patentability discussed in Chapters 3–6 (*i.e.,* the disclosure, novelty, nonobviousness, and utility requirements already operate to prevent a patent from issuing on an idea or law of nature, which is typically neither new nor fully disclosed when discovered) or whether something else is at play. As the Senate Report to section 101 states: "A person may have 'invented' a machine or manufacture, which may include anything under the sun that is made by man, *but it is not necessarily patentable under section 101 unless the conditions of the title are fulfilled.*" S. Rep. No. 82–1979, reprinted in 1952 U.S.C.C.A.N. 2394, 2399 (emphasis added).

Some trace the statutory classes far back into legal history. The English Statute of Monopolies of 1624, which was discussed in Chapter One, referred to patents for "manufactures." The term "manufactures" was broadly construed by the English courts as embracing "not merely a vendible product of inventive skill, but also a method of applying physical forces to the production of physical effects" (*i.e.,* processes as well as products).[7] The first United States Patent Act in 1790 covered "any useful art, manufacture, engine, machine, or device, or any improvement therein." Three years later, the language was altered to read "any art, machine, manufacture, or composition of matter, or any new and useful improvement ..." These four classes have been called the "great and distinct classes of invention"[8] and "as complete as the subject will permit."[9] While the courts consistently interpreted "art" to mean "process," as a matter of clarification, the Patent Act of 1952 changed the language from "art" to "process" and defined "process" as meaning "process, art or method." These categories have been interpreted so as to cover most of the new technologies that evolved during the last 200 years.

Some suggest that the purpose of having statutory classes of subject matter is to limit patent protection to the field of applied technology, and on this view that is why the United States Constitution refers to "the useful arts." If so, no patents should be available for discoveries, however practical and useful, in nontechnological arts, such as liberal arts, the social sciences, theoretical mathematics, and business and management methodology. But since 1980, case law in the Supreme Court and the Federal Circuit has viewed the statutory list of classes to be merely representative, and indeed has included "anything under the sun made by man."[10]

It is interesting to compare the approach of section 101 under United States law with the provisions of the European Patent Convention (EPC). Section 101 defines subject matter eligibility positively, and leaves the exclusions to the common law, whereas the EPC itself sets forth both a

---

7. 1 W. Robinson, The Law of Patents for Useful Inventions 106 (1890).

8. *Ex parte Blythe*, 1885 Comm'n Dec. 82, 86 (Comm'r Pat 1885).

9. Robinson, Law of Patents, *supra* note 7, at 230.

10. *Diamond v. Chakrabarty,* 447 U.S. 303 (1980). *See also State Street Bank, supra* note 3; *AT & T Corp. v. Excel Communications, Inc.,* 172 F.3d 1352 (Fed.Cir.1999). *Cf.,* John R. Thomas, *The Patenting of the Liberal Professions*, 40 B.C. L. Rev. 1139 (1999).

positive and negative definition of patentable subject matter. For example, Article 52 of the EPC provides generally that patents "shall be granted for any inventions which are susceptible of industrial application." Article 57 provides that "an invention shall be considered as susceptible of industrial application if it can be made or used in any kind of industry, including agriculture." But the EPC goes on to specify several exceptions. For example, Article 52(2) excludes from patent protection: "(a) discoveries, scientific theories and mathematical methods; (b) aesthetic creations; (c) schemes, rules and methods for performing mental acts, playing games or doing business, and programs for computers; and (d) presentations of information" *but only* insofar as the patent "relates to such subject-matter or activities as such." Moreover, Article 53(a) excludes from patent protection "inventions the publication or exploitation of which would be contrary to *'ordre public'* or morality ..." and 53(b) excludes "plant or animal varieties or essentially biological processes for the production of plants or animals," but notes that "this provision does not apply to microbiological processes or the products thereof."

The exceptions to patent eligibility of Articles 52(2) (software and business methods, in particular) and 53 will be explored in greater detail below, but for present purposes it is important to note that in 2003, the European Parliament, after making several amendments to a European Commission draft directive,[11] voted to make software and business methods ineligible for patent protection. (It was thought this directive was needed because the European Patent Office continued to issue software and business method patents, despite Article 52(2)'s exclusion.) The outcome of this directive remains uncertain because the amended directive has to be approved by the Council of Ministers, which represents the EU member states. On the biotechnology front, the European Parliament, concerned about a robust American biotechnology industry, adopted a directive in 1998 codifying patent protection for biotech-related inventions,[12] which has been adopted by twenty-seven EU member states. These legislative initiatives will be discussed in more detail below.

One more digression before we return to section 101 of the American patent code. The "TRIPS" Agreement, that is, the 1994 Agreement on the "Trade–Related Aspects of Intellectual Property," is binding on countries that are members of the World Trade Organization (WTO). WTO members include the United States and most of the countries of the world. The TRIPS Agreement establishes *minimum* standards for intellectual property protection, including patents. Article 27 of TRIPS addresses "patentable subject matter" and dictates that "patents shall be available ... without discrimination as to ... field of technology." The Article goes on to permit member countries to "exclude from patentability" certain inventions. But

---

11. A "directive" is a form of EU legislation that is "binding in terms of the results to be achieved and are addressed to the member states, which are free to choose the best forms and methods of implementation." *See* http://www.eurunion.org/infores/euguide/Chapter2. htm#Chapter% 202:

12. *See* Directive 98/44/EC of the European Parliament and the Council of 6 July 1998 on the Legal Protection of Biotechnological Inventions, art. 3, 1998 O.J. (L 213) 13, 18.

the list of permissible exclusions includes many, but not all of the exclusions under the European Patent Convention.

Let's return to section 101 of the American patent code. To better grasp the topic of patentable subject matter in general, it is helpful to gain a basic understanding of the terminology used for what are generally seen to be the four classes of statutory subject matter.

Patent claims directed to machines, manufactures, or compositions of matter are collectively referred to as product claims. The term apparatus is often used to refer to both machines and devices.[13] The distinction between these two classes is that manufactures are generally considered to be static while machines are generally considered to include some moving part. In either case, the elements of an apparatus claim are typically the essential structural components of the claimed apparatus. Just as the elements of an apparatus claim are typically structural in nature, the elements of a composition claim are typically chemical in nature; such as the essential ingredients of a claimed composition. A composition of matter may be a new compound *per se*, or a new combination of existing and/or new compounds. Taken together, the three product classes cover essentially any-*thing* that is made by humans. The distinctions among them are entirely a matter of nomenclature, without substantive or procedural legal significance. A patent applicant need not designate a particular class of statutory subject matter, nor is the particular class an issue in litigation.

Having reviewed the basic terminology, we now turn to the numerous, and more difficult, normative questions concerning patentable subject matter that have arisen in recent years due to the scientific and industrial booms in two particular fields of technology: biotechnology and computer science. In the field of biotechnology, the question is often asked, if a drug is patentable, then why not an organism? Why not genes and proteins? In the field of computer science, the question is often asked, if computer hardware is patentable subject matter, then why not a general purpose piece of hardware programmed for a specific purpose? And for that matter, why not software? And how about methods of doing business, whether implemented with or without software?

The Supreme Court and the Federal Circuit have largely answered most of these questions in the affirmative; but only after a long and tortuous evolution in thought. Thus, as a matter of positive law today—*i.e.*, describing the present state of applicable statutes and case law—the materials in this Chapter can be boiled down to a simple nugget: after the *Chakrabarty* case, discussed *infra*, living organisms are patentable subject matter; and after the *Diehr* and *State Street Bank* cases, also discussed *infra*, computer programs and business methods are patentable subject matter, too. The more interesting issues that are explored at length in this Chapter are those concerning policy, theory, and the implications of these decisions.

---

13. The term device is synonymous with the terms "manufacture" and "article of manufacture." See *In re Hruby*, 373 F.2d 997 (CCPA 1967); *In re Hadden*, 20 F.2d 275 (D.C.Cir.1927).

STATUTORY PROVISIONS: 35 U.S.C. §§ 100(b) and 101

A.   BIOTECHNOLOGY–RELATED INVENTIONS

The issue explored in this section is whether inventions relating to biotechnology raise special problems when analyzed for statutory subject matter. As the materials below show in some detail, the bottom line is that although biotechnology inventions have indeed raised a number of unique issues, it is not clear as a matter of positive law whether they actually do today. When studying the materials that follow the reader should carefully consider at least two important questions: (1) whether the debates raise arguments that are unique to biotechnology; and (2) whether areas of patent law other than the statutory subject matter requirement can, do, or should, respond to those issues.

Diamond v. Chakrabarty

447 U.S. 303 (1980).

■ MR. CHIEF JUSTICE BURGER delivered the opinion of the Court.

We granted certiorari to determine whether a live, human-made micro-organism is patentable subject matter under 35 U.S.C. § 101.

I

In 1972, respondent Chakrabarty, a microbiologist, filed a patent application, assigned to the General Electric Co. The application asserted 36 claims related to Chakrabarty's invention of "a bacterium".... This human-made, genetically engineered bacterium is capable of breaking down multiple components of crude oil. Because of this property, which is possessed by no naturally occurring bacteria, Chakrabarty's invention is believed to have significant value for the treatment of oil spills.[2]

Chakrabarty's patent claims were of three types: first, process claims for the method of producing the bacteria; second, claims for an inoculum comprised of a carrier material floating on water, such as straw, and the new bacteria; and third, claims to the bacteria themselves. The patent examiner allowed the claims falling into the first two categories, but rejected claims for the bacteria. His decision rested on two grounds: (1) that micro-organisms are "products of nature," and (2) that as living things they are not patentable subject matter under 35 U.S.C. § 101.

Chakrabarty appealed the rejection of these claims to the Patent Office Board of Appeals, and the Board affirmed the Examiner on the second

---

2. At present, biological control of oil spills requires the use of a mixture of naturally occurring bacteria, each capable of degrading one component of the oil complex. In this way, oil is decomposed into simpler substances which can serve as food for aquatic life. However, for various reasons, only a portion of any such mixed culture survives to attack the oil spill. By breaking down multiple components of oil, Chakrabarty's micro-organism promises more efficient and rapid oil-spill control.

ground.[3] Relying on the legislative history of the 1930 Plant Patent Act, in which Congress extended patent protection to certain asexually reproduced plants, the Board concluded that § 101 was not intended to cover living things such as these laboratory created micro-organisms.

The Court of Customs and Patent Appeals, by a divided vote, [in an opinion by Judge Rich,] reversed on the authority of its prior decision in *In re Bergy*, 563 F.2d 1031, 1038 (1977), which held that "the fact that microorganisms ... are alive ... [is] without legal significance" for purposes of the patent law. Subsequently, we granted the Acting Commissioner of Patents and Trademarks' petition for certiorari in *Bergy*, vacated the judgment, and remanded the case "for further consideration in light of *Parker v. Flook*, 437 U.S. 584 (1978)." 438 U.S. 902 (1978). The Court of Customs and Patent Appeals then vacated its judgment in *Chakrabarty* and consolidated the case with *Bergy* for reconsideration. After re-examining both cases in the light of our holding in *Flook*, that court, with one dissent, [again through Judge Rich,] reaffirmed its earlier judgments. 596 F.2d 952 (1979).

The Commissioner of Patents and Trademarks again sought certiorari, and we granted the writ as to both *Bergy* and *Chakrabarty*. 444 U.S. 924 (1979). Since then, *Bergy* has been dismissed as moot, 444 U.S. 1028 (1980), leaving only *Chakrabarty* for decision.

II

The Constitution grants Congress broad power to legislate to "promote the Progress of Science and useful Arts, by securing for limited Times to Authors and Inventors the exclusive Right to their respective Writings and Discoveries." Art. I, § 8, cl. 8. The patent laws promote this progress by offering inventors exclusive rights for a limited period as an incentive for their inventiveness and research efforts. *Kewanee Oil Co. v. Bicron Corp.*, 416 U.S. 470, 480–481 (1974); *Universal Oil Co. v. Globe Co.*, 322 U.S. 471, 484 (1944). The authority of Congress is exercised in the hope that "[t]he productive effort thereby fostered will have a positive effect on society through the introduction of new products and processes of manufacture into the economy, and the emanations by way of increased employment and better lives for our citizens." *Kewanee, supra*, 416 U.S., at 480.

The question before us in this case is a narrow one of statutory interpretation requiring us to construe 35 U.S.C. § 101, which provides:

> Whoever invents or discovers any new and useful process, machine, manufacture, or composition of matter, or any new and useful improvement thereof, may obtain a patent therefor, subject to the conditions and requirements of this title.

Specifically, we must determine whether respondent's micro-organism constitutes a "manufacture" or "composition of matter" within the meaning of the statute.[5]

---

3. The Board concluded that the new bacteria were not "products of nature," because Pseudomonas bacteria containing two or more different energy-generating plasmids are not naturally occurring.

5. This case does not involve the other "conditions and requirements" of the patent laws, such as novelty and nonobviousness. 35 U.S.C. §§ 102, 103.

III

In cases of statutory construction we begin, of course, with the language of the statute. *Southeastern Community College v. Davis*, 442 U.S. 397, 405 (1979). And "unless otherwise defined, words will be interpreted as taking their ordinary, contemporary common meaning." *Perrin v. United States*, 444 U.S. 37, 42, 100 S.Ct. 311, 314 (1979). We have also cautioned that courts "should not read into the patent laws limitations and conditions which the legislature has not expressed." *United States v. Dubilier Condenser Corp.*, 289 U.S. 178, 199 (1933).

Guided by these canons of construction, this Court has read the term "manufacture" in § 101 in accordance with its dictionary definition to mean "the production of articles for use from raw or prepared materials by giving to these materials new forms, qualities, properties, or combinations, whether by hand-labor or by machinery." *American Fruit Growers, Inc. v. Brogdex Co.*, 283 U.S. 1, 11 (1931). Similarly, "composition of matter" has been construed consistent with its common usage to include "all compositions of two or more substances and ... all composite articles, whether they be the results of chemical union, or of mechanical mixture, or whether they be gases, fluids, powders or solids." *Shell Development Co. v. Watson*, 149 F.Supp. 279, 280 (D.C.1957) (citing 1 A. Deller, Walker on Patents § 14, p. 55 (1st ed. 1937)). In choosing such expansive terms as "manufacture" and "composition of matter," modified by the comprehensive "any," Congress plainly contemplated that the patent laws would be given wide scope.

The relevant legislative history also supports a broad construction. The Patent Act of 1793, authored by Thomas Jefferson, defined statutory subject matter as "any new and useful art, machine, manufacture, or composition of matter, or any new or useful improvement [thereof]." Act of Feb. 21, 1793, § 1, 1 Stat. 319. The Act embodied Jefferson's philosophy that "ingenuity should receive a liberal encouragement." 5 Writings of Thomas Jefferson 75–76 (Washington ed. 1871). See *Graham v. John Deere Co.*, 383 U.S. 1, 7–10 (1966). Subsequent patent statutes in 1836, 1870, and 1874 employed this same broad language. In 1952, when the patent laws were recodified, Congress replaced the word "art" with "process," but otherwise left Jefferson's language intact. The Committee Reports accompanying the 1952 Act inform us that Congress intended statutory subject matter to "include anything under the sun that is made by man." S.Rep. No.1979, 82d Cong., 2d Sess., 5 (1952); H.R.Rep.No.1923, 82d Cong., 2d Sess., 6 (1952).[6]

This is not to suggest that § 101 has no limits or that it embraces every discovery. The laws of nature, physical phenomena, and abstract ideas have been held not patentable. See *Parker v. Flook*, 437 U.S. (1978); *Gottschalk v. Benson*, 409 U.S. 63, 67 (1972); *Funk Brothers Seed Co. v. Kalo Inoculant Co.*, 333 U.S. 127, 130 (1948); *O'Reilly v. Morse*, 15 How.

---

6. This same language was employed by P. J. Federico, a principal draftsman of the 1952 recodification, in his testimony regarding that legislation: "[U]nder section 101 a person may have invented a machine or a manufacture, which may include anything under the sun that is made by man...." Hearings on H.R. 3760 before Subcommittee No. 3 of the House Committee on the Judiciary, 82d Cong., 1st Sess., 37 (1951).

62, 112–121 (1854); *Le Roy v. Tatham*, 14 How. 156, 175 (1852). Thus, a new mineral discovered in the earth or a new plant found in the wild is not patentable subject matter. Likewise, Einstein could not patent his celebrated law that E=mc2; nor could Newton have patented the law of gravity. Such discoveries are "manifestations of . . . nature, free to all men and reserved exclusively to none." *Funk, supra*, 333 U.S., at 130.

Judged in this light, respondent's micro-organism plainly qualifies as patentable subject matter. His claim is not to a hitherto unknown natural phenomenon, but to a nonnaturally occurring manufacture or composition of matter—a product of human ingenuity "having a distinctive name, character [and] use." *Hartranft v. Wiegmann*, 121 U.S. 609, 615 (1887). The point is underscored dramatically by comparison of the invention here with that in *Funk*. There, the patentee had discovered that there existed in nature certain species of root-nodule bacteria which did not exert a mutually inhibitive effect on each other. He used that discovery to produce a mixed culture capable of inoculating the seeds of leguminous plants. Concluding that the patentee had discovered "only some of the handiwork of nature," the Court ruled the product nonpatentable:

> Each of the species of root-nodule bacteria contained in the package infects the same group of leguminous plants which it always infected. No species acquires a different use. The combination of species produces no new bacteria, no change in the six species of bacteria, and no enlargement of the range of their utility. Each species has the same effect it always had. The bacteria perform in their natural way. Their use in combination does not improve in any way their natural functioning. They serve the ends nature originally provided and act quite independently of any effort of the patentee. 333 U.S., at 131.

Here, by contrast, the patentee has produced a new bacterium with markedly different characteristics from any found in nature and one having the potential for significant utility. His discovery is not nature's handiwork, but his own; accordingly it is patentable subject matter under § 101.

IV

Two contrary arguments are advanced, neither of which we find persuasive.

(A)

The petitioner's first argument rests on the enactment of the 1930 Plant Patent Act, which afforded patent protection to certain asexually reproduced plants, and the 1970 Plant Variety Protection Act, which authorized protection for certain sexually reproduced plants but excluded bacteria from its protection. [Footnote omitted] In the petitioner's view, the passage of these Acts evidences congressional understanding that the terms "manufacture" or "composition of matter" do not include living things; if they did, the petitioner argues, neither Act would have been necessary.

We reject this argument. Prior to 1930, two factors were thought to remove plants from patent protection. The first was the belief that plants, even those artificially bred, were products of nature for purposes of the patent law. This position appears to have derived from the decision of the patent office in *Ex parte Latimer*, 1889 Dec.Com.Pat. 123, in which a patent claim for fiber found in the needle of the Pinus australis was rejected. The Commissioner reasoned that a contrary result would permit "patents [to] be obtained upon the trees of the forest and the plants of the earth, which of course would be unreasonable and impossible." Id., at 126. The *Latimer* case, it seems, came to "se[t] forth the general stand taken in these matters" that plants were natural products not subject to patent protection. Thorne, Relation of Patent Law to Natural Products, 6 J. Pat.Off.Soc. 23, 24 (1923).[8] The second obstacle to patent protection for plants was the fact that plants were thought not amenable to the "written description" requirement of the patent law. See 35 U.S.C. § 112. Because new plants may differ from old only in color or perfume, differentiation by written description was often impossible.

In enacting the Plant Patent Act, Congress addressed both of these concerns. It explained at length its belief that the work of the plant breeder "in aid of nature" was patentable invention. S.Rep.No.315, 71st Cong., 2d Sess., 6–8 (1930); H.R.Rep.No.1129, 71st Cong., 2d Sess., 7–9 (1930). And it relaxed the written description requirement in favor of "a description ... as complete as is reasonably possible." 35 U.S.C. § 162. No Committee or Member of Congress, however, expressed the broader view, now urged by the petitioner, that the terms "manufacture" or "composition of matter" exclude living things. The sole support for that position in the legislative history of the 1930 Act is found in the conclusory statement of Secretary of Agriculture Hyde, in a letter to the Chairmen of the House and Senate Committees considering the 1930 Act, that "the patent laws ... at the present time are understood to cover only inventions or discoveries in the field of inanimate nature." See S.Rep.No.315, *supra*, at Appendix A; H.R.Rep.No.1129, *supra*, at Appendix A. Secretary Hyde's opinion, however, is not entitled to controlling weight. His views were solicited on the administration of the new law and not on the scope of patentable subject matter—an area beyond his competence. Moreover, there is language in the House and Senate Committee Reports suggesting that to the extent Congress considered the matter it found the Secretary's dichotomy unpersuasive. The Reports observe:

> There is a clear and logical distinction *between the discovery of a new variety of plant and of certain inanimate things*, such, for example, as a new and useful natural mineral. The mineral is created wholly by nature unassisted by man.... On the other hand, a plant discovery resulting from cultivation is unique, isolated, and is not repeated by nature, nor can it be reproduced by nature unaided by man.... (emphasis added).

Congress thus recognized that the relevant distinction was not between living and inanimate things, but between products of nature, whether living or not, and human-made inventions. Here, respondent's micro-

---

8. Writing three years after the passage of the 1930 Act, R. Cook, Editor of the Journal of Heredity, commented:

It is a little hard for plant men to understand why [Art. I, § 8] of the Constitution should not have been earlier construed to include the promotion of the art of plant breeding. The reason for this is probably to be found in the principle that natural products are not patentable. Florists Exchange and Horticultural Trade World, July 15, 1933, p. 9.

organism is the result of human ingenuity and research. Hence, the passage of the Plant Patent Act affords the Government no support.

Nor does the passage of the 1970 Plant Variety Protection Act support the Government's position. As the Government acknowledges, sexually reproduced plants were not included under the 1930 Act because new varieties could not be reproduced true-to-type through seedlings. Brief for Petitioner 27, n. 31. By 1970, however, it was generally recognized that true-to-type reproduction was possible and that plant patent protection was therefore appropriate. The 1970 Act extended that protection. There is nothing in its language or history to suggest that it was enacted because § 101 did not include living things.

In particular, we find nothing in the exclusion of bacteria from plant variety protection to support the petitioner's position. The legislative history gives no reason for this exclusion. As the Court of Customs and Patent Appeals suggested, it may simply reflect congressional agreement with the result reached by that court in deciding *In re Arzberger*, 112 F.2d 834 (1940), which held that bacteria were not plants for the purposes of the 1930 Act. Or it may reflect the fact that prior to 1970 the Patent Office had issued patents for bacteria under § 101.[9] In any event, absent some clear indication that Congress "focused on [the] issues . . . directly related to the one presently before the Court," *SEC v. Sloan*, 436 U.S. 103, 120–121 (1978), there is no basis for reading into its actions an intent to modify the plain meaning of the words found in § 101.

(B)

The petitioner's second argument is that micro-organisms cannot qualify as patentable subject matter until Congress expressly authorizes such protection. His position rests on the fact that genetic technology was unforeseen when Congress enacted § 101. From this it is argued that resolution of the patentability of inventions such as respondent's should be left to Congress. The legislative process, the petitioner argues, is best equipped to weigh the competing economic, social, and scientific considerations involved, and to determine whether living organisms produced by genetic engineering should receive patent protection. In support of this position, the petitioner relies on our recent holding in *Parker v. Flook*, 437 U.S. 584 (1978), and the statement that the judiciary "must proceed cautiously when . . . asked to extend patent rights into areas wholly unforeseen by Congress." *Id.*, at 596.

It is, of course, correct that Congress, not the courts, must define the limits of patentability; but it is equally true that once Congress has spoken it is "the province and duty of the judicial department to say what the law is." *Marbury v. Madison*, 1 Cranch 137, 177, 2 L.Ed. 60 (1803). Congress has performed its constitutional role in defining patentable subject matter in § 101; we perform ours in construing the language Congress has

---

9. In 1873, the Patent Office granted Louis Pasteur a patent on "yeast, free from organic germs of disease, as an article of manufacture." And in 1967 and 1968, immediately prior to the passage of the Plant Variety Protection Act, that Office granted two patents which, as the petitioner concedes, state claims for living micro-organisms. See Reply Brief for Petitioner 3, and n. 2.

employed. In so doing, our obligation is to take statutes as we find them, guided, if ambiguity appears, by the legislative history and statutory purpose. Here, we perceive no ambiguity. The subject-matter provisions of the patent law have been cast in broad terms to fulfill the constitutional and statutory goal of promoting "the Progress of Science and the useful Arts" with all that means for the social and economic benefits envisioned by Jefferson. Broad general language is not necessarily ambiguous when congressional objectives require broad terms.

Nothing in *Flook* is to the contrary. That case applied our prior precedents to determine that a "claim for an improved method of calculation, even when tied to a specific end use, is unpatentable subject matter under § 101." 437 U.S., at 595, n. 18. The Court carefully scrutinized the claim at issue to determine whether it was precluded from patent protection under "the principles underlying the prohibition against patents for 'ideas' or phenomena of nature." *Id.*, at 593. We have done that here. *Flook* did not announce a new principle that inventions in areas not contemplated by Congress when the patent laws were enacted are unpatentable per se.

To read that concept into *Flook* would frustrate the purposes of the patent law. This Court frequently has observed that a statute is not to be confined to the "particular application[s] . . . contemplated by the legislators." *Barr v. United States*, 324 U.S. 83, 90 (1945). Accord, *Browder v. United States*, 312 U.S. 335, 339 (1941); *Puerto Rico v. Shell Co.*, 302 U.S. 253, 257 (1937). This is especially true in the field of patent law. A rule that unanticipated inventions are without protection would conflict with the core concept of the patent law that anticipation undermines patentability. See *Graham v. John Deere Co.*, 383 U.S., at 12–17. Mr. Justice Douglas reminded that the inventions most benefiting mankind are those that "push back the frontiers of chemistry, physics, and the like." *Great A. & P. Tea Co. v. Supermarket Corp.*, 340 U.S. 147, 154 (1950) (concurring opinion). Congress employed broad general language in drafting § 101 precisely because such inventions are often unforeseeable.

To buttress his argument, the petitioner, with the support of *amicus*, points to grave risks that may be generated by research endeavors such as respondent's. The briefs present a gruesome parade of horribles. Scientists, among them Nobel laureates, are quoted suggesting that genetic research may pose a serious threat to the human race, or, at the very least, that the dangers are far too substantial to permit such research to proceed apace at this time. We are told that genetic research and related technological developments may spread pollution and disease, that it may result in a loss of genetic diversity, and that its practice may tend to depreciate the value of human life. These arguments are forcefully, even passionately, presented; they remind us that, at times, human ingenuity seems unable to control fully the forces it creates—that with Hamlet, it is sometimes better "to bear those ills we have than fly to others that we know not of."

It is argued that this Court should weigh these potential hazards in considering whether respondent's invention is patentable subject matter under § 101. We disagree. The grant or denial of patents on microorganisms is not likely to put an end to genetic research or to its attendant risks. The large amount of research that has already occurred when no researcher had sure knowledge that patent protection would be available suggests that legislative or judicial fiat as to patentability will not deter the scientific mind from probing into the unknown any more than Canute could command the tides. Whether respondent's claims are patentable may determine whether research efforts are accelerated by the hope of reward or slowed by want of incentives, but that is all.

What is more important is that we are without competence to entertain these arguments—either to brush them aside as fantasies generated by fear of the unknown, or to act on them. The choice we are urged to make is a matter of high policy for resolution within the legislative process after the kind of investigation, examination, and study that legislative bodies can provide and courts cannot. That process involves the balancing of competing values and interests, which in our democratic system is the business of elected representatives. Whatever their validity, the contentions now pressed on us should be addressed to the political branches of the Government, the Congress and the Executive, and not to the courts.

We have emphasized in the recent past that "[o]ur individual appraisal of the wisdom or unwisdom of a particular [legislative] course ... is to be put aside in the process of interpreting a statute." *TVA v. Hill*, 437 U.S., at 194. Our task, rather, is the narrow one of determining what Congress meant by the words it used in the statute; once that is done our powers are exhausted. Congress is free to amend § 101 so as to exclude from patent protection organisms produced by genetic engineering. Cf. 42 U.S.C. § 2181(a), exempting from patent protection inventions "useful solely in the utilization of special nuclear material or atomic energy in an atomic weapon." Or it may choose to craft a statute specifically designed for such living things. But, until Congress takes such action, this Court must construe the language of § 101 as it is. The language of that section fairly embraces respondent's invention.

Accordingly, the judgment of the Court of Customs and Patent Appeals is *AFFIRMED*.

■ MR. JUSTICE BRENNAN, with whom MR. JUSTICE WHITE, MR. JUSTICE MARSHALL, and MR. JUSTICE POWELL join, dissenting.

I agree with the Court that the question before us is a narrow one. Neither the future of scientific research, nor even, the ability of respondent Chakrabarty to reap some monopoly profits from his pioneering work, is at stake. Patents on the processes by which he has produced and employed the new living organism are not contested. The only question we need decide is whether Congress, exercising its authority under Art. I, § 8, of the Constitution, intended that he be able to secure a monopoly on the living organism itself, no matter how produced or how used. Because I believe the Court has misread the applicable legislation, I dissent.

The patent laws attempt to reconcile this Nation's deep seated antipathy to monopolies with the need to encourage progress. *Deepsouth Packing Co. v. Laitram Corp.*, 406 U.S. 518, 530–531 (1972); *Graham v. John Deere Co.*, 383 U.S. 1, 7–10 (1966). Given the complexity and legislative nature of this delicate task, we must be careful to extend patent protection no further than Congress has provided. In particular, were there an absence of legislative direction, the courts should leave to Congress the decisions whether and how far to extend the patent privilege into areas where the common understanding has been that patents are not available.[1] Cf. *Deepsouth Packing Co. v. Laitram Corp., supra.*

In this case, however, we do not confront a complete legislative vacuum. The sweeping language of the Patent Act of 1793, as re-enacted in 1952, is not the last pronouncement Congress has made in this area. In 1930 Congress enacted the Plant Patent Act affording patent protection to developers of certain asexually reproduced plants. In 1970 Congress enacted the Plant Variety Protection Act to extend protection to certain new plant varieties capable of sexual reproduction. Thus, we are not dealing—as the Court would have it—with the routine problem of "unanticipated inventions." *Ante.* In these two Acts Congress has addressed the general problem of patenting animate inventions and has chosen carefully limited language granting protection to some kinds of discoveries, but specifically excluding others. These Acts strongly evidence a congressional limitation that excludes bacteria from patentability.[2]

First, the Acts evidence Congress' understanding, at least since 1930, that § 101 does not include living organisms. If newly developed living organisms not naturally occurring had been patentable under § 101, the plants included in the scope of the 1930 and 1970 Acts could have been patented without new legislation. Those plants, like the bacteria involved in this case, were new varieties not naturally occurring.[3] Although the Court, *ante*, rejects this line of argument, it does not explain why the Acts were necessary unless to correct a pre-existing situation.[4] I cannot share the Court's implicit assumption that Congress was engaged in either idle exercises or mere correction of the public record when it enacted the 1930 and 1970 Acts. And Congress certainly thought it was doing something significant. The Committee Reports contain expansive prose about the previously unavailable benefits to be derived from extending patent protec-

---

1. I read the Court to admit that the popular conception, even among advocates of agricultural patents, was that living organisms were unpatentable. See *ante*, n. 8 [and accompanying text].

2. But even if I agreed with the Court that the 1930 and 1970 Acts were not dispositive, I would dissent. This case presents even more cogent reasons than *Deepsouth Packing Co.* not to extend the patent monopoly in the face of uncertainty. At the very least, these Acts are signs of legislative attention to the problems of patenting living organisms, but they give no affirmative indication of congressional intent that bacteria be patentable. The caveat of *Parker v. Flook*, 437 U.S. 584, 596 (1978), an admonition to "proceed cautiously when we are asked to extend patent rights into areas wholly unforeseen by Congress," therefore becomes pertinent. I should think the necessity for caution is that much greater when we are asked to extend patent rights into areas Congress has foreseen and considered but has not resolved.

3. The Court refers to the logic employed by Congress in choosing not to perpetuate the "dichotomy" suggested by Secretary Hyde. *Ante*, at 2209. But by this logic the bacteria at issue here are distinguishable from a "mineral . . . created wholly by nature" in exactly the same way as were the new varieties of plants. If a new Act was needed to provide patent protection for the plants, it was equally necessary for bacteria. Yet Congress provided for patents on plants but not on these bacteria. In short, Congress decided to make only a subset of animate "human-made inventions," *ibid.*, patentable.

4. If the 1930 Act's only purpose were to solve the technical problem of description referred to by the Court, *ante*, at 2209, most of the Act, and in particular its limitation to asexually reproduced plants, would have been totally unnecessary.

tion to plants.[5] H.R.Rep. No. 91–1605, pp. 1–3 (1970), U.S.Code Cong. & Admin.News 1970, p. 5082; S.Rep.No.315, 71st Cong., 2d Sess., 1–3 (1930). Because Congress thought it had to legislate in order to make agricultural "human-made inventions" patentable and because the legislation Congress enacted is limited, it follows that Congress never meant to make items outside the scope of the legislation patentable.

Second, the 1970 Act clearly indicates that Congress has included bacteria within the focus of its legislative concern, but not within the scope of patent protection. Congress specifically excluded bacteria from the coverage of the 1970 Act. 7 U.S.C. § 2402(a). The Court's attempts to supply explanations for this explicit exclusion ring hollow. It is true that there is no mention in the legislative history of the exclusion, but that does not give us license to invent reasons. The fact is that Congress, assuming that animate objects as to which it had not specifically legislated could not be patented, excluded bacteria from the set of patentable organisms.

The Court protests that its holding today is dictated by the broad language of § 101, which cannot "be confined to the 'particular application [s] ... contemplated by the legislators.'" *Ante*, quoting *Barr v. United States*, 324 U.S. 83, 90 (1945). But as I have shown, the Court's decision does not follow the unavoidable implications of the statute. Rather, it extends the patent system to cover living material even though Congress plainly has legislated in the belief that § 101 does not encompass living organisms. It is the role of Congress, not this Court, to broaden or narrow the reach of the patent laws. This is especially true where, as here, the composition sought to be patented uniquely implicates matters of public concern.

NOTES

1. *Everything Under the Sun Except*.... Why are laws and products of nature not patentable? If the concern is that the claim would not be supported by the disclosure, then why does not Section 112 address the problem? More specifically, if the claim is adjudged to be supported by the disclosure under Section 112, why should Section 101 present a similar but somehow higher hurdle relating to disclosure? If the concern is that the claim would cover something that is in the prior art, then why do not Sections 102 and 103 address the problem? More specifically, if the claim is adjudged to be new under Section 102 and nonobvious under Section 103, why should Section 101 present a similar but somehow higher hurdle relating to prior art? Indeed, in *Chakrabarty*, all that the Court decided was

5. Secretary Hyde's letter was not the only explicit indication in the legislative history of these Acts that Congress was acting on the assumption that legislation was necessary to make living organisms patentable. The Senate Judiciary Committee Report on the 1970 Act states the Committee's understanding that patent protection extended no further than the explicit provisions of these Acts:

Under the patent law, patent protection is limited to those varieties of plants which reproduce asexually, that is, by such methods as grafting or budding. No protection is available to those varieties of plants which reproduce sexually, that is, generally by seeds. S.Rep.No.91–1246, p. 3 (1970).

Similarly, Representative Poage, speaking for the 1970 Act, after noting the protection accorded asexually developed plants, stated that "for plants produced from seed, there has been no such protection." 116 Cong.Rec. 40295 (1970).

that the claimed invention was not excluded from patent protection under Section 101.

Some suggest that the problem is that laws and products of nature are discovered, not made. But the words "discoveries" and "discovers" are expressly recited in Article I, Section 8, Clause 8 of the Constitution and 35 U.S.C. § 101. In addition, as Judge Jerome Frank pointed out, there is a certain irony in the patent law's denial of a reward to the discoverers of general scientific principles:

> Epoch-making "discoveries" or "mere" general scientific "laws," without more, cannot be patented.... So the great "discoveries" of Newton or Faraday could not have been rewarded with such a grant of monopoly. Interestingly enough, apparently many scientists like Faraday care little for monetary rewards; generally the motives of such outstanding geniuses are not pecuniary.... Perhaps (although no one really knows) the same cannot be said of those lesser geniuses who put such discoveries to practical uses.

Katz v. Horni Signal Mfg. Corp, 145 F.2d 961, 961 (2d Cir.1944). Nevertheless, in his well-known 19th century patent law treatise, Albert H. Walker, in his discussion of "discoveries" vis-á-vis "inventions," writes:

> The word "discovery" does not have, either in the Constitution or the statute, its broadest signification. It means invention, in those documents, and in them it means nothing else. The "discoveries" of inventors are inventions. The same man may invent a machine, and may discover an island or law of nature. For doing the first of these things, the patent laws may reward him, because he is an inventor in doing it; but those laws cannot reward him for doing either of the others, because he is not an inventor in doing either.

ALBERT H. WALKER, TEXT-BOOK OF THE PATENT LAWS OF THE UNITED STATES OF AMERICA, § 2, at 2–3 (2d ed. 1889). The problem of shifting standards relating to matters of both utility and statutory subject matter under Section 101 is not trivial. The result [can be] bleak and remarkably reminiscent of the one described by Dickens:

> At the Patent Office in Lincoln's Inn, they made 'a draft of the Queens bill', of my invention, and a 'docket of the bill'. I paid five pound, ten, and six, for this. They 'engrossed two copies of the bill; one for the Signet Office, and one for the Privy–Seal Office'. I paid one pound, seven, and six, for this. Stamp duty over and above, three pound. The Engrossing Clerk of the same office engrossed the Queen's bill for signature. I paid him one pound, one. Stamp-duty again, one pound, ten. I was next to take the Queen's bill to the Attorney–General again, and get it signed again. I took it, and paid five pound more. I fetched it away, and took it to the Home Secretary again. He sent it to the Queen again. She signed it again. I paid seven pound thirteen, and six, more, for this. I had been over a month at Thomas Joy's. I was quite wore out, patience and pocket.

F. Scott Kieff, *The Case for Registering Patents and the Law and Economics of Present Patent Obtaining Rules*, 45 B. C. L. REV. 55, 106 (quoting Charles Dickens, A Poor Man's Tale of a Patent, in Charles Dickens and the 'Poor Man's Tale of a Patent' 15, 18–19, 29 (Jeremy Phillips ed., 1984) (including appendices about the "circumlocution office" described to be ("as everybody knows without being told) the most important Department under Government")).

2. *The Dissent.* The participants in the dissent in Chakrabarty were in large part the majority in the earlier cases on computer hardware and software patenting that are discussed *infra* in the section that follows. One argument that is raised in the dissent is based on the statutory construction approach: *expressio unius est exclusio* *alterius*, which means "to express or include one thing implies the exclusion of the other." BLACK'S LAW DICTIONARY (7th ed. 1999). According to the dissent in *Chakrabarty*, living matter is not expressly listed in Section 101 and was not considered to be patentable until Congress enacted the 1930 and 1970 plant acts; and since Congress only spoke to plants in those statutes, all living matter other than plants, such as microorganisms, are still not patentable. This argument was also made below, unsuccessfully. *See In re Bergy*, 596 F.2d 952, 999 (CCPA 1979) (Miller J., dissenting) (stating that "the Plant Protection Act of 1930 and the Plant Variety Protection Act of 1970, along with their accompanying legislative history, clearly establish that Congress did not intend that any organisms ... other than the plants covered by those Acts, be within the scope of section 101"). Another argument raised by the dissent is based on the view that express Congressional action was needed before patents could be extended to areas of technology that could not have been foreseen by the Founders. Do you think the majority adequately addressed these concerns?

3. *DNA, Proteins, and Products of Nature.* A leading product of nature case is *Funk Bros. Seed v. Kalo Inoculant*, 333 U.S. 127 (1948), which is discussed in *Chakrabarty*. The patent in question concerned inoculants of the bacteria genus Rhizobium. The bacteria enabled leguminous plants to fix nitrogen from air. Different species of the genus were effective for different types of plant crops. Prior to the patent in question, manufactures sold only single species inoculants since different species produced an inhibitory effect on each other. Thus farmers had to procure and use separate inoculants for each type of crop. The patentee discovered that certain strains of each species were mutually non-inhibitive with certain strains of other species. He thus produced a mixed culture of Rhizobia bacteria capable of inoculating several groups of plants. The patent contained both process claims and the method of making such mixed cultures and product claims to such cultures.

The Court, in an opinion by Justice Douglas, declined to allow a patent "on one of the ancient secrets of nature now disclosed:"

> [The patentee] does not create a state of inhibition or of non-inhibition in the bacteria. Their qualities are the work of nature. Those qualities are of course not patentable. For patents cannot issue for the discovery of the phenomena of nature.... The qualities of these bacteria ... are part of the storehouse of knowledge of all men.

333 U.S. at 130. But it would seem that the claim in *Funk Bros.* was not in fact for a true product of nature. The claimed mixture did not exist in natural form. In fact, is the patent any different than the patent in *Chakrabarty* in this regard? Could the patentee in *Funk Bros.* have claimed a *purified* or *isolated* mixture of the naturally existing bacteria? In 1873, the Patent Office granted Louis Pasteur a patent on "yeast, free from organic germs of disease, as an article of manufacture." See footnote 9 of the opinion. If a properly drafted purified-type claim would have been valid under the reasoning of *Chakrabarty*, then is *Funk Bros.* still good law after *Chakrabarty*? In a concurring opinion Justice Frankfurter was poignantly critical of the majority opinion:

> It only confuses the issue ... to introduce such terms as "the work of nature" and the "laws of nature." For these are vague and malleable terms infected with too much ambiguity and equivocation. Everything that happens may be deemed "the work of nature." ... Not can it be contended that there was not invention because the composite has no new properties other than its ingredients in isolation.

Id. at 134–35.

The view that purified naturally occurring substances are not patentable did not begin with *Funk Bros. See, e.g., American Wood–Paper Co. v. Fibre Disintegrating Co.*, 90 U.S. 566 (1874) (In response to the patentee's argument that the patented subject matter (*i.e.,* cellulose) was purified, the Court stated, rather skeptically: "There are many things well known and valuable in medicine or in the arts which may be extracted from diverse substances. But extract is the same, no matter from what it has been taken.... Whether a slight difference in the degree of purity of an article produced by several processes justifies denominating the products different manufactures, so that different patents may be obtained for each, may well be doubted, and it is not necessary to decide"). But it is not clear that it even lasted up to *Funk Bros.*

As the chemical arts progressed, the law began to evolve and became much more receptive to arguments based on human intervention and purification. Perhaps the most significant case in this regard, a case that has provided support for patenting purified DNA sequences and proteins, is *Parke–Davis & Co. v. H.K. Mulford Co.*, 189 Fed. 95 (S.D.N.Y. 1911). This case involved a patent on an adrenalin compound derived from the suprarenal glands of certain animals. It had been previously known that suprenal gland in powdered form had "hemostatic, blood pressure raising and astringent properties," but could not be used for those purposes in its gross form. The patentee, Takamine, produced a substance possessing the desired characteristics in pure and stable form. Judge Learned Hand framed the issue as whether the new compound differed from the natural one in kind or merely in degree:

> [E]ven if it were merely an extracted product without change, there is no rule that such products are not patentable. Takamine was the first to make it available for any use by removing it from the other gland-tissue in which it was found, and, while it is of course possible logically to call this a purification of the principle, it became for every practical purpose a new thing commercially and therapeutically.... Everyone, not already saturated with scholastic distinctions, would recognize that Takamin's crystals were not merely the old dried glands in a purer state, nor would his opinion change if he learned that the crystals were obtained from the glands by a process of eliminating the inactive organic substances. The line between different substances and degrees of the same substance is to be drawn rather from the common usages of men than from nice considerations of dialectic.

Id. at 103. Judge Hand's emphasis on therapeutic novelty and purification was seen as very important and has come to be relied upon by other courts. *See, e.g., Merck & Co. v. Olin Mathieson Chemical Corp.*, 253 F.2d 156 (4th Cir.1958) (upholding validity of patent on purified vitamin B_{12}, which occurred naturally); *In re Bergy*, 563 F.2d 1031 (CCPA 1977) (fining eligible for patent protection a process for preparing the lincomycin); *Amgen, Inc. v. Chugai Pharmaceutical Co., Ltd.*, 13 U.S.P.Q.2d 1737, 1759 (D.Mass.1989), *aff'd in part, rev'd in part, vacated in part*, 927 F.2d 1200 (Fed.Cir.1991) (in upholding the validity of U.S. Patent No. 4,703,008, a patent relating to recombinant human erythropoietin (EPO), the court stated that the "invention claimed in the patent ... is not ... the DNA sequence encoding human EPO since that is a nonpatentable natural phenomenon 'free to all men and reserved exclusively to none.' ... Rather the invention as claimed ... is the 'purified and isolated' DNA sequence encoding erythropoietin"). *See also,* Rebecca Eisenberg, *Re–Examining the Role of Patents in Appropriating the Value of DNA Sequences*, 49 EMORY L.J. 783, 786 (2000) ("Patents have ... issued on 'isolated and purified' DNA sequences, separate from the chromosomes in which they occur in nature, or on DNA sequences that have been spliced into recombinant vectors or introduced into recombinant cells of a sort that do not exist in nature. This is consistent with longstanding practice, even prior to the advent of modern biotechnology, of allowing patents to issue on isolated and purified chemical products that exist in nature only in an impure state, when human intervention has made them available in a new and useful form"). This view is presently reflected in the PTO's utility guidelines: a gene as it exist in the human body is not subject to patent protection, but a gene "isolated from its natural state and processed through purifying steps that separate the gene from other molecules naturally associate with it" is eligible for patent protection under § 101. *See* United States Patent & Trademark Office, *Utility Examination Guidelines*, 66 Fed. Reg. 1092, 1093 (Jan. 5, 2001). Importantly, one could argue that this entire mode of analysis is more related to the rules about prior art in Sections 102 and 103 than it is about statutory subject matter in Section 101.

4. *Muticellular Organisms*. The Board of Patent Appeals and Interferences held that a man-made animal life form constituted patentable subject matter in *Ex parte Allen*, 2 U.S.P.Q.2d 1425 (Bd. Pat. App. & Int'f 1987). In *Allen*, the applicants developed a method for producing polyploid Pacific oysters (those of the species *Crassostrea gigas*). The advantage of such sterile oysters is that they do not devote significant portions of their body weight to reproduction, thereby remaining edible year around. The examiner allowed the applicants' method claims, but rejected the product-by-process claims on the ground that the claimed subject matter was directed to "living entities" and therefore beyond the scope of Section 101. The Board reversed, relying on *Chakrabarty*:

> The issue ... in determining whether the claimed subject matter is patentable under Section 101 is simply whether that subject matter is made by man. If the claimed subject matter occurs naturally, it is not patentable subject matter under Section 101. The fact, as urged by the examiner, that the oysters produced by the claimed method are "controlled by the laws of nature" does not address the issue of whether the subject matter is a non-naturally occurring manufacture or composition of matter. The examiner has presented no evidence that the claimed polyploid oysters occur naturally without the intervention of man, nor has the examiner urged that polyploid oysters occur naturally.

Id. at 1426–27. Of note, the Board affirmed rejection of the claims on obviousness grounds under Section 103. This rejection was affirmed by the Federal Circuit in an unpublished opinion. *See In re Allen*, 846 F.2d 77 (Fed.Cir.1988).

In what is more of an administrative law case, *Animal Legal Defense Fund v. Quigg*, 932 F.2d 920 (Fed.Cir.1991), the Federal Circuit held that plaintiffs, animal rights advocate organizations, farmers, and animal husbandry organizations, lacked standing to seek judicial review of the PTO's April 21, 1987, notice that it "now considers non-naturally occurring, non-human multicellular organisms, including animals, to be patentable subject matter...." The court held that the notice was interpretive, not substantive, under the Administrative Procedures Act, Section 553(b):

> The genesis and effect of the Notice demonstrates that it represents no change in the law effect by the Commissioner and that, in reality, it is merely "interpretive" of prior decisional precedent.... The Notice clearly corresponds with the interpretations of Section 101 set out by the Board in *Allen* and *Hibberd*, in reliance on *Chakrabarty*, with the only caveat being the statement that Section 101 does not extend to humans....

Id. at 927–29.

5. *Transgenic Animals*. An example of a transgenic animal is the Harvard onco-mouse, a mouse that was created to have a genetic predisposition to breast cancer and was designed to study the relationship between genes and cancer. This mouse was patented in the United States (U.S. Patent No. 4,736,866 (titled "Transgenic Non–Human Mammals")) in 1988 (a first on a new variety of animal) and the European Patent Office ("EPO") (European Patent No. 0 169 672) in 1992, although the EPO was less receptive and there was significant opposition based on notions of public order and morality (see note 5, *infra*). In response to a public morality challenge, based on European Patent Convention ("EPC") EPC Article 53(a), the Examining Division stated that the onco-mouse:

> cannot be considered immoral or contrary to public order. The provision of a type of test animal useful in cancer research and giving rise to a reduction in the amount of testing on animals together with a low risk connected with the handling of the animals by qualified staff can generally be regarded as beneficial to mankind. A patent should therefore not be denied for the present invention on the ground of Article 53(a) EPC.

Harvard/Onco-mouse, 1992 O.J. E.P.O. at 593 (Examining Div.).

The onco-mouse has been patented in several countries. But interestingly, the Supreme Court of Canada refused to extend patent protection to the onco-mouse because, in the court's opinion, a higher life form is not a "composition of matter" or "article of manufacture" under Section 2 of the Canadian Patent Act. *See Commissioner of Patents v. President and Fellows of Harvard College*, [2002] D.L.R. (4th) 577, 578–79. Notably, a majority of the court, unlike the dissent, was expressly unpersuaded by *Chakrabarty* and its well known language that Congress intended statutory subject matter to "include anything under the sun that is made by man."

An example of the successful application of the EPC Article 53(a) morality provision is the "Edinburgh" patent opposition proceeding. This patent (No. 0695351), so coined because it is owned by the University of Edinburgh, is entitled "Isolation, selection and propagation of animal transgenic stem cells." The patent issued in 1999, but during prosecution, the EPO failed to limit the term "animal," which can include humans and human embryonic stem cells. No fewer than 14 parties, including the governments of Italy, Germany, and the Netherlands, filed an opposition in March 2000. Largely because of Article 53(a), the opposition proceeding resulted in the patent maintaining its validity in amended form. That is, the patent "no longer includes human or animal embryonic stem cells, but still covers modified human and animal stem cells other than embryonic stem cells." EPO Press Release, July 24, 2002.

6. *Biotechnology Patents in Europe and the EU's Biotechnology Directive.* In 1998, the European Parliament, concerned about the competitive threat of a robust American biotech industry, issued a biotechnology directive codifying patent protection for biotech-related inventions, including DNA sequences. *See* Directive 98/44/EC Legal Protection of Biotechnological Inventions. The directive was over ten years in the making and has been, as of this writing, adopted by only a minority of European Community member states, despite a deadline of July 30, 2000. One of the principal points of contention among several countries (*e.g.*, Netherlands) and political parties (*e.g.*, the Green Party) in adopting the directive continues to be the patenting of DNA sequences, which is stridently opposed on grounds of public morality. In an attempt to address this concern, Article 6(1) of the directive states that inventions are "unpatentable where their commercial exploitation would be contrary to *ordre public* or morality." This section mirrors EPC Article 53(a), which excludes from patent protection "inventions the publication or exploitation of which would be contrary to *ordre public* or morality."

The public morality argument is all but a whisper in American patent law circles. But while this argument commands greater attention in Europe, it is interesting to note that prior to the biotech directive, the European Patent Office

(EPO) issued (and continues to issue) patents on human DNA. For instance, in 1995, the EPO granted a patent on a DNA sequence encoding for a protein used during childbirth, Hormone Relaxin, 1995 O.J. E.P.O. 388 (Opp. Div.). The Opposition Division relied on the fact that the DNA sequence was "isolated from its surroundings." Perhaps the reason the biotech directive has been adamantly opposed is that directives are binding on member states in terms of results to be achieved. Therefore, an EU directive would require every EC member state to recognize patents on DNA sequences. This controversy becomes clearer when the procedural mechanism of the EU and American patent systems are compared. Contrary to the American system, a patent granted by the EPO matures into individual national patents (as designated by the applicant), which are governed by their respective national laws. There is no such thing, in other words, as a European patent that is valid throughout the entire EU. Member states, which often have divergent interpretations of the EPC, retain jurisdiction over issues of infringement and scope of patent protection, thus increasing the likelihood of disparate enforcement. *See* EPC Articles 64 and 138. As such, a directive would lead to greater uniformity.

7. *Medical Procedures.* Medical and surgical procedures are patentable subject matter under section 101. This is different than in Europe, where the European Patent Convention categorically excludes "[m]ethods for treatment of the human or animal body by surgery or therapy and diagnostic methods," EPC Article 52(4). But, in the name of concerns raised by medical professionals over patents issued on surgical techniques, such as those for performing cataract eye surgery (see U.S. Patent No. 5.080,111), Congress in 1996 enacted 35 U.S.C. § 287(c). This section provides that the remedies against patent infringement shall not apply to medical practitioners and related health entities for performance of a medial activity. In other words, the patent cannot be enforced. "Medical activity" is defined rather narrowly, however, "as the performance of a medical or surgical procedure on a body, but ... not ... (i) the use of a patented machine, manufacture, or composition of matter in violation of such patent, (ii) the practice of a patented use of a composition of matter in violation of such patent, or (iii) the practice of a process in violation of a biotechnology patent."

8. *Ongoing Debates about Life.* Debates about patents having to do with life have continued to be vibrant. At the time of this book's writing, on appeal before the Federal Circuit is the grant of a declaratory judgment of invalidity under § 101 in *Association for Molecular Pathology v. USPTO and Myriad Genetics,* which involves several patents related to the genes known as BRCA1 & 2 that are associated with breast and ovarian cancer.

SIDE BAR

Diamond v. Chakrabarty: A Historical Perspective

Ananda M. Chakrabarty*

The beginning of the application for a patent on an oil-eating microorganism (Pseudomonas species), mentioned in the above supreme court decision, dates back to my postdoctoral days at the University of Illinois at Urbana–Champaign during 1966–1971 when I was working in the laboratory of Professor I.C. Gunsalus on the genetic basis of nutritional versatility in microorganisms, particularly in members of the *Pseudomonas* species. Many of these pseudomonads were known to utilize as a nutiritional source such exotic compounds as terpenes, aliphatic, aromatic or polynuclear aromatic hydrocarbons, lignin-derived monomers, etc. The question I was interested in was how much genetic material (DNA) they had in order to exhibit such high nutritional versatility. We demonstrated that at least for terpene or aliphatic hydrocarbon degradation, the pseudomonads had the appropriate genes on plasmids. Many plasmids (that is, extrachromosomal elements that replicate separately from the chromosome) were known to be transmissible. They could be transferred from one cell to another by a process requiring cell-cell contact called conjugation (or sometimes even by naked DNA or phage-mediated transfer called transformation or transduction). These studies were primarily basic academic exercises and no potential application was foreseen.

In May, 1971, I moved to General Electric (GE) Corporate R & D center in Schenectady, N.Y., where I was assigned with a group to develop microorganisms capable of utilizing the undigested ligno-cellulosic components of cow manure. Since most microorganisms are 70 to 80% protein, growth on the ligno-cellulosic components of cow manure not only led to the loss of such components but also to an enrichment with microbial biomass of 70 to 80% protein. This work was, however, highly applied and I missed the opportunity to work on a more exciting system such as the organization and regulation of degradative genes in pseudomonads. However, an opportunity soon presented itself. In the late sixties and during 1970/71, in some parts of the world such as the Middle East, crude oil was cheap but protein was expensive. Several corporations in Europe were therefore interested in making protein from petroleum, much the same way we at GE were trying to make protein from cow manure for use as cattle feed. For degrading crude oil with consequent enrichment of protein, most of the companies were using specific yeast strains. Yeasts are good at eating the straight-chain aliphatic components (alkanes) of crude oil but are notoriously slow with the aromatic or polynuclear aromatic components. The conversion efficiency was therefore low. Since I missed working on degradative plasmids of pseudomonads, I started experimenting on new plasmids after my official work hours or during weekends. Indeed, I published a paper in 1972 from GE showing that the degradation of aromatic compounds such as salicylate was specified by plasmid-borne genes in yet another pseudomonad. Thus it occurred to me that one way to extend the substrate range of the pseudomonads to allow simultaneous degradation of a number of components of crude oil was to bring together plasmids from several naturally-occurring pseudomonads to a single pseudomonad (resulting in the so-called multi-plasmid pseudomonad). I previously observed that the enzymes encoded by the plasmid-borne genes had a broad substrate specificity. The presence of a number of plasmids in a single organism will allow rapid degradation of a number of hydrocarbon components of crude oil. A single culture is easier to grow and maintain than a mixed culture and is easier to study with respect to its pathogenicity or nutritional composition. Additionally, plasmids can be transferred to any appropriate pseudomonad isolated from a given environment, say Alaska, where it might survive better because of its fitness. Thus multi-plasmid organisms could be constructed from any indigenous population, and its survival ensured in that given environment. I also demonstrated that the multi-plasmid pseudomonad I constructed could grow much more rapidly with crude oil than the parent single-plasmid strains I used for plasmid transfer. Feeding such multi-plasmid bacterium, after they have grown on crude oil, to marine aquatic creatures which are subsequently used as food for fish, did not cause any detrimental effect to the fish.

While this research was going reasonably well, the price of oil was rising. It no longer made much sense to make protein from petroleum, since petroleum was already getting expensive. During a lunch time discussion with my colleagues, it was pointed out to me that even though a multi-plasmid oil-eating microorganism may not find a market in the animal feed industry, it could perhaps still be used to clean up oil spills. Such spills are basically eaten up by natural microflora and thus constitute a slow process. A quick laboratory scale experiment on an oil spill in a fish tank appeared to suggest that the genetically-improved multi-plasmid pseudomonad was indeed good at eating oil spills. This was also the time when I got an invitation to talk about hydrocarbon degradative plasmids in an international meeting in Tel Aviv. As required by GE rules, I submitted an abstract of my talk on the construction of oil-eating microorganisms to my management with a letter of invitation from Tel Aviv. This abstract ultimately reached the desk of Dr. Arthur Bueche, our Vice–President at GE. Normally such requests for meeting attendance are received and approved routinely; however, Dr. Bueche seemed intrigued by the report and during a chance meeting asked me If I was serious about this proposition. When I told him that I thought it was an interesting approach based on emerging ideas of plasmids encoding complete degradative pathways, he advised me to seek a patent before giving a formal talk. I was therefore given the go ahead to go to Tel Aviv and attend the meeting, but not present my talk. This was somewhat embarrassing since my name was already in the program and I had to get up and tell the audience why I could not give my talk. The ensuing silence, followed by chuckles, I thought at that time, was deafening. Be as it may, a patent was filed on my behalf on June 7, 1972, serial number 260,563, covering both the process of making multi-plasmid microorganism as well as the product microorganism itself.

In April, 1974, the patent and trademark office (PTO) rejected the product claim but allowed the process claim. They based their rejection on the ground that microorganisms are products of nature and as such cannot be patented. The patent lawyer at GE, Leo I. MaLossi, who had spent his career on patenting mechanical or chemical devices, was miffed at this argument since he was somewhat unfamiliar with the notion of non-patentability of life-forms. He felt that so long as the oil-eating microorganism was improved considerably by a technique that was new and useful, it merited patent protection. On appeal from GE, a three-man board of appeals of the PTO allowed that the multi-plasmid pseudomonad was not a product of nature because of its altered genetic composition, but upheld the rejection of the patent based on the fact that they were living entities.[1] The board argued that granting a patent on a living bacterium with multiple plasmids may not only open a floodgate for new microorganisms generated by the pharmaceutical industry, but to multi-cellular animals, including humans, with new organs such as a transplanted kidney, liver or heart. The board similarly rejected a product patent application from the Upjohn company scientist Malcolm E. Bergy on a purified version of an antibiotic producing strain of *Streptomyces* because of the living nature of the actinomycetes. Both GE as well as Upjohn appealed this decision to the United States Court of Customs and Patent

Appeals (CCPA). In both the cases, the CCPA ruled three-to-two that the patents should be granted since nothing in the patent laws barred the issuance of a patent to an otherwise patentable invention simply because it was alive. Judge Giles S. Rich of the CCPA, on behalf of the majority, delivered a notable and far-reaching opinion on the patentability of the oil-eating microorganisms.

The favorable ruling by the CCPA in early 1978 prompted the patent office to appeal to the U.S. Supreme Court. Initially, the Supreme Court sent back the *Bergy* case to the CCPA for reevaluation in light of an earlier Supreme Court decision (*Parker v. Flook*)[2] on the patentability of a mathematical algorithm. The CCPA was therefore instructed to rule on both the *Bergy* and the *Chakrabarty* cases together in light of *Parker v. Flook*.

In early 1979, Judge Giles Rich, again speaking on behalf of the majority, in *Bergy* and *Chakrabarty*, stressed that biological conversions mediated by microorganisms are basically an application of chemistry and chemical laws, and there is nothing in *Parker v. Flook* that demonstrated otherwise. Thus there is nothing inherently wrong or detrimental in the issuance of a patent on an invention involving living microorganisms.

In the summer of 1979, the patent office again appealed to the Supreme Court to reevaluate the CCPA ruling, which the Supreme Court agreed to review. By now, however, Upjohn lawyers had withdrawn their claim on the product patent, *viz.*, the claim covering the *Streptomyces* producing the antibiotic lyncomycin, thereby effectively removing their case from consideration by the Supreme Court. Ostensibly, this was done with the thought that the genetically-improved *Pseudomonas* strain had a better chance of being approved for patentability. Since Sidney Diamond was the Commissioner of Patents who petitioned the Supreme Court, the case was referred to as *Diamond v. Chakrabarty*.

On June 16, 1980, the U.S. Supreme Court, by a vote of 5 to 4, upheld the patentability of the multi-plasmid oil-eating pseudomonad, thereby subsequently allowing a multitude of genetically-engineered microorganisms, and as it turned out, genetically-engineered multi-cellular organisms including plants and animals, to be secured by patents. Chief Justice Warren Burger, speaking on behalf of the majority, cited all the basic principles that entitled the pseudomonad to be patented, basically along the lines enunciated by Judge Giles Rich of the CCPA.[3]

At the end, the Supreme Court decision was based on a very narrow point that dealt with the patentability of a new product or composition of matter, irrespective of whether it was alive or not. The emphasis was on novelty and human intervention, which meant that any genetically-improved product, alive or not, could be patented so long as it met the other prescribed criteria of patentability.

This decision had a major impact on the biotechnology industry. Indeed, out of ten *amicus* briefs filed to the court by various academic, industrial, foundation and scientific organizations, nine were supportive of the Chakrabarty position. During the decision making time, the PTO had more than 100 patent applications on genetic engineering waiting in the wings, most of which were subsequently granted based on the Supreme Court decision.

There were two major ramifications of the *Diamond v. Chakrabarty* decision. On the one hand, the controversy surrounding the patenting of living organisms galvanized many groups that opposed any form of genetic engineering pertaining to animals and humans. For them, life means something sacred, and nobody should play God by tinkering with the essential constituents of life. Many people were afraid that granting a patent on genetic improvement of a living bacterium is only the first step towards granting patents to animals and ultimately to humans. Thus the social, moral, ethical and potential biohazard issues of genetic engineering were extensively debated and brought to a focus. A casualty of this sharp focus on the potential hazard issue was the oil-eating pseudomonad itself. The genetically-engineered plants grown in fields or microorganisms grown in fermenters for production of valuable commodities presented less dangerous scenarios, since they can be accessed and killed, burned or uprooted if something went wrong. The application of microorganisms for pollution clean up or agricultural productivity in an open environment, however, presented much more complex scenarios since once released, there is no recall for such microorganisms. The legal and financial liability for the release of the oil-eating microorganisms, particularly for a company with substantial resources such as GE, was deemed too great for the industry to field test it in an open oil spill. This problem has not been resolved satisfactorily to date and very few genetically engineered microorganisms are currently being used for environmental restoration or agricultural applications.

On the other hand, the patenting of the oil-eating microorganisms led to a surge of patents being issued to genetically altered life forms including genetically engineered tryptophan-overproducing corn[4] and animals such as an oncomouse.[5] This oncomouse, genetically engineered to enhance its susceptibility to cancer, is the first patented animal that is designed to be used for screening potential carcinogenic materials. Human cells or genes are also being patented, an example being a patent directed to a cell line derived from the spleen of a leukemia patient in California.[6] The ownership of the patent was challenged by the patient who lost in the California courts.[7] Another example is a patent that covers isolated human bone marrow stem cells.[8] Recently, there has been a surge of patents issued for transgenic mammals whose epithelial cells are altered to make them less antigenic or for generating transgenic cattle.[9] Many of these patents that cover human cells or animal organs, or sometimes human disease genes such as the breast cancer genes BRCA1 and BRCA2, are meant for commercial purposes. There is great concern in some circles that increasingly higher forms of life, particularly human life, are losing their sanctity and are becoming parts of the marketplace economy. Reviews concerning patenting of human or animal cells or organs or a review of books dealing with complexities of patenting higher life forms for commercial purposes have now been published,[10] which provide interesting insights to the evolution of the *Diamond v. Chakrabarty* decision to the sphere of patenting all forms of life, including human cells and genes. The recent cloning of Dolly, a lamb obtained by removal of the DNA material from the oocytes of a Blackface ewe and then cloning the genetic material from the differentiated cells of the mammary gland of a 6 year old sheep, or the application for a patent on a yet to be produced hybrid of human and animal embryos,[11] have added significant concerns and confusions with regard to the cloning of humans or even the definition of what constitutes a human being.

A more recent outgrowth of this controversy encompasses the patenting of DNA. Vast amounts of useful DNA sequence information are being generated as part of the human genome project. In many instances, sequences of human genes and their regulatory regions, either whole or partial, are being patented, as part of expressed sequence tags (ESTs) or single nucleotide polymorphisms (SNPs).[12] The functionality of most of these genes or gene fragments is unknown and therefore their utility is not obvious. The patenting of a large number of these sequences is sought because of their potential importance in the detection and screening of diseased genes, which could be excellent diagnostic tests for commercial purposes. The patent office has decided to allow patenting of these ESTs and SNPs because of their potential utility in tracing ancestry, parentage, gene mapping and screening for predisposition to genetic diseases or environmental insults.[13] It is likely that patents issued on animal or human genes or tissues will play increasing roles not only in the commercial arena but also in all spheres of societal and judicial decisions,[14] which will be perhaps an unforeseen outcome of the *Diamond v. Chakrabarty* decision.

* Distinguished University Professor at the University of Illinois at Chicago. This *SIDE BAR* was written specially for PRINCIPLES OF PATENT LAW.

1. An excellent account of this legal controversy is presented in Daniel J. Kevles, *Ananda Chakrabarty wins a patent: Biotechnology, law, and society, 1972–1980*, 25(1) HISTORICAL STUDIES IN THE PHYSICAL AND BIOLOGICAL SCIENCES 111–135 (1994).

2. *Parker v. Flook*, 437 U.S. 584 (1978).

3. *See Kelves, supra*, note 2.

4. K. Hibbard, P. Anderson and M. Barker, US Patent 4, 581, 847, (1986).

5. P. Leder and T. Stewart, US Patent 4, 736, 866, (1988).

6. D. Golde and S. Quan. US Patent 4, 438, 032, (1984).

7. *See, Moore v. Regents of the University of California*, 51 Cal.3d 120, 793 P.2d 479 (Cal.1990).

8. A. Tsukamoto, C. Baum, Y. Aihara and I. Weissman, US Patent 5, 061, 620, (1991).

9. P. Sims, US Patent 5, 705, 732, (1998); H. DeBoer, US Patent 5, 633, 076, (1997); H. DeBoer et al., US Patent 5, 741, 957, (1998).

10. *See*, A. Kimbrell, *Crisis*, pages 43–48, May issue, (1993); M. Gladwell, *The New Yorker*, pages 120–124, November 13 issue, (1995).

11. *See*, Rick Weiss, *Patent Sought on Making Of Part–Human Creatures; Scientist Seeks to Touch Off Ethics Debate*, THE WASHINGTON POST, Section A, April 2, (1998).

12. J.J. Doll, 280 SCIENCE 689–690 (1998).

13. *Id.*

14. 36 JUDGES' JOURNAL 1–96 (1997).

NOTE ON PATENTS, BIOTECHNOLOGY, AND THE BAYH–DOLE ACT

Recent empirical studies have shown that the pharmaceutical and biotechnology industries rely heavily on the patent system. *See* Wesley M. Cohen et al., *Protecting Their Intellectual Assets: Appropriability Conditions and Why U.S. Manufacturing Firms Patent (or Not)*, (Nat'l Bureau of Econ. Research, Working Paper No. 7552, 2000); Robert Mazzoleni and Richard R. Nelson, *"The Benefits and Costs of Strong Patent Protection: A Contribution to the Current Debate,"* 27 Research

Policy 273, 276 (1998) (noting that small and medium size biotechnology firms provide "a striking example of enterprises that would not have come into existence without the prospect of a patent"). For more on the debate about the role of patents in biotechnology generally, consider the materials at the end of Chapter 6, *supra*, as well as the diverse views and perspectives collected in Perspectives on Properties of the Human Genome Project (2003, F. Scott Kieff, ed., Academic Press, an imprint of Elsevier).

The Chakrabarty decision was not the only major change to the biotechnology industry in 1980. To be sure, the decision in that case gave an essential boost to the nascent biotechnology industry. *See, e.g.,* Janice M. Mueller, *No "Dilettante" Affair: Rethinking the Experimental Use Exception to Patent Infringement for Biomedical Research Tools*, 76 Wash. L. Rev. 1, 5 n.23 (stating that *Chakrabarty* "is generally viewed as having given the green light to the U.S. biotechnology industry"); Donald Dunner, *Giles Sutherland Rich*, 9 Fed. Circuit B.J. 71 (noting that *Chakrabarty* "opened the doors to the then-fledgling biotechnology industry"). But that same year, Congress enacted what is known as the Bayh–Dole Act, which allows non-profit organizations, including universities, to "elect to retain title" to inventions derived from federally funded research and to license patents on these inventions. *See* 35 U.S.C. §§ 200–205. Between 1969 and 1986, universities were assigned 0.5% of issued utility patents, whereas in 2000 alone that figure rose to 2.0%. *See* http:www.uspto.gov. The policy and objective of Bayh–Dole is:

> to use the patent system to promote the utilization of inventions arising from federally supported research or development; to encourage maximum participation of small business firms in federally supported research and development efforts; to promote collaboration between commercial concerns and nonprofit organizations, including universities; to ensure that inventions made by nonprofit organizations and small business firms are used in a manner to promote free competition and enterprise without unduly encumbering future research and discovery; to promote the commercialization and public availability of inventions made in the United States by United States industry and labor; to ensure that the Government obtains sufficient rights in federally supported inventions to meet the needs of the Government and protect the public against nonuse or unreasonable use of inventions; and to minimize the costs of administering policies in this area.

35 U.S.C. § 200. The Bayh–Dole has been deemed largely successful in realizing these stated objectives. According to Professor Rebecca Eisenberg:

> Since its passage in 1980 the Bayh–Dole Act has been consistently hailed as an unqualified success in stimulating the commercial development of discoveries emerging from government-sponsored research in universities. Its promoters have cited the dramatic increase in numbers of patents obtained by universities, the superior record of universities, as compared to the federal government, in licensing their patents, and the explosion in collaborative research between universities and industry as evidence that the Bayh–Dole Act works in practice. Subsequent legislation has attempted to duplicate this success for government-sponsored research in other settings, including intramural research, thereby expanding the government's role as patent licensor.

Rebecca S. Eisenberg, *Public Research and Private Development: Patents and Technology Transfer in Government Sponsored Research*, 82 U. Va. L. Rev. 1663, 1708–09 (1996). *See also* Lori Pressman et al., *Pre–Production Investment and Jobs Induced by MIT Exclusive Patent Licenses: A Preliminary Model to Measure the Economic Impact of University Licensing* at http://www.autm.net/pubs/journal/95/

PPI95.html ("The Bayh–Dole Act, allowing the university to grant exclusive licenses, enables the university to make the high-risk investment more attractive to industry: if the company makes the investment and succeeds in developing the product, *exclusive patent protection* will reduce its market risk") (emphasis in original). *See also,* David C. Mowery, Richard R. Nelson, Bhaven N. Sampat, & Arvids A. Ziedonis, *The Growth of Patenting and Licensing by U.S. Universities: An Assessment of the Effects of the Bayh–Dole Act of 1980,* 30 Res. Pol'y 99–100 (2001) (noting the increase in licensing activity by universities after Bayh–Dole). But Bayh–Dole is not without its critics. *See, e.g.,* DEREK BOK, UNIVERSITIES IN THE MARKETPLACE 77 (2003) (While acknowledging the benefits of Bayh–Dole, Bok states that "[u]niversities have paid a price for industry support through excessive secrecy, periodic exposés of financial conflict, and corporate efforts to manipulate or suppress research results").

The top ten American universities receiving the most patents in 2003, according to the PTO, were: University of California (439); California Institute of Technology (139); MIT (127); University of Texas (96); Stanford (85); University of Wisconsin (84); Johns Hopkins (70); University of Michigan (63); Columbia (61); and Cornell and the University of Florida (59).

One of the earliest instances of a university-produced commercially valuable invention came from University of Wisconsin scientist, Henry Steenbock, in 1923–24. Mr. Steenbock discovered how to enrich milk with vitamin D. He Steenbock published his research in the Journal of Biological Chemistry in September 1924, prompting Quaker Oats to offer to buy the invention for $900,000. Although Mr. Steenbock refused to sell to Quaker, he suggested that a foundation be established that would hold title to his patented invention and license such to Quaker Oats. That foundation was the Wisconsin Alumni Research Foundation (WARF), founded in 1925 with the assistance of Quaker's attorneys. Over the next ten years, WARF earned $14 million in licensing revenue from Mr. Steenbock's invention.

The role of patent law and the Bayh–Dole Act in university-based research are discussed in the following *SIDE BAR* by Carl Gulbrandsen, Managing Director of WARF, one of the most prominent and oldest university technology-transfer offices.[14]

SIDE BAR

The Bayh–Dole Act and Universities Under the U.S. Patent System

Carl E. Gulbrandsen*

"Possibly the most inspired piece of legislation to be enacted in America over the past half-century was the Bayh–Dole Act of 1980. Together with amendments in 1984 and augmentation in 1986, this unlocked all the inventions and discoveries that had been made in laboratories throughout the United States with the help of taxpayer's money. More than anything, this single policy measure helped to reverse America's precipitous slide into industrial irrelevance." THE ECONOMIST, January 6, 2003

The Bayh–Dole Act ("The Act") P.L. 96–517 and amendments included in P.L. 98–620, enacted into law in 1984, a uniform patent policy for federally sponsored inventions. The Act permits a university, research

---

14. Thanks to Carl Gulbrandsen for conveying the history of WARF and the role of Henry Steenbock's invention in establishing WARF.

laboratory or small business to elect ownership in inventions arising from federally sponsored research occurring at their institution or small business. Small business can use the patented technology to build their companies. Universities can the license the technology, using the licensing proceeds to fund further research.

The concept of using patented university technology to generate licensing revenues to fund further research has been practiced by the Wisconsin Alumni Research Foundation ("WARF") since 1925. WARF, the patent management organization for the University of Wisconsin started off with a successful vitamin D technology that returned millions of dollars to WARF in the 1930s and early 1940s. This success was followed by the discovery at the university of the blood thinner, coumadin, or Warfarin (named after WARF). The licensing of coumadin brought significant revenues back to WARF throughout the 1950s and 1960s. Warfarin is still the most widely used blood thinner in the world having saved countless of millions of lives. Warfarin is also the most successful rodenticide or rat poison to be marketed. WARF's success and the money it was able to return to the University of Wisconsin, provided and continues to provide the university a "margin of excellence" that allows the university to compete on a global scale.

The early successes of WARF were based on university inventions arising out of research funded by the university or the State. During these early years the federal government was not a significant funder of university research. This changed following World War II, when the federal government greatly increased the amount of federally funded research at universities throughout the United States. Inventions arising from such research, however, were owned by the federal government and universities were not entitled to patent and license such inventions without permission from the funding agency. Obtaining such permission required extensive negotiation and often was unsuccessful. Even if permission was obtained, the requirements placed by the funding agency on how licensing of the technology was to be done often prevented successful licensing from occurring. Most of the inventions arising from federally funded research were retained by the funding agency and remained unlicensed. In 1980 for example, the federal government owned about 28,000 patents covering inventions arising from federally funded research, but only 5% of these were licensed to industry. It was clear that the benefit to the public of federally funded research was not being realized.

Over a twenty year period in the 1960s and 1970s, led by the University of Wisconsin, several universities negotiated institutional patent agreements ("IPAs") with the two largest federal funding agencies, the Department of Health, Education and Welfare (now Health and Human Services) and later the National Science Foundation. Universities that were parties to these agreements could claim ownership in inventions arising from research funded by HEW or NSF, depending on the particular IPA.

Leveraging their experience with the IPA, universities lobbied congress to expand the IPA-concept to cover all federal grants and contracts. Concurrently, policy makers in Washington were looking for a way to stimulate small business formation and growth. These two agendas became aligned in the effort to establish a uniform patent policy for federally funded inventions and on December 12, 1980 the Bayh–Dole Act ("the Act", named for its sponsors, U.S. Senators Birch Bayh and Robert Dole) was enacted.

The policy and objectives of the Act are set out in 35 United States Code (U.S.C.) § 200.

> It is the policy and objective of the Congress to use the patent system to promote the utilization of inventions arising from federally supported research or development; to encourage maximum participation of small business firms in federally supported research and development efforts; to promote collaboration between commercial concerns and nonprofit organizations, including universities; . . . to promote free competition and enterprise without unduly encumbering future research and discovery, . . . commercialization and public availability . . . ensure the Government obtains sufficient rights . . . protect the public against nonuse or unreasonable use . . . minimize the cost of administering policies in this area.

The scope of the Act is broad. It applies to essentially any federal "contract, grant or cooperative agreement with a non-profit organization or small business firm for the performance of experimental, developmental or research work whether the work is funded in full or in part" by the federal agency.

Its definition of what is an "invention" is equally broad. The term "invention" under the Act is defined as "any invention or discovery which is or may be patentable." It is interesting to note that the breadth of this language has expanded as the Court of Appeals for the Federal Circuit has expanded the scope of what is patentable. The Act also states that it applies to inventions that were "conceived or first actually reduced to practice in the performance of work under the funding agreement." So, a researcher could conceive of an invention using federally money and not actually make the invention until after the federal grant had expired and Bayh–Dole would still attach. Conversely, the research could conceive of an invention before a federal grant was given and reduce it to practice or make it during the grant and Bayh–Dole would attach.

The Act requires the institution or small business ("the contractor") that receives federal research funding to disclose to the funding agency within a reasonable time any inventions arising using the federal funds. It also requires that the contractor notify the agency within a specified period of time whether the contractor is electing to own the invention. If the contractor chooses to own the invention, it must file a patent before any statutory bar occurs and provide to the federal government a "nonexclusive, nontransferable, irrevocable, paid-up license to practice or have practiced for or on behalf of the United States any subject invention throughout the world."

To provide incentive to innovate, the Act requires that the contractor share royalties with inventors. What percentage of royalty should be shared with the inventor is not defined but the practice at most universities is to share a percentage of royalties after expenses. At some universities this may be as high as 50% of the net income from licensing. For universities and other non-profits, the residual of royalties after expenses and after paying the inventor must be used to support further research or education.

In keeping with the goal to stimulate small business, the Act requires a preference to licensing to small business. Thus, if a license is to be granted, it must be granted to a small business unless it is shown this is impractical or unfeasible. The Act also requires that if an exclusive license is granted, substantially all of the product licensed must be manufactured in the United States.

The success of the Act is implicit in the numbers. In 1980, about 1% of U.S. patents issued were owned by universities. Today that figure is 3% or higher. For the most part, inventions represented by these patents arise from basic research and form the basis for new products, new processes and even new industries—witness the biotechnology industry. It is estimated that the ability of universities to take title in federally sponsored inventions has resulted in the founding of 2,200 companies (start-ups) based on these inventions. These companies have provided some 260,000 high technology jobs contributing $40 billion to the U.S. economy on annual basis.1

The importance of being able to own the technology and use it to start companies cannot be underestimated. Start-up companies often need the initial guidance and nurture of the faculty member that first made the discovery or invention. WARF today has equity in over 30 start-up companies. All of these companies are based on inventions arising out of federally funded research. All of them pay high salaries to their employees and taxes to our community. This start-up activity is taking place at research universities and hospitals throughout the United States. Were it not for Bayh–Dole Act it is unlikely that any of these companies could have been formed.

The success of the Act has not gone unnoticed outside the borders of the United States. The Act has been studied widely by countries trying to emulate the technology success of the United States. Recently Japan has adopted a version of the Act and policy makers in Great Britain are also calling for similar legislation.

* Managing   Director,   Wisconsin   *Bar* was written specially for Principles of Alumni Research Foundation. This *Side*   Patent Law.

NOTE ON PLANT PATENTS

Compared to utility patents, there are relatively few plant patents issued every year. For instance, in 2001, the U.S. PTO granted 166,039 utility patents (from 326,508 applications) and 584 plant patents (from 944 applications). *See* http://www. uspto.gov/web/offices/ac/ido/oeip/taf/us _ stat.pdf. But plant patents have become extremely important to the agricultural/biotech industry. Proprietary protection for commercially valuable plants is potentially available under three statutory schemes: (1) Plant Patent Act (35 U.S.C. §§ 161–164); (2) Plant Variety Protection Act (7 U.S.C. § 2321 et seq.); and (3) the utility patent statute (35 U.S.C. § 101).

The Plant Patent Act of 1930

Recall in *Diamond v. Chakrabarty*, the Court noted that prior to 1930 patent protection was thought not to be available for plants because of "the belief that plants, even those artificially bred, were products of nature" and that they "were not amenable to the 'written description' requirement" of section 112. Opening up patent law to plants was, as early as the late 19th century, thought to be desirable. In fact, plant patent legislation was proposed in 1892, *see Imazio Nursery, Inc. v. Dania Greehouses*, 69 F.3d 1560, 1562–63 (Fed.Cir.1995), and was supported by prominent inventors such as Thomas Edison, who had argued "[n]othing that Congress could do to help farming would be of greater value and permanence than to give the plant breeder the same status as the mechanical and chemical inventors now have through the law." S. Rep. No. 315, 71st Cong., 2d Sess. 3 (1930) (Senate Report).

It wasn't until 1930, however, that Congress addressed these obstacles to plant patent protection by enacting the Plant Patent Act, which allows patent protection to "[w]hoever invents or discovers and asexually reproduces any distinct and new variety of plant, including cultivated sports, mutants, hybrids, and newly found seedlings, other than a tuber propagated plant or a plant found in an uncultivated state...." 35 U.S.C. § 161. Section 162 addresses the disclosure issue by providing that "[n]o plant patent shall be declared invalid for noncompliance with section 112 ... if the description is as complete as is reasonably possible." And section 163 gives the patent owner the "right to exclude others from asexually reproducing the plant, and from using, offering for sale, or selling the plant so reproduced, or any of its parts, throughout the United States, or from importing the plant so reproduced, or any parts thereof, into the United States."

Section 161 is limited to "asexually" reproduced plant varieties. Asexual reproduction means that the reproduction is done in a manner other than from seeds, such as by budding or grafting. Importantly, section 161 excludes from patent protection "a plant found in an uncultivated state," a plant found in nature so to speak. A variety is a subdivision of a species. For example, the grape varietals Cabernet Sauvignon or Chardonnay (for wine) and Emperor or Perlette (for table grapes) are subdivisions of the grape species *Vitis vinifera*, which in turn, is from the *Vitis* genus. Lastly, section 161 excludes from patent protection uncultivated plants. The Senate and House Committee Reports on the 1930 Act stressed that the Act did not include within its scope "varieties of plants which exists in an uncultivated or wild state, but are newly found by plant explorers or others." S. Rep., *supra*; H.R. Rep. 1129, 71st Cong., 2d Sess. (1930).

The Plant Variety Protection Act of 1970

The Plant Variety Protection Act (PVPA) was enacted by Congress in 1970 and recognizes the ability of plant breeders to produce seeds expressing stable genetic characteristics. In other words, it offers patent-like protection to *sexually* reproduced plants by authorizing the issuance of certificates of plant variety protection. The PVPA was thought to be necessary because it did not make economic sense to asexually reproduce major cash crops such as soybeans and cotton. *See* S. Rep. No. 91–1246 (Oct. 2, 1970) and H.R. No. 91–1605 (Oct. 13, 1970) ("[n]o protection is available to those varieties of plants which reproduce sexually, that is, generally, by seeds. Thus, patent protection is not available with respect to new varieties of most of the economically important agricultural crops such as cotton or soybeans"). Unlike the Plant Patent Act, which is administered by the PTO, the PVPA is administered by the Department of Agriculture. *See* 7 U.S.C. § 2321 et seq. Congress subsequently amended the PVPA in order to conform to international plant patent law and to facilitate U.S. entry into the International Union for the Protection of New Varieties of plants (UPOV).

The certification standards of the PVPA are less rigorous than the standards for utility, design and plant patents. The variety must merely be a "novel variety." There is no required standard of nonobviousness, and the disclosure requirements are not as demanding. But the PVPA contains a research exemption and a save-seed exemption (or "crop exemption"), which allows farmers to save seed from a previous crop for replanting on their own holdings or for noncommercial and private purposes. 7 U.S.C. § 2543. But, since 1994, PVPA certificate holders can preclude the sell of seed for reproductive purposes (known as "brown bag sales"). Also, it is quite common for major PVPA certificate holders to ask farmers to contractually waive the statutory save-seed exemption. These contracts would usually state that the farmer/buyer could use the seed "only for a single season." This type of agreement has been upheld by the Federal Circuit. *See Monsanto v. McFarling*, 302 F.3d 1291, 1298–99 (Fed.Cir.2002) (holding that contract does not violate antitrust laws or patent exhaustion/first sale doctrines). The use of these types of contracts has irritated farmers. *See* N.Y. Times, A–14 (Nov. 2, 2003) (responding to patent owners' enforcement of its single-season contracts, one farmer stated: "It's a God-given right that farmers were given when they were born to save these seeds. All we are is farmers trying to scrape a living out of this dirt").

As agriculture-biotechnology became increasingly lucrative, it became apparent that the PVPA did not offer adequate protection vis-à-vis the Patent Act. It also became apparent that a utility patent for plants was desirable because Title 35 does not have a save-seed exemption and there is no research exemption. *See, e.g., Ex parte Hibberd*, 227 U.S.P.Q. 443 (Bd. Pat. App. & Int'f 1985) (holding utility patent protection available for plant tissue, cells, seeds, or whole plants). The Supreme Court, in what was a wholehearted endorsement of *Chakrabarty's* broad reading of § 101, held that utility patents are available for plants, and that the Plant Patent Act and PVPA were not the only means for protecting plant varieties. *See J.E.M. AG Supply, Inc. v. Pioneer Hi–Bred Int'l, Inc.*, 534 U.S. 124 (2001). Nonetheless, because of ambiguities associated with the exhaustion and first-sale doctrines, owners of plant utility patents frequently employ so-called "seed-wrap" or "bag tag" licenses, which have the effect of limiting the purchased seed to single generation use. *See* Mark D. Janis & Jay P. Kesan, *U.S. Plant Variety Protection: Sound and Fury . . .?*, 39 Hous. L. Rev. 727 (2002). These types of licenses have also been held not to violate the exhaustion and first-sale doctrines. *See Pioneer Hi–Bred International, Inc. v. Ottawa Plant Food, Inc.*, 219 F.R.D. 135 (N.D. Iowa 2003). *See also* the following *Side Bar* by Edmund J. Sease, who successfully argued on behalf of Pioneer Hi–Bred before the Supreme Court.

Side Bar

Plant Patents and the J.E.M. AG Supply Case

Edmund J. Sease*

This case attracted world-wide attention to the issue of patentability of plants under the United States patent laws. Generally amicus briefs of biotech organizations and seed companies were in favor of patent protection and amicus briefs of farmer organizations and representatives of independent inventor groups were against utility patent protection for plants as placing yet another burden on farmers.

Since the 1930 Plant Patent Act (now 35 U.S.C. § 161–164), our Congress has struggled with the appropriate protection for plants. The historical problem had been the inability of patent applicants to meet the written description requirement of 35 U.S.C. § 112 which had been regularly used by examiners to reject utility patent applications for plants. The 1930 Plant Patent Act provided a very limited protection for *asexually* reproduced plants, i.e. those reproduced by means other than from seeds. Thus, for patent eligibility, only plants produced asexually from, for example, rooting of cuttings, layering, budding, in arching, grafting, etc.

were available for patenting. Since the covered plants were only those asexually reproduced, this meant that they were identical genetically to the patented plant. Any deviation from identical genetics was therefore a defense to infringement, and independent development by other means was also a defense, *Imazio Nursery, Inc. v. Dania Greenhouses* (69 F.3d 1560 (Fed.Cir.1995)). In effect, this protection was as limited as copyright protection, *i.e.,* only copying infringes.

Even though the exclusionary power was limited, the patent coverage was welcomed by plant breeders. However, some of the most important domestic crops are reproduced by plant breeders using sexual reproduction, not asexual. Sexual reproduction means that the parent plants each contribute to the formation of the embryo that will develop into the seed and eventually give rise to the plant. Typically this results from the transfer of pollen from an anther to the stigma of the pistil resulting in fertilization. Such common domestic crops as corn, soybeans, cotton, tomatoes and most vegetables are the result of pollination or sexual fertilization. Plant breeders of these very important products thus found the results of their research unprotectable.

In 1970, Congress passed the Plant Variety Protection Act (7 U.S.C. § 2402) to address the huge gap left by disallowing utility patents on sexually reproduced plants. This statute, administered by the United States Department of Agriculture, provided some limited coverage to novel varieties of sexually produced plants. The right to exclude, while somewhat broader than covering only the identical genetic plant (7 U.S.C. § 2541(a)) covered only essentially derived varieties, and had many major exemptions not applicable to regular utility patents. For these reasons, this Act also left plant breeders feeling they were discriminated against in not having access to regular utility patent laws for their inventions.

One can ask, as the lawyers wondered in this case, in view of the decision in *Diamond v. Chakrabarty* (447 U.S. 303 (1980)), why did the Court take this case? Some argued that the very fact the case was taken indicated a likely reversal, and a retraction from the broad basis philosophical endorsement of 35 U.S.C. § 101 patentability, i.e. "anything under the sun made by the hand of man" of *Chakrabarty*. Others took the view that it gave the Court the first opportunity to view a very general broad statutory subject matter statute (35 U.S.C. § 101) in comparison with a very specific narrower statutory regime of protection under the Plant Variety Protection Act, 7 U.S.C. § 2402(a) *et seq.* Of course to companies heavily engaged in plant genetic research, the Plant Variety Protection Act is unsatisfactory. In particular, there is a saved seed exemption, a research exemption and the limited scope of protection not unlike that of copyright law. The broader protection of the general utility patent statutes, where there is no research exemption, no saved seed exemption, and the established doctrine of equivalents results in more enticing protection for the expensive research engaged in by major seed companies such as Pioneer, Monsanto, etc. Their research expenditures are typically hundreds of millions of dollars a year for plant research.

The Court's decision in *J.E.M. Ag Supply vs. Pioneer Hi–Bred International* is a predictable following of the whole hearted endorsement of a broad interpretation of 35 U.S.C. § 101 espoused in *Chakrabarty*. Our appellate team in this case felt the Court would likely endorse the broad view of statutory subject matter in view of the fact that they had denied certiorari in an important and significant Federal Circuit case, *State Street Bank & Trust Co. v. Financial Group, Inc.* (149 F.3d 1368 (Fed.Cir. 1998)). In *State Street*, the Federal Circuit endorsed a broad interpretation of 35 U.S.C. § 101 (citing *Chakrabarty*) to include methods of doing business as patent eligible subject matter.

A contrary holding to the decision in *J.E.M. Ag Supply* might have had little lasting impact, in view of the ingenuity demonstrated by patent attorneys in crafting claims to meet the limits of 35 U.S.C. § 101. An historical view of the way lawyers have crafted claims to successfully distinguish, and ultimately obtain allowed claims for computer software demonstrates the ease with which any individual precedent may be distinguished in claim drafting. For this reason, I believe that the lasting impact of *J.E.M. Ag Supply* may not be the simple statement that plants are patentable subject matter under 35 U.S.C. § 101 and therefore eligible for utility patents, but may be that for the first time the United States Supreme Court endorsed dual regimes of statutory protection for the same "thing". Thus for example, it is conceivable that a plant may be eligible for protection as an asexually reproduced plant, under 35 U.S.C. § 161 *et seq.*, for a utility patent under 35 U.S.C. § 101 and for a Plant Variety Protection Act certificate under 7 U.S.C. § 2402(a). Carrying this a step further, one might well ask why shouldn't a wholly ornamental and different appearing rose, for example, be protectable under the design patent statutes, 35 U.S.C. § 171 *et seq.?* The answer clearly is that such a rose would be available for design patent protection, providing it is a new, ornamental and non-obvious design. To this writer's knowledge, so far no one has yet obtained a design patent on a plant. This will likely change in the future.

In seeking patent protection on plants, and to provide the maximum protection for the genetic research of a breeder, patent attorneys do not limit themselves to claims to the whole plant. Instead, routinely claims are presented for amino acid sequences, for identified genes, for pollen, for traits, and for the seeds.

Perhaps the most broad patents in terms of protection are not those that identify the plant genetically but those that identify the plant based on a set of characteristics or traits. Consider the following claim in U.S. Patent 4,627,192, for genetically altered sunflower seeds that have a different fatty acid profile than naturally occurring sunflower seeds.

1. A sunflower seed having an oleic acid content of approximately 80% or greater, relative to the total fatty acid content of said seed, and a ratio of the amount of linoleic acid in said seed to the amount of oleic acid in said seed of less than about 0.09, said seed being the product of a cross between (A) a first parent from sunflower line which is true-breeding for said oleic acid content and (B) a parent from a second sunflower line.

This claim, at least as approved initially from a patentability standpoint by the Federal Circuit in *In re Sigco Research*, (48 F.3d 1238 (Fed.Cir.1995)), covers a sunflower seed and plant that has a particular fatty acid profile. This is true regardless of how the plant was genetically produced, regardless of its breeding, regardless of its genetic characteristics, and regardless of its lineage. This patent was, of course, issued after *Chakrabarty*, but long before *J.E.M. Ag Supply*. It is submitted that as biological and breeding research techniques become more refined, along with testing systems for identifying genes, the allowance of such broad claims which might be called fingerprint claims (defining a characteristic of something rather than defining what the thing is) will become less routine.

Even in our current environment, the decision in *J.E.M. Ag Supply* has already been effective in promoting the progress of the useful arts, consistent with the U.S. Constitution Article I, Section 8, Clause 8. For example, patents are now issuing for plants that manufacture within themselves edible vaccines, plants that manufacture human drugs, plants that produce higher than normal yields, and even plants that are differing in color from the natural variety, i.e. red sunflowers, black roses, etc. We are, in the plant research field, literally at the beginning of the frontier much like we are on the beginning frontier of space exploration!

To some the flood of litigation that has resulted from the Patent Office's 1985 decision in *Ex Parte Hibberd*, (227 U.S.P.Q. 443 (Bd. Pat. App. & Interf. 1985)), is bad. To others it is analogous to the flood of litigation that occurred in the pharmaceutical field in the 1960's as it adapted a robust patent system. In the end, our patent system has proven a great equalizer, that is to say, it allows the small innovative company to compete with the larger established firms. It is this writer's view that the equalizer effect of a healthy patent system is essential to the field of plants.

The likelihood is that in view of *Chakrabarty*, in view of the refusal to grant certiorari in *State Street* and in view of the ringing endorsement of the broad rules of patentability under 35 U.S.C. § 101 in *J.E.M. Ag Supply*, the Court will not take a statutory subject matter case again in the reasonably near future. Nevertheless, there remains plenty of room for interesting litigation. Just for example, one of the least explored areas, but an inevitable consequence of allowing patenting of living organisms is the area of self-propagation in comparison with traditional rules of infringement. Who is responsible for pollen drift caused by naturally occurring winds developing infringing plants? What are the limits of equivalency to be applied for genetically different plants but nevertheless ones that have the same traits as the patented plant? Finally, a burning question ready for decision is the appropriate use of seed deposits that are made to meet the criteria of 35 U.S.C. § 112. As it now stands, such seeds can be accessed by paying a minor fee and requesting them. Once accessed, they provide the entire genetic map, all self-contained in a manner that can be propagated. Is such propagation a legitimate use or infringing? What if the propagation is only for research breeding purposes? And what if it only occurs for one generation and then the breeder is beyond the scope of the patent? Is this fair? These and other issues remain and will prove interesting topics for judicial decisions that will reflect the genius of our developing patent law.

---

* Edmund J. Sease is a partner in McKee, Voorhees & Sease. Mr. Sease argued before the Supreme Court on behalf of Pioneer Hi–Bred, the prevailing party in *J.E.M. Ag Supply v. Pioneer Hi–Bred International*, 534 U.S. 124 (2001). This Side Bar was written specially for Principles of Patent Law.

B. COMPUTER–RELATED INVENTIONS AND BUSINESS METHODS

The issue explored in this section is whether inventions relating to computers and business methods raise special problems when analyzed for statutory subject matter. As was the case with biotechnology-related inventions, and as the materials below show in some detail, the bottom line for inventions in this area is that although they indeed have raised a number of unique issues, it is not clear as a matter of positive law whether they actually do today. As in the preceding section regarding biotechnology, when studying the materials that follow the reader should carefully consider at least two important questions: (1) whether the debates raise arguments that are unique to computers or business methods; and (2) whether areas of patent law other than the statutory subject matter requirement can, do, or should, respond to those issues.

Gottschalk v. Benson

409 U.S. 63 (1972).

■ Mr. Justice Douglas delivered the opinion of the Court.

Respondents filed in the Patent Office an application for an invention which was described as being related "to the processing of data by program and more particularly to the programmed conversion of numerical information" in general-purpose digital computers. They claimed a method for converting binary-coded decimal (BCD) numerals into pure binary numerals. The claims were not limited to any particular art or technology, to any particular apparatus or machinery, or to any particular end use. They purported to cover any use of the claimed method in a general-purpose digital computer of any type. Claims 8 and 31[2] were rejected by the Patent Office but sustained by the Court of Customs and Patent Appeals, 441 F.2d 682. The case is here on a petition for a writ of certiorari. *Gottschalk v. Benson*, 405 U.S. 915, 92 S.Ct. 934, 30 L.Ed.2d 784.

The question is whether the method described and claimed is a "process" within the meaning of the Patent Act. [Footnote omitted].

A digital computer, as distinguished from an analog computer, operates on data expressed in digits, solving a problem by doing arithmetic as a person would do it by head and hand.[3] Some of the digits are stored as components of the computer. Others are introduced into the computer in a form which it is designed to recognize. The computer operates then upon both new and previously stored data. The general-purpose computer is designed to perform operations under many different programs.

The representation of numbers may be in the form of a time series of electrical impulses, magnetized spots on the surface of tapes, drums, or

---

2. They are set forth in the Appendix to this opinion.

3. See R. Benrey, Understanding Digital Computers 4 (1964).

discs, charged spots on cathode-ray tube screens, the presence or absence of punched holes on paper cards, or other devices. The method or program is a sequence of coded instructions for a digital computer.

* * *

The BCD system using decimal numerals replaces the character for each component decimal digit in the decimal numeral with the corresponding four-digit binary numeral, shown in the right-hand column of the table. Thus decimal 53 is represented as 0101 0011 in BCD, because decimal 5 is equal to binary 0101 and decimal 3 is equivalent to binary 0011. In pure binary notation, however, decimal 53 equals binary 110101. The conversion of BCD numerals to pure binary numerals can be done mentally through use of the foregoing table. The method sought to be patented varies the ordinary arithmetic steps a human would use by changing the order of the steps, changing the symbolism for writing the multiplier used in some steps, and by taking subtotals after each successive operation. The mathematical procedures can be carried out in existing computers long in use, no new machinery being necessary. And, as noted, they can also be performed without a computer.

The Court stated in *MacKay Co. v. Radio Corp.*, 306 U.S. 86, 94, 59 S.Ct. 427, 431, 83 L.Ed. 506 that "(w)hile a scientific truth, or the mathematical expression of it, is not patentable invention, a novel and useful structure created with the aid of knowledge of scientific truth may be." That statement followed the longstanding rule that "(a)n idea of itself is not patentable." *Rubber–Tip Pencil Co. v. Howard*, 20 Wall. (87 U.S.) 498, 507, 22 L.Ed. 410. "A principle, in the abstract, is a fundamental truth; an original cause; a motive; these cannot be patented, as no one can claim in either of them an exclusive right." *Le Roy v. Tatham*, 14 How. (55 U.S.) 156, 175, 14 L.Ed. 367. Phenomena of nature, though just discovered, mental processes, and abstract intellectual concepts are not patentable, as they are the basic tools of scientific and technological work. As we stated in *Funk Bros. Seed Co. v. Kalo Co.*, 333 U.S. 127, 130, 68 S.Ct. 440, 441, 92 L.Ed. 588, "He who discovers a hitherto unknown phenomenon of nature has no claim to a monopoly of it which the law recognizes. If there is to be invention from such a discovery, it must come from the application of the law of nature to a new and useful end." We dealt there with a "product" claim, while the present case deals with a "process" claim. But we think the same principle applies.

Here the "process" claim is so abstract and sweeping as to cover both known and unknown uses of the BCD to pure binary conversion. The end use may (1) vary from the operation of a train to verification of drivers' licenses to researching the law books for precedents and (2) be performed through any existing machinery or future-devised machinery or without any apparatus.

In *O'Reilly v. Morse*, 15 How. (56 U.S.) 62, 14 L.Ed. 601, Morse was allowed a patent for a process of using electromagnetism to produce distinguishable signs for telegraphy. Id., at 111, 14 L.Ed. 601. But the Court denied the eighth claim in which Morse claimed the use of "electro-magnetism, however developed for marking or printing intelligible characters, signs, or letters, at any distances." *Id.*, at 112. The Court in disallow-ing that claim said, "If this claim can be maintained, it matters not by what process or machinery the result is accomplished. For aught that we now know, some future inventor, in the onward march of science, may discover a mode of writing or printing at a distance by means of the electric or galvanic current, without using any part of the process or combination set forth in the plaintiff's specification. His invention may be less compli-cated—less liable to get out of order—less expensive in construction, and in its operation. But yet, if it is covered by this patent, the inventor could not use it, nor the public have the benefit of it, without the permission of this patentee." *Id.*, at 113, 14 L.Ed. 601.

In *The Telephone Cases*, 126 U.S. 1, 534, 8 S.Ct. 778, 782, 31 L.Ed. 863, the Court explained the *Morse* case as follows: "The effect of that decision was, therefore, that the use of magnetism as a motive power, without regard to the particular process with which it was connected in the patent, could not be claimed, but that its use in that connection could." Bell's invention was the use of electric current to transmit vocal or other sounds. The claim was not "for the use of a current of electricity in its natural state as it comes from the battery, but for putting a continuous current, in a closed circuit, into a certain specified condition, suited to the transmission of vocal and other sounds, and using it in that condition for that purpose." *Ibid.* The claim, in other words, was not "one for the use of electricity distinct from the particular process with which it is connected in his patent." *Id.*, at 535, 8 S.Ct., at 782. The patent was for that use of electricity "both for the magneto and variable resistance methods." *Id.*, at 538, 8 S.Ct., at 784. Bell's claim, in other words, was not one for all telephonic use of electricity.

In *Corning v. Burden*, 15 How. (56 U.S.) 252, 267–268, 14 L.Ed. 683, the Court said, "One may discover a new and useful improvement in the process of tanning, dyeing, etc., irrespective of any particular form of machinery or mechanical device." The examples, given were the "arts of tanning, dyeing, making waterproof cloth, vulcanizing India rubber, smelt-ing ores." *Id.*, at 267, 14 L.Ed. 683. Those are instances, however, where the use of chemical substances or physical acts, such as temperature control, changes articles or materials. The chemical process or the physical acts which transform the raw material are, however, sufficiently definite to confine the patent monopoly within rather definite bounds.

Cochrane v. Deener, 94 U.S. 780, 24 L.Ed. 139, involved a process for manufacturing flour so as to improve its quality. The process first separat-ed the superfine flour and then removed impurities from the middlings by blasts of air, reground the middlings, and then combined the product with the superfine. *Id.*, at 785, 24 L.Ed. 139. The claim was not limited to any special arrangement of machinery. *Ibid.* The Court said,

> That a process may be patentable, irrespective of the particular form of the instrumentalities used, cannot be disputed. If one of the steps of a process be that a certain substance is to be reduced to a powder, it may not be at all material what instrument or machinery is used to effect that object, whether a hammer, a pestle and mortar, or a mill. Either may be pointed out; but if the patent is not confined to that particular tool or machine, the

use of the others would be an infringement, the general process being the same. A process is a mode of treatment of certain materials to produce a given result. It is an act, or a series of acts, performed upon the subject-matter to be transformed and reduced to a different state or thing. *Id.*, at 787—788, 24 L.Ed. 139.

Transformation and reduction of an article "to a different state or thing" is the clue to the patentability of a process claim that does not include particular machines. So it is that a patent in the process of "manufacturing fat acids and glycerine from fatty bodies by the action of water at a high temperature and pressure" was sustained in *Tilghman v. Proctor*, 102 U.S. 707, 721, 26 L.Ed. 279. The Court said, "The chemical principle or scientific fact upon which it is founded is, that the elements of neutral fat require to be severally united with an atomic equivalent of water in order to separate from each other and become free. This chemical fact was not discovered by Tilghman. He only claims to have invented a particular mode of bringing about the desired chemical union between the fatty elements and water." *Id.*, at 729, 26 L.Ed. 279.

Expanded Metal Co. v. Bradford, 214 U.S. 366, 29 S.Ct. 652, 53 L.Ed. 1034, sustained a patent on a "process" for expanding metal. A process "involving mechanical operations, and producing a new and useful result," *id.*, at 385–386, 29 S.Ct., at 657, was held to be a patentable process, process patents not being limited to chemical action.

Smith v. Snow, 294 U.S. 1, 55 S.Ct. 279, 79 L.Ed. 721, and *Waxham v. Smith*, 294 U.S. 20, 55 S.Ct. 277, 79 L.Ed. 733, involved a process for setting eggs in staged incubation and applying mechanically circulated currents of air to the eggs. The Court, in sustaining the function performed (the hatching of eggs) and the means or process by which that is done, said:

> By the use of materials in a particular manner, he secured the performance of the function by a means which had never occurred in nature and had not been anticipated by the prior art; this is a patentable method or process. . . . A method, which may be patented irrespective of the particular form of the mechanism which may be availed of for carrying it into operation, is not to be rejected as "functional" merely because the specifications show a machine capable of using it. 294 U.S., at 22, 55 S.Ct., at 278.

It is argued that a process patent must either be tied to a particular machine or apparatus or must operate to change articles or materials to a "different state or thing." We do not hold that no process patent could ever qualify if it did not meet the requirements of our prior precedents. It is said that the decision precludes a patent for any program servicing a computer. We do not so hold. It is said that we have before us a program for a digital computer but extend our holding to programs for analog computers. We have, however, made clear from the start that we deal with a program only for digital computers. It is said we freeze process patents to old technologies, leaving no room for the revelations of the new, onrushing technology. Such is not our purpose. What we come down to in a nutshell is the following.

It is conceded that one may not patent an idea. But in practical effect that would be the result if the formula for converting BCD numerals to pure binary numerals were patented in this case. The mathematical formula involved here has no substantial practical application except in connection with a digital computer, which means that if the judgment below is affirmed, the patent would wholly pre-empt the mathematical formula and in practical effect would be a patent on the algorithm itself.

It may be that the patent laws should be extended to cover these programs, a policy matter to which we are not competent to speak. The President's Commission on the Patent System[4] rejected the proposal that these programs be patentable:[5]

> Uncertainty now exists as to whether the statute permits a valid patent to be granted on programs. Direct attempts to patent programs have been rejected on the ground of nonstatutory subject matter. Indirect attempts to obtain patents and avoid the rejection, by drafting claims as a process, or a machine or components thereof programmed in a given manner, rather than as a program itself, have confused the issue further and should not be permitted.
>
> The Patent Office now cannot examine applications for programs because of a lack of a classification technique and the requisite search files. Even if these were available, reliable searches would not be feasible or economic because of the tremendous volume of prior art being generated. Without this search, the patenting of programs would be tantamount to mere registration and the presumption of validity would be all but nonexistent.
>
> It is noted that the creation of programs has undergone substantial and satisfactory growth in the absence of patent protection and that copyright protection for programs is presently available

If these programs are to be patentable,[6] considerable problems are raised which only committees of Congress can manage, for broad powers of investigation are needed, including hearings which canvass the wide variety of views which those operating in this field entertain. The technological problems tendered in the many briefs before us[7] indicate to us that considered action by the Congress is needed.

REVERSED.

■ MR. JUSTICE STEWART, MR. JUSTICE BLACKMUN, and MR. JUSTICE POWELL took no part in the consideration or decision of this case.

APPENDIX TO OPINION OF THE COURT

Claim 8 reads:

> The method of converting signals from binary coded decimal form into binary which comprises the steps of
>
> (1) storing the binary coded decimal signals in a reentrant shift register,

---

4. "To Promote the Progress of . . . Useful Arts," Report of the President's Commission on the Patent System (1966).

5. *Id.*, at 13.

6. See Wild, *Computer Program Protection: The Need to Legislate a Solution*, 54 CORN.L.REV. 586, 604–609 (1969); Bender, *Computer Programs: Should They Be Patentable?*, 68 COL.L.REV. 241 (1968); Buckman, *Protection of Proprietary Interest in Computer Programs*, 51 J.PAT.OFF.SOC. 135 (1969).

7. Amicus briefs of 14 interested groups have been filed on the merits in this case.

(2) shifting the signals to the right by at least three places, until there is a binary "1" in the second position of said register,

(3) masking out said binary "1" in said second position of said register,

(4) adding a binary "1" to the first position of said register,

(5) shifting the signals to the left by two positions,

(6) adding a "1" to said first position, and

(7) shifting the signals to the right by at least three positions in preparation for a succeeding binary "1" in the second position of said register.

[Claim 13 Omitted]

NOTES

1. *Beyond an Algorithm?* Study claim 8 that was published by the Court in the Appendix to its opinion. Does it recite anything more than an abstract mathematical process? The Court begins by citing *MacKay Co. v. Radio Corp.*, *O'Reilly v. Morse* and *The Telephone Cases* for the proposition that a claim may be so abstract and sweeping as to cover both the "known and unknown." To what extent is this reasoning really either (1) a prior art-based objection to patentability that could be addressed under principles of novelty (35 U.S.C. § 102) and nonobviousness (35 U.S.C. § 103); or (2) an inadequacy of description objection under 35 U.S.C. § 112? The Court then cites *Corning*, *Cochrane*, *Tilghman*, *Expanded Metal*, and *Snow*, to support the reasoning that a patent claim must be sufficiently "tied to a particular" so as not to "wholly preempt the mathematical formula ... [as] a patent on the algorithm itself." Is the Court correct in denying that its reasoning "precludes a patent for any program" or "freeze[s] process patents to old technologies?"

2. *A Look to the Future.* What does *Benson* teach about the all-important boundary that separates ideas and laws of nature from the applied or useful arts? Soon after *Benson*, Judge Rich wrote in dissent in *In re Johnston*, 502 F.2d 765 (CCPA 1974):

> On the authority of *Gottschalk v. Benson*, 409 U.S. 63 (1972), I would affirm the rejection of the claims on appeal which was made by the board under § 101, as requested by the Solicitor for the Patent Office.... The board did not, of course, have the benefit of the Supreme Court's views in *Benson* because the board decision was on October 27, 1971, and *Benson* was not decided by the Supreme Court until November 20, 1972.

> The Supreme Court held the process claims in *Benson* unpatentable under § 101. As the solicitor points out, appellant, in his main brief, ignored the Supreme Court *Benson* decision. In his reply brief he endeavors to deal with it—unsuccessfully, in my view. He attempts to distinguish on the ground that the claims here are directed to machines while *Benson* involved process claims. I think that will not suffice. Appellant has to concede that " ... the only resemblance of this case to *Benson* is that of the use of computer programs to embody the invention." Therein lies the rub, for appellee (The Patent Office) would deny patents for all software-embodied inventions.

> The board, which was dealing with claims of appellant cast in both process and machine form, said the following, with which I agree:

>> We see no essential difference in substance between these apparatus claims which define only broad means for performance of the steps of a data processing method and process claims 25, 26 and 27 which define the steps of the data processing method as being

carried out by any conventional data processing machine. Hence, we consider that both the apparatus and the method claims on appeal must stand or fall together.

I realize that claims 25, 26, and 27 are not on appeal but I do not take the board's comment as being restricted to them among the process claims. The point is that the machine or apparatus and process claims are really directed to the same invention, of which appellant's main brief says:

> ... this invention is being sold as a computer program to banks and to other data processing companies so that they can perform these data processing services for depositors.

What could more clearly reveal the reality that the invention is a program—software—and that is what appellant wants to protect by the appealed "machine system" claims? Appellant did not invent a machine—i.e., "hardware." Appellant's brief further states:

> This machine was reduced to practice in the software form of computer programs....

I am quite familiar with the legal doctrine that a new program makes an old general purpose digital computer into a new and different machine. This court has been through that many times and I am not denying the validity of this principle—which partakes of the nature of a legal fiction when it comes to drafting claims. My problem is that, knowing the invention to be a new program, I must decide whether it is patentable in any claimed form in view of *Benson*, whether claimed as a machine, a "machine system," or otherwise. I am probably as much—if not more—confused by the wording of the *Benson* opinion as many others. What the Court did in its decision reversing the holding of this court that Benson and Tabbot's method claims were patentable subject matter under 101 contains a message that is loud and clear. If those claims are not to patentable subject matter, neither, in my view, are the claims here, regardless of difference in form. Benson et al. had a program invention too and they could have cast their claims in machine system form just as appellant did. Every competent patent draftsman knows how to do that.

It seems to me important to focus on what the Supreme Court did in *Benson*, rather than on the specifics of its explanation of why it did it. I have no idea what was in the collective mind of the six-justice Court in approving the statements:

> It is said that the decision precludes a patent for any program servicing a computer. We do not so hold.... It is said we freeze process patents to old technologies, leaving no room for the revelations of the new, onrushing technology. Such is not our purpose.

These are the comforting words to which some inventors of software and owners of software inventions look for solace. I find it more significant to contemplate the identities of the troops lined up for battle in *Benson* and observe which side obtained the victory. On the one side was the Government, against patenting programs or software, supported by the collective forces of major hardware (*i.e.*, computer) manufacturers and their representative associations who, for economic reasons, did not want patents granted on programs for their machines. On the other side was Benson *et al.* and their assignee and assorted lawyers and legal groups who were in favor of patent protection for programs or software. The anti-patenting forces won the victory—if not an altogether clear one—and on the legal principle that the Benson et al. way of programming a computer to do a particularly useful job of general applicability in the data processing field was the kind of invention the Supreme Court would not approve patenting without prior consideration by and specific authorization from the Congress. The major part of the rather brief and now famous "nutshell" conclusion of the Court's opinion dwells heavily on this point.

I can find no realistic distinction in kind between the Benson *et al.* invention and the invention here and I conclude that the *Benson* decision requires us to affirm the rejection of claims 20–24 as directed to non-patentable subject matter under 35 U.S.C. 101. Holding that view, I find it unnecessary to consider the remaining four grounds of rejection discussed by my colleagues.

It has been suggested that the position I am taking is inconsistent with the position I have taken or the views I have expressed in others of the many carefully reasoned opinions of this court on the statutory subject matter question under 35 U.S.C. 101 which led to *Benson*, none of which was discussed or even recognized in the Supreme Court's *Benson* opinion. As a result, the value of those opinions as precedents has become unsettled.

It may well be that I seem to have been inconsistent. As the author of the opinion of this court in *Benson*, which was wholly reversed, I have not been persuaded by anything the Supreme Court said that we made a "wrong" decision and I therefore do not agree with the Supreme Court's decision. But that is entirely beside the point. Under our judicial system, it is the duty of a judge of a lower court to try to follow in spirit decisions of the Supreme Court—that is to say, their "thrust." I do not deem it to be my province as a judge to assume an advocate's role and argue the rightness or wrongness of what the Court has decided or to participate in what I regard as the inconsistent decision here, supported by a bare majority which tries in vain, and only briefly, to distinguish *Benson* by discussing form rather than substance and various irrelevancies like pre-*Benson* decisions of this court, the banking business, social science, and the liberal arts. I deem it to be the Supreme Court's prerogative to set the limits on *Benson*, which was broadly based. I hope it will do so. As John W. Davis, erstwhile outstanding Solicitor General, once said, "The first requirement of any judicial opinion is utter clarity."[8]

Do you agree with Judge Rich's view that *Benson* was "broadly based" and that it effectively blocked patents on programs in any form?

3. *Criticism of Benson.* Consider Judge Rich's criticism of *Benson* that the Supreme Court's wording caused confusion and his positivist view towards a lower court's duty to exercise judicial restraint. Notice, though, his reminder, or invitation, that it is "the Supreme Court's prerogative to set the limits on *Benson*." Indeed, the reminder did not go unnoticed and *Johnston* itself made its way up to the Supreme Court. Although *Johnston* was reversed by the Supreme Court on other grounds than those discussed by Judge Rich—as urged in the separate dissent by then Chief Judge Markey, the invention was held obvious under 35 U.S.C. § 103. 425 U.S. 219, 96 S.Ct. 1393 (1976)—it is important to note that before reaching the issue of obviousness, the Supreme Court in *Dann v. Johnston*, 425 U.S. at 224, 96 S.Ct. at 1396, did speak on the issue of statutory subject matter:

In *Benson*, the respondent sought to patent as a "new and useful process, [...] a method of programming a general-purpose digital computer to

---

8. Harbaugh, Lawyer's Lawyer, The Life of John W. Davis, Oxford University Press, New York (1973), p. 108.

convert signals from binary-coded decimal form into pure binary form." 409 U.S. at 65, 93 S.Ct. at 254. As we observed: "The claims were not limited to any particular art or technology, to any particular apparatus or machinery, or to any particular end use." *Id*. At 64. Our limited holding, *id*. at 71, 93 S.Ct. at 257, was that respondent's method was not a patentable "process" as that term is defined in 35 U.S.C. § 100(b).

But what was the effect of the *Dann v. Johnston* limit on *Benson*? Almost immediately after the decision in *Dann v. Johnston*, and commenting directly on the Supreme Court's above-quoted statement, Judge Rich wrote, again in dissent, in *In re Chatfield*, 545 F.2d 152, 161–162 (1976):

> That brief observation [by the Supreme Court in *Dann v. Johnston*] adds considerably to the already existing ambiguity inherent in the *Benson* opinion. Does it say Benson's two claims were held non-statutory only because they were not limited to any particular technology, apparatus, or end use?
>
> Does the Supreme Court not regard data processing as a technology, data-processing equipment as apparatus, or the necessary conversion in such apparatus of binary-coded-decimal to pure binary signals as an end use?
>
> The answers to these questions are very important because in the instant case, and in *In re Noll*, the invention relates only to the operation of data-processing equipment ("computers") without reference to any other "technology," "apparatus," or "end use." How, then, can this case be distinguished from *Benson* even when the narrowest possible view of that decision is taken? Just how "limited" was the holding in *Benson* supposed to be? Benson's claims were in fact limited to a method carried out in data-processing apparatus (including a "reentrant shift register," claim 8) and to "A data processing method" (claim 13). Benson did not claim a "formula."
>
> In the *Benson* opinion, the Court states at the outset that "The question is whether the method described and claimed is a 'process' within the meaning of the Patent Act." (Sections 101 and 100(b) were quoted in a footnote to that statement.) But nowhere in the *Benson* opinion have I ever, after many attempts, been able to find an express answer to that question, for which reason, as more fully explained in my dissenting opinion in *Johnston, supra*, I have turned to the competing contentions which were presented to the Supreme Court in *Benson*, to its decision that we erred in holding the claims statutory, which was our only holding, and have concluded that the members of the Court participating in that decision were unanimous in holding that programs for general-purpose digital computers, at least when claimed as a "process," are not within the meaning of that category of inventions in the statute. It is my own view that claiming as a "machine" instead of as a "process" is no distinction at all because it is merely a drafter's choice.
>
> My colleagues of the majority take a narrower view of *Benson* and arrive at an opposite result in these two new cases, as another majority did in *Johnston*. This, to me, signals an urgent need to settle the question of patent protection for software by higher authority than this court so that the Patent and Trademark Office, the Federal judiciary as a whole, and the data-processing industry (hardware and software both) may know what the law on software patentability is. It is a socioeconomic issue with an impact of considerable magnitude, particularly on the practical operation of the Patent and Trademark Office. It is obviously not going to be finally decided in this court. Two Commissioners (Gottschalk and Dann) have obtained

review of our decisions in the Supreme Court and in both instances (*Benson* and *Johnston*) obtained reversals; but here we are in two more cases, three-to-two, reversing findings by the Office that program inventions are non-statutory under § 101. It seems to me like taking the problem of school segregation to court on a case-by-case basis, one school at a time.

4. *Was Benson An Extreme Case?* Were the claims in *Benson* so clearly abstract that the narrow holding of invalidity would not be objectionable even today? Or, as Judge Rich suggests in *Chatfield*, were the claims in *Benson* so limited in concrete ways that the holding of unpatentable subject matter would not be supported today? *Compare* Pamela Samuelson, *Benson Revisited: The Case Against Patent Protection for Algorithms and Other Computer–Related Inventions*, 39 EMORY L. REV. 1025 (1990) (arguing there is a basis in patent law for denying patents on computer program algorithms and other computer-related inventions, and stating "that the computer software industry has grown significantly without patent protection and that many in the industry express opposition to or doubts about patent protection for software innovations suggest that we should be wary of a policy that would grant patents to any computer program-related innovation") and Donald S. Chisum, *The Patentability of Algorithms*, 47 U. PITT. L. REV. 959 (1986) (arguing for the patentability for of algorithms and computer-related inventions). For a nice overview of the case law relating to the patentability of algorithms and computer-related inventions, *see* Robert A. Kreiss, *Patent Protection for Computer Programs and Mathematical Algorithms: The Constitutional Limitations on Patentable Subject Matter*, 29 N.M. L. REV. 31 (1999).

Diamond v. Diehr

450 U.S. 175 (1981).

■ JUSTICE REHNQUIST delivered the opinion of the Court.

We granted certiorari to determine whether a process for curing synthetic rubber which includes in several of its steps the use of a mathematical formula and a programmed digital computer is patentable subject matter under 35 U.S.C. § 101.

I

The patent application at issue was filed by the respondents on August 6, 1975. The claimed invention is a process for molding raw, uncured synthetic rubber into cured precision products. The process uses a mold for precisely shaping the uncured material under heat and pressure and then curing the synthetic rubber in the mold so that the product will retain its shape and be functionally operative after the molding is completed.[1]

Respondents claim that their process ensures the production of molded articles which are properly cured. Achieving the perfect cure depends upon several factors including the thickness of the article to be molded, the temperature of the molding process, and the amount of time that the article is allowed to remain in the press. It is possible using well-known time, temperature, and cure relationships to calculate by means of the

---

1. A "cure" is obtained by mixing curing agents into the uncured polymer in advance of molding and then applying heat over a period of time. If the synthetic rubber is cured for the right length of time at the right temperature, it becomes a usable product.

Arrhenius equation[2] when to open the press and remove the cured product. Nonetheless, according to the respondents, the industry has not been able to obtain uniformly accurate cures because the temperature of the molding press could not be precisely measured, thus making it difficult to do the necessary computations to determine cure time.[3] Because the temperature inside the press has heretofore been viewed as an uncontrollable variable, the conventional industry practice has been to calculate the cure time as the shortest time in which all parts of the product will definitely be cured, assuming a reasonable amount of mold-opening time during loading and unloading. But the shortcoming of this practice is that operating with an uncontrollable variable inevitably led in some instances to overestimating the mold-opening time and overcuring the rubber, and in other instances to underestimating that time and undercuring the product.[4]

Respondents characterize their contribution to the art to reside in the process of constantly measuring the actual temperature inside the mold. These temperature measurements are then automatically fed into a computer which repeatedly recalculates the cure time by use of the Arrhenius equation. When the recalculated time equals the actual time that has elapsed since the press was closed, the computer signals a device to open the press. According to the respondents, the continuous measuring of the temperature inside the mold cavity, the feeding of this information to a digital computer which constantly recalculates the cure time, and the signaling by the computer to open the press, are all new in the art.

The patent examiner rejected the respondents' claims on the sole ground that they were drawn to nonstatutory subject matter under 35 U.S.C. § 101.[5] He determined that those steps in respondents' claims that

---

2. The equation is named after its discoverer Svante Arrhenius and has long been used to calculate the cure time in rubber-molding presses. The equation can be expressed as follows:

$$\ln v = CZ + x$$

wherein ln v is the natural logarithm of v, the total required cure time; C is the activation constant, a unique figure for each batch of each compound being molded, determined in accordance with rheometer measurements of each batch; Z is the temperature in the mold; and x is a constant dependent on the geometry of the particular mold in the press. A rheometer is an instrument to measure flow of viscous substances.

3. During the time a press is open for loading, it will cool. The longer it is open, the cooler it becomes and the longer it takes to reheat the press to the desired temperature range. Thus, the time necessary to raise the mold temperature to curing temperature is an unpredictable variable. The respondents claim to have overcome this problem by continuously measuring the actual temperature in the closed press through the use of a thermocouple.

4. We note that the petitioner does not seriously contest the respondents' assertions regarding the inability of the industry to obtain accurate cures on a uniform basis. See Brief for Petitioner 3.

5. Respondents' application contained 11 different claims. [Representative Claims 1 and 11 provide]

1. A method of operating a rubber-molding press for precision molded compounds with the aid of a digital computer, comprising:

    [a]   providing said computer with a data base for said press including at least,

        [1]   natural logarithm conversion data (ln),

        [2]   the activation energy constant (C) unique to each batch of said compound being molded, and

are carried out by a computer under control of a stored program constituted nonstatutory subject matter under this Court's decision in *Gottschalk v. Benson*, 409 U.S. 63, 93 S.Ct. 253, 34 L.Ed.2d 273 (1972). The remaining [additional] steps—installing rubber in the press and the subsequent closing of the press—were "conventional and necessary to the process and cannot be the basis of patentability." The examiner concluded that respondents' claims defined and sought protection of a computer program for operating a rubber-molding press.

The Patent and Trademark Office Board of Appeals agreed with the examiner, but the Court of Customs and Patent Appeals reversed [in an opinion by Judge Rich]. *In re Diehr*, 602 F.2d 982 (1979). The court noted that a claim drawn to subject matter otherwise statutory does not become nonstatutory because a computer is involved. The respondents' claims were not directed to a mathematical algorithm or an improved method of calculation but rather recited an improved process for molding rubber articles by solving a practical problem which had risen in the molding of rubber products.

The Commissioner of Patents and Trademarks sought certiorari arguing that the decision of the Court of Customs and Patent Appeals was inconsistent with prior decisions of this Court. Because of the importance of the question presented, we granted the writ. 445 U.S. 926, 100 S.Ct. 1311, 63 L.Ed.2d 758 (1980).

II

Last Term in *Diamond v. Chakrabarty*, 447 U.S. 303, 100 S.Ct. 2204, 65 L.Ed.2d 144 (1980), this Court discussed the historical purposes of the patent laws and in particular 35 U.S.C. § 101. As in *Chakrabarty*, we must here construe 35 U.S.C. [§§ 100(b) and 101]....

In cases of statutory construction, we begin with the language of the statute. Unless otherwise defined, "words will be interpreted as taking their ordinary, contemporary, common meaning," *Perrin v. United States*, 444 U.S. 37, 42, 100 S.Ct. 311, 314, 62 L.Ed.2d 199 (1979), and, in dealing with the patent laws, we have more than once cautioned that "courts

---

[3] a constant (x) dependent upon the geometry of the particular mold of the press,

[b] initiating an interval timer in said computer upon the closure of the press for monitoring the elapsed time of said closure,

[c] constantly determining the temperature (Z) of the mold at a location closely adjacent to the mold cavity in the press during molding,

[d] constantly providing the computer with the temperature (Z),

[e] repetitively calculating in the computer, at frequent intervals during each cure, the Arrhenius equation for reaction time during the cure, which is

$$\ln v = CZ + x$$

where v is the total required cure time,

[f] repetitively comparing in the computer at said frequent intervals during the cure each said calculation of the total required cure time calculated with the Arrhenius equation and said elapsed time, and

[g] opening the press automatically when a said comparison indicates equivalence.

[Claim 11 omitted].

'should not read into the patent laws limitations and conditions which the legislature has not expressed.'" *Diamond v. Chakrabarty, supra,* at 308, 100 S.Ct., at 2207 quoting *United States v. Dubilier Condenser Corp.,* 289 U.S. 178, 199, 53 S.Ct. 554, 561, 77 L.Ed. 1114 (1933).

The Patent Act of 1793 defined statutory subject matter as "any new and useful art, machine, manufacture or composition of matter, or any new or useful improvement [thereof]." Act of Feb. 21, 1793, ch. 11, § 1, 1 Stat. 318. Not until the patent laws were recodified in 1952 did Congress replace the word "art" with the word "process." It is that latter word which we confront today, and in order to determine its meaning we may not be unmindful of the Committee Reports accompanying the 1952 Act which inform us that Congress intended statutory subject matter to "include anything under the sun that is made by man." S.Rep.No.1979, 82d Cong., 2d Sess., 5 (1952); H.R.Rep.No.1923, 82d Cong., 2d Sess., 6 (1952), U.S.Code Cong. & Admin.News 1952, pp. 2394, 2399.

Although the term "process" was not added to 35 U.S.C. § 101 until 1952 a process has historically enjoyed patent protection because it was considered a form of "art" as that term was used in the 1793 Act.[7] In defining the nature of a patentable process, the Court stated:

> That a process may be patentable, irrespective of the particular form of the instrumentalities used, cannot be disputed.... A process is a mode of treatment of certain materials to produce a given result. It is an act, or a series of acts, performed upon the subject-matter to be transformed and

---

7. In *Corning v. Burden,* 15 How. 252, 267–268, 14 L.Ed. 683 (1853), this Court explained:

> A process, *eo nomine,* is not made the subject of a patent in our act of congress. It is included under the general term "useful art." An art may require one or more processes or machines in order to produce a certain result or manufacture. The term machine includes every mechanical device or combination of mechanical powers and devices to perform some function and produce a certain effect or result. But where the result or effect is produced by chemical action, by the operation or application of some element or power of nature, or of one substance to another, such modes, methods, or operations, are called processes. A new process is usually the result of discovery; a machine of invention. The arts of tanning, dyeing, making water-proof cloth, vulcanizing India rubber, smelting ores, and numerous others, are usually carried on by processes as distinguished from machines. One may discover a new and useful improvement in the process of tanning, dyeing, & c., irrespective of any particular form of machinery or mechanical device. And another may invent a labor-saving machine by which this operation or process may be performed, and each may be entitled to his patent. As, for instance, A has discovered that by exposing India rubber to a certain degree of heat, in mixture or connection with certain metallic salts, he can produce a valuable product, or manufacture; he is entitled to a patent for his discovery, as a process or improvement in the art, irrespective of any machine or mechanical device. B, on the contrary, may invent a new furnace or stove, or steam apparatus, by which this process may be carried on with much saving of labor, and expense of fuel; and he will be entitled to a patent for his machine, as an improvement in the art. Yet A could not have a patent for a machine, or B for a process; but each would have a patent for the means or method of producing a certain result, or effect, and not for the result or effect produced. It is for the discovery or invention of some practical method or means of producing a beneficial result or effect, that a patent is granted, and not for the result or effect itself. It is when the term process is used to represent the means or method of producing a result that it is patentable, and will include all methods or means which are not effected by mechanism or mechanical combinations.

reduced to a different state or thing. If new and useful, it is just as patentable as is a piece of machinery. In the language of the patent law, it is an art. The machinery pointed out as suitable to perform the process may or may not be new or patentable; whilst the process itself may be altogether new, and produce an entirely new result. The process requires that certain things should be done with certain substances, and in a certain order; but the tools to be used in doing this may be of secondary consequence. *Cochrane v. Deener*, 94 U.S. 780, 787–788, 24 L.Ed. 139 (1876).

Analysis of the eligibility of a claim of patent protection for a "process" did not change with the addition of that term to § 101. Recently, in *Gottschalk v. Benson*, 409 U.S. 63, 93 S.Ct. 253, 34 L.Ed.2d 273 (1972), we repeated the above definition recited in *Cochrane v. Deener*, adding: "Transformation and reduction of an article 'to a different state or thing' is the clue to the patentability of a process claim that does not include particular machines." 409 U.S., at 70, 93 S.Ct., at 256.

Analyzing respondents' claims according to the above statements from our cases, we think that a physical and chemical process for molding precision synthetic rubber products falls within the § 101 categories of possibly patentable subject matter. That respondents' claims involve the transformation of an article, in this case raw, uncured synthetic rubber, into a different state or thing cannot be disputed. The respondents' claims describe in detail a step-by-step method for accomplishing such, beginning with the loading of a mold with raw, uncured rubber and ending with the eventual opening of the press at the conclusion of the cure. Industrial processes such as this are the types which have historically been eligible to receive the protection of our patent laws.[8]

III

Our conclusion regarding respondents' claims is not altered by the fact that in several steps of the process a mathematical equation and a programmed digital computer are used. This Court has undoubtedly recognized limits to § 101 and every discovery is not embraced within the statutory terms. Excluded from such patent protection are laws of nature, natural phenomena, and abstract ideas. See *Parker v. Flook*, 437 U.S. 584, 98 S.Ct. 2522, 57 L.Ed.2d 451 (1978); *Gottschalk v. Benson, supra*, at 67, 93 S.Ct., at 255; *Funk Bros. Seed Co. v. Kalo Inoculant Co.*, 333 U.S. 127, 130, 68 S.Ct. 440, 441, 92 L.Ed. 588 (1948). "An idea of itself is not patentable," *Rubber–Tip Pencil Co. v. Howard*, 20 Wall. 498, 507, 22 L.Ed. 410 (1874). "A principle, in the abstract, is a fundamental truth; an original cause; a motive; these cannot be patented, as no one can claim in either of them an

---

8. We note that as early as 1854 this Court approvingly referred to patent eligibility of processes for curing rubber. See *id.*, at 267; n. 7, *supra*. In *Tilghman v. Proctor*, 102 U.S. 707, 26 L.Ed. 279 (1881) we referred to the original patent Charles Goodyear received on his process for "vulcanizing" or curing rubber. We stated:

That a patent can be granted for a process, there can be no doubt. The patent law is not confined to new machines and new compositions of matter, but extends to any new and useful art or manufacture. A manufacturing process is clearly an art, within the meaning of the law. Goodyear's patent was for a process, namely, the process of vulcanizing india-rubber by subjecting it to a high degree of heat when mixed with sulphur and a mineral salt. The apparatus for performing the process was not patented, and was not material. The patent pointed out how the process could be effected, and that was deemed sufficient. *Id.*, at 722.

exclusive right." *Le Roy v. Tatham*, 14 How. 156, 175, 14 L.Ed. 367 (1853). Only last Term, we explained:

> [A] new mineral discovered in the earth or a new plant found in the wild is not patentable subject matter. Likewise, Einstein could not patent his celebrated law that E = mc2; nor could Newton have patented the law of gravity. Such discoveries are "manifestations of ... nature, free to all men and reserved exclusively to none." *Diamond v. Chakrabarty*, 447 U.S., at 309, 100 S.Ct., at 2208, quoting *Funk Bros. Seed Co. v. Kalo Inoculant Co.*, *supra*, at 130, 68 S.Ct., at 441.

Our recent holdings in *Gottschalk v. Benson*, *supra*, and *Parker v. Flook*, *supra*, both of which are computer-related, stand for no more than these long-established principles. In *Benson*, we held unpatentable claims for an algorithm used to convert binary code decimal numbers to equivalent pure binary numbers. The sole practical application of the algorithm was in connection with the programming of a general purpose digital computer. We defined "algorithm" as a "procedure for solving a given type of mathematical problem," and we concluded that such an algorithm, or mathematical formula, is like a law of nature, which cannot be the subject of a patent.[9]

Parker v. Flook, *supra*, presented a similar situation. The claims were drawn to a method for computing an "alarm limit." An "alarm limit" is simply a number and the Court concluded that the application sought to protect a formula for computing this number. Using this formula, the updated alarm limit could be calculated if several other variables were known. The application, however, did not purport to explain how these other variables were to be determined,[10] nor did it purport "to contain any disclosure relating to the chemical processes at work, the monitoring of process variables, or the means of setting off an alarm or adjusting an alarm system. All that it provides is a formula for computing an updated alarm limit." 437 U.S., at 586, 98 S.Ct., at 2523.

---

9.   The term "algorithm" is subject to a variety of definitions. The petitioner defines the term to mean:

> 1. A fixed step-by-step procedure for accomplishing a given result; usually a simplified procedure for solving a complex problem, also a full statement of a finite number of steps. 2. A defined process or set of rules that leads [*sic*] and assures development of a desired output from a given input. A sequence of formulas and/or algebraic/logical steps to calculate or determine a given task; processing rules.

Brief for Petitioner in *Diamond v. Bradley*, O.T. 1980, No. 79–855, p. 6, n. 12, quoting C. Sippl & R. Sippl, Computer Dictionary and Handbook 23 (2d ed 1972).

> This definition is significantly broader than the definition this Court employed in *Benson* and *Flook*. Our previous decisions regarding the patentability of "algorithms" are necessarily limited to the more narrow definition employed by the Court, and we do not pass judgment on whether processes falling outside the definition previously used by this Court, but within the definition offered by the petitioner, would be patentable subject matter.

10.   As we explained in *Flook*, in order for an operator using the formula to calculate an updated alarm limit the operator would need to know the original alarm base, the appropriate margin of safety, the time interval that should elapse between each updating, the current temperature (or other process variable), and the appropriate weighing factor to be used to average the alarm base and the current temperature. 437 U.S., at 586, 98 S.Ct., at 2523. The patent application did not "explain how to select the approximate margin of safety, the weighing factor, or any of the other variables." *Ibid.*

In contrast, the respondents here do not seek to patent a mathematical formula. Instead, they seek patent protection for a process of curing synthetic rubber. Their process admittedly employs a well-known mathematical equation, but they do not seek to pre-empt the use of that equation. Rather, they seek only to foreclose from others the use of that equation in conjunction with all of the other steps in their claimed process. These include installing rubber in a press, closing the mold, constantly determining the temperature of the mold, constantly recalculating the appropriate cure time through the use of the formula and a digital computer, and automatically opening the press at the proper time. Obviously, one does not need a "computer" to cure natural or synthetic rubber, but if the computer use incorporated in the process patent significantly lessens the possibility of "overcuring" or "undercuring," the process as a whole does not thereby become unpatentable subject matter.

Our earlier opinions lend support to our present conclusion that a claim drawn to subject matter otherwise statutory does not become non-statutory simply because it uses a mathematical formula, computer program, or digital computer. In *Gottschalk v. Benson*, we noted: "It is said that the decision precludes a patent for any program servicing a computer. We do not so hold." 409 U.S., at 71, 93 S.Ct., at 257. Similarly, in *Parker v. Flook*, we stated that "a process is not unpatentable simply because it contains a law of nature or a mathematical algorithm." 437 U.S., at 590, 98 S.Ct., at 2526. It is now commonplace that an application of a law of nature or mathematical formula to a known structure or process may well be deserving of patent protection. See, e.g., *Funk Bros. Seed Co. v. Kalo Inoculant Co.*, 333 U.S. 127, 68 S.Ct. 440, 92 L.Ed. 588 (1948); *Eibel Process Co. v. Minnesota & Ontario Paper Co.*, 261 U.S. 45, 43 S.Ct. 322, 67 L.Ed. 523 (1923); *Cochrane v. Deener*, 94 U.S. 780, 24 L.Ed. 139 (1876); *O'Reilly v. Morse*, 15 How. 62, 14 L.Ed. 601 (1853); and *Le Roy v. Tatham*, 14 How. 156, 14 L.Ed. 367 (1852). As Justice Stone explained four decades ago:

> While a scientific truth, or the mathematical expression of it, is not a patentable invention, a novel and useful structure created with the aid of knowledge of scientific truth may be. *Mackay Radio & Telegraph Co. v. Radio of America*, 306 U.S. 86, 94, 59 S.Ct. 427, 431, 83 L.Ed. 506 (1939).[11]

We think this statement in *MacKay* takes us a long way toward the correct answer in this case. Arrhenius' equation is not patentable in isolation, but when a process for curing rubber is devised which incorporates in it a more efficient solution of the equation, that process is at the very least not barred at the threshold by § 101.

---

11. We noted in *Funk Bros. Seed Co. v. Kalo Inoculant Co.*, 333 U.S. 127, 130, 68 S.Ct. 440, 441, 92 L.Ed. 588 (1948):

> He who discovers a hitherto unknown phenomenon of nature has no claim to a monopoly of it which the law recognizes. If there is to be invention from such a discovery, it must come from the application of the law of nature to a new and useful end.

Although we were dealing with a "product" claim in *Funk Bros.*, the same principle applies to a process claim. *Gottschalk v. Benson*, 409 U.S. 63, 68, 93 S.Ct. 253, 255, 34 L.Ed.2d 273 (1972).

In determining the eligibility of respondents' claimed process for patent protection under § 101, their claims must be considered as a whole. It is inappropriate to dissect the claims into old and new elements and then to ignore the presence of the old elements in the analysis. This is particularly true in a process claim because a new combination of steps in a process may be patentable even though all the constituents of the combination were well known and in common use before the combination was made. The "novelty" of any element or steps in a process, or even of the process itself, is of no relevance in determining whether the subject matter of a claim falls within the § 101 categories of possibly patentable subject matter.[12]

* * *

In this case, it may later be determined that the respondents' process is not deserving of patent protection because it fails to satisfy the statutory conditions of novelty under § 102 or nonobviousness under § 103. A rejection on either of these grounds does not affect the determination that respondents' claims recited subject matter which was eligible for patent protection under § 101.

IV

We have before us today only the question of whether respondents' claims fall within the § 101 categories of possibly patentable subject matter. We view respondents' claims as nothing more than a process for molding rubber products and not as an attempt to patent a mathematical formula. We recognize, of course, that when a claim recites a mathematical formula (or scientific principle or phenomenon of nature), an inquiry must be made into whether the claim is seeking patent protection for that formula in the abstract. A mathematical formula as such is not accorded the protection of our patent laws, *Gottschalk v. Benson*, 409 U.S. 63, 93 S.Ct. 253, 34 L.Ed.2d 273 (1972), and this principle cannot be circumvented by attempting to limit the use of the formula to a particular technological environment. *Parker v. Flook*, 437 U.S. 584, 98 S.Ct. 2522, 57 L.Ed.2d 451 (1978). Similarly, insignificant post-solution activity will not transform an unpatentable principle into a patentable process. *Ibid.*[14] To hold otherwise would allow a competent draftsman to evade the recognized limitations on the type of subject matter eligible for patent protection. On the other hand,

---

12. It is argued that the procedure of dissecting a claim into old and new elements is mandated by our decision in *Flook* which noted that a mathematical algorithm must be assumed to be within the "prior art." It is from this language that the petitioner premises his argument that if everything other than the algorithm is determined to be old in the art, then the claim cannot recite statutory subject matter. The fallacy in this argument is that we did not hold in *Flook* that the mathematical algorithm could not be considered at all when making the § 101 determination. To accept the analysis proffered by the petitioner would, if carried to its extreme, make all inventions unpatentable because all inventions can be reduced to underlying principles of nature which, once known, make their implementation obvious. The analysis suggested by the petitioner would also undermine our earlier decisions regarding the criteria to consider in determining the eligibility of a process for patent protection. See, *e.g.*, *Gottschalk v. Benson*, *supra*; and *Cochrane v. Deener*, 94 U.S. 780, 24 L.Ed. 139 (1876).

14. Arguably, the claims in *Flook* did more than present a mathematical formula. The claims also solved the calculation in order to produce a new number or "alarm limit" and then

when a claim containing a mathematical formula implements or applies
that formula in a structure or process which, when considered as a whole,
is performing a function which the patent laws were designed to protect
(e.g., transforming or reducing an article to a different state or thing), then
the claim satisfies the requirements of § 101. Because we do not view
respondents' claims as an attempt to patent a mathematical formula, but
rather to be drawn to an industrial process for the molding of rubber
products, we affirm the judgment of the Court of Customs and Patent
Appeals.[15]

IT IS SO ORDERED.

■ JUSTICE STEVENS, with whom JUSTICE BRENNAN, JUSTICE MARSHALL, and
JUSTICE BLACKMUN join, dissenting.

---

replaced the old number with the number newly produced. The claims covered all uses of the
formula in processes "comprising the catalytic chemical conversion of hydrocarbons." There
are numerous such processes in the petrochemical and oil refinery industries and the claims
therefore covered a broad range of potential uses, 437 U.S., at 586, 98 S.Ct., at 2523. The
claims, however, did not cover every conceivable application of the formula. We rejected in
Flook the argument that because all possible uses of the mathematical formula were not pre-
empted, the claim should be eligible for patent protection. Our reasoning in *Flook* is in no way
inconsistent with our reasoning here. A mathematical formula does not suddenly become
patentable subject matter simply by having the applicant acquiesce to limiting the reach of the
patent for the formula to a particular technological use. A mathematical formula in the
abstract is nonstatutory subject matter regardless of whether the patent is intended to cover
all uses of the formula or only limited uses. Similarly, a mathematical formula does not
become patentable subject matter merely by including in the claim for the formula token
postsolution activity such as the type claimed in *Flook*. We were careful to note in *Flook* that
the patent application did not purport to explain how the variables used in the formula were
to be selected, nor did the application contain any disclosure relating to chemical processes at
work or the means of setting off an alarm or adjusting the alarm unit. *Ibid.* All the application
provided was a "formula for computing an updated alarm limit." *Ibid.*

    15. The dissent's analysis rises and falls on its characterization of respondents' claims as
presenting nothing more than "an improved method of calculating the time that the mold
should remain closed during the curing process." *Post.* The dissent states that respondents
claim only to have developed "a new method of programming a digital computer in order to
calculate—promptly and repeatedly—the correct curing time in a familiar process." *Post.*
Respondents' claims, however, are not limited to the isolated step of "programming a digital
computer." Rather, respondents' claims describe a process of curing rubber beginning with the
loading of the mold and ending with the opening of the press and the production of a synthetic
rubber product that has been perfectly cured—a result heretofore unknown in the art. See n.
5, *supra.* The fact that one or more of the steps in respondents' process may not, in isolation,
be novel or independently eligible for patent protection is irrelevant to the question of whether
the claims as a whole recite subject matter eligible for patent protection under § 101. As we
explained when discussing machine patents in *Deepsouth Packing Co. v. Laitram Corp.*, 406
U.S. 518, 92 S.Ct. 1700, 32 L.Ed.2d 273 (1972):

> The patents were warranted not by the novelty of their elements but by the novelty
> of the combination they represented. Invention was recognized because Laitram's
> assignors combined ordinary elements in an extraordinary way—a novel union of old
> means was designed to achieve new ends. Thus, for both inventions "the whole in
> some way exceed[ed] the sum of its parts." *Great A. & P. Tea Co. v. Supermarket
> Equipment Corp.*, 340 U.S. 147, 152 [71 S.Ct. 127, 130, 95 L.Ed. 162] (1950). Id., at
> 521–522, 92 S.Ct., at 1703–1704 (footnote omitted).

In order for the dissent to reach its conclusion it is necessary for it to read out of respondents'
patent application all the steps in the claimed process which it determined were not novel or
"inventive." That is not the purpose of the § 101 inquiry and conflicts with the proposition

The starting point in the proper adjudication of patent litigation is an understanding of what the inventor claims to have discovered. The Court's decision in this case rests on a misreading of the Diehr and Lutton patent application. Moreover, the Court has compounded its error by ignoring the critical distinction between the character of the subject matter that the inventor claims to be novel—the § 101 issue—and the question whether that subject matter is in fact novel—the § 102 issue.

* * *

II

As I stated at the outset, the starting point in the proper adjudication of patent litigation is an understanding of what the inventor claims to have discovered. Indeed, the outcome of such litigation is often determined by the judge's understanding of the patent application. This is such a case.

In the first sentence of its opinion, the Court states the question presented as "whether a process for curing synthetic rubber ... is patentable subject matter." *Ante*. Of course, that question was effectively answered many years ago when Charles Goodyear obtained his patent on the vulcanization process.[25] The patent application filed by Diehr and Lutton, however, teaches nothing about the chemistry of the synthetic rubber-curing process, nothing about the raw materials to be used in curing synthetic rubber, nothing about the equipment to be used in the process, and nothing about the significance or effect of any process variable such as temperature, curing time, particular compositions of material, or mold configurations. In short, Diehr and Lutton do not claim to have discovered anything new about the process for curing synthetic rubber.

---

recited above that a claimed invention may be entitled to patent protection even though some or all of its elements are not "novel."

25. In an opinion written over a century ago, the Court noted:

A manufacturing process is clearly an art, within the meaning of the law. Goodyear's patent was for a process, namely, the process of vulcanizing india-rubber by subjecting it to a high degree of heat when mixed with sulphur and a mineral salt.

* * *

The mixing of certain substances together, or the heating of a substance to a certain temperature, is a process. *Tilghman v. Proctor*, 102 U.S. 707, 722, 728, 26 L.Ed. 279 (1880).

See also *Corning v. Burden*, 15 How. 252, 267 (1853). Modern rubber curing methods apparently still are based in substantial part upon the concept discovered by Goodyear:

Since the day 120 years ago when Goodyear first heated a mixture of rubber and sulphur on a domestic stove and so discovered vulcanization, this action of heat and sulphur has remained the standard method of converting crude rubber, with all its limitations, into a commercially usable product, giving it the qualities of resistance to heat and cold in addition to considerable mechanical strength.

Goodyear also conjured up the word "cure" for vulcanization, and this has become the recognized term in production circles. Mernagh, Practical Vulcanization, in The Applied Science of Rubber 1053 (W. Naunton ed. 1961).

See generally Kimmich, Making Rubber Products for Engineering Uses, in Engineering Uses of Rubber 18, 28–34 (A. McPherson & A. Klemin eds. 1956).

As the Court reads the claims in the Diehr and Lutton patent application, the inventors' discovery is a method of constantly measuring the actual temperature inside a rubber molding press.[26] As I read the claims, their discovery is an improved method of calculating the time that the mold should remain closed during the curing process.[27] If the Court's reading of the claims were correct, I would agree that they disclose patentable subject matter. On the other hand, if the Court accepted my reading, I feel confident that the case would be decided differently.

There are three reasons why I cannot accept the Court's conclusion that Diehr and Lutton claim to have discovered a new method of constantly measuring the temperature inside a mold. First, there is not a word in the patent application that suggests that there is anything unusual about the temperature-reading devices used in this process—or indeed that any particular species of temperature-reading device should be used in it.[28] Second, since devices for constantly measuring actual temperatures—on a back porch, for example—have been familiar articles for quite some time. I find it difficult to believe that a patent application filed in 1975 was premised on the notion that a "process of constantly measuring the actual temperature" had just been discovered. Finally, the Patent and Trademark Office Board of Appeals expressly found that "the only difference between the conventional methods of operating a molding press and that claimed in [the] application rests in those steps of the claims which relate to the

---

26. "Respondents characterize their contribution to the art to reside in the process of constantly measuring the actual temperature inside the mold." See *ante*, at 1052.

27. Claim 1 is quoted in full in n. 5 of the Court's opinion, *ante*, at 1052–1053. It describes a "method of operating a rubber-molding press for precision molded compounds with the aid of a digital computer." As the Court of Customs and Patent Appeals noted, the improvement claimed in the application consists of "opening the mold at precisely the correct time rather than at a time which has been determined by approximation or guesswork." *In re Diehr*, 602 F.2d 982, 988 (1979).

28. In the portion of the patent application entitled "Abstract of the Disclosure," the following reference to monitoring the temperature is found:

> An interval timer starts running from the time of mold closure, and the temperature within the mold cavity is measured often, typically every ten seconds. The temperature is fed to a computer. . . . App. to Pet. for Cert. 38a.

In the portion of the application entitled "Background of the Invention," the following statement is found:

> By accurate and constant calculation and recalculation of the correct mold time under the temperatures actually present in the mold, the material can be cured accurately and can be relied upon to produce very few rejections, perhaps completely eliminating all rejections due to faulty mold cure. *Id.*, at 41a.

And, in the "Summary of the Invention," this statement appears:

> A surveillance system is maintained over the mold to determine the actual mold temperature substantially continuously, for example, every ten seconds, and to feed that information to the computer along with the pertinent stored data and along with the elapsed time information. *Ibid.*

Finally, in a description of a simple hypothetical application using the invention described in Claim 1, this is the reference to the temperature-reading device:

> "Thermocouples, or other temperature-detecting devices, located directly within the mold cavity may read the Temperature at the surface where the molding compound touches the mold, so that it actually gets the temperature of the material at that surface." *Id.*, at 45a.

calculation incident to the solution of the mathematical problem or formula used to control the mold heater and the automatic opening of the press."[29] This finding was not disturbed by the Court of Customs and Patent Appeals and is clearly correct.

A fair reading of the entire patent application, as well as the specific claims, makes it perfectly clear that what Diehr and Lutton claim to have discovered is a method of using a digital computer to determine the amount of time that a rubber molding press should remain closed during the synthetic rubber-curing process. There is no suggestion that there is anything novel in the instrumentation of the mold, in actuating a timer when the press is closed, or in automatically opening the press when the computed time expires.[30] Nor does the application suggest that Diehr and Lutton have discovered anything about the temperatures in the mold or the amount of curing time that will produce the best cure. What they claim to have discovered, in essence, is a method of updating the original estimated curing time by repetitively recalculating that time pursuant to a well-known mathematical formula in response to variations in temperature within the mold. Their method of updating the curing time calculation is strikingly reminiscent of the method of updating alarm limits that Dale Flook sought to patent.

Parker v. Flook, 437 U.S. 584, 98 S.Ct. 2522, 57 L.Ed.2d 451 (1978), involved the use of a digital computer in connection with a catalytic conversion process. During the conversion process, variables such as temperature, pressure, and flow rates were constantly monitored and fed into the computer; in this case, temperature in the mold is the variable that is monitored and fed into the computer. In *Flook*, the digital computer repetitively recalculated the "alarm limit"—a number that might signal the need to terminate or modify the catalytic conversion process; in this case, the digital computer repetitively recalculates the correct curing time—a number that signals the time when the synthetic rubber molding press should open.

The essence of the claimed discovery in both cases was an algorithm that could be programmed on a digital computer.[31] In *Flook*, the algorithm

---

29. *Id.*, at 24a.

30. These elements of the rubber-curing process apparently have been well known for years. The following description of the vulcanization process appears in a text published in 1961:

> Vulcanization is too important an operation to be left to human control, however experienced and conscientious. Instrumentation makes controlled cure possible, and in consequence instrument engineering is a highly important function in the modern rubber factory, skilled attention being necessary, not only in the maintenance of the instruments but also in their siting. There are instruments available which will indicate, record or control all the services involved in vulcanization, including time, temperature and pressure, and are capable of setting in motion such operations as the opening and closing of molds and, in general, will control any process variable which is capable of being converted into an electric charge or pneumatic or hydraulic pressure impulse. *Mernagh, supra* n. 25, at 1091–1092.

31. Commentators critical of the *Flook* decision have noted the essential similarity of the two inventions:

made use of multiple process variables; in this case, it makes use of only one. In *Flook*, the algorithm was expressed in a newly developed mathematical formula; in this case, the algorithm makes use of a well-known mathematical formula. Manifestly, neither of these differences can explain today's holding.[32] What I believe does explain today's holding is a misunderstanding of the applicants' claimed invention and a failure to recognize the critical difference between the "discovery" requirement in § 101 and the "novelty" requirement in § 102.[33]

* * *

IV

The broad question whether computer programs should be given patent protection involves policy considerations that this Court is not authorized to address. See *Gottschalk v. Benson*, 409 U.S., at 72–73, 93 S.Ct., at 257–258; *Parker v. Flook*, 437 U.S., at 595–596, 98 S.Ct., at 2528–2529.... Because the invention claimed in the patent application at issue in this case makes no contribution to the art that is not entirely dependent upon the utilization of a computer in a familiar process, I would reverse the decision of the Court of Customs and Patent Appeals.

NOTES

1. *Limiting Benson and Flook.* The majority opinion in *Flook*, by Justice Stevens, held unpatentable a "method for calculating an alarm limit." The dissent, by Justice Stewart, joined by Chief Justice Burger and Justice Rehnquist, argues that

---

> The *Diehr* invention improved the control system by continually remeasuring the temperature and recalculating the proper cure time. The computer would simultaneously keep track of the elapsed time. When the elapsed time equaled the proper cure time, the rubber would be released automatically from the mold.
>
> The facts are difficult to distinguish from those in *Flook*. Both processes involved (1) an initial calculation, (2) continual remeasurement and recalculation, and (3) some control use of the value obtained from the calculation. Novick & Wallenstein, *supra* n. 5, at 326 (footnotes omitted).

32. Indeed, the most significant distinction between the invention at issue in *Flook* and that at issue in this case lies not in the characteristics of the inventions themselves, but rather in the drafting of the claims. After noting that "[t]he *Diehr* claims are reminiscent of the claims in *Flook*," Blumenthal & Riter, *supra* n. 15, at 502–503 (footnote omitted), the authors of a recent article on the subject observe that the Court of Customs and Patent Appeals' analysis in this case "lends itself to an interesting exercise in claim drafting." *Id.*, at 505. To illustrate their point, the authors redrafted the Diehr and Lutton claims into the format employed in the *Flook* application:.... [Redrafted claims omitted]. The authors correctly conclude that even the lower court probably would have found that this claim was drawn to unpatentable subject matter under § 101. *Id.*, at 505–506.

33. In addition to confusing the requirements of §§ 101 and 102, the Court also misapprehends the record in this case when it suggests that the Diehr and Lutton patent application may later be challenged for failure to satisfy the requirements of §§ 102 and 103. See *ante.* This suggestion disregards the fact that the applicants overcame all objections to issuance of the patent except the objection predicated on § 101. The Court seems to assume that §§ 102 and 103 issues of novelty and obviousness remain open on remand. As I understand the record, however, those issues have already been resolved. See Brief for Respondents 11–14; Reply Memorandum for Petitioner 3–4, and n. 4. Therefore, the Court is now deciding that the patent will issue.

the majority is improperly importing into the inquiry under Section 101 concerns that are properly dealt with under Sections 102 and 103. The majority opinion in *Diehr* takes a narrow view of *Benson* and *Flook*. Does *Benson* only stand for the proposition that "[a] mathematical formula is not accorded protection under our patent laws"? Does *Flook* only stand for the proposition that "this principle cannot be circumvented by attempting to limit the use of the formula to a particular technology"? (See text accompanying footnote 14 of the majority opinion). In what way(s) are the holdings of *Benson* and *Flook* broader than these narrow pronouncements?

2. *Ties To Reality?* Carefully consider the claims at issue in *Diehr* and compare them with the claims in *Flook*. In what way are they different? The majority makes much of the non-equation steps in Diehr's claims, especially the steps of opening the press, installing the rubber, closing the press, and monitoring the temperature of the press. But these steps are not in Diehr's claim 1.

3. Is the dissent correct in asserting that the key point of disagreement with the majority is whether Diehr's claims are directed to a method of measuring actual temperature inside a press or merely to a method of calculating time? (See text accompanying footnotes 26–27 of the dissenting opinion).

4. Is the dissent correct in suggesting that the Court has decided the validity of Diehr's claims for good? (See footnote 33 of the dissent). Is it not true that invalidity may always be raised as an affirmative defense in a litigation for patent infringement and a declaratory judgment action for invalidity may also be brought on its own under certain circumstances?

State Street Bank and Trust Co. v. Signature Financial Group, Inc.

149 F.3d 1368 (Fed.Cir.1998).

■ Before RICH, PLAGER, and BRYSON, CIRCUIT JUDGES.

■ RICH, CIRCUIT JUDGE.

Signature Financial Group, Inc. (Signature) appeals from the decision of the United States District Court for the District of Massachusetts granting a motion for summary judgment in favor of State Street Bank & Trust Co. (State Street), finding U.S. Patent No. 5,193,056 (the '056 patent) invalid on the ground that the claimed subject matter is not encompassed by 35 U.S.C. § 101 (1994). See State Street Bank & Trust Co. v. Signature Financial Group, Inc., 927 F.Supp. 502 (D.Mass.1996). We reverse and remand because we conclude that the patent claims are directed to statutory subject matter.

BACKGROUND

Signature is the assignee of the '056 patent which is entitled "Data Processing System for Hub and Spoke Financial Services Configuration." The '056 patent issued to Signature on 9 March 1993, naming R. Todd Boes as the inventor. The '056 patent is generally directed to a data processing system (the system) for implementing an investment structure which was developed for use in Signature's business as an administrator and accounting agent for mutual funds. In essence, the system, identified by the proprietary name Hub and Spoke (R), facilitates a structure whereby mutual funds (Spokes) pool their assets in an investment portfolio (Hub) organized as a partnership. This investment configuration provides the administrator of a mutual fund with the advantageous combination of economies of scale in administering investments coupled with the tax advantages of a partnership.

State Street and Signature are both in the business of acting as custodians and accounting agents for multi-tiered partnership fund financial services. State Street negotiated with Signature for a license to use its patented data processing system described and claimed in the '056 patent. When negotiations broke down, State Street brought a declaratory judgment action asserting invalidity, unenforceability, and noninfringement in Massachusetts district court, and then filed a motion for partial summary judgment of patent invalidity for failure to claim statutory subject matter under § 101. The motion was granted and this appeal followed.

DISCUSSION

On appeal, we are not bound to give deference to the district court's grant of summary judgment, but must make an independent determination that the standards for summary judgment have been met. . . .

The following facts pertinent to the statutory subject matter issue are either undisputed or represent the version alleged by the nonmovant. *See Anderson v. Liberty Lobby, Inc.*, 477 U.S. 242, 255 (1986). The patented invention relates generally to a system that allows an administrator to monitor and record the financial information flow and make all calculations necessary for maintaining a partner fund financial services configuration. As previously mentioned, a partner fund financial services configuration essentially allows several mutual funds, or "Spokes," to pool their investment funds into a single portfolio, or "Hub," allowing for consolidation of, inter alia, the costs of administering the fund combined with the tax advantages of a partnership. In particular, this system provides means for a daily allocation of assets for two or more Spokes that are invested in the same Hub. The system determines the percentage share that each Spoke maintains in the Hub, while taking into consideration daily changes both in the value of the Hub's investment securities and in the concomitant amount of each Spoke's assets.

In determining daily changes, the system also allows for the allocation among the Spokes of the Hub's daily income, expenses, and net realized and unrealized gain or loss, calculating each day's total investments based on the concept of a book capital account. This enables the determination of a true asset value of each Spoke and accurate calculation of allocation ratios between or among the Spokes. The system additionally tracks all the relevant data determined on a daily basis for the Hub and each Spoke, so that aggregate year end income, expenses, and capital gain or loss can be determined for accounting and for tax purposes for the Hub and, as a result, for each publicly traded Spoke.

It is essential that these calculations are quickly and accurately performed. In large part this is required because each Spoke sells shares to the public and the price of those shares is substantially based on the Spoke's percentage interest in the portfolio. In some instances, a mutual fund administrator is required to calculate the value of the shares to the nearest penny within as little as an hour and a half after the market closes. Given the complexity of the calculations, a computer or equivalent device is a virtual necessity to perform the task.

The '056 patent application was filed 11 March 1991. It initially contained six "machine" claims, which incorporated means-plus-function clauses, and six method claims. According to Signature, during prosecution the examiner contemplated a § 101 rejection for failure to claim statutory subject matter. However, upon cancellation of the six method claims, the examiner issued a notice of allowance for the remaining present six claims on appeal. Only claim 1 is an independent claim.

The district court began its analysis by construing the claims to be directed to a process, with each "means" clause merely representing a step in that process. However, "machine" claims having "means" clauses may only be reasonably viewed as process claims if there is no supporting structure in the written description that corresponds to the claimed "means" elements. See *In re Alappat*, 33 F.3d 1526, 1540–41 (Fed.Cir.1994) (in banc). This is not the case now before us.

When independent claim 1 is properly construed in accordance with § 112, ¶ 6, it is directed to a machine, as demonstrated below, where representative claim 1 is set forth, the subject matter in brackets stating the structure the written description discloses as corresponding to the respective "means" recited in the claims.

1. A data processing system for managing a financial services configuration of a portfolio established as a partnership, each partner being one of a plurality of funds, comprising:

(a) computer processor means [a personal computer including a CPU] for processing data;

(b) storage means [a data disk] for storing data on a storage medium;

(c) first means [an arithmetic logic circuit configured to prepare the data disk to magnetically store selected data] for initializing the storage medium;

(d) second means [an arithmetic logic circuit configured to retrieve information from a specific file, calculate incremental increases or decreases based on specific input, allocate the results on a percentage basis, and store the output in a separate file] for processing data regarding assets in the portfolio and each of the funds from a previous day and data regarding increases or decreases in each of the funds, [sic, funds'] assets and for allocating the percentage share that each fund holds in the portfolio;

(e) third means [an arithmetic logic circuit configured to retrieve information from a specific file, calculate incremental increases and decreases based on specific input, allocate the results on a percentage basis and store the output in a separate file] for processing data regarding daily incremental income, expenses, and net realized gain or loss for the portfolio and for allocating such data among each fund;

(f) fourth means [an arithmetic logic circuit configured to retrieve information from a specific file, calculate incremental increases and decreases based on specific input, allocate the results on a percentage basis and store the output in a separate file] for processing data regarding daily net unrealized gain or loss for the portfolio and for allocating such data among each fund; and

(g) fifth means [an arithmetic logic circuit configured to retrieve information from specific files, calculate that information on an aggregate basis and store the output in a separate file] for processing data regarding aggregate year-end income, expenses, and capital gain or loss for the portfolio and each of the funds.

Each claim component, recited as a "means" plus its function, is to be read, of course, pursuant to § 112, ¶ 6, as inclusive of the "equivalents" of the structures disclosed in the written description portion of the specification. Thus, claim 1, properly construed, claims a machine, namely, a data processing system for managing a financial services configuration of a portfolio established as a partnership, which machine is made up of, at the very least, the specific structures disclosed in the written description and corresponding to the means-plus-function elements (a)–(g) recited in the claim. A "machine" is proper statutory subject matter under § 101. We note that, for the purposes of a § 101 analysis, it is of little relevance whether claim 1 is directed to a "machine" or a "process," as long as it falls within at least one of the four enumerated categories of patentable subject matter, "machine" and "process" being such categories.

This does not end our analysis, however, because the court concluded that the claimed subject matter fell into one of two alternative judicially-created exceptions to statutory subject matter.[1] The court refers to the first exception as the "mathematical algorithm" exception and the second exception as the "business method" exception....

The plain and unambiguous meaning of § 101 is that any invention falling within one of the four stated categories of statutory subject matter may be patented, provided it meets the other requirements for patentability set forth in Title 35, i.e., those found in §§ 102, 103, and 112, ¶ 2.[2]

---

1. Indeed, although we do not make this determination here, the judicially created exceptions, i.e., abstract ideas, laws of nature, etc., should be applicable to all categories of statutory subject matter, as our own precedent suggests. See Alappat, 33 F.3d at 1542, 31 U.S.P.Q.2D at 1556; see also In re Johnston, 502 F.2d 765, 183 USPQ 172 (CCPA 1974) (Rich, J., dissenting).

2. As explained in In re Bergy, 596 F.2d 952, 960, 201 USPQ 352, 360 (CCPA 1979) (emphases and footnote omitted):

The first door which must be opened on the difficult path to patentability is § 101.... The person approaching that door is an inventor, whether his invention is patentable or not.... Being an inventor or having an invention, however, is no guarantee of opening even the first door. What kind of an invention or discovery is it? In dealing with the question of kind, as distinguished from the qualitative conditions which make the invention patentable, § 101 is broad and general; its language is: "any ... process, machine, manufacture, or composition of matter, or any ... improvement thereof." Section 100(b) further expands "process" to include "art or method, and ... a new use of a known process, machine, manufacture, composition of matter, or material." If the invention, as the inventor defines it in his claims (pursuant to § 112, second paragraph), falls into any one of the named categories, he is allowed to pass through to the second door, which is § 102; "novelty and loss of right to patent" is the sign on it. Notwithstanding the words "new and useful" in § 101, the invention is not examined under that statute for novelty because that is not the statutory scheme of things or the long-established administrative practice.

The repetitive use of the expansive term "any" in § 101 shows Congress's intent not to place any restrictions on the subject matter for which a patent may be obtained beyond those specifically recited in § 101. Indeed, the Supreme Court has acknowledged that Congress intended § 101 to extend to "anything under the sun that is made by man." *Diamond v. Chakrabarty*, 447 U.S. 303, 309 (1980); *see also Diamond v. Diehr*, 450 U.S. 175, 182 (1981).[3] Thus, it is improper to read limitations into § 101 on the subject matter that may be patented where the legislative history indicates that Congress clearly did not intend such limitations. *See Chakrabarty*, 447 U.S. at 308 ("We have also cautioned that courts 'should not read into the patent laws limitations and conditions which the legislature has not expressed.' " (citations omitted)).

The "Mathematical Algorithm" Exception

The Supreme Court has identified three categories of subject matter that are unpatentable, namely "laws of nature, natural phenomena, and abstract ideas." *Diehr*, 450 U.S. at 185. Of particular relevance to this case, the Court has held that mathematical algorithms are not patentable subject matter to the extent that they are merely abstract ideas. *See Diehr*, 450 U.S. 175, passim; *Parker v. Flook*, 437 U.S. 584 (1978); *Gottschalk v. Benson*, 409 U.S. 63 (1972). In *Diehr*, the Court explained that certain types of mathematical subject matter, standing alone, represent nothing more than abstract ideas until reduced to some type of practical application, *i.e.*, "a useful, concrete and tangible result." *Alappat*, 33 F.3d at 1544.[4]

Unpatentable mathematical algorithms are identifiable by showing they are merely abstract ideas constituting disembodied concepts or truths that are not "useful." From a practical standpoint, this means that to be patentable an algorithm must be applied in a "useful" way. In *Alappat*, we held that data, transformed by a machine through a series of mathematical calculations to produce a smooth waveform display on a rasterizer monitor, constituted a practical application of an abstract idea (a mathematical algorithm, formula, or calculation), because it produced "a useful, concrete and tangible result"—the smooth waveform.

Similarly, in *Arrhythmia Research Technology Inc. v. Corazonix Corp.*, 958 F.2d 1053 (Fed.Cir.1992), we held that the transformation of electrocardiograph signals from a patient's heartbeat by a machine through a series of mathematical calculations constituted a practical application of an abstract idea (a mathematical algorithm, formula, or calculation), because it corresponded to a useful, concrete or tangible thing—the condition of a patient's heart.

---

3. The Committee Reports accompanying the 1952 Act inform us that Congress intended statutory subject matter to "include anything under the sun that is made by man." S.Rep. No. 82–1979 at 5 (1952); H.R.Rep. No. 82–1923 at 6 (1952).

4. This has come to be known as the mathematical algorithm exception. This designation has led to some confusion, especially given the *Freeman–Walter–Abele* analysis. By keeping in mind that the mathematical algorithm is unpatentable only to the extent that it represents an abstract idea, this confusion may be ameliorated.

Today, we hold that the transformation of data, representing discrete dollar amounts, by a machine through a series of mathematical calculations into a final share price, constitutes a practical application of a mathematical algorithm, formula, or calculation, because it produces "a useful, concrete and tangible result"—a final share price momentarily fixed for recording and reporting purposes and even accepted and relied upon by regulatory authorities and in subsequent trades.

The district court erred by applying the *Freeman–Walter–Abele* test to determine whether the claimed subject matter was an unpatentable abstract idea. The *Freeman–Walter–Abele* test was designed by the Court of Customs and Patent Appeals, and subsequently adopted by this court, to extract and identify unpatentable mathematical algorithms in the aftermath of *Benson* and *Flook*. *See In re Freeman*, 573 F.2d 1237 (CCPA 1978) as modified by *In re Walter*, 618 F.2d 758 (CCPA 1980). The test has been thus articulated:

> First, the claim is analyzed to determine whether a mathematical algorithm is directly or indirectly recited. Next, if a mathematical algorithm is found, the claim as a whole is further analyzed to determine whether the algorithm is "applied in any manner to physical elements or process steps," and, if it is, it "passes muster under § 101."

In re Pardo, 684 F.2d 912, 915 (CCPA 1982) (citing *In re Abele*, 684 F.2d 902 (CCPA 1982)).[5]

After *Diehr* and *Chakrabarty*, the *Freeman–Walter–Abele* test has little, if any, applicability to determining the presence of statutory subject matter. As we pointed out in *Alappat*, 33 F.3d at 1543, application of the test could be misleading, because a process, machine, manufacture, or composition of matter employing a law of nature, natural phenomenon, or abstract idea is patentable subject matter even though a law of nature, natural phenomenon, or abstract idea would not, by itself, be entitled to such protection.[6]

---

5. The test has been the source of much confusion. In *In re Abele*, 684 F.2d 902 (CCPA 1982), the CCPA upheld claims applying "a mathematical formula within the context of a process which encompasses significantly more than the algorithm alone." *Id.* at 909. Thus, the CCPA apparently inserted an additional consideration—the significance of additions to the algorithm. The CCPA appeared to abandon the application of the test in *In re Taner*, 681 F.2d 787 (CCPA 1982), only to subsequently "clarify" that the *Freeman–Walter–Abele* test was simply not the exclusive test for detecting unpatentable subject matter. *In re Meyer*, 688 F.2d 789, 796 (CCPA 1982).

6. *See e.g. Parker v. Flook*, 437 U.S. 584, 590 (1978) ("[A] process is not unpatentable simply because it contains a law of nature or a mathematical algorithm."); *Funk Bros. Seed Co. v. Kalo Inoculant Co.*, 333 U.S. 127, 130 (1948) ("He who discovers a hitherto unknown phenomenon of nature has no claim to a monopoly of it which the law recognizes. If there is to be invention from such a discovery, it must come from the application of the law to a new and useful end."); *Mackay Radio & Tel. Co. v. Radio Corp. of Am.*, 306 U.S. 86, 94 (1939) ("While a scientific truth, or the mathematical expression of it, is not a patentable invention, a novel and useful structure created with the aid of knowledge of scientific truth may be.").

> [W]hen a claim containing a mathematical formula implements or applies that formula in a structure or process which, when considered as a whole, is performing a function which the patent laws were designed to protect (e.g., transforming or reducing an article to a different state or thing), then the claim satisfies the requirements of § 101.

The test determines the presence of, for example, an algorithm. Under *Benson*, this may have been a sufficient indicium of nonstatutory subject matter. However, after *Diehr* and *Alappat*, the mere fact that a claimed invention involves inputting numbers, calculating numbers, outputting numbers, and storing numbers, in and of itself, would not render it nonstatutory subject matter, unless, of course, its operation does not produce a "useful, concrete and tangible result." *Alappat*, 33 F.3d at 1544.[7] After all, as we have repeatedly stated,

> every step-by-step process, be it electronic or chemical or mechanical, involves an algorithm in the broad sense of the term. Since § 101 expressly includes processes as a category of inventions which may be patented and § 100(b) further defines the word "process" as meaning "process, art or method, and includes a new use of a known process, machine, manufacture, composition of matter, or material," it follows that it is no ground for holding a claim is directed to nonstatutory subject matter to say it includes or is directed to an algorithm. This is why the proscription against patenting has been limited to mathematical algorithms....

In re Iwahashi, 888 F.2d 1370, 1374 (Fed.Cir.1989).[8]

The question of whether a claim encompasses statutory subject matter should not focus on which of the four categories of subject matter a claim is directed to[9]—process, machine, manufacture, or composition of matter—but rather on the essential characteristics of the subject matter, in particular, its practical utility. Section 101 specifies that statutory subject matter must also satisfy the other "conditions and requirements" of Title 35, including novelty, nonobviousness, and adequacy of disclosure and notice. *See In re Warmerdam*, 33 F.3d 1354, 1359 (Fed.Cir.1994). For purpose of our analysis, as noted above, claim 1 is directed to a machine programmed with the Hub and Spoke software and admittedly produces a "useful, concrete, and tangible result." *Alappat*, 33 F.3d at 1544. This renders it statutory subject matter, even if the useful result is expressed in numbers, such as price, profit, percentage, cost, or loss.

The Business Method Exception

As an alternative ground for invalidating the '056 patent under § 101, the court relied on the judicially-created, so-called "business method"

Diehr, 450 U.S. at 192; *see also In re Iwahashi*, 888 F.2d 1370, 1375 (Fed.Cir.1989); *Taner*, 681 F.2d at 789. The dispositive inquiry is whether the claim as a whole is directed to statutory subject matter. It is irrelevant that a claim may contain, as part of the whole, subject matter which would not be patentable by itself. "A claim drawn to subject matter otherwise statutory does not become nonstatutory simply because it uses a mathematical formula, computer program or digital computer." *Diehr*, 450 U.S. at 187.

7. As the Supreme Court expressly stated in *Diehr*, its own holdings in *Benson* and *Flook* "stand for no more than these long-established principles" that abstract ideas and natural phenomena are not patentable. *Diehr*, 450 U.S. at 185, 101 S.Ct. 1048 (citing *Chakrabarty*, 447 U.S. at 309 and *Funk Bros.*, 333 U.S. at 130).

8. In *In re Pardo*, 684 F.2d 912 (CCPA 1982), the CCPA narrowly limited "mathematical algorithm" to the execution of formulas with given data. In the same year, in *In re Meyer*, 688 F.2d 789, 215 USPQ 193 (CCPA 1982), the CCPA interpreted the same term to include any mental process that can be represented by a mathematical algorithm. This is also the position taken by the PTO in its Examination Guidelines, 61 Fed.Reg. 7478, 7483 (1996).

9. Of course, the subject matter must fall into at least one category of statutory subject matter.

exception to statutory subject matter. We take this opportunity to lay this ill-conceived exception to rest. Since its inception, the "business method" exception has merely represented the application of some general, but no longer applicable legal principle, perhaps arising out of the "requirement for invention"—which was eliminated by § 103. Since the 1952 Patent Act, business methods have been, and should have been, subject to the same legal requirements for patentability as applied to any other process or method.[10]

The business method exception has never been invoked by this court, or the CCPA, to deem an invention unpatentable.[11] Application of this particular exception has always been preceded by a ruling based on some clearer concept of Title 35 or, more commonly, application of the abstract idea exception based on finding a mathematical algorithm. Illustrative is the CCPA's analysis in *In re Howard*, 394 F.2d 869 (CCPA 1968), wherein the court affirmed the Board of Appeals' rejection of the claims for lack of novelty and found it unnecessary to reach the Board's section 101 ground that a method of doing business is "inherently unpatentable." *Id.* at 872.[12]

Similarly, *In re Schrader*, 22 F.3d 290 (Fed.Cir.1994), while making reference to the business method exception, turned on the fact that the claims implicitly recited an abstract idea in the form of a mathematical algorithm and there was no "transformation or conversion of subject matter representative of or constituting physical activity or objects." 22 F.3d at 294 (emphasis omitted).[13]

State Street argues that we acknowledged the validity of the business method exception in *Alappat* when we discussed *Maucorps* and *Meyer*:

> *Maucorps* dealt with a business methodology for deciding how salesmen should best handle respective customers and *Meyer* involved a "system" for

---

10. As Judge Newman has previously stated,

[The business method exception] is ... an unwarranted encumbrance to the definition of statutory subject matter in section 101, that [should] be discarded as error-prone, redundant, and obsolete. It merits retirement from the glossary of section 101.... All of the "doing business" cases could have been decided using the clearer concepts of Title 35. Patentability does not turn on whether the claimed method does "business" instead of something else, but on whether the method, viewed as a whole, meets the requirements of patentability as set forth in Sections 102, 103, and 112 of the Patent Act.

In re Schrader, 22 F.3d 290, 298 (Fed.Cir.1994) (Newman, J., dissenting).

11. *See* Rinaldo Del Gallo, III, Are "Methods of Doing Business" Finally out of Business as a Statutory Rejection?, 38 IDEA 403, 435 (1998).

12. *See also Dann v. Johnston*, 425 U.S. 219 (1976) (the Supreme Court declined to discuss the section 101 argument concerning the computerized financial record-keeping system, in view of the Court's holding of patent invalidity under section 103); *In re Chatfield*, 545 F.2d 152, 157 (CCPA 1976); *Ex parte Murray*, 9 U.S.P.Q.2D 1819, 1820 (Bd.Pat.App & Interf.1988) ("[T]he claimed accounting method [requires] no more than the entering, sorting, debiting and totaling of expenditures as necessary preliminary steps to issuing an expense analysis statement....") states grounds of obviousness or lack of novelty, not of non-statutory subject matter.

13. Any historical distinctions between a method of "doing" business and the means of carrying it out blur in the complexity of modern business systems. *See Paine, Webber, Jackson & Curtis v. Merrill Lynch*, 564 F.Supp. 1358, 218 USPQ 212 (D.Del.1983), (holding a computerized system of cash management was held to be statutory subject matter.).

aiding a neurologist in diagnosing patients. Clearly, neither of the alleged "inventions" in those cases falls within any § 101 category.

Alappat, 33 F.3d at 1541. However, closer scrutiny of these cases reveals that the claimed inventions in both *Maucorps* and *Meyer* were rejected as abstract ideas under the mathematical algorithm exception, not the business method exception. *See In re Maucorps*, 609 F.2d 481, 484 (CCPA 1979); *In re Meyer*, 688 F.2d 789, 796 (CCPA 1982).[14]

Even the case frequently cited as establishing the business method exception to statutory subject matter, *Hotel Security Checking Co. v. Lorraine Co.*, 160 F. 467 (2d Cir.1908), did not rely on the exception to strike the patent.[15] In that case, the patent was found invalid for lack of novelty and "invention," not because it was improper subject matter for a patent. The court stated "the fundamental principle of the system is as old as the art of bookkeeping, i.e., charging the goods of the employer to the agent who takes them." *Id.* at 469. "If at the time of [the patent] application, there had been no system of bookkeeping of any kind in restaurants, we would be confronted with the question whether a new and useful system of cash registering and account checking is such an art as is patentable under the statute." *Id.* at 472.

This case is no exception. The district court announced the precepts of the business method exception as set forth in several treatises, but noted as its primary reason for finding the patent invalid under the business method exception as follows:

> If Signature's invention were patentable, any financial institution desirous of implementing a multi-tiered funding complex modelled (sic) on a Hub and Spoke configuration would be required to seek Signature's permission before embarking on such a project. This is so because the '056 Patent is claimed [sic] sufficiently broadly to foreclose virtually any computer-implemented accounting method necessary to manage this type of financial structure.

927 F.Supp. 502, 516. Whether the patent's claims are too broad to be patentable is not to be judged under § 101, but rather under §§ 102, 103 and 112. Assuming the above statement to be correct, it has nothing to do with whether what is claimed is statutory subject matter.

---

14. Moreover, these cases were subject to the *Benson* era *Freeman–Walter–Abele* test—in other words, analysis as it existed before *Diehr* and *Alappat*.

15. *See also Loew's Drive-in Theatres v. Park-in Theatres*, 174 F.2d 547, 552 (1st Cir.1949) (holding that the means for carrying out the system of transacting business lacked "an exercise of the faculty of invention"); *In re Patton*, 127 F.2d 324, 327–28 (CCPA 1942) (finding claims invalid as failing to define patentable subject matter over the references of record.); *Berardini v. Tocci*, 190 F. 329, 332 (C.C.S.D.N.Y.1911); *In re Wait*, 73 F.2d 982, 983 (CCPA 1934) ("[S]urely these are, and always have been, essential steps in all dealings of this nature, and even conceding, without holding, that some methods of doing business might present patentable novelty, we think such novelty is lacking here."); *In re Howard*, 394 F.2d 869 (CCPA 1968) ("[W]e therefore affirm the decision of the Board of Appeals on the ground that the claims do not define a novel process [so we find it] unnecessary to consider the issue of whether a method of doing business is inherently unpatentable."). Although a clearer statement was made in *In re Patton*, 127 F.2d 324, 327 (CCPA 1942) that a system for transacting business, separate from the means for carrying out the system, is not patentable subject matter, the jurisprudence does not require the creation of a distinct business class of unpatentable subject matter.

In view of this background, it comes as no surprise that in the most recent edition of the Manual of Patent Examining Procedures (MPEP) (1996), a paragraph of § 706.03(a) was deleted. In past editions it read:

> Though seemingly within the category of process or method, a method of doing business can be rejected as not being within the statutory classes. *See Hotel Security Checking Co. v. Lorraine Co.*, 160 F. 467 (2d Cir.1908) and *In re Wait*, 73 F.2d 982 (1934).

MPEP § 706.03(a) (1994). This acknowledgment is buttressed by the U.S. Patent and Trademark 1996 Examination Guidelines for Computer Related Inventions which now read:

> Office personnel have had difficulty in properly treating claims directed to methods of doing business. Claims should not be categorized as methods of doing business. Instead such claims should be treated like any other process claims.

Examination Guidelines, 61 Fed.Reg. 7478, 7479 (1996). We agree that this is precisely the manner in which this type of claim should be treated. Whether the claims are directed to subject matter within § 101 should not turn on whether the claimed subject matter does "business" instead of something else.

CONCLUSION

The appealed decision is reversed and the case is remanded to the district court for further proceedings consistent with this opinion.

Bilski v. Kappos

___ U.S. ___, 130 S.Ct. 3218 (2010).

■ JUSTICE KENNEDY delivered the opinion of the Court, except as to Parts II–B–2 and II–C–2.*

The question in this case turns on whether a patent can be issued for a claimed invention designed for the business world. The patent application claims a procedure for instructing buyers and sellers how to protect against the risk of price fluctuations in a discrete section of the economy. Three arguments are advanced for the proposition that the claimed invention is outside the scope of patent law: (1) it is not tied to a machine and does not transform an article; (2) it involves a method of conducting business; and (3) it is merely an abstract idea. The Court of Appeals ruled that the first mentioned of these, the so-called machine-or-transformation test, was the sole test to be used for determining the patentability of a "process" under the Patent Act, 35 U.S.C. § 101.

I

Petitioners' application seeks patent protection for a claimed invention that explains how buyers and sellers of commodities in the energy market can protect, or hedge, against the risk of price changes. The key claims are claims 1 and 4. Claim 1 describes a series of steps instructing how to hedge

---

* JUSTICE SCALIA does not join Parts II–B–2 and II–C–2.

risk. Claim 4 puts the concept articulated in claim 1 into a simple mathematical formula. Claim 1 consists of the following steps:

> "(a) initiating a series of transactions between said commodity provider and consumers of said commodity wherein said consumers purchase said commodity at a fixed rate based upon historical averages, said fixed rate corresponding to a risk position of said consumers;
>
> "(b) identifying market participants for said commodity having a counter-risk position to said consumers; and
>
> "(c) initiating a series of transactions between said commodity provider and said market participants at a second fixed rate such that said series of market participant transactions balances the risk position of said series of consumer transactions."

The remaining claims explain how claims 1 and 4 can be applied to allow energy suppliers and consumers to minimize the risks resulting from fluctuations in market demand for energy. For example, claim 2 claims "[t]he method of claim 1 wherein said commodity is energy and said market participants are transmission distributors." Some of these claims also suggest familiar statistical approaches to determine the inputs to use in claim 4's equation. For example, claim 7 advises using well-known random analysis techniques to determine how much a seller will gain "from each transaction under each historical weather pattern."

The patent examiner rejected petitioners' application, explaining that it " 'is not implemented on a specific apparatus and merely manipulates [an] abstract idea and solves a purely mathematical problem without any limitation to a practical application, therefore, the invention is not directed to the technological arts.' " The Board of Patent Appeals and Interferences affirmed, concluding that the application involved only mental steps that do not transform physical matter and was directed to an abstract idea.

The United States Court of Appeals for the Federal Circuit heard the case *en banc* and affirmed. The case produced five different opinions. Students of patent law would be well advised to study these scholarly opinions.

Chief Judge Michel wrote the opinion of the court. The court rejected its prior test for determining whether a claimed invention was a patentable "process" under § 101—whether it produces a " 'useful, concrete, and tangible result' "—as articulated in *State Street Bank & Trust Co. v. Signature Financial Group, Inc.*, 149 F.3d 1368, 1373 (1998), and *AT & T Corp. v. Excel Communications, Inc.*, 172 F.3d 1352, 1357 (1999). The court held that "[a] claimed process is surely patent-eligible under § 101 if: (1) it is tied to a particular machine or apparatus, or (2) it transforms a particular article into a different state or thing." *Id.* at 954. The court concluded this "machine-or-transformation test" is "the sole test governing § 101 analyses," *Id.* at 955, and thus the "test for determining patent eligibility of a process under § 101," *Id.* at 956. Applying the machine-or-transformation test, the court held that petitioners' application was not patent eligible. *Id.* at 963–966. Judge Dyk wrote a separate concurring opinion, providing historical support for the court's approach. *Id.* at 966–976.

Three judges wrote dissenting opinions. Judge Mayer argued that petitioners' application was "not eligible for patent protection because it is directed to a method of conducting business." *Id.* at 998. He urged the adoption of a "technological standard for patentability." *Id.* at 1010. Judge Rader would have found petitioners' claims were an unpatentable abstract idea. *Id.* at 1011. Only Judge Newman disagreed with the court's conclusion that petitioners' application was outside of the reach of § 101. She did not say that the application should have been granted but only that the issue should be remanded for further proceedings to determine whether the application qualified as patentable under other provisions. *Id.* at 997.

This Court granted certiorari. 556 U.S. ___ (2009).

II

A

Section 101 defines the subject matter that may be patented under the Patent Act:

> "Whoever invents or discovers any new and useful process, machine, manufacture, or composition of matter, or any new and useful improvement thereof, may obtain a patent therefor, subject to the conditions and requirements of this title."

Section 101 thus specifies four independent categories of inventions or discoveries that are eligible for protection: processes, machines, manufactures, and compositions of matter. "In choosing such expansive terms ... modified by the comprehensive 'any,' Congress plainly contemplated that the patent laws would be given wide scope." *Diamond v. Chakrabarty*, 447 U.S. 303, 308 (1980). Congress took this permissive approach to patent eligibility to ensure that " 'ingenuity should receive a liberal encouragement.' " *Id.* at 308–309 (quoting 5 WRITINGS OF THOMAS JEFFERSON 75–76 (H. Washington ed. 1871)).

The Court's precedents provide three specific exceptions to § 101's broad patent-eligibility principles: "laws of nature, physical phenomena, and abstract ideas." *Chakrabarty*, *supra*, at 309. While these exceptions are not required by the statutory text, they are consistent with the notion that a patentable process must be "new and useful." And, in any case, these exceptions have defined the reach of the statute as a matter of statutory *stare decisis* going back 150 years. *See Le Roy v. Tatham*, 14 How. 156, 174–175 (1853). The concepts covered by these exceptions are "part of the storehouse of knowledge of all men ... free to all men and reserved exclusively to none." *Funk Brothers Seed Co. v. Kalo Inoculant Co.*, 333 U.S. 127, 130 (1948).

The § 101 patent-eligibility inquiry is only a threshold test. Even if an invention qualifies as a process, machine, manufacture, or composition of matter, in order to receive the Patent Act's protection the claimed invention must also satisfy "the conditions and requirements of this title." § 101. Those requirements include that the invention be novel, see § 102, nonobvious, see § 103, and fully and particularly described, see § 112.

The present case involves an invention that is claimed to be a "process" under § 101. Section 100(b) defines "process" as:

"process, art or method, and includes a new use of a known process, machine, manufacture, composition of matter, or material."

The Court first considers two proposed categorical limitations on "process" patents under § 101 that would, if adopted, bar petitioners' application in the present case: the machine-or-transformation test and the categorical exclusion of business method patents.

B

1

Under the Court of Appeals' formulation, an invention is a "process" only if: "(1) it is tied to a particular machine or apparatus, or (2) it transforms a particular article into a different state or thing." 545 F.3d, at 954. This Court has "more than once cautioned that courts 'should not read into the patent laws limitations and conditions which the legislature has not expressed.'" *Diamond v. Diehr*, 450 U.S. 175, 182 (1981). In patent law, as in all statutory construction, "[u]nless otherwise defined, 'words will be interpreted as taking their ordinary, contemporary, common meaning.'" *Diehr, supra*, at 182 (quoting *Perrin v. United States*, 444 U.S. 37, 42 (1979)). The Court has read the § 101 term "manufacture" in accordance with dictionary definitions, *see* Chakrabarty, *supra*, at 308, and approved a construction of the term "composition of matter" consistent with common usage, *see Chakrabarty, supra*, at 308.

Any suggestion in this Court's case law that the Patent Act's terms deviate from their ordinary meaning has only been an explanation for the exceptions for laws of nature, physical phenomena, and abstract ideas. *See Parker v. Flook*, 437 U.S. 584, 588–589 (1978). This Court has not indicated that the existence of these well-established exceptions gives the Judiciary carte blanche to impose other limitations that are inconsistent with the text and the statute's purpose and design. Concerns about attempts to call any form of human activity a "process" can be met by making sure the claim meets the requirements of § 101.

Adopting the machine-or-transformation test as the sole test for what constitutes a "process" (as opposed to just an important and useful clue) violates these statutory interpretation principles. Section 100(b) provides that "[t]he term 'process' means process, art or method, and includes a new use of a known process, machine, manufacture, composition of matter, or material." The Court is unaware of any "'ordinary, contemporary, common meaning,'" *Diehr, supra*, at 182, of the definitional terms "process, art or method" that would require these terms to be tied to a machine or to transform an article. Respondent urges the Court to look to the other patentable categories in § 101—machines, manufactures, and compositions of matter—to confine the meaning of "process" to a machine or transformation, under the doctrine of *noscitur a sociis*. Under this canon, "an ambiguous term may be given more precise content by the neighboring words with which it is associated." *United States v. Stevens*, 559 U.S. ___, ___, 1587 (2010) (internal quotation marks omitted). This canon is inapplicable here, for § 100(b) already explicitly defines the term "process." *See Burgess v. United States*, 553 U.S. 124, 130 (2008) ("When a statute includes an explicit definition, we must follow that definition" (internal quotation marks omitted)).

The Court of Appeals incorrectly concluded that this Court has endorsed the machine-or-transformation test as the exclusive test. It is true that *Cochrane v. Deener*, 94 U.S. 780, 788 (1877), explained that a "process" is "an act, or a series of acts, performed upon the subject-matter to be transformed and reduced to a different state or thing." More recent cases, however, have rejected the broad implications of this dictum; and, in all events, later authority shows that it was not intended to be an exhaustive or exclusive test. *Gottschalk v. Benson*, 409 U.S. 63, 70 (1972), noted that "[t]ransformation and reduction of an article 'to a different state or thing' is the clue to the patentability of a process claim that does not include particular machines." At the same time, it explicitly declined to "hold that no process patent could ever qualify if it did not meet [machine or transformation] requirements." *Id.* at 71. *Flook* took a similar approach, "assum[ing] that a valid process patent may issue even if it does not meet [the machine-or-transformation test]." 437 U.S., at 588, n. 9.

This Court's precedents establish that the machine-or-transformation test is a useful and important clue, an investigative tool, for determining whether some claimed inventions are processes under § 101. The machine-or-transformation test is not the sole test for deciding whether an invention is a patent-eligible "process."

2

It is true that patents for inventions that did not satisfy the machine-or-transformation test were rarely granted in earlier eras, especially in the Industrial Age, as explained by Judge Dyk's thoughtful historical review. *See* 545 F.3d, at 966–976 (concurring opinion). But times change. Technology and other innovations progress in unexpected ways. For example, it was once forcefully argued that until recent times, "well-established principles of patent law probably would have prevented the issuance of a valid patent on almost any conceivable computer program." *Diehr*, 450 U.S., at 195 (Stevens, J., dissenting). But this fact does not mean that unforeseen innovations such as computer programs are always unpatentable. *See Id.* at 192–193 (majority opinion) (holding a procedure for molding rubber that included a computer program is within patentable subject matter). Section 101 is a "dynamic provision designed to encompass new and unforeseen inventions." *J.E.M. Ag Supply, Inc. v. Pioneer Hi–Bred Int'l, Inc.*, 534 U.S. 124, 135 (2001). A categorical rule denying patent protection for "inventions in areas not contemplated by Congress ... would frustrate the purposes of the patent law." *Chakrabarty*, 447 U.S., at 315.

The machine-or-transformation test may well provide a sufficient basis for evaluating processes similar to those in the Industrial Age—for example, inventions grounded in a physical or other tangible form. But there are reasons to doubt whether the test should be the sole criterion for determining the patentability of inventions in the Information Age. As numerous amicus briefs argue, the machine-or-transformation test would create uncertainty as to the patentability of software, advanced diagnostic medicine techniques, and inventions based on linear programming, data compression, and the manipulation of digital signals. *See, e.g.*, Brief for Business Software Alliance 24–25; Brief for Biotechnology Industry Organization et al. 14–27; Brief for Boston Patent Law Association 8–15; Brief for Houston Intellectual Property Law Association 17–22; Brief for Dolby Labs., Inc., et al. 9–10.

In the course of applying the machine-or-transformation test to emerging technologies, courts may pose questions of such intricacy and refinement that they risk obscuring the larger object of securing patents for valuable inventions without transgressing the public domain. The dissent by Judge Rader refers to some of these difficulties. 545 F.3d, at 1015. As a result, in deciding whether previously unforeseen inventions qualify as patentable "process[es]," it may not make sense to require courts to confine themselves to asking the questions posed by the machine-or-transformation test. Section 101's terms suggest that new technologies may call for new inquiries. *See Benson, supra*, at 71 (to "freeze process patents to old technologies, leaving no room for the revelations of the new, onrushing technology[,] . . . is not our purpose").

It is important to emphasize that the Court today is not commenting on the patentability of any particular invention, let alone holding that any of the above-mentioned technologies from the Information Age should or should not receive patent protection. This Age puts the possibility of innovation in the hands of more people and raises new difficulties for the patent law. With ever more people trying to innovate and thus seeking patent protections for their inventions, the patent law faces a great challenge in striking the balance between protecting inventors and not granting monopolies over procedures that others would discover by independent, creative application of general principles. Nothing in this opinion should be read to take a position on where that balance ought to be struck.

C

1

Section 101 similarly precludes the broad contention that the term "process" categorically excludes business methods. The term "method," which is within § 100(b)'s definition of "process," at least as a textual matter and before consulting other limitations in the Patent Act and this Court's precedents, may include at least some methods of doing business. *See, e.g.*, WEBSTER'S NEW INTERNATIONAL DICTIONARY 1548 (2d ed.1954) (defining "method" as "[a]n orderly procedure or process . . . regular way or manner of doing anything; hence, a set form of procedure adopted in investigation or instruction"). The Court is unaware of any argument that the " 'ordinary, contemporary, common meaning,' " *Diehr, supra*, at 182, of "method" excludes business methods. Nor is it clear how far a prohibition on business method patents would reach, and whether it would exclude technologies for conducting a business more efficiently. *See, e.g.*, Hall, *Business and Financial Method Patents, Innovation, and Policy*, 56 SCOTTISH J. POL. ECON. 443, 445 (2009) ("There is no precise definition of . . . business method patents").

The argument that business methods are categorically outside of § 101's scope is further undermined by the fact that federal law explicitly contemplates the existence of at least some business method patents. Under 35 U.S.C. § 273(b)(1), if a patent-holder claims infringement based on "a method in [a] patent," the alleged infringer can assert a defense of prior use. For purposes of this defense alone, "method" is defined as "a method of doing or conducting business." § 273(a)(3). In other words, by allowing this defense the statute itself acknowledges that there may be business method patents. Section 273's definition of "method," to be sure, cannot change the meaning of a prior-enacted statute. But what § 273 does is clarify the understanding that a business method is simply one kind of "method" that is, at least in some circumstances, eligible for patenting under § 101.

A conclusion that business methods are not patentable in any circumstances would render § 273 meaningless. This would violate the canon against interpreting any statutory provision in a manner that would render another provision superfluous. *See Corley v. United States*, 556 U.S. ___, (2009). This principle, of course, applies to interpreting any two provisions in the U.S.Code, even when Congress enacted the provisions at different times. *See, e.g., Hague v. Committee for Industrial Organization*, 307 U.S. 496, 529–530 (1939) (opinion of Stone, J.). This established rule of statutory interpretation cannot be overcome by judicial speculation as to the subjective intent of various legislators in enacting the subsequent provision. Finally, while § 273 appears to leave open the possibility of some business method patents, it does not suggest broad patentability of such claimed inventions.

2

Interpreting § 101 to exclude all business methods simply because business method patents were rarely issued until modern times revives many of the previously discussed difficulties. See *supra*, at 3227–3228. At the same time, some business method patents raise special problems in terms of vagueness and suspect validity. *See eBay Inc. v. MercExchange, L.L.C.*, 547 U.S. 388, 397 (2006) (Kennedy, J., concurring). The Information Age empowers people with new capacities to perform statistical analyses and mathematical calculations with a speed and sophistication that enable the design of protocols for more efficient performance of a vast number of business tasks. If a high enough bar is not set when considering patent applications of this sort, patent examiners and courts could be flooded with claims that would put a chill on creative endeavor and dynamic change.

In searching for a limiting principle, this Court's precedents on the unpatentability of abstract ideas provide useful tools. See *infra*, at 3229–3231. Indeed, if the Court of Appeals were to succeed in defining a narrower category or class of patent applications that claim to instruct how business should be conducted, and then rule that the category is unpatentable because, for instance, it represents an attempt to patent abstract ideas, this conclusion might well be in accord with controlling precedent. See *ibid*. But beyond this or some other limitation consistent with the statutory text, the Patent Act leaves open the possibility that there are at least some processes that can be fairly described as business methods that are within patentable subject matter under § 101.

Finally, even if a particular business method fits into the statutory definition of a "process," that does not mean that the application claiming that method should be granted. In order to receive patent protection, any claimed invention must be novel, § 102, nonobvious, § 103, and fully and particularly described, § 112. These limitations serve a critical role in adjusting the tension, ever present in patent law, between stimulating innovation by protecting inventors and impeding progress by granting patents when not justified by the statutory design.

III

Even though petitioners' application is not categorically outside of § 101 under the two broad and atextual approaches the Court rejects today, that does not mean it is a "process" under § 101. Petitioners seek to patent both the concept of hedging risk and the application of that concept to energy markets. Rather than adopting categorical rules that might have wide-ranging and unforeseen impacts, the Court resolves this case narrowly on the basis of this Court's decisions in *Benson*, *Flook*, and *Diehr*, which show that petitioners' claims are not patentable processes because they are attempts to patent abstract ideas. Indeed, all members of the Court agree that the patent application at issue here falls outside of § 101 because it claims an abstract idea.

In *Benson*, the Court considered whether a patent application for an algorithm to convert binary-coded decimal numerals into pure binary code was a "process" under § 101. 409 U.S., at 64–67. The Court first explained that " '[a] principle, in the abstract, is a fundamental truth; an original cause; a motive; these cannot be patented, as no one can claim in either of them an exclusive right.' " *Id.* at 67 (quoting *Le Roy*, 14 How., at 175). The Court then held the application at issue was not a "process," but an unpatentable abstract idea. "It is conceded that one may not patent an idea. But in practical effect that would be the result if the formula for converting ... numerals to pure binary numerals were patented in this case." 409 U.S., at 71. A contrary holding "would wholly pre-empt the mathematical formula and in practical effect would be a patent on the algorithm itself." *Id.* at 72.

In *Flook*, the Court considered the next logical step after *Benson*. The applicant there attempted to patent a procedure for monitoring the conditions during the catalytic conversion process in the petrochemical and oil-refining industries. The application's only innovation was reliance on a mathematical algorithm. 437 U.S., at 585–586. *Flook* held the invention was not a patentable "process." The Court conceded the invention at issue, unlike the algorithm in *Benson*, had been limited so that it could still be freely used outside the petrochemical and oil-refining industries. 437 U.S., at 589–590. Nevertheless, *Flook* rejected "[t]he notion that post-solution activity, no matter how conventional or obvious in itself, can transform an unpatentable principle into a patentable process." *Id.* at 590. The Court concluded that the process at issue there was "unpatentable under § 101, not because it contain[ed] a mathematical algorithm as one component, but because once that algorithm [wa]s assumed to be within the prior art, the application, considered as a whole, contain[ed] no patentable invention." *Id.* at 594. As the Court later explained, *Flook* stands for the proposition that the prohibition against patenting abstract ideas "cannot be circumvented by attempting to limit the use of the formula to a particular technological environment" or adding "insignificant postsolution activity." *Diehr*, 450 U.S., at 191–192.

Finally, in *Diehr*, the Court established a limitation on the principles articulated in *Benson* and *Flook*. The application in *Diehr* claimed a previously unknown method for "molding raw, uncured synthetic rubber into cured precision products," using a mathematical formula to complete some of its several steps by way of a computer. 450 U.S., at 177. *Diehr* explained that while an abstract idea, law of nature, or mathematical formula could not be patented, "an application of a law of nature or mathematical formula to a known structure or process may well be deserving of patent protection." *Id.* at 187. *Diehr* emphasized the need to consider the invention as a whole, rather than "dissect[ing] the claims into old and new elements and then . . . ignor[ing] the presence of the old elements in the analysis." *Id.* at 188. Finally, the Court concluded that because the claim was not "an attempt to patent a mathematical formula, but rather [was] an industrial process for the molding of rubber products," it fell within § 101's patentable subject matter. *Id.* at 192–193.

In light of these precedents, it is clear that petitioners' application is not a patentable "process." Claims 1 and 4 in petitioners' application explain the basic concept of hedging, or protecting against risk: "Hedging is a fundamental economic practice long prevalent in our system of commerce and taught in any introductory finance class." 545 F.3d, at 1013 (Rader, J., dissenting); *see, e.g.*, D. CHORAFAS, INTRODUCTION TO DERIVATIVE FINANCIAL INSTRUMENTS 75–94 (2008). The concept of hedging, described in claim 1 and reduced to a mathematical formula in claim 4, is an unpatentable abstract idea, just like the algorithms at issue in Benson and *Flook*. Allowing petitioners to patent risk hedging would pre-empt use of this approach in all fields, and would effectively grant a monopoly over an abstract idea.

Petitioners' remaining claims are broad examples of how hedging can be used in commodities and energy markets. *Flook* established that limiting an abstract idea to one field of use or adding token postsolution components did not make the concept patentable. That is exactly what the remaining claims in petitioners' application do. These claims attempt to patent the use of the abstract idea of hedging risk in the energy market and then instruct the use of well-known random analysis techniques to help establish some of the inputs into the equation. Indeed, these claims add even less to the underlying abstract principle than the invention in *Flook* did, for the *Flook* invention was at least directed to the narrower domain of signaling dangers in operating a catalytic converter.

* * *

Today, the Court once again declines to impose limitations on the Patent Act that are inconsistent with the Act's text. The patent application here can be rejected under our precedents on the unpatentability of abstract ideas. The Court, therefore, need not define further what constitutes a patentable "process," beyond pointing to the definition of that term provided in § 100(b) and looking to the guideposts in *Benson, Flook,* and *Diehr.*

And nothing in today's opinion should be read as endorsing interpretations of § 101 that the Court of Appeals for the Federal Circuit has used in the past. *See, e.g., State Street,* 149 F.3d, at 1373; *AT & T Corp.,* 172 F.3d, at 1357. It may be that the Court of Appeals thought it needed to make the machine-or-transformation test exclusive precisely because its case law had not adequately identified less extreme means of restricting business method patents, including (but not limited to) application of our opinions in *Benson, Flook,* and *Diehr.* In disapproving an exclusive machine-or-transformation test, we by no means foreclose the Federal Circuit's development of other limiting criteria that further the purposes of the Patent Act and are not inconsistent with its text.

The judgment of the Court of Appeals is affirmed.

It is so ordered.

■ JUSTICE STEVENS, with whom JUSTICE GINSBURG, JUSTICE BREYER, and JUSTICE SOTOMAYOR join, concurring in the judgment.

In the area of patents, it is especially important that the law remain stable and clear. The only question presented in this case is whether the so-called machine-or-transformation test is the exclusive test for what constitutes a patentable "process" under 35 U.S.C. § 101. It would be possible to answer that question simply by holding, as the entire Court agrees, that although the machine-or-transformation test is reliable in most cases, it is not the exclusive test.

I agree with the Court that, in light of the uncertainty that currently pervades this field, it is prudent to provide further guidance. But I would take a different approach. Rather than making any broad statements about how to define the term "process" in § 101 or tinkering with the bounds of the category of unpatentable, abstract ideas, I would restore patent law to its historical and constitutional moorings.

For centuries, it was considered well established that a series of steps for conducting business was not, in itself, patentable. In the late 1990's, the Federal Circuit and others called this proposition into question. Congress quickly responded to a Federal Circuit decision with a stopgap measure designed to limit a potentially significant new problem for the business community. It passed the First Inventors Defense Act of 1999 (1999 Act), 113 Stat. 1501A–555 (codified at 35 U.S.C. § 273), which provides a limited defense to claims of patent infringement, see § 273(b), for "method[s] of doing or conducting business," § 273(a)(3). Following several more years of confusion, the Federal Circuit changed course, overruling recent decisions and holding that a series of steps may constitute a patentable process only if it is tied to a machine or transforms an article into a different state or thing. This "machine-or-transformation test" excluded general methods of doing business as well as, potentially, a variety of other subjects that could be called processes.

The Court correctly holds that the machine-or-transformation test is not the sole test for what constitutes a patentable process; rather, it is a critical clue.[1] But the Court is quite wrong, in my view, to suggest that any series of steps that is not itself an abstract idea or law of nature may constitute a "process" within the meaning of § 101. The language in the Court's opinion to this effect can only cause mischief. The wiser course would have been to hold that petitioners' method is not a "process" because it describes only a general method of engaging in business transactions—and business methods are not patentable. More precisely, although a process is not patent-ineligible simply because it is useful for conducting business, a claim that merely describes a method of doing business does not qualify as a "process" under § 101.

* * *

VII

The Constitution grants to Congress an important power to promote innovation. In its exercise of that power, Congress has established an intricate system of intellectual property. The scope of patentable subject matter under that system is broad. But it is not endless. In the absence of any clear guidance from Congress, we have only limited textual, historical, and functional clues on which to rely. Those clues all point toward the same conclusion: that petitioners' claim is not a "process" within the meaning of § 101 because methods of doing business are not, in themselves, covered by the statute. In my view, acknowledging as much would be a far more sensible and restrained way to resolve this case. Accordingly, while I concur in the judgment, I strongly disagree with the Court's disposition of this case.

■ JUSTICE BREYER, with whom JUSTICE SCALIA joins as to Part II, concurring in the judgment.

I

I agree with Justice Stevens that a "general method of engaging in business transactions" is not a patentable "process" within the meaning of 35 U.S.C. § 101. This Court has never before held that so-called "business methods" are patentable, and, in my view, the text, history, and purposes of the Patent Act make clear that they are not. I would therefore decide this case on that ground, and I join Justice Stevens' opinion in full.

I write separately, however, in order to highlight the substantial *agreement* among many Members of the Court on many of the fundamental issues of patent law raised by this case. In light of the need for clarity and settled law in this highly technical area, I think it appropriate to do so.

II

In addition to the Court's unanimous agreement that the claims at issue here are unpatentable abstract ideas, it is my view that the following

---

1. Even if the machine-or-transformation test may not define the scope of a patentable process, it would be a grave mistake to assume that anything with a " 'useful, concrete and tangible result,' " *State Street Bank & Trust v. Signature Financial Group, Inc.,* 149 F.3d 1368, 1373 (C.A.Fed.1998), may be patented.

four points are consistent with both the opinion of the Court and Justice Stevens' opinion concurring in the judgment:

First, although the text of § 101 is broad, it is not without limit. "[T]he underlying policy of the patent system [is] that 'the things which are worth to the public the embarrassment of an exclusive patent,' ... must outweigh the restrictive effect of the limited patent monopoly." *Graham v. John Deere Co. of Kansas City*, 383 U.S. 1, 10–11 (1966) (quoting Letter from Thomas Jefferson to Isaac McPherson (Aug. 13, 1813), in 6 WRITINGS OF THOMAS JEFFERSON 181 (H. Washington ed.)). The Court has thus been careful in interpreting the Patent Act to "determine not only what is protected, but also what is free for all to use." *Bonito Boats, Inc. v. Thunder Craft Boats, Inc.*, 489 U.S. 141, 151 (1989). In particular, the Court has long held that "[p]henomena of nature, though just discovered, mental processes, and abstract intellectual concepts are not patentable" under § 101, since allowing individuals to patent these fundamental principles would "wholly pre-empt" the public's access to the "basic tools of scientific and technological work." *Gottschalk v. Benson*, 409 U.S. 63, 67, 72 (1972); *see also, e.g., Diamond v. Diehr*, 450 U.S. 175, 185 (1981); *Diamond v. Chakrabarty*, 447 U.S. 303, 309 (1980).

Second, in a series of cases that extend back over a century, the Court has stated that "[t]ransformation and reduction of an article to a different state or thing is the clue to the patentability of a process claim that does not include particular machines." *Diehr, supra*, at 184 (emphasis added; internal quotation marks omitted); *see also, e.g., Benson, supra*, at 70; *Parker v. Flook*, 437 U.S. 584, 588, n. 9 (1978); *Cochrane v. Deener*, 94 U.S. 780, 788 (1877). Application of this test, the so-called "machine-or-transformation test," has thus repeatedly helped the Court to determine what is "a patentable 'process.'" *Flook, supra*, at 589.

Third, while the machine-or-transformation test has always been a "useful and important clue," it has never been the "sole test" for determining patentability. *Benson, supra*, at 71 (rejecting the argument that "no process patent could ever qualify" for protection under § 101 "if it did not meet the [machine-or-transformation] requirements"). Rather, the Court has emphasized that a process claim meets the requirements of § 101 when, "considered as a whole," it "is performing a function which the patent laws were designed to protect (e.g., transforming or reducing an article to a different state or thing)." *Diehr, supra*, at 192. The machine-or-transformation test is thus an important example of how a court can determine patentability under § 101, but the Federal Circuit erred in this case by treating it as the exclusive test.

Fourth, although the machine-or-transformation test is not the only test for patentability, this by no means indicates that anything which produces a " 'useful, concrete, and tangible result,' " *State Street Bank & Trust Co. v. Signature Financial Group, Inc.*, 149 F.3d 1368, 1373 (C.A.Fed. 1998), is patentable. "[T]his Court has never made such a statement and, if taken literally, the statement would cover instances where this Court has held the contrary." *Laboratory Corp. of America Holdings v. Metabolite Laboratories, Inc.*, 548 U.S. 124, 136 (2006) (Breyer, J., dissenting from dismissal of certiorari as improvidently granted); *see also, e.g., O'Reilly v.*

Morse, 15 How. 62, 117 (1854); *Flook, supra*, at 590. Indeed, the introduction of the "useful, concrete, and tangible result" approach to patentability, associated with the Federal Circuit's State Street decision, preceded the granting of patents that "ranged from the somewhat ridiculous to the truly absurd." *In re Bilski*, 545 F.3d 943, 1004 (C.A.Fed.2008) (Mayer, J., dissenting) (citing patents on, inter alia, a "method of training janitors to dust and vacuum using video displays," a "system for toilet reservations," and a "method of using color-coded bracelets to designate dating status in order to limit 'the embarrassment of rejection' "). To the extent that the Federal Circuit's decision in this case rejected that approach, nothing in today's decision should be taken as disapproving of that determination.

In sum, it is my view that, in reemphasizing that the "machine-or-transformation" test is not necessarily the *sole* test of patentability, the Court intends neither to de-emphasize the test's usefulness nor to suggest that many patentable processes lie beyond its reach.

III

With these observations, I concur in the Court's judgment.

NOTES

1. *Cases in the Wake of* Bilski. As of this writing, the Federal Circuit has rendered two significant post-*Bilski* decisions. In both cases the court has held that the inventions claimed patentable subject matter. In *Research Corp. v. Microsoft Corp.*, the court held that the claimed computer-implemented invention was not an abstract idea. "[T]his court...will not presume to define 'abstract' beyond the recognition that this disqualifying characteristic should exhibit itself so manifestly as to override the broad statutory categories of eligible subject matter and the statutory context that directs primary attention on the patentability criteria of the rest of the Patent Act....this court notes that inventions with specific applications or improvements to technologies in the marketplace are not likely to be so abstract that they override the statutory language and framework of the Patent Act." *Research Corp. v. Microsoft Corp.*, 627 F.3d 859 (Fed.Cir. 2010).

In the second major case to follow *Bilski*, the Federal Circuit upheld the patentability of a diagnostic method patent. "[A]lthough [mental steps] alone are not patent-eligible, the claims are not simply to the mental steps. A subsequent mental step does not, by itself, negate the transformative nature of prior steps." *Prometheus Laboratories, Inc. v. Mayo Collaborative Svcs.*, 628 F.3d 1347 (Fed.Cir. 2010).

Although both of these cases turn out favorably for the patentee, the Supreme Court had initially granted certiorari in *Prometheus* and only remanded to the Federal Circuit in view of the Supreme Court's decision in *Bilski*. Some think that at least some of the justices on the Supreme Court may not have spoken their last word on the case. Indeed, after initially granting certiorari, the Supreme Court dismissed as improvidently granted a writ of certiorari in *Laboratory Corp. of America Holdings* **v.** *Metabolite Laboratories, Inc.*, 548 U.S. 124 (2006), over a dissenting opinion by Justice Breyer, joined by justices Stevens and Souter. The patent in *LabCorp* was directed to a method for helping to diagnose deficiencies of two vitamins.

2. *The Rise and Fall of the Freeman–Walter–Abele Test.* In a series of opinions stretching from *In re Freeman*, 573 F.2d 1237 (CCPA 1978) to *In re Meyer*, 688 F.2d 789 (CCPA 1982), the Court of Customs and Patent Appeals struggled with the implications of the Supreme Court's decisions in *Benson, Flook,* and *Diehr* on computer-related inventions. The CCPA articulated a two-part test. The test poses two inquires. First, does the patent claim recite, directly or indirectly, a mathematical algorithm, formula, or "mental step"? (If no, then the claim is statutory subject matter; if yes, the second inquiry must be reached). Second, does the claim involve *application* of the algorithm, etc. to specific physical elements or processes? (If yes, the claim is statutory subject matter; if no, the claim is not statutory subject matter).

Of course, the *State Street* decision noted that this test "has been the source of much confusion" and "has little, if any, applicability to determining the presence of statutory subject matter." According to the court:

> [A]fter *Diehr* and *Alappat*, the mere fact that a claimed invention involves inputting numbers, calculating numbers, outputting numbers, and storing numbers, in and of itself, would not render it nonstatutory subject matter, unless, of course, its operation does not produce a "useful, concrete and tangible result." *Alappat*, 33 F.3d at 1544. After all, as we have repeatedly stated, every step-by-step process, be it electronic or chemical or mechanical, involves an algorithm in the broad sense of the term. Since § 101 expressly includes processes as a category of inventions which may be patented and § 100(b) further defines the word "process" as meaning "process, art or method, and includes a new use of a known process, machine, manufacture, composition of matter, or material," it follows that it is no ground for holding a claim is directed to nonstatutory subject matter to say it includes or is directed to an algorithm.

149 F.3d at 1374. Although software patents are firmly established in the United States, and have been for some time, the history of software patents is anything but clear. As Professors Cohen and Lemley write:

> Software patents have a convoluted history. Within the legal system, the past three decades have witnessed an about-face on the question of software's eligibility for patent protection. . . . [S]oftware's status as patentable subject matter was first doubted, then grudgingly admitted, and finally embraced.

Julie E. Cohen and Mark A. Lemley, *Patent Scope and Innovation in the Software Industry*, 89 CAL. L. REV. 1, 7 (2001). Indeed, after *State Street,* even so-called pure software is patentable. Some economists have cast doubt on the need for software patents or, worse, assert they are harmful to software innovation. *See, e.g,* James Bessen and Robert M. Hunt, *An Empirical Look at Software Patents*, (Federal Reserve Bank of Philadelphia, Working Paper 03–17, 2003).

3. *How Useful, Concrete, and Tangible Is Money?* The court went from the first step of articulating a standard—that useful, concrete, tangible subject matter is patentable subject matter—to a third step of reaching a conclusion—that the patent in suit, which dealt with the manipulation of financial information, met the standard and is patentable subject matter. The information that is manipulated by the claimed invention at issue in *State Street* may very well be financially useful, but in what way is it concrete and tangible? Isn't it true that as a matter of common discourse and definition, financial information is considered to be *intangible* subject matter? And is financial date or the transformation of data consistent with the "useful arts" as that term is used in the Constitution? *See* John R. Thomas, *The Patenting of the Liberal Professions*, 40 B.C. L. REV. 1139 (1999); Alan L. Durham, *"Useful Arts" in the Information Age*, 1999 B.Y.U. L. REV. 1419. *See also* B. Zorina Khan, *Innovations in Law and Technology, 1790–1920* IN CAMBRIDGE HISTORY OF LAW (2003) (noting that in the 19th century, "[w]hen patents were granted for inventions that seemed to be for contracts or business methods, the were uniformly overturned by the courts, unless the idea or principle could be construed as vest in a tangible medium").

But ask yourself, is a hundred-dollar-bill not concrete and tangible either? How do you feel about the assurance of the Federal Government on a one-hundred-dollar-bill that "THIS NOTE IS LEGAL TENDER FOR ALL DEBTS, PUBLIC AND PRIVATE" to the extent of the amount reflected on the face of the bill–$100.00? Should the paper aspect of the bill be enough to render the full significance of the bill concrete and tangible, given that the bill's financial utility is not a function of the amount of paper—all denominations of U.S. dollar-bills are the same size and use the same amount of paper—but is rather a function of the legally operative writing on the bill? To what extent is the outcome in *State Street Bank* made more palatable by modern legal and economic theories of money? Consider whether a method for converting lead into gold would be patentable subject matter. Then consider whether the method would be patentable subject matter if it made gold out of thin air. And then consider if the method were improved so that it generated hundred-dollar-bills instead of bars of gold—a much easier to carry form of wealth? And then consider if the method avoided the need to carry anything at all, because it generated a book entry on a bank statement rather than generating paper bills or metal bars? Would this method be patentable subject matter? *See* F. Scott Kieff, *Harnessing Law to Promote Corporate Investment: The Expansive Scope of Intellectual Property Subject Matter*, presented to the faculty of the Legal Studies Department, The Wharton School, University of Pennsylvania, April 30, 1997 (on file with the authors). What does such a significant transformation (from nothing into money) suggest about the machine or transformation test used by the Federal Circuit in *Bilski*. How about a method for warning a person who is about to be run over by an oncoming truck? If the truck crushes the person's bones and a new bone screw is invented to fix them, would that invention transform the patient? If instead the invention warns the person to just step aside before being hit does that method transform the person more or less than would the bone screw? After the massive crash of the world economy in 2008, who now does not seriously wish we had available a better tool for spotting market risk?

4. *What is Useful, Concrete, and Tangible?* In *Arrhythmia Research Technology, Inc. v. Corazonix Corp.*, 958 F.2d 1053 (Fed.Cir.1992), the data that was manipulated by the subject matter of the claims at issue *corresponded to* something useful, concrete, and tangible: signals that represent conditions of a human heart. In *In re Alappat*, 33 F.3d 1526 (Fed.Cir.1994), the data that was manipulated by the subject matter of the claims at issue in the case *caused* something useful, concrete, and tangible: the display of a waveform information on a monitor. But in *State Street Bank*, the data that was manipulated by the subject matter of the claims at issue *both corresponded to and caused* something useful, concrete, and tangible: the dollar-value of shares in the fund. Do you agree? What should the result be if the data that is manipulated in the subject matter of the claims at issue in a case merely correspond to some information generated by a second system, or merely generate some information for yet a third system?

In the year following *State Street Bank*, the Federal Circuit addressed these issues when it reversed a district court's holding of invalidity under Section 101 of a claim directed to a method for use in telecommunications systems in which the record for a long-distance call was augmented to include information about whether the maker and the receiver of the call used the same long-distance provider:

> As previously explained, AT & T's claimed process employs subscribers' and call recipients' PICs as data, applies Boolean algebra to those data to determine the value of the PIC indicator, and applies that value through switching and recording mechanisms to create a signal useful for billing

purposes. In *State Street*, we held that the processing system there was patentable subject matter because the system takes data representing discrete dollar amounts through a series of mathematical calculations to determine a final share price—a useful, concrete, and tangible result. . . .

In this case, Excel argues, correctly, that the PIC indicator value is derived using a simple mathematical principle (p and q). But that is not determinative because AT & T does not claim the Boolean principle as such or attempt to forestall its use in any other application. It is clear from the written description of the '184 patent that AT & T is only claiming a process that uses the Boolean principle in order to determine the value of the PIC indicator. The PIC indicator represents information about the call recipient's PIC, a useful, non-abstract result that facilitates differential billing of long-distance calls made by an IXC's subscriber. Because the claimed process applies the Boolean principle to produce a useful, concrete, tangible result without pre-empting other uses of the mathematical principle, on its face the claimed process comfortably falls within the scope of § 101. . . .

Excel argues that method claims containing mathematical algorithms are patentable subject matter only if there is a "physical transformation" or conversion of subject matter from one state into another. The physical transformation language appears in *Diehr*, see 450 U.S. at 184 . . . ("That respondents' claims involve the transformation of an article, in this case raw, uncured synthetic rubber, into a different state or thing cannot be disputed."), and has been echoed by this court in *Schrader*, 22 F.3d at 294, 30 U.S.P.Q.2D at 1458 ("Therefore, we do not find in the claim any kind of data transformation.").

The notion of "physical transformation" can be misunderstood. In the first place, it is not an invariable requirement, but merely one example of how a mathematical algorithm may bring about a useful application. As the Supreme Court itself noted, "when [a claimed invention] is performing a function which the patent laws were designed to protect (e.g., transforming or reducing an article to a different state or thing), then the claim satisfies the requirements of § 101." *Diehr*, 450 U.S. at 192, 101 S.Ct. 1048 (emphasis added). The "e.g." signal denotes an example, not an exclusive requirement.

This understanding of transformation is consistent with our earlier decision in *Arrhythmia*, 958 F.2d 1053 (Fed.Cir.1992). Arrhythmia's process claims included various mathematical formulae to analyze electrocardiograph signals to determine a specified heart activity. . . . The *Arrhythmia* court reasoned that the method claims qualified as statutory subject matter by noting that the steps transformed physical, electrical signals from one form into another form—a number representing a signal related to the patient's heart activity, a non-abstract output. . . . The finding that the claimed process "transformed" data from one "form" to another simply confirmed that Arrhythmia's method claims satisfied § 101 because the mathematical algorithm included within the process was applied to produce a number which had specific meaning—a useful, concrete, tangible result—not a mathematical abstraction. . . .

AT & T Corp. v. Excel Communications, Inc., 172 F.3d 1352 (Fed.Cir.1999). What "specific meaning" does the "PIC" indicator have in *AT & T*? Is the mere fact that it has *some specific meaning* enough? What more would you require? After *AT & T* and *State Street*, is anything left of the "physical transformation" requirement of *Diehr*?

5. *Business Method Patents.* The *State Street* court expressly endorsed the patentability of business methods, and did away with the so-called business exception, an "ill-conceived exception," according to the court. Since *State Street* the PTO has been inundated with business method patent applications, creating concern among some commentators that the PTO is ill-equipped to handle this increased work load. *See, e.g.,* Robert P. Merges, *As Many as Six Possible Patents Before Breakfast: Property Rights for Business Concepts and Patent System Reform,* 14 BERKELEY TECH. L.J. 577 (1999). A high profile example of a controversial business method patent is Amazon.com's patent on its "one-click" ordering method. *See* U.S. Patent No. 5,960,411. Amazon.com successfully obtained a preliminary injunction against Barnes & Noble just before the December holiday season. Although the district court's decision was subsequently vacated by the Federal Circuit due to the patent's questionable validity, *see Amazon.com, Inc. v. Barnesandnoble.com, Inc.,* 239 F.3d 1343 (Fed.Cir.2001) (overturning injunction), the injunction enabled Amazon.com to obtain a competitive advantage over a key competitor at a crucial time of the year. Other noteworthy business method patents are Priceline.com's "reverse auction" patent (U.S. Patent No. 5,794,207), and Doubleclick's patent on Internet advertisements (U.S. Patent No. 5,948,061).

Several scholars have argued that opening up patent protection to business methods will lead to inefficiencies in business operations and the issuance of more invalid patents. According to two commentators:

> Beyond the issue of permissible subject matter, settled by *State Street,* critics raise essentially two objections. First, some BMPs appear to be based on ideas that can not reasonably be considered novel because similar methods have existed in various unprotected forms for some time. For example, Priceline.com's "reverse auction," in which purchasers list a maximum price and the software auctioneer finds a willing supplier, has antecedents in Dutch auctions and other selling methods. Similarly, Barnes & Noble contested the validity of Amazon's "one-click" patent on the grounds that other techniques involving a single operation by the consumer, contingent on the seller's ability to identify the consumer uniquely, were in operation prior to the patent's issuance in 1999. . . .
>
> Second, many patents cover remarkably broad claims that could permit patentees to exclude competition in a wide swath of Internet applications. . . . In brief, [business method patents] are controversial because they provide broad and lengthy exclusivity for inventions that may not be particularly novel or non-obvious.

Keith E. Maskus & Eina Vivian Wong, *Searching For Economic Balance in Business Method Patents,* 8 WASH. U. J.L. & POL'Y 289, 291–92 (2002). Professor Rochelle Dreyfuss nicely captures the view that business method patents "adversely affect innovation:"

> [I]ntellectual property rights generally are basically viewed as solutions to the free rider problem; patents are also valued because they encourage disclosure. . . . But neither the free-rider nor the disclosure rationale justifies business method patents. Businesses are largely practiced in public. Accordingly, there is little need to especially encourage disclosure. Business methods are also hard to free ride on. They depend in strong ways on the social structure within the firms utilizing them—on compensation schemes, lines of reporting, supervising policies, and other business factors. Moreover, as we saw, sticky business methods are their own reward. With lock in, network effects, and even good old fashioned loyalty, lead time (the first mover advantage) goes a long way to assuring returns adequate to recoup costs and earn substantial profit. In sum, while business innovations are

certainly desirable, it is not clear that business method patents are needed to spur people to create them.

On the costs side, matters are even more unfavorable for business method patents. All patents impose social costs. Patented products are more expensive; quantity and quality are less than they would be in a competitive market. Furthermore, there is deadweight loss created as those who would buy the product at the competitive price forgo purchase at the higher patent price.

Rochelle Cooper Dreyfuss, *Are Business Method Patents Bad For Business?*, 16 SANTA CLARA COMPUTER & HIGH TECH. L.J. 263, 274–75 (2000). *See also,* Michael J. Meurer, *Business Method Patents and Patent Floods*, 8 WASH. U. J.L. & POL'Y 309 (2002); John R. Thomas, *Liberty and Property in Patent Law*, 39 HOUS. L. REV. 569 (2002).

But some commentators have argued that the criticism of business method patents lacks empirical support, which has "led to undesirable results." *See, e.g.,* John R. Allison and Emerson H. Tiller, *The Business Method Patent Myth*, http://papers.ssrn.com/sol3/papers.cfm?abstract_id=421980 (July 2003) (comparing Internet business method patents to large random sample of general patents and finding business method patents "actually fare quite well statistically"). Also, some scholars have expressed "[c]oncern[s] about biasing the direction of inventive activity." *See* WILLIAM M. LANDES & RICHARD A. POSNER, THE ECONOMIC STRUCTURE OF INTELLECTUAL PROPERTY LAW 328–29 (2003) (noting that permitting business methods to be patented "goes some way toward correcting the potential distortion in the allocation of resources to inventive activity that arises from limiting patent protection to products of scientific and technological rather than marketing ingenuity").

5. *A Return to Benson, Flook, or Freeman–Walter–Abele?* Most recently, a number of Federal Circuit cases have called into question the approach to 101 subject matter that had its lineage in *Diehr, Chakrabarty, Alappat,* and *State Street Bank,* instead favoring the approach of *Benson, Flook,* or *Freeman–Walter–Abele.* In 2007, the Federal Circuit issued its decision in *In re Stephen W. Comiskey,* 499 F.3d 1365 (Fed. Cir. 2007), which seems to limit the scope of *State Street Bank* by requiring a pure mental process be connected to a machine (e.g., a computer) in order for a claim to recite proper 101 subject matter. If followed, this decision would require patent drafters of claims directed to mental processes to combine a particular technology such as a computer with such mental processes for the subject matter to meet 101. While this seems like an easy decision to draft around, it is strikingly similar to the *Benson, Flook,* or *Freeman–Walter–Abele* case law, which effectively made every software patent subject to discretionary review for being too close to a mental step and therefore invalid. Indeed, in a case handed down the same day as *Comiskey, In re Petrus A.C.M. Nuijten,* 500 F.3d 1346 (Fed.Cir.2007), the Federal Circuit examined the patentability of claims to a digital watermark for a computer data file simply declared it to be not within any patentable subject matter. Later, in *Bilski,* the Federal Circuit embraced a "machine or transformation" test, but that test was rejected by the Supreme Court, which failed to provide its own test, at least beyond that articulated by its prior case law. Do you think this is a type of "know it when you see it" decision making?

6. *Software and Business Method Patents in Europe.* Section 52(2)(c) of the European Patent Convention (EPC) expressly excludes from patent protection methods for "doing business and programs for computers." Article 52(3) states:

The provisions of paragraph 2 shall exclude patentability of the subject-matter or activities referred to in that provision only to the extent to which a European patent application or European patent relates to such subject-matter or activities as such.

While the European Patent Office (EPO) has remained largely faithful to the business method exclusion, it has essentially disregarded the software exception. In fact, it is not uncommon for the EPO to issue software patents as long as the invention possess a "technical character." *See EPO* Guidelines for Substantive Examination, Part C, Chapter IV, §§ 2.1, 2.2. *See also, Computer Program Product/IBM,* T 1173/97–3.5.1 (EPO Bd. of App. July 1, 1998). For instance, 6,856 applications in the "computing" field were filed in 2002, more than double the amount in 1998 (3,306), and more than the number of applications in the fields of biochemistry/genetic engineering, which had 4,427 applications in 2002. *See* EPO 2002 ANNUAL REPORT, (Business Report, Figure 11).

Perhaps the leading EPO case relating to software patents is *Computer Program Product/IBM,* supra. The following is an excerpt from the opinion:

2.   *TRIPS*

[Eds. Note: The EPO Board held that TRIPS is binding only on member states of the WTO, and the EPO is not a member state. Therefore, TRIPS is not binding on the EPO. Nonetheless, the Board noted that it will take TRIPS into consideration]

3.   *The relevant source of substantive patent law*

[T]he only source of substantive patent law for examining European patent applications at this moment is the European Patent Convention [EPC]. The examining division's conclusion in the decision under appeal that the EPC is the only relevant system of substantive law to be taken into account is therefore correct.

* * *

The Board will therefore now investigate what in its view would be the proper interpretation of the exclusion from patentability of programs for computers under Article 52(2) and (3) EPC.

4.   *Exclusion under Article 52(2) and (3) EPC*

4.1   Turning to the exclusion clause itself, the Board notes the following:

Article 52(2)(c) EPC states that programs for computers shall not be regarded as inventions within the meaning of Article 52(1) EPC and are therefore excluded from patentability.

Article 52(3) EPC establishes an important limitation to the scope of this exclusion. According to this provision, the exclusion applies only to the extent to which a European patent application or a European patent relates to programs for computers "as such."

The combination of the two provisions (Article 52(2) and (3) EPC) demonstrates that the legislators did not want to exclude from patentability all programs for computers. In other words the fact that only patent applications relating to programs for computers as such are excluded from patentability may be allowed for patent applications relating to programs for computers where the latter are not considered to be programs for computers as such.

* * *

5.2   *Interpretation of "as such"*

5.1   Within the context of the application of the EPC the technical character of an invention is generally accepted as an essential requirement for its patentability. . . .

5.2 The exclusion from patentability of programs for computers as such (Article 52(2) and (3) EPC) may be construed to mean that such programs are considered to be mere abstract creations, lacking in technical character. The use of the expression "shall not be regarded as inventions" seems to confirm this interpretation.

5.3 This means that programs for computers must be considered as patentable inventions when they have a technical character.

5.4 This conclusion seems to be consistent with the three different provisions concerned:

(a) the exclusion from patentability provided for in Article 52(2) EPC;

(b) the general provision of Article 52(1) EPC, according to which European patents shall be granted for any inventions (therefore having technical features) which are susceptible of industrial application, which are new and which involve an inventive step;

(c) the provision of Article 52(3) EPC, which does not allow a broad interpretation of the scope of the exclusion.

5.5 The main problem for the interpretation of said exclusion is therefore to define the meaning of the feature "technical character," in the present case with specific reference to programs for computers.

6. *Technical Character of programs for computers*

6.1 For the purpose of interpreting the exclusion from patentability of programs for computers under Article 52(2) and (3) EPC, it is assumed that programs for computers cannot be considered as having a technical character for the very reason that they are programs for computers.

6.2 This means that physical modifications of the hardware (causing, for instance, electrical currents) deriving from the execution of the instructions given by programs for computers cannot *per se* constitute the technical character required for avoiding the exclusion of those programs.

6.3 Although such modifications may be considered to be technical, they are a common feature of all those programs for computers which have been made suitable for being run on a computer, and therefore cannot be used to distinguish programs for computers with a technical character from programs for computers as such.

6.4 It is thus necessary to look elsewhere for technical character in the above sense: It could be found in the further effects deriving from the execution (by the hardware) of the instructions given by the computer program. Where said further effects have a technical character or where they cause the software to solve a technical problem, an invention which brings about such an effect may be considered an invention, which can, in principle, be the subject-matter of a patent.

6.5 Consequently a patent may be granted not only the case of an invention where a piece of software manages, by means of a computer, an industrial process or the working of a piece of machinery, but in every case where a program for a computer is the only means, or one of the necessary means, of obtaining a technical effect within the meaning specified above, where, for instance, a technical effect of that kind is achieved by the internal functioning of a computer itself under the influence of said program.

In other words, on condition that they are able to produce a technical effect in the above sense, all computer programs must be considered as inventions within the meaning of Article 52(1) EPC, and may be the subject-matter of a patent if the other requirements provided for by the EPC are satisfied.

6.6   As already indicated in the previous paragraph, said technical effect may also be caused by the functioning of the computer itself on which the program is being run, i.e. by the functioning of the hardware of that computer. It is clear that in this situation too the physical modifications of the hardware deriving from the execution of the instructions given by the program within the meaning indicated under points 6.2 and 6.3 above cannot *per se* constitute the technical character required for avoiding exclusion.

In this case it is only said further technical effect which matters when considering the patentability requirements, and no importance should be attached to the specific further use of the system as a whole. . . .

While it is clear that the EPO issues patents on software-related inventions, despite Article 52 apparent prohibition, there remains a degree of uncertainty due to the lack of a European-wide patent. In other words, there is disparate treatment of software-related patents among the EU member states. Thus, much like the biotechnology industry, the software industry wants to enhance certainty for software patents throughout Europe. To this end, the European Parliament considered a directive on European software patents in 2003. As of this writing, the directive, as amended and passed by the European Parliament, was less receptive of software patents than hoped for by industry. In a study commissioned by the Parliament, the authors wrote that "conclusive evidence supporting a liberalization of existing European patent law and practice in respect of software . . ., on the basis of U.S. experience, does not exist." BNA Patent, Trademark & Copyright Law Daily (September 26, 2003). And some in Parliament sought to write a directive that would force the EPO to adhere more strictly to the exclusions set forth in Article 52 of the EPC. For instance, a senior member of the Parliament's Legal Affairs Committee stated: "Although the patenting of software is supposed to be prohibited by Article 52 of the EPO Convention, Munich [the site of the EPO] has in recent years taken to giving patents on some elements of software. The Parliament's amendments are designed to stop this dangerous drift." *Id. See also* an open letter to the EU Parliament signed by several economists, *An Open Letter to the European Parliament Concerning the Proposed Directive on the Patentability of Computer–Implemented Inventions* (25 August 2003) ("Software patents damage innovation by raising costs and uncertainties") (accessed 9 February 2004). As of this writing, the future of the directive is uncertain as it awaits consideration by the Council of Ministers, which represents the EU member states.

On the business method front, the EPO has been much more stingy with patents. *See, e.g., Pension Benefit Systems Partnership*/T 0931/97 (Sept. 8, 2000), which involved a computer-implemented business method. The EPO held that "methods only involving economic concepts and practices of doing business are not inventions" because they lack a "technical contribution." Thus, the EPO refused to be influenced by *State Street Bank* and distinguished the present case from *Computer Program Product*:

Main request: Method claim

3.   Following [*Computer Program Product/IBM*] the question to be answered in the present case is whether the method according to claim 1

represents a method of doing business as such. If the method is technical or, in other words, has a technical character, it still may be a method for doing business, but not a method for doing business as such.

Claim 1 of the main request is, apart from various computing means mentioned in that claim, directed to a "method for controlling a pension benefits program by administering at least one subscriber employer account." All the features of this claim are steps of processing and producing information having purely administrative, actuarial and/or financial character. Processing and producing such information are typical steps of business and economic methods.

Thus the invention as claimed does not go beyond a method of doing business as such and, therefore, is excluded from patentability under Article 52(2)(c) in combination with Article 52(3) EPC; the claim does not define an invention within the meaning of Article 52(1) EPC.

The appellant referred to the data processing and computing means defined in the method claim, arguing that the use of such means conferred technical character to the method claimed. However, the individual steps defining the claimed method amount to no more than the general teaching to use data processing means for processing or providing information of purely administrative, actuarial and/or financial character, the purpose of each single step and of the method as a whole being a purely economic one.

The feature of using technical means for a purely non-technical purpose and/or for processing purely non-technical information does not necessarily confer technical character to any such individual steps of use or to the method as a whole: in fact, any activity in the non-technical branches of human culture involves physical entities and uses, to a greater or lesser extent, technical means.

* * *

The board therefore concludes that:

Methods only involving economic concepts and practices of doing business are not inventions within the meaning of Article 52(1) EPC.

* * *

A recent case in France highlights European skepticism of business method patents. In *SA Sagem vs. M. Le Directeur de l'INPI*, French high-tech company, Sagem, appealed a ruling by France's top IP authority, the *Institut National de la Propriete Industrielle* (INPI), which denied patent protection for what it characterized as a business method for securing telephone and Internet-based transactions. The appellate court in Paris affirmed the INPI, which is the first such definitive ruling in France on the patentability of business methods. The INPI and the court held that the invention lacked technical effect and was aimed more towards enabling a commercial transaction.

7. *Is There a Need for a Statutory Subject Matter Requirement?* One can fairly read the *State Street* decision as marginalizing the statutory subject matter requirement of § 101 and placing a great deal of reliance on the other patentability provisions. Recall the court noted:

The question of whether a claim encompasses statutory subject matter should not focus on which of the four categories of subject matter a claim is directed to a process, machine, manufacture, or composition of matter—but rather on the essential characteristics of the subject matter, in particular, its practical utility. Section 101 specifies that statutory subject matter must also satisfy the other "conditions and requirements" of Title 35, including novelty, nonobviousness, and adequacy of disclosure and notice.... Whether the patent's claims are too broad to be patentable is not to be judged under § 101, but rather under §§ 102, 103 and 112.

But shouldn't the statutory subject matter requirement have a gatekeeper role? By precluding certain types of inventions and technologies from consideration *ex ante* don't we avoid the messy and difficult novelty and nonobviousness determinations? How easy is it to obtain business method prior art? Or non-patent software prior art? On the other hand, is there a danger that this gatekeeper role can be used to shut the door on technology that has yet to be created, or on existing technology, the use of which is presently unknown?

8. *How About Sports?* While most commentators are satisfied with the financial services' claim to patentable status, others have pushed the envelope even further to debate IP rights in sports moves. See F. Scott Kieff, Robert G. Kramer, and Robert M. Kunstadt, *It's Your Turn, But It's My Move: Intellectual Property Protection For Sports "Moves,"* 25 SANTA CLARA COMPUTER & HIGH TECH. L.J. 765 (2009); Richard B. Schmitt, *Effort Is Under Way To Put New Meaning On Moves In Sports*, WALL ST. J., May 10, 1996, at A5, col. 1; Christopher Simon, *Man With a Patented Putt Hopes Someone Shows Him the Green*, WALL ST. J., August 18, 1997, at B1, col. 1; Robin Jacob, *Industrial Property—Industry's Enemy*, THE INTELLECTUAL PROPERTY QUARTERLY (Sweet & Maxwell), 1997, pp. 3–15.

CHAPTER EIGHT

INFRINGEMENT

> A man ... has no right whatever to take, if I may so say, a leaf out of his neighbor's book.
>
> —Chief Justice Tindal[1]

> The claim is thus the life of the patent so far as the rights of the inventor are concerned, and by it the letters-patent, as a grant of an exclusive privilege, must stand or fall.
>
> —William C. Robinson[2]

INTRODUCTION

A patent grant gives the patentee several rights. A good place to begin the exploration of these rights is sections 154 and 271(a) of the patent code. Section 154(a)(1) states that a

> patent shall contain ... a grant ... of the right to exclude others from making, using, offering for sale, or selling the invention throughout the United States or importing the invention into the United States....[3]

In addition, for applications filed on or after November 29, 2000, the patent applicant enjoys provisional rights beginning on the date the application is published pursuant to 35 U.S.C. § 122(b) and ending on the date the patent issues. 35 U.S.C. § 154(d). These rights are against a third party who makes, uses, offers for sale, or sells in the United States the invention claimed in the published application. 35 U.S.C. § 154(d)(1)(A)(i). The patentee must prove that the third party had actual notice subsequent to publication and the invention claimed in the patent is "substantially identical to the invention as claimed in the published patent application." 35 U.S.C. § 154(d)(2).[4] The remedy for pre-grant use of the invention is a "reasonable royalty."

---

1. Walton v. Potter, 1 Webster 585, 587 (C.P. 1841).

2. William C. Robinson, 2 THE LAW OF PATENTS § 505 (1890). William Robinson, a law professor at Yale University, was a prominent patent law scholar, and his treatise, THE LAW OF PATENTS, was very influential in the late 19th and early 20th centuries. In fact, it is not uncommon to consult Professor Robinson's treatise today. Other important 19th century patent law treatises include, George Ticknor Curtis, A TREATISE ON THE LAW OF PATENTS FOR USEFUL INVENTIONS (1867) and Thomas G. Fessenden, ESSAY ON THE LAW OF PATENTS FOR NEW INVENTIONS (1810)

3. As we read in Chapter One, the patent grant does not give the patentee a right to make, use, or sell the patented invention. Indeed, one may obtain a patent on an invention and still infringe another patent.

4. With respect to PCT applications, § 154(d)(4) states that,

The other significant enforcement section is 271(a), which provides that:

> whoever, without authority makes, uses, offers to sell, or sells any patented invention within the United States or imports into the United States any patented invention during the term of the patent therefor, infringes the patent.

Thus, under §§ 154 and 271 a patentee has five basic rights of exclusion: (1) making; (2) using, (3) selling; (4) offering for sale; and (5) importing.[5]

Patent claims are the touchstone of patent protection and it is the claims that set forth the patentee's proprietary boundaries. Section 271 defines patent infringement as the unauthorized practice of the "patented invention."[6] The "patented invention" of Section 271 is that which the inventor has particularly pointed out and distinctly *claimed* as required under Section 112, paragraph 2.[7] As Judge Rich reminds us in his Foreword to this book, the claims are not "the measure of what was invented," but rather *"the claims are the measure of the patentee's right to exclude."* (Emphasis in original). In other words, the claims serve to circumscribe a property right by setting forth the metes and bounds of the patentee's right to exclude.

The Supreme Court has emphasized for over a century that the claims of a patent should be clear and should control the determination of infringement. In an 1877 decision, for example, the Court stressed that "nothing can be more just and fair both to the patentee and to the public, than that the former should understand and correctly describe just what he has invented and for what he claims a patent." *Merrill v. Yeomans*, 94 U.S. 568 (1877). The process whereby the courts determine the precise meaning of a patent claim is called *claim construction* or *claim interpretation*. Construing the claims is always the first step in an infringement or validity analysis.

A patentee may enforce his patent rights by filing a patent infringement suit in federal district court. The causes of action for patent infringement can be divided into two broad categories: (1) *direct infringement*; and (2) *indirect infringement*. The difference between direct and indirect infringement is entirely a matter of *who* the patentee is able to sue. Under the theory of direct infringement, the patentee may bring an action against a defendant who himself is committing acts (*e.g.,* making a product or

---

> The right ... to obtain a reasonable royalty based upon the publication under the treaty defined in section 351(a) of an international application designating the United States shall commence on the date on which the [PTO] receives a copy of the publication under the treaty of the international application, or, if the publication under the treaty of the international application is in a language other than English, on the date on which the [PTO] receives a translation of the international application in the English language.

5. The "importing" and "offering for sale" provisions became effective on January 1, 1996 and were added to sections 154 and 271(a) as part of the Uruguay Round Agreement of GATT on Trade Related Aspects of Intellectual Property.

6. The reach of the patentee's rights of exclusion under Section 271 are discussed in this chapter.

7. The disclosure requirements, including the requirement of particularly pointing out and distinctly claiming, are the subject of Chapter Three.

practicing a process) that infringe in and of themselves. Under the theory of indirect infringement, the patentee may bring an action against a defendant whose acts do not infringe in and of themselves, but that contribute to or induce acts of direct infringement by some third party.

Direct patent infringement is said to occur where there is either *literal* infringement or infringement under the *doctrine of equivalents*. Literal infringement of a patent is very basic and occurs when "every limitation recited in the claim is found in the accused device." *Engel Industries, Inc. v. Lockformer Company*, 96 F.3d 1398, 1405 (Fed.Cir.1996). For example, patentee X has a patent claiming a product comprising elements A, B, and C and competitor Y makes a product comprising A, B, and C. It would then be said that patentee X's patent claim "reads on" competitor Y's product. Literal infringement is analogous to anticipation. Recall from Chapter Four, that to anticipate a patent, a prior art reference must disclose each and every claim limitation. In an infringement context, however, it is the accused device, not a prior art reference, that must embody each and every claim limitation. Thus, the fundamental patent law maxim: "that which infringes, if later, would anticipate, if earlier." *See Peters v. Active Mfg. Co.*, 129 U.S. 530, 537 (1889). *See also*, DONALD S. CHISUM, CHISUM ON PATENTS § 3.02[1] (1997).

The patentee bears the burden of pleading and proving infringement, and the burden of proof is the ordinary burden in civil litigation, which is known as "preponderance of the evidence." That burden is generally conceived of as having convinced the fact finder that it is more likely than not that the alleged fact actually occurred. The Federal Circuit has also reminded that ordinary inferences and uses of circumstantial evidence can be used in patent cases. For example, "if a district court construes the claims and finds that the reach of the claims includes any device that practices a[n industry] standard, then this can be sufficient for a finding of infringement [by devices that conform to the standard]." Fujitsu Ltd. v. Netgear Inc., 620 F.3d 1321, 1327 (Fed.Cir.2010).

Recent debates have emerged around the question of whether direct infringement must have been conducted by a single person in order to constitute patent infringement. For example, infringement of a method patent is generally considered to require that the defendant either perform every step of the claimed method or have another party perform steps on its behalf; and collective performance of the steps by independent actors would then not constitute infringement. *See Muniauction, Inc. v. Thomson Corp.*, 532 F.3d 1318 (Fed.Cir.2008); *Golden Hour Data Sys., Inc. v. emsCharts, Inc.*, 614 F.3d 1367 (Fed.Cir.2010). Yet, in *Centillion Data Sys. v. Qwest Comm. Int'l*, 631 F.3d 1279 (Fed.Cir.2011), the court seemed to apply a different test for "system" claims and method claims, and appeared to hold that for system claims one person need not perform every element of the claim.

In addition, even the *Muniauction* cases seem to focus on principles of agency when deciding that a core issue is control when deciding whether one person is liable for the actions of another. But in other areas of law courts have long viewed agency theories as just one category of approaches to finding joint infringement. Put differently, while the Federal Circuit's

Muniauction line of cases does provide helpful guidance about one path for proving joint infringement, which is by showing that one party directed or controlled the actions of another, and that when taken together their combined actions constitute infringement. *See e.g., Muniauction; see also* RESTATEMENT OF TORTS (SECOND) § 877 "Directing or Permitting Conduct of Another," such guidance along one path does not foreclose others. In contrast, the Federal Circuit has never held that this is the "only" way joint infringement can be proven. Do you think that a party that wants to show joint infringement should be able to use other well-established pathways for imposing joint liability so long as that party merely satisfies the ordinary legal elements long understood to lie along those pathways? Such a party would of course have to be prepared to plead and prove these elements. For example, joint liability for a tort like infringement has long been recognized to lie where a party can show that two entities "acted in concert" to cause the infringement. *See* RESTATEMENT OF TORTS (SECOND) § 876. "Persons Acting in Concert". Parties are acting in concert when they act in accordance with an agreement to cooperate in a particular line of conduct or to accomplish a particular result. The agreement need not be expressed in words and may be implied and understood to exist from the conduct itself. *See id.* (Comments to Clause (a)). Similarly joint liability also has long been recognized to lie where parties are acting in concert by acting in accordance with an agreement to cooperate in a particular line of conduct or to accomplish a particular result. See Uniform Partnership Act § 6 (defining partnership as an "association of two or more persons to carry on as co-owners a business for profit"); REVISED UNIFORM PARTNERSHIP ACT § 202(a) (defining a partnership as an "association of two or more persons to carry on as co-owners a business for profit … whether or not the persons intend to form a partnership"); *see also Texaco Inc. v. Dagher,* 547 U.S. 1 (2006) (reaffirming definition of "joint venture" and holding that two parties acting together as a joint venture to set prices is qualitatively different from the behavior of two or more separate parties acting to do the same thing and as a result is ineligible for treatment as a per se antitrust violation for price fixing). These traditional rules of joint liability apply when the acts of each of two or more parties, standing alone, would not be wrongful, but together they cause harm to the patentee. *See* RESTATEMENT OF TORTS (SECOND) § 875 "Contributing Tortfeasors—General Rule"; PROSSER & KEETON ON TORTS § 52, at 354 (5th ed. 1984).

Courts have not always confined patentees to the literal meaning of their claims, sometimes finding infringement when an accused infringing device (or process) is an "equivalent" to that claimed in the patent. The rubric under which courts extend the scope of a patentee's right to exclude beyond the literal language of the patent claims has come to be known as the *doctrine of equivalents* (or "DOE"). The doctrine of equivalents is tempered by a related doctrine called *prosecution history estoppel,* which was formerly known as file wrapper estoppel.

The patent term is for 20 years from the earliest filing date. But prior to June 8, 1995 (the effective date of the GATT–TRIPs legislation), the term for a United States patent was 17 years from the date the patent issued.[8] In April 1994, the United States and several other countries concluded the Uruguay Round trade negotiation under the General Agreement on Tariffs and Trade (GATT), which included an "Agreement on Trade–Related Aspects of Intellectual Property" (TRIPs). The TRIPs patent section provided: "The term of protection available shall not end before the expiration of a period of twenty years counted from the filing date."[9]

The Clinton Administration submitted to Congress a comprehensive bill on GATT to "take effect on the date that is 6 months after the date of enactment." Title V of this legislation, pertaining to intellectual property, established a 20–year patent term from date of filing. Congress passed the bill in late 1994, and President Clinton signed it into law on December 8, 1994,[10] thus making June 8, 1995, the effective date of the legislation. In turn, § 154(a)(2) of the Patent Code was amended to read:

> Term.—Subject to the payment of fees under this title, such grant shall be for a term beginning on the date on which the patent issues and ending 20 years from the date on which the application for the patent was filed in the United States, or, if the application contains a specific reference to an earlier filed application or applications under section 120, 121, or 365(c) of this title, from the date on which the earliest such application was filed.

The TRIPs legislation also affects patent applications filed before June 8, 1995. The patent term for applications filed *before* June 8, 1995, is (1) 17 years from date of issuance; *or* (2) 20 years measured from the filing date of the earliest referenced application, whichever is greater. For applications filed *on* or *after* June 8, 1995, the patent term is 20 years measured from the earliest referenced application filing date. Earlier referenced applications, which are discussed in Chapter Two, may include continuation applications under 35 U.S.C. § 120, divisional applications under 35 U.S.C. § 121, or Patent Cooperation Treaty (PCT) applications under 35 U.S.C. § 365(c).

In the Patent Term Guarantee Act of 1999, Congress amended Section 154(b) on term extensions. In addition to providing term extensions, the Act requires the PTO to adopt rules allowing applicants to continue prosecution of an application without the need to file a continuing application or "continued prosecution application." The amendment removes a five-year limitation on the maximum extension.[11] It adds as grounds for

---

8. The patent term of the Patent Act of 1790 was "for any term not exceeding fourteen years." The term of fourteen years was derived from the English Statute of Monopolies, which provided a patent term of fourteen years that was equivalent to two apprenticeships of seven years. *See* DONALD S. CHISUM, 5 CHISUM ON PATENTS 16–186 (1997); *See also, Rite–Hite Corp. v. Kelley Co., Inc.*, 56 F.3d 1538, 1562 n. 12 (Fed.Cir.1995) (Nies, J., dissenting in part: "The original period of exclusivity was 14 years. Why that term was provided is unknown. It may have some relationship to the terms of successive apprenticeships."). It wasn't until the Patent Act of 1861 that the 17 year term was established. For an economic analysis of patent term, see Machlup, *An Economic Review of the Patent System,* Study No. 15, Subcomm. Pat. Trademark & Copyright, Jud. Comm., 85th Cong., 2d Sess 9 (1958); Gilbert and Shapiro, *Optimal Patent Length and Breadth,* 21 RAND JOURNAL OF ECONOMICS 106 (1990).

9. The patent term for design patents was not affected and remains 14 years from date of issuance. 35 U.S.C. § 173.

10. Pub. L. 103–465, 108 Stat. 4809 (Dec. 8, 1994).

11. Congress considered but rejected a ten (10) year cap on extensions:

extension delays occasioned by the failure of the PTO to take certain actions within certain time periods.

The amendment takes effect six months after its enactment date of November 29, 1999. It provides that: "except for a design patent application filed under chapter 16 of title 35, United States Code, [the amendment to Section 154(b)] shall apply to any application filed on or after the date that is 6 months after the date of the enactment of this Act."[12]

The Act sets for three grounds for extension:

1. *PTO Response Times.* Section 154(b)(1)(A) provides for extension when the PTO fails to (1) provide a Section 132 notification (a rejection or an objection) or a notice of allowance within 14 months of the filing of a non-provisional application; (2) respond to an applicant's Section 132 reply to an office action or to an appeal within 4 months; (3) act on an application "in which allowable claims remain in the application" within 4 months of a Board or court decision in an appeal; or (4) issue a patent within 4 months of payment of the issue fee. The restoration is on a day-to-day basis, that is, one day for each day after the period specified until the action is taken.

2. *Greater Than Three–Year Pendency.* Section 154(b)(1)(B) provides for extension when the PTO fails to issue a patent within three (3) years after an application's "actual filing date ... in the United States."[13]

Excluded under 35 U.S.C. § 154(b)(1)(B)(i–iii) are (1) "time consumed by continued examination of the application requested by the applicant under section 132(b);" (2) "time consumed by a proceeding under section 135(a), ... by the imposition of an order under section 181, or ... appellate review by the Board of Patent Appeals and Interferences or by a Federal court;" and (3) "any delay in the processing of the application by the United States Patent and Trademark Office requested by the applicant

---

The provisions that were initially included only provided adjustments for up to 10 years for secrecy orders, interferences, and successful appeals. Not only are these adjustments too short for some cases, but no adjustments were provided for administrative delays caused by the PTO that were beyond the control of the applicant. Accordingly, Title III removes the 10–year caps from existing provisions, adds a new provision to compensate applicants fully for PTO-caused administrative delays, and, for good measure, includes a new provision guaranteeing diligent applicants at least a 17–year term by extending the term of any patent not granted with three years of filing. Thus, no patent applicant diligently seeking to obtain a patent will receive a term of less than the 17 years as provided under the pre-GATT ... standard; in fact, most will receive considerably more. Only those who purposely manipulate the system to delay the issuance of their patents will be penalized under Title III, a result that the Committee believes entirely appropriate.

H.R. No. 106–287(1), 106th Cong., 1st Sess. (1999). *See also* H.R. Conf. Rep. No. 106–464, 106th Cong., 1st Sess. (Nov. 9, 1999).

12. PL 106–113, § 4405(a), 113 Stat. 1501, 1501A–560 (Nov. 29, 1999).

13. The House Report comments on the phrase "actual date of the application in the United States:"

This language was intentionally selected to exclude the filing date of an application under the Patent Cooperation Treaty (PTC).... Otherwise, an applicant could obtain up to a 30–month extension of a U.S. patent merely by filing under PCT, rather than directly in the PTO, gaining an unfair advantage in contrast to strictly domestic applicants.

except as permitted by paragraph (3)(C)." The extension is on a day-to-day basis, that is, a day for each day after the three year period until the patent is issued.

3. *Interferences, Secrecy Orders, and Appeals.* Section 154(b) continues to provide for extension in cases of (1) "a proceeding under section 135(a)," that is, an interference; (2) "the imposition of an order under section 181," that is, a secrecy order; and (3) "appellate review by a Federal court in a case in which the patent was issued under a decision in the review reversing an adverse determination of patentability." The extension is on a day-to-day basis, that is, a day for each day after the three year period until the patent is issued.

A patent is effective and enforceable only upon issuance.[14] As the Supreme Court stated over one hundred years ago, "[u]ntil a patent is issued there is no property right in it, that is, no such right as the inventor can enforce."[15] Just as a patent is unenforceable prior to issuance, it is unenforceable after it expires.[16] What about a third party who *prepares* to make, use, or sell the claimed invention *prior* to the expiration of the patent with the ultimate plan of making, using, and selling *after* expiration? The Federal Circuit, in *Joy Technologies, Inc. v. Flakt, Inc.*,[17] reversed the district court's issuance of an injunction enjoining the defendant from entering into contracts during the term of the patent to build plants designed to perform the patented process because the plants would not be completed until after the expiration of the patent.

In another Federal Circuit case, *Paper Converting Machine Co. v. Magna–Graphics Corp.*,[18] decided several years after *Joy Technologies*, the court held that the defendant infringed the patent when it *made the parts* for a machine claimed in the patent, tested the machine during various stages of assembly (but never tested a complete machine), and thereafter delivered the *parts* to a customer with an understanding that the customer was not to assemble and use the machine until after the patent expired. The defendant did not make, use, or sell the patented machine during the term of the patent. But the court based its decision on policy grounds:

> If without fear of liability a competitor can assemble a patented item past the point of testing, the last year of the patent becomes worthless whenever it deals with a long lead-time article. Nothing would prohibit the unscrupulous competitor from aggressively marketing its own product and constructing it to all but the final screws and bolts.... Because an "operable assembly" of components was tested, this case is distinguishable

---

14. The patentee's provisional rights pursuant to § 122(b) become enforceable upon issuance.

15. *Marsh v. Nichols*, 128 U.S. 605, 612 (1888); *see also GAF Building Materials Corp. v. Elk Corp. of Dallas*, 90 F.3d 479, 483 (Fed.Cir.1996) ("[A] patent does not exist until it is granted.... Patent rights are created only upon the formal issuance of the patent; thus, disputes concerning patent validity and infringement are necessarily hypothetical before patent issuance.").

16. But it should be pointed out that the expiration of a patent during pending litigation does not deprive the court of jurisdiction. *See Beedle v. Bennett*, 122 U.S. 71 (1887).

17. 6 F.3d 770 (Fed.Cir.1993).

18. 745 F.2d 11 (Fed.Cir.1984), *aff'd after remand*, 785 F.2d 1013 (Fed.Cir.1986).

from *Interdent Corp. v. United States*, 531 F.2d 547, 552 (Ct.Cl.1976) (omission of a claimed element from the patented combination avoids infringement) and *Decca Ltd. v. United States*, 640 F.2d 1156, 1168 (Ct.Cl.1980) (infringement does not occur until the combination has been constructed and available for use). Where, as here, significant, unpatented assemblies of elements are tested during the patented term, enabling the infringer to deliver the patented combination in parts to the buyer, without testing the entire combination together as was the infringer's usual practice, testing the assemblies can be held to be in essence testing the patented combination and, hence, infringement.[19]

One remaining issue is whether a court should issue an injunction after the patent expires prohibiting activity that constituted infringement during the term of the patent. The Federal Circuit seems to suggest that a post-expiration injunction lacks statutory authority. In the famous Kearns intermittent windshield wiper saga, the court, in addressing Kearns' request for post-expiration injunctive relief, stated:

> [35 U.S.C.] 283 relief is available only to "prevent the violations of any right secured by patent." Thus, when the rights secured by a patent are no longer protectable by virtue of expiration or unenforceability, entitlement to injunctive relief becomes moot because such relief is no longer available.

> An invention claimed in a patent passes into the public domain upon termination of the patent's ... statutory term. Because the rights flowing from a patent exist only for the term of the patent, there can be no infringement once the patent expires. Granting the relief requested by Kearns would impermissibly extend the statutory term beyond that established by Congress.[20]

Accordingly, "there is nothing in statute or common law giving [a patentee] the right to an injunction against practicing the disclosures in an expired patent."[21]

Statutory Provisions—35 U.S.C. §§ 154, 271

A.   Claim Interpretation

Ideally, patent claim language would be so clear and unambiguous that there could be no dispute as to its meaning, but this goal is difficult to achieve. This is perhaps due to the fact that claims are written by people hampered by various human imperfections, including, in many instances, a necessarily incomplete understanding of the precise nature of the invention, the prior art, or the future market for potentially infringing products. In addition, the limitations of language and the importance the patent

---

19. *Id.* at 19–20. *Cf. de Graffenried v. United States*, 25 Cl.Ct. 209, 214–15 (Cl.Ct.1992) ("The general rule is that until a device covered by a patent is actually assembled, the device has not been 'manufactured,'.... In *Paper Converting Co.*, the court articulated what amounts to a narrow exception to that general rule.... [In *Paper Converting Co.*, the] court labeled [the defendant's] plan a 'scheme to avoid patent infringement,'.... Herein, plaintiff has not demonstrated any analogous 'scheme to avoid infringement.' ").

20. *Kearns v. Chrysler Corp.*, 32 F.3d 1541, 1550 (Fed.Cir.1994), *cert. denied*, 488 U.S. 1007 (1995).

21. *Id.* at 1549.

system assigns to claims combine to further frustrate the goal of absolute clarity. As a result, the meaning of words used in a patent is often the focus of patent litigation, whether the issue is one of validity or infringement.[22]

Consider the remarks made by some courts on the absurdity that may result from the zealous efforts some parties mount when arguing over claim language. In the famous patent case over instant photography, U.S. District Judge Rya W. Zobel quoted Lewis Carroll in her opinion, addressing claim scope:

> "When *I* use a word," Humpty Dumpty said, ... "it means just what I choose it to mean—neither more nor less."
>
> "The question is," said Alice, "whether you *can* make words mean so many different things."
>
> "The question is," said Humpty Dumpty, "which is to be master—that's all."

Polaroid Corp. v. Eastman Kodak Co., 641 F.Supp. 828, 838 n. 8 (D.Mass. 1985), *aff'd*, 789 F.2d 1556 (Fed.Cir.1986) (quoting LEWIS CARROLL, ALICE'S ADVENTURES IN WONDERLAND & THROUGH THE LOOKING-GLASS, 186 (1960)). *See also*, *In re Cooper*, 480 F.2d 900, 902 n.* (CCPA 1973). Indeed, the problem of clarity in claim language has been long recognized:

> Claims cannot be clear and unambiguous on their face. A comparison must exist. The lucidity of a claim is determined in light of what ideas it is trying to convey. Only by knowing the idea, can one decide how much shadow encumbers the reality.
>
> The very nature of words would make a clear and unambiguous claim a rare occurrence. . . .
>
> An invention exists most importantly as a tangible structure or a series of drawings. A verbal portrayal is usually an afterthought written to satisfy the requirements of patent law. This conversion of machine to words allows for unintended idea gaps which cannot be satisfactorily filled. Often the invention is novel and words do not exist to describe it. The dictionary does not always keep abreast of the inventor. It cannot. Things are not made for the sake of words, but words for things. To overcome this lag, patent law allows the inventor to be his own lexicographer. . . .
>
> Allowing the patentee verbal licensee only augments the difficulty of understanding the claims. The sanction of new words or hybrids from old ones not only leaves one unsure what a rose is, but also unsure whether a rose is a rose. Thus we find that a claim cannot be interpreted without going beyond the claim itself. No matter how clear a claim appears to be, lurking in the background are documents that may completely disrupt initial views on its meaning. [footnote omitted]
>
> The necessity of a sensible and systematic approach to claim interpretation is axiomatic. The Alice-in-Wonderland view that something means whatever one chooses it to mean makes for enjoyable reading, but bad law.

Autogiro Co. of America v. United States, 384 F.2d 391, 396–97 (Ct.Cl. 1967). The so-called "Alice-in-Wonderland" view is taken to refer to *post-hoc* explanations of ambiguous terms. The law remains that a patentee may

---

22. *See SmithKline Diagnostics, Inc. v. Helena Labs. Corp.*, 859 F.2d 878, 882 (Fed.Cir. 1988) ("the claims must be interpreted and given the same meaning for purposes of both validity and infringement analyses.").

be "his own lexicographer." But a patent drafter must be careful to create a lexicon when necessary—for the patentee may bear substantial risk from imprecision, especially if it could have been avoided. Where there is ambiguous language in a patent claim, subject to both a narrow and a broad reading, some suggest the ambiguity should be resolved against the patentee by choosing the narrower meaning, while others suggest the ambiguity should be resolved against the patentee by holding the claim invalid for indefiniteness. *See Athletic Alternatives, Inc. v. Prince Manufacturing, Inc.*, 73 F.3d 1573 (Fed.Cir.1996) (compare majority and dissenting opinions). Thus, when possible, many patentees choose to be up front and explicit, defining terms in the initially filed application.

Claim interpretation requires more than determining the dictionary or technically-accepted meanings of words used in the claim. Meaning may be derived from the context in which language is used. This context includes the claim itself, the other claims, the written description, the drawings, and often the prosecution history. Importantly, "a technical term used in a patent document is interpreted as having the meaning that it would be given by persons experienced in the field of the invention." *Hoechst Celanese Corp. v. BP Chemicals, Ltd.*, 78 F.3d 1575, 1578 (Fed.Cir.1996); *Multiform Desiccants, Inc. v. Medzam, Ltd.*, 133 F.3d 1473, 1477 (Fed.Cir. 1998) ("It is the person of ordinary skill in the field of the invention through whose eyes the claims are construed").

Patent drafting, and particularly, patent claim drafting is a complex business subject to many pitfalls.[23] It is a topic that lies beyond the scope of this book, well deserving of its own course, or courses.[24] For purposes of this book, however, it is sufficient to recognize that even common and seemingly synonymous phrases, for example, "consisting of" and "comprising" have distinct and precise meanings in patent law.[25] Indeed, disputed language in patent claims may take many forms. Some representative examples follow.

(1) *Specialized technical terms, such as "sputter-deposited dielectric." See Southwall Technologies, Inc. v. Cardinal IG Co.*, 54 F.3d 1570 (Fed.Cir. 1995);

(2) *Elementary nontechnical words, such as "on" or the indefinite article ("a"). See, e.g., North American Vaccine, Inc. v. American Cyanamid Co.*, 7 F.3d 1571 (Fed.Cir.1993) ("While it is generally accepted in patent parlance that 'a' can mean one or more," *see* ROBERT C. FABER, LANDIS ON MECHANICS OF PATENT CLAIM DRAFTING 531 (3d ed. 1990) ("In a claim, the indefinite article A or AN connotes 'one or more.'), there is no indication in the patent specification that the inventors here intended it to have other than its normal singular meaning."). *Senmed, Inc. v. Richard–Allan Medical Industries, Inc.*, 888 F.2d 815 (Fed.Cir.1989) ("on" an anvil surface

23. *See, e.g.*, Chapter Three "Disclosure Requirements", Section D "Particularly Pointing Out and Distinctly Claiming".

24. For a good introduction to the art of claim drafting, *see* ROBERT C. FABER, LANDIS ON MECHANICS OF PATENT CLAIM DRAFTING (4th ed., 1996).

25. A claim employing the phrase "consisting of" to introduce certain elements covers devices having the recited elements, and no more; whereas, in patent law, the term "comprising" has come to mean "including the following elements but not excluding others." *See* FABER, LANDIS ON MECHANICS OF PATENT CLAIM DRAFTING, §§ 7–8 (4th ed., 1996).

means "in physical contact with" that surface, as opposed to "juxtaposed" over or near that surface); *Read Corp. v. Portec, Inc.*, 970 F.2d 816 (Fed.Cir.1992) (in a patent claim requiring that a device's end be "close . . . to the ground", "to" means sufficiently close to achieve the functions disclosed in the specification and argued during the patent's prosecution, not actually on the ground as in the patentee's commercial embodiment);

(3) *Spatial and relational concepts, such as "integral." See, e.g., Carroll Touch, Inc. v. Electro Mechanical Systems, Inc.*, 15 F.3d 1573 (Fed.Cir. 1993) (properly interpreted in light of a patent's specification and prosecution history, its claim requiring that two surfaces be "spaced apart" means that the surfaces must be "spaced apart over the entirety of their respective surface areas, without any intersection."); *Advanced Cardiovascular Systems, Inc. v. Scimed Life Systems, Inc.*, 887 F.2d 1070 (Fed.Cir.1989) (the patent claim to balloon dilation catheters required that there be a balloon portion *"formed integral with"* the tube portion (emphasis added); the accused catheter had a separate balloon segment, which was glued to a tube segment; a disputed fact issue as to the meaning of "integral" arose, in part, because the patentee cited a dictionary definition of "integral" as including "essential to completeness" as well as "formed as a unit with another part," "composed of integral parts" and "lacking nothing essential."); and

(4) *Approximations, such as "about" and "substantial." See, e.g., Modine Mfg. Co. v. U.S. Intern. Trade Comm'n*, 75 F.3d 1545 (Fed.Cir.1996) (such "broadening usages as 'about' must be given reasonable scope; they must be viewed by the decisionmaker as they would be understood by persons experienced in the field of the invention. . . . Although it is rarely feasible to attach a precise limit to 'about,' the usage can usually be understood in light of the technology embodied in the invention. When the claims are applied to an accused device, it is a question of technologic fact whether the accused device meets a reasonable meaning of 'about' in the particular circumstances."); *Conopco, Inc. v. May Department Stores Co.*, 46 F.3d 1556 (Fed.Cir.1994) (a patent claim to a cosmetic emulsion comprising two ingredients in a ratio "of from about 40:1 to about 1:1" cannot literally encompass an accused product with the ingredients in a 162.9:1 ratio; "That would imply an expansion of the term 'about' to encompass over a fourfold increase in the specified numerical ratio and thus would ignore the ordinary meaning of that term."; "According to Webster's Third New International Dictionary, the term means: 'with some approach to exactness in quantity, number, or time: APPROXIMATELY four feet of snow.' "); *Uniroyal, Inc. v. Rudkin–Wiley Corp.*, 837 F.2d 1044 (Fed.Cir. 1988) ("substantially" and "approximately" "must be interpreted in light of the specification and prosecution history to determine the literal coverage of the claims with respect to height and position.").

A fundamental issue in claim construction is the procedure that courts use to construe a claim. In particular, two central procedural issues are presented: (1) who (*i.e.*, judge or jury) should construe the claim; and (2) which interpretive tools (*e.g.*, the written description, technical texts, or expert testimony) may be used in claim construction? These are issues of great importance because the meaning given to claim language may very well be determinative as to validity and infringement.[26] Each of these issues

---

26. *See Lucas Aerospace, Ltd. v. Unison Indus. L.P.*, 890 F.Supp. 329, 332 n. 3 (D.Del.1995) ("[C]laim construction more often than not determines the outcome on infringe-

remains the subject of rapidly evolving legal precedent, and is discussed in turn below.

But before turning to the complex legal issues surrounding claim interpretation, consider its various strategic implications, as discussed in the following *SIDE BAR*.

SIDE BAR

*The Successful Patent Litigator Must Learn the Way of Strategy:** *The Opportunities and Risks of Claim Construction*

Matthew D. Powers, Eric K. Laumann and Maureen K. Toohey[**]

Strategy is particularly important to the successful patent litigator because much of patent law reflects the fundamental dilemma that "the stronger a patent the weaker it is and the weaker a patent the stronger it is."[1] The dilemma is the result of the inherent tension among issues of claim construction, infringement, and validity.[2] This inherent tension is explored by the late Federal Circuit Judge Giles S. Rich, in his discussion of the dilemma:

> To explain, a patent that is strong in that it contains broad claims which adequately protect the invention so they are hard to design around is weak in that it may be easier to invalidate and is therefore less likely to stand up in court because the claims are more likely to read on prior art or be broader than the disclosed invention, and for other reasons defense lawyers can devise. On the other hand, the patent with narrow claims of the kind the Patent Office readily allows quickly without a contest is weak as protection and as incentive to invest but strong in that a court will not likely invalidate it.[3]

As litigation is a form of warfare, a successful patent litigator must heed Sun Tzu's ancient adage that: "He who knows when he can fight and when he cannot will be victorious."[4] Thus, the savvy litigator must decide whether to confront or avoid patent law's fundamental dilemma in implementing his tactical plan.

If the litigator chooses to confront the dilemma, she must fully understand the specific prior art and the allegedly infringing products at issue in a particular case before taking a position on claim construction, because as Sun Tzu teaches, "know the enemy and know yourself; in a hundred battles you will never be in peril."[5] Indeed, in order to propose a truly successful claim construction, the litigator must understand the infringement and validity case on the element-by-element level. Only then can she choose a claim construction for each limitation that allows her to make the arguments she needs to make on infringement without preventing her from making the arguments she also needs to make on validity. Thus, even if the court signals that it will decide issues of claim construction early in the case but reserve resolution of issues of validity and infringement until late in the case (*e.g.*, at trial), as a practical matter the prudent patent litigator must already have a fully developed picture of her

---

ment"); *MCV, Inc. v. King–Seeley Thermos Co.*, 870 F.2d 1568, 1570 (Fed.Cir.1989) ("Although we do not reach it, the dispositive issue on the merits would be the definition of the invention.").

invalidity and infringement case in order to prevent an ill advised claim construction position from adversely constraining later arguments about infringement or validity. The importance of earlier development of a party's offensive and defensive positions in patent litigation therefore cannot be overemphasized.

If the litigator wants to avoid the dilemma, she may attempt to remove issues of validity from the case. The clever patentee may achieve this by moving before claim construction for summary judgment that her patent is not invalid based on the prior art presented by the defendant, assuming invalidity has been pled as a defense, as is typically the case, and assuming that the court has signaled that claim construction will not be decided until at or shortly before trial.[6] We have successfully made such a motion. When successful, such a summary judgment motion effectively removes the invalidity restraints usually placed on claim construction, thereby allowing the party asserting a patent to argue for the broadest claim construction, which in turn increases the chances of her proving infringement.[7] This is a simple implementation of Sun Tzu's principle that "a victorious army wins its victories before seeking battle."[8]

Using a summary judgment motion as a means of avoiding the dilemma is especially attractive because the patent holder enjoys a reduced evidentiary burden on such a motion since she does not bear the ultimate burden of proof on validity.[9] When the party bringing summary judgment does not bear the burden of proof, the showing required to be successful is greatly reduced. Thus, under *Celotex Corp. v. Catrett*, 477 U.S. 317, 325 (1986), the patent holder need only point to an absence of evidence supporting her opponent's invalidity position, at which point the burden shifts to the party opposing the motion to come forward with actual evidence supporting each element of her invalidity position that is sufficient to raise a genuine issue of material fact as to each such element.

Once the litigator understands that much of patent law requires careful navigation between the horns of a dilemma, it becomes apparent that, as in war, strategy is the path to victory on the battlefield of patent litigation.

* Miyamato Musashi, A BOOK OF FIVE RINGS, 34 (Victor Harris trans., Overlook Press 1974) (1645) (this samurai strategy book begins: "I have been many years training in *the Way of strategy*, called Ni Ten Ichi Ryu, and now I think I will explain it in writing for the first time.") (emphasis added).

** Matthew D. Powers is a patent trial attorney and the managing partner of the Silicon Valley Office of Weil, Gotshal, & Manges LLP. At the time this SIDE BAR was written, Eric K. Laumann specialized in patent litigation as a senior associate in the Silicon Valley office of Weil, Gotshal & Manges LLP and Maureen K. Toohey, a former law clerk to Judge Randall R. Rader on the U.S. Court of Appeals for the Federal Circuit, also specialized in patent litigation as a senior associate in the Sil-

icon Valley office of Weil, Gotshal & Manges LLP. This SIDE BAR was written specially for PRINCIPLES OF PATENT LAW.

1. Giles S. Rich, *The Proposed Patent Legislation: Some Comments*, 35 GEO. WASH. L. REV. 641, 644 (1967) (responding to proposed legislation S. 1042 and H.R. 5924, 90th Cong., 1st Sess. (1967) and Report of the President's Commission on the Patent System (1966)).

2. We note that patent law is rife with tensions other than the infringement/validity tension discussed here. These include, for example, the tension that is present whenever a patentee is attempting to overcome simultaneous validity challenges stemming from both an alleged statutory bar under § 102(b) and an alleged prior invention by another under § 102(g). The presence of these two threats to validity may pressure the patentee to simultaneously argue that the claimed invention was not "ready for patenting" until a later date, to avoid the triggering of the bar, but at the same time argue that the claimed invention was fully conceived and reduced to practice by an earlier date, to maintain priority over the other alleged inventor. Thus, the savvy litigator should decide early in the case which issue is the winner, because pursuing all issues means that, as to issues in tension, she is necessarily doing something that could harm the issue that is the ultimate winner. The winning strategy is to drive the facts toward the winning issue. A tactic could be to file a "sacrificial pawn" summary judgment motion on an issue that the litigator does not think will be a winner in order to use the opponent's own arguments in the opposition brief or the court's findings in the decision on the motion, to support the movant's argument on the issue the litigator does expect and want as the winner.

3. Giles S. Rich, *supra*, note 1, at 644.

4. Sun Tzu, THE ART OF WAR 82 (Samuel B. Griffith trans., Oxford University Press 1963).

5. *Id.* at 84.

6. As discussed later in this Chapter, in the *SIDE BAR* by U.S. District Judge Roderick R. McKelvie, district courts have taken quite different approaches as to

when in the course of a litigation is the best time to do claim construction. If claim construction were being decided earlier in the case, the court would likely deny a pre-claim construction validity motion when it could simply wait until after it had resolved claim construction before addressing the claim construction issues ordinarily inherent in resolving a validity motion.

7. If it turns out that the items of prior art that were the basis of the validity challenges rejected by the summary judgment happen to be the "best" available items of prior art, then the partial summary judgment of no invalidity over that particular art may have the same practical effect as a summary judgment that the patent is valid over all of the prior art—it simply may turn out that there are no other items of prior art that a challenger is likely to find and assert against the patent. Such a judgment might be powerful indeed. However, it is not clear what impact such a judgment would have on third parties; and a discussion of the potential preclusive effect(s) of such a ruling is beyond the scope of this *SIDE BAR*.

8. Sun Tzu, *supra* note 4, at 87.

9. *See* 36 U.S.C. § 282 ("A patent shall be presumed valid.... The burden of establishing invalidity of a patent or any claim thereof shall rest on the party asserting such invalidity.").

1. PROCEDURE: JUDGE, JURY, AND APPELLATE REVIEW

In the courts, the issue of claim construction came to center stage in the context of questions concerning the proper standard of appellate review for district court claim construction decisions. Although standard of review may appear arcane on first glance, these questions brought with them entirely practical questions of procedure, especially concerning the allocation of decision-making power and authority in patent cases among juries, trial judges, and appellate courts.

The question of proper appellate review for district court claim construction decisions was presented to the Federal Circuit sitting *en banc* in the case of *Markman v. Westview Instruments, Inc.*, 52 F.3d 967 (Fed.Cir. 1995) (*Markman I*). The majority opinion of the court, written by then Chief Judge Archer, concluded that claim construction "is properly viewed solely as a question of law" for the court, and that "the construction given the claims is reviewed *de novo* on appeal." *Id.* at 979, 983–84. Concurring opinions were written by then Circuit, now Chief, Judge Mayer and by

Circuit Judge Rader. A dissenting opinion was written by Circuit Judge Newman. According to Judge Mayer, claim construction may be a mixed question of law and fact; and "any facts found in the course of interpreting the claims must be subject to the same standard by which we review any other factual determinations: for clear error in facts found by the court; for substantial evidence to support a jury's verdict." *Id.* at 991. Judge Rader argued that the question of subsidiary fact issues underlying claim construction was not properly before the court. *Id.* at 998. Focusing mainly on the Seventh Amendment right to a jury trial, Judge Newman concluded that the court's decision "denies the critical values of the trial, and moves the Federal Circuit firmly out of the juridical mainstream." *Id.* at 1026.

The Supreme Court granted *certiorari* to address this Seventh Amendment issue and agreed with the majority in *Markman I* that claim interpretation is an issue to be decided by the court. *Markman v. Westview Instruments, Inc.*, 517 U.S. 370 (1996) (*Markman II*). But the Supreme Court was less than clear in its endorsement of *Markman I's* characterization of claim interpretation as a question of law. For a few years, this ambiguity caused some confusion in the context of the proper standard of appellate review culminating in *Cybor Corp. v. FAS Technologies, Inc.* (see note 3, *infra* following *Markman II*).

Markman v. Westview Instruments, Inc. (Markman II)

517 U.S. 370 (1996).

■ JUSTICE SOUTER delivered the opinion of the Court.

The question here is whether the interpretation of a so-called patent claim, the portion of the patent document that defines the scope of the patentee's rights, is a matter of law reserved entirely for the court, or subject to a Seventh Amendment guarantee that a jury will determine the meaning of any disputed term of art about which expert testimony is offered. We hold that the construction of a patent, including terms of art within its claim, is exclusively within the province of the court.

Petitioner in this infringement suit, Markman, owns United States Reissue Patent No. 33,054 for his "Inventory Control and Reporting System for Dry Cleaning Stores." The patent describes a system that can monitor and report the status, location, and movement of clothing in a dry-cleaning establishment. The Markman system consists of a keyboard and data processor to generate written records for each transaction, including a bar code readable by optical detectors operated by employees, who log the progress of clothing through the dry-cleaning process. Respondent Westview's product also includes a keyboard and processor, and it lists charges for the dry-cleaning services on bar-coded tickets that can be read by portable optical detectors.

Markman brought an infringement suit against Westview and Althon Enterprises, an operator of dry-cleaning establishments using Westview's products (collectively, Westview). Westview responded that Markman's patent is not infringed by its system because the latter functions merely to record an inventory of receivables by tracking invoices and transaction totals, rather than to record and track an inventory of articles of clothing.

Part of the dispute hinged upon the meaning of the word "inventory," a term found in Markman's independent claim 1, which states that Markman's product can "maintain an inventory total" and "detect and localize spurious additions to inventory." The case was tried before a jury, which heard, among others, a witness produced by Markman who testified about the meaning of the claim language.

After the jury compared the patent to Westview's device, it found an infringement of Markman's independent claim 1 and dependent claim 10. The District Court nevertheless granted Westview's deferred motion for judgment as a matter of law, one of its reasons being that the term "inventory" in Markman's patent encompasses "both cash inventory and the actual physical inventory of articles of clothing." 772 F.Supp. 1535, 1537–1538 (E.D.Pa.1991). Under the trial court's construction of the patent, the production, sale, or use of a tracking system for dry cleaners would not infringe Markman's patent unless the product was capable of tracking articles of clothing throughout the cleaning process and generating reports about their status and location. Since Westview's system cannot do these things, the District Court directed a verdict on the ground that Westview's device does not have the "means to maintain an inventory total" and thus cannot " 'detect and localize spurious additions to inventory as well as spurious deletions therefrom,' " as required by claim 1. *Id.,* at 1537.

Markman appealed, arguing it was error for the District Court to substitute its construction of the disputed claim term "inventory" for the construction the jury had presumably given it. The United States Court of Appeals for the Federal Circuit affirmed, holding the interpretation of claim terms to be the exclusive province of the court and the Seventh Amendment to be consistent with that conclusion. 52 F.3d 967 (1995). Markman sought our review on each point, and we granted certiorari. 515 U.S. 1192(1995). We now affirm.

II

The Seventh Amendment provides that "[i]n Suits at common law, where the value in controversy shall exceed twenty dollars, the right of trial by jury shall be preserved...." U.S. Const., Amdt. 7. Since Justice Story's day, *United States v. Wonson,* 28 F. Cas. 745, 750 (No. 16,750) (CC Mass. 1812), we have understood that "[t]he right of trial by jury thus preserved is the right which existed under the English common law when the Amendment was adopted." *Baltimore & Carolina Line, Inc. v. Redman,* 295 U.S. 654, 657, 55 S.Ct. 890, 891, 79 L.Ed. 1636 (1935). In keeping with our long-standing adherence to this "historical test," Wolfram, *The Constitutional History of the Seventh Amendment,* 57 MINN. L.REV. 639, 640–643 (1973), we ask, first, whether we are dealing with a cause of action that either was tried at law at the time of the Founding or is at least analogous to one that was, *see, e.g., Tull v. United States,* 481 U.S. 412, 417, 107 S.Ct. 1831, 1835, 95 L.Ed.2d 365 (1987). If the action in question belongs in the law category, we then ask whether the particular trial decision must fall to the jury in order to preserve the substance of the common-law right as it existed in 1791. *See infra* ...[3]

3. Our formulations of the historical test do not deal with the possibility of conflict between actual English common law practice and American assumptions about what that

A

As to the first issue, going to the character of the cause of action, "[t]he form of our analysis is familiar. 'First we compare the statutory action to 18th-century actions brought in the courts of England prior to the merger of the courts of law and equity.' " *Granfinanciera, S.A. v. Nordberg*, 492 U.S. 33, 42, 109 S.Ct. 2782, 2790, 106 L.Ed.2d 26 (1989) (citation omitted). Equally familiar is the descent of today's patent infringement action from the infringement actions tried at law in the 18th century, and there is no dispute that infringement cases today must be tried to a jury, as their predecessors were more than two centuries ago. *See, e.g., Bramah v. Hardcastle*, 1 Carp. P.C. 168 (K.B.1789).

B

This conclusion raises the second question, whether a particular issue occurring within a jury trial (here the construction of a patent claim) is itself necessarily a jury issue, the guarantee being essential to preserve the right to a jury's resolution of the ultimate dispute. In some instances the answer to this second question may be easy because of clear historical evidence that the very subsidiary question was so regarded under the English practice of leaving the issue for a jury. But when, as here, the old practice provides no clear answer, *see infra*, at 1391–1392, we are forced to make a judgment about the scope of the Seventh Amendment guarantee without the benefit of any foolproof test.

The Court has repeatedly said that the answer to the second question "must depend on whether the jury must shoulder this responsibility as necessary to preserve the 'substance of the common-law right of trial by jury.' " . . . " 'Only those incidents which are regarded as fundamental, as inherent in and of the essence of the system of trial by jury, are placed beyond the reach of the legislature.' " . . . .

The "substance of the common-law right" is, however, a pretty blunt instrument for drawing distinctions. We have tried to sharpen it, to be sure, by reference to the distinction between substance and procedure. . . . We have also spoken of the line as one between issues of fact and law.

* * *

But the sounder course, when available, is to classify a mongrel practice (like construing a term of art following receipt of evidence) by using the historical method, much as we do in characterizing the suits and actions within which they arise. Where there is no exact antecedent, the best hope lies in comparing the modern practice to earlier ones whose allocation to court or jury we do know, . . . seeking the best analogy we can draw between an old and the new, *see Tull v. United States*, [481 U.S.] at 420–421, 107 S.Ct., at 1836–1837 (we must search the English common law for "appropriate analogies" rather than a "precisely analogous common-law cause of action").

* * *

---

practice was, or between English and American practices at the relevant time. No such complications arise in this case.

III

Since evidence of common law practice at the time of the Framing does not entail application of the Seventh Amendment's jury guarantee to the construction of the claim document, we must look elsewhere to characterize this determination of meaning in order to allocate it as between court or jury. We accordingly consult existing precedent[10] and consider both the relative interpretive skills of judges and juries and the statutory policies that ought to be furthered by the allocation.

A

The two elements of a simple patent case, construing the patent and determining whether infringement occurred, were characterized by the former patent practitioner, Justice Curtis.[11] "The first is a question of law, to be determined by the court, construing the letters-patent, and the description of the invention and specification of claim annexed to them. The second is a question of fact, to be submitted to a jury." *Winans v. Denmead*, 15 How., at 338; *see Winans v. New York & Erie R. Co.*, 21 How., at 100; *Hogg v. Emerson, supra*, at 484; *cf. Parker v. Hulme, supra*, at 1140.

In arguing for a different allocation of responsibility for the first question, Markman relies primarily on two cases, *Bischoff v. Wethered*, 9 Wall. 812, 19 L.Ed. 829 (1870), and *Tucker v. Spalding*, 13 Wall. 453, 20 L.Ed. 515 (1872). These are said to show that evidence of the meaning of patent terms was offered to 19th-century juries, and thus to imply that the meaning of a documentary term was a jury issue whenever it was subject to evidentiary proof. That is not what Markman's cases show, however.... [N]either *Bischoff* nor *Tucker* indicates that juries resolved the meaning of terms of art in construing a patent, and neither case undercuts Justice Curtis's authority.

B

Where history and precedent provide no clear answers, functional considerations also play their part in the choice between judge and jury to define terms of art. We said in *Miller v. Fenton*, 474 U.S. 104, 114, 106 S.Ct. 445, 451, 88 L.Ed.2d 405 (1985), that when an issue "falls somewhere between a pristine legal standard and a simple historical fact, the fact/law distinction at times has turned on a determination that, as a matter of the sound administration of justice, one judicial actor is better positioned than another to decide the issue in question." So it turns out here, for judges, not juries, are the better suited to find the acquired meaning of patent terms.

---

10. Because we conclude that our precedent supports classifying the question as one for the court, we need not decide either the extent to which the Seventh Amendment can be said to have crystallized a law/fact distinction, *cf. Ex parte Peterson*, 253 U.S. 300, 310, 40 S.Ct. 543, 546, 64 L.Ed. 919 (1920); *Walker v. New Mexico & Southern Pacific R. Co.*, 165 U.S. 593, 597, 17 S.Ct. 421, 422, 41 L.Ed. 837 (1897), or whether post–1791 precedent classifying an issue as one of fact would trigger the protections of the Seventh Amendment if (unlike this case) there were no more specific reason for decision.

11. *See* 1 A MEMOIR OF BENJAMIN ROBBINS CURTIS, L L. D., 84 (B. Curtis ed. 1879); *cf. O'Reilly v. Morse*, 15 How. 62, 63, 14 L.Ed. 601 (1854) (noting his involvement in a patent case).

The construction of written instruments is one of those things that judges often do and are likely to do better than jurors unburdened by training in exegesis. Patent construction in particular "is a special occupation, requiring, like all others, special training and practice. The judge, from his training and discipline, is more likely to give a proper interpretation to such instruments than a jury; and he is, therefore, more likely to be right, in performing such a duty, than a jury can be expected to be." *Parker v. Hulme*, 18 F. Cas., at 1140. Such was the understanding nearly a century and a half ago, and there is no reason to weigh the respective strengths of judge and jury differently in relation to the modern claim; quite the contrary, for "the claims of patents have become highly technical in many respects as the result of special doctrines relating to the proper form and scope of claims that have been developed by the courts and the Patent Office." Woodward, *Definiteness and Particularity in Patent Claims*, 46 Mich.L.Rev. 755, 765 (1948).

Markman would trump these considerations with his argument that a jury should decide a question of meaning peculiar to a trade or profession simply because the question is a subject of testimony requiring credibility determinations, which are the jury's forte. It is, of course, true that credibility judgments have to be made about the experts who testify in patent cases, and in theory there could be a case in which a simple credibility judgment would suffice to choose between experts whose testimony was equally consistent with a patent's internal logic. But our own experience with document construction leaves us doubtful that trial courts will run into many cases like that. In the main, we expect, any credibility determinations will be subsumed within the necessarily sophisticated analysis of the whole document, required by the standard construction rule that a term can be defined only in a way that comports with the instrument as a whole. *See Bates v. Coe*, 98 U.S. 31, 38, 25 L.Ed. 68 (1878); 6 Lipscomb § 21:40, at 393; 2 Robinson, *supra*, § 734, at 484; Woodward, *supra*, at 765; *cf. U.S. Industrial Chemicals, Inc. v. Carbide & Carbon Chemicals Corp..*, 315 U.S. 668, 678, 62 S.Ct. 839, 844, 86 L.Ed. 1105 (1942); *cf.* 6 Lipscomb at § 21:40, at 393. Thus, in these cases a jury's capabilities to evaluate demeanor, *cf. Miller, supra*, at 114, 117, 106 S.Ct., at 451, 453, to sense the "mainsprings of human conduct," *Commissioner v. Duberstein*, 363 U.S. 278, 289, 80 S.Ct. 1190, 1198, 4 L.Ed.2d 1218 (1960), or to reflect community standards, *United States v. McConney*, 728 F.2d 1195, 1204 (C.A.9 1984) (*en banc*), are much less significant than a trained ability to evaluate the testimony in relation to the overall structure of the patent. The decisionmaker vested with the task of construing the patent is in the better position to ascertain whether an expert's proposed definition fully comports with the specification and claims and so will preserve the patent's internal coherence. We accordingly think there is sufficient reason to treat construction of terms of art like many other responsibilities that we cede to a judge in the normal course of trial, notwithstanding its evidentiary underpinnings.

C

Finally, we see the importance of uniformity in the treatment of a given patent as an independent reason to allocate all issues of construction to the court. As we noted in *General Elec. Co. v. Wabash Appliance Corp.*, 304 U.S. 364, 369, 58 S.Ct. 899, 902, 82 L.Ed. 1402 (1938), "[t]he limits of a patent must be known for the protection of the patentee, the encouragement of the inventive genius of others and the assurance that the subject of the patent will be dedicated ultimately to the public." Otherwise, a "zone of uncertainty which enterprise and experimentation may enter only at the risk of infringement claims would discourage invention only a little less than unequivocal foreclosure of the field," *United Carbon Co. v. Binney & Smith Co.*, 317 U.S. 228, 236, 63 S.Ct. 165, 170, 87 L.Ed. 232 (1942), and "[t]he public [would] be deprived of rights supposed to belong to it, without being clearly told what it is that limits these rights." *Merrill v. Yeomans*, 94 U.S. 568, 573, 24 L.Ed. 235 (1877). It was just for the sake of such desirable uniformity that Congress created the Court of Appeals for the Federal Circuit as an exclusive appellate courts for patent cases, H.R.Rep. No. 97–312, pp. 20–23 (1981), observing that increased uniformity would "strengthen the United States patent system in such a way as to foster technological growth and industrial innovation." *Id.*, at 20.

Uniformity would, however, be ill served by submitting issues of document construction to juries. Making them jury issues would not, to be sure, necessarily leave evidentiary questions of meaning wide open in every new court in which a patent might be litigated, for principles of issue preclusion would ordinarily foster uniformity. *Cf. Blonder–Tongue Laboratories, Inc. v. University of Ill. Foundation*, 402 U.S. 313, 91 S.Ct. 1434, 28 L.Ed.2d 788 (1971). But whereas issue preclusion could not be asserted against new and independent infringement defendants even within a given jurisdiction, treating interpretive issues as purely legal will promote (though it will not guarantee) intrajurisdictional certainty through the application of *stare decisis* on those questions not yet subject to interjurisdictional uniformity under the authority of the single appeals court.

* * *

Accordingly, we hold that the interpretation of the word "inventory" in this case is an issue for the judge, not the jury, and affirm the decision of the Court of Appeals for the Federal Circuit.

It is so ordered.

NOTES

1. *The Markman Hearing.* The question of claim construction involving issues of fact affects more than the standard of appellate review. It also significantly affects the process by which a patent case is litigated at trial. In response to the Federal Circuit's *Markman* decision, and especially following the Supreme Court's affirmance, many district courts began holding special hearings to help them construe claims during patent cases. These hearings immediately became known as *Markman* hearings.

The decision to hold a *Markman* hearing, however, leaves several procedural questions unanswered, including: (1) when during the trial should the court construe the patent claim?; (2) what input may the court properly receive to help in claim construction?; and (3) how may the court use this input? Indeed, these questions exist whether or not the trial court conducts a special *Markman* hearing.

These questions are inherent in the claim construction process and are a reason why today practically every aspect of the claim construction process is the topic of debate.

The courts themselves have provided some excellent tools to help study these difficult procedural questions.

The Northern District of California is venue to many high technology litigations, especially in the fields of biotechnology and computer hardware and software. The complexity of the technological issues in these cases presents especially difficult problems in claim construction. To help manage the deluge of issues, the Northern District of California adopted several special local rules for patent cases, which, in effect, imposed more detailed pleading and disclosure rules than are generally mandated by the Federal Rules of Civil Procedure. Local Rule 16–9(a) requires patentees asserting infringement to prepare and serve a "Claim Chart;" and the allegedly infringing parties must file a "Response Chart". A claim chart sets forth in detail:

(1) Each claim of any patent in suit which the party alleges was infringed;

(2) The identity of each apparatus, product, device, process, method, act or other instrumentality of each opposing party which allegedly infringes each claim;

(3) Whether such infringement is claimed to be literal or under the doctrine of equivalents;

(4) Where each element of each infringed claim is found within each apparatus, product, device, process, method, act or other instrumentality; and

(5) If a party claiming patent infringement wishes to preserve the right to rely on its own apparatus, product, device, process, method, act or other instrumentality as evidence of commercial success, the party must identify, separately for each claim, each such apparatus, product, device, process, method, act or other instrumentality that incorporates or reflects that particular claim.

In addition to the claim charts, Local Rule 16–10(a) requires the patentee to serve a "Proposed Claim Construction Statement," with the following information:

(1) Identification of any special or uncommon meanings of words or phrases in the claim;

(2) All references from the specification that support, describe, or explain each element of the claim;

(3) All material in the prosecution history that describes or explains each element of the claim; and

(4) Any extrinsic evidence that supports the proposed construction of the claim, including, but not limited to, expert testimony, inventor testimony, dictionary definitions and citations to learned treatises, as permitted by law.

The local rule requires allegedly infringing parties to file a "Response" setting forth:

(1) Identification of any special or uncommon meanings of words or phrases in the claim in addition to or contrary to those disclosed pursuant to Civil L.R. 16–10(a)(1);

(2) All references from the specification that support, describe, or explain each element of the claim in addition to or contrary to those disclosed pursuant to Civil L.R. 16–10(a)(2);

(3) All material in the prosecution history that describes or explains each element of the claim in addition to or contrary to those disclosed pursuant to Civil L.R. 16–10(a)(3); and

(4) Any extrinsic evidence that supports the proposed construction of the claim, including, but not limited to, expert testimony, inventor testimony, dictionary definitions and citations to learned treatises, as permitted by law.

The exchanging of special papers is not the only change imposed by the local rules. Local Rule 16–11 sets forth several requirements leading up to and governing a "Claim Construction Hearing":

(a) Meet and Confer. No later than 21 days after the "Responses to Proposed Claim Construction Statement" has been served, all parties shall meet and confer for the purpose of preparing a Joint Claim Construction Statement pursuant to Civil L.R. 16–11(b).

(b) Joint Claim Construction Statement. No later than 15 days after the parties meet and confer pursuant to Civil L.R. 16–11(a) the parties must complete and file a Joint Claim Construction Statement, which shall contain the following information:

(1) The construction of those claims and terms on which the parties agree;

(2) Each party's proposed construction of each disputed claim and term, supported by the same information that is required under Civil L.R. 16–10 (a) and (b);

(3) The jointly agreeable dates for a claims construction hearing on all disputed issues of claim construction. The suggested dates shall take into consideration the briefing schedule pursuant to Civil L.R. 16–11(d) and the calendar of the assigned judge; and

(4) For any party who proposes to call one or more witnesses at the claims construction hearing, the identity of each such witness, the subject matter of each witness' testimony and an estimate of the time required for the testimony.

(c) Claim Construction Hearing. No later than 30 days after the parties have filed their Joint Claims Construction Statement, the court will send a notice of the date and time of a Claim Construction Hearing. Unless the notice states otherwise, the parties shall be prepared to call at the hearing all the witnesses they identified under Civil L.R. 16–11(b)(4).

(d) Briefing Schedule. With respect to a Claim Construction Hearing, the parties shall comply with the following briefing schedule:

(1) Not less than 35 days before the hearing, the party claiming patent infringement must serve and file its opening brief and supporting evidence;

(2) Not less than 21 days before the hearing, each opposing party must serve and file its responsive brief and supporting evidence; and

(3) Not less than 14 days before the hearing, the party claiming patent infringement must serve and file any reply brief and any evidence

directly rebutting the supporting evidence contained in an opposing party's response.

At least some of the procedural devices implemented by the Northern District of California are subject to opposing views. Concerning the timing issue, for example, some district judges maintain that *Markman* hearings are premature if held early in the litigation, especially if before the close of discovery. Some conduct a *Markman* hearing at the summary judgment phase of the litigation, and others wait until after hearing all of the evidence at trial. Consider Judge William Young's thoughtful discussion in *Amgen, Inc. v. Hoechst Marion Roussel, Inc.*, 126 F.Supp.2d 69, 79–81 (D.Mass.2001):

> It is appropriate to pause for a moment to emphasize the particular procedural approach that this Court used in conducting the *Markman* hearing. District courts have differed significantly in the timing and procedure for *Markman* hearings—some engaging in claim construction prior to trial and others after hearing all of the evidence at trial. . . .

> Here, however, I want more specifically to emphasize that when the *Markman* hearing is conducted at the summary judgment stage, it is also important to conduct the two hearings independently of each other—the *Markman* hearing being held prior to and entirely independently of the summary judgment hearing. This is exactly the procedure that the Court followed in the case at hand, although other courts have chosen to address the issues raised with respect to claim construction in the context of the motion for summary judgment and hence conduct the *Markman* hearing in conjunction with the hearings on summary judgment.

> This Court's *Markman* procedure turns on what this Court sees as the crucial distinction between construing patent claims in the context of considering motions for summary judgment as opposed to construing the patent claims without regard to the alleged infringement issue presented in the summary judgment motion. With this distinction in mind, this Court scrupulously kept the issues separate in order to avoid conflating the legal explication required by *Markman* with the fact finding that the Seventh Amendment ultimately reserves for the American jury.

> * * *

> Judges are expected to be objective and analytic in their role as law definer, and I daily seek to meet this standard. Moreover, I do not even mean to suggest that the outcome of this case would have somehow been different had this Court followed the approach that other courts apply and mixed the questions of claim construction into the hearing on summary judgment. But the risk that this procedure creates of conflating issues of fact and law is simply too high in my eyes. Let us not forget that the Seventh Amendment requires that infringement cases be tried to a jury. *Markman v. Westview Instruments, Inc.*, 517 U.S. 370, 377 (1996). The judiciary has recently mandated other procedural hurdles that seem to fly in the face of efficiency in the sole effort to preserve the role of the American jury. Believing in the benefits of such a simple prophylactic measure—considering claim construction without regard to infringement—I made careful efforts to follow this procedure consistently. The result is an honest effort to give meaning to the true spirit of *Markman* and the due consideration that it gave to the role of the jury in patent litigation.

For an additional well-informed view on the timing of *Markman* hearings, consider District Judge Roderick McKelvie's remarks in *Lucas Aerospace, Ltd. v. Unison Industries, L.P.*, 890 F.Supp. 329, 332 n. 3 (D.Del.1995):

How does the Court construe claims as a matter of law at the close of evidence without disrupting the jury? For example, in this case the evidence phase of the trial took 11 days and over 2900 pages of trial transcript. Much of the trial testimony consisted of competing expert explanations of claim constructions. To construe the claims before giving the case to the jury requires immediate access to a trial transcript, *i.e.,* daily copy which creates a not insignificant expense to the parties (an important factor whenever non-Fortune 500 inventors brush up against a deep pocket defendant), rapid briefing by the parties, and hopefully an opinion by the court. In this case it probably would have taken no less than five days for the parties to file helpful briefs and the court to memorialize its holdings on claim construction in a meaningful manner. If the jury were sent home during this period, there is a very real chance that many of the facts important to resolving the infringement issues will have been forgotten. Twenty-one years of trial experience convinces me that any jury hiatus should be avoided if at all possible. One can argue that one should take less time with claim construction, but is that fair to the litigants when claim construction more often than not determines the outcome on infringement?

See also Judge McKelvie's SIDE BAR, *infra.*

2. *Interlocutory Appeal.* The interpretation of a claim sets the framework for litigation of a patent dispute, determining what facts must be proved and what evidence is relevant. The parties may waste considerable effort and resources if a trial judge does not interpret the claims early in the litigation or if a case is tried based on a trial judge's interpretation that the Court of Appeals reverses. The general rule is that appeals can only be taken from a final judgment. Should there be a mechanism whereby a party can take an interlocutory appeal from a trial court's claim construction to get a definitive interpretation from the Federal Circuit? *See* Craig Allen Nard, *Process Considerations in the Age of* Markman *and* Mantras, 2001 ILLINOIS L. REV. 101 (discussing approaches to facilitate interlocutory review by the Federal Circuit of trial court claim constructions). Although there is no interlocutory appeal as of right on the issue of claim interpretation, the Federal Circuit may, "in its discretion," grant such an appeal if the district court initially certifies the interlocutory order. *Id.* But the Federal Circuit has thus far refused to exercise its discretion and grant an interlocutory appeal on the issue of claim interpretation; and has shown little inclination to do so.[27] *See Kollmorgen Corp. v. Yaskawa Elec. Corp.,* 147 F.Supp.2d 464, 467 (W.D.Va. 2001) (stating that "even if a District Judge certifies an appeal, the Federal Circuit consistently declines to review patent claim interpretations"). This reluctance may simply reflect the more general fact that the court wants a more complete record or that interlocutory appeals pursuant to section 1292(b) are rarely granted. *See* Michael E. Solimine, *Revitalizing Interlocutory Appeals in the Federal Courts,* 58 GEO. WASH. L. REV. 1165, 1193 (1990) (asserting that "[m]uch of the blame is attributable to the narrow construction given the statute by some courts, as well as the fear that relaxing the use of the

---

27. In declining to grant an interlocutory appeal, the court simply cites the legislative history of 28 U.S.C. § 1292 (b), which states that:

> The granting of the appeal is also discretionary with the court of appeals which may refuse to entertain such an appeal in much the same manner that the Supreme Court today refuses to entertain applications for writs of certiorari.

> It should be made clear that if application for an appeal from an interlocutory order is filed with the court of appeals, the court of appeals may deny such application without specifying the grounds upon which such a denial is based.

S.Rep. No. 2434, 85th Cong. 2d Sess 3. *See also In re Convertible Rowing Exerciser Patent Litigation,* 903 F.2d 822, 822 (Fed.Cir.1990).

statute will open the floodgates to appeals''); Howard B. Eisenberg & Alan B. Morrison, *Discretionary Appellate Review*, 1 J. App. Prac. & Process 285, 292 (1999) (''[C]ourts of appeals decline to hear approximately two-thirds of the cases certified by district courts for interlocutory appeal.''). But as claim interpretation is almost invariably dispositive of validity and infringement, some judges on the Federal Circuit have questioned the court's reluctance.[28]

3. *Appellate Review of Claim Interpretation*. The Supreme Court, in *Markman*, did not explicitly address the issue of appellate review for claim construction. Indeed, the grant of *certiorari* and the precise holding of the opinion were both narrowly tailored to the Seventh Amendment issue (right to a jury trial). But the Supreme Court was not silent on the distinction between ''fact'' and ''law.'' The Court did refer to claim construction as a ''mongrel practice'' that ''falls somewhere between a pristine legal standard and a simple historical fact.'' 116 S.Ct. at 1390, 1395. This is important because the characterization of a disputed question, such as the proper construction of a word or phrase in a patent claim, as one of law or fact may determine whether a decision on that issue is reviewed on appeal *de novo* (as a legal question), for clear error (as a fact found in a bench trial), or for substantial evidence (as a fact found by a jury). Thus, one might wonder whether or not the Court's *Markman* opinion left the field unsettled.

Any uncertainty was put to rest in *Cybor Corp. v. FAS Technologies, Inc.*, 138 F.3d 1448, 1456 (Fed.Cir.1998) (*en banc*). In *Cybor*, the Federal Circuit held that claim interpretation is a question of law subject to *de novo* review. According to the majority,

> [W]e conclude that the standard of review in *Markman I*, as discussed above, was not changed by the Supreme Court's decision in *Markman II*, and we therefore reaffirm that, as a purely legal question, we review claim construction de novo on appeal including any allegedly fact-based questions relating to claim construction. Accordingly, we today disavow any language in previous opinions of this court that holds, purports to hold, states, or suggests anything to the contrary.

There are many competing policy arguments concerning the proper standard of appellate review for claim construction determinations. Two policy concerns in particular are: (1) the need for uniformity; and (2) the need for early certainty.

When speaking about uniformity, the Supreme Court was concerned with ''the importance of uniformity in the treatment of a given patent.'' What implications does this uniformity concern have for the standard of review in claim construction? Consider the following scenario:

> The '111 patent is owned by patentee X. X files a patent infringement suit in the Southern District of New York asserting that defendant Y is infringing the '111 patent. Shortly thereafter, X files another patent infringement action in the Northern District of Texas claiming that defendant Z is infringing the '111 patent. Both district court judges, relying

---

28. As noted by Judge Newman:

Although the district courts have extended themselves, and so-called ''*Markman* hearings'' are common, this has not been accompanied by interlocutory review of the trial judge's claim interpretation. The Federal Circuit has thus far declined all such certified questions ... [thereby] resulting in two untoward consequences; first, the district court has had to conduct a perhaps unnecessary trial; and second, the eventual issuance of a new claim interpretation by the Federal Circuit, on appeal after final judgment, has sometimes required a second trial of the issue of infringement.

Cybor, 138 F.3d at 1479 (Newman, J., additional views).

heavily on expert testimony in interpreting the claims of the '111 patent, arrive at different interpretations. One interpretation leads to a finding that the '111 patent is not invalid; and the other to a finding of invalidity.

As appeals from both cases would be to the Federal Circuit, that court will, for the most part, have the last word on claim interpretation. Therefore, won't uniformity be promoted by the application of a *de novo* standard of review? If the Federal Circuit employed a more deferential standard of review (*e.g.*, clearly erroneous) to the claim interpretation of each district court, particularly with respect to expert testimony, the Federal Circuit may have no choice but to uphold both district court decisions, which in this case would lead to divergent claim interpretations for the same patent.

But with respect to certainty in this context, the concern is for *early* certainty in the interpretation of any given patent claim. A more deferential standard of appellate review would make the district court's claim interpretation less suscepti-ble to reversal, thereby introducing a heightened level of predictability to the law suit at the trial level. This may promote early settlement and decrease litigation costs. Furthermore, the doctrine of issue preclusion, when available, addresses the uniformity issue at the district level. *See TM Patents v. International Business Machines*, 72 F.Supp.2d 370 (S.D.N.Y.1999) (applying issue preclusion to claim interpretation); *Abbott Laboratories v. Dey, L.P.*, 110 F.Supp.2d 667 (N.D.Ill.2000); *but see Kollmorgen Corp. v. Yaskawa Elec. Corp.*, 147 F.Supp.2d 464 (W.D.Va. 2001) (declining to follow *TM Patents*); *Graco Children's Products, Inc. v. Regalo Interna-tional, LLC*, 77 F.Supp.2d 660 (E.D.Pa.1999) (same). *See also,* Craig Allen Nard, *Process Considerations in the Age of Markman and Mantras*, 2001 Ill. L. Rev. 355, 379–80, 382:

> [T]he Federal Circuit's uniqueness is largely irrelevant in a situation where the new and independent asserts issue preclusion against the patentee in a subsequent litigation. Under this scenario, the doctrine of issue preclusion fosters uniformity at the district court level. The applica-tion of issue preclusion in the context of claim interpretation is consistent with *Markman II*. Recall Justice Souter's language that "principles of issue preclusion ... ordinarily foster uniformity." Thus, the Supreme Court envisioned that the Federal Circuit would promote uniformity in claim construction when issue preclusion is *unavailable* as where the patentee seeks to assert issue preclusion against a new and independent defendant.

> The application of the doctrine of issue preclusion in the context of claim interpretation is nicely illustrated in *TM Patents v. IBM* [72 F.Supp.2d 370 (S.D.N.Y. 1999) (McMahon, J.)].... Judge McMahon stated:

After *Markman*, with its requirement that the Court construe the patent for the jury as a matter of law, it is inconceivable that a fully-litigated determination after a first *Markman* hearing would not be preclusive in subsequent actions involving the same disputed claims under the same patent. The nature of the *Markman* proceeding is such that finality is its aim.

> The point to be made here is that when two or more district court judges hold a *Markman* hearing and are willing to invoke collateral estoppel, the Federal Circuit's ability to promote uniformity in claim meaning is no greater than that of a district court—even if the district court judge applying collateral estoppel does not agree with his fellow judge's prior construction. In fact, de novo review delays certainty, wastes trial court resources, and leads to costly appeals. Ironically, from the *Markman I* majority's vantage point, the characterization of claim con-struction as a question of law renders the determination a separate legal

issue susceptible to collateral estoppel, thus enhancing the power of the district court judge.

SIDE BAR

Markman v. Westview and Procedures for Construing Claims

The Honorable Roderick R. McKelvie*

In *Markman v. Westview Instruments*, 517 U.S. 370 (1996), the Supreme Court held that the interpretation of the words of a patent claim is a matter for the court, not the jury. This holding has required trial judges to come up with a procedure for resolving claim construction issues before juries are asked to resolve the remaining issues in a patent trial. In developing such a procedure, I have found it difficult to decide the stage of the proceedings at which claim construction issues should be resolved.

In the typical criminal or civil case, the judge will defer decision on these types of issues until trial. For example, the judge may defer a decision on the admissibility of a coconspirator's statement under Federal Rule of Evidence 801(d) until evidence as to the conspiracy and the declarant's role comes in during the trial. At this point, the judge makes appropriate findings and instructs the jury accordingly. Similarly, where the parties dispute the interpretation of words in a claim in a patent, a trial judge might resolve the dispute at trial and incorporate his or her interpretation into the final instructions given to the jury at the close of evidence pursuant to Fed.R.Civ.P. 51.

For the first three patent jury trials I had after the Federal Circuit's decision in *Markman*, I took this approach. The parties would identify the words in dispute and their proposed constructions in the draft pretrial order, prepared pursuant to Fed R. Civ. P. 16. I then deferred decision until trial. Towards the end of the trial, as part of the final conferences on the form for the jury instructions, I heard argument from the parties and announced my construction of the disputed terms from the bench. I then incorporated that construction into the jury instructions.

The benefit of this approach was that it was efficient and moved the cases to a prompt trial. However, some lawyers were uncomfortable with it, because they could not rely upon a specific claim construction until nearly the end of the trial. Furthermore, I found the process difficult as a judge. I missed having the time to sit and quietly read the prosecution history, and I felt that I would do a better job if I had the opportunity to write out the basis for my decision. I also felt that the parties would benefit from a more thorough explanation of my construction, and from having time to incorporate my construction into their trial strategy.

I began inviting lawyers to suggest alternative approaches for hearing and resolving claim construction issues, so that they might be resolved at some time prior to trial. I have since considered these issues in such contexts as a hearing on a motion for a preliminary injunction, a hearing scheduled mid-way through discovery, a hearing after discovery and before parties filed case dispositive motions, and in briefing on a motion for summary judgment.

Each of these alternative approaches seems to have two principle disadvantages. First, with the time it takes for briefing, a claim construction or *Markman* hearing and an opinion, these procedures tend to add at least a month or two to the time required to resolve these cases. Second, once I have separated claim construction from other issues, I find I am uncomfortable resolving those issues without having a sense of how they fit in the context of the entire case. Claim construction disputes make more sense when one understands the significance of a particular construction to the infringement claims, or the contention that the claims are indefinite or invalid as obvious.

Recently, one of our district judges left me a problem that may turn out to be the solution. He had taken a patent case through discovery, set it for trial and then took senior status. I inherited the case with a relatively prompt trial date and no claim construction. After the parties expressed a preference to hold on to the trial date, I scheduled the pretrial conference for two weeks before trial and a separate hearing on claim construction pursuant to Fed.R.Civ.P. 42(b), to be held one week before trial.

This approach ended up solving the two principle problems I have had with a separate *Markman* hearing. We avoided an additional delay getting the case to the jury. And after reading the draft pretrial order submitted by the parties, I felt comfortable that I could put the claim construction disputes in context. The two weeks between the pretrial and trial was sufficient time to write a short opinion on claim construction. While the parties did not use the construction to support a motion for summary judgment of infringement or noninfringement, the defendant did rethink and abandon certain defenses. This in turn simplified the issues that were presented to the jury, while offering the parties more time to plan out their trial strategies.

* Former United States District Judge, United States District Court for the District of Delaware. The views expressed herein are solely the views of the author and do not necessarily reflect those of the court. This *Side Bar* was written specially for PRINCIPLES OF PATENT LAW.

2.   PROCEDURE: INTERPRETIVE APPROACHES AND EVIDENTIARY SOURCES

While the question of who should interpret a patent claim is one topic of debate, what interpretive aids a court may use in interpreting a patent claim is also a question of great importance that remains subject to substantially divergent views.

In *Markman I*, the Federal Circuit majority drew a distinction between the treatment of *intrinsic evidence* and *extrinsic evidence*. The patent documents themselves—including the claims, the written description, the drawings, and the prosecution history—are considered intrinsic evidence. On the other hand, "all evidence external to the patent and prosecution history, including expert and inventor testimony, dictionaries, and learned treatises" are considered extrinsic evidence. 52 F.3d at 980. Extrinsic evidence "may be helpful to explain scientific principles, the meaning of technical terms, and terms of art that appear in the patent and prosecution history." *Id.* The Federal Circuit suggested that extrinsic evidence may only be used " 'to aid the court in coming to a correct conclusion' as to the 'true meaning of the language employed' in the patent," and the "evidence is to be used for the court's understanding of the patent, not for the purpose of varying or contradicting the terms of the claims." *Id.* at 980–81 (*quoting Seymour v. Osborne*, 78 U.S. (11 Wall.) 516, 546 (1870)).

On *certiorari*, the Supreme Court did not address the actual process of claim construction at great length. The closest it came was in responding to the argument that a "jury's forte" includes the ability to resolve questions of "meaning peculiar to a trade or profession," where the Court noted:

> It is, of course, true that credibility judgments have to be made about the experts who testify in patent cases, and in theory there could be a case in which a simple credibility judgment would suffice to choose between experts whose testimony was equally consistent with a patent's internal logic. But our own experience with document construction leaves us doubtful that trial courts will run into many cases like that. In the main, we expect, any credibility determinations will be subsumed within the necessarily sophisticated analysis of the whole document, required by the standard construction rule that a term can be defined only in a way that comports with the instrument as a whole.

517 U.S. 370, 388 (1996). After the Supreme Court's *Markman* decision there remained uncertainty over the proper methods and sources courts should employ to receive extrinsic evidence, as well as the proper use for such evidence. The following Federal Circuit panel decision, and the notes and SIDE BAR that follow it, highlight many of the contrasting views towards the use of expert testimony and other forms of "extrinsic evidence."

Nevertheless, each of these contrasting views has its roots in what is generally seen as the "basic recipe" for performing a claim construction analysis, which was set forth in the opinion of the Federal Circuit in *Markman I* before the Supreme Court's affirmance:

> The patent is a fully integrated written instrument. By statute, the patent must provide a written description of the invention that will enable one of ordinary skill in the art to make and use it. 35 U.S.C. § 112, para. 1. Section 112, para. 2, also requires the applicant for a patent to conclude the specification with claims "particularly pointing out and distinctly claiming the subject matter which the applicant regards as his invention." It follows, therefore, from the general rule applicable to written instruments that a patent is uniquely suited for having its meaning and scope determined entirely by a court as a matter of law.

* * *

> To ascertain the meaning of claims, we consider three sources: The claims, the specification, and the prosecution history. Expert testimony, including evidence of how those skilled in the art would interpret the claims, may also be used. In construing the claims in this case, all these sources, as well as extrinsic evidence in the form of Westview's sales literature, were included in the record of the trial court proceedings.

> Claims must be read in view of the specification, of which they are a part. The specification contains a written description of the invention that must

enable one of ordinary skill in the art to make and use the invention. For claim construction purposes, the description may act as a sort of dictionary, which explains the invention and may define terms used in the claims. As we have often stated, a patentee is free to be his own lexicographer. The caveat is that any special definition given to a word must be clearly defined in the specification. The written description part of the specification itself does not delimit the right to exclude. That is the function and purpose of claims.

To construe claim language, the court should also consider the patent's prosecution history, if it is in evidence. This undisputed public record of proceedings in the Patent and Trademark Office is of primary significance in understanding the claims. The court has broad power to look as a matter of law to the prosecution history of the patent in order to ascertain the true meaning of language used in the patent claims:

> The construction of the patent is confirmed by the avowed understanding of the patentee, expressed by him, or on his half [sic], when his application for the original patent was pending.... [W]hen a patent bears on its face a particular construction, inasmuch as the specification and claim are in the words of the patentee, ... such a construction may be confirmed by what the patentee said when he was making his application.

Although the prosecution history can and should be used to understand the language used in the claims, it too cannot enlarge, diminish, or vary the limitations in the claims.

Extrinsic evidence consists of all evidence external to the patent and prosecution history, including expert and inventor testimony, dictionaries, and learned treatises. This evidence may be helpful to explain scientific principles, the meaning of technical terms, and terms of art that appear in the patent and prosecution history. Extrinsic evidence may demonstrate the state of the prior art at the time of the invention. It is useful to show what was then old, to distinguish what was new, and to aid the court in the construction of the patent.

The court may, in its discretion, receive extrinsic evidence in order to aid the court in coming to a correct conclusion as to the true meaning of the language employed in the patent.

Extrinsic evidence is to be used for the court's understanding of the patent, not for the purpose of varying or contradicting the terms of the claims. When, after considering the extrinsic evidence, the court finally arrives at an understanding of the language as used in the patent and prosecution history, the court must then pronounce as a matter of law the meaning of that language. This ordinarily can be accomplished by the court in framing its charge to the jury, but may also be done in the context of dispositive motions such as those seeking judgment as a matter of law.

Through this process of construing claims by, among other things, using certain extrinsic evidence that the court finds helpful and rejecting other evidence as unhelpful, and resolving disputes *en route* to pronouncing the meaning of claim language as a matter of law based on the patent documents themselves, the court is *not* crediting certain evidence over other evidence or making factual evidentiary findings. Rather, the court is looking to the extrinsic evidence to assist in its construction of the written document, a task it is required to perform. The district court's claim construction, enlightened by such extrinsic evidence as may be helpful, is still based upon the patent and prosecution history. It is therefore still construction, and is a matter of law subject to *de novo* review.

* * *

Moreover, ideally there should be no "ambiguity" in claim language to one of ordinary skill in the art that would require resort to evidence outside the specification and prosecution history. Section 112 of Title 35 requires that specifications "contain a written description of the invention, and of the manner and process of making and using it, in such *full, clear, concise, and exact* terms as to enable any person skilled in the art to which it pertains, or with which it is most nearly connected, to make and use the same ..." and requires that the specification "shall conclude with one or more claims *particularly pointing out and distinctly claiming* the subject matter which the applicant regards as his invention." 35 U.S.C. § 112 (emphasis added). This statutory language has as its purpose the avoidance of the kind of ambiguity that allows introduction of extrinsic evidence in the contract law analogy. Patent applications, unlike contracts, are reviewed by patent examiners, quasi-judicial officials trained in the law and presumed to have some expertise in interpreting the [prior art] references and to be familiar from their work with the level of skill in the art and whose duty it is to issue only valid patents. If the patent's claims are sufficiently unambiguous for the PTO, there should exist no factual ambiguity when those same claims are later construed by a court of law in an infringement action.

This does not mean there is never a need for extrinsic evidence in a patent infringement suit. A judge is not usually a person conversant in the particular technical art involved and is not the hypothetical person skilled in the art to whom a patent is addressed. Extrinsic evidence, therefore, may be necessary to inform the court about the language in which the patent is written. But this evidence is not for the purpose of clarifying ambiguity in claim terminology. It is not ambiguity in the document that creates the need for extrinsic evidence but rather unfamiliarity of the court with the terminology of the art to which the patent is addressed.

Markman v. Westview Instruments, Inc. (Markman I), 52 F.3d 967, 978–79 (Fed.Cir.1995) (Archer, C.J., joined by Rich, Nies, Michel, Plager, Lourie, Clevenger, and Schall, JJ) (footnotes and internal citations omitted).

Vitronics Corp. v. Conceptronic, Inc.

90 F.3d 1576 (Fed.Cir.1996).

■ Before MICHEL and LOURIE, CIRCUIT JUDGES, and FRIEDMAN, SENIOR CIRCUIT JUDGE.

■ MICHEL, CIRCUIT JUDGE.

Vitronics Corporation ("Vitronics") appeals the September 27, 1995 order of the United States District Court for the District of New Hampshire, ... entering judgment as a matter of law that Vitronics did not prove that Conceptronic, Inc. ("Conceptronic") infringed claim 1 of U.S. Patent No. 4,654,502 ("the '502 patent").... Because we conclude that the specification of the '502 patent dictates a claim interpretation in accordance with the plaintiff's proposed construction, and that, so construed, the '502 patent may have been infringed, we reverse the trial court's decision and remand for further proceedings.

BACKGROUND

The Patented Invention

Vitronics and Conceptronic both manufacture ovens used in the production of printed circuit boards. The ovens are used to solder electrical devices (such as resistors, capacitors and integrated circuits) to the boards. Several methods of soldering devices to boards have been developed; the '502 patent, assigned to Vitronics, is directed to one of those methods.

Specifically, the '502 patent is directed to a method for the reflow soldering of surface mounted devices to a printed circuit board in which the circuit board is moved by a conveyor through a multizone oven. In this process, a solder paste is placed on the circuit board and the devices to be soldered (with attached connectors) are placed on the paste. The circuit board is then placed on what is basically a conveyor belt running through an oven and passing through several different heating zones. In the final and hottest zone, the solder paste melts and forms a connection between the device and the circuit board. The boards remain in the last heating zone for only a short duration, allowing the solder to reach a temperature high enough to cause the solder to melt and reflow while maintaining the devices themselves below the solder reflow temperature. Due to this temperature differential, the solder flows up the device connectors to form a solid connection.

Claim 1 of the '502 patent, the only claim at issue in this appeal, reads as follows (with added emphasis on the disputed terms):

1.   A method for reflow soldering of surface mounted devices to a printed circuit board comprising:

moving a printed circuit board having solder and devices disposed on a surface thereof through a first zone and in close proximity to a first emitting surface of at least one nonfocused infrared panel emitter, said first emitting surface being at a first panel temperature;

moving said board through a second zone and in close proximity to a second emitting surface of at least one nonfocused infrared panel emitter, said second emitting surface being at a second panel temperature lower than said first panel temperature; and

moving said board through a third zone and in close proximity to a third emitting surface of at least one nonfocused infrared panel emitter, said third emitting surface being at a third panel temperature higher than said second panel temperature, said third emitting surface heating said board and said solder to *a solder reflow temperature* for a period of time sufficient to cause said solder to reflow and solder said devices to said board while maintaining the temperature of said devices below *said solder reflow temperature*.

Proceedings Before the District Court

* * *

Vitronics, by way of a request for a jury instruction, asked the court to construe the meaning of the "solder reflow temperature" limitation. The specific instruction sought by Vitronics was as follows:

In considering the question of whether the '502 method patent has been infringed by the Mark and HVC Series ovens, you have to decide whether, in use, those ovens maintain the temperature of the devices below the solder reflow temperature. The phrase "solder reflow temperature" in the '502 patent means the temperature reached by the solder during the period it is reflowing during the final stages of the soldering process, sometimes referred to as the "peak solder reflow temperature." It does not mean the "liquidus temperature," the temperature at which the solder first begins to melt. Thus, if the temperature of the devices stays below that of the solder, the '502 method patent is infringed by the Mark and HVC Series ovens.

Thus, Vitronics contended that, as used in the claim, solder reflow temperature means peak reflow temperature, *i.e.*, a temperature approximately 20° C above the liquidus temperature, at which the solder is completely melted and moves freely. Conceptronic, on the other hand, contended that solder reflow temperature means 183° C, *i.e.*, the liquidus temperature of a particular type of solder known as 63/37 (Sn/Pb) solder.[3]

The district court delayed construing the disputed language until the close of testimony, at which time it ruled in favor of Conceptronic and concluded that the term solder reflow temperature as used in claim 1 refers to 183° C. Vitronics then conceded that the court was required to grant judgment as a matter of law in favor of Conceptronic, as Vitronics had not presented any evidence of infringement under the court's interpretation of solder reflow temperature. This appeal followed.

* * *

The Patent Specification

Vitronics relied heavily upon the patent itself to support its asserted claim construction. Although Vitronics conceded that the term "solder reflow temperature" may be ambiguous when considered in isolation, it argued that the specification clearly shows that, as used in the claim, solder reflow temperature means peak reflow temperature rather than the liquidus temperature. In particular, Vitronics pointed to that part of the specification that describes a preferred embodiment:

A preferred embodiment of the invention for reflow soldering of surface mounted devices to printed circuit boards will now be described. The printed circuit boards are typically made of epoxy-glass, such as fire retardant 4(FR–4), or polyamide glass. These boards typically degrade above temperatures of 225° C. The solder may be, for example, 60/40 (Sn/Pb), 63/37 (Sn/Pb), or 62/36/2 (Sn/Pb/Ag), all of which have a liquidus temperature (*i.e.* begin to melt) of about 190° C. and a peak reflow temperature of about 210°–218° C. Thus, to effect reflow soldering without damaging the board, the solder must be allowed to reach a temperature of at least 210° C., but the board cannot reach a temperature of 225° C.

---

3. The specification of the '502 patent describes three exemplary types of solder which can be used in the solder reflow process—60/40 (Sn/Pb), 63/37 (Sn/Pb) and 62/36/2 (Sn/Pb/Ag)—each of which, it indicates, has a liquidus temperature of about 190° C and a peak reflow temperature of about 210° to 218° C. At trial, the parties appear to have discussed only 63/37 (Sn/Pb) solder, which has a liquidus temperature of 183° C. However, the claims are not limited to that particular solder or a solder with that particular liquidus temperature.

. . . .

> The board is then sent into a fifth zone 5 to bring the temperature of the board up to a temperature of approximately 210° C., the devices up to approximately 195° C., and the solder up to approximately 210° C. for a period of time of from about 10 to about 20 seconds to cause the solder to flow. Because the devices are cooler than the board, the solder flows up the devices. . . . The board spends approximately 60 seconds in the fifth zone, but only about 10 to 20 seconds at 210° C. Thus, the board is at the solder reflow temperature for only a short period of time and the devices never reach the solder reflow temperature.

Vitronics pointed out that, in the example described as the preferred embodiment, the temperature of the solder is raised to 210° C, the peak reflow temperature, and the temperature of the devices is raised to 195° C, 5° above the 190° C liquidus temperature. Thus, as argued by Vitronics, the term "solder reflow temperature" must be construed so that it refers to the peak reflow temperature because the claim requires that the temperature of the devices be maintained below "said solder reflow temperature"; if solder reflow temperature were construed to refer to liquidus temperature, the preferred embodiment would not be covered by the patent claims.

Expert Testimony

Conceptronic relied heavily on the expert testimony of Dr. Rothe. Dr. Rothe testified that the meaning of the term "solder reflow temperature" in claim 1 is synonymous with liquidus temperature. Dr. Rothe further testified that the solder reflow temperature for 63/37 (Sn/Pb) is 183° C. Dr. Rothe likewise testified at trial that several technical articles written by those skilled in the art supported his view that solder reflow temperature refers to liquidus temperature.

The Testimony of Mr. Hall

Conceptronic also relied on the testimony of Mr. Hall, the Chief Engineer at Vitronics. At trial, Mr. Hall confirmed that during his deposition he had testified that the reflow temperature of solder was 183° C. Mr. Hall also testified that, during his deposition, he had used solder reflow temperature to refer to liquidus temperature. However, at another point in his trial testimony, Hall explained that, while in his earlier deposition testimony he had used solder reflow temperature to refer to liquidus temperature, he did not suggest that was how the term was used in the patent. Rather, Hall testified the patent uses the term to refer to the peak reflow temperature.

Paper Written By Former Vitronics Employee

Conceptronic also introduced into evidence a paper written by Phillip Zarrow, a former employee of Vitronics, defining solder reflow temperature in the following manner: "As the temperature of the solder paste on the interconnect passes the solder alloy's melting point and the solder enters a molten state, the assembly enters the reflow region of the process. For 63 Sn/37 Pb, a eutectic solder and the most common SMT alloy, reflow occurs at 183° C." Phillip Zarrow, *Convection/Infrared and Convection Dominant Reflow Soldering of Fine Pitch SMT Devices*, § 10.3.3 (1994). However, that same paper later describes the solder reflow process as taking the temperature of the solder above liquidus: "Most solder manufacturers recommend bringing the interconnection temperature approximately 15 to 25° C above the alloy melting point to achieve full liquidus and assure good solder flow and aid fillet formation." *Id.*

Memorandum of Plaintiff Vitronics Corporation in Opposition to Motion for Summary Judgment of Defendant Conceptronic Corporation and In Support of Plaintiff's Cross–Motion for Summary Judgment of Patent Validity and Infringement

In its brief supporting its proposed construction of claim 1, both at the trial court level and here on appeal, Conceptronic similarly relied on a memorandum written by Vitronics which contains the following language: "Tin/lead solders commonly used by the electronic products industry have a 'liquidus' or 'reflow' temperature in the order of 183° C, or about 361° F. However, this phrase is in the background section of the memorandum and later in the same memorandum, Vitronics discussed the issue of infringement as being whether the temperature of the devices was maintained below the temperatures of the leads at which the solder is reflowing."

Without indicating which evidence it relied upon, the district court simply ruled that solder reflow temperature meant 183° C.

ANALYSIS

The Use of Intrinsic and Extrinsic Evidence in Claim Construction

A literal patent infringement analysis involves two steps: the proper construction of the asserted claim and a determination as to whether the accused method or product infringes the asserted claim as properly construed.... The first step, claim construction, is a matter of law, which we review *de novo*.... Claim construction is the only step in the infringement analysis at issue in this appeal.[4]

In determining the proper construction of a claim, the court has numerous sources that it may properly utilize for guidance. These sources have been detailed in our previous opinions, as discussed below, and include both intrinsic evidence (*e.g.*, the patent specification and file history) and extrinsic evidence (*e.g.*, expert testimony).

It is well-settled that, in interpreting an asserted claim, the court should look first to the intrinsic evidence of record, *i.e.*, the patent itself, including the claims, the specification and, if in evidence, the prosecution history. *See Markman*, 52 F.3d at 979, 34 U.S.P.Q.2D at 1329. Such intrinsic evidence is the most significant source of the legally operative meaning of disputed claim language.

First, we look to the words of the claims themselves, both asserted and nonasserted, to define the scope of the patented invention.... Although words in a claim are generally given their ordinary and customary meaning, a patentee may choose to be his own lexicographer and use terms in a manner other than their ordinary meaning, as long as the special definition

---

4. No assertion was made that defendant infringed under the doctrine of equivalents.

of the term is clearly stated in the patent specification or file history. *Hoechst Celanese Corp. v. BP Chems. Ltd.*, 78 F.3d 1575, 1578, 38 U.S.P.Q.2D 1126, 1129 (Fed.Cir.1996) ("A technical term used in a patent document is interpreted as having the meaning that it would be given by persons experienced in the field of the invention, unless it is apparent from the patent and the prosecution history that the inventor used the term with a different meaning.") (citations omitted); *Hormone*, 904 F.2d at 1563, 15 U.S.P.Q.2D at 1043 ("It is a well-established axiom in patent law that a patentee is free to be his or her own lexicographer and thus may use terms in a manner contrary to or inconsistent with one or more of their ordinary meanings.") (citations omitted).

Thus, second, it is always necessary to review the specification to determine whether the inventor has used any terms in a manner inconsistent with their ordinary meaning. The specification acts as a dictionary when it expressly defines terms used in the claims or when it defines terms by implication. *Markman*, 52 F.3d at 979, 34 U.S.P.Q.2D at 1330. As we have repeatedly stated, "[c]laims must be read in view of the specification, of which they are a part." *Id.* at 979, 52 F.3d 967, 34 U.S.P.Q.2D at 1329. The specification contains a written description of the invention which must be clear and complete enough to enable those of ordinary skill in the art to make and use it. Thus, the specification is always highly relevant to the claim construction analysis. Usually, it is dispositive; it is the single best guide to the meaning of a disputed term.

Third, the court may also consider the prosecution history of the patent, if in evidence. *Id.* at 980, 52 F.3d 967, 34 U.S.P.Q.2D at 1330; *Graham v. John Deere*, 383 U.S. 1, 33, 86 S.Ct. 684, 701–02, 15 L.Ed.2d 545, 148 USPQ 459, 473 (1966). This history contains the complete record of all the proceedings before the Patent and Trademark Office, including any express representations made by the applicant regarding the scope of the claims. As such, the record before the Patent and Trademark Office is often of critical significance in determining the meaning of the claims. *See Markman*, 52 F.3d at 980, 34 U.S.P.Q.2D at 1330; *Southwall Tech., Inc. v. Cardinal IG Co.*, 54 F.3d 1570, 1576, 34 U.S.P.Q.2D 1673, 1676 (Fed.Cir. 1995) ("The prosecution history limits the interpretation of claim terms so as to exclude any interpretation that was disclaimed during prosecution.") (citations omitted). Included within an analysis of the file history may be an examination of the prior art cited therein. *Autogiro Co. of America v. United States*, 181 Ct.Cl. 55, 384 F.2d 391, 399, 155 USPQ 697, 704 (1967) ("In its broader use as source material, the prior art cited in the file wrapper gives clues as to what the claims do not cover.").

In most situations, an analysis of the intrinsic evidence alone will resolve any ambiguity in a disputed claim term. In such circumstances, it is improper to rely on extrinsic evidence. . . . In those cases where the public record unambiguously describes the scope of the patented invention, reliance on any extrinsic evidence is improper. The claims, specification, and file history, rather than extrinsic evidence, constitute the public record of the patentee's claim, a record on which the public is entitled to rely. In other words, competitors are entitled to review the public record, apply the established rules of claim construction, ascertain the scope of the patentee's claimed invention and, thus, design around the claimed invention.... Allowing the public record to be altered or changed by extrinsic evidence introduced at trial, such as expert testimony, would make this right meaningless.... The same holds true whether it is the patentee or the alleged infringer who seeks to alter the scope of the claims.

The Proper Construction of the Claim Term "Solder Reflow Temperature"

As can be readily seen from those portions of the specification set forth above, the meaning of the disputed term "solder reflow temperature" in claim 1 of the '502 patent is clear from a reading of the claim itself and the patent specification. The "peak reflow temperature" and "liquidus temperature" are clearly defined in the specification as having distinctly different meanings. Specifically, for the solders described in the specification, liquidus temperature is about 190° C and the peak reflow temperature is about 210° to 218° C. Moreover, in the preferred embodiment described in the patent, the solder is heated to a temperature of 210° C but the temperature of the devices is maintained at approximately 195° C, *i.e.*, below the peak reflow temperature (210° C) but above the liquidus temperature (190° C). Therefore, in order to be consistent with the specification and preferred embodiment described therein, claim 1 must be construed such that the term solder reflow temperature means the peak reflow temperature, rather than the liquidus temperature. Indeed, if "solder reflow temperature" were defined to mean liquidus temperature, a preferred (and indeed only) embodiment in the specification would not fall within the scope of the patent claim. Such an interpretation is rarely, if ever, correct and would require highly persuasive evidentiary support, which is wholly absent in this case....

The District Court's Reliance on Extrinsic Evidence

Since the claim, read in light of the patent specification, clearly uses the term "solder reflow temperature" to mean the peak reflow temperature, rather than the liquidus temperature, that should have been the end of the trial court's analysis.[5] Only if there were still some genuine ambiguity in the claims, after consideration of all available intrinsic evidence, should the trial court have resorted to extrinsic evidence, such as expert testimony, in order to construe claim 1. Moreover, even if the judge permissibly decided to hear all the possible evidence before construing the claim, the expert testimony, which was inconsistent with the specification and file history, should have been accorded no weight....

Here, the trial judge considered not only the specification, but also expert testimony and other extrinsic evidence, such as the paper written by the former Vitronics employee. No doubt there will be instances in which intrinsic evidence is insufficient to enable the court to determine the meaning of the asserted claims, and in those instances, extrinsic evidence, such as that relied on by the district court, may also properly be relied on to understand the technology and to construe the claims. *See Markman*, 52 F.3d at 979, 34 U.S.P.Q.2D at 1329. Extrinsic evidence is that evidence which is external to the patent and file history, such as expert testimony,

---

5. The file history was apparently not put into evidence.

inventor testimony, dictionaries, and technical treatises and articles.[6] *Id.* at 980, 34 U.S.P.Q.2D at 1330. However, as we have recently re-emphasized, extrinsic evidence in general, and expert testimony in particular, may be used only to help the court come to the proper understanding of the claims; it may not be used to vary or contradict the claim language. *Id.* at 981, 52 F.3d 967, 34 U.S.P.Q.2D at 1331. Nor may it contradict the import of other parts of the specification. Indeed, where the patent documents are unambiguous, expert testimony regarding the meaning of a claim is entitled to no weight. *Southwall*, 54 F.3d at 1578, 34 U.S.P.Q.2D at 1678. "Any other rule would be unfair to competitors who must be able to rely on the patent documents themselves, without consideration of expert opinion that then does not even exist, in ascertaining the scope of a patentee's right to exclude." *Id.* at 1578, 34 U.S.P.Q.2D at 1678–79. Nor may the inventor's subjective intent as to claim scope, when unexpressed in the patent documents, have any effect. Such testimony cannot guide the court to a proper interpretation when the patent documents themselves do so clearly.

In addition, a court in its discretion may admit and rely on prior art proffered by one of the parties, whether or not cited in the specification or the file history. This prior art can often help to demonstrate how a disputed term is used by those skilled in the art. Such art may make it unnecessary to rely on expert testimony and may save much trial time. As compared to expert testimony, which often only indicates what a particular expert believes a term means, prior art references may also be more indicative of what all those skilled in the art generally believe a certain term means. Once again, however, reliance on such evidence is unnecessary, and indeed improper, when the disputed terms can be understood from a careful reading of the public record.... Nor may it be used to vary claim terms from how they are defined, even implicitly, in the specification or file history.

Unfortunately, here the trial judge did use the extrinsic evidence to vary or contradict the manifest meaning of the claims. The trial judge was presented with expert testimony and other evidence that some of those skilled in the relevant art, including certain Vitronics employees, sometimes used the term "solder reflow temperature" and "liquidus temperature" interchangeably. He apparently relied on this testimony in reaching his conclusion that, as used in claim 1, solder reflow temperature meant 183° C.[7] However, regardless of how those skilled in the art would interpret a term in other situations, where those of ordinary skill, on a reading of the patent documents, would conclude that the documents preclude the term being given the meaning propounded by the expert witnesses, we must give

---

6. Although technical treatises and dictionaries fall within the category of extrinsic evidence, as they do not form a part of an integrated patent document, they are worthy of special note. Judges are free to consult such resources at any time in order to better understand the underlying technology and may also rely on dictionary definitions when construing claim terms, so long as the dictionary definition does not contradict any definition found in or ascertained by a reading of the patent documents.

7. Although the trial judge's reasoning does not appear in the record, he must have relied on the testimony presented by Conceptronic that "solder reflow temperature" and "liquidus temperature" were synonymous and the undisputed testimony that the liquidus temperature of 63/37 (Sn/Pb) solder is 183° C.

it the meaning indicated by the patentee in the patent claim, specification and file history. Thus, expert testimony tending to show that those skilled in the art would, in certain circumstances, understand "solder reflow temperature" to mean the solder liquidus temperature is entitled to no weight in light of the clear contrary meaning shown in the specification.... Because the specification clearly and unambiguously defined the disputed term in the claim, reliance on this extrinsic evidence was unnecessary and, hence, legally incorrect.

Had the district court relied on the expert testimony and other extrinsic evidence solely to help it understand the underlying technology, we could not say the district court was in error. But testimony on the technology is far different from other expert testimony, whether it be of an attorney, a technical expert, or the inventor, on the proper construction of a disputed claim term, relied on by the district court in this case. The latter kind of testimony may only be relied upon if the patent documents, taken as a whole, are insufficient to enable the court to construe disputed claim terms. Such instances will rarely, if ever, occur. Indeed, this case did not present such an instance. Even in those rare instances, prior art documents and dictionaries, although to a lesser extent, are more objective and reliable guides. Unlike expert testimony, these sources are accessible to the public in advance of litigation. They are to be preferred over opinion testimony, whether by an attorney or artisan in the field of technology to which the patent is directed. Indeed, opinion testimony on claim construction should be treated with the utmost caution, for it is no better than opinion testimony on the meaning of statutory terms. *See Markman*, 52 F.3d at 983, 34 U.S.P.Q.2D at 1332–33 ("First, the testimony of Markman and his patent attorney on the proper construction of the claims is entitled to no deference.... This testimony about construction, however, amounts to no more than legal opinion—it is precisely the process of construction that the court must undertake.").

* * *

NOTES

1. *The Role of the Specification in Interpreting Claims.* It is well settled that claims are not to be construed by reference to the accused device. *See NeoMagic Corp. v. Trident Microsystems, Inc.*, 287 F.3d 1062, 1074 (Fed.Cir.2002). Rather, claims are to be interpreted in view of the specification. As the Federal Circuit pithily noted: "Specifications teach. Claims claim." *SRI Int'l v. Matsushita Elec. Corp.*, 775 F.2d 1107, 1121, n.14 (Fed.Cir.1985). But this patent law tenet is restrained by two complimentary caveats, both of which flow from the fundamental principle that "it is the function and purpose of claims, not the written description part of the specification itself," to "delimit the right to exclude." *Markman*, 52 F.3d at 980. *See also, Johnson & Johnston Associates v. R.E. Service Co.*, 285 F.3d 1046, 1052 (Fed.Cir.2002) ("Consistent with its scope definition and notice functions, the claim requirement presupposes that a patent applicant defines his invention in the claims, not in the specification. After all, the claims, not the specification, provide the measure of the patentee's right to exclude").

First, it is improper to import (*i.e.*, "read in") a limitation from the specification's general discussion, embodiments, and examples. Second, it is improper to eliminate or ignore (*i.e.*, "read out") a claim limitation in order to extend a patent to subject matter disclosed, but not claimed. In other words, all claim limitations are material. We will talk more about this second caveat in Part B, *infra*.

The Federal Circuit has recognized that "there is sometimes a fine line between reading a claim in light of the specification, and reading a limitation into the claim from the specification." *Comark Communications, Inc. v. Harris Corp.*, 156 F.3d 1182, 1186 (Fed.Cir.1998). In *Renishaw PLC v. Marposs Societa' Per Azioni*, 158 F.3d 1243 (Fed.Cir.1998), the court discussed at length the following canons of claim construction: (a) one must not read a limitation into a claim from the written description; and (b) a claim must be read in view of the specification. According to the court:

> [T]hese two rules share two underlying proposition. First, it is manifest that a claim must explicitly recite a term in need of definition before a definition my enter the claim from the written description. This is so because the claims define the scope of the right to exclude; the claim construction inquiry, therefore, begins and ends in all cases with the actual words of the claim....

> The other clear point provided by these two canons covers the situation in which patent applicant has elected to be a lexicographer by providing an explicit definition in the specification for a claim term. In such a case, the definition selected by the patent applicant controls....

> Absent a special and particular definition created by the patent applicant, terms in a claim are to be given their ordinary and accustomed meaning.... Thus, when a claim term is expressed in general descriptive words, we will not ordinarily limit the term to a numerical range that may appear in the written description or in other claims. Nor may we, in the broader situation, add a narrowing modifier before an otherwise general term that stands unmodified in a claim. For example, if an apparatus claim recites a general structure (e.g., a noun) without limiting that structure to a specific subset of structures (e.g., with an adjective), we will generally construe the claim to cover all known types of that structure that are supported by the patent disclosure.

Id. at 1249–50. These competing canons played out recently in *Alloc, Inc. v. International Trade Commission*, 342 F.3d 1361 (Fed.Cir.2003). The patentee owned patents on systems and methods of joining floor panels. The claims did not recite or expressly require "play" or spacing between the floor panels, but the court read the specification as requiring such:

> [T]his court recognizes that it must interpret the claims in light of the specification, yet avoid impermissibly importing limitations from the specification. That balance turns on how the specification characterizes the claimed invention. In this respect, this court looks to whether the specification refers to a limitation only as a part of less than all possible embodiments or whether the specification read as a whole suggests that the very character of the invention requires the limitation be a part of every embodiment. For example, it is impermissible to read the one and only disclosed embodiment into a claim without other indicia that the patentee so intended to limit the invention. On the other hand, where the specification makes clear at various points that the claimed invention is narrower than the claim language might imply, it is entirely permissible and proper to limit the claims. *SciMed Life Sys., Inc. v. Advance Cardiovascular Sys., Inc.*, 242 F.3d 1337, 1345 (Fed.Cir.2001).... Here [as in *SciMed*], the [patent] specification read as a whole leads to the inescapable conclusion that the claimed invention must include play in every embodiment....

[T]he patent specification indicates that the invention is indeed exclusively directed toward flooring products including play. Moreover, unlike the patent-at-issue in *SunRace [Roots Enters. Co. v. SRAM Corp.*, 336 F.3d 1298 (Fed.Cir.2003)], the [patent] specification also distinguished the prior art on the basis of play.

Id. at 1370–71.

2. *Extrinsic Evidence and the Role of the Artisan.* The *Vitronics* court held that intrinsic evidence includes the claims, specification, and prosecution history. Also part of the intrinsic record is prior art cited in the patent or prosecution history. *See Tate Access Floors, Inc. v. Interface Architectural Res., Inc.*, 279 F.3d 1357, 1371–72 n.4 (Fed.Cir.2002) (noting that prior art not considered by the examiner is extrinsic evidence). Given § 112's admonition to distinctly claim and particularly point out one's invention, it is understandable why *Vitronics* emphasized the need for a clear public record on patent claim scope and restricted the use of extrinsic evidence, such as expert testimony. According to the court:

> [E]xtrinsic evidence in general, and expert testimony in particular, may be used only to help the court come to the proper understanding of the claims; it may not be used to vary or contradict the claim language. Nor may it contradict the import of other parts of the specification. Indeed, where the patent documents are unambiguous, expert testimony regarding the meaning of a claim is entitled to no weight. (citations omitted)

90 F.3d 1576, at 1584. *See also Trilogy Communications v. Times Fiber Communications*, 109 F.3d 739, 744 (Fed.Cir.1997) ("[E]xtrinsic evidence may be relied on when needed to interpret claims, but only when it does not contradict the intrinsic record consisting of the claims themselves, the [remainder of the] specification [*i.e.,* the written description], and the prosecution history"); *Bell & Howell Document Management v. Altek Sys.*, 132 F.3d 701, 706 (Fed.Cir.1997) (testimony about claim interpretation often "amounts to more than legal opinion—it is precisely the process of construction that the court must undertake") (quoting *Markman*, 52 F.3d at 983).

But do *Vitronics* and its progeny ignore the central role of the person having ordinary skill in the art? As stated in Note 1, *supra*, it is a basic tenet of patent law that claims are to be construed through the eyes of the artisan. *See Markman*, 52 F.3d at 999 (Newman, J.) ("[p]atents are technologic disclosures, written by and for the technologically experienced: those 'of skill in the art' "). Moreover, is there a concern with judicial presumptions about the meaning of technological descriptions without the aid of technical experts, particularly when words of degree (e.g., "substantial" or "about") are used? *See BJ Services Co. v. Halliburton Energy Services, Inc.*, 338 F.3d 1368, 1372 (Fed.Cir.2003) (noting that when words of degree are employed, the "question becomes whether one of ordinary skill in the art would understand what is claimed when the claim is read in light of the specification"). *See also Liquid Dynamics Corp. v. Vaughan Co., Inc.*, 355 F.3d 1361 (Fed.Cir.2004) ("The term 'substantial' is a meaningful modifier implying 'approximate,' rather than 'perfect.' . . . '[W]ords of approximation, such as "generally" and "substantially," are descriptive terms commonly used in patent claims to avoid a strict numerical boundary to the specified parameter' ").

Some trial judges were less than enthusiastic about the Federal Circuit's *Markman* decision as it applied to claim interpretation and especially as applied to cases in which the trial is lengthy or the technology surrounding the patent is more complex than the relatively simple systems at issue in *Markman*. *See, e.g., Lucas Aerospace, Ltd. v. Unison Industries, L.P.*, 890 F.Supp. 329, 332 n.3, 333–34 n. 7 (D.Del.1995), *further order*, 899 F.Supp. 1268 (D.Del.1995):

As I understand *Markman*, because claim construction presents a purely legal question, trial judges must ignore all non-transcribable courtroom occurrences.... When two experts testify differently as to the meaning of a technical term, and the court embraces the view of one, the other, or neither while construing a patent claim as a matter of law, the court *has* engaged in weighing evidence and making credibility determinations. If those possessed of a higher commission which to rely on a cold written record and engage in *de novo* review of all claim constructions, that is their privilege. But when the Federal Circuit Court of Appeals states that the trial court does not do something that the trial court does and must do to perform the judicial function, the court knowingly enters the land of sophistry and fiction.

See also Elf Atochem North Am., Inc. v. Libbey–Owens–Ford Co., 894 F.Supp. 844, 857 (D.Del.1995) (McKelvie, J.).

The Federal Circuit has, to some extent, retreated from the *Markman I–Vitronics* interpretive approach. For example, in *Pitney Bowes, Inc. v. Hewlett–Packard Co.*, 182 F.3d 1298, 1308 (Fed.Cir.1999)

Vitronics does not prohibit courts from examining extrinsic evidence, even when the patent document is itself clear.... Moreover, *Vitronics* does not set forth any rules regarding the admissibility of expert testimony into evidence. Certainly, there are no prohibitions in *Vitronics* on courts hearing evidence from experts. Rather, *Vitronics* merely warned courts not to rely on extrinsic evidence in claim construction to contradict the meaning of claims discernible from thoughtful examination of the claims, the written description, and the prosecution history—the intrinsic evidence. *See id.*, 90 F.3d at 1583 ("In most situations, an analysis of the intrinsic evidence alone will resolve any ambiguity in a disputed claim term. In such circumstances, it is improper to rely on extrinsic evidence. In those cases where the public record unambiguously describes the scope of the patented invention, reliance on any extrinsic evidence is improper.").

See also Merck & Co. v. Teva Pharmaceuticals USA, Inc., 347 F.3d 1367 (Fed.Cir. 2003) (noting that "it is not prohibited to provide the opinions and advice of experts to explain the meaning of terms as they are used in patents and as they would be perceived and understood in the field of an invention"); *Verve v. Crane Cams, Inc.*, 311 F.3d 1116, 1119 (Fed.Cir.2002) ("While reference to intrinsic evidence is primary in interpreting claims, the criterion is the meaning of words as they would be understood by persons in the field of the invention. Patent documents are written for persons familiar with the relevant field; the patentee is not required to include in the specification information readily understood by practitioners, lest every patent be required to be written as a comprehensive tutorial and treatise for the generalist, instead of a concise statement for persons in the field"); *Key Pharmaceuticals v. Hercon Laboratories Corp.*, 161 F.3d 709, 716 (Fed.Cir.1998) ("This court has made strong cautionary statements on the proper use of extrinsic evidence, *see Vitronics*, which might be misread by some members of the bar as restricting a trial court's ability to hear such evidence. We intend no such thing. To the contrary, trial courts generally can hear expert testimony for background and education on the technology implicated by the presented claim construction issues, and trial courts have broad discretion in this regard."); *Ferguson Beauregard/Logic Controls v. Mega Systems, LLC*, 350 F.3d 1327 (Fed.Cir.2003) (Rader, J., concurring) (emphasizing the importance of "customary meaning" and "context").

For a discussion of the competing interpretive approaches to claim construction, see Craig Allen Nard, *A Theory of Claim Interpretation*, 14 HARV. J. L. & TECH. 1 (2001); John R. Thomas, *On Preparatory Text and Proprietary Technologies: The*

Place of Prosecution Histories in Patent Claim Interpretation, 47 UCLA L. REV. 183 (1999); Douglas Y'Barbo, *Is Extrinsic Evidence Ever Necessary to Resolve Claim Construction Disputes?*, 81 J. PAT. & TRADEMARK OFF. SOC'Y 567 (1999). For an empirical look at the Federal Circuit's claim interpretation jurisprudence, see R. Polk Wagner & Lee Petherbridge, Is the Federal Circuit Succeeding? An Empirical Assessment of Judicial Performance, *152 U. PA. L. REV. 1105 (2004)* (available online at www.claimconstruction.com).

3. *The Dictionary as Interpretative Tool.* Recall that the *Vitronics* court stated that dictionaries, although extrinsic evidence, are "worthy of special note" and permitted judges to consult them to construe claim language as long as the dictionary did not contradict the claim definition found in the intrinsic record. 90 F.3d at 1584 n.6. In *Texas Digital Systems, Inc. v. Telegenix, Inc.*, 308 F.3d 1193 (Fed.Cir.2002), the Federal Circuit elaborated on the importance of dictionaries:

> When a patent is granted, prosecution is concluded, the intrinsic record is fixed, and the public is placed on notice of its allowed claims. Dictionaries, encyclopedias and treatises, publicly available at the time the patent is issued, are objective resources that serve as reliable sources of information on the established meanings that would have been attributed to the terms of the claims by those of skill in the art. Such references are unbiased reflections of common understanding not influenced by expert testimony or events subsequent to the fixing of the intrinsic record by the grant of the patent, not colored by the motives of the parties, and not inspired by litigation. Indeed, these materials may be the most meaningful sources of information to aid judges in better understanding both the technology and the terminology used by those skilled in the art to describe the technology. . . . Thus, categorizing them as "extrinsic evidence" or even a "special form of extrinsic evidence" is misplaced and does not inform the analysis. . . .
>
> If more than one dictionary definition is consistent with the use of the words in the intrinsic record, the claim terms may be construed to encompass all such consistent meanings. The objective and contemporaneous record provided by the intrinsic evidence is the most reliable guide to help the court determine which of the possible meanings of the terms in question was intended by the inventor to particularly point out and distinctly claim the invention.
>
> Moreover, the intrinsic record also must be examined in every case to determine whether the presumption of ordinary and customary meaning is rebutted. [T]he presumption in favor of a dictionary definition will be overcome where the patentee, acting as his or her own lexicographer, has clearly set forth an explicit definition of the term different from its ordinary meaning. Further, the presumption also will be rebutted if the inventor has disavowed or disclaimed scope of coverage, by using words or expressions of manifest exclusion or restriction, representing a clear disavowal of claim scope.
>
> Consulting the written description and prosecution history as a threshold step in the claim construction process, before any effort is made to discern the ordinary and customary meanings attributed to the words themselves, invites a violation of our precedent counseling against importing limitations into the claims. . . . [I]f the meaning of the words themselves would not have been understood to persons of skill in the art to be limited only to the examples or embodiments described in the specification, reading the words in such a confined way would mandate the wrong result and would violate our proscription of not reading limitations from the specification into the claims.

> By examining relevant dictionaries, encyclopedias and treatises to ascertain possible meanings that would have been attributed to the words of the claims by those skilled in the art, and by further utilizing the intrinsic record to select from those possible meanings the one or ones most consistent with the use of the words by the inventor, the full breadth of the limitations intended by the inventor will be more accurately determined and the improper importation of unintended limitations from the written description into the claims will be more easily avoided.

Id. at 1203–04.

4. *Claim Construction and § 112.* A basic canon of claim construction is that "[c]laims should be so construed, if possible, as to sustain their validity." *Carman Indus., Inc. v. Wahl,* 724 F.2d 932, 937 n. 5 (Fed.Cir.1983); *Whittaker Corp. v. UNR Indus., Inc.,* 911 F.2d 709, 712 (Fed.Cir.1990) ("[C]laims are generally construed so as to sustain their validity, if possible"). This axiom is derived from two Supreme Court cases, *Turrill v. Michigan Southern & Northern Indiana Railroad,* 68 U.S. (1 Wall.) 491 (1863), and *Klein v. Russell,* 86 U.S.(19 Wall.) 433, 22 L.Ed. 116 (1873). The *Turrill* Court endorsed the rule that patents "are to receive a liberal construction, and under the fair application of *ut res magis valeat quam pereat,* are, if practicable, to be so interpreted as to uphold and not to destroy the right of the inventor." *Id. at* 510. But the *Klein* Court cabined this rule by stating that liberal construction with an eye towards validity are permissible *"if this can be done consistently with the language which he has employed."* 86 U.S. at 466. Thus, the canon of liberal construction is subservient to § 112's disclosure requirements. As the Federal Circuit has stated, "if the only claim construction that is consistent with the claim's language and the written description renders the claim invalid, then the axiom does not apply and the claim is simply invalid." *Rhine v. Casio, Inc.,* 183 F.3d 1342, 1345 (Fed.Cir.1999).

5. *The Doctrine of Claim Differentiation.* The "claim differentiation" doctrine is a specific application of the general principle that in construing the language of one claim of a patent, due consideration must be given to the language in the remainder of the specification, including the other claims. The doctrine embodies the common sense notion that ordinarily language of one claim should not be so interpreted as to make another claim, such as a claim dependent on the first claim, identical in scope. In short, the doctrine presumes there is a difference in scope among the claims, and that the limitations of one claim should not be read into another claim. *See Karlin Tech., Inc. v. Surgical Dynamics, Inc.,* 177 F.3d 968, 971–72 (Fed.Cir.1999).

6. *Process Claims.* Do process (or method) claims have to be performed in the order in which the steps are presented? The Federal Circuit applies a two-part test. First, the court looks to the claim language to discern if "as a matter of logic or grammar, they must be performed in the order written." If not, the court looks "to the rest of the specification to determine whether *it* 'directly or implicitly requires such a narrow construction.'" *See Altiris, Inc. v. Symantec Corp.,* 318 F.3d 1363, 1369–70 (Fed.Cir.2003) (quoting *Interactive Gift Express, Inc. v. Compuserve Inc.,* 256 F.3d 1323, 1343 (Fed.Cir.2001)).

7. *The Preamble as an Interpretive Tool.* The preamble to the claim, the introductory language that we first saw in Chapter Two, can be used as an interpretive aid or act as limiting language. Sometimes courts may not treat it as limiting. The test for whether the preamble will be limiting seem to be that "if the body of the claim sets out the complete invention, and the preamble is not necessary to give life, meaning and vitality to the claim, then the preamble is of no significance to claim construction because it cannot be said to constitute or explain a claim limitation." *Schumer v. Laboratory Computer Systems, Inc.,* 308 F.3d 1304, 1310 (Fed.Cir.2002). More recently, the Federal Circuit provided this guidance on the issue:

Generally, we have said, the preamble does not limit the claims. Nonetheless, the preamble may be construed as limiting if it recites essential structure or steps, or if it is necessary to give life, meaning, and vitality to the claim. A preamble is not regarded as limiting, however, when the claim body describes a structurally complete invention such that deletion of the preamble phrase does not affect the structure or steps of the claimed invention. If the preamble is reasonably susceptible to being construed to be merely duplicative of the limitations in the body of the claim (and was not clearly added to overcome a [prior art] rejection), we do not construe it to be a separate limitation. We have held that the preamble has no separate limiting effect if, for example, the preamble merely gives a descriptive name to the set of limitations in the body of the claim that completely set forth the invention.

Am. Med. Sys., Inc. v. Biolitec, Inc., 618 F.3d 1354, 1358–59 (Fed.Cir.2010) (citations and quotations omitted).

8. *Disclaimers*. What limiting effect, if any, should the court give language in the written description or prosecution history that appear to *disclaim* an interpretation of words used in the claim? Substantial Federal Circuit case law suggests that because a patentee may be his own lexicographer, any such statements may actually operate to limit the claims. But to what extent is this improperly reading a limitation into the claim? *See, e.g., Renishaw PLC v. Marposs Societa' per Azioni*, 158 F.3d 1243, 1249, n.3 (Fed.Cir.1998) (in a "situation where the patent applicant has elected to be his own lexicographer by providing an explicit definition in the specification for a claim term ... the definition selected by the patent applicant controls.... Likewise, any interpretation that is provided or disavowed in the prosecution history also shapes claim scope."); *see also, Spectrum Int'l, Inc. v. Sterilite Corp.*, 164 F.3d 1372, 1378–79 (Fed.Cir.1998) (holding that explicit statements made by an applicant during prosecution to distinguish a claimed invention over the prior art narrow the scope of the claims, even if the claim could be construed more broadly based on its language viewed in isolation).

9. *Issues of Validity in Limiting Claims*. What limiting effect, if any, should the court give to issue of validity, when interpreting claims; or should such issues only be considered when deciding issues of validity? Should disclosure issues under Section 112 limit the scope of a claim? *See, e.g., Gentry Gallery, Inc. v. Berkline Corp.*, 134 F.3d 1473, 1478 (Fed.Cir.1998) ("the scope of the right to exclude may be limited by a narrow disclosure" under Section 112, paragraph 1); *Athletic Alternatives, Inc. v. Prince Mfg., Inc.*, 73 F.3d 1573, 1581 (Fed.Cir.1996) (holding that were claims are amenable to more than one construction they should when reasonably possible be interpreted under Section 112, Paragraph 2 to preserve their validity); *Modine Mfg. Co. v. U.S. Int'l Trade Com'n*, 75 F.3d 1545, 1557 (Fed.Cir.1996) (same) *Ethicon Endo–Surgery, Inc. v. United States Surgical Corp.*, 93 F.3d 1572, 1581 (Fed.Cir.1996) (same). How about issues of novelty under Section 102 or obviousness under Section 103?

10. *Phillips en Banc, and the Debate Continues*. The debate about how exactly to conduct claim construction continues to thrive. A recent pronouncement on the issue is the court's en banc decision in *Phillips v. AWH Corp.*, 415 F.3d 1303 (Fed. Cir. 2005) (en banc), in which the court essentially decided: (1) to overrule the line of cases stemming from *Texas Digital Systems, Inc. v. Telegenix, Inc.*, 308 F.3d 1193 (Fed.Cir.2002), which had focused on dictionaries in claim construction, and instead urged that focus be on the intrinsic evidence. The court rejected the notions that the patentee is entitled to the full range of dictionary definitions, that dictionary definitions are presumed to be correct, and that the patent's own written description should only be consulted if the dictionary definition(s) is(are) unclear. The court also reaffirmed that claim terms can be defined "by implication," or through use, in the patent, in contrast with a requirement for an express statement of definitional intent, that it is appropriate to consider dictionary definitions, and that claim construction would be reviewed de novo, as discussed in *Markman v. Westview Instruments*, 517 U.S. 370, 116 S.Ct. 1384 (1996), and *Cybor Corp. v. FAS Technologies, Inc.*, 138 F.3d 1448 (Fed.Cir.1998) (en banc). In addition, the court noted that interpreting the claims to uphold their validity was "of limited value."

SIDE BAR

Vitronics—Some Unanswered Questions

The Honorable Paul R. Michel and Lisa A. Schneider*

In *Vitronics Corporation v. Conceptronic, Inc.*, 90 F.3d 1576 (Fed.Cir. 1996), the Federal Circuit emphasized the distinctions among various types of evidence used in construing claims, dividing the types into two broad categories: (1) intrinsic evidence, such as the written description, the drawings, other claims, and the file history; and (2) extrinsic evidence, such as expert testimony, dictionaries, and technical treatises and articles. *Vitronics* reiterated that the preferred materials are those found in the patent documents themselves, *i.e.*, intrinsic. *Id.* at 1582. Relying on *Markman v. Westview Instruments, Inc.*, 52 F.3d 967, 981 (Fed.Cir.1995) (*en banc*), the opinion also reiterated the settled rule that extrinsic evidence may never be relied on to vary or contradict the plain meaning of claim terms, noting that extrinsic evidence therefore may only be relied on where the claim language remains ambiguous after an examination of the intrinsic evidence. *Vitronics* at 1583–84. *Vitronics* reflects a predominant theme of notice and reliance: competitors are entitled to rely on the official, public record to determine claim scope and no materials outside of that record can enlarge that scope. *Id.* The *Vitronics* opinion, however, left many questions unanswered, most of which concern the differences among, and definitions of, the types of evidence.

First, what is the proper categorization of prior art cited in the file history? The *Vitronics* opinion appears internally inconsistent. Initially, *Vitronics* states that "[i]ncluded within the analysis of the file history may be an examination of the prior art cited therein." *Id.* at 1583. Later, however, *Vitronics* states that reliance on prior art, "whether or not cited in the specification or the file history", is improper when the disputed claim terms "can be understood from a careful reading of the public record." *Id.* at 1584. Considering the opinion's theme of notice and reliance, however, perhaps cited prior art fits more logically into the intrinsic evidence category. A list of prior art is in every file history. Thus, an argument can be made that competitors are on notice and should be expected to review such material before reaching any conclusion as to claim scope.

Second, what is the proper categorization of prior art not cited in the file history? Although *Vitronics* classified uncited prior art as extrinsic evidence, such art may not belong in the same category as expert testimony. Indeed, *Vitronics* distinguished prior art (both cited and uncited) from expert testimony, noting that a review of prior art may make it unnecessary to rely on expert testimony and that prior art may be more indicative of what those skilled in the art thought a term meant. *Id.*

Unlike expert testimony, uncited prior art is available to competitors throughout the life of the patent. Moreover, it is fixed, objective (at least with respect to the lawsuit) and not litigation induced. Perhaps then courts should freely rely on such evidence and competitors should be expected to undertake a prior art search before construing a claim. As a corollary, what about other publicly available documentary information not found in the patent? For example, technical treatises and dictionaries, although not official documents, are publicly available and competitors are aware of them. Indeed, the *Vitronics* opinion comments that although technical treatises and dictionaries fall within the category of extrinsic evidence, they are "worthy of special note" and may always be used to understand the underlying technology. *Id.* at 1584. They are to be preferred to testimony, which can be varying, subjective and litigation inspired. It may be then that the law should recognize a third category of evidence somewhere between intrinsic and extrinsic evidence: a category for pertinent art, including technical dictionaries.

Third, which experts may testify? Generally, the only appropriate expert regarding claim construction is one of ordinary skill in the art, as that is the viewpoint from which the claims must be interpreted. However, parties often inappropriately rely on patent attorneys to explain the technical claim language. In addition, inventors are too often permitted to testify about what they subjectively intended the claims to cover *See, e.g., Bell & Howell Document Management Products Co. v. Altek Systems*, 132 F.3d 701, 706 (Fed.Cir.1997) ("The testimony of an inventor and his attorney concerning claim construction is thus entitled to little or no consideration."); *Markman*, 52 F.3d at 983 ("This testimony about construction, however, amounts to no more than legal opinion—it is precisely the process of construction that the court must undertake."). Some might argue that testimony from patent attorneys is appropriate only in very limited circumstances. For instance, a patent attorney may explain the meaning of non-technological claim terms with a special legal meaning, such as "comprising." Yet, most such terms are adequately defined by the case law, which should be preferred to expert testimony. Others might argue that a patent attorney may testify on claim construction where the attorney is knowledgeable about drafting claims in the pertinent art. Rarely, however, will such a patent attorney qualify as one of skill in the art. Therefore, patent attorney testimony should be viewed with the "utmost caution." *Vitronics*, 90 F.3d at 1585. Perhaps the most useful role for attorney testimony concerns the examination procedures and resulting documentation in the Patent and Trademark Office. Again, however, official, documentary sources may provide enough guidance, which should be preferred.

Fourth, when are experts truly necessary? *Vitronics* insists that expert testimony may only be relied on where intrinsic evidence alone is insufficient to construe the claim. Yet the opinion also suggests that it is within the district judge's discretion to admit all of the possible types of evidence. 90 F.3d at 1584, 1585. Thus, the mere admission of expert testimony will rarely, if ever, be reversible error. However, in the majority of cases where expert testimony is admitted, its appropriate role is not as factual evidence on the claim construction issue, but rather merely to educate the judge regarding the technology. Courts should take care to rely on such testimony only as background information that can aid in understanding the intrinsic evidence and not in deciding the dispute itself. Indeed, district courts should be encouraged to exercise restraint in even admitting expert testimony. Where the claims can be construed in light of the intrinsic evidence, it is not enough that a court simply concludes that the proffered expert testimony has some scientific validity. *See Daubert v. Merrell Dow Pharmaceuticals, Inc.*, 509 U.S. 579, 597 (1993). Rather, district courts could choose to admit expert testimony only after considering the intrinsic evidence and concluding expert testimony was truly "necessary," especially given that *Vitronics* stated that where reliance on expert testimony is "unnecessary" it is "legally incorrect." 90 F.3d at 1585. In addition, as *Vitronics* indicates, expert testimony is the least-preferred source of assistance, only to be resorted to after not only the intrinsic evidence but also all other forms of extrinsic evidence have been exhausted without result. In light of this, presumably the number of cases that turn on a so-called "battle of the experts" should diminish.

Fifth, what is the proper role of trial counsel at an oral hearing on claim construction? Although trial counsel may never testify but only argue, they may play a significant role nevertheless. For instance, during argument trial counsel could explain the client's proffered claim construction in light of specified language in the asserted claim, the written description, the other claims, and the file history. This is hardly objectionable and may be quite helpful, so long as the district court ultimately relies on the intrinsic evidence to support its construction, rather than just the attorney's argument.

Finally, where those skilled in the art credibly assert that a disputed claim term meant different things to ordinary artisans in the pertinent art, should the claim be invalidated as indefinite? As explained in *Markman*, "ideally there should be no 'ambiguity' in claim language to one of ordinary skill in the art that would require resort to evidence outside the specification and prosecution history" because 35 U.S.C. § 112 requires both that a patent application contain a written description of the invention " 'in such full, clear, concise, and exact terms as to enable any person skilled in the art to which it pertains, or with which it is most nearly connected, to make and use the same . . .' " and also requires "that the specification 'shall conclude with one or more claims particularly pointing out and distinctly claiming the subject matter which the applicant regards as his invention.' " 52 F.3d at 986. If those of skill in the art honestly disagree as to claim meaning after review of the specification and file history, then perhaps the claim is indefinite. That is not to say an alleged infringer could defeat a claim of infringement or invalidate a patent simply by introducing expert testimony that contradicts the patentee's expert testimony; rather, the court must be convinced that the term was subject to multiple understandings among artisans.

One possible resolution of this issue appears in *Athletic Alternatives, Inc. v. Prince Mfg., Inc.*, where the court suggested that "[w]here there is an equal choice between a broader and a narrower meaning of a claim, and there is an enabling disclosure that indicates that the applicant is at least entitled to a claim having the narrower meaning, we consider the notice function of the claim to be best served by adopting the narrower meaning." 73 F.3d 1573, 1581 (Fed.Cir.1996). However, Judge Nies took the view in dissent that such a solution "eviscerates the requirement of section 112, ¶ 2 for the patentee to particularly point out and distinctly claim his invention while purporting to rely on it." *Id.* at 1583. The majority view may nevertheless better promote the theme of notice and reliance. Moreover, that view employs a procedure that maintains the validity of the patent, a desirable goal.

* Paul R. Michel is a Retired Circuit Judge on the United States Court of Appeals for the Federal Circuit. Lisa A. Schneider is a partner in the Chicago office of the law firm Sidley & Austin, and a former law clerk to Judge Michel. The views expressed herein are solely those of the authors and do not necessarily reflect those of the United States Court of Appeals for the Federal Circuit, Sidley & Austin, or the firm's clients. This *Side Bar* was written specially for Principles of Patent Law.

B. The Doctrine of Equivalents and Prosecution History Estoppel

1. The Doctrine of Equivalents

Although the courts have consistently recognized the importance of the requirement that patentees particularly point out and distinctly claim their invention, they have not always confined patentees to the literal meaning of their claims. The courts have found infringement when an accused infringing device (or process) is an "equivalent" to that claimed in the patent. The rubric under which courts extend the scope of a patentee's right to exclude beyond the literal language of the patent claims has come to be known as the *doctrine of equivalents* (or "DOE").

Judge Learned Hand referred to the doctrine as an "anomaly:"

[A]fter all aids to interpretation have been exhausted, and the scope of the claims has been enlarged as far as the words can be stretched, on proper occasions courts make them cover more than their meaning will bear. If they applied the law with inexorable rigidity, they would never do this, but would remit the patentee to his remedy of re-issue, and that is exactly what they frequently do. Not always, however, for at times they resort to the "doctrine of equivalents" to temper unsparing logic and prevent an infringer from stealing the benefit of the invention. No doubt, this is, strictly speaking, an anomaly; but it is one which courts have frankly faced and accepted almost from the beginning.

Royal Typewriter Co. v. Remington Rand, Inc., 168 F.2d 691, 692 (2d Cir.1948).

The doctrine has received both criticism and praise and has repeatedly divided the Federal Circuit. In part, the doctrine is controversial because of the underlying policy dilemma that is inherent in any patent system that requires a fixed, written description of the invention, but wishes to avoid undue rigidity. On the one hand, there is an interest in providing a clear definition of the scope of the patent right because lack of clarity can impede legitimate investment in technology-based products and services. As Judge Bryson of the Federal Circuit noted:

Patent counselors should be able to advise their clients, with some confidence, whether to proceed with a product or process of a particular kind. The consequences of advice that turns out to be incorrect can be devastating, and the costs of uncertainty—unjustified caution or the devotion of vast resources to the sterile enterprise of litigation—can be similarly destructive.

Litton Systems, Inc. v. Honeywell, Inc., 87 F.3d 1559, 1580 (Fed.Cir.1996) (Bryson, J., concurring in part and dissenting in part).

On the other hand, strict and literal adherence to the written claim in determining the scope of protection can invite unfair subversion of a valuable right, which would substantially diminish the economic value of patents. Therefore, where exactly to strike an optimal balance of claim scope is one of the most, if not the most, important questions in patent law. Both an overly broad or narrow approach can adversely affect technological innovation.

This conundrum was confronted in Europe in the 1970's during the process of harmonizing the patent laws of the European nations. Traditionally, the United Kingdom focused heavily on claim language while Germany emphasized the nature of the underlying invention. Reconciling these views was a considerable problem in the drafting of the European Patent Convention. Article 69 of the convention provides that the "extent of the protection conferred by a European patent . . . shall be determined by the terms of the claims" and that "nevertheless the description and drawings shall be used to interpret the claims." The parties adopted a "Protocol on the Interpretation of Article 69 of the Convention," which reads:

Article 69 should not be interpreted in the sense that the extent of the protection conferred by a European patent is to be understood as that defined by the strict literal meaning of the wording used in the claim, the description and drawings being employed only for the purpose of resolving an ambiguity found in the claims. Neither should it be interpreted in the sense that the claims serve only as a guideline and that the actual protection conferred may extend to what from a consideration of the description and drawings by a person skilled in the art, the patentee has contemplated. On the contrary, it is to be interpreted as defining a position between these extremes which combines a fair protection for the patentee with a reasonable degree of certainty for third parties.

Article 69 and its Protocol address claim interpretation rather than the doctrine of equivalents. But the Protocol's goal—to combine "a fair protection for the patentee with a reasonable degree of certainty for third parties"—is what historically, the better-reasoned court decisions in the United States have sought to achieve. A House of Lords case that influenced Article 69 was *Catnic v. Hill and Smith*, [1982] RPC 183 (HL). In his opinion, Lord Diplock stressed that a patent's specification should be given a purposive, rather than a literal interpretation, which meant that a patent should be construed through the eyes of a person skilled in the art.

In the U.S., the conundrum is confronted through the evolution of several legal limits on the DOE. Chief among them is the doctrine called *prosecution history estoppel*. As discussed in Chapter Two ("Obtaining the Patent Grant"), the process by which an inventor applies for and obtains a patent is called *patent prosecution*. The record of the proceedings that led to the issuance of the patent is called the *prosecution history*. The prosecution history serves a dual function in infringement analyses. First, it may act as an interpretive tool for construing patent claims. Second, certain aspects of the prosecution history (e.g., claims narrowed by amendment) may operate to limit the scope of equivalents that may be asserted in later litigation. This limit on the scope of equivalents is called *prosecution history estoppel* because the prosecution history is used to estop the patentee from expanding the scope of his claims.

A review of that history of the DOE may help elucidate the issues surrounding the doctrine today. The exact date of the DOE is difficult to discern, but it clearly has its roots in the early 19th century. *See, e.g., Odiorne v. Winkley*, 18 F.Cas. 581, 582 (C.C.D. Mass. 1814) (Story, J.) ("Mere colorable differences, or slight improvements, cannot shake, the right of the original inventor"); *Barrett v. Hall*, 2 F.Cas. 914, 921 (C.C.D. Mass. 1818) (Story, J.) ("Slight or colorable differences will not protect the defendants in their infringement, or defeat the right of the patentee"). The first opinion to use the phrase, "doctrine of equivalents," was *McCormick v. Talcott*, 61 U.S. 402, 405 (1857). And while a number of Supreme Court decisions incorporated the concept of infringement by equivalency, *see e.g. Continental Paper Bag Co. v. Eastern Paper Bag Co.*, 210 U.S. 405 (1908), two decisions, handed down almost a century apart, have been particularly influential in shaping the doctrine: *Winans v. Denmead*, 56 U.S. (15 How.) 330 (1853), the first major pronouncement by the Court, and *Graver Tank v. Linde Air Prods. Co.*, 339 U.S. 605 (1950), the leading modern decision on the doctrine until *Warner–Jenkinson Company v. Hilton Davis Chemical, Inc.* was decided by in the Supreme Court in 1995.

The Winans' patent was directed to a new type of railroad car to carry coal. Prior to Winans' invention, cars were constructed with a rectangular floor plan. Winans perceived that the shape of the car resulted in an uneven dispersion of the force of the coal, thus requiring substantial reinforcement of the car. He designed a conically-shaped car which evenly distributed the pressure of the coal and facilitated its discharge through an aperture in the bottom. This shape enabled the patentee to build cars with a much greater load weight compared to the weight of the car. In his patent, Winans set forth the following claim:

> What I claim as my invention, and desire to secure by letters patent, is making the body of a car for the transportation of coal, etc., in *the form of a frustum of a cone*, substantially as herein described, whereby the force exerted by the weight of the load presses equally in all directions, and does not tend to change the form thereof, so that every part resists its equal proportion, and by which, also, the lower part is so reduced as to pass down within the truck frame and between the axles, to lower the center of gravity of the load without diminishing the capacity of the car as described.

Denmead, the alleged infringer and the defendant in the suit, constructed railroad cars that were "octagonal and pyramidal" in shape, rather than "cylindrical and conical" as provided in Winans' patent. In the infringement suit, all the evidence indicated that the defendant's car achieved substantially all the advantages of the Winans' car. It also indicated that the plaintiff and defendant were competitors and that the defendant's design was directly inspired by the plaintiff's product. Nevertheless, the trial judge instructed the jury that there could be no infringement since the defendant's car was rectilinear and the patent claim required a conical shape.

A sharply-divided Supreme Court reversed. Justice Curtis, writing for the majority, relied on a presumption that the patentee claimed all that he was entitled to claim. He noted that it would be unreasonable to apply the term "cone" literally because "neither the patentee nor any other constructor has made, or will make, a car exactly circular." The majority focused on the principle underlying Winans' patent, and noted that reasonably interpreted, the claim required only that the car "be so near to a true circle as substantially to embody the patentee's mode of operation, and thereby attain the same kind of result as was reached by his invention." 56 U.S. (15 How.) at 343–44.

Four justices dissented in an opinion by Justice Campbell, who emphasized that the patentee confined his claim to the conical form and may have been "unwilling to expose the validity of his patent, by the assertion of a right to any other." The Patent Act required patentees to "specify and point out" what they claim as an invention. Requiring less than precision and particularity in claims would be "mischievous" and "productive of oppressive and costly litigation, of exorbitant and unjust pretensions and vexatious demands." *Id.* at 347.

Nearly a century later, the Court grappled with many of the same arguments.

Graver Tank v. Linde Air Prods. Co.

339 U.S. 605 (1950).

■ MR. JUSTICE JACKSON delivered the opinion of the Court.

[Linde Air Products Co. owned a patent for certain electric welding compositions known as fluxes, which facilitated the fusing of metals. Two sets of claims were involved. One set of claims described a major element as any "silicate." The other set of claims, which were narrower, described the element as any "alkaline earth metal silicate." The Supreme Court held the first set of claims invalid for undue breadth. The narrower claims were held not invalid and the question became whether these claims were infringed.]

* * *

At the outset it should be noted that the single issue before us is whether the trial court's holding that the four flux claims have been infringed will be sustained. Any issue as to the validity of these claims was unanimously determined by the previous decision in this Court and attack on their validity cannot be renewed now by reason of limitation on grant of rehearing. The disclosure, the claims, and the prior art have been adequately described in our former opinion and in the opinions of the courts below.

In determining whether an accused device or composition infringes a valid patent, resort must be had in the first instance to the words of the claim. If accused matter falls clearly within the claim, infringement is made out and that is the end of it.

But courts have also recognized that to permit imitation of a patented invention which does not copy every literal detail would be to convert the protection of the patent grant into a hollow and useless thing. Such a limitation would leave room for—indeed encourage—the unscrupulous copyist to make unimportant and insubstantial changes and substitutions in the patent which, though adding nothing, would be enough to take the copied matter outside the claim, and hence outside the reach of law. One who seeks to pirate an invention, like one who seeks to pirate a copyrighted book or play, may be expected to introduce minor variations to conceal and shelter the piracy. Outright and forthright duplication is a dull and very rare type of infringement. To prohibit no other would place the inventor at the mercy of verbalism and would be subordinating substance to form. It would deprive him of the benefit of his invention and would foster concealment rather than disclosure of inventions, which is one of the primary purposes of the patent system.

The doctrine of equivalents evolved in response to this experience. The essence of the doctrine is that one may not practice a fraud on a patent. Originating almost a century ago in the case of *Winans v. Denmead*, 15 How. 330, 14 L.Ed. 717, it has been consistently applied by this Court and the lower federal courts, and continues today ready and available for utilization when the proper circumstances for its application arise. "To temper unsparing logic and prevent an infringer from stealing the benefit of the invention" a patentee may invoke this doctrine to proceed against the producer of a device "if it performs substantially the same function in substantially the same way to obtain the same result." *Sanitary Refrigerator Co. v. Winters*, 280 U.S. 30, 42, 50 S.Ct. 9, 13, 74 L.Ed. 147. The theory on which it is founded is that "if two devices do the same work in substantially the same way, and accomplish substantially the same result, they are the same, even though they differ in name, form or shape." *Union Paper–Bag Machine Co. v. Murphy*, 97 U.S. 120, 125, 24 L.Ed. 935. The doctrine operates not only in favor of the patentee of a pioneer or primary invention, but also for the patentee of a secondary invention consisting of a combination of old ingredients which produce new and useful results, *Imhaeuser v. Buerk*, 101 U.S. 647, 655, 25 L.Ed. 945, although the area of equivalence may vary under the circumstances. *See Continental Paper Bag Co. v. Eastern Paper Bag Co.*, 210 U.S. 405, 414–415, 28 S.Ct. 748, 749, 52 L.Ed. 1122, and cases cited; *Seymour v. Osborne*, 11 Wall. 516, 556, 20 L.Ed. 33; *Gould v. Rees*, 15 Wall. 187, 192, 21 L.Ed. 39. The wholesome realism of this doctrine is not always applied in favor of a patentee but is sometimes used against him. Thus, where a device is so far changed in principle from a patented article that it performs the same or a similar function in a substantially different way, but nevertheless falls within the literal words of the claim, the doctrine of equivalents may be used to restrict the claim and defeat the patentee's action for infringement. *Westinghouse v. Boyden Power–Brake Co.*, 170 U.S. 537, 568, 18 S.Ct. 707, 722, 42 L.Ed. 1136. In its early development, the doctrine was usually applied in cases involving devices where there was equivalence in mechanical components. Subsequently, however, the same principles were also applied to compositions, where there was equivalence between chemical ingredients. Today the doctrine is applied to mechanical or chemical equivalents in compositions or devices.

What constitutes equivalency must be determined against the context of the patent, the prior art, and the particular circumstances of the case. Equivalence, in the patent law, is not the prisoner of a formula and is not an absolute to be considered in a vacuum. It does not require complete identity for every purpose and in every respect. In determining equivalents, things equal to the same thing may not be equal to each other and, by the same token, things for most purposes different may sometimes be equivalents. Consideration must be given to the purpose for which an ingredient is used in a patent, the qualities it has when combined with the other ingredients, and the function which it is intended to perform. An important factor is whether persons reasonably skilled in the art would have known of the interchangeability of an ingredient not contained in the patent with one that was.

A finding of equivalence is a determination of fact. Proof can be made in any form: through testimony of experts or others versed in the technology; by documents, including texts and treatises; and, of course, by the disclosures of the prior art. Like any other issue of fact, final determination requires a balancing of credibility, persuasiveness and weight of evidence. It is to be decided by the trial court and that court's decision, under general principles of appellate review, should not be disturbed unless clearly erroneous. Particularly is this so in a field where so much depends upon familiarity with specific scientific problems and principles not usually contained in the general storehouse of knowledge and experience.

In the case before us, we have two electric welding compositions or fluxes: the patented composition, Unionmelt Grade 20, and the accused composition, Lincolnweld 660. The patent under which Unionmelt is made claims essentially a combination of alkaline earth metal silicate and calcium fluoride; Unionmelt actually contains, however, silicates of calcium and magnesium, two alkaline earth metal silicates. Lincolnweld's composition is similar to Unionmelt's, except that it substitutes silicates of calcium and manganese—the latter not an alkaline earth metal—for silicates of calcium and magnesium. In all other respects, the two compositions are alike. The mechanical methods in which these compositions are employed are similar. They are identical in operation and produce the same kind and quality of weld.

The question which thus emerges is whether the substitution of the manganese which is not an alkaline earth metal for the magnesium which is, under the circumstances of this case, and in view of the technology and the prior art, is a change of such substance as to make the doctrine of equivalents inapplicable; or conversely, whether under the circumstances the change was so insubstantial that the trial court's invocation of the doctrine of equivalents was justified.

Without attempting to be all-inclusive, we note the following evidence in the record: Chemists familiar with the two fluxes testified that manganese and magnesium were similar in many of their reactions (R. 287, 669). There is testimony by a metallurgist that alkaline earth metals are often found in manganese ores in their natural state and that they serve the same purpose in the fluxes (R. 831—832); and a chemist testified that "in the sense of the patent" manganese could be included as an alkaline earth metal (R. 297). Much of this testimony was corroborated by reference to recognized texts on inorganic chemistry (R. 332). Particularly important, in addition, were the disclosures of the prior art, also contained in the record. The Miller patent, No. 1,754,566, which preceded the patent in suit, taught the use of manganese silicate in welding fluxes (R. 969, 971). Manganese was similarly disclosed in the Armor patent, No. 1,467,825, which also described a welding composition (R. 1346). And the record contains no evidence of any kind to show that Lincolnweld was developed as the result of independent research or experiments.

It is not for this Court to even essay an independent evaluation of this evidence. This is the function of the trial court. And, as we have heretofore observed, "To no type of case is this … more appropriately applicable than to the one before us, where the evidence is largely the testimony of experts as to which a trial court may be enlightened by scientific demonstrations. This trial occupied some three weeks, during which, as the record shows, the trial judge visited laboratories with counsel and experts to observe actual demonstrations of welding as taught by the patent and of the welding accused of infringing it, and of various stages of the prior art. He viewed motion pictures of various welding operations and tests and heard many experts and other witnesses."

The trial judge found on the evidence before him that the Lincolnweld flux and the composition of the patent in suit are substantially identical in operation and in result. He found also that Lincolnweld is in all respects equivalent to Unionmelt for welding purposes. And he concluded that "for all practical purposes, manganese silicate can be efficiently and effectively substituted for calcium and magnesium silicates as the major constituent of the welding composition." These conclusions are adequately supported by the record; certainly they are not clearly erroneous.

It is difficult to conceive of a case more appropriate for application of the doctrine of equivalents. The disclosures of the prior art made clear that manganese silicate was a useful ingredient in welding compositions. Specialists familiar with the problems of welding compositions understood that manganese was equivalent to and could be substituted for magnesium in the composition of the patented flux and their observations were confirmed by the literature of chemistry. Without some explanation or indication that Lincolnweld was developed by independent research, the trial court could properly infer that the accused flux is the result of imitation rather than experimentation or invention. Though infringement was not literal, the changes which avoid literal infringement are colorable only. We conclude that the trial court's judgment of infringement respecting the four flux claims was proper, and we adhere to our prior decision on this aspect of the case.

Dissenting Opinion

■ Mr. Justice Black, with whom Mr. Justice Douglas concurs, dissenting.

I heartily agree with the Court that "fraud" is bad, "piracy" is evil, and "stealing" is reprehensible. But in this case, where petitioners are not charged with any such malevolence, these lofty principles do not justify the Court's sterilization of Acts of Congress and prior decisions, none of which are even mentioned in today's opinion.

R.S. § 4888, as amended, 35 U.S.C. § 33, 35 U.S.C.A. § 33, provides that an applicant "shall particularly point out and distinctly claim the part, improvement, or combination which he claims as his invention or discovery." We have held in this very case that this statute precludes invoking the specifications to alter a claim free from ambiguous language, since "it is the claim which measures the grant to the patentee." *Graver Mfg. Co. v. Linde Co.*, 336 U.S. 271, 277, 69 S.Ct. 535, 538, 93 L.Ed. 672. What is not specifically claimed is dedicated to the public. *See, e.g., Miller v. Brass Co.*, 104 U.S. 350, 352, 26 L.Ed. 783. For the function of claims under R.S. § 4888, as we have frequently reiterated, is to exclude from the patent monopoly field all that is not specifically claimed, whatever may appear in the specifications. *See, e.g., Marconi Wireless Co. v. United States*, 320 U.S. 1, 23, 63 S.Ct. 1393, 1403, 87 L.Ed. 1731, and cases there cited. Today the Court tacitly rejects those cases. It departs from the underlying principle which, as the Court pointed out in *White v. Dunbar*, 119 U.S. 47, 51, 7 S.Ct. 72, 74, 30 L.Ed. 303, forbids treating a patent claim "like a nose of wax, which may be turned and twisted in any direction, by merely referring to the specification, so as to make it include something more than, or something different from, what its words express.... The claim is a statutory requirement, prescribed for the very purpose of making the patentee define precisely what his invention is; and it is unjust to the public, as well as an evasion of the law, to construe it in a manner different from the plain import of its terms." Giving this patentee the benefit of a grant that it did not precisely claim is no less "unjust to the public" and no less an evasion of R.S. § 4888 merely because done in the name of the "doctrine of equivalents."

In seeking to justify its emasculation of R.S. § 4888 by parading potential hardships which literal enforcement might conceivably impose on patentees who had for some reason failed to claim complete protection for their discoveries, the Court fails even to mention the program for alleviation of such hardships which Congress itself has provided. 35 U.S.C. § 64, 35 U.S.C.A. § 64, authorizes reissue of patents where a patent is "wholly or partly inoperative" due to certain errors arising from "inadvertence, accident, or mistake" of the patentee. And while the section does not expressly permit a patentee to expand his claim, this Court has reluctantly interpreted it to justify doing so. *Miller v. Brass Co.*, 104 U.S. 350, 353–354, 26 L.Ed. 783. That interpretation, however, was accompanied by a warning that "Reissues for the enlargement of claims should be the exception and not the rule." 104 U.S. at page 355, 26 L.Ed. 783. And Congress was careful to hedge the privilege of reissue by exacting conditions. It also entrusted the Patent Office, not the courts, with initial authority to determine whether expansion of a claim was justified,[3] and barred suits for retroactive in-

---

3. This provision was inserted in the law for the purpose of relieving the courts from the duty of ascertaining the exact invention of the patentee by inference and conjecture, derived

fringement based on such expansion. Like the Court's opinion, this congressional plan adequately protects patentees from "fraud," "piracy," and "stealing." Unlike the Court's opinion, it also protects business men from retroactive infringement suits and judicial expansion of a monopoly sphere beyond that which a patent expressly authorizes. The plan is just, fair, and reasonable. In effect it is nullified by this decision undercutting what the Court has heretofore recognized as wise safeguards. *See Milcor Steel Co. v. Fuller Co.*, 316 U.S. 143, 148, 62 S.Ct. 969, 972, 86 L.Ed. 1332. One need not be a prophet to suggest that today's rhapsody on the virtue of the "doctrine of equivalents" will, in direct contravention of the Miller case *supra*, make enlargement of patent claims the "rule" rather than the "exception."

■ Mr. Justice Douglas, dissenting [omitted].

NOTES

1. *Some Views On Graver Tank. Graver Tank* became a key judicial precedent, perhaps because the Supreme Court did not address the subject again for almost 50 years. The Court focuses primarily on concerns about fairness in patent protection, almost completely ignoring concerns about certainty in determining the scope of that protection. One can argue that the emphasis on fairness is supported by the existence in the patent of broader claims (*i.e.*, any "silicate") that clearly did cover the defendant's flux. Though held invalid for undue breadth, these broader claims provided a warning to the defendant as to the general nature of the claimed invention. Thus, one can argue that the court did not expand the narrow set of claims into "dedicated" or completely unclaimed territory. In addition, the infringer's product used a species actually disclosed in the patentee's specification, a species that was literally covered by invalidated generic claims.

But as Justice Black noted in his dissent, "What is not specifically claimed is dedicated to the public." Isn't it a convincing argument that while the infringer's product was once claimed, it was invalidated, and therefore, "not specifically claimed?" In fact, the Federal Circuit has since adopted such a rule—what has been characterized as the "public dedication rule." *See Johnson & Johnston Associates Inc. v. R.E. Service Co., Inc.*, 285 F.3d 1046, 1054 (Fed.Cir.2002) ("[W]hen a patent drafter discloses but declines to claim a subject matter, . . . this action dedicates that unclaimed subject matter to the public"). But *Johnson & Johnston* distinguished *Graver* because in *Graver* "the patentee had initially claimed the 'equivalent' subject matter, even if the Court eventually held the relevant claims too broad." Therefore, the court in *Johnson & Johnston* stated that "the patentee [in *Graver*] had not dedicated unclaimed subject matter to the public." *Id.* at 1053.

Another question is, couldn't the patentee have specifically claimed the alternative embodiment or species of silicate of *manganese*? Perhaps not. At the time of *Graver Tank*, PTO policy restricted an inventor to no more than three species

---

from a laborious examination of previous inventions, and a comparison thereof with that claimed by him. This duty is now cast upon the Patent Office. There his claim is, or is supposed to be, examined, scrutinized, limited, and made to conform to what he is entitled to. If the office refuses to allow him all that he asks, he has an appeal. But the courts have no right to enlarge a patent beyond the scope of its claim as allowed by the Patent Office, or the appellate tribunal to which contested applications are referred. When the terms of a claim in a patent are clear and distinct (as they always should be), the patentee, in a suit brought upon the patent, is bound by it. *Merrill v. Yeomans*, 94 U.S. 568, 24 L.Ed. 235. *Keystone Bridge Co. v. Phoenix Iron Co.*, 95 U.S. 274, 278, 24 L.Ed. 344.

claims if a claim to a genus were allowed—a fact that may have strengthened the patentee's equitable position. Again, however, silicate of manganese was not part of the claim.

Yet another interesting point is that the prior art taught the use of manganese silicate in welding fluxes. Thus, did the Court's interpretation of the claims impermissibly read on the prior art? Again, probably not. The patentee most likely *combined* manganese with other elements in a manner not disclosed in the prior art.

Perhaps Justice Black's strongest argument is the availability of reissue. This argument was stronger after the 1952 Act was passed because, as Justice Black noted, the patent statute prior to 1952 did not permit one to expand claims through reissue. But the 1952 Act expressly provided for reissues to broaden claims within two years from issuance. In this regard, see Paul M. Janicke, *Heat of Passion: What Really Happened in Graver Tank*, 24 AIPLA Q.J. 1 (1997) (suggesting reissue-like procedures for use in enlarging the scope of claims under certain circumstances as an alternative to the doctrine of equivalents). In this article, Professor Janicke also provides an excellent history of *Graver Tank*. For a detailed discussion of economic theory of DOE from a judicial perspective, see Judge Newman's concurring opinion in *Hilton Davis Chemical Co. v. Warner–Jenkinson Company*, 62 F.3d 1512, 1529–36 (Fed.Cir.1995) (Newman, J., concurring).

2. *Federal Circuit Decisions After Graver–Tank.* The Federal Circuit first addressed the important issues of the doctrine of equivalents and prosecution history estoppel in the 1983 decision of *Hughes Aircraft Co. v. United States*, 717 F.2d 1351 (Fed.Cir.1983). Begun in 1973, the *Hughes* litigation over a patent claiming an orbiting satellite has stretched on for decades. In a panel decision dealing with the case's damage phase, the judges discussed whether the *Hughes* interpretation of the doctrine of equivalents had been undermined by later Federal Circuit decisions. *See Hughes Aircraft Co. v. United States*, 86 F.3d 1566 (Fed.Cir.1996). After *Warner–Jenkinson*, the Supreme Court remanded *Hughes* for further consideration. *See* 140 F.3d 1470 (Fed.Cir.1998). Soon thereafter it became clear that judges on the court held differing views about how to resolve difficult questions concerning the doctrine of equivalents. Despite attempts to resolve the issue *en banc* in *SRI International v. Matsushita Electric Corp. of America*, 775 F.2d 1107 (Fed.Cir.1985) (of the 11 participating judges, five joined one opinion, five joined an opposing opinion, the eleventh took a middle position in a concurring opinion) and in *Pennwalt Corp. v. Durand–Wayland, Inc.*, 833 F.2d 931 (Fed.Cir.1987), the cases merely served to produce multiple dissenting and concurring opinions. It was evident that the court had not reached a comfortable consensus.

Federal Circuit panel decisions after 1987 developed two schools of thought about the doctrine, reflecting the majority and dissenting views in *Graver Tank*. One school leaned toward fair protection; the other toward clear notice.

The first school held that (1) the doctrine was a "second prong" for determining infringement, if literal infringement is absent, potentially available in every case unless restricted by prosecution history estoppel or the prior art; (2) the test for equivalency was whether the accused product or process performed substantially the same function, way and result as the claimed invention (the "triple identity" test); and (3) a genuine dispute between a patentee and accused infringer over whether the accused product or process met the triple identity test was resolvable as a question of fact by a jury in infringement if one party properly demanded trial by jury. *See, e.g., Miles Laboratories, Inc. v. Shandon Inc.*, 997 F.2d 870 (Fed.Cir. 1993); *Read Corp. v. Portec, Inc.*, 970 F.2d 816 (Fed.Cir.1992); *Sun Studs, Inc. v. ATA Equipment Leasing, Inc.*, 872 F.2d 978 (Fed.Cir.1989).

The second school asserted that (1) the doctrine applied only in "exceptional cases"; (2) the triple identity test was not the exclusive test but rather was supplemented by other "equitable" factors, including whether the accused infringer knew of and copied the patented invention, which favors finding equivalency, or developed the accused product or process independently, which favors finding no equivalency; and (3) the judge must determine whether the equitable "threshold" for applying the doctrine and extending the patent's claims beyond their literal scope has been established, either before or after submitting any factual issues on equivalency to the jury. *See International Visual Corp. v. Crown Metal Manufacturing Co., Inc.*, 991 F.2d 768 (Fed.Cir.1993) (Lourie concurring); *Charles Greiner & Co., Inc. v. Mari–Med Mfg., Inc.*, 962 F.2d 1031 (Fed.Cir.1992); *London v. Carson Pirie Scott & Co.*, 946 F.2d 1534 (Fed.Cir.1991). *Cf. Perkin–Elmer Corp. v. Westinghouse Electric Corp.*, 822 F.2d 1528 (Fed.Cir.1987); *Great Northern Corp. v. Davis Core & Pad Co., Inc.*, 782 F.2d 159 (Fed.Cir.1986).

The triple identity test itself came under scrutiny. The test's abstract character diminished its value as an objective determinant of equivalency. In litigation, patentees characterized function, way, and result broadly to show similarity between the patented invention and the accused product; accused infringers characterized them narrowly to show substantial differences. In addition, some Judges, such as Judge Alan D. Lourie of the Federal Circuit, have criticized the triple identity test, also referred to as "FWR", as inadequate, especially when directed to chemical compounds, because it focuses on function even though the claimed invention is a structure: very different structures can perform the same function in the same way to achieve the same result. *See Genentech, Inc. v. Wellcome Foundation Ltd.*, 29 F.3d 1555 (Fed.Cir.1994).

Warner–Jenkinson Company, Inc. v. Hilton Davis Chemical Co.

520 U.S. 17 (1997).

■ Justice Thomas delivered the opinion of the Court.

Nearly 50 years ago, this Court in *Graver Tank & Mfg. Co. v. Linde Air Products Co.*, 339 U.S. 605, 70 S.Ct. 854, 94 L.Ed. 1097 (1950), set out the modern contours of what is known in patent law as the "doctrine of equivalents." Under this doctrine, a product or process that does not literally infringe upon the express terms of a patent claim may nonetheless be found to infringe if there is "equivalence" between the elements of the accused product or process and the claimed elements of the patented invention.... Petitioner, which was found to have infringed upon respondent's patent under the doctrine of equivalents, invites us to speak the death of that doctrine. We decline that invitation. The significant disagreement within the Court of Appeals for the Federal Circuit concerning the application of *Graver Tank* suggests, however, that the doctrine is not free from confusion. We therefore will endeavor to clarify the proper scope of the doctrine.

I

The essential facts of this case are few. Petitioner Warner–Jenkinson Co. and respondent Hilton Davis Chemical Co. manufacture dyes. Impurities in those dyes must be removed. Hilton Davis holds United States Patent No. 4,560,746 ('746 patent), which discloses an improved purification process involving "ultrafiltration." The '746 process filters impure dye through a porous membrane at certain pressures and pH levels,[1] resulting in a high purity dye product.

The '746 patent issued in 1985. As relevant to this case, the patent claims as its invention an improvement in the ultrafiltration process as follows:

> In a process for the purification of a dye ... the improvement which comprises: subjecting an aqueous solution ... to ultrafiltration through a membrane having a nominal pore diameter of 5–15 Angstroms under a hydrostatic pressure of approximately 200 to 400 p.s.i.g., at a pH from approximately 6.0 to 9.0, to thereby cause separation of said impurities from said dye.... App. 36–37 (emphasis added).

The inventors added the phrase "at a pH from approximately 6.0 to 9.0" during patent prosecution. At a minimum, this phrase was added to distinguish a previous patent (the "Booth" patent) that disclosed an ultrafiltration process operating at a pH above 9.0. The parties disagree as to why the low-end pH limit of 6.0 was included as part of the claim.[2]

In 1986, Warner–Jenkinson developed an ultrafiltration process that operated with membrane pore diameters assumed to be 5–15 Angstroms, at pressures of 200 to nearly 500 p.s.i.g., and at a pH of 5.0. Warner–Jenkinson did not learn of the '746 patent until after it had begun commercial use of its ultrafiltration process. Hilton Davis eventually learned of Warner–Jenkinson's use of ultrafiltration and, in 1991, sued Warner–Jenkinson for patent infringement.

As trial approached, Hilton Davis conceded that there was no literal infringement, and relied solely on the doctrine of equivalents. Over Warner–Jenkinson's objection that the doctrine of equivalents was an equitable doctrine to be applied by the court, the issue of equivalence was included among those sent to the jury. The jury found that the '746 patent was not invalid and that Warner–Jenkinson infringed upon the patent under the doctrine of equivalents. The jury also found, however, that Warner–Jenkinson had not intentionally infringed, and therefore awarded only 20% of the damages sought by Hilton Davis. The District Court denied Warner–Jenkinson's post-trial motions, and entered a permanent injunction prohibiting Warner–Jenkinson from practicing ultrafiltration below 500 p.s.i.g.

---

1. The pH, or power (exponent) of Hydrogen, of a solution is a measure of its acidity or alkalinity. A pH of 7.0 is neutral; a pH below 7.0 is acidic; and a pH above 7.0 is alkaline. Although measurement of pH is on a logarithmic scale, with each whole number difference representing a ten-fold difference in acidity, the practical significance of any such difference will often depend on the context. Pure water, for example, has a neutral pH of 7.0, whereas carbonated water has an acidic pH of 3.0, and concentrated hydrochloric acid has a pH approaching 0.0. On the other end of the scale, milk of magnesia has a pH of 10.0, whereas household ammonia has a pH of 11.9. 21 Encyclopedia Americana 844 (Int'l ed.1990).

2. Petitioner contends that the lower limit was added because below a pH of 6.0 the patented process created "foaming" problems in the plant and because the process was not shown to work below that pH level. Brief for Petitioner 4, n. 5, 37, n. 28. Respondent counters that the process was successfully tested to pH levels as low as 2.2 with no effect on the process because of foaming, but offers no particular explanation as to why the lower level of 6.0 pH was selected. Brief for Respondent 34, n. 34.

and below 9.01 pH. A fractured *en banc* Court of Appeals for the Federal Circuit affirmed. 62 F.3d 1512 (C.A.Fed.1995).

The majority below held that the doctrine of equivalents continues to exist and that its touchstone is whether substantial differences exist between the accused process and the patented process. *Id.*, at 1521–1522. The court also held that the question of equivalence is for the jury to decide and that the jury in this case had substantial evidence from which it could conclude that the Warner–Jenkinson process was not substantially different from the ultrafiltration process disclosed in the '746 patent. *Id.*, at 1525.

There were three separate dissents, commanding a total of 5 of 12 judges. Four of the five dissenting judges viewed the doctrine of equivalents as allowing an improper expansion of claim scope, contrary to this Court's numerous holdings that it is the claim that defines the invention and gives notice to the public of the limits of the patent monopoly. *Id.*, at 1537–1538 (Plager, J., dissenting). The fifth dissenter, the late Judge Nies, was able to reconcile the prohibition against enlarging the scope of claims and the doctrine of equivalents by applying the doctrine to each element of a claim, rather than to the accused product or process "overall." *Id.*, at 1574 (Nies, J., dissenting). As she explained it, "[t]he 'scope' is not enlarged if courts do not go beyond the substitution of equivalent elements." *Ibid.* All of the dissenters, however, would have found that a much narrowed doctrine of equivalents may be applied in whole or in part by the court. *Id.*, at 1540–1542 (Plager, J., dissenting); *id.*, at 1579 (Nies, J., dissenting).

We granted *certiorari*, 516 U.S. ___, 116 S.Ct. 1014, 134 L.Ed.2d 95 (1996), and now reverse and remand.

II

* * *

A

Petitioner's primary argument in this Court is that the doctrine of equivalents, as set out in *Graver Tank* in 1950, did not survive the 1952 revision of the Patent Act, 35 U.S.C. § 100 *et seq.*, because it is inconsistent with several aspects of that Act. In particular, petitioner argues: (1) the doctrine of equivalents is inconsistent with the statutory requirement that a patentee specifically "claim" the invention covered by a patent, 35 U.S.C. § 112; (2) the doctrine circumvents the patent reissue process—designed to correct mistakes in drafting or the like—and avoids the express limitations on that process, 35 U.S.C. §§ 251; (3) the doctrine is inconsistent with the primacy of the Patent and Trademark Office (PTO) in setting the scope of a patent through the patent prosecution process; and (4) the doctrine was implicitly rejected as a general matter by Congress' specific and limited inclusion of the doctrine in one section regarding "means" claiming, 35 U.S.C. § 112, ¶ 6. All but one of these arguments were made in *Graver Tank* in the context of the 1870 Patent Act, and failed to command a majority.[3]

---

3. *Graver Tank* was decided over a vigorous dissent. In that dissent, Justice Black raised the first three of petitioner's four arguments against the doctrine of equivalents. *See* 339 U.S.,

The 1952 Patent Act is not materially different from the 1870 Act with regard to claiming, reissue, and the role of the PTO. Compare, *e.g.*, 35 U.S.C. § 112 ("The specification shall conclude with one or more claims particularly pointing out and distinctly claiming the subject matter which the applicant regards as his invention") with The Consolidated Patent Act of 1870, ch. 230, § 26, 16 Stat. 198, 201 (the applicant "shall particularly point out and distinctly claim the part, improvement, or combination which he claims as his invention or discovery"). Such minor differences as exist between those provisions in the 1870 and the 1952 Acts have no bearing on the result reached in *Graver Tank*, and thus provide no basis for our overruling it. In the context of infringement, we have already held that pre–1952 precedent survived the passage of the 1952 Act. *See Aro Mfg. Co. v. Convertible Top Replacement Co.*, 365 U.S. 336, 342, 81 S.Ct. 599, 602– 603, 5 L.Ed.2d 592 (1961) (new section defining infringement "left intact the entire body of case law on direct infringement"). We see no reason to reach a different result here.[4]

Petitioner's fourth argument for an implied congressional negation of the doctrine of equivalents turns on the reference to "equivalents" in the "means" claiming provision of the 1952 Act.... Because § 112, ¶ 6 was enacted as a targeted cure to a specific problem, and because the reference in that provision to "equivalents" appears to be no more than a prophylactic against potential side effects of that cure, such limited congressional action should not be overread for negative implications. Congress in 1952 could easily have responded to *Graver Tank* as it did to the *Halliburton* decision. But it did not. Absent something more compelling than the dubious negative inference offered by petitioner, the lengthy history of the doctrine of equivalents strongly supports adherence to our refusal in *Graver Tank* to find that the Patent Act conflicts with that doctrine. Congress can legislate the doctrine of equivalents out of existence any time it chooses. The various policy arguments now made by both sides are thus best addressed to Congress, not this Court.

---

at 613–614, 70 S.Ct., at 858–859 (doctrine inconsistent with statutory requirement to "distinctly claim" the invention); *id.*, at 614–615, 70 S.Ct., at 859–860 (patent reissue process available to correct mistakes); *id.*, at 615, n. 3, 70 S.Ct., at 859, n. 3 (duty lies with the Patent Office to examine claims and to conform them to the scope of the invention; inventors may appeal Patent Office determinations if they disagree with result).

Indeed, petitioner's first argument was not new even in 1950. Nearly 100 years before *Graver Tank*, this Court approved of the doctrine of equivalents in *Winans v. Denmead*, 15 How. 330, 14 L.Ed. 717 (1854). The dissent in *Winans* unsuccessfully argued that the majority result was inconsistent with the requirement in the 1836 Patent Act that the applicant "particularly 'specify and point' out what he claims as his invention," and that the patent protected nothing more. Id., 15 How. at 347 (Campbell, J., dissenting).

4. Petitioner argues that the evolution in patent practice from "central" claiming (describing the core principles of the invention) to "peripheral" claiming (describing the outer boundaries of the invention) requires that we treat *Graver Tank* as an aberration and abandon the doctrine of equivalents. Brief for Petitioner 43–45. We disagree. The suggested change in claiming practice predates *Graver Tank*, is not of statutory origin, and seems merely to reflect narrower inventions in more crowded arts. Also, judicial recognition of so-called "pioneer" patents suggests that the abandonment of "central" claiming may be overstated. That a claim describing a limited improvement in a crowded field will have a limited range of permissible equivalents does not negate the availability of the doctrine vel non.

B

We do, however, share the concern of the dissenters below that the doctrine of equivalents, as it has come to be applied since *Graver Tank*, has taken on a life of its own, unbounded by the patent claims. There can be no denying that the doctrine of equivalents, when applied broadly, conflicts with the definitional and public-notice functions of the statutory claiming requirement. Judge Nies identified one means of avoiding this conflict:

> [A] distinction can be drawn that is not too esoteric between substitution of an equivalent for a component *in* an invention and enlarging the metes and bounds of the invention *beyond* what is claimed.
>
> * * *
>
> Where a claim to an invention is expressed as a combination of elements, as here, "equivalents" in the sobriquet "Doctrine of Equivalents" refers to the equivalency of an *element* or *part* of the invention with one that is substituted in the accused product or process.
>
> * * *
>
> This view that the accused device or process must be more than "equivalent" *overall* reconciles the Supreme Court's position on infringement by equivalents with its concurrent statements that "the courts have no right to enlarge a patent beyond the scope of its claims as allowed by the Patent Office." [Citations omitted.] The "scope" is not enlarged if courts do not go beyond the substitution of equivalent elements. 62 F.3d, at 1573–1574 (Nies, J., dissenting) (emphasis in original).

We concur with this apt reconciliation of our two lines of precedent. Each element contained in a patent claim is deemed material to defining the scope of the patented invention, and thus the doctrine of equivalents must be applied to individual elements of the claim, not to the invention as a whole. It is important to ensure that the application of the doctrine, even as to an individual element, is not allowed such broad play as to effectively eliminate that element in its entirety. So long as the doctrine of equivalents does not encroach beyond the limits just described, or beyond related limits to be discussed infra, at 1047–1048, 1053, n. 8, and 1054–1055, we are confident that the doctrine will not vitiate the central functions of the patent claims themselves.

III

Understandably reluctant to assume this Court would overrule *Graver Tank*, petitioner has offered alternative arguments in favor of a more restricted doctrine of equivalents than it feels was applied in this case. We address each in turn.

A

Petitioner first argues that *Graver Tank* never purported to supersede a well-established limit on non-literal infringement, known variously as "prosecution history estoppel" and "file wrapper estoppel." *See Bayer Aktiengesellschaft v. Duphar Int'l Research B.V.*, 738 F.2d 1237, 1238 (C.A.Fed.1984). According to petitioner, any surrender of subject matter during patent prosecution, regardless of the reason for such surrender, precludes recapturing any part of that subject matter, even if it is equivalent to the matter expressly claimed. Because, during patent prosecution, respondent limited the pH element of its claim to pH levels between 6.0 and 9.0, petitioner would have those limits form bright lines beyond which no equivalents may be claimed. Any inquiry into the reasons for a surrender, petitioner claims, would undermine the public's right to clear notice of the scope of the patent as embodied in the patent file.

We can readily agree with petitioner that *Graver Tank* did not dispose of prosecution history estoppel as a legal limitation on the doctrine of equivalents. But petitioner reaches too far in arguing that the reason for an amendment during patent prosecution is irrelevant to any subsequent estoppel. In each of our cases cited by petitioner and by the dissent below, prosecution history estoppel was tied to amendments made to avoid the prior art, or otherwise to address a specific concern—such as obviousness—that arguably would have rendered the claimed subject matter unpatentable. Thus, in *Exhibit Supply Co. v. Ace Patents Corp.*, Chief Justice Stone distinguished inclusion of a limiting phrase in an original patent claim from the "very different" situation in which "the applicant, in order to meet objections in the Patent Office, based on references to the prior art, adopted the phrase as a substitute for the broader one" previously used. 315 U.S. 126, 136, 62 S.Ct. 513, 518, 86 L.Ed. 736 (1942) (emphasis added). Similarly, in *Keystone Driller Co. v. Northwest Engineering Corp.*, 294 U.S. 42, 55 S.Ct. 262, 79 L.Ed. 747 (1935), estoppel was applied where the initial claims were "rejected on the prior art," *id.*, at 48, n. 6, 55 S.Ct., at 265, n. 6, and where the allegedly infringing equivalent element was outside of the revised claims and within the prior art that formed the basis for the rejection of the earlier claims, id., at 48, 55 S.Ct., at 264–265.[5]

It is telling that in each case this Court probed the reasoning behind the Patent Office's insistence upon a change in the claims. In each instance, a change was demanded because the claim as otherwise written was viewed as not describing a patentable invention at all—typically because what it described was encompassed within the prior art. But, as the United States informs us, there are a variety of other reasons why the PTO may request a change in claim language. Brief for United States as Amicus Curiae 22–23 (counsel for the PTO also appearing on the brief). And if the PTO has been requesting changes in claim language without the intent to limit equivalents or, indeed, with the expectation that language it required would in many cases allow for a range of equivalents, we should

---

5. *See also, Smith v. Magic City Kennel Club, Inc.*, 282 U.S. 784, 788, 51 S.Ct. 291, 293, 75 L.Ed. 707 (1931) (estoppel applied to amended claim where the original "claim was rejected on the prior patent to" another); *Computing Scale Co. of America v. Automatic Scale Co.*, 204 U.S. 609, 618–620, 27 S.Ct. 307, 311–312, 51 L.Ed. 645 (1907) (initial claims rejected based on lack of invention over prior patents); *Hubbell v. United States*, 179 U.S. 77, 83, 21 S.Ct. 24, 26–27, 45 L.Ed. 95 (1900) (patentee estopped from excluding a claim element where element was added to overcome objections based on lack of novelty over prior patents); *Sutter v. Robinson*, 119 U.S. 530, 541, 7 S.Ct. 376, 381–382, 30 L.Ed. 492 (1886) (estoppel applied where, during patent prosecution, the applicant "was expressly required to state that [the device's] structural plan was old and not of his invention"); *cf. Graham v. John Deere Co. of Kansas City*, 383 U.S. 1, 33, 86 S.Ct. 684, 701–702, 15 L.Ed.2d 545 (1966) (noting, in a validity determination, that "claims that have been narrowed in order to obtain the issuance of a patent by distinguishing the prior art cannot be sustained to cover that which was previously by limitation eliminated from the patent").

be extremely reluctant to upset the basic assumptions of the PTO without substantial reason for doing so. Our prior cases have consistently applied prosecution history estoppel only where claims have been amended for a limited set of reasons, and we see no substantial cause for requiring a more rigid rule invoking an estoppel regardless of the reasons for a change.[6]

In this case, the patent examiner objected to the patent claim due to a perceived overlap with the Booth patent, which revealed an ultrafiltration process operating at a pH above 9.0. In response to this objection, the phrase "at a pH from approximately 6.0 to 9.0" was added to the claim. While it is undisputed that the upper limit of 9.0 was added in order to distinguish the Booth patent, the reason for adding the lower limit of 6.0 is unclear. The lower limit certainly did not serve to distinguish the Booth patent, which said nothing about pH levels below 6.0. Thus, while a lower limit of 6.0, by its mere inclusion, became a material element of the claim, that did not necessarily preclude the application of the doctrine of equivalents as to that element. *See Hubbell v. United States*, 179 U.S. 77, 82, 21 S.Ct. 24, 26, 45 L.Ed. 95 (1900) (" '[A]ll [specified elements] must be regarded as material,' " though it remains an open " 'question whether an omitted part is supplied by an equivalent device or instrumentality' " (citation omitted)). Where the reason for the change was not related to avoiding the prior art, the change may introduce a new element, but it does not necessarily preclude infringement by equivalents of that element.[7]

We are left with the problem, however, of what to do in a case like the one at bar, where the record seems not to reveal the reason for including the lower pH limit of 6.0. In our view, holding that certain reasons for a claim amendment may avoid the application of prosecution history estoppel is not tantamount to holding that the absence of a reason for an amendment may similarly avoid such an estoppel. Mindful that claims do indeed serve both a definitional and a notice function, we think the better rule is to place the burden on the patent-holder to establish the reason for an amendment required during patent prosecution. The court then would decide whether that reason is sufficient to overcome prosecution history estoppel as a bar to application of the doctrine of equivalents to the element added by that amendment. Where no explanation is established, however, the court should presume that the PTO had a substantial reason related to patentability for including the limiting element added by amendment. In those circumstances, prosecution history estoppel would bar the application

---

6. That petitioner's rule might provide a brighter line for determining whether a patentee is estopped under certain circumstances is not a sufficient reason for adopting such a rule. This is especially true where, as here, the PTO may have relied upon a flexible rule of estoppel when deciding whether to ask for a change in the first place. To change so substantially the rules of the game now could very well subvert the various balances the PTO sought to strike when issuing the numerous patents which have not yet expired and which would be affected by our decision.

7. We do not suggest that, where a change is made to overcome an objection based on the prior art, a court is free to review the correctness of that objection when deciding whether to apply prosecution history estoppel. As petitioner rightly notes, such concerns are properly addressed on direct appeal from the denial of a patent, and will not be revisited in an infringement action. *Smith v. Magic City Kennel Club, Inc., supra*, 282 U.S. at 789–790, 51 S.Ct., at 293–294. What is permissible for a court to explore is the reason (right or wrong) for the objection and the manner in which the amendment addressed and avoided the objection.

of the doctrine equivalents as to that element. The presumption we have described, one subject to rebuttal if an appropriate reason for a required amendment is established, gives proper deference to the role of claims in defining an invention and providing public notice, and to the primacy of the PTO in ensuring that the claims allowed cover only subject matter that is properly patentable in a proffered patent application. Applied in this fashion, prosecution history estoppel places reasonable limits on the doctrine of equivalents, and further insulates the doctrine from any feared conflict with the Patent Act.

Because respondent has not proffered in this Court a reason for the addition of a lower pH limit, it is impossible to tell whether the reason for that addition could properly avoid an estoppel. Whether a reason in fact exists, but simply was not adequately developed, we cannot say. On remand, the Federal Circuit can consider whether reasons for that portion of the amendment were offered or not and whether further opportunity to establish such reasons would be proper.

B

Petitioner next argues that even if *Graver Tank* remains good law, the case held only that the absence of substantial differences was a necessary element for infringement under the doctrine of equivalents, not that it was sufficient for such a result. Brief for Petitioner 32. Relying on *Graver Tank*'s references to the problem of an "unscrupulous copyist" and "piracy," 339 U.S., at 607, 70 S.Ct., at 855–856, petitioner would require judicial exploration of the equities of a case before allowing application of the doctrine of equivalents. To be sure, *Graver Tank* refers to the prevention of copying and piracy when describing the benefits of the doctrine of equivalents. That the doctrine produces such benefits, however, does not mean that its application is limited only to cases where those particular benefits are obtained.

Elsewhere in *Graver Tank* the doctrine is described in more neutral terms. And the history of the doctrine as relied upon by *Graver Tank* reflects a basis for the doctrine not so limited as petitioner would have it. In *Winans v. Denmead*, 15 How. 330, 343, 14 L.Ed. 717 (1854), we described the doctrine of equivalents as growing out of a legally implied term in each patent claim that "the claim extends to the thing patented, however its form or proportions may be varied." Under that view, application of the doctrine of equivalents involves determining whether a particular accused product or process infringes upon the patent claim, where the claim takes the form—half express, half implied—of "X and its equivalents."

Union Paper–Bag Machine Co. v. Murphy, 97 U.S. 120, 125, 24 L.Ed. 935 (1878), on which *Graver Tank* also relied, offers a similarly intent-neutral view of the doctrine of equivalents:

> [T]he substantial equivalent of a thing, in the sense of the patent law, is the same as the thing itself; so that if two devices do the same work in substantially the same way, and accomplish substantially the same result, they are the same, even though they differ in name, form, or shape.

If the essential predicate of the doctrine of equivalents is the notion of identity between a patented invention and its equivalent, there is no basis for treating an infringing equivalent any differently than a device that infringes the express terms of the patent. Application of the doctrine of equivalents, therefore, is akin to determining literal infringement, and neither requires proof of intent.

Petitioner also points to *Graver Tank*'s seeming reliance on the absence of independent experimentation by the alleged infringer as supporting an equitable defense to the doctrine of equivalents. The Federal Circuit explained this factor by suggesting that an alleged infringer's behavior, be it copying, designing around a patent, or independent experimentation, indirectly reflects the substantiality of the differences between the patented invention and the accused device or process. According to the Federal Circuit, a person aiming to copy or aiming to avoid a patent is imagined to be at least marginally skilled at copying or avoidance, and thus intentional copying raises an inference—rebuttable by proof of independent development—of having only insubstantial differences, and intentionally designing around a patent claim raises an inference of substantial differences. This explanation leaves much to be desired. At a minimum, one wonders how ever to distinguish between the intentional copyist making minor changes to lower the risk of legal action, and the incremental innovator designing around the claims, yet seeking to capture as much as is permissible of the patented advance.

But another explanation is available that does not require a divergence from generally objective principles of patent infringement. In both instances in *Graver Tank* where we referred to independent research or experiments, we were discussing the known interchangeability between the chemical compound claimed in the patent and the compound substituted by the alleged infringer. The need for independent experimentation thus could reflect knowledge—or lack thereof—of interchangeability possessed by one presumably skilled in the art. The known interchangeability of substitutes for an element of a patent is one of the express objective factors noted by *Graver Tank* as bearing upon whether the accused device is substantially the same as the patented invention. Independent experimentation by the alleged infringer would not always reflect upon the objective question whether a person skilled in the art would have known of the interchangeability between two elements, but in many cases it would likely be probative of such knowledge.

Although *Graver Tank* certainly leaves room for petitioner's suggested inclusion of intent-based elements in the doctrine of equivalents, we do not read it as requiring them. The better view, and the one consistent with *Graver Tank*'s predecessors and the objective approach to infringement, is that intent plays no role in the application of the doctrine of equivalents.

C

Finally, petitioner proposes that in order to minimize conflict with the notice function of patent claims, the doctrine of equivalents should be limited to equivalents that are disclosed within the patent itself. A milder version of this argument, which found favor with the dissenters below, is that the doctrine should be limited to equivalents that were known at the time the patent was issued, and should not extend to after-arising equivalents.

As we have noted ... with regard to the objective nature of the doctrine, a skilled practitioner's knowledge of the interchangeability between claimed and accused elements is not relevant for its own sake, but rather for what it tells the fact-finder about the similarities or differences between those elements. Much as the perspective of the hypothetical "reasonable person" gives content to concepts such as "negligent" behavior, the perspective of a skilled practitioner provides content to, and limits on, the concept of "equivalence." Insofar as the question under the doctrine of equivalents is whether an accused element is equivalent to a claimed element, the proper time for evaluating equivalency—and thus knowledge of interchangeability between elements—is at the time of infringement, not at the time the patent was issued. And rejecting the milder version of petitioner's argument necessarily rejects the more severe proposition that equivalents must not only be known, but must also be actually disclosed in the patent in order for such equivalents to infringe upon the patent.

IV

The various opinions below, respondents, and amici devote considerable attention to whether application of the doctrine of equivalents is a task for the judge or for the jury. However, despite petitioner's argument below that the doctrine should be applied by the judge, in this Court petitioner makes only passing reference to this issue. *See* Brief for Petitioner 22, n. 15 ("If this Court were to hold in *Markman v. Westview Instruments, Inc.*, No. 95–26, 1996 WL 12585 (argued Jan. 8, 1996), that judges rather than juries are to construe patent claims, so as to provide a uniform definition of the scope of the legally protected monopoly, it would seem at cross-purposes to say that juries may nonetheless expand the claims by resort to a broad notion of 'equivalents' "); Reply Brief for Petitioner 20 (whether judge or jury should apply the doctrine of equivalents depends on how the Court views the nature of the inquiry under the doctrine of equivalents).

Petitioner's comments go more to the alleged inconsistency between the doctrine of equivalents and the claiming requirement than to the role of the jury in applying the doctrine as properly understood. Because resolution of whether, or how much of, the application of the doctrine of equivalents can be resolved by the court is not necessary for us to answer the question presented, we decline to take it up. The Federal Circuit held that it was for the jury to decide whether the accused process was equivalent to the claimed process. There was ample support in our prior cases for that holding. *See, e.g., Union Paper–Bag Machine Co. v. Murphy*, 97 U.S., at 125 ("in determining the question of infringement, the court or jury, as the case may be, ... are to look at the machines or their several devices or elements in the light of what they do, or what office or function they perform, and how they perform it, and to find that one thing is substantially the same as another, if it performs substantially the same function in substantially the same way to obtain the same result"); *Winans v. Denmead*, 15 How., at 344 ("[It] is a question for the jury" whether the accused device was "the same in kind, and effected by the employment of [the patentee's] mode of operation in substance"). Nothing in our recent *Markman* decision necessitates a different result than that reached by the Federal Circuit. Indeed, *Markman* cites with considerable favor, when discussing the role of judge and jury, the seminal *Winans* decision. *Markman v. Westview Instruments, Inc.*, 517 U.S. 370, ___, 116 S.Ct. 1384, 1392–1393, 134 L.Ed.2d 577 (1996). Whether, if the issue were squarely presented to us, we would reach a different conclusion than did the Federal Circuit is not a question we need decide today.[8]

V.

All that remains is to address the debate regarding the linguistic framework under which "equivalence" is determined. Both the parties and the Federal Circuit spend considerable time arguing whether the so-called "triple identity" test—focusing on the function served by a particular claim element, the way that element serves that function, and the result thus obtained by that element—is a suitable method for determining equivalence, or whether an "insubstantial differences" approach is better. There seems to be substantial agreement that, while the triple identity test may be suitable for analyzing mechanical devices, it often provides a poor framework for analyzing other products or processes. On the other hand, the insubstantial differences test offers little additional guidance as to what might render any given difference "insubstantial."

In our view, the particular linguistic framework used is less important than whether the test is probative of the essential inquiry: Does the accused product or process contain elements identical or equivalent to each claimed element of the patented invention? Different linguistic frameworks may be more suitable to different cases, depending on their particular facts. A focus on individual elements and a special vigilance against allowing the concept of equivalence to eliminate completely any such elements should reduce considerably the imprecision of whatever language is used. An analysis of the role played by each element in the context of the specific patent claim will thus inform the inquiry as to whether a substitute

---

8. With regard to the concern over unreviewability due to black-box jury verdicts, we offer only guidance, not a specific mandate. Where the evidence is such that no reasonable jury could determine two elements to be equivalent, district courts are obliged to grant partial or complete summary judgment. See Fed.Rule Civ.Proc. 56; *Celotex Corp. v. Catrett*, 477 U.S. 317, 322–323, 106 S.Ct. 2548, 2552–2553, 91 L.Ed.2d 265 (1986). If there has been a reluctance to do so by some courts due to unfamiliarity with the subject matter, we are confident that the Federal Circuit can remedy the problem. Of course, the various legal limitations on the application of the doctrine of equivalents are to be determined by the court, either on a pretrial motion for partial summary judgment or on a motion for judgment as a matter of law at the close of the evidence and after the jury verdict. Fed.Rule Civ.Proc. 56; Fed.Rule Civ.Proc. 50. Thus, under the particular facts of a case, if prosecution history estoppel would apply or if a theory of equivalence would entirely vitiate a particular claim element, partial or complete judgment should be rendered by the court, as there would be no further material issue for the jury to resolve. Finally, in cases that reach the jury, a special verdict and/or interrogatories on each claim element could be very useful in facilitating review, uniformity, and possibly postverdict judgments as a matter of law. *See* Fed.Rule Civ.Proc. 49; Fed.Rule Civ.Proc. 50. We leave it to the Federal Circuit how best to implement procedural improvements to promote certainty, consistency, and reviewability to this area of the law.

element matches the function, way, and result of the claimed element, or whether the substitute element plays a role substantially different from the claimed element. With these limiting principles as a backdrop, we see no purpose in going further and micro-managing the Federal Circuit's particular word-choice for analyzing equivalence. We expect that the Federal Circuit will refine the formulation of the test for equivalence in the orderly course of case-by-case determinations, and we leave such refinement to that court's sound judgment in this area of its special expertise.

* * *

NOTES

1. *The Objective Standard for Equivalency.* The overall message of *Warner–Jenkinson* is that a theoretically imprecise standard of equivalency will not create excessive uncertainty if, in applying the doctrine, the courts are sensitive to the underlying policies and insist that any theory of equivalence put forth by a patentee not operate to "eliminate completely" the technological substance behind a claim limitation and thereby undermine the "definitional and notice" functions of claims.

Thus, the Court was concerned with an unwieldy DOE and sought to limit its application without undermining the doctrine's role in patent law's incentive dynamic. There are three principal constraints on the DOE: (1) All–Limitations Rule; (2) Public Dedication Rule; and (3) Prosecution History Estoppel. The first two are discussed here, and the third in the next section, B.2.

a. *The All–Limitations Rule.* As an initial matter, it should be noted that the Federal Circuit has expressed a preference for the word "limitation" (instead of "element") when referring to claim language, and "element" when referring to the accused device. *See Festo Corp. v. Shoketsu Kinzoku Kogyo Kabushiki Co., Ltd.*, 234 F.3d 558, 563 n.1 (Fed.Cir.2000) (*en banc*) ("In our prior cases, we have used both the term 'element' and the term 'limitation' to refer to words in a claim. It is preferable to use the term 'limitation' when referring to claim language and the term 'element' when referring to the accused device"). To this end, the court has also noted that the "All Elements rule might better be called the All–Limitations rule." *Ethicon Endo–Surgery, Inc. v. U.S. Surgical Corp.*, 149 F.3d 1309, 1317 n.* (Fed.Cir.1998). *See also* Raj S. Davé, *A Mathematical Approach to Claim Elements and the Doctrine of Equivalents*, 16 HARV. J.L. & TECH. 507, 532 n.133, quoting Judge Paul Michel as follows:

> I like to call it [referring to the "all-elements rule"] the "all-limitations rule," because I don't know what an element is. And every time I've had to debate with someone, it's clear that they have a slightly different idea of what an element is than what I think it is. Once you get past atomic elements, I don't think it's a useful word.

Therefore, we will employ the word "limitation" when referring to claim language and the phrase the "All Limitations Rule."

The Supreme Court's all limitations approach to equivalency was adopted earlier by the 1987 Federal Circuit *en banc* decision *Pennwalt Corp. v. Durand–Wayland, Inc.*, 833 F.2d 931 (Fed.Cir.1987), and adhered to in subsequent panel decisions. But the question of what constitutes an "limitation" remains unanswered.

b. *What is a "Limitation?"* There is some confusion as to what constitutes a limitation, largely because of seemingly conflicting precedent. For example, in

Corning Glass Works v. Sumitomo Electric U.S.A., 868 F.2d 1251 (Fed.Cir.1989),[29] the court recognized that the all-limitations rule has led to

> confusion . . . because of misunderstanding or misleading uses of the term "element" in discussing claims. "Element" may be used to mean a single limitation, but it has also been used to mean a series of limitations which, taken together, make up a component of the claimed invention.

Id. at 1259. Decisions subsequent to *Corning Glass* have carefully confined its scope. For example, in *Dolly, Inc. v. Spalding & Evenflo Companies, Inc.*, 16 F.3d 394 (Fed.Cir.1994), the court, referring to the *Corning Glass* language noted above, court stated:

> This language in *Corning Glass* did not substitute a broader limitation-by-limitation comparison for the doctrine of equivalents than the element-by-element comparison in *Pennwalt*. Rather, the *Corning Glass* court merely clarified the meaning of the term "element" in the context of the *Pennwalt* rule. *Corning Glass* reaffirmed that the rule requires an equivalent for every limitation of the claim, even though the equivalent may not be present in the corresponding component of the accused device.

Id. at 399. And, in *Forest Labs v. Abbott Labs*, 239 F.3d 1305, 1313 (Fed.Cir.2001), the Federal Circuit, in no uncertain terms, stated that "[i]n *Corning Glass*, we did not dispense with the need for one-to-one correspondence of limitations and elements."

What is the status of the all-elements rule after *Warner–Jenkinson*? Is there a risk that the all-elements rule may be applied with excessive strictness, causing the result in particular cases to turn more on formal distinctions than on substance and leading to unfairness to patentees without any significant increase in the level of certainty concerning patent scope? If the all-elements rule is applied strictly as an analytic tool rather than as a general direction, it may not operate as an effective and fair means for limiting the doctrine of equivalents and increasing certainty, as the Supreme Court in *Warner–Jenkinson* assumes. What would be the effect of how the technological substance of a patent claim breaks down into "elements" or "limitations"? Isn't it dependent on both what constitutes an element and the form that a claim drafter uses?

To illustrate, simplistically, how dependent on formal claim drafting the "all elements" rule is, consider a claim to a snuffbox with six sides. The drafter could claim (1) "a snuffbox consisting of a first side, a second side, a third side, a fourth side, a fifth side, and a sixth side" or (2) "a six-sided snuffbox." Both claims define exactly the same literal scope. Does a *five*-sided snuffbox infringe under the doctrine of equivalents? The all elements rule, applied woodenly, would exclude infringement with the first claim because there is a "missing" side element, but would allow equivalency infringement of the second claim if it were shown that five sides was substantially the same as six sides. Is it possible to circumvent or control the all-elements rule by reducing the number of elements and grouping elements together in the accused product?

    c. *What Does it Mean to Vitiate a Claim Limitation?* The Supreme Court and the Federal Circuit have repeatedly stated that claim limitations cannot be ignored. In *Forest Labs*, *supra*, for example, the patentee, Abbott, claimed certain water percentages, but, relying on *Corning Glass*, argued that these percentages were irrelevant in determining whether there was infringement under the doctrine of

---

29. The *Corning Glass* opinion was written by the late Judge Helen Nies, whose analysis of Supreme Court precedent as requiring an element-by-element approach was later expressly adopted by the Supreme Court in *Warner–Jenkinson*.

equivalents. The Federal Circuit disagreed, noting that "[a] statement that water is 'irrelevant' does not establish that an unknown percentage of water is equivalent to the claimed water percentages. If we accepted this testimony and treated the water limitation as irrelevant, we would be vitiating that limitation." 239 F.3d at 1313.

But is a claim element vitiated when the accused product has a single element that performs the same function as two claim elements? Or, when an accused device has two elements that perform the same function as a single claim element? In *Eagle Comtronics, Inc. v. Arrow Communication Laboratories, Inc.*, 305 F.3d 1303, 1317 (Fed.Cir.2002), the court addressed these questions:

> While a claim limitation cannot be totally missing from an accused device, whether or not a limitation is deemed to be vitiated must take into account that when two elements of the accused device perform a single function of the patented invention, or when separate claim limitations are combined into a single element of the accused device, a claim limitation is not necessarily vitiated, and the doctrine of equivalents may still apply if the differences are insubstantial.

2. *The Public Dedication Rule: Equivalency of Disclosed But Unclaimed Embodiments.* Another limitation on the DOE is the "Disclosure–Dedication Rule." Recent Federal Circuit decisions, following an 1881 Supreme Court decision, *Miller v. Bridgeport Brass Co.*, 104 U.S. 350, 352 (1881) ("the claim of a specific device or combination, an omission to claim other devices or combinations apparent on the face of the patent are, in law, a dedication to the public of that which is not claimed."), apply a theory of dedication by unclaimed disclosure to bar a finding of equivalency when the alleged equivalent is expressly disclosed but not literally claimed in the patent itself. For example, in *Maxwell v. J. Baker, Inc.*, 86 F.3d 1098 (Fed.Cir.1996), the patent concerned a system for attaching mated pairs of shoes. The patent's claims required an "extended separate tab" arrangement. An accused product used an "under the sock lining" arrangement. The patent disclosed an "under the sock lining" arrangement as an alternative embodiment. The Federal Circuit, in an opinion by Judge Lourie, reversed a judgment of infringement based on a jury verdict. It reasoned that to allow an equivalency finding in such a case would permit patentees to file broad disclosures and then escape PTO examination by presenting only narrow claims. It noted that a patentee who claims too narrowly can seek reissue within two years of the patent's issuance.

In *Maxwell*, Judge Lourie carefully distinguished the Supreme Court's *Graver Tank* decision, in which the alleged equivalent element (manganese silicate) was disclosed in the specification. In *Graver Tank*, the patent contained both a broad claim that included manganese silicates generically and a narrower claim that was limited to alkaline earth silicates, which excluded manganese silicates. The Supreme Court held that the broader claim was invalid but that the narrower claim was valid and infringed under the doctrine of equivalents. Thus, as Judge Lourie noted, the disclosed equivalent was not in fact "unclaimed" and could not be said to have been dedicated by the patentee. *See also Moore U.S.A., Inc. v. Standard Register Co.*, 229 F.3d 1091, 1107 (Fed.Cir.2000) ("In *Maxwell* we explained the contrary principle that 'subject matter disclosed in the specification, but not claimed, is dedicated to the public' in determining infringement under the doctrine of equivalents. Having fully disclosed two distinct embodiments, one in which the first and second longitudinal strips extend a majority of the length of the longitudinal marginal portions, and one in which they do not, Moore is not entitled to 'enforce the unclaimed embodiment as an equivalent of the one that was claimed.' ")

But in *YBM Magnex, Inc. v. ITC*, 145 F.3d 1317, 1320–21 (Fed.Cir.1998), the court stated that: "The Supreme Court's guidance in *Warner–Jenkinson* and *Graver Tank* does not permit the blanket rule that everything disclosed but not claimed is barred from access to the doctrine of equivalents, whatever the facts, circumstances, and evidence. *Maxwell* accords with the Court's precedent only when its decision is understood and applied in light of its particular facts.... Some factual situations may indeed warrant rejection of an asserted equivalent on this ground, as the Federal Circuit held in *Maxwell*; but to enlarge *Maxwell* to a broad and new rule of law, as did the Commission, is not only an incorrect reading of *Maxwell* but would bring it into direct conflict with Supreme Court precedent."

In *Warner–Jenkinson* the Supreme Court did not directly address the issue of dedication by unclaimed disclosure. It did reject the opposite argument: that equivalents should be *limited* to equivalents disclosed in the patent. The dedication theory relies in part on the view that equivalency subverts the claiming, examination, and reissue provisions of the patent. *Warner–Jenkinson* rejects the argument that those provisions completely abolished the doctrine of equivalents, but, should those provisions be looked to as a reason for imposing a more specific, policy-based limitation on the doctrine? What is the difference between an alternative embodiment and a description of the patented invention?

The Federal Circuit granted en banc review to resolve the *Maxwell/YBM* conflict. In *Johnson & Johnston, Inc. v. R.E. Service Co.*, 285 F.3d 1046, 1054 (Fed.Cir.2001), the court sided with *Maxwell*:

> As stated in *Maxwell*, when a patent drafter discloses but declines to claim subject matter, as in this case, this action dedicates that unclaimed subject matter to the public. Application of the doctrine of equivalents to recapture subject matter deliberately left unclaimed would "conflict with the primacy of the claims in defining the scope of the patentee's exclusive right." [citations omitted]

> Moreover, a patentee cannot narrowly claim an invention to avoid prosecution scrutiny by the PTO, and then, after patent issuance, use the doctrine of equivalents to establish infringement because the specification discloses equivalents. "Such a result would merely encourage a patent applicant to present a broad disclosure in the specification of the application and file narrow claims, avoiding examination of broader claims that the applicant could have filed consistent with the specification." By enforcing the *Maxwell* rule, the courts avoid the problem of extending the coverage of an exclusive right to encompass more than that properly examined by the PTO.

For dedication to occur, does the information simply have to be disclosed, or must the disclosure be enabling? In *PSC Computer Products, Inc. v. Foxconn Intern., Inc.*, 355 F.3d 1353, 1360 (Fed.Cir.2004), the Federal Circuit addressed how specific a disclosure in the written description must be to dedicate subject matter to the public. According to the court:

> [I]f one of ordinary skill in the art can understand the unclaimed disclosed teaching upon reading the written description, the alternative matter disclosed has been dedicated to the public. This "disclosure-dedication" rule does not mean that any generic reference in a written specification necessarily dedicates all members of that particular genus to the public. The disclosure must be of such specificity that one of ordinary skill in the art could identify the subject matter that had been disclosed and not claimed.

Thus, for public dedication to occur, a person having ordinary skill in the art (PHOSITA) must be able to "understand" and/or "identify" the subject matter. Is "identify" the same as "understand?" Do these terms equate with "enablement;"

that is, for instance, does "understand" mean that a PHOSITA must be able to "understand" the subject matter without "undue experimentation?"

3.   *Time of Infringement Approach and After–Arising Technology.* According to the Supreme Court, infringement for DOE purposes is measured at the "time of infringement," rejecting arguments that equivalency should be limited to either "equivalents that are disclosed within the patent itself" or to "equivalents that were known at the time the patent was issued." 520 U.S. at 41. The infringement inquiry is an objective one: does the accused product or process conform to the language of the claim, literally or in substance? Other subjective or time-variable issues, such as when or how the accused infringer developed the accused product or process, are not determinative.

Potentially, questions could be asked as to what is meant by the "time of infringement," especially when the infringement occurs over a lengthy period of time during which the state of the art evolves. Why do we focus on "time of infringement" as opposed to time of issuance? The Federal Circuit has noted that DOE is applied at the time of infringement because of the cumulative and unforeseeable nature of complex and ramified technologies, whereby one inventor opens a door for a subsequent inventor, a door which was perhaps not foreseeable at the time the first inventor filed for a patent, yet was eventually made possible because of the first inventor's patent disclosure. An example can be found in *Hughes Aircraft Co. v. United States*, 717 F.2d 1351 (Fed.Cir.1983). An employee of Hughes, Williams, invented a means of controlling the attitude of a synchronous communications satellite. The claim specified that the satellite have means for receiving and directly executing control signals from a ground control station on earth. After the patent issued, satellites were developed that did not respond directly to control signals, as required by the claim, because they utilized on-board microprocessors that received control signals and then executed them after processing. Such microprocessors were unknown at the time the patent application was filed. The court found there was infringement, noting that "partial variation in technique, an embellishment made possible by post-Williams technology, does not allow the accused spacecraft to escape the web of infringement." *Id.* at 1365. In other words, the inventor is not required to predict all future developments that enable the practice of his invention in substantially the same way. *See also Pennwalt Corp. v. Durand–Wayland, Inc.*, 833 F.2d 931, 941–42 (Fed.Cir.1987) (*en banc*) ("It is clear that an equivalent can be found in technology known at the time of the invention, as well as in subsequently developed technology"); *Chiuminatta Concrete Concepts, Inc. v. Cardinal Industries*, 145 F.3d 1303, 1310 (Fed.Cir.1998) ("The doctrine of equivalents is necessary because one cannot predict the future. Due to technological advances, a variant of an invention may be developed after the patent is granted, and that variant may constitute so insubstantial a change from what is claimed in the patent that it should be held to be an infringement. Such a variant, based on after-developed technology, could not have been disclosed in the patent."). The *Warner–Jenkinson* Court cited a portion of the United States *amicus* brief in its discussion of prosecution history estoppel. The *amicus* brief, in the cited portion, contains, in a footnote, an argument and an example concerning later-developed equivalents:

> Of course, when an accused equivalent (meeting the objective standard of insubstantiality) could not have been known because it was developed or discovered only after the patent issued, the case for application of the doctrine of equivalents becomes especially clear. For example, a claim to a chemical composition might include an inactive filler as a minor, unimportant ingredient. After the patent issues, a competitor of the patentee might manufacture a composition exactly as claimed but use a different, inactive filler, unknown in the art at the time the patent application was filed, that

performs exactly as those literally covered by the claim. Such a substitution, once it became available, might be known to persons of skill in the relevant art to be interchangeable with the claimed filler, and yet it would not have been possible to include the accused element in the patent because it did not exist at the time of issue.

1996 WL 172221, *23 n.8.

Second, when is "time of infringement?" Is it the date at which the accused product or process was designed? When the first infringing act occurred? Can the same product or process infringe at one point in time but not at another because of changing knowledge in the art as to how an alleged equivalent element functions and hence whether it is equivalent? Is equivalency, for purposes of the doctrine of equivalents, treated as an objective fact, provable at trial, just like literal infringement? The issue is not whether the equivalency of a substituted element was known in or obvious from the art at any point in time. The Court noted that the "known interchangeability of substitutes for an element of a patent is one of the express objective factors noted by *Graver Tank* as bearing upon whether the accused device is substantially the same as the patented invention." 520 U.S. at 36. This indicates the knowledge and the state of the art is a "factor" that "bears upon" substantial similarity but is not the ultimate test of substantial similarity or equivalency. Later, the Court again stressed that *"a skilled practitioner's knowledge of the interchangeability between claimed and accused elements is not relevant for its own sake*, but rather for what it tells the fact-finder about the similarities or differences between those elements." 520 U.S. at 37 (emphasis added).

The Court did not address directly the related, difficult issue of whether the patentability of a later-developed accused device or method is relevant to equivalency. It is well-settled that a patent on an accused product or process does not give the owner of the patent a right to exploit the product or process by using without authority an earlier patentee's technology. Existence of a patent provides no defense to literal infringement of a claim. For example, in *Bio–Technology General Corp. v. Genentech, Inc.*, 80 F.3d 1553 (Fed.Cir.1996), Genentech's patent claiming a recombinant process for producing a hormone read literally on the accused infringer's process. The accused infringer argued that its process involved a unique, patented purification method. The court dismissed the argument: "That [the accused infringer] patented its unique purification method is irrelevant: '[T]he existence of one's own patent does not constitute a defense to infringement of someone else's patent.' 'It is elementary that a patent grants only the right *to exclude others* and confers no right on its holder to make, use, or sell.' " 80 F.3d at 1559.

Some Federal Circuit decisions suggest that a patent on the accused device may be relevant to the substantiality of the difference between the patent claim and the accused device, at least when the patent in suit was cited and considered by the PTO in issuing the subsequent patent. *See Zygo Corp. v. Wyko Corp.*, 79 F.3d 1563 (Fed.Cir.1996); *Hoganas AB v. Dresser Industries, Inc.*, 9 F.3d 948 (Fed.Cir.1993). Other decisions limit the significance of the subsequent patenting. *See Hoechst Celanese Corp. v. BP Chemicals Ltd.*, 78 F.3d 1575 (Fed.Cir.1996); *National Presto Industries, Inc. v. West Bend Co.*, 76 F.3d 1185 (Fed.Cir.1996). Moreover, the patenting of the accused product leads one to ask if there are any parallels between the insubstantial differences test for the DOE and the test for nonobviousness. *See Roton Barrier, Inc. v. Stanley Works*, 79 F.3d 1112, 1128 (Fed.Cir.1996) (Nies, J. additional views: "It is a truism that the fact that an accused device is itself patented does not preclude a finding that such device infringes an earlier patent of another. However, the fact of a second patent, depending on its subject matter, may be relevant to the issue of whether the changes are substantial. If the second patent requires practice of the first i.e., the second merely adds an element 'D' to a patented combination A + B + C, the combination A + B + C + D clearly infringes. Conversely, if the second patent is granted for A + B + D over one claiming A + B + C, the change from C to D must not have been obvious to be validly patented. Evidence of a patent covering the change, in my view, is clearly relevant unless the patent is invalid. A substitution in a patented invention cannot be both nonobvious and insubstantial. I would apply nonobviousness as the test for the 'insubstantial change' requirement of *Hilton Davis*.'').

The Supreme Court's adoption in *Warner–Jenkinson* of an objective test of substantial equivalency at the time of infringement strongly suggests that patentability, which turns on the state of the art prior to an invention, may be of only limited relevance.

4. *Does the After–Arising Time Frame for DOE Conflict with the Disclosure Requirements?* Should it be of concern that enablement is measured at time of filing and DOE infringement at time of infringement? Recall that the enablement requirement is properly viewed as a claim limiting tool: the claims and specification must be commensurate. By measuring DOE at the time of infringement, a patentee can capture subject matter that is not enabled. It would seem to follow that, to the extent that the meaning of a patent claim depends on the state of the art or on tests, standards or measurements established in the art, the time framework should be the filing date. *See, e.g., Leggett & Platt, Inc. v. Hickory Springs Mfg. Co.*, 285 F.3d 1353, 1357 (Fed.Cir.2002) ("An infringement analysis requires the trial court to determine the meaning and scope of the asserted patent claims.... To discern accepted meaning, ... the construing court consults the specification and relevant prosecution history to provide context for understanding the meaning of the terms to one of skill in the art at the time of invention"); *Markman v. Westview Instruments, Inc.*, 52 F.3d 967, 968 (Fed.Cir.1995) (en banc) ("[T]he focus in construing disputed terms in claim language is not the subjective intent of the parties to the patent contract when they used a particular term. Rather the focus is on the objective test of what one of ordinary skill in the art at the time of the invention would have understood the term to mean."), *aff'd,* 517 U.S. 370, 116 S.Ct. 1384 (1996).

5. *DOE's Linguistic Framework.* The Federal Circuit *Hilton Davis* majority adopted "insubstantial differences" as the "ultimate test", retaining the triple identity (function-way-result) as a permissible formulation in particular cases. The Supreme Court suggested that insubstantial differences offers "little additional guidance" in determining equivalency and urged the Federal Circuit to formulate further tests "in the orderly course of case-by-case determinations." Given this free rein, did the Supreme Court provide *any* guidance? As 150 years of judicial experience with the doctrine of equivalents has failed to evolve an acceptable, precise "linguistic framework," one might be skeptical whether satisfactory general standards or rules exist, and whether it may be a waste of intellectual energy to search for and refine an analytic test of equivalency, just as some commentators suggest it has been for the related "obviousness" standard of patentability. *See* CHISUM ON PATENTS § 5.04[5] (1997).

6. *"Pioneer" Inventions and the DOE.* The term "pioneer" was defined by the Supreme Court in *Boyden Power–Brake Co. v. Westinghouse*, 170 U.S. 537, 561–62 (1898):

> This word, although used somewhat loosely, is commonly understood to denote a patent covering a function never before performed, a wholly novel device, or one of such novelty and importance as to mark a distinct step in the progress of the art, as distinguished from a mere improvement or perfection of what had gone before. Most conspicuous examples of such

patents are the one to Howe of the sewing machine; to Morse of the electrical telegraph; and to Bell of the telephone.

So-called "pioneer" inventions by definition have very little, if any, prior art. Because of this fact and because of the significant technologic advance, courts have given "pioneer" inventions broader claim scope under the DOE. *See, e.g., Continental Paper Bag Co. v. Eastern Paper Bag Co.*, 210 U.S. 405, 415 (1908) (" '[A] greater degree of liberality and a wider range of equivalents are permitted where the patent is of a pioneer character than when the invention is simply an improvement, may be the last and successful step, in the art theretofore partially developed by other inventors in the same field.' " (quoting *Cimiotti Unhairing Co. v. American Fur Ref. Co.*, 198 U.S. 399, 406 (1905))); *Miller v. Eagle Mfg. Co.*, 151 U.S. 186, 207 (1894) ("The range of equivalents depends upon the extent and nature of the invention. If the invention is broad or primary in its character, the range of equivalents will be correspondingly broad, under the liberal construction which the courts give to such inventions"); *Perkin–Elmer Corp. v. Westinghouse Electric Corp.*, 822 F.2d 1528, 1532 (Fed.Cir.1987) ("A pioneer invention is entitled to a broad range of equivalents"); *In re Hogan*, 559 F.2d 595 (CCPA 1977) (noting pioneer inventions entitled to broad claim scope).

The pioneer status of an invention, while judicially recognized, seems to have lost some of its force. For example, the Federal court has downplayed the importance of pioneer status, noting that such does not translate into a lower enablement standard. *See Plant Genetic Systems, N.V. v. DeKalb Genetics Corp.*, 315 F.3d 1335, 1339–41 (Fed.Cir.2003) (dismissing statements in *Hogan* that pioneer inventors "deserve broad claims to the broad concept" as "unconvincing" and "extended dicta").

7. *Effect of the Prior Art and the Hypothetical Claim.* It is well settled that the doctrine of equivalents cannot be used to encompass a product or process that is identical to or an obvious variation of the prior art. Whether and to what extent prior art may restrict the range of equivalents are difficult questions. In *Wilson Sporting Goods Co. v. David Geoffrey & Associates*, 904 F.2d 677 (Fed.Cir.1990), the court, in an attempt to answer these questions, thought it would be "helpful to conceptualize the limitation on the scope of equivalents by visualizing a hypothetical patent claim, sufficient in scope to literally cover the accused product." 904 F.2d at 684. Armed with what has come to be known as a *phantom claim*, the "pertinent question then becomes whether that . . . claim could have been allowed by the PTO over the prior art. If not, then it would be improper to permit the patentee to obtain that coverage in an infringement suit under the doctrine of equivalents. If the hypothetical claim could have been allowed, then prior art is not a bar to infringement under the doctrine of equivalents." *Id.*

What is the limiting effect of the prior art on the doctrine of equivalents after *Warner–Jenkinson*? Is there anything in the Court's analysis of equivalents that undermines the rule, recognized in several Federal Circuit decisions that the doctrine of equivalents cannot be used to encompass or ensnare the prior art? See *Id.*; *Lemelson v. General Mills, Inc.*, 968 F.2d 1202 (Fed.Cir.1992); *We Care, Inc. v. Ultra–Mark International Corp.*, 930 F.2d 1567 (Fed.Cir.1991). A Federal Circuit panel stressed in *Conroy v. Reebok International, Ltd.*, 14 F.3d 1570 (Fed.Cir.1994), that the standard of comparison is between the accused device as a whole and the prior art; "the mere existence of an element in the prior art" does not "automatically preclude[] a patentee from asserting a scope of equivalency sufficient to encompass the corresponding element in the accused device." This ensnarement defense is generally treated as a legal limitation on the scope of the doctrine of equivalents. Once a prima facie case of infringement under the doctrine of equivalents has been made, the accused infringer may invoke the "ensnarement" defense by showing how the broadened scope of the claims under the doctrine of equivalents would "ensnare" the prior art, and that therefore the scope of the claims must not be so expanded under the DOE. *See Depuy Spine, Inc. v. Medtronic Sofamor Danek, Inc.*, 567 F.3d 1314 (Fed.Cir.2009).

What will be the effect of the Supreme Court's mention in a footnote of the special status of "pioneer" inventions under the doctrine of equivalents in the course of rejecting an argument that "the evolution in patent practice from 'central' claiming (describing the core principles of the invention) to 'peripheral' claiming (describing the outer boundaries of the invention)" required treating *Graver Tank* and the doctrine of equivalents as an "aberration"?

> [J]udicial recognition of so-called "pioneer" patents suggests that the abandonment of "central" claiming may be overstated. That a claim describing a limited improvement in a crowded field will have a limited range of permissible equivalents does not negate the availability of the doctrine *vel non*.

520 U.S. at 27 n. 4.

Is the doctrine of equivalents like the law of nuisance in real property, which supplements formal, hard-edged rights to exclude with more context-specific standards for very important matters (noise, odors, etc.) not well handled by the basic regime? See, e.g., Henry E. Smith, *Intellectual Property as Property: Delineating Property Rights in Information*, 116 Yale L.J. 1742, 1807 (2007). If increased reliance on considerations outside the patent specification—as in the doctrine of equivalents—leads to more costly interpretation by third parties, are the problems of hard-to-foresee but similar technologies worth the extra costs? *Cf.* Christopher A. Cotropia, *Patent Claim Interpretation and Information Costs*, 9 Lewis & Clark L. Rev. 57 (2005).

8. *"Procedural Improvements": Summary Judgment, Verdict Forms, and Linking Evidence and Argument in Jury Presentations.* In *Warner–Jenkinson*, the Supreme Court clearly empathized with the concerns expressed by the dissenting Federal Circuit judges about abuses in assertions of equivalency, especially "the concern over unreviewability due to black-box jury verdicts." In addition to requiring a stricter substantive equivalency standard that precludes vitiation of claim limitations, the Court discussed "procedural improvements" in footnote 8.

Footnote 8 directs the district courts to entertain favorably motions for summary judgment to dismiss equivalency claims when (1) "no reasonable jury could determine two elements to be equivalent"; or (2) a "legal limitation" on equivalency applies, including (a) prosecution history estoppel, or (b) "a theory of equivalence would entirely vitiate a particular claim element, partial or complete judgment should be rendered by the court, as there would be no further material issue for the jury to resolve."

If a district court declines to grant summary judgment, the decision is normally not appealable. But the Supreme Court in *Warner–Jenkinson* suggested "[i]f there has been a reluctance to [grant summary judgment] by some courts due to unfamiliarity with the subject matter, we are confident that the Federal Circuit can remedy the problem," and one can expect the Federal Circuit, in response to the Supreme Court's urging, to find means to encourage district courts to grant proper motions.

A line of Federal Circuit decisions approving of summary judgment against groundless equivalency claims predates *Warner–Jenkinson. See, e.g., Gentex Corp. v. Donnelly Corp.*, 69 F.3d 527, 530 (Fed.Cir.1995); *Wolverine World Wide, Inc. v. Nike, Inc.*, 38 F.3d 1192 (Fed.Cir.1994). Indeed, the granting of summary judgment against equivalency has become a regular occurrence. *See, e.g., Monroe Engineering*

Products, Inc. v. J.W. Winco, Inc., 915 F.Supp. 901 (E.D.Mich.1996); *Soil Solutions, Inc. v. Spraying Devices, Inc.*, 40 U.S.P.Q.2d 1321 (E.D.Cal.1996).

In the course of ruling on claim construction, the court must necessarily become familiar with the patent and the technology. Would it be a logical and practical extension of "*Markman* hearings" to include the threshold legal issues concerning assertion of infringement under the doctrine of equivalents?

In footnote 8, the Supreme Court also suggested that district courts use in jury trials on equivalency "a special verdict and/or interrogatories on each claim element", which "could be very useful in facilitating review, uniformity, and possibly post-verdict judgments as a matter of law." In the past, Federal Circuit decisions did not mandate the use of special verdicts or interrogatories.

To obtain greater predictability, especially when infringement is tried to a jury, the *Lear Siegler* and *Malta* decisions did impose a special proof standard, requiring a patentee to provide evidence and "linking" argument on all three FWR (triple identity) prongs (function, way, result). *See Malta v. Schulmerich Carillons, Inc.*, 952 F.2d 1320 (Fed.Cir.1991) (the district court correctly granted a noninfringement judgment notwithstanding a contrary jury verdict; the patentee's testimony failed to provide "a sufficient explanation of both *why* the overall function, way, and result of the accused device are substantially the same as those of the claimed device and *why* the [accused devices' element that did not literally conform to a specific claim limitation] is the equivalent of [that limitation]." (Emphasis in original.)); *Lear Siegler, Inc. v. Sealy Mattress Company of Michigan, Inc.*, 873 F.2d 1422 (Fed.Cir.1989). *See also Genentech, Inc. v. Wellcome Foundation Ltd.*, 29 F.3d 1555 (Fed.Cir.1994). Recent Federal Circuit panel decisions expressed opposing views on whether the *Lear Siegler—Malta* requirement survived the *en banc Hilton Davis* decision. *Compare Texas Instruments Inc. v. Cypress Semiconductor Corp.*, 90 F.3d 1558, 1566–67 (Fed.Cir.1996) (in *Hilton Davis*, "we did not eliminate the need to prove equivalency on a limitation-by-limitation basis.... Nor did we overrule precedent requiring equivalency to be proven with 'particularized testimony and linking argument.' *See Lear Siegler, Inc. v. Sealy Mattress Co.... Malta v. Schulmerich Carillons, Inc....*"; "a patentee must still provide particularized testimony and linking argument as to the 'insubstantiality of the differences' between the claimed invention and the accused device or process, or with respect to the function, way, result test when such evidence is presented to support a finding of infringement under the doctrine of equivalents. Such evidence must be presented on a limitation-by-limitation basis.") *with National Presto Industries, Inc. v. West Bend Co.*, 76 F.3d 1185, 1191 (Fed.Cir.1996) (the infringer's argument that the patentee "did not provide sufficiently explicit witness testimony and 'linking attorney argument' on each of four factual questions of function, way, result, and 'why,' citing *Lear Siegler, Inc. v. Sealy Mattress Co.* ... and the concurring opinion in *Malta v. Schulmerich Carillons, Inc.....* as requiring this formulaic exposition by witnesses and lawyers" lacks merit: "The court's *en banc* decision in *Hilton Davis* made clear that no specific formulation of evidence and argument is required. Thus this argument is without substance, and indeed neither *Lear Siegler* nor *Malta* requires any particular formulation."). While the Supreme Court encouraged procedural improvements to assure reviewability of jury verdicts, these cases illustrate that micro-management of the presentation of evidence may not always be appropriate.

9. *Claim Interpretation, Prosecution History, and the Doctrine of Equivalents.* It is well settled that the claims must be interpreted in view of the specification of which they are a part, as well as the prosecution history. Courts have recognized the policy importance of ensuring that all "players in the marketplace are entitled to rely on the record made in the Patent Office in determining the meaning and scope" of the patentee's right to exclude, *see Lemelson v. General Mills, Inc.*, 968 F.2d 1202, 1208 (Fed.Cir.1992). Sometimes the patent documents may assign a particular characteristic or function to a claim element that is not expressly stated in the claim. What is the effect of such a characteristic or function on the scope of the patentee's right to exclude?

Consider a case where the prosecution history "may reveal the identification of a specific function relating to claim structure." *Vehicular Tech. Corp. v. Titan Wheel Int'l, Inc.*, 141 F.3d 1084 (Fed.Cir.1998). To what extent should this language in the prosecution history influence claim interpretation? To what extent should it influence the doctrine of equivalents? If it does influence the claim interpretation analysis, should it also influence the analysis under the DOE? If the court restricts its influence under claim interpretation, should it be given more weight in the analysis under DOE? In the end, does it make a difference whether the prosecution history language plays a role in either claim interpretation or equivalents, as long as it plays a role in one of them? For an example of opposing views on this issue, *see* the debate between the majority and dissenting opinions in *Vehicular, supra* (collecting cases).

2.   PROSECUTION HISTORY ESTOPPEL

The "prosecution history" of a patent, as we learned in Chapter Two, is the record of proceedings in the PTO on the application upon which the patent was issued. After a patent issues, the entire prosecution history of the patent is open to public inspection and it is common practice for the prosecution history to be introduced into evidence in an infringement trial.

The doctrine of *prosecution history estoppel* ("PHE") precludes a patent owner in an infringement proceeding from obtaining a construction of a claim that would in effect resurrect subject matter surrendered (through, for example, amendment or cancellation) during the course of proceedings in the PTO. To the extent that it applies, prosecution history estoppel supersedes the doctrine of equivalents. PHE's rationale is based on the notice function of the claim and on third-party detrimental reliance. As the Supreme Court noted in *Warner–Jenkinson,* PHE is linked to both "the role of claims in defining an invention and providing public notice" and to the "primacy of the PTO in ensuring that the claims allowed cover only subject matter that is properly patentable in a proffered patent application." *Warner–Jenkinson* 520 U.S. at 33–34.

But *Warner–Jenkinson* created ambiguity regarding two issues: (1) What types of amendments give rise to PHE; and (2) if PHE is invoked, what effect does it have on the scope of the Doctrine of Equivalents; that is, does PHE completely bar application of DOE or simply limit the range of DOE.

With respect to *types* of amendments, the Court referred alternatively to amendments not relating "to the prior art" and amendments not relating to "patentability." It did not indicate whether "patentability" referred solely to prior art based reasons (novelty and nonobviousness under Sections 102 and 103) or extended to other statutory grounds, such as non-enablement or lack of written description (Section 112, first paragraph) or indefiniteness (Section 112, second paragraph). On the issue of the *effect* of PHE on the doctrine of equivalents, the Court created a rebuttable presumption that DOE does not apply if no reason is given for an amendment.

After *Warner–Jenkinson*, the Supreme Court granted certiorari, vacated and remanded to the Federal Circuit three major cases in which Federal Circuit panels had affirmed findings of infringement under the doctrine of equivalents. The three cases were *Litton Systems, Inc. v. Honeywell, Inc.*, 140 F.3d 1449 (Fed.Cir.1998); *Hughes Aircraft Co. v. United States*, 140 F.3d 1470 (Fed.Cir.1998); and *Festo Corp. v. Shoketsu Kinzoku Kogyo Kabushiki Co., Ltd.*

In *Litton* and *Hughes Aircraft*, three-judge panels held that *Warner–Jenkinson* did *not* dictate a "complete bar"—that is, the patentee is not precluded from asserting DOE. But other Federal Circuit precedent was more restrictive in its approach. *See Kinzenbaw v. Deere & Co.*, 741 F.2d 383 (Fed.Cir.1984).

So there was uncertainty regarding what types of amendments invoked estoppel and whether PHE should give rise to a flexible or complete bar. With this conflicting background in mind, the Federal Circuit heard arguments en banc in the third case that was remanded, *Festo Corp. v. Shoketsu Kinzoku Kogyo Kabushiki Co., Ltd.*, 234 F.3d 558 (Fed.Cir.2000). The Federal Circuit addressed the following questions:

> **Question One**: For the purposes of determining whether an amendment to a claim creates prosecution history estoppel, is "a substantial reason related to patentability," *Warner–Jenkinson Co. v. Hilton Davis Chem. Co.*, 520 U.S. 17, 33 (1997), limited to those amendments made to overcome prior art under § 102 and § 103, or does "patentability" mean any reason affecting the issuance of a patent?
>
> **Answer**: For the purposes of determining whether an amendment gives rise to prosecution history estoppel, a "substantial reason related to patentability" is not limited to overcoming or avoiding prior art, but instead includes any reason which relates to the statutory requirements for a patent. Therefore, a narrowing amendment made for any reason related to the statutory requirements for a patent will give rise to prosecution history estoppel with respect to the amended claim element.
>
> **Question Two**: Under *Warner–Jenkinson*, should a "voluntary" claim amendment—one not required by the examiner or made in response to a rejection by an examiner for a stated reason—create prosecution history estoppel?
>
> **Answer**: Voluntary claim amendments are treated the same as other amendments. Therefore, a voluntary amendment that narrows the scope of a claim for a reason related to the statutory requirements for a patent will give rise to prosecution history estoppel as to the amended claim element.
>
> **Question Three**: If a claim amendment creates prosecution history estoppel, under *Warner–Jenkinson* what range of equivalents, if any, is available under the doctrine of equivalents for the claim element so amended?
>
> **Answer**: When a claim amendment creates prosecution history estoppel with regard to a claim element, there is no range of equivalents available

for the amended claim element. Application of the doctrine of equivalents to the claim element is completely barred (a "complete bar").

Question Four: When "no explanation [for a claim amendment] is established," *Warner–Jenkinson*, 520 U.S. at 33, thus invoking the presumption of prosecution history estoppel under *Warner–Jenkinson*, what range of equivalents, if any, is available under the doctrine of equivalents for the claim element so amended?

Answer: When no explanation for a claim amendment is established, no range of equivalents is available for the claim element so amended.

Of all of the questions posed and answered by the Federal Circuit, questions one and three were noteworthy. But the most significant in terms of innovation policy and how patent attorneys draft patent claims is question three. This question pertained to the range of equivalents, if any, when a claim amendment creates prosecution history estoppel. In answering this question, the court adopted a "complete bar" approach. This holding was based on the importance of "the notice function of the patent claim" and the "need for certainty as to the scope of patent protection." A vigorous dissent was filed in *Festo*, and the Supreme Court granted certiorari.

Festo Corporation v. Shoketsu Kinzoku Kogyo Kabushiki Co., Ltd.

535 U.S. 722 (2002).

■ JUSTICE KENNEDY delivered the opinion of the Court.

This case requires us to address once again the relation between two patent law concepts, the doctrine of equivalents and the rule of prosecution history estoppel. The Court considered the same concepts in *Warner–Jenkinson Co. v. Hilton Davis Chemical Co.*, 520 U.S. 17 (1997), and reaffirmed that a patent protects its holder against efforts of copyists to evade liability for infringement by making only insubstantial changes to a patented invention. At the same time, we appreciated that by extending protection beyond the literal terms in a patent the doctrine of equivalents can create substantial uncertainty about where the patent monopoly ends. *Id.*, at 29. If the range of equivalents is unclear, competitors may be unable to determine what is a permitted alternative to a patented invention and what is an infringing equivalent.

To reduce the uncertainty, *Warner–Jenkinson* acknowledged that competitors may rely on the prosecution history, the public record of the patent proceedings. In some cases the Patent and Trademark Office (PTO) may have rejected an earlier version of the patent application on the ground that a claim does not meet a statutory requirement for patentability. 35 U.S.C. § 132 (1994 ed., Supp. V). When the patentee responds to the rejection by narrowing his claims, this prosecution history estops him from later arguing that the subject matter covered by the original, broader claim was nothing more than an equivalent. Competitors may rely on the estoppel to ensure that their own devices will not be found to infringe by equivalence.

In the decision now under review the Court of Appeals for the Federal Circuit held that by narrowing a claim to obtain a patent, the patentee surrenders all equivalents to the amended claim element. Petitioner asserts this holding departs from past precedent in two respects. First, it applies estoppel to every amendment made to satisfy the requirements of the Patent Act and not just to amendments made to avoid pre-emption by an earlier invention, *i.e.,* the prior art. Second, it holds that when estoppel arises, it bars suit against every equivalent to the amended claim element. The Court of Appeals acknowledged that this holding departed from its own cases, which applied a flexible bar when considering what claims of equivalence were estopped by the prosecution history. Petitioner argues that by replacing the flexible bar with a complete bar the Court of Appeals cast doubt on many existing patents that were amended during the application process when the law, as it then stood, did not apply so rigorous a standard.

We granted certiorari to consider these questions.

I

Petitioner Festo Corporation owns two patents for an improved magnetic rodless cylinder, a piston-driven device that relies on magnets to move objects in a conveying system. The device has many industrial uses and has been employed in machinery as diverse as sewing equipment and the Thunder Mountain ride at Disney World. Although the precise details of the cylinder's operation are not essential here, the prosecution history must be considered.

Petitioner's patent applications, as often occurs, were amended during the prosecution proceedings. The application for the first patent, the Stoll Patent (U.S. Patent No. 4,354,125), was amended after the patent examiner rejected the initial application because the exact method of operation was unclear and some claims were made in an impermissible way. (They were multiply dependent.) 35 U.S.C. § 112 (1994 ed.). The inventor, Dr. Stoll, submitted a new application designed to meet the examiner's objections and also added certain references to prior art. 37 CFR § 1.56 (2000). The second patent, the Carroll Patent (U.S. Patent No. 3,779,401), was also amended during a reexamination proceeding. The prior art references were added to this amended application as well. Both amended patents added a new limitation—that the inventions contain a pair of sealing rings, each having a lip on one side, which would prevent impurities from getting on the piston assembly. The amended Stoll Patent added the further limitation that the outer shell of the device, the sleeve, be made of a magnetizable material.

After Festo began selling its rodless cylinder, respondents (whom we refer to as SMC) entered the market with a device similar, but not identical, to the ones disclosed by Festo's patents. SMC's cylinder, rather than using two one-way sealing rings, employs a single sealing ring with a two-way lip. Furthermore, SMC's sleeve is made of a nonmagnetizable alloy. SMC's device does not fall within the literal claims of either patent, but petitioner contends that it is so similar that it infringes under the doctrine of equivalents.

SMC contends that Festo is estopped from making this argument because of the prosecution history of its patents. The sealing rings and the magnetized alloy in the Festo product were both disclosed for the first time in the amended applications. In SMC's view, these amendments narrowed the earlier applications, surrendering alternatives that are the very points of difference in the competing devices—the sealing rings and the type of alloy used to make the sleeve. As Festo narrowed its claims in these ways in order to obtain the patents, says SMC, Festo is now estopped from saying that these features are immaterial and that SMC's device is an equivalent of its own.

The United States District Court for the District of Massachusetts disagreed. It held that Festo's amendments were not made to avoid prior art, and therefore the amendments were not the kind that give rise to estoppel. A panel of the Court of Appeals for the Federal Circuit affirmed. 72 F.3d 857 (1995). We granted certiorari, vacated, and remanded in light of our intervening decision in *Warner–Jenkinson v. Hilton Davis Chemical Co.*, 520 U.S. 17 (1997). After a decision by the original panel on remand, 172 F.3d 1361 (1999), the Court of Appeals ordered rehearing en banc to address questions that had divided its judges since our decision in *Warner–Jenkinson.* 187 F.3d 1381 (1999).

The en banc court reversed, holding that prosecution history estoppel barred Festo from asserting that the accused device infringed its patents under the doctrine of equivalents. The court held, with only one judge dissenting, that estoppel arises from any amendment that narrows a claim to comply with the Patent Act, not only from amendments made to avoid prior art. *Id.,* at 566. More controversial in the Court of Appeals was its further holding: When estoppel applies, it stands as a complete bar against any claim of equivalence for the element that was amended. *Id.,* at 574–575. The court acknowledged that its own prior case law did not go so far. Previous decisions had held that prosecution history estoppel constituted a flexible bar, foreclosing some, but not all, claims of equivalence, depending on the purpose of the amendment and the alterations in the text. The court concluded, however, that its precedents applying the flexible-bar rule should be overruled because this case-by-case approach has proved unworkable. In the court's view a complete-bar rule, under which estoppel bars all claims of equivalence to the narrowed element, would promote certainty in the determination of infringement cases.

Four judges dissented from the decision to adopt a complete bar. *Id.,* at 562. In four separate opinions, the dissenters argued that the majority's decision to overrule precedent was contrary to *Warner–Jenkinson* and would unsettle the expectations of many existing patentees. Judge Michel, in his dissent, described in detail how the complete bar required the Court of Appeals to disregard 8 older decisions of this Court, as well as more than 50 of its own cases. 234 F.3d, at 601–616.

We granted certiorari.

II

The patent laws "promote the Progress of Science and useful Arts" by rewarding innovation with a temporary monopoly. U.S. Const., Art. I, § 8, cl. 8. The monopoly is a property right; and like any property right, its boundaries should be clear. This clarity is essential to promote progress, because it enables efficient investment in innovation. A patent holder should know what he owns, and the public should know what he does not. For this reason, the patent laws require inventors to describe their work in "full, clear, concise, and exact terms," 35 U.S.C. § 112, as part of the delicate balance the law attempts to maintain between inventors, who rely on the promise of the law to bring the invention forth, and the public, which should be encouraged to pursue innovations, creations, and new ideas beyond the inventor's exclusive rights. *Bonito Boats, Inc. v. Thunder Craft Boats, Inc.,* 489 U.S. 141, 150 (1989).

Unfortunately, the nature of language makes it impossible to capture the essence of a thing in a patent application. The inventor who chooses to patent an invention and disclose it to the public, rather than exploit it in secret, bears the risk that others will devote their efforts toward exploiting the limits of the patent's language:

> An invention exists most importantly as a tangible structure or a series of drawings. A verbal portrayal is usually an afterthought written to satisfy the requirements of patent law. This conversion of machine to words allows for unintended idea gaps which cannot be satisfactorily filled. Often the invention is novel and words do not exist to describe it. The dictionary does not always keep abreast of the inventor. It cannot. Things are not made for the sake of words, but words for things. *Autogiro Co. of America v. United States,* 181 Ct.Cl. 55 (1967).

The language in the patent claims may not capture every nuance of the invention or describe with complete precision the range of its novelty. If patents were always interpreted by their literal terms, their value would be greatly diminished. Unimportant and insubstantial substitutes for certain elements could defeat the patent, and its value to inventors could be destroyed by simple acts of copying. For this reason, the clearest rule of patent interpretation, literalism, may conserve judicial resources but is not necessarily the most efficient rule. The scope of a patent is not limited to its literal terms but instead embraces all equivalents to the claims described. See *Winans v. Denmead,* 56 U.S. (15 How.) 330, 347 (1854). It is true that the doctrine of equivalents renders the scope of patents less certain. It may be difficult to determine what is, or is not, an equivalent to a particular element of an invention. If competitors cannot be certain about a patent's extent, they may be deterred from engaging in legitimate manufactures outside its limits, or they may invest by mistake in competing products that the patent secures. In addition the uncertainty may lead to wasteful litigation between competitors, suits that a rule of literalism might avoid. These concerns with the doctrine of equivalents, however, are not new. Each time the Court has considered the doctrine, it has acknowledged this uncertainty as the price of ensuring the appropriate incentives for innovation, and it has affirmed the doctrine over dissents that urged a more certain rule. When the Court in *Winans v. Denmead, supra,* first adopted what has become the doctrine of equivalents, it stated that "[t]he exclusive right to the thing patented is not secured, if the public are at liberty to make substantial copies of it, varying its form or proportions." *Id.,* at 343. The dissent argued that the Court had sacrificed the objective of "[f]ul[l]ness, clearness, exactness, preciseness, and particularity, in the description of the invention." *Id.,* at 347 (opinion of Campbell, J.).

The debate continued in *Graver Tank & Mfg. Co. v. Linde Air Products Co.,* 339 U.S. 605, (1950), where the Court reaffirmed the doctrine. *Graver Tank* held that patent claims must protect the inventor not only from those who produce devices falling within the literal claims of the patent but also from copyists who "make unimportant and insubstantial changes and substitutions in the patent which, though adding nothing, would be enough to take the copied matter outside the claim, and hence outside the reach of law." *Id.* at 607. Justice Black, in dissent, objected that under the doctrine of equivalents a competitor "cannot rely on what the language of a patent claims. He must be able, at the peril of heavy infringement damages, to forecast how far a court relatively unversed in a particular technological field will expand the claim's language...." *Id.,* at 617.

Most recently, in *Warner–Jenkinson,* the Court reaffirmed that equivalents remain a firmly entrenched part of the settled rights protected by the patent. A unanimous opinion concluded that if the doctrine is to be discarded, it is Congress and not the Court that should do so:

> [T]he lengthy history of the doctrine of equivalents strongly supports adherence to our refusal in *Graver Tank* to find that the Patent Act conflicts with that doctrine. Congress can legislate the doctrine of equivalents out of existence any time it chooses. The various policy arguments now made by both sides are thus best addressed to Congress, not this Court. 520 U.S., at 28.

III

Prosecution history estoppel requires that the claims of a patent be interpreted in light of the proceedings in the PTO during the application process. Estoppel is a "rule of patent construction" that ensures that claims are interpreted by reference to those "that have been cancelled or rejected." *Schriber–Schroth Co. v. Cleveland Trust Co.,* 311 U.S. 211, 220–221 (1940). The doctrine of equivalents allows the patentee to claim those insubstantial alterations that were not captured in drafting the original patent claim but which could be created through trivial changes. When, however, the patentee originally claimed the subject matter alleged to infringe but then narrowed the claim in response to a rejection, he may not argue that the surrendered territory comprised unforeseen subject matter that should be deemed equivalent to the literal claims of the issued patent. On the contrary, "[b]y the amendment [the patentee] recognized and emphasized the difference between the two phrases[,] ... and [t]he difference which [the patentee] thus disclaimed must be regarded as material." *Exhibit Supply Co. v. Ace Patents Corp.,* 315 U.S. 126, 136–137 (1942).

A rejection indicates that the patent examiner does not believe the original claim could be patented. While the patentee has the right to appeal, his decision to forgo an appeal and submit an amended claim is taken as a concession that the invention as patented does not reach as far as the original claim. See *Goodyear Dental Vulcanite Co. v. Davis,* 102 U.S. 222, 228 (1880) ("In view of [the amendment] there can be no doubt of what [the patentee] understood he had patented, and that both he and the commissioner regarded the patent to be for a manufacture made exclusively of vulcanites by the detailed process"); *Wang Laboratories, Inc. v. Mitsubishi Electronics America, Inc.,* 103 F.3d 1571, 1577–1578 (C.A.Fed.1997) ("Prosecution history estoppel ... preclud[es] a patentee from regaining, through litigation, coverage of subject matter relinquished during prosecution of the application for the patent"). Were it otherwise, the inventor might avoid the PTO's gatekeeping role and seek to recapture in an infringement action the very subject matter surrendered as a condition of receiving the patent.

Prosecution history estoppel ensures that the doctrine of equivalents remains tied to its underlying purpose. Where the original application once embraced the purported equivalent but the patentee narrowed his claims to obtain the patent or to protect its validity, the patentee cannot assert that he lacked the words to describe the subject matter in question. The doctrine of equivalents is premised on language's inability to capture the essence of innovation, but a prior application describing the precise element at issue undercuts that premise. In that instance the prosecution history has established that the inventor turned his attention to the subject matter in question, knew the words for both the broader and narrower claim, and affirmatively chose the latter.

A

The first question in this case concerns the kinds of amendments that may give rise to estoppel. Petitioner argues that estoppel should arise when amendments are intended to narrow the subject matter of the patented invention, for instance, amendments to avoid prior art, but not when the amendments are made to comply with requirements concerning the form of the patent application. In *Warner–Jenkinson* we recognized that prosecution history estoppel does not arise in every instance when a patent application is amended. Our "prior cases have consistently applied prosecution history estoppel only where claims have been amended for a limited set of reasons," such as "to avoid the prior art, or otherwise to address a specific concern—such as obviousness—that arguably would have rendered the claimed subject matter unpatentable." 520 U.S., at 30–32. While we made clear that estoppel applies to amendments made for a "substantial reason related to patentability," *id.,* at 33, we did not purport to define that term or to catalog every reason that might raise an estoppel. Indeed, we stated that even if the amendment's purpose were unrelated to patentability, the court might consider whether it was the kind of reason that nonetheless might require resort to the estoppel doctrine. *Id.,* at 40–41.

Petitioner is correct that estoppel has been discussed most often in the context of amendments made to avoid the prior art. See *Exhibit Supply Co., supra,* at 137; *Keystone Driller Co. v. Northwest Engineering Corp.,* 294 U.S. 42, 48 (1935). Amendment to accommodate prior art was the emphasis, too, of our decision in *Warner–Jenkinson, supra,* at 30. It does not follow, however, that amendments for other purposes will not give rise to estoppel. Prosecution history may rebut the inference that a thing not described was indescribable. That rationale does not cease simply because the narrowing amendment, submitted to secure a patent, was for some purpose other than avoiding prior art.

We agree with the Court of Appeals that a narrowing amendment made to satisfy any requirement of the Patent Act may give rise to an estoppel. As that court explained, a number of statutory requirements must be satisfied before a patent can issue. The claimed subject matter must be useful, novel, and not obvious. 35 U.S.C. §§ 101–103 (1994 ed. and Supp. V). In addition, the patent application must describe, enable, and set forth the best mode of carrying out the invention. § 112 (1994 ed.). These latter requirements must be satisfied before issuance of the patent, for exclusive patent rights are given in exchange for disclosing the invention to the public. See *Bonito Boats,* 489 U.S., at 150–151. What is claimed by the patent application must be the same as what is disclosed in the specification; otherwise the patent should not issue. The patent also should not issue if the other requirements of § 112 are not satisfied, and an applicant's failure to meet these requirements could lead to the issued patent being held invalid in later litigation.

Petitioner contends that amendments made to comply with § 112 concern the form of the application and not the subject matter of the invention. The PTO might require the applicant to clarify an ambiguous term, to improve the translation of a foreign word, or to rewrite a dependent claim as an independent one. In these cases, petitioner argues, the applicant has no intention of surrendering subject matter and should not be estopped from challenging equivalent devices. While this may be true in some cases, petitioner's argument conflates the patentee's reason for making the amendment with the impact the amendment has on the subject matter.

Estoppel arises when an amendment is made to secure the patent and the amendment narrows the patent's scope. If a § 112 amendment is truly cosmetic, then it would not narrow the patent's scope or raise an estoppel. On the other hand, if a § 112 amendment is necessary and narrows the patent's scope—even if only for the purpose of better description—estoppel may apply. A patentee who narrows a claim as a condition for obtaining a patent disavows his claim to the broader subject matter, whether the amendment was made to avoid the prior art or to comply with § 112. We must regard the patentee as having conceded an inability to claim the broader subject matter or at least as having abandoned his right to appeal a rejection. In either case estoppel may apply.

B

Petitioner concedes that the limitations at issue—the sealing rings and the composition of the sleeve—were made for reasons related to § 112, if not also to avoid the prior art. Our conclusion that prosecution history estoppel arises when a claim is narrowed to comply with § 112 gives rise to the second question presented: Does the estoppel bar the inventor from asserting infringement against any equivalent to the narrowed element or might some equivalents still infringe? The Court of Appeals held that prosecution history estoppel is a complete bar, and so the narrowed element must be limited to its strict literal terms. Based upon its experience the Court of Appeals decided that the flexible-bar rule is unworkable because it leads to excessive uncertainty and burdens legitimate innovation. For the reasons that follow, we disagree with the decision to adopt the complete bar.

Though prosecution history estoppel can bar challenges to a wide range of equivalents, its reach requires an examination of the subject matter surrendered by the narrowing amendment. The complete bar avoids this inquiry by establishing a *per se* rule; but that approach is inconsistent with the purpose of applying the estoppel in the first place—to hold the inventor to the representations made during the application process and to the inferences that may reasonably be drawn from the amendment. By amending the application, the inventor is deemed to concede that the patent does not extend as far as the original claim. It does not follow, however, that the amended claim becomes so perfect in its description that no one could devise an equivalent. After amendment, as before, language remains an imperfect fit for invention. The narrowing amendment may demonstrate what the claim is not; but it may still fail to capture precisely what the claim is. There is no reason why a narrowing amendment should be deemed to relinquish equivalents unforeseeable at the time of the amendment and beyond a fair interpretation of what was surrendered. Nor is there any call to foreclose claims of equivalence for aspects of the invention that have only a peripheral relation to the reason the amendment was submitted. The amendment does not show that the inventor suddenly had more foresight in the drafting of claims than an inventor whose application was granted without amendments having been submitted. It shows only that he was familiar with the broader text and with the difference between the two. As a result, there is no more reason for holding the patentee to the literal terms of an amended claim than there is for abolishing the doctrine of equivalents altogether and holding every patentee to the literal terms of the patent.

This view of prosecution history estoppel is consistent with our precedents and respectful of the real practice before the PTO. While this Court has not weighed the merits of the complete bar against the flexible bar in its prior cases, we have consistently applied the doctrine in a flexible way, not a rigid one. We have considered what equivalents were surrendered during the prosecution of the patent, rather than imposing a complete bar that resorts to the very literalism the equivalents rule is designed to overcome. *E.g., Goodyear Dental Vulcanite Co.,* 102 U.S., at 230; *Hurlbut v. Schillinger,* 130 U.S. 456, 465 (1889).

The Court of Appeals ignored the guidance of *Warner–Jenkinson,* which instructed that courts must be cautious before adopting changes that disrupt the settled expectations of the inventing community. See 520 U.S., at 28. In that case we made it clear that the doctrine of equivalents and the rule of prosecution history estoppel are settled law. The responsibility for changing them rests with Congress. *Ibid.* Fundamental alterations in these rules risk destroying the legitimate expectations of inventors in their property. The petitioner in *Warner–Jenkinson* requested another bright-line rule that would have provided more certainty in determining when estoppel applies but at the cost of disrupting the expectations of countless existing patent holders. We rejected that approach: "To change so substantially the rules of the game now could very well subvert the various balances the PTO sought to strike when issuing the numerous patents which have not yet expired and which would be affected by our decision." *Id.*, at 32, n. 6; see also *id.*, at 41 (GINSBURG, J., concurring) ("The new presumption, if applied woodenly, might in some instances unfairly discount the expectations of a patentee who had no notice at the time of patent prosecution that such a presumption would apply"). As *Warner–Jenkinson* recognized, patent prosecution occurs in the light of our case law. Inventors who amended their claims under the previous regime had no reason to believe they were conceding all equivalents. If they had known, they might have appealed the rejection instead. There is no justification for applying a new and more robust estoppel to those who relied on prior doctrine.

In *Warner–Jenkinson* we struck the appropriate balance by placing the burden on the patentee to show that an amendment was not for purposes of patentability:

> Where no explanation is established, however, the court should presume that the patent application had a substantial reason related to patentability for including the limiting element added by amendment. In those circumstances, prosecution history estoppel would bar the application of the doctrine of equivalents as to that element. *Id.* at 33.

When the patentee is unable to explain the reason for amendment, estoppel not only applies but also "bar[s] the application of the doctrine of equivalents as to that element." *Ibid.* These words do not mandate a complete bar; they are limited to the circumstance where "no explanation is established." They do provide, however, that when the court is unable to determine the purpose underlying a narrowing amendment—and hence a rationale for limiting the estoppel to the surrender of particular equivalents—the court should presume that the patentee surrendered all subject matter between the broader and the narrower language.

Just as *Warner–Jenkinson* held that the patentee bears the burden of proving that an amendment was not made for a reason that would give rise to estoppel, we hold here that the patentee should bear the burden of showing that the amendment does not surrender the particular equivalent in question. This is the approach advocated by the United States, see Brief for United States as *Amicus Curiae* 22–28, and we regard it to be sound. The patentee, as the author of the claim language, may be expected to draft claims encompassing readily known equivalents. A patentee's decision to narrow his claims through amendment may be presumed to be a general disclaimer of the territory between the original claim and the amended claim. *Exhibit Supply,* 315 U.S., at 136–137 ("By the amendment [the patentee] recognized and emphasized the difference between the two phrases and proclaimed his abandonment of all that is embraced in that difference"). There are some cases, however, where the amendment cannot reasonably be viewed as surrendering a particular equivalent. The equivalent may have been unforeseeable at the time of the application; the rationale underlying the amendment may bear no more than a tangential relation to the equivalent in question; or there may be some other reason suggesting that the patentee could not reasonably be expected to have described the insubstantial substitute in question. In those cases the patentee can overcome the presumption that prosecution history estoppel bars a finding of equivalence.

This presumption is not, then, just the complete bar by another name. Rather, it reflects the fact that the interpretation of the patent must begin with its literal claims, and the prosecution history is relevant to construing those claims. When the patentee has chosen to narrow a claim, courts may presume the amended text was composed with awareness of this rule and that the territory surrendered is not an equivalent of the territory claimed. In those instances, however, the patentee still might rebut the presumption that estoppel bars a claim of equivalence. The patentee must show that at the time of the amendment one skilled in the art could not reasonably be expected to have drafted a claim that would have literally encompassed the alleged equivalent.

IV

On the record before us, we cannot say petitioner has rebutted the presumptions that estoppel applies and that the equivalents at issue have been surrendered. Petitioner concedes that the limitations at issue—the sealing rings and the composition of the sleeve—were made in response to a rejection for reasons under § 112, if not also because of the prior art references. As the amendments were made for a reason relating to patentability, the question is not whether estoppel applies but what territory the amendments surrendered. While estoppel does not effect a complete bar, the question remains whether petitioner can demonstrate that the narrowing amendments did not surrender the particular equivalents at issue. On these questions, respondents may well prevail, for the sealing rings and the composition of the sleeve both were noted expressly in the prosecution history. These matters, however, should be determined in the first instance by further proceedings in the Court of Appeals or the District Court.

The judgment of the Federal Circuit is vacated, and the case is remanded for further proceedings consistent with this opinion.

NOTES

1. *From Flexibility to Rigidity to Flexibility . . . Almost.* Recall that perhaps the most significant portion of the Federal Circuit's *Festo* decision (*Festo VII*) with respect to innovation policy was the court's adoption of the "complete bar" rule. In discussing this rule, the court held "that prosecution history estoppel acts as a complete bar to the application of the doctrine of equivalents when an amendment has narrowed the scope of a claim for a reason related to patentability."

Although the Supreme Court in *Festo* (*Festo VIII*) acknowledged the importance of certainty in a rights-based system such as patent law, the Court, based on the inherent descriptive limitations of language and a recognition that literalism would "greatly diminish[]" the value of patents, rejected the "complete bar" rule and, adopted a modified version of the "flexible bar" rule. The Court candidly noted that the patent system must tolerate some "uncertainty as the price of ensuring the appropriate incentives for innovation."

2. *A Few Obstacles*. Although the Court reinstated the "flexible bar" approach to the Doctrine of Equivalents, it threw a few obstacles in the way of those patentees wishing to invoke the DOE.

a. *Presumptions and Burdens*. Most significantly, the Court reaffirmed and expanded upon the presumption it established in *Warner–Jenkinson* that "[w]hen the patentee is unable to explain the reason for amendment, estoppel not only applies but also 'bar[s] the application of the doctrine of equivalents as to that element.'" In *Festo*, the Supreme Court broadened this presumption, holding that the decision of the patentee to file a narrowing amendment "may be presumed to be a general disclaimer of the territory between the original and the amended claim;" that is, "the territory surrendered is not an equivalent of the territory claimed." This presumption led the Court to impose a burden on the patentee "of showing that the amendment does not surrender the particular equivalent in question." In particular,

> The patentee must show that at the time of the amendment one skilled in the art could not reasonably be expected to have drafted a claim that would have literally encompassed the alleged equivalent.

What can the patentee submit that would overcome the presumption that the amendment surrenders an equivalent? According to the Court, "[1] [t]he equivalent may have been unforeseeable at the time of the application; [2] the rationale underlying the amendment may bear no more than a tangential relation to the equivalent in question; or [3] there may be some other reason suggesting that the patentee could not reasonably be expected to have described the insubstantial substitute in question." The Supreme Court maintained that its "presumption is not … just the complete bar by another name." Do you agree? What incentives does the Court's presumption and burden create for patent applicants? Is the Court inviting more litigation by injecting forseeability and the skilled artisan into the analysis?

b. *Beyond Prior Art—Defining "Substantial Reasons Related to Patentability."* The Supreme Court agreed the with the Federal Circuit that estoppel can arise from amendments "made to satisfy any requirement of the Patent Act" and not just prior art based rejections. According to the Court, "[e]stoppel arises when an amendment is made to secure the patent and the amendment narrows the patent's scope." This approach may deter applicants from using § 112 rejections or objections to make substantive (on non-cosmetic) claim amendments, but when you think of "reasons related to patentability," do you think of anything other than prior art rejections? The Federal Circuit, on remand, emphasized that "voluntary" amendments also give rise to PHE. *Festo IX*, 344 F.3d 1359, 1366 (Fed.Cir.2003).

3. *The Federal Circuit On Remand: Clarification and Elaboration*. On remand, the Federal Circuit cleaned up a few things from Supreme Court *Festo* and elaborated on others.

a. *Time of Amendment or Application*. The Supreme Court discussed unforeseeability both at the time of application and time of amendment. The Federal Circuit held:

> We clarify that the time when the narrowing amendment was made, and not when the application was filed, is the relevant time for evaluating unforeseeability, for that is when the patentee presumptively surrendered the subject matter in question and it is at that time that foreseeability is relevant.

Festo IX, 344 F.3d at 1365 n.2.

b. *Is Rebuttal of Surrender a Question of Law or Fact?* Yet another interesting question is that given the nature of a forseeability inquiry and what a skilled artisan would "reasonably be expected to have drafted," does prosecution history estoppel remain a question of law? Recall that the Supreme Court in *Warner–Jenkinson* stated that prosecution history estoppel is a "legal limitation on the doctrine of equivalents." *Warner–Jenkinson*, 520 U.S. at 30; and the Federal Circuit subsequently held "[p]rosecution history estoppel is a legal question subject to de novo review on appeal." *Cybor Corp. v. FAS Technologies, Inc.*, 138 F.3d 1448, 1460 (Fed.Cir.1998) (en banc).

The Federal Circuit, in *Festo IX*, held that whether PHE applies and the rebuttal of the presumption of surrender are questions of law, while acknowledging there are underlying questions of fact. According to the court: "We have stated on numerous occasions that whether prosecution history estoppel applies, and hence whether the doctrine of equivalents may be available for a particular claim limitation, presents a question of law." *Festo IX*, 344 F.3d 1359, 1367–68.

c. *Retroactivity*. Does the *Festo VIII* presumption of surrender and rebuttal apply to extant patents and litigation? Yes. *See Festo IX*, 344 F.3d 1370 n.4 ("Consistent with Supreme Court precedent, the holdings of that Court and our own regarding the *Festo* presumption of surrender and its rebuttal apply to all granted patents and to all pending litigation that has not been concluded with a final judgment, including appeals").

d. *Some Thoughts on Warner–Jenkinson, Festo, and the Rebuttal Factors*. On remand, the Federal Circuit offered some guidance on the three rebuttal factors:

> [T]he *Warner–Jenkinson* and *Festo* presumptions operate together in the following manner: The first question in a prosecution history estoppel inquiry is whether an amendment filed in the Patent and Trademark Office ("PTO") has narrowed the literal scope of a claim. *Pioneer Magnetics, Inc. v. Micro Linear Corp.*, 330 F.3d 1352, 1356 (Fed.Cir.2003). If the amendment was not narrowing, then prosecution history estoppel does not apply. But if the accused infringer establishes that the amendment was a narrowing one, then the second question is whether the reason for that amendment was a substantial one relating to patentability. *See id.* When the prosecution history record reveals no reason for the narrowing amendment, *Warner–Jenkinson* presumes that the patentee had a substantial reason relating to patentability; consequently, the patentee must show that the reason for the amendment was not one relating to patentability if it is to rebut that presumption. *See id.* (citing *Warner–Jenkinson*, 520 U.S. at 33, 117 S.Ct. 1040). In this regard, we reinstate our earlier holding that a patentee's rebuttal of the *Warner–Jenkinson* presumption is restricted to the evidence in the prosecution history record. *Festo VI*, 234 F.3d at 586 & n. 6; *see also Pioneer Magnetics*, 330 F.3d at 1356 (stating that only the prosecution history record may be considered in determining whether a patentee has overcome the *Warner–Jenkinson* presumption, so as not to undermine the public notice function served by that record). If the patentee successfully establishes that the amendment was not for a reason of patentability, then prosecution history estoppel does not apply.

> If, however, the court determines that a narrowing amendment has been made for a substantial reason relating to patentability—whether based on a reason reflected in the prosecution history record or on the patentee's failure to overcome the *Warner–Jenkinson* presumption—then the third question in a prosecution history estoppel analysis addresses the scope of the subject matter surrendered by the narrowing amendment. *See Pioneer Magnetics*, 330 F.3d at 1357. At that point *Festo VIII* imposes the presumption that the patentee has surrendered all territory between the original claim limitation and the amended claim limitation. *See Festo VIII*, 535 U.S.

at 740, 122 S.Ct. 1831. The patentee may rebut that presumption of total surrender by demonstrating that it did not surrender the particular equivalent in question according to the criteria discussed below. Finally, if the patentee fails to rebut the *Festo* presumption, then prosecution history estoppel bars the patentee from relying on the doctrine of equivalents for the accused element. If the patentee successfully rebuts the presumption, then prosecution history estoppel does not apply and the question whether the accused element is in fact equivalent to the limitation at issue is reached on the merits.

Because we cannot anticipate all of the circumstances in which a patentee might rebut the presumption of surrender, we believe that discussion of the relevant factors encompassed by each of the rebuttal criteria is best left to development on a case-by-case basis. . . .

The first criterion requires a patentee to show that an alleged equivalent would have been "unforeseeable at the time of the amendment and thus beyond a fair interpretation of what was surrendered." This criterion presents an objective inquiry, asking whether the alleged equivalent would have been unforeseeable to one of ordinary skill in the art at the time of the amendment. Usually, if the alleged equivalent represents later-developed technology (*e.g.,* transistors in relation to vacuum tubes, or Velcro® in relation to fasteners) or technology that was not known in the relevant art, then it would not have been foreseeable. In contrast, old technology, while not always foreseeable, would more likely have been foreseeable. Indeed, if the alleged equivalent were known in the prior art in the field of the invention, it certainly should have been foreseeable at the time of the amendment. By its very nature, objective unforeseeability depends on underlying factual issues relating to, for example, the state of the art and the understanding of a hypothetical person of ordinary skill in the art at the time of the amendment. Therefore, in determining whether an alleged equivalent would have been unforeseeable, a district court may hear expert testimony and consider other extrinsic evidence relating to the relevant factual inquiries.

The second criterion requires a patentee to demonstrate that "the rationale underlying the narrowing amendment [bore] no more than a tangential relation to the equivalent in question." In other words, this criterion asks whether the reason for the narrowing amendment was peripheral, or not directly relevant, to the alleged equivalent. *See The American Heritage College Dictionary* 1385 (3d ed.1997) (defining "tangential" as "[m]erely touching or slightly connected" or "[o]nly superficially relevant; divergent"); 2 *The New Shorter Oxford English Dictionary* 3215–16 (1993) (defining "tangential" as "merely touch[ing] a subject or matter; peripheral"). Although we cannot anticipate the instances of mere tangentialness that may arise, we can say that an amendment made to avoid prior art that contains the equivalent in question is not tangential; it is central to allowance of the claim. Moreover, much like the inquiry into whether a patentee can rebut the *Warner–Jenkinson* presumption that a narrowing amendment was made for a reason of patentability, the inquiry into whether a patentee can rebut the *Festo* presumption under the "tangential" criterion focuses on the patentee's objectively apparent reason for the narrowing amendment. As we have held in the *Warner–Jenkinson* context, that reason should be discernible from the prosecution history record, if the public notice function of a patent and its prosecution history is to have significance. *See id.* at 1356 ("Only the public record of the patent prosecution, the prosecution history, can be a basis for [the reason for the amendment to the claim]. Otherwise, the public notice function of the patent record would be undermined.")... Moreover, whether an amendment was merely tangential to an alleged equivalent necessarily requires focus on the context in which the amendment was made; hence the resort to the prosecution history. Thus, whether the patentee has established a merely tangential reason for a narrowing amendment is for the court to determine from the prosecution history record without the introduction of additional evidence, except, when necessary, testimony from those skilled in the art as to the interpretation of that record.

The third criterion requires a patentee to establish "some other reason suggesting that the patentee could not reasonably be expected to have described the insubstantial substitute in question." This category, while vague, must be a narrow one; it is available in order not to totally foreclose a patentee from relying on reasons, other than unforeseeability and tangentialness, to show that it did not surrender the alleged equivalent. Thus, the third criterion may be satisfied when there was some reason, such as the shortcomings of language, why the patentee was prevented from describing the alleged equivalent when it narrowed the claim. When at all possible, determination of the third rebuttal criterion should also be limited to the prosecution history record. For example, as we recently held in *Pioneer*, 330 F.3d 1352 (Fed.Cir.2003), a patentee may not rely on the third rebuttal criterion if the alleged equivalent is in the prior art, for then "there can be no other reason the patentee could not have described the substitute in question." *Id.* at 357. We need not decide now what evidence outside the prosecution history record, if any, should be considered in determining if a patentee has met its burden under this third rebuttal criterion.

Festo IX, 344 F.3d 1369–70.

4. *When Is an Amendment "Narrowing"?* Under *Festo*, a patent applicant desiring to maintain a right to resort to equivalency will try to avoid amendments or arguments that narrow the scope of the asserted claims. A traditional approach to presenting claims in a patent application is to present a set of claims consisting of a very broad claim followed by a series of claims, some dependent, that progressively limit the broadest claim. The type of amendment that was submitted in *Warner–Jenkinson*, where the patent applicant amended its upper pH range to 9 in the light of prior art is a classic narrowing amendment. But what about an applicant who cancels a rejected independent claim and replaces it with an unaltered, but narrower, dependent claim? Is this new independent claim (once a dependent) a narrowing event, thus invoking the *Festo* presumption of surrender? The Federal Circuit has stated that "the correct focus is on whether [the] amendment surrendered subject matter that was originally claimed for reasons related to patentability." *Deering Precision Instruments, L.L.C. v. Vector Distribution Systems, Inc.*, 347 F.3d 1314, 1325 (Fed.Cir.2003).

With this in mind, consider the following example. An applicant may present the following original claims:

1. A therapeutic composition comprising a combination of aspirin and Viagra, the aspirin comprising less than 20% of the composition by weight.

2. The composition of claim 1 in which the aspirin comprises less than 5%.

An examiner allows claim 2, but rejects claim 1 as obvious in view of a reference, which discloses an example of combining aspirin and Viagra, the aspirin comprising 15%. The applicant cancels claim 1 and rewrites dependent claim 2 in independent form. The patent issues and is later asserted against an accused composition that comprises 10% aspirin.

Note that application claim 2, which became patent claim 1, was not actually rejected or limited, and it was only amended in a formal way (*i.e.*, to make it independent) that did not change its substantive scope. Nevertheless, the *Festo* court's discussion of the Stoll patent makes clear that cancellation of a broad claim in favor of a narrower one may have the same effect as an amendment of the broad claim. So, an estoppel may arise as to patent claim 1, and there will be no assertion of equivalency as to the 5% limitation by the accused product, which contains 10% aspirin. *See also Mycogen Plant Science, Inc. and Agrigenetics, Inc. v. Monsanto Co.*, 261 F.3d 1345, 1349 (Fed.Cir.2001) (replacing rejected and cancelled independent claim with narrower dependent claim is a narrowing event); *Ranbaxy Pharmaceuticals Inc. v. Apotex, Inc.*, 350 F.3d 1235 (Fed.Cir.2003) ("In this case the surrender is particularly clear. While Apotex was merely rewriting a dependent claim into independent form, the effect on the subject matter was substantial. The dependent claims that were redrafted into independent form did more than simply add an additional limitation; they further defined and circumscribed an existing limitation for the purpose of putting the claims in condition for allowance").

Moreover, the *Festo* presumption applies to unamended claims (*i.e.*, allowed as originally filed) that contain the limitation that was added through amendment to other claims—claims that were narrowed through the addition of the limitation. For example, applicant files two independent claims. Claim 1 originally recites a marine deck having a solid casing. Claim 2 originally recites a marine deck having a concrete casing surrounding a buoyant core. The Examiner rejects claim 1 in light of prior art disclosing a marine deck having a wooden casing. Applicant amends claim 1 by including the concrete casing limitation of claim 2. The Examiner allows both claims. Competitor makes a marine deck having a steel casing surrounding a buoyant core.

The *Festo* presumption applies to claim 1 because claim 1 was narrowed for reasons related to patentability. Does the presumption apply to claim 2, which was not amended during prosecution? Yes according to the Federal Circuit, because claim 2 contains the limitation (*i.e.*, concrete casing) that was added to claim 1 to render claim 1 allowable. In other words, prosecution history estoppel precludes the patentee from interpreting claim 2 to encompass that which was relinquished in claim 1—a "solid casing"—even though claim 2 was never amended. In *Builders Concrete, Inc. v. Bremerton Concrete Products Company*, 757 F.2d 255 (Fed.Cir. 1985), the Federal Circuit rejected the patentee's (Builders Concrete, Inc.) assertion that "file wrapper estoppel cannot arise without an amendment." *Id.* at 259. According the court:

> The district court concluded that the prosecution history estopped Builders Concrete from interpreting application claim 11 (patent claim 10) to encompass that which was relinquished in the successful argument for patentability of amended claim 1. Although claim 10 is the only claim in suit, the prosecution history of all claims is not insulated from review in connection with determining the fair scope of claim 10. To hold otherwise would be to exalt form over substance and distort the logic of this jurisprudence, which serves as an effective and useful guide to the understanding of patent claims. The fact that the "passage" clause of patent claim 10 was not itself amended during prosecution does not mean that it can be extended by the doctrine of equivalents. To cover the precise subject matter that was relinquished in order to obtain allowance of claim 1. It is clear from the prosecution history that the allowance of claim 1, the

broadest claim ... depended on the amendment narrowing its "passage" definition to that of claim 10.

Id. at 260.

5. *Estoppel by Argument.* Estoppel can arise by an argument during prosecution even when the claims are not amended. The possibility of estoppel by argument may become more critical in the future if applicants, aware of the estoppel effect of any narrowing amendment under *Festo,* elect not to amend claims in response to rejections but, instead, to dispute the basis for an examiner's rejection of the claims.

One position would be that an argument creates an estoppel precluding equivalency of an element only when the prosecution history has the effect of limiting the meaning (that is, literal scope) of the claim. Federal Circuit case law on the effect of prosecution history arguments on claim construction suggests that it can be difficult to predict when arguments will have such a limiting effect. For example, in *Watts v. XL Systems, Inc.,* 232 F.3d 877 (Fed.Cir.2000), an argument had a limiting effect. Two patents concerned a "connection for joints of oilwell tubing." The patents' claims contained a "sealingly connected" limitation:

" '... each joints of pipe having a first end with no increase in wall thickness relative to the average pipe wall thickness and formed with tapered internal threads; the joints each having a *second end formed with tapered external threads dimensioned such that one such joint may be sealingly connected directly with another such joint.*' "

Id. at 879 (Emphasis in original). In the patents' specification, the structure for performing the sealing function was performed by "misaligned taper angles." In an infringement suit, the patent owner and an accused infringer stipulated that the accused structure did not use "misaligned taper angles" or any structure that is "insubstantially different" from such angles. The court held the "sealingly connect-ed" element did not have its broad, ordinary meaning but rather was limited to misaligned taper angles. The misaligned taper angles were the only method for achieving a seal described in the patents' specification. That a person of ordinary skill in the art may have been aware of "myriad ways to effect a sealing connection" did "not overcome the fact that the specification specifies that the invention uses misaligned taper angles." Also, in remarks during prosecution of the first of the two patents, the patent owner limited the invention by "distinguish[ing] the primary reference based on the invention's misaligned taper angles."

Compare *Watts* with *Vanguard Products Corp. v. Parker Hannifin Corp.,* 234 F.3d 1370 (Fed.Cir.2000), in which an argument did *not* have a limiting effect. The patent at issue concerned a gasket shield. The patent's claims required a thick layer and a thin layer "integral therewith." The patent's specification taught a "co-extrusion" method for forming a composition of two materials. Co-extrusion en-tailed forcing the materials through dies. The accused product used a "dip-coating" method for applying one layer to the other. The Federal Circuit majority, in an opinion by Judge Newman, held that a district court properly gave the term "integral" its broad, ordinary meaning, based on a dictionary definition. The term was not limited to co-extrusion. During prosecution, the inventor "extolled the economy of manufacture and superior product made by co-extrusion" but did not expressly disclaim claim scope beyond products made by co-extrusion. Judge Mayer dissented, noting that "[t]he arguments distinguishing the amended claims over the prior art are part of the prosecution history that the public has a right to rely on in determining the scope of the claims."

Is the majority's "no workable" reasoning persuasive? Can you articulate a standard for determining the scope of surrender? Note that the pre-*Festo Litton* panel decision suggested the following standards for determining scope:

When prosecution history estops a patentee, the court ascertains the scope of the estoppel in several ways. First, "a patentee is estopped from recovering through equivalency that which was deemed unpatentable in view of the prior art." *Pall Corp. v. Micron Separations, Inc.*, 66 F.3d 1211, 1219 (Fed.Cir.1995). In other words, when an applicant, in response to an examiner's prior art rejection, amends a claim by substituting one limitation for another, the applicant cannot later assert that the original limitation is an equivalent of the substituted limitation. Thus, the doctrine prevents the applicant from completely recapturing the subject matter rejected by the examiner.

In addition, when an applicant narrows a claim element in the face of an examiner's rejection based on the prior art, the doctrine estops the applicant from later asserting that the claim covers, through the doctrine of equivalents, features that the applicant amended his claim to avoid. A patentee is also estopped to assert equivalence to "trivial" variations of such prior art features. *See Southwall Techs., Inc. v. Cardinal IG Co.*, 54 F.3d 1570, 1580, 34 U.S.P.Q.2D 1673, 1680 (Fed.Cir.1995). Depending on the facts of the case, an amendment may also limit the patentee to its literal claim scope. *See Wang Lab., Inc. v. Toshiba Corp.*, 993 F.2d 858, 867–68 (Fed.Cir.1993); *Wang Lab., Inc. v. Mitsubishi Elecs. America*, 103 F.3d 1571, 1577–78 (Fed.Cir.1997).

In addition, as noted earlier, an applicant's arguments may constitute a clear and unmistakable surrender of subject matter. Such arguments preclude recapture of that subject matter. *See Texas Instruments*, 988 F.2d at 1174–75 (holding that applicants had clearly represented that "same-side gating" did not work and could not be asserted as an equivalent). As noted above, this type of estoppel can arise regardless of the *Warner–Jenkinson* presumptions. . . . Of course, applicants commonly make arguments in combination with an amendment, as in this case. In such circumstances, the scope of estoppel is a product of the effects of both factors working in concert.

6. *In the Final Analysis, Do We Want the DOE?* Having reviewed in some detail the extent to which courts attempt to expand and contract the scope of DOE, including through the use of limiting doctrines like prosecution history estoppel, and others, an important question to ask is whether DOE is really desired, even by patentees. In this connection it is worth noting that a principal drafter of the present system, Judge Rich, joined two of the dissenting opinions in Hilton Davis Chemical Co. v. Warner–Jenkinson Co. that objected to the DOE in its entirety. 62 F.3d 1512, 1536 (1995) (Plager, J., dissenting, joined by Archer, C.J., and Rich & Lourie, JJ.), rev'd, 520 U.S. 17 (1997); id. at 1545 (Lourie, J., dissenting, joined by Rich & Plager, JJ.). For a theoretical perspective consider the following:

> An understanding of incentive for individual patentees to get patent scope "just right" provides some guidance on the ongoing battle over the DOE, which allows a patentee to win an infringement suit against something that is not literally covered by the claims. Allowing the patentee recourse to this doctrine is bad in that it weakens the important self-disciplining effect [that the rules for patentability exert on the claims]; eliminating the doctrine would be good in that it would accentuate this incentive

> Importantly, this criticism of the DOE is not merely driven by concerns about absolute crispness, or advantages of rules over standards. Rather, the core argument is a matter of comparative institutional economics.

> To understand the intuition of the argument it may help to first consider that the DOE is structurally at odds with the basic approach to claims

under the present positive law rules of the patent system, which together yield an approach known as "peripheral claiming"—as distinct from "central claiming"—in which the function of the patent claim is not to set forth the heart of the protected subject matter but rather to set forth its outer bounds. A determination of infringement under a central claiming approach requires the court to determine the heart of the invention and whether the putative infringement is close enough to that heart to justify a judgment of infringement. A determination under peripheral claiming requires the court to determine only the outer bounds of the claim. Anything within those bounds infringes and anything outside does not. The DOE in the present patent system, even though not provided for in the statute, is an odd exception to the peripheral nature of our present peripheral claiming system precisely because it allows the patentee to capture something outside of the claim.

Although the DOE has some general intuitive attraction because it gives some flexibility, the registration theory shows how the patentee can achieve even greater flexibility in a manner that is not only less costly to the patentee but also to all third parties by simply drafting a better patent disclosure at the outset. Under the disclosure rules of patent law, the patentee at the time of filing can draft a disclosure that will support claims of varying scope.

It may be possible that the information-forcing benefits of a system with no DOE would be outweighed by the added costs it may encourage some patent applicants to incur as a precaution. But, on a per-patent basis, the direct costs to patentees of this drafting effort (largely legal fees) are substantially less than those associated with litigating DOE issues later in court. In addition, the indirect costs of having to decide whether this extra flexibility on scope is worth such direct costs will be cabined to some extent by the small size of the potential gain from avoiding the direct costs themselves. Even if it turned out that putative patentees, on average, do not make at least roughly appropriate decisions about which of their own patents deserve more or less attention at the drafting stage, a significant moral hazard problem certainly would arise if decisions on application of the DOE were understood to turn on this type of error by individual patentees. Moreover, the DOE imposes substantial litigation costs on competitors of the patentee. The general uncertainty arising out of the DOE can also chill business transactions of all sorts, including commercialization efforts by competitors and downstream developers as well as by business partners of even the patentee.

It also may be possible that the information-forcing benefits of a system with no DOE would be outweighed by other costs to the system. One major component of these countervailing costs will be the decreased commercialization benefits to society that would be associated with those inventions protected by patents whose patentees, at the time of filing, elected to spend too little on patent drafting. But once again, a significant moral hazard problem certainly would arise if decisions on application of the DOE were understood to turn on this type of error by individual patentees as well.

Alternatively, as Douglas Lichtman suggests, information forcing may be of no benefit if, at the time of filing, the patentee may not be able to draft an application that could convey appropriate patent scope given the inevitably changing state of technological vocabularies. [Douglas Lichtman, Rethinking Prosecution History Estoppel 27–28 (Univ. of Chi., John M. Olin Law & Econ., Working Paper No. 200, 2003), available at http://ssrn.com/

abstract=455380]. But to the extent it suggests that a patentee somehow deserves the broader scope captured by the DOE, this view of what is an appropriate patent scope would seem to be based on a version of a reward theory and would fail to account for the focus on minimizing social cost that is central to positive law rules for patentability—especially the disclosure rules—as elucidated by the registration theory.

In addition, it is not clear whether such concerns about changes in technology actually obtain, as a practical matter, under a peripheral claming system. Under a peripheral claiming approach, each claim can be viewed as a simple logical list in which each word, or element, in the claim is considered a required item in the list. This list of elements can be compared against the allegedly infringing product or process in much the same way it was compared against the prior art.... Patent infringement occurs when each and every element of the claim can be found in the allegedly infringing product or process. According to such a comparison, the more elements there are, the harder it is to infringe. Instead of trying to determine and then recite in the claim every particular use by potential future infringers, a prudent patentee under such a system tries to determine the general nature of these potential uses and then recites them as a class in the claim. For example, rather than drafting a claim that recites, among other elements, a list of specific expected fastener technologies such as nails, screws, and Velcro®, a prudent patentee might recite "a fastener" as a claim element and then elsewhere in the patent provide a careful disclosure of what is meant by this term including a qualitative description and representative examples.

This approach to claiming and drafting deals well with even unknowable future technologies. Put simply, this is the job of a good patent lawyer and one reason why patents are legal documents drafted by lawyers for interpretation by judges and lawyers, not technical documents evaluated by peer review. The standard for satisfaction of the disclosure rules' written description requirement is merely whether the disclosure as filed conveys to a PHOSITA that the inventor had possession of the claimed invention at that time; ipsis verbis disclosure is not needed. As a result, a prudent drafter easily can employ claim elements that are disclosed to be a "genus and its constituent species" (or a class of constituent members) without having to identify in the disclosure every single species (or member), as long as the disclosure provides a clear indication of how to determine membership in the genus (or class).... To be sure, the crafting of a disclosure that complies with these rules may itself be difficult; and no disclosure will be perfect. Recent opinions of the various Federal Circuit judges evidence a particular tension about whether this disclosure standard is so fixed, and whether it can be satisfied. Thus, the disclosure rules themselves to some extent raise many of the same concerns as the DOE. In the final analysis of the tension between the effort to achieve flexibility through either the DOE or the disclosure requirements, the registration theory's contribution is to highlight, as a matter of comparative institutional economics, why reliance on the disclosure rules is less likely to trigger these important concerns as extensively.

F. Scott Kieff, *The Case for Registering Patents and the Law and Economics of Present Patent–Obtaining Rules*, 45 B.C. L. Rev. 55, 109–114 (2003) (footnotes omitted).

C. INFRINGEMENT OF MEANS PLUS FUNCTION CLAIMS—35 U.S.C. § 112, ¶ 6

Paragraph six of § 112 provides that an "element in a claim for a combination may be expressed as a means or step for performing a specified function." Such elements are known as "means-plus-function" elements. The paragraph also directs that a claim with such an element "shall be construed to cover the corresponding structure, material, or acts described in the specification and equivalents thereof." What constitutes a means-plus-function element and how equivalency is determined under § 112 ¶ 6 are explored in *Al–Site Corporation v. VIS International.*

Al–Site Corporation v. VSI International, Inc.

174 F.3d 1308 (Fed.Cir.1999).

■ Before MAYER, CHIEF JUDGE, RICH, AND RADER, CIRCUIT JUDGES

■ RADER, CIRCUIT JUDGE

After the United States District Court for the Southern District of Florida interpreted the claims, a jury found that VSI International, Inc. (VSI) had infringed several patents claiming specific hangers for displaying non-prescription eyeglasses. Although Al–Site Corporation, now Magnivision, Inc. (Magnivision), prevailed on infringement, it appeals the district court's claim construction. On review, this court discerns errors in claim construction. Under a correct claim construction, the record contains substantial evidence that VSI infringed Magnivision's patents. Therefore, this court affirms the patent infringement finding.

I.

Magnivision and VSI both sell non-prescription eyeglasses. Magnivision is the assignee of U.S. Patent Nos. 4,976,532 (the '532 patent), 5,144,345 (the '345 patent), 5,260,726 (the '726 patent), and 5,521,911 (the '911 patent). These patents claim technology for displaying eyeglasses on racks. The claimed inventions allow consumers to try on eyeglasses and return them to the rack without removing them from their display hangers. [The '911 patent is a continuation of the '726 patent, which is a continuation of the '345 patent, which in turn is a continuation of the '532 patent.]

Magnivision sued VSI, as well as its chairman and CEO, Myron Orlinsky, in his individual capacity, for infringement of the Magnivision patents. Six years after filing, the district court conducted a jury trial. After interpreting the claims, the district court instructed the jury to apply its construction of the claims to determine infringement.

The jury determined that one of VSI's products (the Version 1 hanger tag) literally infringed the '532 patent. The jury also determined that a second VSI product (the Version 2 hanger tag) did not literally infringe the '345, '726, and '911 patents, but did infringe those patents under the doctrine of equivalents.

Following the jury verdict, Magnivision moved for judgment as a matter of law that the Version 2 hanger tag literally infringed the '345,- '726, and '911 patents. VSI's post-trial motion sought to reverse all of the jury's determinations. The district court denied both motions and both parties appeal. Specifically, Magnivision challenges the district court's claim construction of the '345, '726, and '911 patents, arguing that the claims, if properly construed, would have been literally infringed by VSI's Version 2 hanger tag. VSI, on the other hand, contends that the district court's claim construction was correct but challenges the jury's determinations for lack of substantial evidence to support a verdict.

II.

* * *

Infringement of the '345, '726, and '911 Patents

The jury determined that VSI's Version 2 hanger tag and display rack did not literally infringe claims 1 and 2 of the '345 patent; claims 1 and 2 of the '726 patent; or claims 1, 2, and 3 of the '911 patent. The jury nevertheless found infringement of each of these claims under the doctrine of equivalents. Magnivision argues that the district court misconstrued these claims, and that, under the proper claim construction, VSI's products literally infringe these claims as a matter of law. VSI, on the other hand, embraces the district court's claim construction and argues that prosecution history estoppel precludes a finding of infringement under the doctrine of equivalents.

Claim 1 of the '345 patent and claim 1 of the '726 patent are similar. Both claim "[t]he combination of an eyeglass display member and an eyeglass hanger member." In each of these claims, this combination includes a "display member" with "cantilever support means" and "an eyeglass hanger member for mounting a pair of eyeglasses." Both claims further define the structure of the eyeglass hanger member. Claim 1 of the '345 patent describes the eyeglass hanger member as "made from flat sheet material," and having an "opening means formed ... below [its] upper edge." According to claim 1 of the '726 patent, the eyeglass hanger member has "an attaching portion attachable to a portion of said frame of said pair of eyeglasses to enable the temples of the frame [to be opened and closed]." Similarly, claim 2 of the '726 patent encompasses a "method of displaying eyeglass/hanger combinations ... the eyeglass hangers having an attaching portion attached to a portion of the frame of an associated pair of eyeglasses."

Claims 1, 2, and 3 of the '911 patent encompass a "combination of an eyeglass display member and an eyeglass contacting member." The '911 patent further describes the structure of the "eyeglass contacting member" as "having an encircling portion adapted to encircle a part of said frame of said pair of eyeglasses."

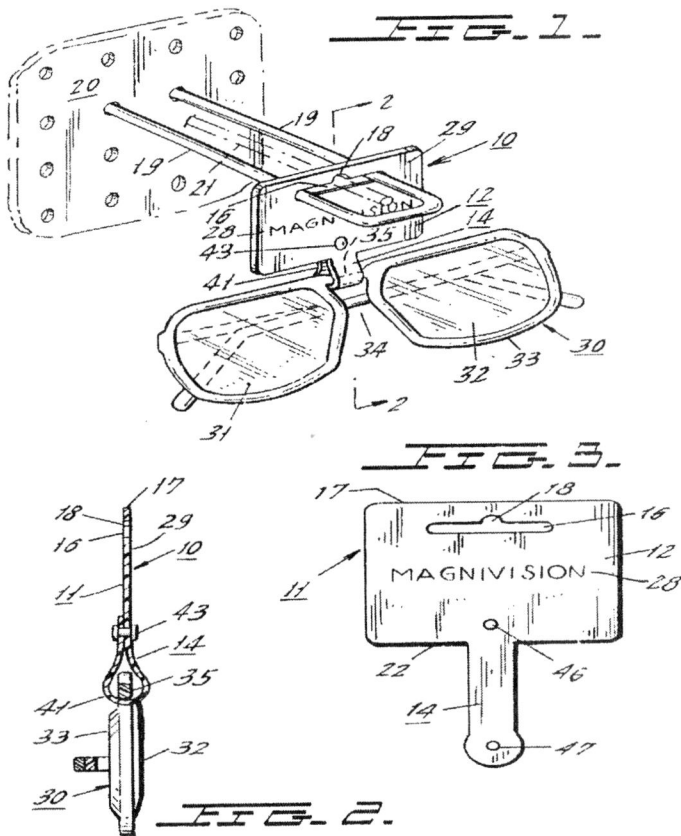

[FIG. 1-3 of '345, '726, and '911 Patents]

[Now referring particularly to FIGS. 1, 2, and 3. Hanger **10**, constructed in accordance with a first embodiment of the instant invention, includes main element **11** (FIG. 3) which is a single sheet of relatively stiff resilient plastic material, typically a polythene. Element **11** consists of rectangular relatively wide main section or body **12** and relatively narrow extension **14**. It is intended that front surface **29** of body **12** is provided with elongated aperture section **16** that is substantially longer than the width of extension **14**, and is disposed in the vicinity of and extends parallel to edge **17**. Centered between the ends of aperture section **16** and extending therefrom toward edge **17** is notch-like aperture section **18**. Elongated section **16** is adapted to receive a cantilevered support comprising spaced parallel arms **19**, **19**, which project horizontally from wall **20**, while notch section **18** is adapted to receive a cantilevered support consisting of single horizontal arm **21**. Extension **14** is centered along edge **22** of main section **12** and is centered with respect to the length of aperture **16**. Edge **17** is parallel to edge **22** and prior to formation of loop **41** (FIG. 2), the entire extension **14** projects from edge **22** away from edge **17**. (Col. 2, ll. 46 to Col. 3, l. 2)]

The district court construed the "eyeglass hanger member" element of the '345 patent as a means-plus-function claim element subject to § 112, ¶ 6. Accordingly, the district court instructed the jury that "[t]he 'eyeglass hanger member for mounting a pair of eyeglasses' [in claim 1 of the '345 patent] is the body of the hanger disclosed in the '345 patent and its drawings and the structural equivalents thereof." The district court similarly interpreted the "eyeglass hanger member" element of the '726 patent. The district court instructed the jury that "[t]he 'eyeglass hanger member for mounting a pair of eyeglasses' [in claim 1 of the '726 patent] is the hanger disclosed in the '726 patent and its drawings as having a body, an aperture, and an attaching portion and the structural equivalents thereof."

With respect to the '911 patent, the district court concluded that the "eyeglass contacting member" was a means-plus-function element. The district court therefore instructed the jury that the "eyeglass contacting member" is "the hanger disclosed in the '911 patent and its drawings having a body and an aperture and an 'encircling portion', and the structural equivalents thereof."

This court reviews the district court's claim interpretation without deference. *See Cybor Corp. v. FAS Technologies, Inc.*, 138 F.3d 1448, 1454–56 (Fed.Cir.1998) (en banc). This court has delineated several rules for claim drafters to invoke the strictures of 35 U.S.C. § 112, ¶ 6. Specifically, if the word "means" appears in a claim element in combination with a function, it is presumed to be a means-plus-function element to which § 112, ¶ 6 applies. *See Sage Prods., Inc. v. Devon Indus., Inc.*, 126 F.3d 1420, 1427 (Fed.Cir.1997). Nevertheless, according to its express terms, § 112, ¶ 6 governs only claim elements that do not recite sufficient structural limitations. Therefore, the presumption that § 112, ¶ 6 applies is overcome if the claim itself recites sufficient structure or material for performing the claimed function. *See Sage*, 126 F.3d at 1427–28 ("[W]here a claim recites a function, but then goes on to elaborate sufficient structure, material, or acts within the claim itself to perform entirely the recited function, the claim is not in means-plus-function format.").

Although use of the phrase "means for" (or "step for") is not the only way to invoke § 112, ¶ 6, that terminology typically invokes § 112, ¶ 6 while other formulations generally do not. Therefore, when an element of a claim does not use the term "means," treatment as a means-plus-function claim element is generally not appropriate. *See Mas–Hamilton Group v. LaGard, Inc.*, 156 F.3d 1206, 1213–15 (Fed.Cir.1998). However, when it is apparent that the element invokes purely functional terms, without the additional recital of specific structure or material for performing that function, the claim element may be a means-plus-function element despite the lack of express means-plus-function language. *See, e.g., Cole*, 102 F.3d at 531 ("[M]erely because an element does not include the word 'means' does not automatically prevent that element from being construed as a means-plus-function element."); *Mas–Hamilton*, 156 F.3d at 1213–15 (interpreting "lever moving element" and "movable link member" under § 112, ¶ 6).

Under this established analytical framework, the "eyeglass hanger member" elements in the claims of both the '345 and the '726 patents do not invoke § 112, ¶ 6. In the first place, these elements are not in traditional means-plus-function format. The word "means" does not appear within these elements. Moreover, although these claim elements include a function, namely, "mounting a pair of eyeglasses," the claims themselves contain sufficient structural limitations for performing those functions. As noted above, claim 1 of the '345 patent describes the eyeglass hanger member as "made from flat sheet material" with an "opening means formed . . . below [its] upper edge." This structure removes this claim from the purview of § 112, ¶ 6. Similarly, according to claim 1 of the '726 patent, the eyeglass hanger member has "an attaching portion attachable to a portion of said frame of said pair of eyeglasses to enable the temples of the frame [to be opened and closed]." This structure also precludes treatment as a means-plus-function claim element. The district court therefore improperly restricted the "eyeglass hanger member" in these claims to the structural embodiments in the specification and their equivalents.

* * *

For reasons similar to those discussed above with respect to the claim elements of the '345 and the '726 patents, the "eyeglass contacting member" element of the '911 patent claims is also not a means-plus-function element. Again, this claim element is not in traditional means-plus-function form. Furthermore, the claim itself recites sufficient structure for performing the recited function. Specifically, claim 1 of the '911 patent describes the "eyeglass contacting member" as "having an encircling portion adapted to encircle a part of said frame of said pair of eyeglasses to enable the temples of the frame to be selectively [opened and closed]." Similarly, claim 3 of the '911 patent describes the "eyeglass contacting member" as "having an attaching portion attachable to a portion of said frame of said eyeglasses." Therefore, the district court erred by applying § 112, ¶ 6 to these claim elements.

Magnivision also complains that the district court erred in its construction of the language "means for securing a portion of said frame of said eyeglasses to said hanger member" in claim 1 of the '345 patent. With respect to this element, the district court instructed the jury that "[t]he 'means for securing' limitation is a mechanically fastened loop that goes around the nose bridge of the glasses . . . or an equivalent thereof." The district court went on, however, to instruct the jury that "[t]he means for securing can be formed from a separate extension or integral extension and includes either the rivet fastener or the button and hole fastener." Magnivision argues that the district court should have included the phrase "or equivalents thereof" after "button and hole fastener" in its instruction to the jury. Absent this and the other claimed errors in the district court's interpretation of claim 1 of the '345 patent, Magnivision argues that the jury would have found literal infringement rather than infringement under the doctrine of equivalents.

The "means for securing" claim element is in conventional means-plus-function format without specific recital of structure and therefore invokes § 112, ¶ 6. The jury's finding of infringement of claim 1 of the '345 patent under the doctrine of equivalents indicates that the jury found every element of the claim literally or equivalently present in the accused device. The question before this court, therefore, is whether the jury's finding that the accused structure was equivalent to the "means for securing" element under the doctrine of equivalents, also indicates that it is equivalent structure under § 112, ¶ 6.

This court has on several occasions explicated the distinctions between the term "equivalents" found in § 112, ¶ 6 and the doctrine of equivalents. *See, e.g., Valmont Indus., Inc. v. Reinke Mfg. Co.*, 983 F.2d 1039, 1042–44 (Fed.Cir.1993); *Chiuminatta*, 145 F.3d at 1310; *Alpex Computer Corp. v. Nintendo Co.*, 102 F.3d 1214, 1222 (Fed.Cir.1996). Indeed, the Supreme Court recently acknowledged distinctions between equivalents as used in § 112, ¶ 6 and the doctrine of equivalents. *See Warner–Jenkinson Co. v. Hilton Davis Chem. Co.*, 520 U.S. 17, 27 (1997) ("[Equivalents under § 112, ¶ 6] is an application of the doctrine of equivalents in a restrictive role, narrowing the application of broad literal claim elements. [Section 112, ¶ 6] was enacted as a targeted cure to a specific problem.... The added provision, however, is silent on the doctrine of equivalents as applied where there is no literal infringement.").

Section 112, ¶ 6 recites a mandatory procedure for interpreting the meaning of a means-or step-plus-function claim element. These claim limitations "shall be construed to cover the corresponding structure, material, or acts described in the specification and equivalents thereof." 35 U.S.C. § 112, ¶ 6. Thus, § 112, ¶ 6 procedures restrict a functional claim element's "broad literal language ... to those means that are 'equivalent' to the actual means shown in the patent specification." *Warner–Jenkinson*, 117 S.Ct. at 1048. Section 112, ¶ 6 restricts the scope of a functional claim limitation as part of a literal infringement analysis. *See Pennwalt Corp. v. Durand–Wayland, Inc.*, 833 F.2d 931, 934 (Fed.Cir.1987). Thus, an equivalent under § 112, ¶ 6 informs the claim meaning for a literal infringement analysis. The doctrine of equivalents, on the other hand, extends enforcement of claim terms beyond their literal reach in the event "there is 'equivalence' between the elements of the accused product or process and the claimed elements of the patented invention." *Warner–Jenkinson*, 117 S.Ct. at 1045.

One important difference between § 112, ¶ 6 and the doctrine of equivalents involves the timing of the separate analyses for an "insubstantial change." As this court has recently clarified, a structural equivalent under § 112 must have been available at the time of the issuance of the claim. *See Chiuminatta*, 145 F.3d at 1310. An equivalent structure or act under § 112 cannot embrace technology developed after the issuance of the patent because the literal meaning of a claim is fixed upon its issuance. An "after arising equivalent" infringes, if at all, under the doctrine of equivalents. *See Warner–Jenkinson*, 117 S.Ct. at 1052; *Hughes Aircraft Co. v. U.S.*, 140 F.3d 1470, 1475 (Fed.Cir.1998). Thus, the temporal difference between patent issuance and infringement distinguish an equivalent under § 112 from an equivalent under the doctrine of equivalents. *See Chiuminatta*, 145 F.3d at 1310. In other words, an equivalent structure or act under § 112 for literal infringement must have been available at the time of patent issuance while an equivalent under the doctrine of equivalents may arise after patent issuance and before the time of infringement. *See Warner–Jenkinson*, 117 S.Ct. at 1053. An "after-arising" technology could thus infringe under the doctrine of equivalents without infringing literally as a § 112, ¶ 6 equivalent.[2] Furthermore, under § 112, ¶ 6, the accused device must perform the identical function as recited in the claim element while the doctrine of equivalents may be satisfied when the function performed by the accused device is only substantially the same.

Although § 112, ¶ 6 and the doctrine of equivalents are different in purpose and administration, "a finding of a lack of literal infringement for lack of equivalent structure under a means-plus-function limitation may preclude a finding of equivalence under the doctrine of equivalents." *Chiuminatta*, 145 F.3d at 1311. Both equivalence analyses, after all, apply "similar analyses of insubstantiality of the differences." *Id.* This confluence occurs because infringement requires, either literally or under the doctrine of equivalents, that the accused product or process incorporate each limitation of the claimed invention. Therefore, if an accused product or process performs the identical function and yet avoids literal infringement for lack of a § 112, ¶ 6 structural equivalent, it may well fail to infringe the same functional element under the doctrine of equivalents. *See Chiuminatta*, 145 F.3d at 1311. This same reasoning may be applied in reverse in certain circumstances. Where, as here, there is identity of function and no after-arising technology, a means-plus-function claim element that is found to be infringed only under the doctrine of equivalents due to a jury instruction failing to instruct on § 112, ¶ 6 structural equivalents is also literally present in the accused device.

VSI's Version 2 hanger tag has a central body and two arms, with one arm extending from each side of the body. Each arm has a hole near the end for receipt of an eyeglasses temple. The body also has an aperture through which a cantilever rod can be placed so the hanger tag can be hung from a display rack. VSI's Version 2 hanger tag is the subject of U.S. Patent No. 5,141,104 (the '104 patent).

As noted above, the doctrine of equivalents and structural equivalents under § 112, ¶ 6, though different in purpose and administration, can at times render the same result. In this case, the jury found infringement under the doctrine of equivalents. This finding presupposes that the jury found an equivalent for each element of the claimed invention, including the "means for securing." The holes in the arms of VSI's Version 2 hanger

---

2. These principles, as explained in *Chiuminatta Concrete Concepts, Inc. v. Cardinal Indus., Inc.*, 145 F.3d 1303 (Fed.Cir.1998), suggest that title 35 will not produce an "equivalent of an equivalent" by applying both § 112, ¶ 6 and the doctrine of equivalents to the structure of a given claim element. A proposed equivalent must have arisen at a definite period in time, i.e., either before or after patent issuance. If before, a § 112, ¶ 6 structural equivalents analysis applies and any analysis for equivalent structure under the doctrine of equivalents collapses into the § 112, ¶ 6 analysis. If after, a non-textual infringement analysis proceeds under the doctrine of equivalents. Patent policy supports application of the doctrine of equivalents to a claim element expressed in means-plus-function form in the case of "after-arising" technology because a patent draftsman has no way to anticipate and account for later developed substitutes for a claim element. Therefore, the doctrine of equivalents appropriately allows marginally broader coverage than § 112, ¶ 6.

tag secure a portion of the eyeglasses frame (the temples) to the hanger member and therefore perform the identical function of the claim element in question. The jury was instructed that the "means for securing" disclosed in the '345 patent "is a mechanically fastened loop that ... can be formed from a separate extension or integral extension and includes either the rivet fastener or the button and hole fastener." Based on this instruction, the jury found that the holes in the arms of the Version 2 hanger tag were equivalent to the mechanically fastened loop of the '345 patent under the doctrine of equivalents.

The parties do not dispute that the holes in the arms of the accused device perform a function identical to the extension of the patented device. Furthermore, the holes do not constitute an after-arising technology. Because the functions are identical and the holes are not an after-arising technology, the jury's finding of infringement under the doctrine of equivalents indicates that the jury found insubstantial structural differences between the holes in the arms of the Version 2 hanger tag and the loop of the '345 patent claim element. That finding is also sufficient to support the inference that the jury considered these to be structural equivalents under § 112, ¶ 6. For these reasons, any perceived error in the district court's jury instruction regarding the "means for securing" is, at most, harmless.

* * *

In sum, the district court erred by interpreting several of the claim elements in the '345, '726 and '911 patents as means-plus-function elements subject to § 112, ¶ 6. Because, properly construed, these claims do not call for interpretation under § 112, ¶ 6, the district court's reading unnecessarily limited their scope. This court has cautioned against incorporating unwarranted functional or structural limitations from the specification into the claims. *See Transmatic, Inc. v. Gulton Indus., Inc.*, 53 F.3d 1270, 1277 (Fed.Cir.1995). Despite the district court's unwarranted restriction of the claims, the jury found infringement under the doctrine of equivalents. Although a reasonable dispute as to the application of the correctly interpreted claims to the accused structure prevents a determination of literal infringement as a matter of law, because the jury found infringement under the trial court's more restricted reading of the claims, this court need not remand for an infringement determination according to this court's broader claim interpretation. Proceeding claim element by claim element, the jury has already found infringement. This court's correction of the claim scope does not disturb that determination.

* * *

IV.

In conclusion, although the district court erred in its construction of the claims of the '345, '726 and '911 patents, these errors were harmless because of the jury's finding of infringement under the doctrine of equivalents. This court therefore affirms the district court's decision not to grant judgment as a matter of law of non-infringement....

NOTES

1. *Some History Behind Means–Plus–Function Claims.* The 1946 Supreme Court case of *Halliburton Oil Well Cementing Co. v. Walker*, 329 U.S. 1 (1946), held that functionally-defined claims were prohibited:

> The language of the claim thus describes this most crucial element in the "new" combination in terms of what it will do rather than in terms of its own physical characteristics or its arrangement in the new combination apparatus. We have held that a claim with such a description of a product is invalid as a violation of [the patent code].

Id. at 9. The *Halliburton* decision prompted the drafters of the 1952 Patent Act to include § 112, ¶ 6. The Federal Circuit, in *Valmont Industries, Inc. v. Reinke Manufacturing Co., Inc.*, 983 F.2d 1039 (Fed.Cir.1993), recited the purpose underlying § 112, ¶ 6:

> Congress added this language to the Patent Act of 1952 to change the doctrine enunciated in *Halliburton Oil Well Cementing Co. v. Walker*, 329 U.S. 1 (1946). *See* P.J. Federico, *Commentary on the New Patent Act*, Preface to 35 U.S.C.A. 25 (1954)(Commentary).... In particular, the Supreme Court feared that means-plus-function language was overbroad and ambiguous.
>
> Congress decided to permit broad means-plus-function language, but provided a standard to make the broad claim language more definite. The 1952 Patent Act included a new section 112. This new language permits a patent applicant to express an element in a combination claim as a means for performing a function. The applicant need not recite structure, material, or acts in the claim's means-plus-function limitation. With this new section, the 1952 Act rendered *Halliburton* obsolete. *Commentary* at 25.
>
> The second clause of the new paragraph, however, places a limiting condition on an applicant's use of means-plus-function language.... A claim limitation described as a means for performing a function, if read literally, could encompass any conceivable means for performing the function.... The applicant must describe in the patent specification some structure which performs the specified function. Moreover, a court must construe the functional claim language "to cover the corresponding structure, material, or acts described in the specification and equivalents thereof."

Id. at 1041–42.

2. *Invoking § 112, ¶ 6.* Although it is not absolutely necessary to use "means for" language to invoke § 112, ¶ 6, it is certainly the most effective way. As noted by the Federal Circuit in *Greenberg v. Ethicon Endo–Surgery, Inc.*, 91 F.3d 1580, 1584 (Fed.Cir.1996):

> We do not mean to suggest that section 112(6) is triggered only if the claim uses the word "means." The Patent and Trademark Office has rejected the argument that only the term "means" will invoke section 112(6), see 1162 O.G. 59 n. 2 (May 17, 1994), and we agree, see Raytheon Co. v. Roper Corp., 724 F.2d 951, 957 (Fed.Cir.1983), (construing functional language introduced by "so that" to be equivalent to "means for" claim language). Nonetheless, the use of the term "means" has come to be so closely associated with "means-plus-function" claiming that it is fair to say that the use of the term "means" (particularly as used in the phrase "means for") generally invokes section 112(6) and that the use of a different formulation generally does not.

See also Cole v. Kimberly–Clark Corp., 102 F.3d 524, 531 (Fed.Cir.1996) ("To invoke this statute, the alleged means-plus-function claim element must not recite a definite structure which performs the described function. Patent drafters conventionally achieved this by using only the words 'means for' followed by a recitation of the function performed. Merely because a named element of a patent claim is followed by the word 'means,' however, does not automatically make that element a means-plus-function" element under ¶ 35 U.S.C. § 112, ¶ 6.).

3. *Common Law Equivalents v. § 112, ¶ 6 Equivalents.* Infringement of a means-plus-function claim is considered to be literal infringement if the relevant structure of the accused device performs the *identical function* set forth in the means-plus-function claim. Once there is identity of function, the next step is to determine whether the accused structure is identical or equivalent to the disclosed structure set forth in the specification. But, as the Federal Circuit has noted, § 112, ¶ 6, "requires two structures to be equivalent, but it does not require them to be 'structurally equivalent,' i.e., it does not mandate an equivalency comparison that necessarily focuses heavily or exclusively on physical structure." *IMS Technology, Inc. v. Haas Automation, Inc.*, 206 F.3d 1422, 1436 (Fed.Cir.2000). The *IMS court* gave the following example, first articulated by Judge Rich, to illustrate this point:

> A claim includes part A, part B, and "means for securing parts A and B together in a fixed relationship." The written description discloses that parts A and B are made of wood and are secured together by nails. For purposes of the invention, it does not matter how parts A and B are secured; nails are not a critical part of the invention. A screw is not a nail, but for purposes of § 112, ¶ 6, it is equivalent structure in the context of the invention, though it is not the "structural equivalent" of a nail.

Id. n. 3.

An equivalence analysis under § 112, ¶ 6 is essentially a common law equivalence analysis (*i.e.*, insubstantial differences) in a limited role because the identity of function is a prerequisite to application of a statutory equivalence analysis to determine if the accused structure and disclosed structure are equivalent. *See Warner–Jenkinson Co., Inc. v. Hilton Davis Chem. Co.*, 520 U.S. 17, 28 (1997) (asserting the equivalence under § 112, ¶ 6 is "an application of the doctrine of equivalents ... in a restrictive role."). As such, the requirement of identity of function, application of the function/way/result test is reduced to insubstantial differences between "way" and "result." Consider the following explanation:

> Structural equivalence under § 112, ¶ 6 is, as noted by the Supreme Court, "an application of the doctrine of equivalents ... in a restrictive role." Warner–Jenkinson Co., Inc. v. Hilton Davis Chem. Co., 520 U.S. 17, 28 (1997). As such, "their tests for equivalence are closely related," Chiuminatta, 145 F.3d at 1310, involving "similar analyses of insubstantiality of differences." *Al–Site*, 174 F.3d at 1321. In the [common law] doctrine of equivalents context, the following test is often used: if the "function, way, or result" of the assertedly substitute structure is substantially different from that described by the claim limitation, equivalence is not established. As we have noted, this tripartite test developed for the doctrine of equivalents is not wholly transferable to the § 112, ¶ 6 statutory equivalence context. Instead, the statutory equivalence analysis, while rooted in similar concepts of insubstantial differences as its doctrine of equivalents counterpart, is narrower. This is because, under § 112, ¶ 6 equivalence, functional identity is required; thus the equivalence (indeed, identity) of the "function" of the assertedly substitute structure, material, or acts must be first established in order to reach the statutory equivalence analysis. *See* ¶ 35 U.S.C. § 112, ¶ 6. The content of the test for insubstantial differences

under § 112, ¶ 6 thus reduces to "way" and "result." That is, the statutory equivalence analysis requires a determination of whether the "way" the assertedly substitute structure performs the claimed function, and the "result" of that performance, is substantially different from the "way" the claimed function is performed by the "corresponding structure, acts, or materials described in the specification," or its "result." Structural equivalence under § 112, ¶ 6 is met only if the differences are insubstantial; that is, if the assertedly equivalent structure performs the claimed function in substantially the same way to achieve substantially the same result as the corresponding structure described in the specification.

Odetics Inc. v. Storage Technology Corp., 185 F.3d 1259, 1267 (Fed.Cir.1999).

Furthermore, there is a temporal distinction as to the applicability of common law equivalents and 112 ¶ 6 equivalents. If the technology embodied in the accused product was available at the time the patent issued then infringement of a 112 ¶ 6 claim is deemed *literal* infringement because the "literal meaning of a claim is fixed upon issuance." However, if the accused technology was developed after the patent issued, infringement exists, if at all, under the common law doctrine of equivalents. Thus, literal infringement of a 112 ¶ 6 claim requires the accused technology to have been available at the time the patent issued; whereas "after-arising technology could infringe under the [common law] doctrine of equivalence without infringing literally." 174 F.3d at 1320. In short, a threshold determination must be made as to when the technology embodied in the accused product was available—pre-or post-issuance.

Lastly, we must ask: What if the claimed function is not literally found in the accused product? In such an instance, there can be no literal infringement and "112 6 equivalency is not involved" and "112 6 plays no role in determining whether an equivalent function is performed by the accused device under the doctrine of equivalents." *Pennwalt Corp. v. Durand–Wayland, Inc.*, 833 F.2d 931, 934 (Fed.Cir. 1987) (*en banc*). Instead, common law equivalents applies to determine if the accused function, as well as structure, is equivalent to the claimed function and disclosed structure. This distinction was explained in *Interactive Pictures Corp. v. Infinite Pictures*, 274 F.3d 1371, 1381–82 (Fed.Cir.2001):

> In *Chiuminatta*, we held that a finding that a component of an accused product is not a structure "equivalent" to the corresponding structure of a means-plus-function limitation for purposes of literal infringement analysis precludes a finding that the same *structure* is equivalent for purposes of the doctrine of equivalents, unless the component constitutes technology arising after the issuance of the patent. *Id.* at 1311. However, when a finding of noninfringement under 35 U.S.C. §§ 112, paragraph 6, is premised on an absence of identical *function,* then infringement under the doctrine of equivalents is not thereby automatically precluded. *WMS Gaming, Inc. v. Int'l Game Tech.*, 184 F.3d 1339, 1353 (Fed.Cir.1999). That is because infringement under the doctrine of equivalents may be premised on the accused and the patented component having *substantially* the same function, whereas structure corresponding to the disclosed limitation in a means-plus-function clause must perform the *identical* function.

4. *"Corresponding Structure."* Section 112, 6 states that a means-plus-function claim "shall be construed to cover the corresponding structure ... described in the specification." What does "corresponding" mean? A structure is corresponding "only if the specification or prosecution history clearly links or associates that structure to the function recited in the claim. This duty to link or associate structure to function is the *quid pro quo* for the convenience of employing § 112, ¶ 6." *B. Braun Med., Inc. v. Abbott Labs.*, 124 F.3d 1419, 1424 (Fed.Cir.1997). This definition is consistent with the written description requirement that an applicant provide an adequate disclosure of his invention. *See In re Donaldson*, 16 F.3d 1189, 1195 (Fed.Cir.1994). The Federal Circuit in *Medical Instrumentation and Diagnostics Corp. v. Elekta AB*, 344 F.3d 1205, 1211 (Fed.Cir.2003) put it this way:

> Section 112, paragraph 6 was intended to allow the use of means expressions in patent claims without requiring the patentee to recite in the claims all possible structures that could be used as means in the claimed apparatus.... However, "[t]he price that must be paid for use of that convenience is limitation of the claim to the means specified in the written description and equivalents thereof." ... If the specification is not clear as to the structure that the patentee intends to correspond to the claimed function, then the patentee has not paid the price but rather is attempting to claim in functional terms unbounded by any reference to structure in the specification. Such is impermissible under the statute.

In the context of a "means-plus-function claim in which the disclosed structure is a computer, or microprocessor, programmed to carry out an algorithm, the disclosed structure is not the general purpose computer, but rather the special purpose computer programmed to perform the disclosed algorithm." *WMS Gaming, Inc. v. International Game Technology*, 184 F.3d 1339, 1349 (Fed.Cir.1999). *See also In re Alappat*, 33 F.3d 1526, 1545 (Fed.Cir.1994); *Intel Corp. v. VIA Technologies. Inc.*, 319 F.3d 1357 (Fed.Cir.2003).

The Federal Circuit also has been skeptical of efforts to look to prior art patents incorporated by reference into a patent application in order to find the corresponding structure of a means-plus-function element. In *Pressure Prods. Med. Supplies, Inc. v. Greatbatch Ltd.*, 599 F.3d 1308, 1317 (Fed.Cir.2010), the court wrote: "Simply mentioning prior art references in a patent does not suffice as a specification description to give the patentee outright claim to all of the structures disclosed in those references."

5. *Means and Indefiniteness*. The Federal Circuit has sometimes found means-plus-function claims indefinite, particularly in the computer-implemented invention context. *See Aristocrat Technologies Australia v. International Game Technology*, 521 F.3d 1328 (Fed.Cir.2008); *Blackboard, Inc. v. Desire2Learn Inc.*, 574 F.3d 1371 (Fed.Cir.2009); *Halliburton Energy Services, Inc. v. M–I LLC*, 514 F.3d 1244 (Fed. Cir. 2008).

6. *Element By Element Approach Impermissible Under § 112, ¶ 6*. The Federal Circuit has also noted that the *Warner–Jenkinson* and *Pennwalt* decisions, which concerned common law equivalents, do not lead to the conclusion that an element-by-element approach to infringement is applicable in a § 112, ¶ 6 context. Instead, the claim limitation is the *overall structure* corresponding to the claimed function. *See Odetics, Inc. v. Storage Technology Corp.*, 185 F.3d 1259, 1268 (Fed.Cir.1999) ("The individual components, if any, of an overall structure that corresponds to the claimed function are not claim limitations. Rather, the claim limitation is the overall structure corresponding to the claimed function. This is why structures with different numbers of parts may still be equivalent under § 112, ¶ 6, thereby meeting the claim limitation."); *Caterpillar Inc. v. Deere & Co.*, 224 F.3d 1374, 1380 (Fed.Cir.2000).

7. *Means v. Lexicons*. We know that a patentee may be his own lexicographer. We also know there are many problems associated with means-plus-function language in claims. The interaction of these two points has caused some practitioners to suggest that the express inclusion of a "definitions" section in a patent application may relieve some of the pressure drafters may feel to use means language. Consider this approach and the ways it might be implemented. What are its advantages and disadvantages?

D. Indirect Infringement

1. Active Inducement

In addition to direct infringement, the Patent Act, under §§ 271(b) and (c), imposes liability for indirect infringement. As discussed in *Hewlett–Packard v. Bausch & Lomb*, § 271(b) pertains to *active inducement*, that is, where a party encourages or aids another to directly infringe a patent by, for example, providing instructions on how to practice a patented invention. The courts have consistently held that a party must harbor some level of intent to induce direct infringement in order for liability to arise under an inducement claim.

Hewlett–Packard Company v. Bausch & Lomb, Inc.

909 F.2d 1464 (Fed.Cir.1990).

■ Before Rich and Newman, Circuit Judges, and Cowen, Senior Circuit Judge.

■ Rich, Circuit Judge.

Bausch & Lomb Incorporated (B & L) appeals from the September 13, 1989 Judgment of the United States District Court for the Northern District of California, holding U.S. Pat. No. 4,384,298 (LaBarre) valid and infringed by B & L. *Hewlett–Packard Co. v. Bausch & Lomb Inc.*, 722 F.Supp. 595, 13 U.S.P.Q.2D 1105 (N.D.Cal.1989). Hewlett–Packard Company (HP) cross-appeals from that portion of the Judgment holding that B & L had not actively induced infringement of the LaBarre patent subsequent to September of 1985. We affirm.

Background

Two patents are discussed extensively throughout this opinion. The first is the patent in suit, LaBarre, which is assigned to HP. The second is U.S. Pat. No. Re 31,684 (Yeiser), which is assigned to B & L and which is the sole piece of prior art argued by B & L to invalidate the LaBarre patent. Both patents relate to X–Y plotters used to create a two-dimensional plot, such as a chart or a graph, on a sheet of paper. Such plotters can be broadly divided into two categories: one in which the paper is held stationary and a pen is attached to a gantry movable in one direction (the Y-direction) and a carriage movable in a second, orthogonal direction (the X-direction); and another in which the paper is moved in the Y-direction, while the pen is attached to a carriage movable in the X-direction. Both LaBarre and Yeiser relate to this second type of plotter, and both show that the movement of the paper in the Y-direction can be effectuated by one or more pairs of pinch rollers between which the paper is placed.

In order to draw accurate plots, it is critical in devices like those disclosed in Yeiser and LaBarre that the paper be moved back and forth without slippage between the paper and the pinch rollers. With this in mind, Yeiser teaches that at least one of the pinch wheels should have a surface with a high coefficient of friction formed "by knurling or by a layer of rubber or the like." LaBarre, on the other hand, teaches that an efficient way to effectively eliminate slippage between the rollers and the paper is to simply cover one of the pinch wheels with silicon carbide grit. The grit not only increases the friction between the pinch wheels and the paper, but also causes small indentations to be formed in the paper. These indentations repeatedly mate with the grit as the paper is moved back and forth in the Y-direction, thus further inhibiting slippage between the pinch wheels and the paper. Due to this mating effect between the grit and the indentations in the paper, HP urges that the LaBarre printer should be considered to be a "positive drive" plotter, wherein the paper is drawn along using "teeth" (*i.e.*, the grit) which engage in "holes" (*i.e.*, the indentations) in the paper, as opposed to a "friction drive" plotter, wherein the moving force on the paper is caused simply by the friction between the wheels and the paper.

Claims 1 and 3 of the LaBarre patent are asserted against B & L, but only claim 1 is relevant to this opinion. It reads as follows:

1. An X–Y plotter system for forming images on a web comprising:

  first means being coupled to at least one edge of said web for imparting motion thereto to provide a first degree of motion during plotting onto said web in response to a first applied signal;

  second means for forming selected visual images on said web and being movable to provide a second degree of motion in response to a second applied signal; and

  third means responsive to a third applied signal for imparting motion to said second means;

  said first means including first drive means having at least one powered drive wheel contacting the web, and an idle wheel opposite to each of said drive wheels to form a pinch roller assembly with the web between the drive and idler wheels, one of said at least one drive and idler wheels having a rough surface, and said drive and idler wheels additionally being spring biased together to cause the rough surface to make a series of indentations along the driven edge of the web to minimize slippage with these indentations repeatedly mating with the rough surface of the drive wheel as the web is driven back and forth, wherein the rough surface on one of said at least one powered drive and idler wheels of the first drive means has a random pattern, size, and height of rough spots.

B & L, through a division called Houston Instruments, began selling plotters having grit-covered pinch wheels ("grit wheel plotters") sometime in late 1982 or early 1983. However, in September of 1985, B & L entered into a "PURCHASE AGREEMENT" with Ametek, Inc. (Ametek) pursuant to which B & L sold the Houston Instruments division (including all "assets, properties, rights and business") to Ametek for a total purchase price of $43,000,000. Concurrent with execution of the PURCHASE AGREEMENT, B & L and Ametek also entered into an "AGREEMENT WITH RESPECT TO PATENTS," in which the parties agreed that, among other things, (1) B & L would grant Ametek a license under the Yeiser patent; (2) B & L would indemnify Ametek against liability for infringing the LaBarre patent up to a cap of $4.6 million; (3) B & L and Ametek would jointly work toward developing a plotter which would not infringe the LaBarre patent; and (4) Ametek would comply with a so-called "gag order;" (*i.e.*, would not communicate with HP concerning the LaBarre patent).

HP brought the present suit against B & L in May of 1986, accusing B & L of direct infringement of the LaBarre patent for the time period prior to the sale of Houston Instruments to Ametek, and of active inducement of infringement under 35 U.S.C. § 271(b) for the period subsequent to the sale of Houston Instruments. As to the charge of direct infringement, B & L admitted infringement, but defended on the grounds that, among other things, the asserted claims of LaBarre were invalid for obviousness under 35 U.S.C. § 103 in view of the Yeiser patent. In particular, B & L argued that the knurled wheel taught by Yeiser would inherently create indentations which would mate with the rough surface of the knurled wheel, as required by the claims of LaBarre. As to the charge of inducing infringement, B & L denied that its activities surrounding the sale of Houston Instruments to Ametek in September of 1985 constituted active inducement of infringement.

The district court, in an extensive Findings of Fact, Conclusions of Law and Order Thereon, found claim 1 of LaBarre would not have been obvious in view of Yeiser and that B & L was liable for infringement prior to the sale of Houston Instruments in September of 1985. However, the district court further found that B & L did not actively induce infringement of the LaBarre patent by Ametek under 35 U.S.C. § 271(b), and so found no liability subsequent to the 1985 sale. These appeals followed.

Opinion

* * *

B.   *Active Inducement—35 U.S.C. § 271(b)*

Section 271(b) provides that "Whoever actively induces infringement of a patent shall be liable as an infringer." At the outset, we feel that it is necessary to make clear the distinction, often confused, between active inducement of infringement under § 271(b) and contributory infringement under § 271(c). Prior to the enactment of the Patent Act of 1952, there was no statute which defined what constituted infringement. However, infringement was judicially divided into two categories: "direct infringement," which was the unauthorized making, using or selling of the patented invention, and "contributory infringement," which was any other activity where, although not technically making, using or selling, the defendant displayed sufficient culpability to be held liable as an infringer. *See, e.g., Henry v. A.B. Dick Co.*, 224 U.S. 1, 33–34, 32 S.Ct. 364, 373, 56 L.Ed. 645 (1912); *Thomson–Houston Elec. Co. v. Ohio Brass Co.*, 80 F. 712, 721 (6th Cir.1897). Such liability was under a theory of joint tortfeasance, wherein one who intentionally caused, or aided and abetted, the commission of a tort by another was jointly and severally liable with the primary tortfeasor. *Thomson–Houston*, 80 F. at 721; *Tubular Rivet & Stud Co. v. O'Brien*, 93 F. 200, 202–05 (C.C.D.Mass.1898).

The most common pre–1952 contributory infringement cases dealt with the situation where a seller would sell a component which was not itself technically covered by the claims of a product or process patent but which had no other use except with the claimed product or process. In such cases, although a plaintiff was required to show intent to cause infringement in order to establish contributory infringement, many courts held that such intent could be presumed because the component had no substantial non-infringing use. *See Henry v. A.B. Dick,* 224 U.S. at 48, 32 S.Ct. at 379.

The legislative history of the Patent Act of 1952 indicates that no substantive change in the scope of what constituted "contributory infringement" was intended by the enactment of § 271. *See* S.Rep. No. 1979, 82d Cong., 2d Sess. 8, 28 (1952), U.S.Code Cong. & Admin.News 1952, p. 2394; *Aro Mfg. Co. v. Convertible Top Replacement Co.,* 377 U.S. 476, 485–86, 84 S.Ct. 1526, 1531–32, 12 L.Ed.2d 457 (1964) ("*Aro II*"). However, the single concept of "contributory infringement" was divided between §§ 271(b) and 271(c) into "active inducement" (a type of direct infringement) and "contributory infringement," respectively. Section 271(c) codified the prohibition against the common type of contributory infringement referred to above, and made clear that only proof of a defendant's knowledge, not intent, that his activity cause infringement was necessary to establish contributory infringement. Section 271(b) codified the prohibition against all other types of activity which, prior to 1952, had constituted "contributory infringement."

That, however, leaves open the question of what level of knowledge or intent is required to find active inducement under § 271(b). On its face, § 271(b) is much broader than § 271(c) and certainly does not speak of any intent requirement to prove active inducement. However, in view of the very definition of "active inducement" in pre–1952 case law and the fact that § 271(b) was intended as merely a codification of pre–1952 law, we are of the opinion that proof of actual intent to cause the acts which constitute the infringement is a necessary prerequisite to finding active inducement.[5] And it is proof of that intent which is missing in the present case. Looking at the totality of events surrounding the sale of Houston Instruments, it is clear that B & L was merely interested in divesting itself of Houston Instruments at the highest possible price. B & L had no interest in what Ametek did with Houston Instruments and certainly did not care one way or the other whether Houston Instruments, under Ametek's ownership, continued to make grit wheel plotters. HP attempts to make much of the fact that part of the sale of Houston Instruments included the sale of specific plans for making grit wheel plotters as well as key personnel knowledgeable in this area. However, this is simply a result of the fact that Houston Instruments was sold "lock, stock and barrel" (*i.e.* with all "assets, properties, rights and business" included). B & L had no interest in nor control over what Ametek chose to do with the plans or the personnel. In this regard, it should also be kept in mind that grit wheel plotters constituted only a portion of Houston Instruments' sales. The PURCHASE AGREEMENT between B & L and Ametek indicates that Houston Instruments was also in the business of developing, manufactur-

---

5. *See Water Technologies v. Calco, Ltd.,* 850 F.2d 660, 668 (Fed.Cir.1988), holding such intent is necessary and that it may be shown by circumstantial evidence.

ing and selling analog and digital recorders, digitizers, computer-assisted drafting equipment, and other products.

We do not find any of the remaining details of the agreement between B & L and Ametek to be sufficiently probative of intent to induce infringement. The grant of a license from B & L to Ametek under the Yeiser patent is not probative of any intent to induce infringement. The license agreement between B & L and Ametek did not purport to give Ametek the right to make, use and sell X–Y plotters; it merely freed Ametek from whatever bar the Yeiser patent would have been to such activity. Both parties clearly knew, as evidenced by their discussion of the LaBarre patent in the AGREEMENT WITH RESPECT TO PATENTS, that other patents could still be a bar to making, using and selling X–Y plotters. The agreement between B & L and Ametek to work together to find a way to avoid infringement of the LaBarre patent establishes, if anything, an intent by B & L not to induce infringement by helping Ametek to develop a plotter which would not infringe.

The most troubling aspect of the agreement between B & L and Ametek is the indemnification clause. Cases have held that an indemnification agreement will generally not establish an intent to induce infringement, but that such intent can be inferred when the primary purpose is to overcome the deterrent effect that the patent laws have on would-be infringers. *See* Miller, "Some Views on the Law of Patent Infringement by Inducement," 53 J.Pat.Off.Soc'y 86, 150–51 (1971), and the cases cited therein. While overcoming the deterrent of the patent laws might have been the ultimate effect of the indemnification agreement in the present case, we cannot say that that was its purpose. We are once again led back to our conclusion that what B & L really wanted out of this agreement was the sale of Houston Instruments at the greatest possible price. Therefore B & L agreed that, if Ametek should wish to continue the manufacture and sale of grit-wheel plotters, B & L would bear the risk of those plotters ultimately being found to infringe the LaBarre patent. The indemnification agreement certainly facilitated the sale of Houston Instruments at the particular price at which it was sold, but we cannot agree that B & L used it to induce infringement by Ametek.

NOTES

1. *Proving Active Inducement.* Two elements must be established to show inducement of infringement: *direct infringement* and *intent* to cause the acts which constitute the infringement. *See Water Tech. Corp. v. Calco, Ltd.*, 850 F.2d 660, 668 (Fed.Cir.1988). What type of evidence do you think should be required to show either element: direct or circumstantial? *See Water Tech.*, 850 F.2d at 668. Some courts have noted that "circumstantial evidence is not only sufficient, but may also be more certain, satisfying, and persuasive than direct evidence." *Moleculon Research Corp. v. CBS, Inc.*, 793 F.2d 1261, 1272 (Fed.Cir.1986), *cert. denied*, 479 U.S. 1030 (1987), *and on remand to* 666 F.Supp. 661(D.Del.1987), *rev'd on other grounds*, 872 F.2d 407 (Fed.Cir.1989). For example, in *Water Technologies* the court, in finding the requisite intent, relied on the fact that the alleged inducer helped the direct infringer make the infringing product and prepared "consumer use instructions," and "exerted control" over the direct infringer's manufacture of the infringing product. In contrast, the court in *Bausch & Lomb* found that "B & L had no interest in nor control over what Ametek chose to do with the plans or the personnel." Does this make sense? If direct evidence were required, what form might one expect it to take in the typical case?

The Federal Circuit recently held that in inducement of patent infringement, as in inducement of copyright infringement, "evidence that the accused indirect infringer successfully communicated a message of encouragement to the alleged direct infringer...is not necessary." *Ricoh Co., Ltd. v. Quanta Computer Inc.*, 550 F.3d 1325, 1341 (Fed.Cir.2008) (citing *MGM, Inc. v. Grokster, Ltd.*, 545 U.S. 913 (2005)). The Federal Circuit has also emphasized that while selling a device that performs a patented method (e.g., software) is not direct infringement under § 271(a), the seller may be liable under a theory of indirect infringement. *See Ricoh Co. Ltd. v. Quanta Computer Inc.*, 550 F.3d 1325 (Fed. Cir. 2008). Similarly, the court has also pointed out that corporate officers may be personally liable for their company's patent infringement despite the protections of the corporate veil, as where the elements of an inducement claim have been proven. *See Wordtech Sys., Inc. v. Integrated Networks Solutions, Inc.*, 609 F.3d 1308 (Fed.Cir.2010).

2. *Active Inducement and Intent.* Unlike § 271(c), § 271(b) does not use the word "knowing." But it is clear from the case law and legislative history that there is a knowledge requirement. As the Federal Circuit stated in *Manville Sales Corp. v. Paramount Systems, Inc.*, 917 F.2d 544, 552 (Fed.Cir.1990):

> It must be established that the defendant possessed specific intent to encourage another's infringement and not merely that the defendant had knowledge of the acts alleged to constitute infringement. The plaintiff has the burden of showing that the alleged infringer's actions induced infringing acts *and* that he knew or should have known his actions would induce actual infringements.

Reading an intent component into § 271(b) makes sense, given the fact that §§ 271(b) and (c) were intended to be complimentary provisions, together codifying the basic common law pre–1952 principle of contributory infringement.

What types of circumstantial evidence of intent might one expect?

a. What if the product was purposefully designed for use in the patented method? *See Water Tech. Corp. v. Calco*, 850 F.2d at 668; *EWP*, 221 USPQ at 554 ("product is especially designed, intended, and in a vast majority of cases used [in practicing the patented method]"); *Dennison Mfg. Co. v. Ben Clements and Sons, Inc.*, 467 F.Supp. 391, 428 (S.D.N.Y.1979) ("defendant sells a product that is obviously designed to function and be used in a specific manner, knows it is so designed and intends it to be used in an infringing manner"); *Oak II*, 726 F.Supp. at 1543; *Mendenhall I*, 14 U.S.P.Q.2D at 1137.

b. What if sales personnel actively encouraged use of the product in an infringing manner? *See H.B. Fuller Co. v. National Starch and Chem. Corp.*, 689 F.Supp. 923, 945 (D.Minn.1988); *Oak II*, 726 F.Supp. at 1543.

c. What if documentation were prepared and disseminated to teach the use of the patented method? *See Water Tech. Corp. v. Calco*, 850 F.2d at 668; *Mendenhall II*, 13 U.S.P.Q.2D at 1953–54 (intent found even where defendant did not provide *specific* instructions, but knew that infringement by his customers was likely given his general advice and the customers' typical use of the product); *Moleculon*, 793 F.2d at 1272.

The Federal Circuit provided a convenient overview of its recent case law on the intent element of an inducement claim in *Kyocera Wireless Corp. v. International Trade Com'n*, 545 F.3d 1340, 1353–54 (Fed.Cir.2008):

> To prevail on inducement, "the patentee must show, first that there has been direct infringement, and second that the alleged infringer knowingly induced infringement and possessed specific intent to encourage another's infringement." *Minn. Mining & Mfg. Co. v. Chemque, Inc.*, 303 F.3d 1294, 1304–05 (Fed.Cir.2002) (citation omitted). In *DSU Med. Corp. v. JMS Co.*, this court clarified en banc that the specific intent necessary to induce infringement "requires more than just intent to cause the acts that produce direct infringement. Beyond that threshold knowledge, the inducer must have an affirmative intent to cause direct infringement." 471 F.3d 1293, 1306 (Fed.Cir.2006) (en banc review of intent requirement)....This specific intent may, of course, be demonstrated by circumstantial evidence ... *DSU*, 471 F.3d at 1306.

But more recently, the Federal Circuit held that "deliberate indifference of a known risk is not different from actual knowledge, but is a form of actual knowledge." SEB SA v. Montgomery Ward & Co., Inc., 594 F.3d 1360, 1377 (Fed.Cir.2010). Thus, deliberate indifference to the existence of a patent may be sufficient to satisfy the knowledge requirement of active inducement. *Id*. The Supreme Court granted certiorari in this case, *see Global–Tech Appliances, Inc. v. SEB SA*, ___ U.S. ___, 131 S.Ct. 458 (2010), and will likely speak to the level of intent required to show inducement. The petitioner's brief sets forth the question presented as: "Whether the legal standard for the state of mind element of a claim for actively inducing infringement under 35 U.S.C. § 271(b) is 'deliberate indifference of a known risk' that an infringement may occur, as the Court of Appeals for the Federal Circuit held, or 'purposeful, culpable expression and conduct' to encourage an infringement, as this Court taught in *MGM Studios, Inc. v. Grokster, Ltd.*, 545 U.S. 913, 937 (2005)?"

3. *The Relationship Between Sections 271(b) and 271(c)*. Section 271 does not expressly indicate the relationship between §§ 271(b) on active inducement and 271(c) on contributory infringement. But legislative history indicates that the two sections were intended as complementary provisions, together codifying the basic principles of contributory infringement developed by the courts prior to 1952.

The one troublesome area in the relationship between §§ 271(b) and (c) is the sale of a staple item with the specific exemption stated in § 271(c). Can such a sale constitute active inducement under § 271(b)? A number of decisions indicate that such liability can be established, provided the defendant takes active steps to induce infringement through advertising, instruction or the like. However, mere sale of a staple with knowledge of the buyer's intended use does not constitute such active inducement.

4. *Defenses*. What defenses will be successful against a claim of inducement? Because intent will be determined in the light of all the circumstances, even a warning label "disclaimer" included on a package insert or in advertisements may fail to insulate a defendant from inducement liability. *See Lifescan, Inc. v. Can–Am Care Corp.*, 859 F.Supp. 392, 395 (N.D.Cal.1994) (warning label alone was not sufficient to support summary judgment of no inducement). This is especially so where the product is designed for use in an infringing manner and there is no evidence the warning will actually have any effect on the consumers. *See American Standard Inc. v. Pfizer Inc.*, 722 F.Supp. 86, 103 (D.Del.1989). In some cases, the warnings may even be a back-handed teaching. *See Wells v. La Point*, No. 93–CV–7647, slip. op. at 6 (N.D. Ohio opinion of June 20, 1996, final order of September 20, 1996), *aff'd without opinion* 121 F.3d 726 (Fed.Cir.1997) (inducement of infringement of a patent on a CB radio antenna tuning device involving two concentric conductive rings where defendant sold an antenna having one of the concentric rings and then defendant's customers were told by defendant's technical support personnel to "put a hose clamp on the antenna where the instructions tell you not to, and slide the clamp up and down to [tune the CB]"). What if the inducer argues that the allegedly infringing acts are not themselves infringing because of particular exceptions to infringement, like governmental use or experimental use?[30] To the extent these defenses are available in cases of direct infringement, should they be considered purely personal defenses? What about one who induces a billion cases of *de minimis*, or experimental uses, and earns one penny profit from each? Such an inducer would still be earning ten million dollars in profits from inducing these infringements.

2.   Contributory Infringement

Section 271(c) pertains to *contributory infringement*, and concerns itself with the sale of a component of a patented device or composition or the sale of a component for use in practicing a patented process. The component must be a non-staple item that is not "suitable for substantial noninfringing use." A seller under § 271(c) must have knowledge that the component is "especially made or especially adapted for use in an infringement of" a patent. The case of *C.R. Bard v. Advanced Cardiovascular Systems* explores § 271(c) and the doctrine of contributory infringement.

C.R. Bard, Inc. v. Advanced Cardiovascular Systems, Inc.

911 F.2d 670 (Fed.Cir.1990).

■ Before Nies, Chief Judge, and Michel and Plager, Circuit Judges.

■ Plager, Circuit Judge.

This is a case of claimed infringement of a method patent for a medical treatment. Defendant–Appellant Advanced Cardiovascular Systems, Inc. (ACS) was marketing the only perfusion catheter approved by the United States Food and Drug Administration for use in coronary angioplasty. Plaintiff–Appellee C.R. Bard, Inc. (Bard) sued ACS for alleged infringement of U.S. Patent No. 4,581,017 ('017), application for which was filed in 1983 and which issued to Harvinder Sahota in 1986; Bard had purchased all rights to the '017 patent as of December 31, 1986. The '017 patent relates to a *method* for using a catheter in coronary angioplasty. On July 28, 1989, the United States District Court for the Central District of California

---

30. The defense of governmental use has generally been applied only where infringement occurred during the performance of a contract to supply the government with specific goods. *See, e.g., John J. McMullen Assoc., Inc. v. State Bd. of Higher Educ.*, 268 F.Supp. 735 (D.Or.1967); *aff'd*, 406 F.2d 497 (9th Cir.1969); *cert. denied*, 395 U.S. 944 (1969). Generally, when the federal government infringes a patent, it is said to be performing a Fifth Amendment-type taking of a license and in 28 U.S.C. § 1498. The government has waived immunity from suit for recovery of "reasonable and entire compensation." The defense of experimental use is a judge-made exception to patent infringement. Under this theory, an act that is purely for experimentation, philosophical inquiry, amusement, or to satisfy idle curiosity may in certain cases be excepted from infringement. *See Roche Prods., Inc. v. Bolar Pharmaceutical Co.*, 733 F.2d 858, 863 (Fed.Cir.1984), *cert. denied*, 469 U.S. 856 (1984). Both of these defenses are affirmative defenses, and as with any affirmative defense, the burden of proving the defense is on the defendant. *See Manville*, 917 F.2d at 555 (governmental use); *Roche v. Bolar*, 733 F.2d at 862–63 (experimental use).

granted plaintiff Bard summary judgment against ACS determining that the '017 patent was not invalid as obvious, and finding infringement of claim 1 of the '017 patent. We reverse the grant of summary judgment and remand the case for further proceedings.

* * *

II. Discussion

* * *

B.

* * *

Bard alleges that under 35 U.S.C. § 271(b), (c) (1988), ACS has both (1) induced infringement of method claim 1 in the '017 patent and (2) contributorily infringed. Of course, a finding of induced or contributory infringement must be predicated on a direct infringement of claim 1 by the users of the ACS catheter. *Aro Mfg. Co. v. Convertible Top Co.*, 365 U.S. 336, 341, 81 S.Ct. 599, 602, 5 L.Ed.2d 592 (1961).

Bard argues that by selling its catheter for use by surgeons in angioplasty procedures, ACS is a contributory infringer of Bard's method claim 1 in the '017 patent. Section 271 of Title 35, United States Code, deals with infringement of patents; subsection (c) specifies what is necessary to be a contributory infringer. For purposes of this case, the statute requires that ACS sell a catheter for use in practicing the '017 process, which use constitutes a material part of the invention, knowing that the catheter is especially made or adapted for use in infringing the patent, and that the catheter is not a staple article or commodity of commerce suitable for substantial noninfringing use. In asserting ACS's contributory infringement of claim 1, Bard seeks to establish the requisite direct infringement by arguing that there is no evidence that any angioplasty procedures using the ACS catheter would be noninfringing.

* * *

Bard argues that the prior art '725 patent teaches the use of the catheter with the inlets (side openings) where the blood enters the tube placed only in the aorta, whereas the '017 method in suit involves insertion of the catheter into the coronary artery in such a manner that the openings "immediately adjacent [the] balloon fluidly connect locations within [the] coronary artery surrounding [the] proximal and distal portions of [the] tube." Thus, Bard argues, a surgeon, inserting the ACS catheter into a coronary artery to a point where an inlet at the catheter's proximal end draws blood from the artery, infringes the '017 patent.

To fully understand this difference, it is important to note that the ACS catheter has a series of ten openings in the tube near, and at the proximal end of, the balloon. The first of these openings—the one closest to the balloon—is approximately six millimeters (less than 1/4 inch) from the edge of the proximal end of the balloon. The remainder are located along the main lumen at intervals, the furthest from the balloon being 6.3 centimeters (approximately 2 1/2 inches) away.

It would appear that three possible fact patterns may arise in the course of using the ACS catheter during a PTCA [percutaneous transluminal coronary angioplasty]. The first pattern involves positioning the catheter such that all of its side openings are located only in the aorta. This is clearly contemplated by the prior art '725 patent cited by the examiner; claims to this method were expressly given up by inventor Sahota during patent prosecution and are not now available to Bard.

In the second of the possible fact patterns, all of the side openings are located within the coronary artery. This situation appears to have been contemplated by the '017 patent, the method patent at issue. In this situation, it correctly can be said that blood flowing through the main lumen will "fluidly connect locations within [the] coronary artery surrounding [the] proximal and distal portions of [the] tube."

In the third fact pattern, some of the side openings are located in the aorta and some are located in the artery. The trial judge concluded,

> [t]hat ACS has added extra holes further from the balloon does not affect the conclusion of infringement, as the patent does not require that *all* holes be "immediately adjacent" the balloon, nor that the blood flowing through the balloon come *solely* from the coronary artery.

(emphasis in original).

There is evidence in the record that 40 to 60 percent of the stenoses that require angioplasty are located less than three centimeters from the entrance to the coronary artery. ACS argues that therefore the ACS catheter may be used in such a way that all of the openings are located in the aorta. Even assuming that the trial judge's conclusion is correct that claim 1 is applicable to the third of the fact patterns, it remains true that on this record a reasonable jury could find that, pursuant to the procedure described in the first of the fact patterns (a noninfringing procedure), there are substantial noninfringing uses for the ACS catheter.

Whether the ACS catheter "has no use except through practice of the patented method," *Dawson Chemical Co. v. Rohm & Haas Co.*, 448 U.S. 176, 199, 100 S.Ct. 2601, 2614, 65 L.Ed.2d 696 (1980), is thus a critical issue to be decided in this case. As the Supreme Court recently noted, "[w]hen a charge of contributory infringement is predicated entirely on the sale of an article of commerce that is used by the purchaser [allegedly] to infringe a patent, the public interest in access to that article of commerce is necessarily implicated." *Sony Corp. v. Universal City Studios, Inc.*, 464 U.S. 417, 440, 104 S.Ct. 774, 788, 78 L.Ed.2d 574 (1983). Viewing the evidence in this case in a light most favorable to the nonmoving party, and resolving reasonable inferences in ACS's favor, it cannot be said that Bard is entitled to judgment as a matter of law. The grant of summary judgment finding ACS a contributory infringer under § 271(c) is not appropriate.

* * *

NOTES

1. *Contributory Infringement—The Early Cases.* The first case to recognize contributory infringement is *Wallace v. Holmes*, 29 F.Cas. 74 (C.C.D.1871). In *Wallace*, the patentee claimed an improved lamp comprising a burner and a chimney. Although the chimney was necessary to the operability of the lamp, "the distinguishing feature of the invention" was the burner. The alleged infringer sold the burner without the chimney; however, customers could easily acquire the chimney from a glass manufacturer. The defendant argued that infringement was lacking because one of the claimed limitations (*i.e.,* the chimney) was missing from the accused device. The judge was not persuaded:

> It cannot be, that, where a useful machine is patented as a combination of parts, two or more can engage in its construction and sale, and protect themselves by showing that, though united in an effort to produce the same machine, and sell it, and bring it into extensive use, each makes and sells one part only, which is useless without the others, and still another person, in precise conformity with the purpose in view, puts them together for use. It were so, such patents would, indeed, be of little value. In such case, all are tort-feasors, engaged in a common purpose to infringe the patent, and actually, by their concerted action, producing that result.... Here, the actual concert with others is a certain inference from the nature of the case, and the distinct efforts of the defendants to bring the burner in question into use, which can only be done by adding the chimney. The defendants have not, perhaps, made an actual pre-arrangement with any particular person to supply the chimney ... but, every sale they make is a proposal to the purchaser to do this, and his purchase is a consent with the defendants that he will do it, or cause it to be done.

Id. at 80. Liability was usually found where the defendant made a component that had no non-infringing use; however, the issue of liability was complicated where the component had both infringing and non-infringing use. In *Saxe v. Hammond,* 21 F. Cas 593 (C.C.D.Mass.1875), the plaintiff had a patent on an improved organ. The defendant made a particular type of fan to be installed in organs, one of which was the plaintiff's. The court refused to find infringement, stating:

> ... [I]n order to render one who makes and sells parts of a patented combination liable for infringement, the parts manufactured must be useless in any other machine, and they must be sold and manufactured with the understanding or intention that the remaining parts are to be supplied by another.... It would be too violent an interference with trade and the rights of merchants and manufacturers, to confine the right of making and selling such articles to the plaintiff and his agents....

Id. at 594.

2. *Direct Infringement Required.* As with active inducement under § 271(b), direct infringement is required for a finding of contributory infringement. In *Aro Manufacturing Co., Inc. v. Convertible Top Replacement Co., Inc.,* 365 U.S. 336 (1961), cited in *C.R. Bard,* the Supreme Court made it clear that there can be no contributory infringement without direct infringement. According to the Court:

> It is plain that § 271(c)—a part of the Patent Code enacted in 1952—made no change in the fundamental precept that there can be no contributory infringement in the absence of a direct infringement. That section defines contributory infringement in terms of direct infringement—namely the sale of a component of a patented combination or machine for use "in an infringement of such patent."

Aro, 365 U.S. at 341–42. But "it is not clear whether *Aro* requires proof of an actual act of direct infringement." DONALD S. CHISUM, V CHISUM ON PATENTS 17–52 (1997). As one court noted, the *Aro* decision "can be read to require nothing more than a showing that a purchaser from the alleged contributory infringer *would* infringe if he used his purchase." *Nordberg Mfg. v. Jackson Vibrators, Inc.*, 153 U.S.P.Q. 777, 783 n. 8 (N.D.Ill.1967), *rev'd on other grounds*, 393 F.2d 192 (7th Cir.1968).

3. *Knowledge and Intent.* Section 271(c) requires that the alleged contributory infringer sell his component "*knowing* the same adapted for use in an infringement of such patent." (Emphasis added). Decisions prior to 1952 often stated that the sale of an unpatented component must have been with both knowledge and intent to contribute to direct infringement. *See, e.g., Henry v. A.B. Dick Co.*, 224 U.S. 1 (1912). But they presumed the intent element whenever the component sold had no noninfringing use. It was unclear whether the knowledge element meant knowledge of the use to which the component would be put or knowledge of both the character of the use and the existence of a patent and a claim of infringement. The legislative history of § 271(c) is equally unclear as to the intended meaning of "knowing." In *Aro Mfg. Co. v. Convertible Top Replacement Co.*, 377 U.S. 476 (1964) (*Aro II*), the Supreme Court stated that "§ 271(c) does require a showing that the alleged contributory infringer knew that the combination for which his component was especially designed was both patented and infringing." *Id.* at 488–90. *See also Lummus Ind., Inc. v. D.M. & E. Corp.*, 862 F.2d 267, 272 (Fed.Cir.1988) ("A person commits contributory infringement when he makes and sells a component of a patented machine for use in practicing a patented process if such component constitutes a material part of the invention, and the person knows that this component is especially made or especially adapted for use in an infringement of the patent and the component is not a staple article or commodity of commerce suitable for substantial noninfringing use.")

4. *Noninfringing Use and the "Wheels of Commerce."* Section 271(c) codifies prior case law which refused to find contributory infringement where the component sold had a noninfringing use. As the Supreme Court stated, "Undoubtedly a bare supposition that by a sale of an article which, though adopted to an infringing use, is also adopted to other and lawful uses, is not enough to make the seller a contributory infringer. Such a rule would block the wheels of commerce." *Sioney Henry v. A.B. Dick Co.*, 224 U.S. 1, 48 (1912). The statute uses the phrase "substantial noninfringing use,"which "relates ... to whether the portion of the invention supplied by the contributory infringer ... has a use other than to be combined with other items that together fall within the metes and bounds of the claims of the patent." *Lucas Aerospace, Ltd. v. Unison Indus.*, 899 F.Supp. 1268, 1287 (D.Del.1995). Whether a component is capable of a substantially noninfringing use is a question of fact. The noninfringing use must not be "farfetched" or "illusory." *See D.O.C.C. Inc. v. Spintech Inc.*, 36 U.S.P.Q.2d 1145, 1155 (S.D.N.Y. 1994) ("Contributory infringement liability is not meant for situations where noninfringing uses are common as opposed to farfetched, illusory, impractical or merely experimental."); *see also, Alcon Laboratories Inc. v. Allergan, Inc.*, 17 U.S.P.Q.2d 1365, 1369 (N.D.Tex.1990) ("a theoretical capability does not suffice.").

However, "even if the article has some significant noninfringing use, a manufacturer's knowledge that the component is to be used by an owner of an infringing system is sufficient to meet the burden under Section 271(c)." *Preemption Devices Inc. v. Minnesota Mining & Mfg. Co.*, 630 F.Supp. 463, 471 n. 10 (E.D.Pa.1985), *aff'd in part, vacated in part, and remanded*, 803 F.2d 1170 (Fed.Cir.1986). The Federal Circuit recently affirmed this view, holding that "[an alleged infringer] should not be permitted to escape liability as a contributory infringer merely by embedding [the claimed invention] in a larger product with some additional, separable feature before importing and selling it. If we were to hold otherwise, then so long as the resulting product, as a whole, has a substantial non-infringing use *based solely on the additional feature,* no contributory liability would exist despite the presence of a component that, if sold alone, plainly would incur liability." *Ricoh*

Co., Ltd. v. Quanta Computer Inc., 550 F.3d 1325, 1337 (Fed.Cir.2008) (emphasis in original).

E.   Geographic Scope of the Patent Grant and Foreign Activity

As the world becomes increasingly connected, especially for digital technologies, it is becoming increasingly possible to structure business methods that otherwise would have infringed a US patent to avoid infringement by conducting some of their steps outside of the US. The Federal Circuit addressed this issue recently in the case of *NTP, Inc. v. Research In Motion, Ltd.*, 418 F.3d 1282 (Fed. Cir. 2005), which, after rehearing, treated the "system" claims as infringed, but the "method" claims as not infringed. Wrestling with the "within the US" restriction of Section 271(a), and relying *Decca v. United States*, 544 F.2d 1070 (Ct. Cl. 1976), the court concluded that a "system" is "used" where the system as a whole is put into service. Focusing on where control is exercised and beneficial use is obtained, both of which were the US in this case to at least some extent, the court affirmed a finding of infringement on the system claims. But for the method claims the court pointed out that not all steps were performed within the US and so no infringement could be found.

A product sold "free on board" abroad and then shipped to the United States is an infringing *sale* of the product under § 271(a). *Litecubes, LLC v. Northern Light Prods., Inc.*, 523 F.3d 1353, 1370 (Fed.Cir.2008). "Since the American customers were in the United States when they contracted for the accused cubes, and the products were delivered directly to the United States, under *North American Philips* and *MEMC* there is substantial evidence to support the jury's conclusion that GlowProducts sold the accused cubes within the United States." *Litecubes*, 523 F.3d at 1371. The Federal Circuit has also held that "an offer which is made in Norway by a U.S. company to a U.S. company to sell a product within the U.S., for delivery and use within the U.S. constitutes an offer to sell within the U.S. under § 271(a)." *Transocean Offshore Deepwater Drilling, Inc. v. Maersk Contractors USA, Inc.*, 617 F.3d 1296, 1309 (Fed.Cir.2010).

Another issue that arises when portions of an infringing business are sent offshore from the US is largely independent of digital technologies. This issue essentially arises when the acts of direct infringement occur off shore but are the clear focus of a domestic business. Put differently, the issue here is analogous to cases of indirect infringement but where the underlying acts of direct infringement happen to be offshore. This is the topic of 35 U.S.C. § 271(f), and the text of Subsection 1, below.

The text in Subsection 2, below, addresses yet a different issue relating to foreign use. This is the problem facing patented methods that are practiced off shore to yield products shipped into the US market, which is addressed by 35 U.S.C. § 271(g).

1.   Foreign Activity and Export Control—§ 271(f)

Clearly, a person who makes a patented invention in the United States and exports it for use or sale infringes the patent because the act of making in this situation is itself an infringement under United States patent law (the product was actually made in the U.S.). A more difficult scenario is where a person makes an incomplete version of the patented product for export or only makes the parts of a patented machine and thereafter exports them for assembly abroad. Does infringement arise in these situations?

As the word "make" is not defined in the patent act, the task of giving it meaning has been left to the courts. The Supreme Court, in *Deepsouth Packing Co. v. Laitram Corp.*,[31] addressed this issue. The defendant in *Deepsouth* manufactured the parts of the patented machine (a machine to devein shrimp) and shipped them to customers in a foreign country where the customers would then assemble an entire machine. The Court, in reversing the Fifth Circuit, ruled for the defendant, stating that "a combination patent protects only against the operable assembly of the whole and not the manufacture of its parts."[32] A maker of unassembled parts can be liable only as a contributory infringer (*see* Part D–2, *infra*). However, contributory infringement can only be found when there is direct infringement, and the manufacture, sale, or use outside the United States does not constitute infringement. After *Deepsouth,* competitors of the patentee could manufacture, with impunity, the parts of a patented machine in the United States and export them to a foreign country for assembly.

In 1984, Congress responded to *Deepsouth* and this apparent loophole in the patent code by adding subsection (f) to section 271. Section 271(f) makes the supply of *unassembled* components an act of infringement. The legislative history nicely sets forth the purpose and policies behind the change:

> The ... change ... will prevent copiers from avoiding U.S. patents by supplying components of a patented product in this country so that the assembly of the components may be completed abroad. This proposal responds to the United States Supreme Court decision in *Deepsouth Packing Co. v. Laitram Corp.*, 406 U.S. 518 (1972), concerning the need for a legislative solution to close a loophole in patent law.
>
> In this regard, section 101 adds a new subsection 271(f) to the patent law. Subsection 271(f) makes it an infringement to supply components of a patented invention, or to cause components to be supplied, that are to be combined outside the United States. In order to be liable as an infringer under paragraph (f)(1), one must supply or cause to be supplied "all or a substantial portion" of the components in a manner that would infringe the patent if such a combination occurred in the United States. The term "actively induce" is drawn from existing subsection 271(b) of the patent law, which provides that whoever actively induces patent infringement is liable as an infringer.
>
> Under paragraph (f)(1) the components may be staple articles or commodities of commerce which are also suitable for substantial non-infringing use, but under paragraph (f)(2) the components must be especially made or adapted for use in the invention. The passage in paragraph (f)(2) reading "especially adapted for use in an infringement of such patent, and not a

---

31.   406 U.S. 518 (1972)

32.   *Id.* at 528

staple article or commodity of commerce suitable for substantial non-infringing use" comes from existing section 271(c) of the patent law, which governs contributory infringement. Paragraph (f)(2), like existing subsection 271(c), requires the infringer to have knowledge that the component is especially made or adapted. Paragraph (f)(2) also contains a further requirement that infringers must have an intent that the components will be combined outside of the United States in a manner that would infringe if the combination occurred within the United States.[33]

Some commentators have argued that section 271(f) "goes beyond a mere reversal of" *Deepsouth*:

> In *Deepsouth*, the defendant produced all of the parts of a patented combination machine and shipped them abroad for easy assembly by customers according to the defendant's instructions. New subsection (f) would reach such a situation as the evidence clearly indicated "active inducement." "Active inducement" should always be viewed as present if the assembly abroad is either under the direct control of the export supplier or carried out with the benefit of the supplier's express instructions (as was the case in *Deepsouth*). New subsection (f) goes beyond *Deepsouth* in reaching exportation of less than all the component parts of a patented combination. Thus, under 271(f)(1), exportation of a "substantial portion of the components" will suffice if the export supplier actively induces someone to assemble the whole combination.

Donald S. Chisum, V Chisum on Patents 16–96 (1997). *See W.R. Grace & Co. v. Intercat, Inc.*, 60 F.Supp.2d 316 (D.Del.1999) (discussing 35 U.S.C. § 271(f)). *See also Rotec Industries, Inc. v. Mitsubishi Corp.*, 215 F.3d 1246 (Fed.Cir.2000), where the Federal Circuit refused to find liability under § 271(f) because there was no evidence that defendant, although offering components of the invention for sell, "supplied or caused to be supply" components of the patented invention in or from the United States. Although recognizing that Congress enacted § 271(f) to overrule *Deepsouth*, the court noted that *Deepsouth* is still good law under § 271(a), and a defendant will not be liable for infringement under § 271(a) unless it made or sold a complete invention.

In *Waymark Corp. v. Porta Systems Corp.*, 245 F.3d 1364 (Fed.Cir. 2001), the Federal Circuit reversed the district court's finding of noninfringement of components under § 271(f)(2). The Federal Circuit noted that liability under § 271(f)(2) requires only that the infringer "intend[ ] that such component will be combined" and that "[a]t no point does the statutory language require or suggest that the infringer must actually combine or assemble the components." According to the court:

> [Section] 271(f)(2) does not incorporate the doctrine of contributory infringement. Section 271(f)(2) states that whoever meets its requirements shall be liable as an infringer. In contrast, 271(c), a contributory infringement subsection, states that whoever meets its requirements shall be liable as a contributory infringer, thereby making infringement under 271(c) dependent on an act of direct infringement. Thus, title 35 does make some acts of indirect infringement dependent on a separate act of direct infringement, but 271(f)(2) does not include language with that meaning. Accord-

---

33. "Section-by-Section Analysis of H.R. 6286, Patent Law Amendments Act of 1984," Congressional Record, Oct. 1, 1984, H10525–26.

ingly, the statutory language in this section does not require an actual combination of the components, but only a showing that the infringer shipped them with the intent that they be combined. The history of the enactment of 271(f)(2) also does not show that the statutory language requires actual combination of shipped components. Although the legislative history accompanying enactment of 271(f)(2) suggests that this section was a response to the *Deepsouth* decision, see, e.g., S.Rep. No. 98–663, at 2–3 (1984), this history does not address whether 271(f)(2) requires actual assembly. Without requiring actual assembly of shipped components, 271(f)(2) already requires a result different from the *Deepsouth* decision. Moreover isolated comments about assembly in reference to 271(f)(2) do not address actual, as opposed to intended, combination. See, e.g., 130 Cong. Rec. H28069 (1984) (Subsection 271(f) makes it an infringement to supply components of a patented invention, or to cause components to be supplied, that are to be combined outside the United States.).

Admittedly, infringement without a completed infringing embodiment is not the norm in patent law, but it is reasonable in the context of 271(f)(2). If 271(f)(2) required actual assembly abroad, then infringement would depend on proof of infringement in a foreign country. This requirement would both raise the difficult obstacle of proving infringement in foreign countries and pose the appearance of giving extraterritorial effect to United States patent protection

Waymark Corp., 245 F.3d at 1368.

In *Eolas Technologies Inc. v. Microsoft Corp.*, 399 F.3d 1325 (Fed. Cir. 2005), the Federal Circuit concluded that so-called "golden master disks" of computer software that are shipped overseas to be used there for installing software on computers there are treated as infringing "components" under 271(f)(1); although in *NTP, Inc. v. Research in Motion, Ltd.*, 418 F.3d 1282 (Fed. Cir. 2005), the court refused to extend this reasoning of *Eolas* to reach method claims. Then, in *Microsoft Corp. v. AT & T Corp.*, 550 U.S. 437 (2007) the Supreme Court determined that it is the actual copy of computer software, not the software itself in the abstract, which qualifies as a "component" within meaning of section of § 271(f)(1) and that as a result the section was not triggered where computer software was first sent from the US to a foreign computer manufacturer on a master disk, or by electronic transmission, and then copied by the foreign recipient for installation on computers made and sold abroad, since the copies, as "components" installed on the foreign made computers, were not supplied from the US. While the present case law on § 271(f) appropriately focuses on the precise language of the statute, do you think it makes sense for that statutory language to be kept as it is? Put differently, if the goal of § 271(f) was to reach acts of indirect infringement that are only unavailable under § 271(b) or (c) because the acts of direct infringement occur outside the US, would it make sense to draft §§ 271(f)(1) and (2) to use broader language expressly tied to §§ 271(b) and (c)?

In *Microsoft v. AT & T* the Supreme Court reserved judgment on whether "an intangible method or process ... qualifies as a 'patented invention' under § 271(f)," *Microsoft*, 550 U.S. at n.13. In *Cardiac Pacemakers, Inc. v. St. Jude Medical Inc.*, 576 F.3d 1348 (Fed.Cir.2009) (en banc), the Federal Circuit overturned *Union Carbide Chemicals & Plastics Technology Corp. v. Shell Oil Co.*, 425 F.3d 1366 (Fed.Cir.2005) and held that § 271(f) does not cover method claims. Judge Newman dissented, arguing that "The statutory term 'patented invention' in § 271(f) has the same meaning in this subsection as in every other part of Title 35: it is the general term embracing all of the statutory classes of patentable invention. The court's interpretation of § 271(f) to exclude all process inventions is contrary to the text of the statute, ignores the legislative history, is without support in precedent, and defeats the statutory purpose." *Cardiac Pacemakers*, 576 F.3d at 1366 (Newman, J., dissenting in part).

2.   Foreign Activity and Import Control—§ 271(g)

There are two primary issues that we must address with respect to importation. The first pertains to the importation, *in and of itself*, into the United States of a product that is covered by a United States patent. The second issue relates to the importation, into the United States, of an *un*patented product made by a process that is patented in the United States.

With respect to the first, prior to January 1, 1996, the importation, *in and of itself*, of a patented invention was not an infringing act. However, the April 1994 Uruguay Round agreement on Trade Related Aspects of Intellectual Property (TRIPs) added the right to exclude importation into the United States to the bundle of patent rights. Thus, to conform to TRIPS, the United States amended section 154 so as to make "importing the invention into the United States" by itself an act of infringement.

The more technical issue pertaining to importation is whether it is an act of infringement to import into the United States an *un*patented product made by a patented process practiced in a foreign country. Prior to February 23, 1989, such activity was not an act of infringement because the process was practiced in a foreign country, where, for whatever reason, the owner of the patented product did not have process patent protection. In these situations, the patent owner could petition the U.S. International Trade Commission under § 337 of the Tariff Act of 1930 for an exclusionary order, but this remedy, for various reasons, was inadequate.[34] Therefore, Congress enacted the Patent Process Amendments Act of 1988 (PPAA—effective February 23, 1989),[35] which allows a patentee to exclude

---

34. *See* S. Rep. No. 100–83, 100th Cong. 1st Sess., 2 (1987). Generally speaking, bringing an action in the FTC has several advantages and disadvantages over an action in District Court. The central advantages include speed (ITC cases typically proceed from inception through trial within six months and often receive a decision within nine months after that); broad relief (an exclusion order prohibiting imports and a cease and desist order blocking sales of those goods already imported); experienced Administrative Law Judges (ALJs) who hear primarily patent cases; and a discovery process that some see as more efficient in that the ALJs tend to be more directly involved than district judges. An additional advantage is that the exceptions in 35 USC 271(g)(1) and (2) do not apply as defenses to ITC actions. See *Kinik v. ITC*, 362 F.3d 1359 (Fed. Cir. 2004). The central disadvantages include lack of money damages; potential need to re-litigate issues (an ITC determination is not a "claim" or "issue" for purposes of res judicata and collateral estoppel); additional pre-filing investigation (allegations of infringement must be substantially more detailed); and the "domestic industry" requirement (the patent holder must be practicing the subject matter claimed in the patent within the US).

35. Pub. L. No. 100–418, §§ 9001–9101, 102 Stat. 1107.

others from importing into the United States, or using or selling through-out the United States, an *un*patented product made by a patented process practiced in a foreign country. This new right is easier stated than enforced, for there are a plethora of conditions and limitations. One such condition or limitation is that the unpatented product must be "made by" the patented process. Section 271(g) provides, in part:

> A product which is made by a patented process will . . . not be considered to be so made after—(1) it is materially changed by subsequent processes; or (2) it becomes a trivial and nonessential component of another product.

Thus, to the extent Congress did define "made by," it was only in the negative. In the end, Congress left it to the courts to interpret "made by" in the light of the PPAA's policy to give meaningful patent protection to process patent owners. With this in mind, let's take a look at the *Eli Lilly* case, which considered the "materially changed" language of § 271(g).

Eli Lilly and Company v. American Cyanamid Company

82 F.3d 1568 (Fed.Cir.1996).

■ Before CLEVENGER, RADER, and BRYSON, CIRCUIT JUDGES.

■ Opinion for the court filed by CIRCUIT JUDGE BRYSON. Concurring opinion filed by CIRCUIT JUDGE RADER.

■ BRYSON, CIRCUIT JUDGE.

The ongoing struggle between "pioneer" drug manufacturers and generic drug distributors has once more come before our court. Eli Lilly and Company (Lilly), the "pioneer" drug manufacturer in this case, has filed suit for patent infringement against the appellees, who are involved in various ways in the distribution of a particular generic drug. Lilly sought a preliminary injunction, arguing that the importation and sale of the generic drug in this country infringed Lilly's patent on a process for making a related compound. After a hearing, the United States District Court for the Southern District of Indiana denied Lilly's request for a preliminary injunction. The court found that Lilly had failed to show that it was likely to prevail on the merits of its infringement claim and had failed to show that it would suffer irreparable harm in the absence of preliminary injunctive relief. *Eli Lilly & Co. v. American Cyanamid Co.*, 896 F.Supp. 851, 36 U.S.P.Q.2D 1011 (S.D.Ind.1995). Because Lilly has failed to overcome the substantial hurdle faced by a party seeking to overturn the denial of a preliminary injunction, we affirm.

I

The pharmaceutical product at issue in this case is a broad-spectrum antibiotic known as "cefaclor." Cefaclor is a member of the class of cephalosporin antibiotics, all of which are based on the cephem nucleus. Although there are many different cephem compounds, only a few have utility as antibiotic drugs. Each of the known commercial methods for producing cefaclor requires the production of an intermediate cephem compound known as an enol. Once the desired enol cephem intermediate is obtained, it is then subjected to several processing steps in order to produce cefaclor.

A

Lilly developed cefaclor and patented it in 1975. Until recently, Lilly has been the exclusive manufacturer and distributor of cefaclor in this country. In addition to its product patent on cefaclor, Lilly obtained several patents covering different aspects of the manufacture of cefaclor, including processes for producing enol cephem intermediates. Many of those patents have now expired.

In 1995, Lilly purchased the patent at issue in this case, U.S. Patent No. 4,160,085 (the '085 patent). Claim 5 of that patent defines a method of producing enol cephem compounds, including what is called "compound 6," an enol cephem similar to the one Lilly uses in its process for manufacturing cefaclor. The '085 patent will expire on July 3, 1996.

Compound 6 differs from cefaclor in three respects. Although both compound 6 and cefaclor are based on the cephem nucleus, compound 6 has a hydroxy group at the 3–position on the cephem nucleus, a para-nitrobenzyl carboxylate ester at the 4–position, and a phenylacetyl group at the 7–position. Cefaclor has different groups at each of those positions: it has a chlorine atom at the 3–position, a free carboxyl group at the 4–position, and a phenylglycyl group at the 7–position. Each of those differences between compound 6 and cefaclor contributes to the effectiveness of cefaclor as an orally administered antibiotic drug. The free carboxyl group at the 4–position is believed important for antibacterial activity; the chlorine increases cefaclor's antibiotic potency; and the phenylglycyl group enables cefaclor to be effective when taken orally.

To produce cefaclor from compound 6 requires four distinct steps. First, the hydroxy group is removed from the 3–position and is replaced by a chlorine atom, which results in the creation of "compound 7." Second, compound 7 is subjected to a reaction that removes the phenylacetyl group at the 7–position, which results in the creation of "compound 8." Third, a phenylglycyl group is added at the 7–position, which results in the creation of "compound 9." Fourth, the para-nitrobenzyl carboxylate ester is removed from the 4–position, which results in the creation of cefaclor.

B

On April 27, 1995, defendants Zenith Laboratories, Inc., (Zenith) and American Cyanamid Company (Cyanamid) obtained permission from the Food and Drug Administration to distribute cefaclor in this country. Defendant Biocraft Laboratories, Inc., (Biocraft) had applied for FDA approval to manufacture and sell cefaclor in the United States but had not yet obtained that approval. All three have obtained large quantities of cefaclor that were manufactured in Italy by defendant Biochimica Opos, S.p.A. (Opos).

On the same day that Zenith and Cyanamid obtained FDA approval to sell cefaclor in this country, Lilly obtained the rights to the '085 patent and filed suit against Zenith, Cyanamid, Biocraft, and Opos. In its complaint, Lilly sought a declaration that the domestic defendants' importation of cefaclor manufactured by Opos infringed Lilly's rights under several patents, including the '085 patent. Lilly also requested a preliminary injunction, based on the alleged infringement of claim 5 of the '085 patent, to bar the defendants from importing or inducing the importation of cefaclor manufactured by Opos.

The district court held a three-day hearing on the motion for a preliminary injunction. Following the hearing, the court denied the motion in a comprehensive opinion. The court devoted most of its attention to the question whether Lilly had met its burden of showing that it was likely to prevail on the merits of its claim that the defendants were liable for infringing claim 5 of the '085 patent.

Based on the evidence presented at the hearing, the district court concluded that Lilly had shown that it was likely to prevail on the issue of the validity of the '085 patent. With respect to the infringement issue, however, the court held that Lilly had not met its burden of showing that it was likely to prevail.

The district court correctly framed the issue as whether, under the Process Patent Amendments Act of 1988, Pub.L. No. 100–418, §§ 9001–07, the importers of cefaclor infringed claim 5 of the '085 patent, which granted U.S. patent protection to the process that Opos used to make compound 6. The Process Patent Amendments Act makes it an act of infringement to import, sell, offer to sell, or use in this country a product that was made abroad by a process protected by a U.S. patent. 35 U.S.C. § 271(g). The Act, however, does not apply if the product made by the patented process is "materially changed by subsequent processes" before it is imported. 35 U.S.C. § 271(g)(1).

The district court found that compound 6 and cefaclor differ significantly in their structure and properties, including their biological activity. Citing the Senate Report on the Process Patent Amendments Act, the district court found that, because the processing steps necessary to convert compound 6 to cefaclor " 'change the physical or chemical properties of the product in a manner which changes the basic utility of the product,' " 896 F.Supp. at 857, 36 U.S.P.Q.2D at 1016 (citing S.Rep. No. 83, 100th Cong., 1st Sess. 50 (1987)), Lilly was not likely to succeed on its claim that the defendants infringed Lilly's rights under claim 5 of the '085 patent by importing and selling cefaclor.

The district court also found that Lilly had failed to prove that it would suffer irreparable harm in the absence of a preliminary injunction. The presumption of irreparable harm that is available when a patentee makes a strong showing of likelihood of success on the merits was not available here, the court held, because of Lilly's failure to make such a showing on the issue of infringement. In addition, the court was not persuaded by Lilly's arguments that it faced irreparable economic injury if it were not granted immediate equitable relief. Under the circumstances of this case, the district court found that an award of money damages would be an adequate remedy in the event that Lilly ultimately proves that the importation of cefaclor made by the Opos process infringes the '085 patent. In light of Lilly's failure to establish either a likelihood of success on the merits or irreparable harm, the court found it unnecessary to articulate findings regarding the other factors bearing on the propriety of preliminary injunctive relief—the balance of the hardships and the effect of the court's action on the public interest.

II

The Process Patent Amendments Act of 1988 was enacted to close a perceived loophole in the statutory scheme for protecting owners of United States patents. Prior to the enactment of the 1988 statute, a patentee holding a process patent could sue for infringement if others used the process in this country, but had no cause of action if such persons used the patented process abroad to manufacture products, and then imported, used, or sold the products in this country. In that setting, the process patent owner's only legal recourse was to seek an exclusion order for such products from the International Trade Commission under section 337a of the Tariff Act of 1930, 19 U.S.C. § 1337a (1982). By enacting the Process Patent Amendments Act, the principal portion of which is codified as 35 U.S.C. § 271(g), Congress changed the law by making it an act of infringement to import into the United States, or to sell or use within the United States "a product which is made by a process patented in the United States . . . if the importation, sale, or use of the product occurs during the term of such process patent."

A concern raised during Congress's consideration of the process patent legislation was whether and to what extent the new legislation would affect products other than the direct and unaltered products of patented processes—that is, whether the new statute would apply when a product was produced abroad by a patented process but then modified or incorporated into other products before being imported into this country. Congress addressed that issue by providing that a product that is "made by" a patented process within the meaning of the statute "will . . . not be considered to be so made after—(1) it is materially changed by subsequent processes; or (2) it becomes a trivial and nonessential component of another product." 35 U.S.C. § 271(g).

That language, unfortunately, is not very precise. Whether the product of a patented process is a "trivial and nonessential component" of another product is necessarily a question of degree. Even less well defined is the question whether the product of a patented process has been "materially changed" before its importation into this country. While applying that statutory language may be relatively easy in extreme cases, it is not at all easy in a closer case such as this one.

A

Lilly argues that the "materially changed" clause of section 271(g) must be construed in light of its underlying purpose, which is to protect the economic value of U.S. process patents to their owners. Prior to the enactment of the Process Patent Amendments Act, the value of a U.S. process patent could be undermined by a manufacturer who used the process abroad and then imported the product into this country. Because the purpose of the process patent legislation was to protect against such subversion of protected economic rights, Lilly argues that the statute should be read to apply to any such scheme that undercuts the commercial value of a U.S. process patent. In Lilly's view, the product of a patented process therefore should not be considered "materially changed" if the principal commercial use of that product lies in its conversion into the product that is the subject of the infringement charge. Because cefaclor is the only product of compound 6 that is sold in the United States market, Lilly argues, the change in compound 6 that results in cefaclor—no matter how significant as a matter of chemical properties or molecular structure— is not a "material change" for purposes of section 271(g).

Although we are not prepared to embrace Lilly's argument, we acknowledge that it has considerable appeal. Congress was concerned with the problem of the overseas use of patented processes followed by the importation of the products of those processes, and a grudging construction of the statute could significantly limit the statute's effectiveness in addressing the problem Congress targeted. That is especially true with respect to chemical products, as to which simple, routine reactions can often produce dramatic changes in the products' structure and properties.

Nonetheless, while the general purpose of the statute informs the construction of the language Congress chose, purpose cannot displace language, and we cannot stretch the term "materially changed" as far as Lilly's argument would require. The problem is that the language of the statute refers to changes in the product; the statute permits the importation of an item that is derived from a product made by a patented process as long as that product is "materially changed" in the course of its conversion into the imported item. The reference to a "changed" product is very hard to square with Lilly's proposed test, which turns on the quite different question of whether the use or sale of the imported item impairs the economic value of the process patent.

The facts of this case demonstrate how far Lilly's test strays from the statutory text. While Lilly notes that there are only four steps between compound 6 and cefaclor, and that all four steps involve relatively routine chemical reactions, Lilly does not suggest any limiting principle based on the structure of the intermediate product or the nature of the steps necessary to produce the imported product. Thus, even if there were ten complex chemical reactions that separated compound 6 from cefaclor, Lilly's test would characterize the two compounds as not "materially" different as long as the primary commercial use of compound 6 in this country was to produce cefaclor.

Besides not responding to the natural meaning of the term "changed," Lilly's construction of the "materially changed" clause would create a curious anomaly. Lilly's value-based construction of the clause turns in large measure on Lilly's contention that the only commercial use for compound 6 in this country is to produce cefaclor; that is, Lilly views compound 6 and cefaclor as essentially the same product because compound 6 has no commercial use in the U.S. market except to produce cefaclor. Under that approach, however, the question whether compound 6 was "materially changed" in the course of its conversion to cefaclor would depend on whether and to what extent other derivative products of compound 6 are marketed in this country. Thus, under Lilly's theory compound

6 would become materially different from cefaclor if and when compound 6 came to have other commercial uses in the United States, even though the respective structures and properties of the two compounds remained unchanged.

That is asking the statutory language to do too much work. We cannot accept the argument that the question whether one compound is "materially changed" in the course of its conversion into another depends on whether there are other products of the first compound that have economic value. We therefore do not adopt Lilly's proposed construction of section 271(g). We look instead to the substantiality of the change between the product of the patented process and the product that is being imported.

In the chemical context, a "material" change in a compound is most naturally viewed as a significant change in the compound's structure and properties. Without attempting to define with precision what classes of changes would be material and what would not, we share the district court's view that a change in chemical structure and properties as significant as the change between compound 6 and cefaclor cannot lightly be dismissed as immaterial. Although compound 6 and cefaclor share the basic cephem nucleus, which is the ultimate source of the antibiotic potential of all cephalosporins, the cephem nucleus is common to thousands of compounds, many of which have antibiotic activity, and many of which are dramatically different from others within the cephem family. Beyond the cephem nucleus that they have in common, compound 6 and cefaclor are different in four important structural respects, corresponding to the four discrete chemical steps between the two compounds. While the addition or removal of a protective group, standing alone, might not be sufficient to constitute a "material change" between two compounds (even though it could dramatically affect certain of their properties), the conversion process between compound 6 and cefaclor involves considerably more than the removal of a protective group. We therefore conclude that the statutory text of section 271(g) does not support Lilly's contention that it is likely to prevail on the merits of its infringement claim.

B

In aid of their differing approaches to the issue of statutory construction, both sides in this dispute seek support for their positions in the legislative history of the 1988 statute. As is often the case, there is something in the legislative history for each side. On Lilly's side, for example, are characterizations of the legislation as creating process patent protection that is "meaningful and not easily evaded," H.R.Rep. No. 60, 100th Cong., 1st Sess. 13 (1987), and as excluding products only if they "cease to have a reasonable nexus with the patented process," S.Rep. No. 83, 100th Cong., 1st Sess. 36 (1987). On the other side are directions for applying the statute to chemical intermediates—directions that suggest a narrower construction of the statute than Lilly proposes. On balance, while we do not find the legislative history dispositive, we conclude that it does not unequivocally favor Lilly's position and thus does not raise doubts about the district court's statutory analysis as applied to the facts of this case.

* * *

■ RADER, CIRCUIT JUDGE, concurring.

I concur in the result reached by the majority because Lilly did not show irreparable harm. On that basis, the district court did not abuse its discretion. I depart from the court's reasoning and conclusion about the "material change" standard under 35 U.S.C. § 271(g).

I

The court's majority places great emphasis on the legislative history to resolve the meaning of "material change"—a curious approach given its recognition that the legislative history contains "something . . . for each side." The enactment history is far from dispositive in this case. The record of the enactment of this provision evinces a bitter battle between the pharmaceutical industry and its generic industry competitors.

* * *

II

Sadly this decision will create another massive loophole in the protection of patented processes. This decision will, in effect, deny protection to holders of process patents on intermediates as opposed to "final" products. This decision denies protection to a patented process anytime it is not the only way to make an intermediate, even if it is the most economically efficient way to produce the intermediate.

In view of the purpose of the statute, compound 6 and cefaclor are essentially the same product. Compound 6 has no commercial use in the U.S. market except to make cefaclor. The patented process is thus in use to make compound 6–a product only four simple, well-known steps from cefaclor. The record shows no other current commercial use of compound 6. Rather than attempting to distill an elixir from this intoxicating witches brew of enactment history, this court should interpret "material change" consistent with the overriding purpose of the Act—to provide protection to process patent holders. With its eye firmly fixed on the purpose of the Act, this court would avoid eliminating processes for intermediates from the protections of the 1988 Act.

NOTES

1. *Why Was the PPAA Needed?* Process patents have significant economic value, especially in the biotechnology and pharmaceutical industries. Often, the product made by a patented process was either not patentable or the patent has since expired. If one were able to import into the United States the unpatented product for use or sale, the commercial value of the patented process would be greatly diminished. Prior to the enactment of the PPAA, a process patent owner would have to invoke section 337 of the Tariff Act of 1930 before the International Trade Commission (ITC) in order to prevent the importation of the unpatented product. However, to recover under section 337, a patent owner had to jump through several complex and burdensome hoops. Consider the following language taken from the PPAA's Senate Report:

> In order to ... [recover] from the ITC, the complainants must show that their patented processes were used in manufacturing the imported products, that an efficiently and economically operated industry utilizing the patent exists in the United States, and that the imported product had the effect or tendency of destroying or substantially injuring the domestic industry. After making these findings the ITC must in addition decide that enjoining the importation of the infringing goods is in the public interest.

SENATE COMM. ON THE JUDICIARY, PROCESS PATENTS AMENDMENTS ACT OF 1987, S. REP. NO. 100–83, at 37. Section 337 offered inadequate protection, but, compared to a patent infringement action, the proceeding itself was relatively quick. Therefore, the PPAA was created to supplement the Tariff Act, rather than replace it.

The policy rationale for including products made by a patented process within the scope of rights afforded by a process patent was nicely articulated in a memorandum prepared by the International Bureau of the World Intellectual Property Organization:

> The extension (to product of the process) seems to be an exception to the principle that the protection conferred by a patent or another title of protection for an invention is defined by the object of the invention. In the case of a process invention, a strict application of the said principle would mean that the owner of a process patent could only exclude others from using the patented process. The legal provisions which extend process protection to products obtained by the patented process are based on practical economic considerations. A process which leads to a specific product presents an economic value only through the product. However, it is not always possible to obtain a patent for the product; for example, the product may not be new or may—although new—lack inventive step [*i.e.,* the invention is obvious]. The invention of a new and inventive process for the production of such a product which is not patentable constitutes an important technological advance but the reward granted through a process patent is not important because—without an extension to the product—the process patent would be difficult to enforce (since infringement of the process is difficult to prove) and could even be circumvented by use of the process in another country where the process is not protected. In order to make patent protection of a process meaningful, it is therefore necessary to consider the patented process and the resulting product as a whole, with the consequence that process protection is automatically extended to the resulting product even if the said product has not been claimed.

S. REP. 100–83, at 30–31. The enactment of the PPAA brought the United States into closer conformity with the countries of the European Patent Convention.

Section 271(g) prohibits the *importation* into the United States of a product made abroad even if the product was made abroad with authority. *See Ajinomoto Co. v. Archer–Daniels–Midland Co.*, 228 F.3d 1338, 1348 (Fed.Cir.2000) ("Section 271(g) by its terms applies to unauthorized actions within the United States; it is irrelevant that the product was authorized to be produced outside the United States. When the process used abroad is the same as the process covered by a United States patent, liability for infringement arises only upon importation, sale or offers, or use in the United States as set forth in Section 271(g)"). But liability under 271(g) requires that the patent be issued and in force at the time the process is practiced. *See Mycogen Plant Science, Inc. v. Monsanto Co.*, 252 F.3d 1306 (Fed.Cir.2001).

Moreover, § 271(g) only applies to the importation of a *physical* object, not information acquired or generated by the patented process. *See Bayer AG v. Housey Pharmaceuticals, Inc.*, 340 F.3d 1367 (Fed.Cir.2003) ("[I]n order for a product to have been 'made by a process patented in the United States' it must have been a physical article that was 'manufactured' and that the production of information is not covered"). And the actual patented process must be employed to invoke § 271(g). As the court noted in *Bayer*, the "statute requires that the allegedly infringing product have been 'made *by* a process patented in the United States.' The pertinent dictionary definitions of 'by' are 'through the means or instrumentality of[;] . . . through the direct agency of [;] . . . through the medium of[;] . . . through the work or operation of.' Thus, the process must be used directly in the manufacture of the product, and not merely as a predicate process to identify the product to be manufactured." *Id.* at 1377–79. *See also Bio–Technology General Corp. v. Genentech, Inc.*, 80 F.3d 1553 (Fed.Cir.1996).

2. *"Materially Changed."* There will be no cause of action under § 271(g) if the "product which is made by the patented process . . . is materially changed by subsequent processes." Many foreign countries do not provide the leeway that "materially changed" allows the patentee and would only find infringement when the product is made "directly" from the patented process. However, Congress explicitly rejected the "directly" language as too restrictive:

> [T]he Committee decided against including the word "directly" in the statute out of concern that the word "directly" might have been construed too broadly and possibly exempt too many products that have been altered in insignificant ways after manufacture by the patented process. These products ought to be treated as infringing under the bill.

S. REP. No. 100–83, at 49. The phrase "materially changed" was therefore created to obviate the "concern that the word 'directly' might have been construed too broadly." But what does "materially changed" mean?

Congress set forth a two-part test in the legislative history. A product that is made by a patented process is not materially changed:

> 1. If it would not be possible or commercially viable to make [a] product but for the use of the patented process.

> 2. If the additional processing steps . . . do not change the physical or chemical properties of the product in a manner which changes the basic utility of the product by the patented process.

Id. at 50–52.

3. *Eli Lilly and Cefacor.* Do you agree with the majority in the *Eli Lilly* case that Cyanamid's product was "materially changed" from compound 6? Do you agree with Eli Lilly and Judge Rader that in the light of the underlying policies of the PPAA in protecting the economic value of U.S. process patents and because the only commercially viable use of compound 6 in the United States is to make cefacor, compound 6 is essentially the same product as that which Cyanamid imported? Was there a change in the "basic utility" between compound 6 and the imported product? Can one argue that the imported product derived its "basic utility" from compound 6?

4. *"Trivial and Nonessential."* Section 271 precludes an infringement action where the product made from the patented process "becomes a trivial and nonessential component of another product." Determining what is trivial and nonessential is as difficult as ascertaining whether a product is "materially changed." Monetary value and functionality seem to be inappropriate tests. With respect to the former, "one can imagine a situation in which a component made from a patented process is relatively inexpensive when compared to the cost of a product of which it is a part. Nevertheless, the component may be vital with respect to the operability of the product" such as a spark plug for an automobile or a reed for a clarinet. *See* David L. Hitchcock and Craig Allen Nard, *The Patent Process Amendments Act: The Labyrinth*, 4 Fordham Ent., Media, & Intell. Prop. L.F. 441, 453 (1993). As to functionality, "[e]very component of a product would be essential in the sense that it provided some function, although relatively minor when compared to the functions other components perform." *Id.* Consider the following standard suggested by Professor Jay Dratler:

> Where components are made using a patented process, determining whether they are "trivial and nonessential" in a particular product should require analyzing their advantages *in that product* relative to commercially available substitutes.

Jay Dratler, Intellectual Property Law: Commercial, Creative and Industrial Property § 3.02[2] (1991). Should the approach one takes in determining whether a product is "materially changed" be the same or similar to a "trivial and nonessential" determination?

Side Bar

International Enforcement

The Honorable Mr. Justice Robin Jacob*

Once upon a time the world was agreed that patents were local and could only be enforced by action in the local courts. ICI could not, for instance, sue Du Pont in England for infringing a US patent in Wilmington. They could sue Du Pont in England for importing a material patented in England. They could sue the importer, and, if Du Pont themselves had somehow conducted acts within the jurisdiction, they could be joined too. In theory this meant that a patentee would have to sue in as many countries as there were infringements going on. And in each country that country's legal procedures had to be used. All this was consistent with the strict territoriality of patent rights—which of course had to be applied for separately in each country.

In practice things were not as bad as they seemed. First, it turned out to be unnecessary for most kind of inventions to take out patents in each country. For Europe for instance, the UK, Germany, and France often would do.[1] Second, it was not normally necessary to sue in too many countries. You might find actions in the US, the UK, and Germany only, when the patentee could have sued in several others too. There were exceptions when there were multiple parallel suits, but they were rare.

That global position has recently come under challenge in Europe. It has done so for several reasons. First, the European Patent Convention has meant that, for patents granted throughout that system, the patents granted in each designated state have in principle had identical scope and their validity is judged by identical laws. Second, within Europe there is a convention[2] which governs where you can sue in contract and tort and it may[3] apply to patents. It seems it does apply to unregistered IP rights. Third, with the increasing tendency of markets to become supranational, even global, it makes less sense for patent rights to be purely national. Given all these things, the Dutch courts made the first[4] move. They say that, as a matter of Dutch law, they can enforce foreign IP rights. This assertion goes beyond Europe. The Dutch courts say, for instance, that they can enforce a US patent. There has to be a parallel infringement in Holland, though quite why that matters I am not sure.

This bold action may, perhaps, infringe international law. It may amount to an interference in the affairs of another country. Consider, for example, what the good folks of Kansas City might think of a foreign court (using its own procedures—which will definitely not include a jury trial) ordering a Kansas factory to close down. It potentially can create a different sort of chaos—for if the Dutch can do it so can everyone else. So I do not think the Dutch solution can work in the long run. What then is to be done?

For myself I think we, in Europe, are now set on an inescapable path—the creation of a European patent court. The only alternative is to go back to purely national rights and enforcement, which, for all the above reasons, is increasingly unsuitable. The task is monumental; involving as it does vastly different legal cultures. We are going to have to make European amalgam of these. If you ask me to guess what this will include I say as follows. We will have some discovery in some cases (but not as much as the English and no-where near as much as the Americans). We will have some oral evidence and cross-examination, but no-where near as much as is used in England. We will use specialist judges and court of appeal of specialist judges. There will certainly be no jury.[5] We will not allow cases to drag on (avoiding the problems of a number of continental jurisdictions and the European Patent Office). We will have different scales of procedure depending on the size of the case. Where will the court (or court of appeal) sit? My preference is for places such as the Great Hall at Versailles, the Doges' Palace, the Council Chamber of the Stadhus in Stockholm, and so on. Actually, we may find courts sitting in cyberspace for some if not all of the time.

Perhaps one of the most difficult questions is that of language. What language(s) will the court use? If all European languages can be used it may be unworkable. My own guess it that a number of languages will be used in principle, but in practice the main language will be English. I know there are formidable objections to this—quite apart from the cultural imperative, why should a man be subject to orders of a court which carries on business in a foreign language? But the reality is that increasingly English is the language of the patent system internationally. It is not the English speakers who will be demanding English, it will be business. A French or Spanish patentee who wants any sort of international protection no more wants to pay for translation into many languages than anyone else. And he will have to read English to understand the prior art, which is very likely to be in English.

All in all we are set for exciting times in Europe as we press on in this venture. It is not uninteresting that, for the first time, the European judges themselves have decided that they can and should get involved. I am hoping to have a lot of fun!

* Royal Courts of Justice, London, England. The views expressed herein are solely the views of the author and do not necessarily reflect those of the court. This

SIDE BAR was written specially for PRINCIPLES OF PATENT LAW.

1. Pharmaceuticals are an exception. Generally speaking it is so easy to make them that there is a copyist in every gap in the patent armoury.

2. The Convention on Jurisdiction and the Enforcement of Judgments (The "Brussels Convention").

3. The point is going to the European Court of Justice in the *Fort Knox* case.

4. Not quite the first—British courts had, in the case of passing off, but not other IP rights, long asserted a right to enforce parallel foreign laws.

5. All Europeans are united in their views of the use of juries for patent cases! Putting it bluntly, we think it is daft.

F. COMPLEX TECHNOLOGIES–CHEMICAL INVENTIONS

Just as complex contemporary technologies—like chemistry, biotechnology, electronics, and computer hardware—may present particularly difficult disclosure and nonobviousness problems, they also present interesting problems in the context of claim construction and infringement, especially concerning infringement under the doctrine of equivalents. The following materials and representative case highlight some of the special problems presented by complex technologies.

Exxon Chemical Patents, Inc. v. Lubrizol Corp.

64 F.3d 1553 (Fed.Cir.1995).

■ Before NIES, PLAGER, and CLEVENGER, CIRCUIT JUDGES.

■ CLEVENGER, CIRCUIT JUDGE.

Lubrizol Corporation (Lubrizol) appeals the February 5, 1993 judgment of the United States District Court for the Southern District of Texas, Houston Division, inter alia holding that U.S. Patent No. 4,867,890 assigned to Exxon Chemical Patents, Inc. (Exxon) is not invalid under 35 U.S.C. § 102 or § 103 (1988) and is enforceable, and that Lubrizol willfully infringed the claims of the '890 patent. We reverse the judgment of infringement.[1] We vacate the award of attorneys' fees and costs to Exxon, the injunction entered against Lubrizol, and the damage award entered on February 15, 1994.

I

After extensive discovery, this patent infringement case was tried to a jury. Following the jury's verdict of willful infringement, the judge concluded that the case was exceptional under 35 U.S.C. § 285 (1988) and awarded Exxon its attorneys' fees and costs. Lubrizol's post trial motion for judg-

---

1. The judgment is limited to literal infringement of Exxon's claims. The jury was charged solely with respect to literal infringement, directly or by inducement or contribution, and whether such literal infringement was willful. Although Exxon initially proposed a jury charge on infringement under the doctrine of equivalents, its counsel consented to the deletion of the doctrine of equivalents from the infringement charge given to the jury. Lubrizol's brief notes that "Exxon asserted only literal infringement", and Exxon does not contest that statement. The dissenting opinion raises a question of whether Exxon is now entitled to a jury trial on infringement under the doctrine of equivalents. That issue was not briefed or argued to the panel, and consequently we, unlike Judge Nies, express no view on that question.

ment as a matter of law or for a new trial was denied by the judge, and Lubrizol timely brought this appeal. . . .

The central issue in this appeal is claim interpretation. Exxon's claims are to a lubricating oil composition suitable for use as a crankcase lubricant in internal combustion engines. The claimed composition is defined as comprising—meaning containing at least—five specific ingredients. Exxon contends that its patent claims a "recipe" of ingredients that extends to any product made by using the claimed ingredients, even if the product itself—as a result of chemical complexing—fails to include one of the claimed ingredients. Lubrizol argues that since Exxon claims a composition product—not a process for making a product or a product made by a claimed process—the '890 patent only extends to final products that include the specified claimed ingredients.

The trial judge, candidly expressing considerable difficulty in understanding the chemistry and law involved in the case, treated the issue of claim interpretation as a matter of deciding which of the two parties offered the correct meaning of the claims. The jury was charged according to Exxon's preferred claim interpretation.

The duty of the trial judge is to determine the meaning of the claims at issue, and to instruct the jury accordingly. *Markman v. Westview Instruments, Inc.*, 52 F.3d 967, 970 (Fed.Cir.1995). In the exercise of that duty, the trial judge has an independent obligation to determine the meaning of the claims, notwithstanding the views asserted by the adversary parties. The pursuit of that obligation in this case would have resulted in a determination that Exxon's preferred claim interpretation is incorrect, and that Lubrizol's is only partly correct. As we explain below, under a jury charge stating the correct interpretation of the claims, no jury could reasonably have found—on the evidence submitted by Exxon—that Lubrizol's accused products literally infringe Exxon's claims. Because of Exxon's failure of proof, Lubrizol is entitled to judgment as a matter of law. . . . Accordingly, we reverse the final judgment on liability entered on the jury verdict and vacate the order awarding attorneys' fees and costs and the injunction entered against Lubrizol. The judgment of the District Court which is the subject of Lubrizol's companion appeal challenging the award of damages is vacated. . . .

II

Exxon and Lubrizol manufacture crankcase lubricating oil compositions and concentrate compositions which are mixed with oil basestock to produce lubricating oils for motor vehicle engines. Such products typically contain the following components as additives: (1) a dispersant, which suspends impurities to prevent sludge and varnish deposits on engine parts, (2) ZDDP, a zinc-containing compound that inhibits engine wear and produces antioxidant results for the oil, (3) a detergent, which helps prevent engine deposits, and (4) a supplemental antioxidant, necessary because use of ZDDP is limited by environmental concerns. Oxidation of the oil component substantially shortens the life of lubricating oils. Oxidation results in increased acidity of the lubricant, which can enhance corrosion of engine parts and increase viscosity of the product, thereby degrading its lubricant qualities.

Exxon's '890 patent seeks enhanced antioxidant results by the addition of a small amount of copper as the supplemental antioxidant to the other typical ingredients of the product. The prosecution history of Exxon's patent emphasized the beneficial synergistic effects caused by the added copper when in the presence of an ashless dispersant.

III

We have recently concluded *en banc* that claim interpretation is a matter of law, and that the trial judge alone has the duty and responsibility to interpret the claims at issue. *Markman*, 52 F.3d at 970. After close of the evidence in this case, the judge heard argument from the parties on the meaning of Exxon's claims. During that argument, Lubrizol argued that the meaning of the claims should be left to the jury for decision, if the court failed to agree with Lubrizol's preferred claim interpretation. The judge correctly refused to submit the issue to the jury, and instead decided which of the two proffered interpretations seemed most correct. It may well be that in some cases one side or the other will offer the correct claim interpretation to the judge. More often, however, it is likely that the adversaries will offer claim interpretations arguably consistent with the claims, the specification and the prosecution history that produce victory for their side. In any event, the judge's task is not to decide which of the adversaries is correct. Instead the judge must independently assess the claims, the specification, and if necessary the prosecution history, and relevant extrinsic evidence, and declare the meaning of the claims. No matter when or how a judge performs the *Markman* task, on appeal we review the issue of claim interpretation independently without deference to the trial judge.

IV

Representative of the claims of the '890 patent, claim 1 is directed to "[a] lubricating oil composition suitable as a crankcase lubricant in internal combustion engines comprising" (1) a major amount of lubricating oil, (2) an ashless dispersant (*i.e.* one that neither contains nor is complexed with metal) in specified amounts of "about 1 to 10 wt. %", (3) from about 0.01 to 5.0 parts by weight of oil soluble ZDDP, (4) 5 to 500 parts per million by weight of added copper in the form of an oil soluble copper compound, and (5) magnesium or calcium detergent.[3]

The subject of claim interpretation was argued to the judge at the close of Exxon's case and was considered again in extensive argument at the close of all the evidence. At the conclusion of the arguments, the judge

---

3. The full text of claim 1 is set forth in the appendix to this opinion. Claim 61 of the '890 patent is drawn to a lubricating oil concentrate composition suitable for use in preparing crankcase lubricants. That claim, like claim 1, has specific quantity limitations for the ingredients, including the ashless dispersant ingredient. However, claim 61 does not require a "major amount" of lubricating oil (it requires "a lubricating oil," without specific amount), and it requires 10 to 60 wt. of ashless dispersant. Both claims were submitted to the jury.

decided that Exxon was correct in its view of the claims' meaning. The parties did not contend that the claims of the '890 patent are process claims drawn to a specified manner of manufacture, and the claims as written could not have such meaning. Nor are the claims said to be, or could they be, product-by-process claims. The claims of the '890 patent are drawn to a particular composition: they are product claims. According to Exxon, its claims cover any product that is made by using the specific ingredients identified in the limitations of claim 1.[4] During the trial, Exxon's claims were thus said to be to a "recipe" for making the composition. Whether the specified ingredients could be found in the actual composition produced by mixing the ingredients is, according to Exxon, simply irrelevant to the meaning of the claims. To emphasize this point, Exxon's counsel stated— both to the trial judge and this court—that Exxon's claims will cover a composition that has the added copper regardless of whether any ashless dispersant can be found in the mixture. In short, in Exxon's view the claimed "recipe" for making the claimed product is the claimed product.

The trial judge charged the jury accordingly:

> I instruct you that Exxon's claims cover the ingredients which go into the composition. If you find that Exxon has proved that a Lubrizol product is made by using the starting ingredients in the amounts called for in one or more of Exxon's claims, then that product directly infringes.

The issue of claim interpretation had been raised first by Lubrizol in its motion for a directed verdict at the close of Exxon's case, which the judge denied. The issue was raised again by Lubrizol's motion for judgment as a matter of law at the close of all the evidence, also denied by the judge. The charge to the jury on claim interpretation was also challenged by Lubrizol, both before the case was submitted to the jury and by the post trial motion for judgment as a matter of law.

As noted above, Exxon's claims are drawn to a specific product which has particularly defined ingredients. Nothing in the claims, the specification, or the prosecution history suggests that Exxon's claims are not drawn to a product that contains particular ingredients. Indeed, to the contrary, the title to the '890 patent reads, with the emphasis added, "Lubricating Oil Compositions Containing Ashless Dispersant, [ZDDP], Metal Detergent and a Copper Compound". *See Titanium Metals Corp. of Am. v. Banner*, 778 F.2d 775, 780, 227 USPQ 773, 777–78 (Fed.Cir.1985) (referring to patent's title as interpretative aid). The language of claim 1 refers to "added" copper and to a detergent "additive." The specification demonstrates that those claim references aim at a chemical composition to which ingredients are being introduced. We must give meaning to all the words in Exxon's claims. *In re Sabatino*, 480 F.2d 911, 913, 178 USPQ 357, 358

---

4. If the claim is defined solely by the starting ingredients, a product actually containing all the specified ingredients would seem to escape at least literal infringement if produced by the combination of different ingredients. Such is at odds with the doctrine that a product claim is infringed by any product containing every claim limitation, regardless of how the product is made. *See Laitram Corp. v. Rexnord, Inc.*, 939 F.2d 1533, 1535, 19 U.S.P.Q.2D 1367, 1369 (Fed.Cir.1991); see also 2 DONALD S. CHISUM, PATENTS § 8.05 at 8–79 (1994) (collecting cases). Under Exxon's view, its claims also would seem not to reach a product made with a non-ashless dispersant starting ingredient that is somehow rendered ashless during manufacture, if such a rendering is chemically possible.

(CCPA 1973) ("Claim limitations defining the subject matter of the invention are never disregarded.") In addition, the text of the '890 specification includes over twenty references to "containing" in reference to the ingredients claimed in the composition. Furthermore, during prosecution of the applications that resulted in the '890 patent, Exxon repeatedly emphasized that the genius of its invention lay "in the previously unknown synergism of this material [copper] with ZDDP in the presence of an ashless dispersant of the type described in the application. . . ."

In sum, a review of the claims, the specification, and the prosecution history all point to the conclusion that Exxon claims a product, not merely a recipe for making whatever product results from the use of the recipe ingredients. This conclusion respects that which is claimed, namely a chemical composition. The chemical composition exists at the moment the ingredients are mixed together. Before creation of the mixture, the ingredients exist independently. The particular proportions specified in the claims simply define the characteristics of the claimed composition.

Under Lubrizol's view of the claims, as asserted at trial and on appeal, the composition claimed by Exxon is limited to the final product made and ready for use in the engine environment. Lubrizol is correct that the claims read on a product, not simply a recipe, but Lubrizol errs in thinking that the claims read only on end product compositions. Lubrizol thus asserts a claim meaning that depends upon the time at which one views the composition claimed. The specification as a whole, and the claims in particular, contain no temporal limitation to the term "composition." Indeed, claim 61 reads on a concentrate for preparing lubricants, which is hardly a product ready for consumer end use. The composition of claim 1, once its ingredients are mixed, is a composition existing during manufacture that is being used to produce the end product. Consequently, as properly interpreted, Exxon's claims are to a composition that contains the specified ingredients at any time from the moment at which the ingredients are mixed together. This interpretation of Exxon's claims preserves their identity as product claims, and recognizes as a matter of chemistry that the composition exists from the moment created. Although Lubrizol is correct in taking Exxon's claims to read on a product, its interpretation of Exxon's claims is too narrow. Exxon is entitled to a broader scope that is not time-limited, one that reads on any product at any time that contains the claimed proportions of ingredients. The correct interpretation simply affords Exxon a wider range of product on which to assert infringement. Indeed, Exxon even took advantage of the correct interpretation during trial. When defending its case under Lubrizol's claim interpretation, Exxon did not introduce evidence that Lubrizol's final product infringed. Instead of offering evidence that analyzed the components of Lubrizol's final product, Exxon's witnesses testified to the reaction that occurs when the Lubrizol product is in the process of being made into the final product. According to Exxon's witnesses, that reaction did not result in complete elimination of ashless dispersant in the product. Exxon thus did not focus on Lubrizol's final product to prove infringement. Exxon adopted the broader view and described the infringing activity as occurring while the claimed ingredients were undergoing chemical reactions, necessarily a time before the final product, ready for sale, exists.

We thus hold that the judge erred as a matter of law in giving Exxon's preferred claim interpretation to the jury, and in using that interpretation in ruling on Lubrizol's post trial motion. Under the proper charge, the jury would not have been asked if Lubrizol used Exxon's starting ingredients. Instead, the jury would have been asked to find whether Exxon had proved by a preponderance of the evidence that Lubrizol's products at some time contained each of the claimed recipe ingredients in the amounts specifically claimed.

V

Given the correct interpretation of Exxon's claims, the dispositive question before us is whether any jury could reasonably have found that Lubrizol's accused products literally infringe the claims of the '890 patent as properly construed.... Literal infringement requires that every limitation in Exxon's claims be found in the accused product.... Exxon's burden is thus to prove by a preponderance of the evidence, among other things, that Lubrizol's products contained at some time ashless dispersant in the amounts specifically claimed.

From the beginning of the trial, Exxon was on notice that Lubrizol's view of claim interpretation required Exxon to prove that Lubrizol's products contained ashless dispersant in the amounts specified. Exxon was also aware from discovery that Lubrizol would defend against the charge of infringement by proof that its products as manufactured contained no ashless dispersant. Exxon thus had the choice of simply proving infringement under its view of the claims, or in addition proving infringement under Lubrizol's view as well. Exxon chose to do both. Lubrizol's defense on its view of the claims is based on its evidence that, when one mixes the ingredients specified in Exxon's claims, (1) the soluble copper compound reacts with ZDDP to form a zinc compound and CuDDP and (2) zinc then bonds to the formerly ashless dispersant to render it non-ashless, inasmuch as, after the reaction, it is complexed with a metal. According to Lubrizol, the reactions are immediate and the bond formed between the dispersant and zinc is firm, and as a result, its product lacks the ashless dispersant specified as a necessary ingredient in Exxon's claims.

At trial, Exxon sought to prove its case, under Lubrizol's claim interpretation, with testimony that the bond formed between the zinc and the dispersant was a weak one. The bond was described as unstable, with the molecules bonding, unbonding and rebonding constantly. The process was described variously as analogous to a square dance with partners swapping around, to hand-holding and unholding, and to hats being taken on and off. The bonding and unbonding, also described as a "dynamic equilibrium," occurs an infinite number of times. According to Exxon, the weak bond—with its constant reversal and rebonding—proved that Lubrizol's dispersant was not always non-ashless, and therefore sometimes ashless. Exxon's proof was supplied by expert opinion and did not include any scientific measurements resulting from tests of Lubrizol's accused products. Exxon's proof did not relate to infringement by Lubrizol's final products. Instead, its proof was aimed at the presence of ashless dispersant during manufacture of the end product.

Lubrizol's expert witnesses countered with their opinion that the bond created between the zinc and the dispersant was a strong complex, and that the dispersant remained non-ashless 99.999% of the time. The testimony of Lubrizol's witnesses relied on nuclear magnetic resonance tests performed by Lubrizol on its products, and concluded that there is no ashless dispersant in Lubrizol's accused products after blending their starting ingredients.

We may assume for purposes of this appeal that a jury hearing such evidence could reasonably have concluded that—at some time—during the manufacture of the product or in its manufactured state—ashless dispersant is found in Lubrizol's product.[5] That assumption, however, is not dispositive of Lubrizol's post trial motion for judgment as a matter of law. It is not enough for Exxon to prove that some of the dispersant in Lubrizol's product is ashless even if momentarily. Lubrizol's motion is only thwarted if Exxon has supplied testimony from which a reasonable jury could conclude that Lubrizol's products contain ashless dispersant in the specific amounts claimed. Exxon offered no testimony on the amounts of ashless dispersant present in Lubrizol's products. Nor did Exxon provide the jury with direct evidence from which it could have inferred that the required percentages are found in the composition after it is created out of its specified starting ingredients. In its briefs to this court, Lubrizol emphasized Exxon's failure of proof with regard to the quantities of the ingredients contained in the accused products. Exxon did not respond with assertions that the record included proofs of the quantities of ingredients present in the accused products. Instead, Exxon argued only that "Lubrizol started with the requisite amount of ashless dispersant and, even under its theory, ashless dispersant is still present in Lubrizol's final product, albeit in ever-changing form." In order to prevail under properly interpreted claims, Exxon was obliged to prove both the presence of ashless dispersant and presence of the required quantity. Exxon's failure as to the latter requires us to conclude as a matter of law in Lubrizol's favor.

Post-trial motion practice entails, *inter alia*, ascertainment of whether correct law has been applied to the facts presented at trial in reaching a verdict or judgment. When a trial judge determines on a post-verdict motion what the law correctly is, the judge then determines whether any juror could reasonably have reached—on the evidence presented at trial—the verdict challenged by the post-verdict motion. If the answer is no, the trial judge reverses the jury verdict for failure of proof on the correct legal standard, and denies the loser a second trial on the correct law. That is what happened at trial in *Markman*, and we affirmed that disposition *en banc*, 52 F.3d 967, 973, 989.

---

5. On the record before this court, it is not clear that the trial judge meant for the jury to consider the testimony about the nature of the bond between the zinc and the ashless dispersant. In discussions with counsel, the judge stated clearly that he would charge the jury as Exxon wanted, and under Exxon's view of the claims what "happens in the pot" during or after manufacture of the composition, and Lubrizol's nuclear magnetic resonance evidence, is simply irrelevant. Under the claim interpretation charge given, there was no reason for the jury to consider the evidence of both parties going to whether Lubrizol infringes under its view of the claims. To find infringement as charged, all the jury had to find is that Lubrizol used Exxon's claimed starting ingredients in the amount claimed, an essentially uncontested fact.

When we determine on appeal, as a matter of law, that a trial judge has misinterpreted a patent claim, we independently construe the claim to determine its correct meaning, and then determine if the facts presented at trial can support the appealed judgment. If not, we reverse the judgment below without remand for a second trial on the correct law. . . .

On the facts of this case, we perceive no reason to deviate from, or reject, the settled law that compels reversal. The correct meaning of Exxon's claims is but a slight variance from that urged vigorously and continuously by Lubrizol. That Lubrizol sought to hold Exxon to proof of infringement of product claims hardly comes, or came, out of the blue. Exxon was fully aware that Lubrizol stood on a claim meaning that would require Exxon to prove the presence of specified amounts of claimed ingredients in some Lubrizol product. In fact, Exxon attempted to prove infringement under the interpretation we give to its claims. We have noted that Exxon chose not to introduce proofs of the contents of Lubrizol's final products. Rather, its proof of the presence of some ashless dispersant, evidence that we credit in testing the denial of the post verdict motion, relates to product in pre-final states. Nothing precluded Exxon from arguing and seeking to prove that a Lubrizol product, at some time after its creation, contained the specified ingredients in the claimed amounts. We have emphasized that Exxon's error was in failure of proof as to the claimed amounts, without which it could not prove infringement under Lubrizol's claim meaning. The trial judge did not interpret the claims until all the evidence was in, just before the case was submitted to the jury. Exxon—knowing Lubrizol's defense—knew that it would lose on Lubrizol's claim meaning unless it could show the presence of the claimed ingredients in the claimed amounts in some Lubrizol product. Exxon was free to choose the moment at which it would identify with proof that a Lubrizol product infringed. Thus, Exxon could have argued and sought to prove that ashless dispersant is present in the claimed percentages, along with the other claimed ingredients in their specified amounts, at any time from the moment of creation of Lubrizol's product. Exxon cannot now claim surprise from our variation on Lubrizol's claim meaning and cry foul in not having a second chance to prove what it was free to prove at trial. Consequently, on the facts of this case, we discern no reason to carve an exception into the settled law in order to provide Exxon an opportunity to escape from the flaws in its claim drafting (as described in Judge Plager's concurring opinion) and trial strategy. We therefore disagree with Judge Nies's view that our reversal without remand for a second trial is improper. . . .

REVERSED.

APPENDIX

Claim 1 of the '890 patent reads as follows:

1. A lubricating oil composition suitable as a crankcase lubricant in internal combustion engines comprising:
   A. a major amount of lubricating oil;
   B. a dispersing amount of lubricating oil dispersant selected from the group consisting of:
       (1) ashless nitrogen or ester containing dispersant compounds selected from the group consisting of:

(a) oil soluble salts, amides, imides, oxazolines, esters, and mixtures thereof, of long chain hydrocarbon substituted mono-and discarboxylic acids or their anhydrides;

(b) long chain aliphatic hydrocarbons having a polyamine attached directly thereto; and

(c) Mannich condensation products formed by condensing about a molar proportion of long chain hydrocarbon substituted phenol with from about 1 to 2.5 moles of formaldehyde and from about 0.5 to 2 moles of polyalkylene polyamine; wherein said long chain hydrocarbon group is a polymer of a C_2 to C_5 monoolefin, said polymer having a molecular weight of from about 700 to about 5000;

(2) nitrogen or ester containing polymeric viscosity index improver dispersants which are selected from the group consisting of:

(a) polymers comprised of C_4 to C_{24} unsaturated esters of vinyl alcohol or of C_3 to C_{10} unsaturated mono-or dicarboxylic acid with unsaturated nitrogen containing monomers having 4 to 20 carbons,

(b) copolymers of C_2 to C_{20} olefin with C_3 to C_{10} mono-or dicarboxylic acid neutralized with amine, hydroxy amine or alcohols, and

(c) polymers of ethylene with a C_3 to C_{20} olefin further reacted either by grafting C_4 to C_{20} unsaturated nitrogen containing monomers thereon or by grafting an unsaturated acid onto the polymer backbone and then reacting said carboxylic acid groups with amine, hydroxy amine or alcohol; and

(3) mixtures of (1) and (2); wherein when said lubricating oil dispersant (1) is present, then said dispersing amount of (1) is about 1 to 10 wt. %, and when said lubricating oil dispersant (2) is present, then said dispersing amount of (2) is from about 0.3 to 10 wt. %;

C. from about 0.01 to 5.0 parts by weight of oil soluble zinc dihydrocarbyl dithiophosphate wherein the hydrocarbyl groups contain from 1 to 18 carbon atoms;

D. an antioxidant effective amount, within the range of from about 5 to about 500 parts per million by weight, of added copper in the form of an oil soluble copper compound; and

E. a lubricating oil detergent additive which comprises at least one magnesium or calcium salt of a material selected from the group consisting of sulfonic acids, alkyl phenols, sulfurized alkyl phenols, alkyl salicylates and naphthenates, wherein said parts by weight are based upon 100 parts by weight of said lubricating composition and said weight is based on the weight of said lubricating composition.

■ PLAGER, CIRCUIT JUDGE, concurring.

I join in the reversal of the trial court's judgment of infringement, based on what I consider to be the correct claim interpretation as advanced by Judge Clevenger, and the consequences that flow therefrom.

There is testimony in the record that indicates that it is not known exactly how the chemical complexing, described in the opinion, actually works. If this is so, then Exxon's burden, to prove that the chemical ingredients exist at some point in the accused composition in the claimed proportions, may be impossible of accomplishment. That could be said to argue in favor of an alternative construction of the claims, that what was meant was a process or product-by-process claim.

The difficulty with that argument is that the claims, as the opinion well demonstrates, are unquestionably composition of matter claims. In retrospect, it would appear that Exxon wishes it had product-by-process claims, and thus a "recipe." But we are not free to read the claims as they might have been drafted, even if as drafted they do not accomplish what the inventor may have intended.

Claim drafting is itself an art, an art on which the entire patent system today depends. The language through which claims are expressed is not a nose of wax to be pushed and shoved into a form that pleases and that produces a particular result a court may desire. The public generally, and in particular, the patentee's competitors, are entitled to clear and specific notice of what the inventor claims as his invention. That is not an easy assignment for those who draft claims, but the law requires it, and our duty demands that we enforce the requirement. There is no room in patent claim interpretation for the equivalent of the cy pres doctrine; that would leave the claiming process too indefinite to serve the purposes which lie at the heart of the patent system.

■ NIES, CIRCUIT JUDGE, dissenting.

Contrary to conventional wisdom in the art, Exxon discovered that small amounts of copper in automobile motor oil acts as an antioxidant, and it developed a highly successful commercial product using that discovery. The record discloses that Lubrizol learned of the presence of copper in Exxon's motor oil from Exxon's U.K. patent application and used the disclosure to prepare a competitive product. Both companies now use copper in the vast majority of their passenger car motor oil formulations. Following this phase of the litigation finding Lubrizol liable for infringement of Exxon's U.S. Patent No. 4,867,890, Exxon was awarded $48,000,000 in damages which were doubled for willfulness and $8,700,000 in interest plus $23,700,000 in attorney fees. . . .

The issue of infringement essentially comes down to whether Exxon drafted a claim in its U.S. patent that covers its invention. The majority interprets the claims to require that each of the listed additives to a motor oil must retain its pre-mix identity, to the extent that each must be present in the claimed proportions at some point after mixing. Because Exxon failed to prove that the additives remained identifiable (in those proportions) in Lubrizol's product at some time during or after mixing, the majority reverses the judgment of infringement. I agree with the trial court that Lubrizol infringes. Lubrizol's motor oil contains the required additives in the required amounts. To hold that the final product does not "comprise" those ingredients because of their possible reaction with each other upon mixing seems to me nothing short of double speak. The claims can be interpreted as the majority does only by reading them in isolation from the context of the patent. Moreover, the majority's interpretation gratuitously provides grounds for invalidation of the patent under section 112, because the specification does not describe nor enable one skilled in the art to make a product containing the claimed ingredients in the claimed amounts except as starting ingredients, not mixed ingredients. . . .

The majority focuses principally on the claimed "ashless dispersant" which must remain in its view "ashless" in the required amount in the composition. I interpret "ashless dispersant" as simply the name or designation of an ingredient required as one of the additives. It does not mean the ingredient must remain inert.

As stated in *United States v. Adams*, 383 U.S. 39, 49, 86 S.Ct. 708, 713, 15 L.Ed.2d 572, 148 USPQ 479, 482 (1966), "it is fundamental that claims are to be construed in light of the specifications and both are to be read with a view to ascertaining the invention." Moreover, claims should be "construed, if possible, as to sustain their validity." *North American Vaccine, Inc. v. American Cyanamid Co.*, 7 F.3d 1571, 1577, 28 U.S.P.Q.2D 1333, 1337 (Fed.Cir.1993).

Applying those precepts warrants an affirmance in this case. My concern is, however, not merely this case. The majority mandates technical rules for how chemical compositions must be claimed which I reject.

I.

* * *

I agree with the trial judge's interpretation of the claims that one skilled in the art, upon reviewing the patent specification, claims, prosecution history, and testimony, would interpret claims 1 and 61 as covering a lubricating oil composition comprising the product resulting from a combination of the required five ingredients, in the claimed amounts, regardless of any unknown reactions, or metal complexes formed between those ingredients that occurs upon mixing. With that interpretation, literal infringement is admitted.

A. *Claim Interpretation In General*

To determine the meaning of claims, we must examine the patent specification, other claims, and the prosecution history.... Resort to testimony of those knowledgeable in the art might also be helpful to the court inasmuch as claims are interpreted from the perspective of one of ordinary skill in the art....

B. *The Specification and Claims*

The patent specification discusses the invention in terms of an additive for motor oil which does not interfere with the function of other additives. The particular focus is on addition of the copper compound as an antioxidant and the amount of it that is employed. Moreover, the amounts specified in the working examples and other parts of the specification are identified as the amount of the additives, not the amounts in the final product after mixing. There is no analysis anywhere in the specification of the identity of intermediate or final "complexation" products produced by combining the ingredients specified in the claims, or of their amounts. In light of those omissions, to say that one of ordinary skill in the art would nevertheless conclude that the proportions must be measured in the pot is divorced from reality.

* * *

C. *Prosecution History*

As does the specification, the prosecution history focuses on the additives as starting ingredients, not on any reaction products (and the amounts in a final or intermediate product). As an example, the Examiner's

Answer prepared with respect to appeal of the examiner's rejection of the claims in Application Ser. No. 362,114 (which was the grandparent of Application Ser. No. 49,712, the application resulting in the '890 patent), states:

> The claims are believed to be directed to the composition comprising known additives, combined at conventional levels of additions for their combined attendant functions.

* * *

Exxon's interpretation is also supported by the following episode. SN 362,114 included both claim 37, which referred to a "copper compound," and claim 38, which was to a "composition according to claim 37, said copper compound being oil soluble." Claim 38 was rejected because it duplicated claim 37.... The examiner took the position that the copper compound must be oil soluble—hence, "copper compound" and "oil soluble copper compound" are the same. The applicants, however, argued that "[o]ne can have a solution of a dispersant complexed with an oil insoluble copper compound, or can have an oil soluble [copper] compound" (emphasis added). Similar debate transpired during prosecution of Application SN 177, 367, the parent of SN 362,114. The Board agreed with applicants....

The argument made during prosecution that some of the claims read on embodiments wherein the copper complexes with the ashless dispersant is probative of Exxon's claim interpretation as well as that of the examiner. Specifically, it shows the claim is directed to a product with "ashless" dispersant as a starting ingredient, inasmuch as some of the claims covered formation of a complex between that dispersant and metal, a formation that would render the dispersant "non-ashless". Significantly, the examiner found no flaw in claiming a motor oil product with additives as set out in Exxon's claim here (and I note in its foreign applications as well).

D. *Other Considerations*

The record includes testimony by Exxon witnesses that it is not known how copper serves as an antioxidant in the environment of the claimed composition, that certain reactions are not predictable in that environment, even though they might be predictable in a model, that it is uncertain whether zinc or phosphorus of ZDDP undergoes interaction, and in general, that no one was certain of the exact identity of the final composition or what was happening in the pot. Despite that, the majority holds applicants responsible for knowing about the formation of a complex between the five ingredients required by the claims. In effect, therefore, the majority opinion penalizes applicants for not knowing or caring about exactly how their invention works.

But, "it is axiomatic that an inventor need not comprehend the scientific principles on which the practical effectiveness of his invention rests." *Fromson v. Advance Offset Plate, Inc.*, 720 F.2d 1565, 1570, 219 USPQ 1137, 1140 (Fed.Cir.1983); *accord In re Isaacs*, 347 F.2d 887, 892, 146 USPQ 193, 197 (CCPA 1965). As stated in *Diamond Rubber Co. v. Consolidated Rubber Tire Co.*, 220 U.S. 428, 435–36, 31 S.Ct. 444, 447, 55 L.Ed. 527 (1911):

And how can it take from his merit that he may not know all of the forces which he has brought into operation? It is certainly not necessary that he understand or be able to state the scientific principles underlying his invention, and it is immaterial whether he can stand a successful examination as to the speculative items involved. [Citations omitted.]

In that respect, Frank Johmann, who helped prosecute the relevant applications for Exxon, stated:

[When looking at an invention like this with a number of components, to determine infringement] . . . you look at what is combined to make the product. The reason for that is that the patent law doesn't require that you understand what happens to that final product. All that is necessary is how you obtain the result. And it is sort of like baking a cake. You mix them together. And what happens chemically in the oven, you are not concerned with. With these compositions, what happens in the engine no one really knows and it is not a consideration.

Mr. Johmann stated that he has "seen probably literally thousands of lubricant patents over the years, and this is like a standard format for a composition." *Id.* Thus, claiming the composition in terms of amounts of additives is "a typical way it is done in connection with motor oil additives." *Id.* Though Mr. Johmann was a patent practitioner, as opposed to a scientist skilled in the art, he adds to the record the perspective of one who has seen many patents in this field, and by shedding some light on how claims have been written in the field, he helps illuminate how one skilled in the art would read the '890 claims.

Furthermore, when Lubrizol asked its own employee, Mr. Pindar, in 1988 to determine whether certain of its products infringed the European counterpart of '890, he performed the analysis by comparing the starting ingredients, not the final or intermediate products. . . . Mr. Pindar, who was a scientific advisor to Lubrizol, read the claims as a person of skill in the art would read the claims. Moreover, Dr. Salomon, a lubricant formulator working for Lubrizol, testified (although not in the specific context of interpreting claim language) that her concern as a formulator is "what goes in the pot."

Lubrizol argues that Exxon's omission of the word "mixture" from the '890 claims precludes interpretation of the claims as a list of starting ingredients. This is indeed a slender reed on which to lean. "Mixture" is implied in the composition claims at issue, because by listing five "additives," the claim implies that coverage is for a mixture of those. Thus, Exxon is claiming a "composition of matter," which:

"... is an instrument formed by the intermixture of two or more ingredients, and possessing properties which belong to none of these ingredients in their separate state. . . . The intermixture of ingredients in a composition of matter may be produced by mechanical or chemical operations, and its result may be a compound substance resolvable into its constituent elements by mechanical processes, or a new substance which can be destroyed only by chemical analysis." [Footnote omitted.]

Walker notes that "this class is a very broad one and embraces chemical compounds, mechanical or physical mixtures, alloys and a great variety of things." [Footnote omitted.] 1 Chisum, PATENTS, § 1.02[2] at 1–10 (1995) (quoting from W. Robinson, The Law of Patents for Useful Inventions 278–79 (1890)).

E. *Conclusion*

Lubrizol added to its motor oil the ingredients taught by the specification, and articulated in the claims, of Exxon's '890 patent. Lubrizol then sought to avoid infringement by arguing at trial that the claims are not literally infringed because metal ions from some of the ingredients complex with the ashless dispersant specified in the claims, converting "ashless dispersant" to non-ashless dispersant. That argument was unsuccessful under the district court's claim interpretation, but it has succeeded on appeal under the majority's claim interpretation.

The majority and concurring opinions seem to be of the view that, if Exxon wanted to claim a lubricating oil composition formed by combining the five ingredients specified in the claims, it made a technical error in writing the claims. The majority would require a product by process claim to cover a product comprising a formula of starting ingredients even though the claim requires no particular method of mixing or particular process steps. It is not a "recipe" with specific directions for making the product. Certainly the examiner found nothing technically wrong with the claim as a list of additives for motor oil. In the view of an experienced claim drafter, Mr. Johmann, this is a standard form for such a product. I am of the view that, to one of ordinary skill in the art, the claims as written cover a product, not a method.[10] Consequently, I disagree with the majority and would affirm the district court's judgment of liability.

II.

I would add that the majority's reversal is an extraordinary disposition assuming its interpretation were correct. This appeal challenges the district court's ruling on Lubrizol's renewed motion for JMOL under Fed.R.Civ.P. 50. The majority holds that the district court's ruling on the merits of Lubrizol's motion was correct. Lubrizol's argument for JMOL—that the claims define the final product—is rejected. If Lubrizol had attempted to advance the position of the majority in this appeal, we would have rejected the argument as outside the grounds asserted in the JMOL motions, before submission to the jury, as well as after the verdict was returned.... The issue on appeal is not the global question "What do Exxon's claims mean?" but rather "Did the district court err in denying Lubrizol's JMOL?" It is not unusual to see a case where a party failed to raise a defense on which it might have prevailed. However, our review of a trial court's ruling on a motion for JMOL is limited to the grounds asserted.... The authority of an appellate court to enter a judgment rather than remand is severely circumscribed....

The wisdom of Rule 50 cannot be gainsaid. By advocating a different interpretation of the claim sua sponte, the majority required Exxon to

---

10. The majority, in its footnote 3, questions whether the claims as so interpreted would be literally infringed if one of the "starting ingredients" is made in situ. That issue is not before us, but it appears to me that there would be literal infringement in such a circumstance because the product formed "in situ" itself can be considered a "starting ingredient".

litigate during trial not only its opponent's position but also the unknowable position of the appellate court. Exxon has been deprived of a jury trial on an unasserted and untried theory. The majority decision comes out of the blue. The majority opines that the requirement that Exxon prove infringement of a product claim does not come out of the blue, and that Exxon, therefore, is not entitled to escape the flaw of its claim drafting by a second trial. This reflects the majority's view, not Exxon's, that a list of additives for motor oil is an invention for a process or for a product made by a process. Exxon never asserted that its claim was for anything but a product. Without pointing to any rule set by the statute or a regulation or by the MANUAL OF PATENT EXAMINING PROCEDURE, the majority decides that Exxon's standard type of claim is poorly drafted.

The majority then states that Exxon attempted to prove infringement under the majority's claim interpretation by evidence of what happened chemically in the pot in pre-final states. This evidence "is credited" in determining the post-trial motion. The record discloses that Lubrizol attempted to prove that its final product did not contain ashless dispersant because of what happened in the pot. Lubrizol's theory was that its dispersant, although ashless to begin with, complexed with metal so as to become non-ashless in the final product. Exxon countered with evidence that such complexation was transient. To rule for Lubrizol, the majority must assume that the absence of proof by Exxon, for example, that for a few moments after mixing no complexation occurred—which would satisfy the majority's claim interpretation—means that that fact could not be proved. Whether or not Exxon was precluded from such proof is debatable. That issue was not part of Exxon's or Lubrizol's theory of the case. But precluded or not, there was no reason for Exxon to evaluate any intermediate product.

The majority notes its claim interpretation is broader than that of Lubrizol and, therefore, it is easier to prove infringement, but Exxon is denied that opportunity. In my view this is untenable. I read nothing in *Markman v. Westview Instruments, Inc.*, 52 F.3d 967, 34 U.S.P.Q.2D 1321 (Fed.Cir.1995) which sanctions this procedure. *Markman* upheld a ruling on a JMOL motion. Exxon cannot conceivably have waived the issue of infringement under the majority's broader claim construction, as the majority rules. Exxon proposed deletion of an instruction on infringement by equivalents in the final version of the instructions, but this revision occurred only after the district court adopted Exxon's claim interpretation in its instructions. Exxon did not waive this issue in connection with Lubrizol's or the majority's different interpretation of the claim. The most the majority could say, as a matter of law, is that there is no possibility of proof of literal infringement. However, the question of infringement under the doctrine of equivalents is a jury question under the recent decision of this court *en banc. Hilton Davis Chem. Co. v. Warner–Jenkinson Co.*, 62 F.3d 1512, 1520–21 (per curiam) (Fed.Cir.1995). The majority simply cuts Exxon off from its right to have the issue of infringement under the majority's claim interpretation tried to a jury.

For the foregoing reasons, I dissent to the merits and to the procedure adopted by the majority.

NOTES

1. *Attorney Choices on Prosecution and Litigation Strategy.* Assuming, as all the judges in *Exxon* did, that the patent disclosed truly breakthrough technology with beneficial results and great commercial value and that the defendant plainly copied that technology for its product, it seems at least odd that the patent owner came away with no recovery after (judging by the size of the trial court's attorney fee award) spending more than $23,000,000 in legal fees. Is it a satisfactory answer to the question—how could such a thing happen?—that clients, in law generally but especially in patent law, must live with the choices and work-product of their lawyers? In this instance, in the preparation and prosecution of the application leading to the patent, the attorneys chose to draft the claims as ones for a composition defined by a listing of ingredients—when, as hindsight demonstrates, they should have drafted the claims more clearly as for a composition resulting from a mixing of those ingredients. In the litigation, the attorneys representing the patentee chose to rely only on a theory of literal infringement after obtaining a favorable interpretation of the patent's claims from the trial judge (*see* footnote 1 of the majority opinion)—when, again, as hindsight demonstrates, they should have submitted additional evidence and an alternative theory of infringement under the doctrine of equivalents as a hedge against the possibility that the Court of Appeals might disagree with the trial court's claim interpretation.

2. *Implications for Chemical Practice.* Consider the opinion by Circuit Judge Newman dissenting from the denial of rehearing *en banc* in this case:

> The court's decision in the case of *Exxon Chem. Patents, Inc. v. Lubrizol Corp.*, 64 F.3d 1553, 35 U.S.P.Q.2D 1801 (Fed.Cir.1995), creates important new law governing the claiming of chemical compositions. Adopted by split panel decision, it is gravely incorrect. It is incorrect as a matter of law, as a matter of chemistry, and as a matter of patent practice. The panel majority's new rule of "claim construction" will cast a cloud upon many thousands of existing patents, and major classes of chemical invention will confront unclear, unnecessary, confusing, expensive, and perhaps impossible scientific requirements.
>
> The panel majority holds that a claim to a chemical formulation composition can not be infringed if there is interaction between any of the ingredients after they are added to the composition, such that any ingredient changes in chemical form or ratio from that listed in the claim. Thus any chemical change or interaction within the composition, even loose "complexing" as appears to happen between ingredients of this composition, renders the claim useless. The panel majority holds that it does not matter that the Lubrizol composition is identical to the claimed composition: the purported changes inside the composition after it is made is held by the panel majority to negate infringement.
>
> This is a new and incorrect rule of claim construction. It is not necessary to state the myriad interactive changes that occur in chemical solutions or dispersions, in order to describe this lubricant formulation clearly and unambiguously. Many thousands of chemical patents are written in the simple combination style here found fatally wanting. Consider Exxon's claim 1 shown in the margin, [footnote omitted, see claim1, above] a straightforward list of the ingredients of the composition, all of which are known lubricating oil additives except the copper component, which is listed at "D" in the claim.
>
> Most or all chemicals interact to some extent in solution, wherein ions and molecules rearrange based on forces of various kinds. Under the

court's new law, table salt dissolved in water will not be an adequate description of the composition for infringement purposes, since the sodium chloride molecule no longer "exists": in dissolution the sodium and chloride ions will have broken their bonds to each other, in interaction with molecules of water. For the Exxon lubricant composition the interactions in the pot were exceedingly complex. However, like salt in water, there is no uncertainty as to what was made and what was infringed. When the invention is adequately described and claimed by listing the ingredients of the composition, and is understood by persons of skill in the field of the invention, the law demands no more. To require inventors to identify and include in their claims the chemical interaction products formed in such a complex mixture is not necessary in order distinctly to state what the inventor regards as his invention. 35 U.S.C. § 112 ¶ 2:

> The specification shall conclude with one or more claims particularly pointing out and distinctly claiming the subject matter which the applicant regards as his invention.

The court's holding that a chemical composition claim that is written by listing the ingredients can not be enforced against the identical composition made by combining the identical ingredients in the identical ratio, unless none of the ingredients interact when they are placed together, is simply bad law. It is without precedent, and it is contrary to the way that chemical formulation composition claims are understood within the chemical and the legal communities. This sua sponte transformation of the patent law does not bode well for this court's implementation of its Markman role as de novo construer of patent claims.

Despite the serious disruption of chemical patent-dependent activity flowing from this decision and the massive taint upon existing property rights, the court has declined *en banc* review. Thus I write to explain why I believe that the panel majority has made an error of major consequence, an error that transcends the interests of these parties and this patent.

Chemical Formulation Compositions Are Correctly Claimed by Their Ingredients

The standard way of claiming chemical compositions is by their ingredients. Naming the chemicals and their amounts is the clearest, most accurate, and most comprehensible way of describing such inventions. Often there is no other way of describing chemical compositions. In Robert C. Faber, Landis on Mechanics of Patent Claim Drafting (3d ed. 1990) the author explains the pervasiveness of this type of claim in chemical inventions:

> As in the other classes, most composition claims are combination claims except where a new compound or molecule per se is claimed.

> * * *

> Composition of matter claims list the chemical ingredients (compounds, elements, or radicals) making up the composition or compound. The ingredients or elements may be claimed narrowly (specific named components), with intermediate scope (a group of similar elements functionally equivalent), or broadly as to function performed, where the prior art permits. Where necessary to novelty, etc., the proportions or other conditions or parameters of the compound are stated, usually in ranges of concentration of ingredients.

Id. at 145, 148 (emphases added). Chemical compositions that are mixtures of ingredients are routinely claimed by listing the ingredients. Such a composition is easy to describe with precision, easy to search and to examine for patentability, easy to understand, and unambiguous in content and scope. Whether there is interaction among the ingredients after they are placed in the container does not affect the specificity of the description of what has been invented. It is not necessary to know what physical or chemical interactions occur in the container in order to describe this invention, which resides in the combination of listed ingredients.

The law requires that the claims "reasonably apprise those skilled in the art both of the utilization and scope of the invention," and that "the language is as precise as the subject matter permits." *Shatterproof Glass Corp. v. Libbey–Owens Ford Co.*, 758 F.2d 613, 624, 225 USPQ 634, 641 (Fed.Cir.1985). That requirement was plainly met by the claims in suit, for they were written as lubricant formulators would write them and understand them, by listing the ingredients of the composition. Whatever the scientific nature of the chemical interactions inside the container, the established and probably only way of describing such formulations is by their ingredients. The court creates a scientific burden that is totally unnecessary and perhaps impossible[2] to meet. There was extensive evidence at trial, presented by witnesses on behalf of both Exxon and Lubrizol, concerning what happens when these ingredients are put in the same container. Noted scientists debated the issue. The trial judge recognized that it was not possible to know what was happening inside the pot.

The court's holding that such claims are not infringed if changes occur within the composition after the ingredients are combined, simply means that such compositions can no longer be patented in this way. The court's requirement that the patentee must state in the claim the products of chemical interaction that occur in the mixing pot, simply means that failure to do so leaves a useless patent that can not be enforced against the identical composition made from the identical ingredients in the identical ratios.

The court's ruling will impose disorder and uncertainty upon many fields of applied chemistry, for this claim form is the standard way of claiming new formulation inventions. The treatises teach the routine nature of such claims, recognizing that the components of a chemical composition are not a "mere aggregation," but cooperate in "joint action":

A composition or product is patentable when it involves (1) a new and useful result and this result is a product of the combination and not the mere aggregation of several results; (2) a different result in the combined forces or processes from that given by their separate parts and a new result is produced by their union; (3) a result which is not the mere aggregate of separate contributions but is due to the joint and cooperating action of all

---

2. Exxon's expert witness, Dr. Ingold, testified as to the scientific possibility of proving what the panel requires:

Q Do you know of any other technique which would allow a chemist to determine precisely what is going on with respect to these hand-holding type interactions [the witness' description of the loose bonds the parties referred to as complexing] in a modern motor oil package?

A Dr. Barrett, there is no such technique available today, nor is there any combination of techniques available today that would let one say what was present after you have mixed all four of those components.

the elements; and (4) several elements which produce by their joint action a new and useful result.

3 ANTHONY W. DELLER, PATENT CLAIMS (2d ed. 1971) § 465 at 48 (citing *Colgate–Palmolive Co. v. Carter Products, Inc.*, 230 F.2d 855 (4th Cir.1956)) (emphases added). Deller's and other treatises provide many examples of such compositions, all claimed by listing their ingredients.

I conducted a rough survey in the Official Gazette of the Patent and Trademark Office for December 26, 1995, which announced the issuance during the preceding week of 608 patents classified as "chemical." About a hundred of these patents were for chemical compositions that were claimed by listing their ingredients. For example, there were patents on a pollution control composition, a dye transfer inhibiting composition, a shampoo composition, a paint stripper composition, a polyol composition for polyurethane foams, a cold water detergent composition, a granular detergent composition, a wood preservative, an adhesive composition, photosensitive and radiation-sensitive resin compositions, an x-ray film developer composition, a radiation-absorbing glass composition, and many more. All were claimed by listing the ingredients.

The invention of all such compositions is well described by the ingredients that are combined. Whatever interactions occur within the container holding the composition is irrelevant to the specificity and clarity of the claim and its understanding by persons in the field of the invention. The patent statute requires that the subject matter be described so that persons in the field know what has been invented. 35 U.S.C. § 112 ¶ 1:

> The specification shall contain a written description of the invention and of the manner and process of making and using it, in such full, clear, concise, and exact terms as to enable any person skilled in the art to which it pertains, or with which it is most nearly connected, to make and use the same, and shall set forth the best mode contemplated by the inventor of carrying out his invention.

It is basic chemistry that most organic and inorganic molecules when placed in solution interact in various ways. Such interactions may produce improved properties, thus providing the commercial value that inventors seek to secure through the patent system. Indeed, as stated by Deller in Patent Claims, supra, the patent office will not grant a patent on compositions where the properties are simply an aggregation of the known properties of the separate ingredients.

It was interesting to learn that the distinguished chemists who testified for both sides did not know with scientific certainty the interactions occurring in this complex lubricant formulation. The following exchange occurred during argument to the trial judge concerning "claim construction":

> Exxon counsel: ... We have Dr. Ingold's testimony about them [the chemical ingredients] coming together and breaking apart. We have Dr. Schroeck admitting that was true. But under cross, he admitted yes, they break apart. These phantom compounds that nobody can find.

>   * * *

> LeSuer, although Mr. Adelman didn't remember it, says I don't know exactly what this is but it is definitely a stable linkage.... That is totally different from Dr. Schroeck saying that they are breaking apart

all the time and Dr. Cotton saying these compounds are going back and forth, they are complexing and uncomplexing.

* * *

District Court: ... I wanted to know if there is any way to find out what is in that composition, and you can't. Only a fool would try.

A lubricant composition described and claimed by listing the ingredients is appropriate to an invention that is indeed a combination of ingredients. A patent attorney testified that he has seen ''literally thousands of lubricant patents'' described and claimed, as in the Exxon patent in suit, by listing the ingredients. The panel majority's new requirement is contrary to chemical and practical reality, as is its speculation that Exxon could not prove infringement even under the court's new theory: the reason given for denying Exxon the chance to do so. Chemists know that all chemical reactions have a reaction time and a reaction threshold. Chemists understand the concepts of chemical reactivity and measurement of activity coefficients. Studies of chemical equilibria and thermodynamic principles as applied to chemical reactions, the basics of ionic forces in solution, and principles such as the Law of Mass Action (relating chemical equilibrium and concentration), are elementary tools of classical chemistry. Chemists know that when chemicals are placed in solution or dispersion they interact with the solvent or dispersant; they may form new bonds, or respond to attractive or repulsive forces, or form loose or tight complexes, or be subject to a variety of other interactions, often a combination of interactions in dynamic equilibrium, in a constantly fluctuating swirl of chemical complexity. Dr. Ingold explained these interactions at the trial:

> And the thing to try and remember about this is these weak [interactions] can break apart quite easily. So that this association between the dispersants and some molecule X can simply come apart and give you the detergent again plus the molecule X in free solution. And X can, of course, recombine. And this can happen thousands of millions of times. You don't in any way destroy the molecule in the dispersant nor do you affect X.

He further explained these interactions as they occur among the constituents of the additive packages:

> Q Dr. Ingold, do all of these components interact in the same associated way that we have discussed for the ZDDP and the ashless dispersant? Do they all interact that way?
>
> A Yes, Dr. Barrett, they interact with one another. They also interact with themselves. Everything is interacting with everything else. It is associating. They are associating and breaking up. It is a grand mixture as the molecules come together and associate and then fall apart again and—or take a new partner and reassociate.

Dr. Cotton, Lubrizol's chemistry expert, analogized these kinds of bonds to a square dance, where molecules release one partner and reattach to another and continue releasing and reattaching in a condition of equilibrium.

When the invention is the combination of ingredients, the occurrence of interactions in the pot does not defeat the adequacy of the description of the invention to persons in the art. The patenting of formulation compositions by identifying the components of the composition is legally sound, simple, and serviceable, and permits infringement or noninfringement to be readily determined, for it is necessary only to ascertain whether the listed ingredients are combined in the listed ratios.

The Patent Grant Encompasses Making, Using, or Selling the Patented Invention

The patent act states that "whoever without authority makes, uses, offers to sell or sells any patented invention," 35 U.S.C. § 271(a), infringes the patent. That statutory requirement is satisfied when the "recipe" of the claims is followed. Thus the panel majority has erred in applying the law, for the patented composition is made when the ingredients are combined.

The Exxon specification states that "modern lubricants are complex mixtures of various additives each serving a particular purpose." Col. 1 line 67 to col. 2 line 5. The specification describes the purpose of the various additives that are listed in the claim. It was testified at trial that the concern of lubricant formulators is "what goes into the pot," in the words at trial of Lubrizol's formulation chemist Dr. Salomon. An inventor need not understand the scientific mechanism in order to place an invention into the patent system. *See Newman v. Quigg*, 877 F.2d 1575, 1581, 11 U.S.P.Q.2D 1340, 1345 (Fed.Cir.1989) (observing that "it is not a requirement of patentability that an inventor correctly set forth, or even know, how or why the invention works"); *Fromson v. Advance Offset Plate, Inc.*, 720 F.2d 1565, 1570, 219 USPQ 1137, 1140 (Fed.Cir.1983) ("[I]t is axiomatic that an inventor need not comprehend the scientific principles on which the practical effectiveness of his invention rests."). The suggestion by the panel majority that Exxon's patent attorney did not know how to write claims is misdirected. These claims are written in the clearest, simplest, and most accurate way in which a formulation can be described: by listing the ingredients. I can discern no justification for the court's departure from this long-standing and reasonable claim practice.[3]

Indeed, the panel majority's concurring opinion suggests that if Exxon's ingredients remain sufficiently uncomplexed or unreacted for a period of time after mixing (an hour? a minute? a nanosecond?) the claim would be infringed even on the majority's interpretation. However, the majority denied Exxon the opportunity to prove such fact.

Justice Requires Remand When this Court Creates a New Law of Claim Construction

Having adopted a claim construction that neither party proposed and that is without legal precedent, the panel majority nonetheless declined the patentee's request for remand so that the patentee could present factual evidence or argument relevant to this new "law" as applied to this case.

Fair procedure has been compromised by the court's refusal to remand to the trial court for the presentation of evidence or argument on the new factual issues raised by this court's new law of claim construction. *See Weade v. Dichmann, Wright & Pugh Inc.*, 337 U.S. 801, 808–09, 69 S.Ct.

---

3. The panel majority recognized that compliance with its new "law" of claim construction may not be scientifically feasible, and suggested that claim-writing gimmickry should have been invoked. Thus the panel majority proposes that a patentee might overcome the court's newly created obstacles with a "product-by-process" claim—although this invention is neither a process nor a product, but a mixture of ingredients to form a composition. I will not speculate on whether the court's ruling can be made less pernicious by creative claim-writing, or how the patent examining process will implement this new law governing composition claims.

1326, 1330, 93 L.Ed. 1704 (1949) (remand required to consider alternative theory of liability).

It is inappropriate for the appellate court to make its own scientific finding that such proof is not possible on the court's new criterion. Although the district court stated during discussion of the jury charge that what is in the composition can not be determined, see *supra*, apparently there was no discussion concerning whether there was a transient existence in the mixture of the uncombined ingredients, for that was not an issue. The district court did not discuss whether the "complexing and uncomplexing" described by Dr. Cotton, and the other interactions postulated by other witnesses, might permit the patentee to prove that the ingredients have at least a transient existence in the ratios stated in the claim. The rate of association or complexing is not discussed in the portion of the record provided us, and does not appear to have been at issue.

As a matter of procedural justice, a litigant is entitled to present its case when the court changes the law. *See Neely v. Martin K. Eby Constr. Co.*, 386 U.S. 317, 325, 87 S.Ct. 1072, 1078, 18 L.Ed.2d 75 (1967) (appellate court "may not order judgment where ... the record reveals a new trial issue which has not been resolved"); *Brinley v. Commissioner of Internal Revenue*, 782 F.2d 1326, 1336 (5th Cir.1986) (justice requires the opportunity to present evidence in light of new legal rule established on appeal). Although the appellate court need not remand for a futile trial, *Boyle v. United Technologies Corp.*, 487 U.S. 500, 513–514, 108 S.Ct. 2510, 2519, 101 L.Ed.2d 442 (1988), it is apparent from the record that such a condition does not here exist. Thus, on the claim construction of the panel majority,[4] the patentee is entitled to develop the facts for application of our new law. Even as this court declined to correct *en banc* the panel's claim construction, the case should have been remanded for application of this new rule of law to the evidence. Thus, respectfully, I dissent from the court's denial of rehearing *en banc*.

Exxon Chemical Patents, Inc. v. Lubrizol Corp., 77 F.3d 450, 451–57 (Fed.Cir.1996) (Newman, J., dissenting from denial of petition for rehearing and suggestion for rehearing *en banc*).

SIDE BAR

The Jury Trial of Patent Cases Involving Complex Technologies

William F. Lee*

The trial of patent issues to a jury involves an inherent tension. In any case tried to a jury (whether patent or otherwise), only three or four basic themes can be effectively communicated at one trial. These themes must be simple and clear, and are most persuasive when the jury can relate them to their own experience. Simultaneously, however, the trial lawyer must build an evidentiary record for the Court of Appeals for the Federal Circuit (the "CAFC") which will review the jury's verdict from a substantially different perspective. Unlike the jury, the CAFC will be

---

4. I can not reconcile the Response's suggestion of today that the theory it adopted was presented at the trial, with the statement in the majority opinion "that Exxon's preferred claim interpretation is incorrect, and that Lubrizol's is only partly correct." 64 F.3d at 1555, 35 U.S.P.Q.2D at 1802.

capable of and interested in the complex and difficult technological and legal issues.

Thus, the jury trial lawyer in patent cases must try his/her case to two very different audiences at the same time. Here, we will focus upon the effective communication of basic themes to a jury in a patent case.

A.   *The Effective Communication of the Technology at Issue.*

One of the most difficult issues in a patent jury trial is communicating the basic technology to a jury. In most cases, the members of the jury have, on average, the equivalent of a high school education. Many have had little scientific training and more than a few decided many years ago that technical issues were not a strength or interest. We have been involved in "debriefing" jurors after verdicts have been rendered, and, on more than one occasion, jurors have communicated their disinterest and (in a few cases) affirmative dislike for technical issues.

The difficulty in communicating background technology is particularly acute in electrical and chemical cases. In biotechnology and mechanical cases, the jury can frequently visualize the manner in which the invention is working. In contrast, in electrical cases, for example, much of what is occurring seems to be a mathematical "black box" which is and remains a complete mystery.

The question then is how can you get the jury's interest and effectively communicate the technical basics of your case.

1.   A critical decision is the selection of the witness or witnesses who will be communicating the technology to the jury. The jury's interest in and willingness to understand the technical issues can be heavily dependent upon the "believability" or "credibility" of your expert witnesses. Judge Farnan, the Chief Judge of the United States District Court for the District of Delaware, has adopted a practice of asking jurors, post verdict, to complete a questionnaire concerning the trial of patent cases. The results of Judge Farnan's questionnaire indicate the following:

a.   The most believable and credible expert witness can be your inventor. If the inventor is an attractive, truthful and straightforward witness, the jury will credit what he himself or she herself has to say about the invention and the technology underlying it more than any other witness.

b.   The next most "believable" category of witnesses is members of the academic community. Juries tend to credit academics with greater integrity and a more dispassionate point of view.

c.   Next in effectiveness are "in-house" experts. Although witnesses employed by a party have an inherent and obvious bias, a likable, credible witness who has "hands on" experience with a technology can be an extraordinarily effective witness.

d.   Last in order are paid consultants from consulting companies specializing in expert testimony. Juries bring a great deal of practical judgment to bear on the decisions before them and are quickly able to recognize "hired guns." The testimony of such consultants, particularly when accompanied by substantial financial remuneration, will be viewed as inherently suspect.

2. In "teaching the jury" fundamental technical concepts, you must start at the most basic level and build only to the level which is essential for you to communicate your three or four basic themes. Most jurors take the task before them very seriously and are, within the limits their technical inclinations, interested in learning what a case is about and deciding that case fairly. The trial lawyer who recognizes this and identifies and teaches those basic technical concepts which will be important and understandable to the jury will have a substantial advantage over the opponent who descends into a level of detail which few lawyers and no jurors will comprehend.

3. Technical issues must be communicated to a jury with a variety of visual aids. Recent studies have indicated that a juror who is interested in and listening to the oral testimony of a witness will comprehend approximately 10–20% of what that witness is saying. In contrast, an interested juror who is watching a demonstration of the "technology at work" on a television screen will comprehend as much as 70% of that which is being communicated. The use of chalks and models is an absolute necessity. Of increasing importance are computer simulations of the "technology at work." While many courts have historically evidenced great caution in admitting computer simulations, the use and admissibility of computer simulations is clearly on the rise.

B. *The Jury Trial by the Patent Owner.*

In general, the presentation of the patent owner should be concise, straightforward and simple. The patent carries the presumption of validity and the opposing party must carry its burden of demonstrating invalidity by clear and convincing evidence. 35 U.S.C. § 282. Jury research has indicated that almost one out of every three jurors is unwilling to undertake a task which they view the Patent and Trademark Office to have already accomplished. While almost all jurors on *voir dire* will honestly state that they are willing to look behind that which the Patent Office has done, many (if not most) will resort to the presumption of validity once the issues become complicated or difficult. This strong bias has resulted in the substantial number of jury verdicts for patent owner plaintiffs in many jurisdictions.

Rather than focusing on detailed technical and legal issues, the effective plaintiff's patent case adheres to the following basic guidelines:

1. You must try the importance of your invention. If the invention has been accorded substantial scientific acclaim, this will be important to the jury. Similarly, if the invention has resulted in a commercially successful product or process, this fact will be convincing to the jury. Juries are practical and pragmatic. If an invention has real world significance, they are much more likely to reject any validity attack.

2. The expert witnesses who are called on behalf of the patent owner should focus upon the importance of the invention rather than attempting to address in great detail technical issues. These expert witnesses will, of course, have to provide sufficient testimony to establish a record for the Court of Appeals. For the jury, however, you must focus the testimony of your witness on establishing the significance of what you claim to be an invention.

3.   The testimony of your inventor is of critical importance. If believed, the inventor's testimony will carry you far towards a favorable liability verdict. If, on the other hand, the jury finds the inventor to be inherently not credible, you have substantial problems. The inventor is the person who should describe in detail the thought process which led to the invention and the time and effort required to bring the invention to fruition. If the jury believes that the inventor has invested substantial time and effort and has made a real scientific advance, your hand will be strengthened.

4.   If you have evidence of copying, you must emphasize it. Many jurors believe (notwithstanding whatever instructions the court may give) that copying is an essential element of proof in a patent case. Even if the jury correctly understands that copying is not necessary, evidence of copying goes far towards demonstrating that the defendant has not made any independent scientific advance and has done nothing more than improperly appropriated the benefits of the scientific work of your patent owner.

5.   Be brief and concise. If your inventor is a good witness and the invention has some scientific or commercial success, the jury will want to be with you. Jurors do not like lawyers or clients who take too long to tell a story. A patent owner's case in particular should not require much time.

C.   *The Accused Infringer's Defense Before a Jury.*

The task of attacking a patent before a jury is a formidable one for the reasons articulated earlier. In general, jurors have difficulty understanding complicated patent concepts such as anticipation, obviousness and enablement. Jurors do, however, have substantial common sense and are capable of understanding basic themes which are predicated upon the policies which underlie validity attacks based upon 35 U.S.C. § 101, *et seq.* The question is how to present a case which appeals to the jurors' common sense. Again, a few basic guidelines.

1.   If you have a good non-infringement defense, focus upon it. Juries are collections of individuals with different perspectives who, when in the jury room, often are in search of compromise. A verdict of non-infringement but valid is a compromise which leaves the accused infringer in business but does not deprive the inventor of his patent. This is, of course, a perfectly acceptable compromise for a defendant.

2.   Communicate your validity attacks in common sense terms. For example, let us assume that a principal defense is nonenablement. A presentation to the jury which relies upon expert testimony couched in the technical terms of 35 U.S.C. § 112 is unlikely to be persuasive. However, a case which focuses upon that which the inventor actually invented and that which the inventor actually describes in the patent specification and suggests to the jury that the inventor is now trying to extend his invention beyond that which he actually invented can be very effective. While juries are interested in rewarding a true inventor for that which he or she has accomplished, they are unwilling to extend the scope of patent protection beyond that which they view as fair and reasonable.

Similarly, an obviousness attack which is presented in the form of a conclusory expert opinion and complicated technical discussion will be ineffective. Instead, an obviousness attack should be built by describing in simple terms incremental advances in the technology, and ultimately demonstrating that the invention claimed was only a small (and logical) step. While the jury may not fully comprehend the issue of obviousness, it is capable of identifying those circumstances in which an advance is small and insignificant.

4. Jurors are extremely concerned with rendering verdicts which will eliminate legitimate competition. If the accused infringer and the patent owner (or its assignee) are competitors, the defense must communicate that the end result of a finding of validity and infringement will be to eliminate competition.

5. When the plaintiff is not a competitor of the defendant, a different dynamic is presented. The defendant, in that instance, cannot focus upon the suppression of competition. That does not leave the defendant without a practical theme to pursue. In that circumstance, the defendant should make much of the plaintiff's inability to effectively develop and commercialize the technology which it claims to have invented. This can have two beneficial effects. First, the plaintiff's failure to commercialize an invention undermines the suggestion that the plaintiff has made a substantial scientific advance. Second, the fact that a defendant has brought a successful commercial product to market and the plaintiff has not can lead the jury to conclude that the defendant's product must be different from that which is claimed in the patent.

6. You must communicate the time, effort and expense expended by your client in independently developing its product. A jury which believes that a defendant has independently and in good faith expended substantial resources to develop its own technology is much more likely to find a patent invalid or not infringed.

D. *Conclusion.*

Simplify, simplify, simplify. A jury presentation should be clear, concise and practical. While juries are not always legally or technically correct in the results they reach, they are more often than not fair and practical. Your case must appeal to these basic attributes of our jury system.

* Managing Partner, Hale & Dorr LLP and John A. Reilly, Visiting Professor from Practice at Harvard Law School. The views expressed herein are solely the views of the author and do not necessarily reflect those of Harvard Law School, Hale and Dorr, LLP or the firm's clients. This SIDE BAR was written specially for PRINCIPLES OF PATENT LAW.

As the above SIDE BAR suggests, good communication skills can help avoid many of the difficulties often perceived to be inherent in trial of a patent case because such a case typically involves complex law and complex technological facts, both of a type that does not typically find itself before district judges and juries. But as the following article and SIDE BAR suggest, diligent counsel should also consider employing a number of legal tools that are available throughout civil litigation, generally.[1]

---

1. A related set of normative questions often arise in any discussion such as this about the extent to which our current systems of justice are adapted to or adaptable to the trial of

Latent Cures for Patent Pathology: Do Our Civil Juries Promote Science and the Useful Arts?

S. Leslie Misrock and F. Scott Kieff.

Science and law are commonly perceived to be radically different in their realms and in the ways they approach the world. To be sure, among jurists and philosophers of law, scholars of the approaches called moral realism and natural law would not agree: they argue instead that there is no philosophical distinction between the disciplines of science and of morality or law—that moral and legal truths exist in nature just as scientific truths exist, and that moral and legal thinking should be conducted using what is commonly called a scientific process. But our current legal system is not controlled by these, or any other single school of legal philosophy. In contrast with those in science, American legal controversies are not resolved by collective experimentation and analysis of resulting data in the search for a single truth. Rather, the American legal system is an adversarial one, where opposing sides are represented by zealous advocates before neutral decision makers. Scientific and legal processes are different; regardless of one's theory of legal reasoning—be it realism, positivism, or relativism—one must agree, at least descriptively, that contemporary American law and science have a tumultuous coexistence.

Law controls science directly, through regulation of scientific experiments including, for example, recombinant DNA research, animal testing, and human drug trials. Law monitors science through administrative and civil policing of scientific fraud and other misconduct. Law must resolve many problems that science generates. Consider those raised by products such as Agent Orange, Bendectin, the Dalkon Shield, asbestos, and breast implants, to name only a conspicuous few. The resulting mass-tort lawsuits shifted traditional theories of causation and burdens of proof under modern tort law. The large number of potential plaintiffs and defendants required new procedural rules to consolidate cases fairly and efficiently, form class actions, and give preclusive effect to issues and claims already decided. The vast damage awards in many such tort judgments drove large firms to seek bankruptcy protection and thereby created chaos among the different classes of creditors. Tort victims, labor, management, business contractors, and shareholders each put science on trial, as each urged a different view of the scientific and economic principles at play. In addition, the law uses science as new technologies give rise to new forms of evidence, such as elaborate blood and other tissue typing, DNA fingerprinting, mass spectrometry, and digital cryptography. In 1990, the Federal Courts Study Committee noted "[e]conomic, statistical, technological, and social scientific data are becoming increasingly important in both routine and complex litigation."[2]

---

complex cases like patent cases. In such a debate, one might ask how patent cases differ from other technologically or legally complex cases? How significant is the jury's unique ability to reflect community standards and determine veracity of specific witness testimony in a patent case? *See*, Richard A. Posner, *Juries on Trial*, COMMENTARY, March 1, 1995, at 49; *Markman*, 116 S.Ct. at 1395. In what other areas of commercial litigation do veracity and community standards play such subordinate roles? In what areas are they important?

2. Judicial Conference of the United States, Report of the Federal Courts Study Committee, 97 (1990).

While each of these areas of administrative, regulatory, and civil law involves interactions between science and law, nowhere is this interaction more naked, notorious, and economically important than the government's promotion of science through intellectual property law, and in particular, patent law. Intellectual property is an increasingly critical component of United States capital and foreign trade; more than in other areas of law, intellectual property is about economics and psychology. It's about incentives.

Article I of the Constitution grants Congress the power to "promote the progress of science and the useful arts, by securing for limited times to authors and inventors the exclusive right to their respective writings and discoveries."[3] United States patent laws exist to achieve this end, but today there is a crisis at this interface of science and law. Our patent system fails to work the way it should and could. The supposedly fixed and reliable public grant of a patent is often reshaped, like a nose of wax, by civil juries in a way that is both unpredictable and divorced from the scientific merits of the case. Each of the participants in the vast market for technological innovation—researchers, inventors, developers, investors, producers, and copiers—suffers from the resulting ambiguous property rights that cause inefficient use of the fuel that drives market transactions.[4] This inefficiency is pathological and requires a cure.

Because invention and technological change are major forces in the growth of national economies, we must cure the pathology of the patent system. Research over the past sixty years has amply demonstrated this causal link and has shown that changes in the law can be used deliberately to promote innovation and national economic development.[5] A classic example of such a change is the 1980 Supreme Court decision in *Diamond v. Chakrabarty*, which held that a new, genetically engineered bacterium was patentable subject matter even though it was a living thing.[6] Yet, before we can know which laws to change, we must determine which are problematic.

As we search the law for the root of this crisis, we make a troubling discovery: much of the pathology that infects patent law today springs from

3. U.S. Const. art. I, § 8, cl. 8.... [remainder of footnote omitted].

4. *See*, Ronald Coase, *The Problem of Social Cost*, 2 J.L. Econ. 1, 25 (1959) (the classic paper for which Professor Coase was awarded the Nobel Prize and in which he described the importance of rules for fixing the initial allocation of resources over which parties can then bargain in order to increase joint profits).

5. *See generally* R & D, Patents and Productivity (Zvi Griliches ed., 1984) (discussing evidence for this causal link). A listing of the seminal works in the field would include Joseph A. Schumpeter, Business Cycles (1939); Simon Kuznets, Secular Movements in Production and Prices (1936); Robert K. Merton, *Fluctuations in the Rate of Industrial Innovation*, Q.J. of Econ., (May 1935); Robert M. Solow, *Technical Change and the Aggregate Production Function*, 39 Rev. Econ. & Stat. 312, 320 (1957) (the classic study on the determinants of economic growth for which professor Solow was awarded the Nobel Prize and in which he concluded that most of the economic growth in the United States in the first half of this century could be explained by investments in research and development and education rather than by increases in capital and labor); and Zvi Grilliches, *Productivity, R & D, and Basic Research at the Firm Level in the 1970's*, 76 Am. Econ. Rev. 141 (1986). For a review of the field, *see* Geoffrey Wyatt, The Economics of Invention (1968).

6. *Diamond v. Chakrabarty*, 447 U.S. 303 (1980).

the role that juries have assumed here, as throughout civil litigation. In most civil litigation, the jury has become an unreliable, time-consuming, costly, and incomprehensible black box. A civil jury trial takes, on average, twice as long as a bench trial.[7] Even then, rather than penetrating to the truth of the matter before them, juries seem too often to respond only to the sexy or popular. A classic example is the award to Pennzoil in 1985 of $10.5–billion in a contract interference case against Texaco over the acquisition of Getty Oil. After that trial, the jurors explained "that they added $1 billion to the award for each of the Texaco lawyers they had most despised."[8] Of even greater concern is the inability of courts to review jury decisions effectively because the underlying reasons are often concealed behind the secrecy of the jury room. In short, unpredictable and unreviewable jury decisions wreak havoc with our technology industries and ultimately erode one of our greatest national economic resources: our talent for creating and exploiting new technology.

To blame juries is troublesome, however, because they are so central to the American experience. Not only is the jury system hallowed in American law, it is protected by the Sixth and Seventh Amendments to our Constitution. And so, like a patient whose cancer has invaded a vital organ, we feel trapped: the cancer must be removed but the organ must stay. Fortunately, in the case of patent law, the cure is safe because no excision is needed. The cancer is not actually part of the organ.

Close scrutiny of patent law's constitutional standing suggests a cure—simple, safe, and in harmony with tradition. Patent suits are civil, not criminal suits. Therefore, the Seventh Amendment[9] applies, not the Sixth.[10] Importantly, the amendments differ in two respects. First, unlike the Sixth Amendment, the Seventh makes no statement about the type of people who must form the jury. Second, unlike the Sixth Amendment, the Seventh does not grant a right—rather, it merely preserves those rights that had evolved at common law by the time the Bill of Rights was enacted. By taking advantage of these two distinguishing features of the Seventh Amendment, we propose changes that avoid any excision from the right it protects. The changes pass constitutional muster because they remove something that was never part of the vital organ.

To demonstrate the need for change, we begin by discussing remedies for the problems of the jury that are now sometimes employed. Each remedy has deficiencies in principle; and in practice they do not seem to have worked. We then discuss two stronger cures: the use of blue-ribbon juries, and the elimination of juries altogether from patent cases. Both cures are entirely consistent with early common-law practice, and as such

---

7. Richard A. Posner, *Juries on Trial*, Commentary, March 1, 1995, at 49.

8. From, Stephen J. Adler, The Jury: Trial and Error in the American Courtroom (1995), as reviewed in Richard A. Posner, *Juries on Trial*, Commentary, March 1, 1995, at 49.

9. "In suits at common law, . . . the right of trial by jury shall be preserved. . . ." U.S. Const. amend. VII.

10. "In all criminal prosecutions, the accused shall enjoy the right to a speedy and public trial, by an impartial jury of the State and district wherein the crime shall have been committed. . . ." U.S. Const. amend. VI.

are latent cures inherent early in our patent system. We now suggest they be dusted off and put back to work.

It is true that much can be done under the current rules to mitigate the damage caused by the black-box jury verdict. Various procedural devices may be used to educate the jury, to probe the jury's reasoning, to prevent certain easily resolved issues from reaching the jury, and—with mutual consent—to escape the jury altogether. Although currently available, these devices are not especially effective. Some have turned out not to be practicable, some courts decline to use them, and some are available only by consent, which the parties will not often give.

In the first place, we have cures that might be possible under the Federal Rules of Civil Procedure—the rules that govern the process by which lawsuits are brought and tried in federal court. For quite some time, judges on the United States Court of Appeals for the Federal Circuit have been reminding practitioners that there is much a lawyer can do under the rules of procedure to make the black box of the jury more translucent.[11] The Federal Circuit's late Chief Judge Emerita Helen W. Nies told us that she is "constantly frustrated by the lack of challenge to [jury] instructions."[12] She reminded lawyers that jury instructions should be fact and case specific, rather than general and abstract, and that objections to them can be proper even if the instruction does not misstate the law. For example, rather than tell the jury "the parties dispute whether the accused device infringes," the judge should instruct that "the parties dispute that the accused device contains the widget G as required by the claim."[13] Judge Nies and the Federal Circuit's Judge Paul R. Michel both have emphasized that parties should be alert to the attempts to send a legal issue to the black box of the jury without detailed guidance.[14] Both have cited the circuit's decision in 1983 in *Connell v. Sears, Roebuck & Co.*, a patent case in which the court analyzed the allocation of decision-making power between judge and jury.[15]

In *Connell*, the Federal Circuit's then Chief Judge Howard T. Markey provided a litigator's guide to the Federal Rules of Civil Procedure and recited the many "safeguards and alternatives" to the general verdict in

---

11. The Federal Circuit's late Chief Judge Emerita Helen W. Nies spoke on this issue several times over the last several years, including her speech to the District of Columbia Bar Association on December 5, 1995, and then again at the Federal Circuit Judicial Conference on May 23, 1996. Judge Paul R. Michel of the Federal Circuit offered similar advice in his speech to the Patent Lawyers Club of Washington, D.C. on April 30, 1996 and at the Federal Circuit Judicial Conference on May 23, 1996. Judges Nies and Michel both cite the detailed advice given in the opinions of the Federal Circuit's Chief Judge Emeritus Howard T. Markey. [Casebook editors' Note: *Also see generally*, Stephen S. Korniczky and Don W. Martens, *Verdict Forms—A Peek into the "Black Box"*, 23 AM. INTELL. PROP. L. ASSOC. Q. J. 617 (1996).]

12. Judge Helen Nies, Address at the D.C. Bar Association, p.3 (December 5, 1995) (citing *Structural Rubber Prods. Co. v. Park Rubber Co.*, 749 F.2d 707 (Fed.Cir.1984)).

13. *Id.* at 7.

14. In *Connell*, there was no objection to sending the legal issue of obviousness to the jury. Writing for the Federal Circuit, Chief Judge Markey held that it was not reversible error *per se*, to send the legal issue to the jury—with proper instructions—because the judge could review the verdict by Judgment as a Matter of Law.

15. *Connell v. Sears, Roebuck & Co.*, 722 F.2d 1542 (Fed.Cir.1983).

civil cases.[15] These include in their current incarnations a number of points that may appear somewhat technical in wording but are important in principle.

Special verdict (Rule 49(a)). A special verdict is one that is more detailed than a general verdict, which would simply report "guilty" or "not guilty." Because the special verdict requires the jury to answer specific questions of fact, it can more logically parse, and thereby reveal, the jury's decision-tree. Once revealed, each portion of the verdict can be analyzed independently and may even stand independently. Imagine a hypothetical case where the judge has held a patent claim to require a widget X and a widget G mounted at Y degrees. The components of a special verdict in such a case might include "the device has a widget G," "the widget G is mounted at Y degrees" and "the device also has a widget X." On appeal, such a verdict could be meaningfully affirmed even if the appellate court determined at the same time that the claim does not require widget X.

General verdict accompanied by jury answers to interrogatories (Rule 49(b)). A general verdict is easier for the trial court and the jury than a special verdict, but at the same time the court may want the jury to answer one or more written interrogatories. These interrogatories operate in much the same way as the specific questions in the special verdict. Under this approach, the jury must provide specific answers to the factual question posed in each interrogatory. Much like a special verdict, a general verdict that is backed by jury answers to interrogatories is strengthened because the reasoning behind the verdict is revealed by the jury's responses.

Judgment as a matter of law before submission to the jury (Rule 50(a)). A judge may prevent certain easily resolved issues from reaching the jury by ruling one way on a particular issue where there is no legally sufficient evidentiary basis for a reasonable jury to find otherwise.

Renewed motion for judgment as a matter of law and alternative motion for new trial (Rule 50(b)). After the jury has reached a verdict, one side or the other may bring a renewed motion for a judgment as a matter of law or in the alternative for a new trial. The standards for granting the motion are the same as if brought in advance of the verdict. A favorable ruling results in either the impaneling of a new jury for a new trial or a decision on the issue directly from the judge.

Jury instructions and objections thereto (Rule 51). Another way to guide or probe the jury's reasoning, depending upon whether one is in trial or on appeal, is through detailed jury instructions. As mentioned above, Judge Nies reminded lawyers that jury instructions should be fact and case specific, rather than general and abstract, and that objections are proper even if the instruction does not misstate the law. Importantly, as she further pointed out, jury instructions must be in plain English and may use examples and analogies. One such—convenient and frequently used—is to analogize the scope of a patent claim to an imagined fence around a hypothetical piece of real estate and compare the question of patent infringement to the more palpable notion of trespass.[16]

---

15. 722 F.2d at 1546.

16. Nies December Speech at 11.

Specific findings of fact (Rule 52). Sometimes, and for various reasons, cases or parts of cases are tried to a judge without a jury or to a judge with an advisory jury. In such instances, the parties may request that the judge give specific findings of fact. Like juries, even a trial judge might appear to have done some black-box decision-making. These specific findings operate substantially the same as special verdicts or jury interrogatories.

Motion for new trial (Rule 59). As a catch-all provision, when a case is winding up, either party may move for a new trial for any of the reasons for which new trials have been granted in the courts of the United States. Such reasons, however, are severely limited in number and frequency.

Notwithstanding such potential remedies, the role of the jury in patent cases today is almost limitless—as a matter of practice, that is, not necessarily as a matter of law. A great theoretical debate is now under way about the proper role of juries in patent cases. The law on this point may soon be changing. The Supreme Court has responded to the debate by recently granting *certiorari* in three patent cases involving this issue: *In re Lockwood* in 1995 (which we will look at again briefly), and in 1996, *Markman v. Westview* and *Hilton Davis v. Warner–Jenkinson*.[17] Each of these cases has to do with the allocation of decision-making power between judge and jury. The net result of this trilogy is yet to be worked out, but it may substantially alter the frequency and extent to which solutions under the Federal Rules of Civil Procedure are implemented.

Until these issues are put to rest, trial courts are likely to hesitate to take aggressive steps under the various procedural rules outlined above. Some trial judges facing uncertainty on the judge-versus-jury issue might rationally insure against reversal by impaneling a jury for at least an advisory opinion. Others might forge ahead, rationally ignoring the theoretical benefits of the procedural rules in favor of the short-term convenience of the black-box verdict. Either way, the potential gains from these procedural devices have certainly not been realized.

The Federal Rules of Evidence offer their own solution as well. Just as the rules of procedure govern the process by which lawsuits are tried in federal court, the rules of evidence govern the admissibility of evidence there. While all irrelevant evidence is inadmissible, not all relevant evidence is admitted.[18] The rules guide the judge to keep out evidence that is, among other things, prejudicial, redundant, confusing, unreliable, or privi-

---

17. *In re Lockwood*, 115 S.Ct. 2274 (1995) (granting *certiorari*); *Markman v. Westview*, 116 S.Ct. 1384 (1996); *Hilton Davis Chem. Co. v. Warner–Jenkinson Co.*, 116 S.Ct. 1014 (1996) (granting *certiorari*), *Warner–Jenkinson Co. v. Hilton Davis Chem. Co.*, 117 S.Ct. 1040 (1997) (reversing and remanding to the Federal Circuit to refine the substantive doctrine at issue in the case, non-literal infringement, also called infringement under the doctrine of equivalents). Interestingly, in *Warner–Jenkinson v. Hilton Davis*, the Supreme Court refused to directly analyze the allocation of decision-making authority between judge and jury because resolution of that issue was not necessary to the Court's decision on the narrow substantive question that was presented. 117 S.Ct. at 1053. The Court skirted concerns over "the unreviewability due to black-box jury verdicts ... offer[ing] guidance, not a specific mandate." *Id.*, at 1053, n.8. Instead, the Court briefly reviewed the various Federal Rules of Civil Procedure discussed in the text above, "leav[ing] it to the Federal Circuit how best to implement procedural improvements to promote certainty, consistency, and reviewability to this area of the law." *Id.*

18. FED. R. EVID. 402.

leged. Rule 706 expressly permits the use of court-appointed experts to eliminate venality, to procure a higher caliber of expert, to assist in settlement, and most importantly to help the jury reach a meaningful decision.[19] Commentators recognize that in cases with highly technical facts, it is naive to expect the trier of fact—especially if it is a jury— meaningfully to assess diametrically opposed testimony from the parties' witnesses. Indeed, in cases with esoteric technologies, the judge himself may be in dire need of the expert. In 1993, the Supreme Court decided in *Daubert v. Merrel Dow Pharmaceutical* that under the Federal Rules of Evidence the judge must play a gatekeeping role by ensuring "that any and all scientific testimony or evidence admitted is not only relevant, but reliable."[20] *Daubert* is a landmark case, if ever there was one, for it applies not just to patent cases but to civil litigation of every sort where scientific experts testify. It imposes crucial and difficult new responsibilities on trial judges. Simply put, *Daubert* says that junk science is not admissible. But how is the judge, not himself an expert, to spot junk science?

In theory, the benefits of court-appointed experts are obvious, if limited. But theory is not always implemented in practice. We come back to the fundamental fact that the American legal system is adversarial, with advocates for each side presenting opposing views of contested facts before a neutral decision maker or makers. As a figure directly aiding the decision maker in receiving and evaluating evidence, the court-appointed expert can circumvent the adversarial nature of this process to some extent. Thus, commentators doubt that Rule 706 will be exploited, citing trial judges' commitment to adversarial responsibility for presenting evidence.[21]

Another set of options is presented by what are called alternative dispute-resolution methods. These included arbitration and mediation. For patent suits, they are attractive in several respects. For instance, arbitration provides a private (that is, unreported), non-precedential, cost-effective, conclusive, and relatively prompt way of resolving disputes before a neutral decision-maker(s) who can be selected for having legal and technological expertise most relevant to the disputed issues. Federal patent law expressly permits arbitration of patent disputes among private parties in litigations[22] and also in interferences, the quasi-litigation proceedings before the Patent Office in which priority of invention is decided between two or more who claim inventorship.[23] A review of civil actions against the Commissioner of Patents to obtain a patent[24] shows that they often end with the commissioner agreeing to settlement, having been reminded by the Court of Customs and Patent Appeals of his authority to do so. In addition, an Executive Order issued on February 5, 1996, entitled "Civil Justice Reform," urged the use of alternative dispute-resolution methods in civil suits involving agencies of the executive branch of the federal govern-

---

19.   3 WEINSTEIN'S EVIDENCE ¶ 706[01].

20.   *Daubert v. Merrell Dow Pharm., Inc.*, 509 U.S. 579, 589 (1993).

21.   3 WEINSTEIN'S EVIDENCE ¶ 706[01].

22.   35 U.S.C. § 294.

23.   35 U.S.C. § 135(d).

24.   35 U.S.C. § 145.

ment.[25] This recent shift in executive policy may herald the arrival of a new use for such methods in patent disputes: civil actions against the Patent and Trademark Office in the person of the commissioner. By such means, alternative dispute-resolution thus can achieve the desired cure. The problem is that it requires approval by all parties to the litigation.[26] Not surprisingly, a party who is clearly wrong will prefer the gamble of a jury to the certainty of judgment as a matter of law.[27]

Such remedies attempt to provide more supervision of juries or to allow the parties to agree to a non-jury forum. Some courts, however, desire a more extreme approach and tackle the problem head-on. They suggest removing complex cases from juries altogether. This complexity exception to the Seventh Amendment right to a jury trial was contemplated by Alexander Hamilton in *The Federalist*:

> [T]he circumstances that constitute cases proper for courts of equity are in many instances so nice and intricate that they are incompatible with the genius of trials by jury. They require often such long, deliberate and critical investigation as would be impracticable to men called from their occupations, and obliged to decide before they were permitted to return to them.[28]

While discussed in *The Federalist*, the complexity exception has its modern roots in footnote 10 of a case the Supreme Court decided in 1970, *Ross v. Bernhard*, in which a corporation's stockholders were suing over a matter of corporate law.[29] In that note, the Court set forth a three-factor test for questions involving the right to a jury trial, which included consideration of "the practical abilities and limitations of juries."[30]

In 1980, the Third Circuit took this analysis one step further in the convoluted *Japanese Electronic Products* antitrust case by pointing out that in very complex cases, the Seventh Amendment right to a jury trial may conflict with the Fifth Amendment right to due process.[31] The court reasoned that as the factual and legal issues in a case become increasingly technical, "[t]he probability is not remote that a jury will become overwhelmed and confused by a mass of evidence and issues and will reach erroneous decisions."[32] Obviously, the goals of the jury system are not advanced when verdicts become completely arbitrary and unpredictable. In reversing the ruling of the trial court, the Third Circuit held that a jury trial is not proper "when a jury will not be able to perform its task of

---

25. Executive Order 12988, 61 FR 4729 (February 5, 1996).

26. Often in the form of an arbitration clause in a contract executed many years before the litigation.

27. For a more thorough discussion of the expected impact of this executive order, *see*, Charles E. Miller, F. Scott Kieff and Bart J. van den Broek, "Executive Order Allows PTO Action Arbitration—ADR Can Resolve Civil Claims By Private Parties Against The PTO," *National Law Journal*, C18–19 (Jan. 27, 1997).

28. Alexander Hamilton, *The Federalist* No. 83 at 505.

29. 396 U.S. 531, 538 at n. 10.

30. *Id*. The other two factors are the nature of the remedy sought and the historical treatment of the issue before the merger of the courts of law and equity in England.

31. *In re: Japanese Electronic Products Antitrust Litigation*, 631 F.2d 1069 (3d Cir.1980).

32. *Id*. at 1086.

rational decision-making with a reasonable understanding of the evidence and the relevant legal standards."[33]

Although the reasoning behind the *Japanese Electronic Products* holding is compelling, federal courts have not rushed to adopt the complexity exception. Some judges cite the lack of a clear-cut test to determine when a case is too complex for a jury.[34] The greatest obstacle, however, seems to be an overly cautious fear of infringing the constitutional rights of litigants that arises in many cases involving Seventh Amendment questions. As one district court judge stated in 1987, denying a motion to strike a demand for a jury: "If I have erred, . . . then I have erred on the side of protecting an important constitutional right, fundamental to the fair administration of justice."[35] Understandably, trial-court judges are reluctant to generate an unmanageable volume of constitutional appeals by granting motions to strike jury demands. As a result, until judges have more confidence in the doctrine, the complexity exception will not be a workable cure.

With all the uncertainty and mayhem in the patent-jury system, we think it may be time for a paradigm shift. An Omnibus Innovation Act ("the Act") could do the trick. The Act could overhaul the system with only a few key changes. Note well that we are suggesting nothing new. Rather, we reintroduce that which is latent and old, though apparently forgotten. The Act could make two major changes. First, we suggest a rebirth of blue-ribbon juries, like those used by Lord Mansfield, the famous jurist on the King's Bench in late eighteenth-century England. Second, we suggest securing a jurisdictional toe-hold in the equity realm so we may reapply the jurisprudence of early Supreme Court patent cases that recognized equity's jurisdiction to adjudicate co-pending claims at law. The distinction here is between courts of law, in which there was a right to a jury trial, and courts of equity, in which there was no right to a jury trial. The two regimes of law and equity traditionally offered separate remedies. The Chancery courts of equity generally imposed duties directly on the parties, subjecting them to contempt sanctions for disobeying the court. Typical equitable remedies included mandatory or prohibitory injunctions, and constructive trusts. The King's (or Queen's) courts of law, on the other hand, generally afforded monetary remedies, like damages, that could be enforced by court officers with or without the cooperation of the parties. While courts of law and equity have been merged for almost a century in the United States, the distinction between the two remains an important instrument in American Constitutional analysis.

History notes that the development and use of what were called merchant juries represented Lord Mansfield's most constructive use of the jury system.[36] After receiving the law mercantile and the law of contracts into the common law, Lord Mansfield quickly recognized that what was

---

33. *Id.*

34. *Davis–Watkins Co. v. Service Merchandise Co., Inc.*, 500 F. Supp. 1244, 1251 (M.Dist. Tenn. 1980).

35. *Educational Testing Services v. Katzman*, 1 U.S.P.Q.2D 1799, 1804 (D.N.J.1987), applying the three-pronged *Ross* test in denying a motion to strike a jury demand.

36. THE MANSFIELD MANUSCRIPTS AND THE GROWTH OF ENGLISH LAW IN THE EIGHTEENTH CENTURY, (James Oldham ed., 1992), at 93.

called the "special jury" understood evidence and testimony very well, knew more about the subject than anyone else present, and successfully formed their judgment from their own notions and experience.[37] In addition to special juries, those having any relevant special background, Lord Mansfield pioneered the use of so-called "merchant juries," that is, those having a particularly specialized background in commerce and trade.[38] Not surprisingly, it took little time for barristers and businessmen to appreciate the benefits of Mansfield's special juries, particularly the merchant juries.[39] Indeed, a review of Mansfield's patent cases reveals that the vast majority were tried to a special jury,[40] even though in every such case one or both of the parties had to pay for the jury.[41]

Borrowing from Lord Mansfield, the Act could require the use of special blue-ribbon juries in patent cases, perhaps formed of doctors, engineers, or scientists. These juries would satisfy the literal language of the Seventh Amendment because the right to jury at common law, as it then existed, would not be diminished. The Act would only reintroduce a device that existed at the time of the Bill of Rights. The spirit of the amendment would also be satisfied. Some might argue that the Seventh Amendment implies a right to a jury of one's peers. However, unlike the Sixth Amendment, the Seventh makes no statement about the type of people, *i.e.*, one's peers, who must form the jury. Because this clause appears in a neighboring amendment, its absence here is by implication intended. Thus, the spirit of the amendment imposes no peer requirement; as a result, the use of blue-ribbon juries would be in harmony with the spirit as well as the text.

One further obstacle might be raised against blue-ribbon juries, but once raised it is easily discarded or avoided. The Jury Selection and Service Act of 1968 does require that juries be selected from a "fair cross section of the community."[42] But existing authority interpreting this statute supports the argument that special juries would not violate the cross-section requirement so long as the special nature of the jury were rationally based on education or skill rather than on some more invidious factor like race or socioeconomic status.[43] Importantly, even if case law did not discard this obstacle, the Omnibus Innovation Act could easily avoid it by carving a patent-law exception into the jury-selection statute.

The use of blue-ribbon juries presents an effective treatment for the jury pathology—a treatment by which a jury's decision-making resources are still available to the parties and the court. Even experienced critics of the current jury system recognize that juries usually comprise conscien-

---

37. *Id.*, at 94.

38. *Id.*, at 95.

39. *Id.*, at 98.

40. *Id.*, at 738–771.

41. *Id.*, at 98.

42. 28 U.S.C. § 1861 (1994).

43. *See*, Rita Sutton, *A More Rational Approach To Complex Litigation In The Federal Courts: The Special Jury*, 1990 U. CHI. LEGAL F. 575 (1990); and Note, *The Case For Special Juries In Complex Litigation*, 89 YALE L. J. 1115 (1980).

tious citizens, and that when they go astray, they often do so simply because the case is too difficult for lay people to understand.[44] When a case turns on which witnesses are lying, the lay jury seems to do well; but not all civil cases turn on the issue of lying.[45] The cognitive limitations of the jury are particularly clear and costly in cases with important issues of complex technologies.[46] As seen by Lord Mansfield and also by proponents of alternative dispute resolution, a blue-ribbon panel would drastically improve the scientific-truth-value of the jury verdict, while keeping the decision-making burden spread among more than one individual.

While the use of blue-ribbon juries appears unconventional today, an even more radical cure would be to avoid juries completely. The Omnibus Innovation Act could effectively remove juries from patent cases by revising the statutes to take advantage of century-old Supreme Court jurisprudence that recognizes circumstances under which a court of equity may decide claims otherwise decided properly only by a court of law. The distinction between law and equity is of great importance in Seventh Amendment analysis, because the amendment only preserves the right of jury trial as it existed at the time the amendment was written, and only to the extent it existed in courts of law, not equity. In 1881, in the case of *Root v. Railway Co.*,[47] the Supreme Court expressly acknowledged that while a bill in equity for a naked legal claim cannot be sustained, an equitable claim having incidental legal aspects was properly before a court of equity. Therefore, if the Act expressly ensured that an equitable remedy was always available to a patent holder, then the patent holder could always avoid a jury trial by demanding such an equitable remedy along with other legal remedies, such as damages.

The facts of *Root* are simple. A patent holder brought suit over a patent in a court of equity after the patent had expired. Because the patent had expired, no injunction was available, needed, or sought. The patent owner did, however, want the infringer to account for and surrender the profits he had made while infringing. The patent owner urged the court to view the infringer as a constructive trustee of the infringement profits, because trust cases could be brought in a court of equity. The Supreme Court disagreed, refusing to view the infringer as a trustee.[48] The Court found the claim to be one sounding in law, for damages, and affirmed the lower court's dismissal for lack of jurisdiction in a court of equity.[49]

Unlike the facts, the rule of *Root* is complex. The Court's holding was narrow, as we saw, acknowledging that a naked legal claim cannot properly be brought before a court in equity.[50] But in a lengthy discussion surrounding the holding, the Supreme Court analyzed several exceptions where a

---

44.   Richard A. Posner, *Juries on Trial*, COMMENTARY, March 1, 1995, at 49.

45.   *Id.*; *see also, Markman*, 116 S.Ct. at 1395.

46.   *Id.*

47.   105 U.S. 189 (1881); *see also, Beedle v. Bennett*, 122 U.S. 71 (1886).

48.   105 U.S. at 214.

49.   *Id.*

50.   *Id.*, at 215–216.

court of equity would have jurisdiction over legal claims.[51] The Court used the rule from England, as written in *Smith v. London & Southwestern R.R.*: where a party is entitled to an equitable remedy, like an injunction, the court in equity will also grant legal damages.[52] The Court in *Root* then recited the rule of *Smith* in its list of exceptions to the narrow holding. Thus, *Root* teaches that in 1881 courts of equity in the United States as well as in England had proper jurisdiction to decide both legal and equitable claims in cases where the equitable claims established a jurisdictional beach-head in the court of equity and where the legal claims were incidental. Under *Root*, legal claims in a patent case could constitutionally be decided without a jury. The catch, though, is that the case must be brought as one seeking at least some equitable relief.

Most patent cases today already include the equitable remedy of a temporary or permanent injunction. But as in *Root*, an injunction is improper where the patent has expired. So the question becomes, what other equitable relief might a patent holder seek? The answer we present is once again hardly novel: an inventor's moral right of attribution. Such a right has already been incorporated for authors into the law of copyrights.[53] In 1990, when the United States became a signatory to the Berne Convention, the leading international treaty on copyright protection, the United States copyright laws were amended to give authors moral rights of attribution and integrity. Moral rights under copyright law include the right of an author or artist to prevent misattribution of authorship, the right of attribution, as well as unauthorized intentional distortion, mutilation or destruction of his work, the right of integrity.

The Act could expand the patent statute to give inventors a similar moral right of attribution. With this addition to the statute, all patent suits could plead equitable claims for attribution, even after the expiration of the patent. For example, a post-expiration suit might seek a mandatory injunction compelling the infringer to announce publicly that the infringing products were made using the inventor's previously patented technique. Under *Root*, such a suit could properly have been brought in a court of equity, even if it also contained claims for legal damages. Therefore, following contemporary Seventh Amendment analysis, there would be no right to a jury trial in such a case.[54] Because of *Root* and its progeny, on passage of the Act, every patent suit brought could avoid a jury trial by demanding at least some equitable remedy, such as the right of attribution provided by the Act.

It is noteworthy that the Federal Circuit summarily distinguished *Root* in its opinion in *Lockwood*, one of the three recent patent cases accepted by the Supreme Court concerning the allocation of decision-making power between judge and jury.[55] *Lockwood* involved the right to a jury trial in a

---

51. *Id.*

52. *Id.*, at 209, citing *Smith v. London & Southwestern R.R.* (Kay, 408).

53. 17 U.S.C. § 106A.

54. *Cf., Chauffeurs, Teamsters & Helpers Local No. 391 v. Terry*, 494 U.S. 558, 570–573 (1989).

55. 50 F.3d at 978.

case where the only issue to be resolved was the validity of the governmentally issued patent. The Federal Circuit held, by a divided court, that there was a right to a jury trial, but the Supreme Court agreed to review the matter.[56] Curiously, the jury issue in *Lockwood* was then settled at the district-court level by a withdrawal of the jury demand. The Supreme Court then dismissed *Lockwood* as moot, vacated the Federal Circuit's judgment, and remanded the case for the district court to proceed without a jury.[57] Therefore, as Judge Nies keenly noted, "the only extant decision on that issue is the opinion of the *Lockwood* district court denying a jury."[58]

Yet, even if *Root* were properly distinguished by the Federal Circuit or the Supreme Court, or overturned by the Supreme Court, the careful practitioner could still benefit from its lessons. A typical court's analysis of patent infringement involves two steps. First, there is claim construction to determine the meaning of the patent claims. Second, there is the infringement analysis itself, to determine whether the properly construed claims encompass the accused device. Today, after *Markman*, the construction of a patent claim is a matter for judge, not jury.[59] There remains some uncertainty, however, whether the comparison of the claim to the device must go to a jury in all cases. A practitioner who is quick to bring suit, before potential damages accrue to any significant extent, may request only an injunction, and not damages, without forgoing a great deal. Such a suit would be entirely analogous to the old injunction suits, which were brought before courts of equity where there was no jury. Therefore, under contemporary Seventh Amendment analysis, there would be no right to a jury trial in such a case and the patentee-plaintiff will escape the jury altogether. Even if another case like *Lockwood* were to be decided by the Federal Circuit as before, and not reversed by the Supreme Court, then the clear case of infringement may still be tried quickly and without a jury by motion to a judge for judgment as a matter of law.

Chief Judge Richard A. Posner of the United States Court of Appeals for the Seventh Circuit often points out that the continued salience of the jury in American civil adjudication contrasts starkly with the rest of the world: we got the system from England, yet England has virtually abandoned it. *See*, Richard A. Posner, *Juries on Trial*, COMMENTARY, March 1, 1995, at 49. Perhaps, at least for patents, it is time for us to abandon it, too. We found the cures for our ailment to have been before us all along. Tradition and history provide convenient solutions that are compatible with the Seventh Amendment. The time has come to put these latent devices to use once again. Blue-ribbon juries and patent suits in equity may help resolve the inefficient ambiguity caused by modern civil juries. While we only discuss these cures in the context of patent cases, they are readily available and easy to implement: perhaps the experience we gain from their use in the patent system could support efforts to expand their application

---

56.   50 F.3d at 980 (Circuit Judge Nies, joined by Chief Judge Archer and Circuit Judge Plager, dissenting opinion from order denying motion to rehear the case *in banc*, before the whole court, to reconsider the opinion of the original three-judge panel).

57.   116 S.Ct. 29 (1995).

58.   (December Speech, at 11).

59.   116 S.Ct. 1384, at 1394–6.

throughout complex civil litigation. Perhaps then, as science becomes more integrated into law, the interface between the two could present a more constructive force for each.

SIDE BAR

Alternative Dispute Resolution of Patent Cases

Tom Arnold*

A dispute is a problem to be solved together, not a combat to be won.

Court dispute resolution, is very poor on average.

We in America have so refined the judicial process that it earned this quote from its highest officer, from Mr. Chief Justice Warren E. Burger:

Our litigation system is too costly, too painful, too destructive, to inefficient, for a civilized people.

Would you recommend to your client a system of dispute resolution so schlocky as to beget that quote from its highest officer?

Do I believe that quote? Yes, in spades. I can cite dozens of examples. *E.g.*, *Hughes Aircraft* after 24 years in the courts, in 1997 was ordered back to the Court of Appeals that decided infringement 14 years earlier, for a redetermination of infringement. 24 years and counting, and no decision, after many tens of millions of total litigation cost. I had a case continue for 27 years, others for 15 years. The average cost of resolving a patent infringement dispute, total to both parties, is now about $2.4 million, enough to drown many an infringement dispute, but the total was nearly $100,000,000 for both sides together in *Polaroid v. Kodak*. Etc.

And the reversal rate in precedential opinions from the Federal Circuit is variously reported but at the January 1998 American Intellectual Property Law Association conference, one judge of that court reported 27% complete reversals and 26% partial reversals for a 53% total of non-affirmances.[1] Since lawyers' opinions are more biased than neutral judges' opinions, and are written before discovery is complete whereas judges have the benefit of full discovery and experts on both sides, lawyer's opinions are surely over 10% less reliable than trial judge opinions. For the cost of a beer at a local tavern (I will buy the beer and lend the coin), we can flip a coin and get results which are just as responsible as pre-litigation attorney opinions, or even trial judge opinions, so why spend those millions in any case, but particularly, why on modest value cases. Etc.

Yes, I believe Burger. "Too costly, too painful, too destructive, too inefficient for a civilized people" may be an understatement for half of all court IP cases.

What are the alternatives?

If court process is too costly, too painful, too destructive, too inefficient, what kinds of alternatives are available out there for us to use? In a paper of mine entitled *A Vocabulary of ADR Procedures*,[2] I undertake to describe and define over twenty such processes, most of them utilizing either or both of mediation and arbitration as a central theme.

Arbitration is not inherently safe from horror stories of time, money and inefficiency, but (a) the arbitration horror stories run perhaps one third as bad as the corresponding litigation stories, and (b) if the arbitration process is intelligently defined, perhaps in a mediation effort to design the process explicitly to fit the dispute and its worth, an additional major saving is available.

And mediation *is* inherently, substantially safe—no real horror stories even though there is no guarantee a party won't waste a couple of days of time in a mediation effort. When a mediation does not settle a case, it usually pays for itself in savings it inherently produces in the ongoing arbitration or litigation process.

Recall, however, that ADR processes are a creature of your contract: You can have what ever you or your ADR expert have skill enough to draft and negotiate with the other party. And for license disputes, it is clear that MEDALOA, MEDiation And Last Offer Arbitration, is the process of choice. It also works very well, if somewhat imperfectly, in most other IP cases.

Do we really know that ADR is Best?

Yes. Some form of ADR is better than Court dispute resolution in all but a very few IP cases.[3] Proved best not just in laboratory tests, but in full scale operations of major corporations like Motorola, Chevron, major insurance companies, who studied the processes in actual use.

Motorola did a careful study and reported "Better dispute resolution results at one quarter the cost." Who doesn't want a piece of that action? A major insurance company reports saving $80,000,000 per year in determining the size of the checks it cuts each year for claimants, without increasing the total. Would you call it malpractice for your purchasing department to blow $80 million a year because they did not know any better, and simply did not bother to find out? Have *you* bothered really to find out?

Some surveys have pointed out that more than twice as many parties to mediations are satisfied with the result and the process as with court result and process. More than four times as many are satisfied with the cost of mediation as with the cost of court process, and a majority do not feel the court process was essentially fair. Does that tell us anything? Is not party perceived satisfaction a meaningful factor to consider?

Ways that ADR is best?

Ten good reasons why some form ADR is best for your case, include:

1.   *Control.* In some forms of ADR, the parties don't abdicate their interests to some stranger who decides the case, but retain full control—nothing happens the party does not approve of.

2.   *Money.* Some poorly structured or performed arbitrations are expensive horror stories even when cheaper than the corresponding court horror stories, but on average ADR processes can save tons of money over court process cases. An early mediation, prior to 75% of the routine discovery expense, settles half of the cases. You can cheaply mediate again later, if need be.

3.   *Time.* On average, save tons of time. Indeed, burdens of time and money are in some cases a reason, perchance an unethical one, that a

party opposes some ADR process. Remember, settlement rates in very early mediations differ from those later mediations by only very small amounts over 50% still settle.

4. *"Judges" with expertise.* In ADR you can select your neutrals to be folks with experience and expertise in the relevant law, business, or technology, or in all three, in lieu of submitting the case to strangers who likely have no background for the subject IP case: friends of Senators we call trial judges,[4] and miscellaneous residents who are mostly poorly educated for a patent law case that we call jurors. To most folks who are dedicated to responsible results rather than extortion, that makes good sense.

5. *Preserve relationships.* Good mediation processes put oil on the troubled waters, offer a good chance of a preservation of licensor-licensee relationships, joint venture relationships, etc., that adversarial court litigation almost inevitably injures or destroys.

6. *Privacy, confidentiality.* It is not automatic, but if you play the process right the parties can usually have a very important degree of confidentiality about their dispute and its resolution, that is not obtainable in court process.

7. *Win-win creative business solutions.* Frequently, a business-interests-based negotiation in a mediation looking to future relationships and profits, will afford some solution that is better for *each* party than any judgment a court of law could determine in any law-bound litigation which of course looks only backward to past acts to determine rights at law, and which usually treats future relationships as irrelevant.

8. *Flexible, rational results in mediation.* As an example: When parties in making a contract overlook some key circumstance, like new governmental controls on international currency exchange or new import controls that frustrate the intent of the contract, the backward looking court process essentially never can generate as fair a result as a forward looking renegotiation of future relationships in light of the new circumstance. There are many such situations where a mediation has provided a better result to *each* party than a court could grant to either pursuant to law.

9. *Avoid litigation in the other party's biased home forum.* In many international cases it is very important to resolve your dispute as by arbitration in some neutral forum, rather that be forced to litigation in the other party's home forum. Would you prefer Switzerland, Bosnia, Iraq?

10. *Easy international enforcement.* Over 115 nations have adhered to the New York Convention affording easy enforcement of arbitration awards. There is no corresponding treaty to which the U.S. adheres for the enforcement of court judgments. Whereby arbitration awards are easier to enforce and much preferred to court judgments at enforcement time.

* * *

ADR is not perfect, not even excellent in most cases. Only better on average than the court process that is as much as I can guarantee to you.

There is no space here to develop and teach avoidance of the booby traps that plague the unwary in ADR practice. But as a package do those values and wants which I have listed seem at least interesting to consider knowledgeably beside the court alternative that is "too costly, too painful, too destructive, too inefficient, for a civilized people"?

A dispute is a problem to be solved together, not a combat to be won.

* Founder, Arnold White & Durkee. Co-author of books including *Patent Alternative Dispute Resolution*, *Licensing Law Handbook*, and *Patent Law for Engineers*, among others. Former President/Chairman of each American Intellectual Property Law Association, IP Section of the American Bar Association, National Council of Patent Law Associations, Houston Bar Association, Houston Executives Association, A. A. White Dispute Resolution Institute, and others. AAA Panel for Large Complex Cases; Advisory Board, Institute for Transnational Arbitration, Fellow, and Executive Committee of the North American Branch, of the Chartered Institute of Arbitrators, London; Advisor to CPR, AAA, and WIPO on alternative dispute resolution matters. The views expressed herein are solely the views of the author and do not necessarily reflect those of Arnold White & Durkee, the firm's clients, or any other of the listed affiliated organizations. This *SIDE BAR* was written specially for PRINCIPLES OF PATENT LAW.

1. This is not a criticism of our judges who are generally among our better and best legal minds; the problem is inherent in our generalized and adversarial system where our legal standards are unavoidably vague (*e.g.* "equivalent", "enablement", and "obvious") and our issues are often legally and technologically quite specialized and complex.

2. *Vocabulary of ADR Procedures*, a three-part series in the American Arbitration Association's Dispute Resolution Journal, 1996.

3. A patentee may have a questionable patent; a Federal Circuit decision of valid and infringed may cause the entire industry to respect it, whereas an arbitration award to the same effect may not deter the challengers. This is a real and common bias to prefer litigation, but lawyers tend to be driven by it to insane, nonsensical degrees, where this factor is not nearly worth the difference in cost, time, risk, etc.

4. Usually selected from the top 20% of the Bar, but typically without patent or technology experience.

CHAPTER NINE

DEFENSES AND LIMITATIONS

> [D]uring the present generation a deeper research and a more exact discrimination have dispelled ... ignorance [of the patent law], and though obscurities of detail still remain, yet whenever questions of Patent Law are now presented to our courts the factors of the problem lie before them, certain and intelligible, requiring only careful distinctions and accurate reasonings to attain impregnable results.
>
> —William C. Robinson[1]

INTRODUCTION

Having just reviewed the vast dimensions of the rights conferred by the patent grant, one might justly wonder whether the patentee faces any limits at all. Section 282 of the Patent Code generally sets forth defenses that may be raised to avoid liability for patent infringement:

The following shall be defenses in any action involving the validity or infringement of a patent and shall be pleaded:

(1) Noninfringement,[2] absence of liability for infringement or unenforceability,

---

1. WILLIAM C. ROBINSON, 1 THE LAW OF PATENTS v (1890).

2. A little used defense relating to non-infringement is the reverse doctrine of equivalents, which has the effect of limiting claim scope. The Federal Circuit has defined this doctrine as follows:

> [The reverse doctrine of equivalents] might better be called a doctrine of non-equivalence. Its invocation requires both that (1) there must be apparent literal infringement of the words of the claims; and (2) the accused device must be sufficiently different from that which is patented that despite the apparent literal infringement, the claims are interpreted to negate infringement....

> The reverse doctrine of equivalents is invoked when claims are written more broadly than the disclosure warrants. The purpose of restricting the scope of such claims is not only to avoid a holding of infringement when a court deems it appropriate, but often is to preserve the validity of claims with respect to their original intended scope.

Texas Instruments Inc. v. U.S. Int'l Trade Comm'n, 805 F.2d 1558 (Fed.Cir.1986), *opinion on denial of rehearing*, 846 F.2d 1369, 1372 (Fed.Cir.1988). But the court has not been sympathetic to this doctrine. *See Tate Access Floors, Inc. v. Interface Architectural Resources, Inc.*, 279 F.3d 1357, 1368 (Fed.Cir.2002):

> Not once has this court affirmed a decision finding noninfringement based on the reverse doctrine of equivalents. And with good reason: when Congress enacted 35 U.S.C. §§ 112, after the decision in *Graver Tank*, it imposed requirements for the written description, enablement, definiteness, and means-plus-function claims that are co-extensive with the broadest possible reach of the reverse doctrine of equivalents.

(2) Invalidity of the patent or any claim under [under §§ 101–103],

(3) Invalidity of the patent or any claim in suit for failure to comply with any requirement of sections 112 or 252 of this title,

(4) Any other fact or act made a defense by this title.

The most commonly asserted defenses other than non-infringement, are those based on the rules of patent validity, such as § 102 (lack of novelty and statutory bars), § 103 (obviousness), and § 112 (failure to comply with one or more of the disclosure requirements). These invalidity defenses generally raise no new issues beyond those already studied in earlier chapters; and the substantive legal tests for assessing invalidity in court are essentially the same as for assessing patentability before the Patent Office. A central issue that does arise in litigation but not during initial examination is what import to give to the issued patent's presumption of validity. Section 282 tells us that patents are to be presumed valid; and the Federal Circuit has long interpreted this presumption to be both procedural (the party challenging validity must plead and prove it) and substantive, in that the burden of proof is by "clear and convincing evidence." *See, e.g., American Hoist & Derrick Co.* v. *Sowa & Sons, Inc.,* 725 F.2d 1350, 1359 (Fed.Cir.1984). The clear and convincing burden is somewhat heavier than the relatively lighter burden known as "the preponderance of the evidence" standard that is widely used for other issues in commercial law, including patent infringement. The Supreme Court has decided to review this issue in the presently pending case of *Microsoft v. i4i,* in which Microsoft is asking the Court to extend the lighter burden to invalidity challenges as well, perhaps for all issues of invalidity and perhaps for those not explicitly discussed in the record of examination before the Patent Office. *See __ US __,* 131 S.Ct. 647 (2010) (granting certiorari). *Cf, Uniroyal, Inc. v. Rudkin–Wiley Corp.,* 837 F.2d 1044, 1050 (Fed.Cir.1988) (applying the clear and convincing burden when the invalidity defense is based on prior art evidence that was not in the examination record).

But there are numerous other defenses and doctrines that have evolved through both statutory and judge-made law to limit the reach of the patent grant. In this chapter, we discuss several of these defenses, including: (A) the doctrine of inequitable conduct; (B) the doctrine of patent misuse; (C) antitrust; (D) the doctrines of first sale, implied license, and repair/reconstruction; (E) preemption as a limitation on actual or potential owners of intellectual property; (F) other limitations on contractual provisions; (G) inventorship and ownership; (H) first inventor defense under 35 U.S.C. § 273; (I) the experimental use exception for abbreviated new drug applications; and (J) governmental immunity.

For a general discussion on the reverse doctrine of equivalents, *see* Robert P. Merges, *Intellectual Property Rights and Bargaining Breakdown: The Core of Blocking Patents,* 62 TENN. L. REV. 75 (1994).

The Federal Circuit recently affirmed that the "reverse doctrine of equivalents" is very infrequently successful: "The reverse doctrine of equivalents is rarely applied, and this court has never affirmed a finding of non-infringement under the reverse doctrine of equivalents." *Roche Palo Alto LLC v. Apotex Inc.,* 531 F.3d 1372 (Fed.Cir.2008).

But before exploring each of these defenses in detail, it is important to consider the strategic implications discussed in the following SIDE BAR that any defense can raise for both patentee and potential alleged infringer.

SIDE BAR

Declaratory Judgment Jurisdiction: A Dance On the Razor's Edge

Thomas G. Pasternak, Erick Ottoson and Karen J. Nelson*

Issues of patent invalidity, unenforceability, and noninfringement have diverse factual and legal underpinnings but remarkably similar practical impact as limitations on a patentee. Each can provide a complete defense to a complete defense to a patent infringement suit brought by the patentee. Each can also provide independent subject matter jurisdiction for a declaratory judgment ("DJ") action against the patentee. It is in this second role, as foundation for a DJ action, that the impact of these issues may be most surprising for both the patentee and the alleged infringer. In the ordinary patent infringement suit, the patentee is the plaintiff, having picked the forum and timing for the litigation. In the typical declaratory judgment suit, the putative infringer is the plaintiff, and has picked the forum and timing for the suit. Litigation is a battle, and as every warrior knows, the ability to pick the time and place for a battle can have enormous tactical and strategic impact.[1]

The pre-suit interactions between patentee and putative infringer often resemble a complex dance, with each partner making both aggressive and gentle overtures. There are a number of reasons why the patentee might want to signal to the putative infringer that its behavior may be infringing. For example, the patentee may want to enter into licensing negotiations; or the patentee may want to increase the likelihood that if a judgment of infringement is eventually obtained it will be found to have been willful and thereby support the remedies of treble damages and attorney fees.[2] Conversely, the putative infringer may want to signal a willingness to negotiate while avoiding any admission about liability. Or, the putative infringer may want to buy time to fully investigate matters and make an informed business decision about whether to proceed with the technology at issue.

Concerns have often arisen that this dance may go too far or take on too much of an antagonistic air. The law governing willful infringement controls the behavior of the putative infringer. But you might wonder, what controls the behavior of the patentee? In response to concerns just such as this, Congress passed the Declaratory Judgment Act, 28 U.S.C. § 2201 ("the Act"). The Act allows those other than the patentee to test the validity, enforceability, or infringement of patents that are being used as what Learned Hand has called "scarecrows."[3] According to the Federal Circuit:

> [Such cases] present a type of the sad and saddening scenario that led to enactment of [the Act].... In the patent version of that scenario, a patent owner engages in a *danse macabre*, brandishing a Damoclean threat with a sheathed sword.... Guerilla-like, the patent owner attempts extra-judicial patent enforcement with scare-the-customer-and-run tactics that infect the competitive environment of the business community with uncertainty and

insecurity.... Before the Act, competitors victimized by that tactic were rendered helpless and immobile so long as the patent owner refused to grasp the nettle and sue. After the Act, those competitors were no longer restricted to an *in terrorem* choice between the incurrence of a growing potential liability for patent infringement and abandonment of their enterprises; they could clear the air by suing for a judgment that would settle the conflict of interests. The sole requirement for jurisdiction under the Act is that the conflict be real and immediate, i.e., that there be a true, actual "controversy" required by the Act.[4]

As Congress intended, the DJ Act enables a putative infringer not certain of his rights to chose to file a suit to obtain an early adjudication, without having to wait for his adversary to see fit to bring the suit, which might not have been until after damages had accrued.[5]

Thus, today, a patentee's dance with a putative infringer may be a dance on the razor's edge. A patentee engaged in aggressive behavior may find itself the defendant in a DJ suit brought at a time and place not likely to be most convenient.[6] Use of a DJ action can allow a party who is engaged (or prepared to engage) in arguably infringing activities to take matters into its own hands and file suit first, in a jurisdiction of its own choosing. Such patent DJ actions are just what was contemplated by those who framed the Act; indeed, patents are a major source of DJ litigation.

I. The Basic Test for Jurisdiction

The basic test for DJ jurisdiction stems from the enabling legislation itself, which provides in pertinent part:

> In a case of actual controversy within its jurisdiction ... any court of the United States, upon the filing of an appropriate pleading, may declare the rights and other legal relations of any interested party seeking such declaration, whether or not further relief is or could be sought.[7]

The Act's "actual controversy" requirement parallels Article III of the Constitution, which provides for federal jurisdiction only over "cases and controversies."[8]

Until quite recently, long-established Federal Circuit caselaw held that the controversy requirement was satisfied in patent DJ cases when two conditions were met: (1) the defendant's conduct must have created on the part of the plaintiff a "reasonable apprehension" that it would face an infringement suit; and (2) the plaintiff must have been engaged in activity which could constitute infringement or concrete steps taken with the intent to conduct such activity.[9] "The first prong look[ed] to the patentholder's conduct, and the second prong look[ed] to the potential infringer's conduct."[10] In 2005, the Federal Circuit modified the test to require "reasonable apprehension of *imminent* suit."[11]

In early 2007, however, the Supreme Court's *MedImmune* decision rejected the "reasonable apprehension" test as inconsistent with a number of prior Supreme Court decisions.[12] The proper standard, according to the Supreme Court, can be summarized as follows: "whether the facts alleged, under all the circumstances, show that there is a substantial controversy, between parties having adverse legal interests, of sufficient immediacy and reality to warrant the issuance of a declaratory judgment."[13] Thus, this area of the law is currently in flux, as both the Federal Circuit and lower courts attempt to sort through the impact of

MedImmune. The discussion below first reviews a number of issues that arose under the reasonable apprehension standard, and then examines *MedImmune* and its aftereffects.

A.   Pre–*MedImmune*

1.   Reasonable Apprehension of Suit

Under the pre-*MedImmune* standard, it was clear that a party fearing potential infringement liability as a result of its past or present acts could be placed in reasonable apprehension of a suit for patent infringement by direct threats of litigation.[14] It was also clear that something less than a direct threat could be sufficient to create reasonable apprehension. However, in the absence of a direct threat, the combination of facts needed to confer jurisdiction was a gray area of the law. Courts found DJ jurisdiction in at least the following situations:

- Where there has been a history of litigation between the parties (a pending infringement action against a third party) and threatening letters to the declaratory judgment plaintiff.[15]

- Where a patentee initiated license negotiations, sent a letter referring to its inclination to "turn the matter over to" its litigation counsel "for action," and urged a preliminary licensing discussion "perhaps avoiding this matter escalating into a contentious legal activity." According to the Federal Circuit, this letter "made it reasonably clear that [patentee] intended to resort to litigation if it were not satisfied with the results" of the negotiations. The court saw this language as evidence of a predisposition to litigate. When coupled with high demands for a licensing offer, the court found that litigation of this matter was extremely likely, thus creating the necessary actual controversy.[16]

- Where a patentee wrote three letters: one to a customer of its competitor stating the belief that the competitor may be infringing its patent; a letter to the competitor stating that it "had reason to believe" that the competitor was an infringer; and a letter to the competitor stating that it had litigated is patent in the past.[17] The Federal Circuit found that the statements of intent to enforce, coupled with prior actual enforcement, were sufficient for an actual controversy, even without a specific charge of infringement.[18]

- Where a licensee brought a declaratory judgment action against the patent holder before terminating an existing licensing arrangement.[19] The licensee had stopped paying royalties, but the licensor did not terminate the license, going so far as to state in an affidavit that he had no intention of terminating the license.[20] The court held that even though the license had not been terminated, subject matter jurisdiction was proper.[21] This ruling was based on a finding that the licensor defendant could have terminated the license agreement at any time since the royalties remained unpaid.[22] The court found that this uncertainty led to a reasonable apprehension of suit sufficient to establish subject matter jurisdiction.[23]

Conversely, courts found reasonable apprehension of suit to be lacking in the following situations:

- Where a patentee's defensive statements about his patent even combined with responses to questions about its view on infringement and its willingness to enforce made in licensing negotiations prompted by the declaratory judgment plaintiff and in response to remarks by the declaratory judgment plaintiff.[24]

- Where the patentee refused to offer a license.[25]

- Where license negotiations are ongoing and have not been terminated and one party requests further information during the negotiations.[26]

- Where a patentee entered into a covenant not to sue for 12 months with a provision that, if it brought suit after 12 months, it would not sue for any prior infringement.[27]

- Where a patentee repeatedly asserted that it had no intention of suing.[28]

- Where a patentee sent a letter to the alleged infringer stating a belief of infringement, but told the alleged infringer to take its time to consider its position on infringement and licensing.[29]

- Where, in a case involving two competitors in the field of plastics manufacturing, each with its own patented technology, the declaratory judgment plaintiff argued that its own customers' decision not to infringe was because they were afraid of being sued by the competitor. The Federal Circuit affirmed the district court's decision to dismiss. The Federal Circuit noted that the mere existence of a patent is not enough to create declaratory judgment jurisdiction, distinguishing the customer's fear of doing infringing acts from the fear of suit for infringement.[30]

- Where the DJ plaintiff essentially admitted that it did not have reasonable apprehension of an infringement suit, but instead feared that it could not sell its product without subjecting its customers to such a suit.[31]

- Where the pendency of a reissue application covering the same subject matter as the patent for which no declaratory judgment jurisdiction lies is insufficient to give rise to an actual controversy.[32]

Thus, the case law concerning reasonable apprehension required more than the "nervous state of mind of a possible infringer"[33]—it required objective circumstances involving certain aggressive behavior.

2. Activity by Plaintiff

The second prong of the pre-*MedImmune* test for DJ jurisdiction was not as controversial. This part of the test required that the putative infringer's present activity place it at risk of infringement liability. This essentially meant that the accused infringer must have actually produced, or been prepared to produce, an allegedly infringing product.[34]

In general, courts gave this prong a relatively straightforward interpretation, finding the level of activity sufficient to create DJ jurisdiction in at least the following infringement situations:

- Where the alleged infringer is making, using, or selling an allegedly infringing product or process.[35]

- Where there is present contributing to or inducement of allegedly infringing activity.[36]

- Where the allegedly infringing activity is not immediate, but where intent and ability are present.[37]

Although the case law in this area was sparse, it seemed to indicate that almost any *actual efforts* by a putative infringer would be sufficient to trigger this prong of the test for DJ jurisdiction. But like every rule, there are exceptions, and the Federal Circuit has recognized that:

> A patentee defending against [a DJ action] can divest the trial court of jurisdiction over the case by filing a covenant not to assert the patent at issue against the putative infringer with respect to any of its past, present, or future acts. . . . The legal effect of [the patentee's] promise not to sue is the heart of the matter. . . .

Super Sack Mfg. Corp. v. Chase Packaging Corp., 57 F.3d 1054, 1058–59 (Fed.Cir.1995). Thus, A "residual possibility of a future infringement suit based on [the would-be-infringer's] future acts is simply too speculative a basis for jurisdiction," and a promise not to sue for past or present acts extinguishes DJ jurisdiction.[38]

II. *MedImmune* and its Impact

The Supreme Court's recent decision in *MedImmune, Inc. v. Genentech, Inc.*[39] rejected the Federal Circuit's "reasonable apprehension of suit" standard for determining patent DJ jurisdiction. The specific issue decided in *MedImmune* was whether Article III's limitation of federal courts' jurisdiction to "cases" and "controversies," as embodied in the DJ Act's "actual controversy" requirement, requires a patent licensee to terminate or breach the license agreement before it can seek a DJ of invalidity, unenforceability, or noninfringement.[40] Holding that no such requirement exists, the Court pointed out that federal courts have long accepted jurisdiction over DJ suits filed by plaintiffs who are effectively being coerced into abstaining from conduct that would, if undertaken, expose them to government prosecution or a civil lawsuit.[41] For example, in a 1943 case, *Altvater v. Freeman*,[42] the Court held that a licensee's failure to cease payment of royalties (under the compulsion of an injunction decree) did not render non-justiciable a dispute over the validity of the patent. The fact that the royalties were being paid did not mean that the dispute over the patent's validity was "of a hypothetical or abstract character."[43]

In dicta, the Court then noted that its *Altvater* decision "contradict[s] the Federal Circuit's 'reasonable apprehension of suit' test," and that "[a] licensee who pays royalties under compulsion of an injunction has no more apprehension of imminent harm than a licensee who pays royalties for fear of treble damages and an injunction."[44] The Court also cited several additional decisions in which DJ jurisdiction obtained despite the absence of any risk of a lawsuit.[45]

Post–*MedImmune*, the general standard for DJ jurisdiction in patent cases (as in other types of cases) is the following:

> that the dispute be "definite and concrete, touching the legal relations of parties having adverse legal interests"; and that it be "real and substantial" and "admi[t] of specific relief through a decree of a conclusive character, as distinguished from an opinion advising what the law would be upon a hypothetical state of facts." . . . "Basically, the question in each case is whether the facts alleged, under all the circumstances, show that there is a substantial controversy, between parties having adverse legal interests, of sufficient immediacy and reality to warrant the issuance of a declaratory judgment."[46]

At the time this article was written, only a handful of Federal Circuit decisions have addressed the impact of *MedImmune*. However, it is quite clear that the bar for establishing DJ jurisdiction in patent cases has been lowered. In a March 2007 decision, the Federal Circuit acknowledged that "*MedImmune* represents a rejection of our reasonable apprehension of suit test."[47] It then held that "where a patentee asserts rights under a patent based on certain identified ongoing or planned activity of another party, and where that party contends that it has the right to engage in the accused activity without license, an Article III case or controversy will arise and the party need not risk a suit for infringement by engaging in the identified activity before seeking a declaration of its legal rights."[48] A few months later, the Federal Circuit reversed a district court's dismissal of a patent DJ suit for lack of jurisdiction, finding that jurisdiction was present where the patentee had provided the plaintiff with a detailed infringement analysis, and the plaintiff had identified specific prior art references that it believed rendered the claims invalid.[49] In both of these cases, the Federal Circuit rejected the notion that a patentee's willingness to continue with ongoing licensing negotiations would defeat jurisdiction.[50]

III. Strategic Lessons for the Litigator

Before *MedImmune*, patentees wishing to approach potential infringers without triggering a DJ suit had to focus on whether their statements and conduct would create an objectively reasonable apprehension of suit. Thus, the challenge facing such patentees was to effectively communicate the idea that the other party's activities constituted infringement, while carefully avoiding an overly adversarial posture by, for example, refraining from direct threats to sue, and conveying a desire to resolve the matter amicably through negotiations. Post–*MedImmune*, avoiding threats and being willing to negotiate remain prudent practices for the patentee wishing to avoid a DJ suit. But *MedImmune* and subsequent Federal Circuit cases have made clear that such steps will not, alone, preclude DJ jurisdiction. The bar has been lowered: DJ jurisdiction can now be established simply on the basis that a patentee asserts that another party's ongoing or planned activities constitute infringement, while that party contends that it has the right to engage in the activity without a license.[51] As a result, it is now not entirely clear what steps a patentee *can* take without triggering DJ jurisdiction, because almost any contact with a potential infringer—e.g., an invitation to take a license, or a letter notifying them of the existence of the patent—carries with it at least the implicit representation that the recipient is engaged in infringing conduct. Undoubtedly, lower courts will sort through the outer boundaries of the post-*MedImmune* standard in the years to come. In the meantime, patentees, and their attorneys, are well-advised to approach infringers with a good deal of caution.

One strategy often undertaken in dancing on the razor's edge, by either party, is to file, but not serve a complaint. By not serving the complaint (which would trigger the other party's need to file an answer), the plaintiff may endeavor to preserve its choice forum while waiting to see how the chips fall. This strategy is often undertaken; but it is not foolproof. A first-filed suit may be dismissed if it is perceived to have been brought for improper reasons. The general rule in patent cases is that the first-filed action is favored over a second-filed suit.[52] Without this rule, the patentee would automatically be granted his choice of forum, which is contrary to the purpose of the Declaratory Judgment Act.[53] However, if a court views forum-shopping to be the sole purpose (perhaps likely when the complaint is filed but not served absent other reasons for not serving), the first-filed suit could be dismissed in favor of the second-filed.[54] This could be a major setback for the party seeking to litigate on his terms. If, on the other hand, the first-filed suit is filed in a forum more convenient to the plaintiff, there are stronger grounds to avoid dismissal for improper filing. Filing in a more convenient forum is not the type of forum shopping that is condemned because it does not show a motive for seeking out a forum where the law or judiciary is more favorable to one's cause than in another.[55]

In conclusion, a party contemplating pre-suit interactions should be wary of the behavior it engages in—or it may find itself defending unanticipated patent litigation on the turf and time schedule set by someone else. A party dancing on the razor's edge should do so with care.

* Thomas G. Pasternak specializes in patent litigation as a partner in the Chicago office of Steptoe & Johnson LLP. Erick Ottoson specializes in patent litigation as an attorney in the Phoenix office of Osborn Maledon. Karen J. Nelson, who co-authored an earlier version of this SIDE BAR, is a Patent Counsel for Abbott Laboratories. This SIDE BAR was written specially for PRINCIPLES OF PATENT LAW, and does not necessarily express the views of the authors' employers or clients.

1. Sun Tzu, THE ART OF WAR, The Denam Translation Group (2001) at 20 ("One who takes the position first at the battleground and awaits the enemy is at ease. One who takes position later at the battleground and hastens to do battle is at labor. Thus one skilled at battle summons others and is not summoned by them.").

2. For more on remedies, see the materials in Chapter Ten, *infra*.

3. *Bresnick v. United States Vitamin Corp.*, 139 F.2d 239, 242 (2d Cir.1943).

4. *Arrowhead Industrial Water, Inc. v. Ecolochem, Inc.*, 846 F.2d 731, 734–35 (Fed.Cir.1988). *Arrowhead* was decided under the Federal Circuit's "reasonable apprehension of suit" test, which, as discussed below, was abrogated by the Supreme Court in *MedImmune, Inc. v. Genentech, Inc.*, 549 U.S. 118 (2007).

5. *See E. Edelmann & Co. v. Triple—A Specialty Co.*, 88 F.2d 852 (7th Cir.1937), *cert. denied*, 300 U.S. 680 (1937).

6. Although personal jurisdiction for DJ actions is not a subject of this SIDE

BAR, a patentee can probably rest assured that the act of sending a cease and desist letter into defendant's forum does not by itself give rise to personal jurisdiction there, because this does not constitute a purposeful availment of the benefits and protections of that forum's laws. *See, e.g., Graphic Controls Corp. v. Utah Medical Products, Inc.*, 149 F.3d 1382, 1387 (Fed. Cir.1998).

7. 28 U.S.C. § 2201(a).

8. *SanDisk Corp. v. STMicroelectronics NV*, 480 F.3d 1372, 1378 (Fed.Cir. 2007); *Aetna Life Ins. Co. v. Haworth*, 300 U.S. 227, 239–41 (1937).

9. *Plumtree Software, Inc. v. Datamize, LLC*, 473 F.3d 1152, 1158 (Fed. Cir. 2006); *see also C.R. Bard, Inc. v. Schwartz*, 716 F.2d 874, 879–82 (Fed. Cir. 1983) (early Federal Circuit decision applying reasonable apprehension of suit standard). The reasonable apprehension standard predates the Federal Circuit. *See, e.g., Japan Gas Lighter Ass'n v. Ronson Corp.*, 257 F.Supp. 219, 237 (D.N.J. 1966), *cited in C.R. Bard*, 716 F.2d at 879.

10. *Sierra Applied Sciences, Inc. v. Advanced Energy Indus., Inc.*, 363 F.3d 1361, 1373 (Fed.Cir.2004).

11. *Teva Pharm. USA, Inc. v. Pfizer, Inc.*, 395 F.3d 1324, 1333 (Fed.Cir.2005).

12. *MedImmune*, 127 S.Ct. at 774 n.11.

13. *Id.* at 771.

14. *Agridyne Techs. v. W.R. Grace & Co.*, 863 F.Supp. 1522, 1525 (D. Utah 1994).

15. *Goodyear Tire & Rubber Co. v. Releasomers, Inc.*, 824 F.2d 953, 956 (Fed. Cir.1987); *see also Plumtree*, 473 F.3d at 1159–60 (finding reasonable apprehension of suit where patentee had sued DJ plaintiff on a related patent two years before the DJ suit was filed, had subsequently sued nine other defendants on the patents that were the subject of the DJ suit, and had stated in an interrogatory response in that case that the DJ plaintiff was infringing those patents).

16. *EMC Corp. v. Norand Corp.*, 89 F.3d 807, 812–13 (Fed.Cir.1996).

17. *Arrowhead Indus. Water, Inc. v. Ecolochem, Inc.*, 846 F.2d 731, 733 (Fed. Cir.1988).

18. *Id.*, at 738–39.

19. *See, e.g., C.R. Bard*, 716 F.2d at 880.

20. *See id.* at 877.

21. *See id.* at 882.

22. *See id.* at 881–82.

23. *See id.; see also Grid Sys. Corp. v. Texas Instruments Inc.*, 771 F.Supp. 1033, 1042–43 (N.D.Cal.1991) (holding that TI had repeatedly asserted that Tandy infringed its patents and had a history of filing suits to assert its patent rights against Tandy and other companies that made products similar to Tandy's); *American Hosp. Supply Corp. v. Damon Corp.*, 597 F.Supp. 445, 447 (N.D.Ill.1984) (holding that "where the parties and their actions dispute the validity of the patent in question, there is sufficient controversy for jurisdiction, under the patent statute or under the diversity statute which turns on the same considerations").

24. *Shell Oil Co. v. Amoco Corp.*, 970 F.2d 885, 889 (Fed.Cir.1992).

25. *Cygnus Therapeutics Sys. v. ALZA Corp.*, 92 F.3d 1153, 1160–61 (Fed. Cir.1996).

26. *Phillips Plastics Corp. v. Kato Hatsujou Kabushiki Kaisha*, 57 F.3d 1051, 1053–54 (Fed.Cir.1995).

27. *Leatherman Tool Group Inc. v. Bear MGC Cutlery Inc.*, 50 U.S.P.Q.2d 1856, 1858–59 (D.Ore.1998).

28. *CAE Screenplates, Inc. v. Beloit Corp.*, 957 F.Supp. 784, 791–92 (E.D.Va. 1997).

29. *Waters Corp. v. Hewlett–Packard Co.*, 999 F.Supp. 167, 172 (D.Mass.1998).

30. *BP Chemicals Ltd. v. Union Carbide Corp.*, 4 F.3d 975, 978–80 (Fed. Cir.1993).

31. *Microchip Technology Inc. v. Chamberlain Group, Inc.*, 441 F.3d 936, 942 (Fed.Cir.2006).

32. *Spectronics Corp. v. H.B. Fuller Co.*, 940 F.2d 631, 637–38 (Fed.Cir.1991).

33. *Phillips Plastics Corp. v. Kato Hatsujou Kabushiki Kaisha*, 57 F.3d 1051, 1053–54 (Fed.Cir.1995).

34. *Id.* at 1052; *Spectronics Corp. v. H.B. Fuller Co., Inc.*, 940 F.2d 631, 633–34 (Fed.Cir.1991); *Arrowhead*, 846 F.2d. at 736; *Cordis Corp. v. Medtronic Inc.*, 835 F.2d 859, 862 (Fed.Cir.1987).

35. *Arrowhead Indus. Water, Inc. v. Ecolochem, Inc.*, 846 F.2d 731, 738 (Fed. Cir.1988).

36. *Ciba–Geigy Corp. v. Minnesota Min. & Mfg. Co.*, 439 F.Supp. 625 (D.R.I. 1977); *see also Pin/Nip, Inc. v. Platte Chemical Co.*, 2006 WL 3302847, at *2–3 (D. Idaho 2006).

37. *Arrowhead*, 846 F.2d 731 at 730.

38. *Id.; see also, Matsushita Battery Industrial Co. v. Energy Conversion Devices, Inc.*, 1997 WL 811563, *6–7 (D.Del. 1997) (holding no DJ jurisdiction where there was a release from liability as to prior conduct and where the alleged infringer represented that the development of the prior allegedly infringing products was terminated, because the possibility that the alleged infringer might begin to make other putatively infringing products was considered by the court to be simply too speculative).

39. 549 U.S. 118 (2007).

40. *Id.* at 767.

41. *Id.* at 772–73.

42. 319 U.S. 359 (1943).

43. *Id.*

44. 127 S.Ct. at 774 n.11.

45. *Id.*

46. *Id.* (citing *Aetna Life Ins. Co. v. Haworth*, 300 U.S. 227 (1937) and *Maryland Casualty Co. v. Pacific Coal & Oil Co.*, 312 U.S. 270 (1941)).

47. *SanDisk*, 480 F.3d at 1380.

48. *Id.* at 1381.

49. *SanDisk*, 480 F.3d at 1382; *Sony*, 497 F.3d at 1286; *contra Phillips Plastics Corp.*, 57 F.3d at 1053 (pre-*Med-*

Immune decision stating that "[w]hen there are proposed or ongoing license negotiations, a litigation controversy normally does not arise until the negotiations have broken down").

50. *Sony Electronics, Inc. v. Guardian Media Technologies, Ltd.*, 497 F.3d 1271, 1285–86 (Fed.Cir.2007).

51. *Sony*, 497 F.3d at 1286.

52. *Genentech, Inc. v. Eli Lilly and Co.*, 998 F.2d 931, 937 (Fed.Cir.1993).

53. *Id.*

54. *Id.* at 938; *see also Kahn v. General Motors*, 889 F.2d 1078, 1081 (Fed.Cir. 1989).

55. *Roadmaster Corp. v. Nordictrack, Inc.*, 29 U.S.P.Q.2d 1699, 1700 (N.D.Ill.1993).

A. INEQUITABLE CONDUCT

Since the mid-1940s, the Supreme Court has endorsed the idea that a patent applicant's conduct during the application process may give rise to a defense to a charge of infringement. *See Hazel–Atlas Glass Co. v. Hartford–Empire Co.*, 322 U.S. 238 (1944) (dictum); *Precision Instrument Mfg. Co. v. Automotive Maintenance Mach. Co.*, 324 U.S. 806 (1945). Such a defense arises from the applicant's duty of candor in dealing with the PTO. Although this defense has always included conduct more easily proven than common-law fraud, the defense had traditionally been labeled "fraud on the Patent Office." But in *J.P. Stevens & Co. v. Lex Tex Ltd.*, 747 F.2d 1553 (Fed.Cir.1984), the Federal Circuit referred to the defense as a charge of *inequitable conduct* before the PTO. Common law fraud is generally seen as having four basic elements: (1) misrepresentation of material fact; (2) intent; (3) justifiable or reasonable reliance; and (4) injury. In contrast, inequitable conduct before the PTO is generally seen as having only the first two elements.

The punishment for "inequitable conduct before the PTO" is harsh. A successful defense renders all the claims of the asserted patent unenforceable for the life of the patent. Proof of this defense requires establishing that inequitable conduct by the applicant (or those aligned with him) occurred during the application process of the asserted patent. Such conduct can include a wide range of actions such as submitting false information, submitting misleading information, misrepresenting information, and not disclosing information. 6 DONALD S. CHISUM, CHISUM ON PATENTS § 19.03[2] (1999).

In *J. P. Stevens*, the Federal Circuit established a two-step process for analyzing inequitable conduct before the PTO. First, at least threshold levels of materiality and intent to deceive must be proven. Then, "[o]nce the thresholds of materiality and intent are established, the court must balance them and determine as a matter of law whether the scales tilt to a conclusion that inequitable conduct occurred." *See J.P. Stevens*, 747 F.2d at 1559–60. A high level of materiality can offset a low level of intent, and vice versa. *See Halliburton Co. v. Schlumberger Tech. Corp.*, 925 F.2d 1435, 1439 (Fed.Cir.1991); *American Hoist & Derrick Co. v. Sowa & Sons*, 725 F.2d 1350, 1363 (Fed.Cir.1984).

This section is divided into two parts: (1) Intent and (2) Materiality. Though these issues must both be taken into account in any determination of inequitable conduct, they are easier to conceptualize when addressed separately.

REGULATION—37 C.F.R. § 1.56 (1999).

1. INTENT

To be guilty of a breach of the duty of candor, the patent applicant must have some culpable state of mind with respect to a misrepresentation or omission. The *Kingsdown Medical Consultants v. Hollister* case discusses the requisite level of "intent" for a charge of inequitable conduct.

Kingsdown Med. Consultants, Ltd. v. Hollister, Inc.

863 F.2d 867 (Fed.Cir.1988).

■ Before MARKEY, CHIEF JUDGE, SMITH and ARCHER, CIRCUIT JUDGES

■ MARKEY, CHIEF JUDGE.

Kingsdown Medical Consultants, Ltd. and E.R. Squibb & Sons, Inc., (Kingsdown) appeal from a judgment of the United States District Court for the Northern District of Illinois, No. 84 C 6113, holding U.S. Patent No. 4,460,363 ('363) unenforceable because of inequitable conduct before the United States Patent and Trademark Office (PTO). We reverse and remand.

BACKGROUND

Kingsdown sued Hollister Incorporated (Hollister) for infringement of claims 2, 4, 5, 9, 10, 12, 13, 14, 16, 17, 18, 27, 28, and 29 of Kingsdown's '363 patent.[1] The district court held the patent unenforceable because of Kingsdown's conduct in respect of claim 9 and reached no other issue.

The invention claimed in the '363 patent is a two-piece ostomy appliance for use by patients with openings in their abdominal walls for release of waste.

The two pieces of the appliance are a pad and a detachable pouch. The pad is secured to the patient's body encircling the abdominal wall opening. Matching coupling rings are attached to the pad and to the pouch. When engaged, the rings provide a water tight seal. Disengaging the rings allows for removal of the pouch.

A. *The Prosecution History*

Kingsdown filed its original patent application in February 1978. The '363 patent issued July 17, 1984. The intervening period of more than six-and-a-half years saw a complex prosecution, involving the submission, rejection, amendment, re-numbering, etc., of 118 claims, a continuation

---

1. Claims 1, 9 and 27 are independent. Claims 2, 4, and 5 depend from claim 1. Claims 10, 12–14, and 16–18 depend from claim 9. Claims 28 and 29 depend from claim 27.

application, an appeal, a petition to make special, and citation and discussion of 44 references.

* * *

Thirty-four claims were filed with the continuation application.... In prosecuting the continuation, a total of 44 references, including 14 new references, were cited and 29 claims were substituted for the 34 earlier filed, making a total of 63 claims presented. Kingsdown submitted a two-column list, one column containing the claim numbers of 22 previously allowed claims, the other column containing the claim numbers of the 21 claims in the continuation application that corresponded to those previously allowed claims. That list indicated, incorrectly, that claim 43 in the continuation application corresponded to allowed claim 50 that had been rejected for indefiniteness under § 112. Claim 43 was renumbered as the present claim 9 in the '363 patent. [This oversight, namely failure to properly copy the allowed version of claim 50 for claim 43, which eventually became claim 9, was the basis for the district court's finding of inequitable conduct before the PTO. As stated in the case, the original claim 50 had been rejected because of indefiniteness.]

* * *

B.   *The District Court*

The district court rendered its opinion and announced its decision orally from the bench.

Having examined the prosecution history, the district court found that the examiner could have relied on the representation that claim 43 corresponded to allowable claim 50 and rejected Kingsdown's suggestion that the examiner must have made an independent examination of claim 43, because: (1) in the Notice of Allowance, the examiner said the claims were allowed "in view of applicant's communication of 2 July 83."[2]

The district court found the materiality element of inequitable conduct, because allowability of claim 50 turned on the amendment overcoming the § 112 rejection in the parent application. Kingsdown's knowledge of materiality was inferred from claim 50's having been deemed allowable in the parent application only after the change in claim language.

The court found the deceitful intent element of inequitable conduct, because Kingsdown was grossly negligent in not noticing the error, or, in the alternative, because Kingsdown's acts indicated an intent to deceive the PTO.

The court found that Kingsdown's patent attorney was grossly negligent in not catching the misrepresentation because a mere ministerial review of the language of amended claim 50 in the parent application and of claim 43 in the continuing application would have uncovered the error, and because Kingsdown's patent attorney had had several opportunities to make that review.

* * *

---

2.   As the district court stated, and all agreed, the correct date was 2 July 1982. The only "communication" filed on that date was the continuation application accompanied by an extensive preliminary amendment which included the two columns of claim numbers.

ISSUE

Whether the district court's finding of intent to deceive was clearly erroneous, rendering its determination that inequitable conduct occurred an abuse of discretion.[3]

OPINION

We confront a case of first impression, in which inequitable conduct has been held to reside in an incorrect inclusion in a continuation application of a claim that contained allowable subject matter, but had been rejected as indefinite in the parent application.

Inequitable conduct resides in failure to disclose material information, or submission of false material information, with an intent to deceive, and those two elements, materiality and intent, must be proven by clear and convincing evidence. *J. P. Stevens & Co., Inc.* v. *Lex Tex Ltd., Inc.*, 747 F.2d 1553, 1559 (Fed.Cir.1984), *cert. denied*, 474 U.S. 822 (1985). The findings on materiality and intent are subject to the clearly erroneous standard of Rule 52(a) Fed.R.Civ.P. and are not to be disturbed unless this court has a definite and firm conviction that a mistake has been committed. *J. P. Stevens*, 747 F.2d at 1562.

"To be guilty of inequitable conduct, one must have intended to act inequitably." *FMC Corp.* v. *Manitowoc Co., Inc.*, 835 F.2d 1411, 1415 (Fed.Cir.1987). Kingsdown's attorney testified that he was not aware of the error until Hollister mentioned it in March 1987, and the experts for both parties testified that they saw no evidence of deceptive intent. As above indicated, the district court's finding of Kingsdown's intent to mislead is based on the alternative grounds of: (a) gross negligence; and (b) acts indicating an intent to deceive. Neither ground, however, supports a finding of intent in this case.

a. *Negligence*

The district court inferred intent based on what it perceived to be Kingsdown's gross negligence. Whether the intent element of inequitable conduct is present cannot always be inferred from a pattern of conduct that may be described as gross negligence. That conduct must be sufficient to require a finding of deceitful intent in the light of all the circumstances. We are not convinced that deceitful intent was present in Kingsdown's negligent filing of its continuation application or, in fact, that its conduct even rises to a level that would warrant the description "gross negligence."

It is well to be reminded of what actually occurred in this case—a ministerial act involving two claims, which, because both claims contained allowable subject matter, did not result in the patenting of anything anticipated or rendered obvious by anything in the prior art and thus took nothing from the public domain. In preparing and filing the continuation

---

3. Because of our decision on intent, it is unnecessary to discuss materiality. *Allen Archery, Inc.* v. *Browning Mfg. Co.*, 819 F.2d 1087, 1094 (Fed.Cir.1987); *FMC Corp.* v. *Manitowoc Co.*, 835 F.2d 1411, 1415–16 (Fed.Cir.1987).

application, a newly-hired counsel for Kingsdown had two versions of "claim 50" in the parent application, an unamended rejected version and an amended allowed version. As is common, counsel renumbered and transferred into the continuation all (here, 22) claims "previously allowed". In filing its claim 43, it copied the "wrong", *i.e.*, the rejected, version of claim 50. That error led to the incorrect listing of claim 43 as corresponding to allowed claim 50 and to incorporation of claim 43 as claim 9 in the patent.[6] In approving the continuation for filing, Kingsdown's regular attorney did not, as the district court said, "catch" the mistake.

In view of the relative ease with which others also overlooked the differences in the claims, Kingsdown's failure to notice that claim 43 did not correspond to the amended and allowed version of claim 50 is insufficient to warrant a finding of an intent to deceive the PTO. Undisputed facts indicating that relative ease are: (1) the similarity in language of the two claims; (2) the use of the same claim number, 50, for the amended and unamended claims; (3) the multiplicity of claims involved in the prosecution of both applications; (4) the examiner's failure to reject claims using "encircled" in the parent application's first and second office actions, making its presence in claim 43 something less than a glaring error; [The word "encircled" was the basis of the examiner's § 112 rejection in claim 50. However, the examiner did not object to an identical use of "encircled" in two other claims.] (5) the two-year interval between the rejection/amendment of claim 50 and the filing of the continuation;[7] (6) failure of the examiner to reject claim 43 under § 112 or to notice the differences between claim 43 and amended claim 50 during what must be presumed, absent contrary evidence, to have been an examination of the continuation; and (7) the failure of Hollister to notice the lack of correspondence between claim 43 and the amended version of claim 50 during three years of discovery and until after it had carefully and critically reviewed the file history 10 to 15 times with an eye toward litigation. That Kingsdown did not notice its mistake during more than one opportunity of doing so, does not in this case, and in view of Hollister's frequent and focused opportunities, establish that Kingsdown intended to deceive the PTO.

We do not, of course, condone inattention to the duty of care owed by one preparing and filing a continuation application. Kingsdown's counsel may have been careless, but it was clearly erroneous to base a finding of intent to deceive on that fact alone.

* * *

Thus the first basis for the district court's finding of deceitful intent (what it viewed as "gross negligence") cannot stand.

b. *Acts*

The district court also based its finding of deceitful intent on the separate and alternative inferences it drew from Kingsdown's acts in

---

6. In filing claim 58 in the continuation, Kingsdown also erroneously copied unamended and rejected claim 51 in place of amended and allowed claim 51. The erroneously copied claim 51 became claim 24 of the patent.

7. There was no evidence that counsel's awareness of the rejection/amendment coincided in time with the filing of the continuation application.

viewing the Hollister device, in desiring to obtain a patent that would "cover" that device, and in failing to disclaim or reissue after Hollister charged it with inequitable conduct. The district court limited its analysis here to claim 9 and amended claim 50.

It should be made clear at the outset of the present discussion that there is nothing improper, illegal or inequitable in filing a patent application for the purpose of obtaining a right to exclude a known competitor's product from the market; nor is it in any manner improper to amend or insert claims intended to cover a competitor's product the applicant's attorney has learned about during the prosecution of a patent application. Any such amendment or insertion must comply with all statutes and regulations, of course, but, if it does, its genesis in the marketplace is simply irrelevant and cannot of itself evidence deceitful intent. *State Indus., Inc. v. A.O. Smith Corp.*, 751 F.2d 1226, 1235 (Fed.Cir.1985).

The district court appears to have dealt with claim 9 in isolation because of Hollister's correct statement that when inequitable conduct occurs in relation to one claim the entire patent is unenforceable. *J.P. Stevens*, 747 F.2d at 1561. But Hollister leapfrogs from that correct proposition to one that is incorrect, *i.e.*, that courts may not look outside the involved claim in determining, in the first place, whether inequitable conduct did in fact occur at all. Claims are not born, and do not live, in isolation. Each is related to other claims, to the specification and drawings, to the prior art, to an attorney's remarks, to co-pending and continuing applications, and often, as here, to earlier or later versions of itself in light of amendments made to it.[9] . . .

Faced with Hollister's assertion that an experienced patent attorney would knowingly and intentionally transfer into a continuing application a claim earlier rejected for indefiniteness,[10] without rearguing that the claim was not indefinite, the district court stated that "how an experienced patent attorney could allow such conduct to take place" gave it "the greatest difficulty." A knowing failure to disclose and knowingly false statements are always difficult to understand. However, a transfer of numerous claims *en masse* from a parent to a continuing application, as the district court stated, is a ministerial act. As such, it is more vulnerable to errors which by definition result from inattention, and is less likely to result from the scienter involved in the more egregious acts of omission and commission that have been seen as reflecting the deceitful intent element of inequitable conduct in our cases.[11]

---

9. The district court alluded to the absence from claim 9 of a specific recitation of a "connecting point" between the coupling and the pad. It is clear from the specification that those elements are connected. Whether claim 9 is invalid under § 112, because of the absence of a specific recitation of a connecting point, may or may not be a matter for consideration in determining the issue of validity on remand. It has no bearing on our decision here.

10. Indefiniteness has to do with validity, not infringement. A claim may be infringed, but the infringer would not be liable if the claim is invalid for indefiniteness under § 112.

11. It is not possible to counter the "I didn't know" excuse with a "should have known" accountability approach when faced with a pure error, which by definition is done unintentionally.

More importantly, however, the district court's focus on claim 9 caused it to disregard the effect of other claims. In addition to claim 9 and its dependent claims, Kingsdown claimed infringement of claims 2, 4, 5, and 27. The first three of those claims were each broader in some respects than claim 9. The first portion of claim 27, *supra*, corresponded precisely with the amended language of claim 50 on which the district court focused.[12] Claim 27 was allowed, when presented and without amendment, as claim 55 in the parent application. The district court expressly stated that it "did not decide the issue of infringement." Because there has been no decision on whether any of claims 2, 4, 5, and 27 are infringed by Hollister's product, or on whether Kingsdown could have reasonably believed they are, it cannot at this stage be said that Kingsdown *needed* claim 9 to properly bring suit for infringement.[13] If it did not, the district court's implication of sinister motivation and the court's inference of deceptive intent from Kingsdown's acts would collapse.[14]

The district court, in finding intent, made a passing reference to Kingsdown's continuation of its suit after Hollister charged inequitable conduct. Hollister vigorously argues before us that Kingsdown's continuing its suit while failing to disclaim or reissue is proof of bad faith. A failure to disclaim or reissue in 1987, however, would not establish that Kingsdown acted in bad faith when it filed its continuation application in 1982. Moreover, a suggestion that patentees should abandon their suits, or disclaim or reissue, in response to every charge of inequitable conduct raised by an alleged infringer would be nothing short of ridiculous. The right of patentees to resist such charges must not be chilled to extinction by fear that a failure to disclaim or reissue will be used against them as evidence that their original intent was deceitful. Nor is there in the record any basis for expecting that any such disclaimer or reissue would cause Hollister to drop its inequitable conduct defense or refrain from reliance on such remedial action as support for that defense. Kingsdown's belief in its innocence meant that a court test of the inequitable conduct charge was inevitable and appropriate. A requirement for disclaimer or reissue to avoid adverse inferences would merely encourage the present proliferation of inequitable conduct charges.[15]

We are forced to the definite and firm conviction that a mistake has been committed, amounting to an abuse of discretion. The district court's finding of deceitful intent was clearly erroneous.

---

12. Claim 27 contains a number of additional limitations, but the language from which the district court thought Kingsdown was attempting to flee is identical.

13. One of Hollister's attorneys rendered an opinion in which the amended language of claim 50 was not seen as freeing Hollister's device of infringement.

14. That would remain true even if the district court were ultimately to determine that claim 9 is actually indefinite.

15. "(T)he habit of charging inequitable conduct in almost every major patent case has become an absolute plague". *Burlington Indus., Inc.* v. *Dayco Corp.*, 849 F.2d 1418, 1422 (Fed.Cir.1988).

RESOLUTION OF CONFLICTING PRECEDENT[16]

"Gross Negligence" and The Intent Element of Inequitable Conduct

Some of our opinions have suggested that a finding of gross negligence compels a finding of an intent to deceive. *In re Jerabek*, 789 F.2d 886, 891 (Fed.Cir.1986); *Driscoll v. Cebalo*, 731 F.2d 878, 885 (Fed.Cir.1984). Others have indicated that gross negligence alone does not mandate a finding of intent to deceive. *FMC Corp. v. Manitowoc Co.*, 835 F.2d 1411, 1415 n. 9 (Fed.Cir.1987).

"Gross negligence" has been used as a label for various patterns of conduct. It is definable, however, only in terms of a particular act or acts viewed in light of all the circumstances. We adopt the view that a finding that particular conduct amounts to "gross negligence" does not of itself justify an inference of intent to deceive; the involved conduct, viewed in light of all the evidence, including evidence indicative of good faith, must indicate sufficient culpability to require a finding of intent to deceive. *See Norton v. Curtiss*, 433 F.2d 779 (CCPA 1970).

Nature of Question

Some of our opinions have indicated that whether inequitable conduct occurred is a question of law. *In re Jerabek*, 789 F.2d at 890 (Fed.Cir.1986). In *Gardco Mfg. Inc. v. Herst Lighting Co.*, 820 F.2d 1209, 1212 (Fed.Cir. 1987) (citing *Precision Instrument Mfg. Co. v. Automotive Maintenance Mach. Co.*, 324 U.S. 806 (1945)), the court indicated that the inequitable conduct question is equitable in nature. We adopt the latter view, *i.e.*, that the ultimate question of whether inequitable conduct occurred is equitable in nature.

Standard of Review

As an equitable issue, inequitable conduct is committed to the discretion of the trial court and is reviewed by this court under an abuse of discretion standard. We, accordingly, will not simply substitute our judgment for that of the trial court in relation to inequitable conduct. "To overturn a discretionary ruling of a district court, the appellant must establish that the ruling is based upon clearly erroneous findings of fact or a misapplication or misinterpretation of applicable law or that the ruling evidences a clear error of judgment on the part of the district court." *PPG Indus. v. Celanese Polymer Specialties Co.*, 840 F.2d 1565, 1572 (Fed.Cir. 1988) (Bissell, J., additional views) (discussing *Seattle Box Co. v. Industrial Crating & Packing Inc.*, 756 F.2d 1574 (Fed.Cir.1985); *Amstar Corp. v. Envirotech Corp.*, 823 F.2d 1538, 1542 (Fed.Cir.1987); *Heat & Control, Inc. v. Hester Indus., Inc.*, 785 F.2d 1017 (Fed.Cir.1986)).

Effect of Inequitable Conduct

When a court has finally determined that inequitable conduct occurred in relation to one or more claims during prosecution of the patent applica-

---

16. Because precedent may not be changed by a panel, *South Corp. v. United States*, 690 F.2d 1368, 1370 n. 2 (Fed.Cir.1982) (*in banc*), this section has been considered and decided by an *in banc* court formed of MARKEY, CHIEF JUDGE, RICH, SMITH, NIES, NEWMAN, BISSELL, ARCHER, MAYER, and MICHEL, CIRCUIT JUDGES.

tion, the entire patent is rendered unenforceable. We, *in banc*, reaffirm that rule as set forth in *J.P. Stevens & Co.* v. *Lex Tex Ltd.*, 747 F.2d 1553, 1561 (Fed.Cir.1984), *cert. denied*, 474 U.S. 822 (1985).

CONCLUSION

Having determined that the district court's finding of intent is clearly erroneous, the panel reverses the judgment based on a conclusion of inequitable conduct before the PTO and remands the case for such further proceedings as the district court may deem appropriate.

Reversed and Remanded.

NOTES

1. *The Intent Prong of the Inequitable Conduct Test.* Direct proof of an intent to mislead or deceive the PTO is rarely available. *See Merck & Co. v. Danbury Pharmacal, Inc.*, 873 F.2d 1418, 1422 (Fed.Cir.1989). In simple terms, a "smoking gun" is almost never found in the files of a patent attorney. What considerations might tempt a patent applicant or his attorney to withhold a damaging reference from the PTO? Is there a reasonable expectation that another party would not find the damaging reference in litigation? What advantages could be gained from owning a patent which could easily be invalidated by a damaging reference?

Though direct evidence of intent to deceive is rare, such an intent may be inferred from circumstantial evidence. *See Hewlett–Packard Co. v. Bausch & Lomb, Inc.*, 882 F.2d 1556, 1562 (Fed.Cir.1989). Nevertheless, as the *Kingsdown* court held, circumstantial evidence consisting solely of conduct amounting to gross negligence does not, by itself, justify drawing an inference of intent to deceive. *See Kingsdown Med. Consultants, Ltd. v. Hollister Inc.*, 863 F.2d 867, 876 (Fed.Cir. 1988). This holding overruled *J. P. Stevens'* holding that gross negligence was sufficient to draw an inference of an intent to deceive. The Federal Circuit in *Molins PLC v. Textron, Inc.* 48 F.3d 1172, 1181 n. 11 (Fed.Cir.1995), followed the ruling in *Kingsdown* that gross negligence was insufficient to establish the intent prong of inequitable conduct. But "[w]here an applicant knows of information the materiality of which may so readily be determined, he or she cannot intentionally avoid learning of its materiality, even through gross negligence; in such cases the district court may find that the applicant should have known of the materiality of the information." *Brasseler, U.S.A. I, L.P. v. Stryker Sales Corp.*, 267 F.3d 1370, 1380 (Fed.Cir.2001).

The court in *Kingsdown* also stated that when making a finding regarding intent to deceive the PTO, all circumstances, including those indicating good faith, must be considered. *See Kingsdown Med. Consultants*, 863 F.2d at 876. Generally, regarding drawing the inference of intent to mislead and good faith of the patentee, the Federal Circuit has stated:

> No single factor or combination of factors can be said always to *require* an inference of intent to mislead; yet a patentee facing a high level of materiality and clear proof that it knew or should have known of that materiality, can expect to find it difficult to establish "subjective good faith" sufficient to prevent the drawing of an inference of intent to mislead. A mere denial of intent to mislead (which would defeat every effort to establish inequitable conduct) will not suffice in such circumstances.

FMC Corp. v. Manitowoc Co., Inc., 835 F.2d 1411, 1416 (Fed.Cir.1987). Is this consistent with *Kingsdown*, or should it be deemed overruled by the later *en banc* decision? (*See Quikrete Cos. v. Nomix Corp.* 874 F.Supp. 1362, 1368–69 (N.D.Ga. 1993), *aff'd without op.*, 34 F.3d 1078 (Fed.Cir.1994), wherein the district court found inequitable conduct, stating that although gross negligence was insufficient to infer intent to deceive, significant circumstantial evidence of lack of intent is required to overcome a high level of materiality.)

In *Semiconductor Energy Laboratory Co., Ltd. v. Samsung Electronics Co., Ltd.*, 204 F.3d 1368 (Fed.Cir.2000), the Federal Circuit further explored the metes and bounds of the intent prong of inequitable conduct. In this case, the inventor, Dr. Yamazaki, was well aware of the requirements of disclosure set forth in § 1.56. When Dr. Yamazaki provided a 29–page Japanese language reference to the PTO, he also composed a concise English-language summary (Dr. Yamazaki was fluent in Japanese and English) of the reference which he included in his disclosure to the PTO. But in his summary, he omitted a portion of the reference that was material to the patent application. The Federal Circuit affirmed the District Court's finding of intent on the part of Dr. Yamazaki because he fully understood a) the reference, b) his duty of disclosure and c) the concise summary provided to the PTO. The effect of this case is to raise the bar for patent applicants who place foreign language references before the Patent and Trademark Office and have the ability to easily translate the references but neglect to do so.

2. *Threshold Levels of Materiality and Intent Always Required.* The Federal Circuit in *Kingsdown* reinforced their holding, established in *J.P. Stevens*, that at least a threshold level of materiality must be established as well as a threshold level of intent to mislead the PTO. *See Kingsdown Med. Consultants*, 863 F.2d at 872. If the threshold levels of materiality and intent are met, the court balances the actual level of materiality and the actual level of intent and determines whether inequitable conduct before the PTO has occurred.

The Federal Circuit's "Resolution of Conflicting Precedent" concerning inequitable conduct located at the end of court's decision in *Kingsdown* also reinforced the position that materiality and intent are factual issues and equitable in nature, as opposed to being issues of law. Thus, one is not entitled to a jury trial on the ultimate issue of inequitable conduct.

The fact-sensitiveness of this determination limits the predictability of a court's finding as to inequitable conduct before the PTO. In *Kingsdown*, the Federal Circuit, by reversing a district court's findings of inequitable conduct, showed how difficult it can be to satisfy the balancing test of inequitable conduct. Indeed, in *Purdue Pharma L.P. v. Endo Pharm. Inc.*, 410 F.3d 690 (Fed. Cir. 2005), the Federal Circuit affirmed the trial court's decision of inequitable conduct based on statements made during prosecution about the unexpectedly high efficacy of the patented drug in response to an obviousness rejection and despite a lack of specific evidence to support those statements. But, on rehearing, the Federal Circuit issued a new opinion superseding its initial opinion, this time determining there was not a sufficient showing of intent to support the judgment of inequitable conduct because the trial court has not given sufficient weight to the substantial evidence of lack of intent that had been offered by the patentee and had overlooked the relatively low level of materiality. *Purdue Pharma L.P. v. Endo Pharm. Inc.*, 438 F.3d 1123 (Fed. Cir. 2006).

The Federal Circuit has recently taken up the issue of inequitable conduct *en banc* in *Therasense Inc. v. Becton, Dickinson and Co.*, in which the court is reconsidering the entire framework of the doctrine, including materiality, intent, and their interaction.

3. *Clear and Convincing Evidence.* In *J.P. Stevens* and again in *Kingsdown*, the Federal Circuit held that the separate elements of materiality and intent must be proven by clear and convincing evidence to support a ruling of inequitable conduct. A party alleging inequitable conduct must plead with particularity "the specific who, what, when, where, and how of the material misrepresentation or omission committed before the PTO." *Exergen Corp. v. Wal–Mart Stores, Inc.*, 575 F.3d 1312, 1327 (Fed.Cir.2009).

4. *Fairness and Inequitable Conduct.* Much of the discussion in inequitable conduct cases seems to turn on arguments based on putatively unfair behavior of a patentee. For example, the patentee is often portrayed as having taken unfair advantage of the *ex parte* nature of the patent examination process. Do you think it fair for an infringer of a *valid* patent to be exonerated because of activity that triggers the test for inequitable conduct? As will be discussed at more length in the section that follows, because the materiality prong of the test for inequitable conduct sets a low bar that is easily overcome, inequitable conduct can be found even where the information that was withheld from the PTO does not destroy validity.

One type of fairness that has not been commonly discussed in inequitable conduct cases in the past relates to the decision by a patentee to add claims during prosecution for the purpose of "covering" a particular competitor's product or process. This was done in *Kingsdown*, but as seen in the above excerpt from the case, the court expressly pointed out that it is not "in any manner improper to amend or insert claims intended to cover a competitor's product." More recently, the Federal Circuit has found, under what many consider to be extreme facts, that such strategic amending combined with great delay in issuance of the patent caused by the patentee may indeed support a judgment of so-called "prosecution laches" against the patentee. *Symbol Tech. v. Lemelson*, 277 F.3d 1361 (Fed.Cir.2002) (holding that defense was available, and remanding); *Symbol Tech. v. Lemelson*, 422 F.3d 1378 (Fed.Cir.2005) (holding that district court's determination of unenforceability for prosecution laches was not an abuse of discretion), *amended on rehearing in part by* 429 F.3d 1051 (Fed. Cir. 2005) (extending unenforceability to all 14 asserted patents). Because the *Symbol Tech. v. Lemelson* case involved a patent that was filed before the GATT amendments to Title 35, the patent in that case enjoyed an effective term that was 17 years as measured from issue date. For patents issued from applications filed after June 8, 1995 the effective patent term will be 20 years measured from filing date. As a result, delay before the PTO will have its own impact on term. It is not clear to what extent a "prosecution estoppel" defense will also be available against those patents.

2. MATERIALITY

A misrepresentation or omission must be "material" in order to constitute inequitable conduct. Materiality is defined in 37 C.F.R. § 1.56 and discussed in the *Critikon v. Becton Dickinson* case.

Critikon Inc. v. Becton Dickinson Vascular Access Inc.

120 F.3d 1253 (Fed.Cir.1997).

■ Before ARCHER, CHIEF JUDGE, and RICH and MAYER, CIRCUIT JUDGES.

■ RICH, CIRCUIT JUDGE.

Becton Dickinson Vascular Access, Inc. (Becton Dickinson) appeals from the April 10, 1995 judgment of the United States District Court for the District of Delaware, No. 93–108–JJF, issuing a permanent injunction in favor of Critikon, Inc. (Critikon) enjoining Becton Dickinson from making, using, selling or offering to sell its infringing safety catheter products in the United States based on U.S. Patent Nos. 4,952,207, reissued as RE34,416, and 4,978,344 (the patents). Following a bench trial, the district court held that: (1) the patents were not invalid; (2) Becton Dickinson had infringed the patents, both literally and under the doctrine of equivalents; (3) the infringement was not willful; (4) Critikon did not engage in inequitable conduct; and (5) Critikon was eligible for injunctive relief. Becton Dickinson appeals the holdings on validity, infringement and inequitable conduct underlying the permanent injunction. Critikon cross-appeals the finding that infringement was not willful. We affirm-in-part and reverse-in-part and remand.

BACKGROUND

The patents and relevant claims in suit are claims 8, 21, and 56 of U.S. Patent No. RE34,416 (Lemieux reissue patent) and U.S. Patent No. 4,952,-207, (original Lemieux patent) and claims 18 and 19 of U.S. Patent No. 4,978,344, (Dombrowski patent). These patents are in the field of intravenous (IV) catheters. IV catheters are thin tubes that are inserted into a vein for the administration of fluids and the like. A needle is used to insert the tube into the vein and then the needle is withdrawn, leaving the tube in the vein. The patents are specifically directed to safety IV catheters, designed to protect health care workers from accidental needle sticks. They feature a needle guard that automatically moves into position over the tip of the needle as the needle is withdrawn from the IV catheter. For ease of reference, we will refer to the reissue and original Lemieux patents collectively as the "Lemieux patents." Claims were added by the reissue.

Through a series of amended complaints, Critikon filed an infringement action against Becton Dickinson based on the Lemieux patents and the Dombrowski patent. The first such complaint alleged infringement of claim 8 of the original Lemieux patent and subsequently included a motion for preliminary injunction to enjoin Becton Dickinson from making, using or selling its catheter product for the pendency of the suit. On July 16, 1993, the district court granted the motion for preliminary injunction based on claim 8 of the original Lemieux patent. Becton Dickinson immediately filed a notice of appeal and moved us to stay the preliminary injunction pending its appeal. On August 26, 1993, we denied that motion.

In the interim, Critikon amended its complaint to assert a claim for infringement of the Dombrowski patent and, subsequently, the Lemieux reissue patent. Further, Becton Dickinson amended its answer to add the defense that the Lemieux patents were unenforceable because of Critikon's allegedly inequitable conduct during the course of prosecution.

Having obtained a trial date, Becton Dickinson withdrew its appeal to us of the preliminary injunction and, on November 1, 1993, the parties commenced a two week bench trial on liability and damages issues. The district court issued a Memorandum Opinion on July 18, 1994, finding, *inter alia*, that Becton Dickinson's catheter products infringed claims 8, 21, and 56 of the Lemieux patents and claims 18 and 19 of the Dombrowski patent. Further, the district court held the patents valid and enforceable. Critikon moved for a permanent injunction, and, on April 10, 1995, the district court issued the order enjoining Becton Dickinson that is the subject of this appeal.

DISCUSSION

1. Infringement/Validity

We review a district court's judgment for errors of law and clearly erroneous findings of fact. Fed.R.Civ.P. 52(a). The district court found the patents-in-suit not invalid and infringed, both literally and under the doctrine of equivalents. After careful consideration, we discern no clear error in the court's findings of fact or error in its conclusions of law and affirm the district court's findings of no invalidity and infringement.

2. Inequitable Conduct

On appeal, Becton Dickinson argues that Critikon's failure to disclose U.S. Patent No. 4,834,718 (the McDonald patent) during both the prosecution of the original Lemieux patent and the Lemieux reissue patent constituted inequitable conduct. Becton Dickinson argues that the district court's failure to find intent is contrary to the weight of the evidence. We agree. We hold that the McDonald patent was material to patentability and Critikon should have disclosed it to the Patent and Trademark Office (PTO). But, more importantly, during the reissue proceedings, Critikon should have disclosed that the original Lemieux patent was concurrently involved in the present litigation and that claims of invalidity and inequitable conduct were asserted against the patent. Failure to disclose the McDonald patent and the fact that the Lemieux patent was in litigation was done with an intent to mislead or deceive and rises to the level of inequitable conduct.

A determination of inequitable conduct is committed to a district court's discretion. Accordingly, the court's ultimate determination is reviewed for abuse of discretion; the subsidiary factual questions are reviewed for clear error and are not to be disturbed unless we have a definite and firm conviction that a mistake has been committed. *Amgen, Inc. v. Chugai Pharmaceutical Co.*, 927 F.2d 1200, 1215 (Fed.Cir.1991).

A patent applicant's duty to disclose material information to the PTO arises under the general duty of candor, good faith, and honesty embodied in 37 C.F.R. Section 1.56(a) (1996). Specifically, applicants have a duty to disclose to the PTO information of which they are aware which is material to the examination of the application. 37 C.F.R. Section 1.56(a) (1996). This duty is also applicable to reissue proceedings. 37 C.F.R. Section 1.175 (a)(7) (1996).

However, a breach of the disclosure duty alone does not render the patent unenforceable. There must be a showing of inequitable conduct. Inequitable conduct resides in the failure to disclose material information with an intent to deceive or mislead the PTO. *J.P. Stevens & Co. v. Lex Tex, Ltd.*, 747 F.2d 1553, 1559–60 (Fed.Cir.1984). Once thresholds of materiality and intent have been established, the court conducts a balancing test and determines whether the scales tilt to a conclusion that "inequitable conduct" occurred. *Halliburton Co. v. Schlumberger Tech. Corp.*, 925 F.2d 1435, 1440 (Fed.Cir.1991). The more material the omission or the misrepresentation, the lower the level of intent required to establish inequitable conduct, and vice versa. *Akzo N.V. v. United States Int'l Trade Comm'n*, 808 F.2d 1471 (Fed.Cir.1986).

* * *

B. Materiality

Information must be disclosed when it is material to patentability. The starting point in determining materiality is the definition of the PTO, which recites, in part, as follows: "information is material to patentability when it is not cumulative to information already of record or being made of record in the application, and … [i]t refutes, or is inconsistent with, a position the applicant takes in: … [a]sserting an argument of patentability." 37 C.F.R. 1.56 (b)(2)(ii) (1996).

The district court found the McDonald patent was not material because it was substantially different from the claimed invention. The court was "persuaded by the testimony of both expert witnesses that the McDonald [ ] patent teaches a device that is substantially different than that contemplated by the Lemieux patents." However, the court did not explicitly outline the evidence that it relied upon in drawing this conclusion nor did it address Critikon's failure to disclose the ongoing litigation during the Lemieux reissue proceedings.

The court apparently failed to recognize that although overall the Lemieux device may be substantially different from McDonald, the McDonald patent teaches two features, which the examiner considered central in the prosecution of the Lemieux patents. Briefly, the protective housing of the McDonald device is designed to automatically cover the needle tip for the purpose of preventing accidental needle sticks. The housing is comprised of a long barrel and a guard hub. As the needle is withdrawn from the catheter, the proximal end of the housing engages with a groove on the handle and automatically releases the needle guard that sheaths the needle. Specifically, it teaches a "retaining means" and an automatically, albeit passively, engaged protective housing.

As noted above, the examiner specifically relied on the "retaining means" as a point of novelty. The use of the "retaining means" to achieve automatic positioning is disclosed only in the uncited McDonald patent; it is not disclosed in any other prior art considered by the examiner. Furthermore, there was testimony from Mr. Fischell, Becton Dickinson's expert, to the effect that the McDonald patent is the most relevant art to the "retaining means" limitation.

Specifically, Mr. Fischell indicated that the retaining means were integral to the automatic positioning. In addition, Mr. Fischell indicated that the key features of McDonald were the automatic positioning and the "retaining means." Mr. Colletti reflected this position, and Critikon's knowledge thereof, when he testified that he could not recall any prior art considered by the examiner who allowed the original Lemieux patent that describes a catheter device with the "retaining means". And yet Mr.

Colletti relied on the novelty of the "retaining means" and the automatic positioning of the protective housing in his arguments to gain allowance of the patent application. It would appear that the "retaining means" and the automatic positioning aspects of McDonald would have been material to a reasonable patent examiner under the PTO standard.

Critikon argues that the McDonald device is significantly different for three primary reasons: (1) the McDonald device operates differently; (2) the McDonald device does not feature automatic positioning; and (3) the McDonald device requires a two step procedure while the Lemieux patent requires the protective housing to function without intervention. The first reason is of no moment. A device that operates differently, assuming the McDonald patent operates differently, may nonetheless have relevant features. With regard to the second and third reasons, there is unrefuted testimony that the catheter may be inserted with one hand and, furthermore, the Lemieux patent only requires that the catheter function without intervention in its preferred embodiment. Thus, we find Critikon's arguments without merit.

The district court did not consider whether the litigation relating to the Lemieux patents was material to the Lemieux reissue proceedings. A patent applicant's duty to disclose is not limited to disclosing prior art. A patent applicant must disclose any material information to the PTO. 37 C.F.R. Section 1.56(a) (1996). There seems little doubt that the litigation involving the patent in question would be relevant to its reissue proceeding. According to the Manual of Patent Examining Procedure, relevant litigation includes the defenses raised against validity of the patent, or charges of fraud or inequitable conduct in litigation, which would normally be material to the reissue application. MPEP 2001.06(c) (1994).

Where the patent for which reissue is being sought is, or has been, involved in litigation which raised a question material to patentability of the reissue application, such as the validity of the patent, or any allegations of "fraud", "inequitable conduct", or "violation of duty of disclosure", the existence of such litigation must be brought to the attention of the Office by the applicant.... [T]he defenses raised against validity of the patent, or charges of "fraud" or "inequitable conduct" in the litigation, would normally be "material to patentability" of the reissue application.... As a minimum, the applicant should call the attention of the Office to the litigation, the existence and the nature of any allegations relating to validity and/or "fraud", or "inequitable conduct" relating to the original patent, and the nature of the litigation materials relating to these issues. MPEP 2001.06(c) (1994); see also, MPEP 1442.04 (1994). In the interests of consistent claim interpretation, it may be appropriate to suspend such proceedings until such litigation is resolved.

In summary, Critikon failed to disclose the McDonald patent, which it should have known was material, but, more importantly, it failed to disclose the ongoing litigation in the reissue proceedings. Given the materiality and the failure at any point to offer a good faith explanation of the pattern of nondisclosure, an intent to mislead may be inferred. We reverse the district court's finding with regard to inequitable conduct and hold the original Lemieux patent and the Lemieux reissue patent unenforceable.

* * *

CONCLUSION

In conclusion, we affirm the district court's holding that the Lemieux patents and the Dombrowski patent are not invalid and infringed. We reverse the court's holding that the Lemieux patents are enforceable and hold them unenforceable because of inequitable conduct. We reverse the holding that infringement was not willful. We remand to the district court for further proceedings in accordance with this opinion. AFFIRMED–IN–PART, REVERSED–IN–PART, AND REMANDED.

NOTES

1. *Inequitable Conduct—The Test.* The Federal Circuit has set forth the inequitable conduct analysis as follows:

> Applicants for patents have a duty to prosecute patent applications in the PTO with candor, good faith, and honesty. *Molins PLC v. Textron, Inc.*, 48 F.3d 1172, 1178 (Fed.Cir.1995); *see also* § 37 C.F.R. § 1.56. A breach of this duty, which breach can include affirmative misrepresentations of material facts, failure to disclose material information, or submission of false material information, coupled with an intent to deceive, constitutes inequitable conduct. In determining whether inequitable conduct occurred, a trial court must determine whether the party asserting the inequitable conduct defense has shown by clear and convincing evidence that the alleged nondisclosure or misrepresentation occurred, that the nondisclosure or misrepresentation was material, and that the patent applicant acted with the intent to deceive the PTO. *Glaxo Inc. v. Novopharm Ltd.*, 52 F.3d 1043, 1048 (Fed.Cir.1995). The nondisclosure or misrepresentation must meet threshold levels of both materiality and intent. *Molins*, 48 F.3d at 1178. We review all of these underlying factual determinations for clear error. *Glaxo*, 52 F.3d at 1048.
>
> Once the threshold levels of materiality and intent have been established, the trial court must weigh materiality and intent to determine whether the equities warrant a conclusion that inequitable conduct occurred. *Id.* The more material the information misrepresented or withheld by the applicant, the less evidence of intent will be required in order to find that inequitable conduct has occurred. *N.V. Akzo v. E.I. DuPont de Nemours*, 810 F.2d 1148, 1153 (Fed.Cir.1987). We review the trial court's ultimate determination of inequitable conduct under an abuse of discretion standard. *Kingsdown Med. Consultants, Ltd. v. Hollister Inc.*, 863 F.2d 867, 876 (Fed.Cir.1988).

Li Second Family v. Toshiba Corp., 231 F.3d 1373, 1378 (Fed.Cir.2000).

2. *Materiality.* The standard for materiality is stated in 37 C.F.R. § 1.56(a) of the Patent and Trademark Office (PTO), which the Federal Circuit has said "is an appropriate starting point for any discussion of materiality, for it appears to be the broadest ... and because that materiality boundary most closely aligns with how one ought to conduct business with the PTO." *American Hoist & Derrick Co. v. Sowa & Sons*, 725 F.2d 1350, 1363 (Fed.Cir.1984). As the Federal Circuit has cautioned, in "[c]lose cases, the question of materiality should be resolved by disclosure." *LaBounty Mfg., Inc.* v. *United States Int'l Trade Comm'n*, 958 F.2d 1066, 1076 (Fed.Cir.1992). To this end, note that the prior art patent in *Critikon* was material even though it did not pose a threat to the claimed invention under §§ 102 or 103.

Prior to March 1992, § 1.56 provided that information would be deemed material if a reasonable examiner would have considered the information important in deciding whether to allow the application to issue as a patent. The scope of materiality was made considerably more precise in 1992 with the revision of § 1.56. After March 1992, as per 37 C.F.R. § 1.56, information is deemed material "when it is not cumulative to information already of record or being made of record," and

(1) It establishes, by itself or in combination with other information, a prima facie case of unpatentability of a claim; or

(2) It refutes, or is inconsistent with, a position the applicant takes in:

(i) Opposing an argument of unpatentability relied on by the Office, or

(ii) Asserting an argument of patentability.

37 C.F.R. § 1.56(b) (1999).

The court, in *Dayco Products, Inc.* v. *Total Containment, Inc.*, 329 F.3d 1358, 1363–64 (Fed.Cir.2003), had this to say about the new test for materiality:

In 1992 ... the Patent Office amended its rules to provide a different standard for materiality. The new rule "was not intended to constitute a significant substantive break in the previous standard." *Hoffmann–La Roche, Inc.* v. *Promega Corp.*, 323 F.3d 1354, 1366 n. 2 (Fed.Cir.2003). The new rule reiterated the preexisting "duty of candor and good faith," but more narrowly defined materiality, providing for disclosure where the information establishes either "a prima facie case of unpatentability" or "refutes, or is inconsistent with a position the applicant takes." 37 C.F.R. § 1.56 (1992) ("Rule 56"). In promulgating the new regulation, the Patent Office noted that: "Section 1.56 has been amended to present a clearer and more objective definition of what information the Office considers material to patentability. The rules do not define fraud or inequitable conduct which have elements both of materiality and of intent." Duty of Disclosure, 57 Fed.Reg.2021, 2024 (Jan. 17, 1992). In response to a comment suggesting that courts might interpret the duty of "candor and good faith" to require more than Patent Office rules require, the Patent Office stated that the rule was "modified to emphasize that there is a duty of candor and good faith which is broader than the duty to disclose material information." *Id.* at 2025. Thus, the extent, if any, to which the Patent Office rulemaking was intended to provide guidance to the courts concerning the duty of disclosure in the context of inequitable conduct determinations is not clear.

Since the time of the 1992 amendment we have continued to apply the reasonable examiner standard, but only as to cases that were prosecuted under the earlier version of Rule 56.

Although the Federal Circuit in *Dayco* noted that the court had "not decided whether it should adhere to the preexisting standard for inequitable conduct in prosecutions occurring after the effective date of the new rule" [citing *Molins PLC*], *Molins* stated that the new § 1.56 applies only to applications and reexamination proceedings pending or filed after March 16, 1992. *See Molins PLC v. Textron, Inc.*, 48 F.3d 1172, 1179 n. 8 (Fed.Cir.1995).

In *Critikon, Inc.* v. *Becton Dickinson Vascular Access, Inc.*, 120 F.3d 1253 (Fed.Cir.1997), the court cited the new § 1.56 as a starting point for a determination on materiality. The court presumably used the new § 1.56 standard because the Lemieux reissue application was prosecuted after the revision of § 1.56. However, the court also used language that harked back to the old § 1.56, stating, "[i]t would appear that the [information] would have been material to a reasonable patent examiner under the PTO standard." 120 F.3d at 1258. One way to answer the seeming contradiction in the language of the court is to say that the two different applications of § 1.56 are directed at two different periods of prosecution; one under the old standard and one under the new standard. In any case, it seems that the question of which of the two standards for § 1.56 was not an issue in this case, because under both standards the McDonald application would have been considered material.

The Federal Circuit has cautioned, however, in "[c]lose cases, the question of materiality should be resolved by disclosure, not unilaterally by the applicant." *LaBounty Mfg., Inc. v. United States Int'l Trade Comm'n*, 958 F.2d 1066, 1076 (Fed.Cir.1992). But the courts continue to recognize the *Kingsdown* requirement that materiality must be proven by clear and convincing evidence.

3. *Cumulative References.* Section 1.56 specifies that information is material "when it is not cumulative to information already of record or being made of record." This rule codified a common law rule that was in existence before the revision of the § 1.56. *See, e.g., Engel Indus. v. Lockformer Co.*, 946 F.2d 1528, 1534 (Fed.Cir.1991).

The Federal Circuit, in *Elk Corp. of Dallas v. GAF Bldg. Materials Corp.*, 168 F.3d 28 (Fed.Cir.1999), examined the validity of a design patent based on this rule. The court determined that the patent in the case was unenforceable because non-cumulative references were known to the applicants but were not cited to the examiner during prosecution. Because this rule codifies a common law rule that existed prior to the revision of § 1.56, no difference in analysis under this rule exists between the periods before and after the revision of § 1.56.

4. *Understanding Critikon v. Becton–Dickinson.* The district court found the prior art, *i.e.*, the McDonald patent, was not material to the prosecution of the Lemieux patents because "it (the device in McDonald) was substantially different from the claimed invention." Therefore, the district court ruled that the patentee was not required to disclose the McDonald patent to the Patent and Trademark Office during prosecution of the Lemieux patents.

But the Court of Appeals for the Federal Circuit reversed the district court and ruled that the patentee committed inequitable conduct by not disclosing the McDonald patent. The Court held that the McDonald patent taught two features, which the examiner considered central in the prosecution of the Lemieux patents and, therefore, should have been disclosed, even though these features were taught in a different device. The Federal Circuit further supported its finding of inequitable conduct stating that defenses raised against validity of the patent in a related litigation would normally be material to patentability of the reissue application and should have been disclosed in the reissue application. *See* MPEP § 2001.06(c) (7th ed. 1998). The patentee had not disclosed the litigation concerning the validity of the original Lemiuex patent in the reissue proceeding.

Interestingly, the Federal Circuit found the Lemiuex patents were valid, yet unenforceable. This indicated that the McDonald patent was insufficient as prior art to invalidate the Lemieux patents. However, the Federal Circuit also determined the McDonald patent sufficiently material to the prosecution of the Lemiuex patents that failure to disclose it was inequitable conduct. Thus, the Lemieux patents were ruled valid, but unenforceable. What point was the Federal Circuit trying to bring out by ruling that the Lemieux patents were valid over the prior art, if it could not be enforced?

B. MISUSE AND § 271(d)

The commission of inequitable conduct is not the only way to render a patent unenforceable. Misuse of a patent can also lead to unenforceability; and such unenforceability will continue until the misuse is purged; that is, there is a cessation of the improper activity and the effects of the misuse have dissipated. *See generally, Morton Salt Co. v. G. S. Suppiger Co.*, 314 U.S. 488 (1942). The doctrine of patent misuse, which is closely related to antitrust law, was born into the field of patent law as an equitable defense where the patentee had attempted to extend the patent beyond what the courts considered to be the patent's lawful scope.

Such allegedly unlawful extensions have included so-called tying and price-fixing arrangements, as well as patentees' post-sales restrictions on patented goods such as contractual field-of-use restrictions and grantback clauses. Each of these behaviors has been viewed with significant criticism. But each can also be viewed through a rosier lens. A patentee engaging in such behavior may be doing so as a way to engage in a technique called price discrimination. Price discrimination means charging different buyers different prices, such as when airlines charge a low price for a 14–day-advance-purchase fare, but a high price for a last-minute-fare. For price discrimination to be successful, the seller must be able to prevent arbitrage among all buyers. Sellers may try to do this by having the buyer agree in the sale contract to only use the good once, or to not transfer it to others. Some may feel that price discrimination is bad because it allows different buyers to be treated differently. Others have argued that, paradoxically, the patent owner's power to restrict use when combined with the ability to price discriminate will actually give the patentee a strong financial incentive to push increased use of the patented product to the same levels one would see in a fully competitive market, as compared with a monopoly market.[3] To achieve this result, price discrimination must be legal. It is for this reason that some have argued that any provisions in the patent laws that would permit the patentee to elect to restrictively license without committing misuse should be considered as normatively good.[4] Such a view may also help reveal some benefits to any provision in the law that facilitates a patentee's ability to price discriminate, including, for example, the law governing the areas of misuse, antitrust, first sale, implied license, repair/reconstruction, limitations on a patentee's contract provisions, and preemption, each of which is discussed in turn in this section and in the next several sections that follow.

Indeed, because misuse is tied to the courts' general policy-based perception of a patent's lawful scope, the defense of misuse has changed over time as our policies about the lawful scope of a patent have changed. Eventually, the defense of misuse was taken to the extreme and had been used to effectively eliminate the doctrines of contributory infringement and

---

3. *See* F. Scott Kieff, *Property Rights and Property Rules for Commercializing Inventions*, 85 MINN. L. REV. 697, 727–732 (2001) (collecting sources).

4. *Id.* at text accompanying notes 165–167, 182–183.

inducement of infringement. In response, the 1952 Patent Act revived these doctrines and clarified permissible patent use. Both tasks were taken in concert, with sections 271(b) and (c) codifying actions for induced and contributory infringement; and section 271(d) giving the patentee limited statutory shelter from the defense of misuse. Thus, the advent of Section 271 in the 1952 Patent Act in many ways superceded the cases that are often cited in arguments for a finding of misuse, such as *Morton Salt*, and careful arguments today will avoid undue reliance on such case law regardless of whether it is designated as "overruled" or "reversed" in citation services. The law governing the appropriate use of the patent grant is the subject of this section.

Dawson Chemical v. Rohm and Haas

448 U.S. 176 (1980).

■ MR. JUSTICE BLACKMUN delivered the opinion of the Court.

This case presents an important question of statutory interpretation arising under the patent laws. The issue before us is whether the owner of a patent on a chemical process is guilty of patent misuse, and therefore is barred from seeking relief against contributory infringement of its patent rights, if it exploits the patent only in conjunction with the sale of an unpatented article that constitutes a material part of the invention and is not suited for commercial use outside the scope of the patent claims. The answer will determine whether respondent, the owner of a process patent on a chemical herbicide, may maintain an action for contributory infringement against other manufacturers of the chemical used in the process. To resolve this issue, we must construe the various provisions of 35 U.S.C. § 271, which Congress enacted in 1952 to codify certain aspects of the doctrines of contributory infringement and patent misuse that previously had been developed by the judiciary.

I

The doctrines of contributory infringement and patent misuse have long and interrelated histories. The idea that a patentee should be able to obtain relief against those whose acts facilitate infringement by others has been part of our law since *Wallace v. Holmes*, 29 F.Cas. 74 (No. 17,100) (CC Conn. 1871). The idea that a patentee should be denied relief against infringers if he has attempted illegally to extend the scope of his patent monopoly is of somewhat more recent origin, but it goes back at least as far as *Motion Picture Patents Co. v. Universal Film Mfg. Co.*, 243 U.S. 502, 37 S.Ct. 416, 61 L.Ed. 871 (1917). The two concepts, contributory infringement and patent misuse, often are juxtaposed, because both concern the relationship between a patented invention and unpatented articles or elements that are needed for the invention to be practiced.

Both doctrines originally were developed by the courts. But in its 1952 codification of the patent laws Congress endeavored, at least in part, to substitute statutory precepts for the general judicial rules that had governed prior to that time. Its efforts find expression in 35 U.S.C. § 271 ... Of particular import to the present controversy are subsections (c) and (d).

The former defines conduct that constitutes contributory infringement; the latter specifies conduct of the patentee that is not to be deemed misuse.

A

The catalyst for this litigation is a chemical compound known to scientists as "3, 4–dichloropropionanilide" and referred to in the chemical industry as "propanil." In the late 1950's, it was discovered that this compound had properties that made it useful as a selective, "post-emergence" herbicide particularly well suited for the cultivation of rice. If applied in the proper quantities, propanil kills weeds normally found in rice crops without adversely affecting the crops themselves. It thus permits spraying of general areas where the crops are already growing, and eliminates the necessity for hand weeding or flooding of the rice fields. Propanil is one of several herbicides that are commercially available for use in rice cultivation.

* * *

Rohm & Haas' efforts to obtain a propanil patent began in 1958. These efforts finally bore fruit when, on June 11, 1974, the United States Patent Office issued Patent No. 3,816,092 (the Wilson patent) to Harold F. Wilson and Dougal H. McRay. [footnote omitted] The patent contains several claims covering a method for applying propanil to inhibit the growth of undesirable plants in areas containing established crops. [footnote omitted] Rohm & Haas has been the sole owner of the patent since its issuance.

Petitioners, too, are chemical manufacturers. They have manufactured and sold propanil for application to rice crops since before Rohm & Haas received its patent. They market the chemical in containers on which are printed directions for application in accordance with the method claimed in the Wilson patent. Petitioners did not cease manufacture and sale of propanil after that patent issued, despite knowledge that farmers purchasing their products would infringe on the patented method by applying the propanil to their crops. Accordingly, Rohm & Haas filed this suit, in the United States District Court for the Southern District of Texas, seeking injunctive relief against petitioners on the ground that their manufacture and sale of propanil interfered with its patent rights.

The complaint alleged not only that petitioners contributed to infringement by farmers who purchased and used petitioners' propanil, but also that they actually induced such infringement by instructing farmers how to apply the herbicide. See 35 U.S.C. §§ 271(b) and (c). Petitioners responded to the suit by requesting licenses to practice the patented method. When Rohm & Haas refused to grant such licenses, however, petitioners raised a defense of patent misuse and counterclaimed for alleged antitrust violations by respondent. The parties entered into a stipulation of facts, and petitioners moved for partial summary judgment. They argued that Rohm & Haas has misused its patent by conveying the right to practice the patented method only to purchasers of its own propanil.

The District Court granted summary judgment for petitioners. 191 USPQ 691 (1976). It agreed that Rohm & Haas was barred from obtaining relief against infringers of its patent because it had attempted illegally to extend its patent monopoly. The District Court recognized that 35 U.S.C. § 271(d) specifies certain conduct which is not to be deemed patent misuse. The court ruled, however, that "[t]he language of § 271(d) simply does not encompass the totality of [Rohm & Haas'] conduct in this case." 191 USPQ, at 704.

* * *

The United States Court of Appeals for the Fifth Circuit reversed. 599 F.2d 685 (1979).

* * *

We granted *certiorari*, 444 U.S. 1012, 100 S.Ct. 659, 62 L.Ed.2d 640 (1980), to forestall a possible conflict in the lower courts [footnote omitted] and to resolve an issue of prime importance in the administration of the patent law.

B

For present purposes certain material facts are not in dispute. First, the validity of the Wilson patent is not in question at this stage in the litigation. [footnote omitted] We therefore must assume that respondent is the lawful owner of the sole and exclusive right to use, or to license others to use, propanil as a herbicide on rice fields in accordance with the methods claimed in the Wilson patent. Second, petitioners do not dispute that their manufacture and sale of propanil together with instructions for use as a herbicide constitute contributory infringement of the Rohm & Haas patent. Tr. of Oral Arg. 14. Accordingly, they admit that propanil constitutes "a material part of [respondent's] invention," that it is "especially made or especially adapted for use in an infringement of [the] patent," and that it is "not a staple article or commodity of commerce suitable for substantial noninfringing use," all within the language of 35 U.S.C. § 271(c). [footnote omitted] They also concede that they have produced and sold propanil with knowledge that it would be used in a manner infringing on respondent's patent rights. To put the same matter in slightly different terms, as the litigation now stands, petitioners admit commission of a tort and raise as their only defense to liability the contention that respondent, by engaging in patent misuse, comes into court with unclean hands.[7]

As a result of these concessions, our chief focus of inquiry must be the scope of the doctrine of patent misuse in light of the limitations placed upon that doctrine by § 271(d). On this subject, as well, our task is guided by certain stipulations and concessions. The parties agree that Rohm & Haas makes and sells propanil; that it has refused to license petitioners or any others to do the same; that it has not granted express licenses either to retailers or to end users of the product; and that farmers who buy propanil from Rohm & Haas may use it, without fear of being sued for direct infringement, by virtue of an "implied license" they obtain when Rohm &

---

7. See *Thomson–Houston Electric Co. v. Ohio Brass Co.*, 80 F. 712, 721 (C.A.6 1897) (contributory infringement a tort); *Morton Salt Co. v. G. S. Suppiger Co.*, 314 U.S. 488, 492–494, 62 S.Ct. 402, 405–406, 86 L.Ed. 363 (1942) (patent misuse linked to equitable doctrine of "unclean hands").

Haas relinquishes its monopoly by selling the propanil. See App. 35–39. See also *United States v. Univis Lens Co.*, 316 U.S. 241, 249, 62 S.Ct. 1088, 1092, 86 L.Ed. 1408 (1942); cf. *Adams v. Burke*, 17 Wall. 453, 21 L.Ed. 700 (1873). The parties further agree that §§ 271(d)(1) and (3) permit respondent both to sell propanil itself and to sue others who sell the same product without a license, and that under § 271(d)(2) it would be free to demand royalties from others for the sale of propanil if it chose to do so.

The parties disagree over whether respondent has engaged in any additional conduct that amounts to patent misuse. Petitioners assert that there has been misuse because respondent has "tied" the sale of patent rights to the purchase of propanil, an unpatented and indeed unpatentable article, and because it has refused to grant licenses to other producers of the chemical compound. They argue that § 271(d) does not permit any sort of tying arrangement, and that resort to such a practice excludes respondent from the category of patentees "otherwise entitled to relief" within the meaning of § 271(d). Rohm & Haas, understandably, vigorously resists this characterization of its conduct. It argues that its acts have been only those that § 271(d), by express mandate, excepts from characterization as patent misuse. It further asserts that if this conduct results in an extension of the patent right to a control over an unpatented commodity, in this instance the extension has been given express statutory sanction.

II

Our mode of analysis follows closely the trail blazed by the District Court and the Court of Appeals. It is axiomatic, of course, that statutory construction must begin with the language of the statute itself. But the language of § 271 is generic and freighted with a meaning derived from the decisional history that preceded it. The Court of Appeals appropriately observed that more than one interpretation of the statutory language has a surface plausibility. To place § 271 in proper perspective, therefore, we believe that it is helpful first to review in detail the doctrines of contributory infringement and patent misuse as they had developed prior to Congress' attempt to codify the governing principles.

As we have noted, the doctrine of contributory infringement had its genesis in an era of simpler and less subtle technology. Its basic elements are perhaps best explained with a classic example drawn from that era. In *Wallace v. Holmes*, 29 F.Cas. 74 (No. 17,100) (CC Conn.1871), the patentee had invented a new burner for an oil lamp. In compliance with the technical rules of patent claiming, this invention was patented in a combination that also included the standard fuel reservoir, wick tube, and chimney necessary for a properly functioning lamp. After the patent issued, a competitor began to market a rival product including the novel burner but not the chimney. *Id.*, at 79. Under the sometimes scholastic law of patents, this conduct did not amount to direct infringement, because the competitor had not replicated every single element of the patentee's claimed combination. Cf., e.g., *Prouty v. Ruggles*, 16 Pet. 336, 341, 10 L.Ed. 985 (1842). Yet the court held that there had been "palpable interference" with the patentee's legal rights, because purchasers would be certain to complete the combination, and hence the infringement, by adding the glass chimney. 29 F.Cas., at 80. The court permitted the patentee to enforce his rights against the competitor who brought about the infringement, rather than requiring the patentee to undertake the almost insuperable task of finding and suing all the innocent purchasers who technically were responsible for completing the infringement. *Ibid.* See also *Bowker v. Dows*, 3 F.Cas. 1070 (No. 1,734) (CC Mass. 1878).

The *Wallace* case demonstrates, in a readily comprehensible setting, the reason for the contributory infringement doctrine. It exists to protect patent rights from subversion by those who, without directly infringing the patent themselves, engage in acts designed to facilitate infringement by others. This protection is of particular importance in situations, like the oil lamp case itself, where enforcement against direct infringers would be difficult, and where the technicalities of patent law make it relatively easy to profit from another's invention without risking a charge of direct infringement. See *Thomson–Houston Electric Co. v. Ohio Brass Co.*, 80 F. 712, 721 (C.A.6 1897) (Taft, Circuit Judge); Miller, *Some Views on the Law of Patent Infringement by Inducement*, 53 J.Pat.Off.Soc. 86, 87–94 (1971).

* * *

The contributory infringement doctrine achieved its high-water mark with the decision in *Henry v. A. B. Dick Co.*, 224 U.S. 1, 32 S.Ct. 364, 56 L.Ed. 645 (1912). In that case a divided Court extended contributory infringement principles to permit a conditional licensing arrangement whereby a manufacturer of a patented printing machine could require purchasers to obtain all supplies used in connection with the invention, including such staple items as paper and ink, exclusively from the patentee. The Court reasoned that the market for these supplies was created by the invention, and that sale of a license to use the patented product, like sale of other species of property, could be limited by whatever conditions the property owner wished to impose. *Id.*, at 31–32, 32 S.Ct., at 373. The *A. B. Dick* decision and its progeny in the lower courts led to a vast expansion in conditional licensing of patented goods and processes used to control markets for staple and nonstaple goods alike. [footnote omitted]

This was followed by what may be characterized through the lens of hindsight as an inevitable judicial reaction. In *Motion Picture Patents Co. v. Universal Film Mfg. Co.*, 243 U.S. 502, 37 S.Ct. 416, 61 L.Ed. 871 (1917), the Court signaled a new trend that was to continue for years thereafter.[10] The owner of a patent on projection equipment attempted to prevent competitors from selling film for use in the patented equipment by attaching to the projectors it sold a notice purporting to condition use of the machine on exclusive use of its film. The film previously had been patented but that patent had expired. The Court addressed the broad issue whether a patentee possessed the right to condition sale of a patented machine on the purchase of articles "which are no part of the patented machine, and

---

10. In addition to this judicial reaction, there was legislative reaction as well. In 1914, partly in response to the decision in *Henry v. A. B. Dick Co.*, 224 U.S. 1, 32 S.Ct. 364, 56 L.Ed. 645 (1912), Congress enacted § 3 of the Clayton Act, 38 Stat. 731, 15 U.S.C. § 14. See *International Business Machines Corp. v. United States*, 298 U.S. 131, 137–138, 56 S.Ct. 701, 704, 80 L.Ed. 1085 (1936).

which are not patented." *Id.*, at 508, 37 S.Ct., at 417. Relying upon the rule that the scope of a patent "must be limited to the invention described in the claims," *Id.*, at 511, 37 S.Ct., at 419, the Court held that the attempted restriction on use of unpatented supplies was improper:

> Such a restriction is invalid because such a film is obviously not any part of the invention of the patent in suit; because it is an attempt, without statutory warrant, to continue the patent monopoly in this particular character of film after it has expired, and because to enforce it would be to create a monopoly in the manufacture and use of moving picture films, wholly outside of the patent in suit and of the patent law as we have interpreted it. *Id.*, at 518, 37 S.Ct., at 421.

By this reasoning, the Court focused on the conduct of the patentee, not that of the alleged infringer. It noted that as a result of lower court decisions, conditional licensing arrangements had greatly increased, indeed, to the point where they threatened to become "perfect instrument[s] of favoritism and oppression." *Id.*, at 515, 37 S.Ct., at 420. The Court warned that approval of the licensing scheme under consideration would enable the patentee to "ruin anyone unfortunate enough to be dependent upon its confessedly important improvements for the doing of business." *Ibid.* This ruling was directly in conflict with *Henry v. A. B. Dick Co.*, *supra*, and the Court expressly observed that that decision "must be regarded as over-ruled." 243 U.S., at 518, 37 S.Ct., at 421.

The broad ramifications of the *Motion Picture* case apparently were not immediately comprehended, and in a series of decisions over the next three decades litigants tested its limits. In *Carbice Corp. v. American Patents Corp.*, 283 U.S. 27, 51 S.Ct. 334, 75 L.Ed. 819 (1931), the Court denied relief to a patentee who, through its sole licensee, authorized use of a patented design for a refrigeration package only to purchasers from the licensee of solid carbon dioxide ("dry ice"), a refrigerant that the licensee manufactured. [footnote omitted] The refrigerant was a well-known and widely used staple article of commerce, and the patent in question claimed neither a machine for making it nor a process for using it. *Id.*, at 29, 51 S.Ct., at 334. The Court held that the patent holder and its licensee were attempting to exclude competitors in the refrigerant business from a portion of the market, and that this conduct constituted patent misuse. It reasoned:

> Control over the supply of such unpatented material is beyond the scope of the patentee's monopoly; and this limitation, inherent in the patent grant, is not dependent upon the peculiar function or character of the unpatented material or on the way in which it is used. Relief is denied because the [licensee] is attempting, without sanction of law, to employ the patent to secure a limited monopoly of unpatented material used in applying the invention. *Id.*, at 33–34, 51 S.Ct., at 336.

* * *

Although none of these decisions purported to cut back on the doctrine of contributory infringement itself, they were generally perceived as having that effect, and how far the developing doctrine of patent misuse might extend was a topic of some speculation among members of the patent bar. The Court's decisions had not yet addressed the status of contributory infringement or patent misuse with respect to nonstaple goods, and some courts and commentators apparently took the view that control of nonstaple items capable only of infringing use might not bar patent protection against contributory infringement. [footnote omitted] This view soon received a serious, if not fatal, blow from the Court's controversial decisions in *Mercoid Corp. v. Mid–Continent Investment Co.*, 320 U.S. 661, 64 S.Ct. 268, 88 L.Ed. 376 (1944) (*Mercoid I*), and *Mercoid Corp. v. Minneapolis–Honeywell Regulator Co.*, 320 U.S. 680, 64 S.Ct. 278, 88 L.Ed. 396 (1944) (*Mercoid II*). In these cases, the Court definitely held that any attempt to control the market for unpatented goods would constitute patent misuse, even if those goods had no use outside a patented invention. Because these cases served as the point of departure for congressional legislation, they merit more than passing citation.

Both cases involved a single patent that claimed a combination of elements for a furnace heating system. Mid–Continent was the owner of the patent, and Honeywell was its licensee. Although neither company made or installed the furnace system, Honeywell manufactured and sold stoker switches especially made for and essential to the system's operation. The right to build and use the system was granted to purchasers of the stoker switches, and royalties owed the patentee were calculated on the number of stoker switches sold. Mercoid manufactured and marketed a competing stoker switch that was designed to be used only in the patented combination. Mercoid had been offered a sublicense by the licensee but had refused to take one. It was sued for contributory infringement by both the patentee and the licensee, and it raised patent misuse as a defense.

In *Mercoid I* the Court barred the patentee from obtaining relief because it deemed the licensing arrangement with Honeywell to be an unlawful attempt to extend the patent monopoly. The opinion for the Court painted with a very broad brush. Prior patent misuse decisions had involved attempts "to secure a partial monopoly in supplies consumed . . . or unpatented materials employed" in connection with the practice of the invention. None, however, had involved an integral component necessary to the functioning of the patented system. 320 U.S., at 665, 64 S.Ct., at 271. The Court refused, however, to infer any "difference in principle" from this distinction in fact. *Ibid.* Instead, it stated an expansive rule that apparently admitted no exception:

> The necessities or convenience of the patentee do not justify any use of the monopoly of the patent to create another monopoly. The fact that the patentee has the power to refuse a license does not enable him to enlarge the monopoly of the patent by the expedient of attaching conditions to its use. . . . The method by which the monopoly is sought to be extended is immaterial. . . . When the patentee ties something else to his invention, he acts only by virtue of his right as the owner of property to make contracts concerning it and not otherwise. He then is subject to all the limitations upon that right which the general law imposes upon such contracts. The contract is not saved by anything in the patent laws because it relates to the invention. If it were, the mere act of the patentee could make the distinctive claim of the patent attach to something which does not possess the quality of invention. Then the patent would be diverted from its statutory purpose and become a ready instrument for economic control in

domains where the anti-trust acts or other laws not the patent statutes define the public policy. *Id.*, at 666, 64 S.Ct., at 271.

The Court recognized that its reasoning directly conflicted with *Leeds & Catlin Co. v. Victor Talking Machine Co., supra,* and it registered disapproval, if not outright rejection, of that case. 320 U.S., at 668, 64 S.Ct., at 272. It also recognized that "[t]he result of this decision, together with those which have preceded it, is to limit substantially the doctrine of contributory infringement." *Id.*, at 669, 64 S.Ct., at 273. The Court commented, rather cryptically, that it would not "stop to consider" what "residuum" of the contributory infringement doctrine "may be left." *Ibid.*

Mercoid II did not add much to the breathtaking sweep of its companion decision. The Court did reinforce, however, the conclusion that its ruling made no exception for elements essential to the inventive character of a patented combination. "However worthy it may be, however essential to the patent, an unpatented part of a combination patent is no more entitled to monopolistic protection than any other unpatented device." 320 U.S., at 684, 64 S.Ct., at 280.

What emerges from this review of judicial development is a fairly complicated picture, in which the rights and obligations of patentees as against contributory infringers have varied over time. We need not decide how respondent would have fared against a charge of patent misuse at any particular point prior to the enactment of 35 U.S.C. § 271. Nevertheless, certain inferences that are pertinent to the present inquiry may be drawn from these historical developments.

First, we agree with the Court of Appeals that the concepts of contributory infringement and patent misuse "rest on antithetical underpinnings." 599 F.2d, at 697. The traditional remedy against contributory infringement is the injunction. And an inevitable concomitant of the right to enjoin another from contributory infringement is the capacity to suppress competition in an unpatented article of commerce. See, e.g., *Thomson–Houston Electric Co. v. Kelsey Electric R. Specialty Co.,* 72 F. 1016, 1018–1019 (CC Conn. 1896). Proponents of contributory infringement defend this result on the grounds that it is necessary for the protection of the patent right, and that the market for the unpatented article flows from the patentee's invention. They also observe that in many instances the article is "unpatented" only because of the technical rules of patent claiming, which require the placement of an invention in its context. Yet suppression of competition in unpatented goods is precisely what the opponents of patent misuse decry.[14] If both the patent misuse and contributory infringement doctrines are to coexist, then, each must have some separate sphere of operation with which the other does not interfere.

---

14. Even in the classic contributory infringement case of *Wallace v. Holmes,* 29 F.Cas. 74 (No. 17,100) (CC Conn. 1871), the patentee's effort to control the market for the novel burner that embodied his invention arguably constituted patent misuse. If the patentee were permitted to prevent competitors from making and selling that element, the argument would run, he would have the power to erect a monopoly over the production and sale of the burner, an unpatented element, even though his patent right was limited to control over use of the burner in the claimed combination.

Second, we find that the majority of cases in which the patent misuse doctrine was developed involved undoing the damage thought to have been done by *A. B. Dick*. The desire to extend patent protection to control of staple articles of commerce died slowly, and the ghost of the expansive contributory infringement era continued to haunt the courts. As a result, among the historical precedents in this Court, only the *Leeds & Catlin* and *Mercoid* cases bear significant factual similarity to the present controversy. Those cases involved questions of control over unpatented articles that were essential to the patented inventions, and that were unsuited for any commercial noninfringing use. In this case, we face similar questions in connection with a chemical, propanil, the herbicidal properties of which are essential to the advance on prior art disclosed by respondent's patented process. Like the record disc in *Leeds & Catlin* or the stoker switch in the *Mercoid* cases, and unlike the dry ice in *Carbice* or the bituminous emulsion in *Leitch*, propanil is a nonstaple commodity which has no use except through practice of the patented method. Accordingly, had the present case arisen prior to *Mercoid*, we believe it fair to say that it would have fallen close to the wavering line between legitimate protection against contributory infringement and illegitimate patent misuse.

III

The *Mercoid* decisions left in their wake some consternation among patent lawyers [footnote omitted] and a degree of confusion in the lower courts. Although some courts treated the *Mercoid* pronouncements as limited in effect to the specific kind of licensing arrangement at issue in those cases, others took a much more expansive view of the decision. [footnote omitted] Among the latter group, some courts held that even the filing of an action for contributory infringement, by threatening to deter competition in unpatented materials, could supply evidence of patent misuse. *See, e.g., Stroco Products, Inc. v. Mullenbach*, 67 USPQ 168, 170 (S.D.Cal.1944). This state of affairs made it difficult for patent lawyers to advise their clients on questions of contributory infringement and to render secure opinions on the validity of proposed licensing arrangements. Certain segments of the patent bar eventually decided to ask Congress for corrective legislation that would restore some scope to the contributory infringement doctrine. With great perseverance, they advanced their proposal in three successive Congresses before it eventually was enacted in 1952 as 35 U.S.C. § 271.

A

The critical inquiry in this case is how the enactment of § 271 affected the doctrines of contributory infringement and patent misuse. Viewed against the backdrop of judicial precedent, we believe that the language and structure of the statute lend significant support to Rhom & Haas' contention that, because § 271 (d) immunizes its conduct from the charge of patent misuse, it should not be barred from seeking relief. The approach that Congress took toward the codification of contributory infringement and patent misuse reveals a compromise between those two doctrines and their competing policies that permits patentees to exercise control over nonstaple articles used in their inventions.

Section 271(c) identifies the basic dividing line between contributory infringement and patent misuse. It adopts a restrictive definition of contributory infringement that distinguishes between staple and nonstaple articles of commerce. It also defines the class of nonstaple items narrowly. In essence, this provision places materials like the dry ice of the *Carbice* case outside the scope of the contributory infringement doctrine. As a result, it is no longer necessary to resort to the doctrine of patent misuse in order to deny patentees control over staple goods used in their inventions.

The limitations on contributory infringement written into § 271(c) are counterbalanced by limitations on patent misuse in § 271(d). Three species of conduct by patentees are expressly excluded from characterization as misuse. First, the patentee may "deriv[e] revenue" from acts that "would constitute contributory infringement" if "performed by another without his consent." This provision clearly signifies that a patentee may make and sell nonstaple goods used in connection with his invention. Second, the patentee may "licens[e] or authoriz[e] another to perform acts" which without such authorization would constitute contributory infringement. This provision's use in the disjunctive of the term "authoriz[e]" suggests that more than explicit licensing agreements is contemplated. Finally, the patentee may "enforce his patent rights against . . . contributory infringement." This provision plainly means that the patentee may bring suit without fear that his doing so will be regarded as an unlawful attempt to suppress competition. The statute explicitly states that a patentee may do "one or more" of these permitted acts, and it does not state that he must do any of them.

In our view, the provisions of § 271(d) effectively confer upon the patentee, as a lawful adjunct of his patent rights, a limited power to exclude others from competition in nonstaple goods. A patentee may sell a nonstaple article himself while enjoining others from marketing that same good without his authorization. By doing so, he is able to eliminate competitors and thereby to control the market for that product. Moreover, his power to demand royalties from others for the privilege of selling the nonstaple item itself implies that the patentee may control the market for the nonstaple good; otherwise, his "right" to sell licenses for the marketing of the nonstaple good would be meaningless, since no one would be willing to pay him for a superfluous authorization. *See* Note, 70 YALE L.J. 649, 659 (1961).

Rohm & Haas' conduct is not dissimilar in either nature or effect from the conduct that is thus clearly embraced within § 271(d). It sells propanil; it authorizes others to use propanil; and it sues contributory infringers. These are all protected activities. Rohm & Haas does not license others to sell propanil, but nothing on the face of the statute requires it to do so. To be sure, the sum effect of Rohm & Haas' actions is to suppress competition in the market for an unpatented commodity. But as we have observed, in this its conduct is no different from that which the statute expressly protects.

The one aspect of Rohm & Haas' behavior that is not expressly covered by § 271(d) is its linkage of two protected activities—sale of propanil and authorization to practice the patented process—together in a single transaction. Petitioners vigorously argue that this linkage, which they characterize pejoratively as "tying," supplies the otherwise missing element of misuse. They fail, however, to identify any way in which this "tying" of two expressly protected activities results in any extension of control over unpatented materials beyond what § 271(d) already allows.

B

Petitioners argue that the legislative materials indicate at most a modest purpose for § 271. Relying mainly on the Committee Reports that accompanied the "Act to Revise and Codify the Patent Laws" (1952 Act), 66 Stat. 792, of which § 271 was a part, petitioners assert that the principal purpose of Congress was to "clarify" the law of contributory infringement as it had been developed by the courts, rather than to effect any significant substantive change. They note that the 1952 Act undertook the major task of codifying all the patent laws in a single title, and they argue that substantive changes from recodifications are not lightly to be inferred. *See United States v. Ryder*, 110 U.S. 729, 739–740, 4 S.Ct. 196, 201, 28 L.Ed. 308 (1884). They further argue that, whatever the impact of § 271 in other respects, there is not the kind of "clear and certain signal from Congress" that should be required for an extension of patent privileges. *See Deepsouth Packing Co. v. Laitram Corp.*, 406 U.S. 518, 531, 92 (1972). We disagree with petitioners' assessment. In our view, the relevant legislative materials abundantly demonstrate an intent both to change the law and to expand significantly the ability of patentees to protect their rights against contributory infringement.

The 1952 Act was approved with virtually no floor debate. Only one exchange is relevant to the present inquiry. In response to a question whether the Act would effect any substantive changes, Senator McCarran, a spokesman for the legislation, commented that the Act "codif[ies] the patent laws." 98 Cong.Rec. 9323 (1952). He also submitted a statement, which explained that, although the general purpose of the Act was to clarify existing law, it also included several changes taken "[i]n view of decisions of the Supreme Court and others." *Ibid.* Perhaps because of the magnitude of the recodification effort, the Committee Reports accompanying the 1952 Act also gave relatively cursory attention to its features. Nevertheless, they did identify § 271 as one of the "major changes or innovations in the title." H.R.Rep.No. 1923, 82d Cong., 2d Sess., 5 (1952).[17] In explaining the provisions of § 271, the Reports stated that they were intended "to codify in statutory form the principles of contributory infringement and at the same time [to] eliminate ... doubt and confusion" that had resulted from "decisions of the courts in recent years." *Id.* at 9. The Reports also commented that §§ 271(b), (c), and (d) "have as their main purpose clarification and stabilization." *Ibid.*

These materials sufficiently demonstrate that the 1952 Act did include significant substantive changes, and that § 271 was one of them.

The principal sources for edification concerning the meaning and scope of § 271, however, are the extensive hearings that were held on the

---

17. The House and Senate Committee Reports in their significant parts were identical. See S.Rep.No. 1979, 82d Cong., 2d Sess. (1952) U.S.Code Cong. & Admin.News 1952, p. 2394. We confine the citations in the text, therefore, to the House Report.

legislative proposals that led up to the final enactment. In three sets of hearings over the course of four years, proponents and opponents of the legislation debated its impact and relationship with prior law. Draftsmen of the legislation contended for a restriction on the doctrine of patent misuse that would enable patentees to protect themselves against contributory infringers. Others, including representatives of the Department of Justice, vigorously opposed such a restriction.

Although the final version of the statute reflects some minor changes from earlier drafts, the essence of the legislation remained constant. References were made in the later hearings to testimony in the earlier ones.[18] Accordingly, we regard each set of hearings as relevant to a full understanding of the final legislative product.... Together, they strongly reinforce the conclusion that § 271(d) was designed to immunize from the charge of patent misuse behavior similar to that in which the respondent has engaged.

1. The 1948 Hearings. The first bill underlying § 271 was H.R. 5988, proposed to the 80th Congress. During the hearings on this bill its origin and purpose were carefully explained. The New York Patent Law Association, which had supervised drafting of the legislation, submitted a prepared memorandum that candidly declared that the purpose of the proposal was to reverse the trend of Supreme Court decisions that indirectly had cut back on the contributory infringement doctrine. Hearings on H.R. 5988, etc., before the Subcommittee on Patents, Trade–Marks, and Copyrights of the House Committee on the Judiciary, 80th Cong., 2d Sess., 4 (1948) (1948 Hearings). The memorandum explained the rationale behind contributory infringement, and it gave as one example of its proper application the protection of a patent for use of a chemical:

> [O]ne who supplies a hitherto unused chemical to the public for use in a new method is stealing the benefit of the discovery of the property of this chemical which made the new method possible. To enjoin him from distributing the chemical for use in the new method does not prevent him from doing anything which he could do before the new property of the chemical had been discovered. *Ibid.*

It criticized several decisions, including *Leitch* and *Carbice* as well as the two *Mercoids*, on the ground that together they had effectively excluded such "new-use inventions" from the protections of the patent law. 1948 Hearings, at 4–5. It went on to explain that the proposed legislation was designed to counteract this effect by providing that "the mere use or enforcement of the right to be protected against contributory infringement ... shall not be regarded as misuse of the patent." *Id.*, at 6. This approach, the memorandum stated, "does away with the ground on which the Supreme Court has destroyed the doctrine of contributory infringement" and "is essential to make the rights against contributory infringers which are revived by the statute practically useful and enforceable." Ibid.

Testimony by proponents of the bill developed the same theme. Giles Rich, then a prominent patent lawyer, was one of the draftsmen. He

---

18. See, e.g., Hearings on H.R. 3760 before Subcommittee No. 3 of the House Committee on the Judiciary, 82d Cong., 1st Sess., 150–151 (1951) (1951 Hearings) (testimony of Giles Rich).

highlighted the tension between the judicial doctrines of contributory infringement and patent misuse. He stated that early patent misuse decisions "seem to us now to have been just," but that "this doctrine has been carried too far—so far that it . . . has practically eliminated from law the doctrine of contributory infringement as a useful legal doctrine." *Id.*, at 9. To illustrate this point, he contrasted the *Carbice* and *Mercoid* cases, and noted that the latter had involved an item without any noninfringing use. Because it incorporated a staple-nonstaple distinction in the definition of contributory infringement, Mr. Rich argued that the bill would "correct [the] situation" left by *Mercoid* "without giving sanction to practices such as those in the *Carbice* case." 1948 Hearings, at 11.

* * *

The bill attracted opponents as well, some of whom defended the result of the Mercoid decisions. [footnote omitted] In addition, Roy C. Hackley, Jr., Chief of the Patent Section, Department of Justice, made an appearance on behalf of the Department. He took the position that statutory clarification of the scope of contributory infringement was desirable, but he warned Congress against using language that might "permit illegal extension of the patent monopoly." 1948 Hearings, at 69. On this ground he opposed the portion of the proposed bill that included language substantially similar to what is now § 271(d). *Ibid.*

2.   The 1949 Hearings. The 1948 bill did not come to a vote, but the patent bar resubmitted its proposal in 1949. Again, there were fairly extensive hearings, with debate, and again Rich led the list of favorable witnesses. He renewed his attempt to explain the legislation in terms of past decisions of this Court. The result in the *Carbice* case, he argued, was proper because the patentee had tried to interfere with the market in an old and widely used product. On the other hand, he cited the *Mercoid* cases as examples of a situation where "[t]here is no practical way to enforce that patent, except through a suit for contributory infringement against the party who makes the thing which is essentially the inventive subject matter [and] which, when put into use, creates infringement." Hearings on H.R. 3866 before Subcommittee No. 4 of the House Committee on the Judiciary, 81st Cong., 1st Sess., 11 (1949) (1949 Hearings).

To restore the doctrine of contributory infringement where it was most needed, Rich argued, it was essential to restrict *pro tanto* the judicially created doctrine of patent misuse:

> "I would like to recall that we are dealing with a problem which involves a conflict between two doctrines, contributory infringement and misuse.
>
> "It is crystal clear, when you have thoroughly studied this subject, that the only way you can make contributory infringement operative again as a doctrine, is to make some exceptions to the misuse doctrine and say that certain acts shall not be misuse. Then contributory infringement, which is there all the time, becomes operative again.
>
> "Contributory infringement has been destroyed by the misuse doctrine; and to revive it you do not have to do anything with contributory infringement itself. You go back along the same road until you get to the point where you have contributory infringement working for you again." *Id.*, at 13–14.

Rich warned against going too far. He took the position that a law designed to reinstate the broad contributory infringement reasoning of *Henry v. A. B. Dick Co.*, 224 U.S. 1, 32 S.Ct. 364, 56 L.Ed. 645 (1912), "would kill itself in time." 1949 Hearings, at 17. The proposed legislation, however, "stopped short of that" and "said that you can control only things like the switches in the *Mercoid* case, which are especially made or adapted for use in connection with such patent and which are not suitable for actual, commercial, noninfringing use." *Ibid.*

In the 1949 Hearings, the Department of Justice pressed more vigorous opposition to the contributory infringement proposal than it had in 1948. Represented by John C. Stedman, Chief, Legislation and Clearance Section, Antitrust Division, the Department argued that legislation was unnecessary because the *Mercoid* decisions were correct, because they had not produced as much confusion as the proponents of the new legislation claimed, and because the legislation would produce new interpretative problems. 1949 Hearings, at 50–56. Stedman defended the result of the *Mercoid* decisions on the ground that marketing techniques employed in those cases were indistinguishable in effect from tying schemes previously considered by the Court. He took the view that the staple-nonstaple distinction should be irrelevant for purposes of patent misuse. "If the owner of the patent is using his patent in a way to prevent the sale of unpatented elements, then the misuse doctrine would apply." 1949 Hearings, at 54. Stedman added that the effect of the legislation would be to revive the *Leeds & Catlin* decision, a result the Department of Justice opposed. 1949 Hearings, at 59. Later in the hearings, he offered several methods of exploiting patent rights that arguably would eliminate the need for the contributory infringement doctrine, and he stated that a suit for contributory infringement could involve patent misuse, even if there were no conditional licensing of patent rights. *Id.*, at 76–77.

After Stedman's opening testimony, Rich was recalled for further questioning. Rich agreed with Stedman's assessment of the effect that the legislation would have, but argued that the Justice Department's arguments ignored the bill's limitation of contributory infringement to nonstaple articles. To clarify the effect of the statute, Rich declared:

> [I]t is absolutely necessary, to get anywhere in the direction we are trying to go, to make some exception to the misuse doctrine because it is the conflict between the doctrine of contributory infringement and the doctrine of misuse that raises the problem. *Id.*, at 67.

He added:

> The exception which we wish to make to the misuse doctrine would reverse the result in the *Mercoid* case; it would not reverse the result in the *Carbice* case. *Ibid.*

In response to questioning, Rich agreed that the bill would preserve both the contributory infringement and misuse doctrines as they had existed in this Court's cases prior to the *Mercoid* decisions. 1949 Hearings, at 68. He asserted that the method by which the patentee's invention was exploited in *Mercoid* was necessary given the nature of the businesses involved. 1949 Hearings, at 69. When asked whether the proposed legislation would allow that kind of licensing activity, Rich responded with an unqualified "Yes." *Ibid*.

3. The 1951 Hearings. By the time the proposal for a statutory law of contributory infringement and patent misuse was presented to the 82d Congress, the battle lines of the earlier hearings had solidified substantially, and the representatives of the patent bar once again found themselves faced with the formidable opposition of the Department of Justice.

In his opening remarks before the 1951 Hearings, Rich reminded the congressional Subcommittee that, as a practical matter, it was necessary to deal with the contributory infringement and the misuse doctrines as a unit "if we are to tackle the problem at all." 1951 Hearings, at 152. He urged on the Subcommittee the need to eliminate confusion in the law left by the *Mercoid* decisions by drawing a "sensible line" between contributory infringement and patent misuse that would be "in accordance with public policy as it seems to exist today." 1951 Hearings, at 152. Rich also attempted to play down the controversiality of the proposal by arguing that a restrictive definition of contributory infringement had been incorporated into the bill. *Id.*, at 153–154.

When questioned about the effect of the bill on present law, Rich replied that it would not extend the contributory infringement doctrine unless "you take the point of view that there is no such things [sic] as contributory infringement today." Id., at 158. He rejected the suggestion that the legislation would return the law of contributory infringement to the *A. B. Dick* era, and he reminded the Subcommittee that the law "would not touch the result of the *Carbice* decision." 1951 Hearings, at 161. Rich concluded his opening testimony with this explanation of subsection (d):

> It deals with the misuse doctrine, and the reason it is necessary is that the Supreme Court has made it abundantly clear that there exist in the law today two doctrines, contributory infringement on the one hand, and misuse on the other, and that, where there is a conflict, the misuse doctrine must prevail because of the public interest inherently involved in patent cases.
>
> Other decisions following *Mercoid* have made it quite clear that at least some courts are going to say that any effort whatever to enforce a patent against a contributory infringer is in itself misuse. . . . Therefore we have always felt—we who study this subject particularly—that to put any measure of contributory infringement into law you must, to that extent and to that extent only, specifically make exceptions to the misuse doctrine, and that is the purpose of paragraph (d).
>
> It goes with, supports, and depends upon paragraph (c). *Id.*, at 161–162.

The Department of Justice, now represented by Wilbur L. Fugate of the Antitrust Division, broadly objected to "writing the doctrine of contributory infringement into the law." *Id.*, at 165. Its most strenuous opposition was directed at what was to become § 271(d). Fugate warned that this provision "would have the effect of wiping out a good deal of the law relating to misuse of patents, particularly with reference to tying-in clauses." *Ibid.* He repeatedly asserted that the language of subsection (d) was unclear, and that it was impossible to tell how far it would serve to insulate patentees from charges of misuse. *See id.*, at 167–169. But as the Department construed it, the subsection would "seriously impair the doctrine of misuse of patents in favor of the doctrine of contributory infringements." *Id.*, at 168. Fugate would not say that any of the three acts protected by subsection (d) were per se illegal, but he felt that they could become evidence of misuse in some contexts. *Id.*, at 168–169.

When Representative Crumpacker challenged Fugate's interpretation of the statute, Fugate replied that Rich had advanced the same construction, and he called upon Rich to say whether he agreed. *Id.*, at 169. The following colloquy then took place:

> Mr. RICH: I will agree with [Mr. Fugate's interpretation] to this extent: That as I testified it is necessary to make an exception to misuse to the extent that you revive contributory infringement in paragraph (c), and this whole section (d) is entirely dependent on (c). Where (d) refers to contributory infringement, it only refers to contributory infringement as defined in (c) and nothing more.

> Mr. CRUMPACKER: In other words, all it says is that bringing an action against someone who is guilty of contributory infringement is not a misuse of the patent.

> Mr. RICH: That is true. *Ibid.*

Rich and Fugate then discussed the law in the courts before and after the *Mercoid* decisions. In an effort to clarify the intendment of the statute, Congressman Rogers asked Rich to identify misuse decisions exemplifying the acts specified in the three parts of subsection (d). Rich identified the *Leitch* and *Carbice* cases as examples of situations where deriving revenue from acts that would be contributory infringement was held to be evidence of misuse; he stated that the *Mercoid* cases exemplified misuse from licensing others; and he referred to *Stroco Products, Inc. v. Mullenbach, supra*, as an example of a case where the mere bringing of an action against contributory infringers was found to exemplify misuse. 1951 Hearings, at 174–175. He again reminded the Subcommittee that the scope of subsection (d) was implicitly limited by the restrictive definition of contributory infringement in subsection (c), and he assured the Subcommittee that "[i]f [a patentee] has gone beyond those and done other acts which could be misuse, then the misuse doctrine would be applicable." *Id.*, at 175. As an example of such "other acts," he suggested that a patentee would be guilty of misuse if he tried to license others to produce staple articles used in a patented invention. *Ibid.*

C

Other legislative materials that we have not discussed bear as well on the meaning to be assigned to § 271(d); but the materials that we have culled are exemplary, and they amply demonstrate the intended scope of the statute. It is the consistent theme of the legislative history that the statute was designed to accomplish a good deal more than mere clarification. It significantly changed existing law, and the change moved in the direction of expanding the statutory protection enjoyed by patentees. The responsible congressional Committees were told again and again that contributory infringement would wither away if the misuse rationale of the *Mercoid* decisions remained as a barrier to enforcement of the patentee's rights. They were told that this was an undesirable result that would deprive many patent holders of effective protection for their patent rights. They were told that Congress could strike a sensible compromise between the competing doctrines of contributory infringement and patent misuse if it eliminated the result of the *Mercoid* decisions yet preserved the result in *Carbice*. And they were told that the proposed legislation would achieve this effect by restricting contributory infringement to the sphere of nonstaple goods while exempting the control of such goods from the scope of patent misuse. These signals cannot be ignored. They fully support the conclusion that, by enacting §§ 271(c) and (d), Congress granted to patent holders a statutory right to control nonstaple goods that are capable only of infringing use in a patented invention, and that are essential to that invention's advance over prior art.

We find nothing in this legislative history to support the assertion that respondent's behavior falls outside the scope of § 271(d). [footnote omitted] To the contrary, respondent has done nothing that would extend its right of control over unpatented goods beyond the line that Congress drew. Respondent, to be sure, has licensed use of its patented process only in connection with purchases of propanil. But propanil is a nonstaple product, and its herbicidal property is the heart of respondent's invention. Respondent's method of doing business is thus essentially the same as the method condemned in the *Mercoid* decisions, and the legislative history reveals that § 271(d) was designed to retreat from *Mercoid* in this regard.

There is one factual difference between this case and *Mercoid*: the licensee in the *Mercoid* cases had offered a sublicense to the alleged contributory infringer, which offer had been refused. *Mercoid II*, 320 U.S., at 683, 64 S.Ct., at 280. Seizing upon this difference, petitioners argue that respondent's unwillingness to offer similar licenses to its would-be competitors in the manufacture of propanil legally distinguishes this case and sets it outside § 271(d). To this argument, there are at least three responses. First, as we have noted, § 271(d) permits such licensing but does not require it. Accordingly, petitioners' suggestion would import into the statute a requirement that simply is not there. Second, petitioners have failed to adduce any evidence from the legislative history that the offering of a license to the alleged contributory infringer was a critical factor in inducing Congress to retreat from the result of the *Mercoid* decisions. Indeed, the *Leeds & Catlin* decision, which did not involve such an offer to license, was placed before Congress as an example of the kind of contributory infringement action the statute would allow. Third, petitioners' argument runs contrary to the long-settled view that the essence of a patent grant is the right to exclude others from profiting by the patented invention. 35 U.S.C. § 154; *see Continental Paper Bag Co. v. Eastern Paper Bag Co.*, 210 U.S. 405, 424–425, 28 S.Ct. 748, 753–754, 52 L.Ed. 1122 (1908); *Zenith Radio Corp. v. Hazeltine Research, Inc.*, 395 U.S. 100, 135, 89 S.Ct. 1562, 1582, 23 L.Ed.2d 129 (1969). If petitioners' argument were accepted, it would force patentees either to grant licenses or to forfeit their statutory protection against contributory infringement. Compulsory licensing is a rarity in our patent system,[20] and we decline to manufacture such a requirement out of § 271(d).

* * *

■ MR. JUSTICE WHITE, with whom MR. JUSTICE BRENNAN, MR. JUSTICE MARSHALL, and MR. JUSTICE STEVENS join, dissenting.

For decades this Court has denied relief from contributory infringement to patent holders who attempt to extend their patent monopolies to unpatented materials used in connection with patented inventions. The Court now refuses to apply this "patent misuse" principle in the very area in which such attempts to restrain competition are most likely to be successful. The Court holds exempt from the patent misuse doctrine a patent holder's refusal to license others to use a patented process unless they purchase from him an unpatented product that has no substantial use except in the patented process. The Court's sole justification for this radical departure from our prior construction of the patent laws is its interpretation of 35 U.S.C. § 271, a provision that created exceptions to the misuse doctrine and that we have held must be strictly construed "in light of this Nation's historical antipathy to monopoly," *Deepsouth Packing Co. v. Laitram Corp.*, 406 U.S. 518, 530, 92 S.Ct. 1700, 1708, 32 L.Ed.2d 273 (1972). The Court recognizes, as it must, that § 271 does not on its face exempt the broad category of nonstaple materials from the misuse doctrine, yet construes it to do so based on what it has gleaned from the testimony of private patent lawyers given in hearings before congressional Committees and from the testimony of Department of Justice attorneys opposing the bill. The Court has often warned that in construing statutes, we should be "extremely wary of testimony before committee hearings and of debates on the floor of Congress save for precise analyses of statutory phrases by the sponsors of the proposed laws." *S & E Contractors, Inc. v. United States*, 406 U.S. 1, 13, n. 9, 92 S.Ct. 1411, 1418, n. 9, 31 L.Ed.2d 658 (1972). We have expressed similar reservations about statements of the opponents of a bill: "The fears and doubts of the opposition are no authoritative guide to the construction of legislation. It is the sponsors that we look to when the meaning of the statutory words is in doubt." *Schwegmann Bros. v. Calvert Distillers Corp.*, 341 U.S. 384, 394–395, 71 S.Ct. 745, 750–751, 95 L.Ed. 1035 (1951). *NLRB v. Fruit Packers*, 377 U.S. 58, 66, 84 S.Ct. 1063, 1068, 12 L.Ed.2d 129 (1964). Here, nothing in support of the Court's novel construction is to be found in the Committee Reports or in the statements of those Congressmen or Senators sponsoring the bill. The Court focuses only on the opposing positions of nonlegislators, none of which I find sufficient to constitute that "clear and certain signal from Congress" that

---

20. Compulsory licensing of patents often has been proposed, but it has never been enacted on a broad scale. See, e.g., Compulsory Licensing of Patents under some Non–American Systems, Study of the Subcommittee on Patents, Trademarks, and Copyrights of the Senate Committee on the Judiciary, 85th Cong., 2d Sess., 1, 2 (Comm. Print 1959). Although compulsory licensing provisions were considered for possible incorporation into the 1952 revision of the patent laws, they were dropped before the final bill was circulated. See House Committee on the Judiciary, Proposed Revision and Amendment of the Patent Laws: Preliminary Draft, 81st Cong., 2d Sess., 91 (Comm. Print 1950).

is required before construing the 1952 Patent Act to extend the patent monopoly beyond pre-existing standards.

* * *

■ Mr. Justice Stevens, dissenting.

This patentee has offered no licenses, either to competing sellers of propanil or to consumers, except the implied license that is granted with every purchase of propanil from it. Thus, every license granted under this patent has been conditioned on the purchase of an unpatented product from the patentee. This is a classic case of patent misuse. As Mr. Justice WHITE demonstrates in his dissenting opinion, nothing in 35 U.S.C. § 271(d) excludes this type of conduct from the well-established misuse doctrine.

The Court may have been led into reaching the contrary, and in my view erroneous, conclusion by the particular facts of this case. It appears that it would not be particularly profitable to exploit this patent by granting express licenses for fixed terms to users of propanil or by granting licenses to competing sellers. Under these circumstances, the patent may well have little or no commercial value unless the patentee is permitted to engage in patent misuse. But surely this is not a good reason for interpreting § 271(d) to permit such misuse. For the logic of the Court's holding would seem to justify the extension of the patent monopoly to unpatented "nonstaples" even in cases in which the patent could be profitably exploited without misuse. Thus, for example, it appears that the Court's decision would allow a manufacturer to condition a long-term lease of a patented piece of equipment on the lessee's agreement to purchase tailormade—*i.e.*, nonstaple—supplies or components for use with the equipment exclusively from the patentee. Whether all of the five Members of the Court who have joined today's revision of § 271(d) would apply their "nonstaple" exception in such a case remains to be seen. In all events, I respectfully dissent for the reasons stated in Mr. Justice WHITE's opinion, which I join.

NOTES

1. *What is Misuse?* The case law suggests that the misuse doctrine is available when a patentee has somehow expanded the scope of the patent grant with anticompetitive effect, using a rule of reason test. See *Virginia Panel Corp. v. MAC Panel Co.*, 133 F.3d 860, 868–69 (Fed.Cir.1997). Regrettably, the case law does not indicate what exactly this means. Misuse charges that have been successful to varying degrees in matters including: efforts to sue or threaten to sue for indirect infringement; efforts to license those who could be sued for indirect infringement; and efforts to license in a way that touches activities that do not directly infringe. This last group includes: where patentee receives compensation after the patent term expires (which some say looks like post-expiration royalties); where the licensee agrees to do something that would not be actionable for direct infringement (which some say looks like tying); and where the licensee agrees not to do something that would not be actionable (which some say looks like a refusal to deal, a restriction in output, or waste). One of the fundamental problems with this area of law is that is based on the notion that there is a "proper scope" of the patent grant that is definable without reference to the patent claims and the patent statute. Many think of this as a problem of objectionable breath in the patentee's reach. But as explored in the Side Bar by Justice Robin Jacob at the end of this subsection, there may also be a problem of "objectionable narrowness."

2. *What is Not Misuse?* In response to the great deal of judge-made law in this area, Congress has twice acted to make clear that certain acts shall not constitute misuse. First, in the 1952 Patent Act itself, Congress expressly provided in Section 271:

> (d) No patent owner otherwise entitle to relief for infringement or contributory infringement of a patent shall be denied relief for deemed guilty of misuse or illegal extension of the patent right by reason of his having done one or more of the following:
>
> (1) derived revenue from acts which if performed by another without his consent would constitute contributory infringement of the patent;
>
> (2) licensed or authorized another to perform acts which if performed without his consent would constitute contributory infringement of the patent;
>
> (3) sought to enforce his patent rights against infringement or contributory infringement [;]

Second, in 1988, Congress amended Section 271(d) to add two new subsections (4 and 5) to the list of acts that shall not constitute misuse:

> (4) refused to license or use any rights to the patent; or
>
> (5) conditioned the license of any rights to the patent or the sale of the patented product on the acquisition of a license to rights in another patent or purchase of a separate product, unless, in view of the circumstances, the patent owner has market power in the relevant market for the patent or patented product on which the license or sale is conditioned.

With respect to subsection (d)(4), it is well settled that a patent owner has no duty to practice the invention claimed in the patent, and indeed the patent gives him the right to exclude all others from practicing it as well, what some call "patent suppression." See *Continental Paper Bag Co. v. Eastern Paper Bag Co.*, 210 U.S. 405 (1908). Nevertheless, as discussed in the materials that follow on antitrust, refusals to deal and efforts to tie *may* trigger some antitrust issues—for reasons unrelated to patent law and indeed often in cases where the presence or absence of patents are irrelevant. The central lesson to take from the materials here is that these are no longer to be considered matters that are *per se* misuse or *per se* antitrust violations, as they have been in the past by some courts. Consistent with this view, in *Illinois Tool Works Inc. v. Independent Ink, Inc.*, 547 U.S. 28 (2006), the Supreme Court expressly held that the mere fact that a tying product is patented does not support a presumption of market power in a patented product, abrogating *Morton Salt Co. v. G.S. Suppiger Co.*, 314 U.S. 488 (1942), *International Salt Co. v. United States*, 332 U.S. 392 (1947), *United States v. Loew's Inc.*, 371 U.S. 38 (1962), and *Jefferson Parish Hospital Dist. No. 2 v. Hyde*, 466 U.S. 2 (1984); that in all cases involving a tying arrangement, the plaintiff must prove that the defendant has market power in the tying product; and that a patent did not give rise to presumption that patentee had market power.

The Federal Circuit has held that it is not patent misuse when a patentee offers to license a patent and induces a third party not to license its separate, competitive technology. *Princo Corp. v. International Trade Comm'n*, 616 F.3d 1318, 1331 (Fed.Cir.2010) (*en banc*).

3. *Interactions Between Misuse and Antitrust.* The Doctrine of Misuse is an affirmative defense that has its origins in equity. Like inequitable conduct, a finding of misuse renders the patent unenforceable, not invalid; but, unlike inequitable conduct, unenforceability due to misuse only lasts until the misuse is purged, *C.R. Bard, Inc. v. M3 Systems, Inc.*, 157 F.3d 1340, 1372 (Fed.Cir.1998), that is, there is a cessation of the improper activity and the effects of the misuse have dissipated. *Virginia Panel Corp. v. MAC Panel Co.*, 133 F.3d 860, 864 (Fed.Cir.1997). Moreover, unlike an antitrust violation, a judgment of misuse does not result in an award of damages to the accused infringer. See *B. Braun Medical, Inc. v. Abbott Laboratories, Inc.*, 124 F.3d 1419, 1427 (Fed.Cir.1997). Thus, one can think of misuse as a shield and antitrust as a sword. Lastly, it is not clear to what extent the two issues—misuse and antitrust—are co-extensive. To be sure, the aggressive party who wins, or think she will win, a misuse defense as a shield may be tempted to turn around and use the same as a sword in an antitrust matter because antitrust causes of action may provide access to fee shifting and damages.

4. *Unpacking History and the Interactions Patents Has With Misuse, Antitrust, Contracts, and Preemption.* Many find the complex history of cases reviewed in *Dawson*, discussed earlier, to be unsatisfying in that it appears to be driven by outcomes and compromise; but not mode of analysis. For this reason, the following excerpt from a recent working paper is included to show how many of these complex cases can be reconciled analytically using the basic principles of the positive law. This is not to suggest that the outcomes the courts did reach are wrong; and indeed in many cases this "basics matters" approach leads to the same outcome as those courts. But learning how to conduct the proper analysis under the basic outline of the positive law is important because it will help the reader understand how patent law interacts with a number of other areas of law, including misuse, antitrust, contracts, and preemption.

The Basics Matter: At the Periphery of Intellectual Property

F. Scott Kieff & Troy A. Paredes.

Stanford Law School John M. Olin Program in Law and Economics

Working Paper No. 275, February 2004*

Applying the basics to prototypical cases at the periphery of IP law, including price discrimination, restrictive licensing arrangements, and suits against indirect infringers, provides a set of rules that are useable *ex ante* by all market participants in a way that helps them order their affairs while at the same time being fair and efficient. The "basics matter" approach has important normative implications, in that judicial fidelity to the basics ultimately affords parties greater freedom and ability to structure their interactions in welfare-enhancing ways.

The cases we explore are appropriately viewed as prototypical for several reasons. They involve fact patterns that are representative. They have actual historical significance through their contribution to the case law. And the primary architect of the present patent system—the 1952 Patent Act—wrote a five-part series of articles about these cases before drafting the statute designed to fundamentally change the way courts applying the law would look to the issues raised by the cases.[32]

---

* Available on-line at http://papers.ssrn.com/paper.taf?abstract_id=501142.

32. *See* Giles S. Rich, *The Relation Between Patent Practices and the Anti–Monopoly Laws* (pts. 1–5), 24 J. Pat. Off. Soc'y 85, 159, 241, 328, 422 (1942). As suggested [earlier], this is one reason why Rich's views have been so influential.

As discussed more fully below, the cases can be fairly divided into two sets. Importantly, a review of both sets of cases shows that the "basics matter" approach is not merely a veiled effort to promote pro-patent or pro-copyright—or more generally, pro-business—positions. Rather, the basics framework is offered as a coherent approach that more predictably can be engaged *ex ante* and that reflects fidelity to, and respect for, separate areas of the law. Although we focus on patents, since the core features of other areas of IP law largely derive from patent law, the basics framework and the essence of the following analysis extend to copyrights and other forms of IP as well.

INDIRECT INFRINGEMENT VS. BREACH OF CONTRACT

The first set of cases involves the tension between indirect infringement and indirect participation in a breach of contract. Indirect infringement may be actionable as a matter of IP law, as discussed earlier. Indirect participation in a breach of contract may be actionable as a matter of contract law under doctrines such as tortious interference with contract, as in the famous multi-billion dollar judgment from the *Texaco, Inc. v. Pennzoil, Co.* litigation.[33] However, the happenstance that a contract relates to patents should not transform interference with that contract into patent infringement. The facts that need to be proven are different under these different frameworks. The potential remedies are different as well.[34]

Wallace, the classic case of indirect infringement, involved a patent on an oil lamp having a new burner, together with a standard fuel reservoir, wick, and chimney.[35] In the case, a competitor of the patent owner had sold a rival product, which included the new burner and other lamp parts but not the chimney. The court reasoned that the defendant had contributed to infringement on the part of its customers, because they would inevitably add a chimney. A judgment of contributory infringement makes sense under the "basics matter" approach because the intended and actual impact of the competitor's efforts were to make sure that its customers acted in an infringing manner. Indeed, *Wallace* is the case that gave rise to the entire doctrine of indirect infringement throughout all of IP law.

By way of comparison, if the plaintiff-patentee in *Wallace* instead had entered into arrangements with its customers obligating them to buy chimneys from the patentee, the analysis under the basics of IP law would be different. A rival seller of chimneys might be liable for tortious interference with contract, or the tying arrangement might violate the antitrust laws. However, the competing chimney seller would not be liable for contributory infringement under the basics of IP law.

The *Heaton* case is an example of just this type of arrangement. *Heaton* involved a patentee who sold a patented machine with a label license under

---

33. Texaco, Inc. v. Pennzoil, Co., 729 S.W.2d 768 (Tex.App. 1987).

34. The transformation of breach of contract into patent infringement is significant. At least one essential difference between patent infringement and breach of contract is that the remedies for infringement include a right to exclude (*i.e.*, property rule protection), whereas a contract is generally viewed as little more than a promise either to perform or to breach and pay actual damages (*i.e.*, liability rule protection).

35. Wallace v. Holmes, 29 F.Cas. 74 (No. 17,100) (C.C.D. Conn. 1871).

the patent that restricted the machine's use to certain unpatented inputs (staples, literally)—a tying arrangement—and a defendant who sold competing inputs.[36] The court seemed to reason that by providing its staples for use in the machine, the defendant was contributing to breach of the label contract, which had given the permission through the label patent license to use the machine. Once that license under the patent was gone, the use of the machine became infringing. Rather than sue for interference with the contract, the plaintiff sued for indirect infringement of the patent under patent law. The court decided that the defendant was, indeed, committing contributory infringement of the patent. But this turned a case about indirect participation in breach of contract into patent infringement. By deciding the case the way it did under IP law, the court in effect extended the scope of IP rights. A collateral consequence of the court's reasoning in *Heaton*, of course, would be to immunize potentially anticompetitive licensing arrangements from the antitrust laws.

The "basics matter" approach rejects the analysis of *Heaton*. Under the "basics matter" approach, and as pointed out by Rich, this decision was inappropriate because it "transformed the law of contracts into 'patent law.'"[37] It may have been appropriate for the plaintiff to consider an interference with contract argument, if sufficient facts could be proven to substantiate the claim under contract law.[38] It may even have been appropriate for the defendant to consider an antitrust tying argument, if the case could be proven under antitrust law.[39] By not addressing these contract and antitrust arguments head on, cases like *Heaton* allow parties, and judges, to selectively mix features of various bodies of law and to extrapolate from them to forge new hybrid doctrines of law that run afoul of the basics of each area.[40]

---

36. Heaton–Peninsular Button–Fastener Co. v. Eureka Specialty Co., 77 F. 288 (C.C.A. 6 1896) (opinion by Lurton, C.J.) (also known as the *"Button Fastener Case"*).

37. Rich, *supra* note 1, at 251. The successful argument in *Heaton*—offered by Frederick P. Fish, founding partner of the law firm formerly known as Fish, Richardson, & Neave, which later became the firms of Fish & Richardson and Fish & Neave—held out the sales of the staples as proxies, or counters, for measuring use of the patented machine. They may have been, and such an arrangement would likely have been efficient. But the cause of action against the defendant, if any, would then be some form of interference with contract, not patent infringement. Depending on the ultimate interpretation of the label contract, the plaintiff may have had a cause of action against the party who was a customer of both the plaintiff and the defendant for both breach of contract and patent infringement.

38. The court opinion suggests there may have been sufficient facts to mount such an argument.

39. The court opinion does not discuss these facts, but it is likely there was no evidence of market power, which would have been required to mount an antitrust argument. It is curious that the court did not discuss the antitrust argument, because, as Rich pointed out, the opinion was written against a background in which antitrust law was recently very active: "The Sherman Act had been passed six years before!" Rich, *supra* note 1, at 254 (punctuation emphasis in original).

40. In many instances, such selective application of the law leads to doctrines, such as misuse, that erode IP rights. In other cases, such as *Heaton* or those cases in which courts have subjected transactions involving IP to less scrutiny under antitrust law, the new doctrines can work to expand IP rights. What is more, in all cases, the courts totally fail to give any meaningful test for determining when those IP rights should be so eroded or expanded.

The Supreme Court applied the same approach as *Heaton* in the *A.B. Dick* case, which involved a patent on a mimeograph machine sold with a label restriction limiting the brand of unpatented ink that could be used in the machine,.[41] As in *Heaton*, the Court agreed with the plaintiff-patentee in *A.B. Dick*, and held that there was contributory infringement of the patent. Because this was a Supreme Court case, its reasoning had a longer lasting impact in pushing IP law in a direction that did not reflect fidelity to the basics.

The "basics matter" approach rejects the reasoning of *A.B. Dick* for the same reason it rejects the reasoning of *Heaton*. Indeed, eventually, these cases were effectively overturned. As Rich pointed out later in his testimony before Congress concerning the provisions he drafted on indirect infringement in the 1952 Patent Act, any effort to follow this body of law "would kill itself in time."[42]

An understanding of the basics suggests why *Heaton*, *A.B. Dick*, and their progeny were not sustainable over the long run. The problem is not merely one of courts going too far one way (e.g., effectively extending the scope of IP rights to anything connected to IP and simultaneously immunizing all transactions involving IP from serious antitrust scrutiny) or the other (e.g., eliminating the doctrine of indirect infringement, thereby eroding IP rights). The problem is more fundamental. Namely, cases like *Heaton* and *A.B. Dick* ignore the basics of each implicated body of law—IP law, antitrust law, and the general law of property and contracts. As a

---

41. Henry v. A.B. Dick Co., 224 U.S. 1 (1912).

42. As the Supreme Court later pointed out in *Dawson*, when he was testifying in support of what became Section 271 of the 1952 Patent Act, "Rich warned against going too far [and] took the position that a law designed to reinstate the broad contributory infringement reasoning of [*A.B. Dick*] 'would kill itself in time.'" Dawson Chem. v. Rohm and Haas Co., 448 U.S. 176, 208 (1980) (citing Hearings on H.R. 3866 before Subcommittee No. 4 of the House Committee on the Judiciary, 81st Cong., 1st Sess., 17 (1949) (testimony of Giles Rich)).

As the Court also pointed out in *Dawson*, *A.B. Dick* "was followed by what may be characterized through the lens of hindsight as an inevitable judicial reaction." *Dawson*, 448 U.S. at 191 (citing *Motion Picture Patents Co. v. Universal Film Mfg. Co.*, 243 U.S. 502 (1917) (reaching result opposite to *A.B. Dick* on similar facts involving a patent on a film projector and a restrictive label contract limiting use to certain film)). *Compare Motion Picture Patents*, 243 U.S. at 519–21 (Holmes, J., dissenting) (arguing that the patentee should be entitled to capture all the market generated by the invention and expressing concerns about the transactions that had been entered in reliance on the rule of *A.B. Dick*).

The law continued to fluctuate after *Motion Picture Patents*. In *United States v. United Shoe Machinery*, 247 U.S. 32 (1918) ("*Shoe Machinery I*"), a case also argued for the patentee by Frederick P. Fish, the Court returned to reasoning similar to that in *A.B. Dick* to permit a complex leasing arrangement. Soon thereafter, the Clayton Act was passed, in part, in response to cases like *A.B. Dick* and *Shoe Machinery I*, and its Section 3 was directed to sales and leases of articles of commerce "whether patented or unpatented." 15 U.S.C. § 14. Not surprisingly, in *United States v. United Shoe Machinery*, 258 U.S. 451 (1922) ("*Shoe Machinery II*"), the Court found that the leases violated the Clayton Act. Similarly, in *International Business Machines Corp. v. United States*, 298 U.S. 131 (1936) ("*IBM*"), the Court found a set of complex leasing arrangements accompanied by sales of punch cards to violate the Clayton Act.

This brief review of the evolution from *A.B. Dick* to *IBM* is provided here only for historical context. A significantly more complete treatment is provided in Rich, *supra* note 1, at 241–283.

result, they lack coherence and, in the name of IP law, encroach upon the boundaries of other well-established bodies of law that reflect more nuanced and time-tested doctrines and rules that have staying power and that are perfectly capable of resolving the disputes on their own terms.

Infringement under IP Law vs. Sui Generis Law

The second set of prototypical cases involves the question of what body of law should govern determinations of infringement: the body of organic IP law—patent, copyright, or trademark—or some special *sui generis* body of law. In many of the cases involving charges of indirect infringement and misuse—which are admittedly somewhat difficult doctrines—too many courts and commentators have ignored the basics and instead tried to rehash the normative case for IP to develop new specialized approaches in these doctrinally difficult cases that they hope will get IP scope just right. The fundamental problem with these specialized approaches is that they recast the entire legal institutional framework for IP in a way that has pernicious ripple effects throughout IP law by ignoring the many choices that have been made over IP law's development.

One basic trap into which these courts and commentators have fallen when adopting such *sui generis* approaches to IP is focusing on the wrong party when considering whose behavior should matter in cases of possible indirect infringement. The behavior of the putative indirect infringer to facilitate or encourage direct infringement is relevant to the analysis under both inducement of infringement and contributory infringement. The behavior of the patentee—in the sense of the patentee engaging in conduct that leverages his IP rights with the goal of extracting value—is not relevant to inducement or contributory infringement. Indeed, in such instances, the patentee is simply exercising his rights to exclude and to use, as the basics of IP law and the general law anticipate. Put simply, the question of a putative defendant's infringement should not turn on whether or not the patentee was trying to get as much out of the patent as possible through some restrictive licensing arrangement, tie-in, or otherwise. If the patentee, or any property owner for that matter, behaves in a way that antitrust law or contract law properly prohibit, then that is a matter of antitrust law or contract law.

The modern trend towards *sui generis* analysis of infringement—as compared with an analysis based in IP law—has its most visible roots in the Supreme Court's *Leeds & Catlin* decision. Just like the classic indirect infringement case of *Wallace*, discussed previously, *Leeds & Catlin* involved a patentee's competitor selling something that had no substantial non-infringing use.[43] In *Leeds & Catlin*, the defendant-infringer sold specially grooved records that could only be used in a patented record player known as a "Victrola." The Supreme Court reasoned that the defendant's selling of the records was infringement because the records were the "distinction [or key element] of the invention."[44] This reasoning is entirely flawed.

---

43. Leeds & Catlin Co. v. Victor Talking Mach. Co. 213 U.S. 325 (1909).

44. *Id.* at 335.

Although the "basics matter" approach might reach the same result—a finding of contributory infringement—it would do so for an entirely different reason than offered by the Court. Under the basics of patent law, there is no "distinction," or key element, of subject matter claimed under the patent. The patent system operates using what is known as "peripheral claiming"—as distinct from "central claiming"—in which the function of the patent claim is not to set forth the heart of the protected subject matter but rather to set forth its outer bounds.[45] Direct infringement is measured against these outer bounds. Indirect infringement is premised upon some occurrence of direct infringement. But the reach of indirect infringement does not turn on whether the putative defendant is targeting some key element of the claim. Rather, as discussed earlier, for a proper analysis of contributory infringement under the basics, a key question is instead whether there were any substantial non-infringing uses for the grooved records. Because there were no such uses in *Leeds & Catlin*, and because the other elements of contributory infringement were established (*i.e.*, direct infringement and knowledge of the patent), applying the basics would have resulted in a finding of contributory infringement.

Hanging determinations of indirect infringement on the factors outlined earlier in our discussion of the basics—such as intent for induced infringement and absence of non-infringing substitutes for contributory infringement—may seem like an effort to exalt form over substance. After all, the reasoning the Court adopted in *Leeds & Catlin* seems to strike at the heart of substance by focusing on the key element. But the Court fails to give any instruction on how to determine which element is key, and neither has any other court or commentator. The tests for indirect infringement have the essential advantage of being comparatively easy to administer. They look to facts well within the control of the putative infringer and are strongly biased in favor of the putative infringer in the types of errors one would expect the tests to generate. The intent requirement under an inducement analysis and the broad and readily identifiable safe harbors under a contributory analysis ensure these important biases and that the doctrines are easy to administer.

Importantly, the improper reasoning of the Court in *Leeds & Catlin* is not mere harmless error. The approach courts—especially the Supreme Court—adopt matters, even if the results are the same in a particular case.

---

45. For more on peripheral claiming, see F. Scott Kieff, *Perusing Property Rights in DNA, in* F. SCOTT KIEFF, PERSPECTIVES ON PROPERTIES OF THE HUMAN GENOME PROJECT 135 (2003). A determination of infringement under a central claiming system requires the court to determine the heart of the invention and whether the putative infringement is close enough to that heart to justify a judgment of infringement. A determination under peripheral claiming requires the court to determine only the outer bounds of the claim. Anything within those bounds infringes and anything outside does not. The so-called "doctrine of equivalents" that exists under the present patent system, even though not provided for in the statute, is an odd exception to the peripheral nature of our present peripheral claiming system because it allows the patentee to capture something outside of the claim. Although some commentators like this doctrine because it gives some flexibility, they fail to see how the patentee can achieve this same flexibility in a manner that is not only less costly to the patentee but also to all third parties by simply drafting a better patent disclosure at the outset. F. Scott Kieff, *The Case for Registering Patents and the Law and Economics of Present Patent–Obtaining Rules*, 45 B.C. L. REV. 55 (forthcoming 2003).

By suggesting in *Leeds & Catlin* that the case turned on the heart of the invention, the Court advanced a line of precedent that focused on the wrong issues in patent cases. One of the most pernicious cases in this line of precedent was *Carbice*, in which the Court denied relief to a patentee after reasoning that the patentee was trying to extend the patent beyond the key elements of the claim.[46] The plaintiff-patentee in *Carbice* had a patent on a packaging method using dry ice. What troubled the Court was that the patentee had a practice of entering into licensing arrangements obligating the licensee to use only certain containers for packaging products with the dry ice.

The facts of *Carbice* are somewhat similar to those of *Leeds & Catlin* with one important difference: the defendant sold a product—dry ice—that was a staple article of commerce usable in many non-infringing manners other than in the patented ice-cream packaging. The "basics matter" approach would again yield the same result as the Court's analysis—in this case, no contributory infringement—but again for a different reason. Instead of focusing on the patentee's alleged extension of the patent beyond its key elements, the "basics matter" approach would turn on the many non-infringing uses for dry ice. As Rich emphasized, it is the behavior of the putative contributory infringer that is relevant to a determination of contributory infringement, not that of the patentee.[47] Under the "basics matter" approach it makes sense that the organic IP law—in this case patent law—has evolved to focus on the behavior of the putative infringer precisely because it is comparatively easy to judge.

Furthermore, an IP holder should not be denied relief for contributory infringement—or even direct infringement—simply because the IP holder is exercising his rights to exclude and to use through a tying arrangement or restrictive license. Such conduct is properly a subject for antitrust law and contract law, but should have no bearing on a court's analysis of indirect (or direct) infringement under patent law. Courts should not recast such conduct as an effort by the IP holder to "extend" his patent rights for the purpose of transforming a matter for antitrust and contract law into a matter for some new and contrived version of IP law.

To be sure, the Court did not always reach the right result, as it did in *Leeds & Catlin* and *Carbice*. Because the Court continued to misplace its focus on the putatively key elements of patent claims, by the time of the *Mercoid* cases, the entire doctrine of indirect infringement had been almost entirely eliminated as a result of judicial reasoning that precluded any action for indirect infringement. In essence, because by its nature every indirect infringement case involves a defendant who is not triggering at least one element of the patent claim—direct infringement occurs when all elements are satisfied—the focus on "key element" in Court's reasoning

---

46. Carbice Corp. v. American Patents Corp., 283 U.S. 27, 33 (1931). A similar approach was followed in *Lietch Mfg. v. Barber Co.*, 302 U.S. 458 (1938) (also known generally as "*Barber*") (Brandeis, J.) (patentee "attempting . . . to employ the patent to secure a limited monopoly of unpatented material").

47. Rich *supra* note 1, at 345 (describing the opinions of the Court in *Carbice* and *Barber* as revealing "a very significant preoccupation by the Court with the *objective of the plaintiffs* rather than with the doings of the defendant") (emphasis in original).

allowed every putative indirect infringer to argue that the missing element was the one that was "key" and therefore no action for indirect infringement could lie.[48]

In response, Rich drafted what became Section 271 of the 1952 Patent Act to statutorily overrule cases like *Mercoid* and to revive indirect infringement.[49] Under this established basic framework of patent law after the 1952 Act, the essential inquiry for indirect infringement is on the comparatively easy to administer framework discussed earlier. While it may be appropriate to debate the benefits and costs of allowing actions for indirect infringement, the above review is designed to show at least two important things. First, *sui generis* attempts to re-hash the proper scope of an organic IP right when addressing cases of misuse or indirect infringement will yield a test that is comparatively more difficult to administer, that eliminates the doctrine, or both. Second, unlike prior approaches commentators have offered for addressing issues at the periphery of IP law—many of which urge a nearly impossible *ex post* balancing of dynamic and allocative efficiency that inappropriately emphasizes reward to inventers as opposed to commercialization—the "basics matter" approach provides a set of clearer rules and doctrines that market participants can better rely on *ex ante* in structuring their affairs.

OTHER PERNICIOUS RIPPLE EFFECTS

The "basics matter" approach has important implications for resolving matters involving at least two current and controversial issues found at the periphery of IP law: patent and copyright misuse and restrictive licensing arrangements.[50] Applying the basics today to these and other tough cases that simultaneously implicate IP law, antitrust law, and contract law

---

48. Mercoid Corp. v. Mid–Continent Investment Co., 320 U.S. 661 (1944) (*"Mercoid I"*), and Mercoid Corp. v. Minneapolis–Honeywell Regulator Co., 320 U.S. 680 (1944) (*"Mercoid II"*) (patent on new furnace stoker switch). The same approach was used earlier in *American Lecithin Co. v. Warfield Co.*, 105 F. 2d 207 (C.C.A. 7, 1939) (also known generally as *"Warfield"*) (patent on use of lecithin as an emulsifier in chocolates to improve its properties by, for example, preventing "whitening" after only a few days).

49. *See, e.g.*, Dawson Chem. v. Rohm and Haas Co., 448 U.S. 176, 214 (1980) ("Respondent's method of doing business is thus essentially the same as the method condemned in the *Mercoid* decisions, and the legislative history reveals that § 271(d) was designed to retreat from *Mercoid* in this regard."). Section 271 achieved this result by codifying in subsections (a), (b), and (c) those acts that would constitute direct, induced, and contributory infringement, respectively; while at the same time codifying in subsection (d) that it would not be misuse for a patentee to sue or license anyone who could be sued under subsections (a), (b), or (c).

50. Although properly a topic of a separate paper because of the many complex approaches the Court has taken on it, the doctrine of preemption is another of the serious pernicious ripple effects caused by approaches that ignore the basics. In essence, the preemption cases can generally be "seen as efforts to place limits on the ability for [IP owners] to avail themselves of various State laws." [Donald S. Chisum, Craig Allen Nard, Herbert F. Schwartz, Pauline Newman & F. Scott Kieff, Principles of Patent Law (2001)] at 1155. *See generally id.* at 1155–96 (reviewing preemption). This makes no sense because the IP rights confer rights on IP owners, not additional restrictions. For more on the conflict between preemption and the basics of IP law, see F. Scott Kieff, *Contrived Conflicts: The Supreme Court vs the Basics of Intellectual Property Law*, 30 WM. MITCHELL L. REV. 1717 (2004) (invited piece for symposium entitled "The United States Supreme Court's Effect on Intellectual Property Law This Millennium" at William Mitchell College of Law held April 24, 2004).

avoids a host of pernicious ripple effects—namely, undercutting innovation and the commercialization of IP—that arise from more specialized approaches to disputes and transactions involving IP.

Concerning the misuse doctrine, the "basics matter" approach is not compatible with the Federal Circuit's present view of patent misuse, which seems to leave a broad and vaguely defined space for misuse.[51] In *Virginia Panel*, the Federal Circuit suggested the following test for determining whether a patentee has misused his patent: "[w]hen a practice alleged to constitute patent misuse is neither *per se* patent misuse nor specifically excluded from a misuse analysis by Section 271(d) [of the Patent] Act], a court must determine if that practice is reasonably within the patent grant."[52] But importantly, the patent statutes make no provision for *per se* misuse.[53] [Rather, Section 271(d) provides specific safe harbors for conduct that is not misuse. Further, it is a misnomer to suggest that some use of a patent is not within its scope, since patents only give a right to exclude. The right to use is derived from sources external to IP law.

If the basics are applied, other bodies of law, such as antitrust law, provide the proper legal lens through which to inspect a patentee's use of a patent and the subject matter it covers, especially when it comes to putative misuse, the basic thrust of which is that an IP holder should be denied relief for infringement when he has used his IP in some allegedly anticompetitive way. As discussed earlier, patentees and copyright holders, like other property owners, are subject to antitrust law, because patents and copyrights give only a right to exclude, not a right to be free from the constraints of other laws. In brief, the pernicious effect of the misuse doctrine is that it erodes IP rights, at least at the margin, and risks rooting out procompetitive and competitively-neutral behavior that the antitrust

---

51. The U.S. Court of Appeals for the Federal Circuit Court has jurisdiction over most appeals in patent cases. *See* Federal Courts Improvement Act of 1982, P.L. 97–164, 96 Stat. 25 (Apr. 2, 1982) (creating a uniform forum for patent appeals in the Federal Circuit by merging the Court of Claims with the Court of Customs and Patent Appeals and transferring to the new court jurisdiction over appeals from patent cases that were tried in the district courts). Patent cases for purposes of making this jurisdictional decision are those in which the well-pleaded complaint alleges a claim arising under federal patent law. Holmes Group, Inc. v. Vornado Air Circulation Systems, Inc., 535 U.S. 826, (2002).

52. Virginia Panel Corp. v. MAC Panel Co., 133 F.3d 860, 869 (Fed.Cir.1997) (internal citations omitted).

53. According to the Federal Circuit in *Virginia Panel*:

The courts have identified certain specific practices as constituting per se patent misuse, including so-called "tying" arrangements in which a patentee conditions a license under the patent on the purchase of a separable, staple good, *see, e.g.,* Morton Salt Co., 314 U.S. 488, 491 (1942), and arrangements in which a patentee effectively extends the term of its patent by requiring post-expiration royalties, *see, e.g.,* Brulotte v. Thys Co., 379 U.S. 29, 33 (1964). Congress, however, has established that other specific practices may not support a finding of patent misuse. *See* 35 U.S.C. § 271(d) (1994); Dawson Chem. Co. v. Rohm & Haas Co., 448 U.S. 176, 202 (1980) (construing earlier version of § 271(d)). A 1988 amendment to § 271(d) provides that, *inter alia,* in the absence of market power, even a tying arrangement does not constitute patent misuse. *See* 35 U.S.C. § 271(d)(5) (1994) (added by Pub.L. No. 100–703, § 201, 102 Stat. 4676 (1988)).

133 F.3d at 869 (internal citations shortened).

laws recognize as such and permit.[54] If the antitrust laws are too lax, the appropriate remedy is to fix the antitrust laws. As Rich pointed out in commenting on the unfortunate habit of courts to treat potential antitrust concerns as some how more serious and in greater need of policing when IP is involved:

> The patent right is not the only form of property subject to such misuse. But it is so little understood, as compared to other forms of property, that much mystery attaches to it and much confusion surrounds it.... [Practices that restrain trade are] not due to the patent law.... [They are] due to failure to enforce the anti-monopoly laws. The advocates of reform would do well to restrict the attack to the latter aspect and not confuse the issue by abortive attempts to emasculate the patent law....[55]

Concerning restrictive licensing arrangements, the "basics matter" approach suggests that courts should generally enforce restrictive licenses involving IP as long as they are enforceable under contract law and do not run afoul of the antitrust laws. Indeed, affording IP holders the right to carve up interests in their IP and the subject matter it covers is consistent with the basics of property law and the right to use enjoyed by owners of tangible property. Courts adopted the "basics" reasoning in considering the validity of restrictive licenses of copyrights in the *ProCD*[56] case and of patents in the *Mallinckrodt* case.[57] Even when a potential or actual IP owner tries to extract payments for activities that fall outside the protection of IP,[58] courts should enforce these contracts to pay as long as the arrangement—which may amount to little more than an effort to ease either the risk burden or the financial liquidity burden of the transaction—is properly enforceable under contract law.[59] By way of contrast, courts that

---

54. For an expanded discussion of this point in the context of copyright misuse, which derives from patent misuse, see [Troy Paredes, *Copyright Misuse and Tying: Will Courts Stop Misusing Misuse?*, 9 HIGH TECH. L.J. 271 (1994)].

55. [Giles S. Rich, *The Relation Between Patent Practices and the Anti–Monopoly Laws* (pt. 4), 24 J. PAT. OFF. SOC'Y 328, 330 (1942)], at 245.

56. ProCD, Inc. v. Zeidenberg, 86 F.3d 1447 (7th Cir.1996) (non-commercial use restriction in shrink-wrap copyright license for computer program held valid and enforceable as a contractual limit on use).

57. Mallinckrodt, Inc. v. Medipart, Inc., 976 F.2d 700 (Fed.Cir.1992) (single use restriction in label license held valid and enforceable limit on grant of authority so that unauthorized acts may support suit for infringement).

58. For example, the payment may be for an activity that is not protectable by IP generally, happens not to have been protected by any particular piece of IP, or was formerly protected by some particular piece of IP.

59. Chief Justice Burger, writing for the majority of the Court, even allowed a promise to pay royalties to reach activity that was never patented so long as at the time the contract was executed it reflected both parties' reasoned assessment of the likelihood and payoff of the different states of the world under which patent rights might or might not materialize. Aronson v. Quick Point Pencil Co., 440 U.S. 257 (1979) (contract to pay royalty on a technology was enforceable even though no patent ever issued on the technology where at the time the contract was entered into the technology might have been patented and the contract provided a low royalty rate for the case where no patent issued and a higher rate for the case where a patent did issue). To be sure, there nevertheless remains deep skepticism in the courts towards contracts that happen to be tied to royalty payments beyond patent term, even though the economic justification for this skepticism is lacking. *See, e.g.*, Scheiber v. Dolby Labs., Inc., 293 F.3d 1014 (7th Cir.2002) (Posner, J.) (discussing at length the strength of the

do not stick to the basics will often err by finding that restrictive licensing arrangements, including tie-ins, constitute some sort of impermissible extension of IP rights.

Side Bar

Objectionable Narrowness of Claim

The Honorable Mr. Justice Robin Jacob*

I wish to throw open a problem that has long niggled me. Can a claim be too narrow and if not, does it matter? If it matters, what is the legal objection to the claim?

The paradigm and most general form of the claim I have in mind is: "the World[1] when supporting my invention?" A more concrete example runs as follows: claim 1 is to an improved steam whistle. It is a perfectly ordinary sort of claim, specifying by integers (or "features" in the new European terminology) the new whistle. But claim 2 is to a battleship fitted with the new steam whistle. Claim 3 is to a navy which includes one or more such battleships. Claim 4 is to a navy which includes any ship fitted with such a whistle. And so on.

It is not all that easy to find a good objection to such a claim. Assume that the whistle is new and non-obvious. Further, there are perfectly good instructions on how to construct the whistle. The skilled man already knows how to construct battleships and navies. The claim is not ambiguous. The ordinary everyday grounds of attack are irrelevant. Nor can you say that the claims are too wide. On the contrary, claims 2 and 3 are *narrower* than claim 1, which is itself unobjectionable. In England we used to have an objection that the claim was "not fairly based" on the matter disclosed in the specification. It was intended to be a codification of the Common Law. But it seldom worked—and when it did it was in circumstances where the claim was too wide. In the case of battleships and so on you could easily disclose the idea of fitting the whistle to a battleship. There is no recorded instance under the old law of a claim having been defeated for being too narrow. There is nothing in the European Patent Convention which seems directly on point and I know of no European case which deals with the point. I am not a US lawyer, but I

---

reasoning of the dissenting opinion of Justice Harlan in *Brulotte v. Thys* Co., 379 U.S. 29, 34 (1964) (Harlan, J., dissenting), but nonetheless following the majority opinion in that case in refusing to enforce a properly formed IP licensing contract—indeed, a settlement agreement from prior litigation—among commercial parties simply because some payments happened to extend beyond patent term at the request of the licensee). The case at the root of this line of precedent, *Brulotte*, involved a patentee who sold a hop-picking machine to farmers and who had several patents that would be infringed by such a machine. The machines were not sold for a simple one-shot price. Instead, payment was to be made over time and based on the actual economic advantage the machine generated for the farmer over alternative hop-picking approaches. Because this meant that payment would extend beyond the last of the patent terms, the Court held the contract to be unenforceable beyond that term in an opinion written by Justice Douglas, who was well known for his dislike of patents. In dissent, Justice Harlan pointed out that this holding would make unenforceable deals that were actually advantageous to farmers who either were liquidity constrained at the time of purchase or who were skeptical of the economic value of such capital equipment.

would be surprised if you have anything either.[2] The problem needs thinking out from first principles.

Should there be an objection that a claim is too narrow? Testing this pragmatically, how could it matter? Does a man who has claim 1 get any advantage from claims 2 or 3? He gets nothing by way of strengthened validity: if claim 1 fell, claims 2–4 would go with it.

However remedies may possibly be affected by this kind of claim, I do not suppose that the level of damages would be affected by infringement of claim 3 rather that claim 1 in the rather absurd steam whistle case. But a steam kettle might be different. You can have a claim to an improved kettle (an obvious example is the invention of the gadget which turned it off when it boiled). Can you have a claim to tea when made from water boiled in the improved kettle? If so the patentee would want to claim damages on (or perhaps profits from) the tea as well as the kettle. Could he sell his kettle with a limited license requiring royalties on tea?**

The last example is not so unreal. Some years ago the patentee of the device for electrostatic (paint) spraying was clever enough to include claims for the use of his device also. He made money not only from the selling of the device but from the licensing of its use—he charged by amount of paint consumed. That is close to charging for articles painted with his process.***

I have an uneasy feeling that somehow the patentee ought not to be better off by this sort of claim but that he could be. It may be that he could not get any more damages directly out of a court (he'd have trouble with me, for instance). But there would be other advantages: it would probably be easier to assert claims against people down the line (cafe proprietors) for instance. And the patentee might be in a better position vis-a-vis anti-trust law. For example, he would say, in charging royalties on tea (or painted articles), that he was doing no more than claiming them on what he had actually patented. Thus he would avoid any charge of "bundling" unpatented articles with patented ones. Moreover, it might be easier to justify what are in reality unreasonable royalty rates.

So I think there should be an objection. What is wanted is one directed at including within a claim that which has no, or no sufficient, nexus to what the patentee has really invented. Whether such an objection can be constructed out of existing laws is, I think, something of a challenge. I leave it to the reader to consider the problem further.

---

* Royal Courts of Justice, London, England. The views expressed herein are solely the views of the author and do not necessarily reflect those of the court. This SIDE BAR was written specially for PRINCIPLES OF PATENT LAW.

1. I suppose "the universe containing ... 'is even more general and even narrower.' "

2. If you do, let me know: rjacob@lix.compulink.co.uk.

** Casebook Editors' Note: compare Judge Rich's discussion reviewing and quoting the dissenting opinion of Justice Holmes in the *Motion Picture Patents* case, in which Holmes wrote that if you have a patent on a tea pot, he does not see why you can't license it by requiring purchase from you of the tea used in it. *See* Giles S. Rich, *The Relation Between Patent Practices and the Anti–Monopoly Laws*, 24 J. Pat. Off. Soc'y 241, 268–270 (1942) (quoting *Motion Picture Patents Co. v. Universal Film Mfg. Co.*, 243 U.S. 502, 521–523 (1917) (dissenting opinion by Mr. Justice O.W. Holmes, joined by Justices McKenna and Van Devanter)).

*** Casebook Editors' Note: compare Judge Rich's review of discussions about the "counters" argument to Chief Circuit Judge Lurton by Frederick P. Fish (founding partner in the firm Fish, Richardson & Neave) which succeeded in the *Button Fasteners Case*, and ultimately led to the opinion by *Justice* Lurton (the same man) in the *A.B. Dick* case, also argued by Fish. The "counters" argument offered the unpatented staples sold by the patentee at a substantial profit as convenient proxies used to count the number of infringing uses by purchasers of the patented stapling machine—which was sold by the patentee at or below cost. *See* Giles S. Rich, *The Relation Between Patent Practices and the Anti–Monopoly* Laws, 24 J. Pat. Off. Soc'y 241 (1942) (citing *Heaton–Peninsular Button–Fastener Co. v. Eureka Specialty Co.*, 77 Fed. 288 (C.C.A.6 1896) (Opinion by Lurton, C.J.) (the *"Button Fastener Case"*), and *Henry v. A.B. Dick Co.*, 224 U.S. 1 (1912) (Opinion by Lurton, J.)).

C. ANTITRUST

Around the beginning of the 20th century, with the growth of technology and industry, a large body of case law evolved to consider the enforceability of numerous patent license and sales practices. Early decisions were rooted in the then recently promulgated antitrust laws. Over time, antitrust approaches in the patent context, as in many others, have been limited to some extent by the so-called *Noerr–Pennington* doctrine, which may preclude antitrust liability where private parties legitimately solicit government action to exercise legal rights, even if such conduct may have an anticompetitive effect.[5] Nevertheless, antitrust issues continue to play an important role in the modern patent system and various antitrust theories have evolved in the context of patents. Several of these are discussed in some detail in the materials that follow.

Nobelpharma AB v. Implant Innovations, Inc.

141 F.3d 1059 (Fed.Cir.1998).

■ Before RICH, PLAGER and LOURIE, CIRCUIT JUDGES.

■ LOURIE, CIRCUIT JUDGE.

Nobelpharma AB and Nobelpharma USA, Inc. (collectively, NP) appeal from the judgment of the United States District Court for the Northern District of Illinois holding that ... (3) NP was not entitled to JMOL or, in the alternative, a new trial following the jury verdict in favor of 3I [Implant Innovations Inc.] on its antitrust counterclaim against NP, Dr. Per–Ingvar Branemark, and the Institute for Applied Biotechnology. We conclude that the district court did not err in ... denying NP's motion for JMOL or a new trial on the antitrust counterclaim. Accordingly, the decision of the district court is affirmed.

5. *See Eastern R. Conf. v. Noerr Motor*, 365 U.S. 127 (1961) and *United Mine Workers v. Pennington*, 381 U.S. 657 (1965). An example is where a patent applicant seeks to obtain a patent from the PTO or a patentee seeks to enforce his patent rights in federal court. This doctrine is grounded in First Amendment principles that place restraints on the exercise of Congressional power limiting the petitioning of government.

Background

Drs. Branemark and Bo–Thuresson af Ekenstam are the named inventors on the '891 patent, the application for which was filed in 1980 and claimed priority from a Swedish patent application that was filed in 1979. The patent claims "an element intended for implantation into bone tissue." This "element," when used as part of a dental implant, is placed directly into the jawbone where it acts as a tooth root substitute. The implants described and claimed in the patent are preferably made of titanium and have a network of particularly-sized and particularly-spaced "micropits." These micropits, which have diameters in the range of about 10 to 1000 nanometers or, preferably, 10 to 300 nanometers, allow a secure connection to form between the implant and growing bone tissue through a process called "osseointegration."

Branemark is also one of the authors of a book published in 1977, entitled "Osseointegrated Implants in the Treatment of the Edentulous Jaw Experienced from a 10–Year Period" (hereinafter "the 1977 Book"). As its title suggests, this book describes a decade-long clinical evaluation of patients who had received dental implants. The 1977 Book includes a single page containing four scanning electron micrographs (SEMs) of titanium implants that exhibit micropits. The caption describing these SEMs reads, in part: "Irregularities are produced during manufacturing in order to increase the retention of the implants within the mineralized tissue." 3I determined, based on measurements and calculations that it presented to the trial court, that the micropits shown in the 1977 Book have diameters within the range claimed in the '891 patent. However, the 1977 Book does not specifically refer to "micropits."

In preparing to file the Swedish patent application, af Ekenstam submitted a draft written description of the invention to the inventors' Swedish patent agent, Mr. Barnieske. This draft referred to the 1977 Book in the following translated passage:

> In ten years of material pertaining to titanium jaw implants in man, Branemark et al. [in the 1977 Book] have shown that a very high frequency of healing, as stated above, can be achieved by utilizing a carefully developed surgical technique and adequately produced implants.

However, Barnieske deleted all reference to the 1977 Book from the patent application that was ultimately filed in Sweden. Similarly, the 1977 Book is not mentioned in the U.S. patent application filed by Barnieske on behalf of Branemark and af Ekenstam.

In June 1980, while the U.S. patent application was pending, Branemark entered into an exclusive license agreement with NP covering the claimed technology. Barnieske kept NP informed of the prosecution of the U.S. patent application and received assistance from NP's U.S. patent agent. The '891 patent issued in 1982; NP has since asserted it in at least three patent infringement suits.

In July 1991, while Branemark was a member of NP's Board of Directors, NP brought this suit alleging that certain of 3I's dental implants infringed the '891 patent. 3I defended on the grounds of invalidity, unenforceability, and non-infringement. 3I also brought an antitrust counterclaim, based in part on the assertion that NP attempted to enforce a patent that it knew was invalid and unenforceable. Specifically, 3I alleged that when NP brought suit, NP was aware that the inventors' intentional failure to disclose the 1977 Book to the U.S. Patent and Trademark Office (PTO) would render the '891 patent unenforceable.

During its case-in-chief, NP introduced portions of a deposition of Branemark that apparently was conducted several years before this trial began in connection with a lawsuit involving neither NP nor 3I. NP also introduced into evidence portions of that deposition that were counter-designated for introduction by 3I. Branemark's deposition testimony included his admissions that one "could consider" the procedure used to manufacture the micropitted surface a trade secret, and "it might be" that there are details "important to making" the micropitted surface that are not disclosed in the patent. At the close of NP's case-in-chief, the district court granted 3I's motion for JMOL of invalidity and non-infringement. The court held that the patent was invalid under § 112, ¶ 1, for failure to disclose the best mode and that NP had failed to prove infringement. The court then denied NP's motion for JMOL on 3I's antitrust counterclaim, proceeded to inform the jury that the court had held the patent invalid, and allowed 3I to present the counterclaim to the jury.

After trial limited to the antitrust issue, the jury found in special verdicts, *inter alia*, that 3I had proven that (1) "the inventors or their agents or attorneys obtained the '891 patent through fraud," (2) NP "had knowledge that the '891 patent was obtained by fraud at the time this action was commenced against 3I," and (3) NP "brought this lawsuit against 3I knowing that the '891 patent was either invalid or unenforceable and with the intent of interfering directly with 3I's ability to compete in the relevant market." The jury awarded 3I approximately $3.3 million in compensatory damages, an amount the court trebled pursuant to section 4 of the Clayton Act, 15 U.S.C. § 15 (1994). The court declined to rule on whether the patent was unenforceable for inequitable conduct, concluding that its judgment of invalidity rendered the issue of enforceability moot.

The court then denied NP's renewed motion for JMOL on the counterclaim or, in the alternative, for a new trial on both the counterclaim and the infringement claim. In denying NP's post-verdict motion for a new trial on the issue of infringement, the district court again concluded that the patent was invalid for failure to disclose the best mode. The court also concluded that NP was not entitled to JMOL on the counterclaim because, inter alia, "NP, as the assignee of the patent, maintained and enforced the patent with knowledge of the patent's fraudulent derivation." The court denied NP's motion for a new trial on the counterclaim, holding, *inter alia*, that it did not err in its evidentiary rulings or in refusing to instruct the jury that in order to impose antitrust liability against NP, it must find NP's lawsuit "objectively baseless." Id. at 1264.

NP appealed to this court, challenging the district court's grant of 3I's motion for JMOL of invalidity and non-infringement and its denial of the post-verdict motion for JMOL or a new trial.

Discussion

* * *

B. Antitrust Liability

I.

After the jury returned its verdict in favor of 3I on its counterclaim that NP violated the antitrust laws by bringing suit against 3I, the court denied NP's motion for JMOL or, in the alternative, for a new trial under Fed.R.Civ.P. 50(b). In denying NP's motion, the district court held that the verdict was supported, *inter alia*, by the jury's factual findings that the patent was obtained through "NP's knowing fraud upon, or intentional misrepresentations to, the [PTO]" and that "NP maintained and enforced the patent with knowledge of the patent's fraudulent derivation" and with the intent of interfering directly with 3I's ability to compete in the relevant market. The court further held, based on these findings, that the jury need not have considered whether NP's suit was "objectively baseless."

In support of its position that the court erred in denying its renewed motion for JMOL, NP argues that there was a lack of substantial evidence to support the jury's findings that the patent was obtained through "fraud" and that NP was aware of that conduct when it brought suit against 3I. NP also argues that these findings, even if supported by substantial evidence, do not provide a legal basis for the imposition of antitrust liability. Finally, NP argues that it is entitled to a new trial because the court failed to instruct the jury that bringing a lawsuit cannot be the basis for antitrust liability if that suit is not "objectively baseless."

3I responds that the jury's explicit findings that the patent was procured through fraudulent conduct and that NP knew of that conduct when it brought suit were supported by substantial evidence, and that these findings provide a sound basis for imposing antitrust liability on NP. Responding to NP's arguments for a new trial, 3I argues that an "objectively reasonable" or "objectively baseless" jury instruction was not necessary because the district court required that 3I prove that NP had actual knowledge of the fraud when it brought suit and that even if such an instruction had been necessary, NP waived this argument by failing to propose a jury instruction relating to an "objectively baseless" standard. We agree with 3I that the court did not err in denying NP's motion for JMOL because substantial evidence supports the jury's findings that the patent was fraudulently obtained and that NP sought to enforce the patent with knowledge of its fraudulent origin. Similarly, the court did not err in denying NP's motion for a new trial because NP was not prejudiced by any legally erroneous jury instruction.

II.

* * *

Whether conduct in the prosecution of a patent is sufficient to strip a patentee of its immunity from the antitrust laws is one of those issues that clearly involves our exclusive jurisdiction over patent cases. It follows that whether a patent infringement suit is based on a fraudulently procured patent impacts our exclusive jurisdiction.

Moreover, an antitrust claim premised on stripping a patentee of its immunity from the antitrust laws is typically raised as a counterclaim by a defendant in a patent infringement suit. *See Argus Chem. Corp. v. Fibre Glass–Evercoat Co.*, 812 F.2d 1381, 1383 (Fed.Cir.1987) ("*Walker Process*, like the present case, was a patent infringement suit in which an accused infringer filed an antitrust counterclaim"). Because most cases involving these issues will therefore be appealed to this court, we conclude that we should decide these issues as a matter of Federal Circuit law, rather than rely on various regional precedents. We arrive at this conclusion because we are in the best position to create a uniform body of federal law on this subject and thereby avoid the "danger of confusion [that] might be enhanced if this court were to embark on an effort to interpret the laws" of the regional circuits. *Forman v. United States*, 767 F.2d 875, 880 n. 6 (Fed.Cir.1985). Accordingly, we hereby change our precedent and hold that whether conduct in procuring or enforcing a patent is sufficient to strip a patentee of its immunity from the antitrust laws is to be decided as a question of Federal Circuit law.[4] This conclusion applies equally to all antitrust claims premised on the bringing of a patent infringement suit. Therefore, *Cygnus*, 92 F.3d at 1161, *Loctite*, 781 F.2d at 875, and *Atari*, 747 F.2d at 1438–40, are expressly overruled to the extent they hold otherwise. However, we will continue to apply the law of the appropriate regional circuit to issues involving other elements of antitrust law such as relevant market, market power, damages, etc., as those issues are not unique to patent law, which is subject to our exclusive jurisdiction.

III.

A patentee who brings an infringement suit may be subject to antitrust liability for the anti-competitive effects of that suit if the alleged infringer (the antitrust plaintiff) proves (1) that the asserted patent was obtained through knowing and willful fraud within the meaning of *Walker Process Equipment, Inc. v. Food Machinery & Chemical Corp.*, 382 U.S. 172, 177 (1965), or (2) that the infringement suit was "a mere sham to cover what is actually nothing more than an attempt to interfere directly with the business relationships of a competitor," *Eastern R.R. Presidents Conference v. Noerr Motor Freight, Inc.*, 365 U.S. 127, 144 (1961); *California Motor Transp. Co. v. Trucking Unlimited*, 404 U.S. 508, 510 (1972) (holding that *Noerr* "governs the approach of citizens or groups of them ... to courts, the third branch of Government"). *See Professional Real Estate Investors, Inc. v. Columbia Pictures Indus., Inc.*, 508 U.S. 49, 62 n. 6 (1993) (PRE) (declining to decide "whether and, if so, to what extent *Noerr* permits the imposition of antitrust liability for a litigant's fraud or other misrepresentations").

---

4. Because precedent may not be changed by a panel, *see South Corp. v. United States*, 690 F.2d 1368, 1370 n. 2, 215 USPQ 657, 658 n. 2 (Fed.Cir.1982) (in banc), the issue of "choice of circuit" law set forth in this Section B.II. has been considered and decided unanimously by an in banc court consisting of Mayer, Chief Judge, Rich, Newman, Michel, Plager, Lourie, Clevenger, Rader, Schall, Bryson, and Gajarsa, Circuit Judges.

In *Walker Process*, the Supreme Court held that in order "to strip [a patentee] of its exemption from the antitrust laws" because of its attempting to enforce its patent monopoly, an antitrust plaintiff is first required to prove that the patentee "obtained the patent by knowingly and willfully misrepresenting facts[5] to the [PTO]." 382 U.S. at 177. The plaintiff in the patent infringement suit must also have been aware of the fraud when bringing suit. *Id.* at 177 & n. 6. The Court cited prior decisions that involved the knowing and willful misrepresentation of specific facts to the Patent Office: *Precision Instrument Manufacturing v. Automotive Maintenance Machinery Co.*, 324 U.S. 806 (1945) (misrepresenting that the inventor had conceived, disclosed, and reduced to practice the invention on certain dates); *Hazel–Atlas Glass Co. v. Hartford–Empire Co.*, 322 U.S. 238 (1944) (misrepresenting that a widely known expert had authored an article praising the invention); and *Keystone Driller Co. v. General Excavator Co.*, 290 U.S. 240 (1933) (involving an agreement to suppress evidence in the course of litigation). These cases indicate the context in which the Court established the knowing and willful misrepresentation test.

Justice Harlan, in a concurring opinion, emphasized that to "achiev[e] a suitable accommodation in this area between the differing policies of the patent and antitrust laws," a distinction must be maintained between patents procured by "deliberate fraud" and those rendered invalid or unenforceable for other reasons. *Walker Process*, 382 U.S. at 179–80. He then stated:

> [T]o hold, as we do not, that private antitrust suits might also reach monopolies practiced under patents that for one reason or another may turn out to be voidable under one or more of the numerous technicalities attending the issuance of a patent, might well chill the disclosure of inventions through the obtaining of a patent because of fear of the vexations or punitive consequences of treble-damage suits. Hence, this private antitrust remedy should not be deemed available to reach [Sherman Act] § 2 monopolies carried on under a nonfraudulently procured patent.

Id. at 180.

Consistent with the Supreme Court's analysis in *Walker Process*, as well as Justice Harlan's concurring opinion, we have distinguished "inequitable conduct" from *Walker Process* fraud, noting that inequitable conduct is a broader, more inclusive concept than the common law fraud needed to support a *Walker Process* counterclaim. *See, e.g., Hewlett–Packard Co. v. Bausch & Lomb Inc.*, 882 F.2d 1556, 1563 (Fed.Cir.1989); *FMC Corp. v. Manitowoc Co.*, 835 F.2d 1411, 1417–18, (Fed.Cir.1987); *J.P. Stevens & Co. v. Lex Tex Ltd.*, 747 F.2d 1553, 1559 (Fed.Cir.1984) ("Conduct before the PTO that may render a patent unenforceable is broader than common law fraud."). Inequitable conduct in fact is a lesser offense than common law

---

5. The alleged misrepresentation in that case involved the patentee's sworn statement "that it neither knew nor believed that its invention had been in public use in the United States more than one year prior to filing its patent application when, in fact, [it] was a party to prior use within such time." *Walker Process*, 382 U.S. at 174. The PTO does not currently require inventors to file a sworn statement regarding such knowledge or belief. See 35 U.S.C. § 115 (1994); 37 C.F.R. § 1.63 (1996).

fraud, and includes types of conduct less serious than "knowing and willful" fraud.

In *Norton v. Curtiss*, 433 F.2d 779, 792–94 & n. 12 (1970), our predecessor court explicitly distinguished inequitable conduct from "fraud," as that term was used by the Supreme Court in *Walker Process*. The court noted that

> the concept of "fraud" has most often been used by the courts, in general, to refer to a type of conduct so reprehensible that it could alone form the basis of an actionable wrong (e.g., the common law action for deceit.)....
> Because severe penalties are usually meted out to the party found guilty of such conduct, technical fraud[6] is generally held not to exist unless the following indispensable elements are found to be present: (1) a representation of a material fact, (2) the falsity of that representation, (3) the intent to deceive or, at least, a state of mind so reckless as to the consequences that it is held to be the equivalent of intent (scienter), (4) a justifiable reliance upon the misrepresentation by the party deceived which induces him to act thereon, and (5) injury to the party deceived as a result of his reliance on the misrepresentation. *See, e.g.*, W. Prosser, Law of Torts, §§ 100–05 (3d ed.1964); 37 C.J.S. Fraud § 3 (1943).

Id. at 792–93; *see also J.P. Stevens*, 747 F.2d at 1559 (citing *Norton*). The court then contrasted such independently actionable common law fraud with lesser misconduct, including what we now refer to as inequitable conduct, which "fail[s], for one reason or another, to satisfy all the elements of the technical offense." *Norton*, 433 F.2d at 793. Regarding such misconduct, "the courts appear to look at the equities of the particular case and determine whether the conduct before them ... was still so reprehensible as to justify the court's refusing to enforce the rights of the party guilty of such conduct." *Id.*

Inequitable conduct is thus an equitable defense in a patent infringement action and serves as a shield, while a more serious finding of fraud potentially exposes a patentee to antitrust liability and thus serves as a sword. *See Korody–Colyer Corp. v. General Motors Corp.*, 828 F.2d 1572, 1578 (Fed.Cir.1987); *see also Norton*, 433 F.2d at 796 ("Where fraud is committed, injury to the public through a weakening of the Patent System is manifest."). Antitrust liability can include treble damages. *See* 15 U.S.C. § 15(a) (1994). In contrast, the remedies for inequitable conduct, while serious enough, only include unenforceability of the affected patent or patents and possible attorney fees. *See* 35 U.S.C. §§ 282, 285 (1994). Simply put, *Walker Process* fraud is a more serious offense than inequitable conduct.

In this case, the jury was instructed that a finding of fraud could be premised on "a knowing, willful and intentional act, misrepresentation or omission before the [PTO]." This instruction was not inconsistent with various opinions of the courts stating that omissions, as well as misrepresentations, may in limited circumstances support a finding of *Walker Process* fraud. *See, e.g., Rolite, Inc. v. Wheelabrator Envtl. Sys., Inc.*, 958 F.Supp. 992, 1006 (E.D.Pa.1997) (finding an allegation of "fraud by omis-

---

6. We understand from the enumeration of elements that the term "technical fraud" was used by the court to mean common law fraud.

sion" in a *Walker Process* claim sufficient to overcome defendant's motion to dismiss); *United States v. Ciba–Geigy Corp.*, 508 F.Supp. 1157, 1170 (D.N.J.1979) (stating, in the context of *Walker Process*: "A misrepresentation is material if the patent would not have issued 'but for' the omission"). We agree that if the evidence shows that the asserted patent was acquired by means of either a fraudulent misrepresentation or a fraudulent omission and that the party asserting the patent was aware of the fraud when bringing suit, such conduct can expose a patentee to liability under the antitrust laws. We arrive at this conclusion because a fraudulent omission can be just as reprehensible as a fraudulent misrepresentation. In addition, of course, in order to find liability, the necessary additional elements of a violation of the antitrust laws must be established. *See Walker Process*, 382 U.S. at 178.

Such a misrepresentation or omission must evidence a clear intent to deceive the examiner and thereby cause the PTO to grant an invalid patent. *See id.* at 794 ("[T]he fact misrepresented must be 'the efficient, inducing, and proximate cause, or the determining ground' of the action taken in reliance thereon.") (quoting 37 C.J.S. Fraud § 18 (1943)). In contrast, a conclusion of inequitable conduct may be based on evidence of a lesser misrepresentation or an omission, such as omission of a reference that would merely have been considered important to the patentability of a claim by a reasonable examiner. *See J.P. Stevens*, 747 F.2d at 1559.[7] A finding of *Walker Process* fraud requires higher threshold showings of both intent and materiality than does a finding of inequitable conduct. Moreover, unlike a finding of inequitable conduct, *see, e.g., Molins PLC v. Textron, Inc.*, 48 F.3d 1172, 1178–79 (Fed.Cir.1995), a finding of *Walker Process* fraud may not be based upon an equitable balancing of lesser degrees of materiality and intent. Rather, it must be based on independent and clear evidence of deceptive intent together with a clear showing of reliance, i.e., that the patent would not have issued but for the misrepresentation or omission. Therefore, for an omission such as a failure to cite a piece of prior art to support a finding of *Walker Process* fraud, the withholding of the reference must show evidence of fraudulent intent. A mere failure to cite a reference to the PTO will not suffice.

IV.

The district court observed that the Supreme Court, in footnote six of its *PRE* opinion, "left unresolved the issue of how '*Noerr* applies to the ex parte application process,' and in particular, how it applies to the *Walker Process* claim." 930 F.Supp. at 1253 (quoting James B. Kobak, Jr., Professional Real Estate Investors and the Future of Patent–Antitrust Litigation, 63 Antitrust L.J. 185, 186 (1994)). The court also accurately pointed out that we have twice declined to resolve this issue. *See FilmTec Corp. v. Hydranautics*, 67 F.3d 931, 939 n. 2 (Fed.Cir.1995). Therefore, after reviewing three opinions from the Ninth and District of Columbia Circuit Courts

---

7. We recognize that this criterion reflects an older PTO rule in effect at the time the instant patent was prosecuted and that the current PTO rule defines materiality differently. *See Critikon, Inc. v. Becton Dickinson Vascular Access, Inc.*, 120 F.3d 1253, 1257 (Fed.Cir. 1997) (quoting 37 C.F.R. § 1.56(b)(2)(ii) (1996)).

of Appeals, the district court made its own determination that *PRE's* two-part test for a sham is inapplicable to an antitrust claim based on the assertion of a patent obtained by knowing and willful fraud. We do not agree with that determination. *PRE* and *Walker Process* provide alternative legal grounds on which a patentee may be stripped of its immunity from the antitrust laws; both legal theories may be applied to the same conduct. Moreover, we need not find a way to merge these decisions. Each provides its own basis for depriving a patent owner of immunity from the antitrust laws; either or both may be applicable to a particular party's conduct in obtaining and enforcing a patent. The Supreme Court saw no need to merge these separate lines of cases and neither do we.

Consequently, if the above-described elements of *Walker Process* fraud, as well as the other criteria for antitrust liability, are met, such liability can be imposed without the additional sham inquiry required under *PRE*. That is because *Walker Process* antitrust liability is based on the knowing assertion of a patent procured by fraud on the PTO, very specific conduct that is clearly reprehensible. On the other hand, irrespective of the patent applicant's conduct before the PTO, an antitrust claim can also be based on a *PRE* allegation that a suit is baseless; in order to prove that a suit was within *Noerr's* "sham" exception to immunity, an antitrust plaintiff must prove that the suit was both *objectively* baseless and *subjectively* motivated by a desire to impose collateral, anti-competitive injury rather than to obtain a justifiable legal remedy. *PRE*, 508 U.S. at 60–61. As the Supreme Court stated:

> First, the lawsuit must be objectively baseless in the sense that no reasonable litigant could realistically expect success on the merits. If an objective litigant could conclude that the suit is reasonably calculated to elicit a favorable outcome, the suit is immunized under *Noerr*, and an antitrust claim premised on the sham exception must fail. Only if challenged litigation is objectively meritless may a court examine the litigant's subjective motivation. Under this second part of our definition of sham, the court should focus on whether the baseless lawsuit conceals "an attempt to interfere *directly* with the business relationships of a competitor," through the "use [of] the governmental *process*—as opposed to the *outcome* of that process—as an anticompetitive weapon." ... Of course, even a plaintiff who defeats the defendant's claim to *Noerr* immunity by demonstrating both the objective and the subjective components of a sham must still prove a substantive antitrust violation. Proof of a sham merely deprives the defendant of immunity; it does not relieve the plaintiff of the obligation to establish all other elements of his claim.

Id. (footnotes and internal citations omitted). Thus, under *PRE*, a sham suit must be both subjectively brought in bad faith and based on a theory of either infringement or validity that is objectively baseless. Accordingly, if a suit is not objectively baseless, an antitrust defendant's subjective motivation is immaterial. *Id.* In contrast with a *Walker Process* claim, a patentee's activities in procuring the patent are not necessarily at issue. It is the bringing of the lawsuit that is subjectively and objectively baseless that must be proved.

V.

As for the present case, we conclude that there exists substantial evidence upon which a reasonable fact finder could strip NP of its immunity from antitrust liability. In particular, there exists substantial evidence that the 1977 Book was fraudulently kept from the PTO during patent prosecution.[8] The jury could reasonably have found that the 1977 Book was fraudulently withheld and that it disclosed the claimed invention. First, the jury could reasonably have concluded that Branemark, through his Swedish patent agent, Barnieske, withheld the 1977 Book with the requisite intent to defraud the PTO. The initial disclosure to Barnieske, provided by Branemark's co-inventor, af Ekenstam, indicated that the studies described in the 1977 Book verified the utility of the claimed invention. While Barnieske did testify that he did not recall his thoughts during the prosecution of the patent and that he would have submitted the 1977 Book to the PTO if he had considered it relevant, the jury was free to disbelieve him. Barnieske could not explain, even in retrospect, why he deleted all reference to the 1977 Book. Importantly, the 1977 Book was thought by at least one inventor to be relevant, as evidenced by the initial disclosure to the patent agent, but it was inexplicably not later disclosed to the PTO. Also, as the author of the 1977 Book and an inventor, Branemark presumably knew of the book's relevance to the invention and could have directed Barnieske not to disclose the book to the PTO. Thus, the jury could properly have inferred that Branemark had the requisite intent to defraud the PTO based on his failure to disclose the reference to the PTO. Such a scheme to defraud is the type of conduct contemplated by *Walker Process*.

Second, substantial evidence upon which a reasonable jury could have relied also indicates that the 1977 Book was sufficiently material to justify a finding of fraud. 3I's expert witness, Dr. Donald Brunette, testified that the SEMs of the 1977 Book depict dental implants having all the elements of the claims asserted by NP. Specifically, he explained how he had determined that the SEMs depict a "biologically flawless material" suitable for use as a dental implant. He also explained how he determined that the depicted micropits have diameters within the claimed range of approximately 10 to 1000 nanometers. Even Branemark, in this deposition testimony, conceded that it would not have been difficult to calculate the size of the micropits depicted in the 1977 Book, given the magnification factors provided in the captions to the SEMs. Accordingly, a reasonable jury could have found, based on the unambiguous claim language, that the 1977 Book anticipated the patent and that the examiner would not have granted the patent if he had been aware of the 1977 Book.

Third, the record indicates that a reasonable jury could have found that NP brought suit against 3I with knowledge of the applicants' fraud. A reasonable jury could have found that two of NP's then-officers, Dr. Ralph Green, Jr. and Mr. Mats Nilsson, were aware of the fraud based on Green's

---

8. Because we consider the conduct relating to the 1977 Book sufficient to uphold the jury's finding of fraud, we need not discuss 3I's allegations that Branemark fraudulently misrepresented the causal relationship between the claimed micropitted surface and osseointegration and fraudulently concealed the best mode of making and using the claimed invention from the PTO.

testimony that Nilsson told him: "[I]f the Patent Office did not receive a copy of [the 1977 Book], and if that were true, then we would have a larger problem and that was fraud." Green's testimony also indicates that NP was aware that the 1977 Book was highly material and, in fact, likely rendered the patent invalid. Green testified that he, Nilsson, and Mr. George Vande Sande obtained a legal opinion from NP's attorney, Mr. David Lindley, who indicated that if "we were to sue anyone on the patent we would lose in the first round.... [T]here was prior art, not the least of which was this textbook [the 1977 Book] that would invalidate the patent."

Regarding NP's motion for a new trial, we have concluded that the court's instructions to the jury regarding fraud, to which NP did not object, substantially comport with the law. Specifically, the court emphasized to the jury that to strip NP of its immunity from the antitrust laws, 3I "must prove that the '891 patent was fraudulently ... obtained by clear and convincing 'evidence.'" The court also pointed out that only "knowing, willful and intentional acts, misrepresentations or omission" may support a finding of fraud and that the jury should approach such a finding with "great care." As to reliance, the court instructed the jury that "[m]ateriality is shown if but for the misrepresentation or omission the '891 patent would not have been issued." These instructions were not legally erroneous.

Because we conclude that the finding of *Walker Process* fraud was supported by substantial evidence and was based upon a jury instruction that was not legally erroneous or prejudicial, we affirm the denial of NP's motion for JMOL. NP was properly deprived of its immunity from the antitrust laws under *Walker Process*, and it could not have benefited from additional jury instructions regarding *PRE* or *Noerr*. The court's refusal to so instruct the jury therefore does not require a new trial.

We have also considered NP's alternative arguments in support of its motion for a new trial, including its assertions that the district court erred in permitting Green to testify, in prohibiting Dr. Hodosh and Messrs. Vande Sande and Martens from testifying, in allowing 3I to present a theory of joint venture liability to the jury, and in impugning the credibility of NP's arguments before the jury. We do not find these arguments persuasive. The district court did not abuse its discretion or misapply the law of attorney-client privilege in making its evidentiary rulings, nor did it prejudice NP's substantive rights by allowing the jury to consider a joint venture theory of liability or by commenting on NP's arguments during the trial. Accordingly, the court did not abuse its discretion in denying NP's motion for a new trial.

Conclusion

The district court did not err ... in denying NP's motion for JMOL or a new trial on 3I's antitrust counterclaim. A reasonable jury, applying the correct law, could have found that the facts of this case were sufficient to constitute fraud within the meaning of *Walker Process*.

NOTES

1. *Patents, Market Power, and Monopolies.* The Supreme Court has defined market power as "the ability to raise prices above those that would be charged in a competitive market." *NCAA v. Board of Regents*, 468 U.S. 85, 108 n.38 (1984). Other definitions include "the ability of a single seller to raise price and restrict output," *Eastman Kodak Co. v. Image Technical Services, Inc.*, 504 U.S. 451, 464 (1992), and "the power to control prices or exclude competition." *United States v. E.I. du Pont de Nemours* Co., 351 U.S. 377, 391 (1956). In a patent context specifically, the Court has stated that "a patent holder has no market power in any relevant sense if there are close substitutes for the patented product. Similarly, a high market share indicates market power only if the market is properly defined to include all reasonable substitutes for the product." *Jefferson Parish Hospital Dist. No. 2 v. Hyde*, 466 U.S. 2, 38 n.7 (1984). Thus, a patent alone does not necessarily create market power and convert a patentee into a "prohibited monopolist." *Abbott Lab. v. Brennan*, 952 F.2d 1346, 1354 (Fed.Cir.1991). *See also C.R. Bard, Inc. v. M3 Sys., Inc.*, 157 F.3d 1340, 1368 (Fed.Cir.1998) ("It is not presumed that the patent-based right to exclude necessarily establishes market power in antitrust terms"); U.S. Department of Justice and Federal Trade Commission, *Antitrust Guidelines for the Licensing of Intellectual Property* § 2.2 (1995) ("Although the intellectual property right confers the power to exclude with respect to the *specific* product, process, or work in question, there will often be sufficient actual or potential close substitutes for such product, process, or work to prevent the exercise of market power"); HERBERT HOVENCAMP ET AL., IP AND ANTITRUST 4–9 (2002) (asserting that a "patent grant creates antitrust 'monopoly' only if it succeeds in giving me the exclusive right to make something for which there are not adequate market alternatives, and for which consumers would be willing to pay a monopoly prices"); WILLIAM M. LANDES AND RICHARD A. POSNER, THE ECONOMIC STRUCTURE OF INTELLECTUAL PROPERTY LAW 374–75 (2003) ("The *average* patent ... confers too little monopoly power on the patentee in a meaningful economic sense to interest a rational antitrust enforcer, and sometimes it confers no monopoly power at all") (emphasis in original); Edmund W. Kitch, *Elementary and Persistent Errors in the Economic Analysis of Intellectual Property*, 53 VAND. L. REV. 1727, 1729–30 (2000) ("Patents ... are the intellectual property right most plausibly characterized as a monopoly. But this is true only if the claims cover all of an economically relevant market, i.e., there is no alternative way for competitors to provide the same economic functionality to their customers without infringing the claims").

2. *The Basics of Antitrust.* Before considering the special case of patents and antitrust, it may help to consider some basics of antitrust law and policy in general:

> Antitrust law is designed to root out unreasonable restraints of trade and transactions that substantially lessen competition or tend to create monopoly. But it is well established that antitrust law does not prohibit market power as such. Nor does antitrust law prohibit a monopoly, if it is achieved by having lawfully outcompeted other competitors. As Judge Learned Hand famously put it, "The successful competitor, having been urged to compete, must not be turned upon when he wins." [United States v. Aluminum Co. of America, 148 F.2d 416, 430 (2d Cir.1945)]. And increasingly, antitrust law takes account of dynamic efficiency, as well as allocative efficiency. Even specific types of conduct that are often associated with restraining trade and that partly drove the passage of the federal antitrust laws—such as price discrimination, tying, and exclusive dealing—are not prohibited in every instance. Rather, such conduct generally is prohibited only to the extent it unreasonably restrains trade. Indeed, many such practices are procompetitive. The usual test for unreasonableness in this context is highly fact-dependent and generally is based on a "rule of reason" analysis as opposed to treating such conduct as an antitrust violation *per se*. Furthermore, antitrust law generally allows unilateral refusals to deal. As Justice Holmes and then-attorney Rich also pointed out, it makes no sense

to tell a property owner that she can absolutely exclude others on the one hand but that she cannot on the other hand be more generous and allow limited access to her property, without giving away the entire store.[15] Accordingly, restrictive licensing arrangements also generally are permitted. To use a simple analogy, as a homeowner, I have the right to exclude you entirely from my house or to sell you my house, lease you a room for a limited period of time, or grant you a limited easement across my front yard. Even though refusals to deal and restrictive licenses might technically restrain trade, they do not do so unreasonably and may by procompetitive.

F. Scott Kieff & Troy A. Paredes, *The Basics Matter: At the Periphery of Intellectual Property*, Stanford Law School John M. Olin Program in Law and Economics Working Paper No. 275, February 2004, at 7–8, available on-line at http://papers. ssrn.com/paper.taf?abstract _ id=501142 (some footnotes and citations omitted). *See also*, CHARLES J. GOETZ & FRED S. McCHESNEY, ANTITRUST LAW: INTERPRETATION AND IMPLEMENTATION (2nd 2002).

3. *The Role of Antitrust in Patent Law.* There are two instances, independent of each other, where the improper obtainment and exercise of patent rights can lead to a violation of the antitrust laws. These instances are known as *Walker Process* claims and *Handgards* claims. *See Walker Process Equipment, Inc. v. Food Machinery & Chemical Corp.*, 382 U.S. 172, 177 (1965); *Handgards, Inc. v. Ethicon, Inc.*, 601 F.2d 986 (9th Cir.1979). While both claims possess different elements and seek to address different problems, a crucial element common to both is proof that the patent owner has market power or is likely to obtain market power. This finding is essential under section 2 of the Sherman Act.

    a. *Walker Process Claim.* A *Walker Process* claim concerns the enforcement of a fraudulently obtained patent by a patent owner with market power. The fraud needed to prove a *Walker Process* violation is narrower and more serious than inequitable conduct fraud. The court in *Nobelpharma* noted that *Walker Process* fraud "must evidence a clear intent to deceive the examiner and thereby cause the PTO to grant an invalid patent," whereas "a conclusion of inequitable conduct may be based on evidence of a lesser misrepresentation or omission, such as omission of a reference that would merely have been considered important to the patentability of a claim by a reasonable examiner." *Nobelpharma* 141 F.3d at 1070. Thus, *Walker Process* fraud is but-for causation.

---

    15. From *Motion Picture Patents Co. v. Universal Film Mfg.*, 243 U.S. 502, 519–20 (Holmes, J., dissenting) (citations omitted):

    "I suppose that a patentee has no less property in his patented machine than any other owner, and that, in addition to keeping the machine to himself, the patent gives him the further right to forbid the rest of the world from making others like it. In short, for whatever motive, he may keep his device wholly out of use. So much being undisputed, I cannot understand why he may not keep it out of use unless the licensee, or, for the matter of that, the buyer, will use some unpatented thing in connection with it. Generally speaking, the measure of a condition is the consequence of a breach, and if that consequence is one that the owner may impose unconditionally, he may impose it conditionally upon a certain event. . . . The domination [over a material used in a patented device] is one only to the extent of the desire for the [patented device]."

See also Giles S. Rich, *The Relation Between Patent Practices and the Anti–Monopoly Laws* (pt. 4), 24 J. PAT. OFF. SOC'Y 328, 330 (1942) (citing same and providing English translation from Latin for the Justinian Maxim cited by Holmes: "[one] to whom the greater is lawful ought not to be debarred from the less as unlawful").

In addition to fraudulent conduct in obtaining the patent, a *Walker Process* plaintiff must prove enforcement of the patent or some other behavior that adversely affects the market (e.g., threatening to sue competitors) *and*, to satisfy Section 2 of the Sherman Act, evidence that the patent owner has market power or will likely obtain market power. *See* Note 1 for a discussion of market power.

b. *Handgards Claim.* A *Handgards* claim relates to the filing of an infringement suit that was "a mere sham to cover what is actually nothing more than an attempt to interfere directly with the business relationships of a competitor." The concern here is with the enforcement of a patent, though properly obtained (*i.e.*, no inequitable conduct or fraud), is believed by the patent owner to be invalid or not infringed.

To prove that an infringement suit is a "mere sham," an "antitrust plaintiff must show that the suit was both objectively baseless and subjectively motivated by a desire to impose collateral, anti-competitive injury rather than to obtain a justifiable legal remedy." *Nobelpharma*, 141 F.3d at 1071. *See Professional Real Estate Investors, Inc. v. Columbia Pictures Industries, Inc.*, 508 U.S. 49 (1993) (*PRE*). In *PRE*, the Supreme Court stated that "objectively baseless" means "that no reasonable litigant could realistically expect success on the merits." Regarding "subjective motivation," the focus is on "whether the baseless lawsuit conceals 'an attempt to interfere directly with the business relationships of a competitor,' through the 'use [of] the governmental *process*—as opposed to the *outcome* of that process—as an anticompetitive weapon.' " *Id.* at 60–1 (emphasis in original).

As with a *Walker Process* claim, a *Handgards* plaintiff, under Section 2 of the Sherman Act, must prove patent owner has market power or is likely to obtain market power.

4. *Reverse Payments.* "Reverse payments" are payments made by a patentee to potential competitors as part of an agreement not to challenge the validity of the patent or compete in the market for the patented product. The Federal Circuit has held that such payments should be judged under a "rule of reason" analysis. *In re Ciprofloxacin Hydrochloride Antitrust Litigation*, 544 F.3d 1323 (Fed.Cir.2008). *See also* Henry N. Butler and Jeffrey Paul Jarosch, *Policy Reversal on Reverse Payments: Why Courts Should Not Follow The New DOJ Position on Reverse–Payment Settlements of Pharmaceutical Patent Litigation*, 96 Iowa L. Rev. 57 (2010); Keith N. Hylton and Sungjoon Cho, *The Economics of Injunctive and Reverse Settlements*, 12 Am. L. & Econ. Rev. 181 (2010); Carl Shapiro, *Antitrust Limits to Patent Settlements*, 34 RAND J. Econ. 391 (2003).

5. *Patent Licensing and Antitrust.* It is common practice for patent owners to license their rights to third parties. Several reasons exist for this practice, including the patentee's inability or unwillingness to manufacture or sell the patented good or its desire to focus on a particular geographic market while permitting third parties to exploit other markets. As a general matter, economists encourage patent licensing because economic theory suggests the market will direct the patent right to the most productive or efficient entity. *See* U.S. Department of Justice and Federal Trade Commission, *Antitrust Guidelines for the Licensing of Intellectual Property* § 2.3 (1995) (recognizing pro-competitive effects of licensing)

Although licensing is generally encouraged, there are certain forms of licensing restrictions and practices that may raise potential antitrust concerns. For instance, (1) patent term extension provisions, *see Brulotte v. Thys Co.*; (2) field-of-use restrictions, *see Mallinckrodt, Inc. v. Medipart, Inc.*; (3) grantback clauses; and (4) cross-licensing and pooling arrangements. One form of the grantback clause requires the licensee to assign or license rights in any improvement the licensee may make to the licensor's claimed invention. Another form only precludes the licensee from suing the licensor from practicing the improvement. Grantback clauses, particularly nonexclusive clauses, can be pro-competitive and reduce transaction costs. But such clauses may also reduce or eliminate competition by licensees or reduce the incentive for licensees to invest in improvement activity. Cross-licensing and pooling arrangements, which are both responses to blocking patent scenarios, may also have pro-and anti-competitive effects. *See id.* § 5.5.

6. *Refusals To Deal.* It is well settled that a patent owner has no duty to practice his invention, and he is within his rights to suppress the invention. *See Continental Paper Bag Co. v. Eastern Paper Bag Co.*, 210 U.S. 405 (1908). And a patentee, perhaps with one caveat discussed in the next several paragraphs, may refuse to sell or license its patented product without violating the antitrust laws. *See In re Independent Service Organizations Antitrust Litigation v. Xerox*, 203 F.3d 1322, 1325 (Fed.Cir.2000) *(ISO II)* ("[n]o patent owner otherwise entitled to relief ... shall be denied relief or deemed guilty of misuse or illegal extension of the patent right by reason of his having ... refused to license or use any rights to the patent....").

But the more controversial notion is the refusal to license patented products to gain a monopoly in a market beyond the scope of the patent. The facts and holding of *ISO II* are worth exploring here. In *ISO II*, Xerox adopted a policy of not selling patented parts (for its copiers) to independent service organizations. (Xerox wanted to protect its ability to price discriminate, thus it sought to prevent arbitrage by refusing to sell patented components.) One such organization, CSU, charged that Xerox had violated the antitrust laws by leveraging its market power acquired through patent rights into a separate market for the service of Xerox's copiers. CSU relied on a footnote in *Eastman Kodak Co. v. Image Technical Services, Inc.*, 504 U.S. 451, 480 n. 29 (1992) *(Kodak I)*, wherein the footnote read: "[t]he Court has held many times that power gained through some natural and legal advantage such as a patent ... can give rise to liability if 'a seller exploits his dominant position in one market to expand his empire into the next.' " 203 F.3d at 1326–27. The Federal Circuit distinguished *Kodak I* by noting that it was a "tying case," and in the present case, there are no assertions "of illegally tying the sale of Xerox's patented parts to unpatented products." *Id.* at 1327. According to the Federal Circuit, the footnote in *Kodak I* "can be interpreted as restating the undisputed premise that the patent holder cannot use his statutory right to refuse to sell patented parts to gain a monopoly in a market beyond the scope of the patent." *Id.*

CSU also relied on the Ninth Circuit's holding in *Kodak II*, which was a decision from remand of *Kodak I*. Specifically, CSU relied on *Kodak II* for the proposition that the court must evaluate the patentee's subjective motivation for refusing to sell or license its patented products. The Federal Circuit "declined to follow" *Kodak II*, stating:

> We have held that "if a [patent infringement] suit is not objectively baseless, an antitrust defendant's subjective motivation is immaterial." [citing *Nobelpharma*]. We see no more reason to inquire into the subjective motivation of Xerox in refusing to sell or license its patented works than we found in evaluating the subjective motivation of a patentee in bringing suit to enforce that same right. In the absence of any indication of illegal tying, fraud in the [PTO], or sham litigation, the patent holder may enforce the statutory right to exclude others from making, using, or selling the claimed invention free from liability under the antitrust laws. We therefore will not inquire into his subjective motivation for exerting his statutory rights, even though his refusal to sell or license his patented invention may have an anticompetitive effect, so long as that anticompetitive effect is not illegally extended beyond the statutory patent grant.

203 F.3d at 1327–28. The court's analysis focuses heavily on the patent right, which includes the right not to practice or license the patented product. But does the court give insufficient weight to anticompetitive effects resulting from the refusal to deal?

The Supreme Court denied certiorari in *ISO II. See CSU, L.L.C. v. Xerox Corp.*, 531 U.S. 1143 (2001). In its brief arguing against a grant of certiorari, the government asserted that the extent of the inter-circuit conflict "is not clear," and that *ISO II* is subject to a narrower reading than that put forth by the ISOs. Thus, according to the government, the Supreme Court should permit this issue "to percolate further in the courts of appeals." Of note, however, is that that government said that it "would have serious concerns" if the Federal Circuit in *ISO II* "had clearly held that a refusal to sell or license property protected by a valid patent may never be an antitrust violation except in the circumstances of an illegal tying arrangement." ISO *II* has been criticized by some commentators as inconsistent with *Kodak I* and *Kodak II*, most notably, by the then Chairman of the Federal Trade Commission, Robert Pitofsky, in an address at the 2000 conference of the American Antitrust Institute. *See* www.ftc.gov/speeches/pitofsky/000615speech.htm.

7. *Applicable Law.* As a general proposition, when reviewing antitrust issues the Federal Circuit will apply the law of the regional circuit in which the district court sits. *Nobelpharma*, 141 F.3d at 1068. But in the interest of creating a uniform body of law, the court will apply its own law when the issue is one that involves the court's exclusive jurisdiction (*e.g.*, patent law). *Id.* ("Whether conduct in procuring or enforcing a patent is sufficient to strip a patentee of its immunity from the antitrust laws is to be decided as a question of Federal Circuit law."); *Midwest Indus., Inc. v. Karavan Trailers, Inc.*, 175 F.3d 1356, 1360 (Fed.Cir.1999) (*en banc*) ("*Pro–Mold* and *Nobelpharma* make clear that our responsibility as the tribunal having sole appellate responsibility for the development of patent law requires that we do more than simply apply our law to questions of substantive patent law."). So, for example, if there are antitrust claims arising out of allegedly improper use of copyrighted material and patented products, the Federal Circuit will apply regional circuit law to the former and Federal Circuit law to the latter. *See In re Independent Service Organizations*, 203 F.3d at 1325.

8. For a discussion on the intersection between patent law and antitrust, *see* Louis Kaplow, *The Patent–Antitrust Intersection: A Reappraisal*, 97 HARV. L. REV. 1815 (1984); Michael A. Carrier, *Unraveling the Patent–Antitrust Paradox*, 150 U. PA. L. REV. 761 (2001); WARD S. BOWAN, JR., PATENT AND ANTITRUST LAW: A LEGAL AND ECONOMIC APPRAISAL (1973). *See also* Department of Justice and Federal Trade Commission *Antitrust Guidelines for Licensing Intellectual Property*, issued April 6, 1995 at http://www.usdoj.gov/atr/public/guidelines/ipguide.htm and the FTC/DOJ Joint Hearings, which are available on-line at www.ftc.gov/opp/intellect/index.htm. Also, volume 69 of the Antitrust Law Journal is devoted the "Federal Circuit and Antitrust."

SIDE BAR

**At the Intersection of Patent Law and Antitrust Law—
Some Questions Raised, Some Questions Answered**

The Honorable Arthur J. Gajarsa and Joseph S. Cianfrani*

One of the biggest problems in applying antitrust law in the context of intellectual property has been the "bad press" patents have received as "monopolies." Patents have historically been criticized for providing a governmental sanction to the "odious monopolies that cause people to have to pay more for virtually every item they use."[1] The Supreme Court has even stated at one time that it must recognize and accommodate the "differing policies of the patent and antitrust laws."[2] However, the benefits of the patent system in rewarding innovation and thereby promoting competition have since been realized by both the courts and Congress. The Federal Circuit has stated that "because the underlying goal of the antitrust laws is to promote competition, the patent and antitrust laws are complementary."[3] Despite the acceptance of patent law as a complement to the antitrust laws, much disagreement still exists over at what point bad faith litigation to enforce patents becomes a violation of § 2 of the Sherman Act. In many patent infringement cases, especially where inequitable conduct is asserted as a defense, a § 2 allegation of attempted monopolization and bad faith litigation is also routinely asserted.

There are many reasons a patent infringement defendant might want to bring an antitrust counterclaim. The counterclaim generally serves to raise the stakes of the suit to the plaintiff and may thereby improve the settlement posture of the defendant. Also, a defendant asserting a claim of bad faith patent enforcement before a jury may be able to erode the patent holder's "aura of respectability" in the minds of the jurors. While some have argued that the threat of a § 2 antitrust counterclaim is a significant chill on the efforts of patentees to vindicate the public interest by bringing patent infringement suits, the probability of winning on an antitrust counterclaim has historically been quite low.

The case law applying the antitrust laws to bad faith patent enforcement is somewhat sparse. In 1965, the Supreme Court reversed a decision of the 7th Circuit in *Walker Process v. Food Machinery Corp.*, 382 U.S. 172 (1965), and announced that attempts to enforce a fraudulently obtained patent could qualify as a § 2 antitrust violation if the other requisite elements could also be proven. However, many questions were not addressed by the Supreme Court. What did it mean to fraudulently obtain a patent? What is the difference between inequitable conduct and an antitrust violation? How did the *Walker Process* decision affect *Noerr–Pennington* immunity? At the time, these issues did not seem to directly concern the Supreme Court which stated only that it was furthering a "paramount interest in seeing that patent monopolies spring from backgrounds free from fraud or other inequitable conduct and that such monopolies are kept within their legitimate scope."[4]

The Federal Circuit has since clarified some of these issues. In *Argus Chemical Corp. v. Fibre Glass–Evercoat Co.*, 812 F.2d 1381 (Fed.Cir.1987), the Federal Circuit stated that there is a difference between inequitable conduct and conduct that will support a § 2 antitrust violation. The level of proof necessary to support a finding of inequitable conduct did not necessarily also rise to a level that would support an antitrust counterclaim. Chief Judge Nies pointed out in additional views that in her view there are three levels of patent misconduct: (1) inequitable conduct making a patent unenforceable; (2) inequitable conduct making the patent unenforceable and justifying attorney's fees; and (3) inequitable conduct sufficient to prove a § 2 Sherman Act claim. *Id.* at 1387 (Nies, J. additional views). However, there was no explanation of what types of conduct justified each category. In *Atari Games v. Nintendo of America*, 897 F.2d 1572 (Fed.Cir.1990), the Federal Circuit explained that the difference between inequitable conduct and an antitrust violation depended on whether the antitrust counterclaimant was using the misconduct to protect itself from a claim of infringement, or whether it was using misconduct as an offensive weapon to obtain treble damages, the latter requiring a more stringent standard of proof. *Id.* at 1576. Inequitable conduct depends on the intent of the applicant and the materiality of the offense.[5] Thus, while some may still argue that a particularly severe act of gross negligence could constitute misuse if the level of materiality is sufficiently high, the Federal Circuit has made clear that even gross negligence cannot rise to the level of fraud under *Walker Process. See Argus Chem. Corp.*, 812 F.2d at 1384.

In addition to fraud before the Patent and Trademark Office (PTO), there are other types of actions that can also constitute an antitrust violation. Even though there may have been no fraud before the PTO, if the patentee knew the patent was invalid and still attempted to enforce the patent, an antitrust counterclaim may still lie against the plaintiff.[6] This was the fact situation presented in *Handgards*. While the 9th Circuit recognized the patentee's right to "test the validity of their patents in court through actions against alleged infringers" under the *Noerr–Pennington* doctrine, the 9th Circuit stated that "infringement actions initiated and conducted in bad faith contribute nothing to the furtherance of the policies of either the patent law or the antitrust law." *Id.* at 993.

A third type of antitrust counterclaim related to *Handgards* and *Walker Process* claims was brought in *Loctite Corp. v. Ultraseal Ltd..*, 781 F.2d 861 (Fed.Cir.1985). In *Loctite*, the Federal Circuit extended § 2 liability to situations in which the patent was valid, but was asserted against a device the plaintiff knew to be noninfringing. On remand, the Federal Circuit instructed the district court to determine whether bad faith had been found by clear and convincing evidence despite the fact that the general standard for proving the elements of an antitrust claim is preponderance of the evidence. The court stated that there was a need "to erect such barriers to antitrust suits as are necessary to provide reasonable protection for the honest patentee who brings an infringement action." *Id.* at 876.

The most recent controversy in defining the application of the antitrust laws to intellectual property involved so-called "sham" litigation and the *Noerr–Pennington* doctrine. The *Noerr–Pennington* doctrine derives its name from two cases that essentially stand for the proposition that under the 1st Amendment, petitions to influence government action are generally exempt from the antitrust laws unless the activity is merely a "sham."[7] Under the "sham" exception to the *Noerr–Pennington* doctrine, activity "ostensibly directed toward influencing governmental action" does not quality for immunity if it "is a mere sham to cover . . . an attempt to interfere directly with the business relationship of a competitor." *Noerr*, 365 U.S. at 144. As such, any legal attempts to influence the government are automatically immune from antitrust attack under Noerr unless the litigation is so baseless as to fit within the "sham" exception. In *United Mine Workers of America v. Pennington*, 381 U.S. 657 (1965), *Noerr* immunity was extended to all petitions before government in legislative or administrative proceedings.

The Supreme Court's most recent review of the *Noerr–Pennington* doctrine came in 1993 in the case of *Professional Real Estate Investors v. Columbia Pictures Indus., Inc. (PRE)*, 508 U.S. 49 (1993). In *PRE*, the Supreme Court was asked to determine when a litigation was a "sham" under the *Noerr–Pennington* doctrine and therefore not entitled to antitrust immunity. The decision had serious implications for *Walker Process* type claims which had long since viewed fraud before the PTO as qualifying as "sham" activity.

In *PRE*, the Supreme Court announced a two part test that determined whether a litigation rose to the level of a "sham." This two part test consisted of an objective prong and a subjective prong. Defining the objective prong of the test, the Court stated that "an objectively reasonable effort to litigate cannot be a sham regardless of subjective intent." *PRE*, 508 U.S. at 57. An antitrust plaintiff must therefore satisfy a court that the litigation was objectively baseless before any evidence may be introduced on the defendant's subjective intent. This would apparently overrule the methodology used in the *Handgards* and *Loctite* cases which treated the question as purely subjective. *Walker Process* and its progeny were not directly addressed by the Supreme Court in *PRE*, and were only indirectly mentioned in what some have called "mysterious footnote 6." The Federal Circuit has since interpreted footnote 6 to mean that *PRE* left unanswered how *Noerr* affects *Walker Process* claims.[8] It is logical to assume that enforcement of a patent known to be procured by fraud would pass the objective part of the *PRE* test since objectively, a litigant could not hope to prevail in such an action absent some error by the court.

The Federal Circuit recently addressed the relationship of *Walker Process* and *PRE* in the case of *Nobelpharma AB v. Implant Innovations, Inc.*, 129 F.3d 1463 (Fed.Cir.1997) [superseded by 141 F.3d 1059 (Fed.Cir. 1998)]. In that case, the Federal Circuit again stated that *Walker Process* was not affected by *PRE* because the two cases each provide their own legal grounds under which a patentee may be stripped of *Noerr* immunity. The court finally laid to rest its interpretation of *PRE*'s effect on *Walker Process* stating that:

> PRE and Walker Process provide alternative legal grounds on which a patentee may be stripped of its immunity from the antitrust laws; both legal theories may be applied to the same conduct. Moreover, we need not find a way to merge these decisions. Each provides its own basis for depriving a patent owner of immunity from the antitrust laws. The Supreme Court saw no need to merge these separate lines of cases and neither do we.

Id. at 1471–72. In *Nobelpharma*, the Federal Circuit has made clear its position that *Walker Process* claims may be prosecuted as they have always been, and that *Walker Process* is unaffected by *PRE* because *PRE* provides alternative legal grounds upon which to base an antitrust counterclaim. While the dissent in *Nobelpharma* seems to dispute what types of conduct are sufficient to constitute "fraud" within the meaning of *Walker Process*, both the majority and the dissent seem to agree that *Walker Process* antitrust claims are alive and well despite the perceived "narrowing" of the "sham" exception in *PRE*.

Although the question of how *PRE* applies to *Walker Process* claims appears to be settled for now, whether the same reasoning also applies to *Handgards* and *Loctite* type cases has been left open. As is common in law, answering one question raises others. This question, at least for now, seems to have been left for another day.

* Arthur J. Gajarsa is a Circuit Judge on the United States Court of Appeals for the Federal Circuit. Joseph S. Cianfrani is a partner with Knobe, Martens, Olson & Bear, Newport Beach, California; and former law clerk to U.S. Circuit Judge Arthur J. Gajarsa. The views expressed herein are solely those of the authors and do not necessarily reflect those of the United States Court of Appeals for the Federal Circuit. This *SIDE BAR* was written specially for PRINCIPLES OF PATENT LAW.

1. The Law Times, Oct. 21, 1871, p. 424.

2. *Walker Process v. Food Mach. Corp.*, 382 U.S. 172, 179 (1965) (Harlan, J. concurring).

3. *See Loctite Corp. v. Ultraseal Ltd..*, 781 F.2d 861 (Fed.Cir.1985).

4. *Walker Process*, 382 U.S. at 350 (quoting *Precision Instrument Mfg. v. Automotive Maintenance Mach. Co.*, 324 U.S. 806, 816 (1945)).

5. *See Critikon, Inc. v. Becton Dickinson Vascular Access, Inc.*, 120 F.3d 1253, 1256 (Fed.Cir.1997).

6. *Handgards, Inc. v. Ethicon, Inc.*, 601 F.2d 986, 994–96 (9th Cir.1979).

7. *See Eastern R.R. Presidents Conference v. Noerr Motor Freight, Inc.*, (*Noerr*) 365 U.S. 127 (1961); *United Mine Workers of Am. v. Pennington*, 381 U.S. 657 (1965).

8. *See Carroll Touch v. Electro Mechanical Sys.*, 15 F.3d 1573, 1583 (Fed. Cir.1993); *see also FilmTec v. Hydranautics*, 67 F.3d 931 (Fed.Cir.1995).

D. THE DOCTRINES OF FIRST SALE, IMPLIED LICENSE, AND REPAIR/RECONSTRUCTION

Acts cannot infringe unless they are carried out "without authority." 35 U.S.C. § 271(a)—even though they may otherwise fall within the scope of a patent claim and within the reach of the right to exclude granted by 35 U.S.C. § 154. The clearest grant of authority is an express grant from the patentee in a contract in the form of a license, *see McCoy v. Mitsuboshi Cutlery, Inc.*, 67 F.3d 917 (license is a contract governed by ordinary principles of state contract law), or even a settlement agreement following a suit for patent infringement, *see Gjerlov v. Schuyler Labs*, 131 F.3d 1016 (Fed.Cir.1997) (suit for breach of settlement agreement is matter of state contract law and treble damages under patent law are unavailable).

But the grant of authority need not be express. At least three distinct theories exist to create authority by less than express contractual grant: (1) the legal doctrine of first sale, under which a patentee's first sale of the patented article may be deemed to include an implied term giving buyers a license to use and sell that article; (2) the equitable doctrine of implied license, under which a patentee's acquiescence or conduct, or the general equities of the circumstances, may permit a court to imply a license granting some or all of the patentee's authority; and (3) the legal doctrine of repair/reconstruction, which is really a corollary to the first-sale doctrine, and which permits the buyer with a license to use and sell a particular article purchased from the patentee (the license obtained under the first-sale doctrine) to repair, but not reconstruct, that particular article. Each of these theories is discussed below.

The First–Sale Doctrine

A long-established default rule derived from general principles of contract law has applied in the context of contracts for the sale of patented articles to provide that absent clouding circumstances or agreement to the contrary, a patentee's unrestricted voluntary introduction of a patented article into commerce may prevent the patentee from exercising his right to exclude others from the article so introduced. This is the so-called first-sale doctrine.

The first-sale doctrine can be traced back to cases as old as *Adams v. Burke* 84 U.S. (17 Wall.) 453 (1873); but most of the first-sale cases of the 20th century rely heavily on *United States v. Univis Lens Co.*, 316 U.S. 241 (1942). Readers of these cases must remember that *Univis* was written in the tumultuous legal environment of the post-depression New Deal era during which intellectual property laws and other industrial practices were markedly affected by new and expanding antitrust doctrines. The 1952 Patent Act revived contributory infringement, substantially narrowed patent misuse, and thereby statutorily overruled cases doctrinally related to *Univis. See Dawson, discussed supra.* And it is likely that *Univis* would be decided differently today. *See* 35 U.S.C. § 271(d)(5) (1994); *State Oil v. Khan*, 522 U.S. 3 (1997); *Virginia Panel Corp. v. MAC Panel Co.*, 133 F.3d 860 (Fed.Cir.1997). In fact, the strict holding of *Univis* may be rather narrow. The law before *Univis* essentially was that when the patentee sells a chattel, as the Supreme Court stated in *Adams v. Burke*, "in the essential nature of things, ... [t]he article passes without the limit[s] of the monopoly." 84 U.S. at 456. As previously mentioned, this is the origin of the first-sale doctrine. Thus, a strict reading of *Univis* suggests that the most the case can be considered to have accomplished is a slight expansion of this doctrine in that the first-sale doctrine may be equally applicable whether "the patented article [is sold] in its completed form or ... before completion for the purpose of enabling the buyer to finish and sell it." *Univis*, 316 U.S. at 252.

The Supreme Court recently returned to *Univis* in *Quanta Computer, Inc. v. LG Elec., Inc.*, 553 U.S. 617 (2008). In that case, the Court held that the exhaustion doctrine applies to method patents and that "[t]he authorized sale of an article that substantially embodies a patent exhausts the patent holder's rights and prevents the patent holder from invoking patent law to control postsale use of the article." *Quanta*, 553 U.S. at 638. *See also Transcore, LP v. Electronic Transaction Consultants Corp.*, 563 F.3d 1271 (Fed. Cir. 2009). For a more in-depth discussion of *Quanta* and its implications see F. Scott Kieff, Quanta v. LG Electronics: *Frustrating Patent Deals by Taking Contracting Options off the Table?*, 2007–2008 Cato S. Ct. Rev. 315 (2008). The Federal Circuit noted in a subsequent case that *Quanta* did not disturb the territoriality requirement of the first sale rule. *Fujifilm Corp. v. Benun*, 605 F.3d 1366, 1371 (Fed.Cir.2010). Thus, the authorized sale of a patented product in a foreign country does not trigger the first sale doctrine for purposes of later importation into the United States.

While the first-sale doctrine's precise logical underpinnings remain somewhat obscured, a careful parsing of the interaction between patent and contract law reveals a great deal. One might view the first-sale doctrine as a legal doctrine governing certain terms that may be reasonably implied into a contract for sale of a patented article. Implied-in-fact terms may be found as a matter of interpretation from evidence of the parties' intent. Implied-in-law terms are a matter of construction and are imposed in the interest of fairness to ensure that both parties receive the rights for which they bargained. Under this view, the first-sale doctrine operates by making explicit the terms that are implicit in most simple contracts for sale of goods: typical customers buy goods so they may enjoy their use without restriction. The first-sale doctrine operates to imply a term into the contracts for such sales of patented goods giving buyers a license to use and sell that article. Of course, restrictive terms expressly included in a contract for sale of a patented article may operate under standard principles of contract law to permit the patentee to in some way restrict even the buyer in a first sale, unless those terms are objectionable on grounds applicable to contracts in general—for example, if they violate a rule of positive law; if they are adhesionary, or unconscionable. See *Mallinckrodt v. Medipart*, 976 F.2d 700 (Fed.Cir.1992) (single use restriction in label license held valid and enforceable limit on grant of authority so that unauthorized acts may support suit for infringement); *ProCD, Inc. v. Zeidenberg*, 86 F.3d 1447 (7th Cir.1996) (non-commercial use restriction in shrink-wrap copyright license for computer program held valid and enforceable as a contractual limit on use); *B. Braun Medical, Inc. v. Abbott Laboratories*, 124 F.3d 1419, 1426 (Fed.Cir.1997) (stating that the "exhaustion doctrine ... does not apply to an expressly conditional sale or license. In such a transaction, it is more reasonable to infer that the parties negotiated a price that reflects only the value of the 'use' rights conferred by the patentee. As a result, express conditions accompanying the sale or license of a patented product are generally upheld"). For example, the following language was held to be a legitimate condition on the doctrine of first sale:

> Opening this package or using the patented cartridge inside confirms your acceptance of the following license/agreement ... Following the initial use, you agree to return the empty cartridge only to Lexmark for remanufacturing and recycling.

Arizona Cartridge Remanufacturers Association, Inc. v. Lexmark International Inc., 290 F.Supp.2d 1034 (N.D.Cal.2003).

Students should also note that the first-sale doctrine is sometimes called the "exhaustion" doctrine, particularly outside of the United States. As the SIDE BAR that follows discusses, the exhaustion or first-sale doctrine varies from country to country or country to "economic community" (e.g., European Union). Importantly, TRIPS is silent on the exhaustion issue. *See* TRIPS Article 6 ("nothing in this agreement shall be used to address the issue of the exhaustion of intellectual property rights"). Yet the issue of exhaustion is particularly germane to the issue of pharmaceutical patents, parallel imports, and the availability of patented drugs to developing countries.

Although the term "exhaustion" is used frequently in the literature, especially abroad, as a synonym for the term "first sale," there is some debate about whether the terms are really equivalent. As Judge Rich pointed out, the term "exhaustion" may not be accurate:

> "Patent exhaustion" is a misnomer. To think clearly about this fact, one must consider two things: (1) the meaning of "exhaustion"; and (2) the nature of the patent right. "Exhaustion" means the state of having been drained or used up completely. It assumes there was something there to begin with that could be used up. The patent right, as recognized by the Supreme Court in *Bloomer v. McQuewan*, 55 U.S. (14 How.) 539 (1852), and as more recently defined in 35 U.S.C. § 154, is the right to exclude others from making, using, offering for sale, or selling the patented invention. When a patentee of a patented article sells the article, how is he in any way exercising his patent right to exclude others from doing so? Clearly he is not. If he is, therefore, not using it at all—let alone using it up—how can he be exhausting it?

Luncheon Address by Judge Giles S. Rich, Sixth Annual Conference on International Intellectual Property Law & Policy, Fordham University, April 16, 1998. Importantly, the distinction here is not merely a matter of which label is more descriptive. The substantive implication of the two terms is different. The term "exhaustion" conveys a position of relatively weak strength that has been achieved, and so in the literature is often used to describe a rule that operates as immutable—no opt-out possible. The term "first-sale" merely conveys that an initial transaction has taken place, and so in the literature is often used to describe a rule that operates merely as a default—it applies absent agreement otherwise.

SIDE BAR

National and International Exhaustion of Patent Rights

Christopher Heath*

1. Around the globe there is no uniform rule on national or international exhaustion in the field of patent law. Germany with its clear-cut stance on national exhaustion as an inherent limitation of patent law on the one side,[1] and no recognition of international exhaustion on the other,[2] comes close to the US doctrine in this respect. Such a clear distinction between (recognised) national and (not recognised) international exhaustion can also be found in other countries, e.g., France.[3] A number of countries recognise international exhaustion to some extent (see below).

The reasons for recognising exhaustion as such differ. Even wider is the doctrinal gap when it comes to arguing international exhaustion. On the level of national law, basically three approaches are conceivable.

(1) The first is the English common law approach.

Under English common law,

> it is open to the patentee, by virtue of his statutory monopoly, to make a sale *sub modo*, or accompanied by restrictive conditions which would not apply in the case of ordinary chattels; ... the imposition of these conditions in the case of sale is not presumed, but, on the contrary, a sale having

occurred, the presumption is that the full right of ownership was meant to be vested in the purchaser while ... the owner's rights in a patented chattel would be limited, if there is brought home to him the knowledge of conditions imposed, by the patentee or those representing the patentee, upon him at the time of sale.[4]

In other words, the patentee is allowed to impose limited conditions when selling his goods, while an ordinary vendor of goods may not.

Apparently this rule applies both to domestic sales and sales abroad. Parallel importation of goods produced abroad is permissible if these goods were produced with the consent of the domestic patent owner and subsequently sold without any clear notice of restriction. This rule applies regardless of the existence of any patent rights in the exporting country[5] and was recently confirmed by a decision of the English Patents Court.[6] This so-called "common law exhaustion" basically leaves the matter to contract law and the proper notification of commerce. Should the patentee not wish his patented products manufactured abroad to be imported and sold, he has to impose a contractual restriction at the point of sale. In order for such restriction to survive further acts of sale, proper notification has to be given also to subsequent purchasers. In the absence thereof, such purchasers can assume to obtain the same rights as with the purchase of other, non patented articles: The right to commercialise the purchased item by export, import, sale or distribution. The same rules now apply to Japan according to a Supreme Court decision[7]:

"If the patented products were marketed abroad, then it can be naturally expected that such goods may be imported into Japan if the patentee puts such goods into circulation abroad without any reservations at the time of transfer. The transferee or any other subsequent purchaser is understood to have purchased the product without any restrictions that might apply to such products in Japan."

This approach has the benefit of simplicity and may therefore be particularly attractive to developing countries whose judiciary might not yet be so familiar with intellectual property rights. The decision of lawfulness of importation depends on the presence or absence of a proper notice on the goods, in other words something easy to detect both for purchasers and judges.

(2) Outside the sphere of common law, the question of international exhaustion is perceived as a basic question of intellectual property law, too important to be left to contractual stipulation. Approaches (2) and (3) therefore interpret the rules for exhaustion from absolute, in-built limits to the patent system. Approach (2) is taken by the European Court of Justice (ECJ) for the intra-European rule of exhaustion. According to the ECJ,

"the substance of a patent right lies essentially in according the inventor an exclusive right to put the product on the market for the first time, thereby allowing him a monopoly in exploiting his product and enabling him to obtain the reward for his creative effort, without, however, guaranteeing such reward in all circumstances ... it [is] for the holder of the patent to decide, in the light of all circumstances, under what conditions he would market his product, including the possibility of marketing it in a [state] where the law did not provide patent protection ..."[8]

In other words, exhaustion under this rule depends on the patentee's consent to market the patented products abroad, regardless of whether he had or could have obtained a patent right there or not. While the latter possibility is becoming increasingly remote due to the TRIPS requirements, it is not uncommon for a patentee to produce or sell his goods in countries where no patent right has been obtained. Decisive for this theory, however, is the voluntary choice to market the goods, and the Thai provision says as much. The rule does not apply if the products are manufactured without the patentee's consent, e.g., in countries where no patent has been obtained, or where a third party produces under a compulsory license.[9] The ECJ's approach of consented marketing has also been adopted by a number of other countries which permit international exhaustion on such condition, e.g., Thailand,[10] Argentina,[11] and South Africa.[12]

(3) The third theory takes the function of patent law as guaranteeing a reward under a monopolistic right as a starting point. The patentee should receive one chance to market his product under monopolistic conditions, thereby exhausting the patent's potential value with respect to such product. This rule is different from above (2), as it does not allow for parallel importation in cases where the goods have been marketed by the patentee in a country where no patent protection has been obtained. Here, the patentee could not market his products under monopolistic conditions (as everyone else can also manufacture the goods lawfully), and therefore could not have obtained the rewards under a monopolistic right. Theory (3) further does not necessarily require the patentee's consent in marketing the products in order to exhaust the right. If, say, the patentee has decided to commercialise his patent by selling it to an unrelated third party, he has received one form of compensation for the right in toto, and therefore also for all goods subsequently produced under such right. Theory (3) was advanced by the Tokyo High Court (modified on appeal by the Supreme Court to theory (1)):

"There is no difference to the case of national exhaustion where the patent holder puts goods into circulation abroad and can determine the prices for the patented products of his own free will as a remuneration for the disclosure of his invention. This means, the opportunity of the patent holder to receive compensation for the disclosure of his invention is limited to one opportunity. Under the material aspect of the above-cited doctrine of national exhaustion in accordance with economic development, it does not make any particular difference whether the putting into circulation takes place within this country or abroad."[13]

Theory (3) is also preferable for the fact that it does not require the patentee to apply for patent protection in every country where future marketing is likely—often, the commercial potential of an invention cannot be properly assessed at the filing date, or even within the priority period prescribed by the Paris Convention. This approach has found some following in academic circles, particularly in Japan[14] and Germany,[15] though has not been endorsed by legislation or jurisdiction in any country yet.

2. It has been mentioned above that English common law basically makes no distinction between national and international exhaustion, save perhaps for the fact that the validity of a condition that would limit

national exhaustion has never quite been tested. Theories that base national exhaustion on the inherent limits of patent rights (theories (2) and (3) above) nonetheless sometimes strive to distinguish between the domestic and foreign marketing of patented products. The reasons brought forward in this respect are basically these:

(1) The costs of a patentee to register the patent right in different countries;[16]

(2) The patentee's legitimate right to obtain maximum profits for his right by separating national markets;[17]

(3) The Japanese Supreme Court has further argued that a domestic exhaustion would not necessarily correspond to an international one because "it cannot be argued that all those selling the product under a parallel patent would receive a double reward, or that it may qualify as an act of use of the domestic patent right";[18]

(4) The Appeal Court of Paris found that under French law, the absence of any contractual limit on the patented product did not indicate any form of consent, and further that the doctrine of international exhaustion did not have any clear basis in national or community law;[19]

(5) Further, the Swiss Supreme Court decided by majority that allowing for parallel imports in the field of patents would require an explicit legal provision;[20]

(6) A marketing abroad would not give the domestic patentee the same reward as a domestic marketing.[21]

The argument under (1) would be convincing if patent rights in other countries were rendered worthless by the possibility of parallel imports. Yet this is not the case. Even when allowing parallel imports, patent rights in other countries would still serve their main—and perhaps only—purpose of granting absolute rights against the use, manufacture and sale of infringing products originating from other sources. Yet it is questionable if it is the function of patent law—and perhaps intellectual property rights in general—to protect the patentee against his own dealings, which would amount to the protection of economic self-denial. Argument (2) above either stands to reason (any patentee should be allowed to fully enjoy those rights granted under patent law) or is unconvincing. Since patents have always been a compromise between the inventor and the public at large for the purpose of stimulating inventive activity, system and structure of patent rights has never been "unlimited". It suffices to note that patent rights are limited in time—20 years from the filing date. Therefore, interpreting patent law in conformity with its underlying purpose would be more consistent with the system of patent rights than an interpretation that disregarded the patent system as a proper compromise between the patentee and the public.

The decisions of the Japanese and French courts are certainly clear in stating that the rules for national exhaustion could not be applied to goods marketed abroad. Yet the material question is *why* this should be so, and this question is left unanswered by the court.[22]

Finally, the Swiss Supreme Court is certainly correct in pointing out that a clear provision in the law would help the interpretation of the exhaustion question. Still, the verdict reached begs two questions. First, why the lack of any clear provision in the law should not lead to the assumption that parallel imports are *permitted* rather than prohibited. Only this would be in accordance with the principle that intellectual property rights as exceptions to the rules of free competition cannot be interpreted beyond the scope granted by law. In the absence of any provision to the contrary, and in the absence of any result that can be deduced from the rationale of patent law as such, the rules of free competition should be applied. Second, one could argue that a decision to limit free international trade requires an unambiguous statement in the form of legislation, particularly for member states of the WTO agreement.

As to the argument of insufficient reward, the law is only interested in the opportunity for reward as such, not the actual sum of money. For that reason it is not important if the patentee could make a better or worse profit by the sale in another country, but that the patentee had the chance to market the product under the same conditions as domestically, that is, under the same monopolistic right. This is not the case if the product was sold abroad by the patentee or with his consent, yet without the existence of a patent right there.

3. A different line has been taken by some courts and academics in arguing that the international exhaustion of patent rights would either be a contravention of the principle of territoriality as expressed in Art. 4[bis] of the Paris Convention,[23] or even the TRIPS Agreement.[24]

As to the Paris Convention, domestic patent rights, so the argument goes, because of their territorial scope cannot be limited by acts committed outside such scope. In other words, a Japanese patent could not become exhausted because patented products were marketed in Germany, which is outside the scope of the Japanese patent right. Such an argumentation, however, misinterprets the intention of wording of Art. 4[bis] of the Paris Convention.[25] Historically, some countries—particularly France—made the existence of a French patent right obtained under the priority of a foreign patent right dependent upon the existence of the latter.[26] Other countries refused to grant a subsequently filed patent a longer term of protection than that of the original one (Brazil, France, U.S.A., Belgium, Italy, and Spain). This principle of dependence of patents, also applied to trade marks under the Madrid Agreement, was found undesirable and indeed contravening the original spirit of the Paris Convention. For this reason, Art. 4[bis] of the Paris Convention was adopted at the Brussels Conference in 1901, and subsequently clarified at the Washington Conference in 1911.[27] The present wording makes clear that the independence of patents concerns "grounds for invalidation and forfeiture and as regards their normal duration". However, there is nothing in the provision to suggest that developments abroad cannot influence patent rights at all. It is now standard practice that patents are only granted on condition of absolute novelty. Absolute novelty, however, requires taking into account the world-wide state of the art, not only the national one. In a similar fashion, national patent law may decree that foreign acts of marketing may have an effect on the exercise of the patent right with regard to particular goods marketed abroad. Article 4[bis] of the Paris Convention is concerned with the existence of a domestic patent right, while the exhaustion doctrine concerns acts that "exhaust" further economic exploitation with regard to specific goods marketed under a patent. Under the exhaustion doctrine, the limits of economic exploitation are defined, and the Paris Convention in fact never dealt with this problem in the first place.

Also the well-known US precedent Emile Boesch v. Albert Gräff[28] is a misguided application of the rule on the independence of patents (although preceding the respective provision in the Paris Convention): Here, the Supreme Court held that the exhaustion of patent rights over goods sold abroad (here: Germany) could not automatically trigger the exhaustion of the corresponding patent rights in the US. This is correct, and Art. 4[bis] Paris Convention would teach as much. But the approach is incorrect: Domestic patent rights in the importing country are not automatically exhausted because they have been exhausted abroad, but rather: Marketing abroad may be a circumstance that could trigger domestic exhaustion. It is not that domestic patent rights must follow what the foreign law of the exporting country decrees, but rather that domestic law must be interpreted in order to determine what acts abroad, if any, can trigger domestic exhaustion. Domestic law is and must be independent of any limitations of the law abroad if and because acts of foreign marketing may be taken into account in order to determine domestic exhaustion. In the US decision, the goods had been marketed in Germany under a compulsory license the conditions of which did not apply to the US market. Under these circumstances, the patentee had not consented to the marketing of the goods, and this could well be a reason for denying domestic exhaustion. The US court, however, did not interpret domestic law, but (correctly) ruled that foreign exhaustion could not impose domestic one. But it is a doubtful precedent to argue that no acts abroad can trigger domestic exhaustion of patent rights: The US courts have never examined a case where the goods were marketed abroad by the patentee or with his consent, after all.

As to the TRIPS Agreement, it would be expected from a treaty covering all aspects of intellectual property rights that the matter of parallel importation is also included. Not so. Although it was recognised that parallel importation would indeed fit nicely within the objective of international free trade advocated by GATT,[29] agreement could not be reached to allow generally for parallel importation. In order to overcome this stalemate situation, Art. 6 of the TRIPs Agreement now provides that "for the purposes of dispute settlement under this Agreement, ... nothing ... shall be used to address the issue of exhaustion of intellectual property rights." The dispute settlement mechanism in general allows every member to bring an action against another state if there is insufficient compliance with the principles of the GATT/WTO Agreement in general. Yet according to Art. 6, whatever national stance is taken on the matter of exhaustion, no complaint can be heard in this respect. While this certainly means that no country can be put in the dock for deciding for or against international exhaustion, it does not necessarily mean that the TRIPs Agreement as such would not favour either one or the other position.[30]

As this exception relates to procedural matters, it only means that members of the GATT/WTO Agreement cannot be made subject to sanctions, no matter how they decide on international exhaustion. Nevertheless, the agreement may favour explicitly or implicitly a certain solution to the issues of international exhaustion and parallel imports.

One aspect that has been particularly mentioned in this respect is the obligation of members to grant patentees a specific right of importation along with other exclusive rights such as for production and sale. However, to conclude that "[t]his means that substantive patent law under the TRIPs Agreement amounts to a barrier to international exhaustion",[31] is both rash and wrong. An importation right is certainly useful once it comes to preventing counterfeit products entering the country. Without an importation right, the patentee would have to wait until the counterfeit products are put on the market in order to obtain relief. This is certainly undesirable and inadequate. However, it is difficult to argue that the right of importation should follow different rules from the rights of production and sale. The importation right concerns an aspect of economic exploitation equal to that of production and sale. If, under the classical doctrine of exhaustion, further rights in commercial exploitation are exhausted upon the first sale of a patented article, and if such exhaustion is also assumed when such patented article is marketed abroad, then the exhaustion relates to all aspects of other commercial exploitation including importation. The correctness of this argument becomes particularly obvious in the case of re-imports. If a patented article is put on the market in, say, Japan, by the patentee or with his consent, then further acts of economic exploitation are "exhausted". If the patentee therefore would not be able to prevent further acts of sale and distribution, then it is difficult to see how and why the patentee should be able to exert any influence over this article once it has been exported into another country and subsequently re-imported. If a patentee is granted a bundle of rights under his patent, such as production, sale and importation, then upon the act of first sale, the whole bundle becomes "exhausted" once and for all. Consequently, no importation right can be invoked later on for the very article that has been marketed previously, regardless where this took place.[32]

Concerning the doctrine of common law exhaustion as outlined by the above-mentioned English and Japanese decisions, there is nothing in the TRIPS Agreement to suggest that the importation right cannot be made subject to certain conditions such as giving proper notice to the public about any restrictions in this respect.

The above analysis would only merit a different evaluation once national patent rights were rendered worthless by permitting parallel importation. Such might be the case if the patentee could not object to the importation of products produced in third countries where no patent rights were obtained, since, in theory and practice, this would require a patentee to apply for patents in all possible countries in order to receive at least once proper compensation for putting the goods on the market. However, as yet, no country has permitted parallel imports under these circumstances.

As to the general principles of the GATT/TRIPS Agreement, it should be borne in mind that, first, the GATT/WTO Agreement as such is concerned with removing rather than erecting trade barriers, and, second, that the TRIPS Agreement, far from giving one-sided favours to intellectual property owners, is meant to promote "the mutual advantage of producers and users of technological knowledge in a manner conducive to social and economic welfare, and to a balance of rights and obligations" (Art. 7 TRIPS Agreement).

To read a prohibition of parallel imports into an agreement that is meant to "ensure that measures and procedures to enforce intellectual property rights do not themselves become barriers to legitimate trade", requires a lot of imagination indeed. The so-called Doha Declaration on Public Health that was adopted by the WTO Member States on 14 November 2001 has clarified that "the effect of the provisions in the TRIPs Agreement that are relevant to the exhaustion of intellectual property rights is to leave each member free to establish its own regime for such exhaustion without challenge, subject to the MFN and national treatment provisions". While it is quite clear that industrialised countries wanted to protect their own industries from competition by their own goods marketed elsewhere, "it is astonishing that the WTO Agreement should still consider it to be compatible with fair world trade for consumers in different countries to be played off against each other."[33]

4. As international agreements make no mention of the question of exhaustion and parallel imports, answers have to be found within the framework of domestic law. Particularly developing countries which are in the course of overhauling their patent systems in order to properly comply with TRIPS, have inserted specific provisions mostly in favour of international exhaustion. While this has not been received well by the pharmaceutical industry, the USTR and the European Commission in Brussels, it is a completely legitimate decision for any country to take.

---

* Head of the Asian Department, Max–Planck Institute for Foreign and International Patent, Copyright and Competition Law, Munich, Germany. This SIDE BAR was written specially for PRINCIPLES OF PATENT LAW.

1. German Reichsgericht, 26 March 1902, RGZ 51, 139—"Duotal".

2. German Bundesgerichtshof, 3 June 1976, 8 IIC 64 [1977]—"Tylosin".

3. Tribunal de Grande Instance de Paris, 3 May 1997—"Dupont de Nemours"; Cour d'Appel de Paris, 29 May 1999—"Phyteron".

4. Privy Council, *National Phonograph Company of Australia Ltd. v. Menck*, 3 February 1911, [28] R.P.C. 229, 248.

5. English Court of Appeal, *Betts v. Willmott*, [1871] LR 6 Ch. App. 239.

6. English Patents Court, *Roussel–Uclaf v. Hockley International*, 9 October 1995, [1996] R.P.C. 441.

7. Japanese Supreme Court, 1 July 1997, 29 International Review of Industrial Property and Copyright Law (IIC) 331 [1998]—"BBS Car Wheels III".

8. ECJ, *Merck & Co. v. Stephar*, 14 July 1981, 13 IIC 70 [1982]; confirmed by

ECJ, *Merck & Co. v. Primecrown*, 5 December 1996, 28 IIC 184 [1998].

9. ECJ, *Pharmon v. Hoechst*, 9 July 1985, 17 IIC 357 [1986].

10. Sec. 36(3)(vii) Thai Patent Act as of 27 March 1999.

11. According to Sec. 36 Argintinean Patent Act, "The right granted by any patent shall not have effect against: . . . (c) any person that acquires, uses, imports or commercialises in any way the product patented or obtained by the patented process, *once such product has been lawfully marketed in any country*". This provision, of course, goes way beyond the above consent rule, as it basically obliges any patentee to obtain patents in all countries of the world to obtain proper protection. In the author's opinion, this is difficult to justify within the framework of the TRIPs Agreement.

12. The relevant provision cannot be found in South Africa's Patent Act, but in Sec. 15C(a) of the Medicines and Related Substances Control Act of 1965, as amended in 1997. The amendment has not yet come into force due to questions of the compatibility of compulsory licensing provisions with the TRIPs requirements.

The explicit purpose of the 1997 amendment was to ensure the proper supply of the South African population with pharmaceuticals, particularly against the AIDS virus.

13. Tokyo High Court, 23 March 1995, 27 IIC 550 [1996]—"BBS Car Wheels II".

14. E.g., N. *Tatsumi, Shôhin ryûtsû to chiteki zaisanken no hôteki kôsei,* 21 Tokkyo Kenkyû 52 [1996]; N. *Nakayama, Tokkyo seihin no heikô yunyû,* 1064 Jurist 31 [1995]; Y. *Tamura, Heikô yunyû to chiteki zaisanken,* 1064 Jurist 45 [1995].

15. H.-G. *Koppensteiner, Urheber- und Erfinderrechte beim Parallelimport geschützter Waren,* RIW/AWD 1971, 357; C. *Heath, Zur Paralleleinfuhr patentierter Erzeugnisse,* RIW 1997, 541.

16. D. *Reimer, Der Erschöpfungsgrundsatz im Urheberrecht und gewerblichen Rechtsschutz unter Berücksichtigung der Rechtsprechung des Europäischen Gerichtshofs,* GRUR Int. 1972, 221.

17. F.K. *Beier, Zur Zulässigkeit von Parallelimporten patentierter Erzeugnisse,* GRUR Int. 1996, 1.

18. Japanese Supreme Court, 1 July 1997, 29 IIC 334 [1998]—"BBS Wheels III".

19. Cour d'Appel de Paris, 29 May 1999—"Phyteron".

20. Swiss Supreme Court, decision 4C.24/99 of 7 December 1999. The decision was reached by a verdict of 3 to 2.

21. Argued particularly by *Bernhardt/Krasser, Lehrbuch des Patentrechts,* 4th ed. 1986, 582.

22. Interestingly enough, it is also left unanswered by a good many academics, e.g., H. *Isay, Patentgesetz,* 4th ed. 1926, 221 and J. *Kohler, Handbuch des deutschen Patentrechts,* 1900, 455.

23. F.K. *Beier, Zur Zulässigkeit von Parallelimporten patentierter Erzeugnisse,*

GRUR Int. 1996, 1. N. P. de Carvalho, The TRIPS Regime of Patent Rights, Kluwer Law International 2002.

24. J. *Straus,* in Beier/Schricker (eds.), *From GATT to TRIPS,* 191 (1986).

25. *See* F.K. *Beier, Territoriality of Trademark Law and International Trade,* 1 IIC 48 [1970].

26. S. *Ladas, Patents, Trademarks and Related Rights,* 505 *et seq.* (1975).

27. Actes de la Conference de Bruxelles 311 (1901); Actes de la Conference de Washington 22, 49 (1911).

28. U.S. Supreme Court, 3 March 1890, Emile Boesch v. Albert Gräff, 133 U.S. 787–792.

29. T. *Cottier, The Prospects for Intellectual Property in GATT,* 28 CMLR 401 (1991). Some authors even go as far as arguing that the interpretation of the TRIPs Agreement in the light of the overall WTO structure should lead to the conclusion that the free trade rule should prevail: S.K. *Verma, Exhaustion of Intellectual Property Rights and Free Trade,* 29 IIC 534 [1998].

30. M. *Bronckers, The Impact of TRIPs: Intellectual Property Protection in Developing Countries,* 31 CMLR 1267 (1994); J. *Straus,* in Beier & Schricker (eds.), *From GATT to TRIPs,* 191 (1996).

31. J. *Straus* at 192.

32. This result seems to be common ground by now. See, e.g., M. *Bronckers, The Exhaustion of Patent Rights Under WTO Law,* 32 (5) Journal of World Trade 137 [1998].The above example of a re-import product is only meant to highlight the fact that the importation right in general is part of the bundle of economic rights which may become exhausted upon first sale. So to speak, it does not lead a life of its own to become exhausted only upon first importation.

33. Ullrich (above fn. 31) 385.

The first-sale doctrine is sometimes mistakenly referred to as creating a type of implied license. While this is conceptually correct in a certain way—the first-sale doctrine may create a limited implied license to use—it is also misleading because the term "implied license," as it is used in patent law, is a term of art that happens to have evolved through the case law in a quite different context from the first-sale doctrine. Indeed, the differences between these two doctrines are several and important. The first-sale doctrine can be viewed as a legal doctrine providing a default rule under which certain terms that may be reasonably implied are inserted into a contract for sale of a patented article. The doctrine steps in to add a term that otherwise does not exist. In contrast, the doctrine of implied license is really an equitable doctrine governing certain types of estoppel. This doctrine is used to prevent, or bar, the patentee from asserting a right that otherwise does exist. For instance, an implied license to make or use a patented device may arise when the patentee does not sell the device but sells a component designed to be used to construct the device.

The Doctrine of Implied License

The implied-license doctrine in patent law refers to long-established rules derived from general principles of equity that have been applied in certain circumstances to create implied licenses under a patent. After all, in the context of a patent case, an implied license is simply a waiver of the patentee's right to exclude, and "[a]s a result, courts and commentators relate that implied licenses arise by . . . equitable estoppel (estoppel in pais), or by legal estoppel." *Wang Laboratories v. Mitsubishi Electronics*, 103 F.3d 1571, 1578–82 (Fed.Cir.1997). Therefore, any conclusion of implied license may only be reached if required by an analysis that is guided by these general principles of equity.

In the case of *Wang Labs. v. Mitsubishi Elecs.*, 103 F.3d 1571 (Fed.Cir. 1997), the court held there to have been an implied license that was in the nature of equitable, rather than legal, estoppel. According to the court, "[l]egal estoppel refers to a narrower category of conduct encompassing scenarios where a patentee has licensed or assigned a right, received consideration, and then sought to derogate from the right granted." 103 F.3d at 1581. The court found there to be an implied license by equitable estoppel because:

> The record shows that Wang tried to coax Mitsubishi into the SIMM market, that Wang provided designs, suggestions, and samples to Mitsubishi, and that Wang eventually purchased SIMMs from Mitsubishi, before accusing Mitsubishi years later of infringement. We hold, as a matter of law, that Mitsubishi properly inferred consent to its use of the invention of Wang's patents.

103 F.3d at 1582. Under the doctrine of equitable estoppel explored in *Wang*, the focus is on the entire course of conduct and requires that conduct of the patentee led the other to act.

In *Met–Coil Systems Corp. v. Korners Unlimited, Inc.*, 803 F.2d 684, 686 (Fed.Cir.1986), the Federal Circuit recited "two requirements for the grant of an implied license by virtue of a sale of nonpatented equipment used to practice a patented invention. . . . First, the equipment involved must have no noninfringing uses. Second, the circumstances of the sale must 'plainly indicate that the grant of a license should be inferred.'" *Id.* Thus, in *Bandag, Inc. v. Al Bolser's Tire Stores*, 750 F.2d 903 (Fed.Cir. 1984), a case involving the purchase of a retreading machine from a going-out-of-business sale of a franchisee of the patentee, the Federal Circuit held that the district court had erred in each facet of its reasoning by failing to consider the countervailing evidence. On appeal, once the countervailing evidence was included in the analysis, the Federal Circuit concluded that the retreader failed to meet its burden of showing implied license under the doctrine of equitable estoppel and, therefore, concluded that there was no license as a matter of law. Concerning the first prong of the district court's analysis, alternative noninfringing uses, one can agree that the use should at least be commercially viable. But it seems equally improper to conclude that the use must be in the same market as, and cost-competitive with, the patented method. In *Bandag*, for example, the alternative use was as disassembled pieces for sale in the market for replacement parts. Concerning the second prong, the circumstances of the sale, the court in *Bandag* found insufficient nexus between the retreader and the patentee because there was no evidence the retreader knew of or relied upon any of the patentee's conduct until after the time that the retreader acted to his detriment.

In contrast, in *Met–Coil Systems*, the Federal Circuit affirmed the district court's holding that a patent owner's unrestricted sale of a machine useful only in practicing the claimed inventions presumptively carries with it an implied license under the patent. The patentee in *Met–Coil* attempted to distinguish *Bandag* by relying on its affirmative acts, as patentee, to ward off any impression that the grant of a license should be implied. The Federal Circuit rejected this distinction, because the warnings were made *after* the purchase of the machines. Whereas *Bandag* held there was no evidence of reliance, *Met–Coil* held that the district court's conclusion of reliance was not unreasonable given the lack of relevant evidence showing no reliance. *See also, Glass Equip. Dev., Inc. v. Besten, Inc.*, 174 F.3d 1337, 1342 (Fed.Cir.1999) (reversing district court's finding of implied license because district court "improperly limited its analysis of the existence of noninfringing uses to the time of the summary judgment hearing" and "applied an overly restrictive profitability or 'commercial viable' requirement to the noninfringing uses").

The Doctrine of Repair/Reconstruction

The doctrine of repair/reconstruction (permissible repair versus impermissible reconstruction) is a corollary to the first-sale doctrine. Remember, the patent gives the right to exclude anyone from making, using, selling, or offering for sale the patented article. Under the first-sale doctrine, the buyer may be given authority to use and sell the particular article. Thus, the repair/reconstruction doctrine further unpacks the details of the first-sale doctrine and permits the buyer to *repair* the article, as part of his right to use and even sell it, but does not give the buyer the authority to *reconstruct* the patented article any more than the purchasing of one patented article from a patentee gives the buyer the authority to independently manufacture or sell large numbers of the patented articles in competition with the patentee. The case law on repair/reconstruction is not generally considered to give the clearest guidance to parties, especially when considered in the context of the first-sale cases discussed above. Read the following *Side Bar*, and the case and notes that follow and then decide for yourself.

To Repair or Not to Repair? That Is the Question

The Honorable Arthur J. Gajarsa and Evelyn Mary Aswad*

The patent statute provides that "whoever without authority makes, uses, offers to sell or sells any patented invention, within the United States . . . during the term of the patent therefor, infringes the patent." 35 U.S.C. § 271(a). Patentees are typically considered to have given to the purchasers of their patented devices the authority to use such devices. Such authority generally also includes the ability to repair the device. However, this grant of authority does not include an unrestricted license to "make" another device. At some point, repairs may be so extensive that they constitute a reconstruction, or unauthorized "making," of the patented device. Developing a framework for a principled analysis of what constitutes permissible repair instead of impermissible reconstruction has presented a great challenge to courts for many years.

In the first Supreme Court case dealing with the repair/reconstruction distinction, the Court held that the replacement of cutting knives from a patented wood planing machine when the knives wore out after several months constituted permissible repair.[1] The Court's reasoning, which is still considered authoritative on this subject, was that:

> When the wearing or injury [to the patented device] is partial, then repair is restoration, and not reconstruction. . . . And it is no more than that, though it shall be a replacement of an essential part of a combination. . . . But if, as a whole, [the combination patented device] should happen to be broken, so that its parts could not be readjusted, or so much worn out as to be useless, then a purchaser cannot make or replace it by another, but he must buy a new one. . . . But if another constituent part of the combination is meant to be only temporary in the use of the whole, and to be frequently replaced, because it will not last as long as the other parts of the combination, its inventor cannot complain [that the purchaser replaces the temporary parts].[2]

About thirty years later, the Supreme Court held that alleged repairs were really reconstructions.[3] The plaintiffs had patents for a metallic cotton-bale tie that was comprised of a metal band and a buckle. The buckle was stamped with the words "Licensed to use once only." The band would remain around the bale of cotton until it was cut, at which point the tie was discarded. The defendants purchased the buckle and band as scrap-iron, recreated the bands, and sold new ties. The Court reasoned that this was reconstruction because "[t]he band was voluntarily severed by the consumer at the cotton-mill because the tie had performed its function of confining the bale of cotton in its transit. . . . Its capacity for use as a tie was voluntarily destroyed."[4] Basically, it appears that the Court believed the patented device could only be used once and any repair after this first and final use was a reconstruction.[5]

In 1961, the Supreme Court faced the issue of whether replacing the spent fabric which formed the top of convertible cars constituted infringing reconstruction of a patent that covered the combination of flexible top fabric, supporting structures, and a mechanism for sealing the fabric against the car.[6] This patent covered a combination of unpatentable parts. In determining whether reconstruction or repair had occurred, the Court seemed to rely on a "practical test" espoused by Learned Hand: " 'The (patent) monopolist cannot prevent those to whom he sells from . . . reconditioning articles worn by use, unless they in fact make a new article.' "[7] In concluding that replacing the spent fabric was permissible repair, the Court explained:

> No element, *not itself separately patented*, that constitutes one of the elements of the combination patent is entitled to patent monopoly, however essential it may be to the patented combination and no matter how costly or difficult replacement may be. . . . Mere replacement of individual unpatented parts, *one at a time, whether the same part repeatedly or different parts successively*, is no more than the lawful right of the owner to repair his property.[8]

The Court therefore clearly rejected the "heart of the invention" test, i.e. analyzing whether the most essential element is being replaced. The Court also seemed to say that there would be no impermissible reconstruction by replacing components of a patented device unless the individual component was separately patented or the entire device was rebuilt at one time.

In *Wilbur*, the Supreme Court again found no reconstruction with regard to the restoration of a fish-canning machine.[9] The patent in this case also covered a combination of unpatentable components. The purchaser of the patented machine retained a repairperson to clean and sandblast his rusted machines and to *resize* six of the 35 elements to enable the machines to pack fish into a different size of can. The court reasoned that:

> [The] machines were not spent; they had years of usefulness remaining though they needed cleaning and repair. . . . When six of the 35 elements of the combination patent were resized or relocated, no invasion of the patent resulted, for . . . the size of the cans serviced by the machine was no part of the invention. . . . Petitioners in adapting the old machines to a related use were doing more than repair in the customary sense; but what they did was kin to repair for it bore on the useful capacity of the old combination in which the royalty had been paid.[10]

Although it appeared that it would be difficult to prove reconstruction under such Supreme Court precedent, the Federal Circuit has recently identified an example of impermissible reconstruction in *Sandvik Aktiebolag v. E.J. Co.*[11] In *Sandvik*, the patents regarded a drill with a shank portion and a unique carbide tip geometry. Over time, the drill tip would dullen and need resharpening. The drill tip was not separately patented and Sandvik issued guidelines explaining how to resharpen the tip. Sandvik did not allege that resharpening the tip was infringement. Rather, Sandvik alleged that retipping the drill when the tip could not be sharpened because it was damaged constituted reconstruction. In determining that replacing the drill tip was reconstruction, some of the factors noted by the court included: (1) the drill was spent when the drill tip could no longer be resharpened, unless it was retipped, (2) retipping required a complex procedure of breaking the damaged tip and creating a completely new tip, (3) the drill tip was not a detachable part like the knives in *Wilson* and was not intended to have a shorter life than the drill shank, (4) there is no evidence of a substantial drill retipping market, which would tend to show there would be a reasonable expectation that the tip would require frequent replacement, and (5) the patentee did not intend its drills to be retipped.

This case raises numerous interesting questions: With regard to the second factor noted by the *Sandvik* court, didn't *Aro I* state that replacing even an essential element at high cost and difficulty was not necessarily indicative of a reconstruction?[12] Is *Sandvik* implicitly using the "heart of the invention" test that was rejected by *Aro I*? With regard to the second and third factors, can this case be distinguished from the reconfiguration that occurred in *Wilbur*, where the Supreme Court found permissible repair? Wasn't the fifth factor explicitly held to be irrelevant in *Hewlett–Packard* when the Federal Circuit stated "The question is not whether the patentee at the time of sale intended to limit the purchaser's right to modify the product.... A noncontractual intention is simply the seller's hope or wish, rather than an enforceable restriction."[13] Why should the patentee's noncontractual intention be given any weight in the repair/reconstruction analysis? Is the only way to distinguish *Sandvik* from the prior caselaw based on the *Sandvik* court's finding that both parties conceded that that once the drill tip could no longer be resharpened, then the *entire* drill was spent? But using this logic, wasn't the *entire* convertible top spent in *Aro I* when the fabric was spent?

Overall, many questions remain regarding the jurisprudence flowing from the evolution of the repair/reconstruction doctrine. Are the courts acting in a principled manner when determining if restoring a product is merely a repair rather than an infringing reconstruction? Or is the "practical test" advocated by the Supreme Court merely a "we know a reconstruction when we see it" test? Is the balancing of numerous factors a useful framework or would a bright-line test be better?[14] Does the current framework provide enough notice to the public of what is permissible repair? Given the state of the law, what should happen if a repair business reasonably errs in judging its own activities as permissible? Remember, to err (and even repair) is human, but to reconstruct is infringement.

---

* Arthur J. Gajarsa is a Circuit Judge on the United States Court of Appeals for the Federal Circuit. Evelyn Mary Aswad is an Attorney–Advisor, Office of the Legal Advisor, U.S. Department of State; and former law clerk to U.S. Circuit Judge Arthur J. Gajarsa. The views expressed herein are solely those of the authors and do not necessarily reflect those of the United States Court of Appeals for the Federal Circuit or the United States Department of State. This *SIDE BAR* was written specially for PRINCIPLES OF PATENT LAW.

1. See *Wilson v. Simpson*, 50 U.S. 109, 9 How. 109 (1850).

2. *Id*. at 123–25.

3. See *American Cotton–Tie Co. v. Simmons*, 106 U.S. 89 (1882).

4. *Id*. at 94.

5. Can *Sage Products, Inc. v. Devon Industries, Inc.*, 45 F.3d 1575 (Fed.Cir. 1995) be reconciled with *American Cotton–Tie*? Sage's patented device was a system for disposing of contaminated items that was comprised of an outer enclosure and a removable inner container. The inner container, which was an unpatentable element of the device, was marked "BIO-HAZARD—SINGLE USE ONLY." Sage stated in the patent specification that users should remove and discard the inner container when it was full. Devon manufactured inner containers that could be used with the Sage system and Sage brought suit for infringement. Sage argued that, because it was physically possible to reuse the inner containers after their first use, there was a disputed material fact as to whether the inner containers were spent and therefore the grant of summary judgment was inappropriate.

The Federal Circuit dismissed this argument in light of Sage's own warnings to customers to use the inner container only once. The Federal Circuit ultimately held that replacing the inner containers was permissible.

Given the holding in *American Cotton-Tie*, why wasn't replacing the damaged inner container viewed as reconstruction in the same way that replacing the band in the tie was held to be reconstruction? Is a distinguishing factor between *American Cotton-Tie* and *Sage* that in *American Cotton-Tie* the purchasers of the patented product were not asking to have the product repaired whereas in *Sage* the purchasers wanted to repair the containers for their own future use? Are the courts merely balancing the equities between the patentee and the purchasers and therefore, because no purchaser was involved in *American Cotton-Tie*, the patentee won?

6. *See Aro Manufacturing Co., Inc. v. Convertible Top Replacement Co., Inc.,* 365 U.S. 336 (1961) ("*Aro I*").

7. *Id.* at 343.

8. *Id.* at 345–46 (emphasis added).

9. *See Wilbur–Ellis Co. v. Kuther,* 377 U.S. 422 (1964).

10. *Id.* at 424–45.

11. *See Sandvik Aktiebolag v. E.J. Co.,* 121 F.3d 669 (Fed.Cir.1997).

12. *See Aro I,* 365 U.S. at 345–46.

13. *Hewlett–Packard Co. v. Repeat–O–Type Stencil Manufacturing Corp., Inc.,* 123 F.3d 1445, 1453 (Fed.Cir.1997). This case was decided about a week after *Sandvik*.

14. The Federal Circuit has declined to formulate a bright-line test, noting the analysis of the First Circuit that: "It is impracticable, as well as unwise, to attempt to lay down any rule on [the repair/reconstruction distinction], owing to the number and indefinite variety of patented inventions. Each case, as it arises, must be decided in light of all the facts and circumstances presented, and with an intelligent comprehension of the scope, nature, and purpose of the patented invention, and the fair and reasonable intention of the parties. . . . [the question of whether restoration is repair] should be determined less by definitions or technical rules than by the exercise of sound common sense and intelligent judgment." *FMC Corp. v. Up–Right, Inc.,* 21 F.3d 1073, 1079 (Fed.Cir.1994) (citing *Goodyear Shoe Machinery Co. v. Jackson,* 112 Fed. 146, 150 (1st Cir.1901)).

Husky Injection Molding Systems Ltd. v. R & D Tool & Engineering Co.

291 F.3d 780 (Fed.Cir.2002).

■ Before Michel, Lourie, and Dyk, Circuit Judges.

■ Dyk, Circuit Judge.

Husky Injection Molding Systems Ltd. ("Husky") appeals from the decision of the United States District Court for the Western District of Missouri, granting the motion of R & D Tool & Engineering Co. ("R & D") for summary judgment of non-infringement of U.S. Patent No. Re. 33,237 (the " '237 patent"). Because we find that there were no genuine issues of material fact regarding infringement of the '237 patent and that the district court correctly concluded that R & D's replacement of the mold and carrier plate of the injection molding system was more akin to repair than reconstruction, we affirm.

BACKGROUND

Husky manufactures and sells injection molding systems (the "X-series systems") that produce hollow plastic articles known as preforms. These preforms are subsequently reheated and blow molded into hollow plastic containers.

Husky is the assignee of the '237 patent, entitled "Apparatus for Producing Hollow Plastic Articles," which is directed to an injection molding machine that includes a carrier plate containing at least two sets of cavities for cooling the hollow plastic articles. The molds and carrier plates are not separately patented.

Generally preforms are made by injecting molten plastic into molds. One half of the mold contains at least one cavity [Fig. 2, 11]; the other half [Fig. 1, 12] contains a number of cores [Fig. 1, 14] corresponding to the number of cavities. '237 patent at col. 3, l. 65 col. 4, l. 4. The cores engage with their respective cavities [Fig. 2, 13] to form a closed mold and produce the shape of the hollow plastic articles. *Id.* at col. 4, ll. 4–7. To prevent damage to the preforms, each article must be adequately cooled before it is handled. *Id.* at col. 3, ll. 26–30. Traditionally the preforms were cooled in the molding machine, which was a time-consuming process. Having a lengthy cooling time in the molding machine was the limiting step in the production process of the articles and was at odds with the "high rate of production [that] is important in commercial operations...." *Id.* at col. 1, ll. 20–24. Other injection molding systems have increased the speed of the molding cycle, although there have been corresponding increases in costs or risks of damage to the articles. *Id.* at col. 1, ll. 66–68, col. 2, ll. 21–23. According to the summary of the invention of the patent, the present invention economically allows a high rate of production while permitting the preforms to cool for an extended period of time inside the cavities [Fig. 2, 21–23] of the carrier plate [Figs. 1 and 2, 20], rather than in the injection molds of the molding machine. *Id.* at col. 3, ll. 20–26.

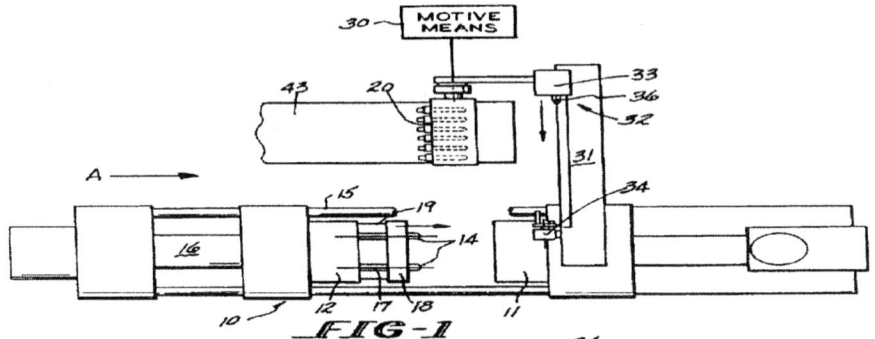

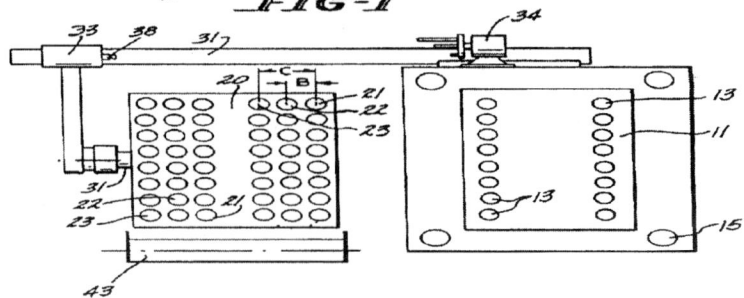

FIG-1

FIG-2

When a customer wishes to make a change in the preform design, it generally must buy a substitute mold and corresponding carrier plate in order to operate the Husky injection molding system as it was designed. Customers change the preform design on average after three to five years. When a system owner wants to make a different type of plastic article, it may purchase a replacement mold and carrier plate combination from Husky.

The alleged contributory infringer, R & D, makes molds and carrier plates, which substitute for components of Husky's injection molding system. To make the substitute molds and carrier plates, R & D purchased Husky's X-series system in 1997 without the mold or the carrier plate. At the time of the sale, R & D informed Husky's salesman of its intent to use the Husky system to make substitute molds. Moreover, all sales of X-series systems were without contractual restriction on the future purchase of molds or carrier plates.

In the summer of 2000, R & D shipped to Grafco, the owner of a Husky system, a new mold and carrier plate to allow Grafco to produce a different preform design. On June 9, 2000, Husky sued R & D for infringement of the '237 patent, urging that R & D had contributed to the infringement of the '237 patent. Husky concedes that the sale of the molds alone did not constitute contributory infringement because the molds were staple items. But Husky urged that R & D's sales to Husky's customers of a mold and carrier plate combination constituted contributory infringement because the substitution of a new carrier plate amounted to reconstruction of Husky's patented invention. R & D did not argue that the products it sold were outside the scope of the claims, but instead defended on the ground that its sales were akin to repair, and alternatively that Husky granted R & D an implied license to make and sell molds and carrier plates.

On September 8, 2000, R & D filed a motion for summary judgment of non-infringement, which the district court granted on March 30, 2001. Based on Husky's own admission that "no reconstruction occurs if the customer replaces the combination for repair purposes," the Court focused on whether substitution of a new mold and carrier plate combination for an unspent combination constituted reconstruction. In light of *Wilbur–Ellis Co. v. Kuther,* 377 U.S. 422 (1964), the district court held that "the use of R & D's retrofit mold/carrier plate assembly to substitute for an unspent original mold/carrier plate assembly does not rise to the level of impermissible reconstruction set out by the Supreme Court in [*Aro Manufacturing Co. v. Convertible Top Replacement Co.,* 365 U.S. 336 (1961) ('*Aro I*')]." The court noted that *Wilbur–Ellis* supports the holding that changing the shape of components to produce a different preform design is more akin to repair than reconstruction. *Id.* at 7. The district court further held that "the use of a substitution mold/carrier plate assembly offered by R & D is within the rights of purchasers of a Husky X-series due to the Plaintiff's admission of its awareness of a replacement mold market...." *Id.* at 8. Alternatively, the court concluded that Husky's customers had an implied license to substitute the mold/carrier plate assembly in order to produce different preform designs because Husky had sold its system without restriction. *Id.* at 11.

DISCUSSION

II.

Here Husky alleges that R & D is a contributory infringer. The law of contributory infringement is well settled. Section 271 of title 35 provides in pertinent part:

(a) Except as otherwise provided in this title, whoever *without authority makes, uses, offers to sell, or sells any patented invention,* within the United States or imports into the United States any patented invention during the term of the patent therefor, *infringes the patent.*

* * *

(c) Whoever offers to sell or sells within the United States or imports into the United States a component of a patented machine, manufacture, combination or composition, or a material or apparatus for use in practicing a patented process, constituting a *material part of the invention, knowing the same to be especially made or especially adapted for use in an infringement of such patent,* and *not a staple article* or commodity of commerce suitable for substantial noninfringing use, shall be liable as a contributory infringer.

35 U.S.C. § 271 (1994) (emphases added).

Thus, a seller of a "material part" of a patented item may be a contributory infringer if he makes a non-staple article that he knows was "especially made or especially adapted for use in an infringement of such patent." *Id.; Dawson Chem. Co. v. Rohm & Haas Co.,* 448 U.S. 176, 219 (1980). For R & D to be liable as a contributory infringer, Husky's customers who purchased the replacement parts from R & D must be liable for direct infringement. 35 U.S.C. § 271(c) (1994); *Aro I,* 365 U.S. at 34, 81 S.Ct. 5991. Both an alleged direct infringer and an alleged contributory infringer benefit from the permissible repair exception.

III.

The Supreme Court and this court have struggled for years to appropriately distinguish between repair of a patented machine and reconstruction. *See* Donald S. Chisum, 5 *Chisum on Patents* § 16.03[3], at 16–159 (1997) ("The line between permissible 'repair' and impermissible 'reconstruction' is a difficult one to draw and is the subject of numerous cases."). Based on those decisions, we can identify at least three primary repair and reconstruction situations.

First, there is the situation in which the entire patented item is spent, and the alleged infringer reconstructs it to make it useable again. This situation was first considered by the Supreme Court in *American Cotton–Tie Co. v. Simmons,* 106 U.S. (16 Otto) 89 (1882). *Cotton–Tie* involved a metallic cotton-bale tie consisting of a band and a buckle. *Id.* at 91. After the cotton-bale tie was cut, it became scrap iron. *Id.* The defendants subsequently purchased the scrap iron, riveted the pieces together, and recreated the bands. *Id.* Although the defendants reused the original buckle, the Court found that the defendants "reconstructed [the band]," *id.* at 94, and thereby infringed the patent, *id.* at 95. Moreover, in *Morgan Envelope Co. v. Albany Perforated Wrapping Paper Co.,* 152 U.S. 425

(1894), the Court explained its decision in *Cotton–Tie*. Specifically, the Court noted that "the use of the tie was intended to be as complete a destruction of it as would be the explosion of a patented torpedo. In either case, the repair of the band or the refilling of the shell would be a practical reconstruction of the device." *Morgan Envelope*, 152 U.S. at 434.

Second, there is the situation in which a spent part is replaced. The Supreme Court first addressed this situation in *Wilson v. Simpson*, 50 U.S. (9 How.) 109 (1850). *Wilson* involved the replacement of cutter-knives in a wood-planing machine. In concluding that replacement of the cutter-knives was permissible repair, the Court stated that

> repairing partial injuries, whether they occur from accident or wear and tear, is only refitting a machine for use. And it is no more than that, though it shall be a replacement of an essential part of a combination. It is the use of the whole of that which a purchaser buys, when the patentee sells to him a machine; and when he repairs the damages which may be done to it, it is no more than the exercise of that right of care which every one may use to give duration to that which he owns, or has a right to use as a whole.

Id. at 123 . . . .

Subsequently, the Supreme Court set forth a definitive test in *Aro Manufacturing Co. v. Convertible Top Replacement Co.*, 365 U.S. 336 (1961) (*"Aro I"*). *Aro I* involved a combination patent on a convertible folding top of an automobile. *Id.* at 337. The fabric of the convertible top had a shorter useful life than the other parts of the patented combination. *Id.* at 337–38. In reaching the conclusion that replacement of the worn-out fabric of the convertible top was permissible repair, *id.* at 346, the Supreme Court adopted a bright-line test, *id.* at 345. Specifically, the Court concluded that replacement of a spent part of a combination patent, which is not separately patented, is not impermissible reconstruction no matter how "essential it may be to the patented combination and no matter how costly or difficult replacement may be." *Id.* In adopting this bright-line test, the majority rejected Justice Brennan's suggestion in his concurrence that a multi-factor fact intensive test was appropriate to distinguish repair from reconstruction. Even if the owner sequentially replaces all of the worn-out parts of a patented combination, this sequential replacement does not constitute reconstruction. *See FMC Corp. v. Up–Right, Inc.*, 21 F.3d 1073, 1077 (Fed.Cir.1994). Moreover, in *Sage Products, Inc. v. Devon Industries, Inc.*, we held that replacement was not limited to worn out articles, but also included articles that were effectively spent. 45 F.3d 1575, 1578 (Fed.Cir. 1995).

Third, there is the situation in which a part is not spent but is replaced to enable the machine to perform a different function. This is a situation "kin to repair." In *Wilbur–Ellis*, the Supreme Court addressed whether changing the size of cans in fish-canning machines constituted reconstruction when the fish-canning machines were not spent, although they needed cleaning and repair. 377 U.S. at 424. The Court concluded that the "[p]etitioners in adapting the old machine to a related use were doing more than repair in the customary sense; but what they did was kin to repair for it bore on the useful capacity of the old combination. . . ." *Id.* at 425. This form of adaptation was within the scope of the purchased patent rights because the size of the cans was not "part of the invention." *Id.* at 424.

This court has followed the holding of *Wilbur–Ellis* when addressing replacement of unpatented parts of a combination patent. For example, in *Surfco* we recently addressed a similar situation involving the modification of a surfboard. Surfco manufactured fins that had an additional safety feature and were interchangeable with the patentee's releasable fins on its surfboard. *Surfco,* 264 F.3d at 1064 (Fed.Cir.2001). This safety feature created an incentive to replace the patentee's fins with Surfco's fins. Once again we reiterated that permissible repair encompasses the situation where parts are replaced. *Id.* at 1065.

IV.

Despite the number of cases concerning repair and reconstruction, difficult questions remain. One of these arises from the necessity of determining what constitutes replacement of a part of the device, which is repair or akin to repair, and what constitutes reconstruction of the entire device, which would not be repair or akin to repair. Some few situations suggest an obvious answer. For example, if a patent is obtained on an automobile, the replacement of the spark plugs would constitute permissible repair, but few would argue that the retention of the spark plugs and the replacement of the remainder of the car at a single stroke was permissible activity akin to repair. Thus, there may be some concept of proportionality inherent in the distinction between repair and reconstruction.

Nonetheless, in *Aro I,* the Supreme Court explicitly rejected a "heart of the invention" standard, noting that no matter how essential an element of the combination is to the patent, "no element, separately viewed, is within the [patent] grant." *Aro I,* 365 U.S. at 344. Similarly, in *Dawson Chemical Co. v. Rohm & Haas Co.,* the Court noted that in *Aro I* it had "eschewed the suggestion that the legal distinction between 'reconstruction' and 'repair' should be affected by whether the element of the combination that has been replaced is an 'essential' or 'distinguishing' part of the invention." 448 U.S. 176, 217 (1980).

However, *Aro I* itself was clearly dealing with "replaceable" parts, and we have interpreted *Aro I* as merely defining permissible repair in the context of "replaceable" parts, and as not foreclosing an inquiry into whether a particular part is replaceable. In *Sandvik Aktiebolag v. E.J. Co.,* the defendant offered a drill repair service that retipped the drill when it could no longer be resharpened. 121 F.3d 669, 671 (Fed.Cir.1997), *cert. denied,* 523 U.S. 1040 (1998). In that case, retipping did not involve "just attach[ing] a new part for a worn part," but instead required "several steps to replace, configure and integrate the tip onto the shank." *Id.* at 673. We concluded that retipping the drill was impermissible reconstruction, applying the following test:

> There are a number of factors to consider in determining whether a defendant has made a new article, after the device has become spent, including the nature of the actions by the defendant, the nature of the device and how it is designed (namely, whether one of the components of

the patented combination has a shorter useful life than the whole), whether a market has developed to manufacture or service the part at issue and objective evidence of the intent of the patentee.

Id. In reaching the conclusion that reconstruction occurred, we noted that "[t]he drill tip was not manufactured to be a replaceable part;" "[i]t was not intended or expected to have a life of temporary duration in comparison to the drill shank;" and "the tip was not attached to the shank in a manner to be easily detachable." *Id.* at 674. Difficult questions may exist as to the line between *Sandvik Aktiebolag* and *Wilbur–Ellis* where readily replaceable parts are not involved. We need not resolve those questions here. At a minimum, repair exists if the part being repaired is a readily replaceable part. *See generally,* Donald S. Chisum, 5 *Chisum on Patents* § 16.03[3], at 16–163 (1997) ("Many decisions finding 'repair' involved soft or temporary parts clearly intended to be replaceable.").

We conclude that the same safe harbor exists where activity "akin to repair" is involved as when repair is involved. In both cases, there is no infringement if the particular part is readily "replaceable." For example, in *Surfco,* the patents in suit were directed to a surfboard having releasable fins. *Surfco,* 264 F.3d at 1064. In describing *Aro I,* this court noted that "the concept of permissible 'repair' is directed primarily to the replacement of broken or worn parts. *However, permissible 'repair' also includes replacement of parts that are neither broken nor worn." Surfco,* 264 F.3d at 1065 (emphasis added). Accordingly, we held that "[t]he patented surf craft [was] not 'recreated' by the substitution of a different set of fins, even when the new fins [were] specifically adapted for use in the patented combination." *Id.* at 1066. Having determined that a part is readily replaceable, it is irrelevant whether the part was an essential element of the invention. We reject Husky's attempt to revive the heart of the invention standard in different words. *See, e.g., Aro I,* 365 U.S. at 344.

Husky also urges that the owner of a patented combination has no right to voluntarily replace an unspent part, unless there is a valid public policy justification for the replacement such as increased safety. This argument is directly inconsistent with both *Wilbur–Ellis* and *Surfco.*

In *Wilbur–Ellis,* the replacement of the 1 pound cans with 5 ounce cans did not enhance safety. In *Surfco,* we addressed whether a part needed to be spent or broken before there was a right to replace or modify it. *Surfco,* 264 F.3d at 1066. We concluded that it was not a reconstruction to substitute different fins, even if the original fins were not in need of repair or replacement. *Id.* Although the fins provided enhanced safety features, our holding in *Surfco* was not based on this policy justification, but instead on the right of a purchaser to modify a machine. *Id.* A purchaser is within its rights to modify a machine by substituting a readily replaceable part whether or not the replacement served some public policy purpose.

V.

Here there is no question that the particular parts were readily "replaceable" parts. The design of the injection molding machine allowed replacement of the mold and carrier plates. Typically, after three to five years, a customer purchases a new mold and carrier plate in order to change the preform design. Moreover, Husky sold substitute molds and carrier plates, and provided separate quotations for the injection molding system and the mold/carrier plate assembly. We conclude that the carrier plates were readily replaceable.

In this case, the carrier plate is just one element of the patented combination and not separately patented, and selling replacement parts cannot constitute contributory infringement. We conclude that Husky's customers did not directly infringe the patent by replacing the molds and carrier plates; thus, R & D did not contributorily infringe the '237 patent.

NOTES

1. *Supreme Court Views on Repair/Reconstruction.* The germinal case on repair and reconstruction is *Wilson v. Simpson*, 50 U.S. (9 How.) 109 (1850). The defendant *Wilson* lawfully obtained a planing machine covered by the plaintiff's patent. Thereafter and without authority of the plaintiff, the defendant replaced cutting knives, which typically wore out after sixty to ninety days of use. The Court held that such a replacement was within the category of permissible repair rather than that of impermissible reconstruction.

More than 100 years later, the Court decided *Aro Mfg. Co. v. Convertible Top Replacement*, 365 U.S. 336 (1961). The plaintiff (Convertible Top Replacement Co.) was assignee of the Mackie–Duluk patent on a convertible top mechanism for automobiles consisting of a flexible top fabric, supporting structures, and a sealing mechanism, all mounted on the automobile body. The fabric element normally deteriorated in about three years from wear and tear. The rest of the elements normally lasted for the life of the automobile. The defendant (Aro Mfg.) manufactured and sold replacement fabrics designed for automobiles fitted with the Mackie–Duluk combination. The plaintiff sued the defendant for infringement and contributory infringement.

The Court, in an opinion written by Justice Whittaker, reversed a finding of infringement below. First, the Court noted that the defendant did not *directly* infringe because the fabrics were unpatented elements of a patented combination. Second, it noted that the defendant could not *contributorily* infringe unless its ultimate customers (owners of automobiles) directly infringed when they replaced the fabrics on their convertibles. This in turn depended on "whether such a replacement by the car owner is infringing 'reconstruction' or permissible 'repair.'"

The Court rejected a test suggested by the plaintiff that would consider the relative durability and expense of the replaced part and whether the part represented the "essential" or "distinguishing" element of the patented combination. In holding that "maintenance of the 'use of the whole' of the patented combination through replacement of a spent, unpatented element" does not constitute reconstruction, the Court cited Judge Learned Hand's statement of the "distilled essence" of *Wilson v. Simpson*:

> [R]econstruction of a patented entity, comprised of unpatented elements, is limited to such a true reconstruction of the entity as to "in fact make a new article," *United States v. Aluminum Co. of America* ..., after the entity, viewed as a whole, has become spent. In order to call the monopoly, conferred by the patent grant, into play for a second time, it must, indeed, be a second creation of the patented entity. Mere replacement of individual unpatented parts, one at a time, whether of the same part repeatedly or different parts successively, is no more than the lawful right of the owner to repair his property.

365 U.S. at 346. Justice Harlan wrote a dissenting opinion in which two other justices concurred. Justice Harlan concluded that "the issue of reconstruction *vel non* turns not upon any single factor, but depends instead upon a variety of circumstances." 365 U.S. at 376. He disagreed with the Court's view that reconstruction is limited to "where the patented combination has been rebuilt de novo from the ground up." *Id.*

2. *Distinction Between Repair and Reconstruction.* A central issue that is present in just about every repair/reconstruction case is the distinction between repair and reconstruction. As Judge Newman noted in *Mallinckrodt, infra,*

> Although the rule is straightforward its implementation is less so, for it is not always clear where the boundary lies: how much "repair" is fair before the device is deemed reconstructed. *See, e.g., Everpure, Inc. v. Cuno, Inc.,* 875 F.2d 300, 10 U.S.P.Q.2D 1855 (Fed.Cir.), *cert. denied,* 493 U.S. 853, 110 S.Ct. 154, 107 L.Ed.2d 112 (1989).

If the repair/reconstruction doctrine is viewed as something that further unpacks the details of the first-sale doctrine, then it makes sense to look to the first-sale doctrine, and its theoretical underpinnings, to elucidate the distinction between repair and reconstruction. Since the first-sale doctrine exists as a gap filling rule to make explicit terms that are implicit in the contract for sale of a patented article, perhaps the investigation into repair/reconstruction should begin by peering into that same contract. In other words, perhaps the repair/reconstruction analysis should focus on the intent of the parties at the time they contracted for sale of the patented article. If so, what evidence should be considered, and what factors would be most relevant? Or, should there be an all-things-considered analysis? In *Sandvik Aktiebolag v. E. J. Company,* 121 F.3d 669 (Fed.Cir.1997), the Federal Circuit noted that:

> There are a number of factors to consider in determining whether a defendant has made a new article, after the device has become spent, including the nature of the actions by the defendant, the nature of the device and how it is designed (namely, whether one of the components of the patented combination has a shorter useful life than the whole), whether a market has developed to manufacture or service the part at issue and objective evidence of the intent of the patentee. Under the totality of the circumstances, we hold in this case that E.J.'s actions are a reconstruction.

What if the patented product is modified to have different properties, different features, and different performance characteristics? What if the modification to the patented article was merely to "soup it up" or "scale it down?" *See Wilbur–Ellis Co. v. Kuther,* 377 U.S. 422 (1964). Consider the following hypothetical: the patentee has two patents—a first patent on a low performance, inexpensive device, and a second on a high performance expensive device. The patentee sells the low performance devices marked with the first patent and the high performance devices marked with the second patent. Suppose that the low performance devices can be modified to function as high performance devices, but the cost of this modification is much less than the difference in cost between the low and high performance devices if purchased through ordinary sales channels. If a company enters the business of buying new low performance devices, immediately modifying them, and selling them in competition with new high performance devices, would you find the company liable for patent infringement? If so, what would be your reasoning? More particularly, would you hold the modification to be "kin to repair," or would you consider it to be "reconstruction" or even "construction?" For a helpful discussion of patent law's "unquestionably idiosyncratic" repair/reconstruction doctrine, *see* Mark D. Janis, *A Tale of the Apocryphal Axe: Repair, Reconstruction, and the Implied License in Intellectual Property Law,* 58 Md. L. Rev. 423 (1999).

3. *The Importance (or Not) of Being Spent and Replaceable.* The *Husky* court identified three repair/reconstruction scenarios. First, the entire patented item is spent, and the defendant reconstructs it to make it usable again. This scenario usually leads to a finding of reconstruction. Second, a spent part is replaced. The court, citing *Aro Manufacturing Co. v. Convertible Top Replacement Co.*, 365 U.S. 336 (1961) (*Aro I*), concluded that the replacement of a spent part, "which is not separately patented, is not impermissible reconstruction no matter how 'essential it may be to the patented combination and no matter how costly or difficult replacement may be.'" Moreover, replacement is not limited to worn out components. *See Sage Products, Inc. v. Devon Industries, Inc.*, 45 F.3d 1575, 1578 (Fed.Cir.1995) ("This court has never said that an element is spent only when it is impossible to reuse it. . . . [W]e believe that when it is neither practical nor feasible to continue using an element that is intended to be replaced, that element is effectively spent"). Third, there are the "kin to repair" cases, which involves a part that is not spent but is replaced to enable the machine to perform a different function. The courts have found that this type of activity is permissible repair. *See, e.g., Surfco Hawaii v. Fin Control Sys. Pty., Ltd.*, 264 F.3d 1062, 1064 (Fed.Cir.2001) (finding repair when Surfco manufactured fins that had an additional safety feature and were interchangeable with the patentee's releasable fins on its surfboard).

Therefore, there is an important distinction between replacement of a part of the device, no matter how essential the part may be, and reconstruction of an entire device. The former is permissible if the part is "readily replaceable" (e.g., meant to be replaced), and the latter is impermissible. Where to draw the line between these two can be difficult. A properly drafted contract, however, can render this inquiry irrelevant. *See Kendall Co. v. Progressive Medical Tech., Inc.*, 85 F.3d 1570, 1575 (Fed.Cir.1996) ("[A]s long as reconstruction does not occur or a contract is not violated, nothing in the law prevents a purchaser of a device from prematurely repairing it or replacing un unpatented component. Premature repair is the business of the purchaser of the product, who owns it, rather than the patentee, who sold it"). Another way to prevent a repair/reconstruction issue is to patent, if available, the various components of the device.

But it is not entirely clear how successful a strategy it is to merely seek more patents. This just begs the additional question about how detailed the later contract terms must be. That is, must the sale contract mention every patent claim specifically? Every patent then owned? Every patent application that is pending? Patents that may later be acquired from third parties? In the case of *Hewlett–Packard v. Repeat–O–Type Stencil*, 123 F.3d 1445 (Fed.Cir.1997), the patentee has claims to both ink-jet cartridges themselves and to the process of making cartridges. The defendant sold refilled cartridges. The court wrote:

> Even accepting that ROT's actions constitute a "making" of the accused cartridges, they were made from new and unused HP cartridges purchased from a legitimate source, and the property of ROT; the HP cartridges were certainly not spent. . . . ROT has only modified an unused cartridge that HP sold without restriction.

Id. at 1452. The question here may be seen as one of burden or presumption. Is it the patentee who must be specific in saying what is not licensed or the defendant in saying what has been licensed. In evaluating this question remember that patents, and some patent applications, are public documents, available to all for free from many on-line sources including the PTO web page. When discussing HP's method patent, the court does seem to indicate that the burden extends to all claims of all patents owned by the patentee that cover the specific article:

Moreover, a license was impliedly granted under the patent for the additional reason that it contained apparatus claims as well as process claims covering use of the cartridges.

Id. at 1445. But, ultimately the holding of the court on this issue seemed to be based on HP's failure of proof:

Finally, HP has not met its burden of showing the existence of an issue of material fact with regard to the asserted method claims of the '295 patent.

Id.

Mallinckrodt v. Medipart

976 F.2d 700 (Fed.Cir.1992).

■ Before NEWMAN, LOURIE, and CLEVENGER, CIRCUIT JUDGES.

■ NEWMAN, CIRCUIT JUDGE.

This action for patent infringement and inducement to infringe relates to the use of a patented medical device in violation of a "single use only" notice that accompanied the sale of the device. Mallinckrodt sold its patented device to hospitals, which after initial use of the devices sent them to Medipart for servicing that enabled the hospitals to use the device again. Mallinckrodt claimed that Medipart thus induced infringement by the hospitals and itself infringed the patent.

The district court held that violation of the "single use only" notice can not be remedied by suit for patent infringement, and granted summary judgment of noninfringement. [footnote omitted]

* * *

[T]he district court held that no restriction whatsoever could be imposed under the patent law, whether or not the restriction was enforceable under some other law, and whether or not this was a first sale to a purchaser with notice. This ruling is incorrect, for if Mallinckrodt's restriction was a valid condition of the sale, then in accordance with *General Talking Pictures Corp. v. Western Electric Co.*, 304 U.S. 175 *aff'd on reh'g*, 305 U.S. 124 (1938), it was not excluded from enforcement under the patent law.

On review of these issues in the posture in which the case reaches us:

1.   The movant Medipart did not dispute actual notice of the restriction. Thus we do not decide whether the form of the restriction met the legal requirements of notice or sufficed as a "label license", as Mallinckrodt calls it, for those questions were not presented on this motion for summary judgment.

2.   Nor do we decide whether Mallinckrodt's enjoined subsequent notice cured any flaws in the first notice, for that issue was not reached by the district court.

We conclude, however, on Mallinckrodt's appeal of the grant of this injunction, that the notice was improperly enjoined.

3.   We also conclude that the district court misapplied precedent in holding that there can be no restriction on use imposed as a matter of law,

even on the first purchaser. The restriction here at issue does not per se violate the doctrine of patent misuse or the antitrust law. Use in violation of a valid restriction may be remedied under the patent law, provided that no other law prevents enforcement of the patent.

4. The district court's misapplication of precedent also led to an incorrect application of the law of repair/reconstruction, for if reuse is established to have been validly restricted, then even repair may constitute patent infringement.

Background

The patented device is an apparatus for delivery of radioactive or therapeutic material in aerosol mist form to the lungs of a patient, for diagnosis and treatment of pulmonary disease. Radioactive material is delivered primarily for image scanning in diagnosis of lung conditions. Therapeutic agents may be administered to patients suffering various lung diseases.

The device is manufactured by Mallinckrodt, who sells it to hospitals as a unitary kit that consists of a "nebulizer" which generates a mist of the radioactive material or the prescribed drug, a "manifold" that directs the flow of oxygen or air and the active material, a filter, tubing, a mouthpiece, and a nose clip. In use, the radioactive material or drug is placed in the nebulizer, is atomized, and the patient inhales and exhales through the closed system. The device traps and retains any radioactive or other toxic material in the exhalate. The device fits into a lead-shielded container that is provided by Mallinckrodt to minimize exposure to radiation and for safe disposal after use.

The device is marked with the appropriate patent numbers, [footnote omitted] and bears the trademarks "Mallinckrodt" and "UltraVent" and the inscription "Single Use Only". The package insert provided with each unit states "For Single Patient Use Only" and instructs that the entire contaminated apparatus be disposed of in accordance with procedures for the disposal of biohazardous waste. The hospital is instructed to seal the used apparatus in the radiation-shielded container prior to proper disposal. The hospitals whose activities led to this action do not dispose of the UltraVent apparatus, or limit it to a single use.

Instead, the hospitals ship the used manifold/nebulizer assemblies to Medipart, Inc. Medipart in turn packages the assemblies and sends them to Radiation Sterilizers Inc., who exposes the packages to at least 2.5 mega-rads of gamma radiation, and returns them to Medipart. Medipart personnel then check each assembly for damage and leaks, and place the assembly in a plastic bag together with a new filter, tubing, mouthpiece, and nose clip. The "reconditioned" units, as Medipart calls them, are shipped back to the hospitals from whence they came. Neither Radiation Sterilizers nor Medipart tests the reconditioned units for any residual biological activity or for radioactivity. The assemblies still bear the inscription "Single Use Only" and the trademarks "Mallinckrodt" and "UltraVent".

Mallinckrodt filed suit against Medipart, asserting patent infringement and inducement to infringe. . . .

The district court granted Medipart's motion on the patent infringement counts, holding that the "Single Use Only" restriction could not be enforced by suit for patent infringement. The court also held that Medipart's activities were permissible repair, not impermissible reconstruction, of the patented apparatus. . . .

The district court also enjoined Mallinckrodt *pendente lite* from distributing a new notice to its hospital customers. The proposed new notice emphasized the "Single Use Only" restriction and stated that the purpose of this restriction is to protect the hospital and its patients from potential adverse consequences of reconditioning, such as infectious disease transmission, material instability, and/or decreased diagnostic performance; that the UltraVent device is covered by certain patents; that the hospital is licensed under these patents to use the device only once; and that reuse of the device would be deemed infringement of the patents.

Mallinckrodt appeals the grant of summary judgment on the infringement issue, and the grant of the preliminary injunction.

I

The Restriction on Reuse

Mallinckrodt describes the restriction on reuse as a label license for a specified field of use, wherein the field is single (*i.e.*, disposable) use. On this motion for summary judgment, there was no issue of whether this form of license gave notice of the restriction. Notice was not disputed. Nor was it disputed that sale to the hospitals was the first sale of the patented device. The issue that the district court decided on summary judgment was the enforceability of the restriction by suit for patent infringement. The court's premise was that even if the notice was sufficient to constitute a valid condition of sale, violation of that condition can not be remedied under the patent law.

Mallinckrodt states that the restriction to single patient use is valid and enforceable under the patent law because the use is within the scope of the patent grant, and the restriction does not enlarge the patent grant. Mallinckrodt states that a license to less than all uses of a patented article is well recognized and a valid practice under patent law, and that such license does not violate the antitrust laws and is not patent misuse. Mallinckrodt also states that the restriction here imposed is reasonable because it is based on health, safety, efficacy, and liability considerations and violates no public policy. Thus Mallinckrodt argues that the restriction is valid and enforceable under the patent law. Mallinckrodt concludes that use in violation of the restriction is patent infringement, and that the district court erred in holding otherwise.

Medipart states that the restriction is unenforceable, for the reason that "the *Bauer* trilogy and *Motion Picture Patents* clearly established that *no* restriction is enforceable under patent law upon a purchaser of a sold article." (Medipart's emphasis). The district court so held. The district court also held that since the hospitals purchased the device from the patentee, not from a manufacturing licensee, no restraint on the use of the device could lawfully be imposed under the patent law.

* * *

The enforceability of restrictions on the use of patented goods derives from the patent grant, which is in classical terms of property: the right to exclude.

> 35 U.S.C. § 154. Every patent shall contain ... a grant ... for the term of seventeen years ... of the right to exclude others from making, using, or selling the invention throughout the United States....

This right to exclude may be waived in whole or in part. The conditions of such waiver are subject to patent, contract, antitrust, and any other applicable law, as well as equitable considerations such as are reflected in the law of patent misuse. As in other areas of commerce, private parties may contract as they choose, provided that no law is violated thereby:

> [T]he rule is, with few exceptions, that any conditions which are not in their very nature illegal with regard to this kind of property, imposed by the patentee and agreed to by the licensee for the right to manufacture or use or sell the [patented] article, will be upheld by the courts.

E. Bement & Sons v. National Harrow Co., 186 U.S. 70, 91 (1902).

The district court's ruling that Mallinckrodt's restriction on reuse was unenforceable was an application of the doctrine of patent misuse, although the court declined to use that designation. The concept of patent misuse arose to restrain practices that did not in themselves violate any law, but that drew anticompetitive strength from the patent right, and thus were deemed to be contrary to public policy. The policy purpose was to prevent a patentee from using the patent to obtain market benefit beyond that which inheres in the statutory patent right.

The district court's holding that Mallinckrodt's restriction to single patient use was unenforceable was, as we have remarked, based on "policy" considerations. The district court relied on a group of cases wherein resale price-fixing of patented goods was held illegal, viz. *Bauer & Cie. v. O'Donnell*, 229 U.S. 1 (1913); *Straus v. Victor Talking Machine Co.*, 243 U.S. 490 (1917); *Boston Store of Chicago v. American Graphophone Co.*, 246 U.S. 8 (1918), ("the *Bauer* trilogy"), and that barred patent-enforced tie-ins, viz. *Motion Picture Patents Co. v. Universal Film Mfg. Co.*, 243 U.S. 502 (1917).

* * *

These cases established that price-fixing and tying restrictions accompanying the sale of patented goods were per se illegal. These cases did not hold, and it did not follow, that all restrictions accompanying the sale of patented goods were deemed illegal. In *General Talking Pictures* the Court, discussing restrictions on use, summarized the state of the law as follows:

> That a restrictive license is legal seems clear. *Mitchell v. Hawley* [83 U.S.], 16 Wall. 544 (1873). As was said in *United States v. General Electric Co.*, 272 U.S. 476, 489 (1926), the patentee may grant a license "upon any condition the performance of which is reasonably within the reward which the patentee by the grant of the patent is entitled to secure"....

The practice of granting licenses for restricted use is an old one, *see Rubber Company v. Goodyear* [76 U.S.] 9 Wall. 788, 799, 800 (1870); *Gamewell Fire–Alarm Telegraph Co. v. Brooklyn*, 14 F. 255 [C.C.N.Y. (1882)]. So far as it appears, its legality has never been questioned. 305 U.S. at 127.

In *General Talking Pictures* the patentee had authorized the licensee to make and sell amplifiers embodying the patented invention for a specified use (home radios). The defendant had purchased the patented amplifier from the manufacturing licensee, with knowledge of the patentee's restriction on use. The Supreme Court stated the question as "whether the restriction in the license is to be given effect" against a purchaser who had notice of the restriction. The Court observed that a restrictive license to a particular use was permissible, and treated the purchaser's unauthorized use as infringement of the patent, deeming the goods to be unlicensed as purchased from the manufacturer.

The Court, in its opinion on rehearing, stated that it

> [did not] consider what the rights of the parties would have been if the amplifier had been manufactured under the patent and had passed into the hands of a purchaser in the ordinary channels of trade.

305 U.S. at 127, 59 S.Ct. at 117. The district court interpreted this reservation as requiring that since the hospitals purchased the UltraVent device from the patentee Mallinckrodt, not from a manufacturing licensee, no restraint on the purchasers' use of the device could be imposed under the patent law. However, in *General Talking Pictures* the Court did not hold that there must be an intervening manufacturing licensee before the patent can be enforced against a purchaser with notice of the restriction. The Court did not decide the situation where the patentee was the manufacturer and the device reached a purchaser in ordinary channels of trade. 305 U.S. at 127.

The UltraVent device was manufactured by the patentee; but the sale to the hospitals was the first sale and was with notice of the restriction. Medipart offers neither law, public policy, nor logic, for the proposition that the enforceability of a restriction to a particular use is determined by whether the purchaser acquired the device from a manufacturing licensee or from a manufacturing patentee. We decline to make a distinction for which there appears to be no foundation. Indeed, Mallinckrodt has pointed out how easily such a criterion could be circumvented. That the viability of a restriction should depend on how the transaction is structured was denigrated as "formalistic line drawing" in *Continental T.V., Inc. v. GTE Sylvania, Inc.*, 433 U.S. 36, 57–59 (1977), the Court explaining, in overruling *United States v. Arnold, Schwinn & Co.*, 388 U.S. 365 (1967), that the legality of attempts by a manufacturer to regulate resale does not turn on whether the reseller had purchased the merchandise or was merely acting as an agent of the manufacturer. The Court having disapproved reliance on formalistic distinctions of no economic consequence in antitrust analysis, we discern no reason to preserve formalistic distinctions of no economic consequence, simply because the goods are patented.

The district court, holding Mallinckrodt's restriction unenforceable, described the holding of *General Talking Pictures* as in "some tension" with the earlier price-fixing and tie-in cases. The district court observed that the Supreme Court did not cite the *Bauer, Boston Store,* or *Motion Picture Patents* cases when it upheld the use restriction in *General Talking Pictures.* That observation is correct, but it should not be remarkable. By the time of *General Talking Pictures,* price-fixing and tie-ins were generally prohibited under the antitrust law as well as the misuse law, while other conditions were generally recognized as within the patent grant. The prohibitions against price-fixing and tying did not make all other restrictions per se invalid and unenforceable. [footnote omitted] Further, the Court could not have been unaware of the *Bauer* trilogy in deciding *General Talking Pictures,* because Justice Black's dissent is built upon those cases.

Restrictions on use are judged in terms of their relation to the patentee's right to exclude from all or part of the patent grant, *see, e.g.,* W.F. Baxter, *The Viability of Vertical Restraints Doctrine,* 75 Calif.L.Rev. 933, 935 (1987) ("historically, legal prohibition began with [resale price control and tie-in agreements] and, with rare exceptions, now continues only with those devices"); and where an anticompetitive effect is asserted, the rule of reason is the basis of determining the legality of the provision. In *Windsurfing International, Inc. v. AMF, Inc.,* 782 F.2d 995, 228 USPQ 562 (Fed.Cir.), *cert. denied,* 477 U.S. 905, 106 S.Ct. 3275, 91 L.Ed.2d 565 (1986), this court stated:

> To sustain a misuse defense involving a licensing arrangement not held to have been per se anticompetitive by the Supreme Court, a factual determination must reveal that the overall effect of the license tends to restrain competition unlawfully in an appropriately defined relevant market.

Id. 782 F.2d at 1001–1002, 228 USPQ at 567 (footnote omitted). *See also Continental T.V. v. GTE Sylvania,* 433 U.S. at 58–59, 97 S.Ct. at 2561–62 (judging vertical restrictions under the rule of reason); *Business Electronics Corp. v. Sharp Electronics Corp.,* 485 U.S. 717, 735–36, 108 S.Ct. 1515, 1525, 99 L.Ed.2d 808 (1988) (vertical non-price restraints are not per se illegal). The district court, stating that it "refuse[s] to limit *Bauer* and *Motion Picture Patents* to tying and price-fixing not only because their language suggests broader application, but because there is a strong public interest in not stretching the patent laws to authorize restrictions on the use of purchased goods", *Mallinckrodt,* 15 U.S.P.Q.2D at 1119, 1990 WL 19535, has contravened this precedent.

In support of its ruling, the district court also cited a group of cases in which the Court considered and affirmed the basic principles that unconditional sale of a patented device exhausts the patentee's right to control the purchaser's use of the device; and that the sale of patented goods, like other goods, can be conditioned. The principle of exhaustion of the patent right did not turn a conditional sale into an unconditional one.

* * *

Viewing the entire group of these early cases, it appears that the Court simply applied, to a variety of factual situations, the rule of contract law that sale may be conditioned. *Adams v. Burke* and its kindred cases do not stand for the proposition that no restriction or condition may be placed upon the sale of a patented article. It was error for the district court to derive that proposition from the precedent. Unless the condition violates some other law or policy (in the patent field, notably the misuse or antitrust law, *e.g.*, *United States v. Univis Lens Co.*, 316 U.S. 241 (1942)), private parties retain the freedom to contract concerning conditions of sale. As we have discussed, the district court cited the price-fixing and tying cases as reflecting what the court deemed to be the correct policy, viz., that no condition can be placed on the sale of patented goods, for any reason. However, this is not a price-fixing or tying case, and the per se antitrust and misuse violations found in the *Bauer* trilogy and *Motion Picture Patents* are not here present. The appropriate criterion is whether Mallinckrodt's restriction is reasonably within the patent grant, or whether the patentee has ventured beyond the patent grant and into behavior having an anticompetitive effect not justifiable under the rule of reason.

Should the restriction be found to be reasonably within the patent grant, *i.e.*, that it relates to subject matter within the scope of the patent claims, that ends the inquiry. However, should such inquiry lead to the conclusion that there are anticompetitive effects extending beyond the patentee's statutory right to exclude, these effects do not automatically impeach the restriction. Anticompetitive effects that are not per se violations of law are reviewed in accordance with the rule of reason. Patent owners should not be in a worse position, by virtue of the patent right to exclude, than owners of other property used in trade. *Compare Tripoli Co. v. Wella Corp.*, 425 F.2d 932, 936–38 (3d Cir.) (en banc), *cert. denied*, 400 U.S. 831 (1970) (in a non-patent action, restriction on resale of certain potentially dangerous products does not violate antitrust laws where motivation was prevention of injury to public and protection against liability risk) with *Marks, Inc. v. Polaroid Corp.*, 237 F.2d 428, 436 (1st Cir.1956), *cert. denied*, 352 U.S. 1005 (1957) (single use only restriction based on safety concerns not patent misuse, and enforceable by suit for patent infringement).

We conclude that the district court erred in holding that the restriction on reuse was, as a matter of law, unenforceable under the patent law. If the sale of the UltraVent was validly conditioned under the applicable law such as the law governing sales and licenses, and if the restriction on reuse was within the scope of the patent grant or otherwise justified, then violation of the restriction may be remedied by action for patent infringement. The grant of summary judgment is reversed, and the cause is remanded.

* * *

III.

The Injunction

The district court enjoined Mallinckrodt from issuing a new notice that stated, *inter alia*, that violation of the single patient use restriction would be deemed patent infringement.

A patentee that has a good faith belief that its patents are being infringed violates no protected right when it so notifies infringers:

> Patents would be of little value if infringers of them could not be notified of the consequences of infringement or proceeded against in the courts. Such action, considered by itself cannot be said to be illegal.

Virtue v. Creamery Package Mfg. Co., 227 U.S. 8, 37–38 (1913). *See Concrete Unlimited, Inc. v. Cementcraft, Inc.*, 776 F.2d 1537, 1539 (Fed.Cir.

1985), *cert. denied*, 479 U.S. 819 (1986) (patentee has the right to enforce its patent and notify alleged infringers).

> [I]t is not an actionable wrong for one in good faith to make plain to whomsoever that it is his purpose to insist upon what he believes to be his legal rights, even though he may misconceive what those rights are.

Kaplan v. Helenhart Novelty Corp., 182 F.2d 311, 314 (2d Cir.1950). Nor should an accused infringer be insulated from knowledge and fair warning of potential liability, or deprived of the opportunity to respond to threatened litigation.

* * *

NOTES

1. *Conditional Sales, Misuse, and First Sale/Exhaustion.* The court in *Mallinckrodt*, noted that "the sale of patented goods, like other goods, can be conditioned." *Mallinckrodt*, 976 F.2d at 706. *See also, B. Braun Med., Inc. v. Abbott Labs.*, 124 F.3d 1419, 1426 (Fed.Cir.1997) (noting the exhaustion doctrine "does not apply to an expressly conditional sale or license"). This is a reminder that the first sale/exhaustion doctrine is indeed a default rule around which parties can otherwise agree—in this case for a so-called field-of-use restriction. *See Mallinckrodt*, 976 F.2d at 706 (stating that "[t]he principle of exhaustion of the patent right did not turn a conditional sale into an unconditional one"). The use of this restrictive contract term in that case was adjudicated to be both (1) enforceable; and (2) not misuse.

It is not clear whether all such efforts will be so successful. That is, although "express conditions accompanying the sale or license of a patented product are generally upheld," *Braun*, 124 F.3d at 1426, "[s]uch express conditions ... are contractual in nature and are subject to antitrust, patent, contract, and any other applicable law, as well as equitable considerations such as patent misuse." *Id. See also, Braun*, 124 F.3d at 1426 ("The key inquiry under this fact-intensive doctrine is whether, by imposing the condition, the patentee has 'impermissibly broadened the "physical or temporal" scope of the patent grant with anticompetitive effect' "). Thus, the "basics matter" for each area of law—for example antitrust law and contract law. See F. Scott Kieff & Troy A. Paredes, The Basics Matter: At the Periphery of Intellectual Property Stanford Law School John M. Olin Program in Law and Economics, Working Paper No. 275, February 2004, Available on-line at http://papers.ssrn.com/paper.taf?abstract_id=501142.

2. *The Absence of a Contract.* Recall in *Husky* the court noted that the "X-series systems were without contractual restriction on the future purchase of molds or carrier plates." What result if Husky contractually required the molds and carrier plates to be purchased from Husky? Would Grafco be a direct infringer and R & D a contributory infringer? Does *Mallinckrodt* help your analysis? In *Mallinckrodt*, the court noted that a breach of an enforceable contract of sale may result in a finding of infringement on the part of the breaching party. *Mallinckrodt*, 976 F.2d at 709. *See also, Kendall Co. v. Progressive Medical Tech., Inc.*, 85 F.3d 1570 (Fed.Cir.1996) (noting that in a "single use" contract case such as *Mallinckrodt*, there is " 'no need to choose between repair and reconstruction' because 'even repair of an unlicensed device constitutes infringement' "). Some have asserted that the "repair-reconstruction distinction has nothing to do with patent policy;" rather, "[i]t is solely a matter of interpreting the license." WILLIAM M. LANDES AND RICHARD A. POSNER, THE ECONOMIC STRUCTURE OF INTELLECTUAL PROPERTY 381–82 (2003).

In *Kendall*, there was a contract with a "Single Patient Use Only" provision similar to *Mallinckrodt*, but unlike the patentee in *Mallinckrodt*, who required its customers to purchase the entire patented device from the patentee, the *Kendall* patentee (*i.e.*, the Kendall Company) neither required its customers to purchase the entire device, nor the unpatented replacement parts. In this regard, the Kendall Company is like Husky. Perhaps patent protection was not available to Husky and the Kendall Company for the replacement parts, but one would think that a properly drafted contract would have helped both patentees.

3. Consider the result in part III of the *Mallinckrodt* opinion. When can a patentee threaten suit for patent infringement? Who can be threatened: direct infringers; inducers or contributory infringers; or government contractors?

E.   PREEMPTION AS A LIMITATION ON PATENTEES

Article I, Section 8, clause 8 of the Constitution (the so-called patent and copyright clause)* grants Congress the power to promote "the Progress of Science and useful Arts" through the promulgation of patent and copyright laws. Article VI, clause 2 of the Constitution (the so-called Supremacy Clause) requires that federal law "be the supreme Law of the Land", and, thereby, preempt any interfering state laws. In this section, we will explore the extent to which federal patent law preempts various state laws.

While studying this section, one might keep a watchful eye for the impact on patentees of the various arguments about the supremacy of patent law. Do the patent preemption cases turn on notions of efficiency and Federalism, or do they turn on more basic American notions of free enterprise and competition? If the former, then preemption seems an apt label. If the latter, then perhaps the real battle lines are not between the federal and state governments, but rather are among the various forms of substantive competition law that may be available to any government. Perhaps the often-called preemption cases, which on first blush might appear to exalt the patent system as the supreme law of the land, can also be seen as efforts to place limits on the ability for patentees to avail themselves of various state laws.

CONSTITUTIONAL PROVISIONS—U.S. CONST. ART. I, § 8, CL. 8; ART. VI, CL. 2

1.   THE BASICS OF PREEMPTION

Cover v. Sea Gull Lighting
83 F.3d 1390 (Fed.Cir.1996).

■ Before RICH, MICHEL and PLAGER, CIRCUIT JUDGES.

■ RICH, CIRCUIT JUDGE.

Appellant Hydramatic Packing Co. (Hydramatic) appeals from the judgment of the United States District Court for the Eastern District of

---

* The patent and copyright clause of the Constitution is sometimes mistakenly referred to as "the intellectual property clause." This label is not correct for a number of reasons. First, federal trademark and unfair competition laws have their constitutional origins in Article 1, Section 8, clause 3 (the so-called commerce clause), which grants Congress the power to "regulate Commerce with foreign Nations, and among the several States, and with the Indian Tribes." Second, as this chapter demonstrates, a range of intellectual property laws have existed at the state level. To be sure, some have been held preempted by federal patent (or other) law. Many, however, have been upheld and remain an important component of the diverse body of American competition law.

Pennsylvania concluding that Hydramatic's state law claim against Appellee Sea Gull Lighting, Inc. (Sea Gull) is precluded because the state statute is preempted by federal patent law. *Cover v. Hydramatic Packing Co. & Sea Gull Lighting, Inc.*, No. 93–6400, 1995 WL 596778 (E.D.Pa.,1995) . We
reverse and remand.

BACKGROUND

Plaintiff Craig H. Cover (Cover) commenced this case in late 1993 as a patent infringement action in which he sued Hydramatic for contributory infringement and Sea Gull for direct infringement of his U.S. Patent No. 4,605,992 ('992 patent). Hydramatic counterclaimed, seeking a declaratory judgment that the '992 patent was unenforceable due to inequitable conduct before the Patent and Trademark Office. Hydramatic also filed a cross-claim against Sea Gull for indemnification under § 2312(c) of the Uniform Commercial Code, which Pennsylvania has adopted.

The '992 patent describes a lighting fixture system having a batt of thermal insulation to protect the wiring from heat produced by a bulb. Hydramatic manufactures insulation products based on the specifications of its customers. Sea Gull, a lighting fixture manufacturer, produced certain lighting fixtures that incorporated multi-layered batts of insulation manufactured to its specifications by Hydramatic. Cover's infringement action was premised on Sea Gull's manufacture of lighting fixtures containing the insulation parts obtained from and manufactured by Hydramatic.

On January 21, 1986, Cover entered into an exclusive license arrangement with Pacor to commercialize the '992 patent. Thereafter, Pacor began to supply multi-layered batts of insulation to Sea Gull, which designated these insulation units as part numbers 6254 and 6255. Of particular relevance is the fact that Pacor did not mark the insulation units with the number of the '992 patent in accordance with 35 U.S.C. § 287 (1988). Pacor sold these insulation units to Sea Gull until 1993.

In July of 1988, however, Sea Gull began furnishing Hydramatic with drawings and specifications to make Sea Gull part numbers 6254 and 6255. Hydramatic produced these parts in accordance with Sea Gull's specifications from July 1988 until late 1993. In 1989, Cover learned that Sea Gull was not obtaining all of its insulation units from Pacor, Cover's exclusive licensee. Rather, Cover discovered that Sea Gull was ordering insulation units from Hydramatic. As a result, Cover wrote a cease and desist letter to Hydramatic on June 5, 1989. Shortly thereafter, on October 9, 1989, Cover wrote a letter to Sea Gull, stating, in relevant part:

> To purchase these patented parts from a known violator [Hydramatic] of the patents is in itself a violation of the patents, and I trust that your company would not have intentionally done so.

The district court found that the October 9, 1989 letter to Sea Gull did not constitute notice of infringement. Therefore, according to the district court, since Pacor did not mark its insulation units sold to Sea Gull in accordance with 35 U.S.C. § 287(a), Sea Gull was not liable for damages, if at all, until after the complaint was filed by Cover on December 3, 1993.

Cover settled with Sea Gull before trial, and the case between them was dismissed with prejudice. Sea Gull agreed to pay Cover $75,000. Hydramatic also settled with Cover and agreed to pay him $175,000 in liquidated compensatory damages. Furthermore, Hydramatic and Cover stipulated that Hydramatic would not contest the validity, infringement, or enforceability of the '992 patent. As a result of these settlement agreements, the only claim remaining for trial was Hydramatic's cross-claim against Sea Gull for indemnification under § 2312(c).

With respect to Hydramatic's cross-claim, the district court stated that "[f]ederal law preempts state law where simultaneous compliance with state and federal law is impossible or would frustrate the purpose of federal law." On the assumption that Sea Gull was not liable for damages because it did not have notice of infringement until the complaint was filed in December of 1993, the district court held that "Hydramatic's state law claim seeking to impose liability on Sea Gull is preempted." Thus, according to the district court, compliance with § 2312(c) of the Pennsylvania commercial code would frustrate the purpose of § 287(a) of the federal patent code.

Hydramatic appealed to this court. We have jurisdiction over this appeal under 28 U.S.C. § 1295.

DISCUSSION

Under the Supremacy Clause, U.S. Const., Art. VI, cl. 2, state laws are invalid if they "interfere with, or are contrary to the laws of [C]ongress, made in pursuance of the [C]onstitution." *Gibbons v. Ogden*, 22 U.S. (9 Wheat.) 1, 6 L.Ed. 23 (1824); *Wisconsin Pub. Intervenor v. Mortier*, 501 U.S. 597, 604, 111 S.Ct. 2476, 2481, 115 L.Ed.2d 532 (1991). Inherent in our patent system is a "tension between the desire to freely exploit the full potential of our inventive resources and the need to create an incentive to deploy those resources" by granting the right to exclude to those who promote the progress of the useful arts. *Bonito Boats, Inc. v. Thunder Craft Boats, Inc.*, 489 U.S. 141, 152, 109 S.Ct. 971, 978, 103 L.Ed.2d 118 (1989). In other words, there are public costs associated with the right to exclude, and our patent system seeks to maintain an efficient balance between incentives to create and commercialize and public costs engendered by these incentives.[2] Where this balance between free exploitation of knowledge and the aforesaid incentives is clear, states may not intervene and provide protection to subject matter that is statutorily unprotected by our patent laws. *Id.* On the other hand, "states are free to regulate the use of ... intellectual property in any manner not inconsistent with federal law." *Aronson v. Quick Point Pencil Co.*, 440 U.S. 257, 262, 99 S.Ct. 1096, 1099, 59 L.Ed.2d 296 (1979).

---

2. Public costs include (1) inflated prices, invariably absorbed by the consumer, which frequently accompany exclusive rights; and (2) overinvestment. See RICHARD A. POSNER, ECONOMIC ANALYSIS OF THE LAW 36–37 (3d ed.1986).

This case, one of first impression, requires us to assess the relationship between the federal patent code and Pennsylvania commercial law. Specifically, we are faced with the question of whether 35 U.S.C. § 287(a) of the patent code pre-empts § 2312(c) of the Uniform Commercial Code. Section 287(a) states, in relevant part:

> In the event of failure . . . to mark [the patented article], no damages shall be recovered by the patentee in any action for infringement, except on proof that the infringer was notified of the infringement and continued to infringe thereafter, in which event damages may be recovered only for infringement occurring after such notice.

The state law warranty provision, § 2312(c), is as follows:

> Warranty of merchant regularly dealing in goods. Unless otherwise agreed a seller who is a merchant regularly dealing in goods of the kind warrants that the goods shall be delivered free of the rightful claim of any third person by way of infringement or the like *but a buyer who furnishes specifications to the seller must hold the seller harmless against any such claim which arises out of compliance with the specifications.*

13 Pa.C.S.A. § 2312(c) (1995) (emphasis added). The emphasized final provision controls here.

Although in determining whether a state statute is pre-empted, "there can be no one crystal clear distinctly marked formula," *Hines v. Davidowitz*, 312 U.S. 52, 67, 61 S.Ct. 399, 404, 85 L.Ed. 581 (1941), the Supreme Court has set forth three grounds for pre-emption: (1) Explicit pre-emption, whereby Congress explicitly provided for pre-emption of state law in the federal statute, *Jones v. Rath Packing Co.*, 430 U.S. 519, 525, 97 S.Ct. 1305, 1309, 51 L.Ed.2d 604 (1977); (2) Field pre-emption, wherein "the scheme of federal regulation is so pervasive as to make reasonable the inference that Congress left no room for the States to supplement it," *Gade v. National Solid Wastes Management Ass'n*, 505 U.S. 88, 98, 112 S.Ct. 2374, 2383, 120 L.Ed.2d 73 (1992) (quoting *Rice v. Santa Fe Elevator Corp.*, 331 U.S. 218, 230, 67 S.Ct. 1146, 1152, 91 L.Ed. 1447 (1947)); and (3) Conflict pre-emption, "where 'compliance with both federal and state regulations is a physical impossibility,' . . . or where state law 'stands as an obstacle to the accomplishment and execution of the full purposes and objectives of Congress,'" *Gade*, 505 U.S. at 98, 112 S.Ct. at 2383 (quoting *Florida Lime & Avocado Growers, Inc. v. Paul*, 373 U.S. 132, 142–43, 83 S.Ct. 1210, 1217, 10 L.Ed.2d 248 (1963), and *Hines*, 487 U.S. at 138).

Applying these tests to the case at hand, it is rather clear upon reading § 287(a) of the patent code that Congress did not explicitly pre-empt state commercial law. With respect to field pre-emption, Title 35 occupies the field of patent law, not commercial law between buyers and sellers. Therefore, field pre-emption does not apply here. We are left with conflict pre-emption. Thus, we must ask ourselves whether there is such a direct conflict between § 287(a) of the patent code and § 2312(c) of Pennsylvania's commercial law that compliance with both the patent law and state law is a "physical impossibility," or whether the state law "stands as an obstacle to the accomplishment and execution of the full purposes and objectives of Congress" in enacting § 287(a). *Gade*, 505 U.S. at 98, 112 S.Ct. at 2383. We hold that there is no conflict pre-emption in that

Pennsylvania's commercial law neither renders compliance with the patent code a "physical impossibility" nor "stands as an obstacle to the accomplishment and execution" of the patent laws.

The patent law defines rights between the patentee and persons who wish to make, use, sell or offer for sale the patented invention. Inasmuch as Sea Gull and Hydramatic settled with the patentee, the patentee and the patent code are no longer in the picture. Sea Gull and Hydramatic remain, and their legal relationship is defined and governed by § 2312(c) of the UCC, which has nothing to do with the liability of Sea Gull and Hydramatic under the patent laws, which are simply irrelevant at this point.

Sea Gull asserts that for § 2312(c) to apply there has to be a "rightful claim" of infringement. Because the patentee, argues Sea Gull, did not mark his goods in accordance with § 287(a), there was no "rightful claim," thus saving Sea Gull from patent liability. As such, Pennsylvania's commercial code cannot impose patent liability where the patent law forbids it. This argument misses the point. By focusing on the phrase "rightful claim" in § 2312(c) and asking us to equate "rightful claim" with patent liability, Sea Gull, in essence, is making a statutory construction argument, which has the effect of avoiding the pre-emption issue.

However, pre-emption is the issue, and the focus of our inquiry is on the interaction, if any, between § 287(a) and § 2312(c). Once the patentee left the picture, so did § 287(a). There is simply nothing on the face of § 287(a) that pertains to anyone but the infringer and the patentee. At issue, therefore, is the legal relationship between two contracting parties, and it is § 2312(c) which defines this relationship. On its face, § 2312(c) shifts all costs, including attorney fees, to the buyer who furnishes a seller with specifications that leads to a "rightful claim" of infringement. This state law, unlike the state laws in previous patent pre-emption cases, does not purport to provide exclusive property rights to "creations which would otherwise remain unprotected under federal law." In short, we cannot discern any conflict between §§ 287(a) and 2312(c).

Furthermore, to adopt Sea Gull's "rightful claim" argument would not lead to judicious public policy inasmuch as parties would eschew settlement and be forced to go to trial to discern whether a "rightful claim" exists under federal patent law. We cannot lend our imprimatur to such a policy.

Therefore, we reverse the district court's judgment based on its holding that compliance with Pennsylvania's commercial law would frustrate the damages limitations set forth in 35 U.S.C. § 287. We remand for further proceedings consistent with our decision.

NOTES

1. The *Sea Gull* case dealt with a contract that was not directly related to the patent or the patentee. Should the analysis differ if the contract at issue is directly tied to the patent or the patentee, or both? Consider the facts and reasoning of *Mallinckrodt, Inc. v. Medipart, Inc.*, 976 F.2d 700 (Fed.Cir.1992):

Before NEWMAN, LOURIE, and CLEVENGER, CIRCUIT JUDGES.

PAULINE NEWMAN, CIRCUIT JUDGE.

This action for patent infringement and inducement to infringe relates to the use of a patented medical device in violation of a "single use only" notice that accompanied the sale of the device. Mallinckrodt sold its patented device to hospitals, which after initial use of the devices sent them to Medipart for servicing that enabled the hospitals to use the device again. Mallinckrodt claimed that Medipart thus induced infringement by the hospitals and itself infringed the patent.

The district court held that violation of the "single use only" notice can not be remedied by suit for patent infringement, and granted summary judgment of noninfringement.

The district court did not decide whether the form of the "single use only" notice was legally sufficient to constitute a license or condition of sale from Mallinckrodt to the hospitals. Nor did the district court decide whether any deficiencies in the "single use only" notice were cured by Mallinckrodt's attempted subsequent notice, the release of which was enjoined by the district court on the ground that it would harm Medipart's business. Thus there was no ruling on whether, if the initial notice was legally defective as a restrictive notice, such defect was cured in the subsequent notice. The district court also specifically stated that it was not deciding whether Mallinckrodt could enforce this notice under contract law. These aspects are not presented on this appeal, and the factual premises were not explored at the summary judgment proceeding from which this appeal is taken.

Instead, the district court held that no restriction whatsoever could be imposed under the patent law, whether or not the restriction was enforceable under some other law, and whether or not this was a first sale to a purchaser with notice. This ruling is incorrect, for if Mallinckrodt's restriction was a valid condition of the sale, then in accordance with *General Talking Pictures Corp. v. Western Electric Co.*, 304 U.S. 175, 58 S.Ct. 849, 82 L.Ed. 1273, 37 USPQ 375, *aff'd on reh'g*, 305 U.S. 124, 59 S.Ct. 116, 83 L.Ed. 81, 39 USPQ 329 (1938), it was not excluded from enforcement under the patent law.

* * *

Mallinckrodt describes the restriction on reuse as a label license for a specified field of use, wherein the field is single (*i.e.*, disposable) use. On this motion for summary judgment, there was no issue of whether this form of license gave notice of the restriction. Notice was not disputed. Nor was it disputed that sale to the hospitals was the first sale of the patented device. The issue that the district court decided on summary judgment was the enforceability of the restriction by suit for patent infringement. The court's premise was that even if the notice was sufficient to constitute a valid condition of sale, violation of that condition can not be remedied under the patent law.

Mallinckrodt states that the restriction to single patient use is valid and enforceable under the patent law because the use is within the scope of the patent grant, and the restriction does not enlarge the patent grant. Mallinckrodt states that a license to less than all uses of a patented article is well recognized and a valid practice under patent law, and that such license does not violate the antitrust laws and is not patent misuse. Mallinckrodt also states that the restriction here imposed is reasonable because it is based on health, safety, efficacy, and liability considerations and violates no public policy. Thus Mallinckrodt argues that the restriction is valid and enforceable under the patent law. Mallinckrodt concludes that use in violation of the restriction is patent infringement, and that the district court erred in holding otherwise.

* * *

We conclude that the district court erred in holding that the restriction on reuse was, as a matter of law, unenforceable under the patent law. If the sale of the UltraVent was validly conditioned under the applicable law such as the law governing sales and licenses, and if the restriction on reuse was within the scope of the patent grant or otherwise justified, then violation of the restriction may be remedied by action for patent infringement. The grant of summary judgment is reversed, and the cause is remanded.

2. *Comparison With Copyright.* Must the preemption analysis be uniform across all laws promulgated pursuant to Article I, Section 8, clause 8 of the Constitution? Consider the opinion by Circuit Judge Easterbrook, joined by Circuit Judges Coffey and Flaum, in *ProCD, Inc. v. Zeidenberg*, 86 F.3d 1447 (7th Cir.1996), holding so-called shrink-wrap licenses entered into under state contract law not to be preempted by federal copyright law:

> Must buyers of computer software obey the terms of shrinkwrap licenses? The district court held not, for two reasons: first, they are not contracts because the licenses are inside the box rather than printed on the outside; second, federal law forbids enforcement even if the licenses are contracts. 908 F.Supp. 640 (W.D.Wis.1996). The parties and numerous amici curiae have briefed many other issues, but these are the only two that matter and we disagree with the district judge's conclusion on each. Shrinkwrap licenses are enforceable unless their terms are objectionable on grounds applicable to contracts in general (for example, if they violate a rule of positive law, or if they are unconscionable). Because no one argues that the terms of the license at issue here are troublesome, we remand with instructions to enter judgment for the plaintiff.

I

> ProCD, the plaintiff, has compiled information from more than 3,000 telephone directories into a computer database. We may assume that this database cannot be copyrighted, although it is more complex, contains more information (nine-digit zip codes and census industrial codes), is organized differently, and therefore is more original than the single alphabetical directory at issue in *Feist Publications, Inc. v. Rural Telephone Service Co.*, 499 U.S. 340, 111 S.Ct. 1282, 113 L.Ed.2d 358 (1991). See Paul J. Heald, *The Vices of Originality*, 1991 Sup.Ct. Rev. 143, 160–68. ProCD sells a version of the database, called SelectPhone (trademark), on CD–ROM discs. (CD–ROM means "compact disc-read only memory." The "shrinkwrap license" gets its name from the fact that retail software packages are covered in plastic or cellophane "shrinkwrap," and some vendors, though not ProCD, have written licenses that become effective as soon as the customer tears the wrapping from the package. Vendors prefer "end user license," but we use the more common term.) A proprietary method of compressing the data serves as effective encryption too. Customers decrypt and use the data with the aid of an application program that ProCD has written. This program, which is copyrighted, searches the database in response to users' criteria (such as "find all people named Tatum in Tennessee, plus all firms with 'Door Systems' in the corporate

name"). The resulting lists (or, as ProCD prefers, "listings") can be read and manipulated by other software, such as word processing programs.

The database in SelectPhone (trademark) cost more than $10 million to compile and is expensive to keep current. It is much more valuable to some users than to others. The combination of names, addresses, and SIC codes enables manufacturers to compile lists of potential customers. Manufacturers and retailers pay high prices to specialized information intermediaries for such mailing lists; ProCD offers a potentially cheaper alternative. People with nothing to sell could use the database as a substitute for calling long distance information, or as a way to look up old friends who have moved to unknown towns, or just as an electronic substitute for the local phone book. ProCD decided to engage in price discrimination, selling its database to the general public for personal use at a low price (approximately $150 for the set of five discs) while selling information to the trade for a higher price. It has adopted some intermediate strategies too: access to the SelectPhone (trademark) database is available via the America Online service for the price America Online charges to its clients (approximately $3 per hour), but this service has been tailored to be useful only to the general public.

If ProCD had to recover all of its costs and make a profit by charging a single price that is, if it could not charge more to commercial users than to the general public it would have to raise the price substantially over $150. The ensuing reduction in sales would harm consumers who value the information at, say, $200. They get consumer surplus of $50 under the current arrangement but would cease to buy if the price rose substantially. If because of high elasticity of demand in the consumer segment of the market the only way to make a profit turned out to be a price attractive to commercial users alone, then all consumers would lose out and so would the commercial clients, who would have to pay more for the listings because ProCD could not obtain any contribution toward costs from the consumer market.

To make price discrimination work, however, the seller must be able to control arbitrage. An air carrier sells tickets for less to vacationers than to business travelers, using advance purchase and Saturday-night-stay requirements to distinguish the categories. A producer of movies segments the market by time, releasing first to theaters, then to pay-per-view services, next to the videotape and laserdisc market, and finally to cable and commercial tv. Vendors of computer software have a harder task. Anyone can walk into a retail store and buy a box. Customers do not wear tags saying "commercial user" or "consumer user." Anyway, even a commercial-user-detector at the door would not work, because a consumer could buy the software and resell to a commercial user. That arbitrage would break down the price discrimination and drive up the minimum price at which ProCD would sell to anyone.

Instead of tinkering with the product and letting users sort themselves for example, furnishing current data at a high price that would be attractive only to commercial customers, and two-year-old data at a low price ProCD turned to the institution of contract. Every box containing its consumer product declares that the software comes with restrictions stated in an enclosed license. This license, which is encoded on the CD ROM disks as well as printed in the manual, and which appears on a user's screen every time the software runs, limits use of the application program and listings to non-commercial purposes.

Matthew Zeidenberg bought a consumer package of SelectPhone (trademark) in 1994 from a retail outlet in Madison, Wisconsin, but decided to ignore the license. He formed Silken Mountain Web Services, Inc., to resell the information in the SelectPhone (trademark) database. The corporation makes the database available on the Internet to anyone willing to pay its price which, needless to say, is less than ProCD charges its commercial customers. Zeidenberg has purchased two additional Select-Phone (trademark) packages, each with an updated version of the database, and made the latest information available over the World Wide Web, for a price, through his corporation. ProCD filed this suit seeking an injunction against further dissemination that exceeds the rights specified in the licenses (identical in each of the three packages Zeidenberg purchased). The district court held the licenses ineffectual because their terms do not appear on the outside of the packages. The court added that the second and third licenses stand no different from the first, even though they are identical, because they might have been different, and a purchaser does not agree to and cannot be bound by terms that were secret at the time of purchase. 908 F.Supp. at 654.

II

Following the district court, we treat the licenses as ordinary contracts accompanying the sale of products, and therefore as governed by the common law of contracts and the Uniform Commercial Code. Whether there are legal differences between "contracts" and "licenses" (which may matter under the copyright doctrine of first sale) is a subject for another day. See *Microsoft Corp. v. Harmony Computers & Electronics, Inc.*, 846 F.Supp. 208 (E.D.N.Y.1994). Zeidenberg does not argue that Silken Mountain Web Services is free of any restrictions that apply to Zeidenberg himself, because any effort to treat the two parties as distinct would put Silken Mountain behind the eight ball on ProCD's argument that copying the application program onto its hard disk violates the copyright laws. Zeidenberg does argue, and the district court held, that placing the package of software on the shelf is an "offer," which the customer "accepts" by paying the asking price and leaving the store with the goods. *Peeters v. State*, 154 Wis. 111, 142 N.W. 181 (1913). In Wisconsin, as elsewhere, a contract includes only the terms on which the parties have agreed. One cannot agree to hidden terms, the judge concluded. So far, so good but one of the terms to which Zeidenberg agreed by purchasing the software is that the transaction was subject to a license. Zeidenberg's position therefore must be that the printed terms on the outside of a box are the parties' contract except for printed terms that refer to or incorporate other terms. But why would Wisconsin fetter the parties' choice in this way? Vendors can put the entire terms of a contract on the outside of a box only by using microscopic type, removing other information that buyers might find more useful (such as what the software does, and on which computers it works), or both. The "Read Me" file included with most software, describing system requirements and potential incompatibilities, may be equivalent to ten pages of type; warranties and license restrictions take still more space. Notice on the outside, terms on the inside, and a right to return the software for a refund if the terms are unacceptable (a right that the license expressly extends), may be a means of doing business valuable to buyers and sellers alike. See E. Allan Farnsworth, 1 FARNSWORTH ON CONTRACTS 4.26 (1990); Restatement (2d) of Contracts 211 comment a (1981) ("Standardization of agreements serves many of the same functions as standardization of goods and services; both are essential to a system of mass production and distribution. Scarce and costly time and skill can be devoted to a class of transactions rather than the details of individual transactions."). Doubtless a state could forbid the use of standard contracts in the software business, but we do not think that Wisconsin has done so.

Transactions in which the exchange of money precedes the communication of detailed terms are common. Consider the purchase of insurance. The buyer goes to an agent, who explains the essentials (amount of coverage, number of years) and remits the premium to the home office, which sends back a policy. On the district judge's understanding, the terms of the policy are irrelevant because the insured paid before receiving them. Yet the device of payment, often with a "binder" (so that the insurance takes effect immediately even though the home office reserves the right to withdraw coverage later), in advance of the policy, serves buyers' interests by accelerating effectiveness and reducing transactions costs. Or consider the purchase of an airline ticket. The traveler calls the carrier or an agent, is quoted a price, reserves a seat, pays, and gets a ticket, in that order. The ticket contains elaborate terms, which the traveler can reject by canceling the reservation. To use the ticket is to accept the terms, even terms that in retrospect are disadvantageous. See *Carnival Cruise Lines, Inc. v. Shute*, 499 U.S. 585, 111 S.Ct. 1522, 113 L.Ed.2d 622 (1991); *see also Vimar Seguros y Reaseguros, S.A. v. M/V Sky Reefer*, 515 U.S. 528, 115 S.Ct. 2322, 132 L.Ed.2d 462 (1995) (bills of lading). Just so with a ticket to a concert. The back of the ticket states that the patron promises not to record the concert; to attend is to agree. A theater that detects a violation will confiscate the tape and escort the violator to the exit. One could arrange things so that every concertgoer signs this promise before forking over the money, but that cumbersome way of doing things not only would lengthen queues and raise prices but also would scotch the sale of tickets by phone or electronic data service.

Consumer goods work the same way. Someone who wants to buy a radio set visits a store, pays, and walks out with a box. Inside the box is a leaflet containing some terms, the most important of which usually is the warranty, read for the first time in the comfort of home. By Zeidenberg's lights, the warranty in the box is irrelevant; every consumer gets the standard warranty implied by the UCC in the event the contract is silent; yet so far as we are aware no state disregards warranties furnished with consumer products. Drugs come with a list of ingredients on the outside and an elaborate package insert on the inside. The package insert describes drug interactions, contraindications, and other vital information but, if Zeidenberg is right, the purchaser need not read the package insert, because it is not part of the contract.

Next consider the software industry itself. Only a minority of sales take place over the counter, where there are boxes to peruse. A customer may place an order by phone in response to a line item in a catalog or a review in a magazine. Much software is ordered over the Internet by purchasers who have never seen a box. Increasingly software arrives by wire. There is no box; there is only a stream of electrons, a collection of information that includes data, an application program, instructions, many limitations ("MegaPixel 3.14159 cannot be used with BytePusher 2.718"), and the terms of sale. The user purchases a serial number, which activates the software's features. On Zeidenberg's arguments, these unboxed sales are unfettered by terms so the seller has made a broad warranty and must pay consequential damages for any shortfalls in performance, two "promises" that if taken seriously would drive prices through the ceiling or return transactions to the horse-and-buggy age.

According to the district court, the UCC does not countenance the sequence of money now, terms later. (Wisconsin's version of the UCC does not differ from the Official Version in any material respect, so we use the regular numbering system. Wis. Stat. § 402.201 corresponds to UCC § 2–201, and other citations are easy to derive.) One of the court's reasons that by proposing as part of the draft Article 2B a new UCC § 2–203 that would explicitly validate standard-form user licenses, the American Law Institute and the National Conference of Commissioners on Uniform Laws have conceded the invalidity of shrinkwrap licenses under current law, see 908 F.Supp. at 655–56 depends on a faulty inference. To propose a change in a law's text is not necessarily to propose a change in the law's effect. New words may be designed to fortify the current rule with a more precise text that curtails uncertainty. To judge by the flux of law review articles discussing shrinkwrap licenses, uncertainty is much in need of reduction although businesses seem to feel less uncertainty than do scholars, for only three cases (other than ours) touch on the subject, and none directly addresses it. *See Step–Saver Data Systems, Inc. v. Wyse Technology*, 939 F.2d 91 (3d Cir.1991); *Vault Corp. v. Quaid Software Ltd.*, 847 F.2d 255, 268–70 (5th Cir.1988); *Arizona Retail Systems, Inc. v. Software Link, Inc.*, 831 F.Supp. 759 (D.Ariz.1993). As their titles suggest, these are not consumer transactions. *Step–Saver* is a battle-of-the-forms case, in which the parties exchange incompatible forms and a court must decide which prevails. See *Northrop Corp. v. Litronic Industries*, 29 F.3d 1173 (7th Cir.1994) (Illinois law); Douglas G. Baird & Robert Weisberg, *Rules, Standards, and the Battle of the Forms: A Reassessment of § 2–207*, 68 Va. L.Rev. 1217, 1227–31 (1982). Our case has only one form; UCC § 2–207 is irrelevant. *Vault* holds that Louisiana's special shrinkwrap-license statute is preempted by federal law, a question to which we return. And *Arizona Retail Systems* did not reach the question, because the court found that the buyer knew the terms of the license before purchasing the software.

What then does the current version of the UCC have to say? We think that the place to start is § 2–204(1): "A contract for sale of goods may be made in any manner sufficient to show agreement, including conduct by both parties which recognizes the existence of such a contract." A vendor, as master of the offer, may invite acceptance by conduct, and may propose limitations on the kind of conduct that constitutes acceptance. A buyer may accept by performing the acts the vendor proposes to treat as acceptance. And that is what happened. ProCD proposed a contract that a buyer would accept by using the software after having an opportunity to read the license at leisure. This Zeidenberg did. He had no choice, because the software splashed the license on the screen and would not let him proceed without indicating acceptance. So although the district judge was right to say that a contract can be, and often is, formed simply by paying the price and walking out of the store, the UCC permits contracts to be formed in other ways. ProCD proposed such a different way, and without protest Zeidenberg agreed. Ours is not a case in which a consumer opens a package to find an insert saying "you owe us an extra $10,000" and the seller files suit to collect. Any buyer finding such a demand can prevent formation of the contract by returning the package, as can any consumer who concludes that the terms of the license make the software worth less than the purchase price. Nothing in the UCC requires a seller to maximize the buyer's net gains.

Section 2–606, which defines "acceptance of goods", reinforces this understanding. A buyer accepts goods under § 2–606(1)(b) when, after an opportunity to inspect, he fails to make an effective rejection under § 2–602(1). ProCD extended an opportunity to reject if a buyer should find the license terms unsatisfactory; Zeidenberg inspected the package, tried out the software, learned of the license, and did not reject the goods. We refer to § 2–606 only to show that the opportunity to return goods can be important; acceptance of an offer differs from acceptance of goods after delivery, see *Gillen v. Atalanta Systems, Inc.*, 997 F.2d 280, 284 n. 1 (7th Cir.1993); but the UCC consistently permits the parties to structure their relations so that the buyer has a chance to make a final decision after a detailed review.

Some portions of the UCC impose additional requirements on the way parties agree on terms. A disclaimer of the implied warranty of merchantability must be "conspicuous." UCC § 2–316(2), incorporating UCC § 1–201(10). Promises to make firm offers, or to negate oral modifications, must be "separately signed." UCC §§ 2–205, 2–209(2). These special provisos reinforce the impression that, so far as the UCC is concerned, other terms may be as inconspicuous as the forum-selection clause on the back of the cruise ship ticket in *Carnival Lines*. Zeidenberg has not located any Wisconsin case for that matter, any case in any state holding that under the UCC the ordinary terms found in shrinkwrap licenses require any special prominence, or otherwise are to be undercut rather than enforced. In the end, the terms of the license are conceptually identical to the contents of the package. Just as no court would dream of saying that SelectPhone (trademark) must contain 3,100 phone books rather than 3,000, or must have data no more than 30 days old, or must sell for $100 rather than $150 although any of these changes would be welcomed by the customer, if all other things were held constant so, we believe, Wisconsin would not let the buyer pick and choose among terms. Terms of use are no less a part of "the product" than are the size of the database and the speed with which the software compiles listings. Competition among vendors, not judicial revision of a package's contents, is how consumers are protected in a market economy. *Digital Equipment Corp. v. Uniq Digital Technologies, Inc.*, 73 F.3d 756 (7th Cir.1996). ProCD has rivals, which may elect to compete by offering superior software, monthly updates, improved terms of use, lower price, or a better compromise among these elements. As we stressed above, adjusting terms in buyers' favor might help Matthew Zeidenberg today (he already has the software) but would lead to a response, such as a higher price, that might make consumers as a whole worse off.

III

The district court held that, even if Wisconsin treats shrinkwrap licenses as contracts, § 301(a) of the Copyright Act, 17 U.S.C. § 301(a), prevents their enforcement. 908 F.Supp. at 656–59. The relevant part of § 301(a) preempts any "legal or equitable rights [under state law] that are equivalent to any of the exclusive rights within the general scope of copyright as specified by section 106 in works of authorship that are fixed in a tangible medium of expression and come within the subject matter of copyright as specified by sections 102 and 103". ProCD's software and data are "fixed in a tangible medium of expression", and the district judge held that they are "within the subject matter of copyright". The latter conclusion is plainly right for the copyrighted application program, and the judge thought that the data likewise are "within the subject matter of copyright" even if, after Feist, they are not sufficiently original to be copyrighted. 908 F.Supp. at 656–57. *Baltimore Orioles, Inc. v. Major League Baseball Players Ass'n*, 805 F.2d 663, 676 (7th Cir.1986), supports that conclusion, with which commentators agree. E.g., Paul Goldstein, III COPYRIGHT § 15.2.3 (2d ed.1996); Melville B. Nimmer & David Nimmer, NIMMER ON COPYRIGHT § 101[B] (1995); William F. Patry, II COPYRIGHT LAW AND PRACTICE 1108–09 (1994). One function of § 301(a) is to prevent states from giving special protection to works of authorship that Congress has decided should be in the public domain, which it can accomplish only if "subject matter of copyright" includes all works of a type covered by sections 102 and 103, even if federal law does not afford protection to them. *Cf. Bonito Boats, Inc. v. Thunder Craft Boats, Inc.*, 489 U.S. 141, 109 S.Ct. 971, 103 L.Ed.2d 118 (1989) (same principle under patent laws).

But are rights created by contract "equivalent to any of the exclusive rights within the general scope of copyright"? Three courts of appeals have answered "no." *National Car Rental System, Inc. v. Computer Associates International, Inc.*, 991 F.2d 426, 433 (8th Cir.1993); *Taquino v. Teledyne Monarch Rubber*, 893 F.2d 1488, 1501 (5th Cir.1990); *Acorn Structures, Inc. v. Swantz*, 846 F.2d 923, 926 (4th Cir.1988). The district court disagreed with these decisions, 908 F.Supp. at 658, but we think them sound. Rights "equivalent to any of the exclusive rights within the general scope of copyright" are rights established by law rights that restrict the options of persons who are strangers to the author. Copyright law forbids duplication, public performance, and so on, unless the person wishing to copy or perform the work gets permission; silence means a ban on copying. A copyright is a right against the world. Contracts, by contrast, generally affect only their parties; strangers may do as they please, so contracts do not create "exclusive rights." Someone who found a copy of SelectPhone (trademark) on the street would not be affected by the shrinkwrap license though the federal copyright laws of their own force would limit the finder's ability to copy or transmit the application program.

Think for a moment about trade secrets. One common trade secret is a customer list. After Feist, a simple alphabetical list of a firm's customers, with address and telephone numbers, could not be protected by copyright. Yet *Kewanee Oil Co. v. Bicron Corp.*, 416 U.S. 470, 94 S.Ct. 1879, 40 L.Ed.2d 315 (1974), holds that contracts about trade secrets may be enforced precisely because they do not affect strangers' ability to discover and use the information independently. If the amendment of § 301(a) in 1976 overruled Kewanee and abolished consensual protection of those trade secrets that cannot be copyrighted, no one has noticed though abolition is a logical consequence of the district court's approach. Think, too, about everyday transactions in intellectual property. A customer visits a video store and rents a copy of Night of the Lepus. The customer's contract with the store limits use of the tape to home viewing and requires its return in two days. May the customer keep the tape, on the ground that § 301(a) makes the promise unenforceable?

A law student uses the LEXIS database, containing public-domain documents, under a contract limiting the results to educational endeavors; may the student resell his access to this database to a law firm from which LEXIS seeks to collect a much higher hourly rate Suppose ProCD hires a firm to scour the nation for telephone directories, promising to pay $100 for each that ProCD does not already have. The firm locates 100 new directories, which it sends to ProCD with an invoice for $10,000. ProCD incorporates the directories into its database; does it have to pay the bill? Surely yes; *Aronson v. Quick Point Pencil Co.*, 440 U.S. 257, 99 S.Ct. 1096, 59 L.Ed.2d 296 (1979), holds that promises to pay for intellectual property may be enforced even though federal law (in *Aronson*, the patent law) offers no protection against third-party uses of that property. See also *Kennedy v. Wright*, 851 F.2d 963 (7th Cir.1988). But these illustrations are what our case is about. ProCD offers software and data for two prices: one for personal use, a higher price for commercial use. Zeidenberg wants to use the data without paying the seller's price; if the law student and Quick Point Pencil Co. could not do that, neither can Zeidenberg.

Although Congress possesses power to preempt even the enforcement of contracts about intellectual property or railroads, on which see *Norfolk & Western Ry. v. Train Dispatchers*, 499 U.S. 117, 111 S.Ct. 1156, 113 L.Ed.2d 95 (1991) courts usually read preemption clauses to leave private contracts unaffected. *American Airlines, Inc. v. Wolens*, 513 U.S. 219, 115 S.Ct. 817, 130 L.Ed.2d 715 (1995), provides a nice illustration. A federal statute preempts any state "law, rule, regulation, standard, or other provision ... relating to rates, routes, or services of any air carrier." 49 U.S.C.App. § 1305(a)(1). Does such a law preempt the law of contracts so that, for example, an air carrier need not honor a quoted price (or a contract to reduce the price by the value of frequent flyer miles)? The Court allowed that it is possible to read the statute that broadly but thought such an interpretation would make little sense. Terms and conditions offered by contract reflect private ordering, essential to the efficient functioning of markets. 513 U.S. at 228–231, 115 S.Ct. at 824–25. Although some principles that carry the name of contract law are designed to defeat rather than implement consensual transactions, *id.* at 233 n. 8, 115 S.Ct. at 826 n. 8, the rules that respect private choice are not preempted by a clause such as § 1305(a)(1). Section 301(a) plays a role similar to § 1301(a)(1): it prevents states from substituting their own regulatory systems for those of the national government. Just as § 301(a) does not itself interfere with private transactions in intellectual property, so it does not prevent states from respecting those transactions. Like the Supreme Court in *Wolens*, we think it prudent to refrain from adopting a rule that anything with the label "contract" is necessarily outside the preemption clause: the variations and possibilities are too numerous to foresee. *National Car Rental* likewise recognizes the possibility that some applications of the law of contract could interfere with the attainment of national objectives and therefore come within the domain of § 301(a). But general enforcement of shrinkwrap licenses of the kind before us does not create such interference.

Aronson emphasized that enforcement of the contract between Aronson and Quick Point Pencil Company would not withdraw any information from the public domain. That is equally true of the contract between ProCD and Zeidenberg. Everyone remains free to copy and disseminate all 3,000 telephone books that have been incorporated into ProCD's database. Anyone can add SIC codes and zip codes. ProCD's rivals have done so. Enforcement of the shrinkwrap license may even make information more readily available, by reducing the price ProCD charges to consumer buyers. To the extent licenses facilitate distribution of object code while concealing the source code (the point of a clause forbidding disassembly), they serve the same procompetitive functions as does the law of trade secrets. *Rockwell Graphic Systems, Inc. v. DEV Industries, Inc.*, 925 F.2d 174, 180 (7th Cir.1991). Licenses may have other benefits for consumers: many licenses permit users to make extra copies, to use the software on multiple computers, even to incorporate the software into the user's products. But whether a particular license is generous or restrictive, a simple two-party contract is not "equivalent to any of the exclusive rights within the general scope of copyright" and therefore may be enforced.

REVERSED AND REMANDED.

3. *Contracts and IP Leveraging Federal Law Issues Into State Court.* The *Sea Gull, Mallinckrodt,* and *ProCD* cases each dealt with some issues that were purely matters of state law (*i.e.,* contracts), and some issues that were purely matters of federal law. Many real world transactions could give rise to a similar mix, and the shrewd lawyer must identify and evaluate their many potential strategic implications. Consider for example a contract that gives a license to do something otherwise excludable by a federal intellectual property right (*i.e.,* a patent, a copyright, or a trademark). Should the lawyer representing the owner of the intellectual property right advise her client to consider suing the licensee for breach of the license agreement as a matter of state contract law or should the suit be one for infringement of the federal intellectual property right?

More particularly, consider what impact there might be depending on whether the suit sounds in an area of state law or federal law. Consider the different remedies: so-called efficient breach theory in contract suggests that injunctions might not be available and that damages might be punitive while the federal patent, copyright, and trademark statutes each provide for injunctions and in some cases for treble damages. Also consider the different impacts on forum: state contract law cases may also be brought under the diversity jurisdiction of the federal district courts and appealed through the regional federal courts of appeals; and federal patent, copyright, and trademark cases may be brought in federal district courts and appealed through the regional federal courts of appeals if they are copyright or trademark cases or through the Federal Circuit if they are patent cases.

You should also consider the Supreme Court's recent decision in *Holmes Group, Inc. v. Vornado Air Circulation Sys., Inc.*, 535 U.S. 826 (2002). The *Holmes* case considered "whether the Federal Circuit has jurisdiction over a case in which the complaint does not allege a claim arising under federal patent law, but the answer contains a patent-law counterclaim." The Court's majority opinion, by Justice Scalia, began its analysis by noting that pursuant to 28 U.S.C. § 1295(a)(1), the Federal Circuit has appellate jurisdiction over any matter in which the district court jurisdiction was based, in whole or in part, on 28 U.S.C. § 1338, which in turn provides federal district court jurisdiction for "any civil action arising under any Act of Congress relating to patents." The "arising under" language of Section 1338 has been interpreted the same as the "arising under" language in the general federal question jurisdiction statute, 28 U.S.C. § 1331. *Id. Accord, Christianson v. Colt Indus.,* 486 U.S. 800, 808 (1988). The Court, therefore, looked to the generally applicable "well pleaded complaint rule," which provides that the Court must look to the "plaintiff's statement of his own claim." *Holmes Group,* 535 U.S. at 830. Because the plaintiff's complaint in *Holmes* did not assert any claim arising under federal patent law the Court decided that the Federal Circuit did not have jurisdiction. The Court rejected the argument that a counterclaim could serve as the basis for the "arising under" appellate jurisdiction of the Federal Circuit under patent because it had rejected similar arguments when applying the general "arising under" test for general federal question jurisdiction, which gives substantial deference to the plaintiff, who the Court treats as "the master of the complaint." *Id.* at 831. In doing so, the Court also relied on a need for linguistic consistency to reject the argument that the "arising under" test for determining Federal Circuit jurisdiction should be treated differently from the arising under test for general federal question jurisdiction. Therefore, the Court ordered that the case be transferred to the otherwise pertinent regional circuit, the Tenth Circuit.

Justice Ginsburg, joined by Justice O'Connor, concurred in the result because the patent claim had not been adjudicated below, but otherwise disagreed with the reasoning of the majority and instead agreed with the reasoning of Chief Judge Markey writing for the unanimous en banc Federal Circuit in *Aerojet–General Corp. v. Machine Tool Works*, 895 F.2d 736 (Fed.Cir.1990). Accordingly, Justices Ginsburg and O'Connor would have extended the analysis to compulsory counterclaims.

Justice Stevens concurred in the result and in part with the reasoning of the majority but also pointed out: "the jurisdiction of the court of appeals is not 'fixed' until the notice of appeal is filed." *Holmes*, Slip Op. at 1 (Stevens, J.) (concurring) (quoting *Griggs v. Provident Consumer Discount Co.*, 459 U.S. 56, 58–59 (1982)). Justice Stevens thereby provides important advice for a patentee otherwise dissatisfied with the impact of *Holmes*.

The full impact of the *Holmes* decision will not be understood for some time. In general, it will be interesting to see what patent issues make their way to the regional circuits. Which ones do you think will?

2.   UNFAIR COMPETITION LAW

Bonito Boats v. Thunder Craft Boats

489 U.S. 141 (1989).

■ JUSTICE O'CONNOR delivered the opinion of the Court.

We must decide today what limits the operation of the federal patent system places on the States' ability to offer substantial protection to utilitarian and design ideas which the patent laws leave otherwise unprotected. In *Interpart Corp. v. Italia*, 777 F.2d 678 (1985), the Court of Appeals for the Federal Circuit concluded that a California law prohibiting the use of the "direct molding process" to duplicate unpatented articles posed no threat to the policies behind the federal patent laws. In this case, the Florida Supreme Court came to a contrary conclusion. It struck down a Florida statute which prohibits the use of the direct molding process to duplicate unpatented boat hulls, finding that the protection offered by the Florida law conflicted with the balance struck by Congress in the federal patent statute between the encouragement of invention and free competition in unpatented ideas. 515 So.2d 220 (1987). We granted certiorari to resolve the conflict, 486 U.S. 1004, 108 S.Ct. 1727, 100 L.Ed.2d 192 (1988), and we now affirm the judgment of the Florida Supreme Court.

I

In September 1976, petitioner Bonito Boats, Inc. (Bonito), a Florida corporation, developed a hull design for a fiberglass recreational boat which it marketed under the trade name Bonito Boat Model 5VBR. App. 5. Designing the boat hull required substantial effort on the part of Bonito. A set of engineering drawings was prepared, from which a hardwood model was created. The hardwood model was then sprayed with fiberglass to create a mold, which then served to produce the finished fiberglass boats for sale. The 5VBR was placed on the market sometime in September 1976.

There is no indication in the record that a patent application was ever filed for protection of the utilitarian or design aspects of the hull, or for the process by which the hull was manufactured. The 5VBR was favorably received by the boating public, and "a broad interstate market" developed for its sale.

In May 1983, after the Bonito 5VBR had been available to the public for over six years, the Florida Legislature enacted Fla.Stat. § 559.94 (1987). The statute makes "[i]t ... unlawful for any person to use the direct molding process to duplicate for the purpose of sale any manufactured vessel hull or component part of a vessel made by another without the written permission of that other person." § 559.94(2). The statute also makes it unlawful for a person to "knowingly sell a vessel hull or component part of a vessel duplicated in violation of subsection (2)." § 559.94(3)....

On December 21, 1984, Bonito filed this action in the Circuit Court of Orange County, Florida. The complaint alleged that respondent here, Thunder Craft Boats, Inc. (Thunder Craft), a Tennessee corporation, had violated the Florida statute by using the direct molding process to duplicate the Bonito 5VBR fiberglass hull, and had knowingly sold such duplicates in violation of the Florida statute. Bonito sought "a temporary and permanent injunction prohibiting [Thunder Craft] from continuing to unlawfully duplicate and sell Bonito Boat hulls or components," as well as an accounting of profits, treble damages, punitive damages, and attorney's fees. App. 6, 7. Respondent filed a motion to dismiss the complaint, arguing that under this Court's decisions in *Sears, Roebuck & Co. v. Stiffel Co.*, 376 U.S. 225, 84 S.Ct. 784, 11 L.Ed.2d 661 (1964), and *Compco Corp. v. Day–Brite Lighting, Inc.*, 376 U.S. 234, 84 S.Ct. 779, 11 L.Ed.2d 669 (1964), the Florida statute conflicted with federal patent law and was therefore invalid under the Supremacy Clause of the Federal Constitution.

On appeal, a sharply divided Florida Supreme Court agreed with the lower courts' conclusion that the Florida law impermissibly interfered with the scheme established by the federal patent laws. The majority read our decisions in *Sears* and *Compco* for the proposition that "when an article is introduced into the public domain, only a patent can eliminate the inherent risk of competition and then but for a limited time."

II

* * *

From their inception, the federal patent laws have embodied a careful balance between the need to promote innovation and the recognition that imitation and refinement through imitation are both necessary to invention itself and the very lifeblood of a competitive economy. The novelty requirement of patentability is presently expressed in 35 U.S.C. §§ 102(a) and (b). Sections 102(a) and (b) operate in tandem to exclude from consideration for patent protection knowledge that is already available to the public. They express a congressional determination that the creation of a monopoly in such information would not only serve no socially useful purpose, but would in fact injure the public by removing existing knowledge from public use. Even if a particular combination of elements is "novel" in the literal sense of the term, it will not qualify for federal patent protection if its contours are so traced by the existing technology in the field that the "improvement is the work of the skillful mechanic, not that of the inventor." *Hotchkiss v. Greenwood*, 11 How. 248, 267, 13 L.Ed. 683 (1851). In 1952, Congress codified this judicially developed requirement in 35 U.S.C. § 103, which refuses protection to new developments where "the differences between the subject matter sought to be patented and the prior art are such that the subject matter as a whole would have been obvious at the time the invention was made to a person of ordinary skill in the art to which said subject matter pertains." Taken together, the novelty and nonobviousness requirements express a congressional determination that the purposes behind the Patent Clause are best served by free competition and exploitation of either that which is already available to the public or that which may be readily discerned from publicly available material. *See Aronson v. Quick Point Pencil Co.*, 440 U.S. 257, 262, 99 S.Ct. 1096, 1099, 59 L.Ed.2d 296 (1979) ("[T]he stringent requirements for patent protection seek to ensure that ideas in the public domain remain there for the use of the public").

* * *

The attractiveness of such a bargain, and its effectiveness in inducing creative effort and disclosure of the results of that effort, depend almost entirely on a backdrop of free competition in the exploitation of unpatented designs and innovations. The novelty and nonobviousness requirements of patentability embody a congressional understanding, implicit in the Patent Clause itself, that free exploitation of ideas will be the rule, to which the protection of a federal patent is the exception. Moreover, the ultimate goal of the patent system is to bring new designs and technologies into the public domain through disclosure. State law protection for techniques and designs whose disclosure has already been induced by market rewards may conflict with the very purpose of the patent laws by decreasing the range of ideas available as the building blocks of further innovation. The offer of federal protection from competitive exploitation of intellectual property would be rendered meaningless in a world where substantially similar state law protections were readily available. To a limited extent, the federal patent laws must determine not only what is protected, but also what is free for all to use.

* * *

Thus our past decisions have made clear that state regulation of intellectual property must yield to the extent that it clashes with the balance struck by Congress in our patent laws. The tension between the desire to freely exploit the full potential of our inventive resources and the need to create an incentive to deploy those resources is constant. Where it is clear how the patent laws strike that balance in a particular circumstance, that is not a judgment the States may second-guess. We have long held that after the expiration of a federal patent, the subject matter of the patent passes to the free use of the public as a matter of federal law. Where the public has paid the congressionally mandated price for disclosure, the

States may not render the exchange fruitless by offering patent-like protection to the subject matter of the expired patent. "It is self-evident that on the expiration of a patent the monopoly created by it ceases to exist, and the right to make the thing formerly covered by the patent becomes public property."

In our decisions in *Sears, Roebuck & Co. v. Stiffel Co.*, 376 U.S. 225 (1964), and *Compco Corp. v. Day–Brite Lighting, Inc.*, 376 U.S. 234 (1964), we found that publicly known design and utilitarian ideas which were unprotected by patent occupied much the same position as the subject matter of an expired patent. The *Sears* case involved a pole lamp originally designed by the plaintiff Stiffel, who had secured both design and mechanical patents on the lamp. Sears purchased unauthorized copies of the lamps, and was able to sell them at a retail price practically equivalent to the wholesale price of the original manufacturer. *Sears, supra*, 376 U.S., at 226, 84 S.Ct., at 786. Stiffel brought an action against Sears in Federal District Court, alleging infringement of the two federal patents and unfair competition under Illinois law. The District Court found that Stiffel's patents were invalid due to anticipation in the prior art, but nonetheless enjoined Sears from further sales of the duplicate lamps based on a finding of consumer confusion under the Illinois law of unfair competition. The Court of Appeals affirmed, coming to the conclusion that the Illinois law of unfair competition prohibited product simulation even in the absence of evidence that the defendant took some further action to induce confusion as to source.

This Court reversed, finding that the unlimited protection against copying which the Illinois law accorded an unpatentable item whose design had been fully disclosed through public sales conflicted with the federal policy embodied in the patent laws. The Court stated:

> In the present case the "pole lamp" sold by Stiffel has been held not to be entitled to the protection of either a mechanical or a design patent. An unpatentable article, like an article on which the patent has expired, is in the public domain and may be made and sold by whoever chooses to do so. What Sears did was to copy Stiffel's design and sell lamps almost identical to those sold by Stiffel. This it had every right to do under the federal patent laws. 376 U.S., at 231, 84 S.Ct., at 789.

The pre-emptive sweep of our decisions in *Sears* and *Compco* has been the subject of heated scholarly and judicial debate. Read at their highest level of generality, the two decisions could be taken to stand for the proposition that the States are completely disabled from offering any form of protection to articles or processes which fall within the broad scope of patentable subject matter. Since the potentially patentable includes "anything under the sun that is made by man," *Diamond v. Chakrabarty*, 447 U.S. 303, 309 (1980), the broadest reading of *Sears* would prohibit the States from regulating the deceptive simulation of trade dress or the tortious appropriation of private information.

That the extrapolation of such a broad pre-emptive principle from *Sears* is inappropriate is clear from the balance struck in *Sears* itself. The *Sears* Court made it plain that the States "may protect businesses in the use of their trademarks, labels, or distinctive dress in the packaging of goods so as to prevent others, by imitating such markings, from misleading purchasers as to the source of the goods." *Sears, supra,* 376 U.S., at 232. Trade dress is, of course, potentially the subject matter of design patents. Yet our decision in *Sears* clearly indicates that the States may place limited regulations on the circumstances in which such designs are used in order to prevent consumer confusion as to source. Thus, while *Sears* speaks in absolutist terms, its conclusion that the States may place some conditions on the use of trade dress indicates an implicit recognition that all state regulation of potentially patentable but unpatented subject matter is not ipso facto pre-empted by the federal patent laws.

* * *

At the heart of *Sears* and *Compco* is the conclusion that the efficient operation of the federal patent system depends upon substantially free trade in publicly known, unpatented design and utilitarian conceptions. In *Sears,* the state law offered "the equivalent of a patent monopoly," in the functional aspects of a product which had been placed in public commerce absent the protection of a valid patent. While, as noted above, our decisions since *Sears* have taken a decidedly less rigid view of the scope of federal pre-emption under the patent laws, *e.g., Kewanee, supra,* 416 U.S., at 479–480, we believe that the *Sears* Court correctly concluded that the States may not offer patent-like protection to intellectual creations which would otherwise remain unprotected as a matter of federal law. Both the novelty and the nonobviousness requirements of federal patent law are grounded in the notion that concepts within the public grasp, or those so obvious that they readily could be, are the tools of creation available to all. They provide the baseline of free competition upon which the patent system's incentive to creative effort depends. A state law that substantially interferes with the enjoyment of an unpatented utilitarian or design conception which has been freely disclosed by its author to the public at large impermissibly contravenes the ultimate goal of public disclosure and use which is the centerpiece of federal patent policy. Moreover, through the creation of patent-like rights, the States could essentially redirect inventive efforts away from the careful criteria of patentability developed by Congress over the last 200 years. We understand this to be the reasoning at the core of our decisions in *Sears* and *Compco,* and we reaffirm that reasoning today.

III

We believe that the Florida statute at issue in this case so substantially impedes the public use of the otherwise unprotected design and utilitarian ideas embodied in unpatented boat hulls as to run afoul of the teaching of our decisions in *Sears* and *Compco.* It is readily apparent that the Florida statute does not operate to prohibit "unfair competition" in the usual sense that the term is understood. The law of unfair competition has its roots in the common-law tort of deceit: its general concern is with protecting consumers from confusion as to source. While that concern may result in the creation of "quasi-property rights" in communicative symbols, the focus is on the protection of consumers, not the protection of producers as an incentive to product innovation....

* * *

In contrast to the operation of unfair competition law, the Florida statute is aimed directly at preventing the exploitation of the design and utilitarian conceptions embodied in the product itself. The sparse legislative history surrounding its enactment indicates that it was intended to create an inducement for the improvement of boat hull designs. See Tr. of Meeting of Transportation Committee, Florida House of Representatives, May 3, 1983, reprinted at App. 22 ("[T]here is no inducement for [a] quality boat manufacturer to improve these designs and secondly, if he does, it is immediately copied. This would prevent that and allow him recourse in circuit court"). To accomplish this goal, the Florida statute endows the original boat hull manufacturer with rights against the world, similar in scope and operation to the rights accorded a federal patentee. Like the patentee, the beneficiary of the Florida statute may prevent a competitor from "making" the product in what is evidently the most efficient manner available and from "selling" the product when it is produced in that fashion. The Florida scheme offers this protection for an unlimited number of years to all boat hulls and their component parts, without regard to their ornamental or technological merit. Protection is available for subject matter for which patent protection has been denied or has expired, as well as for designs which have been freely revealed to the consuming public by their creators.

In this case, the Bonito 5VBR fiberglass hull has been freely exposed to the public for a period in excess of six years. For purposes of federal law, it stands in the same stead as an item for which a patent has expired or been denied: it is unpatented and unpatentable. See 35 U.S.C. § 102(b). Whether because of a determination of unpatentability or other commercial concerns, petitioner chose to expose its hull design to the public in the marketplace, eschewing the bargain held out by the federal patent system of disclosure in exchange for exclusive use. Yet, the Florida statute allows petitioner to reassert a substantial property right in the idea, thereby constricting the spectrum of useful public knowledge. Moreover, it does so without the careful protections of high standards of innovation and limited monopoly contained in the federal scheme. We think it clear that such protection conflicts with the federal policy "that all ideas in general circulation be dedicated to the common good unless they are protected by a valid patent." *Lear, Inc. v. Adkins*, 395 U.S., at 668.

That the Florida statute does not remove all means of reproduction and sale does not eliminate the conflict with the federal scheme. In essence, the Florida law prohibits the entire public from engaging in a form of reverse engineering of a product in the public domain. This is clearly one of the rights vested in the federal patent holder, but has never been a part of state protection under the law of unfair competition or trade secrets. See *Kewanee*, 416 U.S., at 476 ("A trade secret law, however, does not offer protection against discovery by . . . so-called reverse engineering, that is by starting with the known product and working backward to divine the process which aided in its development or manufacture"). The duplication of boat hulls and their component parts may be an essential part of innovation in the field of hydrodynamic design. Variations as to size and combination of various elements may lead to significant advances in the field. Reverse engineering of chemical and mechanical articles in the public domain often leads to significant advances in technology. If Florida may prohibit this particular method of study and recomposition of an unpatented article, we fail to see the principle that would prohibit a State from banning the use of chromatography in the reconstitution of unpatented chemical compounds, or the use of robotics in the duplication of machinery in the public domain.

Moreover, as we noted in *Kewanee*, the competitive reality of reverse engineering may act as a spur to the inventor, creating an incentive to develop inventions that meet the rigorous requirements of patentability. 416 U.S., at 489–490, 94 S.Ct., at 1889–1890. The Florida statute substantially reduces this competitive incentive, thus eroding the general rule of free competition upon which the attractiveness of the federal patent bargain depends. The protections of state trade secret law are most effective at the developmental stage, before a product has been marketed and the threat of reverse engineering becomes real. During this period, patentability will often be an uncertain prospect, and to a certain extent, the protection offered by trade secret law may "dovetail" with the incentives created by the federal patent monopoly. In contrast, under the Florida scheme, the would-be inventor is aware from the outset of his efforts that rights against the public are available regardless of his ability to satisfy the rigorous standards of patentability. Indeed, it appears that even the most mundane and obvious changes in the design of a boat hull will trigger the protections of the statute. See Fla.Stat. § 559.94(2) (1987) (protecting "any manufactured vessel hull or component part"). Given the substantial protection offered by the Florida scheme, we cannot dismiss as hypothetical the possibility that it will become a significant competitor to the federal patent laws, offering investors similar protection without the quid pro quo of substantial creative effort required by the federal statute. The prospect of all 50 States establishing similar protections for preferred industries without the rigorous requirements of patentability prescribed by Congress could pose a substantial threat to the patent system's ability to accomplish its mission of promoting progress in the useful arts.

Finally, allowing the States to create patent-like rights in various products in public circulation would lead to administrative problems of no small dimension. The federal patent scheme provides a basis for the public to ascertain the status of the intellectual property embodied in any article in general circulation. Through the application process, detailed information concerning the claims of the patent holder is compiled in a central location....

The Florida scheme blurs this clear federal demarcation between public and private property. One of the fundamental purposes behind the Patent and Copyright Clauses of the Constitution was to promote national uniformity in the realm of intellectual property. See The Federalist No. 43, p. 309 (B. Wright ed. 1961). Since the Patent Act of 1800, Congress has lodged exclusive jurisdiction of actions "arising under" the patent laws in the federal courts, thus allowing for the development of a uniform body of law in resolving the constant tension between private right and public access. See 28 U.S.C. § 1338; *see also* Chisum, *The Allocation of Jurisdiction Between State and Federal Courts in Patent Litigation*, 46 WASH.L.REV.

633, 636 (1971). Recently, Congress conferred exclusive jurisdiction of all patent appeals on the Court of Appeals for the Federal Circuit, in order to "provide nationwide uniformity in patent law." H.R.Rep. No. 97–312, p. 20 (1981). This purpose is frustrated by the Florida scheme, which renders the status of the design and utilitarian "ideas" embodied in the boat hulls it protects uncertain. Given the inherently ephemeral nature of property in ideas, and the great power such property has to cause harm to the competitive policies which underlay the federal patent laws, the demarcation of broad zones of public and private right is "the type of regulation that demands a uniform national rule." Absent such a federal rule, each State could afford patent-like protection to particularly favored home industries, effectively insulating them from competition from outside the State.

Petitioner and its supporting amici place great weight on the contrary decision of the Court of Appeals for the Federal Circuit in *Interpart Corp. v. Italia*. In upholding the application of the California "antidirect molding" statute to the duplication of unpatented automobile mirrors, the Federal Circuit stated: "The statute prevents unscrupulous competitors from obtaining a product and using it as the 'plug' for making a mold. The statute does not prohibit copying the design of the product in any other way; the latter if in the public domain, is free for anyone to make, use or sell." 777 F.2d, at 685. The court went on to indicate that "the patent laws 'say nothing about the right to copy or the right to use, they speak only in terms of the right to exclude.' " *Ibid.*, quoting *Mine Safety Appliances Co. v. Electric Storage Battery Co.*, 56 C.C.P.A. (Pat.) 863, 864, n. 2, 405 F.2d 901, 902, n. 2 (1969).

We find this reasoning defective in several respects. The Federal Circuit apparently viewed the direct molding statute at issue in *Interpart* as a mere regulation of the use of chattels. Yet, the very purpose of antidirect molding statutes is to "reward" the "inventor" by offering substantial protection against public exploitation of his or her idea embodied in the product. Such statutes would be an exercise in futility if they did not have precisely the effect of substantially limiting the ability of the public to exploit an otherwise unprotected idea. As amicus [Charles E. Lipsey, by appointment of the Court in support of affirmance] points out, the direct molding process itself has been in use since the early 1950s.... It is difficult to conceive of a more effective method of creating substantial property rights in an intellectual creation than to eliminate the most efficient method for its exploitation. *Sears* and *Compco* protect more than the right of the public to contemplate the abstract beauty of an otherwise unprotected intellectual creation they assure its efficient reduction to practice and sale in the marketplace.

* * *

Our decisions since *Sears* and *Compco* have made it clear that the Patent and Copyright Clauses do not, by their own force or by negative implication, deprive the States of the power to adopt rules for the promotion of intellectual creation within their own jurisdictions. *See Aronson*, 440 U.S., at 262, 99 S.Ct., at 1099; *Goldstein v. California*, 412 U.S. 546, 552–561, 93 S.Ct. 2303, 2307–2312, 37 L.Ed.2d 163 (1973); *Kewanee*, 416

U.S., at 478–479, 94 S.Ct., at 1884–1885. Thus, where "Congress determines that neither federal protection nor freedom from restraint is required by the national interest," *Goldstein, supra*, 412 U.S., at 559, 93 S.Ct., at 2311, the States remain free to promote originality and creativity in their own domains.

Nor does the fact that a particular item lies within the subject matter of the federal patent laws necessarily preclude the States from offering limited protection which does not impermissibly interfere with the federal patent scheme. As *Sears* itself makes clear, States may place limited regulations on the use of unpatented designs in order to prevent consumer confusion as to source. In *Kewanee*, we found that state protection of trade secrets, as applied to both patentable and unpatentable subject matter, did not conflict with the federal patent laws. In both situations, state protection was not aimed exclusively at the promotion of invention itself, and the state restrictions on the use of unpatented ideas were limited to those necessary to promote goals outside the contemplation of the federal patent scheme. Both the law of unfair competition and state trade secret law have coexisted harmoniously with federal patent protection for almost 200 years, and Congress has given no indication that their operation is inconsistent with the operation of the federal patent laws.

Indeed, there are affirmative indications from Congress that both the law of unfair competition and trade secret protection are consistent with the balance struck by the patent laws. Section 43(a) of the Lanham Act, 60 Stat. 441, 15 U.S.C. § 1125(a), creates a federal remedy for making "a false designation of origin, or any false description or representation, including words or other symbols tending falsely to describe or represent the same...." Congress has thus given federal recognition to many of the concerns that underlie the state tort of unfair competition, and the application of *Sears* and *Compco* to nonfunctional aspects of a product which have been shown to identify source must take account of competing federal policies in this regard. Similarly, as Justice Marshall noted in his concurring opinion in *Kewanee*: "State trade secret laws and the federal patent laws have co-existed for many, many years. During this time, Congress has repeatedly demonstrated its full awareness of the existence of the trade secret system, without any indication of disapproval. Indeed, Congress has in a number of instances given explicit federal protection to trade secret information provided to federal agencies." *Kewanee, supra*, 416 U.S., at 494, 94 S.Ct., at 1892 (concurring in result) (citation omitted). The case for federal pre-emption is particularly weak where Congress has indicated its awareness of the operation of state law in a field of federal interest, and has nonetheless decided to "stand by both concepts and to tolerate whatever tension there [is] between them." The same cannot be said of the Florida statute at issue here, which offers protection beyond that available under the law of unfair competition or trade secret, without any showing of consumer confusion, or breach of trust or secrecy.

* * *

Congress has considered extending various forms of limited protection to industrial design either through the copyright laws or by relaxing the restrictions on the availability of design patents. Congress explicitly refused to take this step in the copyright laws, and despite sustained criticism for a number of years, it has declined to alter the patent protections presently available for industrial design. It is for Congress to determine if the present system of design and utility patents is ineffectual in promoting the useful arts in the context of industrial design. By offering patent-like protection for ideas deemed unprotected under the present federal scheme, the Florida statute conflicts with the "strong federal policy favoring free competition in ideas which do not merit patent protection." *Lear, Inc.*, 395 U.S., at 656, 89 S.Ct., at 1903. We therefore agree with the majority of the Florida Supreme Court that the Florida statute is preempted by the Supremacy Clause, and the judgment of that court is hereby affirmed.

NOTES

1. How does the law against unfair competition interfere with patent law? To what extent do they regulate the same or different behaviors? What other types of State laws interfere with patent law under the reasoning of *Bonito Boats*? Consider laws designed to impede, but not prevent direct appropriation of another's commercial advantage. To what extent does *Bonito Boats* reveal a fundamental tension between substantive patent law and substantive unfair competition law, whether of State or federal origin? As we saw in Chapter Seven, there is a substantial debate over the *types* of things that may be protected under patent law. Perhaps there is a similar debate over the types of things that may be protected under trademark law and unfair competition law. Commentators note that federal unfair competition law has greatly expanded in this century, from the creation of the Lanham Act in 1947 as predominantly a trademark statute to the substantial increase in the use of the Lanham Act in the 1970s in areas previously considered to be State unfair competition law. *See* J. Thomas McCarthy, McCarthy on Trademarks and Unfair Competition § 1:17, citing generally, Charles E. McKenney and George F. Long, III, Federal Unfair Competition: Lanham Act § 43(A), Ch. 1. But the reach of unfair competition law has been curtailed most recently, especially when it comes into contact with patent law. Consider, for example, the discussion by the Supreme Court in the recent case of *TrafFix Devices, Inc. v. Marketing Displays, Inc.*, 532 U.S. 23, 28–32 (2001):

> [T]he Court of Appeals took note of a split among Courts of Appeals in various other Circuits on the issue whether the existence of an expired utility patent forecloses the possibility of the patentee's claiming trade dress protection in the product's design. *Compare Sunbeam Products, Inc. v. West Bend Co.*, 123 F.3d 246 (5th Cir.1997) (holding that trade dress protection is not foreclosed), *Thomas & Betts Corp. v. Panduit Corp.*, 138 F.3d 277 (7th Cir.1998) (same), and *Midwest Industries, Inc. v. Karavan Trailers, Inc.*, 175 F.3d 1356 (Fed.Cir.1999) (same), with *Vornado Air Circulation Systems, Inc. v. Duracraft Corp.*, 58 F.3d 1498, 1500 (10th Cir.1995) ("Where a product configuration is a significant inventive component of an invention covered by a utility patent . . . it cannot receive trade dress protection").

* * *

The principal question in this case is the effect of an expired patent on a claim of trade dress infringement. A prior patent, we conclude, has vital significance in resolving the trade dress claim. A utility patent is strong evidence that the features therein claimed are functional. If trade dress protection is sought for those features the strong evidence of functionality based on the previous patent adds great weight to the statutory presumption that features are deemed functional until proved otherwise by the party seeking trade dress protection. Where the expired patent claimed the features in question, one who seeks to establish trade dress protection must carry the heavy burden of showing that the feature is not functional, for instance by showing that it is merely an ornamental, incidental, or arbitrary aspect of the device.

* * *

These statements made in the patent applications and in the course of procuring the patents demonstrate the functionality of the design. MDI does not assert that any of these representations are mistaken or inaccurate, and this is further strong evidence of the functionality of the dual-spring design.

2.   In what way do the patent laws grant permission to copy unpatented articles? Where in Title 35 is there a grant of the right to copy? Is it correct to view patent law as entirely directed to rights of exclusion, with the non-imposition of those rights in cases of unpatentability or patent invalidity, and the lifting of those rights in cases of patent expiration? Consider the opinion by Circuit Judge Rich, joined by Circuit Judges Friedman and Bissell, in *Interpart Corp. v. Italia*, 777 F.2d 678 (Fed.Cir.1985):

> This appeal is from the judgment entered July 30, 1984, by the United States District Court for the Central District of California granting summary judgment to appellee Interpart Corporation (Interpart) and holding that United States Design Patent No. 263,130 for "Rear View Mirror," assigned to appellant Imos Italia, Vitaloni, S.p.A., et al. (Vitaloni), is invalid and not infringed by Interpart; that Interpart's manufacture and sale of automobile mirrors does not constitute unfair competition within the meaning of § 43(a) of the Lanham Act, 15 U.S.C. § 1125(a) or within the meaning of §§ 17200, 17300, and 17500 of the California Business and Professions Code; and that Interpart is entitled to an award of attorney fees from Vitaloni for defending the patent infringement action. We affirm-in-part, reverse-in-part, and remand.

Background

> Interpart produces and distributes automobile rear view mirrors in the automobile aftermarket throughout the United States under the styles and trademarks "Interpart," "Mirrari 1," "Mirrari 2," "Mirrari 3," "Mirrari Oval," "Mirrari ERC," and "Mirrari VT." Imos Italia sells automobile rear view mirrors manufactured by Vitaloni in the same aftermarket under the styles and trademarks "Vitaloni," "Tornado Van," "Baby Tornado," and others. Torino exclusively assembles, distributes, and sells the Vitaloni mirrors throughout the United States. Interpart admits that it copied Vitaloni's mirrors, claiming the right to do so.

* * *

II.   Copying of the Vitaloni Mirrors Absent Valid Patent Rights

A.   The Lanham Act, § 43(a)

* * *

> Vitaloni's attempt to recover under § 43(a) for unfair competition by claiming that it need show only nonfunctionality, secondary meaning, and likelihood of confusion would be successful if the facts were not, as they are

here, that Interpart clearly indicated the source of its mirrors. The district court found that Interpart did not falsely describe the origin of its mirrors and that there was no evidence that Interpart did not "clearly designate itself as the manufacturer and/or clearly designate the product as one of the Mirrari line." The court had before it the boxes in which Interpart sold its mirrors. There was testimony during the proceedings, with cross examination, that Interpart used boxes that designated Interpart as the source and indicated that the contents were Mirrari mirrors for retail sales, and that plain boxes were used for sales from Sears and Montgomery Ward's catalogs. The evidence was uncontroverted that every mirror, regardless of how it was sold, had a silver and black mylar label on it that read "Interpart Mirrari"; Interpart did not compete unfairly within the meaning of § 43(a) of the Lanham Act. We therefore affirm the district court's judgment on this issue.

* * *

III. California Business and Professions Code
§ 17300: The Plug Molding Statute

A. Versus the Patent Law

Whether California's plug molding statute is preempted by federal law involves a consideration, under Ninth Circuit law, see *Cable Electric Products, Inc. v. Genmark, Inc.*, 770 F.2d 1015, 1033, 226 USPQ 881, 893 (Fed.Cir.1985), of whether that law "stands as an obstacle to the accomplishment and execution of the full purposes and objectives of Congress." *Kewanee Oil Co. v. Bicron Corp.*, 416 U.S. [470] 474, 94 S.Ct. 1879, 1882, 40 L.Ed.2d 315 (1974) (quoting *Hines v. Davidowitz*, 312 U.S. 52, 67, 61 S.Ct. 399, 404, 85 L.Ed. 581 (1941)). The state law must fail if it "clashes with the objectives of the federal patent laws." *Sears, Roebuck & Co. v. Stiffel Co.*, 376 U.S. 225, 231, 84 S.Ct. 784, 788, 11 L.Ed.2d 661 (1964).

Congress was granted the power to legislate in the areas of patents and copyrights by the Constitution to "promote the Progress of Science and useful Arts." The patent law, in order to promote the useful arts, grants to inventors the right, limited in time, to exclude others from making, using, or selling their patented inventions.

The California plug molding statute, to the contrary, proscribes use of the product itself for a pattern or "plug" in a direct molding process. In that process, the product is entirely coated with a mold-forming substance that sets and which is then removed from the product and used as the mold for making numerous replicas of the product. This process is substantially less expensive than developing a mold from scratch, something the original product manufacturer has to do. The statute reads:

§ 17300. Unlawful acts; duplication for sale; sale

(a) It shall be unlawful for any person to duplicate for the purpose of sale any manufactured item made by another without the permission of that other person using the direct molding process described in subdivision (b) [sic, (c)].

(b) It shall be unlawful for any person to sell an item duplicated in violation of subdivision (a).

(c) The direct molding processes subject to this section is [sic] any direct molding process in which the original manufactured item was itself used as a plug for the making of the mold which is used to manufacture the duplicate item.

(d) The provisions of this section shall apply only to items duplicated using a mold made on or after January 1, 1979.

California Business and Professions Code (West Supp.1985). It is clear from the face of the statute that it does not give the creator of the product the right to exclude others from making, using, or selling the product as does the patent law. The statute does not preclude one from photographing, measuring, or in any way utilizing the concept of the design of the product. It does not preclude copying the product by hand, by using sophisticated machinery, or by any method other than the direct molding process. This is clear from a review of the record which includes much material bearing on the constitutionality of the statute.

The statute prevents unscrupulous competitors from obtaining a product and using it as the "plug" for making a mold. The statute does not prohibit copying the design of the product in any other way; the latter, if in the public domain, is free for anyone to make, use, or sell.

Moreover, as a predecessor of this court once stated, the patent laws "say nothing about the right to copy or the right to use, they speak only in terms of the right to exclude." *Mine Safety Appliances v. Electric Storage Battery*, 405 F.2d 901, 902 n. 2, 160 USPQ 413, 414 n. 2 (CCPA 1969). The California law does not "clash" with the federal patent law; the two laws have different objectives. Absent an existing patent right, we see nothing in the federal patent statutes that conflicts with California's desire to prevent a particular type of competition which it considers unfair. This California statute is not preempted by federal law, contrary to the district court's conclusion.

* * *

3. What did the state statutes in *Bonito Boats* and *Interpart* really do? Did they prevent copying? Or were they merely designed to impede, but not prevent, direct appropriation of another's commercial advantage to ensure the "maintenance of standards of commercial ethics and the encouragement of invention," in the words of Chief Justice Burger in *Kewanee*? Consider a state law against breaking into a company's "trade secret safe". What if technology or social norms change so that it is now possible to peer into an opponents trade secret safe from one's own factory? Surely it is much easier to peer over the shoulders of one's opponent than to solve a business problem independently. Now return to the state law at issue in *Bonito Boats* and *Interpart*, a law that prevented the easiest form of copying, but not other forms of copying, and certainly not independent creation. How is a law against theft different from a law against snatching up what is left unwittingly exposed? To be sure, as noted by Chief Justice Burger in *Kewanee*, there are social costs associated with the self help that might arise in a world where theft was not prevented. But is the elimination of those social costs the only reason to permit trade secret protection? How about the creation of incentives for individual firms to do a certain amount of individual work, because that seems to be a good thing in its own right?

4. General notions of Federalism are emphasized in the *Bonito Boats* opinion: "allowing the States to create patent-like rights in various products in public circulation would lead to administrative problems of no small dimension." The opinion cites the importance of patent law's centralized recording and public marking requirements. Would the opinion have come out differently if the state laws at issue similarly required centralized recording and public marking? Remember, such coordinated recording and notice requirements are common at the state level under various provisions of the Uniform Commercial Code.

5.   When do you think a state should be allowed to regulate behavior of its own citizens in its own market places without being considered to run into the preemptive power of the federal patent system (putting aside the preemptive power of the Commerce Clause and so-called Dormant Commerce Clause, which are studied in depth in classes on Constitutional Law)? Should the result be any different if it is the federal government regulating the market activity (again putting aside the preemptive power of the Commerce Clause and so-called Dormant Commerce Clause)? Today, as long as the law does not offer patent-like protection, it seems that courts will apply a so-called extra-element test to determine whether the state law can survive. Consider, for example, the following discussion by the Federal Circuit in *Dow Chemical Co. v. Exxon Corp.*, 139 F.3d 1470, 1473 (Fed.Cir.1998):

> The principal problem presented to the court is whether state courts, or federal courts adjudicating state law claims, may hear a state law tort claim for intentional interference with actual and prospective contractual relations that implicates the patent law issue of inequitable conduct or, alternatively, whether such a claim is preempted by the federal patent law. We hold that such a state law tort claim is not preempted by the federal patent law, even if it requires the state court to adjudicate a question of federal patent law, provided the state law cause of action includes additional elements not found in the federal patent law cause of action and is not an impermissible attempt to offer patent-like protection to subject matter addressed by federal law.

See also Hunter Douglas, Inc. v. Harmonic Design, Inc., 153 F.3d 1318, 1336–37 (Fed.Cir.1998) (no conflict-type preemption of various state law claims based on publicizing an allegedly invalid and unenforceable patent in the marketplace as long as the claimant can show that the patent holder acted in bad faith in publication of the patent). Concerning federal competition law, compare the above discussion with the following discussion by the Federal Circuit in *Zenith Electronics Corp. v. Exzec, Inc.*, 182 F.3d 1340, 1353–54 (Fed.Cir.1999):

> Accordingly, we conclude that, before a patentee may be held liable under § 43(a) for marketplace activity in support of its patent, and thus be deprived of the right to make statements about potential infringement of its patent, the marketplace activity must have been undertaken in bad faith. This prerequisite is a function of the interaction between the Lanham Act and patent law, and is in addition to the elements required by § 43(a) itself, as § 43(a) alone does not require bad faith, *see, e.g., Seven–Up Co.*, 86 F.3d at 1383 n. 3; *Brandt Consol.*, 801 F.Supp. at 174 ("bad faith is not an element of this [§ 43(a)] cause of action"); *Procter & Gamble Co. v. Chesebrough–Pond's, Inc.*, 747 F.2d 114, 119 (2d Cir.1984) (plaintiff need not prove bad faith to establish § 43(a) liability).

> Requiring bad faith in this context is closely analogous to the conclusion we reached in *Hunter Douglas*—i.e., that, to impose state tort liability against a patentee for publicizing its patent, bad faith in publication of the patent must be established to avoid preemption by patent law, regardless of whether the state cause of action otherwise requires bad faith. *See Hunter Douglas*, 153 F.3d at 1336–37.

> By adding a bad faith requirement to a § 43(a) claim in the context of this case, we give effect both to the rights of patentees as protected by the patent laws under ordinary circumstances, and to the salutary purposes of the Lanham Act to promote fair competition in the marketplace. As thus understood, there is no conflict between the demands of the Lanham Act

and the Patent Act, and a patentee is easily able to comply with both Acts. Furthermore, patent law is not frustrated because bad faith marketplace statements concerning patents do not further the purposes of the patent law. *Cf. Handgards*, 601 F.2d at 993 ("[I]nfringement actions initiated and conducted in bad faith contribute nothing to the furtherance of the policies of either the patent law or the antitrust law.").

3. TRADE SECRET LAW

Kewanee Oil Co. v. Bicron

416 U.S. 470 (1974).

■ MR. CHIEF JUSTICE BURGER delivered the opinion of the Court.

We granted certiorari to resolve a question on which there is a conflict in the courts of appeals: whether state trade secret protection is pre-empted by operation of the federal patent law. In the instant case the Court of Appeals for the Sixth Circuit held that there was pre-emption. The Courts of Appeals for the Second, Fourth, Fifth and Ninth Circuits have reached the opposite conclusion.

I

Harshaw Chemical Co., an unincorporated division of petitioner, is a leading manufacturer of a type of synthetic crystal which is useful in the detection of ionizing radiation. In 1949 Harshaw commenced research into the growth of this type crystal and was able to produce one less than two inches in diameter. By 1966, as the result of expenditures in excess of $1 million, Harshaw was able to grow a 17–inch crystal, something no one else had done previously. Harshaw had developed many processes, procedures, and manufacturing techniques in the purification of raw materials and the growth and encapsulation of the crystals which enabled it to accomplish this feat. Some of these processes Harshaw considers to be trade secrets.

The individual respondents are former employees of Harshaw who formed or later joined respondent Bicron. While at Harshaw the individual respondents executed, as a condition of employment, at least one agreement each, requiring them not to disclose confidential information or trade secrets obtained as employees of Harshaw. Bicron was formed in August 1969 to compete with Harshaw in the production of the crystals, and by April 1970, had grown a 17–inch crystal.

Petitioner brought this diversity action in United States District Court for the Northern District of Ohio seeking injunctive relief and damages for the misappropriation of trade secrets. The District Court, applying Ohio trade secret law, granted a permanent injunction against the disclosure or use by respondents of 20 of the 40 claimed trade secrets until such time as the trade secrets had been released to the public, had otherwise generally become available to the public, or had been obtained by respondents from sources having the legal right to convey the information.

The Court of Appeals for the Sixth Circuit held that the findings of fact by the District Court were not clearly erroneous, and that it was evident from the record that the individual Respondents appropriated to the benefit of Bicron secret information on processes obtained while they were employees at Harshaw. Further, the Court of Appeals held that the District Court properly applied Ohio law relating to trade secrets. Nevertheless, the Court

of Appeals reversed the District Court, finding Ohio's trade secret law to be in conflict with the patent laws of the United States. The Court of Appeals reasoned that Ohio could not grant monopoly protection to processes and manufacturing techniques that were appropriate subjects for consideration under 35 U.S.C. § 101 for a federal patent but which had been in commercial use for over one year and so were no longer eligible for patent protection under 35 U.S.C. § 102(b).

We hold that Ohio's law of trade secrets is not preempted by the patent laws of the United States, and, accordingly, we reverse.

II

Ohio has adopted the widely relied-upon definition of a trade secret found at Restatement of Torts § 757, comment b (1939). *B. F. Goodrich Co. v. Wohlgemuth*, 117 Ohio App. 493, 498, 192 N.E.2d 99, 104 (1963); *W. R. Grace & Co. v. Hargadine*, 392 F.2d 9, 14 (C.A.6 1968). According to the Restatement,

> (a) trade secret may consist of any formula, pattern, device or compilation of information which is used in one's business, and which gives him an opportunity to obtain an advantage over competitors who do not know or use it. It may be a formula for a chemical compound, a process of manufacturing, treating or preserving materials, a pattern for a machine or other device, or a list of customers.

The subject of a trade secret must be secret, and must not be of public knowledge or of a general knowledge in the trade or business. This necessary element of secrecy is not lost, however, if the holder of the trade secret reveals the trade secret to another "in confidence, and under an implied obligation not to use or disclose it." These others may include those of the holder's "employees to whom it is necessary to confide it, in order to apply it to the uses for which it is intended." Often the recipient of confidential knowledge of the subject of a trade secret is a licensee of its holder. *See Lear, Inc. v. Adkins*, 395 U.S. 653, 89 S.Ct. 1902, 23 L.Ed.2d 610 (1969).

The protection accorded the trade secret holder is against the disclosure or unauthorized use of the trade secret by those to whom the secret has been confided under the express or implied restriction of nondisclosure or nonuse.[4] The law also protects the holder of a trade secret against disclosure or use when the knowledge is gained, not by the owner's volition, but by some "improper means," Restatement of Torts § 757(a), which may

---

4.   Ohio Rev. Code Ann. § 1333.51(C) (Supp. 1973) provides:

No person, having obtained possession of an article representing a trade secret or access thereto with the owner's consent, shall convert such article to his own use or that of another person, or thereafter without the owner's consent make or cause to be made a copy of such article, or exhibit such article to another.

Ohio Rev.Code Ann. § 1333.99(E) (Supp.1973) provides:

Whoever violates section 1333.51 of the Revised Code shall be fined not more than five thousand dollars, imprisoned not less than one nor more than ten years, or both.

include theft, wiretapping, or even aerial reconnaissance. A trade secret law, however, does not offer protection against discovery by fair and honest means, such as by independent invention, accidental disclosure, or by so-called reverse engineering, that is by starting with the known product and working backward to divine the process which aided in its development or manufacture.

Novelty, in the patent law sense, is not required for a trade secret. "Quite clearly discovery is something less than invention." *A. O. Smith Corp. v. Petroleum Iron Works Co.*, 73 F.2d 531, 538 (C.A.6 1934), *modified to increase scope of injunction*, 74 F.2d 934 (1935). However, some novelty will be required if merely because that which does not possess novelty is usually known; secrecy, in the context of trade secrets, thus implies at least minimal novelty.

The subject matter of a patent is limited to a "process, machine, manufacture, or composition of matter, or ... improvement thereof," 35 U.S.C. § 101, which fulfills the three conditions of novelty and utility as articulated and defined in 35 U.S.C. §§ 101 and 102, and nonobviousness, as set out in 35 U.S.C. § 103. [footnote omitted] If an invention meets the rigorous statutory tests for the issuance of a patent, the patent is granted, for a period of 17 years, giving what has been described as the "right of exclusion," This protection goes not only to copying the subject matter, which is forbidden under the Copyright Act, 17 U.S.C. § 1 et seq., but also to independent creation.

III

The first issue we deal with is whether the States are forbidden to act at all in the area of protection of the kinds of intellectual property which may make up the subject matter of trade secrets.

Article I, § 8, cl. 8, of the Constitution grants to the Congress the power

> (t)o promote the Progress of Science and useful Arts, by securing for limited Times to Authors and Inventors the exclusive Right to their respective Writings and Discoveries ...

In the 1972 Term, in *Goldstein v. California*, 412 U.S. 546, 93 S.Ct. 2303, 37 L.Ed.2d 163 (1973), we held that the cl. 8 grant of power to Congress was not exclusive and that, at least in the case of writings, the States were not prohibited from encouraging and protecting the efforts of those within their borders by appropriate legislation. The States could, therefore, protect against the unauthorized re-recording for sale of performances fixed on records or tapes, even though those performances qualified as "writings" in the constitutional sense and Congress was empowered to legislate regarding such performances and could pre-empt the area if it chose to do so. This determination was premised on the great diversity of interests in our Nation-the essentially non-uniform character of the appreciation of intellectual achievements in the various States. Evidence for this came from patents granted by the States in the 18th century. 412 U.S., at 557, 93 S.Ct., at 2310.

Just as the States may exercise regulatory power over writings so may the States regulate with respect to discoveries. States may hold diverse viewpoints in protecting intellectual property to invention as they do in protecting the intellectual property relating to the subject matter of copyright. The only limitation on the States is that in regulating the area of patents and copyrights they do not conflict with the operation of the laws in this area passed by Congress, and it is to that more difficult question we now turn.

IV

The question of whether the trade secret law of Ohio is void under the Supremacy Clause involves a consideration of whether that law "stands as an obstacle to the accomplishment and execution of the full purposes and objectives of Congress." We stated in *Sears, Roebuck & Co. v. Stiffel Co.*, 376 U.S. 225, 229, 84 S.Ct. 784, 11 L.Ed.2d 661 (1964), that when state law touches upon the area of federal statutes enacted pursuant to constitutional authority, "it is 'familiar doctrine' that the federal policy 'may not be set at naught, or its benefits denied' by the state law. This is true, of course, even if the state law is enacted in the exercise of otherwise undoubted state power."

The laws which the Court of Appeals in this case held to be in conflict with the Ohio law of trade secrets were the patent laws passed by the Congress in the unchallenged exercise of its clear power under Art. I, § 8, cl. 8, of the Constitution. The patent law does not explicitly endorse or forbid the operation of trade secret law. However, as we have noted, if the scheme of protection developed by Ohio respecting trade secrets "clashes with the objectives of the federal patent laws," *Sears, Roebuck & Co. v. Stiffel Co., supra*, 376 U.S., at 231, 84 S.Ct. at 789, then the state law must fall. To determine whether the Ohio law "clashes" with the federal law it is helpful to examine the objectives of both the patent and trade secret laws.

The stated objective of the Constitution in granting the power to Congress to legislate in the area of intellectual property is to "promote the Progress of Science and useful Arts." The patent laws promote this progress by offering a right of exclusion for a limited period as an incentive to inventors to risk the often enormous costs in terms of time, research, and development. The productive effort thereby fostered will have a positive effect on society through the introduction of new products and processes of manufacture into the economy, and the emanations by way of increased employment and better lives for our citizens. In return for the right of exclusion—this "reward for inventions," the patent laws impose upon the inventor a requirement of disclosure. To insure adequate and full disclosure so that upon the expiration of the 17–year period "the knowledge of the invention enures to the people, who are thus enabled without restriction to practice it and profit by its use, the patent laws require [footnote omitted] that the patent application shall include a full and clear description of the invention and of the manner and process of making and using it" so that any person skilled in the art may make and use the invention. 35 U.S.C. § 112. When a patent is granted and the information contained in it is circulated to the general public and those especially skilled in the trade, such additions to the general store of knowledge are of such importance to the public weal that the Federal Government is willing to pay the high price of 17 years of exclusive use for its disclosure, which disclosure, it is assumed, will stimulate ideas and the eventual development of further significant advances in the art. The Court has also articulated another policy of the patent law: that which is in the public domain cannot be removed therefrom by action of the States.

> (F)ederal laws requires that all ideas in general circulation be dedicated to the common good unless they are protected by a valid patent. *Lear, Inc. v. Adkins*, 395 U.S., at 668, 89 S.Ct., at 1910.

The maintenance of standards of commercial ethics and the encouragement of invention are the broadly stated policies behind trade secret law. "The necessity of good faith and honest, fair dealing, is the very life and spirit of the commercial world." *National Tube Co. v. Eastern Tube Co.*, 3 Ohio Cir.Cr.R., N.S. at 462. In *A. O. Smith Corp. v. Petroleum Iron Works Co.*, 73 F.2d, at 539, the Court emphasized that even though a discovery may not be patentable, that does not

> destroy the value of the discovery to one who makes it, or advantage the competitor who by unfair means, or as the beneficiary of a broken faith, obtains the desired knowledge without himself paying the price in labor, money, or machines expended by the discover.

Having now in mind the objectives of both the patent and trade secret law, we turn to an examination of the interaction of these systems of protection of intellectual property established by the Congress and the other by a State to determine whether and under what circumstances the latter might constitute "too great an encroachment on the federal patent system to be tolerated." *Sears, Roebuck & Co. v. Stiffel Co.*, 376 U.S., at 232, 84 S.Ct., at 789.

As we noted earlier, trade secret law protects items which would not be proper subjects for consideration for patent protection under 35 U.S.C. § 101. As in the case of the recordings in *Goldstein v. California*, Congress, with respect to nonpatentable subject matter, "has drawn no balance; rather, it has left the area unattended, and no reason exists why the State should not be free to act." *Goldstein v. California, supra*, 412 U.S., at 570, 93 S.Ct. at 2316 (footnote omitted).

Since no patent is available for a discovery, however useful, novel, and nonobvious, unless it falls within one of the express categories of patentable subject matter of 35 U.S.C. § 101, the holder of such a discovery would have no reason to apply for a patent whether trade secret protection existed or not. Abolition of trade secret protection would, therefore, not result in increased disclosure to the public of discoveries in the area of nonpatentable subject matter. Also, it is hard to see how the public would be benefited by disclosure of customer lists or advertising campaigns; in fact, keeping such items secret encourages businesses to initiate new and individualized plans of operation, and constructive competition results. This, in turn, leads to a greater variety of business methods than would otherwise be the case if privately developed marketing and other data were passed illicitly among firms involved in the same enterprise.

Congress has spoken in the area of those discoveries which fall within one of the categories of patentable subject matter of 35 U.S.C. § 101 and which are, therefore, of a nature that would be subject to consideration for a patent. Processes, machines, manufactures, compositions of matter and improvements thereof, which meet the tests of utility, novelty, and nonobviousness are entitled to be patented, but those which do not, are not. The question remains whether those items which are proper subjects for consideration for a patent may also have available the alternative protection accorded by trade secret law.

Certainly the patent policy of encouraging invention is not disturbed by the existence of another form of incentive to invention. In this respect the two systems are not and never would be in conflict. Similarly, the policy that matter once in the public domain must remain in the public domain is not incompatible with the existence of trade secret protection. By definition a trade secret has not been placed in the public domain.

The more difficult objective of the patent law to reconcile with trade secret law is that of disclosure, the quid pro quo of the right to exclude. We are helped in this stage of the analysis by Judge Henry Friendly's opinion in *Painton & Co. v. Bourns, Inc.*, 442 F.2d 216 (C.A.2 1971). There the Court of Appeals thought it useful, in determining whether inventors will refrain because of the existence of trade secret law from applying for patents, thereby depriving the public from learning of the invention, to distinguish between three categories of trade secrets:

> (1) the trade secret believed by its owner to constitute a validly patentable invention; (2) the trade secret known to its owner not to be so patentable; and (3) the trade secret whose valid patentability is considered dubious. *Id.*, at 224.

Trade secret protection in each of these categories would run against breaches of confidence—the employee and licensee situations—and theft and other forms of industrial espionage.

As to the trade secret known not to meet the standards of patentability, very little in the way of disclosure would be accomplished by abolishing trade secret protection. With trade secrets of nonpatentable subject matter, the patent alternative would not reasonably be available to the inventor. "There can be no public interest in stimulating developers of such (unpatentable) knowhow to flood an overburdened Patent Office with applications (for) what they do not consider patentable." *Ibid*. The mere filing of applications doomed to be turned down by the Patent Office will bring forth no new public knowledge or enlightenment, since under federal statute and regulation patent applications and abandoned patent applications are held by the Patent Office in confidence and are not open to public inspection.

Even as the extension of trade secret protection to patentable subject matter that the owner knows will not meet the standards of patentability will not conflict with the patent policy of disclosure, it will have a decidedly beneficial effect on society. Trade secret law will encourage invention in areas where patent law does not reach, and will prompt the independent innovator to proceed with the discovery and exploitation of his invention.

Competition is fostered and the public is not deprived of the use of valuable, if not quite patentable, invention.

Even if trade secret protection against the faithless employee were abolished, inventive and exploitive effort in the area of patentable subject matter that did not meet the standards of patentability would continue, although at a reduced level. Alternatively with the effort that remained, however, would come an increase in the amount of self-help that innovative companies would employ. Knowledge would be widely dispersed among the employees of those still active in research. Security precautions necessarily would be increased, and salaries and fringe benefits of those few officers or employees who had to know the whole of the secret invention would be fixed in an amount thought sufficient to assure their loyalty. Smaller companies would be placed at a distinct economic disadvantage, since the costs of this kind of self-help could be great, and the cost to the public of the use of this invention would be increased. The innovative entrepreneur with limited resources would tend to confine his research efforts to himself and those few he felt he could trust without the ultimate assurance of legal protection against breaches of confidence. As a result, organized scientific and technological research could become fragmented, and society, as a whole, would suffer.

Another problem that would arise if state trade secret protection were precluded is in the area of licensing others to exploit secret processes. The holder of a trade secret would not likely share his secret with a manufacturer who cannot be placed under binding legal obligation to pay a license fee or to protect the secret. The result would be to hoard rather than disseminate knowledge. Instead, then, of licensing others to use his invention and making the most efficient use of existing manufacturing and marketing structures within the industry, the trade secret holder would tend either to limit his utilization of the invention, thereby depriving the public of the maximum benefit of its use, or engage in the time-consuming and economically wasteful enterprise of constructing duplicative manufacturing and marketing mechanisms for the exploitation of the invention. The detrimental misallocation of resources and economic waste that would thus take place if trade secret protection were abolished with respect to employees or licensees cannot be justified by reference to any policy that the federal patent law seeks to advance.

Nothing in the patent law requires that States refrain from action to prevent industrial espionage. In addition to the increased costs for protection from burglary, wire-tapping, bribery, and the other means used to misappropriate trade secrets, there is the inevitable cost to the basic decency of society when one firm steals from another. A most fundamental human right, that of privacy, is threatened when industrial espionage is condoned or is made profitable; the state interest in denying profit to such illegal ventures is unchallengeable.

The next category of patentable subject matter to deal with is the invention whose holder has a legitimate doubt as to its patentability. The risk of eventual patent invalidity by the courts and the costs associated with that risk may well impel some with a good-faith doubt as to patentability not to take the trouble to seek to obtain and defend patent protection for their discoveries, regardless of the existence of trade secret protection. Trade secret protection would assist those inventors in the more efficient exploitation of their discoveries and not conflict with the patent law. In most cases of genuine doubt as to patent validity the potential rewards of patent protection are so far superior to those accruing to holders of trade secrets, that the holders of such inventions will seek patent protection, ignoring the trade secret route. For those inventors "on the line" as to whether to seek patent protection, the abolition of trade secret protection might encourage some to apply for a patent who otherwise would not have done so. For some of those so encouraged, no patent will be granted and the result

> will have been an unnecessary postponement in the divulging of the trade secret to persons willing to pay for it. If (the patent does issue), it may well be invalid, yet many will prefer to pay a modest royalty than to contest it, even though Lear allows them to accept a license and pursue the contest without paying royalties while the fight goes on. The result in such a case would be unjustified royalty payments from many who would prefer not to pay them rather than agreed fees from one or a few who are entirely willing to do so. *Painton & Co. v. Bourns, Inc.*, 442 F.2d, at 225.

The point is that those who might be encouraged to file for patents by the absence of trade secret law will include inventors possessing the chaff as well as the wheat. Some of the chaff—the nonpatentable discoveries—will be thrown out by the Patent Office, but in the meantime society will have been deprived of use of those discoveries through trade secret-protected licensing. Some of the chaff may not be thrown out. This Court has noted the difference between the standards used by the Patent Office and the courts to determine patentability. *Graham v. John Deere Co.*, 383 U.S. 1, 18, 86 S.Ct. 684, 694, 15 L.Ed.2d 545 (1966). In *Lear, Inc. v. Adkins*, 395 U.S. 653, 89 S.Ct. 1902, 23 L.Ed.2d 610 (1969), the Court thought that an invalid patent was so serious a threat to the free use of ideas already in the public domain that the Court permitted licensees of the patent holder to challenge the validity of the patent. Better had the invalid patent never issued. More of those patents would likely issue if trade secret law were abolished. Eliminating trade secret law for the doubtfully patentable invention is thus likely to have deleterious effects on society and patent policy which we cannot say are balanced out by the speculative gain which might result from the encouragement of some inventors with doubtfully patentable inventions which deserve patent protection to come forward and apply for patents. There is no conflict, then, between trade secret law and the patent law policy of disclosure, at least insofar as the first two categories of patentable subject matter are concerned.

The final category of patentable subject matter to deal with is the clearly patentable invention, i.e., that invention which the owner believes to meet the standards of patentability. It is here that the federal interest in disclosure is at its peak; these inventions, novel, useful and nonobvious, are "the things which are worth to the public the embarrassment of an exclusive patent." *Graham v. John Deere Co.*, supra, at 9, 86 S.Ct., at 689 (quoting Thomas Jefferson). The interest of the public is that the bargain of 17 years of exclusive use in return for disclosure be accepted. If a State, through a system of protection, were to cause a substantial risk that holders of patentable inventions would not seek patents, but rather would rely on the state protection, we would be compelled to hold that such a system could not constitutionally continue to exist. In the case of trade secret law no reasonable risk of deterrence from patent application by those who can reasonably expect to be granted patents exists.

Trade secret law provides far weaker protection in many respects than the patent law. While trade secret law does not forbid the discovery of the trade secret by fair and honest means, e.g., independent creation or reverse engineering, patent law operates "against the world," forbidding any use of the invention for whatever purpose for a significant length of time. The holder of a trade secret also takes a substantial risk that the secret will be passed on to his competitors, by theft or by breach of a confidential relationship, in a manner not easily susceptible of discovery or proof. *Painton & Co. v. Bourns, Inc.*, 442 F.2d, at 224. Where patent law acts as a barrier, trade secret law functions relatively as a sieve. The possibility that an inventor who believes his invention meets the standards of patentability will sit back, rely on trade secret law, and after one year of use forfeit any right to patent protection, 35 U.S.C. § 102(b), is remote indeed.

Nor does society face much risk that scientific or technological progress will be impeded by the rare inventor with a patentable invention who chooses trade secret protection over patent protection. The ripeness-of-time concept of invention, developed from the study of the many independent multiple discoveries in history, predicts that if a particular individual had not made a particular discovery others would have, and in probably a relatively short period of time. If something is to be discovered at all very likely it will be discovered by more than one person. Even were an inventor to keep his discovery completely to himself, something that neither the patent nor trade secret laws forbid, there is a high probability that it will be soon independently developed. If the invention, though still a trade secret, is put into public use, the competition is alerted to the existence of the inventor's solution to the problem and may be encouraged to make an extra effort to independently find the solution thus known to be possible. The inventor faces pressures not only from private industry, but from the skilled scientists who work in our universities and our other great publicly supported centers of learning and research.

We conclude that the extension of trade secret protection to clearly patentable inventions does not conflict with the patent policy of disclosure. Perhaps because trade secret law does not produce any positive effects in the area of clearly patentable inventions, as opposed to the beneficial effects resulting from trade secret protection in the areas of the doubtfully patentable and the clearly unpatentable inventions, it has been suggested that partial pre-emption may be appropriate, and that courts should refuse to apply trade secret protection to inventions which the holder should have patented, and which would have been, thereby, disclosed. However, since there is no real possibility that trade secret law will conflict with the federal policy favoring disclosure of clearly patentable inventions partial pre-emption is inappropriate. Partial pre-emption, furthermore, could well create serious problems for state courts in the administration of trade secret law. As a preliminary matter in trade secret actions, state courts would be obliged to distinguish between what a reasonable inventor would and would not correctly consider to be clearly patentable, with the holder of the trade secret arguing that the invention was not patentable and the misappropriator of the trade secret arguing its undoubted novelty, utility, and nonobviousness. Federal courts have a difficult enough time trying to determine whether an invention, narrowed by the patent application procedure and fixed in the specifications which describe the invention for which the patent has been granted, is patentable. Although state courts in some circumstances must join federal courts in judging whether an issued patent is valid, *Lear, Inc. v. Adkins, supra*, it would be undesirable to impose the almost impossible burden on state courts to determine the patentability—in fact and in the mind of a reasonable inventor—of a discovery which has not been patented and remains entirely uncircumscribed by expert analysis in the administrative process. Neither complete nor partial pre-emption of state trade secret law is justified.

Trade secret law and patent law have co-existed in this country for over one hundred years. Each has its particular role to play, and the operation of one does not take away from the need for the other. Trade secret law encourages the development and exploitation of those items of lesser or different invention than might be accorded protection under the patent laws, but which items still have an important part to play in the technological and scientific advancement of the Nation. Trade secret law promotes the sharing of knowledge, and the efficient operation of industry; it permits the individual inventor to reap the rewards of his labor by contracting with a company large enough to develop and exploit it. Congress, by its silence over these many years, has seen the wisdom of allowing the States to enforce trade secret protection. Until Congress takes affirmative action to the contrary, States should be free to grant protection to trade secrets.

■ MR. JUSTICE DOUGLAS, with whom MR. JUSTICE BRENNAN concurs, dissenting.

Today's decision is at war with the philosophy of *Sears, Roebuck & Co. v. Stiffel Co.*, 376 U.S. 225, 84 S.Ct. 784, 11 L.Ed.2d 661 and *Compco Corp. v. Day–Brite Lighting, Inc.*, 376 U.S. 234, 84 S.Ct. 779, 11 L.Ed.2d 669. Those cases involved patents—one of a pole lamp and one of fluorescent lighting fixtures each of which was declared invalid. The lower courts held, however, that though the patents were invalid the sale of identical or confusingly similar products to the products of the patentees violated state unfair competition laws. We held that when an article is unprotected by a patent, state law may not forbid others to copy it, because every article not covered by a valid patent is in the public domain. Congress in the patent laws decided that where no patent existed, free competition should prevail; that where a patent is rightfully issued, the right to exclude others should obtain for no longer than 17 years, and that the States may not "under some other law, such as that forbidding unfair competition, give protection of a kind that clashes with the objectives of the federal patent laws,"[1] 376 U.S., at 231, 84 S.Ct. at 789.

---

1. Here as in *Lear, Inc. v. Adkins*, 395 U.S. 653, 674, 89 S.Ct. 1902, 1913, 23 L.Ed.2d 610, which held that a licensee of a patent is not precluded by a contract from challenging the patent, for if he were, that would defeat the policy of the patent laws: "enforcing this

The product involved in this suit, sodium iodide synthetic crystals, was a product that could be patented but was not. Harshaw the inventor apparently contributed greatly to the technology in that field by developing processes, procedures, and techniques that produced much larger crystals than any competitor. These processes, procedures, and techniques were also patentable; but no patent was sought. Rather Harshaw sought to protect its trade secrets by contracts with its employees. And the District Court found that, as a result of those secrecy precautions, "not sufficient disclosure occurred so as to place the claimed trade secrets in the public domain"; and those findings were sustained by the Court of Appeals.

The District Court issued a permanent injunction against respondents, ex-employees, restraining them from using the processes used by Harshaw. By a patent which would require full disclosure Harshaw could have obtained a 17–year monopoly against the world. By the District Court's injunction, which the Court approves and reinstates, Harshaw gets a permanent injunction running into perpetuity against respondents. In *Sears*, as in the present case, an injunction against the unfair competitor issued. We said: "To allow a State by use of its law of unfair competition to prevent the copying of an article which represents too slight an advance to be patented would be to permit the State to block off from the public something which federal law has said belongs to the public. The result would be that while federal law grants only 14 or 17 years' protection to genuine inventions, see 35 U.S.C. §§ 154, 173, States could allow perpetual protection to articles too lacking in novelty to merit any patent at all under federal constitutional standards. This would be too great an encroachment on the federal patent system to be tolerated." 376 U.S., at 231–232, 84 S.Ct. at 789.

The conflict with the patent laws is obvious. The decision of Congress to adopt a patent system was based on the idea that there will be much more innovation if discoveries are disclosed and patented than there will be when everyone works in secret. Society thus fosters a free exchange of technological information at the cost of a limited 17–year monopoly.

A trade secret, unlike a patent, has no property dimension. That was the view of the Court of Appeals, 478 F.2d 1074, 1081; and its decision is supported by what Mr. Justice Holmes said in *DuPont de Nemours Powder Co. v. Masland*, 244 U.S. 100, 102, 37 S.Ct. 575, 576, 61 L.Ed. 1016:

> The word property as applied to trade-marks and trade secrets is an unanalyzed expression of certain makes some rudimentary requirements of good faith. Whether the plaintiffs have any valuable secret or not the defendant knows the facts, whatever they are, through a special confidence that he accepted. The property may be denied but the confidence cannot be. Therefore the starting point for the present matter is not property or due process of law, but that the defendant stood in confidential relations with the plaintiffs, or one of them. These have given place to hostility, and the first thing to be made sure of is that the defendant shall not fraudulently abuse the trust reposed in him. It is the usual incident of confiden-

contractual provision would undermine the strong federal policy favoring the full and free use of ideas in the public domain."

tial relations. If there is any disadvantage in the fact that he knew the plaintiffs' secrets he must take the burden with the good.

The difference between the two things, letters-patent and copyright, may be illustrated by reference to the subjects just enumerated. Take the case of medicines. Certain mixtures are found to be of great value in the healing art. If the discoverer writes and publishes a book on the subject (as regular physicians generally do), he gains no exclusive right to the manufacture and sale of the medicine; he gives that to the public. If he desires to acquire such exclusive right, he must obtain a patent for the mixture as a new art, manufacture, or composition of matter. He may copyright his book, if he pleases; but that only secures to him the exclusive right of printing and publishing his book. So of all other inventions or discoveries. *Baker v. Selden*, 101 U.S. 99, 102–103, 25 L.Ed. 841.

A suit to redress theft of a trade secret is grounded in tort damages for breach of a contract a historic remedy, *Cataphote Corp. v. Hudson*, 5 Cir., 422 F.2d 1290. Damages for breach of a confidential relation are not pre-empted by this patent law, but an injunction against use is pre-empted because the patent law states the only monopoly over trade secrets that is enforceable by specific performance; and that monopoly exacts as a price full disclosure. A trade secret can be protected only by being kept secret. Damages for breach of a contract are one thing; an injunction barring disclosure does service for the protection accorded valid patents and is therefore pre-empted.

From the findings of fact of the lower courts, the process involved in this litigation was unique, such a great discovery as to make its patentability a virtual certainty. Yet the Court's opinion reflects a vigorous activist anti-patent philosophy. My objection is not because it is activist. This is a problem that involves no neutral principle. The Constitution in Art. I, § 8, cl. 8, expresses the activist policy which Congress has enforced by statutes. It is that constitutional policy which we should enforce, not our individual notions of the public good.

NOTES

1.   The *Kewanee* opinions are replete with incentive-based analyses. Compare them to the discussion earlier in this book in Chapter One, Section C, "Economics of Patent Law." Take the incentive to disclose theory, for example, and consider whether the primary goal under that theory should be a disclosure that *teaches*, or a disclosure that gives *notice* that is both fixed and public so as to facilitate bargaining and the transfer of technology?

2.   Consider the possible problems of a world without trade secret protection. They feature prominently in the reasoning of the majority opinion. Should the merits of trade secret protection be directly relevant to an analysis focused entirely on preemption?

3.   The majority opinion asserts that trade secret protection is weaker than patent protection, and then relies on this assertion to support the opinion. Do you agree with the assertion itself? Do you think it is "the rare inventor" who would opt for trade secret protection despite having a patentable invention? Consider an invention that can be maintained as a secret for a great length of time, far in excess of the 20 year patent term. This may be because its commercial embodiment can not be reverse engineered, or because the original invention was such a fluke that independent invention is not likely in the near future. Surely trade secret protection would be much more attractive than patent protection for the inventor in such a case. Would this not be especially true if the invention can be marketed around the world? Trade secrecy can be maintained and effective against the entire world if there is local protection against pirating; by definition a secret is not known to anyone. In contrast, patent protection is domestic in scope. A patent in one country does not give protection in another. Indeed, because of patent disclosure requirements, residents of one country can benefit freely from the published teachings in the patents of another country. As noted in Chapter One, recent empirical studies have shown that some industries rely quite heavily on trade secret protection even though patent protection is available. *See, e.g.,* Wesley M. Cohen et al., *Protecting Their Intellectual Assets: Appropriability Conditions and Why U.S. Manufacturing Firms Patent (or Not)* 24 (Nat'l Bureau of Econ. Research, Working Paper No. 7552, 2000). Should trade secrecy be preempted if it turns out to be stronger than patent protection?

4. Consider the dissent by Justice Douglas, joined by Justice Brennan. Did *Sears/Compco* hold that "every article not covered by a valid patent is in the public domain"? What about a truly secret invention that happens not to be patentable because it is non-statutory subject matter. Would it not be judicial slight of hand to assert that such a secret is in the public domain? Perhaps it should be placed there, but can one credibly assert that it *is* there? Consider the dissent's efforts to distinguish between a suit for breach of a *confidential* relationship and a suit for theft of a trade secret. In what way are these tort theories different?

F. OTHER LIMITATIONS ON CONTRACTUAL PROVISIONS

Although not provided by statute (patent or antitrust), required by the Constitutional doctrine of preemption, or implied by the conduct of the parties to a contract (like first sale, implied license, and repair/reconstruction), some additional limitations have been imposed on patentees and their contracting parties through judge-made law over the years. Two sets of these are discussed in this section. The first relates to agreements not to challenge the validity of a patent and arise from the *Lear* case. The second relates to agreements that touch some activity that is outside of patent term or otherwise not patented, and arise from the *Brulotte* case. Although neither present nor future judicial attitudes towards these cases is clear, the shifts in this area have tended to correspond with the shifts on statutory subject matter, misuse, antitrust, and preemption which are discussed through this Chapter and in Chapter 7, and at least at present are more in-line with a "basics matters" approach to the law, in which contract terms that are otherwise enforceable as a matter of contract law, antitrust law, etc, are likely to be enforceable when relating to patents as well.[6] That being said, at least two "danger" zones do remain: contractual terms that will receive the most scrutiny are those that promise to (1) not challenge a patent and (2) make a payment after patent term for something related to a patent royalty.

---

6. See F. Scott Kieff & Troy A. Paredes, The Basics Matter: At the Periphery of Intellectual Property Stanford Law School John M. Olin Program in Law and Economics, Working Paper No. 275, February 2004, Available on-line at http://papers.ssrn.com/paper.taf? abstract _ id=501142.

1.   THE LICENSEE'S RIGHT TO CHALLENGE THE VALIDITY OF A PATENT

Lear, Inc. v. Adkins

395 U.S. 653 (1969).

■ MR. JUSTICE HARLAN delivered the opinion of the Court.

In January of 1952, John Adkins, an inventor and mechanical engineer, was hired by Lear, Incorporated, for the purpose of solving a vexing problem the company had encountered in its efforts to develop a gyroscope which would meet the increasingly demanding requirements of the aviation industry. The gyroscope is an essential component of the navigational system in all aircraft, enabling the pilot to learn the direction and altitude of his airplane. With the development of the faster airplanes of the 1950's, more accurate gyroscopes were needed, and the gyro industry consequently was casting about for new techniques which would satisfy this need in an economical fashion. Shortly after Adkins was hired, he developed a method of construction at the company's California facilities which improved gyroscope accuracy at a low cost. Lear almost immediately incorporated Adkins' improvements into its production process to its substantial advantage.

The question that remains unsettled in this case, after eight years of litigation in the California courts, is whether Adkins will receive compensation for Lear's use of those improvements which the inventor has subsequently patented. At every stage of this lawsuit, Lear has sought to prove that, despite the grant of a patent by the Patent Office, none of Adkins' improvements were sufficiently novel to warrant the award of a monopoly under the standards delineated in the governing federal statutes. Moreover, the company has sought to prove that Adkins obtained his patent by means of a fraud on the Patent Office. In response, the inventor has argued that since Lear had entered into a licensing agreement with Adkins, it was obliged to pay the agreed royalties regardless of the validity of the underlying patent.

The Supreme Court of California unanimously vindicated the inventor's position. While the court recognized that generally a manufacturer is free to challenge the validity of an inventor's patent, it held that "one of the oldest doctrines in the field of patent law establishes that so long as a licensee is operating under a license agreement he is estopped to deny the validity of his licensor's patent in a suit for royalties under the agreement. The theory underlying this doctrine is that a licensee should not be permitted to enjoy the benefit afforded by the agreement while simultaneously urging that the patent which forms the basis of the agreement is void."

Almost 20 years ago, in its last consideration of the doctrine, this Court also invoked an estoppel to deny a licensee the right to prove that his licensor was demanding royalties for the use of an idea which was in reality a part of the public domain. *Automatic Radio Manufacturing Co. v. Hazeltine Research, Inc.*, 339 U.S. 827, 836 (1950). We granted certiorari in the present case, 391 U.S. 912, 88 S.Ct. 1810, 20 L.Ed.2d 651, to reconsider the validity of the *Hazeltine* rule in the light of our recent decisions emphasizing the strong federal policy favoring free competition in ideas which do not merit patent protection. *Sears, Roebuck & Co. v. Stiffel Co.*, 376 U.S. 225 (1964); *Compco Corp. v. Day–Brite Lighting, Inc.*, 376 U.S. 234 (1964).

I.

At the very beginning of the parties' relationship, Lear and Adkins entered into a rudimentary one-page agreement which provided that although "(a)ll new ideas, discoveries, inventions, etc., related to . . . vertical gyros become the property of Mr. John S. Adkins," the inventor promised to grant Lear a license as to all ideas he might develop "on a mutually satisfactory royalty basis." As soon as Adkins' labors yielded tangible results, it quickly became apparent to the inventor that further steps should be taken to place his rights to his ideas on a firmer basis. On February 4, 1954, Adkins filed an application with the Patent Office in an effort to gain federal protection for his improvements. At about the same time, he entered into a lengthy period of negotiations with Lear in an effort to conclude a licensing agreement which would clearly establish the amount of royalties that would be paid.

These negotiations finally bore fruit on September 15, 1955, when the parties approved a complex 17–page contract which carefully delineated the conditions upon which Lear promised to pay royalties for Adkins' improvements. The parties agreed that if "the U.S. Patent Office refuses to issue a patent on the substantial claims (contained in Adkins' original patent application) or if such a patent so issued is subsequently held invalid, then in any of such events Lear at its option shall have the right forthwith to terminate the specific license so affected or to terminate this entire Agreement. . . ."

. . . . The [Patent Office] regulations do not require the Office to make a final judgment on an invention's patentability on the basis of the inventor's original application. While it sometimes happens that a patent is granted at this early stage, it is far more common for the Office to find that although certain of the applicant's claims may be patentable, certain others have been fully anticipated by the earlier developments in the art. In such a situation, the Patent Office does not attempt to separate the wheat from the chaff on its own initiative. Instead, it rejects the application, giving the inventor the right to make an amendment which narrows his claim to cover only those aspects of the invention which are truly novel. . . .

The progress of Adkins' effort to obtain a patent followed the typical pattern. In his initial application, the inventor made the ambitious claim that his entire method of constructing gyroscopes was sufficiently novel to merit protection. The Patent Office, however, rejected this initial claim, as well as two subsequent amendments, which progressively narrowed the scope of the invention sought to be protected. Finally, Adkins narrowed his claim drastically to assert only that the design of the apparatus used to achieve gyroscope accuracy was novel. In response, the Office issued its 1960 patent, granting a 17–year monopoly on on this more modest claim.

During the long period in which Adkins was attempting to convince the Patent Office of the novelty of his ideas, however, Lear had become convinced that Adkins would never receive a patent on his invention and that it should not continue to pay substantial royalties on ideas which had not contributed substantially to the development of the art of gyroscopy. In 1957, after Adkins' patent application had been rejected twice, Lear announced that it had searched the Patent Office's files and had found a patent which it believed had fully anticipated Adkins' discovery. As a result, the company stated that it would no longer pay royalties on the large number of gyroscopes it was producing at its plant in Grand Rapids, Michigan (the Michigan gyros). Payments were continued on the smaller number of gyros produced at the company's California plant (the California gyros) for two more years until they too were terminated on April 8, 1959.

[The California Supreme Court] rejected the District Court of Appeal's conclusion that the 1955 license gave Lear the right to terminate its royalty obligations in 1959. Since the 1955 agreement was still in effect, the court concluded, relying on the language we have already quoted, that the doctrine of estoppel barred Lear from questioning the propriety of the Patent Office's grant. The court's adherence to estoppel, however, was not without qualification. After noting Lear's claim that it had developed its Michigan gyros independently, the court tested this contention by considering "whether what is being built by Lear (in Michigan) springs entirely" (emphasis supplied) from the prior art. Applying this test, it found that Lear had in fact "utilized the apparatus patented by Adkins throughout the period in question," and reinstated the jury's $888,000 verdict on this branch of the case.

II.

* * *

A.

While the roots of the doctrine have often been celebrated in tradition, we have found only one 19th century case in this Court that invoked estoppel in a considered manner. And that case was decided before the Sherman Act made it clear that the grant of monopoly power to a patent owner constituted a limited exception to the general federal policy favoring free competition....

In the very next year, this Court found the doctrine of patent estoppel so inequitable that it refused to grant an injunction to enforce a licensee's promise never to contest the validity of the underlying patent. "It is as important to the public that competition should not be repressed by worthless patents, as that the patentee of a really valuable invention should be protected in his monopoly...." *Pope Manufacturing Co. v. Gormully*, 144 U.S. 224, 234 (1892).

Although this Court invoked an estoppel in 1905 without citing or considering Pope's powerful argument, *United States v. Harvey Steel Co.*, 196 U.S. 310 the doctrine was not to be applied again in this Court until it was revived in *Automatic Radio Manufacturing Co. v. Hazeltine Research, Inc., supra*, which declared, without prolonged analysis, that licensee estoppel was "the general rule." 339 U.S., at 836. In so holding, the majority ignored the teachings of a series of decisions this Court had rendered during the 45 years since Harvey had been decided. During this period, each time a patentee sought to rely upon his estoppel privilege before this Court, the majority created a new exception to permit judicial scrutiny into the validity of the Patent Office's grant. Long before *Hazeltine* was decided, the estoppel doctrine had been so eroded that it could no longer be considered the "general rule," but was only to be invoked in an ever narrowing set of circumstances.

* * *

III.

The uncertain status of licensee estoppel in the case law is a product of judicial efforts to accommodate the competing demands of the common law of contracts and the federal law of patents. On the one hand, the law of contracts forbids a purchaser to repudiate his promises simply because he later becomes dissatisfied with the bargain he has made. On the other hand, federal law requires, that all ideas in general circulation be dedicated to the common good unless they are protected by a valid patent. *Sears, Roebuck v. Stiffel Co., supra*; *Compco Corp. v. Day–Brite Lighting, Inc., supra*. When faced with this basic conflict in policy, both this Court and courts throughout the land have naturally sought to develop an intermediate position which somehow would remain responsive to the radically different concerns of the two different worlds of contract and patent. The result has been a failure. Rather than creative compromise, there has been a chaos of conflicting case law, proceeding on inconsistent premises. Before renewing the search for an acceptable middle ground, we must reconsider on their own merits the arguments which may properly be advanced on both sides of the estoppel question.

A.

It will simplify matters greatly if we first consider the most typical situation in which patent licenses are negotiated. In contrast to the present case, most manufacturers obtain a license after a patent has issued. Since the Patent Office makes an inventor's ideas public when it issues its grant of a limited monopoly, a potential licensee has access to the inventor's ideas even if he does not enter into an agreement with the patent owner. Consequently, a manufacturer gains only two benefits if he chooses to enter a licensing agreement after the patent has issued. First, by accepting a license and paying royalties for a time, the licensee may have avoided the necessity of defending an expensive infringement action during the period when he may be least able to afford one. Second, the existence of an unchallenged patent may deter others from attempting to compete with the licensee.

Under ordinary contract principles the mere fact that some benefit is received is enough to require the enforcement of the contract, regardless of the validity of the underlying patent. Nevertheless, if one tests this result by the standard of good-faith commercial dealing, it seems far from satisfactory. For the simple contract approach entirely ignores the position of the licensor who is seeking to invoke the court's assistance on his behalf. Consider, for example, the equities of the licensor who has obtained his patent through a fraud on the Patent Office. It is difficult to perceive why good faith requires that courts should permit him to recover royalties despite his licensee's attempts to show that the patent is invalid. Compare *Walker Process Equipment, Inc. v. Food Machinery & Chemical Corp.*, 382 U.S. 172 (1965).

Even in the more typical cases, not involving conscious wrongdoing, the licensor's equities are far from compelling. A patent, in the last analysis, simply represents a legal conclusion reached by the Patent Office. Moreover, the legal conclusion is predicated on factors as to which reasonable men can differ widely. Yet the Patent Office is often obliged to reach its decision in an ex parte proceeding, without the aid of the arguments which could be advanced by parties interested in proving patent invalidity. Consequently, it does not seem to us to be unfair to require a patentee to defend the Patent Office's judgment when his licensee places the question in issue, especially since the licensor's case is buttressed by the presumption of validity which attaches to his patent. Thus, although licensee estoppel may be consistent with the letter of contractual doctrine, we cannot say that it is compelled by the spirit of contract law, which seeks to balance the claims of promisor and promisee in accord with the requirements of good faith.

Surely the equities of the licensor do not weigh very heavily when they are balanced against the important public interest in permitting full and free competition in the use of ideas which are in reality a part of the public domain. Licensees may often be the only individuals with enough economic incentive to challenge the patentability of an inventor's discovery. If they are muzzled, the public may continually be required to pay tribute to would-be monopolists without need or justification. We think it plain that the technical requirements of contract doctrine must give way before the demands of the public interest in the typical situation involving the negotiation of a license after a patent has issued.

We are satisfied that *Automatic Radio Manufacturing Co. v. Hazeltine Research, Inc.*, supra, itself the product of a clouded history, should no longer be regarded as sound law with respect to its "estoppel" holding, and that holding is now overruled.

B.

The case before us, however, presents a far more complicated estoppel problem than the one which arises in the most common licensing context. The problem arises out of the fact that Lear obtained its license in 1955, more than four years before Adkins received his 1960 patent. Indeed, from the very outset of the relationship, Lear obtained special access to Adkins' ideas in return for its promise to pay satisfactory compensation.

Thus, during the lengthy period in which Adkins was attempting to obtain a patent, Lear gained an important benefit not generally obtained by the typical licensee. For until a patent issues, a potential licensee may not learn his licensor's ideas simply by requesting the information from the Patent Office. During the time the inventor is seeking patent protection, the governing federal statute requires the Patent Office to hold an inventor's patent application in confidence. If a potential licensee hopes to use the ideas contained in a secret patent application, he must deal with the inventor himself, unless the inventor chooses to publicize his ideas to the world at large. By promising to pay Adkins royalties from the very outset of their relationship, Lear gained immediate access to ideas which it may well not have learned until the Patent Office published the details of Adkins' invention in 1960. At the core of this case, then, is the difficult question whether federal patent policy bars a State from enforcing a contract regulating access to an unpatented secret idea.

Adkins takes an extreme position on this question. The inventor does not merely argue that since Lear obtained privileged access to his ideas before 1960, the company should be required to pay royalties accruing before 1960 regardless of the validity of the patent which ultimately issued. He also argues that since Lear obtained special benefits before 1960, it should also pay royalties during the entire patent period (1960—1977), without regard to the validity of the Patent Office's grant. We cannot accept so broad an argument.

Adkins' position would permit inventors to negotiate all important licenses during the lengthy period while their applications were still pending at the Patent Office, thereby disabling entirely all those who have the strongest incentive to show that a patent is worthless. While the equities supporting Adkins' position are somewhat more appealing than those supporting the typical licensor, we cannot say that there is enough of a difference to justify such a substantial impairment of overriding federal policy.

Nor can we accept a second argument which may be advanced to support Adkins' claim to at least a portion of his post-patent royalties, regardless of the validity of the Patent Office grant. The terms of the 1955 agreement provide that royalties are to be paid until such time as the "patent . . . is held invalid," § 6, and the fact remains that the question of patent validity has not been finally determined in this case. Thus, it may be suggested that although Lear must be allowed to raise the question of patent validity in the present lawsuit, it must also be required to comply with its contract and continue to pay royalties until its claim is finally vindicated in the courts.

The parties' contract, however, is no more controlling on this issue than is the State's doctrine of estoppel, which is also rooted in contract principles. The decisive question is whether overriding federal policies would be significantly frustrated if licensees could be required to continue to pay royalties during the time they are challenging patent validity in the courts.

It seems to us that such a requirement would be inconsistent with the aims of federal patent policy. Enforcing this contractual provision would give the licensor an additional economic incentive to devise every conceivable dilatory tactic in an effort to postpone the day of final judicial reckoning. We can perceive no reason to encourage dilatory court tactics in this way. Moreover, the cost of prosecuting slow-moving trial proceedings and defending an inevitable appeal might well deter many licensees from attempting to prove patent invalidity in the courts. The deterrent effect would be particularly severe in the many scientific fields in which invention is proceeding at a rapid rate. In these areas, a patent may well become obsolete long before its 17–year term has expired. If a licensee has reason to believe that he will replace a patented idea with a new one in the near future, he will have little incentive to initiate lengthy court proceedings, unless he is freed from liability at least from the time he refuses to pay the contractual royalties. Lastly, enforcing this contractual provision would undermine the strong federal policy favoring the full and free use of ideas in the public domain. For all these reasons, we hold that Lear must be permitted to avoid the payment of all royalties accruing after Adkins' 1960 patent issued if Lear can prove patent invalidity.

C.

Adkins' claim to contractual royalties accruing before the 1960 patent issued is, however, a much more difficult one, since it squarely raises the question whether, and to what extent, the States may protect the owners of unpatented inventions who are willing to disclose their ideas to manufacturers only upon payment of royalties. The California Supreme Court did not address itself to this issue with precision, for it believed that the venerable doctrine of estoppel provided a sufficient answer to all of Lear's claims based upon federal patent law. Thus, we do not know whether the Supreme Court would have awarded Adkins recovery even on his pre-patent royalties if it had recognized that previously established estoppel doctrine could no longer be properly invoked with regard to royalties accruing during the 17–year patent period. Our decision today will, of course, require the state courts to reconsider the theoretical basis of their decisions enforcing the contractual rights of inventors and it is impossible to predict the extent to which this reevaluation may revolutionize the law of any particular State in this regard. Consequently, we have concluded, after much consideration, that even though an important question of federal law underlies this phase of the controversy, we should not now attempt to define in even a limited way the extent, if any, to which the States may properly act to enforce the contractual rights of inventors of unpatented secret ideas. Given the difficulty and importance of this task, it should be undertaken only after the state courts have, after fully focused inquiry, determined the extent to which they will respect the contractual rights of such inventors in the future. Indeed, on remand, the California courts may well reconcile the competing demands of patent and contract law in a way which would not warrant further review in this Court.

NOTES

1. *Licensee Estoppel and Lear.* Under the doctrine of *Lear v. Adkins*, 395 U.S. 653 (1969), a party to a patent license is not precluded by estoppel or express agreement from contesting the validity of a patent as a defense to a charge of infringement or breach of contract. Under this view, the public interest in ferreting out invalid patents overrides the general principles of contract law. In *Lear*, the Supreme Court abolished as inconsistent with federal patent and antitrust policy the doctrine that a licensee was estopped from contesting the validity of a patent. After reviewing the history of the licensee estoppel doctrine, the Court concluded that "the uncertain status of licensee estoppel in the case law is a product of judicial efforts to accommodate the competing demands of the common law of contracts and the federal law of patents." According to the Court:

> One the one hand, the law of contracts forbids a purchaser to repudiate his promises simply because her later becomes dissatisfied with the bargain he has made.... On the other hand, federal patent law requires that all ideas in general circulation be dedicated to the common good unless they are protected by a valid patent.

Id. at 668. Do you agree with the Court that patent law requires anything be available for all to use unless protected by a valid patent? Where in the Patent Act is there a requirement that anything be available to others for use?

One important caveat to *Lear* relates to the "Challenge Rule." One charged with inducing breach of a patent license contract may defend by challenging the validity of the patent. Under the "Challenge Rule," a licensee must, to avoid continuing license royalty obligations, do more than simply cease paying the royalty. In *Studiengesellschaft Kohle, m.b.H v. Shell Oil Co.*, the Federal Circuit addressed the following question:

> Where the Court has found the relevant patent claims invalid, may the Licensor recover damages for breach of contract for past royalties due on processes allegedly covered by such claims, from the date of the alleged breach until the date that the Licensee first challenged validity of the claims?

112 F.3d 1561, 1562 (Fed.Cir.1997). The court distinguished *Lear* and answered affirmatively, noting that the licensee cannot continue using the technology without informing the licensor: "[A] licensee ... cannot invoke the protection of the *Lear* doctrine until it (i) actually ceases payment of royalties, and (ii) provides notice to the licensor that the reason for ceasing payment of royalties is because it has deemed the relevant claims to be invalid." *Id.* at 1568. Enforcement of a license to this extent, "does not frustrate patent policy;" indeed, a party's breach of a license by failing to notify the patentee of its use of the patented technology "is itself more likely to frustrate federal policy than enforcement of the contract." *Id.*

2. *Judgments, Consent Decrees, and Settlements.* The question arises after *Lear* whether a party to a judgment, consent decree, stipulated dismissal or settlement agreement that recognizes the validity of a patent may thereafter raise the question of validity anew. The policies at play in *Lear* related to whether a patent licensee could challenge the validity of the licensed patent for royalties set forth in a contract. Thus, *Lear* emphasized the public interest in facilitating challenges to invalid patents and was concerned with the policy favoring the free use of ideas and protecting the public domain. But in this area there are countervailing policies favoring voluntary resolution of disputes, principles of res judicata, collateral estoppel and conservation of judicial resources that are arguably stronger than the general contract principles considered in *Lear*. The policies set forth in *Lear* must be balanced against the public policies of preserving the finality of judgments and encouraging settlements, policies that *Lear* did not consider.

Perhaps the most difficult area is consent decrees, which have the "same force and effect as judgments entered after a trial on the merits." *Hallco Mfg. Co., Inc. v. Foster*, 256 F.3d 1290, 1294–95 (Fed.Cir.2001). Can a patentee enforce a consent decree (thereby preventing a defendant from challenging the patent) wherein the defendant recognized the validity of the patent? The Federal Circuit discussed this question in *Ecolab, Inc. v. Paraclipse, Inc.*, 285 F.3d 1362, 1376–77 (Fed.Cir.2002):

> We interpret consent judgments in accordance with the general principles of contract law, *Diversey Lever, Inc. v. Ecolab, Inc.*, 191 F.3d 1350, 1352 (Fed.Cir.1999), such that "the scope of a consent decree is limited to its

terms and ... its meaning should not be strained." *Foster v. Hallco Mfg. Co.,* 947 F.2d 469, 481 (Fed.Cir.1991). Moreover, "provisions in a consent judgment asserted to preclude litigation of the issue of validity in connection with a new claim must be construed narrowly." *Id.; Diversey Lever,* 191 F.3d at 1352 ("Any surrender of the right to challenge validity of a patent is construed narrowly."). Thus, a party does not waive its right to challenge the validity of a patent as to future accused products absent a clear intent to do so. To determine whether to give the consent judgment in this case preclusive effect, we therefore turn to the language of the agreement itself. In *Foster,* we found that the alleged infringer was not precluded from challenging the validity of the patent where the consent decree merely stated that the patents were "valid and enforceable in all respects." *Foster,* 947 F.2d at 481. We found that that language standing alone was insufficient to bar the alleged infringer from challenging validity. In that situation, a future validity challenge would have been precluded only if the devices in the two suits were "essentially the same," that is, if the accused product in the second suit was "essentially the same" as the specific device that was before the court in the first suit. *Foster,* 947 F.2d at 479–480.

In *Diversey Lever,* we found that the language standing alone in the agreement at issue was sufficient to bar the alleged infringer from challenging validity, where the alleged infringer, in addition to agreeing that the patents were "valid and enforceable," further agreed that it would not "directly or indirectly aid, assign, or participate in any action contesting the validity" of the patents. *Diversey Lever,* 191 F.3d at 1352. We noted that "*Foster* requires more for a waiver of the invalidity defense as to future accused products," *id.,* and found the "something more" in this additional language. Here, the consent judgment is more analogous to the agreement in *Foster* than *Diversey Lever.* Paraclipse merely agreed in the consent judgment that "the '690 patent is a valid patent." Greater clarity than this is required to foreclose a validity defense in a new infringement suit involving a new product. Because the language of the consent judgment does not, standing alone, preclude the validity challenge, we must determine whether the products are "essentially the same." The record shows that the Insect Inn IV trap differs from the Insect Inn II trap in that (1) it lacks a reflector located between the bulb and the outer wall of the housing, (2) the inside of the outer walls of the housing are black in color, and (3) it has two elements that were not present in the Insect Inn II trap: a shiny black reflector plate immediately below the light bulb and a Mylar strip on the vertical back wall of the housing. Thus, the record demonstrates to our satisfaction that the Insect Inn II and IV devices are not "essentially the same."

The Federal Circuit has also distinguished *Lear* and upheld non-challenge provisions in settlement agreements. *See Hemstreet v. Spiegel, Inc.,* 851 F.2d 348 (Fed.Cir.1988) ("The law strongly favors settlement of litigation, and there is a compelling public interest and policy in upholding and enforcing settlement agreements voluntarily entered into.... *Lear,* however, did not involve a settlement of litigation, but only the right of a patent licensee to challenge the validity of the licensed patent. The enforcement of settlement of litigation involves another public policy totally absent in *Lear:* the encouragement of settlement of litigation and the need to enforce such settlements in order to encourage the parties to enter into them"); *Flex–Foot, Inc. v. CRP, Inc.,* 238 F.3d 1362, 1369 (Fed.Cir.2001) (citing *Hemstreet* and noting that noting that "while the federal patent laws favor full and free competition in the use of ideas in the public domain over the technical requirements of contract doctrine, settlement of litigation is more strongly favored by the law").

3. *Assignor Estoppel.* The doctrine of assignor estoppel prevents an inventor/ assignor of a patent and his company, who are sued for infringement of the patent, from challenging the validity of the patent previously assigned by him as an employee to the assignee. Before *Lear*, the law on assignor estoppel was as uncertain as the law on licensee estoppel, with some courts holding that the *Lear* no-estoppel rule should apply to an assignor of a patent. But the Federal Circuit has taken a different view. The court sees assignor estoppel as distinguishable from licensee estoppel abolished in *Lear*. Unlike a licensee who, absent *Lear*, would have to continue to pay royalties on an invalid patent, an assignor has already been fully compensated for the patent rights he assigned. *See Diamond Scientific Co. v. Ambico, Inc.*, 848 F.2d 1220, 1224 (Fed.Cir.1988). In *Diamond*, the court identified four justifications for the doctrine of assignor estoppel:

> (1) to prevent unfairness and injustice; (2) to prevent one [from] benefit-ting from his own wrong; (3) by analogy to estoppel by deed in real estate; and (4) by analogy to a landlord-tenant relationship. . . . Courts that have expressed the estoppel doctrine in terms of unfairness and injustice have reasoned that an assignor should not be permitted to sell something and later to assert that what was sold is worthless, all to the detriment of the assignee.

Id. at 1224. Though equitable in nature, assignor estoppel is not governed by the traditional elements of equitable estoppel. Rather, it is the functional equivalent of estoppel by deed, which is a legal estoppel. Because of the equities involved, the court has stressed that there is a "presumption" that assignor estoppel applies and that presumption can be rebutted only by "exceptional circumstances." *Mentor Graphics Corp. v. Quickturn Design Systems, Inc.*, 150 F.3d 1374, 1378 (Fed.Cir. 1998).

A few others questions relating to assignor estoppel must be considered. First, where it is the new employer of the assignor who is challenging the validity of the patent, the requirement of privity between of the new employer and the assignor must be met before assignor estoppel can be applied. The deciding the privity question, the court looks to the "balance of the equities." That is, it depend[s] on the equities dictated by the relationship between the inventor and company B in light of the act of infringement. The closer that relationship, the more the equities will favor applying the doctrine to company B. *Shamrock Technologies, Inc. v. Medical Sterilization, Inc.*, 903 F.2d 789, 793 (Fed.Cir.1990). An important determi-nation is "whether the ultimate infringer availed itself of the inventor's 'knowledge and assistance' to conduct infringement." *Intel Corp. v. U.S. Intern. Trade Com'n.*, 946 F.2d 821, 839 (Fed.Cir.1991). *But see, Earth Resources Corp. v. United States*, 44 Fed.Cl. 274 (Fed.Cl. 1999) ("A contractual relationship, alone, is not enough to establish privity in the context of assignor estoppel. Federal Circuit precedents indicate that a degree of financial interconnectedness is significant to determining whether there is privity. . . . [But] [w]hile indemnification is some evidence of privity, indemnification alone does not mandate a finding of privity").

Lastly, other defenses remain even though assignor estoppel applies. For example, the estopped party can argue for a narrow claim interpretation or that the accused devices are within the prior art and therefore cannot infringe. *See Mentor*, 150 F.3d at 1380.

2.   POST-EXPIRATION ROYALTIES AND RESTRAINTS

Brulotte v. Thys Co.

379 U.S. 29 (1964).

■ MR. JUSTICE DOUGLAS delivered the opinion of the Court.

Respondent, owner of various patents for hop-picking, sold a machine to each of the petitioners for a flat sum [footnote omitted] and issued a license for its use. Under that license there is payable a minimum royalty of $500 for each hop-picking season or $3.33 1/3 per 200 pounds of dried hops harvested by the machine, whichever is greater. The licenses by their terms may not be assigned nor may the machines be removed from Yakima County. The licenses issued to petitioners listed 12 patents relating to hop-picking machines;[5] but only seven were incorporated into the machines sold to and licensed for use by petitioners. Of those seven all expired on or before 1957. But the licenses issued by respondent to them[6] continued for terms beyond that date.

Petitioners refused to make royalty payments accruing both before and after the expiration of the patents. This suit followed. One defense was misuse of the patents through extension of the license agreements beyond the expiration date of the patents. The trial court rendered judgment for respondent and the Supreme Court of Washington affirmed. 62 Wash.2d 284. The case is here on a writ of certiorari. 376 U.S. 905.

We conclude that the judgment below must be reversed insofar as it allows royalties to be collected which accrued after the last of the patents incorporated into the machines had expired.

The Constitution by Art. I, § 8 authorizes Congress to secure "for limited times" to inventors "the exclusive right" to their discoveries. Congress exercised that power by 35 U.S.C. § 154 which provides in part as follows:

> Every patent shall contain a short title of the invention and a grant to the patentee, his heirs or assigns, for the term of seventeen years, of the right to exclude others from making, using, or selling the invention throughout the United States, referring to the specification for the particulars thereof. . . .

The right to make, the right to sell, and the right to use "may be granted or conferred separately by the patentee." *Adams v. Burke*, 17 Wall. 453, 456. But these rights become public property once the 17–year period expires. *See Singer Mfg. Co. v. June Mfg. Co.*, 163 U.S. 169, 185; *Kellogg Co. v. National Biscuit Co.*, 305 U.S. 111, 118. As stated by Chief Justice Stone, speaking for the Court in *Scott Paper Co. v. Marcalus Mfg. Co.*, 326 U.S. 249, 256:

> . . . any attempted reservation or continuation in the patentee or those claiming under him of the patent monopoly, after the patent expires, whatever the legal device employed, runs counter to the policy and purpose of the patent laws.

The Supreme Court of Washington held that in the present case the period during which royalties were required was only "a reasonable amount of time over which to spread the payments for the use of the patent." 62 Wash.2d, at 291, 382 P.2d, at 275. But there is intrinsic

---

5. All but one of the 12 expired prior to the expiration of the license agreements. The exception was a patent whose mechanism was not incorporated in these machines.

6. Petitioners purchased their machines from prior purchasers under transfer agreements to which respondent was a party.

evidence that the agreements were not designed with that limited view. As we have seen, [footnote omitted] the purchase price in each case was a flat sum, the annual payments not being part of the purchase price but royalties for use of the machine during that year. The royalty payments due for the post-expiration period are by their terms for use during that period, and are not deferred payments for use during the pre-expiration period. Nor is the case like the hypothetical ones put to us where non-patented articles are marketed at prices based on use. The machines in issue here were patented articles and the royalties exacted were the same for the post-expiration period as they were for the period of the patent. That is peculiarly significant in this case in view of other provisions of the license agreements. The license agreements prevent assignment of the machines or their removal from Yakima County after, as well as before, the expiration of the patents.

Those restrictions are apt and pertinent to protection of the patent monopoly; and their applicability to the post-expiration period is a telltale sign that the licensor was using the licenses to project its monopoly beyond the patent period. They forcefully negate the suggestion that we have here a bare arrangement for a sale or a lease at an undetermined price based on use. The sale or lease of unpatented machines on long-term payments based on a deferred purchase price or on use would present wholly different considerations. Those arrangements seldom rise to the level of a federal question. But patents are in the federal domain; and "whatever the legal device employed" (*Scott Paper Co. v. Marcalus Mfg. Co., supra*, 326 U.S., at 256) a projection of the patent monopoly after the patent expires is not enforceable. The present licenses draw no line between the term of the patent and the post-expiration period. The same provisions as respects both use and royalties are applicable to each. The contracts are, therefore, on their face a bald attempt to exact the same terms and conditions for the period after the patents have expired as they do for the monopoly period. We are, therefore, unable to conjecture what the bargaining position of the parties might have been and what resultant arrangement might have emerged had the provision for post-expiration royalties been divorced from the patent and nowise subject to its leverage.

In light of those considerations, we conclude that a patentee's use of a royalty agreement that projects beyond the expiration date of the patent is unlawful per se. If that device were available to patentees, the free market visualized for the post-expiration period would be subject to monopoly influences that have no proper place there.

Automatic Radio Co. v. Hazeltine, 339 U.S. 827, is not in point. While some of the patents under that license apparently had expired, the royalties claimed were not for a period when all of them had expired.[5] That license covered several hundred patents and the royalty was based on the licen-

---

5. The petition for certiorari did not in the questions presented raise the question of the effect of the expiration of any of the patents on the royalty agreement. Also, the Hazeltine license, which covered many patents, exacted royalties for patents never used. But that aspect of the case is likewise not apposite here for the present licensees are farmers using the machines, not manufacturers buying the right to incorporate patents into their manufactured products.

see's sales, even when no patents were used. The Court held that the computation of royalty payments by that formula was a convenient and reasonable device. We decline the invitation to extend it so as to project the patent monopoly beyond the 17–year period.

A patent empowers the owner to exact royalties as high as he can negotiate with the leverage of that monopoly. But to use that leverage to project those royalty payments beyond the life of the patent is analogous to an effort to enlarge the monopoly of the patent by tieing the sale or use of the patented article to the purchase or use of unpatented ones. *See Ethyl Gasoline Corp. v. United States*, 309 U.S. 436; *Mercoid Corp. v. Mid– Continent Inv. Co.*, 320 U.S. 661, 664–665, and cases cited. The exaction of royalties for use of a machine after the patent has expired is an assertion of monopoly power in the post-expiration period when, as we have seen, the patent has entered the public domain. We share the views of the Court of Appeals in *Ar–Tik Systems, Inc. v. Dairy Queen, Inc.*, 3 Cir., 302 F.2d 496, 510, that after expiration of the last of the patents incorporated in the machines "the grant of patent monopoly was spent" and that an attempt to project it into another term by continuation of the licensing agreement is unenforceable.

Reversed.

■ MR. JUSTICE HARLAN, dissenting.

The Court holds that the Thys Company unlawfully misused its patent monopoly by contracting with purchasers of its patented machines for royalty payments based on use beyond the patent term. I think that more discriminating analysis than the Court has seen fit to give this case produces a different result.

The patent laws prohibit post-expiration restrictions on the use of patented ideas; they have no bearing on use restrictions upon nonpatented, tangible machines. We have before us a mixed case involving the sale of a tangible machine which incorporates an intangible, patented idea. My effort in what follows is to separate out these two notions, to show that there is no substantial restriction on the use of the Thys idea, and to demonstrate that what slight restriction there may be is less objectionable than other post-expiration use restrictions which are clearly acceptable.

I.

It surely cannot be questioned that Thys could have lawfully set a fixed price for its machine and extended credit terms beyond the patent period. It is equally unquestionable, I take it, that if Thys had had no patent or if its patent had expired, it could have sold its machines at a flexible, undetermined price based on use; for example, a phonograph record manufacturer could sell a recording of a song in the public domain to a juke-box owner for an undetermined consideration based on the number of times the record was played.

Conversely it should be equally clear that if Thys licensed another manufacturer to produce hop-picking machines incorporating any of the Thys patents, royalties could not be exacted beyond the patent term. Such royalties would restrict the manufacturer's exploitation of the idea after it falls into the public domain, and no such restriction should be valid. To give another example unconnected with a tangible machine, a song writer could charge a royalty every time his song—his idea—was sung for profit during the period of copyright. But once the song falls into the public domain each and every member of the public should be free to sing it.

In fact Thys sells both a machine and the use of an idea. The company should be free to restrict the use of its machine, as in the first two examples given above. It may not restrict the use of its patented idea once it has fallen into the public domain. Whether it has done so must be the point of inquiry.

Consider the situation as of the day the patent monopoly ends. Any manufacturer is completely free to produce Thys-type hop-pickers. The farmer who has previously purchased a Thys machine is free to buy and use any other kind of machine whether or not it incorporates the Thys idea, or make one himself if he is able. Of course, he is not entitled as against Thys to the free use of any Thys machine. The Court's opinion must therefore ultimately rest on the proposition that the purchasing farmer is restricted in using his particular machine, embodying as it does an application of the patented idea, by the fact that royalties are tied directly to use.

To test this proposition I again put a hypothetical. Assume that a Thys contract called for neither an initial flat-sum payment nor any annual minimum royalties; Thys' sole recompense for giving up ownership of its machine was a royalty payment extending beyond the patent term based on use, without any requirement either to use the machine or not to use a competitor's. A moment's thought reveals that, despite the clear restriction on use both before and after the expiration of the patent term, the arrangement would involve no misuse of patent leverage.[1] Unless the Court's opinion rests on technicalities of contract draftsmanship and not on the economic substance of the transaction, the distinction between the hypothetical and the actual case lies only in the cumulative investment consisting of the initial and minimum payments independent of use, which the purchaser obligated himself to make to Thys. I fail to see why this distinguishing feature should be critical. If anything the investment will encourage the purchaser to use his machine in order to amortize the machine's fixed cost over as large a production base as possible. Yet the gravamen of the majority opinion is restriction, not encouragement, of use.

II.

The essence of the majority opinion may lie in some notion that "patent leverage" being used by Thys to exact use payments extending beyond the patent term somehow allows Thys to extract more onerous payments from the farmers than would otherwise be obtainable. If this be the case, the Court must in some way distinguish long-term use payments from long-term installment payments of a flat-sum purchase price. For the danger which it seems to fear would appear to inhere equally in both, and as I read the Court's opinion, the latter type of arrangement is lawful

---

1. Installment of a patented, coin-operated washing machine in the basement of an apartment building without charge except that the landlord and his tenants must deposit 25 cents for every use, should not constitute patent misuse.

despite the fact that failure to pay an installment under a conditional sales contract would permit the seller to recapture the machine, thus terminating—not merely restricting—the farmer's use of it. Furthermore, since the judgments against petitioners were based almost entirely on defaults in paying the $500 minimums and not on failures to pay for above minimum use,[2] any such distinction of extended use payments and extended installments, even if accepted, would not justify eradicating all petitioners' obligations beyond the patent term, but only those based on use above the stated minimums; for the minimums by themselves, being payable whether or not a machine has been used, are precisely identical in substantive economic effect to flat installments.

In fact a distinction should not be accepted based on the assumption that Thys, which exploits its patents by selling its patented machines rather than licensing others to manufacture them, can use its patent leverage to exact more onerous payments from farmers by gearing price to use instead of charging a flat sum. Four possible situations must be considered. The purchasing farmer could overestimate, exactly estimate, underestimate, or have no firm estimate of his use requirements for a Thys machine. If he overestimates or exactly estimates, the farmer will be fully aware of what the machine will cost him in the long run, and it is unrealistic to suppose that in such circumstances he would be willing to pay more to have the machine on use than on straight terms. If the farmer underestimates, the thought may be that Thys will take advantage of him; but surely the farmer is in a better position than Thys or anyone else to estimate his own requirements and is hardly in need of the Court's protection in this respect. If the farmer has no fixed estimate of his use requirements he may have good business reasons entirely unconnected with "patent leverage" for wanting payments tied to use, and may indeed be willing to pay more in the long run to obtain such an arrangement. One final example should illustrate my point:

At the time when the Thys patent term still has a few years to run, a farmer who has been picking his hops by hand comes into the Thys retail outlet to inquire about the mechanical pickers. The salesman concludes his description of the advantages of the Thys machine with the price tag—$20,000. Value to the farmer depends completely on the use he will derive from the machine; he is willing to obligate himself on long credit terms to pay $10,000, but unless the machine can substantially outpick his old hand-picking methods, it is worth no more to him. He therefore offers to pay $2,000 down, $400 annually for 20 years, and an additional payment during the contract term for any production he can derive from the machine over and above the minimum amount he could pick by hand. Thys accepts, and by doing so, according to the majority, commits a per se misuse of its patent. I cannot believe that this is good law.[3]

---

2. Petitioner Charvet was indebted to Thys only to the extent of the minimums; petitioner Brulotte was in default approximately $4,500 of which $3,210 was attributable to minimums.

3. The Court also adverts to the provisions in the license agreements prohibiting "assignment of the machines or their removal from Yakima County" during the terms of the agreements. Such provisions, however, are surely appropriate to secure performance of what

Furthermore, it should not be overlooked that we are dealing here with a patent, not an antitrust, case, there being no basis in the record for concluding that Thys' arrangements with its licensees were such as to run afoul of the antitrust laws.

III.

The possibility remains that the Court is basing its decision on the technical framing of the contract and would have treated the case differently if title had been declared to pass at the termination instead of the outset of the contract term, or if the use payments had been verbally disassociated from the patent licenses and described as a convenient means of spreading out payments for the machine. If indeed the impact of the opinion is that Thys must redraft its contracts to achieve the same economic results, the decision is not only wrong, but conspicuously ineffectual.

I would affirm.

NOTES

1. *Post–Expiration Royalties and Patent Misuse.* The *Brulotte* Court did not invoke the misuse doctrine, but it did use the phrase "unlawful per se" and it is clear now that term extension is patent misuse. *See Mallinckrodt, Inc. v. Medipart, Inc.*, 976 F.2d 700 (Fed.Cir.1992) (noting that patent term extension is patent misuse). *See also, Rocform Corp. v. Acitelli–Standard Concrete Wall, Inc.*, 367 F.2d 678 (6th Cir.1966). *Brulotte* has also been applied to foreign patent license agreements. *See, e.g., The Administrators of Tulane v. Debio Holding, S.A.*, 177 F.Supp.2d 545, 550–51 (E.D.La.2001) (and cases cited therein).

What is left of *Brulotte* after the 1988 amendments to § 271(d), namely subsection (5), which holds that:

> No patent owner otherwise entitled to relief for infringement or contributory infringement of a patent shall be denied relief or deemed guilty of misuse or illegal extension of the patent right [if he]

> conditioned the license of any rights to the patent or the sale of the patented product on the acquisition of a license to rights in another patent or purchase of a separate product, unless, in view of the circumstances, the patent owner has market power in the relevant market for the patent or patented product on which the license or sale is conditioned.

The *Brulotte* decision has been widely criticized. *See, e.g.*, Rochelle Cooper Dreyfuss, *Dethroning Lear: Licensee Estoppel and the Incentive to Innovate*, 72 VA. L. REV. 677, 709 (1986) (noting that the *Brulotte* decision is "vulnerable on several grounds"). Building of Justice Harlan's dissent, Professor William Landes and Judge Richard Posner write:

> After the patent expires, anyone can make the patented process or product without being guilty of patent infringement. As the patent can no longer be used to exclude anybody from such production, expiration has accomplished what is was supposed to accomplish. If the licensee agrees to continue paying royalties after the patent expires, the royalty rate will be lower during the period before expiration. The duration of the patent fixes the limit of the patentee's power to extract royalties; it is a detail whether

---

are in effect conditional sales agreements and they do not advance the argument for patent misuse.

he extracts them at a higher rate over a shorter period of time or at a lower rate over a longer period of time.

WILLIAM M. LANDES AND RICHARD A. POSNER, THE ECONOMIC STRUCTURE OF INTELLECTUAL PROPERTY LAW 380 (2003). Indeed, Judge Posner applied a relatively strong, and anti-patent and anti-contract, reading of *Brulotte* in *Scheiber v. Dolby*, 293 F.3d 1014 (7th Cir. 2002), which included a very detailed and strong criticism of that logic. Commentators saw this as an effort to follow Supreme Court precedent while hoping to encourage the Court to grant certiorari and reverse that case law on the strength of Posner's reasoning. But the plan seems to have backfired, since the Court did not review the case, leaving a particularly strong reading of *Brulotte* as the governing law of the 7th Circuit.

2. *Installment Sales.* Does *Brulotte* apply to all royalty schemes under which payments fall due after expiration of the patent? The Court emphasized in its opinion that the royalties were based on use of the patented machine after expiration, that the royalty rate was unaffected by expiration of the patent, and that a lump sum was paid for "title" to the machine itself. Thus, the decision leaves open the question of the legality of a bona fide installment sale; or an arrangement whereby the royalties accrue only on sales made prior to the expiration of the patent. Consider a provision in a patent license contract that extends beyond the term of the licensed patent but is expressly described in the contract to be part of a "payment plan" that allows the cash-strapped licensee to pay the full royalty for the length of patent term, but to allocate that total amount over a time period that happened to extend beyond the term of the patent. How would this provision be treated by the Court in *Brulotte*? By Justice Harlan?

3. Another interesting question is whether *Brulotte* applies to a trade secret license on subject matter that could have been patented or to a license conferring both patent rights and trade secret information? This issue was addressed in *Aronson v. Quick Point Pencil Co.*

Aronson v. Quick Point Pencil Co.

440 U.S. 257 (1979).

■ MR. CHIEF JUSTICE BURGER delivered the opinion of the Court.

We granted certiorari, 436 U.S. 943, to consider whether federal patent law pre-empts state contract law so as to preclude enforcement of a contract to pay royalties to a patent applicant, on sales of articles embodying the putative invention, for so long as the contracting party sells them, if a patent is not granted.

(1)

In October 1955 the petitioner, Mrs. Jane Aronson, filed an application, Serial No. 542677, for a patent on a new form of keyholder. Although ingenious, the design was so simple that it readily could be copied unless it was protected by patent. In June 1956, while the patent application was pending, Mrs. Aronson negotiated a contract with the respondent, Quick Point Pencil Co., for the manufacture and sale of the keyholder.

The contract was embodied in two documents. In the first, a letter from Quick Point to Mrs. Aronson, Quick Point agreed to pay Mrs. Aronson a royalty of 5% of the selling price in return for "the exclusive right to make and sell keyholders of the type shown in your application, Serial No.

542677." The letter further provided that the parties would consult one another concerning the steps to be taken "[i]n the event of any infringement."

The contract did not require Quick Point to manufacture the keyholder. Mrs. Aronson received a $750 advance on royalties and was entitled to rescind the exclusive license if Quick Point did not sell a million keyholders by the end of 1957. Quick Point retained the right to cancel the agreement whenever "the volume of sales does not meet our expectations." The duration of the agreement was not otherwise prescribed.

A contemporaneous document provided that if Mrs. Aronson's patent application was "not allowed within five (5) years, Quick Point Pencil Co. [would] pay ... two and one half percent (2 1/2%) of sales ... so long as you [Quick Point] continue to sell same."[1]

In June 1961, when Mrs. Aronson had failed to obtain a patent on the keyholder within the five years specified in the agreement, Quick Point asserted its contractual right to reduce royalty payments to 2 1/2% of sales. In September of that year the Board of Patent Appeals issued a final rejection of the application on the ground that the keyholder was not patentable, and Mrs. Aronson did not appeal. Quick Point continued to pay reduced royalties to her for 14 years thereafter.

The market was more receptive to the keyholder's novelty and utility than the Patent Office. By September 1975 Quick Point had made sales in excess of $7 million and paid Mrs. Aronson royalties totaling $203,963.84; sales were continuing to rise. However, while Quick Point was able to pre-empt the market in the earlier years and was long the only manufacturer of the Aronson keyholder, copies began to appear in the late 1960's. Quick Point's competitors, of course, were not required to pay royalties for their use of the design. Quick Point's share of the Aronson keyholder market has declined during the past decade.

(2)

In November 1975, Quick Point commenced an action in the United States District Court for a declaratory judgment, pursuant to 28 U.S.C. § 2201, that the royalty agreement was unenforceable. Quick Point asserted that state law which might otherwise make the contract enforceable was preempted by federal patent law. This is the only issue presented to us for decision.

Both parties moved for summary judgment on affidavits, exhibits, and stipulations of fact. The District Court concluded that the "language of the agreement is plain, clear and unequivocal and has no relation as to whether or not a patent is ever granted." Accordingly, it held that the agreement

---

1. In April 1961, while Mrs. Aronson's patent application was pending, her husband sought a patent on a different keyholder and made plans to license another company to manufacture it. Quick Point's attorney wrote to the couple that the proposed new license would violate the 1956 agreement. He observed that "your license agreement is in respect of the disclosure of said Jane [Aronson's] application (not merely in respect of its claims) and that even if no patent is ever granted on the Jane [Aronson] application, *Quick Point Pencil Company is obligated to pay royalties in respect of any keyholder manufactured by it in accordance with any disclosure of said application*." (Emphasis added.)

was valid, and that Quick Point was obliged to pay the agreed royalties pursuant to the contract for so long as it manufactured the keyholder.

The Court of Appeals reversed, one judge dissenting. 567 F.2d 757. It held that since the parties contracted with reference to a pending patent application, Mrs. Aronson was estopped from denying that patent law principles governed her contract with Quick Point. Although acknowledging that this Court had never decided the precise issue, the Court of Appeals held that our prior decisions regarding patent licenses compelled the conclusion that Quick Point's contract with Mrs. Aronson became unenforceable once she failed to obtain a patent. The court held that a continuing obligation to pay royalties would be contrary to "the strong federal policy favoring the full and free use of ideas in the public domain," *Lear, Inc. v. Adkins*, 395 U.S. 653, 674 (1969). The court also observed that if Mrs. Aronson actually had obtained a patent, Quick Point would have escaped its royalty obligations either if the patent were held to be invalid, *see ibid.*, or upon its expiration after 17 years, *see Brulotte v. Thys Co.*, 379 U.S. 29 (1964). Accordingly, it concluded that a licensee should be relieved of royalty obligations when the licensor's efforts to obtain a contemplated patent prove unsuccessful.

(3)

On this record it is clear that the parties contracted with full awareness of both the pendency of a patent application and the possibility that a patent might not issue. The clause de-escalating the royalty by half in the event no patent issued within five years makes that crystal clear. Quick Point apparently placed a significant value on exploiting the basic novelty of the device, even if no patent issued; its success demonstrates that this judgment was well founded. Assuming, arguendo, that the initial letter and the commitment to pay a 5% royalty was subject to federal patent law, the provision relating to the 2 1/2% royalty was explicitly independent of federal law. The cases and principles relied on by the Court of Appeals and Quick Point do not bear on a contract that does not rely on a patent, particularly where, as here, the contracting parties agreed expressly as to alternative obligations if no patent should issue.

Commercial agreements traditionally are the domain of state law. State law is not displaced merely because the contract relates to intellectual property which may or may not be patentable; the states are free to regulate the use of such intellectual property in any manner not inconsistent with federal law. *Kewanee Oil Co. v. Bicron Corp.*, 416 U.S. 470, 479 (1974); *see Goldstein v. California*, 412 U.S. 546 (1973). In this as in other fields, the question of whether federal law pre-empts state law "involves a consideration of whether that law 'stands as an obstacle to the accomplishment and execution of the full purposes and objectives of Congress.' *Hines v. Davidowitz*, 312 U.S. 52, 67 (1941)." *Kewanee Oil Co., supra.*, 416 U.S., at 479. If it does not, state law governs.

In *Kewanee Oil Co., supra*, at 480–481, we reviewed the purposes of the federal patent system. First, patent law seeks to foster and reward invention; second, it promotes disclosure of inventions, to stimulate further innovation and to permit the public to practice the invention once the patent expires; third, the stringent requirements for patent protection seek to assure that ideas in the public domain remain there for the free use of the public.

Enforcement of Quick Point's agreement with Mrs. Aronson is not inconsistent with any of these aims. Permitting inventors to make enforceable agreements licensing the use of their inventions in return for royalties provides an additional incentive to invention. Similarly, encouraging Mrs. Aronson to make arrangements for the manufacture of her keyholder furthers the federal policy of disclosure of inventions; these simple devices display the novel idea which they embody wherever they are seen.

Quick Point argues that enforcement of such contracts conflicts with the federal policy against withdrawing ideas from the public domain and discourages recourse to the federal patent system by allowing states to extend "perpetual protection to articles too lacking in novelty to merit any patent at all under federal constitutional standards," *Sears, Roebuck & Co. v. Stiffel Co.*, 376 U.S. 225, 232 (1964).

We find no merit in this contention. Enforcement of the agreement does not withdraw any idea from the public domain. The design for the keyholder was not in the public domain before Quick Point obtained its license to manufacture it. *See Kewanee Oil Co., supra*, 416 U.S. at 484. In negotiating the agreement, Mrs. Aronson disclosed the design in confidence. Had Quick Point tried to exploit the design in breach of that confidence, it would have risked legal liability. It is equally clear that the design entered the public domain as a result of the manufacture and sale of the keyholders under the contract.

Requiring Quick Point to bear the burden of royalties for the use of the design is no more inconsistent with federal patent law than any of the other costs involved in being the first to introduce a new product to the market, such as outlays for research and development, and marketing and promotional expenses. For reasons which Quick Point's experience with the Aronson keyholder demonstrate, innovative entrepreneurs have usually found such costs to be well worth paying.

Finally, enforcement of this agreement does not discourage anyone from seeking a patent. Mrs. Aronson attempted to obtain a patent for over five years. It is quite true that had she succeeded, she would have received a 5% royalty only on keyholders sold during the 17–year life of the patent. Offsetting the limited terms of royalty payments, she would have received twice as much per dollar of Quick Point's sales, and both she and Quick Point could have licensed any others who produced the same keyholder. Which course would have produced the greater yield to the contracting parties is a matter of speculation; the parties resolved the uncertainties by their bargain.

(4)

No decision of this Court relating to patents justifies relieving Quick Point of its contract obligations. We have held that a state may not forbid the copying of an idea in the public domain which does not meet the requirements for federal patent protection. *Compco Corp. v. Day–Brite*

Lighting, Inc., 376 U.S. 234 (1964); *Sears, Roebuck & Co. v. Stiffel Co.*, *supra*. Enforcement of Quick Point's agreement, however, does not prevent anyone from copying the keyholder. It merely requires Quick Point to pay the consideration which it promised in return for the use of a novel device which enabled it to pre-empt the market.

In *Lear, Inc. v. Adkins*, 395 U.S. 653 (1969), we held that a person licensed to use a patent may challenge the validity of the patent, and that a licensee who establishes that the patent is invalid need not pay the royalties accrued under the licensing agreement subsequent to the issuance of the patent. Both holdings relied on the desirability of encouraging licensees to challenge the validity of patents, to further the strong federal policy that only inventions which meet the rigorous requirements of patentability shall be withdrawn from the public domain. *Id.*, at 670–671, 673–674. Accordingly, neither the holding nor the rationale of *Lear* controls when no patent has issued, and no ideas have been withdrawn from public use.

Enforcement of the royalty agreement here is also consistent with the principles treated in *Brulotte v. Thys Co.*, 379 U.S. 29 (1964). There, we held that the obligation to pay royalties in return for the use of a patented device may not extend beyond the life of the patent. The principle underlying that holding was simply that the monopoly granted under a patent cannot lawfully be used to "negotiate with the leverage of that monopoly." The Court emphasized that to "use that leverage to project those royalty payments beyond the life of the patent is analogous to an effort to enlarge the monopoly of the patent...." *Id.*, at 33. Here the reduced royalty which is challenged, far from being negotiated "with the leverage" of a patent, rested on the contingency that no patent would issue within five years.

No doubt a pending patent application gives the applicant some additional bargaining power for purposes of negotiating a royalty agreement. The pending application allows the inventor to hold out the hope of an exclusive right to exploit the idea, as well as the threat that the other party will be prevented from using the idea for 17 years. However, the amount of leverage arising from a patent application depends on how likely the parties consider it to be that a valid patent will issue. Here, where no patent ever issued, the record is entirely clear that the parties assigned a substantial likelihood to that contingency, since they specifically provided for a reduced royalty in the event no patent issued within five years.

This case does not require us to draw the line between what constitutes abuse of a pending application and what does not. It is clear that whatever role the pending application played in the negotiation of the 5% royalty, it played no part in the contract to pay the 2 1/2% royalty indefinitely.

Our holding in *Kewanee Oil Co.* puts to rest the contention that federal law pre-empts and renders unenforceable the contract made by these parties. There we held that state law forbidding the misappropriation of trade secrets was not pre-empted by federal patent law. We observed:

"Certainly the patent policy of encouraging invention is not disturbed by the existence of another form of incentive to invention. In this respect the two systems [patent and trade secret law] are not and never would be in conflict." 416 U.S., at 484.

Enforcement of this royalty agreement is even less offensive to federal patent policies than state law protecting trade secrets. The most commonly accepted definition of trade secrets is restricted to confidential information which is not disclosed in the normal process of exploitation. *See* RESTATE-MENT OF TORTS § 757, Comment b, p. 5 (1939). Accordingly, the exploitation of trade secrets under state law may not satisfy the federal policy in favor of disclosure, whereas disclosure is inescapable in exploiting a device like the Aronson keyholder.

Enforcement of these contractual obligations, freely undertaken in arm's-length negotiation and with no fixed reliance on a patent or a probable patent grant, will

> "encourage invention in areas where patent law does not reach, and will prompt the independent innovator to proceed with the discovery and exploitation of his invention. Competition is fostered and the public is not deprived of the use of valuable, if not quite patentable, invention." 416 U.S., at 485.

The device which is the subject of this contract ceased to have any secrecy as soon as it was first marketed, yet when the contract was negotiated the inventiveness and novelty were sufficiently apparent to induce an experienced novelty manufacturer to agree to pay for the opportunity to be first in the market. Federal patent law is not a barrier to such a contract.

Reversed.

■ MR. JUSTICE BLACKMUN, concurring in the result.

For me, the hard question is whether this case can meaningfully be distinguished from *Brulotte v. Thys Co.*, 379 U.S. 29 (1964). There the Court held that a patent licensor could not use the leverage of its patent to obtain a royalty contract that extended beyond the patent's 17–year term. Here Mrs. Aronson has used the leverage of her patent application to negotiate a royalty contract which continues to be binding even though the patent application was long ago denied.

The Court . . . asserts that her leverage played "no part" with respect to the contingent agreement to pay a reduced royalty if no patent issued within five years. Yet it may well be that Quick Point agreed to that contingency in order to obtain its other rights that depended on the success of the patent application. The parties did not apportion consideration in the neat fashion the Court adopts.

In my view, the holding in *Brulotte* reflects hostility toward extension of a patent monopoly whose term is fixed by statute, 35 U.S.C. § 154. Such hostility has no place here. A patent application which is later denied temporarily discourages unlicensed imitators. Its benefits and hazards are of a different magnitude from those of a granted patent that prohibits all competition for 17 years. Nothing justifies estopping a patent-application licensor from entering into a contract whose term does not end if the application fails. The Court points out, ante, that enforcement of this contract does not conflict with the objectives of the patent laws. The United

States, as *amicus curiae*, maintains that patent-application licensing of this sort is desirable because it encourages patent applications, promotes early disclosure, and allows parties to structure their bargains efficiently.

On this basis, I concur in the Court's holding that federal patent law does not pre-empt the enforcement of Mrs. Aronson's contract with Quick Point.

NOTES

1. *Step–Downs in Royalty Rates.* Do you agree with Justice Blackman that *Brulotte* and *Aronson* are potentially in conflict? Did *Aronson* effectively overrule *Brulotte*? In both cases, a royalty payment was agreed to for use of "public domain" material; in *Brulotte*, the patent expired and in *Aronson*, a patent never issued. Did Jane Aronson, with a patent pending, or Thys, with a patent issued, have greater bargaining leverage?

After *Aronson*, it seems that the safe approach for parties wishing to have the terms of their technology license agreements upheld is for the text of the agreement itself to clearly show that the parties have fully identified, and evaluated the different possible states of the world with respect to the legal status of any protection for the licensed technology. Such a detailed agreement may be especially likely to be enforced if the royalty rates step down on the expiration or invalidity of each formal intellectual property right that is licensed.

2. *"Hybrid" Patent–Trade Secret Licenses. Aronson* did not address the issue of post-expiration royalties on a "hybrid" patent-trade secret license. In *Pitney–Bowes, Inc. v. Mestre*, 517 F.Supp. 52 (S.D. Fla. 1981), the Southern District Court of Florida recognized that "there may be instances in which, given a hybrid trade secret and patent agreement providing clearly separate forms of protection, the trade secret protection might have a separate legal viability and might survive the expiration of a patent." The court indicated that the agreement must have "explicit language ... differentiating between the two forms of protection underlying the royalty obligation" and must also provide a division or allocation of royalties. *Id.* at 61, 63. The court also noted that issuance of a patent on the subject matter of a trade secret agreement will not transform that agreement into a patent license unless the later issuance of patent rights was "a subject of the agreement and a basis of the bargain." On appeal, the Eleventh Circuit agreed that a "hybrid" patent-trade secret license lasting past the expiration of the patent was invalid under federal law, at least absent a clause explicitly allocating payments between trade secrets and patent rights. The court left open the question whether such allocation clause would in fact cure the improper extension problem.

3. *Accommodation Consideration.* Consider a provision in a technology license agreement that expressly states that the payment provisions of the agreement that extend beyond the term of any patents licensed by the agreement are supported by consideration other than a license under those patents, such as some form of technical support. Should this consideration be valid? Or is this consideration merely included to accommodate the reasoning of a case like *Brulotte*, and be rejected as a sham? How about a technology license agreement in which there are no patents or even trade secrets? *See e.g. Apfel v. Prudential–Bache Securities Inc.*, 81 N.Y.2d 470, 600 N.Y.S.2d 433, 616 N.E.2d 1095 (N.Y. 1993) (pointing out that because adequacy of consideration is not a proper subject of judicial scrutiny absent fraud or unconscionability, a sales contract for certain techniques for issuing municipal securities without paper by using a book-entry approach was enforceable even though the system was not patented and may not even have been new).

Consider your parent's contract to pay your childhood piano teacher for teaching services despite the fact that what was being taught was not patented, copyrighted, trademarked, new, and may not even have been unique in any way. Should that contract be enforceable?

4. *Payment Plans.* Consider a provision in a patent license contract that extends beyond the term of the licensed patent but is expressly described in the contract to be part of a "payment plan" that allows the cash-strapped licensee to pay the full royalty for the length of patent term, but to allocate that total amount over a time period that happened to extend beyond the term of the patent. How would this provision be treated by the Court in *Brulotte*? By Justice Harlan? By Chief Justice Burger and the majority in *Aronson*? How would you treat it today?

G. INVENTORSHIP AND OWNERSHIP

It is important to distinguish the issue of *inventorship* for patent law purposes from the issue of *ownership* of patent rights in an invention. Patent law requires that the true and original inventor or inventors be named in the application for a patent, and United States patent law requires that a patent issue to the correct inventive entity, that is, the individual(s) who actually invented the claimed subject matter, not the entity who owns the patent right. Failure to satisfy this requirement may lead to the invalidation of the patent. Because of this potential sanction, the patent law provides for the correction of non-deceptive misjoinder and nonjoinder of inventors. See 35 U.S.C. §§ 116 and 256.

Inventorship provides the starting point for determining ownership of patent rights. Absent some effective transfer or other obligation to assign patent rights, the individual inventor owns the right to apply for and obtain a patent. There can be either a sole inventor or joint inventors, and joint inventors jointly own the patent right.

To be sure, invention is often driven by collaborative efforts that are in the contract sense so-owned, such as a common employer. Indeed, assignment of patent rights is quite common. Federal law explicitly provides that patents have the attributes of personal property, and that both patents and applications for patents are assignable. And, importantly, there is a recording statute for patents; so the chain of title should be searched before any assignment is executed. 35 U.S.C. § 261 (ownership and assignment).

Ethicon, Inc. v. United States Surgical Corp.

135 F.3d 1456 (Fed.Cir.1998).

■ Before NEWMAN, CIRCUIT JUDGE, SKELTON, SENIOR CIRCUIT JUDGE, and RADER, CIRCUIT JUDGE.

■ RADER, CIRCUIT JUDGE.

In this patent infringement action, Dr. InBae Yoon (Yoon) and his exclusive licensee, Ethicon, Inc. (Ethicon), appeal from the judgment of the United States District Court for the District of Connecticut. In 1989, Yoon and Ethicon sued United States Surgical Corporation (U.S. Surgical) for infringement of U.S. Patent No. 4,535,773 (the '773 patent). In 1993, the parties stipulated to the intervention of Mr. Young Jae Choi (Choi) as defendant-intervenor. Choi claimed to be an omitted co-inventor of the '773 patent and to have granted U.S. Surgical a retroactive license under that patent. On U.S. Surgical's motion to correct inventorship of the '773 patent under 35 U.S.C. § 256, the district court ruled that Choi was an omitted co-inventor of two claims, *see* 937 F.Supp. 1015 (D.Conn.1996), and subsequently granted U.S. Surgical's motion to dismiss the infringement complaint. Because the district court's determination of co-inventorship was correct, and because Choi is a joint owner of the '773 patent who has not consented to suit against U.S. Surgical, this court affirms.

I. BACKGROUND

The '773 patent relates to trocars, an essential tool for endoscopic surgery. A trocar is a surgical instrument which makes small incisions in the wall of a body cavity, often the abdomen, to admit endoscopic instruments. Trocars include a shaft within an outer sleeve. One end of the shaft has a sharp blade. At the outset of surgery, the surgeon uses the blade to puncture the wall and extend the trocar into the cavity. The surgeon then removes the shaft, leaving the hollow outer sleeve, through which the surgeon may insert tiny cameras and surgical instruments for the operation.

Conventional trocars, however, pose a risk of damage to internal organs or structures. As the trocar blade punctures the cavity wall, the sudden loss of resistance can cause the blade to lunge forward and injure an internal organ. The '773 patent claims a trocar that alleviates this danger. In one embodiment, the invention equips the trocar with a blunt, spring-loaded rod. As the trocar pierces the cavity wall, the rod automatically springs forward to precede the blade and shield against injury. A second embodiment has a retractable trocar blade that springs back into a protective sheath when it passes through the cavity wall. The patent also teaches the use of an electronic sensor in the end of the blade to signal the surgeon at the moment of puncture.

Yoon is a medical doctor and inventor of numerous patented devices for endoscopic surgery. In the late 1970s, Yoon began to conceive of a safety device to prevent accidental injury during trocar incisions. Yoon also conceived of a device to alert the surgeon when the incision was complete. In 1980, Yoon met Choi, an electronics technician, who had some college training in physics, chemistry, and electrical engineering, but no college degree. Choi had worked in the research and development of electronic devices.

After Choi had demonstrated to Yoon some of the devices he had developed, Yoon asked Choi to work with him on several projects, including one for safety trocars. Choi was not paid for his work.

In 1982, after collaborating for approximately eighteen months, their relationship ended. Choi believed that Yoon found his work unsatisfactory and unlikely to produce any marketable product. For these reasons, Choi withdrew from cooperation with Yoon.

In the same year, however, Yoon filed an application for a patent disclosing various embodiments of a safety trocar. Without informing Choi, Yoon named himself as the sole inventor. In 1985, the Patent and Trademark Office issued the '773 patent to Yoon, with fifty-five claims. Yoon thereafter granted an exclusive license under this patent to Ethicon. Yoon did not inform Choi of the patent application or issuance.

In 1989, Ethicon filed suit against U.S. Surgical for infringement of claims 34 and 50 of the '773 patent. In 1992, while this suit was still pending, U.S. Surgical became aware of Choi, and contacted him regarding his involvement in Yoon's safety trocar project. When Choi confirmed his role in the safety trocar project, U.S. Surgical obtained from Choi a "retroactive license" to practice "Choi's trocar related inventions." Under the license, Choi agreed to assist U.S. Surgical in any suit regarding the '773 patent. For its part, U.S. Surgical agreed to pay Choi contingent on its ultimate ability to continue to practice and market the invention. With the license in hand, U.S. Surgical moved to correct inventorship of the '773 patent under 35 U.S.C. § 256, claiming that Choi was a co-inventor of claims 23, 33, 46, and 47. Following an extensive hearing, the district court granted U.S. Surgical's motion, finding that Choi had contributed to the subject matter of claims 33 and 47.

U.S. Surgical next moved for dismissal of the infringement suit, arguing that Choi, as a joint owner of the patent, had granted it a valid license under the patent. By its terms, the license purported to grant rights to use the patent extending retroactively back to its issuance. The district court granted U.S. Surgical's motion and dismissed the suit.

Ethicon appeals the district court's finding of co-inventorship and its dismissal of the complaint. Specifically, Ethicon contends that (1) Choi supplied insufficient corroboration for his testimony of co-invention; (2) Choi presented insufficient evidence to show co-invention of claims 33 and 47 clearly and convincingly....

II. CO–INVENTORSHIP

Patent issuance creates a presumption that the named inventors are the true and only inventors. *See Hess v. Advanced Cardiovascular Sys., Inc.*, 106 F.3d 976, 980 (Fed.Cir.), *cert. denied*, 520 U.S. 1277 (1997). Inventorship is a question of law, which this court reviews without deference. *See Sewall v. Walters*, 21 F.3d 411, 415 (Fed.Cir.1994). However, this court reviews the underlying findings of fact which uphold a district court's inventorship determination for clear error. See *Hess*, 106 F.3d at 980.

A patented invention may be the work of two or more joint inventors. *See* 35 U.S.C. § 116 (1994). Because "[c]onception is the touchstone of inventorship," each joint inventor must generally contribute to the conception of the invention. *Burroughs Wellcome Co. v. Barr Lab., Inc.*, 40 F.3d 1223, 1227–28 (Fed.Cir.1994). "Conception is the 'formation in the mind of the inventor, of a definite and permanent idea of the complete and operative invention, as it is hereafter to be applied in practice.' " *Hybritech, Inc. v. Monoclonal Antibodies, Inc.*, 802 F.2d 1367, 1376, 231 USPQ 81, 87 (Fed.Cir.1986) (quoting 1 *Robinson on Patents* 532 (1890)). An idea is sufficiently "definite and permanent" when "only ordinary skill would be necessary to reduce the invention to practice, without extensive research or experimentation." *Burroughs Wellcome,* 40 F.3d at 1228.

The conceived invention must include every feature of the subject matter claimed in the patent. *See Sewall,* 21 F.3d at 415. Nevertheless, for the conception of a joint invention, each of the joint inventors need not "make the same type or amount of contribution" to the invention. 35 U.S.C. § 116. Rather, each needs to perform only a part of the task which produces the invention. On the other hand, one does not qualify as a joint inventor by merely assisting the actual inventor after conception of the claimed invention. *See Sewall,* 21 F.3d at 416–17; *Shatterproof Glass Corp. v. Libbey–Owens Ford Co.,* 758 F.2d 613, 624 (Fed.Cir.1985) ("An inventor 'may use the services, ideas and aid of others in the process of perfecting his invention without losing his right to a patent' "). One who simply provides the inventor with well-known principles or explains the state of the art without ever having "a firm and definite idea" of the claimed combination as a whole does not qualify as a joint inventor. See *Hess,* 106 F.3d at 981. . . .

Furthermore, a co-inventor need not make a contribution to every claim of a patent. *See* 35 U.S.C. § 116. A contribution to one claim is enough. *See SmithKline Diagnostics, Inc. v. Helena Lab. Corp.,* 859 F.2d 878, 888 (Fed.Cir.1988). Thus, the critical question for joint conception is who conceived, as that term is used in the patent law, the subject matter of the claims at issue.

35 U.S.C. § 256 provides that a co-inventor omitted from an issued patent may be added to the patent by a court "before which such matter is called in question." To show co-inventorship, however, the alleged co-inventor or co-inventors must prove their contribution to the conception of the claims by clear and convincing evidence. *See Hess,* 106 F.3d at 980. However, "an inventor's testimony respecting the facts surrounding a claim of derivation or priority of invention cannot, standing alone, rise to the level of clear and convincing proof." *Price v. Symsek,* 988 F.2d 1187, 1194 (Fed.Cir.1993). The rule is the same for an alleged co-inventor's testimony. *See Hess,* 106 F.3d at 980. Thus, an alleged co-inventor must supply evidence to corroborate his testimony. *See Price,* 988 F.2d at 1194. Whether the inventor's testimony has been sufficiently corroborated is evaluated under a "rule of reason" analysis. *Id.* at 1195. Under this analysis, "[a]n evaluation of *all* pertinent evidence must be made so that a sound determination of the credibility of the [alleged] inventor's story may be reached." *Id.*

Corroborating evidence may take many forms. Often contemporaneous documents prepared by a putative inventor serve to corroborate an inventor's testimony. *See id.* at 1195–96. Circumstantial evidence about the inventive process may also corroborate. *See Knorr v. Pearson,* 671 F.2d 1368, 1373 (CCPA 1982). Additionally, oral testimony of someone other than the alleged inventor may corroborate. *See Price,* 988 F.2d at 1195–96.

A.   Claim 33

The district court determined that Choi contributed to the conception of the subject matter of claim 33. Claim 33 (with emphasis to highlight relevant elements) reads:

A surgical instrument for providing communication through an anatomical organ structure, comprising:

> means having an abutment member and *shaft longitudinally accommodatable within an outer sleeve,* longitudinal movement of said shaft inside said sleeve being limited by contact of said abutment member with said sleeve, said shaft having a distal end with a distal blade surface tapering into a sharp distal point, *said distal blade surface being perforated along one side by an aperture,* for puncturing an anatomical organ structure when subjected to force along the longitudinal axis of said shaft;

> *means having a blunt distal bearing surface, slidably extending through said aperture, for reciprocating through said aperture* while said abutment member is in stationary contact with said sleeve;

> means positionable between said puncturing means and said reciprocating means for biasing a distal section of said reciprocating means to protrude beyond said aperture and permitting said distal section of said reciprocating means to recede into said aperture when said bearing surface is subject to force along its axis . . .; and

> *means* connectible to the proximal end of said puncturing means *for* responding to longitudinal movement of said reciprocating means relative to said puncturing means and *creating a sensible signal* having one state upon recision of said distal section of said reciprocating means into said aperture and another state upon protrusion of said distal section of said reciprocating means from said aperture.

To determine whether Choi made a contribution to the conception of the subject matter of claim 33, this court must determine what Choi's contribution was and then whether that contribution's role appears in the claimed invention. If Choi in fact contributed to the invention defined by claim 33, he is a joint inventor of that claim.

Figures 18 and 19 of the '773 patent illustrate an embodiment of claim 33. These figures show a trocar blade with an aperture through which a blunt rod can extend. When the trocar blade penetrates the inner wall of a cavity, a spring releases the rod, which juts out past the end of the trocar blade and prevents the blade from cutting further. The embodiment also includes a structure that gives the surgeon aural and visual signals when the blade nears penetration.

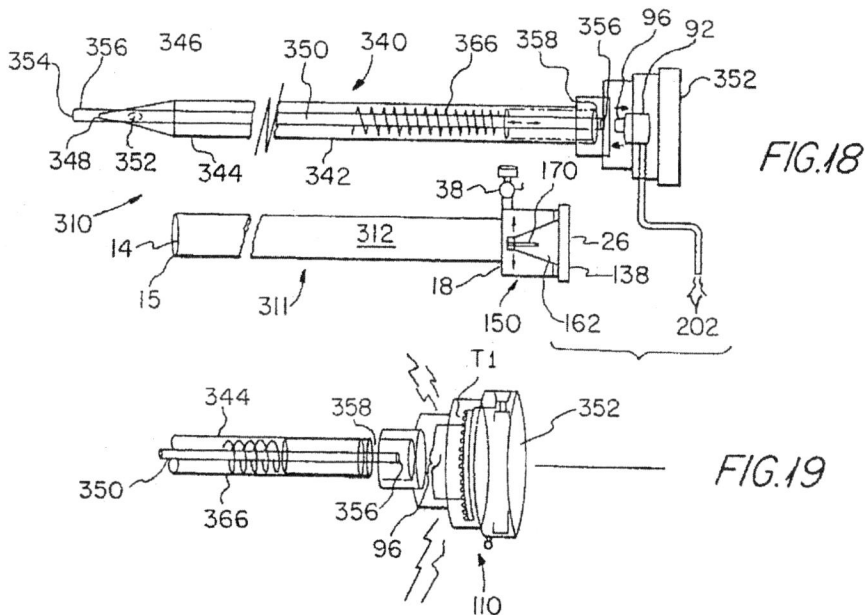

FIG.18

FIG.19

The district court found that Yoon conceived of the use of a blunt probe. However, the court found that Choi conceived of and thereby contributed two features contained in the embodiment shown in figures 18 and 19: first, Choi conceived of locating the blunt probe in the trocar shaft and allowing it to pass through an aperture in the blade surface; second, Choi conceived of the "means ... for ... creating a sensible signal."

If Choi did indeed conceive of "locating the blunt probe in the shaft and allowing it to pass through an aperture in the blade surface," he contributed to the subject matter of claim 33. Claim 33 requires that the "distal blade surface" be "perforated along one side by an aperture" and requires the "shaft" to be "longitudinally accommodatable within [the] outer sleeve." Properly construed, claim 33 includes the elements that Choi contributed to the invention according to the district court's findings.

In making this finding, the district court relied extensively on Choi's testimony. Choi testified that the idea of extending the blunt probe through an aperture in the trocar blade itself was his idea. To corroborate this testimony, Choi produced a series of sketches he created while working with Yoon. One sketch shows a probe inside the shaft of a trocar blade, extending through an opening in the side of the end of the blade.

To rebut Choi's showing, Yoon presented a drawing dated July 1973, which disclosed elements of claim 33. The district court determined, however, that Dr. Yoon had altered this drawing. In fact, according to the district court, it had originally depicted a device from an entirely different patent. Due to its suspicious origins, the trial court rejected it as unreliable.

The court also discounted Yoon's testimony for lack of credibility. Indeed the record supports the trial court's conclusion that Yoon altered and backdated documents to make it appear that he had independently invented trocars, shields, and electronics. Moreover, Yoon's trial testimony clashed with his earlier deposition testimony. For instance, before learning of Choi's role in the case, Yoon falsely testified at his deposition that (1) he had worked with Choi as early as 1975 and (2) the sketches at issue in this case had been drawn completely by him. However, the two did not meet until 1980, and when later questioned about authorship of the documents, Yoon replied, "If I said [that] at that time, then maybe I was confused." The district court justifiably discounted Yoon's testimony.

In sum, after full consideration of the relevant evidence, the district court determined that Choi conceived part of the invention recited in claim 33. This court detects no cause to reverse this determination.

B.   Claim 47

The district court also determined that Choi contributed to the conception of the subject matter of claim 47. Claim 47 (with emphasis to highlight relevant elements) reads:

A surgical instrument for providing communication through an anatomical organ structure, comprising:

* * *

means interposed between said puncturing means proximal end and said interior bore assuming a normally protruding position for determining [sic: detaining] said puncturing means proximal end extended from said interior cavity in opposition to said biasing means.

To determine whether Choi made a contribution to the conception of the subject matter of claim 47, this court must determine what Choi's contribution was and then construe the claim language to determine if Choi's contribution found its way into the defined invention.

Figures 34, 35, and 36 illustrate the invention in claim 47. In these embodiments, a cocked spring pulls the trocar back into a protective sheath as soon as the blade has punctured the inner wall. Release of the detaining means triggers the retracting spring action. The two detaining means disclosed in the specification are (1) a detent extending radially outward from the trocar through a hole in the sheath and (2) a rod extending horizontally from the proximal end of the trocar that butts against an off-center, but slidable, bar with a hole in its center. In the case of the detent detaining means, when a sensor detects that the trocar blade has pierced the wall of a cavity, the plunger of a solenoid pushes the detent out of the hole in the sheath. In the case of the rod detaining means, the solenoid plunger positions the bar so that the hole in its center aligns with the rod.

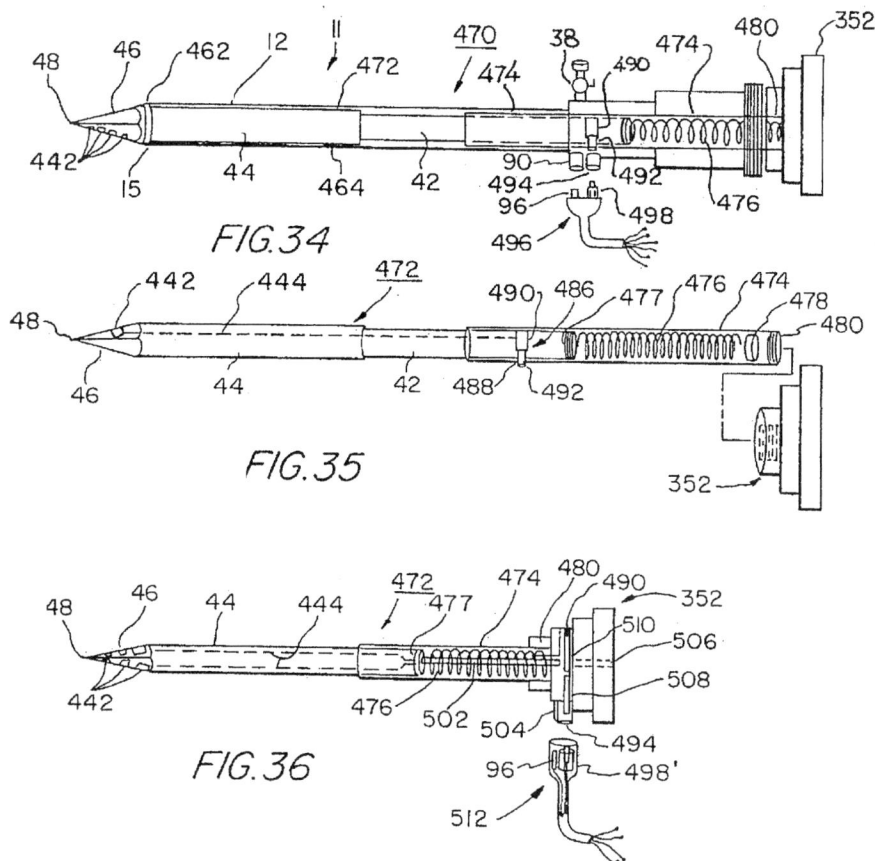

FIG. 34

FIG. 35

FIG. 36

The district court concluded that Yoon generally invented the retractable trocar, but that Choi invented both of the detaining means disclosed in the specification. In addition to oral testimony of the parties, the district court cited Choi's sketches, one of which clearly shows the rod detaining means. However, the sketch in which the district court would find the detent detaining means appears to work differently than the embodiment described in the '773 patent. Instead of a detent that extends radially outward through a hole in the sheath, the sketch illustrates the use of the solenoid plunger itself as a detent, extending radially *inward* through a hole in the sheath. Thus, the record does not show that Choi contributed to the detent detaining means. Therefore, this court affirms the district court's finding that Choi contributed the rod detaining means, but determines that the trial court clearly erred in finding that Choi contributed the detent detaining means.

In this instance, however, claim 47 recites a "means ... for [detaining]." The use of the word "means" gives rise to "a presumption that the inventor used the term advisedly to invoke the statutory mandates for means-plus-function clauses." *York Prods., Inc. v. Central Tractor Farm & Family Ctr.*, 99 F.3d 1568, 1574 (Fed.Cir.1996).... Thus applying section 112, paragraph 6 to interpret this claim, the language adopted the two structures in the specification to define the means for detaining.

Choi showed contribution to one of these alternative structures. The contributor of any disclosed means of a means-plus-function claim element is a joint inventor as to that claim, unless one asserting sole inventorship can show that the contribution of that means was simply a reduction to practice of the sole inventor's broader concept. *See Sewall,* 21 F.3d at 416 (holding that the designer of one disclosed means was not a joint inventor). Although the district court found that Yoon first conceived of a retractable trocar generally, Yoon did not show that Choi's contribution was simply a reduction to practice of the broader concept of using any detaining means commensurate with the scope of claim 47. Thus, Choi showed entitlement to the status of co-inventor for this claim as well.

C. Corroboration

* * *

Taken together, the alleged co-inventor's testimony and the corroborating evidence must show inventorship "by clear and convincing evidence." This requirement is not to be taken lightly. Under the "rule of reason" standard for corroborating evidence, *Holmwood v. Sugavanam,* 948 F.2d 1236, 1238–39 (Fed.Cir.1991), the trial court must consider corroborating evidence in context, make necessary credibility determinations, and assign appropriate probative weight to the evidence to determine whether clear and convincing evidence supports a claim of co-inventorship. Accordingly, there need not be corroboration for every factual issue contested by the parties. . . .

In this case, Choi's sketches show the invention. The parties agree that Choi made the sketches. The contest involves whether Choi conceived of the material in the sketches or merely drew what Yoon conceived. The district court noted many circumstantial factors further corroborating Choi's conception claim: (1) Yoon's need for a person with expertise in electronics; (2) Choi's background in electronics, (3) Yoon's proposal that he and Choi should work together to develop new products, including safety trocars, (4) their informal business relationship, (5) the length of time they worked together, (6) the absence of any pay to Choi for his work, (7) the similarity between Choi's sketches and the patent figures, and (8) the letter in which Choi stated that he could no longer be a "member" of Yoon's business. Additionally, U.S. Surgical introduced expert testimony that some of the sketches dealt with sophisticated concepts that only an electrical engineer or technician would understand. Consequently, the district court found that Choi was presenting ideas to Yoon as the sketches were drawn, rather than the other way around.

On appeal, this court declines to reweigh the evidence. Instead, this court determines that the record shows that corroboration evidence in this case satisfies the "rule of reason."

* * *

IV. SCOPE OF THE CHOI–U.S. SURGICAL LICENSE

Questions of patent ownership are distinct from questions of inventorship. *See Beech Aircraft Corp. v. EDO Corp.,* 990 F.2d 1237, 1248 (Fed.Cir.

1993). In accordance with this principle, this court has nonetheless noted that "an invention presumptively belongs to its creator." *Teets v. Chromalloy Gas Turbine Corp.*, 83 F.3d 403, 406 (Fed.Cir.), *cert. denied*, 519 U.S. 1009 (1996).

Indeed, in the context of joint inventorship, each co-inventor presumptively owns a pro rata undivided interest in the entire patent, no matter what their respective contributions. Several provisions of the Patent Act combine to dictate this rule. 35 U.S.C. § 116, as amended in 1984, states that a joint inventor need not make a contribution "to the subject matter of every claim of the patent." In amending section 116 as to joint inventorship, Congress did not make corresponding modifications as to joint ownership. For example, section 261 continues to provide that "patents shall have the attributes of personal property." This provision suggests that property rights, including ownership, attach to patents as a whole, not individual claims. Moreover, section 262 continues to speak of "joint owners of a patent," not joint owners of a claim. Thus, a joint inventor as to even one claim enjoys a presumption of ownership in the entire patent.

This rule presents the prospect that a co-inventor of only one claim might gain entitlement to ownership of a patent with dozens of claims. As noted, the Patent Act accounts for that occurrence: "Inventors *may* apply for a patent jointly even though ... each did not make a contribution to the subject matter of every claim." 35 U.S.C. § 116 (emphasis added). Thus, where inventors choose to cooperate in the inventive process, their joint inventions may become joint property without some express agreement to the contrary. In this case, Yoon must now effectively share with Choi ownership of all the claims, even those which he invented by himself. Thus, Choi had the power to license rights in the entire patent.

* * *

V. RETROACTIVE LICENSURE

Finally, Ethicon argues that even if the license agreement is enforceable as to the entire patent, it should still be allowed to proceed against U.S. Surgical to recover damages for pre-license infringement. Ethicon contends that to hold otherwise would contravene the decision in *Schering Corp. v. Roussel–UCLAF SA*, 104 F.3d 341 (Fed.Cir.1997). This court agrees with Ethicon's challenge to the retroactive effect of Choi's license, but must affirm the dismissal of the case based on Choi's refusal to join as plaintiff in the suit.

In *Schering,* Roussel and Schering, the two co-owners of the patent in suit, entered into an agreement whereby each granted the other a unilateral right to sue third parties for infringement. Schering then sued to enjoin Zeneca, Inc. from proceeding with planned sales of an allegedly infringing product. Schering joined Roussel in the action as an involuntary plaintiff. Two weeks later, Roussel granted Zeneca a license to practice the patented invention. The district court dismissed Schering's suit. Schering appealed.

On appeal, Schering argued that because Roussel had granted Schering a unilateral right to sue, Roussel could not now grant a license to Zeneca. Schering contended that one grant was incompatible with the other. The court rejected Shering's argument, reasoning that "[t]he right to license and the unilateral right to sue are . . . not incompatible, and the granting of one does not necessarily imply the relinquishment of the other." *Id.* at 345. This court acknowledged the critical distinction that a license to a third party only operates prospectively. Absent agreement to the contrary, a co-owner cannot grant a release of another co-owner's right to accrued damages. Consequently, a co-owner who has granted a unilateral right to sue to another co-owner may also license a third party. Nevertheless, by virtue of the unilateral right to sue, the second co-owner can still force the first co-owner to join an infringement action against the licensee to recover the second co-owner's accrued damages for past infringement. Thus, a prospective license is not per se incompatible with a unilateral right to sue, and, barring any other applicable contractual provision, Schering could not prevent Roussel from granting a license to Zeneca:

> [T]he grant of a license by one co-owner cannot deprive the other co-owner of the right to sue for accrued damages for past infringement. That would require a release, not a license, and the rights of a patent co-owner, absent agreement to the contrary, do not extend to granting a release that would defeat an action by other co-owners to recover damages for past infringement.

Id. at 345.

Thus, Choi's "retroactive license" to U.S. Surgical attempts to operate as the combination of a release and a prospective license. Nonetheless Choi cannot release U.S. Surgical from its liability for past accrued damages to Ethicon, only from liability to himself.

One more settled principle governs this case, however. An action for infringement must join as plaintiffs all co-owners. *See Waterman v. Mackenzie,* 138 U.S. 252, 255 (1891) ("The patentee or his assigns may, by instrument in writing, assign, grant, and convey, either (1) the whole patent . . .; or (2) an undivided part or share of that exclusive right; or (3) the exclusive right under the patent within and throughout a specified part of the United States. A transfer of either of these three kinds of interests is an assignment, properly speaking, and vests in the assignee a title in so much of the patent itself, with a right to sue infringers. In the second case, *jointly with the assignor.* In the first and third cases, in the name of the assignee alone." (emphasis added)); *Moore v. Marsh,* 74 U.S. (7 Wall.) 515, 520 (1868) ("[W]here [an] assignment is of an undivided part of the patent, the action should be brought for every infringement committed subsequent tothe assignment, in the joint names of the patentee and assignee, as representing the entire interest.").

Further, as a matter of substantive patent law, all co-owners must ordinarily consent to join as plaintiffs in an infringement suit.[9] Conse-

---

9. Two established exceptions exist. First, when any patent owner has granted an exclusive license, he stands in a relationship of trust to his licensee and must permit the licensee to sue in his name. *See Independent Wireless Telegraph Co. v. Radio Corp. of Am.,* 269 U.S. 459, 469 (1926). Second, the obligation may arise by contract among co-owners. If, by agreement, a co-owner waives his right to refuse to join suit, his co-owners may subsequently force him to join in a suit against infringers. *See Willingham v. Lawton,* 555 F.2d 1340, 1344–45 (6th Cir.1977).

quently, "one co-owner has the right to impede the other co-owner's ability to sue infringers by refusing to voluntarily join in such a suit." *Schering,* 104 F.3d at 345.

This rule finds support in section 262 of the Patent Act:

> In the absence of any agreement to the contrary, each of the joint owners of a patent may make, use, offer to sell, or sell the patented invention within the United States, or import the patented invention into the United States, without the consent of and without accounting to the other owners.

This freedom to exploit the patent without a duty to account to other co-owners also allows co-owners to freely license others to exploit the patent without the consent of other co-owners. *Schering,* 104 F.3d at 344 ("Each co-owner's ownership rights carry with them the right to license others, a right that also does not require the consent of any other co-owner."). Thus, the congressional policy expressed by section 262 is that patent co-owners are "at the mercy of each other." *Willingham v. Lawton,* 555 F.2d 1340, 1344 (6th Cir.1977).

Although in this case, the result is effectively no different than if Choi could grant a release to U.S. Surgical of any liability to Ethicon, it should be emphasized that the principle that governs this case is not incompatible with the principle enunciated in *Schering.* In *Schering,* this court noted that the granting of a unilateral right to sue is not incompatible with the right to grant a license. Similarly, this court notes that the inability to grant a release is not incompatible with the right to refuse to consent to an infringement suit. It is true that, in some circumstances, the decision of one co-owner to not join an infringement suit may have the same effect as granting a release, but this is not true in all cases. For example, when co-owners have granted each other a unilateral right to sue, each has waived his right not to join an infringement suit, and either of them can force the other to join a suit to collect accrued infringement damages.

Because Choi did not consent to an infringement suit against U.S. Surgical and indeed can no longer consent due to his grant of an exclusive license with its accompanying "right to sue," Ethicon's complaint lacks the participation of a co-owner of the patent. Accordingly, this court must order dismissal of this suit.

Affirmed.

■ Pauline Newman, Circuit Judge, dissenting.

I respectfully dissent, for whether or not Mr. Choi made an inventive contribution to two of the fifty-five claims of the '773 patent, he is not a joint owner of the other fifty-three claims of the patent. Neither the law of joint invention nor the law of property so requires, and indeed these laws mandate otherwise.

. . . . My primary concern is with the failure of the court to recognize, in deciding ownership rights, the effect on these rights of the 1984 amendment of 35 U.S.C. § 116, which markedly changed the law of naming inventors on patents, and authorized the "joint invention" here adjudicated.

Before the statutory change made in 1984 Mr. Choi could not have been named a "joint inventor" of the '773 patent, for he had not jointly conceived and contributed to the entire invention. It is not disputed that his contribution is limited to elements of two of the fifty-five patent claims. Such a person was not a "joint inventor" under pre–1984 law. That law required that joint invention be the "simultaneous production of the genius and labor of both parties." *Stearns v. Barrett,* 22 F. Cas. 1175, 1181 (C.C.D.Mass.1816) (Story, J.). Joint ownership, in turn, was based on this principle of joint invention.

Those assistants who worked on an invention at the behest of the originator of the idea did not achieve the legal status of "joint inventor." Having no legal status as an inventor, such assistants acquired no property right in the invention by virtue of their contributions. *See Collar Co. v. Van Dusen,* 90 U.S. (23 Wall.) 530, 563–64 (1874) (ancillary discoveries of assistant belong to person who conceived original principle unless they "constitute the whole substance of the improvement"); *Agawam Co. v. Jordan,* 74 U.S. (7 Wall.) 583, 602–4 (1868) (same). In *Agawam* the Court explained that one less than a true joint inventor was forbidden from "appropriat[ing] to himself the entire result of the ingenuity and toil of the originator, or put[ting] it in the power of any subsequent infringer to defeat the patent." 74 U.S. at 604.

The 1984 amendment of 35 U.S.C. § 116 permitted the naming as an inventor of all persons who assisted in the development of an idea, or parts thereof, that originated with others. Such naming, however, does not automatically endow the assistant with full and common ownership of the entire invention, including the contributions of all others including the originator. That is not a reasonable consequence of the change in the law of naming inventors that occurred in 1984.

A.   The Law of Joint Invention

The purpose of the amendment of § 116 was to remedy the increasing technical problems arising in team research, for which existing law, deemed to require simultaneous conception as well as shared contribution by each named inventor to every claim, was producing pitfalls for patentees, to no public purpose. As stated in its legislative history, the amendment to 35 U.S.C. § 116 "recognizes the realities of modern team research." 130 Cong. Rec. 28,069–71 (1984) (statement of Rep. Kastenmeier).

Before 1984 precedent did not permit naming as an inventor a person who did not share in the conception of the invention and who did not contribute to all of the claims of the patent. *See In re Sarett,* 51 C.C.P.A. 1180, 327 F.2d 1005, 1010 n. 7 (CCPA 1964) ("It should be clear that the patent could not *legally* contain a claim to Sarett's *sole* invention under existing law because it would not have been the invention of the *joint* patentees." (emphases in original)); *In re Hamilton,* 17 C.C.P.A. 833, 37 F.2d 758, 759, *op. den. reh'g,* 17 C.C.P.A. 914, 38 F.2d 889, 890 (CCPA 1930) (joint patent could not issue on portion of invention made by single inventor). If different persons made an inventive contribution to various parts of an invention or to different claims of a patent, the legalistic problems that arose were not readily soluble, even by the complex, expensive, and often confusing expedient of filing separate patent applications on separate claims.

The progress of technology exacerbated the inventorship problems. Patents were invalidated simply because all of the named inventors did not contribute to all the claims; and patents were also invalidated when there were contributors to some of the claims who were not named. *See Jamesbury Corp. v. United States,* 207 Ct.Cl. 516, 518 F.2d 1384, 1395 (1975) (inclusion of more or less than the true inventors renders patent void and invalid). . . .

As team research increased with the growth of technology-based industry, so did the dilemma, for the rules of joint inventorship were not readily adaptable to the development of complex inventions. It became apparent that legislative remedy was needed. The amendment of 35 U.S.C. § 116 provided a simple solution to a complex problem:

> § 116 [second sentence] Inventors may apply for a patent jointly even though (1) they did not physically work together or at the same time, (2) each did not make the same type or amount of contribution, or (3) each did not make a contribution to the subject matter of every claim of the patent.

Pub.L. 98–622, § 104, 98 Stat. 3384, Nov. 8, 1984. The amendment identified the three major pitfalls that had arisen, and removed them.

This amendment did not also deal with the laws of patent ownership, and did not automatically convey ownership of the entire patent to everyone who could now be named as an inventor, whatever the contribution. The amendment simply permitted persons to be named on the patent document, whether as minor contributors to a subordinate embodiment, or full partners in the creation and development of the invention. The ownership relationships among the persons who, under § 116, could now be recognized as contributors to the invention, is irrelevant to the purpose of the amendment of § 116, and to its consequences. Section 116 has nothing to do with patent ownership.

B.   The Law of Joint Ownership

The pre–1984 rule of joint ownership of joint inventions can be readily understood in its historical context, for a legally cognizable "joint invention" required mutuality of interaction and a real partnership in the creation and development of the invention. On this foundation, a "joint inventor" was also, justly and legally, an equal owner of the idea and of any patent thereon. *Pointer,* 177 F.2d at 157–58 ("as the cases just cited show clearly, in order that an invention be truly called a joint invention, it must appear by clear and convincing proof that the two inventors collaborated in evolving the patented device"); *see* 1 Donald S. Chisum, *Chisum on Patents* § 202[2] & n.2 (rel. May 1987) ("Only where the same single, unitary idea of means is the product of two or more minds, working *pari passu,* and in communication with each other, is the conception truly joint and the result a joint invention," quoting 1 William C. Robinson, *The Law of Patents for Useful Inventions* § 396 (1890)).

The law of patent ownership has its roots in the common law of property—although a patent has its own peculiar character, for it deals with intangibles. *See Crown Die & Tool Co. v. Nye Tool & Machine Works,* 261 U.S. 24, 40 (1923) (a patent is a creature of statute); *Gayler v. Wilder,* 51 U.S. (10 How.) 477, 494 (1850). Certain incidents of patent ownership have been created or clarified by statute, *see* 35 U.S.C. § 262, yet the common law provided the basic rules, as manifested in the concepts of tenancy in common and undivided interests that courts have drawn upon in patent ownership disputes.

The jurisprudence governing property interests is generally a matter of state law. Even when the property is the creation of federal statute, private rights are usually defined by state laws of property. This has long been recognized with respect to patent ownership and transfers. *See Jim Arnold Corp. v. Hydrotech Sys., Inc.,* 109 F.3d 1567, 1572 (Fed.Cir.1997) ("the question of who owns the patent right and on what terms typically is a question exclusively for state courts").... It is equally established that inventorship and patent ownership are separate issues. *Beech Aircraft Corp. v. EDO Corp.,* 990 F.2d 1237, 1248–49 (Fed.Cir.1993).

Most of the disputes concerning patent ownership that reached the Supreme Court dealt not with joint invention, but assignments and other transfers. The oft-cited case of *Waterman v. Mackenzie,* 138 U.S. 252 (1891) dealt with a dispute among the inventor's spouse and various assignees concerning ownership of the fountain pen patent, not inventorship. Occasionally an issue of ownership of patent property arose based on whether the claimant actually shared fully in the creation of the invention. In such cases, as cited *supra,* the decision on "joint invention" also decided the issue of ownership, for a person who had fully shared in the creation of the invention was deemed to be a joint owner of the entire patent property. On this premise each joint inventor was deemed to occupy the entirety of the patented subject matter, on a legal theory of tenancy in common. See 7 Richard R. Powell, *Powell on Real Property* ¶ 602[5] (1997) ("undivided fractional shares held by tenants in common are usually equal and are presumed equal unless circumstances indicate otherwise"). As patent property became viewed more precisely as personal property, *see* 35 U.S.C. § 261, the concept of tenancy in common was adjusted to that of an undivided interest, although with no substantial change in legal rights.

After the major change that the 1984 amendment to § 116 made in "joint invention," by authorizing the naming of any contributor to any claim of a patent, the legal premise that each named person had made a full and equal contribution to the entire patented invention became obsolete. *See SmithKline Diagnostics, Inc. v. Helena Labs. Corp.,* 859 F.2d 878, 888–89 (Fed.Cir.1988) (collecting cases). It is not an implementation of the common law of property, or its statutory embodiments, to treat all persons, however minor their contribution, as full owners of the entire property as a matter of law. The law had never given a contributor to a minor portion of an invention a full share in the originator's patent.

By amending § 116 in order to remove an antiquated pitfall whereby patents were being unjustly invalidated, the legislators surely did not intend to create another inequity. Apparently no one foresaw that judges might routinely transfer pre–1984 ownership concepts into the changed inventorship law. I have come upon no discussion of this anomaly in various scholarly articles on the amended § 116. . . .

In the case at bar, the district court recognized that Dr. Yoon originated the fundamental concept and the major aspects of its implementation. The court, however, construed the law as requiring that since Mr. Choi was named as a "joint inventor" (in accordance with the retroactivity legislated for the amendment to § 116) he automatically owned an undivided interest in the entire patent, and had the unencumbered and unfettered right to alienate an interest in the entire patent. Thus Mr. Choi, who would not pass the pre–1984 test of joint inventor, was nonetheless awarded full property rights in the entire invention and patent, as if he had been a true joint inventor of all the claims.

The panel majority, confirming this error, holds that Mr. Choi's contribution to two claims means and requires that Yoon "must now effectively share with Choi ownership of all the claims, even those which he invented by himself." That is incorrect. As I have discussed, the law of shared ownership was founded on shared invention, a situation that admittedly does not here prevail. Whether or not Mr. Choi is now properly named under § 116 because of his contribution to two claims, he is not a joint owner and he does not have the right to grant a license under all fifty-five claims. No theory of the law of property supports such a distortion of ownership rights. Thus I must, respectfully, dissent from the decision of the panel majority.

C.   Issues of Joinder, Rule 19

The panel majority holds that although Mr. Choi's grant of a license under all fifty-five claims of the '773 patent does not have retroactive effect and thus does not relieve U.S. Surgical of liability for past infringement, Dr. Yoon is powerless to recover for past infringement because Mr. Choi as joint inventor refuses to join in the suit. Precedent and the Federal Rules do not support this ruling. *Schering Corp. & Roussel–Uclaf S.A. v. Zeneca, Inc.,* 104 F.3d (Fed.Cir.1997), relied on by the panel majority, does not bar Dr. Yoon's suit for past infringement and does not bar the joinder of Mr. Choi as an involuntary party in accordance with Fed.R.Civ.P. 19. Nor do *Waterman v. Mackenzie,* 138 U.S. at 255, *Moore v. Marsh,* 74 U.S. (7 Wall.) 515, 520 (1868), or the other cases cited by the majority. There is no barrier to the involuntary joinder of a joint inventor and/or co-owner under Rule 19, if such is needed to bring before the court all persons deemed necessary to the suit. *See also Howes v. Medical Components, Inc.,* 698 F.Supp. 574, 576 (E.D.Pa.1988) ("Rule 19 'makes inappropriate any contention that patent co-owners are per se indispensable in infringement suits' "). Further, Mr. Choi is already before the court as a party, having voluntarily intervened, by general appearance.

Thus I must also dissent from this ruling of my colleagues.

NOTES

1. *Inventorship Entity.* Patent law requires that the patent property the inventors of the claimed invention. There is a rebuttable presumption that the inventors named on an issued patent are correct. To help prove that the claimed subject matter was invented by the named inventor(s), the "theory of inventorship entity" is applied. *See* DONALD D. CHISUM, 1 CHISUM ON PATENTS § 3.08[2] (1996):

> Under the theory [of inventorship entity], the joint work of two or more persons is treated as being by an "inventorship entity" separate and distinct from the work of each person solely or in other joint entities. Thus with two individuals (A and B), three entities or persons for purposes of patent law are possible: A alone; B alone; and A and B jointly.

This requirement does not mean that joint inventors must make equal contributions or that each inventor must contribute to the subject matter in each and every claim. Section 116 of Title 35, as amended in 1984, reads:

> When an invention is made by two or more persons jointly, they shall apply for patent jointly and each make the required oath, ... Inventors may apply for a patent jointly even though (1) they did not physically work together or at the same time, (2) each did not make the same type or amount of contribution, or (3) each did not make a contribution to the subject matter of every claim of the patent.[1]

How much of an inventive contribution is enough to satisfy § 116? Consider the following discussion:

> "Inventors may apply for a patent jointly even though (1) they did not physically work together or at the same time, (2) each did not make the same type or amount of contribution, or (3) each did not make a contribution to the subject matter of every claim of the patent." 35 U.S.C. § 116 (1994). All that is required of a joint inventor is that he or she (1) contribute in some significant manner to the conception or reduction to practice of the invention, (2) make a contribution to the claimed invention that is not insignificant in quality, when that contribution is measured against the dimension of the full invention, and (3) do more than merely explain to the real inventors well-known concepts and/or the current state of the art. *See Fina Oil & Chem. Co. v. Ewen*, 123 F.3d 1466, 1473 (Fed.Cir.1997); *see also Ethicon, Inc. v. United States Surgical Corp.*, 135 F.3d 1456, 1460 (Fed.Cir.1998).

Pannu v. Iolab Corp., 155 F.3d 1344, 1351 (Fed.Cir.1998)

2. *Correction of Inventorship.* Two provisions of the Patent Code, Sections 116 and 256, allow correction of pending applications and issued patents. The third paragraph of § 116 allows correction of an inventorship error, which "arose without any deceptive intention," by misjoinder or nonjoinder in a pending application by amendment. Section 256 allows correction of an inventorship error, committed without "deceptive intention," after the patent issues.

3. *Inventorship, Ownership, and Rights of the Employee.* Although inventorship and ownership are separate concerns, determining who is the inventor of the claimed subject matter has implications not only for drafting and filing the patent application, but also for determining who owns the patent rights in the subject matter. This is because ownership of the patent right vests in the inventor. *See Teets v. Chromalloy Gas Turbine* Corp., 83 F.3d 403, 407 (Fed.Cir.1996); *Beech Aircraft Corp. v. EDO Corp.*, 990 F.2d 1237, 1248 (Fed.Cir.1993).

The inventor owns his invention even if he conceived or reduced to practice in the course of his employment. *Teets*, 83 F.3d at 407; *Banks v. Unisys Corp.*, 228

---

1. Prior to 1984, courts applied the "all-claims rule," which required each named inventor to contribute to every claim. The 1984 Amendments to § 116 changed this requirement.

F.3d 1357 (Fed.Cir.2000). But most employees agree to assign ownership rights in the invention to their employer as part of an express contract; or, absent an express contract, the employer may own the invention under an implied-in-fact contract if the employee was "hired to invent something or solve a particular problem." *Banks*, 228 F.3d at 1359. This latter scenario is known as the "employed to invent" exception. Under this exception, "a court must examine the employment relationship at the time of the inventive work to determine if the parties entered an implied-in-fact contract to assign patent rights." *Id*; *Teets*, 83 F.3d at 407. Furthermore, an employer may obtain a "shop right" in the employee's invention where the employer contributed to the development of the invention. A "shop right" is a common law doctrine that allows an employer to use an invention patented by one or more of its employees without liability for infringement. *McElmurry v. Arkansas Power & Light Co.*, 995 F.2d 1576, 1580 (Fed.Cir.1993). Some of the factors endorsed by the Federal Circuit in determining whether a "shop right" exists are (1) the contractual nature of the relationship between employer and employee, (2) whether the employee consented to the employer's use of the invention, and (3) whether the employee induced, acquiesced in, or assisted the employer in the use of the invention. If the employer usually has a strong case for shop rights if he financed the employee's invention whether by providing wages, tools, or a work place. *Id.* at 1581.

For two competing views on the issue of employer/employee inventions, *see* Robert P. Merges, *The Law and Economics of Employee Inventions*, 13 HARV. J. L. & TECH. 1 (1999), and Ann Bartow, *Inventors of the World, Unite!*, 37 SANTA CLARA L. REV. 673 (1997).

4. *Joint Inventorship and Joint Ownership.* An additional important implication of a decision on inventorship is that joint inventors are also joint owners, and under 35 U.S.C. § 262 in the absence of any agreement to the contrary, each joint owner of a patent can practice the claimed invention or license others to do so without the consent of and even without accounting to the other owners. Thus, anyone interested in owning a patent must be very careful to get an assignment from each and every individual who contributed to the conception of any claim in that patent.

5. *Ownership, Chain of Title, and Standing to Sue.* As stated at the outset of this Section, the Patent Act does have its own recording act, as set forth in 35 U.S.C. § 261, ¶ 3:

> An assignment, grant or conveyance shall be void as against any subsequent purchaser or mortgagee for a valuable consideration, without notice, unless it is recorded in the Patent and Trademark Office within three months from its date or prior to the date of such subsequent purchase or mortgage.

This is a notice type of recording statute having a three-month grace period. Alice Haemmerli, *Insecurity Interests: Where Intellectual Property and Commercial Law Collide*, 96 COLUM. L. REV. 1645, 1701 n.282 (1996) (labeling Section 261 as "notice" type, not "race-notice" type). Under such a notice-type of recording statute, a subsequent bona fide purchaser for value will win against a prior purchaser unless the subsequent purchaser has actual, constructive, or inquiry notice; and the recording of an interest gives constructive, or "record" notice. *See* Thomas W. Merrill and Henry E. Smith, PROPERTY: PRINCIPLES AND POLICIES 921 (Foundation Press 2007). One basic lesson from such a recording act is that it is very wise to record any property interest in a patent, including, for example, assignments, exclusive licenses, and security interests. *See* 37 C.F.R. § 3.11 (a) ("Other documents ... affecting title to applications, patents, or registrations, will be recorded as provided in this part or at the discretion of the Director."). Another basic lesson from any recording act is that it is important to search the Patent Office records for a patent's chain of title.

One practical question that sometimes arises when dealing with assignments is whether particular contractual language creates an obligation to assign, in the future, or itself has the effect of having accomplished an assignment. For example, in *Abraxis Bioscience, Inc. v. Navinta LLC*, 625 F.3d 1359 (Fed.Cir.2010), the majority opinion pointed to a set of cases that draw a distinction between declarations of accomplished fact, which are effective in assigning patent rights, and promises to do so in the future, which are merely promissory in nature. *Id.* at 1364–65. The Federal Circuit has also addressed so-called *nunc pro tunc* assignments (meaning now for then), which are designed to be effective as of an earlier date than when executed. In a case in which ownership had not been perfected before the suit was filed, *Enzo Apa & Son, Inc. v. Geapag A.G.*, 134 F.3d 1090, 1093 (Fed.Cir.1998), the court determined that the particular behavior surrounding the *nunc pro tunc* assignment was not sufficient.

The opposite timing question arises with a contract to assign patent rights that may be created in the future. In *FilmTec Corp. v. Allied–Signal Inc.* 939 F.2d 1568 (Fed.Cir.1991), in an opinion written by Judge Plager, who specialized in property law when he was a law professor, the Federal Circuit pointed out that an assignment of an expected interest in a future invention gives the assignee equitable title immediately, and then legal title transfers by operation of law when the invention is made. *Id.* at 1572. In that case the court was unable to determine on the minimal record developed before a preliminary injunction was issued whether the plaintiff had a reasonable likelihood of showing, as a matter of fact that: (1) the work being carried out by the inventors was done after they moved to the plaintiff, FilmTec, from their prior employers, or (2) FilmTec purchased the assignment of the inventions from the inventors without notice of the prior assignment and therefore holds title under the recording act having recorded first. Because the case turned on these key factual questions the appellate court remanded for further development of the factual record. In a later related case involving the same patent and plaintiff, *FilmTec Corp. v. Hydranautics*, 982 F.2d 1546 (Fed.Cir.1992), the Federal Circuit in an opinion by Judge Lourie decided that title was vested in the government pursuant to a prior assignment that the court determined was accomplished by a federal statute that set up some of the invention's underlying funding. Because a statute that accomplishes such an assignment is public, like any statute, it presumably put the subsequent purchaser, FilmTec, on notice, which may be why the notice issue is not even explored in the *Hydranautics* opinion.

In addition, as explored later in this chapter in the section on EXPERIMENTAL USE—35 U.S.C. § 271(e), the Hatch–Waxman Act created a special type of paper patent infringement in which the mere filing of an application for drug approval from the Food and Drug Administration can be treated as an act of patent infringement, in which case the patentee must bring an infringement suit within a specified period of time. Defendants in these cases have sought to argue that if the patentee does not have perfect title to the patent then the suit must be dismissed for lack of standing. In *Abraxis*, the majority decided that because the underlying contract contained promissory language, it was not effective in making a transfer of title and that as a result the suit had to be dismissed for lack of standing. Judge Newman dissented, writing that "It is beyond cavil that parties to a contract can set the effective date of their agreement." 625 F.3d at 1370 (Newman, J., dissenting).

The holding of cases like *Abraxis* may be very limited to the facts of their contract language and surrounding events. For example, the majority in *Abraxis* focused on the promissory nature of the language of one of the putative assignment documents; while the dissent focused on its temporal effect.

It would be interesting to see how the court would respond to broader arguments about contract law and property law. For example, 35 U.S.C. § 261, ¶ 2 is a straight-forward statute of frauds that requires only that assignments be in writing. As well recognized throughout contract law in the US, an ordinary statute of frauds like this can easily be satisfied, so long as the putative writing (or even writings, in plural) identifies the subject matter of the contract (the patent), the party against whom the contract is to be enforced (the assignee), and any other material terms (such as the fact that the contract is to assign, and the assignee). *See, e.g., Crabtree v. Elizabeth Arden Sales Corp.*, 110 N.E.2d 551 (N.Y.1953); RESTATEMENT (SECOND) OF CONTRACTS § 132. Although the Federal Circuit has taken the position that for purposes of determining standing to bring a patent case questions about a patent assignment are matters of federal law, *see Speedplay, Inc. v. Bebop, Inc.*, 211 F.3d 1245, 1253 (Fed.Cir.2000), the approach throughout contract law in the US is to treat the writing requirement of a statute of frauds very liberally, which is why that view is ensconced in the Restatement. Nevertheless, it does not appear that these issues were raised by the patentee in *Abraxis*.

Nor was the *Abraxis* majority pushed to consider a possible conflict with long-standing principles of the law of property, generally. While it might be nice to notice that all of the parties in the chain of title on a patent may be on the same side of a particular patent litigation case, all that really matters for purposes of determining whether a suit can be brought by one of them is that for each of them their relationship to the defendants in the suit would be only as either plaintiffs or third parties. Since Roman times, up through the English Common Law, and throughout property law in the United States, under the legal doctrine known as "the rejection of the *jus tertii* defense," courts in our legal tradition have long rejected a defendant's efforts to raise the rights of a putative third-party owner as a defense against a suit by one seeking to prevent the defendant's infringement or taking of a property right. *See* Thomas W. Merrill and Henry E. Smith, PROPERTY: PRINCIPLES AND POLICIES 226–27 (Foundation Press 2007) (excerpting leading representative cases such as *Anderson v. Gouldberg*, 53 N.W. 636 (Minn.1892); *Clark v. Maloney*, 3 Del. 68 (Del. Super.1840); Jeffries v. Great Western Ry, 119 Eng.Rep. 680 (Q.B. 1856); *Armory v. Delamirie*, 1 Strange 505 (K.B.1722)). See also Edward H. Warren, *Qualifying as Plaintiff in an Action for a Conversion*, 49 HARV. L. REV. 1084 (1936) (providing more in depth discussion). The doctrine rejecting the *jus tertii* defense makes sense because it allows gatekeepers of property rights to make sure that the value of the property to society is preserved through the maintenance of lawsuits against wrongful infringers. That is one reason why Justice Story while riding circuit in *Dobson v. Campbell*, 7 F. Cas. 783, 785, found that a plaintiff had standing to sue to enforce a patent even though ordinary formalities needed to transfer legal title were not followed. See Adam Mossoff, *Who Cares What Thomas Jefferson Thought about Patents? Reevaluating the Patent "Privilege" in Historical Context*, 92 CORNELL L. REV. 953, 997 (2007).

Federal Circuit cases like *Abraxis* just cannot be read to disturb the wisely entrenched legal doctrine that rejects the *jus tertii* defense To the contrary, such cases are only properly read as dealing with the more mundane problems about contract language, since the issues presented to the court in that case were limited to those topics. Indeed, in the *FilmTec v. Allied–Signal* decision mentioned earlier in this note, Judge Plager explicitly pointed out:

> The question of FilmTec's right to maintain the action against Allied should not be confused with the question of whether Allied could defend by arguing that title to the patent was in a third party-the Government-and therefore Allied has a good defense against any infringement suit. The plea in *jus tertii* (title in a third person) as it was known at common law was held in some early cases to be a good defense to a possessory action,

although more recent cases reject the defense and allow recovery on a prior possession. But the issue here is not whether title lies in the Government or some other third party; it is rather whether FilmTec has made a sufficient showing to establish reasonable likelihood of success on the merits, which includes a showing that title to the patent and the rights thereunder are in FilmTec.

939 F.2d at 1572–73 (citing J. Cribbet & C. Johnson Principles of the Law of Property 13 (3d ed.1989)). Put differently, Judge Plager was reminding readers of the opinion that they should not confuse its outcome (favoring the defendant) with a return of the *jus tertii* defense.

SIDE BAR

Ownership and Employees' Inventions—The German Approach

Heinz Goddar*

1. Principles of German Employees' Inventions Law

Whilst in many—if not most—other countries, worldwide as well as in Europe, employers and employees can determine by employment contract whether inventions made by the employee in the course of its employment under certain provisions, usually to be freely agreed, become the property of the employer—in most instances even without any specific remuneration of considerable height for the employee—, the legal situation in Germany is totally different. German Law, particularly the so-called "Law relating to Inventions made by Employees", in the following designated as "The Law", unavoidably and bindingly determines that inventions made by employees first of all belong to them, and only by a special act and against a special remuneration can become the property of the employer.

The Law has to do with inventions made by employees. Accordingly, one has to determine first what, in the sense of The Law, is an invention, furthermore, what is an employee, and finally, what kind of inventions made by employees are subject of the provisions of The Law.

Inventions in the sense of The Law are only technical inventions which in principle can be protected under German Law by a patent or by a utility model, the latter in this sense and for the purpose of this paper being considered as a kind of a patent (for small inventions). The Law is not related to other creations of employees, which may be protected by design, copyright etc., and accordingly creations of the aforementioned kind are not subject of the binding regulations of The Law.

Only such inventions are ruled by The Law which are made by employees. Employees are persons employed with an employer in the sense of German Labour Law and jurisdiction. It is, in view of the summarizing character of this paper, difficult to positively define what an employee in this sense is under German Law, but negatively one can say that e.g. representatives of legal entities, like managing directors of companies, i.e. all persons which have a employer-like position, are not employees, so that The Law does not apply to inventions made by such persons.

Specific Aspects of The Law relate to inventions made in public service, particularly in universities.

Not all inventions made by employees, even employees in private practice, are subject of The Law. Rather The Law makes a distinction between so-called service inventions, namely a kind of inventions which are bindingly regulated by The Law, and free inventions. Service Inventions are such inventions which either originate from the regular work of the employee he is doing in a company because of its employment contract, e.g. when a chemist working in research and development of a pharmaceutical company invents a new pharmaceutical, or which essentially are based on experiences of the company. All other inventions are free inventions.

When talking about "inventions" in the following, in connection with The Law, usually "service inventions" are meant, if not otherwise stated.

2. Acquisition of Ownership by Employer

Whenever a "normal" employee, whether in private practice or in public service, has made an invention, certain duties must be fulfilled in relation to the employer, depending on the character of the invention.

In case of service inventions, the employee has the duty to immediately and completely notify any such invention made by it to the employer in writing. At that time, the invention is still the property of the employee, and also by the notification to the employer the property and title in the invention do not change. The notification must be complete i.e., must enable the employer to get knowledge of the invention, including of the state of the art the invention is based on, the problem which is solved by the invention, the solution proposed by the invention, the contribution of the internal knowledge inside the company to the creation of the invention, and also the contribution of possible co-inventors.

In case of free inventions, or of inventions from which the inventor believes that they are free inventions, the employee has to inform the employer in a manner which enables the employer to make up its own mind whether the respective invention is a free or a service invention.

After receipt of a notification of a Service Invention a four months term begins during which the employer has the possibility to get certain rights in the invention—or to lose them finally, as explained in the following.

One of the possibilities the employer has during the aforementioned binding four months term is to declare unrestricted claiming of the invention to the employee. By this unilateral act of the employer with factual effect the property of the invention goes to the employer, and from that moment onwards the invention does no longer belong to the employee, but to the employer.

Another possibility, often used by employers when they believe that the respective invention is not important enough for the company to be unrestrictedly claimed, is that the employer declares a limited claiming of the invention. This limited claiming has the effect that the property of the invention remains with the employee, that the employee has the right to protect the invention, e.g. by a patent application at its own cost and in its own name, and that the employee is entitled to make use of the invention by, e.g. licensing it out to a third party. In any such cases, however, the employer, by its limited claiming of the invention, has the right non-exclusively to use the invention should in future the employer come to the decision that such use for the employer's company would be useful.

If, finally, the employer does not react within the above mentioned four months term, the invention becomes free, and this has the same effect as if the employer within the four months term would explicitly declare to the employee that the invention should be free.

3. Obligations of Employer after Acquisition of Ownership

3.1. Protection of Invention

After acquiring full ownership of an employee's invention, the employer has the duty immediately to file a respective patent or utility model application in Germany. According to recent jurisdiction, such application in Germany can be replaced by a European patent application designating Germany or by a PCT (Patent Cooperation Treaty) application designating Germany either directly or via EPC (European Patent Convention). The employer is obliged to inform the inventor of any details of such application, and to keep the inventor informed of its further fate.

The employer is obliged well before the end of the priority year according to the Paris Convention to inform the inventor in which countries the employer wishes to file foreign applications, simultaneously giving the inventor the possibility to file, at the inventor's own cost and in the inventor's own name, foreign applications within the priority term. In such case, the employer is entitled, simultaneously with giving the respective information to the employee, to retain a right of non-exclusively using the invention in such foreign countries where the inventor may file a patent application in its own name.

Should the employer intend at any time to give up a domestic or foreign application for the invention, before finally giving up the respective application or patent the employer must give the employed inventor the possibility to take over the application and patent, respectively, by assignment, for further prosecution in the own name of the inventor. Also in such case, the employer may retain a right of non-exclusive use, with similar provisions, as discussed in relation to foreign applications, in case that the retained right of non-exclusive use of the employer may be considered as an undue burden to the employee. In cases where the employer does not wish to file a patent application for an invention duly unrestrictedly claimed, the employer may make, at its sole discretion, the decision to keep the respective invention company secret. The employer has duly to notify the employee in this case. The aforementioned decision of the employer is only possible, however, if simultaneously with the notification to the inventor that the invention is considered a company secret, the employer declares that principally it does not deny the patentability of subject matter involved, with the consequence that remuneration—to be discussed later on—will have to be paid as if the invention would be protected by a patent.

3.2. Inventor's Remuneration

The second duty which the employer has after acquiring ownership of an invention by unrestricted claiming, in addition to protecting it or considering it in principle as protectable and handling it as a company secret, as discussed above, is that the inventor is entitled in a specific remuneration for the respective invention.

The principle, as expressed in The Law, is insofar that the inventor is entitled in the justified participation in the specific advantages the employer gets from the specific invention. Principally, The Law provides for three methods in which a remuneration can be calculated.

One of these methods consists in the so-called license analogy, in which case the inventor gets a certain percentage, based on the net sales made by the employer, of a reasonable royalty which the employer in a case where a license would have been taken from a third party would ordinarily pay. This method is by far most used in Germany in practice.

Another possibility, specifically used when an invention is related to, e.g., a certain kind of manufacturing which does not modify the products finally sold by the employer, but relates to improvements inside the company, is that the employee gets a certain percentage of the internal cost savings which the employer achieves by using the invention.

A third possibility, finally, is a free estimation of the value of the invention, in which the inventor has the right to participate. Such method is used, e.g., in cases of cross-licensing without real royalty income or purchase price income to the employer.

4. Solution of Disputes

The Law provides for a unique possibility of solving disputes between employee and employer in case of inventions made by employees.

For this purpose, at the German Patent Office there exists a so-called Arbitration Committee, consisting of a legal member (judge-like) as chairman and two members with technical experience. These technical members are examiners of the Patent Office chosen for the specific case according to the subject matter in question.

Whenever an employee and an employer, during a still pending employment agreement, have disputes in relation to claims based on The Law, they are obliged, before going to Court, to present the case to the Arbitration Committee. The Arbitration Committee then makes a proposal, e.g., as in most instances, in relation to a justified remuneration. If the parties do not object to that proposal within one month after notification, the proposal becomes binding. Otherwise, the proposal is null and void, and the parties can go to Court.

Also after termination of an employment agreement the parties still have the possibility to go to the Arbitration Committee, but are no longer bound to do so, rather they can go to Court directly.

The Arbitration Committee plays an important role also in the case of determining whether certain inventions to be considered by the employer as company secret are patentable or not, as already discussed above.

5. The European Future

The provisions of The Law as discussed above are unique for Germany, for the time being. Most European countries, however, during the harmonization of, amongst other provisions, social and labour law provisions in Europe are harmonizing their laws with the result of coming to similar provisions as they now exist in Germany, though with simplification of certain formalities, particularly with regard to acquisition of ownership.

* Partner, Boehmert & Boehmert, Munich, Germany; and associate judge at the Senate for Patent Attorneys Matters at the German Federal Supreme Court. This *Side Bar* was written specially for Principles of Patent Law.

H. First Inventor Defense—35 U.S.C. § 273

In the First Inventor Defense Act of 1999, Congress amended the Patent Act to add Section 273, which provides a "first inventor" defense to infringement.[7] Section 273 provides a limited personal defense for conduct that would otherwise constitute infringement of a patent. The defense must be contrasted with prior use or invention under 35 U.S.C. Section 102, which may be grounds for finding a patent invalid.[8] The section is effective as of its enactment date, November 29, 1999, but does "not apply to any action for infringement that is pending on such date of enactment or with respect to any subject matter for which an adjudication of infringement, including a consent judgment, has been made before such date of enactment."[9]

Section 273 contains critical definitions and qualifications, and the courts will be required to interpret its scope and meaning.

A. *Elements of the Defense.* Section 273(b)(1) sets forth the elements of the defense. It creates "a defense to an action for infringement under section 271 of this title."[10]

1. *Method Claims.* The defense is "with respect to any subject matter that would otherwise infringe one or more *claims for a method in the patent* being asserted against a person."[11] Thus, literally, the defense is limited to "method" claims.[12] This limitation is further restricted by the definition of

---

7. PL 106–113, 113 Stat. 1501, 1501A–555–557 (Nov. 29, 1999).

8. 35 U.S.C. § 102. See Chisum on Patents § 3.01 *et seq.*

9. PL 106–113, § 4303, 113 Stat. 1501, 1537 (Nov. 29, 1999).

10. 35 U.S.C. § 273(b)(1).

11. 35 U.S.C. § 273(b)(1).

12. Early versions of Section 273 referred to methods that "were *or could have been* claimed in a patent in the form of a process." *See* H.R. No. 106–287(I), 106th Cong., 1st Sess. (1999) (emphasis added) (noting that "An invention is considered to be a process or method if it is used in connection with the production of a useful end-product or-service and is or could have been claimed in the form of a business process or method in a patent. A software-related invention, for example, that was claimed by the patent draftsman as a programmed machine when the same invention could have been protected with process or method patent claims is a process or method for purposes of § 273."). This language was deleted from the enacted version.

For a discussion of what constitutes a "process" for purposes of the Process Patents Amendments Act, 35 U.S.C. § 271(g), see Chisum on Patents § 16.02[6][d][iii]. For a discussion of process claims as statutory patentable subject matter, see Chisum on Patents § 1.03.

"method" in Section 273(a), which provides: "the term 'method' means a method of doing or conducting business."[13] The interpretation of "doing or conducting business" is discussed below.

2. *Requisite Acts*. Section 273(b)(1) provides that the defense applies only if the person raising the defense "acting in good faith, actually reduced the subject matter to practice at least 1 year before the effective filing date of such patent, and commercially used the subject matter before the effective filing date of such patent."[14]

a. *Actual Reduction to Practice*. "Actual reduction to practice" is a basic concept of invention priority law, and the case law addressing what constitutes an actual reduction to practice for priority purposes will, presumably, apply to the interpretation of Section 273.[15] Notably, a conception on a date, which is followed by diligence to a reduction to practice after the conception date, is an invention date for most patent law purposes,[16] but will not satisfy Section 273(b)(1)'s requirement that there be an actual reduction to practice.[17]

b. *Commercial Use in United States*. "Commercial use" is defined in Section 273(a)(1).[18] "Commercial use" includes certain uses by "nonprofit" laboratories and entities.[19] The use must be "in the United States."[20]

For a discussion of issues regarding the patentability of method claims, *see* Chisum on Patents § 5.04[8], § 8.05, § 12.03[2][d].

13. 35 U.S.C. § 273(a)(3).

14. 35 U.S.C. § 273(b)(1).

15. For a discussion of actual reduction to practice, *see* Chisum on Patents § 10.06.

16. *See* Chisum on Patents § 5.03[3][c][vi][D].

17. *Compare Pfaff v. Wells Electronics, Inc.*, 525 U.S. 55 (1998) ("The primary meaning of the word 'invention' in the Patent Act unquestionably refers to the inventor's conception rather than to a physical embodiment of that idea. The statute does not contain any express requirement that an invention must be reduced to practice before it can be patented.").

18. 35 U.S.C. § 273(a)(1): "(1) the terms 'commercially used' and 'commercial use' mean use of a method in the United States, so long as such use is in connection with an internal commercial use or an actual arm's-length sale or other arm's-length commercial transfer of a useful end result, whether or not the subject matter at issue is accessible to or otherwise known to the public, except that the subject matter for which commercial marketing or use is subject to a premarketing regulatory review period during which the safety or efficacy of the subject matter is established, including any period specified in section 156(g), shall be deemed 'commercially used' and in 'commercial use' during such regulatory review period...."

19. 35 U.S.C. § 273(a)(2):

"in the case of activities performed by a nonprofit research laboratory, or nonprofit entity such as a university, research center, or hospital, a use for which the public is the intended beneficiary shall be considered to be a use described in paragraph (1), except that the use—

(A) may be asserted as a defense under this section only for continued use by and in the laboratory or nonprofit entity; and

(B) may not be asserted as a defense with respect to any subsequent commercialization or use outside such laboratory or nonprofit entity...."

20. Interesting questions may arise as to what constitutes use in the United States, especially when the subject matter is a business method used in a global telecommunications systems such as the "Internet."

"Uses" within the definition include "an internal commercial use" and "an actual arm's-length sale or other arm's-length commercial transfer of a useful end result, whether or not the subject matter at issue is accessible to or otherwise known to the public."[21] Subject matter undergoing a "pre-marketing regulatory review period" is deemed to be in commercial use during the regulatory review period.[22]

3. *Effective Filing Date.* The "effective filing date" is a concept that is of importance in a number of patentability contexts.[23] Section 273(a)(4) defines a patent's "effective filing date" as "the earlier of the actual filing date of the application for the patent or the filing date of any earlier United States, foreign, or international application to which the subject matter at issue is entitled under section 119, 120, or 365 of this title."[24]

4. *Good Faith.* It is not clear whether the "good faith" requirement qualifies only the actual reduction to practice or both the reduction to practice and the subsequent commercial use. A person might have reduced to practice an invention in good faith and with no knowledge of another inventor's work but start commercial use after acquiring such knowledge.[25] It is also not clear what "good faith" means in these two contexts, especially as another provision in Section 273 precludes the defense in cases of derivation.[26]

B. *Exhaustion of Right.* Section 273(b)(2) provides for "exhaustion of right:"

For discussions of other patent law requirements that activity be "in the United States," *see* Chisum on Patents § 3.05[5], § 6.02[5][d], § 6.02[6][d], § 10.03[3], § 16.05.

For a discussion of personal jurisdiction based on transnational activity, *see* Chisum on Patents § 21.02[3].

21. 35 U.S.C. § 273(a)(1).

Case law interpreting "known or used" in 35 U.S.C. Section 102(a) generally requires that knowledge or use be accessible to the public. See Chisum on Patents § 3.05[5]. On the other hand, secret commercial use of an invention by a party who later applies for a patent on the invention may constitute a barring "public" use or "on sale" act. See Chisum on Patents § 6.02[5][b].

22. The statute references 35 U.S.C. § 156(g), which defines "regulatory review period" for determining patent term extension.

23. *See* Chisum on Patents § 6.02[9], § 13.01, § 14.05[4].

24. 35 U.S.C. § 273(a)(4).

25. The House Report, in discussing the proposed Section 273 defense, appears to link "good faith" only to the actual reduction to practice.

"Subsection (b)(1) of proposed § 273 establishes a general defense against infringement under § 271 of the Patent Act. Specifically, a person will not be held liable with respect to any subject matter that would otherwise infringe one or more claims to a business process or method in another party's patent if the person:

(1) acting in good faith, actually reduced the subject matter to practice at least one year before the effective filing date of the patent; and

(2) commercially used the subject matter before the effective filing date of the patent."

H.R. No. 106–287(I), 106th Cong., 1st Sess. (1999). *See also* H.R. Conf. Rep. No. 106–464, 106th Cong., 1st Sess. (Nov. 9, 1999).

26. *See* 35 U.S.C. § 273(b)(3)(B).

"The sale or other disposition of a useful end product produced by a patented method, by a person entitled to assert a defense under this section with respect to that useful end result shall exhaust the patent owner's rights under the patent to the extent such rights would have been exhausted had such sale or other disposition been made by the patent owner."[27]

Thus, for example, if a patentee **P** holds a patent claiming a method, a prior inventor/user **U** establishes a Section 273 defense by actually reducing to practice the method a year prior to **P**'s effective filing date and beginning commercial use of the method before **P**'s effective filing date, and **U** uses the method to make a "useful end product" **UEP** in a manner protected by the Section 273 defense, **U**'s sale of the **UEP** to a customer **C** will "exhaust" **P**'s exclusive rights as to that specific **UEP** product. **P** will not be able to assert infringement by **C**'s subsequent use or resale of the specific product **UEP** sold by **U**.

C. *Limitations and Qualifications.* Section 273(b)(3) imposes "limitations and qualifications" on the defense created by Section 273.[28]

1. *Method Invention.* First, Section 273(b)(3)(A) states that "[a] person may not assert the defense under this section unless the invention for which the defense is asserted is for a method."[29] This language is peculiar in that it refers to "the invention" for which the defense is asserted being "for a method." This contrasts with the basic definition of the defense, which requires that a patent *claim* be for a method.[30] The language is unclear as to the antecedent of "invention": is it the invention of the patentee *or* that reduced to practice and commercially used by the accused infringer?[31] Is it possible that a prior inventor/user can invent and commercially use subject matter that is a machine, manufacture or composition of matter but not a method and yet later be infringing a method claim? An example might be where a prior inventor/user **U**'s invention is a composition, and the patentee **P**'s patent claims as a method a new use or application of the composition that **U** did not reduce to practice or commercially use before the filing date.[32]

---

27. 35 U.S.C. § 273(b)(2). See H.R. No. 106–287(I), 106th Cong., 1st Sess. (1999) ("Subsection (b)(2) states that the sale or other lawful disposition of a product or service produced by a patented process or method, by a person entitled to assert a § 273 defense, exhausts the patent owner's rights with respect to that product or service to the same extent such rights would have been exhausted had the sale or other disposition been made by the patent owner. For example, if a purchaser would have had the right to resell a product if bought from the patent owner, the purchaser has the same right if the product is purchased from a person entitled to a § 273 defense.").

For a discussion of "exhaustion" in patent law, *see* Chisum on Patents § 16.03[2][a].

28. 35 U.S.C. § 273(b)(3).

29. 35 U.S.C. § 273(b)(3)(A).

30. *See* 35 U.S.C. § 273(b)(1) ("otherwise infringe one or more claims for a method").

31. *See* H.R. No. 106–287(I), 106th Cong., 1st Sess. (1999) ("a person may not assert the defense unless the invention for which the defense is asserted is for a business process or method, the exclusive purpose of which is to produce a useful end product or service; that is, the defense will not be available if the subject matter itself is a useful end product or service that constitutes one or more claims in the patent.")

32. For a discussion of the patentability of "new uses," *see* Chisum on Patents § 1.03[8].

2. *No Derivation.* Second, Section 273(b)(3)(B) states that "[a] person may not assert the defense under this section if the subject matter on which the defense is based was derived from the patentee or persons in privity with the patentee."[33]

3. *Scope.* Third, Section 273(b)(3)(C) states that "[t]he defense asserted by a person under this section is not a general license under all claims of the patent at issue."[34] Rather the defense "extends only to the specific subject matter claimed in the patent with respect to which the person can assert a defense under this chapter."[35] But Section 273 makes an exception: "the defense shall also extend to variations in the quantity or volume of use of the claimed subject matter, and to improvements in the claimed subject matter that do not infringe additional specifically claimed subject matter of the patent."[36]

D. *Burden of Proof.* Section 273(b)(4) allocates and defines the burden of proof on the defense: "A person asserting the defense under this section shall have the burden of establishing the defense by clear and convincing evidence."[37]

E. *Abandonment of Use.* Section 273(b)(5) addresses "abandonment of use": "A person who has abandoned commercial use of subject matter may not rely on activities performed before the date of such abandonment in establishing a defense under this section with respect to actions taken after the date of such abandonment."[38]

F. *Personal Defense.* Section 273(b)(6), which is entitled "personal defense," restricts transfers of the defense.

> The defense under this section may be asserted only by the person who performed the acts necessary to establish the defense and, except for any transfer to the patent owner, the right to assert the defense shall not be licensed or assigned or transferred to another person except as an ancillary and subordinate part of a good faith assignment or transfer for other reasons of the entire enterprise or line of business to which the defense relates.[39]

---

33. 35 U.S.C. § 273(b)(3)(B).

34. 35 U.S.C. § 273(b)(3)(C).

35. 35 U.S.C. § 273(b)(3)(C).

36. 35 U.S.C. § 273(b)(3)(C).

37. 35 U.S.C. § 273(b)(4).

38. 35 U.S.C. § 273(b)(5). *See* H.R. No. 106–287(I), 106th Cong., 1st Sess. (1999) ("Subsection (b)(5) establishes that the person who abandons the commercial use of subject matter may not rely on activities performed before the date of such abandonment in establishing the defense with respect to actions taken after the date of abandonment. Such a person can rely only on the date when commercial use of the subject matter was resumed.").

39. 35 U.S.C. § 273(b)(6). *See* H.R. No. 106–287(I), 106th Cong., 1st Sess. (1999):

> "Subsection (b)(6) notes that the defense may only be asserted by the person who performed the acts necessary to establish the defense, and, except for transfer to the patent owner, the right to assert the defense cannot be licensed, assigned, or transferred to a third party except as an ancillary and subordinate part of a good-faith assignment or transfer for other reasons of the entire enterprise or line of business to which the defense relates. To illustrate, a person is lawfully entitled to assert the defense as it relates to the operation of a specific piece of machinery. The person owns

G. *Limitation on Sites*. Section 273(b)(7) provides a "limitation on sites" when a defense is acquired as part of a transfer.

A defense under this section, when acquired as part of a good faith assignment or transfer of an entire enterprise or line of business to which the defense relates, may only be asserted for uses at sites where the subject matter that would otherwise infringe one or more of the claims is in use before the later of the effective filing date of the patent or the date of the assignment or transfer of such enterprise or line of business.[40]

H. *Attorney Fees*. Section 273(b)(8) provides for a mandatory award of attorney fees against an infringer who pleads the defense, is found to infringe, and then "subsequently fails to demonstrate a reasonable basis for asserting the defense."[41]

I. *Invalidity—Prior Knowledge, Use, Sale*. Section 273(b)(9) provides that "A patent shall not be deemed to be invalid under section 102 or 103 of this title solely because a defense is raised or established under this section."[42]

The subsection recognizes that at least some instances of pre-filing date reduction to practice and commercial use will be sufficient to establish the Section 273(b)(9) defense but will *not* be sufficient to invalidate a patent on the basis of prior knowledge or use under 35 U.S.C. Section

---

several other pieces of machinery that perform distinct functions which, taken together, comprise the person's business. That person may not transfer the defense as it relates to the specific piece of machinery to a third party unless the entire commercial establishment is transferred as well."

40. 35 U.S.C. § 273(b)(7). *See* H.R. No. 106–287(I), 106th Cong., 1st Sess. (1999):

"Subsection (b)(7) limits the sites for which the defense may be asserted when the defense has been transferred along with the enterprise or line of business to which the defense relates, as permitted by subsection (b)(6). Specifically, when the enterprise or line of business to which the defense relates has been transferred, the defense may be asserted only for uses at those sites where the subject matter was used before the later of the patent filing date or the date of transfer of the enterprise or line of business. A site is a factory site or other major facility in which an enterprise or line of business has made a significant capital investment, and does not include, for example, offsite locations for development of software components or manufacture of parts or ingredients."

41. 35 U.S.C. § 273(b)(8).

42. 35 U.S.C. § 273(b)(9). *See* H.R. No. 106–287(I), 106th Cong., 1st Sess. (1999):

"Subsection (b)(9) specifies that the successful assertion of the defense does not mean that the affected patent is invalid. Paragraph (9) eliminates a point of uncertainty under current law concerning the validity of patents, and strikes a balance between the rights of a later inventor who obtains a patent and an earlier inventor who continues to use its method or process in the conduct of its business. Under current law, although the matter has seldom been litigated, a party who commercially used an invention in secrecy before the patent filing date and invented the subject matter before the patent owner's invention may argue that the patent is invalid under § 102 (g) of the Patent Act. Arguably, commercial use of an invention in secrecy is not suppression or concealment of the invention within the meaning of § 102(g), and therefore the party's earlier invention will invalidate the patent.... The bill provides that a party who uses a process or business method commercially in secrecy before the patent filing date and establishes a § 273 defense is not an earlier inventor for purposes of invalidating the patent."

See also H.R. Conf. Rep. No. 106–464, 106th Cong., 1st Sess. (Nov. 9, 1999).

102(a), "on sale" and "public use" activity under 35 U.S.C. Section 102(b), or prior invention by another under 35 U.S.C. Section 102(g).[43]

Possible situations in which conduct might establish a Section 273(b) defense but not constitute invalidating prior art include (1) instances in which the patentee's invention date predates the accused infringer's actual reduction to practice and the accused infringer's commercial use activity is either insufficiently public to constitute a Section 102(b) bar or is less than one year before the patentee's effective filing date; and (2) instances in which the accused infringer's reduction to practice predates that of the patentee, but the accused infringer abandons, suppresses or conceals the invention, thereby ceding invention priority to the patentee, but later begins commercial use before the patentee's effective filing date.[44]

J. *Doing and Conducting "Business."* The interpretation of the phrases "doing" business and "conducting" business will be critical to determining the scope of the Section 273 defense.

1. *Broad Literal Scope.* Given broad literal scope, "conducting" business includes all methods a commercial enterprise uses to "conduct" its business. A broad interpretation of "conducting" business is supported by provisions in Section 273 that refer to covered methods resulting in the "sale or other disposition of a useful end product." These provisions suggest that the defined methods can include processes creating products.[45]

2. *Narrowing Circumstances.* On the other hand, the timing of Section 273's enactment, and discussions in its legislative history, may support a narrow reading of doing and conducting business.

a. *State Street Bank.* Enactment came soon after a landmark Federal Circuit decision, *State Street Bank & Trust Co. v. Signature Financial Group Inc.* (1998),[46] which emphasized that "[w]hether the claims [of a patent] are directed to subject matter within § 101 should not turn on whether the claimed subject matter does 'business' instead of something else."[47]

b. *Prior Assumptions About Unpatentability of Business Methods.* Based on *State Street Bank,* and on a contemporaneous proliferation of patents on "business methods," one might argue that Section 273 is confined to methods of doing or conducting business in a narrow sense, for example, methods of arranging financial matters, methods for controlling inventory, and methods for marketing products or services, and does not extend to methods, such as methods for manufacturing products, that have been more traditionally the subject of patents.

---

43. For discussions of whether, under the law prior to the enactment of Section 273, a prior trade secret user could claim a personal defense that did not invalidate the patent, *see* Chisum on Patents § 3.05[2][a].

44. Some court decisions suggest that secret commercial use of an invention negates abandonment, suppression, and concealment. *See* Chisum on Patents § 10.08[4].

45. *See* 35 U.S.C. § 273(a)(1) (commercial use includes "an actual arm's-length sale or other arm's-length commercial transfer of a useful end result").

46. State Street Bank & Trust Co. v. Signature Financial Group, Inc., 149 F.3d 1368 (Fed.Cir.1998), *cert. denied,* 525 U.S. 1093 (1999).

47. 149 F.3d at 1377, 47 U.S.P.Q.2d at 1604.

One of the purposes of the patent system is to encourage prompt disclosure of new innovations. Innovators who decline to seek patents on innovations and, instead, utilize them as trade secrets can be said to act contrary to that purpose. However, commercial enterprises that practiced innovative *business* methods as trade secrets could reasonably have believed that such methods were not patentable subject matter. Hence, it can be argued that such users, unlike other users who eschewed the patent system in favor of trade secrecy, did not consciously act contrary to the purposes of the patent system. Therefore, it can be credibly argued that Congress' intent in restricting the "first inventor" defense to business methods was to give special consideration to those using business methods as trade secrets and to withhold such consideration from users of other, more traditional technologies.

    c. *House Committee Reports.* A discussion of the language on conducting and doing business in a House Committee Report on the provision that became Section 273 supports this confined interpretation.[48] There is a similar discussion in a later House Conference Committee Reports.[49] For a discussion of prior user rights in the United States, *see* David H. Hollander, *The First Inventor Defense: A Limited Prior User Rights Finds Its Way Into U.S. Patent Law*, 30 AM. INTELL. PROP. L. ASSN. Q.J. 37 (2002); Pierre Jean Hubert, *A Prior User Right of H.R. 400: A Careful Balancing of Competing Interests*, 14 SANTA CLARA COMPUTER & HIGH TECH. L.J. 189 (1998).

I. EXPERIMENTAL USE—35 U.S.C. § 271(e)

Mere use of a patented product constitutes infringement under § 271(a). But there is a line of authority suggesting that use of a patented product for non-commercial, experimental purposes may not be an act of infringement. The conflict between these two approaches came to a head in a battle concerning the pharmaceutical industry in the case of *Roche v. Bolar*, discussed below. In that case, Bolar, a generic drug manufacturer, wanted to sell a patented drug immediately upon expiration of the patent claiming the drug, and wanted to begin the lengthly FDA approval process, which involved making and using the generic drug so it could be tested and studied, before the patent expired. The issue in the case, therefore, became whether such activity constituted infringement.

1. *ROCHE V. BOLAR* AND CONGRESS' RESPONSE

In *Roche Products, Inc. v. Bolar Pharmaceutical Co.*, 733 F.2d 858 (Fed.Cir.1984), the defendant, a generic drug company, obtained a quantity of a patented drug from a foreign source and began testing it to obtain the necessary FDA data. The patent owner thought the defendant's use of the patented drug in this manner constituted patent infringement. The Federal Circuit agreed. The court held that the experimental use doctrine did not apply to "limited use of a patented drug for testing and investigation

48. *See* H.R. No. 106–287(I), 106th Cong., 1st Sess. (1999).

49. *See* H.R. Conf. Rep. No. 106–464, 106th Cong., 1st Sess. (Nov. 9, 1999).

strictly related to FDA drug approval requirements during the last 6 months of the term of the patent." *Id.* at 861. According to the court, the defendant's use was

> solely for business reasons and not for amusement, to satisfy idle curiosity, or for strictly philosophical inquiry.... [The defendant] may intend to perform "experiments," but unlicensed experiments conducted with a view to the adaption of the patented invention to the experimentor's business is a violation of the rights of the patentee to exclude others from using his patented invention.

Id. at 863.

Shortly after *Roche* was decided, Congress responded. At the time of *Roche*, the FDA imposed rigorous requirements on those entities seeking FDA approval for a product, which was often subject to patent protection. The process for approval took several years, resulting in a loss of patent life on the particular product being reviewed. Furthermore, given the lengthy approval process and the *Roche* decision, generic equivalents, which must also be approved by the FDA, would not become publicly available until long after the patent expired, thus giving patent owners coverage beyond the patent term and depriving the public of competitively priced drugs. In an attempt to streamline the FDA approval process and respond to *Roche*, Congress, in 1984, enacted the Drug Price Competition and Patent Term Restoration Act of 1984, also known as the Hatch–Waxman Act, which added section 271(e) to the patent code.

The Act amended both FDA law and the patent law and accomplished several things. First, it abrogated the holding in *Roche*. Section 271(e)(1) hastened the introduction of generic equivalents into the marketplace by exempting from infringement the making, using, or selling of "a patented invention ... solely for uses *reasonably related* to the development and submission of information under a Federal law which regulates the manufacture, use, or sale of drugs." (Emphasis added). Second, the Act created the "abbreviated new drug application" or ANDA, a steamlined application process for entities seeking FDA approval and wishing to market a generic equivalent of an FDA approved patented product. Third, the Act, under section 271(e)(2), provides a patent owner with a special infringement remedy against entities filing an ANDA seeking FDA approval to market a generic equivalent *before* expiration of the patent. Lastly, it provided for extensions of patent terms that result from delays and the rigors of the FDA approval process. For a discussion of the interrelationship between the Hatch–Waxman Act provisions on patent term extension, exemption of FDA data gathering for generic equivalents, and the filing of ANDAs, *see Eli Lilly and Co. v. Medtronic, Inc.*, 496 U.S. 661 (1990) (holding that § 271(e)(i) covers medical devices as well as drugs).

The Hatch–Waxman Act struck a balance between the interests of patentees of brand-name pharmaceuticals and the generic pharmaceutical industry, as well as the interests of the general public in competitively priced pharmaceuticals. In short, the act was designed to promote technological innovation while at the same time enhance the public welfare, a balancing act that is at the very heart of the patent system. A 1992 Federal Circuit opinion nicely reflected upon the policies of the Act:

The Drug Price Competition and Patent Term Restoration Act of 1984 ... addressed two distinct problems created by the legal requirements for premarket FDA approval of drugs and medical devices, and the lengthy delays often attendant on this approval. For products utilizing patented inventions, the approval process created problems at both ends of the patent term.

At the front end, a patent owner's effective patent term was shortened by the time spent obtaining approval, because a medical product using the patented invention could not be marketed without FDA approval.... In 1984, when the amendment was added, the approval process was taking an average of seven to ten years from the time the patent was issued.... The product thus could be unmarketable for a substantial part of the life of the patent.... To avoid this unintended distortion of the purposes of the Patent Act, Congress provided for extending the patent term of patents related to certain products that could not be marketed before undergoing a lengthy regulatory approval process.

At the other end, the delay attendant on obtaining FDA approval for a competing product that utilized the patented invention had the same effect in some situations of extending the patentee's exclusive rights beyond the patent term.... Since a competing product utilizing the invention could not be made or used while the patent was still in effect without infringing, *Roche Products Inc. v. Bolar Pharmaceutical Co.* ..., the process of obtaining FDA approval for the competing product could not be undertaken until the original patent expired. As a practical matter there would be no competing products, such as generic versions of a brand name drug, on the market until long after the patent on the original invention had expired.

To avoid this second unintended distortion, Congress enacted 21 U.S.C. § 355(j), which provided expedited approval for generic drugs through abbreviated new drug applications, and 35 U.S.C. § 271(e).... One effect of § 271(e) was to make the rule of *Roche Products* no longer operative.

Telectronics Pacing Systems, Inc. v. Ventritex, Inc., 982 F.2d 1520, 1525 (Fed.Cir.1992). Let's now turn to some of the specific provisions in § 271(e).

2. The § 271(e)(1) Exemption and "Reasonably Related" Uses

The language of § 271(e) exempting certain activities from infringement is awkward to say the least. Recall, infringement is not present when the activity is "solely for uses reasonably related to the development and submission of information" under federal food and drug laws. Should the focus be on "solely" or "reasonably related," and how should the courts construe these terms.

In *Intermedics, Inc. v. Ventritex, Inc.*, 775 F.Supp. 1269 (N.D.Cal.1991), *aff'd*, 991 F.2d 808 (Fed.Cir.1993), an influential district court opinion, the court held that any commercial uses that exceeded the confines of § 271(e)(1) (*e.g.*, trade shows and demonstrations to non-clinical investigators) were *de minimis*, and that a patent owner may not eradicate the § 271(e)(1) exemption by merely demonstrating that the accused infringer "*intends* to commercialize the device *before* the expiration of the allegedly infringed patent," and (2) the exemption "is not lost simply as a result of a showing that the [accused infringer] has engaged in *non*-infringing acts whose 'uses' fall outside those permitted by the statute." *Id.* at 1273, 1278.

The Federal Circuit, in *Telectronics Pacing, supra*, approved of *Intermedics'* reasoning in holding that the § 271(e)(1) exemption is not lost when the accused infringer, who has used the patented invention solely for FDA data collection, disseminates the data for business and fund-raising purposes. In *Teletronics*, the accused infringer, who was authorized to sell its device (an implantable defibrillator) to gather the necessary FDA information, displayed and demonstrated the device to physicians and to non-physicians at medical conferences and described its clinical trial results to investors, analysts, and journalists. Upon rejecting the patent owner's assertion that the accused infringer's demonstrations exceeded the § 271(e)(1) exemption, the court stated:

> Absent some showing that [the accused infringer's] purpose is disputed, ... such demonstrations constitute an exempt use reasonably related to FDA approval, because device sponsors are responsible for selecting qualified investigators and providing them with the necessary information to conduct clinical testing.... The fact that some non-physicians may have seen the device at the conferences is merely incidental and of minimal import, since only physicians can implant the device. Observation of the device at medical conferences by non-physicians does not impair the conclusion that such uses satisfy the requirements of § 271(e)(1).

Id. at 1523. The court further opined that

> [i]t would strain credulity to imagine that Congress was indifferent to the economics of developing and marketing drugs and medical devices when it enacted § 271(e)(1). The legislative history of the 1984 amendments attests to the costs, and rewards, of success in this highly competitive market ... Congress could not have been unaware of the need of competitors to raise funds for developing and testing competing products, and for preparing to enter the market once controlling patents had expired.

Id. at 1525.

In *Integra Lifesciences I, Ltd. v. Merck*, 331 F.3d 860, 865 (Fed.Cir. 2003), the court considered "whether the pre-clinical research conducted under the Scripps–Merck agreement is exempt from liability for infringement of Integra's patents under 271(e)(1)." The court found the 271(e)(1)'s safe harbor provision was not invoked:

> At the outset, this statutory language strictly limits the exemption "solely" to uses with a reasonable relationship to FDA procedures. The term "solely" places a constraint on the inquiry into the limits of the exemption. The exemption cannot extend at all beyond uses with the reasonable relationship specified in § 271(e)(1).

> The 1984 Act further specifies the subject of the reasonable relationship test. The exemption covers uses "reasonably related to the development and submission of information" to the FDA. Thus, to qualify at all for the exemption, an otherwise infringing activity must reasonably relate to the development and submission of information for FDA's safety and effectiveness approval processes. The focus of the entire exemption is the provision of information to the FDA. Activities that do not directly produce information for the FDA are already straining the relationship to the central

purpose of the safe harbor. The term "reasonably" permits some activities that are not themselves the experiments that produce FDA information to qualify as "solely for uses reasonably related" to clinical tests for the FDA. Again, however, the statutory language limits the reach of that relationship test.

In this case, the Scripps work sponsored by Merck was not clinical testing to supply information to the FDA, but only general biomedical research to identify new pharmaceutical compounds. The FDA has no interest in the hunt for drugs that may or may not later undergo clinical testing for FDA approval. For instance, the FDA does not require information about drugs other than the compound featured in an Investigational New Drug application. Thus, the Scripps work sponsored by Merck was not "solely for uses reasonably related" to clinical testing for FDA.

The reach of the reasonable relationship test as applied in this case receives further confirmation from the context of the 1984 Act. The meaning of the phrase "reasonably related to the development and submission of information" as set forth in § 271(e)(1) is clearer in the context of the role of the 1984 Act in facilitating expedited approval of a generic version of a drug previously approved by the FDA.

As discussed above, the express objective of the 1984 Act was to facilitate the immediate entry of safe, effective generic drugs into the marketplace upon expiration of a pioneer drug patent. The 1984 Act thus permits filing of an ANDA (abbreviated new drug application) to expedite FDA approval of a generic version of a drug already on the market. *Bayer AG v. Elan Pharm. Research Corp.,* 212 F.3d 1241 (Fed.Cir.2000). This expedited approval process requires the generic drug company to perform safety and effectiveness tests on its product before expiration of the patent on the pioneer drug if the generic is to be available immediately upon patent expiration. As noted, however, this court had ruled that those pre-expiration tests infringe the patent on the pioneer drug. *Roche,* 733 F.2d at 858. Therefore, the 1984 Act enacted § 271(e)(1) to create a safe harbor for those pre-expiration tests necessary to satisfy FDA requirements. As also noted, the legislative record shows as well that the 1984 Act narrowly tailored the § 271(e)(1) exemption to have only a *de minimis* impact on the patentee's right to exclude. Therefore, the § 271(e)(1) safe harbor covers those pre-expiration activities "reasonably related" to acquiring FDA approval of a drug already on the market. Within this framework and language of the 1984 Act, the district court correctly confined the § 271(e)(1) exemption to activity that "would contribute (relatively directly)" to information the FDA considers in approving a drug. *Intermedics,* 775 F.Supp. at 1280.

The exemption viewed in this context does not endorse an interpretation of § 271(e)(1) that would encompass drug development activities far beyond those necessary to acquire information for FDA approval of a patented pioneer drug already on the market. It does not, for instance, expand the phrase "reasonably related" to embrace the development of new drugs because those new products will also need FDA approval. Thus, §§ 271(e)(1) simply does not globally embrace all experimental activity that at some point, however attenuated, may lead to an FDA approval process. The safe harbor does not reach any exploratory research that may rationally form a predicate for future FDA clinical tests.

As noted, the text of § 271(e)(1) limits the exemption "solely" to activities "reasonably related to the development and submission of information" to the FDA. Moreover, the context of this safe harbor keys its use to facilitating expedited approval of patented pioneer drugs already on the market. Extending § 271(e)(1) to embrace new drug development activities would ignore its language and context with respect to the 1984 Act in an attempt to exonerate infringing uses only potentially related to information for FDA approval. Moreover, such an extension would not confine the scope of § 271(e)(1) to *de minimis* encroachment on the rights of the patentee. For example, expansion of § 271(e)(1) to include the Scripps Merck activities would effectively vitiate the exclusive rights of patentees owning biotechnology tool patents. After all, patented tools often facilitate general research to identify candidate drugs, as well as downstream safety-related experiments on those new drugs. Because the downstream clinical testing for FDA approval falls within the safe harbor, these patented tools would only supply some commercial benefit to the inventor when applied to general research. Thus, exaggerating § 271(e)(1) out of context would swallow the whole benefit of the Patent Act for some categories of biotechnological inventions. Needless to say, the 1984 Act was meant to reverse the effects of *Roche* under limited circumstances, not to deprive entire categories of inventions of patent protection.

Because the language and context of the safe harbor do not embrace the Scripps Merck general biomedical experimentation, this court discerns no error in the district court's interpretation of 35 U.S.C. § 271(e)(1). This court affirms that aspect of the district court's decision.

Id. at 866–68.

In *Proveris Scientific Corp. v. Innovasystems, Inc.*, the Federal Circuit held that an optical spray analyzer (OSA) that was used by a competitor, that had been used in development of FDA regulatory submissions, but was not itself subject to FDA premarket approval process, was not immunized by the safe harbor provision that sought to eliminate de facto patent term extension:

> Because the [patented] device is not subject to FDA premarket approval, and therefore faces no regulatory barriers to market entry upon patent expiration, [the patentee] is not a party who, prior to enactment of the Hatch–Waxman Act, could be said to have been adversely affected by the [distortion caused by the requirement to seek FDA approval in order to enter the market to compete with patentees]. For this reason, we do not think Congress could have intended that the safe harbor of section 271(e)(1) apply to it. Put another way, insofar as its OSA device is concerned, Innova is not within the category of entities for whom the safe harbor provision was designed to provide relief.

536 F.3d 1256, 1265 (Fed.Cir.2008).

3. INFRINGEMENT UNDER § 271(e)(2)

Section 271(e)(2) makes it an act of infringement to submit an ANDA "for a drug claimed in a patent or the use of which is claimed in a patent ... if the purpose of such submission is to obtain approval ... to engage in the commercial manufacture, use, or sale of [the patented invention] ... before the expiration of such patent." Section 271(e)(4) sets forth the appropriate remedies. These two sections provide a counterweight to § 271(e)(1)'s exemption. On the one hand, it is not an act of infringement to make, use, or sale a patented drug "to the extent it is necessary for the preparation and submission of an ANDA." On the other hand, if the party seeking FDA approval of an ANDA "wants to market the drug prior to the expiration of the patent, the patent owner can seek to prevent approval" by instituting an infringement suit. *See Bristol–Myers Squibb Co. v. Royce Laboratories, Inc.*, 69 F.3d 1130, 1132 (Fed.Cir.1995). Let's examine this dynamic more closely by looking at Justice Scalia's explanation of these two sections in *Eli Lilly and Co. v. Medtronic, Inc.*, 496 U.S. 661, 676–78 (1990):

> The function of [Sections 271(e)(2) and (4)] is to define a new (and somewhat artificial) act of infringement for a very limited and technical purpose that relates only to certain drug applications. As an additional means of eliminating the *de facto* extension at the end of the patent term in the case of drugs, and to enable new drugs to be marketed more cheaply and quickly, § 101 of the 1984 Act amended § 505 of the FDCA, 21 U.S.C. § 355, to authorize abbreviated new drug applications (ANDAs), which would substantially shorten the time and effort needed to obtain marketing approval.
>
> * * *
>
> These abbreviated drug-application provisions incorporated an important new mechanism designed to guard against infringement of patents relating to pioneer drugs. Pioneer drug applicants are required to file with the FDA the number and expiration date of any patent which claims the drug that is the subject of the application, or a method of using such drug.... ANDAs and paper NDAs are required to contain one of four certifications with respect to each patent named in the pioneer drug application: (1) "that such patent information has not been filed," (2) "that such patent has expired," (3) "the date on which such patent will expire," or (4) "that such patent is invalid or will not be infringed by the manufacture, use, or sale of the new drug for which the application is submitted." 21 U.S.C. §§ 355(b)(2)(A), 355(j)(2)(A)(vii).
>
> This certification is significant, in that it determines the date on which approval of an ANDA or paper NDA can be made effective, and hence the date on which commercial marketing may commence. If the applicant makes either the first or second certification, approval can be made effective immediately. See 21 U.S.C. §§ 355(c)(3)(A), 355(j)(4)(B)(i). If the applicant makes the third certification, approval of the application can be made effective as of the date the patent expires. See 21 U.S.C. §§ 355(c)(3)(B), 355(j)(4)(B)(ii). If the applicant makes the fourth certification, however, the effective date must depend on the outcome of further events triggered by the Act. An applicant who makes the fourth certification is required to give notice to the holder of the patent alleged to be invalid or not infringed, stating that an application has been filed seeking approval to engage in the commercial manufacture, use, or sale of the drug before the expiration of the patent, and setting forth a detailed statement of the factual and legal basis for the applicant's opinion that the patent is not valid or will not be infringed. See 21 U.S.C. §§ 355(b)(3)(B), 355(j)(2)(B)(ii). Approval of an ANDA or paper NDA containing the fourth certification may become effective immediately only if the patent owner has not initiated a lawsuit for infringement within 45 days of receiving notice of the certification. If the owner brings such a suit, then approval may not be made effective until the court rules that the patent is not infringed or until the expiration of (in general) 30 months, whichever first occurs. See 21 U.S.C. §§ 355 (c)(3)(C), 355(j)(4)(B)(iii).

This scheme will not work, of course, if the holder of the patent pertaining to the pioneer drug is disabled from establishing in court that there has been an act of infringement. And that was precisely the disability that the new § 271(e)(1) imposed, with regard to use of his patented invention only for the purpose of obtaining premarketing approval. Thus, an act of infringement had to be created for these ANDA and paper NDA proceedings. That is what is achieved by § 271(e)(2)—the creation of a highly artificial act of infringement that consists of submitting an ANDA or a paper NDA containing the fourth type of certification that is in error as to whether commercial manufacture, use, or sale of the new drug (none of which, of course, has actually occurred) violates the relevant patent. Not only is the defined act of infringement artificial, so are the specified consequences, as set forth in paragraph (e)(4). Monetary damages are permitted only if there has been "commercial manufacture, use, or sale." 35 U.S.C. § 271(e)(4)(C). Quite obviously, the purpose of (e)(2) and (e)(4) is to enable the judicial adjudication upon which the ANDA and paper NDA schemes depend.

In *Bayer AG v. Elan Pharmaceutical Research Corp.*, 212 F.3d 1241, 1244–45 (Fed.Cir.2000), the Federal Circuit discussed the ANDA process:

As this court has described before, the Hatch–Waxman Act (the "Act") amended the Federal Food, Drug, and Cosmetic Act, Pub.L. No. 52–675, 52 Stat. 1040 (1938) (codified as amended at 21 U.S.C. §§ 301 et. seq. (1994)) (the "FDCA"), as well as the patent laws. *See Bristol–Myers Squibb Co. v. Royce Lab., Inc.*, 69 F.3d 1130, 1131–32, (Fed.Cir.1995); *DuPont Merck Pharm. Co. v. Bristol–Myers Squibb Co.*, 62 F.3d 1397, 1399–1401 (Fed.Cir. 1995). Under the FDCA, as amended by the Act, a pharmaceutical manufacturer submits an ANDA when seeking expedited FDA approval of a generic version of a drug previously approved by the FDA (a "listed drug"). *See* 21 U.S.C. § 355(j). An ANDA can be filed if the generic drug manufacturer's active ingredient is the "bioequivalent" of the listed drug. *See* 21 U.S.C. § 355(j)(2)(A)(iv). When submitting an ANDA, a manufacturer must certify one of four statements concerning the applicable listed drug: (i) the listed drug is not patented (a "Paragraph I certification"); (ii) the listed drug's patent has expired (a "Paragraph II certification"); (iii) the expiration date of the listed drug's patent (a "Paragraph III certification"); or (iv) the listed drug's patent "is invalid or . . . it will not be infringed by the manufacture, use, or sale of the new drug" covered by the ANDA (a "Paragraph IV certification"). 21 U.S.C. § 355(j)(2)(A)(vii)(I)–(IV). If an ANDA is certified under Paragraph IV, the applicant must notify the patent's owner of the certification. *See* 21 U.S.C. § 355(j)(2)(B).

An ANDA certified under Paragraphs I or II is approved immediately after meeting all applicable scientific and regulatory requirements. *See* 21 U.S.C. §§ 355(j)(5)(A), (B)(i). An ANDA certified under Paragraph III must, even after meeting all applicable scientific and regulatory requirements, wait for approval until the listed drug's patent expires. *See* 21 U.S.C. §§ 355(j)(5)(A), (B)(ii). An ANDA certified under Paragraph IV is approved immediately after meeting all applicable scientific and regulatory requirements unless the listed drug's patent owner brings suit for infringement under 35 U.S.C. § 271(e)(2)(A) within forty-five days of receiving the notice required under 21 U.S.C. § 355(j)(2)(B). *See* 21 U.S.C. § 355(j)(5)(B)(iii). If suit is brought, the FDA is required to suspend approval of the ANDA, and the FDA cannot approve the ANDA until the earliest of three dates: (i) the date of the court's decision that the listed drug's patent is either invalid or not infringed; (ii) the date the listed drug's patent expires, *see* 35 U.S.C.

§ 271(e)(4)(A), if the court finds the listed drug's patent infringed; or (iii) subject to modification by the court, the date that is thirty months from the date the owner of the listed drug's patent received notice of the filing of a Paragraph IV certification. See 21 U.S.C. § 355(j)(5)(B)(iii)(I)–(III).

The Act modified the patent laws to provide that "[i]t shall not be an act of infringement to make, use, or sell ... a patented invention ... solely for uses reasonably related to the development and submission of information under a Federal law which regulates the manufacture, use, or sale of drugs." 35 U.S.C. § 271(e)(1). A Paragraph IV certification, however, is deemed to be an act of infringement "if the purpose of such a submission is to obtain approval under the [FDCA] to engage in the commercial manufacture, use, or sale of a drug ... claimed in a patent or the use of which is claimed in a patent before the expiration of such a patent." 35 U.S.C. § 271(e)(2)(A); *see also Glaxo, Inc. v. Novopharm, Ltd.*, 110 F.3d 1562, 1567 (Fed.Cir.1997). "If the court determines that the patent is not invalid and that infringement would occur, and that therefore the ANDA applicant's [P]aragraph IV certification is incorrect, the patent owner is entitled to an order that FDA approval of the ANDA containing the [P]aragraph IV certification not be effective until the patent expires." *Royce Lab.*, 69 F.3d at 1135 (emphasis omitted).

The full reach of the 271(e)(2) exemption remains an open question. Keep in mind that the common law research use exemption was reaffirmed recently to be extremely narrow in exempting only those uses that are "for amusement, to satisfy idle curiosity, or for strictly philosophical inquiry." *Madey v. Duke University*, 307 F.3d 1351 (Fed. Cir. 2002). For academic researchers, who do much if not all of their work in furtherance of philosophical inquiry, the legal test in essence allows only for a very limited amount of research to be conducted on patented technologies to confirm whether they work as described in the patent. It does not allow for the user of a patented technology to be legally exempt from infringing simply because their use has to do with research or is for research purposes. The distinction here is between researching with and researching on, which basically distinguishes between a business purpose that would not be exempt and a purely philosophical interest that could be. The bottom line is that only a limited number of uses to genuinely test whether a patented technology works will be good candidates for the common law exemption.

Nevertheless, and despite the clear legislative intent to limit the Hatch–Waxman Act's exemption for infringement, the Supreme Court in the recent *Merck* case treated the statutory exemption so broadly that the Court gave a free pass from infringement for work relating to preclinical studies of a new drug seeking FDA approval. *Merck KGaA v. Integra Lifesciences I, Ltd.* 545 U.S. 193 (2005). A careful reading of the *Merck* decision would probably not extend its impact beyond the narrow facts of the case. Any other view may be seen by some as an overly strained reading of the opinion that would undercut the important policies of the patent system. But the language of the *Merck* opinion seems to suggest that the statutory exemption now is not limited only to the development of information for submission to the FDA and that instead Congress "exempted from infringement all uses of patented compounds 'reasonably related' to the process of developing information for submission under any federal law regulating the manufacture, use, or distribution of drugs." 545 U.S. at 206.

This language seems to cover almost any use by any company that is in some way regulated by the government, and which therefore may reasonably be anticipating submitting data to a regulatory body.

4. PATENT TERM EXTENSION

Given the regulatory delays associated with FDA approval, the Hatch–Waxman Act, in addition to creating section 271(e), added section 156 to the patent code which provides for an extension of a patent term under certain circumstances.

Section 156 is complex and requires a determination from both the FDA and PTO. Generally speaking, one can begin by focusing on two time periods, sometimes called: "experimental" and "administrative." While the statue does not provide these labels, they come from an article by Dr. Paul D. Levin that provides a helpful method for calculating the available extension. Paul D. Levin, *On the Inappropriate Inclusion of Medical Devices within the Hatch–Waxman Act*, 89 J. PAT. & TRADEMARK OFF. SOC'Y 456 (2007). If the patent covers a drug, then the "experimental" period is the time between the Investigation New Drug (IND) filing and the New Drug Application (NDA) filing. See 35 U.S.C. § 156(g)(1)(B)(i) (2006). If a device, then the "experimental" period is the time between the start of any clinical investigation and the filing of a Pre–Market Approval (PMA). See 35 U.S.C. § 156(g)(3)(B)(i) (2006). For both, the "administrative" period is the time needed to get approval once in the agency. See 35 U.S.C. § 156(g)(1)(B)(ii), § 156(g)(3)(B)(ii) (2006). To calculate the amount of term extension, begin by adding the half of the "experimental" time to all of the "administrative" time. See 35 U.S.C. § 156(c)(2) (2006). But, note that the amount of "experimental" period that is counted for this purpose can be reduced if the FDA can show that the manufacturer did not use "due diligence" in conducting the trial, 35 U.S.C. § 156(c)(1) (2006). And in any event, the total amount of extension is capped at five years. See 35 U.S.C. § 156(g)(4)(A) (2006). Other limitations also apply, such as if the total term counting the extension would exceed 14 years from the date the extension is granted. See 35 U.S.C. § 156(c)(3) (2006).

Section 156 is limited to patents on products (or processes of making or using the same) that are human drug products, medical devices, food additives, and color additives subject to regulation under the Federal Food, Drug and Cosmetic Act. *See* DONALD S. CHISUM, V CHISUM ON PATENTS § 16.04[5] (1997). A patent owner must apply for an extension "within the 60 day period beginning on the date the product received permission under the provision of law under which the applicable regulatory review period occurred for commercial marketing or use." 35 U.S.C. § 156(a)(3), (d).

It should be noted that the restoration period does not cover the entire period lost due to regulatory review by the FDA. *See Merck & Co., Inc. v. Kessler*, 80 F.3d 1543, 1547 (Fed.Cir.1996). According to *Merck*, the patent term restoration process had the following limitations: First, "[r]egardless of the time lost, if a patent was issued and testing began before the 1984 enactment of the Hatch–Waxman Act the total extension period may not exceed two years ...; otherwise the restoration period is limited to no more than five years." Furthermore, "the effective patent term including the restoration period may not exceed 14 years following FDA approval of the new drug." In addition, "the term of the patent may be given only on *restoration* extension.... If the term of the patent has received such an extension, the patent may not be given another restoration extension even for another drug covered by the patent whose marketing also is delayed by reasons of FDA procedures." Lastly, "the restoration period of the patent does not extend to all products protected by the patent but only to the product on which the extension was based." *Id.* at 1546–47.

Side Bar

Personal Jurisdiction in ANDA Patent Infringement Cases

Gerald Sobel*

The ability to bring a suit for infringement based on the mere filing of an ANDA with the appropriate certification raises some interesting issues of personal jurisdiction. Most important among these is whether such a ministerial act—the filing of the document—should be considered sufficient to trigger personal jurisdiction over the person filing the document in the location where the document is filed, Maryland, even if that person has no other ties to Maryland. Personal jurisdiction is important because, as the *Side Bar* on Declaratory Judgement Jurisdiction at the beginning of this Chapter points out, the ability to pick the place of a battle can have enormous tactical and strategic impact.

The Basic Requirements for Personal Jurisdiction Over a Non–Resident Defendant

It is well-settled that "[i]n order to determine whether personal jurisdiction exists [as to a non-resident defendant] ... the court must determine whether jurisdiction lies under both the applicable state long-arm statute and the Due Process Clause of the Federal Constitution." *Viam Corp. v. Iowa Export–Import Trading Co.*, 84 F.3d 424, 427 (Fed.Cir. 1996).[1] Typically, the long-arm statute has been held to reach to the limits of due process,[2] and it is only necessary to analyze whether the exercise of jurisdiction comports with due process. *Helicopteros Nacionales de Colombia, S.A. v. Hall*, 466 U.S. 408, 413 (1984); *Viam*, 84 F.3d at 427.[3]

The United States Supreme Court has held that the "Due Process Clause protects an individual's liberty interest in not being subject to the binding judgments of a forum with which he has established no meaningful 'contacts, ties, or relations,' " *Burger King Corp. v. Rudzewicz*, 471 U.S. 462, 471–72 (1985), *quoting International Shoe Co. v. Washington*, 326 U.S. 310, 319 (1945), and requires that "individuals have 'fair warning that a particular activity may subject [them] to the jurisdiction of a foreign sovereign.' " *Id.* at 472 (citation omitted). Due process is thus satisfied when the non-resident defendant has engaged in "certain minimum contacts with [the forum] such that the maintenance of the suit does not offend 'traditional notions of fair play and substantial justice.' " *International Shoe*, 326 U.S. at 316 (citations omitted).

In *Helicopteros Nacionales de Colombia, S.A. v. Hall*, 466 U.S. 408, 414–15 (1984), the Supreme Court's analysis of personal jurisdiction over non-resident defendants distinguished between "general jurisdiction" and "specific jurisdiction." General jurisdiction comports with due process only when the defendant's contacts with the forum constitute "continuous and systematic general business contacts." 466 U.S. at 416.[4] Specific jurisdiction is properly exercised when the cause of action arises out of or is related to the defendant's contacts with the forum. *Id.* at 414 n.8.

The due process analysis for specific jurisdiction requires a sufficient nexus between the non-resident defendant's contact with the forum and the asserted cause of action. "Where a forum seeks to assert specific jurisdiction over an out-of-state defendant who has not consented to suit there, [the] 'fair warning' requirement is satisfied if the defendant has 'purposefully directed' his activities at residents of the forum ... and the litigation results from alleged injuries that 'arise out of or relate to' those activities." *Burger King*, 471 U.S. at 472 (internal citations omitted). *See also Akro*, 45 F.3d at 1545. "Nevertheless, minimum requirements inherent in the concept of 'fair play and substantial justice' may defeat the reasonableness of jurisdiction even if the defendant has purposefully engaged in forum activities." 471 U.S. at 477–78.[5]

Specific Jurisdiction for Patent Infringement

Patent infringement is spoken of "loosely" as a tort. *See, e.g., North American Philips Corp. v. American Vending Sales, Inc.,* 35 F.3d 1576, 1579 (Fed.Cir.1994). In a tort context, personal jurisdiction has been upheld where the only contact of a defendant is *"purposeful direction"* of a foreign act *"having effect in the forum state." Roth v. Garcia Marquez,* 942 F.2d 617, 620 (9th Cir.1991) (emphasis added); *Haisten v. Grass Valley Medical Reimbursement Fund, Ltd.,* 784 F.2d 1392, 1397 (9th Cir.1986); *see Beverly Hills Fan Co. v. Royal Sovereign Corp.,* 21 F.3d 1558, 1564 (Fed.Cir.1994). As stated by the U.S. Supreme Court in *Burger King*, "the 'purposeful' availment requirement ensures that a defendant will not be hauled into a jurisdiction solely as a result of 'random', 'fortuitous', or 'attenuated' contacts, or the unilateral activity of another party or a third person." 471 U.S. at 475.

The Federal Circuit has relied upon infringing sales in the jurisdiction to uphold personal jurisdiction. For purposes of determining specific jurisdiction, the Federal Circuit in patent infringement cases has used a three-part test. The non-resident defendant must "purposefully avail" itself of or "direct its activities at" the forum, the claim must "arise out of" or "relate to" the defendant's forum-related activities, and the exercise of jurisdiction must be "reasonable." *Dainippon Screen Mfg. Co. v. CFMT, Inc.,* 142 F.3d 1266 n. 2 (Fed.Cir.1998) (specific jurisdiction in California over an out-of-state holding company, CFMT, was premised on CFMT's conduct of patent licensing negotiations with the plaintiff, although they ultimately reached no agreement; 46 USPQ2d at 1618); *Haisten,* 784 F.2d at 1397.

In *Beverly Hills Fan*, the Federal Circuit held that "indirect shipments through the stream of commerce" were sufficient to confer personal jurisdiction in Virginia, over a Chinese company, Ultec, despite the fact that it "has no assets or employees located in Virginia; has no agent for the service of process in Virginia; does not have a license to do business in Virginia; and has not directly shipped the accused [product] into Virginia." 21 F.3d at 1560, 1564. "The situs of the injury is the location, or locations, at which the infringing activity directly impacts on the interests of the patentee, here the place of the infringing sales in Virginia." *Id.* at 1571 n.33.

In *North American Philips*, decided later the same year as *Beverly Hills Fan*, the Federal Circuit overturned the district court's denial of jurisdiction. *North American Philips Corp. v. American Vending Sales, Inc.*, 35 F.3d 1576, 1581 (Fed.Cir.1994). "[35 U.S.C. § 271(a)] on its face clearly suggests the conception that the 'tort' of patent infringement occurs where the offending act is committed and not where the injury is felt.... We hold that to sell an infringing article to a buyer in Illinois is to commit a tort there (though not necessarily only there)." *Id.* at 1579.

Patent Infringement by Filing an Infringing ANDA as a Basis for Jurisdiction

In the case of a generic drug manufacturer seeking FDA approval to market a generic product, the only infringing activity occurs with the filing of an ANDA application at the FDA headquarters in Rockville, Maryland. The Hatch–Waxman Act states that such an application "shall be an act of infringement." 35 U.S.C. § 271(e)(2)(A).[6] Sales are not permitted until FDA approval occurs. 21 U.S.C. § 355(a). By analogy to the cases where personal jurisdiction is predicated on the place of an infringing sale, one might infer that specific personal jurisdiction can be at the place where the FDA is located; it is there that the act of patent infringement occurred.

The Government Contacts Exception and Its Bases

A "government contacts exception" has been developed by the courts of the District of Columbia, and embraced for the FDA in Maryland. In the seminal case, the Court of Appeals for the D.C. Circuit held that maintaining a correspondent to gather news in Washington did not subject a Philadelphia newspaper to jurisdiction under the "doing business" standard of the District's long-arm statute. *Neely v. Philadelphia Inquirer Co.*, 62 F.2d 873, 874 (D.C.Cir.1932). The plaintiff sued the paper for allegedly libelous material published in its paper. In refusing to exercise jurisdiction, the court stated:

> As the seat of national government, Washington is the source of much news of national importance, which makes it desirable in the public interest that many newspapers should maintain vigilant correspondents here. If the employment of a Washington correspondent, the announcement of his address, and the payment of his office rent, subjects a nonresident newspaper corporation to legal process in Washington for matter appearing in its paper at home, it would bring in nearly every important newspaper in the nation, and many foreign publishing corporations, which in our opinion the present statute does not do.

62 F.2d at 875. *Accord, Layne v. Tribune Co.*, 71 F.2d 223 (D.C.Cir.1934), *cert. denied*, 293 U.S. 572 (1934).

The Court of Appeals later applied the same principle to a nonresident maintaining an office in the District of Columbia for the purpose of gathering information from and communicating with the federal government.[7] *Mueller Brass Co. v. Alexander Milburn Co.*, 152 F.2d 142 (D.C.Cir.1945).

In *Environmental Research Intl., Inc. v. Lockwood Greene Engineers, Inc.*, 355 A.2d 808, 813 (1976) (*en banc*),[8] the only contact the defendant had with the District of Columbia involved petitioning the EPA for a construction grant. *Id.* at 811–12. The court held that these contacts should not be considered in determining whether a party is subject to jurisdiction under the District's long-arm statute. *Id.* at 814. The court explained:

> To permit our local courts to assert personal jurisdiction over nonresidents whose sole contact with the District consists of dealing with a federal instrumentality not only would pose a threat to free public participation in government, but would also threaten to convert the District of Columbia into a national judicial forum.

Id. at 813. To infringe upon the right to free access to the federal government would place "an impermissible burden on the First Amendment 'right of the people ... to petition the Government for redress of grievance.'" *Id.* at 813 n.11. *Accord, Founding Church of Scientology v. Verlag,* 536 F.2d 429, 433 (D.C.Cir.1976) ("in minimum contact situations, the First Amendment protects newsgathering activities in the nation's capital and weighs against the assumption of personal jurisdiction over a nonresident publisher."); *Naartex,* 722 F.2d at 787 (1983) (defendants appeared before the Interior Department to protect their proprietary interest from an adverse regulatory decision).[9]

Nevertheless, in *Calder v. Jones,* 465 U.S. 783 (1984), the Supreme Court upheld jurisdiction in a libel action where the accused newspaper was circulated in the District and rejected "the suggestion that First Amendment concerns enter into jurisdictional analysis." *Id.* at 789. This caused the D.C. Court of Appeals to "conclude that the newsgathering exception is not based upon first amendment considerations but is based upon an interpretation of Congress' intent with respect to what type of 'business' in the District will subject a non-resident corporation to jurisdiction here." *Moncrief v. Lexington Herald–Leader,* 807 F.2d 217, 224 (D.C.Cir.1986).

The Government Contacts Exception in the ANDA Setting

An ANDA filing involves petitioning a government agency, in particular, the FDA, as in *Environmental Research.* Because it presents patent infringement as an issue, the Federal Circuit has jurisdiction. In a two-to-one decision the Federal Circuit held that personal jurisdiction does not lie in Maryland against a generic drug manufacturer based on an "act of infringement" under § 271(e)(2) predicated on an ANDA filing with the FDA in Rockville. *Zeneca Ltd. v. Mylan Pharmaceuticals, Inc.,* 173 F.3d 829 (Fed.Cir.1999), *reh'g en banc denied,* (June 3, 1999). The two concurring judges stated that mere filing of an ANDA did not warrant subjecting the filer to personal jurisdiction, but disagreed on the basis. Judge Gajarsa relied on the government contacts exception and Judge Rader relied on a traditional due process analysis. Judge Rich dissented without offering a written opinion.[10]

Judge Gajarsa applied the government contacts exception as stated in *Environmental Research.* Notwithstanding *Calder* and *Moncrief,* which disclaimed the First Amendment, he referred to the First Amendment and Due Process underpinnings of the doctrine. *Id.* at 831. According to Judge Gajarsa, the exception should apply because an ANDA applicant is "petitioning the government for the right to market its generic drug.... It seems obvious that Mylan's contact with Maryland arose out of the mere fortuity that the government agency that must receive the Petition is located in Maryland." *Id.* at 832. "The submission of the Petition clearly falls within the First Amendment right to petition." *Zeneca*, 173 F.3d at 832.

Application of the government contacts exception, Judge Gajarsa said, would avoid creation of an ANDA "supercourt" in Maryland and would preserve the public's right to freely participate in government. *Id.* at 833. Moreover, denial of jurisdiction in Maryland would not deprive Zeneca of a forum in which to seek relief since it had already established that jurisdiction would lie in the district court in Pennsylvania. *Zeneca Ltd. v. Mylan Pharmaceuticals, Inc.*, 968 F.Supp. 268 (W.D.Pa.1997).

Judge Rader's concurring opinion declined to apply the government contacts exception; instead, jurisdiction was held lacking because it would not comport with "traditional notions of fair play and substantial justice." *Id.* at 836. He observed that Mylan's contacts were not actually with Maryland but with the federal government. *Id.* at 835.[11] Mylan directed its activities at the FDA, not, according to the Court, at the state of Maryland or its residents. *Id.* "The plaintiff's interest and the state's interest in adjudicating the dispute in the forum are so attenuated that they are clearly outweighed by the burden of subjecting the defendant to litigation within the forum." *Id.* (*quoting Beverly Hills Fan Co. v. Royal Sovereign Corp.*, 21 F.3d 1558, 1568 (Fed.Cir.1994)).

In the only other decision addressing the government contacts exception in the ANDA context, the District Court of Maryland held that an applicant's contacts with the Maryland forum based on filing an ANDA with the FDA in Maryland should not be considered in the jurisdictional analysis. *Zeneca Ltd. v. Pharmachemie B.V.*, 42 U.S.P.Q.2d 1212, 1216 (D.Md.1996) (*citing Nichols v. G.D. Searle & Co.*, 783 F.Supp. 233, 242–45 (D.Md.1992)). According to the court, the defendant "has a strong First Amendment interest in petitioning the government through its ANDA filing in an effort to 'advance its commercial or proprietary interests.'" *Zeneca v. Pharmachemie*, 42 U.S.P.Q.2d at 1216. The court initially held Pharmachemie subject to jurisdiction under the stream of commerce theory, but pointed out that "[a]s per the government contacts rule, this jurisdictional determination is in no way based on Pharmachemie's ANDA filing with the Food and Drug Administration." *Id.* at 1216. (The court later vacated the judgment and transferred the case to the District of Massachusetts, without regard to ANDA-related activities. *Id.* at 1217, 1220.)

In view of the on again, off again role of a First Amendment underpinning and the relevance of the availability of jurisdiction elsewhere for a plaintiff-patentee,[12] the exception from personal jurisdiction for an ANDA filing may not be ironclad. For example, it is worthwhile to pose the question of whether an infringement suit in Maryland based on an ANDA filing might survive the government contacts exception where personal jurisdiction elsewhere is doubtful.

* Senior Partner, Kaye Scholer LLP. This *Side Bar* was written specially for Principles of Patent Law.

1. The Court of Appeals for the Federal Circuit has held that it will apply Federal Circuit law, rather than that of the regional circuits, when deciding issues of personal jurisdiction. *Akro Corp. v. Luker*, 45 F.3d 1541, 1543 (Fed.Cir.1995).

2. As to the District of Columbia, for example, *Hummel v. Koehler*, 458 A.2d 1187, 1190 (D.C.App.1983) (*quoting Mouzavires v. Baxter*, 434 A.2d 988, 992 (D.C.App.1981) (*en banc*), *cert. denied*, 455 U.S. 1006 (1982)); *Smith v. Jenkins*, 452 A.2d 333, 336 (D.C.App.1982) (D.C. long-arm statute), the District of Columbia's long-arm statute provides in pertinent part: "A District of Columbia Court may exercise personal jurisdiction over a person, who acts directly or by an agent, as to a claim for relief arising from ... *transacting any business* in the District of Columbia." D.C. Code Ann. § 13–423(a)(1) (emphasis added).

3. The Federal Circuit has held that, although in patent cases it is the Due Process Clause of the Fifth Amendment that applies, the analysis is the same as that applied by the Supreme Court under the Fourteenth Amendment's Due Process Clause. *Akro*, 45 F.3d at 1544–45; *Viam*, 84 F.3d at 427 n.2.

4. "[T]he Supreme Court has upheld general jurisdiction only once, and lower courts have evinced a reluctance to assert general jurisdiction over non-resident defendants or foreign corporations even when the contacts with the forum state are quite extensive." MOORE'S FEDERAL PRACTICE § 108.41[3] (Matthew Bender 3d ed. 1997) (footnotes omitted). In *Helicopteros*, the Court found the exercise of general jurisdiction over a defendant corporation inappropriate notwithstanding the fact that it had considerable contacts with the forum state. The defendant had sent its chief executive officer to the forum for a contract negotiation, purchased helicopters, equipment and training services from the forum, accepted checks drawn at a bank within the forum and sent personnel to the forum for training. 466 U.S. at 416. Nevertheless, the Supreme Court held that the defendant's contacts with the forum did not "constitute the kind of systematic general business contacts" necessary "to satisfy the Due Process Clause of the Fourteenth Amendment." *Id.* at 418–19.

5. In *Viam*, the Federal Circuit articulated this test, listing the *Burger King* factors as follows:

> The test of unreasonableness is a multifaceted balancing test that weighs any burdens on the defendant against various countervailing considerations, including plaintiff's interest in a convenient forum and the forum state's interest in resolving controversies flowing from in-state events.
>
> The inquiry under this test includes a balancing of (1) the burden on the defendant; (2) the interests of the forum state; (3) the plaintiff's interest in obtaining relief; (4) the interstate judicial system's interest in obtaining the most efficient resolution of controversies; and (5) the interest of the states in furthering their social policies.

84 F.3d at 429 (citation omitted).

6. 271(e)(2)(A) provides: "It shall be an act of infringement to submit an application under section 505(j) of the Federal Food, Drug and Cosmetic Act or described in section 505(b)(2) of such Act for a drug claimed in a patent or the use of which is claimed in a patent."

7. The defendant's agent spent "less than 5% of his time ... in connection with the sale of company's products for delivery within the District." *Id.* at 143.

8. Two years after the *en banc* decision in *Environmental Research,* a panel of the D.C. Court of Appeals appeared to narrow the exception to only those cases implicating a party's assertion of First Amendment rights. *Rose v. Silver*, 394 A.2d 1368, 1374 (D.C.App.1978), *en banc hearing denied*, 398 A.2d 787 (D.C.App. 1979). The court stated that "the First Amendment provides the only principled basis for exempting a foreign defendant from suit in the District of Columbia, when its contacts are covered by the long-arm statute and are sufficient to withstand a traditional due process attack." 394 A.2d at 1374. In *Naartex Consulting Corp. v. Watt,* 722 F.2d 779, 786 (D.C.Cir. 1983), the D.C. Court of Appeals followed *Environmental Research* and expressed doubt as to whether the *Rose* panel could overturn that *en banc* decision.

9. The District Court of Maryland recognizes an exception to the government contacts exception for fraudulent representations to government agencies. *Nichols v. G.D. Searle & Co.*, 783 F.Supp. 233, 243 (D.Md.1992), *aff'd*, 991 F.2d

1195 (4th Cir.1993). "Where there are 'credible and specific allegations in the district court that the [defendant] had used the proceedings as an instrumentality of the alleged fraud,' the government contacts rule does not bar a court from finding jurisdiction," noting that "there is no constitutional value in false statements of fact." *Id.* at 243 n.11, *quoting Naartex*, 722 F.2d at 787. However, to protect Maryland courts from "an unrelenting wave of litigation ... the Court will only permit the use of this fraud exception where plaintiffs have not merely alleged fraud but have established a prima facie case of fraud." *Id.*

10. Judge Rich died on June 9, 1999, two months after the decision was handed down.

11. *But see Burger King*, 471 U.S. at 472 (holding that a forum may assert specific jurisdiction over an out-of-state defendant where the defendant has "purposefully directed" its activities at forum residents and the litigation "arises out of or relates to those activities"). It is arguable that patent infringement under § 271(e)(2)(A) arises out of filing the ANDA.

12. *See, e.g., Viam Corp. v. Iowa Export–Import Trading Co.*, 84 F.3d 424, 429 (Fed.Cir.1996).

J.   Governmental Immunity

1.   Federal Government—28 U.S.C. § 1498

When the United States government makes or uses a patented invention, the patent owner's *exclusive* remedy resides in the United States Court of Federal Claims, not federal district court. According to 28 U.S.C. § 1498(a):

> Whenever an invention described in and covered by a patent of the United States is used or manufactured by or for the United States without license of the owner thereof or lawful right to use or manufacture the same, the owner's remedy shall be by action against the United States in the United States Court of Federal Claims for the recovery of his reasonable and entire compensation for such use and manufacture.

> * * *

> For the purpose of this section, the use or manufacture of an invention described in and covered by a patent of the United States by a contractor, a subcontractor, or any person, firm, or corporation for the Government and with the authorization or consent of the Government, shall be construed as use or manufacture for the United States.

Some courts have suggested that section 1498 is actually based on taking jurisprudence, wherein the government is exercising its power of eminent domain. For example, *W.L. Gore & Associates, Inc. v. Garlock, Inc.*, 842 F.2d 1275, 1283 (Fed.Cir.1988), the Federal Circuit stated that "[t]he patentee takes his patent from the United States subject to the government's eminent domain rights to obtain what it needs from manufacturers and to use the same. The government has graciously consented, in the same statute, to be sued in the Claims Court for reasonable and entire compensation, for what would be infringement if by a private person." *See also, Chew v. California*, 893 F.2d 331, 336 (Fed.Cir.1990).

The second paragraph of § 1498(a) states that the "use or manufacture" of a patented invention by an entity "with the authorization and consent of the Government shall be construed as use or manufacture for the United States." This requirement that the use or manufacture have the "authorization and consent" of the government depends on whether the infringement relates "(1) to a product manufactured for actual delivery to the United States or (2) to a product, machine, or process used by a contractor or subcontractor doing work for the United States." DONALD S. CHISUM, V CHISUM ON PATENTS § 16.06[3][a] (1997). In the first situation, courts have held that acceptance by the government of a patented product manufactured by a contractor or subcontractor invokes § 1498. In *TVI Energy Corp. v. Blane*, 806 F.2d 1057 (Fed.Cir.1986), the Federal Circuit held that a demonstration of a product pursuant to a Government bidding procurement scheme was covered by § 1498, despite the fact that the government had not issued an "authorization and consent" letter. According to the court:

> Authorization or consent by the Government can be expressed in a form other than such a letter.... In proper circumstances, Government authorization can be implied. In this case, for instance, Government authorization was expressed by the specific requirement that [the defendant] demonstrate, under the guidelines of the bidding procedure, the allegedly infringing targets.... The mere fact that the Government specifications for the targets did not absolutely require [the defendant] to infringe [the] patent at that demonstration does not extinguish the Government's consent. To limit the scope of § 1498 only to instances where the Government requires by specification that a supplier infringe another's patent would defeat the Congressional intent to allow the Government to procure whatever it wished regardless of possible patent infringement. The coverage of § 1498 should be broad so as not to limit the Government's freedom in procurement by considerations of private patent infringement.

Id. at 1059.

> The second situation poses greater difficulties:

> [t]he standard clause in United States Government supply contracts is limited, extending authorization and consent only where the invention is "utilized in the machinery, tools, or methods the use of which necessarily results from compliance by the Contractor or the using subcontractor with (a) specifications or written provisions now or hereafter forming a part of this contract, or (b) specific written instructions given by the Contracting Officer directing the manner of performance." On the other hand, in contracts for research and development, the government extends "greater latitude," extending authorization and consent for "all use and manufacture of any patented invention in the performance" of the contract.

DONALD S. CHISUM, V CHISUM ON PATENTS § 16.06[3][c] (1997).

Some think that in *Zoltek Corp. v. United States*, 442 F.3d 1345 (Fed.Cir.2006), the Federal Circuit may have limited the ability for patentees to enforce their rights against the Federal Government. Although the specific holding of the case may have only modest impact, the language of the court's *per curiam* opinion could suggest a broader impact that could be troubling both as a matter of theory and practice. The *per curiam* opinion described the case as follows:

> The United States appeals the order of the Court of Federal Claims holding that it could assert jurisdiction over Zoltek Corporation's ("Zoltek")'s patent infringement allegations by treating the action as a Fifth

Amendment taking under the Tucker Act. Zoltek cross-appeals the trial court's ruling that 28 U.S.C. § 1498(c) bars this action as arising in a foreign country. The Court of Federal Claims certified the rulings under 28 U.S.C. § 1292(d)(2), and this court accepted jurisdiction. *See Zoltek Corp. v. United States*, No. 96–166 C (Fed.Cl. Feb. 20, 2004) (certification); *see generally Zoltek Corp. v. United States*, 58 Fed.Cl. 688 (2003), *Zoltek Corp. v. United States*, 51 Fed.Cl. 829 (2002).

We conclude that under § 1498, the United States is liable for the use of a method patent only when it practices every step of the claimed method in the United States. The court therefore affirms the trial court's conclusion that § 1498 bars Zoltek's claims. However, we reverse the trial court's determination that it had jurisdiction under the Tucker Act based on a violation of the Fifth Amendment.

The more troubling text appears elsewhere in the *per curiam* opinion, where it suggests that patents can't be subject to a takings analysis because they are merely "a creature of federal law." 442 F.3d at 1352. However, a close look at the set of opinions issued in that case, as a set, suggests that the reach of the *per curiam* decision may not be so broad. None of the three judges on the panel signed onto the court's opinion, which is why it was issued *per curiam*. This suggests that the only aspect of the court's opinion on which the majority could agree was the outcome. And the outcome of non-infringement in that case may simply have rested on the more mundane aspect of the case: that some of the steps of the claimed process were carried on outside of the United States, in a foreign country. Each of the three judges wrote separately, Judge Plager in dissent, and Judges Gajarsa and Dyk in concurrence. Judge Plager presented a Constitutional analysis, explaining why the Court of Federal Claims had jurisdiction under the Constitution and the Tucker Act, and also disagreeing with the interpretation of the infringement issue. *See* 442 F.3d 1345, 1370–85 (Plager, S.J., dissenting). Judges Gajarsa and Dyk were in agreement that there was no infringement because of the offshore practice, with Judge Gajarsa specifically pointing out that "even if one assumes for the sake of argument" that Judge Plager was correct on the Constitutional issue, the patentee loses. *See* 442 F.3d 1345, 1353–67 (Gajarsa, J., concurring). Judge Dyk also directly disagreed with Judge Plager on the Fifth Amendment. *See* 442 F.3d 1345, 1367–70 (Dyk, J., concurring). For a discussion of the problems that could flow from a broader reading of *Zoltek*, see Adam Mossoff, *How The "New GM" Can Steal From Toyota*, 13 GREEN BAG 2d 399 (2010). For a more general discussion of patent takings and other approaches to compulsory licensing of patents, see Richard A. Epstein and F. Scott Kieff, *Questioning the Frequency and Wisdom of Compulsory Licensing for Pharmaceutical Patents*, 78 U. CHI. L. REV. ___ (2011).

2. STATE GOVERNMENT—11TH AMENDMENT AND § 271(h)

Generally speaking, state governments and their agencies are subject to the patent law. However, Eleventh Amendment immunity issues present significant impediments to an infringement suit. The 11th Amendment states:

> The Judicial power of the United States shall not be construed to extend to any suit in law or equity, commenced or prosecuted against one of the

United States by Citizens of another State, or by Citizens or Subjects of any Foreign State.

In 1992, Congress enacted the Patent and Plant Variety Protection Remedy Clarification Act (Patent Remedy Act). The Patent Remedy Act added § 271(h) and abrogated state immunity as it relates to the patent law. Four years later, however, the Supreme Court decided *Seminole Tribe of Florida v. Florida*, 517 U.S. 44, 116 S.Ct. 1114 (1996), which, although not dealing with intellectual property, casts the constitutionality of the 1992 amendment into question. In *Seminole Tribe*, the Court addressed the Indian Gaming Regulatory Act, which was "passed by Congress under the Indian Commerce Clause [which, according to the Court, is not distinguishable from the Interstate Commerce Clause], U.S. Const., Art I, § 8, cl. 3." The Act "imposes upon the States a duty to negotiate in good faith with an Indian tribe toward the formation of a compact, . . . and authorizes a tribe to bring suit in federal court against a State in order to compel performance of that duty." The Court held that Congress' attempt to abrogate the state of Florida's immunity was not passed pursuant to a valid exercise of Congressional power, and was therefore unconstitutional. According to the Supreme Court, the only legitimate avenue available to Congress in abrogating State immunity was the Fourteenth Amendment:

> Even when the Constitution vests in Congress complete law-making authority over a particular area, the Eleventh Amendment prevents congressional authorization of suits by private parties against unconsenting States. . . . The Eleventh Amendment restricts the judicial power under Article III, and Article I cannot be used to circumvent the constitutional limitations placed upon federal jurisdiction.

Id. at 1131–32.

Thus, for our purposes, the question is: Was the 1992 Patent Remedy Act, which abrogated state immunity, passed pursuant to the Fourteenth Amendment or some Article I power? If the former, one can argue that the Patent Remedy Act is constitutional; if the latter, *Seminole Tribe* dictates that the Act is *un*constitutional.

The Federal Circuit addressed this issue in *College Savings Bank v. Florida Prepaid Postsecondary Ed. Expense Bd.*, 148 F.3d 1343 (Fed.Cir. 1998), and found that Congress intended to abrogate state immunity for patent infringement suits. However, the Supreme Court, in a 5–4 decision, overruled the Federal Circuit, and held the Patent Remedy Act unconstitutional under the 11th Amendment. *See Florida Prepaid Postsecondary Ed. Expense Bd. v. College Savings Bank*, 527 U.S. 627 (1999).

NOTE ON 11TH AMENDMENT IMMUNITY AND BIOTECHNOLOGY[50]

What do you think would happen to the domestic biotechnology industry if it were decided that 11th Amendment immunity applied to patent cases? To help

---

50. The material in this Note is adapted from F. Scott Kieff, *Patent Harmonization and the U.S. Biotechnology Industry* (Position Statement of the Association of Biotechnology Companies Submitted to the Congressional Biotechnology Caucus and the House Subcommittee on Intellectual Property) (1992).

answer this question, let us begin by reviewing some important features of this industry itself.

Biotechnology, unlike many other successful technology fields, was born out of and remains anchored in the laboratories of American research universities. To be sure, significant evidence suggests that university scientists would invent and discover without any patent protection whatsoever, as long as they earned an adequate salary[51] and received adequate funding for their research. Indeed, the United States' lead in biotechnology is due in large part to strong government support for basic research in biological and biomedical sciences.[52] Yet, while the United States has had the largest commitment to basic research in the biological sciences worldwide, in both absolute and relative amounts, the vast majority of Federal support in this area goes to university scientists conducting basic research, whereas applied research and development has always been considered the responsibility of industry.[53]

Moreover, targeting basic research in biotechnology alone, cannot assure increased competitiveness. The United States must also maintain the industrial capacity to convert this basic research into products.[54] The current "choke-point" is the ability of start-up companies to raise the money necessary to move forward into development, testing, and marketing of products, the most expensive parts of the process.[55] The pharmaceutical industry, in particular, is

> a global, competitive, high-risk, and high-return industry that develops and sells innovative, high-value-added products in a tightly regulated process. . . . Barriers to entry in the pharmaceutical industry related to R & D are not so much a result of the demands for resources to conduct research, but rather, for development.[56]

Funding for this development is provided in large part by the United States private sector venture capital pool; a pool which is unmatched in the world.[57] This reliance on the private sector has been compounded by the decline in the growth of Federal funding for biotechnology during the 1970s and 80s, which induced universities to turn to the private sector for additional basic research support.

Recognizing the importance of innovation in biotechnology, the Federal government passed laws to further encourage the privatization of research. Non-profit organizations and small businesses are now permitted to retain title to inventions arising out of government research.[58] In addition, governmental agencies are now authorized to form consortia with private concerns.[59]

However, the most striking institution to be created as a result of the biotechnology boom is the startup company formed by entrepreneurs and university

---

51. The actual amount of that salary would depend on the amount of non monetary reward derived from the job (personal satisfaction, ego, etc.) and the amount of monetary and non monetary rewards available from other professions. *Ex ante* career choices might also include the amount of school (work and tuition) required to become a scientist as compared with the requirements of other professions.

52. Office of Technology Assessment, *Biotechnology in a Global Economy*, 89 (OTA–BA–495 U.S. Government Printing Office, Washington, DC, 1991).

53. *Id.*, at 249.

54. *Id.*, at 22.

55. *Id.*, at 67.

56. *Id.*, at 81–83.

57. *Id.*, at 67.

58. *See* 35 U.S.C. § 202 (1991).

59. *See,* 35 U.S.C. § 207 (1991).

professors and funded by venture capital. Biotechnology was developed almost entirely in academia and in no other industry have university scientists—acting as scientist, manager, or director—played such all encompassing roles in startup companies.

In fact, the university association with industry in the field of biotechnology is not limited to the start up company. Nearly half of all biotechnology firms support research in universities through the use of university-industry research relationships (UIRRs).[60] UIRRs account for approximately one fifth of all biotechnology R & D funds available to universities, as compared with the average of three to four percent for all technological areas combined.[61] Industry therefore provides a much larger proportion of the university budget for R & D in biotechnology than in most other fields.[62] In addition, twenty percent of non Fortune–500 companies involved in UIRRs reported funding faculty who held significant equity in the company.[63] The UIRR has also been a great success for the investing company, yielding over four times as many patent applications as company laboratories.[64] Importantly, for any 11th Amendment analysis, many of the university components in UIRRs are state universities.[65]

Some scholars argue that the UIRR has seriously injured the university scientific community, the birthplace of the biotechnology industry.[66] Commercialization of biotechnology is argued to be an affront to the very norms of science. Most importantly among these norms are communism, disinterestedness, and organized skepticism.[67] Communism refers to the idea that science should be pursued for the benefit of societal enlightenment. A corollary of this norm is that the widespread publication and use of research results will accelerate scientific progress. Disinterestedness suggests that scientists should seek objective truths about nature rather than personal gain. Organized skepticism means that scientific claims are to be scrutinized by others in the field. A corollary of this last norm is that such scrutiny requires the complete disclosure of new claims to putative discoveries in order to facilitate the access needed for peer review. An additional concern of the scientific community is that commercial interests will cause a change in the direction of research paths and a shirking of academic duties.[68]

In contradistinction, however, as argued by Dr. William Raub of the National Institutes of Health, "many biological scientists, perhaps most, regard the patent process as a means of institutionalized secrecy, whereas it is in fact a time-tested way to assure broad and ready access to proprietary information."[69] Furthermore,

---

60. David Blumenthal, *et. al.*, *Industrial Support of University Research in Biotechnology*, 231 SCIENCE 242, 244.

61. *Id.*

62. *Id.*

63. *Id.*

64. *Id.*

65. Even private universities may be considered in certain circumstances to be instrumentalities of the states, or state actors, where the financial or administrative ties to the state are sufficient.

66. This material is reviewed in Rebecca S. Eisenberg, *Property Rights and the Norms of Science in Biotechnology Research*, 97 YALE L. J. 178 (1987).

67. *Id.* at 183 (citing ROBERT MERTON, *The Normative Structure of Science, in* THE SOCIOLOGY OF SCIENCE (1973)).

68. David Blumenthal *et al.*, *University–Industry Research Relationships in Biotechnology: Implications for the University*, 232 Science 1361 (1986).

69. *Commercialization of Academic Biomedical Research: Hearings before the Subcomm. on Investigations and Oversight and the Subcomm. on Science, Research and Technology of the*

the universities benefit directly from the UIRRs. Twenty three percent of university faculty in the field of biotechnology receive some industry support.[70] Faculty with industry support were more than twice as likely to be involved in biotechnology research that led to patents, as compared with faculty without such support.[71] Moreover, despite concerns to the contrary, studies reveal that "[c]ontrolling for other factors, faculty ... who were receiving industry support tended to publish more, patent more, earn more, serve in more administrative roles, and teach just as much as faculty without industry funds."[72] While the most obvious explanation for this result is that industry chooses to support only the most successful faculty, the study does reveal that the scientific and academic norms are not sacrificed by the faculty member's involvement with the UIRR.

So, the UIRR appears to be a good thing for the United States: our industry, investors, universities, and research agendas, all seem to benefit. We must ask, then, how the UIRR will be affected by a decision to apply 11th Amendment immunity in patent cases. Issues arise on both sides of the potential lawsuits. Who is the patentee in the UIRR: the state university faculty member, or the private corporate partner? Who is the infringer: some other state university faculty member, or her private corporate partner? If the UIRR signals such a blurring of the distinction between state and private actors, then how will these relationships affect the 11th Amendment analysis? And how will the 11th Amendment analysis affect these relationships?

House Comm. on Science and Technology, 97th Cong. 1st Sess. (1981) (testimony of Dr. William Raub) *cited in* Eisenberg, *supra* note 20, at 184.

70. Blumenthal, *supra* note 11, at 1362.

71. *Id.* at 1363.

72. *Id.* at 1364.

CHAPTER TEN

REMEDIES

> From the character of the right of the patentee we may judge of his remedies.
>
> —Justice McKenna[1]

> It is of course possible to imagine an invention for a machine, or composition, or process, which is a complete innovation, emerging, full grown, like Athene, from its "parent's" head. It would then be easy to say that profits were to be attributed wholly to the invention. Such inventions are however mythological. All have a background in the past, and are additions to the existing stock of knowledge which infringing articles embody along with the invention. It is generally impossible to allocate quantitatively the shares of the old and the new, and the party on whom that duty falls, will usually lose. If the patentee is required to assess the contribution of his invention to profits, he will find it impossible; vice versa, if this is demanded of the infringer. The burden of proof in such cases is the key to the result.
>
> —Judge Learned Hand[2]

INTRODUCTION

Infringement is the most common violation of a patent owner's rights under the patent laws.[3] Remedies for infringement are designed to accomplish two goals. One infringement-remedy goal is to compensate for past infringement. The remedies that are designed to accomplish this goal are money damages and interest. The other infringement-remedy goal is to prevent future infringement. The remedies that are designed to accomplish this goal are injunctions, punitive damages, and attorney fees.

In an ideal world, lawmakers and judges would be able to craft remedies that do exactly what is necessary to compensate fully for all past infringement and to prevent all future infringement, but that go no

---

1. *Continental Paper Bag Co. v. Eastern Paper Bag Co.*, 210 U.S. 405, 430 (1908).

2. *Cincinnati Car Co. v. New York Rapid Transit Corp.*, 66 F.2d 592, 593 (2d Cir.1933).

3. Infringement is a violation of a patent owner's right to exclude others from doing specific acts. *See* 35 U.S.C. §§ 154 (exclusive rights) and 271 (infringement). Since 2000, patent law also gives patent owner's certain provisional rights. 35 U.S.C. § 154(d). The remedy for a provisional-rights violation is a reasonable royalty. *Id.* Additionally, patent law provides patent owners with numerous rights against the Patent Office. For example, the patent owner has the right to reissue the patent under certain circumstances and the right to disclaim a portion of the patent term. 35 U.S.C. §§ 251 and 253, respectively. To the extent that rights like these are violated, the wrong is done by the Patent Office and the remedy is specific performance.

further. When studying each of the compensation and prevention remedies that exist today, ask yourself: How close are we to the ideal? If you believe that the ideal has not been obtained, ask yourself: How can it be improved? To help you think about this more basic question, perhaps begin by asking, Is the law today workable and does in go too far in favoring either the patent owner or the infringer?

STATUTORY PROVISION—35 U.S.C. § 284

A.   REMEDIES THAT COMPENSATE FOR PAST INFRINGEMENT: MONEY & INTEREST

There are two remedies that compensate for past infringement. The first remedy is money damages, which are awarded to compensate for the damage that the patent owner suffered as a result of the infringement. The second remedy is interest, which is awarded to compensate for the delay in obtaining payment for past infringement. While compensatory remedies can have an effect on preventing infringement (i.e., the possibility of high awards may deter future infringement and the possibility of low awards may encourage infringement), the only intended purpose of these remedies is to compensate fully for past infringement.

1.   MONEY DAMAGES

The law relating to money damages in patent cases is easy to state. It is not easy to apply, though. Additionally, it is not entirely logical. To understand this body of law, it is best to start at the beginning.

In the beginning, compensatory remedies were very general. Specifically, in 1790, infringers simply were required to pay damages assessed by a jury. In 1793, the damage award was changed so that the infringer had to pay a sum at least three times the price at which the patent owner licensed. Because some patent owners sold instead of licensed, this remedy was inadequate. So, in 1800, the law was changed so that an infringer had to pay at least three times the actual damages sustained by the patent owner. 7 DONALD S. CHISUM, CHISUM ON PATENTS § 20.02 (2003). *See generally* Roger D. Blair & Thomas F. Cotter, *Rethinking Patent Damages*, 10 TEX. INTELL. PROP. L.J. 1, 5–7 (2001).

In 1836, Congress dropped the requirement for trebling damages, and a patent owner's compensatory remedy was recovering only his actual damages. At this time, however, a patent owner had an alternative monetary remedy, i.e., he could bring a suit in a court of equity to disgorge the profits of the infringer. A problem with these two monetary remedies, though, was that each was available in mutually exclusive forums. Specifically, a patent owner's actual damages could only be recovered in a court of law and an infringer's profits could only be disgorged by a court of equity.[4]

---

4. A bigger problem was that an injunction could only be obtained from a court of equity. Thus, a patent owner who wanted to obtain injunctive relief had to settle for the infringer's profits as the compensatory relief.

Thus, at that time, a patent owner could obtain as compensatory relief his damages or the infringer's profits, but this left patentees having to predict which might be greater. Congress solved this problem in 1870.

In 1870, Congress changed the damages law and allowed a patent owner to recover both his damages and the infringer's profits in a court of equity. Courts interpreted this change as allowing recovery of the greater of the two amounts, not two awards. A problem that remained, however, was that a patent owner who could not establish equity jurisdiction and who had not suffered economic loss because of the infringement, could recover only nominal damages. In 1922, consistent with existing case law, Congress allowed a patent owner who could not prove his damages or an infringer's profits to be awarded a "reasonable sum." *Id.*

In 1946, Congress again changed the law in a way that was later interpreted by the Supreme Court to eliminate effectively the patentee's right to obtain the infringer's profits. *See Aro Mfg. Co. v. Convertible Top Replacement Co.*, 377 U.S. 476, 505–507 (1964) (interpreting the Act of 1946 §§ 67 and 70). Nevertheless, the infringer's profits may be at least relevant to a damages calculation under the present law. *See Kori Corp. v. Wilco Marsh Buggies & Draglines, Inc.*, 761 F.2d 649, 653–56 (Fed.Cir. 1985).

The present damages provisions are part of the over-all statutory framework of the 1952 Patent Act. The central damages provision of the '52 Act, 35 U.S.C. § 284, essentially allows the patentee to recover either its own lost profits or no less than a reasonable royalty, as discussed in more detail below.

The law relating to patent damages has changed considerably over time. It continues to change. For at least the past decade and probably longer, the law of patent remedies, especially compensatory damages, has been considerably influenced by economic principles and economic justifications. The scholarly literature in this area raises many fundamental questions about the very nature of patent damages. The highwater mark to date of the influence of economic analysis on compensatory patent remedies is *Grain Processing Corp. v. American Maize–Prods. Co.*, 185 F.3d 1341 (Fed.Cir.1999), which is presented later in this section.

a. AN OVERVIEW OF MONEY DAMAGES

Money damages awarded under Section 284 are traditionally measured in two ways. First, if the patent owner and the infringer compete in the same market, the patent owner's lost profits are traditionally the appropriate measure of damages. Second, if the patent owner does not compete with the infringer or if the patent owner cannot sufficiently prove lost profits, the appropriate measure of damages is a royalty (either established or hypothetical). *See Del Mar Avionics, Inc. v. Quinton Instrument Co.*, 836 F.2d 1320, 1326–28 (Fed.Cir.1987); *Polaroid Corp. v. Eastman Kodak Co.*, 16 U.S.P.Q.2d 1481, 1484 (D.Mass.1990). *See generally Comair Rotron, Inc. v. Nippon Densan Corp.*, 49 F.3d 1535, 1540–41 (Fed.Cir.1995) (Rader, J., concurring).

Under the patent statute, a patent owner is entitled to damages "adequate to compensate for the infringement." Absent a complete failure of proof, in no case may a patent owner be awarded less than a reasonable

royalty. *See Crystal Semiconductor Corp. v. TriTech Microelectronics Int'l, Inc.*, 246 F.3d 1336 (Fed.Cir.2001). A damages award may be mixed, i.e.,
lost profits may be the measure of damages on part of an infringer's sales and a reasonable royalty the measure of damages on the remainder. Examples of situations where a mixed award may be appropriate are where the patent owner chose to sell to some but not all of the infringer's customers, where the patent owner chose to compete in some but not all of an infringer's geographic sales territory, and where damages calculated by a reasonable royalty exceed lost profits in some, but not all years. *See* HERBERT F. SCHWARTZ, PATENT LAW AND PRACTICE (5th ed.), 226–27 (BNA 2003).

b. LOST PROFITS

Infringement may cause a patent owner to lose profits. Profits may have been lost because of infringement-induced lost sales, reduced prices, or increased costs. Determining whether infringement caused profits to be lost amounts to examining two basic questions. First, if there had been no infringement, what would the infringer's customers have done? Second, if there had been no infringement, what would the patent owner have done?

The modern legal framework for answering these two questions was set forth in *Panduit Corp. v. Stahlin Bros. Fibre Works*:

> To obtain as damages the profits on sales he would have made absent the infringement, i.e., the sales made by the infringer, a patent owner must prove: (1) demand for the patented product, (2) the absence of acceptable noninfringing substitutes, (3) his manufacturing and marketing capability to exploit the demand, and (4) the amount of the profit he would have made.

575 F.2d 1152, 1156 (6th Cir.1978). *Panduit* elements (1) and (2) relate to what the infringer's customer would have done. *Panduit* elements (3) and (4) relate to what the patent owner would have done.

In 1999, in *Grain Processing*, the Federal Circuit substantially altered the modern lost-profits analysis. Instead of examining how the patent owner was damaged by the infringement that actually occurred, the Federal Circuit sought to determine the market value of the right to exclude in a hypothetical world where the infringement never happened. In essence, *Grain Processing* added a third question to lost-profits analysis: If there had been no infringement, what else would the infringer have done?

i. What Would the Infringer's Customers Have Done?

BIC Leisure Products, Inc. v. Windsurfing International, Inc.

1 F.3d 1214 (Fed.Cir.1993).

■ Before NIES, CHIEF JUDGE, SMITH, SENIOR CIRCUIT JUDGE, and RADER, CIRCUIT JUDGE.

■ RADER, CIRCUIT JUDGE.

* * *

Background

BIC infringed Windsurfing's Reissue Patent No. 31,167, which covers sailboards. Windsurfing seeks damages from BIC for the period from

March 8, 1983 (the reissue date of Windsurfing's patent) to September 30, 1985 (the date the district court enjoined BIC from further infringement).

Windsurfing primarily manufactured and marketed sailboards embodying its patented invention for the "One–Design Class." The One–Design Class refers to a uniform competition class as defined by a sailboarding association. A sailboarding association sponsors regattas in which sailboarders compete against each other on boards of uniform weight and shape. Most of Windsurfing's sailboards fit within the weight and shape requirements for the One–Design competition class.

One–Design sailboards lost favor with most sailboarders, however, with the advent of faster, more maneuverable, and more versatile "funboards" and "wave boards." These newer boards had a lighter hull design. Despite the rising popularity of these newer boards in the early 1980s, Windsurfing decided to continue to concentrate on its One–Design boards.

Windsurfing licensed its patented technology extensively.... All of the U.S. licensees, as well as some of the European licensees, competed against Windsurfing in the United States.

.... Windsurfing controlled 29.2% of the sailboard market in 1983, 25.6% in 1984, and 13.6% in 1985.

BIC began selling sailboards in 1981.... BIC did not sell sailboards with the One Design hull form. Rather, BIC's sailboards differed from Windsurfing's products. BIC instead sold boards at the lower end of the market's price spectrum, reflecting its decision to target the entry level segment of the sailboard market.

In comparison, Windsurfing priced its sailboards at the upper end of the sailboard price spectrum. During the years covered by the damages period, U.S. sailboard dealers charged the following average prices:

1983		1984		1985	
Marker	837	Brockhaus	753	Mistral	804
Brockhaus	753	Mistral	741	Marker	774
Mistral	750	Marker	674	Brockhaus	750
Windsurfing	670	SAN/Romney	623	SAN	623
SAN/Romney	643	Windsurfing	589	Schutz	575
Alpha	574	Schutz	575	Windsurfing	571
Wayler	550	HiFly	527	HiFly	570
HiFly	518	Wayler	500	Wayler	500
SAN/Schaeffer	441	Alpha	450	O'Brien	477
O'Brien	436	O'Brien	412	Alpha	450
BIC	407	SAN/Schaeffer	388	AMF Inc.	380
AMF Inc.	377	AMF Inc.	384	BIC	312
Ten Cate	366	BIC	335	Ten Cate	253
AMF Mares	244	Ten Cate	299	AMF Mares	244
		AMF Mares	234		

* * *

The district court applied the *Panduit* test to determine whether Windsurfing lost profits. BIC I, 761 F. Supp. at 1034. The district court required Windsurfing to show (1) a demand for the patented product, (2) the absence of acceptable noninfringing substitutes, (3) its capacity to exploit the demand, and (4) the profits lost due to the infringement. *See Panduit Corp. v. Stahlin Bros. Fibre Works, Inc.*, 575 F.2d 1152, 1156 (6th Cir.1978). The district court modified the *Panduit* test by presuming that Windsurfing would have captured a share of BIC's sales in proportion to Windsurfing's share of the sailboard market. *BIC I*, 761 F. Supp. at 1035–37. Relying on *State Industries, Inc. v. Mor–Flo Industries, Inc.*, 883 F.2d 1573, 12 USPQ 1026 (Fed.Cir.1989), *cert. denied*, 493 U.S. 1022, 110 S.Ct. 725, 107 L.Ed. 2d 744 (1990), the district court awarded Windsurfing lost profits based upon its pro rata percentage of BIC's sales for each year of the damages period. *BIC I*, 761 F. Supp. at 1035–37, 1039. . . .

* * *

Discussion

* * *

To recover lost profits as opposed to royalties, a patent owner must prove a causal relation between the infringement and its loss of profits. The patent owner must show that "but for" the infringement, it would have made the infringer's sales. *Water Technologies Corp. v. Calco Ltd.*, 850 F.2d 660, 671, 7 USPQ2d 1097, 1106 (Fed.Cir.), cert. denied, 488 U.S. 968, 109 S.Ct. 498, 102 L.Ed.2d 534 (1988). An award of lost profits may not be speculative. Rather the patent owner must show a reasonable probability that, absent the infringement, it would have made the infringer's sales. *Id.* at 671.

The district court clearly erred by failing to apply the "but for" test before awarding lost profits. The record in this case does not evince a reasonable probability that Windsurfing would have made its pro rata share of BIC's sales had BIC not been in the market. During the period in question, at least fourteen competitors vied for sales in the sailboard market with prices ranging from $234 to $837. BIC's boards sold for $312 to $407; Windsurfing's boards sold for $571 to $670—a difference of over $250 or about 60–80% above BIC's selling range. Because Windsurfing concentrated on the One Design class hull form and BIC did not, Windsurfing's boards differed fundamentally from BIC's boards.

The record contains uncontradicted evidence that demand for sailboards is relatively elastic. The record further contains uncontradicted evidence that the sailboard market's entry level, in which BIC competed, is particularly sensitive to price disparity. By purchasing BIC sailboards, BIC's customers demonstrated a preference for sailboards priced around $350, rather than One–Design boards priced around $600. Therefore, without BIC in the market, BIC's customers would have likely sought boards in the same price range.

Several manufacturers offered sailboards at prices much closer to BIC than to Windsurfing. At least two of Windsurfing's licensees, O'Brien and HiFly, sold boards resembling BIC's in the same distribution channels as BIC. On this record, Windsurfing did not show with reasonable probability that BIC's customers would have purchased from Windsurfing in proportion with Windsurfing's market share. The record shows rather that the vast majority of BIC's customers would have purchased boards from O'Brien or HiFly if BIC's boards had not been available. The district court erred in assuming that, without BIC in the market, its customers would have redistributed their purchases among all the remaining sailboards, including Windsurfing's One Design boards at a price $200 to $300 more than BIC's. *See Water Technologies*, 850 F.2d at 673 (district court erred in awarding lost profits when patent owner's product differed significantly from and cost significantly more than infringer's product); *cf. Dobson v. Dornan*, 118 U.S. 10, 17–18, 6 S.Ct. 946, 30 L.Ed. 63 (1886).

Moreover, Windsurfing's sales continued to decline after the district court enjoined BIC's infringement. This aspect of the record shows as well that Windsurfing did not capture its market share of the sales replacing BIC's market sales. According to the record, the principal beneficiary of BIC's exit appears to be O'Brien.

The district court applied the *Panduit* test for lost profits. Properly applied, the *Panduit* test is an acceptable, though not an exclusive, test for determining "but for" causation. *State Indus.*, 883 F.2d at 1577. The *Panduit* test, however, operates under an inherent assumption, not appropriate in this case, that the patent owner and the infringer sell products sufficiently similar to compete against each other in the same market segment. If the patentee's and the infringer's products are not substitutes in a competitive market, *Panduit*'s first two factors do not meet the "but for" test—a prerequisite for lost profits.

The first *Panduit* factor—demand for the patented product—presupposes that demand for the infringer's and patent owner's products is interchangeable. Under this assumption, evidence of sales of the infringing product may suffice to show *Panduit*'s first factor, "demand for the patented product." *E.g., Gyromat Corp. v. Champion Spark Plug Co.*, 735 F.2d 549, 552, 222 USPQ 4, 6 (Fed.Cir.1984). This analysis assumes that the patent owner and the infringer sell substantially the same product. In *Gyromat*, for instance, the patent owner's and the infringer's products were similar in price and product characteristics. *Gyromat*, 735 F.2d at 550–51, 553–54. If the products are not sufficiently similar to compete in the same market for the same customers, the infringer's customers would not necessarily transfer their demand to the patent owner's product in the absence of the infringer's product. In such circumstances, as in this case, the first *Panduit* factor does not operate to satisfy the elemental "but for" test.

Similarly, the second *Panduit* factor—absence of acceptable, noninfringing alternatives—presupposes that the patentee and the infringer sell substantially similar products in the same market. To be acceptable to the infringer's customers in an elastic market, the alleged alternative "must not have a disparately higher price than or possess characteristics significantly different from the patented product." *Kaufman Co. v. Lantech, Inc.*, 926 F.2d 1136, 1142, 17 USPQ2d 1828, 1832 (Fed.Cir.1991) (citing *Gyromat*, 735 F.2d at 553). In *Kaufman*, for instance, the patent owner and the infringer sold substantially the same product. *Kaufman*, 926 F.2d at 1143. Thus *Panduit*'s second factor, properly applied, ensures that any proffered alternative competes in the same market for the same customers as the infringer's product. *See Yarway Corp. v. Eur–Control USA, Inc.*, 775 F.2d 268, 276, 227 USPQ 352, 357 (Fed.Cir.1985) (alternative products did not possess features of the patent owner's and the infringer's products, nor compete in the same " 'special niche' or mini-market").

This court has held that a patent owner may satisfy the second *Panduit* element by substituting proof of its market share for proof of the absence of acceptable substitutes. *State Indus.*, 883 F.2d at 1578. This market share approach allows a patentee to recover lost profits, despite the presence of acceptable, noninfringing substitutes, because it nevertheless can prove with reasonable probability sales it would have made "but for" the infringement. Like *Panduit*'s second prong, however, this market share test also assumes that the patent owner and the infringer compete in the same market. In *State Industries*, for instance, the patent owner, infringer, and the other manufacturers sold substantially similar products. Id. at 1576. This similarity of products is necessary in order for market share proof to show correctly satisfaction of *Panduit*'s second factor.

The assumption underlying *Panduit*, *Gyromat*, and *State Industries* is not appropriate in this case. Instead, the record reveals that during the damages period the sailboard market was not a unitary market in which every competitor sold substantially the same product. Windsurfing and BIC sold different types of sailboards at different prices to different customers. As noted, their sailboards differed significantly in terms of price, product characteristics, and marketing channels. On the facts of this case, Windsurfing did not show "but for" causation under a correct application of *Panduit* or otherwise. The district court erred in awarding lost profits.

NOTES

1. *If There had Been No Infringement, What Would The Infringer's Customers Have Done?* For the patent owner to recover damages for lost profits due to lost sales, the patent owner must show a reasonable probability that one or more of the infringer's customers would have bought the patent owner's product. *Crystal Semiconductor Corp.*, 246 F.3d at 1353; *Fiskars, Inc. v. Hunt Mfg. Co.*, 221 F.3d 1318, 1324–25 (Fed.Cir.2000); *Livesay Window Co. v. Livesay Indus., Inc.*, 251 F.2d 469, 471–72 (5th Cir.1958). *See generally Pandrol USA, LP v. Airboss Ry. Prods., Inc.*, 320 F.3d 1354, 1368 (Fed.Cir.2003).

The best proof of what customers would have done is actual testimony from the customers. While such proof may be possible in some cases (e.g., where there were very few infringing sales), acceptable proof of what a customer would have done can be supplied in other ways. Two other ways to show what customers would have done are the *Panduit* way and the *State Industries* way, which are discussed below.

2. *The Panduit Way.* Although the Federal Circuit has approved the *Panduit* test as a method for proving lost profits, the court has noted that it is not necessarily the only way to prove lost profits. *Carella v. Starlight Archery & Pro Line Co.*, 804

F.2d 135, 141 (Fed.Cir.1986); *Gyromat Corp. v. Champion Spark Plug Co.*, 735 F.2d 549, 552 (Fed.Cir.1984). Nonetheless, as seen above in *BIC*, this standard is usually the starting point for any analysis of lost profits damage. *See also, e.g., Micro Chem., Inc. v. Lextron, Inc.*, 318 F.3d 1119, 1122 (Fed.Cir.2003); *Tate Access Floors, Inc. v. Maxcess Techs., Inc.*, 222 F.3d 958, 971 (Fed.Cir.2000); *Kaufman Co. v. Lantech, Inc.*, 926 F.2d 1136 (Fed.Cir.1991); *Standard Havens Prods., Inc. v. Gencor Indus., Inc.*, 953 F.2d 1360 (Fed.Cir.1991).

Pursuant to *Panduit*, acceptable proof that all of the infringer's customers would have bought the patent owner's products usually exists when the patent owner proves *Panduit* elements (1) and (2). In other words, the patent owner usually can show that all of the infringer's customers would have bought the patent owner's products by showing both demand for the patented product and the absence of acceptable noninfringing substitutes. As made clear above in *BIC*, though, one cannot use the *Panduit* way of proving what the infringer's customers would have done unless the patent owner and the infringer sell products that are sufficiently similar to compete in the same market segment. Regarding the relevant market, *see Micro Chem., Inc. v. Lextron, Inc.*, 318 F.3d 1119, 1124–25 (Fed.Cir.2003). *See also Polaroid Corp. v. Eastman Kodak Co.*, 16 U.S.P.Q.2d 1481, 1506–09 (D.Mass. 1990).

Regarding the first *Panduit* element (demand), significant sales—by either the patent owner or the infringer—are deemed compelling evidence of demand. The reasoning for this is simple: if there had been no demand for the patented product, it never would have sold in the marketplace. As a result of its low threshold of proof, evidence of demand for a product is seldom contested vigorously. *See* Herbert F. Schwartz *et al., Monetary Remedies in Patent Cases*, I–11 (UNIV. OF HOUSTON INTELLECTUAL PROPERTY PROGRAM 1993). Further, under *Panduit* the demand need not be based on the patented feature itself; demand for the product that includes the patented feature is sufficient. *Depuy Spine, Inc. v. Medtronic Sofamor Danek, Inc.*, 567 F.3d 1314, 1329–31 (Fed.Cir.2009).

Regarding the second *Panduit* element (absence of acceptable noninfringing substitutes), this element has evolved into a requirement that the patent owner show, "either that (1) the purchasers in the marketplace generally were willing to buy the patented product for its advantages, or (2) the specific purchasers of the infringing product purchased on that basis." *Standard Havens Prods., Inc.*, 953 F.2d at 1373. It is worth noting that the second *Panduit* element "accounts for more appellate litigation . . . than any other aspect of patent damages law." *See* Paul M. Janicke, *Contemporary Issues in Patent Damages*, 42 AM. U. L. REV. 691, 701 (1993).

The *Panduit* way of proving what the infringer's customers would have done if there had been no infringement is most useful to the patent owner when the patent owner and a single infringer are the only parties supplying products to the relevant market. Under such circumstances, the first two *Panduit* elements are presumed to be satisfied. In other words, it is reasonable to presume that when the patent owner and the infringer are the only suppliers, all of the infringer's customers would have bought from the patent owner if there had been no infringement. *See Micro Chem., Inc.*, 318 F.3d at 1124–25 (infringer can rebut the presumption by proving that it sold other noninfringing products).

The *Panduit* way of proving what the infringer's customers would have done if there had been no infringement is less useful to a patent owner when there are more than two parties supplying products to the relevant market. When there are more than two suppliers, the proofs concerning the absence of acceptable noninfringing substitutes can get quite complex. Imagine the difficulties that would arise for the parties and the court if the issue of infringement had to be decided for all the companies that sold products in the relevant market. A way to avoid the multi-party complexity problem was approved by the Federal Circuit in *State Indus., Inc. v. Mor–Flo Indus., Inc.*, 883 F.2d 1573 (Fed.Cir.1989).

3. *The State Industries Way.* State Industries (the patent owner) and Mor–Flo (the infringer) sold energy-efficient, residential gas water heaters. State Industries had 40% of the national market for that product and the remaining 60% of the market was divided between Mor–Flo and other companies. Instead of trying to prove that there were no acceptable noninfringing substitutes available in the relevant market (and, thus, that all of Mor–Flo's customers would have transferred their demand to State Industries if there had been no infringement), State Industries offered proof of its market share and claimed lost profits for only that percentage of Mor–Flo's sales. The Federal Circuit approved this approach to determining lost profits. *State Indus., Inc.*, 883 F.2d at 1573.

The justification for allowing a patent owner to substitute proof of its market share for proof of the absence of acceptable noninfringing substitutes is two-fold. First, given that the patent owner is not attempting to recover lost sales for 100% of the infringer's sales, it should not have to meet the *Panduit* standard that allows for recovery of 100% of the infringer's sales. Second, if the infringement had not occurred, it is not unreasonable to presume that the infringer's customers would have bought in a manner that mirrors national market behavior. Of course, as seen in *BIC*, market-share analysis cannot be used if the patent owner and the infringer do not sell products that are sufficiently similar to compete in the same market segment. *See also Crystal Semiconductor*, 246 F.3d at 1356, 1360.

Can the patent owner's market share be calculated with the infringer factored out of the market? For example, assume the patent owner has a 30% share of the relevant product market, the infringer has a 60% share, and two other sellers each have a 5% share. Pursuant to *State Indus.*, the patent owner could seek lost profits for 30% of the infringer's sales. Can the patent owner successfully argue that, even under a market-share analysis, it should be entitled to a higher percentage? Specifically, can the patent owner argue that, if there had been no infringement, 75% of the infringer's customers would have bought from the patent owner because that was the patent owner's share of the market if you take the infringer away? Does your opinion depend on the infringer's percentage of the market?

ii. *What Would the Patent Owner Have Done?*

Put simply, to recover damages for profits lost due to sales lost to the infringer, the patent owner must show that he or she would have been able to sell more products profitably. If the patent owner cannot show that it would have profitably sold to the infringer's customers, damages for lost profits are not appropriate.

Pursuant to *Panduit*, to recover damages for lost profits due to lost sales, the patent owner must sufficiently prove that it had the marketing and manufacturing capabilities to make the infringer's sales (the third *Panduit* element) and what its profits would have been it that situation (the fourth *Panduit* element).

The patent owner can meet the third *Panduit* element by proving that he or she possessed adequate manufacturing and marketing capability to meet the additional demand. If the patent owner did not have sufficient manufacturing capacity to meet the demand, proof of an ability to expand to meet the additional demand is adequate. *See Fonar Corp. v. General Elec. Co.*, 107 F.3d 1543, 1553 (Fed.Cir.1977); *Kearns v. Chrysler Corp.*, 32 F.3d 1541, 1551–52 (Fed.Cir.1994); *Bio–Rad Labs., Inc. v. Nicolet Instru-*

ment Corp., 739 F.2d 604, 616 (Fed.Cir.1984); *Yarway Corp. v. Eur–Control USA, Inc.*, 775 F.2d 268, 276–77 (Fed.Cir.1985); *Livesay Window Co.*, 251 F.2d at 473. For an in-depth discussion regarding proving marketing and production capability, *see Polaroid Corp.*, 16 U.S.P.Q.2d at 1510–25.

The patent owner can meet the fourth *Panduit* element with accounting and economic evidence of what its profits would have been if there had been no infringement. The simplest determination of how much the patent owner would have made is represented by the following equation:

LOST PROFITS = LOST SALES REVENUES − INCREMENTAL COSTS

The evidence required to determine lost profits can be quite complex. For example, there are potentially difficult issues relating to costs and pricing.

Incremental costs are those costs that would have increased with an increase in sales volume. *See generally Paper Converting Mach. Co. v. Magna–Graphics Corp.*, 745 F.2d 11, 22 (Fed.Cir.1984). Assume, for example, the patent owner make and sells plastic cups and would have sold twice as many cups if there had been no infringement. In this situation, the patent owner needs twice as much plastic to turn into cups, so the cost of plastic is an incremental cost. If the patent owner would have had to hire extra workers to produce the double volume, then the cost of direct labor is also an incremental cost. It is unlikely, however, that the patent owner's property tax would change. What do you think will happen to the patent owner's insurance costs, management costs, and sales costs?

If the patent owner does not seek to prove that he or she would have charged higher prices, lost sales revenue is usually determined by multiplying the patent owner's historical pre-infringement prices by the additional units that would have been sold if there had been no infringement. Preinfringement prices are generally used in calculating lost revenue so that the patent owner is not penalized because of price erosion caused by the infringer's unlawful competition. A patent owner might have been able to charge higher prices, though, if there had been no infringement. As the following case demonstrates, sufficiently proving those higher prices can be difficult.

Crystal Semiconductor Corporation v. TriTech Microelectronics Int'l, Inc.

246 F.3d 1336 (Fed.Cir.2001).

■ Before MAYER, CHIEF JUDGE, CLEVENGER, and RADER, CIRCUIT JUDGE.

■ RADER, CIRCUIT JUDGE.

* * *

Crystal, a subsidiary of Cirrus Logic, Inc., is the assignee of the '483,- '841, and '899 patents. All three patents involve analog-to-digital (A/D) converter technology. A/D converters convert sound (or analog input voltage information) into digital information and are commonly used in the compact disc burners or sound cards of personal computer (PC) systems.

* * *

By 1994, Apple and Intel/Windows PCs included audio systems with stereo sound. These audio systems used a CODEC—a combination A/D converter and digital-to-analog converter on a single chip. The CODEC transforms analog sound signals into digital form for processing on a PC, and also decodes the digital form back into analog sound so the user can hear it. Crystal incorporated it's a/D converter technology, covered by the three patents-in-suit, into CODEC audio chips, and began selling the chips in the audio PC market in 1991. . . .

TriTech, a company with facilities in Singapore and California, designs, manufactures, and sells audio chips. In 1994, TriTech began manufacturing sixteen-bit audio CODECs in Singapore and selling the chips worldwide. TriTech sold some of these chips to OPTi, which in turn sold these audio chips under the name "Model 931" to the U.S. PC market.

* * *

Price Erosion

Crystal alleged additional loss of profits on a theory of price erosion. The Supreme Court opened the door for price erosion damages in 1886: "Reduction of prices, and consequent loss of profits, enforced by infringing competition, is a proper ground for awarding of damages. The only question is as to the character and sufficiency of the evidence in the particular case." *Yale Lock Mfg. Co. v. Sargent*, 117 U.S. 536, 551, 6 S. Ct. 934, 29 L. Ed. 954 (1886). This court has since explained that "the question as to the character and sufficiency of the evidence" places the burden on the patentee to show that "but for" infringement, it would have sold its product at higher prices. See *BIC Leisure*, 1 F.3d at 1220. Moreover, in a credible economic analysis, the patentee cannot show entitlement to a higher price divorced from the effect of that higher price on demand for the product. In other words, the patentee must also present evidence of the (presumably reduced) amount of product the patentee would have sold at the higher price. Thus, in harmony with the Supreme Court's requirement in *Yale Lock*, the patentee's price erosion theory must account for the nature, or definition, of the market, similarities between any benchmark market and the market in which price erosion is alleged, and the effect of the hypothetically increased price on the likely number of sales at that price in that market.

To make out its theory of price erosion, Crystal used the expert testimony of Mr. Stephen Knowlton. Mr. Knowlton used a "benchmark methodology" to assess price erosion. Under this method, Mr. Knowlton selected a product similar to the patented product and compared the performance of that benchmark in a market free of infringement with the performance of the patented product in the market affected by infringement.

Mr. Knowlton selected as his benchmark Crystal's audio CODEC sales to the separate Apple Computer market. These CODECs featured technology similar to the chips Crystal sold in the IBM and IBM compatible (PC) market. However, neither TriTech nor OPTi sold any product to the Apple Market. In fact, the only manufacturers of CODECs for the Apple market were Crystal and National Semiconductor (National). These two companies worked jointly to develop CODECs for the Apple market and had an agreement with Apple to sell their CODECs on a pro rata basis. Specifically, Crystal supplied 70% of Apple's CODECs, and National 30%.

Mr. Knowlton next compared the performance of chips in the Apple market to nine of Crystal's products in the PC market between the years 1994 and 1998. Mr. Knowlton determined that CODECs sold in the benchmark market had an approximate 49.8% gross margin and decreased about 10% in price over the 17 quarters between 1994 and 1998. Mr. Knowlton then calculated a hypothetical selling price based on the Apple market gross margin for Crystal's products sold in the PC market, and, taking the 10% decrease in price to the Apple market into account, determined the average decrease in Crystal's PC audio CODEC selling prices from the hypothetical price. Mr. Knowlton attributed the entire decrease in Crystal's CODEC selling prices to TriTech/OPTi's infringement.

Mr. Knowlton's calculation resulted in an upper price erosion amount of $1.94 per unit and a lower amount of 89per unit. Multiplying the lower price erosion figure of 89per unit by the total CODEC units sold by Crystal between 1994 and 1998 would yield price erosion damages of $34,700,000. After deliberating, the jury returned with a verdict of $26,649,766 in price erosion damages.

In granting TriTech's JMOL motion to remit Crystal's damages, the district court found Mr. Knowlton's expert testimony, and particularly Mr. Knowlton's "benchmark methodology," unreliable. The court also held that even if Mr. Knowlton's expert opinion could be found reliable, the testimony did not provide "substantial evidence to support Crystal's claims for any price erosion at all." *Crystal*, slip op. at 11.

Upon review, this court affirms the trial court's judgment that Mr. Knowlton's methodology used an inappropriate benchmark, resulting in an inadequate foundation for Crystal's entire price erosion theory. The Apple market differed from the PC CODEC market in several important ways. Most importantly, the Apple CODEC market had characteristics of an oligopoly while the PC CODEC market was competitive.

The Apple CODEC market had only two suppliers—Crystal and National. These two suppliers cooperated with one another as demonstrated by their joint development of audio CODECs for the Apple market and their pro rata supply agreements with Apple. Their amicable relationship and desire to maintain profits, together with the fact that they sold nearly identical products, may well have created a less than competitive market for Crystal and National. The pro rata agreements also may have formed a barrier to expansion for National and made demand static, thereby further decreasing competition in the market. Additionally, as Mr. Knowlton pointed out, competitors such as Yamaha and ADI attempted to enter this market and failed. This evidence suggests the presence of barriers to entry into the Apple market. In sum, the Apple market hardly resembles a market with the same demand characteristics as the PC CODEC market in this case.

The PC market was much larger and more competitive than the Apple market. Crystal faced great price competition from many other CODEC manufacturers besides the alleged infringers. Indeed, the record shows that some of Crystal's competitors beat Crystal to the market with better integrated products. Additionally, the evidence shows that CODEC manufacturers felt great pressure from PC manufacturers to lower chip prices as the price for PCs themselves dropped. In other words, the record amply underscores the district court's determination that the Apple CODEC market did not resemble the PC market in demand characteristics. To repeat the colloquial phrase of the district court, Mr. Knowlton's use of the Apple CODEC market as a benchmark was like comparing apples and oranges. *Crystal*, slip op. at 13.

Crystal argues that TriTech's and OPTi's experts were unable to identify a better benchmark for comparison with the PC CODEC market. However, just because the marketplace does not supply another market for comparison, a poor benchmark cannot supply sufficient evidence to show the likely reaction of this PC market "but for" infringement. Economists can define hypothetical markets, derive a demand curve, and make price erosion approximations without relying on inapposite benchmarks. *See, e.g., Brooktree*, 977 F.2d at 1579–80 (price erosion calculated based on the selling price of the same product before the infringer entered the market); *Minnesota Mining & Mfg. Co., v. Johnson & Johnson Orthopaedics*, 976 F.2d 1559, 1579, 24 USPQ2d 1321, 1337 (Fed.Cir.1992) (price erosion was calculated based on pre-infringement prices because the patentee and infringer occupied almost the entire market).

Even if Mr. Knowlton's testimony and benchmark analysis were correct, the record does not contain sufficient evidence to show the reaction of the market if, "but for" infringement, Crystal would have tried to charge at least 89more per CODEC. All markets must respect the law of demand. *See* Paul A. Samuelson, *Economics* 53–55 (11th ed. 1980). According to the law of demand, consumers will almost always purchase fewer units of a product at a higher price than at a lower price, possibly substituting other products. *Id.* at 55. For example, if substitution of a product were impossible and the product were a necessity, elasticity of demand would be zero—meaning consumers would purchase the product at identical rates even when the price increases. This very rare type of market is called inelastic. *Id.* at 360. On the other side of the spectrum, if any price increase would eradicate demand, elasticity of demand would be infinite—meaning consumers would decline to purchase another single product if the price increases by any amount. This very rare type of market is called perfectly elastic. *Id.* Markets typically have an elasticity greater than zero and less than infinity.

Thus, in a competitive market, sales quantity reacts to price changes. The record shows that the PC CODEC market was competitive. Therefore, according to basic tenets of economics, because Crystal is in a competitive market, if Crystal raised prices, Crystal's sales would have fallen.

In *BIC*, this court held that the infringer's product and the patentee's product had to compete in the same market in order to establish "but for" causation for lost profits due to lost sales. 1 F.3d at 1220. Price erosion requires an analogous showing. To show causation with reliable evidence, a patentee must produce credible economic evidence to show the decrease in sales, if any, that would have occurred at the higher hypothetical price.

Most of the CODECs Crystal sold were priced at under $10 per unit. A minimum 89price increase would have translated to an approximate 10% increase in selling price. Because Crystal was competing in a competitive market, a 10% price increase would have likely caused customers to substitute the CODECs of other manufacturers for Crystal's CODECs. Crystal, however, presented no evidence of the elasticity of demand of the PC sound card CODEC market. Nor did Crystal make any estimates as to the number of sales it would have lost or kept had it increased its prices by 89per unit. Thus, Crystal did not make a showing of "but for" causation of price erosion.

At oral argument, Crystal's counsel asserted that because CODECs are relatively cheap parts in an overall expensive machine, an increase in price of the CODECs would not affect the number of units sold. This argument is unavailing. Although the proportion of consumer income spent on a good, or in this case the proportion of total PC cost attributed to a sound card CODEC, affects the price elasticity of demand, a low proportion does not nullify elasticity. *See* Ernest Gellhorn, *An Introduction to Antitrust Economics*, 1 DUKE L.J. 19–22 (1975).

Crystal also argues that the fact that audio chips were included in nearly all personal computers indicates that the "astounding" demand for these chips would not have waned with a "small" price increase. Crystal's assertion does not overcome its failure to supply reliable evidence of price erosion. This market featured both a large demand for the chips and competition. Without adequate record support for Crystal's theories, this court cannot discern whether, if Crystal had increased its prices, the competitors might have expanded their production to meet market demand at a lower price. Likewise, new competitors might have entered the market to supply demand at a lower price. Crystal cannot assert that demand for its CODECs would not have waned with an increase in price without evidence of barriers to entry and expansion that would have prevented competitors from taking over Crystal's supply.

Furthermore, Crystal did not present any evidence of how a hypothetical increase in price would have affected Crystal's profits due to lost sales. Lost sales and price erosion damages are inextricably linked. *Panduit Corp. v. Stahlin Bros. Fibre Works*, 575 F.2d 1152, 1157 (6th Cir.1978) ("The right to damages caused by price reduction stands on the same ground as that to damages caused by lost sales."). To prevent inconsistent results, this court will not venture to evaluate price erosion and lost profits damages separately. *See* Christopher S. Marchese, *Patent Infringement and Future Lost Profits Damages*, 26 ARIZ. ST. L.J. 885, 747–752 (1994).

As this court explained in *BIC*, lost profits due to lost sales depend on how the patentee and infringer interact in the market. 1 F.3d at 1218. If the patentee and infringer do not sell their products in the same market segment, "but for" causation cannot be demonstrated. *Id.* at 1218–19. In *BIC*, the patentee's sailboards were priced at the upper end of the sailboard price spectrum while the infringer's sailboards were priced at the lower end. *Id.* at 1216–17. This court, therefore, held that even without the infringer in the market, the infringer's customers would have likely sought boards in the same price range and would not have purchased more of Windsurfing's boards. *Id.* at 1218.

In the present case, Crystal did not present any evidence of whether any of its suggested hypothetical price increases, in a world without TriTech and OPTi, would have left Crystal's CODECs in the same market. Crystal presented evidence that the market was already segmented into high quality and low quality market segments according to sound quality instead of price. However, Crystal presented no evidence about whether the market would have been further segmented with greater price differences between the different CODECs. Crystal seeks lost profits because Tri-Tech/OPTi sold CODECs in the same market segment as Crystal. Yet, Crystal also seeks price erosion damages without showing that a higher CODEC price would have allowed Crystal to sell its CODECs in that same market segment. Without economic evidence of the resulting market for higher priced CODECs, Crystal cannot have both lost profits and price erosion damages on each of those lost sales. The district court correctly denied Crystal's price erosion damages for lack of adequate record support.

NOTES

1. *Recovery for Price Erosion.* As noted in *Crystal*, the Supreme Court laid the foundation for the recovery of profits lost because of price erosion in *Yale Lock Mfg. Co. v. Sargent*, 117 U.S. 536, 552–53 (1886):

> The turning-bolt was the essential feature of the Sargent lock. The defendant adopted Sargent's [the plaintiff] arrangement, and then reduced the price of the lock, forcing Sargent to do the same, in order to hold his trade. The evidence shows that the reduction of prices by Sargent was solely due to the defendant's infringement. The only competitor with Sargent in the use of his turning-bolt arrangement, during the period covered by the accounting, was the defendant.

As indicated in *Yale Lock*, price erosion is most apparent in a two-company market. Based on the "two-company market" theory, the Federal Circuit affirmed the award of damages for price erosion in *Amstar Corp. v. Envirotech Corp.*, 823 F.2d 1538, 1543 (Fed.Cir.1987). The Court stated that in a two-company market, where the patent owner and the infringer were the only source of the patented product, "one may infer that the patentee would have ... charged higher prices but for the infringing competition." This inference, though, is not conclusive. For example, in *Polaroid*, the court rejected Polaroid's price erosion claim in part on the grounds that Polaroid had historically reduced its camera prices over time and would have done so absent Kodak's infringement. 16 U.S.P.Q.2d at 1505.

The *Amstar* inference notwithstanding, most courts require some proof as to what the patent owner would have done. *See Brooktree Corp. v. Advanced Micro Devices, Inc.*, 977 F.2d 1555, 1579–81 (Fed.Cir.1992). In an economy that possesses a yearly inflation rate of ten, five, or even three percent, is it really necessary for the patent owner to show that he or she actually reduced prices to compete with the infringer, or is it sufficient that the patent owner kept prices the same over a substantial amount of time? *See TWM Mfg. Co., infra*, 789 F.2d at 902 (price erosion may be taken into account where prices would have increased in the absence of infringement).

In *Crystal*, the patent owner failed to present evidence of the elasticity of demand of the PC sound card CODEC market. How would a patent owner go about showing elasticity? *See generally* James F. Nieberding, *The Importance of Price Elasticity of Demand in Computing Total Lost Profits in Patent Infringement Cases,* 85 J. PAT. & TM. OFF. SOC'Y 835 (2003).

2. *Generally, How Much Proof Is Needed To Recover Lost Profits?* The patent owner bears the burden of proving by a preponderance of the evidence the profits lost and cannot meet this burden with guesswork and speculation. *Oiness v. Walgreen Co.*, 88 F.3d 1025, 1029–31 (Fed.Cir.1996). *See also Riles v. Shell Exploration & Prod. Co.*, 298 F.3d 1302, 1311 (Fed.Cir.2002). Uncertainties that arise from the infringer's failure to keep accurate records, though, are resolved in favor of the patent owner. *Beatrice Foods Co. v. New England Printing & Lithographing Co.*, 899 F.2d 1171, 1175–76 (Fed.Cir.1990). After the patent owner has established a reasonable view of the incremental costs, it is up to the infringer to show that the patent owner's proofs are unreasonable. *See Paper Converting Mach.*, 745 F.2d at 21; *John O. Butler Co. v. Block Drug Co.*, 620 F.Supp. 771, 778–79 (N.D. Ill. 1985) (defendant did not establish that the testimony of plaintiff's damages expert was improper in any significant way).

3. *The Infringer's Profits.* The claim for lost profits is based on profits lost by the patent owner rather than profits made by the infringer. *See Aro Mfg. Co. v. Convertible Top Replacement Co.*, 377 U.S. 476, 502–07 (1964). Nonetheless, it is often difficult to formulate an exact figure for damages without taking the infringer's profits into account. In light of this, the Federal Circuit affirmed a district court decision that assessed lost profits for infringement of a patent for an "Amphibious Marsh Craft" by comparing the patent owner's claimed damages with the infringer's profits on the sale of the infringing craft. *See Kori Corp. v. Wilco Marsh Buggies & Draglines, Inc.*, 761 F.2d 649, 653–55 (Fed.Cir.1985).

iii.   What Else Would the Infringer Have Done?

Grain Processing Corp. v. American Maize–Products Co.

185 F.3d 1341 (Fed.Cir.1999).

■ Before RADER, CIRCUIT JUDGE, FRIEDMAN, SENIOR CIRCUIT JUDGE, and BRYSON, CIRCUIT JUDGE.

■ RADER, CIRCUIT JUDGE.

* * *

This appeal culminates the lengthy and complex history of this case, spanning more than eighteen years and eight prior judicial opinions, three by this court. The patent featured in this infringement suit involves maltodextrins, a versatile family of food additives made from starch. Commercial food manufacturers purchase hundreds of millions of pounds of maltodextrins annually from producers such as Grain Processing and American Maize.

Maltodextrins serve well as food additives because they are bland in taste and clear in solution. They do not affect the natural taste or color of other ingredients in food products. Maltodextrins also improve the structure or behavior of food products. For instance, they inhibit crystal growth, add body, improve binding and viscosity, and preserve food properties in low temperatures. Consequently, food manufacturers use maltodextrins in a wide variety of products such as frostings, syrups, drinks, cereals, and frozen foods.

Maltodextrins belong to a category of chemical products known as "starch hydrolysates." Producers make starch hydrolysates by putting starch through hydrolysis, a chemical reaction with water. Hydrolysis breaks down the starch and converts some of it to dextrose. . . .

Maltodextrins are starch hydrolysates that have a "dextrose equivalence" of less than 20. Dextrose equivalence (D.E.) is a percentage measurement of the "reducing sugars content" of the starch hydrolysate. D.E. reflects the degree to which the hydrolysis process broke down the starch and converted it into dextrose. Converting more starch into dextrose increases the D.E. of the resulting starch hydrolysate. Hence, pure starch has a D.E. of zero, pure dextrose a D.E. of 100. The D.E. value indicates functional properties of a maltodextrin. A 15 D.E. maltodextrin, for example, is slightly sweeter and more soluble than a 5 D.E. maltodextrin. On the other hand, the 5 D.E. maltodextrin has more prevalent binding, bodying, and crystal inhibiting properties.

Grain Processing is the assignee of the '194 patent, "Low D.E. Starch Conversion Products," which claims maltodextrins with particular attributes, and processes for producing them . . . .

Grain Processing has manufactured and sold a line of maltodextrins under the "Maltrin" brand name since 1969. The Maltrin line includes "Maltrin M100," a 10 D.E. maltodextrin. . . .

American Maize began selling maltodextrins in 1974. It made and sold several types of maltodextrins, including "Lo–Dex 10," a 10 D.E. waxy starch maltodextrin. American Maize sold Lo–Dex 10 . . . during the entire time Grain Processing owned the '194 patent rights, from 1979 until the patent expired in 1991. During this time, however, American Maize used four different processes for producing Lo–Dex 10. The changes in American Maize's production processes, and the slight chemical differences in the Lo–Dex 10 from each process, are central to the lost profits issue in this appeal.

American Maize used a first process (Process I) from June 1974 to July 1982. In Process I, American Maize used a single enzyme (an alpha amylase) to facilitate starch hydrolysis. American Maize controlled the reaction to produce a starch hydrolysate with the desired properties, including D.E. value.

Grain Processing sued American Maize for infringement on May 12, 1981. . . .

In August 1982, while the suit was pending, American Maize reduced the amount of alpha amylase enzyme in its process to lower its production costs. . . . American Maize used this process (Process II) exclusively to produce Lo–Dex 10 from August 1982 to February 1988. Grain Processing asserted in its lawsuit that Process II Lo–Dex 10 also infringed the '194 patent.

* * *

Following a bench trial, the district court held that Lo–Dex 10 did not infringe any of the claims. . . . This court reversed. . . . The district court subsequently entered an injunction on October 21, 1988, prohibiting American Maize from making or selling Lo–Dex 10. . . .

In response to the injunction, American Maize developed yet another process for producing Lo–Dex 10. In this new process (Process III), American Maize used more alpha amylase, adjusted the temperature and pH, and reduced the reaction time. American Maize used Process III exclusively to produce Lo–Dex 10 from March 1988 to April 1991.

* * *

[Editor's note: After three more judicial decisions, it was clear that Lo–Dex 10 made by Process III was also infringing. So,] American Maize then adopted a fourth process (Process IV) for producing Lo–Dex 10. In Process IV, American Maize added a second enzyme, glucoamylase, to the reaction. . . .

From the time American Maize began experimenting with the glucoamylase-alpha amylase combination, or the "dual enzyme method," it took only two weeks to perfect the reaction and begin mass producing Lo–Dex 10 using Process IV. *See Grain Processing VI*, 893 F. Supp. at 1391. According to the finding of the district court, this two-week development and production time is "practically instantaneous" for large-scale production. *Id.* American Maize simply experimented with different combinations of glucoamylase and alpha amylase, along with pH, heat, and time of the reaction. *See id.* American Maize did not change any equipment, source starches, or other ingredients from Process III. *See id.* Glucoamylase has been commercially available and its effect in starch hydrolysis widely known since the early 1970's, before the '194 patent issued. *See id.* American Maize had not used Process IV to produce Lo–Dex earlier because the high cost of glucoamylase makes Process IV more expensive than the other processes. *See id.* at 1392.

The parties agree that Process IV yielded only noninfringing Lo–Dex 10 and that consumers discerned no difference between Process IV Lo–Dex 10 and Lo–Dex 10 made by Processes I–III. American Maize used Process IV exclusively to produce Lo–Dex 10 from April 1991 until the '194 patent expired in November 1991, and then switched back to the cheaper Process III.

* * *

The trial court determined that Grain Processing could not establish causation for lost profits, because American Maize "could have produced" a noninfringing substitute 10 D.E. maltodextrin using Process IV. *Grain Processing VI*, 893 F. Supp. at 1391–92. "With infringing Lo–Dex 10 banned, the customers' substitute is non-infringing Lo–Dex 10." *Id.* at 1392 (emphasis added). American Maize did not actually produce and sell this noninfringing substitute until April 1991, seven months before the '194 patent expired, but the district court nevertheless found that its availability "scotches [Grain Processing's] request for lost-profits damages." *Id.*

* * *

Grain Processing appealed the district court's denial of lost profits, alleging that American Maize cannot escape liability for lost profits on the basis of "a noninfringing substitute that did not exist during, and was not developed until after, the period of infringement." *Grain Processing VII*, 1997 WL 71726, at **1. This court reversed and remanded. *Id.* This court observed that "[t]he [district] court denied [Grain Processing's] request for lost profits because [American Maize] developed a new process of producing Lo–Dex 10 in 1991 [after years of infringement] that did not infringe the '194 patent." *Id.* This court noted, however, that the mere fact of "switching to a noninfringing product years after the period of infringement [does] not establish the presence of a noninfringing substitute during the period of infringement." *Id.* at **2 (citing *State Indus., Inc. v. Mor–Flo Industries, Inc.*, 883 F.2d 1573, 1579, 12 USPQ2d 1026, 1030 (Fed.Cir. 1989); *Panduit Corp. v. Stahlin Brothers Fibre Works, Inc.*, 575 F.2d 1152, 1160–62, 197 USPQ 726, 734–35 (6th Cir.1978)). This court noted that a product or process must be "available or on the market at the time of infringement" to qualify as an acceptable non-infringing substitute. *Grain Processing VII*, 1997 WL 71726, at **2 (emphasis added).

On remand, the district court again denied Grain Processing lost profits. The district court found that Process IV was "available" throughout the period of infringement. *Grain Processing VIII*, 979 F. Supp. at 1235. This factual finding, the district court explained, was not based merely on "the simple fact of switching [to Process IV]" but rather on several subsidiary factual findings regarding the technology of enzyme-assisted starch hydrolysis and the price and market structure for the patentee's and accused infringer's products. *Id.* at 1234–35. The trial court found that American Maize could obtain all of the materials needed for Process IV, including the glucoamylase enzyme, before 1979, and that the effects of the enzymes in starch hydrolysis were well known in the field by that time. *Id.* American Maize also had all of the necessary equipment, know-how, and experience to implement Process IV whenever it chose to do so during the time of infringement. *See id.* "The sole reason [American Maize did not use Process IV to produce Lo–Dex 10 prior to 1991] was economic: glucoamalyse is more expensive than the alpha amylase enzyme that [American Maize] had been using." *Id.* . . .

* * *

Grain Processing appeals the district court's decision.

* * *

To recover lost profits, the patent owner must show "causation in fact," establishing that "but for" the infringement, he would have made additional profits. *See King Instruments Corp. v. Perego*, 65 F.3d 941, 952, 36 USPQ2d 1129, 1137 (Fed.Cir.1995). When basing the alleged lost profits on lost sales, the patent owner has an initial burden to show a reasonable probability that he would have made the asserted sales "but for" the infringement. *See id.*; *Rite–Hite*, 56 F.3d at 1545. Once the patent owner establishes a reasonable probability of "but for" causation, "the burden then shifts to the accused infringer to show that [the patent owner's 'but for' causation claim] is unreasonable for some or all of the lost sales." Id. at 1544.

At trial, American Maize proved that Grain Processing's lost sales assertions were unreasonable. The district court adopted Grain Processing's initial premise that, because Grain Processing and American Maize competed head-to-head as the only significant suppliers of 10 D.E. maltodextrins, consumers logically would purchase Maltrin 100 if Lo–Dex 10 were not available. *See Lam, Inc. v. Johns–Manville Corp.*, 718 F.2d 1056, 1065, 219 USPQ 670, 675 (Fed.Cir.1983) (holding that the patent owner may satisfy his initial burden by inference in a two-supplier market). However, the district court found that American Maize proved that Process IV was available and that Process IV Lo–Dex 10 was an acceptable substitute for the claimed invention. In the face of this noninfringing substitute, Grain Processing could not prove lost profits. *See Grain Processing VIII*, 979 F.Supp. at 1234–35.

American Maize concedes that it did not make or sell Lo–Dex 10 from Process IV until 1991, after the period of infringement. However, an alleged substitute not "on the market" or "for sale" during the infringement can figure prominently in determining whether a patentee would have made additional profits "but for" the infringement. As this court stated in Grain Processing VII, "to be an acceptable non-infringing substitute, the product or process must have been available *or* on the market at the time of infringement." *Grain Processing VII*, 1997 WL 71726, at **2 (emphasis added). This statement is an apt summary of this court's precedent, which permits available alternatives—including but not limited to products on the market—to preclude lost profits damages.

In *Aro Manufacturing*, the Supreme Court stated that the statutory measure of "damages" is "the difference between [the patent owner's] pecuniary condition after the infringement, and what his condition would have been if the infringement had not occurred." *Aro Mfg Co. v. Convertible Top Replacement Co.*, 377 U.S. 476, 507, 84 S. Ct. 1526, 1543, 12 L. Ed. 2d 457, 141 USPQ 681, 694 (1964) (plurality opinion), quoting *Yale Lock Mfg. Co. v. Sargent*, 117 U.S. 536, 552, 6 S. Ct. 934, 942, 29 L. Ed. 954 (1886). The determinative question, the Supreme Court stated, is: "had the Infringer not infringed, what would the Patent Holder–Licensee have made?" *Aro*, 377 U.S. at 507, 84 S. Ct. 1526 (quoting *Livesay Window Co. v. Livesay Indus., Inc.*, 251 F.2d 469, 471, 116 USPQ 167, 168 (5th Cir.1958)); *see also Brooktree Corp. v. Advanced Micro Devices, Inc.*, 977 F.2d 1555, 1579, 24 USPQ2d 1401, 1418 (Fed.Cir.1992). The "but for" inquiry therefore requires a reconstruction of the market, as it would have developed absent the infringing product, to determine what the patentee "would ... have made." *See Grain Processing VIII*, 979 F.Supp. at 1236.

Reconstructing the market, by definition a hypothetical enterprise, requires the patentee to project economic results that did not occur. To prevent the hypothetical from lapsing into pure speculation, this court requires sound economic proof of the nature of the market and likely outcomes with infringement factored out of the economic picture. *See Oiness v. Walgreen Co.*, 88 F.3d 1025, 1029–30, 39 USPQ2d 1304, 1307 (Fed.Cir.1996); *Water Technologies Corp. v. Calco, Ltd.*, 850 F.2d 660, 673,

7 USPQ2d 1097, 1107–08 (Fed.Cir.1988). Within this framework, trial courts, with this court's approval, consistently permit patentees to present market reconstruction theories showing all of the ways in which they would have been better off in the "but for world," and accordingly to recover lost profits in a wide variety of forms. . . . In sum, courts have given patentees significant latitude to prove and recover lost profits for a wide variety of foreseeable economic effects of the infringement.

By the same token, a fair and accurate reconstruction of the "but for" market also must take into account, where relevant, alternative actions the infringer foreseeably would have undertaken had he not infringed. Without the infringing product, a rational would-be infringer is likely to offer an acceptable noninfringing alternative, if available, to compete with the patent owner rather than leave the market altogether. The competitor in the "but for" marketplace is hardly likely to surrender its complete market share when faced with a patent, if it can compete in some other lawful manner. Moreover, only by comparing the patented invention to its next-best available alternative(s)—regardless of whether the alternative(s) were actually produced and sold during the infringement—can the court discern the market value of the patent owner's exclusive right, and therefore his expected profit or reward, had the infringer's activities not prevented him from taking full economic advantage of this right. *Cf. Westinghouse Elec. & Mfg. Co. v. Wagner Elec. & Mfg. Co.*, 225 U.S. 604, 614–15, 32 S. Ct. 691, 694, 56 L. Ed. 1222 (1912); *Mowry v. Whitney*, 81 U.S. (14 Wall.) 620, 651, 20 L. Ed. 860 (1871); *King Instrument Corp. v. Otari Corp.*, 767 F.2d 853, 865, 226 USPQ 402, 410–11 (Fed.Cir.1985). Thus, an accurate reconstruction of the hypothetical "but for" market takes into account any alternatives available to the infringer. . . .

* * *

This court next turns to the district court's findings that Process IV was in fact "available" to American Maize for producing Lo–Dex 10 no later than October, 1979, and that consumers would consider Process IV Lo–Dex 10 an acceptable substitute. This court reviews these factual findings for clear error. *See Gargoyles*, 113 F.3d at 1573; *Slimfold*, 932 F.2d at 1458.

The critical time period for determining availability of an alternative is the period of infringement for which the patent owner claims damages, *i.e.*, the "accounting period." *See State Indus.*, 883 F.2d at 1579; *Panduit*, 575 F.2d at 1162. Switching to a noninfringing substitute after the accounting period does not alone show availability of the noninfringing substitute during this critical time. *See Panduit*, 575 F.2d at 1152. When an alleged alternative is not on the market during the accounting period, a trial court may reasonably infer that it was not available as a noninfringing substitute at that time. *Cf. Rite–Hite*, 56 F.3d at 1545. The accused infringer then has the burden to overcome this inference by showing that the substitute was available during the accounting period. *Cf. id.* Mere speculation or conclusory assertions will not suffice to overcome the inference. After all, the infringer chose to produce the infringing, rather than noninfringing, product. Thus, the trial court must proceed with caution in assessing proof of the availability of substitutes not actually sold during the period of infringement. Acceptable substitutes that the infringer proves were available during the accounting period can preclude or limit lost profits; substitutes only theoretically possible will not. *See Minco*, 95 F.3d at 1119.

In this case, the district court did not base its finding that Process IV was available no later than October 1979 on speculation or possibilities, but rather on several specific, concrete factual findings, none of which Grain Processing challenges on appeal. The district court found that American Maize could readily obtain all of the materials needed for Process IV, including the glucoamylase enzyme, before 1979. The court also found that the effects of the enzymes in starch hydrolysis were well known in the field at that time. *Grain Processing VI*, 893 F. Supp. at 1391; *Grain Processing VIII*, 979 F. Supp. at 1235. Furthermore, the court found that American Maize had all of the necessary equipment, know-how, and experience to use Process IV to make Lo–Dex 10, whenever it chose to do so during the time it was instead using Processes I, II or III. *Grain Processing VIII*, 979 F. Supp. at 1235. American Maize "did not have to 'invent around' the patent," the district court observed; "all it had to do was use a glucoamylase enzyme in its production process." *Id*.

The trial court also explained that "the sole reason [American Maize did not use Process IV prior to 1991] was economic: glucoamylase is more expensive than the alpha amylase enzyme American Maize had been using," and American Maize reasonably believed it had a noninfringing product. *Grain Processing VIII*, 979 F. Supp. at 1235. While the high cost of a necessary material can conceivably render a substitute "unavailable," the facts of this case show that glucoamylase was not prohibitively expensive to American Maize. The district court found that American Maize's "substantial profit margins" on Lo–Dex 10 were sufficient for it to absorb the 2.3% cost increase using glucoamylase. *Id*. at 1392.

* * *

Whether and to what extent American Maize's alleged alternative prevents Grain Processing from showing lost sales of Maltrin 100 depends not only on whether and when the alternative was available, but also on whether and to what extent it was acceptable as a substitute in the relevant market. *See King Instruments*, 65 F.3d at 952. Consumer demand defines the relevant market and relative substitutability among products therein. *See BIC*, 1 F.3d at 1218; *cf. United States v. E.I. du Pont de Nemours & Co.*, 351 U.S. 377, 392–95, 76 S. Ct. 994, 1005–07, 100 L. Ed. 1264 (1956). Important factors shaping demand may include consumers' intended use for the patentee's product, similarity of physical and functional attributes of the patentee's product to alleged competing products, and price. *See Fonar Corp. v. General Elec. Co.*, 107 F.3d 1543, 1553, 41 USPQ2d 1801, 1808–09 (Fed.Cir.1997); *BIC*, 1 F.3d at 1218. Where the alleged substitute differs from the patentee's product in one or more of these respects, the patentee often must adduce economic data supporting its theory of the relevant market in order to show "but for" causation. *See BIC*, 1 F.3d at 1218.

* * *

Market evidence in the record supports the district court's uncontroverted findings and conclusions on acceptability. First, for example, American Maize's high profit margin on Lo–Dex 10 and the consumers' sensitivity to price changes support the conclusion that American Maize would not have raised the price of Process IV Lo–Dex 10 to offset the cost of glucoamylase. Further, American Maize's sales records showed no significant changes when it introduced Process IV Lo–Dex 10 at the same price as previous versions, indicating that consumers considered its important properties to be effectively identical to previous versions. Witness testimony supported this market data. Thus, this court discerns no clear error in the district court's finding that Process IV Lo–Dex 10 was an acceptable substitute in the marketplace.

It follows from the district court's findings on availability and acceptability that Grain Processing's theory of "but for" causation fails. As the district court correctly noted, "[a]n [American Maize] using the dual-enzyme method between 1979 and 1991 ... would have sold the same product, for the same price, as the actual [American Maize] did ..." and consequently would have retained its Lo–Dex 10 sales. *Grain Processing VI*, 893 F. Supp. at 1392. Grain Processing did not present any other evidence of lost profits, such as individual lost transactions as in *Rite–Hite Corp. v. Kelley Co.*, 774 F. Supp. 1514, 1525–26, 1528–29, 21 USPQ2d 1801 (E.D.Wis. 1991), *aff'd in part and vacated on other grounds*, 56 F.3d 1538. Thus, the district court properly determined that, absent infringing Lo–Dex 10, Grain Processing would have sold no more and no less Maltrin 100 than it actually did.

IV.

In summary, this court requires reliable economic proof of the market that establishes an accurate context to project the likely results "but for" the infringement. *See, e.g., Oiness*, 88 F.3d 1025; *BIC*, 1 F.3d 1214; *Water Technologies*, 850 F.2d 660. The availability of substitutes invariably will influence the market forces defining this "but for" marketplace, as it did in this case. Moreover, a substitute need not be openly on sale to exert this influence. Thus, with proper economic proof of availability, as American Maize provided the district court in this case, an acceptable substitute not on the market during the infringement may nonetheless become part of the lost profits calculus and therefore limit or preclude those damages.

This court concludes that the district court did not err in considering an alternative not on the market during the period of infringement, nor did it clearly err in determining that the alternative was available, acceptable, and precluded any lost profits. Accordingly, the district court did not abuse its discretion in denying lost profits. This court affirms the district court's decision.

NOTES

1. *What Else Would the Infringer Have Done?* American Maize used an infringing process to make a product that competed directly with Grain Processing's product. Because of that improper competition, Grain Processing lost sales and profits. Instead of measuring the value of the damage done to Grain Processing by that improper competition, the Federal Circuit asked if the competition could have been proper. If the competition could have been proper (*i.e.*, noninfringing) and the competitive results would have been the same (*i.e.*, customers would have stayed with the infringer), then the Federal Circuit held that the patent owner's damages should not be measured by profits lost.

Is it "fair" to ask what the infringer could have done? In *Grain Processing*, the Federal Circuit justified its decision on that basis. According to the court, since existing lost-profits law allowed the patent owner to show what it would have done if there had been no infringement, "a fair and accurate reconstruction of the 'but for' market also must take into account, where relevant, alternative actions the infringer foreseeably would have undertaken had he not infringed." *Grain Processing*, 185 F.3d at 1350–51. Do you agree with the court? Is a sound basis for distinguishing between the patent owner and the infringer the fact that the patent owner did nothing wrong while the infringer acted unlawfully?

2. *When is a Noninfringing Alternative Available to the Infringer?* To defeat the patent owner's claim for lost-profit damages, the noninfringing alternative that the infringer allegedly would have used or sold must have been available during the time for which damages are sought. As *Grain Processing* holds, a product or process may be available even thought it is not sold or used in the marketplace. The infringer bears the burden of showing that the alternative product or process was available. Regarding an infringer that could not meet that burden, see *Micro Chem., Inc. v. Lextron, Inc.*, 318 F.3d 1119, 1123 (Fed.Cir.2003):

> The record shows that Lextron did not have the necessary equipment, know-how, and experience to make the Type 5 machine at the time of infringement. Lextron expended 984 hours to design the Type 5 machine and another 330 to test it. Charles Hoff, a Lextron engineer, worked full-time for several months on the design of the Type 5 machine. Thereafter, he continued to work part-time on the project, estimating that he tested and rejected five potential design changes. Lextron took over four months to convert all of its infringing Type 2 machines to Type 5 machines.

> The effects of the changes also were not well known or readily available. Lextron hired consultants to help it consider the impact and effectiveness of the new designs. Lextron hired a firm to consider "alternative designs." Additionally, Lextron retained a Ph.D. nutritionist "to assure the effectiveness of the new designs in delivering the microingredients to the animal feed."

> The summary judgment record also shows that the materials for the alleged substitutions were not readily available. Lextron requested a 120–day extension to delay the injunction on the use of its Type 2 machines because the "parts required for the conversion" were "difficult to obtain in bulk, particularly since some must be specially fabricated according to our specifications and most are not maintained in inventory." Thus, in Lextron's own words, the needed materials and equipment were "difficult to obtain in bulk," "specially fabricated," and "not maintained in inventory." This record shows that the Type 5 machine was not available at the time of infringement.

An infringer who waits until after trial to disclose and market its allegedly available noninfringing alternative runs the risk that the court will not consider the alternative. *Fiskars, Inc. v. Hunt Mfg. Co.*, 279 F.3d 1378, 1382–83 (Fed.Cir.2002). What does it mean for a non-infringing substitute to be available? Why did the infringer elect the infringing version?

3. *Is The Market Value Of The Exclusive Right The Proper Measure?* The purpose of a compensatory remedy is to compensate for a wrong that has occurred. Do you find it odd that, to value compensation for patent infringement, *Grain Processing* creates a hypothetical world wherein no wrong occurred? The *Grain Processing* justification for using an infringement-free hypothetical world is

> only by comparing the patented invention to its next best available alternative(s) ... can the court discern the market value of the patent owner's exclusive right, and therefore his expected profit or reward, had the infringer's activities not prevented him from taking full economic advantage of this right.

Grain Processing Corp., 185 F.3d at 1351. Is the market value of the patent owner's exclusive right the appropriate measure of damages for patent infringement? Why isn't the market value of the violation of the patent owner's exclusive right (*i.e.*, the market value of the infringement) the proper measure?

In addition to the legal inability to award the infringer's profits as damages, a reason that the market value of the exclusive right (or the market value of the invention) has become the focus of compensatory damages may be rooted in a decades-long debate over the perception and treatment of property rights. But

> Simply deciding that patents should be property rights does not necessarily settle the question of whether they should be enforced as property rules rather than liability rules. [See Guido Calabresi & A. Douglas Melamed, *Property Rules, Liability Rules, and Inalienability: One View of the Cathedral*, 85 Harv. L. Rev. 1089, 1092 (1972)]. An entitlement enjoys the protection of a property rule if the law condones its surrender only through voluntary exchange. The holder of such an entitlement is allowed to enjoin infringement. An entitlement has the lesser protection of a liability rule if it can be lost lawfully to anyone willing to pay some court-determined compensation. The holder of such an entitlement is only entitled to damages caused by infringement.

F. Scott Kieff, *Property Rights and Property Rules for Commercializing Inventions*, 85 Minn. L. Rev. 697, 732 (2001). When it comes to damages in particular, property rule treatment usually involves some form of enhanced damages to deter infringement while liability rule treatment usually involves a limit to merely compensatory damages. Some scholars suggest that liability rule treatment for patent rights will help the most efficient practitioner of the claimed subject matter gain access to by infringing. See, e.g., Ian Ayres & Paul Klemperer, Limiting Patentees' Market Power Without Reducing Innovation Incentives: The Perverse Benefits of Uncertainty and Non–Injunctive Remedies, 97 Mich. L. Rev. 985 (1999); Abraham Bell & Gideon Parchomovsky, Pliability Rules, 101 Mich. L. Rev. 1 (2002). Other scholars suggest that property rule treatment for patent rights can be essential for facilitating commercialization of inventions because private parties have a comparative advantage over courts in evaluating patents and inventions. *See* Kieff, *Property Rights*, *supra*; Robert P. Merges, Of Property Rules, Coase, and Intellectual Property, 94 Colum. L. Rev. 2655, 2664 (1994).

c. REASONABLE ROYALTY

Promega Corp. v. Lifecodes Corp.

53 U.S.P.Q.2d 1463 (D.Utah 1999).

■ Tena Campbell, District Judge.

FINDINGS OF FACT AND CONCLUSIONS OF LAW

Plaintiff Promega Corporation ("Promega") has brought this action against defendant Lifecodes Corporation ("Lifecodes") for willful infringement of U.S. Patent No. 4,963,663 ("White Patent") which relates to DNA probes for use in human genetic identification. Lifecodes has admitted both the validity of the White Patent and that it has infringed the patent. Therefore, the only issues for resolution are those that relate to the amount of damages Lifecodes owes Promega.

* * *

FINDINGS OF FACT

A. *The Patent*

The White Patent is directed to nucleotide probes used to isolate particular regions of DNA for human identity purposes. The patent was issued in 1990 to Dr. Raymond L. White, a professor and scientist at the University of Utah, ("the University"). The patent was then assigned to the University.

B. *The Technology*

Promega has alleged that Lifecodes infringed two of the White Probes: YNH24 and MLJ14.... YNH24 is the stronger, and hence, the most valuable of the two White Probes. Genetic testing requires the use of several probes and, although YNH24 is generally one of the probes, other probes are used with YNH24 in conducting tests. YNH24 is used on most samples in forensic and paternity testing; MLJ14 is used less frequently. A Lifecodes probe, V1, is also a commonly used probe.

Reagents are used with probes in the testing process. Probes can be used interchangeably with reagents because the reagents do not interact with the probes themselves. In a test, the reagents cut the DNA into fragments which can then bind to the probes.

In 1988, when Lifecodes first began selling the White Probes, it offered them in "kits." A kit contained a White Probe and the reagents necessary to carry out identity testing. By 1991, the sale of kits had dwindled as Lifecodes' customers became more sophisticated in the use of the materials and began purchasing reagents apart from the probe, frequently on the basis of price. By 1990, dozens of companies, not all of which also sold probes, sold the reagents used in identity testing.

Lifecodes also sold the White Probes in "cocktails." A cocktail contained several probes in addition to the White Probes; some cocktails contained Lifecodes' own probes.

The probes sold by Lifecodes had certain "value added" features, not found in the probes sold by Promega. These features included the prelabeling of probes with a radioactive composition that made the DNA bands visible when exposed to x-ray film. Another feature was a database, developed by Lifecodes for use in genetic testing. Customers of Lifecodes were given access, without charge, to the database.

* * *

D. *Agreements to License the White Technology*

On May 13, 1988, the University granted Genmark (then know[n] as "Westgene") an exclusive license to make, sell, and use the technology that would later be covered by the White Patent (the "White Technology"). The parties believed that the White Technology would eventually be covered by a patent and, when that occurred, Genmark would pay 6% of the net sales of the probes until sales of $10,000,000 were reached; the royalty rate would then increase to 8% of the net sales of the probes. Until a patent issued, the royalty rate was one-half of the rate to be paid under a patent.

In 1989, Genmark and Promega entered into a sales agency agreement for the White Technology. This agreement marked Promega's entry into the area of genetic identity. Under this agreement, Promega became Genmark's exclusive sales agent with the right "to sell and distribute PROBE PRODUCTS solely for use in manual procedures that have applications in human paternity testing and forensic identification." . . . Genmark reserved the right to manufacture the probes. Promega paid an 18% royalty to Genmark on all sales of probes and on unpatented reagents used with the probes (e.g., enzymes and buffers). Genmark had the right to change Promega's agency from an exclusive agency to a nonexclusive agency. In that event, the royalty rate would be decreased to 9%.

In July 1990, Genmark and Promega entered into a second agreement ("the 1990 Agreement") which replaced their earlier agreement. Under the 1990 Agreement, Promega held an exclusive sublicense to the White Technology, including the right to manufacture and modify the probes. Promega paid Genmark a $60,000 execution fee and a 30% royalty on the sale of the probes. The parties believed that a patent would soon issue, and Promega was given the right to keep its sublicense should a patent issue. The term of the agreement was five years, and would end in July 1995.

On February 1, 1991, Genmark granted Cetus Corporation a nonexclusive license for a limited use that had been specifically exempted from the 1990 Agreement between Genmark and Promega. Cetus was given the right to develop, manufacture, and sell the probes in conjunction with Cetus' own proprietary technology. The parties agreed that Cetus would pay a 5% royalty rate on probe sales.

On July 31, 1991, Genmark granted Biosystems, Inc. a limited use license that was co-exclusive with the license Genmark had granted Cetus. The royalty rate was 5%.

E. *The First Lawsuit*

* * *

On July 9, 1991, the State of Utah, the University of Utah, and Genmark joined as plaintiffs in a lawsuit against Lifecodes, claiming that two of the probes manufactured and sold by Lifecodes, the "White Probes," infringed the claims of the White Patent. . . .

* * *

On December 9, 1991, the University, Genmark and Lifecodes settled the lawsuit. As part of the settlement, Genmark assigned to Lifecodes its exclusive license under the White Patent for $600,000. Lifecodes agreed to assume all of Genmark's rights and obligations under the 1990 agreement between Promega and Genmark.[2]

* * *

G.   *The Second Lawsuit*

On February 19, 1993, Promega filed this patent infringement action against Lifecodes and filed a motion to enjoin Lifecodes' continued infringement of the White Patent. In the proceedings for a preliminary injunction, Lifecodes did not contest that its sales of Lifeprint Identity Probe D2S44 and Lifeprint Identity Probe D14S13 infringed the White Patent. . . . On May 17, 1993, Judge Winder granted Promega's Motion for a Preliminary Injunction. . . .

* * *

CONCLUSIONS OF LAW

* * *

C.   *A Reasonable Royalty*

Promega is entitled to "damages adequate to compensate for the infringement, but in no event less than a reasonable royalty for the use made of the invention. . . ." 35 U.S.C. § 284. Promega claims that a reasonable royalty would be 40% to 49%. . . . Lifecodes does not dispute that Promega is entitled to a reasonable royalty on Lifecodes' infringing sales of White Probes; however, Lifecodes argues that a reasonable royalty rate would be 10%. . . .

* * *

2.   *The Royalty Rate*

To determine the royalty rate due Promega, the court must now engage in what the Federal Circuit has described as "a difficult judicial chore, seeming often to involve more the talents of a conjurer than those of a judge. Lacking adequate evidence of an established royalty, the court [is] left with the judge-created methodology described as 'hypothetical negotiations between willing licensor and willing licensee.' " *Fromson v. Western Litho Plate & Supply Co.*, 853 F.2d 1568, 1574 [7 USPQ2d 1606] (Fed.Cir. 1988). The court can consider a variety of factors in determining what rate would have been agreed upon in this hypothetical negotiation. In *Georgia–Pacific Corp. v. United States Plywood Corp.*, 318 F. Supp. 1116 [166 USPQ

---

2. On July 16, 1998, this court held that because Promega was not a party to the 1991 litigation, it was not bound by the terms of the settlement between Genmark and Lifecodes.

235] (S.D.N.Y. 1970), *modified and aff'd*, 446 F.2d 295 [170 USPQ 369] (2d Cir.1971), the court gave a list "of [fifteen] evidentiary facts relevant, in general, to the determination of the amount of a reasonable royalty for a patent license . . ." *Id.* at 1120.

> These factors generally fall into two groups. One group relates to the specific and general market conditions in the pertinent industry. These include (i) prior and existing licenses under the patent, (ii) industry custom and licenses on comparable patents, and (iii) the patent owner's licensing policy and the relation between the parties. The other group of factors relates to the anticipated profitability of the product or process made, used, or sold by the infringer and covered by the patent. These include (iv) infringer's anticipated profits, (v) comparative utility and noninfringing alternatives, (vi) collateral benefits and convoyed sales, (vii) improvements, small parts and apportionment, (viii) state of development and commercial success, and (ix) duration of the patent. The second group of factors in a sense sets the range of feasible rates since a willing patent owner would demand a greater than minimum rate for a profitable invention and a willing user would concede no more than the expected amount of profit (adjusted for the uncertainty as to its realization). The first group of factors points to the rate that the parties would have adopted within that range.

7 Donald S. Chisum, (*Chisum on Patents*) 20–170–71 (1998).

The court has considered all of the fifteen *Georgia–Pacific* factors and will analyze all those that are applicable here, by the grouping suggested by Chisum:

   a. *The specific and general market conditions in the pertinent industry*

The relationship between Promega and Lifecodes deviates from the usual willing licensor-willing licensee situation. By virtue of the 1990 Agreement, the injured party, Promega, is the licensee of Lifecodes, the infringer.[8] This unique relationship would certainly have an impact on the hypothetical negotiations. However, the court concludes that Promega's obligation to pay Lifecodes a 30% royalty would be eliminated during the negotiations. Dr. Dimond testified that the 1990 Agreement would have to be "cleared out" by the new hypothetical license between Promega and Lifecodes. . . . Still, the duration of any license granted to Lifecodes would undoubtedly be dictated by the 1990 Agreement. The negotiations would occur in October, 1990, when the White Patent issued. Yet in 1995, before the expiration of the White Patent, Promega's rights under the 1990 Agreement would end, and all the rights under the patent would revert to Lifecodes.

The court must also take into account the vigorous competition existing between Lifecodes and Promega. The two companies competed directly for the same sales and had the same customers. As Dr. Dimond explained:

---

   8. Although Lifecodes did not actually assume Genmark's role under the 1990 Agreement until December 9, 1991, more than a year after the hypothetical negotiation, courts are given some leeway in relying on events that occur later. *See* 7 Chisum, *supra*, at 20–161–62. And as Dr. Dimond testified when he explained that he had analyzed the hypothetical negotiation as if Lifecodes had already stepped into Genmark's shoes, "otherwise you end up with a three-party negotiation and it's just more complicated to think about." . . . .

Clearly both companies are in the market. Clearly both companies have the ability to reach all segments of the market. It would have been my belief going into the hypothetical negotiation that in fact we were in contact with the same set of customers. I don't believe there's any customers that Promega had that Lifecodes didn't know about or probably wasn't sending market literature to and vice versa would also be true. . . .

Both companies not only competed in selling products to the same customers, both manufactured the White probes in sufficient quantity to satisfy the entire market. Thus, it was Dr. Dimond's belief that he would enter the hypothetical negotiations with the assumption that any sales that Lifecodes would make in the market would be at Promega's expense in the market. . . .

Moreover, Dr. Dimond testified that by 1990, Promega had the general policy of not granting licenses for any of the patents it held. . . .

Importantly, there is no evidence that Promega has licensed the White Patent to a direct competitor. The two limited field licenses granted by Promega [sic], one to Cetus and one to Applied Biosystems, differed significantly from any license Promega would have granted Lifecodes. Cetus and Applied Biosystems were not direct competitors of Promega, and the licenses they received were for limited uses, in fields in which Promega was not competing.

Given the fact that Promega and Lifecodes were direct competitors, both able to fill the same market for White Probes, and in view of Promega's general policy against granting licenses for the patents it held, the court concludes that the hypothetical license would be a coexclusive license, that is, with only Promega and Lifecodes having the right to manufacture and sell the White Probes. These factors also weigh in favor of a higher royalty rate. *See Super Sack Mfg. Co. v. Bulk-Pack, Inc.*, 1992 WL 96863 (E.D. Tex. 1992) ("Given the competitive commercial relationship between [the parties] . . . [the patentee] would seek a higher reasonable royalty if it elected to license the patent to another manufacturer.").

Although the Cetus and Applied Biosystems licenses are of little probative value here; the earlier licenses of the White Technology granted by the University and by Genmark do shed some light on the hypothetical negotiations: "Courts give considerable weight to actual prior and existing licenses granted under the patent in suit even though such licenses fail to meet the standards for an established royalty." 7 Chisum, *supra* at 20–171.

The first such license is the license given to Genmark (Westgene) by the University in May 1988. The royalty rate was 3 to 4%, to be doubled to 6% when a patent issued. This agreement offers little guidance primarily because it was negotiated before the patent issued and before the parties knew what commercial success, if any, the White Probes would enjoy.

The 1989 and 1990 Agreements between Genmark and Promega . . . are of more significance here despite the apparent differences between them and the hypothetical license. The 1989 Agreement reflected Genmark's intention at the time to manufacture the probes itself; Promega would be the exclusive sales agent for the probes. Importantly, the royalty rate was 18% and would decrease to 9% if Genmark changed the Promega's agency to a nonexclusive agency. The royalty rate reached during the hypothetical negotiations would be higher than the 18% rate because it would be for a coexclusive license, not for an exclusive sales agency with the possibility of being converted to a nonexclusive agency. Further, when the 1989 Agreement was struck, there was virtually no commercial market for DNA probes. By 1990, the time of the hypothetical negotiations, the parties were well aware that a profitable market existed for the probes.

Under the 1990 Agreement, Promega paid a 30% royalty. Promega's damage expert, Todd Nielsen, in his written report, concluded that this was the proper rate for the hypothetical Promega/Lifecodes license. Dr. Dimond was emphatic that Promega would never consider a royalty rate of less than 30% because Promega would be giving up its exclusive rights to the White Probes: "I don't know of any rationale for why I would pay them less than what I have to pay under the 1990 Agreement." . . . However, the hypothetical license would not confer on Lifecodes the same exclusive rights given to Promega by the 1990 Agreement: Promega and Lifecodes would be sharing the rights. Lifecodes might be less willing to pay a 30% royalty rate for a coexclusive license than Promega was willing to pay for its exclusive license. . . .

b. *The profitability of the White Probes*

Much of Lifecodes' proof at trial was directed to demonstrating that, at the time of the hypothetical negotiations, Lifecodes was well-established in the human identity industry, independent of the White Patents, and that certain of its own probes, notably the V–1, enjoyed considerable success. Although the court accepts these facts, the evidence made clear that there was no acceptable substitute for YNH24; it was used in almost all human identity tests. Both Promega and Lifecodes had made their entrance into the human identity market primarily through the strength of YNH24. By the time of the hypothetical negotiations, both Lifecodes and Promega knew that the FBI would use the White Probes in their testing. In short, the White Probes, in particular YNH24, was a dominant probe in the human identity business and was clearly a commercial success. Lifecodes would be far more likely to pay a higher royalty rate for the White Probes because of the lack of an acceptable substitute for YNH24 and because of the success of the White Probes.

Lifecodes would also be willing to pay a higher royalty rate because, at the time of the hypothetical negotiations, Lifecodes was firmly committed to manufacturing, using, and selling the White Probes. Lifecodes, in fact, had incorporated the White Probes into its identity data base. Even though once the 1990 Agreement ended, Lifecodes would have the legal right to the White Probes, Lifecodes did not and, perhaps could not wait for July 1995, but persisted in using the White Probes, even when it knew it had no right to do so.

Dr. Dimond testified that in conducting the hypothetical negotiations, he would have focused on "the strengths and weaknesses of each party and tr[ied] to determine what is a fair division of profits." . . . . Dr. Dimond assumed that because Promega's profit margin on the sale of White probes was 98%, Lifecodes' profit margin was also 98%. He also assumed that, but for Lifecodes' infringement, Promega would have made every sale of a

White Probe that Lifecodes made. According to Dr. Dimond, Promega would have had to receive a royalty rate of 40 to 49% (depending on whether unpatented products were included in the royalty base), to recoup 50% of Promega's lost profits.

Not surprisingly, Lifecodes does not agree with Dr. Dimond's assessment. Among other disagreements Lifecodes has with this analysis is its contention that because one vial of White Probes sold by Lifecodes did not equal one vial of White Probes sold by Promega, a reasonable royalty rate would have to be adjusted to account for that difference.[10] . . . . According to Lifecodes, because Lifecodes made seven times the profit per vial that Promega made, even had Promega made all of Lifecodes sales, it would only have made 1/7 of Lifecodes' profit. Therefore, the theory goes, a reasonable royalty rate would be 4%. However, even Lifecodes appeared to not fully accept its own theory, because it later suggested that 10%, not 4% was a reasonable royalty rate.

Weighing all of the above factors, the court concludes that Lifecodes and Promega would have agreed upon a reasonable royalty rate of 22%. This is less than the 30% royalty rate under the 1990 Agreement, primarily because the sublicense to Lifecodes would be coexclusive, not exclusive. Also, the court gives some weight, although not a great deal, to the fact that the concentrations of the Promega and the Lifecodes vials differed. The court rejects Lifecodes' argument that a reasonable royalty rate would be 10% because such a rate does not take into account the considerable success and value of the White Patent, the competitive relationship between Lifecodes and Promega, and Promega's general policy of not licensing the White Patent.

NOTES

1. *When Is It Appropriate To Determine Damages Based on a Reasonable Royalty?* Lost profits are usually the first choice of the patent owner because they usually provide greater recovery. In general, if lost profits are not claimed or proved, a reasonable royalty measure of damages is appropriate.

2. *Established Royalty.* If the patent owner has an established royalty for licensing the patent, that royalty is often the best measure of what would have been a "reasonable" royalty. What makes a royalty established, though? Is the royalty rate in a single license sufficient? *See Trell v. Marlee Elecs. Corp.*, 912 F.2d 1443, 1446 (Fed.Cir.1990). Are multiple offers to license at a particular rate sufficient? Does it matter if those offers were made after infringement began? Is the royalty rate paid to settle an infringement suit sufficient? *See Hanson v. Alpine Valley Ski Area, Inc.*, 718 F.2d 1075, 1078 (Fed.Cir.1983). How relevant (if at all) are licenses negotiated with other parties after infringement began? *See generally Odetics, Inc. v. Storage Tech. Corp.*, 185 F.3d 1259, 1276–77 (Fed.Cir.1999). Further, for an existing royalty to be relevant, there must be some similarity between the existing license and the situation of the infringer. For example, in *Promega*, the court found that the limited licenses to Cetus and Applied Biosystems were "of little probative value."

---

10. Lifecodes sold a vial of White Probes for $350; the Lifecodes vial had sufficient probe to test 50 samples. The Promega vial sold for $400; 400 hundred samples could be tested from one Promega vial. According to Lifecodes, customers were willing to pay this increased price because of the "value added" features, such as the radioactive labeling.

The Federal Circuit recently held that a reasonable royalty calculation should not take into account past licenses unless there is also "evidence of a link between the...licenses and the claimed invention." *ResQNet.com, Inc. v. Lansa, Inc.*, 594 F.3d 860, 871 (Fed.Cir.2010). Judge Newman dissented, arguing that the patentee's damages expert and the district court took into account the link between the licenses and the claimed invention as well as the proportion of the value of each license attributable to the claimed invention. *ResQNet.com*, 594 F.3d at 876–77 (Newman, J., dissenting in part).

Even if there is an established royalty, do you see any problems with making the damages award equal to that royalty? What message do you send to potential or actual licensees, if all that they will pay if they lose an infringement suit is the license rate they could have taken prior to suit? *See generally Nickson Indus., Inc. v. Rol Mfg. Co.*, 847 F.2d 795, 798 (Fed.Cir.1988). Given that patent law requires damages be adequate to compensate for the infringement, the court has the power to increase an inadequate royalty rate. *Maxwell v. J. Baker, Inc.*, 86 F.3d 1098, 1110 (Fed.Cir.1996). *See generally, Fromson v. Citiplate, Inc.*, 699 F.Supp. 398, 407 (E.D.N.Y.1988), *aff'd*, 886 F.2d 1300 (Fed.Cir.1989). *See, e.g., Polaroid Corp. v. Eastman Kodak Co.*, 16 U.S.P.Q.2d 1481, 1534–35 (D. Mass.1990).

3. *The Factors Relevant to a Hypothetical Negotiation.* The most cited case in the area of reasonable royalty is *Georgia–Pacific Corp. v. United States Plywood Corp.*, 318 F.Supp. 1116 (S.D.N.Y. 1970), *modified and aff'd sub nom. Georgia–Pacific Corp. v. U.S. Plywood–Champion Papers, Inc.*, 446 F.2d 295 (2d Cir.1971). In *Georgia–Pacific*, the court assembled a list of factors that courts had used to determine a reasonable royalty in the past. These were:

1. the royalties received for licensing the patent in suit, proving or tending to prove an established royalty;

2. the royalty rates for comparable technologies;

3. the nature and scope of the license (*e.g.*, exclusive versus nonexclusive or territorial restrictions);

4. the patent owner's policy and marketing practice of refusing to grant licenses;

5. the commercial relationship between the patent owner and the infringer (*e.g.*, whether they are competitors);

6. the value of the invention as a generator of sales of the patent owner's other products (referred to as convoyed and derivative sales);

7. the duration of the patent and term of the license;

8. the established profitability of the product made under the patent, its commercial success, and its current popularity;

9. the advantages of the patented invention over modes or devices previously used;

10. the nature of the invention and benefits to users of the invention;

11. the extent to which the infringer has made use of the invention, and any evidence probative of the value of that use;

12. the percentage of the profit or selling price normally allowed for use of the invention or analogous inventions in the particular business or in comparable businesses;

13. the portion of the profit that can be credited to the invention as opposed to nonpatented features;

14. the expert testimony; and

15. the amount that a licensor (such as the patentee) and a licensee (such as the infringer) would have agreed upon (at the time the infringement began) if both had been reasonably and voluntarily trying to reach an agreement; that is the amount which a prudent licensee—who desired, as a business proposition, to obtain a license to manufacture and sell a particular article embodying the patented invention—would have been willing to pay as a royalty and yet be able to make a reasonable profit and which amount would have been acceptable by a prudent patentee who was willing to grant a license.

318 F.Supp. at 1120.

For the last thirty years, these factors have dominated most reasonable royalty determinations. Not every factor is relevant in a particular case and the factors can be described differently. The fifteenth factor—what a willing licensor and a willing licensee would have done—has become the typical framework for determining a hypothetical royalty.

4. *Willing Licensor—Willing Licensee Negotiation.* Some courts determine a reasonable royalty by comparison to an established royalty (if one exists), by imagining a hypothetical negotiation between a willing licensor and a willing licensee. Under this approach, the hypothetical royalty is based on a supposed arm's length negotiation, which takes place at the time infringement began, between a willing licensor and a willing licensee. It is assumed that both parties know that the patent will be sustained as valid and infringed, if litigated. See generally *Wang Labs., Inc. v. Toshiba Corp.*, 993 F.2d 858, 869–70 (Fed.Cir.1993); *Integra Lifesciences I, Ltd. v. Merck KGaA*, 331 F.3d 860, 869–70 (Fed.Cir.2003); *Riles v. Shell Exploration & Prod. Co.*, 298 F.3d 1302, 1311, 1313 (Fed.Cir.2002); *Unisplay, S.A. v. American Elec. Sign Co.*, 69 F.3d 512, 518–19 (Fed.Cir.1995).

While it is said that a reasonable royalty should leave an infringer with a reasonable profit, this hypothetical profit must be determined at the time of the hypothetical negotiations. Thus, it is irrelevant that, taking into consideration subsequent events, the infringer actually made little or no profit, or that the reasonable royalty yields a damage award larger than an infringer's actual profits. *See generally Radio Steel & Mfg. Co. v. MTD Prods., Inc.*, 788 F.2d 1554, 1557 (Fed.Cir.1986); *Hanson v. Alpine Valley Ski Area, Inc.*, 718 F.2d 1075, 1081 (Fed.Cir.1983); *State Indus., Inc. v. Mor–Flo Indus., Inc.*, 883 F.2d 1573, 1580 (Fed.Cir.1989); *Fromson v. W. Litho Plate & Supply Co.*, 853 F.2d 1568, 1578 n.18 (Fed.Cir.1988).

While patent law no longer allows an infringer's profits to be awarded as damages, a court may rely on internal memoranda created before infringement began that projects anticipated sales or profits. *See, e.g., Interactive Pictures Corp. v. Infinite Pictures, Inc.*, 274 F.3d 1371, 1384–85 (Fed.Cir.2001); *TWM Mfg. Co. v. Dura Corp.*, 789 F.2d 895, 900 (Fed.Cir.1986); *Polaroid Corp. v. Eastman Kodak Co.*, 16 U.S.P.Q.2d 1481, 1534 (D.Mass.1990). Do you believe that a court should also be allowed to examine an infringer's actual profits as probative of anticipated profits? *See Trans–World Mfg. Corp. v. Al Nyman & Sons, Inc.*, 750 F.2d 1552, 1568 (Fed.Cir.1984); *TWM Mfg. Co.*, 789 F.2d at 899.

Availability to the infringer of acceptable alternatives to the patented device may decrease the royalty rate. *Riles*, 298 F.3d at 1312; *Minco, Inc. v. Combustion Eng'g, Inc.*, 95 F.3d 1109, 1119 (Fed.Cir.1996). The infringer's election to infringe and its withdrawal from the business after enforcement of an injunction, though, are evidence of the absence of noninfringing alternatives. *TWM Mfg. Co.*, 789 F.2d at 900. Is an alternative that was not available at the time of the hypothetical negotiation relevant? *See Micro Chem., Inc. v. Lextron, Inc.*, 317 F.3d 1387, 1393–94 (Fed.Cir.2003).

One central problem with an approach premised on there having been a willing licensor and willing licensee, also sometimes known as a willing buy and willing seller, is that the fact of the litigation demonstrates that at least one of the parties was not actually willing. Put differently, adopting this approach goes a long way towards treating the patent as though it is being enforced with a liability rule rather than a property rule.

5. *An Infringing Patent Owner.* Because an exclusive license promises that nobody, not even the patent owner, will be allowed to infringe the patent, it is possible for a patent owner to be liable as an infringer. Do your opinions about compensatory damages change when the patent owner is the infringer?

6. *Burden of Proof.* While the Federal Circuit has recognized that the reasonable royalty determination encompasses elements of "fantasy," the patent owner still has the burden of putting forth satisfactory evidence on the amount of a reasonable royalty. *Fromson v. Western Litho Plate and Supply Co.*, 853 F.2d 1568, 1575 (Fed.Cir.1988). *See, e.g., Riles*, 298 F.3d at 1311–12; *Transclean Corp. v. Bridgewood Servs., Inc.*, 290 F.3d 1364, 1376–77 (Fed.Cir.2002); *Unisplay, S.A.*, 69 F.3d at 517–19; *Lindemann Maschinenfabrik GmbH v. American Hoist & Derrick Co.*, 895 F.2d 1403, 1407 (Fed.Cir.1990).

7. *Is Determining Compensation by Means of a Willing Licensor—Willing Licensee Negotiation Inherently Flawed in Some Cases?* A problem with basing damages on a willing licensor—willing licensee negotiation approach was discussed in *Panduit Corp. v. Stahlin Bros. Fibre Works*, 575 F.2d 1152 (6th Cir.1978). In that case, the court noted that basing a damages award on what a willing patent owner and a willing licensee would do, in addition to pretending that the patent owner's rights were never violated, makes infringement "a handy means for competitors to impose a 'compulsory license' policy upon every patent owner." *Id.* at 1158. In other words, a damages award that is adequate to compensate for the infringement might not be the same as a hypothetical royalty that was based on willing parties. More pointedly, it may understate the reservation price of the patentee—or how willing he actually is. In essence, the willing buyer/willing seller rule treats the patent as a liability rule, not a property rule. For example, if the patent owner sells a product but cannot prove entitlement to lost profits, the hypothetical royalty might be less than adequate compensation. One attempt to solve this problem is referred to as the analytical approach to determining reasonable royalties.

8. *The Analytical Approach.* The "analytical approach" to reasonable royalty determination attempts to allocate a portion of the infringer's actual or anticipated profits to the patent owner as a reasonable royalty. *See, e.g., TWM Mfg. Co. v. Dura Corp.*, 789 F.2d 895 (Fed.Cir.1986). In *TWM*, the infringer had projected a gross profit of 53%. From this figure, the court subtracted the infringer's projected overhead, and the industry's standard net profit and was left with 30%. The court awarded the patent owner that 30% as a reasonable royalty. This approach enforces the patent with more of a property rule than a liability rule.

9. *The 25% Rule.* Some courts have used a 25% "rule of thumb" for determining a reasonable royalty, and until recently the Federal Circuit had never squarely confronted its use. Recently, however, the Federal Circuit rejected this approach, instructing courts to use evidence tied to the case in order to determine a reasonable royalty:

> This court now holds as a matter of Federal Circuit law that the 25 percent rule of thumb is a fundamentally flawed tool for determining a baseline royalty rate in a hypothetical negotiation. Evidence relying on the 25 percent rule of thumb is thus inadmissible under *Daubert* and the Federal Rules of Evidence, because it fails to tie a reasonable royalty base to the facts of the case at issue.

Uniloc USA, Inc. v. Microsoft Corp., 632 F.3d 1292, 1315 (Fed.Cir. 2011).

d. LIMITATIONS ON AWARDING MONEY DAMAGES

In addition to the limitations on awarding money damages that result from the requirements relating to proving entitlement to lost profits or royalties, Congress and the judiciary have imposed additional limitations. The judicial limitations are the foreseeability requirement and the entire-market-value rule. The Congressional limitations are the six-year rule and the notice requirement.

i.   *Foreseeability*

Rite–Hite Corp. v. Kelley Co., Inc.

56 F.3d 1538 (Fed.Cir.1995).

■ Before Archer, Chief Judge, Rich, Circuit Judge, Smith, Senior Circuit Judge, and Nies, Newman, Mayer, Michel, Plager, Lourie, Clevenger, Rader, and Schall, Circuit Judges.

■ Opinion of the court filed by Circuit Judge Lourie, in which Circuit Judges Rich, Michel, Plager, Clevenger, and Schall join.

■ Lourie, Circuit Judge.

* * *

BACKGROUND

On March 22, 1983, Rite–Hite sued Kelley, alleging that Kelley's "Truk Stop" vehicle restraint infringed Rite–Hite's U.S. Patent 4,373,847 ("the '847 patent"). [Footnote omitted.] The '847 patent, issued February 15, 1983, is directed to a device for securing a vehicle to a loading dock to prevent the vehicle from separating from the dock during loading or unloading. Any such separation would create a gap between the vehicle and dock and create a danger for a forklift operator.

* * *

. . . [T]he damage issues were tried to the court. Rite–Hite, 774 F. Supp. at 1514, 21 USPQ2d at 1801. Rite–Hite sought damages calculated as lost profits for two types of vehicle restraints that it made and sold: the "Manual Dok–Lok" model 55 (MDL–55), which incorporated the invention covered by the '847 patent, and the "Automatic Dok–Lok" model 100 (ADL–100), which was not covered by the patent in suit. The ADL–100 was the first vehicle restraint Rite–Hite put on the market and it was covered by one or more patents other than the patent in suit. The Kelley Truk Stop restraint was designed to compete primarily with Rite–Hite's ADL–100. Both employed an electric motor and functioned automatically, and each sold for $1,000–$1,500 at the wholesale level, in contrast to the MDL–55, which sold for one-third to one-half the price of the motorized devices. Rite–Hite does not assert that Kelley's Truk Stop restraint infringed the patents covering the ADL–100.

Of the 3,825 infringing Truk Stop devices sold by Kelley, the district court found that, "but for" Kelley's infringement, Rite–Hite would have made 80 more sales of its MDL–55; 3,243 more sales of its ADL–100; and 1,692 more sales of dock levelers, a bridging platform sold with the restraints and used to bridge the edges of a vehicle and dock. The court awarded Rite–Hite as a manufacturer the wholesale profits that it lost on lost sales of the ADL–100 restraints, MDL–55 restraints, and restraint-leveler packages. . . .

On appeal . . . Kelley argues that (1) the patent statute does not provide for damages based on Rite–Hite's lost profits on ADL–100 restraints because the ADL–100s are not covered by the patent in suit. . . .

* * *

I. Lost Profits on the ADL–100 Restraints

The district court's decision to award lost profits damages pursuant to 35 U.S.C. § 284 turned primarily upon the quality of Rite–Hite's proof of actual lost profits. The court found that, "but for" Kelley's infringing Truk Stop competition, Rite–Hite would have sold 3,243 additional ADL–100 restraints and 80 additional MDL–55 restraints. The court reasoned that awarding lost profits fulfilled the patent statute's goal of affording complete compensation for infringement and compensated Rite–Hite for the ADL–100 sales that Kelley "anticipated taking from Rite–Hite when it marketed the Truk Stop against the ADL–100." *Rite–Hite*, 774 F. Supp. at 1540. The court stated, "[t]he rule applied here therefore does not extend Rite–Hite's patent rights excessively, because Kelley could reasonably have foreseen that its infringement of the '847 patent would make it liable for lost ADL–100 sales in addition to lost MDL–55 sales." *Id* . . . .

Kelley maintains that Rite–Hite's lost sales of the ADL–100 restraints do not constitute an injury that is legally compensable by means of lost profits. It has uniformly been the law, Kelley argues, that to recover damages in the form of lost profits a patentee must prove that, "but for" the infringement, it would have sold a product covered by the patent in suit to the customers who bought from the infringer. Under the circumstances of this case, in Kelley's view, the patent statute provides only for damages calculated as a reasonable royalty. Rite–Hite, on the other hand, argues that the only restriction on an award of actual lost profits damages for patent infringement is proof of causation-in-fact. A patentee, in its view, is entitled to all the profits it would have made on any of its products "but for" the infringement. Each party argues that a judgment in favor of the other would frustrate the purposes of the patent statute. Whether the lost profits at issue are legally compensable is a question of law, which we review *de novo*.

Our analysis of this question necessarily begins with the patent statute. *See General Motors Corp. v. Devex Corp.*, 461 U.S. 648, 653–54 (1983). Implementing the constitutional power under Article I, section 8, to secure to inventors the exclusive right to their discoveries, Congress has provided in 35 U.S.C. § 284 as follows:

> Upon finding for the claimant the court shall award the claimant damages adequate to compensate for the infringement, but in no event less than a

> reasonable royalty for the use made of the invention by the infringer, together with interest and costs as fixed by the court.

35 U.S.C. § 284 (1988). The statute thus mandates that a claimant receive damages "adequate" to compensate for infringement. Section 284 further instructs that a damage award shall be "in no event less than a reasonable royalty"; the purpose of this alternative is not to direct the form of compensation, but to set a floor below which damage awards may not fall. *Del Mar Avionics, Inc. v. Quinton Instrument Co.*, 836 F.2d 1320, 1326 (Fed.Cir.1987). Thus, the language of the statute is expansive rather than limiting. It affirmatively states that damages must be adequate, while providing only a lower limit and no other limitation.

The Supreme Court spoke to the question of patent damages in *General Motors*, stating that, in enacting § 284, Congress sought to "ensure that the patent owner would in fact receive full compensation for 'any damages' [the patentee] suffered as a result of the infringement." *General Motors*, 461 U.S. at 654; *see also* H.R. Rep. No. 1587, 79th Cong., 2d Sess., 1 (1946) (the Bill was intended to allow recovery of "any damages the complainant can prove"); S. Rep. No. 1503, 79th Cong., 2d Sess., 2 (1946) (same). Thus, while the statutory text states tersely that the patentee receive "adequate" damages, the Supreme Court has interpreted this to mean that "adequate" damages should approximate those damages that will *fully compensate* the patentee for infringement. Further, the Court has cautioned against imposing limitations on patent infringement damages, stating: "When Congress wished to limit an element of recovery in a patent infringement action, it said so explicitly." *General Motors*, 461 U.S. at 653, 103 S. Ct. 2061 (refusing to impose limitation on court's authority to award interest).

In *Aro Mfg. Co. v. Convertible Top Replacement Co.*, 377 U.S. 476 (1964), the Court discussed the statutory standard for measuring patent infringement damages, explaining:

> The question to be asked in determining damages is "how much had the Patent Holder and Licensee suffered by the infringement. And that question [is] primarily: had the Infringer not infringed, what would the Patentee Holder–Licensee have made?"

377 U.S. at 507 (plurality opinion) (citations omitted). This surely states a "but for" test. In accordance with the Court's guidance, we have held that the general rule for determining actual damages to a patentee that is itself producing the patented item is to determine the sales and profits lost to the patentee because of the infringement....

* * *

... Kelley argues that damages for the ADL–100, even if in fact caused by the infringement, are not legally compensable because the ADL–100 is not covered by the patent in suit.

Preliminarily, we wish to affirm that the "test" for compensability of damages under § 284 is not solely a "but for" test in the sense that an infringer must compensate a patentee for any and all damages that proceed from the act of patent infringement. Notwithstanding the broad language of § 284, judicial relief cannot redress every conceivable harm that can be traced to an alleged wrongdoing. See Associated General Contractors, Inc. v. California State Council of Carpenters, 459 U.S. 519, 536 (1983).[4] For example, remote consequences, such as a heart attack of the inventor or loss in value of shares of common stock of a patentee corporation caused indirectly by infringement are not compensable. Thus, along with establishing that a particular injury suffered by a patentee is a "but for" consequence of infringement, there may also be a background question whether the asserted injury is of the type for which the patentee may be compensated.

Judicial limitations on damages, either for certain classes of plaintiffs or for certain types of injuries have been imposed in terms of "proximate cause" or "foreseeability." *See Consolidated Rail Corp. v. Gottshall*, 512 U.S. 532, ___, 114 S. Ct. 2396, 2406 (1994). Such labels have been judicial tools used to limit legal responsibility for the consequences of one's conduct that are too remote to justify compensation. *See Holmes v. Securities Investor Protection Corp.*, 503 U.S. 258 (1992). The general principles expressed in the common law tell us that the question of legal compensability is one "to be determined on the facts of each case upon mixed considerations of logic, common sense, justice, policy and precedent." *See* 1 Street, *Foundations of Legal Liability* 110 (1906) (quoted in W. Page Keeton *et al.*, *Prosser & Keeton on the Law of Torts* § 42, at 279 (5th ed. 1984)). [Footnote omitted.]

We believe that under § 284 of the patent statute, the balance between full compensation, which is the meaning that the Supreme Court has attributed to the statute, and the reasonable limits of liability encompassed by general principles of law can best be viewed in terms of reasonable, objective foreseeability. If a particular injury was or should have been reasonably foreseeable by an infringing competitor in the relevant market, broadly defined, that injury is generally compensable absent a persuasive reason to the contrary. Here, the court determined that Rite–Hite's lost sales of the ADL–100, a product that directly competed with the infringing product, were reasonably foreseeable. We agree with that conclusion. Being responsible for lost sales of a competitive product is surely foreseeable; such losses constitute the full compensation set forth by Congress, as interpreted by the Supreme Court, while staying well within the traditional meaning of proximate cause. Such lost sales should therefore clearly be compensable.

Recovery for lost sales of a device not covered by the patent in suit is not of course expressly provided for by the patent statute. Express language is not required, however. Statutes speak in general terms rather than

---

4. As succinctly summarized by Keeton et al.:

In a philosophical sense, the consequences of an act go forward to eternity, and the causes of an event go back to the dawn of human events, and beyond. But any attempt to impose responsibility upon such a basis would result in infinite liability for all wrongful acts, and would "set society on edge and fill the courts with endless litigation." As a practical matter, legal responsibility must be limited to those causes which are so closely connected with the result and of such significance that the law is justified in imposing liability. Some boundary must be set to liability for the consequences of any act, upon the basis of some social idea of justice or policy.

W. Page Keeton *et al.*, *Prosser & Keeton on the Law of Torts* § 41, at 264 (5th. ed. 1984) (citation and footnote omitted).

specifically expressing every detail. Under the patent statute, damages should be awarded "where necessary to afford the plaintiff full compensation for the infringement." *General Motors*, 461 U.S. at 654. Thus, to refuse to award reasonably foreseeable damages necessary to make Rite–Hite whole would be inconsistent with the meaning of § 284.

Kelley asserts that to allow recovery for the ADL–100 would contravene the policy reason for which patents are granted: "[T]o promote the progress of . . . the useful arts." U.S. Const., art. I, § 8, cl. 8. Because an inventor is only entitled to exclusivity to the extent he or she has invented and disclosed a novel, nonobvious, and useful device, Kelley argues, a patent may never be used to restrict competition in the sale of products not covered by the patent in suit. In support, Kelley cites antitrust case law condemning the use of a patent as a means to obtain a "monopoly" on unpatented material . . . . .

These cases are inapposite to the issue raised here. The present case does not involve expanding the limits of the patent grant in violation of the antitrust laws; it simply asks, once infringement of a valid patent is found, what compensable injuries result from that infringement, *i.e.*, how may the patentee be made whole. Rite–Hite is not attempting to exclude its competitors from making, using, or selling a product not within the scope of its patent. The Truk Stop restraint was found to infringe the '847 patent, and Rite–Hite is simply seeking adequate compensation for that infringement; this is not an antitrust issue. Allowing compensation for such damage will "promote the Progress of . . . the useful Arts" by providing a stimulus to the development of new products and industries. *See* 1 Ernest B. Lipscomb III, *Walker on Patents* 65 (3d ed. 1984) (quoting Simonds, *Summary of the Law of Patents* 9 (1883)) ("The patent laws promote the progress in different ways, prominent among which are by protecting the investment of capital in the development and working of a new invention from ruinous competition till the investment becomes remunerative."). [Footnote omitted.]

Kelley further asserts that, as a policy matter, inventors should be encouraged by the law to practice their inventions. This is not a meaningful or persuasive argument, at least in this context. A patent is granted in exchange for a patentee's disclosure of an invention, not for the patentee's use of the invention. There is no requirement in this country that a patentee make, use, or sell its patented invention. See *Continental Paper Bag Co. v. Eastern Paper Bag Co.*, 210 U.S. 405, 424–30 (1908) (irrespective of a patentee's own use of its patented invention, it may enforce its rights under the patent). If a patentee's failure to practice a patented invention frustrates an important public need for the invention, a court need not enjoin infringement of the patent. *See* 35 U.S.C. § 283 (1988) (courts may grant injunctions in accordance with the principles of equity). . . . Whether a patentee sells its patented invention is not crucial in determining lost profits damages. Normally, if the patentee is not selling a product, by definition there can be no lost profits. However, in this case, Rite–Hite did sell its own patented products, the MDL–55 and the ADL–100 restraints.

* * *

Kelley has thus not provided, nor do we find, any justification in the statute, precedent, policy, or logic to limit the compensability of lost sales of a patentee's device that directly competes with the infringing device if it is proven that those lost sales were caused in fact by the infringement. Such lost sales are reasonably foreseeable and the award of damages is necessary to provide adequate compensation for infringement under 35 U.S.C. § 284. Thus, Rite–Hite's ADL–100 lost sales are legally compensable and we affirm the award of lost profits on the 3,283 sales lost to Rite–Hite's wholesale business in ADL–100 restraints. [Footnote omitted.]

* * *

■ NIES, CIRCUIT JUDGE, with whom ARCHER, CHIEF JUDGE, SMITH, SENIOR CIRCUIT JUDGE, and MAYER, CIRCUIT JUDGE join, Dissenting-in-Part.

SUMMARY

The majority uses the provision in 35 U.S.C. § 284 for "damages" as a tool to expand the property rights granted by a patent. I dissent.

No one disputes that Rite–Hite is entitled to "full compensation for any damages suffered as a result of the infringement." *General Motors Corp. v. Devex Corp.*, 461 U.S. 648, 653–54 (1983). "Damages, 'however, is a word of art.'" "Damages in a legal sense means the compensation which the law will award for an injury done." *Recovery in Patent Infringement Suits: Hearings on H.R. 5231 [later H.R. 5311] Before the Committee on Patents*, 79th Cong., 2nd Sess. 9 (1946) (statement of Conder C. Henry, Asst. Comm'r of Patents) (hereinafter "House Hearings"). Thus, the question is, "What are the injuries for which full compensation must be paid?".

The majority divorces "actual damages" from injury to patent rights.[1] The majority holds that a patentee is entitled to recover its lost profits caused by the infringer's competition with the patentee's business in ADL restraints, products not incorporating the invention of the patent in suit but assertedly protected by other unlitigated patents. Indeed, the majority states a broader rule for the award of lost profits on any goods of the patentee with which the infringing device competes, even products in the public domain.

I would hold that the diversion of ADL–100 sales is not an injury to patentee's property rights granted by the '847 patent. To constitute legal injury for which lost profits may be awarded, the infringer must interfere with the patentee's property right to an exclusive market in goods embodying the invention of the patent in suit. The patentee's property rights do not extend to its market in other goods unprotected by the litigated patent. Rite–Hite was compensated for the lost profits for 80 sales associated with

---

1. The term "actual damages" is used to distinguish from an award based on a hypothetical reasonable royalty. In the majority view, this dissent "confuses" the patent right to exclude with the separate determination of actual damages for patent infringement. Contrary to the majority, both determinations depend on injury to patent rights. The patent defines the metes and bounds of legal injury. As the Supreme Court stated in *Continental Paper Bag Co. v. Eastern Paper Bag Co.*, 210 U.S. 405, 430 (1908): "From the character of the right of the patentee we may judge of his remedies." The majority and the dissent do not merely quibble over "line-drawing" by reason of "remoteness" of an injury but rather fundamentally disagree over the legal scope of the market protected by a patent.

the MDL–55, the only product it sells embodying the '847 invention. That is the totality of any possible entitlement to lost profits. Under 35 U.S.C. § 284, therefore, Rite–Hite is entitled to "damages" calculated as a reasonable royalty on the remainder of Kelley's infringing restraints.

* * *

C. *Property Rights Granted by Patent*

An examination of pre–1946 Supreme Court precedent discloses that the legal scope of actual damages for patent infringement was limited to the extent of the defendant's interference with the patentee's market in goods embodying the invention of the patent in suit. This limitation reflects the underlying public policy of the patent statute to promote commerce in new products for the public's benefit. More importantly, it protects the only property rights of a patentee which are protectable, namely those granted by the patent. The patentee obtained as its property an exclusive market in the patented goods. . . .

In *Continental Paper Bag Co. v. Eastern Paper Bag Co.*, 210 U.S. 405, 430 (1908), the Supreme Court advised: "From the character of the right of the patentee we may judge of his remedies." Until the Act of 1952, the right granted to a patentee was stated in terms of the exclusive right to make and use and vend the protected invention. [Footnote omitted.] This language tracks the English Statute of Monopolies (1624) under which the Crown did give a monopoly to an inventor to make and work certain new manufactures within the realm for a limited period. [Footnote omitted.] The term "invention" itself meant the establishment of a new trade or industry. Thus, under the Statute of Monopolies, an "inventor" was anyone who developed an industry previously *unknown in England.* The period of exclusivity was given for the inventor to reap his reward in the marketplace without competition while thereby training others to make and use his invention at the end of the patent term. [Footnote omitted.] Indeed, failure to exploit in England was a basis for cancellation of the grant.

In contrast, in the United States, the grant of a patent did not convey to the inventor a right to make, use and vend his invention despite the statutory language originally to that effect. In interpreting a patentee's rights in *Crown Die & Tool Co. v. Nye Tool & Machine Works*, 261 U.S. 24, 26 (1923), the Supreme Court explained that an inventor has a natural right to make, use and sell his invention, and that a patent augments an inventor's position by making that natural right *exclusive* for a limited time. The statutory language was interpreted to give a right to *preclude others* from interfering with the patentee's exclusivity in providing the patented goods to the public. *Id.* at 34. . . .

An inventor is entitled to a patent by meeting the statutory requirements respecting disclosure of the invention. Prior commercialization of the invention has never been a requirement in our law to *obtain* a patent. An inventor is merely required to teach others his invention in his patent application. Thus, when faced with the question of whether a patentee was entitled to enjoin an infringer despite the patentee's failure to use its invention, the Supreme Court held for the patentee. *Continental Paper Bag*, 210 U.S. at 424–430. Congress provided a right to exclusive use and to deny that privilege would destroy that right. *Id.* at 430. An injunction preserves the patentee's exclusive right to market embodiments of the patented invention.

These clearly established principles, however, do not lead to the conclusion that the patentee's failure to commercialize plays no role in determining damages. That the *quid pro quo* for *obtaining* a patent is disclosure of the invention does not dictate the answer to the question of the legal scope of damages. The patent system was not designed merely to build up a library of information by disclosure, valuable though that is, but to get new products into the marketplace during the period of exclusivity so that the public receives full benefits from the grant. The Congress of the fledgling country did not act so quickly in enacting the Patent Act of 1790 merely to further intellectual pursuits. . . .

* * *

Thus, a patentee may withhold from the public the benefit of use of its invention during the patent term, and the public has no way to withdraw the grant for nonuse. Like the owner of a farm, a patentee may let his property lay fallow. In doing so, "he has but suppressed his own." *Bement*, 186 U.S. at 90. But it is anomalous to hold that Congress, by providing an incentive for the patentee to enter the market, intended the patentee to be rewarded the same for letting his property lay fallow during the term of the patent as for making the investment necessary to commercializing a new product or licensing others to do so, in order that the public benefits from the invention. The *status quo* may serve the patentee's interest, but that is not the only consideration. The patent grant "was never designed for [an inventor's] exclusive profit or advantage." *Kendall v. Winsor*, 62 U.S. (21 How.) 322, 328 (1858).

* * *

G. *"Foreseeability" is not the Test for Patent Damages*

* * *

Nothing in the statute supports the majority's "foreseeability" rule as the sole basis for patent damages. To the contrary, no-fault liability is imposed on "innocent" infringers, those who have no knowledge of the existence of a patent until suit is filed. Damages are recoverable for up to six years of unknowing infringement before suit. 35 U.S.C. § 286 (1988). "Foreseeability" is a wholly anomalous concept to interject as the basis for determining legal injury for patent infringement. While unknowing infringers cannot "foresee" any injury to the patentee, they are subject to liability for damages, including lost profits, for competition with the patentee's patented goods. Now they will be liable for diverting sales of the patentee's unprotected competitive products as well.

* * *

The majority goes on to find the award of damages for lost sales of ADL–100s a *foreseeable* injury for infringement of the '847 patent. This is a remarkable finding. The facts are that Rite–Hite began marketing its ADL–100 motorized restraint in 1980. Kelley put out its Truk Stop restraint in June 1982. There is no dispute in this case [footnote omitted] that Kelley "designed around" the protection afforded by any patent related to the ADL–100 with which Kelley's Truk Stop restraint was intended to compete. Two years later, the '847 patent in suit issued on the later-developed alternative hook technology used in the MDL–55. Kelley would have to have had prescient vision to foresee that it would be held an infringer of the unknown claims of the subsequently issued '847 patent and that its *lawful competition* with the ADL–100 would be transformed into a compensable injury.

Kelley would also have had to foresee that, for the first time in over 200 years of patent infringement suits, a court would extend protection to a part of a patentee's business which is not dependent on the patentee's use of the patented technology. . . .

NOTES

1. *Should A Patent Owner Have To Practice Claimed Invention To Be Entitled To Lost Profits?* As the opinions in *Rite–Hite* show, one's views on appropriate compensatory remedies is informed by one's views on the purpose of the patent laws. For the dissenters, full disclosure of the patented invention to the public is not a sufficient *quid pro quo* for a non-practicing patent owner to have access to the full range of compensatory remedies. Do you agree with the dissenters? If you agree with the dissenters, are you also in favor of compulsory licensing? *See generally* Note, *The Nonmanufacturing Patent Owner: Toward a Theory of Efficient Infringement*, 86 CAL. L. REV. 179 (1998).

Even if you generally accept that a patent owner who does not practice the claimed invention may be entitled to the full range of compensatory remedies, would you make an exception based upon the reason that the patent owner does not work the patent? For example, is there a legally meaningful difference between (a) the patent owner who does not sell a patented invention because that invention would have competed against another product that the patent owner sells and (b) the patent owner who does not sell a patented invention because he or she simply underestimated the demand for that invention? *See generally* Roger D. Blair & Thomas F. Cotter, *Rethinking Patent Damages*, 10 TEX. INTELL. PROP. L.J. 1, 74–84 (2001), which argues that, from an economic point of view, the two situations are quite different.

2. *Foreseeability As A Limitation On Damages.* As *Rite–Hite* holds, patent infringement can result in some damages that are just too remote to be compensable. Examples of such damages, given in dicta in *Rite–Hite*, are an inventor's heart attack and the loss of value in common stock of a patent owning corporation. *See also Interactive Pictures Corp. v. Infinite Pictures, Inc.*, 274 F.3d 1371, 1386 (Fed.Cir.2001).

The test for compensability is reasonable, objective foreseeability. *See also Micro Chem., Inc. v. Lextron, Inc.*, 318 F.3d 1119, 1125–26 (Fed.Cir.2003); *Minco, Inc. v. Combustion Eng'g, Inc.*, 95 F.3d 1109, 1118 (Fed.Cir.1996). In *Rite–Hite*, the majority held that it was reasonably forseeable that Kelly's infringement would cause Rite–Hite to lose sales of a product that, while not the invention of the patent in suit, competed directly with Kelley's infringing product. Do you agree that this was, or should have been, reasonably foreseeable to Kelley?

ii. The Entire–Market–Value Rule

Regardless of how damages are determined (*i.e.*, lost profits or royalties), two important issues may arise. These issues relate to apportionment and complementary products. The apportionment issue arises when a patented device is part of a larger product. For example, the patent owner may have invented a new car headlight. If a car dealer sold a sports car with the infringing headlight, when (if ever) should damages be determined based on the entire market value of the car? The complementary products issue arises when the use of a patented invention causes an increased demand for unpatented products. For example, a newly invented digital camera may increase the sales of (a) memory cards that store digital images, (b) printers that print digital pictures, and (c) paper on which to print the pictures. When (if ever) should damages for the sale of infringing cameras be based on the entire market value of all the complementary products. The entire-market-value rule answers these questions.

Pursuant to the entire-market-value rule, when the patented feature makes up only a portion of the product (the apportionment issue), the entire market value of the entire product is used to compute damages if the patent-related feature is the basis for customer demand. *See, e.g., Bose Corp. v. JBL, Inc.*, 274 F.3d 1354, 1361 (Fed.Cir.2001), where the court stated:

> [T]he invention of the '721 patent improved the performance of the loudspeakers and contributed substantially to the increased demand for the products in which it was incorporated. Bose presented unrebutted evidence that the invention of the '721 patent ... improved bass tones. JBL's marketing executive also acknowledged that improved bass performance was a prerequisite for JBL's decision to go forward with manufacturing and selling certain loudspeakers. Bose presented evidence detailing its efforts to market the benefits of its loudspeakers using the invention of the '721 patent and provided testimony on its increased sales in the year following the introduction of its speakers containing the invention.

Can you imagine a buyer purchasing a sports car because of the headlight?

Pursuant to the entire-market-value rule, when a physically separate product is sold together with the patented invention (the complementary products issue), the entire market value of both items is used to compute damages if the physically separate product functions together with the patented invention in some manner so as to produce a desired end product or result. The entire market value of both products is not used to compute damages if the separate product is sold together with the patented invention only as a matter of convenience or business advantage. *See, e.g., Rite–Hite Corp.*, 56 F.3d at 1550–51, where Rite–Hite sought to recover damages for dock levelers and the court stated:

> The dock levelers operated to bridge the gap between a loading dock and a truck. The patented vehicle restraint operated to secure the rear of the truck to the loading dock. Although the two devices may have been used together, they did not function together to achieve one result and each could effectively have been used independently of each other.... The dock

levelers were ... sold by Kelley with the restraints only for marketing reasons, not because they essentially functioned together.

If a patent owner invented a new digital camera and sought to recover damages for lost sales of (a) memory cards, (b) printers, and (c) paper, the entire market value of which items (if any) do you believe would be included when assessing damages?

Lucent Technologies Inc. v. Gateway, Inc.

509 F.Supp.2d 912 (S.D.Cal.2007).

■ Hon. Rudi M. Brewster, U.S. Senior District Judge.

* * *

VII.   DAMAGES

By statute, the damages for infringement are set at an amount "adequate to compensate for the infringement, but in no event less than a reasonable royalty for the use made of the invention by the infringer." An award of damages by the jury "must be upheld unless the amount is grossly excessive or monstrous, clearly not supported by the evidence, or based only on speculation or guesswork." *Monsanto Co. v. Ralph*, 382 F.3d 1374, 1383 (Fed. Cir. 2004) (quoting *Brooktree Corp. v. Advanced Micro Devices, Inc.*, 977 F.2d 1555, 1580 (Fed. Cir. 1992)).

Microsoft sets forth several grounds on which it argues that the jury's damages verdict should be overturned as a matter of law and/or a new trial should be granted: (1) the royalty rate and the royalty base used to calculate a reasonable royalty;

* * *

These are each reviewed below.

A.   The Royalty Base—Application of the Entire Market Value Rule

Lucent presented a damages model based on a reasonable royalty for the patent; the model presented was a 0.5% royalty rate applied to the average price of a personal computer over the relevant years. Microsoft now argues that there was insufficient evidence to support the application of the entire market value rule on which Lucent predicated the royalty base on the cost of the entire computer.

The entire market value rule is applicable where patented and unpatented components are sold together as a functional unit "so as to produce a desired end product or result." *Rite–Hite Corp. v. Kelley Co., Inc.*, 56 F.3d 1538, 1550 (Fed.Cir.1995). Moreover, the patented component must be "the basis for customer demand" or "substantially create the value of the component parts." *Id.* at 1549.

Two major problems arise in applying the entire market value rule here. The first is the failure of the evidence to establish a link between the cost of the *computers* (rather than the operating system, Windows Media Player, the MP3 codec or some other "unit") and the customer demand or value of the patented technology. The second and probably even more troublesome problem is the failure to establish that the patented features themselves produced any customer demand or value of the product.

The accused products were the HQ and fast encoders present in Windows Media Player. Lucent failed to establish at trial that a commercial necessity and/or desirability of these features was required in computers. Instead, Lucent established at most that there was a desirability that personal computers carry MP3 capabilities. Thobias Jones, a software design engineer at Microsoft, testified that MP3 was a popular request from users who desired Windows Media Player. (Trial Tr. vol. IV, 14:1–13, Feb. 1, 2007.) Dell representative Leonard Zwik testified that Windows Media Player was an integrated function of the computer's operating system and that Dell would not sell a Windows operating system without Windows Media Player. (*Id.* at 72:5–73:1.) He also testified that there was no customer demand for the version of Windows (XP–N) that lacked Windows Media Player. (*Id.* 73:2–74:10.) Witness David Fester, general manager of the Microsoft Windows Digital Media Division testified that MP3 was a feature which attracted users to Windows Media Player. (*Id.* at 85:23–86:7). Finally, Microsoft employee Geoff Harris, responsible for the development of the Windows Media Player product, testified that there was a market need and consumer demand for MP3 encoding capabilities. (*Id.* at 112:16–113:2.) The sum of this evidence establishes at most a market demand for an operating system containing Windows Media Player with MP3 capabilities. It does not establish that the demand for *computers* is based on Microsoft's Windows Media Player and/or MP3 technology.

Even more problematically, however, is the lack of evidence showing that the patented features set forth in the claims of the '457 and/or '080 patents were the basis for customer demand and/or the substantial value of the product sold. Importantly, neither the '457 patent nor the '080 patent covers MP3 capability per se. Rather, each patent relates to a particular *feature* of MP3 capability.[1] Hence, to apply the entire market value rule, the evidence must show that these features were the basis of the customer demand or substantially created the value of the product. *See e.g., Fonar Corp. v. General Elec. Co.*, 107 F.3d 1543, 1549, 1553 (Fed. Cir. 1997) (the multi-angle oblique (MAO) imaging feature claimed in the patent was emphasized as a selling feature in the device found to infringe and thus a reasonable royalty was correctly based on the cost of the entire device); *Bose Corp. v. JBL. Inc.*, 274 F.3d 1354, 1361 (Fed. Cir. 2001) (entire loudspeaker cost was the proper royalty base where the patented feature functioned as one unit with the other components to provide the desired audible performance, the patented feature improved the performance of the

---

1. Lucent's own witness Dr. Jayant, testified that MP3 technology originated from many sources and is composed of many features, including the bit stream syntax (how the bit stream is interpreted and meaningfully decoded to play back the audio signal), features of the decoder and some features of the encoder. (Trial Tr. vol. II, 121:11–23, 123:2–22, Jan. 30, 2007.) In contrast, the claims at issue related to only particular features that could be used in conjunction with MP3 encoders. The '457 patent relates to the methods of audio coding using a tonality value and a masking threshold. The '080 patent relates to methods and apparatus for audio coding which incorporates the use of an absolute hearing threshold in conjunction with a masking threshold.

loudspeaker, and the improved performance was the basis for the customer demand); *Tec Air, Inc. v. Denso Mfg. Michigan Inc.*, 192 F.3d 1353, 1362 (Fed. Cir. 1999) (damages based on entire assembly of motor, radiator and condensor where the performance of the whole assembly was important to the customer, the fan was required for the assembly and the patented method of balancing the fan was critical to the function of the assembly and important to customer demand for the assembly); *compare e.g., Imonex Services, Inc. v. W.H. Munzprufer Dietmar Trenner GMBH*, 408 F.3d 1374, 1380 (Fed. Cir. 2005) (insufficient evidence for the entire market rule where the patented feature, which differentiated which coins were put into the machine, was not shown to be the basis for the customer demand of the entire laundry machine); *Medtronic, Inc. v. Catalyst Research Corp.*, 547 F. Supp. 401, 414 (D.C. Minn. 1982) (the cost of entire pacemaker could not be the royalty base where value of the pacemaker was not substantially due to the patented features of the battery).

Here, the Court finds no evidence adduced at trial that establishes that the patented features of either the '457 or the '080 patents were critical to MP3 or that they established the basis for the customer demand or value of MP3, let alone were critical or provided value to the whole computer. The evidence cited by Lucent from the trial record shows only that MP3 capabilities *overall* were a commercially important feature. According to Lucent's expert Dr. Jayant, MP3 technology originated from many sources and the MP3 standard specifies many aspects of audio compression. (Trial Tr. vol. II, 121:11–123–22, Jan 30, 2007.) Although Jayant pointed out what he considered important in the MP3, the key technology he identified related to the decoding of the bit stream syntax (which allows decoders from different manufactures to interpret and play back the audio signal); he did not identify either the invention of the '080 patent or the '457 patent as critical to MP3. (*Id.* at 123:2–22.) Additionally, the evidence demonstrated that although the inventions of these patents could be used with the MP3 standard, they were not required or critical to practice the MP3 standard.

Finally, Lucent's assertion that even absent application of the entire market value rule, the use of the computers as a royalty base was correct because Microsoft has joint and several liability for Dell's and Gateway's infringement, is misplaced. Although an indirect infringer may be liable for all damages attributable to infringing sales. *Water Tech. v. Calco, Ltd.*, 850 F.2d 660, 669 (Fed. Cir. 1988); *Glenayre v. Jackson*, 443 F.3d 851 (Fed. Cir. 2006), simply because Dell and Gateway sell computers does not automatically designate the computer as the royalty base. The same foundation for application of the entire market value rule would have been required even if Lucent had been in direct litigation with Dell and Gateway. In the absence of this nexus, Lucent may only recover damages for the value of the patented technology itself, regardless of the named defendant.

In sum, the Court finds that there was insufficient evidence to establish the required nexus between the patented features and the value of the entire computer and therefore, the jury's application of the entire market value rule to the computer was unsupported as a matter of law. On this basis, Microsoft's motion for judgment as a matter of law on the damages award is GRANTED.

NOTE

What about repair parts? Do you believe that it might be reasonably foreseeable that selling an infringing product would deprive the patent owner of sales of repair parts? Under what circumstances (if any) should the entire market value of repair or spare parts be used in calculating damages? *See Carborundum Co. v. Molten Metal Equip. Innovations, Inc.*, 72 F.3d 872, 881–82 (Fed.Cir.1995). *See also King Instrument Corp. v. Otari Corp.*, 767 F.2d 853, 865 (Fed.Cir.1985).

iii. The Six–Year Rule—35 U.S.C. § 286

Section 286 of Title 35 states that "no recovery shall be had for any infringement committed more than six years prior to the filing of the complaint or counterclaims for infringement." Importantly, § 286 is not a statute of limitations. It does not preclude a patent owner from bringing suit. Section 286 only precludes a patent owner from recovering for infringement that occurred more than six years before the suit was filed. This six-year limitation on damages has been part of patent law since 1897. *A.C. Aukerman Co. v. R.L. Chaides Constr. Co.*, 960 F.2d 1020, 1030 (Fed.Cir.1992).

Even if some damages are precluded by Section 286, the patent owner is not barred by this statute from recovering for infringement that occurred within the six years prior to the filing of the suit. *Standard Oil Co. v. Nippon Shokubai Kagaku Kogyo Co.*, 754 F.2d 345, 347–48 (Fed.Cir.1985). What about contributory infringers whose actions occurred more than six years before the suit but the direct infringement to which they contributed occurred within the six years before the suit? Are contributory infringers in such a situation liable for damages? *Id.* at 348–49. Do you believe that the six-year period should be extended if the patent owner was incapacitated or deceived by an infringer's fraud? *See A. Stucki Co. v. Buckeye Steel Castings Co.*, 963 F.2d 360, 363 n.3 (Fed.Cir.1992).

iv. Laches

Separate from the six-year rule, and indeed even without a specific statutory provision, courts have generally recognized that patent infringement suits may be barred under the equitable doctrine called "laches," in cases where the plaintiff has failed to act in a reasonably prudent manner to protect and enforce rights, and when a perceived injustice to the defendant would result if later enforcement were allowed. The Federal Circuit has recognized that the laches defense remains today. *See, e.g., A.C. Aukerman Co. v. R.L. Chaides Constr. Co.*, 960 F.2d 1020 (Fed.Cir.1992) (en banc) (patent infringement claim may be barred under the doctrine of laches). As the court recently described:

> To successfully invoke laches, a defendant must prove that the plaintiff delayed filing suit an unreasonable and inexcusable length of time after the plaintiff knew or reasonably should have known of its claim against the defendant and that the delay resulted in material prejudice to the defendant. *Gasser Chair Co., Inc. v. Infanti Chair Mfg. Corp.*, 60 F.3d 770, 773

(Fed.Cir.1995). Once those factual premises are established, the court weighs the equities in order to assess whether laches should apply to bar those damages that accrued prior to suit. *See Advanced Cardiovascular Sys., Inc. v. SciMed Life Sys., Inc.*, 988 F.2d 1157, 1161 (Fed.Cir.1993); *Aukerman*, 960 F.2d at 1041.

State Contracting & Engineering Corp. v. Condotte America, Inc., 346 F.3d 1057, 1065–66 (Fed.Cir. 2003). The laches period cannot begin to run until the patent issues. *See Meyers v. Asics Corp.*, 974 F.2d 1304, 1307 (Fed.Cir. 1992). Prejudice may be presumed after a laches period has run for six years. *Aukerman*, 960 F.2d at 1035–36. Otherwise, the prejudice must be shown to be either economic (harm outside of court) or evidentiary (harm to the ability to mount a case in court). *Aukerman*, 960 F.2d at 1033. It must also be shown to be "because of and as a result of the delay." *Hemstreet v. Computer Entry Sys. Corp.*, 972 F.2d 1290, 1294 (Fed.Cir. 1992). *See also Gasser Chair*, 60 F.3d at 775 ("[T]he evidence of record showed that [the alleged infringer] was indifferent to whether [the patentee] would sue because of his personal belief that the patent was invalid."); *Meyers v. Brooks Shoe, Inc.*, 912 F.2d 1459, 1463 (Fed.Cir.1990) (failure to show prejudice from delay in filing suit when evidence indicated that the accused infringer would have continued its activity anyway; "From all that appears, [the accused infringer] would have followed the same course regardless of what [the plaintiff] did or did not do."); *Hemstreet*, 972 F.2d at 1294 (the infringer's prejudice argument was "severely undercut" by the patentee's provision of notice of other litigation and "implicit suggestion that CES would soon face litigation if it refused to license.").

Importantly, the doctrine of laches differs from the other equitable estoppel doctrine discussed in Chapter 9, in that laches focuses more directly on the patentee's behavior while equitable estoppel focuses on the relationship between a (mis)representation by the plaintiff and reliance by the alleged infringer. *See A.C. Aukerman Co. v. R.L. Chaides Constr. Co.*, 960 F.2d 1020, 1041 (Fed.Cir.1992) (en banc) ("laches focuses on the reasonableness of the plaintiff's delay in suit . . . [while] equitable estoppel focuses on what the defendant has been led to reasonably believe from the plaintiff's conduct").

v.   The Notice Requirement—35 U.S.C. § 287(a)

John L. Rie, Inc. v. Shelly Bros., Inc.

366 F.Supp. 84 (E.D.Pa.1973).

■ GORBEY, DISTRICT JUDGE.

This is an action for patent infringement brought pursuant to 28 U.S.C. § 1338, seeking an injunction against further infringement and seeking damages for the past infringement. Plaintiff is the assignee of Patent No. 3,002,240, granted October 3, 1961, to Maxime Laguerre, plaintiff's assignor. The device is called a closure device and is used in sealing plastic bags. Defendant is a candy manufacturer, who plaintiff alleges was knowingly using an infringing device supplied to it by Union Paper Company, of Providence, Rhode Island.

* * *

FINDINGS OF FACT

1. United States Letters Patent No. 3,002,240 were granted for a closure device to Maxime Laguerre on October 3, 1961.

2. The Laguerre patent was assigned to plaintiff John L. Rie, Inc. . . .

* * *

21. Plaintiff's patented devices came in two pieces, a bridle member and a collar member. During the period in question, plaintiff's device was available in three sizes, small, medium and large.

22. The notice "PAT PEND." was applied directly to the bridle member of plaintiff's patented bag closure prior to the issuance of plaintiff's patent.

23. After issuance of plaintiff's patent on October 3, 1961, and at least through 1967, plaintiff's patented bag closures continued to carry on the bridle member the notice, "PAT PEND."

24. Plaintiff's devices also carried the following inscription on the bridle member: "JOHN L. RIE, INC. YONKERS, N. Y."

25. Both of these inscriptions were clearly visible on plaintiff's large and medium size clips and were easily visible to the naked eye upon close inspection of plaintiff's smallest size clips.

26. The carton in which plaintiff shipped these clips in lots of 5,000 contained the following inscription: "KISCO BIP PLASTICLIPS U.S. PATENT #3,002,240".

* * *

DAMAGES

* * *

First, defendant asserts that if there was any infringement for which the plaintiff has the right to sue, plaintiff is not entitled to any damages for such infringement, because he has failed to comply with the marking requirements in the patent laws (35 U.S.C. § 287). . . .

In response to this, plaintiff claims that the devices in question were too small to clearly mark and that the marking on the cartons in which the devices were shipped was sufficient to satisfy the requirements of § 287. We cannot agree with this proposition. An inspection of the devices reveals that the bridle members are marked "PAT PEND." and also that they contain the inscription "JOHN L. RIE, INC. YONKERS, N. Y." Even on the smallest device, these inscriptions are legible. Plaintiff has not put forth any arguments as to how the inscription "PAT PEND." differs from a required inscription such as "PAT 3002204" or why such inscription could not be placed on the collar member.

The statute is clear that only when "from the character of the article this cannot be done" is affixing the required marking on the package acceptable; and the law is clear that these marking provisions *must be strictly complied with*. (Emphasis added) T. C. Weygandt Co. v. Van Emden, 40 F.2d 938 (S.D.N.Y.1930). Plaintiff has put forth no plausible reason why the proper marking could not have been placed on this device.

Accordingly, we hold that plaintiff has not complied with § 287 of the patent laws, and thus, is not entitled to recover any damages for infringement prior to the point where it can show that defendant Shelly Bros., Inc. had actual notice of the patent in suit. This notice is contained in the letter dated February 22, 1967 from John L. Rie, Jr. to Shelly Bros., Inc. Accordingly, plaintiff cannot recover any damages for infringement occurring prior to that date and the record does not contain any evidence of infringement subsequent to that date; the last sale being dated December 1, 1966.

NOTES

1. *Why Require Marking or Actual Notice as a Prerequisite to Obtaining Damages?* By pre-conditioning the ability to collect damages on compliance with the marking requirements, patent law creates an incentive for patent owners to mark their products, which thereby places the world on notice of the existence of the patent. *Amsted Indus. Inc. v. Buckeye Steel Castings Co.*, 24 F.3d 178, 185 (Fed.Cir.1994); *American Med. Sys., Inc. v. Medical Eng'g Corp.*, 6 F.3d 1523, 1538 (Fed.Cir.1993). Marking also aids the public in identifying what articles are patented, which helps avoid innocent infringement. *Nike, Inc. v. Wal–Mart Stores, Inc.*, 138 F.3d 1437, 1443 (Fed.Cir.1998). Section 287(a) provides strong incentive. For example, as *John L. Rie* shows, when infringement has stopped before actual notice was given, failure to mark precludes all damages.

2. *When Can a Patent Owner Use a Label?* Section 287(a) allows for the use of an attached label, if marking upon the object cannot be done. As *John L. Rie* demonstrates, if the patent owner uses a label instead of marking on the product, he or she had better have a good reason. What might a court accept as a good reason for using a label? *See generally Rutherford v. Trim–Tex, Inc.*, 803 F.Supp. 158, 162–64 (N.D.Ill.1992).

3. *Must Every Product Be Marked?* Marking must be substantially consistent and continuous, but there is no time by when it must begin. *Am. Med. Sys.*, 6 F.3d at 1537 (Fed.Cir.1993). *See also Maxwell v. J. Baker, Inc.*, 86 F.3d 1098, 1111 (Fed.Cir.1996). In other words, a patent owner who initially fails to mark still has a strong incentive to begin marking. If there are no products for the patent owner to mark, though, Section 287(a) does not apply. *Texas Digital Sys., Inc. v. Telegenix, Inc.*, 308 F.3d 1193, 1219–20 (Fed.Cir.2002) (patent owner did not make or sell the patented product). What if there is an error in the marking? *See Allen Eng'g Corp. v. Bartell Indus., Inc.*, 299 F.3d 1336, 1355–56 (Fed.Cir.2002) (a manifestly obvious typographical error in the patent number is not a failure to mark when interested members of the public are not prevented from discerning the number).

4. *What if the Patented Invention is a Method?* Section 287(a) does not apply to patents that only claim processes or methods. *Crystal Semiconductor Corp. v. TriTech Microelectronics, Int'l, Inc.*, 246 F.3d 1336, 1353 (Fed.Cir.2001). What if the patent claims both products and methods? *See Am. Med. Sys.*, 6 F.3d at 1538–39.

5. *What are the Standards for Determining if There Has Been Actual Notice?* Damages may be recovered from the time when marking began or from the time actual notice was given, whichever came first. Actual notice sufficient to satisfy Section 287(a) "requires the affirmative communication of a specific charge of infringement by a specific accused product or device." *Amsted Indus. Inc. v. Buckeye Steel Castings Co.*, 24 F.3d 178, 187 (Fed.Cir.1994). *See, e.g., M–S Cash Drawer Corp. v. Block and Co.*, 26 U.S.P.Q.2d 1472 (C.D.Cal.1992). The patent owner need not assert that there is infringement, actual notice occurs if the communication is sufficiently specific regarding the patent owner's belief that there may be infringement. *Gart v. Logitech, Inc.*, 254 F.3d 1334, 1346 (Fed.Cir.2001). That the infringer knew of the patent, or knew that he or she was infringing, is not relevant to determining whether there has been actual notice because that determination is made by focusing on the actions of the patent owner, not by focusing on the knowledge of the infringer. *Amsted Indus. Inc.*, 24 F.3d at 187. *See also Gart*, 254 F.3d at 1346. May notice come from somebody closely associated with the patent owner? *See Lans v. Digital Equip. Corp.*, 252 F.3d 1320, 1326–28 (Fed.Cir.2001).

6. *Is The Patent Owner Responsible for the Failure of a Licensee to Mark?* When there is a failure to mark by one other than the patent owner, a rule of reason approach is used and substantial compliance may be sufficient. *Maxwell*, 86 F.3d at 1111–12. In such situations, the decision-maker may consider whether the patent owner made reasonable efforts to ensure compliance with Section 287(a). *Id.*

7. *False Marking.* An example of false marking is marking, for the purpose of deceiving the public, a product with the words "patent pending" when no patent is pending. Another example is marking, for the purpose of deceiving the public, an unpatented product with the word "patent." For every item falsely marked, a fine of not more than $500 is mandatory. Any person may sue for the penalty. One half of the recovery goes to the United States, and the other half to the person suing. *See* 35 U.S.C. § 292. *See generally Clontech Labs., Inc. v. Invitrogen Corp.*, 263 F.Supp.2d 780, 791–93 (D.Del.2003). False marking may also give rise under appropriate circumstances to a cause of action for false advertising under section 43(a) of the Lanham Act.

2. COMPENSATION FOR DELAYED PAYMENT—INTEREST

Section 284 of Title 35 states that "[u]pon finding for the claimant the court shall award ... damages adequate to compensate for the infringement, ... together with interest ... as fixed by the court." For each act of infringement for which the patent owner was not compensated, the patent owner lost an opportunity to invest the profits or royalties that should have been paid at the time of infringement. Patent law compensates for those delayed payments by awarding interest. Interest can be awarded both for prejudgment infringement and for postjudgment delay in paying the compensatory damages award. The interest award can be substantial. For an extreme example, see *Polaroid Corp. v. Eastman Kodak Co.*, 17 U.S.P.Q.2d 1711, 1714 (D. Mass. 1991), where the interest award exceeded $430 million.

Postjudgment interest, which has always been available to compensate for an infringer's delay in paying the court's damages award, is completely regulated by statute. 28 U.S.C. § 1961. Section 1961 provides that postjudgment interest be calculated from the date of the entry of the judgment to the date of payment. The interest rate is based on 52–week T-bills and is compounded annually. Because this rate is set by statute, courts are not free to choose other postjudgment interest rates. *Goodwall Constr. Co. v. Beers Constr. Co.*, 991 F.2d 751, 759 (Fed.Cir.1993). In contrast to postjudgment interest, important discretion is given to the courts in fixing a prejudgment interest award.

a. A HISTORY OF PREJUDGMENT INTEREST

Prior to 1946, the patent statute had no reference to prejudgment interest. *See generally*, 35 U.S.C. §§ 67, 70 (1940). At that time and before, courts generally held that awards of prejudgment interest were restricted to "exceptional circumstances," such as bad faith by the infringer. *See, e.g., Duplate Corp. v. Triplex Safety Glass Co. of N. Am.*, 298 U.S. 448, 459 (1936); *Tilghman v. Proctor*, 125 U.S. 136 (1888). In 1946, the patent statute was amended, and an unrestricted authorization to award interest appeared. 35 U.S.C. §§ 67, 70 (1946).

Despite the unrestricted language of the amended statute, the regional Courts of Appeal conflicted in their application of that section to the award of prejudgment interest. Some courts continued to apply the "exceptional circumstances" standard. *E.g., Columbia Broad. Sys., Inc. v. Zenith Radio Corp.*, 537 F.2d 896, 897 (7th Cir.1976). Other courts held that Congress changed the law. *E.g., Georgia–Pacific Corp. v. United States Plywood–Champion Papers, Inc.*, 446 F.2d 295, 302 (2d Cir.1971) (trial Court has discretion to award prejudgment interest from the date of the last infringement); *Trio Process Corp. v. L. Goldstein's Sons, Inc.*, 638 F.2d 661, 662–64 (3d Cir.1981) (affirming an award of prejudgment interest in order to fully compensate plaintiff). The conflict was resolved by the Supreme Court in *General Motors Corp. v. Devex Corp.*, 461 U.S. 648 (1983).

In *Devex Corp.*, the Supreme Court held that a court's authority to award prejudgment interest is not restricted to exceptional circumstances. *Id.* at 653. As to the proper standard, the Court stated that "prejudgment interest should ordinarily be awarded where necessary to afford the plaintiff full compensation for the infringement." *Id.* at 654. In light of that purpose, the Court made clear that prejudgment interest should ordinarily be awarded, absent some justification for withholding such an award. *Id.* at 657.

What would be an appropriate justification for withholding prejudgment interest? Is delay by the patent owner sufficient? *See Crystal Semiconductor Corp. v. TriTech Microelectronics Int'l, Inc.*, 246 F.3d 1336, 1361–62 (Fed.Cir.2001). What if the delay prejudices the infringer? *See Lummus Indus., Inc. v. D.M. & E. Corp.*, 862 F.2d 267, 275 (Fed.Cir.1988). What if the case was stayed? Should the award of interest depend on whether the patent owner sought or opposed the stay? Compare *Uniroyal, Inc. v. Rudkin–Wiley Corp.*, 939 F.2d 1540, 1546 (Fed.Cir.1991) with *Allen Archery, Inc. v. Browning Mfg. Co.*, 898 F.2d 787, 791–92 (Fed.Cir.1990).

b.   CALCULATING PREJUDGMENT INTEREST

The calculation of prejudgment interest depends on three factors: (1) the principal amount to which interest is applied, (2) the interest rate; and (3) the method used to accrue interest (*i.e.*, periodic compounding or simple interest). *See generally* Michael S. Kroll, *A Primer on Prejudgment Interest*, 75 TEX. L. REV. 293 (1996).

i.   *The Principal Amount*

Because the purpose of interest is to compensate, the principal amount to which interest is applied consists of the compensatory damages awarded and not any punitive damages that may have been awarded. *Lam, Inc. v. Johns–Manville Corp.*, 718 F.2d 1056, 1066 (Fed.Cir.1983). As to the compensatory damages, prejudgment interest is equally appropriate for damages determined by royalty or lost-profits. *Gyromat Corp. v. Champion Spark Plug Co.*, 735 F.2d 549, 554–55 (Fed.Cir.1984). Additionally, however, the patent owner may be awarded prejudgment interest on an award of attorney fees. *Mathis v. Spears*, 857 F.2d 749, 760–61 (Fed.Cir.1988).

Prejudgment interest should be applied to damages as they would have accrued (*i.e.*, as sales are made or accounted for). *Dragan v. L.D. Caulk Co.*, 12 U.S.P.Q.2d 1081, 1091 (D.Del.1989), *aff'd without op.*, 897 F.2d 538 (Fed.Cir.1990); *H.B. Fuller Co. v. National Starch & Chem. Corp.*, 689 F.Supp. 923, 954 (D. Minn. 1988); *Bandag, Inc. v. Al Bolser Tire Stores, Inc.*, 228 U.S.P.Q. 211, 212 (W.D. Wash. 1985), *aff'd without op.*, 809 F.2d 788 (Fed.Cir.1986); *Paper Converting Mach. Co. v. Magna–Graphics Corp.*, 576 F.Supp. 967, 979 (E.D. Wis. 1983), *aff'd in part, vacated in part*, 745 F.2d 11 (Fed.Cir.1984); *Trans–World Mfg. Corp. v. Al Nyman & Sons, Inc.*, 633 F.Supp. 1047, 1057 (D.Del.1986).

ii. *Selecting The Rate*

The Federal Circuit has not attempted to create a uniform method for determining prejudgment interest rates. Thus, district courts have broad discretion to select an interest rate. *Datascope Corp. v. SMEC, Inc.*, 879 F.2d 820, 829 (Fed.Cir.1989).

If the patent owner affirmatively demonstrates that a higher rate should be used, the prejudgment interest rate can be higher than the generally established commercial rates (*i.e.*, T-bill or prime). *Lam, Inc.*, 718 F.2d at 1066. This demonstration often will require proof of the rate the patent owner would have received for investing the compensatory damage award. *Micro Motion, Inc. v. Exac Corp.*, 761 F.Supp. 1420, 1436 (N.D. Cal. 1991) (appropriate prejudgment interest rate was the rate the patent owner yielded from accounts into which all its received cash was placed during the period of infringement); *Beckman Instruments, Inc. v. LKB Produkter AB*, 703 F.Supp. 408, 410 (D. Md. 1988) (appropriate prejudgment interest rate was the rates patent owner had invested other funds during the period of infringement, *i.e.*, commercial paper rates in some years and Eurodollar time deposit rates for the other years), *aff'd in part on other grounds*, 892 F.2d 1547 (Fed.Cir.1989).

The patent owner may also obtain a prejudgment interest rate above the prime rate by demonstrating that it was required to borrow money at a higher interest rate during the period of the infringement. *Lam, Inc.*, 718 F.2d at 1065–66; *Smith Corona Corp. v. Pelikan, Inc.*, 784 F.Supp. 452, 484 (M.D. Tenn. 1992) (court applied the demonstrated average interest rate incurred by plaintiff for outstanding debt), *aff'd without op.*, 1 F.3d 1252 (Fed.Cir.1993); *Bott v. Four Starr Corp.*, 229 U.S.P.Q. 241, 250 (E.D. Mich. 1985) (court awarded prime plus one-half percent because that was at the rate that patent owner "would likely have had to pay were they borrowers"), *aff'd in part on other grounds*, 807 F.2d 1567 (Fed.Cir.1986); *see generally In re Mahurkar Double Lumen Hemodialysis Catheter Patent Litig.*, 831 F.Supp. 1354, 1394–95 (N.D.Ill.1993), *aff'd*, 71 F.3d 1573 (Fed. Cir.1995).

In the absence of a demonstration of the rate at which the patent owner would have invested or borrowed, some courts have exercised their discretion and selected the T–bill rate. The rationale for choosing the T-bill rate is that it represents a risk-free rate of return. Because the patent owner has not demonstrated that it would have invested its money on some more risky, higher yielding, investment, its recovery may be limited to this risk-free rate. *See* Bradley J. Hulbert & Mary S. Consalvi, *De-vexing Prejudgment Interest Awards In Patent Cases—At What Point Interest?*, 67 J. PAT. & TM. OFF. SOC'Y 103, 121–22 (1985); Franklin M. Fisher, *Janis Joplin's Yearbook and the Theory of Damages*, in INDUSTRIAL ORGANIZATION, ECONOMICS, AND THE LAW 392 (1991). A number of cases have used the T-bill rate based, at least impliedly, on this rationale. *Fonar Corp. v. General Elec. Co.*, 902 F.Supp. 330, 354 (E.D.N.Y. 1995), *aff'd in part, rev'd in part*, 107 F.3d 1543 (Fed.Cir.1997); *BIC Leisure Prods., Inc. v. Windsurfing Int'l, Inc.*, 774 F.Supp. 832, 837 (S.D.N.Y. 1991); *TP Orthodontics, Inc. v. Professional Positioners, Inc.*, 20 U.S.P.Q.2d 1017, 1026 (E.D. Wis. 1991) (court awarded interest at the T-bill rate because that rate most closely reflected patent owner's actual practice of investing excess cash in short-term CDS), *aff'd without op.*, 980 F.2d 743 (Fed.Cir.1992); *Polaroid Corp. v. Eastman Kodak Co.*, 16 U.S.P.Q.2d 1481, 1540–41 (D.Mass.1990).

In the absence of a demonstration of the rate at which the patent owner would have invested or borrowed, other courts have exercised their discretion and selected the prime rate for corporate borrowers, which is typically several percentage points higher than the T-bill rate. The apparent rationale for using the prime rate is that it is a convenient benchmark rate of return on capital which is at some risk of loss. *See generally, Gorenstein Enters., Inc. v. Quality Care–USA, Inc.*, 874 F.2d 431, 436–37 (7th Cir.1989) (trademark case). It is assumed that the patent owner either would have invested its money to yield this rate of return, or could have avoided borrowing funds which carry this interest rate. A number of courts have approved the use of the prime rate, many without stating a specific rationale. *Mars, Inc. v. Conlux USA Corp.*, 818 F.Supp. 707 (D. Del. 1993); *Amsted Indus. Inc. v. Buckeye Steel Castings Co.*, 28 U.S.P.Q.2d 1352, 1362 (N.D. Ill. 1993), *aff'd in part, vacated in part*, 24 F.3d 178 (Fed.Cir.1994); *Andrew Corp. v. Gabriel Elecs., Inc.*, 785 F.Supp. 1041, 1054 (D. Me. 1992); *Lemelson v. Mattel, Inc.*, 1990 WL 16785 (N.D. Ill. 1990), *rev'd on other grounds sub nom.*, *Lemelson v. General Mills*, 968 F.2d 1202, 1206 (Fed.Cir. 1992).

Rather than focusing solely on how the patent owner would have invested money or on the patent owner's rate of borrowing, courts have also awarded prejudgment interest at the prime rate after considering the infringer's credit-worthiness as a matter of economic theory. In an opinion in a trademark case, the court considered the risk of the infringer's default on its damages obligation. *Gorenstein Enters.*, 874 F.2d at 436–37. The court found that the T-bill rate of prejudgment interest was too low because it assumed no risk of the infringer's default. The optimum rate was said to be the rate the infringer actually paid for unsecured borrowing. In the absence of proof, however, the prime rate was chosen as an easily ascertainable figure that takes into account the infringer's risk of default. This rationale has been followed in patent infringement cases. *Rite–Hite Corp. v. Kelley Co.*, 774 F.Supp. 1514, 1542 (E.D.Wis.1991), *aff'd in part, vacated in part*, 56 F.3d 1538 (Fed.Cir.1995) (applying the prime rate);

Amsted Indus. Inc., 28 U.S.P.Q.2d at 1355 (applying the prime rate); *Lemelson*, 1990 WL 16785, at *13–*16. *See also Ziggity Sys., Inc. v. Val Watering Sys.*, 769 F.Supp. 752, 831 (E.D.Pa.1990).

iii. Accrual Method

In addition to the interest rate, the total amount of prejudgment interest will be affected significantly by the method used to accrue interest. Compounding interest (*i.e.*, adding interest accrued in prior periods to the principal amount upon which interest is computed in later periods) results in higher total awards than the application of simple interest. Because the Federal Circuit has not held that compounding is required, courts have broad discretion in deciding whether to award compound or simple interest. *Gyromat Corp.*, 735 F.2d at 557; *Bio–Rad Labs., Inc. v. Nicolet Instrument Corp.*, 807 F.2d 964, 969 (Fed.Cir.1986).

Compound interest may be more appropriate in a particular case, though. For example, in *Dynamics Corp. of Am. v. United States*, 766 F.2d 518, 519–20 (Fed.Cir.1985), the Federal Circuit reversed a Claims Court's decision to award simple interest under 28 U.S.C. § 1498. The Federal Circuit, limiting its holding to "the facts and circumstances in a particular case" before it, stated that "compound interest may more nearly fit with the policy 'to accomplish complete justice as between the plaintiff and the United States.'" *Id.* at 520. *See also ITT Corp. v. United States*, 11 U.S.P.Q.2d 1657, 1658–93 (Cl. Ct. 1989); *Branning v. United States*, 784 F.2d 361, 364 (Fed.Cir.1986).

What about taxes? *See generally Electro Scientific Indus., Inc. v. General Scanning Inc.*, 247 F.3d 1341, 1354 (Fed.Cir.2001). In at least four cases, the infringer has argued that compounding would result in an inequitable windfall to the patent owner, unless the interest is diminished to account for the hypothetical taxes the patent owner would have paid on the interest as it was hypothetically accruing. *Polaroid Corp.*, 16 U.S.P.Q.2d at 1540–41. *Micro Motion*, 761 F.Supp. at 1436; *Lemelson*, 1990 WL 60696; *ITT Corp.*, 11 USPQ2d at 1692–93. In those case, the court did not compound on an after-tax basis. In *Lemelson*, the court held that it is contrary to legal authority to take taxes into account when determining prejudgment interest. *Lemelson*, 1990 WL 60696, at *1–*3.

The argument for compounding prejudgment interest on an after-tax basis is that, if earlier-accrued interest is not diminished to account for taxes before compounding, the patent owner will earn additional interest on earlier-accrued interest that would have been paid in hypothetical taxes and on which the patent owner could not have earned interest. *See* Franklin M. Fisher, *Janis Joplin's Yearbook and the Theory of Damages*, in INDUSTRIAL ORGANIZATION, ECONOMICS, AND THE LAW 392. As one can imagine, complications arise when the court and the parties attempt to determine the amount of the hypothetical tax to subtract. For example, the court should consider evidence of steps that the patent owner might have taken to shelter additional income from taxes. Calculating a patent owner's hypothetical marginal effective tax rate adds an additional level of complexity and speculation to the already complicated determination of damages.

Polaroid Corp., 16 U.S.P.Q.2d at 1541; *Schnadig Corp. v. Gaines Mfg. Co.*, 620 F.2d 1166, 1169–71 (6th Cir.1980).

B. REMEDIES THAT PREVENT OR DETER FUTURE INFRINGEMENT: INJUNCTIONS, PUNITIVE DAMAGES & ATTORNEYS FEES

There are basically two ways to prevent future infringement. One way is to make it impossible for individuals to infringe in the future. The other way is to deter individuals from infringing in the future.

While one cannot make it impossible for all individuals to infringe in the future, one could make future infringement impossible for particular individuals. For example, if adjudicated infringers were imprisoned for the life of the patent, these individuals would not have the opportunity to infringe again. Similarly, if corporate infringers were dissolved, these corporations would not be able to infringe again. Although they may be available in extreme cases for failure to comply with a court order, patent law itself has never authorized such drastic criminal-law-like measures. Why not? There are criminal laws relating to copyright, trademark, and trade secrets. See generally Computer Crime and Intellectual Property Section of the Department of Justice, Prosecuting Intellectual Property Crimes (2001). Is the wrongfulness of patent infringement substantially different from the wrongfulness of other intellectual property violations? If so, what is the difference?

Instead of making future infringement by others impossible, patent law seeks to prevent it through deterrence. Again, while it could be argued that future patent infringement could be deterred by appropriate criminal laws against patent infringement, Congress has not chosen to go that route. Patent law seeks to deter future patent infringement by use of injunctions, punitive damages, and awards of attorney fees to the prevailing party.[5]

1. INJUNCTIONS

Section 283 of Title 35 states that the "courts ... may grant injunctions in accordance with the principles of equity to prevent the violation of any right secured by patent, on such terms as the court deems reasonable." And section 401 of Title 18 states that a "court of the United States shall have power to punish by fine or imprisonment, or both, at its discretion, such contempt of its authority ... as ... (3) Disobedience ... to its lawful ... order, rule, decree, or command."

---

5. For infringement, patent owners also have recourse to remedies provided by statutory law other than patent law. Specifically, under appropriate circumstances, infringing goods can be kept out of the country by an exclusionary order issued by the International Trade Commission (ITC) pursuant to the Tariff Act of 1930. The ITC can also issue cease-and-desist orders against infringing products already imported into the country. There are many restrictions and procedural requirements related to obtaining such relief. *See generally* DONALD K. DUVALL ET AL., UNFAIR COMPETITION AND THE ITC (West 2003).

Injunctions are court orders commanding that one or more acts be done, or not be done. In the case of patent infringement, an injunction typically would be worded so as to deter specific future infringement. Injunctions are not issued to compensate for past infringement or to punish the infringer. Violation of an injunction, however, can result in compensation being awarded to the patent owner and punishment being inflicted on the infringer.

Injunctions can be permanent or preliminary. Permanent injunctions are issued after infringement has been determined by a final judgment. These injunction are not really permanent. They last only for the life of the infringed patent. Preliminary injunctions, which are sometimes called temporary injunctions, are issued after a lawsuit has been commenced, but before a final judgment of infringement. The purpose of a preliminary injunction in a patent case is to prevent an irreparable injury from occurring before the court can finally decide the patent owner's infringement claim.

a. PERMANENT INJUNCTIONS

Although permanent injunctive relief has almost always been available to a patent owner in federal court to at least some extent,[6] the justification for such relief has varied. An early justification for allowing patent owners to obtain injunctions to prevent future infringement of their patents was practical. *See, e.g., Motte v. Bennett*, 17 F. Cas. 909, 910–11 (C.C. D.S.C. 1849):

> The principle upon which courts of equity have jurisdiction in patent cases, and upon which injunctions are granted in them, is not that there is no legal remedy, but that the law does not give a complete remedy to those whose property is invaded; for if each infringement of the patent were to be made a distinct cause of action, the remedy would be worse than the evil. The inventor ... might be ruined by the necessity of perpetual litigation, without ever being able to have a final establishment of his rights.

While practical considerations were not forgotten, a rights-based justification came to dominate. *See, e.g., Continental Paper Bag Co. v. Eastern Paper Bag Co.*, 210 U.S. 405, 423–25, 430 (1908):

> It may be well, however, before considering what remedies a patentee is entitled to, to consider what rights are conferred upon him. The source of the rights is, of course, the law, and we are admonished at the outset that we must look for the policy of a statute, not in matters outside of it—not to circumstances of expediency and to supposed purposes not expressed by the words. The patent law is the execution of a policy having its first expression in the Constitution, and it may be supposed that all that was deemed necessary to accomplish and safeguard it must have been studied and provided for. It is worthy of note that all that has been deemed necessary for that purpose, through the experience of years, has been to provide for an exclusive right to inventors to make, use and vend their inventions.... And it was further said in [*United States* v. *Bell Telephone Company*, 167 U.S. 224, 249] ... "Counsel seem to argue that one who has made an

---

6. The only exception was that such relief was not available between 1790 and 1819, if the parties in litigation were from the same state. 3 William C. Robinson, The Law of Patents for Useful Inventions § 1082–83 (1890).

invention and thereupon applies for a patent therefor occupies, as it were, the position of a quasi-trustee for the public; that he is under a sort of moral obligation to see that the public acquires the right to the free use of that invention as soon as is conveniently possible. We dissent entirely from the thought thus urged. The inventor is one who has discovered something of value. It is his absolute property. He may withhold a knowledge of it from the public, and he may insist upon all the advantages and benefits which the statute promises to him who discloses to the public his invention."

... whenever this court has had occasion to speak it has decided that an inventor receives from a patent the right to exclude others from its use for the time prescribed in the statute. . . .

* * *

From the character of the right of the patentee we may judge of his remedies. It hardly needs to be pointed out that the right can only retain its attribute of exclusiveness by a prevention of its violation. Anything but prevention takes away the privilege which the law confers upon the patentee.

Indeed, in *Smith Int'l, Inc. v. Hughes Tool Co.*, the Federal Circuit stated:

Without this injunctive power of the courts, the right to exclude granted by the patent would be diminished, and the express purpose of the Constitution and Congress, to promote the progress of the useful arts, would be seriously undermined. The patent owner would lack much of the "leverage," afforded by the right to exclude, to enjoy the full value of his invention in the market place. Without the right to obtain an injunction, the right to exclude granted to the patentee would have only a fraction of the value it was intended to have, and would no longer be as great an incentive to engage in the toils of scientific and technological research.

718 F.2d 1573, 1577–78 (Fed.Cir.1983).

eBay Inc. v. MercExchange, LLC

547 U.S. 388 (2006).

■ THOMAS, JUSTICE

Ordinarily, a federal court considering whether to award permanent injunctive relief to a prevailing plaintiff applies the four-factor test historically employed by courts of equity. Petitioners eBay Inc. and Half.com, Inc., argue that this traditional test applies to disputes arising under the Patent Act. We agree and, accordingly, vacate the judgment of the Court of Appeals.

I

Petitioner eBay operates a popular Internet Web site that allows private sellers to list goods they wish to sell, either through an auction or at a fixed price. Petitioner Half.com, now a wholly owned subsidiary of eBay, operates a similar Web site. Respondent MercExchange, L.L.C, holds a number of patents, including a business method patent for an electronic market designed to facilitate the sale of goods between private individuals by establishing a central authority to promote trust among participants.

See U.S. Patent No. 5,845,265. MercExchange sought to license its patent to eBay and Half.com, as it had previously done with other companies, but the parties failed to reach an agreement. MercExchange subsequently filed a patent infringement suit against eBay and Half.com in the United States District Court for the Eastern District of Virginia. A jury found that MercExchange's patent was valid, that eBay and Half.com had infringed that patent, and that an award of damages was appropriate.

Following the jury verdict, the District Court denied MercExchange's motion for permanent injunctive relief. 275 F.Supp.2d 695 (E.D.Va.2003). The Court of Appeals for the Federal Circuit reversed, applying its "general rule that courts will issue permanent injunctions against patent infringement absent exceptional circumstances." 401 F.3d 1323, 1339 (Fed.Cir. 2005). We granted certiorari to determine the appropriateness of this general rule. 546 U.S. ___ (2005).

II

According to well-established principles of equity, a plaintiff seeking a permanent injunction must satisfy a four-factor test before a court may grant such relief. A plaintiff must demonstrate: (1) that it has suffered an irreparable injury; (2) that remedies available at law, such as monetary damages, are inadequate to compensate for that injury; (3) that, considering the balance of hardships between the plaintiff and defendant, a remedy in equity is warranted; and (4) that the public interest would not be disserved by a permanent injunction. See, *e.g.*, *Weinberger v. Romero–Barcelo*, 456 U.S. 305, 311–313 (1982); *Amoco Production Co. v. Gambell*, 480 U.S. 531, 542 (1987). The decision to grant or deny permanent injunctive relief is an act of equitable discretion by the district court, reviewable on appeal for abuse of discretion. See, *e.g.*, *Romero–Barcelo*, 456 U.S., at 320.

These familiar principles apply with equal force to disputes arising under the Patent Act. As this Court has long recognized, "a major departure from the long tradition of equity practice should not be lightly implied." *Ibid.*; see also *Amoco, supra*, at 542. Nothing in the Patent Act indicates that Congress intended such a departure. To the contrary, the Patent Act expressly provides that injunctions "may" issue "in accordance with the principles of equity." 35 U.S.C. § 283.[2]

* * *

Neither the District Court nor the Court of Appeals below fairly applied these traditional equitable principles in deciding respondent's motion for a permanent injunction. Although the District Court recited the traditional four-factor test, 275 F. Supp. 2d, at 711, it appeared to adopt certain expansive principles suggesting that injunctive relief could not issue in a broad swath of cases. Most notably, it concluded that a "plaintiff's willingness to license its patents" and "its lack of commercial activity in practicing the patents" would be sufficient to establish that the patent

---

2. Section 283 provides that "[t]he several courts having jurisdiction of cases under this title may grant injunctions in accordance with the principles of equity to prevent the violation of any right secured by patent, on such terms as the court deems reasonable."

holder would not suffer irreparable harm if an injunction did not issue. *Id.*, at 712. But traditional equitable principles do not permit such broad classifications. For example, some patent holders, such as university researchers or self-made inventors, might reasonably prefer to license their patents, rather than undertake efforts to secure the financing necessary to bring their works to market themselves. Such patent holders may be able to satisfy the traditional four-factor test, and we see no basis for categorically denying them the opportunity to do so. To the extent that the District Court adopted such a categorical rule, then, its analysis cannot be squared with the principles of equity adopted by Congress. The court's categorical rule is also in tension with *Continental Paper Bag Co. v. Eastern Paper Bag Co.*, 210 U. S. 405, 422–430 (1908), which rejected the contention that a court of equity has no jurisdiction to grant injunctive relief to a patent holder who has unreasonably declined to use the patent.

In reversing the District Court, the Court of Appeals departed in the opposite direction from the four-factor test. The court articulated a "general rule," unique to patent disputes, "that a permanent injunction will issue once infringement and validity have been adjudged." 401 F.3d, at 1338. The court further indicated that injunctions should be denied only in the "unusual" case, under "exceptional circumstances" and " 'in rare instances ... to protect the public interest.' " *Id.*, at 1338–1339. Just as the District Court erred in its categorical denial of injunctive relief, the Court of Appeals erred in its categorical grant of such relief. Cf. *Roche Products* v. *Bolar Pharmaceutical Co.*, 733 F.2d 858, 865 (Fed.Cir.1984) (recognizing the "considerable discretion" district courts have "in determining whether the facts of a situation require it to issue an injunction").

Because we conclude that neither court below correctly applied the traditional four-factor framework that governs the award of injunctive relief we vacate the judgment of the Court of Appeals, so that the District Court may apply that framework in the first instance. In doing so, we take no position on whether permanent injunctive relief should or should not issue in this particular case, or indeed in any number of other disputes arising under the Patent Act. We hold only that the decision whether to grant or deny injunctive relief rests within the equitable discretion of the district courts, and that such discretion must be exercised consistent with traditional principles of equity, in patent disputes no less than in other cases governed by such standards.

Accordingly, we vacate the judgment of the Court of Appeals, and remand for further proceedings consistent with this opinion.

It is so ordered.

■ CHIEF JUSTICE ROBERTS, with whom JUSTICE SCALIA and JUSTICE GINSBURG join, concurring.

I agree with the Court's holding that "the decision whether to grant or deny injunctive relief rests within the equitable discretion of the district courts, and that such discretion must be exercised consistent with traditional principles of equity, in patent disputes no less than in other cases governed by such standards," *ante*, at 5, and I join the opinion of the Court. That opinion rightly rests on the proposition that "a major departure from the long tradition of equity practice should not be lightly implied." *Weinberger v. Romero–Barcelo*, 456 U.S. 305, 320 (1982); see *ante*, at 3.

From at least the early 19th century, courts have granted injunctive relief upon a finding of infringement in the vast majority of patent cases. This "long tradition of equity practice" is not surprising, given the difficulty of protecting a right to *exclude* through monetary remedies that allow an infringer to *use* an invention against the patentee's wishes—a difficulty that often implicates the first two factors of the traditional four-factor test. This historical practice, as the Court holds, does not *entitle* a patentee to a permanent injunction or justify a *general rule* that such injunctions should issue. The Federal Circuit itself so recognized in *Roche Products, Inc. v. Bolar Pharmaceutical Co.*, 733 F.2d 858, 865–867 (1984). At the same time, there is a difference between exercising equitable discretion pursuant to the established four-factor test and writing on an entirely clean slate. "Discretion is not whim, and limiting discretion according to legal standards helps promote the basic principle of justice that like cases should be decided alike." *Martin v. Franklin Capital Corp.*, 546 U.S. __, __ (2005) (slip op., at 6). When it comes to discerning and applying those standards, in this area as others, "a page of history is worth a volume of logic." *New York Trust Co. v. Eisner*, 256 U. S. 345, 349 (1921) (opinion for the Court by Holmes, J.).

■ JUSTICE KENNEDY, with whom JUSTICE STEVENS, JUSTICE SOUTER, and JUSTICE BREYER join, concurring.

The Court is correct, in my view, to hold that courts should apply the well-established, four-factor test—without resort to categorical rules—in deciding whether to grant injunctive relief in patent cases. THE CHIEF JUSTICE is also correct that history may be instructive in applying this test. *Ante*, at 1–2 (concurring opinion). The traditional practice of issuing injunctions against patent infringers, however, does not seem to rest on "the difficulty of protecting a right to *exclude* through monetary remedies that allow an infringer to *use* an invention against the patentee's wishes." *Ante*, at 1 (ROBERTS, C. J., concurring). Both the terms of the Patent Act and the traditional view of injunctive relief accept that the existence of a right to exclude does not dictate the remedy for a violation of that right. *Ante*, at 3–4 (opinion of the Court). To the extent earlier cases establish a pattern of granting an injunction against patent infringers almost as a matter of course, this pattern simply illustrates the result of the four-factor test in the contexts then prevalent. The lesson of the historical practice, therefore, is most helpful and instructive when the circumstances of a case bear substantial parallels to litigation the courts have confronted before.

In cases now arising trial courts should bear in mind that in many instances the nature of the patent being enforced and the economic function of the patent holder present considerations quite unlike earlier cases. An industry has developed in which firms use patents not as a basis for producing and selling goods but, instead, primarily for obtaining licensing fees. See FTC, To Promote Innovation: The Proper Balance of Competition and Patent Law and Policy, ch. 3, pp. 38–39 (Oct. 2003), available at http://www.ftc.gov/os/2003/10/innovationrpt.pdf (as visited May 11, 2006, and available in Clerk of Court's case file). For these firms, an injunction, and the potentially serious sanctions arising from its violation, can be employed as a bargaining tool to charge exorbitant fees to companies that seek to buy licenses to practice the patent. See *ibid*. When the patented invention is but a small component of the product the companies seek to produce and the threat of an injunction is employed simply for undue leverage in negotiations, legal damages may well be sufficient to compensate for the infringement and an injunction may not serve the public interest. In addition injunctive relief may have different consequences for the burgeoning number of patents over business methods, which were not of much economic and legal significance in earlier times. The potential vagueness and suspect validity of some of these patents may affect the calculus under the four-factor test.

The equitable discretion over injunctions, granted by the Patent Act, is well suited to allow courts to adapt to the rapid technological and legal developments in the patent system. For these reasons it should be recognized that district courts must determine whether past practice fits the circumstances of the cases before them. With these observations, I join the opinion of the Court.

NOTES

1. *Four Factor Test?* The Supreme Court in *eBay* goes to some effort to declare the inappropriateness of applying a "general rule" in favor of injunctions. Is it also inappropriate to apply a "general rule" against them? How do you think the Court would react to a "general tendency" by lower courts towards, or against, awarding injunctions? Rejecting a "general rule," the Court embraced what many see as the traditional four factor test for injunctions: (1) irreparable harm; (2) inadequacy of money damages; (3) balance of the hardships; and (4) the public interest. Despite the Court's invocation of "well-established principles of equity," there never was a four-factor test for injunctions (although something closer to it characterized the standard for preliminary injunctions). *See* John M. Golden, *Principles for Patent Remedies*, 88 Tex. L. Rev. 505 (2010); Doug Rendleman, *The Trial Judge's Equitable Discretion Following* eBay v. MercExchange, 27 Rev. Litig. 63, 76 n.71 (2007) ("Remedies specialists had never heard of [*eBay*'s] four-point test."). Interestingly, the Court is starting to apply the four-factor test outside patent law. *Monsanto Co. v. Geertson Seed Farms*, 130 S.Ct. 2743 (2010) (applying the four-factor test in a case involving administrative and environmental law).

Courts have long struggled with how automatic injunctions should be in the case of land (trespass, nuisance), and apparently patent law now faces these questions. Although, as the Court notes, injunctive relief is discretionary, elaborate rules of thumb have developed that make injunctions more or less presumptively available in certain contexts. In the case of land, injunctions were for a long time unavailable ("equity will not enjoin a mere trespass"), but the exceptions (for repeated trespass, willful trespass, etc.) eventually made injunctive relief fairly routine. Nuisance law at one time had a rule of almost automatic injunctions, which has been pared back. Overall, equitable principles point toward rebuttable presumptions for injunctions for certain kinds of violations with safety valves to relieve the hardship on good faith mistaken violators. Might this be the solution to the "troll problem"? *See* Henry E. Smith, *Institutions and Indirectness in Intellectual Property*, 157 U. Pa. L. Rev. 2083, 2125–32 (2009). Surprisingly, courts after eBay have not made the issuance of an injunction turn on the willfulness or bad faith of the infringer. *See Andrew Beckerman–Rodau, The Aftermath of* eBay v. MercExchange, 126 S.Ct. 1837 (2006): A Review of Subsequent Judicial Decisions, 89 J. Pat. & Trademark Off. Soc'y 631, 656 (2007). For an example of a case in which the court denied an injunction even though the defendant had willfully infringed the patent, see, e.g., *z4 Technologies, Inc. v. Microsoft Corp.*, 434 F.Supp.2d 437, 438 (E.D.Tex.2006).

Moreover, the balancing of the hardships according to equitable principles involved relieving a violator of the consequences of "grossly disproportionate hardship," and not inquiring which party suffers "more" hardship. *Id.* at 2131; Herbert F. Schwartz, *Injunctive Relief in Patent Infringement Suits*, 112 U. PA. L. REV. 1025, 1045–46 (1964). Similarly, traditional invocations of the public interest were rather narrow, centering on public health concerns. *See, e.g.*, City of Milwaukee v. Activated Sludge, Inc., 69 F.2d 577 (7th Cir.1934) (dissolving an injunction against an infringing sewage-disposal system).

2. *Injunctions and property rights.* To what extent is injunctive relief inherent in the notion of a property right? Should it be? When a patent has been adjudicated to be both valid and infringed and the infringement is ongoing, how can the first two prongs of the test not be met if the patent is to be seen as a right to exclude? To the extent that damages substitute for injunctions, does the owner no longer have a right to exclude, or does the owner have a right to exclude with a different, perhaps lesser, remedy? *See, e.g.*, Shyam Balganesh, *Demystifying the Right to Exclude: Of Property, Inviolability, and Automatic Injunctions*, 31 HARV. J.L. & PUB. POL'Y 593 (2008).

3. *Do permanent injunctions deter future infringement?* It would seem so. Relative to the number of final adjudications of infringement, there are very few cases concerning violations of permanent injunctions in patent cases. For some infringers, the reason that the injunction is followed may be respect for or fear of the authority of the court. For other infringers, the injunction may be followed to avoid the sanctions that follow injunction violations. In other words, the true deterrent may be contempt proceedings. Ex ante, do injunctions or damages lead to more cooperative behavior? Do damages reward non-cooperative behavior?

4. *Who gets injunctions?* Since *eBay* many district courts have granted permanent injunctions to patent holders who are seeking to prevent a competitor from infringing. *See e.g., Transocean Offshore Deepwater Drilling Inc. v. GlobalSantaFe Corp.*, 2006 WL 3813778 (S.D. Tex. 2006); *Black & Decker Inc. v. Robert Bosch Tool Corp.*, 2006 WL 3446144 (N.D. Ill. Nov. 29, 2006); *Telequip Corp. v. Change Exch.*, 2006 WL 2385425 (N.D.N.Y. 2006); *Wald v. Mudhopper Oilfield Servs.*, 2006 WL 2128851 (W.D. Okla. 2006); *z4 Techs., Inc. v. Microsoft Corp.*, 434 F.Supp.2d 437 (E.D. Tex. 2006). *But see Praxair, Inc. v. ATMI, Inc.*, 479 F.Supp.2d 440, 443–44 (D.Del.2007). The Federal Circuit has also upheld such injunctions. *See i4i Ltd. Partnership v. Microsoft Corp.*, 598 F.3d 831 (Fed.Cir.2010); *Acumed LLC v. Stryker Corp.*, 551 F.3d 1323 (Fed.Cir.2008).

However, other district courts have denied injunctive relief when the infringer was not a competitor of the patentee. *See e.g., MercExchange, L.L.C. v. eBay, Inc.*, 500 F.Supp.2d 556 (E.D.Va.2007); *Visto Corp. v. Seven Networks, Inc.*, 2006 WL 3741891 (E.D. Tex. 2006); *Finisar Corp. v. DirecTV Group, Inc.*, 416 F.Supp.2d 512 (E.D. Tex. 2006). *And see Commonwealth Scientific & Indus. Research Org. v. Buffalo Tech., Inc.*, 492 F.Supp.2d 600 (E.D.Tex.2007) (granting injunctive relief to a non-competing licensor against a manufacturer). *But see Voda v. Cordis Corp.*, 536 F.3d 1311 (Fed.Cir.2008) (holding that a patent owner seeking an injunction must demonstrate irreparable injury to the patent owner, not to an exclusive licensee).

Paice LLC v. Toyota Motor Corp.

504 F.3d 1293 (Fed.Cir.2007).

■ Before LOURIE, RADER and PROST, CIRCUIT JUDGES.

■ Opinion for the court filed by CIRCUIT JUDGE PROST. Opinion concurring in the result filed by CIRCUIT JUDGE RADER.

* * *

Finally, we address the district court's ongoing-royalty order, which allows Toyota to continue using the invention of the '970 patent at a cost of $25 per accused vehicle.[3]

The district court's order reads:

> Defendants are hereby ORDERED, for the remaining life of the '970 patent, to pay Plaintiff an ongoing royalty of $25.00 per infringing Prius II, Toyota Highlander, or Lexus RX400H (the "infringing vehicles"). Royalties shall be paid quarterly and shall be accompanied by an accounting of the sales of infringing vehicles. Payments shall begin three months after the date of signing this judgment and shall be made quarterly thereafter. The first payment shall include royalties for all infringing vehicles sold that were not accounted for in the jury's verdict. Payments not made within 14 days of the due date shall accrue interest at the rate of 10%, compounded monthly. Plaintiff shall have the right to request audits. It is anticipated that the parties may wish to agree to more comprehensive and convenient terms. The parties shall promptly notify the Court of any such agreement. The Court maintains jurisdiction to enforce this portion of the Final Judgment.

J.A. 110. Paice argues that the district court did not have the statutory authority to issue this order, and that, even if the court did have such authority, Paice was denied its right to a jury trial under the Seventh Amendment to determine the amount of the ongoing royalty rate.[4]

We begin with the language of 35 U.S.C. § 283, which provides in relevant part:

> The several courts having jurisdiction of cases under this title may grant injunctions in accordance with the principles of equity to prevent the violation of any right secured by patent, on such terms as the court deems reasonable.

Perhaps the most apparent restriction imposed by § 283 is that injunctions granted thereunder must "prevent the violation of any right secured

---

3. We use the term ongoing royalty to distinguish this equitable remedy from a compulsory license. The term "compulsory license" implies that *anyone* who meets certain criteria has congressional authority to use that which is licensed. *See, e.g.,* 17 U.S.C. § 115 ("When phonorecords of a nondramatic musical work have been distributed ... under the authority of the copyright owner, *any other person* ... may, by complying with the provisions of this section, obtain a compulsory license to make and distribute phonorecords of the work." (emphasis added)). By contrast, the ongoing-royalty order at issue here is limited to one particular set of defendants; there is no implied authority in the court's order for any other auto manufacturer to follow in Toyota's footsteps and use the patented invention with the court's imprimatur.

4. Paice also argues that the ongoing royalty inhibits Paice's ability to grant an exclusive license under its patent. To the extent Paice's inability to grant an exclusive license is a valid consideration, the fact that § 283 is permissive indicates that concerns regarding exclusivity do not outweigh other equitable factors. The district court considered this factor and rejected it, concluding that "other potential licensees would [not] be less likely to take a license if this case ends with monetary damages instead of equitable relief." J.A. 100. This finding is supported by substantial evidence.

by patent." We have previously held that this statutory language limits the scope of activities that may be enjoined. *See, e.g., Joy Techs, v. Flakt, Inc.*, 6 F.3d 770, 777 (Fed. Cir. 1993) (holding that noninfringing acts may not be enjoined). The more difficult question raised by this case, however, is whether an order *permitting* use of a patented invention in exchange for a royalty is properly characterized as *preventing* the violation of the rights secured by the patent.

Under some circumstances, awarding an ongoing royalty for patent infringement in lieu of an injunction may be appropriate. In *Shatterproof Glass Corp. v. Libbey–Owens Ford Co.*, 758 F.2d 613, 628 (Fed. Cir. 1985), this court upheld a 5% court-ordered royalty, based on sales, "for continuing operations." Although the parties in that case contested the amount of the royalty, styled a "compulsory license" by the court, there was no dispute as to the district court's authority to craft such a remedy. *See id.* In the context of an antitrust violation, "mandatory sales and reasonable-royalty licensing" of relevant patents are "well-established forms of relief when necessary to an effective remedy, particularly where patents have provided the leverage for or have contributed to the antitrust violation adjudicated." *United States v. Glaxo Group Ltd.*, 410 U.S. 52, 59(1973).

But, awarding an ongoing royalty where "necessary" to effectuate a remedy, be it for antitrust violations or patent infringement, does not justify the provision of such relief as a matter of course whenever a permanent injunction is not imposed. In most cases, where the district court determines that a permanent injunction is not warranted, the district court may wish to allow the parties to negotiate a license amongst themselves regarding future use of a patented invention before imposing an ongoing royalty. Should the parties fail to come to an agreement, the district court could step in to assess a reasonable royalty in light of the ongoing infringement.

In this case, the district court, after applying the four-factor test for a permanent injunction and declining to issue one, imposed an ongoing royalty sua sponte upon the parties. But, the district court's order provides no reasoning to support the selection of $25 per infringing vehicle as the royalty rate. Thus, this court is unable to determine whether the district court abused its discretion in setting the ongoing royalty rate. Accordingly, we think it prudent to remand the case for the limited purpose of having the district court reevaluate the ongoing royalty rate. Upon remand, the court may take additional evidence if necessary to account for any additional economic factors arising out of the imposition of an ongoing royalty.[5] The district court may determine that $25 is, in fact, an appropriate royalty rate going forward. However, without any indication as to why that rate is appropriate, we are unable to determine whether the district court abused its discretion. *Cf. Hensley v. Eckerhart*, 461 U.S. 424, 437 (1983) ("It [is] important ... for the district court to provide a concise but clear explanation of its reasons for the fee award."). The district court should also take

---

5. This process will also, presumably, allow the parties the opportunity to present evidence regarding an appropriate royalty rate to compensate Paice and the opportunity to negotiate their own rate prior to the imposition of one by the court, as the concurrence suggests.

the opportunity on remand to consider the concerns Paice raises about the terms of Toyota's permissive continuing use.

■ RADER, CIRCUIT JUDGE, concurring.

I agree with the court's judgment in this matter, with respect to both Toyota's appeal and Paice's cross-appeal. But, I write separately to express my opinion that in remanding to the district court for reevaluation of the "ongoing royalty" rate, this court should do more than suggest that "the district court *may* wish to allow the parties to negotiate a license amongst themselves . . . before imposing an ongoing royalty." Slip op. at 34 (emphasis added). Instead, this court should *require* the district court to remand this issue to the parties, or to obtain the permission of both parties before setting the ongoing royalty rate itself.

District courts have considerable discretion in crafting equitable remedies, and in a limited number of cases, as here, imposition of an ongoing royalty may be appropriate. Nonetheless, calling a compulsory license an "ongoing royalty" does not make it any less a compulsory license. To avoid many of the disruptive implications of a royalty imposed as an alternative to the preferred remedy of exclusion, the trial court's discretion should not reach so far as to deny the parties a formal opportunity to set the terms of a royalty on their own. With such an opportunity in place, an ongoing royalty would be an ongoing royalty, not a compulsory license.

In this case, because the court imposed an ongoing royalty on the parties *sua sponte* after denying injunctive relief, the parties had no meaningful chance to present evidence to the district court on an appropriate royalty rate to compensate Paice for Toyota's *future* acts of infringement. Evidence and argument on royalty rates were, of course, presented during the course of the trial, for the purposes of assessing damages for Toyota's *past* infringement. But pre-suit and post-judgment acts of infringement are distinct, and may warrant different royalty rates given the change in the parties' legal relationship and other factors. When given choices between taking additional evidence or not, and between remanding to the parties or not, a district court may prefer the simplest course— impose its own compulsory license. This simplest course, however, affords the parties the least chance to inform the court of potential changes in the market or other circumstances that might affect the royalty rate reaching into the future.

In most cases, the patentee and the infringer should receive an opportunity at least to set license terms that will apply to post-suit use of the patented invention. This general principle has deep roots in both law and policy. Projecting the costs to be incurred for what would otherwise be future acts of infringement is necessarily a speculative exercise, even for the most stable markets and technologies. As licenses are driven largely by business objectives, the parties to a license are better situated than the courts to arrive at fair and efficient terms. After all, it is the parties, rather than the court, that will be bound by the terms of the royalty. Particularly in the case of the patentee, who has proven infringement of its property right, an opportunity to negotiate its own ongoing royalty is a minimal protection for its rights extending for the remainder of the patent term.

For these reasons, I would require the district court to allow the parties an opportunity to set the ongoing royalty rate, or, at least to secure the permission of both parties before setting the rate itself. Of course, if the parties cannot reach agreement, the court would retain jurisdiction to impose a reasonable royalty to remedy the past and ongoing infringement.

NOTES

1. *How do courts set price when they deny an injunction?* Some prefer denying injunctions because they would prefer a court to set the price of infringement. What information does a court need to make this calculation; who has it; and how should it be evaluated? If courts set the price too low too often, there would be strong incentives to infringe rather than use prior or new noninfringing technologies and rather than reaching an agreement to license the patent. If courts price too high too often, then the parties are left facing the same impasse problems that would have been caused by an injunction; but the time and expense of litigation have been lost. While price is an important part of many deals, damages award boil everything down to price, even though most technology deals are reduced to writing in detailed contract documents that contain a plethora of important and complex terms other than price.

2. *What can a patentee do when an injunction is being violated?* When a permanent injunction appears to have been violated, i.e., the enjoined party appears to be continuing to infringe, the patent owner has two options. The first option is to file a new lawsuit for infringement. The second option is to seek relief through a contempt proceeding. Because contempt can be found summarily, i.e., without a full trial, patent owners would always prefer the second option. The second option is not available, however, if there is fair ground of doubt about whether the injunction has been violated. Fair ground of doubt exists when it is not clear that the product sold or process used after the injunction was entered is infringing. In other words, whether an injunction has been violated cannot be determined in a contempt proceeding if the new product or process raises substantial questions about infringement. The Federal Circuit sitting en banc is currently considering when contempt hearings are appropriate in cases of redesigned devices accused of infringement in violation of an injunction. *See TiVo Inc. v. EchoStar Corp.*, 2010 WL 1948577 (Fed.Cir. 2010) (granting rehearing en banc).

When it is appropriate to employ a contempt proceeding, the issue to be decided in that proceeding is whether the new accused product or process infringes. Invalidity is not a defense in the contempt proceeding. The standard of proof for infringement in a contempt proceeding is clear and convincing evidence. *See KSM Fastening Sys. v. H.A. Jones Co.*, 776 F.2d 1522, 1524–37 (Fed.Cir.1985). *See also Additive Controls & Measurement Sys., Inc. v. Flowdata, Inc.*, 154 F.3d 1345, 1349–51 (Fed.Cir.1998) (a new claim construction issue does not necessarily raise a substantial question).

Sanctions in a civil contempt proceeding can serve two purposes. One purpose is to compensate the patent owner for the post-injunction infringement. In such a case, sanctions would be a fine payable to the patent owner in an amount based on actual harm, potentially including attorney fees and costs. The second purpose of a civil contempt proceeding is to coerce compliance with the court's order. In this situation, the sanction (which could be fine or imprisonment) would be conditional, i.e., the sanction could be avoided by complying with the sanction order. *See Spindelfabrik Suessen–Schurr v. Schubert & Salzer Maschinenfabrik Aktiengesellschaft*, 903 F.2d 1568, 1578–80 (Fed.Cir.1990). Although punitive damages are usually not available in a civil contempt proceeding, in appropriately flagrant circumstances, the Federal Circuit has affirmed civil contempt awards to the patent owner that included punitive damages of the kind traditionally available in patent litigation. *See, e.g., Stryker Corp. v. Davol Inc.*, 234 F.3d 1252, 1260 (Fed.Cir.2000). See generally James C. Nemmers, Enforcement of Injunctive Orders and Decrees in Patent Cases, 7 IND. L. REV. 287 (1973). Criminal contempt proceedings are available when it is appropriate to punish the injunction violator.

b.   PRELIMINARY INJUNCTIONS

In most areas of law in the U.S., including patents, there has long been a view that equitable remedies, such as injunctions, should only be available where no legal remedy, such as damages, would be adequate. As a result, the general test for obtaining equitable relief, such as an injunction, is (A) irreparable harm; (B) no adequate remedy at law; (C) the balancing the hardships between the parties weighs in favor of granting; and (D) insufficient adverse impact on the public. Where the relief is temporary pending a final adjudication, such as a temporary restraining order (which is usually for a matter of days until a preliminary hearing can be held) or a preliminary injunction (which can last as long as trial), an additional and preliminary prong to the general test is added: (E) a reasonable likelihood that the party seeking the temporary relief will ultimately succeed on the merits and receive permanent relief. A basic understanding of this general test will help students understand the evolution of the case law as it applies to a number of specific areas in patent law including: preliminary injunctions, permanent injunctions, and stays pending appeal.

For almost 100 years in patent cases up until 1983, patentees were not able to show irreparable harm in preliminary injunction cases if the alleged infringer was financially solvent. Preliminary injunctive relief was usually denied in that situation because it was believed that a patent owner who could be compensated financially for the infringement that occurred during litigation was not irreparably harmed by that infringement. *See generally* Note, *Injunctive Relief in Patent Infringement Suits*, 112 U. PENN. L. REV. 1025, 1026–35 (1964); Herbert F. Schwartz, *Injunctive Relief in Patent Cases*, 50 ALBANY L. REV. 565, 567–68 (1986). In its second year of existence, the Federal Circuit adopted a new rule regarding showing irreparable harm in *Smith Int'l, Inc. v. Hughes Tool Co.*, 718 F.2d 1573 (Fed.Cir.1983).

In *Smith Int'l*, while maintaining the requirement for a showing of irreparable harm by the applicant for a preliminary injunction, the Federal Circuit held:

> The very nature of the patent right is the right to exclude others. Once the patentee's patents have been held to be valid and infringed, he should be entitled to the full enjoyment and protection of his patent rights. The infringer should not be allowed to continue his infringement in the face of such a holding. A court should not be reluctant to use its equity powers once a party has so clearly established his patent rights. We hold that where validity and continuing infringement have been clearly established . . . immediate irreparable harm is presumed. To hold otherwise would be contrary to the public policy underlying the patent laws.

Smith Int'l, Inc., 718 F.2d at 1581 (footnotes omitted).

Subsequent to the decision in *Smith Int'l*, there was a dramatic increase in the number of preliminary injunctions granted in patent cases.

Despite the increase, preliminary injunctions remain a drastic and extraordinary remedy. An example of the impact of the *Smith Int'l* holding regarding irreparable harm can be seen in the following case.

Sanofi–Synthelabo v. Apotex, Inc.

470 F.3d 1368 (Fed.Cir.2006).

■ Before Lourie and Bryson, Circuit Judges, Clevenger, Senior Circuit Judge.

■ Lourie, Circuit Judge.

Apotex, Inc. and Apotex Corp. (collectively referred to as "Apotex") appeal from the decision of the United States District Court for the Southern District of New York granting a preliminary injunction in favor of Sanofi–Synthelabo, Sanofi–Synthelabo, Inc., and Bristol–Myers Squibb ("BMS") Sanofi Pharmaceuticals Holding Partnership (collectively referred to as "Sanofi"). Because we conclude that the district court did not abuse its discretion in granting the preliminary injunction, we affirm.

BACKGROUND

Sanofi markets Plavix(R), a platelet aggregation inhibiting agent used to reduce thrombotic events such as heart attacks and strokes. The active ingredient in Plavix(R) is clopidogrel bisulfate, which is covered by Sanofi's patent, U.S. Patent 4,847,265 ("the '265 patent"), which will expire on November 17, 2011.

In November 2001, Apotex filed an Abbreviated New Drug Application ("ANDA") pursuant to the Hatch–Waxman Act seeking U.S. Food and Drug Administration ("FDA") approval to manufacture and sell a generic version of clopidogrel bisulfate. Apotex filed a Paragraph IV certification with its ANDA, pursuant to 21 U.S.C. § 355(j)(2)(A)(vii)(IV), asserting that the '265 patent is invalid. In response, Sanofi sued Apotex on March 21, 2002, claiming that the filing of the ANDA infringed the '265 patent. Apotex counter claimed, asserting that the patent is invalid and unenforceable. A thirty-month stay of FDA approval for the ANDA was triggered when the suit was filed in the district court, pursuant to 21 U.S.C. § 355(j)(5)(B)(iii). The stay expired May 17, 2005, and on January 20, 2006, the FDA approved the ANDA.

Several days before the ANDA was approved, Sanofi and Apotex began settlement negotiations in an effort to resolve the litigation. On March 17, 2006, the parties reached a first settlement agreement that was subject to the approval of the Federal Trade Commission and a consortium of state attorneys general pursuant to an order issued in another litigation involving BMS. In May 2006, the state attorneys general notified the parties that they would not approve the settlement. The parties negotiated a second agreement ("the May agreement"). The May agreement included provisions specifying, *inter alia*, actions that could be taken by the parties in the event that the settlement failed to receive regulatory approval. In July 2006, the state attorneys general again informed the parties that they would not approve the settlement. Apotex then declared "regulatory denial" on July 31, 2006, as permitted under the settlement agreement, which meant, *inter alia*, "a denial of approval by either the FTC or a state attorney general as to which neither party seeks further review." Under the agreement, litigation would resume in the event of "regulatory denial."

Pursuant to the aforementioned agreement, Apotex launched its generic clopidogrel bisulfate product on August 8, 2006. In accordance with the provisions in the settlement agreement, Sanofi notified Apotex of its intent to move for a preliminary injunction in the time frame permitted by the agreement, *viz.*, five business days after the generic launch. Sanofi filed its motion for a preliminary injunction on August 15, 2006, and requested a recall of Apotex's products that were already distributed. After a two-day evidentiary hearing, the district court granted the motion for injunctive relief on August 31, 2006, but denied the request for recall. During the period between the generic launch and the entry of the preliminary injunction, Apotex shipped a six-month supply of its product to distributors in the United States.

In reaching its decision, the district court applied the established four-factor test for preliminary injunctive relief, and found that the factors weighed in favor of an injunction. Regarding the likelihood of success on the merits, the court noted that Apotex conceded that its accused products infringe claim 3 of the '265 patent. The court then found that Apotex failed to establish a likelihood of proving invalidity at trial—rejecting its anticipation, obviousness, and obviousness-type double patenting invalidity defenses. The court also determined that Apotex failed to raise a substantial question as to whether the '265 patent is unenforceable due to inequitable conduct. Additionally, the court found that the remaining three factors of the test favored issuance of a preliminary injunction. As for Apotex's other defenses, the court concluded that the doctrine of laches was inapplicable, and it rejected Apotex's unclean hands defense. The court set bond in the amount of $400 million. Trial is scheduled to commence on January 22, 2007.

Apotex moved for a stay of the injunction, which we denied on September 21, 2006, and it filed its appeal from the district court's grant of the preliminary injunction. An expedited briefing schedule was set, and oral argument was heard on October 31, 2006. We have jurisdiction pursuant to 28 U.S.C. § 1292(c) in view of §§ 1292(a) and 1295(a)(1).

DISCUSSION

A decision to grant or deny a preliminary injunction pursuant to 35 U.S.C. § 283 is within the sound discretion of the district court, and we review such a decision for an abuse of discretion. *Amazon.com, Inc. v. Barnesandnoble.com, Inc.*, 239 F.3d 1343, 1350 (Fed. Cir. 2001). Thus, a decision granting a preliminary injunction will be overturned on appeal only if it is established "that the court made a clear error of judgment in weighing relevant factors or exercised its discretion based upon an error of law or clearly erroneous factual findings." *Genentech, Inc. v. Novo Nordisk A/S*, 108 F.3d 1361, 1364 (Fed. Cir. 1997). To the extent the court's decision is based upon an issue of law, we review that issue *de novo*. *Tate Access Floors, Inc. v. Interface Architectural Res., Inc.*, 279 F.3d 1357, 1364 (Fed.Cir.2002).

Sanofi, as the moving party, may be entitled to a preliminary injunction if it establishes four factors: "(1) a reasonable likelihood of its success on the merits; (2) irreparable harm if an injunction is not granted; (3) a balance of hardships tipping in its favor; and (4) the injunction's . . . impact on the public interest." *Amazon.com*, 239 F.3d at 1350.

A. *Likelihood of Success on the Merits*

In order to satisfy the first element of the test, Sanofi must demonstrate that, "in light of the presumptions and burdens that will inhere at trial on the merits," *Amazon.com*, 239 F.3d at 1350, Sanofi will likely prove that Apotex's product infringes the '265 patent and that it will withstand Apotex's challenges to the validity and enforceability of the '265 patent. Because Apotex stipulated to infringement, only the second inquiry is at issue in this case. Thus, the first element was properly found satisfied if Apotex failed to raise a "substantial question" with regard to the validity or enforceability of the '265 patent—or, if it succeeded in doing so, Sanofi demonstrated that those defenses "lack substantial merit." Genentech, 108 F.3d at 1364. On appeal, Apotex challenges the district court's rulings with respect to anticipation, obviousness, obviousness-type double patenting, and enforceability.

1. *Validity of the '265 Patent*

a. *Anticipation*

We first consider whether the district court clearly erred in its determination that Sanofi will likely withstand Apotex's challenge to the validity of the '265 patent based on anticipation. Apotex asserted that U.S. Patent 4,529,596 ("the '596 patent") anticipates claim 3 of the '265 patent. The district court rejected Apotex's argument on two grounds. First, the court found that the '596 patent does not describe clopidogrel bisulfate. Second, the court determined that the '596 patent does not enable a person of ordinary skill in the art to make clopidogrel bisulfate without undue experimentation.

As a preliminary matter, we note that the '596 patent was before the Examiner during prosecution, which makes Apotex's burden of proving invalidity at trial "especially difficult." *Glaxo Group Ltd. v. Apotex, Inc.*, 376 F.3d 1339, 1348 (Fed. Cir. 2004). Thus, in light of the deferential standard we apply in reviewing grants or denials of preliminary injunctions, and mindful that "a patent is presumed valid, and this presumption exists at every stage of the litigation," *Canon Computer Sys., Inc. v. Nu–Kote Int'l, Inc.*, 134 F.3d 1085, 1088 (Fed. Cir. 1998), we conclude that the district court did not clearly err in finding that Apotex's anticipation defense lacks substantial merit.

A determination that a patent is invalid as being anticipated under 35 U.S.C. § 102 requires a finding that "each and every limitation is found either expressly or inherently in a single prior art reference." *Celeritas Techs. Ltd. v. Rockwell Int'l Corp.*, 150 F.3d 1354, 1361 (Fed. Cir. 1998). Claim 3 of the '265 patent reads as follows:

> 3. Hydrogen sulfate of the dextrorotatory isomer of methyl alpha–5 (4,5,6,7–tetrahydro (3,2–c) thienopyridyl) (2–chlorophenyl)—acetate substantially separated from the levo-rotatory isomer.

'265 patent col.12 ll.37–40. Thus, the claim consists of the following key limitations: 1) the d-enantiomer; 2) of the compound MATTPCA; 3) the bisulfate salt; and 4)Êsubstantial separation from the levorotatory isomer.

Claim 2 of the '596 patent, in contrast, reads as follows:

2. Methyl   [alpha]-(4,5,6,7–tetrahydro–thieno(3,2–c)–5–pyridyl)-o.chloro-phenyl-acetate.

'596 patent, col. 13, ll.20–21. Thus, the plain language of claim 2 only recites the free base, MATTPCA, and does not expressly describe the dextrorotatory or levorotatory enantiomers or any salt. Because claim 2 fails to describe each and every limitation of claim 3 on its face, claim 2 does not anticipate claim 3.

Apotex argues that the two missing limitations, *viz.*, the d-enantiomer and the bisulfate salt, are inherently disclosed in the claim. With regard to the bisulfate salt limitation, Apotex seeks to import into the scope of claim 2 a statement in the specification that the invention includes "addition salts with pharmaceutically acceptable mineral or organic acids." *Id.*, col.1 ll.42–43. Apotex further argues that the '596 patent discloses a preference for bisulfate salt.

The district court, however, considered that argument and rejected it. After careful consideration of the record before it, the court found that a person of ordinary skill in the art would not be led to the bisulfate salt for several reasons. Based on the testimony of Sanofi's expert, Dr. Byrn, the court noted that a chemist would actually be dissuaded from preparing the bisulfate salt in light of Example 1, which describes the hydrochloride salt of the racemate, because a chemist would believe that the hydrochloride, as opposed to the bisulfate, is the preferred salt for clopidogrel. The court also credited Dr. Byrn's additional testimony that salt formation with a new compound is an "unpredictable exercise." In addition, the court noted that a chemist theoretically had at least fifty different pharmaceutically acceptable salts from which he could have chosen for formulation. Based on that evidence, the court found that "disclosing bisulfate in the '596 patent was insufficient to disclose a single enantiomer of a compound as a bisulfate salt." *Sanofi–Synthelabo*, 488 F. Supp.2d 317, 333. Because we find that the district court did not clearly err in its fact-finding as to this issue, we reject Apotex's argument that claim 2 of the '596 patent inherently discloses the bisulfate salt.

We therefore reject Apotex's assertion that clopidogrel bisulfate is a species of the genus in claim 2 of the '596 patent, and that the district court clearly erred by failing to so find. In light of this holding, we need not address the enablement issue. Accordingly, we conclude that the district court did not clearly err in finding no substantial merit to Apotex's assertion that claim 3 of the '265 patent is anticipated by the '596 patent.

b. *Obviousness*

We next consider Apotex's assertion that claim 3 of the '265 patent is invalid as obvious. Apotex argues that the district court erred in concluding that its obviousness defense failed to raise a substantial question with regard to the validity of the '265 patent. Apotex primarily argues that it would have been obvious to a person of ordinary skill in the art to prepare clopidogrel bisulfate based on the disclosure of the '596 patent. Additionally, Apotex asserts that the "unexpected results" upon which Sanofi relied to establish the nonobviousness of clopidogrel bisulfate were not "unexpected" to a person of ordinary skill in the art. Moreover, Apotex contends that the court erred by failing to cite *Adamson* in its obviousness analysis—a case that, according to Apotex, stands for the proposition that enantiomers are prima facie obvious over disclosures of their racemates.

Sanofi responds that the district court correctly concluded that it would not have been obvious to prepare clopidogrel bisulfate in view of the '596 patent, particularly in light of the effort Sanofi actually had to expend in developing clopidogrel bisulfate, including the four years and millions of dollars that were allocated to the development of the racemate before efforts were redirected toward isolating the d-enantiomer. Sanofi further argues that any prima facie obviousness resulting from the disclosure of the racemate in the prior art was rebutted by the unexpected properties of clopidogrel bisulfate—specifically, high pharmacological activity and low toxicity—two properties that are not necessarily generally associated with one enantiomer.

We agree with Sanofi that the court did not clearly err in finding that Apotex failed to raise a substantial question in its obviousness defense. First, we reject Apotex's contention that it would have been obvious to a person of ordinary skill in the art to prepare clopidogrel bisulfate based on the disclosures of the '596 patent. The district court rejected that position after considering extensive argument, testimony, and references presented by both parties. In reaching that determination, the district court noted that there was "nothing obvious about arriving at clopidogrel bisulfate by separating the enantiomers of [MATTPCA] and preparing the dextrorotatory [enantiomer] as a bisulfate salt." *Sanofi–Synthelabo*, 488 F. Supp.2d at 336. The court determined that nothing existed in the prior art that would make pursuing the enantiomer of MATTPCA an obvious choice, particularly in light of the unpredictability of the pharmaceutical properties of the enantiomers and the potential for enantiomers to racemize in the body.

The court also found that the extensive time and money Sanofi spent developing the racemate before redirecting its efforts toward the enantiomer, and the unpredictability of salt formation, were indicators of nonobviousness. The court credited the testimony of Apotex's own expert, Dr. McClelland, who agreed that salt formation was an unpredictable exercise that would require a chemist "to engage in experimentation to determine which salt would in fact be suitable." *Id.* 488 F. Supp.2d 317. The court also noted that a named inventor, Dr. Badorc, tested twenty different salts before discovering that bisulfate had the most desirable properties. Thus, the court found that it would not have been obvious to a person of ordinary skill in the art to prepare clopidogrel bisulfate from reading the '596 patent in light of the extensive experimentation that was required to arrive at that particular compound. We discern no clear error with respect to those factual determinations or the legal conclusion.

We also reject Apotex's assertion that a person of ordinary skill in the art would have been led to the active enantiomer of MATTPCA after reading the '596 patent. Apotex merely asserts that one would have been motivated "because the patent directs [a person of ordinary skill in the art] to enantiomers and pharmaceutical salts." We have noted that it is insufficient to merely identify each element in the prior art to establish unpatentability of the combined subject matter as a whole. *Abbott Labs. v. Andrx Pharms., Inc.*, 452 F.3d 1331, 1336 (Fed. Cir. 2006). Instead, "a party alleging invalidity due to obviousness must articulate the reasons one of ordinary skill in the art would have been motivated to select the references and to combine them to render the claimed invention obvious." *Id.* Apotex's conclusory assertion that the '596 patent directs a chemist to the enantiomers and salts is insufficient to satisfy this requirement. Certainly nothing directed a chemist to the particular enantiomer and salt, clopidogrel bisulfate, which is the limited subject matter of claim 3.

Second, while Apotex disagrees with the district court's assessment of the evidence relating to the "unexpected results" obtained with clopidogrel bisulfate, we review that assessment, which is based on factual findings made by the district court, for clear error. Based on the record before us, we find no basis to conclude that the district court clearly erred in its evaluation of that evidence.

Based on the preliminary record before us, we thus find that the district court did not err in determining that Apotex failed to raise a substantial question as to the validity of claim 3 based on obviousness.

c. *Obviousness–Type Double Patenting*

In the district court, Apotex also challenged the validity of claim 3 of the '265 patent based on obviousness-type double patenting. Apotex argues that the court committed clear error in concluding that the double patenting inquiry was subsumed by the broader obviousness inquiry, and by failing to specifically address this claim. Apotex asserts that an obviousness inquiry is distinct from the double patenting inquiry and should have been independently analyzed. Sanofi responds that the court correctly concluded that nothing in the prior art, including the '596 patent, rendered claim 3 obvious. Claim 2 of the '596 patent especially did not render claim 3 obvious.

While Apotex asserts that the court erred by failing to separately address its double patenting defense, Apotex fails to set forth any arguments on appeal that raise a substantial question with respect to the validity of claim 3 based on that defense. Accordingly, we reject Apotex's argument that the grant of the preliminary injunction should be reversed on that basis.

2. *Enforceability of the '265 Patent*

Apotex argues that the district court abused its discretion in finding that Apotex failed to raise a substantial question as to the enforceability of the '265 patent. Apotex identifies separate bases upon which it asserts inequitable conduct should have been found. They include incorrect inventorship, concealment of research regarding other compounds that were tested by Sanofi, and purported false statements concerning the "unexpected results" of clopidogrel bisulfate and the "less well-tolerated" statement referring to the l–enantiomer. Sanofi responds to each of Apotex's assertions, explaining why none of Apotex's arguments raises a substantial question as to the '265 patent's enforceability.

"A patent may be rendered unenforceable for inequitable conduct if an applicant, with intent to mislead or deceive the examiner, fails to disclose material information or submits materially false information to the PTO during prosecution." *Digital Control, Inc. v. Charles Mach. Works*, 437 F.3d 1309, 1313 (Fed. Cir. 2006). "The party asserting inequitable conduct must prove a threshold level of materiality and intent by clear and convincing evidence." *Id.* Further, "materiality does not presume intent, which is a separate and essential component of inequitable conduct." *GFI, Inc. v. Franklin Corp.*, 265 F.3d 1268, 1274 (Fed. Cir. 2001) (quoting *Manville Sales Corp. v. Paramount Sys., Inc.*, 917 F.2d 544, 552 (Fed. Cir. 1990)).

While Apotex devotes a significant portion of its briefs to argue its inequitable conduct contentions, virtually none of its discussion is devoted to identifying any evidence that would support a finding of deceptive intent. Apotex's evidence of intent is limited to a statement in Apotex's reply brief that the inventors' declaration, which excluded Dr. Maffrand as an inventor, is evidence of intent. Moreover, Apotex suggests that intent can be inferred because "Sanofi was motivated to extend its patent monopoly beyond the '596 patent term by patenting the enantiomer, and it needed to conjure up 'unexpected' results." Such generalized allegations lack the particularity required to meet the threshold level of deceptive intent necessary for a finding of inequitable conduct. Thus, based on the record before us, Apotex clearly fails to raise a substantial question as to the enforceability of the '265 patent. Accordingly, we find no abuse of discretion with regard to that issue.

B. *Other Preliminary Injunction Factors*

We next consider the remaining elements of the preliminary injunction test. The district court applied a presumption of irreparable harm in light of its conclusion that Sanofi established a likelihood of success on the merits. The court also found that Sanofi proffered substantial evidence establishing other forms of irreparable harm, including irreversible price erosion, loss of good will, potential lay-offs of Sanofi employees, and the discontinuance of clinical trials that are devoted to other medical uses for Plavix(R).

Apotex argues that the district court clearly erred in concluding that Sanofi would suffer irreparable harm in the absence of an injunction. According to Apotex, the settlement agreement entered into by Sanofi and Apotex negated any finding of irreparable harm. Apotex contends that Sanofi quantified in the May agreement the measure of harm it would suffer in the event Apotex marketed a generic product-specifically, 40%–50% of Apotex's net sales. Additionally, Apotex challenges the court's findings with regard to the other kinds of irreparable harm established by Sanofi.

In response, Sanofi argues that it did not contractually surrender its right to prove irreparable harm by entering into the May agreement. Moreover, Sanofi asserts that the court did not clearly err by crediting the evidence it proffered establishing the additional kinds of irreparable harm it would suffer if Apotex were allowed to continue selling its generic product.

We conclude that the district court did not clearly err in finding that Sanofi satisfied this factor. We are not persuaded by Apotex's assertion that Sanofi contracted away its right to prove irreparable harm by entering into the May agreement, which includes a provision that capped damages for infringement by Apotex. In support of this argument, Apotex refers to the following provision:

> 14. In the event of Regulatory Denial, the litigations will be resumed as further described in paragraph 15 hereof, and:
>
> * * *
>
> (ii) If the litigation results in a judgment that the '265 patent is not invalid or unenforceable, Sanofi agrees that its actual damages for any past infringement by Apotex, up to the date on which Apotex is enjoined, will be 50% of Apotex's net sales of clopidogrel products if Sanofi has not launched an authorized generic and 40% of Apotex's net sales if Sanofi has launched an authorized generic. Sanofi further agrees that it will not seek increased damages under 35. U.S.C. § 284.

May agreement, P14.

We think that the above provision favors Sanofi, not Apotex. We disagree with Apotex that by entering into that agreement, Sanofi bargained away its right to seek preliminary injunctive relief, and thus its right to prove irreparable harm, in the event the settlement was not approved. The above provision itself contemplates an injunction in referring to "up to the date on which Apotex is enjoined" and speaks only of damages for past infringement. In addition, based on other provisions in the agreement, it is clear that the parties contemplated the possibility of a preliminary injunction in the event of regulatory denial. Paragraph 15 of the agreement, for example, sets forth the procedural steps the parties must follow when seeking a preliminary injunction. Moreover, merely because a patentee is able to identify a monetary amount that it deems sufficient to avoid or end litigation does not necessarily mean that it automatically foregoes its right to seek a preliminary injunction or that any potential irreparable injury ceases to exist if infringement resumes. Thus, Apotex's argument is unsound.

Further, we reject Apotex's assertion that the district court abused its discretion in concluding that Sanofi would suffer irreversible price erosion if an injunction were not entered. Based on the evidence Sanofi adduced, including the testimony of its economics expert, Professor Hausman, and a declaration from a Sanofi executive, Hugh O'Neill, the court found that Sanofi would suffer irreversible price erosion in light of a complex pricing scheme that is directly affected by the presence of the generic product in the market. In particular, the court found that since Apotex's generic product entered the market, Sanofi has been forced to offer discounted rates and price concessions to third-party payors, such as health maintenance organizations, in order to keep Plavix(R) on a favorable pricing tier, which governs what consumers pay for that drug. The court found that the availability of a generic product encourages third party payors to place Plavix(R) on a less favorable tier, thereby requiring consumers to pay a higher co-pay, and perhaps deterring them from purchasing Plavix(R). The court identified additional consequences of unfavorable tier placement, including a decrease in demand for Plavix(R). According to Sanofi, it is nearly impossible to restore Plavix(R) to its pre-launch price since the generic product entered the market.

Apotex does not argue that price erosion is not a valid ground for finding irreparable harm, but rather challenges the district court's findings as to price erosion. We conclude that the district court did not clearly err in its evaluation of the evidence relating to price erosion. While Apotex asserts that price erosion had already occurred, and thus an injunction is not necessary because it cannot ameliorate Sanofi's position, Apotex fails to identify clear errors in the district court's analysis, and fails to proffer evidence of its own sufficient to rebut the court's findings. Apotex also fails to demonstrate that the court clearly erred in its findings with respect to the additional factors that established irreparable harm, including loss of good will, the potential reduction in work force, and the discontinuation of clinical trials. Accordingly, we conclude that the district court did not clearly err in finding irreparable harm.[9]

As to the third factor of the test, Apotex argues that the court erred in balancing the hardships because it ignored the harm Apotex would face if an injunction were granted, particularly in light of the settlement agreement which, according to Apotex, demonstrates that the harms Sanofi would suffer are a result of its own conduct. Sanofi responds that the court did not abuse its discretion in finding that that factor favored Sanofi, particularly because it was Apotex's own decision to engage in an at-risk launch that would trigger its 180–day exclusivity period before reaching the merits of the case. Based on the record on appeal, we conclude that the court did not clearly err in finding that Apotex's harms were "almost entirely preventable" and were the result of its own calculated risk to launch its product prejudgment. *Sanofi–Synthelabo*, 488 F. Supp.2d at 345. Accordingly, the court did not abuse its discretion in finding that the balance of hardships tipped in Sanofi's favor.

The fourth factor we consider is the public interest, which the court found tips in favor of Sanofi, albeit slightly. Apotex, as well as amici, argue that the district court erred in failing to consider certain public harms that would result if an injunction issues. Apotex, in particular, contends that if the generic products were removed from the market, consumers would be inclined not to purchase their medication because of the accompanying price increase for the brand name drug, leading to possible deaths. Apotex further argues that significant consumer confusion may ensue because of the six-month supply that was shipped to the American market, which was not equally distributed among vendors. Sanofi responds that the court did

---

9. Apotex also argues that the district court erred by applying a presumption of irreparable harm because Sanofi established a likelihood of success on the merits. Apotex contends that applying such a presumption is in direct contravention of the Supreme Court's decision in *eBay Inc. v. MercExchange, L.L.C.*, 126 S. Ct. 1837, 164 L. Ed. 2d 641 (2006). Because we conclude that the district court did not clearly err in finding that Sanofi established several kinds of irreparable harm, including irreversible price erosion, we need not address this contention.

not clearly err in finding that the interest in encouraging pharmaceutical research and development outweighed the public interest advanced by Apotex.

We agree with Sanofi. While Apotex raises legitimate concerns, the district court did not abuse its discretion in concluding that those concerns were outweighed by the public interests identified by Sanofi. We have long acknowledged the importance of the patent system in encouraging innovation. Indeed, the "encouragement of investment-based risk is the fundamental purpose of the patent grant, and is based directly on the right to exclude." *Patlex Corp. v. Mossinghoff*, 758 F.2d 594, 599 (Fed. Cir. 1985). The district court relied on the testimony of Dr. Hausman in finding that the average cost of developing a blockbuster drug is $800 million. Importantly, the patent system provides incentive to the innovative drug companies to continue costly development efforts. We therefore find that the court did not clearly err in concluding that the significant "public interest in encouraging investment in drug development and protecting the exclusionary rights conveyed in valid pharmaceutical patents" tips the scales in favor of Sanofi. Sanofi–Synthelabo, 488 F. Supp.2d at 345.

D.   *Bond*

Lastly, Apotex challenges the court's decision to set bond in the amount of $400 million, which it asserts fails to provide sufficient security because it represents only 10% of the annual market and ignores Apotex's loss of market share. Sanofi responds that the amount far exceeds any damage Apotex may face, particularly in light of the fact that there was no recall of Apotex's generic product after it launched its product on August 8, 2006.

The posting of a bond is governed by Federal Rule of Civil Procedure 65(c) which provides that:

> No restraining order or preliminary injunction shall issue except upon the giving of security by the applicant, in such sum as the court deems proper, for the payment of such costs and damages as may be incurred or suffered by any party who is found to have been wrongfully enjoined or restrained.

Fed.R.Civ.P. 65(c). The amount of a bond is a determination that rests within the sound discretion of a trial court. *Doctor's Assocs., Inc. v. Distajo*, 107 F.3d 126, 136 (2d Cir. 1997) (noting that a district court has wide discretion under Rule 65(c) in setting the amount of a bond). The court based its determination on evidence presented before the court that concerned Apotex's "potential lost profits, lost market share and associated costs of relaunch" in the event of wrongful enjoinment. *Sanofi–Synthelabo*, 488 F. Supp.2d at 349. We find no basis for disturbing the court's assessment of the facts, and thus conclude that the court did not abuse its discretion in setting the bond amount.

CONCLUSION

We have considered Apotex's remaining arguments with respect to the myriad of issues it has raised on appeal and find them unpersuasive. We therefore conclude that the district court did not abuse its discretion in granting preliminary injunctive relief. Accordingly, for the foregoing reasons, we affirm the district court's grant of the preliminary injunction. We wish to note that, while we have carefully considered all of the arguments presented to us in reviewing the district court's grant of the preliminary injunction, we have done so in the context of the standard of review applicable to grant of preliminary injunctions, and that the district court is not bound to its earlier conclusions on full trial on the merits. We leave to that court the conduct of any further proceedings.

AFFIRMED.

NOTES

1. *Four factor test.* As noted in *Apotex*, there are four factors that must be considered when deciding that a patent owner is entitled to a preliminary injunction. These factors are: (1) whether the patent owner has sufficiently established a reasonable likelihood of success on the merits; (2) whether the patent owner would suffer irreparable harm if the injunction were not granted (note that some might also separately ask whether there is no adequate legal remedy); (3) whether the balance of hardships tips in the patent owner's favor; and (4) what impact will the injunction have, if any, on the public interest. Each factor must be weighed against the other factors and against the form and magnitude of the relief sought. *Tate Access Floors v. Interface Architectural Res.*, 279 F.3d 1357, 1365 (Fed.Cir.2002).

2. *Whether the Patent Owner Has Sufficiently Established a Reasonable Likelihood of Success on the Merits.* To obtain a preliminary injunction, a patent owner must show a reasonable likelihood of success on the merits. Such a showing will made if, in light of the presumptions and burdens that apply during trial, the patent owner shows that (a) the patent owner will likely prove infringement and (b) the patent owner's claim of infringement will likely withstand a challenge to the validity and enforceability of the patent. *See Anton/Bauer, Inc. v. PAG, Ltd.*, 329 F.3d 1343, 1348 (Fed.Cir.2003); *Vehicular Techs. Corp. v. Titan Wheel Int'l, Inc.*, 141 F.3d 1084, 1087–88 (Fed.Cir.1998).

The presumption of validity is not evidence that can be weighed when determining whether the patent owner has a reasonable likelihood of success on the merits. Nevertheless, if the alleged infringer does not challenge the patent's validity with evidence, the patent owner does not have to establish that the patent is valid. If the alleged infringer challenges validity, however, the patent owner must show that the invalidity defense lacks substantial merit. *New England Braiding Co. v. A.W. Chesterton Co.*, 970 F.2d 878, 882–83 (Fed.Cir.1992).

The court's decision regarding the likelihood-of-success factor may be based on a tentative claim construction. *International Communication Materials, Inc. v. Ricoh Co.*, 108 F.3d 316 (Fed.Cir.1997). *See also Oakley, Inc. v. Sunglass Hut Int'l*, 316 F.3d 1331, 1345 n.3 (Fed.Cir.2003).

3. *Whether the Patent Owner Would Suffer Irreparable Harm If the Injunction Were Not Granted.* The rebuttable presumption of irreparable harm established in *Smith Int'l* is raised only by a clear showing of validity and infringement. *Hybritech Inc. v. Abbott Labs.*, 849 F.2d 1446, 1456 (Fed.Cir.1988); *H.H. Robertson Co. v. United Steel Deck, Inc.*, 820 F.2d 384, 390 (Fed.Cir.1987). *See also Eli Lilly & Co. v. American Cyanamid Co.*, 82 F.3d 1568, 1578 (Fed.Cir.1996).

Circumstances that have been considered when determining if the presumption of irreparable harm has been rebutted include the patent owner's delay in bringing suit, the patent owner's licensing of the patent in suit, whether the patent owner practices the claimed invention, and the patent owner's large market share in comparison to the alleged infringer's market share. *Rosemount, Inc. v. United States Int'l Trade Comm'n*, 910 F.2d 819, 821 (Fed.Cir.1990); *Hybritech, Inc.*, 849 F.2d at

1456–57; *T.J. Smith & Nephew Ltd. v. Consolidated Med. Equip., Inc.*, 821 F.2d 646, 648 (Fed.Cir.1987); *Roper Corp. v. Litton Sys., Inc.*, 757 F.2d 1266, 1273 (Fed.Cir.1985); *B.F. Goodrich FlightSystems, Inc. v. Insight Instruments Corp.*, 22 U.S.P.Q.2d 1832, 1844 (S.D. Ohio 1992). The fact that the alleged infringer can afford to pay damages if he loses at trial, does not preclude the grant of a preliminary injunction. *Roper Corp.*, 757 F.2d at 1269 n.2. What should the result be if the alleged infringer will *not* be able to pay damages if it loses?

Should any of the following situations rebut the presumption of irreparable harm: that the patent owner elects to sue one infringer and chooses not to sue other infringers, thereby allowing the other infringers to continue to infringe; that the market for goods covered by the patent is small; or that the patent owner is inexperienced in business? *See Polymer Techs., Inc. v. Bridwell*, 103 F.3d 970, 974–76 (Fed.Cir.1996).

4. *Whether the Balance of Hardships Tips in the Patent Owner's Favor.* Regarding the third factor, the court must balance the harm that will occur to the patent owner from the denial of the preliminary injunction against the harm to the alleged infringer if the injunction is entered. *See Hybritech Inc.*, 849 F.2d at 1457. This balancing requires that the court carefully compare the situations of the patent owner and the infringer, and the effect that the injunction would have on each. The factors that the court includes in its determination are: the effect of further infringement on the patent owner's market share, business reputation, and goodwill; and the effect of an injunction on the alleged infringer's overall sales and its employees. *See, e.g., Illinois Tool Works, Inc. v. Grip–Pak, Inc.*, 906 F.2d 679, 683–84 (Fed.Cir.1990); *Atlas Powder Co. v. Ireco Chems.*, 773 F.2d 1230, 1234 (Fed.Cir. 1985); *Critikon, Inc. v. Becton Dickinson Vascular Access Inc.*, 28 U.S.P.Q.2d 1362, 1371 (D.Del.1993); *Tensar Corp. v. Tenax Corp.*, 24 U.S.P.Q.2d 1605, 1614 (D.Md. 1992).

Should the length of the time remaining on the infringed patent's term play a significant part in the balancing test? Put another way, if the patent will soon expire, does that tip the balance in favor of the patent owner or the alleged infringer? *See generally Atlas Powder Co.*, 773 F.2d at 1234 ("Patent rights do not peter out as the end of the patent term ... is approached.").

5. *What Impact Will the Injunction Have (If Any) On the Public Interest?* Regarding the fourth factor, the focus is typically on whether there exists some critical public interest that would be harmed by the grant of an injunction. *Hybritech Inc.*, 849 F.2d at 1458. *See also PPG Indus., Inc. v. Guardian Indus. Corp.*, 75 F.3d 1558, 1567 (Fed.Cir.1996); *Critikon, Inc.*, 28 U.S.P.Q.2d at 1370–71.

6. *An Adequate Bond Must Be Posted.* Because preliminary injunctions are issued before final determination of infringement, there is a significant chance that the final determination will reveal that the party previously believed to be infringing is not actually an infringer. To compensate for the costs incurred and the damages suffered by the preliminarily enjoined party should it turn out that the party was wrongfully enjoined, Rule 65(d), Fed.R.Civ.P., requires the posting of a bond before a preliminary injunction can issue. Typically, the patent owner will want the amount of the bond to be low and the accused infringer will want the amount to be high. The court must determine the amount adequate to compensate a wrongfully enjoined party. *See, e.g., Oakley, Inc. v. Sunglass Hut Int'l*, 61 U.S.P.Q.2d 1658, 1668 (C.D.Cal.2001) ($100,000), *aff'd*, 316 F.3d 1331 (Fed.Cir.2003); *Schawbel Corp. v. Conair Corp.*, 122 F.Supp.2d 71, 85 (D.Mass.2000) ($1 million); *3M Unitek Corp. v. Ormco Co.*, 96 F.Supp.2d 1042, 1052 (C.D.Cal.2000) ($500,000); *Alcon Labs. Inc. v. Bausch & Lomb Inc.*, 52 U.S.P.Q.2d 1927, 1934–35 (N.D.Tex.1999) ($2.9 million).

i. Who Cannot Be Enjoined

It is important to remember the limitations relating to government immunity that were discussed in more detail in Chapter 9. The federal government has granted a limited waiver of its sovereign immunity under 28 U.S.C. § 1498 to allow suits for just compensation, but not and injunction; and the states are essentially immune from suit under the 11th Amendment, although under *Ex Parte Young*, 209 U.S. 123 (1908), injunctions may be available against specific state officials.

In addition, although injunctions are issued to prevent future infringement, they are not issued to prevent any and all possible future infringement by any and all persons. Consistent with the requirements of Rule 65(d), Fed.R.Civ.P., that every order granting an injunction shall be specific and describe in reasonable detail the acts sought to be restrained, injunctions are properly limited to the particular product or process found to be infringing and products or processes that are merely colorably different. *KSM Fastening Sys., Inc. v. H.A. Jones Co.*, 776 F.2d 1522, 1525–27 (Fed.Cir.1985). Additionally, pursuant to Rule 65(d), the injunction is "binding only upon the parties to the action, their officers, agents, servants, employees, and attorneys, and upon those persons in active concert or participation with them who receive actual notice" of the injunction. Successor corporations are also bound. *Additive Controls & Measurement*, 154 F.3d at 1351–65. Regarding affiliated corporations, *see Tegal Corp. v. Tokyo Electron Co., Ltd.*, 248 F.3d 1376 (Fed.Cir.2001).

ii.   Stay of Injunction Pending Appeal

Prior to the creation of the Federal Circuit, it was fairly common in patent infringement cases, for a stay to be granted pending appeal by the posting of an adequate bond. This trend reversed early in 1985. In *Shiley, Inc. v. Bentley Labs., Inc.*, 601 F.Supp. 964 (C.D.Cal.1985), *aff'd*, 794 F.2d 1561 (Fed.Cir.1986); *S.C. Johnson, Inc. v. Carter–Wallace, Inc.*, 225 U.S.P.Q. 968 (S.D.N.Y. 1985) (order denying motion for stay pending appeal), stay pending appeal denied, 781 F.2d 198 (Fed.Cir.1986); and *Crucible, Inc. v. Stora Kopparbergs Bergslags AB*, 226 U.S.P.Q. 842 (W.D.Pa.1985) the respective district courts declined to stay injunctions during the appeals. However, the district courts in *Shiley* and *S.C. Johnson* did allow each defendant a transition period during which the defendant could seek a stay in the court of appeals or comply with the injunction. In both of these cases, the defendants made motions in the Federal Circuit seeking a stay of the injunction, and in both the court declined to grant a stay. *See Shiley*, 782 F.2d at 992; *S.C. Johnson*, 781 F.2d 198 (Fed.Cir. 1986) (order denying motion for stay pending appeal).

Probably the most well-known case in which the Federal Circuit declined a stay of injunction is *Polaroid Corp. v. Eastman Kodak Co.*, 641 F.Supp. 828 (D.Mass.1985), *aff'd*, 789 F.2d 1556 (Fed.Cir.1986). As you read the following order, notice the transition period granted the defendant, Kodak, to adapt to the denial of the stay.

Polaroid Corp. v. Eastman Kodak Co.

641 F.Supp. 828 (D. Mass. 1985).

■ ZOBEL, DISTRICT JUDGE

At a hearing to determine the form of judgment, the parties agreed substantially on the language to be used and on Polaroid's right to injunctive relief. Kodak does not seriously contest the issuance of an order enjoining further violation of those patents judged valid and infringed. It urges, however, that the injunction be stayed pending final resolution of all issues on appeal. For the reasons stated herein, Polaroid's request for injunctive relief is granted, and Kodak's motion for a stay pending appeal is denied. So that Kodak may have time to respond to this order, the injunction will take effect ninety days from today's date, on January 9, 1986.

The Standard

A party seeking to stay an injunction pending appeal must make a strong showing that it (1) is likely to succeed on the merits of the appeal; and a showing that (2) unless a stay is granted, it will suffer irreparable injury, that (3) no substantial harm will come to other interested parties, and that (4) a stay will do no harm to the public interest. *Reserve Mining Co. v. United States*, 498 F.2d 1073, 1076–77 (8th Cir.), *motion denied*, 419 U.S. 802 (1974), *motion denied*, 420 U.S. 1000 (1975). *See also, Crucible, Inc. v. Stora Kopparbergs Bergslags, A.B.*, ___ F.Supp. ___, 226 USPQ 842 (W.D. Pa. 1985). In practice this test reduces to a two-part analysis: courts are to assess the movant's chances for success on appeal and weigh the equities as they affect the parties and the public at large.

Likelihood of Success

The sensible administration of justice demands that "a stay should not ordinarily be granted if the court determines that the injunction will ultimately take effect in any event." *Reserve Mining Co.*, 498 F.2d at 1077. On appeal of this case an injunction will almost certainly issue.

This assessment neither overprizes this Court's conclusions nor disparages Kodak's continuing legal claims. Kodak plainly has—as it insists—"serious legal issues" to raise on appeal, even issues which "could well be ultimately decided by the Court of Appeals in a manner that is not consistent with this Court's decision." The mere existence of a set of viable claims, however, is not an index of Kodak's likelihood of success on appeal. To avoid an injunction, Kodak must prevail not on one or two or even several legal issues but rather on each one of seventeen claims decided by this Court in Polaroid's favor. This case involved eleven separate film and camera patents covering integrally-related aspects of the technology of instant photography. This Court judged Kodak to have infringed valid claims under five of the film, and two of the camera, patents.

At oral argument Kodak pointed out that one of the two infringing cameras—the EK–4—was found to infringe only a single claim (No. 8) of a single patent (the '211). Kodak suggested, therefore, that if this Court were reversed as to that one claim, no injunction against the EK–4 would issue. By the same logic, Kodak's EK–6 camera could escape an injunction if this Court's findings were overturned as to the two patents ('392 and '211) and five claims it was found to have infringed. Although this reasoning appears to ease Kodak's burden on appeal, it misses the point that the infringing film and cameras are inextricably bound together. If, for example, this Court's judgment is upheld as to any one of the five film patents judged infringed, Kodak could not continue marketing even noninfringing instant cameras, since they would be useless without infringing film. Conversely, even if Kodak managed to win reversal of all findings as to the film patents, the survival of a single finding of infringement on a camera patent would impel the Court of Appeals to enjoin the marketing of the noninfringing film so as not to induce use of the infringing camera. Under the circumstances, it is unlikely that Kodak will avoid an injunction altogether.

The Equities

Kodak's claims of irreparable harm—to its name, its employees, and to the camera-toting public—are seductive.

Kodak argues, first, that an injunction pending appeal will cause irreparable harm to its goodwill and severely disrupt its business. Kodak has sold more than 16 million instant cameras. To enjoin production and sale of its instant film, Kodak points out, will render its cameras useless, "since neither Polaroid nor any other company has film on the market that can be substituted for Kodak's." Such an outcome, Kodak insists, is particularly damaging to a company whose "reputation and goodwill are based in part on the fact that Kodak does not desert its customers...."

Not only will an injunction injure Kodak customers and goodwill, it will also, according to Kodak, cause a "major disruption" of business. If and when Kodak is forced to shut down its instant camera production, 800 full-time and 3700 part-time employees will lose their jobs, and the company will lose its $200–million investment in plant and equipment.

I am not unmindful of the hardship an injunction will cause—particularly to Kodak customers and employees. It is worth noting, however, that the harm Kodak will suffer simply mirrors the success it has enjoyed in the field of instant photography. To the extent Kodak has purchased that success at Polaroid's expense, it has taken a "calculated risk" that it might infringe existing patents. *Smith International, Inc. v. Hughes Tool Co.*, 718 F.2d 1573, 1581 (Fed.Cir.), *cert. denied*, 464 U.S. 996, 220 USPQ 385 (1983). As one court has observed, the infringer "should not be heard to complain" when it loses its gamble and reaps predictable results. *Crucible, Inc.*, 226 USPQ at 845.

Kodak argues, second, that whereas it will be damaged irreparably if an injunction issues, Polaroid will suffer "no significant additional harm" beyond "additional money damages and interest on account of additional sales of instant cameras and film." As to that injury, Kodak urges, it is "fully capable of responding in money."

Kodak's final argument considers the public interest and finds that it "weighs heavily against granting Polaroid's request for an injunction pending appeal." Kodak's concern for the sixteen million owners of its cameras is well-taken. However, as Polaroid has pointed out, those cameras carried an implied warranty to the purchasing public that they were free from infringement. *See* A. Squillante and J. Fonseca, *Williston on Sales*, § 15–15, at 378 (4th ed. 1974). In Polaroid's words: "That fact having been disproved in this action, it now properly falls upon Kodak to make whole any customer who complains.''

Kodak's characterization of the public interest not only misallocates risk, it also misconstrues the very concept of public benefit. The public policy at issue in patent cases is the "protection of rights secured by valid patents." *Smith International*, 718 F.2d at 1581. Courts grant—or refuse to stay—injunctions in order to safeguard that policy, even if those injunctions discommode business and the consuming public:

> On balance, I find that the public interest will not be disserved by issuance of an injunction ... and that the public interest to be served by protection of the nation's patent system outweighs any temporary inconvenience or one-time costs associated with staff training or other costs associated with changeover to another model.

Shiley, 601 F.Supp. at 971 (citing *Smith International*, 718 F.2d at 1581). As the Court in *S.C. Johnson* observed of another defendant, Kodak's belated "attempt to denominate itself a public benefactor ... [is] misplaced. Public policy favors the innovator, not the copier." 225 USPQ at 972.

NOTES

1. *What Happened in the 90–Day Window*. As mentioned in the Order, the district court declined to stay the injunction but set its effective date to be 90 days hence, thereby giving Kodak time to appeal or to stop infringing the Polaroid patents. Kodak made a motion in the Federal Circuit to stay the injunction pending an appeal on the merits. At the request of the court, the case was fully briefed on an accelerated schedule and argued on the merits two days before the injunction was to take effect. One day after the hearing and final submission to the court on the merits, Kodak's motion to stay the injunction was denied. *Polaroid Corp. v. Eastman Kodak Co.*, 833 F.2d 930 (Fed.Cir.1986). On the following day, Kodak sought relief from the U.S. Supreme Court, and it was denied. *Eastman Kodak Co. v. Polaroid Corp.*, 833 F.2d 930 (Fed.Cir.1986) (Powell, J.) (denying application to stay injunction). The Federal Circuit ultimately affirmed the district court's decision on the merits in an extensive opinion. *Polaroid Corp.*, 789 F.2d 1556.

2. *Why Have Such Windows?* A variety of things can occur in such windows of opportunity. The infringer may use the time to wind down the infringing activities. This may mean getting out of the business, or it may mean deploying non-infringing substitutes. The time also may facilitate settlement. The time may help essential negotiators overcome both logistical and emotional obstacles.

TiVo, Inc. v. EchoStar Communications Corp.

Order, in 2006–1574 (Fed.Cir., Oct. 3, 2006).

■ Before LOURIE, CIRCUIT JUDGE, CLEVENGER, SENIOR CIRCUIT JUDGE, and BRYSON, CIRCUIT JUDGE.

Order

EchoStar Communications Corporation et al. (EchoStar) move for a stay, pending appeal, of the permanent injunction entered by the United States District Court for the Eastern District of Texas. TiVo, Inc. opposes.

EchoStar replies. TiVo moves to strike a portion of EchoStar's reply, or, in the alternative, for leave to file a surreply. EchoStar moves for leave to respond to TiVo's motion. Tivo replies.

TiVo sued EchoStar for infringement of its patent related to hardware and software components of a digital video recorder (DVR). After a jury verdict of infringement of the hardware and software claims, the district court entered a judgment and issued a permanent injunction. EchoStar appeals and moves for a stay, pending appeal, of the injunction.

To obtain a stay, pending appeal, a movant must establish a strong likelihood of success on the merits or, failing that, nonetheless demonstrate a substantial case on the merits provided that the harm factors militate in its favor. *Hilton v. Braunskill*, 481 U.S. 770, 778 (1987). In deciding whether to grant a stay, pending appeal, this court "assesses the movant's chances of success on the merits and weighs the equities as they affect the parties and the public." *E.I. duPont de Nemours & Co. v. Phillips Petroleum Co.*, 835 F.2d 277, 278 (Fed.Cir.1987). *See also Standard Havens Prods. v. Gencor Indus.*, 897 F.2d 511 (Fed.Cir.1990).

Because EchoStar's DVR was found to infringe both the hardware and software claims, to obtain a stay of the injunction, EchoStar must show that it is likely to prevail on its arguments concerning both sets of claims. Based upon our review of the motions papers, and without prejudicing the ultimate determination of this case by the merits panel, EchoStar has met its burden of showing that there is a substantial case on the merits and that the harm factors militate in its favor. Thus, the motion for a stay is granted. *Hilton*, 481 U.S. at 778.

Accordingly,

IT IS ORDERED THAT:

(1) EchoStar's motion for a stay is granted.

(2) TiVo's motion to strike is denied. TiVo's motion for leave to file a surreply is granted.

(3) EchoStar's motion for leave to file a response is granted.

NOTE

Injunctions Pending Appeals. As you can see from *TiVo*, since the U.S. Supreme Court decided in *Ebay*, the Federal Circuit has been changing its view as to the propriety of stays of injunctive relief pending appeal. Do you think the court should issue or deny stays of such injunctions? What factors should be considered?

2.   Punitive Damages

Section 284 of Title 35 permits a court to "increase the damages up to three times the amount found or accessed." Congress has given district court judges the discretion to award punitive damages for patent infringement. Specifically, the court has the authority to increase the compensatory damages up to three times. 35 U.S.C. § 284. For example, if the compensatory damages were $30,000, then the court has the authority to award damages in any amount between $30,000 and $90,000. The amount awarded over $30,000 is punitive, not compensatory. Because increased damages are punitive, an award of increased damages must be based on culpable conduct. The type of conduct that can justify increased damages is usually referred to as willful infringement.

In re Seagate Technology, LLC

497 F.3d 1360 (Fed.Cir. 2007).

■ Before NEWMAN, MAYER, LOURIE, RADER, SCHALL, BRYSON, GAJARSA, LINN, DYK and PROST, CIRCUIT JUDGES.

■ Opinion for the court filed by CIRCUIT JUDGE MAYER, in which CIRCUIT JUDGES NEWMAN, LOURIE, RADER, SCHALL, BRYSON, GAJARSA, LINN, DYK and PROST join. Concurring opinion filed by CIRCUIT JUDGE GAJARSA, in which CIRCUIT JUDGE NEWMAN joins. Concurring opinion filed by CIRCUIT JUDGE NEWMAN.

■ MAYER, CIRCUIT JUDGE.

Seagate Technology, LLC ("Seagate") petitions for a writ of mandamus directing the United States District Court for the Southern District of New York to vacate its orders compelling disclosure of materials and testimony that Seagate claims is covered by the attorney-client privilege and work product protection. We ordered en banc review, and now grant the petition. We overrule *Underwater Devices Inc. v. Morrison–Knudsen Co.*, 717 F.2d 1380 (1983), and we clarify the scope of the waiver of attorney-client privilege and work product protection that results when an accused patent infringer asserts an advice of counsel defense to a charge of willful infringement.

Background

Convolve, Inc. and the Massachusetts Institute of Technology (collectively "Convolve") sued Seagate on July 13, 2000, alleging infringement of U.S. Patent Nos. 4,916,635 ("the '635 patent") and 5,638,267 ("the '267 patent"). Subsequently, U.S. Patent No. 6,314,473 ("the '473 patent") issued on November 6, 2001, and Convolve amended its complaint on January 25, 2002, to assert infringement of the '473 patent. Convolve also alleged that Seagate willfully infringed the patents.

Prior to the lawsuit, Seagate retained Gerald Sekimura to provide an opinion concerning Convolve's patents, and he ultimately prepared three written opinions. Seagate received the first opinion on July 24, 2000, shortly after the complaint was filed. This opinion analyzed the '635 and '267 patents and concluded that many claims were invalid and that Seagate's products did not infringe. The opinion also considered Convolve's pending International Application WO 99/45535 ("the '535 application"), which recited technology similar to that disclosed in the yet-to-be-issued '473 patent. On December 29, 2000, Sekimura provided an updated opinion to Seagate. In addition to his previous conclusions, this opinion concluded that the '267 patent was possibly unenforceable. Both opinions noted that not all of the patent claims had been reviewed, and that the '535 application required further analysis, which Sekimura recommended postponing until a U.S. patent issued. On February 21, 2003, Seagate received a third opinion concerning the validity and infringement of the by-then-issued '473 patent. There is no dispute that Seagate's opinion counsel operated separately and independently of trial counsel at all times.

In early 2003, pursuant to the trial court's scheduling order, Seagate notified Convolve of its intent to rely on Sekimura's three opinion letters in defending against willful infringement, and it disclosed all of his work product and made him available for deposition. Convolve then moved to compel discovery of any communications and work product of Seagate's other counsel, including its trial counsel. On May 28, 2004, the trial court concluded that Seagate waived the attorney-client privilege for all communications between it and any counsel, including its trial attorneys and in-house counsel, concerning the subject matter of Sekimura's opinions, i.e., infringement, invalidity, and enforceability. It further determined that the waiver began when Seagate first gained knowledge of the patents and would last until the alleged infringement ceased. Accordingly, the court ordered production of any requested documents and testimony concerning the subject matter of Sekimura's opinions. It provided for *in camera* review of documents relating to trial strategy, but said that any advice from trial counsel that undermined the reasonableness of relying on Sekimura's opinions would warrant disclosure. The court also determined that protection of work product communicated to Seagate was waived.

Based on these rulings, Convolve sought production of trial counsel opinions relating to infringement, invalidity, and enforceability of the patents, and also noticed depositions of Seagate's trial counsel. After the trial court denied Seagate's motion for a stay and certification of an interlocutory appeal, Seagate petitioned for a writ of mandamus. We stayed the discovery orders and, recognizing the functional relationship between our willfulness jurisprudence and the practical dilemmas faced in the areas of attorney-client privilege and work product protection, sua sponte ordered en banc review of the petition.

Because patent infringement is a strict liability offense, the nature of the offense is only relevant in determining whether enhanced damages are warranted. Although a trial court's discretion in awarding enhanced damages has a long lineage in patent law, the current statute, similar to its predecessors, is devoid of any standard for awarding them.[6] Absent a statutory guide, we have held that an award of enhanced damages requires a showing of willful infringement. *Beatrice Foods Co. v. New England Printing & Lithographing Co.*, 923 F.2d 1576, 1578 (Fed. Cir. 1991); *see*

---

6. The current statute, enacted in 1952 and codified at 35 U.S.C. § 284, provides:

Upon finding for the claimant the court shall award the claimant damages adequate to compensate for the infringement, but in no event less than a reasonable royalty for the use made of the invention by the infringer, together with interest and costs as fixed by the court.

When the damages are not found by a jury, the court shall assess them. In either event the court may increase the damages up to three times the amount found or assessed. Increased damages under this paragraph shall not apply to provisional rights under section 154(d) of this title.

The court may receive expert testimony as an aid to the determination of damages or of what royalty would be reasonable under the circumstances.

also Jurgens v. CBK. Ltd., 80 F.3d 1566, 1570 (Fed. Cir. 1996) (holding that bad faith infringement, which is a type of willful infringement, is required for enhanced damages). This well-established standard accords with Supreme Court precedent. *See Aro Mfg. Co. v. Convertible Top Replacement Co.*, 377 U.S. 476, 508 (1964) (enhanced damages were available for willful or bad faith infringement); *see also Dowling v. United States*, 473 U.S. 207, 227 n.19 (1985) (enhanced damages are available for "willful infringement"); *Seymour v. McCormick*, 57 U.S. 480, 489 (1853) ("wanton or malicious" injury could result in exemplary damages). But, a finding of willfulness does not require an award of enhanced damages; it merely permits it. *See* 35 U.S.C. § 284; *Odetics, Inc. v. Storage Tech. Corp.*, 185 F.3d 1259, 1274 (Fed. Cir. 1999); *Jurgens*, 80 F.3d at 1570.

This court fashioned a standard for evaluating willful infringement in *Underwater Devices Inc. v. Morrison–Knudsen Co.*, 717 F.2d 1380, 1389–90 (Fed. Cir. 1983): "Where . . . a potential infringer has actual notice of another's patent rights, he has an affirmative duty to exercise due care to determine whether or not he is infringing. Such an affirmative duty includes, *inter alia*, the duty to seek and obtain competent legal advice from counsel *before* the initiation of any possible infringing activity." (citations omitted). This standard was announced shortly after the creation of the court, and at a time "when widespread disregard of patent rights was undermining the national innovation incentive." *Knorr–Bremse Systeme Fuer Nutzfahrzeuge GmbH v. Dana Corp.*, 383 F.3d 1337, 1343 (Fed. Cir. 2004) (en banc) (citing Advisory Committee on Industrial Innovation Final Report, Dep't of Commerce (Sep. 1979)). Indeed, in *Underwater Devices*, an attorney had advised the infringer that "[c]ourts, in recent years, have—in patent infringement cases—found [asserted patents] invalid in approximately 80% of the cases," and on that basis the attorney concluded that the patentee would not likely sue for infringement. 717 F.2d at 1385. Over time, our cases evolved to evaluate willfulness and its duty of due care under the totality of the circumstances, and we enumerated factors informing the inquiry. *E.g., Read Corp. v. Portec, Inc.*, 970 F.2d 816, 826–27 (Fed.Cir.1992); *Rolls–Royce Ltd. v. GTE Valeron Corp.*, 800 F.2d 1101, 1110 (Fed.Cir.1986).

In light of the duty of due care, accused willful infringers commonly assert an advice of counsel defense. Under this defense, an accused willful infringer aims to establish that due to reasonable reliance on advice from counsel, its continued accused activities were done in good faith. Typically, counsel's opinion concludes that the patent is invalid, unenforceable, and/or not infringed. Although an infringer's reliance on favorable advice of counsel, or conversely his failure to proffer any favorable advice, is not dispositive of the willfulness inquiry, it is crucial to the analysis. *E.g., Electro Med. Sys., S.A. v. Cooper Life Scis., Inc.*, 34 F.3d 1048, 1056 (Fed. Cir. 1994) ("Possession of a favorable opinion of counsel is not essential to avoid a willfulness determination; it is only one factor to be considered, albeit an important one.").

Since *Underwater Devices*, we have recognized the practical concerns stemming from our willfulness doctrine, particularly as related to the attorney-client privilege and work product doctrine. For instance, *Quantum*

Corp. v. Tandon Corp., 940 F.2d 642, 643 (Fed. Cir. 1991), observed that "[p]roper resolution of the dilemma of an accused infringer who must choose between the lawful assertion of the attorney-client privilege and avoidance of a willfulness finding if infringement is found, is of great importance not only to the parties but to the fundamental values sought to be preserved by the attorney-client privilege." We cautioned there that an accused infringer "should not, without the trial court's careful consideration, be forced to choose between waiving the privilege in order to protect itself from a willfulness finding, in which case it may risk prejudicing itself on the question of liability, and maintaining the privilege, in which case it may risk being found to be a willful infringer if liability is found." *Id.* at 643–44. We advised that *in camera* review and bifurcating trials in appropriate cases would alleviate these concerns. *Id.* However, such procedures are often considered too onerous to be regularly employed.

Recently, in *Knorr–Bremse*, we addressed another outgrowth of our willfulness doctrine. Over the years, we had held that an accused infringer's failure to produce advice from counsel "would warrant the conclusion that it either obtained no advice of counsel or did so and was advised that its [activities] would be an infringement of valid U.S. Patents." *Knorr–Bremse*, 383 F.3d at 1343 (quoting *Kloster Speedsteel AB v. Crucible Inc.*, 793 F.2d 1565, 1580 (Fed. Cir. 1986)). Recognizing that this inference imposed "inappropriate burdens on the attorney-client relationship," *id.*, we held that invoking the attorney-client privilege or work product protection does not give rise to an adverse inference, *id.* at 1344–45. We further held that an accused infringer's failure to obtain legal advice does not give rise to an adverse inference with respect to willfulness. *Id.* at 1345–46.

More recently, in *Echostar* we addressed the scope of waiver resulting from the advice of counsel defense. First, we concluded that relying on in-house counsel's advice to refute a charge of willfulness triggers waiver of the attorney-client privilege. *Echostar*, 448 F.3d at 1299. Second, we held that asserting the advice of counsel defense waives work product protection and the attorney-client privilege for all communications on the same subject matter, as well as any documents memorializing attorney-client communications. *Id.* at 1299, 1302–03. However, we held that waiver did not extend to work product that was not communicated to an accused infringer. *Id.* at 1303–04. *Echostar* did not consider waiver of the advice of counsel defense as it relates to trial counsel.

In this case, we confront the willfulness scheme and its functional relationship to the attorney-client privilege and work product protection. In light of Supreme Court opinions since *Underwater Devices* and the practical concerns facing litigants under the current regime, we take this opportunity to revisit our willfulness doctrine and to address whether waiver resulting from advice of counsel and work product defenses extend to trial counsel. *See Knorr–Bremse*, 383 F.3d at 1343–44.

I. Willful Infringement

The term willful is not unique to patent law, and it has a well-established meaning in the civil context. For instance, our sister circuits have employed a recklessness standard for enhancing statutory damages for copyright infringement. Under the Copyright Act, a copyright owner can elect to receive statutory damages, and trial courts have discretion to enhance the damages, up to a statutory maximum, for willful infringement. 17 U.S.C. § 504(c). Although the statute does not define willful, it has consistently been defined as including reckless behavior. *See, e.g., Yurman Design, Inc. v. PAJ, Inc.,* 262 F.3d 101, 112 (2d Cir. 2001) ("Willfulness in [the context of statutory damages for copyright infringement] means that the defendant 'recklessly disregarded' the possibility that 'its conduct represented infringement.' ") (quoting *Hamil Am., Inc. v. GFI, Inc.,* 193 F.3d 92, 97 (2d Cir. 1999) (additional citations omitted)); *Wildlife Express Corp. v. Carol Wright Sales,* 18 F.3d 502, 511–12 (7th Cir. 1994) (same); *RCA/Ariola Int'l. Inc. v. Thomas & Grayston Co.,* 845 F.2d 773, 779 (8th Cir. 1988) (same); *see also eBay Inc. v. MercExchange, LLC.,* 126 S.Ct. 1837, 1840 (2006) (noting with approval that its resolution of the permanent injunction standard in the patent context created harmony with copyright law).

Just recently, the Supreme Court addressed the meaning of willfulness as a statutory condition of civil liability for punitive damages. *Safeco Ins. Co. of Am. v. Burr,* 551 U.S. ___, Nos. 06–84,–100, slip op. (June 4, 2007). *Safeco* involved the Fair Credit Reporting Act ("FCRA"), which imposes civil liability for failure to comply with its requirements. Whereas an affected consumer can recover actual damages for negligent violations of the FCRA, 15 U.S.C. § 1681o(a), he can also recover punitive damages for willful ones, 15 U.S.C. § 1681n(a). Addressing the willfulness requirement in this context, the Court concluded that the "standard civil usage" of "willful" includes reckless behavior. *Id.,* slip op. at 7; *accord McLaughlin v. Richland Shoe Co.,* 486 U.S. 128, 132–33 (1988) (concluding that willful violations of the Fair Labor Standards Act include reckless violations); *Trans World Airlines, Inc. v. Thurston,* 469 U.S. 111, 128 (1985). Significantly, the Court said that this definition comports with the common law usage, "which treated actions in 'reckless disregard' of the law as 'willful' violations." *Id.,* slip op. at 7 (citing W. Keeton, D. Dobbs, R. Keeton, & D. Owen, *Prosser and Keeton on Law of Torts* § 34, p. 212 (5th ed. 1984)).

In contrast, the duty of care announced in *Underwater Devices* sets a lower threshold for willful infringement that is more akin to negligence. This standard fails to comport with the general understanding of willfulness in the civil context, *Richland Shoe Co.,* 486 U.S. at 133 ("The word 'willful' ... is generally understood to refer to conduct that is not merely negligent."), and it allows for punitive damages in a manner inconsistent with Supreme Court precedent, *see, e.g., Safeco,* slip op. at 6–7,18–19, 21 n.20; *Smith v. Wade,* 461 U.S. 30, 39–49 (1983). Accordingly, we overrule the standard set out in *Underwater Devices* and hold that proof of willful infringement permitting enhanced damages requires at least a showing of objective recklessness. Because we abandon the affirmative duty of due care, we also reemphasize that there is no affirmative obligation to obtain opinion of counsel.

We fully recognize that "the term [reckless] is not self-defining." *Farmer v. Brennan,* 511 U.S. 825, 836 (1994). However, "[t]he civil law generally calls a person reckless who acts ... in the face of an unjustifiably high risk of harm that is either known or so obvious that it should be known." *Id.* (citing Prosser and Keeton § 34, pp. 213–14; *Restatement (Second) of Torts* § 500 (1965)). Accordingly, to establish willful infringement, a patentee must show by clear and convincing evidence that the infringer acted despite an objectively high likelihood that its actions constituted infringement of a valid patent. *See Safeco*, slip op. at 19 ("It is [a] high risk of harm, objectively assessed, that is the essence of recklessness at common law."). The state of mind of the accused infringer is not relevant to this objective inquiry. If this threshold objective standard is satisfied, the patentee must also demonstrate that this objectively-defined risk (determined by the record developed in the infringement proceeding) was either known or so obvious that it should have been known to the accused infringer. We leave it to future cases to further develop the application of this standard.[7]

Finally, we reject the argument that revisiting our willfulness doctrine is either improper or imprudent, as Convolve contends. The ultimate dispute in this case is the proper scope of discovery. While it is true that the issue of willful infringement, or even infringement for that matter, has not been decided by the trial court, it is indisputable that the proper legal standard for willful infringement informs the relevance of evidence relating to that issue and, more importantly here, the proper scope of discovery. *See United States Nat'l Bank of Or. v. Indep. Ins. Agents of Am., Inc.*, 508 U.S. 439, 447 (1993) ("[A] court may consider an issue 'antecedent to . . . and ultimately dispositive of' the dispute before it, even an issue the parties fail to identify and brief." (quoting *Arcadia v. Ohio Power Co.*, 498 U.S. 73, 77 (1990))); *see also* Fed. R. Civ. Pro. R. 26(b) (limiting discovery to relevant, not necessarily admissible, information); *accord Singleton v. Wulff*, 428 U.S. 106, 121 (1976) ("The matter of what questions may be taken up and resolved for the first time on appeal is one left primarily to the discretion of the courts of appeals, to be exercised on the facts of individual cases."); *Forshey v. Principi*, 284 F.3d 1335, 1355–59 (Fed.Cir.2002) (*en banc*). Accordingly, addressing willfulness is neither hypothetical nor advisory.

II.   Attorney–Client Privilege

We turn now to the appropriate scope of waiver of the attorney-client privilege resulting from an advice of counsel defense asserted in response to a charge of willful infringement. Recognizing that it is "the oldest of the privileges for confidential communications known to the common law," we are guided by its purpose "to encourage full and frank communication between attorneys and their clients and thereby promote broader public interests in the observance of law and administration of justice." *Upjohn Co. v. United States*, 449 U.S. 383, 389 (1981). The privilege also "recognizes that sound legal advice or advocacy serves public ends and that such advice or advocacy depends upon the lawyer's being fully informed by the client." *Id.*

The attorney-client privilege belongs to the client, who alone may waive it. *E.g., Knorr–Bremse*, 383 F.3d at 1345; *Am. Standard. Inc. v.*

---

7. We would expect, as suggested by Judge Newman, *post* at 2, that the standards of commerce would be among the factors a court might consider.

Pfizer, Inc., 828 F.2d 734, 745 (Fed. Cir. 1987). "The widely applied standard for determining the scope of a waiver ... is that the waiver applies to all other communications relating to the same subject matter." *Fort James Corp. v Solo Cup Co.*, 412 F.3d 1340, 1349 (Fed. Cir. 2005). This broad scope is grounded in principles of fairness and serves to prevent a party from simultaneously using the privilege as both a sword and a shield; that is, it prevents the inequitable result of a party disclosing favorable communications while asserting the privilege as to less favorable ones. *Echostar*, 448 F.3d at 1301; *Fort James*, 412 F.3d at 1349. Ultimately, however, "[t]here is no bright line test for determining what constitutes the subject matter of a waiver, rather courts weigh the circumstances of the disclosure, the nature of the legal advice sought and the prejudice to the parties of permitting or prohibiting further disclosures." *Fort James*, 412 F.3d at 1349–50.

In considering the scope of waiver resulting from the advice of counsel defense, district courts have reached varying results with respect to trial counsel. Some decisions have extended waiver to trial counsel, *e.g., Informatica Corp. v. Bus. Objects Data Integration, Inc.*, 454 F. Supp. 2d 957 (N.D. Cal. 2006), whereas others have declined to do so, *e.g., Collaboration Props., Inc. v. Polycom, Inc.*, 224 F.R.D. 473, 476 (N.D. Cal. 2004); *Ampex Corp. v. Eastman Kodak Co.*, 2006 WL 1995140 (D. Del. July 17, 2006). Still others have taken a middle ground and extended waiver to trial counsel only for communications contradicting or casting doubt on the opinions asserted. *E.g., Intex Recreation Corp. v. Team Worldwide Corp.*, 439 F. Supp. 2d 46 (D.D.C. 2006); *Beneficial Franchise Co., Inc. v. Bank One, N.A.*, 205 F.R.D. 212 (N.D. Ill. 2001); *Micron Separations, Inc. v. Pall Corp.*, 159 F.R.D. 361 (D. Mass. 1995).

Recognizing the value of a common approach and in light of the new willfulness analysis set out above, we conclude that the significantly different functions of trial counsel and opinion counsel advise against extending waiver to trial counsel. Whereas opinion counsel serves to provide an objective assessment for making informed business decisions, trial counsel focuses on litigation strategy and evaluates the most successful manner of presenting a case to a judicial decision maker. And trial counsel is engaged in an adversarial process. We previously recognized this distinction with respect to our prior willfulness standard in *Crystal Semiconductor Corp. v. TriTech Microelectronics International, Inc.*, 246 F.3d 1336, 1352 (Fed. Cir. 2001), which concluded that "defenses prepared [by litigation counsel] for a trial are not equivalent to the competent legal opinion of non-infringement or invalidity which qualify as 'due care' before undertaking any potentially infringing activity." Because of the fundamental difference between these types of legal advice, this situation does not present the classic "sword and shield" concerns typically mandating broad subject matter waiver. Therefore, fairness counsels against disclosing trial counsel's communications on an entire subject matter in response to an accused infringer's reliance on opinion counsel's opinion to refute a willfulness allegation.

Moreover, the interests weighing against extending waiver to trial counsel are compelling. The Supreme Court recognized the need to protect trial counsel's thoughts in *Hickman v. Taylor*, 329 U.S. 495, 510–11 (1947):

[I]t is essential that a lawyer work with a certain degree of privacy, free from unnecessary intrusion by opposing parties and their counsel. Proper preparation of a client's case demands that he assemble information, sift what he considers to be the relevant from the irrelevant facts, prepare his legal theories and plan his strategy without undue and needless interference. That is the historical and the necessary way in which lawyers act within the framework of our system of jurisprudence to promote justice and to protect their clients' interests.

The Court saw that allowing discovery of an attorney's thoughts would result in "[i]nefficiency, unfairness and sharp practices," that "[t]he effect on the legal profession would be demoralizing" and thus "the interests of the clients and the cause of justice would be poorly served." *Id.* at 511. Although *Hickman* concerned work product protection, the attorney-client privilege maintained with trial counsel raises the same concerns in patent litigation. In most cases, the demands of our adversarial system of justice will far outweigh any benefits of extending waiver to trial counsel. *See Jaffee v. Redmond*, 518 U.S. 1, 9 (1996) ("Exceptions from the general rule disfavoring testimonial privileges may be justified, however, by a 'public good transcending the normally predominant principle of utilizing all rational means for ascertaining the truth.'" (quoting *Trammel*, 445 U.S. 40, 50 (1980) (quoting *Elkins v. United States*, 364 U.S. 206 (1960) (Frankfurter, J., dissenting)))) (additional internal quotation marks omitted).

Further outweighing any benefit of extending waiver to trial counsel is the realization that in ordinary circumstances, willfulness will depend on an infringer's prelitigation conduct. It is certainly true that patent infringement is an ongoing offense that can continue after litigation has commenced. However, when a complaint is filed, a patentee must have a good faith basis for alleging willful infringement. Fed. R. Civ. Pro. 8, 11(b). So a willfulness claim asserted in the original complaint must necessarily be grounded exclusively in the accused infringer's pre-filing conduct. By contrast, when an accused infringer's post-filing conduct is reckless, a patentee can move for a preliminary injunction, which generally provides an adequate remedy for combating post-filing willful infringement. *See* 35 U.S.C. § 283; *Amazon.com, Inc. v. Barnesandnoble.com, Inc.*, 239 F.3d 1343, 1350 (Fed. Cir. 2001). A patentee who does not attempt to stop an accused infringer's activities in this manner should not be allowed to accrue enhanced damages based solely on the infringer's post-filing conduct. Similarly, if a patentee attempts to secure injunctive relief but fails, it is likely the infringement did not rise to the level of recklessness.

We fully recognize that an accused infringer may avoid a preliminary injunction by showing only a substantial question as to invalidity, as opposed to the higher clear and convincing standard required to prevail on the merits. *Amazon.com*, 239 F.3d at 1359 ("Vulnerability is the issue at the preliminary injunction stage, while validity is the issue at trial. The showing of a substantial question as to invalidity thus requires less proof than the clear and convincing showing necessary to establish invalidity itself."). However, this lessened showing simply accords with the requirement that recklessness must be shown to recover enhanced damages. A substantial question about invalidity or infringement is likely sufficient not only to avoid a preliminary injunction, but also a charge of willfulness based on post-filing conduct.

We also recognize that in some cases a patentee may be denied a preliminary injunction despite establishing a likelihood of success on the merits, such as when the remaining factors are considered and balanced. In that event, whether a willfulness claim based on conduct occurring solely after litigation began is sustainable will depend on the facts of each case.

Because willful infringement in the main must find its basis in prelitigation conduct, communications of trial counsel have little, if any, relevance warranting their disclosure, and this further supports generally shielding trial counsel from the waiver stemming from an advice of counsel defense to willfulness. Here, the opinions of Seagate's opinion counsel, received after suit was commenced, appear to be of similarly marginal value. Although the reasoning contained in those opinions ultimately may preclude Seagate's conduct from being considered reckless if infringement is found, reliance on the opinions after litigation was commenced will likely be of little significance.

In sum, we hold, as a general proposition, that asserting the advice of counsel defense and disclosing opinions of opinion counsel do not constitute waiver of the attorney-client privilege for communications with trial counsel. We do not purport to set out an absolute rule. Instead, trial courts remain free to exercise their discretion in unique circumstances to extend waiver to trial counsel, such as if a party or counsel engages in chicanery. We believe this view comports with Supreme Court precedent, which has made clear that rules concerning privileges are subject to review and revision, when necessary. *See Jaffee*, 518 U.S. at 9 (noting that federal courts are "to 'continue the evolutionary development of testimonial privileges.' " (quoting *Trammel*, 445 U.S. at 47)).

III. Work Product Protection

An advice of counsel defense asserted to refute a charge of willful infringement may also implicate waiver of work product protection. Again, we are here confronted with whether this waiver extends to trial counsel's work product. We hold that it does not, absent exceptional circumstances.

The work product doctrine is "designed to balance the needs of the adversary system: promotion of an attorney's preparation in representing a client versus society's general interest in revealing all true and material facts to the resolution of a dispute." *In re Martin Marietta Corp.*, 856 F.2d 619, 624 (4th Cir. 1988). Unlike the attorney-client privilege, which provides absolute protection from disclosure, work product protection is qualified and may be overcome by need and undue hardship. Fed. R. Civ. Pro. 26(b)(3). However, the level of need and hardship required for discovery depends on whether the work product is factual, or the result of mental processes such as plans, strategies, tactics, and impressions, whether memorialized in writing or not. Whereas factual work product can be discovered solely upon a showing of substantial need and undue hardship, mental process work product is afforded even greater, nearly absolute, protection. *See id.; Upjohn Co. v. United States*, 449 U.S. 383, 400 (1981); *Holmgren v. State Farm Mut. Auto. Ins.*, 976 F.2d 573, 577 (9th Cir. 1992) (holding that work product "may be discovered and admitted when mental impressions are *at issue* in a case and the need for the material is compelling"); *see also Office of Thrift Supervision v. Vinson & Elkins, LLP*, 124 F.3d 1304, 1307 (D.C.Cir.1997) ("virtually undiscoverable"). *But see Nat'l Union Fire Ins. Co. v. Murray Sheet Metal Co.*, 967 F.2d 980, 984 (4th Cir. 1992) ("'absolutely' immune from discovery").

Like the attorney-client privilege, however, work product protection may be waived. *United States v. Nobles*, 422 U.S. 225, 239 (1975). Here, the same rationale generally limiting waiver of the attorney-client privilege with trial counsel applies with even greater force to so limiting work product waiver because of the nature of the work product doctrine. Protecting lawyers from broad subject matter of work product disclosure "strengthens the adversary process, and . . . may ultimately and ideally further the search for the truth." *Martin Marietta*, 856 F.2d at 626; *accord Echostar*, 448 F.3d at 1301 ("[W]ork-product immunity . . . promotes a fair and efficient adversarial system. . . ."); *Coastal States Gas Corp. v. Dep't of Energy*, 617 F.2d 854, 864 (D.C. Cir. 1980) ("The purpose of the privilege, however, is not to protect any interest of the attorney . . . but to protect the adversary trial process itself. It is believed that the integrity of our system would suffer if adversaries were entitled to probe each other's thoughts and plans concerning the case."). In addition, trial counsel's mental processes, which fall within Convolve's discovery requests, enjoy the utmost protection from disclosure; a scope of waiver commensurate with the nature of such heightened protection is appropriate. *See Martin Marietta*, 856 F.2d at 625–26.

The Supreme Court has approved of narrowly restricting the scope of work product waiver. In *United States v. Nobles*, a criminal case, an accused armed robber presented the testimony of an investigator in an attempt to discredit the two eyewitnesses. When they testified for the prosecution, the defense attorney relied on the investigator's report in cross-examining the eyewitnesses. 422 U.S. at 227. After the prosecution rested, the defense attempted to call the investigator to testify. The trial court, however, ruled that if the investigator testified, his affirmative testimony would mandate disclosure of the portions of his report relating to his testimony. *Id.* at 229. The Supreme Court agreed that the investigator's affirmative testimony waived work product protection, but it approvingly noted the "quite limited" scope of waiver imposed by the trial court and its refusal to allow a general "fishing expedition" into the defense files or even the investigator's report. *Id.* at 239–40. Similarly, Convolve has been granted access to the materials relating to Seagate's opinion counsel's opinion, and he was made available for deposition. The extent of this waiver accords with the principles and spirit of *Nobles*.

Accordingly, we hold that, as a general proposition, relying on opinion counsel's work product does not waive work product immunity with respect to trial counsel. Again, we leave open the possibility that situations may arise in which waiver may be extended to trial counsel, such as if a patentee or his counsel engages in chicanery. And, of course, the general principles of work product protection remain in force, so that a party may obtain discovery of work product absent waiver upon a sufficient showing of need and hardship, bearing in mind that a higher burden must be met to obtain that pertaining to mental processes. *See* Fed. R. Civ. Pro. 26(b)(3).

Finally, the work product doctrine was partially codified in Rule 26(b)(3) of the Federal Rules of Civil Procedure, which applies work product protection to "documents and tangible things." Courts continue to apply *Hickman v. Taylor*, 329 U.S. 495, to "nontangible" work product. *See, e.g., In re Cendant Corp. Sec. Litig.*, 343 F.3d 658, 662–63 (3d Cir. 2003); *United States v. One Tract of Real Property*, 95 F.3d 422, 428 n.10 (6th Cir. 1996). This is relevant here because Convolve sought to depose Seagate's trial counsel. We agree that work product protection remains available to "nontangible" work product under *Hickman*. Otherwise, attorneys' files would be protected from discovery, but attorneys themselves would have no work product objection to depositions.

Conclusion

Accordingly, Seagate's petition for a writ of mandamus is granted, and the district court will reconsider its discovery orders in light of this opinion.

■ GAJARSA, CIRCUIT JUDGE, concurring, with whom CIRCUIT JUDGE NEWMAN joins.

I agree with the court's decision to grant the writ of mandamus; however, I write separately to express my belief that the court should take the opportunity to eliminate the grafting of willfulness onto section 284. As the court's opinion points out, although the enhanced damages clause of that section "is devoid of any standard for awarding [such damages]," *ante* at 6, this court has nevertheless read a willfulness standard into the statute, *see, e.g., Beatrice Foods Co. v. New England Printing & Lithographing Co.*, 923 F.2d 1576, 1578 (Fed.Cir.1991); *Leesona Corp. v. United States*, 599 F.2d 958, 969 (Ct.Cl.1979). Because the language of the statute unambiguously omits any such requirement, *see* 35 U.S.C. § 284 ("[T]he court may increase the damages up to three times the amount found or assessed."), and because there is no principled reason for continuing to engraft a willfulness requirement onto section 284, I believe we should adhere to the plain meaning of the statute and leave the discretion to enhance damages in the capable hands of the district courts. Accordingly, I agree that *Underwater Devices, Inc. v. Morrison–Knudsen Co.*, 717 F.2d 1380 (Fed.Cir.1983), should be overruled and the affirmative duty of care eliminated. I would also take the opportunity to overrule the *Beatrice Foods* line of cases to the extent those cases engraft willfulness onto the statute. I would vacate the district court's order and remand for the court to reconsider its ruling in light of the clear and unambiguous language of section 284.

■ NEWMAN, CIRCUIT JUDGE, concurring.

I join the court's holding that a voluntary waiver of the attorney-client privilege and work product protection as to patent opinion counsel is not a waiver of any privilege or protection as to litigation counsel. I also agree with the separate decision to overrule *Underwater Devices*, but only because that case has been misapplied, in the *extremis* of high-stakes litigation, to mean that "due care" requires more than the reasonable care that a responsible enterprise gives to the property of others. The obligation to obey the law is not diminished when the property is "intellectual." However, experience, and the exhortations of the *amici curiae*, have persuaded me that we should reduce the opportunities for abusive gamesmanship that the "due care" standard apparently has facilitated.

The thrust of *Underwater Devices* was that patent property should receive the same respect that the law imposes on all property. Industrial innovation would falter without the order that patent property contributes to the complexities of investment in technologic R & D and commercialization in a competitive marketplace. The loser would be not only the public, but also the nation's economic vigor. So I am sympathetic when told of the disproportionate burdens that a rigorous reading of *Underwater Devices* has placed on otherwise law-abiding commercial enterprise. Thus, to the extent that *Underwater Devices* has been applied as a *per se* rule that every possibly related patent must be exhaustively studied by expensive legal talent, lest infringement presumptively incur treble damages, I agree that the standard should be modified.

Although new uncertainties are introduced by the court's evocation of "objective standards" for such inherently subjective criteria as "recklessness" and "reasonableness," I trust that judicial wisdom will come to show the way, in the common-law tradition. The standards of behavior by which a possible infringer evaluates adverse patents should be the standards of fair commerce, including reasonableness of the actions taken in the particular circumstances. It cannot be the court's intention to tolerate the intentional disregard or destruction of the value of the property of another, simply because that property is a patent; yet the standard of "recklessness" appears to ratify intentional disregard, and to reject objective standards requiring a reasonable respect for property rights.

The remedial and deterrent purposes of multiplied damages, and their measure for a particular case, are best established by the district court in light of the original purposes of 35 U.S.C. § 284, as set forth in Judge Gajarsa's concurring opinion. The fundamental issue remains the reasonableness, or in turn the culpability, of commercial behavior that violates legally protected property rights.

NOTES

1. *Obtaining an Opinion of Counsel After* Seagate. Must you get an opinion? No. Should you get an opinion? Depends. With the scope of waiver curtailed, there are fewer downsides to relying on an opinion. In *Safeco*, the Supreme Court left open the possibility an opinion of counsel could be used to rebut objective recklessness. This question must be addressed on a case-by-case basis

What are the advantages of an opinion after *Seagate*? Will it help to rebut showing of objective recklessness.

What if your client does not have an opinion? What might they consider doing? Get an expert to testify about objective risk, and/or what was reasonable to know—if the expert will be allowed to testify? Get a fact witness (or witnesses) to show accused infringer's behavior was reasonable?

2. *Exculpatory Opinions of Counsel.* One factor that is relevant to determining if infringement was willful is whether the infringer relied on legal advice. While seeking (or not seeking) competent legal advise prior to beginning possibly infringing activities is relevant, it is not necessarily determinative. For example, lack of an opinion from counsel does not mandate a finding of willfulness, *Biotec Biologische Naturverpackungen GmbH & Co. v. Biocorp, Inc.*, 249 F.3d 1341, 1355–56 (Fed.Cir. 2001).

Given that the issue of willful infringement only needs to be resolved if the infringer's counsel was wrong, the focus is not on the legal correctness of the opinion, but instead on whether the opinion was sufficient to instill a belief in the infringer that a court might reasonably hold the patent invalid, not infringed, or unenforceable. Relevant facts include when the infringer sought the advice; what the infringer knew about counsel's independence, skill, and competence to provide the opinion; what the infringer knew about the nature and extent of the analysis performed by counsel; and what the infringer knew and had concluded about the credibility, value, and reasonableness of the opinion. *Johns Hopkins Univ. v. CellPro, Inc.*, 152 F.3d 1342, 1364 (Fed.Cir.1998); *Ortho Pharm. Corp. v. Smith*, 959 F.2d 936, 944 (Fed.Cir.1992); *Thorn Emi N. Am., Inc. v. Micron Tech., Inc.*, 837 F.Supp. 616, 620 (D.Del.1993).

Factors that bear on the competency of an opinion letter include whether counsel examined the file history of the patent, whether the opinion was oral or written, whether the opinion came from inside or outside counsel, whether the opinion came from a patent attorney, whether the opinion was detailed or merely conclusory, and whether material information was withheld from the attorney. *See, e.g., Comark Communications, Inc. v. Harris Corp.*, 156 F.3d 1182, 1190–93 (Fed. Cir.1998); *Read Corp.*, 970 F.2d at 829; *Ortho Pharm. Corp.*, 959 F.2d at 944–45; *Minnesota Mining & Mfg. Co. v. Johnson & Johnson Orthopaedics, Inc.*, 976 F.2d 1559, 1580–81 (Fed.Cir.1992); *Uniroyal, Inc. v. Rudkin–Wiley Corp.*, 939 F.2d 1540, 1546–47 (Fed.Cir.1991); *Studiengesellschaft Kohle, m.b.H. v. Dart Indus., Inc.*, 862 F.2d 1564, 1574–79 (Fed.Cir.1988). Some lawyers now devote their entire practice to preparing patent opinions. *See* San Francisco Daily Journal 1 (Oct. 28, 2003), which tells the story of a seven-lawyer firm that specializes in such opinions. On average, a noninfringement opinion regarding one patent costs between $20,000 and $50,000, and an invalidity opinion regarding one patent costs up to $100,000. *Id.*

Individual lawyers not careful to follow these guidelines for a proper opinion of counsel should take particular heed of the opinions of the district court and the Federal Circuit on the issue of willfulness in *Johns Hopkins Univ. v. CellPro, Inc.*, 978 F.Supp. 184 (D.Del.1997), *aff'd* 152 F.3d 1342 (Fed.Cir.1998). In *CellPro*, the defendant company's legal advisor, who was a member of the company's board of directors, was not only an experienced patent lawyer and former Patent Office Examiner, but had also previously been a partner in the law firm with the lawyer who authored the opinion that was found to be insufficient to insulate the defendant from a finding of willfulness. The district court issued a long and critical opinion that extensively discussed both lawyers by name as well as the name of the law firm, and held that the opinion of counsel was "so obviously deficient, one might expect a juror to conclude that the only value they had to CellPro in the world outside the courtroom would have been to file them in a drawer until they could be used in a cynical effort to try and confuse or mislead what CellPro, its Board, and counsel must have expected would be an unsophisticated jury." 978 F.Supp. at 193. The Federal Circuit affirmed on this issue, with a somewhat shorter opinion that also critically discussed both lawyers by name as well as the name of the law firm. 152 F.3d at 1364. No lawyer or law firm wishes to be so discussed in judicial opinions; and the wise lawyer will learn the obvious lessons from any mistakes made by those in *CellPro*.

3. *One Cannot Willfully Infringe a Patent of Which One Is Not Aware.* The duty to diligently ascertain whether one is infringing another's patent only arises if one has actual notice of that patent. Actual notice has been found where the patent owner offered the infringer a license, where verbal notice of infringement was accompanied by presentation of a copy of the patent, and where there was notification by a third party. *See, e.g., Great N. Corp. v. Davis Core & Pad Co.*, 782 F.2d 159, 167 (Fed.Cir.1986); *American Original Corp. v. Jenkins Food Corp.*, 774 F.2d 459, 465 (Fed.Cir.1985); *Ralston Purina Co. v. Far–Mar–Co.*, 772 F.2d 1570, 1577 (Fed.Cir. 1985).

3. Attorney Fees

Section 285 of Title 35 allows a court, "in exceptional cases," to "award reasonable attorney fees to the prevailing party." In the United States, the general rule is that each party bears its own litigation expenses, including attorney fees. Since the mid–1800s, there have been exceptions to this general rule. One of those exceptions was added to the patent laws in 1946. 35 U.S.C. § 70 (1946). This exception was designed to "discourage infringement of a patent by anyone thinking that all he would be required to pay if he loses the suit would be a royalty." S. Rep. No. 1503, 79th Cong., 2d Sess. 1, 2, *reprinted in* 1946 U.S.C.C.S. 1386, 1387. However, Congress did not intend that the recovery of attorney fees would become an ordinary occurrence, *id.*, and decisions under the 1946 statute did not routinely awarded attorney fees. Instead, awards of attorney fees were only made upon

> a finding of unfairness or bad faith in the conduct of the losing party, or some other equitable consideration of similar force, which makes it grossly unjust that the winner of the particular law suit be left to bear the burden of his own counsel fees which prevailing litigants normally bear.

Rohm & Haas Co. v. Crystal Chem. Co., 736 F.2d 688, 691 (Fed.Cir.1984) (emphasis and footnote omitted) (*quoting Park–In Theatres, Inc. v. Perkins*, 190 F.2d 137, 142 (9th Cir.1951)).

The Patent Act of 1952 revised the provision for awarding attorney fees to better reflect Congressional intent and to codify the post–1946 case law. The revision added the language that a court may award attorney fees only "in exceptional cases." S. Rep. No. 1979, 82d Cong., 2d Sess., *reprinted in* 1952 U.S.C.C.A.N. 2394, 2423. As the Federal Circuit has explained:

> Allowance of fees only in exceptional cases is based on the premise that courts should attempt to strike a balance between the interest of the patentee in protecting his statutory rights and the interest of the public in confining such rights to their legal limits.

Machinery Corp. of Am. v. Gullfiber AB, 774 F.2d 467, 471 (Fed.Cir.1985).

There are three requirements for an award of attorney fees: (1) the case must be exceptional, (2) the fees must be reasonable, and (3) fees may be awarded only to a prevailing party. If the requirements are met, the court has the discretion to decide how much, if anything, of a reasonable fee to award to a prevailing party in an exceptional case. *Gentry Gallery, Inc. v. Berkline Corp.*, 134 F.3d 1473, 1480 (Fed.Cir.1998). *See generally Waner v. Ford Motor Co.*, 331 F.3d 851, 857 (Fed.Cir.2003).

a. THE EXCEPTIONAL–CASE REQUIREMENT

There must be clear-and-convincing evidence that a case is exceptional. *Mach. Corp. of Am.*, 774 F.2d at 470–72. Consistent with the statute's initial purpose of deterring infringement, a case may be exceptional because of the conduct of the infringer. Because the statute was never limited to an infringer's conduct, though, a case may be exceptional because of the conduct of the patent owner, too.

An example of conduct by an infringer that can make a case exceptional is willful infringement. *Rohm & Haas Co.*, 736 F.2d 688, 690. It is important to note, though, that a finding of willful infringement does not necessitate a finding that the case is exceptional. *Cybor Corp. v. FAS Techs., Inc.*, 138 F.3d 1448, 1461 (Fed.Cir.1998) (en banc). However, the court must explain its reason for denying attorney's fees when there has been willful infringement. *Virginia Panel Corp. v. MAC Panel Co.*, 133 F.3d 860, 867 (Fed.Cir.1997). What should lead a court to find that a case is not exceptional even after a finding that infringement has been willful?

An example of conduct by a patent owner that can make a case exceptional is inequitable conduct during the prosecution of the asserted patent. *See, e.g., Tarkett, Inc. v. Congoleum Corp.*, 156 F.R.D. 608, 613–15 (E.D. Pa. 1994). As with willful infringement, a finding of inequitable conduct cannot be ignored, but it does not necessitate a finding that a case is exceptional. *Pharmacia & Upjohn Co. v. Mylan Pharms., Inc.*, 182 F.3d 1356, 1359–60 (Fed.Cir.1999) (inequitable conduct must be considered); *Frank's Casing Crew & Rental Tools, Inc. v. PMR Techs., Ltd.*, 292 F.3d 1363, 1377–78 (Fed.Cir.2002) (inequitable conduct, but not an exceptional case). What might lead a court to find that a case is not exceptional even after a finding that the patent owner committed inequitable conduct during the prosecution of the asserted patent? Do you believe that a case can be exceptional if, even though the patent owner did not commit inequitable conduct during prosecution in the Patent Office, the patent owner attempted to enforce its patent in bad-faith? *See generally Mach. Corp. Of Am.*, 774 F.2d at 473. Do you believe that a case can be exceptional if the patent owner's pre-suit bad faith led to a holding of equitable estoppel? *See generally Forest Labs., Inc. v. Abbott Labs.*, 339 F.3d 1324 (Fed.Cir.2003).

Both the patent owner and the infringer can make a case exceptional by litigation misconduct. *Rambus Inc. v. Infineon Techs. Ag*, 318 F.3d 1081, 1105–06 (Fed.Cir.2003). *See generally McNeil–PPC, Inc. v. L. Perrigo Co.*, 337 F.3d 1362, 1371–73 (Fed.Cir.2003). If litigation misconduct is the only basis for finding the case exceptional, the amount of the fees awarded must bear some relationship to the extent of the misconduct. *Id.* What if there are multiple infringers? Should all infringers be jointly liable for an award of attorney fees if only one committed misconduct? *See Frank's Casing Crew & Rental Tools, Inc. v. PMR Techs., Ltd.*, 292 F.3d 1363, 1369 (Fed.Cir.2002). It should be noted that, independent of the patent laws, the court has the inherent authority to award attorney fees because of litigation misconduct. *See generally Aptix Corp. v. Quickturn Design Sys., Inc.*, 269 F.3d 1369, 1378 (Fed.Cir.2001).

b. THE REASONABLE–FEE REQUIREMENT

In all cases where an award of attorney fees is authorized to a prevailing party, the Supreme Court has held that "[t]he most useful starting point for determining the amount of a reasonable fee is the number of hours reasonably expended on the litigation multiplied by a reasonable hourly rate." *Hensley v. Eckerhart,* 461 U.S. 424, 433 (1983). This amount is known as the lodestar amount.

Generally, a reasonable hourly rate is determined by the established value in the relevant community. This established value generally reflects the training, background, experience, and skill of an attorney in that community. The relevant community is usually the place where the case was tried. The cost of patent litigation can vary considerably from one region of the country to another. For example, in the non-metro southeast region, the 2003 reported median total cost of a single patent case where the value at risk is between one and twenty-five million dollars is $725,000. In California, the 2003 reported median total cost for such a case is $3 million. AIPLA, REPORT OF THE ECONOMIC SURVEY (2003) (total cost includes more than attorney fees). If the party had a good reason for using non-local counsel, though, the relevant community may be somewhere else. For example, in *Howes v. Medical Components, Inc.,* 761 F.Supp. 1193, 1195 (E.D. Pa. 1990), the court found New York City to be the relevant community in determining the reasonable hourly rate even though the case was tried in Philadelphia. The court stated:

> I believe that a party should be entitled to retain the most competent counsel available, particularly in the highly specialized area of complex patent litigation and particularly when its local counsel suggests using an out-of-state law firm for the purpose of litigation.

Id. at 1196.

In considering the number of hours reasonably expended, courts will note the number of attorneys who participated in the matter and their cumulative hours. Because it is not uncommon for patent cases to last for many years, the number of attorneys and their total fees can be quite large. For example, in *Howes,* there were three partners and twenty-three associates at the trial counsel law firm who worked on the case during the case's six year history. The *Howes* court declined to reduce the number of hours even though three attorneys were present at each day of trial and two to three attorneys were present at each deposition. In all, the attorney fees awarded in that 1990 case were just under $2 million. What if a case involved both patent and non-patent claims? When, if ever, would it be appropriate to award the fees that related to the non-patent issues? *See Gjerlov v. Schuyler Labs., Inc.,* 131 F.3d 1016, 1025 (Fed.Cir.1997).

Once the court has determined the reasonable hourly rate and the reasonable number of hours expended on the litigation simple multiplication provides the lodestar amount. Additional factors are then considered in determining whether the lodestar amount should be adjusted upward or downward. These adjustment factors include: the fixed or contingent nature of the fee, the novelty or difficulty of the issue, the legal expertise necessary to properly perform the services, the forbearance of other employment or opportunities by the attorney who handled the case, and the undesirability of the case. *Exxon Chem. Patents, Inc. v. Lubrizol Corp.*, 26 U.S.P.Q.2d 1871 (S.D. Tex. 1993) (reasonable attorney fees award was almost $18 million).

c.   THE PREVAILING–PARTY REQUIREMENT

The party who "has prevailed on the merits of at least some of his claims" is a "prevailing party." *Hanrahan v. Hampton*, 446 U.S. 754, 758 (1980) (non-patent case). A patent owner who recovers damages or has an injunction entered has prevailed. *See Gentry Gallery, Inc. v. Berkline Corp.*, 134 F.3d 1473, 1480 (Fed.Cir.1998). An alleged infringer who has the patent declared invalid has also prevailed. *Manildra Milling Corp. v. Ogilvie Mills, Inc.*, 76 F.3d 1178, 1182–83 (Fed.Cir.1996). Where neither party has unilaterally prevailed, courts have been given discretion to allow in part or deny attorney fees. *See Beckman Instruments, Inc. v. LKB Produkter AB*, 892 F.2d 1547, 1553–54 (Fed.Cir.1989) ("the amount of fees awarded to the 'prevailing party' should bear some relation to the extent to which that party actually prevailed"). Accord *Slimfold Mfg. Co., Inc. v. Kinkead Indus., Inc.*, 932 F.2d 1453, 1459 (Fed.Cir.1991).

d.   THE COURT'S DISCRETION

As stated above, even if all the requirements for awarding attorney fees to a prevailing party have been met, the court has the discretion to decide how much of a reasonable fee to award to a prevailing party in an exceptional case. The Federal Circuit has explained the district court's discretion as follows:

> Even an exceptional case does not require in all circumstances the award of attorney fees. Many factors could affect this result. The trial judge is in the best position to weigh considerations such as the closeness of the case, the tactics of counsel, the conduct of the parties, and any other factors that may contribute to a fair allocation of the burdens of litigation as between winner and loser.

> The exercise of discretion, although granting a broad scope to the trial court, is not unrestrained. The court's choice of discretionary ruling should be in furtherance of the policies of the laws that are being enforced, as informed by the court's familiarity with the matter in litigation and the interest of justice.

S.C. Johnson & Son, Inc. v. Carter–Wallace, Inc., 781 F.2d 198, 201 (Fed.Cir.1986). *See also Superior Fireplace Co. v. Majestic Prods. Co.*, 270 F.3d 1358, 1378 (Fed.Cir.2001).[7]

e.   VEXATIOUS AND BAD FAITH LITIGATION

As a final matter, patent litigants must remember that patent law does not exist in a vacuum, and the tools that are available to cabin attorney and party conduct throughout civil litigation in the federal courts, are

---

7. Courts also have discretion to award costs. Recoverable litigation-related costs (*e.g.*, the cost of preparing some trial exhibits might be recovered) usually amount to far less than the attorney fees. If the patent owner prevails, an award of costs is governed by 35 U.S.C § 284. If the infringer prevails, an award of costs is governed by Rule 54(d), F.R.Civ.P. *Delta–X Corp. v. Baker Hughes Prod. Tools, Inc.*, 984 F.2d 410, 413–14 (Fed.Cir.1993).

equally available in patent cases. These tools include Rule 11 of the Federal Rules of Civil Procedure as well as the so-called vexatious litigation statute, which is 28 U.S.C. § 1927. Of particular note is Rule 11, which requires any party to a federal civil suit to conduct a pre-filing investigation to determine whether the positions it is about to take in litigation are well-grounded in fact. A trial court's decision to grant or deny Rule 11 sanctions is discretionary, but in the remarkable decision of *Judin v. U.S. and Hewlett–Packard Company*, 110 F.3d 780 (Fed.Cir.1997), the Federal Circuit held that the trial court had abused its discretion when it held the pre-filing inquiry that was made by Judin and his attorney was reasonable. As noted by the Federal Circuit, prior to filing the complaint, Judin and his attorney had observed an accused device from a distance while it was in use at a post office, but neither Judin nor his attorney had attempted to obtain a device from the Postal Service or the manufacturer so that they could more closely observe the device, nor did they make any attempt to dissect or "reverse-engineer" a sample device. *Id.* at 784. All that Judin's attorney did, was "reviewed one of the patent claims and stated that he 'saw no problem with it.' " *Id.* In other words, the Federal Circuit found that Judin and his attorney had conducted virtually no investigation in order to determine whether Judin's claims had any foundation. *Id.* This, said the Federal Circuit, violated Rule 11. *Id.* Importantly, for lawyers, the Federal Circuit in *Judin* went on hold that the trial court must on remand conduct further proceedings to decide how to apportion the sanctions among the party *and* trial *and* appellate *counsel. Id.* at 785.

INDEX

References are to pages.

1341

CLAIMS—Cont'd
Narrow claims—Cont'd
  Broadening reissues, 874
  Too narrow claims problem, 1059
Narrowing amendments
    Generally, 236
    Definition, 911
    Prosecution history estoppel, 897
    Voluntary and involuntary, 897
New uses, method or process claims describing, 93
Notice function, 241, 898
Novelty, rejections of claims lacking in application process, 105
Number of claims, patent value correlation, 80
Obvious, rejections of claims as in application process, 105
Optimal claim scope, 164
Parent and continuing applications, 109
Patent value correlation to number of claims, 80
Patentability amendments, 896
Peripheral and central claiming distinguished, 156, 283
Phantom claims, doctrine of equivalents analysis, 893
Pioneer inventions, 183
Pioneer patents, central claiming, 878, 894
Policy considerations, optimal claim scope, 164
Preambles
    Generally, 90
  Use in claim interpretation, 860
Prior art, claims reading on, 828
Prior art defining amendments, 908
Process Claims, this index
Product claims, statutory subject matter, 731
Product-by-process claims, 94
Prophetic claiming
    Biotechnology inventions, 492
    Written description, 277
Prosecution histories, interpretation influences, 236, 846, 896
Public dedication rule, doctrine of equivalents tensions, 873
Public use bar determinations, claim by claim evaluation, 324
Reissues
    Broadening, 874
    Claim enlarging through, 131
    Continuity of claims, 137
Rejections of claims during application process, 105
Representations during prosecution, 102
Risks of claim construction, 828
Scope ambiguities, 92
Scope disclosure, enablement through
    Generally, 168
    Breadth as trailing edge or leading edge issue, 183
    Economics analysis, 165
    Optimal claim scope, 164
Second applications, 108

CLAIMS—Cont'd
Sequences in process claims, 93
Specialized technical terms, use of, 826
Specifications
    Claims in, 73
    Claims not supported by, 219
    Role in interpreting, 855
Statutory requirements, evolution of, 90
Statutory subject matter and, 728
Strategies of claim construction, 828
Substantial reasons related to patentability amendments, 908
Surrenders of claims, recapture doctrine
    Generally, 146
    Material surrendered by argument, 150
System claims, foreign activity infringement, 941
Three elements, 90
Timing of claim construction, 830
Too narrow claims problem, 1059
Transition phrases, 90
Unsupported subject matter, claims dominating, 219
Uses as elements of claims, 93
Vagueness, rejections of claims for in application process, 105
Validity issues in interpretation of limiting claims, 861
Validity presumption, 860
Validity vs infringement interpretations, 283
Voluntary and involuntary narrowing amendments and prosecution history estoppel, 897
Written descriptions and
    Generally, 73
    Correspondence, application, 106
    Prophetic claiming, 277
    Use in claim interpretation, 861

CLASSIFICATIONS
International Patent Classification symbol, 126
PTO classifications and subclasses, 103

COMBINATION PATENTS
  Generally, 609
History of patent law, 22
Means plus functions claims, 917
Nonobviousness, 608, 609

COMMERCIAL LAW
See Contract Law, this index

COMMERCIAL SALE
See On-Sale Bar, this index

COMMERCIAL SUCCESS
Nonobviousness, commercial success as factor, 597, 602, 614

COMMERCIAL VIABILITY
Reduction to practice distinguished, 470

COMMERCIALIZATION THEORY
  Generally, 69
Biotechnology research, 1232

ON-SALE BAR—Cont'd
Development state of invention as factor, 344
Experimental use doctrine and, 329, 339
Experimentation uses, 302
First Inventor Defense Act of 1999, 1210
Grace period trigger, 341
Grace periods, 301
History of doctrine, 345
History of patents, 300
Imputed third-party experimental use, 365
Novelty distinguished, 371
Offers to sell, 336
On hand doctrine, 346
Policy considerations, 345
Public use bar distinguished, 328
Ready-for-patenting test
      Generally, 335, 342, 345
   Substantially complete test compared, 349
Reduction to practice requirement, 346
Related entities, offers and sales between, 340
Substantially complete test
      Generally, 330, 348, 349
   Ready-for-patenting test compared, 349
Third-party activity
      Generally, 302, 354, 358
   Consent or allowance of applicant, 364
   Imputed third-party experimental use, 365
   Pirated inventions, 365
   Secret use by third party, 363
Timely Products standard, 347
Trigger of, 333
Two-part test, 335, 342

OPEN-SOURCE SOFTWARE
Economics of patent law, 65

OPERABILITY
Affidavits and declarations as to, application process, 106

OPPOSITIONS
European Patent Convention, 115
Publication and, 112

ORDINARY SKILL IN THE ART
See Person Having Ordinary Skill in the Art, this index

OWNERSHIP
      Generally, 1180 et seq.
All claims rule, 1196
Assignments of Ownership, this index
Co-inventors and joint inventors, 1180
Defenses, this index
Employed to invent exception, 1197
Employee rights
      Generally, 1196
   Assignments by, 1197
   Policy considerations, 1200
First Inventor Defense Act, this index
Harmonization of patent law, 1203
Inventorship and, relationships, 1180
Inventorship distinguished, 1188

OWNERSHIP—Cont'd
Nunc pro tunc assignments, 1198
Shop rights of employers, 1197

PANDUIT FACTORS
Lost profits damages, 1240

PARIS CONVENTION
Antidiscrimination provision, 438
Discrimination as to patent rights, 438
Territoriality, 1087

PARTIES
      Generally, 1195
Co-inventors, 1181
Injunctions, parties plaintiff, 1299
Joint inventors, party status
      Generally, 1181, 1195
   Jus tertii defense, 1199

PATENT AGENTS
Definition, 193

PATENT AND TRADEMARK OFFICE (PTO)
      Generally, 72
Appeals from rejections, 107
Application Process, this index
Board of Patent Appeals and Interferences, 107
Classification system for applications, 103
Evolution of patent prosecution, 74
Examinations, this index
Filing requirements, 81
Filings, 72
General requirements for practitioners, 73
Guidelines, utility, 706
History of agency, 102
Inequitable conduct before, 1010
Manual of Patent Examining Procedure, 85
Numbering system, 103
Office actions
      Generally, 105
   See also Application Process, this index
Patentability, 130
Practitioners, registration requirements, 73
Prior art disclosure, PTO rules, 77
Prior art searches, 103
Public Search Room, 81
Registration to practice before, 73
Rejections,appeals from, 107
Rules of Practice, 85
Searches of prior art, 122
Solicitors, registration requirements, 73
Term of patent, extensions for PTO delay, 822
Thoroughness of procedures, modern trends, 77
Utility guidelines, 706

PATENT APPLICATIONS
See Application Process, this index

PATENT COOPERATION TREATY (PCT)
Applications as prior art, 290

†